2 Bunhill Row
London
EC1Y 8HQ

BLACKSTONE'S

CIVIL PRACTICE

THE COMMENTARY

BLACKSTONE'S
CIVIL PRACTICE
THE COMMENTARY
2017

EDITOR-IN-CHIEF

THE RT HON SIR MAURICE KAY

Formerly a Lord Justice of Appeal

EDITORS

STUART SIME
DEREK FRENCH

EDITORIAL ADVISORY BOARD

STUART BRIDGE
MICHAEL WALKER
IVOR WEINTROUB

CONTRIBUTORS

HANNAH AMBROSE, JULIE BROWNE, ADRIAN KEANE

LISA LAURENTI, ANDREW LIDBETTER, GERARD MCMEEL

VANESSA NAISH, ALAN OWENS, ANNA PERTOLDI

CHARLES SCOTT, CHRIS TAYLOR

OXFORD
UNIVERSITY PRESS

OXFORD
UNIVERSITY PRESS

Great Clarendon Street, Oxford, OX2 6DP,
United Kingdom

Oxford University Press is a department of the University of Oxford.
It furthers the University's objective of excellence in research, scholarship,
and education by publishing worldwide. Oxford is a registered trade mark of
Oxford University Press in the UK and in certain other countries

© Oxford University Press 2017

The moral rights of the authors have been asserted

First Edition published in 2011
Sixth Edition published in 2017

Impression: 1

Published in the United States of America by Oxford University Press
198 Madison Avenue, New York, NY 10016, United States of America

British Library Cataloguing in Publication Data
Data available

ISBN 978–0–19–879552–0

Printed in Italy by
L.E.G.O. S.p.A.

Preface

NEW TO THE 2017 EDITION

Blackstone's Civil Practice 2017 is up to date to 3 October 2016, and includes rule changes which came into effect on 3 October 2016. The work incorporates rule amendments up to the Civil Procedure (Amendment No. 3) Rules 2016 and the 86th Update. Among the revisions to *Blackstone's Civil Practice* for this edition are:

- New Financial List
- Electronic communications in all courts under the replacement PD 5B, and the electronic working scheme in the Rolls Building in the new PD 51O
- Changes made by the 2016 versions of the Court Guides for the Queen's Bench and Chancery Divisions
- Case law on deliberately understating the value of the claim to avoid paying the full issue fee
- Replacement of PD 4 on court forms
- *Gate Gourmet Luxembourg IV Sàrl v Morby* on effecting personal service
- Developments on setting aside default judgments, including *Gentry v Miller*
- Developments on service outside the jurisdiction, including the Hague Choice of Court Convention
- Revised rules on costs budgeting and the introduction of budget discussion reports
- Developments on sanctions, including *Thevarajah v Riordan* and *Abdulle v Commissioner of Police of the Metropolis*
- *Nursing and Midwifery Council v Harrold* on the court's inherent jurisdiction to make civil restraint orders
- Revisions to the practice relating to Tomlin Orders
- New CPR provisions on charging orders and attachment of earnings
- Revisions to the routes of appeal by the replacement of the Destination of Appeals Order in 2016
- New Part 52 on appeals, together with revisions to the practice directions on appeals

These changes have resulted in substantial revisions to the chapters on enforcement and appeals, as well as extensive amendments throughout the book.

An online resource centre for *Blackstone's Civil Practice 2017* will also be available with regular updates and useful reading. This can be found at: www.oup.com/blackstones/civil.

Blackstone's Civil Practice 2017 provides the civil litigation practitioner with a comprehensive and authoritative work covering every topic which the practitioner can reasonably expect to encounter in everyday practice. The objective of the publishers and the editorial team has been to produce a single volume of manageable size and expense.

Blackstone's Civil Practice occupies a unique place in the civil litigation practitioner's library. It is a complete treatise on all aspects of the law and practice relating to the progress of a civil claim, from funding the litigation to enforcing the judgment. It provides a complete commentary on the Civil Procedure Rules and practice directions, the text of which is set out in appendix 1. There are chapters providing comprehensive but condensed summaries of the law of evidence, judicial review, human rights, sale of goods and unfair contracts. There is commentary on specialist proceedings including arbitration, mortgage possession, company, insolvency and director disqualification.

A team of highly experienced and respected authors has ensured that each subject is given authoritative and specialist attention. The authors and editors have sought to provide a text which is sufficiently comprehensive, clear and up to date to enable a practitioner easily to assimilate a topic on which he or she may have little knowledge, while at the same time providing a depth of analysis and information which will enable those with greater experience of a subject to research in greater detail.

Comprehensive and up-to-date appendices include not only the Civil Procedure Rules, practice directions and pre-action protocols, but also the court fees orders and some of the statutes most commonly needed in civil litigation. Procedural checklists, which are step-by-step guides to various aspects of civil procedure, can be found at the front of the book, beginning on page 1. These provide quick and practical guidance on how to comply with the requirements of the rules.

It has been the foresight and enthusiasm of its publishers which has enabled this work to come to fruition. The editors would, in particular, like to thank Heather Saward and Jeremy Stein, and remember the late Alistair MacQueen, of Blackstone Press, because this work would not have seen the light of day without their vision and enthusiasm. We also extend our thanks to Fiona Sinclair and Andy Redman of Oxford University Press for their guidance, encouragement and total support. We also warmly thank the contributors who have provided authoritative material on their subjects and met a tight schedule notwithstanding their other important commitments.

The editors
3 October 2016

Contributors

Hannah Ambrose, MA Hons (Jurisprudence), Merton College, Oxford (chapters 72, 73 and 80). Hannah is a Professional Support Consultant at Herbert Smith Freehills LLP, working with clients and colleagues globally on complex issues relating to arbitration, dispute resolution and the enforcement of arbitral awards and judgments. She also advises on public international law, in particular on state immunity, investment protection and investor-state dispute settlement (ISDS). Hannah is an editor of the firm's arbitration and PIL blogs and an author and editor of various other internal and external publications.

Stuart Bridge, MA (Cantab), Barrister (editorial advisory board). Stuart was a Lecturer in Law at the University of Cambridge from 1990 until 2012. He served as a Law Commissioner for England and Wales from 2001 until 2008, and he has been one of Her Majesty's Circuit Judges, based on the South Eastern Circuit, since 2012. He is a Bencher of the Middle Temple and a Life Fellow of Queens' College, Cambridge. He has recently co-authored the eighth edition of *Megarry and Wade's Law of Real Property*.

Julie Browne, LLB, Barrister (chapters 2, 3, 11 to 15, 17, 18, 20 and 88). Julie Browne is a deputy course director of the bar vocational course at the City Law School, where she teaches advocacy, civil litigation, drafting, company law and commercial law. She was called to the Bar in 1989 and during 10 years in full-time practice, she undertook a wide variety of general civil and commercial work, including insolvency, company and property litigation. She is the series editor of the 14 bar vocational manuals and co-author of *A Practical Approach to Alternative Dispute Resolution* and the *Jackson ADR Handbook*, all published by Oxford University Press. She is also an experienced CPD trainer in advocacy, evidence, case preparation, drafting and litigation.

Derek French, BSc (editor; chapters 81 to 86 and 92 and appendices). Derek French is co-author of *Mayson, French and Ryan on Company Law* and *Blackstone's Guide to the Civil Justice Reforms 2013* and author of *Applications to Wind Up Companies, Model Articles of Association for Companies* and *How to Cite Legal Authorities*. He is editor of *Blackstone's Statutes on Company Law* and has also written on insolvency law, accountancy and management.

The Right Honourable Sir Maurice Kay (editor-in-chief). Sir Maurice Kay was a Lord Justice of Appeal and Vice President of the Court of Appeal (Civil Division). He was a professor of law before being called to the Bar in 1975 where he practised until becoming a High Court Judge in 1995.

Professor Adrian Keane, LLB, Barrister (chapters 49 and 53). Adrian Keane is Emeritus Professor of Law at The City Law School, City University. Previously, he was Dean of the Inns of Court School of Law. He is a contributor to *Blackstone's Criminal Practice* and his many publications include *The Modern Law of Evidence*.

Lisa Laurenti, LLB, Solicitor (non-practising) (chapters 23 to 30). Lisa Laurenti is Deputy Course Director of the Bar Professional Training Course at the City Law School, teaching drafting, civil litigation, professional negligence and opinion writing. When in private practice, she was a partner in a Legal 500 firm where she specialised in professional indemnity and civil fraud work.

Andrew Lidbetter, MA (Oxon), BCL, Solicitor (chapters 77, 78 and 91). Andrew Lidbetter is a litigation partner at Herbert Smith Freehills LLP specialising in public law including judicial review and human rights. He is the author of *Company Investigations and Public Law*, is on the advisory board of *Judicial Review*, and frequently writes and speaks on public law.

Gerard McMeel, MA (Oxon), BCL, Barrister (chapters 89 and 90). Gerard McMeel is Professor of Commercial Law at the University of Manchester, where he teaches contract law, sale and supply of goods, banking law and carriage of goods by sea. He is the author of *The Construction of Contracts* (Oxford University Press; 2nd edn, 2011; 3rd edn, 2017, forthcoming), and a co-author of *The Law of Personal Property* (Sweet & Maxwell; 2013; 2nd edn, 2017, forthcoming) and *McMeel and Virgo on Financial Advice and Financial Products* (Oxford University Press; 3rd edn, 2014). He has authored numerous contributions in edited collections and journal articles on contract law, commercial law, financial services law and regulation, and unjust enrichment. He is also a Barrister, England and Wales.

Vanessa Naish, MA Hons (History), Clare College, Cambridge (chapters 72, 73 and 80). Vanessa is a Professional Support Consultant at Herbert Smith Freehills LLP, working with clients and colleagues globally on complex issues relating to arbitration, dispute resolution and the enforcement of arbitral awards and judgments. She also advises on public international law, in particular on state immunity, investment protection and investor-state dispute settlement (ISDS). Vanessa is an editor of the firm's arbitration and PIL blogs and an author and editor of various other internal and external publications.

Alan Owens, LLB, Solicitor (chapters 5 and 6). Alan Owens is a partner in the commercial litigation and arbitration department at the London Office of DWF, with extensive international experience across a wide range of contentious disputes. He has lectured widely on civil procedure and is an editor of the *Civil Court Service Newsletter*.

Anna Pertoldi, LLB, LLM, Solicitor Advocate (chapters 16 and 19). Anna Pertoldi is a litigation partner at Herbert Smith Freehills LLP with responsibility for know-how management in the central litigation team. She is editor of her firm's litigation notes blog as well as the author and editor of other of its litigation publications. She has wide-ranging experience of commercial litigation, particularly in the context of international fraud, and has lectured on both substantive and procedural law.

Charles Scott, LLB, Barrister (chapter 4). Charles Scott practises in civil law at 42 Bedford Row. He edits chapter 4 authored by the late Evan Ashfield and is a contributor to the Bar vocational manuals published by Oxford University Press.

Professor Stuart Sime, LLB, Barrister (editor; chapters 1, 7, 8, 9, 10, 21, 22, 31 to 48, 50, 51, 52, 54 to 71, 74, 75, 76 and 79). Stuart Sime is the course director of the full-time Bar Professional Training Course at the City Law School, where he teaches civil litigation, commercial and company law. He was a practising barrister until 2005. In his early career he spent a number of years in the litigation department of the Treasury Solicitor's Office. He is the author of *A Practical Approach to Civil Procedure* and co-author of *A Practical Approach to ADR*, the *Jackson ADR Handbook* and *Blackstone's Guide to the Civil Justice Reforms 2013*.

Chris Taylor, LLB, Solicitor (chapter 87). Chris is Head of Litigation Training at CPD Training (UK) Limited and a Consultant Solicitor at Drydensfairfax solicitors in Leeds. Prior to leaving full-time practice Chris was a partner and Head of Residential Recoveries at Optima Legal, before moving to Drydensfairfax as Head of Secured Recoveries. As well as continuing to practise, Chris now trains qualified solicitors and other legal professionals in litigation skills.

Michael Walker, CBE (consultant editor). Michael Walker was a District Judge from April 1994 to October 2016. Before his appointment to the bench he was a partner in a South London firm of high street, legal aid solicitors. From 1994 to 2007 he sat full time at Wandsworth County Court with a mixed workload of civil and family cases but from September 2007 he was seconded to the Senior Presiding Judge's office at the Royal Courts of Justice. Between 2000 and 2011 he was Honorary Secretary of the Association of Her Majesty's District Judges.

From April 2008 to September 2016 he was one of the judicial members of the board of what is now known as Her Majesty's Courts and Tribunals Service.

Ivor Weintroub, LLB (editorial advisory board). Ivor Weintroub is a Civil and Family Recorder of the Crown and County Courts and previously sat as a District Judge in Bournemouth County Court. He is also an Honorary Visiting Lecturer to the Business and Law department of Bournemouth University LPC course. He has lectured and been a tutor judge on civil and family courses for the Judicial Studies Board. Before appointment as a District Judge he was a partner in a High Street practice with offices in Southampton and Hampshire and was a member of the Law Society Child Care and Mental Health Review Tribunal Panels.

The tables and index were compiled by Moira Greenhalgh BSc MCLIP FSI and updated by Penny Dickman (tables) and Debbie Harris (index).

Contents Summary

Contents

Procedural Checklists

A   GENERAL MATTERS

B   FUNDING LITIGATION

D COMMENCEMENT

F SOLICITORS

G STATEMENTS OF CASE

Contents

Contents

Contents

Q INSOLVENCY PROCEEDINGS AND COMPANIES MATTERS

APPENDICES

Please note that the following appendix materials can be found in Blackstone's Civil Practice 2017, *the hardback version, which includes complete provisions of the full Civil Procedure Rules and Practice Directions, Pre-action Protocols, selected legislation, and court fees orders. These materials can also be found in the public domain.*

Contents

Guide to *Blackstone's Civil Practice The Commentary*

CHAPTERS AND APPENDICES

Blackstone's Civil Practice: The Commentary has 92 chapters and four appendices. The chapters are grouped into 22 parts, A to V. For a list of the parts, chapters and appendices see the **Contents** starting on page xiii.

Chapters are divided up by numbered headings. The first heading in chapter 1 is numbered **1.1**, the second is **1.2** and so on. The number of a heading is printed in the margin against the first line of text after the heading. Each chapter begins with a list of its numbered headings. The numbers are used for cross-references throughout the book.

ORGANISATION OF THE SUBJECT MATTER

Subject-focused chapters

The chapters of *Blackstone's Civil Practice* are subject-focused, dealing with all the law on a topic, wherever the source of the law may be in statutes, rules, practice directions or cases. General points are discussed in part A (**chapters 1 to 4**), then parts B to P (**chapters 5 to 81**) describe the progress of a civil claim in the County Court or the High Court in England and Wales, from consideration of how to fund it (part B) to the methods of enforcing judgment (part P). Part Q (**chapters 82 to 86**) deals with procedure in insolvency proceedings and companies matters in the County Court and High Court. Other special procedures in the County Court and High Court are considered in **chapter 72** (arbitration claims), **chapter 77** (judicial review, which is conducted in the High Court only), **chapter 87** (mortgage possession claims) and **chapter 88** (anti-social behaviour and harassment, which are dealt with in the County Court only). Parts T and U of *Blackstone's Civil Practice* contain compact summaries of some topics of particular importance to practitioners: sale of goods and unfair contracts (part T) and human rights (part U). Part V lists the changes of terminology in civil proceedings which have occurred from 1998 onwards.

Blackstone's Civil Practice does not deal with family proceedings or with civil proceedings ancillary to criminal matters.

Procedural checklists

Starting on page 1 there are 38 procedural checklists which summarise the steps to be taken in the most commonly encountered stages of a civil claim.

Contents, index, cross-references and useful references section

Research in *Blackstone's Civil Practice* can be started either from a subject focus or a source focus, because of the comprehensive indexing and cross-referencing of the book.

The index at the end of *Blackstone's Civil Practice* is an in-depth subject index of chapters 1 to 92 and of the Civil Procedure Rules and practice directions. The index is usually the best way of finding where a particular topic is discussed in chapters 1 to 92 of *Blackstone's Civil Practice* and which rules or practice directions are concerned with that topic.

At the beginning of *Blackstone's Civil Practice* there is a **Table of Cases**, a **Table of Statutes** and a **Table of Rules, Practice Directions, Protocols, Other Secondary Legislation and Court Guides**. These tables list all the headings (by number) under which each case, statute etc. is mentioned.

On the inside covers there is a **Useful References** section. This comprises a list of important and useful paragraphs which often need to be accessed in a hurry.

ONLINE RESOURCE CENTRE

This will alert practitioners to key developments taking place during the life cycle of this edition. It will be available to all *Blackstone's Civil Practice 2017* subscribers. Please visit <www.oup.com/blackstones/civil> and bookmark the site.

Abbreviations

ADR	alternative dispute resolution
ASBO	anti-social behaviour order
ATE	after-the-event
Brussels I Regulation	Regulation (EC) No. 44/2001
BTE	before-the-event
CCMCC	County Court Money Claims Centre
CCR	County Court Rules 1981 (SI 1981/1687) as amended, or as re-enacted in CPR, sch. 2
CDDA 1986	Company Directors Disqualification Act 1986
CFA	conditional fee agreement
CJEU	Court of Justice of the European Union
CJJA 1982	Civil Jurisdiction and Judgments Act 1982
CLS	Community Legal Service
CMA	Competition and Markets Authority
CNF	claim notification form
COMI	centre of main interests
CPFO	Civil Proceedings Fees Order 2008 (SI 2008/1053)
CRA 2015	Consumer Rights Act 2015
CRU	Compensation Recovery Unit
CPR	Civil Procedure Rules 1998 (SI 1998/3132)
DBA	damages-based agreement
DWP	Department for Work and Pensions
ECHR	European Court of Human Rights
EEO	European enforcement order
EL/PL Protocol	Pre-Action Protocol for Low Value Personal Injury (Employers' Liability and Public Liability) Claims
EOP	European order for payment
ESCP	European small claims procedure
Final Report	Lord Woolf, *Access to Justice. Final Report* (London: HMSO, 1996)
GLO	group litigation order
GMC	General Medical Council
HMCTS	Her Majesty's Courts and Tribunals Service
Interim Report	Lord Woolf, *Access to Justice. Interim Report* (London: Lord Chancellor's Department, 1995)
IR 1986	Insolvency Rules 1986 (SI 1986/1925)
IVA	individual voluntary arrangement

Jackson Report	Sir Rupert Jackson's *Review of Civil Litigation Costs: Final Report* (London: TSO, 2010)
LA 1980	Limitation Act 1980
LAA	Legal Aid Agency
LEI	legal expenses insurance
LSC	Legal Services Commission
MF	McKenzie friend
MIB	Motor Insurers' Bureau
ord.	order
para.	paragraph
paras	paragraphs
PCO	protective costs order
PCOL	Possession Claim Online
PD	Practice Direction. PD followed by a number is a practice direction supplementing the Part of the CPR with that number.
PD Directors Disqualification Proceedings	Practice Direction — Directors Disqualification Proceedings
PD Insolvency Proceedings	Practice Direction — Insolvency Proceedings
PD Pre-action Conduct	Practice Direction — Pre-action Conduct
PD Pre-action Conduct and Protocols	Practice Direction — Pre-action Conduct and Protocols
QOCS	qualified one-way costs shifting
r.	rule
RCJ	Royal Courts of Justice
recast Brussels I Regulation	Regulation (EU) No. 1215/2012
Recommendations to national courts	CJEU Recommendations to national courts and tribunals in relation to the initiation of preliminary ruling proceedings [2012] OJ C338, p. 1
rr.	rules
RSC	Rules of the Supreme Court 1965 (SI 1965/1776) as amended, or as re-enacted in CPR, sch. 1
RTA	road traffic accident
RTA Protocol	Pre-action Protocol for Low Value Personal Injury Claims in Road Traffic Accidents
s.	section
SCCO	Senior Courts Costs Office
sch.	schedule
SCR	Supreme Court Rules 2009 (SI 2009/1603)
Service Regulation	Regulation (EC) No. 1393/2007
SoGA 1979	Sale of Goods Act 1979
ss.	sections

Taking of Evidence Regulation	Regulation (EC) No. 1206/2001
TCC	Technology and Construction Court
TFEU	Treaty on the Functioning of the European Union
TPF	third-party funding
UCTA 1977	Unfair Contract Terms Act 1977
WFO	worldwide freezing order
Woolf Report	Lord Woolf, *Access to Justice: Final Report* (London: HMSO, 1996)

Table of Cases

Table of Cases

Table of Cases

Table of Cases

Table of Statutes

(including European and International legislation)

European legislation

Table of Rules, Practice Directions, Protocols, Other Secondary Legislation and Court Guides

Procedural Checklists

Procedural checklist 1   Pre-action Protocol for Personal Injury Claims

See **8.16** to **8.27**.

All references are to the **Pre-action Protocol for Personal Injury Claims** unless otherwise indicated.

Soon after being retained	Solicitor should consider whether an informal notification of the possible claim should be made to the defendant. This will not start the protocol timetable (**para. 2.6**).
Letter before claim	This should be sent at least six months before the expiry of limitation period to give time for compliance before limitation expires. Two copies of the letter should be sent to the defendant, or one to the defendant and one to the insurer (**paras 2.7** and **3.1**). For detailed contents of the letter, see **paras 3.2** to **3.5** and **annex A**.
21 days from letter before claim	Defendant should reply with name of insurer, or the insurer should acknowledge (**para. 3.6**). The period is up to 42 days if the accident was outside England and Wales (**para. 3.8**).
Failure to acknowledge	If there is no acknowledgment within 21 days, proceedings may be issued (**para. 3.6**).
Three months from acknowledging letter before claim	Defendant should have completed investigations. Defendant must reply stating if liability is admitted or denied (**paras 2.12** and **3.7**). If liability is denied or if contributory negligence is alleged, the defendant should give reasons and provide documents on liability (**paras 3.7, 3.10** to **3.12**). Standard disclosure lists are in **annex B**. No charge is to be made for providing copy documents (**para. 3.13**).
Before issuing proceedings	If contributory negligence has been alleged, the claimant should respond to those allegations (**para. 3.12**).
As soon as possible after defendant's response	Claimant sends defendant a schedule of special damages and documents in support. This is particularly important where liability has been admitted (**para. 3.14**). Both sides must consider the claimant's rehabilitation needs (**para. 4.1**).
No time limit, but usually shortly after the defendant's response	Either party may send the other a list of suggested experts for each field of expertise (**para. 3.15**). The letter should also state the basis of the proposed instruction (otherwise this procedure results in the joint selection of experts rather than joint instruction, see **54.19**).
No time limit	Claimant organises access to relevant medical records (**para. 3.16**).
14 days after list of experts	Other side may raise objections to the suggested experts (**para. 3.17**).
Objection to all suggested experts	Both parties are free to instruct their own experts. This may be penalised in costs later if either side has acted unreasonably (**para. 3.18**).
No complete objection	First party selects an expert from those left, and sends a letter of instruction in accordance with the standard letter (**annex C**).
Receipt of report	First party decides whether to send copy to the other side (see **54.19**). Both parties consider sending questions to clarify the report to the expert. The second party should send its questions via the first party's solicitors (**para. 3.20**).
Before proceedings	Both parties should consider sending Part 36 offers to the other side. Both parties should also consider whether mediation or ADR might be appropriate (**paras 2.16, 5.2**, and **8.7**; see **68.19** and **73.23**).
14 days before issue	Claimant should ask the defendant's insurers to nominate solicitors, and both parties should carry out a stocktake of the issues and evidence (**para. 2.17**).

Procedural checklist 2   Pre-action procedure where no protocol applies

See **8.9** to **8.14**.

All references are to **PD Pre-action Conduct and Protocols.**

Letter of claim	Letter of claim is sent to the defendant with concise details of the claim. The letter should include the basis on which the claim is made, the remedies sought, and, in a money claim, how the amount claimed is calculated (**para. 6(a)**)
Defendant's response	Defendant must respond within a reasonable time (**para. 6(b)**). What is reasonable depends on the complexity of the case. The response should include whether the claim is accepted or denied; if denied, the reasons why, with an explanation of which facts and parts of the claim are disputed. The response should include details of any counterclaim.
Documents	Both parties are required to disclose key documents relevant to the issues in dispute (**para. 6(c)**).
Expert evidence	If expert evidence is required, the parties should consider the costs and the fact that court permission will be required. In low value claims in particular a single joint expert may be appropriate (**para. 7**).
Stocktake	Before issuing proceedings the parties should review their respective positions, consider whether proceedings can be avoided, or seek to narrow the issues (**para. 12**).

Procedural checklist 3   Issue and service where service of the claim form is to be effected by the court

See **chapters 12** and **15**.

Where the court is to effect service the procedure is as follows:

(a)   The claimant sends or takes to court one copy of the claim form and a copy for each defendant to be served, together with the issue fee (**CPFO, fee 1**). Claimants in the RCJ can get the court to seal a 'claimant's copy' claim form, if convenient.

(b)   The court issues the claim form by entering the issue date on the claim form, affixing the court seal to the claim form and allocating a number to the claim. It creates a case management file, in which it files its copy of the claim form and, if supplied, notice of funding of claim. The claimant's copy of the claim form (if any) will be returned.

(c)   The court serves the claim form. It is for the court to decide which method of service to choose, although the method will normally be by first-class post (**CPR, r. 6.4(2)**; **PD 6A, para. 8.1**).

(d)   Where particulars of claim are contained in the claim form or are to be served with it, court staff will add to the documents for service a response pack consisting of forms for admitting and for defending the claim and for acknowledging service (**CPR, r. 7.8(1)**). Where the particulars of claim are to be served later, these documents do not accompany the claim form.

(e)   The court will send the claimant a notice of issue (form N205A or N205B), which will include the date when the claim form is deemed to be served under **r. 6.14** (**r. 6.17(1)**).

(f)   Where the court sends the claim form by post and it is returned to the court, or where there is an unsuccessful attempt to effect bailiff service, it must notify the claimant (**rr. 6.18(1)** and **6.19**).

(g)   A claimant who receives a notice of ineffectual bailiff service should take steps to effect service of the claim form himself. If the court sent the claim form by first-class post to the correct address for service, there is an irrebuttable presumption of due service (**r. 6.18(2)**).

Procedural checklist 4   Issue and service where service of the claim form is to be effected by the claimant

See **chapters 12** and **15**.

Where the claimant is to effect service the procedure is as follows:

(a)   The claimant sends or takes to court one copy of the claim form for the court, and a copy for each defendant to be served, together with the issue fee. Claimants in the RCJ can get the court to seal a 'claimant's copy' claim form, if convenient. There must be a notification to the court that the claimant wishes to effect service. If applicable, a notice of funding of claim must be filed.

(b)   The court issues the claim form by entering the issue date on the claim form, affixing the court seal to the claim form and allocating a number to the claim. It creates a case management file, which will include the court's copy of the claim form and, if supplied, copy of public funding certificate.

(c)   The claimant's copy of the claim form (if any) and the copies for service on the defendants will be returned.

(d)   The claimant will effect service, in one of the ways specified in **CPR, r. 6.3**. If a notice of funding of claim form N251 was filed, it must be served with the claim form. Where particulars of claim are contained in the claim form or are to be served with it, the claimant must also serve the forms for acknowledging service, for admitting and for defending the claim (**r. 7.8(1)**). Where the particulars of claim are to be served later, these documents do not accompany the claim form.

(e)   The claimant must file a certificate of service (form N215) within 21 days of service of the particulars of claim, unless all defendants have acknowledged service. The certificate must give the details set out in **r. 6.17(3)** (**r. 6.17(2)(a)**).

Procedural checklist 5   Claim under standard Part 8 procedure

See **chapter 13**.

Issue	Issue claim on form N208 (**PD 8A, para. 4.2**). At same time, file evidence in support of claim (**CPR, r. 8.5(1)**; **PD 8A, para. 7.1**).
Fee	Part 8 claims are likely to be non-money claims for which the fee is £528 in the High Court, £308 in the County Court (**CPFO, fee 1.5**).
Service	Serve claim form (form N208), form for acknowledging service (form N210), and evidence in support of claim (**CPR, r. 8.5(4)**). Forms for defending or admitting the claim are not required (**rr. 7.8(2)** and **8.9(b)(ii)**). Usual rules for service, set out in **Part 6** apply.
Time for service	The claim must be served within four months after issue, if it is served in the jurisdiction, or six months after issue, if it is served out of the jurisdiction (**r. 7.5**).
Acknowledgment	Defendant should file acknowledgment (form N210), verified by a statement of truth (**r. 22.1(1)(d)**) within 14 days after service of claim form, and serve copies of form N210 on other parties at the same time (**r. 8.3(1)**).
Objecting to Part 8 procedure	At same time as filing acknowledgment, defendant may file and serve statement of reasons for objecting to Part 8 procedure (**CPR, r. 8.8(1)**; **PD 8A, para. 5.3**).
Responding to claim	At the same time as acknowledging service, the defendant should file and serve evidence in opposition to the claim (**CPR, r. 8.5(3)** and **(4)**). If he fails to do this, he may participate in the hearing only if the court gives permission. However, judgment in default may not be entered against him (**rr. 8.1(5)** and **8.4**).
Evidence in reply	Within 14 days after service of defendant's evidence, claimant may file and serve evidence in reply (**r. 8.5(5)** and **(6)**).

Form of evidence	Evidence may be in the form of an affidavit or witness statement, or in the case of the claimant's evidence in support, in the claim form itself, provided it is verified by a statement of truth (**PD 8A, para. 7.2**).
Extending time for service of evidence	Parties may agree in writing to extensions of time for service of the defendant's evidence, and of the claimant's evidence in reply, of up to 14 days. A copy of the agreement to extend time for the defendant's evidence must be filed with the defendant's acknowledgment (**PD 8A, para. 7.5(2)(a)**). Any longer extensions may only be granted by the court (**PD 8A, para. 7.4**).
Case management	Part 8 claims are automatically allocated to the multi-track and parties do not need to complete directions questionnaires (**CPR, r. 8.9(c)**). Directions (including fixing a hearing date) will be given by the court either when the claim is issued or after the acknowledgment has been filed (**PD 8A, para. 6**).
Hearing fee	A multi-track hearing fee of £1,090 is payable (**CPFO, fee 2.1(a)**). Usually this fee is payable by the claimant on filing the pre-trial checklist.
Hearing	Most claims will be disposed of at a hearing based on the written evidence.

Procedural checklist 6   Approval of settlement or compromise involving a child or protected party, where sole purpose of claim is to obtain court approval

See **14.22**.

Part 8 claim form	Issue Part 8 claim form, including request for approval of the settlement and either set out the terms of the settlement or attach a draft consent order in form N292 (**PD 21, para. 5.1**).
Contents of Part 8 claim form	The claim form must include the following information (**PD 21, para. 5.1**): • whether and to what extent the defendant admits liability; • the age and occupation (if any) of the child or protected party; • the litigation friend's approval of the proposed settlement; • in a personal injury case only, the circumstances of the accident, any medical reports, a schedule of damages, any evidence or police reports in any related criminal proceedings or inquest and details of any prosecution; • where the settlement provides for periodical payments, the terms of the settlement or compromise. Alternatively the draft consent order should be attached to the claim form.
Part 8 Procedure	See **procedural checklist 5**.
Opinion on the merits	An opinion on the merits by counsel or solicitor should normally be supplied to the court (**PD 21, para. 5.2**).
Hearing	In proceedings involving a child, the application will normally be heard by a Master or District Judge (**PD 21, para. 5.6(1)**). In proceedings involving a protected party, the proceedings will normally be heard by a Master, Designated Civil Judge or his nominee (**PD 21, para. 5.6(2)**). In the Chancery Division, the application will be heard by a judge if the amount exceeds £100,000 (**PD 2B, para. 5.1 (a)**).
Privacy	The hearing of the application to approve the settlement may be in private where it involves the interests of a child or protected party (**CPR, r. 39.2(3)(d)**; **PD 39A, para. 1.6**).

Procedural checklist 7   Claims to controlled or executed goods

See **14.75** to **14.79**.

(a) Notice to enforcement agent or officer: preliminary steps

Notice to enforcement agent or officer	The person claiming ownership of goods taken or intended to be taken by the enforcement agent or officer should notify the enforcement agent or officer of his claim, and give his address for service (**CPR, rr. 85.4(1), 85.6(1)**).

Enforcement agent's or officer's notice to judgment creditor	Enforcement agent or officer must notify judgment creditor and any other person making a claim to the goods within three days of receipt of notice of claim (**rr. 85.4(2)**, **85.6(2)**).
Response from judgment creditor	Within seven days, judgment creditor and any other person making a claim to the goods must give notice in writing to the enforcement agent or officer whether he admits or disputes the claim (**rr. 85.4(3)**, **85.6(3)**). The enforcement agent or officer then notifies the claimant within three days of receiving this notice whether the claim is disputed or admitted (**rr. 85.4(4)**, **85.6(4)**). If the claim is disputed, the claimant must apply to the court.

(b) Application to the court

Application	Application is made by application notice (form N244) (**r. 85.3**). Claimant to controlled goods must also make required payments in accordance with Tribunals, Courts and Enforcement Act 2007, sch. 12, para. 60(4)(a) (**CPR, r. 85.5(6)**).
Fee	£155 (**CPFO, fee 2.4**).
Evidence in support	A witness statement must be filed and served: • specifying the money or goods claimed; • specifying the grounds for the claim; and • enclosing copies of any supporting documents (**CPR, rr. 85.5(2)**, **85.7(2)**).
Service	The application notice and supporting witness statement and documents must be served on all persons asserting a claim to the property and the enforcement agent or officer.
Court hearing	The application will be referred to a Master or District Judge for hearing (**rr. 85.5(7)** and **(8)**, **35.7(5)** and **(6)**).

Procedural checklist 8   Stakeholder claims and applications

See **14.78**.

Jurisdiction	A person ('the stakeholder'), who is under a liability in respect of a debt, money, goods or chattels to which competing claims are made by two or more persons may apply for a direction from the court as to whom the debt or money should be paid or the goods or chattels given (**CPR, rr. 86.1** and **86.2**).
Application	Application is made by a Part 8 Claim form if there are no existing proceedings, or by application notice in an existing claim. The application must be supported by a witness statement showing that the applicant: • claims no interest in the subject matter in dispute, other than for charges or costs; • does not collude with any of the claimants to the subject matter of the application; and • is willing to pay or transfer that subject matter into court or to dispose of it as the court may direct (**r. 86.2(4)**).
Service	The stakeholder must serve the claim form or application notice (**r. 86.2(5)**).
Respondent's evidence	The respondent served with the application notice must serve on the stakeholder a witness statement specifying the goods claimed and the grounds for the claim (**r. 86.2(6)**).
Hearing	The application will then be referred to a Master or District Judge for directions and hearing (**rr. 86.2(7)** and **86.3** to **86.5**).

Procedural checklist 9   Application for joinder

See **14.82 to 14.85.**

Timing	If joinder is sought before service of claim form, the court's permission is not required. If joinder is sought after service of the claim form, application must be made for the court's permission.
Application notice	Form N244. Apply for new party to be added as claimant/defendant, or for new party to be substituted for existing party, or for existing party to be removed and also, in each case, for permission to amend statement of case. Attach draft of order sought and draft of proposed amended statement of case. Set out brief reasons for application.
Consent of new party	Where party to be added or substituted is a claimant, file and serve, with the application notice, the signed written consent of the new party (**PD 19A, para. 2.1**).
Evidence	Application to add or substitute a party must be supported by evidence setting out the proposed new party's interest in or connection with the claim (**PD 19A, para. 1.3**). The evidence must be filed and served with the application notice.
Fee	£155 (**CPFO, fee 2.4**); for consent application £50 (**CPFO, fee 2.5**).
Service	The application notice, attachments and evidence in support must be served on all existing parties and any proposed new party as soon as practicable after filing and at least three clear days before the hearing date (**CPR, r. 23.7**).
Costs	In contested applications, parties should file and serve costs schedules in form N260 24 hours before hearing (**PD 44, para. 9.5**).
Hearing	Consent applications may be dealt with without a hearing.
After the hearing	Comply with directions. If permission is given, these will normally require the applicant to file the amended claim form and particulars of claim within 14 days of the order, to serve the new defendant with the existing statements of case, the amended claim form and particulars of claim, a response pack and a copy of the order.
Limitation	A new defendant does not become a party to the proceedings for the purpose of the Limitation Act 1980 until served with the claim form (**PD 19A, para. 3.3**).

Procedural checklist 10   Application to extend time for service of claim form

See **15.30.**

Application notice	Form N244. The application is for the period within which the claim form may be served to be extended to a specific date. Brief reasons for the application should be included in form N244.
Evidence in support	Evidence in support must be filed with form N244 and will usually either be set out in the notice of application itself or in a witness statement. The evidence must state all the circumstances relied on; the date of issue of the claim; the expiry date of any extension already granted under **CPR, r. 7.6**; and a full explanation of why the claim form has not been served (**PD 7A, para. 8.2**). Where the application is without notice, the evidence must also state why notice has not been given (**CPR, r. 25.3(3)**).
Without notice	Application will usually be made without notice, as the defendant is not yet on the record (**CPR, r. 7.6(4)(b)**). Because the application is without notice to the defendant, the claimant must make full and frank disclosure of all relevant facts.

Fee	£50 (**CPFO, fee 2.5**).
Hearing	As the application is made without notice, there will not normally be a hearing. However, where the application is made shortly before expiry of the period for service of the claim form and where the cause of action has become time-barred since the date of issue of the claim form, it is desirable that the application should be dealt with by an urgent hearing.
Service of order	A copy of any order made without notice to the defendant, whether extending time for service of the claim form or refusing to do so, must be served on the defendant, together with form N244 and any evidence in support. The order should contain a statement of the defendant's right to apply to set aside or vary the order within seven clear days of service of the order (**CPR, r. 23.9**).

Procedural checklist 11   Application for permission to serve claim form out of jurisdiction

See **16.44**.

Claim form	Claimant has the choice of whether to issue the claim form before or after seeking permission to serve outside the jurisdiction (see **16.44**).
Application	If a claim form is issued first, the application is for permission to serve outside the jurisdiction, and **fee 2.5(a)** (see 'Fee' below) is payable on the application. If a claim form is not issued first, the application is for permission to issue and to serve the claim form, and **fee 1.8(a)** (see 'Fee' below) is payable on the application.
Application notice	Form N244. Apply for permission under **CPR, r. 6.36**, to serve the defendant at his address out of the jurisdiction because [state grounds of **PD 6B, Para. 3.1**, relied on; claimant believes his claim has a reasonable prospect of success; state defendant's address, or where it is believed he is, or it is likely he may be. Where **PD 6B, para. 3.1(3)**, is relied on state also that it is believed that there is a real issue which it is reasonable for the court to try between the claimant and an existing defendant]. Indicate that the claimant wishes to have the matter dealt with without a hearing, and that no notice should be given to the defendant.
Evidence in support	Evidence in form of witness statement must be filed with form N244. Evidence must show which paragraph of **PD 6B, para. 3.1** applies to the claim; that the claimant has a reasonable prospect of success; why England and Wales is the proper place to bring the claim and state the defendant's address, or at least the country in which he may be found. Where **PD 6B, para. 3.1(3)**, is relied on set out evidence for belief that there is a real issue which it is reasonable for the court to try between the claimant and an existing defendant (**CPR, r. 6.37**).
Without notice to defendant	Application will be made without notice to the defendant. In the RCJ, Queen's Bench Division, leave the application notice and supporting evidence in the Queen's Bench Masters' Support Unit, room E07. In the Chancery Division, all papers should be filed at Counter 6 (Rolls Building, Masters' appointments section). The papers will be placed before a Master or District Judge, who will note the order on the papers and on the court file. In the Commercial and Mercantile courts, all papers should be filed at Counter 10 (Judges' Listing). Because the application is made without notice to the defendant, the claimant must make full and frank disclosure of all relevant facts.
Fee	For permission to issue and serve: £55 (**CPFO, fee 1.8(a)**). If claim form has already been issued: £100 (**Fee 2.5(a)**).
Hearing	As the application is made without notice, there will not normally be a hearing.

Procedural checklist 12   Admitting a claim and requesting time to pay

See **chapter 17.**

Type of claim and admission	Step to be taken by defendant	Step to be taken by claimant where claimant accepts defendant's offer	Step to be taken by claimant where claimant rejects defendant's offer
Specified sum. Admitted in whole; defendant seeking time to pay (**CPR, r. 14.9**).	Return form N9A to claimant (**r. 14.4(2)**) within 14 days after service of the particulars of claim (**r. 14.2**).	File request for judgment, form N225, reflecting defendant's offer for payment. No fee is payable (**CPFO, notes to fee 2.5**). Court will enter judgment for the amount of the claim and costs, and for payment at the time and rate specified in defendant's request for time to pay (**r. 14.9**).	File request for judgment form N225, and N9A giving notice that claimant does not accept defendant's offer. No fee is payable (**CPFO, notes to fee 2.5**). Court will enter judgment for the amount of the claim and decide time and rate for payment (**r. 14.10(2) and (4)**), and will issue decision on form N30(2). Either party can object to the determination within 14 days after receipt of form N30(2).
Specified sum. Admitted in whole; defendant not seeking time to pay (**r. 14.4**).	Return form N9A to claimant (**r. 14.4(2)**) within 14 days after service of the particulars of claim (**r. 14.2**).	Claimant files request for judgment (form N225) and specifies the times and rates for payment. No fee is payable (**CPFO, notes to fee 2.5**). The court enters judgment as requested by claimant (**r. 14.4(4) to (6)**).	
Specified sum. Admitted in part, but defendant seeks time to pay (**r. 14.5**).	Return forms N9A and N9B to the court (**r. 14.5(2)**) within 14 days after service of the particulars of claim (**r. 14.2**). Court sends forms N9A, N9B and N255A to claimant, requiring claimant to notify response to the court within 14 days (**r. 14.5(3)**). If defendant does not reply within 14 days, claim stayed (**r. 14.5(5)**).	Within 14 days of receipt of forms N9A, N9B and N255A, from court, file request for judgment (form N255A), reflecting defendant's offer for payment. Court will enter judgment for the amount admitted and costs, and for payment at the time and rate specified in defendant's request for time to pay (**r. 14.9**).	Within 14 days of receipt of court notice, file request for judgment (form N255A), giving notice either: • that claimant does not accept defendant's partial admission, in which case the claim will proceed as a defended claim, or • that claimant accepts the partial admission in settlement of the claim but does not accept defendant's proposals for payment. The court will then enter judgment for the amount admitted and will calculate a rate of payment. It will notify the parties of its decision in form N30(2). Either party can object to the determination within 14 days after receipt of form N30(2) (**rr. 14.10 to 14.13**).

Specified sum. Admitted in part; defendant does not seek time to pay (**r. 14.5**).	Return forms N9A and N9B to the court (**r. 14.5(2)**) within 14 days after service of the particulars of claim (**r. 14.2**). Court sends forms N9A, N9B and N255A, requiring claimant to notify response to court within 14 days (**r. 4.5(3)**). If defendant does not reply within 14 days, claim stayed (**r. 14.5(5)**).	Within 14 days of receipt of forms N9A, N9B and N255A, file request for judgment (form N225A), reflecting defendant's offer for payment. No fee is payable (**CPFO, notes to fee 2.5**). Court enters judgment for amount offered by defendant and costs to be paid by the date or at the rate specified in form N255A (**r. 14.5(7)** to (**9**)).	File form N255A at court, indicating that partial admission is rejected and case will proceed as a defended claim.
Unspecified sum. Defendant admits liability without saying how much is admitted (**r. 14.6**).	Return form N9C to court (**r. 14.6(2)**) within 14 days after service of the particulars of claim (**r. 14.2**). Court will forward form N9C to claimant, together with form N226 (notice of admission) (**r. 14.6(3)**). If claimant does not respond within 14 days, claim will be stayed (**r. 14.6(5)**).	Within 14 days of receipt of forms N9C and N226, file completed N226 asking the court to enter judgment for an amount to be decided by the court and costs. No fee is payable (**CPFO, notes to fee 2.5**). Court will enter judgment and give directions, either allocating the claim to the small claims track or directing a disposal hearing (**r. 14.6(6)**).	
Unspecified sum. Defendant admits liability and offers a fixed sum in settlement of it, without seeking time to pay (**r. 14.7**).	Return form N9C to court (**r. 14.7(2)**) within 14 days after service of the particulars of claim (**r. 14.2**). Court will forward form N9C to claimant, together with form N226 (notice of admission).	Within 14 days of receipt of notice from the court, file form N226, accepting the offer. No fee is payable (**CPFO, notes to fee 2.5**). Court will enter judgment in accordance with the offer (**r. 14.7(6)** to (**8**)). Failing to file N226 results in a stay (**r. 14.7(4)**).	Within 14 days of receipt of notice from the court, file form N226, notifying court that offer of sum in settlement of claim rejected. No fee is payable (**CPFO, notes to fee 2.5**). Judgment will be entered for an amount to be decided by the court and costs. The court will give case management directions (**rr. 14.7(9) and 14.8**).
Unspecified sum. Defendant admits liability, offers a fixed sum in settlement and asks to pay by instalments or at a future date (**r. 14.7**).	Return form N9C to court (**r. 14.7(2)**) within 14 days after service of the particulars of claim (**r. 14.2**). Court will forward form N9C to claimant, together with form N226 (notice of admission). If claimant does not respond within 14 days, claim will be stayed (**r. 14.7(4)**).	If the offer is accepted in full, including the proposals for payment, file request for payment (form N226) and court will enter judgment for amount offered and costs at the time and rate specified in defendant's request for time to pay (**r. 14.9**). No fee is payable (**CPFO, notes to fee 2.5**).	If claimant rejects the amount offered, file request for judgment form N226. No fee is payable (**CPFO, notes to fee 2.5**). Court enters judgment for an amount to be decided by the court and costs (**r. 14.7(9)**). If claimant accepts the amount offered, but not the proposals for payment, file form N226. The court will enter judgment and calculate the rate of payment, and will notify the parties of its decision in form N30(2). Either party can object within 14 days after receipt of form N30(2) (**r. 14.10**).

Procedural checklist 13 Time limits for responding to claim by acknowledging service and/or filing a defence

See **chapter 18**.

Step to be taken	Place of service of claim form	Time limit
Acknowledgment to be filed at court	Within the jurisdiction.	14 days after service of particulars of claim (whether or not particulars of claim served with claim form) (**CPR, r. 10.3(1)**).
	Out of the jurisdiction under **r. 6.32** or **6.33** in Scotland or Northern Ireland, or in a Convention territory within Europe or a member State.	21 days after service of particulars of claim (**r. 6.35(2)** and **(3)**).
	Out of the jurisdiction under **r. 6.33** in a Convention territory outside Europe.	31 days after service of particulars of claim (**r. 6.35(4)**).
	Out of the jurisdiction with permission under **r. 6.36**.	Court will specify the time for acknowledging service, calculated by reference to the table at the end of **PD 6B** (**CPR, r. 6.37(5)**; **PD 6B, para. 6.2**).
Filing of defence at court, where no acknowledgment filed	Within the jurisdiction.	14 days after service of particulars of claim (**CPR, r. 15.4(1)(a)**).
	Out of the jurisdiction under **r. 6.32** or **6.33** in Scotland or Northern Ireland, or in a Convention territory within Europe or a member State.	21 days after service of particulars of claim (**r. 6.35(2)** and **(3)**).
	Out of the jurisdiction under **r. 6.33** in a Convention territory outside Europe.	31 days after service of particulars of claim (**r. 6.35(4)**).
	Out of the jurisdiction with permission under **r. 6.36**.	Court will specify the time for acknowledging service, calculated by reference to the table at the end of **PD 6B** (**CPR, r. 6.37(5)**; **PD 6B, para. 6.2**).
Filing of defence at court, following filing of acknowledgment	Within the jurisdiction.	28 days after service of particulars of claim (**CPR, r. 15.4(1)(b)**).
	Out of the jurisdiction under **r. 6.32** or **6.33** in Scotland or Northern Ireland, or in a Convention territory within Europe or a member State.	35 days after service of particulars of claim (**r. 6.35(2)** and **(3)**).
	Out of the jurisdiction **r. 6.33** in a Convention territory outside Europe.	45 days after service of particulars of claim (**r. 6.35(4)**).
	Out of the jurisdiction with permission under **r. 6.36**.	Court will specify the time for acknowledging service, calculated by reference to the table at the end of **PD 6B**, plus an additional 14 days (**CPR, r. 6.37(5)**; **PD 6B, para. 6.2**).

Procedural checklist 14 Procedure for disputing the court's jurisdiction

See **chapter 19**.

Acknowledgment	File acknowledgment of service within 14 days after service of particulars of claim, if served in the jurisdiction, within 21 days after service of the particulars of claim, if served in Europe under **CPR, r. 6.33**, or within the period given in the court order, if served out of the jurisdiction with the court's permission, under **r. 6.36** (**r. 11(2)**). Tick only the 'intention to contest the jurisdiction' box. See **procedural checklist 13**.

Application — time	Within 14 days after filing an acknowledgment (28 days in the Commercial and Mercantile Courts) make an application under **Part 23** for an order that the court has no jurisdiction to try the claim (**rr. 11(4), 58.7, 59.6**).
Extension of time	If more time is needed, apply under **r. 3.1(2)(a)** for an extension of the time limit laid down in **r. 11(4)**. An extension of time for service of the defence will not carry with it an extension of time for an application to dispute the jurisdiction (*Montrose Investments Ltd v Orion Nominees Ltd* [2001] CP Rep 109).
Application notice	Form N244. Where service out of the jurisdiction is contested, application is for any order giving permission for service out of the jurisdiction under **r. 6.36** to be set aside, for service of the claim form to be set aside and for the proceedings to be stayed.
Evidence in support	Must be filed and served with form N244.
Fee	£155 (**CPFO, fee 2.4**).
Service	On defendant as soon as practicable after filing application notice, and at least three days before hearing (**CPR, r. 23.7(1)**).
Costs	Both parties should file and serve costs schedules in form N260 24 hours before hearing (**PD 44, para. 9.5**).
Defence	Do not file defence before hearing (**CPR, r. 11(9)(a)**). If the application is unsuccessful, the defendant must file a further acknowledgment of service if intending to take part in the proceedings, and then the court must give directions for filing and service of the defence (**r. 11.7(c)**). Claimant cannot enter default judgment (**r. 12.3**).

Procedural checklist 15   Request for entry of judgment in default

See **chapter 20**, especially **20.3** to **20.6**.

Claim form	Serve claim form on defendant in accordance with **CPR, r. 6.3**.
Certificate of service of claim form	If claim form is served by claimant rather than court, file certificate of service of claim form, within 21 days after service of claim form (**r. 6.17(2)(a)**), unless all defendants have filed acknowledgments within that time, in which case there is no need to file a certificate of service.
Particulars of claim	Serve particulars of claim, either with claim form or within 14 days after service of claim form, and within period of validity of the claim form (**r. 7.4(1)** and **(2)**).
Filing particulars of claim	Unless a copy of the particulars of claim has already been filed, within seven days of service of the particulars on the defendant, file a copy of the particulars (**r. 7.4(3)**).
Failure to respond: request for judgment	Wait 14 days after service of particulars of claim (whether served with claim form or later) (**rr. 10.3** and **15.4**). (For time limits where service effected out of the jurisdiction, see **procedural checklist 13**.) If neither acknowledgment of service nor defence filed by then, file request for default judgment in form N205A or N225 (for specified sum) or N205B or N227A (for unspecified sum) (**r. 12.4(1)(a)**; **PD 12, para. 3**). No fee is payable (**CPFO, notes to fee 2.5**).
Failure to file defence: request for judgment	If acknowledgment filed within 14 days after service of particulars of claim, wait until 28 days after service of particulars of claim (**CPR, rr. 10.3** and **15.4**). (For time limits where service effected out of the jurisdiction, see **procedural checklist 13**.) If defence not filed by then, file request for default judgment inform N205A or N225 (for specified sum) or N205B or N227A (for unspecified sum) (**r. 12.4(1)(b)**; **PD 12, para. 3**). No fee is payable (**CPFO, notes to fee 2.5**).
Calculating time	The periods of 14 and 28 days above should be calculated to exclude the date of service of the particulars of claim but to include the date of filing of the acknowledgment or service of the particulars of claim (**CPR, r. 2.8(3)(b)**), and must take into account the deemed dates of service in **rr. 6.14** and **6.26** (see **15.36** and **15.42**).

Procedural checklist 16   Application for entry of judgment in default

See **chapter 20**, especially **20.8** to **20.9**.

When required	Claims for costs (other than fixed costs); claims for delivery up (where the defendant has not offered the alternative of paying the value of the goods claimed); claims by one spouse or civil partner against the other in tort and claims against children and protected parties. Also, the following cases where the defendant has not filed an acknowledgment: claims where service has been effected out of the jurisdiction under **CPR, r. 6.32** or **6.33**, or on a defendant domiciled in a Convention territory or Regulation State; claims against States, diplomats and bodies granted immunity under the International Organisations Acts 1968 and 1981.
Preliminary steps	• Serve claim form and particulars of claim and file certificate of service **(procedural checklist 15)**. • In an application against a child or protected party, apply for a litigation friend to be appointed under **CPR, r. 21.6**.
Time	Wait 14 days after service of particulars of claim (whether served with claim form or later) **(rr. 10.3** and **15.4)**. If neither acknowledgment of service nor defence filed by then, make application under **Part 23**. If acknowledgment filed within 14 days after service of particulars of claim, wait until 28 days after service of particulars of claim **(rr. 10.3** and **15.4)** before making application under **Part 23**. Time limits to be calculated as in **procedural checklist 15**. (For time limits where service effected out of the jurisdiction, see **procedural checklist 13**.)
Application notice	Form N244. Application is for judgment to be entered against the defendant on the ground that he has not filed an acknowledgment of service or defence, as the case may be. Where application not on notice, state on form N244 that claimant wishes to have the matter dealt with without a hearing. Where the defendant is an individual, state his/her date of birth, if known.
Evidence in support	An application must be supported by evidence if it is for default judgment • against a child or protected party; • in a claim in tort between spouses or civil partners; • against a State; • against a defendant who was served outside the jurisdiction, or inside the jurisdiction when domiciled in a Convention territory or Regulation State, and who has not acknowledged service (see **r. 12.11(4)(a)**) **(r. 12.11(3)** and **PD 12, para. 4)**.
Service of evidence	Evidence in support need not be served on defendant who failed to file an acknowledgment of service **(CPR, r. 12.11(2))**.
Notice	Generally the application is with notice, but will be without notice where the claim was served under the **Civil Jurisdiction and Judgments Act 1982** or the Brussels I Regulation or where application is made against a State and in either case the defendant has failed to file an acknowledgment **(CPR, r. 12.11(4)** and **(5))**.
Fee	£155 for application on notice **(CPFO, fee 2.4)**; £50 where application without notice **(CPFO, fee 2.5)**.
Service of N244	Where application on notice, serve defendant as soon as practicable after filing application notice, and at least three days before hearing **(CPR, r. 23.7(1))**.
Costs	Where application on notice, both parties should file and serve costs schedules in form N260 24 hours before hearing **(PD 44, para. 9.5)**. The court will not summarily assess the costs of a child or protected party, unless the solicitor acting for the child or protected party has waived the right to further costs **(PD 44, para. 9.9(1))**.
Hearing	Normally before Master or District Judge. Where the application is made without notice, there will not normally be a hearing.

Procedural checklist 17   Counterclaim (Part 20)

See **chapter 28**.

Timing	Generally, at the same time as filing the defence in order to avoid the need for permission (**CPR, r. 20.4(2)**). Can be made up to trial, but obtaining permission gets progressively more difficult.
Forms	N211. Simple counterclaims can be made on forms N9B or N9D.
Title	Must comply with **PD 20, paras 7.1** to **7.11**.
Issue	Issue fee is payable when the counterclaim is filed (**CPFO, fee 1.7**).
Pleading	Particulars of the counterclaim, verified by a statement of truth, can be set out in a counterclaim, but if the defendant also intends to defend the main proceedings, the defence and counterclaim should normally form one document with the counterclaim following the defence (**PD 20, para. 6.1**).
Counterclaim against a person other than the claimant	Most counterclaims are made against the claimant, but it is possible to bring a counterclaim against a person other than a claimant (**CPR, r. 20.5**). Permission is always required (**r. 20.5(1)**), and, unless the court otherwise directs, the application is made without notice (**r. 20.5(2)**). The new party is added as an additional party (**r. 20.5(1)**).
Permission to issue	Required if a defendant wishes to file a counterclaim after filing a defence (**r. 20.4(2)**). Issue application notice with written evidence in support: <ul><li>stating the stage the main proceedings have reached;</li><li>stating the nature of the counterclaim;</li><li>summarising the facts on which the counterclaim is based;</li><li>stating the name and address of the defendant to the counterclaim;</li><li>explaining any delay where this is a factor; and</li><li>providing a timetable of the steps in the claim to date.</li></ul> As **rr. 20.5(2)** and **20.7(5)** do not apply to this situation, the application is made on notice to the claimant.
Documents to be served	Claim form; counterclaim or defence and counterclaim.
Service	**CPR, Part 6**, applies (**chapter 15**).
Response	Acknowledgment of service (**Part 10**) does not apply (**r. 20.4(3)**). The claimant should file and serve a defence to counterclaim or a reply and defence to counterclaim within 14 days of deemed service of the counterclaim (**rr. 15.4(1)**, **20.3(1)**).
Default judgment	May be entered (**CPR, r. 12.3(2)**; **PD 20, para. 3**).
Directions	The effect of **rr. 20.3(2)(c)** and **20.13**, together with **PD 20, para. 5.1**, is that the relevant directions governing counterclaims are (unless the court gives special directions for the counterclaim) those given in the main proceedings.

Procedural checklist 18   Additional claim (against third party)

See **chapter 29**.

Timing	Generally, before or at the same time as filing the defence in order to avoid the need for permission (**CPR, r. 20.7(3)**). Can be made up to trial, but obtaining permission gets progressively more difficult.
Form	Additional claim form, form N211.
Title of claim	Must comply with **PD 20, paras 7.1** to **7.11**.
Issue	Issue fee is the same as for Part 7 claim forms (see **CPFO, fee 1**). Issue takes place when the claim form is sealed and on the date entered by the court on the claim form (**CPR, r. 20.7(2)** and **r. 7.2(2)**).

Pleading	Particulars of the additional claim must be contained in or served with the claim form (**r. 20.7(4)**), and must be verified by a statement of truth in the form '[I believe] [the defendant believes] that the facts stated in this statement of case are true.' (**PD 20, para. 4.2**).
Permission to issue	Required if a defendant wishes to issue an additional claim after filing a defence (**CPR, r. 20.7(3)**).
	Issue application notice (see **procedural checklist 19**) with written evidence in support:
	• stating the stage the main proceedings have reached;
	• stating the nature of the additional claim, question or relief;
	• summarising the facts on which the additional claim is based;
	• stating the name and address of the third party;
	• explaining any delay where this is a factor; and
	• providing a timetable of the steps in the claim to date.
	Unless the court otherwise directs, the application is made without notice (**r. 20.7(5)**).
Documents to be served on third party	Additional claim form (N211); notes for defendant on replying to the additional claim form (N211C); particulars of the additional claim (either contained in or served with the claim form) (**r. 20.7(4)**); forms for defending and admitting the claim (forms N9A and N9B or N9C and N9D as appropriate); form for acknowledging service (form N213) (**r. 20.12(1)**); copies of every statement of case previously served (**r. 20.12(1)(d)(i)**); and such other documents as the court may direct (**r. 20.12(1)(d)(ii)**).
Service	**CPR, Part 6**, applies (**chapter 15**).
Time to serve	An additional claim issued without permission must be served within 14 days after the additional claim is issued by the court (**r. 20.8(1)(b)**).
	Any order for permission will give directions for service (**r. 20.8(3)**).
Effect of service	Third party becomes a party to the proceedings on being served (**r. 20.10(1)**).
Service on other parties	Copies of the additional claim form must be served on all existing parties (**r. 20.12(2)**).
Response	Third party must acknowledge service or file a defence within 14 days of deemed service (**rr. 6.14**, **7.5**, **9.2**, **10.3**, **14.2**, **15.4** and **20.3(1)**).
Defence	A defence to the additional claim must be filed within 14 days of deemed service of the additional claim, or within 28 days if an acknowledgment of service is filed (**r. 15.4**). Time may be extended by consent for up to 28 days (**r. 15.5**). A copy of the defence to the additional claim must be served on every other party (**r. 15.6**). It must be verified by a statement of truth (**PD 15, paras 2.1**, **2.2**).
Default judgment	Subject to **r. 20.11(2)**, default judgment is not available (**r. 20.3(3)**). Instead, if there is no response within the prescribed period, the third party is deemed to admit the additional claim and is bound by any judgment or decision in the main proceedings (**r. 20.11(2)(a)**). If default judgment is given against the defendant and if the defendant satisfies that judgment, the defendant can enter default judgment for a contribution or indemnity against the third party by filing a request (**r. 20.11(3)**). Otherwise, default judgment against a third party is possible only with permission (**r. 20.11(3)**, **(4)**).
Directions	After a defence to an additional claim is filed the court will list the matter for case management directions (**r. 20.13(1)** and **PD 20, para. 5.1**). The court:
	• will ensure, so far as practicable, that the main proceedings and additional claim are managed together (**r. 20.13(2)**);
	• may treat the hearing as a summary judgment hearing (**PD 20, para. 5.3**);
	• may dismiss the additional claim;
	• may require the additional claim to be dealt with separately from the main proceedings (**CPR, r. 20.9(1)(c)**);
	• may give directions about the way the claim should be dealt with (**PD 20, para. 5.3**);
	• may give directions as to the third party's involvement at trial; and
	• may give directions about the extent to which the third party will be bound by any judgment or decision in the main proceedings.

Procedural checklist 19   Interim application without notice

See **chapter 32**, especially **32.7** to **32.11**.

Application notice	Issue and file form N244, stating whether a hearing is sought (**CPR, r. 23.6**). Interim injunction applications should be on form N16A.
Evidence in support	Normally required. In addition to covering evidence required for the order sought (**PD 25A, para. 3.3**), written evidence must: • state reasons why notice was not given (**CPR, r. 25.3(3)**); • where secrecy is not essential, state what steps have been taken to give informal notice to the respondent (**PD 25A, para. 4.3(3)**).
	Usually in the form of witness statements, but affidavits are required for freezing and search orders (**PDA 25A, para. 3.1**).
	Applicant is under a duty of full and frank disclosure, which includes a duty to disclose adverse matters which could be discovered on making reasonable inquiries.
Fee	£50 (**CPFO, fee 2.5**).
Draft order	Usually required for without notice applications as most are complex. If application is for an interim injunction, use form PF 39 CH (intended actions) or PF 40 CH (after issue). Freezing and search orders should follow the standard forms in **PD 25A**.
Undertakings	Should be incorporated into the order as required (e.g. to issue and serve a claim form (**CPR, r. 25.2(3)**), to file and serve written evidence, to pay damages (injunctions)).
Skeleton argument	Required for most High Court applications dealt with by judges. Should state how the requirements for the relief sought are satisfied. File two clear days before the hearing (if possible).
Arrange hearing	Urgent applications: emergency telephone number for the High Court is (020) 7947 6000. See **37.6** and **PD 25A, para. 4.5**.
Hearing	Explain, among other things: • why without notice; • whether any informal notice has been given, and why; • points relevant to the duty of full and frank disclosure; • any variations on standard-form orders.
Note of hearing	Advocate should produce note of the hearing (see **32.8**).
Order	Should include a statement of the respondent's right to apply to set aside (**CPR, r. 23.9(3)**). It also often provides for listing a hearing to review to be heard on notice. Application notice, evidence in support and note of the hearing should be served with the order (see **32.8**).

Procedural checklist 20   Interim application with notice

See **chapter 32**, especially **32.12** to **32.31**.

Timing	As soon as it becomes apparent that it is desirable or necessary (**PD 23A, para. 2.7**). Other than urgent applications, they can only be made once applicant has come on the record. Applications can be made after judgment (**CPR, r. 25.2**).
Application notice	Form N244, which must be filed (**r. 23.3**). It must state the order sought and the reason for applying (**r. 23.6**) and provide a time estimate. Interim injunction applications should be on form N16A.
Draft order	Not required for simple applications. Drafts of more complex orders should be brought to the hearing (**PD 23A, para. 12.1**) together with a copy on electronic storage device.
Evidence in support	Consider whether evidence is required. If so, consider whether to use the box in question 10 of N244, witness statements, affidavits or statements of case. Must be served and filed (if not already done) with the N244.

Combined applications	Are encouraged (**CPR, r. 1.4(2)(i)**), and should be combined with any existing case management hearing (**PD 23A, para. 2.8**).
Fee	£155 (**CPFO, fee 2.4**).
Service	On respondent as soon as practicable after N244 is filed, and at least three clear days before hearing (**CPR, r. 23.7(1)**) (unless some other period is prescribed, such as for summary judgment and interim payments).
Cross-applications	Respondent may issue a cross-application returnable at the same hearing date as the applicant's application. This may require relisting of both applications if the original time estimate is insufficient for both.
Directions	Sometimes directions are made for filing and serving evidence and skeleton arguments in the application (**PD 23A, para. 9.2**).
Respondent's written evidence	Serve and file in accordance with directions, if any, or as soon as possible (**PD 23A, para. 9.4**) and in sufficient time to avoid the need to adjourn.
Applicant's evidence in reply	Serve and file in accordance with directions, if any, or as soon as possible (**PD 23A, para. 9.5**) and in sufficient time to avoid the need to adjourn.
Application bundles	In substantial applications bundles of material documents should be prepared (usually at least two clear days before the hearing, see **32.17**).
Skeleton arguments	Not mandatory for applications before Circuit Judges, Masters and District Judges, but if used should be served and filed the day before the hearing. Usually required for applications before High Court judges, where they should be filed two clear days before the hearing (see **32.18**).
Costs schedules	Both parties should file and serve costs schedules in form N260 24 hours before the hearing (**PD 44, para. 9.5**). (But see **paras 9.8** and **9.9**, where the receiving party is publicly funded, or a child or protected party.)
Hearing	Most applications should be listed for hearing by a Master or District Judge. Injunctions should usually be heard by judges. Search orders should normally be dealt with by High Court judges. Most applications are heard in chambers even if technically they are dealt with in public. The court may review the case and give case management directions (**PD 23A, para. 2.9**).
Costs orders	If the hearing is less than a day, usually there will be a summary assessment (**PD 44, para. 9.2**).

Procedural checklist 21   Application for striking out

See **chapter 33**.

General procedure	Follow **procedural checklist 20**.
Application notice	E.g.: 'for an order that the particulars of claim be struck out under **CPR, r. 3.4**, and judgment be entered for the defendant with costs because the particulars of claim disclose no reasonable grounds for bringing the claim [is an abuse of the court's process] [is likely to obstruct the just disposal of the proceedings]'.
Combined application	It is common to combine the various grounds in **CPR, r. 3.4**, in a single application, and also to seek summary judgment in the alternative.
Fee to Costs orders	See **procedural checklist 20**.
Claim totally without merit	If the court strikes out a claimant's statement of case and considers it is totally without merit, it must record that fact in the order (**r. 3.4(5)**), and consider making a civil restraint order (see **14.55**).

Procedural checklist 22   Application by party for summary judgment

See chapter 34.

Timing	After acknowledgment of service or filing defence (**34.2**).
	Generally before filing directions questionnaire (**PD 26, para. 5.3(1)**).
Application notice	Form N244. Apply for 'summary judgment under **CPR, Part 24**, and costs because the [claimant has no real prospect of succeeding on the claim/issue] or [defendant has no real prospect of successfully defending the claim/issue] and the applicant knows of no other reason why disposal of the claim or issue should await trial' (**PD 24, para. 2(3)**). If the application relates to specific issues, these must be identified (**CPR, r. 24.4(3)(b)**). Also add to the N244: 'Take notice that if the respondent wishes to rely on written evidence at the hearing, he must file and serve the written evidence at least seven days before the summary judgment hearing' (**PD 24, para. 2(5)**).
Evidence in support	Must be served and filed with the N244.
Combined applications	It is common to combine a summary judgment application with an application for striking out under **CPR, r. 3.4**, or for interim payment under **r. 25.7**.
Fee	£155 (**CPFO, fee 2.4**).
Service	On respondent at least 14 days before hearing (**CPR, r. 24.4(3)**).
Respondent's written evidence	Serve and file at least seven days before hearing (**r. 24.5(2)**).
Applicant's evidence in reply	File and serve at least three days before the hearing (**r. 24.5(2)**).
Main proceedings	No need to file defence (**r. 24.4(2)**). Claimant cannot enter default judgment if defendant is applying for summary judgment (**r. 12.3(3)(a)(ii)**). Court will not normally allocate to a track before hearing application to strike out (**PD 26, para. 5.3(2)**).
Costs	Both parties should file and serve costs schedules in form N260 24 hours before the hearing (**PD 44, para. 9.5**).
Hearing	Normally before Master or District Judge (**PD 24, para. 3(1)**). In addition to determining the application, the court usually gives directions (**CPR, r. 24.6**).

Procedural checklist 23   Proposal by court for order for summary judgment

See 34.5.

Notice of date for hearing	At least 14 days before the hearing.
Written evidence	Both sides file and (unless the court otherwise orders) serve written evidence at least seven days before the hearing (**CPR, r. 24.5(3)(a)**).
Evidence in reply	Both sides may file and (unless the court otherwise orders) serve written evidence in reply at least three days before the hearing (**r. 24.5(3)(b)**).
Costs	Both parties should file and serve costs schedules in form N260 24 hours before the hearing (**PD 44, para. 9.5**).

Procedural checklist 24   Application for an order for interim payment

See **chapter 36**.

Timing	After period for filing acknowledgment of service (**CPR, r. 25.6(1)**). More than one application can be made (**r. 25.6(2)**).
Application notice	Form N244. Apply for 'an interim payment under **CPR, r. 25.7**, and costs because the [defendant has admitted liability] [the claimant has obtained judgment for damages to be assessed] [if the claim went to trial the claimant would obtain judgment for a substantial amount of money (other than costs) against the defendant] [the claim is for possession of land and if the claim went to trial the defendant would be held liable to pay the claimant a sum of money for occupation and use of the land while the claim is pending]'.
Evidence in support	Must be served and filed with the N244. It must deal with the matters set out in **PD 25B, para. 2.1**, and exhibit all documents in support, including (in personal injuries claims) medical reports (**para. 2.2**).
Combined applications	Interim payment applications are commonly combined with applications for summary judgment.
Fee	£155 (**CPFO, fee 2.4**).
Service	On respondent at least 14 days before hearing (**CPR, r. 25.6(3)**).
Respondent's written evidence	Serve and file at least seven days before hearing (**r. 25.6(4)**).
Applicant's evidence in reply	File and serve at least three days before the hearing (**r. 25.6(5)**).
Costs	Both parties should file and serve costs schedules in form N260 24 hours before the hearing (**PD 44, para. 9.5**).
Hearing	Normally before Master or District Judge (**PD 24, para. 3(1)**). In addition to determining the application, the court may give directions (**PD 23A, para. 2.9**).
Instalments	If an interim payment is payable by instalments, the order must comply with **PD 25B, para. 3**.
Trial	The fact that an interim payment has been made should not be mentioned to the trial judge until all questions on liability and quantum have been decided (**CPR, r. 25.9**), unless the defendant agrees.
Final judgment	Where an interim payment has previously been made, the final judgment must include details in a preamble, deduct the interim payments from the amount of the judgment, and make any necessary adjustments or orders for repayment (**PD 25B, para. 5**; **PD 40B, para. 6**).

Procedural checklist 25   Standard disclosure

See **chapter 50**, especially **50.4** to **50.9**. For menu disclosure see **50.10**.

When first retained	Inform clients of their duty to retain disclosable documents (*Rockwell Machine Tool Co. Ltd v E. P. Barrus (Concessionaires) Ltd* [1968] 1 WLR 693; **PD 31B, para. 7**).
Pre-action	Preliminary disclosure of documents should often take place in accordance with **PD Pre-action Conduct and Protocols** and any pre-action protocol applicable to the claim (**chapter 8**). This is not standard disclosure, but a means of providing the other side with the key documents to inform them of the nature and strength of the case.

Before first case management conference	Parties and legal representatives discuss use of technology in managing electronic documents (**PD 31B, para. 8**) and disclosing them (**para. 9**).
Timing for standard disclosure	In accordance with directions made by the court. In most fast track and multi-track claims directions are made when the claim is allocated to a track (**CPR, rr. 28.2(1), 28.3, 29.2(1)(a) and PD 29, para. 4**) or at the first case management conference (**CPR, r. 29.2(1)(b)**). These typically include directions for standard disclosure in fast track claims and personal injuries claims on the multi-track.
Normal directions	(1) Standard disclosure by 4 weeks after directions (**PD 28, para. 3.12**). (2) Requests for inspection of listed documents within seven days thereafter (**CPR, r. 31.15(a)**). (3) Inspection of documents, or provision of copies, within seven days thereafter (**r. 31.15(b) and (c)**).
Documents to be disclosed	Standard disclosure covers (**r. 31.6**) documents in a party's control (**r. 31.8**): (a) on which the disclosing party relies; (b) which adversely affect his own case; (c) which adversely affect another party's case; (d) which support another party's case; and (e) which are specified by a PD.
Documents	Anything on which information of any description is recorded (**r. 31.4**). Includes papers (whether written, pictures or photographs); video and sound recordings; computer records, files, mobile phone texts and emails; metadata; inscriptions on metal, wood and stone.
Control	A document is in a party's control (**r. 31.8**) if: (a) it is or was in his physical possession; (b) he has or has had a right to possession of it; or (c) he has or has had a right to inspect or take copies of it.
Search	Each party must make a reasonable search for disclosable documents (**r. 31.7**).
Method of giving disclosure	Usually by serving a list of documents (**r. 31.10(2)**, form N265). Parties may agree in writing to give disclosure without making a list or without a disclosure statement (**r. 31.10(8)**). Parties may agree in writing, or the court may direct, that disclosure and/or inspection should take place in stages (**r. 31.13**). Parties may use the electronic documents questionnaire (**PD 31B, paras 10 to 13**).
List of documents	The list (N265) must (**r. 31.10**): (a) Identify the documents concisely and in a convenient order. (b) Identify privileged documents, stating the grounds on which it is claimed there is a right or duty to withhold inspection (**r. 31.19(3)**). (c) Identify documents no longer in the party's control, stating what has happened to them. (d) Include a disclosure statement in the form set out in the **annex to PD 31A** (**PD 31A, para. 4.1**).
Signing disclosure statement	(a) Should normally be signed by the party (**r. 31.10(6)**: exceptions are set out in **r. 31.10(7) to ((9)**). (b) Legal representative must ensure person signing understands the duty of disclosure in **Part 31** (**PD 31A, para. 4.4**). (c) Companies, firms etc. sign by a duly authorised officer. The disclosure statement must include that person's name and address, the office or position held, and explain why he or she is an appropriate person to make the statement (**CPR, r. 31.10(7)** and **PD 31A, para. 4.3**). (d) An insurer, or the Motor Insurers' Bureau, may sign if they have a financial interest in the claim (**PD 31A, para. 4.7**). An electronic documents questionnaire has a statement of truth (**PD 31B, para. 11**).

Inspection	The party seeking to inspect must give written notice (by letter) (**CPR, r. 31.15(a)**), which must be complied with within seven days.
	(a) Inspection may take place by attendance at the other side's offices or solicitor's office (**r. 31.15(b)**).
	(b) Inspection usually takes place by making a written request for photocopies, with the inspecting party undertaking to pay reasonable copying costs (**r. 31.15(c)**).
	Electronic documents should be provided in native format, preserving metadata (**PD 31B, para. 33**).
Continuing duty	Each party has a continuing duty to disclose documents subsequently coming into their control. If this happens they must immediately notify the other parties (**r. 31.11**) by serving a supplemental list (**PD 31A, para. 3.3**).

Procedural checklist 26   Specific disclosure

See **chapter 50**, especially **50.40** and **50.42**.

Timing	Usually after standard disclosure.
	A request for the documents to be sought in the application should be made first by letter.
Application	Application notice (form N244). Wording for question 3:
	'An order that the [claimant/defendant] do give specific disclosure of documents because [the claimant/defendant] [has failed to give full standard disclosure] [further disclosure is necessary in order to investigate this claim fully]'.
Form of order	(1) The [claimant/defendant] do give specific disclosure of documents by filing and serving a supplementary list of documents in form N265 by 4 p.m. on [date] specifying whether each of the [documents] and/or [classes of documents] specified in the schedule to this order are presently in its control, and if not, specifying which of those [documents] and/or [classes of documents] are no longer in its control (and indicating what has happened to such documents), and also specifying which of those [documents] and/or [classes of documents] it claims a right or duty to withhold inspection of.
	(2) The [claimant/defendant] do make any request for inspection in writing within seven days after service of the list of documents.
	(3) The [claimant/defendant] do provide the [claimant/defendant] with copies of the requested documents within seven days of receipt of the request.
	A schedule attached to the application, or to a draft order, should set out concisely and in a convenient order the documents and classes of documents sought from the other side.
Written evidence	Is required (**PD 31A, para. 5.2**), and is typically given in a witness statement (although the box in question 10 of the N244 can be used). The evidence should:
	(a) Exhibit the lists of documents provided by the other side.
	(b) Exhibit relevant correspondence.
	(c) Deal with each document or class of document in the schedule to the application:
	(i) explaining why it is believed to be in the control of the other side; and
	(ii) explaining why it should be disclosed (because it is relevant to an issue in the case, and should have been disclosed under standard disclosure, or because it is a 'train of inquiry' document, explaining the value of the document in investigating the claim).
Issue application	See **procedural checklist 20**, and **CPR, Part 23**. Fee £155 (**CPFO, fee 2.4**).
Serve application	At least three clear days before the return day (**CPR, rr. 23.7(1)** and **2.8(3)**).

Procedural checklist 27   Non-party disclosure

See **50.90** to **50.95**.

Timing	At any time after proceedings are issued (Senior Courts Act 1981, s. 34(2); County Courts Act 1984, s. 53(2); **CPR, r. 31.17(1)**).
	A request for the documents to be sought in the application should be made first by letter.
Application	Application notice (form N244). Wording for question 3:
	'An order pursuant to the [Senior Courts Act 1981, s. 34(2)] [County Courts Act 1984, s. 53(2)] that [name of person with the documents] give non-party disclosure of documents because it has in its control documents which are likely to support the [claimant's/defendant's] case and disclosure is necessary in order to dispose fairly of the claim or to save costs'.
Form of order	(1) [Name of person with the documents] do by 4 p.m. on [date] serve on the [claimant's/defendant's] solicitors a list of documents in form N265 specifying whether each of the [documents] and/or [classes of documents] specified in the schedule to this order are presently in its control, and if not, specifying which of those [documents] and/or [classes of documents] are no longer in its control (and indicating what has happened to such documents), and also specifying which of those [documents] and/or [classes of documents] it claims a right or duty to withhold inspection of.
	(2) The [claimant/defendant] do make any request for inspection of the documents disclosed by [name of person with the documents] in writing within seven days after service of the list of documents.
	(3) [Name of person with the documents] do provide the [claimant/defendant] with copies of the requested documents within seven days of receipt of the request.
	A schedule attached to the application, or to a draft order, should set out concisely and in a convenient order the documents and classes of documents sought from the non-party.
Written evidence	Is required (**r. 31.17(2)**), and is typically given in a witness statement (although the box in question 10 of the N244 can be used). The evidence should:
	(a) Exhibit relevant correspondence.
	(b) Deal with each document or class of document in the schedule to the application:
	(i) explaining why it is believed to be in the control of the non-party;
	(ii) explaining how it is likely to support the case of the applicant or adversely affect the case of another party (**r. 31.17(3)(a)**);
	(iii) explaining why disclosure is necessary in order to dispose fairly of the claim or to save costs (**r. 31.17(3)(b)**).
Issue application	See **procedural checklist 20**, and **Part 23**. Fee £155 (**CPFO, fee 2.4**).
Serve application	At least three clear days before the return day (**rr. 23.7(1)** and **2.8(3)**).

Procedural checklist 28   Trial preparation

See **chapter 61**.

Item	Timing	Action
Witness availability	Before listing for trial	Communicate with lay and expert witnesses, and also counsel, to obtain available dates (and reasons). See **61.8**.

Witness abroad or incapacitated	Several months before trial	Consider best means of adducing evidence from the witness: (a) Hearsay statement (**chapter 53**). (b) Letter of request (**58.8** to **58.12**). (c) Video link (**58.11**). (d) Deposition (**58.2** to **58.7**).
Listing for trial	In accordance with case management directions	See **61.2** to **61.6**.
Inform witnesses	Receipt of trial date or window	Write to lay and expert witnesses confirming trial date or window and seeking confirmation of the witness's availability.
Pre-trial review (if directed in case management directions)	8–10 weeks before trial	Most common in multi-track claims. Brief trial advocate to attend. May result in further directions, settling a statement of issues, and fixing a trial timetable (see **47.23**).
Statement of issues	As directed	May need to be settled and agreed between the parties after a pre-trial review (see **61.13**).
Brief counsel	Sufficient time before trial	Prepare counsel's brief and supporting trial bundles or papers for the trial bundle. Agree fees with counsel's clerk. Even for simple cases counsel should be briefed at least a week in advance because counsel has to prepare a skeleton argument. In complex claims a period of months may be required. Counsel will also often advise on further pre-trial preparation that may be required.
Witness summonses	At least 2 weeks before trial	Issue witness summonses for unwilling witnesses (see **57.2**, form N20). Fee £50 (**CPFO, fee 2.6**). Serve at least seven clear days (**rr. 2.8(2)** and **34.5(1)**) before the date the witness is required to attend, bearing in mind deemed dates of service (**r. 6.26**). Include witness expenses (see **57.6**).
Reading guide and time estimates	Before lodging trial bundle	In QBD and ChD reading lists and time estimates signed by counsel must be lodged with trial bundles (Practice Direction (Royal Courts of Justice: Reading Lists and Time Estimates) [2000] 1 WLR 208), see **59.8**.
Trial bundles	c. 14 days before trial	Defendants should notify claimant of documents they wish to be included.
	Three to seven days before trial	Copies for judge, witness box and all parties.
	At least seven days before ChD trials	Paginated and prepared in accordance with **PD 39A**, see **chapter 59**.
Skeleton argument (required in the High Court, often directed or desirable in the County Court)	As directed two clear days before HC trials	Usually simultaneous exchange, but directions may provide for sequential exchange (see **32.17** and **61.13**). Lodge at list office (Queen's Bench Guide, para. 7.11.11) or with judge's clerk (Chancery Guide, para. 7.25).

Statement of costs (fast track trials)	Two days before trial	Form N260. **PD 44, para. 9.2**, see **71.4**.
Authorities	4 p.m. day before trial	Advocates should exchange lists of authorities (e.g. Chancery Guide, para. 7.34).
	9 a.m. trial day	Provide usher with list of authorities (Queen's Bench Guide, para. 7.11.8; Chancery Guide, para. 7.33). Authorities are usually supplied as photocopies.
Adjournment	As soon as need arises	Immediately inform court and other parties in writing, seeking adjournment. If not dealt with administratively, issue application in accordance with **Part 23** (see **r. 3.1(2)(b)** and **61.7**).

Procedural checklist 29   Offer to settle

See **chapter 66**.

Timing	Can be made before or after issue of proceedings. Should be made once an appraisal has been made of the merits and value of the claim. Should be made, if possible, more than 21 days before the trial.
Method	Form N242A is the prescribed form, but is not obligatory, and the offer can be made by letter.
Relevant period	Normally, this is the period of not less than 21 days after the offer is made specified as the period within which the defendant will be liable for the claimant's costs if the Part 36 offer is accepted. If the offer is made less than 21 days before trial, the relevant period ends with the end of the trial (**CPR, r. 36.3(g)**).
Form	(a) Must be in writing (**r. 36.5(1)(a)**).
	(b) Must make clear it is made pursuant to **Part 36** (**r. 36.5(1)(b)**).
	(c) If made at least 21 days before trial, it must specify a period of not less than 21 days within which the defendant will be liable for the claimant's costs in accordance with **r. 36.13** or **36.20** if the offer is accepted (**rr. 36.5(1)(c)** and **36.5(2)**).
	(d) Must state whether it relates to the whole claim or part or to an issue, and if so, which (**r. 36.5(1)(d)**).
	(e) Must state whether it takes into account any counterclaim (**r. 36.5(1)(e)**).
	(f) Needs to state the proposed terms of compromise.
Additional requirements	(a) Money claims. Must offer a single sum of money (**r. 36.6(1)**), which is treated as inclusive of interest until the end of the relevant period (**r. 36.5(4)**, see **66.9**).
	(b) Personal injury claims. Must set out the position on deductible amounts/State benefits and lump sum payments under the Social Security (Recovery of Benefits) Act 1997 (see **r. 36.22** and **66.10**), unless the offer is made after the certificate of benefits has been requested but before it arrives. In the latter situation, the defendant is required to clarify the offer within seven days after receipt of the certificate (**r. 36.22(7)**).
	(c) Personal injury claims for future pecuniary loss. There are additional requirements in **r. 36.18**, see **66.11**.
	(d) Provisional damages claims. There are additional requirements in **r. 36.19**, see **66.12**.
Making a Part 36 offer	A Part 36 offer is made when it is served on the offeree (**r. 36.7(2)**). The offer should be served on the legal representative of a person who is legally represented (**PD 36, para. 1.2**). A certificate of service in form N215 should be filed.
Clarification	Can be sought, using the **Part 23** procedure (see **66.23**). See **procedural checklist 20**.

Withdrawal	There are restrictions on withdrawing or reducing a **Part 36** offer during the relevant period (**r. 36.10**). Thereafter, permission is not required, but the offer can be withdrawn or reduced only if it has not been accepted (**r. 36.9(1)**). Notice of withdrawal must be in writing (**r. 36.9(2)**) and should clearly identify the offer being withdrawn (*Gibbon v Manchester City Council* [2010] EWCA Civ 726, [2010] 1 WLR 2081).
Acceptance	By serving written notice of acceptance on the offeror (**r. 36.11(1)**) and filing notice of acceptance at court (**PD 36, para. 3.1**).
Late acceptance	If a Part 36 offer has not been withdrawn, it may be accepted even after the relevant period (**r. 36.11(2)**).
Effect of acceptance	(a) The claim is stayed (**r. 36.14(1)**). (b) If accepted within the relevant period, the defendant is liable to pay the claimant's standard-basis costs to the date of acceptance (**r. 36.13(1) and (3)**). This is subject to four exceptions, see **66.26** to **66.30**. (c) If accepted after the relevant period, the parties may agree costs, but if they do not, the court will make an order for costs (**r. 36.13(4)(b)**).
Trial	A Part 36 offer is treated as 'without prejudice save as to costs' (**r. 36.16(1)**). It must not be communicated to the trial judge, and must not be included in the trial papers, until the case has been decided (**r. 36.16(2)**).
Non-acceptance	The question is whether the offeree can obtain a result on judgment which is more advantageous than the terms of the offer (**r. 36.17**). If not: (a) if the offer was made by the defendant, the claimant will normally be ordered to pay the defendant's costs from the end of the relevant period (**r. 36.17(3)**); (b) if the offer was made by the claimant, the court has a discretion to order enhanced interest at up to 10 per cent above base rate, indemnity-basis costs, and enhanced interest on those costs, from the end of the relevant period (**r. 36.17(4)**), together with an additional amount (**r. 36.17(4)(d)**).
Appeal proceedings	Need a separate **Part 36** offer. A **Part 36** offer made in the proceedings at first instance only relates to the proceedings at first instance (**r. 36.4**).

Procedural checklist 30   Summary assessment of costs

See 71.4 to 71.6.

When required	Unless the court orders otherwise, costs will be assessed summarily (**PD 44, para. 9.2**): (1) at the conclusion of a trial on the fast track; (2) at the conclusion of an interim hearing lasting no more than one day. In these cases the summary assessment covers the interim costs only, unless the whole proceedings are disposed of, in which event the summary assessment may deal with the costs of the whole claim; and (3) at the conclusion of interim hearings within appeals and appeals listed for one day or less.
Statement of costs	Form N260. Should be filed and served 24 hours before the hearing (**PD 44, para. 9.5(4)**).
Failure to serve statement of costs 24 hours in advance	Court may (see **32.30**): (1) give the paying party a brief (minutes or hours) adjournment, and then proceed with the summary assessment; (2) stand over for a detailed assessment; (3) stand over for a summary assessment at a later date; (4) if both sides agree, stand over for a summary assessment to be dealt with in writing.

Procedural checklist 31   Arbitration claim

See **chapter 72**.

Commence an arbitration claim under **CPR, Part 62**, using arbitration claim form N8.	Claim form must:
	• include a concise statement of remedy claimed;
	• include any questions on which the claimant seeks the decision of the court;
	• give details of any arbitration award challenged by the claimant, identifying which part or parts of the award are challenged and specifying the grounds for the challenge;
	• show statutory requirements have been met;
	• specify under which section of the Arbitration Act 1996 the claim is made;
	• identify against which (if any) defendants a cost order is sought;
	• specify either:
	  – the persons on whom the arbitration claim form is to be served, stating their role in the arbitration and whether they are to be defendants; or
	  – that the claim is made without notice under the Arbitration Act 1996, s. 44(3), and the grounds relied on.
	(**CPR, r. 62.4(1)**).
	Where required, evidence in support must be filed with the arbitration claim form.

Issue	Claim form may be issued in one of the following courts: • Admiralty and Commercial Registry; • Technology and Construction Court Registry; • District Registry of the High Court (where a Mercantile Court is established) (Mercantile List); or • District Registry of the High Court (arbitration claim form must be marked 'Technology and Construction Court' in the top right-hand corner) (TCC List) (**PD 62, para. 2.3(1)**). Claim form relating to a landlord and tenant or partnership dispute must be issued in the High Court, Chancery Division (**PD 62, para. 2.3(2)**).
Service	Claim form must be served by the claimant within one month from the date of issue unless court orders otherwise (**CPR, r. 62.4(2)**). Once served, the claimant must file the certificate of service within seven days of service (**PD 62, para. 3.2**).
Service out of the jurisdiction	The court may give permission to serve a claim form out of the jurisdiction in the following circumstances: • When a claimant seeks to challenge an arbitration award or appeal on a question of law arising out of an arbitration award made within England and Wales. • The claim is for an order under the Arbitration Act 1996, s. 44. The court can give permission for service out of the jurisdiction notwithstanding the only remedy sought is in respect of proceedings taking place outside England and Wales. • Any other situation where the claimant seeks a remedy or requires a question to be determined by the court which affects an arbitration (whether started or not), an arbitration agreement or an arbitration award. Seat of the arbitration must be in England and Wales. Where the seat is not in England and Wales the court can still give permission as long as the seat has not been designated or, by reason of connection with England and Wales or Northern Ireland, the court is satisfied it is appropriate to do so (**CPR, r. 62.5(1)**). Application must be supported by written evidence and: • state the grounds on which the application is made; and • show in what place or country the person to be served is, or probably may be, found (**CPR, r. 62.5(2)**). **CPR, rr. 6.40** to **6.46** (which regulate service of claim forms abroad), apply to the service of arbitration claim forms out of the jurisdiction (**r. 62.5(3)**). The order giving permission to serve out of the jurisdiction must specify the period within which the defendant has to file the acknowledgment of service (**r. 62.5(4)**).

Acknowledgment of service	Generally within 14 days after service of the arbitration claim form (**r. 10.3(1)(b)**) by using form N15 or, alternatively in the commercial court, form N210(CC) (Admiralty and Commercial Courts Guide, para. O5.1(b)).
Defendant's written evidence	Must be filed and served within 21 days after the date by which the defendant is required to acknowledge service or, if not required to file an acknowledgment, within 21 days after the service of the arbitration claim form (**PD 62, para. 6.2**).
Claimant's written evidence in reply	Evidence in reply to the defendant's written evidence must be filed or served within seven days after service of the defendant's evidence (**PD 62, para. 6.3**).
Preparation for hearing	Agreed indexed and paginated bundles of all evidence and other documents to be used at the hearing should be prepared by the claimant (**PD 62, para. 6.4**). Estimates for length of the hearing and a complete set of documents should be filed no later than five days before the hearing date (**PD 62, para. 6.5**).
Main hearing	The claimant must file and serve no later than two days before the hearing: • chronology of relevant events cross-referenced to a bundle of documents; • list of persons involved; and • skeleton argument (**PD 62, para. 6.6**). The defendant must file and serve its skeleton argument not later than the day before the hearing date. Where an application is likely to last more than half a day it should be filed and served one clear day before the hearing date (Admiralty and Commercial Courts Guide, para. O6.16(b)). The skeleton arguments for both claimant and respondent must list: • issues which arise for decision; • the grounds for relief to be relied upon; • submissions of fact to be made with references to the evidence; and • submissions of law with references to the relevant authorities (**PD 62, para. 6.7**). Hearing generally in private save for claims to determine a preliminary point of law (Arbitration Act 1996, s. 45) or appeal on a question of law arising out of an award (Arbitration Act 1996, s. 69) (**CPR, r. 62.10(3)**).

Procedural checklist 32 Appeals within the County Court and High Court

See **chapter 74**.

Timing	At the end of the hearing in the lower court, permission to appeal should be sought (see **74.13**). An appellant's notice in form N161 must be filed (unless time is extended, see **71.20**) no later than 21 days from the date of the decision of the lower court (**CPR, r. 52.4(2)(b)**).
Permission	Required for all civil appeals (**r. 52.3**) other than those involving personal liberty and from decisions of authorised court officers in detailed assessments (see **71.12**).
Seeking permission	Initially sought orally from the lower court (**r. 52.3(2)**). If refused, can renew application for permission to the appeal court (**r. 52.3(3)**). Permission from the appeal court is initially sought in the appellant's notice (form N161), and is normally considered without a hearing (**PD 52A, para. 4.2**).
Reconsideration of permission	Where the appeal court refuses permission without a hearing, it may reconsider granting permission at a hearing (**CPR, r. 52.3(4)**). There is no jurisdiction to consider an appeal from an appeal court's refusal to grant permission (**Access to Justice Act 1999, s. 54(4)**).

Appeal court	(1) From County Court District Judge appeal to Circuit Judge.
	(2) From County Court Circuit Judge appeal to High Court judge.
	(3) From High Court Master, District Judge or Registrar appeal to High Court judge.
	See **74.4**. The above applies equally to deputies and part-time judges fulfilling the above roles.
	By way of exceptions to the above:
	(a) Final decisions in multi-track claims are appealed to the Court of Appeal (**Destination of Appeals Order, art. 4**).
	(b) Final decisions in specialist claims are appealed to the Court of Appeal (**Destination of Appeals Order, art. 4**).
	(c) Second appeals are appealed to the Court of Appeal (**Destination of Appeals Order, art. 5**). This applies where a County Court District Judge's decision is appealed to the Circuit Judge, whose decision is subject to a second appeal (which is taken to the Court of Appeal).
Extending time to appeal	Can only be granted by the appeal court (not by consent) (**CPR, r. 52.6**), although the lower court can direct some period other than 21 days for filing the appellant's notice (**r. 52.4(2)(a)**). Applications to extend time are made in the appellant's notice (**PD 52B, para. 3.2**).
Appellant's notice	Form N161. Must be filed with the appeal court no more than 21 days after the decision of the lower court (or as directed or extended) (**CPR, r. 52.4(2)(b)**). It must:
	(a) set out the grounds of the appeal;
	(b) give reasons why the lower court's decision is wrong or unjust through serious procedural or other irregularity and state whether each ground is on a point of law or against a finding of fact (**PD 52B, para. 4.2(d); PD 52C, para. 5.1**);
	(c) include any application for permission to appeal (**PD 52A, para. 4.2**);
	(d) include any application to appeal out of time (**PD 52B, para. 3.2**);
	(e) include any application for a transcript of the judgment of the lower court at public expense (**PD 52B, para. 4.3**);
	(f) include information about any issue raised or remedy sought under the Human Rights Act 1998 (**PD 16, para. 15.1**).
	The N161 may include applications for interim relief (**PD 52B, para. 4.3**), including any stay of execution.
Fee	£120 for small claims appeal; £140 for other appeals in the County Court (**CPFO, fee 2.3**); £240 for appeals in the High Court (**CPFO, fee 2.2**).
Documents to be filed	At the same time as filing the appellant's notice, the appellant must file (**PD 52B, para. 4.2; PD 52C, para. 3(3)**):
	(a) two additional copies of the appellant's notice for the court and one for each respondent;
	(b) the same number of copies of the appellant's skeleton argument;
	(c) a sealed copy of the order of the court below;
	(d) any orders giving or refusing permission to appeal together with the reasons for each decision;
	(e) any written evidence in support of any interim application within the appeal;
	(f) a paginated appeal bundle complying with **PD 52B, para. 6.3**; and
	(g) a transcript (or agreed note, see **71.30**) of the judgment under appeal (**PD 52B, para. 6.2**).
	Where it is not possible to file any of the above, the appellant must state which items are not being filed and why.

Skeleton argument	Form N163. Should be filed with the appellant's notice, or, if impractical, within 14 days of filing the notice. Only required if issues are complex or if skeleton will assist in respects not readily apparent from the papers in the appeal (see **PD 52B, para. 8.3**).
Transcripts of evidence	Are requested, if required, after permission to appeal is granted (see **74.30**). Transcripts of judgments are required before permission.
Service of appellant's notice	As soon as practicable, and within seven days of being filed the appellant must serve the appellant's notice and skeleton argument on the respondents (**CPR, r. 52.4(3)**). The appellant must then file a certificate of service (form N215).
Service of supporting documents	Appeal bundles, orders in the court below and for permission etc. (a) where permission to appeal is being sought, need not be served unless and until permission is given; (b) where permission is granted by the lower court (or not required), supporting documents must be served with the appellant's notice (**PD 52B, para. 6.5(a)**). Where permission is granted by the appeal court, service is required within seven days of receiving the order granting permission (**para. 6.5(b)**).
Permission granted	Court sends order and any directions to the parties (**PD 52C, para. 15(1)**) together with date for the appeal hearing or listing window. The appellant must add the order and other documents to the appeal bundle. Appeal questionnaires are optional in the High Court.
Respondent's notice	Respondent's notice (form N162) is required (**r. 52.5(2)**) where the respondent: (a) seeks permission to appeal against the decision in the court below; (b) wishes the appeal court to uphold the decision of the court below for different or additional reasons to those given by the court below. In circumstances (a) and (b), there is a fee of £120 for a small claims appeal or £140 for any other appeal in the County Court (**CPFO, fee 2.3**); £240 in the High Court (**CPFO, fee 2.2**).
Filing respondent's notice	As directed, otherwise within 14 days of: (a) service of appellant's notice if permission to appeal was not required or if permission was given to the appellant by the court below; (b) service of notification of permission to appeal; or (c) service of notification that permission and the substantive appeal are to be heard together. With the respondent's notice, the respondent must file two additional copies of the notice for the court and one for every other party (**PD 52C, para. 10**).
Additional documents	The respondent must make every effort to agree any additional documents for the appeal bundle with the appellant. If they cannot agree, the respondent should prepare a supplementary bundle, to be served and filed with the respondent's notice (**PD 52B, para. 8.2**).
Service of respondent's notice	As soon as practicable, and within seven days of being filed (**r. 52.5(6)**).
Respondent's skeleton argument	May be included in the respondent's notice, or served within 14 days of filing the respondent's notice (**PD 52C, para. 9**; but see **PD 52B, para. 8.3**).
Authorities	In the County Court authorities must be brought to the hearing. In the High Court lists of authorities must be provided to the head usher by 5.30 p.m. on the working day before the hearing (see **71.51**) or copies should be included in the appeal bundles (Queen's Bench Guide, para. 7.11.9).
Summary assessment of costs	In appeals from case management decisions and appeals listed for one day or less, statements of costs should be filed 24 hours before the appeal hearing (**PD 44, para. 9.5(4)(b)**).

Procedural checklist 33 Appeals to the Court of Appeal

See **chapter** 74.

Timing	At the end of the hearing in the lower court, permission to appeal should be sought (see **74.13**). Any request for the provision of a transcript at public expense (on the ground of poor financial circumstances) should be made at the hearing. An appellant's notice in form N161 must be filed (unless time is extended, see **74.20**) no later than 21 days from the date of the decision of the lower court (**CPR, r. 52.4(2)(b)**).
Permission	Required for all civil appeals (**r. 52.3**) other than those involving personal liberty and from decisions of authorised court officers in detailed assessments (see **74.11**).
Fee	£235 if permission and/or an extension of time is required (**CPFO, fee 13.1(a)**); £465 if permission is not required or was granted by the lower court (**CPFO, fee 13.1(b)**).
Seeking permission	Initially sought orally from the lower court (**r. 52.3(2)**). If refused, can renew application for permission to the appeal court (**r. 52.3(3)**). Except that in second appeals to the Court of Appeal permission can only be sought from the Court of Appeal (**r. 52.13(1)**). Permission from the Court of Appeal is initially sought in the appellant's notice (form N161), and is normally considered without a hearing (**PD 52C, para. 15**).
Reconsideration of permission	Where the Court of Appeal refuses permission without a hearing, it may reconsider granting permission at a hearing (**CPR, r. 52.3(4)**). If represented, the appellant's advocate must file and serve a brief written statement at least four days before the hearing identifying the points proposed to be raised and his reasons why permission should be granted (**PD 52C, para. 14**). There is no jurisdiction to consider an appeal from a refusal by the Court of Appeal to grant permission (**Access to Justice Act 1999, s. 54(4)**).
Appeals taken to the Court of Appeal	(a) Final decisions in multi-track claims (**Destination of Appeals Order, art. 4**). (b) Final decisions in specialist claims (**Destination of Appeals Order, art. 4**). (c) Second appeals in the County Court (**Destination of Appeals Order, art. 5**). This applies where a County Court District Judge's decision is appealed to the Circuit Judge, whose decision is subject to a second appeal (which is taken to the Court of Appeal). See **74.15**. (d) Appeals from High Court judges.
Extending time to appeal	Can only be granted by the appeal court (not by consent) (**CPR, r. 52.6**), although the lower court can direct some period other than 21 days for filing the appellant's notice (**r. 52.4(2)(a)**). Applications to extend time are made in the appellant's notice (**PD 52C, para. 4(1)(b)**).
Appellant's notice	Form N161. Must be filed with the appeal court no more than 21 days after the decision of the lower court (or as directed or extended) (**CPR, r. 52.4(2)(b)**). It must: (a) set out the grounds of the appeal; (b) identify as concisely as possible the respects in which the lower court's decision is wrong or unjust through serious procedural or other irregularity and state whether each ground is on a point of law or against a finding of fact (**PD 52C, para. 5(1)**); (c) include any application for permission to appeal (**PD 52A, para. 4.2**); (d) include any application to appeal out of time (**PD 52C, para. 4(1)(b)**); (e) include information about any issue raised or remedy sought under the Human Rights Act 1998 (**PD 16, para. 15.1**). The N161 may include applications for interim relief (**PD 52B, para. 4.3**), including any stay of execution.

Documents to be filed	At the same time as filing the appellant's notice, the appellant must file (**PD 52C, para. 3(3)**): (a) three copies of the appellant's notice for the court and one for each respondent; (b) a sealed copy of the order of the court below; (c) any orders giving or refusing permission to appeal together with the reasons for each decision; (d) any written evidence in support of any interim application within the appeal; and (e) in a second appeal, the first-instance order, reasons and appellant's notice; (f) a copy of the order allocating the case to a track (if any); (g) the appellant's skeleton argument; (h) approved transcript of the judgment. Where it is not possible to file any of the above, the appellant must state which items are not being filed and why (**PD 52C, para. 6**).
Skeleton argument	Form N163. Should be filed with the appellant's notice.
Transcripts	Transcripts of evidence are requested, if required, after permission to appeal is granted (see **74.30**). Transcripts of judgments are required before permission.
Service of appellant's notice	As soon as practicable, and within seven days of being filed (**CPR, r. 52.4(3)**). Served by the appellant (**PD 52C, para. 7.1**), who must file a certificate of service (**PD 52B, para. 6.1**).
Permission granted	Court sends order and any directions to the parties (**PD 52C, para. 21**), together with listing window notification.
Proposed appeal bundle index	Served by appellant seven days after date of listing window notification (**PD 52C, paras 21** and **27**).
Respondent's notice	Form N162. Fee of £235 (**CPFO, fees 13.1(a)** and **13.2**). Required if (**CPR, r. 52.5(2)**) the respondent: (a) seeks permission to appeal against the decision below (in which event the time for the respondent's notice is 21 days from the lower court's decision); (b) wishes the appeal court to uphold the decision of the court below for different or additional reasons to those given by the court below (in which event it is required 14 days after the grant of permission to appeal to the appellant).
Respondent's skeleton argument	Respondent who has filed a respondent's notice must lodge and serve its skeleton argument within 14 days of filing a respondent's notice (**PD 52C, para. 9**).
Appeal questionnaire	Filed and served on every respondent 14 days after date of listing window notification (**PD 52C, paras 21** and **23**).
Disagreement with time estimate	If a respondent disagrees with the appellant's time estimate, seven days after service of the appeal questionnaire the respondent must file and serve its own time estimate (**PD 52C, paras 21** and **24**).
Appeal skeleton	Appellant serves appeal skeleton on each respondent 21 days after listing window (**PD 52C, paras 21** and **31**).
Agree bundle	21 days after date of listing window notification (**PD 52C, paras 21** and **27**). If there is no agreement in relation to particular documents, they must be placed in a supplementary bundle.
Respondent's skeleton argument (no respondent's notice)	Respondent who has not filed a respondent's notice must lodge and serve its skeleton argument within 42 days of filing a respondent's notice (**PD 52C, paras 13** and **21**).
Lodge appeal bundles	Not later than 42 days before the appeal hearing (**PD 52C, paras 21** and **27**).
Appellant's replacement skeleton argument	Not later than 14 days before the appeal hearing (**PD 52C, paras 21** and **31**).
Respondent's replacement skeleton argument	Not later than seven days before the appeal hearing (**PD 52C, para. 21**).
Bundles of authorities	Not later than seven days before the appeal hearing (**PD 52C, paras 21** and **29**).

| Every document needed for the appeal | If not already lodged or filed, every document needed for the hearing must be lodged or filed not later than seven days before the appeal hearing (**PD 52C, para. 21**). |
| Summary assessment of costs | For appeal hearings estimated at no more than one day, statements of costs (form N260) should be filed 24 hours before the appeal hearing (**PD 44, paras 9.2(b)** and **9.5(4)**). |

Procedural checklist 34   Claim for judicial review

See **chapter** 77.

Pre-action protocol	The **Pre-action Protocol for Judicial Review** requires that, where applicable, before making a claim, the claimant should send a letter to the defendant identifying issues in dispute and establishing whether litigation can be avoided. Copies of the letter should be sent to all interested parties for information. The defendant should normally respond within 14 days to the letter before claim. Response should be sent to all interested parties identified by the claimant and contain details of any other parties who the defendant considers also have an interest. Parties should try to comply with the Pre-action Protocol even in cases when short time limits for commencing the claim apply.
Timing	Claim form must normally be filed promptly and in any event not later than three months after the grounds to make the claim first arose (**CPR, r. 54.5(1)**), although case law disapplies promptness but not three months when advancing European Union law grounds. In planning and procurement cases, the time limit is six weeks from when the grounds first arose and 30 days from when the claimant first knew or ought to have known about the grounds respectively (**r. 54.5(5)** and **(6)**). There must be good reason before this time limit will be extended. This time limit may not be extended by agreement between the parties (**r. 54.5(2)**).
Claim form	Form N461. The claim form must specify: • the name and address of any person considered to be an interested party, • that permission is sought to proceed with a judicial review claim, and • any remedy (including any interim remedy) being claimed. The claim form must include or be accompanied by: • a detailed statement of the claimant's grounds for bringing the claim, • a statement of facts relied on, • any application to extend the time limit for filing the claim form, and • any application for directions (**PD 54A, para. 5.6**). In addition the claim form must be accompanied by: • any written evidence in support of the claim or application to extend time, • a copy of any order that the claimant seeks to have quashed, • where the claim relates to a decision of a court or tribunal, an approved copy of the reasons for reaching that decision, • copies of any documents on which the claimant proposes to rely, • copies of any relevant statutory material, and • a list of essential documents for advance reading by the court (with page references to the passages relied on) (**PD 54A, para. 5.7**). Where it is not possible to file all the above documents, the claimant must indicate which documents have not been filed and the reasons why they are not currently available (**PD 54A, para. 5.8**).
Urgent procedure	Form N463. Claimant must state the reasons for urgency, the proposed timescale for consideration of the permission application, a justification for any delay in making the application and the date by which the full hearing of the merits should take place if permission is granted. A claimant who applies for an interim injunction must also provide a draft order and a statement of the grounds on which the injunction is sought. The application must be served by fax and post, along with the claim form, on the defendant and interested parties. The defendant and interested parties must be advised that they may make representations on the application.

Fee	£154 when claim form is issued, £385 if requesting an oral renewal hearing to consider permission, and a further £770 if permission to proceed is granted (**CPFO, fee 1.9**).
Service	The claim form must be served on the defendant and any person the claimant considers to be an interested party within seven days of issue (**CPR, r. 54.7**).
Acknowledgment of service	Form N462. Any person served with the claim form who wishes to take part in the proceedings must file an acknowledgment of service (A/S) in the Administrative Court Office within 21 days after service of the claim form. Where person filing A/S intends to contest the claim, the A/S must set out a summary of his grounds for doing so. The A/S must also be served on the claimant and interested persons named on the claim form not later than seven days after it is filed (**CPR, r. 54.8**).
Permission	The court's permission to proceed is required in a judicial review claim (**CPR, r. 54.4**). If permission is granted, the court may give directions (**r. 54.10**). The court will serve the permission decision on the claimant and defendant and on any other person who filed an A/S (**r. 54.11**).
Defendant's and other interested parties' detailed grounds of opposition/ support	The defendant and any other interested person has 35 days after service of the permission order to file detailed grounds for contesting the claim or supporting it on additional grounds and any written evidence (**CPR, r. 54.14**).
Skeleton arguments	The claimant must file and serve a skeleton argument not less than 21 working days before the date of the hearing (or the warned date) (**PD 54A, para. 15.1**). The defendant and other relevant parties wishing to make representations must file and serve a skeleton argument not less than 14 working days before the hearing (or warned date) (**PD 54A, para. 15.2**).
Substantive hearing	Substantive judicial review applications in civil matters are generally heard by a single judge sitting in open court. The court may determine the claim without a hearing where all parties agree (**CPR, r. 54.18**).

Procedural checklist 35   Application by a creditor whose debt is presently payable to wind up a company incorporated in England and Wales

See **chapter 82**.

Pre-action	Check that the amount of the creditor's claim is at least £750 and that there is no substantial dispute about the amount or about whether it is due and payable. Check that there is no substantial cross-claim which would reduce the balance owed to the creditor to less than £750. Check that an appropriately clear demand for payment has been made and that no payment has been received. Consider whether serving a statutory demand (form 4.1) or other action short of petitioning might induce payment.
Preparation	Check the company's correct name and details required for the petition (form 4.2) at Companies House. Check at the Central Registry of Winding-up Petitions that no other petition has been presented (go to the Rolls Building ground floor or telephone 0906 754 0043). If a petition has already been presented, do not present a second petition, but notify the existing petitioner of intention to support.
	In order to complete the petition, ascertain whether the company appears to be an insurance undertaking, credit institution, investment undertaking providing services involving the holding of funds or securities for third parties, or a collective investment undertaking, and ascertain whether the company's centre of main interests is outside the United Kingdom.

Appropriate court	High Court, or, if company's paid-up capital is £120,000 or less, the County Court hearing centre which deals with winding up for the district where the company's registered office is located. If the company's registered office is in the London insolvency district, proceedings can only be started in the High Court.
	If the company's centre of main interests is in another EU State (apart from Denmark) and it has no establishment in the United Kingdom (see **82.9** to **82.13**), proceedings must be started in the country where the centre of main interests is located, not in England and Wales.
Form of petition	Form 4.2, which must be verified by statement of truth complying with IR 1986, r. 4.12. For details see **82.19** to **82.24**. At least three copies will be required for filing (one for the court, one for service on the company, one for the petitioner). Extra copies are required if the company has a liquidator in a voluntary winding up, an administrator, an administrative receiver or a supervisor of a voluntary arrangement.
Fees	A court fee of £280 (**CPFO, fee 3.3**) and a deposit of £1,600 for the official receiver's fee must be paid when filing.
Filing	All required copies are sealed and endorsed with the venue for hearing the petition. One copy is retained by the court, the others are returned to the petitioner.
Service	On the company at its registered office:
	• by handing it to a person who there and then acknowledges him or herself to be, or to the best of the server's knowledge, information and belief is, a director or other officer, or employee, of the company, or
	• by handing it to a person who there and then acknowledges him or herself to be authorised to accept service on the company's behalf, or
	• if no individual meeting these criteria is available, by depositing it at or about the registered office in such a way that it is likely to come to the notice of a person attending at the office.
	• If service at the registered office is not practicable, see **82.35** and **82.36**.
	Copies of the petition must also be sent (by post or personal delivery) to the company's voluntary liquidator, administrator, supervisor of a voluntary arrangement or administrative receiver.
Certificate of service	Certificate of service (see **82.37**) on company must be filed as soon as reasonably practicable after service and not less than five business days before the hearing.
Notice	Petition must be advertised in the *London Gazette*, but not until seven business days after service on the company. There must be no other publicity for the petition until this advertisement appears. Advertisement must appear at least seven days before the date appointed for hearing the petition.
Track	Automatically multi-track.
Provisional liquidator	An application may be made for the appointment of a provisional liquidator (see **82.44** to **82.53**).
Evidence	The petition and verifying statement of truth will usually be the only evidence in the case. The company may file evidence in opposition, a copy of which must be sent to the petitioner, not less than five business days before the hearing. No further evidence may be filed unless the court directs.
Certificate of compliance	Certificate of compliance (form 4.7) must be filed, with a copy of the advertisement, at least five business days before the hearing.

List of persons appearing	Form 4.10 must be completed and handed to the court before the hearing commences.
Heard by	Registrar or District Judge in public.
Decision	Court may make order applied for, dismiss the petition, adjourn (conditionally or unconditionally), make an interim order, or any other order it thinks fit. Registrar or District Judge may refer case to judge.
Perfection	If court makes winding-up order, it will notify the official receiver, who becomes liquidator. All documents necessary to enable the order to be completed must be left at the court by the next business day. Court draws up the order. Official receiver notifies the order in the *London Gazette*.

Procedural checklist 36   Application by a creditor whose debt is presently payable for a bankruptcy order

See **chapter 83**.

Pre-action	Check that the amount of the creditor's claim is at least £5,000 and that there is no substantial dispute about the amount. Check that the claim is unsecured and is for a liquidated debt payable immediately and there is no substantial dispute that it is due and payable. Check that there is no substantial cross-claim which would reduce the balance owed to the creditor to less than £5,000. Check that an appropriately clear demand for payment has been made and that no payment has been received. If judgment has been obtained for the debt, consider whether to execute: partly or wholly unsatisfied execution is a ground for a bankruptcy petition.
Statutory demand	Unless there is a partly or wholly unsatisfied execution for the debt, a statutory demand must be served on the debtor. Prescribed form is form 6.1, or form 6.2 if the debt is a judgment debt for which execution has not been issued. If practicable, there must be personal service of a statutory demand, by leaving it with the debtor (**CPR, r. 6.5(3)**). Steps specified in **PD Insolvency Proceedings, para. 13.3.4(1)**, must be followed. If that fails to effect service, the steps specified in **para. 13.3.4(2), (3)** and **(4)**, which may involve substituted service by first-class post or insertion through a letter box, must be followed. If the debt is a judgment debt, service may be by newspaper advertisement if the debtor has absconded or is avoiding service and there is no real prospect of successful execution. Certificate of service, using form 6.11 or, for substituted service, 6.12, must be filed with the petition.
	The debtor has three weeks to comply with the statutory demand and may apply for it to be set aside, see **83.8**.
	A petition may be presented before the three weeks expire if there is a serious possibility that the debtor's property or the value of any of it will be significantly diminished during the three weeks. The petition must state that possibility.
Preparation	In order to complete the petition, ascertain whether the debtor appears to be carrying on business as an insurance undertaking, credit institution, investment undertaking providing services involving the holding of funds or securities for third parties, or a collective investment undertaking, and ascertain whether the debtor's centre of main interests is outside the United Kingdom.
Appropriate court	County Court hearing centre which deals with bankruptcy for the district in which the debtor resided or carried on business in the previous six months. All petitions assigned to the London insolvency district are dealt with at the RCJ, either in the County Court at Central London if the petition debt is less than £50,000 or in the High Court if it is £50,000 or more. See **83.4**.

	If the debtor's centre of main interests is in another EU State (apart from Denmark) and the debtor has no establishment in the United Kingdom (see **82.9** to **82.12**), proceedings must be started in the country where the centre of main interests is located, not in England and Wales.
Form of petition	Form 6.7, or form 6.9 if the petition is based on partially or wholly unsatisfied execution. The petition must be verified by statement of truth in form 6.13A. See **83.9** and **83.10**. Two copies will be required for filing (one for the court, one for service on the debtor).
Fees	A court fee of £280 (**CPFO, fee 3.1(b)**) and a deposit of £990 for the official receiver's fee must be paid when filing.
Filing	Two copies of the petition must be filed and, if the petition relies on non-compliance with a statutory demand, a certificate of service of the demand. Both copies of the petition are sealed and endorsed with the venue for hearing the petition. One copy is retained by the court, the other is returned to the petitioner for service on the debtor.
Service	Personal service of the petition by leaving it with the debtor (**CPR, r. 6.5(3)**) is required. **PD Insolvency Proceedings, para. 13.3.4**, sets out the steps which should be taken before concluding that personal service cannot be effected so that an application for substituted service is justified.
Certificate of service	Certificate of service on the debtor (form 6.17A for personal service; form 6.18A for substituted service) must be filed as soon as reasonably practicable after service, and not less than five business days before the hearing of the petition.
Track	Automatically multi-track.
Interim receiver	An application may be made by the debtor or any creditor for the appointment of an interim receiver (see **83.16**).
Evidence	The petition and verifying statement of truth will usually be the only evidence in the case. If the debtor intends to oppose the petition, he or she must, not later than five business days before the hearing, file in court a notice specifying the grounds of objection and send a copy to the petitioner.
List of persons appearing	Form 6.20 must be completed and handed to the court before the hearing commences.
Decision	Court may make order applied for if satisfied that the statements in the petition are true, and that the debt on which it is founded has not been paid, or secured or compounded for.
Perfection	The court settles a bankruptcy order. Two sealed copies are sent to the official receiver, who sends one to the bankrupt. Official receiver notifies the order in the *London Gazette*.

Procedural checklist 37   Residential mortgage possession claims

See **chapter 87**.

Protocol	**Pre-Action Protocol for Possession Based on Mortgage or Home Purchase Plan Arrears in Respect of Residential Property**: required behaviour of mortgage lenders includes initial pre-proceedings letter giving the borrower regulatory information sheet or equivalent and the following account information: amount of arrears, the outstanding balance and what interest charges are to be added to the account (**para. 5.1**). If an agreement for repayment is made, 15 business days' notice must be given of intention to commence court action (**para. 5.7**). Consideration to be given to postponing possession claim (**paras 6, 7** and **8**).

Which court	County Court hearing centre for district of property address (**CPR, r. 55.3(1)**); unless exceptionally High Court (**CPR, r. 55.3(2)** and **(3)**; **PD 55A, paras 1.3, 1.4, 1.6**; County Courts Act 1984, s. 21). Or online (see below).
Intended parties	All parties to mortgage deed: consider status of persons with overriding interests.
Commencement	Claim form (N5) and particulars of claim (N120) filed and served together. See **CPR, rr. 55.3, 55.4**, and **PD 55A, para. 2.5**; and **PD 16, para. 7.3**.
	Specific contents of particulars of claim (**PD 55A, paras 2.1, 2.5, 2.5A**). Fee is £355 in the County Court, £528 in the High Court (**CPFO, fees 1.4(a)** and **(b)**).
Online	PCOL system. Combined claim form and particulars of claim. See **CPR, r. 55.10A**, and **PD 55B**. No filing of mortgage deed (**PD 55B, para. 6.2**). Specific contents of online form (**PD 55B, paras 6.3, 6.3A, 6.3B**). Fee is £325 (**CPFO, fee 1.4(c)**). Deemed served fifth day after issue. Not more than seven days after issue, claimant serves full arrears history if online form had only a summary (**PD 55B, para. 6.3C**).
Defence	Form N11M. Must be filed within 14 days after service of particulars of claim (**CPR, rr. 15.4** and **55.7(3)**). In Consumer Credit Act 1974 case may apply for time order in defence (**PD 55A, para. 7.1**) or can make later **Part 23** application.
Notices to tenants and others	Within five days of receiving hearing date, claimant sends notice of hearing to tenants/occupiers at the property, to local housing authority and other mortgagees (**CPR, r. 55.10(2)**).
Evidence	Witness statements served at least two days before hearing updating figures to hearing date (**CPR, r. 55.8(4)**).
Pre-hearing adjournment	Application by consent. No fee if made more than 14 days pre-hearing, otherwise £100 (**CPFO, fee 2.5**).
Hearing	Date fixed at issue. Is 28 days or more after issue and 21 days or more after service (**CPR, r. 55.5**), unless time abridged under **CPR, r. 3.1(2)(a)** or **(b)**. At hearing claimant produces office copy Land Registry entries and search, Protocol checklist (N123) with copy for defendant and, if not already filed, copy mortgage, conditions and certificate of service of **CPR, r. 55(10)**, notice (unless in witness statement). Oral update of key figures.
Allocation	If substantial dispute, allocation to track (**CPR, Part 26** and **rr. 55.8(2)** and **55.9**) — potentially proceeds to multi-track trial.

Procedural checklist 38 Enforcement of possession orders

See 87.48 to 87.57.

Warrant of possession	14 days' notice to tenants etc. (**CPR, r. 83.26(5)**). Request for warrant of possession (within 6 years of order) (**rr. 83.2(3)(a)** and **83.26**). Form N325. Fee is £121 (**CPFO, fee 8.6**).
Stay or suspension	Defendant's application to stay, suspend or vary possession order, or application by unauthorised tenant to stay or suspend order for two months. Form N244. See **CPR, Part 23**. Fee is £50 (**CPFO, fee 2.7**). Hearing listed.
Forcible re-entry	Application for permission for warrant of restitution (and witness statement) (**CPR, r. 83.26(8)** and **(9)**). Form N244. Fee is £55 for the application (**CPFO, fee 1.8(a)**) plus £121 for the warrant (**CPFO, fee 8.6**).

PART A

General Matters

Chapter 1   The Overriding Objective and Sources
of Procedural Law

Commentary

INTRODUCTION

This chapter will consider the various sources of the law governing civil proceedings, and will **1.1** also give general guidance on the interpretation of the main source, the Civil Procedure Rules 1998 ('CPR'). Specific consideration of the detailed provisions of the CPR and related statutory sources and case law can be found in **chapters 2 to 81**. These are supplemented by the procedural checklists starting on page 1. The full text of the CPR, and their related practice directions, can be found in **appendix 1**. Pre-action protocols are in **appendix 2**. Court fees orders are in **appendix 3**. Statutes governing civil proceedings are in **appendix 4**. **Chapters 82 to 89** contain text on:

(a) insolvency proceedings and companies matters (**82 to 86**);
(b) mortgage possession claims (**chapter 87**);
(c) anti-social behaviour and harassment (**chapter 88**); and
(d) human rights law (**chapter 89**).

SOURCES OF PROCEDURAL LAW

Inherent jurisdiction

1.2   Being the successor to the pre-1875 common law courts, the High Court has inherent juris-
diction to control its procedures to ensure its proceedings are not abused to achieve injustice.
As Lord Diplock said in *Bremer Vulkan Schiffbau und Maschinenfabrik v South India Shipping
Corporation Ltd* [1981] AC 909 at p. 977, the High Court has:

> a general power to control its own procedure so as to prevent its being used to achieve injustice. Such a
> power is inherent in its constitution as a court of justice.... it would stultify the constitutional role of
> the High Court as a court of justice if it were not armed with power to prevent its process being misused
> in such a way as to diminish its capability of arriving at a just decision of the dispute.

Before the introduction of the CPR, much of the law relating to striking out as a sanction, and
the initial development of the jurisdiction to grant freezing injunctions and search orders, was
based on the High Court's inherent jurisdiction. Once an area has been codified, the need for
recourse to the inherent jurisdiction recedes or disappears, see *Harrison v Tew* [1990] 2 AC 523, in
which it was held that the inherent jurisdiction to order the assessment by the court of a solicitor's
bill of costs had been ousted by subsequent statutory codification. Likewise, there is no residual
inherent discretion where there are express provisions of the CPR (*Raja v Van Hoogstraten (No. 9)*
[2008] EWCA Civ 1444, [2009] 1 WLR 1143). In his Hamlyn lecture, 'The inherent jurisdiction of the
court' ([1970] Current Legal Problems 23, 50–1), Sir Jack Jacob said the powers of the court
under its inherent jurisdiction: 'are complementary to its powers under rules of court; one set of
powers supplements and reinforces the other... where the usefulness of the powers under the rules
ends, the usefulness of the powers under the inherent jurisdiction begins.' Professor Dockray
('The inherent jurisdiction to regulate civil proceedings' (1997) 113 LQR 120, 128) said: 'the
inherent jurisdiction may supplement but cannot be used to lay down procedure which is contrary to or inconsistent with a valid rule of [court]'. See also *Moore v Assignment Courier Ltd* [1977] 1
WLR 638 at pp. 644–5; *Langley v North West Water Authority* [1991] 1 WLR 697 at p. 709; *Raja v Van
Hoogstraten (No. 9)* at [74]–[78]). As a new procedural code (**CPR, r. 1.1(1)**), the CPR are intended
to be comprehensive. If there is any lacuna, any exercise of the inherent jurisdiction should be in
a way which is consistent with the rules (*Raja v Van Hoogstraten (No. 9)* at [85]).

In *Al Rawi v Security Service* [2011] UKSC 34, [2012] 1 AC 531, the point is made that in some circumstances procedure is as important as substantive law. As Professor Dockray said in his article:

> Major innovations in procedural law should therefore be recognised as an institutional responsibility,
> not a matter on which individual judges should respond to the pleas of particular litigants. Procedural
> revolutions should appear first in statutes or in the Rules of Court, not in the law reports.

It is probably the case that the County Court, being the creature of statute, has no inherent jurisdic-
tion. There is direct authority to the contrary in *Langley v North West Water Authority* [1991] 1 WLR 697,
in which it was held (before the enactment, in the Civil Procedure Act 1997, of the County Courts
Act 1984, s. 74A) that the County Court had inherent jurisdiction to issue a local practice direction.
See also the family cases of *D v D (County Court Jurisdiction: Injunctions)* [1993] 2 FLR 802 and *Devon County
Council v B* [1997] 1 FLR 591, which probably turn on the effect of the Children Act 1989. The wide
scope of the legislation governing County Court proceedings now allows practically no scope or
necessity for the exercise of the County Court's inherent jurisdiction even if it has one.

Statutory sources

1.3   The primary source of law governing procedure in the High Court and Court of Appeal is the
Senior Courts Act 1981 (formerly the Supreme Court Act 1981). The County Court is governed
by the County Courts Act 1984. These statutes are the primary source of the jurisdiction exercised
by the civil courts in England and Wales. Both statutes are often expressed in very wide terms,

leaving the detailed mechanics of many of the procedures used in the courts to be set out in rules of court. The power to make court rules is granted by the Civil Procedure Act 1997. The **Access to Justice Act 1999** made provision for funding litigation, and also contains provisions dealing with appeals, courts, judges and civil proceedings. Various other statutes also govern aspects of civil procedure. For example, the Administration of Justice Act 1969 provides for leapfrog appeals to the Supreme Court, certain enforcement procedures are governed by the Charging Orders Act 1979 and the Attachment of Earnings Act 1971, and limitation is governed by the Limitation Act 1980.

There are a number of important statutory instruments. The main source of procedural law is the **Civil Procedure Rules 1998 (SI 1998/3123)** (which are amended several times each year), see **1.5**. Jurisdiction between the High Court and the County Court is mainly dealt with by the **High Court and County Courts Jurisdiction Order 1991 (SI 1991/724)** (see **appendix 4**). Court fees are laid down by the **Civil Proceedings Fees Order 2008 (SI 2008/1053)** (CPFO) (see **appendix 3**).

The international dimension is becoming increasingly important in civil procedure. A fundamental change in the approach to many issues, such as the right to a fair trial, has been brought in by the **Human Rights Act 1998**, which incorporates the provisions of the European Convention on Human Rights into English law (see **chapter 89** and **appendix 4**). Also important are European Community Regulations dealing with jurisdiction and service of proceedings. Extracts from **Regulation (EU) No. 1215/2012** and the **Civil Jurisdiction and Judgments Act 1982** can be found in **appendix 4**.

Former Rules of the Supreme Court and County Court Rules

Until April 1999, rules governing civil procedure were the Rules of the Supreme Court 1965   **1.4** (RSC) which covered proceedings in the High Court and the Civil Division of the Court of Appeal (these were an extensively revised version of rules set out in sch. 1 to the Supreme Court of Judicature Act 1875, which were themselves in part distilled from pre-existing procedures), and the County Court Rules 1981 (CCR) which covered proceedings in the County Court. The fact that the CCR differed in many respects from the RSC added to the complexity of the old civil justice system, and the production of a unified set of rules is one of the main improvements introduced by the **Civil Procedure Rules 1998**.

Civil Procedure Rules

By the Civil Procedure Act 1997, s. 2, a Civil Procedure Rule Committee was established,   **1.5** with the power to make rules governing the practice and procedure to be followed in:

(a) the civil division of the Court of Appeal;
(b) the High Court; and
(c) the County Court.

The committee is required, by s. 1(3), to exercise its power to make rules 'with a view to securing that the civil justice system is accessible, fair and efficient'. Pursuant to this power, with effect from 26 April 1999, civil proceedings in England and Wales have been governed by a unified set of procedural rules, the **Civil Procedure Rules 1998 (SI 1998/3123)**. These rules brought into effect the proposals for reform of the civil justice system set out in the *Final Report* compiled by Lord Woolf (*Access to Justice. Final Report* (London: HMSO, 1996)). They embody the most radical reform of civil litigation since the Judicature Acts 1873 to 1875. The full text of the CPR, as amended (apart from rules concerning civil proceedings which are ancillary to criminal proceedings and investigations), can be found in **appendix 1**.

Schedule rules

When the CPR were introduced, quite substantial sections of the old RSC and CCR were   **1.6** retained (with minor revisions) in **CPR, sch. 1** (the preserved provisions of the RSC) and **sch. 2** (the preserved provisions of the CCR). These provisions continue in force by virtue of **CPR, Part 50**. Since 1998 many provisions of the old rules in the schedules have been replaced by new rules in the main body of the CPR. So the number of Parts of the CPR has increased, with corresponding deletions from the schedules.

The rules re-enacted in the schedules are of two general types. First, a number of general procedural rules are retained, such as some of the rules on enforcement of judgments. Secondly, there are provisions from the old rules dealing with the County Court's special jurisdiction under three statutes (see **CPR, sch. 2, CCR, ord. 44** and **ord. 49**) and rules concerning proceedings, under various statutes, which are ancillary to criminal proceedings and investigations, which are not considered in *Blackstone's Civil Practice*. **CPR, r. 50(2)**, provides that the CPR apply in relation to the proceedings to which the schedules apply, subject to the provisions in the schedules and the relevant practice directions. This means that the overriding objective (see **1.12**) applies to applications made under these re-enacted provisions from the old rules.

Practice directions

1.7   As permitted by the Civil Procedure Act 1997, ss. 1 and 5, and sch. 1, para. 6, the CPR are supplemented by practice directions (PDs). The general scheme is that individual areas of civil procedure are governed by Parts of the CPR, with almost every Part being supplemented by one or more PDs. Practice directions set out details of procedure that it is felt do not need to be set out in statutory instruments (as required for amendments to the CPR), which allows for flexible amendment in the light of experience. The full text of the PDs can be found in **appendix 1**. Each PD is printed after the Part of the CPR which it supplements.

Practice directions may be given either in accordance with the Constitutional Reform Act 2005, sch. 2, part 1, or with the approval of either the Lord Chancellor or Lord Chief Justice (Civil Procedure Act 1997, s. 5). Judges are bound to follow, and have no power to alter, PDs made under s. 5. Judges have no authority to lay down PDs which change rules laid down in the CPR or PDs promulgated by the Ministry of Justice, and any such purported practice direction has no effect (*Bovale Ltd v Secretary of State for Communities and Local Government* [2009] EWCA Civ 171, [2009] 1 WLR 2274). Practice directions are 'directions as to the practice and procedure of any court' (s. 9(1) and (2)). Guidance on the application and interpretation of the law (which is often given in judicial decisions, and often includes guidance on how the rules and PDs work) does not come within this definition (s. 9(5)). A judgment of the court which suggests a procedure to fill a gap in the rules was held not to be a practice direction in *Bovale Ltd v Secretary of State for Communities and Local Government*.

Pre-action protocols

1.8   Pre-action protocols have been formulated for clinical negligence, disease and illness, personal injury, construction and engineering, housing disrepair, dilapidations, rent arrears, mortgage repossession, defamation, professional negligence and judicial review claims, and low value personal injury claims arising from road traffic accidents, employers' liability or public liability. Each protocol contains detailed rules for stating the allegations being made and the reasons for any denial of liability, and for disclosure of documents. **PD Pre-action Conduct and Protocols** sets out the similar approach required in cases not covered by specific pre-action protocols. The protocols are intended to enable parties to obtain relevant information at an early stage, and to promote settlement of the dispute (see **chapter 8**). The CPR enable the court to take into account compliance or non-compliance with **PD Pre-action Conduct and Protocols** or any relevant protocol when giving directions for the management of proceedings (**CPR, rr. 3.1(4)** and **(5)** and **3.9(1)(e)**) and when making orders for costs (**r. 44.3(5)(a)**). The text of the protocols can be found in **appendix 2**.

Court guides

Practical guidance on the conduct of proceedings in the specialist courts and in the main Divisions **1.9** of the High Court have been published. Court guides were first published before the introduction of the CPR. The first edition of the Chancery Guide, for example, was issued in April 1995. The present editions of the guides have been written so as to comply with the provisions of the CPR and relevant PDs. They can be seen at the Ministry of Justice website, http://www.justice.gov.uk.

The court guides draw attention to important matters of practice, common errors and failings, give detailed information about forms to use, provide courtroom and telephone numbers for the use of practitioners, and generally supplement the provisions of the CPR and PDs. Court guides have no formal status, and provide no more than guidance (*Bovale Ltd v Secretary of State for Communities and Local Government* [2009] EWCA Civ 171, [2009] 1 WLR 2274; *Brown v Innovatorone plc* [2009] EWHC 1376 (Comm), [2010] 2 All ER (Comm) 80 at [30]). They are not designed to define the court's jurisdiction, are not to be taken as replacements for the CPR, and are not to be read as if they were statutes (*Vitpol Building Service v Samen* [2008] EWHC 2283 (TCC), [2009] Bus LR D65). Nor can they override the PDs (*Carnegie v Giessen* [2005] EWCA Civ 191, [2005] 1 WLR 2510 at [20]).

Forms

Numerous standard forms have been promulgated to assist practitioners and court users. Many **1.10** are prescribed forms, made under the authority of statutory instruments, and can be identified by the letter 'N' in their designations (e.g. form N244 is the standard application notice). Others are 'practice forms', issued under the authority of the masters of the High Court, which can be identified by the letters 'PF' in their designations. Some PDs contain important precedents, such as the standard-form freezing injunctions and search orders in the annex to **PD 25A**. Forms that are to be completed by parties can be downloaded, in versions that can be completed on-screen, from the Court Form Finder at http://hmctsformfinder.justice.gov.uk/HMCTS/FormFinder.do.

THE CIVIL PROCEDURE RULES 1998

Scope of the Civil Procedure Rules

The general rule is that the Civil Procedure Rules 1998 apply to all proceedings in the County **1.11** Court, the High Court and the Civil Division of the Court of Appeal (**r. 2.1(1)**). Seven types of civil proceedings are taken outside the scope of the CPR by **r. 2.1(2)**. These cover insolvency, non-contentious probate, Prize Court, Court of Protection, family, adoption and election proceedings. The exceptions are mostly covered by their own specific procedural rules, such as the Insolvency Rules 1986 (SI 1986/1925), the Court of Protection Rules 2007 (SI 2007/1744) and the Family Procedure Rules 2010 (SI 2010/2955).

The CPR established an entirely new procedural code (**CPR, r. 1.1(1)**). As a result authorities under the old rules must be applied with considerable caution when interpreting the CPR (see **1.21**). At one level this is because all procedural decisions made under the CPR have to be in accordance with the overriding objective of dealing with cases justly (see **1.12**), whereas there was no specific statement to this effect in the old rules of court. While superficially attractive, this is not the real reason why old cases are not authoritative under the CPR. Making the CPR a new 'code' means that a new start was made. The CPR are not merely a more modern restatement of the old rules, but a complete replacement of those rules. **Rule 1.1(1)** specifically refers to the CPR as being a 'procedural' code. However, there is a clear distinction between procedure (or how the court system operates) and practice (the principles applied when dealing with procedural problems). **Rule 1.1(1)** does not say, perhaps deliberately, that the CPR are to be regarded as being a new codification of the practice to be adopted by the courts when making procedural decisions. Nor does **r. 1.1** override existing rules of evidence (see *McPhilemy v Times Newspapers Ltd (No. 2)* [2000] 1 WLR 1732).

While **r. 2.1(1)** provides that the CPR apply to all proceedings in the County Court, High Court and the Civil Division of the Court of Appeal, they derive their authority as subordinate legislation, and therefore do not oust the effect of Acts of Parliament. This is sometimes stated in terms in the CPR (such as **r. 6.1(a)**, which says Part 6 applies except where any other enactment makes other provision), but also applies generally as a matter of principle (*Mucelli v Government of Albania* [2009] UKHL 2, [2009] 1 WLR 276 at [74]).

Overriding objective

1.12   The ethos of the CPR is encapsulated in **r. 1.1**, which provides:

(1) These Rules are a new procedural code with the overriding objective of enabling the court to deal with cases justly and at proportionate cost.

(2) Dealing with a case justly and at proportionate cost includes, so far as is practicable—

   (a) ensuring that the parties are on an equal footing;

   (b) saving expense;

   (c) dealing with the case in ways which are proportionate—

      (i)   to the amount of money involved;

      (ii) to the importance of the case;

      (iii) to the complexity of the issues; and

      (iv) to the financial position of each party;

   (d) ensuring that it is dealt with expeditiously and fairly;

   (e) allotting to it an appropriate share of the court's resources, while taking into account the need to allot resources to other cases; and

   (f) enforcing compliance with rules, practice directions and orders.

The court is required to give effect to this overriding objective of dealing with cases justly and at proportionate cost when exercising any power under the rules, or when interpreting any rule (**r. 1.2**). Modifications are made to the overriding objective in respect of certain counter-terrorism and national security situations to ensure that information is not disclosed contrary to the public interest or contrary to the national interest (see **50.80** to **50.83**), namely:

(a) control order proceedings under the Prevention of Terrorism Act 2005 (which are governed by CPR, Part 76, and in particular r. 76.2 — the Prevention of Terrorism Act 2005 was repealed by the Terrorism Prevention and Investigation Measures Act 2011, s. 1, subject to transitional provisions in s. 29 and sch. 8);

(b) financial restrictions proceedings under the Counter-Terrorism Act 2008 (which are governed by CPR, Part 79, and in particular r. 79.2);

(c) terrorism prevention and investigation measures proceedings (known as 'TPIM proceedings') under the Terrorism Prevention and Investigation Measures Act 2011 (which are governed by CPR, Part 80, and in particular r. 80.2);

(d) closed material applications under the Justice and Security Act 2013 (which are governed by CPR, Part 82, and in particular r. 82.2); and

(e) temporary exclusion orders under the Counter-Terrorism and Security Act 2015 (which are governed by CPR, Part 88).

Parties to litigation are required to help the court to further the overriding objective (**r. 1.3**).

Interpretation

1.13   The CPR have been promulgated in a statutory instrument, so they must be interpreted in accordance with the provisions of the Interpretation Act 1978 (Interpretation Act 1978, ss. 5 and 11; *Collier v Williams* [2006] EWCA Civ 20, [2006] 1 WLR 1945 at [32]). Reference can be made to the headings to the rules as an aid to interpretation (*Brown v Innovatorone plc* [2009] EWHC 1376 (Comm), [2010] 2 All ER (Comm) 80). Headings may be taken into account in interpreting primary legislation provided due account is taken of the fact that headings are intended to provide brief but necessarily inexact guides to the contents of the relevant provisions and that headings in legislation are not included in a Bill for debate but for ease of reference (*R v Montila*

[2004] UKHL 50, [2004] 1 WLR 3141 at [34]). However, headings are available for consideration by the Civil Procedure Rule Committee, so the last point does not apply when considering headings in the CPR (*Brown v Innovatorone plc* at [17]).

Amendments are made to the CPR (also by statutory instrument) several times each year. Detailed notes on the amendments made to the CPR can be found in **appendix 1**, immediately after the text of the schedules to the CPR. Amendment rules usually have transitional provisions, but the underlying principle is that amendments to the CPR have immediate effect even on existing litigation, so the presumption against retrospection does not apply (*Wagenaar v Weekend Travel Ltd* [2014] EWCA Civ 1105, [2015] 1 WLR 1968).

By **CPR, r. 1.2**, the CPR must be interpreted so as to give effect to the overriding objective (in **r. 1.1**, see **1.12**) of enabling the court to deal with cases justly and at proportionate cost. This is modified in terrorism and closed material proceedings in order to ensure sensitive materials are not disclosed contrary to the public interest or the interests of national security (rr. 76.2, 79.2, 80.2 and 82.2; see **1.12**). Where there are no express words in the CPR dealing with a situation, the court is bound to consider which interpretation best reflects the overriding objective when construing the rules (*Totty v Snowden* [2001] EWCA Civ 1415, [2002] 1 WLR 1384 at [34]). As a result, the old 'quasi-statutory' approach to interpretation, based upon a close analysis of the language used in an attempt to find the true intention of the rules, might be thought to be a thing of the past. Lord Woolf commented in the *Final Report*, ch. 14, para. 5, that:

judges exercising appellate functions will have a significant part to play in giving effect to the new system of case management... by laying down principles to be followed in exercising the new powers of case management. It should be borne in mind, however, that management decisions are pre-eminently matters of discretion with which an appeal court would seldom interfere.

Purposive interpretation

Lord Woolf himself made clear in the *Final Report* how the overriding objective must be used to interpret the rules. At paras 10–11 of ch. 20 he stated: **1.14**

Every word in the rules should have a purpose, but every word cannot sensibly be given a minutely exact meaning. Civil procedure involves more judgment and knowledge than the rules can directly express. In this respect, rules of court are not like an instruction manual for operating a piece of machinery. Ultimately their purpose is to guide the court and the litigants towards the just resolution of the case. Although the rules can offer detailed directions for the technical steps to be taken, the effectiveness of those steps depends upon the spirit in which they are carried out. That in turn depends on an understanding of the fundamental purpose of the rules and of the underlying system of procedure.

In order to identify that purpose at the outset, I have placed at the very beginning of the rules a statement of their overriding objective.

In other words, interpretation is to be purposive rather than a matter of close analysis of the meaning of individual words without taking into account their context.

Plain meaning of the rules

The CPR have been deliberately drafted in a plain English style in order to make them intelligible to lay people using the courts. When construing the rules the courts primarily seek to find the natural meaning of the words used. Although the court must seek to give effect to the overriding objective when interpreting any rule (**CPR, r. 1.2(b)**), this does not enable the court to hold that provisions of the CPR which have a plain meaning should be construed contrary to that meaning, nor that the plain meaning should be ignored (*Vinos v Marks and Spencer plc* [2001] 3 All ER 784 at [20]). The court cannot, therefore, assume a discretion in order to assist a deserving case where there is no jurisdiction to make an order, even by resorting to the overriding objective (*Godwin v Swindon Borough Council* [2001] EWCA Civ 1478, [2002] 1 WLR 997 at [45]).   **1.15**

May, must, should, shall and will

1.16   There is a clear distinction between a rule that says a court 'may' do something, thereby giving the court a discretion (which ought to be exercised in accordance with the overriding objective), and a rule which says something 'must' be done (which is obligatory). An example is **CPR, Part 13**. Where a default judgment has been entered prematurely or otherwise in circumstances where the claimant is not entitled to judgment, **r. 13.2** provides that the default judgment must be set aside. On the other hand, where there has been compliance with the rules relating to entering a default judgment, setting aside the judgment is a matter of discretion, **r. 13.3** providing that the court 'may' set it aside. Most of the powers given to the courts under the CPR are given in discretionary form.

Most of the steps to be taken by the parties in the course of proceedings are expressed in mandatory terms. This is frequently made clear by use of the word 'must'. For example, **PD 7A, para. 3.5**, which applies where a claim is to be served outside the jurisdiction under **Regulation (EC) No. 44/2001**, provides that a prescribed endorsement 'must' be included on the claim form. In the past 'should' or 'shall' have been used interchangeably with the word 'must' in a number of provisions in the CPR, but most of these were changed to 'must' by the Civil Procedure (Amendment) Rules 2008 (SI 2008/2178). Subsequent amendments to the CPR, and Ministry of Justice updates to the practice directions, have made various changes such as 'may' to 'will', and 'shall' to 'will', with the intention of ensuring the relevant requirements are treated as mandatory. These changes were made after cases such as *Choudhury v Kingston Hospital NHS Trust* [2006] EWHC 90057 (Costs), LTL 7/9/2006, and *Metcalfe v Clipston* [2004] EWHC 9005 (Costs) held that 'should' is not mandatory. **PD 2D** says that from 1 October 2014 new rules and amendments to the **CPR** will generally provide that the court 'must' do a required action rather than 'will'. **PD 2D** closes by saying: 'Occasionally in the future, it may still be appropriate to use the word "will", for example in a statement of future intent, and on those occasions, "will" will be used.'

Problems with mandatory and discretionary language

1.17   The word 'may' is, in certain contexts, used in a mandatory rather than a discretionary sense. An example is **CPR, r. 24.4(1)**, which provides that a claimant 'may' not apply for summary judgment until the defendant has filed an acknowledgment of service or a defence.

Sometimes there are problems in determining who has the power to exercise a discretion created by use of the word 'may'. An example is **r. 32.5(5)**, which provides that if a party who has served a witness statement does not call the witness or use the statement at trial, 'any other party may put the witness statement in as hearsay evidence'. A natural reading of the rule would indicate that the discretion is vested in the other party to the proceedings. Remarkably, in *McPhilemy v Times Newspapers Ltd (No. 2)* [2000] 1 WLR 1732 it was held that the court has a discretion to refuse permission to use such a statement (see **51.23**).

Sometimes the word 'should' is interpreted to mean 'ought, but may do something else'. The prime example of this is *Bloomsbury Publishing Group Ltd v News Group Newspapers Ltd* [2003] EWHC 1205 (Ch), [2003] 1 WLR 1633, in which it was held that it is possible to issue a claim against 'person or persons unknown'. **PD 7A, para. 4.1(3)**, provides that the title of a claim form must contain a title which 'should' state the full name of each party. Use of the word 'should' was contrasted by the court with the word 'must', and was held to justify an interpretation allowing proceedings to be issued against persons unknown.

Different meanings given to different expressions

1.18   In a number of cases the courts have held that different expressions appearing in a single rule have to be given different meanings. An example is the difference between 'day' and 'business day' where they appear in **CPR, r. 6.26**. 'Business day' is defined by **r. 6.2(b)** as excluding Saturdays, Sundays and bank holidays (including Christmas Day and Good Friday). In

Anderton v Clwyd County Council (No. 2) [2002] EWCA Civ 933, [2002] 1 WLR 3174 it was held that 'day' had to bear a different meaning, and was interpreted as meaning any calendar day, including weekends and bank holidays etc.

This is based on a literalistic approach to interpretation, and is hard to reconcile with the intended purposive approach advocated by Lord Woolf (see **1.14**).

Interpretation and human rights

The **Human Rights Act 1998, s. 3(1)**, provides that, so far as it is possible to do so, primary   **1.19** legislation and subordinate legislation (which includes the CPR) must be read and given effect in a way which is compatible with the rights set out in the European Convention on Human Rights. In *Goode v Martin* [2001] EWCA Civ 1899, [2002] 1 WLR 1828, s. 3(1) of the Act and **art. 6(1)** of the Convention were used by the court as a basis for reading additional words into **CPR, r. 17.4**, so that it would not prevent the claimant bringing her real claim to trial. The **Human Rights Act 1998, s. 2(1)** provides that a court determining a question which arises in connection with a Convention right must take into account any judgment, decision, declaration or advisory opinion of the European Court of Human Rights. Although lawyers must take a responsible attitude to raising human rights points (*Daniels v Walker* [2000] 1 WLR 1382), such points do arise on occasion when courts are considering procedural applications, and the CPR and practice directions have been drafted with a view to being compatible with the Convention.

Reliance on court staff

In *Sayers v Clarke Walker* [2002] EWCA Civ 645, [2002] 1 WLR 3095, the appellant's solicitors said   **1.20** that a breach of the rules had occurred because they had relied on misleading advice given by court staff. It was held to be wrong for solicitors to attempt to rely on conversations with court staff for the purpose of interpreting civil practice, and that being solicitors they should be expected to know such matters themselves. Likewise, no reliance can be placed on indications given by court staff as to the decision to be made by a judge (*City and General (Holborn) Ltd v Structure Tone Ltd* [2009] EWHC 2139 (TCC), [2009] BLR 541).

Old case law: generally redundant

As a general rule, advocates should not resort to decisions under the old rules for assistance in   **1.21** interpreting the CPR. In *Biguzzi v Rank Leisure plc* [1999] 1 WLR 1926 the Court of Appeal (Lord Woolf MR, Brooke LJ, Robert Walker LJ) held that the pre-CPR cases on abuse of process in the form of wholesale disregard of court rules (such as *Arbuthnot Latham Bank Ltd v Trafalgar Holdings Ltd* [1998] 1 WLR 1426) are not binding or persuasive authorities on the exercise of the court's discretion under the CPR. The Court of Appeal said the position under the CPR is fundamentally different from under the old system. It pointed out that under **r. 1.1** the CPR are a 'new procedural code', and compliance with court orders would be regarded as more important than under the previous system. Lord Woolf made it clear that, 'Earlier authorities are no longer generally of any relevance once the CPR applies' ([1999] 1 WLR 1926 at p. 1934). Counsel in *Vinos v Marks and Spencer plc* [2001] 3 All ER 784 had made submissions by reference to authorities under the old rules. May LJ said, at [17]:

these submissions are not in point. The CPR are a new procedural code, and the question for this court in this case concerns the interpretation and application of the relevant provisions of the new procedural code as they stand untrammelled by the weight of authority that accumulated under the former Rules.

In *SSQ Europe SA v Johann & Backes OHG* [2002] 1 Lloyd's Rep 465 the court commented that decisions under similar (but not identical) provisions of the RSC should be treated 'with caution'. While this is the position in all courts up to and including the Court of Appeal, the Supreme Court frequently reviews case law of some antiquity when deciding important points of principle (see for example, *Summers v Fairclough Homes Ltd* [2012] UKSC 26, [2012] 1 WLR 2004).

Old cases as a guide to exercise of discretion

1.22   Where the CPR and previous rules have similar or identical wording, and where it can be shown that the operation of old authorities is consistent with the requirement to further the overriding objective as it applies in the particular case, the court may be prepared to take them into account or at least be persuaded by arguments based on principles established in pre-CPR cases. In *Purdy v Cameran* [1999] CPLR 843 May LJ stated:

> Lord Woolf in *Biguzzi v Rank Leisure plc* [1999] 1 WLR 1926 was not saying that the underlying thought processes of previous decisions should be completely thrown overboard. It is clear in my view, that what Lord Woolf was saying was that reference to authorities under the former rules is generally no longer relevant. Rather it is necessary to concentrate on the intrinsic justice of a particular case in the light of the overriding objective.

Previous jurisprudence, for example, on the exercise of the court's discretion to discharge orders for service out of the jurisdiction made without notice, is not binding, although it may still be illuminating (*Bua International Ltd v Hai Hing Shipping Co. Ltd* [2000] 1 Lloyd's Rep 300). Likewise, although prejudice is no longer an essential prerequisite for an order to strike out for delay — as the decision depends on the justice in all the circumstances of the individual case — the courts will consider prejudice as part of the general inquiry into what is just in the circumstances (*Axa Insurance Co. Ltd v Swire Fraser Ltd* [2000] CPLR 142; *Annodeus Entertainment Ltd v Gibson* (2000) *The Times*, 3 March 2000). When dealing with excusing delay in filing a defence, in *Thorn plc v Macdonald* [1999] CPLR 660, Brooke LJ and Robert Walker LJ applied the pre-CPR principles established in *Mortgage Corporation Ltd v Sandoes* [1997] PNLR 263 and *Finnegan v Parkside Health Authority* [1998] 1 WLR 411 (although it ought to be mentioned that these cases were decided with a view to the forthcoming implementation of the Woolf reforms).

Pre-CPR cases were applied as authoritative on striking out a claim with no basis (*Nomura International plc v Granada Group Ltd* [2007] EWHC 642 (Comm), [2008] Bus LR 1), on pleading practice (*Taranissi v British Broadcasting Corporation* [2008] EWHC 2486 (QB), LTL 24/10/2008), on the principles to be applied on applications for permission to amend (*Swain-Mason v Mills and Reeve LLP* [2011] EWCA Civ 14, [2011] 1 WLR 2735) and on the question whether a judge should withdraw after a premature disclosure of a Part 36 offer (*Garratt v Saxby* [2004] EWCA Civ 341, [2004] 1 WLR 2152). The Court of Appeal in *Nasser v United Bank of Kuwait* [2001] EWCA Civ 556, [2002] 1 WLR 1868, said that the coming into force of the CPR meant that applications for security for costs are now governed by different principles, whereas in *Vedatech Corporation v Seagate Software Information* [2001] EWCA Civ 1924, LTL 29/11/2001, a differently constituted Court of Appeal held that the judge below had been wrong in not applying a principle derived from pre-CPR case law.

Old cases as a guide to principle

1.23   Sometimes, it is entirely sensible to have regard to the old authorities. In *Harrison v Bloom Camillin* (1999) *The Independent*, 28 June 1999, Neuberger J said that although the court had to be careful in relying on old cases, in the context of the application he was dealing with (to set aside a witness summons) some regard was to be paid to the authorities under the old rules. Another example is *Hertfordshire Investments Ltd v Bubb* [2000] 1 WLR 2318, in which the Court of Appeal held that the principles set out in *Ladd v Marshall* [1954] 1 WLR 1489, concerning the reception of new evidence on appeal, continue to be relevant as factors which must be considered, rather than as strict rules (the court must also consider the overriding objective, *Gillingham v Gillingham* [2001] EWCA Civ 906, LTL 8/6/2001).

In *Nomura International plc v Granada Group Ltd* [2007] EWHC 642 (Comm), [2008] Bus LR 1, the claim form had been issued merely to protect the claimant's position at a time when the claimant had not decided to pursue a claim against the defendant. Cooke J reiterated the point that while pre-CPR authorities are not generally of relevance under the CPR, it is different where a CPR provision follows the same form and has the same intention as a provision in the RSC. In that situation the court should have regard to the principles that had informed the case law on the equivalent provision in the RSC. A similar approach was taken in *Adelson v Associated Newspapers Ltd* [2007] EWCA Civ 701, [2008] 1 WLR 585, in the context of an application to substitute a party after the expiry of limitation under **CPR, r. 19.5(3)(a)**. This gives effect to the Limitation Act 1980, s. 35, with the same intention as the old provision in RSC, ord. 20, r. 5. Post-CPR cases (*Morgan Est (Scotland) Ltd v Hanson Concrete Products Ltd* [2005] EWCA Civ 134, [2005] 1 WLR 2557; *Weston v Gribben* [2006] EWCA Civ 1425, [2007] CP Rep 10), which sought to lay down principles free of the pre-CPR case law, were doubted, and the court followed the principles laid down by the pre-CPR authorities. To the same effect is *City and Country Properties Ltd v Kamali* [2006] EWCA Civ 1879, [2007] 1 WLR 1219, in relation to the address for service of a defendant while temporarily out of the jurisdiction. The Court of Appeal overruled *Chellaram v Chellaram (No. 2)* [2002] EWHC 632 (Ch), [2002] 3 All ER 17, para. [47], as inconsistent with *Rolph v Zolan* [1993] 1 WLR 1305.

Reference to old rules and other procedural rules

Because the CPR are a new procedural code, the courts usually refuse to look at equivalent   **1.24**
provisions in the RSC or CCR as an aid to interpretation. *Omega Engineering Inc. v Omega SA* [2003] EWHC 1482 (Ch), *The Times,* 29 September 2003, is an exception. **CPR, r. 3.1(2)(a)**, which provides a general power to extend or abridge time, was construed by reference to the equivalent provision in the RSC, to avoid an unnecessarily restrictive interpretation being placed on the present rule. A more striking example is *Carnegie v Giessen* [2005] EWCA Civ 191, [2005] 1 WLR 2510. In this case the Court of Appeal said that the pre-CPR **Queen's Bench Masters' Practice Direction (11)** (see **63.18**) is to be treated as remaining in effect, because the CPR do not contain express reference to the enforcement of judgments in foreign currency.

Adopting practice from family proceedings, which have a different procedural framework, is generally unsound (see *Roult v North West Strategic Health Authority* [2009] EWCA Civ 444, [2010] 1 WLR 487).

Rules of practice

As mentioned at **1.11**, there is a distinction between matters of procedure and matters of   **1.25**
practice. Quite a few areas of practice have developed in a way that reflects the substantive law (such as the 'cheque rule' and the rules relating to set-offs in summary judgment applications, see **34.40** to **34.44**) or statutory provisions (such as the Senior Courts Act 1981, s. 37, on injunctions) which have not been changed by the introduction of the CPR. The practice in such areas has not been changed by the introduction of the CPR.

Unreported, unopposed and first-instance decisions

An important point is the extent to which the courts should look at unreported first-instance   **1.26**
decisions on the procedure under the CPR and similar decisions reported in the legal periodicals. Often such reports are very short, they are often misleading when compared with the full transcripts, and there is also a worrying tendency for cases which are in fact contrary to the rules to be the subject of such reports. The danger in citing such cases, especially when they are at first instance, is that they can distract the court from applying the overriding objective and the spirit and intention of the CPR in general and the provisions that directly apply to a case. They also add to the length and expense of hearings.

To combat this, Practice Direction (Citation of Authorities) [2001] 1 WLR 1001 prohibits the use of reports of applications attended by one party only, applications for permission to appeal, applications to decide whether the application is arguable, and County Court cases (other than to illustrate damages or where no higher authorities are available). Excessive citation of authorities and reliance on summaries of cases which may not have been prepared by professional lawyers will not be tolerated (*Hamblin v Field* [2000] BPIR 621). Reference to judgments with no authoritative value and which are no more than examples of the exercise of judicial discretion was deprecated by Leveson LJ in *Heron v TNT (UK) Ltd* [2013] EWCA Civ 469, [2014] 1 WLR 1277 at [35].

Commentary

APPLICATION OF THE OVERRIDING OBJECTIVE

Dealing with cases justly

1.27   The main concept in the overriding objective (**CPR, r. 1.1**) is that the primary concern of the court is to do justice. Ultimately the function of the court is to resolve issues between the parties. It does not have the power to dismiss a claim simply on the ground that the claim (or the issue left in a claim) has a relatively trivial value which will inevitably be exceeded by the costs (*Devaraja v Roy* [2008] EWHC 464 (QB), LTL 3/6/2008). Before the Jackson Reforms, shutting a litigant out through a technical breach of the rules was not regarded as consistent with doing justice, because the primary purpose of the civil courts is to decide cases on their merits, not to reject them for procedural default. An example of this is *Jones v Telford and Wrekin Council* (1999) *The Times,* 29 July 1999, where service had been delayed beyond the period of validity because the claiman's solicitors had problems in obtaining psychiatric reports for service with the particulars of claim. The Court of Appeal upheld an extension of time largely because there were no previous authorities dealing with this situation, Lord Woolf MR commenting that the court must not lose sight of the fact that its primary concern is doing justice.

In *Gilbart v Thomas Graham* [2008] EWCA Civ 897, LTL 24/6/2008, the Court of Appeal overturned a decision to refuse an adjournment of the trial date, in order to give effect to the overriding objective. The defendant had applied for the adjournment 21 days before the date for the trial, on realising that the claimant had not disclosed crucial documents. 21 days was an unrealistically short time for the defendant to obtain specific disclosure from the claimant and to instruct an expert or a loss of profits claim. In *Ratiopharm (UK) Ltd v Alza Corporation* [2008] EWHC 1182 (Ch), LTL 1/5/2008, six months was regarded as enough time to prepare a patent infringement claim for trial (the party seeking to avoid the trial date having received a letter with the allegations in the litigation 13 months before the trial date). Firmer case management control is called for where litigation has taken longer than might otherwise have been hoped for, and where there is a danger that costs will become disproportionate (*Multiplex Construction (UK) Ltd v Cleveland Bridge UK Ltd* [2008] EWHC 231 (TCC), LTL 9/5/2008). A stronger stance is expected following the reforms introduced on 1 April 2013, and there will be cases which are dismissed for procedural default, because courts do not exist for the purpose of providing justice at disproportionate cost.

In *Adan v Securicor Custodial Services Ltd* [2004] EWHC 394 (QB), [2005] PIQR P79 the claimant asked the court to use **r. 3.1(2)(i)** so that his claim for medical expenses in a personal injuries claim could be dealt with at a later date if and when the claimant was discharged from long-term hospital care. The application was refused as contrary to the overriding objective. It would have exposed the defendant's insurers to an uncertain liability for an indefinite period, which was oppressive and undesirable. Standing down witnesses in advance of an application for an adjournment was regarded as failing to act justly in *Albon v Naza Motor Trading Sdn Bhd (No. 5)* [2007] EWHC 2613 (Ch), [2008] 1 WLR 2380, because it precluded the court from determining the merits of the application.

In *Chilton v Surrey County Council* [1999] CPLR 525 the Court of Appeal indicated that dealing with a claim justly involved dealing with the real claim, and allowed the claimant to rely on a revised statement of past and future loss and expense quantifying the claim at about £400,000 rather than the original statement, which indicated a claim value of about £5,000.

In *Cala Homes (South) Ltd v Chichester District Council* (1999) 79 P & CR 430, the principle of dealing with cases justly was invoked in refusing to strike out a claim which was wrongly started in the Central Office of the High Court instead of in the Crown Office. A party who starts a claim using the wrong form, or relying on the wrong statutory provision, is likely to be granted permission to amend in order to deal with the claim justly (particularly if the defendants are not misled by the mistake) (*Thurrock Borough Council v Secretary of State for the Environment, Transport and the Regions* [2001] 1 PLR 94). In *Hannigan v Hannigan* [2000] 2 FCR 650, it was held that although proceedings were instituted using the wrong form, and although the form used contained numerous defects, the substance of the claim was fully known to the defendant. The administration of justice would have been better served had the defendants' solicitors pointed out the defects rather than attempted to take a technical point. *Re Osea Road Camp Sites Ltd* [2004] EWHC 2437 (Ch), [2005] 1 WLR 760, where proceedings were struck out because the claimant issued a claim form rather than presenting a petition, turns on the different code governing unfair prejudice petitions.

Even where one of a number of joint claimants makes a fraudulent claim, unless the fraud makes the trial unfair, dealing with the claim justly means that the other claimants should be awarded remedies in accordance with the evidence, rather than having their claims struck out (*Summers v Fairclough Homes Ltd* [2012] UKSC 26, [2012] 1 WLR 2004, and see the cases discussed at **33.14**). When a case is being considered on appeal, dealing with the case justly includes giving weight to the public interest in the finality of the decision at trial, see *Evans v Tiger Investments Ltd* [2002] EWCA Civ 161, [2002] 2 BCLC 185.

Proportionality: the rule

The overriding objective of dealing with cases justly is defined in terms that include ensuring that justice is achieved at proportionate cost. This is expanded by **CPR, r. 1.1(2)**, which provides that dealing with a case justly and at proportionate cost includes dealing with it in ways which are proportionate to the importance of the case (**r. 1.1(2)(c)(ii)**) and allotting to it an appropriate share of the court's resources, while taking into account the need to allot resources to other cases (**r. 1.1(2)(e)**). An assessment of the importance of the case appears to require consideration of factors other than the amount of money involved and the complexity of the issues, which are mentioned separately (**r. 1.1(2)(c)(i) and (iii)**) Proportionality in relation to costs includes considering any additional work generated by the conduct of the other party, and any wider factors, such as reputation and public importance (**r. 44.3(5)(d) and (e)**). It is submitted that the importance which is to be considered may be either an exceptional significance to one of the parties or an importance to the public in general or a section of the public (for example, if it is a test case). The court resources to be considered will include not merely available finance but also the availability of judiciary or judicial time to deal with a case. **1.28**

Proportionality and costs

With effect from 1 April 2013 a number of measures may be used by the courts to ensure litigation is conducted at proportionate cost as required by **CPR, r. 1.1(1)**. These include: **1.29**

(a) making prospective costs capping orders (see **chapter 44**);
(b) making protective costs orders (see **chapter 44**);
(c) costs management in most multi-track claims (see **chapter 43**);
(d) the agreement or approval of costs budgets in most multi-track claims (see **chapter 43**);
(e) having regard to costs budgets when making case management decisions (see **chapter 42**);
(f) having regard to, or holding parties to, agreed or approved costs budgets when assessing costs (see **chapter 71**);
(g) assessing costs on the standard basis in accordance with **r. 44.3**, and disallowing or reducing costs which are disproportionate even if they were reasonably or necessarily incurred; and
(h) making wasted costs orders (see **68.67**).

Examples of case management decisions made before 1 April 2013 which were designed to keep costs proportionate include:

(i) permitting a defendant to file and serve a single defence to two related claims in order to save costs (*Rosenberg v Nazarov* [2008] EWHC 812 (Ch), LTL 10/4/2008);

(ii) making summary assessments of both sides' costs in a low-value case to avoid the costs that would have been incurred on a detailed assessment (*Gould v Armstrong* [2002] EWCA Civ 1159, LTL 23/7/2002).

Proportionality: examples

1.30 Proportionality lies at the heart of the rules on sanctions (see **chapter 48**), where the court aims to impose punishments which fit the crime. Thus, striking out for failing to file a pre-trial checklist and being late for a case management hearing was regarded as disproportionate in *Lambeth London Borough Council v Onayomake* [2007] EWCA Civ 1426, *The Times*, 2 November 2007. Setting aside an order granting permission to serve outside the jurisdiction on the ground that the claim form and witness statement were not signed was regarded as disproportionate in *Colliers International Property Consultants v Colliers Jordan Lee Jafaar Sdn Bhd* [2008] EWHC 1524 (Comm), [2008] 2 Lloyd's Rep 368. Proportionality may influence various case management decisions, such as limiting the issues to be tried, or even disallowing some issues entirely (see **42.65**). Likewise, proportionality may be taken into account in deciding to restrict the expert evidence the parties may call at trial (see **54.12**).

The need to conduct litigation efficiently and proportionately requires that routine case management decisions and other routine applications should be disposed of without hearings under **CPR, r. 23.8** (*Collier v Williams* [2006] EWCA Civ 20, [2006] 1 WLR 1945 at [29]). Pursuing allegations on collateral matters and events relied upon as similar fact evidence (see **49.74**) may, depending on the circumstances of the case and the probative value of the evidence, be disproportionate (*Guerrero v Monterrico Metals plc* [2010] EWHC 3228 (QB), LTL 20/12/2010).

The concept of proportionality will not be applied to prevent a party from instructing lawyers chosen by that party, even if it means one side is represented by far more eminent lawyers than the other (*Maltez v Lewis* (1999) 16 Const LJ 65). Neuberger J said that the right to choose a legal representative, although not absolute, was a fundamental and well-established ingredient in any free society. In *Ali v Naseem* (2003) *The Times*, 3 October 2003, it was held that a writ *ne exeat regno* (see **38.42**) would only be granted if proportionate and necessary to secure the ends of justice. The importance of the proportionality principle was underlined by *South Bucks District Council v Porter* [2003] UKHL 26, [2003] 2 AC 558, where the House of Lords used the expression 'just and proportionate' to describe the circumstances in which an interim injunction should be granted rather than the conventional 'just and convenient' formula.

Equal footing

1.31 Ensuring the parties are on an equal footing is primarily concerned with the unfair exploitation of superior resources, rather than issues such as a failure to provide information (*Henry v News Group Newspapers Ltd* [2013] EWCA Civ 19, [2013] CP Rep 20). The case management powers of the court will be exercised so as to ensure, so far as possible, that where the parties have very different financial means the costs thought to be unreasonably incurred by the more affluent party should be paid by that party in any event. In *Maltez v Lewis* (1999) 16 Const LJ 65, it was held that the court had the power to ensure a 'level playing field' by using its case management powers to allow a smaller firm more time, or to require a larger firm to prepare court bundles even though the responsibility would otherwise be that of the smaller firm. However, the fact that one party is better informed or better advised, or has stronger evidence than the other, will not normally justify a conclusion that a fair trial is not possible, or that there is an inequality of arms, unless the inequality is very substantial and very prejudicial (*Henley v Bloom* [2010] EWCA Civ 202, [2010] 1 WLR 1770).

In *McPhilemy v Times Newspapers Ltd* [1999] 3 All ER 775 Lord Woolf MR said that a party which wanted the court to restrain the activities of another party with the object of achieving greater equality must demonstrate that it is itself conducting the proceedings with a desire to limit expense so far as practical. However, the powers of the court to restrain excess do not extend to preventing a party from putting forward allegations which are central to its case. That said, it is open to the court to attempt to control how those allegations are litigated with a view to limiting costs.

Ensuring the parties are on an equal footing is not an absolute requirement. For example, the tests on striking out and summary judgment will not be adjusted even where one party is suffering from an inequality of arms (*Bank of Tokyo-Mitsubishi UFJ Ltd v Baskan Gida Sanayi ve Pazarlama AS* [2008] EWHC 659 (Ch), LTL 17/4/2008). The requirement applies so far as practicable, and may be displaced by other considerations, such as proportionality or dealing with the case justly. This may result, for example, in one party being given permission to call more expert witnesses than the other side (*Kirkman v Euro Exide Corporation (CMP Batteries Ltd)* [2007] EWCA Civ 66, [2007] CP Rep 19). Putting the parties on an equal footing may mean that the court ought to allow a party to call more than one expert in a single area of expertise where the other side is able to deploy an independent witness and a number of factual witnesses who are professionally qualified (*ES v Chesterfield and North Derbyshire Royal Hospital NHS Trust* [2003] EWCA Civ 1284, [2004] Lloyd's Rep Med 90).

It is an elementary rule of the administration of justice that none of the parties to proceedings can communicate with the court without simultaneously alerting other parties to that fact (*R (Mohamed) v Secretary of State for Foreign and Commonwealth Affairs (No. 2)* [2010] EWCA Civ 158, [2011] QB 218 at [6]). Not providing the opposite party with a letter sent to the judge, and thereby failing to give the other side an opportunity to respond to it, was a serious procedural irregularity within the meaning of **CPR, r. 52.21(3)**, and a breach of the *audi alteram partem* principle (*National Westminster Bank plc v Rushmer* [2010] EWHC 554 (Ch), [2010] 2 FLR 362).

The case management powers of the court will be exercised so as to ensure, so far as possible, that where the parties have very different financial means the costs thought to be unreasonably incurred by the more affluent party should be paid by that party in any event. In *Maltez v Lewis* (1999) 16 Const LJ 65, it was held that the court had the power to ensure a 'level playing field' by using its case management powers to allow a smaller firm more time, or to require a larger firm to prepare court bundles even though the responsibility would otherwise be that of the smaller firm. However, the fact that one party is better informed or better advised, or has stronger evidence than the other, will not normally justify a conclusion that a fair trial is not possible, or that there is an inequality of arms, unless the inequality is very substantial and very prejudicial (*Henley v Bloom* [2010] EWCA Civ 202, [2010] 1 WLR 1770).

In *McPhilemy v Times Newspapers Ltd* [1999] 3 All ER 775 Lord Woolf MR said that a party which wanted the court to restrain the activities of another party with the object of achieving greater equality must demonstrate that it is itself conducting the proceedings with a desire to limit expense so far as practical. However, the powers of the court to restrain excess do not extend to preventing a party from putting forward allegations which are central to its case. That said, it is open to the court to attempt to control how those allegations are litigated with a view to limiting costs.

Dealing with cases expeditiously and saving expense

In *Cadogan Properties Ltd v Mount Eden Land Ltd* (1999) LTL 29/6/99 the court at first instance had made an order for substituted service in circumstances where there were no grounds for doing so. That order was set aside on appeal, with the result that proceedings had not been served and the period of validity had expired. The Court of Appeal relied on **CPR, r. 1.1(2)(d)**, and the need to deal with cases fairly and expeditiously, and also on the need for proportionality (**r. 1.1(2)(c)**), to justify making an order extending the validity of the originating process. The   **1.32** defendant was aware of the proceedings, and suffered no significant prejudice by the course adopted by the court. A court may refuse to hear the merits of an application on the ground of dealing with the case justly, expeditiously and economically where the application will bring no proportionate benefit to the claim as a whole (*Norwich Union Linked Life Assurance Ltd v Mercantile Credit Co. Ltd* [2003] EWHC 3064 (Ch), LTL 6/1/2004). Where appropriate and available, parties should use technology, such as videoconferencing, to reduce costs (*Black v Pastouna* [2005] EWCA Civ 1389, [2006] CP Rep 11). In *Re Hoicrest Ltd* [2000] 1 WLR 414 it was held that, because there was a dispute about crucial facts, the claimant's application under what is now the Companies Act 2006, s. 125, for rectification of a company's register of members, could not proceed under **CPR, Part 8**. The claimant had known all along about the factual dispute and it was his fault for starting the proceedings in the wrong way. The Court of Appeal held that the overriding objective would be furthered by actively managing the case, with appropriate directions, which would be likely to be more cost-effective than striking it out and requiring the claimant to start fresh proceedings. The court may, under its inherent jurisdiction, decline to continue with a trial which has been delayed by the court's own fault (*Re Rocksteady Services Ltd* [2001] BCC 467).

Allotting an appropriate share of the court's resources

1.33   In *S. B. J. Stephenson Ltd v Mandy* [1999] CPLR 500 the defendant appealed against an interim order restraining him from breaching a restrictive covenant in his contract of employment. The appeal against the interim order came before the Court of Appeal on 30 June, but the trial of the main proceedings had been fixed for 20 July. Given the short period before the trial and the fact that the claimant had given the usual undertaking in damages, the court decided that considering the merits of the appeal would not be in accordance with the overriding objective. Expense would not be saved by hearing the appeal, and, given the short time to trial, hearing the appeal would not be a good use of the court's resources.

An appeal was also dismissed (with costs on the indemnity basis) in *Adoko v Jemal* (1999) *The Times*, 8 July 1999, in very different circumstances, on the ground of allotting to it no more than an appropriate share of the court's resources. In this case the appellant had failed to correct the notice of appeal despite a warning from the respondent that it was seriously defective, and had failed to comply with the directions relating to appeal bundles. The Court of Appeal spent over an hour trying to sort out the position, and then decided it was inappropriate that any further share of the court's resources should be allocated to the appeal.

Cooperating

1.34   In *Chilton v Surrey County Council* [1999] CPLR 525, referred to above at **1.27**, the Court of Appeal decided against the defendant partly because it seemed to be attempting to take tactical advantage of a mistake by the claimant's solicitors in overlooking to serve the revised statement of past and future loss and expense rather than cooperating with the claimant's solicitors to put matters right. Similar reasoning informed *Hertsmere Primary Care Trust v Administrators of Balasubramanium's Estate* [2005] EWHC 320 (Ch), [2005] 3 All ER 274. The claimant made a Part 36 offer, and was then told by counsel for the defendant that the offer was defective. Despite requests, the defendant declined to explain why. Solicitors for the claimant wrote to ask why, but got no reply. It transpired there was an obvious, but technical, defect. The defendant's conduct was held to be a refusal to cooperate, and the court treated the offer as if it had been in the proper form.

Even in litigation with serious allegations it is essential that the parties and their legal teams put to one side their understandable feelings of outrage and hostility and cooperate in the process of preparing the case for trial (*Lexi Holdings v Pannone and Partners* [2010] EWHC 1416 (Ch), LTL 21/6/2010). In *Hateley v Morris* [2004] EWHC 252 (Ch), [2004] 1 BCLC 582, a striking-out order made by the registrar was overturned on appeal despite an eight-month delay when neither side applied to relist a case management conference. One of the reasons given by the court was that either side could have relisted the matter, and both sides have a duty to cooperate in progressing proceedings.

PRACTICAL IMPACT

Culture

The civil justice system is essentially adversarial in nature, with the legal profession performing its traditional adversarial role in a managed environment governed by the courts. The CPR encourage cooperation between the parties in the preparation of cases for trial. The rules discourage the taking of technical points and obstructive tactics, and promote the identification and speedy trial of relevant issues only. The parties are required to exhibit openness and cooperation from the outset, to assist the expeditious resolution of their dispute. This requirement is supported by pre-action protocols, the need to consider ADR, and a system of judicial case management to scrutinise the conduct, cost, and progress of litigation.

Any system of justice needs to have appropriate powers to impose sanctions to ensure that parties keep to the timetable and ensure they are ready for trial when the time comes. Failure to enforce compliance results in delay, expense and vexation. While procedural defaults vary widely in their seriousness and consequences, in the period between the introduction of the CPR in 1999 and implementation of the Civil Justice Reforms in 2013 it had become clear that the courts were taking a far too tolerant approach to compliance with timetable requirements. *Mitchell v News Group Newspapers Ltd* [2013] EWCA Civ 1537, [2014] 1 WLR 795 (see **chapter 48**), sent what was intended to be a clear message that the courts would insist on a new ethos of strict compliance, backed up by a robust but fair approach to sanctions.

Mitchell v News Group Newspapers Ltd did not meet with universal acclaim. There was academic criticism of the decision, largely on the basis that it placed too much emphasis on delay and court resources, and not enough on justice, proportionality and party cooperation. The profession was concerned that *Mitchell v News Group Newspapers Ltd* emphasised the importance of ensuring the efficient use of court resources, to the detriment of the efficient use of resources by the parties' legal representatives. To meet that criticism, the Court of Appeal in *Denton v T. H. White Ltd* [2014] EWCA Civ 906, [2014] 1 WLR 3926, issued revised guidance on how courts should deal with procedural default, producing a more balanced approach, which was intended to reduce satellite litigation and promote party cooperation. Included in the *Denton* guidance is a requirement on non-defaulting parties to consent to applications for relief from sanctions where it is obvious that relief would be granted by the court, with costs sanctions for parties seeking to take tactical advantage of defaults.

There are cases that suggest the *Mitchell* and *Denton* principles apply beyond applications under **CPR, r. 3.9**. *Norseman Holdings Ltd v Warwick Court (Harold Hill) Management Co. Ltd* [2013] EWHC 3868 (QB), LTL 12/12/2013, which was about the status of an undertaking intimated to the court on behalf of a solicitor by counsel, is an instance of *Mitchell v News Group Newspapers Ltd* being used as authority for the general proposition that in the post-Jackson era parties have to conduct litigation in accordance with the rules. *R (Hysaj) v Secretary of State for the Home Department* [2014] EWCA Civ 1633, [2015] 1 WLR 2472, held there is an implied sanctions doctrine that applies the *Denton* guidelines to applications to extend time for bringing an appeal. While this may be justifiable in the context of appeals (see **48.12** and **74.22**), there are decisions, such as *Elliott v Stobart Group Ltd* [2015] EWCA Civ 449, [2015] CP Rep 36, that unhelpfully appear to extend the implied sanctions doctrine into other areas. One problem with this approach is that it elevates many normal directions and provisions in the rules into 'unless orders', contrary to the guidance given in *Denton* itself at [44].

1.35

Commentary

Case management

1.36   Judicial case management effectively removes control of the timescale of litigation from the parties. Procedural judges seek to identify the relevant issues at an early stage, and control the extent to which a party can inflate the costs of the litigation. Particular issues are the curtailment of the rights of parties to adduce expert evidence and to require others to disclose documents. The CPR require the parties to do a substantial amount of work investigating and disclosing information and documents early in the litigation process, and this results in the front-loading of costs.

The cost of litigation should be affordable, predictable and proportionate to the value, or to the complexity, of individual cases. Proceedings are therefore allocated by the court to the small claims track, the fast track or the multi-track, depending on the complexity of the matters to be tried, and the amount in issue. These tracks have different timetables and pre-trial procedures. Small claims track cases (see **chapter 45**) are generally given directions requiring minimal pre-trial preparation, and early trial dates. In non-complex proceedings involving between £10,000 and £25,000 (which are allocated to the fast track, **chapter 46**), there are fixed timetables of no more than 30 weeks between track allocation and trial. Strict sanctions are normally applied to parties who do not comply with the procedures or timetables. More complex cases (assigned to the multi-track, **chapter 47**) usually require more judicial attention during the preparation stages, and there are usually a number of case management hearings to ensure they are prepared in an efficient manner. They are usually tried at civil trial centres which have the required resources, including specialist judges.

Active management of the more complex and substantial cases assigned to the multi-track requires practitioners to investigate the facts, research the legal principles and identify the issues at an earlier stage. At case management conferences the judge can ask searching questions about a party's case with the objective of narrowing the issues to be tried, and may eliminate minor issues which are of little or no relevance to the substance of the dispute. In all cases, litigation practitioners must comply with a rigorous timetable, with a regime of real sanctions on default.

Role of the client

1.37   Even if a solicitor is retained, clients have a number of rights and obligations under the CPR. All statements of case must be verified by a statement of truth, declaring the belief of the party that the contents are true and accurate (see **23.13** to **23.17**). A party giving disclosure (**chapter 50**) is required to make a statement setting out the extent of the search which has been made to locate documents which he is required to disclose, and certifying that he understands his duty to disclose and that to the best of his knowledge he has complied with that duty (**CPR, r. 31.10(6)**). The court may order that a judgment or order be served on a party in person as well as any solicitor acting for the party (**r. 40.5**). A solicitor is under a duty to notify a client against whom a costs order is made, if the client was not present when the costs order was made (**r. 44.2**). When deciding what order to make in respect of costs, the court should have regard not only to which party succeeded, but also to the conduct of the parties, including the manner in which a claim was pursued or defended, and whether a claim was exaggerated (**r. 44.3(4)**). Additionally, the conduct of the parties before, as well as during, the proceedings, and efforts made, if any, before or during the proceedings to resolve the dispute, are factors to be taken into account in deciding the amount of costs (**r. 44.3(5)**).

Close involvement of clients in solicitors' work is one of the objectives of the SRA Code of Conduct 2011. A solicitor is obliged to ensure clients are in a position to make informed decisions about the services they need and the options open to them (O 1.12) and receive the best possible information about the likely overall cost of a case (O 1.13). Solicitors should also discuss with the client whether the likely outcome justifies the expense or risk (including the risk of paying the other side's costs). Solicitors must also give their clients a clear explanation of the issues raised, and keep them properly informed about progress in the case.

Role of the solicitor

The Legal Services Act 2007, s. 188(2), provides that any person exercising a right of audience before any court has 'a duty to the court to act with independence in the interests of justice' and that the duty 'shall override' any other obligation with which it is inconsistent (other than an obligation under the criminal law) (s. 188(3)). Further, the SRA Code of Conduct 2011, O 5.1, requires that a solicitor must not attempt to deceive or knowingly or recklessly mislead the court. If a solicitor is instructed by a client to conduct a case without regard to the overriding objective of the CPR (such as a well-heeled client instructing his solicitor to incur disproportionate expenditure when acting against a client of limited means), the solicitor must warn the client of the potential sanctions in costs that may be incurred as a result. There will be an infringement of the duty in **CPR, r. 1.3**, to assist the court to further the overriding objective if a solicitor advances a case which the solicitor does not regard as properly arguable (*Richard Buxton v Mills-Owen* [2010] EWCA Civ 122, [2010] 1 WLR 1997). If the client insists on the unarguable case being advanced, the solicitor will have a good reason for terminating the retainer (see **22.6**).

1.38

Role of the barrister

A barrister is under a duty to assist the court in the administration of justice and must not deceive or knowingly or recklessly mislead the court (Code of Conduct of the Bar of England and Wales, oC2 and rC3.1).

1.39

Confidentiality and the overriding objective

Conflict may occur between the overriding objective and the duty of a practitioner not to disclose confidential information. For example, **CPR, r. 29.3(2)**, provides for a representative to attend a case management conference 'with sufficient authority to deal with any issues that are likely to arise'. During a case management conference, it is possible that the court may seek information, the disclosure of which would involve a waiver of privilege. The court may well ask about the costs expended to date, the relative financial standing of the parties (one of the issues to be taken into account in meeting the overriding objective), and details of the funding arrangements for the litigation. It is clear the court does not have power to order a representative to disclose privileged information (see **50.53**), but there is an obvious tension between obtaining information for active case management purposes and client confidentiality. If the client is not to attend the case management conference, specific authority will be required to disclose the information which is likely to be sought.

1.40

Advice to clients

It is important that every client should be advised at an early stage, not only about the general duties to promote the overriding objective, but also other matters, including:

(a) the wide-ranging costs and interest sanctions available to the court (see **chapter 48**);
(b) the client's duty in relation to a statement of truth (see **23.15**);
(c) the client's duties of search in relation to disclosure of documents (see **50.4, 50.13** and **50.15**);
(d) the duties to the court of an expert witness (see **54.10**).

1.41

Chapter 2   Court Organisation

INTRODUCTION

2.1   Civil proceedings in England and Wales may be conducted in magistrates' courts, the County Court and the High Court. Magistrates' courts have only limited jurisdiction in relation to civil matters, and will not be considered further in *Blackstone's Civil Practice*. Appeals in civil matters are taken to the Court of Appeal, Civil Division, and the Supreme Court of the United Kingdom (before October 2009, the House of Lords). Appeals are considered in **chapters 74 to 76**. A wide range of civil disputes are also determined by various tribunals, including employment tribunals and the various chambers of the First-tier Tribunal, which have their own rules of procedure and will not be considered further in this work.

This chapter looks at the composition and organisation of the High Court and the County Court and considers the different court personnel and their powers. The rules governing venue, allocation of business and transfer between the High Court and the County Court are dealt with in **chapter 11**.

COUNTY COURT

2.2   The County Court derives its jurisdiction and powers from statute, principally the County Courts Act 1984. Up until 22 April 2014 there were about 180 county courts in England and Wales, each exercising its powers for a limited geographical district (County Courts Act 1984, s. 1). With effect from 22 April 2014, the Crime and Courts Act 2013, s. 17 and sch. 9, amended the County Courts Act 1984 (see s. 1A of the 1984 Act) to create a single County Court with a national jurisdiction for the whole of England and Wales. The County Court now has a single seal and a single identity to indicate its national jurisdiction. It exercises the jurisdiction and powers conferred on it by the County Courts Act 1984. Any judgment, order, warrant or direction of a county court before 22 April 2014 is to have the same effect on or after that date as if made by the single County Court established under the County Courts Act 1984, s. A1 (Crime and Courts Act 2013 (Commencement No. 10 and Transitional Provision) Order 2014 (SI 2014/954), art. 3; see also the Civil Procedure (Amendment No. 4) Rules 2014 (SI 2014/867), r. 25(5)). Sittings of the County Court may be held anywhere in England and Wales, on a continuous, intermittent or occasional basis and the court may adjourn cases from place to place at any time (County Courts Act 1984, s. 3). The court houses in which the County Court convenes act as hearing centres. County Court offices (including offices serving County Court hearing centres, the County Court Money Claims Centre and the Production Centre) are situated at such places as the Lord Chancellor directs for the transaction of the court's business (**PD 2A, para. 3.1**). The Court Finder at the Ministry of Justice website, https://courttribunalfinder.service.gov.uk/, provides a complete list of the County Court hearing centres with contact details and location maps.

The principal judicial officers of the County Court are Circuit Judges and District Judges, although the persons listed in the County Courts Act 1984, s. 5(2) (including Recorders and Deputy District Judges), are also ex officio judges of the County Court. Circuit Judges must be solicitors or barristers of at least seven years' standing and with at least seven years' relevant legal experience (see Courts Act 1971, s. 16). Most (but not all) Circuit Judges sit in the Crown Court as well as the County Court, and may be supplemented by Recorders, who are part-time judges and who, with limited exceptions, exercise the full powers of a Circuit Judge (County Courts Act 1984, s. 5(2)(k)). Circuit Judges conduct most County Court trials, sitting alone, and also hear appeals from decisions of District Judges. It is preferred for such appeals to be heard by a full-time rather than part-time judge, but this is not always possible.

A Circuit Judge or Recorder may be specifically requested (or 'ticketed'), under the Senior Courts Act 1981, s. 9, to sit in the High Court (see **2.7**) or, under s. 68, in the Technology and Construction Court (see **2.16**). Where a Circuit Judge, without being aware she was not duly authorised, heard a High Court case which had not been properly released to her for trial, there was an error of procedure falling within **CPR, r. 3.10** (*Fawdry and Co. v Murfitt* [2002] EWCA Civ 643, [2003] QB 104). The court applied the de facto doctrine, which is that a person who has acted as a judicial tribunal while believing him or herself to have the necessary judicial authority, and who is believed by the parties to have that authority, is regarded in law as possessing the authority. This meant the error could be remedied, and the result of the trial would stand unless the appeal court so ordered. The result would have been different if the judge had known she was not authorised to hear the case. *Fawdry and Co. v Murfitt* was applied in *Coppard v Commissioners of Customs and Excise* [2003] EWCA Civ 511, [2003] QB 1428, in which it was held that the de facto doctrine does not offend against the European Convention on Human Rights, **art. 6(1)**. *Fawdry and Co. v Murfitt* and *Coppard v Commissioners of Customs and Excise* were both applied in *Baldock v Webster* [2004] EWCA Civ 1869, [2006] QB 315, in which the de facto doctrine was invoked to uphold the decision of a recorder at the trial of a High Court case which he had not been authorised to hear under the Senior Courts Act 1981, s. 9, and which he had dealt with in the mistaken belief that it was proceeding in the County Court.

District Judges, who must be solicitors or barristers of at least five years' standing and with at least five years' relevant legal experience (County Courts Act 1984, s. 9), deal with most interim applications made in the County Court, and normally try all small claims track, and many fast track cases. The allocation of business to different levels of judiciary in the County Court is dealt with in **2.3** to **2.6**. Deputy District Judges can be appointed under the County Courts Act 1984, s. 8. A Deputy District Judge has the same powers as a District Judge, except the power to act in a District Registry of the High Court (s. 8(1C)).

The correct mode of address for Circuit Judges and Recorders is 'Your Honour'. District Judges are addressed as 'Sir' or 'Madam'. Full-time judiciary are addressed as 'Judge', when not formally sitting in court, or in private.

The administrative staff of the County Court are civil servants. The administrative staff draw up and issue court documents, and arrange for them to be served. They also maintain court records.

A County Court enforcement officer is responsible for enforcing judgments by process of execution and serving documents personally. Unlike a High Court enforcement officer, a County Court enforcement officer is a civil servant.

Every County Court office and hearing centre will usually be open to the public between 10.00 a.m. and 4.00 p.m., although precise times do vary. The hours during which each County Court office is open can be found in the Court Finder section of Her Majesty's Courts and Tribunals Service website http://courttribunalfinder.service.gov.uk. The County Court is open every day of the year except weekends, bank holidays and one or two other days specified in **PD 2A, para. 3.2** (the same days as those on which the Senior Courts are closed; see **2.7**). HMCTS identifies the County Court hearing centre or office which serves the address of a claimant, a defendant, or a place of business or a property by reference to the party's or the property's postcode. The hearing centre which serves the address of a party or a property can be found using the Court Finder tool available on Gov.uk at https://courttribunalfinder. service.gov.uk/. Money Claim Online is an internet-based service and it may be used outside normal business hours.

Allocation of business to levels of judiciary in the County Court

2.3   **Trials**   Circuit Judges and District Judges may exercise any jurisdiction conferred on the County Court or on a judge of the County Court (**PD 2B, para. 1.1A**). For the purposes of **PD 2B**, in the County Court, the terms 'Circuit Judge' and 'District Judge' mean the individuals specified in **PD 2B, para. 1.3. PD 2B, Section III**, sets out the matters that will be allocated to a Circuit Judge as well as those that are normally allocated to a District Judge. Circuit Judges may exercise the full powers of the County Court. By **PD 2B, para. 11.1**, District Judges can deal with all small claims and fast track cases, and may also hear cases for the recovery of land, the assessment of damages without any financial limit, and Part 8 claims allocated to the multi-track (with some exceptions listed in **PD 2B, para. 11.1(a)**). Other claims may be allocated to a District Judge only with the permission of the Designated Civil Judge or Supervising Judge or Supervising Judge's nominee (**PD 2B, para. 11.1(d)**). Cases allocated to the small claims track may only be assigned to a Circuit Judge with his or her consent (**PD 2B, para. 11.2**). A District Judge may not try a case in which an allegation of indirect discrimination is made against a public authority under the Race Relations Act 1976, s. 19B (which made it unlawful for a public authority to perform a discriminatory act in carrying out its functions but has been repealed and replaced by the Equality Act 2010) (**PD 2B, para. 15**).

2.4   **Injunctions, anti-social behaviour injunctions, committal and freezing orders**   The general rule is that Circuit Judges and District Judges may exercise any jurisdiction conferred on the County Court or on a Judge of the County Court (**PD 2B, para. 1.1A**). PD 2B, Section III, sets out the matters that will be allocated to a Circuit Judge as well as those that may, or will normally, be allocated to a District Judge. Applications for orders and interim applications which may not be made or granted by a District Judge in the High Court may not be allocated to a District Judge in the County Court (**PD 2B, para. 8.1**). In the first instance, the following applications for any interim orders and remedies, including an injunction, will be allocated to a District Judge:

(a) any proceedings which have been allocated to a District Judge under **PD 2B, para. 11.1** (see **2.3**) (**PD 2B, para. 8.1(a)**);

(b) in a money claim which has not yet been allocated to a track, provided the amount claimed is not greater than the fast track limit of £25,000 (**PD 2B, para. 8.1(b); CPR, r. 26.6(4)(b)**);

(c) under the Housing Act 1996, ss. 153A, 153B or 153D (anti-social behaviour injunctions), the Protection from Harassment Act 1997, s. 3 (an order restraining a person from conduct which amounts to harassment) or the Policing and Crime Act 2009, ss. 34, 40 or 41 (injunctions to prevent gang-related violence) or the Anti-Social Behaviour, Crime and Policing Act 2014, part 1 (**PD 2B, para. 8.1(c)**).

An application under the Crime and Disorder Act 1998, ss. 1B or 1D (anti-social behaviour), the Anti-Social Behaviour Act 2003, ss. 26A, 26B or 26C (parenting orders) and the Violent Crime Reduction Act 2006, s. 4 or 9 (drink banning orders) may be allocated to a District Judge (**PD 2B, para. 8.1A**). An application for an order varying or discharging an injunction or an undertaking given to the court may be allocated to a District Judge (**para. 8.2**). An application for a freezing order will be allocated to a Circuit Judge (**para. 8.4**). If a freezing order is made, and a person has been ordered to make a witness statement or affidavit about his assets, any cross-examination on its contents can take place in front of a District Judge, or if the District Judge directs, before an examiner of the court (**paras 7 and 8.4(2)**).

A District Judge cannot make a committal order or attach a power of arrest to an injunction or remand a person, unless the committal order, power of arrest or remand is made pursuant to the Attachment of Earnings Act 1971, s. 23, the County Courts Act 1984, ss. 14 or 118 (but only in relation to proceedings before a District Judge), the Housing Act 1996, ss. 153C, 153D and 154 to 158 and sch. 15, the Policing and Crime Act 2009, ss. 36, 40 to 45 and 48 and sch. 15 or the Anti-Social Behaviour, Crime and Policing Act 2014, part 1, and the relevant rules (**PD 2B, para. 8.3**; see also **85.11**). It is preferable for committal applications to be heard by a Circuit Judge rather than a Recorder, but this is not always possible.

A District Judge will normally hear a claim brought under **PD 8B** and the **Pre-action Protocol for Low Value Personal Injury Claims in Road Traffic Accidents** (**PD 8B, para. 1.2**).

Distribution of business between Circuit and District Judges   Where both Circuit and District Judges have jurisdiction, the Designated Civil Judge may make arrangements distributing business between them, including assigning particular cases to individual District Judges (**PD 2B, paras 13 and 14**). **2.5**

Case management   By virtue of **PD 29, para. 3.10**, a District Judge or a Circuit Judge may deal with case management issues in respect of cases proceeding in the County Court. **2.6**

HIGH COURT

The High Court is one part of the Senior Courts of England and Wales. The other parts are the Crown Court, the Senior Courts Costs Office and the Court of Appeal. The High Court's main administrative offices and court facilities are located at the Royal Courts of Justice (RCJ), Strand, London. In addition, there are about 130 District Registries, which are established by the Senior Courts Act 1981, ss. 99 to 102. **2.7**

Most trials in the High Court are conducted by High Court judges (puisne judges), who must either be practitioners of at least seven years' standing and with at least seven years' relevant legal experience or have been a Circuit Judge for at least two years (Senior Courts Act 1981, s. 10). Most interim applications are dealt with in the RCJ by judicial officers known as Masters, or by District Judges in cases proceeding in the District Registries. The allocation of business to different levels of judiciary in the High Court is dealt with in detail in **2.8 to 2.13**.

Under the Senior Courts Act 1981, s. 9(1) and (2), the Lord Chief Justice may request a Circuit Judge or Recorder (or a person within s. 1ZB) to act as a High Court judge: when so acting such a judge is informally known as a section 9 judge. A request may be made only after consulting the Lord Chancellor (s. 9(2B)) and only with the concurrence of the Judicial Appointments Commission in the case of a request to a Circuit Judge to act as a judge of the Court of Appeal (s. 9(2D)). The Lord Chief Justice, after consulting the Lord Chancellor, may

Commentary

appoint as a deputy High Court judge, for a certain period or to sit on certain occasions, any person who is qualified for appointment as a puisne judge (s. 9(4)).

High Court District Judges are often also County Court District Judges. Masters and District Judges must be practitioners of at least five years' standing and with at least five years' relevant legal experience (Senior Courts Act 1981, s. 88 and sch. 2).

The correct mode of address for a High Court judge is 'My Lord' or 'My Lady'. Masters are addressed as 'Master'. District Judges are addressed as 'Sir' or 'Madam'.

As in the County Court, the administrative work of the High Court is performed by civil servants. Enforcement is conducted by enforcement officers who are self-employed practitioners.

The High Court consists of three Divisions, namely the Chancery Division, the Family Division and the Queen's Bench Division. Each High Court judge is attached to a particular Division, by direction of the Lord Chief Justice under the Senior Courts Act 1981, s. 5(2), but may occasionally act as an additional judge of another Division, by direction of the Lord Chief Justice under s. 5(3). Under s. 5(1)(a), the Chancellor of the High Court is president of the Chancery Division. Under s. 5(1)(b), the Lord Chief Justice is a judge of the Queen's Bench Division by virtue of his office and there are also a president and a vice-president of that Division. There is a president of the Family Division (s. 5(1)(c)). Each Division has its own administrative offices for issuing claim forms, arranging interim hearings and trials and for dealing with enforcement. Further, specialist courts exist within the Queen's Bench Division and the Chancery Division to deal with particular classes of cases. These include the Admiralty Court, the Commercial Court, and the Technology and Construction Court in the Queen's Bench Division and the Companies Court, the Patents Court and the Intellectual Property Enterprise Court in the Chancery Division (see further **2.15** to **2.21**). Each of these specialist courts also has its own judges and administrative offices. In addition, public law matters, particularly applications for judicial review, are dealt with separately in the Administrative Court (see **2.22**).

By **PD 2A, para. 2.1(1)**, the offices of the Senior Courts are open on every day of the year except:

(a) Saturdays and Sundays;
(b) Good Friday;
(c) Christmas Day;
(d) a further day over the Christmas period determined in accordance with the table annexed to **PD 2A** which is based on the day of the week on which Christmas Day falls and is designed to ensure consistency between the various civil courts round the country;
(e) Bank Holidays in England and Wales under the Banking and Financial Dealings Act 1971; and
(f) such other days as the Lord Chancellor, with the concurrence of the Heads of Division, may direct.

Opening hours for the offices of the Senior Courts at the Royal Courts of Justice and Rolls Building are 10.00 a.m. to 4.30 p.m. and such other hours as the Lord Chancellor, with the concurrence of the Heads of Division may direct (**PD 2A, para. 2.1(2)**). Opening hours for a District Registry are (in the absence of any specific direction from the Lord Chancellor) the same as those for the County Court offices of which it forms part (see **2.2**) (**PD 2A, para. 2.1(3)**).

Allocation of cases to different levels of the judiciary in the High Court

2.8   **PD 2B, paras 2 to 7B.4**, state how hearings are allocated between the different levels of the judiciary in the High Court. **PD 2B** does not apply to proceedings in the Family Division, save to the extent that they can also be dealt with in the Chancery Division (**PD 2B, para. 1.1C**).

Trials   CPR, r. 2.4, provides that Judges, Masters and District Judges may exercise any func-   **2.9**
tion of the court except where an enactment, rule or practice direction provides otherwise. In
the High Court, **PD 2B, Section II**, sets out the matters over which Masters and District
Judges do not have jurisdiction or which they can deal with only on certain conditions. A
Master or District Judge may only give directions for early trial after consulting the Head of
the relevant Division or a Judge nominated by the Head of Division (**PD 2B, para. 4.1**).
A bankruptcy registrar has jurisdiction to make third party debt orders (*Thakerar v Lynch Hall and
Hornby (No. 2)* [2005] EWHC 2752 (Ch), [2006] 1 WLR 1513).

Deputy High Court judges, Masters and District Judges cannot try claims under the **Human
Rights Act 1998** in respect of judicial acts or for declarations of incompatibility (**PD 2B, para. 7A**).

Injunctions and interim remedies   Applications for freezing injunctions (including orders   **2.10**
for disclosure of assets which may become the subject of an application for a freezing injunction) and search orders must be made to a judge (**PD 2B, para. 2**). Masters and District Judges
may grant ordinary injunctions in terms agreed by the parties, or in connection with charging
orders and appointments of receivers and in aid of execution of judgments (**PD 25A,
para. 1.2**). In any other case, any judge who has jurisdiction to conduct the trial of the action
has the power to grant an injunction in that action (**PD 25A, para. 1.3**). Examinations made
under freezing orders will usually be dealt with by a Master or District Judge, or before an
examiner they have appointed (**PD 2B, para. 7**). **PD 2B, para. 3.1**, lists a number of orders a
Master or District Judge may not make. These include orders relating to the liberty of a subject, and relating to judicial review claims (except that Queen's Bench Division Masters may
make orders on interim applications in judicial review claims).

Masters of the Crown Office or Administrative Court have power under **PD 2B, para. 3.1A**,
to make interim orders in judicial review proceedings (including judicial review proceedings
relating to criminal cases, extradition appeals, and applications to vary bail conditions provided in the latter case the prosecutor consents), costs orders in judicial review cases and
orders in applications under the Senior Courts Act 1981, s. 42, for permission to start or
continue a judicial review claim.

Chancery proceedings   PD 2B, para. 7B.1, contains a list of Chancery applications that must   **2.11**
be dealt with by a judge rather than a Master or District Judge, unless the Chancellor of the
High Court consents. These include granting an indemnity for costs out of the assets of a company on the application of minority shareholders bringing a derivative claim and, subject to
some specified exceptions, making orders in proceedings in the Patents Court. **PD 2B, para.
7B.2**, sets out other applications in the Chancery Division that a District Judge may not deal
with without the consent of the Supervising Judge for the region in which the District Judge is
sitting. These include approving compromises on behalf of a person under a disability, where the
value of the claim exceeds £100,000; giving permission to executors, administrators or trustees
to bring or defend proceedings or to continue the prosecution or defence of proceedings or to
grant an indemnity for costs out of the trust estate; and granting an indemnity for costs out of
the assets of a company on the application of minority shareholders bringing a derivative claim.
For the practice in the Chancery Division concerning allocation of interim applications to
Masters and Judges see **32.3, 37.2** and **42.5**. For the possibility of a trial by a Master see **61.26**.

Assignment of claims to Masters and transfers between Masters   PD 2B, paras 6.1 and 6.2,   **2.12**
empower the Senior Master and Chief Master to assign claims in the RCJ to individual Masters,
or to transfer an assigned case from one Master to another. The fact that a case has been assigned
to one Master does not prevent it being dealt with by another Master, where necessary.

Case management   By virtue of **PD 29, para. 3.10**, Masters will generally deal with case   **2.13**
management issues in respect of cases proceeding in the RCJ, and District Judges in respect of
cases proceeding in the District Registries.

High Court Divisions

2.14 Business is allocated between the three High Court Divisions by the Senior Courts Act 1981, s. 61 and sch. 1. However, the jurisdiction of the High Court is exercisable by all three Divisions alike (Senior Courts Act 1981, s. 5(5)). Thus, business not specifically allocated to a particular Division may be dealt with by any. In practice, the Divisions have developed their own areas of expertise. The broad position is as follows:

(a) The Queen's Bench Division is usually the most appropriate Division for dealing with claims seeking common law remedies (debt, damages, recovery of land, recovery of goods), including most claims in contract and tort. It will deal, for example, with all personal injury and clinical negligence claims proceeding in the High Court. The Queen's Bench Division has been assigned all cases involving applications for writs of habeas corpus (save those relating to a child, which would be dealt with by the Family Division), applications for judicial review, the proceedings specified in s 30(1)c of the Terrorism Prevention and Investigation Measures Act 2011, financial restrictions proceedings under the Counter-Terrorism Act 2008, s. 65, and Admiralty claims and claims being dealt with in the Commercial Court (Senior Courts Act 1981, sch. 1).

(b) The Chancery Division sits in the Rolls Building. It has been assigned all cases involving the sale, exchange or partition of land; mortgages; execution of trusts; administration of estates; bankruptcy; taking of partnership accounts; rectification etc. of deeds; probate; intellectual property; the appointment of a guardian of a child's estate; and applications under the enactments relating to companies (Senior Courts Act 1981, sch. 1). It can also deal with other areas, such as actions in contract and tort not specifically assigned to other divisions. Any claim which raises an issue under the EC Treaty, art. 81 (anti-competitive agreements) or art. 82 (abuse of a dominant market position) (now the Treaty on the Functioning of the European Union, arts 101 and 102), or the equivalent UK statutory provisions, chapter 1 or 2 of part 1 of the Competition Act 1998, which is not proceeding in the Commercial or Admiralty Court must be transferred to the Chancery Division at the RCJ (**CPR, r. 30.8**). For more information on Chancery business see **11.6**.

(c) The Family Division has been assigned all matrimonial matters including matters relating to children, such as adoption, legitimacy and guardianship; non-contentious or common form probate business proceedings under the Family Law Act 1986, the Children Act 1989 and the Child Abduction and Custody Act 1985, Council Regulation (EC) No. 2201/2003, the Hague Convention 1996, proceedings under the Childcare Act 2006, s. 79, or the Family Law Act 1996, parts 4 or 4A, and the Human Fertilisation and Embryology Act 2008, s. 54, as well as proceedings under the Gender Recognition Act 2004, or applications under the Civil Partnership Act 2004 (Senior Courts Act 1981, sch. 1). Proceedings which invoke the jurisdiction of the High Court to grant declarations as to the best interests of incapacitated adults (such as permanent vegetative state cases and sterilisation of persons unable to give consent) are civil proceedings to which the CPR apply. Although they are not allocated to any Division, they are more suitable for the Family Division (Practice Direction (Declaratory Proceedings: Incapacitated Adults) [2002] 1 WLR 325). Cases which only involve issues of public law, even though they are concerned with the welfare of children or incompetent adults, are properly litigated by way of a claim for judicial review in the Administrative Court (*A v A Health Authority* [2002] EWHC 18 (Fam/Admin), [2002] Fam 213). Human rights challenges to care plans and placements of children should be heard in the Family Division, preferably by judges with experience of administrative law (*C v Bury Metropolitan Borough Council* [2002] EWHC 1438 (Fam), [2002] 2 FLR 868).

The Family Court deals with all family cases with the exception of two classes of case that are reserved for the Family Division (reserved work), those being (a) cases invoking the inherent jurisdiction of the High Court, whether in relation to children (wardship) or incapacitated or vulnerable adults; and (b) international cases involving applications for relief under either the Hague Convention 1996 or the Brussels II Regulation. The judiciary of the Family Court includes High Court judges, Circuit Judges, Recorders, District Judges and Magistrates. Except for

reserved work, cases that require to be heard by a High Court judge are heard in the Family
by a High Court judge, and cases are not transferred to the High Court Family Divis
the grounds of complexity. The procedure relating to family proceedings is not consid
this work.

SPECIALIST COURTS

Within the High Court there are several specialist courts which deal with special ty
claim. Some of these courts have issued guides to their own procedure. These court guid
be seen at the Ministry of Justice website, http://www.justice.gov.uk.

The jurisdiction of these specialist courts is dealt with at **11.7**. The types of case suitable f
specialist courts, and a brief outline of the procedure to be followed in them is set out bel

Technology and Construction Court

The Technology and Construction Court (TCC) sits in the Rolls Building. It consists of
judges and other officers nominated under the Senior Courts Act 1981, s. 68, to exercise the
jurisdiction of the High Court in TCC claims, as defined in **CPR, r. 60.1** and **PD 60,
para. 2.1**. Nomination is by the Lord Chief Justice after consulting the Lord Chancellor.
CPR, Part 60, and **PD 60** set out the practice relating to TCC claims. They are supplemented
by the Technology and Construction Court Guide, 2nd ed., revised on 3 March 2014. All
TCC cases started in or transferred to London will be classified as suitable for determination
either by a High Court judge or a senior Circuit Judge, and will be assigned to a particular
TCC judge, and all statements of case and applications should be marked with the name of
the assigned judge and any communications about case management should be made to the
assigned judge's clerk (Technology and Construction Court Guide, para. 3.7). The TCC deals
with technically complex matters, with particular emphasis on construction cases. TCC
claims in the High Court outside London may be issued in any District Registry, but preferably
in one where a TCC judge will usually be available, namely, Birmingham, Bristol, Cardiff,
Chester, Exeter, Leeds, Liverpool, Manchester, Mold, Newcastle upon Tyne and Nottingham
(**PD 60, para. 3.3**). The County Court also has hearing centres in Birmingham, Bristol,
Cardiff, Central London, Chester, Exeter, Leeds, Liverpool, Newcastle, Nottingham and
Salford which can hear TCC cases (**PD 60, para. 3.4**).

A claim in the TCC will be assigned to a named TCC judge who will have primary responsibility for the case management of the claim (**PD 60, para. 6.1**). The trial will usually be
conducted by the assigned judge (**para. 11.1**).

Commercial Court

The Commercial Court is part of the Queen's Bench Division and sits in the Rolls Building. **2.17**
The judges of the Commercial Court are High Court judges who are nominated to be commercial judges (Senior Courts Act 1981, s. 6). Nomination is by the Lord Chief Justice after
consulting the Lord Chancellor. **CPR, Part 58**, and **PD 58** govern proceedings in the
Commercial Court. The Commercial Court hears commercial claims, as defined in **CPR,
r. 58.1** (Senior Courts Act 1981, s. 62(3)). Claim forms should be marked with the words
'Queen's Bench Division, Commercial Court' (**PD 58, para. 2.3**). All claims in the commercial list are allocated to the multi-track and therefore the rules relating to directions questionnaires and track allocation do not apply to them (**CPR, r. 58.13(1)**), and generally all pre-trial
applications are dealt with by a High Court judge, rather than by a Master or District Judge
(**PD 58, para. 1.3**). The Admiralty and Commercial Courts have published a guide which is
designed to ensure effective management of proceedings in the Commercial Court, without
prejudice to provisions of the CPR and practice directions. The Admiralty and Commercial
Courts Guide was updated in March 2013.

miralty Court

he Admiralty Court, which sits in the Rolls Building, is the part of the Queen's Bench Division which exercises the High Court's Admiralty jurisdiction, as defined in the Senior Courts Act 1981, s 20, and the High Court's jurisdiction as a prize court (s. 62(2)). The judges of the Admiralty Court are High Court judges who are nominated to be Admiralty judges (**s. 6**). Nomination is by the Lord Chief Justice after consulting the Lord Chancellor. All Admiralty proceedings must be commenced in the High Court (Civil Courts (Amendment) (No. 2) Order 1999 (SI 1999/1011)). **CPR, Part 58** (Commercial Court), applies to claims in the Admiralty Court except where **Part 61** provides otherwise (**r. 61.1(3)**). **CPR, Parts 58** and **61**, and **PD 61** are the principal sources for the practice of the Admiralty Court and are supplemented by the Admiralty and Commercial Courts Guide.

Mercantile Courts

2.19   A commercial or business claim, in a broad sense, not specifically required to be brought in the Chancery Division or another specialised court may be brought in one of the Mercantile Courts (**CPR, r. 59 1(2)**), but only if it will benefit from the expertise of one of the judges (known as Mercantile judges: **r. 59.1(3)**) authorised to sit in Mercantile Courts (**PD 59, para. 2.1**). Thus, the ambit of mercantile claims is wider than that of commercial claims. There are Mercantile Courts in the Birmingham, Bristol, Cardiff, Chester, Leeds, Liverpool, Manchester, Mold, and Newcastle upon Tyne District Registries of the High Court. There is also a Mercantile List in the Commercial Court of the Queen's Bench Division at the Royal Courts of Justice, called the London Mercantile Court. A claim proceeding in a Mercantile Court is known as a mercantile claim (**CPR, r. 59.1(3)**). Procedure in the Mercantile Courts is governed by **CPR, Part 59**, and **PD 59**. The Mercantile Courts have published an overall guide to their procedure (Mercantile Court Guide 2012). This largely adopts the Admiralty and Commercial Courts Guide, although the procedure is simpler as befits the size, value and type of case commonly heard in the Mercantile Courts. It is updated regularly and available at the Ministry of Justice website, http://www.justice.gov.uk.

Companies Court

2.20   The Companies Court, which sits in the Rolls Building, is part of the Chancery Division and exercises the High Court's jurisdiction under the enactments relating to companies, including petitions and applications under the Companies Acts and the Insolvency Act 1986 (see **chapters 82, 84, 85** and **86**).

Patents Court and Intellectual Property Enterprise Court

2.21   The Patents Court sits in the Rolls Building. It hears patents cases within the jurisdiction conferred on it by the Patents Act 1977 (Senior Courts Act 1981, s. 62(1)). The Intellectual Property Enterprise Court is a specialist list established within the Chancery Division of the High Court by **CPR, r. 63.1(2)(g)**. Patents and other intellectual property claims are governed by **CPR, Part 63**, and **PD 63**, supplemented by the Patents Court Guide. Patents and registered designs that come within **CPR Part 63, Section I**, are dealt with either in the Patents Court of the Chancery Division or the Intellectual Property Enterprise Court (**CPR, r. 63.2(1)** and **(2)**). Claims in the Patents Court form a specialist list (**r. 63.3**). Claims in respect of registered trade marks and other intellectual property rights that come within **CPR, Part 63, Section II**, and **PD 63, Section II** (see **PD 63, para. 16.1**), must be started in the Chancery Division, the Intellectual Property Enterprise Court or, unless **PD 63** provides otherwise, a County Court hearing centre where there is also a Chancery District Registry. There are Chancery District Registries at Birmingham, Bristol, Caernarfon, Cardiff, Leeds, Liverpool, Manchester, Mold, Newcastle upon Tyne and Preston, although the County Court hearing centres at Caernarfon, Mold and Preston have no jurisdiction in relation to registered or Community trade marks (**PD 63, paras 16.2** and **16.3**). The judges of the Patents Court in the Chancery Division are High Court judges who are nominated to be patents judges (Senior Courts Act 1981, s. 6). Nomination is by the Lord Chief Justice after consulting the Lord Chancellor. General guidance in relation to procedure and practice in the Patents Court is contained in the Patents Court Guide (October 2015) and Practice Statement: Listing of Cases for Trial in the Patents Court (7 December 2015). Guidance on proceedings in the Intellectual Property Enterprise Court can be found in the Intellectual Property Enterprise Court Guide (April 2014), the Intellectual Property Enterprise Court (Multi Track) Practice Note (17 December 2015), and the Guide to the Intellectual Property Enterprise Court Small Claims Track.

Administrative Court and Planning Court

The Administrative Court is the part of the Queen's Bench Division which hears judicial review proceedings, which are governed by **CPR, Part 54**, and **PD 54A, PD 54C** and **PD 54D**. There is detailed consideration of judicial review proceedings in **chapter 77**. The Administrative Court also hears habeas corpus applications and some appeals in criminal cases.

2.22

Judicial reviews and statutory challenges relating to planning and similar matters are allocated to the Planning Court (**CPR, rr. 54.21 to 54.24; PD 54E**). See **77.63**.

Commentary

Chapter 3   Computing Time

APPLICATION OF THE RULES

3.1 **CPR, rr. 2.8 to 2.11**, deal with calculating time. **Rule 2.8** (see **3.2**, **3.3** and **3.5**) applies to periods of time specified by the CPR, any practice direction or any judgment or order of the court. **Rules 2.9** (see **3.6**) and **2.10** (see **3.4**) apply to any judgment, order, direction or document, but not to the CPR or to practice directions. **Rule 2.11** (see **3.7**) applies to a time specified in the CPR or by the court, but is not relevant to practice directions.

Rules 2.8 and **2.9** apply when calculating the time for 'doing any act' specified in the documents or court orders to which they apply. It was held in *Anderton v Clwyd County Council (No. 2)* [2002] EWCA Civ 933, [2002] 1 WLR 3174, that they do not apply when calculating a time which is not a time by which an act is to be done. **Rules 2.8** and **2.9** therefore apply to calculations of time for doing acts such as filing statements of case, serving application notices, complying with mandatory orders, and most other steps required by the CPR, practice directions and court orders. They do not, however, apply to calculating deemed dates of service, because nothing is to be 'done' by the deemed date.

Rules 2.8 and **2.9** also do not apply to the computation of statutory time limits (see, for example, *Hinde v Rugby Borough Council* [2011] EWHC 3684 (Admin), [2012] JPL 816, and *R (Blue Green London Plan) v Secretary of State for the Environment, Food and Rural Affairs* [2015] EWHC 495 (Admin), LTL 23/3/2015). The construction of the time limit will depend on the exact wording of the statute. Thus it was held in *Barker v Hambleton District Council* [2012] EWCA Civ 610, [2012] CP Rep 36, that a statutory time limit which read that an application 'must be made within six weeks from the relevant date' meant that the first day to be counted was the day after the relevant date. This was to be distinguished from a period for doing an act 'starting with' the relevant day, in which case the first day to be counted was the relevant day itself.

DAYS

Clear days

3.2 A period of time, for doing an act, expressed as a number of days must be computed as 'clear days' (**CPR, r. 2.8(2)**). This means that if an act must be done a specified number of days before an event occurs, the day on which the act is done and the day on which the event occurs are not counted when calculating whether the required period has elapsed (**r. 2.8(3)**).

For example, if service must be effected at least three days before a hearing on Friday, 18 October, the last date for service is Monday, 14 October.

Five days or less

3.3 If the period of time for doing any act is five days or less, the following days within the period do not count: Saturday, Sunday, a bank holiday, Christmas Day, Good Friday (**CPR, r. 2.8(4)**).

For example, if service must be effected at least three days before a hearing on Monday, 21 October, the last date for service is Tuesday, 15 October.

Rule 2.8(4)(b), which excludes Saturdays, Sundays and bank holidays when calculating periods of five days or less, does not apply when calculating the deemed date for service of a claim form under **r. 6.14** or of other documents under **r. 6.26** (*Anderton v Clwyd County Council (No. 2)* [2002] EWCA Civ 933, [2002] 1 WLR 3174, applied in *R (Frezghi Semere) v Asylum and Immigration Tribunal* [2009] EWHC 335 (Admin), LTL 4/3/2009). This is because the deemed dates of service as set out in **rr. 6.14** and **6.26** for these methods of service are not periods 'for doing any act' as required for **r. 2.8(1)** to apply. What **rr. 6.14** and **6.26** do is to lay down rules for calculating artificial dates when those documents will be taken as having been received by the other party as a matter of law (**rr. 6.14** and **6.26** create an irrebuttable presumption of law), and so fall outside of **r. 2.8**.

MONTHS

In the CPR, 'month' means calendar month (Interpretation Act 1978, ss. 5 and 22 and sch. 1) and **CPR, r. 2.10**, applies the same definition to any judgment, order, direction or other document.   **3.4**

COURT OFFICE CLOSED

Where a period for doing any act at the court office, such as filing a document, ends on a day when the office is closed, the act will be done in time if done on the next day on which the office is open (**CPR, r. 2.8(5)**). **Rule 2.8(5)** is expressed to apply to a period specified by the CPR, a practice direction, a judgment or a court order. It does not apply to a time limit prescribed by statute (*Adesina v Nursing and Midwifery Council* [2012] EWHC 2615 (Admin), LTL 1/10/2012). However, there is a common law rule to the same effect, which applies, for example, if the court office is closed on the day when a limitation period under the Limitation Act 1980 expires (*Pritam Kaur v S. Russell and Sons Ltd* [1973] QB 336) or the day when a statutory time limit for bringing an appeal expires (*Mucelli v Government of Albania* [2009] UKHL 2, [2009] 1 WLR 276, approving *Pritam Kaur v S. Russell and Sons Ltd*) or the day when a statutory time limit for making an application expires (*R (Modaresi) v Secretary of State for Health* [2011] EWCA Civ 1359, LTL 23/11/2011 and *Nottingham City Council v Calverton Parish Council* [2015] EWHC 503 (Admin)). This common law rule is not limited to acts, such as issuing a claim form, which require something to be done by court staff to make them complete (*R (Modaresi) v Secretary of State for Health*).   **3.5**

When the period specified for doing an act at a court office ends on a day on which the office is open, the act may be done after office hours on that day, provided nothing has to be done by court staff to make the act complete (*Van Aken v Camden London Borough Council* [2002] EWCA Civ 1724, [2003] 1 WLR 684, where the relevant act was filing a document at court, which does not require any action by court staff).

If a claim form is filed during office hours on the last day of a limitation period, it does not matter that the court staff do not issue the claim until a later day (see *Barnes v St Helens Metropolitan Borough Council* [2006] EWCA Civ 1372, [2007] 1 WLR 879, discussed at **12.5**).

PD 2A, paras 2.1 and **3.2** to **3.3**, give details of the opening days and times of the RCJ, the District Registries of the High Court and of the County Court.

By **PD 5A** and **PB 5B**, the parties can also file documents by fax or email where the Electronic Working Scheme is not used. In such cases, a document filed at court by fax or email after 4 p.m. is treated as filed on the next day the court office is open (**PD 5A, para. 5.3(6)**; **PD 5B, para. 4.2**).

PD 51O (The Electronic Working Pilot Scheme) allows parties who register for an account for Electronic Working to issue proceedings and file documents online 24 hours a day every day of the year, with some limited exceptions. The Pilot Scheme is in force for 12 months from 16 November 2015.

TIME LIMITS IN COURT ORDERS

3.6   In a court order, judgment or direction which imposes a time limit for doing any act, the last date for compliance must, wherever practicable, be expressed as a calendar date and include a time on that date by which the act must be done (CPR, r. 2.9(1)). For example, an order should be drafted to state that an act must be done 'by 4 p.m. on 22 February 2016', rather than 'no later than 14 days after the date of this order'.

When the date by which an act must be done is inserted in any document, the date must, wherever practicable, be expressed as a calendar date (r. 2.9(2)).

VARIATION BY CONSENT

3.7   CPR, r. 2.11, makes clear that parties may, by written agreement, vary any deadline specified in the CPR or by the court, unless forbidden to do so by a court order, the CPR or a practice direction. This extends to agreements for extensions of time for service of the claim form (*Thomas v Home Office* [2006] EWCA Civ 1355, [2007] 1 WLR 230). **Rule 3.8(3)** forbids extension of time by agreement if the consequence of failure to comply with the deadline is specified in the rule, practice direction or court order creating it. This is, however, subject to r. 3.8(4), which permits variation of the time for doing any act specified in a rule, practice direction or order by prior written agreement of the parties for up to a maximum of 28 days, provided the agreed extension does not put at risk any hearing date and provided the court does not order otherwise. **Rule 3.8(3)** applies to deadlines set in practice directions, implying that a practice direction deadline which does not specify the consequence of failure to comply can be varied by agreement without the limitations provided in r. 3.8(4). However, authority to vary practice direction deadlines is not given expressly by r. 2.11, unless they can be taken to be covered by the phrase 'specified... by the court'. In *Hallam Estates Ltd v Baker* [2014] EWCA Civ 661, [2014] CP Rep 38, the Court of Appeal, anticipating r. 3.8(4), encouraged parties to cooperate in agreeing reasonable extensions of time. A party asked to agree an extension of time should agree, if sensible reasons are given, future hearing dates are not imperilled and there is no other disruption to the conduct of litigation. The parties have a duty under r. 1.3 to help the court to further the overriding objective, including allotting an appropriate share of the court's resources to an individual case. This can be done by avoiding the need for a contested application for an extension. Unreasonable refusal to agree an extension may be punished by draconian costs penalties (*Denton v T. H. White Ltd* [2014] EWCA Civ 906, [2014] 1 WLR 3926 at [43]). Similarly the courts should not refuse, and r. 1.1(2)(f) does not require them to refuse, to grant reasonable extensions of time in such circumstances.

The meaning of a 'written agreement of the parties' was considered by the Court of Appeal in *Thomas v Home Office*. The court held that there must be a document, or exchange of documents, which is intended to constitute the agreement or to confirm or record an oral agreement. An oral agreement between two solicitors recorded in a letter sent by one solicitor to the other but not replied to by the other cannot constitute a 'written agreement of the parties'. Similarly, an oral agreement between two solicitors, evidenced by an internal confirmatory note by one solicitor, or even by each of the solicitors, cannot constitute a written agreement unless the internal notes are exchanged (or in some way confirmed in writing to each other). On the facts of the case, an oral agreement confirmed by one party in writing to the other and by that party in writing to their expert witness (even though this letter was copied to the first party) could not constitute a 'written agreement of the parties' under **r. 2.11**.

An example of the CPR restricting agreement by the parties is **r. 15.5(1)**, which allows an agreement to extend the time for service of a defence by a maximum of 28 days.

The date specified in a notice of proposed allocation for compliance with specified matters (including filing directions questionnaires) cannot be varied by agreement between the parties (**r. 26.3(6A)**). In a fast track claim, the parties are not allowed to vary by consent the date for the return of pre-trial checklists, the trial date or trial window, or any other directions which would impinge on these dates (**r. 28.4**). In a multi-track claim, the parties are not allowed to vary by consent the dates for any case management conference, pre-trial review, the return of pre-trial checklists, the trial date or trial period, or any other directions which would impinge on these dates (**r. 29.5**).

Where parties agree changes to the case management timetable under **r. 2.11**, they need not file the written agreement at court (**PD 28, para. 4.5; PD 29, para. 6.5**).

VARIATION BY THE COURT

The court has power under **CPR, r. 3.1(2)(a)**, to extend or shorten the time for compliance **3.8** with any rule, practice direction or court order. This power does not extend, however, to statutory time limits, such as the time for filing notices of appeal to the High Court under the many provisions listed in **PD 52D** (*Mucelli v Government of Albania* [2009] UKHL 2, [2009] 1 WLR 276, applied in *Mitchell v Nursing and Midwifery Council* [2009] EWHC 1045 (Admin), LTL 28/5/2009, *Harrison v General Medical Council* [2011] EWHC 1741 (Admin), LTL 8/6/2011, and *Reddy v General Medical Council* [2012] EWCA Civ 310, [2012] CP Rep 27, which confirms that *Mucelli* is of general application, not just of relevance to extradition cases). However an ostensibly non-extendable time limit has to be read so as to comply with Article 6 of the European Convention on Human Rights, which may allow the court a discretion to extend time, in exceptional circumstances, and where the appellant personally had done all that he or she could to bring the appeal timeously (see *Pomiechowski v Poland* [2012] UKSC 20, [2012] 1 WLR 1604; *Adesina v Nursing and Midwifery Council* [2013] EWCA Civ 818, [2013] 1 WLR 3156; *Heron Bros Ltd v Central Bedfordshire Council* [2015] EWHC 604 (TCC), [2015] PTSR 1146; *Daniels v Nursing and Midwifery Council* [2015] EWCA Civ 225, [2015] Med LR 255).

In *Hallam Estates Ltd v Baker* [2014] EWCA Civ 661, [2014] CP Rep 38, it was held (applying *Robert v Momentum Services Ltd* [2003] EWCA Civ 299, [2003] 1 WLR 1577, and *Re Guidezone Ltd* [2014] EWHC 1165 (Ch), [2014] 1 WLR 3728) that an application for an extension of time is not an application for relief from sanctions, provided the application notice is filed before expiry of the relevant time period. This is so even if the court deals with the application after expiry of the relevant period. The case law under **CPR, r. 3.9** (see **chapter 48**), does not apply to such an application.

The court has power under **r. 3.1(2)(a)** to extend the time for compliance with a court order made with the consent of the parties (*Pannone LLP v Aardvark Digital Ltd* [2011] EWCA Civ 803, [2011] 1 WLR 2275). Whether the court will permit variation of a time limit specified in a consent order will depend on the nature of the agreement and the order. The court is likely to place more weight on the consent of the parties to a time limit specified in a compromise agreement than procedural agreements made about case management. See also *Safin (Fursecroft) Ltd v Estate of Badrig* [2015] EWCA Civ 739, [2016] L & TR 11 where, on reviewing the authorities, the Court of Appeal upheld an order extending the time for payment of arrears of rent and service charge in a consent order in proceedings for forfeiture of a lease.

Commentary

Chapter 4   Remedies

INTRODUCTION

4.1 Many kinds of remedy may be asked for in civil proceedings, with the aim of establishing or changing a legal status, determining legal rights and duties, or rectifying an infringement or denial of legal rights. The remedy which the court decides to grant is embodied in its judgment, which is usually phrased as, and is often called, an 'order'. The remedy sought by a claimant must be specified in the claim form (**CPR, r. 16.2(1)(b)**), though this statement does not limit the remedies which the court may award (**r. 16.2(5)**) (see **23.7**). There is nothing to prevent the court giving a merely declaratory judgment stating what parties' rights are without giving any other remedy (**r. 40.20**) (see **4.19**).

Pending a court's decision on what its judgment may be at the trial or final hearing of a claim, it may make interim orders providing what are usually called 'interim remedies', which are discussed in **chapters 32** and **36** to **41**.

Remedies can be granted only in accordance with established principles of law or under statutory authority: the court does not have an inherent jurisdiction to make any order necessary to ensure that justice is done (*Wicks v Wicks* [1999] Fam 65 at pp. 76–8 and 88–9).

The principal remedies which are available in civil proceedings generally are examined in this chapter, consisting of legal remedies (debt and damages), which are available as of right on proof of infringement of the claimant's legal rights, and equitable remedies (injunction, specific performance, rectification and account), which the court may award, at its discretion, when a legal remedy would be inadequate or unavailable. The discretion to award equitable remedies is exercised in accordance with established principles. In particular, an equitable remedy will not be awarded where it would be inequitable to do so, for example, in the light of the claimant's previous bad behaviour in relation to the subject matter of the claim (the rule that the claimant must come to the court with clean hands), or where the claimant has delayed in claiming the remedy, to the defendant's detriment (the rule against laches, see **10.40**).

Numerous other remedies are available in special types of proceedings, such as the discretionary remedies available in judicial review proceedings (see **chapter 77**), the discretionary remedy of rescission of contract, and many orders created by statute (see **4.23**).

Methods of enforcing judgments are considered in **chapters 79** to **81**.

EFFECT OF JUDGMENTS

A judgment or order of a court in civil proceedings takes effect from the day when it is given **4.2** or made (**CPR, r. 40.7(1)**) and this means from the first moment of that day (*Shelley's Case* (1582) 1 Co Rep 93b). The court may specify a later date on which its judgment or order is to take effect (**r. 40.7(1)**). There are special rules in **r. 40.10** concerning default judgments against foreign States.

It is in the public interest that legal proceedings brought to resolve a dispute should result in a final answer to that dispute. The parties must put their whole case before the court and are not permitted to relitigate the questions which the court decides (see **33.15** to **33.20**).

Judgments are traditionally divided into:

(a) those which are *in personam*, that is, determinative of the rights of the parties to the proceedings, and not challengeable by those parties in other proceedings, but not binding on anyone else, and

(b) those which are *in rem*, that is, determinative of legal status and not challengeable in any proceedings before any tribunal which recognises the jurisdiction of the court which gave the judgment (though it may be possible to question the court's jurisdiction).

A judgment by a court of competent jurisdiction binds the parties even if a judgment of a higher court in other proceedings shows that it was wrong in law (*Watt v Ahsan* [2007] UKHL 51, [2008] 1 AC 696).

The finality of a judgment or order is subject to three qualifications:

(a) A person who was not a party to the proceedings in which the judgment or order was made, but who is directly affected by it, may apply under **r. 40.9** for it to be set aside or varied.

(b) Any accidental slip or omission in a judgment or order may be corrected by the court under **r. 40.12** (see **63.44**).

(c) It may be possible to appeal against the judgment or order, see **chapters 74 to 77**.

(d) In insolvency proceedings, the court may be asked to review, rescind or vary its order (see **84.7 to 84.11**).

Merger of cause of action into judgment

When judgment is given, the original cause of action is treated as merged with the judgment, **4.3** so that no further proceedings can be brought on that cause of action. Where an event gives rise to more than one cause of action, not all of which are litigated, the ones which have not been litigated do not merge in the judgment given on those that were. For example, a claim in contract will not merge with a judgment on a tortious claim which arose from the same event. Merger does not apply to successive causes of action, so that judgment for specific instalments of debt or rent will not bar a claim for further instalments. Merger does apply where the court gives judgment on the merits on one of two mutually exclusive alternative bases for the claim (*Balgobin v South West Regional Health Authority* [2012] UKPC 11, [2013] 1 AC 582).

Res judicata

The parties to a claim that is determined by a judgment of the court on the merits of the claim **4.4** are estopped from bringing further similar claims. This estoppel, known as *res judicata* (a thing or matter that has been decided), takes three distinct forms. First, there is a narrow form of estoppel flowing from the merger of the cause of action in the judgment which provides that the issues between the parties which were actually adjudicated by the court have been finally resolved between them. Second, there is a wider form of estoppel known as cause of action estoppel, which is founded on the rule in *Henderson v Henderson* (1843) 3 Hare 100. This rule is based on encouraging finality in litigation and (unless the decision was secured by fraud or collusion) prevents any party to a claim in which judgment has been given from raising in other proceedings any issue which was resolved or could have been raised and resolved in the adjudicated claim (see *Arnold v National Westminster Bank* [1991] 2 AC 93 and *R (Coke-Wallis) v Institute of Chartered Accountants in England and Wales* [2011] UKSC 1, [2011] 2 AC 146, and **33.15**). The third form of estoppel, known as issue estoppel, is based on the same public policy (see **33.16**). The doctrine of issue estoppel is that if, after judgment is delivered in civil proceedings, two of the parties to those proceedings, or their successors in title, are parties to further civil proceedings, then one of those parties cannot repeat, as against the other, in the second proceedings, an assertion which was found to be incorrect by the court in the first proceedings (*Mills v Cooper* [1967] 2 QB 459 per Diplock LJ at pp. 468–9). The doctrine applies only to an assertion — whether of fact, opinion (*Humberclyde Finance Group Ltd v Hicks* (2001) LTL 19/11/2001) or the legal consequences of facts or opinions — which was an essential element of the asserting party's cause of action or defence in the first proceedings. The doctrine affects a party whether the party was an original claimant or defendant in the first proceedings or was joined to those proceedings, but it only affects parties who appear in the same capacity in both sets of proceedings (*Humberclyde Finance Group Ltd v Hicks*). Issue estoppel does not prevent a party repeating an assertion if further material, which is relevant to the correctness or incorrectness of the original assertion in the previous proceedings, has become available and it could not in the exercise of reasonable diligence have been deployed in the previous proceedings.

Where a claimant brings proceedings against more than one defendant, entering summary judgment against one defendant may amount to an election to abandon the claim against the other defendants (*Morel Brothers and Co. Ltd v Earl of Westmorland* [1903] 1 KB 64). A default judgment is entered without investigating the merits, unlike summary judgment. Consequently, entering a default judgment against one defendant does not, without more, amount to an election to abandon the claim against the other defendant (*Pendleton v Westwater* [2001] EWCA Civ 1841, LTL 28/11/2001). In order to make an effective election to abandon a claim against another defendant, a claimant claiming two or more remedies must decide to follow one of them at the expense of the others and must communicate that choice to the defendant against whom the remedy is claimed in terms which make clear a deliberate preference for that remedy over any other. Those requirements were not satisfied where the claimant entered judgment in default against D2 for damages to be assessed for personal injury in reliance on an allegation by D1 that D2 was the claimant's employer at the same time as pursuing her claim that D1 was in truth her employer (*Balgobin v South West Regional Health Authority* [2012] UKPC 11, [2013] 1 AC 582).

In *Johnson v Gore Wood and Co.* [2002] 2 AC 1 the House of Lords reviewed the circumstances in which public policy permitted a second claim (in this case brought by the majority shareholder of a company after the claim by the company had been compromised) to proceed. The test is whether, taking into account all the public and private interests involved and the facts of the case, a claimant is misusing or abusing the process of the court (see **33.15** to **33.19**).

MONEY JUDGMENTS

4.5   The most common judgment given is for payment of a sum of money. The money due will usually be a debt (or other liquidated sum) or damages. The distinction between a debt (or other liquidated claim) and damages is no longer as important as it was in the past, as is reflected in the CPR by the distinction drawn in several places between claims for specified amounts and claims for unspecified amounts. Interest may be awarded on a money judgment (see **chapter 64**), but this is relief ancillary to the principal remedy of a money judgment, rather than an independent remedy (*Bank voor Handel en Scheepvaart NV v Slatford* [1953] 1 QB 248 at p. 278).

Set-off

If two parties to proceedings make monetary claims against each other (a claim and a **4.6**
cross-claim), and both claim and cross-claim are upheld, the court will deduct the smaller of
the amounts found due from the larger and give only one judgment for the balance, if the
claim and the cross-claim can be set off. There are two sets of rules governing whether a claim
and a cross-claim can be set off: one creates a legal set-off, the other an equitable set-off.

In a claim for a liquidated sum the defendant can assert a legal set-off of any liquidated debt
or money demand cross-claimed by it from the claimant, whether or not the mutual debts
arise from the same transaction, provided both the claimant's claim and the defendant's
cross-claim can be quantified with certainty at the time of filing a defence (see *Hanak v Green*
[1958] 2 QB 9 per Morris LJ at p. 17; *Axel Johnson Petroleum AB v MG Mineral Group AG* [1992] 1
WLR 270; *B. Hargreaves Ltd v Action 2000 Ltd* [1993] BCLC 1111; **CPR, r. 16.6**).

Equitable set-off (also called equitable defence) permits a cross-claim by the defendant to be set
off against the claimant's claim if it arises out of the same transaction or is closely connected with
that transaction and is so closely connected with those demands that it would be manifestly
unjust to allow the claimant to enforce payment without taking the defendant's claim into
account (per Lord Denning MR in *Federal Commerce and Navigation Co. Ltd v Molena Alpha Inc.* [1978]
QB 927 at pp. 974–5 and Goff LJ at p. 987, point not considered on appeal; *Geldof Metaalconstructie
NV v Simon Carves Ltd* [2010] EWCA Civ 667, [2010] 4 All ER 847). Equitable set-off is not available
against a claim for freight (*Aries Tanker Corporation v Total Transport Ltd* [1977] 1 WLR 185) or for payment of a bill of exchange (*Nova (Jersey) Knit Ltd v Kammgarn Spinnerei GmbH* [1977] 1 WLR 713).

A defendant who has an unquantified cross-claim against the claimant which is not connected
with the claimant's claim is not entitled to either legal or equitable set-off.

It is possible for the contract governing payment of a debt to prevent the debtor from exercising a right of set-off against the creditor even in legal proceedings brought to enforce payment
of the debt (*Coca-Cola Financial Corporation v Finsat International Ltd* [1998] QB 43; *Re Kaupthing
Singer and Friedlander Ltd* [2009] EWHC 740 (Ch), [2009] 2 Lloyd's Rep 154).

For more on set-off see **34.37** to **34.39**.

DAMAGES

Damages are a monetary payment as the legal remedy for infringement of legal rights. The **4.7**
amount to be paid primarily reflects the compensation required by the claimant for loss caused by
the defendant's wrongdoing (compensatory damages), though the court may increase this compensation because of the additional hurt caused by the objectionable way in which the defendant
acted (aggravated damages). In limited circumstances the court, representing the public interest,
may mark its disapproval of the defendant's behaviour by adding a penalty element to the damages (exemplary damages). Where there has been a breach of contract, the contract itself may
provide how damages for the breach are to be calculated (liquidated damages). An infringement
of a legal right which has caused no compensable loss may result in only nominal damages.

Nominal damages

Nominal damages are awarded where there has been an infringement of a legal right but it has **4.8**
not resulted in any loss for which compensation may be claimed (*The Mediana* [1900] AC 113).

If actual damage to the claimant is an essential element of a cause of action (as it is, for example, for tortious negligence) then failure to prove any damage to the claimant will result in the
dismissal of the claim. If actual damage to the claimant is not an essential element of a cause
of action (as is the case, for example, with breach of contract or trespass to land), the claimant

Commentary

will be given judgment on proof of the matters that are essential, but cannot be awarded damages beyond a nominal amount.

Aggravated damages

4.9 Aggravated damages are defined in the CPR Glossary as 'Additional damages which the court may award as compensation for the defendant's objectionable behaviour'. A claim for aggravated damages must be made separately in the particulars of claim (**CPR, r. 16.4(1)(c)**). Aggravated damages compensate for injury to feelings caused by the manner in which the wrong was committed, and cannot be awarded to a company, which has no feelings to be injured (*Collins Stewart Ltd v Financial Times Ltd* [2005] EWHC 262 (QB), [2006] EMLR 5). Aggravated damages are quite distinct from exemplary damages and in a suitable case both may be awarded. The most common situation in which both are awarded is unlawful eviction (if statutory damages are not claimed or awarded).

Exemplary damages

4.10 Exemplary damages are defined in the CPR Glossary as 'Damages which go beyond compensating for actual loss and are awarded to show the court's disapproval of the defendant's behaviour'. A claim for exemplary damages must be made separately in the particulars of claim (**CPR, r. 16.4(1)(c)**). Exemplary damages can be awarded only in very limited circumstances. The House of Lords in *Rookes v Barnard* [1964] AC 1129 recognised only three categories. They are:

(a) oppressive, arbitrary or unconstitutional behaviour by government servants;

(b) cases where the conduct of the defendant is calculated to make a profit which will be in excess of the compensatory damages which are payable; and

(c) where an award of exemplary damages is expressly authorised by statute.

In *Kuddus v Chief Constable of Leicestershire Constabulary* [2002] 2 AC 122 the House of Lords overruled the decision of the Court of Appeal in *AB v South West Water Services Ltd* [1993] QB 507 with the result that the categories of claim which can give rise to an award of exemplary damages are not now limited to those in which awards were made prior to 1964. It now seems that it is the behaviour complained of rather than the precise cause of action which the court must consider. Awards of exemplary damages are certainly available in claims for trespass to the person or property, defamation, false imprisonment and private nuisance. It is now arguable that awards may be made in other categories of case such as misfeasance in public office (the cause of action in *Kuddus*).

Damages may be awarded as exemplary damages even though they have been quantified by reference to specific losses by the claimant (*Borders (UK) Ltd v Commissioner of Police of the Metropolis* [2005] EWCA Civ 197, [2005] Po LR 1).

Liquidated damages

4.11 A claim for liquidated damages is a claim for the sum agreed in a contract between the parties as payable in the event of a specified breach of that contract which has in fact occurred. In many cases the amount payable has to be calculated by reference to the circumstances of the breach, such as the number of days' delay in performance. A sum which is a genuine pre-estimate by the parties of the loss occasioned by the breach of contract will be recoverable as liquidated damages. A sum which exceeds the amount of any loss likely to be occasioned by the breach complained of will also be recoverable as liquidated damages provided it is not out of all proportion to any legitimate interest of the innocent party in the performance of the contract. Otherwise, the clause will be a void penalty clause and the innocent party will retain their right to sue for recoverable damage caused by the breach. The rules applied in identifying a penalty clause set out in *Dunlop Pneumatic Tyre Co. Ltd v New Garage and Motor Co. Ltd* [1915] AC 79 are matters for the court to consider and not immutable rules of law (*Cavendish Square Holding BV v Makdessi* [2015] UKSC 67, [2015] 3 WLR 1373).

Compensatory damages

Compensatory damages can be divided into pecuniary and non-pecuniary damages. Pecuniary **4.12** damages compensate the claimant for measurable financial losses caused by the defendant's wrongdoing. Non-pecuniary damages (often called 'general' damages) are awarded in recognition of suffering which that wrongdoing has caused the claimant. The amount to award as non-pecuniary damages must be assessed according to the court's sense of what would be appropriate in the case before it, in the light of what has been awarded in comparable cases. Information about appropriate awards for pain, suffering and loss of amenity in personal injuries claims is given by the Judicial College in *Guidelines for the Assessment of General Damages in Personal Injury Cases*, 13th edn. (Oxford: OUP, 2015). Conventionally a claimant does not specify the amount sought as non-pecuniary damages, though an estimate of what is likely to be awarded must be made in order to decide which court to start the claim in (see **11.4**). In personal injury claims, pecuniary damages sought must be specified in a schedule of past and future expenses and losses attached to the particulars of claim (**PD 16, para. 4.2**; see **chapter 25**).

Traditionally, an award for pecuniary loss is based on the loss which the claimant has sustained and not on what it would be fair or reasonable for the defendant to pay (*General Tire and Rubber Co. v Firestone Tyre and Rubber Co. Ltd* [1975] 1 WLR 819). However, in exceptional cases, where it is just to do so, the court may make orders to ensure that the defendant in a claim for breach of contract retains no benefit from the breach (*Attorney General v Blake* [2001] 1 AC 268), or, in cases of misuse of property, to award a sum which it would be reasonable for the defendant to pay for that use (*Experience Hendrix LLC v PPX Enterprises Inc.* [2003] EWCA Civ 323, [2003] 1 All ER (Comm) 830).

In tortious claims the aim is to award a sum of money which will restore the claimant's position to what it would have been but for the wrong for which the damages are being awarded (*Livingstone v Rawyards Coal Co.* (1880) 5 App Cas 25). Compensatory damages in tort can include heads of loss which have been aggravated by the claimant's impecuniosity (*Lagden v O'Connor* [2003] UKHL 64, [2003] 1 AC 1067, overruling *Liesbosch Dredger (Owners of) v Owners of SS Edison* [1933] AC 449 on this point).

Claims for damages for breach of contract may be made on two different bases:

(a) to restore the claimant's position to what it would have been had the contract been properly performed (loss of bargain); or
(b) to compensate for expenditure rendered futile by the breach (reliance loss).

The claimant can choose the basis on which to claim (*CCC Films (London) Ltd v Impact Quadrant Films Ltd* [1985] QB 16).

DELIVERY UP OF GOODS

A final judgment ordering delivery up of goods may take one of the three forms permitted by **4.13** the Torts (Interference with Goods) Act 1977, s. 3(2):

(a) an order for the delivery of the goods and payment of any consequential damages;
(b) an order for delivery of the goods but giving the defendant the alternative of paying the stated value of the goods together, in either case, with the consequential damages; or
(c) judgment for damages.

An order in form (a) is discretionary (s. 3(3)(b)), and tends to be made only where the goods are rare or have some special value, or where they are not readily available on the market (*Howard E. Perry and Co. Ltd v British Railways Board* [1980] 1 WLR 1375). If an order in form (a) is obtained but not complied with, the person in whose favour the judgment was given can return to court and the court can revoke the order and make an order for the payment of damages by reference to the value of the goods (s. 3(4)). Payment of a judgment for the value of the goods extinguishes the claimant's title to those goods (s. 5).

INJUNCTIONS

4.14 An injunction may be either mandatory (requiring some act to be done) or prohibitory (requiring some conduct to stop, or prohibiting threatened conduct). Injunction is an equitable remedy awarded at the court's discretion where a legal remedy would be inadequate (see **4.1**).

The general power to grant injunctions has been given statutory form in the Senior Courts Act 1981, s. 37 (which applies also in the County Court by virtue of the County Courts Act 1984, s. 38). This provides that injunctions, whether final or interim, 'may' (emphasising that this is a discretionary power) be granted where it is 'just and convenient'. In cases where rights under the European Convention on Human Rights may be engaged, the test may better be expressed as 'just and proportionate' (see *South Bucks District Council v Porter* [2003] UKHL 26, [2003] 2 AC 558). There are also specific statutory powers to grant injunctions, for example, in the Housing Act 1996, ss. 153A and 153B (see **88.2** to **88.14**). Power to grant an injunction in judicial review claims is conferred by the Senior Courts Act 1981, s. 31(2) (see **77.58**).

The discretion to grant an injunction must be exercised judicially, taking into account all the relevant circumstances. Factors include the importance of curbing the defendant's activities, whether breaches of the claimant's rights or the law will continue unless restrained, whether the court would be prepared to impose the sanctions available for breach of the injunction (fining and imprisonment, see **chapter 81**), and, in the case of specific statutory powers to grant injunctions, the purpose for which the power was given (*South Bucks District Council v Porter* at [29] and [32]). The inability to order imprisonment is the reason why injunctions are rarely imposed against children (*G v Harrow London Borough Council* [2004] EWHC 17 (QB), LTL 23/1/2004). When granting an injunction the court does not contemplate that it will be disobeyed (*Castanho v Brown and Root (UK) Ltd* [1981] AC 557 at p. 574). Concern that a defendant might disobey an injunction should not therefore deter a court from granting it. As Lord Bingham of Cornhill said in *South Bucks District Council v Porter* at [32], there is not one law for the law-abiding and another for the lawless and truculent. Consequently, a final injunction was granted in *Mid Bedfordshire District Council v Brown* [2004] EWCA Civ 1709, [2005] 1 WLR 1460, where the defendants had moved on to land in breach of an interim order, because the public interest in upholding court orders far outweighed the factors favouring suspension of the injunction.

When a public body applies for an injunction in pursuance of its public functions, one factor which the court may take into account is the lawfulness of the decision to make the application. But this is not the only factor to be taken into account and, in deciding whether to grant the injunction, the court is exercising an original rather than a supervisory jurisdiction (*South Bucks District Council v Porter* at [27]).

The court may award damages in addition to or in lieu of an injunction (Senior Courts Act 1981, s. 50; County Courts Act 1984, s. 38). It is possible to award both an injunction ordering cessation of a breach of the claimant's rights and damages for injury to those rights during the time that the injunction will be in force, for example, where it is clear that the injunction will be evaded (*Brazier v Bramwell Scaffolding (Dunedin) Ltd* [2001] UKPC 59, LTL 20/12/2001). However, if the claimant has established that the claim is one in which the court would usually grant an injunction, the court may not, of its own motion, instead award nominal damages (*Nelson v Nicholson* (2000) LTL 1/12/2000).

When drafting a final injunction it is important that the wording is clear and specific. The order must state what is to be done and when, or what is not to be done from a particular date and time. This is because disobedience of an injunction is contempt of court, for which punishments such as committal and sequestration may be imposed (see **81.7**). Injunction orders should be endorsed with a penal notice (see **81.6**) and follow any relevant form in the CPR, practice directions or court guides. Forms for a final injunction order can be based on the interim injunction forms with the omission of the parts that are relevant to an interim injunction.

SPECIFIC PERFORMANCE

An order for specific performance requires the performance of the obligations of a party to a contract. An order for specific performance is an equitable remedy awarded at the court's discretion where a legal remedy would be inadequate (see **4.1**). In most cases an order for specific performance is asked for as a remedy for a breach of an obligation, but it is also possible to make an order for specific performance in anticipation of a breach. Specific performance is asked for most often in claims for the enforcement of agreements relating to land, but it can also be ordered for the sale of goods, particularly those which are rare or unique such as an original work of art or an heirloom.

4.15

Certain obligations will not be specifically enforced, including illegal contracts, unenforceable contracts (e.g. sale of land without the necessary written contract), voluntary obligations, contracts for personal skill or work, and obligations which require constant supervision (*Ryan v Mutual Tontine Westminster Chambers Association* [1893] 1 Ch 116). The claimant must show that he is ready, willing and able to perform his part of the obligation or contract. Specific performance may be refused where there has been a misrepresentation by the claimant, where there has been a serious mistake or misdescription, and in cases of severe hardship.

The court may award damages in addition to or in lieu of specific performance (Senior Courts Act 1981, s. 50; County Courts Act 1984, s. 38).

An order for specific performance must state what is to be done and when. The contract or obligation does not merge completely into the order, but further performance is subject to the control of the court.

RECTIFICATION

Rectification (alteration of a document to reflect the parties' true intentions) is a discretionary equitable remedy (see **4.1**). It is not the bargain which is rectified, but the written record of the transaction. Rectification is not required where the true meaning is revealed by the ordinary rules of construction of written agreements. Where applying those rules of construction to the document shows that it does not reflect the agreement of the parties, the document may be rectified. An order for rectification has retrospective force so that the document is treated as if it was in the rectified form from the date it was signed or created. Rectification will not be ordered in the absence of convincing evidence of what the parties agreed or intended and of the erroneous recording of their agreement or intention in the written document.

4.16

RESCISSION

Rescission is a discretionary equitable remedy (see **4.1**) by which a party may be entitled to set aside a contract or other transaction entered into with another party in reliance on a misrepresentation or in consequence of a breach of a fiduciary duty on the part of that other party. Under the Misrepresentation Act 1967, s. 2(2), the court may affirm the contract or transaction and award damages in lieu of rescission where the misrepresentation was innocent or negligent. The damages awarded are compensatory. In the case of fraudulent

4.17

misrepresentation the claimant is entitled to rescission as of right. There is no general right to relief by way of rescission simply because it would be equitable to do so. A contract terminated by the acceptance of a repudiatory breach may often be said to have been 'rescinded' but that is not a proper use of the true meaning of the word or the relevant remedy.

ACCOUNTS

4.18   The power of the court to order an account to be taken is considered at **63.38**. Accounts are a common remedy in claims between principal and agent, claims between partners and claims involving jointly owned property. The first stage is to establish that an account should be taken by the court. An account will not be ordered where the parties have already settled the balance between themselves by an account stated or a settled account. As an account is an equitable remedy, the court may refuse to order an account if it would be unjust to do so, for example where the party in default was entirely innocent or the claimant has unjustifiably delayed in bringing the claim (*Hollister Inc. v Medik Ostomy Supplies Ltd* [2012] EWCA Civ 1419, [2013] Bus LR 428). If the limitation period for the claim has expired, an account will not be ordered to avoid that limitation period. At the second stage, the court should give directions for the taking of the account, which may involve disclosure and inspection. The party liable to account will usually be ordered to prepare the first account. The receiving party can then raise objections to items in that account. Those disputed items can then be determined by the court.

In cases of jointly owned real property where one party has left the property and the other has remained in occupation until sale, the court may try to avoid taking detailed accounts as the cost of doing so can exceed the sums involved. The party remaining in occupation will have to pay an occupation rent assessed as the fair rental value of the property. If, as is often the case, that person has paid all the outgoings, those will have to be credited. The result in many cases is that the court will refuse to order an account on the ground that the outgoings paid will be broadly the same as the occupation rent (*Bernard v Josephs* [1982] Ch 391; *Dennis v McDonald* [1982] Fam 63).

An account may also be sought (as an alternative to damages) where there has been an infringement of a proprietary right (e.g. misuse of confidential information, or intellectual property rights). A claimant must elect whether to seek damages (based on the loss he can show he has suffered) or an account (based on the net profits made by the defendant). Proving damage is often extremely difficult, so that an account of the profit made by the defendant may be a more attractive remedy. An account of profits does not involve a consideration of the loss suffered by the innocent party as a result of the unlawful conduct giving rise to the obligation to account. In assessing the profit made by the party in default, the court should disregard general overheads or expenditure incurred by the defaulting party, but may have regard to overheads or expenditure directly referable to the defaulting party's unlawful conduct. The burden of proof lies on the defaulting party (*Hollister Inc. v Medik Ostomy Supplies Ltd*). The claimant may elect between two alternative remedies, such as an account of profits or damages, at any time before judgment is entered for the claimant. The claimant ought not to be required to elect between the two until he has been provided with all the available information required for him to make an informed choice (*Island Records Ltd v Tring International plc* [1996] 1 WLR 1256; *Ramzan v Brookwide Ltd* [2011] EWCA Civ 985, [2011] 2 P & CR 22).

DECLARATIONS

Final declarations

4.19   The power to make binding final declarations can be found in **CPR, r. 40.20**, and the power to make interim declarations is in **r. 25.1(1)(b)**. Power to make a declaration in judicial review claims is conferred by the Senior Courts Act 1981, s. 31(2) (see 77.59). When deciding whether to make a declaration the court should take into account justice to the claimant, justice to the defendant, whether the declaration will serve a useful purpose, and any special reasons affecting the decision (*Financial Services Authority v Rourke* [2002] CP Rep 14). A declaration about the lawfulness of future conduct will not be granted unless the circumstances are truly exceptional (*R (Rusbridger) v Attorney General* [2003] UKHL 38, [2004] 1 AC 357). In deciding whether this test is met, according to *Blackland Park Exploration Ltd v Environment Agency* [2003] EWCA Civ 1795, [2004] Env LR 33, the court will consider the following criteria:

(a) the absence of any genuine dispute about the subject matter;

(b) whether the case is fact-sensitive; and

(c) whether there is a cogent public or individual interest that will be advanced by making the declaration.

A declaration may make findings of fact as well as declaring legal rights (*Compagnie Noga d'Importation et d'Exportation SA v Abacha (No. 3)* [2002] EWCA Civ 1142, LTL 31/7/2002).

Interim declarations

4.20 The inclusion of the power to grant an interim declaration in **CPR, r. 25.1(1)(b)**, means that such an order is no longer 'a contradiction in terms'. It was recognised in *NHS Trust v T (Adult Patient: Refusal of Medical Treatment)* [2004] EWHC 1279 (Fam), [2005] 1 All ER 387, that there are still difficulties, but:

(a) the power to grant interim declarations is not restricted to judicial review claims;

(b) interim declarations can be granted for a one-off medical procedure, for example, a Caesarean section or an amputation (at [44]);

(c) a material change of circumstances can found a reconsideration.

In the case of interim relief in relation to medical treatment of a person said to lack mental capacity, Charles J said the patient should be given an opportunity to make representations. It is for the judge to decide on capacity, then to decide on the best interests of the patient applying the usual civil standard on the best evidence then available.

RESTITUTION

4.21 Claims for restitution can be made at law and in equity and are based on the principle of unjust enrichment. The claim is for repayment of the benefit received by the defendant and not the loss suffered by the claimant. The claim will be particularly important where the claimant's damages are less than the benefit received by the defendant, where the claimant may have difficulty proving his damages and where the claimant made a bad bargain. Thus, where a car is purchased without obtaining good title, the purchaser will normally prefer to reclaim the entire purchase price rather than damages based on the lower value of the car when the defect in title is discovered.

Where a claimant seeks restitution of something given to the defendant in return for something received, there is no principle or rule of practice which requires the claim to include an offer of full counter-restitution. It is for the court to decide at trial what form of counter-restitution should be ordered so as to do practical justice between the parties (*Halpern v Halpern (Nos. 1 and 2)* [2007] EWCA Civ 291, [2008] QB 195; *Ruttle Plant Ltd v Secretary of State for the Environment and Rural Affairs* [2007] EWHC 2870 (TCC), [2008] 2 All ER (Comm) 264).

The most common claims in restitution are for repayment of money had and received which covers both money paid under a mistake and money paid where there has been a total failure of consideration. A claim in restitution may also be made in some tortious actions, particularly those involving interference with proprietary rights. If a defendant takes the claimant's goods and sells them for an advantageous price, it will be more attractive to claim the money received by the defendant rather than the value of the goods. The remedy in tort and the restitutionary remedy are alternatives and the claimant must elect which remedy he seeks. If a claimant seeks restitution he waives the commission of the tort.

POSSESSION

4.22   The court may order a person who has ceased to be entitled, or never has been entitled, to occupation or possession of land or property to give up possession to the person who is entitled to it. This may happen on the termination of a lease or licence, or other right of occupation or possession, e.g., as a mortgagor, or where the defendant occupies land or property as a trespasser (**chapter 35**). An order for possession is an order *in rem*. It relates to the land or property and can be expressly assigned or transferred by the claimant with his title to the land or property. A person in occupation or possession who was not a party to the claim may apply to the court to have the order set aside. Enforcement of the order may be stayed or suspended (see, for example, **87.29** and **87.49** in the context of mortgage possession proceedings). In the absence of such an application the order for possession may be enforced against a non-party occupier in the same way as any party named in the order.

STATUTORY REMEDIES

4.23   A large number of statutory provisions allow the court to grant special statutory remedies in specified circumstances. In each case the requirements to be satisfied before the court has any special power and the criteria for the exercise of that power have to be considered. Statutory remedies include:

(a)   winding-up and administration orders (**chapter 82**);

(b)   bankruptcy orders (**chapter 83**);

(c)   orders regulating the affairs of companies (**chapter 85**);

(d)   director disqualification orders (**chapter 86**);

(e)   various orders and injunctions to control anti-social behaviour and harassment (**chapter 88**);

(f)   orders declaring that legislative provisions are incompatible with the European Convention on Human Rights (**91.4**).

PART B

Funding Litigation

Chapter 5 Funding Litigation

INTRODUCTION

There is no doubt that civil litigation, particularly in England and Wales, is expensive. **5.1**
Potential parties to a claim have to consider their solicitors' fees (which in England are some
of the highest in the world), their barristers' fees, court fees and, depending on the case,
experts' fees. An unsuccessful party can end up paying legal fees twice over or more if he also
has to meet a substantial proportion of each of his opponent's costs. What that means in practice is that every hour spent pursuing a claim can cost one or more of the parties many hun-
dreds, or even thousands, of pounds.

That cumulative cost means that, aside from the relatively rich, many cannot afford to bring
cases unless they receive some type of financial support from a third party. For those with very
low income and limited savings, the State might be prepared to assist through the provision
of legal aid, although that has now been restricted to only a very few categories of litigation.
Other options are for litigants to share the financial risk of litigation with their lawyers,
an insurer and/or a third-party funder.

Conditional fee agreements (CFAs) enable lawyers to share the risk of the litigation with
their clients by offering a number of variations on 'no win, no fee' arrangements. Essentially,
the lawyer agrees not to charge the client if the claim fails, but will charge at their normal
hourly rates, usually with an additional 'success fee' calculated as a percentage of those normal fees, if the claim succeeds. Damages-based agreements (DBAs) are similar, in that they
are 'no win, no fee' agreements, but the success element is based on a percentage of the
amount recovered in the proceedings rather than on the normal fees of the lawyer. The
insurance and investment markets can assist parties by underwriting some or all of the costs
of litigation in return for a premium, a multiple of the funding assistance given, or a share
of any proceeds.

CFAs and various insurance products have dominated personal injury litigation for many
years. In other civil proceedings the use of CFAs and insurance products has risen steadily
following the **Access to Justice Act 1999**. That Act restricted the scope of public funding but
encouraged the use of CFAs, backed by insurance, in a number of ways. In particular, the
uplift on the lawyer's fees which becomes payable by the party if the case is won, and which
was intended to cover the cost of unsuccessful CFA cases run by the same lawyer, could then
be recovered from the losing party, as could any insurance premiums paid to cover the party's
risk of paying his opponent's costs.

It is perhaps not surprising that when CFAs led to both an increase in the number of claims and the level of costs payable in those claims, a substantial body of satellite litigation relating to the enforceability of CFAs and the recoverability of success fees and insurance premiums followed. While solicitors and clients became more familiar both with the concept and practical requirements of 'risk sharing', the consequent uncertainty caused considerable disquiet amongst lawyers, judges, insurance companies and claims management companies. Ongoing reform, aimed at ensuring that CFAs were workable and fair, led to the introduction of 'predictable costs' in bulk litigation markets, the revocation of the Conditional Fee Agreements Regulations 2000 (SI 2000/692) in 2005, and changes to the Solicitors' Practice Rules 1990.

Of course the question 'Who pays?' is quickly followed by 'How much?' Retrospective assessment of the level of costs became increasingly influenced, and sometimes circumscribed, by prospective, court-approved, budgeting and by predictable and fixed cost regimes (for costs budgeting see **chapter** 43, and for fixed costs see the now revoked CPR, rr. 45.15 to 45.22).

The ever increasing cost of litigation in the English courts, fuelled by the widespread use of recoverable success fees and insurance premiums, attracted sustained criticism from the judiciary and insurers, and prompted a number of reviews. The most significant and comprehensive review was Sir Rupert Jackson's *Review of Litigation Costs: Final Report* (2009), which was commissioned by the Ministry of Justice. That report proposed a 'coherent package of interlocking reforms, designed to control costs and promote access to justice' and led to the very significant reforms in litigation funding (alongside many other civil procedure changes) in April 2013.

JACKSON FUNDING REFORMS

5.2 The essential elements of the civil justice reforms of 2013, which were introduced on 1 April 2013, are:

- The elimination of recoverable CFA success fees and recoverable ATE premiums. This is subject to some technical savings and delays in implementation in relation to mesothelioma claims, insolvency proceedings and publication and privacy claims. These areas are the subject of further reviews. Details of the transitional provisions can be found in *Blackstone's Guide to the Civil Justice Reforms 2013*, Sime and French (Oxford: OUP, 2013), ch. 2.
- The extension of the range of funding mechanisms available to parties, by use of:
  - contingency fees ('damages-based agreements'), where:
    - in personal injury claims, there is a 25 per cent cap (excluding damages for future care and loss); and
    - for all non-personal injury claims (excluding employment tribunal cases), there is a 50 per cent cap.
  - third-party funding; and
  - 'contingent legal aid funds'.
- The banning of referral fees in personal injury cases.

Primary legislation giving effect to these reforms was enacted in the Legal Aid, Sentencing and Punishment of Offenders Act 2012. The primary legislation is supplemented by a number of statutory instruments, and extensive amendments to the CPR and practice directions, all of which came into force on 1 April 2013.

Although a current assessment of the impact of the reforms is difficult, the report prepared for the Civil Justice Council Cost Forum (21 March 2014), *Impact of the Jackson Reforms: Some Emerging Themes* by Professor John Peysner, provides some interesting reading based on focused anecdotal research.

GLOSSARY OF KEY FUNDING TERMS

after-the-event (ATE) insurance. Insurance which is purchased when litigation is contem-   **5.3**
plated or started and which covers the risk of having to pay the opponent's costs. It can be
extended to include cover for the insured's own legal costs and expenses.

before-the-event (BTE) insurance, also known as legal expenses insurance (LEI). An
insurance product (often, but not always, linked to other insurance, such as a household
or motor policy) which is purchased on a subscription basis prior to any litigation being
contemplated or started and which usually pays all of the insured's legal costs and the
risk of having to pay the opponent's costs, subject to a financial limit written into the
policy. The limit for non-business cases is often, as a rough guide, between £25,000 and
£100,000.

conditional fee agreement (CFA). A written agreement between a solicitor and his client, or
between a barrister and a solicitor, relating to a particular claim, typically providing that if the
case is lost, no fees are payable, but if the case is won, the costs will be calculated by reference
to a normal hourly rate plus a percentage uplift (a success fee) which is agreed at the outset.
For example, a 100 per cent success fee will double the agreed hourly rate. 100 per cent is the
maximum success fee allowed and is the appropriate uplift for a case with a 50–50 chance
of success.

damages-based agreement (DBA), also known as a contingency fee agreement. An agreement
between a solicitor and his client, typically providing that the solicitor's fees for a claim will be
calculated by reference to a pre-agreed percentage of the damages recovered. The amount of time
the solicitor may spend on the case is irrelevant. Until 1 April 2013 this type of agreement was
illegal for court proceedings, but lawful for non-contentious work and tribunal proceedings (see
5.19). DBAs became lawful across a wide range of civil litigation on 1 April 2013.

detailed assessment. A line-by-line assessment by the court, at the end of a case, of the level
of legal costs of a party. This is often undertaken by specialist costs judges.

disbursements. The expenses in a claim, including court fees, travel costs, experts' fees etc.

indemnity principle. The principle that a party who is ordered to pay another party's costs
does not have to pay amounts which the receiving party has no enforceable obligation to pay
to his own lawyers.

public funding (also known as legal aid). Funding by the State of a person's legal costs, subject to reimbursement from what is recovered in the proceedings. In England and Wales
public funding of civil claims is now very restricted. An assisted party has substantial protection against having to pay his opponent's costs even if the case is lost.

ready reckoner. The usual formula for calculating success fees in CFAs, namely, the chances
of losing divided by the chances of winning. For example, in a case where the chances of winning are 50 per cent, the success fee would be 100 per cent, and in a case where the chances
of winning are 75 per cent, the success fee would be 33 per cent (i.e. 25/75).

statutory charge. A charge on property or damages recovered or preserved in publicly funded
legal proceedings, as security for the payment of costs which are not recovered from the losing party.

success fee. The percentage uplift payable under a CFA on top of a solicitor's (or barrister's)
base hourly rate costs in the event of a successful outcome.

third-party funding (TPF). A funding arrangement under which commercial third parties fund the costs of litigation in return for a percentage of damages recovered or a

Commentary

multiple of their investment, most readily obtained for high-value cases with good prospects of success.

DUTY TO ADVISE CLIENTS ON FUNDING

5.4   Solicitors are under a professional duty to ensure their clients know the funding options available to them and that they understand the main features of different funding methods. The SRA Code of Conduct sets out 'outcomes-focused' conduct requirements, providing greater flexibility for individual firms to decide how best to meet and 'uphold the intention' of the Code, with reference to 'indicative behaviours'. In funding matters the Code provides as follows:

Outcomes

You must achieve these outcomes: ...

O(1.6) you only enter into fee agreements with your clients that are legal, and which you consider are suitable for the client's needs and take account of the client's best interests; ...

O(1.12) clients are in a position to make informed decisions about the services they need, how their matter will be handled and the options available to them;

O(1.13) clients receive the best possible information, both at the time of engagement and when appropriate as their matter progresses, about the likely overall cost of their matter;

O(1.14) clients are informed of their right to challenge or complain about your bill and the circumstances in which they may be liable to pay interest on an unpaid bill;

O(1.15) you properly account to clients for any financial benefit you receive as a result of your instructions;

Indicative behaviours

Acting in the following way(s) may tend to show that you have achieved these outcomes and therefore complied with the Principles:

Dealing with the client's matter

... IB(1.4) explaining any arrangements, such as fee sharing or referral arrangements, which are relevant to the client's instructions;

IB(1.5) explaining any limitations or conditions on what you can do for the client, for example, because of the way the client's matter is funded; ...

Fee arrangements with your client

IB(1.13) discussing whether the potential outcomes of the client's matter are likely to justify the expense or risk involved, including any risk of having to pay someone else's legal fees;

IB(1.14) clearly explaining your fees and if and when they are likely to change;

IB(1.15) warning about any other payments for which the client may be responsible;

IB(1.16) discussing how the client will pay, including whether public funding may be available, whether the client has insurance that might cover the fees, and whether the fees may be paid by someone else such as a trade union;

IB(1.17) where you are acting for a client under a fee arrangement governed by statute, such as a conditional fee agreement, giving the client all relevant information relating to that arrangement;

IB(1.18) where you are acting for a publicly funded client, explaining how their publicly funded status affects the costs;

IB(1.19) providing the information in a clear and accessible form which is appropriate to the needs and circumstances of the client;

IB(1.20) where you receive a financial benefit as a result of acting for a client, either:

(a) paying it to the client;

(b) offsetting it against your fees; or

(c) keeping it only where you can justify keeping it, you have told the client the amount of the benefit (or an approximation if you do not know the exact amount) and the client has agreed that you can keep it;

IB(1.21) ensuring that disbursements included in your bill reflect the actual amount spent or to be spent on behalf of the client; ...

Acting in the following way(s) may tend to show that you have not achieved these outcomes and therefore not complied with the Principles:

Accepting and refusing instructions

...IB(1.27) entering into unlawful fee arrangements such as an unlawful contingency fee.

Practical advice on funding

A client must be told about the potential liability for the other side's costs if the claim is **5.5** unsuccessful. The usual rule is that the unsuccessful party in proceedings is ordered to pay the successful party's costs (**CPR, r. 44.2(2)**). The other side's costs generally have to be paid out of the losing party's personal resources, or, if available, a BTE policy. It may be possible to arrange ATE insurance to cover the risk of paying the other side's costs (see **5.15**).

A solicitor must consider whether a client's claim could be funded by someone else's legal expenses insurance, for example, that of the householder where the client lives or the driver of a vehicle in which the client was a passenger. A solicitor should always ask a client to bring to the first consultation all relevant insurance policies, if obtaining them is reasonably practicable. The solicitor's duty may extend to making thorough enquiries and reviewing the relevant insurance documentation (*Garrett v Halton Borough Council* [2006] EWCA Civ 1017, [2007] 1 WLR 554). The nature of the client, the claim and the cost of any ATE policy are relevant to the depth of inquiry required (see also *White v Revell* [2006] EWHC 90054 (Costs), LTL 15/9/2006, and *Choudhury v Kingston Hospital NHS Trust* [2006] EWHC 90057 (Costs), LTL 7/9/2006). If the client's claim is against the policyholder, and both might be funded by the same insurer, the solicitor must advise whether the degree of control given to the intended defendant's insurer makes it unreasonable to rely on the policy; and this will depend on the size and difficulty of the claim. A failure to follow this practice could mean that the claimant's additional liabilities under a pre-April 2013 funding arrangement, such as an ATE insurance premium and/or success fee under a CFA, cannot be recovered. That is on the basis that any additional liability may have been unreasonably incurred and hence not recoverable on an assessment between parties (*Sarwar v Alam* [2001] EWCA Civ 1401, [2002] 1 WLR 125; see also *Barlow v Perks* (2007) SCCO 0606555, LTL 31/10/2007).

Care should be taken when changing the basis of funding. In *Ramos v Oxford University NHS Trust* (2016) SCCO CL1503600, LTL 23/2/2016 it was held that the claimant had been unable to make an informed choice about a change from LSC funding to a CFA arrangement backed by an ATE insurance policy where her solicitor had wrongly advised her that the LSC would not permit the instruction of experts who charged more than £180 per hour, and failed to explain the effect of the 10 per cent uplift under *Simmons v Castle* [2012] EWCA Civ 1039, [2013] 1 WLR 1239 and the risk that the ATE premium might not be recoverable if successfully challenged. Accordingly, there was sufficient doubt about the reasonableness of her decision to render the success fee and ATE premium irrecoverable under **CPR, r. 44.4**. See also *AH v Lewisham Hospital NHS Trust* (2016) LTL 24/2/2016 and *Davis v Wiltshire Primary Care Trust* (2016) LTL 1/2/2016. However, the court in *Milton Keynes NHS Foundation Trust v Hyde* [2016] EWHC 72 (QB), [2016] 1 Costs LR 1 held that a CFA entered into with a client pursuing a clinical negligence claim was enforceable despite the fact that she had a CLS funding certificate which had not been discharged. The costs limitation in the certificate was about to be exhausted, and the claimant's solicitor had reasonably concluded that the work needed to bring the claim to a conclusion could not be carried out without alternative funding.

Commentary

Information about funding should be given to the client not only at the outset of litigation but at appropriate stages throughout. A solicitor should tell his or her client how much the costs are at regular intervals and in appropriate cases the solicitor should deliver interim bills at agreed intervals. The solicitor should explain to the client and confirm in writing any change in circumstances which will, or which are likely to, affect the amount of the costs, the degree of risk involved or the ratio of cost to benefit to the client of continuing with the matter. The client should be informed in writing as soon as it appears that a cost estimate or agreed upper limit may or will be exceeded. There is an ongoing obligation to consider the client's eligibility for public funding if a material change in the client's means comes to the solicitor's attention.

Standard information sent out with solicitors' terms of business has an important role to play in ensuring compliance with the requirements of the Code, but attention must be given to the particular circumstances of each case for each client. Assumptions should not be made, and the solicitor and client should regularly discuss how the litigation is to be funded and whether it deserves funding at all. Not only does that ensure compliance with the Code but it is an essential part of basic client care, and can prevent complaints arising. The unexpectedly large bill at the end of litigation remains a fertile source of client dissatisfaction.

Hourly rates

5.6   Private funding remains a prevalent method of paying for litigation. Usually, the client will pay the solicitor's costs of conducting the case at an agreed hourly rate. Charge-out rates are defined by a competitive market, but are loosely based on the salaries of the staff and fee earners working at the solicitor's office together with an element representing the firm's overheads and profit margins. The usual approach is to fix a single hourly rate for each fee earner (or grade of fee earner) in the firm taking these factors into account, although 'blended' rates are increasingly common. Guideline hourly rates for different grades of fee earners for different parts of the country can be seen in **tables 71.2 to 71.4.**

The client should be informed if the solicitor's charges are likely to be substantially more than a client can expect to recover on an assessment between parties. In *MacDougall v Boote Edgar Esterkin* (2000) SCCO Case Summary No. 15 of 2000 the client agreed to pay the solicitors at the rate of £300 per hour for work done in Manchester from 1992 onwards. Holland J sitting with assessors found that the consent of the client to that rate was not an informed consent. The solicitor had failed to explain the relationship between party and party and solicitor/own client costs and misrepresented what the approach of the costs officer might be. Notwithstanding that the solicitor was held to have given the client 'devoted skilled service on a sustained basis', on a solicitor/own client assessment his hourly rate was substantially reduced.

Disbursements

5.7   In addition to the legal representative's hourly rates, the client will be expected to pay for disbursements. These are sums paid by the firm during the course of litigation such as court, experts' and counsel's fees, travel costs, copies of photographs, and similar expenditure. Some solicitors provide credit for disbursements and in *Secretary of State for Energy and Climate Change v Jones* [2014] EWCA Civ 363, [2014] 3 All ER 956, the Court of Appeal found that the first instance judge had been entitled to award pre-judgment interest, at 4 per cent above base rate, on disbursements paid by a firm of solicitors for their clients. The clients had borrowed money from their solicitors at a fixed rate of interest for the disbursements, and the judge was correct to have regard to the clients' means rather than the solicitors' means when making the order.

In *Flatman v Germany* [2013] EWCA Civ 278, [2013] 1 WLR 2676, the Court of Appeal held that the funding of disbursements in a personal injury claim by a claimant's solicitor did not render the solicitor a 'real party' to the claim, nor did it justify a conclusion that the solicitor had stepped outside his normal role such that he might be exposed to a non-party costs order.

Fixed fees

Hourly rates are not the only basis for charging. Fixed fees, especially for small claims or fast **5.8** track litigation, can be agreed. They do, however, require a substantial amount of overall management by the solicitor both in terms of client expectations and the uncertainty of the defendant's conduct.

Following work by the Civil Justice Council, a regime of predictable costs for various classes of personal injury claims has applied to road traffic accidents from 6 October 2003 (and has been retained in the current **CPR, rr. 45.9** to **45.15**). Similar schemes applied to accidents at work from 1 October 2004 and to employers' liability disease claims from 1 October 2005, but these have been revoked with effect from 1 April 2013.

There is a streamlined claims process for road traffic accident personal injury claims and low value employers' and public liability personal injury claims between £1,000 and £25,000, which, when pursued and settled through the relevant protocol, attract fixed costs (found in **CPR, rr. 45.16** to **45.29**).

In *Rosenblatt v Man Oil Group SA* [2016] EWHC 1382 (QB), LTL 19/4/2016 a solicitors' firm which had agreed a fixed fee with a client, but with a proviso that it could revisit fees if any of the assumptions on which they were based proved to be incorrect, was held to be obliged to notify the client that it intended to change its fee and to seek the client's agreement to that change. The right to revisit the fees was not a right to revert automatically to charging an hourly rate.

Discounted fees

Practitioners must take particular care with private funding arrangements which offer dis- **5.9** counted fees. It is not uncommon, especially when acting for commercial clients, for solicitors to agree, in writing or otherwise, to reduce their normal hourly rate in the event that the litigation is ultimately unsuccessful. Such arrangements are likely to be construed as CFAs and so, to be enforceable, they must comply with the requirements discussed at **6.6**.

Costs forecasts and budgets

Forecasting fees can be extremely difficult, but the Code requires the solicitor to give the 'best **5.10** information possible'. That can include giving a forecast within a possible range of costs or explaining to the client the reasons why it is not possible to fix or give a realistic estimate of the overall costs, and giving instead the best information possible about the costs of the next stage. In cases where proceedings are issued, fees will in any event need to be accurately forecast and budgeted for case management purposes. Particularly in multi-track claims, cost budgets will need to be served and filed as part of usual case management (see **chapter 43**). The client can also be invited to set an upper limit on the firm's costs not to be exceeded without further authority.

Where there is a difference of 20 per cent or more between the costs claimed by a receiving party on a detailed assessment and the costs shown in a costs budget filed by that party, the receiving party will need to be able to provide reasons for the difference (**PD 44, paras 3.5** to **3.7**). If there is no satisfactory explanation for the difference, the court may regard the difference between the costs claimed and the costs shown on the budget as evidence that the costs claimed are unreasonable or disproportionate (**para. 3.7**).

Commentary

Under the pre-Jackson version of these rules, the difference of 20 per cent was taken as a starting point only, and the extent to which the court had regard to any such difference was a matter for its judgment in the individual case (*Mastercigars Direct Ltd v Withers LLP* [2007] EWHC 2733 (Ch), [2009] 1 WLR 881). A solicitor who gave no estimate at all might be able to recover his fees free of any such restriction (*Garbutt v Edwards* [2005] EWCA Civ 1206, [2006] 1 WLR 2907). However, if a complaint of inadequate professional service for not giving an estimate is upheld, the Legal Ombudsman can vary the fee to what was appropriate and impose a fine.

Client care letter

5.11   A client care letter, which should include the funding arrangements and, if possible, an estimate of the future costs, should be sent to the client promptly after the firm is retained. It may be appropriate to ask for a sum on account of costs at this stage, and it is sensible to agree to periodical billing of the client (which avoids the client being taken by surprise by a large bill at the end of the case, and also assists with the firm's cash flow).

PUBLIC FUNDING (LEGAL AID)

5.12   Public funding of legal proceedings (legal aid) is administered on behalf of the Lord Chancellor (see **chapter 7**). The introduction of contracting has reduced the number of solicitors who can undertake publicly funded work. Further restrictions on the scope of public funding were introduced by the Legal Aid, Sentencing and Punishment of Offenders Act 2012.

Publicly funded cases are subject to strict procedural and cost limits which the solicitor must have regard to and advise the client accordingly. When acting for a publicly funded client, a solicitor's compliance with the Principles of the SRA Code of Conduct 2011 is indicated by explaining to the client how their publicly funded status affects costs (IB 1.18).

CONDITIONAL FEE AGREEMENTS

5.13   From 1 April 2013, funding under a CFA continues to be an option (see **chapter 6**), but success fees and additional liabilities under CFAs entered into from 1 April 2013 cease to be recoverable from the unsuccessful party.

In *Sibthorpe v Southwark London Borough Council* [2011] EWCA Civ 25, [2011] I WLR 2111, the Court of Appeal held that a CFA containing an indemnity given by the solicitors against any adverse costs order made in favour of their client did not amount to maintenance or champerty. Lord Neuberger of Abbotsbury MR acknowledged that the indemnity meant that the solicitors had a financial interest in the outcome of the litigation (being the risk of having to pay the defendant's costs if the claim failed, whilst not enjoying any gain if the claim succeeded). However, Lord Neuberger went on to note that there were no cases in which such an arrangement had been held to be champertous and that judicial definitions of champerty all envisaged a gain if the claim succeeded. Lord Neuberger held that it was not appropriate to extend the law of champerty at a time when both the judicial and legislative trends were in favour of its scope being curtailed. Further, public policy favoured such an indemnity being valid, at the very least where it permits access to justice in small cases where ATE insurance is unavailable or prohibitively expensive (such as the instant case). Arrangements such as that in *Sibthorpe v Southwark London Borough Council* are therefore legal.

BEFORE-THE-EVENT INSURANCE

5.14   Before-the-event (BTE) insurance or legal expenses insurance (LEI) provides the policyholder with an indemnity for the cost of legal fees if the policyholder becomes involved in litigation.

It is generally considered a relatively inexpensive mechanism for resolving a range of problems and legal disputes, primarily for consumers.

Sir Rupert Jackson's *Review of Civil Litigation Costs: Final Report* (Ministry of Justice, December 2009) recommended that positive efforts should be made to encourage the take up of BTE insurance by small and medium-sized enterprises in respect of business disputes and by householders as an add-on to insurance policies. Lord Young of Graffham's report, *Common Sense Common Safety* (2010), also endorsed extending BTE insurance as a possible solution to the problem of access to justice.

Legal expenses cover is usually broadly limited to the subject matter of the main policy and to claims of merit, although it is surprising how widely some policies are worded. The level of cover is usually limited to an agreed figure (£25,000 to £100,000 is not unusual) and will cover both the policyholder's liability for their own legal costs, and their liability for an opponent's costs if a case is lost. Legal expenses insurers often require the client's lawyers to provide advice on the merits of the claim from time to time so they can assess whether continuing the litigation can be justified under the terms of the insurance.

Most policies insist that, before the issue of proceedings, the policyholder uses a solicitor selected from a panel appointed by the insurer, who can then retain control over its terms of business with the panel firms. After proceedings have begun the policyholder has a right to instruct a solicitor of his or her choice (Insurance Companies (Legal Expenses Insurance) Regulations 1990, SI 1990/1159). The narrow interpretation of 'proceedings' to exclude pre- issue work, including working through a pre-action protocol, has been endorsed by the Financial Ombudsman Service in a policy statement issued in March 2003 *Ombudsman News,* issue 26). However, in a different context (when considering costs-only proceedings in *Crosbie v Munroe* [2003] EWCA Civ 350, [2003] 1 WLR 2033) Brooke LJ commented, obiter, at [37]:

lower courts are encountering…difficulties over the meaning of the word 'proceedings' as used in PD Protocols, para. 4A.2….it appears to me that…for instance, the dealings between the parties which lead up to the disposal of a clinical negligence claim are to be treated as 'proceedings' for the purposes of that paragraph even if the dispute is settled without the need to issue a claim form.

AFTER-THE-EVENT INSURANCE

5.15 ATE insurance policies are taken out to help cover the cost of litigation once a dispute has already arisen. If the premium is affordable, it can provide some peace of mind against the possibility of having to pay the total litigation costs if the case is lost. A fixed or predictable premium can also provide a certainty of cost exposure which is otherwise missing for a client involved in litigation.

Cover can be obtained to insure both the client's own legal costs, including disbursements, and those of opposing parties. They are commonly, but not exclusively, used in conjunction with full or partial CFAs so that there is risk sharing between both the insurance company and the solicitor. An application for insurance can normally be made at any time in the litigation but many insurance companies encourage applications to be made as early as possible, and preferably before the issue of proceedings. Applications for insurance made late in proceedings are more likely to be unsuccessful, or lead to higher premium quotes.

Whether or not insurance is offered by a particular provider and at what premium will depend primarily on the strength of the case and the level of cover required. As a very rough guide, insurance is generally available for cases with prospects of success greater than 65 per cent. In matters other than personal injury, premiums tend to be about 20 to 30 per cent of the amount of cover required, but that can be much higher in high risk and/or late stage cases.

The solicitor must exercise caution before assuming any responsibility to give 'best or suitable advice' in relation to the products which may be available. Although it may be incumbent upon the solicitor to suggest to the client a suitable policy, the solicitor should not guarantee that the means of funding adopted will necessarily be the most appropriate to the client's needs. A list of insurance providers is updated quarterly in the Law Society's publication, *Litigation Funding*. Specialist ATE insurance brokers exist, and may charge a fee for their service (often refundable when a policy is taken out). Several different types of policy are available. Some providers offer policies which defer payment of the premium until the conclusion of the case and which rebate the premium if the client is unsuccessful. In *Tilby v Perfect Pizza Ltd* (2002) LTL 28/3/2002 Senior Costs Judge Hurst held that there is no reason why an ATE policy premium must be paid when the policy is taken out. Accordingly an ATE policy can provide for payment of the premium on the conclusion of proceedings without being regarded as providing credit and subject to the Consumer Credit Act 1974. Other policies do specifically offer credit schemes allowing clients to borrow money to pay ongoing disbursements or the insurance premium itself.

A non-party costs order under the Senior Courts Act 1981, s. 51, may be made against an ATE funder, though the liability may be capped to the level of funding provided to the opposing party (*Arkin v Borchard Lines Ltd (Nos. 2 and 3)* [2005] EWCA Civ 655, [2005] 1 WLR 3055). Such an order is much less likely to be made if the funder is a 'pure funder' — one with no commercial or financial interest in the outcome — such as those who made donations towards the legal expenses of the unsuccessful claimant in *Hamilton v Al Fayed (No. 2)* [2002] EWCA Civ 665, [2003] QB 1175.

In *Heron v TNT (UK) Ltd* [2013] EWCA Civ 469, [2014] 1 WLR 1277, the Court of Appeal held that a judge had been right to refuse an employer's application for a non-party costs order against its employee's solicitors instructed on a CFA in a personal injury claim he had brought against it. Despite failing to obtain ATE insurance for the employee, the solicitors had not become a 'real party' to the litigation.

In *Beecham Peacock Solicitors LLP v Enterprise Insurance Co. plc* [2014] EWHC 2194 (QB), LTL 17/7/2014, a claim by a firm of panel solicitors against insurance companies to recover disbursements under ATE legal insurance policies incurred on behalf of the firm's clients was not struck out on the basis of lack of privity of contract. It was found that there was a realistic prospect that a direct claim against the insurers would be successful, based on the contracts at issue and on ancillary procedures and documents, such as payment requests and manuals issued by the insurer. Clearly though, each case is likely to differ on its facts.

An ATE insurer may avoid a policy for material misrepresentation and non-disclosure (*Persimmon Homes Ltd v Great Lakes Reinsurance (UK) plc* [2010] EWHC 1705 (Comm), LTL 13/7/2010). In that case, the successful defendant in the underlying proceedings claimed directly against the insolvent claimant's ATE insurer for its costs under the Third Parties (Rights against Insurers) Act 1930. The ATE insurer avoided the policy for material misrepresentations and non-disclosure, based largely on findings in the underlying proceedings, meaning that the defendant was unable to rely on the ATE insurance obtained by the claimant. In *IHC v Amtrust Europe Ltd* [2015] EWHC 257 (QB), LTL 16/2/2015, the ATE insurer was not estopped from relying on a right to avoid a policy of insurance for fraudulent misrepresentation after making an interim payment and increasing the limit of indemnity following an adverse partial summary judgment. These decisions confirm that ATE insurance is not to be treated differently from any other type of insurance with respect to the impact of material misrepresentations and non-disclosure.

In *Guerrero v Monterrico Metals plc* [2009] EWHC 2475 (QB), LTL 26/10/2009, the court held that the amount to be frozen in respect of a worldwide freezing order could include a sum to reflect part of an ATE insurance premium, but it refused to permit the entire premium (which was close to the defendants' agreed costs limit) to be frozen on the basis that this would shift the preponderance of the litigation risk on to the defendant.

ATE is often deployed to meet applications for security for costs, although it can be a matter of some contention whether or not the particular cover does in fact provide adequate security. In *Harlequin Property (SVG) Ltd v Wilkins Kennedy* [2015] EWHC 1122 (TCC), [2015] 3 Costs LR 495, the court considered if an ATE insurance policy taken out by an offshore claimant provided sufficient security for the defendant's costs. The court held that the defendant's status as a third party might leave it unable to recover under the policy in the event of the claimant's liquidation, because the policy proceeds would be payable to the insolvent estate and the defendant would have no greater claim on that money than any other unsecured creditor. While that was a legitimate concern, the parties were encouraged by the court to deal with this point either by the provision of a direct indemnity or an endorsement which provided that any costs ordered to be paid to the defendant would be paid direct, without set-off. ATE insurers will often consider such requests, or seek to find another way of providing suitable security, such as provision of a bank guarantee (albeit often for an additional fee).

When considering a similar point in *GSM Export (UK) Ltd v Commissioners of HM Revenue and Customs* [2014] UKUT 457 (TCC), [2015] STC 504, the Upper Tribunal held that where a company already in administration had taken out an ATE insurance policy to cover HMRC's costs if its appeal failed, any payment made under that policy by way of indemnity might be subject to a *Quistclose* trust and so would not fall into the assets available to creditors. Accordingly the ATE policy represented adequate security.

Recoverability of ATE insurance premiums paid before 1 April 2013

Provided the policy was entered into before 1 April 2013, or relates to proceedings in which recoverability is still allowed, a successful party may claim the premium paid for ATE cover from the other side as part of the costs of the proceedings (**Access to Justice Act 1999, s. 29**, which has been repealed from 1 April 2013 by the Legal Aid, Sentencing and Punishment of Offenders Act 2012, s. 46, subject to some savings). In accordance with the usual rules on the quantification of costs by the court (now to be found in **CPR, rr. 44.3** and **44.4**), to be recoverable in full the premium must have been reasonably incurred and reasonable and proportionate in amount. There is a considerable body of case law, discussed in **71.61**, on the circumstances in which such a premium can be recovered and what amount is reasonable and proportionate.

5.16

In considering whether a premium is recoverable at all, the principal factor is whether there were any real risks against which it was proper to insure at the time of entering into the insurance policy (*Burgess v J. Breheny Contracts Ltd* [2009] EWHC 90131 (Costs)). A premium on an ATE policy taken out at a late stage may be recoverable depending on the circumstances of the case (*Kris Motor Spares Ltd v Fox Williams LLP* [2010] EWHC 1008 (QB), LTL 13/5/2010). Where the policy was entered into after the defendant made an admission of liability, there may still be real risks against which it was reasonable to insure, including the risk of failing to equal a Part 36 offer (*Burgess v J. Breheny Contracts Ltd*). In considering whether a premium is reasonable, the court must have regard to such evidence as there is, or knowledge that experience has provided, of the relationship between the premium and the risk, and the cost of alternative cover (*Callery v Gray (No. 2)* [2001] EWCA Civ 1246, [2001] 1 WLR 2142 at [69]).

In straightforward road traffic claims, only a modest premium is likely to be allowed. Thus in *Callery v Gray (No. 2)* the court allowed a premium of £367.50. Account has also been taken of the predictable cost regime for smaller personal injury cases (see **5.8**). The courts have taken care when considering premiums charged by claims management companies, where the payment described as the 'premium' might cover a basket of services only one of which was the ATE insurance cover. In *Sharratt v London Central Bus Co. Ltd (No. 2)* [2004] EWCA Civ 575, [2004] 3 All ER 325, the Court of Appeal approved the costs judge's approach of investigating how much of the payment in fact related to the cost of the ATE cover. The fees charged by claims management companies for the referral or introduction of a client or potential client attracted criticism in both the *Jackson Report* (2009) and Lord Young of Graffham's report, *Common Sense Common Safety* (2010). Sir Rupert Jackson recommended that referral fees be banned in personal injury claims and this was implemented by the Legal Aid, Sentencing and Punishment of Offenders Act 2012, ss. 56 to 60.

Fixed staged premiums (which increase at defined stages in the litigation process) in large-volume, low-value cases have also been approved. In *Rogers v Merthyr Tydfil County Borough Council* [2006] EWCA Civ 1134, [2007] 1 WLR 808, the Court of Appeal rejected arguments that the proportionality of a staged premium in an individual case should be tested against the damages recovered. Instead the court held that if it is necessary to incur a staged premium, then it should be found to be a proportionate expense. Necessity could be demonstrated 'by the application of strategic considerations which travel beyond the dictates of the particular case and may include the unavoidable characteristics of the market in insurance of this kind'. In *Rogers v Merthyr Tydfil County Borough Council* the Court of Appeal expressly recognised that due regard should be had to an underwriter's ability to rate the risk the insurer faced as judges do not have the expertise to judge the reasonableness of a premium except in very broad-brush terms, and the viability of the ATE insurance market could be undermined if they were to behave as if they did. In *Parker v Seixo* [2010] EWHC 90162 (Costs), Master Wright reiterated that without the assistance of expert evidence the court could not regard itself as better qualified than the underwriter to assess an ATE insurer's financial risk. This meant that the courts were reluctant to interfere with the amount of a premium even if it appeared at first blush to be disproportionate (*Burgess v J. Breheny Contracts Ltd*).

It is nonetheless important for the parties to provide clear evidence of the reasonableness of a premium, and equally a paying party wishing to challenge the level of a premium should be prepared to adduce evidence of the level which they claim is appropriate (*Burgess v J. Breheny Contracts Ltd*). In *Kris Motor Spares Ltd v Fox Williams LLP* [2010] EWHC 1008 (QB), LTL 13/5/2010, the paying party failed to adduce any evidence that a premium of £95,550 for £130,000 cover (a rate of 73.5 per cent) was unreasonable and, accordingly, its appeal on the grounds that the premium was unreasonable was dismissed.

In *Redwing Construction Ltd v Wishart* [2011] EWHC 19 (TCC), [2011] BLR 186, Akenhead J commented that on a summary assessment, particularly in a relatively low value claim, it may be disproportionate to expect in effect expert evidence to be adduced as to the unreasonableness of the premium, and that the court should be able to look at the amount of the premium compared to the amount of cover provided and form some realistic view of the assessment of risk which must have been taken by the insurer. In doing so, Akenhead J concluded that a premium of £8,480 for cover of £20,000 (i.e. 42 per cent of the insured amount) was 'substantially excessive' and only allowed recovery of 20 per cent of the premium.

In *Evans v Arriva Yorkshire Ltd* (County Court, Leeds) LTL 28/11/2013 the claimant's trade union had undertaken to pay his legal fees and any adverse costs order. This 'self-insurance' was held to be a recoverable ATE premium for the purpose of the **Access to Justice Act 1999, s. 30**. The claimed amount (£3,500) would, though, be assessed by reference to evidence of the union's average exposure in fast track employer's liability cases, its average success rate and an estimate of the overheads involved in an individual employer's liability fast track case.

If following evidence and argument there is still a doubt about the reasonableness of the charge, that doubt must be resolved in favour of the paying party (*Kris Motor Spares Ltd v Fox Williams LLP*; *Rogers v Merthyr Tydfil County Borough Council*).

For difficult litigation, premiums can be substantial. In *Sarwar v Alam* (2003) LTL 23/3/2003 the claim was an important test case. A premium of £62,500 subject to a 50 per cent no-claims bonus was allowed in full. The costs judge commented that although the premium was high, it was unlikely that a lower quotation could have been obtained. In practice, solicitors may have to show they have made inquiries to understand prevailing market rates if a significant premium is to be recovered in full from the other side.

Former requirement to notify other parties

Until 1 April 2013, the fact that a party had taken out an ATE insurance policy had be noti- **5.17** fied to the court and every other party (former CPR, r. 44.15; PD 43–48, para. 19, in force before 1 April 2013). Form N251 had to be used. A party was potentially prohibited from recovering the CFA success fee and any ATE insurance premium for any period in the proceedings during which they failed to provide details in connection to the funding arrangement (former CPR, r. 44.15; PD 43–48, para. 19 in force before 1 April 2013). This was illustrated in *Kutsi v North Middlesex University Hospital NHS Trust* [2008] EWHC 90119 (Costs), in which the claimant was unable to recover an ATE insurance premium where her solicitors had mistakenly failed to notify the defendant of the existence of an ATE policy, and only did so after the claim had settled.

THIRD-PARTY FUNDING

For higher-value cases, third-party funding (TPF), in which commercial third parties fund the **5.18** costs of litigation in return for a percentage of damages recovered or for an agreed multiple of the funding provided, has become increasingly well established. TPF is most readily obtained for high-value cases with good prospects of success, but where solicitors' fees and disbursements (such as expert fees) may be very significant, meaning routine CFA and ATE agreements alone may not be sufficient to fund the claim. For instance in *Arkin v Borchard Lines Ltd (Nos. 2 and 3)* [2005] EWCA Civ 655, [2005] 1 WLR 3055, the funder agreed to pay for the claimants' substantial expert accountants' fees (expected to be £600,000 but which ended up at circa £1.3 million) in return for any recovery of the experts' fees from the other party plus 25 per cent of any damages recovered up to £5 million, and 23 per cent of any sum above that. Although the claimant lost, the Court of Appeal approved the arrangement in principle, finding that it was not champertous. The funder was, however, additionally exposed to a non-party costs order in favour of the defendant equal to the amount of the financial assistance given to the claimant, i.e. £1.3 million.

The market for this kind of funding continues to develop, with regular new entrants to (and exits from) the market and relatively high levels of capacity.

A product comparison table of third-party litigation funders and brokers is updated quarterly by the Law Society's publication, *Litigation Funding*.

A prominent example of the operation of TPF is *Stone and Rolls Ltd v Moore Stephens* [2009] UKHL 39, [2009] 1 AC 1391, in which the claimant company brought a substantial (£106 million) professional negligence claim against its former auditors using funding provided by commercial third-party funders (who reportedly stood to receive some 40 per cent of the proceeds if the claim succeeded). The claim was ultimately unsuccessful and the third-party funders accepted liability for the defendant's costs (reported to be in the region of £2.5 million).

The issue whether third-party funders should be liable for adverse costs has been a matter of debate. In *Arkin v Borchard Lines Ltd (Nos. 2 and 3)* Lord Phillips of Worth Matravers MR suggested that potential liability for adverse costs would discourage third-party funders. Sir Rupert Jackson's *Review of Civil Litigation Costs: Final Report* (Ministry of Justice, December

Commentary

2009) considered this issue and concluded that there is no evidence that full liability for adverse costs would stifle TPF and that it is possible for litigation funders to have business models which encompass such liability (as illustrated by *Stone and Rolls Ltd v Moore Stephens*). Sir Rupert therefore recommended that third-party funders should potentially be liable for the full amount of adverse costs, subject to the discretion of the judge. In practice many TPF cases involve the purchase of ATE policies.

The growth of TPF led to debate about whether third-party funders should be regulated or subscribe to a voluntary code. The *Jackson Report* concluded that statutory regulation was not currently necessary, but that a satisfactory voluntary code should be drawn up, to which all litigation funders should subscribe, containing (among other things) effective capital adequacy requirements and restrictions on funders' ability to withdraw support for ongoing litigation.

The Code of Conduct for Litigation Funders was published by the Civil Justice Council (an agency of the Ministry of Justice) in November 2011, with the Association of Litigation Funders now responsible for administering self-regulation of the industry in line with the Code. The Code is updated from time to time, the latest being issued on 14 January 2014.

DAMAGES-BASED AGREEMENTS

5.19   Lawyers can share in the risk of litigation with their clients by agreeing to link the recovery of their fees with the outcome of the litigation. These fee agreements are known as damages-based agreements (DBAs) or 'contingency fees' — the lawyers' fees are contingent on the result obtained.

Contingency fees strictly encompass all types of CFA (where the solicitor charges an uplift on fees if the case is won, and a reduced fee or no fee at all if the case is lost) but generally refer to agreements to charge fees equivalent to a percentage of the damages awarded.

Contingency fee agreements have historically been unenforceable in litigation because they are champertous arrangements, contrary to public policy and the common law. Exceptions were made for funding mediations and First-tier Tribunal cases as these are non-contentious matters for the purposes of the Solicitors Act 1974, s. 57(2).

The position has changed radically in recent years. First, specific statutory authority has been provided for the use of CFAs in all types of litigation since 1998. The whole topic is considered further in **chapter 6**. Secondly, DBAs became legal for all types of proceedings on 1 April 2013 pursuant to the Legal Aid, Sentencing and Punishment of Offenders Act 2012, s. 45.

Requirements for DBAs

5.20   A DBA will be legal and enforceable if:

(a) it is in writing (Courts and Legal Services Act 1990, s. 58AA(4)(a));

(b) it does not relate to proceedings which cannot be the subject of an enforceable CFA (see **chapter 6**) or to proceedings of a description prescribed by the Lord Chancellor (Courts and Legal Services Act 1990, s. 58AA(4)(aa));

(c) it does not provide for a payment above a prescribed amount or for a payment above an amount calculated in a prescribed manner (Courts and Legal Services Act 1990, s. 58AA(4)(b));

(d) its terms and conditions comply with any prescribed requirements (Courts and Legal Services Act 1990, s. 58AA(4)(c)). As provided by the Damages-Based Agreement Regulations 2013 (SI 2013/609), reg. 3, these terms must specify:

(i)   the claim or proceedings or parts of them to which the agreement relates;

(ii)   the circumstances in which the representative's payment, expenses and costs, or part of them, are payable; and

(iii)   the reason for setting the amount of the payment at the level agreed;

(e) the person providing services under the agreement has complied with any prescribed requirements concerning the provision of information (Courts and Legal Services Act 1990, s. 58AA(4)(d)). Requirements to provide information in SI 2013/609, reg. 5 apply only to employment matters.

Prescribed amounts and payments for the purposes of point (c) apply only to claims at first instance (SI 2013/609, reg. 4(4)). First-instance matters fall into two categories in non-employment proceedings:

(a) In respect of non-personal injuries claims, a DBA must not require an amount to be paid by the client other than costs and expenses which are net of any costs and expenses which have been paid by another party to the proceedings (reg. 4(1)). The amount to be paid by the client must not exceed an amount which, including VAT, is equal to 50 per cent of the sums ultimately recovered by the client (reg. 4(3)). These costs and expenses may include disbursements in respect of counsel's fees as well as other types of disbursements (regs 1(2) and 4(1)(a)(ii)). 'Costs' means the total of the representative's time reasonably spent, in respect of the claim or proceedings, multiplied by the reasonable hourly rate of remuneration of the representative (reg. 1(2)).

(b) In a claim for personal injuries (which, by SI 2013/609, reg. 1(2), has the same meaning as in **CPR, r. 2.3**) a DBA must not provide for a payment above an amount which, including VAT, is equal to 25 per cent of the combined sums of:

(i)   general damages for pain, suffering and loss of amenity; and

(ii)   damages for pecuniary loss other than future pecuniary loss,

which are ultimately recovered by the client (SI 2013/609, reg. 4(2)).

The only sums recovered by the client from which the payment may be met are those damages net of any sums recoverable by the Compensation Recovery Unit of the Department for Work and Pensions (reg. 4(2)(a)).

The validity of contingency fee agreements in non-employment First-tier Tribunal cases was confirmed by Senior Costs Judge Master Hurst in *Tel-Ka Talk Ltd v Commissioners of HM Revenue and Customs* [2010] EWHC 90175 (Costs), BAILII, [2011] STC 497.

Although no reliable statistics are currently available, the lack of reported cases suggests DBAs in general civil litigation remain rare, perhaps because of a preference by users to engage with the more mature CFA and ATE models, and the unavailability of partial DBAs, where only a portion of the solicitors' fees are subject to the DBA.

ASSIGNMENT OF CAUSES OF ACTION

Sometimes someone in whom a cause of action is vested will assign it to another person who may be better placed to fund the litigation. Doing so, if effective, will allow that other person to bring (or continue) proceedings based on that cause of action. There may be practical reasons for doing this. For example, a cause of action may be vested in a trustee in bankruptcy, who may be unwilling to prosecute the claim.

5.21

Assignments are sometimes attacked on the ground that they are tainted by champerty or maintenance, particularly in cases involving the assignment of a large number of small claims to a claims management company in exchange for a substantial success fee in the event of a successful claim (see, e.g., *Claims Group Direct Ltd v Lloyds TSB Bank plc* (2009) LTL 11/11/2009, in which such a scheme was found to be champertous). The subject is dealt with in more detail at **14.6** to **14.9**.

Assignments by companies intended to obtain the benefit of public funding and to avoid the risk of having to provide security for costs were upheld by the House of Lords in *Norglen Ltd v Reeds Rains Prudential Ltd* [1999] 2 AC 1. However, 'matters arising out of the carrying on of a business' are now excluded from the scope of public funding by the Legal Aid, Sentencing and Punishment of Offenders Act 2012, sch. 1, part 2, para. 14, and it is difficult to envisage circumstances where public funding will be available following an assignment of this type.

Chapter 6 Conditional Fee Agreements

INTRODUCTION

A conditional fee agreement (CFA) is defined by the **Courts and Legal Services Act 1990,** **6.1**
s. 58(2)(a), as an agreement for advocacy or litigation services which provides that the lawyer's
fees and expenses, or any part of them, will be payable only in specified circumstances. The
basic nature of CFAs, including this definition, is unchanged by the Legal Aid, Sentencing
and Punishment of Offenders Act 2012.

CFAs with success fees are the more familiar arrangements whereby the legal representative
charges nothing if the case is lost but the full fee plus an enhancement — calculated as a percentage uplift on the fee — if the case is won. Removing the recoverability of success fees from
the unsuccessful party was effected by the Legal Aid, Sentencing and Punishment of Offenders
Act 2012, and applies to CFAs entered into on or after 1 April 2013. Recoverability of success
fees and after-the-event (ATE) premiums, were important elements contributing to the popu-
larity of CFAs, particularly with claimants and claims companies. It is possible that the use of
CFAs may diminish in favour of damages-based agreements (DBAs) and/or third party funding (see **5.18** and **5.19**).

CFAs without success fees effectively replace what were *Thai Trading Co. v Taylor* [1998] QB 781
agreements, i.e. agreements where the client is charged nothing, or a reduced fee, if the case is
lost but the full fee where the case is won.

CFAs can be extremely flexible. If the case is lost, the agreement may be that the client will
pay nothing at all, or will pay the solicitor's charges at a reduced hourly rate or even a fixed fee
depending on the stage reached in the litigation. If the case is won, the agreement can provide
for the payment of the solicitor's basic costs without any enhancement, or a percentage uplift
on those fees. CFAs can use any combination of these provisions, and, within certain boundaries, set basic hourly rates and the level of discounts and enhancements.

Since 30 July 1998 (Conditional Fee Agreements Order 1998 (SI 1998/1860)) it has been
possible to enter into CFAs in all types of civil litigation with the exception of family work.
By the **Courts and Legal Services Act 1990, s. 58A(4)**, 'proceedings' for the purposes of CFAs

includes any sort of proceedings for resolving disputes and is not limited to proceedings in court. Nor is the term limited to cases where proceedings are commenced as opposed to contemplated, and it may include pre-action matters, such as enforcing compliance with a pre-action protocol and an application for pre-action disclosure (*Connaughton v Imperial College Healthcare NHS Trust* [2010] EWHC 90173 (Costs), LTL 2/12/2010). CFAs can be used for many kinds of dispute resolution, including arbitration and tribunal matters.

CFAs and champerty

6.2   The concern that it might be possible for an unsuccessful defendant to avoid paying the costs of a claimant on the basis that the legal representative's retainer under a CFA was illegal on the ground of maintenance or champerty (see **14.7**) was removed by *Hodgson v Imperial Tobacco Ltd* [1998] 1 WLR 1056. The Court of Appeal has confirmed in *Sibthorpe v Southwark London Borough Council* [2011] EWCA Civ 25, [2011] 1 WLR 2111, that a CFA containing an indemnity by the solicitors in favour of their client against any adverse costs order does not amount to maintenance or champerty (see **5.13**). An argument that taking a weak case on a CFA is an abuse of process was rejected in *King v Telegraph Group Ltd* [2003] EWHC 1312 (QB), LTL 9/6/2003. In *Tinseltime Ltd v Roberts* [2012] EWHC 2628 (TCC), [2012] 6 Costs LR 1094, the court held that it was not appropriate to make a non-party costs order against a solicitor who acted for an impecunious claimant under a CFA, where the solicitor funded the disbursements and where there was no ATE policy in place.

The **Courts and Legal Services Act 1990, s. 58**, permitted the recovery of success fees from unsuccessful opponents but that recoverability was abolished by the Legal Aid, Sentencing and Punishment of Offenders Act 2012, s. 44, for CFAs entered into on or after 1 April 2013.

CFAs and freedom of expression

6.3   Even before the Legal Aid, Sentencing and Punishment of Offenders Act 2012, the European Court of Human Rights (ECHR) held that the requirement that the newspaper publisher, MGN Ltd, pay success fees to the supermodel Naomi Campbell on costs awarded in respect of proceedings brought by her for breach of confidence violated its right to freedom of expression under the European Convention on Human Rights, **art. 10** in the **Human Rights Act 1998, sch. 1** (*MGN Ltd v United Kingdom* (application 39401/04) (2011) 53 EHRR 5). Ms Campbell had been successful at first instance, but the decision was overturned by the Court of Appeal before being reinstated by a majority of the House of Lords (*Campbell v MGN Ltd* [2004] UKHL 22, [2004] 2 AC 457). MGN was subsequently served with a bill in respect of Ms Campbell's costs for just over £1 million, made up of £850,000 base costs and £365,000 success fees payable under CFAs entered into by Ms Campbell with her solicitors and counsel for the first and second appeals, which provided for success fees of 95 per cent and 100 per cent respectively. MGN appealed to the House of Lords on the basis that its liability to pay the success fees was so disproportionate as to infringe its **art. 10** rights. The House of Lords dismissed the appeal, holding that the CFA regime (including the recoverability of success fees against defendants) was proportionate to the legitimate aim of providing litigants with access to justice, notwithstanding the possible effects on **art. 10** rights (*Campbell v MGN Ltd (No. 2)* [2005] UKHL 61, [2005] 1 WLR 3394). In contrast, the ECHR found that the requirement that MGN pay success fees was disproportionate, exceeding even the broad margin of appreciation accorded to the government in such matters, and constituted a violation of **art. 10**. In support of this conclusion, the ECHR pointed to 'the depth and nature of the flaws in the [current CFA] system', as reflected in Sir Rupert Jackson's *Review of Litigation Costs: Final Report* (2009), which flaws were borne out by the facts of the case, Ms Campbell being wealthy and therefore not in the category of persons who would be excluded from access to justice for financial reasons.

The decision of the ECHR is binding on the UK government, who are obliged to introduce legislation to cure the unlawfulness, at least in defamation and privacy cases where **art. 10** is engaged. However, publication and privacy cases are one of the areas where implementation of the non-recoverability provisions of the Legal Aid, Sentencing and Punishment of Offenders Act 2012 has been delayed pending further government consultation on costs protection provisions for claimants (**CPR, r. 48.2(1)(b)** and **PD 48, para. 3.2**).

In *Eight Representative Claimants v MGN Ltd* [2016] EWHC 855 (Ch), [2016] 3 Costs LO 413 Mann J held that the recovery regime for ATE premiums in defamation and privacy cases was technically different from that for success fees and was not in issue in *Campbell v MGN Ltd (No. 2)*. Accordingly, neither the House of Lords nor the ECHR had ruled on the recovery of those premiums. However, he saw no reason to treat them differently, and on the basis of binding English authority, the English legislative regime which permitted the recovery of additional liabilities was not incompatible with **art. 10** (see also *Miller v Associated Newspapers* [2016] EWHC 397 (QB), [2016] 2 Costs LR 195). In *Lawrence v Fen Tigers Ltd (No. 3)* [2015] UKSC 50, [2015] 1 WLR 3485, the Supreme Court held that, where **art. 10** is not engaged, an order requiring an unsuccessful party to pay a successful party's success fee and ATE insurance (see **6.19**) is not contrary to **art. 6(1)** or **art. 1** of the **First Protocol**, even if the total costs are far in excess of the value of the claim. Such orders cannot be made in relation to CFAs entered into on or after 1 April 2013 where recoverability has been abolished by the Legal Aid, Sentencing and Punishment of Offenders Act 2012.

PRACTICAL CONSIDERATIONS

Although most CFAs are entered into by claimants, there is no reason to prevent defend- **6.4** ants from using them. The definition of 'win' for the purposes of the agreement is a matter for negotiation between the lawyer and the client. When acting for a claimant 'win' will almost always mean an award (but not necessarily recovery of) damages. Lawyers who represent a defendant may agree to a definition of 'win' that relates to the amount of damages paid by the defendant at the conclusion of the claim, whether by settlement or trial. The level of those damages could be set at nil, or a figure relating to the claim put in the claimant's statement of case. A successful defendant will be able to benefit from the rules on recovery of a success fee and insurance premium in the same way as a successful claimant, although there is much less of a market for after-the-event insurance for defendants than for claimants.

CFAs are most prevalent in personal injury litigation where they are commonly used in conjunction with ATE insurance (see **5.15**). They are also popular in libel claims. The use of CFAs in commercial litigation is increasingly led by client demand and is supported by a wide choice of ATE providers and third-party funders. Since the removal of public funding for business-related disputes, CFAs offer a route to funding and progressing meritorious cases when a client may be unable to raise sufficient funds to pay privately. However, disbursements will need funding during the conduct of the claim and there is no statutory protection (unlike in public funding cases) against an adverse order for costs if the claim is unsuccessful. This means that obtaining suitable ATE insurance is often crucial, as is an assessment of the likelihood of being able to recover base costs from the unsuccessful opponent.

CFAs can have an important part to play in the effective management of litigation. Entering into a CFA (and paying for insurance against an adverse costs order) can have tactical advantages to a client. Until 1 April 2013, the client's risk of having to pay legal fees at all could be substantially reduced, or even extinguished. In *Sousa v Waltham Forest London Borough Council* [2011] EWCA Civ 194, [2011] 1 WLR 2197 the court clarified that a claimant who has had the benefit of a full indemnity of costs from his insurer (and was therefore never at risk as to costs) is nonetheless entitled to rely on a CFA with a success fee. CFAs with pre-April 2013 recoverable success fees have the effect of raising the stakes in terms of costs while shifting some of the risk away from the client. Even

Commentary

with the changes that came into force on 1 April 2013, entering into a CFA and sending the message to the opponent that the case is strong enough to attract risk-sharing from the solicitor and/or an insurer might be of assistance to a litigant, if they choose to make that disclosure.

ENTERING INTO A CFA

6.5   The SRA Code of Conduct 2011 sets out 'outcomes-focused' conduct requirements, providing greater flexibility for individual firms to decide how best to meet and 'uphold the intention' of the Code, with reference to 'indicative behaviours'. For CFAs a solicitor must achieve the following outcome:

O(1.6) you only enter into fee agreements with your clients that are legal, and which you consider are suitable for the clients needs and take account of the client's best interests;...

Acting in the following way(s) may tend to show that you have achieved these outcomes and therefore complied with the Principles:

...IB(1.4) explaining any arrangements, such as fee sharing or referral arrangements, which are relevant to the client's instructions;...

IB(1.17) where you are acting for a client under a fee arrangement governed by statute, such as a conditional fee agreement, giving the client all relevant information relating to that arrangement;

IB(1.18) where you are acting for a publicly funded client, explaining how their publicly funded status affects the costs;

IB(1.19) providing the information in a clear and accessible form which is appropriate to the needs and circumstances of the client.

It is clear from *Callery v Gray* [2001] EWCA Civ 1117, [2001] 1 WLR 2112, that the fact that proceedings have not been issued is not a bar to entering into a valid CFA, and that it may be reasonable to enter into a CFA at the outset of the retainer, before the defendant has been approached or has clarified its position. In *Forde v Birmingham City Council* [2009] EWHC 12 (QB), [2009] 1 WLR 2732, Christopher Clarke J held that there is no prohibition against retrospective CFAs and that a retrospective success fee is not contrary to public policy. The case departs from the previous position that retrospective success fees were contrary to public policy (following the decision of Senior Costs Judge Hurst in *King v Telegraph Group Ltd* [2005] EWHC 90015 (Costs)).

It is important, however, that the CFA identifies the correct counterparties. In *Engeham v London and Quadrant Housing Trust Ltd* (Senior Courts Costs Office 22 March 2013) LTL 9/8/2013 the successful claimant's costs were disallowed in a detailed assessment where the terms of her CFA only covered a claim against the first defendant. Since the settlement sum was being paid by the second defendant, the claimant could not be said to have won her claim against the first defendant.

It is not unreasonable to enter into a CFA after admissions have been made on liability and causation, provided a proper risk assessment is made for the purposes of setting the success fee (*Thornley v Ministry of Defence* [2010] EWHC 2584 (QB), [2011] 3 Costs LR 335).

There may be other considerations for the solicitor to bear in mind. In *Cox v Woodlands Manor Care Home Ltd* [2015] EWCA Civ 415, [2015] 3 Costs LO 327, the Court of Appeal held that a CFA which had been entered into during a visit by a solicitor to a client's home was unenforceable under the Cancellation of Contracts Made in a Consumer's Home or Place of Work etc. Regulations 2008 (SI 2008/1816) because no notice had been given of the client's right to cancel.

Requirements for validity of CFAs before 1 April 2013

6.6   A CFA entered into on or after 1 November 2005 but prior to 1 April 2013 must comply with the **Courts and Legal Services Act 1990, ss. 58** and **58A**. This means that a CFA must:

(a) be in writing (**s. 58(3)(a)**);
(b) relate to a type of case that the statute allows to be run on a CFA (**s. 58(3)(b)**); and

(c) specify the success fee, which must not exceed 100 per cent (s. 58(4); Conditional Fee Agreements Order 2000 (SI 2000/823), art. 4).

A failure to comply with any of these basic elements is likely to mean that the CFA is unenforceable.

An additional fee which depends on success but does not form part of the success fee may be allowed even where the success fee is 100 per cent. In *Morris v John Dennis (Barnsley) Ltd* [2008] EWHC 90112 (Costs), an 'administration charge' of £150, payable only in the event of success, was held not to be part of a 100 per cent success fee and did not, therefore, infringe the **Courts and Legal Services Act 1990, s. 58(4)**. The court held that the use of such charges could be policed in the usual way through seeking an assessment of the solicitors' costs under the Solicitors Act 1974, s. 70. In *Hanley v Smith* [2009] EWHC 90144 (Costs) the court confirmed that entering into a CFA will not of itself prevent a party from being awarded interest on costs from the date of judgment under the Judgments Act 1838, s. 17 (on the basis that a party operating under a CFA has not actually had to pay any costs). The decision clarifies that the right to interest on costs under s. 17 exists whether or not a party has a contractual obligation to pay, or has paid, interest on costs to his lawyers.

By the **Courts and Legal Services Act 1990, s. 58A(1)**, the only proceedings which cannot be the subject of an enforceable CFA are criminal proceedings and family proceedings, as defined in **s. 58A(2)**, apart from proceedings under the Environmental Protection Act 1990, s. 82 (proceedings in a magistrates' court to abate a statutory nuisance).

From 1 April 2000 to 30 October 2005, a CFA was not effective unless it complied with the **Courts and Legal Services Act 1990, ss. 58** and **58A**, and with the Conditional Fee Agreements Regulations 2000 (SI 2000/692). Those Regulations have been revoked and do not apply to CFAs entered into on or after 1 November 2005.

Requirements for validity of CFAs from 1 April 2013

A CFA entered into on or after 1 April 2013 that complies with the requirements of the **6.7** **Courts and Legal Services Act 1990, s. 58**, is not unenforceable by reason only that it is a CFA — but any CFA on or after 1 April 2013 not complying with those requirements is unenforceable. The requirements that must be satisfied for a CFA to be effective if entered into on or after 1 April 2013 are laid down by amended **s 58(3), (4A)** and **(4B)**, and fall into two categories: those for non-personal injury CFAs and those for personal injury CFAs.

Non-personal injury CFAs   There are no changes to the requirements for CFAs concerning **6.8** claims other than for personal injury (nor for personal injury claims where the CFA does not include a success fee). In these cases CFAs must, by the **Courts and Legal Services Act 1990, s. 58(3)** and **(4)**, comply with the following conditions:

(a) The agreement must be in writing (**s. 58(3)(a)**).
(b) It must not relate to proceedings which cannot be the subject of an enforceable CFA (**s. 58(3)(b)**). The only type of civil proceedings which cannot be the subject of an enforceable CFA are family proceedings (**s. 58A(1)(b)**). For the purposes of these provisions, the term 'proceedings' includes any sort of proceedings (whether commenced or contemplated) for resolving disputes, and not just proceedings in a court (**s. 58A(4)**).
(c) It must comply with any requirements which may be prescribed by the Lord Chancellor (**s. 58(3)(c)**). At present there are none.
(d) If the agreement includes a success fee, it must:
   (i) relate to proceedings of a description specified by statutory instrument (**s. 58(4)(b)**; all civil proceedings which can be the subject of an enforceable CFA are currently specified, see the Conditional Fee Agreements Order 2013 (SI 2013/689), art. 2); and

(ii) state the percentage uplift ('success fee'), which must not exceed the percentage prescribed by statutory instrument (**Courts and Legal Services Act 1990, s. 58(4)(b) and (c)**), which is currently 100 per cent (SI 2013/689, art. 3).

Solicitors must comply with s. 58 even if they do not go on the record as acting for a party but provide 'behind the scenes' litigation advice (*Rees v Gateley Wareing* [2014] EWCA Civ 1351, [2015] 1 WLR 2179).

6.9   Personal injury CFAs   A CFA in a claim for personal injuries must comply with the following conditions:

(1) The agreement must be in writing (**Courts and Legal Services Act 1990, s. 58(3)(a)**).

(2) It must not relate to proceedings which cannot be the subject of an enforceable CFA (**s. 58(3)(b)**; see **6.8**).

(3) It must comply with any requirements which may be prescribed by the Lord Chancellor (**s. 58(3)(c)**). At present there are none.

(4) If the agreement includes a success fee, it must:

(a) relate to proceedings of a description specified by statutory instrument (**s. 58(4)(a)**); all civil proceedings which can be the subject of an enforceable CFA are currently specified (Conditional Fee Agreements Order 2013 (SI 2013/689), art. 2);

(b) state the percentage uplift ('success fee'), which must not exceed the percentage prescribed by statutory instrument (**Courts and Legal Services Act 1990, s. 58(4)(b) and (c)**), which is currently 100 per cent (SI 2013/689, art. 3);

(c) provide that the success fee is subject to a maximum limit, which must be expressed as a percentage of the descriptions of damages awarded in the proceedings that are specified in the agreement (**Courts and Legal Services Act 1990, s. 58(4A) and (4B)(a) and (b)**). Those descriptions of damages may only include descriptions of damages specified by order made by the Lord Chancellor in relation to the proceedings (**s. 58(4B)(d)**), which by virtue of SI 2013/689, art. 5(2), are:

(i) general damages for pain, suffering and loss of amenity; and

(ii) damages for pecuniary loss, other than future pecuniary loss,

net of any sums recoverable by the Compensation Recovery Unit of the Department for Work and Pensions; and

(d) the maximum limit must not exceed 25 per cent in respect of first-instance proceedings (**Courts and Legal Services Act 1990, s. 58(4A) and (4B)(c)**; SI 2013/689, art. 5(1)(a)) or 100 per cent in respect of appeal proceedings (art. 5(1)(b)).

'Personal injuries' for this purpose has the same meaning, by SI 2013/689, art. 1(2), as it does in **CPR, r. 2.3**. This provides that a 'claim for personal injuries' means proceedings in which there is a claim for damages in respect of personal injuries to the claimant or any other person or in respect of a person's death, and 'personal injuries' includes any disease and any impairment of a person's physical or mental condition.

The requirements remain of practical importance and real care should be taken when new arrangements are, or are purported to be, put in place, or new solicitors instructed. In *Webb v Bromley London Borough Council* (2016) LTL 6/4/2016 a personal injury claimant was unable to claim costs under a CFA where a purported assignment of the agreement from one firm of solicitors to another had in fact been a novation of the agreement, and a CFA entered into with the new solicitors did not comply with the Conditional Fee Agreements Order 2013 (SI 2013/689). In *Budana v Leeds Teaching Hospitals NHS Trust* (County Court 2016) LTL 10/3/2016 the purported transfer of a CFA from one firm of solicitors to another was held to be ineffective where it took place after the transferring firm had terminated its retainer with the client.

In *Garnat Trading & Shipping (Singapore) Pte Ltd v Thomas Cooper* [2016] EWHC 18 (Ch), [2016] 1 Costs LR 45 the solicitors failed to comply with the CFA requirements when they emailed CFA-type terms when the client appealed. The agreement was held to create a single new, and ultimately unenforceable, contract for the entire retainer, including the work done at first instance.

Fortunately for the solicitors it was held that the offending contract could be severed, enabling the original, enforceable retainer to cover everything except the appeal.

Setting the success fee

6.10 Setting the success fee in a CFA is primarily about risk assessment. Claims with very good prospects of success only justify low-level success fees, whereas claims with 50:50 prospects of success might justify a success fee of up to 100 per cent. The former PD 43–48, paras 11.7 to 11.10, in force before 1 April 2013, govern the assessment of what is a 'reasonable' amount for a success fee in a pre-April 2013 CFA. The guidance given is as follows:

(a) The court will have regard to the facts and circumstances as they reasonably appeared to the solicitor or counsel at the time the funding arrangement was entered into or varied (para. 11.7).

(b) The court will assess the level of the success fee by reference to the risk of non-payment of the costs, fees or expenses, the legal representative's liability for any disbursements and what other methods of financing were available (para. 11.8).

(c) The court will not reduce the success fee simply because, when added to otherwise reasonable base costs, the total becomes disproportionate (para. 11.9). In other words, proportionality for the purposes of costs under the CPR is assessed net of any success fee.

Complexity is not to be equated with risk: a complex case may justify a higher hourly rate, but not a higher success fee (*Thornley v Ministry of Defence* [2010] EWHC 2584 (QB), [2011] 3 Costs LR 335).

6.11 **Risk assessment**   To fix a success fee, the solicitor needs to undertake a risk assessment of the case before him and record that assessment carefully. There are broadly two approaches to assessing risk in litigation claims. Risk is ordinarily assessed on a case-by-case basis by looking at the particular features of the individual case and assessing those which have a risk of being lost. An alternative approach is to look at generic types of case and consider statistically how many of each type are successful.

6.12 **Generic risk assessment**   In high-volume, low-value claims a proportionate way of assessing risk is by using a generic model. The generic model fits with the concept of staged success fees, which the Court of Appeal was attracted to in *Callery v Gray* [2001] EWCA Civ 1117, [200] 1 WLR 2112, and which it endorsed later in *Halloran v Delaney* [2002] EWCA Civ 1258, [2003] 1 WLR 28. Lord Woolf in *Callery v Gray* said, 'by way of example the uplift might be 100 per cent, subject to a reduction to 5 per cent should the claim settle before the end of the protocol period'.

In *Halloran v Delaney* the court applied the reduction to 5 per cent to pre-proceedings settlement, subject to a District Judge's discretion to exceed 5 per cent in appropriate cases. Both cases concerned road traffic accident claims. Brooke LJ, who gave the leading judgment in *Halloran v Delaney*, later clarified that the 5 per cent figure only applies to straightforward road traffic accident cases (see *Re Claims Direct Test Cases* [2003] EWCA Civ 136, [2003] 4 All ER 508 at [99] to [101]). He went on to say that it did not require any research evidence or submissions from other parties in the industry to persuade the court that in this type of extremely simple claim a success fee of over 5 per cent was no longer tenable in all the circumstances. He then made it clear that in straightforward road traffic accident cases the prospects of success are virtually 100 per cent and that the 5 per cent is 'to cater for the wholly unexpected risk lurking below the limpid waters of the simplest of claims'.

From 30 April 2010, the RTA Protocol claims process applies in respect of personal injury claims worth between £1,000 and £25,000 resulting from road traffic accidents where liability is admitted (see **8.30** to **8.60**). The applicable success fees for pre-April 2013 CFAs were set out in CPR, r. 45.31, as in force before 1 April 2013, but have been replaced for post-April 2013 cases with fixed costs in **rr. 45.16** to **45.29L**.

Until 1 April 2013 employers' liability accident cases were also subject to fixed success fees, albeit that (again based on statistical research) the levels are higher than those in road traffic

accident cases. Former rr. 45.20 to 45.22 provided that the CFA success fee in personal injury claims against an employer (save for disease and road traffic accident claims: r. 45.20(2)(a)(i) and (iii)) were fixed at 25 per cent for both solicitors and counsel. If a membership organisation provided ATE cover, the percentage was increased to 27.5 per cent. Since 1 April 2013 that regime has been replaced by fixed costs in **rr. 45.16** to **45.29L**.

6.13   **Case-by-case assessment**   In non-routine cases it is usually appropriate to undertake individual risk assessments. For each case common risk areas, such as limitation, evidence, liability, causation, loss and recovery can be identified and assessed. There is necessarily a large element of subjectivity in assessing the risk in any given case, but the more detailed the list of risk factors identified the more likely it is the court will uphold the level of success fee claimed. Complexity does not necessarily increase risk, although it may increase the unknown and therefore unquantifiable factors at the time of assessment. It remains true that even the simplest cases can be lost, for example, because of unforeseen evidential developments.

Risk factors identified as justifying success fees should be real and not fanciful. For instance, if a simple telephone call will resolve any doubt about the identity of a driver, the call should be made before the success fee is fixed (*Atack v Lee* [2004] EWCA Civ 1712, [2005] 1 WLR 2643).

Probability can be a useful tool in assessing risk. For instance, to succeed at trial a claimant will have to succeed on liability and causation and be able to show a loss. To evaluate the probability of succeeding, the chance of proving all of those elements must be assessed.

If the chance of proving liability in a particular case is 70 per cent and, because of different evidential issues, the chance of proving causation and loss is 80 per cent, the chance of winning the case is 70 per cent multiplied by 80 per cent, that is, 56 per cent. If there is a further 5 per cent chance of the defendant becoming insolvent, win or lose, the chance of recovering damages is reduced to 53.2 per cent. A success fee is ordinarily calculated as: the chances of losing divided by the chances of winning. In a case with 60 per cent prospects, the success fee is 40 per cent divided by 60 per cent, which is 66 per cent. An 80 per cent case will have a success fee of 25 per cent (20/80).

Modest percentages (usually 5 per cent per year) can be added to the success fee to take into account the fact that the solicitor cannot bill the client on an interim basis for costs or disbursements. This additional sum can be claimed against the client, but not between the parties.

There is no need to make a separate assessment of the risk relating to the possible need for a detailed assessment of costs when entering into a CFA. The costs of assessment will, in the (probable) absence of a separate success fee, be dealt with in the same way as other base costs in the case (*Crane v Canons Leisure Centre* [2007] EWCA Civ 1352, [2008] 1 WLR 2549).

C v W [2008] EWCA Civ 1459, LTL 19/12/2008, concerned assessment of an appropriate success fee under a CFA where liability had already been admitted in a road traffic accident case. The Court of Appeal found that the risk of losing was very small but the CFA provided for a success fee of 98 per cent. The Court of Appeal found that there was no more than a 5 per cent risk of losing which, when applying the ready reckoner, gave a basic success fee of 5 per cent (i.e. 5/95). The Court of Appeal found that the real difficulty was in assessing the risk that the solicitors might lose the right to recover part of their fees should the client fail to beat a Part 36 offer rejected on the advice of the solicitors. It was acknowledged that making a proper assessment of that risk was difficult and Moore-Bick LJ concluded that the best solicitors can hope to do is to make a broad assessment of the risks associated with a Part 36 offer based on their own experience. However, given the difficulty of making such an assessment, he wondered whether solicitors should consider including in the CFA a two-stage success fee in the form of a provision giving them the right to review the success fee if a Part 36 offer is made. Thomas LJ also suggested that a new regime may be required for cases where liability is admitted. In the final analysis, the Court of Appeal accepted that a reasonable assessment of the risk in overall terms would be 17 per cent, leading to a success fee of 20 per cent.

In *Redwing Construction Ltd v Wishart* [2011] EWHC 19 (TCC), [2011] BLR 186, the court considered the role of CFAs and ATE insurance in adjudication enforcement cases, in which the vast majority of claims are successful and the prospects of success thus inherently very high. Akenhead J noted that, whilst parties are entitled to enter into such funding arrangements in these cases, the court 'will think long and hard about allowing substantial CFA mark-ups, particularly when there is a summary judgment application by the party with the CFA'. Akenhead J reduced the allowable success fee from 100 per cent to 20 per cent on the basis that, at the time the CFA was entered into the claimant was 'virtually bound substantially to "win"' and its solicitors must have been aware of this given they then pursued a summary judgment application.

The Court of Appeal has strongly criticised the use of success fees in CFAs entered into in circumstances involving no risk to the instructed solicitors. In *Pankhurst v White* [2010] EWCA Civ 1445, [2011] 3 Costs LR 392, it considered a CFA entered into two months after a judgment on liability had been obtained, but prior to a separate trial on quantum, which provided for a success fee of 22.5 per cent if the case settled pre-trial and 100 per cent if it went to trial. Success was defined in the CFA as 'any recovery of damages'. Jackson LJ commented that in the circumstances the CFA 'involved no risk whatsoever to the solicitors' and described the arrangement as 'grotesque'.

In *Grant v Bragg* [2009] EWCA Civ 1228, [2010] 1 All ER (Comm) 1166, the Court of Appeal considered the appropriate success fee for an appeal which has a more than real prospect of success. The court acknowledged that the prospects of success on appeal are always 'somewhat speculative', and that the setting of a success fee for appeal proceedings is a 'ticklish issue'. However, a 100 per cent uplift is not appropriate where an appeal has a good prospect of success. The appropriate uplift in such circumstances was assessed to be 60 per cent. The decision is an indication that it is likely to be difficult to justify a success fee of 100 per cent (generally considered appropriate for cases with a 50 per cent prospect of success) whilst at the same time arguing the appeal has a real prospect of success (being one of the grounds on which permission to appeal may be granted). This is particularly so in cases where the success fee is set after permission to appeal has been granted, and the reasons for granting it suggest that the appeal has a very good chance of success.

In *Oliver v Whipps Cross University Hospital NHS Trust* [2009] EWHC 1104 (QB), 108 BMLR 181, Jack J confirmed that a solicitor is entitled to enter into a CFA at an early stage, even though the prospects of success may be uncertain. In that case, the court upheld a success fee of 100 per cent where the solicitor had not had the opportunity to test the credibility of the evidence or assess the relevant facts or expert witnesses at the time the CFA was entered into, and it was therefore impossible to assess the percentage chance of success with any mathematical precision.

In *Hanley v Smith* [2009] EWHC 90144 (Costs) the court assessed the success fees contained in CFAs entered into by a claimant who had suffered serious head injuries in a motorcycle accident. The CFAs for the claimant's solicitors and junior counsel had been entered into at a time when the liability of the first defendant (uninsured) driver had been established, but not the extent of liability in percentage terms, quantum, or the question of whether the claimant was eligible for cover by the second defendant (the Motor Insurers' Bureau). The court rejected an argument put by the defendants that there had already been a 'win' at this stage simply because the issue of liability against the first defendant had been resolved, as there was still every chance that the second defendant could defend the case on the eligibility point. The court held that a 'win' in this case would mean the final disposal of the case in the claimant's favour as against both defendants (rather than obtaining a worthless (but necessary) judgment against the driver). In the result, the court held that the appropriate success fees were 82 per cent for the solicitors (for the risk element only) and 50 per cent for junior counsel (rising to 100 per cent if a trial brief had been delivered). The court reduced the success fee for leading counsel from 82 per cent to 54 per cent on the ground that, by the time that CFA was concluded, the overall risk had declined.

There is a limited amount of guidance from the courts on appropriate success fees in particular cases. The following list may be illustrative, but each case should be considered with reference to its particular facts:

Claim for industrial injury where the employer's liability for negligence is already established and solicitors' fees are covered by the claim handling agreement (*Beresford v Solicitors Regulation Authority* [2009] EWHC 3155 (Admin), LTL 2/12/2009)	0 per cent
Road traffic accident (pre-trial) (former CPR, rr. 45.15 to 45.19 in force before 1 April 2013)	12.5 per cent
Road traffic accident case where settlement occurs before trial, but application is subsequently made to the court to clarify one aspect of an agreed order (for example, in relation to the frequency of periodic payments) (*Hosking v Smallshaw* [2009] EWHC 90137 (Costs), LTL 6/4/2009)	12.5 per cent
Appeal to the Court of Appeal (where it is 'almost certain' that the client will successfully resist the appeal) (*Alfa Begum v Supin Klarit* [2005] EWCA Civ 210, [2005] 3 Costs LR 452)	15 per cent
Straightforward clinical negligence (*Bensusan v Freedman* (2001) LTL 6/11/2001; *Metcalfe v Clipston* [2004] EWHC 9005 (Costs))	20 per cent
Road traffic accident case where liability is admitted but there is a reasonable risk of the rejection of an effective Part 36 offer (*C v W* [2008] EWCA Civ 1459, [2009] 4 All ER 1129; *Gandy v King* [2010] EWHC 90177 (Costs), LTL 2/12/2010)	20 per cent
Personal injury claim against an employer (pre-trial) (former CPR, rr. 45.20 to 45.22 in force before 1 April 2013)	25 per cent
Mesothelioma claim where the claimant does not have a complicated history of employment (*Holliday v E C Realisations Ltd* [2008] EWHC 90103 (Costs))	33.3 per cent
Slip and trip (*Abrew v Tesco Stores Ltd* (2003) LTL 18/6/2003)	50 per cent
Personal injury claim where the claimants have sustained serious injuries and liability was uncertain (*Burton v Kingsley* [2005] EWHC 1034 (QB), [2006] PIQR P2)	50 per cent
Appeal to the Court of Appeal (where the prospects of success are good, particularly where the success fee is set after permission to appeal has been granted and the reasons for granting permission suggest that the appeal has a very good chance of success) (*Grant v Bragg* [2009] EWCA Civ 1228, [2010] 1 All ER (Comm) 1166)	60 per cent
Accident at work (with evidential and causation difficulties) (*Chalk v Hightown Praetorian Housing Association* (Cambridge County Court, 1 October 2002))	63 per cent
Asbestosis claims (*Smiths Dock Ltd v Edwards* [2004] EWHC 1116 (QB), LTL 20/5/2004)	87 per cent
Road traffic accident (which is tried) (former CPR, rr. 45.15 to 45.19 in force before 1 April 2013, and *Callery v Gray* [2001] EWCA Civ 1117, [2001] 1 WLR 2112)	100 per cent
Fatal accident claim against employer (*Peto-Williamson v Ivan Housley Poultry Ltd* (Nottingham County Court, 10 September 2002))	100 per cent
Intellectual property case lost in the Court of Appeal, successful in the House of Lords (*Designer Guild Ltd v Russell Williams (Textiles) Ltd (No. 2)* (HL, 20 February 2003, SCCO Case Summaries No. 4 of 2003))	100 per cent
Clinical negligence claim where CFA entered into at an early stage and the prospects of success are uncertain (*Oliver v Whipps Cross University Hospital NHS Trust* [2009] EWHC 1104 (QB), 108 BMLR 181)	100 per cent

Staged success fees

Staged success fees, starting low and increasing as the case progresses, or starting high and [reduc]ing if admissions of liability are made during the proceedings, are consistent with practica[l experi]ence of how cases are resolved. Inherently strong claims (generically or by reference to the in[dividual] case facts) settle early; the weaker, and therefore riskier, claims often find their way [to trial.]

Staged success fees have been encouraged by the Court of Appeal since *Halloran v Delane[y]* [2002] EWCA Civ 1258, [2003] 1 WLR 28, and were adopted in the fixed success fee schemes [for] traffic accident and employers' liability claims. The court does not have the power to [reduce] a staged success fee retrospectively (*U v Liverpool City Council* [2005] EWCA Civ 475, [2005] [1 WLR] 2657). This is so even after the risks have been substantially reduced, after admissions [and] detailed assessment of costs following the success of the main claim.

A different version of staged success fees was approved in *Benaim (UK) Ltd v Davies Middleto[n &] Davies Ltd* [2004] EWHC 737 (TCC), LTL 29/3/2004, in which the success fee was linked to the amou[nt] awarded to the claimant. The definition of the success fee varied the percentage uplift by stage[s,] from 40 per cent if the recovery was up to £200,000, to 100 per cent if more than £1 million was recovered.

A CFA with a discounted success fee provides for a basic fee at a stated hourly rate, which is discounted to a lower rate if the client loses, but with the CFA (usually) providing that the basic fee plus any success fee will be payable if the client is successful. In deciding whether the success fee is within the maximum 100 per cent uplift, the court compares the success fee with the basic fee, not the discounted fee (*Gloucestershire County Council v Evans* [2008] EWCA Civ 21, [2008] 1 WLR 1883).

NOTIFICATION OF FUNDING ARRANGEMENT

6.15 From 1 October 2009 to 31 March 2013, a potential party to proceedings who, before proceedings were issued, entered into a CFA that provided for a success fee had to inform the other parties of the funding arrangement as soon as possible (former PD Pre-action Conduct, para. 9.3). That is no longer necessary for CFAs (and DBAs) entered into from 1 April 2013 save where the recovery of the success fee can still be sought, such as in insolvency, mesothelioma and defamation cases.

Once proceedings were started, a party who had retained solicitors under a CFA was under a duty to file and serve notice to that effect in form N251 (former CPR, r. 44.15(1); PD 43–48, para. 19.2; both in force before 1 April 2013).

A success fee associated with a funding arrangement was not recoverable where a party failed to notify the other parties of the arrangement in accordance with a practice direction requirement (former CPR, r. 44.3B(1)(d)). Relief from sanctions was granted by the courts in certain circumstances (**CPR, r. 3.9**; former PD 43–48, para. 10.1, in force before 1 April 2013; *Supperstone v Hurst* [2008] EWHC 735 (Ch), LTL 23/4/2008; *Montlake v Lambert Smith Hampton Group Ltd* [2004] EWHC 1503 (Comm), LTL 16/7/2004).

In *Montlake v Lambert Smith Hampton Group Ltd* [2004] EWHC 1503 (Comm), LTL 16/7/2004, the claimant failed to serve a form N251 notice of funding in respect of a CFA and ATE insurance policy on the defendant or its solicitors. However, the letter before claim stated that 'this claim is now being funded by a conditional fee agreement which provides for a success fee'. In fact the CFA was not finally entered into until a month later and costs were claimed only after that date. The court was informed of the existence of the CFA at the first case management conference. The court found that the defendant had from the outset the information (albeit in an irregular form) to which it was entitled and the court could not see any conceivable prejudice to the defendant from the breaches

he rule and practice directions. Accordingly the court granted relief (pursuant to
.9) from the sanction provided for by r. 44.3B(1)(c), ordering that the claimant was
t to be deprived of the opportunity in principle to recover the agreed success fee.
lowever in *Kutsi v North Middlesex University Hospital NHS Trust* [2008] EWHC 90119 (Costs)
relief against sanctions for failing to provide details of an ATE insurance premium was
refused on the ground that the claimant had failed to provide a good explanation for its
failure to comply with the notice requirement. Notably, relief was refused despite the
fact that the claimant's insurers had requested that the claimant not provide details of
the insurance policy to the defendant and the fault for the failure to comply fell squarely
with the claimant's solicitor (who had agreed to this request without checking whether
this was permitted under the CPR).

There was no requirement for a party to inform the opponent of a funding arrangement made
between the solicitor and counsel or the solicitor and a quasi-expert.

If notice of a CFA was given at first instance, there may be no requirement to give separate
notice in respect of an appeal (*Beer v BexBes LLP* [2009] EWCA Civ 628, LTL 26/6/2009). It was
therefore safest to assume (unless expressly informed otherwise) that parties funded by a CFA
at first instance would also be funded on a CFA basis on appeal. However, this should now be
treated with caution, at least where separate CFAs are entered into for each stage of appeal.
Compare *Harrison v Black Horse Ltd* (Senior Courts Costs Office 20 December 2013) LTL 6/1/2014
where relief from sanctions was refused, with *Ultimate Products Ltd v Woolley* [2014] EWHC 2706
(Ch), [2014] 5 Costs LO 787, decided after *Denton v T. H. White Ltd* [2014] EWCA Civ 906, [2014] 1
WLR 3926, where a failure to send a second N251 notice after a change in CFA funding was
regarded as neither serious nor significant. The Court of Appeal in *Mishcon de Reya v Caliendo*
[2015] EWCA Civ 1029, [2015] 5 Costs LR 849 found no justification for interfering with the exercise of a judge's discretion to grant relief from sanctions for a claimant's failure to serve on a
defendant notice of a CFA and an ATE insurance policy. The correct approach to r. 3.9(1)
required a focus on the effect of the breach, not the consequence of granting relief, and the
failure to attach weight to the absence of a good reason for the default did not mean that the
exercise of the judge's discretion was flawed.

SUCCESS

6.16 In *Marley v Rawlings (No. 2)* [2014] UKSC 51, [2015] AC 157, the unsuccessful respondents had
entered into a CFA with their solicitors in relation to an appeal to the Supreme Court concerning a will. The CFA incorporated the Law Society standard CFA, and provided that the
respondents were liable for the solicitors' costs if they recovered any damages or if they 'in any
way…derive benefit from pursuing the claim'; or, if the respondents lost, the solicitors could
require them to pay the solicitors' disbursements. Despite losing the appeal, the Supreme
Court decided that the costs of both the appellant and the respondents would normally have
been paid out of the deceased's estate, but in the circumstances made a non-party costs order
against the non-party's insurers. As the respondents had lost the substantive appeal, it could
not be said that they had derived benefit from the proceedings, and ordering that their costs
were to be paid by the insurers did not change that. As a result the respondents' solicitors were,
on the terms of their CFA, limited to recovering disbursements in relation to the appeal to the
Supreme Court. The respondents' solicitors entered into a separate CFA with counsel they
instructed which provided that success included 'any outcome which has a value…equal to a
minimum of £1' or if 'the opposing party (to include the estate) agrees to pay or the court
orders that they pay your costs'. Losing the appeal meant there was no outcome having any
value to the defendants. Counsel were permitted to recover their base costs, because the
intended costs order was an order within the success term of counsel's CFA, and was recoverable from the insurers as a disbursement within the meaning of the solicitors' CFA. The

Supreme Court was exceedingly unhappy about countenancing that counsel for the losing side might be paid success fees in addition to base costs, and made the order for recovery of counsel's base costs conditional on counsel waiving their success fees.

ASSESSMENT OF CFA COSTS

General

For a CFA entered into before 1 April 2013, assessment by the court of CFA costs is governed **6.17** by the former CPR, r. 44.3A and 44.3B, and PD 43–48, paras 11.4 to 11.10 (party-and-party assessments), and CPR, r. 48.8(3) and (4), and PD 43–48, paras 54.5 to 54.8 (solicitor-and-client assessments), in force before 1 April 2013. For the procedure on assessment of costs generally see **71.10** to **71.29**.

In a successful conditional fee case the solicitor will calculate his or her fees (referred to in the Law Society's model agreement as 'basic costs') and the barrister's fees at the rates set out in the CFA with the client. The solicitor will seek to recover 100 per cent of the basic costs plus the barrister's fees and disbursements from the unsuccessful paying party. The solicitor may in addition recover from the client:

(a) any part of the solicitor's basic costs, counsel's fees and disbursements not recovered from the paying party;

(b) the agreed success fee (which cannot be more than 100 per cent) calculated as a percentage of the basic costs (and as a separate percentage of the barrister's fees).

When a client receives from the solicitor a bill calculated on the above basis the client is entitled to challenge:

(a) the shortfall in full recovery of the solicitor's basic costs and the barrister's fees,

(b) the solicitor's and barrister's success fees.

The procedure to facilitate such a challenge by the client is set out in **PD 46, paras 6.4** and **6.5**.

Assessment of basic costs

For CFAs entered into both before and after 1 April 2013, as the basic costs in a CFA are the **6.18** costs which would have been charged whether or not the solicitor was retained on a conditional fee basis, detailed assessment of them, as between solicitor and client, is governed by the same rules as apply to detailed assessment of any other solicitor's bill, namely, **CPR, r. 46.9**. **Rule 46.9(3)** provides that costs are to be assessed on the indemnity basis, in which costs are presumed:

(a) to have been reasonably incurred if they were incurred with the express or implied approval of the client;

(b) to be reasonable in amount if their amount was expressly or impliedly approved by the client;

(c) to have been unreasonably incurred if:

    (i) they are of an unusual nature or amount and

    (ii) the solicitor did not tell the client that as a result he might not recover all of them from the other party.

Assessment of basic costs between the parties is usually on the standard basis unless an indemnity basis costs order has been made.

The standard-form CFA Conditions published by the Law Society define the basic charges as 'our charges for the legal work we do on your claim for damages'. This is wide enough to cover generic work done for clients on claims covered, or intended to be covered, by a group litigation order (GLO), and there is no need for any collateral agreement between the solicitor and client for such generic costs (*Brown v Russell Young and Co.* [2007] EWCA Civ 43, [2008] 1 WLR 525).

In *Crane v Canons Leisure Centre* [2007] EWCA Civ 1352, [2008] 1 WLR 2549, a collective CFA defined base costs as 'charges for work done by or on behalf of the Solicitors which would have been payable if this agreement did not provide for a success fee, calculated on the basis of the fees allowable for that work in the court in which the [claim] in question is conducted or would be conducted if proceedings were to be issued'. The costs of the detailed assessment, which was actually conducted by costs consultants engaged by the solicitors, were held to be part of the solicitors' base costs, and to attract the success fee on the same footing as the base costs on the substantive claim.

Assessment of additional liabilities between the parties

6.19   For CFAs entered into before 1 April 2013, the **Courts and Legal Services Act 1990, s. 58A(6)**, allowed the CPR to provide that costs orders could include provision requiring the paying party to pay the success fee as well as the basic costs. The **Access to Justice Act 1999, s. 29**, also enabled insurance premiums to be recovered. The insurance premium could be one paid alongside a CFA but the rules were drafted so as to provide for other 'additional liabilities' including stand-alone insurance policies, such as ATE insurance, and even the cost of membership (perhaps of a trade union) as the case may be. The relevant rules are the former CPR, r. 44.3A (costs orders relating to funding arrangements) and r. 44.3B (limits on recovery under funding arrangements), as amplified by PD 43–48, paras 11.4 to 11.10, in force before 1 April 2013.

The effect of these rules, taken together, is that an 'additional liability' (whether a success fee or insurance premium or both) may be recovered provided that:

(a)   the success fee relates to the risk of losing and not to compensating the legal representative for delayed payment (this, incidentally, is why it is crucial for the CFA to split the success fee);

(b)   the additional liability does not relate to a period where information about the funding arrangement has not been provided as required by PD 43–48, para. 19.2, in force before 1 April 2013;

(c)   the reasons justifying the success fee have been disclosed;

(d)   the additional liability is reasonable.

The assessment of the success fee is considered at **6.10** to **6.14**.

In *Abeles v Equitable Life Assurance Society* (2009) LTL 20/4/2009, an application by the defendant for disclosure of the claimants' CFAs following the settlement of litigation and prior to any request for a detailed assessment of costs was refused on the basis that it had been made prematurely and was not necessary to enable the defendant, as the paying party, to properly formulate its points of dispute. The application could be renewed after an application for a detailed assessment hearing had been made.

The Court of Appeal has indicated that it should be the usual practice for a CFA, redacted where appropriate, to be disclosed for the purposes of costs proceedings in which a success fee is claimed. From 6 April 2010, if the CFA is not disclosed, a receiving party is nonetheless required to disclose details of the CFA (including the definition of 'win' and 'lose' and details of the receiving party's liability to pay costs if it wins or loses or fails to obtain a judgment more advantageous than a Part 36 offer), so as to enable the paying party and the court to determine the level of risk undertaken by the solicitor (PD 43–48, para. 32.5(1), in force before 1 April 2013).

Assessment of additional liabilities between solicitor and client

6.20   For CFAs entered into both before and after 1 April 2013, in a detailed assessment of solicitor-and-client costs under a CFA, when the court is considering the percentage increase, it will have regard to all the relevant factors as they reasonably appeared to the solicitor or counsel when the agreement was entered into or varied (current **CPR, r. 46.9(4)**).

SPECIAL ISSUES RELATING TO CONDITIONAL FEES UNDER THE CPR

Children, protected parties and conditional fees

In *Dunn v Mici* [2008] EWHC 90115 (Costs) the court considered a CFA entered into by a 17-year-old claimant 'by his mother and litigation friend'. The CFA had been signed by the claimant's mother at a time when she could only have been a 'proposed litigation friend' (given that a litigation friend is not formally appointed until proceedings are issued). Nonetheless, the court concluded that the mother had been acting as agent for her son, and that the solicitors had correctly inquired about pre-existing legal expenses insurance relating to the claimant, not his mother. The court pointed out that the CFA should make clear on its face that it is made with a child, if necessary acting through an agent. The child may subsequently ratify the CFA (preferably expressly) after turning 18.   **6.21**

A CFA can also be adopted and ratified by a litigation friend in a case of supervening mental incapacity. In *Findley v Jones* [2009] EWHC 90130 (Costs) the claimant had entered into two CFAs with his solicitors and was later found to lack capacity within the meaning of the Mental Capacity Act 2005. The claimant's sister agreed to act as his litigation friend, but did not formally sign a CFA or ratify either of the existing CFAs. Master Hurst held that a litigation friend could adopt the retainer (the simplest course being to formally adopt the CFA). Although the CFA was strictly required to be signed to be enforceable (meaning it could not be adopted by the conduct of the litigation friend), Master Hurst nonetheless concluded that the CFA was enforceable on the basis that to allow the defendant to avoid liability would 'adversely affect the administration of justice'.

From 3 July 2000 the former CPR, r. 48.9(6), provided that in a case where the client in a CFA was a child or a patient, the court could not vary the percentage increase except in accordance with r. 48.9(5). However r. 48.9 was revoked as from 26 March 2001 and no new equivalent provision has been made.

BARRISTERS AND CONDITIONAL FEES

In a claim where the client has entered into a CFA with the solicitor, it is usual for the solicitor   **6.22** to invite any barrister who may be instructed to enter into a CFA on a similar basis. A high level of mutual understanding is necessary between solicitors and barristers working together as a team on a case where both are acting on a conditional-fee basis. Whilst firms and sets of chambers have developed good working relationships on conditional fee cases, the fact remains that barristers are at a disadvantage because, typically, the greatest financial risk is run in claims that have to be determined at trial and much more work is generally required to be done by counsel in cases as they approach trial than at earlier stages. By the time a case reaches this point the solicitor will still be at risk, but may at the same time have spread that risk by settling large numbers of other cases being run on a conditional-fee basis. Even if the barrister has been involved earlier in the case, he or she will tend to have far fewer cases that succeed through negotiation. Some solicitors prefer counsel not to be on a CFA to avoid any conflict when, for instance, an offer of settlement is made. 'Hybrid' agreements may be an acceptable compromise. In *Designer Guild Ltd v Russell Williams (Textiles) Ltd (No. 2)* (HL 20 February 2003, SCCO Case Summaries No. 4 of 2003) counsel was guaranteed half his fees regardless of the outcome. Accordingly his success fee was approved at 50 per cent, where his solicitors were entitled to a 100 per cent success fee.

To assist with uniformity, a model CFA for barristers in personal injury cases has been produced by collaboration between the Association of Personal Injury Lawyers and the Personal Injury Bar Association. This model agreement has also received the approval of the Bar Council and the Law Society, and is known as APIL/PIBA. In addition the Bar Council has produced a guideline manual about conditional fees. This has been distributed to all sets of chambers and is available at www.barcouncil.org.uk. The Chancery Bar Association has produced its own model CFA.

A CFA which provided that a barrister would be able to claim his fees directly from the losing party grants that barrister an equitable assignment of an entitlement to his fees. It does not entitle him to revert to his client for any shortfall where he had already negotiated a full and final settlement in respect of his fees with the losing party, even where the client later negotiated payment of other costs from that party (*French v Hartman* [2014] EWHC 1682 (QB), [2014] 6 Costs LO 829).

EXPERTS AND CONDITIONAL FEES

6.23   A solicitor must not make or offer to make payments to witnesses dependent upon their evidence or the outcome of the case (SRA Code of Conduct 2011, O 5.8; see also *Solicitors Regulation Authority v Uddin* [2014] EWHC 4553 (Admin), LTL 28/10/2014). It is permissible to make a deferred fee arrangement by which the expert (particularly one who does a lot of work for a firm of solicitors) agrees not to render a fee note until the end of the case when, if it is lost, the expert may decide to waive the fee. Provided there is no antecedent agreement that the expert will not charge if the case is lost, the deferred arrangement does not breach the professional conduct rules.

In *R (Factortame Ltd) v Secretary of State for Transport, Local Government and the Regions (No. 8)* [2002] EWCA Civ 932, [2003] QB 381, the enforceability of a contingency arrangement made between a quasi-expert and solicitors was considered. At a relatively late stage of the litigation, accountants had been instructed to provide forensic accountancy services to the claimants' fishing industry experts. This support included the assessment of the claimants' financial losses. The accountants had agreed to act in return for 8 per cent of the final settlement achieved (not in fact a CFA, but a contingency fee arrangement — the losses being calculated not by an uplift on costs incurred, but by reference to the award of damages). Perhaps surprisingly the court held that the arrangement was enforceable. The Courts and Legal Services Act 1990 was held not to apply as that Act only deals with agreements between clients and 'litigators'. The court was quick to emphasise that this was a 'very rare' case and that the court would not normally consent to an expert being instructed on a contingency fee basis. It noted that experts are frequently in a position to influence litigation in a manner that neither the client nor the lawyer can. To allow an expert to have a financial interest in the outcome of a case carries great dangers for the administration of justice. However, in this case the accountants took care to restrict their role to the provision of support services to the experts who were to be called. Accordingly, their conduct did not offend public policy. The court observed that the accountants' prospect of receiving 8 per cent of the recoveries might have provided a motive for them to inflate the calculation of damages, although not to the extent that a larger percentage might have done. However, there were no grounds for suspecting that the accountants, as reputable members of a respectable profession subject to regulation would do anything other than perform their duties in an honest manner. The court also took some comfort from the fact that, in part at least, the accountants were involved in a joint exercise with the defendant's experts.

In *Papera Traders Co. Ltd v Hyundai Merchant Marine Co. Ltd (No. 2)* [2002] EWHC 2130 (Comm), [2002] 2 Lloyd's Rep 692, the claimant sought to recover as part of its damages fees payable to a firm of marine loss adjusters based on 5 per cent of the recovery made in respect of vehicles which were destroyed in a fire on board the defendant's vessel. The loss adjusters were instructed initially on a fee basis to carry out salvage and general average work and then instructed to carry out recovery services on a percentage basis. The defendant's argument that the agreement was champertous was unsuccessful. The court did agree that the claim was not properly categorised as damages, being too remote, but that the loss adjusters' costs could be assessed on the standard basis, with reference to the amount of time spent on each item.

COLLECTIVE CONDITIONAL FEE AGREEMENTS

Collective conditional fee agreements (collective CFAs) are intended to help bulk users of **6.24** CFAs and their solicitors, by allowing the users to enter into a single agreement with solicitors to allow them to run their members' cases. The agreement need not refer to specific proceedings, but will provide for fees to be payable on a common basis in relation to a class of proceedings. Agreements entered into before 1 November 2005 are subject to the Collective Conditional Fee Agreements Regulations 2000 (SI 2000/2988).

A collective CFA is an agreement between a solicitor and a bulk provider of work. If the provider is also the claimant (as in debt recovery work) there is no difficulty in establishing the terms of the retainer between the party to the litigation and the solicitor. That is not the case if the work provider is a referrer of work, such as a trade union or insurance company. In this situation there is an implied retainer between the solicitor and the client, alternatively, the client will be regarded as having ratified the appointment of the solicitor by the funder (*Thornley v Lang* [2003] EWCA Civ 1484, [2004] 1 WLR 378, applying *Adams v London Improved Motor Coach Builders Ltd* [1921] 1 KB 495). This means the client is under a legal obligation to pay the solicitor's bill, even though in practice this may never happen. Consequently, provided there is compliance with the regulations, where they apply, costs incurred under a collective CFA are recoverable from the opposite party.

A clause in a collective CFA requiring the claimants' solicitors to prepare and retain written risk assessments was held to be an innominate term. The Collective Conditional Fee Agreements Regulations 2000 (SI 2000/2988) required compliance with the specified particulars in the form of the agreement, but did not require the actual performance of those specifications (see *Various Claimants v Gower Chemicals Limited* (Cardiff County Court, 8 March 2007) LTL 8/3/2007).

Collective CFAs are often commercially sensitive documents and the parties to them are unlikely to consent to their disclosure in costs assessment proceedings. In *Hollins v Russell* [2003] EWCA Civ 718, [2003] 1 WLR 2487, the Court of Appeal considered CFAs to be generally disclosable unless no success fee is claimed. There is nothing in the judgment which suggests any distinction will be made between CFAs and collective CFAs if the paying party or the court seeks sight of the agreement. However, in practice many collective CFAs do not provide for a success fee, but instead are discounted fee arrangements (see **5.9** and **6.1**).

The Collective Conditional Fee Agreements Regulations 2000 (SI 2000/2988) were revoked on 1 November 2005, leaving no statutory reference to collective CFAs although it is possible that individual cases will continue to be brought under a collective CFA entered into before 1 November 2005. Collective CFAs continue to be a valid form of CFA, so there is no reason why parties should not continue to enter into collective CFAs where appropriate.

Chapter 7   Legal Aid

INTRODUCTION

7.1   The Legal Aid, Sentencing and Punishment of Offenders Act 2012 (LASPO 2012), s. 39(1) and sch. 5, para. 51, repeal the provisions in the Access to Justice Act 1999 on the Community Legal Service. Those provisions are replaced by a new system of legal aid which is administered on behalf of the Lord Chancellor by a civil servant known as the Director of Legal Aid Casework (LASPO 2012, ss. 1 and 4). Many of the concepts of the old legal aid and Community Legal Service systems are retained in the new provisions. The most notable change is that legal aid for clinical negligence has largely been removed (s. 9 and sch. 1). In relation to clinical negligence, legal aid under LASPO 2012 will only be available for claims for severely disabled infants (as defined in sch. 1, para. 23).

It might be thought that the legal aid provisions in LASPO 2012 are part of the Jackson reforms, not least because they appear in the same statute that makes the necessary legislative changes needed for the funding changes recommended by the *Jackson Report*. In fact it was simply legislative convenience that put the legal aid and Jackson reforms into the same statute, a point made by Sir Rupert Jackson in his first implementation lecture (Cambridge Law Faculty, Legal Aid and the Costs Review Reforms (Legal Aid etc Lecture 5), a talk by Lord Justice Jackson to the Cambridge Law Faculty on 5 September 2011). As was made clear in that lecture, abolition of public funding for most clinical negligence claims runs counter to the views expressed in the *Jackson Report*, which were to the effect that maintenance of legal aid at no less than the existing levels makes sound economic sense and is in the public interest (*Jackson Report*, ch. 7, para. 4.2).

Nevertheless, the changes to the legal aid system did come into force on 1 April 2013 at the same time as the Jackson reforms. Public funding has traditionally played an important role in promoting access to justice. With modern constraints on the public finances, that role will be an attenuated one for the foreseeable future.

ABOLITION OF THE LEGAL SERVICES COMMISSION

7.2   Following the recommendations of the *Magee Report* (Sir Ian Magee, *Review of Legal Aid Delivery and Governance* (March 2010)), the Legal Services Commission is abolished (LASPO 2012, s. 38(1)) and, with effect from 1 April 2013, is replaced by the Legal Aid Agency. This is an executive agency of the Ministry of Justice. The day-to-day administration of legal aid is transferred to the Lord Chancellor (ss. 1 to 3), who is required to designate a civil servant as the Director of Legal Aid Casework (s. 4(1)). The Director is obliged to comply with directions from, and must have regard to guidance given by, the Lord Chancellor about the carrying out of the Director's functions under the Act, but the Lord Chancellor is not permitted to give directions or guidance in relation to individual cases (s. 4(4)).

CIVIL LEGAL AID

The Lord Chancellor is under a duty to secure that legal aid ('civil legal services') is made available in accordance with LASPO 2012, part 1 (s. 1(1)). This does not include a duty to provide those services by the means selected by the legally aided person (s. 27(1)), so services could be provided by telephone or electronic means (s. 27(2)). Likewise, in civil cases there is no general obligation for the legal services to be provided by the lawyer selected by the legally aided person (s. 27(3)), who will usually, in effect, be forced to accept the services from a provider who has entered into a contract with the Legal Aid Agency.   **7.3**

Individuals

Legal aid is available only to individuals (LASPO 2012, s. 9(1)). Consequently, it is not generally available to limited liability companies. It may be available to partnerships, though not on matters of partnership law or relating to the carrying on of the firm's business. Corporations may be covered if the Director has made an exceptional case determination (s. 31 and sch. 3, para. 3).   **7.4**

Exclusions

Civil legal services are to be made available to individuals for cases covered by LASPO 2012, sch. 1, part 1, unless excluded or modified by sch. 1, parts 2, 3 or 4 (s. 9). Schedule 1 runs to 31 pages, and covers various family, immigration and other categories of proceedings, often with detailed exclusions. Included within the scheme are judicial review claims (sch. 1, para. 19), habeas corpus (sch. 1, para. 20), abuse of position or power by public authorities (sch. 1, para. 21), breach of rights under the European Convention on Human Rights by public authorities (sch. 1, para. 22), clinical negligence claims for severely disabled infants (sch. 1, para. 23), and various other categories (sch. 1, paras 24 to 46). Most of these are subject to specific exclusions. There continues to be a list of general excluded services (sch. 1, part 2), including the familiar exclusions for claims relating to personal injuries and death, defamation, and matters relating to company and partnership law, but now joined by most clinical negligence claims.   **7.5**

Exceptional case determination

There is provision for civil legal services to be made available on an exceptional case determination by the Director of Legal Aid Casework where this must be done to avoid a breach of an individual's rights under the European Convention on Human Rights, or where any rights of the individual to the provision of legal services are enforceable EU rights (LASPO 2012, s. 10). An exceptional case determination must be made in accordance with the provisions of the Civil Legal Aid (Procedure) Regulations 2012 (SI 2012/3098), which apply to the form of civil legal services which is the subject of the application (reg. 66(2)).   **7.6**

Financial qualifications

There continue to be financial qualifications for legal aid (LASPO 2012, ss. 11(1)(a) and 21). Regulations may, as with the Community Legal Service, provide for the payment of contributions, or even the whole cost of the services (s. 23(2)), by way of periodical payments, one or more lump sums, and out of income or capital (s. 23(8)).   **7.7**

Commentary

Powers to request information about financial resources are contained in the Legal Aid (Information about Financial Resources) Regulations 2013 (SI 2013/628). Detailed rules for determining financial eligibility for legal aid are contained in the Civil Legal Aid (Financial Resources and Payment for Services) Regulations 2013 (SI 2013/480). These contain rules for determining an individual's income and capital, and for determining contributions. The basic rules are that an individual is not eligible for legal aid if their gross monthly income exceeds £2,657 (reg. 7(4)) or if their capital exceeds £8,000 (reg. 6(4)). There are complex rules on the resources that are to be treated as the individual's resources for this purpose. There are also waivers for certain types of proceedings.

There are also rules dealing with determining the financial eligibility of legal persons in the rare cases where legal aid is available to artificial persons as opposed to individuals (Legal Aid (Financial Resources and Payment for Services) (Legal Persons) Regulations 2013 (SI 2013/512)).

Protection against supplementary payment

7.8 Individuals continue to be protected from having to pay for the provision of legal services which are provided under the Act other than as provided in regulations (LASPO 2012, s. 23(1)).

Criteria for funding

7.9 There are detailed rules setting out the criteria for granting the different forms of civil legal services (LASPO 2012, s. 11). These criteria are based on factors such as cost-benefit considerations, the availability of resources to provide legal services, and the importance of the matter (s. 11(3)). These are intended to reflect the requirements of the different levels of service (see **7.11**), and also to ensure that public money is targeted at the cases that deserve or need it.

Merits of the case

7.10 The prospects of success criterion is divided into the following categories (Civil Legal Aid (Merits Criteria) Regulations 2013 (SI 2013/104), reg. 5):

    (a) 'very good', meaning 80 per cent or more;
    (b) 'good', meaning 60 per cent to 80 per cent;
    (c) 'moderate', meaning 50 per cent to 60 per cent;
    (d) 'borderline', meaning that it is not possible, because of disputes of fact, law, or expert evidence, to say that the prospects of success are better than 50 per cent, but the case is not 'unclear';
    (e) 'poor', meaning 20 per cent to 50 per cent;
    (f) 'very poor', meaning less than 20 per cent; and
    (g) 'unclear', meaning there are identifiable investigations that could be carried out, after which a reliable estimate of prospects should be possible.

The merits criterion is usually only met if the prospects are very good, good or moderate (e.g. regs 43, 56, 60, 66–69, 75). In borderline or poor cases, slightly different approaches are taken under these regulations for different areas of work, but the merits criterion tends to be treated as met if this is necessary to prevent a breach of the individual's Convention or EU rights.

FORMS OF CIVIL LEGAL SERVICES

7.11 Different forms of publicly funded legal services have been developed. The purpose is to ensure that the amount of public funding given to a case should be commensurate with its needs, so that limited funding will be given if that is all that is needed, but full public funding will be given to the most deserving cases. Civil legal services may therefore take any of the following forms (Civil Legal Aid (Procedure) Regulations 2012 (SI 2012/3098), reg. 3):

(a) legal help;
(b) help at court;
(c) family help;
(d) family mediation;
(e) help with family mediation;
(f) legal representation; and
(g) other legal services.

Legal help

This is the lowest level of service, and includes providing advice and legal assistance on things like how the law applies to a particular case. It is intended for people on low incomes who need initial advice and to assist with the early investigation of claims, and is intended to provide a limited amount of legal help at a modest cost to the taxpayer.   **7.12**

Help at court

This authorises legal representation for the purposes of a particular hearing, without the lawyer becoming the client's legal representative in the proceedings. Again, the intention is that limited legal assistance will be given, covering no more than is necessary, so as to keep the cost to the taxpayer to the minimum.   **7.13**

Legal representation

This covers individuals contemplating legal proceedings or who are parties to particular proceedings. This will fund 'investigative representation' or 'full representation'. Investigative representation is limited to investigating the strength of contemplated proceedings, issuing proceedings, and conducting proceedings broadly up to obtaining information relevant to advising on the prospects of success. Full representation means legal representation other than investigative representation.   **7.14**

Family help

Family help may be provided in relation to family disputes, and may include assistance in resolving a dispute through negotiation or otherwise. It does not cover representation at a contested final hearing or appeal. It encompasses two levels of service. Family help (lower) is limited to all steps up to issue of proceedings. Family help (higher) can be used to issue proceedings and for representation in such proceedings other than at a contested final hearing.   **7.15**

Specific directions

Other services are not strictly forms of service covered by the main legal aid scheme, but there is some public funding of other cases if a specific order or direction is made. This may happen in important test cases and possibly also in group litigation.   **7.16**

APPLYING FOR AND WITHDRAWING LEGAL AID

Different procedures apply for making and withdrawing different categories of public funding, as set out in the Civil Legal Aid (Procedure) Regulations 2012 (SI 2012/3098). For example, applications for legal representation that is not controlled work or special case work come within what is known as licensed work, and are governed by regs 29 to 49. Applications   **7.17**

Commentary

must be made in the prescribed form, which must be signed by the individual and the proposed provider (reg. 31). There are detailed requirements to be followed. If the Director makes a determination that an individual qualifies for licensed work, the Director is under a duty to issue and send a certificate recording the determination to the individual with a copy to the provider (reg. 37(1)). The determination must specify any contributions payable by the individual (reg. 36), and the certificate must specify the proceedings to which the determination relates and any conditions or limitations on the cover (reg. 37(2)).

Individuals have a reporting obligation if there is any change in circumstances which might affect their qualification for civil legal services (reg. 40(1)). Providers have duties to report various matters, such as any refusal to accept an offer to settle or an offer to use ADR, or any information which might affect the client's continued qualification for civil legal services (reg. 40(3)).

REMUNERATION FOR PROVIDERS

7.18   The Lord Chancellor must pay remuneration to a provider of civil legal services in accordance with the provisions of the Civil Legal Aid (Remuneration) Regulations 2013 (SI 2013/422). These provide for remuneration in accordance with the relevant provider contract, or the fees and rates set out in sch. 1 to the Regulations (reg. 6(2); Civil Legal Aid (Statutory Charge) Regulations 2013, SI 2013/503).

FIRST CHARGE

7.19   By virtue of LASPO 2012, s. 25, the amounts expended by the Lord Chancellor in securing the provision of the services to the client constitute a first charge on any property recovered or preserved in the proceedings or by any settlement or compromise of the dispute. This means that any money, costs or other property recovered in a publicly funded claim automatically become the subject of an unwelcome charge in favour of the State, which can use the damages recovered to reimburse itself for the costs incurred on behalf of the publicly funded client. Regulations may provide for exceptions (s. 25(3)).

The underlying principle is to place a publicly funded party in a similar position to a party privately funding litigation, whose primary responsibility at the end of proceedings is to pay the costs incurred by his or her own solicitors in bringing or defending the claim.

The charge applies only if there is a net liability to the Legal Aid Agency. This means that it is first necessary to calculate the total costs incurred on behalf of the publicly funded client, then deduct any contributions paid by the publicly funded client, and also deduct any costs paid by the other side. The statutory charge will be for the amount, if any, of the balance. The charge attaches to any property recovered or preserved in the claim. This includes, in the case of proceedings concluded by a court order, any property or money which was the subject matter of the proceedings, and in the case of proceedings concluded by a settlement, any property or money received under the settlement, even if it was not claimed in the proceedings (*Van Hoorn v Law Society* [1985] QB 106). Property is 'recovered' if the publicly funded client gains ownership or possession of it through the proceedings. It is 'preserved' if another's claim to ownership or possession is defeated.

Whenever property is recovered or preserved for a publicly funded person, it is the duty of that person's solicitor to inform the Legal Aid Agency immediately so that the charge can be registered and enforced. It can be enforced in the same way as other charges. Enforcement can be postponed if immediate repayment would be unreasonable and if the charge relates to property to be used as a home for the client or his dependants, or, where the relevant proceedings are family proceedings, it relates to money to pay for such a home.

Solicitors have professional duties to advise clients who apply for public funding of the effects of the statutory charge. This should be done both personally and in writing.

COSTS PROTECTION

LASPO 2012, s. 26, substantially reproduces the costs protection rules in favour of assisted **7.20** individuals previously found in the Access to Justice Act 1999, s. 11. Costs ordered against an individual in relevant civil proceedings must not exceed the amount (if any) which it is reasonable for the individual to pay having regard to all the circumstances, including:

(a) the financial resources of all of the parties to the proceedings; and
(b) their conduct in connection with the dispute to which the proceedings relate.

For this purpose, the term 'relevant civil proceedings' means the whole or part of proceedings for which civil legal services have been made available to an individual under LASPO 2012, part 1 (s. 26(2)). The principles are discussed in more detail at **68.54** to **68.56**.

LEGAL AID COSTS ORDERS AND ASSESSMENTS

Regulations may make provision about costs in relation to proceedings for the purposes of **7.21** which civil legal services are made available under LASPO 2012, part 1 (s. 26(5)). Such regulations may specify the principles to be applied in determining the amount of costs which may be awarded to a party with the benefit of civil legal services (s. 26(6)(d) and (e)). Three situations have been provided for:

(a) Costs orders in favour of a successful legally aided party are made in the same way as if the party was not publicly funded. The amount of costs to be paid under a legally aided party's costs order must be determined as if they were not legally aided (Civil Legal Aid (Costs) Regulations 2013 (SI 2013/611), reg. 21(1)).
(b) Legal representatives acting for a publicly funded party need to obtain an order for the court to assess the amount payable to them out of public funds. See **71.21**.
(c) There is jurisdiction to make an order requiring the payment by the Lord Chancellor of the whole or part of any costs incurred by an unassisted party. This is a very exceptional power, which is discussed at **68.57** to **68.60**.

Commentary

PART C

Before Commencing a Claim

Chapter 8   Pre-action Protocols

Commentary

The following procedural checklists are relevant to this chapter:

Procedural checklist 1   Pre-action Protocol for Personal Injury Claims
Procedural checklist 2   Pre-action procedure where no protocol applies

INTRODUCTION

8.1   The conduct the court will normally expect of prospective parties prior to the start of proceedings is set out in **PD Pre-action Conduct and Protocols** and a number of protocols published with the approval of the Head of Civil Justice. There are currently 13 protocols for specific types of dispute. The full text of these protocols is set out in **appendix 2**. **Table 8.1** shows where commentary of each protocol can be found in this work. In addition there is pre-action guidance for claims likely to join the shorter trials scheme for cases in the Rolls Building.

PD Pre-action Conduct and Protocols lays down general guidance on pre-action conduct forming the background to the specific protocols, and also sets out principles governing disputes falling outside the scope of the specific protocols.

Objectives of the protocols are to encourage the exchange of early and full information about prospective legal claims and to enable the parties to avoid proceedings by settling their dispute before a claim is issued. If a dispute is settled through use of a pre-action protocol, the usual expectation is that the defendant will pay the claimant's reasonable costs assessed, if not agreed, on the basis of the case management track which would have been appropriate for the claim had proceedings been issued (*Birmingham City Council v Lee* [2008] EWCA Civ 891, [2009] HLR 15). If settlement is not achieved, the protocols should assist with the efficient case management of the proceedings (**PD Pre-action Conduct and Protocols, para. 3(e)**).

Each protocol includes a description of its own aims, consistent with the introduction to the overall objectives set out above, but tailored to meet the particular type of proceedings

Table 8.1 Pre-action protocols

Protocol	Introduced	Current version	*Blackstone's Civil Practice 2017*
Personal Injury	26 April 1999	6 April 2015	8.16–8.28
Clinical Disputes	26 April 1999	6 April 2015	8.61–8.63
Construction and Engineering	2 October 2000	2 October 2000	8.86–8.87
Defamation	2 October 2000	2 October 2000	8.88
Professional Negligence	16 July 2001	6 April 2015	8.89–8.97
Judicial Review	4 March 2002	6 April 2015	77.32
Disease and Illness	8 December 2003	8 December 2003	8.64–8.70
Housing Disrepair	8 December 2003	6 April 2015	8.71–8.77
Possession Claims by Social Landlords	2 October 2006	6 April 2015	8.81–8.83
Possession Claims for Mortgage Arrears	19 November 2008	6 April 2015	8.84–8.85
Dilapidation of Commercial Property	1 January 2012	1 January 2012	8.78–8.80
Low Value Personal Injury Road Traffic Accident	30 April 2010	Extended 31 July 2013	8.29–8.59
Low Value Personal Injury Employer's and Public Liability	31 July 2013	31 July 2013	8.60
Claims not Covered by Specific Protocols	26 April 1999	6 April 2015	8.9–8.15
Shorter Trials Scheme	1 October 2015	1 October 2015	8.98

Commentary

covered. **PD Pre-action Conduct and Protocols, para. 3**, summarises the general objectives of the protocols as expecting the parties to have exchanged sufficient information to:

(a) understand each other's position;
(b) make decisions about how to proceed;
(c) try to settle the issues without proceedings;
(d) consider a form of ADR to assist with settlement;
(e) support the efficient management of any proceedings; and
(f) reduce the costs of resolving the dispute.

Pre-action protocols must not be used to gain an unfair tactical advantage. Only reasonable and proportionate steps should be taken, which should be aimed at identifying, narrowing and resolving the legal, factual and expert issues (**PD Pre-action Conduct and Protocols, para. 4**). The costs incurred in complying need to be proportionate, otherwise they will not be recoverable (**para. 5**).

Procedural checklist 1 describes how to comply with the **Pre-action Protocol for Personal Injury Claims**. It, like the **Pre-action Protocol for the Resolution of Clinical Disputes** and the **Pre-action Protocol for Disease and Illness Claims**, provides for disclosure before the commencement of proceedings and is designed to avoid the necessity for applications to the court for pre-action disclosure. While disclosure of documents is a common feature of most of the protocols, there are variations. For example, pre-action disclosure is not one of the requirements of the **Pre-action Protocol for Defamation**.

When following a pre-action protocol, care must be taken to observe the time prescribed for the commencement of the proceedings by the Limitation Act 1980 (for example, three years for personal injury claims) or other legislation (see **chapter 10**). This is because statutory limitation periods take precedence over the time needed for compliance with the protocols. If instructions are received late, making it impossible to comply with the requirements of the relevant protocol before the need to issue a claim, the claim must be issued. **PD Pre-action Conduct and Protocols, para.** 17, states that if for any reason proceedings are commenced before the protocol procedures are complied with, the parties are encouraged to agree to apply to the court for a stay of proceedings while they comply with the requirements.

EXPECTATION OF COMPLIANCE WITH THE PROTOCOLS

8.2   The court will expect the parties to have complied with the protocol relevant to the claim (**PD Pre-action Conduct and Protocols, para.** 13). However, compliance with the protocols must not be used as a tactical device to secure an unfair advantage (**para.** 4). The court will be concerned about whether the parties have complied in substance with the terms of the relevant protocol or **PD Pre-action Conduct and Protocols**, and is not likely to be concerned with minor or technical infringements. Circumstances, such as preparing for mediation, may mean that the parties reasonably depart from the letter of the protocol, and should not be penalised for doing so (*Roundstone Nurseries Ltd v Stephenson Holdings Ltd* [2009] EWHC 1431 (TCC), [2009] 5 Costs LR 787).

The overall aims of the protocols are to enable the parties to settle their disputes without the need to start proceedings, and to support the efficient management by the court of matters where proceedings cannot be avoided (**para.** 3). In particular the court will consider whether the parties have exchanged information about the dispute and considered using a form of ADR (**para.** 3(d)). Examples of non-compliance are given in **para.** 14. They include not having supplied sufficient information, not complying with a time limit set by a relevant protocol or unreasonably refusing some form of ADR. The court will take account of any urgency (**para.** 13), and in such cases it will not be concerned with minor or technical infringements. What the court will look for is the impact of non-compliance on the other party before imposing sanctions (**para.** 16).

Strict compliance with the relevant protocol is not insisted on in living mesothelioma claims (see **47.15**), on account of the limited time for getting these cases to trial (**PD 3D, para.** 9). The version of PD Pre-action Conduct, para. 2.2, which applied before 6 April 2015 said it did not apply to:

(a)   applications for consent orders;
(b)   applications where there is no other party for the applicant to engage with;
(c)   most applications for directions by a trustee or other fiduciary;
(d)   applications where informing the other potential party in advance would defeat the purpose of the application (such as freezing injunctions).

The protocols apply to additional claims under **CPR, Part 20**, as well as to normal claims under **Part 7** (*Daejan Investments Ltd v Park West Club Ltd* [2003] EWHC 2872 (TCC), [2004] BLR 223). However, a pragmatic approach is taken, with due leeway being given to the parties bearing in mind that directions may have been given in the main claim fixing the trial date or window (*Orange Personal Communications Services Ltd v Hoare Lea* [2008] EWHC 223 (TCC), [2009] Bus LR D24).

Procedural Checklist 2 sets out the requirements in a non-protocol case. Consideration is given to non-protocol cases at **8.9** to **8.15**.

Whether a sanction should be imposed

8.3   The CPR enable the court to take into account compliance or non-compliance with an applicable protocol when giving directions for the management of proceedings

(**CPR, rr. 3.1(4)** to **(6A)**) and when making orders for costs (**r. 44.2(5)(a)**). A failure to send a letter of claim was taken into account in *Zambia v Meer Care and Desai* [2008] EWCA Civ 754, LTL 9/7/2008, on an application to set aside judgment for non-attendance under **r. 39.3** (see **62.2**). Sanctions, whether in costs or otherwise, should not be imposed where there has been substantial compliance with the relevant protocol (*T. J. Brent Ltd v Black and Veatch Consulting Ltd* [2008] EWHC 1497 (TCC), 119 Con LR 1). Failing to give an adequate response, or giving an evasive response, to the letter before claim may be reflected in the court's order for the costs of the proceedings (*Fox Gregory Ltd v Hamptons Group Ltd* [2006] EWCA Civ 1544, LTL 4/10/2006). **PD Pre-action Conduct and Protocols, para. 15**, provides that where there has been non-compliance the court may order that:

(a) the parties be relieved from the obligation to comply;
(b) the proceedings be stayed to enable compliance. This may simply allow the parties to catch up with the requirements of the protocols, but may also be desirable to improve the prospects of settling the dispute (*Cundall Johnson and Partners v Whipps Cross University Hospital NHS Trust* [2007] EWHC 2178 (TCC), [2007] BLR 520);
(c) sanctions be applied.

Sanctions and orders following non-compliance

The court has a general power to impose sanctions under **CPR, r. 3.1**, where a party has failed   **8.4** to comply with any relevant pre-action protocol, and those sanctions remain effective unless the party in default applies for and obtains relief from sanctions (**rr. 3.8** and **3.9**, see **chapter 48**). According to **PD Pre-action Conduct and Protocols, para. 16**, sanctions that may be imposed for non-compliance with pre-action protocols include:

(a) an order that the party at fault pay the costs of the proceedings, or part of those costs, of the other party or parties;
(b) an order that the party at fault pay those costs on an indemnity basis;
(c) if the party at fault is a claimant who has been awarded a sum of money, an order depriving that party of interest on that sum for a specified period, and/or awarding interest at a lower rate than would otherwise have been awarded;
(d) if the party at fault is a defendant, and the claimant has been awarded a sum of money, an order awarding interest on that sum for a specified period at a higher rate, not exceeding 10 per cent above base rate, than the rate which would otherwise have been awarded.

This list is not exhaustive. General sanctions which the court may impose include:

(a) costs, which may be ordered to be paid forthwith;
(b) an order refusing permission to call evidence from an expert who has been instructed by one or other party without compliance with the relevant protocol;
(c) under **CPR, r. 3.1(5)**, the court may order any party to pay a sum of money into court if that party has without good reason failed to comply with a rule, practice direction or relevant pre-action protocol. If applied to a claimant, this sanction could amount to giving security for costs, and in the case of a defendant, a payment into court in respect of the whole or part of the claim. The court is reluctant to use this sanction unless breaches have been repeated or there has been lack of good faith (*Mealey Horgan plc v Horgan* (1999) *The Times,* 6 July 1999).

The court will look at the overall effect of non-compliance on the other party when deciding whether to impose a sanction (**PD Pre-action Conduct and Protocols, para. 16**). For example, in *Paul Thomas Construction Ltd v Hyland* [2001] CILL 1748 the court ordered the claimant to pay the defendant's costs on the indemnity basis after finding that the claimant had ignored repeated requests for further information and proposals for resolution of the matter by some form of ADR and had commenced wholly unnecessary proceedings.

CPR, r. 44.2(4), lists factors to be taken into account by the court when deciding to make an order for costs. One of them is the conduct of the parties, which is defined in r. 44.2(5) to include 'conduct, before, as well as during the proceedings and in particular the extent to which the parties followed any relevant pre-action protocol'. In *Straker v Tudor Rose* [2007] EWCA Civ 368, [2008] 2 Costs LR 205 (discussed further at **68.5**), the court in effect imposed a 10 to 15 per cent reduction in the costs of the proceedings awarded to the claimant for failing to consider negotiations, in breach of the protocol. This was regarded as a proportionate sanction to reflect the breach.

Heavy-handed correspondence may result in indemnity-basis costs orders (*Excalibur Ventures LLC v Texas Keystone Inc.* [2013] EWHC 4278 (Comm), LTL 4/2/2014, where the correspondence was described as highly aggressive, voluminous and repetitious). In *King v Telegraph Group Ltd* [2004] EWCA Civ 613, [2005] 1 WLR 2282, one of the factors which inclined the court towards making a prospective cost-capping order (see **44.2**) was that the letter before claim was written in a vituperative tone calculated to raise the temperature and inflate the parties' costs.

COSTS OF ISSUES DROPPED AT THE PRE-ACTION STAGE

8.5 It has always been clear that costs incurred in complying with pre-action protocols (and general pre-action work) are recoverable as 'incidental to' proceedings if a claim is subsequently issued (Senior Courts Act 1981, s. 51; *Callery v Gray* [2001] EWCA Civ 1117, [2001] 1 WLR 2112). The costs of such work are therefore recoverable as part of the general costs of the proceedings. In the absence of agreement between the parties, it has always been the case that costs are not recoverable between parties in dispute if proceedings are not issued.

In *McGlinn v Waltham Contractors Ltd* [2005] EWHC 1419 (TCC), [2005] 3 All ER 1126, it was argued that a successful claimant who raised a number of issues in pre-action correspondence, but abandoned some of them before issuing proceedings, was to be treated as only partially successful. A partially successful party is usually awarded just a percentage of the costs of the claim (see **68.11**). It was held that save in exceptional circumstances (such as where there is unreasonable conduct) the costs of the abandoned issues will not be 'incidental to' the subsequent proceedings. It would be contrary to the whole purpose of the pre-action protocols if claimants were routinely penalised if they dropped issues included in their letters before claim. The protocols are designed to narrow the issues, and allow a defendant to persuade a claimant that claims would not succeed.

ALTERNATIVE DISPUTE RESOLUTION

8.6   **PD Pre-action Conduct and Protocols, para. 8**, reminds parties that litigation usually should be the last resort. Lord Dyson, MR, in January 2013 wrote that the effective promotion of ADR is unquestionably in the public interest. Recommendation 76 in the *Jackson Report* was that there should be a single authoritative handbook explaining clearly and concisely what ADR is, which was implemented by what is now the 2nd edition of the *Jackson ADR Handbook*, Blake, Browne and Sime (Oxford: OUP, 2016), which has been issued to all the civil judges to ensure effective and consistent use of ADR. See **chapter 73**.

While it is recognised that no party can or should be forced to enter into any form of ADR, a failure to consider ADR may be taken into account on the issue of costs. If use of ADR has been suggested, the other side will need to say whether they agree with the proposals and if not, they should explain why by reference to the principles in *Halsey v Milton Keynes General NHS Trust* [2004] EWCA Civ 576, [2004] 1 WLR 3002 (see **73.23**). A party's silence in response to an invitation to participate in ADR might be considered to be unreasonable conduct for the purposes of **CPR, r. 44.2**, which could lead to adverse costs consequences (*PGF II SA v OMFS Co. 1 Ltd* [2013] EWCA Civ 1288, [2014] 1 WLR 1386; **PD Pre-action Conduct and Protocols, para. 11**). If proceedings are issued, the parties may be required by the court to provide evidence that ADR has been considered.

Whether ADR costs are incidental to litigation

A key issue is whether alternative dispute procedures adopted by the parties form part of 'the costs of or incidental to the litigation' within the meaning of the Senior Courts Act 1981, s. 51(1) (and so potentially recoverable under a costs order), or whether the ADR procedure is to be treated as a separate process for costs purposes. It is clear that the general costs of complying with a pre-action protocol may be recoverable as costs incidental to the litigation (*McGlinn v Waltham Contractors Ltd* [2005] EWHC 1419 (TCC), [2005] 3 All ER 1126). Recoverability of mediation costs may be expressly agreed between the parties. An agreement that each side shall bear its own costs of mediation makes it clear that the mediation costs are not part of the main litigation costs (*Lobster Group Ltd v Heidelberg Graphic Equipment Ltd* [2009] EWHC 1919 (TCC), LTL 6/8/2009). In the absence of express agreement, the court will have to consider the circumstances and decide whether the parties have implicitly agreed or accepted that the costs of mediation form part of the costs of the proceedings (*Roundstone Nurseries Ltd v Stephenson Holdings Ltd* [2009] EWHC 1431 (TCC), [2009] 5 Costs LR 787). Only the **Pre-action Protocol for Construction and Engineering Disputes** requires a pre-action meeting between the parties (**paras 5.1 to 5.7**; see **8.86**). This meeting is occasionally swept up in a formal mediation process.

8.7

NOTIFICATION OF FUNDING ARRANGEMENT

Whether or not the dispute is governed by a pre-action protocol, the parties should inform each other in the pre-action stages whether they have the benefit of public funding under legal aid or the Community Legal Service. Notification of funding under a conditional fee arrangement is only necessary in the limited number of cases where recovery of the success fee has been retained (see **6.15**).

8.8

CASES NOT SUBJECT TO SPECIFIC PRE-ACTION PROTOCOLS

Where there is no relevant pre-action protocol, the parties should exchange correspondence and information to allow them to understand each other's position and to comply with the objectives set out in **PD Pre-action Conduct and Protocols, para. 3** (see **8.1**). Parties must ensure compliance is proportionate (**paras 4 and 6**). The current version of **PD Pre-action Conduct and Protocols** removes almost all the detailed guidance on the contents of pre-action correspondence, which was in the version that applied before 6 April 2015, in favour of a short general description of what is required.

8.9

Letter before claim

Under **PD Pre-action Conduct and Protocols, para. 6(a)**, the claimant should send a letter before claim setting out concise details of the claim. The letter should include:

8.10

(a) the basis on which the claim is made;

(b) a summary of the facts; and

(c) what the claimant wants from the defendant, and if money, how the amount is calculated.

The requirements set out in PD Pre-action Conduct as it applied before 6 April 2015 are no longer in force, but continue to be good practical guidance. They were that the letter before claim should include:

(a) the claimant's full name and address;
(b) the basis on which the claimant alleges the defendant is liable;
(c) a clear summary of the facts on which the claim is based;
(d) what the claimant wants from the defendant;
(e) if financial loss is claimed, an explanation of how the amount has been calculated;
(f) a list of the essential documents on which the claimant intends to rely;
(g) the form of ADR (if any) that the claimant considers the most suitable and an invitation to the defendant to agree to this;
(h) the date by which the claimant considers it reasonable for a full response to be provided by the defendant;
(i) details of any relevant documents not in the claimant's possession which the claimant wishes the defendant to provide;
(j) unless the defendant is known to be legally represented, an express reference to what is now **PD Pre-action Conduct and Protocols** and in particular to the court's powers to impose sanctions for failure to comply; and
(k) a warning to the defendant that ignoring the letter before claim may lead to the claimant starting proceedings and may increase the defendant's liability for costs.

It is generally inappropriate to commence proceedings without at the very least a letter before claim, unless the matter is one of extreme urgency. A claimant who brings and loses a claim without having sent a letter before claim may be ordered to pay costs on the indemnity basis, even if the claim is not covered by a specific protocol (*Phoenix Finance Ltd v Fédération Internationale de l'Automobile* [2002] EWHC 1242 (Ch), *The Times,* 27 June 2002). In *Reid v Capita Group plc* [2005] EWHC 2448 (Ch), LTL 17/10/2005, the claimant brought proceedings to obtain documents relating to a commercial transaction without having sent a letter before claim, and without having identified the documents sought. It was held the proceedings were premature, and the claimant was ordered to pay the defendant's costs of the proceedings.

In *King v Telegraph Group Ltd* [2004] EWCA Civ 613, [2005] 1 WLR 2282, solicitors who sent a 10-page letter before claim, settled by junior counsel (at [60]), failed to comply with the spirit of cooperation required by the protocols. Among other things it accused the newspaper of cant, reckless falsehood, and a malicious agenda of incriminating misrepresentation. Its effect was to remove the prospect of conciliation between the parties, making litigation almost inevitable.

Defendant's response

8.11 A defendant has a reasonable time in which to respond (**PD Pre-action Conduct and Protocols, para. 6(b)**). This will depend on the nature of the case, but **para. 6(b)** goes on to explain that 14 days may be reasonable in a straightforward case, and no more than three months in a very complex one. The reply should include:

(a) confirmation whether liability for the claim is accepted;
(b) if it is not accepted:
    (i) the reasons why; and
    (ii) an explanation of which facts and parts of the claim are disputed; and
(c) whether the defendant is making a counterclaim, and if so, details of the counterclaim equivalent to a letter before claim (in which case the claimant will need to give a reply equivalent to a defendant's full response).

A reply should be a full response to the letter before claim. It should deal with both liability and remedies.

Documents

Both sides are under an obligation to disclose key documents relevant to the issues in dispute **8.12** (**PD Pre-action Conduct and Protocols, para. 6(c)**). Although **PD Pre-action Conduct and Protocols** no longer says anything expressly about this, documents disclosed pursuant to a specific protocol or **PD Pre-action Conduct and Protocols** are subject to the usual implied undertaking not to use them for collateral purposes (see **50.45** to **50.48**). Other protocols, such as the **Pre-action Protocol for Personal Injury Claims**, say that there should be no charge for providing documents under the protocol (**para. 6.5**).

Experts

Many disputes can be resolved without expert evidence, and even where experts are necessary, **8.13** parties need to be aware that expert evidence can only be used with the court's permission (**CPR, r. 35.4(1)**). Where the evidence of an expert is necessary, the parties should consider making use of a single joint expert (**PD Pre-action Conduct and Protocols, para. 7**).

Stocktake and List of Issues

Where a dispute has not been resolved after following a relevant protocol or **PD Pre-action** **8.14** **Conduct and Protocols,** the parties should review their respective positions (**para. 12**). They should consider the papers and the evidence to see if proceedings can be avoided, and at least seek to narrow the issues in dispute before the claimant issues proceedings.

Limitation

Limitation periods are not suspended while the parties seek to comply with **PD Pre-action** **8.15** **Conduct and Protocols** or any relevant protocol. If there is insufficient time to comply with the protocol, the claimant will need to issue protective proceedings. The parties should then apply to the court for a stay of the proceedings to allow them to comply with the remaining steps of the protocol (**para. 17**).

PERSONAL INJURY CLAIMS PROTOCOL

The **Pre-action Protocol for Personal Injury Claims** is primarily drafted for personal injuries **8.16** claims that are likely to be allocated to the fast track, and to the entirety of those claims, not just the personal injury element (**para. 1.1.1**). The 'cards on the table' approach prescribed by the protocol is equally applicable to higher-value claims, and the spirit of the protocol should be followed in potential multi-track claims (**para. 1.1.2**).

This protocol does not apply to claims covered by the low value RTA and EL/PL protocols, or the clinical disputes or disease and illness protocols (**para. 1.1.1**). Under **para. 1.3**, claims that exit the low value RTA and El/PL protocols because the defendant considers the mandatory information in the CNF is inadequate enter the **Pre-action Protocol for Personal Injury Claims** at **para. 5.1**. Claims leaving the low value RTA or EL/PL protocols because the defendant denies liability or alleges contributory negligence, or does not complete the CNF response, enter the **Pre-action Protocol for Personal Injury Claims** at **para. 5.5**.

The protocol lays down a timetable for the pre-action period, but **para. 1.4.2** envisages that there may be claims where some flexibility in the timetable will be necessary. Arrangements for disclosure and expert evidence may need to be varied to suit the particular circumstances of individual cases. There may be difficulties, for example, in a claim with a modest personal injury element, which is easily resolved, but a substantial claim for vehicle repairs, where the claimant may wish to move expeditiously to have the vehicle examined and repaired or scrapped and replaced. It may well be considered reasonable for the claimant to give the defendant's insurers much less notice of his or her intention in relation to the vehicle, and to insist on an inspect on far more quickly than the timescale indicated by the protocol. It is undesirable for a claimant to be put in the position of wondering whether a defendant's dilatory insurer will or will not accept the claimant's figures for repairs particularly when an alternative vehicle may have to be hired. It is submitted that common sense must prevail in allowing for variations of the timetable set by the protocol.

If it is considered, by either or both parties to a claim, that the detail of the protocol is not appropriate to it, and proceedings are subsequently issued, the court will expect an explanation of why the protocol has not been followed or has been varied (**para. 1.4.2**). A space is provided in the directions questionnaire for giving such an explanation.

The steps required by the protocol are summarised in **procedural checklist 1**, and are discussed in detail in **8.17** to **8.28**.

Early notification

8.17   The **Pre-action Protocol for Personal Injury Claims** promotes early notification of the possibility of a claim to the person against whom it may be made. **Paragraph 3.1** recognises that it may not be possible to provide all the relevant details immediately but it may be that the potential defendant has limited knowledge of the incident giving rise to the claim, or the claimant may want an interim payment. In such cases the defendant should be put on notice by writing an initial letter as soon as it is apparent that a claim is likely to be made. The letter of notification should advise the defendant or its insurer of any relevant information that is available to assist with determining liability or the suitability of the claim for an early interim payment or rehabilitation (**para. 3.2**). An early notification of this kind will not start the timetable for responding.

Letter of claim

8.18   The timetable set by the **Pre-action Protocol for Personal Injury Claims** is initiated by the letter of claim. This should be as detailed as possible and a specimen letter appears at annex B1 to the protocol. The letter should provide sufficient information for the defendant to assess liability and to enable the defendant to estimate the likely size and heads of claim, without necessarily addressing quantum in detail (**para. 5.2**). In a road traffic claim the letter should provide the name and address of the hospital where the claimant was treated, and, if available, the claimant's hospital reference number (**annex B**). The claimant's National Insurance number and date of birth should not be included in the letter of claim (**para. 5.4**). In low-impact road traffic accident cases the claimant's advisers should offer access to the claimant's vehicle and give early disclosure of the claimant's general practitioner and other relevant medical notes (suitably redacted to remove irrelevant passages). This is to enable the defendant's advisers to get hold of the most important evidential material expeditiously and inexpensively, see *Kearsley v Klarfeld* [2005] EWCA Civ 1510, [2006] 2 All ER 303. Normally two copies of a letter before claim are sent to the defendant, who is asked to pass one copy to the insurers responsible (**para. 5.1**). After sending a letter before claim the claimant should do no more work on investigating liability until the defendant responds indicating whether liability is accepted or denied (**para. 5.6**).

Defendant's acknowledgment

8.19   The defendant is required to acknowledge receipt of the letter before claim within 21 calendar days of posting, identifying the insurers, if any (**Pre-action Protocol for Personal Injury Claims, para. 6.2**). If the defendant or the insurers fail to respond within 21 days, the claimant is entitled to issue proceedings (**para. 3.6**). The time for acknowledging is 42 days where the defendant is outside the jurisdiction (**para. 6.4**). Bearing in mind the spirit of reasonable pre-action behaviour, if the defendant delays passing the letter before claim on to the insurers, it would be reasonable to allow the insurers additional time for responding to it.

Investigation and response

Having acknowledged the letter before claim, the defendant (or insurer) then has three **8.20** months to investigate and to reply. This period is six months if the defendant is outside the jurisdiction (**Pre-action Protocol for Personal Injury Claims, para. 6.4**). The response must say whether liability is admitted by admitting the accident occurred, that it was caused by the defendant's breach of duty, that the claimant suffered loss, and that there is no limitation defence. If liability or causation is denied the letter of response must set out the defendant's version of events and should enclose documents in its possession which are material to the issues between the parties and which would be likely to be ordered to be disclosed by the court (**para. 6.5**). A template for the suggested contents of the letter of response can be found in **annex B2**. In low-impact road traffic accident cases the defendant's advisers should make it clear whether they intend to allege that the claimant's injuries could not possibly have been caused by the accident, see *Kearsley v Klarfeld* [2005] EWCA Civ 1510, [2006] 2 All ER 303.

Proceedings should not be issued in this three-month period. For some claims this may not be possible. For example, if the claimant consults a solicitor towards the end of a relevant limitation period, a protective claim form will have to be issued, so as not to deprive the claimant of a remedy. In these circumstances the claimant's solicitor should give as much notice as is practicable and the parties should consider whether the court might be invited to extend the time for service of the claimant's supporting documents and the service of any defence, or alternatively to stay the proceedings while the recommended steps in the protocol are followed. This may only be done where there is an expectation that there is a valid claim to be pursued. In *West Bromwich Building Society v Mander Hadley and Co.* [1998] CLC 814 the Court of Appeal held that the issue of protective proceedings, when a claimant had no intention of prosecuting the claim and was unaware of any valid basis for it, was an abuse of process.

Status of letters of claim and response

Although a letter of claim and the letter of response should be as full as possible, in order to **8.21** meet the 'cards on the table approach', they do not have the same status as formal statements of case (**Pre-action Protocol for Personal Injury Claims, para. 5.7**). It is recognised that various facts may well come to light as a result of investigations after the letter of claim has been sent or after the defendant has responded, especially in a situation where the disclosure of documents takes place outside the recommended three-month period. Circumstances such as these could mean that particulars of claim and/or the defence may present a party's case in a slightly different way than in the letter of claim and/or response, and it would be inconsistent with the spirit of the protocol for a party to take a point on this in the proceedings, provided there was no deliberate intention to mislead (**para. 5.7**). Indeed it is clear from the comments of Lord Woolf MR in *McPhilemy v Times Newspapers Ltd* [1999] 3 All ER 775 that contests over the terms of statements of case are to be avoided.

Disclosure of documents and schedule of special damages

The **Pre-action Protocol for Personal Injury Claims** provides for pre-action disclosure of **8.22** documents, particularly where the defendant denies liability (see **8.20**). Annex C to the protocol lists documents likely to be material to liability in different types of claim. In cases where liability is admitted in full, disclosure under the protocol is limited to documents relevant to quantum (**para. 7.1.3**). No charge is to be made for supplying documents under the protocol (**para. 6.5**).

In cases where liability is admitted, the claimant is required to send the defendant a schedule of past and future expenses and losses as soon as reasonably practicable (**para. 10.1**). The schedule should contain as much detail as practicable, and should identify those losses that are ongoing. A schedule is required even if the figures are necessarily provisional (**para. 8.1.1(b)**), but a detailed schedule may not be required in a low-value claim (**para. 8.2**). If the schedule is likely to be updated, that should be stated. Provided there are no limitation issues, proceedings should not be issued for at least 21 days after sending the schedule to enable the parties to consider whether the claim is capable of settlement (**para. 8.1.2**).

The aim of early disclosure of documents is not to encourage 'fishing expeditions' by the claimant but to promote an early exchange of relevant information to assist in clarifying or resolving the issues in dispute (**paras 2.1(a)** and **7.1.1**). The claimant's solicitors can assist by identifying in the letter of claim or in a subsequent letter the particular categories of documents which they consider are relevant, and why, with a brief explanation of their alleged relevance, if necessary (**para. 7.1.1**).

Experts

8.23   The **Pre-action Protocol for Personal Injury Claims** encourages the joint selection of, and access to, experts (**para. 7.2**). The protocol also promotes the practice of the claimant obtaining a medical report and disclosing it to the defendant, who then has the opportunity to ask questions on the report and/or agree it without the need to obtain his or her own report (**para. 7.2**). The expectation is that the selection and instruction of experts will be largely or wholly accomplished before proceedings are issued (*Edwards-Tubb v J. D. Wetherspoon plc* [2011] EWCA Civ 136, [2011] 1 WLR 1373 at [27]). In most claims this will apply to medical experts, but there may be occasions when it will also apply to others, such as engineers.

Joint selection is initiated by one of the parties providing the other party with a list of names of experts in the relevant area who are considered suitable to instruct (**para. 7.3**). The other side have 14 days to indicate objections to any of the proposed experts (**para. 7.6**). If the list of experts was provided in the letter of claim, the time for objecting is 35 days (21 days to acknowledge the letter of claim, plus 14 days: **para. 7.6**). Provided at least one expert is not objected to, the first party instructs one of the remaining experts, and arranges for access to the claimant's medical records (**para. 7.5**). The party who instructed a jointly selected expert is solely liable to pay the expert's fee (**para. 7.10**). At least initially, only the party who instructed a jointly selected expert is entitled to see the expert's report, which is protected by legal professional privilege unless the instructing party chooses to disclose it (*Carlson v Townsend* [2001] EWCA Civ 511, [2001] 1 WLR 2415). Conditions requiring the disclosure of such reports are considered at **54.17**.

If the other side object to all the listed experts, each side may instruct experts of their own choice (**para. 7.7**). It will then be for the court to decide whether either side acted unreasonably. If the other side do not object to one or more of the nominated experts, they are not entitled to rely on their own expert evidence unless the first party agrees, or the court so directs, or if the first party's expert's report is amended and the first party refuses to disclose the original report (**para. 7.8**).

Any party can send written questions to the expert, via the instructing party's solicitors (**para. 7.9**). Such questions must be put within 28 days of service of the report, and must be only for the purpose of clarification of the report. Answers should be sent simultaneously to each party. The costs of the expert in answering the questions will usually be borne by the party asking the questions (**para. 7.10**).

8.24   **Medical agencies**   Some solicitors have adopted the practice of obtaining medical reports via medical agencies rather than direct from a specific doctor or hospital (**Pre-action Protocol for**

Personal Injury Claims, para. 7.4). The protocol does not discourage this but emphasises that in such a case, the defendant's prior consent should be sought and, if the defendant so requests, the agency should be asked to provide in advance the names of the doctors whom they are considering instructing.

Court control of expert evidence   The court has some (or a great deal of) control over **8.25** experts instructed pursuant to a protocol (see below and **chapter 54**). Such an expert produces a report which has to be addressed to the court, and is to be contrasted with an expert instructed pre-protocol purely to advise a client and at the client's expense. That kind of expert falls outside the definition in **CPR, r. 35.2**, their report remains privileged in the hands of the client and cannot in usual circumstances be made the subject of an *Edwards-Tubb* order (*Edwards-Tubb v J. D. Wetherspoon plc* at [31], and see **54.19**).

A claimant may wish the medical practitioner who provided the medical treatment to be retained as the expert in the claim. This is expressly prohibited for soft tissue claims under the **RTA Protocol**, and is best avoided, as the court may well reach the conclusion that the medical expert is no longer sufficiently objective, because, first, the expert will have developed a relationship with the patient/claimant and secondly, may regard his or her views on prognosis as unchallengeable. It is suggested that the procedure for the joint selection of experts is preferable in order that a mutually acceptable expert can be instructed.

Claimants who choose to instruct their own expert unilaterally may well discover that the court will later refuse permission to call that expert and insist that an expert be jointly instructed (**CPR, r. 35.7**). The consequence of this is that the costs of the first expert will not be recoverable, regardless of the outcome of the case. The question relating to experts in the directions questionnaire asks whether reports have been disclosed and whether it is proposed to use a joint expert. This allows arguments to be put for a separate defence expert and for the court to enquire whether the defendant's position cannot be protected by simply delivering written questions to the claimant's expert.

Furthermore, the protocol does maintain the flexibility for either party to obtain their own expert's report, if necessary, once proceedings have been commenced, but with the permission of the court. It is also for the court to decide whether either party has acted unreasonably (**paras** 7.7 and **7.11**), and whether the costs of more than one expert report should be recoverable (see **CPR, r. 35.4(4)**).

In contrast, if an expert is jointly instructed, both parties are entitled to see his or her report.

Rehabilitation

As early as possible both sides should consider whether the claimant has reasonable needs **8.26** that could be met by rehabilitation treatment or other measures (**Pre-action Protocol for Personal Injury Claims, para. 4.1**). There is a Rehabilitation Code, which can be accessed at the website referred to in **para. 4.2**. An assessment report should be produced using the seven headings set out in para. 5.2 of the Rehabilitation Code. It will not deal with diagnostic criteria, causation or long-term care requirements (Code, para. 5.3). Instead it must deal with short and medium-term rehabilitation treatment, its likely benefits, and cost (Code, para. 5.2). The defendant's insurer will pay for the report within 28 days of receipt (Code, para. 6.5). It is for the parties to agree that any particular regime of rehabilitation or treatment shall be put in place (Code, para. 6.4). Any funds laid out by the insurer for treatment are treated as voluntary interim payments (Code, para. 7.2). Provided the claimant uses such funds for the recommended purpose, the insurer warrants it will not dispute the reasonableness or the agreed cost of the treatment in subsequent proceedings (Code, para. 7.2). Any assessment report must not be used in the litigation except by consent (**Pre-action Protocol for Personal Injury Claims, para. 4.4**). Any notes and reports created in

Commentary

connection with the assessment process shall not be disclosed in any litigation, and any person involved in the preparation of the assessment report shall not be a compellable witness (Code, para. 6.3).

Negotiation, rehabilitation and settlement

8.27   The **Pre-action Protocol for Personal Injury Claims, para. 9.1.1**, requires the parties to consider whether some form of ADR would be more suitable than litigation. Both sides may be required to provide the court with evidence that ADR was considered. Litigation is regarded as a last resort, and proceedings should not be issued while settlement is being actively explored. It is expressly recognised that the parties cannot be forced to mediate or enter into any form of ADR (**para. 9.1.3**), but a failure to comply with the aim of **para. 9.1.1** may be taken into account on costs.

Preparation for proceedings

8.28   Where a claim is not resolved, even though the parties have followed the protocol, each party should review its position and its strengths and weaknesses, prior to the commencement of proceedings (**Pre-action Protocol for Personal Injury Claims, para. 11.1**). The parties should together consider the evidence and the arguments to see whether litigation can be avoided, or, if not, whether the issues can be narrowed.

If the pre-action steps on the defendant's side have been taken by insurers, **para. 11.1** recommends that, seven to 14 days before the intended issue date, the claimant's solicitor should invite the insurers to nominate solicitors to act in the proceedings.

RTA PROTOCOL

8.29   The **Pre-action Protocol for Low Value Personal Injury Claims in Road Traffic Accidents** (the **RTA Protocol**) has to be read together with a number of related provisions in the CPR. The protocol and related provisions are designed to provide a streamlined and swift process for settling by agreement road traffic personal injury claims where liability is admitted and damages are in the range of £1,000 to £25,000. The RTA Protocol (and the similar EL/PL Protocol, see **8.60**), unlike the other protocols, is therefore intended to be an alternative to litigation, rather than a prelude to litigation. The system provided for dealing with these claims is highly regulated, with short, fixed periods for most of the necessary steps, prescribed interim payments, and a regime of fixed costs. The process under the **RTA Protocol** is divided into three stages, which are shown in general terms in **figure 8.1**.

Cases covered by the RTA Protocol

8.30   A claim will be covered by the RTA Protocol if:

(a) the claim is for damages arising from a road traffic accident (**RTA Protocol, para. 4.1(1)**);
(b) the accident was on or after 30 April 2010. Cases where the claim notification form (CNF, see **8.33**) was submitted before 31 July 2013 are governed by the original RTA Protocol (**para. 4.2**); cases where the CNF was submitted on or after 31 July 2013 are governed by the 2013 RTA Protocol, see **para. 4.1(1)**;
(c) the defendant was a road user (**para. 4.5(1)**);
(d) the claim includes damages in respect of personal injury (**para. 4.1(2)**);
(e) the claimant values the claim between £1,000 and £25,000 on a full liability basis (**para. 4.1(3) and (4)**) (for accidents before 31 July 2013 the upper limit was £10,000); and
(f) the claim does not fall into any of the excluded categories (**para. 4.5**).

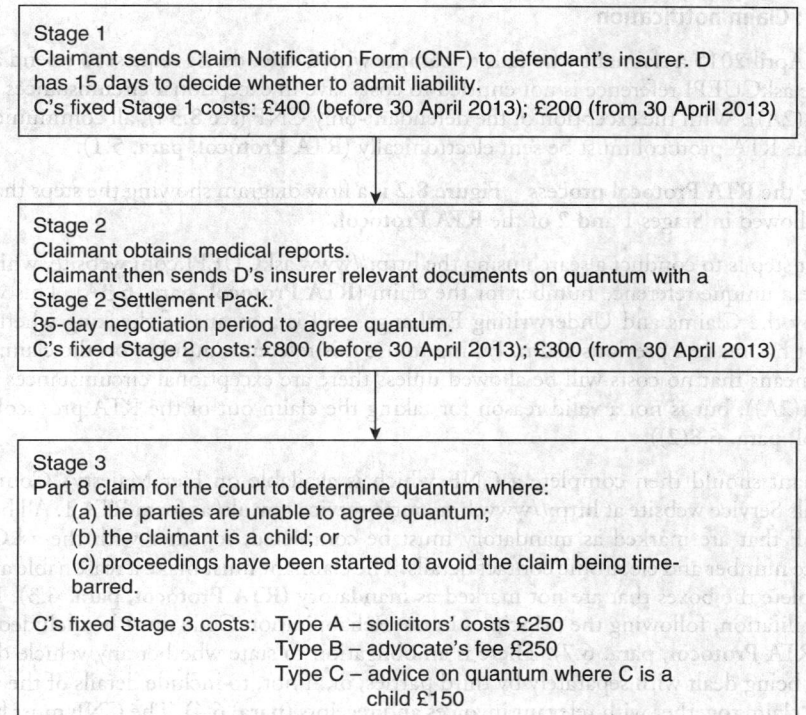

Stage 1
Claimant sends Claim Notification Form (CNF) to defendant's insurer. D has 15 days to decide whether to admit liability.
C's fixed Stage 1 costs: £400 (before 30 April 2013); £200 (from 30 April 2013)

Stage 2
Claimant obtains medical reports.
Claimant then sends D's insurer relevant documents on quantum with a Stage 2 Settlement Pack.
35-day negotiation period to agree quantum.
C's fixed Stage 2 costs: £800 (before 30 April 2013); £300 (from 30 April 2013)

Stage 3
Part 8 claim for the court to determine quantum where:
   (a) the parties are unable to agree quantum;
   (b) the claimant is a child; or
   (c) proceedings have been started to avoid the claim being time-barred.

C's fixed Stage 3 costs: Type A – solicitors' costs £250
                   Type B – advocate's fee £250
                   Type C – advice on quantum where C is a
                              child £150

Figure 8.1 RTA Protocol: the three stages

Commentary

Financial condition

A claim will not be covered by the **RTA Protocol** if the small claims track would be the **8.31** normal track for that claim (**RTA Protocol, para. 4.1(4)**). This is the case where the total value of the claim is not more than £10,000, and where the value of the claim for pain, suffering and loss of amenity is not more than £1,000 (**CPR, r. 26.6(1)**). These claims are excluded from the **RTA Protocol** because the no-costs rule in small claims track cases (see **CPR, r. 27.14**) is inconsistent with the fixed costs regime under the **RTA Protocol**. In deciding whether the claim exceeds the £25,000 upper limit the claimant should:

(a) include pecuniary losses;
(b) exclude the value of vehicle-related damage (**para. 4.4**); and
(c) exclude interest (**para. 1.2(1)**).

Excluded cases

The **RTA Protocol** does not apply (**para. 4.5**) to claims: **8.32**

(a) made to the MIB pursuant to the Untraced Drivers' Agreement 2003 (see **9.5**);
(b) where the claimant or defendant is deceased (see **14.12**);
(c) where the claimant or defendant is a protected party (see **14.15**);
(d) where the claimant is bankrupt (see **14.25**); or
(e) where the defendant's vehicle is registered outside the United Kingdom.

Stage 1: Claim notification

From 6 April 2015 a claimant who fails to comply with a defendant's request to resend a CNF with the askCUEPI reference is not entitled to costs save in exceptional circumstances (**CPR, r. 45.24(2A)**). With the exception of the defendant-only CNF (see **8.34**), all communications under the RTA protocol must be sent electronically (**RTA Protocol, para. 5.1**).

8.33   **Starting the RTA Protocol process**   **Figure 8.2** is a flow diagram showing the steps that have to be followed in Stages 1 and 2 of the **RTA Protocol**.

The first step is to conduct a search using the http://www.askCUEPI.com website, which will generate a unique reference number for the claim (**RTA Protocol, para. 6.3A**). This website is run by the Claims and Underwriting Exchange, and is a means of checking whether the claimant has made a previous claim. Failing to use this reference number on the claim documents means that no costs will be allowed unless there are exceptional circumstances (**CPR, r. 45.24(2A)**), but is not a valid reason for taking the claim out of the RTA protocol (**RTA Protocol, para. 6.8(2)**).

A claimant should then complete a CNF, which is available on Her Majesty's Courts and Tribunals Service website at http://www.hmcourts-service.gov.uk/ as form RTA 1. All boxes in the CNF that are marked as mandatory must be completed, together with the askCUEPI reference number and electronic contact details. The claimant must make a reasonable attempt to complete the boxes that are not marked as mandatory (**RTA Protocol, para. 6.3**). Details of rehabilitation, following the principles in the Rehabilitation Code must be included in the CNF (**RTA Protocol, para. 6.7**). There is an obligation to state whether any vehicle damage claim is being dealt with separately by third parties, or, if not, to include details of the vehicle damage claim together with relevant invoices and receipts (**para. 6.4**). The CNF must be verified by a statement of truth. When completed electronically this requirement is satisfied by entering the name of the person verifying the form in the signature box (**para. 6.6**).

The CNF must be sent electronically to the defendant's insurer. The relevant address should be available on the RTA PI Claims Process website (http://www.claimsportal.org.uk/). To make use of this website it is necessary to register online. At the same time as the CNF is sent to the insurer, or as soon as practicable thereafter, a defendant only CNF (form RTA 2) must be sent to the defendant by first class post (**para. 6.2**).

8.34   **Response by defendant's insurer**   An electronic acknowledgment must be sent by the defendant's insurer on the next business day after receipt of the CNF (**RTA Protocol, para. 6.10**). The insurer has 15 days to investigate liability, and must complete the 'Insurer Response' section of the CNF (the CNF response) and send it to the claimant within 15 business days of receipt of the CNF. The principal question for the insurer is whether liability will be admitted. Secondary questions are whether there will be an allegation of contributory negligence (**para. 6.15**), or an allegation that a low-speed impact could not have caused the alleged injuries (**para. 6.19A**). If liability is denied, brief reasons for that denial must be set out in the CNF response (**para. 6.16**). An admission of liability for the purposes of the RTA Protocol is, by **para. 1.1(1)**, an admission that:

(a)   the accident occurred;

(b)   the accident was caused by the defendant's breach of duty;

(c)   the defendant caused some loss to the claimant, the nature and extent of which is not admitted; and

(d)   the defendant has no accrued defence to the claim under the Limitation Act 1980.

8.35   **CRU certificate**   The defendant must, before the end of Stage 1, apply to the Compensation Recovery Unit (CRU) for a certificate of recoverable benefits (**RTA Protocol, para. 6.12**). Recoupment of State benefits paid to the claimant as a result of a relevant injury is dealt with by the Social Security (Recovery of Benefits) Act 1997.

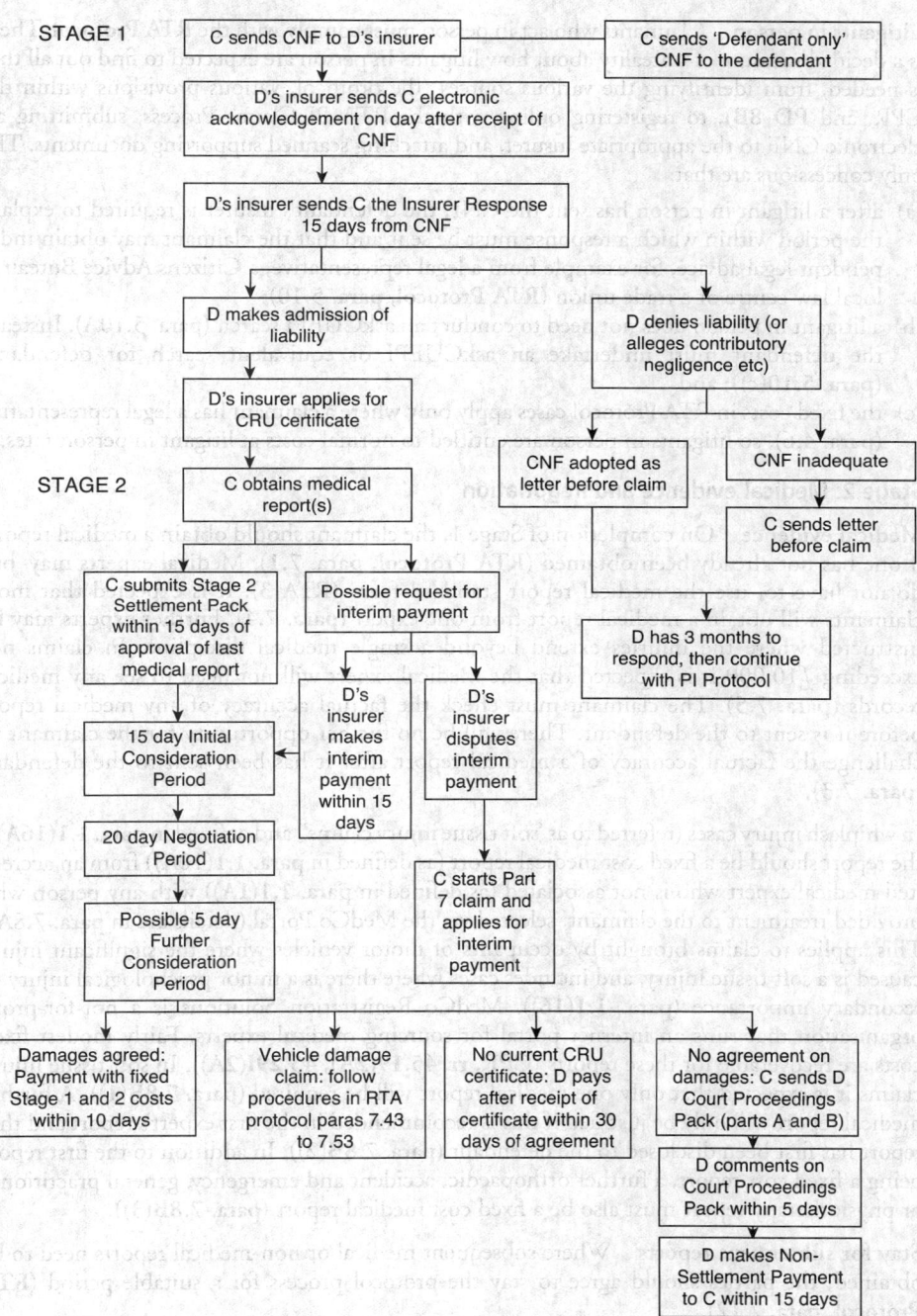

STAGE 1

C sends CNF to D's insurer

C sends 'Defendant only' CNF to the defendant

D's insurer sends C electronic acknowledgement on day after receipt of CNF

D's insurer sends C the Insurer Response 15 days from CNF

D makes admission of liability

D denies liability (or alleges contributory negligence etc)

D's insurer applies for CRU certificate

CNF adopted as letter before claim

CNF inadequate

STAGE 2

C obtains medical report(s)

C sends letter before claim

C submits Stage 2 Settlement Pack within 15 days of approval of last medical report

Possible request for interim payment

D has 3 months to respond, then continue with PI Protocol

15 day Initial Consideration Period

D's insurer makes interim payment within 15 days

D's insurer disputes interim payment

20 day Negotiation Period

C starts Part 7 claim and applies for interim payment

Possible 5 day Further Consideration Period

Damages agreed: Payment with fixed Stage 1 and 2 costs within 10 days

Vehicle damage claim: follow procedures in RTA protocol paras 7.43 to 7.53

No current CRU certificate: D pays after receipt of certificate within 30 days of agreement

No agreement on damages: C sends D Court Proceedings Pack (parts A and B)

D comments on Court Proceedings Pack within 5 days

D makes Non-Settlement Payment to C within 15 days

Figure 8.2 Flow diagram of Stages 1 and 2 under the RTA Protocol

Stage 1 fixed costs   Except where the claimant is a child, the defendant must pay the Stage 1 fixed **8.36** costs in cases where liability is admitted or liability is admitted with an allegation of contributory negligence restricted to the claimant's admitted failure to wear a seat belt (**RTA Protocol, para. 6.18**). These costs must be paid within 10 days after sending the CNF response to the claimant.

145

Commentary

8.37 **Litigants in person** Claimants who act in person must comply with the **RTA Protocol**. There is a decided measure of unreality about how litigants in person are expected to find out all that is needed, from identifying the various sources (the protocol, various provisions within the CPR, and **PD 8B**), to registering online with the RTA PI Claims Process, submitting an electronic CNF to the appropriate insurer, and attaching scanned supporting documents. The only concessions are that:

(a) after a litigant in person has sent the CNF, the defendant's insurer is required to explain the period within which a response must be sent and that the claimant may obtain independent legal advice, for example from a legal representative, a Citizens Advice Bureau, a local law centre or a trade union (**RTA Protocol, para. 5.10**);

(b) a litigant in person does not need to conduct an askCUEPI search (para. 5.10A). Instead, the defendant must undertake an askCUEPI or equivalent search for defendants (**para. 5.10(c)**); and

(c) the fixed costs in RTA Protocol cases apply only where a claimant has a legal representative (**para. 4.6**), so litigants in person are entitled to normal costs at litigant in person rates.

Stage 2: Medical evidence and negotiation

8.38 **Medical evidence** On completion of Stage 1, the claimant should obtain a medical report, if one has not already been obtained (**RTA Protocol, para. 7.1**). Medical experts may, but do not have to, use the medical report standard form (RTA 3). It is expected that most claimants will obtain a medical report from one expert (**para. 7.4**). Further experts may be instructed where the injuries extend beyond a single medical discipline. In claims not exceeding £10,000 it is expected that the medical expert will not need to see any medical records (**para. 7.5**). The claimant must check the factual accuracy of any medical report before it is sent to the defendant. There will be no further opportunity for the claimant to challenge the factual accuracy of a medical report after it has been sent to the defendant (**para. 7.3**).

In whiplash injury cases (referred to as 'soft tissue injury claims', and defined in **para. 1.1(16A)**), the report should be a fixed cost medical report (as defined in **para. 1.1(10A)**) from an accredited medical expert who is not associated (as defined in **para. 1.1(1A)**) with any person who provided treatment to the claimant, selected via the MedCo Portal (details are in **para. 7.8A**). This applies to claims brought by occupants of motor vehicles where the significant injury caused is a soft tissue injury, and includes cases where there is a minor psychological injury of secondary importance (**para. 1.1(16)**). MedCo Registration Solutions is a not-for-profit organisation that runs an internet portal for sourcing medical experts. Fairly modest fixed costs are recoverable for these reports (**CPR, rr. 45.19(2A), 45.29I(2A)**). In soft tissue injury claims it is expected that only one medical report will be required (**para. 7.8B(1)**). A further medical report will only be justified if this is recommended in the first expert's report and that report has first been disclosed to the defendant (**para. 7.8B(2)**). In addition to the first report being a fixed cost report, a further orthopaedic, accident and emergency, general practitioner or physiotherapy report must also be a fixed cost medical report (**para. 7.8B(3)**).

8.39 **Stay for subsequent reports** Where subsequent medical or non-medical reports need to be obtained, the parties should agree to stay the protocol process for a suitable period (**RTA Protocol, para. 7.12**).

8.40 **Interim payment** Where there is a stay for updating reports, the claimant can request an interim payment of £1,000, which generally the defendant's insurer must pay within 10 days (**RTA Protocol, paras 7.13 to 7.18**). A claimant may make a request for an interim payment exceeding £1,000, in which case the defendant's insurer has 15 days to consider the matter. If the defendant fails to make the interim payment, or if the claimant is not satisfied with the defendant's response to the request, the claimant has 10 days to give notice that the claim will no longer be governed by the **RTA Protocol**.

Stage 2 settlement pack   After obtaining the necessary medical reports, the claimant must **8.41** send the defendant's insurers a Stage 2 settlement pack within 15 days of the claimant approving the final medical report and agreeing to rely on the prognosis in that report (**RTA Protocol, para. 7.33**). This pack consists of:

(a) the Stage 2 settlement pack form (form RTA 5). This includes space for the claimant to make an offer of what they will accept in settlement of the claim. Where the defendant alleges contributory negligence because of the claimant's failure to wear a seat belt, the form must give the claimant's suggested percentage reduction (which may be 0 per cent);
(b) a medical report or reports (which in soft tissue injury claims must be fixed cost medical reports, para. 7.32A);
(c) evidence of pecuniary losses;
(d) evidence of disbursements (for example the cost of any medical report);
(e) any non-medical expert report;
(f) any medical records or photographs served with the medical reports; and
(g) any witness statements.

Consideration of claim and negotiation   There is a 35-day period (which can be extended **8.42** by agreement) for consideration of the Stage 2 settlement pack by the defendant (this is called 'the total consideration period': **RTA Protocol, para. 7.35**). The total consideration period includes an initial period of up to 15 days for the defendant to consider the documents and make an offer. Within this period the defendant must either accept the offer made by the claimant on the Stage 2 settlement pack form or make a counter-offer using that form (**para. 7.38**). When making a counter-offer the defendant must propose an amount for each head of damage. Where the defendant has obtained a CRU certificate, the counter-offer must state the name and amount of any deductible amount (**para. 7.42**). If there is no current CRU certificate, a fresh certificate will be needed (**paras 7.49, 7.50, and 7.63**). The defendant must also explain in the counter-offer why a particular head of damage is less than the amount claimed by the claimant. The explanation will assist the claimant when negotiating a settlement and will allow both parties to focus on the areas of the claim that remain in dispute (**para. 7.41**).

Once the initial consideration period has elapsed, the defendant can withdraw the admission of liability only with the claimant's consent (**CPR, r. 14.1B(2)(a)**).

The remaining 20 days of the total consideration period are for any further negotiation between the parties ('the negotiation period'). If there is an offer within five days of the end of the 35-day period, there is an automatic five-day extension to give time for the other side to consider whether to accept the offer (**RTA Protocol, para. 7.37**).

Terms of offers   Any offer to settle made at any stage by either party will automatically **8.43** include, and cannot exclude (**RTA Protocol, para. 7.44**):

(a) the Stage 1 and Stage 2 fixed costs in **CPR, r. 45.18**, and Type C fixed costs of any additional advice on quantum (for which, see **r. 45.23A**, which only applies if the value of the claim exceeds £10,000);
(b) an agreement in principle to pay relevant disbursements under **r. 45.19**; and
(c) in a soft tissue injury claim, the cost of obtaining a fixed cost medical report.

Payment after acceptance of offer   Where the claimant is an adult and the claim is settled **8.44** during Stage 2, under the **RTA Protocol, para. 7.47**, the defendant must pay:

(a) the agreed damages less any deductible amount which is payable to the CRU and any interim payment;
(b) any unpaid Stage 1 and the Stage 2 fixed costs in **CPR, r. 45.18**, and Type C fixed costs of any additional advice on quantum; and
(c) the relevant disbursements under **r. 45.19**.

These sums must be paid within 10 days of the parties agreeing the settlement (**RTA Protocol, para. 7.47**).

8.45   **Failure to compromise**   If the parties do not reach agreement in the total consideration period, the claimant is required by **RTA Protocol, para. 7.64**, to send the defendant's insurer the court proceedings pack (parts A and B) (forms RTA 6 and RTA 7), which must contain:

(a) in part A, the final schedule of the claimant's losses and the defendant's responses, comprising only the figures for the original and additional damages, together with supporting comments and evidence from both parties on any disputed heads of damage; and

(b) in part B, the final offer and counter-offer from the Stage 2 settlement pack form and, where relevant, the offer and any final counter-offer made under **para. 7.53**.

The court proceedings pack (part A) must not raise anything that has not been raised in the Stage 2 settlement pack form (**para. 7.66**). The defendant has five days to make any comments on this pack (**para. 5.67**), and can nominate a legal representative to accept service of court proceedings (**para. 5.68**).

8.46   **Stage 2 payment**   Where the claimant is an adult, by **RTA Protocol, para. 7.70**, the defendant must within 15 days of receipt of the court proceedings pack make a payment to the claimant of:

(a) the final offer of damages made by the defendant in the court proceedings pack, less any deductible amount which is payable to the CRU and any interim payment;

(b) any unpaid Stage 1 and the Stage 2 fixed costs; and

(c) the disbursements listed in CPR, r. 45.19(2), including the fixed fees for soft tissue reports in r. 45.19(2A).

Stage 3: Part 8 claim to determine quantum

8.47   **Procedure under Stage 3**   Figure 8.3 is a flow diagram showing the steps that have to be followed in Stage 3 in cases governed by the **RTA Protocol**. Stage 3 involves a Part 8 claim and the court assessing damages where the claim has not been settled in Stages 1 or 2. The procedure is governed by **PD 8B**, which is a substantially modified version of the normal Part 8 procedure. Most of the provisions of **CPR, Part 8** are disapplied (**PD 8B, para. 2.2**), except for **rr. 8.2** (the Part 8 claim form), **8.4** (consequences of not acknowledging service) and **8.9(a)** and **(b)** (CPR provisions on statements of case and entering judgments on admissions do not apply).

8.48   **Filing and service**   By **PD 8B, para. 6.1**, the claimant must file with the claim form and serve on the defendant:

(a) the court proceedings pack (part A);

(b) the court proceedings pack (part B) (the claimant and defendant's final offers) in a sealed envelope. These are treated as modified Part 36 offers, and must not be communicated to the court until the claim is determined (**CPR, r. 36.28(1)**);

(c) copies of medical reports (which, with a minor exception, must be fixed cost medical reports in soft tissue injury claims (**PD 8B, para. 6.1A**));

(d) evidence of special damages; and

(e) evidence of disbursements.

The claimant can only use documents that have already been sent to the defendant under the **RTA Protocol** (**PD 8B, para. 6.3**).

8.49   **Acknowledgment of service**   The defendant must file and serve an acknowledgment of service in form N210B not more than 14 days after service of the claim form (**PD 8B, para. 8.1**). At the same time the defendant must file a current CRU certificate (**para. 8.2**).

Where the defendant opposes the claim because the claimant has either not followed the **RTA Protocol** or has filed and served additional or new evidence with the claim form that had not been provided under the protocol, the court will dismiss the claim and the claimant may start proceedings under **CPR, Part 7** (**PD 8B, para. 9.1**).

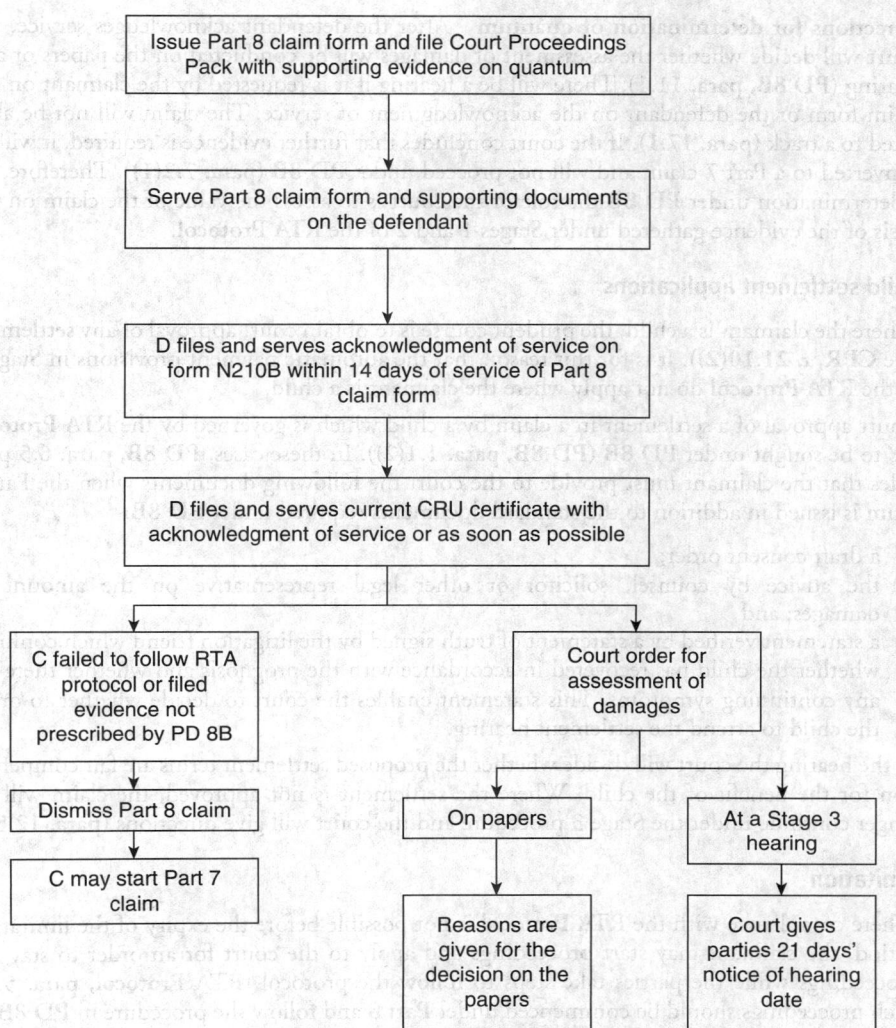

Figure 8.3 Flow diagram of Stage 3 under the RTA Protocol

Changing to or from the PD 8B procedure   The court can order a Part 7 claim to proceed   **8.50**
as if it was governed by the Stage 3 procedure in **PD 8B** (**PD 8B, para. 4.1**). It may also order
a **PD 8B** claim which is unsuitable for the **PD 8B** procedure to continue as if it were a Part 7
claim (**PD 8B, para. 7.2(2)**).

Withdrawal of RTA Protocol admissions and offers   Once the Part 8 claim under **PD 8B**   **8.51**
has been issued, the defendant can only withdraw an admission made under the **RTA Protocol**
with the consent of all the other parties or with the court's permission (**CPR, r. 14.1B(2)(b)**).
An application for permission is made using the Part 23 procedure.

A party may withdraw an RTA Protocol offer after proceedings have started only with the
court's permission (**PD 8B, para. 10.1**). Where the court gives permission, the claim will
no longer continue under the Stage 3 procedure and the court will give directions. The
court will give permission only where there is good reason for the claim not to continue
under Stage 3.

8.52 **Directions for determination of quantum** After the defendant acknowledges service, the court will decide whether the assessment of damages will be conducted on the papers or at a hearing (**PD 8B, para. 11.1**). There will be a hearing if it is requested by the claimant on the claim form or the defendant on the acknowledgment of service. The claim will not be allocated to a track (**para. 17.1**). If the court concludes that further evidence is required, it will be converted to a Part 7 claim and will not proceed under **PD 8B** (**para. 7.2(1)**). Therefore, on a determination under **PD 8B** the role of the court is to assess the value of the claim on the basis of the evidence gathered under Stages 1 and 2 of the **RTA Protocol**.

Child settlement applications

8.53 Where the claimant is a child, the prudent course is to obtain court approval of any settlement (see **CPR, r. 21.10(2)**). It is for this reason that the automatic payment provisions in Stage 2 of the **RTA Protocol** do not apply where the claimant is a child.

Court approval of a settlement in a claim by a child which is governed by the **RTA Protocol** has to be sought under **PD 8B** (**PD 8B, para. 1.1(2)**). In these cases, **PD 8B, para. 6.5** provides that the claimant must provide to the court the following documents when the Part 8 claim is issued in addition to the standard documents required under **PD 8B**:

(a) a draft consent order;
(b) the advice by counsel, solicitor or other legal representative on the amount of damages; and
(c) a statement verified by a statement of truth signed by the litigation friend which confirms whether the child has recovered in accordance with the prognosis and whether there are any continuing symptoms. This statement enables the court to decide whether to order the child to attend the settlement hearing.

At the hearing the court will decide whether the proposed settlement terms are fair compensation for the benefit of the child. Where the settlement is not approved, the claim will no longer continue under the Stage 3 procedure and the court will give directions (**para. 12.5**).

Limitation

8.54 Where compliance with the **RTA Protocol** is not possible before the expiry of the limitation period, the claimant may start proceedings and apply to the court for an order to stay the proceedings while the parties take steps to follow the protocol (**RTA Protocol, para. 5.7**). Such proceedings should be commenced under **Part 8** and follow the procedure in **PD 8B**. If the parties are unable to reach a settlement while the claim is stayed by the end of Stage 2 of the protocol, the claimant must, in order to proceed to Stage 3, apply to lift the stay and request directions in the existing proceedings (**para. 5.8**).

Fixed costs in RTA Protocol cases

8.55 There is a detailed system of fixed costs in RTA Protocol claims. While the claim remains within the RTA Protocol the fixed costs are laid down by **CPR, rr. 45.16 to 45.27** as summarised in **figure 8.1**. For cases where the CNF was submitted on or after 31 July 2013, there is also a fixed costs regime that applies after a claim leaves the RTA Protocol or Stage 3 procedure. This applies also to employers' liability and public liability claims, and effectively introduces a fixed costs regime for most fast track personal injuries claims. The detailed rules are in **CPR, rr. 45.29A to 45.29L**, see **70.17**.

RTA Protocol offers

8.56 There are adjustments to the rules relating to Part 36 offers for RTA claims being dealt with under the **RTA Protocol**, see **CPR, rr. 36.24 to 36.30**. An offer to settle in an RTA Protocol case must be set out in the court proceedings pack (part B) form (**CPR, r. 36.25(2)(a)**).

It should contain the final total amount of the offers from both sides (in accordance with the **RTA Protocol, para. 7.64**). These amounts are treated as exclusive of all interest (**CPR, r. 36.27(a)**). An RTA Protocol offer is deemed to be made on the first business day after the court proceedings pack (parts A and B) is sent to the defendant. It must not be communicated to the court until the claim is determined, at which point the court will examine the RTA Protocol offer (**r. 36.28**). There is an absolute prohibition on any other form of offer being communicated to the court at all (**r. 36.28(b)**).

After a claim leaves the RTA Protocol, Part 36 offers are governed by **rr. 36.20** and **36.21**. Where a Part 36 offer is accepted within the relevant period the claimant is entitled to fixed costs in the relevant table in **Part 45** (**r. 36.20(2)**). Where a Part 36 offer is accepted after the relevant period the claimant is entitled to fixed costs for the stage applicable when the relevant period expired, and the defendant is entitled to its costs thereafter (**r. 36.20(4)**). The defendant's costs cannot exceed the relevant fixed costs (**r. 36.20(12)**).

Failing to obtain a judgment more advantageous than an RTA Protocol offer   Costs consequences for non-acceptance of RTA Protocol offers are set out in **CPR, r. 36.29(1)**, and arise in three different situations: **8.57**

(a) where the determination of the court is less than or equal to the amount of the defendant's RTA Protocol offer (**r. 36.29(1)(a)**). In this case the court will order the claimant to pay the fixed costs under **r. 45.26** and interest on those fixed costs from the first business day after the deemed date of the RTA Protocol offer (**r. 36.29(2)**); or

(b) where the determination of the court is more than a defendant's RTA Protocol offer, but less than the claimant's RTA Protocol offer (**r. 36.29(1)(b)**). In this case the court will order the defendant to pay the fixed costs under **r. 45.20** (**r. 36.29(3)**); or

(c) where the determination of the court is equal or more than the claimant's RTA Protocol offer (**r. 36.29(1)(c)**). In this case the court will order the defendant to pay interest on the whole of the damages at a rate not exceeding 10 per cent above base rate for all or part of the period from the deemed date of the RTA Protocol offer, fixed costs under **r. 45.20**, and interest on those costs at a rate not exceeding 10 per cent above base rate.

Rule 36.21 governs cases where a defendant's Part 36 offer is made after a claim leaves the RTA Protocol but the offer is not accepted and the claimant fails to obtain a judgment more advantageous than the offer. In these cases the claimant is entitled to the relevant fixed costs in **Part 45** for the stage applicable at the end of the relevant period, and the defendant will be entitled to its costs thereafter, which must not exceed the relevant fixed costs (**r. 36.21(2)** and **(9)**).

Success and deductible amounts   CPR, **r. 36.30**, is similar to **r. 36.22(8)** and provides that the amount of a judgment is less than an RTA Protocol offer where the judgment is less than the offer once deductible amounts identified in the judgment are deducted. **8.58**

Cases where the RTA Protocol ceases to apply

The **RTA Protocol** ceases to apply in the following situations: **8.59**

(a) where, at any stage, the claimant notifies the defendant that the claim has now been revalued at more than £25,000 (**RTA Protocol, para. 4.3**);

(b) where the defendant notifies the claimant that it considers that inadequate mandatory information has been provided in the CNF (**paras 6.8** and **6.15(4)(a)**);

(c) where the defendant alleges contributory negligence (other than in relation to the claimant's admitted failure to wear a seat belt) (**para. 6.15(1)**);

(d) where the defendant does not admit liability within the 15 days allowed for sending the CNF response (**para. 6.15(3)**);

(e) where the defendant does not complete and send the CNF response within the 15 days allowed (**para. 6.15(2)**);

Commentary

(f)   where the defendant notifies the claimant that the defendant considers that if proceedings were issued the small claims track would be the normal track for that claim (**para. 6.15(4)(b)**);

(g)   where the defendant fails to pay the Stage 1 fixed costs within the 10-day period specified in **para. 6.18**, and, within 10 days thereafter, the claimant gives the defendant written notice that the claim will no longer continue under the protocol (**para. 6.19**);

(h)   where the claimant is not satisfied with the defendant's response to a request for an interim payment in Stage 2 (**paras 7.28 and 7.29**);

(i)   where the defendant gives notice to the claimant, within the initial 15-day consideration period after receiving the Stage 2 settlement pack, that the defendant considers that the small claims track would be the normal track for that claim (**para. 7.39(a)**);

(j)   where the defendant gives notice to the claimant, within the initial 15-day consideration period after receiving the Stage 2 settlement pack, withdrawing the admission of causation (**para. 7.39(b)**);

(k)   where the defendant does not respond within the initial 15-day consideration period (**para. 7.40**);

(l)   where a party withdraws an offer made in the Stage 2 settlement pack form after the total consideration period (**para. 7.46**);

(m)   where the defendant fails to make the Stage 2 payment (**para. 7.75**); and

(n)   where the claimant gives notice to the defendant that the claim is unsuitable for the protocol (for example, because there are complex issues of fact or law in relation to the vehicle-related damages) (**para. 7.76**).

Where a claim drops out of the RTA Protocol in Stage 1, pre-action conduct should continue under the **Pre-action Protocol for Personal Injury Claims** where appropriate (**RTA Protocol, para. 6.17**). Generally, the CNF will stand as the letter of claim for the purposes of the Personal Injury Protocol (**Pre-action Protocol for Personal Injury Claims, para. 5.5**), unless the CNF is regarded as inadequate. Where a case drops out of the RTA Protocol in Stage 2, further progress is often through starting a Part 7 claim (**RTA Protocol, paras 7.28, 7.29, 7.40, 7.46 and 7.75**). Claims which drop out of the protocol cannot subsequently re-enter the process (**para. 5.11**).

EL/PL PROTOCOL

8.60   The **Pre-action Protocol for Low Value Personal Injury (Employers' Liability and Public Liability) Claims** (the **EL/PL Protocol**) follows the same pattern as the **RTA Protocol** in almost identical terms, and adopts a similar three-stage process. A claim will be covered by the **EL/PL Protocol** if:

(a)   the claim arises from an accident occurring on or after 31 July 2013 (disease cases will be covered if no letter of claim was sent before 31 July 2013);

(b)   the claim includes damages in respect of personal injury;

(c)   the claimant values the claim between £1,000 and £25,000 on a full liability basis (**EL/PL Protocol, para. 4.1(3) and (4)**); and

(d)   the claim does not fall into any of the excluded categories set out in **para. 4.3**. There are 11 excluded categories, including claims where either party acts as a personal representative for a deceased person, clinical negligence claims and mesothelioma cases.

Fixed costs (in **CPR, rr. 45.16 to 45.29** for cases within the **EL/PL Protocol**, and **CPR, rr. 45.28A to 45.29L**, for cases after they leave the protocol or Stage 3 process) apply to EL/PL claims in the same way as they apply to claims in, and which leave, the **RTA Protocol** (see **8.55 and 70.17**). The amounts of the fixed costs are higher for EL and PL claims. The rules on **RTA Protocol** offers (**CPR, rr. 36.20, 36.21 and 36.24 to 36.30**; see **8.56 and 8.57**) also apply to **EL/PL Protocol** claims.

CLINICAL NEGLIGENCE PROTOCOL

The **Pre-action Protocol for the Resolution of Clinical Disputes** applies to all claims against   **8.61**
hospitals, doctors in general practice, dentists and other healthcare providers, whether NHS
or private (**para. 1.1**). The general aims of the protocol are (**para. 2.1**):

(a) to maintain or restore the patient-healthcare provider relationship in an open and
    transparent way;
(b) to reduce delay and ensure costs are proportionate; and
(c) to resolve as many disputes as possible without litigation.

Twelve more specific objectives are set out in **para. 2.2** and include:

(i)   providing an opportunity for healthcare providers to identify whether details of a notifi-
       able safety incident under the Health and Social Care Act 2008 (Regulated Activities)
       Regulations 2014 (SI 2014/2936), reg. 20, should be sent to the claimant;
(ii)   ensuring that sufficient medical and other information is disclosed promptly by both
       parties to enable each to understand the other's perspective and case, and to encourage
       early resolution;
(iii) supporting the efficient management of proceedings where litigation cannot be
       avoided; and
(iv)   discouraging prolonged pursuit of unmeritorious or prolonged defence of meritorious
       claims.

Both the claimant and the defendant are required to consider as early as possible whether the
claimant has reasonable needs that could be met by rehabilitation (**Pre-action Protocol for
the Resolution of Clinical Disputes, para. 3.9**). A defendant is encouraged to make an early
apology if that is appropriate (**para. 2.2(l)**).

Obtaining health records

Any request for health records by a claimant should provide sufficient information to alert the   **8.62**
defendant where there has been a serious adverse outcome, or if it may constitute a notifiable
safety incident. It should also be as specific as possible about the records sought, and include
a request for any relevant guidelines, analyses, protocols or polices and documents created in
relation to an adverse incident, notifiable safety incident or complaint (**Pre-action Protocol
for the Resolution of Clinical Disputes, para. 3.2**). Requests for clinical records should be
made using the approved standard forms in **annex B**.

Records should be provided within 40 days of the request, and for a cost not exceeding that
permissible under the Access to Health Records Act 1990 and/or the Data Protection Act
1998 (**Pre-action Protocol for the Resolution of Clinical Disputes, para. 3.4.1**). An application for pre-action disclosure under CPR, r. 31.16 can be made if the defendant fails to provide the records, or an explanation for any delay (**Pre-action Protocol for the Resolution of
Clinical Disputes, para. 3.7**). At the earliest opportunity the records should be placed in an
indexed and paginated bundle, which should be kept up to date (**para. 3.5**).

Steps required by the Clinical Negligence Protocol

Annex A of the **Pre-action Protocol for the Resolution of Clinical Disputes** set out the stages   **8.63**
to be followed before the commencement of proceedings. Following receipt and analysis of
the clinical records the claimant may wish to send a letter of notification to the defendant and
to the National Health Service Litigation Authority ('NHSLA'), using the template in **Annex
C1** (**paras 3.11.1 and 3.11.2**). This notifies the defendant that a letter of claim may follow
because a possible breach of duty has been identified. An acknowledgement should be sent
within 14 days of receipt identifying who will be dealing with the dispute (**para. 3.12.1**).

Commentary

The letter of claim will follow and it should be as detailed as suitable for the particular circumstances (**paras 3.13, 3.16**). Sufficient information should be provided to enable the defendant to focus its investigations and to put an initial value on the claim (**para. 3.18**). A template for the recommended contents is provided at **annex C2** to the protocol.

The letter of claim should be acknowledged by the healthcare provider within 14 days of receipt (**para. 3.23**). The healthcare provider should identify who will be dealing with the dispute. The healthcare provider then has four months in which to provide a 'reasoned answer', which should follow the suggested contents of the template in **annex C3**. If the claimant has made a Part 36 offer the letter of response should preferably include reasons if the offer is refused. If the defendant makes a Part 36 offer, the defendant should provide sufficient medical or other evidence to allow the claimant to evaluate the offer (**para. 3.26**). **Paragraphs 4.1 to 4.4** seek to encourage proportionality and flexibility over obtaining expert evidence, recognising the cost involved, but that separate expert opinions may be required on breach, causation, condition and prognosis, and for valuing aspects of the claim. Proceedings should not be issued until after four months from the letter of claim, unless there is a limitation problem or the patient's position needs to be protected by early issue.

The parties are encouraged to consider ADR, and **para. 5.2** of the protocol provides details of a number of forms of alternative dispute resolution. A final stocktake should be conducted if proceedings have to be issued (**para. 6**).

DISEASE AND ILLNESS PROTOCOL

8.64   The **Pre-action Protocol for Disease and Illness Claims** applies to all personal injuries claims where the injury takes the form of an illness or disease rather than a physical injury (**para. 2.1**). These tend to be complex cases, and are usually suitable for the multi-track regardless of the value of the claim. The protocol applies to any illness, whether physical or psychological, any disorder, ailment, affliction, complaint, malady or derangement, other than a physical or psychological injury caused solely by an accident or other similar single event (**para. 2.2**). It covers diseases and illnesses occurring in the workplace, and also those caused by, for example, the occupation of premises (where there may be an overlap with the **Pre-action Protocol for Housing Disrepair Cases**) or the use of products (including medications). The Disease and Illness Protocol is not intended to cover cases dealt with as group or class claims (**para. 2.4**). If the claimant's life expectancy is short, it may not be possible to follow the protocol and the defendant is expected to treat the claim with urgency (**para. 2.7**).

Disclosure of occupational and health records, and product data

8.65   Before sending a letter before claim, under the **Pre-action Protocol for Disease and Illness Claims**, the potential claimant is permitted to request copies of any relevant occupational or health records, and also to request copies of product data which may be relevant to a causation issue. The potential defendant should provide copies of the claimant's records within 40 days (**para. 4.3**), and the protocol says it is good practice to provide product data. If a defendant is in difficulties in providing the documents in time, this should be explained, with a reasonable time estimate for compliance (**para. 4.4**). Failure to comply may provide grounds for an application for pre-action disclosure (**para. 4.5, and see chapter 50**).

Records with third parties

8.66   Employment records with previous employers, and general practitioner and hospital records, should, if relevant, be sought by the claimant (**Pre-action Protocol for Disease and Illness Claims, para. 5.1**). If, on considering the records, the claimant decides not to pursue the claim, this decision should be communicated in writing to any defendants previously notified of the claim (**para. 5.3**).

Letter before claim, chronology and schedule of damages

Two copies of a letter before claim, primarily addressing liability issues, should be sent to **8.67** the defendant (one copy is for any insurer) (**Pre-action Protocol for Disease and Illness Claims, paras 6.1 to 6.4**). The standard format for the letter is laid down in **annex B of the protocol**. It should identify relevant documents (**para. 6.6**) and identify any other potential defendants (**para. 6.7**). A chronology, including dates of exposure to the substance alleged to be the cause of the complaint, should be sent with the letter before claim (**para. 6.5**). A schedule of special damages, with copies of supporting documents, should be sent to the defendant as soon as practicable, particularly where the defendant admits liability (**para. 8.1**).

Response

The defendant should send an acknowledgment identifying any liability insurer within **8.68** 21 days of posting of the letter before claim (**Pre-action Protocol for Disease and Illness Claims, para. 7.1**). The response should make clear which insurer is dealing with the claim where there may be multiple defendants, and should give the names of any additional insurers during a work career, which can be important in cases concerning diseases such as asbestosis. The defendant will need to investigate the claim, and must provide a reasoned answer to the letter before claim, stating a number of matters including the extent to which the claim is admitted or denied, within 90 days of the date of the acknowledgment letter (**para. 7.3**). Copies of documents material to the issues should be sent with the reply. If 90 days is insufficient time, the defendant may seek an agreed extension if there is a reasonable justification (**para. 7.5**). If the claimant's life expectancy is short, it may not be possible to follow the protocol and the defendant is expected to treat the claim with urgency (**para. 2.7**).

Experts in disease and illness claims

Expert evidence may be required dealing with: **8.69**

(a) knowledge, fault, causation and apportionment;
(b) the claimant's condition and prognosis; and
(c) valuing aspects of the claim.

The **Pre-action Protocol for Disease and Illness Claims** recognises that it is important to adopt a flexible approach to the decisions that have to be made about obtaining expert evidence in these claims (**paras 9.2 and 9.3**). Joint selection, joint instruction, separate experts, and claimants disclosing medical evidence before defendants take a view on causation are all canvassed in the protocol. Different approaches may be appropriate for different issues within a claim. Care must be taken before the parties decide on instructing their own experts, because the court may subsequently rule that doing so was unreasonable (**para. 9.7**).

Commencing proceedings and negotiations

Proceedings should not be commenced within the three-month investigation period unless **8.70** there is a limitation problem or some other reason for needing to protect the claimant's position (**Pre-action Protocol for Disease and Illness Claims, paras 6.10 and 6.11**). Further, the defendant should be given 21 days from disclosure of reports to allow for attempts to settle the claim without the need for proceedings (**paras 10.1 and 10.3**). **Paragraph 2A.1** requires the parties to consider whether some form of ADR would be more suitable than litigation. Both sides may be required to provide the court with evidence that ADR was considered. Litigation is regarded as a last resort, and proceedings should not be issued while settlement is being actively explored. It is expressly recognised that the parties cannot be forced to mediate or enter into any form of ADR (**para. 2A.4**), but a failure to comply with the aim of **para. 2A.1** may be taken into account on costs.

Before proceedings are commenced the parties should carry out a 'stocktake' of the issues in dispute and the evidence required (**para. 10.2**). If an insurer is acting for the defendant, it is good practice to give the insurer seven to 14 days' notice to nominate solicitors to accept service of the proposed proceedings (**para. 10.5**).

HOUSING DISREPAIR PROTOCOL

8.71   The **Pre-action Protocol for Housing Disrepair Cases** applies to all civil claims arising from the condition of residential premises, and may include a related personal injury claim (**para. 3.1**). If the personal injury element requires an expert report other than a general practitioner's letter, **Pre-action Protocol for Personal Injury Claims** should be followed for that element of the claim (**Pre-action Protocol for Housing Disrepair Cases, para. 3.5**). This protocol does not apply to disrepair claims raised as a counterclaim or set-off (because, by definition, a claim has already commenced, see **para. 3.3**). Where housing disrepair is raised by a counterclaim or set-off, the landlord and tenant will still be expected to act reasonably in exchanging information and trying to settle the claim at an early stage (**para. 3.3**).

The protocol should be followed in all cases, whatever the value of the damages claim (**para. 3.4**). It applies to disrepair claims brought by tenants, members of the tenant's family (**para. 3.1**), and to 'lessees', which is presumably a typographical error for licensees.

Notification to landlord

8.72   As a matter of substantive law (see *O'Brien v Robinson* [1973] AC 912), the tenant must show that the landlord has received sufficient information about the alleged defects to put a reasonable person on inquiry as to whether repairs are necessary. Nothing in the **Pre-action Protocol for Housing Disrepair Cases** avoids this requirement, the protocol being aimed at seeking to resolve cases where the problem persists despite notice.

Where repairs are urgent, the claimant may send a letter notifying the landlord of the claim before the letter of claim is sent (**para. 5.1**).

Tenant's letter of claim

8.73   A tenant's letter of claim should be sent at the earliest reasonable opportunity (**Pre-action Protocol for Housing Disrepair Cases, para. 5.2**). Detailed requirements for the information to be included in this letter, in so far as it has not been given in an early notification letter, are set out in **para. 5.2**, with template letters at **annex A**, a template schedule of disrepair at **annex C**, and a template special damages form at **annex D**. A letter of claim should identify the proposed expert, and enclose a proposed letter of instruction (in the form of the template at **annex B**). Copies of documents the tenant relies upon should also be enclosed, together with a list of the documents the tenant wishes the landlord to disclose (see **para. 5.3**).

Landlord's response

8.74   The landlord should provide a written response within 20 working days of receipt of the first letter from the tenant (**Pre-action Protocol for Housing Disrepair Cases, para. 6.2**). The response should include copies of the records or documents requested by the tenant and a response on appointing an expert (**para. 6.2**). This letter may state whether liability is admitted, take any point about lack of notice or difficulty in gaining access, include a full schedule of intended works, and any offer of compensation or costs, although a response on these points may be delayed until up to 20 working days from receipt of the report of a single joint expert (**para. 6.3**).

Evidence

The **Pre-action Protocol for Housing Disrepair Cases** reminds tenants that photographic and video evidence before and after any works may be useful in disrepair claims (**para. 7.1(c)**).   **8.75**

Experts

There will be some cases where no expert evidence is required (**Pre-action Protocol for Housing Disrepair Cases, para. 7.1(c)**), but generally it is expected that the parties will agree on a single joint expert (**para. 7.2(a)**). The expert should be asked to report on all items of disrepair which the landlord ought reasonably to have known, or which the expert should reasonably report on, and should be asked to prepare a schedule of works and an estimate of the costs of repair, and to list any urgent works (**para. 7.1(d)**). The single joint expert should inspect the property within 20 working days of the landlord's response (**para. 7.4(a)**), and should send copies of his or her report to both parties within 10 working days of the inspection (**para. 7.4(b)**).   **8.76**

If the parties cannot agree joint instructions, the landlord should send the tenant a copy of its letter of instruction (the tenant having already done so, see **8.73**). If it is not possible to agree on a single joint expert, the parties should attempt to agree to a joint inspection of the premises by the different experts each is instructing, to take place at the same time (**para. 7.3(a)**). Where there is a joint inspection, the experts should produce an agreed schedule of works to both parties within 10 working days of the inspection (**para. 7.4(c), (d)**).

The tenant is under a duty to allow the landlord reasonable access for inspection and repairs (**para. 7.6**). Each party should normally pay half the fees of a jointly instructed expert (**para. 7.7**).

Costs, negotiations and proceedings

If the tenant's claim is settled without proceedings on terms that justify raising the claim, the landlord 'will' pay the tenant's reasonable costs (**Pre-action Protocol for Housing Disrepair Cases, para. 11**). Form N260 can be used to inform the landlord of the amount of these costs, which should be calculated according to the track which the claim would have been allocated to if litigation had been started (*Birmingham City Council v Lee* [2008] EWCA Civ 891, [2009] HLR 15). The appropriate order to make is one for costs on the appropriate basis up to the date the repair work is done (*Birmingham City Council v Lee*).   **8.77**

The purpose of the protocol is to prevent unnecessary proceedings, so the parties are required to consider whether some form of ADR would be more suitable than litigation (**para. 4.1**). Both sides may be required to provide the court with evidence that ADR was considered. A number of different ADR procedures that might be appropriate are set out in **para. 4.2**. The parties will be expected to have attempted to agree a schedule of works, a timetable for implementation, and any claim for compensation before a claim is issued. If limitation is an issue, the tenant should ask for an extension of the limitation period in the first letter to the landlord so the parties can comply with the protocol (**para. 10(a)**). Before proceedings are commenced the parties must review their respective positions, and at least try to narrow the issues (**para. 8**).

DILAPIDATIONS (COMMERCIAL PROPERTY) PROTOCOL

Claims for damages for dilapidations against tenants at the termination of commercial tenancies are governed by the **Pre-action Protocol for Claims for Damages in Relation to the Physical**   **8.78**

State of Commercial Property at Termination of a Tenancy, the 'Dilapidations Protocol', which came into effect on 1 January 2012. The nature and extent of the work that may have to be done to demised premises at the end of a lease will depend on the terms of the lease, so expressions such as 'dilapidations', 'repair', 'reinstatement' and 'redecoration' are not defined by the protocol.

Schedule of dilapidations and quantified demand

8.79   A schedule of dilapidations should be compiled by the landlord setting out what the land-lord considers to be the breaches, the works required, and the landlord's costings (**Dilapidations Protocol, para. 3.1**). This takes the form of a Scott schedule, with an add-itional column for the tenant's responses. Slightly different versions of the schedule can be found in **annexes B** and **C** to the **Dilapidations Protocol**. **Annex B** is for use where the schedule is compiled by the landlord's surveyor, and **Annex C** is where it is compiled by the landlord. In compiling and signing the schedule, a surveyor should have regard to the prin-ciples laid down in the Royal Institute of Chartered Surveyors' Guidance Note on Dilapidations (**Dilapidations Protocol, para. 3.5**). The schedule of dilapidations should be sent to the tenant electronically (**para. 3.7**) within 56 days of the termination of the lease (**para. 3.3**). Also within 56 days of the termination of the lease, the landlord should send the tenant a quantified demand setting out all aspects of the dispute and substantiating the monetary sum sought as damages (**paras 4.2.1** and **4.2.3**) supported by invoices or detailed estimates (**para. 4.3**). The quantified demand should confirm the landlord and/or its sur-veyor will attend a meeting or meetings on a without-prejudice basis to seek to agree as many items as possible (**paras 4.2.2** and **7**), and should specify a period, usually within 56 days, by which the tenant should respond.

Response and subsequent steps

8.80   The tenant's response should be set out by using the additional column in the schedule of dilapidations (**Dilapidations Protocol, para. 5.3**). The entries must be in sufficient detail to enable the landlord to understand clearly the tenant's views on each item, and must comply with the principles laid down in the Royal Institute of Chartered Surveyors' Guidance Note on Dilapidations (**Dilapidations Protocol, para. 5.4**). If the tenant considers that items in the schedule of dilapidations are likely to be superseded by works to be carried out by the landlord or by the landlord's intentions for the property, this should be stated in the response with particulars (**para. 5.6**).

The landlord and tenant and/or their respective surveyors should meet within 28 days after the tenant's response on a without-prejudice basis to seek to agree as many items as possible (**para. 7**). They should also consider whether some form of ADR would be more suitable than litigation (**para. 8.1**), and may have to provide evidence that ADR was considered. If proceed-ings are to be issued, the landlord should quantify its loss by providing a detailed breakdown of the issues and consequential losses to the tenant (**para. 9.1**). If a formal diminution valu-ation is required, it should be prepared by a valuer (**para. 9.2**). Details of the landlord's inten-tions must be supplied to the tenant if remedial works have not been carried out (**para. 9.3**). Any diminution valuation from the tenant should be supplied by the tenant to the landlord within 56 days of the landlord's detailed breakdown of issues (**para. 9.6**). A final stocktake, reviewing their respective positions, the state of the papers, the evidence, and any possible narrowing of the issues, should be undertaken before proceedings are issued (**para. 10**).

POSSESSION CLAIMS BY SOCIAL LANDLORDS PROTOCOL

8.81   The **Pre-action Protocol for Possession Claims by Social Landlords** applies to residential possession claims by social landlords and private registered providers of social housing where possession is sought solely on the ground of rent arrears. It does not apply to tenancies involving long leases or where there is no security of tenure (**para. 1.1**).

Pre-action steps under the Possession Claims by Social Landlords Protocol

Where a tenant falls into arrears of rent, the landlord is required to contact the tenant as soon as reasonably possible to discuss the cause of the arrears, the tenant's financial circumstances, the tenant's entitlement to benefits (including housing benefit), and how the arrears are to be paid (**Pre-action Protocol for Possession Claims by Social Landlords, para. 2.1**). Pre-action contact is encouraged, with the aim of seeking to achieve agreement on affordable sums for the tenant to pay towards the arrears (**para. 2.2**). It is recognised that rent arrears cases are often part of a wider debt problem (**para. 2.7**). Where appropriate the landlord should offer to assist the tenant with any claim for housing benefit (**para. 2.5**) and should advise the tenant to seek assistance from citizens' advice or debt advice agencies (**para. 2.7**). Extra care should be taken where the tenant is under 18, unable to read or otherwise vulnerable (**para. 1.6**).

Pre-action correspondence should set out clearly any time limits the landlord wants the tenant to comply with (**para. 2.2**). Upon request, the landlord should provide the tenant with copies of rent statements in a comprehensible form from the date when arrears first arose, and in all cases should provide the tenant with quarterly rent statements covering the previous 13 weeks (**para. 2.3**). Possession proceedings should not be commenced (**para. 2.6**) against a tenant who can demonstrate that:

(a) all the evidence required to process a housing benefit or universal credit (housing element) claim has been provided to the local authority;

(b) there is a reasonable expectation of eligibility for housing benefit or universal credit (housing element); and

(c) other sums not covered by housing benefit or universal credit (housing element) have been paid.

After service of a statutory notice, the landlord should make reasonable attempts to contact the tenant to discuss the amount of arrears, its causes, repayment and the housing benefit or universal credit (housing element) position (**para. 2.8**). Proceedings should be postponed for so long as the tenant keeps to any agreement to pay the current rent and a reasonable amount towards the arrears (**para. 2.9**). If the tenant breaks such an agreement, the landlord should warn the tenant of the intention to bring proceedings, and give the tenant clear time limits within which to comply (**para. 2.9**). ADR should be considered, and litigation should be a last resort (**para. 2.10**).

Litigation steps under the Possession Claims Based on Rent Arrears Protocol

Possession hearings are often marked by the non-attendance of tenants, so the **Pre-action Protocol for Possession Claims Based on Rent Arrears** requires landlords to inform tenants of the date and time of any court hearing, and to have evidence available that they have done so (**para. 2.12(a)**). Another common problem is confusion at the hearing over the exact amount of arrears, so **para. 2.11** requires landlords to provide their tenants with up-to-date rent statements and any information available to the landlord on the housing benefit or universal credit (housing element) position at least 10 days before the hearing. The landlord should agree to postpone court proceedings if the tenant complies with any agreement to pay current rent and a reasonable amount towards the arrears (**para. 2.12(b)**).

Failure by a landlord to comply with the protocol may result in costs sanctions, and may be taken into account when considering whether (if the case is brought on a non-mandatory

8.82

8.83

Commentary

ground) to adjourn, strike out or dismiss the claim (**para. 2.13**). Unreasonable non-compliance by the tenant may be taken into account in deciding whether it is reasonable to make a possession order (**para. 2.14**).

POSSESSION CLAIMS BASED ON MORTGAGE OR HOME PURCHASE PLAN ARREARS PROTOCOL

8.84   The **Pre-action Protocol for Possession Claims Based on Mortgage or Home Purchase Plan Arrears in Respect of Residential Property** applies (see **para. 4.1**) to potential money and/or possession claims based on:

(a) first charge residential mortgages and home purchase plans regulated by the Financial Services Authority under the Financial Services and Markets Act 2000;

(b) second charge mortgages over residential property and other secured loans regulated under the Consumer Credit Act 1974 on residential property; and

(c) unregulated residential mortgages.

Where a borrower falls into arrears the lender must provide the borrower with details of the monthly instalments and amounts paid over the last two years, the amount of arrears, the total capital outstanding, and whether interest or charges will be added (with an estimate) (**para. 5.1**). Where appropriate the lender must also provide the required regulatory information sheet or the National Homelessness Advice Service booklet on mortgage arrears (**para. 5.1(a)**). The lender must advise the borrower to make early contact with the housing department and, where necessary, refer the borrower to appropriate sources of independent debt advice (**para. 5.3**). The parties or their representatives must take all reasonable steps to discuss the causes of the arrears, the borrower's financial circumstances, whether the causes of the arrears are temporary or long term, and whether the borrower may be able to pay the arrears in a reasonable time (**para. 5.4**).

A possession claim should normally be a last resort. The parties should instead consider whether it is reasonable and appropriate (**para. 7.1**) to:

(a) extend the term of the mortgage;

(b) change the type of mortgage;

(c) defer payment of interest due under the mortgage;

(d) capitalise the arrears; or

(e) make use of any government forbearance initiatives in which the lender chooses to participate.

The lender must respond promptly to any proposal for payment, and should give written reasons for any refusal of an offer within 10 business days of the proposal (**para. 5.6**). If the lender makes a proposal for payment, it must include sufficient details to enable the borrower to understand the implications of the proposal, and the borrower must be given a reasonable time to consider the proposals (**para. 5.7**). If the borrower fails to comply with an agreement, the lender should give the borrower 15 business days' notice of intention to start a possession claim unless the borrower remedies the breach (**para. 5.8**).

Postponing the start of a mortgage possession claim

8.85   A lender must consider postponing the commencement of a possession claim where the borrower has submitted a claim under a mortgage payment protection policy or to the Department for Work and Pensions ('DWP') for support for mortgage interest. The borrower will need to demonstrate that all the necessary evidence required to process the claim has been provided to the insurer or DWP, that there is a reasonable expectation of eligibility, and that the borrower is able to pay instalments not covered by the policy or scheme (**Pre-action Protocol for Possession Claims Based on Mortgage or Home Purchase Plan Arrears in Respect of Residential Property, para. 6.1**).

Similarly, the lender must consider postponing the start of possession proceedings if the borrower can demonstrate taking reasonable steps to market the property at an appropriate price (**para. 6.2**). The borrower should provide the lender with a copy of the particulars of sale, the energy performance certificate and details of any purchase offers. The borrower should also provide details of the estate agent dealing with the sale, and authorise the agent to communicate with the lender about the progress of any sale and the borrower's conduct during the process (**para. 6.3**).

If the lender decides not to postpone possession proceedings despite a claim under a payment protection policy, support for mortgage interest, mortgage rescue scheme or proposed sale, the lender must inform the borrower of the reasons at least five business days before starting proceedings (**para. 6.4**). The lender must complete a mortgage pre-action protocol checklist, form N123. Two completed copies of this form will be required for the hearing (**PD 55A, para. 5.5**).

CONSTRUCTION AND ENGINEERING DISPUTES PROTOCOL

The **Pre-action Protocol for Construction and Engineering Disputes** applies to all construction and engineering disputes, including professional negligence claims against architects, engineers and quantity surveyors. It applies to additional claims under **CPR, Part 20** (*Daejan Investments Ltd v Park West Club Ltd* [2003] EWHC 2872 (TCC), [2004] BLR 223), although a pragmatic approach has to be taken as there will often be limited time in which to comply with the protocol, issue the claim and get the case ready for any trial (*Alfred McAlpine Capital Projects Ltd v SIAC (UK) Ltd* [2005] EWHC 3139 (TCC), [2006] BLR 139). It applies to claims for the payment of an engineering firm's fees, even though such a claim could be characterised as a debt recovery case (*Cundall Johnson and Partners v Whipps Cross University Hospital NHS Trust* [2007] EWHC 2178 (TCC), [2007] BLR 520). However, a claimant is not expected to follow the protocol where the proposed proceedings:

8.86

(a) are for the purpose of enforcing an adjudicator's decision under the Housing Grants, Construction and Regeneration Act 1996, s. 108;
(b) include a claim for an interim injunction;
(c) are expected to proceed to an application for summary judgment; or
(d) relate to the same or substantially the same issues as have been the subject of a recent adjudication under the 1996 Act or some other formal ADR procedure.

In additional claims under **CPR, Part 20**, care should be taken before granting a stay of the main proceedings to enable full compliance with the protocol by the parties to the additional claim if that will mean breaking trial directions (*Orange Personal Communications Services Ltd v Hoare Lea* [2008] EWHC 223 (TCC), [2009] Bus LR D24).

The **Pre-action Protocol for Construction and Engineering Disputes** must not be used as a tactical device to secure advantage or to generate unnecessary costs (**para. 1.5**). This means that in lower-value claims the letter before claim and response should be simple, and the costs of both sides should be kept to a modest level.

Requirements of the Construction and Engineering Disputes Protocol

The protocol timetable starts with a letter before claim being sent by the claimant to the proposed defendants (**Pre-action Protocol for Construction and Engineering Disputes, para. 3**). This should include details of all the proposed defendants, a clear summary of

8.87

the facts on which the claim or claims are based, and the allegations forming the basis of each claim. This will include reference to the contractual terms and statutory provisions relied upon, the nature of the relief claimed, and a breakdown of how any damages are quantified or liquidated claim is calculated. It does not have to identify every detail on liability, or the exact amount claimed (*T. J. Brent Ltd v Black and Veatch Consulting Ltd* [2008] EWHC 1497 (TCC), 119 Con LR 1). If a claim has previously been made and rejected, the claimant must explain the reasons for disagreeing with the rejection of the claim. If any experts on whom the claimant wishes to rely have already been instructed, the letter before claim must include their names and state the issues to which the experts' evidence is directed.

The defendants should acknowledge receipt of the letter before claim within 14 days (**para. 4.1**). If there is no response, the claimant becomes entitled to issue proceedings. It may also be necessary for a claimant to issue proceedings at an early stage if the expiry of the limitation period is approaching (**para. 6**).

If a defendant intends to dispute the court's jurisdiction, or allege that the claim should be referred to arbitration, or allege that the wrong defendant has been identified, this should be made clear by a letter of objection which should be sent within 28 days after the letter before claim (**para. 4.2.1**). In *Bovis Homes Ltd v Kendrick Construction Ltd* [2009] EWHC 1359 (TCC), [2009] 5 Costs LR 778, failure to mention a preference for arbitration in the letter of objection resulted in an order that the defendant should pay the costs thrown away when it later sought a stay of proceedings under the Arbitration Act 1996, s. 9. If a letter of objection is sent, there is no need to make a substantive response to the letter before claim (**para. 4.2.2**). If there is no letter of objection, the defendants have to send a letter of response (**para. 4.3.1**). This should normally be sent within 28 days after the letter before claim, although the parties may agree to a longer period of up to four months. A letter of response will set out in detail which parts of the claim are agreed, which parts are rejected and why. If a defendant raises an allegation of contributory negligence, a summary of the facts relied on should be included in the letter of response and the claimant should reply with detailed responses within 28 days (**para. 4.4**). Neither the letter before claim nor the defendant's response are required to resemble pleadings, either in their length or in their detail (*Cundall Johnson and Partners v Whipps Cross University Hospital NHS Trust* [2007] EWHC 2178 (TCC), [2007] BLR 520).

Within 28 days of completion of this correspondence, the parties should normally arrange a without-prejudice meeting to seek to agree what are the main issues, identify the root problem and consider how to resolve matters without recourse to litigation (**para. 5.2**). If litigation cannot be avoided, the parties should seek to agree the steps they should take in accordance with the overriding objective, including how best to obtain any expert evidence that might be necessary, the extent of the disclosure of documents required, and how best to minimise costs and prevent delay (**para. 5.5**). In respect of specific issues, or the dispute as a whole, the parties should consider whether some form of ADR would be more suitable than litigation. It is expressly recognised that no party can, however, be forced to mediate or adopt any other form of ADR (**para. 5.4**). Although pre-action meetings are 'without prejudice', this does not prevent any of the parties disclosing that meetings did or did not take place, any refusal to attend and the result of any agreements made (**para. 5.6**).

DEFAMATION PROTOCOL

8.88 Since the primary limitation period for defamation claims is only one year, it is recognised that time is of the essence regarding pre-action skirmishing in this area. The claimant is, under the protocol, required to notify the defendant in writing of the claim at the earliest reasonable opportunity (**Pre-action Protocol for Defamation, para. 3.1**). The letter before claim should include as much detail as possible, including an identification of the publication or broadcast containing the words complained of, factual inaccuracies, where relevant, any facts tying the claimant to the alleged defamatory statement and any special facts relevant to interpretation, and the nature of the remedies sought (**para. 3.2**). The defendant is required to respond as soon as reasonably possible, and normally within 14 days (**para. 3.4**). The letter of response should say whether or the extent to which the claim is accepted. If the claim is rejected, the defendant should explain why, indicating any facts relied upon in support of any substantive defence. If more information is sought, this should be stated in the response (**para. 3.5**). Both parties are expected to act reasonably so as to keep costs proportionate, and should consider whether the matter could be referred to ADR (**paras 3.6 to 3.9**).

PROFESSIONAL NEGLIGENCE PRE-ACTION PROTOCOL

Introduction

The **Professional Negligence Pre-action Protocol** applies to any claim against a professional, other than a construction professional or healthcare provider, as a result of that professional's alleged negligence or breach of fiduciary duty, although there may be other types of claim for which the protocol is appropriate (**para. 1.1**). It also applies where allegations of professional negligence are raised in response to a claim by the professional for payment of the relevant fees (**para. 1.3**). The protocol is not intended to replace other forms of dispute resolution, and parties are under the usual duty to consider some form of ADR (**paras 2.3 and 12**). The standards set in this protocol will be treated by the courts as the normal, reasonable approach in professional negligence cases (**para. 3.1**). The protocol contains no definition of 'professional'. Should it become an issue whether a defendant is or is not a professional, the version of the protocol which applied before 6 April 2015 (at para. C2.3) reminded parties of the overriding need to act reasonably and rather than argue about the definition of 'professional', recommended that they use the protocol, adapting it where appropriate.

8.89

Preliminary notice

As soon as the claimant decides there is a reasonable chance that a claim will be brought against a professional, the claimant is encouraged to notify the professional by letter, referred to as a preliminary notice (**Professional Negligence Pre-action Protocol, para. 5.1**) informing the recipient of the claimant's identity, a brief outline of the grievance against the professional and, if possible, an indication of the financial value of the claim (**para. 5.2**). The letter should also request the professional to notify his or her professional indemnity insurers, if any (**para. 5.3**). Receipt of the letter is required to be acknowledged by the professional within 21 days (**para. 5.4**). If the claimant does not send any further correspondence to the professional over the next six months, the claimant must notify the professional whether it is intended to pursue the claim (**para. 5.5**).

8.90

Letter of claim

As soon as the claimant considers that there are grounds for a claim against the professional a detailed letter of claim should be sent (**Professional Negligence Pre-action Protocol, para. 6.1**). Normally a letter of claim should not be expressed to be without prejudice and it should include (**para. 6.2**):

(a) the identity of any other parties to the dispute;

(b) a clear chronological summary of the facts on which the claim is based identifying and enclosing copies of key documents;

8.91

(c) any reasonable requests for relevant documents which are held by the professional;

(d) the allegations against the professional, identifying the acts and omissions relied upon;

(e) explanation of how the alleged error has caused the loss claimed;

(f) estimate and calculation of the financial loss together with documentary evidence in support or an explanation of why details of the loss cannot be supplied, if this is the case. Any non-financial redress should also be made clear;

(g) confirmation of whether or not an expert has been appointed and if so, the identity of the expert, his or her discipline and the date of appointment;

(h) request that the letter of claim is immediately forwarded to the professional's insurers.

Although the letter of claim is not intended to have the same status as a statement of case, if it differs materially from a statement of case in subsequent proceedings, the court may decide to impose sanctions (**para. 6.3**). Where the claimant has sent other letters of claim to other parties in relation to this or a related dispute, those letters should also be copied to the professional (**para. 6.4**).

The letter of claim should be acknowledged by the professional in a letter of acknowledgment within 21 days of receipt (**para. 7.1**).

Investigations

8.92   The professional will have three months from the date of the letter of acknowledgment to investigate the claim (**Professional Negligence Pre-action Protocol, para. 8.2**). Any difficulty in complying with that period should be notified to the claimant as soon as possible, together with an explanation of what is being done to resolve the problem and when the professional expects to complete the investigations. The claimant should agree to any reasonable request for an extension of the three-month period (**para. 8.3**). During this stage and throughout, the parties should provide each other with whatever relevant information or documentation is reasonably requested (**para. 8.4**). Any potential third party claim must be notified to the claimant as soon as possible (**para. 8.5**). As with the other protocols, the early exchange of information is considered conducive to early settlement.

Letter of response and letter of settlement

8.93   As soon as the professional's investigations are complete, the claimant should be sent:

(a) a letter of response, or

(b) a letter of settlement, or

(c) both.

These may be contained within a single letter (**Professional Negligence Pre-action Protocol, para. B5.1**).

The letter of response will normally not be expressed to be without prejudice (**para. 9.2.1**). It should be a reasoned answer to the claimant's allegations. If the claim is admitted, the letter of response should say so.

If only part of the claim is admitted, the letter of response should make clear which parts of the claim are admitted and which are denied.

If the claim is denied in whole or in part, the letter of response should include specific comments on the allegations against the professional and, if the claimant's version of events is disputed, the professional should provide his or her version of events.

If the professional is unable to admit or deny the claim, the professional should say why and any further information which is required should be identified.

If the professional disputes the estimate of the claimant's financial loss, the letter of response should set out the professional's estimate. If an estimate cannot be provided, the professional should explain why and should state when it will be possible to provide an estimate. This information should be sent to the claimant as soon as reasonably possible.

Where additional documents are relied upon in the letter of response, copies should be provided.

The letter of response is not intended to have the same formal status as a defence. However, if it differs materially from the defence in subsequent proceedings, the court may decide to impose sanctions (**para. 9.2.2**).

A letter of settlement may be in an open or without-prejudice letter and should be sent if the professional intends to make proposals for settlement (**para. 9.3.1**). It should contain the professional's views on the claim identifying those issues which the professional believes are likely to remain in dispute and those which are not. This information is not required if it is in the letter of response. The letter of settlement should contain a settlement proposal or identify any further information which is required before the professional can formulate proposals. Copies of additional documents should be provided where these are relied upon.

Effect of letter of response and/or letter of settlement

Where the letter of response denies the claim in its entirety and there is no letter of settlement, it is open to the claimant to commence proceedings (**Professional Negligence Pre-action Protocol, para. 9.4.1**). Otherwise, the professional and the claimant should begin negotiations with the aim of reaching a conclusion within six months of the date of the letter of acknowledgment (not from the date of the letter of response) (**para. 9.4.2**). If the claim cannot be resolved within this period, the parties should agree within 14 days of the end of the period whether the period should be extended and, if so, by how long (**para. 9.4.3**). They should also identify the issues which remain in dispute and those which are agreed. If an extension of time for settlement negotiations cannot be agreed, the claimant may commence proceedings.

8.94

Alternative dispute resolution

The **Professional Negligence Pre-action Protocol, para. 12** requires the parties to consider whether some form of ADR would be more suitable than litigation. If proceedings are issued, both sides may be required to provide the court with evidence that ADR was considered. Litigation is regarded as a last resort, and proceedings should not be issued while settlement is being actively explored. A failure to comply may be taken into account on costs.

8.95

Experts

The **Professional Negligence Pre-action Protocol, para. 11.2**, recognises that in professional negligence cases the parties will require flexibility on the issue of experts, leaving it to the parties to cooperate when making decisions on which experts to instruct and whether this should be on a joint or separate basis. It reminds the parties of the duty in **CPR, r. 35.1**, to restrict expert evidence to that which is reasonably required to resolve the dispute, and that permission is required for the use of expert evidence if proceedings are commenced (**r. 35.4**).

8.96

Proceedings

Unless it is necessary, for example, to obtain protection against the expiry of a relevant limitation period, court proceedings should not be commenced until the letter of response denies the claim in its entirety and there is no letter of settlement, or the period for negotiation has come to an end (**Professional Negligence Pre-action Protocol, para. 14.1**). If the claimant

8.97

Commentary

does intend to institute proceedings, where possible 14 days' written notice should be given to the professional, indicating the court within which the claimant is intending to commence litigation (**para. 14.3**). If proceedings are commenced prior to the parties following the procedures in the protocol, they are encouraged to agree to apply to the court for a stay of proceedings while the protocol procedures are followed (**para. 14.2**).

SHORTER TRIALS SCHEME

8.98   Pre-action conduct in claims likely to join the shorter trials scheme (see **42.34**) starts with sending a letter of claim stating the intention to adopt the shorter trials scheme procedure, and giving succinct but sufficient details of the claim to enable the potential defendant to understand and to investigate the allegations (**PD 51N, paras 2.17 and 2.19**). This letter may be dispensed with for good reasons, such as urgency. The defendant should respond within 14 days stating whether they agree or oppose invoking the shorter trial procedure, or stating they have insufficient information to commit to the scheme (**para. 2.20**). There are no other prescribed pre-action requirements, other than an obligation on the claimant to serve the claim form and particulars of claim promptly following the defendant's response (**para. 2.25**).

Chapter 9   Notices before Action

LETTER BEFORE CLAIM

Whether a claim is governed by a specific pre-action protocol or by the general requirements **9.1**
in **PD Pre-action Conduct and Protocols**, generally a letter before claim should be sent before
starting proceedings. The matters to include in the letter before claim will be laid down either
in the specific protocol, or in **PD Pre-action Conduct and Protocols, para. 6**. Exceptional
cases where a letter before claim is dispensed with are where an application needs to be made
urgently or secretly, where there is no other party to engage with, or where the matter is agreed
or non-contentious (see **8.2**). The court has a discretion to order a claimant who issues proceedings without giving warning to the other side to pay indemnity-basis costs (*Phoenix Finance Ltd v
Fédération Internationale de l'Automobile* [2002] EWHC 1242 (Ch), *The Times*, 27 June 2002; and
see **8.10**).

ROAD TRAFFIC CASES

Introduction

A person who sustains injury in a road traffic accident has a cause of action against a negligent **9.2**
driver but not against his or her insurers. Damages may be recovered direct from the insurers
provided the claimant gives the insurers notice of the proceedings against the defendant driver
either before or within seven days after the commencement of the proceedings (Road Traffic
Act 1988, s. 152). The phrase 'commencement of proceedings' has its ordinary meaning (*Silver
v Goodall* [1997] PIQR P451). The **Pre-action Protocol for Personal Injury Claims, para. 3.4**,
states that a letter before claim should ask a potential defendant for insurance details.

Notice must be something more formal than a casual mention of proceedings in conversation
(*Herbert v Railway Passengers Assurance Co.* [1938] 1 All ER 650). However, notice given in a telephone conversation, dealing mainly with obtaining details of the insured driver, with a secretary employed by the insurer was held to be sufficient in *Nawaz v Crowe Insurance Group* [2003]
EWCA Civ 316, [2003] PIQR P27. A loosely written letter may not be sufficient notice (*Weldrick v
Essex and Suffolk Equitable Insurance Society Ltd* (1949) 83 Ll L Rep 91, in which the letter which
purported to give notice was found to be no more than an intimation that proceedings might
be brought).

A pre-action protocol letter before claim is insufficient notification of the proceedings for the
purposes of the Road Traffic Act 1988, s. 152(1)(a) (*Wylie v Wake* [2000] RTR 291). Lack of
notice may be raised as a defence at any stage of the proceedings and the fact that a claim has
been defended on its merits does not constitute a waiver of lack of notice (*Wylie v Wake*).

Motor Insurers' Bureau

9.3   It sometimes happens that a claimant sustains injury in a road traffic accident arising out of the negligence of a driver who is uninsured or untraceable. In return for the business generated by compulsory motor insurance, the insurance industry has set up the Motor Insurers' Bureau (MIB) to enable claimants to obtain compensation in circumstances in which they would be unable to bring effective proceedings. There are two agreements between the MIB and the Minister for Transport, one dealing with uninsured drivers and the other with untraced drivers. The question whether the MIB is an emanation of the State (which is relevant in cases on whether these agreements are a sufficient compliance with the Second Council Directive (84/5/EEC), see **9.4**) has been referred to the Court of Justice of the European Union by the Court of Appeal (*McCall v Poulton* [2008] EWCA Civ 1313, [2009] PIQR P8). See also Donald Williams and Malcolm Johnson, *Guide to Motor Insurers' Bureau Claims*, 10th edn. (London: Law Society, 2012).

Uninsured drivers

9.4   Under the Motor Insurers' Bureau (Compensation of Victims of Uninsured Drivers) Agreement 1999, the claimant must satisfy a number of conditions in order for the MIB to pay an award of damages in respect of an uninsured driver. Provided the claim is one that the MIB is obliged to satisfy and the claimant fulfils the requisite conditions, the MIB will pay any award of damages if the judgment is not satisfied within seven days. Two conditions of the agreement are particularly relevant to pre-action conduct. First, under cl. 13(a) of the agreement, the claimant must have demanded the information, and where appropriate, the particulars, specified in the Road Traffic Act 1988, s. 154, in accordance with that section or, if so required by MIB, have authorised MIB to do so on the claimant's behalf. Section 154 requires the person against whom a claim is made to provide the claimant with details of the name and address of his insurers, details of his insurance and the policy number. This can be dealt with very simply in the letter before claim. The MIB does not have to wait for a judgment to be obtained before intervening in a case. Claimants may wish to apply to the MIB before the commencement of proceedings, but any claim must comply with cl. 7 of the agreement. This means that the claim must be in the form required by the MIB and must give such information about the proceedings and other relevant matters and be accompanied by such documents as the MIB may require. Wherever possible, claims should be made on the MIB application form, accompanied by supporting documents. Using the correct forms is likely to avoid delays occurring in the claim being processed.

A further condition is that the claimant must give written notice of proceedings to the MIB or identified insurer not later than 14 days after commencement of proceedings and that such notice should be accompanied by a copy of the sealed claim form, particulars of claim, schedule of past and future loss and expense, medical report and any other relevant documents, for example, correspondence with the defendant. A pre-action protocol letter before claim is insufficient notification of the proceedings for these purposes (*Wylie v Wake* [2000] RTR 291, a case under the Road Traffic Act 1988, s. 152(1)(a)). The particulars of claim, schedule and medical report may, alternatively, be served within seven days after service on the defendant (cl. 9(3)). Furthermore, notice of service of the claim form must be given to the MIB or identified insurer within seven days of notification by the court (or 14 days of deemed service) (see cl. 10). It is recommended that the claimant's notice, if sent by post, be sent by recorded delivery, which will provide confirmation to the claimant that the notice has in fact been received by the MIB. The MIB does, however, prefer service by fax because it is speedy and can be confirmed equally quickly. Service of documents by DX is not permitted.

A common problem is failing to give the required notice in MIB cases. The purpose of requiring notice is to ensure the MIB is informed so it can intervene and prevent judgment being entered by default (*Richardson v Watson* [2006] EWCA Civ 1662, [2007] RTR 247), although the

MIB believes the reason is to prevent stale claims. Until about 2000, it was common for the MIB to ignore the notice point. More recently, the MIB has been raising want of notice when it arises. A claimant who fails to give notice should, if the point is taken by the MIB, discontinue the defective claim, and issue a second claim giving the necessary notice. Taking this approach is certainly not an abuse of process if the primary limitation period has not expired. *Richardson v Watson* held that issuing a second claim is not an abuse of process even if the primary limitation period has expired. *Horton v Sadler* [2006] UKHL 27, [2007] 1 AC 307, held that in this situation there is jurisdiction under the Limitation Act 1980, s. 33, to make an order disapplying the primary limitation period to the second claim (see **10.19**), and such an order was made in *Richardson v Watson*.

Under cl. 6(1)(e)(ii) of the uninsured drivers' agreement, the MIB is absolved from liability where the injured passenger 'knew or ought to have known' that the vehicle was uninsured. Article 1(4) of the Second Council Directive (84/5/EEC) (to which the uninsured drivers' agreement is intended to give effect) entitles member States to exclude liability only if the injured person 'knew' the vehicle was uninsured. This was held by the House of Lords in *White v White* [2001] 1 WLR 481 to include actual knowledge and cases where the injured party deliberately refrained from asking questions about the insured status of the vehicle. It does not cover cases where the passenger was careless or negligent about whether the vehicle was insured. This exception of the MIB from liability does not apply unless the passenger's presence in the vehicle was voluntary. A passenger who knows the driver is uninsured on entering a vehicle will continue being voluntarily in the vehicle until he or she either gets out or unequivocally requests the driver to stop (*Pickett v Roberts* [2004] EWCA Civ 6, [2004] 1 WLR 2450). The exception only applies to 'the claimant'. In a fatal accident case this is the dependant making the claim, so if he or she was unaware that the driver was not insured the exception does not apply (*Phillips v Rafiq* [2007] EWCA Civ 74, [2007] 1 WLR 1351).

Untraced drivers

The MIB's other agreement with the Minister of Transport seeks to provide compensation for **9.5** any victim of any untraced driver. The current agreement relating to untraced drivers was concluded in 2003 and applies to accidents on or after 14 February 2003. The Court of Justice of the European Union has decided that the untraced drivers' agreement broadly complies with Council Directive 84/5/EEC (*Evans v Secretary of State for the Environment, Transport and the Regions* (case C-63/01) [2005] All ER (EC) 763). The court pointed out, however, that art. 1(4) of the Directive has to be interpreted to mean that compensation awarded under the agreement must take account of the passage of time between the accident and payment. This is now provided for by cl. 9 of the 2003 agreement. Costs need not be included in the scheme, unless reimbursement of costs is necessary to safeguard the rights derived from the Directive (see cl. 10 of the 2003 agreement).

An application arising out of an accident alleged to have been caused by an untraced driver must be made within three years of the accident where the application includes a claim for compensation for personal injuries or death, or within nine months of the accident where the claim is limited to compensation for damage to property (cl. 4(3)(a)). In order to comply with Directive 84/5/EEC, this has to be taken as subject to a similar extension to the time limit for bringing a claim as that contained in the Limitation Act 1980, s. 28. The result is that time does not run against a child until he or she reaches the age of 18 (*Byrne v Motor Insurers' Bureau* [2008] EWCA Civ 574, [2009] QB 66). The applicant must, unless this was not reasonably possible, have reported the accident to the police within 14 days of the accident (within five days if limited to damage to property (cl. 4(3)(c)). When it receives the application, the MIB makes a preliminary investigation (cl. 7(1)(a)) to decide whether the case is one to which the agreement applies and whether there is, in addition to the untraced driver, a second person partly liable for the accident (for which see cl. 13). If the preliminary investigation indicates that the agreement applies and that cl. 13 does not apply, the MIB may notify the applicant that it is using the accelerated procedure in cl. 26 and make an offer to settle the claim. The offer will include reasons for the assessment of the award. The applicant then has six weeks to notify the MIB whether the offer is accepted or rejected. If the offer is accepted, the MIB has to pay the compensation within the next 14 days, and is discharged from all liability under the agreement (cl. 27).

If the accelerated procedure is not adopted by the MIB, or if the applicant rejects an offer made under that procedure, the MIB arranges for a full investigation to be made of the accident by a delegated member of the Bureau. The subsequent report enables the MIB to decide whether an award will be made and if so, the amount of that award. Decisions are based on ordinary principles of negligence and quantification of damage, but with some minor adjustments regarding quantum, as they would apply to the accident (cl. 8).

Under the normal procedure, the MIB's decision is sent, together with reasons, to the claimant (cl. 16). If the claimant does not disagree with the decision or the amount of any award within the period of six weeks from the notice of the decision, the MIB will pay the award to the claimant. An applicant who is unwilling to accept the MIB's decision or determination has six weeks from being notified by the MIB of its decision to send a written notice of appeal to the MIB (cl. 19(1)). The matter will then be referred to arbitration in accordance with cll. 19 to 25 of the agreement.

Procedure on Motor Insurers' Bureau claims

9.6 The agreements are between the MIB and the Minister of Transport. Claimants are not parties to the agreements, though the agreements were clearly made for their benefit and the MIB has never tried to rely on the lack of privity of a claimant as a defence to a claim, because doing so would make the agreements pointless. In *Albert v Motor Insurers' Bureau* [1972] AC 301 Lord Donovan said:

The question immediately suggests itself as to how the appellant as a third party can claim the benefit of this agreement. The point was looked at in *Hardy v Motor Insurers' Bureau* [1964] 2 QB 745 where, at p. 757, Lord Denning MR remarks that the agreement is on the face of it a contract between two parties for the benefit of a third, and that no point was taken by the Bureau that the agreement was not enforceable by the third person.

Diplock LJ also considered the matter in *Gurtner v Circuit* [1968] 2 QB 587, saying that on a number of occasions the court had turned a blind eye to the position and that unless the point were specifically raised the court was 'entitled to proceed upon the assumption that the Bureau has, before action is brought, contracted for good consideration with the [claimant] to perform the obligations specified in its contract with the Minister or has by its conduct raised an estoppel which would bar it from relying on absence of privity of contract'.

As the uninsured drivers agreement was made before the Contracts (Rights of Third Parties) Act 1999 was passed it is not covered by the Act, but it is clear that when it is renewed it will be.

The effective paying party in uninsured drivers cases is the MIB, but the named defendant will be the driver, who will often play no active role in the litigation. It is therefore common practice for the court to grant permission for the MIB to be added as a defendant under what is now **CPR, r. 19.2(2)(a)** (see *Gurtner v Circuit* [1968] 2 QB 587). The same does not apply to untraced drivers (see *White v London Transport Executive* [1971] 2 QB 721).

There is no formal procedure for making claims to the MIB under either of the agreements. The notification of the claim may usually be made in a letter to the MIB from the claimant or the claimant's legal representatives, after which the MIB sends out a claim form which should be completed and returned. The rest is up to the MIB, either in the case of untraced drivers to appoint a member to investigate or in the case of uninsured drivers to make enquiries of anyone such as witnesses and experts who may be able to piece together the accident. In cases where the driver is untraced, there is little a victim can do but apply to the MIB for assistance. In the case of the uninsured driver, however, claimants and those representing them would do well to make their own enquiries to ensure that there was no insurance cover at the time of the accident. The MIB should not be notified unless and until the claimant is aware of the true position, in order to avoid time being wasted and unnecessary expense.

FOURTH MOTOR INSURANCE DIRECTIVE

Directive 2000/26/EC on the approximation of laws of the member States relating to insurance against civil liability in respect of the use of motor vehicles ('the Fourth Motor Insurance Directive') provides the victim of a road traffic accident with a mechanism for dealing with his claim in his own country and in his own language, even though the applicable law may remain that of the country where the accident happened. It applies when a person who is resident in an EU State suffers loss or damage resulting from an accident in another member State and the responsible vehicle is registered and insured with an insurer established in a member State other than his own. It can also apply when the accident is in a non-EU green card signatory country if the offending vehicle is registered and insured in another EU State.   **9.7**

The Directive requires every motor insurer authorised in an EU State to appoint a claims representative in every other member State capable of responding to road traffic claims and paying them where necessary. Every EU State has established an 'information centre' so a victim can, by reference to the registration number of a vehicle, obtain details of its insurance, or the name and address of the owner or user. The Directive is implemented in the United Kingdom by the Motor Insurance (Compulsory Insurance) (Information Centre and Compensation Body) Regulations 2003 (SI 2003/37), and the Motor Insurers' Information Centre is the information centre for the United Kingdom (reg. 3(1)). This should result in the identification of the correct insurer. A claim can then be made, and the insurer's representative must provide a reasoned reply within three months. Under the Fourth Motor Insurance Directive there has to be a direct right of legal action available against insurers. This has been implemented by the European Communities (Rights against Insurers) Regulations 2002 (SI 2002/3061) (see 14.4). A claim is dealt with in accordance with the law of the country where the accident occurred.

Where there is no reasoned response within the three-month period the MIB is the compensation body for the United Kingdom for the purposes of the Fourth Motor Insurance Directive (SI 2003/37, reg. 10). If the insurer's representative corrects the omission, it can continue to handle the claim. Otherwise the claim will be dealt with by the MIB. A claim against the MIB will not be defeated if a trigger event under reg. 6(1) subsequently ends, such as by the subsequent insolvency of the driver's insurer (*Wigley-Foster v Wilson* [2016] EWCA Civ 454, [2016] WLR (D) 271). The MIB will also deal with the claim (reg. 13) where it has proved impossible:

(a) to identify the vehicle the use of which is alleged to have been responsible for the accident; or
(b) within a period of two months after the date of a request, to identify an insurance undertaking which insures the use of the vehicle.

In claims governed by reg. 13, liability and quantum are dealt with in accordance with the law where the accident happened (*Moreno v Motor Insurers' Bureau* [2016] UKSC 52, [2016] 1 WLR 3194).

LANDLORD AND TENANT NOTICES

Various pre-action notices must be given in landlord and tenant disputes. These include: **9.8**

(a) *Notice to quit.* This is a means of terminating a periodic tenancy. At common law, notice to quit could be given orally, but had to be of the correct length (generally that corresponding to a period of the tenancy, although for tenancies from year to year, only six months' notice was required). Difficulties of proof have resulted in notices to quit invariably being given in writing. In relation to residential premises, the notice must set out certain prescribed information.

(b) *Statutory notices in claims for possession of residential property.* There are different statutory codes dealing with security of tenure for residential tenants. Before possession proceedings can be brought, various forms of notice must be served on the tenant.

(c) *Business tenancies.* There is a regime of serving pre-action notices and counter-notices in relation to the termination of business tenancies and seeking new business leases under the Landlord and Tenant Act 1954, part 2.

(d) *Law of Property Act 1925, s. 146.* This section provides that where the landlord seeks to enforce a right of re-entry or forfeiture for breach of covenant or condition (other than non-payment of rent), the landlord must first serve a notice specifying the breach; requiring it to be remedied (if capable of remedy) within a reasonable, specified, time; and requiring the payment of any compensation. For further details, see works on landlord and tenant law.

(e) *Notice of disrepair.* In a claim for housing disrepair, whether brought for breach of the tenancy agreement or in tort, the tenant must show that the landlord has received sufficient information about the alleged defects to put a reasonable person on inquiry as to whether repairs are necessary (*O'Brien v Robinson* [1973] AC 912). A landlord will be assumed to have notice of defects in the common parts of a building as these areas are under the landlord's care and control (*British Telecommunications plc v Sun Life Assurance plc* [1996] Ch 69).

BILLS OF EXCHANGE

Notice of dishonour

9.9   A claim against a person for liability on a bill of exchange which has been dishonoured by non-acceptance or non-payment cannot be made unless notice of dishonour has been given (Bills of Exchange Act 1882, s. 48). Notice must be sent off on the day after dishonour, or, if there is no convenient post on that day, by the next post, unless the person giving, and the person to be given, the notice reside in the same place, in which case notice must be sent off in time to reach the latter on the day after dishonour (s. 49(12)).

Section 50(2) provides several exceptions from the requirement to give notice of dishonour. In particular, it dispenses with the need to give notice of dishonour in practically all instances where a cheque (which is a bill of exchange drawn on a banker payable on demand: s. 73) is dishonoured by non-payment. (There is no need to present a cheque for acceptance: s. 39.) Normally the only person liable on a dishonoured cheque is the drawer and usually it is not necessary to give notice of dishonour to the drawer of a cheque because s. 50(2)(c)(4) provides that notice is dispensed with if the drawee (the bank) is under no obligation (as between drawee and drawer) to pay the cheque, and normally this is the only reason why a cheque is dishonoured. A bank has no obligation to pay its customer's cheque if, for example, there are insufficient funds in the account on which the cheque is drawn, or the customer has countermanded (stopped) payment (ss. 50(2)(c)(5) and 75) or the bank has notice that the customer has died (s. 75). The answer given on the cheque when it is returned by the paying bank will indicate whether any of these apply.

If notice of dishonour of a bill of exchange is not dispensed with by s. 50(2), the notice, in order to be valid and effectual, must be given in accordance with the rules in s. 49.

Notice can be given only by or on behalf of the holder of the bill, or by or on behalf of an endorser who is at the time liable on the bill (s. 49(1)), but written notice need not be signed (s. 49(7)). Notice may be given to a duly authorised agent of the party sought to be made liable (s. 49(8)).

There is no prescribed form of notice, which need not even be written, but it must sufficiently identify the bill and state whether the dishonour was by non-acceptance or non-payment (s. 49(5)). If notice is given of non-acceptance, it is unnecessary to give a further notice of non-payment, unless the bill has been accepted in the meantime (s. 48, proviso (2)). In fact there is no need to present a non-accepted bill for payment (s. 43(2)). Misdescription of the bill does not vitiate the notice unless the recipient of the notice has in fact been misled by it (s. 49(7)). Simply returning the bill to the drawer or an endorser is sufficient notice (s. 49(6)), but in practice it is usual to retain possession of the bill for the purposes of taking proceedings on it.

Notice of dishonour must be given within a reasonable time after the dishonour (s. 49(12)). In the absence of special circumstances, notice is not deemed to have been given within a reasonable time, unless (s. 49(12)):

(a) where the person giving, and the person to receive, notice reside in the same place, the notice is given or sent off in time to reach the latter on the day after the dishonour;
(b) otherwise, the notice is sent off on the day after the dishonour, unless there is no post at a convenient time on that day, in which case it must be sent by the next post.

Whether persons are in the same place for the purposes of s. 49(12)(a) seems to be determined by facilities for travel rather than administrative boundaries (*Hamilton Finance Co. Ltd v Coverley Westry Walbaum and Tosetti Ltd* [1969] 1 Lloyd's Rep 53, in which Upper Brook Street, London W1 and Seething Lane EC3 were held to be in the same place as they are 'a modest bus or tube journey apart, both in the central area').

Where a notice of dishonour is duly addressed and posted, the sender is deemed to have given due notice of dishonour, 'notwithstanding any miscarriage by the post office' (s. 49(15)).

Where a bill which has been dishonoured is in the hands of an agent, for example, a bank collecting payment for its customer, notice of dishonour may be given by the agent either direct to the person liable on the bill or to the agent's principal, who then has a reasonable time (as specified in s. 49(12), see above) to give notice to the person liable (s. 49(13)).

Delay in giving notice of dishonour is excused where the delay is caused by circumstances beyond the control of the party giving notice (s. 50(1)).

Section 50(2) lists circumstances in which notice of dishonour is not required. They are:

(a) when, after the exercise of reasonable diligence, notice as required by the Act cannot be given or does not reach the drawer or endorser sought to be made liable;
(b) where it has been waived (waiver may be express or implied and may be after notice should have been given).

Notice to the drawer is not required where (s. 50(2)(c)):

(a) drawer and drawee are the same person (as with a bank draft);
(b) the drawee is fictitious or has no capacity to contract;
(c) presentation was to the drawer;
(d) as between drawee/acceptor and drawer, the drawee/acceptor is under no obligation to pay/accept the bill (see above, in relation to cheques);
(e) the drawer has countermanded payment.

Notice to an endorser is not required where (s. 50(2)(d)):

(a) at the time of endorsing the bill the endorser was aware that the drawee was fictitious or had no capacity to contract;
(b) presentation was to the endorser;
(c) the bill was drawn or accepted for the accommodation of the endorser.

Notice given by or on behalf of the holder of a bill enures for the benefit of all prior endorsers who have a right of recourse against the person notified, and also for the benefit of any subsequent holder (s. 49(3)). Notice given by or on behalf of an endorser enures for the benefit of the holder and all subsequent endorsers (s. 49(4)).

Protesting foreign bills

9.10   A foreign bill which has been dishonoured by non-acceptance must be protested for non-acceptance, and a foreign bill which is dishonoured by non-payment must be protested for non-payment, unless it has been previously dishonoured by non-acceptance (Bills of Exchange Act 1882, s. 51(2)). A foreign bill is a bill of exchange which is not an inland bill (s. 4) and an inland bill is one which is either (a) both drawn and payable within the British Islands or (b) drawn within the British Islands upon some person resident in the British Islands. The British Islands are the United Kingdom, the Isle of Man and the Channel Islands (s. 4(1)). Failure to protest a foreign bill discharges the liability of the drawer and endorsers. A protest is made by a notary public in the form prescribed in s. 51(7). It is usual to ask a notary to note a dishonoured bill, which must be done on the day of dishonour or the next business day (s. 51(4)), so that a later protest will take effect, under s. 51(4), as from the date of noting. Protest is required in addition to notice of dishonour and is dispensed with in the same circumstances (s. 51(9)).

Letter before claim on a bill of exchange

9.11   Even if a statutory notice of dishonour of a bill of exchange is not required, in a letter before claim sent before proceedings are started, the dishonoured bill should be identified and a photocopy provided, the nature of the dishonour should be stated and the amount claimed should be set out in detail.

DEMANDS IN MONEY CLAIMS

9.12   In the case of a bank owing money to a customer (perhaps being money held to the customer's credit on a current or deposit account), subject to contrary agreement, a demand from the customer is a condition precedent to repayment (*N. Joachimson v Swiss Bank Corporation* [1921] 3 KB 110) and the demand must be made at the branch where the account is kept (*Clare and Co. v Dresdner Bank* [1915] 2 KB 576). In all other situations where money has been borrowed with no time specified for repayment, including lending repayable on demand (such as bank overdrafts, which, subject to contrary agreement, are repayable on demand: *Paget's Law of Banking*, 11th edn. (1996), p. 167, citing *Titford Property Co. Ltd v Cannon Street Acceptances Ltd* (ChD, 22 May 1975)), at common law the demand was not regarded as a condition precedent to repayment (*Re Brown's Estate* [1893] 2 Ch 300; *Bradford Old Bank v Sutcliffe* [1918] 2 KB 833). This meant that the limitation period ran from the time of making the loan. However, the effect of the Limitation Act 1980, s. 6, is that in relation to loans which are not for a fixed term, time only starts running for limitation purposes from the making of a demand. Demands have a further importance in lending cases, because under the terms of any security agreements (such as guarantees and mortgages), resort to the security or the right to appoint a receiver is usually only possible after a demand has been made.

To be effective, a demand must be a clear intimation that payment is required. It must be peremptory in character and unconditional, but the language used is immaterial, and the word 'demand' need not be used (*Re Colonial Finance, Mortgage, Investment and Guarantee Corporation Ltd* (1905) 6 SR (NSW) 6, followed in *Re a Company* [1985] BCLC 37). A demand need not state the amount to be repaid (*Bank of Baroda v Panessar* [1987] Ch 335).

In England and Wales the rule is that a borrower of money repayable on demand must have the money ready to repay at all times, so that the only time that need be allowed between making a demand and regarding the borrower as being in default is the time necessary to effect the mechanics of payment, and if it is known that the borrower has not got the money then no time at all need be allowed (*Sheppard and Cooper Ltd v TSB Bank plc* [1996] 2 All ER 654). The commercially unrealistic mechanics-of-payment test has been rejected in Canada in favour of a reasonable-time test, and may be due for re-examination at appellate level in England (see *Lloyds Bank plc v Lampert* [1999] BCC 507).

A claim for restitution after rescission of a contract cannot be made until notice of rescission has been given, but no demand is necessary before claiming restitution in a case of unjust enrichment (*Fuller v Happy Shopper Markets Ltd* [2001] 1 WLR 1681).

NOTICE OF ASSIGNMENT

Where there has been a legal assignment of a debt or other thing in action, express written notice must be given to the debtor or other person against whom the right can be enforced. See the Law of Property Act 1925, s. 136, and **14.92**.   **9.13**

DIRECTOR DISQUALIFICATION

For pre-action notification of disqualification proceedings see **86.9**.   **9.14**

Commentary

the maturity of payment, and it is known that the borrower has more than the money then so due at all need be allowed (*Shepard Son Co* v *Manley* [1891] ...). The communication is useless because of payment as it has been released in Canada in favour of a reasonable time, and may be due for re-examination at a public trial in England (see *Hyde Bank* ...).

A claim for restitution after rescission of a contract cannot be made until notice of rescission has been given, but no demand is necessary before claiming restitution in a case of unjust enrichment (*Vidler's Property Shop* v *Marcus* [...] [2003] ... WLR ...).

NOTICE OF ASSIGNMENT

3.15 Where there has been a legal assignment of a debt or other claim in action, express written notice must be given to the debtor or other person against whom the debt can be enforced. See the Law of Property Act 1925 s.136 and 1.92.

DIRECTOR DISQUALIFICATION

9.14 For pre-action notification of disqualification proceedings see 8.5.

PART D

Commencement

Chapter 10 Limitation

Commentary

INTRODUCTION

Expiry of a limitation period provides a defendant with a complete defence to a claim. Lord **10.1**
Griffiths in *Donovan v Gwentoys Ltd* [1990] 1 WLR 472 said, 'The primary purpose of the

179

limitation period is to protect a defendant from the injustice of having to face a stale claim, that is a claim with which he never expected to have to deal'. If a claim is brought a long time after the events in question, the likelihood is that evidence which may have been available earlier may have been lost, and the memories of witnesses who may still be available will inevitably have faded or become confused. Further, it is contrary to general policy to keep people perpetually at risk.

Most limitation periods are laid down in the Limitation Act 1980 (LA 1980) as amended. Several other statutes lay down limitation periods, and some procedural rules impose time limits which act rather like limitation periods (see **table 10.1** and **10.65** to **10.68**). The usual rule is that no objection can be taken to a claim started on the last day of the limitation period, but there is a complete defence if proceedings are brought one day late.

There has been a move in recent legislation towards flexible limitation periods for some types of cases, which will be considered in this chapter in the context of the limitation rules affecting different causes of action. Examples are the Latent Damage Act 1986, which provides for limitation to apply as a defence only from the date when a negligence claim was discoverable, and LA 1980, s. 33, which allows the court to disapply the three-year personal injuries time limit where the court considers it equitable to do so. Where flexibility of this kind is available the LA 1980 may be seen as seeking to achieve a balance of justice between the claimant and the defendant.

Limitation is usually a procedural defence (the exceptions relate to limitation periods operating outside the LA 1980). Limitation will not be taken by the court of its own motion, but must be specifically set out in the defence (**PD 16, para. 13.1**). Time-barred cases rarely go to trial. If the claimant is unwilling to discontinue the claim (see **chapter 55**), it is usually possible for the defendant to apply successfully for the claim to be struck out (see **chapter 33**) as an abuse of the court's process.

Normally, the only consequence of the expiry of a limitation period is that the defendant acquires a technical defence to the claim. The claimant still has a cause of action, but one that cannot be enforced. In cases of adverse possession of land and conversion, expiry of the limitation period has the additional consequence of extinguishing the party's title to the land or goods.

Main concepts

10.2 When a limitation issue arises in a claim, the following concepts need to be considered:

(a) The date the cause of action accrued (see **10.4**). Accrual starts time running.

(b) Whether time did not start running when the cause of action accrued. This might be because the cause of action is subject to 'date of knowledge' provisions, which apply to personal injuries claims (see **10.12** to **10.18**) and latent damage claims (see **10.30** to **10.32**), or because the claimant was under a disability (see **10.51**), or because the claimant can take advantage of the provisions dealing with acknowledgments, fraud, concealment or mistake (see **10.55** to **10.58**).

(c) The applicable limitation period (see **10.5**).

(d) The date time stopped running. This is the date the claim is brought, see **10.6**.

(e) Whether the claim is subject to rules analogous to limitation, albeit outside the LA 1980.

Issuing a second claim

10.3 Where proceedings are issued and come to naught through inactivity on the part of the claimant, they can be abandoned or discontinued, and, provided the limitation period has not expired, fresh proceedings can be commenced in respect of the same cause of action. There are

exceptions where the original proceedings are struck out as an abuse of process or as a sanction for non-compliance with the rules or directions (see *Janov v Morris* [1981] 1 WLR 1389 and **33.13**). *Horton v Sadler* [2006] UKHL 27, [2007] 1 AC 307, held that there is jurisdiction to make an order under LA 1980, s. 33, to disapply the primary personal injury limitation period in a second claim after an earlier claim has been discontinued or struck out. The House of Lords applied Practice Statement (Judicial Precedent) [1966] 1 WLR 1234 and reversed the decision in *Walkley v Precision Forgings Ltd* [1979] 1 WLR 606, which had held there is no such jurisdiction. Issuing a second claim in these circumstances is not an abuse of process (*Aktas v Adepta* [2010] EWCA Civ 1170, [2011] QB 894).

ACCRUAL OF CAUSE OF ACTION

Time runs from the day following the day on which the cause of action arose, as parts of a day **10.4** are ignored (*Marren v Dawson Bentley and Co. Ltd* [1961] 2 QB 135).

The rules on accrual fix the date from which time begins to run for limitation purposes. Lindley LJ in *Reeves v Butcher* [1891] 2 QB 509 said: 'it has always been held that the statute runs from the earliest time at which an action could be brought'. In *Read v Brown* (1888) 22 QBD 128 Lord Esher MR defined 'cause of action' as encompassing 'every fact which it would be necessary for the [claimant] to prove, if traversed, in order to support his right to the judgment of the court'. In other words, time runs from the point when facts exist establishing all the essential elements of the cause of action.

A distinction is drawn between the substantive elements and mere procedural requirements. Thus, a solicitor can commence a claim to recover costs from a client only if at least a month has elapsed since a bill for those costs has been delivered to the client (Solicitors Act 1974, s. 69(1)). In *Coburn v Colledge* [1897] 1 QB 702 it was held that the requirement to furnish a bill was only a procedural matter, and time ran from completion of the work as opposed to delivery of the bill. Sometimes this can be a difficult distinction to draw. A 'misfeasance' claim for a summary remedy against a delinquent director for breach of duty to a company under the Insolvency Act 1986, s. 212, accrues with the breach of duty, not when the liquidator is appointed (*Re Eurocruit Europe Ltd* [2007] EWHC 1433 (Ch), [2008] Bus LR 146), because s. 212 is only procedural in nature. Conversely, a claim against a former director under the Insolvency Act 1986, s. 213 (fraudulent trading), which only comes into effect when a company is being wound up, accrues on the date the company is ordered to be wound up (*Re Overnight Ltd* [2009] EWHC 601 (Ch), [2009] Bus LR 1141). *Sevcon Ltd v Lucas CAV Ltd* [1986] 1 WLR 462 concerned the Patents Act 1949, s. 13(4), which contained a proviso: 'Provided that an applicant shall not be entitled to institute any proceedings for infringement until the patent has been sealed'. It was held that the cause of action accrued on the date of the infringement, but could not be enforced until the procedural requirement of sealing was met.

In addition to the elements of the cause of action being present, there must be a party capable of suing and a party liable to be sued. So, if goods are converted after the owner has died intestate, time would run only from the date letters of administration were taken out (*Thomson v Lord Clanmorris* [1900] 1 Ch 718 per Vaughan Williams LJ). However, if it is necessary to restore to the register of companies a company against which a claim is to be made, the date of accrual remains based on the date of the breach (or other element of the cause of action), not on the date of restoration (*Smith v White Knight Laundry Ltd* [2001] EWCA Civ 660, [2002] 1 WLR 616). Although the court has power under the Companies Act 2006, s. 1032(3), to direct that the period between dissolution and restoration shall not count for the purposes of limitation, a direction under this provision should not normally be made unless notice of the application has been served on all parties who could be expected to oppose it. Time continues running

Commentary

during a period in which the defendant is an undischarged bankrupt (*Anglo Manx Group Ltd v Aitken* [2002] BPIR 215).

LIMITATION PERIODS

10.5   Time runs from accrual of the cause of action until the claim form is filed, or, as it is put in the LA 1980, when the claim is brought. **Table 10.1** sets out the limitation periods for the most important classes of cases.

The relevant claim form is the one issued in the present proceedings. An earlier claim form based on the same alleged cause of action which is not proceeded with does not affect the question whether the claim form in the present claim was issued before limitation expired (*Markfield Investments Ltd v Evans* [2001] 1 WLR 1321).

Table 10.1 Limitation periods

Class of claim		Limitation period	*Blackstone's Civil Practice 2017*
1	Fraudulent breach of trust	None (LA 1980, s. 21(1))	**10.36**
2	Recovery of land	12 years (LA 1980, s. 15(1))	**10.41**
3	Recovery of money secured by mortgage	12 years (LA 1980, s. 20(1))	**10.44**
4	Specialty	12 years (LA 1980, s. 8(1))	**10.46**
5	Defective product claims	10 years (Consumer Protection Act 1987, s. 11A(3))	**10.27**
6	Recovery of a sum due under statute	6 years (LA 1980, s. 9(1))	**10.47**
7	Enforcement of a judgment	6 years (LA 1980, s. 24(1))	**10.50**
8	Contract	6 years (LA 1980, s. 5)	**10.35**
9	Recovery of trust property and breach of trust	6 years (LA 1980, s. 21(3))	**10.36**
10	Recovery of arrears of rent	6 years (LA 1980, s. 19)	
11	Enforcement of awards not under seal	6 years (LA 1980, s. 7)	**10.62**
12	Tort (except those listed below)	6 years (LA 1980, s. 2)	**10.7**
13	Defective Premises Act 1972 claims	6 years (Defective Premises Act 1972, s. 1(5))	
14	Personal injuries claims	3 years (LA 1980, s. 11(4))	**10.12**
15	Fatal Accidents Act 1976 claims	3 years (LA 1980, s. 12(2))	**10.29**
16	Personal injuries or damage to property claims under the Consumer Protection Act 1987	3 years (LA 1980, s. 11A)	**10.27**
17	Carriage by Air Act 1961 claims	2 years (Carriage by Air Act 1961, sch. 1)	
18	Claims for personal injuries or damage to vessel, cargo or property or personal injuries to passengers at sea	2 years (Merchant Shipping Act 1995, s. 190(3) and sch. 6, part 1, art. 16)	
19	Disqualification of company directors under the Company Directors Disqualification Act 1986, s. 6	2 years (Company Directors Disqualification Act 1986, s. 7(2))	**86.8**
20	Contribution under the Civil Liability (Contribution) Act 1978	2 years (LA 1980, s. 10(1))	**10.45**
21	Contribution under the Maritime Conventions Act 1911	1 year (Merchant Shipping Act 1995, s. 190(4))	

Table 10.1 (Continued)

Class of claim		Limitation period	*Blackstone's Civil Practice 2017*
22	Carriage of Goods by Road Act 1965 claims	1 year (Carriage of Goods by Road Act 1965, sch., art. 32)	
23	Cargo claims under the Hague–Visby Rules	1 year (Hague–Visby Rules, art. III, rule 6)	
24	Defamation and malicious falsehood	1 year (LA 1980, s. 4A)	**10.33**
25	Late payment of insurance claims	1 year (LA 1980, s. 5A)	
26	Applications for judicial review	3 months (CPR, r. 54.5)	**77.36**
27	Unfair dismissal under the Employment Rights Act 1996	3 months (Employment Rights Act 1996, s. 111(2))	
28	Applications for new business tenancies under the Landlord and Tenant Act 1954, part 2	If made by the tenant, not before 2 months after the tenant's request for a new tenancy under s. 26 (s. 29A(3)), and whether by the tenant or landlord, not after the date specified in any s. 25 notice or the day before the date specified in any s. 26 request (s. 29A(2))	
29	Claims for an account	Period applicable to claim on which account is based (LA 1980, s. 23)	

DATE A CLAIM IS BROUGHT

A claim is time-barred under the LA 1980 if proceedings are not 'brought' (which is the word used in most of the provisions in the Act) before the expiry of the stated limitation period. Traditionally it was thought that a claim was brought for limitation purposes 'when the [claim form] or other originating process is issued by the central office of the High Court and not when it is brought to the knowledge of the defendant by service upon him' (per Lord Diplock in *Thompson v Brown* [1981] 1 WLR 744). *Barnes v St Helens Metropolitan Borough Council* [2006] EWCA Civ 1372, [2007] 1 WLR 879, drew a distinction between the date a claim is 'brought' and the date it is 'issued'. The result is that time stops running for limitation when the claim form and issue fee are delivered to the court (this is the date the claim is 'brought'), which is in the claimant's control, rather than on the date of issue, which the claimant does not control. The same result was achieved for the two-year limitation period under the Company Directors Disqualification Act 1986, s. 6, in *Secretary of State for Trade and Industry v Vohora* [2007] EWHC 2656 (Ch), [2008] Bus LR 161. Likewise, in relation to laying of informations in the magistrates' courts (*Rockall v Department for Environment, Food and Rural Affairs* [2007] EWHC 614 (Admin), [2007] 1 WLR 2666) and the presentation of petitions (*Re Blights Builders Ltd* [2006] EWHC 3549 (Ch), [2007] Bus LR 629). Part 20 proceedings are brought for limitation purposes on the date the Part 20 claim is commenced (LA 1980, s. 35(1)(a)).

10.6

A claimant may send a claim form to the court office for issue. Letters requesting the issue of claim forms will be date-stamped on receipt, and the date of receipt will stop time running for limitation purposes if the court does not issue the claim form on the same day (**PD 7A, paras 5.1 and 5.2**). An inquiry about the date on which a claim form was received by the court should be directed to a court officer (**para 5.3**). **Paragraph 5.4** goes on to say that parties should recognise the importance of establishing the date of receipt if a limitation period is approaching, and should take steps to record the date of receipt. To avoid difficulties in cases where limitation might be a problem, it is usually best to make a personal attendance at court to issue the proceedings.

Commentary

If the court office is closed on the final day of the limitation period, proceedings are deemed to be in time if they are issued on the next day the court office is open (*Pritam Kaur v S. Russell and Sons Ltd* [1973] QB 336).

TORT

General claims in tort

10.7   LA 1980, s. 2, provides:

2. Time Limit For Actions Founded on Tort

An action founded on tort shall not be brought after the expiration of six years from the date on which the cause of action accrued.

The general rule is that in addition to proving the defendant is guilty of some wrongful conduct, liability in tort can only be established on proof of damage. Usually, damage is the final matter to come into existence, so the usual rule is that time runs in tort from the date when damage is sustained. In most situations this is the first date on which the claimant has suffered a measurable loss. This means that a claim against a structural engineer for negligent advice in relation to remedial works required on a building project will accrue when the remedial works failed (*Renwick v Simon and Michael Brooke Architects* [2011] EWHC 874 (TCC), [2011] PNLR 31).

In *Law Society v Sephton and Co.* [2006] UKHL 22, [2006] 2 AC 543, it was alleged that accountants had negligently prepared solicitors' accounts which failed to find misappropriations of clients' money which might have been prevented if the accounts had been prepared properly. Various clients of the solicitors made claims against the Solicitors' Compensation Fund based on the misappropriations. It was held that each misappropriation gave rise to a contingent liability against the Fund, and that the cause of action accrued when the contingency occurred. This was the date each client made a claim against the Fund, because it was at that point that a loss or damage was sustained by the Fund. *Law Society v Sephton and Co.* should not be understood as laying down a general rule that damage only occurs when a claim is made against the party who is now the claimant as a result of the alleged negligence of the defendant. The date when damage is suffered is a fact-specific question. In a claim by an ATE insurer against a solicitor, based on negligent vetting of the prospects of success of personal injuries claims, the insurer suffered measurable loss when the ATE policies were entered into, as this was the time at which the insurer valued the policies erroneously in reliance on the defendant's negligent vetting (*AXA Insurance Ltd v Akther and Darby Solicitors* [2009] EWCA Civ 1166, [2010] 1 WLR 1662).

A claim for damages under the principle in *Francovich v Italy* (cases C-6 and 9/90) [1995] ICR 722) based on an alleged failure of the government to implement EU law accrued when the claimants suffered their personal injuries (*Spencer v Secretary of State for Work and Pensions* [2008] EWCA Civ 750, [2009] QB 358). A similar result was achieved in a claim by Lloyd's underwriters against the Treasury in *Poole v Her Majesty's Treasury* [2006] EWHC 2731 (Comm), [2007] 1 All ER (Comm) 255. There is a principle that time does not run until there has been full implementation of a Directive, but this applies only where the conduct of the member State was responsible for the lapse of time which brought the relevant time bar into operation such as to make it inequitable for the State then to rely on the time bar.

Time will not start running until the claimant has suffered some damage. In *Rothwell v Chemical and Insulating Co. Ltd* [2007] UKHL 39, [2008] 1 AC 281, the claimants had developed pleural plaques, which proved that the claimants' lungs had been penetrated by asbestos fibres. The evidence was that pleural plaques cause no symptoms and do not increase susceptibility to other asbestos-related diseases or shorten life expectancy. Their presence did not amount to an injury such as to set time running.

The important date is the date damage was sustained, not the date on which the claimant discovered the damage (*Cartledge v E. Jopling and Sons Ltd* [1963] AC 758). There are, of course, many cases where measurable damage and its discovery coincide (*Abbott v Will Gannon and Smith Ltd* [2005] EWCA Civ 198, [2005] BLR 195). In *Pirelli General Cable Works Ltd v Oscar Faber and Partners* [1983] 2 AC 1 it was held that a cause of action for negligent design of a chimney arose when cracking in the structure first developed, and not when the damage could have been or was in fact discovered. Likewise, where additional damage is suffered after the tortious act complained of, time continues to run from the original tortious act (*Iqbal v Legal Services Commission* [2005] EWCA Civ 623, LTL 10/5/2005). Latent damage is considered at **10.30**.

Continuing torts

The decision in *Darley Main Colliery v Mitchell* (1886) 11 App Cas 127 on continuing torts is prob-   **10.8**
ably confined to subsidence claims (*Iqbal v Legal Services Commission* [2005] EWCA Civ 623, LTL 10/5/2005). Conversely, it was held in *Phonographic Performance Ltd v Department of Trade and Industry* [2004] EWHC 1795 (Ch), [2004] 1 WLR 2893, that where the tort is one which is not actionable per se, there is a continuing breach of duty and a fresh cause of action every time the claimant suffers loss. Where work done by a developer is defective, and the developer does further work intended to rectify defects but which is also defective, the further work is a fresh cause of action and time starts running again (*Alderson v Beetham Organization Ltd* [2003] EWCA Civ 408, [2003] 1 WLR 1686).

Professional negligence

In a claim against a solicitor for negligent advice, actual damage is suffered when the advice is   **10.9**
acted upon, such as by executing a document (*Forster v Outred and Co.* [1982] 1 WLR 86) or entering into an agreement (*McCarroll v Statham Gill Davis* [2003] EWCA Civ 425, [2003] PNLR 509). Thus, in *Pegasus Management Holdings SCA v Ernst and Young* [2008] EWHC 2720 (Ch), [2009] PNLR 11, a claim against accountants based on alleged failure to advise the client to incorporate a company with subsidiaries accrued when the client acquired shares in the company. A claim against financial advisers, arising from advice to transfer benefits from an occupational pension scheme to a personal pension fund, accrues when the benefits are transferred (*Shore v Sedgwick Financial Services Ltd* [2008] EWCA Civ 863, [2009] Bus LR 42; *Williams v Lishman, Sidwell, Campbell and Price Ltd* [2010] EWCA Civ 418, [2010] PNLR 25). In a claim based on alleged negligence in a conveyancing transaction, if the property is diminished in value on completion due to the negligence, accrual occurs at that point rather than on registration of the transfer (*Nouri v Marvi* [2010] EWCA Civ 1107, [2011] PNLR 7, although there are cases where the cause of action accrues on exchange, such as *Edehomo v Edehomo* [2011] EWHC 393 (Ch), [2011] 1 WLR 2217).

A claim against a solicitor based on alleged negligent advice on inheritance tax accrues when the client relies on the advice (*Daniels v Thompson* [2004] EWCA Civ 307, [2004] PNLR 33). In *Watkins v Jones Maidment Wilson* [2008] EWCA Civ 134, [2008] PNLR 23, negligent advice resulted in an immediate measurable loss because the claimant lost the chance of negotiating a better agreement, which meant the claim was time-barred. Even if the advice given by the solicitor should have included advice to renegotiate the contract, there was a single event amounting to the breach of duty. Where a claimant seeks to sue a solicitor for negligently allowing a claim to be struck out as a sanction for breach of directions or the requirements of the CPR, time runs from the date when the claimant had no arguable basis for avoiding the claim being struck out, not from the date on which it was actually struck out (*Khan v R. M. Falvey and Co.* [2002] EWCA Civ 400, [2002] PNLR 28; *Hatton v Chafes* [2003] EWCA Civ 341, [2003] PNLR 24, disapproving *Hopkins v MacKenzie* (1994) 6 Med LR 26). A related, but different point, was considered in *Cohen v Kingsley Napley* [2006] EWCA Civ 66, [2006] PNLR 22. Pill LJ at [19] said that even if the original claim would have been struck out if an application had been made by the original opponent at the

Commentary

point six years before the present claim was issued against the solicitors, the claim against the solicitors will not be time-barred if:

(a) on the evidence the original opponent would not have applied to strike out at that time;

(b) with the result that the original claim still had some value at the point six years before the current proceedings.

There are not many cases where the first point will be satisfied. *Cohen v Kingsley Napley* was a strike-out application, and the Court of Appeal said it was a matter that could be argued at trial. The court was swayed by the fact the original claim was a counterclaim, so the original opponent was a claimant, and so may have been reluctant to strike out the counterclaim for delay given the claim would also be in danger of being struck out.

Applying the rule that a claim accrues when actual damage is sustained, a professional negligence claim against solicitors based on failing to serve a claim form in time, or based on wrongly relying on an order (later set aside) extending time for service, accrues when the original period of validity of the claim form expires (*Polley v Warner Goodman and Street Solicitors* [2003] EWCA Civ 1013, [2003] PNLR 784). A continuing duty on a solicitor to advise will continually renew the accrual of limitation until the duty to advise ends, usually on termination of the retainer (*Workman v Pannone and Partners* [2002] EWHC 2366 (QB), LTL 18/11/2002).

Where a claim is in respect of a transaction entered into through a breach of duty owed by the defendant to the claimant (such as a loan agreement entered into in reliance on a negligent property valuation), time will run from the date the transaction was entered into if the claimant suffered a loss there and then. If there was no immediate loss, such as where the security for a loan was worth more than the loan when it was first advanced (albeit not as much as the defendant's valuation), time will start running only when the value of the security falls below the amount of the loan (see the discussion in *First National Commercial Bank plc v Humberts* [1995] 2 All ER 673).

The principle that a judicial decision stating what the common law is has retrospective effect meant, in *Awoyomi v Radford* [2007] EWHC 1671 (QB), [2008] QB 793, that time had started running in a claim against a barrister from before the decision in *Arthur J. S. Hall and Co. v Simons* [2002] 1 AC 615, which had removed the immunity from suit previously enjoyed by advocates.

Trespass

10.10   Trespass claims are actionable per se, so time runs from the wrongful act since there is no requirement to prove damage.

Conversion

10.11   Time runs from the date the goods were converted. A number of special rules apply:

(a) where goods are converted more than once, the original six-year period continues to run and is not renewed (LA 1980, s. 3(1));

(b) at the end of the original six-year period the true owner's title is extinguished (s. 3(2));

(c) subject to (d) below, there is no time limit where goods are stolen (s. 4);

(d) where goods are converted (but not stolen) and are then stolen at a later date, proceedings in respect of the theft are barred once the true owner's title is extinguished under s. 3(2) by virtue of the original conversion (s. 4(1)).

Personal injuries claims

10.12   Subsections (1) to (4) of LA 1980, s. 11, provide:

11. Special Time Limit For Actions in Respect of Personal Injuries

(1)   This section applies to any action for damages for negligence, nuisance or breach of duty (whether the duty exists by virtue of a contract or of provision made by or under a statute or independently of any contract or any such provision) where the damages claimed by the plaintiff for the negligence, nuisance or breach of duty consist of or include damages in respect of personal injuries to the plaintiff or any other person.

(1A) This section does not apply to any action brought for damages under section 3 of the Protection from Harassment Act 1997.

(2)   None of the time limits given in the preceding provisions of this Act shall apply to an action to which this section applies.

(3)   An action to which this section applies shall not be brought after the expiration of the period applicable in accordance with subsection (4) or (5) below.

(4)   Except where subsection (5) below applies, the period applicable is three years from—
   (a) the date on which the cause of action accrued; or
   (b) the date of knowledge (if later) of the person injured.

Claims for personal injuries (class 14 in **table 10.1**) comprise all claims in negligence, nuisance and breach of duty (including contractual and statutory duties) where the claim to relief consists of or includes damages in respect of personal injuries to the claimant or any other person (LA 1980, s. 11(1)). Under s. 11(4) the basic limitation period for such claims is three years. An attempt was made to avoid this limitation period in *Letang v Cooper* [1965] 1 QB 232. The claimant was injured when the defendant drove his car over her legs while she was sunbathing on the grass in the car park of a hotel. Proceedings were issued four years afterwards, but the cause of action was pleaded both in negligence and in trespass to the person. The Court of Appeal overruled the trial judge and held the claim was time-barred. Two reasons were advanced. One was that where an injury is inflicted negligently rather than intentionally, the only cause of action is in negligence, so the claimant is unable to rely on the six-year limitation period in trespass (class 12 in **table 10.1**). The second reason was that the phrase 'breach of duty' in what is now s. 11(1) covered a breach of any duty under the law of tort.

A claim by an employee against an employer for failing to advise on the benefits available after suffering a personal injury is a claim for negligent advice (class 12), see *Gaud v Leeds Health Authority* (1999) 49 BMLR 105. On the other hand, a claim in professional negligence against a solicitor arising out of the firm's handling of a divorce ancillary relief claim, which included a claim for anxiety and stress arising out of the firm's alleged mishandling of her claim, became, for that reason, a claim in respect of personal injuries and subject to a three-year limitation period (class 14) rather than the usual six-year period in claims in tort and breach of contract (*Oates v Harte Reade and Co.* [1999] PIQR P120). A negligent failure by an education authority to improve the consequences of the claimant's dyslexia by appropriate teaching, or a negligent failure to treat a physical injury, are both claims for personal injuries (*Adams v Bracknell Forest Borough Council* [2004] UKHL 29, [2005] 1 AC 76).

In *Ackbar v C. F. Green and Co. Ltd* [1975] QB 582 a claim against an insurance broker for damages for breach of contract for failing to effect cover for a passenger who later suffered personal injuries in a road accident was held to be a claim in contract (class 8). A claim for breach of statutory duty to insure a motor vehicle on the road was, in contrast, held to be a claim for personal injuries in *Norman v Ali* [2000] RTR 107.

Deliberate trespass to the person

There is no distinction in LA 1980, s. 11, between negligent breaches of duty resulting in personal injuries (as discussed at **10.12**) and cases involving deliberate trespass to the person. Consequently, civil claims arising out of assaults, battery, rape and indecent assaults etc. are governed by the same three-year limitation period (and the rules in ss. 14 and 33)   **10.13** as claims arising through negligence (*A v Hoare* [2008] UKHL 6, [2008] 1 AC 844). *Stubbings v Webb* [1993] AC 498 (which was confirmed by the European Court of Human Rights in *Stubbings v United Kingdom* (applications 22083/93 and 22095/93) (1996) 23 EHRR 213) was departed from in accordance with Practice Statement (House of Lords: Judicial Precedent) [1966] 1 WLR 1234.

Personal injuries claims: date of knowledge

10.14   Time runs in personal injuries claims from the date the cause of action accrued, or, if later, the date of the claimant's date of knowledge (LA 1980, s. 11(4)). Date of knowledge is defined by s. 14, which provides:

14. Definition of Date of Knowledge for Purposes of Sections 11 and 12

(1) Subject to subsection (1A) below, in sections 11 and 12 of this Act references to a person's date of knowledge are references to the date on which he first had knowledge of the following facts—
   (a) that the injury in question was significant; and
   (b) that the injury was attributable in whole or in part to the act or omission which is alleged to constitute negligence, nuisance or breach of duty; and
   (c) the identity of the defendant; and
   (d) if it is alleged that the act or omission was that of a person other than the defendant, the identity of that person and the additional facts supporting the bringing of an action against the defendant;

and knowledge that any acts or omissions did or did not, as a matter of law, involve negligence, nuisance or breach of duty is irrelevant.

[Subsection (1A) deals with claims for death caused by defective products.]

(2) For the purposes of this section an injury is significant if the person whose date of knowledge is in question would reasonably have considered it sufficiently serious to justify his instituting proceedings for damages against a defendant who did not dispute liability and was able to satisfy a judgment.

(3) For the purposes of this section a person's knowledge includes knowledge which he might reasonably have been expected to acquire—
   (a) from facts observable or ascertainable by him; or
   (b) from facts ascertainable by him with the help of medical or other appropriate expert advice which it is reasonable for him to seek;

but a person shall not be fixed under this subsection with knowledge of a fact ascertainable only with the help of expert advice so long as he has taken all reasonable steps to obtain (and, where appropriate, to act on) that advice.

The provision for time to run from date of knowledge was first introduced in July 1963 by the Limitation Act 1963 and has no application to any claim already time-barred before it was introduced (*McDonnell v Congregation of Christian Brothers Trustees* [2003] UKHL 63, [2003] 1 AC 1101, applying *Arnold v Central Electricity Generating Board* [1988] AC 228).

10.15   **Constructive knowledge**   Time will start running before a claimant has actual knowledge within LA 1980, s. 14(1), if the claimant has constructive knowledge under s. 14(3). A claimant is taken to know facts observable or ascertainable by him or her, and also facts ascertainable with the help of expert advice which it would have been reasonable to obtain (s. 14(3)). The burden of proof under s. 14(3) rests on the defendant (*Norton v Corus UK Ltd* [2006] EWCA Civ 1630, LTL 13/11/2006). Despite this, the issue continues to be argued (*Whiston v London Strategic Health Authority* [2009] EWHC 956 (QB), [2009] LS Law Med 355, in which it was said, at [6], the burden of proof rests on the claimant).

Defining the test for constructive knowledge has proved difficult. Authorities suggesting a substantially subjective test concentrating on the characteristics of the individual claimant (*Davis v City and Hackney Health Authority* (1998) 2 Med LR 366 and *KR v Bryn Alyn Community (Holdings) Ltd* [2003] EWCA Civ 85, [2003] QB 1441) should be treated with caution. A substantially objective test was said to be applicable under s. 14(3)(b) in *Adams v Bracknell Forest Borough*

Council [2004] UKHL 29, [2005] 1 AC 76. However, in *AB v Ministry of Defence* [2012] UKSC 9, [2013] 1 AC 78, it was held that time will start running against a claimant who believes their injury was attributable to the relevant act or omission 'with sufficient confidence to justify embarking on the preliminaries to the issue of a claim form, such as submitting a claim to a proposed defendant, taking legal and other advice, and collecting evidence'. While suspicion is not knowledge within the meaning of s. 14, reasonable belief normally suffices.

In *Forbes v Wandsworth Health Authority* [1997] QB 402, the Court of Appeal doubted the relevance of the claimant's individual characteristics in what is expressed to be an objective test. This means that personal characteristics of the claimant, such as a lack of confidence or wishing to avoid contention, are irrelevant under s. 14. Rather, the court has to consider how a reasonable person in the claimant's situation, suffering from the claimant's medical condition, would have acted. It is to be expected that claimants who have suffered significant injuries will seek professional advice on the cause of their problems, even if they have serious difficulties with reading and writing (*Adams v Bracknell Forest Borough Council*). The way it was put in *Whiston v London Strategic Health Authority* [2010] EWCA Civ 195, [2010] 1 WLR 1582, was that a person who knows he has a significant injury is to be judged against an objective expectation of heightened curiosity to find out what happened. This might include asking his parents about what happened at his birth. The question is whether, having regard to the symptoms the claimant was experiencing, it would have been reasonable to expect him to seek specific advice from his doctor (*White v Eon* [2008] EWCA Civ 1463, LTL 26/11/2008).

A claimant will not have constructive knowledge over a period where her post-operation symptoms are consistent with what she was told before the operation, where she trusts her doctors, and there is nothing to put her on notice that something may have gone wrong (*Rogers v East Kent Hospitals NHS Trust* [2009] EWHC 54 (QB), [2009] LS Law Med 153). Time will, however, run against a claimant from the moment he had information demonstrating a real possibility that his working conditions caused his symptoms, even without information establishing causation (*Kew v Bettamix Ltd* [2006] EWCA Civ 1535, [2007] PIQR P210).

The *Forbes* approach was applied in *Parry v Clwyd Health Authority* [1997] PIQR P1, where in context the knowledge of the 'reasonable man' was regarded as being that of a person who knew no more of the subject than what might have been learnt at school, from parents or friends or the media. A claimant who is clear in her own mind that there was a connection between the defendant's conduct and her injury has sufficient knowledge even if other people would want to get expert advice before making up their minds (*Spargo v North Essex District Health Authority* [1997] PIQR P235). In *Ali v Courtaulds Textiles Ltd* [1999] Lloyd's Rep Med 301 the Court of Appeal held that the claimant in an industrial deafness case could not be said to know his deafness was attributable to his working conditions, as opposed to being age-induced, until after he had been advised by his doctors. A claimant who eventually makes a claim against a drug company in respect of the effects of an allegedly defective drug may well have consulted a doctor at an early stage when possibly drug-related symptoms first became apparent. A doctor is likely to concentrate on a solution to the patient's problems rather than give advice on attributing blame. Therefore, whether the doctor's knowledge about the cause of the claimant's symptoms should be attributed to the claimant depends on whether in the circumstances it would have been reasonable to expect the claimant to have asked the doctor about cause as well as cure (*Nash v Eli Lilly and Co.* [1993] 1 WLR 782).

In *Henderson v Temple Pier Co. Ltd* [1998] 1 WLR 1540 the claimant was injured as she boarded a moored ship. She did not know the identity of the owners. She instructed solicitors about a month after the accident. If they had acted competently, they could have discovered the identity of the defendant from the General Register of Shipping and Seamen fairly soon after they were retained, but in the event they only discovered the defendant's identity about 18 months after the accident. Proceedings were issued 4 years and 3 months after the accident. It was held that the proviso to s. 14(3) was not intended to give an extended period to a person whose solicitor acted in a dilatory manner in obtaining information which is obtainable without particular expertise, and the claimant was fixed with constructive knowledge which her solicitors ought to have acquired. The same reasoning applies where a solicitor fails to identify a defendant through failing to request a copy of a police road accident report (*Copeland v Smith* [2000] 1 WLR 1371), or through declining to see relevant care records (*Pierce v Doncaster Metropolitan Borough Council* [2008] EWCA Civ 1416, [2009] 1 FLR 1189).

10.16   **Significant injury**   The 'injury in question' for the purposes of LA 1980, s. 14(1)(a), is the injury for which the claim is brought (*McManus v Mannings Marine Ltd* [2001] EWCA Civ 1668, LTL 29/10/2001). Therefore, where a claimant sues for the exacerbation of a previous injury following further exposure to hazardous working conditions, time runs from the date the claimant knew the exacerbated injury was significant. It has been held that it is legitimate for a claimant to restrict a claim to post-traumatic stress disorder which arose in a delayed form, and not to include a claim for the alleged underlying (and earlier) physical abuse. In such a case the 'injury in question' for the purposes of s. 14 is the post-traumatic stress disorder, for which the claimant's date of knowledge may be later than for the underlying abuse (*H v Northampton County Council* [2004] EWCA Civ 526, [2005] PIQR P87, per Pill LJ at [18]). The cases relied on, *KR v Bryn Alyn Community (Holdings) Ltd* [2003] EWCA Civ 85, [2003] QB 1441 at [39] and *Stubbings v Webb* [1992] QB 197 at p. 208, have not survived *A v Hoare* [2008] UKHL 6, [2008] 1 AC 844, and so it is unlikely that *H v Northampton County Council* remains good law.

An injury is 'significant' for the purposes of s. 14(1)(a) if the claimant would have considered it sufficiently serious to justify proceedings against a defendant who does not dispute liability and is able to satisfy any judgment (s. 14(2)). The burden of proof on this question rests on the defendant (*Furniss v Firth Brown Tools Ltd* [2008] EWCA Civ 182, LTL 12/3/2008). It could be objected that any injury will satisfy this test. However, it was held in *Stephen v Riverside Health Authority* (1989) *The Times*, 29 November 1989, that the early symptoms of cancer arising from excessive radiation received from a medical X-ray did not amount to a significant injury. A person who alleges rape, whether vaginal or anal, must know objectively, at the time of the assault, that he or she has suffered a significant injury (*Albonetti v Wirral Metropolitan Borough Council* [2008] EWCA Civ 783, LTL 7/7/2008).

Reasons for not bringing proceedings outside the merits of the claim, such as reluctance to sue an employer, have been held to be irrelevant under s. 14, although they can be relevant under s. 33 (see **10.19**) (*McCafferty v Metropolitan Police District Receiver* [1977] 1 WLR 1073). To a similar effect is *McCoubrey v Ministry of Defence* [2007] EWCA Civ 17, [2007] 1 WLR 1544. The key question is whether the claimant knew he or she had suffered a significant injury. The effect of the injury on the claimant's career or private life is irrelevant under s. 14.

The test in s. 14(2) is only 'subjective' to the limited extent that it is applied to what the claimant knows of his or her injury, rather than the injury as it actually is. The claimant's knowledge may have to be supplemented by constructive knowledge under s. 14(3). Otherwise, the test in s. 14(2) sets an entirely impersonal standard. The question is not whether the claimant considered his or her injury was sufficiently serious, but whether the claimant reasonably would have done so. The court needs to find what the claimant knew about the injury, then add any constructive knowledge under s. 14(3). The court must then consider whether a reasonable person with that knowledge would have considered the injury sufficiently serious to justify commencing proceedings against a defendant who did not dispute liability and who was able to satisfy a judgment (*A v Hoare* [2008] UKHL 6, [2008] 1 AC 844, per Lord Hoffmann at [34]). It is not a case of considering whether someone with the claimant's intelligence would have been reasonable if he did not consider the injury sufficiently serious to justify proceedings (*B v Nugent Care Society* [2009] EWCA Civ 827, [2010] 1 WLR 516 at [9]). Once the court has ascertained what the claimant knew and should have known, the

characteristics of the actual claimant (such as intelligence or vulnerability) dro⎫
the picture.

There is a difference between s. 14(3), which turns on what the claimant ought reaso⎫
have done, and s. 14(2), which sets a standard for whether the injury suffered was sig⎫
Under s. 14(3) the court must take into account the injury the claimant has suffer⎫
example, the court will not assume a claimant who has been blinded could reasonab⎫
acquired knowledge by seeing things. Under s. 14(2), on the other hand, the effect⎫
injuries on what the claimant could reasonably be expected to do is irrelevant (*A v H*⎫
[39]). Where the injury suffered has impeded the claimant in bringing a claim (for ex⎫
repressed memories following sexual abuse), the correct approach is to consider the⎫
under s. 33, not s. 14 (at [44], [45]).

James v East Dorset Health Authority (1999) 59 BMLR 196 is a relatively rare case where a pa⎫
who underwent an unsuccessful operation did not realise he might have suffered an in⎫
until he was put on notice that this was a possibility by an independent consultant five yea⎫
later. Time did not start running against the claimant over the subsequent 17 months either⎫
because it was not unreasonable for him to have taken at least that time to obtain confirmation that the original operation had caused him injury. In *Field v British Coal Corporation* [2008]
EWCA Civ 912, LTL 31/7/2008, time did not run against a claimant who alleged he had suffered
industrial deafness while he followed medical advice that his hearing loss was due to wax or
an infection.

Attributable to defendant's conduct   The knowledge mentioned in LA 1980, s. 14(1)(b), is   **10.17**
not knowledge detailed enough to enable the claimant's advisers to draft particulars of claim,
and there is no requirement that the claimant must be aware that the defendant's conduct is
actionable. To hold that this is the case would be contrary to the final words of s. 14(1) that
knowledge that any acts or omissions do or do not constitute negligence as a matter of law is
irrelevant. In *Spargo v North Essex District Health Authority* [1997] PIQR P235, Brooke LJ laid down
the following four principles:

(a) The knowledge required to satisfy s. 14(1)(b) is a broad knowledge of the essence of the
    causally relevant act or omission to which the injury is attributable.
(b) 'Attributable' in this context means 'capable of being attributed to' in the sense of being a
    real possibility.
(c) An injured person has the requisite knowledge when he or she knows enough to make
    it reasonable to begin to investigate whether or not there is a case against the person
    responsible. This will be the case if the injured person so firmly believes that his condi-
    tion is capable of being attributed to an act or omission which he can identify (in broad
    terms) that he goes to a solicitor to seek advice about making a claim for
    compensation.
(d) An injured person will not have the requisite knowledge if he thinks he knows of acts or
    omissions which he should investigate, but in fact is barking up the wrong tree; or if his
    knowledge is so vague or general that he cannot fairly be expected to know what he
    should investigate; or if his state of mind is such that he thinks his condition could be
    attributable to the act or omission alleged to constitute negligence, but he is not sure
    about this, and would need to check with an expert before he could properly be said to
    know that it was.

In *Broadley v Guy Clapham and Co.* [1994] 4 All ER 439 the claimant had gone into hospital for
a knee operation, and left suffering from a condition known as foot drop. It was held that
time started to run when the claimant had both a 'broad knowledge' that the operation had
caused an injury to her foot, and specific knowledge that the operation had been carried
out in such a way as to damage a nerve in her leg (the cause of her foot drop condition).
She had the requisite broad knowledge shortly after the operation, and should have had the

...ic knowledge within a few months after the operation if she had taken the appropriate ...rt advice. In *Dobbie v Medway Health Authority* [1994] 1 WLR 1234 it was alleged that a ...pital carried out a mastectomy without conducting the usual tests, and that the ...eration was entirely unnecessary. The surgeon was alleged to have told the claimant ...fterwards that at least she was fortunate that there was no malignancy. It was held that within days of the operation the claimant had the requisite broad knowledge that she had suffered a significant injury, and time started running from that point, even though it was not until several years later that she realised she could make a claim. In *Whiston v London Strategic Health Authority* [2010] EWCA Civ 195, [2010] 1 WLR 1582, the relevant knowledge in a clinical negligence claim based on being deprived of oxygen at birth was not merely that the claimant knew he had a forceps delivery, but whether he knew his injury was due to a junior doctor's persistence in attempting a forceps delivery, his use of the wrong forceps, and delay in seeking assistance.

Whether the relevant facts could only be known after obtaining an expert's report depends on the complexity of the case (*Hendy v Milton Keynes Health Authority* (1991) 3 Med LR 114). Thus, in *Forbes v Wandsworth Health Authority* [1997] QB 402 the claimant was admitted to hospital for an operation to cure circulation problems in his leg. The operation was not a success, and a fortnight later his leg was amputated. He did not obtain actual knowledge of the default of the hospital that he later relied on in proceedings for medical negligence until he received advice from a consultant 10 years later. It was held that, where an operation was expected to be successful, but ended up with disappointing results, the patient had to be allowed a reasonable time in which to get over the shock and to take stock of the situation before being expected to seek advice for the purpose of bringing a claim. Where the results were serious, as in this case, the taking-stock period would be in the region of 12 to 18 months. From that point the patient would be fixed with constructive knowledge, and time would start running for limitation purposes. The claimant in *Secretary of State for Trade and Industry v Mackie* [2007] EWCA Civ 642, LTL 28/6/2007, was a miner, who took a hearing test in 1992 and was informed he had suffered a 9.98 dB hearing loss. He was aware that other miners were making noise exposure claims based on hearing losses exceeding 10 dB. He was informed by a union official that he did not have a claim. He did not bring proceedings until consulting solicitors in 2003. It was held that time ran from 1992, as the original hearing test was plainly arranged with a view to bringing a claim for damages, and showed an injury which was attributable to his working conditions. Even if the misinformation provided by the union official had displaced that knowledge, it was unreasonable, for the purposes of s. 14(3), for the claimant to do nothing for the next 10 years.

10.18 **Defendant's identity** Typical cases where time is postponed under LA 1980, s. 14(1)(c), are hit-and-run accidents and cases where claimants are rendered unconscious and have no recollection of the accident. Claimants injured at work almost always have immediate knowledge of the identity of their employer. However, there are cases where the exact identity of the claimant's employer does not become clear until some time after an accident. In *Simpson v Norwest Holst Southern Ltd* [1980] 1 WLR 968 time was postponed where the claimant's employer 'hid' (to use the word used by Lawton LJ at p. 974) its identity by calling itself 'Norwest Holst Group'. Time was also postponed in *Cressey v E. Timm and Son Ltd* [2005] EWCA Civ 763, [2005] 1 WLR 3926, where the actual employer was one company in the group (Holdings), but the claimant's pay slips were issued by another company (Limited). Rix LJ made the point (at [29]) that application of s. 14(1)(c) does not depend on deliberate 'hiding' of the defendant's identity. At [35] Rix LJ said that knowing the defendant's 'identity' in s. 14(1)(c) requires something specific enough to enable a person to be identified for the purposes of a claim form. This in turn means that time will run against a claimant who knows who the defendant is, but does not have the defendant's correct name (at [33]).

Personal injuries claims: discretion to disapply limitation period

A wide discretion is given to override the usual three-year limitation period in personal injuries claims by LA 1980, s. 33, which in part provides: **10.19**

33. Discretionary Exclusion of Time Limit for Actions in Respect of Personal Injuries or Death

(1) If it appears to the court that it would be equitable to allow an action to proceed having regard to the degree to which—

    (a) the provisions of section 11 or 11A or 12 of this Act prejudice the plaintiff or any person whom he represents; and

    (b) any decision of the court under this subsection would prejudice the defendant or any person whom he represents;

    the court may direct that those provisions shall not apply to the action, or shall not apply to any specified cause of action to which the action relates....

(3) In acting under this section the court shall have regard to all the circumstances of the case and in particular to—

    (a) the length of, and the reasons for, the delay on the part of the plaintiff;

    (b) the extent to which, having regard to the delay, the evidence adduced or likely to be adduced by the plaintiff or the defendant is or is likely to be less cogent than if the action had been brought within the time allowed by section 11, by section 11A or (as the case may be) by section 12;

    (c) the conduct of the defendant after the cause of action arose, including the extent (if any) to which he responded to requests reasonably made by the plaintiff for information or inspection for the purpose of ascertaining facts which were or might be relevant to the plaintiff's cause of action against the defendant;

    (d) the duration of any disability of the plaintiff arising after the date of the accrual of the cause of action;

    (e) the extent to which the plaintiff acted promptly and reasonably once he knew whether or not the act or omission of the defendant, to which the injury was attributable, might be capable at that time of giving rise to an action for damages;

    (f) the steps, if any, taken by the plaintiff to obtain medical, legal or other expert advice and the nature of any such advice he may have received.

Interpretation of s. 33   The leading authority on LA 1980, s. 33, is *Thompson v Brown* [1981] **10.20** 1 WLR 744, in which the House of Lords held that the court has a discretion unfettered by any rules of practice, that the court must consider all the circumstances of the case, and is not restricted to the matters specifically set out in s. 33(3). Lord Diplock said in that case that a direction under s. 33 is always prejudicial to the defendant, but the extent of the prejudice is related to the strength or otherwise of the claim or defence. 'Equitable' in s. 33 means doing what is fair and just. A tortfeasor only deserves to have his obligation to pay damages removed if the passage of time has significantly compromised his ability to defend the claim (*Cain v Francis* [2008] EWCA Civ 1451, [2009] QB 754).

While the analysis of s. 14 in *KR v Bryn Alyn Community (Holdings) Ltd* [2003] EWCA Civ 85, [2003] QB 1441, is no longer good law given the decision in *A v Hoare* [2008] UKHL 6, [2008] 1 AC 844, Auld LJ's statement of the principles to be applied in applications under s. 33 at [74] remains broadly good law, albeit in need of adjustment to take into account subsequent decisions, in particular *A v Hoare* (*B v Nugent Care Society* [2009] EWCA Civ 827, [2010] 1 WLR 516 at [11] to [26]). As adjusted, Auld LJ's principles on the substantive aspects of applications under s. 33 are as follows:

(a) [In cases where there is more than one claimant], a judge should consider the exercise of his discretion separately in relation to each claim.

(b) The burden of showing that it would be equitable to disapply the limitation period lies on the claimant. [How easy or difficult it is for the claimant to persuade the court to exercise its discretion depends on the facts of the particular case (*Sayers v Hunt* [2012] EWCA Civ 1715, [2013] 1 WLR 1695). In *B v Nugent Care Society* at [20] Lord Clarke of Stone-cum-Ebony MR said that 'it is correct to describe the exercise of the discretion as an exceptional indulgence to the claimant because, but for the exercise of the discretion, his claim will be time-barred.

But it is only exceptional for that reason. The cases stress that the discretion is wide and unfettered.']

(c) Depending on the issues and the nature of the evidence going to them, the longer the delay the more likely, and the greater, the prejudice to the defendant.

(d) Where a judge is minded to grant a long 'extension' he should take meticulous care in giving reasons for doing so.

(e) A judge should not reach a decision effectively concluding the matter on the strength of any one of the circumstances specified in s. 33(3), or on one of any other circumstances relevant to his decision, or without regard to all the issues in the case. He should conduct the balancing exercise at the end of his analysis of all the relevant circumstances and with regard to all the issues, taking them all into account.

(f) [Auld LJ's sub-para. (vii)] Where a judge determines the s. 33 issue along with the substantive issues in the case, he should take care not to determine the substantive issues, including liability, causation and quantum, before determining the issue of limitation and, in particular, the effect of delay on the cogency of the evidence.... To rely on his findings on those issues to assess the cogency of the evidence for the purposes of the limitation exercise would put the cart before the horse. Put another way, it would effectively require the defendant to prove a negative, namely, that the judge could not have found against him on one or more of the substantive issues if he had tried the matter earlier and without the evidential disadvantages resulting from the delay.

(g) [Auld LJ's sub-para. (viii) This deals with the merits of the claim. Auld LJ, relying on *Hartley v Birmingham City District Council* [1992] 1 WLR 968 at pp. 979–80, said the merits are usually a neutral factor. Auld LJ pointed to the exception identified by *Nash v Eli Lilly and Co.* [1993] 1 WLR 782 at p. 804E, that weak claims on liability brought by impecunious claimants do cause prejudice to defendants, which should be taken into account. In *B v Nugent Care Society* the Master of the Rolls at [23] explained that *Hartley v Birmingham City District Council* had been misunderstood. All that Parker LJ intended to say in that case was that the prejudice to the defendant of losing a limitation defence is not the relevant prejudice to be addressed. The relevant prejudice is that which affects the defendant's ability to defend (confirmed by *Cain v Francis* [2008] EWCA Civ 1451, [2009] QB 754). Lord Clarke MR in *B v Nugent Care Society* at [23] said in terms that: 'Clearly the strength of the claimant's case is relevant and was relevant to the decision of Parker and Leggatt LJJ in *Hartley v Birmingham City District Council*.']

The circumstances set out in s. 33(3) are those which experience had indicated were of real importance in considering where the balance of prejudice was likely to lie. The delay referred to in point (a) is the same as that referred to in point (b), namely, the delay after the expiry of the primary limitation period as extended, if appropriate, by the claimant's date of knowledge under s. 14 (*Long v Tolchard and Sons Ltd* [2001] PIQR P2). Overall delay is also relevant as part of all the circumstances of the case (s. 33(3); *McDonnell v Walker* [2009] EWCA Civ 1257, LTL 24/11/2009). The reasons for the delay to be considered are those of the claimant: it is a subjective test (*Coad v Cornwall and Isles of Scilly Health Authority* [1997] 1 WLR 189). Having found what the reason is for the delay, the court must then decide whether the reason is good or bad. The general rule is that the longer the delay, the more likely it is that the balance of prejudice will move away from granting relief to the claimant. While it has been said to be wrong to concentrate mainly on the claimant's reasons for the delay, without sufficient emphasis on the length of the delay (*Buckler v Sheffield City Council* [2004] EWCA Civ 920, [2005] PIQR P36), this was in a case decided before *A v Hoare*. The current approach is to give greater emphasis than formerly, especially in childhood abuse claims, to the 'reasons' for the delay under s. 33(3)(a) (*B v Nugent Care Society*).

The question of cogency in point (b) is only concerned with the loss or adverse effect on evidence through the passage of time. A court is not entitled in an application under s. 33 to find prejudice to the defendant by assuming that omissions or contradictions in the claimant's evidence may be excused by the trial judge (*Nash v Eli Lilly and Co.* [1993] 1 WLR 782). Any prejudice to contribution proceedings, such as tracing witnesses, has to be taken into account under s. 33(3)(b) (*Buckler v Sheffield City Council* [2004] EWCA Civ 920, [2005] PIQR P36).

The period of disability referred to in point (d) is one of mental disability arising after the accrual of the cause of action, and hence one which does not prevent time running (see **10.51**).

Cross-claims against solicitor   One factor not mentioned in LA 1980, s. 33(3), but of considerable importance, is whether the claimant has an alternative claim in negligence against his or her solicitor for failing to issue proceedings in time (*Thompson v Brown* [1981] 1 WLR 744). Possibly negligent discontinuance of the first claim tended towards dismissing an application under s. 33 (*Williams v Johnstone* [2008] EWHC 1334 (QB), LTL 26/6/2008). This factor can be discounted if there is real doubt about the strength of the claim against the solicitor, and in any event the claimant will suffer some prejudice through further delay, instructing unknown solicitors to pursue the new claim, the old solicitors knowing the weaknesses of the original claim, and possible restrictions in obtaining disclosure against the original defendants (see disclosure against non-parties in **chapter 50**). In *Steeds v Peverel Management Services Ltd* [2001] EWCA Civ 419, *The Times,* 16 May 2001, the claimant's solicitors had, through oversight, issued proceedings 49 days after the expiry of limitation. The Court of Appeal held that the judge at first instance had erred in law in assuming that the solicitors' failings were those of the claimant, and in criticising a period of delay after the solicitors were instructed. Despite the strong claim in negligence against the solicitors, if the claim were defeated by the expiry of the limitation period, greater prejudice would be suffered by the claimant than the defendant, and the claim was allowed to proceed.

10.21

Date of notification and forensic prejudice   A second factor not mentioned in LA 1980, s. 33(3), which is always regarded as being of considerable importance, is the delay between the accident and the defendant being informed of the claim. The reason is that a defendant who is informed of the potential claim at an early stage has the opportunity to investigate the facts while the events are still fresh in witnesses' memories, even if proceedings are issued rather late, and hence cannot complain of significant prejudice under s. 33(3)(b). This seems to have been a significant factor in *Thompson v Brown* [1981] 1 WLR 744 and also in *Hartley v Birmingham City District Council* [1992] 1 WLR 968. In early notification cases where there is no defence on liability, financial prejudice to the defendant should not be taken into account (*Cain v Francis* [2008] EWCA Civ 1451, [2009] QB 754). It is unclear whether the court should disregard financial prejudice to the defendant in other cases, although the principle is stated in general terms. *Cain v Francis*, where the limitation period was disapplied despite a one-year delay, must be regarded as a case where there was no forensic prejudice (*McDonnell v Walker* [2009] EWCA Civ 1257, LTL 24/11/2009).

10.22

The length of time since the accident (in *McDonnell v Walker* it was seven years), substantial changes in the nature of the alleged claim since first notification, or the death of witnesses, may mean there is forensic prejudice. In these cases *McDonnell v Walker* says the court must consider:

(a) the cause of the delays (often it is necessary to split the delay into different periods);
(b) whether the delays are excusable;
(c) the effects of the delays in effectively being able to investigate the evidence; and
(d) whether it is still possible to have a fair trial.

In *Donovan v Gwentoys Ltd* [1990] 1 WLR 472 there was a delay in excess of six years before the defendants were given full details of the claim. In fact proceedings were issued only six months late, as the claimant was a child at the date of the accident. She instructed solicitors 19 days before her eighteenth birthday, so she had an alternative claim against her solicitors. It was held that the delay in notifying the defendants was an extremely important consideration, that

Commentary

it would be inequitable to require the defendants to meet such a stale claim, and the claimant would suffer only the slightest prejudice in being required to sue her solicitors. Permission was refused. See also *Kamar v Nightingale* [2007] EWHC 2982 (QB), [2008] PNLR 15. In sexual abuse claims, the date of notification of the claim and, where the claim is brought many years after the alleged events, the possibility of having a fair trial, are important factors (*A v Hoare* [2008] UKHL 6, [2008] 1 AC 844).

10.23   **Merits of substantive claim**   Parker LJ in *Hartley v Birmingham City District Council* [1992] 1 WLR 968 expressed the view that the merits of the claimant's case are of little importance, on the ground that the stronger the merits the greater the prejudice to both the claimant and the defendant of the decision under LA 1980, s. 33, going against them. This is inconsistent with Lord Diplock's speech in *Thompson v Brown* [1981] 1 WLR 744, and contrary to subsequent cases. These include *Nash v Eli Lilly and Co.* [1993] 1 WLR 782, where a finding that the claims were weak was regarded as an important factor in refusing to make orders under s. 33, and *Long v Tolchard and Sons Ltd* [2001] PIQR P2, where it was said that if the claimant has a strong, or even a cast-iron, case against the original tortfeasor, that is an important factor to place into the balance that has to be struck. Unless the claim has no realistic prospect of success (in which event the application should be refused: *TCD v Harrow London Borough Council* [2008] EWHC 3048 (QB), [2009] 1 FLR 719), the strength of the case is not determinative of the application. Where the question of the merits arises at an interim hearing, all the court should do is determine the overall prospects (*Dale v British Coal Corporation (No. 2)* (1992) *The Times*, 2 July 1992), although a determination to the usual civil standard may be appropriate where the matter is raised as a preliminary issue.

10.24   **Second claim cases**   When finding the balance of prejudice under LA 1980, s. 33, in a 'second claim' case, the court has to consider the degree of prejudice in that second claim. In *Richardson v Watson* [2006] EWCA Civ 1662, [2007] RTR 247, following *Horton v Sadler* [2006] UKHL 27, [2007] 1 AC 307, the court disapplied the limitation period. In this case the first claim was brought within the three-year limitation period, but had to be discontinued because of a failure to give the requisite notice under the Uninsured Drivers Agreement (see **9.4**). In *Adams v Ali* [2006] EWCA Civ 91, [2006] 1 WLR 1330, the first claim was started a week outside the three-year limitation period, and was struck out for failure to serve particulars of claim. Liability was not in dispute, and the delay was the fault of the claimant's solicitors. It was held to be equitable to disapply the limitation period under s. 33 in a second claim issued about 13 months after the expiry of limitation.

10.25   **Other factors**   In *Das v Ganju* [1999] PIQR P260 the Court of Appeal held that delays caused by incorrect advice given by the claimant's lawyers should not be laid at the claimant's door, and allowed a claim to continue despite a delay of many years. Conversely, a delay of almost a year after the law was changed by *Horton v Sadler* [2006] UKHL 27, [2007] 1 AC 307 (see **10.3**), tended against disapplying limitation in *Williams v Johnstone* [2008] EWHC 1334 (QB), LTL 26/6/2008. In *Whiston v London Strategic Health Authority* [2010] EWCA Civ 195, [2010] 1 WLR 1582, the judge was held to have placed far too much weight on the claimant's decision not to sue when he was younger and not so badly affected by his cerebral palsy. Once he acquired actual knowledge of the alleged negligence there was no basis for finding he had made a decision not to sue. A fair trial was still possible, and he had a substantial claim which gave him a prospect of having his future needs provided for. It was therefore equitable to allow the claim to proceed.

As mentioned at **10.16**, many reasons for not bringing a claim, such as a reluctance to sue one's present employer, are irrelevant under LA 1980, s. 14. However, they can be important factors under s. 33. So, in *McCafferty v Metropolitan Police District Receiver* [1977] 1 WLR 1073 Lawton LJ said, in relation to an application under s. 33, 'the court should be understanding of men who, after taking an overall view of their situation, come to the conclusion that they would prefer to go on working rather than become involved in litigation'. Also relevant is the defendant's ability to satisfy a judgment, such as by winning the lottery. Claimants should not feel obliged to sue indigent defendants in the hope they might at some later stage become rich enough to pay (*A v Hoare* [2008] UKHL 6, [2008] 1 AC 844; the limitation period was disapplied on the facts when the matter was considered by Coulson J in *A v Hoare* [2008] EWHC 1573 (QB), LTL 15/7/2008). Limitation was disapplied in the sexual abuse claim of *Raggett v Society of Jesus Trust 1929 for Roman Catholic Purposes* [2009] EWHC 909 (QB), 108 BMLR 147, despite a delay of 28 years, whereas a fair trial was felt to be impossible 40 years after the event in the otherwise similar case of *Albonetti v Wirral Metropolitan Borough* [2009] EWHC 832 (QB), LTL 12/5/2009.

Discretionary disapplication of the limitation period under s. 33 has no application in cases governed by the two-year limitation period under the Convention relating to the Carriage of Passengers and their Luggage by Sea (as enacted by the Merchant Shipping Act 1995; class 18 in **table 10.1**), see *Higham v Stena Sealink Ltd* [1996] 1 WLR 1107.

Procedure   In *KR v Bryn Alyn Community (Holdings) Ltd* [2003] EWCA Civ 85, [2003] QB 1441 at **10.26** [74(vi)], Auld LJ suggested that wherever the judge considers it feasible to do so, decisions under LA 1980, s. 33, should be made at preliminary hearings by reference to the statements of case and written witness statements, together with the documents provided through standard disclosure. In *B v Nugent Care Society* [2009] EWCA Civ 827, [2010] 1 WLR 516 at [21], Lord Clarke of Stone-cum-Ebony MR said that in many cases (probably of childhood abuse) the judge may conclude that it is desirable that oral evidence should be heard, because the strength of the claimant's evidence is relevant to the way the discretion under s. 33 should be exercised. It is incumbent on the claimant to disclose all relevant circumstances at the hearing of the application, and if this is breached, the decision may be set aside (*Long v Tolchard and Sons Ltd* [2001] PIQR P2).

Defective products

Claims under the Consumer Protection Act 1987 in respect of personal injuries or damage to **10.27** property accrue on the date of damage or the 'date of knowledge' (LA 1980, s. 11A(4)). By s. 11A(3), proceedings must be instituted against the producer of an allegedly defective product within 10 years. Section 11A provides in part:

11A. Actions in Respect of Defective Products

(3) An action to which this section applies shall not be brought after the expiration of the period of ten years from the relevant time, within the meaning of section 4 of the said Act of 1987; and this subsection shall operate to extinguish a right of action and shall do so whether or not that right of action had accrued, or time under the following provisions of this Act had begun to run, at the end of the said period of ten years.

(4) Subject to subsection (5) below, an action to which this section applies in which the damages claimed by the plaintiff consist of or include damages in respect of personal injuries to the plaintiff or any other person or loss of or damage to any property, shall not be brought after the expiration of the period of three years from whichever is the later of—

  (a) the date on which the cause of action accrued; and
  (b) the date of knowledge of the injured person or, in the case of loss of or damage to property, the date of knowledge of the plaintiff or (if earlier) of any person in whom his cause of action was previously vested.

(5) If in a case where the damages claimed by the plaintiff consist of or include damages in respect of personal injuries to the plaintiff or any other person the injured person died before the expiration of the period mentioned in subsection (4) above, that subsection shall have effect as respects the cause of action surviving for the benefit of his estate by virtue of section 1 of the Law Reform (Miscellaneous Provisions) Act 1934 as if for the reference to that period there were substituted a reference to the period of three years from whichever is the later of—

  (a) the date of death; and
  (b) the date of the personal representative's knowledge.

For substitution of a party after the expiry of the ten-year period under s. 35 see **14.86**.

Fatal accidents: accrual of cause of action

10.28 If a person injured in an accident later dies as a result of those injuries, the cause of action vesting in the injured person's estate under the **Law Reform (Miscellaneous Provisions) Act 1934** accrued at the date of the accident. However, the related cause of action for the benefit of the injured person's beneficiaries under the **Fatal Accidents Act 1976, s. 1**, accrues on the date of death, with the result there are two limitation periods (*Reader v Molesworths Bright Clegg* [2007] EWCA Civ 169, [2007] 1 WLR 1082).

Fatal accidents and death: date of knowledge

10.29 In proceedings brought for the benefit of the deceased's estate under the **Law Reform (Miscellaneous Provisions) Act 1934** time runs from the date of death or the personal representative's 'date of knowledge' (LA 1980, s. 11(5)). Section 11(5) provides:

> If in a case where the damages claimed by the plaintiff consist of or include damages in respect of personal injuries to the plaintiff or any other person the injured person died before the expiration of the period mentioned in subsection (4) above, that subsection shall have effect as respects the cause of action surviving for the benefit of his estate by virtue of section 1 of the Law Reform (Miscellaneous Provisions) Act 1934 as if for the reference to that period there were substituted a reference to the period of three years from whichever is the later of—
>
> (a) the date of death; and
> (b) the date of the personal representative's knowledge.

Time runs in claims brought by dependants under the **Fatal Accidents Act 1976** from the date of death or the 'date of knowledge' (as set out in **10.14**) of the person for whose benefit the proceedings are brought (LA 1980, s. 12). Section 12(1) and (2) provide:

> **12. Special Time Limit for Actions under Fatal Accidents Legislation**
>
> (1) An action under the Fatal Accidents Act 1976 shall not be brought if the death occurred when the person injured could no longer maintain an action and recover damages in respect of the injury (whether because of a time limit in this Act or in any other Act, or for any other reason).
>   Where any such action by the injured person would have been barred by the time limit in section 11 or 11A of this Act, no account shall be taken of the possibility of that time limit being overridden under section 33 of this Act.
> (2) None of the time limits given in the preceding provisions of this Act shall apply to an action under the Fatal Accidents Act 1976, but no such action shall be brought after the expiration of three years from—
>   (a)   the date of death; or
>   (b)   the date of knowledge of the person for whose benefit the action is brought;
>   whichever is the later.

Latent damage

10.30 It follows from the decision in *Pirelli General Cable Works Ltd v Oscar Faber and Partners* [1983] 2 AC 1 noted at **10.7** that it is possible for a claim in tort to be statute barred before the claimant knows that damage has been sustained, because time runs from the date of damage rather than discovery. To mitigate this position the Latent Damage Act 1986 inserted ss. 14A and 14B into the LA 1980:

> **14A. Special Time Limit for Negligence Actions Where Facts Relevant to Cause of Action are Not Known at Date of Accrual**
>
> (1) This section applies to any action for damages for negligence, other than one to which section 11 of this Act applies, where the starting date for reckoning the period of limitation under subsection (4)(b) below falls after the date on which the cause of action accrued.
> (2) Section 2 of this Act shall not apply to an action to which this section applies.
> (3) An action to which this section applies shall not be brought after the expiration of the period applicable in accordance with subsection (4) below.

(4)   That period is either—
    (a)   six years from the date on which the cause of action accrued; or
    (b)   three years from the starting date as defined by subsection (5) below, if that period expires later than the period mentioned in paragraph (a) above.

(5)   For the purposes of this section, the starting date for reckoning the period of limitation under subsection (4)(b) above is the earliest date on which the plaintiff or any person in whom the cause of action was vested before him first had both the knowledge required for bringing an action for damages in respect of the relevant damage and a right to bring such an action.

(6)   In subsection (5) above 'the knowledge required for bringing an action for damages in respect of the relevant damage' means knowledge both—
    (a)   of the material facts about the damage in respect of which damages are claimed; and
    (b)   of the other facts relevant to the current action mentioned in subsection (8) below.

(7)   For the purposes of subsection (6)(a) above, the material facts about the damage are such facts about the damage as would lead a reasonable person who had suffered such damage to consider it sufficiently serious to justify his instituting proceedings for damages against a defendant who did not dispute liability and was able to satisfy a judgment.

(8)   The other facts referred to in subsection (6)(b) above are—
    (a)   that the damage was attributable in whole or in part to the act or omission which is alleged to constitute negligence; and
    (b)   the identity of the defendant; and
    (c)   if it is alleged that the act or omission was that of a person other than the defendant, the identity of that person and the additional facts supporting the bringing of an action against the defendant.

(9)   Knowledge that any acts or omissions did or did not, as a matter of law, involve negligence is irrelevant for the purposes of subsection (5) above.

(10)   For the purposes of this section a person's knowledge includes knowledge which he might reasonably have been expected to acquire—
    (a)   from facts observable or ascertainable by him; or
    (b)   from facts ascertainable by him with the help of appropriate expert advice which it is reasonable for him to seek;
    but a person shall not be taken by virtue of this subsection to have knowledge of a fact ascertainable only with the help of expert advice so long as he has taken all reasonable steps to obtain (and, where appropriate, to act on) that advice.

14B. Overriding Time Limit for Negligence Actions Not Involving Personal Injuries

(1)   An action for damages for negligence, other than one to which section 11 of this Act applies, shall not be brought after the expiration of fifteen years from the date (or, if more than one, from the last of the dates) on which there occurred any act or omission—
    (a)   which is alleged to constitute negligence; and
    (b)   to which the damage in respect of which damages are claimed is alleged to be attributable (in whole or in part).

(2)   This section bars the right of action in a case to which subsection (1) above applies notwithstanding that—
    (a)   the cause of action has not yet accrued; or
    (b)   where section 14A of this Act applies to the action, the date which is for the purposes of that section the starting date for reckoning the period mentioned in subsection (4)(b) of that section has not yet occurred;
    before the end of the period of limitation prescribed by this section.

These provisions apply to claims for negligence other than for personal injuries (s. 14A(1)). They do not apply while the claimant can rely on the defendant's concealment under s. 32 (*Williams v Lishman, Sidwell, Campbell and Price Ltd* [2010] EWCA Civ 418, [2010] PNLR 25). They are restricted to claims in tort, and do not extend to claims for 'contractual negligence' (*Société Commerciale de Réassurance v ERAS (International) Ltd* [1992] 2 All ER 82).

Latent damage: starting date   Two alternative periods of limitation are provided by LA 1980, s. 14A(4), namely, six years from accrual and three years from the 'starting date'. The first of these periods is simply the usual period for claims in tort. Where the claimant was under a disability on the starting date, the period of three years in s. 14A(4)(b) runs from   **10.31**

when he ceased to be under a disability or died (s. 28A). The 'starting date' is the earliest date the claimant knew:

(a) that the relevant damage was sufficiently serious to justify proceedings; and

(b) that the damage was attributable to the alleged negligence; and

(c) the defendant's identity.

These concepts are very similar to those in s. 14 (see **10.14** to **10.18**) and it was accepted in *Hallam-Eames v Merrett* [1995] CLC 173 that the authorities on s. 14 apply to applications under s. 14A. 'Knowledge' in s. 14A means knowing with sufficient confidence to justify embarking on the preliminaries to issuing proceedings (*Haward v Fawcetts* [2006] UKHL 9, [2006] 1 WLR 682s). Regarding condition (b), it is clear the claimant does not need to know he has a cause of action, or that the defendant's acts would be characterised by the law as negligence. It is enough if the claimant has broad knowledge of the facts on which the complaint is based, and knows there is a real possibility that the defendant's acts or omissions caused the damage under condition (a) (*Haward v Fawcetts*). In *Gravgaard v Aldridge and Brownlee* [2004] EWCA Civ 1529, [2005] PNLR 19, the defendant solicitors negligently failed to advise the claimant that it was not necessary for her to transfer the matrimonial home into joint names with her husband before charging it as security to pay her husband's debts. It was held that the claimant did not have actual knowledge for the purposes of condition (b) until she knew that the exposure of her husband's share of the home to her husband's creditors was caused by the solicitors' wrongful advice. In *3M United Kingdom plc v Linklaters and Paines* [2006] EWCA Civ 530, [2006] PNLR 30, which was a negligence claim by a tenant against its solicitors complaining that an assignment of a lease had caused the loss of a break clause, it was held that the tenant had the relevant knowledge when, during negotiations with the landlord, it came to light that the break was no longer exercisable.

The knowledge of a loss adjuster appointed by the claimant's insurer in a subrogated claim can be attributed to the claimant for the purposes of s. 14A(5) (*Graham v Entec Europe Ltd* [2003] EWCA Civ 1177, [2003] 4 All ER 1345).

Section 14A(9) provides that knowledge that any acts or omissions did or did not, as a matter of law, involve negligence is irrelevant for the purposes of the provisions on date of knowledge in s. 14A. In *Bowie v Southorns* [2002] EWHC 1389 (QB), 152 NLJ 1240, it was held that this covers both knowledge of breach and knowledge that the defendant owed a duty of care, both of which are irrelevant for the purposes of date of knowledge under s. 14A(5).

A claimant is fixed with constructive knowledge by LA 1980, s. 14A(10). Knowing there had been large erosions in the capital in a pension scheme should have put the claimants in *Williams v Lishman, Sidwell, Campbell and Price Ltd* [2009] EWHC 1322 (QB), [2009] PNLR 34, on notice of possibly negligent advice by their pension adviser. In s. 14A(10), 'expert advice' means advice from an independent expert rather than one of the parties whose conduct is being called into question (*Williams v Lishman, Sidwell, Campbell and Price Ltd*).

10.32   **Latent damage: longstop**   In order to give some protection to defendants who might otherwise be perpetually at risk, LA 1980, s. 14B, provides a longstop or overriding time limit for bringing proceedings of 15 years from the act or omission alleged to constitute the negligence causing the claimant's damage. *Financial Services Compensation Scheme Ltd v Larnell (Insurances) Ltd* [2005] EWCA Civ 1408, [2006] QB 808, held that the principle in *Re General Rolling Stock Co., Joint Stock Discount Co.'s claim* (1872) LR 7 Ch App 646 (see **10.59**) is not defeated by the longstop provision in s. 14B. The longstop is merely a procedural bar to bringing a claim.

Defamation

10.33   **Libel: accrual**   Libel claims are actionable per se, so time runs from publication. Knowledge of the identity of the publisher is not an essential element of the cause of action (*Edwards v Golding* [2007] EWCA Civ 416, *The Times*, 22 May 2007).

Defamation: discretion to disapply   Where defamation or malicious falsehood proceedings are not commenced within the one-year time limit, the court may direct that the limitation period shall not apply if it appears equitable to allow the claim to proceed, having regard to the balance of prejudice between the claimant and the defendant (LA 1980, s. 32A, as substituted by the Defamation Act 1996, s. 5). LA 1980, s. 32A, is modelled on s. 33, which provides a similar discretion in personal injuries cases, and which is considered in some detail at **10.19** to **10.26**. Permission was granted in *Wood v Chief Constable of West Midlands Police* [2004] EWCA Civ 1638, [2005] EMLR 20, to add an alternative claim for slander four years after the event by way of an amendment at the close of evidence in a libel trial. Permission was also granted in *Gentoo Group Ltd v Hanratty* [2008] EWHC 627 (QB), LTL 11/4/2008, to include claims arising from material published on a website five days beyond the one-year limitation period. The court took into account the connection between the material published outside the limitation period and material published on the same website which came within the primary limitation period, the fact that the relevant evidence was no less cogent through the five-day delay, the seriousness of the alleged libels, and conduct of the defendant in seeking to deflect suspicion that he was responsible for some of the publications.

10.34

The discretion was exercised against the claimant in *Hinks v Channel 4 Television Corporation* (2000) LTL 3/3/2000, principally because the claimant's solicitor had missed the one-year limitation period by relying, in April 1999, on a textbook written in 1994, which was before the limitation period was reduced from three years to one year in 1996. Unexplained delay in issuing an application to disapply after becoming aware of the limitation difficulties is highly relevant under LA 1980, s. 32A(2)(b)(ii) (*Bewry v Reed Elsevier UK Ltd* [2014] EWCA Civ 1411, [2015] 1 WLR 2565). Another case where solicitors overlooked the one-year limitation period is *Steedman v British Broadcasting Corporation* [2001] EWCA Civ 1534, [2002] EMLR 17, in which it was held that an absence of prejudice to the ability to defend by reason of the delay is simply a factor, and in this case it was outweighed by the strong claim against the solicitors. *Steedman v British Broadcasting Corporation* should not be regarded as inconsistent with *Cain v Francis* [2008] EWCA Civ 1451, [2009] QB 754, discussed at **10.22**. Instead, there are different considerations in defamation and personal injuries claims, which are reflected in the shorter limitation period in defamation and an enhanced need to pursue any claim speedily (*Brady v Norman* [2011] EWCA Civ 107, [2011] EMLR 16).

CONTRACT

LA 1980, s. 5, provides:

10.35

5. Time Limit for Actions Founded on Simple Contract

An action founded on simple contract shall not be brought after the expiration of six years from the date on which the cause of action accrued.

Time runs from the breach of contract. When this is depends on the nature of the obligation sued on and the terms of the contract, and also on whether a repudiatory breach is accepted by the claimant. Applying the general rule, causes of action in breach of contract will accrue as follows:

(a) In claims for breach of the implied terms about satisfactory quality etc. in the Sale of Goods Act 1979 (SoGA 1979), time normally starts running on delivery of the goods (*Battley v Faulkner* (1820) 3 B & Ald 288).

(b) In claims for late delivery of goods, time runs from the contractual date for delivery.

(c) In claims based on the implied terms about title to goods sold, time runs from the date of the contract, or, in the case of an agreement to sell, from the date title was to pass (see SoGA 1979, s. 12(1)).

(d) Claims for the price of goods sold accrue on the contractual date for payment (SoGA 1979, s. 49(2)), failing which on the date property in the goods passes to the buyer (s. 49(1)) or the date the buyer is informed that the seller is ready and willing to deliver (s. 28).

(e) In a construction contract where the price is payable by stated instalments at the end of each month, time runs in respect of each instalment from the end of the relevant month (*Henry Boot Construction Ltd v Alstom Combined Cycles Ltd* [2005] EWCA Civ 814, [2005] 1 WLR 3850 at [60]).

(f) In a construction contract where stage and final payments are payable after certification by an architect or engineer, the certificate is a condition precedent to payment, so time runs from the date the certificate is issued or ought to be issued (*Henry Boot Construction Ltd v Alstom Combined Cycles Ltd* [2005] EWCA Civ 814, [2005] 1 WLR 3850 at [23] to [28] and [50]). This case also pointed out that there are separate causes of action based on interim and final certificates, even if the amounts certified are the same (at [56]). Where there is an overpayment following an adjudication under the Scheme for Construction Contracts the cause of action accrues on the date of the overpayment (*Aspect Contracts (Asbestos) Ltd v Higgins Construction plc* [2013] EWCA Civ 1541, [2014] BLR 79).

(g) In claims based on defective building work, time usually starts running on practical or substantial completion (*Tameside Metropolitan Borough Council v Barlow Securities Group Services Ltd* [2001] BLR 113).

(h) Claims for the price of entire contracts for work and services accrue on completion of the work (*Emery v Day* (1834) 1 Cr M & R 245). In many building contracts the parties agree to stage payments, and time starts running in relation to these at the contractual date for payment.

(i) Claims by banks to recover overdrafts from customers normally accrue on service of a demand in writing (LA 1980, s. 6). There is an exception in s. 6 relating to loans where the debtor also enters into a collateral obligation to pay, such as by delivering a promissory note, but most bank overdrafts fall into the main category.

(j) Claims against sureties and guarantors usually accrue on default by the principal debtor (*Parr's Banking Co. v Yates* [1898] 2 QB 460).

(k) Accrual in the case of negotiable instruments is somewhat complicated. Claims against acceptors and makers based on non-payment accrue on the maturity of the instrument, unless it is a bill of exchange which is accepted after maturity, in which case time runs from the date of acceptance (Bills of Exchange Act 1882, s. 10(2)). Bills of exchange often mature on fixed dates, but if they mature (say) a fixed period of time after sight, time starts running that fixed period after acceptance (or after noting or protesting if it is not accepted) (s. 14(3)). A claim against a drawer or endorser after dishonour by non-payment accrues when the bill is duly presented for payment and payment is refused or cannot be obtained, or, if presentment is excused, when the bill is overdue and unpaid (s. 47(2)).

(l) Accrual in claims against insurers depends on the terms of the policy. The general rule is that time starts running at the date of the loss. For example, claims for constructive total loss accrue on the date of the casualty (*Bank of America National Trust v Chrismas* [1994] 1 All ER 401). However, it is open to the parties to displace the general rule by creating conditions precedent to the insured's right to payment. For example, in *Virk v Gan Life Holdings plc* [2000] Lloyd's Rep IR 159 critical illness benefit became payable under a policy if the insured survived 30 days after suffering a stroke. It was held that time started running 30 days after the stroke. Liability under an indemnity policy does not accrue unless and until the existence and amount of the liability to the third party is established (*Post Office v Norwich Union Fire Insurance Society Ltd* [1967] 2 QB 363).

In cases where the claimant has accepted an anticipatory breach as a repudiation, time starts running from the date of acceptance rather than the contractual date for performance of the obligation in question (*Reeves v Butcher* [1891] 2 QB 509). Claims for consequential losses, such as salvage charges arising out of a claim against an insurer based on the loss of a ship, are not separate causes of action, so accrual turns on the date of the underlying cause of action (the casualty) not on the date the consequential loss was incurred (*Bank of America National Trust v Chrismas* [1994] 1 All ER 401). There are several types of contractual obligation that give rise to continuing or repeated breaches. An example of a continuing breach is a failure to comply with a covenant to keep in repair (*Spoor v Green* (1874) LR 9 Ex 99 at p. 111), and an example of a repeated breach is a failure to pay rent

(*Archbold v Scully* (1861) 9 HL Cas 360). In these cases the claimant will be able to succeed in respect of the consequences of breach over the six-year period (12 years for claims on a specialty) before the claim form is issued.

BREACH OF TRUST

Breach of trust: limitation periods

LA 1980, s. 21, provides: **10.36**

21. Time Limit for Actions in Respect of Trust Property

(1) No period of limitation prescribed by this Act shall apply to an action by a beneficiary under a trust, being an action—
   (a) in respect of any fraud or fraudulent breach of trust to which the trustee was a party or privy; or
   (b) to recover from the trustee trust property or the proceeds of trust property in the possession of the trustee, or previously received by the trustee and converted to his use.
(2) Where a trustee who is also a beneficiary under the trust receives or retains trust property or its proceeds as his share on a distribution of trust property under the trust, his liability in any action brought by virtue of subsection (1)(b) above to recover that property or its proceeds after the expiration of the period of limitation prescribed by this Act for bringing an action to recover trust property shall be limited to the excess over his proper share. This subsection only applies if the trustee acted honestly and reasonably in making the distribution.
(3) Subject to the preceding provisions of this section, an action by a beneficiary to recover trust property or in respect of any breach of trust, not being an action for which a period of limitation is prescribed by any other provision of this Act, shall not be brought after the expiration of six years from the date on which the right of action accrued. For the purposes of this subsection, the right of action shall not be treated as having accrued to any beneficiary entitled to a future interest in the trust property until the interest fell into possession.
(4) No beneficiary as against whom there would be a good defence under this Act shall derive any greater or other benefit from a judgment or order obtained by any other beneficiary than he could have obtained if he had brought the action and this Act had been pleaded in defence.

The main limitation periods are six years in claims for breach of trust and to recover trust property (LA 1980, s. 21(3)), and the unlimited period for bringing claims in respect of any fraud or fraudulent breach of trust to which the trustee was party or privy (s. 21(1)(a)) and for claims to recover from a trustee trust property in the possession of the trustee or which was previously received by the trustee and converted to the trustee's use (s. 21(1)(b)). A claim for an account of profits against a director following a deliberate non-disclosure of an interest was held in *Gwembe Valley Development Co. Ltd v Koshy (No. 3)* [2003] EWCA Civ 1478, [2004] 1 BCLC 131, to be a fraudulent breach of trust within s. 21(1)(a), so there was no period of limitation. It was held that a breach of trust is fraudulent if it was dishonest. *J. J. Harrison (Properties) Ltd v Harrison* [2001] EWCA Civ 1467, [2002] 1 BCLC 162, in which it was held that a claim to recover property conveyed to a director who was in breach of fiduciary duty came within s. 21(1)(b) (also resulting in there being no limitation period), was distinguished in *Gwembe Valley Development Co. Ltd v Koshy (No. 3)*. In *Re Pantone 485 Ltd, Miller v Bain* [2002] 1 BCLC 266 it was held that use of a beneficiary's money for the benefit of the fiduciary amounts to a conversion for the use of the fiduciary, and thereby brings the claim within s. 21(1)(b) (so there is no limitation period). Likewise, a claim for an account and payment of amounts found due to the estate from a personal representative were held to fall within s. 21(1)(b) in *Green v Gaul* [2006] EWCA Civ 1124, [2006] 4 All ER 1011.

A trustee who had negligently left trust money with a solicitor, who then embezzled it, but who was not a party to or privy to the solicitor's fraud, was held in *Thorne v Heard* [1894] 1 Ch 599 to be entitled to rely on a limitation defence after six years (class 9 in **table 10.1**). *Halton International Inc. v Guernroy Ltd* [2006] EWCA Civ 801, [2006] WTLR 1241 concerned a voting agreement between shareholders under which one shareholder was given power of attorney to act, in its absolute discretion, as the agent of and to vote the shares of the other shareholders. This was held to give rise to a bare promise, not a trust. A claim based on allegations of a failure to exercise those powers in good faith and not to make secret profits was therefore governed by the usual six-year limitation period, and did not come within LA 1980, s. 21(1)(b).

Breach of fiduciary duty

10.37   In *Nelson v Rye* [1996] 1 WLR 1378 it was held that a claim for breach of fiduciary duty *simpliciter* is outside the provisions of LA 1980, and so is not subject to any limitation period. This case has been called into question by subsequent decisions, particularly *Paragon Finance plc v D. B. Thakerar and Co.* [1999] 1 All ER 400. In *Nelson v Rye* the claimant was a musician and sought accounts from his former manager stretching back 11 years before proceedings were issued. Millett LJ in *Paragon Finance plc v D. B. Thakerar and Co.* pointed out that every agent owes fiduciary duties to his principal, and without something more the claim would have been subject to the usual six-year limitation period. The defendant in *Nelson v Rye* was no more than an accounting party who had failed to account. To have been entitled to a longer limitation period, the claimant would have had to show, among other things, that the defendant owed fiduciary duties in relation to the money.

Constructive trusts

10.38   Millett LJ in *Paragon Finance plc v D. B. Thakerar and Co.* [1999] 1 All ER 400 (and approved by the Supreme Court in *Williams v Central Bank of Nigeria* [2014] UKSC 10, [2014] AC 1189) pointed out that there is a distinction between two categories of constructive trust claim:

(a)   Where the constructive trustee, although not expressly appointed as a trustee, has assumed the duties of a trustee before the events which are alleged to constitute the breach of trust. In this category the defendant is a real trustee, and the provisions of LA 1980, s. 21(1), may apply if the other conditions of the subsection are satisfied, with the result that there may be an unlimited period for bringing proceedings. It also applies to a company director, who owes fiduciary duties to his company (*J. J. Harrison (Properties) Ltd v Harrison* [2001] EWCA Civ 1467, [2002] 1 BCLC 162). In *James v Williams* [2000] Ch 1 it was held on the facts that an executor de son tort, who was one of three surviving adult children of an intestate parent, became a constructive trustee, and consequently there was no limitation period by virtue of s. 21(1).

(b)   Where the constructive trust is merely the creation of the court as a remedy to meet the alleged wrongdoing. This covers cases of ancillary liability, and includes claims alleging knowing receipt and dishonest assistance in the fraudulent breach of trust of another (*Williams v Central Bank of Nigeria* [2014] UKSC 10, [2014] AC 1189). In this category there is no real trust, and usually no prospect of a proprietary remedy. The defendant is merely said to be liable to account as a constructive trustee. In this category the other provisions of the LA 1980 apply, with the result that the period will usually be six years from accrual. An example is *Halton International Inc. v Guernroy Ltd* [2006] EWCA Civ 801, [2006] WTLR 1241, discussed at **10.36**.

When considering the boundary between cases where the defendant is a true trustee under an express or constructive trust, and those where he is not, the key factor is whether there is trust property (*Clarke v Marlborough Fine Art (London) Ltd* (2001) *The Times*, 5 July 2001).

Beneficiaries

10.39   Different types of claims by beneficiaries have no time limits, 12-year and six-year time limits, see LA 1980, ss. 21 and 22. A right of action for non-fraudulent breach of trust does not accrue until a future interest falls into possession (LA 1980, s. 21(3)). Claims to the personal estate of a deceased person accrue on 'the date on which the right to receive the share or interest accrued'. Time was held to run from the end of the executor's year (one year from death) in *Re Loftus* [2005] EWHC 406 (Ch), [2005] 1 WLR 1890.

EQUITABLE REMEDIES, LACHES AND ACQUIESCENCE

LA 1980, s. 36, provides:

10.40

36. Equitable Jurisdiction and Remedies

(1) The following time limits under this Act, that is to say—
    (a) the time limit under section 2 for actions founded on tort;
    (aa) the time limit under section 4A for actions for libel or slander, or for slander of title, slander of goods or other malicious falsehood;
    (b) the time limit under section 5 for actions founded on simple contract;
    (c) the time limit under section 7 for actions to enforce awards where the submission is not by an instrument under seal;
    (d) the time limit under section 8 for actions on a specialty;
    (e) the time limit under section 9 for actions to recover a sum recoverable by virtue of any enactment; and
    (f) the time limit under section 24 for actions to enforce a judgment;
    shall not apply to any claim for specific performance of a contract or for an injunction or for other equitable relief, except in so far as any such time limit may be applied by the court by analogy in like manner as the corresponding time limit under any enactment repealed by the Limitation Act 1939 was applied before 1st July 1940.

(2) Nothing in this Act shall affect any equitable jurisdiction to refuse relief on the ground of acquiescence or otherwise.

Claims for equitable damages or equitable compensation are claims to which s. 36 applies the six-year limitation periods in ss. 2 and 5 by analogy (*Companhia de Seguros Imperio v Heath (REBX) Ltd* [2001] 1 WLR 112). In such cases the question is whether prior to 1 July 1940 a court facing such a case would have applied a limitation period by analogy. However, trawling through ancient authorities to find actual instances where this had been done in the past is deprecated.

In *Clarke v Marlborough Fine Art (London) Ltd* (2001) *The Times*, 5 July 2001, it was said that it is probable that in undue influence claims the only time-related defences available are laches and acquiescence (and presumably, affirmation). The defences of laches and acquiescence are preserved by s. 36(2).

Laches is an equitable doctrine under which delay can bar a claim to equitable relief. Some form of detrimental reliance is usually an essential ingredient, which has to be considered together with the period of the delay and the nature of the acts done during the interval, with the court considering the balance of justice or injustice in either allowing or disallowing the continuation of the proceedings (*Fisher v Brooker* [2009] UKHL 41, [2009] 1 WLR 1764 at [62], [64]). It can only bar equitable relief (at [79]), so on the facts did not bar the claim which was for a declaration as to the long-term existence of a property right despite the passage of 38 years. Further, laches only applies where the defendant can establish prejudice, and even then only if that prejudice is not outweighed by any benefits obtained by the defendant through the delay.

The essence of the defence of acquiescence is that there has been an encouragement or allowance of a party to believe something to his detriment. Principles dealing with this defence were laid down in *Jones v Stones* [1999] 1 WLR 1739, which considered the older cases of *Willmott v Barber* (1880) 15 ChD 96 and *Habib Bank Ltd v Habib Bank AG Zurich* [1981] 1 WLR 1265. The first question is whether one party, by its action or inaction, has encouraged the other party to believe a certain state of affairs. The second question is whether there was reliance on that encouragement. Thirdly, whether in all the circumstances of the case it would be unconscionable for the first party to then insist on its legal right. It is incorrect to concentrate on the period of delay as being enough of itself. Lord Neuberger of Abbotsbury in *Fisher v Brooker* took the view at [62] that acquiescence does not add anything to the established equitable

205

doctrines of laches and estoppel. The classic example of proprietary estoppel (standing by whilst a neighbour builds on one's land believing it to be his property) can be characterised as acquiescence. Similarly, laches (failing to raise or enforce an equitable right for a long period) can also be characterised as acquiescence.

The period of delay likely to give rise to these equitable defences depends on the nature of the relief claimed and the facts of the case. Delay in the context of interim injunctions is considered in **37.62**. For claims to redeem mortgages, a period of 20 years was said to be a convenient guide in *Weld v Petre* [1929] 1 Ch 33. Laches was held to be a defence in *Lynch v James Lynch and Sons (Transport) Ltd* (2000) LTL 8/3/2000 where a shareholder failed to assert his rights for 24 years.

LAND

Accrual in claims for the recovery of land

10.41   For recovery of land cases not governed by the Land Registration Act 2002 (see **10.42**), there are detailed rules dealing with accrual in LA 1980, sch. 1. For adverse possession against Crown land, and the 30-year period in LA 1980, sch. 1, para. 10, see *Hill v Transport for London* [2005] EWHC 856 (Ch), [2005] Ch 379. Broadly, time runs from the taking of adverse possession where the person bringing the claim has a present interest in the land but will be delayed until the determination of the preceding interest in the case of future interests. Use of the phrase 'adverse possession' is well established, but was regretted by the House of Lords in *J. A. Pye (Oxford) Ltd v Graham* [2002] UKHL 30, [2003] 1 AC 419 because it may be misleading. The question is whether the squatter dispossessed the paper owner by going into ordinary possession of the land for the requisite 12 years without the consent of the owner. There are two elements:

(a) Factual possession. This requires an appropriate degree of physical control, which depends on the circumstances, such as the nature of the land and the manner in which such land is commonly used. It has to be shown that the squatter has dealt with the land as an occupying owner might be expected to do, and that no one else has done so. Parking vehicles and delivering goods on the disputed land amounted to no more than use of the land in *Tennant v Adamczyk* [2005] EWCA Civ 1239, [2006] 1 P & CR 28. Anchoring a vessel in a tidal river may be sufficient (*Port of London Authority v Ashmore* [2009] EWHC 954 (Ch), [2009] 4 All ER 665).

(b) Intention to possess. What must be proved is an intention to possess, not a more extensive intention to own, or to acquire ownership, or to exclude the true owner. Lord Browne-Wilkinson described as heretical and wrong the concept, stemming from *Leigh v Jack* (1879) 5 ExD 264, that it must be shown that acts have been done which were inconsistent with the true owner's enjoyment of the land for the purposes for which he intended to use it. What is required is proof of an intention, in the squatter's own name and on his own behalf, to exclude the world at large, including the paper owner so far as was reasonably practicable and so far as the processes of the law would allow. Consequently, evidence that the squatter was willing to pay for his occupation if asked by the paper owner does not prevent time running against the paper owner.

The principles for establishing adverse possession laid down in *J. A. Pye (Oxford) Ltd v Graham* apply in all claims to recover land (*Ofulue v Bossert* [2008] EWCA Civ 7, [2009] Ch 1 (not affected by the further appeal); *Ashe v National Westminster Bank plc* [2008] EWCA Civ 55, [2008] 1 WLR 710). This includes claims by legal mortgagees against mortgagors in possession (*Ashe v National Westminster Bank plc*) and cases where the person claiming adverse possession believed he was a tenant because he had been let into the property by a former tenant (*Ofulue v Bossert*). It also applies in favour of the Crown (Limitation Act 1980, s. 37; *Roberts v Swangrove Estates Ltd* [2008] EWCA Civ 98, [2008] Ch 439). In *Ashe v National Westminster Bank plc* a mortgagee's legal charge was extinguished under the Limitation Act 1980, s. 17, 12 years after the last payment made by the mortgagor.

Registered land   The provisions of the LA 1980 as regards registered land were replaced as **10.42** from 13 October 2003 by the Land Registration Act 2002, sch. 6 and sch. 12. These support the principle under the 2002 Act that the register is to be a complete and accurate record of the state of the title to registered land at any given time, so that it will be possible to investigate title to land online and with the absolute minimum of additional enquiries and inspections. A person claiming adverse possession of registered land for at least 10 years is allowed to apply for registration. The usual evidence of adverse possession is required. Notice of the application is then served on the registered owner, and any chargees and other interested persons, and they may serve counter-notice. If they fail to do so, the applicant will be registered as the registered proprietor in place of the former proprietor, and free from former charges. If counter-notice is served, the application is dismissed unless one of three grounds is established. These are that it would be unfair to dispossess the applicant because of an equity by estoppel; that the applicant has an independent right which suggests he ought to be registered as the owner; or that there has been a reasonable mistake over boundaries. If an exception applies, the applicant is registered in place of the registered proprietor, and this happens notwithstanding objections from registered chargees. However, charges will continue to apply unless as a matter of general law the applicant's rights have priority over the charge. Where prior charges continue to apply, the applicant can apply for an apportionment of the charges between the land acquired by adverse possession and the remainder of the original title.

If an application under the 2002 Act is dismissed, the registered owner then has two years to take action to evict the person claiming adverse possession or otherwise regularise the position. If this is not done, once the two-year period has elapsed the person claiming adverse possession may reapply for registration, and, if still in possession, will be automatically registered in place of the existing registered owner. If this happens, the applicant is registered with a new, separate title, and takes free of any former registered charges.

Extinction of title and the European Convention on Human Rights

The Grand Chamber of the European Court of Human Rights in *J. A. Pye (Oxford) Ltd v United* **10.43** *Kingdom* (application 44302/02) (2007) 46 EHRR 45 held that the extinction of title under the Land Registration Act 1925 and the LA 1980 after 12 years' adverse possession does not infringe **art. 1** of the First Protocol to the European Convention on Human Rights in the **Human Rights Act 1998, sch. 1** (no one shall be deprived of his possessions except in the public interest). The 12-year rule is part of general land law, and is intended to regulate the use and occupation of land between individuals. Similar rules, also without payment of compensation, apply in a large number of other European countries, so the rules cannot be said to be manifestly without reasonable foundation. It was held that a fair balance had been struck between the demands of the general interest and the interests of the individuals concerned. This was so even though the land in question was extremely valuable. Limitation periods, if they are to fulfil their purpose, have to apply regardless of the size of the claim.

Mortgages and deeds

LA 1980, s. 20, provides: **10.44**

20. Time Limit for Actions to Recover Money Secured by a Mortgage or Charge or to Recover Proceeds of the Sale of Land

(1) No action shall be brought to recover—
   (a) any principal sum of money secured by a mortgage or other charge on property (whether real or personal); or
   (b) proceeds of the sale of land;

Commentary

after the expiration of twelve years from the date on which the right to receive the money accrued.

(2) No foreclosure action in respect of mortgaged personal property shall be brought after the expiration of twelve years from the date on which the right to foreclose accrued.

But if the mortgagee was in possession of the mortgaged property after that date, the right to foreclose on the property which was in his possession shall not be treated as having accrued for the purposes of this subsection until the date on which his possession discontinued.

(3) The right to receive any principal sum of money secured by a mortgage or other charge and the right to foreclose on the property subject to the mortgage or charge shall not be treated as accruing so long as that property comprises any future interest or any life insurance policy which has not matured or been determined.

(4) Nothing in this section shall apply to a foreclosure action in respect of mortgaged land, but the provisions of this Act relating to actions to recover land shall apply to such an action.

(5) Subject to subsections (6) and (7) below, no action to recover arrears of interest payable in respect of any sum of money secured by a mortgage or other charge or payable in respect of proceeds of the sale of land, or to recover damages in respect of such arrears shall be brought after the expiration of six years from the date on which the interest became due.

(6) Where—

(a) a prior mortgagee or other encumbrancer has been in possession of the property charged; and

(b) an action is brought within one year of the discontinuance of that possession by the subsequent encumbrancer;

the subsequent encumbrancer may recover by that action all the arrears of interest which fell due during the period of possession by the prior encumbrancer or damages in respect of those arrears, notwithstanding that the period exceeded six years.

(7) Where—

(a) the property subject to the mortgage or charge comprises any future interest or life insurance policy; and

(b) it is a term of the mortgage or charge that arrears of interest shall be treated as part of the principal sum of money secured by the mortgage or charge;

interest shall not be treated as becoming due before the right to recover the principal sum of money has accrued or is treated as having accrued.

A claim for the recovery of the principal due under a mortgage, even after the property has been repossessed and sold, is governed by the 12-year period in LA 1980, s. 20 (class 3 in **table 10.1**), but claims for interest are subject to a six-year limitation period as set out in s. 20(5) (*Bristol and West plc v Bartlett* [2002] EWCA Civ 1181, [2003] 1 WLR 284). A claim to enforce a charge by deed securing moneys guaranteed by the defendant is a claim on a specialty and governed by the 12-year limitation period (*Securum Finance Ltd v Ashton* [2001] Ch 291). It seems from *Global Financial Recoveries Ltd v Jones* [2000] BPIR 1029, that whether a claim for any shortfall after the realisation of mortgaged property (the mortgage being by deed) is one based on simple contract or specialty depends on whether the terms of the mortgage include the consequences of any shortfall.

In *West Bromwich Building Society v Wilkinson* [2005] UKHL 44, [2005] 1 WLR 2303, the defendants bought a property with a loan secured by a legal charge. The charge contained a proviso for redemption in conventional form. It also provided for a power of sale which was exercisable on demand of the money advanced or on five other events of default, including non-payment. Only two of the monthly instalments were paid. Default on the monthly payments, and obtaining and execution of an order for possession, occurred more than 12 years before the present proceedings, which sought judgment on the shortfall after sale of the property. Sale of the property was less than 12 years before the claim was issued. The building society argued that under the charge it had no right to recover the mortgage advance until the shortfall was quantified, which was when the property was sold. The House of Lords held that on the true construction of the charge, the principal money outstanding became payable when the power of sale became exercisable. Although the relevant clause did not in terms say this, the natural meaning of the clause was that the money became payable on making the demand or on the occurrence of any of the other events of default (at [19]). This was more than 12 years before the date of issue, so the claim was time-barred under LA 1980, s. 8.

A charge on a bankrupt's dwelling house in favour of the trustee in bankruptcy created by an order under the Insolvency Act 1986, s. 313, secures a future obligation, with no immediate right to receive any principal sum. Accordingly, time cannot run under LA 1980, s. 20(1), until an order has been made for the sale of the property (*Gotham v Doodes* [2006] EWCA Civ 1080, [2007] 1 WLR 86). Enforcement of a charging order (see **79.29** to **79.34**) is not an 'action brought to recover any principal sum secured by a…charge on property' within LA 1980, s. 20, and is not subject to any limitation period (*Ezekiel v Orakpo* [1997] 1 WLR 340; *Yorkshire Bank Finance Ltd v Mulhall* [2008] EWCA Civ 1156, [2009] 2 All ER (Comm) 164).

INDEMNITY AND CONTRIBUTION CLAIMS

At common law, an indemnity accrued on actual payment to the third party rather than on the event giving rise to the liability to the third party (*Huntley v Sanderson* (1833) 1 Cr & M 467). Equity, on the other hand, allowed a party to preserve its position by claiming an indemnity as soon as the liability was incurred, and to recover once the liability was established or quantified (*British Union and National Insurance Co. v Rawson* [1916] 2 Ch 476). The leading modern case is *Telfair Shipping Corporation v Inersea Carriers SA* [1985] 1 WLR 553. Accrual depends on the construction of the indemnity clause. The key question is usually whether the clause gives rise to the indemnity once primary liability to the third party has been ascertained or established, or whether the indemnity arises only after payment to the third party (*Socony Mobil Oil Co. Inc. v West of England Ship Owners Mutual Insurance Association (London) Ltd (No. 2)* [1989] 1 Lloyd's Rep 239).

10.45

A contribution claim accrues on the date the amount of the underlying liability is fixed, disregarding any possible appeal. If the amount of underlying liability is determined by the court, time runs from judgment (LA 1980, s. 10(3)), which means judgment on quantum, not merely liability (see *Aer Lingus v Gildacroft Ltd* [2006] EWCA Civ 4, [2006] 1 WLR 1173). If the amount of the underlying liability is fixed by agreement, time runs from the date of settlement (s. 10(4)). Where a firm agreement to settle the primary claim is made, time starts running immediately under s. 10(4), and does not start again if the agreement is subsequently recorded in a consent order (*Knight v Rochdale Healthcare NHS Trust* [2003] EWHC 1831 (QB), [2004] 1 WLR 371). However, if the agreement requires the making of a consent order before it takes effect, time starts running from the consent order (*Knight v Rochdale Healthcare*).

STATUTES AND SPECIALTIES

A claim for damages for infringement of a right conferred by EU law amounts to a claim for damages for breach of statutory duty. It is therefore founded on tort and subject to a six-year limitation period under LA 1980, s. 2 (*R v Secretary of State for Transport, ex parte Factortame Ltd (No. 7)* [2001] 1 WLR 942). A claim to recover rent due under a lease under seal is governed by the six-year limitation period in class 10, not the 12 years in class 4 (*Romain v Scuba TV Ltd* [1997] QB 887). Although statutes are specialties, money claims pursuant to statute are governed by the six-year period in s. 9 (class 6) (see *Central Electricity Board v Halifax Corporation* [1963] AC 785 and *Re Farmizer (Products) Ltd* [1997] 1 BCLC 589), whereas claims for other remedies pursuant to statute will be governed by the 12-year period in s. 8 (class 4). Consequently, a claim to reopen an extortionate credit bargain under the Consumer Credit Act 1974, s. 139, has a 12-year limitation period running from the date of the agreement (*Rahman v Sterling Credit Ltd* [2001] 1 WLR 496 confirmed in *Nolan v Wright* [2009] EWHC 305 (Ch), [2009] 3 All ER 823).

10.46

Direct claims against insurers under the Third Parties (Rights against Insurers) Act 2010, s. 1, are governed by the same limitation period, accruing on the same date, as is applicable against the original tortfeasor (*Matadeen v Caribbean Insurance Co. Ltd* [2002] UKPC 69, [2003] 1 WLR 670). Conversely, claims against the Motor Insurers' Bureau under the Motor Vehicles (Compulsory Insurance) (Information Centre and Compensation Body) Regulations 2003

(SI 2003/37), reg. 13, are to recover sums recoverable by virtue of an enactment, so are subject to the six-year limitation period in LA 1980, s. 9 (*Howe v Motor Insurers' Bureau (No. 1)* [2016] EWHC 640 (QB), [2016] 1 WLR 2707). Claims to recover unpaid council tax are subject to the six-year period in the Council Tax (Administration and Enforcement) Regulations 1992 (SI 1992/613), reg. 34(3), which runs from the date the tax fell due (*Bolsover District Council v Ashfield Nominees Ltd* [2010] EWCA Civ 1129, [2011] Bus LR 492).

Money due under statute

10.47 In *Swansea City Council v Glass* [1992] QB 844 the council brought a claim to recover the cost of repairing a house owned by the defendant and let to a tenant where the defendant had failed to effect necessary repairs. The claim was brought under the Housing Act 1957, s. 10(3), and was commenced over six years after the work was done, but less than six years after a demand for payment. It was held that time ran from completion of the work, so the claim was statute barred. A claim to recover sums owed after revocation of a legal aid certificate under the Civil Legal Aid (General) Regulations 1989 (SI 1989/339), reg. 86, accrues on the date of revocation, not the date when the amount to be recovered has been quantified (*Legal Services Commission v Rasool* [2008] EWCA Civ 154, [2008] 1 WLR 2711).

Compulsory purchase compensation claims

10.48 In *Hillingdon London Borough Council v ARC Ltd* [1998] 1 WLR 174 it was held that a cause of action in respect of a claim for compensation under the Compulsory Purchase Act 1965, s. 9, accrues on the date of the acquiring authority's entry on the land. In *Halstead v Manchester City Council* [1998] 1 All ER 33 it was held that the statutory right to recover interest on compensation under the 1965 Act did not accrue until the amount on which interest became due was awarded or agreed.

Competition claims

10.49 A claim under the Competition Act 1998, s. 47A, accrues for the purposes of the Competition Appeal Tribunal Rules 2003 (SI 2003/1372), r. 31, on the 'relevant date', which is the end of the period for appealing to the Court of First Instance against a Commission decision, or, if such an appeal is lodged, the time when the appeal proceedings are determined. Decisions on infringement and the amount of any fine are separate for this purpose, so an appeal against the fine only does not postpone the relevant date (*BCL Old Co. Ltd v BASF SE* [2009] EWCA Civ 434, [2009] Bus LR 1516).

JUDGMENTS

10.50 By LA 1980, s. 24(1), an action may not be brought upon any judgment after the expiration of six years from the date on which the judgment became enforceable. A judgment for costs to be assessed is not enforceable for the purposes of s. 24(1) until the costs have been assessed (*Chohan v Times Newspapers Ltd* [2001] EWCA Civ 964, [2001] 1 WLR 1859). Insolvency proceedings, whether personal or corporate, are not 'actions' within the meaning of s. 24(1). Accordingly, a winding-up petition based on a judgment for costs obtained more than six years before the winding-up petition was held not to be time-barred in *Ridgeway Motors (Isleworth) Ltd v ALTS Ltd* [2005] EWCA Civ 92, [2005] 1 WLR 2871. Similarly, bringing an 'action' on a judgment does not include proceedings by way of execution (*Lowsley v Forbes* [1999] 1 AC 329), or by enforcement of a charging order (*Yorkshire Bank Finance Ltd v Mulhall* [2008] EWCA Civ 1156, [2009] 2 All ER (Comm) 164) or third party debt order (*Westacre Investments Inc. v Yugoimport SDPR* [2008] EWHC 801 (Comm), [2009] 1 All ER (Comm) 780.

A judgment creditor is entitled to bring a second claim seeking a judgment upon an earlier unsatisfied judgment. The juridical basis for the second claim is an implied contract to honour the first judgment (*Kuwait Oil Tanker Co. SAK v Al Bader* [2008] EWHC 2432 (Comm), LTL 23/10/2008). The only defence is that the second claim is an abuse of process. Requiring a fresh judgment to avoid problems in enforcing a judgment more than six years old is not an abuse. The court will impose a condition on the second judgment that permission to enforce it must be sought under **CPR, r. 83.2.** If enforcement proceedings are brought more than six years after judgment, LA 1980, s. 24(2), will limit the interest that can be claimed on the judgment debt to that accrued over six years.

DISABILITY

Subsections (1), (2) and (6) of LA 1980, s. 28, provide: **10.51**

28. Extension of Limitation Period in Case of Disability

(1) Subject to the following provisions of this section, if on the date when any right of action accrued for which a period of limitation is prescribed by this Act, the person to whom it accrued was under a disability, the action may be brought at any time before the expiration of six years from the date when he ceased to be under a disability or died (whichever first occurred) notwithstanding that the period of limitation has expired.

(2) This section shall not affect any case where the right of action first accrued to some person (not under a disability) through whom the person under a disability claims.

(6) If the action is one to which section 11 or 12(2) of this Act applies, subsection (1) above shall have effect as if for the words 'six years' there were substituted the words 'three years'.

There are two categories of persons under disability: children and persons who lack capacity (within the meaning of the Mental Capacity Act 2005) to conduct legal proceedings (LA 1980, s. 38(2)). By virtue of LA 1980, s. 28, time does not run against a child until his or her 18th birthday. Also by virtue of s. 28, time does not run against a person who lacks capacity if that person was under disability at the date the cause of action accrued. Thus, an adult who is immediately deprived of capacity by an accident is not subject to limitation until he or she recovers. The same applies to a child who, though not lacking capacity when a cause of action arises, loses capacity before reaching the age of majority. However, time will continue to run during a period of lack of capacity where a cause of action accrues to an adult who did not lack capacity at the date of accrual.

A potential defendant who is concerned that delay in bringing a claim by a person under disability may prejudice the trial through the evidence becoming stale may force the issue by bringing a claim for a negative declaration as to liability. The person under disability may choose to bring the substantive claim as a counterclaim to those proceedings. The court's decision whether to grant such a negative declaration is a matter of discretion rather than jurisdiction (*Messier Dowty Ltd v Sabena SA* [2000] 1 WLR 2040 as applied in *Eidha v Toropdar* [2008] EWHC 1219 (QB), LTL 6/6/2008).

ACKNOWLEDGMENTS AND PART PAYMENTS

Renewal of limitation period

Under LA 1980, s. 29, acknowledging title to land, acknowledging a debt and making part   **10.52** payments have the effect of renewing the limitation period from the date of acknowledgment or payment. Subsections (1) to (4) deal with acknowledgments relating to land and mortgages. Subsections (5) to (7) provide:

(5) Subject to subsection (6) below, where any right of action has accrued to recover—
   (a) any debt or other liquidated pecuniary claim; or
   (b) any claim to the personal estate of a deceased person or to any share or interest in any such estate;

   and the person liable or accountable for the claim acknowledges the claim or makes any payment in respect of it the right shall be treated as having accrued on and not before the date of the acknowledgment or payment.

(6) A payment of a part of the rent or interest due at any time shall not extend the period for claiming the remainder then due, but any payment of interest shall be treated as a payment in respect of the principal debt.

(7) Subject to subsection (6) above, a current period of limitation may be repeatedly extended under this section by further acknowledgments or payments, but a right of action, once barred by this Act, shall not be revived by any subsequent acknowledgment or payment.

Section 29(5) applies to claims for debts and liquidated pecuniary claims. It does not apply to claims for damages (*City and General (Holborn) Ltd v Royal and Sun Alliance Insurance plc* [2010] EWCA Civ 911, [2010] BLR 639).

Acknowledgments

10.53 A statement of case can amount to an acknowledgment for the purpose of LA 1980, s. 29(5) (*Ofulue v Bossert* [2009] UKHL 16, [2009] 1 AC 990). An acknowledgment must, however, be precisely focused on the disputed right (*Surrendra Overseas Ltd v Sri Lanka* [1977] 1 WLR 565). A letter in which the defendant said he was 'happy to confirm that you suggest the following amounts are owed by me to you' was held to be a sufficient acknowledgment in *Ross v McGrath* [2004] EWCA Civ 1054, LTL 14/7/2004. *Bradford and Bingley plc v Rashid* [2006] UKHL 37, [2006] 1 WLR 2066, was essentially the same as *West Bromwich Building Society v Wilkinson* [2005] UKHL 44, [2005] 1 WLR 2303 (discussed at 10-44). To avoid the claim being time-barred the lender sought to rely on letters sent on behalf of the defendant, one saying: 'at present, he is not in a position to repay the outstanding balance owed to you', and the other saying: 'He is willing to pay approximately £500 towards the outstanding amount as a final settlement'. It was held that both letters amounted to acknowledgments of the debt under s. 29, and started time running again. It did not matter that neither letter acknowledged the amount owed by the debtor. It was sufficient that they acknowledged the liability. It was said in *City and General (Holborn) Ltd v Royal and Sun Alliance Insurance plc* that it was not immediately obvious that an open offer in a small sum in response to a claim for a much larger amount could amount to an acknowledgment of the larger sum. An acknowledgment of a claim without an admission of liability is ineffective to start time running again under s. 29(5). It may amount to an estoppel by convention, for which see *Commissioners of HM Revenue and Customs v Benchdollar Ltd* [2009] EWHC 1310 (Ch), [2009] STC 2342.

Under s. 30 any acknowledgment must be in writing and signed by the person liable or by that person's agent. A typed signature on a telex is a sufficient signature for this purpose (*Good Challenger Navegante SA v Metalexportimport SA* [2003] EWCA Civ 1668, [2004] 1 Lloyd's Rep 67).

Part payments

10.54 Acknowledgments and part payments are explicitly separated and given equal status by LA 1980, s. 29(5). Part payments are not merely a subspecies of acknowledgments (*Ashcroft v Bradford and Bingley plc* [2010] EWCA Civ 223, [2010] 2 P & CR 13). Whether a part payment is 'in respect of' the sum owed is a question of fact. Once it is established that a payment has been made, if there is no other debt owed by the defendant to the claimant, it is permissible to infer that the payment was in respect of the debt sued for. It may be different where the part payment is clearly referable to an admitted part of a debt (*Surrendra Overseas Ltd v Sri Lanka* [1977] 1 WLR 565). All that s. 29(5) does is to enlarge the time for bringing a claim, it does not fix the amount of the debt (*Ashcroft v Bradford and Bingley plc*). The part payment of rent or interest due at any time does not extend the time for claiming the balance (s. 29(6)). However, a payment made outside a repayment schedule has the effect of renewing the limitation period (*International Finance Corporation v Utexafrica Sprl* [2001] CLC 1361).

FRAUD, CONCEALMENT AND MISTAKE

The commencement of a limitation period may be postponed under LA 1980, s. 32, where **10.55** there is fraud, concealment or mistake. Section 32 provides:

32. Postponement of Limitation Period in Case of Fraud, Concealment or Mistake

(1) Subject to subsections (3) and (4A) below, where in the case of any action for which a period of limitation is prescribed by this Act, either—
(a) the action is based upon the fraud of the defendant; or
(b) any fact relevant to the plaintiff's right of action has been deliberately concealed from him by the defendant; or
(c) the action is for relief from the consequences of a mistake;
the period of limitation shall not begin to run until the plaintiff has discovered the fraud, concealment or mistake (as the case may be) or could with reasonable diligence have discovered it. References in this subsection to the defendant include references to the defendant's agent and to any person through whom the defendant claims and his agent.

(2) For the purposes of subsection (1) above, deliberate commission of a breach of duty in circumstances in which it is unlikely to be discovered for some time amounts to deliberate concealment of the facts involved in that breach of duty.

(3) Nothing in this section shall enable any action—
(a) to recover, or recover the value of, any property; or
(b) to enforce any charge against, or set aside any transaction affecting, any property;
to be brought against the purchaser of the property or any person claiming through him in any case where the property has been purchased for valuable consideration by an innocent third party since the fraud or concealment or (as the case may be) the transaction in which the mistake was made took place.

(4) A purchaser is an innocent third party for the purposes of this section—
(a) in the case of fraud or concealment of any fact relevant to the plaintiff's right of action, if he was not a party to the fraud or (as the case may be) to the concealment of that fact and did not at the time of the purchase know or have reason to believe that the fraud or concealment had taken place; and
(b) in the case of mistake, if he did not at the time of the purchase know or have reason to believe that the mistake had been made.

(4A) Subsection (1) above shall not apply in relation to the time limit prescribed by section 11A(3) of this Act or in relation to that time limit as applied by virtue of section 12(1) of this Act.

(5) Sections 14A and 14B of this Act shall not apply to any action to which subsection (1)(b) above applies (and accordingly the period of limitation referred to in that subsection, in any case to which either of those sections would otherwise apply, is the period applicable under section 2 of this Act).

Fraud

In claims based on fraud, the limitation period does not begin to run until the claimant dis- **10.56** covers the fraud or could with reasonable diligence have discovered it (LA 1980, s. 32(1)(a)). Time does not run while a claimant merely suspects the defendant is dishonest (*Barnstaple Boat Co. Ltd v Jones* [2007] EWCA Civ 727, [2008] 1 All ER 1124). Instead, time runs from the date the precise fraud as pleaded was or could have been discovered (*Allison v Horner* [2014] EWCA Civ 117, LTL 12/2/2014). Section 32(1)(a) applies only where fraud is the essence of the claim. An action in conversion where the defendant has incidentally been guilty of fraud or dishonesty does not bring the provision into effect (*Beaman v ARTS Ltd* [1949] 1 KB 550).

Concealment

Where any fact relevant to a claim has been deliberately concealed by the defendant, time does **10.57** not run until the concealment is discovered or with reasonable diligence could have been discovered (LA 1980, s. 32(1)(b)). The normal test for whether a fact is 'relevant' for this purpose is whether that fact should be pleaded in the particulars of claim, although it may be that this test should be modified (*Williams v Lishman, Sidwell, Campbell and Price Ltd* [2010] EWCA Civ 418, [2010] PNLR 25). A concealment may be 'deliberate' even if the defendant is not dishonest (*AIC Ltd v ITS Testing Services (UK) Ltd* [2006] EWCA Civ 1601, [2007] 1 All ER (Comm) 667). For the purposes of s. 32(1)(b), deliberate commission of a breach of duty in circumstances in which it is unlikely to be discovered for some time amounts to deliberate concealment of the facts involved in that breach of duty (s. 32(2)). 'Breach of duty' within the meaning of s. 32(2) includes executing a document to defraud a debtor's creditors contrary to the Insolvency Act 1986, s. 423 (*Giles v Rhind (No. 2)* [2008] EWCA Civ 118, [2009] Ch 191). At one time, LA 1980, s. 32(2), was interpreted by a number of authorities as meaning that time did not run where a professional person deliberately provided a service, even if the professional did not realise that the service was being provided in a negligent way (*Brocklesby v Armitage and Guest* [2002] 1 WLR 598 and *Liverpool Roman Catholic Archdiocese Trustees Inc. v Goldberg* [2001] 1 All ER 182). This line of authorities was overruled by *Cave v Robinson Jarvis and Rolf* [2002] UKHL 18, [2003] 1 AC 384, in which it was held that s. 32(1)(b) deprives a defendant of a limitation defence:

(a) where the defendant has taken active steps to conceal his breach of duty after he has become aware of it; and

(b) where the defendant is guilty of deliberate wrongdoing and conceals or fails to disclose it in circumstances where the wrongdoing is unlikely to be discovered for some time.

However, the mere fact that the defendant intended to do the act complained of does not mean that s. 32(1)(b) applies to prevent time running. If the defendant is unaware of his alleged error or that he may have failed to take proper care, there is nothing for the defendant to disclose, and time is not prevented from running by s. 32(1)(b). Consequently, to use examples referred to in *Cave v Robinson Jarvis and Rolf*, time will run where a surgeon negligently leaves a swab inside a patient; and where an anaesthetist negligently administers the wrong drug; and where a solicitor gives a client negligent advice. Time will not run if the surgeon deliberately left the swab inside the patient, or if the lawyer after giving negligent advice fails to disclose other facts which he is under a duty to disclose to the client which would have alerted the client to the negligent nature of the advice. Thus, there was concealment by a solicitor sued for the negligent conduct of litigation who failed to inform the client that the claim had been compromised and failed to tell the client he had agreed to a consent order (*Williams v Fanshaw Porter and Hazelhurst* [2004] EWCA Civ 157, [2004] 1 WLR 3185). Likewise, time did not run in favour of a testing services company when it failed to reveal to its principal the results of retesting of samples in *AIC Ltd v ITS Testing Services (UK) Ltd* [2006] EWCA Civ 1601, [2007] 1 All ER (Comm) 667.

In *Sheldon v R. H. M. Outhwaite (Underwriting Agencies) Ltd* [1996] AC 102 the claim was governed by a six-year limitation period and was allowed to continue although it was commenced 10 years after accrual. The defendants were alleged to have deliberately concealed material facts two years after accrual, and it was held that s. 32(1)(b) applies both where the concealment of the relevant facts was contemporaneous with the accrual of the cause of action and where it occurred subsequently. Concealment, for the purposes of s. 32(1)(b), will almost inevitably occur after the cause of action has arisen. In *Skerratt v Linfax Ltd* [2003] EWCA Civ 695, LTL 6/5/2003, it was held that there had not been concealment for the purposes of s. 32(1)(b) when, before allowing the claimant to take part in the activity which injured him, the defendant required him to sign a document which misled him to believe that he could not make a claim, and more than three years elapsed before a solicitor advised him that this was not so.

Mistake

10.58   Where a claim is for relief from the consequences of a mistake, time does not run until the mistake is, or could with reasonable diligence have been, discovered (LA 1980, s. 32(1)(c)). In *Kleinwort Benson Ltd v Lincoln City Council* [1999] 2 AC 349 the House of Lords held that LA 1980,

s. 32(1)(c), applies to all mistakes, whether of fact or of law, so that it could apply where the claimant had paid money to the defendant under a mistake of law. Conversely, a restitutionary claim made by a person who makes a payment to HM Revenue and Customs pursuant to an unlawful demand (see *Woolwich Equitable Building Society v Commissioners of Inland Revenue* [1993] AC 70) accrues when the payment is made. These cases were considered in *Deutsche Morgan Grenfell Group plc v Commissioners of Inland Revenue* [2006] UKHL 49, [2007] 1 AC 558, which held that s. 32(1)(c) applies where a taxpayer makes a mistake of law and as a result wrongly pays tax. Time ran against the taxpayer on its restitutionary claim from the date it discovered the mistake, which on the facts was the date of a decision of the Court of Justice of the European Union which clarified the relevant tax law. Lord Hoffmann at [20] to [30] dealt with the question of whether the taxpayer had made a mistake within s. 32(1)(c), or merely had a doubt as to the legal position (the latter does not come within s. 32(1)(c)). Even after the taxpayer became aware that there was a challenge to the English tax provision, the taxpayer took the view that the existing tax statute had to be complied with, which was held to be properly characterised as a mistake.

What amounts to 'reasonable diligence' is a question of fact. In *Peco Arts Inc. v Hazlitt Gallery Ltd* [1983] 1 WLR 1315, a case involving an alleged mistake over whether a 19th-century drawing was an original signed by the artist, it was held that the term meant doing what an ordinary prudent buyer of a valuable work of art would do. Depending on the facts, this might include taking suitable expert advice. See also *West Sussex Properties Ltd v Chichester District Council* (2000) LTL 28/6/2000. By way of exception, none of the provisions in s. 32 applies to the time bar on interest on judgment debts in s. 24(2) (see **10.50**), because execution of a judgment is not an 'action' within the meaning of s. 32 (*Lowsley v Forbes* [1999] 1 AC 329).

Commentary

COMMENCEMENT OF INSOLVENCY

10.59   A claim against a company which is not time-barred when the company goes into liquidation remains alive no matter how much time elapses thereafter (*Re General Rolling Stock Co., Joint Stock Discount Co.'s claim* (1872) LR 7 Ch App 646). In other words, limitation periods cease running from the date of the winding-up order (*Re General Rolling Stock Co.; Re Cases of Taffs Well Ltd* [1992] Ch 179) or resolution for voluntary winding up (*Re Northern Ontario Power Co. Ltd* [1954] 1 DLR 627; *Re Mixhurst Ltd* [1994] 2 BCLC 19). The same applies to claims against an individual when a bankruptcy order is made. Time ceases to run no matter which provision of the LA 1980, including the latent damage provisions in ss. 14A and 14B, preserve the claim at the date of going into liquidation or bankruptcy (*Financial Services Compensation Scheme Ltd v Larnell (Insurances) Ltd* [2005] EWCA Civ 1408, [2006] QB 808). Lloyd LJ's remark in *Financial Services Compensation Scheme Ltd v Larnell (Insurances) Ltd* that the principle in *Re General Rolling Stock Co.* applies in 'all types of insolvency' is obiter and is, it is submitted, a dubious generalisation. The *Re General Rolling Stock Co.* principle cannot apply to administrative receivership and, depending on what the rationale for the rule is, it probably does not apply to any insolvency procedure other than bankruptcy, voluntary winding up and winding up by the court.

AGREEMENT TO EXTEND

10.60   An agreement to extend time for commencing proceedings will be interpreted by applying the principles from *Investors Compensation Scheme Ltd v West Bromwich Building Society* [1998] 1 WLR 896, see *Gold Shipping Navigation Co. SA v Lulu Maritime Ltd* [2009] EWHC 1365 (Admlty), [2009] 2 Lloyd's Rep 484.

ARBITRATION AND ADR

Arbitration and limitation

10.61 The normal limitation periods under the LA 1980 apply to arbitration (Arbitration Act 1996, s. 13(1)). In determining when a cause of action accrued, any provision that an award is a condition precedent to the bringing of legal proceedings (a *Scott v Avery* (1856) 25 LJ Ex 308 clause) is to be disregarded (s. 13(3)). In arbitration proceedings the parties are entitled to agree when the arbitration is to be regarded as having commenced for limitation purposes (s. 14(1)). If there is no such agreement, s. 14(3) to (5), set out three rules for when the arbitration is to be regarded as having commenced depending on how the arbitral tribunal is to be appointed. These are:

(a) where the arbitrator is named or designated in the arbitration agreement, arbitral proceedings are commenced when one party serves on the other party or parties a notice in writing requiring him or them to submit the dispute to the person so named or designated (s. 14(3));

(b) where the arbitrator or arbitrators are to be appointed by the parties, arbitral proceedings are commenced when one party serves on the other party or parties notice in writing requiring him or them to appoint an arbitrator or to agree to the appointment of an arbitrator in respect of the dispute (s. 14(4)); and

(c) where the arbitrator or arbitrators are to be appointed by a person other than a party to the proceedings, arbitral proceedings are commenced when one party gives notice in writing to that person requesting him to make the appointment in respect of the dispute (s. 14(5)).

If an arbitral award is set aside or declared to be of no effect, the court can direct that the period between the commencement of the arbitration and the relevant order is to be excluded (s. 13(2)).

Enforcement of arbitral awards

10.62 Enforcement of an arbitration award under the Arbitration Act 1996, s. 66, or bringing an ordinary claim on an award, are both subject to the six-year limitation period in LA 1980, s. 7 (class 11 in **table 10.1**) (*National Ability SA v Tinna Oils and Chemicals Ltd* [2009] EWCA Civ 1330, [2010] Bus LR 1058).

ADR and limitation

10.63 Where there is a dispute, making use of ADR processes such as negotiation and mediation does not stop time running. **PD Pre-action Conduct and Protocols, para. 17**, recommends that where it is not possible to complete the stages required by the protocols (which may include ADR) before the expiry of limitation, proceedings should be commenced to avoid the claim becoming time-barred, and the parties should seek to agree to apply to the court for a stay so that the remaining steps can be completed.

Limitation periods apply in respect of litigation and arbitration, so probably do not apply to non-adjudicative ADR processes or ADR processes where there is no dispute, such as expert determination (*Braceforce Warehousing Ltd v Mediterranean Shipping Company (UK) Ltd* [2009] EWHC 3839 (QB), LTL 4/6/2009).

Cross-border mediation

10.64 Under LA 1980, s. 33A, where the limitation period would expire between the start and eight weeks after the end of a cross-border mediation, the limitation period will instead expire eight weeks after the mediation ends. Directive 2008/52/EC, art. 2(1), provides that for these purposes a cross-border dispute shall be one in which at least one of the parties is domiciled or habitually resident in a member State other than that of any other party on the date on which:

(a) the parties agree to use mediation after the dispute has arisen;
(b) mediation is ordered by a court;
(c) an obligation to use mediation arises under national law; or
(d) for the purposes of art. 5 an invitation is made to the parties.

Further, by art. 2(2) there is a cross-border dispute where, following a mediation, arbitration or judicial proceedings are initiated in a member State other than that in which the parties were domiciled or habitually resident on the date referred to in art. 2(1)(a), (b) or (c).

CASES OUTSIDE THE LIMITATION ACT 1980

The LA 1980 does not apply to any action or arbitration for which a period of limitation is prescribed by or under any other enactment, whether passed before or after the passing of the LA 1980 (LA 1980, s. 39). Warsaw Convention claims (class 17 in **table 10.1**) and cargo claims under the Hague–Visby Rules (class 23) are subject to substantive as opposed to procedural time bars (*Aries Tanker Corporation v Total Transport Ltd* [1977] 1 WLR 185). The same applies to defective product claims (class 5: *O'Byrne v Aventis Pasteur SA* (case C-358/08) [2010] 1 WLR 1375; *O'Byrne v Aventis Pasteur MSD Ltd* [2010] UKSC 23, [2010] 1 WLR 1412). In these cases the right of action ceases to exist after the expiry of the relevant time bar, which is not suspended, interrupted or extended by anything in the LA 1980 (*Laroche v Spirit of Adventure (UK) Ltd* [2009] EWCA Civ 12, [2009] QB 778 at [70]).

10.65

A claim which is outside the provisions of the LA 1980 (or other enactment creating a time bar) is not subject to a strict period of limitation (*Nelson v Rye* [1996] 1 WLR 1378). It may, however, be subject to a time limit by analogy to the LA 1980 (see s. 36 and *Coulthard v Disco Mix Club Ltd* [1999] 2 All ER 457), or it may be subject to the defences of laches and acquiescence (as in *Nelson v Rye* [1996] 1 WLR 1378, but see the discussion at **10.36**). For example, a claim against a mortgagee for failing to obtain a proper price on the sale of mortgaged property was held to be governed by a six-year limitation period by analogy with s. 2 in *Raja v Lloyds TSB Bank plc* [2001] 2 EGLR 78. In *Companhia de Seguros Imperio v Heath (REBX) Ltd* [2001] 1 WLR 112 a six-year limitation period was imposed on a claim for breach of fiduciary duty, by analogy with ss. 2 and 5.

By way of contrast, the court refused to apply any limitation period (other than laches and acquiescence) to a claim for specific performance of a contract in *P & O Nedlloyd BV v Arab Metals Co. (No. 2)* [2006] EWCA Civ 1717, [2007] 1 WLR 2288. Undue influence claims fall outside the LA 1980 (*Clarke v Marlborough Fine Art (London) Ltd* (2001) *The Times*, 5 July 2001, but see **10.40**). Further, if there is no limitation period, the court may still strike out the proceedings as an abuse of process. In *Taylor v Ribby Hall Leisure Ltd* [1998] 1 WLR 400 an application to commit was delayed by about five years. It was struck out, the court taking into account factors such as the prospects of the court exercising its supervisory powers at the hearing, and the public interest in the efficient administration of justice and the compliance with court orders and undertakings.

Agreement extending Landlord and Tenant Act 1954, part 2, time limits

The statutory period for commencing applications by landlords or tenants for new business tenancies under the Landlord and Tenant Act 1954, s. 24, and by landlords for orders terminating part 2 tenancies under s. 29(2), is set out in s. 29A(2). Where the landlord has given a notice under s. 25, the statutory period ends on the date specified in that notice, and where

10.66

Commentary

the tenant has made a request for a new tenancy under s. 26, it ends immediately before the date specified in the request.

In the period between the landlord's notice under s. 25 or the tenant's request under s. 26 and the expiry of the statutory period, the parties may agree to extend the time for bringing an application under the Act for a specified period (s. 29B(1)). The parties may from time to time agree further, specified, extensions, but such agreements must be made before time has expired under the current agreement (s. 29B(2)).

Judicial review: discretionary extension

10.67   The three-month time limit for bringing a claim for judicial review can be extended if good reasons are shown, see 77.36.

Foreign limitation periods

10.68   Where, in accordance with the rules of private international law, the law of any other country is to be taken into account in any claim in England and Wales, the law of that other country relating to limitation must be applied (Foreign Limitation Periods Act 1984, s. 1(1)). When applying the foreign limitation period the question is whether the defendant can establish on the balance of probabilities that the foreign court would have dismissed the claim on the ground of limitation (*Harley v Smith* [2010] EWCA Civ 78, [2010] CP Rep 33). If so, the claimant may seek to rely on the exceptions in s. 2, which include conflicts with public policy (s. 2(1)) and causing undue hardship (s. 2(2)), for which see *OJSC Oil Co. Yugraneft v Abramovich* [2008] EWHC 2613 (Comm), LTL 3/11/2008. In considering whether a claimant will suffer undue hardship under s. 2(2), problems caused by the fact the claimant's lawyer did not appreciate there was a short foreign limitation period are irrelevant (*Harley v Smith*). It is hardship caused by the application of the foreign limitation period that is relevant, not the effect of wrong legal advice. Further, uncertainty over how limitation is calculated in the foreign jurisdiction is not relevant hardship. In a case where there is uncertainty of this type it behoves those advising the claimant to issue proceedings promptly to avoid the difficulty.

Chapter 11   Where to Start Proceedings

JURISDICTION OF HIGH COURT AND COUNTY COURT

Concurrent jurisdiction

The High Court and the County Court have concurrent jurisdiction over most claims. These include claims:

11.1

(a) in contract and tort (County Courts Act 1984, s. 15) — a claim can be founded in contract within the meaning of s. 15 where there is privity of estate but not privity of contract between a landlord and tenant (*Cussens v Realreed Ltd* [2013] EWHC 1229 (QB), [2014] 1 WLR 275);

(b) for the recovery of land (s. 21);

(c) under the Inheritance (Provision for Family and Dependants) Act 1975 (County Courts Act 1984, s. 25);

(d) for relief from forfeiture (s. 139); and

(e) under the Landlord and Tenant Act 1954, part 2, in relation to the security of tenure of business tenants (Landlord and Tenant Act 1954, s. 63).

Cases where County Court jurisdiction is limited

The jurisdiction of the County Court is limited in certain cases to claims which fall below particular financial limits. For example, the County Court has jurisdiction over claims in equity where the estate, fund or value of property does not exceed £350,000 (County Courts Act 1984, s. 23; County Court Jurisdiction Order 2014 (SI 2014/503)) (parties can in certain cases agree to vary this limit: County Courts Act 1984, s. 24). Other limits to the County Court's jurisdiction are set out in the **High Court and County Courts Jurisdiction Order 1991 (SI 1991/724), art. 2.**

11.2

Where a claimant has a cause of action for more than the County Court limit, the claimant may abandon the excess, in order to bring the claim within the jurisdiction of the County Court, but the claimant cannot recover in that claim an amount exceeding the County Court limit (County Courts Act 1984, s. 17). In certain cases, but not actions which, if commenced in the High Court, would have been assigned to the Chancery or Family Divisions, or have involved the exercise of the High Court's Admiralty jurisdiction, the parties can agree by a signed memorandum that the County Court should have jurisdiction (s. 18).

Further, the following claims may not be conducted in the County Court, whatever their financial value, unless (in the case of paragraphs (c) and (d)) the parties agree in writing:

(a) a claim for judicial review, as the County Court does not have the power to make any of the orders asked for in judicial review claims (County Courts Act 1984, s. 38(3)(a)) except on a claim under the Equality Act 2010 (see **11.3(d)**): judicial review is assigned to the Queen's Bench Division by the Senior Courts Act 1981, sch. 1, para. 2(b) (referred to in **PD 7A, para. 2.6**), and claims are dealt with in the Administrative Court (**PD 54A, para. 2.1**; **PD 54D, para. 2.1**);

(b) an application for a writ of habeas corpus, which must be made in the Administrative Court, Queen's Bench Division (Senior Courts Act 1981, sch. 1, para. 2(a); **PD 7A, para. 2.6**; CPR, r. 87.2(4)), unless it is an application by a parent or guardian of a child in relation to the custody, care or control of the child, in which case it must be made in the Family Division (see the Family Procedure Rules 2010 (SI 2010/2955), r. 12.42A, which incorporate CPR, Part 87, with appropriate modifications);

(c) a claim for libel or slander (County Courts Act 1984, s. 15(2)(c); **PD 7A, para. 2.9**);

(d) a claim in which the title to any toll, fair, market or franchise is in question (County Courts Act 1984, s. 15(2)(b); **PD 7A, para. 2.9**);

(e) applications concerning the decisions of local authority auditors (**High Court and County Courts Jurisdiction Order 1991, art. 6**).

A claim under the **Human Rights Act 1998, s. 7(1)(a)**, in respect of a judicial act may only be brought in the High Court. Any other claims under that section may be brought in any court (**CPR, r. 7.11**).

The County Court no longer has Admiralty jurisdiction as defined in the County Courts Act 1984, s. 27 (Civil Courts (Amendment) (No. 2) Order 1999 (SI 1999/1011)). Most Admiralty claims must be started in the Admiralty Court in the Queen's Bench Division (**CPR, r. 61.2**).

Cases which must be brought in the County Court

11.3 Certain claims must be brought in the County Court:

(a) Claims under the Consumer Credit Act 1974 may only be brought in the County Court, and should normally be made at the County Court hearing centre where the debtor resides or carries on business (**PD 7B, paras 4.1, 4.2, 4.3 and 5.1A**).

(b) Unless exceptional circumstances justify starting a claim in the High Court, a possession claim must be made in the County Court and can be made at any County Court hearing centre. However, if the claim is not made at the hearing centre which serves the address of the property, the claim will be sent to the hearing centre serving that address when it is issued (**CPR, r. 55.3(1)** and **(2)**). To avoid delay, claimants are encouraged to issue the claim at the County Court hearing centre which serves the address where the land is situated (**PD 55A, para. 1.1(2)**). Where a mortgage possession claim relates to a dwelling house and no part of the land is situated in Greater London, no court other than the County Court has jurisdiction to hear and determine the claim unless the proceedings also include a claim for foreclosure or sale (County Courts Act 1985, s. 21(3) and (4)). Exceptional reasons which justify commencing possession claims in the High Court are complex factual disputes or points of law of general importance, or the claim properly requires immediate determination because it is against trespassers and there is a substantial risk of public disturbance or serious harm to persons or property (**CPR, r. 55.3; PD 55A, paras 1.1 and 1.3**). If the claim is commenced in the High Court, the claimant must file with the claim form a certificate stating the reasons for bringing the claim in the High Court verified by a statement of truth (**CPR, r. 55.3(2)**). If a possession claim is started in the High Court which should have been brought in the County Court, it will either be struck out or automatically transferred to the County Court, and the costs of bringing the claim in the High Court and the costs of transfer will not normally be allowed (**PD 55A, para. 1.2**).

(c) Applications under the Access to Neighbouring Land Act 1992, s. 1, must be started in the County Court (**High Court and County Courts Jurisdiction Order 1991, art. 6A**).

(d) Proceedings under the Equality Act 2010 to enforce claims of discrimination arising in the context of premises, education, associations or the provision of services must be brought in the County Court (Equality Act 2010, s. 114). In any such proceedings, the County Court has power make any of the orders which could be granted by the High Court in tort or in judicial review claims (s. 119(2)).

(e) Claims brought under **PD 8B** and the **Pre-action Protocol for Low Value Personal Injury Claims in Road Traffic Accidents** (**PD 8B, para. 1.2**).

(f) Claims under the European Small Claims Procedure, Regulation (EC) No. 861/2007, art. 4, must be brought in the County Court (**High Court and County Courts Jurisdiction Order 1991, art. 6B**).

(g) An application for an adaption order or challenge under the **recast Brussels I Regulation** (**Regulation (EU) No. 1215/2012**), art. 54(2), must be made to the **High Court** (**High Court and County Courts Jurisdiction Order 1991, art. 6G**).

ALLOCATION OF BUSINESS BETWEEN HIGH COURT AND COUNTY COURT

Where the High Court and the County Court have concurrent jurisdiction, business is allocated according to the following rules: **11.4**

(a) A claim for damages or for a specified sum may be issued in the High Court only where the value of the claim is more than £100,000 (**PD 7A, para. 2.1; High Court and County Courts Jurisdiction Order 1991, art. 4A**).

(b) **PD 29, para. 2.2,** restricts a claimant's right to continue proceedings issued in the Central Office or Chancery Chambers of the Royal Courts of Justice (RCJ). Although any money claim worth over £100,000 may be issued in the RCJ, other claims with an estimated value less than £100,000 will generally be transferred to the County Court, unless one of the following exceptions applies:

   (i) The claim is required by statute to be tried in the High Court.

   (ii) The claim falls within a specialist list as defined in **CPR, r. 2.3(2)**. The specialist lists are the lists of proceedings in the Planning Court (**r. 54.22(1)**), the Commercial Court (**r. 58.2(1)**), Mercantile Courts (**r. 59.1(3)(a)**), the Technology and Construction Court (**r. 60.2(1)**), the Intellectual Property Enterprise Court (**r. 63.1(2)(g)**), the Patents Court (**r. 63.3**) and the Financial List (**r. 63A.2(1)**). Claims in the Financial List may be commenced in either the Commercial Court or the Chancery Division (**r. 63A.2(1)**).

   (iii) The claim falls into one of the following categories: professional negligence, fraud or undue influence, defamation, malicious prosecution or false imprisonment, claims against the police, claims under the Fatal Accidents Act 1976, or contentious probate claims (**PD 29, para. 2.6**).

   (iv) The claim is otherwise 'within the criteria of art. 7(5) of the **High Court and County Courts Jurisdiction Order 1991**' (SI 1991/724). This article has in fact been repealed by the High Court and County Courts Jurisdiction (Amendment) Order 1999 (SI 1999/1014). It stated the following criteria: the financial substance of the action; its importance, and in particular whether it raises questions of importance to non-parties or the general public; its complexity; and whether transfer is likely to result in a more speedy trial of the action (although transfer may not be ordered on this ground alone).

(c) A claim for personal injuries must not be started in the High Court unless the value of the claim is £50,000 or more (**PD 7A, para. 2.2; High Court and County Courts Jurisdiction Order 1991, art. 5**).

(d) A claim must be issued in the High Court or County Court, as appropriate, where an enactment requires it (**PD 7A, para. 2.3**).

(e) Insolvency proceedings and companies matters are subject to special rules which are discussed at **82.8** (companies winding up), **83.4** (bankruptcy), **85.1** (companies matters) and **86.6** (director disqualification applications).

(f) Proceedings under the Variation of Trusts Act 1958, s. 1, may be commenced and taken only in the High Court (**High Court and County Courts Jurisdiction Order 1991, art. 6D**).

(g) Claims falling within **CPR, Part 63, Section I** (see **r. 63.2(1)**), must be started in the High Court in the Patents Court or the Intellectual Property Enterprise Court (**r. 63.2(2)**). Claims within **Part 63, Section II** (registered trade marks and other intellectual property claims), must be started in the Chancery Division, the Intellectual Property Enterprise Court or, except as set out in **PD 63**, in a County Court hearing centre where there is also a Chancery District Registry. The Intellectual Property Enterprise Court has replaced the Patents County Court, with effect from 1 October 2013. If the amount or value of the claim exceeds £0.5 million, and the claim is for damages or an account of profits, IPEC does not have jurisdiction unless the parties agree that it shall have (**CPR, r. 63.17A**). Claims started in or transferred to the Intellectual Property Enterprise Court which have a value below £10,000 will normally be allocated to the small claims track (**r. 63.27**).

(h) Subject to paragraphs (a) and (c) above, a claim should be started in the High Court if the claimant believes it should be tried by a High Court judge because of the financial value of the claim and the amount in dispute, its complexity or its importance to the general public (**PD 7A, para. 2.4**). In other words, the £100,000 and £50,000 limits referred to in (a) and (c) above are the lowest thresholds for issuing a claim in the High Court in claims of those types. But, even where a case is worth more than these amounts, the claimant should not issue automatically in the High Court but should go on to consider the factors listed in **para. 2.4** in deciding whether trial by a High Court judge is really necessary.

By **PD 7A, para. 2.2**, the value of a claim is determined in accordance with the **High Court and County Courts Jurisdiction Order 1991, art. 9**. This simply cross-refers to **CPR, r. 16.3(6)**. Thus, the following must all be disregarded:

(a) interest;
(b) costs;
(c) any reduction for contributory negligence against the claimant;
(d) the value of any counterclaim or set-off; and
(e) the recoupment of benefits under the Social Security (Recovery of Benefits) Act 1997.

Table 11.1 Summary of the rules on allocation of business where both the High Court and the County Court have jurisdiction

Nature of claim	Venue
Money claim (i.e. claim for debt or liquidated demand or damages)	May be commenced in the High Court only if the claimant expects to recover more than £100,000.
Other claims issued in the RCJ	May be commenced in the RCJ, but will generally be transferred to the County Court, if worth less than £100,000, unless one of the exceptions stated in **PD 29, para. 2.2**, applies.
Claim for personal injuries	May be commenced in the High Court only if the value of the claim is £50,000 or more.

ALLOCATION OF BUSINESS TO THE QUEEN'S BENCH DIVISION

The following claims must be issued in the Queen's Bench Division of the High Court: **11.5**

(a) applications for a writ of habeas corpus (Senior Courts Act 1981, sch. 1, para. 2(a); **PD 7A, para. 2.6**) except applications by a parent or guardian in relation to a child (see **11.2**);

(b) applications for judicial review (Senior Courts Act 1981, sch. 1, para. 2(b); **PD 7A, para. 2.6**);

(c) the proceedings specified in the Terrorism Prevention and Investigation Measures Act 2011, s. 30(1) (Senior Courts Act 1981, sch. 1, para. 2(bd));

(d) all financial restrictions proceedings within the meaning of the Counter-Terrorism Act 2008, part 6, chapter 2 (Senior Courts Act 1981, sch. 1, para. 2(bb));

(e) matters involving the exercise of the High Court's jurisdiction as a prize court (Senior Courts Act 1981, sch. 1, para. 2(c));

(f) Commercial Court claims (Senior Courts Act 1981, sch. 1, para. 2(d); see further **11.7(d)**).

A claim in the High Court ordered to be tried by jury will be transferred to the Queen's Bench Division, if not already being conducted there (**PD 7A, para. 2.8**).

CHANCERY BUSINESS

Claims involving Chancery business may be dealt with either in the High Court or in the County   **11.6**
Court (**PD 7A, para. 2.5**). The claim form must be marked 'Chancery Division' in the top right corner, if issued in the High Court, and 'Chancery Business' if issued in the County Court (**PD 7A, para. 2.5**). The County Court's jurisdiction over equity claims is limited to £350,000 (County Courts Act 1984, s. 23; County Court Jurisdiction Order 2014 (SI 2014/503)), though parties may agree to vary this in certain types of proceedings (County Courts Act 1984, s. 24).

PD 7A, para. 2.5, defines 'Chancery business' as including any of the matters specified in the Senior Courts Act 1981, sch. 1, para. 1. Those matters are:

(a) the sale, exchange or partition of land, or the raising of charges on land;

(b) the redemption or foreclosure of mortgages;

(c) the execution of trusts;

(d) the administration of the estates of deceased persons;

(e) bankruptcy;

(f) the dissolution of partnerships or the taking of partnership or other accounts;

(g) the rectification, setting aside or cancellation of deeds or other instruments in writing;

(h) probate business, other than non-contentious or common form business;

(i) patents, trade marks, registered designs, copyright or design right;

(j) the appointment of a guardian of a minor's estate;

(k) all causes and matters involving the exercise of the High Court's jurisdiction under the enactments relating to companies.

Within the £350,000 limit in the County Courts Act 1984, s. 23, and the County Court Jurisdiction Order 2014 (SI 2014/503), the County Court can deal with any Chancery business claim except that:

(a) County Court probate claims must be brought in a County Court hearing centre where there is also a Chancery District Registry or in the County Court at Central London (**CPR, r. 57.2(3)**);

(b) County Court claims falling within **Part 63, Section II** (see **r. 63.13(1)(c)**), must be started in a County Court hearing centre where there is also a Chancery District Registry (**r. 63.2(2)**; see **11.4**). The County Court no longer has jurisdiction to deal with claims falling within **Part 63, Section I**, as such claims must be brought in the Patents Court or the Intellectual Property Enterprise Court (**r. 63.2(2)**);

(c) insolvency proceedings in the County Court may only be brought in hearing centres designated for those purposes in the Insolvency (Commencement of Proceedings) and Insolvency Rules 1986 (Amendment) Rules 2014 (SI 2014/817), rr. 2 and 3 and sch. 1 (see **82.8** and **83.4**).

There are 10 Chancery District Registries, at Birmingham, Bristol, Caernarfon, Cardiff, Leeds, Liverpool, Manchester, Mold, Newcastle upon Tyne and Preston (Civil Courts Order 2014 (SI 2014/819); (**PD 63, para. 16.2**). The County Court hearing centres at Caernarfon, Mold and Preston do not have jurisdiction in relation to registered or Community trade marks (**PD 63, para. 16.3**).

This means that there will be claims designated as Chancery business which are commenced in a County Court hearing centre with no Chancery expertise. Detailed guidance on transferring these cases, and also claims from the Chancery Division to the appropriate County Court hearing centre (and in particular to the County Court at Central London Chancery List), is given in the Chancery Guide 2016, paras 14.15 to 14.26.

Any claim which raises an issue under the Treaty on the Functioning of the European Union, arts 101 or 102, or the equivalent UK statutory provisions, chapter 1 or chapter 2 of part 1 of the Competition Act 1998, must be transferred to the Chancery Division at the RCJ if commenced in any court other than the Commercial and Admiralty Court (**CPR, r. 30.8**). If a commercial claim, as defined in **r. 58.1(2)**, which raises a competition issue is commenced in the Queen's Bench Division or a Mercantile Court, any party may apply for the claim to be transferred to the Commercial Court instead of the Chancery Division. If the application to transfer to the Commercial Court is refused, the claim must be transferred to the Chancery Division at the RCJ in the usual way (**r. 30.8(4)**).

SPECIALIST CLAIMS

11.7 Various rules and practice directions regulate the place where the specialist proceedings to which they relate should be started. In brief, the position is as follows:

(a) Probate claims: **CPR, Part 57**, and **PD 57A**. A probate claim to be conducted in the High Court must be issued in the Chancery Division, that is, either Chancery Chambers of the Royal Courts of Justice, or a Chancery District Registry. (Chancery District Registries are to be found at Birmingham, Bristol, Caernarfon, Cardiff, Leeds, Liverpool, Manchester, Mold, Newcastle upon Tyne and Preston.) A probate claim in the County Court can only be brought in a County Court hearing centre where there is also a Chancery District Registry or in the County Court at Central London (**CPR, r. 57.2(3)**).

(b) Companies Acts applications: **PD 49A**. See **85.1** and **85.3**

(c) Technology and Construction Court (TCC): **CPR, Part 60**, and **PD 60**. Claims that involve issues or questions which are technically complex, or for which a trial by a judge of the TCC is desirable, may be issued in the TCC. TCC claims may be brought either in the High Court or in a County Court hearing centre specified in **PD 60**. In the High Court outside London, they may be issued in any District Registry, but preferably in a District Registry where a TCC judge will usually be available. These are: Birmingham, Bristol, Cardiff, Chester, Exeter, Leeds, Liverpool, Manchester, Mold, Newcastle upon Tyne and Nottingham (**PD 60, para. 3.3**). TCC claims may be issued only in the following County Court hearing centres: Birmingham, Bristol, Cardiff, Central London, Chester, Exeter, Leeds, Liverpool, Manchester, Mold, Newcastle upon Tyne and Nottingham (**PD 60, para. 3.4**). In recent years, there has been a significant increase in the work of the TCC in London and the TCC judges wish to ensure that only the most substantial cases are heard at the High Court in London. Accordingly in *West Country Renovations Ltd v McDowell* [2012] EWHC 307 (TCC), [2012] 3 All ER 106 Akenhead J, following consultation with the other TCC judges, stated that TCC claims worth less than £250,000 should be commenced in the County Court or High Court centres outside London that have TCC-designated judges instead of in the TCC in Fetter Lane in London. A non-exhaustive list of exceptions to this general rule is identified, including international claims, adjudications, public procurement cases, claims for an injunction or for a declaration, Part 8 claims, cases involving new or difficult points of law, test cases and complex nuisance claims.

(d) Commercial Court: **CPR, Part 58**, and **PD 58**. Commercial claims as defined by **CPR, r. 58.1(2)**, may be conducted in the commercial list in the Royal Courts of Justice and, if they are, they should be issued out of the Admiralty and Commercial Registry (**PD 58, para. 2.1**). By **CPR, r. 58.1(2)**, any case arising out of trade and commerce in general may be commenced in the Commercial Court, including any case relating to:

(i)   a business document or contract;

(ii)   the export or import of goods;

(iii)   the carriage of goods by land, sea, air or pipeline;

(iv)   the exploitation of oil and gas reserves or other natural resources;

(v)   insurance and reinsurance;

(vi)   banking and financial services;

(vii)   the operation of markets and exchanges;

(viii) the purchase and sale of commodities;

(ix)   the construction of ships;

(x)   business agency; and

(xi)   arbitration.

(e) Mercantile Courts: **CPR, Part 59**, and **PD 59**. Claims which are broadly commercial in nature, and which are not required to proceed in the Chancery Division or in any other specialist list may be issued in a Mercantile Court (**CPR, r. 59.1(2)**; see **2.19**). By **PD 59, para. 2.1**, a claim should only be started in a Mercantile Court if it would benefit from the expertise of a Mercantile judge.

(f) Patents etc.: **CPR, Part 63**, and **PD 63**. The jurisdiction of the Patents Court and the Intellectual Property Enterprise Court is conferred by the statutes concerning intellectual property rights. The Intellectual Property Enterprise Court is designed to deal with simpler and lower-value intellectual property disputes in a more cost-effective way.

(g) Admiralty proceedings: **CPR, Part 61**, and **PD 61**. An Admiralty claim listed in **CPR, r. 61.2(1)**, must be commenced in the Admiralty Court. The County Court has no Admiralty jurisdiction (Civil Courts (Amendment) (No. 2) Order 1999 (SI 1999/1011)).

(h) The business assigned to the Family Division is listed in **2.14**.

(i) Financial List: This was created by **CPR, Part 63A** and **PD 63AA**, with effect from 1 October 2015 for finance cases worth more than £50 million or the equivalent, such as loans, project finance, banking transactions, debt securities, private equity deals, bonds, hedge fund disputes, sovereign debt, clearing or settlement, or claims which require particular expertise in the financial markets or which raise issues of general importance to the financial markets (**CPR, r. 63A.1**). The list is also suitable for cases involving the construction of standard form documentation in such cases (*GSO Credit — A Partners LP v Barclays Bank plc* [2016] EWHC 146 (Comm), LTL 4/2/2016). Claims allocated to the Financial List can be issued in either the Commercial Court or the Chancery Division of the High Court (**r. 63A.2**). Apart from some limited exceptions, proceedings in the Financial List will be allocated to a designated Financial List Judge (**r. 63A.4; PD 63AA, para. 1.2**). An application has to be made to the Financial List Judge before proceedings are issued to determine whether a claim should be brought in the Financial List (**PD 63AA, paras 3.1 to 3.3**). Further guidance is contained in the Guide to the Financial List issued on 1 October 2015.

An application to transfer a claim from one specialist list to another specialist list can be made to a judge dealing with claims in either list (**CPR, r. 30.5(3)**, *Natl Amusements (UK) Ltd v White City (Shepherds Bush) LP* [2009] EWHC 2524 (TCC), [2010] 1 WLR 1181).

APPLICATIONS BEFORE ISSUE

11.8   Applications made before a claim has started should be made to the court where it is likely that the claim to which the application relates will be issued, unless there is good reason to make the application to a different court (**CPR, r. 23.2(4)**). There is no explanation in the rules of what is meant by 'good reason' but one circumstance in which it would be appropriate to make an application in a different court is where a search order (which may be made only by the High Court or a duly authorised judge, see **37.2**) is sought in relation to a claim to be issued in the County court (see the County Court Remedies Regulations 2014 (SI 2014/982), which contain provisions relating to the automatic transfer of proceedings in the County Court to the High Court where an application for a search order has been made to the High Court). An application made in the County Court before a claim has been started may be made at any County Court hearing centre, unless an enactment, rule or practice direction states otherwise (**CPR, r. 23.2(4A)**).

MONEY CLAIMS ONLY

11.9   From 19 March 2012, the administrative functions of the County Court in the early stages of straightforward money claims have been centralised. A claim in the County Court under **CPR, Part 7**, may be made at any County Court hearing centre, unless any enactment, rule or practice direction provides otherwise (**PD 7A, para. 2.4A(1)**). If a claim required to be made at a particular County Court hearing centre is made at the wrong hearing centre, a court officer will send the claim to the correct hearing centre before it is issued (**PD 7A, para. 2.4A(2)**). Restrictions on where proceedings may be started are set out in the practice directions supplementing **CPR, Part 7**. For a claim started in the County Court under **Part 7** which is a claim only for an amount of money, whether specified or unspecified, and to which no special procedures apply, the claim form (form N1) must be sent to the County Court Money Claims Centre (CCMCC), PO Box 527, M5 0BY (**PD 7A, para. 4A.1**). The CCMCC acts as the court office for these claims until they are sent to a County Court hearing centre. The claimant must specify their preferred hearing centre in the claim form (**PD 7A, para 4A.2**). The preferred hearing centre means the County Court hearing centre the claimant has specified in the claim form as the hearing centre to which the proceedings should be sent if necessary (**CPR, r. 2.3(1)**). Claims sent to the CCMCC will be sent by post or DX and it is the responsibility of the claimant to ensure that the claim form is delivered to the CCMCC within the limitation period, accompanied by a request to issue and payment of the appropriate fee (see *Page v Hewetts Solicitors* [2012] EWCA Civ 805, [2012] CP Rep 40).

If at any time a court officer considers that the claim should be referred to a judge for directions, the court officer can send the proceedings to the preferred court or the defendant's home court (that being the County Court hearing centre serving the address at which the defendant resides or carries on business (see **r. 2.3(1)**) or such other court as may be appropriate (**r. 26.2A**). Otherwise, money only claims will remain in the CCMCC until the 'relevant time' as defined by **r. 26.2A(6)**. The relevant time is when all parties have returned their directions questionnaires; when any stay ordered by the court, or period to attempt settlement through mediation, has expired; or, if the claim falls within **PD 7D**, when the defence is filed or enforcement of a default judgment other than by a warrant of control is requested, whichever occurs first. A County Court money claim will also be transferred to the preferred hearing centre if:

(a) the claimant files a request for default judgment under **rr. 12.4** and **12.5** which includes an amount of money to be decided by the court (**r. 12.5A**);

(b) a defendant who is not an individual applies under **r. 13.4** to set aside or vary a default judgment on a claim for a specified sum (**r. 13.4(1B)**);

(c) the claimant files a request for judgment in the CCMCC for an amount of money to be decided by the court in accordance with **r. 14.6** or **14.7** (**r. 14.7A**);

(d) a judge is to determine the time and rate of payment under **r. 14.12** on a judgment entered following an admission of liability and a request from the defendant for time to pay — automatic transfer to the preferred hearing centre under this rule will take place where the claim is for a specified sum only, the defendant is not an individual and the claim has not already been sent to another court (**r. 14.12(2A)**);

(e) the judge is to determine the time and rate of payment at a hearing, the only claim is for a specified amount of money, the defendant is an individual and the claim has not been transferred or sent to another defendant's home court or started in the defendant's home court or started in a specialist list (**r. 14.12(2)**) — transfer under this rule is to the defendant's home court; or

(f) a judge, or a court officer, has determined the time and rate of payment under **r. 14.11** or **14.12** without a hearing and either party makes an application under **r. 14.13** for the decision to be redetermined by a judge. Automatic transfer under this rule will take place either to the defendant's home court if the defendant is an individual and the claim has not been transferred to another defendant's court or started in the defendant's home court, or to the preferred hearing centre where the claim is for a specified sum only, the defendant is not an individual and the claim has not already been transferred to another court (**r. 14.13(3A)**).

In each case, the transfer will happen automatically upon receipt of the request for judgment or application by the CCMCC. Automatic transfer to the defendant's home court is dealt with at **42.9**, and transfer to the claimant's preferred hearing centre is discussed at **42.8**.

COMMENCING IN THE WRONG COURT AND TRANSFER

Generally, when proceedings are commenced in the wrong court, they will be transferred to the correct court using the power under the County Courts Act 1984, ss. 40 to 42, and **CPR, r. 30.2**. The High Court has power under the County Courts Act 1984, s. 40(2), to order transfer of a claim to the County Court. Both the High Court and the County Court have power under the County Courts Act 1984, ss. 41 and 42, to order transfer from the County Court to the High Court. For an example of the exercise of this power, see *Paratus AMC Ltd v Lewis* [2014] EWHC 933 (Ch), LTL 25/2/2014.

11.10

An application to transfer a claim from one County Court hearing centre to another should be made to the County Court hearing centre in which the claim is proceeding, not the hearing centre to which transfer is sought (**CPR, r. 30.2(3)**). Applications for transfer between District Registries of the High Court or from a District Registry to the RCJ should also be made in the court where the claim is proceeding (**r. 30.2(6)**). Applications under **r. 30.5(1)** for transfer from one division to another may be made in either division (*Natl Amusements (UK) Ltd v White City (Shepherds Bush) LP* [2009] EWHC 2524 (TCC), [2010] 1 WLR 1181). Application for a transfer to or from a specialist list must be made to a judge dealing with claims in that list (**r. 30.5(3)**). See Chancery Masters Guidelines for the Transfer of Claims (20 May 2015) for guidance in relation to the transfer of cases from the Chancery Division to a Chancery District Registry or the County Court or another division of the High Court. The objective of the guidance is to ensure that only cases which are suitable for management and trial in the Chancery Division in London are retained there. If a case is to be transferred, this should occur before detailed case management has taken place.

However, **r. 30.5(3)** does not govern transfers of copyright and passing off claims falling within **Part 63, Section II**, from the Patents Court in the High Court to the County Court. For those cases, transfer is instead governed by the County Courts Act 1984, s. 40. Application should therefore be made to the sending court and can be made to a Master rather than being referred to a judge (*DKH Retail Ltd v Republic (Retail) Ltd* [2012] EWHC 877, [2012] Bus LR 1363). The factors to be taken into account in deciding whether to transfer a patents case to or from the

Intellectual Property Enterprise Court are set out at **PD 30, para. 9**, and the Copyright, Designs and Patents Act 1988, s. 289(2)).

The criteria to which the court must have regard when considering whether or not to transfer a case are set out at C?R, r. 30.3. An example of the application of these criteria, in this case to a claim being transferred from the County Court to the TCC, is to be found in *Collins v Drumgold* [2008] EWHC 584 (TCC), [2008] CILL 2585. In deciding whether or not to make an order for transfer from one High Court division to another, the court does not have to decide that it is inappropriate for a case to remain in the division in which it has been issued, although the suitability of the expertise of its judges is the single most important consideration. Where the differences in the suitability of different courts for the particular type of case are less marked, factors such as cost and speed can be taken into account (*Natl Amusements (UK) Ltd v White City (Shepherds Bush) LP*).

It was held in *National Westminster Bank plc v King* [2008] EWHC 280 (Ch), [2008] Ch 385, that the High Court has power to transfer a case under the County Courts Act 1984, s. 40(2), even if the value of the case exceeds the County Court limit. This case involved the enforcement of a charging order for £39,356, where the County Court's jurisdiction was limited to £30,000. In making a transfer order the High Court held that the County Court's jurisdiction effectively derived from the order of transfer. This decision was followed by the Court of Appeal in *Wallace v Crossley* [2009] EWCA Civ 896, LTL 26/8/2009.

The claimant will usually be penalised by being ordered to pay the costs involved in the transfer. In addition, where proceedings which, in the court's opinion, should have been commenced in the County Court have been commenced in the High Court, the court may reduce any award of costs by up to 25 per cent (Senior Courts Act 1981, s. 51(8) and (9)). However, if a claimant brings a claim in the High Court in breach of a requirement that it should be in the County Court (or vice versa), the court may either transfer the claim, or, if it is satisfied that the person bringing the claim knew or ought to have known of the requirement, strike out the proceedings (County Courts Act 1984, ss. 40(1)(b) and 42(1)(b); see *Adshead v Royal Bank of Scotland plc* [2002] EWHC 192 (Ch), LTL 25/2/2002). According to *Restick v Crickmore* [1994] 1 WLR 420, striking out is inappropriate for bona fide mistakes, but would be a proper response to instances where starting in the wrong court was a deliberate attempt to harass a defendant, or a deliberate attempt to run up unnecessary costs, or was done despite the claimant being told by the defendant where the claim should be commenced.

Where a claimant seeks to issue proceedings, and the court manager believes they are being issued in the wrong court, the court should nevertheless accept the papers. Court officials have no power to determine judicially whether the court should accept a claim (*Gwynedd County Council v Grunshaw* [2000] 1 WLR 494). Once the claim is issued, an order for transfer may be made. This is subject to **PD 7A, para. 2.4A**, which provides that if a claim is required to be made at a particular County Court hearing centre, but is made at the wrong hearing centre, a court officer will send the claim to the correct hearing centre before it is issued.

It is desirable to give notice to the court or hearing centre from which transfer is sought of the making of an application under **CPR, r. 30.2**. However, in *Neath Port Talbot County Borough Council v Currie and Brown Project Management Ltd* [2008] EWHC 1508 (TCC), [2008] BLR 464, this procedural irregularity did not prevent the TCC from determining an application for the claim to be transferred to it from the County Court. **PD 60, para. 5**, makes provision for the transfer of cases between the TCC in the High Court and the County Court, but provides no criteria for transfer. *Neath* also provides guidance for the factors to be considered on making applications for transfer to and from the TCC in London. See also *West Country Renovations Ltd v McDowell* [2012] EWHC 307, [2012] 3 All ER 106 (discussed in **11.7**).

Chapter 12   Issuing Proceedings

The following procedural checklists are relevant to this chapter and **chapter 15**:

Procedural checklist 3   Issue and service where service of the claim form is to be effected by the court

Procedural checklist 4   Issue and service where service of the claim form is to be effected by the claimant

METHODS OF COMMENCING CIVIL PROCEEDINGS

Lord Woolf's *Final Report* commented that 'A prime example of [the complexity of the old rules] is the fact that there are four different ways of starting proceedings in the High Court, and another four in the county courts' (ch. 12, para. 1). In order to further the aim of achieving simplicity in civil proceedings, Lord Woolf recommended that there should be a single claim form which could be used for every case (ch. 2, para. 3).   **12.1**

This radical simplification has not worked out in practice. First, during the drafting of the CPR it was realised that it is possible to use a simplified procedure (now in **CPR, Part 8**; see **chapter 13**) for certain classes of proceedings in which it is normal for there to be no disputes over facts. Secondly it was decided to create a special form of process for third-party and other subsidiary claims (**CPR, Part 20**; see **chapters 28** and **29**). Thirdly it was not possible, in time for the introduction of the CPR in April 1999, to assimilate the numerous varieties of specialist proceedings for which special forms of originating process existed under the old rules, and at present they remain exceptions under the CPR. Some of these exceptional procedures are prescribed by statute and some were excluded from the terms of reference of Lord Woolf's inquiry. The current version of **PD 4**, which came into force on 16 April 2016, lists many forms prescribed by practice direction, including those used to commence proceedings, and the forms are arranged both by subject matter and in alphabetical order. Forms can be downloaded from Form Finder at https://hmctsformfinder.justice.gov.uk/HMCTS/FormFinder.do.

There are still at least 15 different ways of commencing claims in civil courts. These are by:

(a) Claim form (form N1; see **chapter 23**), which is the standard method under the CPR. Three special claim forms are prescribed for use in Admiralty claims (ADM 1, ADM 1A and ADM 15); there is a special version of form N1 for use in the Commercial Court (form N1(CC)); a special claim form (N461) is prescribed for judicial review proceedings; and there is also a special claim form for Part 7 claims in the Chancery Division Financial List (N1(CHFL)) and in the Commercial Court Financial List (N1(CCFL)).

(b)   Part 8 claim form (form N208), for use in proceedings in which there are no substantial factual disputes and where required by a practice direction (see **chapter 13**). There is a special version of form N208 for use in the Commercial Court (form N208(CC)) and a special Part 8 claim form (N500) has been prescribed for director disqualification proceedings. There is also a special claim form (N501) for applications under the Company Directors Disqualification Act 1986, s. 8A, and a special claim form for Part 8 claims in the Chancery Division Financial List (N208(CHFL)) and the Commercial Court Financial List (N208(CCFL)).

(c)   Claim form (form N211) for additional claims under CPR, Part 20 (see chapters 28 and 29). There is a special version of form N211 for use in the Commercial Court (form N211(CC)) and for additional claims in the Commercial Court Financial List (N211(CCFL)) and the Chancery Division Financial List (N208(CHFL)).

(d)   Arbitration claim form (form N8), which is used in arbitration applications (see **72.2** and **72.3**).

(e)   Special claim forms for starting a claim for possession of land (N5 and N5B), for relief against forfeiture of a lease (N5A) and for demotion of tenancy (N6).

(f)   Special claim form (N2) for use in probate claims.

(g)   A control order claim form relating to proceedings under the Prevention of Terrorism Act 2005, s. 11.

(h)   A European Small Claims Procedure claim form, which is required for claims under Regulation (EC) No. 861/2007 (see **45.33**) and a European Order for Payment application form, for claims under Regulation (EC) No. 1896/2006 (see **12.11**).

(i)   Petition, which is required by statute or statutory instrument for various proceedings, such as divorce and judicial separation (which are not considered in this work), winding up of companies (see **chapter 82**) and bankruptcy (see **chapter 83**).

(j)   Administration application, to obtain an order appointing an administrator of a company (see **82.96** to **82.111**).

(k)   Application notice, which is required for an application under the Insolvency Act 1986 or the Insolvency Rules 1986 (SI 1986/1925) if it is not in pending proceedings (see **chapter 84**).

(l)   Summons in respect of alleged offences contrary to the County Courts Act 1984, ss. 14, 92, and 124 (**CPR, r. 81.34**), which is a procedure more of a criminal nature than civil.

(m)   Request, such as under the rules for enforcing parking penalties under the Road Traffic Act 1991 (CPR, r. 75.3).

(n)   Some cases can be brought very informally simply by making an application by witness statement or affidavit, examples being an application under the Deeds of Arrangement Act 1914, s. 7 (**PD 8A, para. 12A**, which states that an application may be made either by Part 8 claim form or by witness statement), and an application for confirmation of a creditors' voluntary winding up of a company (Insolvency Rules 1986 (SI 1986/1925), r. 7.62).

The point is made in **PD Pre-action Conduct and Protocols, para. 8**, and in most of the pre-action protocols themselves, that litigation is a last resort (see **chapter 8**). Complaints procedures and other forms of alternative dispute resolution should at least be considered before most forms of litigation are started: even if the whole dispute cannot be resolved by these means, the parties and their legal advisers should resolve the dispute as far as possible without litigation (*R (Cowl) v Plymouth City Council* [2001] EWCA Civ 1935, [2002] 1 WLR 803).

Use of incorrect form

12.2   A party who commences proceedings using the incorrect form is likely to be given permission, under **CPR, r. 3.10**, to rectify the error, applying the principle in **r. 1.1** of dealing with cases justly. Thus, in *Hannigan v Hannigan* [2000] 2 FCR 650, the court allowed the claimant to rectify an error in using the wrong form on the grounds that all the information the defendant needed to understand the case had been provided. Similarly, use of the wrong form to bring an application in insolvency proceedings (see **84.2**) is a formal defect or irregularity which does not invalidate the application unless it has caused substantial injustice which cannot be remedied by any order of the court (Insolvency Rules 1986, r. 7.55). For example, in *Phillips v McGregor-Paterson* [2009] EWHC 2385 (Ch), LTL 8/10/2009, use of a claim form instead of an insolvency ordinary application was excused because it had not caused injustice even though it meant that an insolvency application for summary judgment was not heard by a registrar but by a master, whose decision was reversed on appeal. In *Re Osea Road Camp Sites Ltd* [2004] EWHC 2437 (Ch), [2005] 1 WLR 760, however, an application which had incorrectly been brought by claim form rather than by petition under what is now the Companies Act 2006, s. 994 (see **85.10**), was struck out on the grounds that **CPR, r. 3.10**, gives the court power to cure a defect in procedure under the CPR only.

In *Islam v Secretary of State for Communities and Local Government* [2012] EWHC 1314 (Admin), [2012] JPL 1378, the claimant incorrectly brought an appeal against the refusal of planning permission under s. 288 of the Town and Country Planning Act instead of s. 289. The court refused to permit an appeal under s. 289 out of time because to do so would have the effect of substituting a new claim. (For further discussion of using the incorrect form to initiate proceedings, see **1.27** and **23.4**.). The breadth and operation of **r. 3.10** were considered in *Integral Petroleum SA v SCU-Finanz AG* [2014] EWHC 702 (Comm), LTL 19/3/2014 (decision affirmed on appeal at [2015] EWCA Civ 144, [2015] Bus LR 640).

ISSUING A CLAIM FORM

Under the CPR, unless another method of commencing proceedings is required or permitted (see **12.1**), proceedings are started when the court issues, at the request of the claimant, a claim form (form N1) prepared by or on behalf of the claimant (**r. 7.2(1)**).   **12.3**

Issue, rather than service, is the relevant date for the purposes of the supply of court records of proceedings under **r. 5.4(1)** (*Advance Specialist Treatment Engineering Ltd v Cleveland Structural Engineering (Hong Kong) Ltd* [2000] 1 WLR 558). The date the claim is brought (i.e., the date on which the request for issue is delivered to the court office), as opposed to issued, is the relevant date for limitation (*Barnes v St Helens Metropolitan Borough Council* [2006] EWCA Civ 1372, [2007] 1 WLR 879; *Page v Hewetts Solicitors* [2012] EWCA Civ 805, [2012] CP Rep 40; see **12.5**).

An issue fee is payable in accordance with the CPFO (see **appendix 3**). The court will issue the claim form by affixing the court seal (**CPR, r. 2.6(1)**), which it may do by hand or by printing a facsimile of the seal on the document, electronically or otherwise (**r. 2.6(2)**). There is nothing to prevent a claim being issued with a stated value well below the full value of the damage done, even though the effect may be that a lower issue fee will be payable (*Khiaban v Beard* [2003] EWCA Civ 358, [2003] 1 WLR 1626). However, deliberately underestimating a claim to avoid or defer paying higher court fees on issue is likely to be an abuse of the court's process and may result in an application being made to strike out the claim, or for summary judgment to be awarded on the grounds of limitation (where such claims are issued just before the expiry of the limitation period) as the failure to pay the appropriate fee may mean that the claim is not properly 'brought' for limitation purposes (*Lewis v Ward Hadaway* [2015] EWHC 3503 (Ch), [2016] 4 WLR 6).

The procedure for issuing and serving a claim is summarised in **procedural checklist 3** and **procedural checklist 4**. Those procedural checklists should be read in conjunction with **chapter 15**.

Commentary

Number of copies required

12.4   In order to have a claim form issued, the claimant must take or send to court one copy of the completed claim form for the court and one for each defendant (**CPR, r. 6.4(3)**). The rules do not mention a copy for the claimant's own use. However, a claimant who wants a file copy of the claim form as issued will be required to provide a further copy of the claim form which the court will seal and return to the claimant marked 'claimant's copy' (Queen's Bench Guide, para. 4.1.5).

Time of issue

12.5   For the purposes of the CPR, proceedings are started when the claim form is issued by the court (**CPR, r. 7.2(1)**). The date of issue is entered on the form by the court (**r. 7.2(2)**). For the purposes of the Limitation Act 1980 and other statutes a claim is 'brought' when the claimant's request for the issue of a claim form (together with the court fee) is delivered to the court office. That is also when the court is seised of the claim for the purposes of **Regulation (EU) No. 1215/2012** (the **recast Brussels I Regulation**) (see **16.38**). The Court of Appeal confirmed in *Barnes v St Helens Metropolitan Borough Council* [2006] EWCA Civ 1372, [2007] 1 WLR 879, that the guidance in **PD 7A, para. 5.1**, clarifying **CPR, r. 7.2**, is correct, for the reason that the claimant is not responsible for any shortcomings of the court in failing to issue the claim form promptly and so should not be at risk of his claim being time-barred once the claim form is in the hands of the court (*Page v Hewetts Solicitors* [2012] EWCA Civ 805, [2012] CP Rep 40). In *Barnes v St Helens Metropolitan Borough Council*, the claim form was received by the court office on 4 November 2004 and date stamped by the court with that date. The limitation period expired the following day. Because of industrial action at the court offices, the claim form was not issued until Monday 8 November. The court held that the claim was not time-barred. Where, as here, a claim form is received in the court office on a date earlier than the date on which it is issued by the court, the claim is brought for the purposes of the Limitation Act 1980 on the earlier date (see **3.5** and **10.6**). Court officials will record the date of receipt of the claim form either on the claim form itself, or on its covering letter (**PD 7A, para. 5.2**). However **PD 7A, para. 5.4**, enjoins claimants for whom the date of receipt is crucial to make their own arrangements for recording it.

Notice of issue

12.6   Once the court has issued a claim form, it will assign the claim a number, create a case management file and send a notice of issue to the claimant, using form N205A, N205B or N205C, depending on whether the claim is for a specified or unspecified amount of money or whether it is a non-money claim.

Issue by fax in the Admiralty and Commercial Registry

12.7   Appendix A to PD 58 provides a procedure for claimants to make a request by fax for the issue of a claim form in the Admiralty and Commercial Registry in the RCJ when that registry is closed. Provided the procedure is followed, the claim form is treated as issued at the time when the fax is recorded by the registry as having been received.

CLAIM PRODUCTION CENTRE

12.8   Claim forms in debt recovery claims may be issued and served in bulk from the Production Centre in Northampton. The Centre issues and serves claim forms electronically by the

County Court, in accordance with **PD 7C**. Proceedings may be issued using the Centre only by persons, known as 'centre users', permitted to use it, such as credit card companies and public utilities. Any rule or practice direction requiring documents to be filed is complied with in claim production cases by delivering to the Production Centre data for the document in computer readable form (**PD 7C, para. 1.4(1)**). A code of practice provides for the forms of magnetic media that may be used when delivering data.

Claims that may be issued at the Production Centre are restricted to County Court claims for specified sums, in pounds sterling, up to £100,000 brought against only one defendant (or two if the same sum is claimed from each of them), none of whom has an address for service out of the jurisdiction, where the claimant is not publicly funded and does not have an address for service outside the United Kingdom, and where none of the parties is a child or protected party. The Centre will not deal with claims against the Crown, nor will it issue Part 8 claims. The Centre can deal with cases filed in the Centre from issue, service, entry of default judgment and judgment on admissions, and to the registration of judgment and issuing warrants of control. When a defence is filed the Centre will send a notice to the claimant requiring a reply within 28 days stating whether the claimant wishes the claim to proceed. If no such notification is given the claim will be stayed. If, however, notification is received that the claim is to continue, the proceedings will be transferred to (if the defendant is an individual) the defendant's home court (defined in **CPR, r. 2.3(1)**), or (if the defendant is not an individual) to the County Court hearing centre which serves the claimant's home address (or that of the claimant's solicitors) (**PD 7C, paras 1.3(2)(e) and 5.3**). A claim will also be transferred to the defendant's home court before the parties have filed their directions questionnaires where directions are required or where a hearing is required before judgment, or if the defendant applies to set aside or vary judgment or if either party makes an application which cannot be dealt with without a hearing (**PD 7C, para. 5.4**). Applications for an oral examination or third party debt order must be issued in accordance with **PD 70, paras 9.1 and 11.1**, unless proceedings have already been sent to a County Court hearing centre. A request for a warrant of control to enforce a judgment or order made at the Centre must be made to that office, unless the proceedings have already been sent to a County Court hearing centre (**PD 7C, para. 5.6**).

The claimant can serve particulars of claim separately, once the Centre has issued and served the claim form. But in this case the claim form must state that the particulars will follow and include a brief summary of the claim. The claimant must file a certificate of service (form N215) at the Centre within 14 days of service. There is no requirement to file particulars of claim, unless the defendant files a defence and the claim is transferred to the defendant's home court, in which case the claimant must file a copy of the particulars at the court to which the claim is transferred. The requirement in **PD 16, para. 7.3**, to attach contractual documents to the particulars of claim in breach of contract cases does not apply to claims issued in the Production Centre, unless the particulars of claim are served separately under **PD 7C, para. 5.2 (PD 7C, para. 1.4(3A))**.

From 1 October 2015, **PD 51K** (County Court Legal Advisers Pilot Scheme) permits a legal adviser to exercise the jurisdiction of the County Court in relation to the matters set out in the first column of the schedule to **PD 51K**, subject to the restrictions in column 2. The list in column 1 includes orders to rectify procedural errors, extending the validity of the claim form, amending particulars of claim, adding or substituting a party and setting aside default judgment. Decisions of a legal adviser can be made without a hearing (**PD 51K, para. 3.1**). The parties have the right to have the decision of a legal adviser reconsidered by a District Judge provided the application is made within 14 days after the party is served with notice of the decision (**PD 51K, para. 3.3**). The pilot will run for 12 months from 1 October 2015 until 30 September 2016.

CLAIMS UNDER THE CONSUMER CREDIT ACT 1974: FIXED-DATE CLAIMS

12.9 The court may in certain cases fix a date for a hearing upon issue of a claim form (**CPR, r. 7.9**). The claims for which the court will adopt this procedure are listed in **PD 7B, para. 3**. They are all claims under specified sections of the Consumer Credit Act 1974. A modified procedure applies to these claims, as set out in **PD 7B, para. 5**. It is as follows:

(a) The court will fix a hearing date on the issue of the claim form. Each party must be given at least 28 days' notice of the hearing date. Notice of the hearing date must be served at the same time as the claim form, unless the hearing date is specified in the claim form.

(b) The claimant must serve particulars of the claim with the claim form.

(c) The defendant should not file an acknowledgment of service. A defendant who wishes to defend the claim should file a defence, within 14 days after service of the claim form.

(d) Where the defendant fails to file a defence within 14 days, the claimant may not apply for judgment in default: **CPR, Part 12**, does not apply where the claimant is using the **PD 7B** procedure. The defendant may file a defence after the expiry of the 14-day time limit, but the court may take account of the delay in the costs order it makes.

(e) The court will usually dispose of the claim at the hearing, provided the defendant has not served a defence. If a defence has been served, the court may allocate the claim to a track and give directions.

MONEY CLAIM ONLINE

12.10 A claimant may start a claim by requesting the issue of a claim form electronically via Her Majesty's Courts and Tribunals Service website. Claims started using Money Claim Online will be issued in the County Court Business Centre and will proceed at the County Court Business Centre unless they are sent to a County Court hearing centre. The address for filing any document, application or request, other than one which is filed electronically in accordance with **PD 7E**, is the County Court Business Centre, St Katherine's House, 21–27 St Katherine's Street, Northampton NN1 2LH, DX 702885 Northampton 7, fax 0845 6015889 (**CPR, r. 7.12; PD 7E, paras 1.2(1)** and **1.4**). Once a claim has been started in this way, the claimant can also file electronically a request for judgment in default, or judgment on acceptance of an admission of the whole of the amount claimed or the issue of a warrant of control (**para. 1.2(2)**). The claimant can also view an electronic record of the progress of the claim. The record of each claim will be reviewed and, where necessary, updated every day until the claim is sent from the County Court Business Centre (**para. 13.2**).

By **para. 4**, Money Claim Online may only be used for money claims in sterling which are for less than £100,000. It may not be used where the claimant is a child or protected party, or is funded by the Legal Services Commission. Nor may it be used against more than one defendant (or more than two, where the claim is for a single amount against each of them) or where the defendant is the Crown or a child or protected party. The defendant's address for service must be within England and Wales, and the claimant's address for service must be within the United Kingdom.

The claimant requests the issue of a claim form by completing and sending an online claim form and electronically paying the appropriate issue fee via Her Majesty's Courts and Tribunals Service website (**para. 5.1**). The claim is brought for the purposes of the Limitation Act 1980 on the date on which the online claim form is received by the court's computer system (**PD 7E, para. 5.4**). The court will serve a hard copy of the claim form on the defendant, and will also send the claimant notice of issue by post (**para. 5.5**). The claim form is deemed to be served on the fifth day after issue, whether that day is a business day or not (**para. 5.7**). The claim form includes a unique customer identification number or password to enable the defendant to gain access to the claim at the website.

The claimant may file particulars of claim with the claim form or serve particulars of claim separately to the claim form, provided they comply with the requirements set out at **para. 6.1**. The requirement in **PD 16, para. 7.3**, to attach contractual documents to the particulars of claim in breach of contract cases does not apply to Money Claim Online cases unless the particulars of claim are served separately under **PD 7E, para. 5.2** (**PD 7E, para. 5.2A**). The defendant may then acknowledge service or file a defence and/or counterclaim in the conventional way or by completing and sending the relevant online form at https://www.money-claim.gov.uk. If the defendant files an online form, a hard copy must not be sent in addition, and the form is not filed until it is received by the court, whatever time it is shown to have been sent. An online form received after 4 p.m. will be treated as filed on the next day the court office is open. It is the responsibility of the defendant to ensure that the online form is filed on time (**para 7.2**).

By **para. 12**, where the defendant is an individual and the claim has not been sent to a County Court hearing centre, the claim will be sent to the defendant's home court if the defendant applies to set aside or vary judgment, or if either party makes an application which requires a hearing (**para. 12.1**). If the defendant is not an individual and one of the events in **para. 12.1** arises, the claim will be sent to the County Court hearing centre serving the claimant's address for service which is stated on the claim form (**para. 12.2**). Where a defence is filed and the parties have filed their directions questionnaires, the proceedings will be sent to the relevant County Court hearing centre in accordance with **CPR, r. 26.2A(3) to (6)**.

An application for an oral examination or a third party debt order must be issued in accordance with **PD 70, paras 9.1**, and **11.1**, unless the proceedings have already been sent to a County Court hearing centre. A request for a warrant of control to enforce a judgment or order made at the Centre must be made to the Centre, unless proceedings have since been sent to a County Court hearing centre (**PD 7E, paras 12A.1 and 12A.2**).

With effect from 1 October 2015, **PD 51K** (County Court Legal Advisers Pilot Scheme) allows some applications in relation to claims made using Money Claims Online to be determined by a legal adviser, who can exercise the jurisdiction of the County Court with regard to the matters set out in the first column of the schedule to **PD 51K**, subject to the restrictions in the second column. See **12.8**.

EUROPEAN ORDER FOR PAYMENT

Regulation (EC) No. 1896/2006 of 12 December 2006 (the 'EOP Regulation') created a European order for payment ('EOP') procedure with effect from 12 December 2008. The   **12.11** purpose of the Regulation is to simplify, speed up and reduce the costs of litigation in cross-border cases concerning uncontested pecuniary claims by creating the EOP procedure, and to permit the free circulation of EOPs throughout the member States by laying down a common procedure for establishing liability to pay. Compliance with the EOP procedure renders unnecessary any intermediate proceedings in the member State of enforcement prior to recognition and enforcement (recital 9). The procedure established by the EOP Regulation is intended to serve as an additional and optional means for the claimant, who remains free to resort to a procedure provided for by national law. Accordingly, the Regulation neither replaces nor harmonises the existing mechanisms for the recovery of uncontested claims under national law (recital 10).

The EOP Regulation applies to civil and commercial matters in cross-border cases, whatever the nature of the court or tribunal, but with various exceptions set out in art. 2(1) and (2). For this purpose, a cross-border case is one in which at least one of the parties is domiciled or habitually resident in a member State other than the member State of the court seised (art. 3(1)).

The EOP Regulation lays down detailed procedural rules, and EOP applications are primarily governed by the EOP Regulation. Where the EOP Regulation is silent, the CPR apply with necessary modifications (**PD 78, para. 1.1**). When deciding which courts are to have jurisdiction to issue an EOP, member States should take due account of the need to ensure access to justice (EOP Regulation, recital 12). The procedure is based, to the largest extent possible, on the use of standard forms in any communication between the court and the parties in order to facilitate its administration and enable the use of automatic data processing.

An EOP application form A must be completed in English or accompanied by a translation into English, and filed at court in person or by post (**PD 78, para. 2.1**). An EOP application made to the High Court will be assigned to the Queen's Bench Division, but that will not prevent the application being transferred where appropriate (**para. 2.2**). The court seised of an EOP application must examine, as soon as possible and on the basis of the application form, whether the requirements set out in the EOP Regulation, arts 2, 3, 4, 6 and 7, are met and whether the claim appears to be founded (art. 8). The application will be rejected if the requirements are not met (art. 11). If the requirements are met, the court must issue, as soon as possible and normally within 30 days of the lodging of the application, an EOP using standard form E as set out in annex 5 to the EOP Regulation (art. 12(1)). The 30-day period does not include the time taken by the claimant to complete, rectify or modify the application. In the EOP, the defendant is advised of his options to:

(a) pay the amount indicated in the order to the claimant; or

(b) oppose the order by lodging with the court of origin a statement of opposition, to be sent within 30 days of service of the order on him.

Articles 13 to 15 of the EOP Regulation contain rules on service. Where the EOP Regulation is silent on service, the Service Regulation (Regulation (EC) No. 1393/2007) and the CPR apply as appropriate (**PD 78, para. 4**).

The defendant may lodge a statement of opposition to the EOP with the court of origin using standard form F (as set out in the EOP Regulation, annex 6), which must be supplied to him together with the EOP (art. 16(1)). A statement of opposition has to be sent within 30 days of service of the order on the defendant (art. 16(2)). If a statement of opposition is entered within the time limit laid down in art. 16(2), the proceedings continue before the competent courts of the member State of origin in accordance with the rules of ordinary civil procedure unless the claimant has explicitly requested that the proceedings be terminated in that event (art. 17(1)).

Detailed further provisions can be seen in the EOP Regulation, **CPR, Part 78**, and **PD 78**.

ELECTRONIC WORKING

The current pilot scheme for electronic working is set out in **PD 51O**. It operates in the   **12.12**
Chancery Division of the High Court, the Commercial Court, the Technology and
Construction Court, the Mercantile Court and the Admiralty Court at the RCJ Rolls Building
from 16 November 2015 for two years. It applies to existing claims and to proceedings started
on or after 16 November 2015. Where the provisions of **PD 51O** conflict with those of
PD 5B, **PD 51O** is to take precedence. Electronic working may be used to start or continue
Part 7, Part 8 and Part 20 claims, pre-action applications including applications under **CPR,
r. 31.16**, insolvency proceedings and arbitration claims in the courts in which the scheme
operates (**PD 51O, para. 2.2**).

Anyone wishing to use Electronic Working must first create an account on the Electronic
Working website at https://efile.cefile-app.com (**PD 51O, para. 2.3**). Once that is done,
then under **PD 51O** parties can issue proceedings and file documents online 24 hours a day
every day of the year, including out of normal court office hours and on weekends and bank
holidays except during periods of planned or unplanned 'down-time' (**PD 51O, para. 2.1**).
Proceedings which have not been started by Electronic Working may be continued using
Electronic Working after documents in those proceedings have been converted to PDF format. The proceedings will then continue as if they had been started using Electronic Working
(**PD 51O, paras 3.2 and 3.3**). Proceedings which require original documents to be filed such
as the original will which must be filed in contentious probate proceedings cannot be issued
using Electronic Working unless the court permits (**PD 51O, para. 3.5**). Any document or
form filed electronically must not also be filed in paper format, subject only to the provisions
of **PD 51O, paras 10, 11 and 13**, or the requirements of a rule or practice direction or court
order. Application bundles where a hearing is required, and bundles for case and costs management directions with a hearing scheduled for more than 15 minutes must also be filed in
paper copy, unless otherwise ordered, and trial bundles must also be filed in paper format,
together with an electronic version if the court so orders (**PD 51O, paras 10, 11 and 13**).
Only one copy of the document need be supplied unless further copies are required by court
order, rule or practice direction and it must be in PDF format unless the court specifies otherwise, except for draft orders which should be in 'Word' format. The document should not
exceed 10 megabytes or such other limit as may be specified. If the document exceeds this
limit, the document should be divided into parts and each part should be filed separately
(**PD 51O, paras 5.1 and 5.2**). A party submitting a document electronically will be sent an
automated notification that the document has been submitted and is being reviewed by the
court prior to it being accepted. Any error of procedure can be remedied under **CPR, r. 3.10**
(**PD 51O, para. 5.3**). When the document has been accepted, a notification will appear on
the account of the filing party together with the date and time of issue or filing (**PD 51O,
para. 5.4(4)**). The date and time of filing on acceptance will be deemed to be the date and
time of payment of any court fee required on filing the document, and this will also be the
date of issue for all claim forms and other originating processes, and for all other documents
this date and time will also be the submission date and time for the purpose of complying
with any court order or direction under the Rules (**PD 51O, para. 5.4(1) to (3)**). A claim
form or originating application filed using Electronic Working will be sealed electronically
with the date on which the relevant court fee was paid and this will be the issue date (**PD 51O,
para. 7.1**). However, the date and time of issue or filing will not be delayed by acceptance
unless the document fails to be accepted (**PD 51O, para. 5.4(5)**). The issued claim form
or originating application will be electronically returned to the party's account for service.
Any document filed or issued using Electronic Working has to be served by the party and
not the court (**PD 51O, paras 8.1 and 8.2**). If proceedings which have used Electronic
Working are subsequently transferred to a court not operating Electronic Working, the

provisions of **PD 51O** will no longer apply (**PD 51O, para. 9.1**). HMCTS will send a version of the Electronic Working case file to the receiving court in a format requested by that court (**PD 51O, para. 9.2**). If proceedings are transferred to a court using Electronic Working, all filing after transfer can be made under **PD 51O** after any documents already submitted in those proceedings have been converted to PDF format in accordance with **paras 3.2** and **3.3** (**PD 51O, para. 9.3**).

Chapter 13   Part 8 Claims

The following procedural checklist is relevant to this chapter:

Procedural checklist 5   Claim under standard Part 8 procedure

TYPES OF CLAIM TO WHICH PART 8 APPLIES

Introduction

The Part 8 procedure is intended for cases where the nature of the relief or remedy sought, or **13.1** the lack of factual dispute, would make the standard procedure unnecessarily cumbersome. It provides a speedy mechanism for disposing of claims without the need for particulars of claim (**CPR, rr. 8.9(a)(i)** and **16.1**), a defence (**rr. 8.9(a)(ii)** and **15.1**), or a directions questionnaire (because all Part 8 claims are allocated to the multi-track: **r. 8.9(c)**). Judgment in default is not available (**r. 12.2(b)**). By **r. 8.1(2)** and **(6)**, and **PD 8A, paras 3.1** to **3.3**, a claimant may use the Part 8 procedure to seek the court's decision on a question which is unlikely to involve a substantial dispute of fact (see **13.2**), or where a rule or practice direction requires or permits use of the procedure (see **13.3** and **13.4**).

PD 8B sets out the procedure to be followed in certain situations covered by the **Pre-action Protocol for Low Value Personal Injury Claims in Road Traffic Accidents** (the RTA Protocol) and the **Pre-action Protocol for Low Value Personal Injury (Employers' Liability and Public Liability) Claims** (the EL/PL Protocol). See further **13.4**.

PD 8C sets out the procedure for statutory review of planning matters under the Town and Country Planning Act 1990, ss. 287 and 288; the Planning (Listed Buildings and Conservation Areas) Act 1990, s. 63; the Planning (Hazardous Substances) Act 1990, s. 22; and the Compulsory Purchase Act 2004, s. 113. **CPR, Part 8**, applies to such claims with the modifications set out in **PD 8C**.

General claims unlikely to involve a substantial dispute of fact

Claims for which the Part 8 procedure may be used on the ground that they are unlikely to **13.2** involve a substantial dispute of fact include claims which turn on a question of law, claims relating to the construction of a document or statute and applications for a declaration. However, Part 8 proceedings are wholly unsuitable for a disputed issue of estoppel, because estoppel requires careful pleading. Further, because the issue will be fact sensitive, it will not comply with the requirement in **r. 8.1(2)(a)** that the case should be unlikely to involve a substantial dispute of fact (*ING Bank NV v Ros Roca SA* [2011] EWCA Civ 353, [2012] 1 WLR 472).

239

In some cases, the claimant will have the choice between (a) invoking the Part 8 procedure, and (b) issuing a Part 7 claim form and applying for summary judgment. However, as the Part 8 procedure does not permit the exchange of particulars of claim or defences, it will not be suitable for claims where the parties need to set out their respective cases in complicated or lengthy statements of case. Nor will Part 8 be suitable for a claim where the claimant does not know until the defence is available whether the defendant admits the factual basis of the claim. But where a claim is suitable for determination under Part 8, the claimant may well find it a speedier mechanism for disposing of the claim than issuing proceedings under Part 7, even where these are dealt with by way of summary judgment.

Part 8 is the appropriate procedure for an application for a mediation settlement enforcement order under **r. 78.24(1)(b)(1)** where there are no existing proceedings in the jurisdiction (**PD 78, para. 22.2**). These provisions permit the enforcement of commercial mediation agreements in cross-border disputes under Directive 2008/52/EC.

CPR, Part 8, is also the appropriate procedure for commencing costs-only proceedings under **r. 46.14**, where the parties have reached agreement on the issues, including which party is to pay the costs, but they have failed to agree the amount of those costs. The parties must try to reach agreement on the amount of costs before issuing the Part 8 claim form, otherwise the condition for issuing proceedings set out in **r. 46.14(1)**, that the parties have failed to reach agreement on the amount of costs, will not be satisfied and the proceedings may be stuck out (*Knowles v Goldborn* (2014) LTL 29/1/2014).

Part 8 is also the appropriate mechanism to use where a party wishes to obtain court orders or declarations in relation to a disputed adjudication, although such applications should be the exception rather than the norm and orders should only be made in clear-cut cases (*Dorchester Hotel Ltd v Vivid Interiors Ltd* [2009] EWHC 70 (TCC), [2009] Bus LR 1026). The courts have been prepared to hear such cases under the Part 8 procedure even where there are disputed facts between the parties, provided these are facts which do not require oral evidence to determine. Where oral evidence is required on a limited factual dispute, the court is prepared to be flexible, to the extent of making orders for a hybrid Part 7 and Part 8 procedure which can accommodate oral evidence at the final hearing (*Vitpol Building Service v Samen* [2008] EWHC 2283 (TCC), [2009] Bus LR D65). This hybrid procedure is only suitable where the disputed issue of fact can be determined by a short hearing with a narrow focus and without the need for disclosure (*Forest Heath District Council v ISG Jackson Ltd* [2010] EWHC 322 (TCC), LTL 29/3/2010).

PD 8A, para. 3.1, gives the following examples where the Part 8 procedure may be used:

(a) Where a claim by or against a child or protected party has been settled before the commencement of proceedings and the sole purpose of issuing the claim form is to obtain the approval of the court to the settlement. **CPR, r. 21.10(2)**, says that **Part 8** must be used in these circumstances.

(b) Where a claim for provisional damages has been settled before the commencement of proceedings and the sole purpose of the claim is to obtain a consent judgment.

The Part 8 procedure must be used for the claims and applications listed in the table in **PD 8A, Section B**, as well as for any claim or application required by an Act, rule or practice direction to be commenced by originating summons, originating motion or originating application (**PD 8A, paras 3.2** and **3.3**).

Landlord and tenant claims under **PD 56, para. 2.1** are conducted under a Part 8 procedure, modified by **Part 56** and **PD 56**.

It is the claimant, or the claimant's legal advisers, who must choose whether to use the Part 8 procedure, but the rules enable the court to weed out claims for which the chosen procedure appears to be inappropriate. Where the court receives a Part 8 claim form, a court officer who believes it may not be appropriate for the claim may refer it to a judge for consideration (**PD 8A, para. 3.4**). The court may at any stage order a Part 8 claim to continue using the standard procedure, and give appropriate directions (**CPR, r. 8.1(3)**).

Claims and applications that must be made under Part 8

PD 8A, Section B sets out a table listing the claims and applications which must be made **13.3** using the Part 8 procedure. The claims and applications fall into three categories:

(a) Applications and claims to which special provisions set out in **PD 8A, Section C**, apply, modifying the usual Part 8 procedure. The table cross-refers to the relevant paragraphs of **PD 8A, Section C**. There is no longer a standard, modified Part 8 procedure. Rather, different provisions apply to different applications in this category.

(b) Applications and claims dealt with in schedules 1 and 2 to the CPR (the re-enacted provisions of the RSC and CCR, respectively). The table cross-refers to the relevant schedule rules which modify the usual Part 8 procedure.

(c) Other claims and applications for which the Part 8 procedure must be used, without modification.

The table also specifies the Division to which the application is assigned.

RTA Protocol, EL/PL Protocol and PD 8B

The original RTA Protocol covered road traffic claims for personal injury worth no more than **13.4** £10,000 arising out of accidents occurring on or after 30 April 2010. A new and revised **RTA Protocol** came into effect on 31 July 2013 which applies to claims of no more than £25,000. The 2010 edition of the Protocol continues to apply to all claims submitted before 31 July 2013. From 31 July 2013, the **EL/PL Protocol** was introduced for employers' liability claims for damages arising from an accident or a disease and to public liability claims arising out of an accident. Like the second edition of the **RTA Protocol**, the **EL/PL Protocol** is limited to claims of not more than £25,000. Both the **RTA Protocol** and the **EL/PL Protocol** provide a mechanism for the settlement of claims and the recovery of fixed legal costs under **CPR, Part 45, Section III**, without the need for court proceedings. The pre-action processes which the parties are expected to follow are set out in detail at **8.33** to **8.46**, and are divided into two consecutive stages, Stage 1 and Stage 2. Following an admission of liability under Stage 1 and a negotiation over the amount to pay in Stage 2, the amount of the defendant's final offer, plus disbursements and fixed costs, the ('non-settlement payment') should be paid to the claimant, who may or may not accept it. Where there is no admission of liability, or there is an admission but the defendant fails to make a non-settlement payment, the claimant may issue proceedings under **Part 7** in the usual way. A significant change under the 2013 edition of the **RTA Protocol** and the **EL/PL Protocol** is that successful claimants in cases which cannot be settled under the relevant Protocol and which proceed as a Part 7 claim can only recover the fixed costs set out in **CPR, Part 45, Section IIIA** (see **rr. 45.29A** to **49.29I**). The court may make a different order where the claimant is at fault in not complying or continuing with the process set out in the relevant Protocol (**rr. 45.24** and **45.29A(3)**) or the court considers that there are exceptional circumstances which merit a greater amount of costs (**r. 45.29J**). Proceedings should be issued under **Part 8** where:

(a) parties have complied with the terms of the relevant Protocol but have not agreed quantum; or

(b) the court's approval is sought of a settlement of a claim under the relevant Protocol brought by a child; or

(c) it is not possible to follow the terms of the relevant Protocol before the expiry of the limitation period.

In each of these three cases, a claim under **Part 8** must be started in the County Court and will normally be heard by a District Judge (**PD 8B, para. 1.2**). The procedure to be followed is set out at **8.48** to **8.55**. A settlement offer under the **RTA Protocol** or the **EL/PL Protocol** takes effect as a type of Part 36 offer and **CPR, r. 36.29**, sets out the costs consequences of such an offer (see **8.56** to **8.58**). If the claimant succeeds in recovering more than the amount specified in a claimant's Part 36 offer, the enhanced increase in damages under **r. 36.17(4)(d)** also applies to proceedings commenced by Part 8 claim (**r. 36.29(4)(d)**).

Where proceedings are issued because of the imminent expiry of the limitation period, there is no need to include the documents required under the relevant Protocol. Instead, the claimant should issue a claim form in which he states that his claim is for damages and that a stay of proceedings is sought in order to comply with the relevant Protocol (**PD 8B, para. 16.2**). The court will issue the claim and order an immediate stay which can be lifted in due course if liability is admitted under the relevant Protocol but damages need to be determined by the court (**PD 8B, para. 16.5**).

PART 8 PROCEDURE

13.5   The Part 8 procedure is straightforward (see **procedural checklist 5**). The claim is begun by the issue of a Part 8 claim form. In the County Court, a claim can be issued at any County Court hearing centre, unless an enactment, rule or practice direction provides otherwise (**CPR. r. 8.1(2A)**). However, when a claim is given a hearing date the court may direct that proceedings should be transferred to another hearing centre if appropriate to do so. Claimants are therefore urged to consider the potential delay that may result if a claim is not made at the appropriate hearing centre in the first instance (**PD 8A, para. 4.1(2)**). Evidence in support must be filed and served at the same time as the claim form is issued and served. The defendant responds by filing and serving an acknowledgment of service in form N210 and evidence in opposition, but not a defence. The claimant may then serve evidence in reply. The court will automatically allocate the case to the multi-track, and will give directions for the disposal of the case. In most cases there will be a hearing, usually on written evidence only (but see **13.2** on cases for which a hybrid Part 7 and Part 8 procedure is appropriate).

Issue and service of Part 8 claim

13.6   The claim is issued on claim form N208. The rules on issue and service contained in **CPR, Parts 6 and** 7 (see **chapters 12** and **15**), apply to Part 8 claims, save that the only form which should be served with the claim form when it is served on the defendant is the form for acknowledging service (form N210). Forms for defending or admitting the claim are not required (**rr. 7.8(2)** and **8.9(a)(iv)** and **(b)(ii)**).

As with any other claim form, a Part 8 claim form must be served within four months after issue, or six months where it is served out of the jurisdiction (**r. 7.5**). The provisions of **r. 7.6** permitting a claimant to apply for an extension of time for service of the claim form apply also to Part 8 claims (*Barker v Casserly* (2000) LTL 24/10/2000).

Forms N208(CC) and N210(CC) are special versions of the Part 8 claim and acknowledgment forms for use in the Commercial Court (**PD 58, paras 2.4** and **5.2**).

Contents of Part 8 claim form

13.7   The following requirements for Part 8 claim forms are made by **CPR, r. 8.2**:

(a) The form must state that **Part 8** applies to the claim.
(b) The form must set out the question which the claimant wants the court to decide or the remedy the claimant is seeking, and the legal basis for the remedy claimed.
(c) If the claim is being made under an enactment, the claimant must identify the enactment.
(d) If the claimant is claiming, or the defendant is being sued, in a representative capacity, the claim form must state that fact and state what the capacity is.

In *Szekeres v Alan Smeath and Co.* [2005] EWHC 1733 (Ch), LTL 2/8/2005, a Part 8 claim form which was intended to seek an order for detailed assessment of a solicitor's bills failed to state the question to be decided, did not state the remedy sought, did not refer to the Solicitors Act 1974, did not state that **CPR, Part 8**, applied and did not contain a statement of truth. Despite these defects, it was held that the claim form contained enough information to convey the nature of the claim. That being so, the claim form was sufficient to commence the proceedings and there was no basis on which the court could decline putting the document into formal order.

Because of the nature of the procedure, it is not necessary in a claim started by a Part 8 claim form to serve particulars of claim, and **Part 16** does not apply to Part 8 claims (**r. 8.9(a)(i)**). Instead, any written evidence on which a Part 8 claimant intends to rely must be filed and served with the Part 8 claim form (**r. 8.5(1) and (2)**). Written evidence will usually be in the form of a witness statement or affidavit, but the matters included in the claim form may stand as the claimant's evidence, where the claim form is verified by a statement of truth (which it must be by virtue of **Part 22**) (**PD 8A, para. 7.2**).

Under **CPR, r. 8.2A**, a Part 8 claim form may be issued without naming a defendant, provided the court's permission is obtained first by issuing an application notice, with a copy of the draft claim form. This enables proceedings to be issued under **Part 8** where there is no defendant to a claim, or where the defendant is unascertained. Claim forms which do not name a defendant may be issued for certain proceedings without the court's permission. See the provisions of **PD 49A** discussed at **85.6**; **PD 64A, para. 5**; and **PD 78, para. 22.2**.

Acknowledgment of service

The defendant responds to service of a Part 8 claim form by filing an acknowledgment of **13.8** service, and serving a copy on the claimant and any other parties (**CPR, r. 8.3(1)**). Acknowledgment must be made in the appropriate form (N210) (**PD 8A, para. 5.2**).

An acknowledgment of service in a Part 8 claim must be verified by a statement of truth (**CPR, r. 22.1(1)(d)**).

The acknowledgment must be filed no more than 14 days after service of the claim form (**CPR, r. 8.3**) (unless **r. 10.3(2)** applies: see **18.2**). It is in the nature of the sort of claims which are suitable for determination by the Part 8 procedure, that a pleaded defence is inappropriate. Accordingly, the rules state that the defendant should not file a defence. Rather, any points which the defendant wishes to rely on in reply to the claim should be set out in a witness statement or affidavit. The provisions of **Part 15** in relation to defences do not apply to Part 8 claims (**r. 8.9(a)(ii)**) nor do **rr. 14.4** to **14.7** in relation to judgments on an admission (**r. 8.9(b)(i)**).

In the acknowledgment of service the defendant must:

(a) indicate whether he contests the claim (**r. 8.3(2)(a)**);
(b) if he seeks a different remedy from that set out in the claim form, state what remedy he seeks (**r. 8.3(2)(b)**);
(c) include his address for service (**r. 10.5**).

The acknowledgment must be signed by the defendant or his legal representative (**r. 10.5**). **Paragraphs** 4.2 to 4.4 of **PD 10** specify who should sign the acknowledgment where the defendant is a company, corporation or partnership.

Consequences of failure to file an acknowledgment

Due to the nature of the proceedings, in a Part 8 claim the claimant may not obtain default **13.9** judgment under **CPR, Part 12**, if the defendant fails to acknowledge service in time, or at all (**r. 8.1(5)**). However, a defendant who has not acknowledged service may not take part in the hearing of the claim unless the court gives permission, although he may attend the hearing (**r. 8.4**). Clearly the likelihood of permission being granted will depend on the reasons for the failure, the circumstances of the claim, the nature of the defendant's interest and the speed with which the claimant and the court were notified of the wish to be heard.

In an application under the Town and Country Planning Act, 1990, s. 280, to which **PD 8A, para. 22**, applies, the rules make no provision for an acknowledgment of service to be served or filed by the respondent. Accordingly, in *Morris v Secretary of State for Communities and Local Government* [2009] EWHC 2302, LTL 8/10/2009, the fact that the respondent had not served an acknowledgment did not provide grounds for refusing to hear him. He had served a skeleton argument and copies of relevant documents so it could not be said that the applicant had not had time to consider the respondent's case.

Defendant's evidence

13.10 A defendant to a Part 8 claim who wishes to rely on written evidence (which by **PD 8A, para. 7.2**, may be in the form either of a witness statement or affidavit) should file and serve it when filing and serving the acknowledgment of service (**CPR, r. 8.5(3) and (4)**). If the deadline is missed, the case may proceed without the defendant's evidence. See *Clanbrassil Trust Co. v Clanbrassil (Nominees) Ltd* [2011] EWHC 1163 (Ch), LTL 28/3/2011, for an example of an application for permission to serve evidence late under **r. 8.5** and the court's approach to the exercise of its discretion under r. 3.9 as it was before 1 April 2013 to grant relief from sanctions. A more robust approach is likely to be taken by the court now in considering extensions of time and relief from sanctions in light of the revised **r. 3.9** and the cases discussed in **chapter 48**.

In practice, 14 days may not be long enough to prepare evidence in opposition to the claim. After filing the acknowledgment, a party may apply to the court for an extension of time for filing and service of evidence, or for permission to serve additional evidence (**r. 8.6(1)(b); PD 8A, para. 7.4**). Alternatively, parties can agree an extension of up to 14 days for filing and serving the defendant's evidence. The agreement must be in writing, and a copy of the agreement must be filed at court at the same time as the acknowledgment (**PD 8A, para. 7.5(1) and (2)**).

For a Part 8 claim in the Commercial Court, the rule is modified to provide that the defendant's evidence must be filed and served within 28 days after filing an acknowledgment of service (**CPR, r. 58.12**).

In *Bovale Ltd v Secretary of State for Communities and Local Government* [2009] EWCA Civ 171, [2009] 1 WLR 2274, it was held that although courts have very wide powers to make directions in individual cases (see at [69]), they cannot declare that rules made by delegated legislation are to be disapplied or varied in future cases (in this case the court had sought to declare that time limits for service of evidence under **PD 8A, para. 22**, would be varied in future). See **1.7** on the power to make practice directions.

In *Kensington and Chelsea Royal London, Borough Council v Secretary of State for Communities and Local Government* [2012] EWHC 1785 (Admin), 162 NLJ 963, an interested party to Part 8 proceedings was allowed the costs of filing and serving grounds of defence as well as an acknowledgment of service, even though there is no requirement in **Part 8** to file a defence. There was no objection in principle to the party being awarded costs and it was appropriate in this case because it had a separate interest to the defendant and its defence clarified the issues.

Contesting jurisdiction

13.11 A defendant to a Part 8 claim may contest the jurisdiction of the English courts in the usual way provided for in **CPR, Part 11** (see **chapter 19**), by filing an acknowledgment of service, completing section C, and proceeding to make an application for an order that the court does not have jurisdiction. Any such application must be made within 14 days after filing the acknowledgment of service (**r. 11(4)(a)**).

Objecting to use of the Part 8 procedure

13.12 A defendant to a Part 8 claim who believes that the Part 8 procedure should not be used, should file an acknowledgment of service, completing section D, but at the same time should file and serve a statement of reasons for opposing the procedure (CPR, r. 8.8(1)).

The court has power to order the claim to continue as if it were an ordinary claim not governed by Part 8, and give appropriate directions (CPR, r. 8.1(3)). Upon receipt of the defendant's acknowledgment and evidence opposing the procedure, the court will consider how the claim should continue, and will give directions as to its future management (r. 8.8(2)).

Claimant's evidence in reply

13.13 If the defendant to a Part 8 claim files evidence, the claimant may file and serve evidence in reply within 14 days (CPR, r. 8.5(5) and (6)). Evidence may be served after this deadline with the permission of the court (CPR, r. 8.6(1)(b); PD 8A, para. 7.5). Alternatively, parties can agree an extension of up to 28 days for service of the claimant's evidence in reply. Any such agreement must be in writing (PD 8A, para. 7.5(1) and (3)).

Parties may also apply to the court for permission to serve and file additional evidence (CPR, r. 8.6(1); PD 8A, para. 7.4).

Case management of a Part 8 claim

13.14 Part 8 claims to which the usual procedure applies are automatically treated as allocated to the multi-track (CPR, r. 8.9(c)) and there is no need to complete directions questionnaires. Part 26 does not apply. This implies that Part 8 proceedings will be treated as allocated to the multi-track and so fixed costs will not be restricted to small claims track costs, even when the amount at issue falls within the small claims track financial threshold (see *JR v Turner* (2009) LTL 3/11/2009, following *W v Robinson* [2002] CLY 389, for an application of this principle in child settlement cases). However, at a hearing of a Part 8 claim, the court has power under PD 8A, para. 8.2, to allocate a Part 8 claim to any specific track, in which case CPR, rr. 26.5(3) and (4) and 26.6 to 26.10, apply. Also, under r. 46.13(3) the court may restrict the recoverable costs to those that would have been allowed on the track to which the claim would have been allocated if allocation had taken place.

The court may give directions immediately a Part 8 claim form is issued, either upon application of a party or on its own initiative (PD 8A, para. 6.1). The directions can include fixing a hearing date either where there is no dispute (for example, in child and protected party settlements) or where there is a dispute but it is convenient to give a hearing date (for example, in mortgage possession claims or applications for the appointment of trustees). If it has not fixed a hearing date earlier, the court will give directions for the disposal of the claim as soon as practicable after the defendant has acknowledged service and filed any written evidence or after the time has expired for this to be done (PD 8A, para. 6.2).

CPR, Part 29, does not apply to Part 8 claims that are treated as being allocated to the multi-track by virtue of r. 8.9(c). Part 29 only applies if the court specifically makes an order allocating the Part 8 claim to the multi-track (*Kershaw v Roberts* [2014] EWHC 1037 (Ch), [2015] 1 All ER 734). However, in all cases, the parties should try to agree appropriate directions for the management of the claim. Parties should submit these to the court either at the same time as filing the acknowledgment or at the latest by the time any case management conference is fixed. Where a Part 8 claim is treated as allocated to the multi-track under r. 8.9(c), the costs management provisions in Part 3, **Section II**, and PD 3E will not apply because those provisions only apply to Part 7 multi-track claims, unless the court otherwise orders under CPR, r. 3.12(1A). A costs management order would not be appropriate in many Part 8 claims, but the parties should consider in advance of the first case management

conference whether it would be appropriate to file costs budgets, or even apply for a costs capping order under **r. 3.19** and **PD 3F**.

Hearing of a Part 8 claim

13.15   On the hearing date, the court may proceed to hear the case and dispose of the claim or give case management directions (**PD 8A, para. 8.1**).

Evidence at the hearing of a Part 8 claim will normally be adduced in written form. A party may only rely on evidence served after the time limits specified in **CPR, r. 8.5** (i.e. at the time of service of the claim form or acknowledgment of service, or in reply 14 days thereafter), with the court's permission (**r. 8.6(1)(b)**).

However, the court has power to require or permit oral evidence or to require a witness who has given written evidence to attend for cross-examination (**r. 8.6(2)** and **(3)**). Such an order may be appropriate where there is a limited factual dispute (*Vitpol Building Service v Samen* [2008] EWHC 2283 (TCC), [2009] Bus LR D65).

Additional claims and the Part 8 procedure

13.16   Counterclaims and other additional claims do not sit easily with Part 8 claims. A defendant to a Part 8 claim who wishes to bring any other claim may do so only with the permission of the court (**CPR, r. 8.7**). (See **chapters 28** and **29** on additional claims.)

Chapter 14 Joinder and Parties

Commentary

The following procedural checklists are relevant to this chapter:

Procedural checklist 6   Approval of settlement or compromise involving a child or protected party, where sole purpose of claim is to obtain court approval

Procedural checklist 7   Claims on Controlled and Executed Goods

Procedural checklist 8   Stakeholder claims and applications

Procedural checklist 9   Application for joinder

IDENTIFYING PARTIES WHEN COMMENCING A CLAIM

Description of parties

14.1   Under the CPR the party who makes a claim is known as 'the claimant' (**r. 2.3(1)**). The party against whom proceedings are brought is 'the defendant' (**r. 2.3(1)**). Parties to applications are referred to as 'applicant' and 'respondent' (**r. 23.1**). Parties to petitions are known as the 'petitioner' and the 'respondent'. Before 6 April 2006, parties to additional claims under **Part 20** were known as the 'Part 20 claimant' and 'Part 20 defendant'. From 6 April 2006, parties to additional claims are known by their titles as they appeared in the original claim (if they were claimants or defendants: **PD 20, para. 7.3**), but if they have been brought in under **CPR, Part 20**, they are known as the 'third party', 'fourth party' etc. (**PD 20, para. 7.4**).

The heading of a claim form must include the full name of each party (**PD 16, para. 2.6**). The name of a party who is an individual must include the title by which he or she is known (**para. 2.6(a)**).

The form of words to be used in describing different types of parties in the headings of statements of case and other court documents is considered at **14.10** to **14.50** and in **table 14.1**.

Joinder of causes of action and parties

14.2   The Senior Courts Act 1981, s. 49(2), requires the court to exercise its discretion to ensure that:

as far as possible, all matters in dispute between the parties are completely and finally determined, and all multiplicity of legal proceedings with respect to any of those matters is avoided.

This is reflected in **CPR, r. 7.3**, which states that a single claim form may be used to start all claims which can be conveniently disposed of in the same proceedings. This does not require a claimant to include in his pleaded case all the heads of damage he could possibly argue against a defendant (*Khiaban v Beard* [2003] EWCA Civ 358, [2003] 1 WLR 1626). **Rule 19.1** states that any number of claimants or defendants may be joined as parties to one claim. There must, however, be a cause of action against all those joined (*Douihech v Findlay* [1990] 1 WLR 269, but see *Individual Homes Ltd v Macbream Investments Ltd* (2002) *The Times*, 14 November 2002, where a bank was joined as a party to enable it to recover the costs of complying with a witness summons). Joint claimants must have the same interest in the claim and must be represented by the same solicitors and counsel. The particulars of claim must be contained in or served with the claim form or served on the defendant within 14 days after service of the claim form but no later than the latest time for serving a claim form (**CPR, r. 7.4(1) and (2)**). In *Tetra Pak Ltd v Biddle and Co.* [2010] EWHC 54 (Ch), [2010] 1 WLR 1466, it was held that it would not be inconsistent with the CPR, and in particular **rr. 7.4 and 16.4**, for a claimant to serve separate particulars of claim on different defendants within the same claim. The mere fact that a claimant served particulars of claim against other defendants did not automatically constitute an abandonment of all claims against a defendant who was not served (*Chandra v Brooke North* [2013] EWCA Civ 1559, [2014] TCLR 1).

Rule 19.3 (which does not apply to probate claims: **r. 19.3(3)**) deals with claims in respect of rights held by two or more persons jointly (as opposed to severally held rights, alternative claims and related claims). All persons jointly entitled to a remedy must be parties to the claim, either as joint claimants, if they are willing, or as defendants, if they are not (**r. 19.3(1) and (2)**). When claiming to recover land it is good practice, though not a legal requirement, to name as co-claimants, all the persons in whom title to possession is vested (*Dearman v Simpletest Ltd* (1999) *The Times*, 14 February 2000).

The court may consider the constitution of proceedings, and make appropriate orders of its own initiative, as part of its duty to manage a case. The case management powers given to the court expressly include power to direct that part of a claim (such as a counterclaim) be dealt with separately, power to consolidate (i.e. to order two separate claims to continue and be tried as if they were a single claim), and power to try two or more claims on the same occasion (**r. 3.1(2)**).

No guidance is provided about which claims it might be considered convenient to dispose of in the same proceedings. However, the court will take into account the overriding objective in coming to its decision, in particular the objectives of saving expense and of ensuring that cases are dealt with expeditiously and fairly. Thus claims involving common questions of law or fact between different parties, or different causes of action involving the same parties, should be dealt with in the same proceedings.

Persons unknown

PD 7A, para. 4.1, provides that a claim form must be headed with the title of the proceedings and that the title should include the full name of each party and each party's status in the proceedings (e.g. claimant, defendant, third party). All known forenames and the surname should be used. But a claimant who does not know the identity or name of a defendant may use a description rather than a name, or sue 'Persons Unknown', provided the description is sufficiently clear to identify who is included within it and who is not (*Bloomsbury Publishing Group Ltd v News Group Newspapers Ltd* [2003] EWHC 1205 (Ch), [2003] 1 WLR 1633; approved by the Court of Appeal in *South Cambridgeshire District Council v Persons Unknown* [2004] EWCA Civ 1280, [2004] 4 PLR 88; see also *Eli Lilly and Co. Ltd v Stop Huntington Animal Cruelty* [2011] EWHC 3527 (QB), LTL 31/1/2012). This is of particular application in intellectual property claims where there is a clear case for an injunction against a defendant

14.3

whose identity is not known to the claimant. For possession claims against squatters see chapter 35.

Rights against insurers in road traffic cases

14.4   Under the European Communities (Rights against Insurers) Regulations 2002 (SI 2002/3061), a claimant who is resident in an EEA country (the EU plus Iceland, Liechtenstein and Norway) bringing proceedings in tort arising out of a road accident may issue proceedings against the insurer of the vehicle alleged to be responsible for the accident (reg. 3). An 'accident' for the purposes of the Regulations means an accident on a road or other public place in the United Kingdom caused by, or arising out of, the use of any insured vehicle (reg. 2(1)). A 'vehicle' is any vehicle normally based in the United Kingdom intended for travel on land which is propelled by mechanical power, but not running on rails, and includes any trailer whether or not it is coupled (reg. 2(1)). A vehicle is 'insured' if there is a policy of insurance in force fulfilling the requirements of the Road Traffic Act 1988, s. 145 (SI 2002/3061, reg. 2(3)). If the Regulations apply, the insurer is directly liable to the claimant (reg. 3(2)), and the right to sue the insurer is in addition to the existing right of action against the driver (reg. 3(2)).

Claims for wrongful interference with goods

14.5   A claimant bringing a claim for wrongful interference with goods must state in the particulars of claim the name and address of every person who, to the claimant's knowledge, has or claims an interest in the goods, but who is not a party to the claim (**CPR, r. 19.5A**). The defendant may then apply to the court for any person named to be made a party to the claim. If the defendant makes such an application, but the person sought to be joined fails to attend the hearing of the application or to comply with any directions made, the court may order that person to be deprived of any claim against the defendant in respect of the goods.

This rule gives effect to the provisions of the Torts (Interference with Goods) Act 1977, ss. 7 and 8. These sections deal with the potential wrong of a defendant being doubly liable in damages to competing owners of goods. They deal with this wrong in two ways:

(a) Section 7 of the Act requires any order for relief in proceedings for wrongful interference to which two or more persons interested in goods are parties to be such as to avoid the double liability of the wrongdoer as between those persons. Where only one of two or more persons interested in goods is a party, and receives more from the wrongdoer than is properly due, the overpayment must be passed on to other persons interested or repaid to the defendant.

(b) Section 8 of the Act entitles the defendant to show that a third party has a better right to the goods which are the subject matter of the claim, and to rely on this as a defence to the claim or in reduction of the damages claimed.

ASSIGNMENT OF CAUSES OF ACTION: MAINTENANCE AND CHAMPERTY

Introduction

14.6   It sometimes happens that a litigant's rights and liabilities in a claim are voluntarily transferred to a non-party before judgment has been obtained. Whether such a transfer can be validly made depends on whether the transaction is tainted by maintenance or champerty (see **14.7** to **14.9**). Assignment of a cause of action arising from a contract may be forbidden by the terms of the contract (*Ruttle Plant Ltd v Secretary of State for the Environment and Rural Affairs* [2007] EWHC 2870 (TCC), [2008] 2 All ER (Comm) 264). For a case on a defective assignment, see *Smith v*

Henniker-Major and Co. [2002] EWCA Civ 762, [2003] Ch 182 (applied in *Finlan v Eyton Morris Winfield* [2007] EWHC 914 (Ch), [2007] 4 All ER 143).

Maintenance and champerty

Maintenance is the support of litigation by a stranger without just cause. Champerty is an **14.7** aggravated form of maintenance. The distinguishing feature of champerty is the support of litigation by a stranger with a financial interest in their outcome, such as a share of the proceeds (*Giles v Thompson* [1994] 1 AC 142). Until 1967 champerty and maintenance gave rise to both criminal and tortious liability. The Criminal Law Act 1967 abolished champerty and maintenance as crimes and torts. But s. 14(2) of the Act expressly preserved the common law rule that contracts which are tainted by champerty or maintenance are 'to be treated as contrary to public policy or otherwise illegal'.

The doctrines of maintenance and champerty must be reappraised in light of current notions of public policy (*Trendtex Trading Corporation v Credit Suisse* [1982] AC 679; see also Sir Rupert Jackson's *Review of Civil Litigation Costs* (Ministry of Justice, December 2009)). The bounds of justification for supporting litigation by others have greatly widened in the last 50 years. Support of legal proceedings based on a bona fide community of pecuniary interest, religion, principle, problems or mutual protection is not likely to constitute maintenance (*Martell v Consett Iron Co. Ltd* [1955] Ch 363; *Hill v Archbold* [1968] 1 QB 686).

A contract of maintenance is unenforceable between the parties to it. However, the illegal maintenance of a claim does not give rise to a defence to the claim, or lead to it being stayed or dismissed, unless the proceedings are an abuse of process (*Abraham v Thompson* [1997] 4 All ER 362; *Murphy v Young and Co.'s Brewery plc* [1997] 1 WLR 1591). An order for costs can be made against the maintainer under the Senior Courts Act 1981, s. 51 (see *Flatman v Germany* [2013] EWCA Civ 278, [2013] 1 WLR 2676). In *Media CAT Ltd v Adams* [2011] EWPCC 10, [2011] FSR 29, the court considered that there was a good arguable case that a wasted costs order should be made against solicitors who entered into champertous contingency revenue-sharing agreements which underpinned the whole case and without which the other party to the litigation would not have been sued.

There are two circumstances in which the rule against champerty and maintenance continues to be of relevance:

(a) The rule may still invalidate agreements whereby a stranger to litigation provides funding to enable a party to bring or continue a claim. Historically, this has precluded solicitors from entering into contingency fee arrangements with their clients. The decision of the Court of Appeal in *Thai Trading Co. v Taylor* [1998] QB 781 appeared to remove the prohibition against the type of contingency fee arrangement in which the solicitor agrees with the client not to charge if the claim fails, but to seek costs from the other side if the claim succeeds. Subsequent decisions (*Hughes v Kingston upon Hull City Council* [1999] QB 1193; *Awwad v Geraghty and Co.* [2001] QB 570) preserved the original rule. In *Sibthorpe v Southwark London Borough Council* [2011] EWCA Civ 25, [2011] 1 WLR 2111, the court held that a CFA agreement that included an indemnity clause preventing a party from being liable to pay the opponent's costs if the claim were unsuccessful and if insurance could not be obtained against that risk was not void for champerty and did not undermine the public interest or undermine justice. The court applied *Wallersteiner v Moir (No. 2)* [1975] QB 373 and *Awwad v Geraghty and Co.* [2001] QB 570 and doubted the decision in *Thai Trading Co. v Taylor* [1998] QB 781 as it was per incuriam. In *Rees v Gateley Wareing* [2014] EWCA Civ 1351, [2015] 1 WLR 2179, it was held that a fee agreement made by a solicitor with its client amounted to a CFA that was unenforceable under the Courts and Legal Services Act 1990, s. 58(1). A licence agreement permitting a person to act on behalf of others in relation to alleged breaches of copyright was not an agreement to conduct litigation within the meaning of the *Sibthorpe* case, but was rather a commercial agreement which did not jeopardise the administration of justice (*Golden Eye (International) Ltd v Telefonica UK Ltd* [2012] EWCA Civ 1740, [2013] Bus LR 414). In *Ahmed v Powell*

[2003] PNLR 22 it was held that the basis on which costs negotiators charged fees was champertous. In an arrangement with the defendant's insurers, the costs negotiators were to receive a percentage of the reduction in the amount of costs which they achieved. On the other hand, in *Benaim (UK) Ltd v Davies Middleton and Davies Ltd* [2004] EWHC 737 (TCC), LTL 29/3/2004, the court upheld a CFA which provided for an uplift of up to 100 per cent depending upon the amount of damages recovered. For discussion of the current rules on CFAs see **chapter 6**. In *Westlaw Services Ltd v Boddy* [2010] EWCA Civ 929, [2011] PNLR 4, it was held that a fee-sharing arrangement whereby individuals who obtained work for the firm were to obtain a percentage of the net fees received for that work was void and unenforceable. Since 1 April 2013, contingency fee agreements in the form of damages-based agreements are permitted, provided they comply with statutory requirements (see **Chapter 5**).

(b) The rule may invalidate some assignments of causes of action.

14.8 Scope of maintenance and champerty The scope of the rule against champerty and maintenance, in so far as it affects both funding of litigation and assignments of causes of action, has been progressively narrowed. The current position can be summarised as follows:

(a) Liquidated claims in contract, such as the right to sue for the price of goods sold and delivered for which the defendant had failed to pay, can be assigned (*County Hotel and Wine Co. Ltd v London and North Western Railway Co.* [1918] 2 KB 251).

(b) The fruits of litigation can be validly assigned (*Glegg v Bromley* [1912] 3 KB 474; *Ruttle Plant Hire Ltd v Secretary of State for the Environment, Food and Rural Affairs (No. 2)* [2008] EWHC 238 (TCC), [2009] 1 All ER 448). An assignment of the benefit of a costs order (which required the costs to be assessed) from one party to the other is not likely to be champertous (*Zabihi v Janzemini* [2009] EWHC 3471 (Ch), LTL 29/1/2010).

(c) Assignments of property are permissible (*Dawson v Great Northern and City Railway* [1905] 1 KB 260), as are assignments which are designed to support or enlarge a property interest which the assignee already possesses (*Compañía Colombiana de Seguros v Pacific Steam Navigation Co.* [1965] 1 QB 101). An assignment of a bare right to litigate is also permissible if it is incidental and subsidiary to a transfer of property (*Williams v Protheroe* (1829) 3 Y & J 129; *Offer-Hoar v Larkstore Ltd* [2006] EWCA Civ 1079, [2006] 1 WLR 2926). See also *Pegasus Management Holdings SCA v Ernst & Young* [2012] EWHC 738 (Ch), [2012] PNLR 24.

(d) The status of the assignment of a damages claim in contract or tort is more complex. The current approach of the courts is set out in *Giles v Thompson* [1994] 1 AC 142. The first question the court will ask is whether the contract of assignment has the characteristics of champerty or maintenance and is therefore prima facie unlawful. In other words, has a stranger to the dispute agreed to involve itself in litigation (maintenance) in a way which yields it a financial benefit from a successful outcome (champerty)? If it does, the court will then inquire whether the transaction is validated by the legitimate interest of the person supporting the action in its outcome. A proprietary interest in the subject matter of the litigation has been held to be a sufficient interest (*Alabaster v Harness* [1894] 2 QB 897), as has a genuine commercial interest in the outcome of the litigation (*Trendtex Trading Corporation v Credit Suisse* [1982] AC 679). A bare right to litigate that was not supported by any collateral interest sufficient to justify the pursuit of the proceedings by the third party for its own benefit was champertous and contrary to public policy (*Skywell (UK) Ltd v Commissioners of HM Revenue and Customs* [2012] UKFTT 611 (TC), [2012] STI 3030). However, assignment of a bare right to litigate a contract claim together with the assignment of debts from an individual to a limited liability partnership established by him and two others was not held to be champertous in *JEB Recoveries LLP v Binstock* [2015] EWHC 1063 (Ch), LTL 6/5/2015 (appeal outstanding). A member of a family has been held justified in maintaining a claim by another member of the family (*Bradlaugh v Newdegate* (1883) 11 QBD 1). An agreement granting a company's former majority shareholder the right to bring a claim for damages for breach of contract in the name of the company, on the basis that he received a percentage of damages as additional consideration for the sale of his shares, was not champertous (*Eurocall Ltd v Energis Communications Ltd* [2010] EWHC 1730 (QB), LTL 12/8/2010).

In *Simpson v Norfolk and Norwich University Hospital NHS Trust* [2011] EWCA Civ 1149, [2012] QB 640, the Court of Appeal held that a claim for damages for personal injury is a legal thing in action which is capable of being assigned, but the assignee did not have a sufficient legitimate interest of a kind that the law would recognise as justifying the pursuit of the proceedings for her own benefit. The assignment was therefore void on the grounds of champerty. The assignee's objective was primarily to mount a campaign against the NHS Trust to implement procedures to prevent and control infection. The court noted that the law on maintenance and champerty was open to further development and it was not possible to state definitely what might constitute a sufficient interest to support the assignment of a cause of action in tort for personal injury. Each case will therefore be decided, to some extent, on its own facts.

The court will also look at public policy considerations. It will examine the question of maintenance and champerty in the light of their 'origins as a principle of public policy designed to protect the purity of justice and the interests of vulnerable litigants' (*Giles v Thompson*, per Lord Mustill).

(e) An administrator, administrative receiver or liquidator of a company has a statutory power under the Insolvency Act 1986, sch. 1, para. 2, and sch. 4, para. 6, to sell the company's property, which includes assigning the fruits of a cause of action on terms that the assignees, by way of consideration, will return a share of the recoveries (*Glegg v Bromley* [1912] 3 KB 474; *Grovewood Holdings plc v James Capel and Co. Ltd* [1995] Ch 80; *Norglen Ltd v Reeds Rain Prudential Ltd* [1999] 2 AC 1). A liquidator may assign the fruits of litigation, but not the right to prosecute it, because that is not an asset of the company, but a right conferred on the liquidator by the Insolvency Act 1986 (*Ruttle Plant Hire Ltd v Secretary of State for the Environment, Food and Rural Affairs (No. 2)* [2008] EWHC 238 (TCC), [2009] 1 All ER 448). Property which could be acquired for the company's estate by the exercise of a statutory power to bring proceedings given to a liquidator or administrator by the Insolvency Act 1986, ss. 127, 213, 214, 238, 239, 244 or 245, is not the company's property and cannot be assigned in return for funding the proceedings (*Re Oasis Merchandising Services Ltd* [1998] Ch 170). A trustee in bankruptcy has a similar power under the Insolvency Act 1986, sch. 5, para. 9 (*Grovewood Holdings plc v James Capel and Co. Ltd* [1995] Ch 80). These powers must be exercised in the best interests of the creditors. So, for example, in *Faryab v Smith* [2001] BPIR 246 a trustee in bankruptcy was ordered not to assign a right of action of the bankrupt to the potential defendant without evaluating the claim.

(f) The right to litigate about purely personal claims (e.g. slander) is not assignable (*Trendtex Trading Corporation v Credit Suisse* [1980] QB 629).

Examples   *Giles v Thompson* [1994] 1 AC 142 involved car insurance arrangements, whereby the   **14.9**
insurance company loaned its insured a replacement vehicle at no charge in return for the assignment of the insured's right to claim hire charges against the defendant. The House of Lords considered whether such arrangements would harm the administration of justice or the interests of the motorist. It concluded that they did not, and therefore, that even though the insurance companies had no interest in the outcome of the litigation, the arrangements were not champertous.

This approach was upheld by the Court of Appeal in *R (Factortame Ltd) v Secretary of State for Transport, Local Government and the Regions (No. 8)* [2002] EWCA Civ 932, [2003] QB 381. The question in that case was whether the provision of expert accounting services to the claimants in return for an assignment of 8 per cent of the damages to be received by the claimants was champertous. Lord Phillips of Worth Matravers MR said that:

It is necessary to look at the agreement under attack in order to see whether it tends to conflict with existing public policy that is directed to protecting the due administration of justice with particular regard to the interests of the defendant.

The court held first that the agreement was not in breach of the **Courts and Legal Services Act 1990, s. 58** (which invalidates any conditional fee agreements outside its ambit), as the section applies only to the provision of litigation services by a legal representative, not by an expert. Secondly, the court held that giving evidence on a contingency fee basis gives an expert a significant financial interest in the outcome of the case, which is undesirable. The court would only rarely permit an expert to operate under a contingency fee agreement. However, the court concluded that in this case the agreement was not champertous and did not put justice in jeopardy. The accountants did not perform the role of expert witnesses. Their involvement was limited to assisting the quantification of damages. They had no involvement in the court's decision on the merits of the claim.

In *Stocznia Gdanska SA v Latreefers Inc. (No. 2)* [2001] 2 BCLC 116 the Court of Appeal considered the status of an agreement to fund litigation where the funder had a clear commercial interest in the litigation, but the funding agreement gave it a substantial profit in the form of a division of the damages which was in excess of its preceding loss. Morritt LJ considered the circumstances in which the court would stay a claim on the grounds of champerty or maintenance. He stated that the court was concerned with abuses of the court's process, but that not every abuse will result in a stay. The court was concerned to prevent 'trafficking in litigation'. He declined to define 'trafficking', but continued:

it seems to us to connote unjustified buying and selling of rights to litigation where the purchaser has no proper reason to be concerned with the litigation .... A large mathematical disproportion between any pre-existing financial interest and the potential profit of funders may in particular cases contribute to a finding of abuse, but is not bound to do so.

In this case, the funding agreement did not constitute trafficking in litigation, and there was no abuse of process.

In *Papera Traders Co. Ltd v Hyundai Merchant Marine Co. Ltd (No. 2)* [2002] EWHC 2130 (Comm), [2002] 2 Lloyd's Rep 692, the court considered whether an agreement to pay 5 per cent of the amount recovered in litigation against insurers to a firm of marine loss adjusters was champertous. Again, the question for the court was whether the agreement impugned the integrity of the English legal system and in coming to a decision the court had to consider the precise nature of the loss adjusters' interest in the outcome of the litigation. In this case, the agreement was not champertous as their activities were subject to the control of solicitors and counsel, the agreement was not exclusively concerned with litigation and there was a good commercial reason to retain them.

In *Mansell v Robinson* [2007] EWHC 101 (QB), LTL 9/2/2007, it was held that an agreement to provide investigative services in return for 1 per cent of the proceeds of litigation plus a weekly salary was not champertous. The agreement could not realistically be said to have a tendency to corrupt public justice. In some meritorious cases, it could be a real barrier to justice to insist on an absolute rule preventing a skilled researcher or inquiry agent, whose services were sought by a person with a potential claim, from making an enforceable contract under which he would be partly remunerated by reference to sums recovered.

In *Lediaev v Vallen* [2008] EWHC 1271 (Ch), LTL 1/8/2008, reversed on other grounds, [2009] EWCA Civ 156, LTL 5/3/2009, the court considered whether it could make a finding of champerty of its own motion, when no such claim had been pleaded and neither party had invited the court to hold the agreement illegal. It concluded that it did have the power to do so, as champerty is a matter of public policy. However, it could only make a finding where it could clearly see that it had all the relevant facts and was in a position to take a close look at the circumstances of the individual case, as envisaged by *R (Factortame Ltd) v Secretary of State for Transport, Local Government and the Regions (No. 8)* [2002] EWCA Civ 932, [2003] QB 381. In the present case the court did have access to the facts and it was satisfied that the agreement was not champertous. The fact that the success fee came from a third party and was not a share of the proceeds of the litigation made no difference to whether or not the agreement was illegal.

Properly structured litigation funding agreements by professional funders are not likely to infringe the rules relating to maintenance or champerty (*Arkin v Borchard Lines* [2005] EWCA Civ 655, [2005] 1 WLR 3055). Such funders will usually comply with the Code of Conduct for Third Party Funders and be members of and comply with the Rules of the Association of Litigation Funders in England and Wales. Litigation funders are likely to have a greater role to play under the reformed system of civil litigation costs operating from 1 April 2013.

NAMING PARTIES IN STATEMENTS OF CASE

A claim form must be headed with the title to the proceedings, including the full name of each party (**PD 16, para. 2.6**). **Paragraph 2.6** continues with more detailed rules for different classes of party, which are summarised in **table 14.1** and at **14.11** to **14.50**. The rules on serving different classes of party are discussed at **15.45** to **15.53**.

14.10

Table 14.1 Names of parties

Class of party	Form of words
An individual	His or her full unabbreviated name and the title by which he or she is known, e.g. Mr Richard John Brown
An individual carrying on business in a name other than his own name	The full unabbreviated name of the individual, together with the title by which he is known and the full trading name (e.g. John Smith T/as JS Autos)
A child under 18	Miss Jane Mary Brown (a child by Mr Joe Bloggs her litigation friend)
A child under 18 who is conducting proceedings on his or her own behalf	Master Tim Brown (a child)
A child reaching full age	Ms Jane Mary Brown (formerly a child but now of full age)
An individual who is a protected party within the meaning of the Mental Capacity Act 2005	Mrs Jane Mary Brown (by Mr Joe Bloggs, her litigation friend)
An individual who is trading under another name	Mr John Smith, trading as (or T/as) 'Smith's Groceries'
An individual who is suing or being sued in a representative capacity	Miss Jane Mary Brown, as the representative of Hilda Marion Brown (deceased)
An individual who is suing or being sued in the name of a club or other unincorporated organisation	Miss Jane Mary Brown, suing/sued on behalf of the Northtown Under 16 Football Club
A firm (other than a limited liability partnership)	(a) where partners are being sued in the name of the partnership, the full name by which the partnership is known and the words '(a firm)', e.g. 'Brown & Co. (A Firm)'; (b) where the partners are being sued as individuals, the full unabbreviated name and title of each partner.
A corporation (other than a company)	The full name of the corporation by which it is known, including indication of legal form ('Corporation', 'Incorporated', etc.), where appropriate
A company, whether registered in England and Wales, or an overseas company, or a limited liability partnership	The full registered name, including indication of legal form (plc, Ltd, LLP, etc.)

Commentary

DECEASED PARTIES

Survival of causes of action

14.11   Under the **Law Reform (Miscellaneous Provisions) Act 1934, s. 1(1)**, most causes of action subsisting against or vested in an individual survive his or her death, against or for the benefit of his or her estate. Even a claim for unlawful racial discrimination survives the claimant's death (*Lewisham and Guys Mental Health NHS Trust v Andrews* [2000] 3 All ER 769). The loss of the chance of a death-in-service benefit being paid under an employee pension scheme following the unfair dismissal of the employee one month prior to his death was to be regarded as a pecuniary loss suffered by him for which he could have claimed in proceedings prior to his death (*Fox v British Airways plc* [2013] EWCA Civ 972, [2013] ICR 1257). The principal exception is that a defamation claim comes to an end upon the claimant's death (**Law Reform (Miscellaneous Provisions) Act 1934, s. 1(1)**).

Death of party before claim issued

14.12   If an individual who has a claim dies before the claim is started, it must be brought by the personal representatives of the deceased if they have been granted probate or letters of administration. The capacity of the executor or administrator must be made clear in their description in the claim form, for example, 'Mr Joe Bloggs as the executor of Mrs Sharon Bloggs (deceased)' (**PD 7A, para. 5.5; CPR, r. 19.8(3)(a)**). A claim brought against a person who was in fact dead at its commencement will be treated as if it had been commenced against his or her estate (**r. 19.8(3)(b)**). However, the irregularity must be corrected by the making of an application for a person to represent the deceased for the purposes of the claim. Until that happens there is no defendant with legal personality (*Piggott v Aulton* [2003] EWCA Civ 24, [2003] RTR 540; *Millburn-Snell v Evans* [2011] EWCA Civ 577, [2012] 1 WLR 41).

Where a defendant against whom a claim could have been brought has died, and a grant of probate or administration has been made, the claim must be brought against the persons who are the personal representatives of the deceased (**r. 19.8(2)(a)**). A claimant who wishes to start proceedings against the estate of a deceased defendant before there has been a grant of probate or letters of administration should bring a claim against 'the estate' of the deceased (**r. 19.8(2)(b)(i)**). A claim is treated as having been brought against 'the estate of' the deceased where it is brought against the 'personal representatives' of the deceased but a grant of probate or administration has not been made (**r. 19.8(3)(a)**). However, the claim form may not be served in this form, because it does not identify the defendants upon whom it should be served. So the next step in the claim is for the claimant to apply, within the time limited for service of the claim form (which is four months within the jurisdiction, six months outside), for an order appointing a person to represent the estate of the deceased person for the purpose of the claim and for the action to continue against the representative (**PD 7A, para. 5.5; CPR, r. 19.8(2)(b)(ii)**).

Before making an order, the court may direct notice of the application to be given to any other person with an interest in the claim (**r. 19.8(4)**). Where an order is made, any judgment or order made in the claim is binding on the estate of the deceased (**r. 19.8(5)**).

Before the grant of letters of administration there is a limited power for a person to take essential steps to preserve and protect the deceased's estate. Unless proceedings are necessary for that purpose, a claimant has no right to commence proceedings before the grant, and the court will refuse to give relief to the claimant in such proceedings (*Caudle v LD Law Ltd* [2008] EWHC 374 (QB), [2008] 1 WLR 1540).

Death of party after claim issued

14.13   Where a claimant or defendant dies after the claim has been issued, an order may be obtained under **CPR, r. 19.2(4)**, for the claim to be carried on by or against his or her personal representatives. Application should be made by application notice, with evidence in support, in accordance with the procedure set out **CPR, Part 19**, and **PD 19A** (see **14.83** to **14.92**).

Where a party who has an interest in a claim has died but has no personal representatives, the court may order the claim to proceed in the absence of a person representing the estate, or may order the appointment of a person to represent the estate for the purpose of the proceedings (**CPR, r. 19.8(1)**). This enables the court to dispense with the need for a formal grant of probate or letters of administration. In *Re Berti* [2001] EWCA Civ 2079, LTL 16/11/2001 the Court of Appeal emphasised that a person who wishes to represent a deceased's estate may obtain a representation order under **r. 19.8(1)(b)** as an alternative to being granted probate or letters of administration, and the court should not insist on such a person going to the expense of obtaining probate or administration, especially where the estate is small. **Rule 19.8(1)** does not permit the court to correct deficiencies in the manner in which proceedings were instituted. It only enables the court to make directions for the continued prosecution of proceedings where a person who had an interest in the claim has died. So an action brought by a claimant purportedly as administrator, when he did not have that capacity, was a nullity (*Milbum-Snell v Evans* [2011] EWCA Civ 577, [2012] 1 WLR 41). However, the court may use its powers under **Parts 3** and **17** to allow a claimant to amend a statement of case to perfect a claim brought on behalf of a deceased's estate which would otherwise have failed on the grounds that letters of administration had not been obtained by the claimant at the time the proceedings were issued, particularly where the defendant has acquiesced in the claimant's title to sue despite the lack of any grant (*Meerza v Al Baho* [2015] EWHC 3154 (Ch), LTL 13/11/2015).

The court will require notice of an application under **r. 19.8(1)** to be given to anyone who may have an interest in the deceased's estate (**r. 19.8(4)**). Any judgment or order made in the claim will then bind the estate (**r. 19.8(5)**).

An application for an order to carry on existing proceedings, which were brought before the expiry of limitation in the name of the personal representatives following the death of a party, raises no issues under the Limitation Act 1980, whether the death or application occurs before or after the expiry of limitation (*Roberts v Gill and Co.* [2010] UKSC 22, [2011] 1 AC 240 at [103]–[104]). **CPR, r. 19.5(3)(c)**, therefore probably has no real function (see **14.89**).

Notice of claim to non-parties

In a claim relating to the estate of a deceased person, the court has power under **CPR, r. 19.8A**, to require notice of the claim or a judgment or order in it to be given to any person who is not a party but who may be affected by any judgment. An application for an order under this rule may be made without notice but must be supported by written evidence which includes the reasons why the person to be served should be bound by the judgment in the claim. Notice must be given in form 52, accompanied by a copy of the claim form, a form for acknowledging service and any affidavits, witness statements or statements of case ordered by the court to be served. Once the person served acknowledges service, that person becomes a party to the claim. Even if there is no acknowledgment of service, the person will be bound by any judgment or order made in the claim. If after service of notice of a claim, the claim form is substantially amended so as to alter the relief claimed, the court can direct that a judgment will not bind the notified person unless a further notice, together with the amended claim form, is served on him (**r. 19.8A(7)**).   **14.14**

Any person served with a notice of a judgment or order under **r. 19.8A** is bound by it as if he had been a party to the claim, but may, provided he acknowledges service, apply to the court within 28 days of service, to set aside or vary the judgment or order and take part in any proceedings relating to it (**r. 19.8A(8)**).

CHILDREN AND PROTECTED PARTIES

Introduction

CPR, Part 21, contains special provisions governing proceedings involving children (defined as persons under 18: **r. 21.1(2)**) and protected parties (see **14.16**). **Part 21** does not apply to   **14.15**

certain proceedings, even though one of the parties to the proceedings is a child (**r. 21.1(1)(c)**). Those are proceedings under **Part 75**, enforcement of specified debts by taking control of goods, and applications in relation to the enforcement of specified debts by taking control of goods.

Protected parties

14.16   The term 'protected party' means a party, or an intended party, who lacks capacity within the meaning of the Mental Capacity Act 2005, s. 2(1), to conduct proceedings (**CPR, r. 21.1(2)**). This statutory definition is to be used to decide whether a person is a protected party (*Saulle v Nouvet* [2007] EWHC 2902 (QB), [2008] LS Law Medical 201). It states that a person lacks capacity if at the material time he or she is unable to make a decision for him or herself in relation to a matter because of an impairment of, or a disturbance in, the functioning of the mind or brain. The disturbance could be permanent or temporary, and could cover a range of problems such as psychiatric illness, learning disability, dementia and brain damage. This definition of capacity reflects the common law position (see *Re C (Adult: Refusal of Treatment)* [1994] 1 WLR 290 and *Masterman-Lister v Brutton and Co. (Nos. 1 and 2)* [2002] EWCA Civ 1889, [2003] EWCA Civ 70, [2003] 1 WLR 1511). However, the test of capacity in the Mental Capacity Act 1995 is not appropriate to evaluate if a deceased person had had capacity at the time of making his or her will. The correct and only test of capacity in relation to an issue concerning the validity of a will, is the common law test set out in *Banks v Goodfellow* (1870) LR 5 QB 549 (*Re Walker* [2014] EWHC 71 (Ch), [2015] WTLR 493).

The Mental Capacity Act 2005, s. 1, establishes a number of fundamental principles. The most important is a presumption of capacity. A person must be assumed to have capacity unless it is established that he lacks capacity (s. 1(2)). A person must be presented with all of the options so that his or her capacity to weigh up those options can be fairly assessed. A person who understands the salient features of the available options may have capacity even if there is a lack of understanding of every nuance or point of detail of each respective option (*CC v KK* [2012] EWHC 2136 (COP), LTL 2/11/2012). A person is not to be treated as unable to make a decision unless all practicable steps to help him to do so have been taken without success (s. 1(3); *Re W (Children)* [2008] EWHC 1188 (Fam), [2010] 1 FLR 1176). A person is not to be treated as unable to make a decision merely because he makes an unwise decision (s. 1(4)). The issue is whether the person has the ability to make decisions and, where relevant, to carry out a process of using and weighing up information in order to make a decision whether wise or unwise (*RB (A Patient) v Brighton and Hove City Council* [2014] EWCA Civ 561, [2014] COPLR 629). Treating a person as lacking capacity is an important interference with his or her human rights, and ought only to be done after proper consideration. The burden is on the person alleging incapacity to establish it, on the balance of probabilities, and it is to be determined by the judge, not the experts.

Any act done or decision made under the Act for or on behalf of a person who lacks capacity must be done, or made, in his best interests (s. 1(5)), and s. 4 sets out factors which must be applied in deciding what is in a person's best interests. When determining the best interests of a person lacking capacity pursuant to s. 4, the substituted judgment of the court as to what the decision of the protected person would have been had he not lacked capacity is a relevant factor (*Re G* [2010] EWHC 3005 (Fam), [2011] WTLR 231). Before the act is done or the decision is made, regard must be had to whether the purpose can be achieved in a way that is less restrictive of a person's rights and freedom of action (s. 1(6)). Any determination of what is in a person's best interests under s. 4 has to be considered against the backdrop of that person's rights under the European Convention on Human Rights in the **Human Rights Act 1998, sch. 1**. The correct approach is to make the determination under the Mental Capacity Act 2005, s. 4, then assess whether it violates rights under **art. 8** and, if it does, whether that violation is necessary and proportional (*K v A Local Authority* [2012] EWCA Civ 79, [2012] 1 FCR 441; *An NHS Trust v DE* [2013] EWHC 2562 (Fam), [2013] 3 FCR 343).

The court has power to make declarations about capacity (Mental Capacity Act 2005, s. 15) and decisions on the person's behalf (ss. 16, 17 and 18). The powers of the court are subject to s. 1 (principles) and s. 4 (best interests). Some decisions are excluded (see ss. 27, 28 and 29).

Where apparently irrational comments and instructions lead legal representatives to suspect there is a real risk that their client lacks legal capacity, it is right to take steps (including bringing the matter before the court if there is an impending trial) to ascertain whether it is necessary to appoint a litigation friend (*McFaddens v Platford* [2009] EWHC 126 (TCC), [2009] PNLR 26; *V v R* [2011] EWHC 822 (QB), LTL 23/1/2012).

The court will almost certainly require a medical report before being able to find a party to be under a mental incapacity. In cases where no one recognises the fact that one of the parties is under a mental incapacity, the court can regularise the position retrospectively, provided everyone is acting in good faith. However, **CPR, Part 21**, invalidates a consent order involving a protected party if it has been reached without court approval, and such a consent order will be set aside, even if the individual's lack of capacity was not known at the time of the compromise (*Dunhill v Burgin* [2014] UKSC 18, [2014] 1 WLR 933).

There is a two-stage test to be applied to assess capacity. The first stage, sometimes called the 'diagnostic test', involves determining whether the individual has an impairment of the mind or brain. The second stage, sometimes called the 'functional test' involves determining whether the impairment is such as to prevent the individual from being able to make the decision in question at the time it needs to be made. A person will not lack capacity unless both stages or tests are satisfied (*A Local Authority v TZ* [2013] EWHC 2322 (COP), LTL 14/10/2013). Where it has not been possible to obtain medical evidence, a court has to be cautious before concluding that a litigant is suffering from a disturbance of mind preventing him or her from participating in litigation (*Baker Tilly v Makar* [2013] EWHC 759 (QB), [2013] 3 Costs LR 444). In order to assess the individual's ability to make the decision, the test set out in s. 3(1) must be satisfied. This is that a person lacks capacity if he or she is unable:

(a) to understand information relevant to a decision;
(b) to retain the information;
(c) to use or weigh that information as part of the process of making the decision; or
(d) to communicate the decision (by any means).

A lack of capacity cannot be established merely by reference to a person's age or appearance, or a condition of his, or an aspect of his behaviour, which might lead others to make unjustified assumptions about his capacity (s. 2(3)). A person should not be regarded as unable to understand information if he is able to understand an explanation of it given to him in a way that is appropriate to his circumstances (e.g. using simple language, by visual aids or other means), and he should not be regarded as unable to make a decision because he can only retain information for a short period of time (s. 3(2) and (3)). Profound loss or impairment of memory might be compatible with capacity to make a decision provided the person could retain relevant information for a sufficient period of time to enable him to understand and evaluate it and to form and communicate his decision (*Re S* [2010] EWHC 2405 (COP), BAILLI at [37] to [39]).

The issue of capacity is specific to the issues raised in the proceedings before the court and it is irrelevant whether a person had capacity in other proceedings (*Durkan v Madden* [2013] EWHC 4409 (Ch), LTL 17/9/2013). Assessment of an individual's capacity can be made more difficult if the individual deliberately refuses to engage or cooperate with the process. Lack of engagement or cooperation might contribute to a conclusion that the individual was unable to understand the information relevant to the decision or use or weigh that information within the meaning of s. 3(1)(a) and (e) of the Act. Having regard to these matters, and the factors in s. 4, in *W NHS Trust v P* [2014] EWHC 119 (COP), LTL 3/3/2014, the court held that it was in an uncooperative patient's best interests to have medical investigations carried out whether or not this amounted to a deprivation of his liberty under the European Convention on Human Rights, **art. 5** or **art. 8**, in the **Human Rights Act 1998, sch. 1**.

The question is whether the litigant is capable of understanding, with assistance from his legal representatives and other experts, the issues on which his consent or decision is likely to be necessary in the course of the proceedings. Similar issues arise when considering whether a party has the mental capacity to approve a settlement of liability or quantum, where the enquiry has to be directed to the transaction which is to be approved, and the question is whether the party is able to understand the proceedings and make an informed decision, with the help of any explanation from his or her advisers (*Bailey v Warren* [2006] EWCA Civ 51, [2006] WTLR 753). Capacity is to be judged in relation to the activity or decision in question, and not globally. The proper test of capacity is whether the party could conduct the claim that the party actually has, rather than the claim as formulated by their lawyers (*Dunhill v Burgin* [2014] UKSC 18, [2014] 1 WLR 933).

Where a party loses mental capacity during the course of proceedings, the loss of capacity does not have an immediate and automatic effect of terminating the solicitor's retainer. However, it does remove the solicitor's authority to act on the party's behalf and it might cause a delay in performance of the obligation to give instructions, although the solicitor's authority to act can be restored if the party regains capacity or a deputy or litigation friend is appointed and gives instructions to the solicitor (*Blankley v Central Manchester and Manchester Children's University Hospitals NHS Trust* [2015] EWCA Civ 18, [2015] 1 Costs LR 119).

The overarching principle under the Mental Capacity Act 2005 is that decisions must be made in the best interests of the protected person. This is not the same as asking what that person would have decided if he or she had full capacity, and care must be taken not to conflate the assessment of capacity with the best interests analysis (*CC v KK* [2012] EWHC 2136 (COP), LTL 2/11/2012). The decision-maker must consider all relevant circumstances, follow the steps set out in the Act (including consideration of s. 1(6)), then form a value judgment of his or her own giving effect to the paramount statutory principle that the decision has to be made in the person's best interests. Although the wishes of the protected person must be given great weight, together with the protected person's beliefs, values and other factors that would have influenced his or her own decision, they are simply part of the balance (see *A London Local Authority v JH* [2011] EWHC 2420 (Fam), LTL 28/10/2011). The 'best interest' test in s. 4 requires a person-centred approach rather than considering, in general terms, what is best for a certain group of the population (*AH v Hertfordshire Partnership NHS Foundation Trust* [2011] EWHC 276 (Fam), 14 CCL Rep 301). An unwise decision cannot be made by the decision-maker simply because the protected person would have made it (*Re P* [2009] EWHC 163 (Ch), [2009] 2 All ER 1198; *Re S (Protected Persons)* [2010] 1 WLR 1082). In *Aintree University Hospitals NHS Foundation Trust v James* [2013] UKSC 67, [2013] AC 591, the Supreme Court set out the correct approach to making decisions about whether to give life-sustaining treatment to a person who lacked capacity.

Alongside the Mental Capacity Act 2005, the court has an inherent jurisdiction to protect vulnerable adults who, while not suffering from mental incapacity within the meaning of that Act, are nevertheless unable to make relevant decisions because of vitiating factors such as coercion or undue influence (*Re L (Vulnerable Adults with Capacity: Court's Jurisdiction) (No. 2)* [2012] EWCA Civ 253, [2013] Fam 1).

Litigation friends

14.17   Both protected parties and children (subject, in the latter case to any order by the court to the contrary, see **14.20**) must have a litigation friend to conduct proceedings on their behalf (**CPR, r. 21.2**). The title to a claim where one of the parties is a protected party should read 'AB (a protected party by CD his litigation friend)'. In the case of a child, it should read 'AB (a child, by CD his litigation friend)' (**PD 21, paras 1.1 and 1.2**).

A claimant who sues a child or protected party who has no litigation friend may take no step in a claim without the court's permission, other than issuing and serving the claim form, or making an application for the appointment of a litigation friend (**CPR, r. 21.3(2)**). If a party lacks capacity to continue to conduct proceedings, no further step in the claim may be taken without the court's permission until he or she has a litigation friend (**r. 21.3(3)**). Any step taken before the appointment of the litigation friend has no effect, subject to any order by the court to the contrary (**r. 21.3(4)**).

Default judgment may be entered against a child or protected party only with the court's permission (**r. 12.10(a)(i)**) and only after a litigation friend has been appointed by the court (**PD 12, para. 4.2(1)**). It would seem that a litigation friend appointed out of court under CPR, **r. 21.5** (see **14.19**), is not acceptable.

Who may be a litigation friend?

By **CPR, rr. 21.4(3)** and **21.6**, a litigation friend may be: **14.18**

(a) a person appointed by the court (see **14.19**);
(b) a 'deputy' appointed under the Mental Capacity Act 2005, s. 16(2), with power to conduct specified legal proceedings on the protected party's behalf; or
(c) a person who can fairly and competently conduct proceedings on behalf of the child or protected party and who has no adverse interest in the claim.

A litigation friend who acts for a claimant (but not a defendant) must undertake to pay any costs which the claimant may be ordered to pay (subject to any right that the friend may have to be repaid from the claimant's assets) (**CPR, r. 21.4(3)**). A litigation friend who incurs expenses on behalf of a child or protected party in the course of proceedings is entitled to recoup them out of any money recovered from the opposing party or from a payment into court, provided the expenses are of a reasonable amount and were reasonably incurred (**r. 21.12**). However, costs recoverable under this rule are limited to (a) costs incurred by or on behalf of a child and which have been assessed by way of detailed assessment pursuant to **r. 46.4(2)**; or (b) costs incurred by or on behalf of a child by way of a success fee under a conditional fee agreement or sum payable under a damages-based agreement in a claim for damages for personal injury where the damages agreed or ordered to be paid do not exceed £25,000, where such costs have been assessed summarily pursuant to **r. 46.4(5)** (**r. 21.12(1A)**). The amount which the litigation friend may recover under **r. 21.12(1)** in respect of costs must not (in proceedings at first instance) exceed 25 per cent of the amount of the sum agreed or awarded in respect of (a) general damages for pain, suffering and loss of amenity; and (b) damages for pecuniary loss other than future pecuniary loss, net of any sums recoverable by the Compensation Recovery Unit of the Department for Work and Pensions (**r. 21.12(7)**). By **r. 21.12(6)**, where the child or protected party recovers £5,000 or less from the proceedings, the litigation friend may not recoup more than 25 per cent of the sum recovered to cover expenses, unless the court orders otherwise. Even with a court order, the amount recouped may not exceed 50 per cent. No application should be made under **r. 21.12** for a payment out of the money recovered by the child or protected party until the costs payable to the child or protected party have been assessed or agreed (**r. 21.12(8)**).

Where the litigation friend's expenses are recoverable as *inter partes* costs, where the court has ordered an assessment of costs under **r. 46.4(2)**, the claim for costs or expenses should be made at the detailed assessment hearing. Where the court has made a summary assessment of costs under **r. 46.4(5)(b)**, the litigation friend should make the application for costs or expenses at the conclusion of the hearing at which the damages payable to the child are assessed or at the hearing to approve the compromise or settlement under **Part 21**, or at any time thereafter (**PD 21, para. 11.1(1A)**). If they are not recoverable as costs, the application should be made either at the hearing under **CPR, Part 21** to approve a settlement of the claim or, where no approval is necessary, by separate application under **Part 23**.

Whatever its form, the application must be supported by a witness statement setting out the nature and amount of the expense being claimed and the reason it was incurred (**PD 21, para. 11.2**). Where the application is for payment out of the damages pursuant to **CPR**.

r. 21.12(1A), the witness statement should include, or be accompanied by, a copy of the conditional fee agreement or damages-based agreement, the risk assessment by reference to which the success fee was determined, the reasons why the particular funding model was selected, the advice given to the litigation friend in relation to the funding arrangements, details of any costs agreed, recovered or fixed costs recoverable by the child, and confirmation of the amount of the sum agreed or awarded in respect of general damages for pain, suffering and loss of amenity and damages for pecuniary loss other than future pecuniary loss (**PD 21, para. 11.3**).

In practice, a child's litigation friend will normally be a parent, guardian or other relative who can comply with these requirements. A protected party's litigation friend may be a deputy under the Mental Capacity Act 2005 (particularly where there are assets to be administered) or, where no such person has been appointed, the person with whom the protected party lives or who is caring for the party. If no one is available to be a litigation friend, application can be made to the Official Solicitor for him to act.

In *Nottinghamshire County Council v Bottomley* [2010] EWCA Civ 756, [2010] Med LR 407, the local authority's director of social care was acting as the claimant's litigation friend. It was held she had a conflict of interest between achieving the best outcome for the claimant and the interest of her employer in achieving a result on the question of periodical payments that favoured the local authority. Accordingly, she could not continue in the role of litigation friend.

How is a litigation friend appointed?

14.19 There are two methods in the CPR whereby a litigation friend may be appointed.

First, a person may become a litigation friend without a court order, under **r. 21.5**, by filing either:

(a) in the case of a deputy under the Mental Capacity Act 2005, an official copy of the order of the Court of Protection which confers the deputy's power to act; or

(b) in the case of any other person, a certificate of suitability in form N235. The details of what the certificate must state are set out at **PD 21, para. 2.2**.

These documents must be filed when proceedings are first issued (where the litigation friend acts on behalf of the claimant) or when the litigation friend first takes a step in the proceedings (where acting on behalf of the defendant). A copy of the certificate of suitability must, by **CPR, r. 21.5(4)**, be served on every person on whom the claim form must be served under **r. 6.13** (see **15.45**) and a certificate of service must be filed with the certificate of suitability.

Alternatively, a litigation friend may be appointed by court order under **r. 21.6**. An application for an order under this rule may be made by any person who wishes to be appointed as litigation friend or by any party to the action (**r. 21.6(2)**). The application should be made under the Part 23 procedure. It must, by **PD 21, para. 3.3**, be supported by evidence that the person proposed for appointment:

(a) consents to act;

(b) can conduct proceedings fairly and competently;

(c) has no adverse interest to the child or protected party; and

(d) in the case of a claimant, undertakes to pay any costs order (subject to any right to be repaid from the assets of the child or protected party).

The last three of these conditions are also specified in **CPR, r. 21.4(3)**. Where it is sought to appoint the Official Solicitor as the litigation friend, provision must be made for payment of his charges (**PD 21, para. 3.4**). The courts are reluctant to permit the question of whether a party has the mental capacity to conduct litigation to become unnecessary satellite litigation, and the Court of Appeal has held in *Folks v Faizey* [2006] EWCA Civ 381, *The Independent*, 12 April 2006, that the question is not suitable for determination as a preliminary issue. Although the court must have evidence to support any application for an order appointing a litigation friend, where the protected party and the litigation friend both consent to the appointment, where there is adequate evidence to support the application and where there is no evidence to suggest that the application is anything but a bona fide one, the court should make the order.

The Court of Appeal in *Folks v Faizey* also cast doubt on the need to serve a copy of the notice applying for the appointment of a litigation friend on other parties to the litigation. It commented that an application notice under **CPR, Part 23**, need only be served on the person against whom the order is sought and any other person as the court may direct and that this therefore might not include parties other than the child or protected party. However, in making these comments, it seems to have overlooked the express requirement in **r. 21.8(1)** that an application to appoint a litigation friend must be served on every person on whom the claim form should be served under what is now **r. 6.13** (see **15.45**). An application to appoint a litigation friend for a protected party must also be served on the protected party, unless the court orders otherwise (**r. 21.8(2)**).

On an application under **r. 21.6** the court may, under **r. 21.8(4)** appoint the person proposed in the application or any other person who complies with the conditions in **r. 21.4(3)**.

When may a child conduct proceedings without a litigation friend?

In the case of a child (but not a protected party) the court has a discretion to make an **14.20** order permitting the child to conduct proceedings without a litigation friend (**CPR, r. 21.2(3)**). The order may be made on application by the child, on notice to the litigation friend if the child already has one. The court has power to rescind any such order (**CPR, r. 21.2(3) to (5)**).

The court will only authorise a child to conduct proceedings without a litigation friend where it is satisfied that the child is of sufficient maturity and understanding (*Gillick v West Norfolk and Wisbech Area Health Authority* [1986] AC 112).

Where a child is conducting proceedings on his or her own behalf, the claim should be headed 'A. B. (a child)' (**PD 21, para. 1.2(2)**).

Terminating the appointment of a litigation friend

The court may direct that a person may not act as a litigation friend, or may substitute or **14.21** remove a litigation friend (**CPR, r. 21.7**). An application for an order under r. 21.7 must be supported by evidence (**r. 21.7(2)**).

By **r. 21.8(1)** and **(3)**, an application to substitute or remove a litigation friend must be served on every person on whom the claim form should be served (see **15.45**) and on the person acting, or purporting to act, as litigation friend. A person proposed for substitution as a litigation friend must comply with the conditions specified in **r. 21.4(3)** (see **14.19**) (**r. 21.7(3)**) and must be served with the application, unless he or she is the applicant (**r. 21.8(3)**).

By **r. 21.8(4)**, on an application for substitution the court may appoint the person proposed in the application or any other person who complies with the conditions in **r. 21.4(3)**.

When a child (who is not a protected party) reaches 18, the appointment of his or her litigation friend ceases (**r. 21.9(1)**). No application to the court to terminate the appointment is necessary. The individual for whom the friend has been acting must serve a notice under **PD 21, para. 4.2**, stating that he or she has reached full age and that the litigation friend's appointment has ceased, giving an address for service and stating whether he or she intends to continue the proceedings. The heading in the action then becomes: 'A. B. (formerly a child but now of full age)' (**para. 4.3**). Alternatively, the litigation friend may serve a notice under **para. 4.4**.

When a protected party regains or acquires capacity to conduct the proceedings, an application to court must be made in order to terminate the appointment of the litigation friend

(CPR, r. 21.9(2) and (3)). The application can be made by the former protected party, the litigation friend or a party (r. 21.9(3)). The application must be supported by medical or other suitable expert evidence that the protected party has regained or acquired capacity to conduct the proceedings, a copy of any relevant order of the Court of Protection, and (if the application is made by the protected party) a statement whether or not he or she intends to continue to pursue or defend the proceedings (PD 21, para. 4.6). The former protected party must file in court a notice that the litigation friend's appointment has ceased, giving an address for service and stating whether he or she intends to continue to pursue or defend the proceedings (para. 4.7; CPR, r. 21.9(4)). If a child or protected party does not serve such a notice within 28 days after the day on which the appointment of the litigation friend ceases, the court may, on application, strike out the claim (or defence) of the child or the protected party (r. 21.9(5)). The litigation friend's liability for costs continues until the notice has been served by the child or protected party or the litigation friend serves notice on the parties that his or her appointment has ceased (r. 21.9(6)). Any order made must be served on other parties to the proceedings.

Court approval of settlement of a claim involving a child or protected party

14.22   In a claim by, or on behalf of, or against a child or protected party, no settlement, compromise or payment, and no acceptance of money paid into court, is valid without the court's approval (CPR, r. 21.10(1)). CPR, Part 21 invalidates a consent judgment involving a protected party reached without the appointment of a litigation friend and the approval of the court, even where the individual's lack of capacity was unknown to anyone acting for either party at the time of the compromise (*Dunhill v Burgin* [2014] UKSC 18, [2014] 1 WLR 933). Whether proceedings have been started or not, until a proposed settlement is approved by the court there is no binding contract, and either party may renege on it (*Dietz v Lennig Chemicals Ltd* [1969] 1 AC 170; *Drinkall v Whitwood* [2003] EWCA Civ 1547, [2004] 1 WLR 462). Rule 21.10(1) is intended to enable a defendant to obtain a valid discharge from a claim, and to ensure that any settlement etc. is fair on the child or protected party. The court will weigh the claimant's prospects of success against the likely level of damages, assuming full liability, and decide whether the proposed settlement etc. is in the interests of the child or protected party. Paragraphs 6.2 and 6.3 of PD 21 set out the procedure to be used where the parties have agreed that damages are to be paid periodically. The court must be supplied with an opinion on the merits from counsel or a solicitor, except in a very clear case, and a copy of any financial advice (PD 21, para. 6.4).

An application for approval of a settlement etc. in proceedings is made using the Part 23 procedure (see chapter 32). In the Chancery Division the application will be heard by a judge, not a Master, where the claim exceeds £100,000 or is in respect of absent, unborn or unascertained persons (PD 2B, para. 7B.2(a)). The court cannot use its power to vary or revoke an order under CPR, r. 3.1(7), to vary or revoke an approved settlement order as this would, in effect, permit a judge to hear an appeal from himself (*Roult v North West Strategic Health Authority* [2009] EWCA Civ 444, [2010] 1 WLR 487).

It is possible to bring proceedings solely for the purpose of obtaining the court's approval for a settlement of a claim before it has been issued. Court approval of a settlement reached in these circumstances is necessary to prevent a defendant repudiating the settlement at a later stage (*Drinkall v Whitwood* [2003] EWCA Civ 1547, [2004] 1 WLR 462). Such proceedings should be brought using the Part 8 procedure (see chapter 13) (CPR, r. 21.10(2); PD 8A, para. 3.1). For a summary of the approval procedure see procedural checklist 6. The Part 8 claim form should set out the details of the claim and request the court's approval of the settlement. A draft consent order in form N292 must be attached (PD 21, para. 5.1(1)). The court must satisfy itself that the parties have considered whether payment in instalments is appropriate (para. 5.4). Where periodic payments are included in the settlement, para. 5.5 sets out further information which the parties should provide.

PD 21, para. 5.1, sets out details of other information which must be included in the claim form. This includes whether and to what extent the defendant admits liability, the age and occupation (if any) of the child or protected party, the litigation friend's approval of the proposed settlement, a copy of any relevant financial advice, and, in a personal injury case arising from an accident, the circumstances of the accident, any medical reports, schedules of damages, and details of any relevant criminal proceedings. Except in very clear cases, a legal opinion on the merits of the settlement (including the instructions on which it is given) must be provided to the court (**para. 5.2**).

The apportionment of any claim brought on behalf of dependent children under the **Fatal Accidents Act 1976** must be approved by the court. See **PD 21, para. 7.4,** for the additional information which must be provided to the court in such a claim.

Where the only remedy which a claimant is seeking against a child or protected person is the payment of money, judgment cannot be entered by the claimant on an admission by the defendant (**CPR, r. 14.1(4)(a)**).

Where a child or protected person makes a claim in which the only remedy sought is the payment of money, judgment cannot be entered by the claimant on an admission if it is only an admission under **r. 14.5** of part of the claim for a specified amount or it is an admission under **r. 14.7** of liability for an unspecified amount with an offer of a sum in satisfaction (**r. 14.1(4)(b)**).

For limitations on default judgments see **14.17**.

When making an order approving a settlement, the court can also make an order under the Children and Young Persons Act 1933, s. 39, prohibiting any newspaper report of the proceedings from revealing the name, address or school attended by the child or the inclusion of any information that would lead to the identification of the child. This is regarded as being more acceptable than an anonymity order as it interferes less with the principle of open justice and freedom of expression. The court made such an order in *A (A child) v Cambridge University Hospitals NHS Foundation Trust* [2011] EWHC 454 (QB), [2011] EMLR 18. See also *U v Sarker* (2011) LTL 24/6/2011. In *X (A Child) v Dartford and Gravesham NHS Trust* [2015] EWCA Civ 96, [2015] 1 WLR 3647, the Court of Appeal held that when dealing with an application for approval of a settlement for damages for personal injury, the court should normally make an anonymity order in favour of the claimant prohibiting the publication of the names and addresses of the claimant, the immediate family and the litigation friend without the need for any formal application unless it is satisfied that it is unnecessary or inappropriate to do so. However, the press should be given the chance to make submissions before the order is made, and should normally have to file and serve on the applicant a statement of its case. The hearing should be listed in public, the press and public can be present and observe, and the parties and the press should be invited to make submissions before any anonymity order is made. The press should be free to report the decision of the court, subject to complying with the terms of the anonymity order. The judge should give reasons for making or declining to make an order, and make a copy of the judgment available to the press, on request, as soon as possible.

In relation to protected parties, a distinction must be drawn between ordinary civil proceedings in which a patient or protected party may be involved and proceedings about the compulsory powers of detention, care and treatment of such a person. There is no presumption of anonymity in every case. The question is always whether anonymity is necessary in the interests of the patient or protected party. In proceedings about compulsory powers, the starting point is anonymity, although this may be relaxed. A balance has to be struck between the public's right to know what is going on in court and whether the patient or protected party's treatment could be jeopardised if his or her identity is disclosed (*R (C) v Secretary of State for Justice* [2016] UKSC 2, [2016] 1 WLR 444). Reporting restrictions orders can extend beyond the death of the subject of those proceedings (*Re C (Deceased)* [2016] EWCOP 21, LTL 26/4/2016).

Commentary

Investment of money recovered for a child or protected party

14.23   Any money recovered by or on behalf of a child or protected party, including an accepted payment into court, may be dealt with only as directed by the court (**CPR, r. 21.11**). Before giving directions under **r. 21.11(2)** for the investment or otherwise of that money the court must consider whether the protected party is a protected beneficiary (**r. 21.11(3)**). This is a protected party who lacks capacity to manage and control money he or she recovers in the proceedings (**r. 21.1(2)(e)**). The court has power to appoint the Official Solicitor a guardian of a child's estate (**r. 21.13**). **Paragraphs 8** to **13** of **PD 21** set out details concerning how money recovered for a child or protected party should be applied.

In *Brennan v Eco Composting Ltd* [2006] EWHC 3153 (QB), [2007] 1 WLR 773, the court held that the claimant's entitlement to interest on money paid into court under CPR, old Part 36, which ran from the date of acceptance of the payment in, and no earlier, applied equally to parties under a disability even though the requirement for the payment in to be approved by the court inevitably delayed the date upon which the money could be accepted.

Control of litigation in mental health matters

14.24   The Mental Health Act 1983, s. 139(2), provides that no civil proceedings shall be brought against any person in any court in respect of any act purporting to have been done under the Act without the leave of the High Court. *Seal v Chief Constable of South Wales Police* [2007] UKHL 31, [2007] 1 WLR 1910, held that a failure to obtain leave under s. 139(2), before commencing proceedings based on police action in removing the claimant to a place of safety under s. 136 rendered the proceedings a nullity.

BANKRUPTCY

14.25   A bankrupt's estate becomes vested in the trustee in bankruptcy immediately on the trustee's appointment taking effect (Insolvency Act 1986, s. 306(1)). Property vests in the trustee without the need for any conveyance, assignment or transfer (s. 306(2)). By s. 283, a bankrupt's estate comprises all property belonging to or vested in the bankrupt at the commencement of the bankruptcy, and property which by virtue of the Insolvency Act 1986 is treated as belonging to the bankrupt. There are certain exceptions, such as tools and basic domestic belongings. By s. 436, 'property' includes money, goods, things in action, land and every description of property, and every description of interest in property. Consequently, most causes of action vested in an individual become vested in the trustee in bankruptcy once the trustee is appointed. Even in cases where a trustee in bankruptcy has not yet been appointed and therefore the assets remain vested in the bankrupt, the bankrupt has no interest in the assets and therefore no standing to make an application for a stay of execution pending an appeal (*Dadourian Group International Inc. v Simms* [2008] EWHC 723 (Ch), [2008] BPIR 508). However, personal claims, and in particular claims for defamation and personal injuries, remain vested in the bankrupt notwithstanding the appointment of a trustee in bankruptcy (*Heath v Tang* [1993] 1 WLR 1421), provided the claim is solely of a personal nature (*Ord v Upton* [2000] Ch 352). An appeal against self-assessment which had been settled by agreement between the trustee in bankruptcy and HMRC was not a personal right which remained vested in the bankrupt (*McNulty v Commissioners of HM Revenue & Customs* [2012] UKUT 174 (TCC), [2012] STC 2110). A bare right to appeal against tax assessments is not property within the meaning of s. 436. Adjudication of bankruptcy ends such a right, because the only assets out of which the underlying liability could be met vest in the trustee, not because the right to appeal is a chose in action that vests in the trustee. The trustee has a statutory right, but not an obligation, to exercise any right of appeal that the bankrupt had at the time of the bankruptcy order (*Re GP Aviation Group International Ltd* [2013] EWHC 1447 (Ch), [2014] 1 WLR 166).

Where a claim in negligence gives rise to heads of damage personal to the bankrupt (such as for pain, suffering and loss of amenity) and others which have vested in the trustee (such as for loss of earnings up to the date of discharge from bankruptcy or for loss of reputation), there is an indivisible cause of action and the whole cause of action vests in the trustee, who is therefore the proper claimant (*Ord v Upton* [2000] Ch 352). The trustee does not hold such a mixed cause of action on a bare trust for the bankrupt alone, but for the benefit of both the bankrupt and the creditors (*Mulkerrins v PricewaterhouseCoopers* [2001] BPIR 106, point not considered on appeal). However, in such a case the trustee will hold the damages recovered in respect of the personal heads on a constructive trust for the bankrupt (*Ord v Upton* [2000] Ch 352; see also *Simpson v Norfolk and Norwich University Hospital NHS Trust* [2011] EWCA Civ 1149, [2012] QB 640). A claim for damages for harassment is such a hybrid claim because it seeks both personal and non-personal loss, and where the damage occurred before the date of the bankruptcy, the whole claim will vest in the trustee. However, each further act of harassment after the date of the bankruptcy is a fresh cause of action which vests in the bankrupt (*Hayes v Butters* [2014] EWHC 4557 (Ch), [2015] Ch 495).

Where the trustee refuses to bring proceedings on a cause of action in which part of the damages will be held on trust for the bankrupt, one solution is for the bankrupt (after discharge) to negotiate an assignment of the cause of action from the trustee. It appears there may be jurisdiction for the court to give directions for such an assignment (*Smith and Williamson v Sims Pipes* (2000) LTL 17/3/2000). The bankrupt could also apply to the court under the Insolvency Act 1986, s. 303, for review of the trustee's decision.

For control of litigation against individuals subject to insolvency procedures, see **84.19** and **84.26** to **84.40**.

COMPANIES

A company registered under the Companies Act 2006 or an earlier Companies Act must sue and be sued using the full, registered company name. Where the company is in liquidation, the words '(in liquidation)' should be included in the heading. A company which is not required to end its name with 'Ltd' or 'plc' (or their Welsh equivalents) should be referred to by its name followed by an appropriate description, such as '(a company limited by guarantee)'. The full name of a foreign company should be followed, if helpful, by '(a company incorporated under the law of…)'.

14.26

The articles of association of a registered company usually confer on its directors a general power to manage the business of the company (see, for example, the Companies (Model Articles) Regulations 2008 (SI 2008/3229), sch. 1, art. 3 (private companies limited by shares), and sch. 3, art. 3 (public companies)). The power to litigate in the name of a company is part of this general power of management and so may be exercised by the directors, not the members (shareholders) (*John Shaw and Sons (Salford) Ltd v Shaw* [1935] 2 KB 113; *Breckland Group Holdings Ltd v London and Suffolk Properties Ltd* [1989] BCLC 100; *Mitchell and Hobbs (UK) Ltd v Mill* [1996] 2 BCLC 102). The members may be able to take a decision to litigate in the company's name only if there is no board of directors capable of acting (*Alexander Ward and Co. Ltd v Samyang Navigation Co. Ltd* [1975] 1 WLR 673).

If a company has more than one director, they must take decisions collectively. No one director has authority to act for the company unless the authority arises by implication from his office or the board has delegated authority in accordance with the company's constitution (*Smith v Butler* [2012] EWCA Civ 314, [2012] Bus LR 1836). All actions by the directors of a company must be taken in accordance with their duties to the company which are set out in the Companies Act 2006, ss. 171 to 177.

If directors of a company, in breach of their duty to the company, refuse to agree to it taking legal proceedings, the other directors, even if they do not have a majority of votes in directors' decision-making, may cause the proceedings to be brought in the company's name, and the court will treat the proceedings as properly authorised (*Fusion Interactive Communication Solutions Ltd v Venture Investment Placement Ltd (No. 2)* [2005] EWHC 736 (Ch), [2005] 2 BCLC 571). Alternatively,

Commentary

assuming that the directors who are blocking proceedings cannot be removed from office, a member of the company may:

(a) commence the proceedings as a derivative claim under the Companies Act 2006, ss. 260 to 264 (see **14.27**); or

(b) petition under s. 996 on the ground that the failure to bring the proceedings is unfairly prejudicial conduct of the company's affairs (see **85.9** to **85.20**); or

(c) apply to the court, under the Senior Courts Act 1981, s. 37(1) and (2), for the appointment of a receiver of the company's cause of action.

If a company is in administration, or an administrative receiver has been appointed, the administrator or receiver has a power to bring or defend any claim in the name and on behalf of the company (Insolvency Act 1986, s. 42, sch. B1, para. 60, and sch. 1, para. 5). During administration, any power of the company or its officers, including the power to litigate, that could be exercised in such a way as to interfere with the administrator's exercise of his or her powers is not exercisable except with the consent of the administrator (sch. B1, para. 64).

In *Newhart Developments Ltd v Cooperative Commercial Bank Ltd* [1978] QB 814 it was held that the appointment of a receiver does not divest the directors of their power to institute proceedings in the company's name, provided they do not interfere with the receiver's work of realising the charged assets (cf. *Shanks v Central Regional Council* 1987 SLT 410, affirmed 1988 SLT 212). In *Tudor Grange Holdings Ltd v Citibank NA* [1992] Ch 53 Browne-Wilkinson V-C said that he had substantial doubts that *Newhart Developments Ltd v Cooperative Commercial Bank Ltd* was correctly decided, and thought that, at present, it should only be followed in cases where, as in the *Newhart Developments* case, the directors proposing litigation undertook to meet any award of costs against the company if the litigation should fail. In *Sutton v GE Capital Commercial Finance Ltd* [2004] EWCA Civ 315, [2004] 2 BCLC 662, the Court of Appeal, following the *Newhart Developments* case, held that it was open to the company, acting by its directors, to bring proceedings notwithstanding the appointment of administrative receivers, so long as the proceedings did not impinge prejudicially on the position of the debenture holder.

It is likely that directors do have power to bring proceedings in the company's name to challenge the appointment of the receiver, sue the receiver for breach of duty, or oppose a petition to wind up the company (*Watts v Midland Bank plc* [1986] BCLC 15; *Re Reprographic Exports (Euromat) Ltd* (1978) 122 SJ 400). The directors also retain their office notwithstanding the appointment of a receiver, and they retain their powers and functions in relation to the assets which are not under the control of the receiver, provided this does not prejudice the course of the receivership.

If a company is in voluntary liquidation, its liquidator has a power to bring or defend any claim in the name and on behalf of the company (Insolvency Act 1986, s. 165(3) and sch. 4, para. 4), but in a compulsory liquidation (a winding up by the court) the liquidator must obtain the permission of the court or of the liquidation committee (Insolvency Act 1986, s. 167(l)(a) and sch. 4, para. 4).

For control of litigation against companies subject to insolvency proceedings see **84.19** to **84.25** and **84.30** to **84.40**.

Derivative claims

14.27   Normally, it is not possible for a company's rights to be enforced in proceedings brought in the name of a member of the company (*Foss v Harbottle* (1843) 2 Hare 461), because the company is the proper claimant to enforce its own rights. As an exception to this proper claimant principle, a court may permit proceedings in the name of a member of the company if the company will not commence a claim. The member's claim derives from the company's cause of action and is called a 'derivative claim', which is defined in the Companies Act 2006, s. 260(1), as a proceeding by a member of a company:

(a) in respect of a cause of action vested in the company, and

(b) seeking relief on behalf of the company.

In this provision, 'member' includes a person to whom shares in the company have been transferred, or have been transmitted by operation of law (that is, to a personal representative of a deceased member or the trustee of a bankrupt member), but who is not a member of the company (because of not being registered as the holder of the shares) (s. 260(5)(c)).

A derivative claim may be brought only under the Companies Act 2006, part 11, chapter 1 (ss. 260 to 264), or in pursuance of a court order under s. 996(2)(c) (protection of members against unfair prejudice) (s. 260(2)). The procedure on a derivative claim is governed by **CPR, rr. 19.9 to 19.9F**, but those rules do not apply to a claim authorised by the court under the Companies Act 2006, s. 996(2)(c) (**CPR, r. 19.9(1)(b)**). A derivative claim must be commenced by claim form (**r. 19.9(2)**), which must be headed 'Derivative claim' (**PD 19C, para. 2(1)**). The company must be joined as a co-defendant so that if its rights are vindicated it will be able to enforce the judgment (**CPR, r. 19.9(3)**). Other reasons why the company must be named as a co-defendant in a derivative claim are in order for it to be bound by any judgment (otherwise it could bring its own proceedings in respect of the same wrong), to receive the fruits (if any) of the judgment, and because the claim has not been authorised by its board or general meeting (*Roberts v Gill and Co.* [2010] UKSC 22, [2011] 1 AC 240 at [57]). It is not a requirement that the delinquent director should have profited or benefited from his misconduct.

A statutory derivative claim under the Companies Act 2006, ss. 260 to 264, may be brought only in respect of a cause of action specified in s. 260. The cause of action must be vested in the company (s. 260(1)). It must arise from an actual or proposed act or omission which involves negligence, default, breach of duty or breach of trust by a director, former director or shadow director of the company (s. 260(3) and (5)(a) and (b)). The cause of action may be against the director, or another person or both (s. 260(3)). It may have arisen before the claimant became a member of the company (s. 260(4)).

A member of a company who brings a statutory derivative claim under ss. 260 to 264 must apply to the court for permission to continue it (s. 261(1)). Section 263 gives guidance on how the court should approach deciding whether to give permission. The principal matters to be taken into account are:

(a) the good faith of the derivative claimant (s. 263(3)(a));
(b) the importance that a person acting in accordance with the duty to promote the success of the company would attach to continuing it (s. 263(3)(b));
(c) whether there has been, or could be, authorisation or ratification of the act or omission giving rise to the claim (s. 263(2)(b) and (c) and (3)(c) and (d));
(d) whether the company has decided not to pursue the claim (s. 263(3)(e));
(e) whether the claim is one which the member could pursue in his own right rather than on behalf of the company (s. 263(3)(f));
(f) the views of disinterested members (s. 263(4));
(g) whether the claim would promote the company's success (s. 263(2)(a) and (3)(b)).

The fact that the claimant's primary motivation is to enhance the value of its own shareholding rather than the prosperity of the company does not show that it is acting in bad faith. Permission to continue a derivative claim may be refused if appropriate remedies could be obtained by pursuing an unfair prejudice petition under s. 994 (*Franbar Holdings Ltd v Patel* [2008] EWHC 1534 (Ch), [2009] 1 BCLC 1; *Stimpson v Southern Private Landlords Association* [2009] EWHC 2072 (Ch), [2010] BCC 387; *Kleanthous v Paphitis* [2011] EWHC 2287 (Ch), LTL 21/9/2011), but this is not inevitable, particularly where the applicant is not seeking to be bought out (see *Wishart v Castlecroft Securities Ltd* [2009] CSIH 65, 2010 SC 16; *Stainer v Lee* [2010] EWHC 1539 (Ch), [2011] 1 BCLC 537). There is no need for a derivative claim if the persons bringing it could bring a private claim for their own loss and the claim cannot be regarded as a corporate asset (*Certain Limited Partners in Henderson PFI Secondary Fund II LLP v Henderson PFI Secondary Fund LP* [2012] EWHC 3259 (Comm), LTL 23/11/2012). The court may allow a derivative claim to continue even if a shareholder cannot show that the director's actions did not give rise to a cause of action which the company could pursue in its own right

Commentary

but the derivative claim is being brought as a reasonable response to the defence put forward by the director in the personal claim which the shareholder had brought against him (*Cullen Investments Ltd v Brown* [2015] EWHC 473 (Ch), [2016] 1 BCLC 491). Although it cannot be said that it would never be appropriate for a derivative claim to be brought by a majority shareholder in control of a company, permission to do so would be given only in very exceptional circumstances and it is difficult to imagine what those might be (*Cinematic Finance Ltd v Ryder* [2010] EWHC 3387 (Ch), LTL 21/10/2010). A derivative claim can be brought and may be allowed to continue where the applicant and proposed respondent are each 50 per cent shareholders in the company (*Parry v Bartlett* [2011] EWHC 3146 (Ch), LTL 11/1/2012). An unfair prejudice petition can be brought where a director and shareholder has been unfairly excluded from management of a company which was run as a quasi-partnership and there has been no offer to acquire his shares at a fair value (*Re J and S Insurance and Financial Consultants Ltd* [2014] EWHC 2206 (Ch), LTL 9/7/2014). Although there is no rule that a derivative claim can only be brought where the alleged wrongdoers remain in control, the potential of the company itself to commence proceedings was a relevant consideration. An application for permission to continue a derivative claim may be refused if a procedure exists for instituting a claim on the company's behalf under a company's shareholder agreement (*Bamford v Harvey* [2012] EWHC 2858 (Ch), [2013] Bus LR 589).

The court may take into account other factors, but must pay particular regard to the listed factors (*Franbar Holdings Ltd v Patel*). In *Kiani v Cooper* [2010] EWHC 577 (Ch), [2010] 2 BCLC 427, the court granted permission to continue a derivative claim where the director alleged to be in breach of fiduciary duty had failed to produce any evidence which corroborated his defence to the allegations against him (see also *Phillips v Fryer* [2013] BCC 176). Although it was possible for the applicant to bring a petition under the Companies Act 2006, s. 994, instead of the derivative claim, the existence of this alternative remedy was only one factor which the court should consider. A notional director, acting in accordance with his duties under s. 172 of the Act, would wish to continue with the claim, at least to the stage of disclosure, where corroborative documents might be produced by the respondent. In contrast, in *Kleanthous v Paphitis* [2011] EWHC 2287 (Ch), LTL 21/9/2011, the court refused permission to allow the derivative claim to continue as it was not of such a size and strength (there being a number of limitation and other difficulties) to make it appropriate to grant permission when this was opposed by the companies and the applicant could obtain his preferred remedy (a share buy-out) by the more appropriate course of an Unfair Prejudice petition under the Companies Act, s. 994.

Section 263(3)(b) asks the court to take into account, in particular, the importance that a person (called, in the cases, the 'hypothetical director') acting in accordance with s. 172 (duty to promote the success of the company) would attach to continuing the claim. Section 263(2)(a) requires the court to refuse permission if satisfied the hypothetical director would not seek to continue the claim. The claimant does not have to show that the hypothetical director would undoubtedly continue the claim (*Franbar Holdings Ltd v Patel*). If the hypothetical director would not attach much importance to the claim, permission to continue it will be refused (*Mission Capital plc v Sinclair* [2008] EWHC 1339 (Ch), [2008] BCC 866; *Iesini v Westrip Holdings Ltd* [2009] EWHC 2526 (Ch), [2011] 1 BCLC 498; *Stimpson v Southern Private Landlords Association*; *Bridge v Daley* [2015] EWHC 2121 (Ch), LTL 24/8/2015).

The relationship between s. 263(2)(a) and s. 263(3)(b) was considered in *Iesini v Westrip Holdings Ltd*. Section 263(2)(a) applies only where the court is satisfied that no director acting in accordance with s. 172 would seek to continue the claim. If some directors would, and others would not, seek to continue the claim, then s. 263(3)(b) should be applied, when many of the same considerations will apply.

Permission must be refused where the cause of action arises from an act or omission yet to occur, and that act or omission has been ratified by the company, or is in relation to past acts or omissions which were authorised by the company before they occurred or have been subsequently ratified by the company (s. 263(2)(b) and (c)). The court, applying the mandatory bar in s. 263(2)(c), refused permission to continue a derivative claim against a fellow director and shareholder in respect of excessive dividend and remuneration payments on the grounds that these had either been authorised by the company before they were made or effectively ratified afterwards as the payments were recorded in the accounts which were signed off each year by the board of directors. The real motivation behind the claim was animosity between the parties following a family dispute, and that also justified a refusal of permission under s. 263(3)(a) (*Re Singh Brothers Contractors (North West) Ltd* [2013] EWHC 2138 (Ch), LTL 22/8/2013; [2014] EWCA Civ 103; see also *Brannigan v Style* [2016] EWHC 512 (Ch), LTL 3/2/2016, where permission was refused where the shareholders had ratified a director's conduct by written resolution).

Section 261 requires the court to consider an application for permission to continue a derivative claim in two stages. At the first stage it considers only the evidence presented by the claimant and must dismiss the application if this evidence does not disclose a prima facie case for giving permission (s. 261(2)). The prima facie case to which s. 261(1) refers is a prima facie case for giving permission. There must be a prima facie case that the company has a good cause of action and that cause of action arises out of a director's default, negligence, breach of duty or breach of trust (*Iesini v Westrip Holdings Ltd*). If the court decides that there is a prima facie case, it will give directions for evidence to be provided by the company and for a contested hearing of the application (s. 261(3)). Both stages may be taken together if the parties agree (*Mission Capital plc v Sinclair*; *Franbar Holdings Ltd v Patel*).

In *Stainer v Lee* [2010] EWHC 1539 (Ch), [2011] 1 BCLC 537, the court considered the standard to be applied when considering the provisional merits of the cause of action against the respondents. If the case seemed very strong, it might be appropriate to continue it even if the sums at stake were not large, as such a claim is likely to be settled or result in summary judgment being awarded. On the other hand if the sums at stake were very large, it might be in the company's interests for the claim to be continued even if the court formed the provisional view that the claim was not a strong one. See also *Hughes v Weiss* [2012] EWHC 2363 (Ch), LTL 28/9/2012. A derivative claim may be permitted to continue where the respondent directors fail to produce a convincing explanation in defence to the allegations raised against them (*Philips v Fryer* [2013] BCC 176). In ascertaining whether there is a prima facie case, the court cannot resolve factual disputes at a hearing which does not involve cross-examination of the witnesses. In some cases, a prima facie case may be established if the defendant's evidence is ignored, but would fail at trial if the defendant's evidence is accepted. In such a case, it is still open to the court to hold that the claimant had established a prima facie case because it might not be possible to predict whether the defendant's evidence would be accepted at the trial, and it would be wrong to assume that it would be accepted (*Bhullar v Bhullar* [2015] EWHC 1943 (Ch), [2016] 1 BCLC 106).

When the claim form for a derivative claim is issued, the claimant must file an application notice under **CPR, Part 23**, for permission to continue the claim, together with written evidence in support (Companies Act 2006, s. 261(1); **CPR, r. 19.9A(2)**). The claimant must not take any further step in the proceedings (other than pursuing the permission application) without the court's permission, except for an urgent application for interim relief (r. 19.9(4)).

At the first stage the company must not be made a respondent to the permission application (**r. 19.9A(3)**) but must be given notice of it in accordance with **r. 19.9A(4), (5) and (6)**, and **PD 19C, para. 4**. A witness statement must be filed by the claimant confirming that the company has been notified (**r. 19.9A(6)**). The court may, on a without-notice application by the claimant, order that the company need not be notified of the permission application, if notification would be likely to frustrate some part of the remedy sought (**r. 19.9A(7) and (8)**). An application for an order under **r. 19.9A(7)** must state the reasons for the application and any written evidence in support must be filed with it (**PD 19C, para. 3**).

A permission application in the High Court is assigned to the Chancery Division and will be decided by a judge. In the County Court it will be decided by a Circuit Judge (**PD 19C, para. 6**).

At the first stage, the court must dismiss the permission application if it appears that the application and the supporting evidence do not disclose a prima facie case for giving permission (Companies Act 2006, s. 261(2)). A permission application may be dismissed on this basis without a hearing (**CPR, r. 19.9A(9)**), but if it is, the claimant may, within seven days of being notified of the decision, request an oral hearing to reconsider it (**r. 19.9A(10)**). Such a request must be in writing and must be notified to the company in writing, unless the court orders otherwise (**r. 19.9A(10)**).

A decision at the first stage will normally be made without submissions from the company. If, without invitation by the court, the company volunteers a submission, or appears at an oral hearing, it will not normally be allowed its costs (**PD 19C, para. 5**).

If the court does not dismiss for failure to disclose a prima facie case, it will order that the company, and any other appropriate party, must be made respondents to the application, and give directions for service (**CPR, r. 19.9A(12)**) so that there can be a full hearing.

On a full hearing, the court may give permission to continue the derivative claim on such terms as it thinks fit, or refuse permission and dismiss the claim, or adjourn the proceedings and give such directions as it thinks fit (Companies Act 2006, s. 261(4)).

A person making a derivative claim on behalf of a company may seek indemnification by the company for the costs of the claim (**CPR, r. 19.9E**; see **44.15**). For an example see *Stainer v Lee* [2010] EWHC 1539 (Ch), [2011] 1 BCLC 537.

If a claim vested in a company arises out of facts which also disclose unfairly prejudicial conduct of the company's affairs, a petition by a member under the Companies Act 2006, s. 994 (see **85.9** to **85.20**), may be used as an alternative to a derivative claim (*Re a Company (No. 005287 of 1985)* [1986] 1 WLR 281; *Lowe v Fahey* [1996] 1 BCLC 262; *Clark v Cutland* [2003] EWCA Civ 810, [2004] 1 WLR 783).

The proper claimant principle applies to any association which is capable of suing or being sued in its own name, and **CPR, r. 19.9**, is expressed to apply not only to companies but also to other bodies corporate and trade unions (**r. 19.9(1)(a)** and **r. 19.9C**). A derivative claim may be brought in relation to a foreign company as well as a company incorporated in England and Wales. However, the appropriate forum for such a claim is likely to be the country of incorporation (*Konamaneni v Rolls-Royce Industrial Power (India) Ltd* [2002] 1 WLR 1269; *Music Sales Ltd v Shapiro Bornstein and Co. Inc.* [2005] EWHC 759 (Ch), [2006] 1 BCLC 371; *Reeves v Sprecher* [2007] EWHC 117 (Ch), [2007] 2 BCLC 614; see **16.57**). See also *Novatrust Ltd v Kea Investments Ltd* [2014] EWHC 4061 (Ch), LTL 5/1/2015.

A derivative claim can also be brought in respect of a limited partnership. However, there was no need for a derivative claim to be made by limited partners against the general partner of a limited partnership where the claim was not a partnership asset and each limited partner had its own claim for its own loss. However, a claim against the manager of the partnership was a partnership asset and could not be pursued by any limited partner individually. It was just to allow the derivative claim to be brought because the partnership had no realistic prospects of obtaining redress by any other route (*Certain Limited Partners in Henderson PFI Secondary Fund II LLP v Henderson PFI Secondary Fund LP* [2012] EWHC 3259 (Comm), LTL 23/11/2012).

Derivative claims may also be made by beneficiaries of a trust or beneficiaries under a will. However, a beneficiary under a will may bring a derivative claim only if the circumstances of the case are sufficiently special to make it just for the beneficiary to have the remedy rather than the personal representatives. If a beneficiary is entitled to bring a derivative claim, the personal representatives should also be joined at the outset of the proceedings (*Roberts v Gill and Co.* [2010] UKSC 22, [2011] 1 AC 240). See also *Bayley v SG Associates* [2014] EWHC 782 (Ch), [2014] WTLR 1315, where it was held that a derivative claim by the beneficiaries of a trust could be available against an adviser who provided investment advice to the trustees, where it was difficult for the trustee to act or he refused to act.

The court can entertain a derivative claim even if it does not fall within the provisions of the Companies Act 1996, s. 260, for example because it is a multiple derivative claim (*Re Fort*

Gilkicker Ltd [2013] EWHC 348 (Ch), [2013] Ch 551). However, the claimant must show a prima facie entitlement to the relief sought, and that the claim falls within an exception to the rule in *Foss v Harbottle* (1843) 2 Hare 461. Even if these hurdles can be satisfied, the court will not allow the derivative claim procedure to be used for an improper purpose, such as allowing a claimant to use his shareholding in a parent company to advance his interests as a creditor of a wholly owned subsidiary, thereby providing him with a means of enforcement that would not be available to other creditors (*Abouraya v Sigmund* [2014] EWHC 277 (Ch), [2015] BCC 503).

Continuation of a company's claim as a derivative claim or of a derivative claim with a different claimant

If those with authority to conduct a company's litigation fear a derivative claim, they may try to block it by causing the company to bring a claim but with no intention of genuinely pursuing it. The Companies Act 2006, s. 262, therefore permits a member of a company to apply to the court for permission to take over a claim brought by the company and continue it as a derivative claim on the grounds that:

14.28

(a) the manner in which the company commenced or continued the claim amounts to an abuse of the process of the court;
(b) the company has failed to prosecute the claim diligently; and
(c) it is appropriate for the member to continue the claim as a derivative claim.

There is a similar provision in s. 264 for an existing derivative claim to be taken over by a new claimant on the same grounds.

An application for permission under s. 262 or s. 264 follows the same two-stage process as an application under s. 261 (see **14.27**). **CPR, r. 19.9B**, applies **r. 19.9A** with necessary modifications.

Permission to continue a derivative claim may be given on condition that the claim is not to be discontinued, settled or compromised without the court's permission (**r. 19.9F**). This will be appropriate to ensure that other members of the company are given an opportunity to continue the derivative claim themselves (**PD 19C, para. 7**).

Reflective loss

It follows from the proper claimant principle (**14.27**) that a member holding shares in a company cannot claim any compensation for the diminution in value of those shares which merely reflects a loss which the company could recover (the 'no reflective loss principle'). The diminution in value of the shares due to the company's loss will be reversed when the company recovers compensation for that loss (*Prudential Assurance Co. Ltd v Newman Industries Ltd (No. 2)* [1982] Ch 204 at pp. 222–3; *Johnson v Gore Wood and Co.* [2002] 2 AC 1; *Norcross v Georgallides* [2015] EWHC 1290 (Comm), LTL 21/5/2015). A member of the company also cannot sue for any other losses which merely reflect losses which the company could recover, such as lost dividends and any other payments which the shareholder might have obtained from the company if it had not been deprived of its funds, including payments which might have been made in the shareholder's capacity as an officer or employee of the company. See also *Webster v Sandersons Solicitors* [2009] EWCA Civ 830, [2009] 2 BCLC 542.

14.29

The no reflective loss principle ensures that a defendant can only be sued once for the same loss. It prevents a person other than the company suing even if that person has a cause of action against the defendant and even if that cause of action differs from the company's (*Day v Cook* [2001] EWCA Civ 592, [2002] 1 BCLC 1 at [79]). It applies whether the cause of action lies in common law or equity, and whether the remedy is damages or restitution (*Gardner v Parker* [2004] EWCA Civ 781, [2004] 2 BCLC 554). It applies to prevent a member suing whether the member has a controlling or a minority interest (*Gardner v Parker*, rejecting doubts expressed in *Humberclyde Finance Group Ltd v Hicks* (2001) LTL 19/11/2001 and in *Floyd v John Fairhurst and Co.* [2004] EWCA Civ 604, [2004] PNLR 41 at [77]). See also *Mellor v Partridge* [2013] EWCA Civ 477, LTL 3/5/2013 and *Bank Mellat v HM Treasury* [2016] EWCA Civ 452, LTL 10/5/2016.

The no reflective loss principle is not an infringement of the European Convention on Human Rights, **protocol 1, art. 1** (protection of property), in the **Human Rights Act 1998, sch. 1** (*Humberclyde Finance Group Ltd v Hicks* (2001) LTL 19/11/2001).

Practice relating to reflective loss

14.30   If a company with a right to sue a person, D, to recover a loss fails to recover all or part of that loss, for example because it settles the claim before trial, or refuses to take any action at all, then all or part of members' reflective losses will not be recovered. This does not give the members a right to sue D for the unrecovered amount of the reflective losses, because the shortfall in recovery is caused by the company, not D (*Johnson v Gore Wood and Co.* [2002] 2 AC 1). There is an exception if it is D's wrongdoing which has caused the company to be unable to sue, for example because that wrongdoing has left it without enough money to fund litigation (*Giles v Rhind* [2002] EWCA Civ 1428, [2003] Ch 618).

The mere fact that D has caused a company to suffer loss does not give a holder of shares in that company a right of action to sue for the diminution in share value resulting from that loss. However, it is possible for a company to suffer loss because of something done by D but have no right of action against D while a shareholder does have a right of action against D. In such a case, the shareholder is permitted to claim for loss in value of the shareholding due to a loss which the company itself has no cause of action to recover (*George Fischer (Great Britain) Ltd v Multi Construction Ltd* [1995] 1 BCLC 260; *Gerber Garment Technology Inc. v Lectra Systems Ltd* [1997] RPC 443).

It is possible, when both company and shareholder have causes of action against the same defendant, that some of the shareholder's claims are not for reflective losses and can be pursued by the shareholder personally (see, for example, *R. P. Howard Ltd v Woodman Matthews and Co.* [1983] BCLC 117; *Giles v Rhind*). A secured debenture holder's claim against an administrative receiver it had appointed over the company did not offend the rule against reflective loss. The administrative receiver's primary duty was to the appointing debenture holder and not the company. A secured debenture holder's position was different to that of a shareholder who sought to sue for loss suffered by a company (*International Leisure Ltd v First National Trustee Co UK Ltd* [2012] EWHC 1971 (Ch), [2013] Ch 346).

It has been suggested that a defendant applying to strike out a claim, on the ground that it reflects a loss which a company could have sued for, but did not, must show that the supposed claim by the company would have been likely to succeed (*Perry v Day* [2004] EWHC 1398 (Ch), LTL 18/6/2004, per Rimer J at [65]).

By analogy with the no reflective loss principle, if a defendant's wrongful act is found to have caused both a loss to a claimant and a gain to a company in which the claimant is a shareholder, the claimant's loss and the company's gain must be set off, at least where the claimant effectively owns all the shares in the company (*Floyd v John Fairhurst and Co.* [2004] EWCA Civ 604, [2004] PNLR 41).

If a company has been injured by a breach of the European Convention on Human Rights, a member of the company is not a victim of that breach and so has no standing to apply to the European Court of Human Rights or to bring proceedings under the **Human Rights Act 1998, s. 7** (*Agrotexim v Greece* (application 14807/89) (1995) 21 EHRR 250; *Weir v Secretary of State for Transport* [2005] EWHC 2192 (Ch), LTL 14/10/2005 at [294] to [298]). The European Court of Human Rights has, however, allowed a form of derivative claim, in which a member of a company presents an application in the company's name, where it is clear that it is not possible for those responsible for the company's litigation to make the application (*Credit and Industrial Bank v Czech Republic* (application 29010/95) ECHR 2003-XI at [46] to [52]).

PARTNERSHIPS

Name

14.31   By **PD 7A, para. 5A.3,** claims by and against partners carrying on business within the jurisdiction at the time when the cause of action accrued must be brought in the partnership name, unless it is inappropriate to do so (as to which, no guidance is provided). The name to be used is that at the date of accrual of the cause of action, not at the date when proceedings are issued. For the purpose of para. 5A, 'partners' includes persons claiming to be entitled as partners and persons alleged to be partners (**para. 5A.2**). Partners in a firm which was not carrying on business in England and Wales at the time the cause of action accrued may only sue or be sued individually in their own names.

Where partners are being sued in the name of the partnership the full name of the partnership and the words '(A Firm)' should appear in the title of the claim. Where they are being sued as individuals, the full unabbreviated name of each partner and the title by which he is known should appear (**PD 16, para. 2.6**). It is arguable that bringing proceedings against a named partner and also against the firm in which he was a partner at the relevant time is an irregularity because the partner is effectively being sued twice in the same claim (*Brown v Innovatorone plc* [2009] EWHC 1376 (Comm), [2010] 2 All ER (Comm) 80 at [12]).

Disclosure of partners' names

Any party to a claim may serve a request asking for the partners to provide a partnership membership statement, providing details of the names and last known places of residence of all the partners at the time when the cause of action accrued (**PD 7A, paras. 5B.1** and **5B.2**). It is for the party making the request to specify the date when the relevant cause of action accrued (**para. 5B.3**). If the partners are requested to provide a copy of the partnership membership statement by any party to the claim, the partners must do so within 14 days of receipt of the request (**PD 7A, para. 5B.2**). However, presumably an application for disclosure could be made under **CPR, Part 23**. **14.32**

Enforcement of a judgment debt against partnership property is dealt with at **79.45**.

Limited liability partnerships

A limited liability partnership is a body corporate with legal personality separate from that of its members (Limited Liability Partnerships Act 2000, s. 1(2)). It should be sued in its full registered name, including the expression 'limited liability partnership' or the abbreviation 'llp' or LLP' (or their Welsh equivalents), which must be at the end of the registered name (Limited Liability Partnerships Act 2000, sch. 1, para. 2). **14.33**

SOLE TRADERS

By **PD 7A, para. 5C**, where a claim is brought against an individual carrying on business in the jurisdiction under a business name, the claim may be brought against the business name as if it were the name of a partnership. The provision therefore enables proceedings to be issued against a business even if the name of the person running it is not known. However, if the full name of the sole trader is known, the claim form should state the individual's full unabbreviated name and title, and the full trading name (for example, John Smith trading as (or T/as) JS Autos) (**PD 16, para. 2.6(b)**). **14.34**

OTHER INCORPORATED AND UNINCORPORATED ASSOCIATIONS

Building societies

A building society must be incorporated under the Building Societies Act 1986 and can sue or be sued in its corporate name. **14.35**

Charities

14.36   A charitable corporation, which may sue or be sued in its own name, may be created in a number of ways: by royal charter, by the Charity Commission under the Charities Act 2011, as a registered society, or as a company or community interest company registered at Companies House. Part 11 of the Charities Act 2011 contains provisions for the constitution and registration of charitable incorporated organisations (CIOs). These provisions came into force on 2 January 2013. Where a CIO is constituted and entered on the register of charities maintained by the Charity Commission under Part 4 of the Charities Act 2011, it becomes, by virtue of the registration, a body corporate (Charities Act 2011, s. 210).

Where a charitable institution is unincorporated, proceedings may be brought against it by suing an officer of the charity 'on behalf of the charity [naming it]'. Alternatively, the charity's trustees may be named as parties (*Muman v Nagasena* [2000] 1 WLR 299).

Proceedings under the court's jurisdiction with respect to charities, or with respect to trusts in relation to the administration of a trust for charitable purposes, cannot be brought without the permission of the Charity Commission (Charities Act 2011, s. 115). The Commission will not give permission without special reasons if, in its opinion, it can deal with the matter itself under the 2011 Act (s. 115(3)). If the Commission refuses to give permission, it may be given instead by a judge of the Chancery Division (s. 115(5)). Proceedings commenced without the permission of the court or the Charity Commission will be stayed pending a decision on permission (*Choudhury v Stepney Shahjalal Mosque and Cultural Centre Ltd* [2015] EWHC 743 (Ch), LTL 16/2/2015). For the approach to be followed in applications for permission under s. 115(5), see *Rai v Charity Commission for England and Wales* [2012] EWHC 1111 (Ch), [2012] WTLR 1053. It was not appropriate to grant permission for proceedings to continue where the claim had no real prospect of success and was likely to result in the demise of the charity, which had limited resources (*Rosenzweig v NMC Recordings Ltd* [2013] EWHC 3792 (Ch), [2014] PTSR 261). These rules do not apply to proceedings brought by the Commission itself or by the Attorney General (s. 115(6)).

Applications to the High Court to start charity proceedings, following refusal by the Charity Commission to authorise them, must be brought in accordance with **CPR, Part 64**. Although **CPR, Part 64** continues to refer to the repealed Charities Act 1993, this should be construed as a reference to the Charities Act 2011. An application for permission to start charity proceedings must be made within 21 days after the Commission's refusal to do so (**r. 64.6**). The application is made by issuing a Part 8 claim form, containing the information specified in **PD 64A, para. 9.1**. The Commission must be made a defendant to the claim, and the judge may direct it to file a written statement of the reasons for its decision (**CPR, r. 64.6**). If the Commission has given reasons, a copy of those reasons must be filed with the claim form (**PD 64A, para. 9.2**). The judge may give permission without a hearing or fix a hearing (**r. 64.6(6)**). The Attorney General is a necessary party to all charity proceedings, other than any commenced by the Charity Commission, and must be joined as a defendant if he or she is not the claimant (**PD 64A, para. 7**).

An appeal against an order or decision of the Charity Commission is to the First-tier Tribunal or the Upper Tribunal in accordance with the Charities Act 2011, part 17. The reference in **PD 64A, para. 10**, to appeals to the Court of Appeal is no longer correct.

Trade unions and employers' associations

14.37   A trade union which is not a special register body under the Trade Union and Labour Relations (Consolidation) Act 1992, s. 117, is not a body corporate. However, even if unincorporated, a trade union is capable of suing or being sued in its own name (Trade Union and Labour Relations (Consolidation) Act 1992, s. 10(1)(b)). It may not, however, unless it is a special register body and therefore a body corporate, sue in its own name for damages for defamation. This is because a libel is a wrong to the person and therefore no claim may be brought unless the trade union has a legal personality (*Electrical, Electronic, Telecommunication and Plumbing Union v Times Newspapers Ltd* [1980] QB 585).

An employers' association may be either a body corporate or an unincorporated association. However, even where unincorporated, it may sue or be sued in its own name (Trade Union and Labour Relations (Consolidation) Act 1992, s. 127(2)(b)).

Central government departments

Most central government departments may sue or be sued in their own name: see **14.44** to **14.46**.   **14.38**

Local government bodies

London boroughs (London Government Act 1963, s. 1), metropolitan districts and non-metropolitan counties and districts (Local Government Act 1972, s. 2) are bodies corporate, and may sue or be sued by name.   **14.39**

A local authority (which includes a county council, a district council, a London borough council and a parish council: Local Government Act 1972, s. 270) may institute civil proceedings where it considers it expedient for the promotion or protection of the interests of the inhabitants of its area (Local Government Act 1972, s. 222).

Quasi-governmental public bodies

There are numerous quasi-governmental public bodies which are not formal departments of State. These bodies will usually have an implicit power to bring proceedings to protect their special interests in the performance of their functions (*Broadmoor Special Health Authority v Robinson* [2000] QB 775). See also *R v Rollins* [2010] UKSC 39, [2010] 1 WLR 1922.   **14.40**

Clubs

An unincorporated members' social or sporting club is not a separate legal entity and may not sue or be sued in the name of the club. Thus, in *Oxford University v Webb* [2006] EWHC 2490 (QB), LTL 20/10/2006, it was held that the Animal Liberation Front, an unincorporated association, could not sue or be sued in its own name because it was not a legal person. It could only be joined through representative proceedings under **CPR, r. 19.6**. Nor can the secretary or any other officer of such a club sue or be sued on behalf of the club. Where proceedings are necessary, there are two main options: **14.41**

(a) Bring proceedings against individual members of the club. However, members who are not made parties will have no direct interest in the claim, and any judgment obtained may not be enforced against them.

(b) Bring representative proceedings (see **14.62**) (*Campbell v Thompson* [1953] 1 QB 445; *Artistic Upholstery Ltd v Art Forma (Furniture) Ltd* [1999] 4 All ER 277). A judgment in a representative action binds the members represented, but may not be enforced against any member who is not a party to the proceedings, without the court's permission.

A proprietary club is one where the property and funds of the club belong to the proprietor, who usually conducts it with a view to profit. Where such a club is unincorporated, the proprietor may sue or be sued, either in his or her own name or in the name of the club (*Firmin and Sons Ltd v International Club* (1889) 5 TLR 694). Where it is incorporated, it should sue and be sued in its corporate name.

A costs order against 'London Animal Action', an unincorporated association, was enforced against a bank account in the association's name by a third party debt order. An appeal by London Animal Action, arguing that an order can only be enforced against persons with legal identity, was rejected (*Huntingdon Life Sciences Group plc v Cass* [2005] EWHC 2233 (QB), [2005] 4 All ER 899).

TRUSTS AND TRUSTEES

14.42 A claim by or against a trust is brought by joining its trustees. Trustees should act jointly and all should be named in any proceedings (as defendants, if they will not consent to act as claimants).

It is provided in **CPR, r. 19.7A**, that beneficiaries need not be joined as parties to a claim brought by or against a trust. Any judgment or order made in the claim will bind the beneficiaries unless the court orders otherwise. The predecessor to this rule (RSC, ord. 15, r. 14(1)) empowered the court to order otherwise only because the trustees could not or did not represent the beneficiaries' interests. In practice this is likely to remain the principal reason for ordering that a judgment is not binding on beneficiaries.

In a claim, judgment or order relating to trust property, the court has power under **CPR, r. 19.8A**, to order notice of the claim to be given to anyone who is not a party but who may be affected by it. An application for an order under this rule may be made without notice but must be supported by written evidence which includes the reasons why the person to be served should be bound by the judgment in the claim. Notice must be given in form No. 52, accompanied by a copy of the claim form, a copy of the judgment or order (if relevant), all other statements of case, including written evidence as the court may direct and a form for acknowledging service. The person served becomes a party to the claim on acknowledging service. Even if there is no acknowledgment of service, the person will be bound by any judgment or order made in the claim.

Derivative claim by beneficiaries

14.43 While claims involving the assets of an estate or *inter vivos* trust are ordinarily brought by or against the personal representatives or trustees, in special circumstances it may be possible for beneficiaries to bring a derivative claim. Typical examples of special circumstances are fraud on the part of the trustees, or collusion between the trustees and third parties, or the insolvency of the trustee, although the categories are not closed (*Roberts v Gill and Co.* [2010] UKSC 22, [2011] 1 AC 240 at [45]). See also *Bayley v SG Associates* [2014] EWHC 782 (Ch), [2014] WTLR 1315, where a conflict of interest on the part of the trustee provided the necessary special circumstance for permitting the beneficiaries to bring the derivative claim against the wrongdoers. The availability of public funding to the beneficiary that might not be available to the trustees is not a special circumstance (*Roberts v Gill and Co.* at [75]).

If there are special circumstances, it is necessary to name the trustees or personal representatives as defendants (*Roberts v Gill and Co.* at [56]). The claimant's representative capacity has to be set out in the claim form (**CPR, r. 16.2(3)**), and the special circumstances have to be set out in the particulars of claim (*Roberts v Gill and Co.* at [103]). The detailed rules on company derivative claims in **rr. 19.9 to 19.9F** do not technically apply to derivative claims by beneficiaries, but it is suggested that an application for permission to continue the claim and for directions should be issued at an early stage, perhaps after the acknowledgment of service.

CROWN PROCEEDINGS

Introduction

14.44 Proceedings by and against the Crown are governed by the Crown Proceedings Act 1947 and **CPR, Part 66**. The intention behind the Crown Proceedings Act 1947 is that proceedings involving the Crown should be governed by broadly the same procedure as between private litigants. **CPR, Part 66**, has removed some of the procedural advantages which the Crown had under earlier rules. There are still special rules for Crown proceedings concerning the content of a claim form (see **23.18**), service (**15.52**), venue (**14.45**), forms of relief (**14.47**), default judgment (**20.7**), counterclaims (**28.2**) and enforcement (**79.47**). Crown proceedings cannot be undertaken through the Claim Production Centre (**12.8**) or Money Claim Online (**12.10**).

Venue

The Crown Proceedings Act 1947, s. 20(2), provides that the usual rules on transfer from the County Court to the High Court, or the transfer of proceedings from the High Court to the County Court, apply in relation to proceedings against the Crown. However, **CPR, r. 30.3(2)(h)**, adds to the factors to which the court must have regard in considering whether or not to transfer the claim 'the location of the relevant government department or officers of the Crown and, where appropriate, any relevant public interest that the matter should be tried in London'. A note by the Attorney General to assist judges and practitioners with matters relevant to the venue of Crown proceedings is annexed to **PD 66**. The note points out that whilst a number of government departments have offices outside London, central government bodies are based in London and the Government Legal Service is geared towards processing claims in the RCJ. Where there is a High Court claim, many witnesses as well as lawyers and officials are London based and there may be a disproportionate cost in transferring them to a venue outside London. However, the Crown will not oppose transfer away from the RCJ where it is appropriate, for example, in personal injury disputes.

14.45

Commentary

Parties to the proceedings

Only authorised government departments may sue or be sued in their own name (Crown Proceedings Act 1947, s. 17(2) and (3)). Where a department is not authorised under the Act, proceedings by or against it may be instituted in the name of the Attorney General. **CPR, r. 19.4(4A)**, provides that the Commissioners for HM Revenue and Customs may be added as a party to proceedings only if they consent in writing. The Cabinet Office publishes a list of government departments authorised for the purposes of the Act. The list is annexed to **PD 66**. See also **15.52**.

14.46

In a claim against the Crown, the claim form must give the names of the government departments and officers of the Crown concerned, and brief details of the circumstances in which the alleged liability of the Crown arose (**CPR, r. 16.2(1A)**).

Forms of relief available against the Crown

Apart from the cases set out below, the court has power to grant the same relief against the Crown as it has in proceedings between private litigants. By the Crown Proceedings Act 1947, s. 21, the court may not, however, make an order for any of the following against the Crown:

14.47

(a) an injunction (although the court may require the Crown to provide a cross-undertaking in damages in support of an application for an interim injunction: *F. Hoffmann-La Roche & Co. AG v Secretary of State for Trade and Industry* [1975] AC 295);

(b) specific performance; or

(c) an order for the recovery of land or other property.

In these cases, the court will instead make a declaration against the Crown.

There are procedural restrictions on applications for default judgments (**CPR, r. 12.4(4)**) and summary judgment (**r. 24.4(1A)**) against the Crown.

Human rights: joining minister

14.48   The court cannot make a declaration of incompatibility under the **Human Rights Act 1998, s. 4**, unless 21 days' notice has been given to the Crown (**CPR, r. 19.4A(1)**). The minister, or other person permitted by the Act, is entitled to be joined on giving notice to the court. Where a claim is made for damages in respect of a judicial act under the Human Rights Act 1998, s. 9, notice must again be given to the Crown (**CPR, r. 19.4A(3)**), but in this situation, if the appropriate person does not apply to be joined within 21 days or such other time as may be allowed by the court, the court may join that person as a party (**r. 19.4A(4)**). A notice to the Crown under **r. 19.4A** must be served on the person named in the list published under the **Crown Proceedings Act 1947, s. 17** (**PD 19A, para. 6.4(1)**; the list is annexed to **PD 66**; for more on service on the Crown see **15.52**). In *Poplar Housing and Regeneration Community Association Ltd v Donoghue* [2001] EWCA Civ 595, [2002] QB 48 the Court of Appeal said that, in addition to the formal notice required under **r. 19.4A**, the party intending to raise the issue of incompatibility should also give informal notice of its intention to do so, both to the court and to the Crown, at the earliest possible opportunity. Directions under these provisions will usually be made at the case management conference (**PD 19A, paras 6.2** and **6.6**).

FOREIGN STATES AND DIPLOMATS

Foreign States

14.49   The State Immunity Act 1978 gives foreign States immunity from the jurisdiction of the UK courts for acts of a governmental nature. The Act applies to any foreign or Commonwealth State, and to its government, head of State and governmental departments (s. 14(1)). Entities which are distinct from the executive organs of State are also immune if the proceedings relate to something done by the separate entity in the exercise of sovereign authority and the circumstances are such that a State would have been immune under the Act (s. 14(2)). A certificate issued by the Secretary of State of the Foreign and Commonwealth Office is conclusive evidence as to whether a territory is a State, and as to the person or persons to be regarded as the head of the government or State (s. 21(a)).

The 1978 Act sets out the categories of claims for which a foreign State is not immune. Acts which could be performed by a company or a private individual will not enjoy immunity. These include where the proceedings relate to a commercial transaction (s. 3, the application of which is discussed in *NML Capital Ltd v Argentina* [2011] UKSC 31, [2011] 2 AC 495), to a contract of employment made or to be performed within the United Kingdom (s. 4), to death or personal injury, or damage to or loss of tangible property, caused by an act or omission in the United Kingdom (s. 5), to immovable property within the United Kingdom (s. 6), or to intellectual property rights (s. 7). The House of Lords has held in *Jones v Ministry of the Interior of Saudi Arabia* [2006] UKHL 26, [2007] 1 AC 270, that State immunity extends to the officials, servants and agents of the State. Immunity extended to a State's central bank which was acting to maintain the State's currency reserves, and was therefore to be considered the agent of the State (*Koo Golden East Mongolia v Bank of Nova Scotia* [2007] EWCA Civ 1443, [2008] QB 717).

The European Court of Human Rights has accepted that a plea of State immunity does in principle interfere with rights under **art. 6** of the European Convention on Human Rights in the **Human Rights Act 1998, sch. 1** (e.g. *McElhinney v Ireland* (application 31253/96) (2001) 34 EHRR 13, para. 26; *Fogarty v United Kingdom* (application 37112/97) (2001) 34 EHRR 12, para. 28; and *Al-Adsani v United Kingdom* (application 35763/97) (2001) 34 EHRR 273, para. 52). However, the House of Lords cast doubt on this proposition in *Jones v Ministry of the Interior of Saudi Arabia*. It stated that the rule of international law to which the State Immunity Act 1978 gives effect is that one State has no jurisdiction over another State and therefore a State cannot be said to deny access to its court if it has no access to give. The case involved an allegation of torture against the Kingdom of Saudi Arabia, alleged to have occurred in Saudi Arabia, in respect of which the Kingdom claimed State immunity. The court held that the application of state immunity to a torture claim did not infringe the claimants' rights under the European Convention of Human Rights, **art. 6** in the **Human Rights Act 1998, sch. 1**, as it could not be shown that the prohibition of torture is a peremptory norm which takes precedence over State immunity or a disproportionate restriction on access to a court. See also *Al Malki v Reyes* [2015] EWCA Civ 32, [2015] IRLR 289, where it was held that international law obligations in relation to diplomatic immunity are not incompatible with **art. 6**.

A claim may be brought against a State where it has submitted voluntarily to the jurisdiction. It may do this by filing an acknowledgment of service and not taking any step to contest jurisdiction, or by prior written agreement, or by instituting, or intervening in, proceedings (s. 2).

Foreign diplomats

Both at common law, and under the provisions of the Diplomatic Privileges Act 1964, foreign **14.50** diplomats, their families and their servants are immune from civil or criminal proceedings. A certificate of immunity issued by the Secretary of State will be conclusive (s. 4). Accordingly, service of a claim form on a person with diplomatic immunity is null and void, unless immunity is waived by the defendant filing an acknowledgment of service, and not following it up by an application under **CPR, Part 11**.

VEXATIOUS LITIGANTS

Means of restraining vexatious litigants

A small minority of litigants misuse the freedom of access to the courts by launching large **14.51** numbers of unmeritorious claims or numerous interim applications, wasting court resources and causing a great deal of anxiety, trouble and expense to the persons they litigate against. Following amendments to the CPR made as a consequence of the decision in *Bhamjee v Forsdick* [2003] EWCA Civ 1113, [2004] 1 WLR 88, there are now two mechanisms for restraining the activities of a vexatious litigant. They are:

(a) Civil proceedings and all proceedings orders under the Senior Courts Act 1981, s. 42, made by the Divisional Court on the application of the Attorney General, preventing a vexatious litigant issuing proceedings without permission of the court for an indefinite period (see **14.52**).

(b) One of three kinds of civil restraint orders, as defined in **CPR, r. 2.3(1)**. The procedure for making these is simpler than for orders under the Senior Courts Act 1981, s. 42, and does not require the involvement of the Attorney General. Civil restraint orders can be made by the court acting on its own initiative (**CPR, r. 3.3(7)**). See **14.55** to **14.60**.

The Court of Appeal considered the relationship between the new rules and the court's inherent jurisdiction to regulate its own affairs in *R (Kumar) v Secretary of State for Constitutional Affairs* [2006] EWCA Civ 990, [2007] 1 WLR 536. Here, a general civil restraint order had been made despite the fact that there was no extended civil restraint order in place, contrary to the requirements of **PD 3C, para. 4.1**. The Court of Appeal held that there was no power, under either the CPR or the court's inherent jurisdiction, to make an order in these circumstances. Although the court's inherent jurisdiction to protect its process from abuse has been preserved alongside the powers conferred on it by the CPR, it would be a very rare case in which a judge could rely on the inherent jurisdiction in an area which appears to have been comprehensively covered in the rules.

However, the court also has relevant case management powers under **r. 3.1** which it can invoke to restrain disproportionate and unnecessary litigation. In *Phillips v Symes* [2006] EWHC 2595 (Ch), LTL 17/10/2006, the court upheld an order for a stay of proceedings in order to avoid the costs of litigation and to give the parties an opportunity to negotiate, thereby furthering the overriding objective.

Civil proceedings orders and all proceedings orders

14.52 Where it is proved that a litigant has 'habitually and persistently and without any reasonable ground' instituted vexatious proceedings or applications, whether in the High Court or any inferior court, and this includes tribunals such as the Leasehold Valuation Tribunal (which has now been abolished) (*Attorney General v Singer* [2012] EWHC 326 (Admin), LTL 25/1/2012), the High Court is given power under the Senior Courts Act 1981, s. 42, to make:

(a) a civil proceedings order; or

(b) an all proceedings order applying both to all civil proceedings and applications and specified criminal proceedings.

A person subject to either order is prevented from continuing or commencing a civil claim, or making applications in a civil claim, without the permission of the High Court. The order will remain in force indefinitely, unless it is expressed to be for a specific period. Proceedings commenced in breach of a civil restraint order are a nullity. Accordingly the High Court does not have jurisdiction to hear an application for leave to continue the proceedings, nor can it grant retrospective leave to issue the proceedings (*Attorney General v Edwards* [2015] EWHC 1653 (Admin), LTL 13/5/2015).

An order under the Senior Courts Act 1981, s. 42, does not violate the European Convention on Human Rights, **art. 6(1)**, in the **Human Rights Act 1998, sch. 1** (*Attorney General v Covey* [2001] EWCA Civ 254, *The Times*, 2 March 2001). The Convention requires a fair and reasonable opportunity to address the court, not an unlimited and uncontrolled opportunity. See also *Nowak v Nursing and Midwifery Council* [2013] EWHC 1932 (QB), LTL 30/7/2013, where it was held that an extended civil restraint order did not breach **art. 6**, in particular because the litigant would be granted permission to pursue a properly arguable claim or application.

In considering an application by the Attorney General, the court will not go behind the previous adjudications made on the vexatious litigant's claims. The total litigation picture may merit a civil proceedings order being made under s. 42 with a penal notice attached so that defendants are protected from claims that disclose no intelligible grounds or are abusive (*Attorney General v Ali* [2008] EWHC 1452 (Admin), LTL 25/7/2008; *Attorney General v Ford* [2008] EWHC 2066 (Admin), LTL 28/8/2008). A civil proceedings order under the Senior Courts Act 1981, s. 42, covers proposed judicial review proceedings relating to a criminal cause or matter because the judicial review proceedings are civil (*Ewing v Director of Public Prosecutions* [2010] EWCA Civ 70, [2010] ACD 48).

Applying for orders under the Senior Courts Act 1981, s. 42

14.53 Application for an order under the Senior Courts Act 1981, s. 42, must be made by the Attorney General and is heard by a Divisional Court (**PD 8A, para. 16**). The claim form must be filed at the Administrative Court. It should be accompanied by a witness statement in support and served on the person against whom the order is sought.

Where a vexatious litigant (despite a civil proceedings order being made against him) is likely to conduct litigation in the names of others, acting as a litigation friend, but perhaps using the litigation as a vehicle for his own claims, an order (a '*Noueiri*' order) may be made restraining him from acting or purporting to act for others in legal proceedings unless he has obtained permission from a judge of the High Court or Court of Appeal (*Paragon Finance plc v Noueiri* [2001] EWCA Civ 1402, [2001] 1 WLR 2357; *Attorney General v Branch* [2008] EWHC 2872 (Admin), LTL

7/11/2008). A *Noueiri* order can also be made to prevent a person acting as a McKenzie friend indefinitely, although such an order would not prevent the person from litigating in his or her own name and on his or her own behalf (*Re Baggaley* [2015] EWHC 1496 (Fam), LTL 28/5/2015).

Once an order is made under s. 42, it will not usually be appropriate to allow the person subject to the order to reopen the earlier proceedings even if he wishes to rely on facts that arose in those proceedings in his defence to a fresh claim brought against him by the other party (*University of Southampton v Mohtasham* [2011] EWHC 3979 (QB)).

Permission applications by vexatious litigants

Permission to institute or continue or make an application in any civil proceedings by a person subject to a civil proceedings order will not be granted unless the High Court is satisfied that the proceedings or application are not an abuse of the process of the court and that there are reasonable grounds for bringing the proceedings or application (Senior Courts Act 1981, s. 42(3)). The jurisdiction under s. 42(3) should be exercised with due care and caution or carefully and sparingly. In considering whether the applicant can show that there are reasonable grounds for bringing a claim, the court normally has to consider whether or not the claim is justifiable and has a real prospect of success (*Mathew v Attorney General* [2013] EWHC 3009 (Admin), LTL 16/10/2013). Deciding whether a claim is an abuse of process involves a careful consideration of all the likely issues as well as proportionality and the overriding objective. On an application for permission, the court should take into account all of the information before it, which includes evidence of conduct before and after being categorised a vexatious litigant (*Ewing v News International Ltd* [2008] EWHC 1390 (QB), LTL 29/7/2008). A local authority has standing to make submissions in relation to a vexatious litigant's application for permission to commence proceedings against it under the Senior Courts Act 1981, s. 42(3) (*Ewing v Camden London Borough Council* [2013] EWHC 961 (Admin), [2013] ACD 85).

14.54

The procedure whereby a litigant against whom an order has been made under the Senior Courts Act 1981, s. 42, makes an application for permission to commence or continue a claim is set out in **PD 3A, para. 7**. An application notice should be issued in the High Court and signed by the litigant who is subject to the order. The application notice must state:

(a) the title and reference number of the proceedings in which the order was made;
(b) the full name and address of the litigant;
(c) the order the litigant is seeking; and
(d) briefly, why the order is sought.

Written evidence may be filed in support of the application. Either in the application notice, or the supporting evidence, the litigant must list the previous occasions on which he or she has made an application for permission.

The application will then be placed before a High Court judge, who may:

(a) make an order granting or dismissing the application without the attendance of the applicant;
(b) ask for further written evidence from the litigant; or
(c) give directions for there to be a hearing of the application. Such directions may include an order that the application notice be served on the Attorney General and on anyone against whom the litigant wishes to bring the new claim.

No appeal is possible against a decision refusing permission (Senior Courts Act 1981, s. 42(4)).

If permission is given for a vexatious litigant to commence a new claim, at a hearing of which the proposed defendant was not given notice, the defendant to the new claim may apply to set it aside (**PD 3A, para. 7.9**).

In *R (Ewing) v Office of the Deputy Prime Minister* [2005] EWCA Civ 1583, [2006] 1 WLR 1260, the court considered concurrent applications by a vexatious litigant under the Senior Courts Act 1981, s. 42, for permission to bring proceedings and for permission to seek judicial review. The court stated that a vexatious litigant should not allow his name to be included in a claim form (even as a 'proposed' claimant) unless and until he has obtained the necessary permission, and went on to give guidance on dealing with an application for permission under s. 42 in the context of a proposed judicial review claim. It also held that the procedure under s. 42 is designed to provide a mechanism to ensure that a vexatious litigant has access to the court to pursue his own genuine legal grievances, not to set himself up as a public champion. Where the court considers that the vexatious litigant does not have sufficient standing in the substantive action, it should refuse permission under s. 42 to bring the claim.

The court also has power to vary or discharge an order made under s. 42, but it will usually do so only if the applicant can show a material change of circumstances, which may include demonstrating that he or she has achieved a proper understanding of the unacceptable nature of his or her conduct. The fact that the applicant can show prejudice does not mean that the rationale for the existence of the order has disappeared. The court will not vary or discharge an order if it appears likely that an applicant will continue to pursue vexatious proceedings if unrestrained (*Douglas v Attorney General* [2015] EWHC 4109 (Admin), LTL 17/12/2015).

Civil restraint orders

14.55 By virtue of **CPR, r. 3.11**, and **PD 3C**, the court has power to make civil restraint orders. These provisions give effect to the recommendations in *Bhamjee v Forsdick* [2003] EWCA Civ 1113, [2004] 1 WLR 88, extending the old '*Grepe v Loam*' orders which restrained a party from making further applications in current proceedings (*Grepe v Loam* (1887) 37 ChD 168). **CPR, r. 2.3(1)**, defines three kinds of civil restraint orders:

(a) a limited civil restraint order, restraining a party from making any further applications in current proceedings (see **14.56**);

(b) an extended civil restraint order, restraining a party from issuing particular claims or making particular applications in specified courts (see **14.57** and **14.58**); and

(c) a general civil restraint order, restraining a party from issuing any claim or making any application in specified courts (see **14.59** and **14.60**).

Court orders must record whether any application (including an application for permission to appeal or for permission to apply for judicial review), statement of case or appeal has been struck out or dismissed as being totally without merit. Whenever it makes any such order, the court must go on to consider whether to make a civil restraint order (**rr. 3.3(7), 3.4(6), 23.12** and **52.20(6)**). However, the court is entitled to take into account any proceedings and applications made by the respondent which the court considers to be totally without merit. It is not restricted to proceedings and applications where there was at the time an express finding of a total lack of merit (*R (Kumar) v Secretary of State for Constitutional Affairs* [2006] EWCA Civ 990, [2007] 1 WLR 536). **Rule 3.3(7)** gives the court power to make a civil restraint order on its own initiative and such an order is subject to **r. 3.3**. It is doubtful whether an application as of right under **r. 3.3(5)(a)** to set aside an order made of the court's own initiative is subject to **PD 3C, para. 4.2** (including the provision in **para. 4.2(2)** that permission is required for an application to amend or discharge a general civil restraint order) (*Deeds v Various Respondents* [2013] EWCA Civ 1678, LTL 9/1/2014). Whether there should be an oral hearing of such an application depends on the nature of the order in question. But in a case where a citizen's right of access to the court is at stake, the presumption must be in favour of an oral hearing (*Deeds v Various Respondents*). A civil restraint order made on the court's own initiative without giving notice to the person against whom it is to be made should be an urgent interim measure only (*Deeds v Various Respondents*).

Alternatively, a party to the litigation may make an application for an order using the procedure in **Part 23** (**PD 3C, paras 5.1** and **5.2**). Examples of limited, extended and general restraint orders are annexed to **PD 3C**. In *R (Kumar) v Secretary of State for Constitutional Affairs* [2006] EWCA Civ 990, [2007] 1 WLR 536, the Court of Appeal stressed that where the history of the litigation is complicated, the court should not make an order without giving the litigant an opportunity to prepare resistance to the order. Here, an order had been applied for by the defendant without filing any Part 23 notice, and the claimant against whom the order was sought had not had three clear days' notice of the application. The court held that the application should have been adjourned to give the claimant more time to prepare his case. Where the court is considering making a civil restraint order of its own initiative immediately upon striking out or dismissing a statement of case as being without merit (under **CPR, rr. 3.3(7), 3.4(6), 23.12** or **52.20(6)**) it will need to consider whether the party against whom an order is being considered has had adequate time to prepare opposition to the order. Similarly, in *R (Webster) v West Yorkshire Police* [2008] EWHC 2594, LTL 21/11/2008, the court declined to make a civil restraint order of its own motion and 'on the hoof', even though it had dismissed an application for judicial review as wholly without merit, because it did not have enough information before it to be satisfied that the claimant had persistently issued claims without merit. It required a formal application to be made so that full details of previous applications and claims made by the defendant could be considered with care.

Sometimes the court must go further and protect its staff from a litigant who persists in wasting their time and disturbing the orderly conduct of court business. The appropriate way of doing this is by an injunction prohibiting the litigant from entering the court building unless summoned by the court (*Attorney General v Ebert* [2001] EWHC Admin 695, [2002] 2 All ER 789). See also *Mahajan v Department for Constitutional Affairs* [2004] EWCA Civ 946, *The Times*, 13 July 2004, in which an order was made restraining the claimant from addressing or corresponding with court staff in a rude or abusive manner.

In *Ebert v Venvil* [2000] Ch 484 the Court of Appeal made an extended civil restraint order restraining a party from taking any steps, including the issuing of new proceedings, in any Division of the High Court or any county court, arising out of the same matter. It rejected an argument that this would be contrary to the European Convention on Human Rights, **art. 6**, or the common law approach indicated in *R v Lord Chancellor, ex parte Witham* [1998] QB 575. The same view was taken in *Mahajan v Department for Constitutional Affairs* [2004] EWCA Civ 946, *The Times*, 13 July 2004, in which the Court of Appeal confirmed that, so long as the right of access to the court is not being extinguished, the court is entitled to regulate its affairs so as to protect its process and the interests of other parties against whom vexatious litigation is persistently brought.

An important factor in exercising the discretion to make a civil restraint order once the necessary preconditions are satisfied is whether the unmeritorious applications have been made as part of a vendetta (or similar motivation) or merely through ignorance or lack of funds (*R (Austin) v Portsmouth City Council* [2009] EWHC 1339 (Admin), LTL 22/6/2009).

CPR, r. 3.11, applies to High Court and County Court proceedings only. It does not confer jurisdiction on the High Court to make an order in respect of tribunal proceedings, even though it can take into account unmeritorious claims in a tribunal when deciding whether to make a civil restraint order in the High Court or County Court. Where an inferior court lacks jurisdiction to make a restraint order, the High Court has a power to make a general restraint order which extends to tribunal proceedings under its inherent jurisdiction (*Law Society v Otobo* [2011] EWHC 2264 (Ch), LTL 20/4/2011). In *Nursing and Midwifery Council v Harrold* [2015] EWHC 2254 (QB), [2016] IRLR 30, it was held that the High Court has inherent jurisdiction to make a civil restraint order extending to proceedings before the employment tribunal as that tribunal is an inferior court, and there is clearly a need for inferior courts to be protected from vexatious proceedings, particularly where the inferior tribunal has no power itself to make a civil restraint order. However, an employment tribunal has power to strike out an application where the applicant has acted vexatiously (*Fariba v Pfizer Ltd* (2011) UKEAT/0605/10/CEA, LTL 29/7/2011) and the Employment Appeal Tribunal can make a restriction of proceedings order against a vexatious litigant (see Employment Tribunals Act 1996, s. 33; *Attorney General v Bentley* (2012) UKEAT/0556/11/RN, LTL 14/6/2012).

Limited civil restraint orders

14.56 A limited civil restraint order restrains a party from making any further applications in current proceedings without obtaining the permission of a particular judge specified in the order (**PD 3C, para. 2.2(1)**). An order may be made by a judge of any court, where a party has made two or more applications which are totally without merit (**para. 2.1**). The order will remain in force for the duration of the proceedings (**para. 2.9**). This is the only form of civil restraint order which may be made by a Master, Circuit Judge or District Judge under **PD 3C**. For the position before **PD 3C** came into force see *Wickramaratna v Cambridge University Chemistry Department* [2004] EWCA Civ 1532, LTL 2/11/2004.

A party subject to a limited civil restraint order may apply to vary or discharge the order only with the permission of the judge specified in the order (**para. 2.2(2)**). The restrained party may also appeal against the order, but again only with permission (**para. 2.2(3)**). Making an application without permission will result in automatic dismissal (**para. 2.3(1)**). Where a person who is subject to a civil restraint order makes repeated applications for permission which are totally devoid of merit, by **para. 2.7**, a Court of Appeal judge, a High Court judge or Master, or a Designated Civil Judge or their deputy may make a further order refusing any further right of appeal unless the judge who refused permission to appeal now grants it (**para. 2.3(2)**).

Notice of an application, by a party who is subject to a limited civil restraint order, for permission under **para. 2.2(1)** or (2) must be served by that party on any other parties to the proceedings, setting out the nature and grounds of the application and giving the other parties at least seven days in which to respond. The application must be in writing, must include the other parties' written responses and will be determined without a hearing (**para. 2.6**). Any appeal against the refusal of permission under **para. 2.2(1)** or (2) must also be in writing and will also be determined without a hearing (**para. 2.8**).

Extended civil restraint orders

14.57 An extended civil restraint order restrains a party from issuing claims or applications in specified courts which involve, relate to, touch upon or lead to the proceedings in which the order is made (**PD 3C, para. 3.2(1)**). By **para. 3.1** a Court of Appeal judge, a High Court judge or a Designated Civil Judge or their deputy may make such an order where a party has persistently issued claims or applications which are totally without merit in more than one set of proceedings (*Supperstone v Hurst* [2009] EWHC 1271 (Ch), [2009] 1 WLR 2306). In deciding whether to make an extended civil restraint order the court can take into account all claims and applications issued by a party, including those issued before an earlier extended civil restraint order was made (*Society of Lloyd's v Noel* [2015] EWHC 734 (QB), [2015] 1 WLR 4393). The fact that the party has also made some successful, or partially successful, applications is relevant to the exercise of the discretion to grant an extended civil restraint order, but is not a bar (*Thakerar v Lynch Hall and Hornby* [2005] EWHC 2751 (Ch), [2006] 1 WLR 1511). There is a greater willingness to make these orders in light of the steadily increasing nuisance represented by vexatious litigants (*Bhamjee v Forsdick* [2003] EWCA Civ 1113, [2004] 1 WLR 88; see also *Richardson v Google UK Ltd* [2016] EWHC 1534 (QB), LTL 5/7/2016). Where the claim was the third claim brought by a claimant arising out of the same set of facts, the court ordered that it be struck out, and made an extended civil restraint order against the claimant as there was conduct which established an indifference to court orders and the abuse or misuse of the process of the court (*Karim v Charkham* [2014] EWHC 497 (Admin), LTL 3/3/2014; see also *Winsor v Vale* [2014] EWHC 957 (Ch), LTL 28/1/2014). An extended civil restraint order can also be made against an individual who has made a number of claims which were without merit and disclosed no legally recognisable claim, and where restraining him was necessary to protect court staff and the court system from being bombarded with letters and phone calls, as well as abusive allegations that the judges and court staff involved in handling those claims had been guilty of criminal behaviour (*Wicks v Parkin* [2013] EWHC 3671 (QB), LTL 27/11/2013). An extended civil restraint order cannot curtail a person's communications with others. The order is designed to prevent abuse of the court's process, not harassment of persons (which can be prevented under the Protection from Harassment Act 1997) (*Supperstone v Hurst* [2009] EWHC 1271 (Ch), [2009] 1 WLR 2306). Masters, Circuit Judges and District Judges have no power to make such an order. If they consider that an order should be made in a case before them, they must transfer it to a High Court or Designated Civil Judge (**para. 3.11**). An extended civil restraint order can also be imposed on a non-party to proceedings if that person has been the driving force behind unmeritorious legal proceedings and there is a risk of such litigation occurring in the future (*Hurst v Denton-Cox* (2011) LTL 24/2/2011).

An extended civil restraint order will apply to claims or applications in:

(a) any court, where the order is made by a Court of Appeal judge;
(b) the High Court or the County Court, where the order is made by a High Court judge; or
(c) the County Court where the order is made by a Designated Civil Judge or their appointed deputy.

An extended civil restraint order will remain in force for a specified period not exceeding two years, although it may be extended for periods of up to two years at a time (**paras 3.9** and **3.10**).

Applications by persons subject to extended civil restraint orders

A person subject to an extended civil restraint order may apply to vary or discharge the order **14.58** only with the permission of the judge specified in the order (**PD 3C, para. 3.2(2)**). The restrained person may also appeal against the order, but again only with permission (**para. 3.2(3)**). Issuing a claim or making an application without permission will result in automatic striking out or dismissal (**para. 3.3(1)**). Where a person who is subject to an extended civil restraint order makes repeated applications for permission which are totally devoid of merit, by **para. 3.7**, a Court of Appeal judge, a High Court judge or a Designated Civil Judge or his deputy may make a further order refusing any further right of appeal unless the judge who refused permission to appeal now grants it (**para. 3.3(2)**).

Notice of an application, by a party who is subject to an extended civil restraint order, for permission under **para. 3.2(1)** or **(2)**, must be served by that party on any other parties to the proceedings, setting out the nature and grounds of the application and giving the other parties at least seven days in which to respond. The application for permission must be in writing, must include the other parties' written responses and will be determined without a hearing (**para. 3.6**). Any appeal against the refusal of permission under **para. 3.2(1)** or **(2)** must also be in writing and will be determined without a hearing (**para. 3.8**). In *Forrester Ketley and Co. v Brent* [2008] EWHC 3150 (Ch), LTL 9/1/2009, the court considered the test to be applied in applications under **PD 3C, para. 3.2(2)**. It held that whilst it was not possible to provide a comprehensive list of factors, usually permission would not be granted unless the claim, application or step in the action for which permission was sought had a realistic prospect of success. An order may also be discharged having regard to the length of time that has elapsed since it was made, how the subject of the order has behaved since the order was made and the fact that there had been no further litigation and none was contemplated (*Attorney General v Abiola* [2014] EWHC 4746 (Admin), [2015] ACD 82). Where a civil restraint order has been made against a vexatious litigant, the requirement to pay a fee in accordance with the Civil Proceedings Fees Order 2008, sch. 2 for permission to appeal against the order is not incompatible with **art. 6** of the European Convention on Human Rights (*Senior-Milne v Secretary of State for Justice* [2012] EWHC 3062 (Admin), LTL 14/11/2012).

As an alternative to making any form of civil restraint order, the court may accept an appropriate assurance from the litigant. In *Wilkes v Ballam Delaney Hunt* [2005] EWCA Civ 1104, the court declined to order an extended civil restraint order against a litigant who had given an assurance to the court not to commence fresh proceedings against specified individuals and had kept to his assurance.

An undertaking which is accepted by the court as an alternative to making a civil restraint order should be limited to the same period as a civil restraint order, namely, two years (*R (Austin) v Portsmouth City Council* [2009] EWHC 1339 Admin), LTL 22/6/2009).

General civil restraint orders

14.59 A general civil restraint order restrains a person from issuing any claim or making any application in specified courts without obtaining the permission of a particular judge specified in the order (**PD 3C, para. 4.2(1)**). By **paras 4.2(1)** and **4.1** a Court of Appeal judge, a High Court judge, or a Designated Civil Judge or his deputy may make an order where a person has persistently issued claims or applications which are totally without merit and where an extended civil restraint order would not be sufficient or appropriate. Masters, Circuit Judges and District Judges have no power to make general civil restraint orders. If they consider that an order should be made in a case before them, they must transfer it to a High Court or Designated Civil Judge (**para. 4.11**).

Where a litigant had repeatedly breached an extended civil proceedings order and there was no indication that the extended order had effectively limited his activities, it was appropriate to make a general civil proceedings order against him. This was particularly so, given that he had made applications in relation to third parties to the main litigation (*Carroll v Kynaston* [2005] EWHC 927, LTL 2/6/2005). Similarly, a general restraint order was appropriate to prevent a party bringing proceedings in respect of many different incidents against a number of different defendants, including prison governors and staff, the Ministry of Justice and the Parole Board so that it was not possible to frame an extended civil restraint order which would achieve the necessary protection of the public interest in preventing further abuse (*Douglas v Ministry of Justice* [2013] EWHC 3640 (QB), LTL 28/11/2013 and *R (Hodge) v Information Commissioner* [2014] EWHC 3716 (Admin), LTL 8/12/2014). In *R (Sturgess) v Swansea County Court* [2014] EWHC 608 (Admin), LTL 13/3/2014, a general civil restraint order was made against a claimant who brought several unmeritorious claims without serious allegations against a number of parties within the period covered by an extended civil restraint order. In a borderline case, it is better to make an extended civil restraint order and only make a general order when it is necessary to do so (*West v Taylor-Duncan* [2013] EWHC 4394 (QB), LTL 12/9/2013).

The court can make a civil restraint order of its own initiative under **CPR, r. 3.11** (see **14.55**). Where an extended civil restraint order cannot deal with the issues raised by the respondent because the court would have to speculate about what the next cause of action might be, a general civil restraint order can be made (*R (Salmon) v Secretary of State for the Home Department* [2009] EWHC 760 (Admin), LTL 5/5/2009; see also *Moosun v HSBC Bank plc* [2015] EWHC 3308 (Ch), LTL 3/11/2015, where a general civil restraint order was made against a party who sought repeatedly to relitigate matters that had already been determined by bringing proceedings in various guises).

A general civil restraint order will apply to claims or applications in:

(a) any court, where the order is made by a Court of Appeal judge;

(b) the High Court or the County Court, where the order is made by a High Court judge; or

(c) the County Court where the order is made by a Designated Civil Judge or his deputy (**para. 4.2(1)**).

A general civil restraint order will remain in force for a specified period not exceeding two years, although it may be extended for periods of up to two years at a time (**paras 4.9** and **4.10**). In *Bar Mutual Indemnity Fund v Sheikh* [2011] EWHC 1946 (QB), LTL 28/7/2011, the court extended a general civil restraint order for a further two years as the respondent's behaviour clearly required the order to be continued. See also *Sheikh v Page* [2015] EWHC 1923 (QB), LTL 10/7/2015.

Applications by persons subject to general civil restraint orders

14.60 A person subject to a general civil restraint order may apply to vary or discharge the order only with the permission of the judge specified in the order (**PD 3C, para. 4.2(2)**). The restrained person may also appeal against the order, but again only with permission (**para. 4.2(3)**). Issuing a claim or making an application without permission will result in automatic striking out or dismissal (**para. 4.3(1)**). It is an abuse of process to repeat an application which has already been refused without informing the judge of the previous refusal. An applicant who repeated an application which had already been refused without informing the court either of the previous refusal or that he was subject to a civil restraint order committed an abuse of process (*Anas v King Fahad Academy* [2014] EWHC 1258 (QB), LTL 30/4/2014). Where a person who is subject to a general civil restraint order makes repeated applications for permission which are totally devoid of merit, by **para. 4.7**, a Court of Appeal judge, a High Court judge or a Designated Civil Judge or their appointed deputy may make a further order refusing any further right of appeal unless the judge who refused permission to appeal now grants it (**para. 4.3(2)**).

Notice of an application, by a party who is subject to a general civil restraint order, for permission under **para. 4.2(1)** or **(2)**, must be served by that party on any other parties to the proceedings, setting out the nature and grounds of the application and giving the other parties at least seven days in which to respond. The application for permission must be in writing, must include the other parties' written responses and will be determined without a hearing (**para. 4.6**). Any appeal against the refusal of permission under **para. 4.2(1)** or **(2)** must also be in writing and will also be determined without a hearing (**para. 4.8**).

CONSOLIDATION

The court may order closely connected claims to be consolidated (**CPR, r. 3.1(2)(g)**). **14.61**
After consolidation the claims continue as if they were a single claim. Consolidation is only likely to be ordered where there is a strong overlap of issues of fact or law, or where there is a risk of irreconcilable judgments. Where there is minimal overlap, consolidation is inappropriate (*Law Debenture Trust Corporation (Channel Islands) Ltd v Lexington Insurance Co.* (2001) LTL 12/11/2001). The court will refuse consolidation, even where there is a sufficient overlap, if an order would lead to procedural unfairness and difficulties in case management. In *IXIS Corporate and Investment Bank v WestLB AG* [2007] EWHC 1748 (Comm), LTL 30/7/2007, the court refused an application to consolidate because the two cases concerned were at very different stages: a trial date had been fixed in one whereas the other had not reached the defence stage.

A consolidation order can only be made if all the claims are before the court on the same occasion. Therefore applications will have to be made in each of the claims returnable in the same court (perhaps after some of the claims are transferred) at the same time. Alternatively, a single application can be issued (again after ensuring all claims are proceeding in the same court and Division) stating the titles of all the claims proposed to be consolidated. If the order is made, one of the claims is nominated as the lead claim. After consolidation, the usual rule is that all claimants (if legally represented) must have the same solicitors and counsel.

Where consolidation is inappropriate, similar case management objectives can be achieved by ordering trials of related claims to be listed together. In *Actavis UK Ltd v Eli Lilly and Co. Ltd* [2010] EWCA Civ 43, LTL 13/1/2010, the claimant in the first claim applied for the revocation of the defendant's patent. The claimant in the second claim, being concerned that the parties in the first claim might reach a settlement which would adversely affect its market position, commenced its own proceedings also seeking the revocation of the patent on the same grounds as those set out in the first claim. Case management directions in both claims provided that they be heard simultaneously before the same judge pursuant to **r. 3.1(2)(h)**, and that the expert evidence, experiments and evidence at trial in the first claim would serve as the evidence in the second claim. The Court of Appeal upheld an order that the costs of both claims be split equally because it was impossible to distinguish between the two claims.

REPRESENTATIVE PARTIES

Principles

14.62 Where it is difficult or impossible for all persons affected by a claim to be parties to the proceedings, the court may, under **CPR, rr. 19.6** and **19.7**, order one or more persons to be made party to the claim as representative of persons who are not parties and direct that orders made in the claim are to bind represented persons. **Rule 19.6** also permits a claim to be commenced by or against a representative party without a court order. **Rule 19.6** applies to any kind of claim (but not to claims governed by **r. 19.7**). **Rule 19.7** (see **14.64**) is available only in the kinds of claims listed in **r. 19.7(1)**. The rules provide for two different sorts of 'representative proceedings':

(a) representation under **r. 19.6** of one person by another with the same interest in the claim (see below); and

(b) representation under **r. 19.7** of one person by another, where the person represented cannot be identified (see **14.63**).

An alternative method of dealing with the interests of several persons is by a group litigation order, or 'GLO' (see **14.66**).

It is provided in **CPR, r. 19.6(1)**, that:

Where more than one person has the same interest in a claim—

(a) the claim may be begun; or

(b) the court may order that the claim be continued,

by or against one or more of the persons who have the same interest as representatives of any other persons who have that interest.

In *Duke of Bedford v Ellis* [1901] AC 1 (followed in *Independiente Ltd v Music Trading On-Line (HK) Ltd* [2003] EWHC 470 (Ch), LTL 25/3/2003) it was held that there are three elements to be satisfied in deciding whether the representative party and the persons represented have the same interest:

(a) a common interest;

(b) a common grievance; and

(c) a remedy beneficial to all.

For a review of authorities and principles relevant to **r. 19.6** see *Millharbour Management Ltd v Weston Homes Ltd* [2011] EWHC 661 (TCC), [2011] 3 All ER 1027.

A representation order in respect of a defendant may be made only where everyone within the class has a common interest in the claim. Where different defendants have different defences there is no common interest within **r. 19.6(1)** (*London Association for Protection of Trade v Greenlands Ltd* [1916] 2 AC 15). However, in *Oxford University v Webb* [2006] EWHC 2490 (QB), LTL 20/10/2006, Irwin J held that the fact that different members of a defendant class have different defences will not prevent a representative order being made in all cases. There are two safeguards available to a member of the class affected by a representative action. First, the existence of the representation order and the fact that it binds them should be drawn to the attention of all those in the class. Any person wishing to argue a difference of interest and/or to run a different defence could apply to the court to be joined as a party and run that different defence. Secondly, by **r. 19.6(4)(b)**, a judgment or order may not be enforced against a person who is not a party to the claim without the permission of the court. It was concluded in this case that the Animal Liberation Front was a sufficiently consistent and coherent organisation, even though it deliberately lacked the 'trappings' of an organisation, to make it capable of being represented under **r. 19.6** by its public spokesman.

The court must also take account of the overriding objective. In *National Bank of Greece SA v R. M. Outhwaite 317 Syndicate at Lloyd's* [2001] Lloyd's Rep IR 652 it was held in the Commercial Court that it was proper to begin proceedings against one individual as representative of all members of 39 Lloyd's syndicates which had subscribed an insurance policy, even though the chosen individual was a member of only one of the syndicates and there was no leading underwriter clause in the policy. Andrew Smith J said that the phrase 'the same interest in a claim' in **r. 19.6** is to be interpreted with a view to giving effect to the overriding objective in the CPR. Specifically, it should be interpreted in a way that makes representative proceedings available in cases where they would save expense and enable a matter to be dealt with expeditiously.

The class the claimant seeks to represent must have a common interest in the claim and a common grievance, which must have existed when the claim was begun. If it is impossible to say whether any given person was a member of the class at the time the claim form was issued and throughout the proceedings because the criteria for inclusion in the class depend on the outcome of the litigation itself, then no representation order can be made under **r. 19.6** (*Emerald Supplies Ltd v British Airways plc* [2010] EWCA Civ 1284, [2011] Ch 345).

It is not a purpose of representative orders to shut out a person who is ready and willing to conduct his own case in the litigation, and such a person should ordinarily be added in his own right (*Irish Shipping Ltd v Commercial Union Assurance Co. plc* [1991] 2 QB 206; *Re PD Teesport Ltd* [2009] EWHC 1693 (Ch), LTL 16/7/2009).

Procedure

The representative capacity of the claimant or defendant, and the class of persons represented, must be made clear in the description of the parties in the claim form. For example, 'AB, as representing himself and all other members of the British Phonographic Industry Ltd'.   **14.63**

It is not necessary for a representative claimant to obtain the authority of the represented persons to bring the claim. The authority to bring the proceedings is provided by **CPR, r. 19.6**, itself, *Independiente Ltd v Music Trading On-Line (HK) Ltd* [2003] EWHC 470 (QB), LTL 25/3/2003; *Howells v Dominion Insurance Co. Ltd* [2005] EWHC 552 (QB), LTL 8/4/2005. Nor is it necessary for a claimant to obtain the court's permission to issue a claim form either as a representative of other claimants, or against a representative defendant. But the court is expressly empowered by **CPR, r. 19.6(2)**, to order that a person may not act as a representative. Any party may make an application for such an order.

The representative claimant is fully empowered to choose how to run the litigation on behalf of the class. However, those represented are not parties to the litigation, so, for example, disclosure may be ordered against them only as non-parties (*Ventouris v Mountain* [1990] 1 WLR 1370, QBD). Nor are the persons represented individually liable for costs (*Howells v Dominion Insurance Co. Ltd*), though the representatives may be (*SmithKline Beecham plc v Avery* [2009] EWHC 1924 (QB), LTL 26/8/2009).

By virtue of **r. 19.6**, unless the court orders otherwise, any judgment or order is binding on the persons represented. However, it may not be enforced by or against a person who is not a named party without the court's permission (**r. 19.6(4)(b)**). The requirement for permission is an important protection and the court will consider whether it should be enforced on a case-by-case basis (*Howells v Dominion Insurance Co. Ltd*). Permission to enforce an order may not be granted in advance, without identifying the represented party or parties against whom the order could be enforced. Such a person should have an opportunity to make submissions before any enforcement could occur (*SmithKline Beecham plc v Avery* [2007] EWHC 948 (QB), LTL 9/5/2007; *Huntingdon Life Sciences Group plc v Stop Huntingdon Animal Cruelty (SHAC)* [2007] EWHC 522 (QB), LTL 19/4/2007). A judgment may be enforced against a person represented whether or not that person authorised the litigation (*Howells v Dominion Insurance Co. Ltd*).

Representation of unascertained persons

In claims involving: **14.64**

(a) the estate of a deceased person,

(b) trust property, or

(c) the meaning of a document (including a statute),

the court has power to appoint a representative for another person or class, for the purposes of the claim (**CPR, r. 19.**7). The court may exercise the power where:

(a) the person or persons to be represented are unborn, or cannot be found or easily ascertained; or

(b) in the case of a class, the members of the class have the same interest in the claim and:

(i)   one or more members are unborn, or cannot be found or easily ascertained; or

(ii) appointing a representative would further the overriding objective.

An application for a representation order may be made by any person who seeks to be appointed under the order or by any party to the claim. The application can be made at any time before or after the issue of the claim form (**r. 19.7(3)**). The application must be served on all parties to the claim if it has started, and the person to be appointed (if that person is not already a party to the claim), and any other person directed by the court (**r. 19.7(4)**).

Court approval must be sought to settle a claim in which a party is acting as a representative under **r. 19.7** (**r. 19.7(5)**), and the settlement will be approved only if it is for the benefit of all the represented parties (**r. 19.7(6)**).

If the court does appoint such a representative, any judgments or orders made in the action are binding on the person(s) represented, but may only be enforced by or against a person who is not a party with the permission of the court (**r. 19.7(7)**). It is unlikely that the fact that parties who have no opportunity to be heard personally can be bound by a judgment made against them under **r. 7.7** gives rise to any issue under the European Convention on Human Rights, **art. 6**, in the **Human Rights Act 1998, sch. 1** (*Smithson v Hamilton* [2008] EWCA Civ 996, [2009] ICR 1; *Re PD Teesport Ltd* [2009] EWHC 1693 (Ch), LTL 16/7/2009). Nevertheless, in *Smithson v Hamilton*, the court ordered that the judgment should not be enforced until 28 days after notification to parties who would be affected by it, with liberty to apply in the meantime.

INTERVENTION

14.65 In cases where there is no effective respondent and which raise issues likely to be of wider importance than the immediate interests of the parties, the court may adjourn so that a suitable person, or advocate to the court (*amicus curiae*), be appointed to ensure arguments are raised in the public interest. The Pensions Ombudsman was invited to appear on this basis in *Legal and General Assurance Society Ltd v CCA Stationery Ltd* [2003] EWHC 1491 (Ch), LTL 11/6/2003.

Applications to intervene are made under **CPR, r. 19.2** (see **14.83**). Unmeritorious applications will be dismissed in the court's discretion. In *Nottinghamshire County Council v Bottomley* [2010] EWCA Civ 756, [2010] Med LR 407, the local authority was given permission to intervene. It had a financial interest in the form of the award in the case (whether it should be a lump sum or periodical payments, see **63.30**), which made it desirable to make the order under both **r. 19.2(2)(a)** and **(b)**.

GROUP LITIGATION

Group litigation orders

14.66 Until May 2000, no special provision was made in rules of court for multi-party group litigation, or class actions. Representative proceedings under **CPR, r. 19.7** (see **14.62** to **14.64**) are one way of dealing with multi-party actions, but are not designed for group litigation. In particular, they do not provide an effective mechanism for managing group litigation, for identifying generic issues applicable to the entire group or for resolving cases at a cost which is proportionate to the value of an individual claim. By the early 1990s there was wide agreement that a new approach was needed (see *Nash v Eli Lilly and Co.* [1993] 1 WLR 782). Recommendations by Lord Woolf in ch. 17 of his *Final Report* for a new framework for multi-party actions led (albeit with some differences) to the introduction of **CPR, r. 19.11**, and **PD 19B**. The court may, under **CPR, r. 19.11**, make a 'group litigation order' or 'GLO', where a number of claims give rise to common or related, issues of fact or law. The order may be made upon the application of any party, or by the court acting of its own initiative (**PD 19B, paras 3.1** and **4**). The types of cases suitable for a GLO include mass product liability claims, claims arising out of a public transport disaster, and housing claims involving similar claims by numerous tenants.

The key features of the rules on GLOs are:

(a) Either before or after the commencement of litigation, a party may apply for a GLO.

(b) The GLO will identify the issues to be managed as part of the group litigation (the 'GLO issues'). Any individual claim (a 'GLO claim') must raise these issues to fall under the terms of the order. In *Hobson v Ashton Morton Slack Solicitors* [2006] EWHC 1134 (QB), LTL 26/5/2006, a GLO was refused in part because no group litigation issue had been sufficiently or precisely identified. The GLO issues cannot be phrased so as to exclude the individual circumstances of some of the parties from the scope of the litigation. The GLO issues must properly encapsulate the issues that arise in the litigation (*Tew v BOS (Shared Appreciation Mortgages) No. 1 plc* [2010] EWHC 203 (Ch), LTL 30/4/2010). The case concerned a GLO relating to challenges to the fairness of certain mortgages under the Consumer Credit Act 1974 and the Unfair Terms in Consumer Contracts Regulations 1994 (SI 1994/3159). As questions of fairness involve a one-stage inquiry based on the facts of particular situations, it was decided that the appropriate case management directions would be for the taking of lead cases, rather than trying to identify common issues.

(c) A register will be established for the GLO claims, and a specified court will be given responsibility for managing them.

(d) The managing court is given wide powers to give case management directions to ensure the effective coordination and resolution of the GLO claims (see **14.71**).

(e) Any judgment made on a GLO issue will bind all the GLO claimants (see **14.73**).

Preliminary steps

Solicitors acting for potential applicants for a GLO should contact the Law Society's Multi-Party Action Information Service (telephone 0870 606 2522) to identify other potential claims giving rise to the same issues (**PD 19B, para. 2.1**). (Members of the public should ring Law Society Information Services on 0870 606 2555.) Consideration should also be given to forming a solicitors' group and to identifying a solicitor to lead the application for a GLO and the litigation of the GLO issues. **PD 19B, para. 2.2**, advises that the lead solicitor's role and relationship with other members of the solicitors' group should be defined in writing. In any event, the lead solicitor will be subject to any directions given by the court.   **14.67**

PD 19B, para. 2.3, advises that the applicant should consider whether it would be more appropriate to seek any other order, in particular, an order for claims to be consolidated or for a representative to be appointed under **CPR, rr. 19.6** to **19.9**. In *Hobson v Ashton Morton Slack Solicitors* [2006] EWHC 1134 (QB), LTL 26/5/2006, a GLO was refused in part because insufficient consideration had been given to more cost-efficient means of resolving the dispute, such as bringing a test case, or consolidating the claims.

The Law Society publishes practice guidelines for those conducting or wishing to conduct disaster litigation under a GLO. A copy is available on the Law Society website (http://www.lawsociety.org).

Applying for a GLO

14.68   Application for a GLO, whether before or after issue of the claim, is made by the Part 23 procedure (see **chapter 32**), and can be made by any party to the claim (**PD 19B, para. 3.1**). Alternatively the court may make an order of its own motion (**PD 19B, para.** 4). The application should be made to the Senior Master in the Queen's Bench Division of the High Court, or the Chief Chancery Master in the Chancery Division. For claims likely to proceed in a specialist list (see **11.4**), the application should be made to a senior judge of that list. For claims likely to proceed in a District Registry, application should be made to the presiding judge, or to the supervising Chancery judge. County Court applications should be made to the Designated Civil Judge for the area in which the application notice has been issued (**PD 19B, paras 3.5 to 3.7**).

By **PD 19B, para. 3.2**, either the application notice itself, or the written evidence in support should include the following information:

(a) a summary of the nature of the litigation;
(b) the number and nature of claims already issued;
(c) the number of parties likely to be involved;
(d) the common issues of fact or law ('the GLO issues'); and
(e) whether there are any matters that distinguish smaller groups of claims within the wider group.

The decision whether to make a GLO is a matter for the court's discretion. A GLO requires substantial resources of both the parties and the court and it should not be made unless it is clear that there is a sufficient number of claimants and that they clearly intend to proceed (*Austin v Miller Argent (South Wales) Ltd* [2011] EWCA Civ 928, [2011] Env LR 32, in which it was not established that a sufficient number of claimants intended to proceed).

A GLO may not be made without the consent of the President of the Queen's Bench Division in the case of claims proceeding in the Queen's Bench Division, the Chancellor of the High Court in the case of claims proceeding in the Chancery Division, or the Head of Civil Justice in the case of claims proceeding in the County Court (**PD 19B, para. 3.3**). It is for the court, not the parties, to seek such consent, by sending to the President of the Queen's Bench Division, the Chancellor of the High Court or the Head of Civil Justice, as appropriate, a copy of the application notice, any relevant written evidence in support and a written statement of the reasons a GLO is thought to be desirable. This step may be taken before or after hearing the application. Indeed, in the County Court, the applicant should request the relevant County Court hearing centre to refer the application notice to the Designated Civil Judge as soon as possible to enable him or her to consider seeking the consent of the Head of Civil Justice prior to the hearing of the application (**PD 19B, para. 3.8**).

Nature of the order

14.69   A GLO must, by **CPR, r. 19.11(2)**:

(a) identify the issues which a claim must raise if it is to be managed under the order (the 'GLO issues');
(b) set up a register for such claims; and
(c) specify the court that will manage the claims (the 'management court').

The management court is the court to which any application to vary the GLO should be made (**PD 19B, para. 12.2**).

Once a GLO has been made, a copy should be supplied to the Law Society and to the Senior Master of the Queen's Bench Division (**PD 19B, para. 11**). There is a list of GLOs at http://www.justice.gov.uk/courts/rcj-rolls-building/queens-bench/group-litigation-orders with a link to archived details of lead solicitors and defined issues.

Group register

The group register of claims managed under a GLO is normally maintained by the management court, but that court may direct it to be kept by a solicitor for one of the parties to a case entered on it (normally the lead solicitor) (**PD 19B, para. 6.5**). In this case, the solicitor must permit the register to be inspected by the public during business hours, upon reasonable notice and upon paying an appropriate fee (**PD 19B, para. 6.6(2)**).

14.70

Any party to a case may apply to be entered on or removed from a group register (**PD 19B, paras 6.2** and **9.2; CPR, r. 19.14**). An order for a case to be entered may be made where the case raises at least one of the GLO issues (**PD 19B, para. 6.3**). A claim must be issued before it can be entered on the group register (**PD 19B, para. 6.1A**). However, even where a case does raise a GLO issue, the court has a discretion to refuse registration (or to order the removal of a case from the register) on the grounds that it cannot conveniently be managed with the other cases on the register, or that its inclusion would adversely affect the management of the other cases (**PD 19B, para. 6.4**).

The management court may specify a cut-off date after which no claim may be added to the register without the court's permission (**CPR, r. 19.13; PD 19B, para. 13**). In *Taylor v Nugent Care Society* [2004] EWCA Civ 51, [2004] 1 WLR 1129, the claimant issued separate proceedings arising out of alleged abuse in a children's home, an issue which was the subject of a GLO. He applied unsuccessfully to join the group litigation, some two and a half years after the cut-off date set by the court. The defendant made an application to strike out the claim. The Court of Appeal refused the application on the grounds that it was a disproportionate reaction to the claimant's delay and there were other steps, such as staying the claimant's action pending case management directions, which adequately protected the defendant's interests. The Court of Appeal also considered the relationship between a GLO and a claim on the same issue not included in the group. The court stated that although there is no requirement in **CPR, Part 19**, for a claimant to join a GLO, if he chooses not to do so he is still subject to the management powers of the court. If he brings proceedings in parallel to a GLO, the court is entitled to manage those separate proceedings in a way which takes account of the position of those who have joined the GLO. Those who have joined the GLO are entitled to have their interests given a higher priority than those of a defendant who has not joined. This is partly because of their number but also because by joining the GLO they are cooperating with the proper management of the claim. The court refused to permit 17 claimants to be added to the register in group litigation concerning defective breast implants where their application was made 10 months after the cut-off date and there was no good reason for the delay. The making of an application for permission is an application for relief from a sanction and accordingly **r. 3.9** and the relevant case law decided under that rule applies (*Holloway v Transform Medical Group (CS) Ltd* [2014] EWHC 1641 (QB), LTL 30/5/2014). Cut-off dates are essential to secure good case management of GLOs and to give the parties certainty about how and when to apply their resources. Accordingly, the court will be cautious about extending cut-off dates and extensions should not be regarded as the norm (*Pearce v Secretary of State for Energy and Climate Change* [2015] EWHC 3775 (QB), LTL 15/1/2016).

Managing the GLO claims

After a GLO is made, all existing claims which raise any of the GLO issues will, where necessary, be transferred to the management court, be listed on the group register and, where appropriate (for example, where one claim is proceeding as a test claim or to await group case management directions), be stayed pending further order (**CPR, r. 19.11(3)**). Every claim entered on the group register will automatically be allocated to the multi-track. Any case management directions already given will be set aside and any hearing date already fixed other than for the purpose of the group litigation will be vacated (**PD 19B, para. 7**).

14.71

The management court will normally require all new claims to be commenced in it. Failure to comply with any such order will not invalidate a claim, but the claim should be transferred to

Commentary

the management court and entered on the group register as soon as possible after issue (PD 19B, para. 9).

A GLO claim will be managed by a single assigned judge, assisted by an assigned District Judge or Master and a costs judge (PD 19B, para. 8). Case management directions may be given when the GLO is made, or subsequently. Such directions may include orders for one claim to proceed as a test claim, appointing a lead solicitor and specifying a cut-off date for joining the group, and provision for allocation of costs (CPR, r. 19.13; PD 19B, paras 12 and 13). See *Greenwood v Goodwin* [2013] EWHC 2785 (Ch), LTL 31/7/2013, for an example of the type of case management directions made in such cases.

Directions will normally also address the form that the particulars of claim should take. In particular, PD 19B, para. 14, makes provision for the service of 'group particulars of claim' — i.e. one statement of case which sets out details of all the claims on the group register at the time it is filed. PD 19B suggests that the particulars should contain details of the general allegations common to all claims and a schedule (or a series of questionnaires, in a form approved by the court) setting out specific facts relating to particular claimants on the group register (paras 14.1 and 14.3).

PD 19B, para. 12, does not give the court power to order disclosure and inspection of group litigation claimants' ATE insurance policies, the terms of which are privileged (*Arroyo v BP Exploration Co. (Colombia) Ltd* (2010), LTL 4/6/2010).

The management court may give directions for the trial of the action, addressing how the issues common to the group claims and those raised by particular claims should be dealt with (PD 19B, para. 15.1). While common issues will normally be tried in the management court, the separate issues raised by individual claims may be tried at a court which suits the convenience of the parties to that particular claim (PD 19B, para. 15.2).

Test claims

14.72 If one claim on the group register proceeding as a test claim is settled, the management court may order that another claim on the group register be substituted as the test claim. If such an order is made, any order made in the test claim before the date of substitution is binding on the substituted claim unless the court otherwise orders (CPR, r. 19.15). The court can make an interim payment in favour of a party to group litigation provided the relevant conditions are satisfied and the fact that the applicant is not a test claimant in the group litigation is not a reason for refusing to do so (*Test Claimants in the FII Group Litigation v Commissioners of HM Revenue & Customs (No. 2)* [2012] EWCA Civ 57, [2012] 1 WLR 2375; see also *GKN Holdings plc v Commissioners of HM Revenue and Customs* [2013] EWHC 108 (Ch), [2013] BTC 113).

Judgment

14.73 Subject to any court order to the contrary, any judgment or order made by the court in relation to a GLO issue is binding on the parties to all the other claims which are by then already on the GLO register (CPR, r. 19.12(1)(a)). An appeal against the judgment or order may only be made with the permission of the court (CPR, r. 19.12(2)).

The court may also direct to what extent any order or judgment should bind parties to claims entered subsequently on the GLO register (CPR, r. 19.12(1)(b)). However, in this case, an affected party may apply to the court for an order that the judgment or order is not binding on him (CPR, r. 19.12(3)).

Any document disclosed by a party to any claim on the GLO register is disclosed to all parties to claims on the GLO register at the time disclosure is made and to those subsequently entered (CPR, r. 19.12(4)).

Costs

In assessing costs, the court will need to apportion costs between those relating to common **14.74** issues and those which relate to issues in particular cases. The question of costs in group actions is governed by **CPR, r. 46.6**, and is considered more fully at **68.52**. While recognising that complex funding and costs issues arise in applications in GLO cases, the starting point on interim costs decisions is that the usual single party costs order should be made (adjusted as appropriate) (*AB v Ministry of Defence* [2009] EWHC 1421 (QB), LTL 6/7/2009). A proportionate costs order can be made in group litigation if the claimants do not win on all issues (*Jones v Secretary of State for Energy & Climate Change* [2012] EWHC 3647 (QB), [2013] 2 Costs LR 230).

STAKEHOLDER PROCEEDINGS

Introduction

Stakeholder proceedings are used to determine ownership of disputed property in two **14.75** circumstances:

(a) where a person ('the stakeholder') owes a debt, or has possession of goods or money, and does not claim the property personally, but is being, or expects to be, sued by competing claimants to the property;

(b) where an enforcement agent or officer has seized goods in execution which a person other than the judgment debtor claims to own.

The stakeholder or enforcement agent or officer in effect calls on the competing claimants to claim against each other (before 6 April 2014 this was called 'interpleading') so that title to the property can be decided by the court. The stakeholder or enforcement officer may then dispose of the property in accordance with the court's order, safe from being sued by the competing claimants.

CPR, Part 85, provides for three different kinds of claim that can arise during enforcement:

(a) **Part 85, Section III**, applies to an application to the court asserting that controlled goods taken by enforcement agents executing a writ or warrant of control under the provisions of the Tribunals, Courts and Enforcement Act 2007, sch. 12, and the Taking Control of Goods Regulations 2013 (SI 2013/1894) belong to the applicant and not to the debtor.

(b) **Part 85, Section IV**, applies to an application to the court claiming that goods, money or chattels taken or intended to be taken under a writ of execution or the proceeds or value of such goods belong to the applicant and not to the judgment debtor.

(c) **Part 85, Section V**, sets out the procedure where a debtor makes a claim that some or all of the goods taken under a writ or warrant of control or a writ of execution are exempt goods. In respect of controlled goods, exempt goods are those set out in the Tribunals, Courts and Enforcement Act 2007, sch. 12, para. 3(1), and SI 2013/1894, regs 4 and 5 (**CPR, r. 85.2(1)(k)**). In relation to executed goods, exempt goods has the meaning given in the Courts Act 2003, sch. 7, para. 9(3) (**CPR, r. 85.2(1)(k)**).

CPR, Part 86, applies to all other stakeholder claims and applications that arise outside of the enforcement process.

Participation by a property holder as an applicant in stakeholder proceedings does not ordinarily amount to a submission to the jurisdiction, because the purpose of stakeholder proceedings is to gain the protection of the court from the competing claimants (*Australia v Peacekeeper International FZC UAE* [2008] EWHC 1220 (QB), LTL 9/6/2008).

Procedure for making a claim to controlled or executed goods

CPR, Part 85, distinguishes between controlled and executed goods. **14.76**

Commentary

Controlled goods are goods taken by an enforcement agent under a warrant or writ of control under the Tribunals, Courts and Enforcement Act 2007, sch. 12, that (a) have not been sold or abandoned, (b) if they have been removed, have not been returned to the debtor (unless subject to a controlled goods agreement) and (c) if they are goods of another person, have not been returned to that person (Tribunals Courts and Enforcement Act 2007, sch. 12, para. 3(1)).

Executed goods are goods subject to a writ of execution (**CPR, r. 85.2(1)(j)**). A writ of execution is defined in **r. 85.2(1)(s)** as including a writ of possession, a writ of delivery, a writ of sequestration, writs relating to ecclesiastical property (*fieri facias de bonis ecclesiasticis, sequestrari de bonis ecclesiasticis*), and any further writ in aid of such writs, but does not include a writ of control.

The procedure for asserting a claim against controlled and executed goods is almost identical and it is set out below.

(a) Claimants must give notice in writing of their claim to the enforcement agent who has taken control of the goods, or the enforcement officer who has taken or intends to take the goods. The notice must contain the claimant's full name and address, and confirmation that such address is their address for service, a list of the goods which they assert a claim over and the grounds of their claim in respect of each item. This notice must be given as soon as practicable but in any event within seven days of the goods being removed (**rr. 85.4(1) and 85.6(1)**).

(b) The enforcement agent or enforcement officer must then notify the creditor and any other person making a claim to the controlled or executed goods within three days (**rr. 85.4(2) and 85.6(2)**).

(c) The creditor and any other person making a claim to the controlled or executed goods must, within seven days after receiving the notice of claim, give notice in writing to the enforcement agent or enforcement officer informing them whether the claim is admitted or disputed in whole or in part (**rr. 85.4(3) and 85.6(3)**).

(d) The enforcement agent or officer must, within three days of receiving that notice, notify the claimant whether the claim is admitted or disputed in whole or in part (**rr. 85.4(4) and 85.6(4)**).

(e) A creditor who gives notice admitting a claim is not liable to the enforcement agent or officer for any fees and expenses incurred by them after receipt of that notice (**rr. 85.4(5) and 85.6(5)**).

(f) If the enforcement agent or officer receives a notice from a creditor admitting the claim to the goods, then the enforcement power or the writ of execution ceases to be exercisable in respect of those controlled or executed goods and, if the goods have been removed from where they were found, the enforcement agent or officer must, as soon as reasonably practicable, make the goods available for collection by the claimant (**rr. 85.4(6) and 85.6(6)**).

(g) Where a creditor or other person making a claim to the controlled or executed goods fails to give notice stating whether the claim is admitted or disputed within the seven-day period set out in **rr. 85.4(3) and 85.6(3)**, the enforcement agent or officer may apply to the court for directions and for an order preventing the bringing of a claim against them for taking or failing to take control of the goods (**rr. 85.4(7) and 85.6(7)**). In relation to claims against executed goods, the enforcement officer has to apply to the court that issued the writ of execution.

(h) If the creditor or any other person making a claim to the controlled or executed goods has given notice that the claim or any part of the claim is disputed, the claimant must make an application under **Part 23**, supported by a witness statement which sets out the grounds of their claim to the goods, together with copies of any supporting documents. This must be served on the creditor, any other person making a claim to the goods, and the enforcement officer or enforcement agent. The application should be made to the court which issued the writ or warrant of control or the writ of execution. In respect of a claim to controlled goods, the claimant must also make the required payments in accordance with the Tribunals, Courts and Enforcement Act 2007, sch. 12, para. 60 (**CPR, rr. 85.5 and 85.7**). After receiving notice of an application to the court in relation to controlled goods, the enforcement agent must not sell or dispose of those controlled goods, unless directed by the court. The court can direct the enforcement agent to sell or dispose of the controlled goods if the applicant fails to make or to continue to make the required payments into court, or if the court otherwise considers it appropriate (Tribunals, Courts and Enforcement Act 2007, sch. 12, para. 60(2), (3) and (6)).

(i)   The court will then make orders for the management of the case, including directions for the retention, sale or disposal of the controlled or executed goods and directions for the determination of any issue raised by a claim to those goods (**CPR, rr. 85.5(8) and 85.7(6)**). The enforcement agent will usually request the court to remove him from the litigation so that the claim continues between the claimant, the creditor and if applicable the debtor.

An enforcement agent will not be liable for selling controlled goods in the possession of the judgment debtor which belong to a third party except where the enforcement officer or agent had notice at the time of the sale that the goods did not belong to the debtor and the third party (the lawful claimant to the goods) had made an application to the court claiming an interest in the goods at the time of the sale (Tribunals, Courts and Enforcement Act 2007, sch. 12, para. 63). The enforcement agent will also have no liability for paying out the proceeds of sale of the goods, unless at the time of the payment, he had notice that the goods did not belong to the debtor, or by then the lawful claimant to the goods had made an application to the court claiming an interest in the goods (sch. 12, para. 64). An enforcement agent will be regarded as having notice of something if they could have discovered it by making reasonable enquiries (sch. 12, para. 65).

Procedure for a debtor making a claim to exempt goods

The procedure for a debtor making a claim to exempt goods is set out in **CPR, r. 85.8**. It follows the same steps as for claims against controlled or executed goods described at **14.76**.   **14.77**

Stakeholder claims and applications

CPR, Part 86, governs all other competing claims to goods that are made outside the enforcement process. It applies where a person (the stakeholder) is under a liability in respect of a debt or in respect of any money, goods or chattels and competing claims are made against that person in respect of the debt, money, goods or chattels by two or more persons (**r. 86.1**). In such circumstances, the stakeholder can make an application to the court, by Part 8 claim form or an application notice if the claim is made in existing proceedings, for a direction as to whom he should pay the debt or money or give the goods or chattels (**r. 86.2(1) to (3)**). The claim form or application notice must be supported by a witness statement which confirms that the stakeholder has no interest in the subject matter of the dispute, other than for payment of his charges or costs, does not collude with any of the claimants, and is willing to pay or transfer the subject matter of the dispute into court or dispose of it as the court thinks fit (**r. 86.2(4)**). The stakeholder must serve the claim form or application notice on all persons who assert a claim to the subject matter of the application. A respondent served with the claim form or application notice has to file and serve on the stakeholder a witness statement setting out the grounds of his claim and identifying the money, goods or chattels to which the claim relates (**r. 86.2(6)**). The court will then hear the stakeholder application, and can give directions ordering which party should be claimant and defendant, order an issue to be tried between the parties and give directions for the trial of that issue, and give directions for the retention, sale or disposal of the subject matter of the stakeholder application and for the   **14.78**

payment of any proceeds of sale. The court can also hear the stakeholder application summarily (**rr. 86.3** and **86.4**).

ADDITION AND SUBSTITUTION OF PARTIES

Addition of parties

14.79   The court is given a wide discretion under the CPR to order that a person be added, removed or substituted as a party to a claim, provided that (in the case of adding a party) the limitation period has not yet expired. The court's attitude is permissive, provided the other party can be appropriately protected in costs. The court's power may be exercised upon application by a party, or by a person who wishes to intervene in proceedings to become a party, or by the court acting on its own initiative (**CPR, r. 19.4(2); PD 19A, para. 1.1**). Addition of a party after the expiry of a limitation period is considered at **14.85** to **14.90**.

The Administrative Court held in *River Thames Society v First Secretary of State* [2006] EWHC 2829 (Admin), LTL 22/9/2006, that the provisions of **CPR, Part 19**, do not apply to public law cases. The power to substitute parties in public law cases depends on the inherent jurisdiction of the court. In this case it permitted the vice-president of the claimant society to be substituted for the society itself, which wished to withdraw a challenge under the Town and Country Planning Act 1990, s. 288, because it had adopted a policy of non-involvement in litigation. The court allowed the substitution, applying *Eco-Energy (GB) Ltd v First Secretary of State* [2004] EWCA Civ 1566, LTL 10/1/2005, on the ground that there was sufficient identity of interest between the society and its vice-president so that the substitution would not undermine the principles of s. 288. Where substitution cannot take place because proceedings have been discontinued, the court may allow fresh judicial review proceedings to be brought out of time where they are in substantially the same terms as the original claim (*R (SDR) v Bristol City Council* [2012] EWHC 859 (Admin), LTL 5/4/2012). See also *San Vicente v Secretary of State for Communities and Local Government* [2013] EWCA Civ 817, [2014] 1 WLR 966 (six-week period for challenging the validity of a planning decision under the Town and Country Planning Act 1990, s. 288(3), is not a relevant limitation period for the purpose of **CPR, r. 17.4**, governing the amendment of statements of case after the expiry of the limitation period).

The court is empowered by **CPR, r. 19.2(2)**, to add a party where it is desirable:

(a) to enable it to resolve all the matters in dispute in the proceedings; or

(b) to resolve an issue between an existing party and a proposed new party, which is connected to the matters in dispute in the claim.

Adding a person as a claimant may not be done without the person's written consent, which must be filed at court (**CPR, r. 19.4(4)**). Any order made by the court joining a new claimant will not take effect unless and until the signed, written consent of the person joined has been filed (**PD 19A, para. 2.2**). The Commissioners for HM Revenue and Customs may be added as a party only if they consent (**CPR, r. 19.4(4A)**).

Discretion

14.80   In *United Film Distribution Ltd v Chhabria* [2001] EWCA Civ 416, [2001] 2 All ER (Comm) 865, the Court of Appeal stated that the discretion to add a party under **CPR, r. 19.2(2)**, is as wide as under the predecessors to that paragraph, namely, RSC, ord. 15, rr. 4(1) and 6(2)(b). **CPR, r. 19.2**, is not to be construed in a narrow way. Accordingly, where a party cannot bring himself within **r. 19.2(4)** (substitution where the existing party's interest or liability has passed to a new party), an order for substitution may nevertheless be made under **r. 19.2(2)** and (3) because the language of those rules achieves in two steps what could be achieved in a single step under **r. 19.4(2)**. To limit the power to substitute to circumstances where an interest or liability has passed from the party to the new party under **r. 19.4** would be to read the whole of **r. 19.2** in a way which would not do justice to a number of other situations where it would clearly be desirable to permit a change of party (*Hounslow London Borough Council v Cumar* [2012] EWCA Civ 1426, LTL 7/11/2012). However, claims that are quite separate will not be joined (*Turner v Haworth Associates* [2001] EWCA Civ 370, LTL 23/2/2001). The Court of Appeal confirmed in *Davies v Department of Trade and Industry* [2006] EWCA Civ 1360, [2007] 1 All ER 518, that the court has a very wide discretion to consider joinder under **r. 19.2(2)**. In this case, the interests of existing parties in keeping costs to a minimum outweighed the possible injustice to parties who wished to be added as additional defendants, which might arise from their being prevented from participating in the trial in circumstances when Part 20 proceedings might be brought against them at a later date. A party may be added to a claim under **r. 19.2(2)** even if none of the existing parties to the litigation could assert a substantive claim against the new party (*Dunlop Haywards (DHL) Ltd v Erinaceous Insurance Services Ltd* [2009] EWCA Civ 354, [2009] Lloyd's Rep IR 464). The court's power to add a new defendant is not limited to joining a person against whom the claimant wishes to make a claim or who is needed to complete the claimant's cause of action. **Rule 19.2(2)(b)** is wider than that. For the rule to be engaged, all that is necessary is that there is an 'issue' to be determined, which is 'connected to the matters in dispute in the proceedings', not that the issue forms part of a claim for relief against the new party (*Shetty v Al Rushaid Petroleum Investment Co.* [2011] EWHC 1460 (Ch), LTL 14/6/2011. See also *XYZ v Various Companies* [2014] EWHC 4056 (QB), LTL 9/12/2014).

Where an application is made to re-join a defendant against whom a claim in the same action has previously been struck out, the court should exercise its discretion under **r. 19.2**, in accordance with the test for bringing a second claim on the same facts as a claim struck out, established in *Securum Finance Ltd v Ashton* [2001] Ch 291 (see **33.27**) (*Kent v M and L Management and Legal Ltd* [2005] EWHC 2546 (Ch), LTL 28/11/2005). In *Kent v M and L Management and Legal Ltd* the court refused permission to re-join the defendant because it was no longer possible for him to have a fair trial. He had become mentally ill and could not give live evidence. Further, part of the evidence against him was contained in written statements from his mother who had since died.

In *Kooltrade Ltd v XTS Ltd* (2001) IPD 25018 doubt was cast on whether the power to substitute a new party under **r. 19.2** could be exercised after judgment, because it related to 'matters in dispute in the proceedings'. The Court of Appeal has now clarified the point. In *Dunwoody Sports Marketing v Prescott* [2007] EWCA Civ 461, [2007] 1 WLR 2343, it was held (following *C Inc. plc v L* [2001] 2 Lloyd's Rep 459 and *The Selby Paradigm* [2004] EWHC 1804 (Admlty), [2004] 2 Lloyd's Rep 714) that the power under **r. 19.2** to substitute a new party for an existing party does exist after judgment as well as before. On the facts of the case, the transferee of the claimant's business was substituted even though a final injunction had already been granted. See also *Starlight Shipping Co. v Allianz Marine and Aviation Versicherungs AG* [2011] EWHC 3381 (Comm), LTL 3/1/2012, where permission was granted under **r. 19.2(2)(b)** to add a party to a claim after it had been settled by Tomlin orders which the original defendant was seeking to enforce and which the new party wished to take advantage of.

Under **r. 19.2(2)** the court will add a person who is bound to satisfy any judgment given in the claim, for example, the Motor Insurers' Bureau (*Gurtner v Circuit* [1968] 2 QB 587). But it will not substitute a person who runs the risk of being ordered to pay costs, for example, a person funding one of the parties (see *Hamilton v Al Fayed* (2000) *The Times*, 13 October 2000) or a professional body such as the Medical Defence Union.

Substitution and removal of parties

The court may, by **CPR, r. 19.2(3)**, remove a party if it is not desirable for that person to be   **14.81**
a party to the proceedings.

The court may, by **r. 19.2(4)**, substitute a new party for an existing one if:

(a) the existing party's interest or liability has passed to the new party; and

(b) it is desirable to substitute the new party so that the court can resolve the matters in dispute in the proceedings.

If proceedings were commenced, before the expiry of the relevant limitation period, by a party whose cause of action has since been assigned following insolvency or transmitted on death, an application for an order under **r. 19.2(4)** does not involve raising a new claim under the Limitation Act 1980, s. 35, whether the assignment, death, bankruptcy or application occurs before or after the expiry of limitation (*Roberts v Gill and Co.* [2010] UKSC 22, [2011] 1 AC 240 at [103] to [104]).

Procedure

14.82 A party may only be added, removed or substituted with the permission of the court, unless the claim form has not been served. Thus where an existing party, or the proposed new party, wishes to change the parties to a claim, an application for permission to do so must be made under **CPR, Part 23** (**r. 19.4(1); PD 19A, para. 1.4**). The procedure is summarised in **procedural checklist 9**, and there is detailed commentary at **14.83** to **14.85**.

14.83 **Application** Application is made by filing an application notice in accordance with **CPR, r. 23.3** (**PD 19A, para. 1.4**). The application must be made on notice (except in the case of the substitution of a party following a transfer of interest or liability) and, where it is on notice, a copy of the application notice must be filed and served in accordance with **CPR, rr. 23.3** and **23.4** (**PD 19A, para. 1.4**). An application to add or substitute a party must be supported by evidence setting out the proposed new party's interest in or connection with the claim (**PD 19A, para. 1.3**). Where the application is to substitute a party following the transfer of an interest or liability, the evidence in support must show the stage reached by the proceedings and set out the change which has occurred to cause the transfer of interest or liability (**PD 19A, para. 5.2**). The rules contain no requirement for evidence to be submitted in support of an application to remove a party. The party applying for the amendment will usually be ordered to pay the costs of the application and any additional costs arising from the amendment.

Where the party to be added or substituted is a claimant, a copy of the proposed amended claim form and particulars of claim and the signed written consent of the new party must be filed with the application notice (**PD 19A, para. 2.1**).

14.84 **Hearing** Where all parties (and the proposed new party) agree the change, the application may be dealt with without a hearing (**PD 19A, para. 1.2**). The application must still be approved by a judicial officer, and the procedural judge has a discretion to refuse or allow an agreed order.

14.85 **Order and consequential directions** Where the court makes an order adding or substituting a party it will normally also make consequential directions (**CPR, r. 19.4(6)**). In addition to directions about the management of the proceedings, these will normally include orders that:

(a) the claimant or the party who made the application file the amended claim form and particulars of claim within 14 days (**PD 19A, paras 2.3(3) and 3.2(1)**);

(b) the new party be served with a copy of the existing statements of case (and documents referred to in them) (**paras 2.3(2) and 3.2(3)**);

(c) any new defendant (and, unless the court orders to the contrary, any other defendants) be served with the amended claim form and particulars of claim and the usual response pack (forms for admitting, defending and acknowledging the claim) (**para. 3.2(3)**); and

(d) a copy of the order be served on the parties, and any other person affected by it (**CPR, r. 19.4(5); PD 19A, paras 2.3(1) and 3.2(2)**).

A new defendant does not become a party to the proceedings until served with the amended claim form (**PD 19A, para. 3.3**). Thus it is this step (not the making of the application) which will interrupt the running of the limitation period against that person (*Ketteman v Hansel Properties Ltd* [1987] AC 189). However, in *Blake v Stewart* [2015] EWHC 3241 (Ch), the court expressed doubt as to the correctness of **PD 19A, para. 3.3**, and considered that it was doubtful, reading the rules and **PD 19A** as a whole, whether service of the order was a precondition of becoming a party. Although the defendant added to the claim had not been served with the claim form or the order adding him, the court refused to set aside a judgment order against him as he had been aware of the proceedings, and had inexcusably delayed in applying to have the order set aside.

When a party is removed, the claimant must file in court an amended claim form and particulars of claim, and a copy of the order must be served on every party and on any other person affected (**CPR, r. 19.4(5)**; **PD 19A, para. 4**). The court may give consequential directions about the management of the proceedings (**CPR, r. 19.4(6)**).

The procedure for amending a statement of case is dealt with in **PD 17, para.** 2 (see **chapter 31**).

An order giving permission to amend should normally be drawn up. The court will serve it, unless the parties wish, or the court orders them, to do so (**PD 19A, para. 1.5**).

Addition or substitution of a party after the expiry of the limitation period

14.86 The addition or substitution of parties after the expiry of a limitation period is considered at **14.86** to **14.91**. For the related topic of adding new causes of action after a limitation period has expired see **31.24** to **31.28**. The starting point is the Limitation Act 1980, s. 35, which provides:

35. New Claims in Pending Actions: Rules of Court

(1) For the purposes of this Act, any new claim made in the course of any action shall be deemed to be a separate action and to have been commenced—
   (a) in the case of a new claim made in or by way of third party proceedings, on the date on which those proceedings were commenced; and
   (b) in the case of any other new claim, on the same date as the original action.

(2) In this section a new claim means any claim by way of set-off or counterclaim, and any claim involving either—
   (a) the addition or substitution of a new cause of action; or
   (b) the addition or substitution of a new party;
   and 'third party proceedings' means any proceedings brought in the course of any action by any party to the action against a person not previously a party to the action, other than proceedings brought by joining any such person as defendant to any claim already made in the original action by the party bringing the proceedings.

(3) Except as provided by section 33 of this Act or by rules of court, neither the High Court nor the county court shall allow a new claim within subsection (1)(b) above, other than an original set-off or counterclaim, to be made in the course of any action after the expiry of any time limit under this Act which would affect a new action to enforce that claim.
   For the purposes of this subsection, a claim is an original set-off or an original counterclaim if it is a claim made by way of set-off or (as the case may be) by way of counterclaim by a party who has not previously made any claim in the action.

(4) Rules of court may provide for allowing a new claim to which subsection (3) above applies to be made as there mentioned, but only if the conditions specified in subsection (5) below are satisfied, and subject to any further restrictions the rules may impose.

(5) The conditions referred to in subsection (4) above are the following—
   (a) in the case of a claim involving a new cause of action, if the new cause of action arises out of the same facts or substantially the same facts as are already in issue on any claim previously made in the original action; and
   (b) in the case of a claim involving a new party, if the addition or substitution of the new party is necessary for the determination of the original action.

Commentary

(6)   The addition or substitution of a new party shall not be regarded for the purposes of subsection (5)(b) above as necessary for the determination of the original action unless either—

(a)   the new party is substituted for a party whose name was given in any claim made in the original action in mistake for the new party's name; or

(b)   any claim already made in the original action cannot be maintained by or against an existing party unless the new party is joined or substituted as plaintiff or defendant in that action.

(7)   Subject to subsection (4) above, rules of court may provide for allowing a party to any action to claim relief in a new capacity in respect of a new cause of action notwithstanding that he had no title to make that claim at the date of the commencement of the action.

This subsection shall not be taken as prejudicing the power of rules of court to provide for allowing a party to claim relief in a new capacity without adding or substituting a new cause of action.

(8)   Subsections (3) to (7) above shall apply in relation to a new claim made in the course of third party proceedings as if those proceedings were the original action, and subject to such other modifications as may be prescribed by rules of court in any case or class of case.

Section 35 and **CPR, r. 19.5**, restrict the circumstances in which parties can be added or substituted after the limitation period has expired. The addition or substitution has to be within the terms of the Limitation Act 1980, s. 35 (*Nemeti v Sabre Insurance Co. Ltd* [2013] EWCA Civ 1555, [2014] CP Rep 16). Substitution after expiry of the ten-year limitation period in s. 11A(3) is not generally permitted (*O'Byrne v Aventis Pasteur SA* (case C-358/08) [2010] 1 WLR 1375; *O'Byrne v Aventis Pasteur MSD Ltd* [2010] UKSC 23, [2010] 1 WLR 1412). The Supreme Court had to interpret a passage in the decision of the Court of Justice which said that Council Directive 85/374/EEC, art. 11, did not preclude a national court from allowing substitution after the ten-year limitation period if a claim had been instituted in time against a wholly owned subsidiary of the producer and the putting into circulation of the product had in fact been determined by the parent company which manufactured it. The Supreme Court held that this meant substitution was permitted only if the supplier could itself be sued as a producer within art. 3(1). As that was not the case on the facts, substitution was not permitted. In claims other than for personal injury, the court may grant permission only where the limitation period had not expired when the claim was issued, and the addition or substitution is necessary. It will be 'necessary' only if one of the circumstances discussed in **14.87** to **14.92** exists. In *Martin v Kaisary* [2005] EWCA Civ 594, [2006] PIQR P5, the court held that whether it is 'necessary' to add a defendant depends on whether the claim against the existing defendant can be determined without the addition of the new defendant. Adding an alternative claim against a new defendant is not 'necessary' within the meaning of the rule.

In *Tetra Pak Ltd v Biddle and Co.* [2010] EWHC 54 (Ch), [2010] 1 WLR 1466, it was held that serving separate particulars of claim on different defendants within the same claim did not involve raising a 'new claim' within the meaning of the Limitation Act 1980, s. 35(2) (at [71]), and involved no amendments to the particulars of claim served on the first defendants (at [88]). When deciding whether to allow an amendment after the expiry of the limitation period, the court must compare the proposed amendments with the particulars of claim, not the claim form (*Chandra v Brooke North* [2013] EWCA Civ 1559, [2014] TCLR 1). Where the claimant seeks permission to amend its particulars of claim to add a new cause of action, once the defendant shows a prima facie defence of limitation, the burden is on the claimant to show that the defence is not reasonably arguable. If the availability of the defence of limitation depends on disputed factual issues which can only be resolved at trial, the matter should not be determined summarily. A defendant can only be deprived of a limitation defence at an interlocutory stage if the claimant can demonstrate that the defence was not reasonably arguable (*Bellinger v Mercer Ltd* [2014] EWCA Civ 996, [2014] 1 WLR 3597).

14.87   **Correcting a mistake**   Under **CPR, r. 19.5(3)(a)**, which implements the Limitation Act 1980, s. 35, the court may substitute a new party for an existing party, after the expiry of a relevant limitation period, where the existing party was named in mistake for the new party. **CPR, r. 19.5(3)(a)**, allows the substitution of a new party for an existing party named in error, but not the addition of a new party, and so contemplates only a change in the persons named as parties, not an increase in their number. *Broadhurst v Broadhurst* [2007] EWHC 1828 (Ch), LTL

10/4/2007, makes the point (which must be right, and contradicts *Morgan Est (Scotland) Ltd v Hanson Concrete Products Ltd* [2005] EWCA Civ 134, [2005] 1 WLR 2557 — see below) that the use of 'substituted' in **r. 19.5(3)(a)** as opposed to 'added or substituted' in **r. 19.5(3)(b)** is significant. It means that a pure addition of a party is not permitted under **r. 19.5(3)(a)**. However, if there are two or more distinct claims against a party, substitution is possible under **r. 19.5(3)(a)** in respect of only some of the claims, leaving the others to continue against the original party (*Procter and Gamble (Health and Beauty Care) Ltd v Carrier Holdings Ltd* [2003] EWHC 83 (TCC), [2003] BLR 255; *Ultra Furniture Ltd v KPMG Audit plc* [2003] All ER (D) 302).

The Court of Appeal has stated in *Adelson v Associated Newspapers Ltd* [2007] EWCA Civ 701, [2008] 1 WLR 585, that it is necessary to have regard to the pre-CPR principles in applying **r. 19.5(3)(a)** as the provision is intended to replicate RSC, ord. 20, r. 5. It doubted *Morgan Est (Scotland) Ltd v Hanson Concrete Products Ltd* [2005] EWCA Civ 134, [2005] 1 WLR 2557, and *Weston v Gribben* [2006] EWCA Civ 1425, [2007] CP Rep 10, which sought to lay down principles free of the pre-CPR case law.

It held that in allowing applications under **CPR, r. 19.5(3)(a)**:

(a) The court must be satisfied that the person who makes the mistake, directly or through an agent, was the person responsible for issuing the claim form (**r. 19.5(3)(a)**).

(b) The applicant has to show that, had the mistake not been made, the new party would have been named in the claim form.

(c) The mistake must be about the name of the party rather than the identity of the party (*The Sardinia Sulcis* [1991] 1 Lloyd's Rep 201). Such a mistake in name may exist where the statements of case provided a description of the party, but gave the party the wrong name. A key question to ask is whether it is possible to identify the party by reference to a description more or less specific to the particular case. If the right description is given, but the wrong name is used, there is unlikely to be any doubt about the identity of the party to be sued, but if the wrong description is used, there is likely to be doubt about identity, and an order for substitution is unlikely to be made under **r. 19.5(3)(a)**. That a mistake is about name rather than identity may be demonstrated, for example, if a mistake is made about the group structure or the roles played by members of the group of companies in which the defendant and the new party operate. Often there will be a connection between the party named in the claim form and the party to be substituted (although this is not a requirement), and often the party intended to be substituted will have been aware of the proceedings (again this is not a formal requirement). If the party to be substituted was unaware of the claim, the court is likely to exercise its discretion against granting the application (*Horne-Roberts v SmithKline Beecham plc* [2001] EWCA Civ 2006, [2002] 1 WLR 1662). An application to substitute a director for the company, as it was the former rather than the latter which was the contracting party, failed under **r. 19.5(3)(a)**, because the mistake was as to the identity not the name of the party (*Dewrace Ltd v Brown* [2007] EWHC 3100 (TCC), LTL 20/2/2008).

In *Lockheed Martin Corp v Willis Group Ltd* [2010] EWCA Civ 927, [2010] PNLR 34, a claimant sued the wrong defendant by mistake and applied under **r. 19.5(3)(a)** and the Limitation Act 1980, s. 35(6)(a), to substitute a new party as defendant on the basis that the original party was named in mistake for the new defendant. An appeal was dismissed against an order refusing substitution on the ground that there was no cause of action against the proposed substituted defendant. It could not be said to be necessary to substitute the new party for the existing party when the claimant had no cause of action against the new party. The Court of Appeal also considered whether it was necessary to show that the original party was aware of the identity of the true intended party. It considered the status of the supposed second condition in genuine mistake cases that the true intended party had to be reasonably apparent to the original defendant. It held that this was not an additional formal condition of **CPR, r. 19.5**. This requirement was really an aspect of discretion. In many cases, the justice of the matter would militate against a successful application under **r. 19.5** unless the correct defendant was aware of the complaint before the limitation period expired, although this cannot be stated

Commentary

too firmly as a principle, and may be inconsistent with *Horne-Roberts v SmithKline Beecham plc* [2001] EWCA Civ 2006, [2002] 1 WLR 1662. The element of the test from *The Sardinia Sulcis* [1991] 1 Lloyd's Rep 201 that *Adelson v Associated Newspapers Ltd* [2007] EWCA Civ 701, [2008] 1 WLR 585 requires the court to apply is whether it is possible to identify the intended new party 'by reference to a description which was more or less specific to the particular case'. This phrase has to be interpreted as a reference to what description of the intended party was material, from a legal point of view, to the claim made (*Insight Group Ltd v Kingston Smith* [2012] EWHC 3644 (QB), [2013] PNLR 13). Even when the conditions in **CPR, r. 19.5(3)(a)**, are met, the court retains a discretion to make an order for substitution and it can refuse to do so where there has been delay on the part of the applicant in making the application, and relevant delay also includes delay in issuing and serving the claim form (*American Leisure Group Ltd v Olswang LLP* [2015] EWHC 629 (Ch), [2015] PNLR 21).

Rule 19.5(3)(a) should be read in conjunction with **r. 17.4(3)**, which provides that the court may make an amendment to correct a mistake as to the name of a party, but only where the mistake was genuine and not one which would cause reasonable doubt as to the identity of the party in question. Whether a mistake would cause reasonable doubt about the identity of the party intending to sue must be determined objectively having regard to what is said in the claim form in the light of what was known by the defendant and the context in which the claim was made (*ABB Asea Brown Boveri Ltd v Hiscox Dedicated Corporate Member Ltd* [2007] EWHC 1150 (Comm), LTL 24/5/2007). A description of the role played by the claimant in the particulars of claim attached to the claim form may be sufficiently clear to avoid such doubt (*International Bulk Shipping and Services Ltd v Minerals and Metals Trading Corporation of India* [1996] 1 All ER 1017). In *Gregson v Channel Four Television Corporation* [2000] CP Rep 60 (approved in *Adelson v Associated Newspapers Ltd*), the Court of Appeal considered the relationship between **r. 17.4(3)** and **r. 19.5(2)** and (3). It held that **r. 19.5** deals with cases where the claimant mistakenly names the wrong person as defendant, whereas **r. 17.4** deals with cases where the claimant misnames the defendant. The court made clear that there is no significant conflict between the two rules, thus confirming the decision in *International Distillers and Vintners Ltd v J. F. Hillebrand (UK) Ltd* (1999) *The Times*, 25 January 2000. In *Lockheed Martin Corp v Willis Group Ltd* [2010] EWCA Civ 927, [2010] PNLR 34, the Court of Appeal also noted that there is no further jurisdictional requirement in **r. 19.5(3)(a)** that the mistake was not misleading to the other party or had not caused reasonable doubt as to the identity of the party intended to be sued. Even if such a test had to be applied, it had to be judged objectively by the court. The guidance given in *Welsh Development Agency v Redpath Dorman Long Ltd* [1994] 1 WLR 1409 remains effective (*Chandra v Brooke North* [2013] EWCA Civ 1559, [2014] TCLR 1; *Bellinger v Mercer Ltd* [2014] EWCA Civ 996, [2014] 1 WLR 3597). **Rule 17.4** can be used to correct the description of a party, even though it only refers to correcting the name of a party, in circumstances where it is acceptable to commence proceedings against a party by reference to their description rather than by name (*Maman v Certain Lloyd's Underwriters subscribing to Policy No. DCAL/08230* [2016] EWHC 1327 (QB), LTL 23/6/2016).

14.88   **Claim cannot properly be continued**   The court may add or substitute a new party as claimant or defendant after the expiry of a relevant limitation period if the claim cannot properly be continued without the addition or substitution of the new party (**CPR, r. 19.5(3)(b)**). This rule gives effect to the Limitation Act 1980, s. 35(6)(b). The operation of the equivalent provision in the old rules (RSC, ord. 15, r. 6(6)) was limited to five categories of case in which, for technical reasons, claims were liable to be defeated for want of the correct parties. These were where: the claim concerned property vested in the new party at law or in equity and the claimant had an equitable interest in the property; the claim was vested in the claimant and the new party jointly but not severally; the new party was the Attorney General and the proceedings should have been brought as relator proceedings in his name; the new party was a company in which the claimant was a shareholder whose claim was liable to be defeated by the proper claimant principle (see **14.27**); and the claim should have been brought against new party and the existing defendant jointly. It remains to be seen whether **CPR, r. 19.5(3)(b)**, will be interpreted in a similar, restrictive way, but it is submitted that it should be, so as to accord with the policy of the Limitation Act 1980, s. 35. This view is supported by *Merrett v Babb* [2001] EWCA Civ 214, [2001] QB 1174, where permission to add the claimant's mother as second claimant was granted after the expiry of the limitation period on the ground that the cause of action was vested in them jointly, so the claim could not be maintained by the original claimant without joining her mother. In *Martin v Kaisary* [2005] EWCA Civ 594, [2006] PIQR P5, joinder of a new defendant was not permitted as it was not necessary to establish the liability of the original defendant. The addition of a party could not be said to be necessary within the meaning of **CPR, r. 19.5(2)** and **(3)(b)**, where it was not needed to maintain an existing claim but rather to enable the bringing of a new claim outside the limitation period (*Roberts v Gill and Co.* [2010] UKSC 22, [2011] 1 AC 240).

In *Parkinson Engineering Services plc v Swan* [2009] EWCA Civ 1366, [2010] Bus LR 857, the Court of Appeal distinguished *Adelson v Associated Newspapers Ltd* [2007] EWCA Civ 701, [2008] 1 WLR 585, and *Roberts v Gill and Co.*, and upheld an order permitting a liquidator to be substituted as claimant, instead of the company in liquidation, in proceedings brought against administrators for negligence. The substitution was made so as to prevent the administrators relying on a statutory defence under what is now the Insolvency Act 1986, sch. B1, para. 98, which the court could not disapply in a claim brought by the company, but could, and did, disapply in an application brought by the liquidator under s. 212 (sch. B1, para. 75(6)). The Court of Appeal held that the order for substitution was necessary in the terms of the Limitation Act 1980, s. 35(5)(b), and **CPR, r. 19.5(3)(b)**. The original claim could not properly be carried on by the original party (the company) as it was bound to fail or be struck out because of the statutory defence, but it could be maintained and carried on if the liquidator was substituted.

In *Nemeti v Sabre Insurance Co. Ltd* [2013] EWCA Civ 1555, [2014] CP Rep 16, the claimant originally brought a claim against the proposed defendant's insurers under the European Communities (Rights against Insurers) Regulations 2002 (SI 2002/3061) in respect of injuries he suffered in a road traffic accident. However, as the defendant was uninsured at the time, the Regulations did not apply. The claimant then sought to amend by substituting the personal representatives of the deceased driver as defendants. The court held that this was a new claim, because the original claim against the insurers was derived from statute, namely the Regulations, and the amended claim was based on negligence. The conditions in the Limitation Act 1980, s. 35, for allowing such a claim outside the expiry of the limitation period were not met and the substitution of the new party was not necessary for the determination of the original claim within the meaning of **CPR, r. 19.5(2)(b)**.

While the Supreme Court dismissed the appeal in *Roberts v Gill and Co.* [2010] UKSC 22, [2011] 1 AC 240, the unanimous ground was that there were no special circumstances justifying a derivative claim by the beneficiary. A majority (Lord Collins of Mapesbury JSC, Lord Rodger of Earlsferry JSC and Lord Walker of Gestingthorpe JSC) also held that it would be an abuse of process to allow changes in capacity (from the claimant's personal capacity as a beneficiary to a representative capacity) and the addition of the personal representative of the estate in stages as a device to get around the provisions of the Limitation Act 1980, s. 35 (see [70] to [72], [85] and [95]).

An order substituting a company in place of the company's administrator under **CPR, r. 19.5(3) (b)**, was made in *Irwin v Lynch* [2010] EWCA Civ 1153, LTL 6/10/2010, in a misfeasance claim against its directors. Such a claim cannot be brought by an administrator (Insolvency Act 1986, s. 212(3)), so the claim could not be continued without substituting the company. The court commented that it would not allow the jurisdiction under **r. 19.5(3)(b)** to be used to circumvent the restrictions in **rr. 17.4** and **19.5(3)(a)** where the case really involves a mistake if the additional requirements in those provisions for curing mistakes cannot be satisfied.

Death and bankruptcy   If a party to a claim dies or is adjudicated bankrupt, the court may, **14.89** even if a relevant limitation period has expired, add or substitute as a party the person to whom the deceased or bankrupt party's interest or liability has passed (**CPR, r. 19.5(3)(c)**). In *Morgan*

Est (Scotland) Ltd v Hanson Concrete Products Ltd [2005] EWCA Civ 134, [2005] 1 WLR 2557, the court used **r. 19.5(3)(c)** to permit the addition of a claimant to whom the claim had been assigned, despite the fact that the rule does not refer to transmission by assignment. **Rule 19.5(3)(c)** was included in **Part 19** in order to provide for situations referred to in *Yorkshire Regional Health Authority v Fairclough Building Ltd* [1996] 1 WLR 210 at p. 218. As discussed at **14.81**, this is unnecessary because the transmission of a cause of action following assignment, death or bankruptcy does not raise a new claim under the Limitation Act 1980, s. 35, and these situations should be dealt with under **r. 19.2(4)**. Lord Walker of Gestingthorpe JSC described **r. 19.5(3)(c)** as an 'oddity' in *Roberts v Gill and Co.* [2010] UKSC 22, [2011] 1 AC 240 at [104].

14.90 **Alteration of capacity** The court may, after a relevant limitation period has expired, allow an amendment to alter the capacity in which a party claims, if the new capacity is one which that party had when the proceedings started or has since acquired (**CPR, r. 17.4(4)**). In *Haq v Singh* [2001] EWCA Civ 957, [2001] 1 WLR 1594 the court held that 'capacity' in **r. 17.4(4)** has the same meaning as it has in the Limitation Act 1980, s. 35. Thus the alteration in capacity referred to is an alteration from a representative capacity or personal capacity to another representative capacity, or (in the case of a representative claim) from a representative capacity to a personal capacity. The claimant could not take advantage of **CPR, r. 17.4(4)**, to cure her lack of standing by taking an assignment of the cause of action which had previously been vested in her trustee in bankruptcy. The reality was that the claim was being brought by her in her personal capacity both before and after the assignment. If an amendment after the limitation period requires the addition of a new party as well as a change of capacity, the requirements of **r. 19.5(3)** must be satisfied as well as those of **r. 17.4** (*Roberts v Gill and Co.* [2010] UKSC 22, [2011] 1 AC 240).

The final words in **r. 17.4(4)** ('or has since acquired') give effect to a recommendation of the Law Reform Commission to avoid the anomaly that while the title of an executor relates back, on the grant of probate, to the date of the testator's death, the title of an administrator only relates back to the date of the grant of letters of administration. These words therefore allow alterations in the case of administrators as well as executors (*Roberts v Gill and Co.* [2010] UKSC 22, [2010] 1 AC 240 at [34]).

14.91 **Personal injury claims** CPR, **r. 19.5(4)**, gives the court an additional power in a personal injuries case to add a new party after the expiry of the limitation period:

(a) where it has exercised its discretion under the Limitation Act 1980, s. 33, to override the usual three-year limitation period for a personal injuries claim (Limitation Act 1980, s. 11) or a claim under the fatal accidents legislation (Limitation Act 1980, s. 12); or

(b) where it directs that this issue should be decided at trial.

Procedure for substitution following assignment

14.92 CPR, **r. 19.2(4)**, provides that:

The court may order a new party to be substituted for an existing one if—
(a) the existing party's interest or liability has passed to the new party; and
(b) it is desirable to substitute the new party so that the court can resolve the matters in dispute in the proceedings.

An application for such an order may be made without notice but must be supported by evidence (**r. 19.4(3)**) showing the stage the claim has reached and setting out details of the transfer of interest or liability (**PD 19A, para. 5.2**).

A new claimant must consent in writing to being added as a claimant, and the consent must be filed at court (**CPR, r. 19.4(4)**). The order substituting the new party must then be served on all parties and any other person affected by it (**r. 19.4(5)**). The court will order service of the existing statements of case on the new party.

Chapter 15   Filing and Service

Commentary

The following procedural checklists are relevant to this chapter and **chapter 12**:

Procedural checklist 3   Issue and service where service of the claim form is to be effected by the court
Procedural checklist 4   Issue and service where service of the claim form is to be effected by the claimant

The following procedural checklist is relevant to this chapter:

Procedural checklist 10   Application to extend time for service of claim form

INTRODUCTION

15.1   Service is the process by which one party seeks to bring a document to the attention of another party. The document may be the claim form, service of which notifies the defendant that proceedings have been issued against him, or any other document in the proceedings. As has been stated in previous editions of this work, the rules on service in the CPR were initially among the least successful of the Woolf reforms and generated a large volume of new case law. In *Collier v Williams* [2006] EWCA Civ 20, [2006] 1 WLR 1945, Dyson LJ noted that the rules were proving difficult to understand and apply. He commented with dismay that the intention of reducing cost, complexity and delays in litigation by the introduction of rules which were simple, straightforward and not susceptible to satellite litigation had not been achieved in this area.

For this reason, and because of the fundamental importance of the service rules, the Civil Procedure Rule Committee conducted a comprehensive review of **CPR, Part 6**, leading to the introduction, with effect from 1 October 2008, of a new **CPR, Part 6**, and associated practice directions, **PD 6A** and **PD 6B**. The new rules have been effective in reducing the quantity of satellite litigation on the question of service.

SERVICE OF CLAIM FORM

15.2   **CPR, Part 6**, distinguishes between service of claim forms and service of other documents. **Part 6, Section II**, sets out the rules for service of the claim form in the jurisdiction. The rules governing the service of other documents in the United Kingdom are contained in **Part 6, Section III**, and are dealt with at **15.37** to **15.44**. In practice, there are few differences between the two regimes, the most important being those relating to the rules for deemed service (see **15.36** and **15.42**). **Part 6, Section IV**, governs service of the claim form and other documents out of the jurisdiction (see **chapter 16**). Service of claim forms in Scotland and Northern Ireland is governed by **r. 6.32**. Service of other documents in Scotland and Northern Ireland is covered by **Part 6, Section III** (see **r. 6.38(3)**).

Definition of 'claim form'

15.3   'Claim form' is defined to include petitions and other documents used to commence proceedings as well as documents used to bring pre-action applications (**CPR, r. 6.2(c)**). Thus an application notice for pre-action disclosure under **r. 31.16**, for example, must be served in accordance with **Part 6, Section II**, and **r. 6.14** will determine its deemed date of service.

In *Weston v Bates* [2012] EWHC 590 (QB), [2013] 1 WLR 189, the court considered whether service out of the jurisdiction of a printout of a scan of a photocopy of a claim form was valid, or whether the original, sealed copy of the claim form was required for service. It held that under the CPR what constituted a claim form was a matter of substance and that the words 'claim form' were not a reference to a particular hard copy of the document. Nevertheless, although the court upheld service in this case, practitioners were strongly advised to serve the original, sealed copy to avoid questions being raised about the validity of service. In *Hills Contractors and Construction Ltd v Struth* [2013] EWHC 1693 (TCC), [2014] 1 WLR 1, the court considered the effect of **r. 2.6(1)** (which requires the court to seal the claim form) and **r. 7.2(1)** (which provides that proceedings are commenced when the court issues a claim form) and held that the claim form is the document issued and sealed by the court, and this is the document referred to in **r. 6.3(1)**, which listed the methods by which a claim form may be served. Service of a photocopy of the claim form was therefore not sufficient.

Documents to be served

In most cases, the only document which must be served on the defendant is the claim form itself. Where the Part 8 procedure is being used, the claim form must be accompanied by a form for acknowledging service (**CPR, r. 7.8(2)**) as well as any written evidence on which the claimant intends to rely (**r. 8.5(1) and (2)**).

15.4

The particulars of claim may be included in the claim form, served at the same time but in a separate document, or served subsequently, although **PD 16, para. 3.1**, exhorts practitioners to include the particulars of claim in the claim form if practicable. The response pack required under **CPR, r. 7.8(1)**, accompanies the particulars of claim not the claim form, and so is not needed if the particulars are not included in or served with the claim form. However, in this case the claim form must contain a statement that particulars of claim will follow (**PD 7A, para. 6.2; PD 16, para. 3.3**). Where particulars of claim are served with the claim form, and so must be accompanied by the response pack, failure to include the response pack will not invalidate service. Failure to include the response pack is a matter for the court to take into account under **CPR, r. 13.3(1)(b)**, in considering whether or not to set the judgment aside (*Hart Investments Ltd v Fidler* [2006] EWHC 2857 (TCC), [2007] BLR 30). A similar approach was taken in *Hughes v Alan Dick and Co. Ltd* [2008] EWHC 2695 (QB), LTL 8/1/2009 and *Rajval Construction Ltd v Bestville Properties Ltd* [2010] EWCA Civ 1621, [2011] CILL 2994; see further **20.13**).

There are exceptions in specialised proceedings. For example, in possession claims the particulars of claim must be filed and served with the claim form (**CPR, r. 55.4**). In Commercial Court cases, the documents for responding to the claim must be served with the claim form (**r. 58.5(1)(b)**).

For the documents required to be served with the particulars of claim, see **15.40**.

Who may serve the claim form?

Unless the claimant is required to serve the claim form by a rule, court order or practice direction, the claimant may either serve it himself or ask the court in which it is issued to do so (**CPR, r. 6.4(1)**). In most cases, the court will serve the claim form unless the claimant notifies the court that the claimant wishes to serve it. The court will not serve particulars of claim unless they are to be served with the claim form (**r. 6.21(1)**).

15.5

For several specialist proceedings, the option of court service is not available. The Commercial Court will not serve documents or orders and service must be effected by the parties (**PD 58, para. 9**). Neither the High Court nor the County Court will serve documents in insolvency proceedings, except where otherwise provided by the Insolvency Rules 1986 or required under Regulation (EC) No. 1393/2007 (**PD Insolvency Proceedings, para. 6.2**). Those courts will not serve documents in proceedings under the Companies Acts and related legislation (**PD 49A, para. 28**) or claim forms in directors disqualification proceedings (**PD Directors Disqualification Proceedings, para. 7.1**).

The Civil Appeals Office will not serve documents relating to proceedings before the Court of Appeal (**PD 52C, para. 7.1**).

The court will not serve documents which are filed under the Electronic Working Pilot Scheme (**PD 51O, para. 8.2**). See **12.12** for more detail about this scheme.

Service by the court   A claimant who wishes the court to serve the claim form must file in court a copy of it for service on each defendant, as well as a copy for the court (**CPR, r. 6.4(3)**).

15.6

Commentary

It is then for the court to decide which method of service to use (**CPR, r. 6.4(2)**). The method will normally be first class post (**PD 6A, para. 8.1**).

The court will notify the claimant that the claim form has been served in the notice of issue, which will also indicate the deemed date of service (**CPR, r. 6.17(1)**).

The court will notify the claimant if a claim form which the court has served on the defendant by post is returned undelivered (**r. 6.18**). **Rule 6.18(2)** provides that the claim form will nevertheless be deemed to have been served, unless the defendant's address on the claim form is not the right address under **rr. 6.7 to 6.10**. The court must also notify the party who requested service of a document by the bailiff if the bailiff has been unable to serve it (**r. 6.19**).

Where the court file contains no record that service has taken place, there can be no presumption that service has indeed been effected by the court (*Patel v Smeaton* [2000] WL 1675263). Where a court fails to effect service within the period for service of the claim form, the claimant may apply for an extension of time for serving the claim form under **r. 7.6(3)(a)**.

The procedure is summarised in **procedural checklist 3**.

15.7 **Service by a party**   It is always open to a claimant to make its own arrangements to serve the claim form, instead of using the option of court service. Many practitioners prefer to serve documents themselves, either to retain control over the process, for example, because they do not wish to serve the claim form immediately upon issue, or to take advantage of the wider methods of service available when a party serves.

The claimant should notify the court that it intends to serve the claim form when it files the claim form (**CPR, r. 6.4(1)(b)**). The rules do not specify the form that notification should take. In practice, a party may notify the court informally by letter that it wishes to effect service. In the RCJ, solicitors are invited to indicate at the commencement of proceedings whether they wish to effect service themselves, and if this is done, the file will be marked accordingly and no further application will be necessary.

The claimant must file a certificate of service of the claim form (form N215) within 21 days of service of the particulars of claim, giving the particulars required by **r. 6.17(3)**, unless the defendants have all filed acknowledgments by then, in which case no notification to the court is required (**r. 6.17(2)(a)**). A claimant may not obtain judgment in default under **Part 12** unless a certificate of service has been filed (**r. 6.17(2)(b)**). Failure to file a certificate of service will not automatically lead to a default judgment being set aside, but it may constitute a good reason under **r. 13.3(1)(b)** why the court may set aside judgment (*Henriksen v Pires* [2011] EWCA Civ 1720, LTL 14/2/2012). In this case, as the claimant had held an affidavit of service containing all the information requested by form N215 it was not appropriate to set aside the default judgment.

Service out of the jurisdiction through the Senior Master and through diplomatic channels is service by the claimant and not service by the court (*Chare v Fairclough* [2003] EWHC 180 (QB), LTL 20/01/2003).

The procedure is summarised in **procedural checklist 4**.

On whom may a claim form be served?

15.8 **Service on the defendant**   A claim form should be served on the defendant except where the defendant has nominated a solicitor or European lawyer to accept service on his behalf, in which case service must be effected on the solicitor or European lawyer (see **15.9**). Subject to any requirement for personal service (see **15.11**), service on the defendant may be at the address for service specified (before service) by the defendant. For this purpose, a defendant may specify an address in any part of the United Kingdom or any other EEA State where the defendant resides or carries on business (**r. 6.8**, which is subject to any contrary provision in any rule or practice direction). Service outside England and Wales is subject to the provisions of **Part 6, Section IV**, on service out of the jurisdiction (see **16.58** to **16.69**). Before 6 April 2011, the address had to be within the United Kingdom. Before 1 October 2008, it had to be within England and Wales.

There are special rules specifying the individuals who may validly be served on behalf of companies, partnerships, limited partnerships, children and protected parties. These are dealt with in **15.45** to **15.51**.

Service on the defendant's solicitor or European lawyer Unless personal service on the defendant is required (see **15.11**), a claim form must (**CPR, r. 6.7(1)**) be served at the business address within the jurisdiction of the defendant's solicitor if: **15.9**

(a) the defendant has given written notification that that address is his address for service of the claim form; or

(b) the solicitor has notified the claimant in writing that he has the defendant's instructions to accept service at that address.

Unless personal service on the defendant is required (see **15.11**), a claim form must (**r. 6.7(2)**) be served at the business address in another part of the United Kingdom or in another EEA State of the defendant's solicitor if:

(a) the defendant has given written notification that that address is his address for service of the claim form; or

(b) the solicitor has notified the claimant in writing that he has the defendant's instructions to accept service at that address.

Unless personal service on the defendant is required (see **15.11**), a claim form must (**r. 6.7(3)**) be served on a European lawyer at that lawyer's business address anywhere in the EEA if:

(a) the defendant has given written notification that that address is his address for service of the claim form; or

(b) the European lawyer has notified the claimant in writing that he has the defendant's instructions to accept service at that address.

Service outside England and Wales is subject to the provisions of **Part 6, Section IV**, on service out of the jurisdiction (see **16.58** to **16.69**).

For the purposes of **Part 6**, 'solicitor' has an extended definition, which includes any person who, under the Legal Services Act 2007, is authorised to conduct litigation (**CPR, r. 6.2(d)**). The term 'European lawyer' is defined in the European Communities (Services of Lawyers) Order 1978 (SI 1978/1910), art. 2 (applied by **CPR, r. 6.2(e)**).

Sending the claim form to a solicitor who has been involved in pre-action correspondence with the claimant will not be good service if notification under **r. 6.7** has not been given, even though it will probably result in the claim form coming to the attention of the defendant (*Brown v Innovatorone plc* [2009] EWHC 1376 (Comm), [2010] 2 All ER (Comm) 80).

The wording of **r. 6.7** neatly avoids the confusion under earlier rules which had led to the Court of Appeal holding that, in the case of personal service, notification of the nomination of a solicitor for service had to come from the solicitor not the defendant. The result of this was that personal service on a defendant was valid even where the defendant had notified the claimant that service should be effected on his solicitor, although no other forms of service on the defendant were permitted once such notification had been made (see *Collier v Williams* [2006] EWCA Civ 20, [2006] 1 WLR 1945).

It is likely that jurisprudence under what was then r. 6.5, requiring the solicitor's authority to accept service to relate to the specific claim in which the claim form has been issued, remains valid (*Nagusina Naviera v Allied Maritime Inc.* [2002] EWCA Civ 1147, LTL 10/7/2002; *Firstdale Ltd v Quinton* [2004]

EWHC 1926 (Comm), [2005] 1 All ER 639; *Peacocks Ltd v Chapman Taylor* [2004] EWHC 2898 (TCC), LTL 18/4/2005). Practitioners acting for a claimant should seek written instructions to accept service of each specific claim form, rather than relying on the fact that the defendant's solicitors have accepted service in related proceedings, or have been involved in pre-action correspondence.

METHODS OF SERVING A CLAIM FORM

Prescribed methods of service of the claim form

15.10   The methods of service permitted under **CPR, Part 6**, are listed in **r. 6.3**. They are:

(a)   personal service in accordance with **r. 6.5**;

(b)   first class post, document exchange or other service which provides for delivery on the next business day, in accordance with **PD 6A**;

(c)   leaving the claim form at a place specified in **rr. 6.7, 6.8, 6.9** or **6.10**;

(d)   fax or other means of electronic communication in accordance with **PD 6A**; or

(e)   any method authorised by the court under **r. 6.15**.

Rule 6.3 lists the methods of service of a claim form in the jurisdiction. Alternative methods of service are considered at **15.17** to **15.21**. Whether the list in **r. 6.3** is exhaustive is considered at **15.22**.

The CPR do not define what is meant by service other than prescribing how it may be done. In *Asia Pacific (HK) Ltd v Hanjin Shipping Co. Ltd* [2005] EWHC 2443 (Comm), [2005] 2 CLC 747, the question arose whether a claim form which had been transmitted to a defendant by fax, and therefore in a manner provided for under the rules, was intended to be served or was for information only. The court held that when a claim form was delivered to the recipient in a manner provided for by the rules, it was served unless it was made clear by the person who delivered it that whilst he was delivering the form by such a method he was not in fact serving it. The fact that no response pack was served, that the claim form was marked 'Claimant's copy' and that the fax did not state that the claim form was faxed by way of service did not demonstrate that no service was intended at all. In *Hills Contractors and Construction Ltd v Struth* [2013] EWHC 1693 (TCC), [2014] 1 WLR 1, the claimant sent the defendant a photocopy of the claim form, but as the claimant did not regard this as service of the claim form, it was not followed with service of the particulars of claim. Despite the fact the defendant confirmed that they accepted the photocopy as service of the claim form, the court held, having regard to the whole context, that the claimant's actions could not objectively be construed as an intention to serve the claim form, therefore the time for service of the particulars of claim had not yet commenced, and the judgment that was entered on the defendant's application for default by the claimant in serving the particulars of claim was set aside.

General provisions about methods of service are considered at **15.10** to **15.15**.

There are special rules for service on the Crown (see **15.52**) and service in proceedings for the recovery of land and mortgage possession claims (**Part 55**). There are also special guidelines for service on members of the US Air Force and members of HM Forces in the annex to **PD 6A**.

Personal service

15.11   Personal service has to be used to serve a claim form where a statute, a rule, practice direction or order requires it (**CPR, r. 6.5(1)**). An example of a claim form which is required by a rule to be served personally is a Part 8 claim form for permission to make a committal application (**r. 81.14(2)**).

In other cases, an individual may be served personally except where notice has been given under **r. 6.7** that a solicitor has instructions to accept service on the defendant's behalf. For service on a party's solicitor, see **15.9**.

A document is served personally on an individual by leaving it with that individual (**r. 6.5(3) (a)**). The meaning of 'personal service' was considered in *Ener-G Holdings plc v Hormell* [2012] EWCA Civ 1059, [2012] CP Rep 47. The question arose in the context of the construction of a contract which required a notice to be served by 'delivering it personally'. The court held that this phrase meant personal service, and that personal service required that the notice should be handed to the intended recipient personally. It did not mean delivery in person by a process server (or anyone else) who simply left the notice at the address for service to be found by the defendant.

Personal service may be effected on the defendant wherever he or she happens to be found in the jurisdiction. It is likely that personal service on a reluctant defendant is effective if the individual to be served is informed of what the document is and it is left as nearly as possible in his or her possession or control (*Thompson v Pheney* (1832) 1 Dowl Pr Cas 441). If the person to be served will not accept the document, personal service is validly effected if the person is told what the document contained and it is left with or near him or her, and this includes leaving it with someone who is present with the person to be served, such as a friend. What is important is that the person to be served has a sufficient opportunity of possessing the document to enable him or her to exercise dominion over it (*Gate Gourmet Luxembourg IV Sàrl v Morby* [2016] EWHC 74 (Ch), [2016] Bus LR 218). Once a document which is to be served on an individual has been handed to that individual and the individual knows what it is, the document is served and it makes no difference that the individual gives it back to the process server (*Nottingham Building Society v Peter Bennett and Co.* (1997) *The Times*, 26 February 1997).

Leaving the claim form with a third party who has no authority to accept it on behalf of the defendant does not amount to personal service (*Cherney v Deripaska* [2007] EWHC 965 (Comm), [2007] 2 All ER (Comm) 785). This is so even if the third party hands the documents to the defendant, unless the third party agrees to become the claimant's agent for the purpose of effecting service of the claim form (*Kenneth Allison Ltd v A. E. Limehouse and Co.* [1992] 2 AC 105).

Postal service

Under **CPR, r. 6.3(1)(b)**, service of a claim form within the jurisdiction may be effected by **15.12** first class post, document exchange or other service which provides for delivery on the next business day. Postal service is no longer limited to Royal Mail first class post, as the Royal Mail's postal service monopoly came to an end in 2006.

Exactly how service is effected by post, document exchange (DX) or other service is defined in **PD 6A, para. 3.1**, as:

(a) placing the claim form in a postbox;
(b) leaving it with or delivering it to the relevant service provider; or
(c) having it collected by the relevant service provider.

In addition, by **PD 6A, para. 2.1**, service by DX is only allowed if:

(a) the address at which the party is to be served includes a numbered box at a DX; or
(b) the writing paper of the party who is to be served or of the solicitor acting for that party sets out a DX box number; and (in either case)
(c) the party or the solicitor acting for that party has not indicated in writing that they are unwilling to accept service by DX.

The claim form should be posted to:

(a) the address of the defendant's solicitor or European lawyer under **CPR, r. 6.7**; or
(b) if the defendant has not instructed a solicitor or European lawyer to accept service for him, the address (in the UK or any other EEA State) for service which the defendant has provided under **r. 6.8**; or

(c) if the defendant has provided no address for service, as a last resort, the address specified in the table at **r. 6.9(2)** (see **15.14**). Postal service at this address is valid even if the defendant is out of the jurisdiction at the time of service (*Kamali v City and Country Properties Ltd* [2006] EWCA Civ 1879, [2007] 1 WLR 1219).

Service by leaving the claim form at an address

15.13   Service of a claim form may be effected under **CPR, r. 6.3(1)(c)**, by leaving it at the defendant's solicitor's address, or if he has not instructed a solicitor to accept service for him, at the address for service he has provided, or, if he has provided no such address, as a last resort, at the address specified in the table at **r. 6.9(2)**. See **15.14**.

Where the claim form must be served

15.14   Personal service may be effected on an individual defendant wherever he or she is found within the jurisdiction. Service on a defendant's solicitor should be effected at the solicitor's business address within the United Kingdom or within an EEA State (**CPR, r. 6.7**).

The position in relation to postal service or service by leaving the claim form at an address is more complicated.

In order to identify an address where service may safely be effected, the claimant should ask the defendant for his or her address for service within the United Kingdom or any other EEA State, under **r. 6.8(a)**. Although the rules do not expressly require a claimant to make this enquiry, in *Mersey Docks Property Holdings v Kilgour* [2004] EWHC 1638 (TCC), [2004] BLR 412, the court concluded that the claimant had not taken all reasonable steps to ascertain the defendant's whereabouts because it had taken no steps to communicate with the defendant directly.

If a defendant does not provide any address in response to this enquiry, service should be effected at the address specified in the table in **r. 6.9(2)** (see **table 15.1**). In the case of an individual, the address in the table is that of his or her usual or last known residence. Where the individual is being sued in the name of a business, service may alternatively be effected at the principal or last known place of business. An individual is not sued in the name of a business if he is an employee working in someone else's business. An individual is sued in the name of a business when he is sued in the name of a business which is not his personal name (*Murrills v Berlanda* [2014] EWCA Civ 6, [2014] CP Rep 21). Where the individual is being sued in the name of a partnership, the individual may alternatively be served at the principal or last known place of business of the partnership.

Service at the address specified in **r. 6.9(2)** is effective even though the defendant does not receive the claim form (*Collier v Williams* [2006] EWCA Civ 20, [2006] 1 WLR 1945). To mitigate against this potential unfairness, **r. 6.9(3)** provides that where the claimant has reason to believe that the defendant may no longer reside or carry on business from his or her usual, principal or last known address, the claimant must take reasonable steps to ascertain the address of the defendant's current residence or place of business ('current address'), confirming *Mersey Docks Property Holdings v Kilgour*. In *Re Broadside Colours and Chemicals Ltd* [2012] EWHC 195 (Ch), LTL 22/2/2012, the court decided that a claimant was entitled to rely on the address for a defendant director of a company revealed by a Companies House search, even though the details of the address had been filed six years before the date of service, as the claimant had no reason to believe that the published address was not current. The requirement under **r. 6.9(3)** to make further enquiries was not triggered. As a result, service at that address was good service, even though the defendant no longer lived there and the proceedings did not thereby come to his attention. Where, having taken the reasonable steps required by **r. 6.9(3)**, the claimant ascertains the defendant's current address, the claim form must be served at that address (**r. 6.9(4)(a)**).

Where the claimant, having made reasonable enquiries, cannot ascertain the defendant's current address, the claimant must consider whether the defendant could be served at an alternative place or by an alternative method, and if so make an application under **r. 6.15**.

If all these steps have failed (i.e. the defendant has failed to provide an address for service; the claimant has reason to believe the defendant no longer resides or carries on business at the address specified in the table at **r. 6.9(2)** but reasonable enquiries have not revealed the defendant's current address; service by an alternative method or at an alternative place is not possible), the claimant may effect valid service on the defendant at the address specified in the table at **r. 6.9(2)** even though the claimant knows the defendant no longer resides or carries on business there.

The meaning of 'reasonable steps' in **r. 6.9(3)** is not defined in the rules or practice directions, and will inevitably vary from case to case. It is likely that taking reasonable steps would include checking the defendant's address for service with him (*Mersey Docks Property Holdings v Kilgour*). A rather more difficult judgment is the extent of the steps which should be taken where the defendant's whereabouts are not known, or where the defendant is not cooperating. Of all the new rules in force from 1 October 2008, this perhaps leaves the most scope for uncertainty, in that the claimant will not know when he effects service whether the steps he has taken to ascertain the defendant's current address are reasonable, and so whether service at what he believes to be the defendant's usual or last known address will be treated as good service by the court.

The meaning of 'residence' in the table at **r. 6.9(2)** has proved problematic. In *Varsani v Relfo Ltd* [2010] EWCA Civ 560, [2010] 3 All ER 1045, the Court of Appeal considered the meaning of 'residence' in the context of an international businessman with more than one home. The claim form was left by way of service on the defendant at an address in Middlesex where the defendant's wife, children and extended family lived. The evidence before the court was that the defendant worked in Kenya and visited his family at this address once a year for several weeks. There was no evidence that he was estranged from his family. The court held that it was possible for a person to reside in more than one place at the same time, and that the question before it was whether the quality of occupation was as a home. On the basis that the defendant's address in Middlesex was the home of his wife and children, which he could not share because of his work in Kenya but to which he returned regularly each year, the court held that the address was the defendant's residence. The test to be applied in determining a defendant's usual residence is his pattern of life, taking into account the nature of the use of the premises as well as the duration of the periods of occupation. The facts were to be distinguished from

Table 15.1 Service of claim form if the defendant does not give an address (CPR, r. 6.9(2))

Nature of defendant to be served	Place of service
1. Individual	Usual or last known residence.
2. Individual being sued in the name of a business	Usual or last known residence of the individual; or principal or last known place of business.
3. Individual being sued in the business name of a partnership	Usual or last known residence of the individual; or principal or last known place of business of the partnership.
4. Limited liability partnership	Principal office of the partnership; or any place of business of the partnership within the jurisdiction which has a real connection with the claim.
5. Corporation (other than a company) incorporated in England and Wales	Principal office of the corporation; or any place within the jurisdiction where the corporation carries on its activities and which has a real connection with the claim.
6. Company registered in England and Wales	Principal office of the company; or any place of business of the company within the jurisdiction which has a real connection with the claim.
7. Any other company or corporation	Any place within the jurisdiction where the corporation carries on its activities; or any place of business of the company within the jurisdiction.

Commentary

cases such as *Cherney v Deripaska* [2007] EWHC 965 (Comm), [2007] 2 All ER (Comm) 785, and *OJSC Oil Co. Yugraneft v Abramovich* [2008] EWHC 2613 (Comm), LTL 3/11/2008, where the defendants owned several houses in different countries and their visits to their London houses were sporadic, often for single nights only and for the purpose of business. For recent cases applying the test in *Varsani v Relfo Ltd* see *Moloobhoy v Kanani* [2012] EWHC 1670 (Comm), LTL 9/7/2012 and *Grimason v Cates* [2013] EWHC 2304 (QB), LTL 7/8/2013.

Service by fax or other electronic means

15.15   Service by fax or other electronic means is only permitted in accordance with **PD 6A, para. 4.1.** This provides that the party who is to be served or the solicitor acting for that party must previously have indicated in writing to the party serving:

(a)   that the party to be served or the solicitor is willing to accept service by fax or other electronic means. The following are sufficient written indications for the purpose:

(i)   a fax number set out on the writing paper of the solicitor acting for the party to be served;

(ii)   an email address set out on the writing paper of the solicitor acting for the party to be served but only where it is stated that the email address may be used for service; or

(iii)   a fax number, email address or electronic identification set out on a statement of case or a response to a claim filed with the court; and

(b)   the fax number, email address or other electronic identification to which it must be sent.

The fax number must be either that of the address for service provided by the defendant under **CPR, r. 6.8**, or as set out in the table in **r. 6.9**, or that of the defendant's solicitor instructed to accept service under **r. 6.7**.

Where the claimant wishes to serve the claim form electronically (other than by fax) he must first check whether there are any restrictions on the format in which the claim form may be sent or as to the maximum size of attachments (**PD 6A, para. 4.2**). There is no need to send a hard copy of the claim form (**PD 6A, para. 4.3**).

In *Thorne v Lass Salt Garvin* [2009] EWHC 100 (QB), LTL 5/2/2009, service by fax on a defendant firm of solicitors without their prior consent was not valid service. The fact that they were solicitors and that their fax number appeared on their letterhead did not bring them within **PD 6A, para. 4.1(2)(a)**, as they were not acting for themselves. Nor was the case sufficiently exceptional to justify an order dispensing with service under what is now **CPR, r. 6.16**.

A solicitor is 'acting for' a party within the meaning of **PD 6A, para. 4.1**, only where either the defendant has given written notification that his address for service is that of his solicitor, or the solicitor has notified the claimant in writing that he has the defendant's instructions to accept service (**CPR, r. 6.7**). Faxing a copy of the claim form to the address of a solicitor who has been involved in pre-action correspondence will not be valid service unless notice under **r. 6.7** has been given (*Brown v Innovatorone plc* [2009] EWHC 1376 (Comm), [2010] 2 All ER (Comm) 80). The reference in **PD 6A, para. 4.1**, to 'the solicitor acting for the party' is to a solicitor whose authority to accept service has been notified to the claimant under **CPR, r. 6.7**. In other words, the requirement of **PD 6A, para. 4.2(a)**, simply makes clear that a solicitor is willing to accept service by fax, as a method of service. It does not constitute any representation that a solicitor has the defendant's authority to accept service.

Where a document other than a claim form is served by fax, it must be served at the party's address for service (**CPR, r. 6.23(5)**). This will be the defendant's solicitor's address only if that is the address for service specified by the defendant under **r. 6.23(1)**.

Where a claimant is entitled to serve a defendant out of the jurisdiction under **Part 6, Section IV**, service may be effected by email, provided the defendant's permission for service by this method has been obtained under **PD 6A, para. 4.1**. Where this requirement is not met, an order for service by an alternative method will be needed under **CPR, r. 6.15** (*Bacon* *v Automattic Inc.* [2011] EWHC 1072 (QB), [2011] 2 All ER (Comm) 852). Alternatively, the court may be prepared to treat an error in effecting service by fax or email as an error of procedure under **r. 3.10** and hold that the service is valid (*Integral Petroleum SA v SCU-Finanz AG* [2014] EWHC 702 (Comm), LTL 19/3/2014).

In either case, service by email must be permitted under local law as required by **r. 6.40(3)**.

Service by contractually agreed method

Where a contract contains a provision for service, a claim form containing a claim in respect only of that contract may be served at the place or by the method specified in it (**CPR, r. 6.11(1)**). By **r. 6.11(2)**, the claim form may not be served at a contractually agreed place out of the jurisdiction unless either permission is obtained under **r. 6.36**, or service can be effected without permission under **rr. 6.32** or **6.33**. Only parties to the contract, their transferees and assignees can take advantage of a contractual method of service (*Argo Capital Investors Fund SPC v Essar Steel Ltd* [2005] EWHC 2587, LTL 28/11/2005). **15.16**

SERVICE BY AN ALTERNATIVE METHOD

The court may authorise service of a claim form or any other document by an alternative method, or at a place not otherwise permitted by **CPR, Part 6**, where 'there is a good reason' to do so (**rr. 6.15(1)** and **6.27**). Authorisation can be applied for before or after service has been unsuccessfully attempted (**PD 6A, paras 9.1** and **9.2**). It is not a prerequisite for the making of an order under **CPR, rr. 6.15** or **6.27** (as it was under RSC, ord. 65, r. 4), that service in accordance with the rules is impracticable: it is only necessary that there is a good reason (*Albon v Naza Motor Trading Sdn Bhd (No. 2)* [2007] EWHC 327(Ch), [2007] 1 All ER (Comm) 813). In deciding whether a good reason has been shown, the court will take into account the overriding objective and whether the making of the order will enable the court to deal with the case fairly (*Albon v Naza Motor Trading Sdn Bhd (No. 2)*). The phrase 'good reason' is less stringent than the 'exceptional circumstances' required for the court to make an order dispensing with service under **CPR, r. 6.16** (*Brown v Innovatorone plc* [2009] EWHC 1376 (Comm), [2010] 2 ALL ER (Comm) 80). The court must examine with some care the reason why it is being asked to make an order. The power in **r. 6.15** should not be exercised over-readily, and the mere absence of prejudice to the defendant is unlikely to be enough to justify an order. On the facts of this case, where the claimant's solicitors had left service very late, and no explanation was offered for the lateness, there was no 'good reason' to justify an order. See also *MB Garden Buildings Ltd v Mark Burton Construction Ltd* [2014] EWHC 431 (IPEC), LTL 10/3/2014, where the court refused to rule that there was good service under **rr. 6.15(2)** and **6.27** where the failure to achieve good service within the required time was largely the result of a number of failures on the claimant's part. If the court finds that there is a good reason to justify making an order, it will go on to consider whether it should exercise its discretion to do so, having regard to all the facts including the parties' conduct (*Albon v Naza Motor Trading Sdn Bhd (No. 2)*). In that case it had been right to make an order for service by an alternative method as there was evidence of non-cooperation by the defendant with the claimant's attempts to effect service. Further, making the order saved expense and time and promoted the objective of dealing with the case justly. See also *R (Hanuman) v University of East Anglia* [2015] EWHC 4122 (Admin), LTL 19/5/2015, where an order was made under **r. 6.15** in circumstances where the defendant had been notified of the application by email and had sought to make service difficult by unreasonably refusing to accept service by email. The court refused to make an order for alternative service where there was no good reason other than questions of speed and convenience to justify an order for service by alternative means. There was no evidence to show that the party to be served was evading service or of the efforts made by the claimant to serve by the conventional methods under the rules before applying for an order for alternative service under **r. 6.15(1)** (*Deutsche Bank AG v Sebastian Holdings Inc.* [2014] EWHC 112 (Comm), [2014] 1 All ER (Comm) 733). In *Dunbar Assets plc v BCP Premier Ltd* [2015] EWHC 10 **15.17**

Commentary

(Ch), LTL 19/1/2015, the court refused to make an order that the invalid service of a claim form by email on the last day for service should be permitted as good service under **r. 6.15** as no good reason was shown for not serving the claim form in accordance with the CPR and such an order could potentially deprive the defendant of a limitation defence. In *Power v Meloy Whittle Robinson Solicitors* [2014] EWCA Civ 898, LTL 2/7/2014 the court made an order under **r. 6.15(2)** as the conduct and correspondence between the solicitors was consistent with service having been effected within the period of validity of the claim form. In *Barton v Wright Hassall LLP* [2016] EWCA Civ 177, [2016] CP Rep 29 and *Gee 7 Group Ltd v Personal Management Solutions Ltd* [2016] EWHC 891 (Ch), LTL 7/4/2016 the court refused to grant orders validating service, despite the fact that the claim form in each case had come to the attention of the defendant.

An application under **r. 6.15** can be made at any time, before or after the time limit for service has expired. There is no requirement for the court to adopt a more rigorous approach after the time for service has expired (*Kaki v National Private Air Transport Co.* [2015] EWCA Civ 731, LTL 14/5/2015).

The desirability of serving a defendant in the jurisdiction in order to ensure that England is the jurisdiction first seised of proceedings for the purposes of the Brussels Convention, art. 21, does not constitute a good reason (*Knauf UK GmbH v British Gypsum Ltd* [2001] EWCA Civ 1570, [2002] 1 WLR 907; see also the comments in *Albon v Naza Motor Trading Sdn Bhd (No. 2)* [2007] EWHC 327 (Ch), [2007] 1 All ER (Comm) 813).

Service by an alternative method or at an alternative place on a defendant who is abroad

15.18 The court's power to order service by an alternative method applies to service both within and outside the jurisdiction, despite the fact that **CPR, r. 6.15** appears in **Section II of Part 6** (the rules for service within the jurisdiction). This is because **r. 6.37(5)(b)(i)**, which authorises the court to give directions about the method of service when it gives permission to serve a claim out of the jurisdiction enables it to make orders for alternative service under **r. 6.15** (*Bacon v Automattic Inc.* [2011] EWHC 1072 (QB), [2011] 2 All ER (Comm) 852, following *Cecil v Bayat* [2011] EWCA Civ 135, [2011] 1 WLR 3086, and overturning previous decisions in *Brown v Innovatorone plc* [2009] EWHC 1376 (Comm), [2010] 2 All ER (Comm) 80, and *Amalgamated Metal Trading Ltd v Baron* [2010] EWHC 3207, LTL 4/1/2011).

Where it is sought to serve a defendant who is abroad pursuant to an order under **r. 6.15**, the order may not be used to circumvent the rules on service out of the jurisdiction. So service abroad must be permitted under **Regulation (EU) No. 1215/2012**, the Lugano Convention or the common law rules on jurisdiction (see **chapter 16**). If the case is one to which Regulation (EC) No. 1393/2007 applies, or in which there is a bilateral service convention or treaty, an alternative service order should not be used to subvert the provisions of the relevant Regulation, convention or treaty (*Cecil v Bayat* [2011] EWCA Civ 135, [2011] 1 WLR 3086).

In *Abela v Baadarani* [2013] UKSC 44, [2013] 1 WLR 2043, the Supreme Court held that in a case requiring service out of the jurisdiction, but to which the Hague Service Convention or any bilateral service convention or treaty does not apply, the court should simply ask whether, in all the circumstances of the case, there is a good reason to order that delivery of documents amounts to good service. It is not appropriate to add a gloss to the test by saying that there would only be a good reason in exceptional circumstances. The mere fact that the defendant learned of the claim form does not constitute a good reason for making an order under **r. 6.15(2)**, although this is a crucial factor because exercising the power to validate retrospectively alternative service out of the jurisdiction involves considering whether what was done to attempt service is capable of constituting proper service in the sense that the court can be satisfied that the proceedings have been properly brought to the attention of the defendant. An order for alternative service under **r. 6.15** is only necessary where none of the methods of service in **r. 6.40** can be employed, including any method permitted by the law of the country in which service is to be effected (**r. 6.40(3)(c)**). The only bar to the exercise of the discretion under **r. 6.15(1)** or **(2)**, if appropriate, is that, by **r. 6.40(4)**, nothing in a court order must authorise a person to do anything which is contrary to the law of the country where the claim form is to be served. It is wrong to say that a claimant seeking retrospective validation of alternative service abroad must show that the method used was good service under local law. To impose such a test would render **r. 6.15(1)** and **(2)** otiose. Therefore an order can be made validating service which was not effected in accordance with local law, provided it was not contrary to local law, in the sense of being illegal. It was also held that delay before issue of the claim form is not usually a relevant consideration in deciding whether to grant an order under **r. 6.15**. Other factors which are relevant are the additional delay and expense that could be incurred in trying to effect service through diplomatic channels, and any unwillingness on the part of the party to be served to cooperate in relation to service.

Cases which might justify an order for service abroad by an alternative method are where there are grounds for believing that the defendant is avoiding personal service by the only method permitted by the foreign law, or where there is a need for urgency, although speed of itself will not in general be a sufficient reason for an order. In *Bitumex (HK) Co. Ltd v IRPC Public Co. Ltd* [2012] EWHC 1065, [2012] 2 All ER (Comm) 1131, the court was prepared to make an order under **r. 6.15(2)** retrospectively authorising service by a method which did not comply with Thai law. The reason was not only that service under the Hague Service Convention would take substantially longer but that the order was justified in order to assist the progress of an international arbitration in London which the defendants were seeking to delay by failing to join in the appointment of an arbitrator. In *La Société pour la Recherche, la Production, le Transport, la Transformation et la Commercialisation des Hydrocarbures SPA v Statoil Natural Gas LLC* [2014] EWHC 875 (Comm), [2014] 2 All ER (Comm) 857, the court granted a retrospective order for alternative service under **r. 6.15(2)** where there was no bilateral service treaty between the United Kingdom and Algeria and if service there was possible at all, which was uncertain, it would take at least a year. The court may be prepared to make a retrospective order under **r. 16.5(2)** even if it accepts that a claimant had not taken all reasonable steps to serve a claim form out of the jurisdiction, if overall significant efforts had been made over a prolonged period and the claim form had been brought to the attention of the defendant (*Kaki v National Private Air Transport Co.* [2015] EWCA Civ 731, LTL 14/5/2015). Questions of the legality of service under foreign law do not arise if the court exercises power under **r. 6.15** to order service by an alternative method on a foreign defendant in England (provided of course the relevant jurisdictional gateway is satisfied) *BNP Paribas SA v OJSC 'Russian Machines'* [2012] EWCA Civ 644, [2012] 1 Lloyd's Rep, 649.

Examples of orders which may be made under r. 6.15

PD 6A, para. 9.3, gives some examples of the alternative methods which may be used to serve a document, and the additional evidence required. Where an application is made to serve a third party who knows the person to be served (such as a friend, relative or solicitor acting for the defendant but without instructions to accept service), the application must include evidence that the claim form is likely to reach the person to be served by this method. An application to serve by sending a text message or leaving a voicemail message with details of the place where the claim form, or other document, can be found must be accompanied by evidence that the person to be served uses the relevant telephone number and is likely to receive the message. An application to serve a company by email (other than in accordance with **PD 6A, para 4.1**) must include evidence that the email is likely to come to the attention of a person holding a senior position in that company.

15.19

Other commonly ordered alternatives include newspaper advertisement and service at a place the defendant is known to frequent. An order can be made for service by an alternative method on the insurers of drivers of motor vehicles who have disappeared but are not 'untraced drivers' for the purposes of the Motor Insurers' Bureau agreements (see *Gurtner v Circuit* [1968] 2 QB

587). Similarly, in a claim for professional negligence against a solicitor who had disappeared, service was allowed at the address of the Solicitors' Indemnity Fund in *Abbey National plc v Frost* [1999] 1 WLR 1080. In *South Cambridgeshire District Council v Persons Unknown* [2004] EWCA Civ 1280, [2004] 4 PLR 88, a case involving the eviction of squatters from an illegal caravan site, the court permitted service by documents placed in plastic bags nailed to posts in prominent positions on the site. This reflects one of the methods of service provided for in possession claims under **CPR, r. 55.6**.

Retrospective order for alternative service

15.20   The court is given express power by **CPR, r. 6.15(2)**, to make an order that steps already taken to bring the claim form to the attention of the defendant by an alternative method or at an alternative place are good service. This reverses the effect of the decisions in *Nanglegan v Royal Free Hampstead NHS Trust* [2001] EWCA Civ 127, [2002] 1 WLR 1043, and *Elmes v Hygrade Food Products plc* [2001] EWCA Civ 121, LTL 27/2/2001, to the effect that the court had no retrospective power under the former **r. 6.8** to cure defects in service. Although **r. 6.15** appears in **Section II of Part 6**, it applies to service both within and outside the jurisdiction (*Bacon v Automattic Inc.* [2011] EWHC 1072 (QB), [2011] 2 All ER (Comm) 852, following *Cecil v Bayat* [2011] EWCA Civ 135, [2011] 1 WLR 3086). See also *Abela v Baadarani* [2013] UKSC 44, [2013] 1 WLR 2043, which is discussed at **15.18**.

The applicant for a retrospective order under **r. 6.15** will have to satisfy the court that there is a 'good reason' under **r. 6.15(1)** to make an order in the circumstances. **PD 6A, para. 9.2**, requires retrospective applications for an order to include evidence showing why the order is sought, what alternative method or place was used, when service was attempted by this method, and why the applicant believes that the document in question is likely to have reached the person to be served by the steps taken.

Application for order permitting alternative service

15.21   An application for an order permitting service by an alternative method should be made using the Part 23 procedure. The application may be made without notice to other parties (**CPR, r. 6.15(3)(b)**). The application must be supported by evidence (**r. 6.15(3)(a)**), including evidence showing why the order is sought, what alternative order or place is proposed and why the applicant believes the alternative steps are likely to enable the document to reach the person to be served (**PD 6A, para. 9.1**). Where the court makes an order permitting such service, it will specify the method of service, the deemed date of service and the date for filing an acknowledgment, admission or defence (**CPR, r. 6.15(4)(c)**). If a date for acknowledging service is not specified in an order for alternative service under **r. 6.15(4)**, this means that a defendant is under no obligation to acknowledge service, and judgment in default of an acknowledgment could not be entered against him (*Dubai Financial Group LLC v National Private Air Transport Services* [2016] EWCA Civ 71).

Service by means outside the CPR

15.22   Under the RSC it was possible to effect service by a method outside the rules, provided the defendant had agreed to accept service by the method chosen. In *Kenneth Allison Ltd v A. E. Limehouse and Co.* [1992] 2 AC 105 a process server effected service on the defendant partnership by leaving the writ with the receptionist, who took it only after she had consulted one of the partners and he had authorised her to accept it. The House of Lords held that although service by this method was outside the rules, it was nevertheless valid as it had been effected pursuant to an ad hoc agreement. The decision was followed in *Finn v Girobank plc* (2000) LTL 19/1/2000, which was a case on the old RSC, ord. 10.

The Court of Appeal in *Anderton v Clwyd County Council (No. 2)* [2002] EWCA Civ 933, [2002] 1 WLR 3174, appears to have held that the list of methods for service in what is now **CPR, r. 6.3**, is exhaustive and that provision of the claim form to the defendant by any other method, even where it is effective to bring the existence of the claim to the defendant's attention, does not constitute service under the rules. In that case, the Court of Appeal did not consider the effect of an agreement by the defendant to the use of an alternative method of service. In *Cranfield v Bridgegrove Ltd* [2003] EWCA Civ 656, [2003] 1 WLR 2441, though, it approved, obiter, *Kenneth Allison Ltd v A. E. Limehouse and Co.* as authority for the proposition that an ad hoc agreement for service in a manner outside the CPR is legally effective.

COURT'S POWER TO CURE DEFECTS IN SERVICE

The court has power to make orders retrospectively under **CPR, r. 3.10**, to cure a procedural **15.23** defect in service, and there are no material differences between this rule and RSC, ord. 2, r. 1 (*Phillips v Symes (No. 3)* [2008] UKHL 1, [2008] 1 WLR 180). Attempting to serve at the wrong address is an 'error of procedure' within the meaning of **CPR, r. 3.10**, and the court has power under this rule, and alternatively under **r. 3.1(2)(m)**, to make an order remedying the error (*Nelson v Clearsprings (Management) Ltd* [2006] EWCA Civ 1252, [2007] 1 WLR 962). **Rule 3.10** can apply where the error is made by the court rather than a party (*Stoute v LTA Operations Ltd* [2014] EWCA Civ 657, [2015] 1 WLR 79). So, when the court served the claim form, in disregard of the claimant's notification that the claimant wished to effect service of the claim form itself, an order could be made, under **r. 3.10**, that the service was effective, and consequently **r. 7.6** did not apply on the facts of the case (*Stoute v LTA Operations Ltd*). If there is some important reason in a particular case why service had to be effected by the claimant, an order could be made under **r. 3.10** invalidating the court's service (*Stoute v LTA Operations Ltd*). However, a judgment, wrongly obtained without notice to the defendant and in the absence of a party at trial, cannot be set aside under **r. 3.10**, as that would be inconsistent with the overriding objective and **rr. 39.3(5)** and **13.3**, which apply to judgments entered in these circumstances (*De Ferranti v Execuzen Ltd* [2013] EWCA Civ 592, LTL 10/6/2013). The type of situation where the court might exercise this power is where no question of limitation arises and there is no benefit to the defendant in requiring the claimant to reissue. In these circumstances, it cannot be said that it is in the interests of the overriding objective for the claimant to be required to reissue proceedings for no good purpose. For the application of **r. 3.10** to the service of other documents see **15.43**.

DISPENSING WITH SERVICE

The court may dispense with service of a claim form in exceptional circumstances (**CPR, 15.24 r. 6.16(1)**). An application for an order to dispense with service may be made at any time and without notice (**r. 6.16(2)(b)**). It must be supported by evidence (**r. 6.16(2)(a)**).

Under the predecessor to this rule in force before 1 October 2008 (r. 6.9), the court granted orders dispensing with service both before and after the period for service of the claim form had expired. However, orders would only be made in exceptional circumstances where the time for service of the claim form had expired before the order was sought (*Godwin v Swindon Borough Council* [2001] EWCA Civ 1478, [2002] 1 WLR 997; *Anderton v Clwyd County Council (No. 2)* [2002] EWCA Civ 933, [2002] 1 WLR 3174). The version of the rule now in force preserves the power to make orders at any time, but extends the requirement for exceptional circumstances to all cases. This is a more stringent test than the requirement in **r. 6.15** to show 'good reason' (*Bethell Construction Ltd v Deloitte and Touche* [2011] EWCA Civ 1321, LTL 18/11/2011; *Abela v Baadarani* [2013] UKSC 44, [2013] 1 WLR 2043).

The jurisprudence on the old r. 6.9 sheds light on what is meant by 'exceptional circumstances'. The court's approach under the old rule was strict. The fact that the defendant had actually received the claim form, albeit in a manner which did not comply with the rules, was not of itself exceptional (e.g. *Nathoo v Ashford and St Peter's Hospital Trust* [2004] EWHC 1571 (QB), LTL 24/11/2003). Nor were simple errors in service by the claimant's solicitors likely to amount to exceptional circumstances (e.g. *Kuenyehia v International Hospitals Group Ltd* [2006] EWCA Civ 21, [2006] CP Rep 34, service by fax when the defendant's solicitors had not consented to it). However, the Court of Appeal upheld the decision to dispense with service under the old r. 6.9 in *Olafsson v Gissurarson (No. 2)* [2008] EWCA Civ 152, [2008] 1 WLR 2016, where it did consider that the circumstances were truly exceptional. The facts were that the claimant had sought to serve the defendant in Iceland and had requested service through the appropriate channels. The correct documents were given to the defendant in Iceland, but were not served in accordance with Icelandic law because the defendant was not asked to and did not sign a declaration confirming his receipt of them. The claimant had not taken steps in time to cure the defect by re-serving the proceedings, because he had received a certificate from the British Embassy in Reykjavik stating that the relevant documents had been served.

The court will not make an order dispensing with service in circumstances in which this would enable a party to circumvent the rules on service out of the jurisdiction (*Cherney v Deripaska* [2007] EWHC 965 (Comm), [2007] 2 All ER (Comm) 785, applying *Shiblaq v Sadikoglu* [2004] EWHC 1890 (Comm), [2004] 2 All ER (Comm) 596).

The House of Lords has held in *Mucelli v Government of Albania* [2009] UKHL 2, [2009] 1 WLR 276, that the CPR do not apply to, and so there is no power to dispense with service of documents in, the procedures under the Extradition Act 2003.

The fact that the defendant happens to be a firm of solicitors does not make the case an exceptional one such as to justify dispensing with service under **CPR, r. 6.16** (*Thorne v Lass Salt Garvin* [2009] EWHC 100 (QB), LTL 5/2/2009). Attempting service on the final day of validity, and attempting to serve without prior notification to the defendant, are powerful factors against dispensing with service.

DEFENDANT REQUIRING SERVICE

15.25 Where the claimant has issued but not yet served the claim form, the defendant can serve a notice under **CPR, r. 7.7**, requiring the claimant either to do so, or to discontinue the claim by a date which is at least 14 days after the date of service of the notice. If the claimant fails to comply, the defendant may apply to the court for an order dismissing the claim. This rule enables the defendant to require the claimant to proceed with the claim, rather than wait for the four or six months during which the claim form may be served. In practice, the provision is rarely used.

TIME FOR SERVING A CLAIM FORM IN THE JURISDICTION

Period of validity

15.26 Proceedings are started when the court issues a claim form (see **chapter 12**) at the request of the claimant, on the date entered on the form by the court (**CPR, r. 7.2**). Before 12.00 midnight on the calendar day four months after the date of issue of the claim form, the claimant must take the relevant step specified in **table 15.2** to dispatch or deliver the claim form in the jurisdiction (**r. 7.5**).

The effect of this rule is to give the claimant complete control over compliance with **r. 7.5**, provided he is satisfied he knows the defendant's address. He need not concern himself about whether the claim form gets to the defendant on time. Two business days after the relevant step has been taken, the defendant is deemed served (**r. 6.14**; see **15.36**). In *T & L Sugars Ltd v*

Table 15.2 Service of a claim form within the jurisdiction: steps to be completed before 12.00 midnight on the calendar day four months after the date of issue of the claim form (CPR, r. 7.5)

Method of service	Step required
First class post, document exchange or other service which provides for delivery on the next business day	Posting, leaving with, delivering to or collection by the relevant service provider
Delivery of the document to or leaving it at the relevant place	Delivering to or leaving the document at the relevant place
Personal service under **r. 6.5**	Completing the relevant step required by **r. 6.5(3)**
Fax	Completing the transmission of the fax
Other electronic method	Sending the email or other electronic transmission

Tate & Lyle Industries Ltd [2014] EWHC 1066 (Comm), LTL 17/4/2014, it was held that **rr. 7.5** and **6.14** drew a clear distinction between the date on which service is effected, and the date upon which service is deemed to take place. Service is effected when the step required by **r. 7.5** is completed, and it is the completion of that step which constitutes actual service. The date on which service is deemed to have taken place is two business days later. **Rule 7.5** looks at when actual service took place; **r. 6.14** looks at when service is deemed to take place for the purpose of other steps in the proceedings.

Calculating the period of validity

It is clear from the precise wording used in **CPR, r. 7.5**, that for a claim form issued on 21 July 2015, the relevant step must be taken before midnight on 21 November 2015. When there is no corresponding date in the month in which the period ends it will end on the last day of the month, using the corresponding date rule (*Dodds v Walker* [1981] 1 WLR 1027). So, for a claim form issued on 30 October 2015, the relevant step must be taken before midnight on 29 February 2016. The relevant step may therefore be taken on any day, including Saturdays, Sundays and bank holidays and at any time of day or night.

15.27

Effect on period of validity of applying to serve outside the jurisdiction

Under the pre-October 2008 version of the CPR, the court had power to grant permission for service out of the jurisdiction of a claim form originally issued as one not for service out of the jurisdiction even where the application was made more than four months after the date of issue. In this case the provisions of **CPR, r. 7.6(3)**, did not apply, provided that the application for permission was made no later than six months from the date of issue (*Anderton v Clwyd County Council (No. 2)* [2002] EWCA Civ 933, [2002] 1 WLR 3174). It is unlikely the changes to the CPR have affected this.

15.28

Failure to serve a claim form in time

The consequences of failure to take the relevant steps within the time limits in **CPR, r. 7.5**, particularly when the limitation period for the claim has expired, are extremely dangerous for the claimant and for the claimant's legal advisers. The claim form will have expired and the cause of action will by then be time-barred. Now that control of compliance with the deadline in **r. 7.5** has been given to the claimant, there will be few (if any) acceptable excuses for failure to do so.

15.29

Practitioners can expect little sympathy from the court where they delay service of proceedings, particularly where the claim form was itself issued at the end of the limitation period. The usual position is that the court will not grant an extension of time for service of the claim form if to do so deprives the defendant of a limitation defence (*Cecil v Bayat* [2011] EWCA Civ 135,

Commentary

[2011] 1 WLR 3086; see the discussion in **15.32**). See also *Murrills v Berlanda* [2014] EWCA Civ 6, [2014] CP Rep 21, where the court held that a claimant who commences proceedings close to the expiry of the limitation period must pursue the claim expeditiously. If a claimant delays issuing proceedings and fails to make any enquiries to discover the defendant's usual or last known residence within the time for service of the claim form, there is no justification for any extension of time.

Negligent failure to serve the claim form within the period stipulated in **r. 7.5** does not render the subsequent issue of a second claim form an abuse of process where either the limitation period has not yet expired (see, for example, *Hoddinott v Persimmon Homes (Wessex) Ltd* [2007] EWCA Civ 1203, [2008] 1 WLR 806 at [54]) or, in a personal injury case, in order to seek an extension to the primary limitation period under the Limitation Act 1980, s. 33 (*Aktas v Adepta* [2010] EWCA Civ 1170, [2011] QB 894).

EXTENDING TIME FOR SERVING A CLAIM FORM

Procedure

15.30   If it is not possible to comply with the time limit set out in **CPR, r. 7.5**, the claimant can apply under **r. 7.6** for an extension. (For Part 8 claim forms see **13.6**.) The procedure is summarised in **procedural checklist 10**, and there is detailed commentary from here to **15.35**. Practitioners should beware, however, of relying on this provision where they know time for service of the claim form is running out, but they are not yet ready to proceed. In these circumstances, the appropriate procedure is to serve proceedings and then apply for a stay or an extension of time for the next steps in the action rather than applying for an extension of time to serve the claim form. See, for example, *Hoddinott v Persimmon Homes (Wessex) Ltd* [2007] EWCA Civ 1203, [2008] 1 WLR 806, a case where the particulars of claim were not yet ready, or *Cecil v Bayat* [2011] EWCA Civ 135, [2011] 1 WLR 3086, where the claimants were seeking funding for the litigation.

An application for extending time for serving a claim form should be made using the Part 23 procedure (see **chapter 32**). It may be made without serving a copy of the application notice on the defendant (or any other respondent) (**r. 7.6(4)(b)**). A defendant who is served with an order made without notice, extending time for service of a claim form, has seven days in which to apply for it to be set aside (**r. 23.10**).

The application must be supported by evidence (**r. 7.6(4)(a)**). The evidence will either be set out in the application notice (which must then be verified by a statement of truth) or be in the form of a witness statement (which must also be verified by a statement of truth) (**r. 32.6**).

Alternatively, evidence may be in affidavit form, although any additional cost of producing the evidence in this form may not be recovered from any other party without a court order (**r. 32.15(2)**).

PD 7A, para. 8.2, requires the evidence to include the following details:

(a) all the circumstances relied on;
(b) the date of issue of the claim;
(c) the expiry date of any extension already granted under **CPR, r. 7.6**; and
(d) a full explanation of why the claim form has not been served.

In stating the circumstances relied on the evidence should cover both those relating to the cause of action and the reasons for seeking an extension. The former will include the dates of accrual and expiry of the limitation period. As an application for extending time for service is made without notice, the applicant has a duty of full and frank disclosure, which includes an obligation to make reasonable inquiries into the matters relevant to the application.

An applicant who wishes to have the application dealt with without a hearing should request this in the application notice (**PD 23A, para. 2.1(5)**). The court has the power to dispense with a hearing where it does not consider a hearing appropriate (**CPR, r. 23.8(c)**), for example, where there are clear grounds for granting an extension. In practice, it is very common for these applications to be considered without a hearing and without notice to the defendant. However, in *Collier v Williams* [2006] EWCA Civ 20, [2006] 1 WLR 1945, the Court of Appeal stated that courts should consider whether that is an appropriate way of proceeding. Where the application is made shortly before expiry of the period in **r. 7.5** and where the cause of action has become time-barred since the date on which the claim form was issued, the application is potentially crucial. It is highly desirable that applications of this type, where time is running out, should normally be dealt with by an urgent hearing. Where pressure of business means it is not possible to deal with the application other than on paper, consideration should be given to dealing with it by telephone. In *Hoddinott v Persimmon Homes (Wessex) Ltd* [2007] EWCA Civ 1203, [2008] 1 WLR 806, the Court of Appeal made clear that a claimant who applies for and obtains an extension of time for service of the claim form, without giving notice to the defendant, bears the risk that the order may subsequently be set aside.

Under **PD 51K** (County Court Legal Advisers Pilot Scheme), which applies to claims started in the Production Centre or Money Claims Online, for a period of 12 months from 1 October 2015, a legal adviser may exercise the jurisdiction of the County Court with regard to the matters set out in the schedule to **PD 51K**. A legal adviser can determine an application to extend time for service of the claim form pursuant to **CPR, r. 7.6**, but this is limited to the first application, unless the claim would normally be allocated to the small claims track, and further limited to applications made within the period specified in **r. 7.5** for service of the claim form (item 2 in the schedule to **PD 51K**). Decisions of a legal adviser are made without a hearing, although a party can request a decision to be reconsidered by a District Judge, provided the request is filed within 14 days after the party is served with notice of the decision (**PD 51K, para. 3**).

Order extending time for serving

There is no limit on the length of any extension, or on the number of extensions which a court may grant. It will be for the applicant to justify the length of extension sought. Bearing in mind the court's duty as part of the overriding objective to ensure that cases are dealt with expeditiously it is unlikely that the court will be prepared to grant long or multiple extensions in the absence of good reason (see **15.32**). Under the old rules in the RSC and CCR, the maximum period of any extension was 12 months at a time (this was renewable), but the courts insisted on a justification for the period of any extension sought. **15.31**

Where an order is made (whether granting or dismissing the application) without notice to the defendant, a copy of the order, the application notice and any evidence in support must be served on the defendant, unless the court orders to the contrary (**CPR, r. 23.9**). The order must contain a statement of the defendant's right to apply to have the order set aside or varied (**r. 23.9(3)**). The defendant has seven days from the date of service to apply to the court for the order to be varied or set aside (**r. 23.10**).

Grounds on which the court will grant an extension

A new version of **CPR, r. 7.6**, came into operation on 1 October 2008. It is reworded for consistency with the new **r. 7.5**, but is unchanged in substance. It is likely, therefore, that the jurisprudence on the old version of this rule, which is considered below, will continue to be of relevance, even though the full control given to the claimant to comply with **r. 7.5** will make it harder for orders extending time for service to be obtained. The crucial enquiry will relate to the relevant steps under **r. 7.5** for dispatching the claim form. Dates of deemed service are no longer of any relevance. **15.32**

The general rule is that an application to extend the time for taking the relevant steps under r. 7.5 should be made within the usual period of service (or that period as already extended by the court) (r. 7.6(2)). The application is 'made' when the notice is received by the court, not when it is heard (r. 23.5; *Collier v Williams* [2006] EWCA Civ 20, [2006] 1 WLR 1945). The CPR are silent on the test to be applied in deciding whether to allow an extension under r. 7.6(2), but guidance was given in *Hashtroodi v Hancock* [2004] EWCA Civ 652, [2004] 1 WLR 3206, in which the Court of Appeal made clear that the authorities on extending the period of validity of a writ under RSC, ord. 6, r. 8, no longer apply. *Hashtroodi v Hancock* was clarified by *Collier v Williams*. The approach of the court to applications under r. 7.6(2) should now be as follows:

The crucial enquiry the court must undertake is to evaluate why the claimant did not take the relevant steps under r. 7.5 within the specified period. Whereas under the RSC a plaintiff who was unable to show a good reason for not serving in time failed to satisfy the former threshold condition (*Kleinwort Benson Ltd v Barbrak Ltd* [1987] AC 597), under the CPR a more calibrated approach is adopted, albeit in the context of a generally strict regime, especially where limitation is involved. A defendant should not be deprived of a limitation defence by an extension of time for serving a claim form, save in exceptional circumstances (*Cecil v Bayat* [2011] EWCA Civ 135, [2011] 1 WLR 3086). If there is a good reason for the failure to take the relevant steps within the specified period, an extension of time will usually be granted. The weaker the reason, the readier the court will be to refuse the application and where there is no reason or only a very weak reason the court is most unlikely to grant an extension of time. The fact that the claimant has taken all reasonable steps to try to effect service will be a strong reason to grant the application. Where service has not been effected because of the incompetence of the claimant's legal advisers, that will be a strong reason to refuse the application, even if not an absolute bar.

The good reason must be a difficulty in serving the claim form on the defendant, not other problems which the claimant might have, such as needing more time to prepare the claim. In the latter circumstances, as stated at 15.30, the appropriate procedure is to issue the claim form and apply for a stay or an extension of time for taking the next steps in the action (*Cecil v Bayat*).

In *Collier v Williams*, the reason for the failure to serve in time was the claimant's erroneous belief as to the whereabouts of the defendant's usual or last known residence. So the court needed to consider the reasonableness of that belief. If the claimant had been misled by the defendant as to his residence, the court would be likely to hold that the claimant had reasonable grounds for his belief, that there was a very good reason for the claimant's failure to serve in time and would grant an extension of time under r. 7.6(2). But it is always incumbent on the claimant to take reasonable steps to ascertain the defendant's last known residence. What is reasonable must depend on the circumstances of the case. The claimant in this case had made an assumption about the defendant's address based on little evidence and so there was no good reason to extend the period for service of the claim form. The discretion must be exercised in accordance with the overriding objective. However, the exercise of going through the checklist of factors set out in r. 1.1(2) will often not be necessary. Where there is no good reason justifying the failure to serve the claim form in time (or, now, to take the relevant steps), there should normally be no need to go further. On the facts of the case, the court refused to grant an extension because the reason for failing to serve within the period of validity was the incompetence of the claimant's advisers. The requirement to take reasonable steps to ascertain the defendant's usual or last known residence is now enshrined in r. 6.9(3).

Collier v Williams was applied in *Hoddinott v Persimmon Homes (Wessex) Ltd* [2007] EWCA Civ 1203, [2008] 1 WLR 806. The court again articulated the principle that where there is no good reason for the failure to serve the claim form within the four-month period, the court still has a discretion to grant an extension of time, but is unlikely to do so. In this case, the reason for non-service was that full particulars of the claim were not ready by the last date for service of the claim form. The court held that this was not a good reason. The correct course of action would have been for the claim form to have been served and then agreement obtained from the defendant, or an order from the court, that no further steps be taken in the litigation until the claimant was able to produce particulars of claim. However, the case was not yet time-barred, so if the order were set aside the claimant could simply reissue. The fact that a claim was clearly not time-barred was a relevant consideration, albeit not determinative, to be taken into account in favour of the claimant when the court decided whether to grant an extension of time under r. 7.6(2) (but not r. 7.6(3), where the list of factors specified is exhaustive). Further, the claimant had sent a copy of the claim form to the defendant for information. These two facts together were sufficiently exceptional to justify the extension.

The Court of Appeal has made clear in *Collier v Williams* that while the r. 7.6(3) requirements (see **15.33**) are relevant to the exercise of the discretion given by r. 7.6(2), there is a clear difference between the two paragraphs and the fact that the preconditions stated in r. 7.6(3) are not satisfied is not necessarily determinative of the outcome of an application under r. 7.6(2). In particular, in deciding whether to grant an extension under r. 7.6(2), the court is required to make a judgment about how good a reason there is for the failure to serve in time (assuming that the application is being dealt with after the expiry of the four-month period for service). Under r. 7.6(3) the position is that unless all reasonable steps have been taken, the court cannot extend time. However, more recently, in *Cecil v Bayat*, the Court of Appeal stated that it would be curious if the test to be applied in applications under r. 7.6(2) where the limitation period has expired should be different to applications under r. 7.6(3) where the period of validity of the claim form has expired. At the very least, even if he has not taken *all* reasonable steps, the claimant should have to show that he has taken reasonable steps. Generally, where the limitation period has expired, an extension will not be granted save in exceptional circumstances. This requires the claimant to show that the good reason for failing to serve the claim form in time directly impacts on the limitation problem, as for instance where the claimant can show that he has been delayed in service for reasons for which he does not bear responsibility. In *JSC BTA Bank v Ablyazov* [2011] EWHC 2988 (Comm), LTL 29/11/2011, the long period of time (up to two years) required to effect service under the Hague Service Convention in Russia was a good reason justifying an extension under r. 7.6(2) notwithstanding a small period of delay on the part of the claimants' solicitors. The long delay also surmounted the expiry of the limitation period during this time.

The view taken by the court of the conduct of the claimant's solicitors can be an important factor. In *Imperial Cancer Research Fund v Ove Arup and Partners Ltd* [2009] EWHC 1453 (TCC), LTL 25/6/2009, the court granted an extension where a claim form supported by a statement of truth could not properly be served without expert evidence and the claimant's solicitors had been acting responsibly. This case looks surprising in the light of *Cecil v Bayat*. However, it was not clear that there was a limitation defence. In *City and General (Holborn) Ltd v Structure Tone Ltd* [2010] EWCA Civ 911, [2010] BLR 458, the court set aside an extension obtained without notice where the claim form could in fact have been served, even if loss and damage could not be fully particularised in the particulars of claim. In *F. G. Hawkes (Western) Ltd v Beli Shipping Co. Ltd* [2009] EWHC 1740 (Comm), [2010] 1 Lloyd's Rep 449, an extension was refused when the claimant's solicitors did not make enquiries of the defendant about its address for service until the last month of the six-month period for service of the claim form out of the jurisdiction. The defendant had refused to cooperate with the claimant's enquiries, had notice of the claimant's intention to bring proceedings and would not be prejudiced by a short extension. Further, the claimant had a good arguable case. But none of these factors outweighed the fault of the claimant's advisers in not taking steps to effect service until too late. In *Duckworth v Coates* [2009] EWHC 1936 (Ch), LTL 4/8/2009, five applications were made under r. 7.6(2) for extensions totalling 12 months. All the applications were made without notice and without a hearing. None of the applications

Commentary

after the first drew the court's attention to the fact that previous orders had been made. The applications also contained other errors of fact. Although it was the claimant's responsibility to ensure that all relevant information was brought to the court's attention, the court declined to set the orders aside on the ground that the claimant had failed to comply with its duty to make full and frank disclosure. It did set the orders aside on the ground that it could not find any good reason for the extensions. Although for much of this period the claimant's solicitors were trying to effect service through diplomatic channels (at, it transpired, the wrong address), they had let matters drift. Once they properly instructed a local process server to locate and serve the relevant defendant, service took place within a matter of two weeks.

It is clear from these cases that neither the defendant nor the defendant's solicitors are under any obligation to assist the claimant's solicitors' attempts to serve the defendant, provided that they do not actually obstruct service. In *Malcolm-Green v And So To Bed Ltd* [2013] EWHC 4016 (IPEC), LTL 3/1/2014, an order under **r. 7.6(2)**, granting an extension of time for service of the claim form, was set aside and the claim struck out. The reason advanced for the failure to serve, that there was a lack of a substantive response by the defendant to the complaints which made it difficult or wasteful in costs to draft particulars of claim, did not qualify as a good reason. The court also considered whether there were exceptional reasons which would justify an extension of time, even in the complete absence of a good reason for the failure to serve in time, following *Hoddinott v Persimmon Homes (Wessex) Ltd* [2007] EWCA Civ 1203, [2008] 1 WLR 806. A highly relevant factor was whether the claim would be statute-barred if the claimant were to issue fresh proceedings. The court held that the defendant should not be deprived of a limitation defence, and if it was open to doubt whether a claim would be time-barred, the court should make an assumption in the defendant's favour.

In *Steele v Mooney* [2005] EWCA Civ 96, [2005] 1 WLR 2819, the Court of Appeal considered the relationship between **r. 3.10** (the power to cure an irregularity) and **r. 7.6(2)**. In this case, an application to extend time for service of the particulars of claim had by mistake failed to refer to the claim form, so an application to extend time for service of the claim form had not been made within the four-month period for service. The court held that the error was procedural in nature and did fall within the ambit of **r. 3.10**, which should not be given an artificially restrictive meaning. However, **r. 3.10** should not be used to circumvent something that is prohibited under another rule (an application of the decision in *Vinos v Marks and Spencer plc* [2001] 3 All ER 784 — see **15.34**). The application now fell to be considered under the provisions of **r. 7.6(2)** (not **r. 7.6(3)**, see **15.34**) as the original application for an extension had been made within the usual time limit for service. The application would have succeeded under **r. 7.6(2)** if it had been made correctly, so **r. 3.10** could be used to correct the error now and extend time for service of the claim form. See also *Stoute v LTA Operations Ltd* [2014] EWCA Civ 657, [2015] 1 WLR 79, discussed at **15.23**.

Applications made after the usual period of service has expired

15.33 The rules permit the making of an application after the expiry of time for service of the claim form. But in this case, an order may be made only if (**CPR, r. 7.6(3)**):

(a) the court has failed to serve the claim form, or
(b) the claimant has taken all reasonable steps to comply with **r. 7.5** but has been unable to do so, and
(c) in either case the claimant has acted promptly in making the application.

The application may be made without notice, but must be supported by evidence (**r. 7.6(4)**). For the distinction between this test and the test under **r. 7.6(2)**, see **15.32**. Because of the requirement in applications under **r. 7.6(3)(b)** that the claimant must have taken *all* reasonable steps to comply with **r. 7.5**, it is difficult to see, in practice, how extensions will now be justified, save where the defendant is evading service or where the court has failed to serve the claim form. It is clear from *Latreefers Inc. v Hobson* [2002] EWHC 1586 (Ch), LTL 31/7/2002 (a case on the version of **r. 7.6(3)** in force before 1 October 2008; see **15.32**), that parties will be expected to have used the whole period of **r. 7.5** to attempt to take the relevant steps and that if they wait until the last moment, the court will not be sympathetic. See also *MB Garden Buildings Ltd v Mark Burton Construction Ltd* [2014] EWHC 431 (IPEC) where the court refused to grant a claimant a retrospective extension of time to serve a claim form and particulars of claim under **r. 7.6(3)**, or to rule that there had been good service of the claim form under **rr. 6.15(2)** and **6.27**, where the failure to achieve good service within the relevant time was largely the result of a number of failures on the claimant's part.

'Promptly' is to be construed in accordance with the ordinary meaning of the word, 'readily, quickly, at once' (*Chare v Fairclough* [2003] EWHC 180 (QB), LTL 20/1/2003).

The phrase 'the court has failed to serve the claim form' in **r. 7.6(3)(a)** includes a case where the court overlooks the claim form and makes no attempt to serve it (*Cranfield v Bridgegrove Ltd* [2003] EWCA Civ 656, [2003] 1 WLR 2441). In most cases of court neglect it will be appropriate to grant an extension of time provided the claimant has acted promptly. However, if failures on the part of the claimant or his solicitors are the real reason why the claim form is not served within the period of validity, it will often be inappropriate to grant an extension.

In *Hoddinott v Persimmon Homes (Wessex) Ltd* [2007] EWCA Civ 1203, [2008] 1 WLR 806, the Court of Appeal held that in applications made under **r. 7.6(3)**, the fact that a claim is clearly not yet time-barred (and so the claimant can reissue if the extension is denied) is irrelevant.

Only steps taken within the period of validity of the claim form — not afterwards — are relevant in deciding whether the claimant has taken all reasonable steps to serve the claim form, for the purposes of **r. 7.6(3)(b)** (*Drury v British Broadcasting Corporation* [2007] EWCA Civ 497, [2007] EMLR 24).

Attempts to evade r. 7.6(3)

Under the old version of CPR, **r. 7.6(3)**, in force before 1 October 2008 (see **15.32**), attempts to use **rr. 3.1** (extending time), **3.9** (relief from sanctions) and **3.10** (correcting errors of procedure) to evade the operation of **r. 7.6** were all rejected by the court (see *Vinos v Marks and Spencer plc* [2001] 3 All ER 784; *National Bank of Greece SA v R. M. Outhwaite 317 Syndicate at Lloyd's* [2001] Lloyd's Rep IR 652 and *Kaur v CTP Coil Ltd* (2000) LTL 10/7/2000). Although it now appears, following the decision of the House of Lords in *Phillips v Symes (No. 3)* [2008] UKHL 1, [2008] 1 WLR 180, that the court does have power to make orders retrospectively under **r. 3.10** to cure a procedural defect in service, that case was not one which involved attempted service of a claim form after the expiry of the period for service of the claim form under **r. 7.6**. The court can also use **r. 3.10** to declare whether irregular service by the court within the period of validity of the claim form was or was not valid service before consideration is given to the question of whether an extension is necessary under **r. 7.6**. See *Stoute v LTA Operations Ltd* [2014] EWCA Civ 657, [2015] 1 WLR 79, discussed more fully at **15.23**.

15.34

The rules in force since 1 October 2008 do, however, offer two possible avenues of relief to claimants who have been unable to comply with **r. 7.5** (changing the position which operated previously — see *Elmes v Hygrade Food Products plc* [2001] EWCA Civ 121, LTL 27/2/2001; *Godwin v Swindon Borough Council* [2001] EWCA Civ 1478, [2002] 1 WLR 997; and *Anderton v Clwyd County Council (No. 2)* [2002] EWCA Civ 933, [2002] 1 WLR 3174). First, claimants may make a retrospective application under **r. 6.15(2)** for an order that steps they have already taken are good service. Secondly, they may in exceptional circumstances make an application under **r. 6.16** to dispense with service. See **15.20** and **15.24**. In appropriate circumstances, a claimant may also be able to rely on **r. 3.10** to cure an irregularity in service which occurs within the period of validity of the claim form. See **15.23**.

Agreeing extensions of time for service of the claim form

15.35   In *Thomas v Home Office* [2006] EWCA Civ 1355, [2007] 1 WLR 230, the Court of Appeal considered the question, on which there was no previous authority, of whether the parties could agree extensions of time for service of the claim form under **CPR, r. 2.11**, or whether this rule was effectively excluded by the provisions of **r. 7.6**. The court held that parties could indeed agree extensions of time for service of the claim form under **r. 2.11** and rejected the submission that this enabled parties to extend time virtually indefinitely and meant the court had no mechanism to prevent proceedings stagnating. Rather it was persuaded by the fact that **rr. 7.5** and **7.6** are not included in the list set out at **r. 2.11** of the provisions in the CPR which cannot be varied by agreement between the parties. See **3.7** for what constitutes a 'written agreement of the parties'.

DEEMED DATES OF SERVICE

15.36   Under **CPR, r. 6.14**, a claim form served in the United Kingdom in accordance with **Part 6** is deemed served on the second business day after completion of the relevant step set out in the table in **r. 7.5(1)** (see **table 15.2**). This applies to all forms of service, with the effect that leaving a document with an individual by way of personal service under **r. 6.5(3)** is no longer deemed served immediately. 'Business day' is defined in **r. 6.2(b)** to mean any day except Saturday, Sunday, a bank holiday, Good Friday or Christmas Day. 'Bank holiday' means a bank holiday under the Banking and Financial Dealings Act 1971 in the part of the United Kingdom where service is to take place (**r. 6.2(a)**). **Rule 2.8** (which excludes weekends and public holidays when calculating periods of five days or less) does not apply here (*Anderton v Clwyd County Council (No. 2)* [2002] EWCA Civ 933, [2002] 1 WLR 3174), because nothing is 'done'.

The phrase 'is deemed to be served' in **r. 6.14** creates an irrebuttable presumption that service occurred on the deemed day of service. The presumption cannot be displaced by proving the actual day of receipt (*Godwin v Swindon Borough Council* [2001] EWCA Civ 1478, [2002] 1 WLR 997; *Anderton v Clwyd County Council (No. 2)* [2002] EWCA Civ 933, [2002] 1 WLR 3174; *Cranfield v Bridgegrove Ltd* [2003] EWCA Civ 656, [2003] 1 WLR 2441).

The function of the deemed date of service is to compute with certainty the next steps to be taken in the claim. It is no longer the case that service needs to be deemed to have taken place within the four-month period for service of the claim form in the jurisdiction (**r. 7.5**). The effect of **rr. 7.5(1)** and **6.14** is that, in dispatching or delivering the claim form for service within the period of validity, the claimant does not have to be concerned with how long it takes for the claim form to reach the defendant, or even if it ever does reach the defendant. Also, full use of the periods available means that a claim form may be validly served where deemed service takes effect four months and two business days after issue.

There are different rules for calculating the deemed dates of service of documents other than the claim form (**r. 6.26**, see **15.42**).

SERVICE OF DOCUMENTS OTHER THAN THE CLAIM FORM IN THE UNITED KINGDOM

15.37   The rules relating to service of documents other than the claim form are set out in **CPR, Part 6, Section III**. The term 'other documents' excludes not just claim forms but other documents used to commence proceedings, such as petitions, as well as documents used to issue pre-action applications. These documents are included in the definition of 'claim form' in **r. 6.2(c)** and therefore their service is governed by **Part 6, Section II**. 'Other documents' therefore refers primarily to documents generated in the course of litigation.

The geographical area within which a defendant's nominated address for service can be located has been expanded from England and Wales (before 1 October 2008) to anywhere in the United Kingdom (from 1 October 2008) and now to anywhere in the EEA where the defendant resides or carries on business or where the defendant's solicitor or European lawyer has a business address (from 6 April 2011).

Who may serve documents?

Service by the court   The court will serve documents it has prepared, unless a rule or practice **15.38** direction provides otherwise, the court orders otherwise or the party on whose behalf it is to be served informs the court it wishes to effect service (**CPR, r. 6.21(2)**). This notification may be made at the start of the case, informally by letter. In the RCJ, solicitors are invited to indicate at the commencement of proceedings whether they wish to effect service themselves, and if this is done, the file will be marked accordingly and no further applications will be necessary.

The court will decide which method of service to use (**r. 6.21(3)**). It will usually be first class post (**PD 6A, para. 8.1**). In the minority of cases where the court is serving a document prepared by a party, the party must provide a copy for the court and for each party to be served (**r. 6.21(4)**).

The CPR do not require the court to give notice of service in the case of documents other than the claim form (as defined in **r. 6.2(c)**). Nor do the rules contain any provision requiring the court to notify a party that a document it has served (other than the claim form, as defined) has been returned undelivered.

Service by a party   Parties are required to serve documents they have prepared, unless a rule **15.39** or practice direction provides otherwise or the court orders otherwise (**CPR, r. 6.21(1)**). There is no requirement to notify the court of service of any document other than the claim form (as defined in **r. 6.2(c)**). However, the rules make provision for many documents, including statements of case, to be filed as well as served.

Service of particulars of claim

Particulars of claim must be served within 14 days after serving the claim form (**CPR,** **15.40** **r. 7.4(1)**) and no later than the latest time for serving the claim form (**r. 7.4(2)**). Where a claimant is late in serving the particulars of claim, the court has a general discretion under **r. 3.1(2)(a)** to extend time. Thus, in *Rogers v East Kent Hospitals NHS Trust* [2009] EWHC 54 (QB), [2009] LS Law Med 153, an objection that particulars had been served out of time, because they were faxed one minute after the last time for service (under the current **r. 6.26**, this is 4.30 p.m.) on the last day on which they should have been served, was regarded as being unmeritorious in the absence of prejudice to the defendant. The court exercised its discretion to order a retrospective extension of time for service of the particulars of claim. The court's discretion applies even where the delay extends beyond the period of validity of the claim form, and such applications are not bound by the requirements in **r. 7.6(3)** (see **15.33**) (*Totty v Snowden* [2001] EWCA Civ 1415, [2002] 1 WLR 1384). The court refused an order extending time for service of the particulars of claim in *Venulum Property Investments Ltd v Space Architecture Ltd* [2013] EWHC 1242 (TCC), [2013] 4 Costs LR 596 (which was decided before *Denton v T. H. White Ltd* [2014] EWCA Civ 906, [2014] 1 WLR 3926). The court took into account that the claimant had failed to issue proceedings for five years after becoming aware it had an actionable claim, it had a good or better case against other defendants, there was no good reason for failing to serve the particulars of claim in time, and it was not in accordance with the overriding objective to extend time, particularly taking into account the amendments to **rr. 3.9** and **1.1** effective from 1 April 2013 and the new stricter approach required towards those who fail to comply with the rules since that date.

When the particulars of claim are served separately there is nothing in the CPR which requires a claimant to include all claims against different defendants in a single set of particulars (*Tetra Pak Ltd v Biddle and Co.* [2010] EWHC 54 (Ch), [2010] 1 WLR 1466).

In a case of any complexity, before the Jackson reforms in April 2013, it was held that when a court was considering an application for an extension of time made after the time prescribed for the taking of a step in proceedings has expired, the court had to follow the checklist given in r. 3.9 as it was before 1 April 2013 (*Sayers v Clarke Walker* [2002] EWCA Civ 645, [2002] 1 WLR 3095; see **48.30**). It is not necessary for the court to apply the **r. 3.9** criteria (either before or since 1 April 2013) in an application for an extension of time made before the deadline for service has expired: the court's discretion should be exercised simply by having regard to the overriding objective and the factors listed in **r. 1.1(2)** (*Robert v Momentum Services Ltd* [2003] EWCA Civ 299, [2003] 1 WLR 1577).

Totty v Snowden and *Sayers v Clarke Walker* were applied in *Price v Price* [2003] EWCA Civ 888, [2003] 3 All ER 911, in which the Court of Appeal signalled that the courts should take care not to relax the disciplinary framework created by the CPR. In this case an extension of time for service of particulars of claim was granted, but subject to a condition restricting the value of the claim, using the case management powers under **r. 3.1(2)(a)** and **(3)(a)**.

An intentional delay in serving particulars of claim would, if made out, be highly significant if not determinative of whether to grant relief (*Bournemouth and Boscombe Athletic Football Club Ltd v Lloyds TSB Bank plc* [2003] EWCA Civ 1755, LTL 10/12/2003).

In summary, the effect of these authorities is that applications for extensions of time for service of particulars of claim after the period of validity of the claim form has expired appears to be governed by **r. 3.9**, not **r. 7.4**. In *Associated Electrical Industries Ltd v Istom UK* [2014] EWHC 430 (Comm), the court, applying **r. 3.9**, struck out a claim for late service of the particulars of claim in circumstances where a timely request could have been made for an extension and there was no good reason for the delay. Where application is made before the period of validity of the claim form has expired, the application is governed by the overriding objective and the list of factors in **r. 1.1(2)**.

The particulars of claim must be accompanied by the response pack, which consists of forms for acknowledging service, and for admission, defence and counterclaim (**CPR, r. 7.8(1)**). Where the claim is for a specified sum, forms N9A and N9B should be used. Where the claim is for an unspecified sum, or is a non-money claim, forms N9C and N9D should be used. A default judgment entered where a claimant has failed to serve a response pack may be set aside under **r. 13.3(1)(b)** (*Rajval Construction Ltd v Bestville Properties Ltd* [2010] EWCA Civ 1621, [2011] CILL 2994).

In personal injury claims, the particulars of claim must be accompanied by a medical report and schedule of past and future loss and expense (**PD 16, paras** 4.2 and 4.3). In a claim based upon a written contract, a copy of the contract or documents constituting the agreement, or any relevant general conditions of sale should accompany the particulars of claim (**PD 16, para. 7.3**).

If particulars of claim are served separately from the claim form, a copy of the particulars must be filed within seven days of service on the defendant, unless the claim is proceeding in the Production Centre or in the County Court Business Centre in respect of Money Claims Online (**CPR, r. 7.4(3)**).

Method

15.41   The methods of service of other documents are prescribed by **CPR, r. 6.20**. In essence, they are the same as those to be used for serving claim forms (see **15.10**). As with claim forms, other documents must be served personally where a statute, practice direction or court order requires it (**r. 6.22(1)**). Examples include orders endorsed with a penal notice under **CPR, r. 81.4** and search orders under **PD 25A, para. 7.4(1)**. Personal service cannot be used for service on a party that has provided an address for service under **CPR, r. 6.23**, unless it is required by an enactment, practice direction or court order (**r. 6.22(1) and (2)(a)**).

After proceedings are started, every party to the proceedings must give an address at which that party may be served with documents relating to the proceedings (**r. 6.23(1)**). **Rule 6.23(2)** requires a party's address for service to be within the EEA and to be:

(a) the business address of a solicitor acting for the party; or

(b) the business address of a European lawyer nominated to accept service of documents; or

(c) where there is no solicitor acting for the party or no European lawyer nominated to accept service of documents, an address at which the party resides or carries on business. For the definitions of 'solicitor' and 'European lawyer' see **15.9**.

Where a party has indicated (or is deemed to have indicated) willingness to accept service by fax or email, the fax number must be at the address for service (**r. 6.23(5)**) and the email address is deemed to be there (**r. 6.23(6)**).

If he has not already done so, the defendant will provide an address for service when he completes the acknowledgment of service. Parties must notify the court and all other parties in writing immediately if their address for service changes (**r. 6.24**).

Deemed dates of service

The deemed dates of service of other documents are different for those of claim forms, and are set out at the table in **CPR, r. 6.26**, which is reproduced in **table 15.3**. The table uses the expression 'day' (which means a calendar day) and 'business day', which is defined in **r. 6.2(b)** as any day except Saturday, Sunday, a bank holiday, Good Friday or Christmas Day. 'Bank holiday' means a bank holiday under the Banking and Financial Dealings Act 1971 in the part of the United Kingdom where service is to take place (**r. 6.2(a)**). **Rule 2.8** (which excludes weekends and public holidays when calculating periods of five days or less) does not apply here (*Anderton v Clwyd County Council (No. 2)* [2002] EWCA Civ 933, [2002] 1 WLR 3174), because nothing is 'done'. **15.42**

Examples of how to calculate the deemed dates of service in **r. 6.26** are provided in **PD 6A, para. 10**. Example 6 makes clear that the words 'provided that day is a business day' refer only to the deemed date of service, not to the date of dispatching. Example 6 says: 'Where the document is posted (by first class post) on a bank holiday Monday, the day of deemed service is the following Wednesday (a business day)'.

These deeming provisions apply only where service is effected in the United Kingdom (**CPR, r. 6.26**).

The decision in *Godwin v Swindon Borough Council* [2001] EWCA Civ 1478, [2002] 1 WLR 997, that the deemed dates of service create an irrebuttable presumption that service occurred on the deemed date applies to other documents just as much as to the claim form (*Joyce v West Bus Coach Services Ltd* [2012] EWHC 404 (QB), [2012] 3 Costs LR 540).

Alternative service and dispensing with service

The court has the power to make an order for service of other documents by an alternative method or at an alternative place under **CPR, r. 6.15**, as well as to make an order dispensing with service (**rr. 6.27 and 6.28**). In both cases, the application must be supported by evidence and may be made without notice (**rr. 6.15(3) and 6.28(2)**). In *R (Hanuman) v University of East Anglia* [2015] EWHC 4122 (Admin), LTL 19/5/2015, the court retrospectively ordered service by an alternative method under **rr. 6.27 and 6.15** as the debtor had tried to make service difficult, had refused to accept service by email even **15.43**

Table 15.3 Deemed dates of service of other documents within the United Kingdom (CPR, r. 6.26)

Method of service	Deemed date of service
1. First class post (or other service which provides for delivery on the next business day)	The second day after it was posted, left with, delivered to or collected by the relevant service provider provided that day is a business day; or if not, the next business day after that day.
2. Document exchange	The second day after it was left with, delivered to or collected by the relevant service provider provided that day is a business day; or if not, the next business day after that day.
3. Delivering the document to or leaving it at a permitted address	If it is delivered to or left at the permitted address on a business day before 4.30 p.m., on that day; or in any other case, on the next business day after that day.
4. Fax	If the transmission of the fax is completed on a business day before 4.30 p.m., on that day; or in any other case, on the next business day after the day on which it was transmitted.
5. Other electronic method	If the email or other electronic transmission is sent on a business day before 4.30 p.m., on that day; or in any other case, on the next business day after the day on which it was sent.
6. Personal service	If the document is served personally before 4.30 p.m. on a business day, on that day; or in any other case, on the next business day after that day.

though he resided in Barbados, and refused to give an address in the United Kingdom at which he could be served. The court may be prepared to make an order under **r. 3.10** curing any irregularity in effecting service of any other document (other than a claim form). A wider approach to **r. 3.10** would be justified in relation to documents other than claim forms because the rules relating to service of subsequent documents are concerned only with bringing them to the attention of the other party so as to notify the taking of a procedural step, not with establishing jurisdiction (*Integral Petroleum SA v SCU-Finanz AG* [2014] EWHC 702 (Comm), LTL 19/3/2014).

Certificate of service

15.44 A table at **CPR, r. 6.29**, sets out the information to be included in a certificate of service, where one is required for a document other than a claim form.

PARTICULAR TYPES OF PARTY

Children and protected parties

15.45 **Claim form and application for appointment of litigation friend by court order** Where proceedings are begun against a child (who is not also a protected party), the claim form must be served on one of his or her parents or guardians, or, if there is no such person, on the person with whom the child resides or who has care of the child (**CPR, r. 6.13(1)**).

In the case of a protected party, the claim form must be served on a person with authority in relation to the protected party by virtue of being that party's attorney under a registered enduring power of attorney, the donee of a lasting power of attorney or the protected party's deputy appointed by the Court of Protection. Where there is nobody so authorised, the claim form should be served on an adult with whom the protected party resides or in whose care the protected party is (**r. 6.13(2)**).

There is no requirement for the child or the protected party to be served, or given any other form of notification of the existence of the proceedings, although the court has a discretion to make an order to that effect (**r. 6.13(4)**). Where the court has made an order allowing a child to conduct proceedings without a litigation friend, the usual rules for service on an individual apply (**r. 6.13(7)**).

An application for the appointment of a litigation friend by court order under **r. 21.8**, must be served on every person on whom a claim form must be served, under **r. 6.13** (**r. 21.8(1)**). An application made before proceedings have started falls within the definition of claim form in **r. 6.2(c)** and will have to be served in the same way as a claim form, under **Part 6, Section II**. If the application is made after the claim has started, it will be served in accordance with the provisions of **Part 6, Section III**.

Other documents   Once proceedings have been commenced with a litigation friend act- **15.46** ing on behalf of the child or protected party, any document which would otherwise be served on the child or protected party should be served on his or her litigation friend (**CPR, r. 6.25(2)**).

These rules are subject to any order to the contrary made by the court (**r. 6.25(3)**). Such an order may be made without notice (**r. 6.25(4)**). Where a document has been served on some other person, the court may make an order that service should stand (**r. 6.25(5)**). Where the court has made an order allowing a child to conduct proceedings without a litigation friend, the usual rules for service on an individual apply (**r. 6.25(6)**).

Companies

Service of a claim form in the jurisdiction on a company is governed by **CPR, r. 6.3(2)**. It **15.47** is clear that, in **r. 6.3(2)**, 'company' includes a company registered under the Companies Act 2006 and an overseas company whose particulars have been registered under s. 1046 of the 2006 Act, as express provision for these companies is made in **r. 6.3(2)(b)** (see below and **15.48**). There is separate provision for limited liability partnerships in **r. 6.3(3)**. Elsewhere in **Part 6**, a distinction is made between companies and other corporations (table in **r. 6.9(2)**).

By **CPR, r. 6.3(2)(a)**, a company may be served by any of the methods permitted under **Part 6** (see **15.10**).

Personal service on a company is effected by leaving a document with a person holding a senior position within the company (**r. 6.5(3)(b)**). The following hold a senior position for the purpose of the CPR: a director, secretary, treasurer, chief executive, manager or other officer of the company (**PD 6A, para. 6.2(1)**). Whether a person falls within the ambit of **CPR, r. 6.5(3)(b)**, and **PD 6A, para. 6.2(1)**, is a matter of fact (*Lakah Group v Al Jazeera Satellite Channel* [2003] EWHC 1231 (QB), [2003] EWCA Civ 1781, [2004] BCC 703). The word 'company' in **CPR, r. 6.5(3)(b)**, means a company that is carrying on business within the jurisdiction. Thus serving a claim form on a director of a foreign company not carrying on business in the jurisdiction when he happens to be temporarily visiting, purportedly under **r. 6.5(3)(b)**, is not good service on the company (*SSL International plc v TTK LIG Ltd* [2011] EWCA Civ 1170, [2012] 1 WLR 1842).

If a company registered in England and Wales has not instructed a solicitor or European lawyer to accept service under **r. 6.7** or provided an address for service under **r. 6.8**, service, by any method permitted by **Part 6** other than personal service, may be effected at its principal office or at any place of business of the company within the jurisdiction which has a real connection with the claim (**r. 6.9(2)**).

As an alternative to service under the CPR, a company may be served by any of the methods of service permitted under the Companies Act 2006 (**CPR, r. 6.3(2)(b)**). The Companies Act 2006, s. 1139(1), provides that: 'A document may be served on a company registered under this Act by leaving it at, or sending it by post to, the company's registered office'. A document is sent by post by a person if that person posts a prepaid envelope containing the document (Companies Act 2006, sch. 4, paras 1(1) and 3(2)). This definition is wide enough to cover first and second class post, registered post or the use of postal services other than those provided by the Royal Mail. Unless the contrary is proved, service is deemed to be effected at the time when the letter would be delivered in the ordinary course of post (Interpretation Act 1978, s. 7). Service on a registered company at its registered office takes effect under the Companies Act 2006, s. 1139, and not under the CPR. Service under the Companies Act 2006 and under the CPR are true alternatives. There are the following differences between the two methods. If service of a document is effected by post under the Companies Act 2006, the document will be deemed to have been served, unless the contrary is proved, when the letter would have been delivered in the ordinary course of post (Interpretation Act 1978, s. 7; *Cranfield v Bridgegrove Ltd* [2003] EWCA Civ 656, [2003] 1 WLR 2441). Service by second class post is allowed by the Companies Act 2006, but not by the CPR because second class post does not provide for delivery on the next business day as required by **r. 6.3(1)(b)**. Under the Companies Act 2006 the deemed date of delivery depends on which day the letter is posted and whether first or second class is used, and the deemed date can be displaced by evidence to the contrary.

Service on a company registered in Northern Ireland or Scotland at its registered office will be service outside the jurisdiction (see **chapter 16**). English court process may be served on a Northern Irish or Scottish company by leaving it at, or posting it to, the company's principal place of business in England and Wales, if it carries on business here (Companies Act 2006, s. 1139(4)). The process must be addressed to the manager or other head officer in England and Wales of the company (s. 1139(4)) and a copy must be sent by post to the company's registered office (s. 1139(4)).

Overseas companies

15.48   By **CPR, r. 6.3(2)**, a claim form may be served in the jurisdiction on a company incorporated outside the United Kingdom (known as an 'overseas company': see the Companies Act 2006, s. 1044), whose particulars have been registered under s. 1046. Registration under s. 1046, is governed by the Overseas Companies Regulations 2009 (SI 2009/1801). Whenever an overseas company establishes a branch or other place of business in the United Kingdom, it must, within one month, deliver a return to Companies House complying with part 2 of the Regulations (reg. 4). The return must state the name and service address of every person resident in the United Kingdom authorised to accept service of documents on behalf of the company in respect of the establishment, or a statement that there is no such person (reg. 7(1)(e)). This information is available for inspection at Companies House. In addition, any person with whom the company deals in the course of business may make a written request to the company for the address of any person resident in the United Kingdom authorised to accept service of documents on its behalf (reg. 65(1)). The company must send a written response within five working days of receiving the request (reg. 65(2)). The company may be served:

(a) by any of the methods permitted under **CPR, Part 6** (see **15.10**), including personal service under **r. 6.5(3)(b)** on its directors who happen to be visiting the jurisdiction (*SSL International plc v TTK LIG Ltd* [2011] EWCA Civ 1170, [2012] 1 WLR 1842), or, where the company has not provided an address for service, at any place in the jurisdiction where the company carries on its activities or any place of business of the company in the jurisdiction (**r. 6.9(2)**; *Sea Assets Ltd v PT Garuda Indonesia* [2000] 4 All ER 371); or

(b) under the provisions of the Companies Act 2006, s. 1139(2).

Service will not be valid under **CPR, r. 6.9(2)**, at an address with which the company has no more than a transient or irregular connection (*Lakah Group v Al Jazeera Satellite Channel* [2003] EWHC 1231 (QB), [2004] BCC 703). Where the company has an establishment in the United Kingdom, it can be served there under the Overseas Companies Regulations 2009, reg. 7, even if there is no link between the proceedings served and the company's UK establishment (*Teekay Tankers Ltd v STX Offshore and Shipping Co.* [2014] EWHC 3612 (Comm), [2015] Bus LR 731). Whether a company has a place of business in the jurisdiction, and where that place of business is, are questions of fact (*Rakusens Ltd v Baser Ambalaj Plastik Sanayi Ticaret AS* [2001] EWCA Civ 1820, [2002] 1 BCLC 104 at [8]; *Matchnet plc v William Blair and Co. LLC* [2002] EWHC 2128 (Ch), [2003] 2 BCLC 195). A place may be a company's place of business even if only an ancillary part of the company's business is carried on there (*South India Shipping Corporation Ltd v Export-Import Bank of Korea* [1985] 1 WLR 585; see also *Akzo Nobel NV v Competition Commission* [2014] EWCA Civ 482, [2014] Bus LR 802). A place in the jurisdiction where a person takes orders for a company incorporated outside the United Kingdom, without authority to decide whether to accept or reject them, is not the company's place of business (*Rakusens Ltd v Baser Ambalaj Plastik Sanayi Ticaret AS*; *Harrods Ltd v Dow Jones and Co. Inc.* [2003] EWHC 1162 (QB), LTL 29/5/2003). In *Harrods Ltd v Dow Jones and Co. Inc.* the criteria used to determine whether the place of business of an agent of a foreign company was that company's place of business were the criteria suggested by the Court of Appeal in *Adams v Cape Industries plc* [1990] Ch 433 at pp. 530–1 for determining whether the activities of an agent here of a foreign company make the company subject to the jurisdiction of the courts here. The same approach was taken in *Reuben v Time Inc.* [2003] EWHC 1430 (QB), LTL 3/7/2003.

The Companies Act 2006, s. 1139(2), provides that a document may be served on an overseas company whose particulars are registered under s. 1046:

(a) by leaving it at, or sending it by post to, the registered address of any person resident in the United Kingdom who is authorised to accept service of documents on the company's behalf; or

(b) if there is no such person, or if any such person refuses service or service cannot for any other reason be effected, by leaving it at or sending by post to any place of business of the company in the United Kingdom.

The rules on postal service under s. 1139 are discussed at **15.47**.

If the only address given by an overseas company of a UK resident authorised to accept service is in Northern Ireland or Scotland, service under the Companies Act 2006, s. 1139(2), will be service outside the jurisdiction (see **chapter 16**).

To be served in accordance with s. 1139(2), a document must be addressed to the person resident in the United Kingdom who is authorised to accept service — addressing it to the company and leaving it at the authorised person's address is not sufficient (*Boocock v Hilton International Co.* [1993] 1 WLR 1065).

In *Harrods Ltd v Dow Jones and Co. Inc.* [2003] EWHC 1162 (QB), LTL 29/5/2003 at [32] and [33], it was held that an overseas company that was not required to register under what is now the Companies Act 2006, s. 1046, could not be served either under what is now s. 1139(2) or by any of the methods permitted by **CPR, Part 6**. In particular, it cannot be served, under r. 6.9(2), at a place in the jurisdiction where its activities are carried on. In *Reuben v Time Inc.* [2003] EWHC 1430 (QB), LTL 3/7/2003, Morland J said, at [31], that he agreed with this statement of the law. In *Lakah Group v Al Jazeera Satellite Channel* Gray J, at first instance, thought that **Part 6** allows for service on a wider range of foreign companies than those which can be served under the Companies Act 2006. However, when refusing permission to appeal against Gray J's decision, the Court of Appeal found it unnecessary to discuss the point.

Commentary

Other corporations

15.49 A corporation, incorporated in England and Wales, which cannot be served under the Companies Act 2006, s. 1139(1) (see **15.47**), must be served by one of the methods listed in **CPR, r. 6.3(1)** (see **15.10**). This applies to entities such as building societies and incorporated friendly societies.

Personal service on a corporation is effected by leaving the document to be served with a person holding a senior position within the corporation (**r. 6.5(3)(b)**). The following hold a senior position for this purpose: a director, the treasurer, secretary, chief executive, manager or other officer of the corporation, the mayor, chairman, president, town clerk or similar officer (**PD 6A, paras 6.1** and **6.2**).

Service by any other method under the CPR on a corporation incorporated in England and Wales, which has not instructed a solicitor to accept service under **CPR, r. 6.7**, or provided an address for service under **r. 6.8**, may be effected at either the principal office of the corporation or any place within the jurisdiction where the corporation carries on its activities and which has a real connection with the claim (**r. 6.9(2)**).

Rule 6.9(2) names the place of service (other than personal service) for a company not registered in England and Wales and a corporation (other than a company) not incorporated in England and Wales where no solicitor is acting and no address for service in the jurisdiction has been given. This is 'any place within the jurisdiction where the *corporation* carries on its activities; or any place of business of the *company* within the jurisdiction' (emphasis added).

Partnerships

15.50 Service on a partnership may be effected by any of the methods permitted by **CPR, r. 6.3(1)** (see **15.10**).

Where partners are sued in the firm name, personal service is effected by leaving the document to be served with a partner, or, alternatively, at the firm's principal place of business, with a person having, at the time of service, control or management of the partnership business (**r. 6.5(3)(c)**). Postal service at the usual or last known residence of one partner constitutes good service on the firm, and therefore on his co-partners (*Lexi Holdings plc v Luqman* (2007) LTL 30/10/2007).

Where a firm has not instructed a solicitor to accept service under **r. 6.7** or provided an address for service under **r. 6.8**, service on it by any method other than personal service should be effected by sending the claim form either to the usual or last known residential address of a partner, or to the principal or last known place of business of the firm (**r. 6.9(2)**).

Partners sued in their individual names must be served as individual defendants. This will now be rare, as **PD 7A, para. 5A.3**, requires proceedings by or against a partnership to be brought in the name of the partnership at the time the cause of action accrued 'unless it is inappropriate to do so'. Proceedings against a foreign partnership, however, will still be brought against the individual partners, as **PD 7A, para. 5A.3**, applies only to partnerships 'carrying on business within the jurisdiction' (**PD 7A, para. 5A.1**). When a claim is made against a partnership, any party to the claim may require the partners to provide a 'partnership membership statement', which is a written statement of the names and last known places of residence of all the persons who were partners in the partnership at the time when the cause of action accrued (**PD 7A, para. 5B.1**). The statement must be provided within 14 days of the date of the request (**PD 7A, para. 5B.2**).

By **PD 10, para. 4.4**, where a claim is brought against a partnership, service must be acknowledged in the name of the partnership on behalf of all the partners at the time the cause of action accrued. The acknowledgment may be signed by anyone who was a partner at the time the cause of action accrued or any other person authorised to do so by such a partner.

The mechanism formerly set out in CPR, sch. 1, RSC, ord. 81, r. 4(2), enabling a person who denied he or she was a partner at the time the cause of action accrued to sign an acknowledgment under protest and then apply to have the acknowledgment set aside has been abolished. Someone in this position must now take the point in his or her defence. The CPR also make no provision for the situation where a partner has no actual authority to sign the acknowledgment on behalf of another partner — where, for example, the other partner wishes to conduct his or her defence separately. The problem was recognised in *Brooks v A. H. Brooks and Co.* [2010] EWHC 2720 (Ch), [2011] 3 All ER 982. The court accepted that, although there is no express provision in the CPR, it must still be possible for a partner to acknowledge service on behalf of only some of the partners at the time the cause of action accrued. But it also held that, by virtue of **PD 10, para.** 4.4(2), an acknowledgment signed by a partner at the time the cause of action accrued (or by a person authorised by any such partner) is effective on behalf of all partners at the relevant time, regardless of whether the person signing has actual authority from his or her partners.

For the effect of acknowledging service on enforcement against the assets of individual partners see **79.45**.

Limited liability partnerships

By **CPR, r. 6.3(3)**, a limited liability partnership (LLP) may be served by any of the methods permitted under **Part 6** or by any method permitted under the Companies Act 2006, s. 1139(1) (see **15.47**), as applied to LLPs in modified form by the Limited Liability Partnerships (Application of Companies Act 2006) Regulations 2009 (SI 2009/1804), reg. 75. SI 2009/1804, reg. 75 also applies the Companies Act 2006, s. 1139(2) (in modified form) to Scottish or Northern Irish LLPs, with the effect that where such LLPs carry on business in England and Wales, service of court process can be effected by leaving the document to be served at, or posting it to, the LLP's principal place of business in England and Wales, addressed to the manager or a designated member of the LLP. A copy must then be sent to the registered office of the LLP. **15.51**

Where a limited liability partnership has not instructed a solicitor to accept service under **CPR, r. 6.7**, or provided an address for service under **r. 6.8**, service by any method other than personal service should be effected by sending the claim form either to the principal office of the partnership or any place of business of the partnership within the jurisdiction which has a real connection with the claim (**r. 6.9(2)**).

Crown proceedings

By **CPR, r. 6.5(2)(b)**, documents required to be served on the Crown may not be served personally. Further, **r. 6.10** stipulates that service on the Attorney General must be effected on the Treasury Solicitor and service on a government department must be effected on the solicitor acting for that department as required by the Crown Proceedings Act 1947, s. 18. The method of service in **CPR, r. 6.10**, applies both to claim forms, as defined in **r. 6.2(c)**, and to other documents (**r. 6.23(7)**). The list published under the Crown Proceedings Act 1947, s. 17, is annexed to **PD 66**. **15.52**

Agent of a principal who is overseas

By **CPR, r. 6.12**, a claimant may, with the court's permission, serve a claim form on the agent of a defendant who is out of the jurisdiction, where: **15.53**

(a) the claim relates to a contract entered into within the jurisdiction, with or through the agent; and

(b) at the time of the application for permission, the agent's authority has not been terminated or the agent is still in business relations with the defendant.

Application for permission should be made in accordance with the Part 23 procedure. No notice need be given, but the application must, by **r. 6.12(2)**, be supported by evidence setting out details of the contract, confirming that it was entered into in the jurisdiction or through an agent who is in the jurisdiction and providing the other information specified in **r. 6.12(2)(a)**. Any order made under the rule must give a time limit within which the defendant must respond to the particulars of claim (not the claim form) (**r. 6.12(3)**). For cases proceeding in the Commercial Court or the Mercantile Courts, the court must specify a period for the defendant to respond which runs from the date of service of the claim form, not the particulars of claim (**CPR, rr. 58.6(3) and 59.5(3)**). A copy of the order and of the claim form must be served on the defendant (**r. 6.12(4)**). **Rule 6.12(5)** makes clear that **r. 6.12** does not exclude the court's power to make an order for alternative service under **r. 6.15**.

A Practice Direction (1920) 150 LT Jo 388 was issued in relation to an earlier version of this rule. It contains the following guidance for practitioners, which the courts may still take into account:

(a) The court's power to make an order under the rule is discretionary, and to be exercised with caution. It should not be used where there is no difficulty in getting an order and serving out of the jurisdiction in the usual way.
(b) The court will look at the nature of the agency relationship. If it is 'casual', the court will be less ready to make an order.

FILING DOCUMENTS

15.54   The CPR distinguish between serving a document, which is the procedure whereby a document is brought to the attention of another party and filing a document, which is the procedure whereby the court receives a copy of a document. 'Filing' is defined in **r. 2.3(1)** as: 'delivering [a document], by post or otherwise, to the court office'. A document sent by post is filed when it is delivered to the court, not when it is posted (*Morshead Mansions Ltd v Langford* [2003] EWHC 2023 (QB), LTL 29/8/2003). Filing takes effect immediately documents are put through the court's letter box, even if the court is then closed to the public and there are no officials to take delivery of the document (*Van Aken v Camden London Borough Council* [2002] EWCA Civ 1724, [2003] 1 WLR 684). The problem with this approach is that it will be impossible for court officials to establish the time (and therefore the date) of filing without making further enquiry of the person who delivered the document.

The deeming rules discussed at **15.36** and **15.42** only apply to service, so for filing it is the actual delivery date that counts. The Interpretation Act 1978, s. 7, applies (by s. 23(1) and (2)), so a document filed by post is deemed to be filed at the time at which the letter containing it would be delivered in the ordinary course of post, unless the contrary is proved.

The CPR make clear which documents must be filed, and when. The detailed requirements are addressed at relevant points in this work. The general rule is that a copy of most formal documents generated in the course of a claim must be filed at court. Thus, all statements of case must be filed, and witness statements and experts' reports may be ordered to be filed. The purpose of the requirement is clear: it is only by having access to information about the case as it progresses that the court is able to exercise its case management powers.

Officials will record the date and time when a document was received at court for filing in court records and/or computer systems (**PD 5A, para. 5.2**). The actual date of filing will be stamped on the document itself (**PD 5A, para. 5.1**).

Filing by email or fax

Under **CPR, r. 5.5**, practice directions may provide for filing by fax or other electronic means. Filing by fax is covered by **PD 5A, para. 5.3**, which provides that a fax received after 4 p.m. is treated as filed on the next day that the court office is open. Any court which has published an email address for the filing of documents on Her Majesty's Courts and Tribunals Service website, will accept electronic filing (**PD 5B, para. 1.3**) of specified documents which are listed on that website as a document that may be sent to or filed in that court by email. Many courts now accept filing by email, see **PD 5B**. Electronic filing is used in Money Claim Online (**PD 7E**; see **12.10**). An earlier version of PD 5B made clear that emailing a judge direct does not constitute filing by email in accordance with the rules. Electronic filing is also permitted under **PD 51O**.

15.55

HM Courts and Tribunals Service has published guidance (http://www.justice.gov.uk/courts/email-guidance) about emailing the civil and family courts, which includes information about what may be emailed to which courts and also technical information about which file types the courts will accept.

Inspecting the court file

Public right of access to court register and to court documents   In accordance with the principle of open justice, the CPR make provision for members of the public or the press to be able to apply for copies of particular court documents. Under **CPR, r. 5.4(1)**, the Queen's Bench and Chancery Divisions and the Admiralty and Commercial Court registry in the RCJ keep a register of the claims which they have issued (**PD 5A, para. 4.1**). The register is open to members of the public to search upon payment of the prescribed fee (**CPR, r. 5.4(2)**). There are no registers of claims in any District Registries or other offices of the High Court or the County Court (**PD 5A, para. 4.2**).

15.56

The Attorney General may search, inspect and copy any document on a court file with a view to making an application under the Senior Courts Act 1981, s. 42, or the Employment Tribunals Act 1966, s. 33, for a person to be declared a vexatious litigant (**CPR, r. 5.4A(1)**). The Attorney General must make a request in writing, pay the prescribed fee and name the person who would be the subject of the application (**r. 5.4A(2)**).

A non-party is entitled, under **r. 5.4C**, to obtain from court records:

(a) a copy of a statement of case, but not any documents filed with or attached to it or intended to be served with it (**r. 5.4C(1)(a)**);
(b) a judgment or order given or made in public (whether made at a hearing or not) (**r. 5.4C(1)(b)**);
(c) a copy of any other document filed by a party, or communication between the court and a party or another person, but only if the court gives permission (**r. 5.4C(2)**).

Statements of case are defined in **CPR, r. 2.3(1)** as meaning a claim form, particulars of claim, defence, Part 20 claim or reply as well as any further information given in relation to them either voluntarily or under **CPR, r. 18.1**. It was held in *Various Claimants v News Group Newspapers Ltd* [2012] EWHC 397 (Ch), [2012] 1 WLR 2545, that the reference to statements of case in **r. 5.4C(1)(a)** covers generic particulars of claim, including amended particulars of claim. A notice to admit and a response to that notice were not within the definition. An application for a copy of these documents fell under **r. 5.4C(2)** and could only be granted with the permission of the court. However, the right of access to statements of case under **r. 5.4C(1)(a)** does include the acknowledgment of service and detailed grounds for contesting a claim for judicial review, although not the documents annexed to the acknowledgment or grounds (*R (Corner House Research) v Director of the Serious Fraud Office* [2008] EWHC 246 (Admin), LTL 20/2/2008).

The distinction between private and public hearings is addressed in **PD 39A, para. 1**.

Various documents listed in **CPR, r. 5.4C(1B)**, relating to mediated cross-border disputes subject to Directive 2008/52/EC and **CPR, rr. 78.23** to **78.28**, may be inspected only with the court's permission.

The right to a copy of a statement of case, judgment or order only arises once the defendant has filed an acknowledgment of service or defence (or, where there is more than one defendant, all have done so or at least one has and the court gives permission), or the claim has been listed for hearing or judgment has been entered (**r. 5.4C(3)**). The rules include a measure of protection for those mentioned in statements of case, but not judgments or orders under **r. 5.4C(1)(b)** because they have been given or made in public and the rules reflect the principle of open justice. A party or person identified in a statement of case (which may not have been referred to in open court) has the right under **r. 5.4C(4)** to apply for an order that a non-party may not obtain a copy of a statement of case, or that the categories of person who may obtain a copy should be restricted or that the statement of case should be provided only in edited form, or any other appropriate restriction. However, the presumption is that the public should be entitled to see any statement of case in unredacted form. A restriction may be ordered under **r. 5.4C(4)** where, for example, there is a risk that disclosure of unredacted statements of case will prejudice a criminal trial. In *Associated Newspapers Ltd v Bannatyne* [2015] EWHC 3467 (Ch), LTL 13/12/2015, the court accepted that although there was an implied undertaking of confidentiality relating to disclosure in financial remedy divorce proceedings, the court refused to grant an application to prevent disclosure of statements of case in circumstances where the party concerned had made misleading statements in those documents which he had later corrected. The presumption is reversed in relation to documents which are the subject of an application under **r. 5.4C(2)** which can only be disclosed with the permission of the court. Here, there is no presumption in favour of disclosure, although the court will lean in favour of allowing disclosure of documents which have been read out in open court or documents which have been read by the judge in the course of the decision-making process. The court will look at the reason why the documents are sought, the use to which they will be put and whether they are truly required to understand and report the court proceedings to which they relate (*Various Claimants v News Group Newspapers Ltd* [2012] EWHC 397 (Ch), [2012] 1 WLR 2545 and *Chan U Seek v Alvis Vehicles Ltd* [2004] EWHC 3092 (Ch), [2005] 1 WLR 2965). No distinction can be drawn between documents used at trial and those used at the interim stages of a case (*Various Claimants v News Group Newspapers Ltd* [2012] EWHC 397 (Ch), [2012] 1 WLR 2545, and *Cleveland Bridge UK Ltd v Multiplex Constructions (UK) Ltd* [2005] EWHC 2101 (TCC), LTL 31/8/2005).

For statements of case filed before 2 October 2006, the former **r. 5.4(5)** to **(9)** continue to apply and are reproduced in full in **PD 5A, paras 4A.1** to **4A.9**. Under the old rules, a non-party was entitled to obtain a claim form, subject to a court order to the contrary. However, an application for permission had to be made in order to obtain a statement of case other than the claim form.

A witness statement which stands as the evidence-in-chief of a witness is open for inspection by the public during the trial unless the court directs otherwise (**CPR, r. 32.13**).

In *Dian AO v David Frankel and Mead* [2004] EWHC 2662 (Comm), [2005] 1 WLR 2951, the court considered an application by a non-party for permission to inspect and copy the entire court file. It held that the applicant must identify with reasonable precision the documents or class of documents it wished to search for and explain why it wanted them. The principle of open justice which lies behind the rules must be borne in mind in any application for access to the court file. The court granted permission for specified documents only to be copied and inspected on the grounds that the relevance of those documents on the court file to proceedings in which the applicant was involved abroad constituted a legitimate reason for seeking access to the court file. The principle stated in this case remains good law despite the revision of the rules in 2006 (*ABC Ltd v Y* [2010] EWHC 3176 (Ch), [2011] 4 All ER 113; *Pfizer Health AB v Schwarz Pharma AG* [2010] EWHC 3236 (Pat), [2011] FSR 14).

Rule 5.4C applies both to private law and public law claims. If either a claimant or a defendant wishes to keep matters out of the public domain, they should make a positive application to this effect either in the claim form or acknowledgment (*R (Corner House Research) v Director of the Serious Fraud Office* [2008] EWHC 246 (Admin), [2008] ACD 63). An order for disclosure under **r. 5.4C** may be made where the documents are sought for the purpose of collateral litigation. It is in the interests of justice for disclosure to be made of any documents which will be relevant to the collateral litigation (*R (Taranissi) v Human Fertilisation and Embryology Authority* [2009] EWHC 130 (Admin), LTL 2/2/2009).

In *Glidepath BV v Thompson* [2005] EWHC 818 (Comm), [2005] 2 Lloyd's Rep 549, the court refused to order disclosure of documents filed in court proceedings which had subsequently been stayed pursuant to the Arbitration Act 1996, s. 9. The private and confidential character of proceedings ancillary to the arbitral process ought to be protected. Disclosure should be granted only if all parties consented or if there were an overriding reason in the interests of justice.

The presumption in favour of inspection under the CPR does not apply to documents in bankruptcy proceedings in respect of which an application is made under the Insolvency Rules 1986 (SI 1986/1925), **r. 7.31(4)** (*Mansell v Acton* [2005] EWHC 3048 (Ch), LTL 3/2/2006). The principle of open justice extends to criminal cases. In cases where documents have been placed before a judge and referred to in the course of proceedings, the default position should be that access should be permitted on the open justice principle. The case for allowing access will be particularly strong where it is sought by the press for a proper journalistic purpose (*R (Guardian News and Media Ltd) v City of Westminster Magistrates' Court* [2012] EWCA Civ 420, [2013] QB 618; see also *NAB v Serco Ltd* [2014] EWHC 1225 (QB), LTL 22/4/2014).

Parties' right of access to court documents   Subject to an order to the contrary, **CPR, r. 5.4B(1)**, and **PD 5A, para. 4.2A**, give parties to proceedings the right to obtain copies of the following documents from the court file: **15.57**

(a)   a certificate of suitability of a litigation friend;

(b)   a notice of funding;

(c)   a claim form or other statement of case, together with any documents filed with, or attached to, or intended by the claimant to be served with, it;

(d)   an acknowledgment of service, together with any documents filed with, or attached to, or intended by the party acknowledging service to be served with, it;

(e)   a certificate of service, other than a certificate of service of an application notice or order in relation to a type of application mentioned in sub-paragraph (h)(i) or (ii) below;

(f)   a notice of non-service;

(g)   a directions questionnaire;

(h)   an application notice, other than in relation to:

    (i)   an application by a solicitor for an order declaring that he has ceased to be the solicitor acting for a party; or

    (ii)   an application for an order that the identity of a party or witness should not be disclosed;

(i)   any written evidence filed in relation to an application, other than a type of application mentioned in sub-paragraph (h)(i) or (ii);

(j)   a judgment or order given or made in public (whether made at a hearing or without a hearing);

(k)   a statement of costs;

(l)   a list of documents;

(m)   a notice of payment into court;

(n)   a notice of discontinuance;

(o)   a notice of change; or

(p)   an appellant's or respondent's notice of appeal.

Provision of a copy of any other document filed at court, or of any communication between the court and a party or any other person, requires the court's permission (**CPR, r. 5.4B(2)**).

A party is entitled to copies of documents on the court file not in order to enable the case to be dealt with fairly (it is not a question of disclosure) but in order to ensure the open and transparent administration of justice (*R (Riseborough) v Lands Tribunal* [2009] EWHC 1135 (Admin), LTL 9/6/2009).

Procedure

15.58   A person who wishes to obtain a copy of a document from court records must pay a fee and either file a written request for the document (if the court's permission is not required) or an application notice under **CPR, Part 23** (if the court's permission is required) (**r. 5.4D(1)**). Applications for permission by a party under **r. 5.4B(2)** or a non-party under **r. 5.4C** and applications for restrictions on access under **r. 5.4C** may be made without notice. An application by a non-party under **r. 5.4C(6)** for access to a document on which restrictions have been placed under **r. 5.4C(4)** must be on notice to the person who requested the restrictions (**r. 5.4C(6)**).

Inspecting a document without the court's permission is an interference with the administration of justice, and is a criminal contempt of court if done in the knowledge that the court's permission is required (*Dobson v Hastings* [1992] Ch 394).

Although the current version of **Part 5** no longer makes this explicit, the CPR do contain provisions which restrict access to certain documents. These include:

(a) **r. 57.5(5)**, which provides that, unless the court gives permission, a party to a probate claim may not inspect testamentary documents or written evidence filed by any other party until he has filed his own testamentary documents and evidence;

(b) **PD 62, para. 5.1**, which states that an arbitration claim form may only be inspected with the permission of the court (reflecting the privacy of arbitration proceedings);

(c) PD Application for a Warrant under the Competition Act 1998, paras 3.3 and 3.4, and PD Application for a Warrant under the Enterprise Act 2002, paras 3.3 and 3.4, under which a Part 8 claim form issued on an application by the Competition and Markets Authority (the practice directions still refer to the old Office of Fair Trading) for a warrant under the Competition Act 1998 or the Enterprise Act 2002 may not be inspected by a member of the public unless a High Court judge grants permission.

Chapter 16 Service outside the Jurisdiction

The following procedural checklist is relevant to this chapter:

Procedural checklist 11   Application for permission to serve claim form out of the jurisdiction

INTRODUCTION

16.1   Inevitably, there are a number of complexities where the intended defendant to proceedings is outside the jurisdiction. At common law, an action *in personam* (i.e. an action against a legal person as opposed to an action *in rem* against a ship or other property) could only be brought against a defendant served with process while in England or Wales. This, at least superficially, had the merit of ensuring the courts of this country did not purport to exert an exorbitant jurisdiction over defendants who were not amenable to the coercive powers of the courts. The superficiality stemmed from the fact that jurisdiction could be established by service on a defendant while on a temporary visit to this country (**16.2**) or by a foreign defendant submitting to the jurisdiction (**16.3**). In any event, the restrictive common law rule has been subject to a discretionary power to allow English proceedings against defendants outside the jurisdiction since the enactment of the Common Law Procedure Act 1852. This discretionary power is governed by **CPR, r. 6.36**, and is discussed at **16.42** to **16.57**. These rules will be referred to in this chapter as the common law rules.

If a defendant is domiciled in an EU member State (other than Denmark), the common law rules are replaced by **Regulation (EU) No. 1215/2012** on jurisdiction and the recognition and enforcement of judgments in civil and commercial matters. This lays down a general rule that a defendant domiciled in an EU State must be sued in the courts of that State (**16.16**). This is subject to a number of wide-ranging exceptions, which are discussed in **16.17** to **16.36**.

Regulation (EU) No. 1215/2012 is known as the '**recast Brussels I Regulation**' (and will be referred to as such in this chapter). It applies only to legal proceedings instituted on or after 10 January 2015 (**art. 66**). It is based on and replaces Regulation (EC) No. 44/2001 (the 'Brussels I Regulation'), which in turn was based on, and is substantially the same as, an earlier treaty which all the then member States of the EU agreed to, namely, the Brussels Convention on Jurisdiction and the Enforcement of Judgments in Civil and Commercial Matters (the 'Brussels Convention'). Unlike a Regulation, which has direct effect, the Brussels Convention had to be incorporated into UK law by an Act of Parliament: the **Civil Jurisdiction and Judgments Act 1982** ('CJJA 1982'). The Brussels Convention is set out in sch. 1 to the **CJJA 1982**. The Brussels Convention continues to determine questions of jurisdiction between EU States and Aruba and the French overseas departments (recital (23)).

As between EU States and the EFTA States, Norway, Switzerland and Iceland, questions of jurisdiction and the enforcement of judgments are governed by two versions of the Lugano Convention: the original 1988 Convention, which is in practically the same terms as the Brussels Convention, and the revised 2007 Convention, which is in practically the same terms as the Brussels I Regulation. Norway, Switzerland and Iceland moved to the revised Lugano Convention on 1 January 2010, 1 January 2011 and 1 May 2011 respectively. Proceedings commenced on or after those dates are governed by the 2007 Convention whilst proceedings commenced before those dates are governed by the 1988 Convention.

The States which joined the EU after 1988, apart from Poland, never became parties to the original Lugano Convention but are parties to the revised one. Poland became a party to the original Lugano Convention on 1 February 2000.

Until 1 July 2007, Denmark opted out of the Brussels I Regulation and questions of jurisdiction between Denmark and other EU States continued to be determined by the Brussels Convention. As from 1 July 2007 the Brussels I Regulation applied to Denmark under an agreement (OJ L299, 16/11/2005, pp. 62–7) which was approved on behalf of the EU by Council Decision 2006/325/EC (OJ L120, 5/5/2006, p. 22). Denmark has also notified the European Commission pursuant to art. 3(2) of the agreement that it intends to implement the **recast Brussels I Regulation** (OJ L79, 21/3/2013, p. 4). The implementation date will be notified to the Commission in due course.

In summary, the **recast Brussels I Regulation** applies to proceedings commenced in all EU member States on or after 10 January 2015 other than Denmark. The EU member States are currently Austria, Belgium, Bulgaria, Croatia, Cyprus, Czech Republic, Denmark, Estonia, Finland, France, Germany, Greece, Hungary, Republic of Ireland, Italy, Latvia, Lithuania, Luxembourg, Malta, Netherlands, Poland, Portugal, Romania, Slovakia, Slovenia, Spain, Sweden and the United Kingdom.

The Brussels I Regulation still applies for the time being to proceedings commenced in Denmark. The 2007 Lugano Convention (which is in substantially the same terms as the Brussels I Regulation) applies as between all EU member States (including Denmark) and Norway, Switzerland and Iceland. This chapter concentrates on discussing the **recast Brussels I Regulation** and, unless otherwise stated, references to articles are to articles in that Regulation.

Within the United Kingdom, separate jurisdiction is exercised by the courts of England and Wales, Scotland and Northern Ireland. Under the **CJJA 1982** these three areas are known as 'parts' of the United Kingdom. Allocation of jurisdiction between the courts of the various parts of the United Kingdom is regulated by a modified form of the Brussels I Regulation, which can be found in the CJJA 1982, sch. 4. The substantive provisions of the Brussels Convention are applied as between Gibraltar and the United Kingdom by the Civil Jurisdiction and Judgments Act 1982 (Gibraltar) Order 1997 (SI 1997/2602). But in Gibraltar, the **recast Brussels I Regulation** is applied by the Civil Jurisdiction and Judgments Act 1993 (Gibraltar), ss. 2(1) and 39.

In 2005 the Hague Choice of Court Convention, aimed at giving effect to exclusive jurisdiction agreements between EU and non-EU countries, was concluded. The Convention entered into force on 1 October 2015 between the EU member States (other than Denmark) and Mexico and on 1 October 2016 with Singapore. Ukraine and the United States have signed the Convention but not yet ratified it. For the latest position, the status table at the Hague Conference website should be checked. The necessary amendments to statute and court rules to bring the Convention into effect in this country were made in the Civil Jurisdiction and Judgments (Hague Convention on Choice of Court Agreements 2005) Regulations 2015 (SI 2015/1644).

Where a claim can be brought in the courts of more than one country, there is a general concern that it should be brought in the courts of the most appropriate country. The courts are also concerned that the same dispute should not be litigated in several countries at the same time, with the risk of irreconcilable judgments and difficulties regarding the recognition of judgments for enforcement purposes. These problems are addressed under the common law rules by the courts' powers to refuse permission to serve outside of the jurisdiction, or where proceedings have been served within the jurisdiction, by staying the English proceedings on the ground of *forum non conveniens* (**16.71** to **16.76**). There is also a power to grant injunctions to restrain foreign proceedings (an anti-suit injunction) (**16.77**).

Similar problems in the **recast Brussels I Regulation** cases are dealt with by requirements that courts other than the one first seised of the matter must either decline jurisdiction or stay their proceedings unless the court has exclusive jurisdiction under a jurisdiction agreement (see **16.37** and **16.39**).

Determining the system of law to be applied to resolve an action where one or more of the parties is foreign is a matter of private international law. As such it is outside the scope of this work, and specialist works should be consulted.

SERVICE ON THE FOREIGN DEFENDANT WITHIN THE JURISDICTION

16.2 Under the common law rules, a foreign defendant is amenable to the jurisdiction of the courts in this country if process is served upon the defendant within the jurisdiction. Applying this rule, jurisdiction was established in *Maharanee Seethaderi Gaekwar of Baroda v Wildenstein* [1972] 2 QB 283, where the proceedings were served on the defendant while on a temporary visit to this country to attend the Ascot Races. This rule has been abolished for cases governed by the **recast Brussels I Regulation**, which by **art. 5** provides that jurisdiction against EU defendants can no longer be founded by service during the defendant's temporary presence in this country. The practice is that a claim form with a foreign defendant will be marked 'not for service out of the jurisdiction', unless it is filed with form N510 or an order permitting service abroad is obtained. The intention when this is done is usually either to effect service on the defendant during a temporary visit to this country (unless the defendant lives in the EU) or to secure the defendant's agreement to service within the jurisdiction (often on English solicitors). The period of validity of an originating process served within the jurisdiction is four months, not six. This is so regardless of whether service could instead have been effected outside the jurisdiction (**CPR, r. 7.5**; *American Leisure Group Ltd v Garrard* [2014] EWHC 2101 (Ch), [2014] 1 WLR 4102).

If a domestic claim form has been issued, and it is later discovered that the defendant is outside the jurisdiction, the usual procedure used to be to issue a concurrent claim form. The more usual procedure now, where no defendant has been served, is to issue an amended claim form relying on **r. 17.1**.

It is no longer the case that the defendant must be present in the jurisdiction at the time of actual or deemed service for service to be effective (*Kamali v City and Country Properties Ltd* [2006] EWCA Civ 1879, [2007] 1 WLR 1219, overturning *Chellaram v Chellaram (No. 2)* [2002] EWHC 6323 (Ch), [2002] 3 All ER 17). See *Key Homes Bradford Ltd v Patel* [2015] 1 BCLC 402.

A foreign company which does not carry on business within the jurisdiction is not effectively served by purporting to serve on a director within the jurisdiction (*SSL International plc v TTK LIG Ltd* [2011] EWCA Civ 1170, [2012] 1 WLR 1842).

Where however a director has registered an address for service in the jurisdiction under the Companies Act 2006, s. 1140, it may be possible to serve proceedings against the director at that address, regardless of whether the proceedings concern the company (*Key Homes Bradford Ltd v Patel* [2015] 1 BCLC 402).

Similarly, where an overseas company has registered a UK establishment under the Companies Act 2006, proceedings can be served at its registered address under s. 1139 regardless of whether the proceedings concern that establishment (*Teekay Tankers Ltd v STX Offshore and Shipping Co.* [2014] EWHC 3612 (Comm), [2015] Bus LR 731).

Despite having jurisdiction over a foreign defendant through service within England and Wales, the English court may decide not to exercise that jurisdiction and to grant a stay of proceedings if there is another more appropriate forum to hear the dispute (see **16.71** to **16.76**).

SUBMISSION TO THE JURISDICTION

Regardless of whether the court would otherwise have jurisdiction, a defendant may **16.3** submit to the jurisdiction of the courts of this country. It may be, for example, to save the costs of disputing jurisdiction, that a defendant will agree to English proceedings being served at the offices of a solicitor in England. Alternatively, a domestic claim form may be sent to a defendant outside the jurisdiction in breach of the rules requiring permission to serve (**16.42** to **16.57**) and the defendant may proceed to contest the action on its merits without objecting to the defect in service. In the absence of any express agreement to submit to the jurisdiction, it is a question of whether the defendant's conduct, when viewed objectively in the context of all the circumstances of the case, is inconsistent with maintaining an objection to the jurisdiction of the court. It is always dangerous to do anything more than to acknowledge service and to make an application under **CPR, Part 11**, to contest the jurisdiction (see **chapter 19**). It is easy to submit to the jurisdiction inadvertently by, for example:

(a) instructing a solicitor to accept service in the jurisdiction (*Manta Line Inc. v Sofianites* [1984] 1 Lloyd's Rep 14); or

(b) appearing to contest the merits. An example is *Marc Rich & Co. AG v Società Italiana Impianti PA (No. 2)* [1992] 1 Lloyd's Rep 624, where the defendant was held to have submitted to the jurisdiction of the courts in Italy by delivering a statement of case disputing the merits of the claim. See, also, *SSQ Europe SA v Johann & Backes OHG* [2002] 1 Lloyd's Rep 465, and *Global Multimedia International Ltd v ARA Media Services* [2006] EWHC 3612 (Ch), [2007] 1 All ER (Comm) 1160, which are discussed in **19.3** and **19.4**.

A claimant who has commenced proceedings thereby submits not just the determination of the claim itself to the jurisdiction of the court, but also the incidents of the litigation (*Liberia v Gulf Oceanic Inc.* [1985] 1 Lloyd's Rep 539). Most commonly, this principle means that the court has jurisdiction over a counterclaim brought against the claimant. But a costs order, and an application to commit for contempt for failing to comply with it, are also ordinary incidents of the claim, and as such the court has jurisdiction over them so that the court's permission is not needed to serve the application out of the jurisdiction (*Marketmaker Technology Ltd v CMC Group plc* [2008] EWHC 1556 (QB), LTL 4/9/2008; *Dar Al Arkan Real Estate Development Co. v Majid Al-Sayed Bader Hashim Al-Refai* [2014] EWCA Civ 715, [2015] 1 WLR 135).

A similar principle applies in **recast Brussels I Regulation** cases, where **art. 26(1)** provides that the courts of a member State have jurisdiction where the defendant 'enters an appearance' unless the appearance is entered to contest jurisdiction. The reference to entering an appearance was considered by the Court of Appeal in *Deutsche Bank AG London Branch v Petromena ASA* [2015] EWCA Civ 226, [2015] 1 WLR 4225. Whether an appearance has been entered is to be decided as a matter of national procedural law, provided the result is consistent with the effective operation of the Regulation. There are two different ways in which a defendant might submit to the jurisdiction. The first requires the doing of an act inconsistent with maintaining a challenge to the jurisdiction. Such a waiver must clearly convey an unequivocal renunciation by the defendant of his right to challenge the jurisdiction. The second is where national procedural rules provide that a particular act shall be treated as a submission. So a defence contesting jurisdiction and the merits in the alternative, where that is permitted under the procedural law of the court seised, does not constitute a submission to the jurisdiction (*Elefanten Schuh GmbH v Jacqmain* (case 150/80) [1981] ECR 1671). It is not possible to submit to the jurisdiction of a court where the courts of another country have exclusive jurisdiction under **art. 24**. It is possible to submit even if there is a jurisdiction clause in favour of another State or a non-member State, or the proceedings have been brought in a jurisdiction other than those provided for to protect the weaker party in **arts 10** to **23** (insurance, employment and consumer claims) (**art. 26(2)**; *Česká podnikatelská pojišťovna as, Vienna Insurance Group v Bilas* (case C-111/09) [2010] ECR I-4545; *Taser International Inc. v SC Gate 4 Business SRL* (case C-175/15) ECLI:EU:C:2016:176, [2016] ETMR 28). A weaker party, must, however, be informed by the court of his or her right to contest the jurisdiction of the court and of the consequences of entering or not entering an appearance. This is a new provision in the **recast Brussels I Regulation** (**art. 26(2)**) and it is not clear how the English court will comply with this obligation.

The UK Intellectual Property Office ('IPO') is a court of a member State for the purposes of the **recast Brussels I Regulation** and submission before the IPO amounts to submission to the Intellectual Property Enterprise Court ('IPEC'). Once a party has appeared before a court of a member State, that court and any other court in that State which may hear any stage of the proceedings according to local law has jurisdiction under **art. 26** (*Future New Developments Ltd v B&S Patente und Marken GmbH* [2014] EWHC 1874 (IPEC), [2015] FSR 15).

CASES OUTSIDE THE GENERAL RULES

16.4   Certain types of proceedings affect rights *in rem*. Both under the common law rules and under the **recast Brussels I Regulation** special rules govern where many of these types of proceedings must be litigated. The main policy consideration justifying these special rules is that rights *in rem* are often protected by detailed national laws, and the courts of the country in question are in the best position to apply them. These special rules are considered at **16.5** to **16.13**.

Difficult questions arise where the **recast Brussels I Regulation** applies but the proceedings concern rights *in rem*, or similar rights and a non EU member State is the most appropriate forum. The English court may be prepared to apply the **recast Brussels I Regulation** provisions by analogy or reflexively. This is considered at **16.76**.

Under the common law rules

16.5   **Land disputes**   Claims founded on a dispute as to the title to, or possession of, land must be brought in the courts of the country where the land is situated. The authority for this is *British South Africa Co. v Companhia de Moçambique* [1893] AC 602 as interpreted by later decisions. Where a question as to the title of foreign land is no more than a collateral issue in a claim, the rule does not prevent the courts in this country exercising jurisdiction (see *St Pierre v South American Stores (Gath and Chaves) Ltd* [1936] 1 KB 382 and, in relation to claims for trespass, CJJA 1982, s. 30). It was established by *Penn v Lord Baltimore* (1750) 1 Ves Sen 444 that the rule can be circumvented if the defendant is subject to the general jurisdiction of the courts in this country, such as through presence here, and if the claim can be framed so as to impose a personal obligation on the defendant. An example is a claim for rent due under a lease of foreign land (*St Pierre v South American Stores (Gath and Chaves) Ltd* [1936] 1 KB 382).

16.6   **Intellectual property**   Claims alleging breach of foreign copyright are justiciable in the United Kingdom where the court has personal jurisdiction over the defendant (*Lucasfilm Ltd v Ainsworth* [2011] UKSC 39, [2012] 1 AC 208). It is unclear from the Supreme Court's decision, however, whether cases involving other foreign IP rights are justiciable. Following the approach under the **recast Brussels I Regulation**, claims involving validity of rights which are required to be deposited or registered are unlikely to be justiciable whereas claims of infringement will be. Of particular difficulty will be cases which involve consideration of both validity and infringement.

16.7   **Insolvency proceedings**   The **recast Brussels I Regulation** does not apply to bankruptcy, proceedings relating to the winding up of insolvent companies or other legal persons, judicial arrangements, compositions and analogous proceedings (**art. 1(2)(b)**). Jurisdiction over insolvency proceedings in EU States (apart from Denmark) is subject to Regulation

(EC) No. 1346/2000 (see **82.9** to **82.12** and **83.3**). Service outside the jurisdiction of any document in proceedings under the Insolvency Act 1986 or the Insolvency Rules 1986 is governed by the Insolvency Rules 1986 (SI 1986/1925), r. 12A.20 (see **84.5**). The intention is that the **recast Brussels I Regulation** and Regulation (EC) No. 1346/2000 dovetail completely (*Polymer Vision R&D Ltd v Van Dooren* [2011] EWHC 2951 (Comm), LTL 28/11/2011), but there are some difficulties of classification. Not all claims by or against liquidators or trustees in bankruptcy are excluded from the **recast Brussels I Regulation** by art. 1(2)(b). In order to be excluded, a claim must derive directly from the bankruptcy or winding up and be closely connected with the insolvency proceedings (*Gourdain v Nadler* (case 133/78) [1979] ECR 733). Claims based on pre-insolvency rights, such as a retention of title clause, are unlikely to be excluded (*German Graphics Graphische Maschinen GmbH v Van der Schee* (case C-292/08) [2009] ECR I-8421). Whereas claims brought by or against liquidators exercising their powers for the general body of creditors are likely to be excluded (*Seagon v Deko Marty Belgium NV* (case C-339/07) [2009] ECR I-767). Claims assigned by a liquidator, where the validity of the assignment is not in question, will not come within the exception (*F-Tex SIA v Lietuvos-Anglijos UAB 'Jadecloud-Vilma'* (case C-213/10) [2013] Bus LR 232) nor will claims available to a creditor of an insolvent company outside of the insolvency (*ÖFAB v Koot* (case C-147/12) [2015] QB 20).

Under the recast Brussels I Regulation

Exclusive jurisdiction   Recast Brussels I Regulation, art. 24, allocates exclusive jurisdiction, regardless of the domicile of the parties, over five categories of cases. The courts of the member States are required, of their own motion, to declare they have no jurisdiction in these cases (**art. 27**). The words 'shall have exclusive jurisdiction, regardless of domicile' at the beginning of the Brussels I Regulation, art. 22, were interpreted by the Court of Appeal as applying only as between the courts of member States (*Choudhary v Bhatter* [2009] EWCA Civ 1176, [2010] 2 All ER 1031). They did not create an 'extra-EU jurisdiction' or 'universal international jurisdiction' in the subject-matter jurisdiction cases set out in **art. 22** (*Lucasfilm Ltd v Ainsworth* [2009] EWCA Civ 1328, [2010] Ch 503 at [129], [183]). In *Dar Al Arkan Real Estate Development Co. v Majid Al-Sayed Bader Hashim Al-Refai* [2014] EWCA Civ 715, [2015] 1 WLR 135, Beatson LJ (with whom Briggs and Richards LJJ agreed) expressed the obiter view that *Choudhary v Bhatter* was decided per incuriam and is wrong. **Recital 14** of the **recast Brussels I Regulation** now makes clear that the exclusive jurisdiction provisions are intended to apply regardless of the defendant's domicile.

16.8

Land   Recast Brussels I Regulation, art. 24(1), provides that proceedings which have as their object rights *in rem* in immovable property or tenancies of immovable property are subject to the exclusive jurisdiction of the courts of the member State in which the property is situated. This is subject to an exception in respect of actions concerning tenancies between natural persons domiciled in the same country for temporary private use for periods of up to six months, which may be brought in the country where the defendant is domiciled.

16.9

Regarding rights *in rem*, the article has been interpreted by the Court of Justice of the European Union (CJEU) in *Reichert v Dresdner Bank* (case C-115/88) [1990] ECR 27 as being restricted to actions to determine the extent, content, ownership or possession of immovable property, or the existence of other rights *in rem* therein. In *Webb v Webb* (case C-294/92) [1994] QB 696 an apartment in France had been bought in the defendant's name with money provided by the claimant. An action was brought in England claiming a declaration that the property was held on an express or resulting trust for the claimant. It was held, by reasoning analogous to that in *Penn v Lord Baltimore* (1750) 1 Ves Sen 444 (see **16.5**), that the claim affected the defendant's obligations *in personam* and did not have as its object rights *in rem*, and so was outside the scope of **art. 24**. In *G v G* [2015] EWHC 2101 (Fam), [2016] 4 WLR 22, however, an action seeking an order for sale of a property held in joint names was held to come within

Commentary

art. 24. *Webb v Webb* was distinguished on the basis that the claimant in that case was seeking to establish and acquire rights in immovable property by way of constructive or resulting trust, whereas in this case the claimant already had proprietary rights as co-owner and was seeking to enforce and give effect to those rights.

While the phrase 'rights *in rem*' has generally been construed restrictively, the provision regarding tenancies has in contrast been construed widely. It covers cases where the existence of a lease is disputed (*Sanders v Van der Putte* (case 73/77) [1977] ECR 2383) and to any dispute concerning the respective obligations of the parties under a lease (*Rösler v Rottwinkel* (case 241/83) [1986] QB 33). It therefore applies to claims in respect of unpaid rent and other breaches of covenant under a lease. There are limits, however. In *Jarrett v Barclays Bank plc* [1999] QB 1, claims by consumers against the bank under the Consumer Credit Act 1974 arising out of loans to purchase timeshares in properties in Portugal did not have as their object tenancies in immovable property. The foundation of the claims was the loan agreement, and so the claims were not prevented by **art. 24** from being commenced in England.

16.10   **Companies and associations**   Recast Brussels I Regulation, **art. 24(2)**, provides that proceedings having as their object the validity of the constitution, nullity or dissolution of companies or associations of legal or natural persons, or of their organs, must be brought in the country where the relevant body has its 'seat'. Under the Regulation a court in a member State determines where a company has its seat by applying its rules of private international law (see also **art. 63**). In *Choudhary v Bhatter* [2009] EWCA Civ 1176, [2010] 2 All ER 1031, the Court of Appeal held that the English court had jurisdiction against a company formed in England in 1872, but which had its entire operations in India.

Problems have arisen in practice where there are a number of issues in the case, not all of which come within **art. 24(2)**. The CJEU clarified the position in *Berliner Verkehrsbetriebe (BVG), Anstalt des öffentlichen Rechts v J. P. Morgan Chase Bank NA, Frankfurt Branch* (case C-144/10) [2011] 1 WLR 2087. For **art. 24(2)** to be engaged, the validity of a company's decision must form the subject matter of the dispute, not merely be an ancillary question. **Article 24(2)** therefore does not apply to proceedings in which a company pleads that a contract cannot be relied upon against it because a decision of its organs which led to the conclusion of the contract is supposedly invalid on account of infringement of its statutes.

Unsurprisingly, the CJEU has held that an action seeking compensation for damage resulting from alleged infringements of EU competition law does not constitute proceedings having as their object the validity of the decisions of organs of companies (*flyLAL-Lithuanian Airlines AS v Starptautiskā lidosta Riga VAS* (case C-302/13) [2014] 5 CMLR 27).

16.11   **Public registers**   Recast Brussels I Regulation, **art. 24(3)**, gives exclusive jurisdiction over proceedings concerning the validity of entries in a public register to the courts of the State where the register is kept.

16.12   **Intellectual property**   Recast Brussels I Regulation, **art. 24(4)**, gives exclusive jurisdiction over proceedings concerning the registration or validity of patents, trade marks, designs and similar rights to the courts of the State where the property in question has been registered or where registration has been applied for. This does not extend to claims for infringement, which are claims in tort and may be brought in accordance with **art. 7(2)** (see **16.27**). **Article 24(4)** provides that the courts of a member State have exclusive jurisdiction in proceedings concerned with the registration or validity of a European patent granted for that State. This does not prevent courts in other member States granting interim relief under **art. 35** (*Solvay SA v Honeywell Fluorine Products Europe BV* (case C-616/10) ECLI:EU:C:2012:445).

When the Unified Patent Court (UPC) comes into operation, it will have exclusive jurisdiction in cases concerning the validity or infringement of the patents coming within its remit and **arts 24(4)** and **7(2)** will not apply. The UPC will also have jurisdiction over a defendant from a non-member State in some circumstances where there would be no such jurisdiction under the **recast Brussels I Regulation**. Under its present wording, the UPC Agreement cannot come into force until it has been ratified by the United Kingdom. Only EU States can accede to the Agreement and when this edition went to press, no announcement had been made of what would happen following the UK's decision to leave the EU.

Enforcement of judgments Recast Brussels I Regulation, art. 24(5), gives exclusive jurisdiction in enforcement proceedings to the courts of the State in which the judgment is to be enforced. This may include committal proceedings following breach of a court order (*Dar Al Arkan Real Estate Development Co. v Majid Al-Sayed Bader Hashim Al-Refai* [2014] EWCA Civ 715, [2015] 1 WLR 135). **16.13**

JURISDICTION UNDER THE RECAST BRUSSELS I REGULATION

The **recast Brussels I Regulation** is designed to determine the international jurisdiction of the courts of the member States, to facilitate recognition, and to introduce a simple procedure for securing the international enforcement of judgments. Enforcement under the Regulation is considered in **chapter 80**. **16.14**

The main rule (**16.16**) is that a claim must be brought in the courts of the member State where the defendant is domiciled. However, there are many types of claim that can be brought in other countries (**16.17** to **16.36**). Where the other country is England, English proceedings may be issued and served out of the jurisdiction without permission. As there is a possibility that the courts of more than one country may have jurisdiction over a case, provision has been made for jurisdiction being declined or subsequent claims being stayed (**16.37** and **16.39**).

As the **recast Brussels I Regulation** is an act of the institutions of the Union, the CJEU may give preliminary rulings on its interpretation under the Treaty on the Functioning of the European Union, art. 267. It will not give rulings on a hypothetical basis, nor where the ruling is no longer required in the case referred, but would be relevant in other pending cases (*Antonio Gramsci Shipping Corporation (Order of the Court)* (case C-350/13) ECLI:EU:C:2014:1516) (see **chapter 78**).

Under the 1971 Protocol on the interpretation of the Brussels Convention by the European Court, questions of interpretation of the Brussels Convention can also be referred to the CJEU.

It is important that the Regulation and Convention are interpreted in the same way in all the contracting States. Obviously, there are many differences in the domestic laws applied in the various contracting States, particularly between the civil and common law systems. The CJEU has therefore regularly decided that legal concepts used in the Regulation and the Convention must be given a 'Community meaning'. This involves attempting to discover shared principles, a far from simple task. A number of important CJEU cases involve interpretation of the Brussels Convention. The same principles apply in the interpretation of the **recast Brussels I Regulation**, to the extent the relevant provisions are unchanged.

Scope of the recast Brussels I Regulation

The **recast Brussels I Regulation** applies to civil and commercial proceedings whatever the nature of the court or tribunal (**art. 1**). It does not apply to revenue, customs, social security, insolvency (see **16.7**), arbitration or administrative matters, nor to proceedings relating to the status or legal capacity of natural persons, rights in property arising out of a matrimonial relationship, wills and succession. An action for damages for infringements of EU competition law is a civil and commercial matter (*flyLAL-Lithuanian Airlines AS v Starptautiskā lidosta Riga VAS* (case C-302/13) [2014] 5 CMLR 27). A court of a member State encompasses any tribunal of the **16.15** member State or a tribunal of a place within a member State which may lawfully hear the proceedings (*Future New Developments Ltd v B & S Patente und Marken GmbH* [2014] EWHC 1874 (IPEC), [2015] FSR 15).

The exclusions are often narrower than might first appear to be the case. Proceedings brought by the English tax authorities were not revenue proceedings as the claim was brought in tort for a conspiracy to commit a VAT fraud and did not depend on any special powers given to HMRC (*Commissioners of HM Revenue and Customs v Sunico ApS* (case C-49/12) [2014] 1 QB 391).

Similarly claims brought by an heir to her father's estate were not succession proceedings as the claim made was of a tortious conspiracy and succession was not the principal focus of the claim (*Sabbagh v Khoury* [2014] EWHC 3233 (Comm), LTL 21/10/2014).

For a discussion of the interplay between the wills and succession exclusion and the Succession Regulation (Regulation (EU) No. 650/2012), see *Winkler v Shamoon* [2016] EWHC 217 (Ch), 18 ITELR 818.

For the difficulties in determining whether proceedings are insolvency proceedings, see **16.7**.

For the application of the **recast Brussels I Regulation** to schemes of arrangement under the Companies Act 2006, s. 895, see *Re Van Gansewinkel Groep BV* [2015] EWHC 2151 (Ch), [2015] Bus LR 1046.

Arbitration matters were excluded from the scope of the Brussels Convention because they were already covered by international conventions, particularly the New York Convention, 1958. However, a number of the provisions in the Brussels I Regulation, as interpreted by the CJEU, undermined the exclusion of arbitration. Most significantly, proceedings relating to the incorporation or validity of an arbitration clause were held to be within the scope of the Regulation (*National Navigation Co. v Endesa Generaciün SA* [2009] EWCA Civ 1397, [2010] 1 Lloyd's Rep 193, applying *West Tankers Inc. v Allianz SpA* (case C-185/07) [2009] AC 1138, where the CJEU held that a preliminary ruling on the applicability of an arbitration clause in proceedings in which the main subject of the proceedings was within the Regulation was itself to be categorised as within the Regulation). For legal proceedings instituted on or after 10 January 2015, changes made in the **recast Brussels I Regulation** seek to reverse this gradual encroachment (see in particular **recital 12**).

A claim which is brought by or against a public body acting in the exercise of its public powers is not a 'civil [or] commercial matter' within the meaning of the **recast Brussels I Regulation, art. 1** (*Grovit v De Nederlandsche Bank NV* [2007] EWCA Civ 953, [2008] 1 WLR 51). In this case a decision by the central bank to refuse registration of a money transaction business was held to be a public law decision. Where a fine is imposed to ensure compliance with an order or judgment given in a civil or commercial matter, the fine is also civil and commercial in nature (*Realchemie Nederland BV v Bayer CropScience AG* (case C-406/09) [2012] Bus LR 1825). Conversely, a matter may be a public law matter even where no parties are State entities (*British Airways plc v Sindicato Español de Pilotos de Líneas Aéreas* [2013] EWHC 1657 (Comm), [2013] ILPr 45).

Domicile: the general rule

16.16   The general rule laid down by the **recast Brussels I Regulation** is that proceedings must be brought in the courts of the member State where the defendant is domiciled. **Article 4(1)** provides:

Subject to this Regulation, persons domiciled in a member State shall, whatever their nationality, be sued in the courts of that member State.

Domicile is determined by reference to the internal law of the State concerned (**art. 62**). In the United Kingdom domicile is defined for the purposes of the **recast Brussels I Regulation** by the Civil Jurisdiction and Judgments Order 2001 (SI 2001/3929), sch. 1, paras 9 to 12, as amended by the Civil Jurisdiction and Judgments (Amendment) Regulations (SI 2014/2947).

The domicile of individuals is governed by SI 2001/3929, sch. 1, para. 9, which provides in sub-para. (2):

An individual is domiciled in the United Kingdom if and only if—
(a) he is resident in the United Kingdom; and
(b) the nature and circumstances of his residence indicate that he has a substantial connection with the United Kingdom.

By sub-para. (6) an individual is presumed to have a substantial connection with the United Kingdom after being resident in the United Kingdom for three months unless the contrary is proved. It is domicile at the time of the proceedings which is relevant not domicile at, for example, the time of contracting (*Sherdley v Nordea Life and Pension SA* [2012] EWCA Civ 88, [2012] 2 All ER (Comm) 725).

An individual may have more than one domicile, but ownership of property and business interests in the jurisdiction will not be sufficient to establish domicile here if there is no settled or usual place of abode (*High Tech International AG v Deripaska* [2006] EWHC 3276 (QB), [2007] EMLR 15; *Cherney v Deripaska* [2007] EWHC 965 (Comm), [2007] 2 All ER (Comm) 785; *OJSC Oil Co. Yugraneft v Abramovich* [2008] EWHC 2613 (Comm), LTL 3/11/2008).

Where the defendant's whereabouts are unknown, in spite of attempts to locate him, his last known domicile may be sufficient in some circumstances (*Hypoteční banka as v Lindner* (case C-327/10) [2011] ECR I-11543).

Recast Brussels I Regulation, art. 63(1), provides that a corporation is domiciled where it has its 'statutory seat', central administration or principal place of business. A company's statutory seat is its registered office or, if it does not have one, the place where it was incorporated (**art. 63(2)**). The 'principal place of business' of a company within **art. 63** is the place at the heart of its operations (*King v Crown Energy Trading AG* [2003] EWHC 163 (Comm), [2003] ILPr 28). In *Ministry of Defence and Support for the Armed Forces of Iran v FAZ Aviation Ltd* [2007] EWHC 1042 (Comm), [2008] 1 All ER (Comm) 372, the court stated that the principal place of business is likely to be the place where the corporate authority (shareholders and directors) is to be found and to be the place from which the company is controlled and managed. The place where the company's day-to-day activities are conducted may not be the principal place of business if those activities are subject to the control of senior management located elsewhere. The central administration of a company is where decisions are made and where the entrepreneurial management takes place. This does not mean a subsidiary will, in the ordinary case, be domiciled where its parent is domiciled (*Young v Anglo American South Africa Ltd (No. 2)* [2014] EWCA Civ 1130, [2014] Bus LR 1434).

A corporation may be domiciled in more than one State under the rules in **art. 63**.

A dispute about where a company has its seat is determined on the basis of establishing a good arguable case. This has been said to mean that one side has a much better argument on the material available (*889457 Alberta Inc. v Katanga Mining Ltd* [2008] EWHC 2679 (Comm), [2009] 1 BCLC 189; *OJSC Oil Co. Yugraneft v Abramovich* [2008] EWHC 2613 (Comm), LTL 3/11/2008). However, the Court of Appeal has suggested that the word 'much' does not add anything to the test (*JSC 'Aeroflot-Russian Airlines' v Berezovsky* [2013] EWCA Civ 784, [2013] 2 Lloyd's Rep 242).

The time for judging whether there is a defendant domiciled within the jurisdiction for the purposes of **art. 63** is the date of issue, not the date of service (*Canada Trust Co. v Stolzenberg (No. 2)* [2002] 1 AC 1).

Exceptions to the rule that jurisdiction is based on domicile

Although **recast Brussels I Regulation, art. 4(1)**, lays down the general rule, a claimant often **16.17** has a choice of forum under the Regulation. This is because, in a wide variety of cases, the claimant is given the option of suing in another country. **Article 5(1)** provides that 'Persons domiciled in a member State may be sued in the courts of another member State only by virtue of the rules set out in sections 2 to 7 of this Chapter'. These sections encompass **arts 7 to 26** of the Regulation. **Article 24** was considered at **16.8** to **16.13**. **Articles 7, 8, 10 to 23** and **25** will be considered at **16.18** to **16.36**.

The basic scheme, as confirmed by **CPR, r. 6.33(2)**, is that the courts of England and Wales will have jurisdiction to hear and determine a claim under the Regulation if:

(a) the case falls within one of the provisions set out in **arts 7 to 26**;

(b) there are no proceedings pending involving the same claim in another part of the United Kingdom or another member State; and

(c) the defendant is domiciled in a member State.

If none of the parties are domiciled in a member State but they have agreed to the jurisdiction of the courts of a member State, those courts will have jurisdiction unless under that State's law the agreement is null and void as to its substantive validity (**art. 25(1)**). The defendant no longer needs to be domiciled in a member State in certain claims against employers (**art. 21(2)**), certain claims by consumers against traders (**art. 18(1)**) nor, it seems likely, where the court has exclusive jurisdiction (**art. 24, recital 14**). The Unified Patent Court, when it comes into effect, will also have jurisdiction against defendants domiciled outside the EU in certain circumstances (see **16.12**).

Similar provision is made in relation to Aruba, French overseas departments, Iceland, Norway and Switzerland by **CPR, r. 6.33(1)**.

Contract

16.18   **Main provision**   Recast Brussels I Regulation, **art. 7(1)**, provides in part that a person domiciled in one member State may alternatively 'be sued…in matters relating to a contract, in the courts for the place of performance of the obligation in question'.

In *Kalfelis v Bankhaus Schröder, Münchmeyer, Hengst & Co.* (case 189/87) [1988] ECR 5565 the CJEU laid down the general principle that the special jurisdiction given by **art. 7** must be interpreted restrictively as it derogates from the principle that jurisdiction is vested in the courts of the country where the defendant is domiciled.

16.19   **Scope of article 7(1)**   In *Arcado SPRL v Haviland SA* (case 9/87) [1988] ECR 1539 the CJEU confirmed that, in **recast Brussels I Regulation, art.** 7(1), the phrase 'matters relating to a contract':

is to be regarded as an independent concept which, for the purpose of the application of the Convention, must be interpreted by reference principally to the system and objectives of the Convention in order to ensure that it is fully effective.

The classification of a claim under national law is irrelevant and a claim cannot come within both the contract and tort heads. So in *Brogsitter v Fabrication de Montres Normandes EURL* (case C-548/12) [2014] ILPr 20, a claim of unfair competition which was classified as a tort under German law could be a matter relating to a contract within **art. 7(1)**. The relevant question was whether the interpretation of the contract was indispensable in deciding whether the conduct was lawful or unlawful.

A claim brought under the Contracts (Rights of Third Parties) Act 1999 is a matter relating to a contract within **recast Brussels I Regulation, art.** 7(1) (*WPP Holdings Italy SRL v Benatti* [2007] EWCA Civ 263, [2007] 1 WLR 2316).

There is uncertainty over whether contribution claims are 'matters relating to a contract', 'matters relating to tort' or neither (*XL Insurance Co. SE v Axa Corporate Solutions Assurance* [2015] EWHC 3431 (Comm), LTL 3/12/2015; *Iveco SpA v Magna Electronics Srl* [2015] EWHC 2887 (TCC), [2016] ILPr 18; and *Ergo Insurance SE v If P&C Insurance AS* (cases C-359/14 and C-475/14) ECLI:EU:C:2016:40, [2016] ILPr 20).

In *Martin Peters Bauunternehmung GmbH v Zuid Nederlandse Aannemers Vereniging* (case 34/82) [1983] ECR 987, the CJEU decided that as membership of an association creates close links between members of the same kind as those between the parties to a contract, jurisdiction over a dispute between an association and one of its members could be given by **art. 7(1)**.

In *Česká spořitelna as v Feichter* (case C-419/11) [2013] ILPr 22, a claim under a promissory note was held to be a matter relating to a contract even though under the relevant national law a promissory note was classified as an abstract security, not a contract.

The effect is that **art. 7(1)** can be invoked where either there is a contractual relationship giving rise to an actual contract, or there is a consensual obligation similar to a contract giving rise to a comparable obligation.

In *Kleinwort Benson Ltd v Glasgow City Council* [1999] 1 AC 153, the House of Lords held that restitutionary claims based on void contracts did not fall within **art. 7(1)**. The CJEU has, however, since held that actions seeking the annulment of a contract and the restitution of sums paid but not due on the basis of that contract do constitute 'matters relating to a contract' (*Profit Investment SIM SpA v Ossi* (case C-366/13) ECLI:EU:C:2016:282).

Where the only connection with this country is an alleged non-disclosure or misrepresentation in relation to the making of a contract, jurisdiction may be given by **art. 7(1)**. This is because the word 'obligation' in **art. 7(1)** is not limited to contractual obligation, and in suitable cases the objects of the Convention can be achieved by bringing proceedings where the negotiations in a matter related to a contract were conducted (*Agnew v Länsförsäkringsbolagens AB* [2001] 1 AC 223).

In *Effer SpA v Kantner* (case 38/81) [1982] ECR 825 the CJEU held that **art. 7(1)** applies even where the existence of the contract on which the claim is based is disputed by the defendant. Otherwise, a defendant could oust the jurisdiction granted by **art. 7(1)** merely by saying there is a dispute. There must be evidence from which it would be proper to conclude that a contract existed; mere assertion is not sufficient (*Tesam Distribution Ltd v Schuh Mode Team GmbH* [1990] ILPr 149). **Article 7(1)** can confer jurisdiction where the relief sought is a negative declaration (as can **art. 7(3)** in relation to tort claims: *Folien Fischer AG v Ritrama SpA* (case C-133/11) [2013] QB 523).

Place of performance of obligation   If recast **Brussels I Regulation, art. 7(1)**, applies, proceedings may be brought in the courts of 'the place of performance of the obligation in question'. In *Etablissements A. de Bloos SPRL v SCA Bouyer* (case 14/76) [1976] ECR 1497 the CJEU held that the 'obligation' in **art. 7(1)** refers to the contractual obligation forming the basis of the legal proceedings. Regard must be had to the contractual obligation under consideration, and not to the contract as a whole. The place of performance of that obligation is not necessarily the same as the place where breach occurred.   **16.20**

Where a claimant brings a claim concerning a number of obligations under a single contract, it is the principal obligation that determines jurisdiction under **art. 7(1)** (*Shenavai v Kreischer* (case 266/85) [1987] ECR 239). This was applied in *Union Transport plc v Continental Lines SA* [1992] 1 WLR 15, where the claimant had claims under a voyage charter for failing to nominate a vessel (which was to be performed in England) and for failure to provide a vessel (which was to be performed in the United States). It was held that nominating a vessel was the principal obligation as it triggered the other contractual obligations, and therefore proceedings had validly been brought in England. The place of performance of a warranty as to an existing state of affairs is the place where that state of affairs was required to exist (*Crucial Music Corporation v Klondyke Management AG* [2007] EWHC 1782 (Ch), [2008] Bus LR 327).

A claimant does not have to establish finally and conclusively that the place of performance of the obligation was in England, but does have to establish a 'good arguable case that that was so' (*Boss Group Ltd v Boss France SA* [1997] 1 WLR 351).

Where there is more than one possible place of performance, the claimant may have a choice of where to commence proceedings (*Canyon Offshore Ltd v GDF Suez E&P Nederland BV* [2014] EWHC 3810 (Comm), [2015] Bus LR 578).

The Regulation goes on to provide that the place of performance of the obligation in question shall be, in the case of the sale of goods, the place in a member State where, under the contract, the goods were delivered or should have been delivered, and in the case of the provision of services, the place in a member State where, under the contract, the services were provided or should have been provided (**art. 7(1)(b)**). There is no equivalent provision in the Brussels Convention. The revision was introduced by the Brussels I Regulation to counter criticism that the operation of art. 5(1) of the Brussels Convention tended to give jurisdiction to the courts of the claimant's domicile not the courts of the country with the closest connection to the dispute.

Whether a contract is for the sale of goods or services is an autonomous principle of EU law which depends on whether the characteristic obligation is the supply of goods or of services (*Granarolo SpA v Ambrosi Emmi France SA* (case C-196/15), [2016] ILPr 32).

In a claim relating to the sale of goods where the contract provides for delivery to a number of locations, the place of delivery under **recast Brussels I Regulation, art. 7(1)**, is the place with the closest link with the contract. In general this is the principal place of delivery determined on the basis of economic criteria, which is a matter to be decided by the domestic court seised of the proceedings. If there is no principal place of delivery, each of the delivery points can found the basis for jurisdiction under **art. 7(1)**, giving the claimant a choice of where to litigate (*Color Drack GmbH v Lexx International Vertriebs GmbH* (case C-386/05) [2008] 1 All ER (Comm) 169). In a case involving carriage of goods, the place where the goods were delivered or should have been delivered should be determined on the basis of the provisions of the contract. Where it is impossible to do so, the place of delivery is where the physical transfer of the goods took place, as a result of which the purchaser obtained or should have obtained actual power of disposal over those goods at the final destination of the sales transaction (*Car Trim GmbH v KeySafety Systems Srl* (case C-381/08) [2010] Bus LR 1648). In an FOB contract, risk and property pass to the buyer on shipment, and delivery as a result is effected on shipment by virtue of the Sale of Goods Act 1979, s. 32(1) (*Scottish and Newcastle International Ltd v Othon Ghalanos Ltd* [2008] UKHL 11, [2008] Bus LR 583). Contracts for the manufacture of goods will usually be contracts for the sale of goods within **recast Brussels I Regulation, art. 7(1)**, (*Car Trim GmbH v KeySafety Systems Srl*).

In a claim relating to services provided in different member States, the place of provision is the place with the closest link to the contract, in particular, the place where the main provision of services is to be carried out. Where this is in more than one country, the claimant has a choice of where to sue (*Rehder v Air Baltic Corporation* (case C-204/08) [2009] ILPr 44). In the case of a commercial agency contract, the main place of provision of services depends on the provisions in the contract or, in the absence of such provisions, the actual place of performance or, failing that, the place where the agent is domiciled (*Wood Floor Solutions Andreas Domberger GmbH v Silva Trade SA* (case C-19/09) [2010] 1 WLR 1900).

An exclusive distribution agreement is a contract for the provision of services, not goods (*Corman-Collins SA v La Maison du Whisky SA* (case C-9/12) [2014] QB 431).

16.21   Contracts of employment   Articles 20 to 23 of the **recast Brussels I Regulation** deal with jurisdiction over individual contracts of employment and have no equivalent in the Brussels Convention. The Regulation provides that the employee may be sued by the employer only in the courts of the member State in which the employee is domiciled (save that a counterclaim may be brought against an employee in the courts where the original claim is pending) (**art. 22**). This cannot be departed from by agreement unless the agreement is entered into after the dispute has arisen. A jurisdiction clause will therefore be ineffective as against the employee (*Petter v EMC Europe Ltd* [2015] EWCA Civ 828, [2016] ILPr 3). An employee can submit to the English jurisdiction in circumstances where the court does not otherwise have jurisdiction, but **art. 26(2)** requires the court to ensure the employee is informed of his right to contest the jurisdiction and of the consequences of submitting.

The employer, on the other hand, under **art. 21(1)**, may be sued in:

(a) the courts of the member State where the employer is domiciled; or

(b) in the courts for the place where the employee habitually carries out his or her work, or last did so (see *Powell v OMV Exploration and Production Ltd* UKEAT/131/13, [2014] ICR 63); or

(c) if the employee does not or did not habitually carry out his or her work in any one country, in the courts for the place where the business which engaged the employee is or was situated.

Options (b) and (c) are also now available if the employer is not domiciled in a member State (**art. 21(2)**). An employer who is not domiciled in a member State, but has a branch, agency or other establishment in one of the member States, is deemed to be domiciled in that member State for the purposes of a dispute arising out of the operations of the branch, agency or establishment (**art. 20**, overriding the provisions of **arts 6** and **7(5)**). This includes an embassy of a non-member State (*Mahamdia v Algeria* (case C-154/11) [2013] ICR 1).

An employer can also be sued by the employee in any country given jurisdiction pursuant to a jurisdiction clause in the employment contract and can be joined as a defendant under **art. 8(1)** in appropriate circumstances.

The rights given to employees in the Regulation are in accordance with a policy of protecting the weaker party in contractual relationships. In *Mercury Publicity Ltd v Wolfgang Loerke GmbH* [1993] ILPr 142, the Court of Appeal emphasised that the rule was restricted to relationships of master and servant of a personal nature and refused to extend it to a contract of commercial agency. **Articles 20** to **23** can apply where claims are brought in tort or for breaches of company law. In *Alfa Laval Tumba AB v Separator Spares International Ltd* [2012] EWCA Civ 1569, [2013] 1 WLR 1110 the Court of Appeal held that claims against a former employee for breach of copyright and misuse of confidential information were matters relating to his employment contract. In *Shannon v Global Tunnelling Experts UK Ltd* [2015] EWHC 1267 (QB), LTL 11/5/2015 the court was just about persuaded that a personal injury claim could come within **arts 20** to **23**. In *Holterman Ferho Exploitatie BV v Spies von Büllesheim* (case C-47/14) ECLI:EU:C:2015:574 the CJEU held that claims against an employee who was also a director and alleged to be in breach of Dutch company law provisions came within what are now **arts 20** to **23**. In contrast, in *Arcadia Petroleum Ltd v Bosworth* [2016] EWCA Civ 818, [2016] CP Rep 48, it was held that claims in conspiracy against former senior managers of the claimants did not relate to individual contracts of employment.

Consumer contracts The recast **Brussels I Regulation**, **arts 17** to **19** apply to consumer contracts, ousting the special jurisdiction granted by **art. 7(1)**. As with contracts of employment (see **16.21**), these provisions are designed to protect the weaker party. To qualify as a consumer a party must not have entered into the contract in the course of a trade or profession (**art. 17**). The contract must then be either: **16.22**

(a) for the sale of goods on instalment credit terms; or

(b) for a loan repayable by instalments, or for any other form of credit, made to finance the sale of goods; or

(c) concluded with a person who pursues commercial or professional activities in the member State of the consumer's domicile or, by any means, directs such activities to that member State or to several States including that member State, and the contract falls within the scope of such activities.

In contrast to the employment provisions, only contracts come within the consumer provisions. A consumer with a claim in tort will need to bring himself within **art. 7(2)** (*Kolassa v Barclays Bank plc* (case C-375/13) [2015] ILPr 14).

The circumstances in which the possibility of accessing a website from a member State amounts to directing commercial activities to that State has been considered by the CJEU in *Pammer v Reederei Karl Schlüter GmbH & Co. KG* (case C-585/08) [2010] ECR I-12527 and by the Court of Appeal in *Wood v Hewitsons LLP* [2014] EWCA Civ 1698. Mere accessibility of a website in the consumer's domicile is not sufficient. It is not necessary that the sales contract was entered into at a distance (*Mühlleitner v Yusufi* (case C-190/11) [2012] ILPr 46).

The consumer provisions may apply to a contract which does not come within the scope of the commercial or professional activities directed to a member State if it is closely connected with a contract which does meet that test (*Hobohm v Benedikt Kampik Ltd & Co. KG* (case C-297/14) ECLI:EU:C:2015:844, [2016] QB 616).

By **art. 18** a consumer acting as a claimant may bring proceedings in the courts of the member State where either party is domiciled, regardless now of the domicile of the defendant, but a consumer may generally only be sued in the courts of the country in which he or she is domiciled. A jurisdiction agreement is only effective as against a consumer if entered into after the dispute has arisen or where both parties are domiciled in the same member State and jurisdiction is given to that member State. A consumer can, however, sue in another member State pursuant to a jurisdiction agreement. A consumer can submit to the English jurisdiction in circumstances where the court does not otherwise have jurisdiction, but **art. 26(2)** requires the court to ensure the consumer is informed of his or her right to contest the jurisdiction and of the consequences of submitting. Where a consumer commences proceedings in a member State, a counterclaim can be brought in the same proceedings.

16.23   **Insurance contracts**   Jurisdiction in insurance matters is governed by **recast Brussels I Regulation, arts 10 to 16**, and **art. 7(1)** is ousted. These provisions are designed to protect the insured, who is regarded as being the weaker party in insurance matters. It is not always the case that an insured will be in a weaker negotiating position than the insurer, especially where the insured is a large commercial corporation. Nevertheless, the Court of Appeal held in *New Hampshire Insurance Co. v Strabag Bau AG* [1992] 1 Lloyd's Rep 361 that the concept of 'matters relating to insurance' in these provisions has to be given a literal interpretation, and is not restricted to insurance for domestic or private purposes. However, contract claims between insurers are outside the scope of the provisions (*Youell v La Réunion Aérienne* [2009] EWCA Civ 175, [2009] Bus LR 1504), as are reinsurance contracts (*Universal General Insurance Co. v Group Josi Reinsurance Co. SA* (case C-412/98) [2001] QB 68). There is uncertainty over whether a contribution claim by one insurer against another is a 'matter relating to a contract', 'a matter relating to tort' or neither (see **16.19**).

By **arts 11** and **12** an insurer domiciled (or having a branch, agency or establishment) in a member State may be sued:

(a) in the courts of the State where it is domiciled; or
(b) in the courts of the State where the policyholder, insured or beneficiary is domiciled, provided that State is a member State; or
(c) if there are co-insurers, in the courts of a member State where proceedings have been brought against the leading insurer; or
(d) if the case involves liability insurance or insurance over immovable property, in the courts for the place where the harmful event occurred.

The insured is protected by **art. 14**, which provides that an insurer may bring proceedings only in the courts of the country where the insured is domiciled.

Proceedings can be brought directly against an insurer in England where a direct action is permitted under the substantive law governing the claim. The insured may then also be joined to the action if that is permitted under the substantive law. An injured party may therefore be able to commence proceedings in its own domicile even if no damage is suffered within the jurisdiction (*Mapfre Mutualidad Compañía de Seguros y Reaseguros SA v Hoteles Piñero Canarias SL* [2015] EWCA Civ 598, [2015] CP Rep 39).

Jurisdiction agreements   Recast Brussels I Regulation, art. 25(1) provides: **16.24**

If the parties, regardless of their domicile, have agreed that a court or the courts of a Member State are to have jurisdiction to settle any disputes which have arisen or which may arise in connection with a particular legal relationship, that court or those courts shall have jurisdiction, unless the agreement is null and void as to its substantive validity under the law of that Member State. Such jurisdiction shall be exclusive unless the parties have agreed otherwise. The agreement conferring jurisdiction shall be either—
(a)   in writing or evidenced in writing;
(b)   in a form which accords with practices which the parties have established between themselves; or
(c)   in international trade or commerce, in a form which accords with a usage of which the parties are or ought to have been aware and which in such trade or commerce is widely known to, and regularly observed by, parties to contracts of the type involved in the particular trade or commerce concerned.

Article 25(2) goes on to provide that any communication by electronic means which provides a durable record of the agreement shall be equivalent to 'writing'. This includes so-called 'click wrapping' where a party has to click on an additional link to open the terms and conditions (*El Majdoub v CarsOnTheWeb.Deutschland GmbH* (case C-322/14) [2015] ILPr 32).

It is for the party who is relying on **art. 25** to prove the existence of an agreement which satisfies these requirements (*Konkola Copper Mines v Coromin Ltd* [2006] EWCA Civ 5, [2006] 1 Lloyd's Rep 410). However, as jurisdictional questions are resolved at an interim stage, the standard of proof must be moderated. The general rule is that any fact or matter on which the assumption of jurisdiction by the court depends has to be shown to exist by reference to the test of 'a good arguable case' (*Canada Trust Co. v Stolzenberg (No. 2)* [1998] 1 WLR 547). In the case of **art. 25**, 'good arguable case' has been held to mean the party invoking **art. 25** must show it has much the better of the argument that the requirements as to form are met and that the jurisdiction clause was the subject of consensus between the parties (*Bols Distilleries BV v Superior Yacht Services Ltd* [2006] UKPC 45, [2007] 1 WLR 12) However, the Court of Appeal has suggested that the word 'much' does not add anything to the test (*JSC 'Aeroflot-Russian Airlines' v Berezovsky* [2013] EWCA Civ 784, [2013] 2 Lloyd's Rep 242).

Application of article 25(1)   General words of incorporation might be effective to incorporate a jurisdiction clause for the purposes of **recast Brussels I Regulation, art. 25(1)(a)**, but will do so only if they clearly and precisely demonstrate the existence of a consensus to that effect (*AIG Europe SA v QBE International Insurance Ltd* [2001] 2 All ER (Comm) 622; *Tradigrain SA v Siat SpA* [2002] CLC 574).   **16.25**

In order for **art. 25** to apply the parties must have 'agreed' to give jurisdiction to the courts of a member State. *Dresser UK Ltd v Falcongate Freight Management Ltd* [1992] QB 502 concerned a jurisdiction clause in a bill of lading relied on by a bailor of goods against a sub-bailee. As that relationship does not depend on agreement, the clause did not satisfy the requirements of **art. 25**. In *Powell Duffryn plc v Petereit* (case C-214/89) [1992] ECR I-1745 the CJEU held that a jurisdiction clause in the articles of association of a company was to be regarded as being part of a contract for the purposes of **art. 25** as between the company and the shareholders and also between the shareholders *inter se*. A jurisdiction clause will generally only apply to the parties to the contract. It is not possible to pierce the corporate veil and make non-parties subject to the jurisdiction provisions (*VTB Capital plc v Nutritek International Corporation* [2013] UKSC 5, [2013] 2 AC 337). Nor will a manufacturer be able to rely on a jurisdiction clause in a contract with its buyer when an action is brought against it by a sub-buyer (*Refcomp SpA v AXA Corporate Solutions Assurance SA* (case C-543/10) [2013] 1 All ER (Comm) 1201). The position may be different where the contract is made for the benefit of a non-party (*Gerling Konzern Speziale Kreditversicherungs-AG v Amministrazione del Tesoro dello Stato* (case 201/82) [1983] ECR 2503). A jurisdiction clause in a bond prospectus may be relied upon against purchasers of the bonds on the secondary market where the clause was valid between the issuer and financial intermediary, the purchaser succeeded to the intermediary's rights and obligations and had the opportunity to acquaint himself with the prospectus containing the clause (*Profit Investment SIM SpA v Ossi* (case C-366/13) ECLI:EU:C:2016:282).

Article 25(5) provides that the validity of the agreement conferring jurisdiction cannot be contested solely on the ground that the contract is not valid. **Article 25** may therefore still apply where there is an allegation that the contract is vitiated by mistake, misrepresentation, illegality, lack of authority or lack of capacity. A jurisdiction clause is severable from the main contract. This means that it is only where the clause itself is under attack that jurisdiction may be lost.

Article 25(1) also lays down certain requirements as to the form of jurisdiction clauses. A distinction is drawn between international trading and commercial contracts and, on the other hand, more general contracts. A jurisdiction clause in a general contract must be in writing or evidenced in writing, or else accord with the practices of the parties. The CJEU held in *Colzani v Rüwa* (case 24/76) [1976] ECR 1831 that if the jurisdiction clause is contained in written standard terms, the contract must contain an express reference to those standard terms. In *7E Communications Ltd v Vertex Antennentechnik GmbH* [2007] EWCA Civ 140, [2008] Bus LR 472, jurisdiction under **art. 25** was conferred by a jurisdiction clause contained in standard terms and conditions which were referred to in a contract, even though the defendant had not seen those terms and the reference to the standard terms and conditions did not refer expressly to the jurisdiction clause. It is more difficult to demonstrate that a jurisdiction clause in a separate contract has been incorporated (*Seitz GmbH & Co. KG v Brunner SpA* [2009] ILPr 31; *Africa Express Line Ltd v Socofi SA* [2009] EWHC 3223 (Comm), [2010] 2 Lloyd's Rep 181). Similarly, in *SSL International plc v TTK LIG Ltd* [2011] EWCA Civ 1170, [2012] 1 WLR 1842, there was no evidence of any consensus where the jurisdiction clause was contained in supply conditions which were only mentioned on a website and in purchase orders which were not sent to the defendants. In international trade or commerce, a jurisdiction clause may alternatively be in a form which accords with a widely known usage in that trade or commerce of which the parties are or ought to have been aware.

Problems arise in practice where there are a number of different but connected agreements between the parties containing conflicting provisions in respect of jurisdiction. This has arisen on a number of occasions in recent years, in particular in cases concerning international finance. In these circumstances the court has to undertake a commercially minded construction of the agreements. If a dispute clearly comes within the scope of a particular agreement then effect will be given to this even if this results in a fragmentation of disputes (*Sebastian Holdings Inc. v Deutsche Bank AG* [2010] EWCA Civ 998, [2011] 1 Lloyd's Rep 106). The position is different where a claim involves a number of agreements and commercial parties would not have intended more than one jurisdiction to apply. In those circumstances the parties may be taken to have agreed to refer the dispute to the jurisdiction provided for in the jurisdiction agreement at the commercial centre of the claim (*UBS AG v HSH Nordbank AG* [2009] EWCA Civ 585, [2009] 2 Lloyd's Rep 272). In the case of an arbitration agreement, account must also be taken of the 'one stop' presumption — the assumption that the parties, as rational business people, are likely to have intended any dispute arising out of the relationship into which they have entered to be decided by the same tribunal (*Fiona Trust Holding Corporation v Privalov* [2007] EWHC 1217 (Comm), [2008] 1 Lloyd's Rep 254; *Trust Risk Group SpA v Amtrust Europe Ltd* [2015] EWCA Civ 437, [2015] 2 Lloyd's Rep 154).

International finance agreements also commonly include unilateral jurisdiction options, whereby jurisdiction is given to a particular court but the finance parties have the option to bring proceedings in another country, or refer the dispute to arbitration. It is possible that some member States will not give effect to such clauses (see for example the decisions of the Cour de cassation in France in *Société Banque privée Edmond de Rothschild Europe v Mme X* (11-26.022) 26 September 2012 Bull civ I No. 176 and *Apple Sales International v eBizcuss* ECLI:FR:CCASS:2015:C101053, Cass. 1ère Civ 7 October 2015, 14-16-898). The English courts will give effect to unilateral options (*Mauritius Commercial Bank Ltd v Hestia Holdings Ltd* [2013] EWHC 1328 (Comm), [2013] 2 All ER (Comm) 898).

A jurisdiction clause may be interpreted as giving exclusive jurisdiction to the courts of a particular country even if the word 'exclusive' is not included (*BNP Paribas SA v Anchorage Capital Group LLC* [2013] EWHC 3073, LTL 16/10/2013; *Global Maritime Investments Cyprus Ltd v O.W. Supply & Trading A/S* [2015] EWHC 2690 (Comm), LTL 9/10/2015).

Jurisdiction given by **art. 25** takes precedence over the rules on *lis pendens* and related actions in **arts 29** and **30** (**art. 31**; see **16.37** to **16.39**). It also takes precedence over the provisions of **art. 8(1)** (see **16.35**) (*Hough v P and O Containers Ltd* [1999] QB 834).

Restrictions on jurisdiction clauses　Parties are not completely free to confer jurisdiction by means of jurisdiction clauses. The following restrictions should be noted: **16.26**

(a)　a jurisdiction clause cannot override exclusive jurisdiction conferred by **recast Brussels I Regulation, art. 24** (for which, see **16.8** to **16.13**);

(b)　a jurisdiction clause inserted for the benefit of one party may be waived by that party;

(c)　in actions relating to individual contracts of employment, consumer contracts and insurance contracts, jurisdiction agreements are only effective (in broad terms) if entered into after the dispute has arisen or if invoked by the employee, consumer or insured (see **arts 15, 16, 19** and **23**); *Sherdley v Nordea Life and Pension SA* [2012] EWCA Civ 88, [2012] 2 All ER (Comm) 725);

(d)　submission to the jurisdiction (**16.3**) overrides a jurisdiction clause (*Elefanten Schuh GmbH v Jacqmain* (case 150/80) [1981] ECR 1671).

Tort

A claim in tort may be brought where the harmful event occurred or may occur (**recast Brussels I Regulation, art. 7(2)**). **16.27**

As with jurisdiction in contract under **art. 7(1)**, the claimant must establish a good arguable case on the merits (*Mölnlycke AB v Procter and Gamble Ltd* [1992] 1 WLR 1112).

Meaning of 'tort'　In common with matters relating to contract (**16.18**), it is important that **recast Brussels I Regulation, art. 7(2)**, should be construed consistently in all the member States despite differences in the types of conduct regarded as tortious in the various countries. Accordingly, the CJEU in *Kalfelis v Bankhaus Schröder, Münchmeyer, Hengst & Co.* (case 189/87) [1988] ECR 5565 decided that 'tort' must be regarded as an autonomous concept and, as it is a derogation from jurisdiction based on domicile, it must be interpreted restrictively. **16.28**

'Mainstream' torts, such as negligence, nuisance, defamation and patent infringement, all come within the definition. A claim that the defendant was constructive trustee of money which, with the dishonest assistance of the defendant, had been taken from the claimant by a senior employee in breach of duty was also held to be a matter 'relating to tort, delict or quasi-delict' within **art. 7(2)** in *Casio Computer Co. Ltd v Kaiser* [2001] EWCA Civ 661, [2001] ILPr 43.

There is uncertainty over whether contribution claims are 'matters relating to tort', 'matters relating to a contract' or neither (see **16.19**).

An unfair competition claim, although a tort under German law, would be a 'matter relating to a contract' and therefore subject to **art. 7(1)** rather than **art. 7(2)** if the interpretation of the contract between the parties was indispensable in deciding whether the conduct was lawful or unlawful (*Brogsitter v Fabrication de Montres Normandes EURL* (case C-548/12) [2014] ILPr 20).

16.29 **Harmful event** It was held by the CJEU in *Handelskwekerij G. J. Bier BV v Mines de Potasse d'Alsace SA* (case 21/76) [1978] QB 708 that art. 5(3) of the Brussels Convention (**recast Brussels I Regulation, art.** 7(2)) gives the claimant the option of commencing proceedings either in the country where the wrongful act or omission took place, or in the country where the damage occurred. The place where the wrongful act occurred in the case of negligent misstatement is where the misstatement originated and not where it was received and acted upon (*Domicrest Ltd v Swiss Bank Corporation* [1999] QB 548). If the misstatement is in documents then the harmful act may take place where the documents are sent from or, if they are handed over in a meeting, where the meeting takes place (*McGraw-Hill International (UK) Ltd v Deutsche Apotheker- und Arztebank EG* [2014] EWHC 2436 (Comm), [2014] 2 Lloyd's Rep 523). In the case of a conspiracy to injure by unlawful means, the place of the event giving rise to damage is where the conspiracy was implemented, not where the conspiracy was hatched (*JSC BTA Bank v Ablyazov* [2016] EWHC 230 (Comm), LTL 18/2/2016). In *Future Investments SA v FIFA* [2010] EWHC 1019 (Ch), [2010] ILPr 34, a case concerning causing loss by unlawful means, the place where the harmful event occurred was the place where the contract complained of was signed.

In *Kainz v Pantherweke AG* (case C-45/13) [2014] 1 All ER (Comm) 433, the place where a defective product was manufactured was where the wrongful act occurred.

The alleged wrongful act needs to be that of the defendant, not of other jointfeasors who are not sued (*Melzer v MF Global UK Ltd* (case C-228/11) [2013] QB 1112).

In *Henderson v Jaouen* [2002] EWCA Civ 75, [2002] 1 WLR 2971, the claimant was injured in a road accident in France, and obtained a final award of damages from the civil courts in France. Under French law he was entitled to bring a fresh action, which was regarded in French law as a fresh cause of action, if his injuries subsequently deteriorated. His injuries did deteriorate, and by this time the claimant was living in England. He brought English proceedings based on this deterioration, alleging that the deterioration was a 'harmful event' engaging **art.** 7(2). The Court of Appeal held that this second claim had to be brought in France, because the 'harmful event' was the original 'tort, delict or quasi-delict', which was the original road traffic accident in France. That was a single event, which had no extraterritorial effect. It is the place where the tortious event takes place that matters for **art.** 7(2), not the place where the decision is made to commit the tort (*Anton Durbeck GmbH v Den Norske Bank ASA* [2002] EWHC 1173 (Comm), LTL 17/6/2002, point not considered on appeal).

The place where the damage occurred is not the place where the damage was quantified or where steps were taken to mitigate the effects of the wrongful conduct of the defendant (*Netherlands v Rüffer* (case 814/79) [1980] ECR 3807). It was held in *London Helicopters Ltd v Heliportugal LDA-INAC* [2006] EWHC 108 (QB), [2006] 1 All ER (Comm) 595, that in order to determine the place where the damage had occurred the court needed to establish where the event giving rise to the damage had produced its initial, direct, immediate or physical harmful effect (also see *Dumez France SA v Hessische Landesbank* (case C-220/88) [1990] ILPr 299). It is not generally sufficient to claim financial damage has been suffered where a claimant resides, maintains a bank account or carries on business, as this would give jurisdiction in most cases to the claimant's domicile (see *Kronhofer v Maier* (case C-168/02) [2004] 2 All ER (Comm) 759). Insofar as the CJEU decision in *Kolassa v Barclays Bank plc* (case C-375/13) [2015] ILPr 14 suggests the contrary, at least in terms of its outcome, this may be because the claimant was a consumer but he was unable to rely on the special protections given to consumers in **arts 17** to **19** as there was no contract in place.

In *Deutsche Bahn AG v Morgan Advanced Materials plc* [2013] EWCA Civ 1484, [2014] 1 Bus LR 377, purchasing from a subsidiary of a member of a cartel or an intermediate purchaser did not mean the damage suffered was indirect.

In *Dolphin Maritime and Aviation Services Ltd v Sveriges Ångfartygs Assurans Förening* [2009] EWHC 716 (Comm), [2009] 2 Lloyd's Rep 123, claims for procuring or inducing a breach of contract and conspiracy to use unlawful means came within **art. 7(2)**. They could be brought in England as the damage occurred in England because that is where the claimant would have received money if the underlying contract had been performed. In *Crucial Music Corporation v Klondyke Management AG* [2007] EWHC 1782 (Ch), [2008] Bus LR 327, a case concerning misrepresentation, damage occurred where the contract was entered into, as the agreed price was greater than the price would have been if the true facts had been known.

In *Marzillier, Dr Meier & Dr Guntner Rechtsanwaltsgesellschaft mbH v AMT Futures Ltd* [2015] EWCA Civ 143, [2015] ILPr 20, the damage from inducing breach of an English exclusive jurisdiction clause was suffered in Germany as that was where the proceedings were commenced and costs and expense were incurred in defending those proceedings.

In *Shevill v Presse Alliance SA* (case C-68/93) [1995] 2 AC 18 (CJEU); [1996] AC 959 (HL), the claimants commenced proceedings in England against a French defendant complaining that they had been libelled in one of the defendant's newspapers. The newspaper had a daily circulation of 200,000 copies in France, and about 250 copies in England. The particulars of claim relied only on publication in England. It was held that the action had been validly brought in England, as damage had been suffered there, although the English courts had jurisdiction solely in respect of the harm caused in England. An action to recover in respect of all the harm caused could alternatively have been brought before the courts of the defendant's domicile or the place where the publisher of the defamatory publication was established. In *eDate Advertising GmbH v X* (case C-509/09) [2012] QB 654 the CJEU held that the publication of harmful content on the Internet needed to be treated differently to the circulation of printed media. The wronged party had the option of bringing a claim in respect of all the damage caused either before the courts of the member State in which the publisher of the content was established or before the courts of the member State in which the publisher's centre of interests was based. Alternatively, claims could be brought in the courts for each State in which online content was or had been accessible, but only in respect of damage caused in that territory. An action for trade mark infringement based on an adword (advertising keyword) can be brought in the country of registration or the member State in which the advertiser is established (*Wintersteiger AG v Products 4U Sondermaschinenbau GmbH* (case C-523/10) [2013] Bus LR 150). An action for breach of copyright in respect of works posted online can be brought in any country where the website is accessible, but only in respect of damage suffered in that member State (*Hejduk v EnergieAgentur.NRW GmbH* (case C-441/13) [2015] Bus LR 560). There is no jurisdiction in respect of trade mark infringement if no acts have been committed within the jurisdiction of the court (*Coty Germany GmbH v First Note Perfumes NV* (case C-360/12) [2014] Bus LR 1294).

Article 7(2) confers jurisdiction in an action seeking a declaration of non-liability in tort (*Folien Fischer AG v Ritrama SpA* (case C-133/11) [2013] QB 523).

Criminal compensation

Where a civil claim is made based on an act giving rise to criminal proceedings, jurisdiction is given by **recast Brussels I Regulation, art. 7(3)** to the courts of the country dealing with the criminal proceedings.   **16.30**

Recovery of a cultural object

A civil claim against a person domiciled in a member State for the recovery, based on ownership, of a cultural object (as defined in Directive 93/7/EEC, art. 1(1)) may be brought in the courts for the place where the cultural object is situated at the time when the court is seised (**recast Brussels I Regulation, art. 7(4)**).   **16.31**

Branches, agencies and establishments

16.32   Recast Brussels I Regulation, art. 7(5), provides that alternative jurisdiction is given as regards disputes arising out of the operations of a branch, agency or other establishment to the courts for the place in which the branch, agency or other establishment is situated. This provision has been restrictively interpreted. From the Jenard Report and the opinion of the advocate general in *Etablissements A. de Bloos SPRL v SCA Bouyer* (case 14/76) [1976] ECR 1497 it is accepted that the branch, agency or other establishment referred to must be that of the proposed defendant, and the claimant's arrangements in this respect are irrelevant. Further, the mere fact that some person in the country where the claimant wishes to commence proceedings acted as the proposed defendant's agent for the purposes of the law of agency is not enough, on its own, to satisfy **art.** 7(5). 'Agency' must be interpreted *eiusdem generis* with 'branch' and 'establishment'. The effect is that **art.** 7(5) is dealing with emanations of the defendant's business which are subject to the defendant's control and which give the defendant a corporate presence within the relevant jurisdiction. Even if the defendant does have a branch, agency or establishment within the meaning of **art.** 7(5), it is further necessary that the dispute must arise out of the activities of that branch, agency or establishment. This will comprehend, according to *Somafer SA v Saar-Ferngas AG* (case 33/78) [1978] ECR 2183, the following types of activities by the branch, agency or establishment:

(a)   management matters, such as the local engagement of staff;
(b)   contractual undertakings given in the name of the parent;
(c)   tortious and other non-contractual liability.

If a dispute arises out of the operations of a branch, there is no further requirement that the obligation in question must be performed in the State where the branch is situated. So, in *Lloyd's Register of Shipping v Société Campenon Bernard* (case C-439/93) [1995] ECR I-961 the claimant entered into a contract with the French branch of the defendant under which the defendant agreed to do certain work in Spain. The work was carried out by the defendant's Spanish branch. A dispute arose, and proceedings were commenced in France, the claimant relying on **art.** 7(5). The CJEU held the proceedings had been validly commenced in France, and there was no requirement in **art.** 7(5) for performance to be in the State where proceedings were commenced.

It was held in *Anton Durbeck GmbH v Den Norske Bank ASA* [2003] EWCA Civ 147, [2003] QB 1160, applying *Lloyd's Register of Shipping v Société Campenon Bernard* (case C-439/93) [1995] ECR I-961, that there has to be a nexus between the operations of the branch and the dispute to render it natural to describe the dispute as arising out of the operations of the branch. It is, however, unnecessary for the activities of the branch to bring about the harmful event giving rise to the dispute. It is relevant for the court to consider what connection the branch has with the dispute compared with the connection which the defendant's domicile has. In *McGraw-Hill International (UK) Ltd v Deutsche Apotheker- und Arztebank EG* [2014] EWHC 2436 (Comm), [2014] 2 Lloyd's Rep 523, it was a relevant factor that there was no connection at all with the defendant's domicile. In contract claims the nexus required could be derived from the negotiations giving rise to the contract. Tort claims vary widely, so whether the necessary nexus exists depends on the facts of the particular case.

Trusts

16.33   A settlor, trustee or beneficiary of a trust created by the operation of a statute, or by a written instrument, or created orally and evidenced in writing, may be joined as a party to proceedings brought in the courts of the country where the trust is domiciled (**recast Brussels I Regulation, art.** 7(6)). This form of wording excludes implied and constructive trusts. The word 'trustee' in **art.** 7(6) has to be restrictively construed. It does not extend to persons such as appointors, or protectors, or to any other person with fiduciary powers who does not come within the normal meaning of the expression 'trustee' (*Gómez v Gómez-Monche Vives* [2008] EWCA Civ 1065, [2009] Ch 245). The Court of Appeal in this case also considered the mechanism for determining the domicile of a trust. It held that the court had to apply its rules of private international law (**art. 63(3)**). The relevant rule is that a trust is domiciled in England if English law is the system of law with which the trust has its closest and most real connection (Civil Jurisdiction and Judgments Order 2001 (SI 2001/3929), sch. 1, para. 12(3)). Although a choice of English law might not be conclusive, it was very difficult to see what other circumstances would be sufficient to outweigh it, because of the close connection between a trust and its governing law. Here, the fact that the trust had no other connection with England, that it was administered elsewhere, that the trustees and beneficiaries were resident elsewhere and that the assets were located elsewhere did not outweigh the connection made by virtue of the choice of law. In *G v G* [2015] EWHC 2101 (Fam), [2016] 4 WLR 22, an application seeking an order for sale of an English property held in joint names was held to come within **art. 7(6)** (as well as **art. 24**). A statutory trust was imposed when the house was purchased in joint names and, given the property was located in London and the parties were living in England at the time of its purchase, that trust was clearly domiciled in England.

Salvage and freight

Under **recast Brussels I Regulation, art. 7(7)**, claims for freight or salvage of cargo may be brought where the freight or cargo has been or could be arrested. **16.34**

Co-defendants

It is provided by **recast Brussels I Regulation, art. 8(1)**, that a person domiciled in a member State may also be sued, 'where he is one of a number of defendants, in the courts for the place where any one of them is domiciled'. This is followed by a proviso that the claims must be so closely connected that it is expedient to hear and determine them together to avoid the risk of irreconcilable judgments resulting from separate proceedings. In order to use this provision to join persons domiciled outside England and Wales to a claim against a person domiciled in England and Wales there must, first of all, be a valid claim against the defendant domiciled within the jurisdiction (the 'anchor defendant') (*The Rewia* [1991] 2 Lloyd's Rep 325) and the proposed co-defendant (*Brown v Innovatorone plc* [2010] EWHC 2281 (Comm), [2011] ILPr 9). There is, however, no merits threshold (*JSC 'Aeroflot-Russian Airlines' v Berezovsky* [2013] EWCA Civ 784, [2013] 2 Lloyd's Rep 242). The anchor defendant must have been domiciled here at the time the claim was issued (*Canada Trust Co. v Stolzenberg (No. 2)* [2002] 1 AC 1). It is irrelevant if judgment in default is obtained against the anchor defendant (*Linuzs v Latmar Holdings Corporation* [2013] EWCA Civ 4, [2013] ILPr 19) or, possibly, if the proceedings are discontinued, at least in the case of an honest mistake (*Stewart v Stozenberg* [1997] EWCA Civ 2592). It is then necessary to consider whether the joinder is valid. The nature of the connection justifying joinder of a defendant not domiciled in England is given an independent Community meaning, and it is not necessarily enough that the joinder satisfies **CPR, r. 7.3** (for which see **14.2**) (*Kalfelis v Bankhaus Schröder, Münchmeyer, Hengst & Co.* (case 189/87) [1988] ECR 5565). According to the CJEU, the proper use of art. 6(1) of the Brussels Convention is to avoid the risk of irreconcilable judgments and to prevent related actions proceeding in different contracting States. The proviso added to the Regulation makes this principle explicit. In order for decisions to be regarded as contradictory, it has been held that it is not sufficient that there be a divergence in the outcome of the dispute, that divergence must also arise in the context of the same situation of law and fact (*Roche Nederland BV v Primus* (case C-539/03) [2006] ECR I-6535). A difference in legal basis between the claims brought against a number of defendants is, however, just one factor, it does not preclude the application of **recast Brussels I Regulation, art. 8(1)** (*Painer v Standard VerlagsGmbH* (case C-145/10) [2012] ECDR 6). **16.35**

The Court of Appeal held in *Masri v Consolidated Contractors International (UK) Ltd* [2005] EWCA Civ 1436, [2006] 1 WLR 830, that there is nothing in **art. 8(1)** which requires the close connection to be in relation to a single set of proceedings. In this case, there were two separate sets of proceedings: claim 1, against English domiciled defendants, and claim 2, against a number of defendants who were not domiciled in England. The Court of Appeal upheld the decision of the judge at first instance that the two claims were so closely connected that it was expedient to hear them together and that this was a sufficient basis for **art. 8(1)** to apply and for the two claims to be consolidated.

The CJEU has held in *Freeport plc v Arnoldsson* (case C-98/06) [2008] QB 634) that **art. 8(1)** applies to claims based on different causes of action (e.g. contract and tort). All that is required is that the claims are sufficiently close to make it expedient to determine them together in order to avoid the risk of irreconcilable judgments. The court went on to hold that, provided the necessary connection exists, there is no need for the claimant to establish that the claims have not been brought in order to oust the jurisdiction of the courts where any of the defendants is domiciled. In *Cooper Tire and Rubber Co. v Shell Chemicals UK Ltd* [2009] EWHC 2609 (Comm), [2009] 2 CLC 619, Teare J noted that it was alleged that three of the defendants in a claim had been selected as a tactical device to establish jurisdiction against other defendants. He said that appeared to be likely, but the question was whether it was a tactic which succeeded. On the facts, there was a good arguable case against the anchor defendants, so jurisdiction was established. Alternate or contingent claims also fall within **art. 8(1)**. **Article 8(1)** requires an examination of the claim as a whole and where a contingent or alternate claim is inextricably linked with the anchor claim, it is right to hear them together in order to avoid the risk of inconsistent judgments (*FKI Engineering Ltd v De Wind Holdings Ltd* [2008] EWCA Civ 316, [2009] 1 All ER (Comm) 118).

Article 8(1) does not apply where the claimant seeking to invoke it does not have a claim against the anchor defendant, but another claimant with a similar claim is suing both the anchor defendant and the defendant challenging jurisdiction (*Madoff Securities International Ltd v Raven* [2011] EWHC 3102 (Comm), [2012] 2 All ER (Comm) 634).

In *Gard Marine and Energy Ltd v Tunnicliffe* [2009] EWHC 2388 (Comm), [2010] Lloyd's Rep IR 62, it was held that it did not matter that the defendant domiciled in England had been added subsequently to the proceedings.

The court also has a discretion whether to permit a party to be joined to proceedings, because **arts 8** and **26** do not give an absolute right (see **14.84**; **CPR, r. 19.2**; *Dornoch Ltd v Westminster International BV* [2009] EWHC 201 (Admlty), [2009] Lloyd's Rep IR 540).

Counterclaims and Part 20 proceedings

16.36 By recast Brussels I Regulation, **art. 8(2)** and **(3)**, counterclaims arising from the same contract or facts as those founding the claim, and third-party proceedings, may be brought in the court in which the claimant's claim is or was pending. In the case of third-party proceedings, this does not apply if the initial proceedings were instituted solely with the object of removing the third-party claim from the jurisdiction of the court which would otherwise be competent. The nexus required for bringing claims under **CPR, Part 20** (see **chapter 29**), is likely to be sufficient to justify the special jurisdiction granted by **recast Brussels I Regulation, art. 8(2)** and **(3)** (*Kinnear v Falconfilms NV* [1996] 1 WLR 920) but this will not always be the case (*Waterford Wedgwood plc v David Nagli Ltd* [1998] CLC 1011). It needs to be demonstrated that there is a close connection between the original proceedings and the third-party proceedings so as to fulfil the objective of **art. 8(2)** of securing the rational and efficient disposal of trials and the avoidance of the risk of irreconcilable judgments (*Barton v Golden Sun Holidays Ltd* [2007] EWHC 3455 (QB), [2007] ILPr 57; *Shetty v Al Rushaid Petroleum Investment Co.* [2011] EWHC 1460 (Ch), LTL 14/6/2011). Where there are proceedings between a claimant insured and a defendant insurer, the court may have jurisdiction under **art. 8(2)** in respect of a contribution claim commenced by another insurer against the defendant (*SOVAG v If Vahinkovakuutusyhtiö Oy* (case C-521/14) ECLI:EU:C:2016:41, [2016] 3 WLR 136).

It is not possible to argue that a claim against a defendant is in substance a third party claim (*McGraw-Hill International (UK) Ltd v Deutsche Apotheker- und Arztebank EG* [2014] EWHC 2436 (Comm), [2014] 2 Lloyd's Rep 523) A contribution notice will be set aside if the defendant served with the notice ceases to be a defendant by an order setting aside service on that defendant (*Knauf UK GmbH v British Gypsum Ltd* [2002] EWHC 739 (Comm), [2002] 2 Lloyd's Rep 416).

Lis pendens

Recast Brussels I Regulation, art. 29, provides: **16.37**

(1) Without prejudice to Article 31(2), where proceedings involving the same cause of action and between the same parties are brought in the courts of different member States, any court other than the court first seised shall of its own motion stay its proceedings until such time as the jurisdiction of the court first seised is established.

(2) In cases referred to in paragraph 1, upon request by a court seised of the dispute, any other court seised shall without delay inform the former court of the date when it was seised in accordance with Article 32.

(3) Where the jurisdiction of the court first seised is established, any court other than the court first seised shall decline jurisdiction in favour of that court.

Article 31(2) and (3) provide:

(2) Without prejudice to Article 26, where a court of a member State on which an agreement as referred to in Article 25 confers exclusive jurisdiction is seised, any court of another member State shall stay the proceedings until such time as the court seised on the basis of the agreement declares that it has no jurisdiction under the agreement.

(3) Where the court designated in the agreement has established jurisdiction in accordance with the agreement, any court of another member State shall decline jurisdiction in favour of that court.

These provisions are designed to prevent parallel proceedings before the courts of different contracting States, and to avoid the conflicts that might otherwise result. **Article 31(2) and (3)**, which give priority to a chosen court, are new to the **recast Brussels I Regulation**. **Article 29** is to be interpreted broadly, and covers all situations of *lis pendens*, irrespective of the parties' domicile (*Overseas Union Insurance Ltd v New Hampshire Insurance Co.* (case C-351/89) [1992] QB 434; *West Tankers Inc. v Allianz SpA* (case C-185/07) [2009] AC 1138). **Article 29** envisages that the court will stay the proceedings as a whole, rather than deal with each claim separately (*WMS Gaming Inc. v B Plus Giocolegale Ltd* [2011] EWHC 2620 (Comm), [2012] ILPr 5). The phrase 'proceedings involving the same cause of action' must be given an independent EU meaning (*Gubisch Maschinenfabrik KG v Palumbo* (case 144/86) [1987] ECR 4861). The article obviously covers the situation where a claimant brings identical proceedings in two countries. It also covers the situation where a claimant brings proceedings in one country for a declaration that there has been no breach of a contract and the defendant to that action brings proceedings in another country claiming damages for breach of that contract (see *The Maciej Rataj* (case C-406/92) [1994] ECR I-5439). It even covers a case where one party to a contract brings an action for rescission of a contract and the other party to the contract brings proceedings in another country to enforce the same contract. The key question is whether the two claims have the same cause and object. Competing claims in England and Greece arising out of the same facts but with a different cause of action (breach of contract on the one hand, and tort and breach of statutory duty on the other) did not come within **art. 29** (*Underwriting Members of Lloyd's Syndicate 980 v Sinco SA* [2008] EWHC 1842 (Comm), [2008] 2 CLC 187) and more than common issues are required. **Article 29** only operates to the extent that the parties to the second claim are the same as those in the first. The term 'the same parties' in **art. 29** has an independent EU meaning and in considering whether two entities are the same party, the court will look to the substance, not the form. The same parties can include separate legal entities. Whether they are the same parties for this purpose may depend on whether a judgment against one of them would have the force of *res judicata* as against the other. It will also depend on whether their interests are identical and indissociable. It is for the national court to ascertain whether this is the case (*Kolden Holdings Ltd v Rodette Commerce Ltd* [2008] EWCA Civ 10, [2008] Bus LR 1051; *Cooper Tire and Rubber Co. v Shell Chemicals UK Ltd* [2009] EWHC 2609 (Comm), [2009] 2 CLC 619; *UBS Ltd v Regione Calabria* [2012] EWHC 699 (Comm), [2012] ILPr 22; *Re The Alexandros T* [2013] UKSC 70, [2014] 1 All ER 590).

There is an exception to **art. 29** if a jurisdiction agreement confers exclusive jurisdiction on one of the courts. If that is the case, all the other courts must stay their proceedings until the chosen court declares that it does not have jurisdiction (**art. 31(2)**). If the chosen court has established jurisdiction, the other courts must decline jurisdiction in favour of the chosen court (**art. 31(3)**).

16.38 **Court first seised**   Priority under **recast Brussels I Regulation, art. 29**, is given to the court 'first seised'. An English court becomes seised when a claim form (or other originating process) is lodged at court for issue, unless the claimant fails to effect service (**art. 32(1)(a)**). There is no obligation to serve 'forthwith' or 'as soon as practicable'. The claimant simply has to serve within the time allowed under **CPR, r. 7.5** (*UBS AG v Kommunale Wasserwerke Leipzig GmbH* [2010] EWHC 2566 (Comm), [2010] 2 CLC 499).

Slightly different rules apply in some other member States (**art. 32(1)(b)**) where domestic law requires the originating process to be served before being lodged with the court. In such cases the court becomes seised when the document is received by the authority responsible for service, provided the claimant has not subsequently failed to take any required steps to lodge the document with the court. It is not the case that for a court to be seised of a claim under **art. 32(1)(b)** the defendant must have been validly served (*WPP Holdings Italy SRL v Benatti* [2007] EWCA Civ 263, [2007] 1 WLR 2316). All that is required is that a document capable of being served has been lodged at court, so as to institute proceedings. Thus, the fact that an Italian writ was lodged at the court office for service without the requisite translation did not prevent the Italian court being seised for the purposes of **art. 32(1)(b)** on the date it was filed at court. Non-payment of a court fee can, however, amount to a failure to take a step required for effective service (*Debt Collect London Ltd v SK Slavia Praha-Fotball AS* [2010] EWCA Civ 1250, [2011] 1 WLR 866). Receipt of foreign proceedings by fax at the Foreign Process Service office is sufficient, the postal copy need not have arrived (*Arbuthnot Latham and Co. Ltd v M3 Marine Ltd* [2013] EWHC 1019 (Comm), [2014] 1 WLR 190). Where proceedings are amended to add a new claim or a party is added, it is unclear whether the court will consider the court in which that particular claim was first brought or that party was first sued to be the court first seised, or whether it will be the court where proceedings were first commenced. Case law and academic comment largely support the former interpretation but the Supreme Court had doubts whether that was correct and would have referred the question to the CJEU if it had been necessary for its decision (*Re The Alexandros T* [2013] UKSC 70, [2014] 1 All ER 590). The position is clearer under **art. 30** (see **16.39**) (*Striborg Ltd v FKI Engineering Ltd* [2011] EWCA Civ 622, [2011] Bus LR 1410).

It is unclear what amounts to a 'new claim' in these circumstances. Additional remedies and causes of action may not be new claims if they arise out of the same facts and matters already alleged (*Maxter Catheters SAS v Medicina Ltd* [2015] EWHC 3076 (Comm), [2016] 1 WLR 349).

Conciliation proceedings before a conciliation authority may be proceedings before a court for the purposes of the *lis pendens* rules (*Lehman Brothers Finance AG v Klaus Tschira Stiftung GmbH* [2014] EWHC 2782 (Ch), [2014] 2 CLC 242), as may proceedings seeking to join a civil action to a criminal action before an investigating magistrate (*Aannemingsbedrijf Aertssen NV v VSB Machineverhuur BV* (case C-523/14) ECLI:EU:C:2015:722, [2016] ILPr 16). Proceedings seeking provisional emergency relief will not be sufficient, unless those proceedings may result in determination of the substantive issue between the parties (*Maxter Catheters SAS v Medicina Ltd* [2015] EWHC 3076 (Comm), [2016] 1 WLR 349).

The court has power to make an order in relation to service under **CPR, r. 3.10** (power to remedy an error) and/or **r. 6.16** (power to dispense with service), even if the effect is to give the English court priority (*Phillips v Symes (No. 3)* [2008] UKHL 1, [2008] 1 WLR 180). Such an order is not retrospective validation of service, but a declaration that the previous service was valid and effective. The facts of the case were that the claim form (but not the translation into German) was removed from the service pack by the Swiss court, because it was mistakenly marked 'not for service out of the jurisdiction'. The Swiss defendant challenged service and issued proceedings before the Swiss court for a negative declaration. The House of Lords held that as the error was that of the Swiss court, and had resulted in no prejudice to the defendant, who was able to read the German translation of the claim form, it was appropriate to exercise its discretion under **rr. 3.10 and 6.16** with the result that the English court was seised of the proceedings on the date of service, before proceedings were issued in Switzerland.

Where an action is brought in one country, and the defendant to that action brings a second action in another country and alleges that the courts of the country first seised have no jurisdiction under the **recast Brussels I Regulation**, then, unless **art. 31(2)** applies, the second court may either decline jurisdiction or stay its proceedings to await the outcome of any challenge made to the jurisdiction of the first court. What the second court is not allowed to do is to investigate the jurisdiction of the first court (*Overseas Union Insurance Ltd v New Hampshire Insurance Co.* (case C-351/89) [1992] QB 434; *West Tankers Inc. v Allianz SpA* (case C-185/07) [2009] AC 1138). This is so even where there are excessive delays in the first court (*Erich Gasser GmbH v MISAT Srl* (case C-116/02) [2005] QB 1).

This gave rise to problems in practice as waiting for the court first seised to determine whether it had jurisdiction could cause considerable delay, particularly where there was no mechanism for jurisdiction to be considered as a preliminary issue. For legal proceedings instituted on or after 10 January 2015, **recast Brussels I Regulation, art. 31**, largely resolves this issue. Where there is an exclusive jurisdiction clause in favour of a member State, proceedings brought in another member State must be stayed until the chosen court has ruled upon its jurisdiction. This is regardless of which proceedings are commenced first in time, although proceedings must have actually been commenced before the chosen court. Where there is an agreement to arbitrate, each member State will have the right to refer parties to arbitration, stay or dismiss proceedings and examine whether an arbitration agreement is null, void or inoperative or incapable of being performed. This is regardless of whether it is the court first seised. It may be possible to make a claim for damages where proceedings have been commenced other than in the chosen court (*Starlight Shipping Co. v Allianz Marine & Aviation Versicherungs AG* [2014] EWCA Civ 1010, [2014] 2 Lloyd's Rep 544; *West Tankers Inc. v Allianz SpA* [2012] EWCA Civ 27, [2012] Bus LR 1701; *Barclays Bank plc v Ente Nazionale di Previdenza ed Assistenza dei Medici e degli Odontoiatri* [2015] EWHC 2857 (Comm), [2015] 2 Lloyd's Rep 527).

Related actions

Recast Brussels I Regulation, art. 30, provides: **16.39**

(1) Where related actions are pending in the courts of different member States, any court other than the court first seised may stay its proceedings....

(3) For the purposes of this article, actions are deemed to be related where they are so closely connected that it is expedient to hear and determine them together to avoid the risk of irreconcilable judgments resulting from separate proceedings.

Article 30 deals with the area between situations where two claims are the same (where the second claim must be stayed under **art. 29** if there is no exclusive jurisdiction agreement in favour of that court) and situations where it is right for two claims to proceed at the same time. In considering whether to grant a stay, the court must apply the test set out in the article, which is designed to cover a range of circumstances. The purpose of **art. 30** is to harmonise courts' jurisdiction and avoid irreconcilable judgments (*Sarrio SA v Kuwait Investment Authority* [1999] 1 AC 32).

The court is given a discretion under **art. 30** to assess the degree of connection between the two claims and the risk of inconsistent judgments. The fact that there is some measure of risk does not mean that proceedings are inevitably related. **Article 30** leaves it open to a court to acknowledge a connection, or a risk of inconsistent judgments, but to say that the connection is not sufficiently close, or the risk is not sufficiently great, to make the actions related for the purposes of the article (*Research in Motion UK Ltd v Visto Corporation* [2008] EWCA Civ 153, [2008] 2 All ER (Comm) 560). It would cover a claim *in rem* and a claim *in personam* in respect of the same loss, where technically the parties are not the same (*The Sylt* [1991] 1 Lloyd's Rep 240). It was conceded in *Dresser UK Ltd v Falcongate Freight Management Ltd* [1992] QB 502 that it would cover proceedings for limitation of liability for loss of cargo at sea and a claim for damages for the loss of the same cargo. Once it is held that proceedings are related, the court second seised has a discretion whether to grant a stay. If there is an exclusive jurisdiction clause in favour of the English courts there is still a discretion to stay but it is unlikely to be exercised in most circumstances (*Nomura International plc v Banca Monte dei Paschi di Siena SpA* [2013] EWHC 3187 (Comm), [2014] 1 WLR 1584; *Lehman Brothers Bankhaus AG v CMA CGM* [2013] EWHC 171 (Comm), [2013] 2 All ER (Comm) 557).

It is unclear whether an action which is subject to the **recast Brussels I Regulation** and an action subject to Regulation (EC) No. 1346/2000 on insolvency proceedings can be related for the purposes of **recast Brussels I Regulation, art. 30** (see *Rahman v GMAC Commercial Finance Ltd* [2012] EWCA Civ 1467, [2013] ILPr 5; *Marme Inversiones 2007 SL v Royal Bank of Scotland plc* [2016] EWHC 1570 (Comm), LTL 11/7/2016).

Where proceedings become related by amendment, it seems the court first seised for the purposes of **art. 30** will be the court where the proceedings first in time were commenced (*Striborg Ltd v FKI Engineering Ltd* [2011] EWCA Civ 622, [2011] Bus LR 1410; *Re The Alexandros T* [2013] UKSC 70, [2014] 1 All ER 590; *Maxter Catheters SAS v Medicina Ltd* [2015] EWHC 3076 (Comm), [2016] 1 WLR 349). The position is less clear under **art. 29**, see **16.38**. In *Striborg*, proceedings were commenced in Germany and then subsequently in England. The German proceedings did not include a claim for the purchase price of certain assets when commenced, but were subsequently amended so as to put the payment of the purchase price in issue. This took place after the commencement of the English proceedings which claimed payment of the purchase price. The Court of Appeal decided that the test is not which court was first seised of the issue which makes the claims related as at the date of the application. The test is whether the claims were related as at the date of the application. If so, which action was commenced first in time? Adopting this approach the German court was the court first seised and the English court therefore had the power to stay its proceedings. *Striborg* did not involve a new cause of action or new party, so it is not clear whether the same principles would apply in those circumstances.

It is possible that proceedings which have been stayed, including by means of a Tomlin order following settlement, are still pending and so the court in which they were commenced remains the court first seised (*Re The Alexandros T* [2013] UKSC 70, [2014] 1 All ER 590).

It appears that *lis pendens* arguments should be raised promptly, within the time for challenging the court's jurisdiction where possible and in any event prior to making defence submissions (*Re The Alexandros T* [2013] UKSC 70, [2014] 1 All ER 590; *SET Select Energy GmbH v F and M Bunkering Ltd* [2014] EWHC 192 (Comm), [2014] 1 Lloyd's Rep 652; *Cartier Parfums - Lunettes SAS v Ziegler France SA* (case C-1/13) [2014] ILPr 25; although *Deutsche Bank AG London*

Branch v Petromena ASA [2015] EWCA Civ 226, [2015] CP Rep 27, appears to suggest this is not always necessary).

It is unclear whether there is a power to stay proceedings in favour of a non-member State where an identical or related action is pending there, i.e. whether **arts 29** and **30** can be given so-called reflexive effect. See **16.76** for further consideration of this issue.

Interim relief

Recast Brussels I Regulation, art. 35, allows the courts of a member State to grant provisional, **16.40** including protective, measures in respect of proceedings in another member State.

CJJA 1982, s. 25(1), and the Civil Jurisdiction and Judgments Act 1982 (Interim Relief) Order 1997 (SI 1997/302) confer on the High Court in England power to grant interim relief in the absence of substantive proceedings, provided proceedings have been or will be commenced in any other jurisdiction (see **38.6**).

Section 25 is not confined to freezing injunctions, **subsection** (7) defining 'interim relief' as relief of any kind which the court has power to grant in proceedings within its jurisdiction other than warrants for arrest and orders for obtaining evidence.

PROCEDURE ON COMMENCING PROCEEDINGS PURSUANT TO THE REGULATION OR CONVENTIONS

A claim form may be served on a defendant out of the jurisdiction, without the court's **16.41** permission, if each claim being made against that defendant can be determined by the court under the **CJJA 1982** or the Lugano Convention (**CPR, r. 6.33(1)**), or the **recast Brussels I Regulation** (**CPR, r. 6.33(2)**), or the 2005 Hague Choice of Court Convention (**CPR, r. 6.33(2B)**) or any other enactment (**r. 6.33(3)**). **Rule 6.32** makes separate provision for service of the claim form without permission in Scotland and Northern Ireland.

The only formality is that the claimant must file and serve with the claim form a notice (form N510) containing a statement of the grounds on which the claimant is entitled to serve out of the jurisdiction (**r. 6.34(1); PD 6B, para. 2.1**). This statement replaces the jurisdiction endorsement which until October 2008 was required to be included on a claim form for service out of the jurisdiction. The claim form may not be served out of the jurisdiction until the statement of grounds is filed, unless the court gives permission (**CPR, r. 6.34(2)**). Regard should also be had to the provisions in the Queen's Bench Guide (para. 4.4) and the Commercial Court Guide when the proceedings have been or are to be issued in those courts. Incorrect completion of form N510 will not necessarily mean the claimant is unable to rely on the relevant provisions of the **recast Brussels I Regulation** (*DSG International Sourcing Ltd v Universal Media Corporation (Slovakia) sro* [2011] EWHC 1116 (Comm), [2011] ILPr 33).

The **recast Brussels I Regulation** has extended the jurisdiction of member States over defendants domiciled outside the EU in a number of respects. It is important to remember that those proceedings are now within the Brussels regime and therefore no permission is required to serve outside the jurisdiction. For example, no permission will be required where there is an English jurisdiction clause, regardless of the domicile of the parties. Form N510 has been amended to take account of the additional grounds for taking jurisdiction.

JURISDICTION UNDER THE COMMON LAW RULES

The rules discussed at **16.42** to **16.57** deal with the situation where it is desired to serve **16.42** English proceedings on a defendant outside the jurisdiction in proceedings outside the scope of the **recast Brussels I Regulation**, Brussels I Regulation, the Brussels and Lugano

Conventions and the Hague Convention on Choice of Court Agreements. Permission is required from the court in those circumstances. A claimant may either issue his claim form for service abroad first and then apply for permission to serve (in which case the court will stamp the claim form on issue 'not for service out of the jurisdiction' and the claim form should be amended when permission is granted) or may apply for permission both to issue the claim form and to serve it out of the jurisdiction (Queen's Bench Guide, para. 4.4.23).

Basic principles governing applications for permission

16.43   The requirements that need to be satisfied if the English courts are to grant permission to serve proceedings outside the jurisdiction under the court's assumed jurisdiction were set out by Lord Collins in *Altimo Holdings and Investment Ltd v Kyrgyz Mobil Tel Ltd* [2011] UKPC 7, [2012] 1 WLR 1804. The intending claimant must establish that:

(a) There is a serious issue to be tried on the merits, i.e., a substantial question of fact or law or both. This is the same test as for summary judgment, namely, whether there is a real (as opposed to a fanciful) prospect of success (e.g., *Carvill America Inc. v Camperdown UK Ltd* [2005] EWCA Civ 645, [2005] 2 Lloyd's Rep 457). Where a question of law goes to the existence of jurisdiction, the court will normally decide it, rather than treating it as a question of whether there is a good arguable case (*E. F. Hutton and Co. (London) Ltd v Mofarrij* [1989] 1 WLR 488; *Chellaram v Chellaram (No. 2)* [2002] EWHC 632 (Ch), [2002] 3 All ER 17).

(b) There is a good arguable case that the claim falls within one or more classes of case in which permission to serve out may be given, i.e., it falls within one of the 23 grounds set out in **PD 6B, para. 3.1.** These are discussed at **16.45 to 16.56.** In this context, good arguable case has been held to mean that one side has a much better argument than the other (*Canada Trust Co. v Stolzenberg (No. 2)* [1998] 1 WLR 547, [2002] 1 AC 1; *Bols Distilleries BV v Superior Yacht Services Ltd* [2006] UKPC 45, [2007] 1 WLR 12). However, the Court of Appeal has suggested that the word 'much' does not add anything to the test (*JSC 'Aeroflot-Russian Airlines' v Berezovsky* [2013] EWCA Civ 784, [2013] 2 Lloyd's Rep 242).

(c) In all the circumstances England is clearly or distinctly the appropriate forum for the trial of the dispute and that in all the circumstances the court ought to exercise its discretion to permit service of the proceedings out of the jurisdiction. This is considered further at **16.57.**

Putting a foreigner to the inconvenience of defending an action in this country is a serious matter, so the courts have historically always exercised the power to allow service abroad with caution. More recently, the Supreme Court has warned against considering the power to order service out of the jurisdiction as 'exorbitant'. Litigation between residents of different countries is commonplace and many countries take jurisdiction on a similar basis to the English courts. The decision whether to allow service out of the jurisdiction is essentially a pragmatic one about the efficient conduct of litigation in an appropriate forum (*Abela v Baadarani* [2013] UKSC 44, [2013] 1 WLR 2043).

Procedure on seeking permission

16.44   An application for permission to serve a claim form out of the jurisdiction, or to issue a claim form for service out of the jurisdiction, should be made without notice under **CPR, Part 23.** There will generally be no hearing. There is no requirement in the CPR that the court is provided with draft particulars of claim in addition to the application notice, claim form and evidence but the High Court has said it is desirable that draft particulars are available, as it focuses the minds of the applicant and of the court on what the claim is and what matters need to be disclosed to the court (*Ahuja v Politika Novine I Magazini DOO* [2015] EWHC 3380, [2016] 1 WLR 1414). The papers are lodged in the appropriate court office and the claimant is later notified of the court's decision. A refusal to grant permission can be appealed. If permission is granted and the defendant considers that it should not have been, he can challenge the court's jurisdiction (see **chapter 19**).

The evidence in support of the application for permission must state, according to **CPR, r. 6.37**:

(a) which grounds in **PD 6B, para. 3.1** are relied on in respect of each claim;
(b) that the claimant believes that the claim has a reasonable prospect of success;
(c) the defendant's address, or, if that is not known, in what place the defendant is or is likely to be found;
(d) where the application is made under **PD 6B, para. 3.1(3)** (that the defendant is a necessary or proper party), the grounds for believing that there is a real issue between the claimant and the existing defendant which it is reasonable for the court to try.

The procedure is summarised in **procedural checklist 11**.

Because service out of the jurisdiction is an assertion of extraterritorial jurisdiction which could have international repercussions, it was the rule under RSC, ord. 11, that irregularities should be cured only in exceptional cases (*Camera Care Ltd v Victor Hasselblad AB* [1986] 1 FTLR 348). In *Ophthalmic Innovations International (UK) Ltd v Ophthalmic Innovations International Inc.* [2004] EWHC 2948 (Ch), LTL 4/1/2005, Lawrence Collins J stated that the same principle applies under the CPR. The Supreme Court's decision in *NML Capital Ltd v Argentina* [2011] UKSC 31, [2011] 2 AC 495 (see **16.45**) suggests a more relaxed approach might be taken, although the decision was before *Mitchell v News Group Newspapers Ltd* [2013] EWCA Civ 1537, [2014] 1 WLR 795 and *Denton v T. H. White Ltd* [2014] EWCA Civ 906, [2014] 1 WLR 3926.

As the application is made initially without notice, the claimant is under an obligation to make full and frank disclosure of all material facts. In deciding whether that duty has been complied with, the primary question is whether in all the circumstances the effect of the evidence in support of the application is such as to mislead the court in any material respect concerning its jurisdiction and the discretion under the rules (*BP Exploration Co. (Libya) Ltd v Hunt* [1976] 1 WLR 788). The existence of overlapping proceedings in a foreign jurisdiction between the same or related parties (whether pending or prospective) is likely to be a particularly relevant matter which in normal circumstances must be disclosed, and the non-disclosure of which may well lead to the order for permission being set aside (*Konamaneni v Rolls-Royce Industrial Power (India) Ltd* [2002] 1 WLR 1269). The court will also take into account whether the material non-disclosure was deliberate (*Ahuja v Politika Novine I Magazini DOO* [2015] EWHC 3380, [2016] 1 WLR 1414) and whether, if service is set aside, proceedings will merely be started again, wasting time and costs (*Rawlinson & Hunter Trustees SA v ITG Ltd* [2014] EWHC 3764 (Ch), LTL 22/10/2014).

If a foreign law might be applicable to a claim and under that law the defendant may have a defence to the claim, the Court of Appeal has stated that the claimant would be wise to give full and frank disclosure of this fact in its evidence. There is, however, generally no obligation on a claimant, in order to show there is a serious issue to be tried, to plead the foreign law as an alternative to its primary case. It is enough that the facts alleged disclose a serious issue to be tried as a matter of English law and it is then for the party alleging that some foreign law both applies and was fatal to the claim to plead and prove it (*Erste Group Bank AG London Branch v JSC VMZ Red October* [2015] EWCA Civ 379, [2015] 1 CLC 706).

Grounds for granting permission

General interpretation The grounds in **PD 6B, para. 3**, were formerly in RSC, ord. 11, **16.45** r. 1(1), and have been amended several times over the years. The grounds were reformulated in 1983 and again in 2000, and significant changes were again made in 2015, so some caution is necessary with earlier case law. However, it is likely that case law on the basic principles governing applications for permission to serve a claim form out of the jurisdiction remains valid.

As **PD 6B, para. 3**, allows the court to exercise an exorbitant jurisdiction, historically its provisions have been strictly construed in favour of the foreigner (*The Hagen* [1908] P 189). The Supreme Court's comments in *Abela v Baadarani* [2013] UKSC 44, [2013] 1 WLR 2043 suggest there may be a softening in this approach (see **16.43**).

It appears that in order to establish one of the grounds it is not necessary to come within the 'spirit' as well as the letter of the rule, although this may be relevant to the exercise of discretion if one of the grounds is established (*Sharab v Prince Al-Waleed bin Talal bin Abdal-Aziz-Al-Saud* [2009] EWCA Civ 353, [2009] 2 Lloyd's Rep 160; *Johnson v Taylor Bros and Co.* [1920] AC 144; *Beck v Value Capital Ltd (No. 2)* [1975] 1 WLR 6). Service out is not allowed unless each claim falls into one or other of the grounds set out in the rule (*Holland v Leslie* [1894] 2 QB 346; *Fern Computer Consultancy Ltd v Intergraph Cadworx and Analysis Solutions Inc.* [2014] EWHC 2908 (Ch), [2014] Bus LR 1397) (but note the alternative gateway allowing, in some circumstances, additional claims arising out of the same or closely connected facts, see **16.49**). Although the claimant can choose which ground or grounds to rely on (*Matthews v Kuwait Bechtel Corporation* [1959] 2 QB 57), the claimant must specifically state those grounds in the evidence in support of the application.

Before the CPR came into force, a claimant could not rely on alternative grounds to sustain an order for service out of the jurisdiction in addition to the grounds relied upon to obtain permission, unless, possibly, the alternative basis had been specifically referred to in affidavit evidence (*Metall und Rohstoff AG v Donaldson Lufkin and Jenrette Inc.* [1990] 1 QB 391). The Supreme Court has, however, disapproved of this approach in *NML Capital Ltd v Argentina* [2011] UKSC 31, [2011] 2 AC 495. Although obiter, this approach is now being followed by the lower courts, see for example *Apex Global Management Ltd v Fi Call Ltd* [2013] EWHC 1652 (Ch), LTL 27/6/2013.

An application, made before the end of the six months allowed for service of a claim form, for permission to serve it out of the jurisdiction is governed by **CPR, r. 6.33**, and **PD 6B, para. 3**, not by **CPR, r. 7.6(3)** (*Anderton v Clwyd County Council (No. 2)* [2002] EWCA Civ 933, [2002] 1 WLR 3174).

16.46 **Domicile (PD 6B, para. 3.1(1))** A claim form may be served out of the jurisdiction if the claim is for a remedy against a person domiciled within the jurisdiction (**PD 6B, para. 3.1(1)**). The **recast Brussels I Regulation, art. 4**, permits a person to be sued where domiciled, and, by **CPR, r. 6.31(1)(i)**, domicile for the purposes of **Part 6, Section IV**, is to be determined:

(a) in relation to EU States, in accordance with the **recast Brussels I Regulation** and the Civil Jurisdiction and Judgments Order 2001 (SI 2001/3929), sch. 1, paras 9 to 12, and

(b) in relation to Aruba, French overseas departments, Iceland, Norway and Switzerland, by the rules in the **CJJA 1982, ss. 41 to 46**.

This provision is of little practical significance as in cases coming within the **recast Brussels I Regulation**, Brussels I Regulation or the Brussels or Lugano Conventions permission to serve outside the jurisdiction on defendants domiciled within the jurisdiction is not required.

16.47 **Injunctions and interim relief (PD 6B, para. 3.1(2) and (5))** The injunction referred to in **PD 6B, para. 3.1(2)**, has to be final as opposed to interim (*The Siskina* [1979] AC 210). The injunction must be the real form of relief sought, and must not simply be tacked on in order to found jurisdiction (*Rosler v Hilbery* [1925] Ch 250).

However, the **CJJA 1982, s. 25(1)** (see **16.40**), enables the court to grant interim relief in the absence of substantive proceedings, regardless of whether the defendant is domiciled in a country which is a party to the **recast Brussels I Regulation** or the Brussels or Lugano Conventions. Since **PD 6B, para. 3.1(2)**, applies only to final injunctions, **para. 3.1(5)** enables the court to permit service out of the jurisdiction in such cases where the defendant is not resident in an EU or Convention country.

Necessary or proper party   PD 6B, para. 3.1(3), may be compared with the **recast Brussels I**   **16.48**
Regulation, art. 8(1) (16.35). PD 6B, para. 3.1(3), provides:

(3) A claim is made against a person ('the defendant') on whom the claim form has been or will be
served (otherwise than in reliance on this paragraph) and—
   (a) there is between the claimant and the defendant a real issue which it is reasonable for the court
to try; and
   (b) the claimant wishes to serve the claim form on another person who is a necessary or proper
party to that claim.

It was a requirement under RSC, ord. 11, that the claim form be served before making the
application to join a defendant as a necessary or proper party. This changed in 2004. The
words in parenthesis make clear, however, that **PD 6B, para. 3.1(3)**, only permits the claimant
to join a defendant to proceedings brought against another defendant against whom jurisdiction can be established in reliance on some other provision. It is unclear whether reliance on
para. 3.1(3) in addition to other gateways means a defendant cannot be an anchor defendant.
Walker J in *Standard Bank plc v Just Group LLC* [2014] EWHC 2687 (Comm), LTL 17/10/2014, thought
this was strongly arguable but did not decide the point.

The necessary or proper party head of jurisdiction was considered by the Privy Council in
Altimo Holdings and Investment Ltd v Kyrgyz Mobil Tel Ltd [2011] UKPC 7, [2012] 1 WLR 1804 (and
again in *Nilon Ltd v Royal Westminster Investments SA* [2015] UKPC 2, [2015] 3 All ER 372) and a
number of points, drawing on previous case law, were emphasised. First, this is an anoma-
lous head of jurisdiction as it is not founded upon any territorial connection between the
claim and the jurisdiction of the English courts, so caution is required. In particular, it
should never become the practice to bring in foreign defendants as a matter of course on the
ground that the only alternative requires more than one set of proceedings in different countries. The fact that the anchor defendant is sued only for the purpose of adding the foreign
defendants is a factor in the exercise of discretion and not an element in the question whether
the action was properly brought against the anchor defendant, provided there is a viable
claim against the anchor defendant. As regards the merits, a claim is not properly brought
against the anchor defendant if it is bound to fail. Merits are also relevant to whether there
is a 'serious issue to be tried' against the second defendant. There is no practical difference
between the two tests and they are the same as the test for summary judgment. Questions of
law going to the existence of jurisdiction and the merits should ordinarily be decided
although that will not normally be appropriate where it is a controversial question of law in
a developing area. Finally, the question whether the second defendant is a proper party is
answered by asking: 'Supposing both parties had been within the jurisdiction would they
both have been proper parties to the action?'

The decision in *Altimo Holdings and Investment Ltd v Kyrgyz Mobil Tel Ltd* has to be read alongside
the Court of Appeal decision in *Erste Group Bank AG London Branch v JSC VMZ Red October* [2015]
EWCA Civ 379, [2015] 1 CLC 706, where the court considered the meaning of the requirement
that 'there is between the claimant and the defendant a real issue which it is reasonable for the
court to try'. This test was not satisfied on the facts of that case as the claimant had submitted
its claims to the Russian courts by taking part in the insolvency proceedings underway against
the anchor defendants; there was no utility in the proceedings in that any English judgment
would not be enforceable in Russia and there was very little prospect of a trial on the merits
in England.

By **PD 6B, para. 3.1(4)**, permission may be given to serve a claim form under **CPR, Part 20**,
on persons who are necessary or proper parties to the claim or additional claim (see *CH Offshore
Ltd v PDV Marina SA* [2015] EWHC 595 (Comm), LTL 19/3/2015).

Claims based on same or closely connected facts (PD 6B, para. 3.1(4A))   This is a new   **16.49**
gateway, introduced from 1 October 2015, which may have wide-reaching effects.

Commentary

Where a claim is made against a defendant in reliance on another gateway (with some exceptions, including the necessary or proper party gateway), a further claim can be made against the same defendant which arises out of the same or closely connected facts.

The gateway was introduced following the report of a Chancery Working Group established in 2015 to consider proposals made by the Lord Chancellor's Advisory Committee on Private International law, chaired by Lord Mance. The Working Group's report notes the risk that this new gateway might be considered exorbitant, but expresses the view that the risk is outweighed by the practical advantages of enabling closely related claims against the same defendant to be tried together. The report also notes the safeguard that, as with all gateways, permission is subject to England being the appropriate forum and to the court exercising its discretion.

16.50 **Contract** Claims under PD 6B, para. 3.1(6) and (7), presuppose the existence of a contract between the claimant and the defendant. Claims seeking a declaration that such a contract never existed fall instead under PD 6B, para. 3.1(8).

PD 6B, para. 3.1(6)(a) (a claim in respect of a contract made within the jurisdiction), has no equivalent in the **recast Brussels I Regulation** or the Brussels and Lugano Conventions. Whether a contract was made within the jurisdiction may not depend on general contractual principles. In *Conductive Inkjet Technology Ltd v Uni-Pixel Displays Inc.* [2013] EWHC 2968 (Ch), [2014] 1 All ER (Comm) 654, the High Court considered a contract to have been made for jurisdiction purposes in both England and the United States. A contract made within the jurisdiction which is subsequently amended outside the jurisdiction still comes within **PD 6B, para. 3.1(6)**, unless the amendment substitutes a new contract (*BP Exploration Co. (Libya) Ltd v Hunt* [1976] 1 WLR 788; *Sharab v Prince Al-Waleed bin Talal bin Abdal-Aziz-Al-Saud* [2009] EWCA Civ 353, [2009] 2 Lloyd's Rep 160). The words 'in respect of a contract' in **PD 6B, para. 3.1(6)**, do not require that the claim arose under a contract. They require only that the claim relates to or is connected with the contract. The rule therefore includes a claim in restitution for recovery of alleged overpayments under an oral agreement (*Albon v Naza Motor Trading Sdn Bhd* [2007] EWHC 9 (Ch), [2007] 1 WLR 2489). It also includes a claim for a contribution under the **Civil Liability (Contribution) Act 1978, s. 1**, even where the claimant is not a party to a contract and the claim is not brought for breach of contract. A claim (such as for a contribution) will be a claim 'in respect of a contract' within the meaning of **PD 6B, para. 3.1(6)** and (7), if it has a connection with a contract having one of the attributes in **para. 3.1(6)(a)** to (d) or a contract broken in England within **para. 3.1(7)**. There is no requirement that the claim has to be in respect of a contract between the claimant and the defendant, because that would be adding words to the rules which are not there (*Greene Wood and McLean v Templeton Insurance Ltd* [2009] EWCA Civ 65, [2009] 1 WLR 2013). A claim to enforce a trust which arose from a contract is also a claim in respect of a contract within **PD 6B, para. 3.1(6)** (*Cherney v Deripaska* [2009] EWCA Civ 849, [2009] 2 CLC 408). Claims 'in respect of a contract' probably do not include *quantum meruit* claims if they are restitutionary and do not derive from a contract (*Sharab v Al-Saud* [2012] EWHC 1798 (Ch), [2012] 2 CLC 612). Where there is more than one contract, the court needs to consider which contract the claim is made in respect of. It is not sufficient that a connected contract meets the jurisdictional gateway (*Global 5000 Ltd v Wadhawan* [2012] EWCA Civ 13, [2012] 2 All ER (Comm) 18).

Unlike **recast Brussels I Regulation, art. 7(5)** (see **16.32**), **PD 6B, para. 3.1(6)(b)** (contract made by or through an agent trading or residing within the jurisdiction), is given a wide interpretation, and even includes a case where the defendant's London agent merely sent the claimant the defendant's price list and forwarded the claimant's order to the defendant (*National Mortgage and Agency Co. of New Zealand Ltd v Gosselin* (1922) 38 TLR 832). The 'agent', however, must be that of the defendant, not the claimant (*Union International Insurance Co. Ltd v Jubilee Insurance Co. Ltd* [1991] 1 WLR 415).

There is no equivalent to **PD 6B, para. 3.1(6)(c)**, that the contract is governed by English law, in the **recast Brussels I Regulation** or the Brussels and Lugano Conventions. The law governing the contract will generally be determined in respect of contracts entered into on or after 17 December 2009 by Regulation (EC) 593/2008 (Rome I). For contracts entered into before that date the rules in the Rome Convention apply, incorporated into UK law by the Contracts (Applicable Law) Act 1990. An express choice of English law clause should not cause difficulties in most cases.

An express jurisdiction clause granting jurisdiction to the English courts (**PD 6B, para. 3.1(6)(d)**) will almost always be given effect by the courts (compare **16.24**), but there are sometimes questions as to whether the dispute arises under a particular agreement where there are a number of interlocking contracts. See *UBS AG v HSH Nordbank AG* [2009] EWCA 585, [2009] 2 Lloyds Rep 272 and *Sebastian Holdings Inc. v Deutsche Bank AG* [2010] EWCA Civ 998, [2011] 1 Lloyd's Rep 106. Whether a jurisdiction clause gives exclusive or non-exclusive jurisdiction to the English courts, is a matter of contractual interpretation. The absence of the word 'exclusive' is not necessarily determinative (*Hin-Pro International Logistics Ltd v Compañía Sud Americana de Vapores SA* [2015] EWCA Civ 401, [2016] 1 All ER (Comm) 417; *BNP Paribas SA v Anchorage Capital Group LLC* [2013] EWHC 3073, LTL 16/10/2013; *Global Maritime Investments Cyprus Ltd v O.W. Supply & Trading A/S* [2015] EWHC 2690 (Comm), LTL 9/10/2015).

A court may decide to not give effect to an exclusive jurisdiction clause in a trust document (*Crociani v Crociani* [2014] UKPC 40, [2015] WTLR 975).

The jurisdiction agreement gateway is now of little practical significance as permission is no longer required to serve outside the jurisdiction where the parties have chosen the jurisdiction of the English courts in cases coming within the **recast Brussels I Regulation**, regardless of the domicile of the parties (see **16.24** to **16.26** and **16.41**).

PD 6B, para. 3.1(7), breach within the jurisdiction, should be compared with **recast Brussels I Regulation, art. 7(1)** (see **16.18**). Where the breach consists of a failure to perform a contractual obligation, it is necessary to find the place where performance should have taken place (*Brinkibon Ltd v Stahag Stahl und Stahlwarenhandelsgesellschaft mbH* [1983] 2 AC 34).

Tort Jurisdiction in tort under **PD 6B, para. 3.1(9)**, has been modelled on **recast Brussels I Regulation, art. 7(2)** (see **16.27**), although it has not always been interpreted in the same way. Jurisdiction may be founded either on the basis of damage being suffered in England or through the tortious act being committed in England. It is sufficient if damage has been, or will be, sustained within the jurisdiction. In a case on the meaning of RSC, ord. 11, r. 1(1)(f), predecessor to **PD 6B, para. 3.1(9)**, the Court of Appeal held that it was sufficient if the cause of action in substance arose in England. If separate acts constituting a single tort were committed here and abroad, the question was whether the tort was in substance committed within the jurisdiction (*Metall und Rohstoff AG v Donaldson Lufkin and Jenrette Inc.* [1990] 1 QB 391). In *Booth v Phillips* [2004] EWHC 1437 (Comm), [2004] 1 WLR 3292, the court considered the meaning of the word 'damage' in what is now **PD 6B, para. 3.1(9)**, and stated that it should be given its natural and ordinary meaning. It referred to harm which had been sustained by the claimant, whether physical or economic, and it was sufficient if some damage (not necessarily all of the damage) was sustained within the jurisdiction. There was no requirement that the damage sustained within the jurisdiction should be that which completed the cause of action. Under the **recast Brussels I Regulation** the damage suffered must be direct damage (*Dumez France SA v Hessische Landesbank* (case C-220/88) [1990] ILPr 299). For the purposes of **PD 6B, para. 3.1(9)**, a number of first-instance decisions held that indirect damage was sufficient. The Court of Appeal in *Brownlie v Four Seasons Holdings Inc.* [2015] EWCA Civ 665, [2015] CP Rep 40, has effectively overruled those decisions, holding that indirect or consequential loss is not sufficient to satisfy the tort gateway.

Where a computer server located in London was hacked into from outside the jurisdiction, the damage was sustained and the act was committed within the jurisdiction, satisfying both

16.51

heads of **PD 6B, para. 3.1(9)** (*Ashton Investments Ltd v OJSC Russian Aluminium (RUSAL)* [2006] EWHC 2545 (Comm), [2007] 1 All ER (Comm) 857).

Misuse of private information and breach of the Data Protection Act 1998 are torts and permission to serve out of the jurisdiction can therefore be sought under **PD 6B, para. 3.1(9)** (*Google Inc. v Vidal-Hall* [2015] EWCA Civ 311, [2015] CP Rep 28). There is also a separate gateway for claims involving misuse of private information (see **16.56**).

16.52 **Enforcing judgment or arbitral award**   **PD 6B, para. 3.1(10)**, permits service out of the jurisdiction to enforce a judgment or arbitral award. There is no requirement that assets should be located in the jurisdiction as a prerequisite to an order for service out of the jurisdiction under the rule, although the claimant must show some benefit, even if only an indirect or prospective benefit, accruing to it from the granting of permission (*Tasarruf Mevduatı Sigorta Fonu v Demirel* [2007] EWCA Civ 799, [2007] 1 WLR 2508). Here, the Court of Appeal held that a benefit could be made out by the fact that, unless permission were granted, the defendant would be free to transfer assets into the jurisdiction with impunity after late 2007 when the Turkish judgment which the claimant sought to enforce would become time-barred.

16.53 **Property**   **PD 6B, para. 3.1(11)**, permits service out of the jurisdiction where the whole subject matter of a claim relates to property located within the jurisdiction. 'Property' is not restricted to land.

16.54 **Trusts**   **PD 6B, para. 3.1(12)** to (16), deal with claims concerning trusts. From 6 April 2015, these provisions have been widened so that they expressly apply to trusts governed by English law (**PD 6B, para. 3.1(12)**) and to trusts containing an English jurisdiction clause (**PD6B, para 3.1(12A)**). The provision now in **PD 6B, para. 3.1(15)**, was added in 1990 to allow claims arising from acts committed within the jurisdiction to be brought in England against constructive trustees who cannot be served within the jurisdiction. There is some uncertainty over the acts needed within the jurisdiction to found jurisdiction under this head (see *NABB Brothers International Ltd v Lloyds Bank International (Guernsey) Ltd* [2005] EWHC 405 (Ch), [2005] ILPr 506). Jurisdiction under the **recast Brussels I Regulation, art. 7(6)**, is, in contrast, based on domicile (see **16.33**).

16.55 **Claims under various enactments (PD 6B, para. 3.1(20))**   An unfair prejudice application under the Companies Act 2006, s. 994, may come within this ground (*Apex Global Management Ltd v Fi Call Ltd* [2013] EWHC 1652 (Ch), LTL 27/6/2013), as may a claim that a transaction has been entered into at an undervalue in order to put assets beyond the reach of a claimant (Insolvency Act 1986, s. 423) (*Erste Group Bank AG London Branch v JSC VMZ Red October* [2015] EWCA Civ 379, [2015] 1 CLC 706).

16.56 **Claims for breach of confidence or misuse of private information (PD 6B, para. 3.1(21))**   This gateway was introduced from 1 October 2015. It applies where detriment was suffered, or will be suffered, within the jurisdiction, or detriment which has been or will be suffered results from an act committed or likely to be committed within the jurisdiction.

Prior to the introduction of this gateway, the Court of Appeal held that in a claim involving misuse of private information, permission to serve out of the jurisdiction could be sought under the tort gateway, **PD 6B, para. 3.1(9)** (*Google Inc. v Vidal-Hall* [2015] EWCA Civ 311, [2015] CP Rep 28). Arguably, therefore, no separate gateway was required for misuse of private information. However, given the Supreme Court could take a different view, and as breach of confidence claims required express provision in any event, the view was taken that it made sense to deal explicitly with misuse of private information.

The proper place to bring the claim (*forum conveniens*)

16.57 It is provided in **CPR, r. 6.37(3)**, that the court will not give permission for service out of the jurisdiction 'unless satisfied that England and Wales is the proper place in which to bring the claim', i.e. is the *forum conveniens*. The leading case is *Spiliada Maritime Corporation v Cansulex Ltd* [1987] AC 460. The claimant shipowner sought permission to serve English proceedings on Canadian sulphur exporters, claiming damages in respect of severe corrosion to the hold of the claimant's ship, the *Spiliada*, allegedly caused by a cargo of wet sulphur. An almost identical claim, *The Cambridgeshire*, had just reached trial in England. The defendants in both claims were the same, and the claimants in both claims had the same insurer (through subrogation, the insurer rather than the nominal claimants had the real interest in bringing the actions). *The Cambridgeshire* was in the nature of a test case. The scientific investigations made approached the limits of scientific knowledge. The claimant's experts came from England, whereas the defendant had instructed two English and four foreign experts. A total of 15 counsel were instructed, each being armed with 75 files of evidence and documents, and the trial was estimated for six months. Many of the potential witnesses of fact would be Canadian, but many witnesses would come from other places (the *Spiliada* was registered in Liberia).

Lord Goff of Chieveley laid down the general principle that the court has to identify the forum in which the case can be most suitably tried in the interests of all the parties and for the ends of justice. The burden of proof rests on the claimant to show that England is clearly the most appropriate place for the trial of the action. Factors to be considered by the court when deciding whether to exercise its discretion to grant permission include the residence or place of business of the parties, the ground invoked by the claimant, the applicable law and the residence and availability of factual and expert witnesses. The weight to be attached to the relevant factors depends on all the circumstances of the case. As Lord Goff said:

the defendant's place of residence may be no more than a tax haven to which no great importance should be attached. It is also significant to observe that the circumstances specified in ord. 11, r. 1(1), as those in which the court may exercise its discretion to grant leave to serve proceedings on the defendant outside the jurisdiction, are of great variety, ranging from cases where, one would have thought, the discretion would normally be exercised in favour of granting leave (e.g. where the relief sought is an injunction ordering the defendant to do or refrain from doing something within the jurisdiction) to cases where the grant of leave is far more problematical. In addition, the importance to be attached to any particular ground invoked by the plaintiff may vary from case to case. For example, the fact that English law is the putative law of the contract may be of very great importance (as in *BP Exploration Co. (Libya) Ltd v Hunt* [1976] 1 WLR 788, where, in my opinion, Kerr J rightly granted leave to serve proceedings on the defendant out of the jurisdiction); or it may be of little importance as seen in the context of the whole case.

On the facts, the extent and depth of preparation undertaken in *The Cambridgeshire* proceedings, and the fact that English law was the proper law of the contract, meant that England was the appropriate forum, and permission to serve outside the jurisdiction was granted. The doctrine of *forum non conveniens* is considered further at **16.71** to **16.76**.

An English court may have jurisdiction to hear a derivative claim concerning a foreign company in an appropriate case, and if so, it will give permission for the claim form to be served on the company out of the jurisdiction, because the company is a necessary party to the claim (**PD 6B, para. 3.1(3)**; *Konamaneni v Rolls-Royce Industrial Power (India) Ltd* [2002] 1 WLR 1269). However, the courts of the place of incorporation of a company will almost invariably be the most appropriate forum for determining whether a shareholder may sue on behalf of the company (*Konamaneni v Rolls-Royce Industrial Power (India) Ltd*); *SMAY Investments Ltd v Sachdev* [2003] EWHC 474 (Ch), [2003] 1 WLR 1973. The sort of case where English courts may have jurisdiction to hear a derivative claim concerning a foreign company, are where the company has assets within the jurisdiction, or the acts giving rise to the claim occurred within the jurisdiction. The fact that the claimant lived within the jurisdiction was insufficient to displace the normal rule (*Reeves v Sprecher* [2007] EWHC 117 (Ch), [2007] 2 BCLC 614).

Particular rules aimed at preventing 'libel tourism' apply in respect of defamation proceedings, where the defendant is not domiciled in the United Kingdom, an EU member State or a State bound by the Lugano Convention. Under s. 9(2) of the Defamation Act 2013, the English court will have no jurisdiction to hear the action unless it is satisfied that of all the places in which the statement complained of has been published, England and Wales is clearly the most appropriate place in which to bring a claim in respect of the statement. In practice, this requires a claimant to put forward evidence of the extent of their reputation in each country where publication has taken place, as well as the damage suffered. Where publication is online, evidence of the number of 'hits' in each country may well be required (*Ahuja v Politika Novine I Magazini DOO* [2015] EWHC 3380, [2016] 1 WLR 1414).

In *Novus Aviation Ltd v Onur Air Taşımacılık AŞ* [2009] EWCA Civ 122, [2009] 1 Lloyd's Rep 576, England was held, in 'a finely balanced case' to be the appropriate forum where the only connecting factor was that the contract was governed by English law. The issues in the case included construction of an English language document and evidence of negotiations in English conducted by people who did not have English as their first language. In *Vidal-Hall v Google Inc.* [2014] EWHC 13 (QB), [2014] EMLR 14, one of the factors in favour of English jurisdiction was that the case raised complex issues in a developing area of law. In *Golden Ocean Group v Salgacar Mining Industries Pvt Ltd* [2011] EWHC 56 (Comm), [2011] 1 WLR 2575, it was relevant that the overriding laws of the competing forum would negate the English law principles which would otherwise apply. While the Supreme Court has said (*VTB Capital plc v Nutritek International Corporation* [2013] UKSC 5, [2013] 2 AC 337) that it is generally preferable, all other things being equal, that a case should be tried in the country whose law applies, in practice things are rarely equal, so, generally, the existence of agreements governed by English law will be a factor but not a major factor in favour of English jurisdiction (see *Alliance Bank JSC v Aquanta Corporation* [2012] EWCA Civ 1588, [2013] 1 All ER (Comm) 819).

The English courts were to be preferred where the competing forum was not one which was able to exercise jurisdiction over the defendant as of right and to which, at the time of the hearing, he had not agreed voluntarily to submit, where there was a risk that any judgment from the competing jurisdiction could not be enforced against the defendant's assets in the jurisdiction and where the claimant was entitled to the benefit of having started the proceedings in the jurisdiction (*Sharab v Prince Al-Waleed bin Talal bin Abdal-Aziz-Al-Saud* [2009] EWCA Civ 353, [2009] 2 Lloyd's Rep 160). England was the forum where a claim could be most suitably tried, despite Russia being the natural forum, where there were risks that the claimant would be arrested on trumped-up charges and would not get a fair trial of his claim in Russia (*Cherney v Deripaska* [2009] EWCA Civ 849, [2009] 2 CLC 408). By contrast in *OJSC Oil Co. Yugraneft v Abramovich* [2008] EWHC 2613 (Comm), LTL 3/11/2008, *Erste Group Bank AG v JSC 'VMZ Red October'* [2013] EWHC 2926 (Comm), [2014] BPIR 81, and *Pacific International Sports Clubs Ltd v Soccer Marketing International Ltd* [2009] EWHC 1839 (Ch), LTL 30/7/2009, it was held that a fair trial in Russia and Ukraine respectively would be possible. According to the Privy Council, the claimant needs to show a real risk that justice will not be obtained in the foreign court by reason of incompetence, or lack of independence or corruption (*Altimo Holdings and Investment Ltd v Kyrgyz Mobil Tel Ltd* [2011] UKPC 7, [2012] 1 WLR 1804). There is no rule that the court will not consider whether a foreign court or court system is corrupt or lacking in independence based on act of State doctrine or judicial restraint. Otherwise the paradoxical result would follow that the worse the system of justice, the less it would be permissible to make adverse findings on it. Considerations of international comity will, however, militate against any such finding in the absence of cogent evidence and in practice the test is very difficult to satisfy.

The court may permit oral evidence and cross-examination of witnesses when considering whether there can be a fair trial in the relevant jurisdiction (*Mengiste v Endowment Fund for the Rehabilitation of Tigray* [2013] EWHC 599 (Ch), LTL 28/3/2013).

Delay in the foreign court, absence of funding and difficulties in obtaining representation are factors in determining the appropriate forum (*Pike v Indian Hotels Co. Ltd* [2013] EWHC 4096 (QB), LTL 27/1/2014; *Lungowe v Vedanta Resources plc* [2016] EWHC 975 (TCC), LTL 2/6/2016).

Where the proceedings concern a claim for negative declaratory relief, it is necessary to demonstrate that they serve a useful purpose (contrast *Faraday Reinsurance Co. Ltd v Howden North America Inc.* [2012] EWCA Civ 980, [2012] Lloyd's Rep IR 631, with *Howden North America Inc. v Ace European Group Ltd* [2012] EWCA Civ 1624, LTL 6/12/2012).

The court does not have the power to stay proceedings against a defendant domiciled in the jurisdiction in favour of a court in a non-Regulation State on the basis that it is a more convenient forum, although there may be a power to stay in other limited circumstances (*Owusu v Jackson* (case C-281/02) [2005] QB 801; see **16.76**). Where permission is sought to join non-EU defendants to the proceedings (or a stay is sought of claims against non-EU defendants) the court has had to consider what relevance this has to its decision. A refusal to grant permission to serve out (or the granting of a stay) will inevitably result in two sets of proceedings, with the risk of inconsistent judgments and duplication of time and costs. In *Pacific International Sports Clubs Ltd v Surkis* [2010] EWCA Civ 753, LTL 2/7/2010, the court ordered a stay against all defendants other than an English domiciled company as the Ukraine was the proper forum for a dispute over control of a stake in a Ukrainian football team. The English company had a minor role in the dispute and, as Blackburne J put it at first instance (*Pacific International Sports Clubs Ltd v Soccer Marketing International Ltd* [2009] EWHC 1839 (Ch), LTL 30/7/2009), this would be allowing the tail to wag the dog. In contrast, in *JSC BTA Bank v Granton Trade Ltd* [2010] EWHC 2577 (Comm), [2011] 2 All ER (Comm) 542, a case which concerned an alleged fraud on a Kazakhstan bank carried out in Kazakhstan by two Kazakhstan nationals, the court refused to set aside orders granted for service out of the jurisdiction on non-EU defendants. The English courts had jurisdiction under the Brussels I Regulation, art. 2, over the two individuals who were the alleged architects of the fraud as they had since moved to England, so in this case it would, continuing Blackburne J's metaphor, be allowing the dog to wag the tail. An exclusive jurisdiction clause in favour of a non-member State will be an important factor to weigh in the balance but does not trump all other considerations (*Jong v HSBC Private Bank (Monaco) SA* [2015] EWCA Civ 1057, LTL 22/10/2015). For the issues which arise when the jurisdiction gateway relied upon is 'necessary or proper party' see **16.48**, *Lungowe v Vedanta Resources plc* [2016] EWHC 975 (TCC), LTL 2/6/2016, and *Iiyama (UK) Ltd v Samsung Electronics Co. Ltd* [2016] EWHC 1980 (Ch), LTL 5/8/2016. Caution may also be required where reliance is placed on **PD 6B, para. 3.1(4A)**, as this gateway might be considered exorbitant (see **16.49**).

The court has the power to stay in favour of proceedings in another part of the United Kingdom where no other country is involved. So in *Cook v Virgin Media Ltd* [2015] EWCA Civ 1287, [2016] 1 WLR 1672 English proceedings were stayed in favour of the Scottish courts on the basis that Scotland was the *forum conveniens*.

SERVICE ABROAD

Effecting service abroad

It is provided in **CPR, r. 6.40**, that service abroad must be effected either:

16.58

(a) in accordance with the provisions of the EU Service Regulation (Regulation (EC) No. 1393/2007; see **16.62**) (**CPR, r. 6.40(3)(a)(i)**); or

(b) by a method permitted by the law of the country in which it is to be served (**r. 6.40(3)(c)**); or

(c) through foreign governments, judicial authorities or British consular authorities (see **16.65**) (**r. 6.40(3)(a)(ii)**); or

(d) by a method permitted by a civil procedure convention (see **16.63** and **16.64**) (**r. 6.40(3)(b)**).

Rule 6.40(4) goes on to provide that nothing in the CPR, or a court order, authorises or requires any person to do anything which is contrary to the law of the country where the claim form or other document is to be served. But service does not have to be valid under that law (*Abela v Baadarani* [2013] UKSC 44, [2013] 1 WLR 2043).

The provisions of the EU Service Regulation are mandatory (*Alder v Orłowska* (case C-325/11) ECLI:EU:C:2012:824; *Hornan v Baillie* [2012] EWHC 285 (Ch), [2012] ILPr 29; *Alpha Bank Cyprus Ltd v Dau Si Senh* (case C-519/13) ECLI:EU:C:2015:603, [2016] 1 WLR 1115). There are only two situations outside its scope: where the permanent or habitual residence of the addressee is unknown and where an authorised representative has been appointed in the member State where the judicial proceedings are taking place. You should therefore serve in accordance with the Regulation where it applies (see **16.62**). If a service of process clause in a contract does not accord with the provisions of the Service Regulation, it may be advisable to serve twice, once in accordance with the contractual provision and again in accordance with the Service Regulation. There appears to be no objection to serving twice in this way regardless of which method is first in time (*Tecom Mican SL v Domínguez* (case C-223/14) ECLI:EU:C:2015:744, [2016] 1 WLR 1599).

To decide on the appropriate method of service in any particular case, it may be necessary to consult lawyers in the jurisdiction where service is to be effected and the Foreign Process Section at the RCJ (telephone (020) 7947 6691). The following factors may need to be considered:

(a) The methods available for service in that country (there will usually be a choice).
(b) The speed with which service will be effected. Service can be very slow through governments and consular authorities in particular.
(c) The cost involved. Instructing local lawyers to effect service, where permitted, will be relatively speedy but is likely to cost more than the other methods.
(d) Whether the defendant is likely to seek to evade service. Personal service is likely to be most effective in those circumstances if permitted.
(e) Whether the defendant is likely to appear in the proceedings. If he is not, then proof of service in order to obtain judgment in default of acknowledgment will be of key importance. This may be difficult where service has been effected by post.

A claimant has six months in which to serve a claim form outside the jurisdiction compared with four months where service is within the jurisdiction. The extra time takes into account the difficulties that can be encountered in serving abroad, including obtaining translations where needed. It should not therefore be assumed that the time for service will be extended where such difficulties are encountered, particularly where an extension would deprive the defendant of a limitation defence (*Cecil v Bayat* [2011] EWCA Civ 135, [2011] 1 WLR 3086; *Foran v Secret Surgery Ltd* [2016] EWHC 1029 (QB), LTL 6/5/2016).

16.59 **Alternative service** It was controversial for a period of time whether there was any jurisdiction to order alternative service of proceedings outside the jurisdiction (*Bacon v Automattic Inc.* [2011] EWHC 1072 (QB), [2011] 2 All ER (Comm) 852, sets out the reasons). That controversy has been resolved in favour of the existence of such a jurisdiction (*Cecil v Bayat* [2011] EWCA Civ 135, [2011] 1 WLR 3086; *Abela v Baadarani* [2013] UKSC 44, [2013] 1 WLR 2043). CPR, r. **6.37(5)(b)(i)** therefore authorises the court to make an order for alternative service pursuant to r. **6.15(1)** and also to make an order with retrospective effect pursuant to r. **6.15(2)**. In cases where service cannot be effected under the Hague Service Convention (see **16.63**), the EU Service Regulation or a bilateral service treaty, the claimant needs to show 'good reason' for the order to be made. There is no requirement to show 'exceptional circumstances' (*Abela v Baadarani*). It appears that an order for alternative service may be easier to obtain in respect of arbitration claim forms and claims seeking enforcement of judgments than in other types of case (*Cruz City 1 Mauritius Holdings v Unitech Ltd* [2013] EWHC 1323 (Comm), [2013] 2 All ER (Comm) 1137; *Caucedo Investments Inc. v Saipem SA* [2013] EWHC 3375 (TCC), LTL 12/11/2013; *JSC VTB Bank v Skurikhin* [2013] EWHC 3863 (Comm), LTL 28/06/2013). For further information on alternative service see **15.17**.

Scotland   Proceedings can be served in Scotland and Northern Ireland by the same methods   **16.60**
permitted for service in England (**CPR, r. 6.40(2)**).

Service on a foreign State   Service of a claim form or any other document on a foreign State   **16.61**
must be effected in the manner set out in **CPR, r. 6.44**. A request for service, a copy of the
claim form or other document and any translation of it required under **r. 6.45** must be filed
in the Central Office of the Royal Courts of Justice. The Senior Master will send the documents filed to the Foreign and Commonwealth Office to be transmitted to the Ministry of
Foreign Affairs of the State which is to be served. Service is deemed to have been effected
when the claim form or other document is received at the Ministry (State Immunity Act
1978, s. 12(1)).

A foreign State may agree to an alternative method of service. Where it does, service may be
effected either under the provisions of **CPR, r. 6.44**, or by the agreed method (**r. 6.44(7)**).

Service under the EU Service Regulation

The Service Regulation (Regulation (EC) No. 1393/2007) came into force on 13 November   **16.62**
2008. It repealed Regulation (EC) No. 1348/2000 and binds all EU member States (including
Denmark, see OJ L331, 10.12.2008, p. 21). The Service Regulation applies to service between
member States of documents (including extrajudicial documents) in civil and commercial
matters. As between EU States, the Service Regulation supersedes all earlier treaties including
any earlier bilateral conventions and the Hague Service Convention (Service Regulation,
art. 20). The provisions of the Service Regulation are mandatory (see **16.58**).

The European Commission assessed the application of the Regulation for the period 2008
to 2012 and produced a report (COM (2013) 858). It concluded that in general the
Regulation operates well, but there are areas where it may be further improved, for example
consideration should be given to whether electronic service should be available at cross-border
level. A number of difficulties surrounding service by post and direct service are also identified. A public consultation on the Service Regulation was launched in June 2015 and is due
to report shortly.

The Service Regulation requires member States to establish transmitting and receiving agencies to effect service of judicial documents (art. 2(1) and (2)). Under the Service Regulation,
documents are transmitted directly between courts, without going through a central authority as under the Hague Service Convention. For England and Wales the transmitting and
receiving agency is the Senior Master, Foreign Process Section, room E16, in the RCJ (telephone (020) 7947 6691; foreignprocess.rcj@hmcts.gsi.gov.uk). To achieve service under
the Service Regulation the claimant must file with the claim form, or other document, any
translations and other documents required by the Service Regulation (**CPR, r. 6.41(2)**). The
court officer will then seal the copy of the claim form and forward the documents to the
Senior Master (**r. 6.41(3)**). The documents will then be transmitted to the receiving agency
in the State where they are to be served and that agency will serve them. The CJEU has held
in *Leffler v Berlin Chemie AG* (case C-443/03) [2005] ECR I-9611, that where a claim form is served
without a proper translation, and the defendant has accordingly refused to accept service,
the defect may be remedied by sending the translation through the channels established by
the Service Regulation as soon as possible. In *Alpha Bank Cyprus Ltd v Dau Si Senh* (case C-519/13)
ECLI:EU:C:2015:603, [2016] 1 WLR 1115 the CJEU held that the serving court must inform a
document's addressee of their right to refuse to accept the document in certain circumstances and must do so using the standard form in Annex II to the Service Regulation.
Failure to do so can, however, be remedied and does not mean service is invalid. It may not
be necessary to translate annexes to a document if they have an evidentiary function and are
not necessary to understand the subject matter of the claim and the cause of action
(*Ingenieurbüro Michael Weiss und Partner GbR v Industrie- und Handelskammer Berlin* (case C-14/07)
[2009] ILPr 24).

The Service Regulation attempts to deal with the delays which are often inherent in other methods of service through formal channels by providing that the receiving agency must send a receipt for any document it receives to the transmitting agency as soon as possible, and in any event within seven days of receipt (art. 6(1)). All steps necessary to effect service must be taken as soon as possible, and the receiving agency must notify the transmitting agency if it has not proved possible to effect service within one month of receipt (art. 7(2)).

Article 9 establishes a mechanism for calculating the date of service of a document served under the Service Regulation. Where the document has to be served within a particular time under the law of the sending State, the rules of the sending State will determine the date of service. Otherwise, the date of service will be determined by the law of the receiving State.

Article 19 sets out the conditions which must be satisfied before judgment in default of acknowledgment can be entered against a defendant served under the provisions of the Service Regulation. See **16.70**.

The European Union publishes a manual containing details of the receiving agencies established by the member States under the terms of the Service Regulation, the geographical areas in which they have jurisdiction, the means of receipt of documents available and the languages that may be used for the completion of the standard form for service. It also publishes a glossary, for information purposes only, of the documents which may be served. An updated version of this manual is maintained online at the website of the European Judicial Atlas in Civil Matters, http://ec.europa.eu/justice_home/judicialatlascivil/html/ds_information_en.htm. The necessary forms are available at that website for completion on-screen. The UK section of the manual dealing with receipt of documents for service from other member States provides: 'Documents will be transmitted by fax and post'. Receipt of the documents by fax alone is sufficient to seise the foreign court pursuant to art. 30(2) (*Arbuthnot Latham and Co. Ltd v M3 Marine Ltd* [2013] EWHC 1019 (Comm), [2014] 1 WLR 190).

The Service Regulation applies to 'extrajudicial' documents as well as judicial documents (art. 16). 'Extrajudicial' documents is an autonomous concept of EU law. It includes documents drawn up by notaries (*Roda Golf & Beach Resort SL* (case C-14/08) ECLI:EU:C:2009:395, [2010] All ER (EC) 340) and private documents where the formal transmission to an address abroad is necessary for the purposes of 'exercising, proving or safeguarding a right or a claim in civil or commercial law' (*Tecom Mican SL v Domínguez* (case C-223/14) ECLI:EU:C:2015:744, [2016] 1 WLR 1599).

Service under the Hague Service Convention

16.63   The United Kingdom is one of the 71 contracting States to the Hague Convention on the Service Abroad of Judicial and Extra-judicial Documents in Civil or Commercial Matters (1965) ('the Hague Service Convention'). The member States of the EU (apart from Austria) are also parties to the Hague Service Convention, but as between all of the EU States the provisions of the EU Service Regulation (Regulation (EC) No. 1393/2007, see **16.62**) prevail over the provisions of the Hague Service Convention (Service Regulation, art. 20). The EU Service Regulation also applies to the French overseas departments of French Guiana, Guadeloupe, Martinique and Réunion, which are part of the EU territory. The Netherlands and the United Kingdom have extended the operation of the Hague Service Convention to some of the overseas countries and territories for which they are responsible and which are not part of the EU territory, so that the EU Service Regulation does not apply to them. The countries in which English process may be served under the Hague Service Convention are listed in **table 16.1**. The text of the Convention and the declarations of the contracting States on the details of how it applies in their territories can be seen on the website of the Hague Conference on Private International Law: http://www.hcch.net.

The main method of service under the Hague Service Convention is through a central authority. Under art. 2, each contracting State is obliged to designate a central authority which will undertake to receive requests for service coming from other contracting States. In the United Kingdom the central authority is the Senior Master, the Foreign Process Section, Room E16, Royal Courts of Justice, Strand, London WC2A 2LL (telephone: (020) 7497 6691, email foreignprocess.rcj@hmcts.gsi.gov.uk). Effect is given to this method of service by **CPR, r. 6.42(1)(a)**.

The Hague Service Convention also permits service in some circumstances through a contracting State's diplomatic or consular agents, through consular channels or through diplomatic channels (arts 8 and 9). The procedure is then as set out in **CPR, r. 6.43**.

The Hague Service Convention does not prevent certain other informal methods of service provided the State of destination does not object (art. 10, see **16.66**).

By **CPR, rr. 6.43, 6.45 and 6.46**, and **PD 6B, paras 4.1 and 4.2**, the following documents should be filed at the Foreign Process Section, RCJ, room E02 for onward transmission to the central authority in the receiving country:

(a) request for service;
(b) the claim form, plus a duplicate for every defendant to be served;
(c) particulars of claim, and any documents accompanying them, where these are to be served with the claim form, plus a duplicate of these documents;
(d) the response pack (form N9), or form N1C (notes for defendants) where the claim form is served without particulars of claim — both form N9 and N1C must be amended to show the relevant deadline for filing the acknowledgment and/or the defence;
(e) unless the claim form is to be served in a country where English is an official language or on a British citizen, a certified translation into the language of the jurisdiction where service is to be effected of the claim form, particulars of claim and form N9 or N1C;
(f) an undertaking to be responsible for the expenses incurred by the Foreign and Commonwealth Office; and
(g) any documents required by the country where service is to be effected (e.g. legalisation of documents is required in some countries). Further information is available from the Foreign Process Section, Room E02 at the RCJ.

Where permission to serve out of the jurisdiction has been granted, the order giving permission, and a translation of it where necessary, will also need to be served.

Service under a bilateral civil procedure convention

16.64 The United Kingdom has entered into bilateral conventions for service of proceedings with a number of countries. Details from the Foreign and Commonwealth Office can be found at https://www.gov.uk/guidance/service-of-documents-and-taking-of-evidence. It is also advisable to check with the Foreign Process Section at the RCJ.

A claim form may be served in such countries either through the judicial authorities of that country or through a British consul, subject to any provisions of the applicable convention governing the nationality of a person who may be served by a British consul (**CPR, r. 6.42(1)(b)**).

As in Hague Service Convention cases (see **16.63**), the documents to be served should be filed in the Foreign Process Section for onward transmission. The documents are the same as in Hague Service Convention cases.

Service through diplomatic channels where there is no civil procedure convention

16.65 It is possible for service to be effected through diplomatic channels even where there is no civil procedure convention between the United Kingdom and the country where it is sought to effect service. By **CPR, r. 6.42(2)**, in such cases, provided the law of the relevant jurisdiction permits it, the claim form may be served either:

(a) through the government of that country, where that government is willing to effect service; or

(b) through a British consular authority in that country.

However, given that the receiving country has not bound itself by international treaty to permit service through these channels, there is no guarantee that service will be effective under local law. In practice, the advice of a local lawyer must be sought.

The same documents as in Hague Service Convention cases must be filed at the Foreign Process Section (**r. 6.43(1)**; see **16.63**).

Service cannot be effected through judicial authorities, consular authorities or diplomatic channels in the Isle of Man, the Channel Islands, or any United Kingdom Overseas Territory. Service in any of these places can be effected by the claimant or his agent (**r. 6.42(3)**).

The United Kingdom Overseas Territories are listed in **PD 6B, para. 5.2**: the Hague Service Convention has been extended to most of them (see **table 16.1**).

The same is generally true of Commonwealth States which are not a party to the Hague Service Convention, save that some do require service to be through judicial authorities. A list of these countries can be obtained from the Foreign Process Section at the RCJ (**CPR, r. 6.42(3)(a); PD 6B, para. 5.1**).

Service by informal methods

16.66 In practice, service through diplomatic channels is usually a slow and laborious process. It is often quicker, where permitted under local law, for the claimant to effect service by an informal method, for example, by instructing a local process server to effect service personally on the defendant.

Personal service by the claimant's agent is permitted in most common law countries. The position in civil law countries, where service is seen as a judicial act, is more problematic. However, even here, it is possible in some countries to use a local agent to transmit documents direct to the court official responsible for effecting service of court documents. For service in Scotland and Northern Ireland see **16.60**.

The EU Service Regulation permits service directly through judicial officers, officials or other competent persons of the member State addressed, where such direct service is permitted under the law of that member State (Regulation (EC) No. 1393/2007, art. 15). There is no general acceptance of this method of service of documents (see the Commission's report on

Table 16.1 Countries in which English process may be served under the Hague Service Convention. In case of doubt contact the Foreign Process Section, RCJ, room E10 (telephone (020) 7947 6691; fax (020) 7947 6237), or consult the Hague Conference website, http://www.hcch.net

Albania, Anguilla, Antigua and Barbuda, Argentina, Armenia, Aruba, Australia (including Australian external territories), Bahamas, Barbados, Belarus, Belize, Bermuda, Bosnia and Herzegovina, Botswana, British Virgin Islands, Canada, Cayman Islands, China, Colombia, Costa Rica, Egypt, Falkland Islands and dependencies, Gibraltar, Guernsey, Hong Kong SAR, Iceland, India, Israel, Isle of Man, Japan, Jersey, Kazakhstan, Republic of Korea, Kuwait, Macau SAR, Macedonia, Malawi, Mexico, Moldova, Monaco, Montenegro, Montserrat, Morocco, Norway, Pakistan, Pitcairn, Russian Federation, San Marino, Serbia, Seychelles, Sri Lanka, St Helena and dependencies, St Vincent and the Grenadines, Switzerland, Turkey, Turks and Caicos Islands, Ukraine, United States of America, Venezuela, Vietnam, Virgin Islands.

the Regulation (COM (2013) 858, **16.62**). The Hague Service Convention has similar provisions in art. 10. Where service is pursuant to another civil procedure convention the terms of that bilateral convention would need to be checked.

As regards service by post, the EU Service Regulation permits member States to effect service of judicial documents directly by post on persons residing in another member State by registered letter with acknowledgment of receipt or equivalent (art. 14). It is unclear whether this permits postal service by the claimant or requires service by the member State, but it is probably the latter. In view of this, the courts originally put in place a special procedure for service by the claimant through the Aldwych Post Office. This has now been replaced by a procedure whereby the Foreign Process Section of the court (FPS) effects service after being provided with the following documents by the claimant:

- A completed N224 form which includes an undertaking to pay costs incurred (the postage charges)
- A covering letter for the court, prepared in accordance with a template
- A legible set of documents for service
- Translations and translation certificate where required
- An A4 (or larger if required) envelope

The postage costs must be paid within seven days of invoice at which point a unique reference number is provided to the claimant enabling them to track the documents. Evidence of service is obtained by the claimant conducting their own search via the tracking number and website provided by the FPS. Queries regarding the process should be directed to the FPS on (020) 7947 6488/7786/6691/1741 or by email to foreignprocess.rcj@hmcts.gsi.gov.uk.

There are difficulties serving by post in some member States, see the Commission's report on the Regulation (COM (2013) 858, **16.62**).

Service by post is also permitted under the Hague Service Convention provided the State of destination does not object (art. 10(a)). The FPS process for service by the court set out above should be used in such cases. In the case of a bilateral convention, the specific terms of the convention would need to be checked.

Although service by post is not costly and is quick, problems can arise in establishing whether service has taken place and if so when, for the purposes of entering judgment in default. It may be possible to obtain the necessary information from the equivalent in the country of service of the Royal Mail's Track and Trace system, but this is by no means straightforward. A further question is whether service abroad by the electronic methods now permitted under **CPR, Part 6**, would be good service. In theory, provided that electronic methods of service are not contrary to local law, and in particular to the provisions of any relevant convention, the answer should be yes. In *Molins plc v GD SpA* [2000] 1 WLR 1741 it was held that service by fax effected by an Italian litigant on a defendant in England could have been good service under art. 15 of the Hague Service Convention if the requirements of what is now **PD 6A, para. 4.1** had been met.

For service on a defendant who is abroad under **CPR, r. 6.37** (service by an alternative method or at an alternative place) see **15.17**.

Responding to service

Where a court in England and Wales has jurisdiction under the **recast Brussels I Regulation** or the Brussels or Lugano Convention, or the modified Regulation which applies within the United Kingdom, over a claim against a defendant out of the jurisdiction and the claim form is served on the defendant in a European territory of a contracting State or a Regulation State (or in Scotland or Northern Ireland), the defendant must acknowledge service or file a defence within 21 days after service of the claim form, or, where the claim form states that particulars of claim

16.67

Commentary

are to follow, of the particulars (**CPR, r. 6.35(2) and (3)**). The defendant is not obliged to acknowledge service at all, but where an acknowledgment is filed, the period for filing a defence is extended by 14 days (**PD 6B, para. 6.4(2)**). **Rule 6.35(4)** prescribes a response period of 31 days where a claim form is served in 'a Convention territory outside Europe' (i.e. other than European territory, which is covered in **r. 6.35(3)**). It seems that **r. 6.35(4)** can only ever have referred to the French overseas departments (French Guiana, Guadeloupe, Martinique and Réunion) and the African territories of Portugal (Madeira) and Spain (Canary Islands, Ceuta and Melilla), so that it should refer to Regulation States rather than Convention territories.

Where proceedings are served on a defendant outside the jurisdiction who resides outside the territories of contracting States (either where permission to serve has been obtained, or where arts 16 or 17 of the Conventions apply and the defendant is not in the territory of a contracting State), the period for acknowledging service is set out in the table at the end of **PD 6B**. The periods for acknowledging service or filing an admission in the response pack included with particulars of claim served outside the jurisdiction have to be amended accordingly (**PD 6B, para. 6.6**). After service of the particulars of claim the defence must be served within the number of days set out in the table. But a defendant who has acknowledged service is given an extra 14 days to file the defence (**PD 6B, para. 6.4(2)**).

Service abroad of documents other than a claim form

16.68 Where permission is required to serve a claim form out of the jurisdiction, the claimant must apply for permission to serve any other document in the proceedings which he needs to serve abroad (**CPR, r. 6.38(1)**). Permission is not required, however, to serve particulars of claim abroad where permission has been given to serve a claim form out of the jurisdiction which states that particulars are to follow (**r. 6.38(2)**), or where the defendant has given an address for service in Scotland or Northern Ireland (**r. 6.38(3)**). In practice, as parties will usually provide an address for service within the United Kingdom (no longer just England and Wales) under **r. 6.23**, the necessity to apply for permission will be limited. As regards the method of service, if there is an address for service within the jurisdiction, no special considerations arise. In rare circumstances there may not be such an address. This might be because a defendant has not acknowledged service but the claimant has decided not to seek default judgment (e.g. in a multi-party case with interlinking issues). It may also occur because a party has given as his address for service the address of a solicitor in another EEA State, as permitted under **r. 6.23(2)(a)**. Such cases will need to be considered and dealt with on an individual basis, by agreement or court order.

Where an application notice or order is served out of the jurisdiction, the period for responding is seven days less than the number of days listed in the table set out at the end of **PD 6B** (**PD 6B, para. 7.1**).

Proof of service

16.69 Where service is effected through the central authority designated under the Hague Service Convention or through consular, government or judicial channels, the claimant will be provided with an official certificate of service (which is evidence that service has been effected) and with a note of the expenses incurred (**CPR, r. 6.43(5)**). It is important to check that service has been carried out correctly and in a permitted manner (see *Olafsson v Gissurarson (No. 2)* [2008] EWCA Civ 152, [2008] 1 WLR 2016).

Service may still have been properly effected where the defendant has refused to accept service of documents or has refused to attend a hearing fixed to effect service (*Vis Trading Co. Ltd v Nazarov* [2013] EWHC 491 (QB), LTL 2/4/2013; *Sloutsker v Romanova* [2015] EWHC 545 (QB), [2015] 2 Costs LR 321, both cases concerning service in Russia).

Where service is effected through informal methods, service should be evidenced by a certificate of service (or affidavit or witness statement of service) from the person who effected service.

JUDGMENT IN DEFAULT

No special rule applies in cases of assumed jurisdiction regarding entering judgment in default **16.70** other than the need for waiting the enhanced period laid down by **PD 6B**.

Where service outside the jurisdiction has been effected without permission under **CPR, rr. 6.32** and **6.33**, and the defendant has failed to file an acknowledgment of service, judgment in default can only be entered by application under **CPR, Part 12** (**CPR, r. 12.10(b) (i)** and **(ii)**). These provisions give effect to the **recast Brussels I Regulation, art. 28**, which requires the courts of contracting States to declare of their own motion that they have no jurisdiction where that is the case and the defendant has failed to 'enter an appearance' (i.e. acknowledge service).

Where a hearing date is fixed when a claim is issued, and a defendant who is served with the claim form outside the jurisdiction does not appear at the hearing, the claimant may not take any further step without filing written evidence of service of the claim form (**CPR, r. 6.47**). **Rule 6.47** does not apply where service has been effected under the EU Service Regulation (see **16.62**) (**r. 6.41(4)**).

Where service is effected under the Service Regulation, judgment in default cannot be given until it is established that service was effected by a method prescribed by the internal law of the receiving State or that the documents were actually delivered to the defendant or to the defendant's residence by another method provided by the Regulation and that, in either case, the defendant had sufficient time to defend the claim (Service Regulation, art. 19).

STAYS ON THE GROUND OF *FORUM NON CONVENIENS*

General

English proceedings can be served under the common law as of right on a defendant within **16.71** the jurisdiction irrespective of the degree of connection with this country of the defendant or the cause of action (see **16.2**). A claim form for an Admiralty claim *in rem* may be served within the jurisdiction on a ship or sister ship while at port in the country, even if there is absolutely no other connection with this country.

To prevent completely unsuitable actions proceeding, the courts have a discretion in common law cases (and intra UK cases) to stay English proceedings on the principle of *forum non conveniens*. The leading case is *Spiliada Maritime Corporation v Cansulex Ltd* [1987] AC 460 (see **16.57**). The principles applied are similar to those on applications for permission under **CPR, r. 6.36** (see **16.42** to **16.56**), but the burden of proof is reversed. In an application for a stay there is a two-stage test. The defendant has to show there is another forum which is prima facie the appropriate forum. If he does so, the court considers whether there are special circumstances by reason of which justice requires the trial should take place in England. In contrast, in an application for permission under **CPR, r. 6.36**, or a challenge to permission granted under that rule, the court must be satisfied by the claimant that England is clearly or distinctly the appropriate forum (*VTB Capital plc v Nutritek International Corporation* [2012] EWCA Civ 808, [2012] 2 Lloyd's Rep 313 at [131]).

If at the time the proceedings are first served, there are circumstances which would justify a stay, an application should be made promptly under **CPR, r. 11** (see **chapter 19**). Failure to do so within the time limits in **Part 11** does not mean the defendant has conclusively accepted that the court should exercise its jurisdiction. But an extension of time will be needed and the test for relief from sanctions under r.3.9 will apply. If circumstances arise subsequently which would justify an application for a stay, the application can be made under the court's inherent jurisdiction or **r. 3.1(2)(f)** (*Texan Management Ltd v Pacific Electric Wire and Cable Co.* [2009] UKPC 46, LTL 26/11/2009; *Zumax Nigeria Ltd v First City Monument Bank plc* [2016] EWCA Civ 567, LTL 24/6/2016). The court may also have the power to stay of its own motion, exercising its case management powers (*Cook v Virgin Media Ltd* [2015] EWCA Civ 1287, [2016] 1 WLR 1672, stay of English proceedings as Scotland was the *forum conveniens*).

The court will not grant a stay on the ground of *forum non conveniens* on the application of the claimant, where there has been no challenge to the court's jurisdiction by the defendant, unless there are exceptional circumstances (*Ledra Fisheries Ltd v Turner* [2003] EWHC 1049 (Ch), LTL 15/4/2003; *Insurance Company of the State of Pennsylvania v Equitas Insurance Ltd* [2013] EWHC 3713 (Comm), [2014] Lloyd's Rep IR 195). In *Ledra Fisheries Ltd v Turner* the court also refused the claimant's application for stay of a counterclaim by the defendant.

Appropriate forum

16.72 In *Spiliada Maritime Corporation v Cansulex Ltd* [1987] AC 460 Lord Goff of Chieveley said:

> The basic principle is that a stay will only be granted on the ground of *forum non conveniens* where the court is satisfied that there is some other available forum, having competent jurisdiction, which is the appropriate forum for the trial of the action, i.e. in which the case may be tried more suitably for the interests of all the parties and the ends of justice.

The burden of proof rests on the defendant to show there is some other clearly more appropriate forum. If there is no other more suitable forum, the stay should usually be refused. So, for example, in *The Vishva Abha* [1990] 2 Lloyd's Rep 312 the owners of cargo on board a ship named the *Dias* made a claim *in rem* against the owners of a ship named the *Vishva Apurva*. The collision happened on the high seas. The only connection with England other than the fact that the defendant's ship was arrested here was that the defendant's ships regularly docked in this country. The suggested alternative forum was South Africa, on the ground that the *Dias* had been arrested there in litigation between the owners of the two ships. The only connection with South Africa was that proceedings had been served there while the *Dias* was in port. It was pure chance that litigation was pending in South Africa over the same collision as opposed to any other country, so there was no other distinctly more appropriate forum. In *Catlin Syndicate Ltd v Adams Land and Cattle Co.* [2006] EWHC 2065 (Comm), [2006] 2 CLC 425, the court considered the effect of jurisdiction clauses on the question of *forum conveniens*. The claim arose out of an insurance policy, where the parties had on the face of the insurance slip agreed to English law and jurisdiction, but at the same time they had agreed to an option in the policy itself enabling the insured to require the underwriters to submit to the jurisdiction of the US courts. Thus, the appropriateness of both the English and US courts had been accepted by the parties. The insured had exercised its right to issue proceedings in Nebraska and this gave rise to duplication of proceedings and brought into play the question of *forum conveniens*. The court held that the specific election and the provision which provided for it took precedence over the general law and jurisdiction clause in the context of deciding the appropriate forum.

The existence of proceedings overseas will be a relevant factor, but not conclusive, the strength depending in particular on how far advanced those proceedings are (*MacDermid Offshore Solutions LLC v Niche Products Ltd* [2013] EWHC 1493 (Ch), [2014] FSR 21).

If the parties have provided for non-exclusive English jurisdiction in their contract then the lack of connections to England will be irrelevant (*Cuccolini SRL v Elcan Industries Inc.* [2013] EWHC 2994 (QB), LTL 15/10/2013).

Real and substantial connection

In considering whether there is an alternative forum, the court will look for the country 'with **16.73** which the action has the most real and substantial connection' (*The Abidin Daver* [1984] AC 398 per Lord Keith of Kinkel). Sometimes, the natural forum of the action will be obvious. In *MacShannon v Rockware Glass Ltd* [1978] AC 795, a Scots employee sued his employer, which was registered in England, in respect of an accident in Scotland. All the witnesses lived in Scotland. Clearly, Scotland was the natural forum. *Gulf Oil Belgian SA v Finland Steamship Co. Ltd* [1980] 2 Lloyd's Rep 229 arose from a collision between two ships in Swedish waters caused by a misunderstanding between two Swedish pilots speaking in Swedish by VHF radio. It was patently obvious that the case should be tried in Sweden. The places of residence or business of the parties must be considered. A stay will be more readily granted if service was effected during a temporary visit to England and Wales. On the other hand, where the defendant has an established place of business within the jurisdiction, very clear and weighty grounds must be shown for refusing to exercise jurisdiction (*Banco Atlantico SA v British Bank of the Middle East* [1990] 2 Lloyd's Rep 504). The court will also consider the availability of factual and expert witnesses, the law governing the dispute and whether the parties have conferred jurisdiction on any particular court. The law governing the dispute will be particularly significant if the case involves an issue where the application of that law is not straightforward (*Golden Ocean Group Ltd v Salgaocar Mining Industries Pvt Ltd* [2011] EWHC 56 (Comm), [2011] 1 WLR 2575; *Vidal-Hall v Google Inc.* [2014] EWHC 13 (QB), [2014] EMLR 14). An alternative forum which simply applies its own laws irrespective of the generally accepted rules on the conflict of laws is unlikely to be regarded as a suitable alternative (*Banco Atlantico SA v British Bank of the Middle East* [1990] 2 Lloyd's Rep 504; *Erste Group Bank AG v JSC 'VMZ Red October'* [2013] EWHC 2926 (Comm), [2014] BPIR 81). Convincing reasons must usually be shown before the court will go behind an express agreement between the parties as to jurisdiction (*Kuwait Oil Co. (KSC) v Idemitsu Tankers KK* [1981] 2 Lloyd's Rep 510; *Deutsche Bank AG v Sebastian Holdings Inc.* [2009] EWHC 3069 (Comm), [2009] 2 CLC 949; *Jong v HSBC Private Bank (Monaco) SA* [2015] EWCA Civ 1057, LTL 22/10/2015). The strength of the claimant's case is irrelevant (*Euromark Ltd v Smash Enterprises Pty Ltd* [2013] EWHC 1627 (QB), LTL 9/6/2013).

Reasons of justice

If there is some more appropriate forum, the court may refuse a stay if, in all the circum- **16.74** stances of the case, justice requires that a stay should not be granted (*Spiliada Maritime Corporation v Cansulex Ltd* [1987] AC 460). The burden of proof regarding showing some reason for not granting a stay despite there being some more suitable forum is on the claimant. A stay may be refused, for example, where the claimant can provide cogent evidence of a real risk that justice will not be done in the foreign jurisdiction, by reason of incompetence, lack of independence or corruption (*The Abidin Daver* [1984] AC 398; *Cherney v Deripaska* [2009] EWCA Civ 849, [2009] 2 CLC 408; *Altimo Holdings and Investment Ltd v Kyrgyz Mobil Tel Ltd* [2011] UKPC 7, [2012] 1 WLR 1804; *Erste Group Bank AG v JSC 'VMZ Red October'* [2013] EWHC 2926 (Comm), [2014] BPIR 81; *Mengiste v Endowment Fund for the Rehabilitation of Tigray* [2013] EWHC 599 (Ch), LTL 28/3/2013; *Pike v Indian Hotels Co. Ltd* [2013] EWHC 4096 (QB), LTL 27/1/2014). In a group action, the lack of established procedures for handling such claims together with the strong likeli- hood that funding will be unavailable in the foreign jurisdiction to investigate complex fac- tual and legal issues may mean that substantial justice would not be done there (*Lubbe v Cape plc* [2000] 1 WLR 1545; *Lungowe v Vedanta Resources plc* [2016] EWHC 975 (TCC), LTL 2/6/2016).

Legitimate personal or juridical advantage

There are many cases where a claimant can secure some advantage by commencing proceed- **16.75** ings in one jurisdiction rather than another. Examples include the measure of damages, the vigour of the procedures on disclosure, the power to award interest, the enforceability of the judgment and the length of the limitation period. Generally, an advantage to the claimant will give rise to an equal disadvantage to the defendant. Stays have been granted in cases where

Commentary

doing so deprives the claimant of some advantage, as in *Trendtex Trading Corporation v Credit Suisse* [1982] AC 679. Generally, the court seeks to do 'practical justice' between the parties (see Lord Goff of Chieveley in *Spiliada Maritime Corporation v Cansulex Ltd* [1987] AC 460), being less worried about depriving a claimant of a benefit secured by 'forum shopping'. Any injustice that may be caused by granting a stay may be avoided by making the order subject to conditions. For example, a stay may be granted in favour of a jurisdiction with a shorter limitation period on condition that the defendant waives any limitation defence. Indeed, the parties may try to pre-empt arguments along these lines by voluntarily undertaking not to take advantage of procedural differences in advance of the hearing for the stay.

Recast Brussels I Regulation cases

16.76   Generally, the **recast Brussels I Regulation** provides a complete code, so a stay in favour of the courts of another member State in circumstances not specifically provided for in the Regulation (e.g. **art. 29, art. 31(2)**) would be inconsistent with it. The English courts initially took the approach, in the context of the Brussels Convention, that where the defendant is domiciled in England, but the dispute about jurisdiction was between the courts of this country and the courts of a non-contracting State, English proceedings could be stayed on the ground of *forum non conveniens* (*Re Harrods (Buenos Aires) Ltd* [1992] Ch 72).

In *Owusu v Jackson* [2002] EWCA Civ 877, LTL 19/6/2002, however, the Court of Appeal referred to the CJEU the following question:

(a) whether it is inconsistent with the Brussels Convention, where a claimant contends that jurisdiction is founded on art. 2, for a court of a contracting State to exercise a discretionary power, available under its national law, to decline to hear proceedings brought against a person domiciled in that State in favour of the courts of a non-contracting State if: (i) the jurisdiction of no other contracting State under the Convention is in issue; and (ii) the proceedings have no connecting factors with any other contracting State; and

(b) if the answer to (a)(i) or (a)(ii) is yes, whether it is inconsistent in all circumstances or only in some, and if so, which.

The CJEU held (*Owusu v Jackson* (case C-281/02) [2005] QB 801) in answer to (a) that art. 2 (now art. 4) is mandatory and can be derogated from only by express provision in the Convention. There is therefore no power to stay in those circumstances (for a recent unsuccessful challenge to *Owusu*, see *Lungowe v Vedanta Resources plc* [2016] EWHC 975 (TCC), LTL 2/6/2016). The court declined to answer part (b) of the question, which left it unclear whether there could be a stay in other circumstances. This opened the door to the English courts allowing stays in favour of non-member States by applying certain articles in the Brussels I Regulation by analogy or 'reflexively' in some cases.

So, in *Ferrexpo AG v Gilson Investments Ltd* [2012] EWHC 721 (Comm), [2012] 1 Lloyd's Rep 588, Andrew Smith J held that the Brussels I Regulation, art. 22 (which gives exclusive jurisdiction to particular EU courts in specified cases), should be applied by analogy or 'reflexively', thereby giving the English court a discretion to stay its proceedings in favour of the courts of a non-contracting State in appropriate circumstances. On the facts, the proceedings against English domiciled companies were stayed in favour of the Ukrainian courts as they had as their object the validity of resolutions of a Ukrainian company. Newey J in *Blue Tropic Ltd v Chkhartishvili* [2014] EWHC 2243 (Ch), [2014] ILPr 33, also considered art. 22 could be applied reflexively, although, on the facts, the case did not come within the scope of the article.

Similarly, there are a number of first-instance decisions giving reflexive effect to the Brussels I Regulation, art. 23, so as to allow a stay in favour of proceedings in a non-member State brought pursuant to an exclusive jurisdiction clause in that court's favour (*Plaza BV v Law Debenture Trust Corporation plc* [2015] EWHC 43 (Ch), LTL 22/1/2015; *Konkola Copper Mines plc v*

Coromin [2005] EWHC 898 (Comm), [2005] 2 All ER (Comm) 637; *Winnetka Trading Corporation v Julius Baer International Ltd* [2008] EWHC 3146 (Ch), [2009] Bus LR 1006).

There are conflicting first-instance decisions on whether Brussels I Regulation, arts 27 and 28 (stays where identical or related proceedings are on foot), can be given reflexive effect, so as to allow a stay in favour of proceedings in a non-member State which are identical or related. Recent decisions, however, suggest there is such a power (see *Plaza BV v Law Debenture Trust Corporation* and *Ferrexpo AG v Gilson Investments Ltd* in contrast to *Catalyst Investment Group Ltd v Lewinsohn* [2009] EWHC 1964 (Ch), [2010] Ch 218).

For legal proceedings commenced on or after 10 January 2015, the **recast Brussels I Regulation** gives courts in member States an express power to stay proceedings in favour of non-member States in certain circumstances (**arts 33** and **34, recitals 23** and **24**). The proceedings in the non-member State must be first in time and the stay must be necessary for the proper administration of justice. This entails the court assessing matters such as the connections between the facts of the case and the parties and the non-member State concerned, the stage the proceedings have reached in those courts and whether or not a judgment will be given within a reasonable time (*Re Zavarco plc* [2015] EWHC 1898 (Ch), [2016] Ch 128). The assessment may also include whether the court of the third State has exclusive jurisdiction in circumstances where a court of a member State would have exclusive jurisdiction.

It is unclear whether the court is able to give reflexive effect to articles in the **recast Brussels I Regulation** or whether **arts 33** and **34** set out the only circumstances in which proceedings in a member State can be stayed in favour of proceedings in a non-member State. Can proceedings be stayed, for example, where there is an exclusive jurisdiction agreement in favour of the courts of a non-member State but the proceedings there are commenced second in time? The decision of the CJEU in *Coreck Maritime GmbH v Handelsveem BV* (case C-387/98) [2001] ILPr 39 suggests there should be such a power.

Similarly, it is an open question whether proceedings can be stayed where the proceedings in the non-member State concern, for example, title to land in that State but those proceedings are second in time.

Separately, the court has a general power to order a temporary stay on case management grounds. But the burden on the defendant is heavy and stays will be granted only in rare and compelling cases (*Reichhold Norway ASA v Goldman Sachs International* [2000] 1 WLR 173; *Citigroup Global Markets Ltd v Amatra Leveraged Feeder Holdings Ltd* [2012] EWHC 1331 (Comm), [2012] 2 CLC 279); *Plaza BV v Law Debenture Trust Corporation*). The power to stay on this basis exists even where there is a non-exclusive jurisdiction clause in favour of the English courts and a *forum non conveniens* waiver clause (*Standard Chartered Bank (Hong Kong) Ltd v Independent Power Tanzania Ltd* [2016] EWCA Civ 411, [2016] 2 Lloyd's Rep 25). A *forum non conveniens* waiver clause is an agreement that a defendant will not argue that proceedings commenced in the chosen court or courts are inconvenient and that there is some other more suitable court (the *forum conveniens*) in which the case should be heard. A stay on the grounds of abuse of process is also possible, it seems, where the proceedings pointlessly duplicate other proceedings (*Ferrexpo AG v Gilson Investments Ltd*).

INJUNCTIONS TO RESTRAIN FOREIGN PROCEEDINGS (ANTI-SUIT INJUNCTIONS)

In rare circumstances, an English court may grant an injunction restraining the institution or **16.77** continuance of foreign proceedings. Such an injunction is only granted when it is required for the ends of justice (*Castanho v Brown and Root (UK) Ltd* [1981] AC 557). The injunction is directed to a party, not to the foreign court, so is only available against a party who is amenable to the jurisdiction of the English courts. It is a jurisdiction which must be exercised with a great deal of caution. There are two main categories of case in which an anti-suit injunction will be awarded. First, where the pursuit of the foreign (non-EU) proceedings is vexatious and oppressive and second, in order to restrain proceedings brought in a foreign (non-EU) country in breach of either a jurisdiction or an arbitration agreement between the parties. There is also an exceptional power to grant a worldwide anti-enforcement injunction (*Bank St Petersburg OJSC v Arkhangelsky* [2014] EWCA Civ 593, [2014] 1 WLR 4360; *Ecobank Transnational Inc. v Tanoh* [2015] EWCA Civ 1309, [2016] 1 WLR 2231).

The leading case concerning the first of these categories is *Société Nationale Industrielle Aérospatiale v Lee Kui Jak* [1987] AC 871. The principle laid down was that where a remedy for a particular wrong is available both in England and in a foreign country, an injunction will only be granted to restrain the foreign proceedings if pursuit of those proceedings would be vexatious, oppressive or unconscionable. This presupposes that England is the natural forum for the trial. Account must be taken of the balance of injustice to the parties depending on whether the injunction is either granted or refused, bearing in mind the possibility of removing any injustice by the imposition of suitable terms or the giving of undertakings.

The facts were that the deceased, who had lived in Brunei, was killed in a helicopter crash in Brunei. A government report on the accident concluded that the accident was caused by metal debris in the rotating assembly. The administrators of the deceased's estate started proceedings, *inter alia*, against the manufacturer of the helicopter and the maintenance company in both Brunei and Texas. The maintenance company had been served with a contribution notice in Brunei where they did not object to the jurisdiction of the court, but were vigorously resisting the jurisdiction of the court in Texas. Brunei was obviously the natural forum for the action, but an injunction could only be granted if the proceedings in Texas were vexatious or oppressive. Vexation on the ground that under Texan law there was strict liability and punitive damages was neutralised by undertakings by the claimants that neither of these would be pursued. However, there was a distinct possibility that the defendants would be unable to claim contribution from the maintenance company in Texas, whereas they could in Brunei, with the result that the proceedings in Texas could be described as oppressive. An injunction was granted.

The existence of two concurrent proceedings in different jurisdictions is not of itself 'vexatious and oppressive' and will not alone justify the granting of an anti-suit injunction (*Dornoch Ltd v Mauritius Union Assurance Co. Ltd* [2005] EWHC 1887 (Comm), LTL 30/8/2005; *Deutsche Bank AG v Highland Crusader Offshore Partners LP* [2009] EWCA Civ 725, [2010] 1 WLR 1023; *Insurance Company of the State of Pennsylvania v Equitas Insurance Ltd* [2013] EWHC 3713 (Comm), [2014] Lloyd's Rep IR 195; *Navig8 Pte Ltd v Al-Riyadh Co. for Vegetable Oil Industry* [2013] EWHC 328 (Comm), [2013] 2 All ER (Comm) 145). This is so even where the English proceedings have been commenced in reliance on a non-exclusive English jurisdiction clause (*Deutsche Bank AG v Highland Crusader Offshore Partners LP* [2009] EWCA Civ 725, [2010] 1 WLR 1023; *Dawnus Sierra Leone Ltd v Timis Mining Corporation Ltd* [2016] EWHC 236 (TCC), LTL 17/2/2016).

A litigant's reliance on the availability of enhanced or punitive damages in a jurisdiction having no connection with a dispute may be an indicator that he is acting oppressively, as might misinforming a foreign court about the status of English proceedings (*Royal Bank of Scotland plc v Hicks* [2011] EWHC 287 (Ch), LTL 21/2/2011).

A leading case concerning the second category is *Donohue v Armco Inc.* [2001] UKHL 64, [2002] 1 Lloyd's Rep 425, where it was held that effect should ordinarily be given to an exclusive jurisdiction agreement in the absence of strong reasons for departing from it. In considering whether there are 'strong reasons' the court has to take into account all of the circumstances of the case (*The Eleftheria* [1970] P 94). The fact that a judgment of the chosen court will not be enforceable where the defendant has its assets is potentially a strong reason, but is not conclusive where the risk is foreseen or foreseeable (*Impala Warehousing and Logistics (Shanghai) Co. Ltd v Wanxiang Resources (Singapore) Pte Ltd* [2015] EWHC 811 (Comm), [2015] 2 All ER (Comm) 234).

An application for an anti-suit injunction does not have to be made by a formal claim or counterclaim (*Glencore International AG v Exter Shipping Ltd* [2002] EWCA Civ 528, [2002] 2 All ER (Comm) 1). In this case it was held there was territorial, *in personam* jurisdiction to grant the injunction against a party who had submitted to the jurisdiction, and on the facts there was a clear need to protect the English proceedings.

An anti-suit injunction is not a substantive cause of action requiring a separate basis of jurisdiction. Once the court has jurisdiction over the underlying claim, it has power to make ancillary orders, including anti-suit injunctions, in order to protect the process of the English court (*Masri v Consolidated Contractors International (UK) Ltd (No. 3)* [2008] EWCA Civ 625, [2009] QB 503). Where permission is required to serve out of the jurisdiction, no separate jurisdictional gateway is required (*Golden Endurance Shipping SA v RMA Watanya SA* [2014] EWHC 3917 (Comm), [2015] 1 Lloyd's Rep 266).

An application for an anti-suit injunction should be made promptly. It is unlikely to be granted once judgment has been obtained in the foreign claim, or where it has been allowed to continue almost to the point of judgment (*Toepfer International GmbH v Molino Boschi Srl* [1996] 1 Lloyd's Rep 510). On the other hand, the foreign action must be more than merely anticipated (*Pan American World Airways v Andrews* 1992 SLT 268). Delay also needs to be considered viewed against the stage the proceedings have reached (*REC Wafer Norway AS v Moser Baer Photo Voltaic Ltd* [2010] EWHC 2581 (Comm), [2011] 1 Lloyd's Rep 410; *Essar Shipping Ltd v Bank of China Ltd* [2015] EWHC 3266, [2016] 1 Lloyd's Rep 427).

If a company is in compulsory liquidation in England and Wales, the winding-up court may restrain any person subject to its jurisdiction from taking proceedings outside the jurisdiction which would distort the distribution of the company's assets in accordance with English law (*Re Oriental Inland Steam Co., ex parte Scinde Railway Co.* (1874) LR 9 Ch App 557; *Re Vocalion (Foreign) Ltd* [1932] 2 Ch 196). This may be applied to a voluntary winding up on an application under the Insolvency Act 1986, s. 112 (*Re Jenkins and Co. Ltd* (1907) 51 SJ 715). An anti-suit injunction may also be granted where an administration order has been made (*Bloom v Harms Offshore AHT 'Taurus' GmbH & Co. KG* [2009] EWCA Civ 632, [2010] Ch 187). For a recent discussion of the principles by the Privy Council, see *Stichting Shell Pensioenfonds v Krys* [2014] UKPC 41, [2015] AC 616.

In *OT Africa Line Ltd v Hijazy* [2001] 1 Lloyd's Rep 76 the court considered whether an anti-suit injunction restraining proceedings before a foreign court was a breach of **art. 6** of the European Convention on Human Rights in **Human Rights Act 1998, sch. 1**, in that it would prevent a party's case being considered by an independent and impartial tribunal established by law. The court held that **art. 6** does not give a person an unfettered choice of tribunal in which to pursue or defend civil rights. **Article 6** does not deal with the place where the right to a fair trial is to be exercised by a litigant: it simply requires a fair trial to be available somewhere. Accordingly **art. 6** does not prevent an anti-suit injunction being granted.

An anti-suit injunction may be refused if the applicant does not have clean hands, applying general equitable principles (*Royal Bank of Scotland plc v Highland Financial Partners LP* [2012] EWHC 1278 (Comm), [2012] 2 CLC 109).

Recast Brussels I Regulation cases

An anti-suit injunction could be obtained to restrain proceedings in a non-EU State where the English courts had jurisdiction under the Brussels I Regulation (*Royal Bank of Scotland plc v Hicks* [2011] EWHC 287 (Ch), LTL 21/2/2011). In *Samengo-Turner v J. and H. Marsh and McLennan (Services) Ltd* [2007] EWCA Civ 723, [2007] 2 CLC 104, employers had started proceedings in New York against employees under bonus agreements. The New York court, applying its rules, held it

16.78

had exclusive jurisdiction over the claim. The employees applied to the English courts for an anti-suit injunction restraining the New York proceedings. The Court of Appeal held that the claim related to an employment contract and granted an injunction on the grounds that under the Brussels I Regulation, art. 18, claims relating to a contract of employment had to be brought before the English courts as the employees' courts of domicile. Granting the anti-suit injunction was the only way to give effect to the claimants' statutory rights. See also *Petter v EMC Europe Ltd* [2015] EWCA Civ 828, [2016] ILPr 3. The position is likely to be unchanged under the **recast Brussels I Regulation**.

It was not possible, however, to obtain an anti-suit injunction from the English courts to prevent proceedings continuing in another member State, even where they had been brought in breach of a jurisdiction or arbitration clause.

The CJEU held, in *Turner v Grovit* (case C-159/02) [2005] AC 101, that a court in a country which is a party to the Brussels Convention may not issue an injunction prohibiting another party from commencing or continuing proceedings in another Convention State on the ground that the proceedings are vexatious and oppressive. The reasoning was that an anti-suit injunction constitutes an interference with the jurisdiction of the foreign court and is therefore inconsistent with the system of the Convention. The position was no different in relation to the Brussels I Regulation. In *West Tankers Inc. v Allianz SpA* (case C-185/07) [2009] AC 1138 the CJEU held that it is also incompatible with the Brussels I Regulation for an English court to grant an anti-suit injunction to restrain proceedings in another member State on the ground that those proceedings are inconsistent with an arbitration agreement. It is exclusively for the courts of the member State seised of the original proceedings to determine any objection to its jurisdiction.

The absence of an anti-suit injunction opened up the possibility of tactical use of proceedings: beginning proceedings in country B in breach of a jurisdiction clause in favour of country A or in breach of an arbitration clause in order to delay the substantive consideration of a dispute. It may be possible to claim equitable damages in these circumstances (*West Tankers Inc. v Allianz SpA* [2012] EWHC 854 (Comm), [2012] 2 Lloyd's Rep 103; *Starlight Shipping Co. v Allianz Marine & Aviation Versicherungs AG* [2014] EWCA Civ 1010, [2014] 2 Lloyd's Rep 544). It may also be possible to prevent the recognition of any inconsistent foreign judgment in England by enforcing a declaratory arbitral award under the Arbitration Act 1996, s. 66 (*West Tankers Inc. v Allianz SpA* [2012] EWCA Civ 27, [2012] Bus LR 1701).

For legal proceedings instituted on or after 10 January 2015, **recast Brussels I Regulation, art. 31(2)**, addresses the problems caused by tactical use of proceedings in this way (see **16.38**). It is likely, however, that an anti-suit injunction will still be unavailable where proceedings in another member State are concerned. The position may be different where proceedings are brought in breach of an arbitration agreement (see opinion of Advocate General Wathelet in *'Gazprom' OAO* (case C-536/13) ECLI:EU:C:2014:2414).

Future developments

16.79   The Council of the Hague Conference is setting up a special commission to prepare a draft convention on enforcement of foreign judgments. This follows the completion by a working group of a proposed draft text which would apply to judgments given where the court had jurisdiction on the grounds set out in the convention. These include where the defendant was resident in the country giving judgment and, in the case of contractual obligations, where the performance of the contractual obligation took place or should have taken place. The United Kingdom is taking part in the negotiations. It is likely to be a number of years before any convention is concluded and open for signature.

PART E

Responding to a Claim

Chapter 17   Admitting the Claim and Requesting Time to Pay

The following procedural checklist is relevant to this chapter:

Procedural checklist 12   Admitting a claim and requesting time to pay

DEFENDANT'S OPTIONS ON RECEIVING PARTICULARS OF CLAIM

17.1 A defendant to a claim is not required by the CPR to do anything until particulars of claim are served. On receipt of particulars of claim, **Part 9** provides for three alternative responses:

(a) A defendant who wishes to admit the claim should file a form of admission (see **17.4** to **17.10**).

(b) A defendant who wishes to contest the claim should file a defence within 14 days of service of the particulars of claim (see **18.4** to **18.8**).

(c) A defendant who wishes to contest the claim but needs more than 14 days to prepare the defence, or who wishes to contest the jurisdiction of the court, should file an acknowledgment of service (see **18.1** to **18.3**).

ADMISSIONS MADE BEFORE COMMENCEMENT OF PROCEEDINGS

17.2 It was held in *Sowerby v Charlton* [2005] EWCA Civ 1610, [2006] 1 WLR 568, that the provisions of **CPR, Part 14**, did not apply to an admission of liability made before proceedings were commenced. This decision was followed in *Walley v Stoke-on-Trent City Council* [2006] EWCA Civ 1137, [2007] 1 WLR 352. Brooke LJ, however, added a recommendation that **Part 14** should be extended to cover pre-action admissions in claims governed by a pre-action protocol.

Accordingly, with effect from 6 April 2007, a party who wishes to admit the truth of the whole or any part of another party's case before the commencement of proceedings may do so by giving notice in writing (**r. 14.1A(1)**).

In proceedings to which the **Pre-action Protocols** for **Personal Injury Claims**, for the **Resolution of Clinical Disputes**, and for **Disease and Illness Claims** apply, a pre-action admission may be withdrawn or judgment entered on it if the admission is made after the party making it has received a letter before claim under the protocol or it is made before receipt of any letter before claim and the party making the admission states it to be made under **CPR, Part 14** (**r. 14.1A(2)**). The rules refer to a 'letter before claim' even though the pre-action protocol refers to a 'letter of claim'. Accordingly, the Association of British Insurers, the Association of Personal Injury Lawyers, the Forum of Insurance Lawyers and the Motor Accident Solicitors Society entered into a memorandum of understanding on 2 April 2009 agreeing that the reference to 'letter before claim' in **CPR, r. 14.1A**, should be interpreted as a reference to 'letter of claim' in a protocol. A pre-action admission may only be withdrawn before commencement of proceedings if the person to whom the admission was made agrees or after proceedings have been commenced if all parties consent or with the permission of the court (**r. 14.1A(3)**).

See 17.4 for the court's approach in granting permission to withdraw an admission.

ADMISSION AFTER COMMENCEMENT OF PROCEEDINGS

17.3   Any party may admit the truth of the whole or any part of another party's case at any stage after the commencement of the proceedings (**CPR, r. 14.1(1)**), by giving notice in writing either in a statement of case or by letter (**r. 14.1(2)**). Where a defendant makes an admission by notice under **r. 14.1**, the claimant is then entitled to apply for judgment (**r. 14.3(1)**). The court will enter such judgment as it appears to the court that the applicant is entitled to on the admission (**r. 14.3(2)**). An admission must be clear and unequivocal. An open offer to settle proceedings made without explicit reference to **r. 14.1**, and which makes no explicit or formal admission of any fact or matter, is not likely to amount to a formal admission under **r. 14.1**. A claimant rejecting such an offer is not entitled to apply for judgment on the basis that the offer constituted a formal admission (*Dorchester Group Ltd v Kier Construction Ltd* [2015] EWHC 3051 (TCC), [2016] CILL 3753). A claimant is entitled to enter judgment in respect of a partial admission, made in the defence, of damages due to the claimant, and such an admission will result in reducing the amount in dispute when considering track allocation (*Akhtar v Boland* [2014] EWCA Civ 872, [2015] 1 All ER 644).

WITHDRAWAL OF AN ADMISSION

17.4   There are four sets of rules regulating the withdrawal of an admission:

(a) Admissions made under **CPR, r. 14.1**, after commencement of proceedings may be amended or withdrawn only with the permission of the court (**r. 14.1(5)**).

(b) Pre-action admissions made after 6 April 2007 in cases to which **r. 14.1A(2)** applies may be withdrawn before commencement of proceedings only with the consent of the party to whom the admission was made and after commencement only with all parties' consent or the court's permission (**r. 14.1A(3)**).

(c) Pre-action admissions made before 6 April 2007, or after that date in cases not covered by **r. 14.1A(2)**, continue to be ruled by the decision in *Walley v Stoke-on-Trent City Council* [2006] EWCA Civ 1137, [2007] 1 WLR 352, with the effect that the withdrawal of the admission does not require court approval and can only be challenged by an application to strike out a defence, or part of it, under **r. 3.4(2)** as an abuse of process, for which the claimant will have to demonstrate bad faith on the part of the defendant. (See below.)

(d) Pre-action admissions made in cases covered by the **Pre-action Protocol for Low Value Personal Injury Claims in Road Traffic Accidents** or the **Pre-Action Protocol for Low Value Personal Injury (Employers' Liability and Public Liability) Claims** have their own separate rules (**CPR, r. 14.1B**). See further 17.5.

On any application for permission to withdraw an admission, the court must consider the factors listed at **PD 14, para. 7.2**:

(a) the grounds on which the applicant seeks to withdraw the admission, including whether or not new evidence has come to light which was not available at the time the admission was made;

(b) the conduct of the parties, including any conduct which led the party making the admission to do so;

(c) the prejudice that may be caused to any person if the admission is withdrawn, or, conversely, if the application to withdraw is refused;

(d) the stage in the proceedings at which the application is made, and in particular the proximity of the trial;

(e) the prospects of success, if the admission is withdrawn, of the claim or part of the claim in relation to which the offer was made; and

(f) the interests of the administration of justice.

The approach the court should take in applying the factors in **PD 14, para. 7.2**, has been considered by the Court of Appeal in *Woodland v Stopford* [2011] EWCA Civ 266, [2011] Med LR 237. The existence of fresh evidence is not a threshold test which applies to all applications for permission to withdraw a pre-action admission, and it cannot be said that without new evidence a pre-action admission cannot be withdrawn. The court will need to consider all the factors in **PD 14, para. 7.2**. They are not listed in any hierarchical order and the weight to be given to them will vary from case to case. Thus, the overriding importance attached by the court in *American Reliable Insurance Co. v Willis Ltd* [2008] EWHC 2677 (Comm), LTL 20/11/2008, to the need for fresh evidence, whilst appropriate in that case, is not of general application. **CPR, Part 14**, does not stand alone and the court has to consider the provisions in the context of the overriding objective. It is appropriate to look at an application to withdraw an admission against the background of the more robust approach set out in cases such as *Mitchell v News Group Newspapers Ltd* [2013] EWCA Civ 1537, [2014] 1 WLR 795, and *Denton v T. H. White Ltd* [2014] EWCA Civ 906, [2014] 1 WLR 3926, but it is not the case that such an application necessarily imports the full factors that are relevant when considering relief from sanctions under **r. 3.9**. The fact that the admission was made on the basis of genuine mistake rather than as a result of deliberate conduct is highly relevant and also the fact that the application was made promptly (see *Moore v Worcestershire Acute Hospitals NHS Trust* [2015] EWHC 1209 (QB), LTL 13/2/2015). In *Tchenguiz v Director of the Serious Fraud Office* [2014] EWCA Civ 472, [2014] CP Rep 35, the defendant was permitted, under **CPR, r. 14.1(5)**, to withdraw an admission that it was liable in trespass. The relevant factors were that the defences the defendant now wished to raise were at least arguable, the amounts potentially at stake were significant, there was no reason to suppose the application was made in anything other than good faith, the overriding objective required the court to reach a decision that was correct in law, rather than founded on an admission that might be incorrect as a matter of law, the withdrawal of the admission caused no prejudice to the other parties and no prejudice was caused to them by being required to meet the amended defence, whereas there was considerable prejudice to the SFO if it was prevented from amending. The court did not permit a conditional admission to be withdrawn by a defendant where the claimant had relied on it and would be prejudiced by the withdrawal, the application to withdraw the admission was not made promptly, and if the application was granted the defendant would have to be given permission to amend its defence and rely on a second report from its expert (*Clark v Braintree Clinical Services Ltd* [2015] EWHC 3181 (QB), LTL 2/12/2015). The regime set out in **PD 14, para. 7.2**, applies only to the withdrawal of admissions during rather than after the final determination of proceedings (*Kojima v HSBC Bank plc* [2011] EWHC 611, [2011] 3 All ER 359). Where the admission has resulted in a final judgment, the finality principle means that it cannot be revoked under the power given the court by **CPR, r. 3.1(7)**, to vary or revoke an order (*Roult v North West Strategic Health Authority* [2009] EWCA 444, [2010] 1 WLR 487).

The provisions of **CPR, Part 14**, relating to the withdrawal of admissions do not affect the law relating to the compromise of a claim. The distinction between a bare admission and a binding compromise depends on whether the requirements for the creation of a contract (consideration, intention to create legal relations and clarity as to the terms of the contract) are met. Where they are, the agreement is binding and the provisions of **Part 14** have no application (*Burden v Harrods Ltd* [2005] EWHC 410 (QB), [2005] PIQR P17, in which the acceptance of an admission of liability in return for a 25 per cent reduction in damages for contributory negligence was held to be a binding contract). In *Telling v OCS Group Ltd* (2008) LTL 2/6/2008 (Sheffield County Court), the court held that an admission of liability by the defendant in consideration for which the claimant ended her investigations into the claim was sufficient to create a binding compromise to which **Part 14** did not apply. There is some authority that the provisions of **Part 14** relating to the withdrawal of an admission do not apply to cases proceeding on the fast track. In *Green v Brunel and Family Housing Association Ltd* (2008) LTL 6/6/2008 (Bradford County Court), the judge struck out sections of a defence which sought to resile from a pre-action admission. The court drew a distinction between fast track claims (where the Pre-action Protocol for Personal Injury Claims then in force created a presumption that such admissions would be binding) and multi-track claims. However, the relevant provision no longer appears in the **Pre-action Protocol for Personal Injury Claims**. **Paragraph 5.7** of the current protocol envisages clearly that investigations between the date of pre-action correspondence and statements of case may result in parties' cases being put differently.

In *White v Greensand Homes Ltd* [2007] EWCA Civ 643, [2007] 1 CLC 1001 (a case to which **CPR, r. 14.1A**, did not apply), the Court of Appeal clarified the approach to a difference between a party's pleaded case and that set out in pre-action correspondence. There are two different circumstances to which different principles apply. The first is where a party seeks to amend a statement of case under **CPR, r. 17.1(2)(b)**, where the amendment will have the effect of withdrawing an admission made in an earlier letter sent under a pre-action protocol. In this circumstance, the court must have regard to the factors listed above in **PD 14, para. 7.2**.

The second situation is where an admission is made in pre-action correspondence but not repeated in a statement of case, and the question is whether the statement of case which did not repeat the admission can stand. As **CPR, r. 14.1A**, does not apply here, the court should follow the approach set out in *Walley v Stoke-on-Trent City Council* [2006] EWCA Civ 1137, [2007] 1 WLR 352. An application should be brought under **r. 3.4(2)(b)** to strike out the statement of case on the ground that it is an abuse of the court's process or is otherwise likely to obstruct the just disposal of the proceedings. In order to show abuse, the claimant would normally have to show that the defendant had acted in bad faith.

In *Gunn v Taygroup Ltd* [2010] EWHC 1665 (TCC), LTL 8/7/2010, the court held that where there is no assertion of bad faith, so that it cannot strike out parts of the defence on the grounds of an abuse of process within **r. 3.4(2)(b)**, the court's decision must be founded on the principles of equity and estoppel. The admission cannot be withdrawn if it was relied upon by the party to whom it was made to its substantial detriment. On the facts in this case, there was no prejudice to the claimant. The court rejected the argument that key evidence may have been lost or deteriorated over the passage of time. Further, it would be unfair to hold the defendant to its pre-admission decision in the face of a fivefold increase in the value of the claim between the pre-action admission and the denial of liability in the defence.

There must be good reason why it is in the interests of justice for an admission to be withdrawn close to trial. This will usually be that there is good evidence that the admission is in fact false. The court should go on to consider other factors such as prejudice to the parties caused by permitting the admission to stand only where there is also counter-evidence of the truth of the facts admitted (*Les Laboratoires Servier v Apotex Inc.* [2007] EWHC 591 (Pat), IPD 30030).

Withdrawal of an admission made under the RTA Protocol or the EL/PL Protocol

17.5   The **Pre-action Protocol for Low Value Personal Injury Claims in Road Traffic Accidents** ('the RTA Protocol') covers road traffic claims for personal injury worth no more than £25,000 (£10,000 if the accident occurred on or after 30 April 2010 and before 31 July 2013). The **RTA Protocol** provides a mechanism for the settlement of claims and the recovery of fixed legal costs without the need for court proceedings.

The **Pre-Action Protocol for Low Value Personal Injury (Employers' Liability and Public Liability) Claims** ('the EL/PL Protocol') extends the scheme to employers' liability and public liability claims made on or after 31 July 2013 which are valued at no more than £25,000.

CPR, r. 14.1B, sets out the position relating to the withdrawal of admissions made under Stage 1 or Stage 2 of the **RTA Protocol** or the **EL/PL Protocol**. It distinguishes between admissions of causation and other admissions. Withdrawal of an admission of causation may be made before proceedings are issued during the initial consideration period (defined in the **RTA Protocol, para. 7.35** (formerly para. 7.28), and the **EL/PL Protocol, para. 7.32**, as the period of 15 days which the defendant has for consideration of the Stage 2 settlement pack sent by the claimant) or at any time up to the commencement of the claim if the person to whom it was made agrees (**CPR, r. 14.1B(2)(a)**). After issue of proceedings, an admission of causation, or any pre-action admission, may be withdrawn with all parties' consent or court permission (**r. 14.1B(2)(b) and (3)**). An application for permission must be made under **Part 23** (**r. 14.1B (4)**).

ADMISSION OF A MONEY CLAIM WITHIN 14 DAYS OF SERVICE OF THE PARTICULARS OF CLAIM

In money claims (whether for a specified sum or not), the CPR contain a procedure for the admission of the claim at an early stage. This procedure (which is in addition to the procedure described in **17.3**) is aimed primarily at individual defendants in debt claims (though it is not actually restricted to such defendants). It provides a mechanism whereby the rate and time by which the admitted claim is to be paid can be agreed between the parties or fixed by the court.   **17.6**

There are separate rules for four different categories of admission:

(a) admission of the whole of a claim for a specified sum (**CPR, r. 14.4**; see **17.7**);
(b) admission of part of a claim for a specified sum (**r. 14.5**; see **17.8**);
(c) admission of liability to pay the whole of a claim for an unspecified amount of money (**r. 14.6**; see **17.9**); and
(d) admission of liability to pay the whole of a claim for an unspecified amount of money, where the defendant offers a sum in satisfaction of the claim (**r. 14.7**; see **17.10**).

The claimant may not enter judgment in default under these rules against a child or a protected party, nor may a claimant who is a child or protected party enter judgment where the admission has been made under **r. 14.5** or **r. 14.7** (**r. 14.1(4)**).

Any admission by the defendant under **rr. 14.4 to 14.7** must be made within 14 days after service of the claim form, or, where the claim form states that particulars of claim will follow, within 14 days after service of the particulars of claim (**r. 14.2**). **Rule 14.2(2)** extends this deadline in two cases:

(a) Where the claim form has been served out of the jurisdiction in circumstances where the court's permission is not required, in which case the time limits set out in **r. 6.35** apply. (Where the court's permission is required for service out of the jurisdiction the court's order will specify the time for filing or serving an admission (**PD 6B, para. 6.2**) calculated by reference to the table at the end of PD 6B (**PD 6B, para. 6.2**).)
(b) Where the court makes an order for service on an agent of an overseas principal under **CPR, r. 6.12(3)**, in which case the deadline for filing the acknowledgment will be that specified in the order.

In any event, the defendant may return an admission under **rr. 14.4 to 14.7** after the dead-line specified in **r. 14.2**, provided judgment in default has not already been entered (**r. 14.2(3)**).

When particulars of claim are served on a defendant, the response pack will include a series of forms for responding to the claim. These will include forms for making an admission (**r. 7.8(1); PD 14, para. 2.1**). The defendant will need to choose the correct form from the pack for making his admission.

Admission of the whole of a claim for a specified sum

17.7 Under **CPR, r. 14.4**, a defendant who admits the whole of a claim for a specified sum has three options:

(a) If he is able, he may simply pay the sum claimed in full (together with interest, and the amount of fixed costs (see **chapter 69**) and issue fee endorsed on the claim form) direct to the claimant in full within 14 days after service.

(b) Alternatively, the defendant may ask for time to pay, or ask to pay by instalments (**r. 14.9**), by returning form N9A to the claimant having completed the details sought about his means (**r. 14.4(2)**). Where the claimant accepts the defendant's proposals, he may obtain judgment by filing request form N225 (**r. 14.9(4)**). The court will then enter judgment for payment at the time and rate specified in the defendant's request (**r. 14.9(5) and (6)**). If the claimant does not accept the defendant's proposals, he should still file request form N225, but give notice that he does not accept the proposals (**r. 14.10(2)**). The court will then decide the time and rate at which payment should be made (**r. 14.10(4)**).

(c) The defendant may simply admit the claim without seeking time to pay, by returning form N9A to the claimant. In this case, the claimant may obtain judgment by filing a request for judgment in form N225 (**r. 14.4(3)**). The claimant may specify the date by which the judgment should be paid or the times and rates at which it is to be paid by instalments (**r. 14.4(4)**). Judgment will then be entered by the court in the terms specified by the claimant (**r. 14.4(5) and (6)**).

Admission of only part of a claim for a specified sum

17.8 A defendant who, under **CPR, r. 14.5**, admits part of a claim for a specified sum should complete forms N9A and N9B and return them to the court within 14 days after service. The claimant then has the choice of accepting the partial admission and entering judgment, or refusing the admission altogether, in which case the claim will continue as a defended claim.

On receipt of the defendant's admission, the court will serve notice on the claimant requiring notification to the court within 14 days of whether the claimant wishes to accept the defendant's offer in satisfaction of the claim, reject it or accept the amount of the offer but reject the proposals for payment (**r. 14.5(3)**). If the claimant does not reply within 14 days, the claim will be stayed until the reply is filed (**r. 14.5(4) and (5)**).

The defendant may or may not have asked for time to pay. Where the claimant has accepted the partial admission in principle, the procedure in **17.7(b)** and **(c)** then applies in relation to proposals for payment (except that form N225A is used instead of N225).

The provisions of **r. 14.5** do not apply to claims in the Commercial Court (**r. 58.9(1)**). Instead the claimant should simply apply for judgment on the admission under **r. 14.3**.

Admission of liability on a claim for an unspecified sum

17.9 A defendant who, under **CPR, r. 14.6**, admits liability for the whole of a claim for an unspecified sum without offering to pay a specified amount in satisfaction of the claim should complete form N9C and return it to the court within 14 days after service. This form is then sent by the court to the claimant, who may request the court to enter judgment on liability, with damages to be assessed. If the claimant files a request for judgment in the County Court Money Claims Centre for an amount of money to be decided by the court in accordance with **r. 14.6** (**r. 2.3(1)**), the claim will be sent to the preferred hearing centre (which the claimant has specified in the claim form; see **PD 7A, para. 4A.2**), and once that occurs, any further correspondence should be sent to, and any further applications should be made to the hearing centre to which the claim was sent (**CPR, r. 14.7A**). That hearing centre will then enter judgment and give directions for the assessment of damages. If appropriate, the case may be allocated to a track (**r. 14.8**). The procedure for assessing damages is considered at **42.67 to 42.70**.

If the claimant does not file a request for judgment within 14 days after service of the admission on him, the claim is stayed until the request is filed (**r. 14.6(5)**).

Admission of liability for a claim for an unspecified sum and offer of an amount to satisfy the claim

A defendant who, under **CPR, r. 14.7**, admits liability for a claim for an unspecified sum and **17.10** offers an amount of money to satisfy the claim should complete form N9C and send it to the court within 14 days after service. The court will forward it to the claimant. The claimant may then either accept the amount offered and request judgment to be entered in that amount, or reject the amount offered and request judgment to be entered for an amount to be decided by the court and costs. The claimant's choice must be notified to the court within 14 days of being served with a notice of request. If the claimant does not reply within 14 days, the claim will be stayed until the reply is filed. If the claimant files a request for judgment in the County Court Money Claims Centre for an amount to be decided by the court in accordance with **r. 14.7**, the claim will be sent to the preferred hearing centre specified by the claimant in the claim form. Any further correspondence or applications should then be sent to the hearing centre to which the claim was sent (**r. 14.7A**). The defendant may or may not ask for time to pay under **r. 14.9**. Where the claimant accepts the admission in principle, the procedure in 17.7(b) and (c) then applies in relation to proposals for payment (except that form N226 is used instead of N225).

Court's discretion to postpone payment under r. 14.10

The nature of the court's jurisdiction under **CPR, r. 14.10**, to postpone payment or to order **17.11** payment by instalments where the defendant makes a request for time to pay was considered in *Gulf International Bank v Al Ittefaq Steel Products Co.* [2010] EWHC 2601 (QB), LTL 1/11/2010, there having previously been no authority on the point. The case was an unusual one for the application of the Part 14 rules on admitting a claim and seeking time to pay, in that it involved commercial parties seeking to restructure major loan debt. The defendants admitted the claim under **r. 14.4** and then made a request under **r. 14.9** for postponement of the normal 14-day period for payment, on the basis that there was a real prospect of a rescheduling agreement of its indebtedness, which would benefit all creditors. The court took the view that the same considerations applied as to applications under **r. 40.11** for extensions of time to pay a judgment debt (e.g. *Amsalem v Raivid* [2008] EWHC 3226 (TCC), LTL 27/3/2009). Applying these principles, it refused the application, holding that mere inability to pay would not usually justify the postponement of the normal period for payment, particularly where the parties were business entities. The court will extend time under **r. 14.10** only exceptionally and then only where the judgment debtor is solvent and for a relatively short period of time.

Determination of time and rate of payment

Where the court is to make a determination of the time and rate of payment, this will usually **17.12** be done by a court officer if the amount outstanding is not more than £50,000 and this will take place without a hearing (**CPR, r. 4.11**). Where a judge is to determine the time and rate of payment at a hearing, the proceedings will usually be transferred to the hearing centre serving the defendant's address if the defendant is an individual, the only claim is for a specified amount of money, the claim has not been sent or transferred to another defendant's home court, and the claim was not started in a specialist list. Otherwise, the proceedings will be sent to the preferred hearing centre specified by the claimant in the claim form, if the defendant is not an individual, the only claim is for a specified amount of money, the claim was started in the County Court Business Centre and the claim has not been sent to another court (**r. 14.12**). The parties have a right of redetermination where the time and rate of payment were determined by a court officer or a judge without a hearing (**r. 14.13**). Either party may, on account of a change in circumstances since the date of the decision or redetermination, apply to vary the time and rate of payments still outstanding (**PD 14, para. 6.1**).

Chapter 18 Acknowledging Service and Filing a Defence

The following procedural checklist is relevant to this chapter:

Procedural checklist 13 Time limits for responding to claim by acknowledging service and/or filing a defence

ACKNOWLEDGING SERVICE

18.1 When particulars of claim are served on the defendant, the response pack will include a form (form N9) for acknowledging service of the claim (**CPR, r. 7.8(1)**). Except in the case of Part 8 claims (see **chapter 13**), contentious probate claims and claims issued in the Commercial and Mercantile Courts (see below), a defendant is under no obligation to file an acknowledgment, even if there is an intention to defend the claim. Instead of filing an acknowledgment, a defendant may proceed immediately to file and serve a defence.

By **r. 10.1(3)**, an acknowledgment may be filed in any case where:

(a) the defendant is not able to file a defence within 14 days after service of the particulars of claim; or

(b) the defendant wishes to dispute the court's jurisdiction.

In the latter case, filing an acknowledgment indicating an intention to contest the jurisdiction will not constitute a submission to the jurisdiction (**r. 11(3)**) (see further **chapter 19** on disputing the court's jurisdiction). However, by signing an acknowledgment without indicating an intention to challenge jurisdiction, a party waives any defects in service (see, e.g., *Brooks v A. H. Brooks and Co.* [2010] EWHC 2720 (Ch), [2011] 3 All ER 982).

If the claim has been brought under the Part 8 procedure (in which case the claim form must state that **Part 8** applies), the claim form is accompanied only by a form of acknowledgment of service (**r. 7.8(2)(b)**). The defendant must then file and serve an acknowledgment within 14 days after service of the claim form (**r. 8.3**). See further **chapter 13**.

The general provisions for acknowledging service are modified for claims issued in the Commercial and Mercantile Courts. In those courts the defendant must always file an acknowledgment of service (**rr. 58.6(1) and 59.5(1)**) within 14 days after service of the claim form (whether or not it is accompanied by particulars of claim) (**rr. 58.6(2) and 59.5(2)**). An adapted version of N9 has been approved for use in the Commercial Court (form N9(CC)). The period for acknowledging service is extended in the situations listed in **rr. 58.6(3) and 59.5(3)**. There are special rules for Admiralty claims in **rr. 61.3 and 61.4**.

For acknowledging service in cases under the **Pre-action Protocol for Low Value Personal Injury Claims in Road Traffic Accidents** see **8.49**.

TIME FOR FILING THE ACKNOWLEDGMENT

An acknowledgment of service must, by **CPR, r. 10.3(1)**, be filed: **18.2**

(a) within 14 days after service of the particulars of claim, where the particulars of claim are served after the claim form; or

(b) within 14 days after service of the claim form, where the particulars of claim are included in or served with the claim form.

In contentious probate proceedings, the time limits are 28 days after service of the claim form or particulars of claim, where the particulars are served after the claim form (**r. 57.4**).

In *Coll v Tattum* (2001) *The Times,* 3 December 2001, Neuberger J held that, although the CPR are silent on the point, a defendant who wishes to acknowledge service or file a defence after these time limits have expired but before judgment in default is entered needs either the other side's consent or the court's permission. Granting permission is a matter for the court's discretion, which will normally be exercised in favour of extending time where there is a defence which is apparently bona fide and arguable (see **20.9**). *Coll v Tattum* has been followed in *Boeing Capital Corporation v Wells Fargo Bank Northwest* [2003] EWHC 1364 (Comm), LTL 17/7/2003 and *Lexi Holdings plc v Luqman* [2007] EWHC 2497 (Ch), LTL 26/11/2007. In *ESR Insurance Services Ltd v Clemons* [2008] EWHC 2023 (Comm), LTL 2/9/2008, the court gave permission to a defendant to file an acknowledgment late, and extended time for him to do so, on the grounds that it would be unfair to the defendant to enter default judgment where he had in fact filed an acknowledgment by the time of the application for judgment in default and needed time to take legal advice. However, at the same time it gave permission to the claimant to make a summary judgment application, on the strength of the existing evidence. See also *Taylor v Giovani Developers Ltd* [2015] EWHC 328 (Comm), LTL 24/6/2015, in which the court refused to grant an application for an extension of time for acknowledgment of service by the defendant where the application was not made promptly, but was a response to the claimant's application for judgment in default and the defendant's failure to participate in the proceedings was deliberate because it intended to challenge jurisdiction. See further **18.6**.

These deadlines are extended where the claim form has been served out of the jurisdiction (**r. 10.3(2)(a)**). Where service out of the jurisdiction has been effected without the court's permission, under **rr. 6.32** and **6.33**, the time limits set out in **r. 6.35** apply. Where an order for service out of the jurisdiction has been obtained, it will include the date by which acknowledgment should be filed (**PD 6B, para. 6.2**) calculated by reference to the table at the end of **PD 6B** (**PD 6B, para. 6.2**). In contentious probate proceedings, the time limits for service out of the jurisdiction without permission under **CPR, rr. 6.32** and **6.33**, are extended by a further 14 days (**CPR, r. 57.4(3)**).

Where the court makes an order under **r. 6.12**, for service on an agent of an overseas principal, any acknowledgment of service must be filed within the period specified by the court under **r. 6.12(3)** for responding to particulars of claim (**r. 10.3(2)(b)**).

In judicial review cases, acknowledgment of service must be filed within 21 days after service of the claim form, and must be served on the claimant and any other person named in the claim form (**r. 54.8(2)**).

Naturally, time for filing the acknowledgment does not run during the period of a stay (*Roundstone Nurseries Ltd v Stephenson Holdings Ltd* [2009] EWHC 1431 (TCC), [2009] 5 Costs LR 787).

The court must notify the claimant in writing that an acknowledgment has been filed (**r. 10.4**).

CONTENTS OF THE FORM OF ACKNOWLEDGMENT

The form of acknowledgment of service (form N9) requires the defendant: **18.3**

(a) to indicate the intention to defend all or part of the claim;

(b) to state whether it is intended to contest the jurisdiction; and

(c) if an individual, to state his or her date of birth (**PD 16, para. 10.7**).

If a party seeks to challenge the jurisdiction of the court, the most prudent course is to tick only the second box. See further the discussion at **19.2**.

The acknowledgment must give the defendant's full name, if it is different from the name given on the claim form. It must give an address for service (**CPR, r. 10.5(b)**). If the defendant's legal representative has signed the acknowledgment, the representative's business address will be the defendant's address for service (**PD 10, para. 3.2**).

The acknowledgment must be signed either by the defendant or by the defendant's legal representative (**CPR, r. 10.5(a)**). In the case of a company or other corporation, the acknowledgment must be signed by a person in a senior position. Persons who fall into this category are set out at **PD 10, para. 4.3**. Where the defendant is a partnership, the acknowledgment must be signed in the name of the partnership on behalf of all partners at the time the cause of action accrued. It may be signed by any partner or a person authorised by any partner to sign it (**PD 10, para. 4.4**) (see further **15.50** for a fuller discussion of acknowledging service on behalf of a partnership, and **79.45** for the effect of acknowledgment on enforcement against the personal assets of a partner). A child or protected party may sign an acknowledgment only through his or her litigation friend or solicitor, unless the court orders to the contrary (**PD 10, para. 4.5**).

An acknowledgment of service in a claim begun using the CPR, Part 8, procedure (but not other types of claim) must be verified by a statement of truth (**r. 22.1(1)(d)**).

The same form may be used for two or more defendants, if they are represented by the same solicitor (**PD 10, para. 5.3**).

If the defendant has entered into a funding agreement falling within **CPR, Part 48** (which contains transitional arrangements relating to certain conditional fee agreements and after-the-event insurance policies entered into before 1 April 2013), a notice of funding (form N251) should be filed with the acknowledgment of claim and a copy served on every other party (see **Parts 43 to 44**, and **PD 44, para. 19.2(3)**, as in force before 1 April 2013, which continue to apply to these cases).

An acknowledgment of service may be amended or withdrawn only with permission of the court (**PD 10, para. 5.4**).

Where an acknowledgment is returned by a defendant with the 'I do not intend to defend this claim' box ticked, the proper course for the claimant is to issue an application for judgment to be entered, rather than a request for judgment. This means that the acknowledgment or admission can be considered by the court, rather than being dealt with as an administrative act (*Northern Rock (Asset Management) plc v Chancellors Associates Ltd* [2011] EWHC 3229, [2012] 2 All ER 501).

FILING A DEFENCE

18.4 Save in the case of Part 8 claims (**CPR, r. 15.1**), a defendant who wishes to defend all or part of a claim must file a defence (**r. 15.2**). A defendant's privilege against self-incrimination does not give rise to a right not to plead a defence in civil proceedings (*Versailles Trade Finance Ltd v Clough* [2001] EWCA Civ 1509, [2002] CP Rep 8, and affirmed by the Court of Appeal in *Coogan v News Group Newspapers Ltd* [2012] EWCA Civ 48, [2013] 1 AC 1; *Phillips v News Group Newspapers Ltd* [2012] UKSC 28, [2013] 1 AC 1). If a defence is not filed within the specified period, default judgment (see **chapter 20**) may be entered (**r. 15.3**). A copy of the defence must be served on every other party (**r. 15.6**). **Rule 15.6** does not explicitly state whether it is the court's or the defendant's responsibility to serve the defence, but **r. 6.21(1)** makes clear that the party who has prepared a document must serve it, except where a rule, practice direction or court order provides otherwise.

If the defendant has entered into a funding agreement falling within **CPR, Part 48** (which contains transitional arrangements relating to certain conditional fee agreements and after-the-event insurance policies entered into before 1 April 2013), a notice of funding (form N251) should be filed with the defence, if this is the first document to be filed by the defendant, and a copy served on every other party (see **Parts 43 to 44** and **PD 44, para. 19.2(3)**, as in force before 1 April 2013, which continue to apply to these cases).

None of the rules relating to the filing of defences applies to Part 8 claims (**CPR, r. 15.1**). They do, however, apply to cases where a defence is filed to a counterclaim (**r. 20.3**).

Period for filing a defence

The general rule is that a defence must be filed within 14 days after service of the particulars of claim (**CPR, r. 15.4(1)(a)**). Where a claim form is served which does not include, and is not accompanied by, particulars of claim, the defendant should wait for the particulars, which should be served by the claimant within 14 days after service of the claim form (**r. 7.4**). **18.5**

If more time is needed in which to file and serve a defence, the defendant may file an acknowledgment of service under **Part 10**. The time for filing a defence is then extended until 28 days after service of the particulars of claim (**r. 15.4(1)(b)**).

There are different time limits for filing a defence where the claim form is served out of the jurisdiction without the court's permission, under **rr. 6.32** and **6.33** (see **r. 6.25**). Where an order for service out of the jurisdiction has been obtained, it will include the date by which a defence should be filed (**PD 6B, para. 6.2**) calculated by reference to the table at the end of **PD 6B** (**PD 6B, para. 6.2**). Where a claim form is served on the agent of a principal who is overseas the court will, under **CPR, r. 6.12(3)**, specify the period for responding to the particulars of claim.

There are two further exceptions to the general rule:

(a) A defendant who makes an application disputing the jurisdiction of the court (see **chapter 19**) need not file a defence before the hearing of the application (**r. 11(9)**). However, if any such application is abandoned, the protection of **r. 11(9)** is lost (*Flame SA v Primera Maritime (Hellas) Ltd* [2009] EWHC 1973 (Comm), LTL 29/9/2009).

(b) Where the claimant makes an application for summary judgment under **Part 24** (see **chapter 34**) before the defendant has filed a defence, the defendant need not then do so before the hearing of the application (**r. 24.4(2)**).

If either application is unsuccessful, and the claim continues, the court will make a direction for filing and service of the defence within a stated period. **Rules 11(9)** and **24.4(2)** do not prevent a defendant filing a defence in the period before the hearing of the application.

Naturally, time for filing a defence does not run during the period of a stay (*Roundstone Nurseries Ltd v Stephenson Holdings Ltd* [2009] EWHC 1431 (TCC), [2009] 5 Costs LR 787).

Late filing of the defence

Under **CPR, r. 15.4**, the general rule is that the period for filing a defence is 14 days after service of the particulars of claim. This period can be extended by filing an acknowledgment of service, obtaining the claimant's consent, or obtaining an order for an extension. Once this period has elapsed, the claimant is usually entitled to enter a default judgment under **Part 12**, and the only consequence stated in the CPR as flowing from not filing a defence within the stated time is the danger that the claimant might enter judgment in default (**r. 15.3**). A default judgment may only be entered where the defendant has failed to file an acknowledgment of service or a defence (**r. 12.1**). This means that if the claimant delays in entering judgment in default, the question is which side then acts first. If the claimant enters judgment first, all the defendant can do is to apply to set the judgment aside under **Part 13**. If the defendant files a **18.6** defence first, it is no longer open for the claimant to enter judgment in default because of **r. 12.1**. In this situation, the claim proceeds as normal, but the delay by the defendant may be taken into account on costs or in general case management.

In a number of situations, judgment in default can only be entered after the claimant issues an application for permission to enter judgment (see **20.8** and **20.9**). Typically, these are claims where the relief sought includes equitable remedies. What is the position if the defendant purports to acknowledge service or file a defence in the period between the claimant issuing an application for the entry of default judgment and the hearing of the application? In *Coll v Tattum* (2001) *The Times,* 3 December 2001, Neuberger J said that as the defendant was seeking to file the defence outside the time limit, he needed either the consent of the claimant or the permission of the court. Permission would normally be granted where there was a genuine defence. A similar result was achieved in *Boeing Capital Corporation v Wells Fargo Bank Northwest* [2003] EWHC 1364 (Comm), LTL 17/7/2003, a case like *Coll v Tattum* where the claimant needed permission because the claim was for equitable relief. In *Lexi Holdings plc v Luqman* [2007] EWHC 2497 (Ch), LTL 26/11/2007, the court followed *Coll v Tattum*, and held that a defence which was on its face apparently bona fide and arguable should be permitted to be served out of time after an application for judgment in default had been made. The test applied by the court in deciding whether to enter judgment in default was different to the wider question of whether the defence was susceptible to an application for summary judgment, which should normally be left over to a further application, should the claimant wish to pursue it. However, this approach was a rule of thumb rather than an invariable rule. On the facts of this case, where the defence had been filed late, and it could be shown it was bound to fail in part, judgment in default would be entered on that part (see **34.10**).

Extending the time for service of a defence

18.7   Under **CPR, r. 15.5**, the defendant and the claimant may agree an extension of the time for filing a defence of up to 28 days only. Where they do so, they must notify the court in writing (**r. 15.5(2)**).

A defendant who requires additional time beyond this must make an application, using the **Part 23** procedure, under **r. 3.1(2)(a)**. Guidance on the exercise of the court's discretion when making orders under **r. 3.1(2)(a)** is to be found in *Sayers v Clarke Walker* [2002] EWCA Civ 645, [2002] 1 WLR 3095; *SC DG Petrol SRL v Vitol Broking Ltd* [2013] EWHC 3920 (Comm), [2014] 2 Costs LR 205; *Robert v Momentum Services Ltd* [2003] EWCA Civ 299, [2003] 1 WLR 1577; and *Hallam Estates Ltd v Baker* [2014] EWCA Civ 661, [2014] CP Rep 38 (see **3.8**, **15.40**, **42.46** to **42.52** and **chapter 48**, and in particular **42.23**). However, the court will expect the parties to be reasonable in agreeing appropriate extensions. The court will now scrutinise an extension application more rigorously than it might have done before 1 April 2013 when the overriding objective was amended, and an extension may be disallowed, even if there is no prejudice to the other party. On the other hand, in *Re Atrium Training Services Ltd* [2013] EWHC 1562 (Ch), [2013] 5 Costs LO 707, and *Hallam Estates Ltd v Baker*, the court has noted that it is important that parties should not unreasonably oppose extensions that are applied for or requested in time and which involve no real prejudice. A court hearing involving the preparation of witness statements and exhibits to determine whether an extension should be final or not was inappropriate and a wholly disproportionate waste of time. A future judge could decide if the defendant had had ample time to prepare its defence by the end of the agreed extension, should further time be necessary (*TIP Communications LLC v Motorola Ltd* [2009] EWHC 212 (Pat), LTL 23/2/2009).

Filing and serving a defence in the Commercial Court

18.8   The Commercial Court no longer has special rules on filing and serving defences.

Chapter 19   Disputing the Court's Jurisdiction

The following procedural checklist is relevant to this chapter:

Procedural checklist 14   Procedure for disputing the court's jurisdiction

INTRODUCTION

CPR, Part 11, makes provision for the defendant to challenge the jurisdiction of the English **19.1** court, or to argue that the court should not exercise any jurisdiction which it may have. The rule is not confined to challenges over the court's geographic jurisdiction. It may be invoked where there is any dispute over the court's power or authority to try a claim, including disputes over the bringing of litigation despite an arbitration clause in an agreement between the parties or over service of a claim form after it has expired (*Hoddinott v Persimmon Homes (Wessex) Ltd* [2008] EWCA Civ 1203, [2008] 1 WLR 806). **Part 11** does not, however, extend to disputes over possible limitation defences, whether under the Limitation Act 1980 or under the **Human Rights Act 1998, s. 7(5)** (*Dunn v The Parole Board* [2008] EWCA Civ 374, [2009] 1 WLR 728; *M v Ministry of Justice* [2009] EWCA Civ 419, LTL 19/5/2009). All challenges to the jurisdiction should be brought in one application (*IMS SA v Capital Oil and Gas Industries Ltd* [2016] EWHC 1956 (Comm), LTL 12/8/2016). The rules on jurisdiction are considered in **chapter 16**. The procedure for disputing the court's jurisdiction is considered at **19.3**.

ACKNOWLEDGMENT OF SERVICE

The defendant must first file an acknowledgment of service within the usual time limit **19.2** (i.e. within 14 days after service of the claim form, or of the particulars of claim, if served later, or, where served out of the jurisdiction, the time limits given under **CPR, r. 6.35**, and **PD 6B, para. 6.2**) stating an intention to contest the jurisdiction (**CPR, r. 11(2)**). To avoid any ambiguity about submitting to the jurisdiction, the defendant should tick only the 'intention to contest the jurisdiction' box and not also tick the 'intention to defend' box (see **19.4**). In *Hoddinott v Persimmon Homes (Wessex) Ltd* [2007] EWCA Civ 1203, [2008] 1 WLR 806, the defendant applied to set aside an order extending time for service of the claim form, made without notice to it. Before the application was heard, the claimant served the claim form. In response, the defendant filed an acknowledgment of service in which it ticked the box 'I intend to defend all of this claim', and not the box 'I intend to contest the jurisdiction'. However, it made no application under **Part 11**. The Court of Appeal held that it had abandoned its application to set aside the order extending the time for service. It was reinforced in its conclusion by the fact that the defendant had indicated in the acknowledgment of service that it did not intend to contest jurisdiction and did intend to defend the claim.

APPLICATION DISPUTING JURISDICTION

19.3   Within 14 days after filing an acknowledgment of service, the defendant should make an application for the order sought, using the Part 23 procedure (**CPR, r. 11(4)(a)**). In the Commercial and Mercantile Courts the time limit is 28 days after filing an acknowledgment (**rr. 58.7** and **59.6**). Failure to make the application within this time limit will be taken as a submission to the jurisdiction (**r. 11(5)(b)**). The application must be supported by evidence (**r. 11(4)(b)**). No defence need be served before the hearing of the application (**r. 11(9)**). Indeed, serving a defence may constitute a voluntary submission to the jurisdiction (see **19.4**).

As originally drafted, **r. 11(4)** expressed the time limit for making an application as 'the period for filing a defence'. It became clear in *Monrose Investments Ltd v Orion Nominees Ltd* [2001] CP Rep 109 that it was confusing to express the time limit in this way as the reference was to the time limit in **r. 15.4**, not the time as it might have been extended by the court. The current wording of **r. 11(4)** deals with this problem. It was also held in *Monrose Investments v Orion Nominees* that if a party needs additional time to make an application to contest the jurisdiction, it should make an application for an extension of the time limit laid down in **r. 11(4)** and the court has a discretion under **r. 3.1(2)(a)** to extend it. The decision on this point was followed in *SSQ Europe SA v Johann & Backes OHG* [2002] 1 Lloyd's Rep 465, in which the court confirmed that an extension of time for service of a defence does not carry with it an extension of time for an application to challenge the court's jurisdiction.

The application for an extension of time in which to challenge jurisdiction should be made within the time limit (14 days or 28 days in the Commercial and Mercantile Courts) as a failure to do so may be taken as a submission to the jurisdiction (*Maple Leaf Macro Volatility Master Fund v Rouvroy* [2009] EWHC 257 (Comm), [2009] 2 All ER (Comm) 287 at [187]).

An application to extend the period for making an application to dispute the jurisdiction can be made retrospectively. But the test for relief from sanctions in **r. 3.9** applies, so an extension may not be easy to obtain (*Altomart Ltd v Salford Estates (No. 2) Ltd* [2014] EWCA Civ 1408, [2015] 1 WLR 1825; *Zumax Nigeria Ltd v First City Monument Bank plc* [2016] EWCA Civ 567, LTL 24/6/2016).

Applications disputing jurisdiction should, as a matter of principle, be decided at the earliest reasonable opportunity (*Cooper Tire and Rubber Co. v Shell Chemicals UK Ltd* [2009] EWHC 1529 (Comm), LTL 7/7/2009, where an adjournment was refused, despite a risk that the costs of a complex jurisdictional challenge could prove to be wasted depending on the result of pending appeals in Italy).

The time limits in **CPR, Part 11**, do not apply where a party is seeking a stay under the Arbitration Act 1996, s. 9 (*Bilta (UK) Ltd v Nazir* [2010] EWHC 1086 (Ch), [2010] Bus LR 1634).

Where a party is seeking a stay on *forum non conveniens* grounds in non-EU cases and at the time the proceedings are first served there are circumstances which would potentially justify a stay, the application should be made under **CPR, Part 11** (see **16.71**). Failure to do so within the time limits in **Part 11** does not mean the defendant has conclusively accepted that the court should exercise its jurisdiction, but an application to extend time must be made to which **r. 3.9** will apply. If circumstances arise subsequently which would justify an application for a stay, the application can be made under the court's inherent jurisdiction or **r. 3.1(2)(f)** (*Texan Management Ltd v Pacific Electric Wire and Cable Co.* [2009] UKPC 46, LTL 26/11/2009; *Zumax Nigeria Ltd v First City Monument Bank plc*).

The time limits in **Part 11** probably apply when the defendant is seeking to rely on the **recast Brussels 1 Regulation, arts 29** or **30** (same or related proceedings in another member State) (*Re The Alexandros T* [2013] UKSC 70, [2014] 1 All ER 590; *Cartier Parfums - Lunettes SAS v Ziegler France*

SA (case C-1/13) [2014] ILPr 25; but see *Deutsche Bank AG London Branch v Petromena ASA* [2015] EWCA Civ 266, [2015] CP Rep 27, which appears to suggest this is not always necessary). The court may extend the time for raising *lis pendens* arguments in an appropriate case (*SET Select Energy GmbH v F and M Bunkering Ltd* [2014] EWHC 192 (Comm), [2014] 1 Lloyd's Rep 652).

An application to set aside permission to serve out of the jurisdiction falls to be determined by reference to the position at the time permission is granted, not by reference to circumstances at the time that the application to set aside is heard, although subsequent events may throw light upon considerations which were relevant at that time (*Erste Group Bank AG London Branch v JSC VMZ Red October* [2015] EWCA Civ 379, [2015] 1 CLC 706). A non-party served out of the jurisdiction with an application notice may apply to contest the jurisdiction in relation to the application notice, by virtue of **CPR, r. 6.39(2)**.

SUBMISSION TO JURISDICTION

Acknowledging service does not affect any right the defendant might have to contest the jurisdiction of the court (**CPR, r. 11(3)**). Although the CPR do not address the point explicitly, taking any step in the claim other than acknowledging service and applying under **Part 11** to contest the court's jurisdiction is extremely dangerous. Any such action may constitute a voluntary submission to the jurisdiction of the English courts. It was held in *Monrose Investments Ltd v Orion Nominees Ltd* [2001] CP Rep 109 (applying *Sage v Double A Hydraulics Ltd* (1992) *The Times*, 2 April 1992) that applying for an extension of time for service of a defence, without any reference to an intention to contest the jurisdiction, constituted a submission to the jurisdiction. In *Global Multimedia International Ltd v ARA Media Services* [2006] EWHC 3612 (Ch), [2007] 1 All ER (Comm) 1160, the defendant filed an acknowledgment of service indicating an intention to defend the claim, but not to contest the jurisdiction. The defendant's solicitors also entered into correspondence with solicitors for the claimant over a five-week period seeking an extension of time for service of the defence and entering into discussions as to the merits of the defence. The court held that the test to be applied in considering whether such conduct amounted to a submission was an objective one, and that on the facts this conduct was consistent with an acceptance of the jurisdiction of the English courts. The court advised solicitors who may have little time to decide whether or not to challenge the jurisdiction to tick the box indicating an intention to contest the jurisdiction and then apply for an extension of time under **r. 11(4)**. In *SSQ Europe SA v Johann & Backes OHG* [2002] 1 Lloyd's Rep 465 it was held that service of a defence and counterclaim accompanied by an express challenge to the jurisdiction did not constitute a submission. It did not amount to the unconditional entry of an appearance or unequivocal conduct required by what is now **recast Brussels I Regulation, art. 26** (*Elefanten Schuh GmbH v Jacqmain* (case 150/80) [1981] ECR 1671). In *SMAY Investments Ltd v Sachdev* [2003] EWHC 474 (Ch), [2003] 1 WLR 1973 (followed by *Massey v Glover* [2006] EWHC 2323 (Ch)), it was held that neither (a) ticking both the 'intention to defend' and the 'intention to contest the jurisdiction' boxes on the acknowledgment of service nor (b) obtaining an extension of time for service of the defence and offering undertakings to the court accompanied by an intention to contest the jurisdiction constituted an unequivocal intention to submit to the jurisdiction. Attending before a judge to challenge a freezing injunction obtained without notice does not amount to submitting to the jurisdiction, unless the party agrees to an order regulating his position pending trial (*SMAY Investments Ltd v Sachdev*). See further **16.3**. Participation by a property holder as an applicant in interpleader proceedings does not ordinarily amount to a submission to the jurisdiction because the purpose is to gain the protection of the court from the competing claimants (*Australia v Peacekeeper International FZC UAE* [2008] EWHC 1220 (QB), LTL 9/6/2008). An application under the Bankers' Books Evidence Act 1879 did not amount to a submission to the jurisdiction in *Zumax Nigeria Ltd v First City Monument Bank plc* [2016] EWCA Civ 567, LTL 24/6/2016. The application was made after the defendant had issued an application to challenge the jurisdiction and it did not amount to a wholly unequivocal waiver of the right to challenge.

19.4

Commentary

In *Winkler v Shamoon* [2016] EWHC 217 (Ch), 18 ITELR 818 a **Part 18** request for further information and applications seeking to strike out a claim on the ground that no particulars had been served and to set aside default judgment, were held not to amount to submission. This was in circumstances where it was made clear that the steps being taken were without prejudice to a jurisdictional challenge.

SUSPENSION OF TIME IN MAIN CLAIM

19.5   Making an application to contest the jurisdiction suspends time in the main claim. Thus, a defendant need not file a defence (**CPR, r. 11(9)(a)**); a defendant to a Part 8 claim need not file evidence in opposition (**r. 11(9)(b)**) and in claims in the Commercial or Mercantile Courts where the application has been made before service of the particulars of claim, the claimant need not file particulars of claim (**rr. 58.7** and **59.6**).

ORDERS

19.6   The court may make a declaration that it has no jurisdiction over the claim, or that it will not exercise its jurisdiction. Under **CPR, r. 11(6)**, the order may also:

(a) set aside the claim form;
(b) set aside service of the claim form;
(c) discharge any order made before the claim was commenced or the claim form served;
(d) stay the proceedings.

SECOND ACKNOWLEDGMENT

19.7   Where the court does not make any declaration that it does not have, or should not exercise, jurisdiction, the acknowledgment of service already filed by the defendant will cease to have effect and the defendant should, if it intends to take part in the proceedings, complete and file another form within 14 days or such period as the court may order (**CPR, r. 11(7)**). This acknowledgment will be treated as a submission to the jurisdiction (**r. 11(8)**).

If the defendant wishes to appeal against a decision that the English court has jurisdiction, no further acknowledgment should be filed as this will be treated as a submission, notwithstanding the appeal. To avoid judgment in default being entered against the defendant in these circumstances, an extension of time for acknowledging service pending the appeal should be sought (*Deutsche Bank AG London Branch v Petromena ASA* [2015] EWCA Civ 226, [2015] CP Rep 27). If a further acknowledgment is inadvertently filed, an immediate application should be made to withdraw it supported by evidence under **PD 10, para. 5.4**.

Where the defendant files a further acknowledgement, the court will give directions for the filing and service of the defence, in a Part 7 claim, or for the filing of evidence in a Part 8 claim (**CPR, r. 11(7)(c)**).

In very rare cases the court may hear a summary judgment application immediately following an unsuccessful challenge to the jurisdiction (*Moloobhoy v Kanani* [2013] EWCA Civ 600, LTL 30/5/2013; *Barclays Bank plc v Ente Nazionale di Previdenza ed Assistenza dei Medici e degli Odontoiatri* [2015] EWHC 2857 (Comm), [2015] 2 Lloyd's Rep 527).

Chapter 20   Default Judgment

The following procedural checklists are relevant to this chapter:

Procedural checklist 15   Request for entry of judgment in default
Procedural checklist 16   Application for entry of judgment in default

INTRODUCTION

Failure to file an acknowledgment or a defence within the time limits laid down in the CPR **20.1**
may result under **Part 12** in the claimant entering judgment in default, that is, judgment
without a trial of the claim. In most cases the entry of judgment in default is a purely administrative act, not involving any judicial determination of the merits of the claim. Nevertheless,
a default judgment is a final judgment which can be enforced in the usual way. It is a final
judgment for the purposes of the Housing Act 1996, s. 81 (*Church Commissioners for England v
Koyale Enterprises* (2011) LTL 30/11/2011).

There are two mechanisms under the rules for entering default judgment:

(a) A simple request-for-judgment procedure under **Part 12** is available in money claims
   (**r. 12.4(1)**), which include claims for specified sums, claims for unquantified damages
   and some other types of claim. Under this procedure, judgment is entered over the counter on filing a request for default judgment, without any consideration of the merits of
   the claim. (See **20.4** to **20.7**.) This will apply in the overwhelming majority of cases.
(b) In a claim for a remedy other than a money claim, in a claim only for costs (other than
   fixed costs) and in certain other cases set out in **r. 12.10**, an application for judgment must
   be made using the Part 23 procedure (see **chapter 32**). On an application for the entry of
   a default judgment there will be a hearing and the court will give 'such judgment as it
   appears to the court that the claimant is entitled to on his statement of case'
   (**r. 12.11(1)**). This does not mean that the court will consider the merits of the particular
   claim. Rather, the court's role is to ensure that the claimant is entitled, procedurally, to the
   relief sought (*Football Dataco Ltd v Smoot Enterprises Ltd* [2011] EWHC 973 (Ch), [2011] 1
   WLR 1978). (See **20.8** and **20.9**.)

419

A default judgment obtained using the request procedure in error instead of the application-for-judgment procedure was irregular and capable of being set aside as of right under **r. 13.2** (*Intense Investments Ltd v Development Ventures Ltd* [2005] EWHC 1726 (TCC), [2005] BLR 478 (see further **20.12**).

There is no objection in EU law to issuing a default judgment against a defendant where service has been effected by public notice under local law because the claimant is unable to locate him, provided that all the investigations required by the principles of diligence and good faith to trace the defendant have been undertaken and there is no firm evidence that the defendant is domiciled outside the European Union (*G v de Visser* (case C-292/10) ECLI:EU:C:2012:142).

CASES WHERE DEFAULT JUDGMENT MAY NOT BE ENTERED

20.2   CPR, **r. 12.2**, and PD 12, para. 1.2, provide that judgment in default may not be entered:

(a) on a claim where the Part 8 procedure has been used (see further **13.9**);

(b) on a claim for 'delivery of goods' (i.e. delivery up of goods) subject to an agreement regulated by the Consumer Credit Act 1974; and

(c) in any case where a practice direction provides that a claimant may not obtain a default judgment.

Default judgment cannot be obtained in a possession claim to which **CPR, Part 55** applies (**r. 55.7(4)**) or in a probate claim (**r. 57.10(1)**). In the Admiralty Court the procedure is modified by **r. 61.9** and **PD 61, para. 8.1**. In the Commercial Court, the procedure is modified by **CPR, r. 58.8**, and **PD 58, para. 6**. Default judgment cannot be obtained in arbitration claims under **CPR, Part 62**, because they are brought under the Part 8 procedure (**rr. 62.3(1)** and **62.13(1)**). Nor can default judgment be entered in a case involving a claim for provisional damages, unless the claimant abandons the claim for provisional damages. If the defendant does not file his acknowledgment or defence in time, and the claimant does not wish to abandon the claim for provisional damages, he should apply to the court for directions under **Part 23** (**PD 41A, para. 5.1**).

Where a defendant has made an admission, the correct response is for the claimant to proceed under **CPR, Part 14** (see **chapter 17**), rather than by way of entry of judgment in default.

CONDITIONS FOR ENTERING JUDGMENT IN DEFAULT

20.3   In order to enter judgment in default, the court is required by **CPR, r. 12.3**, and **PD 12, paras 4.1** and **4.2**, to be satisfied:

(a) that the particulars of claim have been served (a certificate of service on the court file will be sufficient evidence where service was effected by the claimant);

(b) that either the defendant has not filed an acknowledgment of service or has not filed a defence, and, in either case, time for doing so has expired;

(c) that the defendant has not satisfied the claim;

(d) that the defendant has not filed or served an admission under **CPR, r. 14.4** or **r. 14.7**, together with a request for time to pay, or an admission of liability in respect of an unspecified claim under **r. 14.6**;

(e) that the defendant has not made an application to strike out the claim or for summary judgment which has not been disposed of; and

(f) where it is sought to enter judgment in default against a child or protected party, that a litigation friend has been appointed.

Point (a) does not have to be satisfied in the Commercial and Mercantile Courts, where default judgment may be entered before the claimant has served particulars of claim (**rr. 58.8** and **59.7**). However, in the Mercantile Courts it is necessary to make an application, rather than a request, for default judgment in these circumstances.

A claimant may not obtain default judgment if notice has been given under **r. 82.21** of a person's intention to make an application for a declaration under the Justice and Security Act 2013, s. 6, in relation to the proceedings, and that application has not been disposed of (**CPR, r. 12.3(3)(d)**).

If the claimant (rather than the court) served the claim form, judgment in default cannot be obtained unless a certificate of service of the claim form has been filed (**r. 6.17**). The purpose of the rule is to ensure there is satisfactory evidence that the claim form has been served, and it was held in *Lombard North Central plc v Hussein* (2011) LTL 7/3/2011 that it would not be in accordance with the overriding objective for a default judgment to be set aside because the certificate of service had been filed one day late, but before the entry of the judgment in default. The court therefore extended time retrospectively under **r. 3.1(2)** in order to validate the certificate of service.

For the purpose of (b) above, the filing of any document purporting to be a defence will prevent the claimant obtaining judgment in default (**PD 12, para. 1.1**). If a purported defence discloses no substantial grounds of defence, the claimant may consider applying to strike it out (see **chapter 33**) or may seek summary judgment (see **chapter 34**).

For the position where service has been effected under Regulation (EC) No. 1393/2007 (the Service Regulation) see **20.19**.

REQUEST FOR DEFAULT JUDGMENT

20.4 The procedure for requesting entry of judgment in default is summarised in **procedural checklist 15**.

By **CPR, r. 12.4**, a claimant may obtain judgment in default by filing a form requesting judgment to be entered where the claim is for:

(a) a specified sum of money (save where the claim is only for costs other than fixed costs);
(b) an amount of money to be decided by the court;
(c) delivery of goods where the claim form gives the defendant the alternative of paying their value; or
(d) any combination of these remedies.

The claimant is not required to give the defendant notice of making a request for default judgment.

Judgment in default can be obtained under **r. 12.4** for a claim which includes a claim or claims for a remedy other than money provided the non-money claims are abandoned in the request form (**r. 12.4(3)**). However, where this is done and default judgment is entered only to be later set aside, the abandoned claim will be restored when judgment is set aside (**r. 13.6**). The court will require a direct and explicit statement that a non-money claim has been abandoned before it permits the entry of default judgment if the claim form includes an application for an injunction. This requirement will not be satisfied simply by completion of the standard wording in the request for judgment form that 'judgment be entered for an amount including costs to be decided by the court' (*Media CAT Ltd v A* [2010] EWPCC 17, BAILII).

The forms used for requesting judgment in default (forms N205A, N205B, N225 and N227A) require the claimant to provide the date of birth (if known) of the defendant, where the defendant is an individual (**PD 12, para. 3.2**). This is because the request procedure applies only where the defendant is an adult. Permission must be sought if the defendant is a child (**CPR, r. 12.10(a)(i)**).

Commentary

Claim for specified sum

20.5   To obtain judgment in default on a claim for a specified sum, the claimant files a request for judgment in form N205A (part of the notice of issue) or N225.

Judgment will be entered for the amount sought in the claim form, plus fixed costs (set out in **table 2** at **CPR, r. 45.4**, and see **chapter 69**). Alternatively, the claimant may give the defendant time to pay or permit the defendant to pay in instalments. This is done by setting out the rate and times of payment acceptable in the request for judgment form. Judgment will then be entered on this basis (**r. 12.5**).

By **r. 12.6**, the default judgment will include interest on claims for specified sums which has accrued due up to the date on which the default judgment was entered, provided that:

(a) full particulars of interest were set out in the particulars of claim;
(b) on a claim for statutory interest, the rate sought is no higher than that payable on judgment debts (currently 8 per cent); and
(c) the request for judgment sets out a calculation of the interest claimed between the date to which interest has been calculated in the claim form, and the date of the request for judgment.

Otherwise, judgment will be entered for interest to be decided by the court (**r. 12.6(2)**).

Claim for unspecified sum

20.6   To obtain judgment in default on a claim for an unspecified sum, the claimant files form N205B (part of the notice of issue) or N227A and judgment will be for an amount to be decided by the court, plus costs (**CPR, r. 12.5(3)**). If the claim is a County Court claim for a specified or unspecified amount of money, receipt of a request from the claimant under **rr. 12.4** and **12.5** for judgment to be entered for an amount to be decided by the court will trigger the automatic transfer of the claim to the preferred hearing centre (this is the hearing centre specified by the claimant in the claim form as the hearing centre to which proceedings should be sent if necessary; see **r. 2.3**). A default judgment on liability for an amount to be decided by the court is conclusive on liability in respect of all matters pleaded. But all questions going to quantification of the damage remain open. Any point may be raised by the defendant at the assessment of damages, provided it is consistent with the judgment on liability. Thus it is not open to the defendant to say that its acts or omissions had not caused any damage, but it could say that its acts or omissions had not caused certain individual items of damage (*Lunnun v Singh* [1999] CPLR 587, followed in *Pugh v Cantor Fitzgerald International* [2001] EWCA Civ 307, *The Times*, 19 March 2001) and approved by the Privy Council in *Strachan v Gleaner Co. Ltd* [2005] UKPC 33, [2005] 1 WLR 3204; see also *New Century Media Ltd v Makhlay* [2013] EWHC 3556 (QB), LTL 29/11/2013). A defendant who wishes to dispute liability must apply to set aside the judgment.

In any case where the court enters judgment for:

(a) an amount to be decided by the court,
(b) the value of goods to be decided by the court, or
(c) interest to be decided by the court,

it will also give any directions it considers appropriate and may allocate the case to a track (**r. 12.7**). However, it will normally only allocate the case (other than in small claims track cases) where there is a substantial dispute between the parties as to the amount payable (**PD 26, para. 12.3**).

The detailed procedure governing the assessment of damages is set out in **PD 26, para. 12**. On the entry of the default judgment, the court will fix an appointment for a disposal hearing, at which it may either give case management directions, or, where it has sufficient information, quantify the claim immediately. Where the value of the claim is below the limit for the small claims track, the court will allocate the case to that track and may treat the disposal hearing as the final hearing of the case (**PD 26, para. 12.4(3)**). The types of case management orders the court may make are set out in **PD 26, para. 12.2**, and include the filing of directions questionnaires and stays for the purpose of ADR. The court may also fix further hearings, and, to enable it to come to a decision on quantum, it might order disclosure, the filing of expert evidence and the exchange of witness statements on the issues which remain live between the parties.

Claims against the Crown

Default judgment in claims against the Crown may now be entered upon filing a request **20.7** for judgment. An application is no longer necessary. However, a request for a default judgment against the Crown must be considered by a Master or District Judge, who must be satisfied that the claim form and particulars of claim have been properly served on the Crown in accordance with the Crown Proceedings Act 1947, s. 18, and **CPR, r. 6.10** (**CPR, r. 12.4(4)**).

APPLICATION FOR DEFAULT JUDGMENT

The procedure for applying for entry of judgment in default is summarised in **procedural** **20.8** **checklist 16**.

CPR, rr. 12.9(1)(b) and **12.10**, and **PD 12, para. 2.3**, specify certain types of claim on which default judgment may only be obtained by making an application under **CPR, Part 23**. Cases where the claimant must make an application are where:

(a) the claim is:
  (i) a claim which consists of or includes any other remedy, rather than simply a money claim (**r. 12.4(2)**);
  (ii) a claim against a child or protected party;
  (iii) a claim in tort by one spouse or civil partner against the other;
  (iv) a claim for costs other than fixed costs;
  (v) for delivery up of goods where the defendant will not be allowed the alternative of paying their value; or

(b) the defendant is:
  (i) a person who has been served with the claim out of the jurisdiction without the court's permission under **rr. 6.32** and **6.33** or is a person domiciled in Northern Ireland, Scotland, another EU state or any other territory to which the Brussels or Lugano Conventions apply;
  (ii) a State;
  (iii) a diplomatic agent who enjoys diplomatic immunity by virtue of the Diplomatic Privileges Act 1964;
  (iv) a person or organisation which enjoys immunity from civil claims under the International Organisations Acts 1968 and 1981.

A claimant who has served a claim form and particulars of claim on a child or protected party cannot apply immediately for default judgment, because no step may be taken in the proceedings (other than issuing and serving a claim form) until a litigation friend has been appointed for the defendant (**CPR, r. 21.3(2)**). Therefore, the correct procedure is to apply for the appointment of a litigation friend under **r. 21.6** before applying for default judgment (**PD 12, para. 4.2(1)**).

Where an acknowledgment is returned by a defendant with the 'I do not intend to defend this claim' box ticked, the proper course for the claimant where there is an admission by the defendant (in this case the admission was made by mistake) is to issue an application for judgment to be entered, rather than a request for judgment. This means that the acknowledgment can be considered by the court, rather than being dealt with as an administrative act (*Northern Rock (Asset Management) plc v Chancellors Associates Ltd* [2011] EWHC 3229 (TCC), [2012] 2 All ER 501).

Commentary

Application procedure

20.9   A notice of application for default judgment must be filed in accordance with the procedure in **CPR, Part 23**. Where the defendant is an individual, the claimant must provide the defendant's date of birth (if known) at para. 10 of the application notice, for use in the registration of judgments (**r. 12.4(2)**). Notice of the application must be given to the defendant, unless the defendant has not acknowledged service and the claim was either served under **r. 6.32** or **r. 6.33** (service out of the jurisdiction for which permission is not required) or is a claim against a foreign State (**r. 12.11(4)**; **PD 12, para. 5.1**).

A defendant who seeks to prevent judgment being entered in default by filing an acknowledgment of service or a defence at or just before the hearing must apply for an extension of time. Whether permission will be granted is a matter for the court's discretion, but normally it will be exercised in favour of extending time where, in the case of late acknowledgment, it is a genuine preliminary to a defence to the claim (*Coll v Tattum* (2001) *The Times,* 3 December 2001, followed in *Boeing Capital Corporation v Wells Fargo Bank Northwest* [2003] EWHC 1364 (Comm), LTL 17/7/2003). Thus a defence which is on its face apparently bona fide and arguable will normally be permitted to be served out of time after the making of an application for judgment in default. The wider question of whether the defence is susceptible to an application for summary judgment will normally be left over to a further application, should the claimant wish to pursue it. In *Lexi Holdings plc v Luqman* [2007] EWHC 2497 (Ch), LTL 26/11/2007, however, the court held that this principle was a rule of thumb rather than an invariable rule. Here, the court entered judgment in default on part of the claim, because not only had the defence been filed late, but it could be shown it was bound to fail on that part. See also *Taylor v Giovani Developers Ltd* [2015] EWHC 328 (Comm), LTL 24/6/2015 and *Almond v Medgolf Properties Ltd* [2015] EWHC 3280 (Comm), LTL 20/5/2015.

There will be a hearing, and judgment will be entered for what it appears to the court that the claimant is entitled to on the statement of case (**CPR, r. 12.11(1)**). The meaning of **r. 12.11(1)** was considered in *Football Dataco Ltd v Smoot Enterprises Ltd* [2011] EWHC 973 (Ch), [2011] 1 WLR 1978. It was held that the rule does not require the court to consider the legal foundation of the cause of action. Rather, the purpose of the requirement is to enable the court to consider the aspects of the case which prompted the need for an application for default judgment instead of a request, e.g. whether the conditions for service out of the jurisdiction have been fully and properly satisfied or what the precise terms of a non-monetary remedy should be. In any event, the existence of an adjourned appeal of a related claim, pending reference to the CJEU, would not be sufficient to prevent entry of the judgment in default.

On an application for default judgment against a child or a protected party or a claim in tort between spouses or civil partners, evidence must be produced to satisfy the court that the claimant is entitled to the judgment claimed (**r. 12.11(3)**; **PD 12, para. 4.2**).

On an application for default judgment in a claim where service was effected under the Civil Jurisdiction and Judgments Act 1982, the Lugano Convention or Regulation (EC) No. 44/2001 or a claim against a foreign State, evidence must establish the points listed in **PD 12, paras 4.3** or **4.4**, respectively, and must be given by affidavit (**para. 4.5**).

TWO OR MORE DEFENDANTS

20.10   If there are two or more defendants, the claimant may obtain a judgment on request against one defendant and proceed with the claim against any other defendants (**CPR, r. 12.8(1)**). However, where a claimant applies for default judgment against some defendants and not others, the court will only enter default judgment where the claim can be dealt with separately from the claim against other defendants (**r. 12.8(2)**). Otherwise, the court must deal with the application for default judgment at the same time as it disposes of the claim against the other defendants (**r. 12.8(2)(b)**).

Rule 12.8 enables the court to deal with the complications that can arise from the common law doctrine of election, whereby judgment against one defendant severally liable with another defendant can discharge the other defendant's liability (*Morel Brothers and Co. Ltd v Earl of Westmoreland* [1903] 1 KB 64). The doctrine has been abolished in the case of joint liability by the Civil Liability (Contribution) Act 1978, s. 3. Entry of a default judgment against one defendant in a case which has been pleaded on a number of different bases does not necessarily amount to an election, because the judgment is entered without an investigation of the merits (*Pendleton v Westwater* [2001] EWCA Civ 1841, LTL 28/11/2001). This approach has been confirmed by the Privy Council in *Balgobin v South West Regional Health Authority* [2012] UKPC 11, [2013] 1 AC 582. For an unequivocal election to have been made, there must be a decision by the person making the election to follow one remedy out of a range of two or more and that choice must be communicated to the other side in a way which will make it clear that there has been a deliberate preference of the chosen alternative over any other. It was not correct to say that the entry of a default judgment could never amount to an unequivocal election, and it was relevant that the judgment had been obtained without any consideration of the merits. The court should be slow to regard the entry of a default judgment as constituting an unequivocal election where, as in this case, it was not intended to be the abandonment of a primary cause of action.

Rule 12.8 is not confined to cases involving truly alternative claims. It applies to any case where the effect of entering a default judgment would be that the claim could not be pursued separately against another defendant (*Crown Aluminium Ltd v Northern and Western Insurance Co. Ltd* [2011] EWHC 277 (TCC), [2011] BLR 355).

Having obtained the default judgment, a claimant may enforce it against only some defendants, save where it is for the possession of land or delivery of goods. Here, the defendant may enforce only after obtaining judgment against all defendants, or where the court gives its permission (**r. 12.8(3)**).

SETTING ASIDE A DEFAULT JUDGMENT

Principles upon which a default judgment will be set aside

A defendant against whom judgment in default has been entered may apply for it to be varied or set aside under **CPR, Part 13**. 20.11

A judgment which has been entered wrongly (as defined in the CPR) must be set aside by the court. In other cases, the court has a discretion to set the judgment aside and it will normally require the defendant to show a real prospect of successfully defending the claim before it will do so.

In any case where the court sets aside a default judgment, it may attach conditions, such as the payment of money into court (**r. 3.1(3)**). See **20.21**.

Where the default judgment was entered wrongly

The court must set aside any judgment entered wrongly (**CPR, r. 13.2**). The phrase 'entered wrongly' is defined precisely under the rules. By **r. 13.2(a)** to (c), it is limited to the following cases: 20.12

(a) time for acknowledging service, or for serving a defence (as the case may be) had not expired by the time the default judgment was entered;

(b) a summary judgment application or an application to strike out the claim made by the defendant was pending when the default judgment was entered; or

(c) the defendant had satisfied the whole claim or, on a money claim, filed an admission and a request for time to pay at the time the default judgment was entered.

It is, therefore, a condition for entering judgment in default that service has been effected. Thus, judgment was set aside as of right under **r. 13.2(a)** in *Credit Agricole Indosuez v Unicof Ltd* [2003] EWHC 77 (Comm), LTL 4/2/2003. The claimant purported to serve the claim form by leaving it with the defendant's company secretary in Kenya, whereas service in Kenya had to be by leaving the claim form at the company's registered office. In *Norcross v Georgallides* [2015] EWHC 4804 (Comm), LTL 21/5/2014 it was held that service of the claim form at the defendant's usual or last known address was not good service under **r. 6.9** where the claimant had reason to believe that the defendant no longer lived there. Accordingly, the defendant was entitled to have the judgment set aside as of right under **r. 13.2**. For a full discussion of the rules on service within and out of the jurisdiction see **chapters 15** and **16**.

Time for acknowledging service or filing a defence does not run for the purposes of **r. 13.2(a)** during the period of a stay (*Roundstone Nurseries Ltd v Stephenson Holdings Ltd* [2009] EWHC 1431 (TCC), [2009] 5 Costs LR 787).

A default judgment obtained using the request procedure in error instead of the application for judgment procedure was irregular and capable of being set aside as of right under **r. 13.2** (*Intense Investments Ltd v Development Ventures Ltd* [2005] EWHC 1762 (TCC), [2005] BLR 478). It is submitted that this decision ignores the constraints of **r. 13.2** which specifies precisely the circumstances in which the court must set aside a default judgment. These do not include using the wrong procedure to enter the default judgment.

What about the case where a judgment has been entered incorrectly, in circumstances other than those set out at **r. 13.2**? In *Northern Rock (Asset Management) plc v Chancellors Associates Ltd* [2011] EWHC 3229 (TCC), [2012] 2 All ER 501, an acknowledgment was returned to the claimant with the 'I do not intend to defend this claim' box ticked in error. The claimant submitted a request for judgment form to court instead of making an application for judgment in default, and, incorrectly, judgment was entered by the court as an administrative act without any judicial consideration of the case. The circumstances clearly fell outside the situations envisaged by **r. 13.2**. The court held that it had jurisdiction under **r. 3.1(2)(m)** to set the judgment aside if it was fair and just to do so, on the grounds that the overriding objective would normally demand that a judgment should be set aside, where it had been obtained irregularly on the basis of an obviously mistaken admission, where there was a properly arguable defence, where the application to set aside was brought reasonably promptly and where there was no prejudice caused by the setting aside.

WHERE THE DEFAULT JUDGMENT WAS NOT ENTERED WRONGLY

20.13   The court has a discretion to set aside a default judgment which was not entered wrongly. It may exercise its discretion if (**CPR, r. 13.3(1)**):

(a) the defendant has a real prospect of successfully defending the claim; or
(b) it appears to the court that there is some other good reason why:
    (i) the judgment should be set aside or varied; or
    (ii) the defendant should be allowed to defend the claim.

In considering whether to set aside or vary a judgment entered under **Part 12**, the matters to which the court must have regard include whether the person seeking to set aside the judgment made an application to do so promptly (**r. 13.3(2)**). The principles in **r. 13.3** also apply to any default judgment that is made at a hearing without notice to the defendant, and such a judgment cannot be set aside as of right, even though the defendant was not properly served with notice of the hearing, as this would be contrary to the overriding objective (*De Ferranti v Execuzen Ltd* [2013] EWCA Civ 592, LTL 10/6/2013; *Nelson v Clearsprings (Management) Ltd* [2006] EWCA Civ 1252, [2007] 1 WLR 962).

Discretion to set aside

In *Rahman v Rahman* (1999) LTL 26/11/99 the court considered the nature of the discretion to set **20.14** aside a default judgment under **CPR, r. 13.3**. It concluded that the elements the judge had to consider were the nature of the defence, the period of delay (i.e. why the application to set aside had not been made before), any prejudice the claimant was likely to suffer if the default judgment was set aside, and the overriding objective.

In *Thorn plc v Macdonald* [1999] CPLR 660 the Court of Appeal approved the following principles:

(a) while the length of any delay by the defendant must be taken into account, any pre-action delay is irrelevant;

(b) any failure by the defendant to provide a good explanation for the delay is a factor to be taken into account, but is not always a reason to refuse to set aside;

(c) the primary considerations are whether there is a defence with a real prospect of success, and that justice should be done; and

(d) prejudice (or the absence of it) to the claimant also has to be taken into account.

It appears that an application to set aside a default judgment is a decision about whether or not to relieve a party from a sanction imposed, or more accurately, impliedly imposed, for its failure to comply with a rule, and so the principles in **r. 3.9(1)** must be considered in applications under **r. 13.3** (*Mid-East Sales Ltd v United Engineering and Trading Co. (Pvt) Ltd* [2014] EWHC 1457 (Comm), [2014] 2 All ER (Comm) 623). This is the so-called implied sanction doctrine, which is considered at **48.12**.

How the doctrine should be applied has proved controversial. Christopher Clarke LJ in *Regione Piemonte v Dexia Crediop SpA* [2014] EWCA Civ 1298, LTL 9/10/2014 at [40] said the considerations relevant under **r. 3.9** were to be taken into account, at least on the question of whether the application to set aside was made promptly. In *Blakemores LDP v Scott* [2015] EWCA Civ 999, [2016] CP Rep 1, at [56]–[61], the Court of Appeal first considered whether there was a defence with a real prospect of success under **r. 13.3(1)(a)**, then considered the three-stage test from *Denton v T. H. White Ltd* [2014] EWCA Civ 906, [2014] 1 WLR 3926 (see **48.32**) with what could be described as a light touch. Important considerations were that there was a 36-day delay in making the application to set aside, but this was explained by the claim arising unexpectedly, the defendant's desire to trace the solicitor previously acting for him (this was a dispute about a solicitor's fees), and unsuccessful attempts to secure fee remission. The default judgment was set aside. *Gentry v Miller* [2016] EWCA Civ 141, [2016] 1 WLR 2696 attempted to reconcile the two tests as follows:

(a) The court must first consider the express requirements for setting aside in **r. 13.3**.

(b) Secondly, the court must apply the three stages of *Denton v T. H. White Ltd* (seriousness and significance of the breach; reasons for the default; all the circumstances of case, including factors (a) and (b) from **r. 3.9(1)**).

According to *Gentry v Miller*, at stage 1 of *Denton*, in applications to set aside default judgments, seriousness etc. relates to the initial delay in acknowledging service or filing the defence. This is the opposite conclusion to that in *Blakemores LDP v Scott*, where the 36-day delay was in issuing the application to set aside, which was analysed at [60] in relation to stage 2, which addresses the reasons for the breach at stage 1.

Again according to *Gentry v Miller*, promptness in making the application to set aside is both:

(a) an express requirement under **r. 13.3(2)**, being one of the factors that the court must take into account when considering discretionary setting aside of default judgments; and

(b) something that needs to be considered as part of all the circumstances of the case at stage 3 of the *Denton* principles.

There are problems with all these authorities. *Regione Piemonte v Dexia Crediop SpA* was an application for permission to appeal, so is not strictly binding. Nor is *Blakemores LDP v Scott*, because the application of the *Denton* principles was conceded by counsel (see [58]). *Gentry v Miller* appears to be a binding Court of Appeal authority. It was cited in argument in *Mohun-Smith v TBO Investments Ltd* [2016] EWCA Civ 403, [2016] 1 WLR 2919 on the related procedure of setting aside judgment after non-attendance under r. 39.3 (see 62.3 and 62.7) (which also arose in *Gentry v Miller* itself), but was not even mentioned in the judgments. The *Denton* principles were not applied in *Mohun-Smith* even though *Denton* was referred to, but for a different point. There are also doctrinal problems with applying the implied sanctions doctrine to applications under r. 13.3. Grafting relief from sanctions principles on to applications to set aside default judgments adds a layer of unnecessary complication (and expense) to these applications, and is contrary to the usual principle that rules governing a specific case (here r. 13.3) displace general rules (here r. 3.9). It is also contrary to the Privy Council set-aside decisions referred to at 48.12. Nevertheless, the most authoritative decision on the relevance of the implied sanctions doctrine to applications to set aside default judgments is *Gentry v Miller*.

The overriding objective set out in r. 1.1 also applies to applications under r. 13.3 (*Samara v MBI Partners UK Ltd* [2014] EWHC 563 (QB), [2014] 3 Costs LR 457).

The Privy Council has held in *Strachan v Gleaner Co. Ltd* [2005] UKPC 33, [2005] 1 WLR 3204, that the court is not deprived of its jurisdiction to set aside a default judgment by the fact that final judgment on quantum has been entered and damages assessed. These factors are, however, relevant to the exercise of the court's discretion in deciding whether to set aside the default judgment as an aspect of, but separate from, the question of delay.

In *Continuity Promotions Ltd v O'Connor's Nenagh Shopping Centre Ltd* [2005] EWHC 3462 (QB), [2006] All ER (D) 39 (Feb), the court considered the impact on the exercise of its jurisdiction to set aside a default judgment of the fact that it did not have jurisdiction over the claim under Regulation (EC) 44/2001. It held that only in an exceptional case should an English court decline to set aside a default judgment entered against a defendant without jurisdiction. However, it declined to do so here, holding that the fact that the defendant had made no application to challenge the jurisdiction despite being advised by solicitors and the delay in bringing the application to set aside amounted to exceptional circumstances.

In *Law v St Margarets Insurance Ltd* [2001] EWCA Civ 30, LTL 18/1/2001, the Court of Appeal allowed judgment in default to be set aside despite the defendant's solicitors' procedural errors in failing to file an acknowledgment of service and in failing to ensure that the statement of truth in relation to the evidence in support of the application was signed by the right person. The overriding objective required that the default judgment be set aside in order to enable the merits of the defence to be determined.

Making the application promptly

20.15   In *Mullock v Price* [2009] EWCA Civ 1222, [2010] CP Rep 10, the Court of Appeal held that 'promptly' in **CPR, r. 13.3(2)**, is an ordinary English word with a plain and obvious meaning. It adopted the definition given in *Regency Rolls Ltd v Carnall* (2000) LTL 16/10/2000, that 'promptly' means to act 'with all reasonable celerity'.

It is clear from the wording of r. 13.3 that promptness is not an absolute requirement for the making of an order withdrawing a default judgment. But it is also clear that an application to set aside default judgment may fail simply on the ground of significant delay in bringing the application, notwithstanding the existence of a defence with a realistic prospect of success (*Standard Bank plc v Agrinvest International Inc.* [2010] EWCA Civ 1400, [2010] 2 CLC 886). Similarly, in *Mullock v Price* [2009] EWCA Civ 1222, [2010] CP Rep 10, the existence of a defence with a real prospect of success did not prevent the failure of the application to set aside judgment. The obligation in **r. 13.3(2)** to bring the application promptly is personal to the defendant *Hussain v Birmingham City Council* [2005] EWCA Civ 1570, LTL 25/11/2005. In *Mullock v Price*, the defendant had delayed for two years in making an application to set aside judgment, in the mistaken belief that his insurers were dealing with the claim. The defendant could not hide behind his representatives' inaction to excuse this period of delay. *Samara v MBI Partners UK Ltd* [2014] EWHC 563 (QB), 164 (7598) NLJ 18 is an example of the implied sanction doctrine. The court refused to set aside a default judgment where the defendant waited 15 months to apply to set it aside and had only done so once the claimant tried to enforce it. In making this decision, the court applied *Mitchell v News Group Newspapers Ltd* [2013] EWCA Civ 1537, [2014] 1 WLR 795, and noted that it was clear that under the new stricter regime in force since 1 April 2013, the need for promptness was given even greater significance than it had been given previously and that relief would be granted much more sparingly. A seven-month delay in applying to set aside was held to be serious and substantial in *Regione Piemonte v Dexia Crediop SpA* [2014] EWCA Civ 1298, LTL 9/10/2014.

In unusual circumstances, though, delay may not necessarily be fatal. In *Hussain v Birmingham City Council* [2005] EWCA Civ 1570, LTL 25/11/2005, the Court of Appeal held that the defendant had not acted promptly in making an application to set aside a default judgment. But it considered it appropriate for the judgment to be set aside on the grounds that the defendant had a real prospect of successfully defending the claim and full participation by the defendant at trial was necessary in order to determine where liability lay between a number of defendants. Similarly, in *Berezovsky v Russian Television and Radio Broadcasting Co.* [2009] EWHC 1733 (QB), LTL 20/7/2009, the court accepted that the defendant had not acted promptly but still set the judgment aside, holding that the delay was outweighed by the need to avoid any suggestion of a 'cover-up' and to investigate the defence fully, which constituted a 'good reason' under **r. 13.3(1)(b)**. In *Wuxi Suntech Power Co. Ltd v Tittmann Solar GmbH* [2011] EWPCC 17, LTL 15/7/2011, the court went further still and allowed default judgment to be set aside despite a delay of six months in making the application, for three months of which there was no proper explanation. It did this despite sufficiently serious reservations about the existence of a defence with a reasonable prospect of success that it made the order conditional upon the defendant paying into court a sum by way of security for the claimant's costs. *Mid-East Sales Ltd v United Engineering and Trading Co. (Pvt) Ltd* [2014] EWHC 1457 (Comm), [2014] 2 All ER (Comm) 623, is another example of the court applying the implied sanction doctrine. Nevertheless, an application to set aside a default judgment was successful despite a seven-month delay on the part of the defendant, largely because there were arguable defences.

If the investigations for the evidence required for an application to set aside are not straightforward, such as where evidence has to be sought from a distant country, an application may be prompt within the meaning of **r. 13.3(2)** even if it is issued some weeks after the default judgment (*Shandong Chenming Paper Holding Ltd v Saga Forest Carriers Intl AS* [2008] EWHC 1055 (Comm), LTL 16/5/2008).

In *Priestley v Dunbar and Co.* [2015] EWHC 987 (Ch), LTL 3/6/2015, it was held that the correct approach is to consider whether the application had been made promptly. If the court concludes it has not been, it should then consider when the application should have been made, otherwise the court has no means of deciding whether the delay is significant. It is necessary to work out the extent of the delay in order to apply the three-stage test in *Denton v T. H. White Ltd* [2014] EWCA Civ 906, [2014] 1 WLR 3926. Although in that case there was a delay of approximately eight weeks in applying to set aside the judgment, when weighed against all the circumstances of the case, including the fact that the defence was arguable and the value of the claim was high, it would have been disproportionate to refuse to set aside the default judgment. Where the delay is occasioned by a conscious decision to ignore the proceedings, it is unlikely that a judgment will be set aside (see *Avanesov v TOO Shymkentpivo* [2015] EWHC 394 (Comm), [2015] 2 Costs LO 289).

Reasonable prospect of success

20.16   The wording of **CPR, r. 13.3(1)(a)**, mirrors the test established in *Alpine Bulk Transport Co. Inc. v Saudi Eagle Shipping Co. Inc.* [1986] 2 Lloyd's Rep 221, that the defendant must have a case with a reasonable prospect of success, and it is not enough to show a merely arguable defence. The approach to be taken by the court was summarised by Moore-Bick J in *International Finance Corporation v Utexafrica Sprl* [2001] CLC 1361: 'A person who holds a regular judgment, even a default judgment, has something of value and in order to avoid injustice he should not be deprived of it without good reason. Something more than a merely arguable case is needed to tip the balance of justice in favour of setting the judgment aside ... the expression "realistic prospect of success" in this context means a case which carries a degree of conviction.' In *E. D. and F. Man Liquid Products Ltd v Patel* [2003] EWCA Civ 472, [2003] CPLR 384, the Court of Appeal confirmed that the test is the same as the test for summary judgment. The only significant difference is that in a summary judgment application the burden of proof rests on the claimant to show that the defendant has no real prospect of success whereas in an application to set aside a default judgment it is for the defendant to show that his defence has a real prospect of success. For this reason it might be harder for a defendant to succeed in an application to set aside than to resist an application for summary judgment. The test was considered in detail in *Swain v Hillman* [2001] 1 All ER 91 (see **34.10**).

In *Lloyds Investment (Scandinavia) Ltd v Ager-Hansen* (2001) LTL 7/11/2001 a default judgment was set aside on the ground that the defendant had a real prospect of success. Although the claimant had raised serious questions about the defendant's credibility, no finding could be made without oral evidence and cross-examination.

Where summary judgment had been refused against defendants who appeared on the application but default judgment had been entered against a defendant who did not appear, the court subsequently set aside the default judgment, because there had been no examination of the evidence against that defendant. Given that the question of a real prospect of successfully defending the claim had been determined in favour of the defendants who had filed defences, it would have been wrong to come to a different conclusion in relation to the defendant who had not participated (*Huntingdon Life Sciences Ltd v Stop Huntingdon Animal Cruelty* [2004] EWHC 3145 (QB), LTL 11/11/2004).

The privilege against self-incrimination does not afford an excuse for failing to serve a defence with a realistic prospect of success, and will not provide grounds for setting aside a judgment in default (*Versailles Trade Finance Ltd v Clough* [2001] EWCA Civ 1509, [2002] CP Rep 8).

There was a real prospect of success in establishing a time-bar defence where there was some documentary evidence in support of an argument that the cause of action accrued just outside the relevant time limit (*Shandong Chenming Paper Holding Ltd v Saga Forest Carriers Intl AS* [2008] EWHC 1055 (Comm) LTL 16/5/2008).

The provisions governing default judgments in Admiralty claims are in **CPR, r. 61.9**. Although **r. 61.9(5)** gives the court power to set aside a default judgment, it does not prescribe the criteria. It was held in *The Selby Paradigm* [2004] EWHC 1804 (Admlty), [2004] 2 Lloyd's Rep 714, that the burden on the defendant is to show that it has a real prospect of success in defending the claim, and is not akin to that imposed on an appellant.

Some other good reason

20.17   There is no definition of what constitutes 'some other good reason' under **CPR, r. 13.3(1)(b)**. However, the authorities establish that the parties' conduct may be relevant (*Hart Investments*

Ltd v Fidler [2006] EWHC 2857 (TCC), [2007] BLR 30). In *Roundstone Nurseries Ltd v Stephenson Holdings Ltd* [2009] EWHC 1431 (TCC), [2009] 5 Costs LR 787, the court held that a claimant's unreasonable conduct in taking advantage of a mutual failure to extend a stay in order to enter judgment in default was a good reason under **r. 13.3(1)(b)** for judgment to be set aside. In the same case, Coulson J also commented that a claimant should not enter judgment in default because he is technically entitled to, where he knows the defendant has a good defence and so would be entitled to set judgment aside. A claimant who enters judgment in these circumstances is at risk of an adverse costs order on the application to set aside. *Roundstone* has been followed in *APP Wholesale plc v Adlink UK Ltd* [2012] EWHC 1806 (QB), LTL 14/5/2012. Here, the defendant posted an acknowledgment of service to the court, but it was never received. The claimant entered judgment in default without notice to the defendant, even though it knew (or could have checked by a simple phone call) that there was a substantial dispute between the parties. Entering judgment in these circumstances was a waste of time and money and was set aside under **r. 13.3(1)(b)**.

In *Berezovsky v Russian Television and Radio Broadcasting Co.* [2009] EWHC 1733 (QB), LTL 20/7/2009, the court set aside the judgment where, although it was not established on the evidence that the defendant had a case with a real prospect of success, it did consider that there was a defence which was not bound to fail and the nature of the allegations (involving fraud and vindication of the claimant's reputation) provided 'some other good reason' for allowing the defendant to defend the claim. However, this decision should not be read as creating a rule that in the event of serious allegations there must be a trial. The existence of such allegations is a relevant consideration, but must be regarded in the light of the other factors in the case. Where the defendant was unable to establish a realistic prospect of successfully defending the claim, had not taken steps open to him to ask for documents so as to be able to investigate and challenge the claim, and it was unlikely that he would be able to defend the claim even if he were able to go into the witness box to deny the allegations made against him, judgment should not be set aside (*Defty v Hirani* [2012] EWHC 1812, LTL 25/5/2012).

In *Latmar Holdings Corp v Media Focus Ltd* [2012] EWHC 262 (Comm), LTL 13/12/2012, the court exercised its discretion under **r. 13.3(1)(b)** to set a judgment aside on the grounds that although the defendants did not reach the threshold required for **r. 13.3(1)(a)** of being able to show a defence with a realistic prospect of success, nevertheless the allegations involved serious allegations of fraud and the value of the claim was relatively large. Further, the period of delay was not inordinate.

In *Messer Griesheim GmbH v Goyal MG Gases Pvt Ltd* [2006] EWHC 79 (Comm), [2006] 1 CLC 283, there was a good reason for setting aside a default judgment under **r. 13.3(1)(b)** where the default judgment was not capable of being enforced in the foreign jurisdiction in which the defendant's assets were located, and so the claim would effectively be lost. As the defendant had no prospect of successfully defending the claim, the court entered summary judgment instead, which was capable of enforcement. Another good reason for setting aside under **r. 13.3(1)(b)** was where a judgment in default had been entered which had the effect of discharging an injunction and the master who had ordered the entry of the default judgment had no power under **PD 2B, para. 2.2**, to discharge the injunction (*Richmond v Burch* [2006] EWHC 921 (Ch), [2007] 1 All ER 658).

The failure by the claimant to include a response pack with the particulars of claim is a matter which may result in a default judgment being set aside under **r. 13.3(1)(b)**, even where the defendant has not shown that they have a reasonable prospect of defending the claim. The requirement to serve the response pack, which includes the acknowledgment of service and guidance for the defendant as to how to proceed next, is an important omission. In *Rajval Construction Ltd v Bestville Properties Ltd* [2010] EWCA Civ 1621, [2011] CILL 2994; *Gulf International Bank BSC v Ekttitab Holding Co. KSCC* (2010) LTL 15/11/2010 **and** *Erol v Global Fashion Links Ltd* [2014]

EWHC 4687 (IPEC), LTL 10/12/2014 the default judgment was set aside under **r. 13.3(1)(b)** on the ground that no response pack had been filed regardless of whether the defendant could show it had a reasonable prospect of defence. However, setting aside a default judgment under **r. 13.3(1)(b)** is a matter of discretion, and so other factors, such as delay and the strength of any possible defence, will weigh in the court's decision. In *Henriksen v Pires* [2011] EWCA Civ 1720, LTL 14/2/2012, the Court of Appeal held that the failure of the claimant to include a response pack did not justify the making of an order under **r. 13.3**. In this case, the failure to include a response pack emerged as a possible ground upon which to seek to set aside judgment only very late in the day and the merits of the defence were not sufficiently strong to justify setting aside the judgment.

In *Henriksen v Pires* [2011] EWCA Civ 1720, LTL 14/2/2012, the Court of Appeal also considered the effect on the default judgment of the claimant's failure to file a certificate of service under **r. 6.17(2)**. It held that this was a free-standing requirement, independent of **r. 12.3**. The failure to file a certificate of service would not lead to a mandatory order setting aside the default judgment but it could constitute a good reason under **r. 13.3(1)(b)** why the court might set aside judgment. Where, as here, the claimant had filed an affidavit of service which contained all the information required of a certificate of service, even if it was not in the relevant practice form (N215), the defendant had not suffered any prejudice and it was not appropriate to make an order setting aside judgment.

In *Paseana Ltd v Lextrex Holdings Ltd* [2010] EWCA Civ 1539, LTL 30/11/2010, the Court of Appeal set aside a default judgment even though there was evidence that the defendants had put forward inaccurate or dishonest statements about the circumstances in which the default judgments had come to be entered. There had been no delay in making the application and the defendants had a defence with a real prospect of success. Applying the overriding objective, it was in the interests of justice that the defendants should be given an opportunity to defend the claim.

Defendant unaware that service has been deemed to have occurred

20.18   Once it is proved (such as by a certificate of service) that proceedings have been served by one of the methods prescribed by the CPR, service is deemed to take effect on the date laid down by **r. 6.14**, and evidence to prove the contrary is not admissible (*Anderton v Clwyd County Council (No. 2)* [2002] EWCA Civ 933, [2002] 1 WLR 3174). Where a default judgment has been entered after the expiry of 14 days from the deemed date of service in a case where the defendant did not in fact receive the proceedings, setting aside is subject to the court's discretion rather than as of right (*Godwin v Swindon Borough Council* [2001] EWCA Civ 1478, [2002] 1 WLR 997). The decisions in *Anderton v Clwyd County Council (No. 2)* and *Godwin v Swindon Borough Council* concerned the effect of the deeming provisions on a claimant who delays serving a claim form until the end of the period for service. However, in *Akram v Adam* [2004] EWCA Civ 1601, [2005] 1 WLR 2762, the Court of Appeal looked at the position of a defendant who says that he had no notice of the proceedings at all until after he heard of the default judgment. The court dismissed the contention that a defendant in this situation should be entitled to have the judgment set aside as of right on the grounds that he had received no notification of the proceedings and was therefore a stranger to them. It also held that the deeming provisions on service in the CPR did not contravene the European Convention on Human Rights, **art. 6** in the **Human Rights Act 1998, sch. 1**. It confirmed that a judgment entered on a claim served in accordance with the rules, but of which the defendant had no notice, has not been entered wrongly and the defendant can have it set aside only on the grounds specified in **CPR, r. 13.3(1)** (see **20.13**). Such a defendant will therefore either have to show a defence with a real prospect of success, or rely on non-service as 'some other good reason' for setting aside the judgment. According to May LJ in *Godwin v Swindon Borough Council* at [49] this may arise where a defendant would have paid instead of having an embarrassing judgment entered, and it may give grounds for departing from the usual rule of the defendant being ordered to pay the costs thrown away (see **table 68.1** at **68.29**). In *Manx Electricity Authority v J P Morgan Chase Bank* [2002] EWHC 867 (Comm), LTL 16/5/2002, the court agreed that a judgment entered in this situation should be set aside under **r. 13.3(1)(b)**. See also *De Ferranti v Execuzen Ltd* [2013] EWCA Civ 592, LTL 10/6/2013, where the court held that an application to set aside a judgment in default (against a defendant who did not have notice of the hearing) must be approached by applying the factors in **r. 13.3**. Doubts about the effectiveness of alternative service in the circumstances of the case appear to have been treated as a factor in setting aside a default judgment in *Black Arrow Finance Ltd v Orderdaily Co. Ltd* [2002] EWCA Civ 289, LTL 31/1/2002.

Setting aside under the Service Regulation

Where service is effected under Regulation (EC) No. 1393/2007 (the Service Regulation), **20.19** judgment in default cannot be given until it is established that service was effected by a method prescribed by the internal law of the receiving State or that the documents were actually delivered to the defendant or to the defendant's residence by another method provided by the Service Regulation and that, in either case, the defendant had sufficient time to defend the claim (**art. 19**). See **16.70**.

Procedure

A defendant must apply for judgment in default to be varied or set aside under the Part 23 **20.20** procedure (see **chapter 32**). An application to set aside a default judgment which has not been entered wrongly must be supported by evidence (**CPR, r. 13.4(3)**). Commonly, a draft defence is attached to a witness statement in support of the application.

Where the claim is for a specified sum of money, has not been started in a specialist list and the judgment is entered against an individual in a court which is not the defendant's home court (defined in **r. 2.3(1)**), the court will automatically transfer the application there (**r. 13.4(1)**).

If the claim is for a specified amount of money, has been started in the County Court Money Claims Centre, is made against a defendant who is not an individual, and has not already been sent to a County Court hearing centre, an application by a defendant to set aside or vary a default judgment will be sent to the preferred hearing centre as defined in **r. 2.3** (**r. 13.4(1B)**). Any further correspondence should be sent to, and any further requests should be made at, the hearing centre to which the claim has been sent (**r. 13.4(1C)**).

Setting aside on conditions

The court may attach conditions to an order to set aside judgment (**CPR, r. 3.1(3)**). In most **20.21** cases the defaulting defendant will be ordered to pay the claimant's costs thrown away. In appropriate cases, the court may also require the defendant to pay money into court to await the final disposal of the claim. Such a condition is commonly imposed where, although the defendant has satisfied the court that it has a defence with a real prospect of success, the defence is 'shadowy' (see **34.34**). However, conditions imposed on setting aside a default judgment are not intended to punish the defendant but to ensure that justice is achieved between the parties (*Hussain v Birmingham City Council* [2005] EWCA Civ 1570, LTL 25/11/2005). Security for costs should not be imposed as a condition unless the requirements in **r. 25.13** are satisfied (*Camden London Borough Council v Makers UK Ltd* [2009] EWHC 605 (TCC), 124 Con LR 32). Nor should the court impose a condition barring the defendant from exercising its statutory right to make use of the adjudication process under the Housing Grants, Construction and Regeneration Act 1996 (see **34.20**) save in exceptional cases (*Camden London Borough Council v Makers UK Ltd*).

Commentary

DEFENDANT NOT SERVED

20.22   The provision formerly in CPR, r. 13.5, which placed a duty on a claimant who had entered default judgment, but subsequently became aware that the particulars of claim had not reached the defendant before judgment was entered, to request that the default judgment be set aside or apply for directions, was revoked as from 30 June 2004. It was inconsistent with the policy that there is an irrevocable presumption of service on the date deemed in what are now **rr. 6.14** and **6.26** (r. 6.7 before 1 October 2008) on proof of service by one of the methods permitted by **Part 6**. See **15.36** and *Anderton v Clwyd County Council (No. 2)* [2002] EWCA Civ 933, [2002] 1 WLR 3174.

An application to set aside a judgment entered after a trial which a defendant, who has been served and so is properly a party to the proceedings, failed to attend is not governed by **Part 13** at all. It should be made under **r. 39.3(5)**. If the defendant did not attend a trial because he was not properly served with notice of it, **r. 39.3(5)** does not apply. In such a case, the defendant is not entitled to have the judgment set aside as of right. Instead the court should approach the application with **r. 13.3** in mind and consider whether the judgment should be set aside in accordance with those provisions (*Nelson v Clearsprings (Management) Ltd* [2006] EWCA Civ 1252, [2007] 1 WLR 962; *De Ferranti v Execuzen Ltd* [2013] EWCA Civ 592, LTL 10/6/2013) (see **62.4**).

DEFAULT JUDGMENT ON AN ADDITIONAL CLAIM

20.23   There are special rules which apply in relation to entering judgment in default on an additional claim. These are dealt with in **29.10**.

PART F

Solicitors

Chapter 21   Acting by a Solicitor

INTRODUCTION

This chapter deals with a number of issues that arise when litigation is conducted, as it often **21.1**
is, by solicitors. A solicitor is an officer of the court, and is therefore under certain duties to
the court and subject to the disciplinary jurisdiction of the High Court. Once proceedings
are issued by a solicitor on behalf of a client, or acknowledged by a solicitor on behalf of a
client, the solicitor will be regarded as being on the record. All further steps taken on behalf
of that client should be taken by that solicitor, and all further documents served on that client
should be served on that solicitor, until formal notice of change has been served. While on
the record the solicitor will have apparent authority (and often actual authority) to take all
steps on behalf of the client, who will be bound by the action taken. A number of other topics
are also considered.

OFFICER OF THE COURT

The Solicitors Act 1974, s. 50, provides as follows: **21.2**

(1) Any person duly admitted as a solicitor shall be an officer of the Senior Courts.
(2) Subject to the provisions of this Act, the High Court, the Crown Court and the Court of
    Appeal respectively, or any division or judge of those courts, may exercise the same jurisdiction
    in respect of solicitors as any one of the superior courts of law or equity from which the Senior
    Courts were constituted might have exercised immediately before the passing of the Supreme
    Court of Judicature Act 1873 in respect of any solicitor, attorney or proctor admitted to
    practise there.
(3) An appeal shall lie to the Court of Appeal from any order made against a solicitor by the High
    Court or the Crown Court in the exercise of its jurisdiction in respect of solicitors under
    subsection (2).

As officers of the court, solicitors are under duties not to mislead the court, to bring to the
court's attention authorities relevant to the case which may go against their clients, and
various other duties conveniently summarised in *Cordery on Solicitors*, 9th edn.
(London: Butterworths, 1995) and the SRA Code of Conduct 2011. Counsel owe similar
duties under the Code of Conduct of the Bar of England and Wales. Solicitors and counsel
must, moreover, be regarded as owing a duty to assist the court in achieving the overriding
objective by reason of **CPR, r. 1.3** (which in fact places the duty on the legal representatives'

clients), and the fact that solicitors are officers of the court. A solicitor who receives a request from another party for pre-action disclosure of its records has no obligation to explain why electronic or paper records have been destroyed. The solicitor's only obligation is to tell the truth (*Beckett Bemrose and Hagen Solicitors v Future Mortgages Ltd* [2010] EWHC 1997 (QB), LTL 12/7/2010).

The High Court has a summary disciplinary jurisdiction over solicitors. In *Myers v Elman* [1940] AC 282 Lord Wright said that the underlying principle of the summary jurisdiction is that the High Court has a right and a duty to supervise the conduct of solicitors, and to impose penalties where the conduct of a solicitor is of such a nature as to tend to defeat justice. The jurisdiction is compensatory rather than punitive, but does have a disciplinary slant. There was formerly a body of case law dealing with applications for costs orders against solicitors pursuant to the court's inherent jurisdiction over them. This particular area is now covered by the detailed rules on wasted costs applications, which are considered further in **chapter 68**.

Disciplinary proceedings against solicitors are currently mainly investigated by the Solicitors Regulation Authority (SRA) under the SRA Disciplinary Procedure Rules 2011 and, where appropriate, are brought before the Solicitors Disciplinary Tribunal under r. 10 of those Rules. The tribunal's procedures are governed by the Solicitors (Disciplinary Proceedings) Rules 2007 (SI 2007/3588) and the Solicitors Disciplinary Tribunal (Appeals and Amendment) Rules 2011 (SI 2011/2346). Powers still exist, however, to apply to the High Court to strike the name of a solicitor off the roll of solicitors, or to answer certain allegations, under the Solicitors Act 1974, ss. 50 to 55. An independent Legal Ombudsman service has been set up under the Legal Services Act 2007. They act as a point of entry for reports of alleged breaches of the SRA Code of Conduct 2011, and work with consumers and very small businesses to resolve legal complaints in a fair and independent way. Members of the Chartered Institute of Legal Executives (CILEx) are subject to the disciplinary procedures laid down by ILEX Professional Standards Ltd (IPS), which carries out on behalf of CILEx its functions and responsibilities as an approved regulator under the Legal Services Act 2007. All members of CILEx must comply with its Code of Conduct. Disciplinary hearings are conducted before the Institute of Legal Executives Appeal Tribunal, whose decisions are amenable to judicial review (*R (Kaur) v Institute of Legal Executives Appeal Tribunal* [2010] EWHC 3321 (Admin), [2011] ACD 25).

SOLICITOR ON THE RECORD

21.3   Every party to litigation must provide an address for service within the United Kingdom (extended to the EEA if acting by a solicitor) (**CPR, r. 6.23(2)**). This will be the business address of the party's solicitor, if there is one (**r. 6.23(2)(a)**). The claim form will identify whether the claimant is acting by a solicitor, and the acknowledgment of service form, defence, or defence and counterclaim, will identify whether the defendant is acting by a solicitor.

Once a solicitor is on the court record as acting for a party, by **rr. 42.1** and **42.2(5)**, that solicitor will be considered to be continuing to act for that party until due notice is given or an order is made in accordance with **Part 42**. The rules on giving notice of change are considered further in **chapter 22**.

ACTING FOR JOINT CLAIMANTS

21.4   Before the introduction of the CPR, the usual rule where there were joint claimants was that they were not allowed to take inconsistent steps (such as by just one of them making an interim application within the proceedings), they had to act by a common firm of solicitors, and be represented at trial and other hearings by the same counsel (*Re Wright* [1895] 2 Ch 747; *Re Mathews* [1905] 2 Ch 460; *Lewis v Daily Telegraph Ltd (No. 2)* [1964] 2 QB 601). Pearson LJ in *Lewis v Daily Telegraph Ltd (No. 2)* said that there may be scope for making a special order for separate representation of joint claimants, but indicated a distinct reluctance to do this. The disinclination against separate representation of joint claimants must be stronger under the CPR, given the elements of the overriding objective relating to saving expense and ensuring that cases are dealt with expeditiously. A defendant faced with separately represented claimants should consider applying for a stay (**chapter 56**).

DUTY OF CONFIDENTIALITY

A solicitor has a duty of single-minded loyalty to his client's interests, and a duty to respect his **21.5** client's confidences (*Hilton v Barker Booth and Eastwood* [2005] UKHL 8, [2005] 1 WLR 567 at [30]). These duties arise primarily from the contractual retainer between the solicitor and client, but there is also usually a fiduciary relationship between the solicitor and client arising from the fact that the client reposes trust and confidence in the solicitor (per Lord Walker of Gestingthorpe at [28] and [29]). This means that the solicitor's duty of confidence need not be coterminous with the retainer (*Conway v Ratiu* [2005] EWCA Civ 1302, [2006] 1 All ER 571 at [71]). The nature of the solicitor's fiduciary duty may have to be moulded and informed by the terms of the retainer, because it has to be consistent and in conformity with the terms of the contract between the parties (*Conway v Ratiu* at [73]). Depending on the facts, a solicitor's fiduciary duty may extend beyond the termination of the retainer (*Longstaff v Birtles* [2001] EWCA Civ 1219, [2002] 1 WLR 470), and may arise without a retainer at all (*Conway v Ratiu* at [73]).

CONFLICTS BETWEEN CLIENTS

No-conflict rule

A solicitor will be unable to act for two or more clients in the same matter (whether as **21.6** claimants or defendants) where there is a conflict of interest between the clients. If the clients whose interests are in conflict are intending claimants, the best course is for them all to go to new solicitors and, if proceedings are necessary, to bring separate proceedings so that they can be separately represented. The original solicitor will have to consider carefully whether he or she is able to act for one of the parties in view of the initial contact with another party, bearing in mind the outcomes and indicative behaviour set out in the SRA Code of Conduct 2011, chapter 3. A solicitor who discovers a conflict of interest in representing a client must inform the client of his or her inability to act, and that the client should seek legal advice from other solicitors, starting afresh and not relying on any advice already given by the solicitor (*Hilton v Barker Booth and Eastwood* [2005] UKHL 8, [2005] 1 WLR 567).

Nor can a solicitor generally act for a client where that client's interests conflict with those of a former client. For example, in *Saminadhen v Khan* [1992] 1 All ER 963 Lord Donaldson of Lymington MR said he could conceive of no circumstances in which it would be proper for a solicitor who had acted for one defendant in criminal proceedings, in which a cut-throat defence had been advanced between two defendants, to act subsequently for the other defendant after the first retainer had terminated. However, the full position is more complicated than this, because the courts dealing with this problem are in fact seeking to balance two conflicting public interests:

(a) The public interest in enabling the client to repose the fullest confidence in the solicitor he retains, and ensuring there is no risk or perception of a risk that confidential information relating to a client will be conveyed to anyone else. The information that the court will seek to protect will have the following characteristics:

(i)   It was originally communicated to the solicitor in confidence.

(ii) It is still confidential, and reasonably capable of being considered capable of being recalled. It might lose this characteristic by becoming common knowledge, or (in certain circumstances) if it has been communicated to an opponent during the course of litigation. Alternatively, it might be so eminently forgettable that it should not be protected. A client complaining that confidential information might be at risk must identify it with some particularity, but the degree of particularity required depends on the facts of the case (*Re a Firm of Solicitors* [1997] Ch 1).

(iii) It is relevant to the subject matter of the subsequent retainer.

(b) The public interest in the freedom of the solicitor to obtain instructions from any member of the public, and for all members of the public to instruct the solicitor of their choice.

A solicitor who continues to act without disclosing a conflict between duty of loyalty to the first client and duty of confidentiality to a second client, is liable for any loss suffered by the first client. The duty of loyalty to the first client is not modified by the fact that complying with it will involve breaching the duty of confidentiality to the second client: the predicament is the solicitor's own fault in allowing the conflict to arise (*Hilton v Barker Booth and Eastwood* [2005] UKHL 8, [2005] 1 WLR 567).

Further, a solicitor cannot simultaneously act for two clients in separate matters if the clients have potentially conflicting interests and there is a reasonable relationship between the two transactions (*Marks and Spencer plc v Freshfields Bruckhaus Deringer* [2004] EWHC 1337 (Ch), [2004] 1 WLR 2331).

As a matter of practice, it is wise for solicitors to run computer conflict checks when instructed and when parties are added to existing proceedings.

Restraining a solicitor from acting

21.7 A solicitor who is possessed of relevant confidential information will be restrained from acting against the former client (*Re a Firm of Solicitors* [1992] QB 959). In the case of a firm previously retained by a client, the partners and employees who are in possession of confidential information may be restrained from acting against the former client, and this extends to them if they change firms. Members and employees of the firm who never had possession of relevant confidential information are in a rather more complex position. While they remain with the firm they will, generally, be precluded from acting against the former client of the firm, but it is possible they may be allowed to act if there is no real (as opposed to fanciful) risk that relevant confidential information may have been communicated to them (*Re a Firm of Solicitors* [1992] QB 959).

Real risk of disclosure

21.8 In *Bolkiah v KPMG* [1999] 2 AC 222 the claimant had retained the defendant firm of accountants in his private capacity to provide extensive litigation support services of a kind commonly provided by solicitors in relation to proceedings he was involved in. In the course of this retainer the defendants became privy to detailed information relating to the claimant's financial affairs, and no less than 168 of the defendants' employees were involved. Some months after the conclusion of the claimant's action, the defendants were retained by the claimant's former employer (the Brunei Investment Agency, BIA) to investigate the location of substantial funds that had been transferred during his period of employment. Aware of a possible conflict of interest, the defendants erected an information barrier (also known as an 'ethical wall' or 'Chinese wall') around the department conducting the BIA investigation. The defendants did not, however, ask for the claimant's consent to them acting for the BIA. It was held that the claimant was entitled to an injunction restraining the defendants from continuing to act in the BIA investigation. Such injunctions will be granted unless the firm produces clear and convincing evidence that effective measures have been taken to ensure that no disclosure of the former client's affairs will be made to the department acting for the new client, and that there is no risk of the former client's information reaching the department acting for the new client. Although, in some cases, ethical walls may be sufficient protection, there is a very heavy burden on the firm to prove this, and it will be very difficult for the firm to do so unless those measures were an established part of the firm's organisational structure. Institution of an ethical wall system and various other precautions to protect the client's confidential information from risk of disclosure were sufficient in *Gus Consulting GmbH v LeBoeuf Lamb Greene and MacRae* [2006] EWCA Civ 683, [2006] PNLR 32, to enable solicitors to act against a former client in an arbitration.

Following *Bolkiah v KPMG* the question is whether there is a real, as opposed to a fanciful, risk of disclosure. Whether there is such a risk is a question of fact. Where a solicitor acted for a party many years before, but neither the solicitor nor the client have any material recollection of the previous matter, there is no material conflict (*Re T and A (Children) (Risk of Disclosure)* [2000] 1 FLR 859). Each case turns on its own facts. There was no real risk of disclosure in *Re Bloomsbury International Ltd, Bloomsbury International Ltd v Holyoake* [2010] EWHC 1150 (Ch), LTL 24/5/2010, where the issue concerned the company's administrators who had previously acted for the company in relation to its tax affairs. The retainer relating to its tax affairs had been terminated, and there was an information barrier between the two teams dealing with the administration and the company's tax affairs. In *Koch Shipping Inc. v Richards Butler* [2002] EWCA Civ 1280, [2002] 2 All ER (Comm) 957, it was held that fears of inadvertent disclosure of confidential information by the solicitor formerly with day-to-day conduct of a case for one side who then joined the firm representing the other side (where she had no dealings with the case) were fanciful.

In *Bodle v Coutts and Co.* [2003] EWHC 1865 (Ch), LTL 17/7/2003, Farrer and Co. ('the solicitors') had acted for the claimant some years previously in matrimonial proceedings. Subsequently, the claimant sued the defendant bank, who were now represented by the solicitors. The claimant had not paid the solicitors, who exerted a lien over her matrimonial papers. An application was made to restrain the solicitors from acting for the bank. The court directed the solicitors to produce the papers (which were not shown to the claimant), and the judge concluded they contained nothing relevant to the present proceedings. This procedure was held not to infringe the European Convention on Human Rights, art. 6(1), as production had been directed by the court, rather than the papers being voluntarily deployed by the solicitors. On the solicitors giving undertakings restricting access to the papers and discussion of their contents, the claimant's application was refused.

Staff moving to new firms

21.9 Once members or employees, who never had possession of confidential information about a former client of a firm, move to new firms, they will be free from constraint. To come into this more favoured class, the burden is on the solicitor to prove not only that he or she did not have possession of relevant confidential information, but that there is no real risk that he or she has such information (*Re a Firm of Solicitors* [1997] Ch 1).

Other examples

21.10 A different problem was considered in *Re Schuppan* [1996] 2 All ER 664. A well-known firm of solicitors had acted for the judgment creditor in hard-fought High Court proceedings involving allegations of fraud and a detailed investigation of the assets of the judgment debtor. The judgment was not satisfied, and the debtor was declared bankrupt. The trustee in bankruptcy retained the solicitors who had been acting for the judgment creditor to act in the bankruptcy. It was held that having a blanket rule that it is never allowable for a creditor's solicitors to act for the trustee in bankruptcy was a counsel of perfection, and this could be allowed if no difficulty was expected in quantifying the provable debts (which generally is the most obvious area of possible conflict of interest), provided there were good reasons for retaining the creditor's solicitors. In this case there were good reasons, as they already had a good grasp of the bankrupt's finances, and it would have been very expensive for any new firm to read into the case. In addition, there were further unresolved issues arising from the original litigation, including a wasted costs application against the creditor's solicitors and an inquiry based on the creditor's undertaking in damages in respect of a discharged freezing order. These issues did give rise to a possible conflict of interest, but it was held that the risk could be averted by a division of responsibility (with another firm being retained to deal with these issues), and then a balancing exercise would be undertaken (which on the facts favoured allowing the creditor's solicitor to act).

In *Re L (Minors) (Care Proceedings: Solicitors)* [2001] 1 WLR 100 Wilson J in the Family Division made a declaration that the solicitor acting for the local authority in care proceedings was not so acting, thus removing her from the record, because the fact of her cohabiting with the solicitor for two of the seven respondents to the proceedings could give rise to an apprehension of bias by lay persons.

There may be a conflict of interest where a solicitor has a financial interest in a transaction which may conflict with the interests of a client (*Hilton v Barker Booth and Eastwood* [2005] UKHL 8, [2005] 1 WLR 567).

Orders available

21.11 Where a party establishes a conflict of interest, the most the court can do is to grant an injunction forbidding the solicitor from continuing to act for the other party and, if necessary, a stay unless and until new solicitors are instructed. There is no power to order a party to instruct new solicitors (*SMC Engineering (Bristol) Ltd v Fraser* [2001] CP Rep 76).

MONEY LAUNDERING

21.12 Where the matter involves a financial or real property transaction, the solicitor must apply customer due diligence measures when establishing a business relationship with the client (Money Laundering Regulations 2007 (SI 2007/2157), regs 3, 5 and 7). There is a similar obligation when an occasional transaction is to be entered into with a value of €15,000 or more. Customer due diligence means identifying the customer and verifying the customer's identity on the basis of documents, data or information obtained from a reliable and independent source, such as a passport, or photo-card driving licence, or birth certificate, and keeping a record of the identification evidence.

AUTHORITY OF SOLICITORS

21.13 A solicitor retained by a client is, of course, the client's agent, and has actual or apparent authority to do all things that may reasonably be expected to arise in litigation being conducted for the client (*Prestwich v Poley* (1865) 18 CB NS 806). As against an opposing litigant, the only limitation on the apparent authority of a solicitor to compromise litigation is that it cannot be taken to include the compromise of matters collateral to the proceedings. A matter will only be regarded as collateral where it really is extraneous to the proceedings (*Waugh v H. B. Clifford and Sons Ltd* [1982] Ch 374). A solicitor with general authority to act for a client may have authority to defend the client against disparagement in the media based on information from the solicitor's own experience rather than being limited to direct instructions from the client (*Regan v Taylor* [2000] EMLR 549; *Khader v Aziz* [2010] EWCA Civ 716, [2010] 1 WLR 2673).

However, as between solicitor and client, there will be a breach of authority by the solicitor unless any action taken (particularly compromising the claim) is within his or her express or implied authority. It may well be that a proposed compromise of a claim will be within the apparent authority of the solicitor as against the other side (because it does not include anything collateral to the claim), but will be outside the actual authority of the solicitor as between himself and his client. The solicitor will generally only be safe in concluding the proposed compromise if the client gives express instructions. See *Waugh v H. B. Clifford and Sons Ltd. Fusion Interactive Communication Solutions Ltd v Venture Investment Placement Ltd (No. 2)* [2005] EWHC 736 (Ch), [2005] 2 BCLC 571, dealt with the effect on a defendant where conflicting letters before claim are sent by different firms of solicitors instructed by the same client. On the facts, compliance with one letter before claim meant that there was no default in respect of the second (and wider) claim as set out in the other letter.

A solicitor with a 'general retainer' in litigation is required to act for the client to the end and to take all necessary steps to bring the claim to a conclusion. Difficulties in obtaining instructions do not affect the authority of solicitors acting under a general retainer (*Euroafrica Shipping Lines Co. Ltd v Żegluga Polska SA* [2004] EWHC 385 (Comm), [2004] 2 BCLC 97).

In general, death of a client will terminate a solicitor's authority. However, where the client is a company, death of its sole shareholder and director will not have this effect, as the company will continue to exist (*Donsland Ltd v Van Hoogstraten* [2002] EWCA Civ 253, [2002] PNLR 26). Supervening mental incapacity of the client will terminate the actual authority of the solicitor (*Drew v Nunn* (1879) 4 QBD 661 at p. 666). If a deputy has been appointed for a solicitor's client, the solicitor, even if acting without the deputy's authority, may have continuing ostensible authority (the situation in *Drew v Nunn* under the old receivership procedure, which has been replaced by deputyship) or might be liable for breach of warranty of authority (as in *Yonge v Toynbee* [1910] 1 KB 215). Termination of actual authority by reason of mental incapacity does not frustrate the underlying retainer contract between the solicitor and client (*Blankley v Central Manchester Hospitals Trust* [2014] EWHC 168 (QB), [2014] 1 WLR 2683).

After the solicitor's retainer has been ended the client has full authority to settle the claim and any costs issues (*Khans Solicitors v Chifuntwe* [2013] EWCA Civ 481, [2014] 1 WLR 1185 at [37]), subject to any restrictions written into the original retainer. Solicitors concerned that a former client may seek to override their lien for unpaid costs should give notice to the other side not to pay the client direct without preserving the lien (see **71.69**).

AUTHORITY OF COUNSEL

In *Swinfen v Lord Chelmsford* (1860) 5 Hurl & N 890 Pollock CB said that a barrister has complete   **21.14**
authority over the conduct of litigation and all that is incidental to it, but not over matters which are collateral to the case. In *Matthews v Munster* (1887) 20 QBD 141 Lord Esher MR said, at p. 143:

when the client has requested counsel to act as his advocate...he thereby represents to the other side that counsel is to act for him in the usual course, and he must be bound by that representation so long as it continues....The request does not mean that counsel is to act in any other character than that of advocate or to do any other act than such as an advocate usually does. The duty of counsel is to advise his client out of court and to act for him in court, and until his authority is withdrawn he has, with regard to all matters that properly relate to the conduct of the case, unlimited power to do that which is best for his client.

A court or tribunal is entitled to rely on the agreement of a party's properly qualified advocate to any proposed procedural course, even one where in the absence of agreement there would be a breach of the rules of natural justice, without having to go behind the advocate to check that the client agrees (*R (Hill) v Institute of Chartered Accountants in England and Wales* [2013] EWCA Civ 555, [2014] 1 WLR 86). In *Worldwide Corporation Ltd v Marconi Communications Ltd* (1999) The

Times, 7 July 1999, an application for permission to amend to set up a different cause of action, leading counsel for the claimant had abandoned the cause of action originally pleaded, in a strategy to try to obtain permission to amend. Permission was refused, with the result that, as the original claim had been abandoned, the claim was dismissed. An attempt was then made on behalf of the claimant to resuscitate the original claim, and new leading counsel was briefed. Although it left open the possibility that there may be exceptional cases, the Court of Appeal held that the court had to be able to rely on counsel, and the client was not able to retreat from the abandonment of the original claim.

WARRANTY OF AUTHORITY

Breach of warranty of authority

21.15   By issuing proceedings a firm of solicitors warrant that they have authority from the claimant to do so. Similarly, by filing a defence or taking any other step in the proceedings a firm purporting to act for a defendant warrant that they have authority to act for the defendant. According to Buxton LJ in *SEB Trygg Liv Holding AB v Manches* [2005] EWCA Civ 1237, [2006] 1 WLR 2276, the solicitor warrants:

(a) that he has a client; and
(b) that the client has instructed him to assert or deny the claims made in the proceedings.

There is no warranty that the solicitor's client has the same name as that used in the proceedings. Otherwise the solicitor would be liable for every misnomer, including typographical errors and changes in company names (*SEB Trygg Liv Holding AB v Manches*).

If solicitors do not have authority to issue proceedings, they will be in breach of warranty of authority and liable to the other parties. This rarely occurs through the deliberate action of the solicitors. However, the cases show that it is no defence that the solicitors acted perfectly innocently and without knowledge of the defect in their authority. Solicitors have been held to be in breach of warranty of authority in the following circumstances:

(a) where the claimant is a child or under a mental disability (*Geilinger v Gibbs* [1897] 1 Ch 479; *Yonge v Toynbee* [1910] 1 KB 215);
(b) where the claimant does not exist (*Simmons v Liberal Opinion Ltd* [1911] 1 KB 966);
(c) where the claimant is a limited company which has no directors or officers with authority to give instructions to the solicitors (*West End Hotels Syndicate Ltd v Bayer* (1912) 29 TLR 92);
(d) where the claimant has died before proceedings were commenced (*Tetlow v Orela Ltd* [1920] 2 Ch 24);
(e) where the claimant is a company that has been dissolved (*Babury Ltd v London Industrial plc* (1989) 139 NLJ 1596).

Being without instructions

21.16   There is a difference between a solicitor being without instructions and being without authority. It is only in the latter case that damages may be awarded against the solicitor for breach of warranty of authority (*Donsland Ltd v Van Hoogstraten* [2002] EWCA Civ 253, [2002] PNLR 26). Where a sole director and shareholder of a company died during the course of proceedings, the company's solicitors, acting under a general retainer, continued to have authority to make applications in those proceedings even though they did not have anyone to give them specific instructions (*Donsland Ltd v Van Hoogstraten*).

Practice after a breach of warranty of authority

21.17   Where a breach of warranty of authority occurs, the court has jurisdiction to make a summary order against the solicitor where the issues are reasonably clear, but where there are real issues of fact or law the injured party should be left to bring the claim by issuing separate proceedings (*Skylight Maritime SA v Ascot Underwriting* [2005] EWHC 15 (Comm), [2005] PNLR 25). In both cases the jurisdiction is compensatory rather than punitive, so proof of loss is essential (*Skylight Maritime SA v Ascot Underwriting*). Where the summary procedure is used, the innocent party should make an application using form N244 seeking an order striking out the claim (or the defence) and that the solicitor should be ordered to pay the costs on the indemnity basis. (The principles established in the old cases are unlikely to have been altered in this respect by the introduction of the CPR. The earlier cases indicate that the solicitor in breach should be ordered to pay its client's costs on the indemnity basis.) The application should be served on the solicitors and on the party (if it exists) for whom the solicitor has purported to act.

There are some breaches that can be cured, such as by the appointment of a litigation friend (*Cooper v Dumnett* [1930] WN 248) or the passing of necessary company resolutions and ratification of the actions of the solicitors (*East Pant Du United Lead Mining Co. Ltd v Merryweather* (1864) 2 Hem & M 254), and in these cases the court may be prepared to grant a stay for these steps to be taken. In some cases there may be a dispute of fact as to whether there was a want of authority. For example, it may be disputed whether the claimant lacks capacity. In these cases the court may dismiss or adjourn the application, and leave the applicant to bring separate proceedings for damages for breach of warranty of authority (*Yonge v Toynbee* [1910] 1 KB 215). Otherwise, an order dismissing the claim (or defence) and for indemnity basis costs follows almost as a matter of course.

SOLICITORS' AGENTS

21.18   It is common practice for solicitors to appoint local agents to deal with court hearings, particularly simple interim applications and short trials. There is also a common practice for provincial firms to appoint London agents for trials and important hearings at the Royal Courts of Justice. In these situations the London or local agent's principal is the firm of solicitors originally retained by the lay client, subject to contrary express agreement. The local or London agents must therefore look to their principals for payment of their costs, rather than the client (*Collins v Griffin* (1734) Barnes 37; *Scrace v Whittington* (1823) 2 B & C 11). If the agent is negligent, the client is able to sue the principal, who will be liable for the acts and omissions of the agent (*Re Ward* (1862) 31 Beav 1). In most such cases the principal could seek a contribution or indemnity from the agent by issuing an additional claim under **Part 20**. As regards the other side, the solicitor agent has apparent authority within the scope of the application under consideration. If that is the trial, the agent has apparent authority to compromise the claim (*Re Newen* [1903] 1 Ch 812), and if an application, to agree terms relevant to the application.

ENFORCING SOLICITORS' UNDERTAKINGS

Binding nature of undertakings

21.19   Undertakings are regularly given by solicitors in a variety of circumstances, and include undertakings that payments will be made, or that things will or will not be done. Holding money on a solicitor's undertaking may give rise to a stakeholder relationship, typically involving two contracts, one between the principals, and the other being a tripartite contract with the stakeholder agreeing terms. Alternatively, such money may be held on trust. The actual relationship depends on the facts and wording of the undertaking (*Tradegro (UK) Ltd v Wigmore Street Investments Ltd* [2011] EWCA Civ 268, LTL 16/3/2011, in which it was held there was no security provided by an undertaking given in place of a freezing injunction). An undertaking will bind

Commentary

not only the individual solicitor giving it, but also his or her firm, if it is made by a partner in the usual way of business of the kind carried on by the firm (see Partnership Act 1890, and *United Bank of Kuwait Ltd v Hammoud* [1988] 1 WLR 1051). Where the underlying transaction is unusual, the other partners will be bound only if they expressly consent (see *Hirst v Etherington* (1999) 149 NLJ 1110).

Failing to implement a solicitor's undertaking is regarded by the courts and the Solicitors Disciplinary Tribunal as professional misconduct, even if the solicitor has not been guilty of dishonourable conduct. As solicitors are officers of the court, the High Court has a general jurisdiction to enforce undertakings given by solicitors in their capacities as solicitors (*United Mining and Finance Corporation Ltd v Becher* [1910] 2 KB 296). This jurisdiction is not limited to undertakings given in the course of litigation. The court also has the power to grant a solicitor relief from an undertaking on sufficient cause being shown (*John Fox v Bannister, King and Rigbeys* [1988] QB 925). It may do so, for example, to give relief from a mistake or where there has been impropriety by the other side.

Practice on enforcing solicitors' undertakings

21.20 In *Udall v Capri Lighting Ltd* [1988] QB 907 Balcombe LJ said there are three ways in which a party seeking to enforce a solicitor's undertaking can proceed:

(a) by an action at law;

(b) by an application to the High Court to exercise its inherent supervisory jurisdiction over solicitors; and

(c) by reporting the solicitor to the SRA or the Legal Ombudsman for disciplinary action.

A claim against the solicitor (option (a)) may be capable of being framed as a breach of trust, such as where the solicitor has not applied money in the way specified in the undertaking (*Global Marine Drillships Ltd v Landmark Solicitors LLP* [2011] EWHC 2685 (Ch), LTL 25/10/2011, applying *Twinsectra Ltd v Yardley* [2002] UKHL 12, [2002] 2 AC 164). The drawback in taking this course is that there may be defences available to the solicitor which will make it difficult to obtain summary judgment (this was the problem in *Global Marine Drillships Ltd v Landmark Solicitors LLP*), whereas invoking the inherent jurisdiction (option (b)) will in many cases produce a simple claim for the enforcement of the solicitor's obligations in the undertaking.

In *Rooks Rider v Steel* [1994] 1 WLR 818 the claimant solicitors acted for a company based in Louisiana in a complex transaction under which the Louisiana company agreed to lend money to a hotel company. The hotel company's solicitors undertook in writing to pay the claimant's fees in connection with the transaction 'whether the matter proceeds to completion or not'. The transaction was never completed, and it transpired the Louisiana company did not have the funds to make the loan, and used the proposed transaction for fraudulent purposes. The defendant solicitors refused to honour their undertaking, relying on the fraud as absolving them from liability. It was found that the claimant solicitors were not involved in their client's fraud. It was accordingly held there was no lawful justification for not complying with the undertaking, and an order was made requiring the defendants to comply. In *Bentley v Gaisford* [1997] QB 627 it was held to be a breach of an undertaking given by the defendant firm to hold documents, which were the subject of a lien against unpaid fees, to the order of the claimant firm, when a partner in the defendant firm, acting in good faith and in what he regarded as his duty to his client, copied all the documents to the client. Doing so rendered the lien worthless.

Where on an application under the supervisory jurisdiction over solicitors it is shown that there has been a breach of an undertaking by a solicitor, the court will usually make an order requiring the solicitor to comply with the undertaking (*Re a Solicitor* [1966] 1 WLR 1604). On the breach by a solicitor of the standard undertaking in a residential property transaction to redeem or discharge existing mortgages or charges, the solicitor is liable to pay any sums required to discharge those instruments at the time redemption is sought (*Angel Solicitors v Jenkins O'Dowd and Barth* [2009] EWHC 46 (Ch), [2009] 1 WLR 1220). There may be a defence if the demand on the undertaking is wholly unreasonable or outside the solicitor's contemplation (*Clark v Lucas Solicitors LLP* [2009] EWHC 1952 (Ch), [2010] PNLR 2). If compliance with the undertaking will be impossible (perhaps because it involves actions which are not within the control of the solicitor), the court may order the solicitor to pay compensation to any person who suffers loss as a result of the breach of undertaking (*Udall v Capri Lighting Ltd* [1988] QB 907). In *Bentley v Gaisford* [1997] QB 627 the court refused to order the defendant solicitors to pay compensation despite their breach of undertaking because the partner who had copied the documents to the client was not guilty of inexcusable conduct meriting reproof.

Option (c), taking disciplinary action, has the drawback that there are limited remedies. There is no disciplinary power to order specific performance, although returning money to clients can be included as part of a regulatory settlement agreement. The SRA may alternatively refer the conduct to the Solicitors Disciplinary Tribunal, which has the disciplinary powers set out in the Solicitors Act 1974, s. 47, which include striking off, suspension and the imposition of penalties.

RESTRAINING STRUCK-OFF SOLICITOR

The statutory scheme regulating solicitors can be found in the Solicitors Act 1974 and other legislation such as the Legal Services Act 2007. A summary of the legislation can be found in *Law Society v Shah* [2014] EWHC 4382 (Ch), [2015] 1 WLR 2094 at [33]–[52]. This case held that the Law Society has standing to seek a High Court injunction to restrain a person who holds himself out as a solicitor or who carries on a reserved legal activity without authorisation. **21.21**

Chapter 22   Change of Solicitor

TERMINATION OF RETAINER

22.1   A retainer to conduct litigation is generally regarded as an entire contract, with the effect that a solicitor once retained must see the litigation through to its conclusion. However, the retainer is subject to an implied term that the solicitor may withdraw if there is good cause and provided reasonable notice is given to the client. The client may terminate the retainer without cause at any time. When a party changes solicitors, or retains a solicitor having previously been acting in person, or starts acting in person having previously retained a solicitor, the other parties and the court need to be informed so that future correspondence and court applications, orders and other documents can be sent to the correct address.

SOLICITOR ON THE RECORD

22.2   **CPR, Part 6**, contains general rules on service of documents. Although there are several refinements (see **chapter 15**), some of the basic rules on where litigation documents should be served are:

    (a) Under **r. 6.23**, each party to litigation must provide an address for service within the United Kingdom or any other EEA State.

    (b) **Rules 6.7** and **6.23(2)** in effect provide that where a solicitor or European lawyer is acting for a party, that party's address for service is the business address of the solicitor or European lawyer. The address of the solicitor or European lawyer may be anywhere in the United Kingdom or any other EEA State.

    (c) The address for service of a party who is acting in person is usually the party's residential address or place of business (**rr. 6.8, 6.9(2)** and **6.23(2)(c)**).

    (d) Any change of address of a party or of a party's solicitor (without changing the identity of the person acting for that party) must be notified in writing to the court and to other parties as soon as the change takes place (**r. 6.24**).

    (e) In recent times the practice has been that if one solicitor acts for a number of parties in a claim, it is sufficient to serve on that solicitor a single copy of any documents that need to be served (see, for example, **PD 10, para. 5.3**).

    The claim form will identify whether the claimant is acting by a solicitor or in person, and the defence or defence and counterclaim will similarly identify whether the defendant is acting in person or by a solicitor. For these purposes 'solicitor' includes any other person who, for the purposes of the Legal Services Act 2007, is an authorised person in relation to the conduct of litigation (**CPR, r. 6.2(d)**). **CPR, Part 42**, contains rules dealing with giving notice of changes relating to representation by solicitors.

PRESUMED CONTINUANCE

22.3   Where the address for service of a party is the business address of the party's solicitor (which for this purpose includes other legal representatives authorised by the Legal Services Act 2007), by

CPR, rr. 42.1 and **42.2(5)**, that solicitor will be considered to be continuing to act for that party until due notice is given or an order is made in accordance with **Part 42**. However, a solicitor appointed solely for the purpose of acting as an advocate at a hearing is not considered to be acting for the client for the purposes of **Part 42** (**PD 42, para. 1.3**).

NOTICE OF CHANGE

By **CPR, r. 42.2**, notice of change stating the change and the new address for service (which **22.4** must be within the United Kingdom or another EEA State, see **r. 6.23(2)**) must be filed at court and served on all other parties whenever:

(a) a party who has been acting by a solicitor changes solicitor;

(b) a party who has been acting in person appoints a solicitor; or

(c) a party who has been acting by a solicitor intends to act in future as a litigant in person.

In the circumstances set out in (a) and (c) above the notice of change must also be served on the former solicitor. The form of notice of change of solicitor is form N434. It should not be filed until every other party has been served (**PD 42, para. 1.2**), and should be filed in the court office in which the claim is proceeding (**para. 2.5**). Where the claim is the subject of an appeal to the Court of Appeal, the notice should also be filed in the Civil Appeals Office (**para. 2.7**). The copy of the notice filed at court must state that it has also been served on the other parties, and, if appropriate, the former solicitor.

REVOCATION OR DISCHARGE OF PUBLIC FUNDING

The retainer of any solicitor acting on behalf of a publicly funded client terminates on the **22.5** withdrawal of a determination that an individual qualifies for licensed work (Civil Legal Aid (Procedure) Regulations 2012 (SI 2012/3098), reg. 41). As soon as the retainer of a solicitor is ended, the solicitor is required by **CPR, r. 42.2(6)(a)**, to cease acting for the formerly funded or assisted litigant. If the litigant wishes to continue the litigation despite the cessation of public funding, a notice of change (see **22.4**) must be given (**r. 42.2(6)(b)**; **PD 42, para. 2.2**), even if the same solicitor is retained (because the previous solicitor is deemed by **CPR, r. 42.2(6)(a)**, to have ceased to act and **r. 42.2(6)(b)(i)** treats the litigant as previously having acted in person). Where a solicitor is appointed the notice of change does not have to be served on the former solicitor (again because **r. 42.2(6)(b)(i)** treats the litigant as previously having acted in person). The notice must give the last known address of the formerly funded or assisted person (**PD 42, para. 2.2**).

COMING OFF THE RECORD

A solicitor's retainer may be terminated by the solicitor if there is a 'good reason' and provided **22.6** the client is given reasonable notice (SRA Code of Conduct 2011, O 1.3 and IB 1.26). There is no comprehensive definition of what amounts to a good reason for this purpose, the question being fact-sensitive. There may be a good reason where the client fails to give instructions, acts unreasonably, or fails or refuses to pay a reasonable sum on account of the past and future costs of the litigation within a reasonable time of a request for payment (Solicitors Act 1974, s. 65(2); *Underwood, Son and Piper v Lewis* [1894] 2 QB 306). The test will be satisfied if the client insists on advancing a case which the solicitor does not regard as properly arguable (*Richard Buxton v Mills-Owen* [2010] EWCA Civ 122, [2010] 1 WLR 1997). This may arise through the use of documents containing contentions that are not properly arguable, or through instructing counsel to advance such contentions. It is recognised that it is difficult to draw the line between weak cases which are and are not properly arguable. A solicitor who withdraws in the

Commentary

absence of good reason is in breach of the contract of retainer, and, as it is an entire contract, will be unable to recover any fees from the client (and may be required to refund fees previously paid).

When a solicitor ceases to act for a client, whether or not there is a breach of contract as between the solicitor and client, the change ought to be entered in the court records by one means or another. In most cases this will be done by the client or any new solicitor retained by the client giving notice of change as discussed in **22.4**. If this does not happen, the former solicitor will in practical terms be obliged to take steps to come off the record. To do this it is necessary to apply for an order under **CPR, r. 42.3**. It is reasonably clear from *Plenty v Gladwin* (1986) 67 ALR 26 (High Court of Australia) that such an application has nothing to do with whether or not the solicitor was right to withdraw, but is simply a matter of ensuring the court's record accords with the reality of whether the solicitor is continuing to act for the client. Unless there are special circumstances to the contrary, orders that a solicitor has ceased to act are generally made as a matter of course when it is shown that the solicitor is no longer acting for the party, and that no notice of change has been given.

An application under **r. 42.3** is made by application notice, which must be served on the client unless the court directs otherwise, and must be supported by evidence, usually by witness statement (see **r. 42.3(2)** and **Part 23**). The application and evidence must not be served on the other parties as it will often contain information which is confidential between the solicitor and client (*Re Creehouse Ltd* [1983] 1 WLR 77).

If an order is made under **r. 42.3** that a solicitor has ceased to act, the order must be served on all the parties to the proceedings, and if the order is not served by the court, the serving party or solicitor must also file a certificate of service in form N215 (**r. 42.3(3)**).

REMOVAL OF SOLICITOR ON APPLICATION
OF ANOTHER PARTY

22.7 Where a solicitor has died, become bankrupt, ceased to practise or gone missing, the court and other parties should be informed and the client's address for service duly altered. Although this is not expressly provided by the CPR, ceasing to practise covers a multitude of circumstances, including retirement, changing professions, and also being struck off the roll of solicitors, failing to take out a practising certificate and being suspended from practising. In the circumstances mentioned in this paragraph there is a strong likelihood of the Solicitors Regulation Authority intervening in the solicitor's practice, under the Solicitors Act 1974, s. 35 and sch. 1.

Normally the client will appoint a new solicitor who will serve and file the appropriate notice of change. However, if no notice of change is served, the position can be regularised on the application of any other party under **CPR, r. 42.4**, for an order declaring the solicitor has ceased acting for the relevant party. Before the CPR came into force, the phrase 'any other party', which appeared in a number of contexts in the RSC and also appears in **CPR, r. 42.4(1)**, was interpreted restrictively by old cases such as *Shaw v Smith* (1886) 18 QBD 193 as limited to opposite parties, with the result that a co-defendant was not included. More recently, in *Manatee Towing Co. v Oceanbulk Maritime SA* [1999] 1 Lloyd's Rep 876, a decision under the RSC, it was held that this restrictive interpretation of the phrase no longer applied to the latest version of the RSC before they were replaced by the CPR. There is no prospect of the old restrictive interpretation being revived to apply to the CPR. The result is that an application under **r. 42.4** may be made by any party other than the party whose solicitor is no longer available.

An application notice seeking a declaration under **r. 42.4** must be supported by evidence (**PD 42, para. 4.2**) and, unless the court otherwise directs, must be served on the client whose solicitor is unavailable. If the declaration is made, a copy of the order must be served on all the other parties, and if the order is not served by the court, the serving party must also file a certificate of service in form N215 (**CPR, r. 42.4(3)**).

An application to make a declaration under r.12.4 must be supported by evidence (PD 12, para. 4.2) and, unless the court otherwise directs, must be served on the client whose solicitor is unavailable. If the declaration is made, a copy of the order must be served on all the other parties and if the order is not served by the court, the serving party must file a certificate of service in form N215 (CPR r.42.1(3)).

PART G

Statements of Case

Chapter 23   Statements of Case and Claim Forms

INTRODUCTION

23.1 The standard method of starting a claim under the CPR is by the court issuing a claim form (form N1), prepared for or by the claimant (the other methods and the circumstances in which they are used are summarised in **12.1**). A claim form is required by the CPR to set out essential details of the claim, including a concise statement of the nature of the cause of action and a statement of the remedy sought. The CPR also require the claimant to provide rather fuller particulars of claim (see **chapter 24**), which must include, among other prescribed matters, a concise statement of the facts on which the claimant relies. If practicable the particulars of claim should be set out in the claim form, though they may be in a separate document either accompanying the claim form or served and filed separately (see **15.40**).

STATEMENTS OF CASE

23.2 Claim forms and separate particulars of claim are examples of what the CPR call 'statements of case', a term which applies to all documents in which a party's case is set out for the other parties and for the court. The former term for statements of case, 'pleadings', is still commonly used. **CPR, r. 2.3(1)**, includes the following definition:

'statement of case'—
(a) means a claim form, particulars of claim where these are not included in a claim form, defence, Part 20 claim, or reply to defence; and
(b) includes any further information given in relation to them voluntarily or by court order under rule 18.1.

This definition excludes winding-up petitions. Although they are not strictly 'statements of case', this does not prevent the court from striking them out under **r. 3.4** (*Investment Invoice Financing Ltd v Limehouse Board Mills Ltd* [2006] EWCA Civ 9, [2006] 1 WLR 985).

The term 'statement of case' within **r. 2.3** extends to the acknowledgment of service and detailed grounds for contesting a claim for judicial review (*R (Corner House Research) v Director of the Serious Fraud Office* [2008] EWHC 246 (Admin), [2008] ACD 63). Scott schedules are also treated as statements of case (*Easygroup IP Licensing Ltd v Easyjet Airline Co. Ltd* [2009] EWHC 1386 (Ch), LTL 13/7/2009 at [2]–[3]).

455

Every statement of case, including a claim form and particulars of claim, must be verified by a statement of truth (see **23.12**). A person who makes a false statement in a document verified by a statement of truth, without an honest belief in its truth, is guilty of a contempt of court (**r. 32.14(1)**). See *Nield v Loveday* [2011] EWHC 2324 (Admin), LTL 14/9/2011, where a claimant who had brought a personal injury claim following a road traffic accident was committed to prison for nine months for contempt as he had verified his statement of claim and witness statement despite knowing that they contained false information which tended to exaggerate the value of his claim. His wife, who had verified false statements to support his claim, admitted her contempt and was given a suspended six-month sentence. Thus there is now a degree of consanguinity between statements of case, witness statements and affidavits.

Statements of case exceeding 25 pages

23.3 There are cases which, on account of their complexity, have to be pleaded at length. Where, exceptionally, a statement of case exceeds 25 pages (excluding schedules), an appropriate short summary must also be filed and served (**PD 16, para. 1.4**). Lengthy statements of case can contribute to excessive costs, as recognised by the Jackson Review of Civil Costs. In the Admiralty and Commercial Courts, statements of case should be limited to 25 pages (Admiralty and Commercial Courts Guide, para. C1.1(b)). This is backed by prohibitions against setting out evidence (para. C1.1(a)) and substantial quotations from documents (para. C1.1(c): where this is necessary the quotations should be included in a schedule). A party seeking to rely on a statement of case exceeding 25 pages in these courts must apply on paper for permission to do so, including a brief statement of the reasons for exceeding the 25-page limit (para. C1.1(b)). In *Tchenguiz v Grant Thornton UK LLP* [2015] EWHC 405 (Comm), [2015] 1 All ER (Comm) 961 the claimants, in breach of the Guide, served particulars of claim that were 94 pages long and only applied for permission from the court to do so after objections from the defendants. Leading and junior counsel were unable to provide a satisfactory explanation for this failure to comply (the former had forgotten permission was needed and the latter did not know of the Guide's requirements). They could not therefore rely on their failure to seek permission at the proper time as a reason why it should be granted retrospectively. Accordingly, the particulars of claim were struck out, the costs of drafting them were disallowed and fresh particulars of no more than 45 pages but otherwise compliant with the Guide were to be served. The Chancery Guide does not require permission for statements of case exceeding 25 pages, but does require the document to be as brief and concise as possible and includes guidance on not pleading evidence or lengthy extracts from documents (Chapter 10).

CONTENTS OF A CLAIM FORM

23.4 Form N1 is the form used to start most proceedings under **CPR, Part 7**. There is a special version of form N1 for use in the Commercial Court (form N1(CC)). There are also special claim forms for Admiralty claims (ADM1, ADM1A and ADM15), arbitration applications (N8, see **chapter 72**), claims for possession of land (N5 and N5B), claims for relief against forfeiture of a lease (N5A), claims for demotion of tenancy (N6), judicial review claims (N461, see **chapter 74**) and probate claims (N2). Part 8 claims (see **chapter 13**) are generally commenced by form N208, but form N208(CC) is used in the Commercial Court, and N500 and N501 are used in director disqualification proceedings (see **chapter 86**). For additional claims under **Part 20** see **chapters 28** and **29**. This chapter is principally concerned with form N1.

It is not appropriate to strike out a claim merely because the wrong form has been used to bring it, even if important elements such as the royal arms have been omitted, provided it is clear to the defendant (or, at least, the defendant's lawyers) what case has to be met and what type of proceedings are being brought (*Hannigan v Hannigan* [2000] 2 FCR 650). In *Hannigan v Hannigan* the mistake was made by the claimant's professional advisers and the

Court of Appeal indicated that its judgment was not to be taken as giving general permission to practitioners not to bother about using correct forms. However, a claimant using the wrong form of originating process may well be granted permission to correct the position in the interests of dealing with the case justly (see *Thurrock Borough Council v Secretary of State for the Environment, Transport and the Regions* [2001] 1 PLR 94). The court does not have any power under the CPR to waive a failure to use a form (such as a petition) prescribed by Act of Parliament (*Re Osea Road Camp Sites Ltd* [2004] EWHC 2437 (Ch), [2005] 1 WLR 760, see **1.27**).

Heading

On page 1 of form N1 there must be stated: **23.5**

(a) The court in which the claimant wishes to issue the claim. If the claim is to be issued in the High Court, the form must specify (a) the Division and (b) whether the claim is to be issued in the Royal Courts of Justice or a named District Registry. The name of the court must be stated on the claim form for a claim in the Commercial Court (**PD 58, para. 2.3**), a Mercantile Court (**PD 59, para. 2.2**) or the Technology and Construction Court (**PD 60, para. 3.2**). In patent claims, **PD 63, para. 3.1(a)**, requires that claim forms must be marked 'Chancery Division Patents Court' or 'Chancery Division Intellectual Property Enterprise Court' in the top right-hand corner below the title of the court, and must state the number of any patent or registered design to which the claim relates. Claims within **CPR, Part 63, Section II**, must be marked 'Intellectual Property' in the top right-hand corner below the title of the court, unless it is started in the Intellectual Property Enterprise Court (**PD 63, para. 17.1**).

(b) The claimant's preferred hearing centre, but only if the claim form (form N1) must be sent to the County Court Money Claims Centre (**PD 7A, paras 4A.1 and 4A.2; see 11.9**). This may be used where the claim needs to be sent to a local court centre, e.g. if the claim is contested, see **CPR, r. 26.2(4)**.

(c) The parties, who should be described as in **table 14.1**. The full unabbreviated names and titles must be given of parties who are individuals (see **PD 16, para. 2.6**). If the claimant is claiming in a representative capacity, the claim form must state what that capacity is (**CPR, r. 16.2(3)**). If the defendant is sued in a representative capacity, the claim form must likewise state what that capacity is (**r. 16.2(4)**).

(d) The addresses of all parties, as specified in **table 15.1** in **15.14**. An address for service must include a full postcode unless the court orders otherwise (**r. 6.6(2)**). Postcode information can be obtained from http://www.royalmail.com. The claimant's address goes under the heading 'Claimant' on page 1. This address must be that at which the claimant resides or carries on business, even if the business address of the claimant's solicitor is the claimant's address for service (**PD 16, para. 2.2**). If the claimant's address for service is different from the address on page 1, it should be entered on page 2 in the box headed 'Claimant's or claimant's solicitor's address'. The defendant's name and address go in the space provided at the foot of page 1. Where the defendant is an individual, the claimant should (if the information is available) include the address at which the defendant resides or carries on business, even though solicitors may have agreed to accept service on the defendant's behalf (**para. 2.3**). A separate claim form must be prepared for each defendant, giving that defendant's name and address in this box.

If a claim form does not include full addresses for either the claimants or defendants, it will still be issued, but will be retained by the court and will not be served (**para. 2.5**). The court will notify the claimant, and will retain the claim form until the claimant provides full addresses including postcodes, or until the court dispenses with the requirement to provide full addresses (**para. 2.5**).

In clinical negligence claims the words 'clinical negligence' must be inserted at the top of every statement of case (**para. 9.3**).

Commentary

Brief details of claim

23.6   Every claim form must contain a concise statement of the nature of the claim (**CPR, r. 16.2(1)(a)**). This should be inserted in page 1 of form N1 under the heading 'Brief details of claim'. It is suggested that, save in the most straightforward cases where the particulars of claim will be included in the claim form, this will be a simple statement such as:

> The claimant's claim is for damages for personal injuries and interest arising out of a collision caused by the defendant's negligence when driving a motor car along Regent Street, London W1 on 1 July 2016.

More precise details of the allegations and issues will be contained in the particulars of claim (see **chapter 24**), and from a drafting standpoint, it would perhaps not be amiss to state that in the brief details. Particulars of claim should be included in the claim form (page 2 of form N1), if practicable (**PD 16, para. 3.1**), but may be in a separate document. If particulars of claim are not set out in the claim form for a claim issued through the Production Centre or Money Claim Online, the claim form must state that the particulars of claim will follow and must include a brief summary of the claim (**PD 7C, para, 5.2(1)**; **PD 7E, para. 5.2(2)**). It is an abuse of process to issue a claim for which no basis is known to the claimant (*Nomura International plc v Granada Group Ltd* [2007] EWHC 642 (Comm), [2008] Bus LR 1). The claim form had been issued at a time when the claimant had not decided to pursue a claim against the defendant, and had issued the claim form merely to protect its position. Cooke J said that **r. 16.2(1)** followed the same form and had the same intention as RSC, ord. 6, r. 2. Therefore, he had regard to the principles that had informed the pre-CPR cases of *Sterman v E. W. and W. J. Moore* [1970] 1 QB 596 and *Marshall v London Passenger Transport Board* [1936] 3 All ER 83. These decided that failing to include a concise statement on what is now the claim form could only be cured if the claimant had a known and genuine cause of action when the claim was issued. Gaining such knowledge by the time the application to strike out was heard was not enough, and the claim was struck out.

In probate cases, the claim form must contain a statement of the nature of the interest that the claimant and each defendant has in the estate (**CPR, r. 57.7(1)**); *O'Brien v Seagrave* [2007] EWHC 788 (Ch), [2007] 1 WLR 2002).

Remedy sought

23.7   Every claim form must specify the remedy which the claimant seeks (**CPR, r. 16.2(1)(b)**). There is no separate heading for this statement in form N1 and so the remedies sought should be included in the section of the claim form dealing with the brief details of claim.

Failure to specify a particular remedy will not limit any power of the court to grant such a remedy if the claimant is entitled to it (**r. 16.2(5)**). Likewise, in *Slater v Buckinghamshire County Council* [2004] EWCA Civ 1478, LTL 10/11/2004, it was held that the trial judge was entitled to make a finding of fact on an issue which had not been specifically pleaded, but which the parties clearly regarded as live and crucial to the case, and which they adequately dealt with at trial. Thus it should not be possible for a defendant to rely on a technical but unmeritorious defence that a particular remedy has not been set out, in order to escape the full scope of the court's powers (but see the cases discussed at **31.10**). It is suggested that the best practice is to set out all the remedies that are being claimed against the defendant, and there may be costs penalties if this is not done.

STATEMENT OF VALUE

23.8   Where the claimant is making a claim for money, the claim form must contain a statement of value (**CPR, r. 16.2(1)(c)**). The term 'claim for money' includes both a claim for a debt or liquidated demand and a claim for damages.

The clear objective of this rule is not merely to ensure precision and avoid ambiguity, but also to enable the court to allocate the case to the appropriate court and track. A statement of value on a claim form does not, however, limit the power of the court to give judgment for the amount to which it considers the claimant to be entitled (**r. 16.3(7)**).

By **r. 16.2(1)(c)**, a statement of value must be in accordance with **r. 16.3**, and additional requirements are set out in **PD 7A, para. 3**. On page 1 of form N1 there is a space headed 'Value'. By **CPR, r. 16.3(2)**, a statement of value must specify:

(a) the amount of money claimed;
(b) that the claimant expects to recover:
   (i) not more than £10,000, or
   (ii) more than £10,000 but not more than £25,000, or
   (iii) more than £25,000 (these are the basic delineations between cases on the small claims track, the fast track, and the multi-track); or
(c) that the claimant cannot say how much is likely to be recovered.

If the claim is one for personal injuries, the claimant must state whether the amount that he or she expects to recover as general damages for pain, suffering and loss of amenity is not more than £1,000 or more than £1,000 (**r. 16.3(3)**; **PD 7A, para. 3.8**). This declaration is in addition to the statement of the overall expected value of the claim required by **CPR, r. 16.3(2)**, as it relates solely to the general damages aspect of the claim value. This may be important if the overall value of the claim is less than £10,000 (in which event it would normally fall to be tried on the small claims track) but where the general damages aspect of the case is expected to be over £1,000, the claim will normally be dealt with on the fast track, by virtue of **r. 26.6(1)(a)**. Curiously, the 'notes for claimant' (form N1A) only require the statement of value for the personal injury claim to be inserted in a case where the overall value does not exceed £5,000, but this guidance is out of date and does not accord with the requirements of **r. 16.3(3)**.

If the claim includes a claim by a tenant of residential premises against his or her landlord seeking an order requiring the landlord to carry out repairs or other work to the premises, the claimant must state whether the estimated cost of those repairs or other work is not more than £1,000 or more than £1,000; and whether or not the claimant expects to recover more than £1,000 in respect of any other claim for damages (**r. 16.3(4)**; **PD 7A, para. 3.9**). This will determine whether the claim can be allocated to the small claims track (see **CPR, r. 26.6(1)(b)**).

For other matters concerning claim forms in specialist jurisdictions, or using special procedures, see **23.18**.

Reason for starting claim in High Court

If the claim form is to be issued in the High Court, it must include an explanation of why it is being filed there, by stating (**CPR, r. 16.3(5)**):

23.9

(a) that the claimant expects to recover more than £100,000; or
(b) that some other enactment provides that the claim may be commenced only in the High Court (stating the relevant enactment); or
(c) if the claim is one for personal injuries, that the claimant expects to recover £50,000 or more; or
(d) that the claim needs to be in one of the specialist High Court lists, stating which list.

The way in which the financial details are to be entered in the claim form is set out in the notes for claimant on form N1A.

Computation of values

In calculating how much it is expected to recover, the following matters should be disregarded (**CPR, r. 16.3(6)**):

23.10

(a) interest;
(b) costs;

459

(c) any potential finding of contributory negligence;

(d) any potential counterclaim or defence of set-off;

(e) any potential payments that the defendant may have to make, out of any award to the claimant, to the Secretary of State for Social Security under the Social Security (Recovery of Benefits) Act 1997, s. 6.

Foreign currency claim

23.11 Where a claim is for a sum of money expressed in a foreign currency, the claim form should expressly state (**PD 16, para. 9.1**):

(a) that the claim is for payment in a specified foreign currency;

(b) why it is for payment in that currency;

(c) the sterling equivalent of the sum at the date of the claim; and

(d) the source of the exchange rate used in calculating the sterling equivalent.

STATEMENT OF TRUTH

Requirements

23.12 By **CPR, r. 2.3(1)**, a claim form and, if separate, the particulars of claim are classified as statements of case. **Rule 22.1(1)(a)** requires every statement of case to be verified by a statement of truth, that is, a statement that the party putting forward the document believes the facts stated in the document are true (**r. 22.1(4)**). The basic format of a statement of truth is (**PD 22, para. 2.1**):

I believe that the facts stated in this [name of document being verified] are true.

It is possible for the legal representative of a party to make a statement of truth verifying a document put forward by that party (**CPR, r. 22.1(6)**), in which event the basic format of the statement is:

The [claimant/defendant] believes that the facts stated in this [name of document being verified] are true.

There is a pro forma statement of truth on form N1 for use when the particulars of claim are included in the claim form.

A statement of truth may be contained in the document it verifies, or it may be in a separate document served subsequently (**PD 22, para. 1.5**). If it is in a separate document, the formalities set out in **PD 22, para. 2.3**, must be observed.

Who may sign a statement of truth

23.13 A statement of truth verifying a document put forward by a party must be signed by the party or his or her litigation friend (**CPR, r. 22.1(6)(a)(i)**). Alternatively it can be signed by the party's legal representative (**r. 22.1(6)(a)(ii)**), provided the capacity in which the representative signs and the name of his or her firm are stated (**PD 22, para. 3.7**). The term 'legal representative' is defined by **CPR, r. 2.3**, as a person who:

(a) has been instructed to act for a party in relation to proceedings; and

(b) is a barrister, solicitor, solicitor's employee, manager of a body recognised under the Administration of Justice Act 1985, s. 9, or a person who, for the purposes of the Legal Services Act 2007, is an authorised person in relation to an activity which constitutes the conduct of litigation (within the meaning of that Act).

A statement of truth signed by a legal representative will refer to the client's belief and not the representative's but must be signed in the representative's own name and not that of his or her firm or employer (**PD 22, para. 3.10**). The individual who signs a statement of truth must print his or her full name clearly beneath the signature (**PD 22, para. 3.9**).

In the case of a company or other corporation, the statement of truth must be signed by one of the persons 'holding a senior position' listed in **PD 22, para. 3.5**, giving his or her position in the organisation (**PD 22, para. 3.4**). The list in **para. 3.5** includes 'manager or other officer of the company or corporation'. A footnote in **para. 3.4** refers to **PD 6A, para. 6.2**, which, however, defines persons holding a senior position in a company or corporation in precisely the same terms as **PD 22, para. 3.5**. A manager signing a statement of truth must be someone who has personal knowledge of the contents of the document being verified or is responsible for managing those who have that knowledge. In a large company this may be the manager of a claims, insurance or legal department. In a small company it may be that the only persons who hold senior positions are the directors. An employee of a company who works in a legal department managed by an employed solicitor is employed by the company, not by the solicitor, and so cannot qualify as the company's legal representative, though, depending on his or her responsibilities, such an employee might be regarded as holding a senior position.

If an insurer or the Motor Insurers' Bureau has a financial interest in the result of the proceedings for which the document is created, the insurer or Bureau may sign the statement of truth verifying the document (**PD 22, para. 3.6A**). A claims manager may be a person holding a senior position who can sign for the insurer (**para. 3.11**). Signature of a statement of truth when insurers are conducting proceedings on behalf of several claimants or defendants, is dealt with in **para. 3.6B**.

When the claimant is a partnership, the statement of truth may be signed by any of the partners or a person having the control or management of the partnership business (**para. 3.6**). It is not thought that there is any significance in the difference between the word 'must' used in **para. 3.4** and 'may' used in **para. 3.6**.

An agent who manages property or investments for a party cannot sign a statement of truth to verify that party's documents (**para. 3.11**).

It is stated in **para. 3.11** that 'Where some or all of the trustees [of a trust] comprise a single party one, some or all of the trustees comprising the party may sign a statement of truth. The legal representative of the trustees may sign it.' It seems that this permits one trustee to sign on behalf of all.

Mechanically reproduced signatures

It is submitted that it is not good practice for a statement of truth to be signed otherwise than by the hand of the person making the statement. If a mechanically reproduced signature is added by the person making the statement and is an assertion that the signatory's mind has been applied to the contents of the verified document, it is highly arguable that **CPR, r. 22.1(6)**, has been complied with, but it is difficult to see why the signature could not have been written. If a mechanically reproduced signature is applied by someone other than the purported signatory, **r. 22.1(6)** has not been complied with (*Birmingham City Council v Hosey* 2002 Legal Action 20). Although the defect is an irregularity which could be cured by order of the court under **r. 3.10**, until that is done, the statement of case cannot be relied on as evidence of any of the matters set out in it (**r. 22.2(1)**; see **23.17**).

23.14

In *Goodman v J. Eban Ltd* [1954] 1 QB 550 it was held that a solicitor's bill of costs accompanied by a letter, on which the solicitor's signature had been rubber-stamped, was 'signed by' the solicitor, as required by what is now the Solicitors Act 1974, s. 69(2), the rubber stamp having been applied by the solicitor himself, but the practice was disapproved by the court. In *Birmingham City Council v Hosey* a statement of truth was rubber-stamped with the name of an employee in the council's legal services department who had never seen the papers, checked

Commentary

the facts or read any of the source documents. He had merely authorised more junior employees to apply the rubber stamp. Judge MacDuff QC held that the statement had not been properly signed, saying that the requirement in **CPR, r. 22.1(6)**, was not a mere technicality or a matter of form only. **Rule 5.3**, which allows a document to be signed by 'computer or other mechanical means' did not apply, because a statement of truth is not a document but a statement in a document.

Liability for a statement of truth

23.15   A person who makes a false statement in a document verified by a statement of truth, or who causes such a statement to be made, without an honest belief in its truth, is guilty of contempt of court (**CPR, r. 32.14(1)**). It must be shown that the person knew (a) that the statement was false, (b) that it was likely to interfere with the course of justice (*Malgar Ltd v R. E. Leach (Engineering) Ltd* [2000] FSR 393; *KK Sony Computer Entertainment v Ball* [2004] EWHC 1984 (Ch), LTL 11/8/2004). Another way of expressing point (a) is that it must be shown that the false statement was made or caused to be made without an honest belief in its truth (*Walton v Kirk* [2009] EWHC 703 (QB), LTL 9/4/2009). It is not enough to find discrepancies between a document verified by a statement of truth and other objectively verifiable evidence. It is the degree of difference and/or the circumstances in which the verified statement was made that matter (*Walton v Kirk*).

The mere fact that the parties have agreed to settle proceedings does not extinguish a contempt committed by making a false statement in those proceedings (*Kirk v Walton* [2008] EWHC 1780 (QB), [2009] 1 All ER 257).

A party to proceedings who believes that there should be an application for committal of another party for making a false statement can make that application themselves only with the permission of the court dealing with the proceedings (**r. 81.18(1)(a)**) or, if the court dealing with the proceedings is the County Court, a single judge of the Queen's Bench Division (**r. 81.18(3)(a)**). Alternatively a request may be made to the Attorney General to make the application (**rr. 81.18(1)(b)** and **81.18(3)(b)**). This is to ensure that proceedings are brought only when required in the public interest. A party wishing to apply for, or persuade the Attorney General to apply for, committal should consider whether the incident complained of does amount to contempt of court and whether such proceedings would further the overriding objective (**PD 81, para. 5.7**). The party should warn the maker of the statement at the earliest suitable opportunity (*KJM Superbikes Ltd v Hinton* [2008] EWCA Civ 1280, [2009] 1 WLR 2406). If the maker of the statement of truth is likely to be a witness at the trial of the claim in which the statement was made, such notification should be delayed until after that evidence has been given, so as to avoid imposing improper pressure on the witness.

An application for permission under **CPR, r. 81.18(1)(a)** or **81.18(3)(a)** is made using the procedure in **r. 81.14** but, if the application is under **r. 81.18(1)(a)**, it is made by Part 23 application notice instead of Part 8 claim form (**rr. 81.18(2)** and **81.18(4)**). **PD 81, para. 5.2**, requires the affidavit evidence in support of the application to identify the statement said to be false and explain why it is false and why the maker knew the statement to be false at the time it was made. The evidence must also explain why contempt proceedings would be appropriate in the light of the overriding objective. The court considering an application for permission may initiate steps to consider if there is a contempt of court and, where there is, to punish it (**para 5.3(2)**) or direct that the matter be referred to the Attorney General with a request to consider whether to bring proceedings for contempt (**para 5.3(3)**; **CPR, r. 81.18(5)**).

The Attorney General prefers a request that comes from the court to one made direct by a party to the claim in which the alleged contempt occurred without prior consideration by the court (**PD 81, para. 5.1**). A request to the Attorney General is not a way of appealing against or reviewing the decision of the judge (**para. 5.1**). A request to the Attorney General must be made in writing and sent to the Attorney General's Office at 20 Victoria Street, London SW1H 0NF (**para. 5.4**). If the request is made at the direction of the court under **para. 5.3(3)**, it must be accompanied by a copy of the court's order (**para. 5.5**). In any case it must include the same statements as are required by **para. 5.2** in the affidavit evidence in support of an application to the court (**para. 5.5**). The applicant must send a copy of the result of the request to the court that will deal with the committal application, and the court will give such directions as it sees fit (**para. 5.6**).

In deciding whether to give permission under **CPR, r. 81.18(1)(a)** or **81.18(3)(a)**, the only question is whether the complaint has sufficient gravity to make it in the public interest for committal proceedings to be brought (*KJM Superbikes Ltd v Hinton*). Permission should be given where there is a serious example of a false statement, because otherwise parties and witnesses will regard the statement of truth as a mere formality. Factors to be taken into account in deciding whether it is in the public interest to proceed include:

(a) the strength of the evidence tending to show the statement was false;
(b) the strength of the evidence showing the maker of the statement knew it was false when the statement was made;
(c) the circumstances in which the statement was made;
(d) the significance of the document in the proceedings;
(e) any evidence of the maker's state of mind, including his understanding of the significance of the document in the proceedings;
(f) the length of time the false statements were persisted in (*Kirk v Walton* [2008] EWHC 1780 (QB), [2009] 1 All ER 257).

The belief stated in a statement of truth (and the consequent responsibility for making a false statement) is that of the party putting forward the document, save in the case where a party is conducting proceedings with the aid of a litigation friend, in which event the statement of belief is that of the litigation friend (**r. 22.1(5)**). Although it could possibly be argued that both a litigation friend and the party on whose behalf such friend is acting, could be jointly or independently responsible for the accuracy of the statement of truth in the (possibly rare) circumstances where it could be shown that the party was aware that the statement was false, this seems to be precluded by the terms of **r. 22.1(5)**.

When a statement of truth verifying a document is signed by a legal adviser of the party putting forward the document, its contents and the consequences of signing it are deemed, by virtue of the signature, to have been explained to the claimant, and the signature will be taken by the court as meaning that the client has authorised the representative to sign (**PD 22, para. 3.8**).

For the position of an insurer or the Motor Insurers' Bureau signing a statement of truth see **PD 22, paras 3.6A** and **3.6B**.

The effect of this rule is to rest the responsibility for the contents of the document squarely on the shoulders of the person putting forward the facts. It is not sufficient for a legal representative to put forward matters in the belief (however genuine) that what his client has told him is the truth — it is incumbent on him to ensure that he has received direct instructions to that effect. This is particularly important in view of the explanation deemed to have been made to the client by **PD 22, para. 3.8**, which, if not actually given, could well lead to an allegation of professional misconduct. Provided that such instructions have been given, the legal representative signing a statement should not incur personal liability in respect of any default, unless he is aware that the contents are false, notwithstanding his instructions to the contrary.

Use of a verified statement of case as evidence

23.16   The principal reason for the requirement for a statement of case to be verified by a statement of truth is to ensure that litigants do not lightly put forward false cases. A secondary purpose is to enable a statement of case to be used as evidence in interim proceedings. By **r. 32.6(2)**, at hearings other than the trial, matters set out in a party's statement of case or application notice may be relied on in support of that party's application, provided that the statement or notice is verified by a statement of truth.

Consequence of failure to verify a statement of case

23.17   If a statement of case is not verified by a statement of truth, it will remain effective unless struck out, but the party putting it forward may not rely on it as evidence of any of the matters set out in it (**CPR, r. 22.2(1)**). The omission simply means that the statement of case cannot be used for the purpose of supporting an application under **r. 32.6(2)**.

Where a statement of case remains unverified, any party may apply either:

(a)   under **r. 22.4** for an order that the statement be verified within such period as the court may specify, or be struck out in default (**PD 22, para. 4.2**); or

(b)   under **r. 22.2(2)** for an order that the statement be struck out.

The costs of such an application will normally be ordered to be paid by the defaulting party in any event, and forthwith (**PD 22, para. 4.3**). It is probable that the majority of such applications will be as a result of oversight on the part of the party putting forward the document, rather than as a result of any deliberate intention to avoid the rule.

The usual order on failing to verify a statement of case is to allow the defaulting party a limited period of time to file a verified statement of case. Setting aside an order granting permission to serve outside the jurisdiction on the ground that the claim form and witness statement were not signed was regarded as disproportionate in *Colliers International Property Consultants v Colliers Jordan Lee Jafaar Sdn Bhd* [2008] EWHC 1524 (Comm), [2008] 2 Lloyd's Rep 368.

OTHER MATTERS TO BE SET OUT IN THE CLAIM FORM

23.18   Special rules concerning claims against the Crown are set out in **CPR, r. 16.2(1A)**.

A claim form must contain such other matters as may be set out in a practice direction (**CPR, r. 16.2(1)(d)**).

For entering fixed costs on a claim form see **70.6**. Where fixed costs do not apply, the words 'to be assessed' should be entered in the box labelled 'Legal representative's costs'.

Paragraphs 14 and 15 of PD 16 specify matters which must be included in a claimant's statement of case and so could either be in the claim form or in the particulars of claim. **Paragraph 14** is concerned with certain proceedings under the Competition Act 1998, and specifies information which must be presented by a claimant intending to rely on a determination of the Competition and Markets Authority. **Paragraph 15** specifies what must be set out in a statement of case by a claimant who seeks to rely on any provision of, or right arising under, the **Human Rights Act 1998**, or seeks a remedy under that Act.

PD Pre-action Conduct and Protocols no longer requires that a claimant should state, either in the claim form or in particulars of claim, whether there has been compliance with the practice direction, or any relevant protocol. However, the parties remain obliged to comply with any such relevant protocol or, where there is none, to exchange correspondence and information that enables them to understand each other's position, decide how to proceed, try to settle issues without proceedings, consider ADR and reduce costs. It is therefore likely that the practice which arose under the former PD Pre-action Conduct, para. 9.7, will continue.

NOTICES TO BE FILED WITH THE CLAIM FORM

If a claim form, which is to be served out of the jurisdiction, is one which the court has **23.19** power to deal with under the **Civil Jurisdiction and Judgments Act 1982** and the **recast Brussels I Regulation**, it must be filed and served with form N510 (CPR, r. 6.34; PD 6B, para. 2.1; PD 7A, para. 3.5; see 16.41).

Chapter 24　Particulars of Claim

REQUIREMENT

24.1　Particulars of claim are required by **CPR, r. 7.4(1)**. They must include the matters specified in **r. 16.4**, the first of which is a concise statement of the facts on which the claimant relies (see **24.3**). Particulars of claim should, if practicable, be set out in the claim form (**PD 16, para. 3.1**). Page 2 of form N1 has a space headed 'Particulars of Claim'. If it is not practicable to state the particulars of claim on the claim form, they may be in a separate document accompanying the claim form, or they may be served and filed separately within the time limits stated in **15.40**. In the **PD 7B** procedure, which applies to most claims under the Consumer Credit Act 1974, particulars of claim must be served with the claim form (**PD 7B, para. 5.2**). In Money Claim Online there is a limit of 1080 characters (including spaces) for particulars of claim in the claim form (**PD 7E, para. 5.2(1)**). If particulars of claim are not set out in a claim form issued through the Claims Production Centre or Money Claim Online, the claim form must state that the particulars of claim will follow and must include a brief summary of the claim (**PD 7C, para, 5.2(1)**; **PD 7E, para. 5.2(2)**).

In *Tetra Pak Ltd v Biddle and Co.* [2010] EWHC 54 (Ch), [2010] 1 WLR 1466, it was held that it would not be inconsistent with the CPR, and in particular **rr. 7.4** and **16.4**, for a claimant to serve separate particulars of claim on different defendants within the same claim.

CPR, Part 8, provides an alternative procedure for bringing claims, and specifically excludes the provisions in **Part 16** on statements of case (**r. 8.9(a)(i)**).

POWER TO DISPENSE WITH STATEMENTS OF CASE

24.2　If a claim form has been properly issued and served on a defendant, the court has the power under **CPR, r. 16.8**, to order that the claim will then continue without any statements of case having to be filed. This will presumably be reserved for cases of considerable urgency where the matter can be dealt with expeditiously without formal disclosure of the respective parties' cases, or matters where the issue is extremely simple, and where the service of statements of case would only add to the delay and expense of the proceedings.

CONTENT

Where the particulars of claim are served separately from the claim form, they must state **24.3**
(PD 16, para. 3.8):

(a) the name of the court in which the claim is proceeding;
(b) the claim number;
(c) the title of the proceedings (parties should be described as in **table 14.1**); and
(d) the claimant's address for service.

The body of the particulars of claim must include:

(a) A concise statement of the facts on which the claimant relies (**CPR, r. 16.4(1)(a)**). Particulars
of claim extending to 109 pages with 162 numbered paragraphs could not be regarded as
concise (*Diamantides v J. P. Morgan Chase Bank* [2005] EWHC 263 (Comm), LTL 5/3/2005 at [10]).
The rules should not be read or interpreted as suggesting that the particulars of claim should
contain evidence. The distinction between material facts (relevant), and the evidence by
which those facts are to be proved (irrelevant) still remains good practice.

The purpose of statements of case is to elucidate the facts. A party is not obliged to particularise or explain its legal arguments in its statements of case (that is the function of skeleton
arguments) (*Trader Publishing Ltd v Autotrader.Com Inc.* [2010] EWHC 142 (Ch), LTL 12/3/2010).

In *Petromec Inc. v Petróleo Brasileiro SA* [2007] EWCA Civ 1371, [2008] 1 Lloyd's Rep 305, the claimant
was seeking to recover reasonably incurred extra costs pursuant to contractual clauses for extra
work carried out to upgrade an oil production platform for the defendant beyond the original
specifications and for alterations specified by the defendant. The claimant could not just assert
the final costs from which the reasonable extra costs could be calculated, instead it was necessary
to identify the work required to effect the changes from the original specification, particularise
what the defendant instructed it to do, the cost incurred and where necessary a causal nexus.

(b) Details of any interest claimed (**CPR, r. 16.4(1)(b) and (2)**). A claimant who is seeking
interest must state whether it is being claimed under the terms of a contract, or under a
specified enactment, or for some other (defined) reason (**r. 16.4(2)(a)**). If the claim is for
a specified sum of money, the particulars of claim should state the percentage rate claimed,
the date from which interest is claimed, the date to which it is calculated (being not later
than the date of issue of the claim form), the amount claimed up until that date, and the
daily rate of interest accruing after that date (**r. 16.4(2)(b)**). Thus, on a specified sum, a
claim for interest 'pursuant to statute' or 'at such rate and for such period as the court shall
deem fit' will not comply with the rule.

(c) Where appropriate, a statement to the effect that aggravated or exemplary damages (or both)
are being claimed; together with the grounds on which they are claimed (**r. 16.4(1)(c)**).

(d) Where appropriate, a statement to the effect that provisional damages are being claimed,
together with the grounds on which they are claimed (**r. 16.4(1)(d)**).

(e) Where a claim is brought to enforce a right to recover possession of goods, a statement
showing the value of the goods (**PD 16, para. 7.2**).

(f) Where a claim is based upon a written agreement, a copy of the contract or contractual
documents should be attached to or served with the particulars of claim; together with
relevant parts of the contract or documents incorporating any general conditions of sale
(**PD 16, para. 7.3**). The requirement to attach contractual documents to the particulars
of claim in breach of contract cases does not apply in Claims Production Centre or Money
Claim Online cases (**PD 7C, para. 1.4(3A); PD 7E, para. 5.2A**), unless the particulars of
claim are served separately in accordance with **PD 7C, para. 5.2**, or **PD 7E, para. 5.2(2)**.
In trespass and injunction cases it is often helpful to illustrate the facts with plans annexed
to the particulars of claim. The original documents should be available at the hearing.

(g) Where a claim is based upon an oral agreement, the contractual words relied upon,
including by whom, to whom, when and where they were spoken (**PD 16, para. 7.4**).

(h) Where a claim is based upon an agreement by conduct, particulars of the conduct relied on, stating by whom, when and where the acts constituting the conduct were done (**PD 16, para. 7.5**).

(i) In a claim issued in the High Court relating to a Consumer Credit Act 1974 agreement, a statement that the action is not one to which s. 141 of the Act applies (**PD 16, para. 7.6**).

(j) Any other matters required by practice directions to be included in respect of certain types of claim (**CPR, r. 16.4(1)(e); PD 16, para. 3.6(2)**).

(k) Where a party seeks to raise a human rights point, the particulars of claim (and any other type of statement of claim or appeal notice filed on behalf of that party) must set out precise details of the Convention right relied upon. It must also give details of the alleged infringement and it must state the relief sought (**PD 16, para. 15.1**).

(l) In a claim for wrongful interference with goods the particulars of claim must state the name and address of every person (who is not a party) who the claimant knows claims an interest in the goods (**CPR, r. 19.5A(1)**).

Additionally, the following specific matters are required by **PD 16, para. 8.2**, to be set out in particulars of claim, if the claimant wishes to rely on them:

(a) any allegation of fraud (see *Rigby v Decorating Den Systems Ltd* [1999] EWCA Civ 986 BAILII, LTL 15/3/99; Chancery Guide, paras 10.1 and 10.2);

(b) the fact of any illegality;

(c) details of any misrepresentation;

(d) details of all breaches of trust;

(e) notice or knowledge of a fact;

(f) details of unsoundness of mind or undue influence;

(g) details of wilful default;

(h) any facts relating to mitigation of loss or damage.

A statement of compliance with requirements concerning pre-action conduct is no longer required by **PD Pre-action Conduct and Protocols**. However, the parties remain obliged to comply with any relevant protocol or, where there is none, to exchange correspondence and information that enables them to understand each other's position, decide how to proceed, try to settle issues without proceedings, consider ADR and reduce costs. It is therefore likely that, if there has been alleged default by the defendant, the practice of addressing this in the particulars of claim which arose under the former PD Pre-action Conduct, para. 9.7, will continue (see **23.18**).

Signature when drafted by legal representative

24.4 Statements of case and other documents drafted by a legal representative must be signed. Documents drafted by counsel must bear counsel's signature, and those drafted by a solicitor must be signed in the name of the firm (**PD 5A, para. 2.1**). In practice, counsel's handwritten signature appears only on the draft as settled by counsel. The version of the document used for service and filing simply has the barrister's name typed in capitals. For the use of mechanically reproduced signatures see **23.14**.

Statement of truth

24.5 The particulars of claim, being a statement of case, must be verified by a statement of truth (**CPR, r. 22.1(1)(a); see 23.12 to 23.17**). The purpose of requiring a statement of truth is to eliminate claims in which a party has no honest belief and to discourage the pleading of claims unsupported by evidence and which are put forward in the hope that something may turn up on disclosure or at trial (*Clarke v Marlborough Fine Art (London) Ltd* [2002] 1 WLR 1731).

Special rules for certain types of claim

24.6 For special requirements in:

(a) personal injury claims, see **PD 16, para. 4**;

(b) fatal accident claims, see **PD 16, para. 5**;

(c) possession claims, see **PD 55A, paras** 2.1 to 2.7;

(d) hire-purchase claims, see **PD 16, para.** 6;

(e) claims under the Consumer Credit Act 1974 to which **PD 7B** applies, see **PD 7B, para.** 7;

(f) defamation claims, see **PD 53, para.** 2;

(g) claims made for an injunction or declaration in respect of land or its possession, see **PD 16, para.** 7.1;

(h) claims for recovery of goods, see **PD 16, para.** 7.2;

(i) cases where a claimant wishes to rely on the provisions of the Civil Evidence Act 1968, s. 11 or s. 12, concerning evidence of conviction of an offence, or a finding of adultery or paternity, see **PD 16, para.** 8.1;

(j) a claim for infringement of a patent or registered design, or an application in which the validity of a patent or registered design is challenged, see **CPR, r. 63.6**, and **PD 63, para.** 4.

Paragraphs 14 and **15** of **PD 16** specify matters which must be included in a claimant's statement of case and so could either be in the claim form or in the particulars of claim. **Paragraph 14** is concerned with certain proceedings under the Competition Act 1998 and specifies information which must be presented by a claimant intending to rely on a determination of the Competition and Markets Authority (the practice direction still refers to the old Office of Fair Trading). **Paragraph 15** specifies what must be set out in a statement of case by a claimant who seeks to rely on any provision of, or right arising under, the Human Rights Act 1998, or seeks a remedy under that Act.

Points of law, witnesses and documents

PD 16, para. 13.3, states that a statement of case may include:　　　　　　　　　　　　　**24.7**

(a) a reference to any point of law on which the party's claim or defence is based;

(b) the name of any witness whom the party proposes to call; and

(c) (by way of service or attachment) a copy of any document which the party considers is necessary to the claim or defence (including any expert's report to be filed in accordance with **Part 35**).

It is interesting that there is no reference to this option in the guidance notes on drafting particulars of claim which are given to claimants on form N1A.

STRUCTURE OF PARTICULARS OF CLAIM

It is not intended to provide precedents of statements of case in this work, as some of the worst **24.8** excesses of the previous system came about as a result of over-reliance on formulaic pleading, to the detriment of clear and objective thought. It is suggested that the basic objective of particulars of claim should be to inform the court and the other side what the case is all about, including (in the vast majority of cases) the duty that was allegedly owed, the fact that it was broken, how it was broken, and the remedies sought as a result. It is hoped that the following advice on structure will be of assistance.

Identification of the parties

It is, of course, essential to ensure that the correct parties appear as claimant(s) and defendant(s). **24.9** Although in most cases these may be self-evident, there are instances in which the correct parties may only be ascertained by reference to the cause of action (for example, where there are special rules as to the parties entitled to claim relief, or against whom relief can be claimed). It may be necessary to sue 'persons unknown', who are identified by description rather than name (see **14.3**).

Commentary

The manner in which a claim form, and every other statement of case should be headed, is now set out specifically in **PD 7A, paras 4.1 and 4.2,** and **PD 16, para. 2.6.** The title should state:

(a) the number of proceedings (i.e. the case number);
(b) the court or Division in which they are proceeding;
(c) each party's full unabbreviated name and title by which he is known;
(d) each party's status in the proceedings (i.e. claimant or defendant).

Where there is more than one claimant and/or defendant, the parties should be described in the title as:

> (1) MR AB
> (2) MISS CD
> (3) MRS EF   <u>Claimants</u>
> — and —
> (1) MR GH
> (2) MS IJ
> (3) Master KL   <u>Defendants</u>

Although it may be helpful for some description of the parties to be given in the first paragraph of the particulars of claim, it is not necessary to do this when their business, profession or relationship to the other parties is not relevant to the claim. If, however, it is necessary to assert the identity and status of the claimant or defendant in order to set out the legal basis on which the claim is being brought, this should be done. Thus, it may be necessary to state the nature of a company's business where a claim is being brought by or against a company arising out of matters concerning its business. Similarly it may be important to set out the fact that a party is a landlord or tenant of premises, or the owner of a particular chattel, or an employer or employee.

Background

24.10   Before turning to the precise nature of the duty owed, it will often (but not invariably) be necessary to 'set the scene', by giving a short description of the circumstances in which the duty came about. This should be done with sufficient precision to enable the defendant precisely to identify what will subsequently be alleged, and to put it into context. This may vary from a short description of the circumstances in which an accident occurred, to the events which ultimately gave rise to a concluded agreement between the parties. In many cases, the CPR or PDs will require the insertion of material here, such as supporting documentation, or particulars of words spoken.

Duty alleged

24.11   The vast majority of claims involve allegations of breaches of duty. It is thus essential first to state what the duty is (and if necessary how it is alleged to have arisen) before alleging the breach or breaches relied on. Often this will be no more than stating the fact that a contract has come into being with various terms. Sometimes the relationship between the parties has given rise to a duty. In road traffic cases, it is conventional not to allege the fact that the presence of a motor vehicle on a road gave rise to a duty of care towards other road users, because that is taken for granted.

Breach of duty

24.12   Once the existence and nature of the duty have been alleged, it is necessary to set out precisely the manner in which it is alleged that the duty has been breached. Inserting 'stock' particulars, which tell little or nothing about the real nature of the claim, is to be avoided. A specimen of such unsatisfactory particulars appears in example 24.3 in **24.20.** Such particulars will almost inevitably be struck out today.

It must be remembered that the objectives of particulars of breach are twofold — first to describe the nature of the breach, and secondly to do so in such a way that it is clear to the defendant and the court how the breach actually took place. In particulars of negligence, for example, it is essential that each particular should not only describe a breach of the duty, but set out the manner and circumstances (singly or collectively) in which that breach occurred. See example 24.1 for an annotated description of properly drafted particulars.

Example 24.1   Properly drafted particulars

<u>PARTICULARS OF NEGLIGENCE</u>

The Defendant was negligent in that he:

1. Drove his car along Litigation Avenue towards the junction with Blackstone Road, at a speed that was excessive in the circumstances.

(The conventional phrase 'drove too fast', says very little if anything about the breach, and often appears to be inserted as a matter of form. It is often incorrectly thought that this allegation means that the Defendant was exceeding the speed limit. The duty is to drive at a safe speed in the circumstances. The manner in which the particulars are set out makes this clear, and also starts to build up the picture which, when all the particulars are complete, will properly identify the Claimant's case, so that it can be answered by the Defendant.)

2. Failed to keep a proper lookout.

(This is a straightforward example of an allegation of breach of a generic duty. It should later be qualified by particulars of how precisely it is alleged that the breach took place.)

3. Failed to see or heed the presence of the Claimant's vehicle, which was in the process of entering into Litigation Avenue from Blackstone Road into the path of the Defendant's car.

(This paragraph comprises specific particulars of the generic allegation made in paragraph 2, and adds further details which, in conjunction with paragraph 1, clarifies the circumstances in which the accident took place. Essentially, this paragraph could be silently prefaced by the words, 'because he failed to keep a proper lookout, he...'.

4. Failed to brake, steer or otherwise manoeuvre his car in order to avoid colliding with the Claimant.

(Again, this paragraph runs logically on from the last one: 'Because he failed to see the Claimant, he failed to brake etc.'. Once again, specific breaches of duty are alleged here in the context of the events that are being described.)

5. Caused his car to collide with that of the Claimant.

(Often, and wrongly, omitted in many particulars, this is the actual breach of duty which gives rise to the claim.)

The above example not merely describes the alleged breaches of duty, but puts them in a context which enables the claimant's case to be understood, so that an appropriate response can be made. This does not, of course mean that the case is unassailable — the defence in the above example may well be to the effect that the claimant was emerging from a minor road and that the defendant had the right of way. He would not, however, be in a position to assert this had the context of the claim not been fully particularised.

In *Uren v First National Home Finance Ltd* [2005] EWHC 2529 (Ch), *The Times*, 17 November 2005, the claim simply pleaded a sequence of events and stated that as a result of those events the defendant had been unjustly enriched. This was struck out. It failed to set out facts which were capable of bringing the claim within one of the established restitutionary categories, or some justifiable extension of them. However, in *Sinclair Investment Holdings SA v Versailles Trade Finance Ltd* [2005] EWCA Civ 722, [2006] 1 BCLC 60, in a claim for breach of fiduciary duty based on an assumption of a duty of loyalty with an alternative claim in constructive trust, although the assumption of loyalty was not expressly pleaded, it was held to be sufficiently pleaded by allegations that the defendant controlled the exercise, or was in a position to control the exercise, of powers over the claimant's money.

While the court will be slow to strike out for failing to give sufficient particulars of negligence, where the claimant has been given the opportunity to provide those particulars and fails to do so, striking out may be appropriate (*S v Chapman* [2008] EWCA Civ 800, [2008] ELR 603). Indeed, the court in *Spencer v Barclays Bank plc* (2009) LTL 30/10/2009 struck out the claim as an abuse of process because the particulars failed to include a concise statement of the facts upon which the claimants were relying, such that neither the court nor the defendant could see the case the defendant was to meet, and further, the claimants clearly had no intention of trying to amend their statement of case to put forward a coherently pleaded and intelligible claim.

Particulars of claim expressed in a general non-specific way may be struck out. See *English, Welsh and Scottish Railway Ltd v Goodman* [2007] EWHC 3463 (QB), LTL 21/8/2007, which was a claim for breach of restrictive covenants against a former employee. The particulars of claim were struck out as far too broad in making claims and allegations which were unfocused and unparticularised. See also *Dunn v Glass Systems (UK) Ltd* [2007] EWHC 1901 (QB), LTL 23/7/2007, in which particulars of claim running to 221 pages were struck out. They were excessively long, which was oppressive, and contained details irrelevant to the cause of action, a large number of terms that were incomprehensible and privileged material.

Where a company director is alleged to have failed to disclose to the board conflicts of interest, it is essential that the transactions affected by the conflicts of interest be pleaded and clearly identified (*Towler v Wills* [2010] EWHC 1209 (Comm), LTL 27/5/2010).

A party is obliged to plead its positive case on an issue, even if the burden of proof rests with the other side (*Baxter Healthcare Corporation v Abbott Laboratories* [2005] EWHC 2878 (Pat), LTL 6/12/2005).

Loss suffered

24.13   Although the claim form N1 contains a section into which the value of the claim has to be inserted (the 'statement of value', see **23.8**), it will normally be necessary to set out what loss has been suffered in consequence of the breaches alleged in the previous paragraph(s). Without this, logically, there will be no sustainable claim, as there is no formal averment that the relief being sought is as a result of the breach previously alleged. Such particulars may well include, for example, brief details of any injury suffered (attaching or serving any evidence from a medical practitioner on which reliance is made: **PD 16, para. 4.3**) as well as details of the effect of the breaches on the claimant, in support of the relief sought at the end of the particulars of claim. Where there is a money claim, it will be necessary to make clear whether it is a claim for general and/or special damages. In many cases it will be necessary to deal with the amount of special damages by means of a schedule attached to the particulars of claim. This must be done when the claim is for personal injury, where the claimant is claiming past and future expenses and losses (**PD 16, para. 4.2**), and in all cases where the damages claimed are anything other than short and straightforward.

Pleading the number of hours worked multiplied by the applicable hourly rates in a claim for unpaid building work was regarded as perfectly clear in *Clancy Consulting Ltd v Derwent Holdings Ltd* [2010] EWHC 762 (TCC), LTL 21/4/2010. However, a claim for lost management time in dealing with the defendant's breach of contract must show the alleged causal link between the cost incurred and the alleged default, and also how the claimant's normal trading routine was disturbed (and hence why additional money had to be spent). See *Clancy Consulting Ltd v Derwent Holdings Ltd*.

Failing to plead losses flowing from specific transactions alleged to have been affected by conflicts of interest was held to be defective in *Towler v Wills* [2010] EWHC 1209 (Comm), LTL 27/5/2010. Similarly, where a claimant relied not on actual damage but on probable damage under the Defamation Act 1952, s. 3(1), he had to give particulars of the nature of the alleged probable damage and the grounds relied on for saying that it was more likely than not. In *Tesla Motors Ltd v British Broadcasting Corporation* [2011] EWHC 2760 (QB), LTL 1/11/2011, a claim for damages for malicious falsehood under s. 3(1) was so lacking in particularity that it could not be allowed to proceed.

As a matter of law, a claimant is not required to give credit against a debt claim for sums saved through not having to complete a contract after the defendant is in repudiatory breach. Such credit is only required for damages claims (*Ram Media Ltd v Ministry of Culture for the Hellenic Republic (Secretariat of Sport)* [2009] EWCA Civ 528, LTL 16/6/2009).

Other relevant matters

Many types of claim require certain information to be inserted in the particulars of claim, and care should be taken to ensure that these requirements are complied with. For example, claims for aggravated or exemplary damages must be specifically set out together with the grounds for claiming them (**CPR, r. 16.4(1)(c)**). Claims for interest must comply with **r. 16.4(2)**. **24.14**

In many cases some of this information will have to be given in previous paragraphs or particulars. In others, it will be sufficient to set them out formally in separate paragraphs. Often it will be a combination of the two (see, for example, the required matters in claims for the recovery of land in **PD 55A, para. 2**, where it is clear that the special requirements will have to be inserted at various places in the particulars of claim). Further special rules are set out in **24.6**.

Names of persons which are known to the claimant who play a significant part in the narrative relating to the claim (such as persons to whom a libel is alleged to have been published) should be included in the particulars of claim (*Freer v Zeb* [2008] EWHC 212 (QB), LTL 21/2/2008). Particulars must be pleaded of any assignment of the cause of action sufficient to show that it is vested in the claimant (*Pickthall v Hill Dickinson LLP* [2008] EWHC 3409 (Ch), [2009] PNLR 10).

General allegations must be supported by particulars. Commonly occurring examples are particulars of negligence, of breach of statutory duty, of breach of contract, and of loss and damage. An allegation of 'systematic overcharging' had to be supported by particulars of the supposed system (*Clyde and Co. LLP v New Look Interiors of Marlow Ltd* [2009] EWHC 173 (QB), LTL 13/2/2009).

Although there is no express requirement for a statement of value to be included in the particulars of claim (**CPR, r. 16.3**, referring specifically to it being set out in the claim form), it may nevertheless be good practice to repeat it in the particulars of claim, particularly when that document is likely to be the principal one referred to in the course of the trial.

Alternative and contradictory claims

The purpose of requiring statements of truth is to deter parties from advancing cases which are inherently untrue or wholly speculative. Nevertheless, if it would further the overriding objective, a party should be allowed to rely on more than one version of the facts (*Binks v Securicor Omega Express Ltd* [2003] EWCA Civ 993, [2003] 1 WLR 2557). There is, therefore, no objection to a claimant advancing alternative claims, provided the alternative sets of facts are clearly set out. Examples are where: **24.15**

(a) The claimant advances one set of facts, and the defence advances a different set of facts. The claimant seeks to amend, saying that even on the defendant's version of the facts liability is established.
(b) The claimant, perhaps because of injuries suffered in the accident, has no personal re-collection of the material events, and has to rely on independent witnesses, who give different versions of those events, each of which is consistent with liability being established.

(c) The claimant, perhaps through having honestly convinced himself of the truth of his version of events as set out in the particulars of claim, gives evidence, but a different version of events emerges from the body of evidence at the trial. Permission may be sought to amend at trial to adopt the version that has emerged at trial.

Subject to the court's discretion based on the overriding objective, a claimant in each of these situations may be given permission to rely on the alternative or new versions of events (*Binks v Securicor Omega Express Ltd*). The claimant's statement of truth has the effect of stating the claimant's honest belief that on either one set of facts or the other the claim is made out (*Clarke v Marlborough Fine Art (London) Ltd* [2002] 1 WLR 1731). It may be necessary to seek the court's permission in cases like the examples set out above to amend without verifying the amended statements of case with a new statement of truth, or to use an amended statement of truth making clear that the primary case is not an assertion of the truth (say) of the defendant's alternative version, but that the defendant's version is relied on as an alternative basis for liability if the court finds the facts to be as pleaded by the defendant (*Binks v Securicor Omega Express Ltd*).

A claimant cannot make a unified claim relying on contradictory allegations of fact, because in such a case the claimant cannot honestly sign a statement of truth (*Clarke v Marlborough Fine Art (London) Ltd*).

Allegations of abuse of process and anti-suit injunctions

24.16   Any allegation of abuse of process should be fully pleaded in the statements of case so that the true nature of the issue can be identified and considered in advance of the trial (*Conlon v Simms* [2006] EWCA Civ 1749, [2008] 1 WLR 484 at [151], [166] and [176]). There is probably a similar obligation to plead any claim for an anti-suit injunction in the particulars of claim (*Albon v Naza Motor Trading Sdn Bhd (No. 4)* [2007] EWCA Civ 1124, [2008] 1 All ER (Comm) 351 at [9]).

It is necessary for allegations of fraud to be separately and distinctly pleaded in order to comply with CPR, r. 16.2(1)(a) (*Berezovsky v Abramovich* [2008] EWHC 1138 (Comm), LTL 30/5/2008).

Foreign law

24.17   CPR, Part 16, does not have an express requirement, unlike RSC, ord. 18, r 8(1)(b), to plead any allegation of foreign law. However, CPR, r. 16.4(1)(a), provides that particulars of claim must include a concise statement of the facts on which the claimant relies. It was held in *Global Multimedia International Ltd v ARA Media Services* [2006] EWHC 3612 (Ch), [2007] 1 All ER (Comm) 1160, that a requirement to plead foreign law that is relied upon can be read into the CPR through r. 16.4(1)(a) or through the application of the overriding objective. A party relying on foreign law must plead the relevant point of foreign law, and must expressly state which system of foreign law is alleged to give rise to the point.

Relief claimed

24.18   The CPR do not require a summary of the relief claimed in particulars of claim. The claim form contains a box for 'brief details of the claim' and another for the value, but it is suggested that it is good practice to provide a list of remedies sought at the end of particulars of claim so that the extent of the claim can be seen at a glance. It is unnecessary to include a claim for costs in this list.

EFFECT OF THE CPR ON DRAFTING STYLE

Is evidence required in a claim form or particulars of claim?

24.19   The requirement set out in CPR, r. 16.2(1)(a), that the claim form must contain a concise statement of the nature of the claim, has led some to take the view that some evidence must be set out in the claim form, and if such evidence is omitted, it would be possible to have the claim struck out for containing insufficient particulars. Support for this argument is gained by the fact that the claim form is required to be verified by a statement of truth (see **23.12**), which, by its very nature, implies that the claim form is to contain matters of evidence.

Nevertheless, it is submitted that the CPR do not impose any additional *requirement* to include evidence in a statement of case, but in making it clear that the claim form must contain a concise statement of the nature of the claim (**r. 16.2(1)(a)**) and that particulars of claim must include a concise statement of the facts on which the claimant relies (**r. 16.4(1)(a)**), the principles of pleading are reaffirmed in mandatory form. In practice, there appear to be few instances of statements of case containing much evidential matter.

The fact that there is no direct rule to the effect that evidence should *not* be contained in a statement of case does not mean that a statement of case is automatically defective if evidence is not included. If that was the intention of the rules, **r. 16.2(1)** would surely say so. Furthermore, although statements of case are required to be verified by a statement of truth, and when so verified can stand as the evidence on interim applications, the notice of application (form N244) provides space for evidence to be inserted separately or attached as witness statements or affidavits, which would be unnecessary if the evidence was required already to have been fully incorporated into the statement of case. It may of course be that in some instances a verified statement of case will contain all the particulars and evidence necessary to entitle an applicant to the remedy sought, but there will be many instances in which it will not.

There has always been a grey area between 'material facts' and 'evidence'. A situation in which particulars would be sufficient to support an interim application, without necessarily involving the inclusion of evidence, is set out in example 24.2.

Example 24.2

1. The Claimant is and was at all relevant times the owner of residential premises known as 1 Acacia Gardens, Boggle, Kent. The premises comprise a house together with a 100 foot back garden.

2. On at least 3 occasions per week since 1 March 2016, the Defendants have unlawfully entered into the Claimant's garden and remained there for periods of up to 2 hours, using the same for football practice. The last 3 occasions on which the Defendants have trespassed into the garden were [a], [b] and [c].

3. Despite being orally requested to leave the garden by the Claimant on several occasions, the Defendants have refused to do so, and the Claimant fears that unless an injunction is granted restraining such acts of trespass, they will be frequently repeated.

4. Further, by reason of the acts of trespass described in paragraph 2, the Claimant has suffered damage to his garden plants and furniture…[particulars etc.].

If the statement of case in example 24.2 was verified by a statement of truth, there seems little doubt that it would be sufficient, on its own, to support an application made in the case (e.g. for an interim injunction under **CPR, Part 25**), yet it would be hard to argue that the statement of case actually contains any evidence. Put another way, the example sets out the relevant material such that the defendants are made aware of the nature and extent of the claimant's case, but not the means by which he intends to prove it. Verification of the particulars by a statement of truth will suffice for the purposes of an interim application, but for a final hearing, the claimant's case must be proved in the conventional manner.

True purpose of statements of case

A good claim or defence should enable the parties and the court to narrow down and identify **24.20** the central issues in dispute. This has always been the case. For example, a defendant is

---

Example 24.3   Unsatisfactory drafting

IN THE COUNTY COURT   Claim No. 6YL 3456

BETWEEN:

MR ADAM BROWN   Claimant

— and —

MR CHARLES DAVIS   Defendant

Brief details of claim: The Claimant claims damages for loss and personal injuries caused in a road traffic accident on 21 May 2015.

Value: more than £10,000 but not more than £25,000. The claim includes a claim for personal injuries and the amount expected to be recovered exceeds £1,000.

Particulars of claim: On 21 May 2015 an accident occurred at the junction of Fairfax Road and Grove Hill, London SW99 between the Claimant's Renoir Nicole RN63 ABC and a Bergman Y456 JKL driven by the Defendant.

The accident was caused by the Defendant's negligence, in that he:

(a) drove too fast;

(b) failed to keep a proper lookout;

(c) failed to brake in time or at all to avoid the accident.

As a result, the Claimant suffered injuries and loss.

(Particulars etc.)

(Statement of truth etc.)

---

entitled to know not merely the cause of action against him, but also the manner in which it is alleged that he was in breach of his duty, thereby causing the claimant to seek redress against him. To achieve that objective requires no more than a properly detailed set of particulars (as opposed to evidence), thereby allowing him to set out his case in response.

Thus a claim or defence which discloses little or nothing about the party's case is liable to be (and almost certainly will be) struck out. Example 24.3 shows a common type of defective claim, which will almost certainly be struck out (relevant parts of the claim only are illustrated).

Similarly a 'block and parry' defence, confining itself merely to admitting, requiring proof of or denying the allegations in the claim, but not containing any particulars of the defendant's case, will also be liable to be struck out.

The ultimate purpose of a party's statement of case is to inform the other party of the case against them. In *Conticorp SA v Central Bank of Ecuador* [2007] UKPC 40, LTL 20/6/2007, the issues were convoluted but were not in doubt; partly because further and better particulars (equivalent to further information under **CPR, Part 18**) had been provided.

Similarly, in *MMI Research Ltd v CellXion Ltd* [2007] EWHC 2611 (Pat), LTL 8/11/2007, a patents case, Warren J, applying *Visx Inc. v Nidek Co. Ltd (No. 2)* [1999] FSR 91, held that whilst a claimant should make real efforts to comply with **PD 63**, a pleading which did not do so to the letter would not necessarily be struck out. Whilst there had to be sufficient particularity, it was a question of degree whether it was a genuine ground for objection to a patent and raised an issue in a way that the other party knew what he had to meet.

Length on its own is not a reason for striking out a statement of case. Complex claims inevitably need to be pleaded with care. If a statement of case is too long, the proper course is for the court to order the party to produce a summary, possibly in schedule form, by reference to the relevant paragraphs in the pleading (*Waite v Denby* [2009] EWCA Civ 592, LTL 29/6/2009). See also **23.3** for the requirement in **PD 16, para. 1.4**, to produce a short summary of any statement of case exceeding 25 pages.

A proposed amendment to include a defence of justification in a libel claim was refused in *Al Rajhi Banking and Investment Corporation v Wall Street Journal Europe Sprl* [2003] EWHC 1358 (QB), LTL 24/6/2003, because the draft amended statement of case lacked clarity and precision.

Good drafting involves the concise and clear identification of the subject matter of the claim, the issues in the case, and the parties' respective positions in respect of those issues.

Drafting language

There is little doubt that the aims and objectives of the CPR militate against much of the previously conventional and archaic language of pleadings. Not only is the use of Latin terms now obsolete, but many of the more 'old-fashioned' English words such as 'hereinbefore' and 'thereafter' are thought to be inconsistent with the objectives of the CPR, though the price of drafting in modern language is frequently a lack of elegance and an increase rather than saving in verbiage.

Court procedure is designed for use by laypersons as well as lawyers, however, the CPR are not intended to encourage sloppy drafting. Although it is clear that the overriding objective does not permit cases to be won or lost on purely technical points of pleading, the need for precision in the drafting of statements of case (particularly in more complex matters) is still paramount.

A short list of some of the conventional Latin and English phrases previously used (and still to be found in some precedents), and possible modern counterparts, appears in **table 24.1**.

24.21

Commentary

Table 24.1 Suggested replacements for traditional legal language

Old term	Suggested equivalent
Aforesaid	Above
Aver	Contend
By reason of the matters aforesaid	Due to the above matters, or As a result of the above
Due to (meaning 'because of')	Because of
Hereinafter set out	Set out below
Hereinbefore set out	Set out above
In the premises	In the circumstances
In so far (or insofar)	To the extent that
Inter alia	Among other things
Material	Relevant
Mutatis mutandis	With all necessary changes
Notwithstanding	Despite (the fact that)
Pursuant to	In consequence of, or as a result of, or in the course of, or under
Seriatim	Individually
Without prejudice to the generality of the foregoing	Without prejudice to the matters set out above

MEANINGS OF COMMON DRAFTING TERMS

At all material times

24.22 'At all material times' is perhaps the most commonly used stock phrase in drafting statements of case. When used in relation to breach by the defendant, it means 'material to the period of the breach' as detailed in the particulars of claim (*Convergence Group plc v Chantrey Vellacott* [2005] EWCA Civ 290, *The Times*, 25 April 2005).

Include, but not limited to

24.23 Where a statement of case is drafted when inquiries are incomplete, it is common to plead such particulars as are known, but prefaced by a phrase such as 'include but are not limited to' the particulars that immediately follow or which are set out in a schedule. This device is used at various times when giving particulars of breach and particulars of loss. Its use prevents the statement of case being treated as deliberately excluding details not specifically set out (*Deutsche Morgan Grenfell Group plc v Commissioners of Inland Revenue* [2005] EWCA Civ 78, [2006] Ch 243 at [257], approved in the House of Lords [2006] UKHL 49, [2007] 1 AC 558, by Lord Walker of Gestingthorpe at [148]). If used, the statement of case should be amended to include the full particulars when these become known. A defendant faced with such an allegation should make a request for further information (see **chapter 30**), rather than applying to strike it out (Lord Walker of Gestingthorpe at [148]).

UNPLEADED ALLEGATIONS

24.24 A judge should not normally make a finding of fact on an issue which depends on evidence and which has not been raised in statements of case, so that all parties did not have a proper opportunity to address it, even if it was raised in correspondence after statements of case have been served (*Sivanandan v Executive Committee of Hackney Action for Racial Equality* [2002] EWCA Civ 111, LTL 25/1/2002). However, if a factual issue has been adequately dealt with at trial and is clearly regarded by all parties as a live issue which is crucial to the case, the judge is entitled to make a finding of fact, even if the issue was not raised in the statements of case, which could have been amended during the trial (*Slater v Buckinghamshire County Council* [2004] EWCA Civ 1478, LTL 10/11/2004). In *Strover v Strover* [2005] EWHC 860 (Ch), [2005] NPC 64, it was held that where the essential allegations to establish proprietary estoppel had not been pleaded, but had formed the central planks in the evidence of the claimant in support of his original plea, the court could grant the relief flowing from the estoppel. An allegation which is not included in the particulars of claim cannot provide a sustainable ground for an appeal (*Dunnett v Railtrack plc* [2002] EWCA Civ 303, [2002] 1 WLR 2434).

While a court should give a fair reading to a statement of case, it was not open to the court below in *Lawrence v Poorah* [2008] UKPC 21, LTL 9/4/2008, to read allegations of undue influence or unconscionable bargain into an imprecisely drawn statement of case. There are limits on the degree to which a judge can intervene, even with the scope of the active case management powers granted by **CPR, Part 1**, in defining a case for a party. Ultimately, the judge must remain scrupulously impartial, and it is wrong to conclude, while giving judgment, that the claimant should succeed on an unpleaded basis.

In *Lombard North Central plc v Automobile World (UK) Ltd* [2010] EWCA Civ 20, LTL 26/1/2010, it was held that the onus is on the party to amend its statement of case if it wishes to advance an unpleaded point. In this case not only was the issue not pleaded, but the defendant also failed to raise it when invited to summarise its main points when the trial started. It was raised for the first time after all the evidence had been taken. The Court of Appeal decided that the trial judge had not made a substantial procedural error in not allowing the defendant to raise the unpleaded point at the trial.

In *JN Dairies Ltd v Johal Dairies Ltd* [2010] EWCA Civ 348, LTL 31/3/2010, the claim was based on an alleged breach of confidence by a former employee. Shortly before the trial the defendant disclosed an affidavit to the effect that the claimant had sought to bribe the former employee to commit perjury, which the claimant responded to by disclosing witness statements to the effect that the former employee had confessed to being paid £40,000 by the defendant to steal confidential documents from the claimant. It was held that both sides should have pleaded these allegations, and both should have applied to the court to list a pre-trial review to deal with amendments, further disclosure and other directions. Both sides had been willing to proceed with the pleadings in their unamended form, so trying the case on that basis was not unfair. In *Investec Bank (UK) Ltd v Zulman* [2010] EWCA Civ 675, LTL 18/5/2010, the court decided whether a written contract had been varied by an oral agreement, even though the issue was not pleaded, because it had surfaced in cross-examination and was covered by closing speeches. If this is not the result that is wanted, an objection must be made at the time.

An appeal against a decision on an unpleaded basis may therefore be dismissed if there is no real injustice in that the evidence would be the same on the new basis of the claim (*Whitecap Leisure Ltd v John H. Rundle Ltd* [2008] EWCA Civ 429, [2008] 2 Lloyd's Rep 216).

Chapter 25   Schedule of Past and Future Loss and Expense

INTRODUCTION

25.1   The purpose of a schedule of past and future loss and expense is to display, in concise and digestible form, the extent of the special damage that the claimant wishes to obtain from the defendant. This is not merely to enable the value of the claim to be appreciated, but also to allow the defendant to agree with or dispute the contents (independently of whether or not liability is admitted), and to draft a counter-schedule indicating any areas of contention. As a result, the parties and court will know the degree and extent to which damages are disputed, and the areas of dispute should clearly be defined. This is, of course, precisely what the system of statements of case is intended to achieve.

In *Tomer v Atlantic Cleaning Service Ltd* [2008] EWHC 1652 (QB), LTL 25/7/2008, particulars of claim which stated that a schedule of past and future loss and expense was 'to follow' were held to include a claim for special damages (which could accordingly be attacked by way of striking out or a request for further information).

CONTENTS OF THE SCHEDULE

25.2   No format for a schedule of past and future loss and expense is prescribed by the CPR or any practice direction. Logic dictates that different heads of damage should be separately calculated in the body of the schedule, and that subtotals should be calculated wherever possible. This will normally cause no problems where specific amounts have already been expended or loss of earnings incurred, but items of alleged future loss may be more difficult to set out. The appropriate manner in which to do this is by reference to the multiplier that it is alleged is appropriate in the particular case, thus making the basis of the calculation quite clear, and enabling the preparation of a counter-schedule in similar format on the defendant's side.

The defendant's counter-schedule must state which items in the claimant's schedule are agreed, in dispute, or neither agreed nor disputed, because of lack of knowledge (**PD 16, para. 12.2(1)**). Where items are disputed, alternative figures, where appropriate, should be supplied (**para. 12.2(2)**).

A schedule or counter-schedule must be verified by a statement of truth (**PD 22, para. 1.4(3)**).

EXAMPLES

25.3   Two examples of a schedule of past and future loss and expense are given below, showing how different heads of loss should be set out.

Example 25.1

<u>IN THE COUNTY COURT</u>   Claim No. 6YL 1234

BETWEEN:

MS ANNA BRIGHT   <u>Claimant</u>

and

(1) MR CHARLES DAVIS

(2) MRS ELEANOR FOWKES   <u>Defendants</u>

SCHEDULE OF PAST AND FUTURE LOSS AND EXPENSE

The calculations in this Schedule are calculated up to 12 February 2016.

A) Past Losses

1. Earnings

Prior to the accident, which occurred on 5 June 2013, the Claimant, who is an Auxiliary Nurse, worked for the Loganberry Nursing Home, Beresford Road, Blackstone BL5 lAB. At the time of the accident the Claimant's average net weekly earnings were £230.61. Since the accident the Claimant has been unable to return to work, and has received no pay from her previous (or any other) employer. The Claimant claims loss of income as follows:

5.6.2013 to 31.12.2013, being 30 weeks at £230.61 per week	£6,918.30
1.1.2014 to 31.12.2014, being 52 weeks at £235.83 per week	£12,263.16
1.1.2015 to 31.12.2015, being 52 weeks at £241.26 per week	£12,545.52
1.1.2016 to 12.2.2016, being 6 weeks at £246.91 per week	£1,481.46
Total claim under this part	£33,208.44

2. Medication

(a) Prescriptions, 2 at £7.85 each	£15.70
(b) Paracetamol. The Claimant takes four paracetamol tablets a day, and has done since the accident. Estimated cost	£100.00
Total claim under this paragraph	£115.70

3. Taxi fares

As a result of her injuries the Claimant has not been as mobile as she was before the accident, and has had to travel by taxi or minicab, whereas before being injured she would have walked or travelled by public transport. The Claimant claims the taxi and minicab fares and/or the difference in costs between the fares and the costs of travel by public transport. The Claimant walks to the supermarket once a week, but has to take a minicab back home with her shopping. This minicab fare is paid out once a week and has been since March 2014.

28.3.2014 to 12.2.2016, being 97 weeks at £5.00 per week	£485.00

4. Care and Assistance

Since the accident the Claimant has received considerable care and assistance from her husband. The Claimant's husband does all the vacuum cleaning in the house. He assists with the washing. The Claimant puts washing in the washing machine a piece at a time but her husband has to empty the machine and hang out the washing. The Claimant is unable to do gardening and her husband now spends about one hour per week keeping weeds under control. He also strips the beds, does the cooking and a little shopping for the Claimant. This assistance amounts to 8 hours per week at £6.04 per hour and the Claimant claims for the period from 5.6.2013 to 12.2.2016, being 140 weeks:

	£6,764.80

Summary of Past Losses

Para. 1	£33,208.44
Para. 2	£115.70
Para. 3	£485.00
Para. 4	£6,764.80
Total	£40,573.94

Together with interest to be assessed

B) Future Losses

1. Earnings

(a) The Claimant will not be able to return to her job or to ever undertake any form of paid employment. Her loss of earnings will continue until the date she would have retired had she not been injured in the accident. The Claimant contends that but for the accident she would have retired on 21 May 2016. From 12 February 2016 her net loss of earnings will be £246.91 per week. The Claimant claims:

12.2.2016 to 21.5.2016, being 15 weeks at £246.91 per week   £3,703.65

(b) The Claimant would have worked part-time from 24 May 2016 for a period of 5 years earning approximately half her pre-retirement income, being £123.45 net per week. Her annual loss of income during this period is therefore £6,419.40. The appropriate multiplier is 4.7 and amounts to: £30,171.18

The Claimant therefore claims total future loss of earnings of   £33,874.83

2. Medication

This loss will continue at the approximate rate of £1.50 per week, equivalent to £78.00 per annum. The appropriate multiplier is 20.3 and the Claimant claims: £1,583.40

3. Taxi Fares

This loss continues at the rate of £5.00 per week, and will continue for the rest of her life. The annual loss is £260.00, and the appropriate multiplier is 20.3. The Claimant therefore claims: £5,278.00

4. Care and Assistance

The Claimant will need assistance for 8 hours per week at an hourly rate of £6.04 for the rest of her life. The annual loss is £2,512.64 and the appropriate multiplier is 20.3. The Claimant therefore claims: £51,006.59

Summary of Future Losses

Para. 1	£33,874.83
Para. 2	£1,583.40
Para. 3	£5,278.00
Para. 4	£51,006.59
Total	£91,742.82

TOTAL CLAIM UNDER THIS SCHEDULE

A) Past Losses	£40,573.94
B) Future Losses	£91,742.82
Total	£132,316.76

STATEMENT OF TRUTH etc.

DATED 12 February 2016

Messrs O'Reilly & Mackman, Bank Chambers, Edinburgh Road, Blackstone BL3 8GC,
Solicitors for the Claimant.

Example 25.2

In this example, various heads of damage are claimed which cannot presently be quantified. The Claimant is aged 30

IN THE COUNTY COURT   Claim No. 6YL 4753

BETWEEN:

MR GARTH HOPKINS   Claimant

and

MR IAN JACKS   Defendant

SCHEDULE OF PAST AND FUTURE LOSS AND EXPENSE

The calculations in this Schedule are made to 12 January 2016

Past Losses

Loss of Earnings

1. At the time of the accident the Claimant was employed by Closestaff Limited as a trainee manager. He was paid at his standard salary rates despite a protracted period off work as a result of his injuries. On 31 January 2014 he was made redundant. His gross average monthly earnings at the time he was made redundant were £1,250, with deductions of £167.83 for tax and £94.00 for National Insurance (net £988.17 per month). Thereafter he was unemployed for 6 months 17 days until he commenced work on 18 August 2014 with Opendoors Limited. He was offered another job with Final Position Limited on 21 August 2015, which he accepted and commenced work on 7 September 2015. His current annual salary is £18,500, so there is no continuing loss of earnings while he remains in this employment.

2. By reason of his injuries the Claimant was unable to apply for jobs in the period between his redundancy and August 2014 which involved an element of manual work and had to restrict himself to office-based jobs. He also would have been able to put more energy into his job search but for the accident. If he had not been injured he would have commenced work about 3 months earlier than he did.

Total claim for loss of earnings:

3 months at £988.17 net per month   £2,964.51

Care and Assistance

3. Before the accident the Claimant lived in his own house. On being discharged from hospital on 21 June 2013 he moved in with his parents because he was totally reliant on them. In particular he needed assistance with washing, shaving and personal hygiene, with dressing and drinking and eating. In the period until 1 November 2013 he was unable to wash or iron his clothes, do his shopping or cooking, and was reliant entirely on his parents. 1 November 2013 was the first occasion on which he was able to assist his mother with preparing meals and some washing-up. The Claimant was unable to drive until 20 December 2013. Until then he was dependent on his parents for lifts to hospital and physiotherapy sessions and for all other purposes. From the beginning of November 2013 until the end of January 2014 the Claimant was given reducing levels of assistance, until he was able to cope with most domestic tasks by himself by the beginning of February 2014. The Claimant required additional assistance in late October and November 2014 when he returned to hospital for removal of the plate and screws in his elbow. The Claimant claims for the care and assistance he has been given.

Damages to be assessed

Gardening, DIY etc.

4. As a result of his injuries the Claimant has been unable to carry out gardening or domestic jobs requiring heavy lifting, and has had to obtain assistance from members of his family. He has also been unable to do any decorating, and will have to seek assistance from his family for decorating and DIY work at his own property and will be restricted in assistance he can give to his parents. He has also been unable to continue doing maintenance work on his car, and has had to seek the help of his brother-in-law. All these are continuing. The annual values for these are:

(a) Gardening	£200.00
(b) Heavy domestic work	£150.00
(c) Decorating	£350.00
(d) DIY	£100.00
(e) Assistance to parents	£150.00
(f) Car maintenance	£100.00
Total	£1,050.00

5. The Claimant therefore claims under this head the value to date of gardening, heavy domestic work, decorating, DIY, assistance to parents and car maintenance from from 12 June 2013 to 12 January 2016 (2 years 7 months) at £1,050.00 per annum: £2,712.50

Accidental Damage

6. Excess	£450.00
7. Loss of use of car and inconvenience from 13 June 2013 to 15 August 2013	£750.00
8. Damage to clothing	£87.00
Total claim under this head	£1,287.00

Other Out-of-pocket Expenses

9. Loss of deposit for holiday	£115.00
10. Loss of deposit for railway ticket	£23.00
11. Miscellaneous expenses for telephone, letters and the like	£70.00
Total claim under this head	£208.00

Travel Costs

12. Taxis

(a) Before 21 November 2013	£39.00
(b) 21 November 2013	£10.00
(c) 10 January 2014	£10.00
(d) 14 November 2014	£5.00
Subtotal	£64.00

13. Driving to hospital, physiotherapy etc. at £0.35 per mile

(a) To Blackstone General Hospital up to 21 November 2013 (13 visits)	£50.00
(b) 7 January 2014 (6 miles)	£2.10
(c) 13 January 2014 (6 miles)	£2.10
(d) 4 February 2014 (6 miles)	£2.10
(e) 30 April 2014 (6 miles)	£2.10

(f) 6 June 2014 (6 miles)	£2.10
(g) 4 July 2014 (6 miles)	£2.10
(h) Parking on 4 July 2014	£1.40
(i) 11 July 2014 (6 miles)	£2.10
(j) 18 July 2014 (6 miles)	£2.10
(k) 10 September 2014 (6 miles)	£2.10
(l) 24 October 2014 (20 miles)	£7.00
(m) 3 December 2014 (10 miles)	£3.50
(n) 7 January 2015 (6 miles)	£2.10
(o) 5 June 2015 (20 miles)	£7.00
(p) 5 visits for physiotherapy (the Claimant walked for the other 26 sessions) at 3 miles each round trip	£5.25
(q) Additional trips to physiotherapy (78 miles)	£27.30
(r) 7 August 2015 (24 miles)	£8.40
Subtotal	£130.85
Total claim under this head	£194.85

Medication

19. To November 2013	£23.55
20. From November 2013 to January 2016 at £12.00 a year	£24.00
Total for this head	£47.55
Total quantified Past Losses	**£6,381.07**

Together with Interest to be assessed

Future Losses

Disadvantage on the Labour Market

21. The Claimant has a 12-month contract in his current employment ending on 9 September 2016.

22. By reason of his elbow injury the Claimant has been left with residual pain and restricted movements which compromise the overall function of his dominant right arm. This substantially limits the amount of physical work he can do with his arms, and also interferes with his driving in that he finds it difficult to steer. He is therefore effectively restricted to purely clerical work, whereas before the accident he could take jobs which included physical work. He is also going to be unable to take jobs involving any substantial amount of driving. He is consequently disadvantaged if he needs to look for work in the future, and he claims:

Damages to be assessed

Gardening, DIY etc.

23. Future value of gardening, heavy domestic work, decorating, DIY, assistance to parents and car maintenance from 12 January 2016 @ £1,050 per annum with a multiplier of 29.6

Total claim under this head   £31,080.00

Power Steering

24. By reason of his elbow injury the Claimant needs to buy cars with power steering. His car at the time of the accident was a Kurosawa Benidorm 1.1, which was replaced by another Benidorm 1.1 registration number LG62 DAB. These cars do not come with power-assisted steering, and there is

Commentary

no practical method of converting them to power steering. In order to buy cars with power steering the Claimant will have to buy cars which are more expensive than if he did not have this restriction. The Claimant estimates the price difference to be about £1,000, and that he will replace his vehicles approximately every 3 years until age 70. His annual loss is therefore about £330. Additional annual cost of buying cars with power steering, with a multiplier of 25.42:

£8,388.60

Future Surgery

25. There is an approximately 30% chance that the Claimant will require either elbow replacement surgery or an arthrodesis of his elbow within the next 30 years. Such an operation is likely to cost about £5,000 to £6,000. The Claimant will give credit for advanced receipt as appropriate.

To be assessed

26. There is an approximately 30% chance that the Claimant will require an arthrodesis of his great toe within the next 30 years. Such an operation is likely to cost about £2,000 to £2,500. The Claimant will give credit for advanced receipt as appropriate.

Medication

27. Continuing need for medications at £12.00 a year, with a multiplier of 29.6. Total claim under this head: £355.20

STATEMENT OF TRUTH etc.

DATED 12 January 2016

Messrs O'Reilly & Mackman, Bank Chambers, Edinburgh Road, Blackstone BL3 8GC,

Solicitors for the Claimant.

Chapter 26 Defending a Claim

Commentary

INTRODUCTION

The principal rules concerning the drafting of the defence can be found in **CPR, Parts 15** and **26.1**
16, and their associated practice directions.

The matters discussed below do not apply where the claimant uses the Part 8 procedure, and
apply with limited effect to specialist claims. They do, however, apply to cases where a defence
is drafted to a counterclaim.

Although it is not mandatory, form N9B (specified amount) or N9D (unspecified amount or
non-money claims) may be used for the purpose of setting out a defence (**PD 15, para. 1.3**).
Copies of the forms are included in the response pack served on the defendant with the particulars of claim.

WHEN A DEFENCE IS REQUIRED

A defendant who wishes to defend all or part of a claim must file a defence (**CPR, r. 15.2**). If a **26.2**
defence is not filed, default judgment (see **chapter 20**) may be entered if the conditions set out
in **Part 12** have been met (**r. 15.3**). The consequences therefore failing to file a defence are
grave. At best the defendant will incur unnecessary expense in applying to set aside the judgment
but he risks being unable to persuade a judge to allow him to defend the claim, or only on satisfaction of conditions. A copy of the defence must be served on every other party (**r. 15.6**).

PERIOD FOR FILING A DEFENCE

The general rule is that a defence must be filed within 14 days after service of the particulars **26.3**
of claim (**CPR, r. 15.4(1)(a)**). Therefore, no defence need be filed where a claim form is
served which does not include, and is not accompanied by, particulars of claim (which can be
served within 14 days thereafter: see 15.40). As the particulars of claim can be contained
within the body of the claim form (as opposed to served with it, or at a later date) care should

therefore be taken to ensure whether the claim form contains the full particulars of claim, or merely the basic information required.

The defendant is allowed to gain an additional 14 days for filing the defence simply by filing the acknowledgment of service form included in the response pack (see **chapter 18**). If this is done, the time for filing a defence is extended to 28 days after service of the particulars of the claim (**r. 15.4(1)(b)**).

There are different periods for filing a defence where the claim form is served out of the jurisdiction (see **r. 15.4(2)(a)**). If the court grants permission for a claim form to be served on the agent of a principal who is overseas, the court will, at the same time, under **r. 6.12(3)**, specify the period for responding.

There are three further exceptions to the above rules:

(a) Where the defendant makes an application disputing the jurisdiction of the court under **Part 11** (see **chapter 19**), the defence need not be filed before the hearing of the application (**r. 11(9)**).
(b) Where the claimant applies for summary judgment under **Part 24** (see **chapter 34**) before the defendant has filed a defence, the defendant need not file a defence before the summary judgment hearing (**r. 24.4(2)**).
(c) Where the defendant has applied for summary judgment under **Part 24**, or for the claimant's statement of case to be struck out under **r. 3.4**, default judgment may not be entered for the claimant until that application has been disposed of (**r. 12.3(3)(a)**).

The words of **r. 15.4** do not appear to prohibit the filing of a defence in the exceptional circumstances should the defendant wish. Where an application for summary judgment has been made by the claimant under **Part 24**, the defendant would appear to have a choice:

(a) His response may be supported by evidence, usually by witness statement, which may exhibit a draft defence. In practice this is usually the simplest and best approach.
(b) Alternatively, under **r. 32.6(2)**, a party may rely on his statement of case in hearings other than the trial, provided that it is verified by a statement of truth. Thus it appears, should the defendant wish to file his defence, he may do so, and then rely on it in addition to any witness statement he may wish to file.

EXTENDING THE TIME FOR SERVICE OF A DEFENCE

26.4   The defendant and the claimant may, under **CPR, r. 15.5**, agree that the period for filing a defence shall be extended by up to 28 days. Where this is done, the defendant must notify the court in writing (**r. 15.5(2)**). Thus there is a strict limit to the degree of 'slippage' which the parties may, by consent, allow. The principle of judicially led case management precludes the parties from agreeing further (or even open-ended) extensions of time. Any party wishing a further extension of time (whether by consent or otherwise) will have to make an application to the court under **r. 3.1(2)(a)**.

STAY OF CLAIM WHERE NO ACTION TAKEN

26.5   Where at least six months have expired since the end of the period for filing a defence, and no defendant has served or filed any admission, defence or counterclaim, and the claimant has not entered or applied for default judgment under **CPR, Part 12**, or summary judgment under **Part 24**, the claim shall be stayed, although any party can apply for such stay to be lifted (**r. 15.11**). The evidence in support of an application to lift the stay must give the reason for the delay in proceeding with or responding to the claim (**PD 15, para. 3.4**).

CONTENTS OF A DEFENCE — GENERAL MATTERS

The defence of a defendant who is an individual must include the defendant's residential or **26.6**
business address, unless it has been correctly given on the claim form (**PD 16, para. 10.4**).
The address must include the postcode unless the court orders otherwise (**para. 10.6**).
Postcode information can be obtained from www.royalmail.com. This address determines
which court location is most convenient for the defendant and must be established even if it
is not the defendant's address for service (**para. 10.5**).

A defendant who is an individual must provide his or her date of birth (if known) in the
defence (or acknowledgment of service, admission, defence and counterclaim, or reply or
other response) (**para. 10.7**). This is primarily to identify the defendant if a judgment is to be
registered (see **63.50**).

Admit, require to prove, deny

A defence to a claim must say which of the allegations in the particulars of claim are admitted, **26.7**
which are denied and which allegations the defendant is unable to admit or deny, but requires
the claimant to prove (**CPR, r. 16.5(1)**). Every allegation made in a claim should be dealt with
in the defence (**PD 16, para. 10.2**).

It may be useful to restate the established principles behind the three possible responses to an
allegation in particulars of claim, and their consequences so far as the claimant is concerned.

If an allegation is *admitted*, the claimant is absolved from any obligation to bring any further
evidence in support of that allegation. This is apart from any other consequences that may
flow from the admission made. Allegations should be admitted if they are accepted by the
defendant or if they make no material difference. A defendant who wishes to admit the truth
of all or part of the other party's case may adopt the admissions procedure set out in **CPR,
Part 14** (see **17.3**). The principles governing applications for permission to withdraw admissions are considered at **34.31**.

A defendant may *require the claimant to prove* an allegation which the defendant is unable to
admit or deny (**r. 16.5(1)(b)**), usually because the defendant does not have sufficient information on the point. Often this will be because the evidence relevant to the allegation is in the
possession of another party or person, or has been lost. Allegations which the claimant is
required to prove are still in issue, but the defendant will not be making a positive alternative
case on the point.

Where an allegation is *denied*, this normally implies that the defendant intends to put up a
positive case to the contrary. Indeed, **r. 16.5(2)** specifically provides that where the defendant
denies an allegation, he must state his reasons for doing so; and if he intends to put forward a
different version of events from that given by the claimant, he must state his own version.

Where a paragraph in a statement of case sets up a contention followed by a number of
sub-paragraphs, each containing allegations of fact, a general response to the main allegation
without responding to the individual sub-paragraphs may be inadequate, depending on the
circumstances and how important the allegations are (*Ciccone v Associated Newspapers Ltd* [2009]
EWHC 1108 (Ch), LTL 12/6/2009, where further particulars were required).

It is inappropriate to require a claimant to prove a matter of which the defendant must have
personal knowledge. Such a matter must either be admitted or denied with reasons (*Ciccone v
Associated Newspapers Ltd*, where it was alleged the defendant 'knowingly and deliberately
infringed [certain copyrights]'). If a party can plead to a matter they should. There is no concept that general non-admissions can be used when a defendant has made all the admissions
they want to (**r. 16.5(1)**; *Ciccone v Associated Newspapers Ltd*).

A defendant who fails to answer a specific allegation will nevertheless be taken to require that allegation to be proved, provided that in his defence, he has set out the nature of his case in relation to the issue to which that allegation is relevant (**r. 16.5(3)**). In such an event, it will presumably be open to the claimant to apply to the court that the defendant give further information under **Part 18**, or for the court to order it of its own volition. However if the defendant totally fails to deal with an allegation, he shall be taken to have admitted it (**r. 16.5(5)**), unless it is an allegation relating to the value of a money claim, in which case he shall be taken to require that any allegation relating to the amount of money claimed by proved, unless he expressly admits the allegation (**r. 16.5(4)**).

Stand-alone defences and positive case

26.8   In addition to responding to the particulars of claim by admitting, requiring proof and denying the allegations made by the claimant, the defendant is obliged to set out his own case in sufficient detail to ensure the claimant can prepare for trial and understand the case which has to be met. This is the effect of **PD 18, para. 1.2**. The obligation extends beyond stating reasons and any alternative version where the defence uses denials (see **26.7**). It means the defence must give full details of:

(a) Any stand-alone defence relied upon. Examples are reliance on limitation periods, exemption and limitation of liability clauses in contracts, and equitable and legal defences, such as laches, delay, consent, illegality, lack of writing etc. The obligation is to set out sufficient facts to establish the elements of the defence based on the circumstances of the case.

(b) Any positive case relied upon by the defendant on an issue, even if the burden of proof rests with the claimant (*Baxter Healthcare Corporation v Abbott Laboratories* [2005] EWHC 2878 (Pat), LTL 6/12/2005). In a building case where there is a claim based on hours worked multiplied by alleged rates, it is for the defendant to set out a positive case in its defence if it wishes to dispute the reasonableness of the claimed rates (*Clancy Consulting Ltd v Derwent Holdings Ltd* [2010] EWHC 762 (TCC), LTL 21/4/2010).

CONTENTS OF A DEFENCE — SPECIFIC MATTERS

Dispute about statement of value

26.9   A claim form is required by **CPR, r. 16.3**, to contain a statement of value (see **23.8**). If this statement is disputed, the defendant must state why he disputes it, and if he can, give his own statement of the value of the claim (**r. 16.5(6)**).

Claims already paid

26.10 Where (apart from costs and interest) the only claim against a defendant is for a specified sum of money, and a defence is filed stating that the sum has been paid to the claimant, the special procedure in **CPR, r. 15.10** applies.

Defendant in representative capacity

26.11 A defendant who is defending in a representative capacity must state that fact in the defence, and also say what that capacity is (**CPR, r. 16.5(7)**).

Address for service

26.12 **CPR, r. 16.5(8)**, requires a defence to contain an address for service, within the United Kingdom (**r. 6.23**), to which documents can be sent to the defendant, if no acknowledgment of service has been filed.

Personal injury claim

26.13 Where a defended claim is one in respect of personal injury, and the claimant has attached a medical report in respect of his or her alleged injuries, **PD 16, para. 12.1**, provides that the defence should state whether the defendant:

(a) agrees with the medical report; or

(b) disputes it (in which event the reasons for doing so should be stated (**para. 12.1(2)**)); or

(c) neither agrees nor disputes it, but has no knowledge of the matters contained in the medical report.

If a medical report has been obtained by the defendant, on which the defendant intends to rely, it should be attached to the defence (**para. 12.1(3)**). It is submitted that 'should' in **PD 16, para. 12.1**, has the same mandatory force as 'must' in **CPR, r. 16.5**, and that no technical distinction should be drawn between the two.

Thus, there is an obligation on a defendant who disputes medical evidence served with the particulars of claim to attach his own medical report to his defence, when it has been obtained by the time the defence is drafted. There is, interestingly, no mandatory requirement to attach a medical report to a defence *whenever* the claimant's report is in dispute, but only where the defendant has already obtained his own medical report at the time of drafting the defence. However, it may well be difficult to dispute the claimant's report (particularly when reasons have to be given) save on grounds obtained as a result of a defence medical report, which is frequently not predicated upon a defence medical examination of the claimant, but upon an examination of medical records. If a defence medical report is not attached to a defence when detailed reasons for dispute are given, it would almost certainly prompt the claimant to question the basis for the response and apply for disclosure of the report. If the defendant has not had the opportunity to obtain his own expert evidence by the time the defence is drafted, it is likely that he would then have to state that he had 'no knowledge of the matters contained in the [claimant's] medical report', under **PD 16, para. 12.1(1)(c)**. Such a situation should be rare. In the vast majority of personal injury claims, and particularly when the amount of damages claimed is less than £25,000 and consequently allocated to the fast track, the parties will have been expected to have complied with the **Pre-action Protocol for Personal Injury Claims, paras 2, 5** and **7** (or the **Low Value Personal Injury RTA or EL/PL Protocols**). By **para. 7.2** of the Personal Injury Protocol, the joint selection of experts is encouraged, and is an almost invariable requirement in fast track cases. Thus it is likely that if the Protocol has been complied with, and proceedings are then issued, the medical report will have been agreed or obtained on a joint basis, and it is unlikely that the defendant will have obtained one of his own. If separate experts are instructed, it will be for the court ultimately to decide whether either party had acted unreasonably (**para. 7.7** of the Protocol). For detailed discussion of the pre-action protocols, see **chapter 8**.

Whole claim alleged to be fraudulent

26.14 There are occasions where the defendant alleges the whole claim is fraudulent or fabricated (Criminal Justice and Courts Act 2015, s. 57, see **63.32** and also **31.09**). A typical example is a low velocity impact road traffic accident. The argument is that the two vehicles collided at such a low speed that it is impossible for the injuries alleged by the claimant to have been caused by the collision. In such a case there is no burden on the defendant to prove fraud, and no obligation on the defendant to plead fraud or fabrication in the defence (*Kearsley v Klarfeld* [2005] EWCA Civ 1510, [2006] 2 All ER 303). It is sufficient simply to set out in the defence the facts from which the defendant will invite the judge to infer that the claimant had not suffered the injuries being claimed (*Cooper v P & O Stena Line Ltd* [1999] 1 Lloyd's Rep

734). In these cases the court will expect the parties to be particularly open and cooperative on matters such as access to the vehicles for expert examination and access to medical notes, and these claims are likely to be suitable for the multi-track even if below the usual threshold (*Kearsley v Klarfeld*).

Limitation defence

26.15   A defendant who relies on the expiry of any limitation period, must give in his defence details of the date on which it is alleged the relevant limitation period expired (**PD 16, para. 13.1**).

Human Rights Act 1998

26.16   A defendant who seeks to rely on any provision of, or right arising under, the **Human Rights Act 1998**, or seeks a remedy under that Act, must state in the defence the matters set out in **PD 16, para. 15.1**.

Defamation

26.17   For particular rules in cases of defamation etc., see **PD 53, para. 2**.

Tender

26.18   For particular rules where the defence is one of tender before claim see **PD 16, para. 13.2**, **CPR, r. 37.2**, and **PD 37, para. 1**.

Competition Act 1998

26.19   In certain proceedings under the Competition Act 1998, a defendant who intends to rely on a determination of the Competition and Markets Authority (the practice direction still refers to the old Office of Fair Trading) must comply with **PD 16, para. 14**.

SET-OFFS

26.20   A defendant who wishes to rely wholly or in part on a defence of set-off (see **34.37**) may, by **CPR, r. 16.6**, include this in the defence, whether or not it will also form the subject of a counterclaim under **Part 20**. Interestingly, the rule does not *require* this to be done, but set-offs continue to be pleaded in the defence.

STATEMENT OF TRUTH

26.21   A defence must be verified by a statement of truth (see **23.13** to **23.17**). The form of statement is (**PD 16, para. 11.2**):

[I believe] [the defendant believes] that the facts stated in the defence are true.

DRAFTING STYLE

26.22   It is as incumbent upon a defendant to state full particulars of his case as it is for the claimant. In addition to stating his position with regard to the allegations made against him, the defendant, when denying an allegation, must state his reasons for doing so, and if he intends to put forward a different version of events from that given by the claimant, he must state his own version (**CPR, r. 16.5(2)**). Defences that concentrate point by point on the allegations set out in the claim, stating whether they are admitted, denied or not admitted, but then wholly neglect to set out the defendant's own case on the issues are in grave danger of being struck out. The incorrect and correct approaches are illustrated in example 26.1.

Example 26.1

Insufficiently set out

It is denied that the Defendant was negligent as alleged or at all.

Insufficiently set out

It is denied that the Defendant drove along Litigation Avenue at an excessive speed, and/or failed to keep a proper lookout, and/or failed to brake or steer his car so as to avoid colliding with the Claimant, as alleged or at all.

Correctly set out

It is denied that the Defendant was negligent in any of the ways set out in the particulars of negligence, or at all. The Defendant was driving at a safe speed down Litigation Avenue, which is a major road. The accident was caused when the Claimant drove his car out of Blackstone Road, which was a minor road, into the path of the Defendant's car, giving the Defendant no opportunity to avoid the collision. In the circumstances, the collision was wholly caused by the negligence of the Claimant, as set out below:

<u>PARTICULARS OF NEGLIGENCE</u>

etc.

Chapter 27   Reply and Subsequent Statements of Case

GENERAL AND PROCEDURAL REQUIREMENTS

27.1   Although a claimant may file a reply to a defence, he does not have to do so, and failure to file a reply must not be taken as an admission of any of the matters raised in the defence (**CPR, r. 16.7(1)**). If a reply is filed, but fails to deal with a matter raised in the defence, the claimant shall nevertheless be taken to require that matter to be proved. Thus, strictly speaking, it is unnecessary for the reply to commence with a statement joining issue with the defendant upon all matters not specifically admitted in the defence, as there is an implied joinder of issue. Where, however, the defence includes a counterclaim to which it is intended to file a defence, it is suggested that a formal reply should also be filed in the conventional manner, joining issue with the defendant on his defence and counterclaim, although the rules do not specifically provide for, or require, this to be done.

When a claimant intends to file a reply, this must be done when he files his directions questionnaire under **r. 26.3(6)**, and the reply must be served on the other parties at the same time as it is filed (**r. 15.8**).

CONTENTS OF A REPLY

27.2   Conventionally, a reply may respond to any matters raised in the defence which were not, and which should not have been, dealt with in the particulars of claim, and exists solely for the purpose of dealing disjunctively with matters which could not properly have been dealt with in the particulars of claim, but which require a response once they have been raised in the defence. It has always been a cardinal principle of pleading (which has certainly not been altered by the CPR) that a claim should not anticipate a potential defence (popularly known as 'jumping the stile'). Once, however, a defence has been raised which requires a response so that the issues between the parties can be defined, a reply becomes necessary for the purpose of setting out the claimant's case on that point. The reply is, however, neither an opportunity to restate the claim, nor is it, nor should it be drafted as, a 'defence to the defence'.

Where the defence takes issue with a fact set out in the particulars of claim, and the claimant accepts that the fact is incorrect, the proper course should be for the claimant to seek to amend his statement of case accordingly (see **chapter 31**), and not to deal with the matter in a reply (**PD 16, para. 9.2**). Thus where, for example, the particulars of claim contain an error as to the quantity of goods ordered, and the correct quantity is set out in the defence, the error should be corrected by way of amendment, rather than reply.

A reply must be verified by a statement of truth (see **23.13** to **23.17**; **CPR, r. 22.1(1)(a)**).

SUBSEQUENT STATEMENTS OF CASE

27.3   A party may not file or serve any statement of case beyond a reply, without the permission of the court (**CPR, r. 15.9**). Such permission should rarely be required, and presumably will rarely be granted. Save in the most exceptional cases the supposed need for additional pleadings normally evidences a failure to plead the case properly in the first place. Problems of this kind can be resolved either by amendment or by requests for further information.

Chapter 28   Counterclaims

The following procedural checklist is relevant to this chapter:

Procedural checklist 17   Counterclaim (Part 20)

INTRODUCTION

28.1   The rules governing counterclaims are contained in **CPR, Part 20**, and **PD 20**. For claims against co-defendants and other parties (which are also covered by **Part 20**) see **chapter 29**.

Any claim other than a claim by a claimant against a defendant, is classed as an 'additional claim', an expression which includes a counterclaim by a defendant (whether against the claimant or against the claimant and some other person) (**r. 20.2(2)**).

The ability to bring a counterclaim within existing proceedings allows a defendant to wrest some of the initiative away from the claimant. Its main purpose, however, is to promote the general policy of ensuring that, so far as convenient, all issues between the parties are resolved together, with a view to saving costs, avoiding a multiplicity of claims, and avoiding the risk of irreconcilable judgments. Under **CPR, r. 3.1(2)(e)** and **(j)**, the court has general case management powers to order part of proceedings to be dealt with as separate proceedings, and to decide the order in which issues are tried. Specific factors that the court should take into account in making such decisions in the context of additional claims like counterclaims are set out in **r. 20.9**.

PERMISSION TO MAKE A COUNTERCLAIM

28.2   Provided it is filed with the defence, the court's permission is not required to make a counterclaim (**CPR, r. 20.4(2)(a)**). However, permission is required for filing a counterclaim after service of the defence (**r. 20.4(2)(b)**), and the procedure and conditions laid down in **Part 20** and **PD 20** will have to be followed. A copy of the proposed counterclaim must be filed together with the application notice seeking permission (**PD 20, para. 1.2**). The evidence in support must state the stage reached in the main proceedings, the nature of the additional claim, a summary of the facts on which the additional claim is based, and the name and address of any proposed additional party (**para. 2.1**). Where possible the applicant should provide a timetable of the proceedings to date (**para. 2.3**).

The permission of the court is required for a counterclaim against the Crown if:

(a) the proceedings were brought in the name of a government department and the counterclaim does not relate to that department (**CPR, r. 66.4(4)**); or

(b) the proceedings were brought in the name of the Attorney General (**r. 66.4(3)**).

A defendant who wishes to counterclaim against a person other than the claimant must apply to the court for an order adding that person as a defendant to the counterclaim (**r. 20.5(1)**).

An application for such an order may be made without notice, unless the court directs otherwise (**r. 20.5(2)**), and if the order is made, the court will at the same time give directions for the management of the case (**r. 20.5(3)**).

The court will refuse permission to add a counterclaim which shows no reasonable prospects of success (*K/S Victoria Street v House of Fraser (Stores Management) Ltd* [2011] EWHC 3179 (Ch), LTL 1/12/2011).

PROCEDURE

A defendant may make a counterclaim against a claimant by filing particulars of the counter- **28.3** claim (**CPR, r. 20.4(1)**). The counterclaim will attract an additional fee, equal to that of starting fresh proceedings (**CPFO, fee 1.7**). A fee of £55 is payable if a party is added to the claim (**CPFO, fee 1.6**). If the issue fee is not paid after due warning by the court, the counterclaim will be struck out automatically (**CPR, r. 3.7A**).

The defence and counterclaim should normally form one document with the counterclaim following on from the defence (**PD 15, para. 3.1; PD 20, para. 6.1**).

The usual rule once judgment has been obtained and fully satisfied is that it is not possible to bring a counterclaim, because there is no subsisting claim against which the counterclaim can be brought. This rule has been held to be subject to an exception where the claim is for possession of land, see *Laib v Aravindan* [2003] EWHC 2521 (QB), *The Times,* 13 November 2003.

In a claim by the Crown for taxes, duties or penalties, the defendant cannot bring a counterclaim or raise a set-off (**CPR, r. 66.4(1)**). Similarly, in a claim by the Crown, the defendant cannot bring a counterclaim or raise a set-off based on a claim for repayment of taxes, duties or penalties (**r. 66.4(2)**).

Where the permission of the court to make a counterclaim is not required, the counterclaim should also be served on every other party when a copy of the defence is served (**r. 20.8(1)(a)**), or within 14 days after the date on which the counterclaim was issued by the court, if it is to be served on a person who is not an existing party (**r. 20.8(1)(b)**). **Rule 20.8(1)(a)** refers to a counterclaim against an 'additional' party only. This is an obvious drafting error (a counterclaim against an additional party only is not a counterclaim at all, but a third party claim), and should refer to a counterclaim against an 'existing' party only. Where the permission of the court is required, the court will give directions as to service (**r. 20.8(3)**). If a counterclaim is made against an additional party, the copy served on that additional party must be accompanied by forms for admitting and defending the counterclaim, and for acknowledging service. Also, that additional party must be served with copies of all statements of case which have been served in the proceedings, together with any other documents which the court may direct (**r. 20.12(1)**). A copy of the additional claim form must be served on every existing party (**r. 20.12(2)**).

HEADING A COUNTERCLAIM

Example 28.1		
IN THE COUNTY COURT AT BLACKSTONE		Claim No. BK16 12345
BETWEEN		
	AB	<u>Claimant</u>
	— and —	
	CD	<u>Defendant</u>
	— and —	
	EF	<u>Third Party</u>

Commentary

28.4   **PD 20** adopts the practice set out in example 28.1. This provides that claimants and defendants in the original claim should always be referred to as such in the title to the proceedings, even if they subsequently acquire an additional procedural status (**para. 7.3**). In a simple counterclaim there is no change in the parties, with the counterclaim being brought by the defendant against the claimant. Where the defendant brings a counterclaim against the claimant and an additional party, the additional party is called the 'third party' (**para. 7.4(c)**), unless there has been an earlier additional claim within the proceedings. In that event there will already be a third party, so the additional party on the counterclaim will be the 'fourth party' (or whatever in accordance with the order in which this person is added to the proceedings, see **para. 7.4**).

A counterclaim brought against the original claimant is simply described as the counterclaim, see example 28.2. A counterclaim brought against the claimant and an additional party has to be described in the title as such. For example, 'Defendant's Counterclaim against Claimant and Third Party' (see **para 7.10**).

Example 28.2

IN THE HIGH COURT OF JUSTICE   Claim No. HQ16X 12345
QUEEN'S BENCH DIVISION
BETWEEN:

MR EDWARD GLOVER   Claimant

— and —

MR RICHARD BULMORE   Defendant

_____

DEFENDANT'S DEFENCE AND

COUNTERCLAIM AGAINST CLAIMANT

_____

STATUS OF A COUNTERCLAIM

28.5   Save where **CPR, Part 20**, states to the contrary, the provisions of the CPR apply to counterclaims as if they were claims (**r. 20.3(1)**). In particular, as **PD 20, para. 3**, points out, the provisions relating to any failure to respond will apply as much to a counterclaim as they do to a claim. **CPR, Part 15**, applies to a defence to a counterclaim. Thus it is, for example, open to a defendant to obtain judgment in default of a defence to a counterclaim, subject to the conditions and procedure laid down in **Part 12**. However, a claimant wishing to defend a counterclaim is not permitted to file an acknowledgment of service (**r. 20.4(3)**), and various consequential rules pertaining to time limits, statements of value for the purposes of issue in the High Court, and preliminary case management under **Part 26** also do not apply (see **r. 20.3(2)** for details).

CONTENTS OF A COUNTERCLAIM

28.6   As a counterclaim is treated as if it was a claim for the purposes of the CPR, it should be set out in the same format, and with the same particularity as particulars of claim. Consequently, counterclaims which do not disclose a reasonable cause of action are liable to be struck out

(*Ikea Ltd v Brown* [2009] EWHC 955 (Comm), LTL 13/5/2009; *RGI International Ltd v Synergy Classic Ltd* [2011] EWHC 3166 (Comm), LTL 8/12/2011; *Jones v Longley* [2016] EWHC 1309 (Ch), LTL 21/6/2016).

For the features which are required of a cross-claim if it is to qualify as a set-off see **28.7**.

The contents of a counterclaim must be verified by a statement of truth (see **23.13** to **23.17**; **CPR, r. 22.1(1)(a)**; **PD 20, para. 4.1**). The form of statement is (**PD 20, para 4.2**; **PD 22, para. 2.1**):

[I believe] [the defendant believes] that the facts stated in this counterclaim are true.

CROSS-CLAIMS

Cross-claims fall into three categories. Where the only answer to the claim is a cross-claim, the nature and effect of the three types are as follows: **28.7**

(a) Cross-claims unconnected with the claim. Here, summary judgment should be entered. An example is *Rotheram v Priest* (1879) 41 LT 558, where the claimant claimed arrears of rent and the defendant counterclaimed in libel. It was held that the counterclaim was totally foreign to the claim, so summary judgment was given to the claimant. The result would be the same under the CPR.

(b) Counterclaims linked to the claim. The appropriate order used to be for judgment subject to a stay of execution pending trial of the counterclaim. In *Drake and Fletcher Ltd v Batchelor* (1986) 130 SJ 285 Sir Neil Lawson said that in considering whether to grant a stay of execution, 'The question is whether the two contracts are so closely linked that it would be fair and equitable to deprive the [claimant] of the fruits of its judgment until resolution of the counterclaim'. The judge said there were three matters which needed to be considered:

   (i) The degree of connection between the claim and the counterclaim.

   (ii) The strength of the counterclaim. The weaker it was, the weaker the case for granting a stay.

   (iii) The claimant's ability to satisfy any judgment on the counterclaim. Any doubt on this matter strengthened the case for granting a stay.

There is some doubt about how cases where the only matter raised by the defendant is a connected counterclaim should be dealt with under the CPR. There is no longer any equivalent to the former RSC, ord. 14, r. 3(2), which provided for a stay of execution in summary judgment applications where there was a connected counterclaim. Early drafts of the CPR had a directly equivalent provision, and the probable consequence of removing it from the final version of the rules is that the court should simply enter judgment for the claimant. If this is correct, there is no longer any practical difference between this type of counterclaim and totally unconnected cross-claims.

(c) Set-offs. Where a counterclaim amounts to a set-off it is a defence to the claim and any summary judgment application should be dismissed, provided the value of the set-off is at least equal to the value of the claim. Where a set-off is not worth as much as the claim, the appropriate order is for summary judgment for the undisputed balance. The nature of set-offs is considered in **28.8**.

Set-offs

The following are established set-off situations: **28.8**

(a) Mutual debts. By virtue of the 18th-century Statutes of Set-off, mutual debts owed between the claimant and the defendant can be set off against each other. There is no need for the transactions giving rise to the debts to be connected other than through the parties. They need not be debts, strictly so-called, but may sound in damages provided they are capable of being ascertained with precision at the time of the application (*Morley v Inglis*

Commentary

(1837) 4 Bing NC 58, applied in *Axel Johnson Petroleum AB v MG Mineral Group AG* [1992] 1 WLR 270). A former partner was held in *Hurst v Bennett* [2001] 2 BCLC 290 to be unable to set off claims for money allegedly owed to him on the taking of partnership accounts against the claim of certain of the former partners to be indemnified against expenses they had incurred on the ground of lack of mutuality.

(b) Sale of goods. By virtue of the Sale of Goods Act 1979, s. 53(1), a buyer may set off counterclaims for breach of the statutory implied conditions about satisfactory quality, fitness for purpose and correspondence to description against a claim by the seller for the price.

(c) On a claim for the price of services, for example, where a builder is suing for the price of building work done, the defendant can set off a counterclaim for damages for poor workmanship in respect of the contract the claimant is suing on (*Basten v Butter* (1806) 7 East 479).

(d) Arrears of rent. Where a landlord brings a claim for arrears of rent, the tenant is allowed to set off a counterclaim for damages against the landlord for breach of a covenant in the lease in respect of which the landlord is claiming (*British Anzani (Felixstowe) Ltd v International Marine Management (UK) Ltd* [1980] QB 137, not following *Hart v Rogers* [1916] 1 KB 646, confirmed by *Agyeman v Boadi* (1996) 28 HLR 558). A tenant does not have a similar right of set-off in respect of a counterclaim for breach of repairing obligations against a claim for service charges as against a manager appointed by the court under the Landlord and Tenant Act 1987, s. 24(1) (*Taylor v Blaquiere* [2002] EWCA Civ 1633, [2003] 1 WLR 379), nor where the tenant's failure to pay has the intended consequence that the landlord will be unable to meet the repairing covenant (*Bluestorm Ltd v Portvale Holdings Ltd* [2004] EWCA Civ 289, [2004] HLR 49).

(e) Equitable set-off.

Mutual debts amount to set-offs whether or not the relevant transactions are connected, but they must be liquidated. Set-offs in categories (b) to (d) above involve liquidated claims and unliquidated cross-claims arising from the same transaction. A defendant relying on an unliquidated cross-claim also has to establish a case with at least a real prospect of success on quantum. An alleged set-off will be ineffective if its value cannot be quantified (*Eilon and Associates Ltd v Easygroup IP Licensing Ltd* (2011) LTL 15/4/2011). If the amount to be set off is less than the amount claimed, it can be effective as a partial defence.

The authorities on equitable set-off were reviewed in *Geldof Metaalconstructie NV v Simon Carves Ltd* [2010] EWCA Civ 667, [2010] 4 All ER 847. There has for a long time been a lack of clarity over when a cross-claim will amount to an equitable set-off (*Aries Tanker Corporation v Total Transport Ltd* [1977] 1 WLR 185). One test, which can be traced back to *Rawson v Samuel* (1841) Cr & Ph 161 (per Lord Cottenham at p. 178), and which was applied in modern authorities such as *Federal Commerce and Navigation Co. Ltd v Molena Alpha Inc.* [1978] QB 927 at pp. 974–5 (not affected by the appeal to the House of Lords), was whether there was an equity which went to impeach the claimant's demands ('the impeachment of title test'). Rix LJ in *Geldof Metaalconstructie NV v Simon Carves Ltd* at [28]–[31] applied Lord Brandon of Oakbrook's reasoning from *Bank of Boston Connecticut v European Grain and Shipping Ltd* [1989] AC 1056 at pp. 1106–10 in concluding that the impeachment of title test has been rejected as of continuing use in the modern world.

The test for whether a cross-claim amounts to an equitable set-off used by Lord Brandon in *Bank of Boston Connecticut v European Grain and Shipping Ltd* was whether the cross-claim 'flows out of and is inseparably connected with the dealings and transactions giving rise to the subject of the claim'. In *Geldof Metaalconstructie NV v Simon Carves Ltd* at [43(vi)] Rix LJ preferred a test based on the discredited passage of Lord Denning MR's judgment in *Federal Commerce and Navigation Co. Ltd v Molena Alpha Inc.*, but with the offending reference to the impeachment of title test removed, as the best modern statement of the test, namely whether the cross-claim is 'so closely connected with [the claimant's] demands that it would be manifestly unjust to allow him to enforce payment without taking into account the cross-claim'.

Care also needs to be taken with this formulation, because 'manifest injustice' was omitted from the formulation of Lord Brandon in *Bank of Boston Connecticut v European Grain and Shipping Ltd*, a matter considered important by Potter LJ in *Bim Kemi v Blackburn Chemicals Ltd* [2001] EWCA Civ 457, [2001] 2 Lloyd's Rep 93 at [38]. Rix LJ in *Geldof Metaalconstructie NV v Simon Carves Ltd* at [43(iv)] concluded that Lord Brandon did not intend to remove the manifest injustice element of the test, which has been emphasised in all the modern cases, including *Bim Kemi v Blackburn Chemicals Ltd* itself. The reason Lord Brandon did not refer to manifest injustice was that in *Bank of Boston Connecticut v European Grain and Shipping Ltd* Lord Brandon was focusing on dethroning the impeachment of title test.

In applying the modern test in *Geldof Metaalconstructie NV v Simon Carves Ltd*, Rix LJ at [43(ii)–(iv)] said there are two elements:

(a) A formal requirement of close connection between the claim and cross-claim. This is to ensure the doctrine of equitable set-off is based on principle and not discretion. There have been various ways in which this has been expressed in the cases: 'so closely connected with [the claimant's] demands that it would be manifestly unjust to allow him to enforce payment without taking into account the cross-claim' (*Federal Commerce and Navigation Co. Ltd v Molena Alpha Inc.*); 'flowing out of and inseparably connected with the dealings and transactions which also give rise to the claim' (*Government of Newfoundland v Newfoundland Railway Co.* (1888) 13 App Cas 199); 'inseparably connected so that the one ought not to be enforced without taking into account the other' (*Dole Dried Fruit and Nut Co. v Trustin Kerwood Ltd* [1990] 2 Lloyd's Rep 309). These should not be regarded as competing tests, but as different ways of expressing the broad concept that there has to be a close connection. This is an area where the courts have wisely refused to get bogged down in nuances of formulation (*Bim Kemi v Blackburn Chemicals Ltd* per Potter LJ at [38] and *Geldof Metaalconstructie NV v Simon Carves Ltd* per Rix LJ at [43(iii)]).

(b) A functional requirement whereby it needs to be unjust to enforce the claim without taking into account the cross-claim. This is the 'manifestly unjust' element of Lord Denning's formulation. Ultimately the rationale of the principle is equity.

At [43(v)] Rix LJ expressly said these requirements are not to be regarded as establishing a two-stage test. Instead, he preferred to say that there is both a formal element in the test and a functional element.

In one-contract cases (where the cross-claim arises out of the alleged breach of the same contract on which the claim is based) the claim and cross-claim will almost certainly have a close connection. A counterclaim for breach of a financial consultant's fiduciary and contractual duties to act in the client's best interests was regarded as capable of being set off against a claim for the consultant's fees in *Eilon and Associates Ltd v Easygroup IP Licensing Ltd* (2011) LTL 15/4/2011 because both claims arose from the same contract. There is, nevertheless, high authority for the proposition that 'there is no universal rule that claims arising out of the same contract may be set off against each other in all circumstances' (per Lord Hobhouse in *Government of Newfoundland v Newfoundland Railway Co.* at p. 212). The exceptions, which in most cases should be regarded as not fulfilling the functional requirement of the test, are probably limited to the traditional categories where the court has taken the strict view that the claimant has the right to be paid a liquidated sum free from any set-off. These were identified by Potter LJ in *Bim Kemi v Blackburn Chemicals Ltd* at [38], including claims for rent, freight and sums due under bills of exchange. To these should be added claims for a solicitor's fees (*Templer v M'Lachlan* (1806) 2 Bos & P NR 136) and cases where there is an effective 'no set-off' clause in the contract (see **34.39**). Other than in these established exceptions, it is difficult to justify refusing to accept a one-contract cross-claim as an equitable set-off.

Lord Denning's principle uses the expression 'without taking into account' the cross-claim. This is deliberately stated in non-quasi-statutory language (Rix LJ in *Geldof Metaalconstructie*

Commentary

NV v Simon Carves Ltd at [43]) to avoid spurious arguments that the doctrine is restricted to one-contract cases. There are various examples of two-contract cases where the doctrine has been applied in the past (examples include *Bankes v Jarvis* [1903] 1 KB 549; *Dole Dried Fruit and Nut Co. v Trustin Kerwood Ltd*; *Bim Kemi v Blackburn Chemicals Ltd*). As Lord Denning said in *Federal Commerce and Navigation Co. Ltd v Molena Alpha Inc.* at pp. 974–5, an equitable set-off may be based on a cross-claim that arises out of the same transaction or which is closely connected with it.

Geldof Metaalconstructie NV v Simon Carves Ltd itself was a two-contract case. Both contracts were between the same parties and related to the construction of a bioethanol plant. One was for goods to be supplied by the claimant ('the supply contract'), and the other for installation work to be done by the claimant ('the installation contract'). The dispute arose after the defendant alleged the claimant was in breach of the installation contract and issued a notice of default, and did not pay the claimant's invoice under the supply contract. The claimant then informed the defendant it would not continue with the installation work until the defendant paid all its outstanding invoices, including the invoice under the supply contract. The defendant then terminated the installation contract. The claimant issued proceedings for part of the contract price of the goods that became payable following delivery, and the defendant cross-claimed for damages for repudiation of an installation contract. It was held that the cross-claim amounted to an equitable set-off. While there were two contracts, they were both dedicated to the construction of the bioethanol plant. Any doubts about the degree of connection were dispelled by the claimant's conduct in insisting on payment of the supply contract invoice as a precondition for its continued performance of the installation contract. While the cross-claim did not arise from the supply contract or the claim for non-payment of the price, it did arise from the use to which the claimant sought to put its supply contract claim.

Geldof Metaalconstructie NV v Simon Carves Ltd was applied in *Addax Bank BSC v Wellesley Partners LLP* [2010] EWHC 1904 (QB), LTL 26/7/2010, where it was held there was a close connection between a claim for a liquidated sum payable under an investment contract and a cross-claim for unpaid invoices raised under an earlier consultancy contract which met the requirements for the cross-claim to amount to an equitable set-off. *Crastvell Trading Ltd v Bozel SA* [2010] EWHC 166 (Comm), LTL 10/3/2010 should be treated with caution. It applies a test of whether the cross-claim actually impugns the claim itself, which is probably a variant on the discredited impeachment of title test.

See also **63.20** on final judgments where there is an effective set-off.

28.9   Parties to set-off   Although set-offs usually arise between the immediate parties to a transaction, this is not always the case. A defendant who has guaranteed payment of a debt owed to the claimant by a principal debtor can rely on set-offs and cross-claims available to the debtor. This principle extends to certain types of bonds entered into in building contracts (whereby the party giving the bond promises to pay a specified sum to the claimant if one of the contractors fails to perform) provided the bond is construed as a guarantee (*Trafalgar House Construction (Regions) Ltd v General Surety and Guarantee Co. Ltd* [1996] AC 199).

Unliquidated damages claims which can be set off as between the original parties can also be set off against an assignee (*Hanak v Green* [1958] 2 QB 9), because an assignee of a chose in action takes subject to all rights of set-off available against the assignor (*Roxburghe v Cox* (1881) 17 ChD 520). A tenant is therefore entitled to set off any damages for disrepair due from the original landlord against a claim for arrears of rent brought by the landlord's assignee (*Smith v Muscat* [2003] EWCA Civ 962, [2003] 1 WLR 2853).

28.10   Excluding rights of set-off   It is open to the parties to a contract to exclude any right to set-off by an express term to that effect (*Hong Kong and Shanghai Banking Corporation v Kloeckner & Co. AG* [1990] 2 QB 514), but it is possible that such a term may be unreasonable and rendered ineffective by virtue of the Unfair Contract Terms Act 1977, as happened in *Stewart Gill Ltd v Horatio Myer and Co. Ltd* [1992] QB 600. Where there is a dispute over the reasonableness of a contractual term excluding the right of set-off the court should either determine whether the clause is effective on the summary judgment application, or order its effectiveness to be tried as a preliminary issue (*Stewart Gill Ltd v Horatio Myer and Co. Ltd* at p. 604G). Making a conditional order is inappropriate because the purpose of such a clause is to enable the claimant to be treated almost as a cash seller, and delaying the issue until trial deprives the claimant of the benefit of the clause.

An example of the opposite of a 'no set-off' clause was a clause in the contract in *Geldof Metaalconstructie NV v Simon Carves Ltd* [2010] EWCA Civ 667, [2010] 4 All ER 847, which provided that the purchaser 'shall be entitled from time to time to set off against the purchase order price any amounts lawfully due from the supplier to the purchaser whether under this purchase order or otherwise'. Such a clause should be given effect in accordance with its terms, and was regarded as effective in *Geldof Metaalconstructie NV v Simon Carves Ltd* (at [48]–[54]).

DEFENCE TO COUNTERCLAIM

General and procedural requirements

A claimant who files a reply and a defence to a counterclaim should normally put them in one **28.11** document, with the reply followed by the defence to counterclaim (**PD 20, para. 6.2**).

Where a defence is filed to a counterclaim, the court must consider the future conduct of the proceedings and give appropriate directions, in the course of which it must ensure that both the main claim and the counterclaim are managed together, so far as is practicable (**CPR, r. 20.13**). For this purpose the court will arrange a case management conference. Normally this will be fixed for the same time as a case management hearing for the original claim and any other additional claims (**PD 20, para. 5.1**).

Contents of defence to counterclaim

A defence to a counterclaim is governed by the same rules as a defence to a claim (see **28.12** **chapter 26**) and must be verified by a statement of truth (see **23.13** to **23.17**).

Chapter 29   Additional Claims under Part 20

The following procedural checklist is relevant to this chapter:

Procedural checklist 18   Additional claim (against third party)

INTRODUCTION

29.1   **CPR, Part 20**, concerns both counterclaims and claims against third parties. Counterclaims have already been discussed in **chapter 28**. This chapter considers claims made by a defendant, either against a co-defendant, seeking a contribution or indemnity, or against a third party. Together with counterclaims, these are generically known as 'additional claims'.

An indemnity is an obligation to reimburse someone, i.e. it is a claim for the fulfilment of an obligation, not for damages for breach of one. A contribution is essentially a partial indemnity.

CONTRIBUTION

29.2   A right to a contribution can arise as between joint tortfeasors, debtors or contractors, or by statute, for example, under the **Civil Liability (Contribution) Act 1978, s. 1(1)**, which provides that where two or more persons are liable to the same claimant for the same damage, each may claim contribution towards that liability from the others. The 'damage' referred to in **s. 1(1)** is the wrong causing the injury: it is not the injury itself (*Jameson v Central Electricity Generating Board* [1998] QB 323). Note also that the word used is 'damage' rather than 'damages' (see *Birse Construction Ltd v Haiste Ltd* [1996] 1 WLR 675). There is no limit or restriction on this concept. For example, a building contractor who remedies defective building work at no cost to the employer can claim a contribution from a consulting engineer based on the value of the remedial work (*Baker and Davies plc v Leslie Wilks Associates* [2005] EWHC 1179 (TCC), [2005] 3 All ER 603). The 1978 Act extends the reach of the contribution principle to cover cases whatever the legal basis of the liability, whether in tort, breach of contract, breach of trust or otherwise (see **s. 6(1)**).

In deciding whether the defendant and the third party are 'liable for the same damage', the words from **s. 1(1)** must be given their natural and ordinary meaning, without any restrictive or expansive gloss (*Royal Brompton Hospital NHS Trust v Hammond* [2002] UKHL 14, [2002] 1 WLR 1397). The words do not cover damage which is merely substantially or materially similar (per

Lord Steyn). The defendants in *Royal Brompton Hospital NHS Trust v Hammond* were architects who were sued by the hospital for negligently issuing certificates to building contractors, the effect of which was to give the contractors a defence to a claim the hospital had against the contractors for breach of contract for delays in completing building work. It was held that the hospital's claims against the contractors and against the architects were different, so the architects could not claim a contribution against the contractors. If the third party has no liability to the claimant, such as through a term in a contract absolving the third party from liability, the defendant cannot claim contribution from the third party (*Cooperative Retail Services Ltd v Taylor Young Partnership Ltd* [2002] UKHL 17, [2002] 1 WLR 1419).

Nationwide Building Society v Dunlop Haywards (DHL) Ltd [2009] EWHC 254 (Comm), [2010] 1 WLR 258, involved a claim by the lender against two defendants, in fraud against a valuer and in negligence against solicitors. In a claim by the solicitors for a contribution from the valuer, it was necessary to leave out of account the losses that arose only because one defendant was fraudulent when identifying the foreseeable losses for which both defendants were liable. For the purposes of the **Civil Liability (Contribution) Act 1978, ss. 1** and **2**, the 'same damage' (also the 'damage in question') in the contribution proceedings was therefore limited to the net amount advanced and lost interest on alternate advances, less the value of the property, and was not the value of the total liability. The 'damage in question' could not mean, as the solicitors asserted, the amount for which they were liable by agreement, having regard to their defences of limitation of liability and contributory negligence, or there would be no scope for the operation of **s. 2(3)**. The court went on to make a reduction for contributory negligence by the claimant to reach the final amount to be apportioned between the defendants. In *Cook v Green* [2009] BCC 204, in apportioning contributions between parties who had personally benefited from the wrong to the claimant and those who had not, the court added the whole of the value of the personal benefit to the amount of the contribution required from those taking that benefit.

A relevant liability under **s. 1** includes a liability under a court order, even if the amount of that liability has not been determined (*Abbey National plc v Matthews and Son* [2003] EWHC 925 (Ch), [2003] 1 WLR 2042, applying *R. A. Lister and Co. Ltd v E. G. Thomson (Shipping) Ltd (No. 2)* [1987] 1 WLR 1614).

An overall settlement, including a sum attributed by the paying party to costs, can found a contribution claim under **s. 1(1)** and **(4)**. A 'contribution' is not limited to a contribution in respect of damages, but includes one based on 'liability for damage' (*Mouchel Ltd v Van Oord (UK) Ltd (No. 2)* [2011] EWHC 1516 (TCC), [2011] BLR 492).

An additional claim under **CPR, Part 20**, was struck out in *Abbey National plc v Matthews and Son* on the ground of circularity. The building society sued solicitors for failing to disclose material relevant to a loan agreement, and the solicitors issued an additional claim against surveyors seeking a contribution on the ground of an alleged negligent valuation. The solicitors settled with the building society, and assigned their additional claim to the building society. By virtue of the settlement arrangements, the building society, using the assigned additional claim, could only claim a contribution from the surveyors if the solicitors were liable to the building society, but the solicitors were only liable to the building society if and to the extent that the building society obtained a contribution order from the surveyors.

The personal innocence of a person vicariously liable for the acts of an employee or partner is not relevant for the purpose of contribution proceedings between that person and another wrongdoer (*Dubai Aluminium Co. Ltd v Salaam* [2002] UKHL 48, [2003] 2 AC 366).

A claim in breach of trust or fiduciary duty is a claim for compensation in respect of any damage within the meaning of the **Civil Liability (Contribution) Act 1978, ss. 1(1)** and **6(1)**, if it is a claim to make good the claimant's loss, whereas a claim for an account of profits falls outside the statute (*Charter plc v City Index Ltd* [2007] EWCA Civ 1382, [2008] Ch 313).

In *Charter plc v City Index Ltd* a claim that a company's auditors and directors had allowed unauthorised transactions to continue in breach of duty to the company was held to be in respect of the same damage as a claim in breach of trust or fiduciary duty against a manager who used the company's funds to finance his personal betting transactions.

A contribution could be claimed under s. 1(1) from the company in fact liable to a former employee where a residuary body mistakenly paid compensation to the former employee (*BRB (Residuary) Ltd v Connex South Eastern Ltd* [2008] EWHC 1172 (QB), [2008] 1 WLR 2867).

INDEMNITY

29.3   Entitlement to an indemnity can arise by contract, under statute, or by virtue of the relationship between the parties. It is reasonably common for commercial and standard-form contracts to include provisions requiring one party to indemnify the other in specified circumstances, such as where one party incurs a liability to another person through the fault or breach of the other contracting party. General principles of contract law apply to such terms.

The principal purpose of a contract of insurance is to provide an indemnity to the assured. It has long been the practice not to allow a defendant to join its insurer as a third party in claims where the defendant is insured against the potential liability. Traditionally this has been because jurors were thought to be unduly influenced by the presence of insurance (*Harman v Crilly* [1943] KB 168), but even today joining an insurer can only be justified in accordance with the overriding objective if the insurer is denying liability under the insurance contract.

Indemnities arising by statute are mostly of a specialised nature.

Indemnities arising out of the relationship between the parties depend on the substantive law. For example, a principal is required to indemnify an agent in respect of liabilities incurred by the agent when acting within the agent's authority (*Adamson v Jarvis* (1827) 4 Bing 66; *Frixione v Tagliaferro and Sons* (1856) 10 Moo PC 175). Similarly, a surety who is sued may claim an indemnity against the principal debtor (*Ascherson v Tredegar Dry Dock and Wharf Co. Ltd* [1909] 2 Ch 401; *Thomas v Nottingham Incorporated Football Club Ltd* [1972] Ch 596).

A contractual clause giving an indemnity for all actions, claims, costs, proceedings and demands was considered in *Lomax Leisure Ltd v Fabric London Ltd* [2003] EWHC 307 (Ch), LTL 19/3/2003.

REQUIREMENT FOR PERMISSION

29.4   The permission of the court is not required in order to bring an additional claim, save in the following circumstances:

   (a) where a defendant wishes to counterclaim against a claimant after having already filed his defence (**CPR, r. 20.4(2)(b)**; see **chapter 28**);
   (b) where a defendant wishes to counterclaim against a person other than the claimant (**r. 20.5(1)**; see **chapter 28**);
   (c) where a defendant wishes to make a claim for contribution or indemnity against a co-defendant, but does not file the notice of claim with his defence (**r. 20.6**);
   (d) where a defendant who has already filed a defence wishes to make a claim for contribution or indemnity against a co-defendant added to the proceedings after the defence was filed, but does not file the notice of claim within 28 days of the filing of the new defendant's defence (**r. 20.6**); and

(e) where a defendant wishes to make a claim (whether for a contribution or indemnity or otherwise) against a person who is not a co-defendant, and where the claim is not a counterclaim, and where such claim is not issued before or at the same time as he files his defence (**r. 20.7(1)** and **(3)**).

It follows that the permission of the court to make an additional claim is not required:

(a) where a defendant wishes to counterclaim against the claimant at the same time that he files his defence (see **chapter 28**);

(b) where a defendant wishes to make a claim against a co-defendant for a contribution or an indemnity at the same time as filing his own defence (**r. 20.6**);

(c) where a defendant who has filed a defence wishes to make a claim for a contribution or an indemnity against a new co-defendant added after the defence was filed and does so within 28 days of the filing of the new co-defendant's defence (**r. 20.6**);

(d) where a defendant wishes to make any claim against a third party before or at the same time as he files his defence (**r. 20.7(3)(a)**). The expression 'defendant' in **r. 20.7(3)** is presumably intended to apply to a third (or fourth) party wishing to make a further claim against a person not already a party. This was perfectly clear on the pre-6 April 2006 wording of **r. 20.7(3)**, because at that time a third party brought in by the original defendant was known as the 'Part 20 defendant'. It is not so clear under the present version of **r. 20.7(3)**, because it is worded on the basis that the 'defendant' means the defendant to the original claim (see **PD 20, paras** 7.3 and 7.4), and the person brought in by the defendant is known as the 'third party'. However, this should not prevent a third party who acts quickly being allowed to issue a fourth party claim without permission. This is because **CPR, r. 20.3(1)**, provides that an additional claim is to be treated as if it were a claim for the purposes of the CPR, and there is no reason to read **r. 20.7(3)** as derogating from that for this purpose.

PROCEDURE FOR COMMENCING AN ADDITIONAL CLAIM WHEN PERMISSION IS NOT REQUIRED

29.5 The claim and particulars must be served on the person against whom it is made within 14 days after the date on which the additional claim is issued by the court (**CPR, r. 20.8(1)(b)**). There is no express provision that copies must also be served on every other party, which apparently only has to be done, under **r. 20.12(2)**, when an additional claim is served on a person who is not already a party (**r. 20.12(2)** refers to 'the additional claim form', referring to the form which is the subject of **r. 20.12(1)**). However, it is suggested that it would be good practice to do so. **Rule 20.8(1)** does not apply to a defendant's claim against a co-defendant for contribution or indemnity, for which see **29.11** (**r. 20.8(2)**).

PROCEDURE FOR FILING AN ADDITIONAL CLAIM WHEN PERMISSION IS REQUIRED

29.6 A party requiring permission to make an additional claim may apply without notice unless the court directs otherwise (**CPR, r. 20.7(5)**). The application notice should be filed together with a copy of the proposed additional claim (**PD 20, para. 1.2**), and the evidence in support should set out (**PD 20, para. 2.1**):

(a) the stage which the proceedings have reached;

(b) the nature of the additional claim, or details of the question or issue which needs to be decided;

(c) a summary of the facts on which the additional claim is based; and

(d) the name and address of any proposed additional party.

Where there has been delay which has caused or contributed to the need to apply for permission an explanation of the delay should be given in the evidence in support (**PD 20, para. 2.2**).

Additionally, where possible, the evidence should include a timetable of the proceedings to date (**PD 20, para. 2.3**).

Relevant considerations in applications for permission to file an additional claim

29.7 When considering whether or not to give permission for the filing of an additional claim, the court clearly has the power either to grant the application, dismiss it, or, under **CPR, r. 3.1(2) (e)**, require the additional claim to be dealt with separately from the claim by the claimant against the defendant. Apart from the question of whether or not it would be proper to allow the claim to be filed on its merits, or when there has been any delay, the court may also, by **r. 20.9(2)**, have regard to:

(a) the connection between the additional claim and the claim made by the claimant against the defendant;

(b) whether the party making the additional claim is seeking substantially the same remedy which some other party is claiming from him;

(c) whether the party making the additional claim wants the court to decide any question connected with the subject matter of the proceedings not only between existing parties, but between existing parties and a third party; or against an existing party in some different capacity in which he may stand, as well as in the capacity in which he is already a party.

The approach of the courts in deciding whether or not to grant permission to bring an additional claim does not differ substantially from the manner in which discretion was exercised under the old rules before the CPR came into force. Under those old rules in *Chatsworth Investments Ltd v Amoco (UK) Ltd* [1968] Ch 665, Russell LJ held that the court had to take a wide approach in exercising its discretion, and had to ask whether the third-party claim accorded with the general functions of third-party proceedings. In *Barclays Bank Ltd v Tom* [1923] 1 KB 221, Scrutton LJ identified these functions as safeguarding against differing results, ensuring the third party is bound by the decision between the claimant and the defendant, ensuring the additional claim is decided close in time to the proceedings commenced by the claimant, and to save the expense of having two trials.

Essentially, therefore, the establishment of some factual, legal or personal connection between the additional claim and the original claim will be helpful in ensuring the success of the application. In *Kazakhstan Kagazy plc v Zhunus* [2016] EWHC 1048 (Comm), [2016] 4 WLR 86 two defendants in a fraud claim were refused permission to make a claim for a contribution against a co-defendant. At that time, the co-defendant had already reached a settlement with the claimants and the draft contribution notice failed to advance a case of fraud or other wrongdoing by the co-defendant.

In *Angel Solicitors v Jenkins O'Dowd and Barth* [2009] EWHC 46 (Ch), [2009] 1 WLR 1220, permission to bring in a third party was refused when the application was heard at the same time as a summary judgment application which resulted in judgment against the only defendant. As the main claim had come to an end, it was more convenient for the third party claim to be brought in fresh proceedings (see [18]).

Permission to make an additional claim for contribution will be refused if no court would order the contribution claimed (*African Strategic Investment (Holdings) Ltd v Main* [2011] EWHC 2223 (Ch), LTL 30/8/2011).

Permission to issue an additional claim may be refused if the application is made after an unjustified delay. In *Borealis AB v Stargas Ltd* [2002] EWCA Civ 757, LTL 9/5/2002, there was a counterclaim against the claimant, and the claimant had sought to bring an additional claim against a non-party, SA, to contribute towards any liability on the counterclaim. The claimant's additional claim was set aside by the House of Lords in March 2001. In September 2001 there was a case management conference and a trial was fixed for July 2002. In March 2002 the defendant, for the first time, sought to bring its own additional claim against SA to contribute towards any liability the defendant might have. Although it was held that the defendant had a good arguable case on its additional claim, permission was refused because there was an inexcusable delay of a year after the House of Lords decision, and granting permission would have resulted in the trial being vacated.

Being a discretionary decision, an appeal court can only interfere with a decision on permission to file an additional claim where the judge either fails to apply the correct principles or makes a decision outside the generous ambit of the discretion (*Walbrook Trustees (Jersey) Ltd v Fattal* [2008] EWCA Civ 427, LTL 11/3/2008).

CONTENTS OF AN ADDITIONAL CLAIM

An additional claim under **CPR, Part 20**, must contain particulars, or particulars must be served with the claim (**r. 20.7(4)**). **Rule 20.7** does not apply to a defendant's claim against a co-defendant for contribution or indemnity, for which see **29.11** (**r. 20.7(1)**). The title of an additional claim should, where there are additional parties, comprise a list of all the parties, describing them by giving each party a separate identification (**PD 20, para 7.2**). This identification should be used throughout. Claimants and defendants in the original claim should be described as such, a position that does not change even if they acquire an additional procedural status (**para. 7.3**). The first party added under **CPR, Part 20**, is called the 'third party'. Subsequently added parties are the 'fourth party', 'fifth party', etc., in the order in which they are joined to the proceedings (**PD 20, para. 7.4**). If an additional claim is brought against more than one party jointly, they are known as the 'first named third party' and 'second named third party' (etc.) (**para. 7.5**). If an additional party ceases to be a party, all the remaining parties retain their existing nominal status (**para. 7.9**).

29.8

The description of an additional claim (traditionally set out in tramlines beneath the names of the parties in the title) must reflect the nature of the document and its relation to the parties. Thus:

(a) A 'defendant's additional claim against third party' is an additional claim brought by the defendant against a single additional party, the third party.

(b) A 'third party's defence to defendant's additional claim' would be the defence filed by the third party in the previous example.

It is established drafting practice to set out in the opening paragraphs of the particulars of an additional claim summaries of the original and any existing additional claims, to state that copies of the previous statements of case are being served with the present statement of case (in compliance with **CPR, r. 20.12**), and a denial of the claim made against the drafting party. This provides a context for the rest of the draft against the new additional party, and also allows certain terms to be defined for use in the rest of the draft. See example 29.1.

In proceedings where there are fourth or subsequent parties, they should be referred to in the text of statements of case, witness statements etc. by name, suitably abbreviated if appropriate (**PD 20, para. 7.11**). If parties have similar names, suitable distinguishing abbreviations should be used.

An additional claim should be verified by a statement of truth (see **23.13** to **23.17**; **CPR, r. 22.1(1)(a)**; **PD 20, para. 4.1**). The form of statement is (**PD 20, para. 4.2**; **PD 22, para. 2.1**):

[I believe] [the [defendant] believes] that the facts stated in this additional claim are true.

PROCEDURE AND CASE MANAGEMENT AFTER FILING

29.9 Although **CPR, Part 12** (obtaining judgment in default of a defence), applies to counterclaims (see **28.3**), it does not apply to other additional claims (**r. 20.3(3)**). Instead, the procedure where no acknowledgment of service or defence is filed to an additional claim is set out in **r. 20.11** (see **29.10**) (which does not apply to a defendant's claim against a co-defendant for contribution or indemnity: **r. 20.11(1)(a)**).

Part 14 (admissions) also does not apply (**r. 20.3(4)**), save for the provisions relating to the ability to admit in writing the truth of another party's case (under **r. 14.1(1)** and (2)), so that the other party can obtain judgment under **r. 14.3**.

Where the court gives permission to make an additional claim it will at the same time give directions as to its service (**r. 20.8(3)**). Service is effected in accordance with **Part 6**, see **r. 20.3(1)** and **chapter 15**.

Example 29.1

IN THE HIGH COURT OF JUSTICE   Claim No. ....

QUEEN'S BENCH DIVISION

BETWEEN:

MR ALAN BEST	Claimant
— and —	
MISS CATHERINE DAY	Defendant
— and —	
MS ELAINE FRASER	Third Party
— and —	
MS GAIL HARVEY	Fourth Party

THIRD PARTY'S ADDITIONAL CLAIM AGAINST FOURTH PARTY

1. In his claim against the Defendant the Claimant claims damages and interest for alleged breach of a contract in writing dated 14 June 2014 ('the third contract') for the sale of a Bergman car registration number ML13 TYS ('the car'). Copies of the third contract, Claim Form and Particulars of Claim are served with these particulars of additional claim.

2. The Defendant denies she is liable to the Claimant on the grounds set out in the Defence, a copy of which is served with these particulars of additional claim.

3. In her additional claim against the Third Party, the Defendant claims damages and interest for alleged breach of a contract in writing dated 4 June 2014 ('the second contract') for the car. Copies of the second contract, Additional Claim Form and Defendant's Additional Claim against Third Party are served with these particulars of additional claim.

4. The Third Party denies she is liable to the Defendant on the grounds set out in the Third Party's Defence to Defendant's Additional Claim, a copy of which is served with these particulars of additional claim. If, contrary to the Third Party's Defence to Defendant's Additional Claim, the Third Party is held liable in whole or in part to the Defendant, the Third Party claims against the Fourth Party ('Ms Harvey') [to be indemnified against] [, alternatively, a contribution towards] [her liability, if any, to the Defendant] [damages and interest for alleged breach of a contract in writing dated 24 May 2014 ('the first contract') for the car] for the reasons set out below.

5. [*Continue with details of the claim against the Fourth Party as in normal particulars of claim.*]

Once an additional claim is served on a person, he either becomes a party if he is not one already, or if he is already a party but the additional claim is served on him for the purpose of requiring the court to decide a question against him in a further capacity, he also becomes a party in such further capacity (**r. 20.10**).

If an additional claim form is served on a person who is not already a party, **r. 20.12(1)** requires it to be accompanied by:

(a) a form for defending the claim (form N9B (specified amount) or form N9D (unspecified amount));

(b) a form for admitting the claim (form N9A (specified amount) or form N9C (unspecified amount));

(c) a form for acknowledging service (form N213);

(d) a copy of every statement of case which has already been served in the proceedings; and

(e) such other documents as the court may direct.

A copy of the additional claim form must also be served on every existing party (**r. 20.12(2)**).

Where a defence is filed to an additional claim, the court must consider the future conduct of the proceedings and give appropriate directions (**r. 20.13(1)**). In order to do so, the court will arrange a hearing to consider case management of the additional claim, and will give notice of the hearing to each party likely to be affected by any order made at the hearing (**PD 20, paras 5.1 and 5.2**). When giving directions, the court must ensure that, so far as practicable, the additional and the main claims are managed together (**CPR, r. 20.13(2)**). An additional claim which is unsuitable for hearing with the main claim may be filtered out at an earlier stage if it requires the court's permission before it can be made (see **29.7**). However, if the permission of the court was not required, the question of the best means by which the two matters should be heard will be decided at this stage.

At the hearing, the court may (**PD 20, para. 5.3**):

(a) treat the matter as a summary judgment hearing (whether on the application of the defendant, third party, or of its own volition);

(b) order that the additional claim be dismissed (presumably as an outcome of (a) above);

(c) give directions as to the manner in which any matter set out in or arising from the additional claim should be dealt with, and as to the part, if any, that the third party will take at the trial of the claim, and the extent to which he is to be bound by any judgment or decision to be made in the claim.

It would be wrong, however, for a judge to conclude that a third party does not require representation at the main trial because he shared a common intention with the defendant. The third party is not just a witness: he is at risk and he needs to be represented by his own lawyers (*Tantera v Moore* [2009] EWCA Civ 1393, LTL 29/10/2009).

Any of the above orders can be made either before or after any judgment in the claim has been entered by the claimant against the defendant (**PD 20, para. 5.4**).

Where an additional claim had proceeded to trial without an order expressly stating that permission had been granted, contrary to **CPR, r. 20.7(3)**, it was held in *Lloyds Bank plc v Ellicott* [2002] EWCA Civ 1333, [2003] BPIR 632, to have been wrong to have struck out the additional claim. Rather, the judge should have exercised his case management powers under **r. 3.10** to cure the irregularity and proceeded on the basis that permission had been granted.

Where third parties were added at a late stage in a case where there were good reasons for not granting an adjournment of the trial of the main claim, the judge was held to have been entitled to order that the third parties would not be added to the trial between the claimant and the defendant (*Powell v Pallisers of Hereford Ltd* [2002] EWCA Civ 959, LTL 1/7/2002). The Court of

Appeal in this case also advised the parties to reach a consensual agreement whereby the third parties were given an opportunity (such as by being allowed to ask questions at trial) to test the defendant's witnesses, with a view to reducing the costs caused by duplication at the later trial of the additional claim.

DEFAULT JUDGMENT IN ADDITIONAL CLAIMS

29.10 Where no acknowledgment of service or defence is filed in respect of an additional claim, the procedure is governed by **CPR, r. 20.11**. The provisions for judgment in default under **Part 12** are not applicable, except in respect of a counterclaim, because a default judgment in an additional claim may depend on the success or otherwise of the principal claim against the defendant.

A failure to file an acknowledgment of service or defence will be deemed to be an admission of the additional claim, and, to the extent that it is relevant, the third party will be bound by any judgment or decision in the main proceedings (**r. 20.11(2)(a)**). The consequences of default are set out in the notes for the third party which are sent with the additional claim.

If a default judgment under **Part 12** is given against a defendant who has made an additional claim, then, if no acknowledgment of service or defence has been filed by the third party, the defendant may, in turn, obtain judgment in respect of the additional claim, by filing a request in the relevant practice form (**r. 20.11(2)(b)**). Until Her Majesty's Courts and Tribunals Service issues a form it is suggested that form N227 may be adapted for this purpose. This may be done without the court's permission, provided that the defendant has satisfied the default judgment against himself, and does not wish to obtain judgment against the third party for any other remedy than a contribution or indemnity (**r. 20.11(3)**). However, if he has not satisfied the judgment against himself, or if he wishes to obtain judgment for some remedy other than a contribution or indemnity, the permission of the court has to be obtained, on an application which can be made without notice, unless the court otherwise directs (**r. 20.11(4)**). Such a judgment can be set aside or varied by the court at any time (**r. 20.11(5)**). The rule requiring prior payment (unless the court's permission is obtained) is presumably to ensure that a defendant does not profit by a default judgment against him, by keeping the proceeds of a default judgment against the third party, and failing to pass it on to the claimant. **Rule 20.11(3)(b)** does not appear to preclude the obtaining of a default judgment against a third party where a claim has been made against him for a remedy in addition to that of a contribution or indemnity, provided that it is not intended to pursue that part of the claim — the rule uses the words 'he wishes to obtain judgment for any remedy' rather than 'the claim is for any remedy'.

DEFENDANT'S CLAIM AGAINST A CO-DEFENDANT FOR CONTRIBUTION OR INDEMNITY

29.11 Under **CPR, r. 20.6**, a defendant may make an additional claim against a co-defendant for contribution or indemnity by:

(a) filing a notice containing a statement of the nature and grounds of the claim; and
(b) serving that notice on the co-defendant against whom the claim is to be made.

Unless this notice is filed with the defendant's defence, the court's permission is required. If the only reason for not filing the notice with the defence is that the co-defendant was not added to the claim until after the defence was filed, the court's permission is not required if the notice is filed and served within 28 days after the new co-defendant's defence is filed.

Rules **20.7** to **20.12** are either irrelevant to or are expressed not to apply to a defendant's claim against a co-defendant for contribution or indemnity. There is apparently no provision for any form of judgment in default of defence. The co-defendant against whom the claim is made will presumably remain a party to the main action (unless he fails to file a defence to that action, in which event judgment in default will presumably be obtained in the main action), and thus all issues will be heard together.

At first instance, it has been held that a contribution notice under **r. 20.6** is not a claim form and cannot be served outside the jurisdiction (*Knauf UK GmbH v British Gypsum Ltd* [2002] EWHC 739 (Comm), [2002] 2 Lloyd's Rep 416). Defendants who are outside the jurisdiction, once they come on the record by acknowledging service or filing a defence, are obliged to provide an address for service within the jurisdiction (**r. 6.23**), which is the address to be used for serving contribution notices.

RESOLVING CLAIMS BETWEEN A DEFENDANT AND A THIRD PARTY

There will be occasions when a claim by a claimant against a defendant is intimately connected with a dispute between the defendant and a third party which involves the same facts or a common point of law, but does not affect the defendant's liability to the claimant. In such an event, the defendant has a choice of either commencing separate proceedings against the third party, or applying that the third party be joined to the existing claim under **CPR, r. 19.2(2)(b)**, on the ground that there is an issue between the defendant and the new party which is connected to the matters in dispute, and that it is desirable to add the new party to resolve that issue. **29.12**

The advantage of the latter procedure is that bringing the claim within existing proceedings will normally provide a speedier and more cost-effective means of resolving the dispute, and will also avoid the potentially difficult situation of different tribunals arriving at different conclusions on what are essentially the same facts and issues. See also **chapter 14**.

Chapter 30　Further Information

PRINCIPLES

30.1　**CPR, Part 18**, and **PD 18** provide procedures by which, subject to any rule of law or procedure to the contrary, one party to proceedings can obtain from any other party:

(a)　clarification of any matter which is in dispute in the proceedings; and/or

(b)　additional information in relation to any such matter.

Initially this is to be done by making a request directly to the other party, under **PD 18**, without the court's involvement. If the other party does not respond to the request, or the response is considered inadequate, an application may be made to the court for an order under **CPR, r. 18.1**, to give further information.

The doctrine of proportionality and the approach to statements of case generally, should mean that requests for further information are used with some caution. Although they can be used to advantage in some claims, considerable care must be taken in selecting the areas to be investigated by a request, and in formulating the questions to be put. Where the responding party's statement of case is already sufficiently pleaded, requests for further information designed for:

(a)　tactical reasons;

(b)　obtaining further explanation of matters clearly put in issue on the existing statements of case;

(c)　an explanation of the responding party's legal arguments; or

(d)　obtaining information that might be useful for bringing separate claims against other persons,

are abuses of **Part 18** and will not be allowed (*Trader Publishing Ltd v Autotrader.Com Inc.* [2010] EWHC 142 (Ch), LTL 12/3/2010). Before making a request for further information a party should consider the other side's statement of case very carefully, and avoid making requests concerning matters that are already adequately particularised or are otherwise unnecessary (*Trader Publishing Ltd v Autotrader.Com Inc.*). The tests of necessity and proportionality in **PD 18, para. 1.2**, mean the procedure is more restrictive than the old procedure for further and better particulars. There is no need to make a request for further information on matters of evidence (statements of case should deal with facts, not evidence) or points which are for argument at trial (these should be in the skeleton arguments), or where the information is readily available (*Lexi Holdings v Pannone and Partners* [2010] EWHC 1416 (Ch), LTL 21/6/2010).

On the other hand, a request for further information may be the proportionate and best way of dealing with a statement of case by an opponent which does not provide full information, rather than the more drastic approach of applying to strike out (*Deutsche Morgan Grenfell Group plc v Commissioners of Inland Revenue* [2006] UKHL 49, [2007] 1 AC 558 at [148]).

REQUEST FOR FURTHER INFORMATION

30.2　A party should not make an application to the court for an order under **CPR, r. 18.1**, without having first served a written request on the party from whom the information or clarification is sought. The request must give a reasonable time to respond, and set a date by which the response should be served (**PD 18, para. 1.1**). Such request should be made, as far as possible, in a single comprehensive document, and not piecemeal (**para. 1.3**). It should be concise, and strictly confined to matters which are reasonably necessary and proportionate to enable the party requesting the information to prepare his own case or to understand the case he has to meet (**para. 1.2**). The requirement of proportionality is, of course, to ensure compliance with the overriding objective in **Part 1**, and provides the recipient with a new ground for refusing to give further information (although, it is suggested, not clarification) even though the request might otherwise be legitimate.

In patent infringement claims, it is unusual for the court to order a party to answer a request for further information to clarify the construction which that party proposes to put on the terms of the patent (*Lux Traffic Controls Ltd v Staffordshire Public Works* [1991] RPC 73). This is not an invariable rule, and it may save costs to order further information where the answers will assist in defining the issues before experts are instructed (*Novartis AG v Johnson and Johnson Medical Ltd* [2008] EWHC 293 (Pat), LTL 5/3/2008).

What constitutes 'a matter in dispute' was liberally construed in relation to requests for information concerning the nature and extent of insurance cover available to meet the claimant's claim in *Harcourt v Griffin* [2007] EWHC 1500 (QB), [2007] PIQR Q177. That claim was likely to be worth over £8 million against an unincorporated association with limited assets. Disclosure was ordered as it would be irrational to devote a great deal of expense to maximise damages if the resources available were limited.

However, this was not followed in *West London Pipeline and Storage Ltd v Total UK Ltd* [2008] EWHC 1296 (Comm), [2008] 1 CLC 935, where it was held there is no jurisdiction to order a party to disclose its insurance position, where it is not a matter in dispute in the proceedings. It is submitted that this is the appropriate line for the court to take. *Arroyo v BP Exploration Co. (Colombia) Ltd* (2010) LTL 4/6/2010 followed this line in refusing a request for the disclosure of the claimant's ATE cover. There is no general right to be informed of an opponent's ability to satisfy a judgment or pay an order for costs. Similarly, a request for further information about the number of times a judge had acted for a particular client while the judge was at the Bar was refused as fishing and failing to relate to any issue in the case in *Mireskandari v Associated Newspapers Ltd* [2010] EWHC 967 (QB), 160 NLJ 695.

Form and content of request

There is no requirement that a request for further information should be in a particular form, **30.3** save that a party who has indicated willingness to be served by email (see **15.15**) should be served with a request by email (**PD 18, para. 1.7**). If the text is brief, and the reply likely to be so as well, it may be made by letter (**PD 18, para. 1.4**). Such a letter should expressly state that it contains a request made under **CPR, Part 18**, and should deal with no matters other than the request (**PD 18, para. 1.5**). It is required to contain the same formalities as a request made in a separate document (**para. 1.6**). These requirements tend to blur the distinction between the two formats to the extent that there seems little advantage in making the request other than by way of a formal separate document.

Whether made by letter or in a separate document, the request must (**PD 18, para. 1.6(1)**):

(a) be headed with the name of the court and the title and number of the claim;
(b) state in its heading that it is a request made under **Part 18**;
(c) identify the party making the request and the party to whom the request is made (referred to in **PD 18** as the 'first party' and the 'second party');
(d) set out in a separate numbered paragraph, each request for information or clarification;
(e) identify any document referred to in the request, and (if relevant) the paragraph or words to which the request relates;
(f) state the date by which the response is expected.

A further advantage of making the request by way of a separate document rather than by letter is that, if convenient, it may be prepared with the numbered paragraphs set out on the left-hand half of each sheet, leaving room for the response to appear on the same document on the right. Thus the entire request and response would appear on the same document. If the request is prepared in this manner, an extra copy should be served for the use of the recipient (**PD 18, para. 1.6(2)**). It may well be, however, that, save in straightforward cases, limitations of space, and word-processing difficulties may make it easier for the 'second party' to adopt the alternative response procedure, where the text of the request is repeated, followed by the response (**PD 18, para. 2.3(1)(c)**) (as was formerly the case when responding to a request for further and better particulars).

Example 30.1 provides some suggestions as to the manner in which a request could be approached. The request need not be verified by a statement of truth, although the response must be (see **23.12** to **23.17**; **CPR, r. 22.1(1)(a)**; **PD 18, para. 3**).

Example 30.1

IN THE COUNTY COURT AT BLACKSTONE   Claim No. BK16 1234

BETWEEN

AB   Claimant

— and —

CD   Defendant

REQUEST FOR FURTHER INFORMATION

ABOUT THE CLAIMANT'S CASE UNDER PART 18

Sought on behalf of the Defendant (the first party) from the Claimant (the second party), and made on 18 March 2016.

[*Example of a straightforward request for clarification of the claim*]

Under Paragraph 2 of the Particulars of Claim

Of: 'It was a term of the agreement between the parties that the propellers would be delivered to the Claimant within 7 working days of receipt of the order by the Defendant'.

Request

1. Please state whether the alleged term was made orally or in writing. If the term was made orally, please give full information as to the parties agreeing the term, the date, time and place that it was allegedly agreed, and the gist of all words spoken. If it is alleged that the term was made in writing, please give the above information with all necessary changes, identifying any document or documents relied on, and attaching a copy of the same to the response.

[*Example of a request not directly referable to the particulars of claim*]

2. Is it not the case:

    (a) that on 21 May 2014 the Claimant was handed a cheque for £2,350 by the Defendant, in the course of a meeting at the Defendant's premises, being a refund in respect of propellers that the Defendant was unable to supply?

    (b) that the Claimant, or some other person on his behalf, subsequently presented the cheque and that it was duly met and cleared through the Defendant's bank account on 4 June 2014?

    (c) that such sum falls therefore to be deducted from the Claimant's claim against the Defendant?

> [*Example of a request referable to a document attached to the particulars of claim*]
>
> Please look at the letter dated 16 May 2014 from the Claimant to the Defendant, attached to the Particulars of Claim.
>
> **Request**
>
> 3. Please state whether it is the Claimant's case:
>
>   (a) that the propellers referred to in the final paragraph on page 1 are of model PDG 234, or PDG 236, or some other, and if so, which model?
>
>   (b) that the signature on the letter is that of the Claimant, or some other person (and if so, please identify the alleged signatory)?
>
> Take notice that these requests must be answered no later than 4.00 p.m. on 8 April 2016
>
> Dated 18 March 2016

FORM AND CONTENT OF RESPONSE

30.4 The response to a request for further information must be in writing and must be dated and signed by the second party or his legal representative (**PD 18, para. 2.1**). It must be verified by a statement of truth (see **23.12** to **23.17**; **CPR, r. 22.1(1)(a)**; **PD 18, para. 3**). Where the request is made by letter, the response may be in like form, or in a formal reply (**para. 2.2(1)**), but if the response is made in a letter it should identify itself as a response, and deal with no matters other than the response (**para. 2.2(2)**). To this extent the format of the letter will be similar to that containing the original request. By analogy, it is submitted, a response to an email request should be sent by email.

If the original request was prepared in the form set out in **para. 1.6(2)** (so that the response could be made on the same form as the request), the second party may choose whether to use it, or to reply in a separate document. If he uses the original form, no additional formalities are required (save for the date, signature and statement of truth). However, if the response is made in a formal document, it must (**para. 2.3(1)**):

(a) be headed with the name of the court and the title and number of the claim;

(b) in its heading, identify itself as a response to the request;

(c) repeat the text of each separate paragraph of the request and set out under each paragraph the response to it;

(d) refer to and have attached to it, a copy of any document not already in the possession of the first party, which forms part of the response.

A second or supplementary response must identify itself as such in its heading (**para. 2.3(2)**).

It seems clear from the practice direction, that where the original request is made in a formal document, the response should not be by way of letter.

The response must be served on all parties (in addition to the first party), and a copy should be filed with the court together with a copy of the request (**para. 2.4**).

OBJECTIONS TO RESPONDING

30.5 The second party appears to be allowed five principal grounds on which to object to part or all of a request:

(a) that it is a request for information or clarification that is unnecessary, irrelevant or improper;

(b)   that he is unable to provide the information or clarification requested;

(c)   that insufficient time has been given to him to formulate a reply;

(d)   that the request can only be complied with at an expense which is disproportionate to the claim, or is otherwise contrary to the overriding objective;

(e)   that he is protected from answering by privilege.

In the event of an objection being taken, the second party must inform the first party promptly, and in any event within the time stipulated in the request (**PD 18, para. 4.1(1)**). Such information may be by letter, or by way of a formal response in a separate document, but in either event must be accompanied by reasons for the objection, and, where relevant, a date by which he expects to be able to comply with the request (**para. 4.1(2)**). Presumably, there is no reason why such objection(s) could not be taken in the course of a response that does answer other requests, although this is not specifically dealt with in **PD 18**.

Where the objection is one of disproportionate expense, it seems that it will not be sufficient for the second party to adopt the above course. Instead, he must serve a reply, and explain in it briefly why he has taken the view (**para. 4.2(2)**). Where the objection is founded on privilege, a reply should be served setting out the nature of the privilege relied upon.

Once the second party has indicated his objection(s) in the appropriate format, there is no need for him to make any application to the court (**para. 4.2(1)**). Upon receipt of the response or objection, it will be for the first party to decide whether or not to make an application to the court for an order that the information be provided.

A 'fishing' request will be improper. A request is fishing where the party making the request does not have evidence supporting the cause of action or defence being put forward, but is hoping that something may turn up in response to the request (*Best v Charter Medical of England Ltd* [2001] EWCA Civ 1588, [2002] EMLR 18).

In *English, Welsh and Scottish Railway Ltd v Goodman* [2007] EWHC 3463 (QB), LTL 21/8/2007, the claim was pleaded in a general and non-specific way. It was struck out partly because the claimant refused to answer a request for further information, on the ground, regarded as inadequate in the circumstances, that the answers would be found in the exchanged witness statements.

COURT ORDER TO PROVIDE FURTHER INFORMATION

30.6   Under **CPR, r. 18.1**, a party to proceedings may ask the court to order another party:

(a)   to clarify any matter which is in dispute in the proceedings; or

(b)   to give additional information in relation to any such matter.

This may be done whether or not the matter is contained in or referred to in a statement of case. The court may exercise the power to make an order under **r. 18.1(1)** at any time, but the power is expressed by **r. 18.1(2)** to be subject to any rule of law to the contrary.

If a party makes no response to a request (in whole or in part) or it is considered that such response as is made is inadequate, an application can be made to the court in the manner laid down in **CPR, Part 23** (see **chapter 32**) for an order under **r. 18.1**. The application notice should set out, or have attached to it, the text of the order sought, and in particular should specify the matter or matters in respect of which the clarification or information is sought (**PD 18, para. 5.2**). In practice, it would presumably be helpful to set out or attach the request (or that part of it that is said still to be unanswered) in the format in which it was originally sent to the 'second party'. If no request had originally been sent to the 'second party', an explanation for this should be set out in the application notice (**PD 18, para. 5.3(1)**), as should any response made by the 'second party' to any request that had been made (**PD 18, para. 5.3**).

If a request has been served, and no response received, the party making the application need not serve the application notice on the second party, and the court may deal with the application without a hearing, provided that at least 14 days have passed since the request was served, and the time stated in it for a response has expired (**PD 18, para. 5.5**). In all other cases, the application notice must be served on the second party and on all other parties to the claim (**PD 18, para. 5.6**).

Both parties to the application (or just the first party if an application notice is not served) should consider whether evidence in support of or in opposition to the application is required (**PD 18, para. 5.4**).

Where an order is made, the party required to provide the clarification or information must file his response and serve it on the other parties within the time specified (**CPR, r. 18.1(3)**). The order itself must be served on all parties to the claim (**PD 18, para. 5.7**), regardless of whether or not notice of the application was originally given. The order may also make a summary assessment of costs (**PD 18, para. 5.8**). If the order makes no reference to costs, no party is entitled to claim them (**PD 18, para. 5.8(2)**).

RESTRICTIONS ON THE USE OF FURTHER INFORMATION

Whether or not further information is given voluntarily or following an order of the court, the court may direct that such information must not be used for any purpose except for that of the proceedings in which it is given (**CPR, r. 18.2**).   **30.7**

Commentary

Chapter 31 Amendments to Statements of Case

INTRODUCTION

31.1 Generally, statements of case can be amended without seeking permission before they are served. After service, amendments are generally either by consent or with permission. Permission is generally granted where there is no prejudice to other parties, and in general there is no prejudice if the other parties are adequately protected by the usual order that the costs of and occasioned by the amendments are paid by the amending party. For the documents that are statements of case see **23.2**. Amendments involving the addition or substitution of parties are considered at **14.79** to **14.92**, and this chapter will consider amendments not involving changes in the parties. There are particular restrictions on amendments sought after the expiry of limitation, see **14.86** to **14.91** and **31.21** to **31.28**.

WHEN PERMISSION IS NOT REQUIRED FOR AMENDMENT

31.2 A party may amend a statement of case at any time before it has been served on any other party (**CPR, r. 17.1(1)**), and in such an event, the permission of the court is not required. However, such an amendment can subsequently be disallowed by the court (**r. 17.2(1)**) on the application, within 14 days of service of the amended statement of case, by the party on whom it is served (**r. 17.2(2)**). The rules do not presently state any specific matters that the court will take into consideration when deciding whether or not to grant such an application, but it is almost certain that the overriding objective and general principles of case management will be applied.

If a statement of case has been served, an amendment can be made without permission of the court, provided the written consent of all the other parties has been obtained (**r. 17.1(2)(a)**).

It will not be sufficient under this rule simply to obtain the consent of the party to whom the statement of case has been directed.

If, however, the application is to amend by removing, adding or substituting a party, the application must be made in accordance with **r. 19.4** (which deals more specifically with the addition and substitution of parties; see **14.79** to **14.85**).

Where an amended statement of case is filed without the need for the permission of the court, it should be endorsed in the following manner (**PD 17, para. 2.1(2)**):

Amended [particulars of claim/defence (or as may be)] under CPR, [rule 17.1(1) or 17.1(2)(a)], dated...

For the format of an amended statement of case, see **31.20**.

APPLICATION FOR PERMISSION TO AMEND

Where a statement of case has been served, and the written consent of all the other parties has not been obtained, or is not forthcoming, a party may apply to the court for permission to make an amendment (**CPR, r. 17.1(2)(b)**). The applicant should file the application notice with the court, together with a copy of the statement of case with the proposed amendments (**PD 17, para. 1.2**). By **PD 17, para. 2.2**, the statement of case in its amended form need not show the original text (see **31.20**), but it is difficult to see how the court will be assisted in making a decision on an application to amend, if the original text is not shown in the copy to be filed with the application.   **31.3**

The application may be dealt with at a hearing, or, where all parties consent, without a hearing (i.e. on written submissions) (**PD 17, para. 1.1**). If permission to amend is given, the court may (not must) give directions as to amendments to be made to any other statement of case, and service of any amendments (**CPR, r. 17.3(1)**). Thus provision can (and it is suggested normally will) be made by the court for the service of any amendments that will have to be made by other parties consequent upon the service of the amended statement of case on them. In any event, the amended statement of case should be filed by the applicant within 14 days of the date of the order, unless the court directs otherwise (**PD 17, para. 1.3**). A copy of the amended statement of case and the order should be served on every party to the proceedings unless the court directs otherwise (**PD 17, para. 1.5**). The court's power to give permission is subject to the rules on change of parties, both before and after the end of a relevant limitation period, set out in **CPR, rr. 19.2** and **19.5**, and to **r. 17.4** dealing with amendments after the expiry of a relevant limitation period (**r. 17.3(2)**).

One of the conditions considered on an application for permission is whether the proposed amended case has a real prospect of success (see **31.13**). This should be addressed in the written evidence in support of the application. The judge may consider the evidence in support and decide that the amended case has a real prospect of success. Alternatively, the judge may grant permission to amend conditionally on supporting evidence being adduced at trial, with permission to amend being subject to disallowance if such evidence is not adduced (*Swain-Mason v Mills and Reeve LLP* [2011] EWCA Civ 14, [2011] 1 WLR 2735 at [81]). Another alternative is to disallow amendments which are not at the time of the application supported by evidence establishing a real prospect of success, but to allow the application to be renewed at trial once the evidence is complete (*Bleasdale v Forster* [2011] EWHC 596 (Ch), LTL 17/3/2011).

Where an amended statement of case is filed with the permission of the court, it should be endorsed in the following manner (**PD 17, para. 2.1(1)**):

Amended [particulars of claim/defence (or as may be)] by order of [Master.../District Judge...or as may be] dated...

PRINCIPLES ON WHICH PERMISSION IS GRANTED

General principles applied on applications to amend

31.4   No criteria are laid down in CPR, rr. 17.1, 17.3 and 19.4, to govern applications for permission to amend. In accordance with the overriding objective, as a general statement of principle, it can be said that amendments should be allowed where this is just and proportionate. (*J. W. Spear and Sons Ltd v Zynga Inc.* [2013] EWHC 1640 (Ch), LTL 21/6/2013). In all cases the proposed amendments must comply with the rules on drafting statements of case (*Hague Plant Ltd v Hague* [2014] EWCA Civ 1609, [2015] CP Rep 14). There are two distinct lines of authority on how this should be applied (see **31.5** and **31.6**).

Amendments which introduce a new cause of action after the expiry of limitation raise special problems which are considered at **31.21** to **31.28**. For addition and substitution of parties see **14.79** to **14.92**. For withdrawal of admissions see **17.4**. On amending to withdraw an offer of amends under the Defamation Act 1996, s. 2, see **66.31**.

Traditional approach

31.5   Under the RSC a permissive approach was taken to applications to amend, which was based on the principle that at trial the court should determine the real issues between the parties. Thus, in *Cropper v Smith* (1883) 26 ChD 700 at pp. 710–11 Bowen LJ said:

> It is a well-established principle that the object of the court is to decide the rights of the parties, and not to punish them for mistakes they make in the conduct of their cases by deciding otherwise than in accordance with their rights. . . . I know of no kind of error or mistake which, if not fraudulent or intended to overreach, the court ought not to correct, if it can be done without injustice to the other party. Courts do not exist for the sake of discipline, but for the sake of deciding matters in controversy, and I do not regard such amendment as a matter of favour or grace. . . . It seems to me that as soon as it appears that the way in which a party has framed his case will not lead to a decision of the real matter in controversy, it is as much a matter of right on his part to have it corrected if it can be done without injustice, as anything else in the case is a matter of right.

This statement is extremely controversial. Bowen LJ's point that courts do not exist for the sake of discipline was quoted with approval by Davis LJ in the context of relief from sanctions in *Chartwell Estate Agents Ltd v Fergies Properties SA* [2014] EWCA Civ 506, [2014] CP Rep 36 at [62], which was itself quoted with apparent approval by the Master of the Rolls in *Denton v T. H. White Ltd* [2014] EWCA Civ 906, [2014] 1 WLR 3926 at [19]. Conversely, Lord Neuberger of Abbotsbury PSC in another sanctions case, *Global Torch Ltd v Apex Global Management Ltd (No. 2)* [2014] UKSC 64, [2014] 1 WLR 4495 at [27], said the approach laid down by *Cropper v Smith* has been overtaken by the CPR.

The rule on the traditional approach was encapsulated by Brett MR in *Clarapede and Co. v Commercial Union Association* (1883) 32 WR 262 at p. 263 as follows:

> However negligent or careless may have been the first omission, and however late the proposed amendment, the amendment should be allowed if it can be compensated by costs.

It is the latter phrase in this quotation that is the guiding concept in the traditional approach. It is the reason why the opening words of PD 17 and of PD 19A are that: 'A party applying for an amendment will usually be responsible for the costs of and arising from the amendment' (see further **31.18**). *Cropper v Smith* and *Clarapede and Co. v Commercial Union Association* have been applied, expressly or by implication, in numerous post-CPR cases. They were described as laying down timeless principles in *Charlesworth v Relay Roads Ltd* [2000] 1 WLR 230. They were restated in a more modern form in *Cobbold v Greenwich London Borough Council* (1999) LTL 24/5/2001. Peter Gibson LJ said that in considering an application to amend the court has to apply the overriding objective of dealing with cases justly, which includes ensuring that cases are dealt with both expeditiously and fairly. His Lordship said:

Amendments in general ought to be allowed so that the real dispute between the parties can be adjudicated upon provided that any prejudice to the other party or parties caused by the amendment can be compensated for in costs, and the public interest in the efficient administration of justice is not significantly harmed....There is always prejudice when a party is not allowed to put forward his real case, provided that that is properly arguable.

On this approach the key questions are whether there is any injustice or prejudice that cannot be compensated in costs, and whether the party seeking to amend can pay the usual costs order. Inconvenience in investigating the amended case after the passage of time since the original pleading is not normally relevant prejudice for this purpose (*P & O Nedlloyd BV v Arab Metals Co.* [2006] EWCA Civ 1300, [2007] 1 WLR 2483 at [22]). Loss of evidence through the death or disappearance of witnesses might be.

Balancing factors approach

The second line of authorities on permission to amend stems from *Worldwide Corporation Ltd v GPT Ltd* [1998] EWCA Civ 1894 (BAILII), LTL 2/1/98, and the cases referred to in the judgment, such as *Ketteman v Hansel Properties Ltd* [1987] AC 189 and *Ashmore v Corporation of Lloyd's* [1992] 1 WLR 446. In *Worldwide Corporation Ltd v GPT Ltd* counsel for the claimant realised that the claim could not succeed on the pleaded basis, so the defendant was notified 11 days before the trial that permission would be sought at the trial to rely on amended points of claim which abandoned large parts of the pleaded case and inserted a different case. Permission was refused. After referring to the passage from *Cropper v Smith* (1883) 26 ChD 700 set out at **31.5**, Waller LJ said:

In the modern era it is more readily recognised that in truth the payment of costs of an adjournment may well not adequately compensate someone who is desirous of being rid of a piece of litigation which has been hanging over his head for some time, and may not adequately compensate him for being totally (and we are afraid there are no better words for it) 'mucked around' at the last moment. Furthermore, the courts are now much more conscious that in assessing the justice of the case the disruption caused to other litigants by last-minute adjournments and last-minute applications have also to be brought into the scales.

The final sentence is fully in line with the guidance on **CPR, r. 3.9**, given in *Denton v T. H. White Ltd* [2014] EWCA Civ 906, [2014] 1 WLR 3926. *Worldwide Corporation Ltd v GPT Ltd* was approved in *Savings and Investment Bank Ltd v Fincken* [2003] EWCA Civ 1630, [2004] 1 WLR 667, where Rix LJ said it gives better effect to the overriding objective by requiring the court to have greater regard to all the circumstances before granting permission to amend. In *Swain-Mason v Mills and Reeve LLP* [2011] EWCA Civ 14, [2011] 1 WLR 2735, *Worldwide Corporation Ltd v GPT Ltd* was held to be the correct modern approach, and reliance on *Cobbold v London Borough of Greenwich* was held to be wrong in law (at [85]). According to Lloyd LJ in *Swain-Mason v Mills and Reeve LLP* at [72], the decision whether to grant permission to amend is always one of balancing the relevant factors.

Swain-Mason v Mills and Reeve LLP was applied at first instance in *Capita Alternative Fund Services (Guernsey) Ltd v Drivers Jonas* [2011] EWHC 1228 (Comm), LTL 25/5/2011, and, in relation to raising a new point of mixed law and fact, on an appeal in *Jones v Environcom Ltd* [2011] EWCA Civ 1152, [2012] PNLR 5.

Choice between the two approaches

It is not entirely clear from *Swain-Mason v Mills and Reeve LLP* [2011] EWCA Civ 14, [2011] 1 WLR 2735, whether the court intended to say that the *Cobbold v Greenwich London Borough Council* (1999) LTL 24/5/2001 approach is always wrong in law (this seems to be the meaning of paras [72] and [85]), or whether it was wrong in law in the circumstances of the case. Like *Worldwide Corporation Ltd v GPT Ltd* [1998] EWCA Civ 1894 (BAILII), LTL 2/1/98, *Swain-Mason*

31.6

31.7

v Mills and Reeve LLP was a late amendment case, where permission to amend was sought on the second effective date of the trial to make a fundamental change to the nature of the claim, albeit one that was not so radical as the change sought in *Worldwide Corporation Ltd v GPT Ltd*. The various cases, including Court of Appeal decisions, that have applied *Cobbold v Greenwich London Borough Council* were not considered in the judgment. *Worldwide Corporation Ltd v GPT Ltd* was expressly decided on the basis of being a late amendment case.

It is submitted that late amendments are the most prominent of a group of situations where proposed amendments have the effect of overreaching the other parties. It is where there is a good arguable case that an amendment will have the effect of overreaching other parties that the balancing of factors approach should be used. In *P & O Nedlloyd BV v Arab Metals Co.* [2006] EWCA Civ 1300, [2007] 1 WLR 2483 at [23], Thomas LJ said it is only where there is some express prejudice that the court has to balance the prejudice against the reasons why the applicant did not advance their new case at the correct time. Overreaching may arise in any of the following circumstances:

(a) the amendment is sought at a very late stage;
(b) the amendment raises a radically different case than that originally pleaded;
(c) the amended case will be difficult to investigate due to the passage of time or the loss of evidence;
(d) the costs incurred in investigating the original case have been substantial and are unlikely to be recoverable from the party seeking to amend;
(e) the amendment is sought for tactical reasons; and
(f) the amendment seeks to replace a case that has been taken to the point of defeat.

Each of these situations involves a value judgment, and the situations will often overlap. *Ketteman v Hansel Properties Ltd* [1987] AC 189 was a case where the amendment was sought during closing speeches to substitute a completely new defence where the case had reached the point where the defence appeared to have been defeated. Permission to amend was refused. Lateness in itself is not a reason for refusing permission to amend, and it is extremely common for amendments to be made at the start and even the end of trials. Where the purpose is to correct the statements of case to ensure that they reflect the way the evidence emerges at the trial, permission is usually granted as this accords with the overriding objective (*Binks v Securicor Omega Express Ltd* [2003] EWCA Civ 993, [2003] 1 WLR 2557).

Where an amendment does not have the effect of overreaching the other parties, it is submitted that the traditional approach of granting permission, almost as a matter of right, but subject to payment of the costs of and arising from the amendment, should continue to apply. This is reflected in the Admiralty and Commercial Courts Guide, para C5.3, which says that questions of amendment, and consequential amendment, should wherever possible be dealt with by consent. A party should consent to a proposed amendment unless he has substantial grounds for objecting to it.

Factors in making the balance

31.8   Where permission to amend is being approached by balancing the relevant factors to find where justice lies (see **31.6** and **31.7**), Lord Griffiths in *Ketteman v Hansel Properties Ltd* [1987] AC 189 at p. 220 said that many and diverse factors will bear upon the exercise of the court's discretion, and that it is not possible or wise to attempt to enumerate them all. Justice cannot always be measured in terms of money. Nevertheless, factors regarded as relevant include:

(a) the strain of litigation, particularly for personal litigants (*Ketteman v Hansel Properties Ltd*);
(b) anxieties caused by needing to face fresh issues (*Ketteman v Hansel Properties Ltd*);
(c) the legitimate expectation that the trial will finally determine the dispute (*Ketteman v Hansel Properties Ltd*);

(d) how late the application is made (*Ketteman v Hansel Properties Ltd*);

(e) the effect on other litigants, and the delays caused to them (*Ketteman v Hansel Properties Ltd; Worldwide Corporation Ltd v GPT Ltd* [1998] EWCA Civ 1894 (BAILII), LTL 2/1/98);

(f) whether the need to amend arose from some recent disclosure or other good reason explaining the delay (*Worldwide Corporation Ltd v GPT Ltd; Hussain v Sarkar* [2010] EWCA Civ 301, LTL 16/4/2010). A reappraisal by the lawyers of the merits of the case is not regarded as a good reason (*Swain-Mason v Mills and Reeve LLP* [2011] EWCA Civ 14, [2011] 1 WLR 2735);

(g) the earlier history of amendment in the case (*Swain-Mason v Mills and Reeve LLP*);

(h) whether the amending party can pay the usual costs order (*Swain-Mason v Mills and Reeve LLP*);

(i) the length of any adjournment of the trial (*Swain-Mason v Mills and Reeve LLP*);

(j) the effect on the length of the trial (*Swain-Mason v Mills and Reeve LLP*);

(k) whether the amendment will prevent the trial taking place on a false or artificial basis (*Swain-Mason v Mills and Reeve LLP*); and

(l) the size or importance of the claim (*Swain-Mason v Mills and Reeve LLP*).

Late amendments

In *Hague Plant Ltd v Hague* [2014] EWCA Civ 1609, [2015] CP Rep 14, Briggs LJ at [32] distinguished between: **31.9**

(a) 'late' amendments, which do not put at risk the trial date, but which risk undermining work already done on the case. In these cases the cost and effort of the potential duplication of work have to be taken into account; and

(b) 'very late' amendments which put at risk the trial date. An example is *Swain-Mason v Mills and Reeve LLP* [2011] EWCA Civ 14, [2011] 1 WLR 2735.

Timing is one of the factors in deciding whether an amendment is in either of these categories. Also relevant are the nature of the amendments, their impact on the progress of the case, and the extent to which the other parties are taken by surprise. An amendment at trial to adopt allegations in the other side's statement of case against them should cause no such surprise, so delay ought not to be a ground for refusing permission (*Bleasdale v Forster* [2011] EWHC 596 (Ch), LTL 17/3/2011).

Amendments can be made during the course of the trial, and even during closing speeches (see **31.10**), Lateness is often combined with related factors, such as impact on the trial date, and whether the party seeking to amend can be criticised for failing to apply earlier because they have known for some time of the material forming the basis of the amended case. In *National Westminster Bank plc v Rabobank Nederland* [2006] EWHC 2108 (Comm), LTL 29/1/2007, the original defence was based on misrepresentation, but the amended pleading expanded on the allegations of misrepresentation and added allegations of negligent misstatement. Permission was granted to amend the misrepresentation allegations on conditions as to the service of additional witness statements, but was refused regarding negligent misstatement as they would have resulted in delay and disruption to the trial timetable.

In the case of last-minute amendments, there is a heavy onus on the party seeking permission to show the strength of the new case and why justice to all the parties and other litigants requires him or her to be able to pursue it (*Worldwide Corporation Ltd v GPT Ltd* [1998] EWCA Civ 1894, LTL 2/1/98; *Swain-Mason v Mills and Reeve LLP*). It is legitimate to consider the impact on court users generally (*Hague Plant Ltd v Hague* at [25]–[27]). Lateness, combined with a weak case, albeit one with some prospect of success (see **31.13**), resulted in permission being denied in *Savings and Investment Bank Ltd v Fincken* [2003] EWCA Civ 1630, [2004] 1 WLR 667. Permission to make an apparently small amendment, which in fact amounted to a complete volte-face by the defendant, sought two weeks before trial in a substantial claim, was refused in *Calenti v North Middlesex NHS Trust* (2001) LTL 10/4/2001.

Commentary

An amendment sought at a late stage in an attempt to save a claim that would otherwise have been struck out as disclosing no reasonable claim was refused in accordance with the overriding objective in *Christofi v Barclays Bank plc* [2000] 1 WLR 937. It is not clear how late the application was made, but it may have been during the appeal hearing itself. On the other hand, amendments were allowed in accordance with the overriding objective in *Finley v Connell Associates* [1999] Lloyd's Rep PN 895. In *Mark v Associated Newspapers Ltd* (2002) LTL 6/2/2002 permission to make amendments was granted even though the amendments represented a complete change of tack and involved allegations which were always open and obvious to the claimant, because permission was sought at an early stage in the proceedings (even though there had been delay before issue) and the amendments would not prejudice the defendant. A careless error resulting in the wrong defendant being named was allowed to be corrected by amendment under what is now **CPR, r. 19.5**, in *Virk v Gan Life Holdings plc* [2000] Lloyd's Rep IR 159 as there was no suggestion of prejudice to the defendant being brought in by the amendment.

A very late amendment was allowed in *Les Laboratoires Servier v Apotex Inc.* [2010] EWCA Civ 279, LTL 12/2/2010, primarily because refusing permission to amend would have given the claimant a large financial windfall. In *Hussain v Sarkar* [2010] EWCA Civ 301, LTL 16/4/2010, permission to amend the defence in an RTA claim to plead that the accident had been staged was sought one week before trial. It had not been possible to amend earlier because it was not until three weeks before trial that the defendant had sufficient evidence to enable counsel to plead fraud in accordance with the Bar Code of Conduct. Permission to amend was granted.

Where a claimant had failed to file an amended schedule of special damages and this had clearly been an obvious mistake and had been foreshadowed, the overriding objective meant that the parties should have cooperated with each other to allow a late amendment at a time where the mistake could have obviated satellite litigation (*Chilton v Surrey County Council* [1999] CPLR 525). Refusal of permission to amend was held to have been wrong in *Kelly v Chief Constable of South Yorkshire Police* [2001] EWCA Civ 1632, LTL 25/10/2001, even though it was sought at the end of the trial and changed the basis of the case against the defendant. Where proposed amendments had been raised in earlier statements of case and affidavits, delay in applying to amend should not, of itself, preclude permission being granted (*Stansburys v Pashley* (2000) LTL 6/4/2000).

Changing basis of case at trial

31.10   A not infrequent occurrence is that a party will seek to rely on a secondary case at trial that is not fully reflected in the way that party's case was previously put in its statement of case. Where this is done to reflect a version of the facts that only emerges with the evidence at the trial, an amendment is generally permitted as this accords with the overriding objective (*Binks v Securicor Omega Express Ltd* [2003] EWCA Civ 993, [2003] 1 WLR 2557). Where the party seeking to amend is aware of the alternative version in advance of the trial, an application to amend should be made a reasonable time before the trial. Likewise, seeking permission to argue a point which is raised for the first time at or shortly before the hearing will generally be granted, as refusing may be an unduly harsh penalty and represent a windfall to the other side (*E. I. Du Pont de Nemours and Co. v S. T. Dupont (No. 2)* [2002] EWHC 2455 (Ch), *The Times,* 28 November 2002). Neuberger J in this case said that permission may be refused if there are special factors, such as the point being raised at a late stage combined with:

(a) the other side needing a significant adjournment to adduce evidence in response; or

(b) the point being new and difficult, again requiring a long adjournment.

An example of a party seeking to amend to rely on a secondary case is *Sturton v Sutherland Holdings plc* (2000) LTL 27/10/2000, in which the counterclaim set out a claim for damages for breach of warranty, relying on one set of accounts. At trial, the defendant sought to rely on a fallback case based on amended accounts, which had not been mentioned in the counterclaim (although they had been referred to in the defence). It was held that the defendant had been under a duty to make clear it was relying on the fallback case well in advance of trial, so that the claimant could answer that case and call appropriate evidence.

Permission to amend the particulars of claim was granted on the first day of the trial in *Airways Aero Associations Ltd v Wycombe District Council* [2010] EWHC 1774 (Ch), LTL 10/8/2010, despite the amendment being very substantial, largely because the amended case was important both within the context of the case and as raising a point of some general importance in other claims. In *Bowerbank v Amos* [2003] EWCA Civ 1161, LTL 31/7/2003, a re-re-re-re-re-amendment was allowed during the course of the trial changing the case from one pleaded in breach of trust to one pleaded in breach of contract. It was held that this was permissible, especially as otherwise a meritorious claim would have been defeated on a pleading point. Once such an amendment was allowed, the judge had to be scrupulous to minimise any prejudice to the other party. The judge had refused permission to recall the claimant for further cross-examination after the amendment was made, so the case was remitted back to the judge to hear the further cross-examination and to reconsider his findings.

In *Hall v Motor Sport Vision Ltd* (2002) LTL 1/5/2002 an appeal was dismissed against a refusal of permission sought at trial to allow amendments and additional evidence. These had the effect of raising certain allegations as separate breaches of the defendant's obligations, whereas in the original particulars of claim they were pleaded only as particulars of breach.

A judge is not permitted to give judgment on the basis of a claim that is not included in the statements of case. If this is done, there may be no option but to order a retrial (*Rosengrenstann Ltd v Ayres* (2001) LTL 22/6/2001).

Substantial amendments

In *Cook v News Group Newspapers Ltd* [2002] EWHC 1070 (QB), LTL 21/6/2002, permission to make **31.11** substantial amendments to the defences in a libel claim was sought five months before trial. The amendments would have entailed substantial amendments to the replies, together with extensive further disclosure and additions to the witness statements. In such cases the court needed to have regard to the public interest in enabling the defendant to deploy the defences it wished to use, while fulfilling the overriding objective. Such applications are therefore considered with great care, being astute to avoid granting permission to allegations which failed to address (in the context of a libel claim) the real sting of the publication. The court would be more accommodating where the proposed amendments related to matters which had only emerged at a late stage with the discovery of evidence which previously had been genuinely unavailable. On the facts, permission was granted restricted to allegations genuinely supporting the central allegations. A similar case, *Morris v Bank of America National Trust and Savings Association* (2001) LTL 11/1/2002, resulted in all the substantial proposed amendments being disallowed, with permission being granted only for one amendment, which narrowed the issues. Late permission to add a single, but important, paragraph to a defence was allowed in *Electronic Data Systems Ltd v National Air Traffic Services Ltd* [2002] EWCA Civ 13, LTL 15/1/2002.

Case management considerations

An amendment may be refused where it will only enlarge the litigation with little potential **31.12** benefit (*Clarke v Bain* [2008] EWHC 2636 (QB), LTL 26/11/2008). Amendments were refused in *Multiplex Construction (UK) Ltd v Cleveland Bridge UK Ltd* [2008] EWHC 231 (TCC), LTL 9/5/2008, in the interests of firm case management. In particular Jackson J disallowed non-essential amendments to the pleadings which either imperilled the trial date or would cause material prejudice to either party in maintaining that date. It is incumbent on a party, particularly in complex litigation, to state clearly the nature of his case (*Law Debenture Trust Corporation (Channel Islands) Ltd v Lexington Insurance Co.* [2002] EWCA Civ 1824, LTL 13/12/2002). It is preferable as a matter of

Commentary

case management to allow amendments which set out details of a party's allegations, rather than simply let matters take their natural course at trial based on general allegations (*Three Rivers District Council v Bank of England* [2003] EWHC 1269 (Comm), LTL 9/6/2003).

An amendment order should not require a party to plead its case in accordance with the judge's view of the law where the party has a different view which is at least arguably correct (*Coflexip SA v Stolt Offshore MS Ltd* [2003] EWCA Civ 296, [2003] FSR 728).

Amendments with no real prospect of success

31.13   A proposed amendment will be refused where the amended case has no real prospect of success (*Oil and Mineral Development Corporation Ltd v Sajjad* (2001) LTL 6/12/2001; *Savings and Investment Bank Ltd v Fincken* (2001) *The Times*, 15 November 2001; *Clarke v Slay* [2002] EWCA Civ 113, LTL 25/1/2002). **CPR, Part 24**, can properly be relied upon to establish this (*Flexitallic Group Inc. v T. and N. Ltd* (2001) LTL 9/1/2002; *Findlay v Cantor Index Ltd* [2007] EWHC 643 (QB), LTL 20/4/2007). Permission to amend a pleading in a way which was speculative, pleading every conceivable cause of action in a scattergun approach, and which sought to reverse the burden of proof, was refused in *Clyde and Co. LLP v New Look Interiors of Marlow Ltd* [2009] EWHC 173 (QB), LTL 13/2/2009. Amendments will not be allowed if they seek to introduce matters covered by issue estoppel, or which will be an abuse of process (see **33.14** to **33.16**) (*Seele Austria GmbH & Co. KG v Tokio Marine Europe Insurance Ltd* [2009] EWHC 255 (TCC), [2009] BLR 261).

In *Hussain v Sarkar* [2010] EWCA Civ 301, LTL 16/4/2010, the first-instance judge had described the evidence in support of a proposed amended case that an RTA had been staged as no more than 'fishing'. This was criticised on appeal. Fishing implies a lack of a factual basis for an allegation which it is hoped will be strengthened either through disclosure or cross-examination. What the first-instance judge had in mind was that there was no hard evidence of the fraud. The Court of Appeal pointed out that there rarely is any direct hard evidence of fraud: it is far more common for fraud to be established by the assembly of circumstantial evidence pointing to the probability of guilt.

Permission to amend was refused in *Groveholt Ltd v Hughes* [2010] EWCA Civ 538, LTL 20/5/2010, because there was an insufficient basis for implying terms into a commercial contract. In *Giles v Rhind* [2007] EWHC 687 (Ch), [2007] Bus LR 1470, the claimant sought to amend the particulars of claim to change the alleged date of a deed which he said set out the proportions held by the parties in certain property. The defence had alleged that the deed as originally pleaded was a sham, or was in fact made six years later, and after the relevant dispute arose. It was held that while there were serious questions as to the reliability and credibility of the claimant's evidence, this was not a case where the amended case was incredible, so permission to amend was granted. In *Hussain v Cuddy Woods and Cochrane* (1999) LTL 19/10/99 an application to amend particulars of claim was refused where the claimant had no prospect of success against the solicitor and barrister defendants in his claim that a settlement reached was inadequate. Similarly, permission will be refused to make an amendment adding a claim which cannot succeed (*Laws v Society of Lloyd's* [2003] EWCA Civ 1887, *The Times*, 23 January 2004; *Collier v Blount Petre Kramer* [2004] EWCA Civ 467, LTL 1/4/2004). In *Multiplex Constructions (UK) Ltd v Cleveland Bridge UK Ltd* [2008] EWHC 569 (TCC), LTL 30/5/2008, the court refused permission to make certain amendments which were regarded as being incomprehensible.

Cause of action accruing after issue

31.14   The modern approach is flexible, with amendments being granted in accordance with the justice of the case. There is no longer any absolute rule of law or practice which precludes an amendment to rely on a cause of action which has arisen after the commencement of the proceedings where otherwise the claim would fail (*Maridive and Oil Services (SAE) v CNA Insurance*

Co. (Europe) Ltd [2002] EWCA Civ 369, [2002] 2 Lloyd's Rep 9). Likewise, amendments may be allowed adding heads of claim which have arisen after the proceedings were commenced (*British Credit Trust Holdings v UK Insurance Ltd* [2003] EWHC 2404 (Comm), LTL 28/10/2003). In *Finlan v Eyton Morris Winfield* [2007] EWHC 914 (Ch), [2007] 4 All ER 143, an amendment was allowed after the expiry of limitation to substitute an assignment of the cause of action which was executed after the claim form was issued.

Abandonment

In *British Credit Trust Holdings v UK Insurance Ltd* [2003] EWHC 2404 (Comm), LTL 28/10/2003, the **31.15** claim form sought damages and declaratory relief. The original particulars of claim only sought damages. It was held that the particulars of claim could be amended to include the declaratory relief, which had not been abandoned. There was no intention to abandon and no detriment.

Deemed amendment

While generally contrary to principle and fraught with difficulties, there are occasions where **31.16** a court deems the pleadings to have been amended without actual production of amended pleadings. An example is *Khan v Rehman* [2008] EWCA Civ 1407, LTL 24/11/2008.

AMENDING IN AN APPEAL COURT

In *Islington London Borough Council v Uckac* [2006] EWCA Civ 340, [2006] 1 WLR 1303, Dyson LJ at **31.17** [36] to [41] said that an appeal court has the power to allow a party to amend in order to deal with a point raised during the course of an appeal. This power may be used, for example, on an appeal from a strike-out application, even if permission to amend had not been sought in the court of first instance. An appeal court should not grant permission to amend if it would have been refused had the point been raised at trial (*Jones v Environcom Ltd* [2011] EWCA Civ 1152, [2012] PNLR 5).

COSTS OF AMENDING

Normally, amendments are allowed with the party making the amendment being ordered **31.18** to pay the costs of and arising from the amendments (**PD 17, introduction; PD 19A, introduction**). Costs arising from an amendment may include the costs of any extension to the length of the trial (*Airways Aero Associations Ltd v Wycombe District Council* [2010] EWHC 1774 (Ch), LTL 10/8/2010). A party who ought to have consented to proposed amendments was ordered to pay the costs of the amendments in *La Chemise Lacoste SA v Sketchers USA Ltd* [2006] EWHC 3462 (Ch), LTL 24/5/2006. Strictly, where consent is unreasonably refused, the correct approach is to order that party to pay the costs of the application to amend, but the costs of and occasioned by the amendments themselves should still be paid by the party seeking to amend. Despite *La Chemise Lacoste SA v Sketchers USA Ltd*, the normal rule is that the applicant should pay the costs of the application to amend (*Lidl UK GmbH v Davies* [2008] EWCA Civ 976, LTL 10/7/2008). Even if costs will not adequately compensate the other party, amendments will be allowed if they are required in the interests of justice (*Gabriel v Hayward* [2004] EWHC 2363 (TCC), LTL 29/10/2004).

CHANGING TRACK AT TRIAL

There are no additional problems if an amendment at trial involves changing between the **31.19** small claims and fast tracks, or from the multi-track to the fast track. However, an amendment

Commentary

involving changing from the fast track to the multi-track may involve having to change judges, because multi-track claims are not tried by District Judges without the consent of the designated civil judge (**PD 2B, para. 11.1(a)** and **(d)**). Having to adjourn (for example, where the new value of the claim is substantially above the normal fast track limit of £25,000) may be a sufficient reason for refusing permission to amend (*Maguire v Molin* [2002] EWCA Civ 1083, [2002] 4 All ER 325). Another option is for the District Judge to allow the amendment without changing tracks (*Maguire v Molin*), but this may lead to an inappropriate fast track costs limitation (see **71.7**).

FORMAT OF AN AMENDED STATEMENT OF CASE

31.20   The amended form of the statement of case need not show the original text, unless the court thinks that it is desirable for it to do so, in which event it may direct that the amendments should be shown either by coloured amendments (either manuscript or computer-generated) or by use of a numerical code in a monochrome computer-generated document (**PD 17, para. 2.2**). (Many word processing packages include the facility to print an amended text automatically showing corrections and deletions.) Where colour is used, the deleted text should be struck through in colour, and any replacement text should be inserted or underlined in the same colour (**PD 17, para. 2.3**). The order for successive amendments is, as has always been the case: red for the first amendment, green for the second, violet for the third, and yellow for the fourth (**PD 17, para. 2.4**).

The court will normally direct whether the original text should be shown together with the amendment at the time that it gives the permission for the amendment to be made. However, if no such permission is required, such a direction would have to be given after service. The principal purpose of displaying the original text has always been to enable the parties and the court to see the degree and extent to which a party has departed from its original stated case. Obviously, if the amendment is comparatively minor, and has been undertaken under **CPR, r. 17.1(1)**, the case for showing the original text is far less persuasive. In cases where it is wished to amend a statement of case after it has been served, there seems no reason why, as a precondition of giving written consent, the other party should not require the amendment to display the original text as well, failing which the 'amending party' will have to apply to the court, which may well be persuaded by the opposing party to order that the original text be shown.

If the substance of the statement of case is changed by reason of the amendment, the statement of case should be re-verified by a statement of truth (**PD 17, para. 1.4**). When a statement of case is amended, the court has a power in **r. 22.1(2)** to dispense with the need to re-verify with another statement of truth. This power may be exercised, or a suitably drafted statement of truth may be used making it clear that there is a primary and a secondary case, where a party relies on the facts asserted by the other side (which are inconsistent with the primary case) as an alternative basis for a finding in his favour (*Binks v Securicor Omega Express Ltd* [2003] EWCA Civ 993, [2003] 1 WLR 2557, and see **24.15**).

AMENDMENT AFTER A RELEVANT LIMITATION PERIOD HAS EXPIRED

Effect of expiry of limitation

31.21   For the purposes of the Limitation Act 1980 (LA 1980), an amendment to add or substitute a new party (a situation discussed at **14.79** to **14.92**) or a new cause of action is deemed to be a separate claim and to have been commenced on the same date as the original claim (LA 1980, s. 35(1) and (2)). The text of s. 35 can be seen at **14.86**. Consequently, if the original claim was commenced within the relevant limitation period, and an amendment is allowed adding a party or cause of action after the expiry of the limitation period, the defendant will be deprived of the limitation defence, and will usually suffer injustice not compensable by an order for costs. The usual rule, therefore, is that such amendments are not permitted (LA 1980, s. 35(3)). There are, however, a number of exceptions which are considered below. It seems that if there is a dispute about whether a limitation period has expired, the test is whether the claim is unarguably time-barred (*Leicester Wholesale Fruit Market Ltd v Grundy* [1990] 1 WLR 107), although in *BP plc v Aon Ltd* [2005] EWHC 2554 (Comm), [2006] 1 Lloyd's Rep 549 at [57], Colman J said the question is whether there is a reasonably arguable case that the claim is time-barred.

The statutory relation back in LA 1980, s. 35(1), only applies to the procedural time bars in the LA 1980. It does not apply to contractual or substantive time limits, like that in the Hague–Visby Rules, art. III, rule 6 (Carriage of Goods by Sea Act 1971, sch.), which have the effect that on expiry of the period laid down the claimant's cause of action ceases to exist (*Payabi v Armstel Shipping Corporation* [1992] QB 907).

Permission to amend after expiry of limitation

Provision is made in **CPR, r. 17.4**, for the problem which can arise when a party wishes to amend a statement of case after a period of limitation has expired. The rule is expressed to apply where a party applies to amend a statement of case under **Part 17**, and a period of limitation has expired under the LA 1980, the Foreign Limitation Periods Act 1984 or other statutory provision (**CPR, r. 17.4(1)**). Public law time limits are not limitation periods for this purpose, so amendments in public law claims are governed by **r. 17.1** rather than **r. 17.4** even after the expiry of a relevant time limit (*San Vicente v Secretary of State for Communities and Local Government* [2013] EWCA Civ 817, [2014] 1 WLR 966).

31.22

Where there is a dispute over whether the limitation period has expired, different approaches are taken depending on whether the application is dealt with as a conventional application for permission to amend, or as the trial of a preliminary issue (*Chandra v Brooke North* [2013] EWCA Civ 1559, [2014] TCLR 1 at [66]). On a conventional application to amend the court will not descend into factual issues (at [67]), but will limit itself to considering whether the defendant has a reasonably arguable case on limitation (*Welsh Development Agency v Redpath Dorman Long Ltd* [1994] 1 WLR 1409 at p. 1425). Provided the defendant can raise a prima facie case on limitation, the burden of persuasion is on the claimant to show the defendant has no reasonably arguable limitation defence to the new claims (*Ballinger v Mercer Ltd* [2014] EWCA Civ 996, [2014] 1 WLR 3597 at [29], [32]).

No provision is made in **r. 17.4** for a situation in which no application is made because a party is entitled to amend without permission. Clearly, if the statement of case has been served, it is unlikely that the other party will give written permission under **r. 17.1(2)(a)**, and an application would have to be made to the court. However, if proceedings are filed immediately before the expiry of the limitation period, but have not been served, and the claimant wishes to amend them before service, no application would ordinarily be made to the court. Of course, the court may disallow the amendment on an application under **r. 17.2**, but it is suggested that **r. 17.4** implies that such an amendment should only be made upon application to the court.

Rule 17.4(1) makes it clear that **r. 17.4** is merely procedural and does not give a power to add or substitute a new case after the expiry of limitation where this is not allowed by the governing statute. Consequently, while such amendments may be made in prescribed circumstances under the LA 1980 (see **14.79** to **14.91** and **31.23** to **31.27**) and the Foreign Limitation Periods Act 1984, they are not permitted under the Hague–Visby Rules (see **31.21**).

New cause of action

In assessing whether proposed amendments in fact amount to a new cause of action for the purposes of LA 1980, s. 35 (rather than a clarification of the existing cause of action), it is necessary to consider the statement of case as a whole (*Leeds and Holbeck Building Society v Ellis*

31.23

(2000) LTL 5/10/2000). To determine whether a proposed amendment introduces a new cause of action for the purposes of LA 1980, s. 35(5)(a), it is necessary to compare the essential factual elements of the existing cause of action with the essential factual elements of the proposed cause of action (*Aldi Stores Ltd v Holmes Buildings plc* [2003] EWCA Civ 1882, [2005] PNLR 9; *Commissioners of HM Revenue and Customs v Noorasa Begum* [2010] EWHC 1799 (Ch), LTL 15/7/2010). In making this assessment the court may take into account any further information provided under **CPR, Part 18** (*Boake Allen Ltd v Commissioners of HM Revenue and Customs* [2006] EWCA Civ 25, [2006] STC 606).

According to Brett J in *Cooke v Gill* (1873) LR 8 CP 107 at p. 116:

'Cause of action' has been held from the earliest time to mean every fact which is material to be proved to entitle the [claimant] to succeed — every fact which the defendant would have a right to traverse.

Robert Walker LJ in *Smith v Henniker-Major and Co.* [2002] EWCA Civ 762, [2003] Ch 182, said that in identifying a new cause of action, it is necessary to compare the bare minimum of essential facts abstracted from the original statement of case with the minimum facts required to constitute the cause of action in the amended statement of case. As Millett LJ said in *Paragon Finance plc v D. B. Thakerar and Co.* [1999] 1 All ER 400 at p. 405, this has to be done 'at the highest level of abstraction'.

In *Evans v Cig Mon Cymru Ltd* [2008] EWCA Civ 390, [2008] 1 WLR 2675, the claimant had contemplated bringing a claim against his former employer for damages following an accident at work together with a claim based on workplace bullying. He decided to pursue only the accident claim, and issued a claim form shortly before the expiry of limitation. After limitation it was noticed that the claim form described the claim as for 'loss and damage arising out of abuse at work'. The supporting medical report and particulars of claim were based on the accident. It was held to be permissible to read the claim form together with the particulars of claim and medical report to determine what the claim was intended to cover. In context, the words 'of abuse' were an obvious clerical error for the phrase 'of an accident', and permission to amend was granted as the amendment did not involve introducing a new claim within the meaning of s. 35(5)(a).

It is necessary to examine the duty alleged, the nature and extent of the breach alleged, and the nature and extent of the damage claimed. Where the only difference between the original case and the case set out in the proposed amendments is a further instance of breach, or the addition of a new remedy, there is no addition of a new cause of action (*Savings and Investment Bank Ltd v Fincken* [2001] EWCA Civ 1639, *The Times,* 15 November 2001). An amendment to plead consequential loss in a professional negligence claim was interpreted as simply adding a new head of damage, so was not a new cause of action in *Harland and Wolff Pension Trustees Ltd v Aon Consulting Financial Services Ltd* [2009] EWHC 1557 (Ch), [2010] ICR 121. Changing from alleging the claimant had a beneficial interest in shares (a concept unknown in Russian law) to an interest based on a joint activity or *sui generis* contract was regarded as just applying a different label, and not to involve a new cause of action, in *Berezovsky v Abramovitch* [2011] EWCA Civ 153, [2011] 1 WLR 2290.

However, making an amendment to justify a claim on a different factual basis amounts to making a new claim even if the sum claimed remains unchanged (*Seele Austria GmbH & Co. KG v Tokio Marine Europe Insurance Ltd* [2009] EWHC 2066 (TCC), [2009] BLR 481). Amendments changing page references from the American edition of a magazine to the European page references were held not to involve making a new claim in *Reuben v Time Inc.* [2003] EWCA Civ 6, LTL 22/1/2003. An amendment adding a new duty or obligation usually raises a new cause of action, whereas pleading additional facts, or better particulars, allegedly constituting a breach of the duty already pleaded usually will not (*Darlington Building Society v O'Rourke James Scourfield* [1999] PNLR 365). An amendment to plead a claim under the law of a different State raises a new claim within s. 35 (*Latreefers Inc. v Hobson* [2002] EWHC 1586 (Ch), LTL 31/7/2002). In *Abbey National plc v John Perry and Co.* [2001] EWCA Civ 1630, LTL 24/10/2001, it was held that deleting the word 'constructive' from a claim, thereby altering the basis of the claim from one in constructive trust to one in implied trust, was a matter of semantics and did not involve the substitution of a new cause of action.

Where a claimant has brought proceedings as an assignee of a claim, a valid assignment is an essential element of the cause of action (*Smith v Henniker-Major and Co.* [2002] EWCA Civ 762, [2003] Ch 182 at [99]). An amendment after limitation to plead an assignment can therefore only be allowed if it comes within s. 35(5)(a). In *Smith v Henniker-Major and Co.* the claim as originally formulated relied on an invalid assignment from a company purportedly signed at an inquorate board meeting. After limitation expired, the claimant procured a resolution from the company purporting to ratify parts of the invalid assignment. Although the amendment to plead the ratification arose out of substantially the same facts as the original claim, permission was refused, because a party seeking to ratify a transaction had to adopt it in its entirety, and because of prejudice to the defendant caused by the delays.

Amendment of causes of action after expiry of limitation

Amendment after a limitation period has expired is governed by LA 1980, s. 35, the text of which can be found at **14.86**. A new cause of action (as opposed to a new party) may be added to an existing claim after the relevant period of limitation has expired in three situations: **31.24**

(a) Where the claim is in respect of personal injuries and the court makes a direction under LA 1980, s. 33 (see **10.19**), that the usual limitation period shall not apply (LA 1980, s. 35(3)).

(b) Where the new cause of action is an original set-off or counterclaim (LA 1980, s. 35(3)). An original set-off or counterclaim is one made by an original defendant who has not previously raised any counterclaim under **CPR, Part 20**, in the claim, and the counterclaim must be made against the original claimant (see *Kennett v Brown* [1988] 1 WLR 582, which is still good law on this point). All that is required to engage this exception is that the party proposing to make the counterclaim has not previously counterclaimed and is on the opposite side of the record to the defendant to the proposed counterclaim (*Law Society v Shah (No. 2)* [2008] EWHC 2515, [2009] 1 WLR 2254). Section 35(3) may be regarded as a procedural quirk, and amendments under this provision may be refused in the court's discretion, for example, where the counterclaim is being used as an offensive weapon, or if it is radically different to the existing causes of action (*Law Society v Shah (No. 2)*). See also *Ernst and Young v Butte Mining plc (No. 2)* [1997] 1 WLR 1485. If bringing a counterclaim in effect evades an accrued limitation period, the claimant should consider making an application to strike out the counterclaim under **CPR, r. 3.4**.

(c) Where the new cause of action arises out of the same facts or substantially the same facts as are already in issue in the original claim (LA 1980, s. 35(5)(a); see **31.25**).

Same or substantially the same facts

Raised by either party LA 1980, s. 35(5)(a), permits rules of court to allow a claimant to add, after a limitation period has ended, a new claim which arises out of the same facts as are already in issue on any claim previously made in the original claim. This includes facts which are put in issue in the defence to the original claim (*Goode v Martin* [2001] EWCA Civ 1899, [2002] 1 WLR 1828; *Lidl UK GmbH v Davies* [2008] EWCA Civ 976, LTL 10/7/2008). It also allows a claimant to adopt facts after the expiry of limitation which had been pleaded by one defendant by amending the particulars of claim against another defendant (*Charles Church Developments Ltd v Stent Foundations Ltd* [2006] EWHC 3158 (TCC), [2007] 1 WLR 1203). **31.25**

CPR, r. 17.4(2), is expressed to allow a new claim to be added only if it arises out of the same facts as the original claim, but it must be read as also allowing a new claim which arises out of

Commentary

the same facts as 'are already in issue on' the original claim, because otherwise the rule would impede a claimant's access to a court for determination of civil rights, contrary to the European Convention on Human Rights, art. 6 (*Goode v Martin*). The court held that words in quotation marks in the previous sentence must be read into **r. 17.4(2)** under the **Human Rights Act 1998, s. 3.** The wording of the rule has not been amended to reflect this. In *Goode v Martin* the claimant had originally alleged that the defendant had negligently caused personal injuries to the claimant in the factual circumstances set out in the claim. The defendant served a defence asserting that the personal injuries happened in different circumstances. After the limitation period had expired the claimant was allowed to add a claim that, even if the defendant's version of events was true, the injuries were caused by the defendant's negligence.

31.26   **The test**   Whether amendments involve the same or substantially the same facts as those already in issue has been said to be largely a matter of impression (*Welsh Development Agency v Redpath Dorman Long Ltd* [1994] 1 WLR 1409 at p. 1418). Tomlinson LJ in *Ballinger v Mercer Ltd* [2014] EWCA Civ 996, [2014] 1 WLR 3597 at [36] said this may be right in borderline cases, but in other cases, which are probably the majority, it is a question of analysis. In deciding whether the new cause of action arises out of substantially the same facts as those originally pleaded it is necessary to identify 'the bare minimum of essential facts abstracted from the original pleading [and to compare them] with the minimum as it would be constituted under the amended pleading' (*P & O Nedlloyd BV v Arab Metals Co.* [2006] EWCA Civ 1300, [2007] 1 WLR 2483 at [14], applying the similar test from *Smith v Henniker-Major and Co.* [2002] EWCA Civ 762, [2003] Ch 182). In *Hoechst UK Ltd v Commissioners of Inland Revenue* [2003] EWHC 1002 (Ch), LTL 11/4/2003, it was held that it is not enough that the background facts of the two claims are the same: the central facts of both causes of action must be the same or based on substantially the same facts. In making this assessment the judge must not confine himself to the original statements of case, but must consider the facts that would have had to be litigated on the original statements of case (*Hemmingway v Roddam* [2003] EWCA Civ 1342, LTL 18/9/2003).

31.27   **Examples**   Spanish fishermen were refused permission to amend their claim to add further claims for compensation for breach of EU law (in being prevented from fishing by unlawful UK legislation) in respect of additional vessels. This was because the facts they needed to prove were largely specific to each boat, and so the additional claims did not arise out of substantially the same facts as were already in issue (*R v Secretary of State for Transport, ex parte Factortame Ltd (No. 7)* [2001] 1 WLR 942). A claim in negligent misrepresentation, which focused on what the defendant should have done, was held in *Law v Society of Lloyd's* [2003] EWCA Civ 1887, *The Times*, 23 January 2004, not to arise out of substantially the same facts as the original case pleaded in fraud (which was based on an allegation that the defendant knew the representations were false). In *BP plc v Aon Ltd* [2005] EWHC 2554 (Comm), [2006] 1 Lloyd's Rep 549, a claim for breach of an insurance contract did not arise out of substantially the same facts as a claim pleaded in negligence. In *Del Grosso v Payne and Payne* [2007] EWCA Civ 340, LTL 1/3/2007, the original claim against the defendant solicitors was based on alleged negligence in failing to advise the client on the effect of a break clause in a lease. It was held that a wide-ranging amendment to the particulars of claim, alleging new beaches of duty, issues relating to the scope of the retainer, and the basis of the alleged financial losses, did not arise out of the same or substantially the same facts as the original claim.

In *Senior v Pearsons and Ward* (2001) LTL 26/1/2001 the claim originally alleged that the defendant solicitors had acted contrary to their instructions. The claimant was permitted to amend the particulars of claim after the expiry of limitation to add allegations of failing to advise fully, as the additional allegations arose out of the same facts, or substantially the same facts, as those originally pleaded. In *Brickfield Properties Ltd v Newton* [1971] 1 WLR 862 the general endorsement on the writ (the equivalent of a claim form giving just a concise statement of the nature of the claim under **CPR, r. 16.2(1)(a)**) claimed damages against an architect for negligent supervision of certain building works. The particulars of claim were served after the expiry of the limitation period, and contained claims both for negligent supervision and negligent design.

It was held that the negligent design claim arose substantially out of the same facts as the negligent supervision claim and in its discretion the court allowed the amendment. In *Hancock Shipping Co. Ltd v Kawasaki Heavy Industries Ltd* [1992] 1 WLR 1025, permission to amend the particulars of claim was sought three years after service of the original statement of case and after the limitation period had expired. In considering whether it is just to allow an amendment in such circumstances, the court held that it had to take into account that granting permission will deprive the defendant of an accrued limitation defence, but could exercise its discretion to allow the amendment in the light of all the relevant factors. An important factor is the degree to which the defendant is prejudiced in being unable to investigate the facts of the new claim through the disappearance of evidence. The Court of Appeal in *Hancock Shipping Co. Ltd v Kawasaki Heavy Industries Ltd* disallowed certain of the proposed amendments on the ground that the defendant would be prejudiced through the loss of evidence, but allowed certain other amendments which were closely related to the claim already made as there was likely to be little prejudice through the loss of evidence.

Amendments after the limitation period affecting accrued rights

A defendant will not be given permission to amend where the effect of the proposed amendment is to transfer responsibility for the claim on to a non-party who cannot be sued by the claimant as a result of the expiry of the relevant limitation period. An example is *Steward v North Metropolitan Tramways Co.* (1886) 16 QBD 556, where the claimant sued the tramway for personal injuries. After the expiry of the limitation period, the defendant sought to amend its defence. The effect of the proposed amendment was to transfer the defendant's liability for the claimant's injuries to the local road authority. Permission to amend was refused, because even an order for costs could not put the claimant into the same position as if the proposed defence had been pleaded at the proper time. This approach was confirmed by *Cluley v R. L. Dix Heating* [2003] EWCA Civ 1595, LTL 31/10/2003, where the court dismissed an argument that the prejudice was caused by the claimant having failed to identify the proper person to bring proceedings against rather than by the defendant seeking, after the expiry of limitation, to withdraw an admission of having entered into a contract with the claimant.

31.28

Much depends on whether the defendant has been at fault in not pleading the proposed defence at the proper time. In *Weait v Jayanbee Joinery Ltd* [1963] 1 QB 239, through no fault of their own, the defendants discovered after the expiry of the limitation period that the claimant's injuries were probably worse than they should have been through the intervening negligence of the doctor who treated the claimant. An amendment to the defence to plead the doctor's negligence was allowed despite the fact that the claimant could not make a claim against the doctor as that claim was time-barred. Further, an amendment blaming a non-party may be allowed if it alleges facts within the knowledge of the claimant, since in such a case the prejudice to the claimant arises from the claimant's own failure to sue the non-party in time, rather than by some line of defence being made known at a late stage. An example is *Turner v Ford Motor Co. Ltd* [1965] 1 WLR 948. The claimant sued the occupier and a building contractor (but not his own employer) for injuries suffered when he was struck by a falling brick. After disclosure of documents by the first defendant, and after the expiry of the limitation period, the second defendant discovered that the claimant had not been wearing a safety helmet at the relevant time, and sought to amend its defence to allege contributory negligence on the part of the claimant. The claimant opposed the amendment on the ground that he was now out of time in suing his employer for failing to provide him with a helmet. The amendment was allowed, because the claimant must have known whether he was wearing a safety helmet at the time of the accident, so the amendment told him nothing he did not know in order to commence his claim. If the first defendant, who had knowledge of the claimant not wearing a helmet, had sought an amendment to plead contributory negligence after the expiry of the limitation period, permission would have been refused.

PART H

Interim Applications

Chapter 32　Applications and Interim Orders

The following procedural checklists are relevant to this chapter:

Procedural checklist 19　Interim application without notice
Procedural checklist 20　Interim application with notice

INTRODUCTION

Interim applications are made when a party to proceedings seeks an order or directions from **32.1** the court prior to the substantive hearing of the claim. Parties seeking interim orders or directions in general have to issue an application notice in form N244, pay a court fee, and often have to provide written evidence in support. The application notice and evidence must in general be served at least three clear days before the return date. Generally, service will be effected by the applicant where the applicant prepares the application notice (**CPR, r. 6.21(1)**).

Chapters 33 to 41 deal with various types of interim application, such as for summary judgment, interim injunctions, freezing injunctions and search orders. Applications for disclosure orders, such as specific disclosure and pre-action disclosure, are dealt with in **chapter 50**. Various other types of application are considered elsewhere, such as applications for alternative service in **15.19** and **15.43**, setting aside default judgments in **20.11** to **20.18**, for further information in **30.6** and for amendment in **chapter 31**. There is a separate code of procedure for applications in insolvency proceedings, which is considered in **chapter 84**.

In most cases there should be a limited need for making interim applications because of the level of involvement of the judiciary in case management. Part of the obligation placed on the courts in furthering the overriding objective is to consider whether the likely benefits of taking a particular step will justify the cost of taking it (**r. 1.4(2)(h)**). The court is also required to deal with as many aspects of the case as is practicable on the same occasion (**r. 1.4(2)(i)**).

In fast track and multi-track cases the procedural judge will scrutinise defended claims shortly after defences are filed, and there will be further judicial consideration of the case at the listing for trial stage (see **chapters 42, 46** and **47**). A party contemplating a particular order may ask the court to consider it during the scrutiny process.

Whenever the parties are notified that an interim hearing, such as a case management conference or listing hearing, has been fixed, they must consider and make any application which may be appropriate for the court to deal with at the hearing (**PD 23A, para. 2.8; PD 28, para. 2.5** (fast track cases); **PD 29, para. 3.5** (multi-track cases)).

Consequently, most interim orders are made as part of the regular case management system. Further, there is a general obligation to make all interim applications as soon as it becomes apparent they are necessary or desirable (**PD 23A, para. 2.7**).

The CPR permit the court to make interim orders on its own initiative, and to hold hearings by telephone or other direct means of communication. Solicitors should keep correspondence with Masters and District Judges to a minimum, and must ensure that opposing parties receive copies (Chancery Guide, para. 15.58). The ordinary rule is that interim hearings are in public, although there are significant exceptions (see **61.21**).

A distinction needs to be drawn between applications for directions and applications for interim remedies. A somewhat more formal approach is taken with applications for interim remedies, which should in almost all cases be supported by written evidence (see **CPR, r. 25.3(2)**). The distinction is between:

(a) case management matters, such as standard disclosure of documents, exchange of factual and expert evidence, and trial directions; and

(b) applications for specific remedies, such as specific disclosure, interim injunctions, interim payments and striking out.

There is a further important distinction between interim applications made without giving notice to any other parties, and those made on notice. This distinction will be considered further at **32.7** and **32.12**.

TO WHICH COURT SHOULD AN APPLICATION BE MADE?

32.2   In general an application must be made to the court where the claim is presently being dealt with. This will be the court where the proceedings were commenced (**CPR, r. 23.2(1)**), unless:

(a) the claim has been transferred, or sent to, another County Court hearing centre, in which case the application must be made there unless there is a good reason (**r. 23.2(2); PD 2C, para. 7.2** and see **42.7**);

(b) the claim has been listed for trial at another court or hearing centre, in which event the application should be made to the trial court (**CPR, r. 23.2(3); PD 2C, para. 7.3**);

(c) the claim has been started in the County Court Money Claims Centre, in which case the application must be made to the County Court Money Claims Centre or the County Court hearing centre where the claim is being dealt with (**PD 2C, para.** 7.6; **PD 23A, para. 5A.1**). A District Judge may consider the application without a hearing, or may transfer the claim to a hearing centre (**para. 5A.2**); or

(d) the application is made after judgment, in which event the application may need to be made to the court or hearing centre dealing with enforcement (**CPR, r. 23.2(5)**; **PD 2C, para. 7.5**).

An application for pre-action remedies (such as some injunction, freezing injunction and search order applications) should be made to the court where the substantive proceedings are likely to be brought, unless there is a good reason for applying to another court (**CPR, r. 23.2(4)**; **PD 2C, para. 7.4**). A pre-action application in the County Court may be made at any County Court hearing centre, unless any enactment, rule or practice direction provides otherwise (**CPR, r. 23.2(4A)**).

Rule 2.7 gives the court a general power to deal with a case at any place that it considers appropriate. This power may be used in courts with shared listing arrangements, and where a court with congested lists arranges to release some cases to another court to reduce listing delays.

WHICH JUDGE SHOULD DEAL WITH AN APPLICATION?

Unless otherwise provided for by an Act, rule or practice direction, interim applications can be dealt with by judges, Masters and District Judges (**CPR, r. 2.4**). Most applications are dealt with by Masters and District Judges, but they may refer particular applications to be dealt with by a judge (**PD 23A, para. 1**). The most significant exceptions are search orders, which are dealt with by High Court judges, and freezing injunctions and ancillary orders under **CPR, r. 25.1(1)(g)** (which are dealt with by High Court judges and Circuit Judges) (**PD 2B, paras 2** and **8.4**). Other High Court interim injunctions can in principle be granted by Masters (because they are not excluded by **PD 2B**), but generally a Master will refer an application for an injunction to a judge (Chancery Guide, para. 15.12). In the County Court, Circuit Judges deal with interim injunction applications in most multi-track claims, but District Judges may hear such applications in small claims and fast track cases, and also in a number of other types of claim (**PD 2B, para. 8.1(c)**; **PD 25A, paras 1.2 to 1.4**). High Court Masters and District Judges may grant interim injunctions by consent, in connection with charging orders and receivers and in aid of execution (**PD 25A, para. 1.2**). In both the High Court and the County Court, Masters and District Judges have jurisdiction to vary or discharge injunctions by consent (**PD 2B, para. 8.2**; **PD 25A, para. 1.4**).

Applications to a High Court judge in the Chancery Division are made to the interim applications judge (Chancery Guide, paras 16.9 and 16.12). An application notice must be used, which should usually state that it is to be heard by 'the interim applications judge'. Chancery Division Masters may only grant Wallersteiner orders (see **44.15**) and certain orders in the Patents Court with the consent of the Chancellor of the High Court (**PD 2B, para. 7B.1**).

In the Chancery and Queen's Bench Divisions there are arrangements for assigning claims to individual Masters. Once assigned a claim may be transferred to another Master, and the fact that a claim has been assigned does not prevent it being dealt with by another Master (**PD 2B, para. 6.2**). However, the usual rule is that once a claim is assigned all applications in that claim will be dealt with by the assigned Master. The role of the Queen's Bench Division 'Practice Master' was abolished with effect from 3 October 2016.

In the County Court Business Centre and the County Court Money Claims Centre certain types of application can be dealt with by a court officer designated as a 'legal adviser' under **PD 51K**, a pilot scheme that operates between 1 October 2015 and 31 March 2017.

32.3

Commentary

TIMING AND EXPEDITION

32.4 An interim application should be made as soon as it becomes apparent that it is necessary or desirable (**PD 23A, para. 2.7**). Applications for interim relief should be dealt with expeditiously, because delay might frustrate the purpose for which the application was made (*E. E. and Brian Smith (1928) Ltd v Hodson* [2007] EWCA Civ 1210, LTL 23/11/2007). In the case of an interim injunction, a delay of three or four weeks in announcing the decision or giving reasons was regarded as too long. There is also a principle, not expressly stated in the CPR, that the court's jurisdiction can only be invoked by a party who has come on to the court record. For a claimant this is when proceedings are issued, and for a defendant it is when service is acknowledged or a defence is filed (**CPR, r. 25.2(2)**).

PRE-ACTION INTERIM REMEDIES

32.5 A claimant may exceptionally make an application for an interim order before the commencement of proceedings (see **CPR, r. 25.2(2)(b)**) if either:

(a) the matter is urgent; or

(b) it is otherwise desirable to grant the interim remedy before the claim is brought in the interests of justice.

The courts may thus entertain pre-commencement applications for urgent interim injunctions (such as some libel cases where publication is threatened within hours of the applicant finding out about the matter) and some applications for freezing injunctions and search orders. If the application is to be served, the rules on service of claim forms apply (**r. 6.2(c)**).

If a pre-action interim remedy is granted, the court should give directions requiring a claim to be commenced (**r. 25.2(3)**). **Rule 25.2(4)** points out that such directions need not be given where an order is made for pre-action disclosure or inspection under the Senior Courts Act 1981, s. 33, or the County Courts Act 1984, s. 52 (see **50.88**). This is because such an order may result in the applicant deciding not to bring substantive proceedings at all, as recognised in *Dunning v United Liverpool Hospitals' Board of Governors* [1973] 1 WLR 586. The same can be said for *Norwich Pharmacal* orders (see **50.100**), which may not result in the true wrongdoer being identified. Normally directions for bringing substantive proceedings are made in other types of pre-action order.

OBLIGATION TO APPLY EARLY

32.6 The obligation to apply early for an interim remedy stems from the overriding objective, which includes ensuring that cases are dealt with expeditiously (**CPR, r. 1.1(2)(d)**).

Parties should normally notify the court of any intention to apply for interim remedies when they file their directions questionnaires (**PD 26, para. 2.2**).

In multi-track cases the appropriate time to consider most forms of interim relief, if possible, is the first case management conference. A party that wishes to invite the court to make directions or orders of types not usually dealt with on case management conferences, and which are likely to be opposed, is required by **PD 29, para. 5.8**, to issue and serve an application returnable at the same time as that set for the case management conference (with a time estimate if it is clear that the time originally allowed for the case management conference will be insufficient, so a fresh date can be fixed). **Paragraph 3.8** expressly says that applications in multi-track cases must be made as early as possible so as to minimise the need to change the directions timetable, and an application to vary a directions timetable laid down by the court (perhaps on its own initiative) must ordinarily be made within 14 days of service of the directions (**para. 6.2**).

There are some express restrictions in the CPR about when some types of application can be made. Examples include summary judgment, which can be applied for only after the defendant has acknowledged service or entered a defence (**r. 24.4(1)**), and interim payments, where a similar restriction applies (**r. 25.6(1)**). Nevertheless, summary judgment (and striking-out) applications should normally be made on or before filing of directions questionnaires (**PD 26, para. 5.3(1)**).

Of course the need for an interim remedy may not become apparent until some later stage. **CPR, r. 25.2(1)(b)**, provides that applications can be made even after final judgment has been given. Where it becomes necessary to make an application shortly before trial, it should be dealt with on the pre-trial review if there will be one (there is a pre-trial review about eight to 10 weeks before the trial in some multi-track cases, see **47.23**). If this is not possible, another option is to make the application at the start of the trial itself.

APPLICATIONS WITHOUT NOTICE

The general rule is that all applications must be made on notice to the other parties (**CPR, r. 23.4(1)**). Exceptions to this rule are only allowed where permitted by a provision in the CPR, a practice direction, or a court order (**r. 23.4(2)**). For example, applications to extend the time for serving a claim form (renewal of process) are permitted without notice (**r. 7.6(4)**), as are applications for permission to issue additional claims after filing of the defence (**r. 20.7(5)**). These are both examples of applications where the opposite party will not be on the court record when the application is made. Other situations where applications may be made without giving notice to the other parties are:

32.7

(a) Where the application arises in urgent circumstances, so there is no practical possibility of giving the required minimum of three clear days' notice to the other side. In cases of this sort informal notification should be given to the other parties unless the circumstances require secrecy (**PD 23A, para. 4.2**). Delay by the applicant cannot make an application urgent (*Bates v Lord Hailsham of St Marylebone* [1972] 1 WLR 1373). Giving only one hour's notice for no good reason, combined with a failure to give full and frank disclosure, resulted in an interim injunction being discharged in *Kulkarni v Milton Keynes Hospital NHS Trust* [2008] EWHC 1861 (QB), [2008] LS Law Medical 494. See also the cases at **37.4**. An alternative is to combine the main application with an application to abridge time under **r. 3.1(2)(a)**. Abridging time may be appropriate where a defendant is repeating behaviour previously adjudicated upon (*Secretary of State for the Environment, Food and Rural Affairs v Meier* [2009] UKSC 11, [2009] 1 WLR 2780 at [82]).

(b) Where a party decides to make an application at a hearing that has already been fixed, but there is insufficient time to serve an application notice. In cases of this sort the applicant should inform the other parties and the court (preferably in writing) as soon as possible of the nature of the application, the reason for it, and then make the application orally at the hearing (**PD 23A, para. 2.10**).

(c) Where the application depends on secrecy for its efficacy, such as most applications for freezing injunctions and search orders.

Procedure on applications without notice

The procedure for an interim application without notice is summarised in **procedural checklist 19**.

32.8

Commentary

Like applications on notice, applications without notice should normally be made by filing an application notice (**CPR, r. 23.3(1)**) in form N244, which must state the order being sought and the reasons for seeking the order (**r. 23.6**). Letters must not be used in place of formal application notices. The prescribed fee is £50 (**CPFO, fee 2.5**). The application notice must also be signed, and include the title of the claim, its reference number and the full name of the applicant. If the applicant is not already a party it should also give the applicant's address for service. If the applicant wants a hearing, that too must be stated (**PD 23A, para. 2.1**). The application should normally be supported by evidence, which should, in addition to setting out the evidence in support of the relief sought, state the reasons why notice was not given (**CPR, r. 25.3(3)**).

By virtue of **r. 39.2**, which applies to all types of hearings, including interim hearings and trials, applications made without notice will in general be held in public. However, sometimes one of the exceptions may apply, such as publicity defeating the object of the application (as in applications for freezing injunctions and search orders) or the application being made without notice and it being unjust to the respondent for there to be a public hearing (**r. 39.2(3)(a)** and (**e**)). In any event, most applications will be heard in chambers even if technically they are being dealt with in public.

Legal representatives acting for the applicant are under a duty to provide full notes of the hearing to all parties affected by the order (*Interoute Telecommunications (UK) Ltd v Fashion Gossip Ltd* (1999) *The Times,* 10 November 1999, freezing injunctions and search orders; *Cinpres Gas Injection Ltd v Melea Ltd* [2005] EWHC 3180 (Pat), [2006] FSR 36, interim injunctions). This is to ensure other parties know exactly what happened, the basis and material on which the order was made, and so they can make an informed decision whether to apply to discharge the order. Applications to set aside or vary are normally made back to the judge who made the original order.

Duty of full and frank disclosure

32.9 Any application made without notice is subject to a duty of full and frank disclosure of matters adverse to the application. These include matters which are known to the applicant and matters which the applicant should have known on making reasonable inquiries. Proper disclosure requires advocates to identify specially all relevant documents for the judge, taking the judge to the particular passages in those documents, and ensuring the judge is aware of the legal significance of the material (*R (Lawer) v Restormel Borough Council* [2007] EWHC 2299 (Admin), [2008] HLR 20). The burden on counsel to ensure that this duty is discharged is all the more onerous on urgent telephone applications (**PD 25A, para. 4.2; 37.6**) where the judge will not have any papers and will know nothing in advance about the case.

The duty is to disclose facts relevant to the matter being decided on the application. What is material depends on the nature of the application. Facts going to granting permission to serve outside the jurisdiction are not relevant on an application for permission to serve by an alternative method (*Albon v Naza Motor Trading Sdn Bhd (No. 2)* [2007] EWHC 327 (Ch), [2007] 1 All ER (Comm) 813 at [47]). While the duty of full and frank disclosure might mean that a without-prejudice document, or the fact it existed, must be disclosed, it was held that failure to make such a disclosure was not a breach of the duty in *Linsen International Ltd v Humpuss Sea Transport Pte Ltd* [2010] EWHC 303 (Comm), LTL 1/3/2010. The defendant had deliberately chosen to withhold information about the without-prejudice negotiation, and neither the fact of the meeting nor what was discussed had any real bearing on the risk of dissipation of assets. The duty is a continuing one, continuing until the application is renewed on notice or until the without notice order is acted upon (*Network Telecom (Europe) Ltd v Telephone Systems International Inc* [2003] EWHC 2890 (QB), LTL 21/10/2003). This duty, and the question of discharging for material non-disclosure, has frequently been an issue in applications for freezing injunctions (see **38.35** for a full discussion), but the principles apply to all applications made without notice.

Applications to set aside or vary

Where an application is made for an order to be made against a person without notice to that person, the order made on the application must be served on the person together (unless the court orders otherwise) with the application notice and any evidence in support (**CPR, r. 23.9(2)**). The order must, by virtue of **r. 23.9(3)**, contain a statement to the effect that the person against whom it is made has a right to apply to set aside or vary the order within seven clear days of service of the order (**rr. 23.9(3)** and **23.10**). In *Dadourian Group International Inc. v Simms* [2005] EWHC 268 (Ch), [2005] 2 All ER 651, affirmed [2006] EWCA Civ 399, [2006] 1 WLR 2499, a without-notice order was not served in accordance with **r. 23.9(2)** and did not contain the notice required by **r. 23.9(3)**. The defendant was a solicitor. It was held at [24] that while the parties must not flout the CPR, the court had to retain a sense of balance in deciding the consequences of any breach, and refused to discharge the order on this ground.

Rules 23.9 and **23.10** apply to applications to set aside without-notice orders whether or not the original application was supported by an application notice (*Raja v Van Hoogstraten (No. 9)* [2008] EWCA Civ 1444, [2009] 1 WLR 1143). The headnote in this case says that under the court's inherent jurisdiction a party affected by 'an order made without notice' is entitled to have it set aside *ex debito justitiae*, in the sense that the order will be set aside unless the right has been lost, for example, by waiver or estoppel. The relevant part of the judgment (at [79]–[85], and particularly [83]) is focused on orders and judgments which ought to have been applied for on notice, but which (perhaps through being misaddressed) did not come to the attention of the respondent before the hearing (or before a default judgment was entered). References to 'affecting the rights of parties' (e.g. at [84]) should be understood as meaning adversely affecting non-parties served with an order. *Raja v Van Hoogstraten (No. 9)* must not be understood as meaning that legitimately obtained orders made under without-notice applications are set aside as of right. A literal application of the comments in *Raja v Van Hoogstraten (No. 9)* would destroy the essential role played by without-notice orders in providing urgent relief, protection where secrecy is essential, and savings in costs on certain (usually) non-controversial applications as prescribed by the CPR.

Renewing without-notice applications

There are cases where an applicant initially asks the court to consider an application without notice on the papers, and then, being disappointed with the resulting order, wishes to challenge that order. Rather than bringing an appeal, the applicant may ask the same court for an order setting aside or varying that order at a renewed application with a hearing. See *Collier v Williams* [2006] EWCA Civ 20, [2006] 1 WLR 1945, discussed at **32.43**.

APPLICATIONS WITH NOTICE

The general rule is that all other parties should be given three clear days' notice of any interim application that may be made (**CPR, rr. 23.4(1)** and **23.7(1)**). While pre-action applications are treated as claim forms for the purposes of the rules on service (**r. 6.2(c)**), applications in pending proceedings are governed by **rr. 6.20** to **6.29**. Advance notice should be given of the grounds on which an interim order is sought. A particular example is an application to discharge a freezing injunction on the ground of material non-disclosure, where specific notice of the grounds of the application must be given (*Bracken Partners Ltd v Gutteridge* (2001) LTL 16/1/2002). The procedure for an interim application with notice is summarised in **procedural checklist 20**, and there is a detailed discussion in **32.13** to **32.31**. Even if an application is misconceived or hopeless, the respondent should not cross-apply to strike out the first application, but should simply oppose it, as issuing such a cross-application wastes costs (*Arkin v Borchard Lines Ltd (No. 2)* (2001) LTL 21/6/2001).

32.10

32.11

32.12

Commentary

There is no requirement to give three days' or any other notice to a party of conditions or orders in the nature of sanctions which the court decides to impose after hearing an application (*Anglo-Eastern Trust Ltd v Kermanshahchi* [2002] EWCA Civ 198, [2002] CP Rep 36; *Olatawura v Abiloye* [2002] EWCA Civ 998, [2003] 1 WLR 275 at [29]).

Documentation

32.13 An interim application should normally be made by filing an application notice stating the order being sought and the reasons for seeking the order (**CPR, rr. 23.3(1) and 23.6**). The application notice must be signed, and should include the title of the claim, its reference number and the full name of the applicant. If the applicant is not already a party it should also give the applicant's address for service. If the applicant seeks a hearing, that must be stated (**PD 23A, para. 2.1**). If the applicant wants the application dealt with by a telephone hearing, that must also be stated (**para. 6.1A**). The application should normally be supported by written evidence setting out the facts justifying the relief sought (**CPR, r. 25.3(2)**). The notice must be filed at court together with the prescribed fee (£155, **CPFO, fee 2.4**), and served as soon as possible thereafter (**r. 23.7(1)**). The standard form of application notice is form N244. On receipt of the application notice the court may either notify the parties of the time and date of the hearing, or notify them that it proposes to consider the application without a hearing (**PD 23A, para. 2.3; CPR, r. 23.8(c)**).

Any application for a court order requires an application notice unless this is dispensed with (**r. 23.3(2)(b)**) or where a rule or practice direction permits an application without an application notice (**r. 23.3(2)(a)**). Unless these exceptions apply it is impermissible to apply by letter (*R (Simmons) v Bolton Metropolitan Borough Council* [2011] EWHC 2729 (Admin), LTL 14/11/2011).

Applications by persons who are not parties

32.14 Persons who are not parties may make applications in existing proceedings in a number of circumstances. These include applications to intervene in the proceedings (see **14.65**) and applications by third parties to vary the terms of injunctions (see **38.31**). In urgent cases an intending claimant may apply for injunctive relief before a claim form is issued (see **37.4** and **37.5**).

A person who is not already a party who issues an application notice must include a postcode in his address for service on the application notice (**PD 23A, para. 2.1(4)**).

Evidence in support

32.15 The general rule is that applications for interim remedies must be supported by evidence (**CPR, r. 25.3(2)**), but evidence in support is not required when applying for case management directions. Some judgment is required from lawyers when deciding whether they need evidence for their applications. **PD 23A, para. 9.1**, specifically mentions that, as a practical matter, the court will often need to be satisfied by evidence of the facts that are relied on in support of, or for opposing, an application. Sometimes the matter will be put beyond doubt if the court gives directions for filing evidence when it fixes a hearing.

The evidence in support must be filed at court, although the exhibits should not be filed unless the court otherwise directs (**PD 23A, para. 9.6**). The evidence (including exhibits) in support must be served with the application (**CPR, r. 23.7(3)**). The comment by Floyd J in *Re Names at Lloyd's represented by Equitas Ltd* [2008] EWHC 2960 (Ch), [2009] Bus LR 509, that it is sufficient if the evidence in support of an interim application is filed by the time 'it is needed' (relying on **rr. 13.4(3) and 21.6(4)**) was made without reference to **r. 23.7(3)**. However, it echoes the provisions in the court guides that documents must be served on other parties in sufficient time to enable them to be prepared (Queen's Bench Guide, para. 9.8.6). Any evidence which a respondent wishes to rely upon must be served as soon as possible, and in any event in accordance with any directions the court may have given (**PD 23A, para. 9.4**). The court will not take kindly to respondents who serve evidence in response at the last minute, particularly if this results in a wasted hearing and a need to adjourn.

Four options are available to the applicant regarding the format of the evidence to be used in support of an interim application. They are:

(a) To provide sufficiently full factual information in support of the application in the body of the application notice itself (**CPR, rr. 22.1(3) and 32.6(2)(b)**), and include a statement of truth in the notice. This is a signed statement that the applicant believes that any facts stated in the application are true (**r. 22.1(4) and (6); PD 22, para. 2.1**). A statement of truth of an application notice which did not disclose any facts on which the application (to strike out or give summary judgment on a claim) could be based was regarded as insufficient in *Vectone Services Ltd v Transport Media Ltd* (2011) LTL 10/6/2011.

(b) To rely on the facts stated in a statement of case filed in the proceedings, provided it contains a statement of truth (**CPR, r. 32.6(2)(a)**). This will usually have been previously served and filed, and if so there is no need to reserve or refile (**r. 23.7(5)**).

(c) To rely on witness statements each with statements of truth signed by the witnesses (**rr. 22.1(4) and 32.6(1)**). The witness statements used may be ones drafted specifically for the interim application, or it may be possible to rely on the main witness statements that have been disclosed on the substantive issues in the case. The general rule is that any fact that needs to be proved at any hearing other than the trial should be proved by the evidence of witnesses in writing (**r. 32.2(1)**), and it is further provided by **r. 32.6(1)** that at hearings other than the trial evidence is to be by witness statement unless the court, a practice direction or any other enactment requires otherwise. Consequently, evidence by witness statement is the primary means of adducing evidence at interim hearings.

(d) To rely on affidavit evidence. **Rule 32.15(2)** allows a witness to give evidence by affidavit at any hearing other than a trial if he or she chooses to do so. This also allows the use of affirmations (**PD 32, para. 1.7**). However, using affidavits may result in the loss of the additional costs over and above the cost of using an ordinary witness statement. There are situations where affidavit evidence is required either by specific court order, or by virtue of a practice direction or other enactment. Affidavits are required, for example, in applications under the Protection from Harassment Act 1997, s. 3(5)(a) (see **88.25**); for certain applications relating to confiscation and forfeiture in connection with criminal proceedings; under the environmental control legislation; and in director disqualification proceedings. **PD 32** and **PD 25A** require affidavit evidence in support of applications for:

(i) search orders,
(ii) freezing injunctions,
(iii) orders to require an occupier to permit another to enter land, and
(iv) orders for contempt of court.

Affidavits are not used in applications for other types of interim injunction unless specifically ordered by the court.

Unless the form which the evidence in support has to take is prescribed, a party to an interim application may choose the method of adducing evidence in support from the above options. This allows flexibility, and should assist in ensuring applications are prepared in a cost-efficient manner. Form N244 requires the applicant to indicate which type of evidence will be relied upon by ticking an appropriate box. It may on occasion be appropriate to use a combination of these methods. It may also be important to place the background facts of the case before the court (which could be done by use of the statement of case), as well as facts relevant solely to the application in hand (which could be adduced by a specifically drawn-up witness statement or affidavit).

Time estimates and judicial pre-reading

32.16 A time estimate has to be included on the N244 when an application is issued. This should cover the entire hearing (submissions by both sides, giving any judgment, and applications for costs and permission to appeal, see Chancery Guide, para. 15.33). For hearings likely to exceed two hours the estimate should be discussed between the parties. Where extensive judicial pre-reading is required the parties must inform the court in advance (*Jacobs UK Ltd v Skidmore Owings and Merrill LLP* [2008] EWHC 2847 (TCC), LTL 1/12/2008).

Bundles of documents

32.17 Sometimes it is appropriate to prepare bundles of documents for interim applications. Often it is sufficient to rely on the application notice, written evidence and exhibits without the need to go to the expense of compiling formal bundles. It is stated in the Queen's Bench Guide, para. 7.10.8, that bundles should be prepared for applications heard by judges whenever more than 25 pages are involved, although it must be said that even in straightforward applications it is easy to exceed this. In the Chancery Division, bundles are required in all cases except those that are very short and straightforward (Chancery Guide, para. 15.34). The whole point of compiling bundles is to save time and expense (as recognised by para. 21.34). If they are used, the general guidance discussed in **chapter 59** should be followed, but bearing in mind that for an interim application it ought to be possible to restrict the number of documents that need to be included. There are plenty of interim applications that do not need all the statements of case, witness statements, etc.

All parties should cooperate in agreeing bundles (see, for example, Chancery Guide, para. 15.35), and should make clear whether they are simply agreeing which documents should be included in the bundles, or whether they are also agreeing that the included documents are to be treated as evidence of the facts stated in them and/or that the documents to be included are agreed to be authentic (**CPR, r. 32.19**).

For applications, the applicant should ensure that one copy of the bundle is lodged at court at least two clear days before the hearing (though for a Queen's Bench Master's appointment, the bundle should be brought to the hearing, unless the Master otherwise directs: Queen's Bench Guide, para. 7.10.9), and that all parties and the court have identical bundles.

Skeleton arguments

32.18 Skeleton arguments are not often used on interim applications before District Judges, Masters and bankruptcy and Companies Court registrars, but are usually required for hearings before High Court judges and are often used for interim hearings before Circuit Judges. It depends on the complexity of the application. Failing to provide a skeleton argument on a striking-out application was described as 'regrettable' in *Vectone Services Ltd v Transport Media Ltd* (2011) LTL 10/6/2011. Even before High Court judges they are not insisted on if the application is likely to be short or if it is so urgent that preparation of a skeleton argument is impracticable. For substantial hearings, and Chancery Masters' appointments, skeleton arguments should be delivered not less than two clear days before the hearing (Chancery Guide, paras 15.34 and 21.77). For shorter applications, or urgent applications, they may be delivered by 10 am the day before the hearing, or even at the hearing.

A skeleton argument should provide a concise summary of the party's submissions on the issues raised by the application, and should be as brief as the nature of the case allows

(Chancery Guide, para. 21.80). There is a general ceiling of 20 pages of double-spaced A4 paper. Longer skeleton arguments are sometimes necessary in complex claims (as recognised in the Chancery Guide, para. 21.78). A skeleton should cite the main authorities relied upon, be divided into numbered paragraphs, be paginated, make use of abbreviations (such as 'C' for claimant, 'A/345' for page 345 of bundle A) and give dates in the form '26.4.2016'. It should not go so far as to argue the case on paper. In more substantial applications it should have a reading list for the judge of the core documents. See also **61.18** and **74.29**. In *Khader v Aziz* [2010] EWCA Civ 716, [2010] 1 WLR 2673, the Court of Appeal deprecated the tendencies:

(a) to produce skeleton arguments that are not skeletal; and

(b) to produce bundles of authorities with unnecessary cases.

The costs of preparing these materials may be disallowed if the guidelines are not followed.

Authorities in skeleton arguments

Practice Direction (Citation of Authorities) [2001] 1 WLR 1001 provides that the following types of authorities should not be cited unless they establish a new principle or extend the law: **32.19**

(a) law reports of applications attended by one party only;

(b) applications for permission to appeal;

(c) applications that only decide the application is arguable; and

(d) County Court cases (other than to illustrate damages in personal injuries claims or to illustrate current authority where no higher authorities are available).

Lawyers were criticised in *Bank of Scotland v Henry Butcher and Co.* [2003] EWCA Civ 67, [2003] 2 All ER (Comm) 557, for using the *All England Law Reports* and *All England Law Reports Reprint* rather than the *Weekly Law Reports* and *English Reports*. BAILII (British and Irish Legal Information Institute) transcripts of judgments, with neutral citations (which are assigned by BAILII if they have not been given by the court), should only be used if no recognised reports are available and then only if the case really needs to be cited (*A City Council v T* [2011] EWCA Civ 17, [2011] 1 WLR 819).

Practice Direction (Citation of Authorities) [2001] 1 WLR 1001 says that skeleton arguments will have to justify reliance on decisions that merely apply decided law to the facts, and also decisions from other jurisdictions. Decisions of the Court of Justice of the European Union and organs of the European Convention on Human Rights are treated as domestic authorities for this purpose. For each authority cited, the skeleton must state the proposition of law the case demonstrates, and refer to the passages in support. Any bundle or list of authorities must contain a certificate by the advocate that these requirements have been complied with.

Practice Direction (Judgments: Form and Citation) [2001] 1 WLR 194 and Practice Direction (Judgments: Neutral Citations) [2002] 1 WLR 346 introduced a method of neutral citation in the format *Smith v Jones* [2001] EWCA Civ 10 at [30], [2001] QB 124. 'EWCA' stands for England and Wales, Court of Appeal. 'Civ 10' stands for Civil Division, 10th case of 2001. 'At [30]' stands for paragraph 30 of the judgments (with the paragraph numbering continuing into the second and subsequent judgments). This is designed to assist publication of judgments on the Internet. Reports cited in court should be taken from the official *Law Reports*, and only from other series if unavailable from the *Law Reports*. **Practice Direction (Citation of Authorities) (2012)** also provides that it is permissible to cite judgments by means of copies reproduced from electronic sources. Such copies should preferably be in 12-point fonts (although 10- or 11-point fonts are acceptable), and the advocate presenting the report must be satisfied that it has not been reproduced in a garbled form. More detailed guidance on the use of authorities in appeals, including the use of *Hansard,* which should also be followed in first-instance skeleton arguments, can be found at **74.52** to **74.53**.

Chronologies

32.20   Skeleton arguments are often accompanied by chronologies. Good chronologies have short entries for the material events, phrased in a non-contentious way to promote agreement with the other parties.

Draft orders

32.21   **Paragraph 12.1** of **PD 23A** says that except in the most simple applications the applicant should bring to the hearing a draft of the order sought. The hard copy brought to court should be double spaced (Queen's Bench Guide, para. 7.11.3). If the order is unusually long or complex, the draft should be supplied on disk as well as on hard copy (**PD 23A, para. 12.1**). Preparing draft orders is particularly important in all types of interim injunction applications, and (although strictly this is turning **PD 23A** on its head) whenever the order is at all complicated or unusual. Draft orders are also useful if a detailed directions timetable needs to be laid down. For almost all other types of application the short particulars of the orders sought normally inserted in the N244 will be sufficient.

Service and three days' notice

32.22   Where the applicant prepares the application notice, as is usual, the applicant must serve it and evidence in support, except where a rule or practice direction provides that the court will serve, or the court orders otherwise (**CPR, r. 6.21(1)**). The usual methods of service may be used (personal service, service through first class post, document exchange or other delivery service that provides for next-day delivery, leaving it at the address for service, fax or electronic service where allowed by **PD 6A**, and alternative service, see **CPR, r. 6.27**). An irrebuttable presumption of due service applies where one of these methods is used in accordance with the table in **r. 6.26** (*Anderton v Clwyd County Council (No. 2)* [2002] EWCA Civ 933, [2002] 1 WLR 3174).

Where the court prepares the application notice, the court will serve it, unless a rule or practice direction provides that a party must serve the document, or the party on whose behalf the document is to be served notifies the court that the party wishes to serve it, or the court orders otherwise (**r. 6.21(2)**). Where the court is to serve a document, it is for the court to decide which method of service is to be used (**r. 6.21(3)**). When the court is to effect service, the applicant must file with the court copies of the evidence in support for service on the respondents and a copy of any draft order prepared on behalf of the applicant. There is no requirement to re-file or re-serve documents which have already been filed or served at an earlier stage (**CPR, r. 23.7(5)**).

Service must be effected as soon as possible after the application is issued, and in any event not less than three days before it is to be heard (**r. 23.7(1)**). In accordance with the general rules on computing time in **r. 2.8**, this means clear days (excluding the date of effective service and the date of the hearing), and, because the period is less than five days, also excluding weekends, bank holidays, Christmas and Good Friday. Take, for example, a hearing which is listed for Wednesday 15 March 2017. Assume the solicitor for the applicant decides to serve the application and evidence in support by document exchange. The three clear days before the hearing are Friday 10 March, Monday 13 March and Tuesday 14 March. The documents must therefore arrive on Thursday 9 March, and given the provision in **r. 6.26** that documents transmitted by DX are deemed to be served on the second day after being left at the document exchange, the latest the documents could be left at the document exchange would be Tuesday 7 March 2017.

Disposal without a hearing

CPR, r. 23.8, provides that the court may deal with an interim application without a hearing if: **32.23**

(a) the parties agree the terms of the order; or

(b) the parties agree that the court should dispose of the application without a hearing (the applicant's view on whether there should be a hearing should be stated in the application notice); or

(c) the court does not consider that a hearing would be appropriate.

A party dissatisfied with any order or direction made without a hearing is able to apply to have it set aside, varied or stayed (**r. 3.3(5)(a)**). Such an application must be made within seven days after service of the order, and the right to make such an application must be stated in the order (**r. 3.3(5)(b) and (6)**). See **42.42** and also renewing interim applications at **32.44**.

In *Irwin Mitchell Solicitors v Patel* [2003] EWCA Civ 633, LTL 15/4/2003, an application for disclosure of documents, which resulted in an 'unless order', was marked to be dealt with without a hearing. Although the respondent should have been served with the application, this was not done. Ultimately, all the orders flowing from the application notice were set aside because of the procedural irregularity.

Hearings by telephone

Active case management in accordance with the overriding objective includes dealing with **32.24** cases without the parties needing to attend court, and by making use of technology (**CPR, r. 1.4(2)(j) and (k)**). Both may be achieved by dealing with some applications by telephone conference calls, which is specifically provided for by **r. 3.1(2)(d)**. The rule enables the court to hold a hearing by telephone or any other method of direct oral communication, so other means of electronic communication may be used as technology develops.

District Registries of the High Court and County Court hearing centres in which telephone conferencing facilities are available are termed 'telephone conference enabled courts' (**PD 23A, para. 6.1**). Contact details for these courts are given in the Court Finder at the Ministry of Justice website, http://www.justice.gov.uk. At a telephone conference enabled court, the following hearings will be conducted by telephone unless the court orders otherwise:

(a) allocation hearings;

(b) listing hearings; and

(c) interim applications, case management conferences and pre-trial reviews with time estimates of less than one hour (**para. 6.2**).

Even in the above cases, telephone hearings will not be used if the application is made without notice, or if all the parties are unrepresented, or if there are more than four parties who wish to take part (**para. 6.3**). A request for a hearing to take place in the normal way rather than by telephone can be made by letter, which should arrive at court at least seven days before the appointed day (**para. 6.4**). Where there is to be a telephone hearing the application notice must be served as soon as practicable after it has been issued and in any event at least five days before the date of the hearing (**para. 4.1A**).

Where **para. 6.2** does not apply, the court may order an application to be dealt with by telephone either of its own initiative or at the request of the parties (**para. 6.5**). The applicant should state in the application notice whether he seeks an order for a telephone hearing (**para. 6.6**). Orders under **para. 6.5** will not normally be made unless all the parties consent (**para. 6.7**).

If an application is to be heard by telephone, normally the directions set out in **para. 6.10** will apply (and see also **para. 6.8**). There will be a 'designated legal representative', who is usually the solicitor for the applicant (**para. 6.1**), who is responsible for setting up the telephone hearing. In multi-track claims, and in other cases if the court so directs, the designated legal

Commentary

representative is required to file and serve a case summary and draft order no later than 4 p.m. two days before the hearing (**paras 6.11** and **6.12**). Any other documents relied upon must be filed and served by the party relying on them within the same time limit (**para. 6.13**). The conference call for the hearing should be fully connected at least 10 minutes before the time for the hearing (**para. 6.10(5)**), with the call being set up with the designated legal representative (and counsel) being called first, then the other parties and their counsel, and finally the judge (**para. 6.10(4)**). No party or representative may attend in person unless every other party agrees (**para. 6.9**).

Orders made on the court's own initiative

32.25   As part of the ethos of active case management, the courts are encouraged to exercise their powers on their own initiative where this is appropriate, and to this end **CPR, r. 3.3(1)**, gives the court the power to make orders of its own initiative. This power is intended to be exercised for the purpose of managing the case and furthering the overriding objective (see **r. 3.1(2)(m)**). Orders made in this way must, by virtue of **r. 3.3(5)(b)** and **(6)**, include a statement that parties who are affected may apply within seven days (or such other period as the court may specify) after service for the order to be set aside, varied or stayed. Failing to make an application to vary or set aside is likely to result in the court assuming the orders or directions made were correct in the circumstances then existing (**PD 28, para. 4.2(2)**, for fast track cases; **PD 29, para. 6.2(2)**, for multi-track cases).

There is a related power enabling the court to make orders on its own initiative after giving the parties an opportunity of making representations on the matter. Where the court proposes to make such an order it will specify a time within which the representations must be made (**CPR, r. 3.3(2)**). If the court on its own initiative strikes out a statement of case or application, and it considers the claim or application was totally without merit, that fact must be recorded in the court's order, and the court must consider whether to make a civil restraint order (see **r. 3.3(7)** and **14.55**).

Hearings convened on the court's own initiative

32.26   In addition, the court has power to fix a hearing for the purpose of deciding whether to make any order it might propose to make of its own initiative. For example, in order to reduce the issues in a case it might convene a summary judgment hearing. Unless some other period is specified in the rules regarding notice, any application convened by the court must be notified to parties likely to be affected by the proposed order at least three clear days in advance (**CPR, r. 3.3(3)**).

Court hearing

32.27   The general rule is that interim hearings will be in public (**CPR, r. 39.2**). In practice the public do not attend most hearings before Masters and District Judges, even if notionally they are heard in public, because most interim applications are conducted in chambers, with limited facilities for accommodating the public. It is sufficient if the door is open, or if there is no sign on the door indicating that the hearing is in private (**PD 39A, para. 1.10**). There is no obligation to provide space for the public, although the judge may, if he or she thinks it appropriate, adjourn to a larger room or court (**para. 1.10**).

In addition to dealing with the specific application that has been made, the court may wish to review the conduct of the case as a whole and give any necessary case management directions. The parties will therefore have to be prepared for this and be able to answer any questions the court may ask (**PD 23A, para. 2.9**). The procedural judge will keep, either by way of a note or a tape recording, brief details of all proceedings, including a short statement of the decision taken at each hearing (**PD 23A, para. 8**).

In most courts applications are given specific hearing times, and are called in one at a time. The main exception are judge's applications in the Chancery Division (see Chancery Guide, para. 16.17). For these the judge sitting has a discretion as to the order in which applications are heard. However, urgent applications and applications affecting the liberty of the subject are given priority, followed by ineffective applications (those which are to be adjourned or have settled), then effective applications usually in order of their time estimates, with the shortest applications being heard earliest. Applications estimated for more than two hours are usually made applications by order. In these cases the applications judge may make a temporary order to preserve the position pending a full hearing of the application. Solicitors or counsel's clerks must then apply to the Chancery Judges' Listing Officer for a date for the hearing of the application. There is also a procedure for interim applications by order by consent. See Chancery Guide, paras 16.23 and 16.24.

Adjournment of applications

An application may be adjourned (**CPR, r. 3.1(2)(b)**). This power is exercised in accordance **32.28** with the overriding objective, and similar considerations to those applicable on applications to adjourn trials (see **61.9** to **61.14**) are taken into account. Dealing with an application justly may make it appropriate to adjourn an application so that a party has the time needed to recover its files (*Financial Services Authority v Anderson* [2010] EWHC 308 (Ch), LTL 1/3/2010).

Standard of proof on disputed facts on interim applications

Imposing the trial standard of proof (on the balance of probabilities) on an issue at an interim **32.29** hearing is erroneous, and in effect would require the premature trial of the issue or premature expression of the court's view on the merits (*Seaconsar Far East Ltd v Bank Markazi Jomhouri Islami Iran* [1994] 1 AC 438). Doing so was said to be completely contrary to principle in *Energy Venture Partners Ltd v Malabu Oil and Gas Ltd* [2014] EWCA Civ 1295, [2015] 1 WLR 2309, per Tomlinson LJ at [53]). It would require at least the cross-examination of the makers of the witness statements, which is strongly discouraged on interim hearings (per Lord Steyn in *Canada Trust Co. v Stolzenberg (No. 2)* [2002] 1 AC 1 at p. 13 and Waller LJ in the same case in the Court of Appeal [1998] 1 WLR 547).

The normal standard of proof in interim applications is therefore whether any disputed fact is established by a good arguable case (per Lord Nicholls in *Re H (Minors) (Sexual Abuse: Standard of Proof)* [1996] AC 563). An applicant must show a good arguable case that the matter falls within one of the grounds for granting permission to serve outside the jurisdiction (**CPR, r. 6.37**), and it applies to disputes on the grounds giving jurisdiction under the **recast Brussels I Regulation** (*Kolden Holdings Ltd v Rodette Commerce Ltd* [2008] EWCA Civ 10, [2008] Bus LR 1051). It applies to the merits of the substantive claim in freezing injunction applications (*Ninemia Maritime Corporation v Trave Schiffahrtsgesellschaft mbH & Co. KG* [1983] 1 WLR 1412), and the maximum amount that can be frozen (*Pacific Maritime (Asia) Ltd v Holystone Overseas Ltd* [2007] EWHC 2319 (Comm), [2008] 1 Lloyd's Rep 371).

The 'good arguable case' test is intended to encapsulate the crucial rule that the court must be as satisfied as it can be, given the limitations of an interim application, that factors exist which give the court jurisdiction or justify the exercise of that jurisdiction. Inevitably, the way the test is applied must vary from case to case (*WPP Holdings Italy Srl v Benatti* [2007] EWCA Civ 263, [2007] 1 WLR 2316).

What amounts to a good arguable case depends on what is required to be shown in any particular situation (*Bols Distilleries BV v Superior Yacht Services Ltd* [2006] UKPC 45, [2007] 1 WLR 12 at [28]). There will be a good arguable case where the judge is able to reach a provisional or tentative conclusion on all the admissible evidence that the claimant is probably right on the disputed facts (*Attock Cement Co. Ltd v Romanian Bank for Foreign Trade* [1989] 1 All ER 1189). A good arguable case is one which is better than barely capable of serious argument, yet not necessarily one which the judge believes to have a better than 50 per cent chance of success (*Ninemia Maritime Corporation v Trave Schiffahrtsgesellschaft mbH & Co. KG* [1983] 2 Lloyd's Rep 600 at p. 605). If the argument on one side is clearly better than the argument on the other, that will normally be sufficient to resolve an issue on this test (*Masri v Consolidated Contractors International (UK) Ltd (No. 2)* [2008] EWCA Civ 303, [2009] QB 450 at [88] per Lawrence Collins LJ). To similar effect, in *Bols Distilleries BV v Superior Yacht Services Ltd* Lord Rodger of Earlsferry said at [28] that the applicant has to show it has a much better argument than the respondent on the material available at the hearing on the matter. See also *Deutsche Bank AG v Asia Pacific Broadband Wireless Communications Inc.* [2008] EWCA Civ 1091, [2009] 2 All ER (Comm) 129 at [16].

For various types of application, or issues in applications, case law, or occasionally provisions in the CPR, lay down different standards of proof. Examples are:

(a) serious question on merits (*American Cyanamid Co. v Ethicon Ltd* [1975] AC 396, see **37.21**);
(b) real prospect of success: see **CPR, r. 6.37** (merits in applications for permission to serve outside the jurisdiction), **r. 13.3(1)(a)** (setting aside default judgment), **r. 24.2(a)** (summary judgment), and **rr. 52.6(1)(a)** and **52.7(2)(a)(i)** (applications for permission to appeal);
(c) real possibility or grave danger of destruction of evidence (search orders, see **39.9**);
(d) much better argument on the material available, which is used where an issue is effectively determinative of whether the court has jurisdiction (*Canada Trust Co. v Stolzenberg (No. 2)* [1998] 1 WLR 547);
(e) extremely strong prima facie case, which is used in relation to the merits of the substantive claim in applications for search orders, see **39.7**;
(f) high degree of assurance (the merits of the claim in applications for interim mandatory injunctions: *Shepherd Homes Ltd v Sandham* [1971] Ch 340);
(g) overwhelming case, which is on occasions applied on interim injunction applications which finally dispose of the case (*Cayne v Global Natural Resources plc* [1984] 1 All ER 225).

On an interim application it is generally inappropriate for an English court to examine the strength of a proposed claim in a different jurisdiction (*Sybron Corporation v Barclays Bank plc* [1985] Ch 299). All that is required is that the overseas claim is not obviously unsustainable (*Vitol SA v Capri Marine Ltd* [2010] EWHC 458 (Comm), [2011] 1 All ER (Comm) 366 at [40]).

Weight attached to written evidence

32.30 The courts will give the same weight to all forms of written evidence whether they have statements of truth or are sworn. It has always been the case that, unless deponents are called for cross-examination, written evidence adduced on an interim application will usually be accepted as correct for the purposes of the application. A court will not normally go behind a witness statement on an interim hearing except in a clear case (*Vestergaard Frandsen A/S v Bestnet Europe Ltd* [2009] EWHC 2662 (Ch), LTL 25/11/2009). Most applications are dealt with on the basis of facts which are not disputed by the respondent, together with the respondent's version of any disputed facts (*Prince of Wales v Associated Newspapers Ltd* [2006] EWCA Civ 1776, [2008] Ch 57). Cases such as *National Westminster Bank plc v Daniel* [1993] 1 WLR 1453 established that the court would only go behind written evidence if its contents are incredible. In *Shyam Jewellers Ltd v Cheeseman* [2001] EWCA Civ 1818, LTL 29/11/2001, it was stated that choosing between witnesses is the function of the trial judge, and it is only permissible for a judge to go behind a witness statement in an interim application if there is some inherent improbability being asserted or there is extraneous evidence contradicting it.

Facts may be inferred on an interim application from a failure to deal adequately with an issue in response to correspondence or the written evidence in an interim application. In *Pattihis v Jackson* [2002] EWHC 2480 (QB), LTL 22/11/2002, an assistant solicitor left his employment with the claimant to work for the second defendant, taking with him a large number of the claimant's client files. The fact of the removal of the files, and the second defendant's failure to demonstrate a right to the files in the two days following demands for the return of the files, enabled the court to find the files were unlawfully in the second defendant's possession.

Evidence from a defendant, who had set up a rival business, to the effect he had not opened certain emails was disregarded in *World Trade Group Ltd v Basanez* (2008) LTL 22/10/2008 given the lack of an explanation of why he had not opened any of his email accounts, and the fact that when examined all the emails in his accounts had been deleted.

Written evidence may be rejected where it is inconsistent with unchallengeable contemporaneous documentation (*Three Rivers District Council v Bank of England (No. 3)* [2001] UKHL 16, [2003] 2 AC 1), or where there has been a failure to include exhibits where the narrative would be expected to be supportable with documentary evidence. Whether exhibits are required depends on the circumstances (*Congentra AG v Sixteen Thirteen Marine SA* [2008] EWHC 1615 (Comm), [2008] 2 Lloyd's Rep 602, where the court regarded an argument that there was no good arguable case on quantum because it was not supported by documents as hopeless).

In *Zappia Middle East Construction Co. Ltd v Clifford Chance* [2001] EWCA Civ 946, in an application for security for costs, there was a conflict of evidence on the claimant's place of residence. The court refused to accept unparticularised second-hand evidence from the claimant's solicitor, the claimant obviously being able to give first-hand and detailed evidence on the matter, and decided the point in a summary way in favour of the applicant.

Facts can also be inferred from the nature of the situation. In *Aims Asset Management Sdn Bhd v Kazakhstan Investment Fund Ltd* [2002] EWHC 3225 (Ch), LTL 23/5/2002, the court found, based on the respondent's location in Kazakhstan but no further evidence, that there was a very substantial, but unquantifiable, risk that enforcement in that country of an English judgment would be extremely difficult and expensive, if not impossible. This comes close to taking judicial notice (see **49.27** to **49.34**) of such facts.

The power to order cross-examination of a witness in an interim application pursuant to **CPR, r. 32.7**, tends to be used only in extreme cases (see *West London Pipeline and Storage Ltd v Total UK Ltd* [2008] EWHC 1729 (Comm), [2008] 2 CLC 258). In an application for a non-party costs order, it was held in *Dweck v Forstater* [2010] EWHC 1874 (QB), LTL 28/7/2010, that a finding that witnesses were, in effect, lying in their witness statements should only have been made after cross-examination of the witnesses.

Summary determination of interim costs

Where an interim application is disposed of in less than a day (which will cover the vast majority of such applications), the court will normally make a summary assessment of the costs of the application immediately after making its order (**PD 44, para. 9.2**). In the absence of a specific order to the contrary, costs assessed summarily are payable within 14 days of the order (**CPR, r. 44.7**). To assist the judge in assessing costs the parties are required by **PD 44, para. 9.5**, to file and serve not less than 24 hours before the interim hearing signed statements of their costs for the interim hearing in form N260 setting out:

(a) the number of hours to be claimed;
(b) the hourly rate to be claimed;
(c) the grade of the earner;
(d) the amount and nature of any disbursements other than counsel's fee for attending the hearing;
(e) the amount of the legal representative's costs for attending or appearing at the hearing;
(f) counsel's fees; and
(g) VAT on the above.

Any failure to file or serve a statement of costs, without reasonable excuse, will be taken into account in deciding the costs order to be made on the application (**PD 44, para. 9.6**). In the absence of any aggravating factors, mere failure to serve a statement of costs in compliance with **para. 9.5** should not result in the successful party being deprived of its costs. Instead, the court should consider whether the failure has resulted in any prejudice to the paying party and

32.31

decide on a proportionate response which will deal with any prejudice found (*MacDonald v Taree Holdings Ltd* [2001] CPLR 439). Options are:

(a) giving the paying party a brief adjournment to consider the statement of costs, then proceeding with the summary assessment, with the judge erring towards a lighter figure;

(b) standing the matter over for a detailed assessment;

(c) standing the matter over for a summary assessment at a later date; and

(d) provided all the parties agree, standing the matter over for the summary assessment to be dealt with in writing.

Immediate summary assessment of costs will be appropriate only where the court decides to order costs in any event. Where the interim costs are to be in the case, assessment will almost certainly be left to the conclusion of the case. In cases where costs are awarded in any event, the court should make a summary assessment there and then, but may decide to give directions for a further hearing to deal with the costs (**PD 44, para. 9.7**). Summary assessment will be unnecessary in cases where the parties have agreed the amount of costs (**para. 9.4**). The court must not make a summary assessment of the costs of a publicly funded party (**para. 9.8**). Nor may it make a summary assessment of the costs of a party under a disability, unless that party's solicitor has waived the right to further costs (**para. 9.9(1)**). These last two sentences do not prevent the court making a summary assessment of any interim costs which it decides are payable by an assisted party or a party under a disability (as reflected in **para. 9.9(2)**), although the court should not make such costs payable immediately (in the case of an assisted paying party) unless it also makes a determination under the **Access to Justice Act 1999, s. 11(1)**, or the Legal Aid, Sentencing and Punishment of Offenders Act 2012, s. 26(1) (for which, see **68.55**).

Non-attendance

32.32   The court may proceed in the absence of any party to an application (**CPR, r. 23.11(1)**). When this happens the court has a general discretion to relist the application (see **62.1**).

GENERAL POWERS REGARDING INTERIM RELIEF AND ORDERS

32.33   CPR, **r. 3.1(2)**, sets out a non-exhaustive list of orders that may be made for the purpose of managing cases, and **r. 25.1(1)** sets out a non-exhaustive list of interim remedies that may be granted by the court. The **r. 3.1(2)** list includes orders:

(a) extending or shortening time for compliance with rules, orders and practice directions (see **42.46** to **42.52**);

(b) adjourning or bringing forward hearing dates (see **61.7** and **61.9**);

(c) requiring a party or a legal representative to attend court;

(d) directing part of proceedings, such as a counterclaim, to be dealt with as separate proceedings;

(e) dealing with part of a case as a preliminary issue (see **61.57**);

(f) staying all or part of the proceedings generally or to a specified date or event (see **chapter 56**);

(g) consolidating two or more claims, or trying two or more claims on the same occasion (see **14.61**);

(h) deciding the order in which issues are to be tried;

(i) excluding an issue from consideration (see **42.65**); and

(j) to require any party to file and exchange a costs budget (see **43.7**).

The **r. 25.1(1)** list of interim remedies includes:

(a) Interim injunctions (see **chapter 37**).

(b) Interim declarations (see **4.20**).

(c) Freezing injunctions, which may also include ancillary disclosure orders (see **chapter 38**).

(d)   Search orders (see **chapter 39**).

(e)   Orders for the detention, custody, preservation, inspection or sale of, taking samples from or carrying out of experiments on relevant property, or for the payment of income from relevant property (see **41.2, 41.3**). The order may include authority to enter land in the possession of a party to the proceedings for one of these purposes. 'Relevant property' means property which is the subject of a claim, or as to which any question may arise in a claim.

(f)   Orders for interim delivery up of goods pursuant to the Torts (Interference with Goods) Act 1977, s. 4 (see **chapter 40**).

(g)   Orders for pre-action disclosure and inspection pursuant to the Senior Courts Act 1981, s. 33, or the County Courts Act 1984, s. 52. For the application of these provisions to disclosure of documents, see **chapter 50**. For their application to inspection of property, see **chapter 41**.

(h)   Disclosure or inspection orders against non-parties pursuant to the Senior Courts Act 1981, s. 34, or the County Courts Act 1984, s. 53. For the application of these provisions relate to disclosure of documents, see **chapter 50**. For their application to inspection of property, see **chapter 41**.

(i)   Interim payment orders (see **chapter 36**).

(j)   An order that a specified fund be paid into court or otherwise secured (see **41.4**).

(k)   An order permitting a party seeking to recover personal property to pay money into court pending the outcome of the case, and directing that if this is done, the property shall be given to the party (see **chapter 40**).

(l)   An order directing a party to prepare and file accounts relating to the dispute or directing an account to be taken or inquiry to be made by the court (see **CPR, r. 25.1(1)(n) and (o)**) (see **34.49** and **chapter 63**).

(m)   An order in intellectual property proceedings under Directive (EC) 2004/48, art. 9, making the continuation of an alleged infringement subject to the lodging of guarantees (see **CPR, r. 25.1(1)(p)**).

Care has to be taken when the court is asked to use its general powers under **r. 3.1** to make orders equivalent to specific orders which are governed by principles laid down elsewhere in the CPR. Generally, the principles governing the specific procedure should be adopted, although it may be appropriate to adjust the strict requirements of the specific procedure. See *Quest Advisors Ltd v McFeely* [2011] EWCA Civ 1517, LTL 9/12/2011 at **36.7** in relation to interim payments, and *Olatawura v Abiloye* [2002] EWCA Civ 998, [2003] 1 WLR 275, and *Huscroft v P & O Ferries Ltd* [2010] EWCA Civ 1483, [2011] 1 WLR 939 at **48.20** in relation to security for costs.

Where an order imposes a time limit for doing any act, the date for compliance must be expressed as a calendar date, and must include the time of day by which the act must be done (**r. 2.9(1)**). Orders may be made subject to conditions, and may, at the court's discretion, specify the consequences of failing to comply (**r. 3.1(3)**).

If the court dismisses an application, and it considers the application was totally without merit, that fact must be recorded in the court's order, and the court must consider whether to make a civil restraint order (see **r. 23.13** and **14.55**).

Relief where there are proceedings in another jurisdiction

The High Court has power under the **Civil Jurisdiction and Judgments Act 1982, s. 25(1)**, to grant interim relief where proceedings have been or are to be commenced in another jurisdiction. This is discussed in relation to freezing injunctions at **38.6**. The principle underpinning **s. 25** is that the High Court should be willing to assist the courts of other jurisdictions by providing interim relief on the same basis as if the High Court was itself seised of the substantive claim (*Kensington International Ltd v Republic of Congo* [2007] EWCA Civ 1128, [2008] 1 WLR 1144).

32.34

CONSENT ORDERS

32.35 Consent orders are divided into those which can be entered on a purely administrative basis, without seeking the approval of a judicial officer, and those that need approval. The court may deal with an application without a hearing if the parties agree on the terms of the order sought (**CPR, r. 23.8(a)**).

Administrative consent orders

32.36 Administrative entry of consent orders is only permitted where none of the parties is a litigant in person (**CPR, r. 40.6(2)(b)**). By **r. 40.6(3)** only the following types of orders may be entered by this process:

   (a) judgments and orders for the payment of money;

   (b) judgments and orders for the delivery up of goods with or without the option of paying the value of the goods or an agreed value;

   (c) orders for the dismissal of the whole or part of proceedings;

   (d) Tomlin orders (for the stay of proceedings on agreed terms, which are usually set out in a schedule to the order) and other stays on agreed terms disposing of the proceedings;

   (e) orders for the stay of enforcement of a judgment, either unconditionally or on condition that the money due under the judgment be paid by specified instalments;

   (f) orders setting aside unsatisfied default judgments;

   (g) orders for the payment out of money paid into court;

   (h) orders for the discharge from liability of any party; and

   (i) orders for the payment, assessment or waiver of costs.

Approved consent orders

32.37 Proposed orders or directions which are agreed between the parties must be submitted to the court for scrutiny if either (a) one or more of them is a litigant in person, or (b) any of the orders or directions fall outside the list set out at **32.3**. The procedural judge has a discretion to allow or refuse agreed orders and directions. The court will be particularly concerned to ensure that orders and directions that may have been agreed between the parties are consistent with the overriding objective and with the case management structure for the case. The parties may agree the terms for interim orders at or shortly before a hearing, and to submit them to the court for approval. As at present the court will usually expect the agreed terms to be reduced into writing before being submitted to the court, which is often done in a fairly informal manner. If there is time, it may be possible to draw up a formal Tomlin order or other suitable order for approval by the court.

Costs in consent orders

32.38 Where the parties agree to an order by consent in an interim application, they should also agree a figure for costs to be inserted in the consent order, or agree that there should be no order for costs (**PD 44, para. 9.4**). If they cannot agree on a figure for costs, they will need to attend on the appointment. If this happens, costs are unlikely to be allowed for the attendance unless good reason can be shown for the failure to agree the figure for the costs.

DRAWING UP INTERIM ORDERS

Drawing up consent orders

32.39 A consent order must be drawn up in the terms that have been agreed, must be expressed to be 'by consent', and must be signed by the legal representatives of all parties (or, if approved by the court, any litigant in person) affected by the order (**CPR, r. 40.6(7)**). Letters sent to the court by the respective parties signifying their consent to a draft order are sufficient (**PD 23A, para. 10.2**). The order is then filed with the court, which will arrange for it to be sealed, entered in the court records, and sent out to the parties.

Drawing up non-consent interim orders

CPR, rr. 40.2(2) and 40.3(1)(c), provide that all interim orders have to be drawn up and **32.40** sealed by the court, unless the court dispenses with the need to do so. Normally the court will take responsibility for drawing up, but:

(a) unless otherwise ordered, every judgment or order in the Queen's Bench Division (including the Admiralty, Commercial, and Technology and Construction Courts, but excluding the Administrative Court) must be drawn up by the parties (**rr. 40.3 and 63.38**);

(b) in any court, the court may order a party to draw up an order; or

(c) a party may, with the permission of the court, agree to draw up an order; or

(d) the court may direct a party to draw up the order subject to checking by the court before it is sealed; or

(e) the court may direct the parties to file an agreed statement of the terms of the order before the court itself draws up the order; or

(f) the order may be entered administratively by consent, in which event the parties will submit a drawn-up version of their agreement for entry.

A party who is required to draw up a judgment is allowed seven days to file it, together with sufficient copies for all relevant parties, failing which any other party may draw it up and file it for sealing (**rr. 40.3(3) and 40.4(1)**).

Every judgment (apart from judgments on admissions, default judgments and consent judgments) must state the name and judicial title of the judge who made it (**r. 40.2(1)**).

Once an order has been drawn up the court will serve sealed copies on the applicant and respondent, and also on any other person the court may order to be served (**r. 40.4(2)**). (Service will not be by the court if one of the exceptions set out in **r. 6.21(2)** applies.) The court is given a specific power by **r. 40.5** to order service on a litigant as well as the litigant's solicitor.

Judgments and orders normally take effect from the day they are given or made, not from the time they are drawn up, sealed or served (**r. 40.7**). However, the court is given the power to specify some later date from which the order shall take effect.

REVIEW OF INTERIM DECISIONS

Additional submissions before judgment

Once a hearing has ended, exceptional circumstances should be shown before advocates seek **32.41** to add to their submissions or introduce additional evidence. It is a long-standing rule of natural justice not to hear one side behind the back of the other. There are exceptions, principally where an advocate has to bring a matter to the court's attention in compliance with the advocate's duty to the court (e.g. so as to ensure the court is not misled, or is aware of an adverse authority, or in compliance with the continuing duty of full and frank disclosure in without-notice applications). Where any post-hearing communication takes place with the judge, the usual principle should be that the other side are provided with copies, and given an opportunity to address the court on those matters.

This is an area on which the CPR are silent. It is a potential source of problems, as illustrated by *Albon v Naza Motor Trading Sdn Bhd (No. 2)* [2007] EWHC 327 (Ch), [2007] 1 All ER

Commentary

(Comm) 813, where counsel sent a plethora of emails to the judge after he had commenced writing his judgment.

Reconsideration

32.42   The court has a power to reconsider its decision in an interim application at any point up to the time the order is drawn up *(Pittalis v Sherefettin* [1986] QB 868; *Charlesworth v Relay Roads Ltd* [2000] 1 WLR 230). This jurisdiction has to be exercised in accordance with the overriding objective, and is not limited to exceptional circumstances *(Thomas Cook Tour Operations Ltd v Louis Hotels SA* [2013] EWHC 2469 (QB), LTL 12/8/2013; *Re L-B (Children) (Care Proceedings: Power to Revise Judgment)* [2013] UKSC 8, [2013] 1 WLR 634).

Varying and revoking orders

32.43   The court has the power to vary or revoke a previous order made under a power conferred by the CPR (**CPR, r. 3.1(7)**). See **42.42**.

Renewing interim applications

32.44   The general principle is that it is incumbent on the parties to bring their whole case to the court at the relevant hearing. If they choose to hold back some of their evidence or arguments, they are not, generally, permitted to have a second attempt, deploying further arguments. There are limits to this general principle:

(a)   Most decisions can be reviewed on appeal (see **chapter 74**). There are restricted grounds on which an appeal can be brought (see **75.6**), and generally permission must be sought if an appeal is to be brought (see **74.11**). Although sometimes fresh evidence can be adduced on an appeal, there are severe restrictions on when this will be permitted (see **75.16**).

(b)   Interim orders can be varied or revoked by a court at the same level as the court that made the original order where there has been a change of circumstances (see **32.42**).

(c)   Where the court makes an order of its own initiative, without hearing the parties or giving them an opportunity to make representations, a party affected by the order may apply, within seven days of being served with it, for it to be set aside, varied or stayed (**CPR, r. 3.3(4)** and **(5)**). Where an application notice includes a request for the application to be dealt with without a hearing, and the court accedes to that request, it is **r. 23.8(c)** that applies rather than **r. 23.8(b)** *(Collier v Williams* [2006] EWCA Civ 20, [2006] 1 WLR 1945 at [30]–[37]). This is because the agreement referred to in **r. 23.8(b)** is one between the parties, rather than an agreement with the court. Consequently, the court will treat this situation as if the eventual order were an order the court made on its own initiative (**PD 23A, para. 11.2**), which means either party may apply to have the order varied or set aside under **r. 3.3(5)** *(Collier v Williams* at [30]). The proper practice is to decide any application under **r. 3.3(5)** at a hearing rather than on paper, to prevent repeat applications *(Collier v Williams* at [37]). In situations where the parties agree the terms of the order (**r. 23.8(a)**) or agree to the application being disposed of without a hearing (**r. 23.8(b)**), it is only the respondent who may apply to have the order set aside or varied (under **r. 23.10**).

(d)   The court has power to adjourn a hearing under **CPR, r. 3.1(2)(b)**, which it can use while a hearing is part-heard to allow a party to return on a future date with additional evidence.

Beyond this, it is submitted, the court should not go. A first-instance decision, *Laemthong International Lines Co. Ltd v ARTIS* [2004] EWHC 2226 (Comm), [2004] 2 All ER (Comm) 797, appears to have taken an additional, forbidden step. Colman J held that a judge has jurisdiction to hear a without notice application for a freezing injunction despite the same application having been heard and dismissed on two previous occasions by two different judges. Plainly, the duty of full and frank disclosure requires an applicant who is renewing an application to disclose to the court all previous unsuccessful attempts (see **32.9**). While Colman J said that another judge will normally dismiss a renewed application, this is not strong enough, and the correct position is that the renewed application must be dismissed unless there has been a material change of circumstances.

Chapter 33   Striking Out

The following procedural checklist is relevant to this chapter:

Procedural checklist 21   Application for striking out

INTRODUCTION

33.1   By **CPR, r. 3.4**, the court has the power to order the whole or any part of a statement of case to be struck out. This power may be resorted to on an application by a party seeking to attack the statement of case drafted by the other side. It may also be used by the court of its own initiative. This may be because of failure to comply with the requirement to give a concise statement of the facts on which the claimant relies (**r. 16.4(1)(a)**) or the requirement to give the reasons for any denial in a defence (**r. 16.5(2)(a)**). A related use of the power is where it is alleged that a statement of case, even if its contents are assumed to be true, does not amount to a sustainable claim or defence as a matter of law. Striking out is also used to prevent the misuse of the right to issue proceedings, on the ground that proceedings are an abuse of process. These facets of the jurisdiction to strike out will be considered in this chapter.

Striking out is also used as a means of enforcing compliance with the general provisions of the CPR, practice directions and court orders and directions as part of the court's case management functions. This aspect of striking out will be considered in **chapter 48**.

Once a claim is struck out there are no subsisting proceedings that can provide a platform for making interim applications (*Mireskandari v Associated Newspapers Ltd* [2010] EWHC 967 (QB), 160 NLJ 695). All that can be done after a claim is struck out is to appeal, assess damages, assess costs, enforce judgment or deal with false statement of truth.

It is recognised in several places in the CPR that striking out under **r. 3.4** is closely related to the jurisdiction to enter summary judgment under **Part 24**, discussed in **chapter 34** (see, for example, **PD 3A, paras 1.2, 1.7** and **6.1**; the note to **CPR, r. 24.2**; and **PD 26, para. 5.2**).

Both powers are used to achieve the active case management aim of summarily disposing of issues that do not need full investigation at trial (**CPR, r. 1.4(2)(c)**). As they are closely related, it is very common for parties to make applications in suitable cases for striking out and summary judgment in the alternative, although in *Clarke v Davey* [2002] EWHC 2342 (QB), LTL 11/11/2002, it was said that the right course is to apply only for summary judgment. In *Three Rivers District Council v Bank of England (No. 3)* [2001] UKHL 16, [2003] 2 AC 1, Lord Hope of Craighead said, that under **r. 3.4** the court generally is only concerned with the statement of case which it is alleged discloses no reasonable grounds for bringing or defending the claim. In *Monsanto plc v Tilly* [2000] Env LR 313 Stuart-Smith LJ said that **r. 24.2** gives a wider scope for dismissing a claim or defence. The court should look to see what will happen at the trial and, if the case is so weak that it has no reasonable prospects of success, summary judgment should be entered. There is an inevitable overlap between the two concepts. Some allegations will be factually weak and aptly described as disclosing no reasonable grounds within the meaning of **r. 3.4**. Procedural judges are under a duty to narrow the issues as part of their case management functions under **Part 1** and have the power to treat an application to strike out as one for summary judgment in order to dispose of issues or claims that do not deserve full investigation at trial (*Three Rivers District Council v Bank of England (No. 3)* at [88]).

THE MAIN RULE

CPR, r. 3.4(2), provides: **33.2**

The court may strike out a statement of case if it appears to the court—

(a) that the statement of case discloses no reasonable grounds for bringing or defending the claim;
(b) that the statement of case is an abuse of the court's process or is otherwise likely to obstruct the just disposal of the proceedings; or
(c) that there has been a failure to comply with a rule, practice direction or court order.

By **r. 3.4(1)** references in **r. 3.4(2)** to a statement of case include references to part of a statement of case. A claim may fall within **r. 3.4(2)(b)** where it is vexatious, scurrilous or obviously ill-founded (**PD 3A, para. 1.5**). While striking out is closely related to summary judgment (see **33.1**), the tests are different. It is wrong for a judge to apply the summary judgment test of no real prospect of success on a striking-out application (*Duce v Worcestershire Acute Hospitals NHS Trust* [2014] EWCA Civ 249, LTL 12/3/2014).

In addition, the High Court retains its power to strike out under its inherent jurisdiction, as **CPR, r. 3.4(5)**, provides that **r. 3.4(2)** does not limit any other power of the court to strike out a statement of case (*Re Abermeadow Ltd* [2000] 2 BCLC 824).

PROCEDURE ON APPLICATIONS MADE BY PARTIES

An application to strike out made by a party should be brought by issuing an application   **33.3**
notice in accordance with the procedure in **CPR, Part 23** (see **chapter 32**). PD 3A, para. 5.2, says that while many applications to strike out can be made without evidence in support (the poor drafting of the statement of case may be self-evident, or the point may be one of law on which no evidence would be required), the applicant should always consider whether facts need to be proved. If so, evidence in support should usually be filed and served, unless the facts relied upon have already been adequately evidenced in, say, a statement of case which included a statement of truth. However, careful consideration should be given before relying on a statement of case in this way.

In accordance with **PD 23A, para. 2.7**, any application to strike out should be made as soon as it becomes apparent that it is desirable to make it. Applications to strike out should

Commentary

normally be made in the period between acknowledgment of service and filing of directions questionnaires (**PD 26, para. 5.3(1)**, and see also **PD 3A, para. 5.1**).

There will be cases where it may be appropriate to seek striking out or summary judgment in the alternative (**PD 3A, para. 1.7**; see **33.1**).

Effect on default and summary judgment and allocation

33.4   If a striking-out application is issued before the defence is filed, default judgment cannot be entered until the striking-out application has been disposed of (**CPR, r. 12.3(3)**). If a striking-out application is dealt with before allocation and the claim survives, the court may be in a position to dispense with the need to file directions questionnaires, and may allocate the case and make case management directions at the end of the striking-out hearing (**PD 26, para. 2.4**). If a striking-out application is contemplated, but has not been dealt with by the time directions questionnaires have to be returned, the intention to make the application should be included as extra information provided when the questionnaire is returned (**PD 26, para. 2.2(3)(a)**).

PD 26, para. 5.3(2), provides that where a party makes an application to strike out before the claim has been allocated to a track the court will not allocate the claim before hearing the application. By **PD 26, para. 5.3(3)** and (4), where a party files a directions questionnaire and states an intention to strike out but has not yet done so, the judge will usually direct that an allocation hearing is listed. The striking-out application may be heard at the allocation hearing if the application notice has been issued and served in sufficient time.

REFERENCES BY COURT OFFICERS

33.5   A claim form that has been lodged for issuing may be referred by a court official to the judge (**CPR, r. 3.2**), and this power may be exercised where it is felt that the claim form (which in context means the particulars of claim) is amenable to being struck out under (see **PD 3A, para. 2.1**). The judge may then make an order designed to ensure that the claim is disposed of, or proceeds, in a way that accords with the rules. The judge has a discretion whether to hear the claimant before making such order as may be appropriate (**para. 2.3**). If an order is made without giving notice to the claimant, **CPR, rr. 23.9** and **23.10**, apply, so that the order has to include a statement that the claimant has the right within seven days after service of the order to apply to vary or set it aside.

One option available to the judge is to order a stay to allow the claimant an opportunity of putting the claim on a proper footing. This may take the form of a simple stay until further order, or an order that the claim form shall not be served until the stay is lifted, or an order that no application to lift the stay shall be made until the claimant files specified further documents, such as amended particulars of claim or a witness statement (**PD 3A, para. 2.4**). If the claimant does what the judge requires, and the stay is lifted, the judge may give directions regarding service of the order and any other documents on the court file (**para. 2.5**). The fact that the judge allows the claim to proceed does not preclude the defendant from making an application to strike out or for summary judgment once proceedings are served (**para. 2.6**).

Similar powers are available where a court official believes a document purporting to be a defence is amenable to being struck out (**para. 3**). A stay would be inappropriate in this situation, but the judge may strike out the defence on his or her own initiative, or allow the defendant an opportunity to file an amended defence, or may require the defendant to provide further information to clarify the defence within a stated time, failing which the judge may order the defence to be struck out. The fact that a judge does not strike out a defence under this power does not prejudice the claimant's right to apply for such an order or any other order.

GENERAL TEST

Under the old rules it was well settled that the jurisdiction to strike out was to be used spar-   **33.6**
ingly. The reason was, and this has not changed, that the exercise of the jurisdiction deprives
a party of its right to a trial, and of its ability to strengthen its case through the process of
disclosure and other court procedures such as requests for further information. Further, it has
always been true that the examination and cross-examination of witnesses often changes the
complexion of a case. It was accordingly the accepted rule that striking out was limited to
plain and obvious cases where there was no point in having a trial.

Under the CPR it is part of the court's active case management role to identify the issues at an
early stage and to decide which issues need full investigation at trial, and to dispose summarily
of the others (**CPR, r. 1.4(2)(b)** and (**c**)). In *Swain v Hillman* [2001] 1 All ER 91 (a summary judgment case), Lord Woolf MR said that Part 24 applications had to be kept within their proper
limits, and were not meant to be used to dispense with the need for a trial where there were
issues which should be considered at trial. The same could be said in relation to striking out
under **r. 3.4**. In the same vein, before using **r. 3.4** to dispose of 'side issues', care should be
taken to ensure that a party is not deprived of the right to trial on issues essential to its case.
In *McPhilemy v Times Newspapers Ltd* [1999] 3 All ER 775, one of the first cases decided under the
CPR, the Master of the Rolls said that the powers of the court to restrain excess do not extend
to preventing a party from putting forward allegations which are central to its case. That said,
it is open to the court to attempt to control how those allegations are litigated with a view to
limiting costs.

The leading case under the old rules was *Williams and Humbert Ltd v W. and H. Trade Marks (Jersey)
Ltd* [1986] AC 368. The claimant's application to strike out the defence took seven days to
argue before the judge, six days in the Court of Appeal, and four days in the House of Lords.
The case reiterated the point that striking out was only appropriate in plain and obvious
cases. Sometimes, a case would only become clear after protracted argument. Lord Templeman
said that:

if an application to strike out involves a prolonged and serious argument the judge should, as a general
rule, decline to proceed with the argument unless he not only harbours doubts about the soundness of
the pleading but, in addition, is satisfied that striking out will obviate the necessity for a trial or will
substantially reduce the burden of preparing for trial or the burden of the trial itself.

A judge may therefore refuse to hear a striking-out application if: (a) the application is unlikely
to succeed; or (b) the application will not be decisive or appreciably simplify the eventual trial
(see *Morris v Bank of America National Trust* [2000] 1 All ER 954). It is generally improper to conduct
what is in effect a mini-trial involving protracted examination of the documents and facts as
disclosed in the written evidence on a striking-out application (*Wenlock v Moloney* [1965] 1 WLR
1238), although such a detailed analysis is sometimes appropriate in striking-out applications
in relation to unfair prejudice petitions under the Companies Act 2006, s. 994 (*Morris v Bank
of America National Trust*).

The principles from *Williams and Humbert Ltd v W. and H. Trade Marks (Jersey) Ltd*, *Wenlock v
Moloney* and *Morris v Bank of America National Trust* were approved in *Three Rivers District
Council v Bank of England (No. 3)* [2001] UKHL 16, [2003] 2 AC 1 at [96]–[97]. No adjustment
is made to the test where one party is suffering from an inequality of arms (*Bank of
Tokyo-Mitsubishi UFJ Ltd v Baskan Gida Sanayi ve Pazarlama AS* [2008] EWHC 659 (Ch), LTL
17/4/2008).

If an application to strike out is unsuccessful, the claim will proceed towards trial. In such
cases it may be considered undesirable for the judge or Master to express any reasons as to why
that decision has been made (*Re Baltic Real Estate Ltd (No. 1)* [1993] BCLC 498).

Commentary

NO REASONABLE GROUNDS FOR BRINGING OR DEFENDING THE CLAIM

33.7   Applications under **CPR, r. 3.4(2)(a)**, may be made on the basis that the statement of case under attack fails on its face to disclose a sustainable claim or defence. Traditionally this has been regarded as restricted to cases which are bad in law, or which fail to plead a complete claim or defence. In practice the rule is regarded as shading into applications for summary judgment, which have traditionally been regarded as a means for attacking cases which are weak on the evidence. For example, in *Freer v Zeb* [2008] EWHC 212 (QB), LTL 21/2/2008, a claim that the defendant was vicariously liable for the actions of certain people was struck out, because all the evidence pointed to them being employed not by the defendant but by a company of which the defendant was a director.

On hearing such an application it will be assumed that the facts alleged by the respondent are true (see *Morgan Crucible Co. plc v Hill Samuel and Co. Ltd* [1991] Ch 295 per Slade LJ). For purists it ought to be unnecessary to seek to undermine the claim or defence with evidence in support of the application. The rules do not, however, contain any express ban on adducing evidence in support: **r. 25.3(2)** provides that applications must be supported by evidence unless the court otherwise orders, and **PD 3A, para. 5.2**, leaves open the option of adducing evidence in support. In claims for breach of written contracts, including cases where the contractual obligations are contained in more than one document, the courts have always been willing to consider the contractual documents to decide whether there is an arguable case on a strike-out application. A counterclaim was struck out on this basis in *Al-Dawood Shipping Lines Ltd v Dynastic Maritime Inc.* [2010] EWCA Civ 104, LTL 19/2/2010.

In deciding whether to strike out, the judge should consider the effect of the order. In *Watson v Ian Snipe and Co.* [2002] EWCA Civ 293, LTL 21/2/2002, there were parallel proceedings against two firms of solicitors, which had successively been retained by the claimants in an unsuccessful claim. It was held to have been inconsistent with sound case management principles to have struck out the claim against one of the firms, because this added to the overall complexity of the proceedings.

A number of examples of statements of case open to attack under **CPR, r. 3.4(2)(a)**, are given by **PD 3A**. A claim may be struck out if it sets out no facts indicating what the claim is about (such as a claim simply saying it is for 'Money owed £5,000'), or if it is incoherent and makes no sense, or if the facts it states, even if true, do not disclose a legally recognisable claim against the defendant. A defence may be struck out if it consists of a bare denial or otherwise fails to set out a coherent statement of facts, or if the facts it sets out, even if true, do not amount in law to a defence to the claim. Many institutional defendants have been in the habit of filing short defences making blanket denials without stating any positive case. These defences ought to be a thing of the past. See **chapters 24** and **26**.

Some prospects of success

33.8   Under the old rules, a cause of action with some prospects of success would not be struck out. Provided the statement of case raised some question fit to be tried, it did not matter that the case was weak or unlikely to succeed (*Wenlock v Moloney* [1965] 1 WLR 1238), one of the leading cases under the old rules, and *Chan U Seek v Alvis Vehicles Ltd* [2003] EWHC 1238 (Ch), *The Times*, 16 May 2003, which adopted the same test under the CPR). Judges often apply the test of whether the claim is bound to fail, so that even a case 'fraught with difficulty' will not be struck out (*Smith v Chief Constable of Sussex* [2008] EWCA Civ 39, [2008] PIQR P12; *K v Central and North West London Mental Health NHS Trust* [2008] EWHC 1217 (QB), [2008] PIQR P19). The apparent implausibility of a case on paper is not in itself enough to justify striking it out (*Merelie v*

Newcastle Primary Care Trust [2004] EWHC 2554 (QB), *The Times*, 1 December 2004). Nor is it appropriate to strike out a claim where the central issues are in dispute (*King v Telegraph Group Ltd* [2003] EWHC 1312 (QB), LTL 9/6/2003). In *Top Layers Interior Ltd v Azure Maritime Holdings SA* [2007] EWHC 2844 (QB), LTL 10/12/2007, a statement of case alleging the parties had orally agreed a term that time was of the essence was regarded as having no prospect of success where there had been no complaints at the time.

According to Potter LJ in *Partco Group Ltd v Wragg* [2002] EWCA Civ 594, [2002] 2 Lloyd's Rep 343 at [46], cases where striking out under **CPR, r. 3.4(2)(a)**, is appropriate include:

(a) where the statement of case raises an unwinnable case where continuing the proceedings is without any possible benefit to the respondent and would waste resources on both sides (*Harris v Bolt Burdon* [2000] CPLR 9); and

(b) where the statement of case does not raise a valid claim or defence as a matter of law (*Price Meats Ltd v Barclays Bank plc* [2000] 2 All ER (Comm) 346).

A cause of action that is unknown to the law will be struck out, such as a claim alleging abuse of civil proceedings (*Ustimenko v Prescot Management Co. Ltd* [2007] EWHC 1853 (QB), LTL 20/8/2007). Subject to the court giving permission to amend, a statement of case will be struck out that omits some material element of the claim or defence. A statement of case ought also to be struck out if the facts set out do not constitute the cause of action or defence alleged, or if the relief sought would not be ordered by the court. A defence may be struck out if it does not answer the claim being made. However, purely technical objections to the form of statements of case will not be entertained, provided the statement of case is sufficient to allow the other side to have a fair trial (*Morris v Bank of America National Trust* [2000] 1 All ER 954).

Sinclair Investment Holdings SA v Versailles Trade Finance Ltd [2005] EWCA Civ 722, [2006] 1 BCLC 60, was a claim for breach of fiduciary duty based on an assumption of a duty of loyalty (as opposed to the more usual director and trustee situations) with an alternative claim in constructive trust. It was held that the assumption of loyalty element was sufficiently pleaded by allegations that the defendant controlled, or was in a position to control, the exercise of powers over the claimant's money. The constructive trust claim was pleaded in novel circumstances, but there was no authority against liability being established on the pleaded facts (which included actual fraud), so this was allowed to proceed.

In *Taylor v Inntrepreneur Estates (CPC) Ltd* (2001) LTL 7/2/2001 the claimant brought a claim seeking a declaration that a lease agreement had come into force, damages for breach of the lease, and damages for misrepresentation resulting from having entered into the alleged lease. On the documents it was clear that throughout the parties had negotiated on a 'subject to contract' basis. It was held that as no written agreement had been signed, no lease had been entered into. It followed that there was no reasonable cause of action, and the claim was struck out. Conversely, in *Cornelius v Hackney London Borough Council* [2002] EWCA Civ 1073, [2003] LGR 178, an application to strike out a misfeasance claim was dismissed because liability turned on whether an official had abused his public office, which was a question of fact. In *Kirk v London Borough of Brent* [2005] EWCA Civ 1701, LTL 8/12/2005, the Court of Appeal said it had been wrong to strike out a nuisance claim which alleged the claimant's property had been damaged by tree roots. While the defendant had been notified of the claim very late, a letter about a similar problem involving a neighbouring property written a year after the damage to the claimant's property had been discovered raised implications about the defendant's state of knowledge which meant the claim was not suitable for striking out.

Points of law

Where the argument involves a substantial point of law which does not admit of a plain and obvious answer, it may be best not to have it determined on a striking-out application. One thing the courts are anxious to avoid is expensive satellite litigation. Instead, sensible case

33.9

management may indicate that it would be better dealt with as a preliminary issue, although dealing with issues in this way sometimes increases costs and delay — see **61.59**.

Where the law is in a state of development, it will usually be inappropriate to decide questions, such as whether a duty of care exists in a novel situation, on hypothetical facts. Such questions are usually best dealt with at trial (*D v East Berkshire Community Health NHS Trust* [2005] UKHL 23, [2005] 2 AC 373, per Lord Bingham of Cornhill at [4]; *Brooks v Commissioner of Police of the Metropolis* [2005] UKHL 24, [2005] 1 WLR 1495, per Lord Bingham of Cornhill at [3]; *Hughes v Richards* [2004] EWCA Civ 266, [2004] PNLR 35).

Claim meriting further investigation

33.10   A similar approach is taken in striking-out applications to that adopted in summary judgment applications (see **34.22**) where the strength of a case may not be clear because it has not been fully investigated. Where there is a real possibility that, on a full investigation of the factual background, any uncertainty on the merits might be remedied, striking out should be refused (*Kyrris v Oldham* [2003] EWCA Civ 1506, [2004] 1 BCLC 305).

Amendment, rectifying errors and disclosure

33.11   The court may allow a party to amend rather than striking out. There have been cases where amendments have been allowed at a very late stage (see, under the old rules, *CBS Songs Ltd v Amstrad Consumer Electronics plc* [1987] RPC 417). An amendment may be allowed on an appeal, even if the amendment has not been raised in the court below (*Islington London Borough Council v Uckac* [2006] EWCA Civ 340, [2006] 1 WLR 1303 at [39]. The power to amend will be exercised in accordance with the overriding objective, and this may militate against giving permission depending on the circumstances of the case (see *Finley v Connell Associates* [1999] Lloyd's Rep PN 895, where permission to amend was granted, and *Christofi v Barclays Bank plc* [2000] 1 WLR 937, where permission was refused). An amendment should only be permitted as an alternative to striking out if there is a real prospect of establishing the amended case (*Charles Church Developments plc v Cronin* [1990] FSR 1; *Savings and Investment Bank Ltd v Fincken* (2001) *The Times*, 15 November 2001).

Where the problem is an error of procedure, the judge has to consider whether to cure the irregularity, which may avoid a striking-out order (*Firth v Everitt* [2007] EWHC 1979 (Ch), LTL 25/9/2007).

Where a claim is arguably so speculative that it discloses no reasonable cause of action or amounts to an abuse of process, instead of striking out the court may be prepared to allow the claim to proceed to enable the claimant to obtain disclosure from the defendant to see whether there is evidence substantiating the claim. If it does not, the defendant would be allowed to reapply for striking out (*Arsenal Football Club plc v Elite Sports Distribution Ltd* [2002] EWHC 3057 (Ch), [2003] FSR 26, where the circumstances pointed towards the defendant having committed some tort, but it was unclear which one).

ABUSE OF PROCESS

33.12   The first half of CPR, r. 3.4(2)(b), gives the court power to strike out a statement of case which is an abuse of the court's process. This is a power 'which any court of justice must possess to prevent misuse of its procedure in a way which, although not inconsistent with the literal application of its procedural rules, would nevertheless be manifestly unfair to a party to litigation before it, or would otherwise bring the administration of justice into disrepute among right-thinking people' (per Lord Diplock in *Hunter v Chief Constable of the West Midlands Police* [1982] AC 529 at p. 536). Applications to strike out for abuse of process should be made shortly after service. Once the defendant has filed a defence and defended on the merits he is taken to have acquiesced, and it is too late to take the point (*Johnson v Gore Wood and Co.* [2002] 2 AC 1; *Coca-Cola Co. v Ketteridge* [2003] EWHC 2488 (Ch), [2004] FSR 29).

Whether there is an abuse of process is a question of judgment to which there is only one correct answer, even though many factors will usually have to be weighed in coming to that judgment. It is not a matter of discretion (*Aldi Stores Ltd v WSP Group plc* [2007] EWCA Civ 1260, [2008] 1 WLR 748).

The court has the power to strike out even a valid claim where there has been an abuse of process, but it is not always correct to do so. Striking out should be the last option. If the abuse can be addressed in some less draconian way, it should be (*Reckitt Benckiser (UK) Ltd v Home Pairfum Ltd* [2004] EWHC 302 (Pat), [2004] FSR 37).

Some striking-out applications are brought on the basis that it is an abuse of process to litigate a very weak claim. It is submitted that this is a misuse of the term 'abuse of process', and that weak claims should be dealt with either as disclosing no reasonable grounds for bringing or defending the claim (see **33.7** to **33.10**) or on an application for summary judgment (**chapter 34**). In so far as there is any validity in striking out on this basis, it was held in *Barrett v Universal-Island Records Ltd* [2003] EWHC 625 (Ch), *The Times*, 24 April 2003, that the court needed to have a high degree of confidence that the claim or defence would not succeed before striking it out as an abuse of process.

General examples of abuse of process

A claim that is issued after the expiry of limitation may be struck out as an abuse of process (alternatively, the limitation point may be determined as a preliminary issue, or at trial, or by way of an application for a direction under the LA 1980, s. 33), but cannot be struck out on the ground of there being no reasonable cause of action. The reason is that limitation is a procedural defence, so does not prevent there being a cause of action. See *Ronex Properties Ltd v John Laing Construction Ltd* [1983] QB 398. **33.13**

Issuing a claim form merely to protect the claimant's position at a time when the claimant had not decided to pursue a claim against the defendant is an abuse of process (*Nomura International plc v Granada Group Ltd* [2007] EWHC 642 (Comm), [2008] Bus LR 1). The relevant provision in the CPR (**r. 16.2(1)**) follows the same form and has the same intention as RSC, ord. 6, r. 2. In these circumstances the court properly had regard to the principles behind the pre-CPR case-law. *Sterman v E. W. and W. J. Moore* [1970] 1 QB 596 and *Marshall v London Passenger Transport Board* [1936] 2 All ER 83 decided that failing to include a concise statement on what is now the claim form could only be cured if the claimant had a known and genuine cause of action when the claim was issued. Gaining such knowledge by the time the application to strike out is heard does not cure the abuse. Generally it is an abuse of process to have simultaneously two active, identical, claims against the same defendant. This is because it is oppressive to force a defendant into defending the same claim in multiple proceedings. A claim is active for this purpose once it is served, and it is a common precaution where there is a technical problem with proceedings to issue a second, protective, claim (which is not served) pending resolution of the objections to the first claim. In *Rosenberg v Nazarov* [2008] EWHC 812 (Ch), LTL 10/4/2008, there were two active claims against the defendant, the only difference between the two particulars of claim being two paragraphs. The court declined to strike out the first claim because it was issued eight months before the second, and there were potential limitation problems with the second claim which would not affect the first, and the court took the view that consolidation would avoid any oppression to the defendant.

In *Jameel v Dow Jones and Co. Inc.* [2005] EWCA Civ 75, [2005] QB 946, the claimant brought a defamation claim in respect of an alleged internet libel which had been accessed (apparently) by five people. While there was a reasonable cause of action because of the presumption of damage, the claim was struck out as an abuse of process. The court sought to keep a balance between the

Commentary

right of freedom of expression under the European Convention on Human Rights, **art. 10**, in the **Human Rights Act 1998, sch. 1**, and the need to protect individual rights. As there was only minimal publication and insignificant damage to the claimant's reputation, it was held there was no 'real and substantial tort', with the result that the claim was disproportionate and an abuse of process. A claim may be struck out on this basis if the claimant has already obtained all he is ever likely to obtain by way of redress (*Ansari v Knowles* [2013] EWCA Civ 1448, [2014] CP Rep 9). The mere fact a claim is small is not enough (*Sullivan v Bristol Film Studios Ltd* [2012] EWCA Civ 570, [2012] CP Rep 34). A strike-out application on the *Jameel v Dow Jones and Co. Ltd* principle is dealt with in a summary way, taking the claim at face value (unless the merits are very clear one way or the other), and must not be allowed to descend into a mini-trial (*Ansari v Knowles*). The *Jameel v Dow Jones and Co. Ltd* principle has been applied most frequently in defamation cases, but it has also been applied in intellectual property claims (*Lilley v DMG Events Ltd* [2014] EWHC 610 (IPEC), LTL 18/3/2014) and it is probably of general application.

Withdrawing in bad faith a pre-action admission of liability may be an abuse of process (*Walley v Stoke-on-Trent City Council* [2006] EWCA Civ 1137, [2007] 1 WLR 352, and see the discussion at **34.30**).

Generally, it is an abuse of process for a claimant complaining about a public authority's infringement of the claimant's public law rights to seek redress by way of an ordinary claim rather than by way of judicial review (see *O'Reilly v Mackman* [1983] 2 AC 237). In considering whether to strike out on this ground, the court will take into account whether the claimant has used the ordinary procedure to obtain some advantage not available in judicial review proceedings, and generally whether striking out accords with the overriding objective (*Clark v University of Lincolnshire and Humberside* [2000] 1 WLR 1988). The prohibition is limited to bringing claims, so there is no restriction on raising public law issues in a defence (*Rhondda Cynon Taff County Borough Council v Watkins* [2003] EWCA Civ 129, [2003] 1 WLR 1864).

In *Barton Henderson Rasen v Merrett* [1993] 1 Lloyd's Rep 540 Saville J said that, as courts exist to determine claims in contentious matters, starting a claim with no intention of pursuing it is an abuse of process. Protracted delay combined with a legitimate concern to avoid costs in the hope of settlement do not amount to this (*Artibell Shipping Co. Ltd v Markel International Insurance Co. Ltd* [2008] EWHC 811 (Comm), LTL 2/5/2008). Similarly, issuing a claim for which the claimant knows no basis is an abuse of process (*Nomura International plc v Granada Group Ltd* [2007] EWHC 642 (Comm), [2008] Bus LR 1), as is advancing a claim making serious charges involving bad faith without adequate particulars (*RGI International Ltd v Synergy Classic Ltd* [2011] EWHC 3166 (Comm), LTL 8/12/2011). 'Parking' proceedings in an attempt to achieve a settlement with other defendants justified striking out with indemnity costs in *Sodeca SA v NE Investments Inc.* [2002] EWHC 1700 (QB), LTL 27/8/2002. Litigating for the purpose of causing expense, harassment or commercial prejudice beyond that normally encountered in the course of properly conducted litigation justifies striking out as an abuse of process (*Wallis v Valentine* [2002] EWCA Civ 1034, [2003] EMLR 8). A claim based on comments made in without-prejudice communications is an abuse of process (*Unilever plc v Procter and Gamble Co.* [2000] 1 WLR 2436).

In *Raja v Van Hoogstraten* [2006] EWHC 1315 (Ch), LTL 20/6/2006, a finding on the trial of a preliminary issue was that the defendant had arranged for the killing of the claimant in order to prevent him giving evidence. Bearing in mind the European Convention on Human Rights, **art. 6**, in the **Human Rights Act 1998, sch. 1**, the defence and counterclaim were struck out. Arranging for the killing of an opponent was a grave form of abuse of process.

According to *McDonald's Corporation v Steel* [1995] 3 All ER 615, it is an abuse of process where the statement of case is incurably incapable of proof. The fact that a party's case may be incapable of proof may become apparent after disclosure of documents or after exchange of witness statements. However, in *McDonald's Corporation v Steel* it was said that striking out on this basis will be fairly unusual, as there are few cases which are sufficiently clearly and obviously hopeless that they deserve the draconian step of being struck out. A clinical negligence claim commenced five years after the event and which was not supported by the medical experts instructed for the claimant was regarded as unwinnable in *Harris v Bolt Burdon* [2000] CPLR 9.

Commencing proceedings knowing that the cause of action is vested in someone else is an abuse of process, as it is only the person with the vested right of action who can bring a claim (*Pickthall v Hill Dickinson LLP* [2009] EWCA Civ 543, [2009] PNLR 31).

Framing a claim in malicious falsehood rather than the more natural cause of action in libel, in order to gain the benefit of public funding for the claim, was not regarded as an abuse of process in *Joyce v Sengupta* [1993] 1 WLR 337. In *R v Richmond upon Thames London Borough Council, ex parte C* [2001] LGR 146, bringing judicial review proceedings relating to obtaining a place for a child in a preferred school in the name of the child rather than his parent in order to obtain public funding was regarded by Kennedy LJ as an abuse of process.

Where a claimant has two reasons for bringing a claim, one legitimate, and one illegitimate, it was held in *JSC BTA Bank v Ablyazov (No. 6)* [2011] EWHC 1136 (Comm), [2011] 1 WLR 2996, that there is no abuse of process. Teare J recognised there is an argument that there would be an abuse of process if the illegitimate reason for bringing the claim was the predominant reason (at [23(iii)] and [53], citing *Metall und Rohstoff AG v Donaldson Lufkin and Jenrette Inc.* [1990] 1 QB 391).

Fraudulent claims

33.14 Making a claim tainted by dishonesty can amount to an abuse of process, but it will rarely result in a claim being struck out. In *Arrow Nominees Inc. v Blackledge* one of the parties admitted tampering with a number of material documents. It was held that where a litigant was guilty of conduct which put the fairness of the trial in jeopardy and prevented the court doing justice, striking out may be appropriate. *Arrow Nominees Inc. v Blackledge* was considered in two Court of Appeal decisions with differing results. In *Ul-Haq v Shah* [2009] EWCA Civ 542, [2010] 1 WLR 616 one of a number of co-claimants made a fraudulent claim with the assistance of the other co-claimants. While the fraudulent claim was dismissed, the other claimants were awarded damages in accordance with the evidence. However, where a party's conduct (such as perjury or presenting fraudulent evidence) so damages the integrity of the case being presented that its continuation would be an affront to justice, it may be struck out as an abuse of process (*Masood v Zahoor* [2009] EWCA Civ 650, [2010] 1 WLR 746). These cases were considered in *Summers v Fairclough Homes Ltd* [2012] UKSC 26, [2012] 1 WLR 2004, where *Masood v Zahoor* was preferred. In *Summers v Fairclough Homes Ltd* the claimant suffered genuine injuries, but gave false evidence about his date of recovery, and signed false statements of truth on his schedules of special damages. It was held that in theory a striking-out order could be made, even at the end of the trial, in such a case. However, this power is likely to be used only rarely for two reasons. First, it will be more appropriate at that stage of the proceedings for the judge to make the necessary findings (probably with wide adverse inferences being drawn against the dishonest party) and for judgment to follow in the usual way. Secondly, the judgment on the genuine part of the claim is a possession within the meaning of the European Convention on Human Rights, First Protocol, art. 1, in the **Human Rights Act 1998, sch.** 1, so should only be lost if striking out performs a legitimate aim and is a proportionate means of achieving that aim. It was held that while this was a case of a serious abuse of process, it would have been wrong to strike it out.

Destruction of evidence before proceedings are commenced in an attempt to pervert the course of justice may result in a claim or defence being struck out. Destruction of evidence after proceedings are issued may be visited by striking out if a fair trial is no longer achievable (*Douglas v Hello! Ltd (No. 2)* [2003] EWHC 55 (Ch), [2003] 1 All ER 1087).

Relitigation amounting to an abuse of process

33.15 Several cases have considered whether a claim which is inconsistent with an earlier claim or evidence given by the claimant in earlier proceedings (such as an affidavit used in an application to discharge a freezing injunction) should be struck out as an abuse of process. Further, a party to litigation must bring forward his whole case, and is generally not permitted to bring later proceedings raising matters that could have been resolved in the earlier proceedings (*Henderson v Henderson* (1843) 3 Hare 100). It is clear from cases such as *Bradford and Bingley Building Society v Seddon* [1999] 1 WLR 1482 that there are two main elements:

(a) that the second claim is one that could have been brought in the first claim, or is in conflict with an earlier claim or evidence; and

(b) an additional element, such as a collateral attack on the earlier decision, or dishonesty, election, or unjust harassment.

Thus, in *Hunter v Chief Constable of the West Midlands Police* [1982] AC 529 a claim against the police was struck out as it was held to be no more than a collateral attack upon the decision of another court of competent jurisdiction. The same principle applies where the earlier decision is a disciplinary finding of a professional regulator (*Baxendale-Walker v Middleton* [2011] EWHC 998 (QB), LTL 20/4/2011). In *Calzaghe v Warren* [2010] EWHC 71 (QB), LTL 9/4/2010, the claimant had brought a first claim against a boxing promoter's company, and in winning that claim had established at trial that the promoter's evidence was dishonest. The company was put into administration, so the judgment on the first claim remained unsatisfied. A second claim was then brought, this time against the promoter in his individual capacity, based on the same facts as the first claim, and alleging that the company was the promoter's alter ego. As the defendants were different in the two claims this was not a case of issue estoppel. Nevertheless it was held to be an abuse of process for the promoter to seek to put in issue the facts found against him as a witness in the first claim, including the finding that his evidence had been dishonest. Summary judgment was entered for the claimant. See also *Taylor Walton v Laing* [2007] EWCA Civ 1146, (2007) 47 EG 169 (CS), where the claim was in substance a complete relitigation of a previous decision at trial.

33.16   **Issue estoppel**   Where the issues raised in an earlier claim are identical to those raised in a later claim, there is an absolute bar on the later proceedings unless fraud or collusion is alleged (*Arnold v National Westminster Bank plc* [1991] 2 AC 93). Where an issue decided in a previous claim between the parties is central to a second claim between the same parties, the whole second claim will be struck out (*Kennecott Utah Copper Corporation v Minet Ltd* [2002] EWHC 1622 (Comm), [2003] PNLR 18). Issue estoppel, like cause of action estoppel, only applies to matters finally decided upon, usually in litigation. It also applies where the same issue has been decided in arbitration (*Arts and Antiques Ltd v Richards* [2013] EWHC 3361 (Comm), [2014] PNLR 10) and where a payment has been accepted under the Financial Ombudsman Scheme (*Clark v In Focus Asset Management and Tax Solutions Ltd* [2014] EWCA Civ 118, [2014] PNLR 19). It applies where an order is made, whether by consent or after argument (*Lennon v Birmingham City Council* [2001] EWCA Civ 435, LTL 27/3/2001). While a consent order is treated like a judgment, if it does not in terms set out the issues compromised, the court needs to consider the circumstances to find the issues implicitly compromised for the purposes of issue estoppel (*South Somerset District Council v Tonstate (Yeovil Leisure) Ltd* [2009] EWHC 3308 (Ch), LTL 14/12/2009). Issue estoppel also prevents a party reopening a liability issue after a judgment for damages to be decided by the court on the assessment of damages (*Item Software (UK) Ltd v Fassihi* (2003) LTL 28/1/2003).

Issue estoppel does not apply where the court declines jurisdiction, or if a claim is struck out as a sanction, or if a claim is discontinued (*Pople v Evans* [1969] 2 Ch 255). Nor does it apply to rulings on interim applications or hearings for directions, because these are not designed to be conclusive (*Autofocus Ltd v Accident Exchange Ltd* [2010] EWCA Civ 788, LTL 14/7/2010). There is no issue estoppel if there is no definitive decision on the issue in the first claim (*Tannu v Moosajee* [2003] EWCA Civ 815, LTL 20/6/2003). Issue estoppel does not apply in criminal proceedings (*Director of Public Prosecutions v Humphreys* [1977] AC 1), subject to a limited exception relating to habeas corpus (*R v Governor of Brixton Prison, ex parte Osman* [1991] 1 WLR 281). Judicial review proceedings cannot found an issue estoppel (*R v Secretary of State for the Environment, ex parte Hackney London Borough Council* [1983] 1 WLR 524). The facts on which a prosecution for murder was based but which resulted in an acquittal can be relied upon in the First-tier Tribunal (Immigration and Asylum) when considering a deportation order to show that the individual facing deportation had in fact committed the murder (*R (V (Colombia)) v Asylum and Immigration Tribunal* [2010] EWCA Civ 491, LTL 27/5/2010). However, where subsequent proceedings are a collateral attack on the findings in judicial review proceedings, they can be struck out as an abuse of process based on relitigating matters found in the judicial review proceedings (*Eco-Power UK Ltd v Transport for London* [2010] EWHC 1683 (Admin), [2010] ACD 69, and see **33.15**).

Where the parties in two claims are not the same, issue estoppel does not apply (*Sweetman v Nathan* [2003] EWCA Civ 1115, [2004] PNLR 7), and the factual findings in the first claim are not admissible evidence in the second (*Hollington v F. Hewthorn and Co. Ltd* [1943] KB 587; see **49.95** and **49.100**). A person claiming title to property is treated as being privy to the interests of those through whom title is claimed, and so will be bound by the decision in proceedings in which any predecessor in title was a party, but only if judgment in those proceedings was given before the presently claimed title was acquired. A person who purchased title before judgment is not regarded as a privy (*Powell v Wiltshire* [2004] EWCA Civ 534, [2005] QB 117).

Issue which should have been raised in earlier proceedings   It is an abuse of process to raise in **33.17** a second claim an issue which should have been raised against someone who was a party to earlier proceedings (*Henderson v Henderson* (1843) 3 Hare 100; *Talbot v Berkshire County Council* [1994] QB 290). Where it is alleged that an issue was or should have been raised in earlier proceedings, it is first necessary to consider whether issue estoppel applies, which can only be negatived by fraud or collusion (see **33.16**). It is only if there is no such estoppel that it is appropriate to consider whether raising the issue now would be an abuse of process under the principle in *Henderson v Henderson* (see *Coflexip SA v Stolt Offshore MS Ltd* [2004] EWCA Civ 213, [2004] FSR 34; *Kennecott Utah Copper Corporation v Minet Ltd* [2003] EWCA Civ 905, [2004] 1 All ER (Comm) 60; *Bim Kemi AB v Blackburn Chemicals Ltd* [2004] EWCA Civ 1490, [2005] EuLR 176). The judge dealing with such an application has to make a decision involving the assessment of a large number of factors to which there is only one answer: it is not a matter of discretion (*Aldi Stores Ltd v WSP Group plc* [2007] EWCA Civ 1260, [2008] 1 WLR 748). An appellate court will be reluctant to allow an appeal where the judge below had balanced the relevant factors (*Stuart v Goldberg* [2008] EWCA Civ 2, [2008] 1 WLR 823; *Challinor v Staffordshire County Council* [2011] EWCA Civ 90, LTL 9/2/2011). There is no distinction between situations where the earlier case is concluded either by settlement or trial (*Aldi Stores Ltd v WSP Group plc*). There can be cases, like *Kotonou v National Westminster Bank plc* [2010] EWHC 1659 (Ch), [2011] 1 All ER (Comm) 1164, where it is an abuse of process to put forward assertions of fact which are contrary to findings in earlier proceedings concerning the same factual matters. In *Johnson v Gore Wood and Co.* [2002] 2 AC 1 the House of Lords held that when considering whether a second claim is an abuse of process a broad, merits-based judgment has to be made, taking into account all the public and private interests involved, and all the facts. A second claim should be struck out only if, in all the circumstances, it should, rather than merely could, have been brought in the first claim. Mr Johnson was a shareholder in a company which had sued the defendant solicitors. That first claim was settled, with the compromise agreement containing a clause seeking to limit the defendants' liability to Mr Johnson personally. Mr Johnson then sued the solicitors in his personal capacity, and the defendants applied to strike out his personal claim as an abuse. Certain heads of claim were struck out, as they merely reflected losses suffered by the company in which Mr Johnson held shares, but others were arguably recoverable by Mr Johnson in his own right, and it was held that even though his personal claim could have been joined with the first claim by the company, it was not on the facts an abuse to have brought the personal claim by separate proceedings. Contrast *Giles v Rhind* [2002] EWCA Civ 1428, [2003] Ch 18, where a shareholder's claim was allowed to proceed because it was not reflective of the company's loss. The question of reflective losses is discussed further at **14.29** and **14.30**.

In *Dexter Ltd v Vlieland-Boddy* [2003] EWCA Civ 14, 147 SJLB 117, the defendant in the second claim was the brother of the defendant in an earlier claim based on the same facts. It was held that the burden was on the defendant to show that the second claim was abusive. Applying a broad merits-based approach, taking into account the fact the defendants were different and that the first claim resulted in an unsatisfied judgment, the second claim was allowed to proceed. In *De Crittenden v Bayliss* [2005] EWCA Civ 1425, LTL 13/10/2005, the claimant became aware of an alternative cause of action after issuing the first claim, and issued a second claim form. It was held that the second claim should have been brought by amending the first claim, so issuing separate proceedings was an abuse of process. Where permission to amend to claim an account of profits was refused in a first action, it was an abuse of process to bring a second claim for damages under the principle in *Wrotham Park Estate Co. Ltd v Parkside Homes Ltd* [1974] 1 WLR 798 (*WWF-World Wide Fund for Nature v World Wrestling Federation Entertainment Inc.* [2007] EWCA Civ 286, [2008] 1 WLR 445).

It will only be an abuse of process to challenge the findings in the earlier claim if it would be manifestly unfair to a party in the later claim for the issues to be relitigated, or if relitigating will bring the administration of justice into disrepute (*Secretary of State for Trade and Industry v Bairstow* [2003] EWCA Civ 321, [2004] Ch 1), or if the later proceedings amount to unjust harassment or oppression of the defendant (*Meretz Investments NV v ACP Ltd* [2006] EWHC 74 (Ch), [2007] Ch 197). *Secretary of State for Trade and Industry v Bairstow* provides a means of circumventing the rule in *Hollington v F. Hewthorn and Co. Ltd* [1943] 1 KB 587 (see **33.16**) on the theory that, if an abuse of process is established, the party against whom the previous finding was made is prevented from asserting facts contrary to the previous finding (*Conlon v Simms* [2006] EWCA Civ 1749, [2008] 1 WLR 484 at [177] per Ward LJ). In applying the principles in *Secretary of State for Trade and Industry v Bairstow* the court should be slower in preventing a party from continuing to deny serious charges after a previous adverse finding by way of defence, than in preventing a party from initiating proceedings for the purpose of launching a collateral attack on such a previous finding (*Conlon v Simms*). In *Conlon v Simms* the court refused to strike out a solicitor's defence in a claim by the solicitor's former partners which alleged they had been induced to enter into partnership with him by fraudulent misrepresentations. It would have been unfair to allow the claimant to raise findings of the Solicitors Disciplinary Tribunal in previous disciplinary proceedings against the solicitor without having to prove its case, which would have been the position if the defence had been struck out as an abuse of process. Where an issue, which is raised on taking accounts following judgment, was before the trial judge, but was not decided definitively, the question is whether a party is misusing or abusing the process of the court in raising the issue again (*Tannu v Moosajee* [2003] EWCA Civ 815, LTL 20/6/2003). Keeping a second claim secret while prosecuting the first claim may well be an abuse. In assessing the balance to be struck it is not significant that large parts of the particulars of claim have been adopted from the first claim. Delay in bringing the second claim is not in itself relevant, nor is weakness on the merits not coming within the test for summary judgment (*Stuart v Goldberg*).

Where the first and second claims are of a different nature, compelling reasons are required before the later claim will be struck out (*Specialist Group International Ltd v Deakin* [2001] EWCA Civ 77, LTL 23/5/2001). In *Heffernan v Grangewood Securities Ltd* [2001] EWCA Civ 1082, LTL 19/6/2001, proceedings were commenced by a mortgagee which were compromised in 1995 on terms that the mortgagors would pay the arrears over the remaining term of the mortgage. In 1997 the mortgagors commenced their own claim seeking a declaration that the original mortgage was not binding. This second claim was struck out because the mortgagors should have raised this issue in the first claim.

33.18 **Estoppel preventing application to strike out** In *Johnson v Gore Wood and Co.* [2002] 2 AC 1 the House of Lords considered whether a court should refuse to strike out a second claim, which is alleged to be an abusive relitigation of an earlier claim, because of the defendant's previous conduct, in particular where the second claim was taken into consideration when reaching a settlement of the first claim. This is best considered as an estoppel by representation, with the key question being whether it would be unconscionable for the defendant to apply for striking out.

Fresh evidence   Claims have been allowed even though they involve questioning the deci- **33.19**
sion of a court of competent jurisdiction if fresh evidence has come to light since the earlier
decision, or where the second claim is a professional negligence claim against the solicitors
acting for the claimant in the first claim, see *Walpole v Partridge and Wilson* [1994] QB 106.
A damages claim was permitted to proceed, subject to stringent conditions, in *Sweetman v
Shepherd* [2000] CPLR 378, despite the fact that it could have been brought by contribution
proceedings in an earlier claim.

Reviving earlier claim   In *Buckland v Palmer* [1984] 1 WLR 1109 it was held to be an abuse of **33.20**
process to commence a second claim in respect of the same cause of action as was raised in an
earlier claim. The claimant's car had been damaged in a motor accident. Repairs cost £1,142.
She claimed on her insurance, and brought proceedings against the defendant claiming the
£50 excess not paid by her insurer. This claim was stayed when she accepted a payment into
court. The insurer then commenced a second claim in the name of the claimant claiming
£1,092, and this claim was struck out as an abuse of process. However, it was possible for the
insurer to apply for the first claim to be revived (as it had not proceeded to judgment) and for
the original claim to be amended to include the full costs of repairs. A comment was made in
Bradford and Bingley Building Society v Seddon [1999] 1 WLR 1482 that abuse of process cases of this
nature will perhaps be less frequent under the CPR, because of the requirement that the
claimant must sign a statement of truth in relation to the second claim, which might be difficult given an earlier, inconsistent, claim.

Settlement acting as a bar to later proceedings

Settling a claim can act as a bar to later proceedings. In *Jameson v Central Electricity Generating* **33.21**
Board [2000] 1 AC 455, the deceased accepted £80,000 from his former employer in 'full and
final settlement and satisfaction of all the causes of action' set out in his statement of claim
against his employer in respect of asbestos-related disease. After his death his widow brought
a claim against the Board as the owner of premises where the deceased had been exposed to
asbestos. It was held, on the assumption that the employer and the Board were concurrent and
not joint tortfeasors, and as the settlement could not be construed as only a partial settlement,
that the compromise with the employer operated to extinguish the claims against all the tortfeasors. The claim against the Board was therefore struck out. *Jameson v Central Electricity
Generating Board* was interpreted by the House of Lords in *Heaton v AXA Equity and Law Life
Assurance Society plc* [2002] UKHL 15, [2002] 2 AC 329, as laying down the following principles:

(a) A claim for unliquidated damages, whether in contract or tort, is capable of being fixed in
    a specific sum of money either on judgment or by agreement.
(b) Although a judgment invariably fixes the full measure of the claimant's loss, whether a
    compromise fixes the full measure depends on the proper construction of the compromise
    agreement. Lord Bingham of Cornhill said that in construing a compromise agreement
    for this purpose one significant factor is whether the claimant has expressly reserved the
    right to sue other persons, although the absence of such a reservation is by no means con-
    clusive in favour of an argument that other claims are extinguished.
(c) If a compromise, on its proper construction, fixes the full measure of the claimant's loss,
    the compromise extinguishes the claim so that other claims for the same damage cannot
    be pursued against other persons, whether in contract or tort.

The question for the court is whether on its true construction the settlement agreement
applies to claims of the type raised in the subsequent proceedings (*Satyam Computer Services Ltd
v Upaid Systems Ltd* [2008] EWCA Civ 487, [2008] 2 All ER (Comm) 465). In *Steenberg v Enterprise Inns
plc* [2010] EWCA Civ 201, LTL 10/3/2010, a nuisance claim arising out of the use of the kitchen
and an extractor fan at a public house was compromised in 2001 with a consent order which
provided it was 'in full and final settlement of all claims by either party howsoever arising of
which either party are aware at the date hereof'. The present claim involved the use of the

kitchen and compressors located outside the kitchen at the same public house. The parties were also the same as in the earlier claim. The actual nuisances complained of, however, all post-dated the 2001 consent order, so they could not have been claims that the claimants were 'aware of' when they signed the consent order, and so the present claim was not barred by the consent order. In *Henley v Bloom* [2010] EWCA Civ 202, [2010] 1 WLR 1770, a consent order 'in full and final settlement' of any claim the claimant might have in respect of improvements he made to a leased flat was held not to act as a bar to a disrepair claim.

Following *Heaton v AXA Equity and Law Life Assurance Society plc*, in *Cape and Dalgleish v Fitzgerald* [2002] UKHL 16, LTL 25/4/2002, it was held that a settlement between the original claimant and the defendant was not intended or understood to represent full compensation, so the original claimant had been able to commence a second claim against another party (Cape). The consequence was that Cape was then entitled, in a third claim, to seek a contribution against the defendant in respect of the damages Cape was ordered to pay the claimant in the second claim.

Although a party can agree to release claims or rights of which he is unaware if appropriate language is used in the agreement, the court will be very slow to accept that this is the effect of a release (*Capital Trust Investments Ltd v Radio Design TJ AB* [2002] EWCA Civ 135, [2002] 2 All ER 159). Express words are required before a settlement agreement will be construed as applying to fraud claims (*Satyam Computer Services Ltd v Upaid Systems Ltd*).

In *Minton v Kenburgh Investments (Northern) Ltd* [2000] CPLR 551 liquidators brought misfeasance proceedings under the Insolvency Act 1986, s. 212, against former directors alleging breach of fiduciary duty, which were compromised with sums payable in full and final settlement of the proceedings. The liquidators then brought proceedings against the company's former solicitors arising out of the same transaction as had formed the basis of the first claim for breach of their duties to the company. It was held that as the causes of action were different in the two claims the *Jameson* principle did not apply.

Impossible to have a fair trial

33.22   In *Al Rawi v Security Service* [2011] UKSC 34, [2012] 1 AC 531, the Supreme Court held that in the absence of statutory authority, or possibly consent by the parties, there is no inherent jurisdiction to permit a closed material procedure (this has subsequently been placed on a statutory footing, see at **50.83**). The claimants alleged the defendants were complicit in their detention and ill-treatment at Guantánamo Bay. The defendants said a great deal of the material relevant to their defence was protected by public interest immunity. It was held there is no inherent jurisdiction to permit material protected in the public interest to be deployed without disclosure to the other side. In such cases both sides are faced with three possibilities:

(a)   proceeding with the case without the material protected by public interest immunity;

(b)   abandoning the claim or conceding liability (depending on which side's case is more severely damaged by the absence of the material); or

(c)   applying to the court to stay or strike out the claim on the ground that through neither side's fault a fair trial is not possible. This alternative was recognised by *Carnduff v Rock* [2001] EWCA Civ 680, [2001] 1 WLR 1786 (where a claim by a police informer for contractual payments was struck out because it would have required evidence of special police operations which were protected by public interest immunity), and approved by Lord Clarke of Stone-cum-Ebony JSC in *Al Rawi v Security Service* at [159].

OBSTRUCTING THE JUST DISPOSAL OF THE PROCEEDINGS

33.23   The second half of CPR, r. 3.4(2)(b), allows the court to strike out a statement of case which obstructs the just disposal of the proceedings. This is expanded upon by **PD 3A, para. 1.5,**

which provides that a claim may come within **r. 3.4(2)(b)** if it is vexatious, scurrilous or obviously ill-founded. Generally, the court will know a claim of this kind when it sees it.

Whether a statement of case is vexatious depends 'on all the circumstances of the case: the categories are not closed and the considerations of public policy and the interests of justice may be very material' (per Stuart-Smith LJ in *Ashmore v British Coal Corporation* [1990] 2 QB 338). The applicant in *Ashmore v British Coal Corporation* was one of 1,500 women claiming they were employed on less favourable terms than certain male comparators. Fourteen cases were selected for determination, and the eventual finding was in favour of the employer. The applicant then sought to proceed with her claim. Although the previous determination was not strictly binding, the applicant's claim was struck out as being frivolous and vexatious. Pleadings under the old system have also been struck out on this ground where a party has been joined merely to obtain disclosure of documents or costs (*Burstall v Beyfus* (1884) 26 ChD 35) or where a claim is a disguised action for gaming debts (*Day v William Hill (Park Lane) Ltd* [1949] 1 KB 632).

Poor drafting

A party confronted with a poorly drafted statement of case cannot insist on it being amended, **33.24** but can take the initiative by applying to have the whole or offending parts of the statement of case struck out. If the statement of case fails to comply with the principles discussed in **chapter 24**, it is likely to obstruct the just disposal of the claim. Statements of case which fail to inform the other side of the case it will have to meet tend to be described as 'embarrassing' (a term that does not appear in the CPR). A statement of case that was unreasonably vague and incoherent was struck out as an abuse of process and for obstructing the just disposal of the claim in *Towler v Wills* [2010] EWHC 1209 (Comm), LTL 27/5/2010.

Rassam v Budge [1893] 1 QB 571 concerned a claim for damages for slander. Instead of pleading to the words alleged by the claimant, the defence set out the defendant's rather different version of what he had said, and alleged the words he alleged he had spoken were true. These allegations were struck out as tending to prejudice the fair trial of the claim, because they left it unclear whether the issue was whether the words complained of by the claimant were spoken and published, or whether those words were true.

In *Philipps v Philipps* (1878) 4 QBD 127 Cotton LJ said, at p. 139:

in my opinion it is absolutely essential that the pleading, not to be embarrassing to the defendants, should state those facts which will put the defendants on their guard and tell them what they have to meet when the case comes on for trial.

Deutsche Morgan Grenfell Group plc v Commissioners of Inland Revenue [2006] UKHL 49, [2007] 1 AC 558, was a claim for restitution of money paid to the Inland Revenue. The particulars of claim sought repayment of sums which 'include but are not limited to' certain payments set out in a schedule. As this only stated part of the sum actually sought, Lord Walker of Gestingthorpe said it was imprecise and unsatisfactory, but the defect could be cured by a request for further information (at [148]). Bearing in mind the overriding objective, an overly pedantic approach should be avoided. As Millett LJ said in *Paragon Finance plc v D. B. Thakerar and Co.* [1999] 1 All ER 400 at p. 405:

The pleading of unnecessary allegations or the addition of further instances or better particulars do not amount to a distinct cause of action. The selection of the material facts to define the cause of action must be made at the highest level of abstraction.

A defence will be struck out if it does not make clear how much of the claim is admitted and how much is denied (*British and Colonial Land Association Ltd v Foster* (1887) 4 TLR 574). Mere prolixity or setting out of inconsistent claims or defences would be unlikely to result in striking out (see, for example, *Re Morgan* (1887) 35 ChD 492), although costs sanctions may be imposed if the case is protracted as a result.

POWERS AFTER A STRIKING-OUT APPLICATION

33.25 When a court strikes out a statement of case it may enter such judgment as the successful party appears entitled to (**PD 3A, para.** 4.2) and make any consequential order it considers appropriate (**CPR, r.** 3.4(3)). If the court strikes out a claimant's statement of case, and it considers the claim was totally without merit, that fact must be recorded in the court's order, and the court must consider whether to make a civil restraint order (see **r.** 3.4(6) and **14.55**). An appeal was designated as being totally without merit where the appellant was seeking to relitigate an issue that had repeatedly been decided against him in *Shepherd v Official Receiver* [2010] EWHC 681 (Ch), LTL 24/3/2010. If a claim survives a striking-out application, the court may dispense with the need to file directions questionnaires, may allocate the claim to a track, and make case management directions (**PD 26, para.** 2.4).

Loss of QOCS protection

33.26 Costs protection under qualified one-way costs shifting (see **chapter 69**) is lost if the claim is struck out as disclosing no reasonable grounds for bringing the proceedings, or if the proceedings are an abuse of process or if the conduct of the claimant or those acting on the claimant's behalf is likely to obstruct the just disposal of the proceedings (**CPR, r.** 44.15). Loss of costs protection under **r.** 44.15 is obligatory (unlike the discretionary loss of costs protection under **r.** 44.16 for claims that are fundamentally dishonest).

COMMENCING A SECOND CLAIM

33.27 In *Janov v Morris* [1981] 1 WLR 1389 it was held to be an abuse of process to commence a second claim after a first claim based on the same cause of action had been struck out for failing to comply with an unless order where no explanation was advanced for the failure to comply with the unless order. As explained by Dunn LJ, the second claim could be an abuse where there had been intentional and contumacious default, for example, disobedience of a peremptory order, or where there had been inordinate and inexcusable delay. Intentional and contumacious default can also be established where there has been a wholesale disregard of court orders (*Arbuthnot Latham Bank Ltd v Trafalgar Holdings Ltd* [1998] 1 WLR 1426). For cases applying these principles in the context of the current rules on sanctions, see **48.52** to **48.54**.

Where a claim is struck out for delay, the claimant is entitled to issue fresh proceedings based on the same cause of action, which will not have been determined on its merits. Such a second claim may be met by an application to strike out if the limitation period has expired. Even if the limitation period has not expired, the court has the power to strike out the second claim as an abuse of process if doing so accords with the overriding objective, particularly on the ground that it constitutes a misuse of the court's resources. See *Securum Finance Ltd v Ashton* [2001] Ch 291, where the second claim raised a different cause of action, and was allowed to continue. In *Collins v CPS Fuels Ltd* [2001] EWCA Civ 1597, LTL 9/10/2001, the first claim was struck out for repeated breaches of orders for disclosure of documents, and because the claimant's solicitors failed to attend two case management conferences. A second claim was then issued, making the same allegations. There were no limitation difficulties because the claimant was a child. The judge balanced the prejudice to the claimant in having to sue her solicitors and the possibility of the original allegations being fairly dealt with, against the conduct giving rise to the first claim being struck out and the effect of the delays, and concluded that the second claim should be struck out. This decision was approved on appeal, where it was held that the decision to strike out has to be made by balancing all the competing arguments and reasons. Putting a gloss on this exercise, by saying (as previous authorities have said) that the claimant has to establish 'special reasons', grounds that are 'good enough' or 'sufficient reasons', was regarded as unhelpful.

It was argued for the defendants in *Aktas v Adepta* [2010] EWCA Civ 1170, [2011] QB 894, that the above principles should, under the CPR, also apply to situations where the claimant failed to serve the first claim in time. Reliance was placed on *Securum Finance Ltd v Ashton* where Chadwick LJ at [34] said:

The position, now, is that the court must address the application to strike out the second action with the overriding objective of the Civil Procedure Rules in mind — and must consider whether the claimant's wish to have a 'second bite of the cherry' outweighs the need to allot its own limited resources to other cases.... It is an abuse because it is a misuse of the court's limited resources.

This was rejected in *Aktas v Adepta*, where Rix LJ concluded that a mere failure to serve a claim form in time is not an abuse of process, and never has been. Real abuse of process cases in the *Janov v Morris* sense require intentional and contumacious default, inordinate and inexcusable delay, or possibly a wholesale disregard of court orders. Negligence in the first claim is not an abuse of process, and to hold otherwise would have been to disregard the decision in *Horton v Sadler* [2006] UKHL 27, [2007] 1 AC 307, that in a personal injuries claim it is possible for the court to disapply the primary limitation period under the Limitation Act 1980, s. 33, in a second claim form case.

Endorsing the rule laid down in *Gardner v Southwark London Borough Council (No. 2)* [1996] 1 WLR 561, **CPR, r. 3.4(4)**, provides that where a claim is struck out and the claimant is ordered to pay the defendant's costs, if the claimant commences a second claim (within the limitation period) arising out of substantially the same facts as those forming the basis of the struck-out claim, the defendant may apply for a stay of the second claim until the costs of the first claim have been paid. In *Investment Invoice Financing Ltd v Limehouse Board Mills Ltd* [2006] EWCA Civ 9, [2006] 1 WLR 985, a creditor company presented a winding-up petition against the present defendant based on unpaid invoices, which was dismissed with an order for costs against the creditor company. The costs order was never paid. The creditor company assigned some of the invoices to the claimant, which brought the present claim against the defendant. This was regarded as equivalent to the situation in *Gardner v Southwark London Borough Council (No. 2)*. The present claim was therefore an abuse of process, and was stayed until the costs of the earlier proceedings were paid. A stay will not be granted where the two sets of proceedings do not have a sufficient degree of similarity (*Star Reefers Pool Inc. v JFC Group* [2011] EWCA Civ 1052, LTL 13/9/2011, a case on what is now **r. 52.18(1)(c)**).

Commentary

Chapter 34   Summary Judgment

The following procedural checklists are relevant to this chapter:

Procedural checklist 22   Application by a party for summary judgment
Procedural checklist 23   Proposal by court for order for summary judgment

INTRODUCTION

34.1   In cases where the defendant fails to defend it is usually possible to enter a default judgment (see **chapter 20**). Where there is no real defence, a defendant may go through the motions of defending in order to delay the time when judgment may be entered. It is possible for defendants to put up the pretence of having a real defence to such an extent that some cases run all the way through to trial before judgment can be entered. The CPR provide several ways of preventing this happening. The court can use its power to strike out (see **chapter 33**) to knock out hopeless defences, such as those that simply do not amount to a legal defence to a claim. Entering summary judgment is a related procedure, and is used where a purported defence can be shown to have no real prospect of success and there is no other compelling reason why the case should be disposed of at trial. Indeed, **PD 3A, para. 1.7**, recognises that there will be cases where applications for summary judgment and striking out may be sought in the alternative. Where a defence includes bare denials, it may be appropriate to strike out the offending paragraphs under **CPR, r. 3.4(2)(a)**, and to grant summary judgment under **r. 24.2** on the parts of the claim denied (*Clancy Consulting Ltd v Derwent Holdings Ltd* [2010] EWHC 762 (TCC), LTL 21/4/2010).

The procedure for entering summary judgment is not limited to use by claimants against defendants. Defendants may apply for summary judgment to attack weak claims brought by claimants. Further, summary judgment can be used by the court of its own initiative to perform the important function of stopping weak cases from proceeding. The procedure can also be used for the purpose of obtaining a summary determination of some of the issues in a case, thereby reducing the complexity of the trial.

Many applications under the Companies Acts are made on a summary basis, usually on the substantive hearing of a Part 8 claim (see **chapter 85**). It is also possible for these applications to be made by way of summary judgment applications (*Oxford Legal Group Ltd v Sibbasbridge Services plc* [2008] EWCA Civ 387, [2008] Bus LR 1244).

TIME AT WHICH THE APPLICATION MAY BE MADE

Summary judgment can be applied for by a claimant or a defendant (see **procedural checklist 22**) or can be proposed by the court of its own initiative (see **34.5** and **procedural checklist 23**). **34.2**

A claimant may apply for summary judgment only after the defendant has filed either an acknowledgment of service or a defence (**CPR, r. 24.4(1)**). If the defendant fails to do either of these within the time limited by the CPR, the claimant may enter a default judgment, which, depending on the nature of the claim, may require the court's permission (see **chapter 20**). By analogy with **r. 25.2(2)(c)**, a defendant likewise can only apply for summary judgment after either filing an acknowledgment of service or a defence.

Where the claimant has failed to comply with **PD Pre-action Conduct and Protocols** or any relevant pre-action protocol, an application for summary judgment will not normally be entertained before the defence has been filed, or the time for doing so has expired (**PD 24, para. 2(6)**).

Applications for summary judgment should normally be made in the period between acknowledgment of service and filing of the applicant's directions questionnaire (**PD 26, para. 5.3(1)**). This is normally the appropriate time, because, if the other side have no realistic prospects of success, entering summary judgment early prevents unnecessary costs being incurred. Question D in the directions questionnaire (form N181) specifically asks whether there is any pending application for summary judgment. If for any reason the application is not made before allocation, there is still a general obligation to apply as soon as it becomes apparent that it is desirable to do so (**PD 23A, para. 2.7**).

Under the old rules there was nothing to prevent a late application for summary judgment (see, for example, *Brinks Ltd v Abu-Saleh (No. 1)* [1995] 1 WLR 1478), but as a practical matter the judge dealing with a late application might well have felt there was a lack of conviction on the part of the applicant if the application was significantly delayed. For summary judgment at trial, see **61.37**.

Summary judgment applications made before filing the defence

34.3   If the application is made after filing an acknowledgment of service, but before filing of the defence, there is no need to file a defence before the hearing (**CPR, r. 24.4(2)**). At that stage the court will give directions, which will include providing a date for filing the defence. The permissive wording of the rule confirms *Natural Resources Inc. v Origin Clothing Ltd* [1995] FSR 280, in which it was held that there is nothing to prevent a defendant from serving a defence in the period before the hearing if the defendant chooses to do so.

Summary judgment applications made before allocation to a track

34.4   PD 26, para. 5.3(2), provides that where a party makes an application for summary judgment before the claim has been allocated to a track the court will not allocate the claim before hearing the application. If a party files a directions questionnaire stating an intention to apply for summary judgment but has not yet made an application, the judge will usually direct the listing of an allocation hearing (**para. 5.3(3) and (4)**). The summary judgment application may be heard at the allocation hearing if the application notice has been issued and served in sufficient time.

Hearings fixed by the court of its own initiative

34.5   The rules specifically mention that the court may fix a summary judgment hearing of its own initiative (**CPR, r. 24.4(3)**), and doing so may further the overriding objective, which includes deciding promptly which issues need full investigation and trial, and accordingly disposing summarily of the others (**r. 1.4(2)(c)**). If the court is minded to make use of this power, it is most likely to do so on the initial scrutiny at the track allocation stage shortly after filing of the defence. If the court uses the power, it will not allocate the case to a track, but instead it will fix a hearing, giving the parties 14 days' notice and informing them of the issues it proposes to decide (**PD 26, para. 5.4**).

DEFENDANT'S APPLICATION FOR SUMMARY JUDGMENT: NO DEFAULT JUDGMENT

34.6   Where a defendant has applied for summary judgment against a claimant, the claimant cannot obtain a default judgment until the summary judgment application has been disposed of (**CPR, r. 12.3(3)(a)**).

EXCLUDED PROCEEDINGS

34.7   Under **CPR, r. 24.3(2)**, an application for summary judgment cannot be brought against the defendant in:

(a)   residential possession proceedings against a mortgagor or a tenant or person holding over whose occupancy is protected by the Rent Act 1977 or the Housing Act 1988; or

(b)   Admiralty claims *in rem*.

The Crown's exemption from summary judgment was repealed by the Civil Procedure (Modification of Crown Proceedings Act 1947) Order 2005, SI 2005/2712, art. 8.

In applications against claimants there are no excluded types of proceedings (**CPR, r. 24.3(1)**).

PROCEDURE

34.8   The general rules on making interim applications (see **chapter 32**) apply on making an application for summary judgment, with certain refinements. The application is made by application notice, which must be supported by evidence (**CPR, r. 25.3(2)**). The evidence in support is most likely to be contained either in the application notice, or in a separate witness statement.

The facts supporting the claim will have been verified by a statement of truth included in the particulars of claim. The evidence in support of an application by a claimant will have to state a belief that there is no defence with a reasonable prospect of success. It may be prudent to go further and to give details of the background facts and to exhibit relevant documentation to show there is no reasonable defence. On an application by the defendant there may or may not be a filed defence. If not, clearly the evidence will have to explain why the claim is unlikely to succeed, and will probably have to go into the background in some detail.

Instead of the usual notice period of three clear days which applies to most types of interim application, the notice period in applications for summary judgment is 14 clear days (**r. 24.4(3)**). The 14-day period of notice may be varied by practice directions (**r. 24.4(4)**), and has been shortened for specific performance claims (see **34.48**).

The respondent must file and serve any evidence in reply at least seven clear days before the hearing (**r. 24.5(1)**). The application notice must inform the respondent of this time limit (**PD 24, para. 2(5)**). If the applicant wishes to respond to the respondent's evidence, the further evidence must be served and filed at least three clear days before the hearing of the application (**CPR, r. 24.5(2)**).

In cases where the hearing is fixed by the court on its own initiative, all parties must file and serve their evidence at least seven clear days before the return day, and if they want to respond to their opponents' evidence, that must be done at least three clear days before the return day (**r. 24.5(3)**). Where there are cross-applications, one challenging the court's jurisdiction, the other seeking summary judgment, the court is entitled to proceed immediately to the summary judgment application after determining the jurisdictional challenge (*Moloobhoy v Kanani* [2013] EWCA Civ 600, LTL 30/5/2013).

ORDERS AVAILABLE

PD 24, para. 5.1, says that the range of orders available on a summary judgment application include: **34.9**

(a) giving judgment on the claim;
(b) striking out or dismissal of the claim — the court cannot dismiss the claim unless the claimant has been given notice and an opportunity to address the court and place before it any relevant material (*P & O Nedlloyd BV v Arab Metals Co. (No. 2)* [2006] EWCA Civ 1717, [2007] 1 WLR 2288, per Moore-Bick LJ at [67]);
(c) dismissal of the application; and
(d) making a conditional order (see **34.34**).

This is not a comprehensive list (note the use of the word 'include' in **PD 24, para. 5.1**), and the court can make other orders. These include:

(e) allowing the claim to continue to trial on condition that a party pay money into court as security for costs (*Olatawura v Abiloye* [2002] EWCA Civ 998, [2003] 1 WLR 275, relying on **r. 3.1(3), (5) and (6)**);
(f) making summary declarations (*BBC Worldwide Ltd v Bee Load Ltd* [2007] EWHC 134 (Comm), *The Times*, 15 March 2007);
(g) entering summary judgment subject to a stay of execution. This may be ordered where there is a counterclaim (not amounting to a set-off) which is linked to the claim (see **34.36**, sub-paragraph (b)). More generally, there needs to be some unresolved matter which may mean it is unjust for payment to be required immediately, particularly where

Commentary

the party required to make the payment may not be able to recover it, for example, because of the likely insolvency of the party receiving the payment. In *Mead General Building Ltd v Dartmoor Properties Ltd* [2009] EWHC 200 (TCC), [2009] BCC 510, it was held that the court could order a stay of execution of summary judgment on a claim to enforce an adjudicator's award (see **34.20**) if the claimant has solvency difficulties (these cases proceed on the principle 'pay now, argue later', so there is always the possibility that the money will have to be paid back). The nature of the claimant's financial difficulties is relevant, as is the question of the extent to which those difficulties have been caused by the defendant's failure to pay on the contract in question;

(h) entering summary judgment for such part of the sum for which there is no defence, with dismissal of the application as to the balance; and

(i) entering summary judgment on particular issues under **CPR, r. 24.2**. This is most appropriate where resolving the issue or issues will resolve or help to resolve the litigation (*Kent v Griffiths (No. 3)* [2001] QB 36 at p. 51). The court must apply the overriding objective, and may consider that where there are connected issues, some of which should go to trial, summary judgment should be refused on the others as well (*Redevco Properties v Mount Cook Land Ltd* [2002] EWHC 1647 (Ch), LTL 30/7/2002). The court should be slow to entertain an application for summary judgment on certain issues where there is going to be a full trial in any event, particularly where dealing with such an application may delay (because of possible appeals) the final disposal of the claim (*Partco Group Ltd v Wragg* [2002] EWCA Civ 594, [2002] 2 Lloyd's Rep 343 at [27]).

In *Costain Ltd v Wilson* [2007] EWHC 713 (QB), LTL 12/4/2007, it was held there was no real prospect of success on D2's defence on a claim to recover sums obtained from the claimant on false invoices, where the proceeds had been divided equally between D1 and D2. The claimant was in the process of negotiating a settlement with D1. In order to avoid double recovery, while the claimant was strictly entitled to judgment in the full amount against D2, summary judgment was entered for half that amount in order to set a realistic unarguable recovery target. It is doubtful whether this is legitimate. Once a decision has been made that there is no prospect of success, the applicant should be given the whole of the remedy that follows as a matter of law.

TEST FOR ENTERING SUMMARY JUDGMENT

34.10 **CPR, r. 24.2**, provides:

The court may give summary judgment against a claimant or defendant on the whole of a claim or on a particular issue if—

(a) it considers that—
  (i) that claimant has no real prospect of succeeding on the claim or issue; or
  (ii) that defendant has no real prospect of successfully defending the claim or issue; and
(b) there is no other compelling reason why the case or issue should be disposed of at a trial.

An application for summary judgment is decided applying the test of whether the respondent has a case with a real prospect of success, which is considered having regard to the overriding objective of dealing with the case justly. This has been said to be consistent with the need for a fair trial under **art. 6(1)** of the European Convention on Human Rights (*Three Rivers District Council v Bank of England (No. 3)* [2001] UKHL 16, [2003] 2 AC 1). Whether there is a real prospect of success is the same test as that applied in applications to set aside default judgments (see **20.13** and *E. D. and F. Man Liquid Products Ltd v Patel* [2003] EWCA Civ 472, [2003] CPLR 384). The question is whether there is a real prospect of success on the case as pleaded in the particulars of claim (*Credit Suisse AG v Arabian Aircraft and Equipment Leasing Co EC* [2013] EWCA Civ 1169, [2014] CP Rep 4). No adjustments are made to the test for summary judgment where one party is suffering from an inequality of arms (*Bank of Tokyo-Mitsubishi UFJ Ltd v Baskan Gida Sanayi ve Pazarlama AS* [2008] EWHC 659 (Ch), LTL 17/4/2008).

In *Swain v Hillman* [2001] 1 All ER 91 Lord Woolf MR said that the words 'no real prospect of succeeding' did not need any amplification as they spoke for themselves. The word 'real' directed the court to the need to see whether there was a realistic, as opposed to a fanciful, prospect of success. The phrase does not mean 'real and substantial' prospect of success. Nor does it mean that summary judgment will only be granted if the claim or defence is 'bound to be dismissed at trial'. Nor does it require compelling evidence, but simply enough evidence to raise a real prospect of a contrary case (*Korea National Insurance Corporation v Allianz Global Corporate and Specialty AG* [2007] EWCA Civ 1066, LTL 30/10/2007).

In *Bee v Jenson* [2006] EWHC 2534 (Comm), [2007] RTR 115, the court adopted the approach explained by Potter LJ in *E. D. and F. Man Liquid Products Ltd v Patel* [2003] EWCA Civ 472, [2003] CPLR 384 at [8]:

I regard the distinction between a realistic and fanciful prospect of success as appropriately reflecting the observation in [*Alpine Bulk Transport Co. Inc. v Saudi Eagle Shipping Co. Inc.* [1986] 2 Lloyd's Rep 221] that the defence sought to be argued must carry some degree of conviction. Both approaches require the defendant to have a case which is better than merely arguable, as was formerly the case under RSC ord. 14.

A claim may be fanciful where it is entirely without substance, or where it is clear beyond question that the statement of case is contradicted by all the documents or other material on which it is based (*Three Rivers District Council v Bank of England (No. 3)*). The judge should have regard to the witness statements and also to the question of whether the case is capable of being supplemented by evidence at trial (*Royal Brompton Hospital NHS Trust v Hammond* [2001] BLR 297). Where the respondent's evidence, taken at its highest, does not raise a possibility of a defence, but is in the realm of a mere (and distinctly improbable) possibility, it is right to enter summary judgment (*Akinleye v East Sussex Hospitals NHS Trust* [2008] EWHC 68 (QB), [2008] LS Law Medical 216). Conversely, where there is some prospect of success, summary judgment should be refused, and the court should not conduct a mini-trial into disputed questions of fact (*Cotton v Rickard Metals Inc.* [2008] EWHC 824 (QB), LTL 25/4/2008).

The question of whether there is a real prospect of success is not approached by applying the usual balance of probabilities standard of proof (*Royal Brompton Hospital NHS Trust v Hammond*). Many cases will succeed at trial, but will be unsuitable for summary judgment because there are complexities, disputes of fact, or further inquiries that need to be resolved through case management and trial before it can be said that the applicant should win on the balance of probabilities. Rather, summary judgment should only be entered where, on the untested written evidence, and whatever further evidence may be found in the future, there is no real prospect of success. Comments in *Director of the Assets Recovery Agency v Woodstock* [2006] EWCA Civ 741, LTL 18/5/2006, to the effect that the onus on the applicant is to establish its version on the balance of probabilities have to be understood in this context. This need for a case which will succeed no matter what further work is done on behalf of the respondent explains why summary judgment was refused in *Director of the Assets Recovery Agency v Woodstock* despite obvious weaknesses in the respondent's case because that case was not bound to be disbelieved. Applying a test of whether the claim is arguable will give grounds for appeal (*Sinclair v Chief Constable of West Yorkshire* (2000) LTL 12/12/2000).

In *E. D. and F. Man Liquid Products Ltd v Patel* Potter LJ at [6] regarded the terms 'real prospect' and 'realistic prospect' as interchangeable. Lord Woolf MR in *Swain v Hillman* said that summary judgment applications have to be kept within their proper role. They are not meant to dispense with the need for a trial where there are issues which should be considered at trial. Further, summary judgment hearings should not be mini-trials. They are simply summary hearings to dispose of cases where there is no real prospect of success. Without allowing the application to become a mini-trial, there are occasions when the court has to consider fairly voluminous evidence in order to understand the facts that are in issue (*Miles v ITV Networks Ltd* [2003] EWHC 3134 (Ch), LTL 9/12/2003).

Commentary

Burden of proof

34.11   In *E. D. and F. Man Liquid Products Ltd v Patel* [2003] EWCA Civ 472, [2003] CPLR 384, Potter LJ said at [9] that the burden of proof is on the applicant to show the respondent's case has no real prospect of success. Strictly this is no more than an obiter dictum, because the learned judge was dealing with an application to set aside a default judgment, and was contrasting his view of the burden of proof on the two types of application. A similar approach was taken in *Director of the Assets Recovery Agency v Woodstock* [2006] EWCA Civ 741, LTL 18/5/2006, where the Court of Appeal said that the onus is on the applicant. Tuckey LJ said that where the applicant establishes a prima facie case against the respondent, there is an evidential burden on the respondent to show a case answering that advanced by the applicant. A respondent who shows a prima facie case in answer should ordinarily be allowed to take the matter to trial.

Complex claims

34.12   Complex claims, cases relying on complex inferences of fact, and cases with issues involving mixed questions of law and fact where the law is complex are likely to be inappropriate for summary judgment (*Three Rivers District Council v Bank of England (No. 3)* [2001] UKHL 16, [2003] 2 AC 1; *Arkin v Borchard Lines Ltd (No. 2)* (2001) LTL 21/6/2001). The high standard of proof required at trial in fraud claims means that it will be difficult to succeed on a summary judgment application in such a case (*Allied Dunbar Assurance plc v Ireland* [2001] EWCA Civ 1129, LTL 12/6/2001).

If an application for summary judgment involves prolonged serious argument, the court should, as a rule, dismiss it without hearing the argument, unless it harbours doubt about the soundness of the statement of case and is satisfied that granting summary judgment would avoid the need for a trial or would substantially reduce the burden of the trial (*Three Rivers District Council v Bank of England (No. 3)*; *Partco Group Ltd v Wragg* [2002] EWCA Civ 594, [2002] 2 Lloyd's Rep 343 at [28]; *Equitable Life Assurance Society v Ernst and Young* [2003] EWCA Civ 1114, [2003] 2 BCLC 603). Despite this, judges do on occasion fully investigate complex applications for summary judgment, particularly where there is a suspicion that the respondent has overloaded the court with documents in an attempt to escape judgment (*Jacobs UK Ltd v Skidmore Owings and Merrill LLP* [2008] EWHC 2847 (TCC), LTL 1/12/2008, where the application took three days). The general rule, however, is that the court cannot expect a party to bring forward its entire case at an interim hearing such as for summary judgment, which is one of the reasons why it may not be appropriate to enter summary judgment in a complicated case (*Groveholt Ltd v Hughes* [2010] EWCA Civ 538, LTL 20/5/2010). Summary judgment was refused in *Apvodedo NV v Collins* [2008] EWHC 775 (Ch), LTL 29/4/2008, where the respondent raised a defence of common mistake which turned on a detailed analysis of a complex factual matrix. Summary judgment is also inappropriate in cases in areas of developing jurisprudence (*Farah v British Airways plc* (1999) *The Times*, 26 January 2000; *Barrett v Enfield London Borough Council* [2001] 2 AC 550), unless the claim is doomed to failure (*K v Central and North West London Mental Health NHS Trust* [2008] EWHC 1217 (QB), [2008] PIQR P19).

Defence on the merits

34.13   In most summary judgment applications the applicant presents its case to the court in the form of witness statements and exhibits, and seeks to persuade the court there is no conceivable defence to the claim. Defendants are invariably invited to state the basis of any dispute they may wish to raise during the course of pre-action correspondence. This is particularly so where the parties are following one of the pre-action protocols. If a defendant has failed to state a defence in pre-action correspondence, or if the purported defence is viewed as merely spurious, the claimant may well be justified in seeking summary judgment.

When faced with an application for summary judgment by a claimant, the defendant may seek to show a defence with a real prospect of success by setting up one or more of the following:

(a) a substantive defence, e.g. *volenti non fit injuria*, frustration or illegality;
(b) a point of law destroying the claimant's cause of action;
(c) a denial of the facts supporting the claimant's cause of action;
(d) further facts answering the claimant's cause of action, e.g. an exclusion clause, or that the defendant was an agent rather than a principal, or that a dispute has been settled by a compromise agreement.

An example under the old rules was *Mercer v Craven Grain Storage Ltd* [1994] CLC 328. The claimant was a farmer who deposited a quantity of grain with the defendant storage company. Later, the claimant requested redelivery, but the defendant was only able to deliver a small fraction of the grain. The defendant alleged that the claimant had entered into an agreement with a marketing company, and that the missing grain had been withdrawn from the store with the authority of the marketing company. By a bare majority it was held that this defence raised triable legal and factual issues, and leave to defend was given. With the change in the test, this case would now perhaps result in a conditional order being made.

Points of law and construction

Although summary judgment applications should not be allowed to turn into mini-trials, **34.14** where the case turns on an issue of construction of a term in a contract the court will usually determine the point and give judgment accordingly (*Wootton v Telecommunications UK Ltd* (2000) LTL 4/5/2000). In *ICI Chemicals and Polymers Ltd v TTE Training Ltd* [2007] EWCA Civ 725, LTL 13/6/2007, it was held that where a short point of construction arises on a summary judgment application and the parties are ready to argue it, the judge should decide the point, unless there is likely to be other evidence available at trial which will shed light on it. This is particularly so where the disputed phrase can be readily construed applying the principles in *Investors Compensation Scheme Ltd v West Bromwich Building Society* [1998] 1 WLR 896 (*Gaetano Ltd v Obertor Ltd* [2009] EWHC 2653 (Ch), LTL 29/10/2009, where the words 'at any time' were given their ordinary meaning). Likewise where there is a short point on whether a disputed term can legitimately be implied into a written contract (*Omega SA v Omega Engineering Inc.* [2011] EWCA Civ 645, [2011] ETMR 40).

Where a clear-cut issue of law is raised by way of defence in an application for summary judgment, the court should decide it immediately. This is so even if the question is, at first blush, of some complexity and therefore will take some time to argue fully (see Lord Greene MR in *Cow v Casey* [1949] 1 KB 474). Not deciding a case once full argument has been addressed to the court on the issue will result in the case going to trial, where the argument will be rehearsed again, with consequent delay and unnecessary expense. Summary judgment may be given where the dispute is largely one of law and any disputed questions of fact are largely peripheral (*Jenson v Faux* [2011] EWCA Civ 423, [2011] 1 WLR 3038). A misconceived 'legal' point does not amount to a triable issue (*National Commercial Bank Jamaica Ltd v Olint Corporation Ltd* [2009] UKPC 16, [2009] 1 WLR 1405 at [7], an injunction case). In *GMAC Commercial Credit Ltd v Dearden* (2002) LTL 31/5/2002 it was held that defences of economic duress had no real prospect of success, the claimant having acted in good faith and its conduct not going beyond what was normal and legitimate in commercial arrangements.

However, it is quite a different matter, per Lord Donaldson of Lymington MR in *R. G. Carter Ltd v Clarke* [1990] 1 WLR 578:

if the issue of law is not decisive of all the issues between the parties or, if decisive of part of the [claimant's] claim or of some of those issues, is of such a character as would not justify its being determined as a preliminary point, because little or no savings in costs would ensue. It is an a fortiori case if the answer to the question of law is any way dependent upon undecided issues of fact.

Summary judgment should also be refused where the point requires protracted argument (*Home and Overseas Insurance Co. Ltd v Mentor Insurance Co. (UK) Ltd* [1990] 1 WLR 153). Summary judgment was refused in *System Control plc v Munro Corporate plc* [1990] BCLC 659, in which it was held that whether the claimants had irrevocably elected to treat a contract as discharged, or whether they could enforce it, was an issue which should be decided at trial. In *I-Way Ltd v World Online Telecom Ltd* [2002] EWCA Civ 413, LTL 8/3/2002, the claimant sued to recover the benefits it alleged were due to it under an oral variation of a written contract. The defendant resisted the claim relying on a clause of the written contract that there was to be no addition or amendment to the contract unless it was in writing and signed by both parties. An application by the defendant for summary judgment against the claimant was dismissed, because there was no direct authority on the issue whether the parties could prevent oral variations of a contract by use of such a clause, and an important point of principle such as the one in issue needed to be tried rather than determined by summary judgment.

Disputes of fact

34.15   Many summary judgment applications are made after a defence has been filed by the defendant. Most of these applications are decided on the basis of the facts which are not disputed by the respondent, together with the respondent's version of the disputed facts (*Prince of Wales v Associated Newspapers Ltd* [2006] EWCA Civ 1776, [2008] Ch 57). Judgment may be entered if there is no, or no real, prospect of the defendant establishing facts sufficient to justify the key elements pleaded in the defence (*P. and S. Amusements Ltd v Valley House Leisure Ltd* [2006] EWHC 1510 (Ch), LTL 4/7/2006). Where there is no dispute of fact, in that the evidence on liability is either admitted or is derived from matters adduced by the respondent, summary judgment may be entered (*Wrexham Association Football Club Ltd v Crucialmove Ltd* [2006] EWCA Civ 237, [2008] 1 BCLC 508). A defence that consists mainly of denials with no explanations may lead the court into concluding the defence has no real prospect of success (*Broderick v Centaur Tipping Services Ltd* (2006) LTL 22/8/2006).

Where there are issues of fact, which, if decided in the respondent's favour, would result in judgment for the respondent, it is inappropriate to enter summary judgment, even if there is substantial evidence in support of the applicant's case (*Munn v North West Water Ltd* (2000) LTL 18/7/2000). Primarily the court will consider the written evidence adduced by the parties, and if it discloses a dispute with a real prospect of success, the summary judgment application will be dismissed. However, there is no rule that summary judgment must always be refused where the respondent puts in written evidence to support its case (*Miller v Garton Shires* [2006] EWCA Civ 1386, LTL 31/10/2006). The court is not always obliged to accept written evidence at face value, and may disregard evidence which is incredible (see **32.30**). There has to be some basis for going behind the respondent's written evidence, and it is not permissible for the judge on a summary judgment application simply to disbelieve the respondent's account (*Mentmore International Ltd v Abbey Healthcare (Festival) Ltd* [2010] EWCA Civ 761, LTL 7/7/2010). Where the respondent's assertion that he retained a beneficial interest in property was unsupported by documentary evidence and where the circumstances (such as no provision for any rental income or how his interest was to be realised) was regarded as fantastic, summary judgment was entered (*Sandhar v Sandhar and Kang Ltd* [2008] EWCA Civ 238, LTL 14/2/2008). It is generally unsafe to base a summary judgment application on second- and third-hand evidence. Such evidence frequently takes on a different character when subjected to cross-examination (*Radiocomms Systems Ltd v Radio Communications Systems Ltd* [2010] EWHC 149 (Ch), LTL 25/2/2010). It is also a risky course to rely on facts set out in a statement of case without more detailed witness statement evidence, particularly in support of an alleged oral agreement (*Korea National Insurance Corporation v Allianz Global Corporate and Specialty AG* [2007] EWCA Civ 1066, LTL 30/10/2007).

In *Public Trustee v Williams* (2000) LTL 10/2/2000 the claimant sought to recover for a deceased's estate the sum of £74,000 which was received by one of the defendants and used by her to buy a house. The evidence of the recipient filed in response to an application for summary judgment was at its best unclear and at its worst confusing as to where she thought the money had come from. However, there was no clear evidence that the money had come from the estate, and it was held it was not a suitable case for summary judgment. In *Bates v Microstar Ltd* (2000) LTL 4/7/2000 summary judgment had been granted based on a purported contract written on hotel notepaper. There were two other documents purporting to be the contract between the parties, and a number of the terms in the hotel notepaper document were arguably too vague. The judgment was set aside on appeal. In *Mehdi v Bates* [2001] EWCA Civ 1948, LTL 3/12/2001, the contractual documentation was unclear on the issue of whether the contract had been entered into by the defendant personally or by the defendant's company. It was held that the judge had not been justified in entering summary judgment against the claimant on the basis that it was unlikely that a businessman would have entered into this contract personally.

Cases involving disputes over whether employers are vicariously liable for the tortious acts of employees who might not be acting in the course of their employment are fact-sensitive and inappropriate for summary judgment (*Cercato-Gouveia v Kiprianou* [2001] EWCA Civ 1887, LTL 30/11/2001).

Where the applicant has the burden of proving a disputed issue, such as the reasonableness of an exclusion clause under the Unfair Contract Terms Act 1977, it will be difficult for the applicant to establish that the respondent has no real prospect of success (see, for example, *Lalji v Post Office Ltd* [2003] EWCA Civ 1873, LTL19/12/2003).

In a proprietary estoppel claim, where the context and meaning of the words used needs to be investigated, summary judgment is inappropriate (*Century (UK) Ltd SA v Clibbery* [2003] EWCA Civ 1374, LTL 17/7/2003). Where there is no arguable evidence on an essential element of the claim (or defence), or where a claimant will be unable to establish any loss flowing from a breach not actionable per se, summary judgment should be entered (*Morshead Mansions Ltd v Langford* [2003] EWHC 2023 (QB), LTL 29/8/2003). In *Shamil Bank of Bahrain EC v Beximco Pharmaceuticals Ltd* [2003] EWHC 2118 (Comm), [2003] 2 All ER (Comm) 849, a defence to a claim by the bank for repayment of moneys lent was that there was an oral agreement suspending payment until a further agreement had been reached. This was dismissed as fanciful, as it made no commercial sense for a bank to enter such an arrangement, because if the parties failed to reach a further agreement the defendants would be released from liability (different issues were raised on the appeal, [2004] EWCA Civ 19, [2004] 1 WLR 1784).

Defamation

Defamation claims are no longer tried by jury, unless the court orders otherwise (Defamation Act 2013, s. 11). This removes former concerns that summary judgment should not be granted in these claims, because issues of fact should be decided by the jury (*Safeway Stores plc v Tate* [2001] QB 1120). Applications for summary judgment in defamation cases will therefore be dealt with on the same basis as other cases.   **34.16**

Claims involving the investigation of the respondent's state of mind, such as the issue of malice or honest opinion, are not suitable for summary judgment (*Hayter v Fahie* [2008] EWCA Civ 1336, LTL 28/10/2008).

In *Creative Resins International Ltd v Glasslam Europe Ltd* [2005] EWHC 777 (QB), LTL 11/5/2005, the claimant sued the second defendant (the solicitors acting for the first defendant) in libel based on a letter sent by the solicitors to one of the claimant's customers. The second defendant applied for summary judgment, arguing that the letter was protected by qualified privilege. The first defendant had not at this point waived legal professional privilege in respect of solicitor and client communications leading up to the allegedly libellous letter. The possibility that legal professional privilege might be waived before trial, combined with the complexity surrounding cases raising qualified privilege, meant this was not a suitable case for summary judgment.

Fraud, deceit and misconduct

34.17   Claims involving allegations of fraudulent or deceitful misconduct which are not admitted and which are not capable of being substantiated by inference from the documentary or written evidence are inappropriate for summary judgment (*Esprit Telecoms UK Ltd v Fashion Gossip Ltd* (2000) LTL 27/7/2000). Conversely, where a challenge to a fraud claim has no real prospects of success, summary judgment may be appropriate (*Sinclair Investment Holdings SA v Cushnie* [2006] EWHC 219 (Ch), LTL 6/2/2006). *Costain Ltd v Wilson* [2007] EWHC 713 (QB), LTL 12/4/2007, was a claim to recover sums obtained from the claimant on false invoices, where the proceeds had been divided equally between a subcontractor and the claimant's accountants. The subcontractor sought to avoid summary judgment by alleging that four of the claimant's employees, whom the subcontractor refused to name, had also benefited from the fraud, and were the alter ego of the claimant. The fact these allegedly corrupt employees were not named, the absence of evidence that they had gained from the fraud, and the fact that it was not a defence to the subcontractor's own wrongdoing, meant this was a hopeless argument.

There is no rule that summary judgment is not available where this involves a finding adverse to the integrity of the respondent (*Wrexham Association Football Club Ltd v Crucialmove Ltd* [2006] EWCA Civ 237, [2008] 1 BCLC 508, where summary judgment was entered in a claim based on a director being in breach of his duty of good faith to his company).

Negligence claims and previous convictions

34.18   Although there is nothing in principle preventing a claimant from applying for summary judgment in claims seeking damages for negligence, such cases invariably involve disputed factual issues, so it is rare for a court to find there is no real defence once liability is denied. It is unlikely to be appropriate to grant summary judgment to a defendant on the basis there was no duty of care in a novel situation (*Bishara v Sheffield Teaching Hospitals NHS Trust* [2007] EWCA Civ 353, LTL 26/3/2007). The question of whether a duty of care is owed often has to be decided in the light of all the facts and evidence (*Caparo Industries plc v Dickman* [1990] 2 AC 605; *Capital and Counties plc v Hampshire County Council* [1997] QB 1004).

An exception was *Dummer v Brown* [1953] 1 QB 710, where summary judgment was given against the defendant, a coach driver, who had previously pleaded guilty of dangerous driving in respect of the accident giving rise to the claim. Even if there is a conviction, summary judgment may be refused if there are good reasons for believing the conviction was erroneous (*McCauley v Vine* [1999] 1 WLR 1977).

Previous disciplinary proceedings

34.19   Adverse findings in disciplinary proceedings against a solicitor may mean the solicitor has no real prospect of success in related proceedings (*Simms v Law Society* [2005] EWCA Civ 849, [2005] ACD 98).

Housing Grants, Construction and Regeneration Act 1996 claims

34.20   The Housing Grants, Construction and Regeneration Act 1996, part 2, provides for the speedy resolution of construction industry disputes. It applies only where the contract is in writing (s. 107) and it does not apply to contracts with residential occupiers (s. 106). A party to a contract to which the Act applies has the right to refer a dispute arising under the contract for adjudication under a procedure that complies with s. 108. To the extent that a construction contract does not do this, the adjudication provisions contained in the Scheme for Construction Contracts (England and Wales) Regulations, SI 1998/649, apply (see s. 108(5)). By s. 108(2) an adjudicator is required to reach a decision within 28 days after a referral, or such longer term as may be agreed by the parties. A clause in a construction contract that provided that the adjudicator's decision was valid even if issued out of time meant that the Housing Grants, Construction and Regeneration Act 1996, s. 108(2)(c) and (d), had not been complied with. This meant that the provisions in the Scheme for Construction Contracts applied to the dispute (*Aveat Heating Ltd v Jerram Falkus Construction Ltd* [2007] EWHC 131 (TCC), 113 Con LR 13). By s. 108(3) the construction contract must provide that the adjudicator's decision is binding until the dispute is finally determined by legal proceedings, by arbitration or agreement. The parties may agree to accept the decision of the adjudicator as finally determining the dispute.

Adjudications are intended to be provisional, but binding, decisions (*Macob Civil Engineering Ltd v Morrison Construction Ltd* [1999] BLR 93 at [14]). The policy is 'pay now, argue later' (*RJT Consulting Engineers Ltd v DM Engineering (Northern Ireland) Ltd* [2002] EWCA Civ 270, [2002] 1 WLR 2344). A party with the benefit of an adjudicator's decision may bring enforcement proceedings by issuing a Part 8 claim form, and then entering default judgment (*Coventry Scaffolding Co. (London) Ltd v Lancsville Construction Ltd* [2009] EWHC 2995 (TCC), LTL 3/12/2009), if there is no acknowledgment of service, or otherwise applying for summary judgment. In most cases it is to be expected that summary judgment will be entered in accordance with the policy of the Act.

Summary judgment will be refused, however, if the defendant advances a properly arguable jurisdictional objection, such as a dispute about whether there was a written construction contract between the parties (*Pegram Shopfitters Ltd v Tally Weijl (UK) Ltd* [2003] EWCA Civ 1750, [2004] 1 WLR 2082), or a dispute that the defendant was a party to the relevant contract (*Estor Ltd v Multifit (UK) Ltd* [2009] EWHC 2108 (TCC), 126 Con LR 40). An issue as to whether an implied term existed does not impact on the question of whether the contract was in writing for the purposes of s. 107 (*Connex South Eastern Ltd v MJ Building Services Group plc* [2004] EWHC 1518 (TCC), [2004] BLR 333). A list of nine questions which are relevant where there is a dispute over an adjudicator's jurisdiction was suggested in *McAlpine PPS Pipeline Systems Ltd v Transco plc* [2004] EWHC 2030 (TCC), [2004] BLR 352. Summary judgment was refused in *Lead Technical Services Ltd v CMS Medical Ltd* [2007] EWCA Civ 316, [2007] BLR 251, because there was a real prospect that the defendant could prove that the original agreement between the parties had been supplanted by a signed deed of appointment which had the effect of depriving the adjudicator of jurisdiction. If the defendant has agreed that the adjudicator can rule on the issue of jurisdiction and that he will be bound by the adjudicator's decision, summary judgment will be entered even if the adjudicator is wrong (*Thomas-Fredric's (Construction) Ltd v Wilson* [2003] EWCA Civ 1494, [2004] BLR 23 at [20]). Summary judgment may also be entered if the defendant has not submitted to the adjudicator's jurisdiction, provided the adjudicator's decision is plainly right (*Thomas-Fredric's (Construction) Ltd v Wilson*).

Summary judgment will also be entered where the defendant has not paid the amount due under an architect's certificate, unless the defendant has given an effective notice of intention to withhold payment under s. 111. This is so even if the certificate might be wrong (*Rupert Morgan Building Services (LLC) Ltd v Jervis* [2003] EWCA Civ 1563, [2004] 1 WLR 1867).

Performance bonds

34.21 A bank which has given a performance bond must honour that obligation according to its terms. The bank cannot rely on issues relating to the relations between the supplier and the customer, or whether the supplier has performed its obligations, or with any question of whether the supplier is in default. The bank must pay according to its guarantee, on demand if so stipulated, without proof or conditions. The only exception is where there is clear fraud of which the bank has notice at the date when payment was due (*Edward Owen Engineering Ltd v Barclays Bank International Ltd* [1978] QB 159 at p. 171). The fraud exception applies where there is clear evidence both of the fraud and the bank's knowledge. There must be a real prospect on the material available that the only realistic inference is that the beneficiary could not have honestly believed in the validity of its demand on its performance bond (*United Trading Corporation SA v Allied Arab Bank Ltd* [1985] 2 Lloyd's Rep 554 as interpreted by *Solo Industries UK Ltd v Canara Bank* [2001] EWCA Civ 1041, [2001] 1 WLR 1800 at [32]). In applying this test the court must be careful not to upset what is in effect a strong presumption in favour of fulfilment of the bank's obligation under a performance guarantee (*Czarnikow-Rionda Sugar Trading Inc. v Standard Bank London Ltd* [1999] 1 All ER (Comm) 890 at p. 913). The effect is that there is a heightened test in relation to the fraud exception in an application for summary judgment against a bank (*Banque Saudi Fransi v Lear Siegler Services Inc.* [2006] EWCA Civ 1130, [2007] 1 All ER (Comm) 67 at [16]).

Conversely, in an application for summary judgment by a bank which has honoured a performance bond against a person who has given the bank a counter-indemnity, the normal 'real prospect of success' test applies (*Banque Saudi Fransi v Lear Siegler Services Inc.* at [18]).

Evidence not yet investigated

34.22   Where the contractual position between the parties needs to be investigated, and disclosure has not taken place, summary judgment should be refused (*Groveholt Ltd v Hughes* [2008] EWHC 1358 (Ch), LTL 27/6/2008). Summary judgment was regarded as inappropriate in *Derksen v Pillar* (2002) LTL 17/12/2002 because evidence was still being acquired or investigated and the claim raised complex issues.

Where an issue requires the court to consider conduct over a period of time, it is unlikely that the issue can be disposed of on an application for summary judgment (*Celador Productions Ltd v Melville* [2004] EWHC 2362 (Ch), 28(1) IPD 10). In *Microsoft Corporation v P4 Com Ltd* [2007] EWHC 746 (Ch), LTL 23/4/2007, the claimant alleged trade mark and copyright infringement during a specific 14-month period. The defendant sought summary judgment, relying on documentary evidence supporting its allegation that it had been a dormant company during that period. Summary judgment was refused, because the evidence adduced was simply that chosen by the defendant. Disclosure and cross-examination could be revelatory and could completely change the picture, and there was evidence that the defendant had operated a website during the relevant period which could have been used for allegedly infringing activities. On the other hand, in *Mancini v Telecommunications UK Ltd* [2003] EWHC 211 (Ch), LTL 16/1/2003, the lack of evidence produced by the claimant resulted in the claim being struck out. It was reasonable to expect the claimant to have numerous documents, and to be able to produce witnesses, to explain what had happened in relation to the key issue. The court was not impressed by the explanation, first raised on appeal, that the documents had been destroyed in a flood, and there was no explanation for not adducing witness statements dealing with the facts.

Case management reasons

34.23   Case management decisions, or the failure to comply with them, may make it plain that one side has no real prospect of success. For example, various paragraphs might be struck out of a statement of case, and the court might grant summary judgment because the remainder may mean there is no real prospect of success. In *Wright v Basildon and Thurrock Hospital NHS Trust* (2011) LTL 8/12/2011, the claimant in a clinical dispute was debarred from relying on all the medical evidence other than a written report, and did not apply to vary or set aside that order. On an application for summary judgment heard three days before the trial it was held the claimant had no real prospect of success, given the heavy burden on a claimant in a clinical dispute, and the fact the report would be untested by cross-examination.

In complex and borderline cases there may be sound case management reasons for adjourning an application for summary judgment to trial. In some cases an appeal against the summary judgment decision will jeopardise the trial date. This may mean it is better to adjourn the summary judgment application to trial (*Monsanto Technology LLC v Cargill International SA* (2006) LTL 13/11/2006; *Doncaster Pharmaceuticals Group Ltd v Bolton Pharmaceutical Co. 100 Ltd* [2006] EWCA Civ 661, [2007] FSR 3).

Conduct in the litigation

In *Penningtons v Abedi* (1999) LTL 13/8/99 there had been ongoing litigation in which the **34.24** defendant had advanced a series of defences, each of which had been shown to be false. An application was made for summary judgment, and it was held that the defendant's conduct of the litigation was such that there was no realistic prospect of her successfully defending the claim.

Contemporaneous documentation

There are cases where the contemporaneous documentation shows that the respondent will **34.25** never be able to establish its case at trial, and in those cases, such as *Collins v Union Bank of Switzerland* (2000) LTL 25/5/2000, summary judgment will be entered. In *Abelene Ltd v Cranbrook Finance Inc.* (2000) LTL 25/8/2000 it was held that although it was open to a court to accept documents produced at the last moment by a respondent to an application for summary judgment, if there was no explanation as to the circumstances in which the documents were executed or why they were not produced at the proper time, it would also be open to the court to be sufficiently suspicious of their genuineness to disregard them. Summary judgment was entered in *Musical Fidelity Ltd v Vickers* [2002] EWCA Civ 1989, LTL 2/12/2002, where the contents of the defendant's website established a clear case of infringement of the claimant's trade mark. Likewise, in *National Westminster plc v Szirtes* (2003) LTL 27/6/2003, the cumulative effect of all the evidence, and in particular the correspondence between the parties, strained the credibility of the defendants' evidence that they were unaware of the guarantees relied upon by the bank to such an extent that they had no real prospect of success. A slightly different formulation was applied in *Hussain v Cuddy Woods and Cochrane* [2001] Lloyd's Rep PN 134, where it was said in a professional negligence claim against a barrister that, from a consideration of the voluminous documentation available, it was 'difficult to see how the claimant could establish' his claim, and summary judgment was entered in favour of the defendant.

In *Vaseeharan v Uthayaranjan* [2010] EWHC 1083 (Ch), LTL 24/5/2010, the key issue between the parties was whether the defendant was an employee (as contended by the claimant) or a partner (as contended by the defendant) of the claimant. There was no contemporaneous documentation of either a contract of employment or a partnership deed or agreement. That was not regarded as surprising in what was plainly an informal arrangement. What made a difference was the complete lack of evidence to show the defendant asked for any annual accounts or payment of his share of the alleged partnership profits for a period of almost five years. Summary judgment was entered for the claimant on this part of the claim.

Amendment

It is inappropriate to subject a pleading to too close a syntactical analysis on an application for **34.26** summary judgment where it is clear on the pleadings overall what the real issues are, and where any defects in the respondent's pleaded case can be saved by amendment (*Landfast (Anglia) Ltd v Cameron Taylor One Ltd* [2008] EWHC 343 (TCC), LTL 23/5/2008). As it was put by Moore-Bick LJ in *P & O Nedlloyd BV v Arab Metals Co. (No. 2)* [2006] EWCA Civ 1717, [2007] 1 WLR 2288 at [62], a respondent to an application for summary judgment cannot be strictly confined to matters set out in his existing statement of case. If the problem with the respondent's case is one of how the case is put rather than of substance, the court has a wide power to allow an amendment to correct the problem, which can be exercised at the hearing (*Stewart v Engel* [2000] 1 WLR 2268) or on an appeal (*Islington London Borough Council v Uckac* [2006] EWCA Civ 340, [2006] 1 WLR 1303 at [39]).

Commentary

ADMISSIONS

34.27 In *E. D. and F. Man Liquid Products Ltd v Patel* [2003] EWCA Civ 472, [2003] CPLR 384, a defence which might have had a real prospect of success was destroyed by clear, written admissions made by the defendant. Likewise, in *Soir Contracting and General Trading Co. v Desai* [2006] EWCA Civ 245, LTL 14/2/2006, despite a lack of documentary evidence substantiating the claim, and an allegation that the defendant was the victim of a dishonest fabrication, clear, signed acknowledgments of the debt by the defendant meant the defence had no real prospect of success. In *Equant SAS v Ives* [2002] EWHC 1992 (Ch), LTL 4/10/2002, the defendant was permitted to resile from an admission in the defence, and on the amended case there were disputes of fact which resulted in summary judgment being refused. A defendant seeking to avoid summary judgment being entered on an admission has to issue an application for permission to amend, otherwise the court is entitled to enter judgment on the unamended statement of case (*Loveridge v Healey* [2004] EWCA Civ 173, [2004] CP Rep 30).

Whether an apparent admission is binding on a party and such as to justify the entry of summary judgment is considered further at **34.29** to **34.33**.

Whether the admission binds the other party

34.28 In the case of parties which are artificial bodies, such as registered companies, an issue arises as to whether the individual said to have made the admission was authorised in fact or in law to bind the party in question in this way. Much depends on the seniority of the individual within the body in question, and on the nature of the relationship between the individual and that body. So, a limited company's directors or solicitor would have authority to bind it when making an admission, whereas an ordinary employee would not in the absence of express authority from the directors. Questions of actual, apparent or ostensible and usual authority of agents may arise, for which see the general works on agency.

Under the general law of evidence, binding admissions can sometimes be made by persons connected with a party. Typical examples are admissions made by partners (see the Partnership Act 1890, s. 15), predecessors in title and referees.

A related question is the extent to which a party is bound by an admission once it has been made. The following distinctions must be drawn between:

(a) formal and informal admissions (see **34.29**). Any fact which is formally admitted is no longer in issue, whereas an informal admission is merely an item of evidence;

(b) admissions made before and after proceedings are issued (see **34.30**). Admissions made before proceedings are issued can only be informal admissions;

(c) pre-action admissions made in fast track personal injuries claims and in other types of claims (see **34.30**). A pre-action admission in a fast track personal injury claim made before 6 April 2007 may bind the person making it;

(d) admissions made in certain personal injuries claims from 6 April 2007, when **CPR, r. 14.1A**, came into force. It restricts the ability of a party to withdraw pre-action admissions in these claims (see **34.30**); and

(e) admissions made with and without a proper understanding of the situation (see **34.32**).

Formal and informal admissions

34.29 Admissions may be formal or informal. As discussed in **chapters 17, 26 and 27**, the statements of case, and in particular the defence and any reply, may well contain admissions. These reduce the area of dispute, and can be very helpful in summary judgment applications. Admissions in statements of case are one example of formal admissions, which have the effect of establishing the facts admitted without the need to call evidence, and which can only be withdrawn with the permission of the court. Other examples of formal admissions are admissions made and recorded at a case management conference or pre-trial review, admissions made in reply to a notice to admit facts (see **49.9**) and admissions made by counsel at trial (for which see *Worldwide Corporation Ltd v Marconi Communications Ltd* (1999) *The Times*, 7 July 1999).

Informal admissions, on the other hand, are merely items of evidence and may be disproved or explained away by other evidence at trial. Informal admissions may be oral statements made by a party or person connected to a party which are at least partially adverse to that party's case, or may be made in correspondence. Admissions made in statements of case in other proceedings, or by witnesses called by a party in other proceedings, are not binding as informal admissions in the present proceedings (*British Thomson-Houston Co. Ltd v British Insulated and Helsby Cables Ltd* [1924] 2 Ch 160). Rather inconsistently, it was held in the old case of *Brickell v Hulse* (1837) 7 Ad & El 454 that reliance on written evidence in earlier proceedings can amount to an informal admission of anything contained in that evidence. Possibly this can be explained on the basis that by relying on written evidence the party is to be taken as adopting it, whereas the details of oral testimony are uncertain until the evidence has been called, and that statements of case are delivered for the purposes of the present litigation only. Admissions made in answers to requests for further information in the present action are probably formal admissions because of the need to include a statement of truth.

Withdrawing and amending admissions

A party may withdraw a pre-action admission if it was made before 6 April 2007 as of right, **34.30** and court permission is not required (*Sowerby v Charlton* [2005] EWCA Civ 1610, [2006] 1 WLR 568). *Gale v Superdrug Stores plc* [1996] 1 WLR 1089, which held that the court could investigate the defendant's explanation for a decision to withdraw a pre-action admission, is no longer good law. *Sowerby v Charlton* was followed by *Walley v Stoke-on-Trent City Council* [2006] EWCA Civ 1137, [2007] 1 WLR 352. A withdrawn pre-action admission is merely an item of evidence. Exceptionally, summary judgment may be available even after a pre-action admission is withdrawn if the other facts in the case mean that any defence has no real prospects of success. It may also be possible to strike out the defence if the withdrawal of the pre-action admission was made in bad faith (*Walley v Stoke-on-Trent City Council*).

Restrictions on withdrawing pre-action admissions are made by **CPR, r. 14.1A**, with effect from 6 April 2007. These restrictions apply if the pre-action admission:

(a) was made after 5 April 2007 (Civil Procedure (Amendment No. 3) Rules 2006 (SI 2006/3435), r. 5);
(b) was made by a notice in writing (**CPR, r. 14.1A(1)**);
(c) was made in one of the types of proceedings listed in **PD 14, para. 1.1(2)**; and
(d) was made either:
    (i) after the party making it had received a letter before claim written in accordance with **PD Pre-action Conduct and Protocols** or any relevant pre-action protocol (**CPR, r. 14.1A(2)(a)**); or
    (ii) before receipt of a letter before claim, but is stated to be made under **Part 14** (**r. 14.1A(2)(b)**).

The proceedings listed in **PD 14, para. 1.1(2)** are claims governed by either the **Pre-action Protocol for Personal Injury Claims** (see **8.16**); the **Pre-action Protocol for the Resolution of Clinical Disputes** (see **8.61**); or the **Pre-action Protocol for Disease and Illness Claims** (see **8.64**). The reference to what is now **PD Pre-action Conduct and Protocols** in CPR, **r. 14.1A(2)(a)**, only describes the nature of the letter before claim. It does not extend the types of relevant proceedings to cases not covered by specific protocols. A note to **PD 14, para. 1.1(2)**, makes it clear that for this purpose the **Pre-action Protocol for Personal Injury Claims** applies to all personal injury claims regardless of the value of the claim.

If these conditions are satisfied, such an admission may be withdrawn before proceedings are issued only with the consent of the person to whom the admission was made (**r. 14.1A(3)(a)**). After proceedings are issued, such an admission may only be withdrawn if all parties consent or if the court gives permission (**r. 14.1A(3)(b)**). Once proceedings are issued, any party may apply for judgment on the pre-action admission, and the party who made it may apply (or cross-apply) for permission to withdraw it (**r. 14.1A(4) and (5)**).

Withdrawal and amendment of post-issue admissions is governed by **r. 14.1(5)**, see **34.31**, and by the rules on amendment of statements of case (see **chapter 31**).

Permission to withdraw or amend admissions

34.31   Once proceedings have been issued, a party seeking to amend or withdraw a pre-action admission made after 5 April 2007 or a post-issue admission should either:

(a)   obtain the consent of all the other parties (**CPR, r. 14.1A(3)(b)** for pre-action admissions; **r. 17.1(2)(a)** for admissions in statements of case); or

(b)   apply or cross-apply for permission (**r. 14.1A(3)(b)** for pre-action admissions; **rr. 14.1(5)** and **17.3** for admissions in statements of case).

In deciding whether to give permission to withdraw an admission, the court is required by **PD 14, para. 7.2**, to have regard to all the circumstances of the case, including:

(a)   the grounds upon which the applicant seeks to withdraw the admission, including whether or not new evidence has come to light which was not available at the time the admission was made;

(b)   the conduct of the parties, including any conduct which led the applicant into making the admission;

(c)   any prejudice that may be caused to any person if the admission is withdrawn;

(d)   the prejudice that may be caused to any person if the application is refused;

(e)   the stage in the proceedings at which the application to withdraw is made, and in particular in relation to the trial date or window;

(f)   the prospects of success (if the admission is withdrawn) of the claim or part of the claim in relation to which the admission was made; and

(g)   the interests of the administration of justice.

Brooke LJ in *Sowerby v Charlton* [2005] EWCA Civ 1610, [2006] 1 WLR 568, a decision before **para. 7.2** was introduced on 6 April 2007, endorsed a number of guidelines suggested by Sumner J in *Basildon and Thurrock University NHS Trust v Braybrook* [2004] EWHC 3352 (Fam), LTL 7/1/2005. These may be of continuing importance. They include seeking to give effect to the overriding objective, whether the application to withdraw the admission is made in good faith, whether any party has been the author of any prejudice he might suffer, and the need to avoid satellite litigation and the disproportionate use of court resources.

In *White v Greensand Homes Ltd* [2007] EWCA Civ 643, [2007] 1 CLC 1001, the defendant consulting engineers admitted an allegation that they had designed the foundations for a building, and defended the claim on other grounds. After reviewing the matter, the engineers found that the design work had been done by another contractor (a company that was dissolved three years before the current application), and applied to amend by withdrawing the admission. The admission in the defence repeated one that had been made in earlier correspondence. The admission in the letter was before the expiry of limitation, the original defence was after the expiry of limitation. If there had been no letter, the amendment would simply have been allowed, because there would have been no claim lost because of the admission. With the letter, there was potential prejudice to the claimant. The amendment should only be allowed if the claimant could be left in no worse a position than if the amended defence had been served at the time of the original defence, and in no better position than if the claimant had applied to strike it out under **CPR, r. 3.4(2)(b)**.

Taking into account the risk of finding liability on a false basis, the chances of the claimant bringing a claim against the other contractor relying on the latent damage provisions, and the risk the other contractor may have been unable to pay at all stages, the balance favoured granting permission to withdraw the admission.

Admissions of limited evidential value

An 'admission' made without knowledge of the facts said to have been admitted has little if **34.32** any evidential value (see *Comptroller of Customs v Western Electric Co. Ltd* [1966] AC 367). Also, the 'admission' must be one of fact, not law. In *Ashmore v Corporation of Lloyd's* [1992] 1 WLR 446, the House of Lords held that statements made by members of the Committee of Lloyd's said to be admissions that the defendants owed a duty of care to 'names' (members of underwriting syndicates) concerned a question of law and so the statements were neither relevant nor admissible.

Obtaining judgment on admissions

There is rarely any doubt about formal admissions, although occasionally points of construc- **34.33** tion are taken in respect of admissions said to have been made in statements of case. Informal admissions, on the other hand, need to be proved. In *Re Beeny* [1894] 1 Ch 499, judgment was entered on the basis of informal oral admissions made by the defendant to the claimant's solicitor. The admissions were proved by an affidavit sworn by the solicitor, the court having to decide whether the admissions were sufficiently proved and sufficiently clear. As North J said in this case:

No doubt, if the alleged admission is only verbal, there is more difficulty in treating it as sufficient, if there be any dispute as to the fact of its having been made.

CONDITIONAL ORDERS

PD 24, para. 4, provides that where it appears to the court possible that a claim or defence **34.34** may succeed but improbable that it will do so, the court may make a conditional order. **Paragraph 5.2** provides that a conditional order is an order which requires a party:

(a) to pay a sum of money into court (which is complied with if a cheque is lodged with the Court Funds Office by the final date specified in the order, even if the cheque does not clear until later: *Petróleo Brasileiro SA v Ene Kos 1 Ltd* [2009] EWCA Civ 1127, [2010] 1 All ER 1099); or

(b) to take a specified step in relation to his claim or defence, as the case may be, and which provides that that party's claim will be dismissed or his statement of case will be struck out if he does not comply.

Conditional orders are appropriate for cases in the grey area between granting judgment and dismissing the application. A conditional order was appropriate where the prospects of success on a defence of *force majeure* or frustration were felt to be remote in *Classic Maritime Inc. v Lion Diversified Holdings Bhd* [2009] EWHC 1142 (Comm), [2010] 1 Lloyd's Rep 59. A conditional order was made against the claimant in *Olatawura v Abiloye* [2002] EWCA Civ 998, [2003] 1 WLR 275, where the claim, which was based on an oral contract, had limited prospects of success. A similar case was *Allen Wilson Joinery Ltd v Privetgrange Construction Ltd* [2008] EWHC 2802 (TCC), 123 Con LR 1, where there were issues as to whether any oral agreement was superseded by a quotation in an email, and whether the eventual contract required working drawings. In *Homebase Ltd v LSS Services Ltd* [2004] EWHC 3182 (Ch), LTL 28/6/2004, the claimant made a claim against the defendant seeking five months' licence fees for occupying a site. The defendant filed a witness statement to the effect that the claimant had orally agreed that the defendant need pay nothing until the claimant had obtained consent from its landlord to assign the land to the defendant.

The claimant denied there was any such agreement. Despite the absence of contemporaneous documents, it could not be said that the defendant's version of events was incredible. Entering summary judgment was therefore inappropriate, but because of the justifiable doubts about the defendant's version, a conditional order was made requiring the whole sum claimed to be paid into court.

Amount to be paid in

34.35   If the court decides to make the respondent to the application pay money into court under a conditional order, it must decide how much should be paid in. The starting point has traditionally been the full amount of the claim. However, the court has a discretion, which it will exercise in accordance with the overriding objective. Obviously, the more uncertain the defence, the more likely it is that the court will order the full amount to be paid in. Another factor is the defendant's ability to pay. Under the old rules (and similar principles are applied under the CPR, see *Sweetman v Shepherd* [2000] CPLR 378), Lord Diplock in *M. V. Yorke Motors v Edwards* [1982] 1 WLR 444 endorsed the following principles:

(a) Defendants seeking to limit a financial condition must make full and frank disclosure of their finances. This is done on affidavit or witness statement. It is common for defendants who realise that a conditional order may be made to produce such written evidence in advance of the summary judgment hearing, and to disclose it to the claimant on the claimant undertaking not to refer to it unless a conditional order is made.

(b) Reliance on a legal aid certificate as evidence of impecuniosity is not enough.

(c) The test is whether it will be impossible for the defendant to comply with the financial condition, as opposed to merely finding it difficult. An impossible condition is tantamount to entering judgment.

M. V. Yorke Motors were suing Mr Edwards for breach of warranty of title in relation to a contract for the sale of a car for £23,520. Conditional leave to defend was given, because the court was sceptical about his defence that he was only acting as the agent for a foreign buyer. By the time of the hearing Mr Edwards was unemployed, living with his father, and in receipt of legal aid with a nil contribution. The House of Lords substituted a condition of bringing £3,000 into court. The 'impossibility' test on the amount to pay in is sometimes modified for the purpose of avoiding a conditional order stifling the defence (see *Kazeminy v Siddiqi* [2010] EWHC 201 (Comm), LTL 2/3/2010).

A claimant who intends to invite the court to make a conditional order if summary judgment is not granted should give the defendant notice of that intention in advance of the hearing. If this is not done, the judge should not make such an order without giving the defendant an opportunity to be heard (and adduce evidence) on questions such as whether the defendant has the means to pay the amount contemplated (*Anglo-Eastern Trust Ltd v Kermanshahchi* [2002] EWCA Civ 198, [2002] CP Rep 36).

Where money is paid into court in compliance with a conditional order, the claimant is a secured creditor for that amount in the event of the defendant's bankruptcy (*Re Ford* [1900] 2 QB 211).

CROSS-CLAIMS

34.36   Cross-claims fall into three categories. Where the only answer to the claim is a cross-claim, the nature and effect of the three types are as follows:

(a) Cross-claims unconnected with the claim. Here, summary judgment should be entered. An example is *Rotheram v Priest* (1879) 41 LT 558, where the claimant claimed arrears of rent, and the defendant counterclaimed in libel. It was held that the counterclaim was totally foreign to the claim, so summary judgment was given to the claimant. The result would be the same under the CPR.

(b) Counterclaims linked to the claim. The appropriate order used to be for judgment subject to a stay of execution pending trial of the counterclaim. In *Drake and Fletcher Ltd v Batchelor* (1986) 130 SJ 285 Sir Neil Lawson said that in considering whether to grant a stay of execution, 'The question is whether the two contracts are so closely linked that it would be fair and equitable to deprive the [claimant] of the fruits of its judgment until resolution of the counterclaim'. The judge said there were three matters which needed to be considered:
   (i) The degree of connection between the claim and the counterclaim.
   (ii) The strength of the counterclaim. The weaker it was, the weaker the case for granting a stay.
   (iii) The claimant's ability to satisfy any judgment on the counterclaim. Any doubt on this matter strengthened the case for granting a stay.

There is some doubt about how cases where the only matter raised by the defendant is a connected counterclaim should be dealt with under the CPR. There is no longer any equivalent to the former RSC, ord. 14, r. 3(2), which provided for a stay of execution in summary judgment applications where there was a connected counterclaim. Early drafts of the CPR had a directly equivalent provision, and the probable consequence of removing it from the final version of the rules is that the court should simply enter judgment for the claimant. If this is correct, there is no longer any practical difference between this type of counterclaim and totally unconnected cross-claims.

(c) Set-offs. Where a counterclaim amounts to a set-off it is a defence to the claim and any summary judgment application should be dismissed, provided the value of the set-off is at least equal to the value of the claim. Where a set-off is not worth as much as the claim, the appropriate order is for summary judgment for the undisputed balance. The nature of set-offs is considered in **34.37**.

Set-offs

The following are established set-off situations: **34.37**

(a) Mutual debts. By virtue of the 18th-century Statutes of Set-off, mutual debts owed between the claimant and the defendant can be set off against each other. There is no need for the transactions giving rise to the debts to be connected other than through the parties. They need not be debts, strictly so-called, but may sound in damages provided they are capable of being ascertained with precision at the time of the application (*Morley v Inglis* (1837) 4 Bing NC 58, applied in *Axel Johnson Petroleum AB v MG Mineral Group AG* [1992] 1 WLR 270). A former partner was held in *Hurst v Bennett* [2001] 2 BCLC 290 to be unable to set off claims for money allegedly owed to him on the taking of partnership accounts against the claim of certain of the former partners to be indemnified against expenses they had incurred on the ground of lack of mutuality.

(b) Sale of goods. By virtue of the Sale of Goods Act 1979, s. 53(1), a buyer may set off counterclaims for breach of the statutory implied conditions about satisfactory quality, fitness for purpose and correspondence to description against a claim by the seller for the price.

(c) On a claim for the price of services, for example, where a builder is suing for the price of building work done, the defendant can set off a counterclaim for damages for poor workmanship in respect of the contract the claimant is suing on (*Basten v Butter* (1806) 7 East 479).

(d) Arrears of rent. Where a landlord brings a claim for arrears of rent, the tenant is allowed to set off a counterclaim for damages against the landlord for breach of a covenant in the lease in respect of which the landlord is claiming (*British Anzani (Felixstowe) Ltd v International Marine Management (UK) Ltd* [1980] QB 137, not following *Hart v Rogers* [1916] 1 KB 646, confirmed by *Agyeman v Boadi* (1996) 28 HLR 558). A tenant does not have a similar right of set-off in respect of a counterclaim for breach of repairing obligations against a claim for

Commentary

service charges as against a manager appointed by the court under the Landlord and Tenant Act 1987, s. 24(1) (*Taylor v Blaquiere* [2002] EWCA Civ 1633, [2003] 1 WLR 379), nor where the tenant's failure to pay has the intended consequence that the landlord will be unable to meet the repairing covenant (*Bluestorm Ltd v Portvale Holdings Ltd* [2004] EWCA Civ 289, [2004] HLR 49).

(e) Equitable set-off.

Mutual debts amount to set-offs whether or not the relevant transactions are connected, but they must be liquidated. Set-offs in categories (b) to (d) above involve liquidated claims and unliquidated cross-claims arising from the same transaction. A defendant relying on an unliquidated cross-claim also has to establish a case with at least a real prospect of success on quantum. An alleged set-off will be ineffective if its value cannot be quantified (*Eilon and Associates Ltd v Easygroup IP Licensing Ltd* (2011) LTL 15/4/2011). If the amount to be set off is less than the amount claimed, it can be effective as a partial defence.

The authorities on equitable set-off were reviewed in *Geldof Metaalconstructie NV v Simon Carves Ltd* [2010] EWCA Civ 667, [2010] 4 All ER 847. There has for a long time been a lack of clarity over when a cross-claim will amount to an equitable set-off (*Aries Tanker Corporation v Total Transport Ltd* [1977] 1 WLR 185). One test, which can be traced back to *Rawson v Samuel* (1841) Cr & Ph 161 (per Lord Cottenham at p. 178), and which was applied in modern authorities such as *Federal Commerce and Navigation Co. Ltd v Molena Alpha Inc.* [1978] QB 927 at pp. 974–5 (not affected by the appeal to the House of Lords), was whether there was an equity which went to impeach the claimant's demands ('the impeachment of title test'). Rix LJ in *Geldof Metaalconstructie NV v Simon Carves Ltd* at [28]–[31] applied Lord Brandon of Oakbrook's reasoning from *Bank of Boston Connecticut v European Grain and Shipping Ltd* [1989] AC 1056 at pp. 1106–10 in concluding that the impeachment of title test has been rejected as of continuing use in the modern world.

The test for whether a cross-claim amounts to an equitable set-off used by Lord Brandon in *Bank of Boston Connecticut v European Grain and Shipping Ltd* was whether the cross-claim 'flows out of and is inseparably connected with the dealings and transactions giving rise to the subject of the claim'. In *Geldof Metaalconstructie NV v Simon Carves Ltd* at [43(vi)] Rix LJ preferred a test based on the discredited passage of Lord Denning MR's judgment in *Federal Commerce and Navigation Co. Ltd v Molena Alpha Inc.*, but with the offending reference to the impeachment of title test removed, as the best modern statement of the test, namely whether the cross-claim is 'so closely connected with [the claimant's] demands that it would be manifestly unjust to allow him to enforce payment without taking into account the cross-claim'.

Care also needs to be taken with this formulation, because 'manifest injustice' was omitted from the formulation of Lord Brandon in *Bank of Boston Connecticut v European Grain and Shipping Ltd*, a matter considered important by Potter LJ in *Bim Kemi v Blackburn Chemicals Ltd* [2001] EWCA Civ 457, [2001] 2 Lloyd's Rep 93 at [38]. Rix LJ in *Geldof Metaalconstructie NV v Simon Carves Ltd* at [43(iv)] concluded that Lord Brandon did not intend to remove the manifest injustice element of the test, which has been emphasised in all the modern cases, including *Bim Kemi v Blackburn Chemicals Ltd* itself. The reason Lord Brandon did not refer to manifest injustice was that in *Bank of Boston Connecticut v European Grain and Shipping Ltd* Lord Brandon was focusing on dethroning the impeachment of title test.

In applying the modern test in *Geldof Metaalconstructie NV v Simon Carves Ltd*, Rix LJ at [43(ii)–(iv)] said there are two elements:

(a) A formal requirement of close connection between the claim and cross-claim. This is to ensure the doctrine of equitable set-off is based on principle and not discretion. There have been various ways in which this has been expressed in the cases: 'so closely connected with [the claimant's] demands that it would be manifestly unjust to allow him to enforce payment without taking into account the cross-claim' (*Federal Commerce and Navigation Co.*

Ltd v Molena Alpha Inc.); 'flowing out of and inseparably connected with the dealings and transactions which also give rise to the claim' (*Government of Newfoundland v Newfoundland Railway Co.* (1888) 13 App Cas 199); 'inseparably connected so that the one ought not to be enforced without taking into account the other' (*Dole Dried Fruit and Nut Co. v Trustin Kerwood Ltd* [1990] 2 Lloyd's Rep 309). These should not be regarded as competing tests, but as different ways of expressing the broad concept that there has to be a close connection. This is an area where the courts have wisely refused to get bogged down in nuances of formulation (*Bim Kemi v Blackburn Chemicals Ltd* per Potter LJ at [38] and *Geldof Metaalconstructie NV v Simon Carves Ltd* per Rix LJ at [43(iii)]).

(b) A functional requirement whereby it needs to be unjust to enforce the claim without taking into account the cross-claim. This is the 'manifestly unjust' element of Lord Denning's formulation. Ultimately the rationale of the principle is equity.

At [43(v)] Rix LJ expressly said these requirements are not to be regarded as establishing a two-stage test. Instead, he preferred to say that there is both a formal element in the test and a functional element.

In one-contract cases (where the cross-claim arises out of the alleged breach of the same contract on which the claim is based) the claim and cross-claim will almost certainly have a close connection. A counterclaim for breach of a financial consultant's fiduciary and contractual duties to act in the client's best interests was regarded as capable of being set off against a claim for the consultant's fees in *Eilon and Associates Ltd v Easygroup IP Licensing Ltd* (2011) LTL 15/4/2011 because both claims arose from the same contract. There is, nevertheless, high authority for the proposition that 'there is no universal rule that claims arising out of the same contract may be set off against each other in all circumstances' (per Lord Hobhouse in *Government of Newfoundland v Newfoundland Railway Co.* at p. 212). The exceptions, which in most cases should be regarded as not fulfilling the functional requirement of the test, are probably limited to the traditional categories where the court has taken the strict view that the claimant has the right to be paid a liquidated sum free from any set-off. These were identified by Potter LJ in *Bim Kemi v Blackburn Chemicals Ltd* at [38], including claims for rent, freight and sums due under bills of exchange. To these should be added claims for a solicitor's fees (*Templer v M'Lachlan* (1806) 2 Bos & P NR 136) and cases where there is an effective 'no set-off' clause in the contract (see **34.39**). Other than in these established exceptions, it is difficult to justify refusing to accept a one-contract cross-claim as an equitable set-off.

Lord Denning's principle uses the expression 'without taking into account' the cross-claim. This is deliberately stated in non-quasi-statutory language (Rix LJ in *Geldof Metaalconstructie NV v Simon Carves Ltd* at [43]) to avoid spurious arguments that the doctrine is restricted to one-contract cases. There are various examples of two-contract cases where the doctrine has been applied in the past (examples include *Bankes v Jarvis* [1903] 1 KB 549; *Dole Dried Fruit and Nut Co. v Trustin Kerwood Ltd*; *Bim Kemi v Blackburn Chemicals Ltd*). As Lord Denning said in *Federal Commerce and Navigation Co. Ltd v Molena Alpha Inc.* at pp. 974–5, an equitable set-off may be based on a cross-claim that arises out of the same transaction or which is closely connected with it.

Geldof Metaalconstructie NV v Simon Carves Ltd itself was a two-contract case. Both contracts were between the same parties and related to the construction of a bioethanol plant. One was for goods to be supplied by the claimant ('the supply contract'), and the other for installation work to be done by the claimant ('the installation contract'). The dispute arose after the defendant alleged the claimant was in breach of the installation contract and issued a notice of default, and did not pay the claimant's invoice under the supply contract. The claimant then informed the defendant it would not continue with the installation work until the defendant paid all its outstanding invoices, including the invoice under the supply contract. The defendant then terminated the installation contract. The claimant issued proceedings for part of the contract price of the goods that became payable following delivery, and the defendant cross-claimed for damages for repudiation of an installation contract. It was held that the cross-claim amounted to an equitable set-off. While there were two contracts, they were both dedicated to the construction of the bioethanol plant. Any doubts about the degree of connection were dispelled by the claimant's conduct in insisting on payment of the supply contract invoice as a precondition for its continued performance of the installation contract. While the cross-claim did not arise from the supply contract or the claim for non-payment of the price, it did arise from the use to which the claimant sought to put its supply contract claim.

Geldof Metaalconstructie NV v Simon Carves Ltd was applied in *Addax Bank BSC v Wellesley Partners LLP* [2010] EWHC 1904 (QB), LTL 26/7/2010, where it was held there was a close connection between a claim for a liquidated sum payable under an investment contract and a cross-claim for unpaid invoices raised under an earlier consultancy contract which met the requirements for the cross-claim to amount to an equitable set-off. *Crastvell Trading Ltd v Bozel SA* [2010] EWHC 166 (Comm), LTL 10/3/2010, should be treated with caution. It applies a test of whether the cross-claim actually impugns the claim itself, which is probably a variant on the discredited impeachment of title test.

See also **63.20** on final judgments where there is an effective set-off.

34.38 **Parties to set-off**   Although set-offs usually arise between the immediate parties to a transaction, this is not always the case. A defendant who has guaranteed payment of a debt owed to the claimant by a principal debtor can rely on set-offs and cross-claims available to the debtor. This principle extends to certain types of bonds entered into in building contracts (whereby the party giving the bond promises to pay a specified sum to the claimant if one of the contractors fails to perform) provided the bond is construed as a guarantee, see *Trafalgar House Construction (Regions) Ltd v General Surety and Guarantee Co. Ltd* [1996] AC 199.

Unliquidated damages claims which can be set off as between the original parties can also be set off against an assignee (*Hanak v Green* [1958] 2 QB 9), because an assignee of a chose in action takes subject to all rights of set-off available against the assignor (*Roxburghe v Cox* (1881) 17 ChD 520). A tenant is therefore entitled to set off any damages for disrepair due from the original landlord against a claim for arrears of rent brought by the landlord's assignee (*Smith v Muscat* [2003] EWCA Civ 962, [2003] 1 WLR 2853).

34.39 **Excluding rights of set-off**   It is open to the parties to a contract to exclude any right to set-off by an express term to that effect (*Hong Kong and Shanghai Banking Corporation v Kloeckner & Co. AG* [1990] 2 QB 514), but it is possible that such a term may be unreasonable and rendered ineffective by virtue of the Unfair Contract Terms Act 1977, as happened in *Stewart Gill Ltd v Horatio Myer and Co. Ltd* [1992] QB 600. Where there is a dispute over the reasonableness of a contractual term excluding the right of set-off the court should either determine whether the clause is effective on the summary judgment application, or order its effectiveness to be tried as a preliminary issue (*Stewart Gill Ltd v Horatio Myer and Co. Ltd* at p. 604G). Making a conditional order is inappropriate because the purpose of such a clause is to enable the claimant to be treated almost as a cash seller, and delaying the issue until trial deprives the claimant of the benefit of the clause.

An example of the opposite of a 'no set-off' clause was a clause in the contract in *Geldof Metaalconstructie NV v Simon Carves Ltd* [2010] EWCA Civ 667, [2010] 4 All ER 847, which provided that the purchaser: 'shall be entitled from time to time to set off against the purchase order price any amounts lawfully due from the supplier to the purchaser whether under this purchase order or otherwise'. Such a clause should be given effect in accordance with its terms, and was regarded as effective in *Geldof Metaalconstructie NV v Simon Carves Ltd* (at [48]–[54]).

The cheque rule

34.40 Cheques are one form of bill of exchange. Where goods or services are paid for by cheque, two contracts are entered into by the parties. The first contract is the underlying contract for the sale of goods or for the provision of services. The second contract is contained in the cheque, whereby the drawer of the cheque undertakes to pay the payee the sum stated. If a cheque is dishonoured, the seller has the option of suing on the underlying contract or on the cheque. If the seller sues on the underlying contract, the buyer is entitled to rely on any set-off that may be available in respect of that contract by way of defence to an application for summary judgment. However, if the seller sues on the cheque, the buyer is permitted to raise only limited defences on an application for summary judgment. The reason probably stems from the unconditional nature of a bill of exchange, as provided by the Bills of Exchange Act 1882, s. 3(1). As Lord Wilberforce said in *Nova (Jersey) Knit Ltd v Kammgarn Spinnerei GmbH* [1977] 1 WLR 713, bills of exchange 'are taken as equivalent to deferred instalments of cash'. Therefore English law does not allow unliquidated cross-claims or defences to be made. The rule is regarded as being of considerable importance to the business community, and the courts will not 'whittle away [the] rule of practice by introducing unnecessary exceptions to it under influence of sympathy-evoking stories' (per Sachs LJ in *Cebora SNC v SIP (Industrial Products) Ltd* [1976] 1 Lloyd's Rep 271). It is only in exceptional circumstances that the court will allow a stay of execution when entering summary judgment for non-payment of a cheque. The fact the claimant is a company in administration is not an exceptional circumstance (*Isovel Contracts Ltd v ABB Building Technologies Ltd* [2002] 1 BCLC 390).

The cheque rule applies to:

(a) cheques and bills of exchange;
(b) direct debits (*Esso Petroleum Co. Ltd v Milton* [1997] 1 WLR 938);
(c) letters of credit (*SAFA Ltd v Banque du Caire* [2000] 2 All ER (Comm) 567); and
(d) performance bonds (*Solo Industries UK Ltd v Canara Bank* [2001] EWCA Civ 1041, [2001] 1 WLR 1800) (see **34.21**).

The cheque rule does not prevent a defendant raising a liquidated cross-claim as a defence. Nor does it apply in the context of statutory demands (*Hofer v Strawson* [1999] 2 BCLC 336, a case which turns on the wording of the Insolvency Rules 1986 (SI 1986/1925), r. 6.5(4)).

There are some exceptional cases where summary judgment will not be given even in respect of unliquidated cross-claims in a claim on a bill of exchange (see **34.42** to **34.44**). Before looking at these it is necessary to consider the nature of the claimant's title to the bill of exchange.

Types of holder of a bill of exchange   Under the Bills of Exchange Act 1882 there are four **34.41** types of holder of a bill of exchange. A mere holder is a person in possession of the bill. Although a mere holder can sue on the bill and give a valid discharge (s. 38), any claim is prone to be defeated for want of consideration. A holder for value is a person in possession of a bill who has given consideration sufficient to support a simple contract, or who derives title directly or indirectly from a previous holder who gave value for the bill (s. 27). A holder for value cannot be defeated on the ground of want of consideration. A holder in due course is broadly a holder of a complete and regular bill who gave value for it in good faith without notice of any defect in the title of the person who negotiated it (s. 29). A holder in due course obtains title to the bill free from equities and defects in the title of the transferor. The fourth type of holder is one who derives title through a holder in due course, and who broadly has all the rights of a holder in due course (s. 29(3)).

An application for summary judgment by a mere holder will always be defeated by a plea of want of consideration, whereas an application by a holder in due course should always succeed as such a holder takes free of equities. If the claimant's title as a holder in due course is challenged by the defendant, judgment will only be given for the claimant if the claim to be a bona fide holder for value is supported by unchallenged or unchallengeable contemporary documents (*Bank für Gemeinwirtschaft AG v City of London Garages Ltd* [1971] 1 WLR 149). Holders for value are the most problematic category. They are also the most numerous, given that an immediate party to a bill cannot be a holder in due course (*R. E. Jones Ltd v Waring and Gillow Ltd* [1926] AC 670).

34.42 **Fraud, duress and illegality** To amount to a defence against a holder for value, an allegation of fraud, duress or illegality must be supported by evidence. A mere allegation in the defendant's written evidence is insufficient (*Bank für Gemeinwirtschaft AG v City of London Garages Ltd* [1971] 1 WLR 149). Such a defence will not, however, avail against a holder in due course (see the Bills of Exchange Act 1882, s. 30(2)).

34.43 **No consideration** As explained in **34.40**, there will be a defence where the claimant is a mere holder who has given no consideration for the bill sued on. A total failure of consideration arises where a buyer lawfully rejects goods sold, the buyer being entitled to recover the price from the seller. Again summary judgment should be refused. Likewise, a liquidated partial failure of consideration is a defence *pro tanto* (*Thoni GmbH & Co. KG v RTP Equipment Ltd* [1979] 2 Lloyd's Rep 282). In *Isovel Contracts Ltd v ABB Building Technologies Ltd* [2002] 1 BCLC 390 the defendant countermanded a cheque given to a subcontractor in payment of the sum due under an interim certificate in a building project. The certificate had been issued by the main contractor, and, before payment of the cheque, had been shown to be wrong, because later certificates showed no money at all was due at the time the cheque was given. The subcontract provided that in this event any overpayment would be deducted from the amounts payable under subsequent interim certificates. It was held that in these circumstances the defendant could not rely on failure of consideration as a defence to an application for summary judgment.

34.44 **Misrepresentation** In *Clovertogs Ltd v Jean Scenes Ltd* [1982] Com LR 88 the Court of Appeal held that an allegation that the claimant had procured two cheques by misrepresentation amounted to a defence in an application for summary judgment. This decision was described as surprising in *Famous Ltd v Ge Im Ex Italia SRL* (1987) The Times, 3 August 1987, and should be regarded as wrongly decided as it is inconsistent with other cases on bills of exchange. Following *SAFA Ltd v Banque du Caire* [2000] 2 All ER (Comm) 567 and *Solo Industries UK Ltd v Canara Bank* [2001] 1 WLR 1800, a distinction needs to be drawn between:

(a) Cases where there is a misrepresentation by a beneficiary which was made directly to induce the execution of the bill of exchange (or other payment obligation covered by the cheque rule). In such cases, provided there is a real prospect of establishing the misrepresentation, summary judgment on the cheque (or other payment obligation) should be refused.

(b) Cases where an allegation of misrepresentation is in reality an allegation relating to the underlying contract of services or sale on which the payment obligation is based. In these cases summary judgment should be entered on the cheque (or other payment obligation), with no stay of execution. The courts need to be particularly astute in ensuring the cheque rule is not diluted by treating cases in this category as ones affecting the cheque or other payment obligation.

International trade

34.45 Irrevocable letters of credit are treated as cash and must be honoured. If the bank refuses to honour such a transaction, the court will grant summary judgment to the claimant (*Power Curber International Ltd v National Bank of Kuwait SAK* [1981] 1 WLR 1233). See also **34.21** on performance bonds. Summary judgment will also be given on a claim for freight even if there is a cross-claim relating to the cargo (*Aries Tanker Corporation v Total Transport Ltd* [1977] 1 WLR 185).

SOME OTHER COMPELLING REASON

34.46 Summary judgment will be refused if there is some other compelling reason why the case should be disposed of at a trial (**CPR, r. 24.2(b)**). An assertion that pleading a defence would infringe the defendant's privilege against self-incrimination does not amount to a compelling reason for a trial, nor for staying or adjourning a summary judgment application (*Versailles Trade Finance Ltd v Clough* [2001] EWCA Civ 1509, [2002] CP Rep 8). The privilege does not amount to a defence in civil proceedings, nor does it provide a right not to plead a defence. It does not, therefore, provide any basis for resisting an application for summary judgment (although the defendant in *Versailles Trade Finance Ltd v Clough* was allowed 14 days to file a full defence). Seeking an adjournment to negotiate with the claimant was not regarded as a compelling reason in *Phonographic Performance Ltd v Planet Ice (Peterborough) Ltd* [2004] EWHC 486 (Ch), LTL 2/2/2004. Reasons for going to trial include:

(a) The respondent is unable to contact a material witness who may provide material for a defence.

(b) The facts are wholly within the applicant's hands. In such a case it may be unjust to enter judgment without giving the respondent an opportunity of establishing a defence in the light of disclosure or after serving a request for further information (*Harrison v Bottenheim* (1878) 26 WR 362). However, summary judgment will not necessarily be refused in cases where the evidence for any possible defence could only lie with the applicant if there is nothing devious or artificial in the claim *State Trading Corporation of India v Doyle Carriers Inc.* [1991] 2 Lloyd's Rep 55).

(c) The case is highly complicated such that judgment should only be given after mature consideration at trial.

(d) Strange factual situations which call for further investigation. An example is *Global Marine Drillships Ltd v Landmark Solicitors LLP* [2011] EWHC 2685 (Ch), LTL 25/10/2011, where £7 million was deposited with a solicitor to pay an insurance premium on a policy that involved the services of a shadowy overseas broker.

(e) The applicant has acted harshly or unconscionably, or the facts disclose a suspicion of dishonesty or deviousness on the part of the applicant such that judgment should only be obtained in the light of publicity at trial. An example is *Miles v Bull* [1969] 1 QB 258, where possession proceedings had the appearance of a device to evict the defendant.

DIRECTIONS ON SUMMARY JUDGMENT HEARING

34.47 If a summary judgment application is dismissed or otherwise fails finally to dispose of the claim, the court will give case management directions for the future conduct of the case (**PD 24, para. 10**), which may include directions for filing and service of a defence (**CPR, r. 24.6**), and may dispense with directions questionnaires and allocate the case to a case management track (**PD 26, para. 2.4**).

SPECIFIC PERFORMANCE, RESCISSION AND FORFEITURE IN PROPERTY CASES

34.48 An even speedier process for obtaining summary judgment is available by virtue of **PD 24, para. 7**, in claims for specific performance and similar claims arising out of the sale, purchase, exchange, mortgage or charge of any property, or for the grant or assignment of a lease or tenancy of any property. Specific performance as a remedy requires an exceptional case (*Cooperative Insurance Society Ltd v Argyll Stores (Holdings) Ltd* [1998] AC 1), and the same applies on an application for summary judgment. Summary judgment for specific performance of a share purchase agreement was ordered in *Gaetano Ltd v Obertor Ltd* [2009] EWHC 2653 (Ch), LTL 29/10/2009, damages not being an adequate remedy for an obligation to transfer shares in an unquoted company due to the lack of a ready market in the shares. The judge is not entitled to enter into a mini-trial on an application for summary judgment, and it is wrong to attempt to resolve disputes of fact on such an application on the balance of probabilities (*North East*

Lincolnshire Borough Council v Millennium Park (Grimsby) Ltd [2002] EWCA Civ 1719, *The Times,* 31 October 2002). Summary judgment was not appropriate in *Greenacre Properties Ltd v Tower Hamlets London Borough Council* (2002) LTL 24/7/2002 where it was arguable that the sale of land was beyond the council's power as it had not obtained ministerial consent.

Where there is no defence, summary judgment can be sought at any time after the claim is served, rather than having to wait until after acknowledgment or defence, and the application can be made even in the absence of particulars of claim. The application notice, evidence in support and a draft order must be served no less than four clear days before the hearing.

SUMMARY ORDERS FOR ACCOUNTS AND INQUIRIES

34.49   By **CPR, r. 25.1(1)(o)**, the court may make an interim order directing accounts to be taken or inquiries to be made. The application notice seeking such an order should ask:

(a) for specified accounts to be taken or specified inquiries to be made;

(b) for directions for the taking of the account or for making the inquiries; and

(c) for payment of the amount found to be due on taking the accounts.

Written evidence is not always required in support, but if the matter is at all contentious such evidence should be filed and served with the application. The court may refuse to make the order if there is a preliminary question that ought to be tried, such as whether the defendant is under a duty to account.

The practice on taking accounts and conducting inquiries is dealt with by **PD 40A**. When making an order for accounts and inquiries the court may also at the same time or later give directions as to how the account is to be taken or the inquiry conducted (**PD 40A, para. 1.1**). Among the directions that may be made are the following:

(a) that the relevant books of account shall be evidence of their contents, subject to the parties having the right to make objections (**para. 1.2**);

(b) that an accounting party must make out his account and verify it by exhibiting it to an affidavit or witness statement (**para. 2(1)**); and

(c) that, if appropriate, and at any stage in the proceedings, the parties must serve points of claim and points of defence (**para. 5**).

A party alleging that an account drawn by an accounting party is inaccurate (or making similar allegations) must give written notice of the objections to the accounting party (**para. 3.1**). These objections must give full particulars, specify the grounds on which it is alleged the account is inaccurate, and be verified by a statement of truth (or exhibited to an affidavit or witness statement).

Unless the court orders otherwise, accounts and inquiries are conducted by a Master or District Judge (**para. 9**). Detailed provisions dealing with inquiries into estates, trusts and for beneficiaries and next of kin can be found in **paras 10 to 15**.

SUMMARY DETERMINATION OF CONSTRUCTION OF WILLS

34.50   The High Court may make an order authorising trustees or personal representatives to act in reliance on an opinion of counsel of 10 years' call on the construction of a will or trust (Administration of Justice Act 1985, s. 48). Applications under s. 48 are made in the Chancery Division without notice supported by written evidence stating the names of all persons who may be affected by the order sought; all admissible surrounding circumstances; counsel's call and experience; the value of the fund; and details of any known dispute. Instructions to counsel, counsel's opinion, and draft minutes of the order sought must be exhibited to the evidence in support. The papers are considered by a judge without hearing argument, who will make the order sought if that order is appropriate and if there appears to be no tenable argument contrary to counsel's opinion.

Claims by trustees seeking orders approving any sale, purchase, compromise or other transaction by a trustee, including a case where the remedy sought is approval of a transaction affected by conflict of interests or duties (**PD 64A, para. 1(2)(b)**), may be determined without a hearing (**para. 1A.1**). Detailed procedural requirements can be found in **para. 1A.3**.

Commentary

Chapter 35   Possession Claims against Trespassers

INTRODUCTION

35.1 Machinery for obtaining possession orders without undue delay against trespassers and similar categories of unauthorised occupiers is provided by **CPR, Part 55.** Landowners seeking possession against squatters frequently do not know the identity of those on their land. One of the main objects of the rules governing claims against trespassers is to avoid the need for the claimant to investigate the identities of the people in unauthorised occupation, and to allow possession orders to be made even against 'persons unknown'. Where the summary procedure against trespassers is not available, ordinary possession proceedings (see **35.15**) should be used.

POLICE

35.2 There are occasions when trespassers enter on to land and refuse to leave. A person entitled to possession who attempts to turn trespassers off the land without the sanction of a court order risks a breach of the peace and may incur civil or criminal liability for doing so. A court order is not needed, however, if the person entitled to the land can make use of the Criminal Law Act 1977, s. 7, as substituted by the Criminal Justice and Public Order Act 1994, s. 73. This makes it an offence for any person who is on premises as a trespasser to fail to leave on being required to do so by the residential occupier or a protected occupier. A constable in uniform may arrest such a trespasser without a warrant. The section only applies to residential property, and not to commercial property or open land.

PROCEDURE ON POSSESSION CLAIMS AGAINST TRESPASSERS

Definition

35.3 Possession claims against trespassers are claims for the recovery of land which is alleged to be occupied by persons who entered or remained on the land without the consent of a person entitled to possession of the land (**CPR, r. 55.1(b)**). They do not include claims against tenants or sub-tenants, whether the defendant's tenancy has terminated or not. These claims can include claims against licensees who remain in occupation after the termination of their licences.

In addition to the obvious situation of the owner in fee simple in possession claiming against a squatter, the summary procedure against trespassers may be used:

(a) By the owner of the premises against a person who had gone into possession as a licensee, but whose licence has expired (*Greater London Council v Jenkins* [1975] 1 WLR 155). This also applies where the occupant is a former employee whose right to remain was terminated on dismissal, even where the employee has applied to an employment tribunal for reinstatement if the employer has expressed an intention not to reinstate in any event (*Whitbread West Pennines Ltd v Reedy* [1988] ICR 807). It can also apply to a claim against a former freehold owner who sold the premises to the claimant and who did not give vacant possession in accordance with the terms of a licence granted by the claimant (*Pritchard v Teitelbaum* [2011] EWHC 1063 (Ch), [2011] 2 EGLR 1).

(b) By a tenant of premises against a person who, while the tenant was absent, was let into occupation with the consent of the landlord (*Borg v Rogers* (1981) 132 NLJ 134).

(c) By a licensee who was not in occupation of the land against a trespasser where possession was necessary to give effect to the licensee's contractual rights of occupation (*Manchester Airport plc v Dutton* [2000] QB 133). The land in this case was owned by the National Trust, and the airport was given a licence in order to fell some trees for purposes connected with the construction of a second runway. The trespassers were protesters. It was held that an order for possession would not interfere with the prior rights of the National Trust.

Situations not amounting to claims against trespassers

35.4 The summary procedure in claims against trespassers cannot be used against a tenant or sub-tenant or a former tenant or sub-tenant holding over at the end of the tenancy (see **CPR, r. 55.1(b)**). In addition, the following situations have been considered by the courts:

(a) Where the defendant was allowed into the premises by a tenant, the landlord was held not to be entitled to use the summary procedure unless the tenancy had been determined or surrendered (*Auto Finance Ltd v Pugh* (unreported, 10 June 1985)).

(b) A number of cases have considered claims brought by councils which may be in breach of statutory duty to provide accommodation for the defendants. It has been held that the fact that the council is in breach of its statutory duty, and that the breach has caused the presence of the defendants on the council's land, does not by itself provide the defendants with any defence (*Southwark London Borough Council v Williams* [1971] Ch 734). However, if the decision to use the summary procedure against trespassers is void on the ground of unreasonableness in the *Wednesbury* sense (see *Associated Provincial Picture Houses Ltd v Wednesbury Corporation* [1948] 1 KB 223), then the defendants can seek to have the possession proceedings struck out (*Bristol District Council v Clark* [1975] 1 WLR 1443). In *Cannock Chase District Council v Kelly* [1978] 1 WLR 1 Megaw J said that overwhelming proof of the unreasonableness would be required. A case in which possession was refused on this basis is *West Glamorgan County Council v Rafferty* [1987] 1 WLR 457.

(c) Where a complicated issue arises as to title (*Cudworth v Masefield* (1984) *The Times,* 16 May 1984) or as to whether there has been a surrender of a tenancy by operation of law (*Cooper v Vardari* (1986) 18 HLR 299), the summary procedure against trespassers may be inappropriate.

(d) A doubtful situation is where a head landlord seeks possession against unlawful sub-tenants. This was held to be a situation where summary possession could be ordered under the old rules before the CPR (*Moore Properties (Ilford) Ltd v McKeon* [1976] 1 WLR 1278), but the words 'or sub-tenant' in **CPR, r. 55.1(b)**, may be regarded as extending even to an unlawful sub-tenant, with the effect that the summary procedure will not be available in such a claim.

County Court or High Court

35.5 In the County Court, possession claims may be started in any County Court hearing centre unless an enactment provides otherwise (**CPR, r. 55.3(1)**). After issue the claim will be sent to the hearing centre which serves the address where the land is situated, which may result in delay (**PD 55A, para. 1.1(2)**). Only exceptional circumstances justify starting possession claims in the High Court (**para. 1.1(1)**). The High Court may be appropriate where there are complicated issues of fact, points of law of general importance, or the claim properly requires immediate determination because it is against trespassers and there is a substantial risk of public disturbance or of serious harm to persons or property (**para. 1.3**). If the claim is started in the High Court when it should have been started in the County Court, the claim will either be struck out or transferred (**para. 1.2**).

Claim form, particulars of claim and evidence in support

35.6 A special claim form (form N5) must be used in claims against trespassers. The claim form should name as defendants all the persons in occupation whose identities are known to the claimant. Where the claimant does not know the names of all the occupiers, the claim is brought against 'persons unknown' in addition to any named defendants. There is nothing to be gained, therefore, by making inquiries as to who might be in occupation, but there will be extra people to serve if some of those in occupation become known to the claimant. Where the claimant is a large organisation, it is important for the solicitor conducting the case to find out what may be known by any of the employees of the claimant, as there have been cases where delays have occurred through the need to amend by adding extra defendants when it later becomes clear that some of the occupiers were known to local employees of the claimant.

The particulars of claim must be in form N121, which is specifically for claims against trespassers. This must identify the land, state whether it is residential property, state the claimant's interest in the property or the basis for claiming possession, the circumstances in which it has been occupied without the claimant's licence or consent, and give details of every person who, to the best of the claimant's knowledge, is in possession of the property (**PD 55A, paras 2.1 and 2.6**). Particulars of claim and witness statements in support must be filed when the claim is issued (**CPR, rr. 55.4 and 57.8(5)**). When the claim is issued the court will fix a date for the hearing, which will usually be just a few days after issue.

Service

35.7 No acknowledgment of service form is required (**CPR, r. 55.7(1)**), so the only documents that need to be served are the claim form, particulars of claim, any additional evidence in support, and any notice of the return day. Service copies of the claim form must be sealed (see **12.3**).

Individually named defendants must be served in accordance with the normal rules on service (see **chapter 15**). Service by the means described below for 'persons unknown' will not suffice for individually named defendants (*Greater London Council v Tully* (1976) 120 SJ 555).

Where the claim is against, or includes, persons unknown, in addition to serving the named defendants in the normal way, the documents must, by **r. 55.6**, be served by:

(a) attaching copies to the main door or some other part of the land so they are clearly visible, and, if practicable, by inserting another set of the documents through the letter box in a sealed transparent envelope addressed to 'the occupiers'; or

(b) attaching copies, contained in sealed transparent envelopes addressed to 'the occupiers', to stakes placed in the land in places where they are clearly visible. This method is used where the trespassers are on open land. Where service is to be effected by the court, the claimant must provide sufficient transparent envelopes and stakes (**PD 55A, para. 4.1**).

In *Westminster City Council v Chapman* [1975] 1 WLR 1112, the County Court bailiff served the proceedings, but did not affix a copy to the main door or other conspicuous part of the premises. The defendants learnt of the matter by reading the copy inserted through the letter box. It was held that service was irregular (rather than a nullity), and as there was no prejudice to the defendants, the irregularity was cured under what is now **CPR, r. 3.10**.

Service must be effected not less than five days before the hearing in the case of residential property, and not less than two days before the hearing in respect of commercial property and open land (**r. 55.5(2)**). Time is calculated from service on each of the various defendants. Time may be shortened under **r. 3.1(2)(a)** and **(b)** where the occupiers have threatened to assault the claimant or to cause serious damage to the property or other property in the locality (**PD 55A, para. 3.2**).

Defence

The form for a defence in a possession claim against trespassers (form N11) simply provides a **35.8** space for giving the reasons for disputing the claim and a statement of truth. However, in possession claims against trespassers, **CPR, r. 15.2**, does not apply, and there is no need for a defendant to file a defence (**r. 55.7(2)**). The provisions on default judgment do not apply (**r. 55.7(4)**).

Application by occupier to be made a party

By **CPR, r. 19.4**, an occupier who is not named as a defendant and who wishes to be heard **35.9** on the return day may apply at any stage to be joined as a defendant. An application notice should be filed and served in accordance with **Part 23** (**PD 19A, para. 1.4**). Such applications are often heard on the day of the hearing. All that need be shown is that the occupier wishes to be heard on whether an order for possession should be made, so permission to join is usually granted quite readily.

Hearing in claims against trespassers

Summary possession hearings are generally heard by Masters in the Royal Courts of Justice **35.10** and by District Judges in the County Court. Unless the court orders otherwise, the facts are placed before the court at the hearing by relying on the evidence in the witness statements served with the claim form (**CPR, r. 55.8(3)**). The fact of service is proved by producing a certificate of service (**r. 55.8(6)** and form N215).

If the defendants need an opportunity to file evidence in reply, the first hearing may be used for giving directions (particularly where there is not much time between service and the return date). If the necessary five or two clear days have not elapsed since service, the court should ordinarily adjourn the hearing to enable the proper time to elapse (*Westminster City Council v Monahan* [1981] 1 WLR 698). If the maker of a witness statement does not attend the hearing, and another party disputes material evidence contained in the statement, the court will normally adjourn the hearing so that oral evidence can be given (**PD 55A, para. 5.4**). Adjournments are usually very short, as the whole point of the procedure is to provide an expeditious means of obtaining possession orders where there is no defence.

The summary procedure against trespassers is only appropriate where the defendants have no real defence. If the court takes the view that the case is not suitable for summary possession, it may dismiss the claim (particularly where it does not come within the scope of the procedure). If the defendants attend and adduce evidence showing a substantial defence, the claim is usually converted into an ordinary possession claim.

Possession orders against trespassers

Normally, if the court is satisfied that there are grounds for granting possession of the land, **35.11** the order will be for possession forthwith. It has been held that where the defendants' original entry on to the land was unlawful, the court has no discretion to make a suspended order in the absence of consent from the landowner (*Swordheath Properties Ltd v Floydd* [1978] 1 WLR 550) and this is not affected by the Housing Act 1980, s. 89 (*Boyland and Son Ltd v Persons Unknown* [2006] EWCA Civ 1860, [2007] HLR 24). Even in this situation it may be necessary to consider whether it is proportionate to make the possession order, and to do so separately against different defendants, under the European Convention on Human Rights, **arts 10** and **11**, in the **Human Rights Act 1998, sch. 1** (*Mayor of London v Hall* [2010] EWCA Civ 817, [2011] 1 WLR 504). If the original occupation was lawful, such as under a service agreement, the court may exercise any power which it could have exercised if possession had been sought in an ordinary possession claim.

Area orders

35.12   Usually the order will grant possession of the land actually occupied by the defendants. This may not provide sufficient protection for the claimant, who may fear (often based on experience) the defendants will simply relocate to a site nearby. Where only part of a single piece of land is occupied by the trespassers, the order can cover the whole piece of land, particularly where it is unrealistic to require the claimant to identify different parts of the land occupied by different trespassers (*Mayor of London v Hall* [2010] EWCA Civ 817, [2011] 1 WLR 504). What the court cannot do is to make an order covering similar areas of land also owned by the claimant but which are wholly detached and separate from the land occupied by the defendants (*Secretary of State for the Environment, Food and Rural Affairs v Meier* [2009] UKSC 11, [2009] 1 WLR 2780). The order made may be supported by an injunction forbidding the defendants from re-entering the occupied site or from entering other sites.

Warrant of possession

35.13   A warrant of possession to enforce a possession order against a trespasser may be issued immediately after the order is made. However, permission to issue a warrant of possession is required if the warrant is not issued within the next three months (**CPR, rr. 83.13(3), 83.26(10)** and **(11)**). Orders for permission to enforce out of time are made on application to the Master or District Judge without notice (unless the court otherwise directs). If permission is granted, the defendants may apply to vary or set it aside by making an application within seven days of service of the order granting permission (**CPR, r. 23.10**).

Interim possession orders

35.14   An interim order for possession can be sought in a claim for possession against trespassers by following the procedure in **CPR, rr. 55.20 to 57.28**. Such an order is available if the following conditions are satisfied:

(a) the only claim in the proceedings is for possession so there can be no money claim;

(b) the claim is in respect of premises (and not open land); and

(c) the claim is made within 28 days of the claimant knowing (or reasonably being able to know) of the wrongful occupation.

The claim must be brought by issuing an application for possession in form N130, supported by written evidence in the prescribed form, and a notice of application for an interim possession order must also be issued (in form N131). Once the proceedings have been issued the court will fix a date for consideration of the application, which must be not less than three days after the proceedings were issued. Service must be effected by the applicant within 24 hours after issue. Service is effected by fixing one set of copies to the main door or other conspicuous part of the premises, and inserting a second set through the letter box in a transparent envelope addressed to 'the occupiers'.

The defendant is permitted to file written evidence in reply, and a standard form for this must be used (form N133). If the court decides to make an interim possession order, the claimant is required to give a number of undertakings set out in **CPR, r. 55.25(1)** including a promise to reinstate the defendant if the court later holds that the interim possession order should not have been made. An interim possession order requires the defendant to vacate within 24 hours of service (**r. 55.25(3)**). A defendant who does not comply commits an offence contrary to the Criminal Justice and Public Order Act 1994, s. 76, punishable by imprisonment for up to six months and/or a fine not exceeding level 5 on the standard scale. The only means of enforcement is under the 1994 Act, which requires the involvement of the police.

After an interim possession order is made there is a second return date when the court will consider whether to make a final order for possession, or to dismiss the claim for possession.

OTHER POSSESSION PROCEEDINGS

Ordinary possession claims

Ordinary possession claims, like possession claims against trespassers, are governed by **CPR, Part 55**, and **PD 55A**. The court has a power to allocate these claims to the fast track or multi-track (**CPR, r. 55.8(2)**), may give case management directions, and may require the facts to be proved by calling witnesses at the trial.   **35.15**

The claim form to be used in possession claims is form N5; the claim form for relief against forfeiture is form N5A; the form for particulars of claim in claims in respect of rented residential premises is form N119; the form for particulars of claim in claims for possession of mortgaged residential premises is form N120; the form for a defence in mortgage possession claims is form N11M; and the form for a defence in claims in respect of rented residential premises is form N11R.

ACCELERATED PROCEDURE FOR ASSURED SHORTHOLD TENANCIES

CPR, rr. 55.11 to 57.19, provide an accelerated procedure for obtaining possession orders to recover possession of residential properties let under assured shorthold tenancies. There are prescribed claim forms and defence forms, and the papers are referred to a District Judge or judge, who may strike out the claim if it discloses no reasonable grounds (**r. 55.16(1)(c)**), or may make an order for possession without requiring the attendance of the parties (**r. 55.17**). Although an application can be made to set aside such an order (**r. 55.19**), the procedure is intended to provide a speedy and inexpensive means of obtaining possession orders in cases where there is unlikely to be any defence.   **35.16**

There is a special claim form (form N5B) for use in accelerated procedure claims in respect of assured shorthold property and it includes the particulars of claim. The form for a defence to such a claim is form N11B.

Chapter 36   Interim Payments

The following procedural checklist is relevant to this chapter:

Procedural checklist 24   Application for an order for interim payment

ORDERS FOR INTERIM PAYMENT

36.1   An order for interim payment is defined in **CPR, r. 25.1(1)(k)**, as an order for payment of a sum of money by a defendant on account of any damages, debt or other sum (except costs) which the court may hold the defendant liable to pay. Such orders are likely to be made in claims where it appears the claimant will achieve at least some success, and where it would be unjust to delay, until after the trial, payment of the money to which the claimant appears to be entitled. The purpose behind this procedure is to alleviate the hardship that may otherwise be suffered by claimants who may have to wait substantial periods of time before they recover any damages in respect of wrongs they may have suffered. In addition to providing resources to the claimant, sometimes making an interim payment will enable the claimant to pay for treatment, or to save assets which would otherwise be lost, or to have an asset repaired earlier than might otherwise be the case, and may thereby reduce the amount of the claim. Further, making an early interim payment will reduce the defendant's liability to pay interest.

Cases on the small claims track are unlikely to be large enough to justify the expense of applications for interim payments, and small claims and fast track cases, unless delayed, are likely to proceed to final hearing with such speed that there will be little point in making an application, unless the hearing results in a judgment for damages to be assessed. Most applications for interim payments are therefore likely to be made in multi-track cases (or cases likely to be allocated to the multi-track when track allocation is considered).

Voluntary interim payments and rehabilitation

36.2   There is nothing to prevent the parties agreeing to voluntary interim payments, and these are quite common in cases where liability is not in dispute but where quantum is still being investigated. Payments made by insurers for intervention or treatment pursuant to the Rehabilitation Code (**Annex D to the Pre-action Protocol for Personal Injury Claims**) are treated as interim payments on account of damages (**Code, para. 7.2**). The permission of the court must be obtained if a voluntary interim payment is being considered where the claimant is a child or protected party (**PD 25B, para. 1.2**).

EU law and informal interim payments under CPR, r. 25.1

In *R (Teleos plc) v Commissioners of Customs and Excise* [2005] EWCA Civ 200, [2005] 1 WLR 3007, **36.3** the company brought judicial review proceedings to challenge a VAT assessment which the Commissioners had levied through a set-off. The Commissioners refused to make an interim payment to the company under the Value Added Tax Act 1994, and it was clear there were no grounds for granting an interim payment under **CPR, r. 25.7**. The company applied for interim relief under **r. 25.1** and/or the court's inherent jurisdiction for an interim payment of 50 per cent of the assessed VAT. Dyson LJ said at [23] that if there were no mechanism for a taxpayer in these circumstances to obtain an interim payment of VAT withheld by the Commissioners, there would be an infringement of the principle of proportionality (see *Garage Molenheide BVBA v Belgium* (cases C-286/94, C-340/95, C-401/95 and C-47/96) [1997] ECR I-7281). This did not apply to the present case, given the Commissioners' power to make interim payments and the right to challenge their decisions through judicial review. Accordingly, it was unnecessary to give a strained interpretation of **CPR, r. 25.1**, to provide such a power, nor did the court need such a power as a consequence of EU law (at [33]).

PROCEDURE

Who may apply

The rules (**CPR, rr. 25.1(1)(k)** and **25.6(1)**) refer to interim payments being applied for by **36.4** claimants against defendants. This should be interpreted as meaning that interim payments may also be applied for by claimants in additional claims, so that defendants may bring interim payment applications against the defendants to their counterclaims, and defendants may seek interim payments against additional parties.

Time for applying

An application for an order for an interim payment cannot be made until the period for filing **36.5** an acknowledgment of service has expired (**CPR, r. 25.6(1)**). However, voluntary interim payments may be made at any time, including the period before proceedings are issued. It is possible to make several applications for interim payments during the life of a claim (**r. 25.6(2)**).

Application and evidence

The procedure for applying for an interim payment is summarised in **procedural checklist 24**. **36.6** Applications for interim payments are made on notice, and must be served at least 14 clear days before the hearing of the application (**CPR, rr. 2.8(2)** and **25.6(3)(a)**). Rather unnecessarily, it is specifically stated as a requirement by **r. 25.6(3)(b)**, that applications for interim payments must be supported by evidence which must be served with the application (**r. 23.7(2)** and **(3)**). **PD 25B, para. 2.1**, provides that the evidence in support should set out all relevant matters including:

(a) the amount sought by way of interim payment;
(b) what the money will be used for (see **36.15**);
(c) the likely amount of money that will be awarded;
(d) the reasons for believing the relevant ground (see **36.7**) is satisfied;
(e) in a personal injuries claim, details of special damages and past and future loss; and
(f) in a claim under the **Fatal Accidents Act 1976**, details of the persons on whose behalf the claim is made and the nature of the claim.

All relevant documents in support should be exhibited. In personal injuries claims these will include the disclosed medical reports.

Commentary

Respondents who wish to rely on written evidence in reply must file and serve their evidence at least seven clear days before the hearing. In personal injuries claims and claims in which damages in respect of a disease for which a lump sum payment within the definition of the Social Security (Recovery of Benefits) Act 1997, s. 1A(2), has been, or is likely to be made, the respondent will need to obtain a certificate of recoverable benefits from the Secretary of State. This is needed for the purposes of framing the order. If the applicant wants to respond to the respondent's evidence, any further evidence must be filed and served at least three clear days before the return day (**CPR, r. 25.6(4) and (5)**).

GROUNDS

36.7   The conditions which must be satisfied before an interim payment order can be made are set out in **CPR, r. 25.7**. Under **CPR, r. 25.7(1)**, an interim payment may be ordered against a specific defendant only if:

(a)   the defendant has admitted liability to pay damages or some other sum of money to the claimant (**r. 25.7(1)(a)**); or

(b)   the claimant has obtained judgment against the defendant for damages or some other sum (other than costs) to be assessed (**r. 25.7(1)(b)**); or

(c)   the court is satisfied that, if the claim went to trial, the claimant would obtain judgment against the defendant from whom the interim payment is sought for a substantial sum of money (other than costs) whether or not that defendant is the only defendant or one of a number of defendants to the claim (**r. 25.7(1)(c)**); or

(d)   the claimant is seeking possession of land, and the court is satisfied that if the case went to trial the defendant would be held liable to pay the claimant a sum of money for use and occupation of the land while the claim is pending (**r. 25.7(1)(d)**).

Where there are two or more defendants and the court, though satisfied that the claimant will obtain judgment, cannot determine which of the defendants will be found liable, **r. 25.7(1)(e)**, which is discussed in **36.11**, provides an alternative ground for granting an interim payment.

There is probably no basis for making an interim payment order outside these categories (*Quest Advisors Ltd v McFeely* [2011] EWCA Civ 1517, LTL 9/12/2011).

Standard of proof

36.8   On an application under **CPR, r. 25.7(1)(c)**, the court has to be satisfied on the balance of probabilities that if the claim went to trial, the claimant would obtain judgment for a substantial amount of money from the respondent (*Test Claimants in the FII Group Litigation v Commissioners of HM Revenue and Customs (No. 2)* [2012] EWCA Civ 57, [2012] 1 WLR 2375 at [36]). 'Substantial' has to be considered in the context of the total claim made, and is to be contrasted with negligible rather than nominal damages (at [39]). It may be that in small claims an applicant can never satisfy the 'substantial amount of money' condition (at [39]). Similar principles, with the necessary changes, should apply to applications under **r. 25.7(1)(d)** and **(e)**, which also apply where the court is satisfied either that the defendant would be liable or that the claimant would obtain judgment.

Establishing the claim would succeed

36.9   In an application under **CPR, r. 25.7(1)(c)**, the judge has to put himself in the hypothetical position of being the trial judge, and, on the material before him on the interim payment application, decide whether the claimant would actually succeed on the claim, and that the claimant would actually obtain judgment for a substantial amount of money (*Test Claimants in the*

FII Group Litigation v Commissioners of HM Revenue and Customs (No. 2) [2012] EWCA Civ 57, [2012] 1 WLR 2375 at [36], [38]). It is open for the court to make an interim payment in respect of only part of the claim (at [48]). In *O2 (UK) Ltd v Dimension Data Network Services Ltd* (2007) LTL 8/11/2007 summary judgment was refused as there was a real prospect that a defence of overcharging and a counterclaim might succeed. However, the court found that the defendant was bound to have to pay something for the services provided by the claimant, and an interim payment was made on that basis.

Under the old rules before the CPR there were several reported cases that considered the question of whether it was possible to make an interim payment order if a summary judgment application was unsuccessful (see, for example, *Schott Kem Ltd v Bentley* [1991] 1 QB 61 and *Andrews v Schooling* [1991] 1 WLR 783). The better view under the old rules was that an interim payment order would not be made in such cases, although it was possible to make an interim payment order if conditional leave to defend (the old equivalent to a conditional order) was granted. With the increased availability of summary judgment under the CPR, there can be no doubt that if summary judgment is refused it would be inconsistent for the court then to decide that the claimant 'would' succeed so as to give grounds for an interim payment. There may even be a little doubt about whether making an interim payment order can be consistent with making a conditional order, again because of the change in the test for summary judgment. If the defence is on the border of having a real prospect of success (the situation where conditional orders are appropriate), it is difficult to see how the court can simultaneously find that the claimant will win for the purposes of making an interim payment order.

MULTIPLE DEFENDANTS

Where the court is satisfied a specific defendant is liable

An interim payment order can be made against a specific defendant if the claimant establishes one of the conditions in **CPR, r. 25.7(1)(a)** to **(d)** to the required standard against that specific defendant. Where this can be done there is no need to satisfy the additional requirements of **CPR, r. 25.7(1)(e)** described at **36.11**. **36.10**

Where the court cannot determine which defendant is liable

By **CPR, 25.7(1)(e)**, an interim payment may be ordered where all the following conditions are satisfied: **36.11**

(a) there are two or more defendants;
(b) the court is satisfied that if the claim went to trial the claimant would obtain judgment for a substantial sum of money (other than costs) against at least one of the defendants;
(c) the court cannot determine under **r. 25.7(1)(c)** which of the defendants will lose; and
(d) all the defendants are either insured, public bodies, or are defendants whose liability will be met by an insurer under the Road Traffic Act 1988, s. 151, or an insurer acting under the Motor Insurers' Bureau Agreement or by the Motor Insurers' Bureau itself.

In **r. 25.7(1)(e)** the term 'defendants' (see points (b) and (d) above) means the defendants against whom the interim payment is sought (*Berry v Ashtead Plant Hire Co. Ltd* [2011] EWCA Civ 1304, [2012] PIQR P6). The provision in **r. 25.7(1)(e)(ii)(b)** (see (d) above) should be construed as including cases where liability will be met by an insurance company under the Domestic Regulations Agreement between the Motor Insurers' Bureau and its members pursuant to the Uninsured Drivers' Agreement (*Sharp v Pereira* [1991] 1 WLR 195, considering a provision in the same form).

If it transpires that the wrong defendant was required to make the interim payment, the requirement that all the defendants must be insured etc. means it should be possible to make effective adjustments (see **36.16**) after the final determination of the case.

EFFECT OF COUNTERCLAIMS AND DEFENCES

36.12   When deciding on an order for interim payment the court 'must take into account' any relevant set-off or counterclaim and any contributory negligence (**CPR, r. 25.7(5)**). From the context of this provision it clearly applies at the second stage of an interim payment application when the court is considering the amount to be ordered by way of an interim payment. Counterclaims and allegations of contributory negligence with reasonable prospects of success obviously affect the likely amount of the final judgment. **Rule 25.7(5)**, however, has no express restriction to quantum. Unlike unconnected cross-claims, set-offs are also defences. Consequently, the existence of a set-off with a reasonable prospect of success should also be taken into account at the first stage when the court is considering the grounds for granting an interim payment, and may prevent the court being satisfied that the claimant will obtain judgment for the purposes of **r. 25.7(1)(c)**. This was the position under the previous rules (see *Shanning International Ltd v George Wimpey International Ltd* [1989] 1 WLR 981).

COMBINED WITH SUMMARY JUDGMENT

36.13   It is quite common to combine applications for summary judgment under **CPR, Part 24** (see **chapter 34**) with applications for interim payments. Summary judgment is available where the defence has no real prospect of success, and interim payments are available where the claimant can show that liability will be established. Obviously these are similar concepts. Further, on the summary judgment application the court may make a 'relevant order' (**PD 26, para. 12.1**) entering judgment for damages to be assessed, which would itself provide grounds for making an order for an interim payment. Another possibility is that the court may make a conditional order on the summary judgment application, with the condition being compliance with an interim payment order.

DISCRETION

36.14   Even if the claimant establishes a ground for making an interim payment, the court retains a discretion whether to make an order. As a general proposition, once an applicant satisfies the conditions in **CPR, r. 25.7**, the court should order an interim payment unless there is a sufficient specific reason not to do so (*Test Claimants in the FII Group Litigation v Commissioners of Revenue and Customs (No. 2)* [2012] EWCA Civ 57, [2012] 1 WLR 2375 at [47]). The discretion is exercised in accordance with the overriding objective, bearing in mind the policy behind the jurisdiction conferred by the Senior Courts Act 1981, s. 32, and the County Courts Act 1984, s. 50, to make interim payment orders. This is essentially to alleviate the hardship that can occur when a claimant is kept out of his money for a protracted period of time. Relevant factors include the time that has elapsed since the cause of action accrued and the estimated time to trial (*Spillman v Bradfield Riding Centre* [2007] EWHC 89 (QB), LTL 13/2/2007), and the effect on the claimant of being kept out of what may turn out to be his money. In one of the old cases (*British and Commonwealth Holdings plc v Quadrex Holdings Inc.* [1989] QB 842) it was said that the court may take into account the respondent's lack of means in either refusing to make an order or in fixing its amount.

AMOUNT TO BE ORDERED

The court is not permitted to order an interim payment of more than a reasonable proportion **36.15** of the likely amount of any final judgment, taking into account any contributory negligence and any relevant set-off or counterclaim (**CPR, r. 25.7(4)** and **(5)**). The judge is obliged to assess the likely amount of the final judgment, and is not permitted to take short cuts such as basing the assessment on offers made by the defendant (*Eeles v Cobham Hire Services Ltd* [2009] EWCA Civ 204, [2010] 1 WLR 409). The issues need to be considered individually, and the judge has to decide whether there is an irreducible minimum sum the claimant will recover in any event (*Chiron Corporation v Murex Diagnostics Ltd (No. 13)* [1996] FSR 578). While most judges err on the side of caution, a reasonable proportion may in an appropriate case be a high proportion, provided the assessment of the likely final award is conservative. The amount payable should not expose the defendant to the risk that the eventual damages would be less than the interim payments that are made (*Osunde v Guy's and St Thomas' Hospital* [2007] EWHC 2275 (Fam), LTL 26/11/2007). In *Spillman v Bradfield Riding Centre* [2007] EWHC 89 (QB), LTL 13/2/2007, 75 per cent of the likely total award was regarded as a 'reasonable proportion' of the likely award in a personal injuries case. The interim payment of £1.7 million (part of which had already been paid voluntarily) which was ordered in a claim with an estimated value of £1.8 million in *FP v Taunton and Somerset NHS Trust* [2009] EWHC 1965 (QB), [2009] LS Law Medical 598, should be regarded as either exceptional or wrong. In a personal injuries claim the amount ordered is not limited to the likely lump sum award, but also includes the capitalised value of any likely award for periodical payments (for which, see **63.30**) (*Braithwaite v Homerton University Hospital NHS Foundation Trust* [2008] EWHC 353 (QB), [2008] LS Law Medical 261). In deciding how much to order by way of interim payment in a personal injuries claim where the claimant had suffered catastrophic injuries, the court in *Mealing v Chelsea and Westminster Healthcare NHS Trust* [2007] EWHC 3254 (QB), [2008] LS Law Medical 236, took into account:

(a) whether there was any likelihood that the amount ordered would pre-empt any decision by the trial judge on any of the issues between the parties;

(b) that ordering too much by way of interim payments could act as a disincentive to the claimant in progressing the claim to trial; and

(c) that if too much were ordered by way of interim payments the amount left to be awarded at trial may be too little to make an effective periodical payments order, or too little to make an effective lump sum award for the necessary capital expenses for the claimant's care.

In the non-personal injuries field, the pre-CPR case of *Andrews v Schooling* [1991] 1 WLR 783 is helpful. This was a claim for damages against builders under the Defective Premises Act 1972. The court ignored the claimant's quantification of the claim at £12,000, but made an order for an interim payment of £7,500 given an estimate of £10,000 for necessary remedial works.

PD 25B, para. 2.1(2), states that the evidence in support of the application must deal with the items or matters in respect of which the interim payment is sought. In general, the claimant's intended use of the money if an interim payment is awarded is irrelevant to the court's decision. As stated in *Schott Kem Ltd v Bentley* [1991] 1 QB 61, commercial people always have a need for money for the purposes of their business interests. Once an interim payment is made they will invest it somewhere. It is generally the same in personal injuries claims (*Stringman v McArdle* [1994] 1 WLR 1653), particularly where the interim payment is limited to an amount based on the damages alleged to have been suffered to the date of the application (*Eeles v Cobham Hire Services Ltd*). The court is not concerned with how a claimant of full capacity spends a final award in damages, and should not try to prescribe what an interim payment is spent on either. Despite the general principle, the rule in *Stringman v McArdle* must not be applied in a mechanical way, and there are cases where the proposed use of the interim payment has a significant bearing on the decision of the court (*Tinsley v Sarkar* [2004] EWCA Civ 1098, LTL 23/7/2004). The intended use of the money may be relevant where the payment may prejudice the trial or the position of the defendant in the proceedings or pre-judge an issue to be determined at the trial (Thorpe LJ at [48]). In periodical payments cases it is essential to establish a real need for the money, and an award will be made only if the judge can confidently predict the trial judge will wish to award a capital sum greater than past special damages and damages for pain, suffering and loss of amenity (*Eeles v Cobham Hire Services Ltd*). Where an interim payment may effectively preclude a periodical payments order at trial, it should be ordered only where the court is satisfied to a high degree of confidence that the interim payment is reasonably necessary (*Preston v City Electrical Factors Ltd* [2009] EWHC 2907 (QB), LTL 16/11/2009). Information on the claimant's proposed use of the money may assist the court in deciding whether the money is needed urgently, or in deciding how much to order.

Judges applying these principles have tended, in cases of catastrophic personal injuries, to award interim payments coming close to the likely lump sum award at trial and covering the likely cost of suitable accommodation and other expenditure which is felt ought not to be postponed until after trial (*Brewis v Heatherwood and Wrexham Park Hospitals NHS Trust* [2008] EWHC 2526 (QB), LTL 3/11/2008; *Pitcher v Headstart Nursery Ltd* [2008] EWHC 2681 (QB), LTL 17/11/2008).

There is a standard interim payment of £1,000 under both the **RTA Protocol (para. 7.13)** and the **EL/PL Protocol (para. 7.12)**, and of £50,000 for mesothelioma claims (**PD 3D, paras 2** and **6.7**).

In personal injuries and lump sum disease claims the defendant will need to obtain a certificate of recoverable benefits from the Secretary of State under the Social Security (Recovery of Benefits) Act 1997. A copy of the certificate should be filed at the hearing, and any order made must set out the amount by which the payment to be made to the claimant has been reduced in accordance with the Act and the Social Security (Recovery of Benefits) Regulations 1997 (SI 1997/2205) (**PD 25B, paras 4.1 to 4.4; PD 40B, paras 5.1 and 5.1A**).

CPR, r. 25.6(7), allows an interim payment order to require payment by instalments. Where this happens, the order should set out the total amount of the interim payment, the amount of each instalment, the number of instalments and the date they are to be paid, and to whom the payments should be made (**PD 25B, para. 3**).

Undertaking for repayment

36.16 In *Ultraframe (UK) Ltd v Eurocell Building Plastics Ltd* [2005] EWHC 2111 (Ch), LTL 30/8/2005, as a condition for granting an interim payment, the claimant and its holding company were required to give a cross-undertaking to repay the interim payment, and to provide a guarantee. Such undertakings are comparatively rare.

FURTHER APPLICATIONS

36.17 The claimant is permitted to make more than a single application for an interim payment (**CPR, r. 25.6(2)**). In practice, a second or subsequent application will have to be justified by a change in circumstances or other cause being shown, such as an increase in the special damages claim through additional loss of income or expenses being incurred, or through unforeseen delays in determining the claim.

NON-DISCLOSURE

36.18 The fact that a defendant has made an interim payment must not be disclosed to the trial judge until all questions of liability and quantum have been determined (**CPR, r. 25.9**), unless the defendant agrees. This is important, as the trial judge may (unwittingly) be influenced by knowing that the court has previously decided that the claimant will win, and that the claim is worth more than the amount of the interim payment. In advance of trial a request should be made to the court office to remove all references to interim payments (and Part 36 offers) from the court file to avoid accidental disclosure to the trial judge. Where a claimant (usually through ignorance) does disclose this information prematurely, the judge will usually abort the trial and consider making a wasted costs order against the lawyer responsible (but compare **66.3**).

ADJUSTMENT

The court has powers to order all or part of an interim payment to be repaid, to vary or dis- **36.19**
charge an interim payment order, and to order a co-defendant to reimburse a defendant who has made an interim payment (provided the defendant who made the interim payment has claimed a contribution, indemnity or other remedy against the co-defendant being ordered to reimburse) (**CPR, r. 25.8**). Reimbursement can also be ordered between co-claimants (*Trebor Bassett Holdings Ltd v ADT Fire and Security plc* [2012] EWHC 3365 (TCC), 145 Con LR 147). Interest may be ordered in favour of the defendant on any overpaid interim payment. These powers are usually exercised, if at all, at trial.

PD 25B, para. 5, and **PD 40B, para. 6**, contain detailed rules on recording the effect of interim payments and any order for adjustment on the final award for damages. **Paragraphs 6.1** and **6.3** of **PD 40B** say that the amount and dates of any interim payments should be set out in a preamble to the judgment whether or not the interim payments exceed the amount awarded at trial, together with the total amount awarded by the judge. If the interim payments are less than the judgment, the total award has to be reduced by the interim payments, with an order for payment of the balance (**para. 6.2**). Where the interim payments exceed the amount awarded at trial, the judgment has to provide for repayment, reimbursement, variation or discharge under **CPR, r. 25.8(2)**, and for interest on the overpayment under **r. 25.8(5)** (**PD 40B, para. 6.4**).

Commentary

Chapter 37   Interim Injunctions

INTRODUCTION

Interim injunctions are temporary orders made with the purpose of regulating the position **37.1** between the parties to an action pending trial. Imposing an interim injunction is a serious matter, and should be restricted to appropriate cases. Such an order is particularly useful where there is evidence that the respondent's alleged wrongdoing will cause irreparable damage to the applicant's interests in the period between issue of process and trial.

Interim injunctions should be distinguished from perpetual injunctions, which are final orders, usually made at trial (but see **37.56**) and which continue with no limitation of time. Further distinctions are:

(a) Injunctions made without notice. These are a form of interim injunction, usually made in circumstances of urgency, which are expressed to continue in force for a limited period, usually a few days, sufficient for the application to be renewed on a hearing with notice being given to the respondent.

(b) Mandatory injunctions require the other side to do specified acts (such as to deliver up documents or to demolish a wall), whereas prohibitory injunctions require the other side to refrain from doing specified acts (such as publishing a libel or breaching a confidence). It is the substance of the order (rather than its wording) which makes it mandatory or prohibitory. Both types of injunction can be granted on an interim basis, but the courts are more wary of granting mandatory orders (see **37.61**).

(c) Where the other side have not yet committed a civil wrong, but have threatened to do so in the future, it is possible to obtain an interim injunction on a *quia timet* basis.

Interim injunctions can be applied for even in claims allocated to the small claims track (**CPR, r. 27.2(1)**).

Any party to proceedings can apply for an interim injunction, and can do so whether or not a claim for the injunction was included in that party's originating process or statement of case (**CPR, r. 25.1(4)**).

JUDGES ABLE TO GRANT INJUNCTIONS

The detailed rules on which judges may make various types of injunction are to be found in **37.2** **PD 25A, paras 1.1** to **1.4**, which have to be read together with **PD 2B**. The effect of the various rules is that applications for search orders must be made to a High Court judge, and applications for freezing injunctions must be made to either a Circuit Judge or High Court judge. While other types of injunctions can be made by any judge, including Masters and District Judges, in the High Court and particularly the Chancery Division interim injunction applications will normally be referred up to the judge unless there are good reasons for an application to be dealt with by a Master (**PD 2B, paras 2** to **3.1A**; Chancery Guide, para. 15.12). In the County Court a freezing injunction can only be granted by a Circuit Judge, not a District Judge (**PD 2B, para. 8.4**). Unfortunately, in relation to other County Court interim injunctions **para. 8.1** seems to be internally contradictory. Its opening words say County Court District Judges cannot make any interim order that cannot be granted by a District Judge in the High Court. Given **para. 3.1**, in which interim injunctions are not listed as orders that cannot be made by High Court District Judges, it is clear that High Court District Judges can make any interim injunction order other than a search order or freezing

Commentary

injunction. However, **para. 8.1(a)** to **(c)** point against County Court District Judges having a general power to make orders for injunctions. They say County Court District Judges have power to grant injunctions in small claims and fast track cases, in cases where the value of the claim does not exceed the fast track limit, and under four specified statutes. There would be no need to set out these specific categories if it is the case (as implied by the opening words of **para. 8.1**) that County Court District Judges have general jurisdiction to grant injunctions other than search orders and freezing injunctions.

PRE-ACTION APPLICATIONS FOR INTERIM INJUNCTIONS

37.3   **CPR, r. 25.2(1)**, empowers the court to grant an interim injunction before a claim form has been issued. An application for an interim injunction at that stage must be made under **Part 23 (PD 23A, para. 5)**. By **CPR, r. 25.2(2)**, an interim injunction can be obtained prior to issue of proceedings provided:

(a) no rule or practice direction prohibits the granting of the order;

(b) the matter is urgent or it is otherwise desirable to make the order in the interests of justice;

(c) in the less common circumstance in which the applicant is an intended defendant, the defendant has obtained the court's permission to make the application. The defendant cannot without this permission apply for an interim remedy prior to the filing of an acknowledgment of service or defence (which can only happen after issue). It seems that the defendant could apply for permission and for the injunction in the same application and at the same hearing.

Urgent cases

37.4   A case is 'urgent' where there is a true impossibility in giving the requisite three clear days' notice or in arranging for the issue of process. There has to be an element of threatened damage, requiring the immediate intervention of the court, which may occur between the without-notice hearing and the hearing of an effective application (*Mayne Pharma (USA) Inc. v Teva UK Ltd* [2004] EWHC 3248 (Ch), LTL 3/12/2004). An 'impossibility' resulting from delay on the part of the claimant will not suffice (*Bates v Lord Hailsham of St Marylebone* [1972] 1 WLR 1373).

Reasons for applying without notice have to be given to the judge. It is especially important to give notice where grave allegations are to be made on the application. Thus, in *Cinpres Gas Injection Ltd v Melea Ltd* [2005] EWHC 3180 (Pat), [2006] FSR 36, a without-notice interim injunction to restrain the defendant from threatening, intimidating or harassing any witnesses was set aside because it should have been made on notice. Although the court will not usually consider an application made without notice where there is no true impossibility in notifying the defendant, there is a suggestion in *Bates v Lord Hailsham of St Marylebone* that the court may do so if the case is overwhelming on the merits. The relief sought on a without-notice application must be necessary and proportionate to the reasons for applying without notice (*Moat Housing Group-South Ltd v Harris* [2005] EWCA Civ 287, [2006] QB 606).

Where a case is urgent, the usual procedural requirements are relaxed in so far as is necessary to do justice between the parties. For example:

(a) The application may be made before issue of process.

(b) The application may be made without notice. However, it is still incumbent on the applicant to give the other side such notice as is possible, such as by telephone or by fax, and it will be rare that short notice cannot be given (*National Commercial Bank Jamaica Ltd v Olint Corporation Ltd* [2009] UKPC 16, [2009] 1 WLR 1405). The exception is where secrecy is essential (such as on applications for search orders and freezing injunctions). A defendant who is notified in this way may decide to attend the hearing, a situation which is known as an 'opposed hearing without notice'.

(c) Informal evidence may be relied on. This may be in the form of an unsworn draft affidavit, or a witness statement, correspondence or even simply facts related to the court by counsel on instructions.

(d) Although very much a last resort, the court may make an order without a draft having been prepared by counsel on behalf of the applicant. It is very rare for there to be no time for anything to be drafted in advance of appearing before the judge.

(e) In particularly urgent cases it is possible to interrupt the judge's list, or even to see the judge out of normal hours or to apply to the judge over the telephone.

Procedure on pre-action applications

For a summary of the procedure, see **procedural checklist 19**.

37.5

The application itself will normally be in a written application notice (**CPR, r. 23.3(1)**), the general requirement for which is that it should set out the order sought and why the order is being sought (**r. 23.6**). In the High Court form N244 should usually be used for the application notice, but in the County Court there is a special form for applying for injunctions (form N16A) which may be used. It must include the title of the proposed claim, the full name of the applicant, and, as the applicant is not yet a party, the applicant's address for service. It should contain a request for a hearing or ask that the application be dealt with without a hearing (**PD 23A, para. 2.1**). It will be very rare for injunctions to be sought without hearings. Dispensing with a hearing is only permissible if the parties agree to the terms of the order sought, or agree that the court should dispose of the application without a hearing, or if the court does not consider a hearing would be appropriate (**CPR, r. 23.8**). None of these is very likely in the case of pre-action injunctions. **PD 25A, para. 2.1**, provides that an application notice for an interim injunction should:

(a) state the order sought, and

(b) give the date, time and place of the hearing.

It is good practice to annex a draft order to the application notice where time allows. Forms N16, N16(1), CH10 and CH11 are available for this purpose.

Many pre-action applications for injunctions are made in cases of real urgency. Drafting and issuing an application notice may delay matters to the detriment of the applicant, and the court may in such cases exercise its power in **CPR, r. 23.3(2)(b)**, to dispense with the requirement for an application notice. If the court dispenses with the application notice, it will usually only do so for the purposes of the initial hearing. **PD 25A, para. 5.1(4)**, provides that in these circumstances the court will, unless it orders otherwise, require an undertaking from the applicant to file an application notice and pay the appropriate fee on the same or the next working day.

An application for an interim remedy must be supported by evidence, unless the court orders otherwise (**CPR, r. 25.3(2)**). The evidence required is discussed further in **37.13**.

The application should be made in the court in which the substantive proceedings are likely to be issued unless 'there is good reason to make the application to a different court' (**CPR, r. 23.2(4)**).

Especially where the terms of the injunction sought are complex, it is good practice to attach a draft of the order to the application notice and to provide it on computer disk (**PD 25A, para. 2.4**).

If the court is to serve the application on the respondent, a suitable number of copies of the application notice and evidence in support must be filed with the court. Unless the court orders otherwise, or an application without service of an application notice can be justified, the application notice should be served as soon as practicable and in any event at least three clear days before the hearing (**CPR, r. 23.7**). Pre-action applications are treated as claim forms for the purposes of the rules on service (**r. 6.2(c)**). Obviously, if three days' notice can be given of an application for an interim injunction, there will be time to issue proceedings. Pre-action applications will therefore always be made without full notice to the respondent. This can only be justified if there are 'good reasons for not giving notice' (**r. 25.3(1)**). Urgency and/or the need for secrecy will be accepted as good reasons.

Arrangements for pre-action injunction hearings

37.6 Pre-action interim injunction applications will almost always be considered at a hearing but without full (or any) notice to the respondent. Such applications will almost certainly be of an urgent nature. If they arise during or shortly before the ordinary times when the court is sitting, the hearing will take place in court as soon as the circumstances permit. This means that generally such applications are heard before other matters that are listed, either as soon as the court sits in the morning or immediately after lunch. The necessary arrangements must be made with the court staff, who will invariably do all they can to ensure urgent applications are dealt with at the first available opportunity. Solicitors should therefore contact the court by telephone as soon as they know they will need to make an urgent application, so as to allow the court time to make the necessary arrangements. Sometimes urgent applications arise during the course of the morning or afternoon in circumstances where it is not possible to wait to the beginning of the next session. If the case is sufficiently urgent the court will invariably interrupt whatever it is doing at a convenient moment so that it can hear the urgent application.

On other occasions the need for a pre-action interim injunction may arise at a time when it is not possible to wait until the next occasion when the court will be sitting. If the application is of extreme urgency it may be dealt with by telephone (**PD 25A, para. 4.2**). If the problem has arisen during business hours, but in circumstances where it will not be possible to go before a judge before the close of business, initially it is necessary to telephone the court (either the High Court on (020) 7947 6000 or the appropriate County Court hearing centre) asking to be put in touch with a High Court judge of the appropriate division or Circuit Judge available to deal with an emergency application (**PD 25A, para. 4.5(1)**).

If the problem has arisen outside office hours, the applicant should telephone either the High Court (on the same number as above) asking to be put in touch with the clerk to the appropriate duty judge (or the appropriate area Circuit Judge where known), or should telephone the urgent court business officer of the appropriate circuit, who will contact the local duty judge.

If the facilities are available, a draft of the order sought will usually be required to be sent by fax to the duty judge who will be dealing with the application.

Telephone hearings are only available if the applicant is acting by solicitors or counsel (**PD 25A, para. 4.5(5)**).

The pre-action order and related matters

37.7 The order should be in form PF 39 CH. If the order is granted, the court may give directions requiring a claim to be commenced (**CPR, r. 25.2(3)**). PD 25A, para. 5.1(5), gives effect to this by providing that an order made before issue of the claim form will, unless the court orders otherwise, include 'an undertaking to issue and pay the appropriate fee on the same or next working day' or contain directions for the commencement of the claim. In other respects the order will follow the same form as other interim injunctions, see **37.63**.

As the application will invariably have been made without notice to the respondent, the order must, by **PD 25A, para. 5.1(2)** and (3), include, unless the court orders otherwise:

(a) an undertaking by the applicant to the court to serve the respondent with the application notice, evidence in support and any order made, as soon as practicable; and

(b) a return date for a further hearing at which the other party can be present.

Counsel and solicitors have a responsibility to take a full note of what is said on a hearing where the respondent is not present, so the respondent can know the case that was made against him. There are too many technical problems in the recording system at the Royal Courts of Justice for lawyers to rely on official transcripts for this purpose (*Cinpres Gas Injection Ltd v Melea Ltd* [2005] EWHC 3180 (Pat), [2006] FSR 36).

Service of pre-action interim injunctions

Generally, pre-action applications for interim injunctions are made without notice to the respondent. Therefore, **CPR, r. 23.9**, applies. This requires a copy of the application notice and any evidence in support to be served with the injunction order on all parties and persons against whom the order was sought or made. The order must contain a statement of the right to apply under **r. 23.10** to set aside or vary the order within seven days after it is served.

37.8

Where possible the claim form should be served with the injunction order (**PD 25A, para. 4.4(2)**).

APPLICATIONS FOR INTERIM INJUNCTIONS DURING THE COURSE OF PROCEEDINGS

Time for applying for general interim injunctions

An application for an interim injunction in proceedings must be made after the claim form commencing the proceedings is issued if applying before issue is prevented by the conditions laid down in **CPR, r. 25.2(2)** (see 37.3). This will be the case where a pre-action application is prohibited by a rule or practice direction, or the matter is not urgent and it is not desirable to grant an injunction before issue in the interests of justice, or the applicant is an intended defendant and the court refuses permission. **Paragraphs 2.7** and **2.8 of PD 23A** say that any application during proceedings should be made as soon as it becomes apparent that it is necessary or desirable, but should preferably be made at a hearing for which a date has already been, or is about to be, fixed. In many cases this means that the right time to apply for an interim injunction will be at the allocation stage, but an earlier, separate hearing would be justified if delay would make it more difficult to preserve the status quo.

37.9

If the applicant is a defendant who has yet to file either an acknowledgment or a defence, the applicant must obtain the court's permission to make the application (**CPR, r. 25.2(2)(c)**).

Procedure on applications during proceedings

The procedure will be as described in 37.5 for pre-action applications except that:

37.10

(a) The application notice need not give the applicant's address for service.

(b) The application will be made:

    (i) to the court in which the substantive proceedings were started (**CPR, r. 23.2(1)**), or

    (ii) to the court in which the proceedings were subsequently transferred or sent (**r. 23.2(2)**), or

    (iii) if a date has been fixed for trial, to the court where the trial is to take place (**r. 23.2(3)**), or

    (iv) if after enforcement proceedings have been started, to the court dealing with enforcement 'unless any rule or practice direction provides otherwise' (**r. 23.2(5)**).

Commentary

(c) The rules for service of documents other than claim forms apply (**rr. 6.20** to **6.29**).

(d) It is good practice, where time allows, to annex to the application notice a draft order using N16, N16(1), CH10 or CH11. An electronic version in Word format should be emailed to the court.

For a summary of the procedure, see **procedural checklist 19** and **procedural checklist 20**.

Where the court is to serve, sufficient copies of the application notice and evidence in support should be provided for the court and each respondent (**PD 25A, para. 2.3**). Service should be effected as soon as possible, and in any event not less than three clear days before the hearing.

Although **PD 23A, para. 2.8**, provides that 'Applications should wherever possible be made so that they can be considered at any other hearing for which a date has already been fixed or for which a date is about to be fixed', clearly an application for an injunction, even where both parties are to appear at the hearing, will very often be of sufficient urgency to make it inappropriate to wait to make it until, say, the case management conference. Given the requirement to save expense (**CPR, r. 1.1(2)(b)**) and to allot to the case an appropriate share of the court's resources, while taking into account the need to allot resources to other cases (**r. 1.1(2)(e)**), an applicant should expect to be called on to justify the need for a separate hearing.

Respondents to applications made on notice are not under any specific duty under the rules to disclose their evidence in reply in advance of the hearings. However, deliberately holding back evidence in reply to the last minute will be a clear breach of the overriding objective. If the minimum of three clear days' notice was given by the applicant, it might be difficult or impossible for a respondent to compile and serve evidence in reply, which is why the CPR require the applicant to serve the application notice and evidence in support as soon as practicable after issue. The greater the notice given to the respondent, the greater is the effective obligation on the respondent to serve evidence in advance of the hearing. The rules seek to avoid multiple hearings (**CPR, r. 1.4(2)(i)**), and although the court may be prepared to give directions as to the service of evidence on the first hearing, it may well impose sanctions if it considers the need to give directions was caused by the default of either party.

Hearing of interim injunction applications in pending proceedings

37.11   Normally the hearing of an application for an interim injunction will be listed in the usual way for disposal in public (see **CPR, r. 39.2**). There are exceptional circumstances in which the hearing will be in private, such as where the hearing involves confidential information, the interests of children or protected parties, or where it would be unjust to proceed in public because the respondent has not been given due notice.

If the application is of an urgent nature justifying giving less than the usual three clear days' notice (see **37.4**), unless secrecy is essential, the applicant should give the respondents informal notice (**PD 25A, para. 4.3(3)**), which should be explained in the evidence in support. If the urgency justifies making the application without first issuing an application notice, a draft order (at least) should be provided at the hearing. Normally the court will direct that an application notice and evidence in support must be filed with the court on the same or the next working day (**PD 25A, para. 4.3(2)**). If possible, even in the case of urgent applications, the application notice, evidence in support and draft order should be filed with the court at least two hours before it is intended to go before the judge (**PD 25A, para. 4.3(1)**).

In cases of extreme urgency, the court may interrupt its list, or conduct the hearing by telephone with the duty judge, in the same way as extremely urgent pre-action applications (see **37.6**).

Where there is to be a hearing, then with consent of all parties (and provided no party is acting in person), the court can order the hearing to be dealt with by telephone (**PD 23A, para. 6.1**) or by video conference (**PD 23A, para. 7**).

Both parties should be prepared to deal with the future case management of the action. **PD 23A, para. 2.9**, warns them that: 'at any hearing the court may wish to review the conduct of the case as a whole and give any necessary case management directions. They should be ready to assist the court in doing so and to answer questions the court may ask for this purpose.' Indeed if the application takes place before allocation, the court may deal with allocation at the hearing (**PD 26, para. 2.4**).

Order obtained without notice

When an interim injunction is obtained in the course of proceedings without notice to the respondent, **CPR, rr. 23.9** and **23.10**, apply as they do to pre-action injunctions (see **37.8**). Lawyers acting for the applicant have to make and serve on the respondent a note of what was said at the without-notice hearing (*Cinpres Gas Injection Ltd v Melea Ltd* [2005] EWHC 3180 (Pat), [2006] FSR 36).   **37.12**

EVIDENCE IN SUPPORT OF AN APPLICATION
FOR AN INTERIM INJUNCTION

An application for an interim injunction must be supported by evidence unless the court orders otherwise (**CPR, r. 25.3(2)**). The evidence must cover the substantive issues and also, if the application is without notice, explain why notice has not been given (**r. 25.3(3)**; **PD 25A, para. 3.4**). If the application is made before the issue of a claim form, the evidence should also address the urgency of the application or why it is 'desirable ... in the interests of justice' to make the order (**CPR, r. 25.2(2)(b)**). The evidence should also address the relevant principles for granting injunctive relief (see below).   **37.13**

PD 25A, para. 3.2, states that unless the court or an Act requires evidence by affidavit, evidence is to be:

(a) by witness statement;
(b) set out in the application, provided it is verified by a statement of truth; or
(c) set out in a statement of case, provided it is verified by a statement of truth.

The provision whereby a statement of case can be relied on as evidence is more likely to be of use where an application for an interim injunction is made during the course of proceedings.

PD 25A, para. 3.3, provides that 'The evidence must set out the facts on which the applicant relies for the claim being made against the respondent, including all material facts of which the court should be made aware.' This provision is not restricted to applications without notice. It appears to import at least some of the concepts of the previous duty of full and frank disclosure in relation to *ex parte* applications. The extent to which there is any duty, in any applications on full notice, to make reasonable inquiries remains obscure. Further, the 'material facts of which the court should be made aware' are likely to be more wide-ranging in an application made without notice than one made with the required three clear days' notice. Nevertheless, this paragraph of the practice direction is clearly intended to make parties address adverse facts in their evidence, even where the application is on notice and the respondent has a clear ability to file evidence and make representations at the hearing.

Where the application is on notice the respondent may, of course, file evidence in opposition (**PD 23A, para. 9.4**).

STATUTORY AUTHORITY

37.14 Like all forms of equitable relief, the granting of interim injunctions is a matter within the discretion of the court. The fundamental principle is contained in the Senior Courts Act 1981, s. 37(1), which (using pre-CPR terminology) provides:

The High Court may by order (whether interlocutory or final) grant an injunction or appoint a receiver in all cases in which it appears to the court to be just and convenient to do so.

The same principle applies in the County Court, where the County Courts Act 1984, s. 38, provides in part:

(1) Subject to what follows, in any proceedings in [the County Court] the court may make any order which could be made by the High Court if the proceedings were in the High Court.
(2) Any order made by [the County Court] may be—
    (a) absolute or conditional;
    (b) final or interlocutory.

With the introduction of the **Human Rights Act 1998**, the test to be applied may be whether granting relief is just and proportionate rather than just and convenient (*South Bucks District Council v Porter* [2003] UKHL 26, [2003] 2 AC 558).

SUBSTANTIVE CAUSE OF ACTION

37.15 Injunctions are only remedies, so can usually only be granted if the applicant has a substantive cause of action. As stated by Lord Diplock in *The Siskina* [1979] AC 210:

A right to obtain an [interim] injunction is not a cause of action. It cannot stand on its own. It is dependent upon there being a pre-existing cause of action against the defendant arising out of an invasion, actual or threatened by him, of a legal or equitable right of the [claimant] for the enforcement of which the defendant is amenable to the jurisdiction of the court. The right to obtain an [interim] injunction is merely ancillary and incidental to the pre-existing cause of action.

In *The Siskina* the claimant had a cause of action against the defendant, but it was only actionable in a foreign country. It was therefore held that the English courts had no jurisdiction to grant an interim injunction to protect the applicant's position. This principle was restated by Lord Brandon of Oakbrook in *South Carolina Insurance Co. v Assurantie Maatschappij 'De Zeven Provincien' NV* [1987] AC 24, where he said that, apart from freezing injunctions and injunctions to restrain foreign proceedings, the court has discretion to grant injunctions in only two situations:

(a) where a party has invaded or threatened to invade a legal or equitable right of another party which is amenable to the jurisdiction of the court;
(b) where a party has behaved or threatened to behave in an unconscionable manner.

Point (a) above has been largely overtaken by well-known exceptions. Lord Brandon himself referred to the established jurisdiction to grant injunctions to restrain foreign proceedings. Further, the High Court has a wide power to grant injunctions in support of overseas proceedings.

Civil Jurisdiction and Judgments Act 1982, s. 25

37.16 The **CJJA 1982, s. 25**, as extended by the Civil Jurisdiction and Judgments Act 1982 (Interim Relief) Order 1997, SI 1997/302, enables the High Court to grant interim relief where proceedings have been or are to be commenced in an overseas jurisdiction. The principle underpinning **CJJA 1982, s. 25**, is that the court should assist the courts of other jurisdictions by providing such interim relief as would be available if it were itself seised of the substantive proceedings (*Refco Inc. v Eastern Trading Co.* [1999] 1 Lloyd's Rep 159; *Kensington International Ltd v Republic of Congo* [2007] EWCA Civ 1128, [2008] 1 WLR 1144). Two key restrictions in the original s. 25 (that the overseas jurisdiction had to be in the EU, and that the substantive proceedings had to come within the scope of what is now the **recast Brussels I Regulation, art. 1**) were removed by the 1997 Order. The only remaining limitation is under **CJJA 1982, s. 25(2)**, that the court may refuse relief if, in the opinion of the court, the fact that the court has no jurisdiction apart from **s. 25** makes it inexpedient for the court to grant the interim relief that is sought.

Examples

Lord Browne-Wilkinson in *Channel Tunnel Group Ltd v Balfour Beatty Construction Ltd* [1993] AC 334 in the House of Lords expressed doubt on whether the law as stated in *The Siskina* [1979] AC 210 (see **37.15**) was correct in restricting the power to grant injunctions to certain exclusive categories. The question was, however, reserved for consideration when it arises.   **37.17**

The *South Carolina Insurance Co.* principles (see **37.15**) were applied in *Ali v Westminster City Council* [1999] 1 WLR 314, in which it was held that the County Court had no jurisdiction to grant an injunction in favour of applicants seeking interim mandatory injunctions to require their local housing authorities to provide them with accommodation pending the resolution of their appeals against decisions that they were not homeless persons within the meaning of the Housing Act 1996.

A company law claim for relief of unfairly prejudicial conduct (see **85.9**) is not in itself a substantive cause of action, and it is only if there is a claim that the directors are in breach of fiduciary duty or some other established cause of action that an injunction can be granted in such proceedings (*Re Premier Electronics (GB) Ltd* [2002] 2 BCLC 634).

A judge should not be deterred from granting an interim injunction on the correct basis where, through the incompetent presentation of the applicant's case, the underlying legal cause of action has not been identified by the applicant's representatives (*Watson v Durham University* [2008] EWCA Civ 1266, LTL 24/10/2008).

Person unknown as defendant

Under the pre-CPR rules it was an almost invariable rule that proceedings and orders could only be granted against named parties (*Friern Barnet Urban District Council v Adams* [1927] 2 Ch 25). The only exception related to claims for summary possession of land.   **37.18**

In a radical decision, *Bloomsbury Publishing Group Ltd v News Group Newspapers Ltd* [2003] EWHC 1087 Ch, [2003] 1 WLR 1633, the claimant was allowed to join 'person or persons unknown' as second defendants to a claim where an interim injunction was granted restraining disclosure of the contents of, or information from, a book prior to its publication date. Laddie J said that if somebody could be identified clearly enough, a court should do what it could to allow injunctive relief to be ordered against him even if it was not possible to identify him by name. **PD 7A, para. 4.1**, merely says that the defendant 'should' be named. If proceedings are started against an unnamed person, they can be remedied under **CPR, r. 3.10**, unless the court thinks otherwise. On the facts, the injunction would be effective against people who, knowing of the order, assisted in its breach or nullified the purpose of a trial. The significance attached in this decision to the use of the word 'should' instead of 'must' in **PD 7A, para. 4.1**, while highly technical, may have been confirmed by the retention of the word 'should' in **para. 4.1** when many other occurrences of the word in the CPR and practice directions were changed to 'must' as from 1 October 2008. *Bloomsbury Publishing Group Ltd v News Group Newspapers Ltd* has been approved by the Court of Appeal in *South Cambridgeshire District Council v Persons Unknown* [2004] EWCA Civ

Commentary

1280, [2004] 4 PLR 88 and *South Cambridgeshire District Council v Gammell* [2005] EWCA Civ 1429, [2006] 1 WLR 658.

Generally, media groups that might be affected by the injunction should be given prior notice of the application. The extent of any prior notification depends on the facts of each case. It may be appropriate to limit prior notification to organisations that are believed to have shown an interest in publishing (*TUV v Person or Persons Unknown* [2010] EWHC 853 (QB), [2010] EMLR 19).

INJUNCTIONS IN SUPPORT OF THE CRIMINAL LAW

37.19   The High Court has jurisdiction to grant injunctions in support of the criminal law. In *Attorney General v Chaudry* [1971] 1 WLR 1614 Lord Denning MR said:

> There are many statutes which provide penalties for breach of them—penalties which are enforceable by means of a fine—or even imprisonment—but this has never stood in the way of the High Court granting an injunction. Many a time people have found it profitable to pay a fine and go on breaking the law. In all such cases the High Court has been ready to grant an injunction…
>
> Whenever Parliament has enacted a law and given a particular remedy for the breach of it, such remedy being in an inferior court, nevertheless the High Court always has reserve power to enforce the law so enacted by way of an injunction or declaration or other suitable remedy. The High Court has jurisdiction to ensure obedience to the law whenever it is just and convenient so to do.

These injunctions are exceptional. The main questions are whether criminal proceedings are likely to be effective to achieve the public-interest purposes of the legislation and whether there are good grounds for believing that compliance would not be secured by prosecution (*Guildford Borough Council v Hein* [2005] EWCA Civ 979, [2005] BLGR 797).

In the 1980s there were cases (*Chief Constable of Kent v V* [1983] QB 34; *West Mercia Constabulary v Wagener* [1982] 1 WLR 127; *Chief Constable of Hampshire v A Ltd* [1985] QB 132; *Chief Constable of Leicestershire v M* [1989] 1 WLR 20) dealing with applications for injunctions brought by chief constables to freeze suspected proceeds of crime in advance of any conviction for the crime in question. In *Chief Constable of Leicestershire v M* it was said that the detailed interventions by Parliament in part 6 of the Criminal Justice Act 1988 (now in the Proceeds of Crime Act 2002) suggested that the civil courts should not indulge in parallel creativity by extension of the common law principles. In *Attorney General v Blake* [2001] 1 AC 268 the claimant sought an injunction restraining the defendant from receiving any payment from a publisher resulting from the defendant's criminal conduct as a spy. The defendant had escaped to Moscow in 1966 and there was no realistic prospect of him returning to the United Kingdom. It was held that there was no common law power to confiscate property (the royalties) without compensation and no statutory confiscatory powers applied, so the court had no jurisdiction to grant the injunction.

THE *AMERICAN CYANAMID* GUIDELINES

37.20   In *American Cyanamid Co. v Ethicon Ltd* [1975] AC 396 Lord Diplock laid down guidelines on how the court's discretion to grant interim injunctions should be exercised in the usual types of cases. They most typically apply in applications for interim prohibitory injunctions. Particular examples of where they apply include applications for interim injunctions in unfair prejudice petitions under the Companies Act 2006, s. 994 (*Re Canterbury Travel (London) Ltd, Collins v Collins* [2010] EWHC 1464 (Ch), LTL 12/7/2010) and to applications relating to the Public Contracts Regulations 2006 (SI 2006/5) (*Exel Europe Ltd v University Hospitals Coventry and Warwickshire NHS Trust* [2010] EWHC 3332 (TCC), LTL 4/1/2011). Although these guidelines are of great authority, they must not be read as if they were statutory provisions, and in practice they are applied with some degree of flexibility. However, it is not unknown for judges to give reasoned judgments in interim injunction cases following the sequence of steps set out by Lord Diplock (for example, *Rottenberg v Monjack* [1993] BCLC 374). The court must also be careful to apply the overriding objective, and to grant an injunction only if it is 'just and convenient'.

The underlying purpose of the guidelines is to enable the court to make an order that will do justice between the parties, whichever way the decision goes at trial, while interfering with the parties' freedom of action to the minimum extent necessary (see *Polaroid Corporation v Eastman Kodak Co.* [1977] RPC 379 per Buckley LJ at p. 395). The guidelines are described in **37.21** to **37.33**, but there are exceptions, which are discussed in **37.34** to **37.53**.

Serious question to be tried

Before *American Cyanamid Co. v Ethicon Ltd* [1975] AC 396, the courts would only grant an interim **37.21** injunction if the applicant could establish a prima facie case on the merits. Consequently, the courts needed to consider the respective merits of the parties' cases in some detail. This encouraged the filing of detailed written evidence supported by voluminous exhibits, and resulted in lengthy interim hearings. As Lord Diplock said at p. 407:

It is no part of the court's function at this stage of the litigation to try to resolve conflicts of evidence on affidavits as to facts on which the claims of either party may ultimately depend nor to decide difficult questions of law which call for detailed argument and mature consideration.

Therefore, the court only needs to be satisfied that there is a serious question to be tried on the merits. A cause of action that can be described as hopeless will not satisfy this test (*National Commercial Bank Jamaica Ltd v Olint Corporation Ltd* [2009] UKPC 16, [2009] 1 WLR 1405 at [11]–[12]). The result is that the court is required to investigate the merits to a limited extent only. All that needs to be shown is that the claimant's cause of action has substance and reality. Beyond that, it does not matter if the claimant's chance of winning is 90 per cent or 20 per cent (*Mothercare Ltd v Robson Books Ltd* [1979] FSR 466 per Megarry V-C at p. 474; *Alfred Dunhill Ltd v Sunoptic SA* [1979] FSR 337 per Megaw LJ at p. 373). Having a weak case does not mean there is no serious issue to be tried (*B2net Ltd v HM Treasury* [2010] EWHC 51 (QB), 128 Con LR 53).

However, if there is no merit in the substantive cause of action, the application does not get past the first stage of the *American Cyanamid* guidelines (*APCOA Parking (UK) Ltd v Westminster City Council* [2010] EWHC 943 (QB), LTL 30/4/2010).

Examples   Convincing the court that the claim brought by an applicant for an interim **37.22** injunction raises a serious question to be tried is not a difficult hurdle to surmount. In *Porter v National Union of Journalists* [1980] IRLR 404, the issue was whether a strike instruction by the union affected a majority of its members. If it did, the union's rule book required a ballot. Neither party adduced accurate figures of the total numbers in the union, nor of the numbers affected by the strike instruction. It was held there was a serious question to be tried.

In *Les Laboratoires Servier v KRKA Polska Sp zoo* [2006] EWHC 2453 (Pat), LTL 3/10/2006, the claimant owned a patent for a pharmaceutical product which it alleged was about to be infringed by the defendant. There was evidence that the patented form of the product had been sold by the claimant before the priority date for the patent, thus potentially depriving the patent of its novelty. This did not mean that the claimant had no case, and it was held there was a serious issue to be tried.

On the other hand, if there is no serious question to be tried on the substantive claim, the injunction must be refused. *Morning Star Co-operative Society Ltd v Express Newspapers Ltd* [1979]

FSR 113 should be regarded as not having passed this hurdle. At the time of the case, the *Daily Star* newspaper was about to be launched. The claimant alleged that it was going to be passed off as the established *Morning Star* newspaper. Apart from the fact that they were both newspapers and had the word 'Star' in their names, they were different in about every other respect. As Foster J commented, 'Only a moron in a hurry would be misled' into thinking that the *Daily Star* was the *Morning Star*, so the claimant had failed to show a serious issue to be tried on the alleged cause of action. A weak claim on the merits combined with relatively little financial harm to the claimant through the defendant's alleged infringement of intellectual property rights resulted in a refusal of relief in *GMG Radio Holdings Ltd v Tokyo Project Ltd* [2005] EWHC 2188(Ch), LTL 21/10/2005.

In *Boobyer v David Holman and Co. Ltd* [1993] 1 Lloyd's Rep 96 the claimant, a name at Lloyd's, applied for an interim injunction to restrain the defendant underwriting agent from paying cash calls on the claimant for being a member of a number of syndicates. Saville J refused the injunction without considering the balance of convenience as the claimant had failed to show even a serious issue to be tried. In *News Datacom Ltd v Satellite Decoding Systems* [1995] FSR 201 the claimant alleged that the defendant was selling a computerised 'smart card' for decoding satellite television programmes by copying the computer program supplied by the claimant to its customers. It was accepted that the defendant's card enabled its customers to decode the claimant's satellite broadcasts. In its application for an interim injunction the claimant exhibited an expert's report in which the expert stated an opinion that the defendant's product must have been copied from the claimant's program. This opinion was based on the complexity of the program and the implausibility of the defendant's product not being a copy, and not on a comparison of the two products. The High Court of Ireland held that as the claimant had failed to adduce evidence comparing the two products it had failed to show a serious question to be tried.

Sometimes there are arguments about whether the claimant's allegations amount to a cause of action known to the law. An example was *Khorasandjian v Bush* [1993] QB 727, in which it was held by a majority that the tort of harassment exists, and on the facts the judge had been entitled to grant an interim injunction restraining the defendant from 'harassing, pestering or communicating' with the claimant. In a related case, it was held in *Burris v Azadani* [1995] 1 WLR 1372 that, when granting an interim injunction to restrain future assaults or harassment, the court has power to impose an exclusion zone at the same time. An injunction to prevent cybersquatting was granted in *Lifestyle Management Ltd v Frater* [2010] EWHC 3258 (TCC), LTL 7/1/2011.

Adequacy of damages to the applicant

37.23   If there is a serious question to be tried on the merits of the substantive claim, the court should then consider whether the applicant will be adequately compensated by an award of damages at trial. The test was stated in the following way by Lord Diplock in *American Cyanamid Co. v Ethicon Ltd* [1975] AC 396 at p. 408:

If damages in the measure recoverable at common law would be an adequate remedy and the defendant would be in a financial position to pay them, no [interim] injunction should normally be granted.

The question is whether it is just that the claimant be confined to its remedy in damages (*Evans Marshall and Co. Ltd v Bertola SA (No. 1)* [1973] 1 WLR 349). Damages will often be an adequate remedy for the claimant in claims for breach of contract, including contracts of employment (see *Ali v Southwark London Borough Council* [1988] ICR 567, but the position regarding claims in respect of contracts of employment is not completely free from doubt, see *Powell v Brent London Borough Council* [1988] ICR 176). A term providing for liquidated damages or excluding a claim for damages may mean damages are not an adequate remedy (*AB v CD* [2014] EWCA Civ 229,

[2015] 1 WLR 771). A claimant bringing an action for breach of copyright or confidence may (depending on the facts) be refused injunctive relief on the ground that damages would be an adequate remedy (*Hubbard v Vosper* [1972] 2 QB 84). However, damages will be inadequate if:

(a) The defendant is unlikely to be able to pay the sum likely to be awarded at trial.

(b) The wrong is irreparable, e.g. suspension from a professional post (*Watson v Durham University* [2008] EWCA Civ 1266, LTL 24/10/2008), loss of the right to vote.

(c) The damage is non-pecuniary, e.g. breach of an arbitration clause (*Starlight Shipping Co. v Tai Ping Insurance Co. Ltd, Hubei Branch* [2007] EWHC 1893 (Comm), [2008] 1 All ER (Comm) 593), libel, nuisance, trade secrets.

(d) There is no available market. In *Howard E. Perry and Co. Ltd v British Railways Board* [1980] 1 WLR 1375 the defendant refused to allow the claimant to remove a consignment of steel during a steelworkers' dispute. The claimant sought an order that the defendant permit the claimant to remove it. As steel was otherwise unobtainable at the time, damages were not an adequate remedy.

(e) Damages would be difficult to assess. Examples are loss of goodwill (*Foseco International Ltd v Fordath Ltd* [1975] FSR 507), disruption of business (*Evans Marshall and Co. Ltd v Bertola SA* [1973] 1 WLR 349) and where the defendant's conduct has the effect of killing off a business before it is established (*Mitchelstown Co-operative Society Ltd v Société des Produits Nestlé SA* [1989] FSR 345). Damages following being excluded from a public procurement exercise were held to be readily capable of calculation in *B2net Ltd v HM Treasury* [2010] EWHC 51 (QB), 128 Con LR 53.

As where the claimant fails to show a serious question to be tried, if damages would be an adequate remedy, that is the end of the matter and the injunction must be refused.

Undertakings in damages

37.24 Subject to some limited exceptions, an undertaking in damages is always required when an interim injunction is granted. The court has a discretion to order an interim injunction subject to a limited undertaking in damages (*RBG Resources plc v Rastogi* [2002] BPIR 1028). By the undertaking the claimant is required to compensate the defendant for any loss incurred by the defendant during the currency of the injunction if it later appears that the injunction was wrongly granted. Its purpose is to provide a safeguard for the defendant who may be unjustifiably prevented from doing something it was entitled to do. As stated in *Wakefield v Duke of Buccleugh* (1865) 12 LT 628, this assists the court 'in doing that which was its great object, viz. abstaining from expressing any opinion on the merits of the case until the hearing'.

Undertakings in damages are not required where the Crown or a local authority is seeking an interim injunction to enforce the law (*Kirklees Metropolitan Borough Council v Wickes Building Supplies Ltd* [1993] AC 227), nor from the Financial Services Authority (*Securities and Investments Board v Lloyd-Wright* [1993] 4 All ER 210) or a foreign regulator (*United States Securities and Exchange Commission v Manterfield* [2009] EWCA Civ 27, [2010] 1 WLR 172) performing its regulatory functions, unless the defendant shows a strong prima facie case that its conduct is lawful (*F. Hoffmann-La Roche & Co. AG v Secretary of State for Trade and Industry* [1975] AC 295).

The modern approach is to require an undertaking in damages in applications for freezing injunctions in aid of enforcement in the same way as other applications (*Banco Nacional de Comercio Exterior SNC v Empresa de Telecomunicaciones de Cuba SA* [2007] EWCA Civ 662, [2008] 1 WLR 1936). Like other injunctions, the undertaking is usually dispensed with in freezing injunctions sought by public authorities to enforce the law (*Financial Services Authority v Sinaloa Gold plc* [2011] EWCA Civ 1158, [2012] CP Rep 4, where the absence of an express provision about

Commentary

cross-undertakings in the Financial Services and Markets Act 2000 was held not to change the position). In *Customs and Excise Commissioners v Anchor Foods Ltd* [1999] 1 WLR 1139 the Commissioners applied to restrain the disposal of certain assets by the defendant. The purpose of the application was to protect funds which the Commissioners contended should be paid to them. Neuberger J said that in these circumstances the presence or absence of an undertaking in damages was a factor to be weighed when considering the balance of convenience, and was only prepared to grant an injunction if the Commissioners gave an undertaking in damages.

An undertaking is also dispensed with where the injunction is in the nature of final relief (*Fenner v Wilson* [1893] 2 Ch 656), and where an injunction is granted in aid of execution after judgment (*Gwembe Valley Development Co. Ltd v Koshy (No. 4)* (2001) *The Times*, 28 February 2002).

37.25   **Fortifying the undertaking in damages**   Where there is doubt about the claimant's solvency and hence the value of the usual undertaking in damages, the claimant may be required to 'fortify the undertaking' by bringing money into court or by providing security. A defendant seeking an order that the claimant must fortify an undertaking needs to satisfy the court that the injunction is likely to cause the defendant significant loss and there must be satisfactory evidence that the claimant may be unable to pay (*Bhimji v Chatwani (No. 2)* [1992] BCLC 387). For procedural requirements, see **37.64**, and in relation to freezing injunctions, **38.16**.

37.26   **Whether the undertaking in damages is an adequate protection for the defendant**   In *American Cyanamid Co. v Ethicon Ltd* [1975] AC 396 Lord Diplock said at p. 408:

> If... damages would not provide an adequate remedy for the [claimant] in the event of his succeeding at the trial, the court should then consider whether, on the contrary hypothesis that the defendant were to succeed at the trial in establishing his right to do that which was sought to be enjoined, he would be adequately compensated under the [claimant's] undertaking as to damages for the loss he would have sustained by being prevented from doing so between the time of the application and the time of the trial. If damages in the measure recoverable under such an undertaking would be an adequate remedy and the [claimant] would be in a financial position to pay them, there would be no reason upon this ground to refuse an [interim] injunction.
>
> It is where there is doubt as to the adequacy of the respective remedies in damages available to either party or to both, that the question of balance of convenience arises.

It is clear from this that, unlike the question whether the claimant would be adequately compensated in damages, the adequacy of the undertaking will rarely be determinative of the application. If it is an adequate protection, that is 'no reason' for refusing the injunction. The court will then consider the balance of convenience, but the fact that the defendant is adequately protected will be a substantial factor in favour of granting the injunction (see *Bunn v British Broadcasting Corporation* [1998] 3 All ER 552). If there is a serious issue to be tried, and the claimant could be prejudiced by the acts or omissions of the defendant pending trial, and the claimant's undertaking in damages would provide the defendant with an adequate remedy if it transpires that his freedom of action should not have been restrained, an interim injunction should ordinarily be granted (*National Commercial Bank Jamaica Ltd v Olint Corporation Ltd* [2009] UKPC 16, [2009] 1 WLR 1405 at [16]). If the undertaking does not adequately protect the defendant, although that is a reason for refusing the injunction, normally the court will go on to consider the balance of convenience.

Even a freezing injunction has been granted in favour of a legally aided claimant (who obviously could not give a valuable undertaking in damages) where otherwise it was a proper case for granting the injunction (*Allen v Jambo Holdings Ltd* [1980] 1 WLR 1252). If the claimant is unable to give an undertaking in damages, care must be exercised before granting an injunction. It was said in *Belize Alliance of Conservation Non-Governmental Organisations v Department of the Environment* [2003] UKPC 63, 63 WIR 42, that it is particularly important to form a view on the merits of the claim in such cases, and to grant an injunction only if the claimant has a strong case. Where defendants in an application for a freezing injunction had failed to put in any evidence of the sort of loss they might suffer as a result of the order, it was held in *Bracken Partners Ltd v Gutteridge* (2001) LTL 16/1/2002 that there was no present basis for regarding the claimant's undertaking in damages as being insufficient.

Refusal of injunction in extreme cases   In extreme cases where the claimant cannot give   **37.27**
an adequate undertaking in damages, the court will refuse the injunction without considering the balance of convenience. *Morning Star Co-operative Society Ltd v Express Newspapers Ltd* [1979] FSR 113 was such a case, referred to at **37.22**. In addition to the weak cause of action, the claimant had assets of £170,000 and liabilities of £260,000, so there was no realistic chance of it being able to honour the undertaking, especially as the defendants were likely to suffer appreciable, unquantifiable, damages. In *Merrell Dow Pharmaceuticals Inc. v N. H. Norton and Co. Ltd* [1994] RPC 1 a patentee would probably have had to make a permanent reduction in its prices as a result of an alleged infringement, which was an ascertainable loss, whereas the defendant had an unascertainable loss represented by the possible market share it would not achieve if the injunction was granted. On this basis the injunction was refused.

Balance of convenience   Most injunction cases are determined on the balance of conveni-   **37.28**
ence. In *American Cyanamid Co. v Ethicon Ltd* [1975] AC 396 Lord Diplock said, at p. 408:

> it would be unwise to attempt even to list all the various matters which may need to be taken into consideration in deciding where the balance lies, let alone to suggest the relative weight to be attached to them. These will vary from case to case.

In other cases, such as *Cayne v Global Natural Resources plc* [1984] 1 All ER 225, the courts have insisted that it is not mere convenience that needs to be weighed, but the risk of doing an injustice to one side or the other. This is often an exercise in seeking to determine whether granting or refusing the injunction will cause irremediable prejudice, and to what extent (*National Commercial Bank Jamaica Ltd v Olint Corporation Ltd* [2009] UKPC 16, [2009] 1 WLR 1405 at [17]–[18]). Among the matters the court may take into account are:

(a) The prejudice the claimant may suffer if no injunction is granted or the defendant may suffer if it is. A claimant can reduce the potential injustice to the defendant by drafting the terms of the injunction as narrowly as is consistent with preserving the claimant's interests, or by offering undertakings to provide extra safeguards for the defendant.
(b) The likelihood of such prejudice actually occurring.
(c) The extent to which it may be compensated by an award of damages or enforcement of the undertaking in damages. Lord Diplock in *American Cyanamid Co. v Ethicon Ltd* said the extent to which the disadvantages to each party would be incapable of being compensated in damages is always a significant factor in assessing where the balance of convenience lies. In *Dyrlund Smith A/S v Turberville Smith Ltd* [1998] FSR 774 the apparent inability of the defendants to meet an award of damages was regarded as the decisive factor in favour of granting an interim injunction.
(d) The likelihood of either party being able to satisfy such an award.
(e) The likelihood that the injunction will turn out to have been wrongly granted or withheld (i.e. the court's view of the relative strengths of the parties' cases). It is submitted that this last matter should only be considered if the other matters are evenly balanced, or where it is possible to form such a view on facts which are clear or not in dispute. The main purpose behind the decision in *American Cyanamid Co. v Ethicon Ltd* [1975] AC 396 was to avoid contentious disputes over the merits of the case on applications for interim injunctions, which is the reason why the threshold is for a serious question to be tried, rather than the earlier prima facie case test.

The fact a court may have decided to order a speedy trial is no more than a factor in assessing the balance of convenience (*Talaris (Sweden) AB v Network Controls International Ltd* [2008] EWHC 2930 (TCC), LTL 5/12/2008).

37.29   Examples   The claimants in *American Cyanamid Co. v Ethicon Ltd* [1975] AC 396 sought an interim injunction to prevent the defendants marketing a surgical suture alleged to be in breach of patent. The claimants' patented suture had recently been introduced, and the claimants were expanding their market. The defendants' product had not at that time been introduced. They asserted that their product did not infringe the claimants' patent, alternatively, that the patent was invalid. If the injunction had been granted no factories would have closed, but if refused the claimants might have failed to increase their market and would effectively have lost the benefit of their patent. Therefore, the balance favoured the claimants. In *Douglas v Hello! Ltd* [2001] QB 967 an interim injunction to restrain a magazine from publishing wedding photographs alleged to infringe the first two claimants' rights of privacy was refused. If the event had been more intimate and private, the court would have been more willing to assist, but the first two claimants had already sold the rights to their wedding photographs to the third claimant, and the third claimant was adequately protected by an award of damages. On the other side, an injunction would have prevented publication of an issue of the defendant's magazine.

Each case turns on its own facts, but matters found to be important include:

(a)   being deprived of employment (*Fellowes and Son v Fisher* [1976] QB 122);

(b)   damage to business through picketing (*Hubbard v Pitt* [1976] QB 142);

(c)   damage to the goodwill of a business (*Associated Newspapers plc v Insert Media Ltd* [1991] 1 WLR 571);

(d)   closing down the defendant's business, and the number of people who might lose their jobs (*Lawrence v Fen Tigers Ltd* [2014] UKSC 13, [2014] AC 822). Closing a factory was described as being catastrophic in *Potters-Ballotini Ltd v Weston-Baker* [1977] RPC 202;

(e)   long-term effects on the price of the claimant's patented products if the defendant and other competitors are able to copy them (*Les Laboratoires Servier v KRKA Polska Sp zoo* [2006] EWHC 2453 (Pat), LTL 3/10/2006);

(f)   whether complying with its mandate would put a bank in breach of the Proceeds of Crime Act 2002 (*K Ltd v National Westminster Bank plc* [2006] EWCA Civ 1039, [2007] 1 WLR 311);

(g)   although the fact that an injunction may result in a company being wound up is a weighty matter, in *Astor Chemicals Ltd v Synthetic Technology Ltd* [1990] BCLC 1 this was outweighed by other considerations, particularly the fact that the company wanted to continue trading on a very speculative venture while hopelessly insolvent;

(h)   interim relief seeking to prolong a state of affairs that is unsustainable in the long term is likely to be refused (*Re Canterbury Travel (London) Ltd, Collins v Collins* [2010] EWHC 1464 (Ch), LTL 12/7/2010, an unfair prejudice case);

(i)   the number of people affected by the defendant's activities (*Lawrence v Fen Tigers Ltd* [2014] UKSC 13, [2014] AC 822);

(j)   disruption to non-parties (*B2net Ltd v HM Treasury* [2010] EWHC 51 (QB), 128 Con LR 53, an application to suspend a public procurement exercise);

(k)   preserving confidential information (*X AG v A Bank* [1983] 2 All ER 464);

(l)   the public benefit of the defendant's activities (*Lawrence v Fen Tigers Ltd* [2014] UKSC 13, [2014] AC 822 (sporting activities); *Roussel-Uclaf v G. D. Searle and Co. Ltd* [1977] FSR 125 (drug with life-saving characteristics));

(m)   preserving a substantial financial investment (*Catnic Components Ltd v Stressline Ltd* [1976] FSR 157);

(n)   a failure by the claimant to respond to a letter from the defendant frankly stating its plans and enclosing sample containers, use of which is alleged by the claimant to amount to passing off (*Dalgety Spillers Foods Ltd v Food Brokers Ltd* [1994] FSR 504).

Status quo

37.30   In *American Cyanamid Co. v Ethicon Ltd* [1975] AC 396 Lord Diplock said at p. 408 that, in considering the balance of convenience: 'Where other factors appear to be evenly balanced it is a counsel of prudence to take such measures as are calculated to preserve the status quo'. From

Garden Cottage Foods Ltd v Milk Marketing Board [1984] AC 130, it appears that the status quo ante is the state of affairs before the defendant started the conduct complained of, unless there has been unreasonable delay, when it is the state of affairs immediately before the application. Therefore, it behoves the claimant to act quickly. An apparently unreasonable delay may be excused if sufficiently explained by the claimant.

Special factors

As Lord Diplock said in *American Cyanamid Co. v Ethicon Ltd* [1975] AC 396 at p. 409, 'there **37.31** may be many special factors to be taken into consideration [in the balance of convenience] in the particular circumstances of individual cases'. If American Cyanamid Co. had been refused interim relief, but had established its claim at trial, it was probable that it would have been commercially impracticable for it to have insisted on Ethicon's sutures then being withdrawn, as doctors would have by then become used to using Ethicon's new sutures.

Merits of the claim

In *American Cyanamid Co. v Ethicon Ltd* [1975] AC 396 Lord Diplock said at p. 409 that, as a last **37.32** resort:

it may not be improper to take into account in tipping the balance the relative strength of each party's case as revealed by the affidavit evidence adduced on the hearing of the application. This, however, should be done only where it is apparent upon the facts disclosed by evidence as to which there is no credible dispute that the strength of one party's case is disproportionate to that of the other party. The court is not justified in embarking upon anything resembling a trial of the action upon conflicting affidavits in order to evaluate the strength of either party's case.

An example of a case where the merits were considered under this principle is *Cambridge Nutrition Ltd v British Broadcasting Corporation* [1990] 3 All ER 523. The merits were considered, because the incompensable damage to each party did not differ widely.

Less formal approaches

Although the *American Cyanamid* principles are well established, there are occasions where **37.33** judges adopt slightly different approaches when deciding whether it is just and convenient (the Senior Courts Act 1981, s. 37, test, see **37.14**) to grant an injunction. There are some judges who, in exceptional cases, will weigh the respective merits of the parties' cases as disclosed in the written evidence and exhibits in deciding whether or not to grant interim injunctive relief. This approach finds expression in the judgment of Laddie J in *Series 5 Software Ltd v Clarke* [1996] 1 All ER 853. In his judgment Laddie J said the following were the guidelines to be adopted on a proper analysis of the *American Cyanamid* decision:

(a) that interim injunctions are discretionary and all the facts of the case must be considered;

(b) there are no fixed rules, and the relief must be kept flexible;

(c) the court should rarely attempt to resolve complex issues of disputed fact or law;

(d) important factors in exercising the jurisdiction to grant interim injunctions are:

   (i) the extent to which damages are likely to be an adequate remedy to either side, and the ability of the other party to pay;

   (ii) the balance of convenience;

   (iii) maintaining the status quo; and

   (iv) any clear view the court may reach about the relative strength of the parties' cases.

In *Carlisle Cumbria United Independent Supporters Society Ltd v Courtnay* (2005) LTL 25/11/2005 the questions asked by Sir Donald Rattee in considering whether to continue an injunction restraining the defendant from acting contrary to an agreement between the parties (a case close to the negative covenant exception discussed at **37.51**) were:

(a) whether the claimant had shown a good arguable case on the merits; and

(b) whether the continuation of the injunction would better preserve the court's ability to do justice between the parties at trial than a refusal to continue the injunction.

EXCEPTIONAL CASES

37.34   There are some well-settled categories of cases where the *American Cyanamid* guidelines (see **37.20** to **37.33**) are not applied. Interim injunctions in pending appeals are considered at **74.47**. The usual difference is that in most exceptional cases the courts will investigate the merits of the cause of action. How these various cases can be reconciled with *American Cyanamid Co. v Ethicon Ltd* [1975] AC 396 is a question of some theoretical controversy. Suggestions are that they are examples of the 'special factors' mentioned by Lord Diplock; that the *American Cyanamid* guidelines only apply where the facts are in dispute; that *American Cyanamid* only applies where a trial is likely; and that the existence of some or all of the categories were not directly considered by Lord Diplock.

Final disposal of the claim

37.35   In *NWL Ltd v Woods* [1979] 1 WLR 1294 Lord Diplock said at p. 1306:

> *American Cyanamid Co. v Ethicon Ltd* [1975] AC 396 ... was not dealing with a case in which the grant or refusal of an injunction at that stage would, in effect, dispose of the action finally in favour of which-ever party was successful in the application, because there would be nothing left on which it was in the unsuccessful party's interest to proceed to trial.

Two questions arise (see *Cayne v Global Natural Resources plc* [1984] 1 All ER 225; *Channel Tunnel Group Ltd v Balfour Beatty Construction Ltd* [1993] AC 334). First, on the assumption that the injunction is refused, and taking into account the likely length of time it will take to get to trial and the probable factual situation at that time, is there any realistic possibility that the claimant will wish to proceed to trial? Assertions by claimants that they will in any event pro-ceed to trial to recover damages may be disregarded if in reality a trial would be a meaningless gesture (*Lansing Linde Ltd v Kerr* [1991] 1 WLR 251). Secondly, on the assumption that the injunc-tion is granted, is there any realistic prospect of the defendant insisting on going to trial to vindicate its defence and having the injunction discharged? Where neither party has a real interest in going to trial, the interim application will finally determine the claim. In such a case, Lord Diplock in *NWL Ltd v Woods* [1979] 1 WLR 1294, said at p. 1307:

> the degree of likelihood that the [claimant] would have succeeded in establishing his right to an injunc-tion if the action had gone to trial, is a factor to be brought into the balance by the judge in weighing the risks that injustice may result from his deciding the application one way rather than the other.

The degree to which the claimant must establish the merits of the case vary with the circum-stances. Thus, in *Cayne v Global Natural Resources plc* [1984] 1 All ER 225, the claimants, who were shareholders in the defendant company, sought injunctions, *inter alia*, to restrain the com-pany from implementing a merger transaction without first obtaining the approval of the company in general meeting. There was no realistic prospect of a trial, because by the time the claim could be tried either the deal would have been implemented or the general meeting would have taken place. The claimants alleged the purpose of the transaction was to main-tain the directors in office. The defendants served evidence which, if true, completely destroyed the claimants' case. Instead of applying the *American Cyanamid* guidelines the court had to apply the broad principle of doing its best to avoid injustice. Eveleigh LJ said, at p. 233:

> it would be wrong to run the risk of causing an injustice to a defendant who is being denied the right to trial where the defence put forward has been substantiated by affidavits and a number of exhibits.

Accordingly, an injunction would only have been granted if the claimants' case was overwhelming on its merits. It was not, so the injunction was refused. The actual standard of proof demanded in final disposal cases depends on the circumstances of each case. The 'high degree of assurance' test (the usual test for interim mandatory injunctions, see **37.61**) was applied in the final disposal case of *Chambers v British Olympic Association* [2008] EWHC 2028 (QB), LTL 18/7/2008. *Lansing Linde Ltd v Kerr* [1991] 1 WLR 251 concerned an application for an injunction to enforce a covenant in restraint of trade. It was not possible for the claim to be tried before the expiry of the period of the restraint; the claimants were not realistically interested in pursuing their claim for damages; so there was no prospect of a trial. Staughton LJ said that in the circumstances justice simply required 'some assessment of the merits...more than merely a serious issue to be tried'. A case just on the other side of the line regarding final disposal was *Astor Chemicals Ltd v Synthetic Technology Ltd* [1990] BCLC 1. The main issue on this aspect of the case was whether the defendant had any real interest in taking the case to trial if the injunction was granted, given that the effect of the injunction was almost certainly to force it into liquidation. It was held that there was some prospect of the liquidator taking the claim to trial for the defendant, so *American Cyanamid Co. v Ethicon Ltd* had to be applied.

Defamation claims at common law

Since *Bonnard v Perryman* [1891] 2 Ch 269, it has been held that interim injunctions will not generally be granted in defamation cases if the defendant intends to defend on the basis that the statement is substantially true under what is now the Defamation Act 2013, s. 2. In *Bestobell Paints Ltd v Bigg* [1975] FSR 421 it was held that this principle is unaltered by *American Cyanamid Co. v Ethicon Ltd* [1975] AC 396, because of the overriding public interest in protecting the right to free speech. In *Greene v Associated Newspapers Ltd* [2004] EWCA Civ 1462, [2005] QB 972, it was held that the rule in *Bonnard v Perryman* is also unaltered by the **Human Rights Act 1998, s. 12(3)** (see **37.37**) or by the **Human Rights Act 1998, s. 6** (which requires public authorities to act in ways compatible with the Convention, see **91.6**). The defamation rule does not, however, apply to trade mark infringement cases, even where the trademark is used in comparative advertising (*Boehringer Ingelheim Ltd v Vetplus Ltd* [2007] EWCA Civ 583, [2007] Bus LR 1456).

37.36

For the *Bonnard v Perryman* exception to apply there are two conditions:

(a) The defendant must state in the evidence in reply that it is intended to set up the defence that the statement is substantially true.
(b) The alleged libel must not be obviously untruthful. The claimant may accordingly adduce evidence to prove the falsity of the words published. However, the burden on the claimant is a heavy one (*Holley v Smyth* [1998] QB 726).

In *Holley v Smyth* the claimants could not discharge the burden of proving that the alleged libel was obviously untruthful, but argued that an injunction should nevertheless be granted on account of the defendant's motive. The defendant alleged that the first two claimants were guilty of fraud and that the third and fourth claimants were guilty of negligence in relation to the fraud. He wrote to the claimants enclosing copies of press releases he proposed publishing if the sums he alleged had been lost were not repaid. It was accepted in the Court of Appeal that his motive was not so much to publish the truth, but the less high-minded one of obtaining the sum he considered he was owed by the claimants. It was held that this was insufficient to allow the court to go behind the principle in *Bonnard v Perryman*. However, if the defendant's conduct had gone further and amounted to the crime of blackmail, an injunction would have been granted.

Similar principles probably apply where the defendant intends to rely on the defences of honest opinion (Defamation Act 2013, s. 3) or public interest (s. 4). This was the position before the Defamation Act 2013 in relation to the defences of fair comment on a matter of public

Commentary

interest (*Fraser v Evans* [1969] 1 QB 349) and qualified privilege (*Harakas v Baltic Mercantile and Shipping Exchange Ltd* [1982] 1 WLR 958). The rule in *Bonnard v Perryman* cannot be evaded by pleading the claim in both libel and breach of confidence, where it is clear that the main claim is in libel (*Woodward v Hutchins* [1977] 1 WLR 760). However, the rule in *Bonnard v Perryman* is ousted where the publication amounts to a contempt of court as well as a libel (*Attorney General v News Group Newspapers Ltd* [1987] QB 1).

Right to freedom of expression

37.37   Article 10(1) of the European Convention on Human Rights provides that everyone has the right to freedom of expression. This right is subject to safeguards in **art. 10(2)**, which include restrictions for the protection of the reputation or rights of others. The **Human Rights Act 1998**, sets out three interlocking provisions to protect the primacy of the right to freedom of expression. First, the applicant is under a duty to take all practical steps to inform the respondent of the application (**s. 12(2)**). Secondly, **s. 12(3)** provides that no relief to restrain publication before trial which might affect the **art. 10(1)** right is to be allowed 'unless the court is satisfied that the applicant is likely to establish that the publication should not be allowed'. In *Cream Holdings Ltd v Banerjee* [2004] UKHL 44, [2005] AC 253, the House of Lords rejected an argument that **s. 12(3)** simply required the applicant to show a 'real prospect of success', even one convincingly established. Instead, a flexible approach has to be taken. To satisfy the test in **s. 12(3)** the applicant must in most cases advance a case which will probably ('more likely than not') succeed at trial (Lord Nicholls of Birkenhead at [22]). The threshold that the applicant needs to pass is a high one (*Viscount Monckton of Brenchley v British Broadcasting Corporation* (2011) LTL 3/2/2011). While the cases may appear to lay down clear principles, applying them is far more difficult. Eady J in *CDE v MGN Ltd* [2010] EWHC 3308 (QB), LTL 11/2/2011, commented that the guidance given in *Cream Holdings Ltd v Banerjee* does not make the task any easier: there are no hard and fast rules, and it is a question of weighing up competing Convention rights and forming a judgment based on the unique facts of each case. The court will then exercise its discretion, taking into account the jurisprudence on **art. 10** and any other relevant matters.

Where this approach does not achieve the legislative intention behind **s. 12(3)**, or fails to give effect to countervailing Convention rights, a lesser degree of likelihood will suffice to satisfy the test. Exceptional cases suggested by Lord Nicholls in *Cream Holdings Ltd v Banerjee* were where the potential adverse consequences of disclosure are particularly grave, and where a short-term injunction is needed to enable the court to give proper consideration to an application for an interim injunction. Damage to reputation is not in itself enough to make a case exceptional for this purpose (*Boehringer Ingelheim Ltd v Vetplus Ltd* [2007] EWCA Civ 583, [2007] Bus LR 1456).

Thirdly, **s. 12(4)** provides that the court must have particular regard to the importance of the Convention right to freedom of expression, and in particular:

(a) whether the material is available to the public; and
(b) whether it is in the public interest for material to be published.

In considering whether a publication is in the public interest for the purposes of **s. 12(4)(b)** the court is obliged to consider any relevant privacy code (*TSE v News Group Newspapers Ltd* [2011] EWHC 1308 (QB), LTL 26/5/2011). Under the Press Complaints Commission Editors' Code of Practice, 'Editors will be expected to justify intrusions into any individual's private life without consent' (cl. 3(ii)). Such intrusions can be justified only where they 'can be demonstrated to be in the public interest'. It is frequently the case that stories newspapers may wish to publish are of great interest to the public, but are not in the public interest (*K v News Group Newspapers Ltd* [2011] EWCA Civ 439, [2011] 1 WLR 1827).

Privacy: new or extended torts

Interim injunctions in proceedings to restrain newspapers from publishing articles that invade **37.38** the claimant's privacy should normally be governed by the *American Cyanamid* guidelines (see **37.20** to **37.33**), as adapted by the **Human Rights Act 1998, s. 12(3)** (see **37.37**). *Douglas v Hello! Ltd* [2001] QB 967, which is discussed at **37.29**, was widely interpreted as opening the door to a new cause of action to protect individual privacy based on the European Convention on Human Rights, **art. 8**, in the **Human Rights Act 1998, sch. 1**. The House of Lords has made clear there is no common law tort of invasion of privacy, with or without the **Human Rights Act 1998** (*Wainwright v Home Office* [2003] UKHL 53, [2004] 2 AC 406). The absence of a legally binding requirement to notify the subject in advance of any publication in the media does not breach **art. 8** (*Mosley v United Kingdom* (application 48009/08) (2011) 53 EHRR 30).

Despite the decision in *Wainwright v Home Office* the courts have been concerned to develop a law of privacy that provides protection of the rights of an individual to 'private and family life, his home and his correspondence' as recognised by **art. 8**. Among the high-profile reported cases are *Prince of Wales v Associated Newspapers Ltd* [2006] EWCA Civ 1776, [2008] Ch 57; *Douglas v Hello! Ltd (No. 3)* [2007] UKHL 21, [2008] 1 AC 1; *Campbell v MGN Ltd* [2004] UKHL 22, [2004] 2 AC 457; *Murray v Express Newspapers plc* [2008] EWCA Civ 446, [2009] Ch 481; and *Donald v Ntuli* [2010] EWCA Civ 1276, [2011] 1 WLR 294. As Lord Neuberger MR said in his *Report of the Committee on Super-Injunctions: Super-Injunctions, Anonymised Injunctions and Open Justice, Judiciary* (20 May 2011) the courts have:

(a) developed the pre-existing tort of breach of confidence; and
(b) started to develop a new tort of misuse of private information.

Confidentiality

Confidentiality cases broadly fall into three categories: those where there is an express prior con- **37.39** fidentiality agreement; those involving conduct which is inconsistent with a pre-existing relationship; and those involving purloining of private information. An express contractual duty of confidentiality should be given more weight than an implied duty arising from the general principles of equity (*London Regional Transport v Mayor of London* [2001] EWCA Civ 1491, [2003] EMLR 4). Stolen private information is more likely to be protected than confidential information arising from a pre-existing relationship (*McKennitt v Ash* [2006] EWCA Civ 1714, [2008] QB 73 at [8]).

Where no Convention rights are engaged, applications to restrain confidential information are decided applying the usual *American Cyanamid* principles (*Lock International plc v Beswick* [1989] 1 WLR 1268). An additional question is whether the information is in the public domain, in which event there will not be a serious question to be tried.

Applications to restrain the use of confidential information often engage either or both of **arts 8** and **10** of the European Convention on **Human Rights in the Human Rights Act 1998, sch. 1**. Where **art. 10** is engaged, the applicant has to satisfy the merits test set out in the **Human Rights Act 1998, s. 12(3)** (see **37.37**). In these cases three issues arise:

(a) whether the information is in principle protected (*McKennitt v Ash*) (if not, there is no case);
(b) whether the information is already in the public domain, so that it has lost its private or confidential nature (*Attorney General v Guardian Newspapers Ltd (No. 2)* [1990] 1 AC 109); and
(c) whether the interest in keeping the information private or confidential should yield to the public interest in freedom of expression (*McKennitt v Ash*).

Protection of private or confidential information

A duty of confidence may arise by statute (such as the Official Secrets Acts 1911 to 1989) or **37.40** through the obligations imposed by a person's professional rules (such as the SRA Code of Conduct 2011 and the Bar Code of Conduct: see also the Legal Services Act 2007, ss. 176 and 188).

Employees, purchasers of businesses, parties involved in arbitrations and mediations, and parties in numerous other situations, may enter into contractual obligations of confidentiality. In these situations there may be little doubt over the duty of confidentiality. The more difficult question may be whether the relevant information or circumstances come within the duty.

There may be a duty of confidentiality where sensitive information is communicated in a letter marked 'private and confidential' (see *Prince of Wales v Associated Newspapers Ltd* [2006] EWCA Civ 1776, [2008] Ch 57).

In other cases the duty arises only if the information is of such a nature and obtained in such circumstances that any reasonable person in the position of the recipient ought to recognise that it should be treated as confidential (*Napier v Pressdram Ltd* [2009] EWCA Civ 443, [2010] 1 WLR 934). This will be satisfied where a reasonable person in the position of the subject of the disclosure would find the publication offensive (*Campbell v MGN Ltd* [2004] UKHL 22, [2004] 2 AC 457). The result of a disciplinary inquiry is not confidential information, nor is the identity of the parties (*Napier v Pressdram Ltd*). The court must bear in mind the jurisprudence under **art. 8**, including *Hannover v Germany* (application 59320/00) (2005) 40 EHRR 1, which decided that activities such as family holidays and sporting activities are part of a person's private recreation time and are protected by **art. 8**. Factors to take into account in deciding whether there was a reasonable expectation of privacy include the attributes of the claimant, what he was doing at the time, where, the nature of the intrusion, whether there was consent, the effect on the claimant and the circumstances of the proposed publication (*Murray v Express Newspapers plc* [2008] EWCA Civ 446, [2009] Ch 481). Depending on the facts, this may mean that photographs taken of a child in a public place may be protected. In *Mosley v News Group Newspapers Ltd* [2008] EWHC 1777 (QB), [2008] EMLR 20, it was held that the clandestine recording of sexual activity on private property engaged **art. 8**. Photographs taken at a private wedding were held to be protected in *Douglas v Hello! Ltd (No. 3)* [2007] UKHL 21, [2008] 1 AC 1. A finding that the information is untrue is not a defence (*McKennitt v Ash* [2006] EWCA Civ 1714, [2008] QB 73).

Information in the public domain

37.41 Once information has become available to the public it loses its confidential nature (*Attorney General v Guardian Newspapers Ltd (No. 2)* [1990] 1 AC 109). An injunction will not be granted to restrain disclosure of information which is already in the public domain (*D v L* [2003] EWCA Civ 1169, LTL 31/7/2003). The 'springboard doctrine' (that an injunction might be granted to restrain continued use of confidential information once the information has ceased to be confidential) has been laid to rest (*Vestergaard Frandsen A/S v Bestnet Europe Ltd* [2009] EWHC 1456 (Ch), [2010] FSR 2). Whether dissemination of the information has resulted in it losing its confidential nature is a qualitative and not merely a quantitative question (*Northern Rock plc v Financial Times Ltd* [2007] EWHC 2677 (QB), LTL 26/11/2007). Publication of the material on some remote or expert website not generally available to the public without a great deal of effort, may mean confidentiality is not lost (*Barclays Bank plc v Guardian News and Media Ltd* [2009] EWHC 591 (QB), LTL 27/3/2009).

Balancing art. 8 and art. 10 rights

37.42 If information is private, the question is whether the interest of its owner, under the European Convention on Human Rights, **art. 8**, in the **Human Rights Act 1998, sch. 1**, should in all the circumstances yield to the right of freedom of expression which the publisher has under **art. 10**. Four principles were extracted from *Campbell v MGN Ltd* [2004] UKHL 22, [2004] 2 AC 457, by Lord Steyn in *Re S (A Child) (Identification: Restrictions on Publication)* [2004] UKHL 47, [2005] 1 AC 593 at [17]:

(a) neither **art. 8** nor **art. 10** has precedence over the other;

(b) where the values under the two articles are in conflict, an intense focus on the comparative importance of the specific rights being claimed in the individual case is necessary;

(c) the justifications for interfering with or restricting each right must be taken into account; and

(d) the proportionality test must be applied to each (also known as the ultimate balancing test).

In *Campbell v MGN Ltd* details of the claimant's drug addiction therapy went beyond the level of detail required to give credibility to the story published in the newspaper. Taking into account all the circumstances, the claimant's right to respect for her private life under **art. 8** outweighed the newspaper's right to freedom of expression under **art. 10**. In *Donald v Ntuli* [2010] EWCA Civ 1276, [2011] 1 WLR 294, it was held there was a reasonable expectation of privacy over salacious details and other details of an intimate nature about a past personal relationship, unless it could be shown that there was a countervailing public interest (such as the relationship between a politician and someone they have appointed to public office).

At this stage the court takes into account whether the publication would be highly offensive to an objective, reasonable person (*Murray v Express Newspapers plc* [2008] EWCA Civ 446, [2009] Ch 48). A particularly weighty factor is the **art. 8** rights of any children who might be harmed by a publication (*K v News Group Newspapers Ltd* [2011] EWCA Civ 439, [2011] 1 WLR 1827). In *Mosley v News Group Newspapers Ltd* [2008] EWHC 1777 (QB), [2009] EMLR 20, it was held that a particularly serious reason was required before clandestine recordings could be published under **art. 10**.

A distinction is drawn between cases where there is and is not a breach of confidence (*Prince of Wales v Associated Newspapers Ltd* [2006] EWCA Civ 1776, [2008] Ch 57, per Lord Phillips of Worth Matravers LCJ). Where there is no breach of confidence, the balance between **arts 8** and **10** usually involves weighing the nature and consequences of the breach of privacy against the public interest, if any, in the disclosure of the information. In cases where there is a breach of confidence, that is in itself a factor capable of justifying restrictions on freedom of expression under **art. 10(2)**. The question is whether a fetter on the right of freedom of expression is in the particular circumstances necessary in a democratic society. A significant element in reaching a proportionate decision on this issue is the importance attached in a democratic society to upholding duties of confidence, as well as considering the nature of the information and the nature of the relationship giving rise to the duty of confidentiality. In *Re A Local Authority (Inquiry: Restraint on Publication)* [2003] EWHC 2746 (Fam), [2004] Fam 96, the balance came down in favour of granting an injunction to restrain publication of a report on fostering children as the **art. 8** rights of the children and vulnerable adults identified in the report outweighed the local authority's right to publish under **art. 10**.

Super-injunctions

The term 'super-injunction' was first used by *The Guardian* newspaper when describing the injunction granted in the *Trafigura* case (*RJW v Guardian News and Media Ltd* [2009] EWHC 2540 (QB)). A super-injunction clause uses words that prohibit the publication or disclosure of the court proceedings and also the fact that an interim injunction has been applied for, to anyone other than the respondent's lawyers. In the *Trafigura* case Maddison J granted an injunction against the newspaper and persons unknown preventing them from publishing or disclosing a privileged report on alleged dumping of toxic waste in the Ivory Coast. The application:

37.43

(a) was made without notice; and

(b) was dealt with at a hearing conducted in private.

The order included clauses which:

(a) anonymised the claimant's name by changing it to a sequence of letters, 'RJW';

(b) adjusted all references to people and places to conceal the identity of the claimant;

Commentary

(c) contained a super-injunction clause;

(d) contained a further clause that 'sealed' the court file for the purposes of **CPR, r. 5.4C**; and

(e) prevented the respondent from disclosing court papers to anyone other than for the purpose of obtaining legal advice.

Detailed guidance on the procedures to be followed, together with precedents for the draft order, can be found in Practice Guidance (Interim Non-disclosure Orders) [2012] 1 WLR 1003. It is the cumulative effect of the above clauses, combined with making the application without notice and at a private hearing, that make super-injunctions controversial. It is the lack of public scrutiny that has caused the main concern. To assess the extent of the problem **PD 40F** requires judges to provide data on all injunctions that involve a derogation from the principle of open justice, and is not restricted to super-injunctions.

The complete abrogation of the open justice principle inherent in strict super-injunction orders means they should only be granted in extremely exceptional situations. This may be the case if it is necessary to ensure the ultimate vindication of the claimant's rights at trial is not undermined by the way the court has processed the interim application (*Donald v Ntuli* [2010] EWCA Civ 1276, [2011] 1 WLR 294). Any restrictions, however, must be the minimum that can be imposed to give the claimant the protection to which they are entitled (at [54]).

Hearing super-injunction applications in private

37.44   The general rule is that litigation is conducted in public (European Convention on Human Rights, **art. 6(1)**, in the **Human Rights Act 1998, sch. 1**; **CPR, r. 39.2(1)**; *Scott v Scott* [1913] AC 417). There are recognised exceptions, a list of which appears in **r. 39.2(3)**. They principally cover situations where it is necessary to depart from the general rule to avoid frustrating or rendering impracticable the administration of justice (*Attorney General v Leveller Magazine Ltd* [1979] AC 440 per Lord Diplock at p. 450).

Where the hearing involves reference to confidential material the parties and the court need to make arrangements to ensure justice is done in as open a manner as is practicable. For example, confidential material could be placed in an annex or separate file in the application bundle, which will allow it to be readily identified by the court and assist in ensuring clarity if the court orders it not to be disclosed (*Ambrosiadou v Coward* [2011] EWCA Civ 409, [2011] 2 FLR 617). When giving judgment the court should consider the extent to which details need to be included which would directly or indirectly reveal confidential information. A carefully constructed judgment may mean there is no need to deliver judgment in private (*Donald v Ntuli* [2010] EWCA Civ 1276, [2011] 1 WLR 294). If the court permits the identity of the applicant to be revealed, it will almost certainly mean that less detail should be included in the judgment than if an anonymity order is made (*H v News Group Newspapers Ltd* [2011] EWCA Civ 42, [2011] 1 WLR 1645). If an order is made permitting only a redacted version of a document to be made public, the parties must ensure the redaction is effective (*Ambrosiadou v Coward*, where the redacted copy could be unredacted using fairly easily available software).

Anonymity orders

37.45   A true super-injunction will invariably include an anonymity clause, but an injunction without the super-injunction clause is not a super-injunction even if it has anonymity provisions. An anonymity order will remove the claimant's name from the court papers and replace them with initials. The initials chosen, for example 'CTB', bear no relation to the actual name of the litigant. This is sometimes referred to as 'alphabet soup'. Anonymity and reporting restriction orders cannot be made by consent, because the parties cannot waive the rights of the public (*H v News Group Newspapers Ltd* [2011] EWCA Civ 42, [2011] 1 WLR 1645).

Anonymising judgments is considered at **63.36**. Questions of necessity and proportionality similar to those relevant to the decision to hold the hearing in private are taken into account when considering whether to anonymise the parties to an interim injunction application (*Donald v Ntuli* [2010] EWCA Civ 1276, [2011] 1 WLR 294, where the application was refused; *CDE v MGN Ltd* [2010] EWHC 3308 (QB), LTL 11/2/2011, where the application was granted). It is necessary to balance the competing interests under **arts 8 and 10**, and the facts and circumstances of the case have to be sufficiently strong to justify encroaching on the cardinal principle of open justice (*H v News Group Newspapers Ltd*). Careful writing up of the judgment may ensure it is in a form suitable for publication (*Donald v Ntuli* at [55]).

Hyper-injunctions

Hyper-injunctions are injunctions which appear to go further than a super-injunction, and prohibit discussion of the case or the order with a constituent's Member of Parliament. They are exceptionally rare. Lord Neuberger MR (*Report of the Committee on Super-Injunctions: Super-Injunctions, Anonymised Injunctions and Open Justice*, Judiciary 20 May 2011) made the point that hyper-injunctions are unnecessary. The standard super-injunction clause prevents publication or disclosure of the order or proceedings to anyone, which includes Members of Parliament (at least outside the Chamber of the House of Commons, because the courts have no jurisdiction to restrain anything said in either Chamber of the Houses of Parliament by virtue of the Bill of Rights 1689, art. 9). The law on discussing cases subject to super-injunctions with Members of Parliament was found to be undeveloped by Lord Neuberger MR when this was discussed in his report. However, a clear view was expressed that a super-injunction order would prevent any such discussion or disclosure, but that such a restriction does not infringe the Bill of Rights, art. 9, because it is not a direct restraint on Parliamentary debates. **37.46**

Anonymising judgments is considered at **63.36**. Similar questions of necessity and proportionality are taken into account when considering whether to anonymise the parties to an interim injunction application (*Donald v Ntuli*, where the application was refused; *CDE v MGN Ltd* [2010] EWHC 3308 (QB), LTL 11/2/2011, where the application was granted). Careful writing up of the judgment may ensure it is in a form suitable for publication (*Donald v Ntuli* at [55]).

Copyright

In *Hubbard v Vosper* [1972] 2 QB 84 Lord Denning MR said that in copyright claims defendants with reasonable defences of fair dealing under what is now the Copyright, Designs and Patents Act 1988, s. 30, should not be restrained by injunctions. The reason is that a defendant with such a defence 'is entitled to publish it: and the law will not intervene to suppress freedom of speech except when it is abused'. **37.47**

Industrial disputes

After *American Cyanamid Co. v Ethicon Ltd* [1975] AC 396, whenever an interim injunction was sought against a trade union that claimed it was acting in contemplation or furtherance of a trade dispute, the courts refused to investigate the respective merits of the case on each side, and tended to concentrate on the balance of convenience. Unions could rarely point to significant inconvenience if they were restrained from striking, whereas employers could readily identify their continuing financial losses. The result was that injunctions were invariably granted against unions involved in trade disputes despite the statutory defences. Legislation was accordingly passed to ensure the merits of the statutory defences are considered before injunctions are granted against trade unions. This legislation is now contained **37.48** in the Trade Union and Labour Relations (Consolidation) Act 1992, s. 221(2), which provides:

Where—

(a) an application for an interlocutory injunction is made to a court pending the trial of an action, and

(b) the party against whom it is sought claims that he acted in contemplation or furtherance of a trade dispute,

the court shall, in exercising its discretion whether or not to grant the injunction, have regard to the likelihood of that party's succeeding at the trial of the action in establishing any matter which would afford a defence to the action under section 219 (protection from certain tort liabilities) or section 220 (peaceful picketing).

Differing views have been expressed on the interpretation of this section. The approach favoured by Lord Scarman in *NWL Ltd v Woods* [1979] 1 WLR 1294 was that the court must consider:

(a) whether the cause of action against the union discloses a serious action to be tried;

(b) the balance of convenience; and

(c) the likelihood of the union establishing the statutory defence.

Lord Fraser of Tullybelton in the same case pointed out that the word 'likelihood' is a word of degree, and the weight to be given to establishing the trade dispute defence varies according to the degree of the likelihood. Where it is highly probable that a trade union will persuade the court that it has complied with the requirements for strike balloting laid down in the Trade Union and Labour Relations (Consolidation) Act 1992, an interim injunction to restrain strike action will be refused (*British Airways plc v Unite the Union* [2010] EWCA Civ 669, [2010] ICR 1316).

Claims against public authorities

37.49 *Smith v Inner London Education Authority* [1978] 1 All ER 411 is authority for the proposition that public authorities should not be restrained from exercising their statutory powers and duties unless the claimant has an extremely strong case on the merits. If the evidence indicates that the authority is exceeding the law, often upholding the rule of law will prevail over administrative inconvenience (*Bradbury v Enfield London Borough Council* [1967] 1 WLR 1311). Most cases of this nature should now be brought by proceedings for judicial review (**chapter** 77). Where interim injunctions are sought in judicial review proceedings, the *American Cyanamid* principles (see **37.20** to **37.33**) will be applied (see *R v Ministry of Agriculture, Fisheries and Food, ex parte Monsanto plc* [1999] QB 1161). The *Monsanto plc* case also considered how those principles ought to be applied in a public law case. An interim injunction may be granted to restrain the enforcement of a UK statute where there are strong grounds for finding that the statute contravenes EU law (*R v Secretary of State for Transport, ex parte Factortame Ltd (No. 2)* (case C-213/89) [1991] 1 AC 603).

In considering an application to disapply national legislation by injunction pending a reference to the CJEU, the Court of Appeal in *R v Her Majesty's Treasury, ex parte British Telecommunications plc* [1994] 1 CMLR 621 said the following factors must be taken into account:

(a) The apparent strength of the Community right asserted. This is not to be considered in depth, as this is a matter for the CJEU. However, if the English court is almost persuaded that the applicant will succeed before the CJEU, albeit having enough doubt to refer the point to the CJEU, an injunction is far more likely to be granted than where the Community right is more speculative.

(b) The importance, in political terms, of the impugned legislation. An injunction is more likely to be granted where the legislation is obscure than where it is a major piece of legislation on which an election was fought.

(c) Other factors include whether the economic survival of the applicant depends on injunctive relief being granted, and the degree to which the applicant can be compensated in damages.

Town and Country Planning Act 1990 injunctions

For the factors to be taken into account in applications for injunctions under the Town and **37.50** Country Planning Act 1990, s. 187B, including the personal circumstances of the persons in occupation, see *South Bucks District Council v Porter (No. 2)* [2004] UKHL 33, [2004] 1 WLR 1953, and *South Cambridgeshire District Council v Gammell* [2005] EWCA Civ 1429, [2006] 1 WLR 658.

Negative covenants and covenants in restraint of trade

A perpetual injunction has been held to issue 'as of course' where it is established that the **37.51** defendant is in breach of a valid express negative covenant (*Doherty v Allman* (1878) 3 App Cas 709). The same principle applies to applications for interim injunctions (*Attorney General v Barker* [1990] 3 All ER 257), which means the balance of convenience test does not apply (*Araci v Fallon* [2011] EWHC 1621 (QB), LTL 3/6/2011).

As a matter of competition law, a negative covenant which is in restraint of trade will not be enforced unless it is in a contract of employment or a contract for the sale of a business and its terms relating to activities restrained, duration and geographical limits are reasonably required to protect the covenantee's legitimate interests. In *Office Overload Ltd v Gunn* [1977] FSR 39, the defendant was the branch manager of the claimant's employment agency in Croydon. In his contract of employment he covenanted not to work for or set up a competing business in the Croydon area for one year after ceasing to work for the claimant. After giving notice the defendant immediately started competing. The claimant applied for an interim injunction. Given that to be valid a covenant has to be for a limited period of time, refusal of interim relief will usually deprive a claimant of the benefit of the covenant. Lord Denning MR accordingly said:

Covenants in restraint of trade are in a special category...if they are prima facie valid and there is an infringement the courts will grant an injunction.

A covenant will be prima facie valid if:

(a) all the facts are before the court; and
(b) the covenant is reasonable in ambit, area and duration.

Restraint of trade cases to which the *American Cyanamid* guidelines apply The rule that an **37.52** interim injunction will be issued to prevent breach of a valid covenant in restraint of trade (*Office Overload Ltd v Gunn* [1977] FSR 39) applies only where there is no sustainable dispute concerning the claimant's cause of action. If there is real doubt about the claimant's case, the *American Cyanamid* guidelines apply. Thus, in *Lawrence David Ltd v Ashton* [1991] 1 All ER 385, the claimant had dismissed the defendant from his employment, and there was a real issue as to whether that amounted to a repudiatory breach of the employment contract (and if so, it could not insist on the covenant being observed). Further, the terms of the covenant were perhaps too wide. Given those two matters, the case was not an open-and-shut one in favour of the claimant, and the *American Cyanamid* guidelines were applied.

As the foundation of this exception is the effective deprivation of the employer of the benefit of the covenant due to the effluxion of time before trial, the exception does not apply if a trial can be arranged before the period of the covenant expires (for example, through ordering a speedy trial) (*Dairy Crest Ltd v Pigott* [1989] ICR 92). An example of what can be done with co-operation from all sides is *Symphony Group plc v Hodgson* [1994] QB 179, where the action was tried six weeks after the employee gave his notice.

Injunctions to restrain breaches of covenants in employment contracts are often combined with injunctions to restrain the misuse of confidential information obtained during the defendant's employment. Injunctions to restrain breach of confidence are decided in accordance with *American Cyanamid* guidelines, see *Lock International plc v Beswick* [1989] 1 WLR 1268, or the guidelines in *McKennitt v Ash* [2006] EWCA Civ 1714, [2008] QB 73, and **37.38**.

37.53   Enforced inactivity ('garden leave')   If a covenant in a contract of employment against working for competitors is too wide and therefore void, the employer may still be able to obtain some injunctive relief if the employee resigns and starts working for a competitor under the principle in *Evening Standard Co. Ltd v Henderson* [1987] ICR 588. In this case the Court of Appeal found that a newspaper production manager, whose contract provided that he had to give a year's notice, was in clear breach of his contract of employment when he purported to give two months' notice after which he intended to work for a competitor. The claimant refused to accept the defendant's repudiation of his contract, and undertook to pay the defendant his full normal salary during his period of notice. Applying the *American Cyanamid* guidelines, an injunction was granted restraining the defendant from working for any competitor for his contractual period of notice, thereby giving the defendant a period of 'garden leave'. It is not always possible to obtain a 'garden leave' injunction even if the employee fails to give the contractual period of notice. The cases fall into two categories (see *Langston v Amalgamated Union of Engineering Workers (No. 2)* [1974] ICR 510). In the first, the employment contract extends to an obligation to permit the employee to do the contractual work. Theatrical engagements usually fall into this category. In these cases the employer needs a provision in the employment contract entitling the employer to send the employee home on garden leave. There will be little scope for implying such a term into the contract. Without such a term, no injunction will be granted. In the second category the employment contract is confined to the employer agreeing to pay wages for the work done. In this category the employer is entitled to send the employee home on garden leave even in the absence of an express or implied term, because there is no contractual obligation to prevent this. Garden leave injunctions are therefore far more likely to be granted in this category. See *William Hill Organisation Ltd v Tucker* [1999] ICR 291. Other decisions have shown that enforcing a period of idleness on the defendant is a factor to be taken into account in the balance of convenience against granting such an injunction (*Euro Brokers Ltd v Rabey* [1995] IRLR 206), and it may be appropriate to impose the injunction for a period shorter than the contractual period of notice where other 'defectors' are on shorter periods of notice than the defendant (*GFI Group Inc. v Eaglestone* [1994] IRLR 119).

Injunction equivalent to specific performance

37.54   The House of Lords in *Scandinavian Trading Tanker Co. AB v Flota Petrolera Ecuatoriana* [1983] 2 AC 694 held that specific performance will not be ordered of a non-demise time charter. Under this type of charterparty the owner provides the ship and the crew, and the charterer provides the cargo. It is therefore a contract for services, which the law never enforces by specific performance. In *Lauritzencool AB v Lady Navigation Inc.* [2005] EWCA Civ 579, [2005] 1 WLR 3686, it was held that nevertheless the court could grant an interim injunction prohibiting a shipowner from employing the vessel in a manner inconsistent with a charterparty. Such an order does not juristically amount to an order for specific performance, even if in practical reality it compels the owner to perform the charterparty.

Arbitration Act 1996 injunctions

37.55   The Arbitration Act 1996, s. 44, provides:

(1) Unless otherwise agreed by the parties, the court has for the purposes of and in relation to arbitral proceedings the same power of making orders about the matters listed below as it has for the purposes of and in relation to legal proceedings.

(2) Those matters are—
    (a) the taking of the evidence of witnesses;
    (b) the preservation of evidence;
    (c) making orders relating to property which is the subject of the proceedings or as to which any question arises in the proceedings...;

    (d) the sale of any goods the subject of the proceedings;

    (e) the granting of an interim injunction or the appointment of a receiver.

(3) If the case is one of urgency, the court may, on the application of a party or proposed party to the arbitral proceedings, make such orders as it thinks necessary for the purpose of preserving evidence or assets.

Econet Wireless Ltd v Vee Networks Ltd [2006] EWHC 1568 (Comm), [2006] 2 Lloyd's Rep 428, held that the purpose of the power to grant injunctions under s. 44 is to provide protection for the period before an arbitrator can be appointed. Nevertheless, there is jurisdiction to grant an anti-suit injunction even if there are no pending or contemplated arbitral proceedings under the principle in *Turner v Grovit* [2001] UKHL 65, [2002] 1 WLR 107 (*AES Ust-Kamenogorsk Hydropower Plant LLP v Ust-Kamenogorsk Hydropower Plant JSC* [2013] UKSC 35, [2013] 1 WLR 1889; **CPR, rr. 62.2** and **62.5**). The steps being taken to appoint an arbitrator must be set out in the evidence in support, and there must be an undertaking to appoint an arbitrator without delay. It was held to be inappropriate to seek an interim injunction in England under s. 44 when the arbitration is to take place in another jurisdiction. In *Cetelem SA v Roust Holdings Ltd* [2005] EWCA Civ 618, [2005] 1 WLR 3555, a dispute arose between parties to a share sale contract containing a London arbitration clause. A condition precedent under the contract was that approval had to be given by the Russian Central Bank. Five weeks before the expiry of the time for obtaining approval, no action had been taken by the defendant, so the claimant applied for an urgent mandatory interim injunction requiring the defendant to lodge the necessary papers in Russia. It was held that such an order could only be made if it was necessary for the preservation of evidence or assets, and there was no jurisdiction to make the order on any wider basis. Nevertheless the injunction satisfied the test. 'Assets' to be preserved under s. 44(3) could include choses in action. In this case the injunction was necessary to preserve the claimant's contractual right to purchase the shares, because the right to purchase them would be lost if no application was made for Russian Central Bank approval.

An application to the court for a freezing injunction in support of arbitration proceedings under the Arbitration Act 1996, s. 44, has the advantages that the court's order will bind third parties and is buttressed by sanctions (*Pacific Maritime (Asia) Ltd v Holystone Overseas Ltd* [2007] EWHC 2319 (Comm), [2008] 1 Lloyd's Rep 371).

Apart from the Arbitration Act 1996, s. 44, the High Court also has an inherent jurisdiction to grant interim injunctions. This jurisdiction can be invoked even if there is an arbitration clause in the contract underlying the dispute which might be invoked at a later stage and lead to a stay of the court proceedings (*Glidepath Holding BV v Thompson* [2004] EWHC 2234 (Comm), [2005] 1 All ER (Comm) 434).

No defence

In *Official Custodian for Charities v Mackey* [1985] Ch 168 Scott J said that the *American Cyanamid* principles: 'are not, in my view, applicable to a case where there is no arguable defence to the [claimant's] claim'. The court will not consider the balance of convenience, but will grant the relief claimed subject to the usual equitable considerations. Injunctions have been granted on this basis in cases of clear trespass (*Patel v W.H. Smith (Eziot) Ltd* [1987] 1 WLR 853) and of clear breach of contract (*Sheppard and Cooper Ltd v TSB Bank plc* [1996] 2 All ER 654). Similarly, if all that is at issue on the merits is a simple point of construction, the court will resolve it and dismiss or grant the application accordingly (*Associated British Ports v Transport and General Workers Union* [1989] 1 WLR 939 at p. 979).

37.56

Alternatively, where there is no defence with real prospects of success the claimant may apply for summary judgment including a final order for an injunction, instead of applying for an interim order (*Viscount Chelsea v Muscatt* [1990] 2 EGLR 48). Summary judgment was entered and an injunction granted in *WWF-World Wide Fund for Nature v World Wrestling Federation Entertainment Inc.* [2002] EWCA Civ 196, [2002] FSR 504, in a claim to enforce a settlement of an earlier trade mark dispute. A settlement is presumed to represent a reasonable division of the parties' trading interests for the purposes of the restraint-of-trade doctrine, and it is for the party seeking to go behind the settlement to show grounds for doing so, such as the settlement being contrived, or there being no reasonable basis for the rights claimed, or the settlement being otherwise contrary to the public interest.

Restraint of legal proceedings

37.57   *American Cyanamid* principles do not govern the exceptional jurisdiction of the courts to restrain the commencement of legal proceedings. This commonly arises in relation to preventing the presentation of petitions to wind up companies (see **82.28** to **82.32**). An injunction may also be sought to restrain foreign proceedings to prevent 'forum shopping', if it can be established that the foreign proceedings would be vexatious or oppressive (*Société Nationale Industrielle Aérospatiale v Lee Kui Jak* [1987] AC 871, see **16.77**). Anti-suit injunctions can also be sought to enforce 'no-action' clauses (prohibiting proceedings other than by a named person) (*Elektrim SA v Vivendi Holdings 1 Corporation* [2008] EWCA Civ 1178, [2009] 1 Lloyd's Rep 59) or to restrain unreasonable or oppressive adjudication proceedings under the Housing Grants, Construction and Regeneration Act 1996, s. 110 (*Mentmore Towers Ltd v Packman Lucas Ltd* [2010] EWHC 457 (TCC), [2010] BLR 393).

According to *Glencore International AG v Exter Shipping Ltd* [2002] EWCA Civ 528, [2002] 2 All ER (Comm) 1 at [42]–[43], the principles applicable when deciding whether an injunction to restrain foreign proceedings should be granted are:

(a) whether the defendant is amenable to the English territorial and personal jurisdiction; and
(b) whether it is just and convenient to grant the injunction under the Senior Courts Act 1981, s. 37(1).

In exercising the discretion factors the court will consider include:

(a) whether the threatened conduct is unconscionable, which primarily refers to conduct which is oppressive, vexatious or unconscionable, or which interferes with the due process of the court;
(b) whether injunctive relief is necessary to protect the applicant's legitimate interest in proceedings in England; and
(c) whether England is the natural forum for the litigation.

The same principles were applied on an application to restrain arbitration proceedings in *Albon v Naza Motor Trading Sdn Bhd (No. 4)* [2007] EWCA Civ 1124, [2008] 1 All ER (Comm) 351. In applying these principles in an arbitration case, Jackson J in *J. Jarvis and Sons Ltd v Blue Circle Dartford Estates Ltd* [2007] EWHC 1262 (TCC), [2007] BLR 439, said at [40]:

(a) the discretion to grant such an injunction is exercised very sparingly and with due regard to the principles on which the Arbitration Act 1996 is expressly based (for which see **72.1**); and
(b) delay by the applicant is material to the court's exercise of its discretion, and in some cases will be fatal to the application.

Worldwide injunctions

37.58   In exceptional cases the courts may make injunctive orders having a worldwide effect. Such orders have been made in a small number of freezing injunction cases (see **38.9**), and also in an application to enforce a covenant of confidentiality against a former employee of the Royal household (*Attorney General v Barker* [1990] 3 All ER 257).

Medical treatment

37.59   In *Re J (A Minor) (Child in Care: Medical Treatment)* [1993] Fam 15 an application was made for an interim injunction to compel doctors to give a child in an intensive care unit a specific form of medical treatment. It was held that there was absolutely no room in such a case for the application of the *American Cyanamid* principles. The proper approach was to consider the options available to the court, and in the proper exercise of its inherent powers to make such orders as would best serve the interests of the child pending a final decision. In future these applications will be dealt with under the Mental Capacity Act 2005.

Anti-social behaviour

It is not just and convenient to grant interim injunctions under the Senior Courts Act 1981, **37.60** s. 37, in circumstances where an anti-social behaviour order (see **chapter 88**) might be available. Such applications have to be brought under the relevant anti-social behaviour legislation, to ensure the prescribed checks and balances are applied (*Birmingham City Council v Shafi* [2008] EWCA Civ 1186, [2009] PTSR 503).

INTERIM MANDATORY INJUNCTIONS

In *National Commercial Bank Jamaica Ltd v Olint Corporation Ltd* [2009] UKPC 16, [2009] 1 WLR 1405 **37.61** at [19], Lord Hoffmann said there is no underlying difference in principle between interim applications for prohibitory and mandatory injunctions. His Lordship's view is that it is often more likely that there will be irremediable prejudice to the defendant if the injunction is mandatory in nature. If the injunction is likely to cause irremediable damage to the defendant, the court should be reluctant to grant the injunction unless it is satisfied that the chances that it will turn out to have been wrongly granted are low. It is for this reason that Megarry J in the leading case of *Shepherd Homes Ltd v Sandham* [1971] Ch 340 said, at p. 351, that such injunctions should be granted only if the court felt a 'high degree of assurance' that at trial it will turn out that the injunction was rightly granted.

In *Leisure Data v Bell* [1988] FSR 367, a dispute arose about the copyright in a computer program developed by the defendant for the claimant. The claimant was granted a mandatory injunction despite the merits being equally arguable either way. Partly this was because the claimant was prepared to give wide-ranging undertakings to protect the defendant's position, and partly because the practical reality of the situation was that of the two parties only the claimant was in a position to make commercial use of the program.

The importance of taking the course carrying the least risk of injustice was emphasised in *Nikitenko v Leboeuf Lamb Greene and Macrae* (1999) *The Times*, 26 January 1999. Pumfrey J in *Incasep Ltd v Jones* (2001) LTL 26/10/2001 said that an application for an interim mandatory injunction requiring a company to reinstate the claimant as an executive director pending the outcome of his unfair prejudice petition (see Companies Act 2006, s. 994) was governed by the *American Cyanamid* guidelines, albeit having regard to particular factors concerning the potential injustice that such injunctions could cause. On the facts the injunction was refused.

DEFENCES

Any of the following equitable defences and bars to relief may be raised on an application for **37.62** an interim injunction:

(a) Acquiescence. This arises where the claimant's conduct (usually inactivity) induces the defendant to believe something to his detriment (*Davies v Marshall* (1861) 10 CB NS 697; *Jones v Stones* [1999] 1 WLR 1739; see **10.40**).

(b) Delay or laches. Simply allowing time to elapse may persuade a court to refuse injunctive relief even if the conduct does not amount to acquiescence. Delay is a more significant factor in interim applications than at trial (*Johnson v Wyatt* (1863) De G J & S 18). The length of delay meriting refusal of relief depends on the nature of the case and whether the defendant has been prejudiced, but usually will need to be measured in months. See, for example,

Century Electronics Ltd v CVS Enterprises Ltd [1983] FSR 1 and *Newport Association Football Club Ltd v Football Association of Wales Ltd* [1995] 2 All ER 87, where the facts were sufficiently exceptional to excuse a two-year delay. Furthermore, what may appear to be an unreasonable delay may be justified by the claimant (*Carroll v Tomado Ltd* [1971] FSR 218). On the other hand, a delay of 20 days was held to bar relief in *Bunn v British Broadcasting Corporation* [1998] 3 All ER 552, where an application to restrain the broadcast of confidential information was made just two working days before the intended date of the broadcast. Delay of over a year was fatal to an application for an interim injunction to restrain trademark infringement and passing off in *Blinkx UK Ltd v Blinkbox Entertainment Ltd* [2010] EWHC 1624 (Ch), LTL 27/10/2010. Delay interrelates with the status quo (for which, see **37.30**).

(c) Hardship. This is taken into account in the balance of convenience.

(d) Clean hands. Inequitable conduct by the claimant may be a bar to equitable relief (*Hubbard v Vosper* [1972] 2 QB 84).

(e) Equity does not act in vain. In *Attorney General v Guardian Newspapers Ltd (No. 2)* [1990] 1 AC 109 an injunction to restrain breach of confidence was refused where there had already been widespread publication.

(f) 'The court will not and ought not to make an order performance or obedience to which it cannot enforce' (per Astbury J in *Amber Size and Chemical Co. Ltd v Menzel* [1913] 2 Ch 239). Injunctions are therefore rarely granted against children, because they cannot be committed to prison and can rarely pay a fine (*G v Harrow London Borough Council* [2004] EWHC 17 (QB), LTL 23/1/2004).

(g) An injunction will be refused if its effect is to enforce an agreement for personal services (e.g. *Warren v Mendy* [1989] 1 WLR 853).

(h) Difficulty in compliance. An injunction was refused in *Unique Pub Properties Ltd v Licensed Wholesale Co. Ltd* (2003) LTL 13/10/2003 as it would have imposed on the defendant a serious obligation to check information given to it by its tenants, any error constituting a breach.

(i) The likelihood of damages being awarded in lieu of an injunction (*Lawrence v Fen Tigers Ltd* [2014] UKSC 13, [2014] AC 822).

THE ORDER

37.63   There are currently four standard forms for interim injunction orders:

(a) PF 39 CH, order for an injunction (intended action);

(b) PF 40 CH, order for interim injunction (for use where substantive proceedings have been issued);

(c) Freezing injunction order (**PD 25A, Annex**);

(d) Search order (**PD 25A, Annex**).

All these forms are for use in the County Court and High Court, and both the Queen's Bench Division and the Chancery Division.

An injunction order may only be enforced by committal proceedings under **CPR, r. 81.4**, if a penal notice is prominently displayed on the front of the copy of the order served on the defendant (**r. 81.9(1)**). A penal notice should be in form N77, and is a warning that disobedience of the order is a contempt of court punishable by imprisonment, a fine or sequestration of assets (see **chapter 81**). For undertakings in lieu of injunctions, see **81.25**.

Undertakings

37.64   Undertakings may be required from either party to ensure there is no injustice as a result of the decision on an application for an interim injunction. Subject to the exceptions referred to at **37.24**, the applicant will always be required to give an undertaking in damages. An impecunious claimant may be required to fortify the undertaking in damages by providing security or paying money into court (**37.25**). An order to fortify the undertaking should not be made unless there is evidence that the respondent is likely to suffer loss as a result of the injunction (*JSC Mezhdunarodniy Promyshlenniy Bank v Pugachev* [2015] EWCA Civ 139, [2016] 1 WLR 160). The general principle is that the amount of security should be based on the highest arguable figure for the likely damage to the defendant that is supported by the evidence (*Business Online Group plc v MCI Worldcom Ltd* [2001] EWCA Civ 1399, LTL 9/8/2001).

Until the standard form injunctions were changed in March 2005, there was no need in most interim injunctions, other than freezing injunctions, to include an undertaking to pay the reasonable costs of any third party incurred as a result of the order (*Miller Brewing Co. v Ruhi Enterprises Ltd* [2003] EWHC 1606 (Ch), [2004] FSR 5). In *SmithKline Beecham plc v Apotex Europe Ltd* [2006] EWCA Civ 658, [2007] Ch 71, the claimant obtained an interim injunction in the pre-2005 form against alleged infringement of patented pharmaceuticals by the original defendants. These defendants were supplied by related companies based in Canada (the additional defendants). The additional defendants were made parties two days before the injunction was discharged, and then sought to recover on the claimant's undertaking in damages. As this was a pre-2005 injunction there was no express undertaking to compensate third parties. At first instance it was held that the additional defendants only took the benefit of the undertaking from the day they were joined, not retrospectively, which was regarded as *de minimis*. It was also held that the injunction could not be corrected under the slip rule (**CPR, r. 40.12**) to include an undertaking to compensate third parties. The slip rule can only be used to correct mistakes on matters which the court or party had in mind. Here no one had thought of including an undertaking to compensate third parties until after the new standard forms were introduced. On appeal it was also held that the third-party companies were not entitled to any remedy against the claimant in restitution or through any estoppel.

Forms PF 39 CH and PF 40 CH contain undertakings to compensate both parties and third parties who suffer loss caused by the order. The additional protection for third parties is not always needed. Under **PD 25A, para. 5.1A**, when the court makes an order for an injunction, it should consider whether to require an undertaking by the applicant to pay any damages sustained by a person other than the respondent, including another party to the proceedings or any other person who may suffer loss as a consequence of the order.

Other undertakings include without-notice undertakings to serve and file evidence etc. (see **37.7**), and other undertakings designed to reduce the possible prejudice to the other side. For example, in *Travel Intelligence v Townsend* [2009] EWHC 726 (QB), LTL 30/4/2009, the defendant was permitted to continue running a business on undertaking to provide the other party with monthly financial statements. In *Watson v Durham University* [2008] EWCA Civ 1266, LTL 24/10/2008, an employee undertook not to attend the employer's premises until the dispute was determined.

Undertakings given by a party may be released or modified if there are special or exceptional circumstances (*Warren v Random House Group Ltd* [2008] EWCA Civ 834, [2009] QB 600). These include:

(a) the context of the agreement in which the undertaking was given;
(b) whether the undertaking was given to the court independently of the agreement of the other party or as part of a collateral agreement; and
(c) whether there are circumstances so different from those contemplated or intended to be governed by the undertaking when it was given that the party should be released.

Operative provisions

The precise form of any injunction depends on the facts of the particular case (*Lawrence v Fen Tigers Ltd* [2014] UKSC 13, [2014] AC 822). The operative part of the order for an interim injunction should not be in terms wider than is necessary to do justice between the parties. In *Moat Housing Group-South Ltd v Harris* [2005] EWCA Civ 287, [2006] QB 606, Brooke LJ said that the relief granted must be limited to that which is necessary and proportionate as a means of avoiding the apprehended harm. In *E. E. and Brian Smith (1928) Ltd v Hodson* [2007] EWCA Civ 1210, LTL 23/11/2007, the order as drawn was too wide in that it prevented the company from fulfilling contracts already entered into, and there was no

37.65

sufficient definition of the information caught by the restrictions, nor any exclusion of information in the public domain. *Hall v Save Newchurch Guinea Pigs (Campaign)* [2005] EWHC 372 (QB), *The Times*, 7 April 2005, was an application under the Protection from Harassment Act 1997, s. 3, for an injunction and an exclusion zone of seven parishes, covering 200 square kilometres. Although there had been extreme conduct in the past, only a prohibitory injunction was granted. The judge said that an exclusion zone might be added later if the initial injunction was not effective.

The injunction should be worded so that the defendant can know with certainty what is and what is not permitted (**PD 25A, para. 5.3**). An injunction to restrain publication must be to the highest degree clear and precise so that no publisher can be in any doubt whether he is infringing or not (*Times Newspapers Ltd v MGN Ltd* [1993] EMLR 443). A provision in an injunction will be too uncertain if there would be issues of fact over whether particular conduct would be a breach (*Staver Co. Inc. v Digitext Display Ltd* [1985] FSR 512). Thus, an order which restrained, among other things, the defendant 'from otherwise infringing' a patent lacked sufficient specificity (*Hepworth Plastics Ltd v Naylor Bros (Clayware) Ltd* [1979] FSR 521). The fact that there is an overlap between different words used in an order does not necessarily establish there is any ambiguity or lack of clarity. There is nothing objectionable about injunctions that restrain 'publishing, communicating or disclosing' or restraining publication of 'any intimate, personal or sexually explicit' details (*Donald v Ntuli* [2010] EWCA Civ 1276, [2011] 1 WLR 294). It is usually best to avoid using legal terms of art, especially the names of torts, which often include matters of degree with the result that the defendant will often not know whether specific conduct will breach the order. A proposed order restraining disclosure of 'confidential information' is oppressive, excessively general and wide. Instead, it needs to be limited to defined confidential information (*Raks Holdings AS v TTPCom Ltd* [2004] EWHC 2137 (Ch), LTL 29/7/2004). An injunction may adopt the precise wording of a contractual provision, because in such a case the order simply requires the defendant to comply with its contractual obligation (*Parallel Media Group plc v Lagardère SCA* [2010] EWHC 27 (QB), LTL 17/2/2010). In *Mid Suffolk District Council v Clarke* [2006] EWCA Civ 71, [2006] Env LR 38, an undertaking was given by a defendant to restrain a nuisance in defined ways whether by himself, his employees or agents 'or otherwise howsoever'. These three words were not too imprecise or uncertain, but were aimed at ensuring the defendant would not carry out the prohibited acts in any way, directly or indirectly. In *Huntingdon Life Sciences Group plc v Stop Huntingdon Animal Cruelty* [2007] EWHC 522 (QB), LTL 19/4/2007, a final injunction was granted restraining animal rights protestors from harassing the claimant's employees. This was done by establishing exclusion zones, imposing a maximum number of protestors, permitting use of megaphones for a maximum of one hour at medium to low amplification for verbal sound, and a protest procession to be allowed every three months. For this purpose 'protestor' was defined as meaning the defendants, whether by themselves, their employees or agents, any other person, whether by himself, his employees or agents, who was acting in concert with the defendant. The order was not to be enforceable against any individual without the express permission of the court.

The judge will have regard to the draft prepared by the claimant, and may initial the draft without amendment. Ultimately, however, the choice of wording is a matter within the discretion of the judge (*Khorasandjian v Bush* [1993] QB 727). It will not usually be appropriate to qualify the terms of an injunction to protect the defendant from the consequences of any misbehaviour by its employees (*British Telecommunications plc v Nextcall Telecom plc* [2000] FSR 679). Where the order is made in the presence of all relevant parties (or at least at a hearing of which they had notice even if they did not attend), it may be expressed to last 'until trial or further order' (**PD 25A, para. 5.2**).

Injunctions affecting third parties

37.66   For undertakings to compensate third parties see **37.64**. Where an injunction will affect a third party who was not present at the hearing, that person may request copies of any materials read by the judge, any documents prepared after the hearing in compliance with directions of the judge, and the note of the hearing (**PD 25A, para. 9.2**). The applicant is required to comply with such a request promptly, unless the court orders otherwise. It may be appropriate to include a restriction in an order that documents requested under **para. 9.2** will be provided only on the third party giving a written undertaking to use the documents only for the purposes of the proceedings (*TUV v Person or Persons Unknown* [2010] EWHC 853 (QB), [2010] EMLR 19).

Suspending the operation of an injunction

The court has the power to suspend the operation of an injunction. This is generally exercised where it is necessary to ensure injunctions operate in a just and convenient (or just and proportionate, see **37.14**) manner. See *Waverley Borough Council v Lee* [2003] EWHC 29 (Ch), LTL 14/1/2003. An injunction was postponed until the end of a school term when otherwise it would have interfered with the defendant's children's schooling in *Tewkesbury Borough Council v Brown* [2006] EWHC 2697 (QB), LTL 7/11/2006. **37.67**

INQUIRY AS TO DAMAGES

Where it transpires that an interim injunction should not have been granted (for example, if the claimant loses at trial) the defendant may seek to enforce the undertaking in damages by applying for an order for an inquiry as to damages. A formal application is required, supported by written evidence (*Euroil Ltd v Cameroon Offshore Petroleum SARL* [2014] EWHC 215 (Comm), LTL 11/2/2014). If a claimant discontinues (for which, see **chapter 55**), the court should consider the circumstances and the reasons why this has been done before ordering an inquiry as to damages (*Goldman Sachs International Ltd v Lyons* (1995) The Times, 28 February 1995). **37.68**

Excessive, inexcusable delay may result in an application for an inquiry as to damages being dismissed (*Barratt Manchester Ltd v Bolton Metropolitan Borough Council* [1998] 1 WLR 1003). An order for an inquiry is not penal and does not depend on fault on the part of the claimant.

Where an interim injunction is discharged before trial, the court has a number of options on an application for an inquiry as to damages. These were identified in *Cheltenham and Gloucester Building Society v Ricketts* [1993] 1 WLR 1545, as being:

(a) To accede to the application and immediately proceed to determine the question of damages. This should be done only in the most straightforward cases. In *Fourie v Le Roux* [2007] UKHL 1, [2007] 1 WLR 320, it was held to have been wrong in principle to order an immediate inquiry into damages on the discharge of a freezing injunction before trial. A second, replacement, injunction had been granted, and there was evidence that the frozen money was either itself, or the proceeds from, assets which had been fraudulently obtained by the defendant. The question of whether to order an inquiry was postponed to trial.

(b) To allow the application, and to order the inquiry by a Master or District Judge. The judge making the order will give directions for the inquiry.

(c) To stand the application over (that is, adjourn it) to a specified time. This is perhaps the usual order where an injunction is discharged during the interim stages of a claim. It is the most appropriate option where matters material to the question whether it is just to order an inquiry are still in issue and will only be determined at trial. The application is most frequently stood over to trial, when all the facts should be known.

(d) To order an inquiry and to direct that the question of liability on the undertaking be determined at the inquiry. This is unusual.

(e) To refuse the application. This is only done in straightforward cases where, for example, it is clear the defendant has suffered no loss as a result of the injunction.

(f) To make an order setting off the sum found on making an inquiry against an earlier judgment. Such an order was made in *Keller v Cowen* [2001] EWCA Civ 1704, LTL 6/11/2001, where the earlier judgment was obtained in a foreign court, and despite there being no mutuality of debts.

Commentary

Example 37.1   High Court interim injunction (form CH11)

IN THE HIGH COURT OF JUSTICE   Claim No. HQ17X 73635
QUEEN'S BENCH DIVISION

BEFORE the Honourable Mr Justice Collier (judge in private) Monday
the 16th day of January 2017

BETWEEN

CASPKEELER PRODUCTS LIMITED   <u>Claimants</u>

— and —

LOAMER TECHTRONICS LIMITED   <u>Defendants</u>

ORDER FOR AN INJUNCTION

Important

NOTICE TO THE DEFENDANTS

(1) This Order prohibits you from doing the acts set out in this Order. You should read it carefully.
You are advised to consult a Solicitor as soon as possible. You have a right to ask the Court to
vary or discharge this Order.

(2) If you disobey this Order you may be guilty of Contempt of Court [and any of your directors]
may be sent to prison or fined [and you may be fined] or your assets may be seized.

Include the words in square brackets in the case of a corporate defendant. This notice is not a
substitute for the endorsement of a penal notice

An Application was made on 16 January 2017 by Counsel for the Claimants in a Claim to the Judge
and was attended by Counsel for the Defendants. The Judge heard the Application and read the
witness statements listed in Schedule 1 to this Order, and accepted the undertakings in Schedule 2
at the end of this Order.

IT IS ORDERED that:

THE INJUNCTION

(1) Until after final judgment in this Claim the Defendants must not:

    (a) license the right to distribute the Loamer Techtron Capacitor anywhere in the world in
the term of six years from 16 September 2013 granted to the Claimants Caspkeeler
Products Limited under an agreement between the Claimants and the Defendants dated
16 September 2013;

    (b) sell Loamer Techtron Capacitors otherwise than through the Claimants Caspkeeler
Products Limited;

    (c) assert or represent to customers that the Claimants Caspkeeler Products Limited are not
the sole distributors of the Loamer Techtron Capacitor.

Costs of the Application

(2) [The Defendant shall pay the Claimant's costs of this Application.] [The costs of this Application
are reserved to be dealt with by the Judge who tries this Claim.] [The costs of this Application are
to be costs in the case.] [The costs of this Application are to be the Claimant's costs in the case.]

Variation or Discharge of This Order

The Defendants may apply to the Court at any time to vary or discharge this Order, but if they wish
to do so they must first inform the Claimants' Solicitors in writing at least 48 hours beforehand.

Name and Address of Claimants' Solicitors

The Claimant's Solicitors are:
Collins, Brown and Heath, of 7 Ingrave Road, Birmingham B5 8EP
Ref: JGB/4663, Telephone: 01212158349.

Interpretation of This Order

(1) In this Order the words 'he' 'him' or 'his' include 'she' or 'her' and 'it' or 'its'.
(2) Where there are two or more Defendants then (unless the contrary appears):
    (a) references to 'the Defendant' mean both or all of them;
    (b) an Order requiring 'the Defendant' to do or not to do anything requires each Defendant to do or not to do it.

The Effect of This Order

(1) A Defendant who is an individual who is ordered not to do something must not do it himself or in any other way. He must not do it through others acting on his behalf or on his instructions or with his encouragement.
(2) A Defendant which is a corporation and which is ordered not to do something must not do it itself or by its directors, officers, employees or agents or in any other way.

Service of This Order

This Order shall be served by the Claimants on the Defendants.
The court has provided a sealed copy of this Order to the serving party:
Collins, Brown and Heath at 7 Ingrave Road, Birmingham B5 8EP
Reference: JGB/4663

SCHEDULE 1

Witness Statements

The Judge read the following witness statements before making this Order:

(1) Rachel Helen Radcliffe, made on 9 January 2017,
(2) Daniel Jordan Loamer, made on 10 January 2017.

SCHEDULE 2

Undertaking given to the Court by the Claimants

If the Court later finds that this Order has caused loss to the Defendants or any other Party served with or notified of this Order and decides that the Defendant or other Party should be compensated for that loss, the Claimants will comply with any Order the Court may make.

All communications to the Court about this Order should be sent to Room 307, Royal Courts of Justice, Strand, London WC2A 2LL quoting the case number. The office is open between 10 a.m. and 4.30 p.m. Monday to Friday. The telephone number is (020) 7936 6148.

Quantification of damages

37.69 An application for an inquiry as to damages made by a successful defendant at the end of the trial will normally only be refused if it is unlikely that the defendant has suffered any provable loss (*McDonald's Hamburgers Ltd v Burgerking (UK) Ltd* [1987] FSR 112). Ordinary contractual principles are applied on causation and quantum, but adjusted to the extent needed to reflect the fact that the exercise is to compensate for the loss caused by the injunction (*Abbey Forwarding Ltd v Hone (No. 3)* [2014] EWCA Civ 711, [2015] Ch 309). It is possible for aggravated or exemplary damages to be awarded in cases where the claimant has acted oppressively (*McDonald's Hamburgers Ltd v Burgerking (UK) Ltd*). Contractual defences are in theory available. A defence based on illegality arising from infringement of a Canadian patent failed in *Les Laboratoires Servier v Apotex Inc.* [2014] UKSC 55, [2015] AC 430.

Where defendants had sought enormous damages and failed, the court was justified in refusing any order rather than seeking out a smaller loss (*Tyco European Metal Framing Ltd v New Systems Ltd*

Commentary

(2001) LTL 7/12/2001). There is a power to strike out an inquiry (*FSL Services Ltd v MacDonald* [2001] EWCA Civ 1008, LTL 21/6/2001). Inquiries are normally conducted by Masters and District Judges.

UNDERTAKINGS GIVEN BY THE DEFENDANT

37.70 Instead of contesting an application for an interim injunction, a defendant may give undertakings in similar terms to the injunction sought by the claimant. Such undertakings have the same force as an injunction ordered by the court, with the result that the defendant will be in contempt of court if the undertakings are broken. Where undertakings are given by a defendant and incorporated into a consent order, the undertakings may be construed as having contractual effect between the parties. In such a case breach of the undertakings may be enforced as breaches of contract, resulting in a claim for damages (*Independiente Ltd v Music Trading On-Line (HK) Ltd* [2007] EWCA Civ 111, [2008] 1 WLR 608). The claimant will be required to give a cross-undertaking in damages to safeguard the defendant.

A defendant can be released from an undertaking only in special circumstances and where this will not occasion an injustice (*Eronat v Tabbah* [2002] EWCA Civ 950, LTL 10/7/2002). In the absence of special circumstances, a claim commenced in breach of an undertaking will be struck out as an abuse of process, unless striking out would not further the overriding objective (*Di Placito v Slater* [2003] EWCA Civ 1863, [2004] 1 WLR 1605).

DISCHARGE

37.71 Applications to vary or discharge injunctions are made by application notice to a judge, often the same judge who granted the initial injunction. The normal practice where there are cross-applications to continue an interim injunction and to discharge the original interim injunction is for both applications to be heard at the same time. However, the court could hear the applications separately (*Network Multimedia Television Ltd v Jobserve Ltd* (2000) *The Times*, 25 January 2001) applying the following factors: the likely delay if they are heard together; prejudice to the defendant if the injunction were to be discharged after being renewed; prejudice to the claimant if the injunction is discharged and later reimposed; the grounds relied upon for discharging the injunction; the interrelationship of the two applications; the circumstances in which the injunction was obtained; and any special facts. Grounds for varying or discharging injunctions include:

(a) Material non-disclosure if the injunction was granted without notice. The importance of the issue, the nature of the undisclosed evidence and the extent of the non-disclosures have to be considered in deciding whether non-disclosures are material (*Millhouse Capital UK Ltd v Sibir Energy plc* [2008] EWHC 2614 (Ch), [2009] Bus LR D33). In *Network Multimedia Television Ltd v Jobserve Ltd (No. 2)* (2001) LTL 9/4/2001 it was found there were non-deliberate material non-disclosures. The injunction obtained without notice was therefore discharged. On a full consideration of the *American Cyanamid* factors (see **37.20** to **37.33**) the judge decided that it was an appropriate case for reimposing an injunction, albeit recognising that this discretion should be used sparingly after a previous injunction had been discharged.

(b) The particulars of claim being inconsistent with the written evidence on an application without notice.

(c) The facts not justifying relief without giving notice.

(d) The claimant's failure to comply with the undertakings incorporated into the order.

(e) The order having an oppressive effect.

(f) Unreasonable interference with the rights of innocent third parties. Affected third parties are entitled to apply for a variation of the order. All the circumstances have to be considered, and it is sometimes within the court's powers to grant an injunction to restrain a defendant from fulfilling a contract already entered into with an innocent third party. An example is where this is necessary in order to protect the claimant's trade secrets (*PSM International plc v Whitehouse* [1992] IRLR 279).

(g) Material change in the circumstances.

(h) A failure to prosecute the substantive claim with due speed.

(i) If the claim is stayed other than by agreement between the parties, any interim injunction, other than a freezing injunction, will be set aside unless the court orders that it should continue in force (**CPR, r. 25.10**).

(j) If the claim is struck out for non-payment of the hearing fee, the interim injunction will lapse 14 days after the claim is struck out. However, if within that 14-day period the claimant applies to reinstate the claim, the injunction will remain in force until the hearing of that application (unless the court otherwise orders) (**r. 25.11**).

Non-disclosure at on-notice hearing

Traditionally, material non-disclosure has only been a ground for discharging an injunction granted without notice (see **37.71**). In *DEG-Deutsche Investitions- und Entwicklungsgesellschaft mbH v Koshy (No. 2)* [2005] EWHC 2896 (Ch), [2005] 1 WLR 2434, a freezing injunction (granted before the introduction of the CPR) was continued after an on-notice hearing. The defendant argued that the facts found by the trial judge showed there had been material non-disclosure by the claimant. It was held that, apart from provision made by rules of court, there is no jurisdiction to discharge a freezing injunction based on alleged non-disclosure at an on-notice hearing. **CPR, r. 3.1**(7), provides, 'A power of the court under these Rules to make an order includes a power to vary or revoke the order'. As the case was decided under the old rules, Hart J did not express an opinion on whether the wording of **r. 3.1**(7) has changed the position. It is doubtful whether it has. The rule is expressed as conferring a jurisdiction to vary or revoke, but does not deal in terms with the grounds for doing so. A provision more likely to assist the argument is **PD 25A, para. 3.3**, which says that the evidence in support of applications for interim injunctions must include 'all material facts of which the court should be made aware'. The counter-argument is that what the court should be made aware of depends on the nature of the application.

37.72

Commentary

BREACH

If a mandatory order is not complied with, the court may direct that the act required by the injunction be done by another person, with the expense of doing so being borne by the disobedient party (**CPR, r. 70.2A**). Breach of an injunction is also a contempt of court punishable by imprisonment or sequestration. Contempt must be proved beyond reasonable doubt. Punishment for contempt of court is considered in more detail in **chapter 81**.

37.73

Clearly, the person against whom the order was made will be in contempt if he or she acts in breach of an injunction after having notice of it (*Z Ltd v A-Z and AA-LL* [1982] QB 558 per Eveleigh LJ). A non-party who aids and abets the defendant in breaching the terms of an injunction, or who acts with the intention of impeding the administration of justice, will also be in contempt of court (*Attorney General v Times Newspapers Ltd* [1992] 1 AC 191). The Attorney General had obtained interim injunctions against a number of national newspapers restraining them from publishing materials from a book (*Spycatcher*) pending trial. The substantive action was based on alleged breach of confidence. The present defendants were not named in the injunction. They obtained serialisation rights in the book, and published their first instalment. The purpose of the injunctions was to prevent publication pending trial. Publication nullified the purpose of the trial by putting into the public domain what was alleged to be confidential material, and thereby impeded or interfered with the administration of justice. As the defendants had acted knowingly, they were in contempt of court. To establish a contempt by a non-party it must be demonstrated both that the non-party's acts defeated, in whole or in part, the court's purpose in granting the injunction, and that the non-party appreciated that what he was doing was what the injunction was intended to prevent. There is no need to prove an intention to thwart the court's purpose (*Attorney General v Punch Ltd* [2002] UKHL 50, [2003] 1 AC 1046).

Attorney General v Times Newspapers Ltd and the Court of Appeal's decision in *Attorney General v Punch Ltd* [2001] QB 1028 were interpreted in *Jockey Club v Buffham* [2002] EWHC 1866 (QB), [2003] QB 462, as only protecting from interference with pending proceedings. On that basis it was held that the *Spycatcher* principle does not extend to final injunctions. *Jockey Club v Buffham* might have been decided differently if the committal had been brought on the basis that the third party had aided and abetted a breach of the injunction rather than on the basis of interfering with the administration of justice (see *Attorney General v Punch Ltd* [2002] UKHL 50, [2003] 1 AC 1046).

EFFECT OF NOT APPLYING FOR INTERIM RELIEF

37.74 Failing to apply for interim relief is a factor in considering at trial whether the claimant is guilty of acquiescence (*Shaw v Appelgate* [1977] 1 WLR 970). It may also provide grounds for awarding damages in lieu of an injunction (*Jaggard v Sawyer* [1995] 1 WLR 269). Delay in issuing proceedings after the claimant is aware of the defendant's breach, and deciding not to apply for an interim injunction to avoid giving an undertaking in damages, were considered by the Court of Appeal in *Mortimer v Bailey* [2004] EWCA Civ 1514, [2005] 2 P & CR 9. These are both matters to be taken into account in considering whether to grant a final injunction, but do not bar granting such an injunction where the claimant has made clear his objection to the defendant's conduct. *Blue Town Investments Ltd v Higgs and Hill plc* [1990] 1 WLR 696, which said that continuing proceedings was an abuse of process after failing to apply for an interim injunction to avoid having to give an undertaking in damages, should be regarded as wrongly decided. (Another first-instance decision, *Oxy-Electric Ltd v Zainuddin* [1991] 1 WLR 115, reached the opposite conclusion.)

Chapter 38　Freezing Injunctions

NATURE OF A FREEZING INJUNCTION

A freezing injunction is an interim order restraining a party from removing assets located **38.1** within the jurisdiction out of the country, or from dealing with assets whether they are located within the jurisdiction or not (**CPR, r. 25.1(1)(f)**). Usually the order will be restricted to assets not exceeding the value of the claim. Until the CPR came into force on 26 April 1999 this form of order was known as a *Mareva* injunction, taking its name from *Mareva Compania Naviera SA v International Bulkcarriers SA* [1980] 1 All ER 213.

The purpose of a freezing injunction is to prevent the injustice of a defendant's assets being salted away so as to deprive the claimant of the fruits of any judgment that may be obtained. However, as Ackner LJ said in *A. J. Bekhor and Co. Ltd v Bilton* [1981] QB 923, the jurisdiction to grant freezing injunctions has not rewritten the law of insolvency, and the imposition of such an order does not give the claimant any priority or security if the defendant becomes insolvent. It is a relief *in personam* which simply prohibits certain acts in relation to the assets frozen.

In *Mareva Compania Naviera SA v International Bulkcarriers SA* [1980] 1 All ER 213 the Court of Appeal refused to consider itself bound by *Lister v Stubbs* (1890) 45 ChD 1, which had held that a defendant could not be compelled to give security before judgment, and decided that what is now the Senior Courts Act 1981, s. 37(1), is wide enough to permit the court to grant an interim injunction restraining the dissipation of assets. Parliament has subsequently acknowledged the jurisdiction in the Senior Courts Act 1981, s. 37(3) and **CPR, r. 25.1(1)(f)**.

It has always been recognised that freezing orders are draconian measures, and they will be granted only if a number of onerous conditions are fulfilled (see **38.4** to **38.29**). The most significant of these conditions is that there must be a real risk that the defendant will dissipate assets to frustrate any judgment the claimant may obtain.

Although freezing injunctions are most commonly sought by claimants, they may be sought by any party, such as a counterclaiming defendant or a defendant against a third party.

PROCEDURE

38.2   For a summary of the procedure, see **procedural checklist 19**.

With effect from 22 April 2014, the County Court has been given jurisdiction to grant freezing injunctions (County Court Remedies Regulations 2014, SI 2014/982). Freezing injunction applications should therefore be made in the court where the claim is proceeding, or where it is anticipated proceedings will be issued (**CPR, r. 23.2**).

Given that a freezing injunction can only be ordered against an unscrupulous defendant who is prepared to dissipate assets to prevent the claimant recovering on any judgment obtained, the application is, in practice, made without informing the defendant to ensure the injunction is effective. They are often sought on an urgent basis (see **37.4**) before proceedings are issued, in which event directions should be given for instituting proceedings for substantive relief (*Fourie v Le Roux* [2007] UKHL 1, [2007] 1 WLR 320 at [36]). Where the claimant had been pursuing the defendant for some time, and there had been other applications for relief in other jurisdictions, it was not wrong to refuse to deal with an application for a freezing order without notice (*Kensington International Ltd v Republic of Congo* [2003] EWCA Civ 709, LTL 13/5/2003). The application is made to a judge sitting in private and is made before service of the claim form so as not to alert the defendant.

Papers in support

38.3   An application for a freezing injunction must be supported by an affidavit making full and frank disclosure of all material facts, including those going against the grant of the order. This type of application is one of the exceptions where affidavits must be used (**PD 25A, para. 3.1**). The affidavit must be clear and fair, and claimants should avoid the temptation to flood the court with voluminous exhibits, particularly where this will tend to obscure the real issues.

A draft claim form, or its overseas equivalent, must be produced in order to identify the substantive claim against the defendant (*Fourie v Le Roux* [2007] UKHL 1, [2007] 1 WLR 320). Counsel must produce a draft minute of the order sought. The form of the order is considered at **38.15** to **38.29**. In urgent cases the application can be made before issue of the proceedings, and may be supported by evidence in draft or referred to orally on instructions, but in such cases the applicant will be required to confirm on affidavit all the evidence presented at the hearing (*Flightwise Travel Services Ltd v Gill* [2003] EWHC 3082 (Ch), *The Times*, 5 December 2003).

The papers must, wherever possible, be delivered to the court at least two hours before the hearing to allow the judge to read them in advance (**PD 25A, para. 4.3(1)**). Further, even on applications without notice and especially where 'worldwide' freezing injunctions (see **38.9**) are sought, counsel should consider drafting a skeleton argument indicating how the requirements for granting the order are made out (see *ALG Inc. v Uganda Airlines Corporation* (1992) *The Times*, 31 July 1992). Judges dealing with freezing injunctions applications made without notice to the respondents must be astute to ensure the provisions of **PD 25A** are complied with, and must be sure that the evidence adduced by the applicant justifies the order in the terms sought (*Thane Investments Ltd v Tomlinson* [2003] EWCA Civ 1272, LTL 29/7/2003).

Paragraph 3 of the standard-form freezing injunction order in the annex to **PD 25A** provides for a return day for a further hearing on notice, which is normally a few days after the without-notice hearing. The respondent must be fully informed of the case against him well in advance of the hearing on notice, including being provided with the evidence and being told of the arguments used (and, if appropriate, any observations made by the judge) at the without-notice hearing (*Flightwise Travel Services Ltd v Gill* [2003] EWHC 3082 (Ch), *The Times*, 5 December 2003). Consequently, a full note of the hearing must be provided to all parties affected by the order to ensure they know exactly what happened, the basis and material on which the order had been made (*Interoute Telecommunications (UK) Ltd v Fashion Gossip Ltd* (1999) *The Times*, 10 November 1999). Full notes must be provided without respondents needing to ask for them (*Thane Investments Ltd v Tomlinson* [2002] EWHC 2972 (Ch), *The Times*, 10 December 2002). A failure to provide notes of the without-notice hearing was not regarded as a strong enough reason to justify discharging the freezing order in *Thane Investments Ltd v Tomlinson*.

A third party who did not attend the hearing at which a freezing injunction was made, but who is served with the order, may request copies of the materials read by the judge, material prepared at the direction of the judge, and the note of the hearing (**PD 25A, para. 9.2**). Unless the court otherwise orders, the applicant must comply promptly with the request.

CONDITIONS FOR GRANTING FREEZING INJUNCTIONS

The jurisdiction to grant freezing injunctions derives from the Senior Courts Act 1981, **38.4** s. 37(1). This section enables the court to grant interim injunctions on such terms and conditions as the court thinks just where it appears 'just and convenient' to do so. The requirements laid down by the courts for granting freezing injunctions are:

(a) a cause of action justiciable in England and Wales;
(b) a good arguable case;
(c) the defendant having assets within the jurisdiction;
(d) a real risk that the defendant may dissipate those assets before judgment can be enforced;
(e) that the defendant will be adequately protected by the claimant's undertaking in damages (the discussion at **37.26** applies equally to freezing injunctions).

These principles cover the general run of cases. Because injunctions are granted where it is just and convenient, the court retains a discretion to refuse relief, and has power to stretch the usual rules in the interests of justice. This power is used only in truly exceptional cases. Otherwise, the above requirements must be established, and it is not sufficient to say that a freezing injunction would involve no immediate and obvious prejudice to the defendant (*Flightwise Travel Services Ltd v Gill* [2003] EWHC 3082 (Ch), *The Times*, 5 December 2003).

Claim justiciable in England and Wales

Since the jurisdiction was first recognised, it has been stated the first condition for granting a **38.5** freezing injunction is that there is a cause of action justiciable in England and Wales (*The Siskina* [1979] AC 210). Traditionally that meant the defendant had to be available for service within the jurisdiction, or otherwise amenable to the jurisdiction of the High Court through the rules on service outside the jurisdiction (now **CPR, r. 6.36**) or submission to the jurisdiction. Today, the High Court has such a wide jurisdiction to grant injunctions in aid of overseas proceedings (see **38.6**) under the **CJJA 1982, s. 25**, that this requirement is satisfied provided there is a claim for substantive relief which can be formulated against the defendant somewhere in the world.

Injunctions in support of foreign proceedings

38.6   If proceedings have been, or are to be, commenced in another jurisdiction, the High Court is empowered by the **CJJA 1982, s. 25**, and the Civil Jurisdiction and Judgments Act 1982 (Interim Relief) Order 1997 (SI 1997/302) to grant interim relief, including freezing injunctions, in support of those foreign proceedings (see **16.40**). *The Siskina* [1979] AC 210 was decided before the CJJA 1982, so could be decided differently today if its facts were to reoccur. The result is that jurisdiction, in the sense of whether the court has power to deal with the application, is no longer an issue. Instead, the focus is on whether the claimant can identify a cause of action against the defendant, which means there must be a formulated claim for substantive relief against the defendant. It does not matter if the substantive claim is to be brought in England and Wales or an overseas jurisdiction (*Fourie v Le Roux* [2007] UKHL 1, [2007] 1 WLR 320 at [35]). Particular caution is shown before granting freezing injunctions under **s. 25** (*Crédit Suisse Fides Trust SA v Cuoghi* [1998] QB 818), because this can result in the English freezing order overlapping with similar orders made in other countries, which can lead to double jeopardy for the defendants and the opportunity for forum shopping by the claimants (*Ryan v Friction Dynamics Ltd* [2001] CP Rep 75).

ICSID arbitration proceedings are not 'proceedings' for the purpose of **s. 25**. This is because the power in **s. 25(3)(c)**, to extend **s. 25** to arbitration proceedings was repealed by the Arbitration Act 1996, and while the Arbitration Act 1996 contains a power to extend the Arbitration Act 1996, s. 44, that power has not been exercised in relation to ICSID arbitration proceedings (*ETI Euro Telecom International NV v Bolivia* [2008] EWCA Civ 880, [2009] 1 WLR 665). Further, the foreign proceedings have to be on the substance of the dispute, so foreign attachment proceedings, being interim in nature, do not come within **s. 25** (*ETI Euro Telecom International NV v Bolivia*).

A court in England and Wales can grant interim relief in aid of foreign courts unless the fact the court has no jurisdiction over the case apart from **s. 25** 'makes it inexpedient' (**s. 25(2)**) for the court to grant relief. According to *Motorola Credit Corporation v Uzan (No. 2)* [2003] EWCA Civ 752, [2004] 1 WLR 113, the following factors are relevant in deciding expediency:

(a) whether making the order would interfere with the management of the case in the primary court;

(b) whether it is the policy in the primary jurisdiction to refuse to make worldwide freezing or disclosure orders;

(c) whether there is a danger that the order would give rise to disharmony or confusion and/or the risk of conflicting, inconsistent or overlapping orders in other jurisdictions;

(d) whether at the time the order is sought there is likely to be potential conflict as to jurisdiction; and

(e) whether the worldwide order could be enforced. In such cases each defendant falls to be considered separately.

It will rarely if ever be expedient to make an order under **s. 25** where the relevant defendants have no connection with the jurisdiction and the relevant assets are not located here either (*Belletti v Morici* [2009] EWHC 2316 (Comm), LTL 28/9/2009). In *Banco Nacional de Comercio Exterior SNC v Empresa de Telecomunicaciones de Cuba SA* [2007] EWCA Civ 662, [2008] 1 WLR 1936, the court made a domestic freezing injunction in support of a judgment obtained in Turin, but refused to make a worldwide order. It is not the policy of the Italian courts to grant worldwide freezing orders. A worldwide order was inexpedient because the judgment debtor was outside the jurisdiction, the original judgment was granted in Italy, any assets within the jurisdiction were covered by the domestic freezing injunction, and granting a worldwide order would be likely to give rise to disharmony and confusion. It was also held that there is no jurisdiction under Regulation (EC) No. 44/2001, art. 47, to grant a worldwide freezing injunction. All this provision says is that a person with a judgment which must be recognised is not prevented from applying for protective measures before registration. By way of contrast, in *Amedeo Hotels Ltd Partnership v Zaman* [2007] EWHC 295 (Comm), LTL 14/6/2007, the non-availability of world-wide freezing orders in New York was regarded as a reason in favour of granting an English worldwide order, rather than as a reason against doing so.

Of course the other basic requirements must also be satisfied (*Refco Inc. v Eastern Trading Co.* [1999] 1 Lloyd's Rep 159). Where it is appropriate to grant a freezing order that overlaps with an order from a foreign court, it is sensible to state in the order which court is to have the primary role in enforcing the overlapping orders, and for the English order, if it is a secondary order, to be in substantially the same terms as the primary foreign order (*Ryan v Friction Dynamics Ltd*).

Lawyers in England and Wales have to exercise extreme caution when instructed to apply for freezing injunctions in aid of foreign proceedings under **CJJA1982, s. 25.** These applications often involve copious and complex financial or commercial information which is difficult to digest, and because the lawyers in this jurisdiction will not be as familiar with the case as the foreign lawyers, it can mean that important features of the case are not covered in the evidence or otherwise not disclosed to the judge (*Lewis v Eliades* [2002] EWHC 335 (QB), [2002] CP Rep 28).

Good arguable case

Regarding the merits of the substantive claim, the minimum threshold for the exercise of the discretion is the establishment of a 'good arguable case' (*Ninemia Maritime Corporation v Trave Schiffahrtsgesellschaft mbH & Co.* [1983] 1 WLR 1412). This imposes a higher merits requirement than the 'serious issue to be tried' test commonly used in applications to amend and in applications applying the *American Cyanamid* principles (*Fiona Trust Holding Corporation v Privalov* [2007] EWHC 1217 (Comm), [2008] 1 Lloyd's Rep 254). According to Mustill J in *Ninemia Maritime Corporation v Trave Schiffahrtsgesellschaft mbH & Co.* [1983] 2 Lloyd's Rep 600 at p. 605, the expression means 'a case which is more than barely capable of serious argument, and yet not necessarily one which the judge believes to have a better than 50 per cent chance of success'. In *Attock Cement Co. Ltd v Romanian Bank for Foreign Trade* [1989] 1 All ER 1189 (a case on service outside the jurisdiction), it was said that a judge considering whether there is a good arguable case must reach a provisional or tentative conclusion on all the admissible material that the claimant is probably right on the disputed question of fact. This test will not be satisfied if the claimant does not have the evidence to substantiate the case relied upon, or if the case is likely to be struck out, and may not be satisfied if there is an arguable defence. Experts' reports supporting the claim, or a body of documentary evidence, might satisfy the test. In *Fiona Trust Holding Corporation v Privalov* matters pointing to a good arguable case included a lack of negotiations in allegedly fraudulent transactions, unconvincing evidence from the defendants to explain their conduct, a letter referring to 'the delicate nature of our exchanges', and attempts to prevent outsiders finding out. Freezing injunctions against directors were refused in an unfair prejudice case (see **85.9**), where there was no personal cause of action against the directors (*Re Premier Electronics (GB) Ltd* [2002] 2 BCLC 634). The courts have on occasion been reluctant to find there is a good arguable case where fraud is alleged, as in *Cheltenham and Gloucester Building Society v Ricketts* [1993] 1 WLR 1545, given the difficulty of proving this particular allegation. An arguable set-off may be taken as reducing or extinguishing the value of the claim. Anticipation that the defendant will be in breach of contract in the future has been held to be insufficient to satisfy this part of the test (*Veracruz Transportation Inc. v VC Shipping Co. Inc.* [1992] 1 Lloyd's Rep 353, overruling *A v B* [1989] 2 Lloyd's Rep 423).

38.7

Commentary

In *Softwarecore Ltd v Pathan* [2005] EWHC 1845 (Ch), LTL 1/8/2005, Pumfrey J used a 'triable issue' test for the merits of the claim, rather than the traditional 'good arguable case' test. This was satisfied on the facts, where the issue was whether the defendant was knowingly involved in certain alleged frauds. The judge took into account the pattern of trading, the lack of any formal written terms of agreement, the lack of investigations into the other parties' creditworthiness, and suspicious figures for profits in various transactions.

Assets

38.8 The requirement of proving that the defendant has assets within the jurisdiction stems from the principle that equity will not act in vain so that if an injunction will not be effective it will not be granted. The claimant must show 'some grounds for believing' that the defendant has assets within the jurisdiction. 'Assets' includes money, shares, securities, insurance money, bills of exchange, motor vehicles, ships, aircraft, trade goods, office equipment, jewellery and paintings. Ownership may be legal or beneficial, but must be in the same capacity as the defendant is or will be a party to the claim.

The existence of an overdrawn bank account was held in one case, *Third Chandris Shipping Corporation v Unimarine SA* [1979] QB 645, to be some evidence of assets within the jurisdiction. This is so particularly where the court can infer that the account is likely to be secured in some way.

Assets in the name of a third party will not usually be included in a freezing injunction unless the claimant establishes a good arguable case that the assets are beneficially owned by the defendant (*TSB Private Bank International SA v Chabra* [1992] 1 WLR 231; approved by the Court of Appeal in *Yukong Line Ltd v Rendsburg Investments Corporation* [2001] 2 Lloyd's Rep 113). In *TSB Private Bank International SA v Chabra* it was clear that the claimant had a good cause of action against the first defendant, and equally clear there was no independent cause of action against the second defendant, a company owned by the first defendant and/or his wife. As there was credible evidence that the assets apparently owned by the second defendant in fact belonged to the first defendant, Mummery J granted a freezing injunction against the second defendant on the ground that it was ancillary and incidental to the claim against the first defendant. See also the discussion on freezing injunctions against third parties at **38.26**.

Worldwide freezing injunctions

38.9 A worldwide freezing order (WFO) operates against assets located outside of England and Wales (with or without a clause covering assets within the jurisdiction). Such an order should not be made where the defendant has sufficient assets within the jurisdiction to satisfy the claim. In any event, it should only be granted in an exceptional case. Typically, exceptional cases are those having the three following characteristics:

(a) the defendant has acted dishonestly or fraudulently on a large scale;

(b) the defendant has the ability to transfer large sums of money around the world quickly; and

(c) the defendant is able to hide assets behind companies or in countries where they are unlikely to be found.

Examples are *Derby and Co. Ltd v Weldon (No. 1)* [1990] Ch 48, and *Republic of Haiti v Duvalier* [1990] 1 QB 202. The power to grant WFOs in support of domestic proceedings or domestic judgments derives from the Senior Courts Act 1981, s. 37(1), not **CJJA 1992, s. 25**, or the recast **Brussels I Regulation, art. 35** (*Masri v Consolidated Contractors International (UK) Ltd (No. 2)* [2007] EWHC 3010 (Comm), [2008] 1 All ER (Comm) 305 at [53]; [2008] EWCA Civ 303, [2009] QB 450 at [92]–[107]). WFOs are readily made against defendants incorporated in the jurisdiction or with a significant presence in the jurisdiction where there is cogent evidence of international fraud (*Mediterranean Shipping Co. v OMG International Ltd* [2008] EWHC 2150 (Comm), LTL 25/9/2008). A WFO may be granted even where the defendant has no assets within the jurisdiction (*Derby and Co. Ltd v Weldon (Nos. 3 and 4)* [1990] Ch 65).

A WFO may be granted under **CJJA 1992, s. 25** (see **38.6**), in support of foreign proceedings (*Credit Suisse Fides Trust SA v Cuoghi* [1998] QB 818). A WFO in aid of foreign proceedings affecting assets outside the jurisdiction will only be granted where the respondent or the dispute has a sufficiently strong link with the jurisdiction, or if there is some other factor justifying the court's intervention despite the lack of such a link (*Mobil Cerro Negro Ltd v Petróleos de Venezuela SA* [2008] EWHC 532 (Comm), [2008] 1 Lloyd's Rep 684).

WFO undertakings   WFOs must include a *Babanaft* proviso that the order will not affect third   **38.10**
parties outside the jurisdiction until, and to the extent that, it has been recognised, registered or enforced by a foreign court. See *Babanaft International Co. SA v Bassatne* [1990] Ch 13 and clause 19 of the standard-form freezing injunction in **PD 25A**. They must also include a 'Baltic' proviso to the effect that third parties served with the order may comply with what they reasonably believe to be their civil and criminal obligations in the country where the assets are located (*Bank of China v NBM LLC* [2001] EWCA Civ 1933, [2002] 1 WLR 844, and clause 20 of the standard-form freezing injunction). The claimant is further required to undertake not to enforce the order in a foreign court without first obtaining permission from the English court (*Derby and Co. Ltd v Weldon (No. 1)* [1990] Ch 48 and sch. B, para. 10, of the standard-form freezing injunction).

In *Re Bank of Credit and Commerce International SA* [1994] 1 WLR 708 the English liquidators of foreign companies had obtained WFOs in proceedings brought against two individuals alleging fraud in connection with the companies' affairs. The defendants sought an undertaking that the liquidators would not commence criminal proceedings against them outside the jurisdiction without the court's permission, but the court refused to impose such an undertaking, because it would impede investigation of the companies' affairs by regulatory and prosecuting authorities which the liquidators had a duty to assist.

Schedule B, para. 10, of the standard-form freezing injunction is an undertaking by the applicant not to seek to enforce the order outside the jurisdiction without the permission of the court. This undertaking takes effect as if it were an injunction, and can be replaced by an express injunction to the same effect (*Grupo Torras SA v Al Sabah* [2005] EWCA Civ 1370, LTL 24/8/2005). In deciding whether to release the claimant from an undertaking not to use information obtained from another party under a WFO in contempt proceedings, the court should consider whether it would be just and convenient to permit use of that information for the purpose of policing or enforcing the WFO (*Dadourian Group International Inc. v Simms (No. 2)* [2006] EWCA Civ 1745, [2007] 1 WLR 2967) (slightly different formulations were given by the three members of the court).

Seeking permission to enforce outside the jurisdiction   Guidance on the procedure to be   **38.11**
followed on an application for permission to enforce a WFO outside the jurisdiction was given in *Dadourian Group International Inc. v Simms* [2006] EWCA Civ 399, [2006] 1 WLR 2499:

(a) Normally the application should be made on notice to the respondent, but in cases of urgency, where it is just to do so, the permission may be given without notice to the party against whom relief will be sought in the foreign proceedings, but that party should be given the earliest opportunity of having the matter reconsidered by the court at a hearing on notice (Arden LJ's guideline 8).

(b) The evidence in support of the application for permission should contain all the information (so far as it can reasonably be obtained in the time available) necessary to enable the judge to make an informed decision. This should include evidence of the applicable law and practice in the foreign court; evidence as to the nature of the proposed proceedings to be commenced; evidence as to the assets believed to be located in the jurisdiction of the foreign court; and the names of the parties by whom such assets are held (Arden LJ's guideline 5).

Commentary

Arden LJ laid down the following guidelines for deciding whether to grant permission to enforce a WFO:

1. The principle applying to the grant of permission to enforce a WFO abroad is that the grant of that permission should be just and convenient for the purpose of ensuring the effectiveness of the WFO, and in addition that it is not oppressive to the parties to the English proceedings or to third parties who may be joined to the foreign proceedings.
2. All the relevant circumstances and options need to be considered. In particular consideration should be given to granting relief on terms, for example terms as to the extension to third parties of the undertaking to compensate for costs incurred as a result of the WFO and as to the type of proceedings that may be commenced abroad. Consideration should also be given to the proportionality of the steps proposed to be taken abroad, and in addition to the form of any order.
3. The interests of the applicant should be balanced against the interests of the other parties to the proceedings and any new party likely to be joined to the foreign proceedings.
4. Permission should not normally be given in terms that would enable the applicant to obtain relief in the foreign proceedings which is superior to the relief given by the WFO.
5. [Deals with evidence in support, see above.]
6. The standard of proof as to the existence of assets that are both within the WFO and within the jurisdiction of the foreign court is a real prospect, that is the applicant must show that there is a real prospect that such assets are located within the jurisdiction of the foreign court in question.
7. There must be evidence of a risk of dissipation of the assets in question.
8. [Deals with applying on notice, see above.]

The court will also consider whether granting permission is appropriate in the interests of justice, and whether information obtained under the injunction is intended to be used for a purpose which is not a purpose of the worldwide injunction (*Bates v Microstar Ltd* [2003] EWHC 661 (Ch), *The Times*, 15 April 2003).

Risk of disposal

38.12   The claimant must establish that there is a real risk that the defendant will dissipate assets if unrestrained (*Ninemia Maritime Corporation v Trave Schiffahrtsgesellschaft mbH & Co. KG* [1983] 1 WLR 1412). There has to be 'solid evidence' of the risk of disposal (*Ninemia Maritime Corporation v Trave Schiffahrts GmbH & Co. KG*; *Dean and Dean v Grinina* [2008] EWHC 927 (QB), LTL 13/5/2008). In *Customs and Excise Commissioners v Anchor Foods Ltd* [1999] 1 WLR 1139 Neuberger J said that what is required is a good and arguable case for a risk of dissipation. This was found to be so where the defendant proposed to dispose of its entire business at a price which had been independently verified by a partner in a leading accountancy firm, because the purchaser was a company controlled by the same people who controlled the defendant and there was contrary valuation evidence (also from very eminent experts) indicating that the price was too low. A real risk of disposal of assets may be established by reference either to previous conduct which tends to show a want of probity or to a course of dealing suggesting the defendant will deal with his assets to make himself judgment-proof, or by raising an inference that such is the case by other evidence (*Re Industrial Services Group Ltd (No. 1)* [2003] BPIR 392). While it may be difficult to establish a real risk of dissipation if the respondent is a well-established business (*Vinprom Rousse v Bulgarian Vintners Co. Ltd* (2000) LTL 8/5/2001), there is a real risk of disposal where even an apparently financially solid company transfers its assets outside the jurisdiction if enforcement overseas would cause extra costs and delays (*Stronghold Insurance Co. Ltd v Overseas Union Insurance Ltd* [1996] IRLR 13). The risk of dissipation has to involve a risk of impairing the claimant's ability to enforce a judgment (*Mobil Cerro Negro Ltd v Petróleos de Venezuela SA* [2008] EWHC 532 (Comm), [2008] 1 Lloyd's Rep 684). It is sufficient if the defendant's actions are unjustifiable (*Ketchum International plc v Group Public Relations Holdings Ltd* [1997] 1 WLR 4 at p. 10) and will have this effect. It is not necessary to show the defendant intends to produce this effect (*Mobil Cerro Negro Ltd v Petróleos de Venezuela SA* at [40]). However, being short of money is not to be equated with an intention to dissipate assets (*Midas Merchant Bank plc v Bello* [2002] EWCA Civ 1496, LTL 14/10/2002).

In *Oaktree Financial Services Ltd v Higham* [2004] EWHC 2098 (Ch), LTL 11/5/2004, one of the solicitors involved in the case wrote to the defendant unwittingly but in effect warning him of the possibility of an application being made for a freezing injunction. Laddie J was almost minded to refuse the injunction on this ground alone, as there was a strong prospect that any funds would have been dissipated once the defendant was put on notice.

At one time it was thought that freezing injunctions could only be granted against foreign defendants. The Senior Courts Act 1981, s. 37(3), now provides that the jurisdiction to grant these orders 'shall be exercisable in cases where [the defendant] is, as well as in cases where he is not, domiciled, resident or present within [the] jurisdiction'. Lord Denning MR in *Third Chandris Shipping Corporation v Unimarine SA* [1979] QB 645 said, at p. 669:

The mere fact that the defendant is abroad is not by itself sufficient... But there are some foreign companies whose structure invites comment. We often see in this court a corporation which is registered in a country where the company law is so loose that nothing is known about it—where it does no work and has no officers and no assets... Judgment cannot be enforced against it. There is no reciprocal enforcement of judgments... In such cases the very fact of incorporation there gives some ground for believing there is a risk that, if judgment or an award is obtained, it may go unsatisfied.

Reciprocal enforcement of judgments is considered in **chapter 80**.

Assessing risk   Factors relevant to the question of risk of dissipation include: **38.13**

(a) The nature of the assets: the more easily disposed of, the easier it is to establish a real risk of disposal.

(b) The location of the respondent's assets. There will be less risk if the respondent has substantial assets within the jurisdiction. If the respondent's assets are overseas, an important factor is whether English judgments are enforceable in the country where those assets are situated (*Montecchi v Shimco (UK) Ltd* [1979] 1 WLR 1180). There will be less risk if the assets are in an EU country on account of the ease of enforcement under the **recast Brussels I Regulation.**

(c) The nature and financial standing of the respondent's business, and the time it has been in existence.

(d) Any intentions expressed by the respondent about dealings with its assets.

(e) Whether the respondent is reputable and accustomed to paying its debts (*Barclay-Johnson v Yuill* [1980] 1 WLR 1259).

(f) Whether the respondent is domiciled or incorporated in a tax haven or country with lax company law.

(g) Whether the evidence supporting the substantive cause of action discloses dishonesty or a suspicion of dishonesty on the part of the respondent. This is a weighty factor when it is present, and this is so whether or not it is pleaded as fraud (*Guinness plc v Saunders* (1987) *The Independent*, 15 April 1987). Alleged or admitted dishonesty is not of itself enough: all the circumstances must be considered (*Thane Investments Ltd v Tomlinson* [2003] EWCA Civ 1272, LTL 29/7/2003). There was a real risk of disposal in *Lawson v Mizzi* [2010] EWHC 55 (Ch), LTL 19/2/2010, where the respondent was an admitted fraudster who misapplied funds over a considerable period, and who had admitted destroying evidence. The fact she made admissions after being caught out did not remove the risk. Lesser allegations, such as of negligence, breach of contract and breach of fiduciary duty, rarely make it appropriate to infer risk of disposal of assets from the nature of the allegation in the substantive cause of action (*Renewable Power and Light plc v Renewable Power and Light Services Inc.* [2008] EWHC 1058 (Ch), LTL 23/5/2008).

(h) Any pattern of evasiveness (*Linsen International Ltd v Humpuss Sea Transport Pte Ltd* [2010] EWHC 303 (Comm), LTL 1/3/2010), the raising of thin defences, or total silence, in the face of the claimant's claim. A good arguable case of perjury was significant in *Congentra AG v Sixteen Thirteen Marine SA* [2008] EWHC 1615 (Comm), [2008] 2 Lloyd's Rep 602.

(i) Whether there is evidence that the respondent has been dishonest, outside the actual cause of action. This includes matters such as contrivances designed to generate an appearance of wealth.

(j) Past incidents of debt default by the respondent, although it is not essential for the claimant to have such evidence (*Third Chandris Shipping Corporation v Unimarine SA* [1979] QB 645).

(k) Evidence that the respondent has already taken steps to remove or dissipate its assets (*Aiglon Ltd v Gau Shan Co. Ltd* [1993] 1 Lloyd's Rep 164).

(l) Any history of non-compliance with court orders and other action by the respondent taken in total disregard of court orders (*Great Future International Ltd v Sealand Housing Corporation* (2002) LTL 16/5/2002).

Discretion

38.14 In its discretion, the court can refuse a freezing injunction even if the usual requirements are made out. In *Rasu Maritima SA v Perusahaan Pertambangan Minyak Dan Gas Bumi Negara* [1978] QB 644 the Court of Appeal refused to grant an order partly because the 'cleanliness' of the claimant's hands was open to question, and partly in the exercise of its discretion. The assets frozen were parts for a fertiliser plant, and were valued at $12 million in the hands of the defendants, but were only worth $0.35 million as scrap. This was regarded as only a 'drop in the ocean' in comparison with the size of the claim.

A freezing order against a defendant bank was discharged in the exercise of the court's discretion in *Polly Peck International plc v Nadir (No. 2)* [1992] 4 All ER 769. The claimants claimed the bank, the fourth defendant, was liable as a constructive trustee in respect of money allegedly misapplied by the first defendant. The freezing injunction covered 60 per cent of the bank's assets, and would almost certainly have severely damaged its day-to-day banking business, and also was likely to result in a loss of confidence among investors with the possibility of a run on its deposits. In those circumstances, the granting of the order was inimical to the purpose for which the freezing injunction jurisdiction existed. Lord Donaldson of Lymington MR said that the judgments in this case should not be taken as meaning that it will never be possible to obtain a freezing injunction against a bank, but the circumstances would have to be unusual. At the other end of the scale, freezing injunctions will not be granted where the assets in question are relatively modest. The defendant in *Indosuez International Finance BV v National Reserve Bank* [2002] EWHC 774 (Comm), LTL 26/4/2002, applied to discharge a freezing injunction in support of a foreign judgment on the ground that sufficient funds had been frozen under a Belgian order also in support of that judgment.

The application was refused, partly because the defendant was strenuously resisting enforcement in Belgium, and partly because the value of the Belgian assets (bonds) was highly volatile, so the Belgian assets were not adequate protection. In *Sions v Price* (1988) *The Independent*, 19 December 1988, an order was refused where the claim was £2,000. The current small claims limit of £5,000 may be a good guide to where the line should be drawn.

CONTENTS OF A FREEZING INJUNCTION

Undertakings

38.15 The following undertakings by the claimant must be given to the court and incorporated into the order (see the standard order in **PD 25A** at sch. B):

(a) As with other interim injunctions, to pay damages to the defendant if it transpires that the order should not have been granted; the court has a discretion to order a freezing injunction subject to a limited undertaking in damages (*RBG Resources plc v Rastogi* [2005] EWHC 994 (Ch), [2005] 2 BCLC 592);

(b) to notify the defendant forthwith of the terms of the order, often by telex or fax, and to serve the defendant with the affidavit and exhibits in support; this is a consequence of applying without notice;

(c) to pay the reasonable costs and expenses incurred by third parties in complying with the order;

(d) to indemnify third parties in respect of any liability incurred in complying with the order.

In urgent cases, the following further undertakings may be required:

(e) to issue a claim form in the terms of the draft used on the application;

(f) to swear and file affidavits deposing to the facts relied on before the judge.

Financial undertakings ((a) and (c) in the above list) are not normally required if the applicant is a public body acting under a public duty (*Financial Services Authority v Sinaloa Gold plc* [2013] UKSC 11, [2013] 2 AC 28).

Under the Senior Courts Act 1981, s. 37(2), interim injunctions can be granted on such terms and conditions as the court thinks fit. A little latitude is permissible. So, in *Allen v Jambo Holdings Ltd* [1980] 1 WLR 1252 the Court of Appeal continued a freezing injunction in favour of a legally aided claimant who could not give a valuable undertaking in damages. The case was unusual in that the defendants had sworn an affidavit blatantly exaggerating the effects of the order and had been less than forthcoming on a number of points. Also, in any event, the defendants could have obtained the release of their frozen aeroplane by providing security.

In the event that the order is discharged, the defendant is entitled to both special and general damages arising from the effects of the order. Special damages might include disruption to the defendant's business and management time in dealing with the order. The scale of the order (particularly if combined with a search order) may of itself be sufficient for the court to be satisfied that there was significant disruption to the defendant's business (*Aerospace Publishing Ltd v Thames Water Utilities Ltd* [2007] EWCA Civ 3, [2007] Bus LR 726; *Al-Rawas v Pegasus Energy Ltd* [2008] EWHC 617 (QB), [2009] 1 All ER 346). In most circumstances evidence is required to support an award for general damages; damages for emotional distress are not recoverable; and exemplary damages are unlikely to be appropriate (*Al-Rawas v Pegasus Energy Ltd*).

Fortifying the undertaking in damages   If the defendant can show it has a good arguable **38.16** case that it will suffer loss in consequence of granting a freezing injunction, the court can order the applicant to fortify the undertaking in damages by paying money into court or providing other security. The court said in *Energy Venture Partners Ltd v Malabu Oil and Gas Ltd* [2014] EWCA Civ 1295, [2015] 1 WLR 2309 at [53] that there are three requirements:

(a) an intelligent estimate needs to be made of the likely amount of any loss which may be suffered by the applicant for fortification (typically the defendant) by reason of the making of the interim order;

(b) there must be a good arguable case that there is a risk of loss arising from the interim order; and

(c) the loss has been or is likely to be caused by the granting of the injunction.

In assessing the likely loss it is important to distinguish between the harm caused by the litigation and the harm caused by the freezing injunction (*Al-Rawas v Pegasus Energy Ltd* [2008] EWHC 617 (QB), [2009] 1 All ER 346). Practical difficulties can also be taken into account: it may be difficult for an administrator to obtain suitable security in cases where a company has a large number of small creditors, whereas the position may be different if the company has a small number of large creditors (*Re Bloomsbury International Ltd, Bloomsbury International Ltd v Holyoake* [2010] EWHC 1150 (Ch), LTL 24/5/2010). Factors that the court should consider are similar to those on applications for security for costs (see **67.16** to **67.24**). Therefore, the court should not usually take into account the merits of the claim, but should consider whether requiring the applicant to fortify the undertaking may stifle a genuine claim (*Sinclair Investment Holdings SA v Cushnie* [2004] EWHC 218 (Ch), LTL 23/3/2004).

Assets covered by the order

38.17 Considered in relation to the assets they cover, freezing injunctions can be divided into three types:

(a) General orders, which cover all the defendant's assets.

(b) Maximum-sum orders, which cover the defendant's assets up to the highest amount, including interest and costs, for which the claimant has a good arguable case (*Pacific Maritime (Asia) Ltd v Holystone Overseas Ltd* [2007] EWHC 2319 (Comm), [2008] 1 Lloyd's Rep 371). An appropriate sum should be included for the applicant's estimated costs (*Fourie v Le Roux* [2005] EWCA Civ 204, [2006] 2 BCLC 531, point not considered on appeal). A slightly different test applies in applications to enforce WFOs outside the jurisdiction, see *Dadourian Group International Inc. v Simms* [2006] EWCA Civ 399, [2006] 1 WLR 2499, in which Arden LJ at [47] said that the applicant must show a real prospect that the assets are located within the jurisdiction of the foreign court.

(c) Orders attaching to specific assets, such as a ship, a cargo or an aeroplane.

Often, orders attaching to specific assets are combined with either general or maximum-sum orders. The choice between general and maximum-sum orders was considered in *Z Ltd v A-Z and AA-LL* [1982] QB 558. Maximum-sum orders are the norm. A general order is likely to provoke an application for a variation down to a maximum-sum order. One drawback with maximum-sum orders is that banks will not necessarily know if they can honour transactions on the defendant's accounts as they will not know the total value of the defendant's assets covered by the order at any particular time. Where such practical difficulties result in a larger sum being 'frozen' than the sum stated in the order, the claimant may be held liable on its undertakings in damages. General orders may accordingly be used where the defendant's assets are not fully known by the claimant, and are also appropriate in fraud cases where the amount of the claim may be unknown.

Where the claimant asks for a freezing injunction to cover assets which the defendant or some third party alleges belong to someone other than the defendant, the court has a wide power to do whatever is just and convenient, including ordering the question of ownership to be tried as an issue between the claimant and the third party (*SCF Finance Co. Ltd v Masri* [1985] 1 WLR 876). Unless specifically excluded, the defendant's assets subject to a freezing order will include assets over which the defendant claims to have only legal title (for example, as executor or bare trustee) as well as assets in respect of which the defendant is beneficial owner (*Federal Bank of the Middle East Ltd v Hadkinson* [2000] 1 WLR 1695).

The extended definition of 'his assets' in para. 6 of the standard freezing injunction order in **PD 25A** is designed to preserve the decision in *Federal Bank of the Middle East Ltd v Hadkinson*, but to make it clear that such assets include assets controlled by the defendant or in which the respondent has beneficial ownership but which are held by third parties (*JSC BTA Bank v Solodchenko* [2010] EWCA Civ 1436, [2011] 1 WLR 888). These may include assets held by a foreign trust or a Liechtenstein *Anstalt*. A debt owed to a company in which the defendant is a director and shareholder is not directly covered by the standard wording of para. 6, and an express extension is required if it can be demonstrated there is a likelihood of the corporate veil being lifted (*Group Seven Ltd v Allied Investment Corporation Ltd* [2013] EWHC 1509 (Ch), [2014] 1 WLR 735, applying *Prest v Prest* [2012] EWCA Civ 1395, [2013] 2 AC 415). The director's shares in such a non-party company, however, will be assets covered by para. 6, and the standard wording will restrain such a director from procuring the non-party company from making dispositions of its assets which are likely to result in a diminution of the value of those shares (*Lakatamia Shipping Co. Ltd v Su* [2014] EWCA Civ 636, [2015] 1 WLR 291). A personal right to draw down on a loan agreement entered into after a standard form freezing injunction is made is also not covered by para. 6, and express words would need to be added to ensure the injunction covered choses in action to achieve this (*JSC BTA Bank v Ablyazov (No. 10)* [2013] EWCA Civ 928, [2014] 1 WLR 1414). It is possible to include assets of which the respondent is the legal owner for the benefit of someone else by including words such as 'whether the respondent is interested in them legally, beneficially or otherwise' (*JSC BTA Bank v Solodchenko*; see **38.26**).

Any dispute about whether the defendant is only a legal owner can be dealt with by trying an issue, as suggested in *SCF Finance Co. Ltd v Masri*. In *C Inc. plc v L* [2001] 2 Lloyd's Rep 459, the claimant obtained judgment against the defendant, and sought a freezing injunction in aid of execution against both the defendant and her husband. On the facts the defendant had an arguable right to an indemnity from her husband in respect of the judgment, and it was held that in those circumstances it was right to add the husband as a party and to extend the freezing injunction to cover his assets. Setting aside a transfer of assets said to have been in breach of a freezing injunction requires a separate originating process (*JSC BTA Bank v Ablyazov (No. 11)* [2014] EWCA Civ 602, [2015] 1 WLR 1287).

Bank accounts

Bank accounts are one of the most common assets covered by freezing injunctions. The following points should be noted: **38.18**

(a) A joint account will not be affected by a freezing injunction unless it is specifically covered by the wording of the order (*SCF Finance Co. Ltd v Masri* [1985] 1 WLR 876).

(b) If the defendant has an account containing money over which the claimant asserts a proprietary interest, mixed with the defendant's own money and/or money held by the defendant on behalf of a third party, the court has jurisdiction to freeze the entire account (*Chief Constable of Kent v V* [1983] QB 34).

(c) The claimant must give the fullest possible details (bank, branch, account name and number) in the affidavit in support. If it is necessary to ask the bank to search for an account, the number of branches involved should be as limited as possible. The claimant will be required to pay the costs of such searches immediately, which may or may not be recoverable from the defendant as costs of the action.

(d) The bank should honour transactions entered into before the order is made. The bank must also honour cheques backed by guarantee cards and irrevocable letters of credit, see, for example, *Cretanor Maritime Co. Ltd v Irish Marine Management Ltd* [1978] 1 WLR 966, and *Lewis and Peat (Produce) Ltd v Almatu Properties Ltd* (1992) *The Times,* 14 May 1992. Cheque cards should be recalled once the order has been served on the bank. Transferring money from a current account to a deposit account is a breach by the bank (*R (Revenue and Customs Prosecution Office) v R* [2007] EWHC 2393 (Admin), LTL 22/11/2007).

(e) A freezing injunction can apply to the *proceeds* of a letter of credit when received (*Z Ltd v A-Z and AA-LL* [1982] QB 558).

(f) A provision must be incorporated into the order to allow any bank served with the order to exercise any right of set-off it may have in respect of facilities given to the defendant before the order (*Oceanica Castelana Armadora SA v Mineralimportexport* [1983] 1 WLR 1294).

Duty owed by banks to the claimant The negligence liability of banks after being notified of freezing orders was considered by the House of Lords in *Commissioners of Customs and Excise v Barclays Bank plc* [2006] UKHL 28, [2007] 1 AC 181. Under its usual practice, the bank would have frozen the defendant's accounts on being notified of a freezing injunction. Due to human error it allowed the defendant to withdraw £2 million two hours after notification. Shortly afterwards the bank wrote to the claimant confirming it would comply with the order. The Court of Appeal ([2004] EWCA Civ 1555, [2005] 1 WLR 2082) held that the three-fold test of foreseeability, proximity and fairness pointed to the imposition of a duty of care, which was not displaced by the apparent lack of any assumption of responsibility, and that the incremental approach supported liability (at [48]). This was reversed by the House of Lords which held the bank did not owe a duty of care. Lord Bingham of Cornhill at [17]–[23] gave six reasons why the reasoning of the Court of Appeal would not be upheld. These include the fact that freezing injunctions do not warn third parties that there might be liability, and that it is illogical to impose a duty of care on a third party when **38.19**

it is already established that a litigant owes no duty of care to an opponent. The imposition of a duty of care in a novel situation turns on a careful analysis of the circumstances of the case. Lord Hoffmann in particular made it clear that deciding whether a duty of care is owed in novel situations cannot be answered by a mechanical application of any of the established tests.

Port authorities

38.20   Where a freezing injunction affects a ship in harbour, the claimant will be required to undertake to reimburse the port authority for lost income, and a proviso will be incorporated into the order giving the port authority a discretion to move the ship for operational reasons (*Clipper Maritime Co. Ltd v Mineralimportexport* [1981] 1 WLR 1262).

Land

38.21   Freezing injunctions can be granted over land, although it may be difficult to prove there is a 'risk of disposal'. An order, if granted, would not be made for the purpose of enforcing a judgment, so would not be registrable as a land charge (*Stockler v Fourways Estates Ltd* [1984] 1 WLR 25).

Living expenses

38.22   A freezing injunction must allow an individual defendant to use a reasonable sum each week or month to pay his or her ordinary living expenses. As decided in *PCW (Underwriting Agencies) Ltd v Dixon* [1983] 2 All ER 158, a defendant is not dissipating his assets by living as he has always lived. It is a misuse of the jurisdiction to grant freezing injunctions to seek to apply pressure on the defendant (perhaps with a view to obtaining a favourable settlement) by unreasonably limiting the money available for ordinary living expenses. A provision requiring an account of expenditure on living expenses does not require the submission of receipts, although that may be the most convenient way of complying. Such a clause does not control the relevant person's expenditure, but merely monitors that expenditure, and is a proportionate invasion of rights under the European Convention on Human Rights, **art. 8(1)**, and the **First Protocol, art. 1**, in the **Human Rights Act 1998, sch. 1** (*R (K) v HM Treasury* [2009] EWHC 1643 (Admin), LTL 22/5/2009).

Living expenses money must not, however, be spent on extraordinary items, such as expensive motor cars (see *TDK Tape Distributor (UK) Ltd v Videochoice Ltd* [1986] 1 WLR 141). More caution must be shown before allowing a defendant to use frozen assets where the claim is a proprietary one, because the allegation is that the frozen assets belong to the claimant (*Halifax plc v Chandler* [2001] EWCA Civ 1750, [2002] CPLR 41). Spending in excess of the living expenses clause is not a breach of the injunction if it is funded by borrowing from another source (*Cantor Index Ltd v Lister* (2001) LTL 23/11/2001). Retrospective variation to allow frozen assets to be used to pay for substantial living expenses is unlikely to be allowed (*Cantor Index Ltd v Lister*).

Trade debts

38.23   A freezing injunction must allow a defendant who is engaged in trade to pay any legitimate trade debts as they would be paid in the ordinary and proper course of the defendant's business (cl. 11(2) of the standard freezing injunction order in **PD 25A**). The philosophy behind this is that a freezing injunction is not intended to confer priority over other trade creditors. A defendant should be allowed to pay a trade debt, if the defendant is acting in good faith and in the ordinary course of business, even if the debt is not strictly enforceable (*Iraqi Ministry of Defence v Arcepey Shipping Co. SA* [1981] QB 65). Ordinary business expenses may usually be paid from frozen funds, and, in the event of a dispute, the court does not usually consider whether the business venture is reasonable nor whether the business expenses are reasonable. Further, it does not balance the strength of the defendant's case against that of the claimant, nor does it take into consideration that money will not be available to the claimant if it gets judgment (*Halifax plc v Chandler* [2001] EWCA Civ 1750, [2002]

CPLR 41). The standard trade debts clause only covers transactions which are consistent with the way the defendant's business has been carried on in the past (*Abbey Forwarding Ltd v Hone* [2010] EWHC 1532 (Ch), LTL 5/7/2010). Payments falling outside this concept require the court's permission. In deciding whether to grant permission the court in *Abbey Forwarding Ltd v Hone* took into account:

(a) the fact this was a conventional freezing injunction rather than an injunction giving effect to a proprietary claim. In conventional freezing injunctions the frozen assets still belong to the defendant;

(b) the prospects of the defendant succeeding at trial;

(c) restrictions on the defendant's related business activities by any insolvency procedures or other practical matters which made it difficult for the defendant to make the payment from other sources.

Whether the defendant should use assets not covered by the order where such are available depends ultimately on the defendant's motive (*Campbell Mussels v Thompson* (1984) 81 LS Gaz 2140, interpreting *A v C (No. 2)* [1981] QB 961). A payment by a defendant as an agent to its principal was accepted as amounting to an abuse of a freezing injunction in *Atlas Maritime Co. SA v Avalon Maritime Ltd (No. 1)* [1991] 4 All ER 769, where the relationship of principal and agent was held not to exist on the facts.

The 'ordinary course of business' proviso is inappropriate in a post-judgment freezing order in respect of bank accounts (*Soinco SACI v Novokuznetsk Aluminium Plant* [1998] QB 406), although it was regarded as appropriate for a post-judgment receivables freezing injunction in *Masri v Consolidated Contractors International Co. SAL* [2008] EWHC 2492 (Comm), LTL 28/10/2008 and for a freezing injunction to enforce an arbitral award in *Mobile Telesystems Finance SA v Nomihold Securities Inc.* [2011] EWCA Civ 1040, [2012] 1 All ER (Comm) 223.

Costs of litigation

A freezing injunction should normally also allow the defendant to pay the ordinary costs of the present proceedings if no other funds are available. Even substantial expenditure, and expenditure on VAT advice which is necessary for the defendant's solicitor to formulate the defence, may be allowed under this proviso (*Furylong Ltd v Masterpiece Technology Ltd* [2004] EWHC 3103 (Ch), LTL 13/7/2004). It does not cover the costs of unnecessary legal advice (*Chantrey Vellacott v Convergence Group plc* (2008) LTL 23/6/2008). A case where the Court of Appeal held there were other funds available to pay the defendant's costs was *Atlas Maritime Co. SA v Avalon Maritime Ltd (No. 3)* [1991] 1 WLR 917. In this case it was found that the defendants' parent company operated the defendants in such a way that all funds received by the defendants were immediately paid to the parent company, and any sums payable by the defendants were paid by the parent company. **38.24**

The permission to use money to pay reasonable legal costs (or living expenses or trade debts) does no more than to permit the expenditure without the defendant being in contempt of court. Thus, where the underlying cause of action asserts a proprietary claim against the defendant, the permission to use money to pay reasonable legal expenses is no guarantee that the recipients of that money will escape a later claim in constructive trust for knowing receipt should the claim be established (*United Mizrahi Bank Ltd v Doherty* [1998] 1 WLR 435).

A freezing injunction should not prevent, and may be varied if it does, bona fide expenditure on the legal costs of litigation other than the case in hand, where the other case has a reasonable prospect of success and was on foot when the freezing injunction was granted (*Halifax plc v Chandler* [2001] EWCA Civ 1750, [2002] CPLR 41).

Disclosure of assets orders

The court has power under **CPR, r. 25.1(1)(g)**, to make ancillary orders for disclosure and answers to requests for further information to ensure the effectiveness of the main freezing injunction. Such an order can be granted where there is a reasonable possibility, based on **38.25** credible evidence, that a freezing injunction application might be made (*Lichter v Rubin* [2008] EWHC 450 (Ch), *The Times*, 18 April 2008). While there is no free-standing power to grant this type of order, it can be made where there is a likelihood of a freezing injunction application (*Parker v CS Structured Credit Fund Ltd* [2003] EWHC 391 (Ch), [2003] 1 WLR 1680). Clause 9(1) of the standard freezing injunction order in **PD 25A** requires the defendant to provide information confirmed on affidavit giving details of all his assets exceeding a specified value. The figure inserted in clause 9(1) in *Cinar Corporation v Panju* [2006] EWHC 2557 (QB), [2007] 1 All ER (Comm) 373, was £1,000. Clause 18 of the standard search order requires the defendant to provide information confirmed on affidavit of the whereabouts of all listed items, the names and addresses of the persons who supplied them or to whom they have been supplied, and dates and quantities of each transaction. Orders may be made requiring disclosure of the nature and whereabouts of all the defendant's assets within the jurisdiction. An order for a company to disclose its assets does not extend to disclosure of the assets of its subsidiaries (*Linsen International Ltd v Humpuss Sea Transport Pte Ltd* [2010] EWHC 303 (Comm), LTL 1/3/2010). A proposed variation on the asset disclosure order in *Intercontinental Bank plc v Akingbola* [2010] EWHC 35 (QB), LTL 3/2/2010, which would have limited the disclosure to the applicant's London-based lawyers, was refused. The practical effect of the proposed variation would have been to prevent the lawyers obtaining effective instructions from the applicant, rendering the order unworkable.

Grupo Torras v Fahad [2004] EWCA Civ 60 held that the court has a discretion to make such an order even if there is a pending application disputing the court's jurisdiction over the substantive claim. *JSC BTA Bank v Ablyazov (No. 3)* [2010] EWCA Civ 1141, [2011] Bus LR D119, went further, and held that it is even possible to make an unless order, with judgment to be entered in default, to secure compliance with a disclosure order in a freezing injunction while there is a pending application challenging the court's jurisdiction.

At the post-judgment stage a disclosure of assets order serves two purposes. One is to assist in the identification of assets which may be covered by the freezing order, and the other is to assist the judgment creditor in locating assets against which enforcement may be sought (*Vitol SA v Capri Marine Ltd* [2010] EWHC 458 (Comm), [2011] 1 All ER (Comm) 366). Post-judgment it is usually just and convenient for the judgment creditor to have full information to assist with execution of the judgment anywhere in the world (*Gidrxslme Shipping Co. Ltd v Tantomar-Transportes Maritimos Lda* [1995] 1 WLR 299). Use in this way is not a collateral purpose within the meaning of **CPR, r. 31.22**, and does not need prior permission from the court (*Vitol SA v Capri Marine Ltd* at [23]).

Defendants should be given a realistic time for compliance (*Oystertec plc v Davidson* [2004] EWHC 627 (Ch), LTL 7/4/2004, where four working days was regarded as extremely short). Seven working days may be reasonable, depending on the circumstances. A judge may be justified in refusing to extend a seven-day order despite a pending application to discharge the injunction (*VTB Capital plc v Malofeev* [2011] EWCA Civ 1252, LTL 4/10/2011). In addition, the defendant's bank may be ordered, even if not a party, to give disclosure of documents relating to the defendant's bank account (*A v C* [1981] QB 956).

Orders requiring disclosure of the nature and whereabouts of all the defendant's assets within the jurisdiction are a standard requirement in freezing injunctions, and are generally required if freezing injunctions are to be effective (*Motorola Credit Corporation v Uzan* [2002] EWCA Civ 989, [2002] 2 All ER (Comm) 945, in which the defendant was required to disclose the whereabouts of his assets notwithstanding a pending application to set aside the freezing order). They can require disclosure before the hearing of an appeal challenging the granting of the freezing injunction (*JSC BTA Bank v Ablyazov* [2009] EWCA Civ 1125, [2010] 1 All ER (Comm) 1029). They are nevertheless regarded as intrusive in that they override the defendant's privacy, and compliance can be burdensome. In the case of freezing injunctions in support of foreign proceedings, they should be used sparingly. Factors are the interests of justice, the nature of the claim against the defendant, whether making the order would be proportionate to the interference with the defendant's rights, and whether it would be oppressive (*Cinar Corporation v Panju*).

There are three major limits on the jurisdiction to make ancillary disclosure orders. First, as with other forms of disclosure, such orders will not be granted if they are merely 'fishing' (see *Faith Panton Property Plan Ltd v Hodgetts* [1981] 1 WLR 927). Essentially, an application for disclosure will be 'fishing' if it is based on no more than suspicion as opposed to some evidence.

Secondly, similar problems arise in relation to the privilege against self-incrimination as can arise in relation to search orders (see **chapter 39**).

Thirdly, there is no free-standing power under **r. 25.1(1)(g)** to order the disclosure of information which might be of assistance in seeking a freezing injunction if the applicant has no material at present justifying an application for a freezing injunction (*Parker v CS Structured Credit Fund Ltd* [2003] EWHC 391 (Ch), [2003] 1 WLR 1680).

Freezing injunction against third party

There is an undoubted jurisdiction to make a freezing injunction against a third party where there is good reason to believe that assets in the name of the third party are really those of the principal defendant (*SCF Finance Co. Ltd v Masri* [1985] 1 WLR 876). This power is ancillary to para. 6 of the standard-form freezing injunction order, which states the order covers assets over which the respondent has a direct or indirect power to dispose of or deal with as if they were his own. Assets held on a bare trust can be frozen up to the amount of the principal defendant's assets (*TSB Private Bank International SA v Chabra* [1992] 1 WLR 231). Likewise, ancillary freezing orders can be made where there is a good arguable case that the principal defendant has hidden assets in offshore trusts and companies in tax havens (*International Credit and Investment Co. (Overseas) Ltd v Adham* [1998] BCC 134). Even where the principal defendant has no strict legal or equitable right to the assets, such as where assets are held under a discretionary trust, an ancillary freezing injunction can be made if the principal defendant has some right in respect of the assets, or has control over them, or other rights of access to them (*Dadourian Group International Inc. v Azuri Ltd* (2005) LTL 26/7/2005), for example, where the defendant has a degree of control over the third party's assets amounting to ownership in all but name (*Yukos Capital Sàrl v OJSC Rosneft Oil Co.* [2010] EWHC 784 (Comm), [2001] 1 All ER (Comm) 172).

38.26

In *Her Majesty's Revenue and Customs v Egleton* [2006] EWHC 2313 (Ch), LTL 20/9/2006, HMRC presented a winding-up petition against a company for unpaid VAT, alleging there had been a large-scale carousel fraud. It was held there was jurisdiction to grant freezing injunctions not only against the company but also against persons alleged to be liable to the company. It was not alleged that HMRC had any direct cause of action against those persons, but that a liquidator appointed in the liquidation of the company would have causes of action against them under the Insolvency Act 1986. An argument that *Her Majesty's Revenue and Customs v Egleton* was inconsistent with *Yukong Line Ltd v Rendsburg Investments Corporation* [2001] 2 Lloyd's Rep 113 was rejected in *Yukos Capital Sàrl v OJSC Rosneft Oil Co.* because when Potter LJ used the phrase 'beneficially entitled' ([2001] 2 Lloyd's Rep 113 at [44]) all he was doing was briefly describing the Chabra-style jurisdiction, and was not limiting it to cases where the principal defendant was beneficially entitled. In fact, the decision in *Yukong Line Ltd v Rendsburg Investments Corporation* showed there is a wider jurisdiction, because it held that specific assets did not have to be identified, and thus no question of beneficial ownership arose (*Yukos Capital Sàrl v OJSC Rosneft Oil Co.* at [17]). In such cases the court has to consider whether it would be just and convenient to freeze the assets held by the further defendants.

Cross-examination as to assets

It is only in exceptional circumstances that cross-examination will be ordered on an affidavit of assets sworn pursuant to a freezing order. However, where the claimant has justifiable concerns as to whether the defendant has made a full disclosure as required by the order, the court

38.27

may order the defendant to be cross-examined (*Den Norske Bank ASA v Antonatos* [1999] QB 271). Following *Den Norske Bank ASA v Antonatos*, while it is legitimate for claimants to have information in order to enable them to trace their money, ancillary orders cannot require the defendant to reveal whether he has obtained bribes other than those identified by the claimant. The purpose of the cross-examination is solely to discover what assets the defendant has, with a view to freezing them, and so will be unnecessary if sufficient assets are known to meet the value of the claim (*Great Future International Ltd v Sealand Housing Corporation* [2001] CPLR 293). It must not be undertaken for an ulterior purpose (*Jenington International Inc. v Assaubayev* [2010] EWHC 2351 (Ch), LTL 17/2/2011).

In the absence of an express order to the contrary, the information gained on the cross-examination is covered by the same undertaking given by the applicant on being granted the freezing injunction not to use the information for the purpose of any civil or criminal proceedings, either in England and Wales or any other jurisdiction, other than the present claim (*British Sky Broadcasting Group plc v Digital Satellite Warranty Cover Ltd* [2011] EWHC 3062 (Ch), [2012] 1 WLR 219).

Where a third party is to be cross-examined as to the assets of a defendant, it is likely to be appropriate to require the claimant to give a cross-undertaking not to use the answers for collateral purposes. In *Dadourian Group International v Simms* [2008] EWHC 186 (Ch), LTL 19/5/2008, an undertaking not to use the answers for the purposes of 'any criminal or committal proceedings, or for the trial of the actions' was held to cover use in a summary judgment application. Similar considerations to those laid down in *Dadourian Group International Inc. v Simms (No. 2)* [2006] EWCA Civ 1745, [2007] 1 WLR 2967 (see **38.10**) were applied in deciding whether to release the claimant from this undertaking. It was also held that two defendants had no standing to object to the lifting of the undertaking as it was given to protect the third party, not them.

The examination will be conducted by a Master or District Judge unless the judge making the order otherwise directs (**PD 2B, para. 7**).

Duration

38.28   A freezing injunction made without notice will remain in force for a limited period until the 'return date', which will be fixed by the judge when the order is granted. So far as practicable, any application to discharge or vary the injunction should be dealt with on the return date. The standard forms of freezing injunction in **PD 25A** contain a clause enabling the defendant or any third party notified of the order to apply to the court at any time (i.e. less than the usual three clear days' notice), but must first notify the claimant's legal representatives. The standard-form freezing injunctions in the annex to **PD 25A** say the orders are to continue 'until further order'. This is a reference to an order which expressly or impliedly discharges the freezing injunction. A freezing injunction does not therefore lapse when final judgment is entered against the defendant (*Cantor Index Ltd v Lister* (2001) LTL 23/11/2001).

Standard-form orders

38.29   A combined standard-form freezing injunction order for domestic freezing injunctions and worldwide freezing injunctions can be found in the annex to **PD 25A**. The current form was revised with effect from 1 October 2005, with minor amendments with effect from 2 October 2006 and 6 April 2010. This form should always be used, with only such modifications as are essential to fit the circumstances of the case. Any substantial variation from the form should be brought to the attention of the judge at the hearing. Wherever possible, a draft of the order sought should be filed with the application notice, with a copy on disk (**PD 25A, para. 2.4**).

EFFECT OF THE ORDER

A defendant or anyone else with notice of a freezing injunction will be in contempt of court **38.30** if they dispose or assist in the disposal or dissipation of enjoined assets (*Z Ltd v A-Z and AA-LL* [1982] QB 558 at p. 572 per Lord Denning MR). A non-party who hands an asset covered by a freezing injunction back to the defendant does not thereby dissipate or dispose of it (*Law Society v Shanks* [1988] 1 FLR 504), unless the non-party knows of a probability that after receiving it the defendant will dispose of it in breach of the order (*Bank Mellat v Kazmi* [1989] 1 QB 541).

A freezing injunction covering unspecified assets has an ambulatory effect (see *Cretanor Maritime Co. Ltd v Irish Marine Management Ltd* [1978] 1 WLR 966 per Buckley LJ). Assets acquired by the defendant after the order is granted will be covered by it, up to the maximum sum (if any) stated in the order (*TDK Tape Distributor (UK) Ltd v Videochoice Ltd* [1986] 1 WLR 141).

VARIATION OR DISCHARGE OF A FREEZING INJUNCTION

Procedure on application to vary or discharge

Applications to vary or discharge freezing injunctions are made to a judge, either pursuant **38.31** to the liberty to apply provision in the order itself, or on the claimant's application to renew the order on the return date. The application will be made in accordance with **CPR, Part 23** (see **chapter 32**). It is inappropriate to entertain an application to discharge a freezing injunction where a defendant has given no warning of an intention to argue that it should be discharged on the ground of material non-disclosure (*Bracken Partners Ltd v Gutteridge* (2001) LTL 16/1/2002).

A non-party who is affected by the terms of a freezing injunction can apply to intervene in the proceedings under **CPR, r. 19.2(2)**, and for the terms of the order to be varied. However, formal intervention may be unnecessary, as Buckley LJ in *Cretanor Maritime Co. Ltd v Irish Marine Management Ltd* [1978] 1 WLR 966 said that a non-party may apply for a variation of a freezing injunction order without intervening provided the non-party had a clear interest. Provided the intervention (whether formal or on the lines indicated by Buckley LJ) is justified, the non-party should be entitled to its costs on the indemnity basis (see *Project Development Co. Ltd SA v KMK Securities Ltd* [1982] 1 WLR 1470).

Grounds for variation

Variations of freezing injunctions may be allowed where the original order is more onerous **38.32** to the defendant than is necessary, or if it imposes unnecessary obligations on a non-party. Examples are failures to include necessary provisos, such as for ordinary living expenses, paying trade debts, allowing banks the usual set-off, or making a general order when a maximum-sum order is appropriate. Hardship to third parties may also give grounds for a variation. In *Camdex International Ltd v Bank of Zambia (No. 2)* [1997] 1 WLR 632 a freezing injunction had caught a large quantity of banknotes for issue in Zambia. It was varied to allow the release of the banknotes, to prevent serious damage being inflicted on the general population of the country.

Discharge where the claim is not one in which a freezing injunction order may be made

A freezing injunction may be discharged on the ground that one of the usual requirements has not **38.33** been made out. This may be on the basis, for example, that the claimant does not have a good arguable case, as in *Cheltenham and Gloucester Building Society v Ricketts* [1993] 1 WLR 1545. Alternatively, what may have appeared to be a good arguable case on the application without

Commentary

notice may be wiped out by an arguable defence or set-off. It may be that evidence concerning the defendant's financial status, business history or links with this country (or other countries where an English judgment would be enforceable) will persuade the court that there is no real risk of the defendant dissipating the enjoined assets in order to frustrate any judgment the claimant may obtain. Further, a change in the management of a company defendant may remove the risk of dissipation and merit a freezing injunction being discharged (*Capital Cameras Ltd v Harold Lines Ltd* [1991] 1 WLR 54).

Discharge on provision of security

38.34   A freezing injunction will cease to have effect where the defendant provides sufficient security for the claim (cl. 11(4) of the standard freezing injunction order). Security can be provided by bond or guarantee, paying money into an account in the joint names of the parties' solicitors or by paying money into court. The standard security provision in a freezing injunction in cl. 11(4) only gives 'security' against the risk of dissipation of assets. It does not confer priority over the defendant's other creditors (*Technocrats International Inc. v Fredic Ltd* [2004] EWHC 2674 (QB), [2005] 1 BCLC 467). Likewise, a payment into a bank account in the joint names of the parties' solicitors was held not to confer any security rights in *Flightline Ltd v Edwards* [2003] EWCA Civ 63, [2003] 1 WLR 1200. For an equitable charge to be created it is necessary for the terms on which the 'security' is given to include an obligation on the debtor to pay the debt out of the fund (*Palmer v Carey* [1926] AC 703). This can be done by including a clause that the respondent has to satisfy any judgment obtained by the applicant out of the moneys in the joint account. Giving security can be to the advantage of the defendant, since it may be that the order 'freezes' an asset worth more to the defendant than the cost of the security being offered, and in any event it is often important for defendants for freezing injunctions to be discharged as such orders carry a significant financial stigma, and usually result in banking facilities being withdrawn.

Discharge on the basis of material non-disclosure

38.35   A consequence of freezing injunction applications being made without notice is that a claimant applying for a freezing injunction is under a duty to give full and frank disclosure of any defence or other facts going against the grant of the relief sought. This duty extends both to facts within the actual knowledge of the claimant, and to facts which would have been known on the making of reasonable inquiries. It also extends to breaches of an advocate's duty to the court (*Memory Corporation plc v Sidhu (No. 2)* [2000] 1 WLR 1443).

To determine whether there has been a material non-disclosure, it is first necessary to consider the affidavit in support to see whether any adverse facts which the applicant either knew or could have discovered have been omitted. All material facts must appear in the affidavit itself, not in documents exhibited to it (see *National Bank of Sharjah v Dellborg* (1992) *The Times*, 24 December 1992). Second, it is necessary to consider whether anything omitted was 'material' in the sense that it would have affected the judgment of a reasonable tribunal when deciding whether to grant the freezing injunction in question (*Lloyds Bowmaker Ltd v Britannia Arrow Holdings plc* [1988] 1 WLR 1337). Facts are material if they are necessary to enable the court to exercise its discretion on a proper basis, bearing in mind the need to act fairly between the parties, the fact that the defendant has not been heard, and the inherent hardship and inconvenience caused by a freezing injunction. There is obviously a distinction between what are material facts and documents for the purposes of the application for the injunction and those which will be relevant at the trial of the action, and a claimant should not feel it is necessary to exhibit more than a few key documents to the *affidavit in support* of the application without notice (*National Bank of Sharjah v Dellborg*

(1992) *The Times,* 24 December 1992). Instances where omitted facts have been held to be material include:

(a) mistakes in framing the cause of action (*Bank Mellat v Nikpour* [1985] FSR 87);

(b) failing to disclose the existence of proceedings in another country (*Behbehani v Salem* [1989] 1 WLR 723) or this country (*Elvee Ltd v Taylor* [2001] EWCA Civ 1943, [2002] FSR 48);

(c) misstating the source of information (*St Merryn Meat Ltd v Hawkins* [2001] CP Rep 116, where the affidavit said that information about the defendants' activities was obtained using a bugged telephone in the claimants' offices, whereas in fact it was obtained using an interception device at one of the defendant's homes);

(d) failing to correct an assertion that the defendant was outside the jurisdiction once the claimant knew that was wrong (*Lombard North Central plc v Bradley* [2002] EWHC 121 (QB), LTL 3/2/2002, but this was an innocent non-disclosure and did not justify discharging a worldwide freezing injunction);

(e) a series of independent breaches which, taken together, result in the court being given a misleading picture of the case against the defendant (*Complete Retreats Liquidating Trust v Logue* [2010] EWHC 1864 (Ch), LTL 27/7/2010);

(f) failing to disclose weaknesses in the claimant's financial position, which are relevant to the value of the claimant's undertaking in damages and to the undertaking to indemnify third parties;

(g) failing to disclose the application is a 'trap' application (where a buyer obtains a without-notice freezing injunction shortly before executing a contract, so the seller in effect walks into a trap when executing the contract) (*Swift-Fortune Ltd v Magnifica Marine SA* [2007] EWHC 1630 (Comm), [2008] 1 Lloyd's Rep 54). If the fact the application is a trap application is disclosed, the court is very unlikely to grant the order.

Delay in objecting to an alleged non-disclosure can be a reason in itself for dismissing an application to discharge (*Indicii Salus Ltd v Chandrasekaran* [2008] EWCA Civ 67, LTL 12/2/2008, a search order case).

Continuing duty of disclosure

38.36 The duty to make full and frank disclosure is a continuing one until the first hearing on notice, so the applicant has a duty to bring to the attention of the court any material changes in the circumstances after a freezing injunction has been granted (*Commercial Bank of the Near East plc v A* [1989] 2 Lloyd's Rep 319). There is a continuing duty on the claimant to draw the defendant's attention to any material change in the claimant's financial position (*Staines v Walsh* [2003] EWHC 1486 (Ch), *The Times,* 1 August 2003).

Discretion to forgive a non-disclosure

38.37 Finding a material non-disclosure is not necessarily the end of the matter. As Lord Denning said in *Bank Mellat v Nikpour* [1985] FSR 87 at p. 90, 'It is not for every omission that the injunction will be automatically discharged. A *locus poenitentiae* may sometimes be afforded.' The court has a discretion to continue the order, or to make a new order on terms (such as on costs or payment of damages) 'if the original non-disclosure was innocent and if an injunction could properly be granted even had the facts been disclosed' (per Glidewell LJ in *Lloyds Bowmaker Ltd v Britannia Arrow Holdings plc* [1988] 1 WLR 1337). 'Innocence' in this connection depends on whether the omission was made intentionally, but, of course, there are degrees of culpability. Much depends on the quality of the facts that have not been disclosed.

In *Millhouse Capital UK Ltd v Sibir Energy plc* [2008] EWHC 2614 (Ch), [2009] Bus LR D33, Christopher Clarke J approved the following principles, which were formulated by Alan Boyle QC

Commentary

sitting as a deputy judge in *Arena Corporation Ltd v Schroeder* [2003] EWHC 1089 (Ch), LTL 15/5/2003 at [213]:

(a) If the court finds that there have been breaches of the duty of full and fair disclosure on the without-notice application, the general rule is that it should discharge the order obtained in breach and refuse to renew the order until trial.

(b) Notwithstanding that general rule, the court has jurisdiction to continue or re-grant the order.

(c) The jurisdiction should be exercised sparingly, and should take account of the need to protect the administration of justice and uphold the public interest in requiring full and fair disclosure.

(d) The court should assess the degree and extent of the culpability with regard to non-disclosure. It is relevant that the breach was innocent, but there is no general rule that an innocent breach will not attract the sanction of discharge of the order. Equally, there is no general rule that a deliberate breach will attract that sanction.

(e) The court should assess the importance and significance to the outcome of the application for an injunction of the matters which were not disclosed to the court. In making this assessment, the fact that the judge might have made the order anyway is of little importance.

(f) The court can weigh the merits of the claimant's claim, but should not conduct a simple balancing exercise in which the merits of the claimant's case are allowed to undermine the policy objective of the principle.

(g) The application of the principle should not be carried to extreme lengths or be allowed to become an instrument of injustice.

(h) The jurisdiction is penal in nature and the court should therefore have regard to the proportionality between the punishment and the offence.

(i) There are no hard and fast rules as to whether the discretion to continue or re-grant the order should be exercised, and the court should take into account all relevant circumstances.

Some facts are so important that the court will readily infer that the non-disclosure was deliberate. For example, in *St Merryn Meat Ltd v Hawkins* [2001] CP Rep 116 the claimants stated in the affidavits in support of the without notice application that certain information was obtained using a bugged telephone in the claimants' offices. It later transpired that the conversations were taped using an interception device at one of the defendant's homes. The order was discharged and not re-granted to mark the gravity of the claimants' conduct. Others, being material but not central to the application, will be more readily forgiven. See the judgment of Woolf LJ in *Behbehani v Salem* [1989] 1 WLR 723. Three incidents of non-disclosure were regarded as not very serious in *Caring Together Ltd v Bauso* [2006] EWHC 2345 (Ch), LTL 13/7/2006, where the injunction was continued because overall there had been a serious and sustained process of frank disclosure.

In deciding what sanctions, if any, to impose for any breach of duty, it is necessary to take into account all the relevant circumstances, including the gravity of the breach, the excuse or explanation offered, the severity and duration of any prejudice occasioned, and whether the consequences of the breach were remediable and had been remedied. The court must also apply the overriding objective and the need for proportionality (*Memory Corporation plc v Sidhu (No. 2)* [2000] 1 WLR 1443). A past record on the part of the defendant of breaking court orders and assisting others to do so for financial gain is a reason for reimposing freezing injunctive relief despite material non-disclosure (*Amedeo Hotels Ltd Partnership v Zaman* [2007] EWHC 295 (Comm), LTL 14/6/2007). It is important that the rule against material non-disclosure does not itself become an instrument of injustice (*Brink's Mat Ltd v Elcombe* [1988] 1 WLR 1350).

Discharge on the basis of unfair conduct

38.38   In *Negocios Del Mar SA v Doric Shipping Corporation SA* [1979] 1 Lloyd's Rep 331 the claimants had agreed to buy a ship from the defendants. Before paying the agreed price, they discovered it was damaged. So they obtained a freezing injunction, which they served immediately on the exchange of the ship for the price. The effect was that the proceeds of the sale were immediately frozen in the hands of the sellers. On appeal, this was regarded as being unfair conduct on the part of the claimants, and the injunction was discharged.

Discharge on the basis of delay

It was stated by Glidewell LJ in *Lloyds Bowmaker Ltd v Britannia Arrow Holdings plc* [1988] 1 WLR 1337 that: **38.39**

a plaintiff who succeeds in obtaining a Mareva injunction is in my view under an obligation to press on with his action as rapidly as he can so that if he should fail to establish liability in the defendant the disadvantage which the injunction imposes upon the defendant will be lessened so far as possible.

A failure to press on with the substantive action will therefore provide grounds for discharging a freezing injunction. A fully and sufficiently explained delay will not result in the injunction being discharged (*Walsh v Deloitte and Touche Inc.* [2001] UKPC 58, 59 WIR 30).

FREEZING INJUNCTIONS AFTER JUDGMENT

There is nothing in the decision in *Lister v Stubbs* (1890) 45 ChD 1 to prevent an injunction being granted *after* judgment to restrain a judgment debtor from disposing of assets in order to prevent the judgment creditor enforcing the judgment that has been obtained. Indeed, it was expressly held in *Orwell Steel (Erection and Fabrication) Ltd v Asphalt and Tarmac (UK) Ltd* [1984] 1 WLR 1097 that a freezing injunction may be granted in aid of the execution of a judgment debt, and in *Faith Panton Property Plan Ltd v Hodgetts* [1981] 1 WLR 927, that a freezing injunction may be granted to restrain the disposal of assets to frustrate the enforcement of an order for costs. In the latter case, the proceedings for the assessment of costs were likely to take about four or five months to complete, but the Court of Appeal held that it was appropriate to grant the injunction under principles established before *Mareva Compania Naviera SA v International Bulkcarriers SA* [1980] 1 All ER 213.   **38.40**

Freezing injunctions after judgment, like freezing injunctions in support of pending proceedings, operate *in personam* rather than *in rem* (*Masri v Consolidated Contractors International (UK) Ltd (No. 2)* [2007] EWHC 3010 (Comm), [2008] 1 All ER (Comm) 305 at [64]–[75]; [2008] EWCA Civ 303, [2009] QB 450 at [92]).

Regarding the principles to be applied on a post-judgment application, provided the judgment is enforceable in England and Wales, the requirements that the claimant must have a cause of action justiciable in England and Wales and a good arguable case are satisfied by the judgment itself. Consequently, the only requirements are that the defendant has assets within the jurisdiction and there is a real risk of those assets being dissipated before judgment can be enforced. A freezing injunction in aid of execution should operate in the same way as a freezing injunction granted in the course of proceedings. So, for example, a bank served with an order freezing a customer's account should still honour routine banking transactions such as bills of exchange or letters of credit (see *Lewis and Peat (Produce) Ltd v Almatu Properties Ltd* (1992) *The Times*, 14 May 1992).

In *Banco Nacional de Comercio Exterior SNC v Empresa de Telecomunicaciones de Cuba SA* [2007] EWCA Civ 662, [2008] 1 WLR 1936, it was held that a domestic freezing injunction granted after registration of a foreign judgment should be varied to include an undertaking in damages. Earlier cases indicating that such an undertaking is not required in post-judgment freezing injunctions (*Gwembe Valley Development Co. Ltd v Koshy (No. 4)* (2001) *The Times*, 28 February 2002; *Oystertec plc v Davidson* [2004] EWHC 2004 (Ch), LTL 6/8/2004) are therefore to be treated as overruled. Whether this is good practice is another matter. The reason why such undertakings are

Commentary

Chapter 39   Search Orders

NATURE OF A SEARCH ORDER

39.1   A search order is a bundle of interim orders which require the respondent to admit another party to premises for the purpose of preserving evidence which might otherwise be destroyed or concealed by the respondent (see **CPR, r. 25.1(1)(h)**). Statutory authority for the jurisdiction is given by the Civil Procedure Act 1997, s. 7. Prior to the introduction of the CPR this form of order was commonly known as an Anton Piller order, taking its name from *Anton Piller KG v Manufacturing Processes Ltd* [1976] Ch 55.

A search order is both injunctive and mandatory in nature. It requires the intended defendant to allow a named supervising solicitor from an independent firm, a partner from the claimant's own solicitors, and a limited number of additional people to enter on to the defendant's premises, and any vehicles in the defendant's control in the vicinity of those premises, so that they can search for, inspect, take photocopies and remove specified items and documents. The specified items and documents are those likely to be probative in the proceedings. The order will also often require the intended defendant to deliver up relevant documents not located at the premises searched, and to verify information on affidavit. The potential oppression inherent in such an order is recognised by the courts, and a search order is regarded as at the extremity of the court's powers. Although the jurisdiction to make search orders may be invoked in any type of claim, it is most frequently encountered in claims for infringement of intellectual property rights in the entertainment industry.

PROCEDURE ON APPLICATIONS FOR SEARCH ORDERS

Court

39.2   By virtue of the County Court Remedies Regulations 2014 (SI 2014/982), reg. 3(1), the County Court has in general no jurisdiction to grant, vary or revoke a search order. The prohibition does not apply to a judge of the Court of Appeal or a High Court judge sitting as a judge of the County Court (reg. 3(2)). Most applications will therefore be made in the High Court, and they are most frequently encountered in intellectual property claims in the Chancery Division. If an application for a search order in an intellectual property case is not made in the Chancery Division (or the Patents Court or the Intellectual Property Enterprise Court as appropriate), the applicant should tell the court that applications should normally be made in the relevant court, and explain why the present application is not being made there (*Elvee Ltd v Taylor* [2001] EWCA Civ 1943, [2002] FSR 48).

Where a search order is sought in a County Court claim (and none of the exceptions in the County Court Remedies Regulations 2014 applies), the application for the search order must be made in the High Court (**High Court and County Courts Jurisdiction Order 1991 (SI 1991/724), art. 3**). Such an application is deemed to include an application for the transfer of the proceedings to the High Court (County Court Remedies Regulations 2014, reg. 4). The application must be made returnable to a judge, and the application notice must (see *Schmidt v Wong* [2005] EWCA Civ 1 506, [2006] 1 WLR 561) carry the following endorsement:

This application is being made in the course of [in anticipation of] proceedings in the County Court pursuant to article 3 of the High Court and County Courts Jurisdiction Order 1991. The County Court has no jurisdiction to grant the relief sought by reason of regulation 3(1) of the County Court Remedies Regulations 2014.

Procedure

Search orders are only obtainable against defendants who are likely to destroy relevant evidence if an application on notice were to be made (see **39.9**). Consequently, secrecy is essential, so the application will be made without notice and the court will sit in private. Many applications are also urgent, and many are made before proceedings are issued. The general procedure for applications for interim injunctions applies, for which see **37.5** to **37.13** and **procedural checklist 19**. Essentially, the claimant must:

39.3

(a) have issued a claim form in respect of the substantive cause of action, unless the application is too urgent to wait for this to be done;
(b) issue an application notice in form N244;
(c) provide affidavit evidence in support (witness statements are not acceptable: **PD 25A, para. 3.1**);
(d) provide a draft order, together with a copy on disk;
(e) provide a skeleton argument in support; and
(f) after the hearing, provide all affected parties with a full note, for which they do not have to ask, of what happened at the hearing, including the basis and materials on which the order was made (*Interoute Telecommunications (UK) Ltd v Fashion Gossip Ltd* (1999) *The Times*, 10 November 1999).

It is very common to combine applications for search orders with other forms of urgent interim relief. It is not unknown, to use the old terminology, to 'pile *Piller* upon *Mareva*' in fraud and pirating claims.

Full and frank disclosure

As the application is made without notice, the claimant has the usual duty of full and frank disclosure. The courts have insisted that this is especially important in applications for search orders, and the claimant should err on the side of excessive disclosure. The supporting affidavit must disclose in very full terms the reason for seeking the order, including the probability that relevant material will disappear if the order is not made (**PD 25A, para. 7.3**).

39.4

Commentary

Supervising solicitor

39.5 The affidavit supporting an application for a search order must state the name and experience of the proposed supervising solicitor, and give the name and address of his or her firm. The proposed supervising solicitor must be someone experienced in the operation of search orders (**PD 25A, para. 7.2**) and must not be a member or employee of the claimant's solicitors (**para. 7.6**). Names of suitable supervising solicitors can be obtained through the Law Society and (for the London area) the London Solicitors Litigation Association. If the court orders that a search order need not be served by the supervising solicitor, the reason for so ordering must be set out in the order (**para. 7.7**). Various undertakings given by the supervising solicitor appear in the standard-form search order in **sch. E**. These include an undertaking by the supervising solicitor to keep the existence of the removed items confidential.

Documents to third parties

39.6 A third party who did not attend the hearing at which a search order was made, but who is served with the order, may request copies of the materials read by the judge, materials prepared at the direction of the judge, and the note of the hearing (**PD 25A, para. 9.2**). Unless the court otherwise orders, the applicant must comply promptly with the request.

PRINCIPLES

39.7 Ormrod LJ in *Anton Piller KG v Manufacturing Processes Ltd* [1976] Ch 55 laid down the following preconditions for granting search orders:

  (a) There must be an extremely strong prima facie case on the merits. It is worth contrasting this with the requirement of merely showing a good arguable case in applications for freezing orders.
  (b) The defendant's activities must be proved to result in very serious potential or actual harm to the claimant's interests.
  (c) There must be clear evidence that incriminating documents or materials are in the defendant's possession.
  (d) There must be a real possibility that such items may be destroyed before any applications on notice can be made. This is considered at **39.9**.
  (e) The defendant will be adequately protected by the claimant's undertaking in damages (the discussion at **37.26** applies equally to search orders).

Insistence on strict compliance

39.8 In the early 1980s it was thought that the conditions set out in **39.7** had been relaxed by *Yousif v Salama* [1980] 1 WLR 1 540 and *Dunlop Holdings Ltd v Staravia Ltd* [1982] Com LR 3. In the former it was inferred that there was a real risk of the defendant disobeying any orders made on applications on notice from evidence that he had forged a signature on a cheque. In the latter, Oliver LJ said:

it has certainly become customary to infer the probability of disappearance or destruction of evidence where it is clearly established on the evidence before the court that the defendant is engaged in a nefarious activity which renders it likely that he is an untrustworthy person. It is seldom that one can get cogent or actual evidence of a threat to destroy material or documents.

The claimant's solicitors in *Columbia Picture Industries Inc. v Robinson* [1987] Ch 38 had applied for some 300 search orders between 1974 and 1985, and none of their applications had been refused.

Since *Booker McConnell plc v Plascow* [1985] RPC 425 there has been a marked change in judicial attitude, and nowadays the courts insist on strict compliance with the principles enunciated by Ormrod LJ in *Anton Piller KG v Manufacturing Processes Ltd* [1976] Ch 55. The order is regarded as a serious stigma on the defendant's commercial reputation, and will often result in banks refusing further credit or even calling in loans. The order itself often allows the claimant's representatives to remove the defendant's stock-in-trade, and the net result is often to drive the defendant out of business. Accordingly, the order is regarded as a remedy of last resort, and should be made only 'when there is no alternative' (per Ormrod LJ in *Anton Piller KG v Manufacturing Processes Ltd*). As Dillon LJ explained in *Booker McConnell plc v Plascow*:

the courts have always proceeded, justifiably, on the basis that the overwhelming majority of people in this country will comply with the court's order, and that defendants will therefore comply with orders to, for example, produce and deliver up documents without it being necessary to empower the [claimants'] solicitors to search the defendant's premises.

Putting the matter slightly differently, Hoffmann J in *Lock International plc v Beswick* [1989] 1 WLR 1268 said at p. 1281: 'there must be *proportionality* between the perceived threat to the [claimant's] rights and the remedy granted'. Before embarking on an application for a search order, it is therefore necessary to consider whether some less draconian measure, such as applying on notice for negative injunctions or for an order that the documents be delivered up to the defendant's solicitor, or even awaiting disclosure in the usual way, would adequately protect the claimant.

REAL RISK OF DESTRUCTION

In *Anton Piller KG v Manufacturing Processes Ltd* [1976] Ch 55 it was said that a search order would **39.9** not be made unless there is 'real possibility' that material evidence will be destroyed if an application for disclosure were to be made on notice to the defendant. This formula has been adopted in numerous cases since then. It is possible that the CPR have made a slight alteration in this requirement. **PD 25A, para. 7.3(2)**, referring to the evidence needed in support of an application for a search order, says it must cover 'the probability' that relevant material would disappear if the order were not made. There is a slight difference between a 'real possibility' and a 'probability', in that the latter expression means that the risk of destruction has to be proved on the balance of probabilities, whereas the earlier expression can be satisfied by evidence coming a little distance short of establishing the risk on the balance of probabilities. However, it is doubtful that **para. 7.3(2)**, which is a provision dealing with the evidence required in support of an application, can have been intended to alter the established conditions for the remedy.

The requirement of showing there is a real risk that the defendant will destroy vital evidence lies at the heart of the jurisdiction to grant search orders. Sometimes it is possible to infer this risk from the nature of the defendant's alleged conduct, for instance, in video pirating claims and commercial fraud actions. Even in these cases, however, the claimant is still obliged to give full and frank disclosure of anything known about the defendant, including past responsible conduct or other matters which tend to show the defendant would obey the court's orders.

Outside the area of actions based directly on dishonesty, it will be rare for the claimant to have evidence of a real risk of destruction. An example is *Lock International plc v Beswick* [1989] 1 WLR 1268, where the claimant alleged the defendants, who were former employees now competing with the claimant, were making use of its trade secrets and confidential information. A search order was executed, and the defendants successfully applied to discharge the order. Hoffmann J said the claimant's evidence:

came nowhere near [establishing] . . . a 'grave danger' or 'real possibility' that the defendants might destroy evidence . . . these defendants were no fly-by-night video pirates. They were former long-service

691

employees with families and mortgages, who had openly said that they were entering into competition and whom the plaintiff knew to be financed by highly respectable institutions.

FORM OF THE ORDER

39.10   A standard form of search order is provided in the annex to **PD 25A** (as refined from time to time). This form is described in **PD 25A, para. 7.11**, as an 'example', and should be used with such modifications as are necessary to fit the circumstances of the case. Any substantial variation from the form should be brought to the attention of the judge at the hearing. All the standard wording should be retained even where the privilege against self-incrimination has been removed by statute (see **39.16**, and **PD 25A, para. 7.9**).

The main provision is clause 6, which provides that the defendant 'must permit [certain named people, referred to as "the search party"] to enter' the defendant's premises. Other clauses in the order are designed to give effect to the basic purpose of the order, which is to allow the search party to enter the defendant's premises and to take documents which might be disclosable in the proceedings or otherwise be relevant, while providing suitable safeguards for the defendant. These include the appointment of an independent supervising solicitor to ensure the order is not misused by the claimant. Clause 22 may be used to set out prohibitory injunctions ancillary to the main part of the order. Schedule B sets out the items that may be seized, and must extend no further than the minimum necessary to preserve the evidence which might otherwise be concealed or destroyed (*Columbia Picture Industries Inc. v Robinson* [1987] Ch 38).

Service of the order

39.11   Since *Universal Thermosensors Ltd v Hibben* [1992] 1 WLR 840 execution of search orders has been subject to oversight by supervising solicitors who are independent of the claimant's usual solicitors. Before this case there was mounting concern about the execution of search orders by enthusiastic but inexperienced persons. Execution by a solicitor related to the claimant or by one of the claimant's directors was deprecated in *Manor Electronics Ltd v Dickson* [1988] RPC 618.

The order must be served personally by the supervising solicitor, unless the court otherwise orders. Together with the order there must be served an application notice for a hearing on notice in respect of the search order (see **39.21**). The affidavits in support and any exhibits capable of being copied must be served at the same time as the order (**PD 25A, para. 7.4(1)**). Confidential exhibits need not be served, but they must be made available for inspection by the defendant in the presence of the claimant's solicitors while the order is being executed. Copies of confidential exhibits may be retained by the defendant's solicitors on their undertaking not to permit the defendant to see them except in their presence, nor to allow the defendant to make or take away any note or record of them (**para. 7.4(2)**). Unless the court otherwise orders, service may only be effected between 9.30 a.m. and 5.30 p.m. Monday to Friday (**para. 7.4(6)**). The reason for this is that the defendant is entitled to seek legal advice, and this will only be effective if the order is executed during office hours. It is recognised that mistakes (on both sides) are less likely to occur if these orders are executed during office hours (for an example, see *Adam Phones Ltd v Goldschmidt* [1999] 4 All ER 486).

Planning is essential for effective execution. If several addresses are included in the order, it is important that execution is simultaneous. To reduce its oppressive effect the order will limit the number of persons who can assist with its execution at each address specified. Further, if the defendant is a woman living alone, a woman must accompany those executing the order (**para. 7.4(5)**). The police will be informed beforehand if there is any prospect of a breach of the peace.

Gaining access and explaining the order

A search order is not a search warrant, and does not authorise the use of force to gain access. **39.12** In cases where the defendant has committed both a civil wrong against the claimant and a criminal offence, a search order must not be executed at the same time as a police search warrant (**PD 25A, para. 7.8**; cl. 8 of the standard form of search order). Clause 6 is a mandatory order that the defendant 'must permit' access to the supervising solicitor. But before entering, the supervising solicitor must explain the terms and effect of the order in everyday language and must inform the defendant that legal advice may be sought before entry is permitted and of the defendant's right to apply to vary or discharge the order.

By **PD 25A, para. 7.4(4)**, the supervising solicitor must also advise the respondent that he may avail himself of:

(a) legal professional privilege; and

(b) the privilege against self-incrimination. Situations where the privilege against self-incrimination do not apply are listed in **para. 7.9** (see **39.16** and **39.17**).

A solicitor who negligently failed to explain the effect of the order to the defendant in a fair and accurate manner was held to be in contempt of court in *VDU Installations Ltd v Integrated Computer Systems and Cybernetics Ltd* [1989] FSR 378. The right to seek legal advice means that the obligation to give permission for entry only arises after a reasonable period of time has elapsed for legal advice to be obtained (*Bhimji v Chatwani* [1991] 1 WLR 989). Thereafter, the defendant must give permission, or else will be in contempt of court. Even if there are grounds for seeking an order for the immediate discharge of the search order, while it subsists it is an order of the court and must be obeyed (*Wardle Fabrics Ltd v G. Myristis Ltd* [1984] FSR 263). However, if entry is refused and the order is successfully discharged shortly thereafter, that will give the court grounds for imposing no penalty on an application to commit for contempt of court. Matters to be taken into account include whether an application to discharge is merely a device to delay the search, and whether the defendant has interfered with the evidence during the delay (*Bhimji v Chatwani*).

Executing the order

There is a heavy duty on the supervising solicitor to comply strictly with the terms of the order **39.13** as to the premises which can be searched and the items which can be removed.

The defendant's premises must not be searched, and no items may be removed, except in the presence of the defendant or a person who appears to be a responsible employee of the defendant (**PD 25A, para. 7.5(2)**). If any of the items covered by the order exist only in computer-readable form, the defendant must immediately give the claimant's solicitors effective access, including any necessary passwords, and arrange for the material to be printed out. The claimant must take all reasonable steps to ensure that no damage is done to the defendant's computer system, and must ensure that the person searching the defendant's system has sufficient expertise to avoid causing damage (**para. 7.5(8)** to **(10)**). Items seized must be recorded by the supervising solicitor in a list, and must be retained by the claimant's solicitors for the minimum time necessary to take copies and in any case for no more than two days, after which they must be returned to their owner (**para. 7.5(3)** and **(6)**). Nothing should be removed until the defendant has had a reasonable opportunity to check it against the list (**para. 7.5(7)**). Where ownership of the material seized is in dispute, the claimant's solicitors should place it in the custody of the defendant's solicitors pending trial on the defendant's solicitors undertaking to retain it in safekeeping and to produce it to the court when required (**para. 7.5(4)**). It may be appropriate for the order to require the claimant to insure the materials seized (**para. 7.5(5)**).

Execution of a search order in an excessive or oppressive manner will render the claimant liable under the undertaking in damages. Seizing documents not specified in the order may be penalised by an award of aggravated damages. An award of £10,000 against the claimant was made on this ground in *Columbia Picture Industries Inc. v Robinson* [1987] Ch 38.

It is important that neither the claimant nor the claimant's employees are allowed to conduct searches for documents belonging to a trade competitor. Safeguards must be built into the order to protect the confidentiality of the defendant's trade secrets.

Additional powers and duties of the supervising solicitor

39.14   It may become apparent that it is impracticable to comply fully with the requirement that the defendant be allowed to check the claimant's list of materials before anything is removed from the premises, or the conditions for accessing material stored on computer. If the supervising solicitor is satisfied that compliance is impracticable, he or she may permit the search to proceed and for items to be removed without full compliance (**PD 25A, para. 7.5(13)**).

Once the search has been completed, the supervising solicitor must provide the claimant's solicitors with a report on the carrying out of the order. The claimant's solicitors must then serve a copy on the defendant and file a copy with the court (**PD 25A, para. 7.5(11) and (12)**).

Contempt by the defendant

39.15   In *Alliance and Leicester Building Society v Ghahremani* (1992) 142 NLJ 313 a search order was executed at the premises of a firm of solicitors. The order required the defendant solicitor to disclose 'documents' of various categories. There was evidence that the defendant erased information stored on computer while the order was being executed. Hoffmann J held that the word 'document' in the order was, in the light of the earlier decision of *Derby and Co. Ltd v Weldon (No. 9)* [1991] 1 WLR 652, wide enough to include information stored on computer, and that the defendant was guilty of contempt of court. It is probable that if the defendant had not been a lawyer the court would have held that the wording was insufficiently clear to found an application for committal. It is for this reason that the standard search order contains specific provision in cl. 17 for copying information stored on computer. In addition to being a contempt of court, 'the refusal to comply may be the most damning evidence against the defendant at the subsequent trial' (per Ormrod LJ in *Anton Piller KG v Manufacturing Processes Ltd* [1976] Ch 55).

On the other hand, a petty breach of a search order in circumstances where the defendant had honestly tried to obey it should be ignored by the parties. Under the CPR, given the emphasis on proportionality, an application to commit for no more than a technicality is likely to be dismissed with costs (*Adam Phones Ltd v Goldschmidt* [1999] 4 All ER 486).

PRIVILEGE AGAINST SELF-INCRIMINATION

39.16   The House of Lords in *Rank Film Distributors Ltd v Video Information Centre* [1982] AC 380 held that where a criminal charge was more than a contrived, fanciful or remote possibility, the defendant could refuse to provide information by relying on the privilege against *self-incrimination*. In many cases where the evidence is strong enough for a search order, it will also amount to a breach of the criminal law. The privilege applies in relation to any piece of information or evidence on which the prosecution might wish to rely in establishing guilt or in deciding whether to prosecute or not (*Den Norske Bank ASA v Antonatos* [1999] QB 271). The precise scope of the privilege has been modified as a result of the incorporation into UK law of the European Convention on Human Rights by the **Human Rights Act 1998.** Consequently, in *C plc v P* [2007] EWCA Civ 493, [2008] Ch 1, it was held that free-standing evidence (in this case images of children found on a computer which had been imaged under the terms of a search order) which was not created in compliance with the terms of the search order could be passed to the police. The scope of the privilege is discussed at **50.51.**

The *Rank* decision threatened to destroy the utility of many search orders, and was swiftly reversed by the Senior Courts Act 1981, s. 72. This is not the only provision making inroads into the privilege against self-incrimination (see **PD 25A, para. 7.9**), the relevant provisions being:

(a) the Senior Courts Act 1981, s. 72, which focuses on the civil cause of action, applying to intellectual property and passing-off civil claims, and removes the privilege in respect of 'related offences' and the recovery of 'related penalties';
(b) the Theft Act 1968, s. 31(1), which removes the privilege in civil proceedings for the recovery or administration of any property, for the execution of any trust, or for an account, notwithstanding that compliance may expose the witness or his spouse to a charge under the Theft Act 1968;
(c) the Fraud Act 2006, s. 13, which operates in a similar way to the Theft Act 1968, s. 31;
(d) the Children Act 1989, s. 98, which removes the privilege in applications relating to the care, supervision or protection of a child;
(e) various statutes and statutory instruments where the privilege has been impliedly removed (see *Bank of England v Riley* [1992] Ch 475).

In cases where the privilege against self-incrimination still applies, it was held in *Tate Access Floors Inc. v Boswell* [1991] Ch 512 that the privilege entitles a defendant served with a search order to refuse:

(a) permission to enter;
(b) to deliver up documents covered by the order; and
(c) to verify information about suppliers and customers.

However, as was also held in *Tate Access Floors Inc. v Boswell*, it is a privilege against *self*-incrimination. The privilege may be relied on by persons ordered to give information whether they are natural persons or artificial persons such as limited companies (for which see *Triplex Safety Glass Co. Ltd v Lancegaye Safety (1934) Glass Ltd* [1939] 2 KB 395) provided they do so on their own behalf. However, one person cannot refuse to give information which might incriminate another, except where the other is the person's spouse. In *Tate Access Floors Inc. v Boswell* the court left open the question whether the connection between the controller of a company and the company might be so strong that they should be allowed to refuse to incriminate each other. In *Sociedade Nacional de Combustiveis de Angola UEE v Lundqvist* [1991] 2 QB 310 the court said that a company officer nominated to transmit the company's information (which in that case was information about assets subject to a freezing injunction) could refuse to transmit evidence which might incriminate him or her, but that the court would immediately nominate another person to transmit the information.

The above problems can be avoided if the risk of the information supplied being used in criminal proceedings can be removed. This can be achieved if the Crown Prosecution Service indicate in writing that they will not make use of the information for the purposes of any criminal prosecution against the defendant or the defendant's spouse, and if a clause stating that no disclosure made in compliance with the order will be used in evidence in the prosecution or any offence committed by the defendant of the defendant's spouse is included in the order (*AT and T Istel Ltd v Tully* [1993] AC 45).

Commentary

Privilege and terms of the search order

39.17   Until *Den Norske Bank ASA v Antonatos* [1999] QB 271 an attempt was sometimes made to add a clause to a search order to the effect that a defendant who claimed to be entitled to the benefit of the privilege against self-incrimination still had to provide the allegedly privileged information to the supervising solicitor, who would hold the information to the order of the court. It was held in *Den Norske Bank ASA v Antonatos* that such a clause is inconsistent with the privilege if it applies, and should no longer be used.

A respondent who wishes to claim that listed documents are protected by privilege may gather them together and hand them over to the supervising solicitor to assess whether they are privileged as claimed (standard search order, cl. 11(1)). On assessing the materials, the supervising solicitor may:

(a) Decide they are privileged (standard search order, cl. 11(2)). In such a case the materials will be excluded from the search. The supervising solicitor will list them for inclusion in his report, and return them to the respondent.

(b) Decide they may be privileged (standard search order, cl. 11(3)). In such a case the supervising solicitor will exclude the material from the search, but will retain it in his possession pending further order of the court.

Clause 11(3) of the standard search order states the same procedure as in (b) above applies 'if the respondent claims to be entitled to withhold production on [the grounds that the documents may be privileged or incriminating]'. It is probable, but not clear from cl. 11(1) and (3), that this applies only where the respondent does not hand the documents over to the supervising solicitor to assess whether they are privileged (under cl. 11(1)). It is possible to read cl. 11(3) as applying also where cl. 11(1) has been invoked and the supervising solicitor has decided the documents are clearly not privileged, but the respondent then claims to be entitled to withhold them.

DISCHARGE AND VARIATION OF SEARCH ORDERS

Discharge of search orders

39.18   Applications to discharge or vary search orders are largely governed by the principles already discussed in relation to freezing injunctions at **38.32** to **38.39**. However, if a search order has been executed, there is a strong argument that it is an unjustified waste of costs and of the court's time to seek its discharge before trial. Doing so was said by Browne-Wilkinson V-C in *Dormeuil Frères SA v Nicolian International (Textiles) Ltd* [1988] 1 WLR 1362 to be little more than an empty gesture, and that the right course was normally to adjourn an application to set aside the order to be dealt with at trial. Where the order had not been complied with at the time of the application to set aside, as in *Arab Monetary Fund v Hashim* [1989] 1 WLR 565, it was necessary to consider whether the order would be made in the light of the full facts. In *Tate Access Floors Inc. v Boswell* [1991] Ch 512 the Vice-Chancellor reconsidered his decision in *Dormeuil Frères SA* in the light of the freezing injunction case of *Behbehani v Salem* [1989] 1 WLR 723. There is a conflict between the public interest in ensuring that applications made without notice are made in good faith, and the public interest in ensuring the courts are not clogged up with long interim hearings. The Vice-Chancellor suggested the solution may be that the circumstances in which an order without notice was obtained should only be investigated at the pre-trial stage if it is clear there has been a material non-disclosure or where the nature of the alleged non-disclosure is so serious as to demand immediate investigation. If the ground for seeking to have the order discharged is that the claimant is guilty of material non-disclosure over a *matter relevant* to the granting of relief without notice, being a matter which has no relevance to the merits of the substantive action (such as the value of the claimant's undertaking in damages), it may be more appropriate to determine the matter immediately rather than waiting until trial.

Further, it is sometimes argued that even if the original order was granted on insufficient grounds, the fruits of the search may indicate that justice was done in the event. Such an argument was rejected in *Manor Electronics Ltd v Dickson* [1988] RPC 618 in the face of a clear material non-disclosure.

A search order was discharged in *Gadget Shop Ltd v Bug.Com Ltd* [2001] FSR 26, for multiple breaches of procedure. Small variations in the standard form of order had not been drawn to the attention of the judge on the initial application; the lack of experience of the supervising solicitor had not been adequately explained in the evidence in support; and the evidence in support did not give adequate full and frank disclosure, for example, that some of the allegedly confidential material said to have been taken by the defendants had been published on the applicant's own website. Conversely, in *Indicii Salus Ltd v Chandrasekaran* [2008] EWCA Civ 67, LTL 12/2/2008, it was held that the fact the applicant's accountants had reservations about its ability to pay their fees did not have to be disclosed on an application for a search order, and that a statement that an asset had a substantial but uncertain value had not been false.

Exclusion of evidence obtained under a discharged search order

39.19 The question of whether any documents seized under a search order which is subsequently discharged should be held to be inadmissible at trial was left open by the Vice-Chancellor in *Tate Access Floors Inc. v Boswell* [1991] Ch 512. The general rule has been that there is no exclusionary discretion in civil cases, and if the documents are otherwise relevant and admissible it should not matter how they were obtained. This has been changed by **CPR, r. 32.1**, as decisively held in *Grobbelaar v Sun Newspapers Ltd* (1999) *The Times,* 12 August 1999. The defendant also has a remedy under the claimant's undertaking in damages.

Variation on grounds of intimidation

39.20 One of the defendants in *Coca-Cola Co. v Gilbey* [1995] 4 All ER 711 argued that he should not be required to disclose the identities of other persons involved with him in a highly organised passing-off operation, and other information, as required by a search order, on the ground that doing so might expose himself and his family to physical violence from those other persons. It was held that, although violence or threats of violence would be legitimate grounds if put forward by innocent parties, when put forward by actual participants, public policy and the interests of the victim carried more weight, and disclosure was ordered forthwith.

AFTER EXECUTION

39.21 After executing the order, the supervising solicitor is required to compile a report of what happened (see **39.14**). The report is served on the defendant. Clause 3 of the model form of search order specifies a return date when there will be a second hearing, this time on notice to the defendant. The applicant's solicitors are required to provide the supervising solicitor with an application for hearing on the return date (sch. D, para. 1(iii)), which will be served on the defendant when the main order is executed by the supervising solicitor.

On the hearing the court will consider the supervising solicitor's report and the defendant may apply to discharge the order. Once a search order has been executed, there is an enhanced duty on the claimant to prosecute the main action without delay. In *Hytrac Conveyors Ltd v Conveyors International Ltd* [1983] 1 WLR 44, the claimant delayed for 10 weeks after obtaining a search order without serving a statement of claim. The claim was dismissed, Lawton LJ saying that claimants 'must not use [search] orders as a means of finding out what sort of charges they could make'.

Commentary

If the claim was transferred to, or commenced in, the High Court for the purposes of applying for a search order, but is otherwise more suitable for the County Court, after the application for the search order has been disposed of the claim will be transferred down to the County Court (County Court Remedies Regulations 2014 (SI 2014/982), reg. 5). The application is not treated as disposed of until any application to set the order aside has been heard, or until the expiry of 28 days during which no such application is made.

COLLATERAL USE OF MATERIAL

39.22   As with other forms of disclosure (see **chapter 50**), the claimant gives an implied undertaking not to use items seized under a search order for any collateral purposes. The court may sanction a relaxation of this undertaking in a proper case. The leading case is *Crest Homes plc v Marks* [1987] AC 829. In 1984 the claimant brought a claim against the defendant seeking injunctions to restrain breach of copyright in certain house designs. In the course of that claim a search order was obtained and executed. In 1985 the claimant commenced a second copyright claim against the defendant in relation to another house design, and obtained and executed a second search order. Some of the documents seized under the second search order were alleged by the claimant to show the defendant had not given full disclosure under the first search order. The claimant therefore sought to use those documents in contempt proceedings in relation to the first search order. The House of Lords held that although there were technically two separate actions, in substance they were a single set of proceedings. As the defendant would suffer no injustice by lifting the implied undertaking, permission was given to allow the claimant to use the documents in the contempt proceedings.

case, and directing that if this is done, the property shall be given up to the party (r. 25.1(1)(m)).

The procedure in **Part 23**, should be followed on making an application under the Torts (Interference with Goods) Act 1977, s. 4 (see **chapter 32** and **procedural checklist 20**). An application notice in form N244 should be issued seeking delivery up of the goods, which must be specified, usually in a schedule to the application notice. It is not uncommon to combine the application with requests for orders for the detention, custody or preservation of the goods under **CPR, r. 25.1(1)(c)**, in the alternative. The application will need to be supported by written evidence (r. 25.3(2)).

Usually, applications for the interim delivery up of goods will be made on notice in the course of pending proceedings. However, if the case is of an urgent nature, the application may be made before the claim form is issued (as recognised in the Torts (Interference with Goods) Act 1977, s. 4(2) itself). If there is reason to believe the defendant may destroy or otherwise dispose of the goods if notice is given, the application may be made without giving notice, but the need for this will have to be justified in the evidence in support, and the usual duty of full and frank disclosure will apply to any application without notice.

Hearings for orders for interim delivery up of goods are usually dealt with by Masters and District Judges (see CPR, r. 2.4, and PD 2B).

PRINCIPLES

40.4   A court considering an application for interim delivery up must first decide whether the goods are or may become the subject matter of proceedings for wrongful interference with goods (see **40.2**), and then consider whether to exercise its discretion to make the order. All that is required at the first stage is an arguable case. In *Patrhis v Jackson* [2002] EWHC 2480 (QB), LTL 22/11/2002, an assistant solicitor left his employment with the claimant to work for the second defendant, taking with him a large number of the claimant's client files. It was held that the second defendant had converted the files when it failed to return them by the third day after receiving a request for their return.

Once it is established that there is an arguable case for one of the forms of wrongful interference with goods, the court has a discretion whether to make an interim delivery-up order. There is no need to show that there is an urgent need for the order, or that there might be a danger or risk that the goods might be lost or destroyed if the order is not made (*Howard E. Perry and Co. Ltd v British Railways Board* [1980] 1 WLR 1375). However, the order may be refused in the court's discretion where there would be no grounds for making an order for specific delivery (for which, see the Torts (Interference with Goods) Act 1977, s. 3, and 4.13), because the order in effect gives an advance order for specific delivery (*Howard E. Perry and Co. Ltd v British Railways Board*).

The discretion is exercised by the balancing of considerations from each side (*Howard E. Perry and Co. Ltd v British Railways Board*).

If the order is refused, the court may make an order for the detention or preservation of the goods, falling short of delivery up, if the application includes this in the alternative. Normally, orders in this form are very readily made, as there are usually few reasons why the subject matter of the claim should not be preserved so it can be available at the trial. Countervailing considerations may be that the defendant has some legitimate reason for selling the goods for business reasons or because the goods are of a perishable nature.

Solicitors' and accountants' liens

40.5   The court will not usually order the delivery up of documents over which an accountant or solicitor is asserting a lien for unpaid fees, but it has a discretion to do so, particularly where

Chapter 40   Interim Delivery Up of Goods

INTRODUCTION

40.1   An order for the interim delivery up of goods operates in a similar way to freezing injunctions, but instead of merely restraining the defendant from disposing of or otherwise dealing with the goods covered by the order, actually requires the defendant to deliver up the goods to the claimant or someone else specified in the order. In the primary legislation the term used is 'delivery up' (see 40.2), whereas in the CPR it is 'giving up' (see 40.3). In this chapter 'delivery up' will be used. These orders are only available in proceedings for wrongful interference with goods.

JURISDICTION

40.2   The jurisdiction to make orders for interim delivery up is conferred by the Torts (Interference with Goods) Act 1977, s. 4, which provides:

(1)   In this section 'proceedings' means proceedings for wrongful interference.

(2)   On the application of any person in accordance with rules of court, the High Court shall, in such circumstances as may be specified in the rules, have power to make an order providing for the delivery up of any goods which are or may become the subject matter of subsequent proceedings in the court, or as to which any question may arise in proceedings.

(3)   Delivery shall be, as the order may provide, to the claimant or to a person appointed by the court for the purpose, and shall be on such terms and conditions as may be specified in the order.

By the Torts (Interference with Goods) Act 1977, orders under s. 4 can be made in County Court claims on the same basis as equivalent orders in the High Court. The power to make s. 4 orders is listed among the interim remedies available to the court under CPR, r. 25.1(1)(e).

'Wrongful interference', for the purpose of the Torts (Interference with Goods) Act 1977, s. 4(1), is defined by s. 1 to mean:

(a)   conversion of goods (a claim in conversion is expanded by s. 2(2) to cover the loss or destruction of goods which a bailee has allowed to happen in breach of his duty to his bailor, to balance the abolition of detinue, see (d) below);

(b)   trespass to goods;

(c)   negligence so far as it results in damage to goods or to an interest in goods; and

(d)   any other tort so far as it results in damage to goods or to an interest in goods (but the tort of detinue was abolished by s. 2(1)).

By the Torts (Interference with Goods) Act 1977, s. 14, for the purposes of the Act the term 'goods' includes all chattels personal other than things in action and money.

PROCEDURE

40.3   Among the interim remedies listed in CPR, r. 25.1, is an interim order permitting a party seeking to recover personal property to pay money into court pending the outcome of the there is a lack of evidence in support of the work alleged to have been done and which is said to give rise to the lien (*Thaper v Singh* 1987 FLR 369).

If a solicitor discharges himself, it is clear there is jurisdiction to make an order under **CPR, r. 25.1(1)(m)**, for the delivery up of the client's papers (*Ismail v Richards Butler* [1996] QB 711, where the client was required to pay the full amount of the solicitor's fees into court). The order should be limited to documents which are the property of the applicant. It will not include memoranda, calculations, draft plans and other documents which a professional person has prepared to assist in carrying out his professional duties (*Gwelhayl Ltd v Midas Construction Ltd* [2008] EWHC 2316 (TCC), [2008] CILL 2637). In *Paragon Finance plc v Rosling King* (2000) LTL 26/5/2000, where the client terminated the retainer, the court refused the order in the exercise of its discretion.

THE ORDER

The order may provide for delivery up to the claimant or to anyone else appointed by the **40.6** court for the purpose (Torts (Interference with Goods) Act 1977, s. 4(3)). The order may have to make provision for how delivery up is to be effected, and whether the claimant is to be allowed to collect the goods himself. The court must consider whether to include in the order similar provisions to those specified in **PD 25A, paras 5.1 to 5.3** (ordinary injunctions) and **paras 7.1 to 7.11** (search orders) for the benefit or protection of the parties (**PD 25A, para. 8.2**). Suitable provisions may well include undertakings in damages, and provisions dealing with the listing, insurance and custody of the goods to be delivered up. The order should provide that the applicant must pay money into court pending the outcome of the proceedings, and direct that if he does so, the property shall be given up to him (**CPR, r. 25.1(1)(m)**).

HYBRID DELIVERY-UP ORDERS

According to the Court of Appeal in *CBS United Kingdom Ltd v Lambert* [1983] Ch 37, the court **40.7** has a power deriving from either its inherent jurisdiction or from the Senior Courts Act 1981, s. 37(1), to order the interim delivery up of assets as an adjunct to a freezing order. The defendant had admitted his involvement in the large-scale counterfeiting of musical recordings, and the evidence pointed to the defendant having deliberately put the proceeds of his activities into easily disposable chattels such as expensive motor cars. It was held to be a clear case for ordering delivery up of his assets. A number of guidelines were laid down for this type of order:

(a) There should be clear evidence that the defendant is likely, unless restrained by order, to dispose of or otherwise deal with the goods in order to deprive the claimant of the fruits of any judgment which may be obtained. The court will be slow to order the delivery up of property belonging to the defendant unless there is some evidence or inference that the property has been acquired as a result of the defendant's alleged wrongdoing.

(b) No order should be made for the delivery up of a defendant's clothes, bedding, furnishings, tools of his trade, farm implements, livestock or machinery (including motor vehicles) or stock-in-trade which it is likely that the defendant uses for the purposes of a lawful business. However, furnishings consisting of *objets d'art* of substantial value which the evidence indicates were bought with the fruits of the wrongdoing may be included in the order.

(c) The order should specify as clearly as possible the goods or classes of goods to be delivered up. If the claimant is unable to identify the goods in question, that points towards refusing an order.

(d) The order must not authorise the claimant to enter the defendant's premises or to seize the defendant's property save with the defendant's permission.

(e) The order should not require delivery up to anyone other than the claimant's solicitor or a receiver appointed by the court. The court will need to be satisfied that the claimant's solicitor, if to be the person taking possession of the goods, has facilities for suitable safe custody.

(f) Suitable safeguards should be built into the order for the protection of the defendant along the lines of freezing injunctions. These will include an undertaking in damages, and provision for the defendant's living expenses.

(g) The order should give the defendant liberty to apply to stay, vary or discharge the order.

Chapter 41   Inspection of Property

INTRODUCTION

By **CPR, r. 25.1(1)(c)**, the High Court and the County Court have powers to make orders, on the **41.1** application of one party to proceedings, for the inspection and preservation of property in the possession of another party. There are ancillary powers to authorise the taking of samples, and conducting experiments on and with property in the possession of the other party. There is a further power to authorise entry on to any land or building in the possession of the other party where the property that needs to be inspected is located (**r. 25.1(1)(d)**). These powers are useful for ensuring that the subject matter of the claim is still in existence when the proceedings reach trial. They are also used to give all sides a fair and proper opportunity to obtain informed expert evidence relevant to the issues in the claim. For example, in a claim arising out of an accident at work it may be necessary for the claimant's engineering expert to be able to inspect and test the machinery involved in the accident, which is likely to be located in the defendant's premises. In a claim arising out of the sale of goods it may be necessary for the seller's expert to take a sample of the goods in question and to test them or comment on their quality, and the goods may well be in the possession of the buyer. In a claim for negligence against a valuer the defendant's expert will almost inevitably have to inspect the claimant's property for the purposes of considering both liability and quantum.

The most usual situation arises where the property that needs to be inspected is in the possession of an opposite party, and the request for inspection arises during the course of proceedings. However, the rules also make provision for inspection (and related orders) before the claim is issued, and for orders for inspection against persons who are not parties to the proceedings.

When making an order for the preservation of property the court must consider whether to include in the order similar provisions to those specified in **PD 25A, paras 5.1 to 5.3** (ordinary injunctions) and **paras 7.1 to 7.11** (search orders) for the benefit or protection of the parties (**PD 25A, para. 8.2**). Suitable provisions are likely to include undertakings in damages, and provisions dealing with the listing, insurance and custody of the property to be preserved.

INSPECTION DURING THE COURSE
OF PROCEEDINGS AGAINST A PARTY

CPR, r. 25.1(1)(c), provides that the courts have power to make orders for: **41.2**

(a) the detention, custody or preservation of relevant property (for the purpose of ensuring that the property is still available at trial); and

(b) the inspection of, taking samples of, carrying out of experiments on or with relevant property (for the purpose of ensuring that experts can provide informed evidence at the trial, and to ensure fairness to both sides).

The order may include authority to enter land in the possession of a party to the proceedings for any of these purposes (**r. 25.1(1)(d)**).

Detention and preservation orders are usually sought where there is some risk that the other side may deliberately or accidentally get rid of the property before trial. If there is some risk, the order should be made quite readily as, unless there is some legitimate reason for the party with possession of the property wishing to sell it or use it up, justice points strongly towards it being preserved for the purposes of the proceedings.

Regarding orders for inspection etc., it is usually unarguably in the interests of justice and in accordance with the overriding objective for such orders to be made. It is usual, given the requirement of cooperation (**r. 1.3**), for the parties to seek consent to any necessary inspections before resorting to the assistance of the court. An order should only be sought if the other side do not respond in a reasonable time, or refuse their consent, or insist on unreasonable conditions.

Meaning of 'property'

41.3   'Relevant property' for the purposes of **CPR, r. 25.1(1)(c)**, means property which is the subject of a claim, or as to which any question may arise in a claim (**r. 25.1(2)**). It covers land and physical items and processes which might need to be preserved, inspected, sampled or experimented upon for the purposes of the litigation. An identified fund or money subject to a trust might be 'property' for this purpose if it is the subject matter of the claim, but money claimed by way of damages, compensation or debt is not (*Sports Network Ltd v Calzaghe* [2008] EWHC 2566 (QB), LTL 3/11/2008 at [49]–[51]). Before the introduction of the CPR it was held that the rules allowing inspection of 'property' did not extend to inspecting the defendant's manufacturing process (*Tudor Accumulator Co. Ltd v China Mutual Steam Navigation Co. Ltd* [1930] WN 200). Nevertheless, under the old system it was held that there was inherent jurisdiction to make such an order (*Ash v Buxted Poultry Ltd* (1989) *The Times,* 29 November 1989). Technical limitations like those identified in *Tudor Accumulator Co. Ltd v China Mutual Co.* are precisely the sorts of restrictions the CPR were intended to sweep away, and inspection of a manufacturing process is almost certainly included within the meaning of 'relevant property' as set out in **r. 25.1(2)**. In *Huddleston v Control Risks Information Services Ltd* [1987] 1 WLR 701 (a case on the related pre-action procedure in the Senior Courts Act 1981, s. 33(1), discussed at **41.6**) it was held that a document could be an item of 'property' for these purposes, but whether it was depended on whether the application sought inspection or detention of the physical document. If the application in substance sought the disclosure of the information recorded on the document, it was a disclosure application (for which, see **chapter 50**) rather than an application relating to 'property'.

Payment into court or securing a specified fund

41.4   The court can make an interim order that a specified fund be paid into court or otherwise secured (**CPR, r. 25.1(1)(l)**). This power is limited to money which forms all or part of a 'specified fund'. This phrase is not a term of art, and is capable of a number of meanings depending on the context. It can include the proceeds from the sale of property, but an order may only be appropriate if the claimant has a proprietary interest in those proceeds. The power cannot be used to order the payment into court of a sum merely representing a debt owed to the claimant (*Myers v Design Inc. (International) Ltd* [2003] EWHC 103 (Ch), [2003] 1 WLR 1642). The opposite conclusion was reached in *Sports Network Ltd v Calzaghe* [2008] EWHC 2566 QB), LTL 3/11/2008 at [53], relying on *Polly Peck International plc v Nadir (No. 2)* [1992] 4 All

ER 769. An order can be made where the claimant establishes a serious issue to be tried on the merits, and if the balance of convenience favours granting the order (*Sports Network Ltd v Calzaghe* at [53]).

Procedure on applications for inspection etc. during proceedings

Where an order for the preservation, detention or inspection of relevant property is required, the proper time for seeking it is at the track allocation stage, if the need for the order can be identified at that time. If so, the terms of the order sought should be provided to the court in the form of a draft order and sent to the court with the directions questionnaire (see **PD 26, para. 2.2(3)(d); PD 28, paras 3.4** and **3.5; PD 29, para. 4.7**). The parties should seek to agree suitable directions, but failing that, the minimum is that the party seeking inspection etc. should send details of the proposed orders to the other side no later than the time the questionnaire is sent to the court. **41.5**

There are cases where the need for preservation, detention or inspection orders only becomes apparent at a later stage. If so, the application should be made at a case management conference or pre-trial review or other hearing, and having a hearing just for this purpose is a last resort. In the latter situation an application notice in form N244 will need to be issued. If a hearing is necessary because of the default of a party, sanctions may be imposed (**PD 28, para. 2.3; PD 29, para. 3.6**).

Written evidence in support is required unless the court otherwise orders (**CPR, r. 25.3(2)**). There will be some cases where the need for the order is so self-evident that no evidence is required. Hearings are generally before a Master or District Judge (**PD 2B**).

INSPECTION BEFORE COMMENCEMENT OF PROCEEDINGS

There is jurisdiction to make orders for the inspection, detention and preservation of relevant property even before proceedings are issued, under the Senior Courts Act 1981, s. 33(1), and the County Courts Act 1984, s. 52(1). The Senior Courts Act 1981, s. 33(1), provides: **41.6**

On the application of any person in accordance with rules of court, the High Court shall, in such circumstances as may be specified in the rules, have power to make an order providing for any one or more of the following matters, that is to say—

(a) the inspection, photocopying, preservation, custody and detention of property which appears to the court to be property which may become the subject matter of subsequent proceedings in the High Court, or as to which any question may arise in such proceedings; and

(b) the taking of samples of any such property as is mentioned in paragraph (a), and the carrying out of any experiment on or with any such property.

The County Courts Act 1984, s. 52(1), is in essentially the same terms, but refers to the power being vested in the County Court.

The only condition laid down by the statutory provisions is that an order for inspection etc. must be in respect of 'property which may become the subject matter of subsequent proceedings'. The discussion of what constitutes 'property' in **41.3** also applies for the purposes of these sections. However, the importance of *Huddleston v Control Risks Information Services Ltd* [1987] 1 WLR 701 has all but disappeared since the jurisdiction to make pre-commencement orders for disclosure of documents (see **chapter 50**) was widened by the Civil Procedure (Modification of Enactments) Order 1998 (SI 1998/2940) to extend these orders to all types of proceedings (and not just personal injuries claims).

There are no other restrictions, apart from the application of the overriding objective. An order may be refused on the grounds of proportionality and saving expense if it is not

Commentary

necessary to obtain the order until after proceedings are issued, or if no attempt has been made to obtain the inspection by consent. Also, it is less likely that the court will be prepared to make an order against someone who is not likely to be a party to the substantive proceedings than a respondent who is the likely opposite party.

Procedure on pre-commencement application for inspection

41.7   The general rules governing applications made before the commencement of proceedings are considered in **chapter 32**, particularly at **32.2** and **32.5**. Pre-commencement inspection orders are applied for by issuing an ordinary application notice in form N244 in the anticipated proceedings, supported by written evidence. **CPR, r. 25.5(2)**, requires the evidence in support of the application to show, if practicable by reference to any statement of case prepared in relation to the anticipated proceedings, that the property:

(a) is or may become the subject matter of such proceedings; or
(b) is relevant to the issues that will arise in relation to such proceedings.

A copy of the application and a copy of the evidence in support must be served on the person against whom the order is sought (**r. 25.5(3)**). If the order is made, the court will probably decide against giving directions requiring a claim to be commenced, as the decision to commence will usually turn on the nature of the evidence gathered from the inspection (see **r. 25.2(3)** and **(4)**).

INSPECTION AGAINST NON-PARTIES

41.8   There is jurisdiction to make orders in pending proceedings for the inspection, detention and preservation of relevant property against persons who are not parties to the substantive claim, under the Senior Courts Act 1981, s. 34(3), and the County Courts Act 1984, s. 53(3). The Senior Courts Act 1981, s. 34(3), provides:

On the application, in accordance with rules of court, of a party to any proceedings, the High Court shall, in such circumstances as may be specified in the rules, have power to make an order providing for any one or more of the following matters, that is to say—

(a) the inspection, photographing, preservation, custody and detention of property which is not the property of, or in the possession of, any party to the proceedings but which is the subject matter of the proceedings or as to which any question arises in the proceedings;

(b) the taking of samples of any such property as is mentioned in paragraph (a) and the carrying out of any experiment on or with any such property.

The County Courts Act 1984, s. 53(3), is in essentially the same terms, but refers to the power being vested in the County Court. Before amendment by the Civil Procedure (Modification of Enactments) Order 1998 (SI 1998/2940), the provisions applied only to personal injuries claims, but now they cover all types of proceedings.

There are two conditions:

(a) substantive proceedings must have been issued before the application is made; and
(b) the property must be the subject matter of the proceedings, or a question relating to the property must arise in the proceedings. The discussion of what constitutes 'property' in **41.3** also applies for the purposes of these sections.

If the conditions are satisfied, the court has a discretion whether to make the order, which will be exercised in accordance with the overriding objective.

Procedure on application for inspection against a non-party

41.9   An order for inspection of property against a non-party is sought by issuing an application notice in form N244 supported by evidence during the course of the proceedings. The fact that such an application is contemplated should be mentioned in further information filed with the directions questionnaire. If possible the application should be made returnable at any case management hearing that may already have been listed. The evidence in support of an application for inspection against a non-party must, by **CPR, r. 25.5(2)**, show, if practicable by reference to any statement of case prepared in relation to the proceedings, that the property in question is the subject matter of the proceedings, or is relevant to the issues that will arise in relation to the proceedings.

A copy of the application notice and a copy of the evidence in support must be served on the person against whom the order is sought and every party to the proceedings other than the applicant (**r. 25.5(3)**).

ORDERS FOR SALE AND IN RELATION TO INCOME

Power is conferred on the civil courts by **CPR, r. 25.1(1)(c)(v)** and (**vi**), to make orders: **41.10**

(a) for the sale of relevant property which is of a perishable nature, or which for any other good reason should be sold quickly; and

(b) for the payment of income from relevant property until the claim is decided.

'Relevant property' means property which is the subject of a claim, or as to which any question may arise in a claim (**r. 25.1(2)**). In *On Demand Information plc v Michael Gerson (Finance) plc* [2002] UKHL 13, [2003] 1 AC 368, an interim order for sale of the subject matter of the proceedings was made under the equivalent provisions of the old rules (RSC, ord. 29, r. 4). The claimants had leased video and editing equipment from the defendants on three-year lease agreements which provided that after expiry of the three-year term the claimants could sell the equipment and retain 95 per cent of the price. The claimants went into receivership, which under the terms of the leases allowed the defendants to terminate the leases. The receiver wished to sell the claimants' business as a going concern, together with the leased equipment, and brought a claim seeking relief from forfeiture (so as to preserve the claimants' right to retain 95 per cent of the proceeds of sale). An interim order was made under what would now be **CPR, r. 25.1(1)(c)(v)**, allowing the equipment to be sold on the ground that there was good reason for it to be sold quickly. At trial it was held that because the equipment had been sold under the interim order, the court no longer had jurisdiction to grant relief from forfeiture, such relief only being available if the relevant asset remained unsold. In the House of Lords it was said that the whole purpose of this type of interim order is to preserve the value of the parties' rights. Once the equipment was sold the proceeds of sale stood in the place of the equipment for the purposes of the litigation, and although relief from forfeiture was no longer possible (because of the sale), the court could still give effect to the respective rights of the parties by formulating an order deciding the proportions in which the parties were entitled to the proceeds of sale.

A party seeking an order under **r. 25.1(1)(c)(v)** or (**vi**) should issue an application notice in form N244 supported by written evidence. The application should, if possible, be listed with any subsisting pending case management hearing.

Commentary

PART I

Case Management

Chapter 42   Case Management

Commentary

INTRODUCTION

42.1   Judicial case management of civil litigation is one of the central planks of the CPR. The *Woolf Report* stressed the idea that ultimate responsibility for the control of litigation should move from the litigants and their advisers to the court. Under the CPR, the legal profession is intended to perform its traditional adversarial role in a managed environment governed by the courts. One of the purposes behind the CPR is to require the parties to focus their efforts on the key issues rather than allowing every issue to be pursued regardless of expense and time. Case management is seen as the principal means by which the judiciary will ensure this happens.

Active case management: *Woolf* and *Jackson*

42.2   As explained by the former Senior Master, Robert Turner in ' "Actively": the word that changed the civil courts' in *The Civil Procedure Rules Ten Years On*, ed. Déirdre Dwyer (Oxford: OUP, 2009), pp. 77–88, including active case management as part of the court's overriding objective effected a revolution in English civil procedure. This single change wrested control of litigation from the parties, and gave it to the judiciary. Instead of judges influencing litigation in a reactive way, under the CPR judges have been expected to intervene in a proactive way. One of the conclusions reached by Sir Rupert Jackson's *Review of Civil Litigation Costs* (2009) was that the revolution had not gone far enough, and an even more radical change of ethos was needed, with judges adopting a robust approach to case management (see *Blackstone's Guide to the Civil Justice Reforms 2013* (Oxford: OUP, 2013), paras 5.01 to 5.06). The change of ethos demands:

(a) a proactive judiciary who engage with the litigation from a very early stage;

(b) courts having regard to whether any of the parties is unrepresented (**CPR, r. 3.1A(2)**); and

(c) lawyers adopting a cooperative stance with the courts and with their opponents.

Robust case management has three elements:

(a) delivery of effective case management directions by a judge with relevant expertise who is on top of the case;

(b) moving the claim along swiftly to settlement or trial; and

(c) firm enforcement of directions once they are given, applying a 'no nonsense' approach.

Case management and the overriding objective

42.3   In exercising their powers to manage cases, the courts seek to secure the overriding objective of ensuring that cases are dealt with justly and at proportionate cost. **CPR, r. 1.1(2)**, provides that this includes ensuring cases are dealt with expeditiously and fairly, allotting to them an appropriate share of the court's resources, and ensuring they are dealt with proportionately bearing in mind factors such as the importance and complexities of the issues and the monetary value of the claim. Conducting litigation expeditiously includes taking steps to enforce compliance with rules, practice directions and court orders (**r. 1.1(2)(f)**).

Rule 1.3, which is discussed at **1.12** and **1.38**, requires the parties to assist the court in furthering the overriding objective. This means that the parties must ensure the court has the information required if effective directions are to be made, and must inform the court of events which may affect directions previously made which cannot be dealt with by the consent of the parties. Examples are case management hearings, permission to call experts, pre-trial checklist dates and the trial date or window. Failure to do so may result in sanctions being imposed, including costs sanctions for any resulting applications and even striking out under **r. 3.4(2)(c)**.

The *Woolf Report*, ch. 1, para. 4, envisaged that active case management would involve procedural judges identifying the issues in the case, summarily disposing of some issues and deciding the order in which other issues are to be resolved, fixing timetables for the procedural steps in preparing cases for trial, and limiting evidence, particularly documentary and expert evidence. These ideas are put into effect by **r. 1.4(1)**, which lists 12 methods that may be adopted to achieve this, a number of which adopt the ideas listed at the beginning of this paragraph. It is accordingly intended that procedural judges should be willing to intervene during the early stages of proceedings to ensure that the issues are narrowed, that cases are prepared economically and speedily, and disposed of fairly and without undue delay or expense.

Proportionate case management

To ensure that case management is proportionate the *Woolf Report* envisaged there would be active judicial intervention only in cases which would require and repay it. Basic management, with a fixed timetable and standard procedure, is used wherever possible, on the multi-track as well as on the fast track. Standard directions are laid down for the small claims track (**PD 27, app. A**), fast track (**PD 28, app.**) and multi-track (**CPR, r. 29.1(2)**). The published standard directions should be the starting point in cases where any of the parties is a litigant in person (**r. 3.1A(3)**). Keeping case management proportionate can, however, prove quite difficult, particularly on the multi-track, or where the parties fail to identify the issues or fail to consider properly the expert evidence required to prove the case.

Directions may be given without hearings and by consent (see **32.23** and **32.35**). The CPR give the courts powers to hold five types of procedural hearing (allocation hearings, case management conferences, costs management conferences, pre-trial reviews and hearings under **rr. 28.5(4)** and **(5)** and **29.6(4)**), which, unless kept under control, could result in substantial increases in the use of court resources and expense to the parties. The overall result is that the majority of defended cases proceed between the filing of a defence and trial with directions in a more or less standard form, but tailored to the needs of the particular case.

Recommendations in Sir Rupert Jackson's *Review of Civil Litigation Costs* (Ministry of Justice, December 2009, the *Jackson Report*) and implemented from 1 April 2013 include:

- measures to assign more cases to designated judges (recommendation 81);
- a menu of standard paragraphs for directions in different types of cases (recommendation 82);
- case management conferences and pre-trial reviews to be more effective, and dealt with on the papers where appropriate (recommendation 83);
- less tolerance of delays, with court monitoring of progress (recommendation 86);
- a standard costs management procedure (recommendation 91, see **chapter 43**).

PROCEDURAL JUDGES

Case management decisions are generally dealt with by Masters for cases proceeding in the Royal Courts of Justice, and by District Judges in High Court District Registry and County Court cases. The governing rule (**CPR, r. 2.4**) in fact gives the courts a great deal of flexibility, allowing performance by any judicial officer, whether a District Judge, Master or judge, subject to any specific contrary provision in any enactment, rule or practice direction. However, **PD 29, para. 3.10**, says (in relation to multi-track cases) that Masters will in general perform case management functions in the Royal Courts of Justice, District Judges in District Registries, and either District Judges or Circuit Judges in County Court cases. Much the same is said, in effect, by **PD 2B, para. 1.1. PD 2B** enables Masters and District Judges to deal with all types of application, but with express exceptions set out in the practice direction. Exceptions include freezing injunctions and search orders. An interim injunction governed by the *American Cyanamid* guidelines will usually be referred forthwith to a judge, unless there are good reasons for a Master to hear the application (Chancery Guide, para. 15.21). Detailed lists of exceptions can be seen in **para. 3.1** (High Court), **paras 7B.1** to **7B.4** (Chancery

42.4

42.5

Division) and **paras 8.1** to **8.4** (County Court); see **2.8** to **2.11** and **37.2**. A County Court District Judge can deal with interim injunctions before allocation (see **para. 8.1(b)**) where the claim has a monetary limit not exceeding the fast track limit, also in cases where District Judges have trial jurisdiction as listed in **para. 11.1**, and under the legislation on protection from harassment and anti-social behaviour (see **chapter 88**).

Cases in the Chancery and Queen's Bench Divisions are assigned to individual Masters (**PD 2B, para. 6.1**), although from time to time hearings may be dealt with by other Masters or deputies as the circumstances may require, and cases may be transferred from one Master to another.

References to Circuit Judges include Recorders and references to Masters and District Judges include deputies (**PD 2B, para. 1.1**).

LITIGANTS IN PERSON

42.6 Many litigants cannot afford legal representation, or choose to represent themselves. Guidelines for lawyers dealing with opponents who are litigants in person were published by the Law Society, CILEX and BSB in June 2015. These recommend adopting a professional, cooperative and courteous approach, with care being taken to avoid legal jargon when communicating with a litigant in person. They also suggest recommending to the litigant in person that they should seek independent legal advice. Lawyers must not take unfair advantage of a litigant in person, but are under no obligation to help a litigant in person run their case, or to take any action on their behalf, unless ordered by the court to do so, or if the lawyer considers doing so is required by their duty to the court. When negotiating with a litigant in person the guidelines advise doing so in the presence of a colleague, and making a note as soon as practicable afterwards. To avoid being unfair they suggest saying something like: 'are you prepared to agree to...' rather than 'the courts in this situation would never agree to X, so I suggest that you agree to...', even if this is legally accurate.

Broadly, the rules of procedure apply equally to represented and unrepresented parties, but with some exceptions. Litigants in person are provided with the directions questionnaire by the court (**CPR, r. 26.3(1B)**). When exercising its case management powers the court must have regard to whether any of the parties is acting in person (**r. 3.1A**). In cases with litigants in person, the starting point for case management directions is the standard directions available on the Ministry of Justice website (**r. 3.1A(3)**). Litigants in person are not required to provide costs budgets (**r. 3.13(1)**), but may claim costs at a special litigants in person rate of £19 per hour (**r. 46.5** and **PD 46, para. 3.4**).

Being a litigant in person with no experience of legal proceedings is not a good reason for not complying with the CPR or court orders (*R (Hysaj) v Secretary of State for the Home Department* [2014] EWCA Civ 1633, [2015] 1 WLR 2472). However, experience shows judges do tend to treat litigants differently depending on the judge's view on how knowledgeable they are of court procedures. There have been cases where judges have said this is wrong. For example, in *Blake v Coote* (2016) LTL 18/4/2016 Sir Alistair MacDuff said being a litigant in person might go to competence, but not understanding procedure does not entitle a litigant in person to extra indulgence. A similar point was made in *Tinkler v Elliott* [2012] EWCA Civ 1289, [2013] CP Rep 4, where it was said that it would be taking sympathy for a litigant in person too far if the court were to forgive a litigant in person for making the wrong type of application. Familiarity with civil procedure is taken into account. An example is *Gentry v Miller* [2016] EWCA Civ 141, [2016] 1 WLR 2698 where Vos LJ said at [34] that the court could not ignore the fact that insurers are professional litigators.

At hearings the court must adopt procedures designed to further the overriding objective. This may include the judge ascertaining from the litigant in person the areas on which witnesses may give evidence-in-chief or which should be covered in cross-examination, and the judge putting, or causing to be put, such questions as the judge considers proper to witnesses (**CPR, r. 3.1A(5)**). Some litigants in person are assisted by McKenzie friends, see **61.32**.

TRANSFER OR SENDING TO APPROPRIATE COURT

Transfers are judicial decisions to move a case to another court or location. The term 'send' is used in the CPR to refer to administrative action in moving cases to different locations of the County Court.

42.7

County Court money claims that are commenced using hard copy documents must be issued in the County Court Money Claims Centre in Salford (**PD 7A, para. 4A.1**). Certain bulk users of the court system are able to have their money claims issued in the County Court using information technology through the Production Centre (**CPR, r. 7.10; PD 7C**). County Court money claims not exceeding £100,000 may also be issued using Money Claim Online, and are commenced in the County Court Business Centre under **PD 7E**. In these three situations the claim is issued in an administrative office which is part of the County Court, but which is not a hearing centre. There are also detailed rules on the allocation of business between the High Court and County Court (see **11.4**). Subject to these rules, a claimant has a free choice of which court to use when commencing a civil claim. The first case management intervention may be to transfer or send the case to the most appropriate court.

General powers to order transfers can be found in the County Courts Act 1984, ss. 40 to 42. The High Court has unlimited power under s. 40(2) to transfer cases to the County Court regardless, in a suitable case, of whether the case is outside the monetary limits of the County Court (*National Westminster Bank plc v King* [2008] EWHC 280 (Ch), [2008] Ch 385). An application for a transfer from the County Court to a specialist list should be made to the receiving court under **CPR, r. 30.5**, with notice to the County Court (*Collins v Drumgold* [2008] EWHC 584 (TCC), [2008] CILL 2585), because transfers to and from specialist lists can only be made by judges dealing with claims in the specialist list (**r. 30.5(2) and (3)**). A transfer between the Chancery Division and a Queen's Bench Division specialist list may only be made with the consent of the Chancellor of the High Court (**r. 30.5(4)**). Allocation of cases to Divisions and specialist courts is discussed in **chapter 11**.

Automatic transfers etc.

Sending County Court money claims to the preferred hearing centre When a County Court money claim, whether for a specified or unspecified amount, is issued, the claimant is required to specify a 'preferred hearing centre' on the claim form to which the proceedings should be sent if necessary (**CPR, r. 2.3; PD 7A, para. 4A.2**). A County Court money claim must be sent to the preferred hearing centre where:

42.8

(a) the claimant files a request for judgment in the County Court Money Claims Centre following an order striking out a statement of case where the request includes an amount of money to be decided by the court in accordance with **CPR, r. 3.5 (r. 3.5A)**; or

(b) the claimant files a request for the entry of judgment in default where the request includes an amount of money to be decided by the court in accordance with **rr. 12.4 and 12.5** (**r. 12.5A**); or

(c) the defendant, not being an individual, applies to set aside a default judgment in a claim that was started in the County Court Money Claims Centre (**r. 13.4(1B)**); or

(d) the claimant files a request for judgment in the County Court Money Claims Centre following an admission of liability where the request includes an amount of money to be decided by the court in accordance with **r. 14.6 or r. 14.7 (r. 14.7A)**; or

Commentary

(e) the court is to determine or redetermine the rate of payment in a claim started in the County Court following an admission by a defendant who is not an individual (**rr. 14.12(2A)** and **14.13(3A)**); or

(f) the claim is a County Court unspecified money claim or the defendant is not an individual, and the 'relevant time' has come (**r. 26.2A(1)**, **(3)** and **(4)**). The 'relevant time' is defined by **r. 26.2A(6)**. With the exception of claims for the recovery of taxes and duties, this is when all the parties have filed their directions questionnaires, or any stay ordered by the court or period to attempt settlement through mediation has expired. In this situation the claimant may specify another hearing centre in his directions questionnaire, and if so the case will be sent to that specified hearing centre (**r. 26.2A(5)(b)**).

42.9 **Transferring or sending claims to the defendant's home court** In County Court claims the defendant's home court is usually the County Court hearing centre serving the address where the defendant resides or carries on business. Multi-track claims started in the County Court Business Centre or the County Court Money Claims Centre are instead sent to the County Court at Central London where the relevant home court or preferred hearing centre is one of the London hearing centres listed in **PD 26, para. 10.4** (**CPR, r. 26.2A(5A)**). For High Court claims, the home court is the District Registry for the district where the defendant resides or carries on business or, where there is no such District Registry (such as where the defendant is outside the jurisdiction), the Royal Courts of Justice (**r. 2.3(1)**).

In the High Court, defended claims for specified sums of money against individuals are automatically transferred to the defendant's home court on receipt by the court of a defence (**r. 26.2**). Where there is more than one defendant, the claim is transferred to the home court of the defendant whose defence is filed first (**r. 26.2(5)**). A High Court claim for a specified amount of money will also be transferred automatically to the defendant's home court if the defendant is an individual and applies to set aside a default judgment (**r. 13.4(1)**), or if the court is to determine or redetermine the rate of payment following an admission by a defendant who is an individual (**rr. 14.12(2)** and **14.13(3)**).

In the County Court, where the defendant is an individual and the claim is for a specified sum of money, at the 'relevant time' as defined by **r. 26.2A(6)** (see **42.8**):

(a) the claim must be sent to the defendant's home court, or, where there are two or more defendants who are individuals, to the home court of the defendant who first files a defence (**r. 26.2A(3)**);

(b) unless the defendant specifies another hearing centre in their directions questionnaire. In this situation the claim must be sent to that specified hearing centre (**r. 26.2A(5)(a)**).

A County Court claim for a specified amount of money will be sent to the defendant's home court if the defendant is an individual and applies to set aside a default judgment (**r. 13.4(1)**), or if the court is to determine or redetermine the rate of payment following an admission by a defendant who is an individual (**rr. 14.12(2)** and **14.13(3)**).

A claim issued in the County Court Money Claims Centre will be transferred to the court where the defendant resides or carries on business for the purposes of any application to obtain further information from the judgment debtor and other forms of enforcement except charging orders and attachment of earnings (**rr. 71.2(2)(b)(ii)**, **72.3(b)(ii)**, **73.3(2)** and **89.3**; **PD 70, paras 8.1 to 11.1**).

A claim issued in the Production Centre is normally sent to the defendant's home court after the parties have filed their directions questionnaires (**PD 7C, para. 1.3(2)(f)**). This will happen earlier if the defendant is an individual and directions are required, or if the defendant files a counterclaim (**para. 1.3(2)(e)**).

Discretionary transfers

Transfers in other cases are governed by **CPR, Part 30**, with criteria for deciding whether to **42.10** transfer being set out in **r. 30.3(2)**. These criteria include the financial value of the claim, and whether it would be more convenient to try the case in another court. The convenience of the defendant is always a strong factor, because the defendant has not chosen to be sued (*Pepin v Taylor* [2002] EWCA Civ 1522, LTL 10/10/2002). Simply inserting a high value on the claim form does not ensure the claim will not be transferred to the County Court (*Kohanzad v Derbyshire Police Authority* [2004] EWCA Civ 1387, LTL 8/10/2004, where the amount was £5 million). For transfers to the Royal Courts of Justice where the Crown is a party, see the Attorney General's note annexed to **PD 66**.

In considering transfers in specialist claims the court must have regard to the availability of specialist judges, and in particular the availability of a specialist judge in an appropriate regional specialist court (**CPR, r. 30.3(2)(c)**). Guidance was given on the allocation of cases between the County Court and the Technology and Construction Court of the High Court by *West Country Renovations Ltd v McDowell* [2012] EWHC 307 (TCC), [2013] 1 WLR 416. Claims with a value up to £250,000 should usually be commenced in the County Court, or will be transferred down if they are commenced in the TCC. The judgment includes a lengthy but non-exhaustive list of exceptions to the general rule. General factors listed by Coulson J in *Collins v Drumgold* [2008] EWHC 584 (TCC), [2008] CILL 2585 were:

(a) whether the dispute arose out of or was connected with a claim of a type set out in **PD 60**, para. 2.1;
(b) the value of the claim and its complexity;
(c) the convenience of the parties;
(d) any costs implications in proceeding in the High Court rather than the County Court (sometimes transferring to a specialist list will save costs).

Transfer to civil trial centre

Cases commenced in courts that are not civil trial centres (such courts are described as 'feeder **42.11** courts') are considered by a procedural judge when defences are filed. If it appears that the case is suitable for allocation to the multi-track, the District Judge will normally make an order allocating the case to the multi-track, will give case management directions, and transfer the claim to a civil trial centre (**PD 26, para. 10.2(5)**). A case may be allocated to the multi-track and be retained in a feeder court, if it is envisaged that there may need to be more than one case management conference and the parties or their legal advisers are located inconveniently far from the designated civil trial centre (**PD 26, para. 10.2(10)**) or where pressure of work in the trial centre has led to the designated civil judge approving retention of the case by the feeder court. If it is not possible to decide whether a case should be allocated to the fast or multi-track, the procedural judge will either hold an allocation hearing at the feeder court, or transfer the case to a civil trial centre for the allocation decision to be made there (**paras 10.2(6)** and **(8)**). Once a case is transferred, a judge will consider the file when it is received at the civil trial centre and give any further directions that appear necessary or desirable (**para. 10.2(9)**).

ALLOCATION

Every defended claim must be allocated to one of the three tracks (small claims track, fast **42.12** track, multi-track). The underlying purpose is to ensure a proportionate amount of resources is devoted to each case based on its value and complexity.

Provisional allocation

42.13   With effect from 1 April 2013, under **CPR, r. 26.3(1)**, if a defendant files a defence, a court officer will provisionally decide the track which appears to be most suitable for the claim, and will serve on each party a notice of proposed allocation.

The notice of proposed allocation will:

(a) specify any matter to be complied with by the date specified in the notice;

(b) require the parties to file a completed directions questionnaire and serve copies on all other parties;

(c) state the address of the court or the court office to which the directions questionnaire must be returned;

(d) inform the parties how to obtain the directions questionnaire; and

(e) if a case appears suitable for allocation to the fast track or multi-track, require the parties to file proposed directions by the date specified in the notice.

There are three forms of notice of proposed allocation:

(i)   N149A, notice of proposed allocation to the small claims track;

(ii) N149B, notice of proposed allocation to the fast track; and

(iii) N149C, notice of proposed allocation to the multi-track.

The effect of **r. 26.3(2)** is that where there are two or more defendants the court will serve the notice of proposed allocation under **r. 26.3(1)** when all the defendants have filed a defence, or when the period for filing the last defence has expired, whichever is the sooner. Where either **r. 14.5** (admission of part of a claim for a specified amount of money) or **r. 15.10** (claimant's notice where the defence is that the money claimed has been paid) applies, **r. 26.3(4)** says the court will not serve the notice of proposed allocation under **r. 26.3(1)** until the claimant has filed a notice requiring the proceedings to continue.

Where there is an interim hearing before the claim is allocated, at that hearing the court may dispense with directions questionnaires, allocate the claim to a track, and make case management directions (**PD 26, para. 2.4(1)**). It may alternatively fix a date for filing directions questionnaires and give other directions (**PD 26, para. 2.4(2)**).

Litigants in person and directions questionnaires

42.14   The court will serve litigants in person with the appropriate directions questionnaire (**CPR, r. 26.3(1B)**). The time when the court does so may be varied by a practice direction in respect of claims issued by the Production Centre (**r. 26.3(7)**), although at present no such variation has been made in **PD 7C**.

DIRECTIONS QUESTIONNAIRES

42.15   There are different forms of directions questionnaire for small claims track claims (N180) and for fast track and multi-track claims (N181).

The questionnaire asks for details of whether the relevant pre-action protocol procedure was complied with. Unjustified failure to follow the protocol may result in sanctions being imposed (see **8.2** to **8.4**). It also asks whether a stay is sought for settlement (see **42.62**), about possible transfer to another court, for the party's view on the appropriate track for the case, for details about disclosure of electronic documents, experts and factual witnesses, and for details of any contemplated application for summary judgment. It should provide information to enable the judge to gauge the value of the claim, to see how many expert witnesses are required, and how long the trial is likely to take. The questionnaire is obviously an important document, and care in completing it will assist the court in deciding whether to transfer the case to a more appropriate venue, on the appropriate track for the case, on the nature of any directions that may be appropriate, and whether a case management conference will be required if the case is allocated to the multi-track. The parties are encouraged to consult one another and cooperate in completing their directions questionnaires, and also in deciding on any additional information, which may include suggested directions (see **42.16**), they may send to the court with their questionnaires (**PD 26, para. 2.3**). A costs budget, budget discussion report (see **chapter 43**) and disclosure report (see **chapter 50**) normally have to be filed in advance of the first case management conference if the claim has been provisionally allocated to the multi-track.

Completion of directions questionnaires

The parties should consult one another and cooperate in completing the directions questionnaires and giving other information to the court (**PD 26, para. 2.3(1)**). They must try to agree the case management directions which they will invite the court to make (**para. 2.3(2)**). The process of consultation must not delay the filing of the directions questionnaire or, where required, the proposed directions (whether or not agreed) (**para. 2.3(3)**). Specimen directions for multi-track claims should be used where applicable (**CPR, r. 29.1(2)**), and are available on the Ministry of Justice website at http://www.justice.gov.uk/courts/procedure-rules/civil. | **42.16**

If a party wishes to give the court further information which is believed to be relevant to allocation or case management it shall be given when the party files the directions questionnaire and must be copied to all other parties (**para. 2.2(1)**). The general rule is that the court will not take such information into account unless the document containing it either confirms that all parties have agreed that the information is correct and that it should be put before the court, or confirms that the party who has sent the document to the court has delivered a copy to all the other parties (**para. 2.2(2)**). Examples of information likely to assist the court are given by **para. 2.2(3)**, and include:

(a) whether any of the parties intends to apply for summary judgment or to strike out or for some other order that might dispose of the case or reduce the amount in dispute or the issues to be decided;

(b) whether any of the parties intends to make an additional claim or to apply to add another party;

(c) information about the steps taken and intended to be taken regarding preparing the evidence for trial; and

(d) suggested case management directions for the case.

FILING DIRECTIONS QUESTIONNAIRES

The date for filing directions questionnaires will be specified in the notice of proposed allocation served by the court under **CPR, r. 26.3(1)**. Once a notice of proposed allocation has been served, by **r. 26.3(6)**: | **42.17**

(a) each party must file at court, and serve on all other parties, the relevant directions questionnaire by no later than the date specified in it; and

(b) the date specified will be:

  (i) if the notice relates to the small claims track, at least 14 days; or

  (ii) if the notice relates to the fast track or multi-track, at least 28 days after the date when it is deemed to be served on the party in question.

The parties are not permitted to vary the date for complying with the notice of proposed allocation by agreement (**r. 26.3(6A)**).

Directions questionnaires: additional items

42.18   Documents that may need to be provided with, or shortly after, the directions questionnaire include:

(a) Any written request for a stay while the parties try to settle using ADR (**CPR, r. 26.4(1)**).

(b) Further information thought to be relevant to allocation or case management (**PD 26, para. 2.2(1)**).

(c) Draft directions (**PD 26, para. 2.2(3)(d); CPR, r. 29.4**).

(d) A list of issues (agreed or not agreed) is required in the Chancery Division (Chancery Guide, para. 15.7) and in Rolls Building cases on the shorter trials scheme (**PD 51N, para. 2.39**), and may be required in other courts.

(e) Any reply to the defence must be filed with the claimant's directions questionnaire (**r. 15.8(a)**). Where a claimant also needs to file a defence to counterclaim, the filing dates for the defence to counterclaim and the reply may differ. In this situation the court will normally order that the defence to counterclaim must be filed by the same date as the reply (**PD 15, para. 3.2A**). If no such order is made, the two statements of case may form separate documents.

(f) Any application to strike out or for summary judgment should be made before or on filing the applicant's directions questionnaire (**PD 26, para. 5.3(1)**).

(g) Where costs budgeting applies (see **chapter 43**) the costs budget will have to be filed either with the directions questionnaire (claims less than £50,000) or not later than 21 days before the first case management conference (claims over £50,000), see **CPR, r. 3.13(1)**.

(h) An agreed budget discussion report must be filed no later than seven days before the first case management conference where cost budgeting applies (**r. 3.13(2)**).

(i) In multi-track claims other than personal injury claims the parties will need to file disclosure reports not less than 14 days before the first case management conference (**r. 31.5(3)**), so should be regarded as part of the work involved in preparing the directions questionnaire.

(j) In shorter trials scheme claims, and some other specialist claims, lists of issues need to be exchanged and discussed before the first case management conference (see **42.34**).

Dispensing with directions questionnaires

42.19   Where a court hearing takes place (for example, on an application for an interim injunction or for summary judgment under **CPR, Part 24**) before the claim is allocated to a track, the court may at that hearing dispense with the need for the parties to file directions questionnaires, treat the hearing as an allocation hearing, make an order for allocation and give directions for case management (**PD 26, para. 2.4(a)**).

Cases where directions questionnaires are not used

42.20   Directions questionnaires are not used in Part 8 claims, because these cases are automatically allocated to the multi-track (see **42.26(f)** and Chancery Guide, para. 9.4). Nor are they, in general, used in specialist cases automatically allocated to the multi-track (the types of cases automatically allocated to the multi-track are mentioned at **42.26(g)**, and see, for example, **CPR, r. 60.6**, for claims in the TCC). Each specialist court has its own procedure dealing with case management at the allocation stage. In the TCC, for example, the court will send the parties a case management information sheet and a case management directions form (see **PD 60, para. 8.2 and app. A and B**). In the Commercial Court, within 14 days after service of the defence, the claimant must apply for a case management conference (**PD 58, para. 10.2**). The legal representatives for each party must liaise for the purpose of preparing a short case memorandum and an agreed list of important issues (with a separate section dealing with matters which are common ground between all or some of the parties), and the claimant's solicitors must prepare a case management bundle (**PD 58, para. 10.8**). Seven days before the case management conference each party must file a completed case management information sheet, in the form set out in the Admiralty and Commercial Courts Guide, app. 6, and it is this form that takes the place of the directions questionnaire (**PD 58, para. 10.7**). On the other hand, directions questionnaires are used in Chancery Division cases (Chancery Guide, para. 17.8).

FAILING TO FILE DIRECTIONS QUESTIONNAIRES

County Court money claims: automatic striking out

CPR, r. 26.3(7A), provides that if in a County Court money claim a party does not comply with the notice served under **r. 26.3(1)** by the date specified: **42.21**

(a) the court will serve a further notice on that party requiring them to comply, within seven days of service; and

(b) if that party fails to comply with the notice served under subparagraph (a), the party's statement of case will be struck out without further order of the court.

This is not the same as the notorious CCR, ord. 17, r. 11(9), under the pre-CPR rules, in that under **r. 26.3(7A)** there are two reminders from the court before striking out takes effect. However, there are obvious risks of satellite litigation over exactly when automatic striking out under **r. 26.3(7A)** takes effect, and on when it would be appropriate to grant relief from the sanction.

Rule 26.3(7A) is also likely to attract attention over whether it complies with the European Convention on Human Rights, **art. 6(1)**, on two grounds:

(a) whether it is both necessary and a proportionate response to the perceived public need; and

(b) striking out under **r. 26.3(7A)(b)**, without any judicial involvement, may be difficult to justify under the European Convention on Human Rights, **art. 6**.

The answer to these points may be that because striking out under **r. 26.3(7A)**, takes place without a hearing, the defaulting party may apply to set aside or revoke (under **r. 3.1(7)**), or to set aside or vary (under **r. 23.10(1)**), the striking out of their statement of case. That there is some such power is plainly assumed by **r. 26.3(10)**, see below. There are a number of problems with this. One is that there is no 'order' under **r. 26.3(7A)**. Striking out takes effect automatically, with no judge making any order, so there is no order to set aside or vary. The wording of **r. 26.3(10)** recognises there is no order when a claim is struck out under **r. 26.3(7A)**, but seems to misfire by simply assuming there is a power to set aside or vary. Secondly, it is possibly the case that **r. 26.3(10)** is contemplating the use of the power to set aside or vary under **r. 3.3(5)**. Again, this depends on the court having made an order on its own initiative (**r. 3.3(4)**).

Where striking out occurs under **r. 26.3(7A)**, the more natural approach for the defaulting party is to apply for relief from sanctions under **r. 3.9**. As discussed in **chapter 48**, a defaulting party is unlikely to meet with a tolerant response from the court.

By the amended **r. 26.3(10)**, where a case has been struck out under **r. 26.3(7A)(b)**, a party who was in default will not normally be entitled to an order for the costs of any application to set aside or vary that order and will, unless the court thinks it unjust to do so, be ordered to pay the costs that the default caused to any other party.

High Court specified money claims: default in filing directions questionnaire

From 22 April 2014, **CPR, r. 26.3(8)**, provides that if a party does not comply with the notice   **42.22**
served under **r. 26.3(1)** in a High Court specified money claim by the date specified, the court will make such order as it considers appropriate, including:

(a) an order for directions;

(b) an order striking out the claim;

(c) an order striking out the defence and entering judgment; or

(d) listing the case for a case management conference.

Where an order has been made under r. 26.3(8), a party who was in default will not normally be entitled to an order for the costs of any application to set aside or vary that order nor of attending any case management conference and will, unless the court thinks it unjust to do so, be ordered to pay the costs that the default caused to any other party (r. 26.3(10)). The court will almost certainly order the costs of the hearing to be paid by the party in default on the indemnity basis, usually with a summary assessment of those costs and an order for them to be paid forthwith or within a stated period (PD 26, para. 6.6(2)).

Non-money claims and High Court damages claims

42.23   From 22 April 2014, the sanctions for not filing directions questionnaires set out in CPR, r. 26.3(7A) and (8) apply to County Court money claims and High Court claims for specified amounts. This means there are no specific sanctions laid down by the CPR for failing to file directions questionnaires by the deadline for non-money claims in both the High Court and County Court or for High Court damages claims. This is probably a drafting error. Between 1 April 2013 and 21 April 2014 r. 26.3(7A) applied to designated money claims, and r. 26.3(8) applied to non-designated money claims, so all civil claims were covered. The drafting defect has arisen through changing the designated money claim terminology in r. 26.3(7A), and by defining the ambit of r. 26.3(8) by reference to r. 26.2, which has been cut down to only covering High Court claims for specified amounts. This means that a sanction for not filing a directions questionnaire in these cases will only arise if the court makes an order with a sanction in an individual case.

ALLOCATION HEARING

42.24   The court may hold an allocation hearing if it thinks it is necessary (CPR, r. 26.5(4); PD 26, para. 6.1). If the solicitors are not local, this is often organised as a telephone hearing. Alternatively, the court may treat any other interim hearing as an allocation hearing, the most likely candidates being applications for summary judgment and interim injunctions. At such a hearing the procedural judge will consider which track will be most suitable for the case, bearing in mind its financial value and the other factors set out at 42.27, and give suitable case management directions. Consequently, the person attending for the parties should, if possible, be the person responsible for the case. In any event, the representative must be familiar with the case, be able to provide the court with the information it is likely to require, and have sufficient authority to deal with any issues that are likely to arise (PD 26, para. 6.5).

If an allocation hearing was listed because one of the parties was in default of the requirement to file a directions questionnaire, and that party fails to attend the hearing, the court will usually make an order specifying the steps which that party is required to take, and providing that unless those steps are taken within stated periods of time that party's statement of case will be struck out (PD 26, para. 6.6(3)).

Allocation at case management conference

42.25   Alternatively, the court may convene a case management conference for the purpose of allocating the claim to a track and for making case management directions. Although it may not be the intention in a particular case, often the need to hold an allocation hearing implies that one or more of the parties are in default in relation to directions questionnaires. Listing the case for a case management conference tends to avoid this implication.

Where a case is listed for a case management conference the parties will also need to comply with:

(a) the costs budgeting requirements in most multi-track claims (see **chapter 43**); and

(b) the requirement to serve and file disclosure reports in non-personal injuries multi-track claims (see **chapter 50**).

TRACK ALLOCATION DECISION

The usual position is that the procedural judge will decide which track to allocate a case to **42.26** when all parties have filed their directions questionnaires, or when giving directions under **CPR, r. 26.3(8)** (**r. 26.5(1)**, and see **42.22**). There are some additional provisions dealing with track allocation in special cases, as follows:

(a) In cases where there is a stay for settlement (see **42.62**), allocation is dealt with at the end of the period of the stay (**r. 26.5(2)**).

(b) In cases which are sent to a County Court hearing centre or automatically transferred, allocation decisions are taken after the transfer takes place and are made by a procedural judge of the destination court.

(c) In cases which could be allocated either to the fast track or to the multi-track, allocation decisions are usually taken in the court where the proceedings are commenced, but occasionally they will be transferred to the appropriate civil trial centre for allocation and directions.

(d) Where a claimant enters a default judgment for an amount of money to be decided by the court or for the value of goods or the amount of interest to be decided by the court, the case will not be 'defended' in that a defence will not have been filed. These cases therefore are not governed by the standard track allocation provisions. Instead, when judgment is entered the court will give any necessary directions and will, if appropriate, allocate the case to one of the three tracks (**r. 12.7(2)(b)**). These cases are considered further at **42.67**.

(e) When judgment is entered for damages to be decided on an admission by the defendant in a claim for money that has not been specified, then, as in (d), the court will give any necessary directions and, if appropriate, allocate the case to one of the three tracks (**r. 14.8**). These cases are also considered at **42.67**.

(f) Part 8 claims are treated as allocated to the multi-track (**r. 8.9(c)**). Nevertheless, the court can allocate a Part 8 claim to a different track when giving directions (see **rr. 8.1(3)** and **8.8(2)** and **PD 8A, para. 8.2**).

(g) Most types of specialist proceedings are treated as allocated to the multi-track. This includes claims in the Commercial Court (**CPR, r. 58.13(1)**), mercantile claims (**r. 59.11(1)**), claims allocated to the Technology and Construction Court (**r. 60.6(1)**), Admiralty Court claims (**r. 61.1(3)**, applying **Part 58**), arbitration claims (**r. 62.7(2)**), claims retained at the Royal Courts of Justice in the Queen's Bench Division (Queen's Bench Guide, para. 6.5.8), intellectual property claims under **CPR, Part 63** (**r. 63.1(3)**), directors disqualification proceedings (**PD Directors Disqualification Proceedings, para. 2.1**) and insolvency proceedings (Insolvency Rules 1986 (SI 1986/1925), **r. 7.51(2)**)). Proceedings under the Companies Acts are governed by **PD 49A**. This does not expressly refer to track allocation. However, most cases governed by **PD 49A** must be commenced by Part 8 claim form (**PD 49A, para. 5**), and so are allocated to the multi-track by **CPR, r. 8.9(c)**.

ALLOCATION RULES

The primary rules for track allocation are based on the financial value of the claim. Claims **42.27** with a value up to £10,000 are usually allocated to the small claims track, claims between £10,000 and £25,000 are allocated to the fast track, and claims valued at over £25,000 are allocated to the multi-track. Monetary values for this purpose are calculated disregarding any amount not in dispute, any claim for interest or costs, and also disregarding any allegation of contributory negligence (**CPR, r. 26.8(2)**). It is for the court to assess the financial value of the claim, though it will take into account the way in which the claim is formulated in the particulars of claim and any information given in the directions questionnaire. Any sum for which the defendant does not admit liability is in dispute, but the court will not regard the following as in dispute (**PD 26, para.** 7.4):

(a) sums for which summary judgment on a part of a claim has been entered;
(b) any distinct items in the claim for which the defendant has admitted liability; and
(c) any distinct items in the claim which have been agreed between the parties.

Generally claims are allocated in accordance with their financial value, but a claim may be allocated to a track which is not the one normally appropriate to its value if the procedural judge decides that it can be dealt with more justly on that other track, taking into account a number of factors set out in **CPR, r. 26.8** (see **42.32**).

Until 1 April 2013 the court had no power to allocate a case to a track lower than that indicated by the claim's financial value unless all the parties consented. **Rule 26.7(3)**, which set this out, was removed from the CPR by the Civil Procedure (Amendment) Rules 2013, r. 7(g). This means that the court can insist on a claim being allocated to a lower track than indicated by its value regardless of the wishes of the parties. It may do so where the claim is a straightforward one and suitable for a lower track despite its financial value. **PD 26, para.** 8.1(2), says the court will not normally allow more than one day for the hearing of a claim which is allocated to the small claims track even though it has a financial value above the small claims track limits set out in **r. 26.6(2)**. The implication is that if a claim needs more than a day for the hearing, normally it will not be allocated to the small claims track.

Small claims track

42.28   The small claims track is intended to provide a proportionate procedure for the most straightforward types of cases, such as consumer disputes, small accident claims, disputes about the ownership of goods, and landlord and tenant cases other than opposed claims under **CPR, Part 56**, disputed claims for possession under **Part 55**, and demotion claims (**PD 26, para.** 8.1(1)(c)). This is the normal track for defended claims with a value not exceeding £10,000 (**CPR, r. 26.6(3)**).

Although most claims under £10,000 will end up in the small claims track, the following types of claim will not normally be allocated there even if they have a value under £10,000:

(a) personal injuries cases where the value of the claim for pain, suffering and loss of amenity exceeds £1,000 (**r. 26.6(1)(a) and (2)**);
(b) claims by tenants of residential premises seeking orders that their landlords should carry out repairs or other works to the premises where the value of the claim exceeds £1,000 (**r. 26.6(1)(b)**);
(c) claims by residential tenants seeking damages against their landlords for harassment or unlawful eviction (**r. 26.7(4)**); and
(d) claims involving a disputed allegation of dishonesty (**PD 26, para.** 8.1(1)(d)).

Even if the claim is worth less than £10,000 there may be other reasons why it should not be allocated to the small claims track. One relates to expert evidence, which is not allowed in small claims track cases, either by calling an expert at the hearing or simply relying on an expert's report, unless the court gives permission (**CPR, r. 27.5**). Although permission may be granted, there are also severe restrictions on the costs recoverable for expert evidence in small claims track cases, including a limit of £750 for each expert's fees (**PD 27, para.** 7.3(2) and see also **CPR, r. 35.4(3A) and (4)**), which may make it unjust for a small case which requires expert evidence to be allocated to the small claims track.

An explanatory note following **PD 26, para. 7.4**, is to the effect that if, in relation to a claim with a value above the small claims limit of £10,000, the defendant makes an admission before allocation reducing the amount in dispute below £10,000, the normal track for the claim will be the small claims track. Where such an admission is made, it may be in the interests of the claimant to apply for judgment on the admission under **CPR, Part 14**, in order to recover costs, although even in such an application recovery of costs will be discretionary (see **r. 44.4(3)**).

If the claim is worth more than £10,000, the parties may consent to it being allocated to the small claims track (**r. 26.7(3)**). However, the court retains control, and may refuse to allocate the case in accordance with the parties' wishes if it feels the case is not suitable for the small claims track (**PD 26, para. 8.1(2)(b)**). For example, it is unlikely to agree to a case being allocated to the small claims track if the hearing is likely to take more than a day (**PD 26, para. 8.1(2)(c)**). If the court agrees with the parties and allocates the case to the small claims track, the small claims track costs provisions apply unless the parties agree that the fast track costs provisions should apply (**CPR, r. 27.14(5)**). Where the parties agree that the fast track costs provisions are to apply, the claim and any appeal will be treated as if it were proceeding on the fast track.

Fast track

The fast track is the normal track for cases broadly falling into the £10,000 to £25,000 **42.29** bracket, and which can be disposed of by a trial which will not exceed a day. For proceedings issued before 6 April 2009, the upper limit of the fast-track bracket is £15,000 (**CPR, r. 26.6(4)(b)(ii)**), and for claims issued before 1 April 2013 the lower threshold is £5,000.

There are two factors for deciding whether the fast track is the normal track for defended cases that are not allocated to the small claims track. The first factor, financial value (**CPR, r. 26.6(1) to (4)**), is to the effect that the following cases will normally be allocated to the fast track:

(a) personal injuries cases with a financial value between £10,000 and £25,000;

(b) personal injuries cases with an overall value under £10,000, but where the damages for pain, suffering and loss of amenity are likely to exceed £1,000;

(c) claims by residential tenants for orders requiring their landlords to carry out repairs or other work to the premises where the financial value of the claim is between £1,000 and £25,000;

(d) claims by residential tenants for damages against their landlords for harassment or unlawful eviction where the financial value of the claim does not exceed £25,000; and

(e) other categories of cases where the financial value of the claim is between £10,000 and £25,000.

The second factor, disposal at trial (**r. 26.6(5)**), is to the effect that cases falling within the normal limits for allocation to the fast track must also be likely to be disposed of by a trial lasting no more than a day, and with oral expert evidence limited to experts in no more than two expert fields and to one expert per party per field of expertise. The possibility that the trial might last longer than a day (which in this context means five hours) is not necessarily a conclusive reason for allocating a case to the multi-track (**PD 26, para. 9.1(3)(c)**), though in practice such cases are almost always so allocated, because on the fast track there will be no costs allowed beyond the first day. The assessment of likely trial length and the nature of the expert evidence necessary usually has to be made in the early stages of the proceedings, although it can arise again on a subsequent application to reallocate the case.

Multi-track

The multi-track is the normal track for claims not falling within the rules in 42.28 and 42.29 **42.30** for allocation to either the small claims or fast tracks (**CPR, r. 26.6(6)**). Typically these will be cases involving claims exceeding £25,000, and cases worth less than that sum where the trial is likely to exceed a day. Complex and important cases may be allocated to the multi-track even if they have a monetary value below £25,000, see the discretionary factors discussed at **42.32**.

Claims with no monetary value

42.31 Claims with no financial value will be allocated to the track which the procedural judge considers to be most suitable to enable it to be dealt with justly, taking into account the factors discussed at **42.32** (**CPR, r. 26.7(2)**). In these cases the importance of careful completion of the directions questionnaire cannot be overemphasised.

Discretionary factors

42.32 In addition to the financial value of the claim (if it has one), when deciding which track to allocate it to the court is required to have regard to the following factors (**CPR, r. 26.8**):

(a) the nature of the remedy sought;

(b) the likely complexity of the facts, law or evidence;

(c) the number of parties or likely parties;

(d) the value of any counterclaim or other additional claim and the complexity of any matters relating to those claims (the court will not aggregate the sums claimed in the claim, counterclaim and so on, but will generally simply look at the value of the largest of the cross-claims: **PD 26, para. 7.7**). Where a claim with a value under the small claims threshold is allocated to the multi-track because of the alleged value of a counterclaim, the defendant may be penalised in costs if the counterclaim is found to be inflated. See *Peakman v Linbrooke Services Ltd* [2008] EWCA Civ 1239, LTL 13/11/2008, where an order that the defendant should pay 50 per cent of the claimant's costs after allocation was substituted for no order as to costs for this reason;

(e) the amount of oral evidence which may be required;

(f) the importance of the claim to persons who are not parties to the proceedings;

(g) the views expressed by the parties, which will be regarded as important, though not binding on the court (**PD 26, para. 7.5**); and

(h) the circumstances of the parties.

These factors are not exclusive, and the court exercises its discretion taking into account all the circumstances including the nature of the case as disclosed by the statements of case and other relevant information provided by the parties. Complex claims are usually allocated to the multi-track, partly for case management reasons, and partly to ensure they are tried by a sufficiently senior judge. In practice, the following types of cases are allocated to the multi-track even if the amount at stake was within the normal financial value for allocation to the fast track:

(a) cases involving issues of public importance;

(b) test cases;

(c) medical negligence cases; and

(d) cases where there is a right to trial by jury, including deceit cases.

Other professional negligence cases and building cases that fall within the financial parameters of the fast track vary considerably in complexity, and should be allocated to the most suitable track depending on the complexity of each case.

From time to time novel issues arise in otherwise fairly usual personal injuries claims which in practice involve considerable case handling complexities. Ultimately it is for the procedural judge to decide on the track allocation for these cases, but it would not be wrong for them to be allocated to the multi-track even if the value of an individual claim is considerably less than £25,000. An example is *Kearsley v Klarfeld* [2005] EWCA Civ 1510, [2006] 2 All ER 303, a low-impact road traffic accident, in which the defendant alleged that the claimant's alleged injuries could not possibly have been caused in a crash where the vehicles were travelling at less than 3 mph.

Chancery Division tracks

42.33 Since 5 March 2015 there have been four case management tracks in the Chancery Division (see *New Case Management Tracks in Chancery* at https://www.judiciary.gov.uk/publications/chancery-division/, referred to in the Chancery Guide at para. 17.9). These are:

(a) case management by a Master or Registrar, with trial by a judge;
(b) full docketing to a particular judge (see **42.54**);
(c) case management and trial by a Master or Registrar; and
(d) partnership management, under which the prospective trial judge works with a specified Master or Registrar.

Shorter trials scheme

42.34 In the Rolls Building courts (the Chancery Division, Commercial Court, London Mercantile Court and TCC) there is a three-year shorter trials pilot scheme running from 1 October 2015 (**PD 51N, paras 1.2** and **2**). For claims in the scheme, **PD 51N** prevails over other provisions of the CPR and PDs (**para. 1.3**). This scheme is usually suitable for cases where the trial will not exceed four days (including reading time) which do not include allegations of fraud or dishonesty, and which do not require extensive disclosure and/or reliance upon extensive witness or expert evidence (**paras 2.3** and **2.4**). There is a shortened pre-action protocol approach for these cases (see **8.98**). Claims may be started in the shorter trials scheme by issuing the claim in the appropriate Rolls Building Registry and marking the claim form in the top right-hand corner with 'Shorter Trials Scheme' after the name of the court (**paras 2.8** and **2.9**). Claims may be transferred into the scheme by making an application (**paras 2.10** to **2.15**).

Particulars of claim in shorter trials scheme cases should normally be no more than 20 pages long (**para. 2.23**). In addition to complying with **CPR, r. 16.4**, particulars of claim should include a brief summary of the dispute and identify the anticipated issues, and a full statement of the relief or remedies claimed with detailed calculations of any sums claimed (**PD 51N, para. 2.22**). The claim form and particulars of claim, accompanied by a bundle of core documents, should be filed and served promptly after the 14-day period for the defendant's response to the letter before claim (**paras 2.20, 2.24** and **2.25**). The defendant is required to file an acknowledgment of service (**para. 2.27**), followed within 28 days of acknowledgment by the defence and any counterclaim (**para. 2.30**). The defence should not exceed 20 pages; must state whether it is agreed the case is suitable for the shorter trials scheme and, where these differ from the claimant's version, a summary of the dispute and the defendant's version of the anticipated issues; and be accompanied by any additional core documents relied upon by the defendant (**paras 2.31** to **2.33**). Any reply and defence to counterclaim must be served within 14 days thereafter (**para. 2.35**). If a case is transferred into the scheme, the court will consider whether it is necessary to order that existing statements of case should be amended to comply with these requirements (**para. 2.15A**).

Promptly after serving the claim form and particulars of claim, the claimant must take steps to fix a case management conference for a date approximately, but not less than, 12 weeks after the date for filing the acknowledgment of service (**para. 2.26**). A designated judge will be allocated to the case at the time of the first case management conference, or earlier if necessary (**para. 2.5**). Normally this will be a full judge, but in the Chancery Division a case may be tried by a Master with the consent of the parties (**para. 2.6(c)**). Before the case management conference the parties must use their best endeavours to discuss and agree a draft list of issues (**para. 2.39**). Approval of this list is one of the functions of the case management conference, as well as giving directions for trial (**para. 2.40**). Save in exceptional circumstances, the court

Commentary

will not permit a party to submit material at trial in addition to that permitted at the case management conference or by later court order (**para. 2.52**). Time limits set by the case management conference may be extended by the parties by agreement by up to seven days. Any extension beyond seven days is by court order and only for good reason (**para. 2.51**). Costs management does not apply to cases on the shorter trials scheme unless the parties otherwise agree (**para. 2.58**).

Menu disclosure (**CPR, r. 31.5(2)**) and the duty to make a reasonable search (**r. 31.7**) do not apply to claims on the shorter trials scheme (**PD 51N, para. 2.41**). Instead, the usual position is that the parties will be ordered to disclose the documents they intend to rely upon (i.e. less than standard disclosure) in a list of documents, together with documents requested by the other side (the court may need to rule on whether such requests are reasonable and proportionate at the case management conference). Applications for specific disclosure are discouraged. See **paras 2.42 to 2.45**.

Witness statements and experts' reports will be limited to the approved issues. Witness statements should, unless there is a good reason, be limited to 25 pages. See **paras 2.46 to 2.48**. A pre-trial review will be fixed at the case management conference. At the pre-trial review the court will fix the timetable for the trial (**paras 2.40(f) and 2.53**).

While the case management conference and pre-trial review will be given oral hearings, other interim applications will usually be dealt with on the papers in accordance with standard directions set out in **para. 2.50**.

Trial judges will manage trials on the scheme to ensure the trial estimate is adhered to (**para. 2.55**). Cross-examination will be strictly controlled, and it is only necessary for parties to put the principal parts of their case to witnesses (unless the court directs otherwise) (**paras 2.55 and 2.56**). Judgments will normally be handed down within six weeks of the trial (**para. 2.57**).

Within 21 days of the conclusion of the trial all the parties are required to file and simultaneously exchange schedules of their costs. These should contain sufficient detail on each of the phases in the usual costs budget (Precedent H) to enable the trial judge to make a summary assessment of costs (**paras. 2.59 to 2.61**).

Flexible trials scheme

42.35   In the Rolls Building courts (the Chancery Division, Commercial Court, London Mercantile Court and TCC) there is a three-year flexible trials pilot scheme running from 1 October 2015 (**PD 51N, paras 1.2 and 3**). An application to join the scheme, or for a variation on the scheme, should be made at the first case management conference (**paras 3.6 and 3.7**). For claims in the scheme, **PD 51N** prevails over other provisions of the CPR and PDs (**para. 1.3**). Standard disclosure is given in cases on the flexible trials scheme, but with documents within **CPR, r. 31.6(b)** and **(c)**, being limited to those known about without the need for a search (**PD 51N, para. 3.9(a)**). Any application for specific disclosure will be determined based on whether the documents are likely to have significant probative value, as well as reasonableness and proportionality (**PD 51N, para. 3.9(b)**). Witness evidence will be limited to identified issues or to identified witnesses, as directed at the case management conference (**para. 3.9(c)**). Expert evidence will be limited to identified issues, or as subsequently agreed by the parties or directed by the court (**para. 3.9(d)**). Submissions at trial will be made in writing with oral submissions and cross-examination subject to time limits (**para. 3.9(e)**). Where an issue is to be determined at trial on the basis of written evidence, it is not necessary for a party to put their case on that issue to the other side's witnesses (**para. 3.9(f)**). Where an issue is to be determined on the basis of oral evidence, it is only necessary for a party to put the principal parts of their case to the witnesses unless the court directs otherwise (**para. 3.9(f)**).

TRIAL IN THE ROYAL COURTS OF JUSTICE

In principle only the most important cases should be managed and tried in the Royal Courts **42.36**
of Justice as opposed to another civil trial centre, because only the most important cases justify
use of the resources of the Royal Courts of Justice. Thus, in general, cases with an estimated
value of less than £100,000 will be transferred out of the Royal Courts of Justice to the
County Court (**PD 29, para. 2.2**). Exceptions are listed in **11.4**.

NOTICE OF ALLOCATION

After the court has decided on the track to which a case is allocated, it will send a notice of **42.37**
allocation to the parties, together with copies of all relevant directions questionnaires and
further information provided by the other parties (**CPR, r. 26.9**). Several forms of notice of
allocation have been devised for different circumstances. There are four different forms for
cases allocated to the small claims track (N157 to N160), one for the fast track (N154) and
one for the multi-track (N155). Each has a space for allocation directions and for the judge's
reasons for the allocation decision.

ALLOCATION DIRECTIONS

The type of directions the court will make at the allocation stage depends on which track the **42.38**
case is allocated to, and the circumstances of the case. Typically the court will make standard
directions in small claims track cases (see **chapter** 45). In fast track and multi-track cases it will
consider making directions covering disclosure of documents, exchange of witness statements,
disclosure of experts' reports and narrowing the expert evidence issues, and listing the claim
for trial (see **chapters** 46 and 47). There are standard directions for fast track claims in the
appendix to **PD 28** and for multi-track claims on the Ministry of Justice website. In multi-track
cases the court will also consider whether to convene a case management conference or a
pre-trial review. Orders and directions imposing time limits must include the time and date
by which the step must be taken (**CPR, r. 2.9(1)**), see **63.8**.

Directions and proportionality

When making directions the court will be astute to apply the overriding objective in all its aspects. It **42.39**
will seek to ensure that the case is prepared properly so that the claim can be determined justly, but it
will also seek to avoid unnecessary expense. As discussed more fully in **chapter** 43, the court will have
regard to any available costs budgets, and will take into account the costs involved in taking each
procedural step, whenever it is making case management decisions (**CPR, r. 3.17(1)**). Information
provided by the parties in their costs budgets will be extremely valuable in assessing what steps are
required, and in what form, in order to progress the claim in a proportionate manner.

Directions timetables

Active case management by the courts, combined with the modern robust approach to **42.40**
compliance with deadlines, means it is essential that the timetable laid down by the court is
realistic. *Sir Rupert Jackson's starting point on enforcement of rules and directions* (*Review of
Civil Litigation Costs: Final Report*, para. 39.6.5) was: 'First, the courts should set realistic
timetables for cases and not impossibly tough timetables in order to give the impression of
firmness'. This was endorsed by Lord Dyson MR in *Denton v T. H. White Ltd* [2014] EWCA Civ
906, [2014] 1 WLR 3926 at [44]:

We should make clear that the culture of compliance that the new rules are intended to promote requires
that judges ensure that the directions that they give are realistic and achievable. It is no use imposing a

Commentary

tight timetable that can be seen at the outset to be unattainable. The court must have regard to the realities of litigation in making orders in the first place.

This marks a departure from previous practice, which was to impose discipline by setting a trial date or window which would not be moved unless there were exceptional circumstances (still present in **PD 28, para. 5.4(1)**, and **PD 29, para. 7.4(1)**), but with the dates for the other steps being little more than markers. Before the Civil Justice Reforms of 2013, dates for lists, witness statements, experts' reports etc. were typically given in conventional 14 and 28-day stages. Often difficulties in keeping to the timetable only become apparent when the parties start the work needed to comply. Where this happens, the duty to cooperate in **CPR, r. 1.4(2)(a)**, should mean that other parties will give their consent to reasonable requests for extensions (*Hallam Estates Ltd v Baker* [2014] EWCA Civ 661, [2014] CP Rep 38). In a climate where the deadline for every step in litigation is regarded as important, and potentially sounding in sanctions for non-compliance, there is an obligation on both the parties and the courts to ensure that proper thought is given to producing realistic deadlines based on the work needed in the case and the availability of experts and witnesses.

Where appropriate the court will seek to narrow the issues, or use its power under **CPR, r. 32.1**, to control the evidence that is prepared. A trial date or window is often set as part of allocation directions. It gives the parties a target date for the trial, enables witnesses (especially expert witnesses) to be warned at an early stage, and emphasises the fact that the court has control over the timetable. **CPR, r. 32.1**, gives the court a wide-ranging power to give directions about the issues on which it requires evidence, the nature of the evidence which it requires to decide those issues, and the way in which the evidence is to be placed before the court. The power under the rule may be used to exclude evidence that would otherwise be admissible (**r. 32.1(2)**; *Grobbelaar v Sun Newspapers Ltd* (1999) *The Times*, 12 August 1999). However, it is primarily a case management power designed to enable the court to stop cases getting out of hand (*Post Office Counters Ltd v Mahida* [2003] EWCA Civ 1583, *The Times*, 31 October 2003). See also the more detailed discussion at **49.9**. For directions in possession claims by local authorities against Gypsies, see *Hillingdon London Borough Council v Collins* [2008] EWHC 3016 (Admin), LTL 16/12/2008.

Powers available in cases of difficulty in compliance

42.41   The courts possess a range of powers to assist with the just disposal of civil claims, and to deal with cases of procedural default. These powers are:

(a) Setting aside, varying and staying orders made on the court's own initiative under **CPR, r. 3.3(5)(a)**, or where a person was not served with the application notice under **r. 23.10(1)**.

(b) Time applications for extending time for complying with provisions in orders, directions, rules and practice directions under **r. 3.1(2)(a)**; see **15.40, 42.46** to **42.52**.

(c) Time applications to abridge time for taking steps in litigation under **r. 3.1(2)(a)**; see **42.49**.

(d) Applications to extend the period of validity of a claim form under **r. 7.6**; see **15.30** to **15.34**.

(e) Miscellaneous case management powers are set out in **rr. 3.1(2)** and **25.1(1)**; see **32.33**.

(f) Applications to cure procedural irregularities under **r. 3.10**; see **15.23, 15.32** and **42.53**.

(g) The slip rule enabling the correction of slips and errors in orders and judgments under **r. 40.12(1)**, see **63.44**.

(h) Relief from sanctions under **r. 3.9**, see **chapter 48**.

(i) Appeals under **Part 52**, see **chapter 74**.

Applications to set aside, vary or stay orders may be made in two circumstances:

(a) when the original order was made by the court of its own initiative without hearing the parties or giving them an opportunity to make representations (**r. 3.3(4)**); and

(b) where a party can establish it did not receive the application notice for the hearing where the directions were made (**r. 23.10(1)**).

A party who is dissatisfied with the directions given in such circumstances must apply for the court to reconsider its decision, and the application will normally be heard by the same judge as gave the original directions (**PD 28, para. 4.3(4)(a)**; **PD 29, para. 6.3(4)(a)**). In both situations there is a seven-day time limit from the date the order is served (**CPR, rr. 3.3(6)(a)** and **23.10(2)**). The court will give the parties at least three clear days' notice of the hearing to reconsider the directions. At the hearing the court may confirm the original directions, or may make such different order as it thinks just.

A party who disagrees with the directions timetable laid down should either appeal or apply to the court for it to reconsider its directions (**PD 28, para. 4.3**; **PD 29, para. 6.3**). This may be necessary because the court will assume for the purposes of any later application that the parties were content that any case management directions given were correct in the circumstances existing when they were given, unless an appeal under **CPR, Part 52**, or application to vary or revoke under **r. 3.1(7)**, is made within 14 days (**PD 28, para. 4.2(2)**; **PD 29, para. 6.2(2)**; *Mitchell v News Group Newspapers Ltd* [2013] EWCA Civ 1537, [2014] 1 WLR 795 at [44]). Regarding appeals, the period should be 21 days. **PD 28** and **PD 29** were not amended when the time for appealing was increased from 14 to 21 days (see **CPR, r. 52.12(2)(b)**), and provisions in practice directions are subordinate to provisions in the **CPR**.

Orders and directions made at hearings attended by a party or his or her representative or regarding which the party was given due notice, should be appealed, whereas an application is necessary in relation to directions made of the court's own initiative (**PD 28, para. 4.3**; **PD 29, para. 6.3**). Where there are no changed circumstances, any review of directions made on notice has to be made by way of appeal (*Jameson v Lovis* [2001] EWCA Civ 1264, LTL 24/7/2001).

VARYING AND REVOKING ORDERS

Application to vary or revoke

The court has the power to vary or revoke a previous order made under a power conferred by the CPR (**CPR, r. 3.1(7)**). This power may be exercised on an application by a party or by the court on its own initiative (**PD 29, para. 3.4**). Applications under **CPR, r. 3.1(7)**, may arise in at least three situations: **42.42**

(a) where the original order was made by the court on its own initiative under **r. 3.3**;

(b) where the parties attended the original hearing, and one of the parties realises almost immediately after the event that the order made is not realistic;

(c) where the need to vary or revoke is based on circumstances arising some time after the original order.

In situation (a), **r. 3.3(5)** and **(6)** provide that an application to set aside, vary or stay an order made on the court's own initiative must be made within seven days after service of the order, or such other period as may be specified by the court. In situation (b), an application to vary or revoke under **r. 3.1(7)** should be made within 14 days (**PD 28, para. 4.2(2)**; **PD 29, para. 6.2(2)**). Some courts expressly abridge this period to seven days after service, to be consistent with **CPR, r. 3.3(5)**. In situation (c), **PD 28, para. 4.2(1)**, and **PD 29, para. 6.2(1)**, say it is essential that any party wanting to vary the directions timetable should take steps to do so as soon as possible.

A delay in making an essential application to vary the timetable may well have the effect of losing all the time used before the application is eventually heard, which is not going to be looked upon favourably given the objective of dealing with cases expeditiously (**CPR, r. 1.1(2)(d)**) and complying with court orders (**r. 1.1(2)(f)**). Obviously, parties should not feel forced into making speculative applications in relation to directions that are based on future events (such as requests for further information and questions to experts), and applications to extend these (and some of the other) time limits are dealt with realistically when the need arises.

Where an application under **r. 3.1(7)** is combined with an application for relief from sanctions under **r. 3.9**, the court should determine the application to vary or revoke first, which may mean there is no need to go on to consider the application for relief from sanctions (*Mitchell v News Group Newspapers Ltd* [2013] EWCA Civ 1537, [2014] 1 WLR 795 at [45]).

Varying or revoking final decisions is considered at **63.46**.

Grounds to vary or revoke

42.43 Upholding the finality of decisions, the policy against giving litigants a second bite of the cherry, and supporting the appeals system, all point towards a restrictive approach to applications under **r. 3.1(7)**. *Tibbles v SIG plc* [2012] EWCA Civ 518, [2012] 1 WLR 2591 (approved in *Thevarajah v Riordan* [2015] UKSC 78, [2016] 1 WLR 76 at [15]) held that a court will normally only exercise this power where:

(a) there has been a material change of circumstances—this should be established by evidence, or possibly argument (*Edwards v Golding* [2007] EWCA Civ 416, *The Times*, 22 May 2007);
(b) the facts on which the original order was made were misstated. This will cover cases of material non-disclosure (see **32.9**). It can also cover inadvertent errors, an example being *Newland Shipping and Forwarding Ltd v Toba Trading FZC* [2014] EWHC 210 (Comm), [2014] 2 Costs LR 279, where an order was varied to reflect the correct figure claimed; and
(c) there has been a manifest mistake on the part of the judge in formulating the original order.

These criteria apply both to an express application to vary or revoke an earlier order, and to an application which effectively requires an earlier order to be varied or rescinded (*Thevarajah v Riordan* [2015] UKSC 78, [2016] 1 WLR 76 at [18]). Courts act with considerable caution before making substantial variations in previous directions (such as cancelling previous directions for the trial of a preliminary issue), because doing so comes close to overruling the decision-making process of the earlier directions hearing. Whether a substantial variation should be allowed depends on the circumstances of the case, and an application of the overriding objective (*Umm Qarn Management Co. Ltd v Bunting* [2001] CPLR 21).

In addition to the three categories identified in *Tibbles v SIG plc*, it is suggested that the power to vary or revoke in **r. 3.1(7)** may also properly be exercised in the following situations:

(a) where the original order was made on a without notice application (see **37.71**);
(b) where a party does not attend (see **62.1**); and
(c) where a third party is adversely affected by an order made in his or her absence (**r. 40.9** and see **37.71** and **38.31**).

It is clear that **r. 3.1(7)** cannot be used to have a second attempt relying on the same evidence as on the first application, or where additional evidence or submissions are to be deployed which were available but for whatever reason not used on the first application (*Collier v Williams* [2006] EWCA Civ 20, [2006] 1 WLR 1945 at [39]–[40]). In such a case the only available route is to appeal (*Jameson v Lovis* [2001] EWCA Civ 1264, LTL 24/7/2001).

Material change of circumstances

42.44 Confirming principle (a) in **42.43**, a court may vary previous directions without the need for an appeal where there has been a change of circumstances (**PD 28, para. 4.4; PD 29,**

para. 6.4). The phrase most commonly used is that there must be a material change of circumstances. If there has been a real change in circumstances there is usually no objection to the court reviewing previous directions, but merely rectifying a previous default is not enough. In *Thevarajah v Riordan* [2015] UKSC 78, [2016] 1 WLR 76, the defaulting parties produced evidence that they had been misled by their former solicitors into believing that the solicitors had complied with an earlier unless order. The Supreme Court held that late compliance with an unless order after the deadline had expired was not a change in circumstances. Neither is realising the consequences of an order (*Apex Global Management v Global Torch Ltd* [2013] EWHC 3478 (Ch), LTL 29/11/2013. This case also reached the Supreme Court as *Global Torch Ltd v Apex Global Management Ltd (No. 2)* [2014] UKSC 64, [2014] 1 WLR 4495). *Bass Taverns Ltd v Carford Catering Equipment Ltd* [2002] EWCA Civ 671, LTL 23/4/2002, which decided that the production of extra evidence was a change of circumstances, will probably only be followed where the applicant is not at fault in not producing the evidence for the earlier hearing.

The change in the approach to procedural default between *Mitchell v News Group Newspapers Ltd* [2013] EWCA Civ 1537, [2014] 1 WLR 795 and *Denton v T. H. White Ltd* [2014] EWCA Civ 906, [2014] 1 WLR 3926 (see **48.31** and **48.32**) was regarded as a material change in circumstances in *Michael Wilson and Partners Ltd v Sinclair* [2015] EWCA Civ 774, [2015] CP Rep 45.

Each case turns on its own facts, with the court seeking to give effect to the overriding objective, but if there has been a change of circumstances it may well be appropriate to interfere with the procedural regime previously laid down (*Umm Qarn Management Co. Ltd v Bunting* [2001] CPLR 21). It is only if there is a significant change in circumstances that a case management decision can be revisited on a later occasion (*Jameson v Personal Representatives of Smith* [2001] EWCA Civ 1264, [2001] CPLR 489). It is incumbent on a party to claim interim relief based on the same facts once and once only (*Halifax plc v Chandler* [2001] EWCA Civ 1750, [2002] CPLR 41, where there were two applications to vary a freezing injunction). In *Leadmill Ltd v Omare* [2002] EWHC 1226 (Ch), LTL 23/4/2002, an interim injunction was granted restraining the defendant from calling his tapas bar 'The Treadmill', being sited close to the claimant's nightclub, 'The Leadmill'. The defendant applied to discharge the order on the basis he intended to change the colour and font of his signs. It was held that the defendant could have raised this at the initial hearing. As afterthoughts are not permitted, the application was refused.

Consequential orders after revocation

Where an order is set aside, the court has a discretion to preserve the effect or protection **42.45** of steps taken between the original order and setting aside (*Raja v Van Hoogstraten (No. 9)* [2007] EWHC 1743 (Ch), *The Times*, 23 August 2007, [2008] EWCA Civ 1444, [2009] 1 WLR 1143 at [104]–[105]).

EXTENDING AND ABRIDGING TIME

Party agreement to extend time

The parties are required to help the court to further the overriding objective (**CPR, r. 1.3**) **42.46** and the court must encourage the parties to cooperate with each other in the conduct of proceedings (**r. 1.4(2)(a)**). If a party falls a little behind on the directions timetable, one would expect the other side to assist by agreeing to a slight revision to the timetable, rather than insisting on strict compliance. The general rule is that agreements to extend the times laid down in directions may be agreed in writing between the parties (**r. 2.11**) without needing to inform the court (**PD 28, para. 4.5(1)**, and **PD 29, para. 6.5(1)**) or to file anything in court. Agreements about changes to disclosure directions under **CPR, rr. 31.5, 31.10(8)** and **31.13**, need to be made in writing and filed at court (**PD 28, para. 4.5(1)**, and **PD 29, para. 6.5(1)**).

Extensions of time requiring court permission

42.47   In the following situations an extension of time under **CPR, r. 3.1(2)(a)**, can only be granted with the court's permission:

(a)   Where a direction (or rule or practice direction) requires a party to do something within a specified time and specifies a consequence for failure to comply, subject to **r. 3.8(4)**, time cannot be extended by agreement between the parties, but only by an order of the court (**r. 3.8(3)**). Under **r. 3.8(4)**, time for compliance with unless orders etc. covered by **r. 3.8(3)** may be extended by consent without the need for court permission provided:
   (i)   the court does not make an order preventing the parties agreeing an extension;
   (ii)   the time for complying with the order has not expired;
   (iii)   the extension is agreed in writing;
   (iv)   the extension does not exceed 28 days; and
   (v)   the extension does not put at risk any hearing date.
(b)   In fast track claims court permission is required to vary the date for the return of a pre-trial checklist, the trial, or the trial period (r. 28.4(1)), or which would make it necessary to vary any of these dates (r. 28.4(2)).
(c)   In multi-track claims court permission is required to vary the date for a case management conference, a pre-trial review, the return of a pre-trial checklist, the trial, or the trial period (r. 29.5(1)), or which would make it necessary to vary any of these dates (r. 29.5(2)).

Paragraphs (b) and (c) above set out what may be described as 'key dates' in fast track and multi-track directions that can only be changed with the court's permission. They are dates which will have been diarised by the court, so the court needs to be involved if they are to be changed.

Consensual variation of 'key dates'

42.48   If the parties agree to a variation of any of the key dates in the case management timetable as laid down by the court, they must apply for an order by consent, file a draft of the order sought, and also file an agreed statement of the reasons why the variation is sought (**PD 29, para. 6.5(2)**). If the procedural judge is satisfied with the stated reasons, an order will be made without a hearing, either in the terms agreed or as thought fit by the procedural judge. Otherwise, the application will be listed for hearing, at which the parties will need to justify their position.

Applying to extend or abridge time

42.49   The court has a general power to extend and abridge time (**CPR, r. 3.1(2)(a)**). The rule expressly says the power can be exercised even if the application is made after the time for compliance has expired. The court can extend time on an application or on its own initiative under **rr. 3.1(2)(a)** and **3.3**, and this is so even where the extension relates to an unless order (*Keen Phillips v Field* [2006] EWCA Civ 1524, [2007] 1 WLR 686). The power to extend time may be exercised even where a rule says a step 'must' be taken within a stated period (*USF Ltd v Aqua Technology Hanson NV/SA* (2001) LTL 31/1/2001). It is wrong to use the **r. 3.1(2)(a)** power to extend time for the purpose of nullifying the effect of a mandatory provision in the CPR (*Walker Residential Ltd v Davis* [2005] EWHC 3483 (Ch), LTL 9/12/2005). There is a general power to impose conditions (**r. 3.1(3)**).

The power to extend time in **r. 3.1(2)(a)** is wide enough to enable the court to extend the time for compliance with the provisions of an order previously made by the same court (*Omega Engineering Inc. v Omega SA* [2003] EWHC 1482 (Ch), *The Times*, 29 September 2003).

Principles on in-time applications to extend time

42.50   There is a fundamental difference between applying for an extension of time before a time limit has expired, and seeking relief from a sanction after the event (*Robert v Momentum Services*

Ltd [2003] EWCA Civ 299, [2003] 1 WLR 1577; *Hallam Estates Ltd v Baker* [2014] EWCA Civ 661, [2014] CP Rep 38). An application is made when the application notice is received by the court, probably with the necessary fee etc., even if the application notice is not issued or heard until later (**CPR, r. 23.5**; *Robert v Momentum Services Ltd*).

No guidance is given in **r. 3.1(2)(a)** on the principles to be applied, which means the court must consider all the circumstances of the particular case. The principle that a discretion must be exercised judicially means that the power must be exercised in a broadly similar way in similar cases (*R (Hysaf) Secretary of State for the Home Department* [2014] EWCA Civ 1633, [2015] 1 WLR 2472 at [24]). On an in-time application for an extension the court will apply the overriding objective, which includes taking into account the need to enforce compliance with rules, practice directions and orders (**r. 1.1(2)(f)**; *Re Guidezone Ltd* [2014] EWHC 1165 (Ch), [2014] 1 WLR 3728). Important considerations are whether there is any prejudice caused to the other side, and whether the date for any hearing will be affected. These applications are not governed by the restrictions in *Mitchell v News Group Newspapers Ltd* [2013] EWCA Civ 1537, [2014] 1 WLR 795 (*Hallam Estates Ltd v Baker*). **Rule 1.1(2)(f)** does not require the court to refuse a reasonable request for an extension of time which neither imperils a hearing date nor disrupts the proceedings (*Hallam Estates Ltd v Baker* at [31]).

Time may be extended where the original order was made by consent. The fact that a deadline was agreed is simply one of the circumstances to be taken into account (*Pannone LLP v Aardvark Digital Ltd* [2011] EWCA Civ 803, [2011] 1 WLR 2275).

Extensions after time has expired

Although an application to extend time under **CPR, r. 3.1(2)(a)**, can be made after the time **42.51** for compliance has expired, such an application may also raise the question of relief from sanctions (see **chapter 48**). Whether this is so depends on whether the order, rule or practice direction imposes a sanction for non-compliance (**rr. 3.8 and 3.9**). Even where there is no express sanction, the need to consider all the circumstances of the case may mean that in some cases the discretion in **r. 3.1(2)(a)** has to be applied in a similar way to applications for relief from sanctions (*R (Hysaf) Secretary of State for the Home Department* [2014] EWCA Civ 1633, [2015] 1 WLR 2472 at [24]). The most obvious example is an application to extend the time for appealing, see **74.22**. There are comments in *Elliott v Stobart Group Ltd* [2015] EWCA Civ 449, [2015] CP Rep 36 at [35] that the need to consider all the circumstances of the case under **r. 3.1(2)(a)** in the context of an application to extend time in the absence of an unless order for disclosure of expert evidence was ultimately little different from the need to consider all the circumstances of the case at stage 3 of the test in *Denton v T. H. White Ltd* [2014] EWCA Civ 906, [2014] 1 WLR 3926 under **r. 3.9(1)**. While the phrases are the same, there is a fundamental difference between the circumstances of a case where no sanction is imposed for breach of the order in question and one where there is. In the latter the sanction is stated to bring home to the parties the particular importance of compliance with that specific requirement, which elevates breach to a higher level (see **48.7**).

Any significant departure from the timetable is likely to be penalised in accordance with the need to enforce compliance with court orders as part of the overriding objective (**r. 1.1(2)(f)**). A party who is late in taking a particular step and who has not yet taken it may be treated differently from a party who has been late in taking a step but has rectified the position.

Impact on trial date

Any party unable to keep to the timetable has to explain to the court why the case may not be **42.52** ready for the set trial date or window and should understand that the court may refuse to vacate the date set for the trial unless there are exceptional circumstances (**PD 28, para. 5.4(1); PD 29, para. 7.4(1)**). An application made very close to the trial may be refused where its effect would be unfair on the other party (*Calenti v North Middlesex NHS Trust* (2001) LTL 10/4/2001). The *Denton* appeal in *Denton v T. H. White Ltd* [2014] EWCA Civ 906, [2014] 1 WLR 3926, was a case where a month before trial the claimant sought to introduce additional witness statements in support of an unpleaded point which had been raised a year earlier in an expert's report. Giving permission to adduce this evidence, which resulted in adjourning the trial, was held to be an impermissible exercise of the court's case management powers (at [53]).

It is made very clear by **PD 28, para. 5.4(6)**, and **PD 29, para. 7.4(6)**, that variations involving loss of the trial date will be considered matters of last resort. Examples include cases where there are significant problems with the evidence, where medical evidence requires re-tracking or further investigation, where there is a change of solicitor, where proceedings are issued at the very end of the limitation period, and in personal injuries cases where the prognosis is uncertain (Woolf Report, ch. 3, para. 19). Listing and adjourning problems caused by the restricted availability of experts are discussed at **61.8**, and the principles governing applications to adjourn at **61.9** to **61.14**. Postponing trial on account of a failure to comply with directions will only be allowed if there are exceptional circumstances (**PD 28, para. 5.4(1)**, and **PD 29, para. 7.4(1)**; see **48.7**).

If there is no option but to postpone the trial, the postponement will be for the shortest possible time, and the court will give directions for taking the necessary steps outstanding as rapidly as possible. In some of these cases the best course may be to have split trials of liability and quantum, or to proceed only on those issues that are ready (**PD 28, para. 5.4(4)**; **PD 29, para. 7.4(4)**). Where this happens the court may disallow the costs of the remaining issues, or order them to be paid by the party in default in any event. If necessary the judge can decide issues while the case is allocated to the fast track, then reallocate the claim, if reallocating the claim immediately would cause substantial disruption to the litigation or unreasonable delay (*Maguire v Molin* [2002] EWCA Civ 1083, [2002] 4 All ER 325).

RECTIFYING DEFECTIVE PERFORMANCE

42.53   On some occasions a default may arise through the defective performance of the requirements of a rule, practice direction or court order. For example, it may be that the wrong form was used, or that it was sent to the wrong address (but still came to the attention of the other side) or that the document used was not completed correctly. These are errors of procedure. By **CPR, r. 3.10**, such errors do not invalidate the step purportedly taken, unless the court so orders. This rule is discussed in the context of extending the period of validity of a claim form at **15.32**. The court may make an order invalidating a step if it was so badly defective that the other side was misled, or where the defects are so great that it would not be right to regard the purported performance as performance at all. Further, by **r. 3.10(b)** the court may make an order to remedy any error of procedure. A defaulting party should consider seeking such an order where there is an objection made regarding defective performance.

Applications under **r. 3.10** may be affected by the implied sanction doctrine (see **48.13**), in which case the following principles will need to be adjusted to incorporate the principles that apply on applications for relief from sanctions.

A key factor in deciding whether to set aside or to rectify any irregularity is whether the other side has suffered any prejudice. In the absence of prejudice it is usual to allow the defaulting party to rectify the defect (*Colliers International Property Consultants v Colliers Jordan Lee Jafaar Sdn Bhd* [2008] EWHC 1524 (Comm), [2008] 2 Lloyd's Rep 368 (failure to serve complete copies of the exhibits with witness statements)). An obvious and technical defect in a Part 36 offer was ignored in *Hertsmere Primary Care Trust v Administrators of Balasubramanium's Estate* [2005] EWHC 320 (Ch), [2005] 3 All ER 274 (and it is submitted would have been cured under **r. 3.10**).

Where a party purports to serve a claim form within its period of validity, but by an incorrect method, or at an incorrect address, the court has a discretion whether to grant relief under r. 3.10, which is exercised in accordance with the overriding objective. On an application for an order remedying such an error in procedure, the court will consider whether the claimant has taken all reasonable steps to put the matter right once the problem was discovered (*Nanglegan v Royal Free Hampstead NHS Trust* [2001] EWCA Civ 127, [2002] 1 WLR 1043, where relief was refused). In *Phillips v Symes (No. 3)* [2008] UKHL 1, [2008] 1 WLR 180, it was thought that r. 3.10 could be used to cure an irregularity in effecting service outside the jurisdiction.

An order rectifying an error in procedure was made in *Fawdry and Co. v Murfitt* [2002] EWCA Civ 643, [2003] QB 104, where a judge, without being aware she was not duly authorised, heard a case which had not been properly released to her for trial.

It is doubtful that r. 3.10 can be used to validate a step (here withdrawing a Part 36 offer) which has not been taken if the result is to invalidate a procedural step (here the offeree's acceptance of the Part 36 offer) that actually has been taken (see *Re Kilopress Ltd* (2010) LTL 22/4/2010).

DOCKETING

Docketing was defined in the *Jackson Report* as the system of assigning a case to one judge from issue up to and including trial. Under docketing, pre-trial case management deadlines and trial dates are crucial. Once set these dates should stay set (Lord Neuberger, 9th Implementation Lecture, para. 19). They should be moved only if there are exceptional circumstances beyond the control of the parties. This should mean that the parties concentrate on what is essential in preparing a case, with what is inessential not being pursued. The result should be that costs are reduced, and the early identification of the issues should promote early settlements.   **42.54**

Having a system for implementing docketing is mainly a matter of court administration and resourcing, and so does not feature in the revisions to the CPR. However, legal representatives should also play a role in identifying cases suitable for docketing, and there may be directions dealing with docketing in individual cases. Normally, small claims and fast track cases will not be suitable for docketing (Lord Neuberger, 9th Implementation Lecture, para. 30). It is likely that in these cases having a single managing judge would increase costs. Docketing is not even right for every multi-track claim. Straightforward multi-track cases are unlikely to benefit from docketing. Generally, it will be the more complex and specialist claims which will be the most suitable for docketing. Complexity for this purpose may be based on the law or the facts. Suitable cases will include many Chancery claims, clinical negligence and complex personal injuries claims. There may be a need to review the position if, for example, a case that initially looked reasonably straightforward develops into something rather more complicated.

Selecting claims for docketing

The Admiralty and Commercial Courts Guide, at section D4, lists the following factors in deciding whether to designate a claim for docketing: **42.55**

i)   the size of or complexity of the case,
ii) the fact that it has the potential to give rise to numerous pre-trial applications,
iii) there is a likelihood that specific assignment will give rise to a substantial saving in costs,
iv) the same or similar issues arise in other cases,
v)   other case management considerations indicate that assignment to a specific judge at the start of the case, or at some subsequent date, is appropriate.

In the Chancery Division docketing is usually a case management decision after filing of directions questionnaires, but may be decided on an application by a party. Factors listed as relevant in *New Case Management Tracks in Chancery* (5 March 2015) are:

Commentary

(a) claims where the trial is estimated to last 15 days or more, and there is potential for reducing the trial length by active case management by the trial judge;

(b) claims involving numerous pre-trial applications which are likely to be heard by a judge;

(c) claims where there is a particular advantage in pre-trial applications being heard by the trial judge;

(d) claims which by their subject-matter require the specialist knowledge of a special judge;

(e) claims subject to GLO and other substantial group claims requiring active case management by the trial judge;

(f) urgent claims requiring determination within weeks or months;

(g) claims with litigants in person and it is considered that docketing will best serve the needs of the parties and the efficient administration of justice.

Procedure relating to docketing

42.56   In the Admiralty and Commercial Courts an application for the appointment of a designated judge should be made in writing to the judge in charge of the list at the time of fixing the case management conference (Admiralty and Commercial Courts Guide, para. D4.2). In appropriate cases the court may assign a designated judge regardless of whether an application is made. If an order is made for allocation to a designated judge, the designated judge will preside at all subsequent pre-trial case management conferences and other hearings. Normally all applications in the case, other than applications for an interim payment, will be determined by the designated judge and he will be the trial judge (para. D4.3). In all cases the Commercial Court listing office will endeavour to ensure a degree of judicial continuity. To assist in this the parties should indicate clearly when lodging the papers the identity of the last judge who considered the case (para. D4.4).

In the Chancery Division docketing decisions may be made by Masters, registrars or judges, but usually in the first instance a Master (Chancery Guide, para. 8.10). Any such decision will be passed to the Chancellor for final approval (*New Case Management Tracks in Chancery* (5 March 2015)).

DIRECT JUDICIAL CONTACT WITH THE PARTIES

42.57   Direct policing of case management directions has been enhanced by the insertion of **CPR, r. 3.1(8)**, with effect from 1 April 2013, which provides that the court may contact the parties from time to time in order to monitor compliance with directions. It also says that the parties must respond promptly to any such enquiries from the court. Perhaps it is not surprising that Sir Rupert Jackson found that experience in overseas jurisdictions suggests that a phone call or email from the court enquiring about progress on a case can have a dramatic effect (5th Implementation Lecture, para 3.3). As Sir Rupert went on to say, securing compliance with directions is far preferable than imposing sanctions for breach.

MAKING USE OF TECHNOLOGY

42.58   The courts are increasingly aware of the savings that can be made by the use of developing technology. In addition to judicial contact with solicitors by telephone or email under **CPR, r. 3.1(8)**, there is provision for holding interim hearings by telephone (see **32.24**). On occasion, the court will go even further, such as by allowing evidence to be given by video conferencing (see **58.11**), or by ordering that substantial parts of the documentation be provided in electronic form, supported by hypertext or other links to enable the judge to move rapidly from one document to another. In *Morris v Bank of America National Trust* [2000] 1 All ER 954, the Court of Appeal stressed that use of technology is acceptable only if it will save time or money, and if it will not unfairly prejudice any of the parties.

With effect from 7 December 2015 it has been possible to file most documents by email (**PD 5B**). This practice direction does not apply to claims in the Rolls Building (which are governed by **PD 51O**, see **42.59**) or to money claims online started under **PD 7E** unless the claim has been sent to a County Court hearing centre (**PD 5B, para. 1.2**). While it is possible to file documents requiring the payment of a fee by email under **PD 5B** in the County Court provided arrangements are made for payment (**para. 2.3**), this is not possible for High Court documents requiring a fee (**para. 2.2(a)**). Where a document needs a signed statement of truth it is sufficient to retain the original and have it ready for production, and to file a version by email with the signatory's name typed underneath the statement of truth, or with a facsimile of the signature (**para. 5.1**).

Various technical requirements that have to be met are set out in **PD 5B**, and further guidance can be found at https://www.justice.gov.uk/courts/email-guidance#canfile. Where proceedings have been started the subject line of the email must contain the case number, the parties' names (which may be abbreviated) and the date of any relevant hearing (**para. 3.6**). The email must include the name and telephone number of the sender, and a contact address (which may be an email address) (**para. 3.1**). No more than 25 pages (50 sides) can be sent, and the email must not exceed 10MB (**para. 2.3**). Prescribed forms must be sent as attachments (**paras 3.3 and 3.4**). The guidance lists the various file formats that the courts will accept. A party filing a document by email must not also send a hard copy (**para. 4.1**). An email received by the court at or after 4.00 pm and before 11.59 pm is deemed to be filed on the next day the court office is open (**para. 4.2(a)**). If an email requires urgent attention, the sender should also contact the court by telephone (**para. 4.5**).

Electronic Working Pilot Scheme

In the Rolls Building jurisdictions (the Chancery Division, Commercial Court, TCC, Mercantile Court and Admiralty Court) an electronic working pilot scheme is in operation from 16 November 2016 for one year (**PD 51O, para. 1.1**). These courts use an electronic court file system (CE-File). Electronic filing applies to claim forms, statements of case, application notices and hearing bundles. This is done by accessing the Electronic Working website run by Her Majesty's Courts and Tribunal Service, and paying the fee online. Details are in the Chancery Guide at para. 6.13 and **PD 51O**. Where **PD 51O** applies, the court will not accept documents by email except where expressly requested by the trial judge or the trial judge's clerk (**para. 3.4(2)**). Documents are filed in PDF form, and one copy only is required (**para. 5.1**). Documents are treated as filed when the fee is paid (**para. 5.4**), and are sealed electronically by the court (**para. 7.1**). Application bundles for hearings exceeding 15 minutes, and trial bundles, must also be filed in paper format corresponding exactly to the electronic version (**paras 10.2, 10.4, 11.2 and 13.1**). The PDF version must have bookmarks for each document (**para. 10.3(b)**). Parties filing documents electronically are required to preserve the original signed versions and any exhibits, and make them available for inspection when required (**para. 4**). Before a hearing the applicant should send a draft order to the court as an email attachment in Word (not PDF) format (Chancery Guide, paras 16.10 and 16.30).

42.59

CHANGING TRACKS

After a claim has been allocated to a track the court may make a subsequent order reallocating it to a different track (**CPR, r. 26.10**). Where a claim was initially allocated to the small claims track, and is later reallocated to another track, the small claims costs restrictions cease to apply from the date of reallocation (**r. 27.15**).

42.60

A party who is dissatisfied with an allocation decision may challenge the decision either by appealing up to the next higher court or by making an application back to the judge who made the initial decision (**PD 26, para. 11.1(1)**). Applications should be used where the decision was made without any hearing of which the party was given due notice or if there has been a material change of circumstances. If the party was present, represented or given due notice of the hearing where the decision was made, the only appropriate route is by way of appeal (**PD 26, paras 11.1** and **11.2**).

If an additional claim is issued, it may be necessary to redetermine the most suitable track for the proceedings. Mere issue of an additional claim will not have this effect, but where a defence to an additional claim has been filed the proceedings will be reconsidered by the procedural judge to determine whether the claim should remain on its existing track (particularly in cases on the small claims and fast tracks) and whether there needs to be any adjustment to the timetable. At the same time the procedural judge will consider whether the additional claim should be dealt with separately from the main claim.

When an amendment increases or reduces the amount of a claim, the court may consider reallocating the case to a different case management track. It will only do so if there is a good reason (*Maguire v Molin* [2002] EWCA Civ 1083, [2002] 4 All ER 325). In addition to the factors in **CPR, r. 26.8** (see **42.32**), the amount by which the claim now exceeds the normal limit for the allocated track is a highly relevant consideration. If the new value is substantially above the normal limit, the case will normally need to be reallocated. Another important factor is whether the trial date will be lost as a result of reallocating the claim (perhaps because of the limited trial jurisdiction of District Judges, see **PD 2B, para. 11.1**), particularly if the amendment is sought after the trial has started (*Maguire v Molin*, where permission to amend was refused).

STAY TO ALLOW FOR SETTLEMENT

Judicial encouragement of ADR

42.61 One of the court's case management functions is to help the parties to settle the whole or part of the case (**CPR, r. 1.4(2)(f)**), and another is to encourage the parties to use alternative dispute resolution procedures if appropriate, and to facilitate the use of such procedures (**r. 1.4(2)(e)**). This includes hearing an early neutral evaluation with the aim of helping the parties to settle the case (**r. 3.1(2)(m)**). Although the court can require the parties to consider ADR, it cannot force them to use it. Since the implementation of the Jackson Reforms on 1 April 2013 the expectation of the judiciary is that some form of ADR should have been attempted in every case that goes to trial. Sir Rupert Jackson commented in the 11th implementation lecture that no rule changes were necessary because the courts already have all the powers they need in this area. What was required was a culture change. Recommendations 75 and 76 in the *Jackson Report* are to the effect that practitioners, parties and the judiciary need to be better informed about the range and effectiveness of ADR processes. To this end, as Lord Dyson, MR, explained in January 2013, *The Jackson ADR Handbook*, Blake, Brown and Sime (Oxford: OUP, now 2nd edn, 2016) was first published in April 2013 under the auspices of the Judicial College, the Civil Justice Council and the Civil Mediation Council as a single authoritative handbook explaining ADR clearly, authoritatively and in an accessible way.

The strength of the encouragement, if any, given by the judge may affect the decision on costs when the claim is finally determined (see *Halsey v Milton Keynes General NHS Trust* [2004] EWCA Civ 576, [2004] 1 WLR 3002). ADR is discussed in **chapter 73**. A simple ADR direction appears as direction 2 in the basic standard directions for multi-track claims on the Ministry of Justice website. Also useful is the somewhat more sophisticated Ungley order, which originated in clinical dispute claims. This provides:

The parties shall by [a date usually about three months before the trial window opens] consider whether the case is capable of resolution by ADR. If any party considers the case is unsuitable for resolution by

ADR that party shall be prepared to justify that decision at the conclusion of the trial, should the trial judge consider that such means of resolution were appropriate, when he is considering the appropriate costs order to make. Such means of ADR as shall be adopted shall be concluded not less than 35 days prior to the trial.

The party considering the case unsuitable for ADR shall, not less than 28 days before the commencement of the trial, file with the court a witness statement, without prejudice save as to costs, giving the reasons upon which they rely for saying that the case is unsuitable. The witness statement shall not be disclosed to the trial judge until the conclusion of the case.

A note to the Ungley order says that 'ADR' includes a round-table conference at which the parties attempt to define and narrow the issues in the case, including those to which expert evidence is directed, early neutral evaluation, mediation and arbitration. The object is to try to reduce the number of cases settled at the door of the court, which are wasteful both of costs and judicial time. Despite the reference to arbitration, in practical terms unless a very contracted procedure is adopted, it will be impossible to arbitrate a dispute in what is effectively a period of less than two months. It is essential that parties use the time efficiently. Giving parties the opportunity to explore settlement of their case is not a good ground for adjourning a fixed date trial (*Fitzroy Robinson Ltd v Mentmore Towers Ltd* [2009] EWHC 3070 (TCC), [2010] CP Rep 15; *Elliott Group Ltd v GECC UK* [2010] EWHC 409 (TCC), LTL 10/3/2010).

Request of stay for ADR

The directions questionnaire allows a party to include a request for the proceedings to be stayed while the parties try to settle the case. If all the parties make such a request, the proceedings will be stayed for one month, and the court will notify the parties accordingly (**CPR, r. 26.4(2)**). The court may, of its own initiative, direct that the proceedings, either in whole or in part, be stayed for one month, or for such specified period as the court considers appropriate (**r. 26.4(2A)**). The court has power to extend the stay for such specified period as it thinks appropriate (**r. 26.4(3)**), which it will generally exercise on receipt of a letter from either party confirming that the extension is sought with the agreement of all the parties and giving a reasonable explanation of the steps being taken and the identity of the mediator or expert assisting with the process (**PD 26, para. 3.1(1)**). Extensions will not usually exceed four weeks at a time unless there are clear reasons to justify a longer time. During the period of such a stay the claimant is under a duty to inform the court if a settlement is reached (**CPR, r. 26.4(4)**). If, by the end of the defined period of the stay, the claimant has not told the court that the case has been settled, the court will often seek a report on progress, and will give such directions for the management of the case as it considers appropriate, including allocating it to an appropriate track (**rr. 26.4(5)** and **26.5(2)**). **42.62**

The periods of stays under the above rules are carefully restricted so as to prevent the procedure being used to secure protracted 'authorised' delays after proceedings are commenced, under the guise of attempting to settle. A substantially longer stay of two years was ordered in *Phillips v Symes* [2006] EWHC 2595 (Ch), LTL 17/10/2006. This order was made pursuant to **r. 1.1** (the overriding objective) and **r. 3.1(2)(m)**, and was made in the context of an extremely expensive piece of litigation with the aim of containing costs and giving the parties time to resolve the dispute.

A complex commercial dispute which could be solved by means going outside the remedies available in a court or in commercial arbitration was particularly suitable for being stayed for the purpose of mediation (*C v RHL* [2005] EWHC 873 (Comm), LTL 12/5/2005).

Judicial ENE

Case management powers available to the court include conducting an early neutral evaluation ('ENE') with the aim of helping the parties settle their litigation (**CPR, r. 3.1(2)(m)**). For ENE, see *The Jackson ADR Handbook*, 2nd edn (Oxford: OUP, 2016), ch. 22. **Rule 3.1(2)(m)** **42.63** gives effect to *Seals v Williams* [2015] EWHC 1829 (Ch), [2015] WTLR 1265. ENE can be particularly useful where the parties have differing views of the issues in dispute and the strength of their respective cases. Norris J said that conducting an ENE, and expressing provisional, non-binding, views on a particular hypothesis or upon the judge's overall impression of the case was an inherent part of the judicial function. An ENE order requires careful directions, with the settlement judge having no further involvement with the case after the ENE.

Small claims mediation scheme

42.64   There is a Small Claims Mediation Service operated by Her Majesty's Courts and Tribunals Service. It applies to claims that would normally be allocated to the small claims track, other than RTA, personal injury and housing disrepair claims (**CPR, r. 26.4A**). When all parties indicate on their directions questionnaires that they agree to mediation, the claim will be referred to the Mediation Service. If this results in the claim being settled, the proceedings will be stayed with permission to apply for judgment for the unpaid balance of the settlement agreement or for the claim to be restored for hearing of the full amount claimed. The settlement agreement must be in form N182 (**PD 26, para. 3A.1**). If the claim is not settled, it will be allocated to a track no later than four weeks after the last directions questionnaire was filed (**CPR, r. 26.5(2A)**).

LIMITING THE ISSUES TO BE TRIED

42.65   The court has power under **CPR, r. 32.1**, to give directions limiting the issues on which it wishes to be addressed, and on the evidence that may be adduced at trial on those issues, despite the fact that doing so may result in the exclusion of material that would otherwise be admissible under the law of evidence, and may take this into account when allocating (**PD 26, para. 9.1(3)(b)**). This power should only be exercised in accordance with the overriding objective. This requires that cases must be dealt with justly and fairly, so limiting evidence should not be so intrusive that it prevents either or both parties from proving their cases at trial. In a complex case, the parties should consider whether seeking a determination of the court on limiting the issues to be tried may turn out to be longer and more costly than allowing the case as pleaded to go to trial (*Korea National Insurance Corporation v Allianz Global Corporate and Specialty AG* [2008] EWCA Civ 1355, [2008] 2 CLC 837). In *McPhilemy v Times Newspapers Ltd* [1999] 3 All ER 775 Lord Woolf MR said that the courts' case management powers to restrain excess do not extend to preventing a party from putting forward allegations which are central to its case. That said, it is open to the court to attempt to control how those allegations are litigated with a view to limiting costs. This means that the procedural judge may cut out peripheral matters, or matters having little significant probative value (*Guerrero v Monterrico Metals plc* [2010] EWHC 3228 (QB), LTL 20/12/2010). In a libel claim this may mean that the judge can decide that a plea even of justification is either central or peripheral: it is essentially a matter within the discretion of the procedural judge (*Tancic v Times Newspapers Ltd* (1999) *The Times*, 12 January 2000). The parties should also keep the issues to be tried under review, and should not be unduly penalised (if at all) if they decide not to advance one of a number of points, even at a very late stage (*D. Pride and Partners v Institute for Animal Health* [2009] EWHC 1617 (QB), LTL 14/7/2009). An alternative approach is to separate certain issues for determination as preliminary issues (*GKR Karate (UK) Ltd v Yorkshire Post Newspapers Ltd* [2000] 1 WLR 2571).

CLINICAL CASE MANAGER

42.66   Clinical case managers are in some cases appointed to assist a severely injured person to deal with a dispute, typically involving litigation. The cost involved in having a clinical case manager is habitually included in any relevant damages claim. A clinical case manager must act in the best interests of his or her client, the injured person, and owes duties to that person, not to the court (*Wright v Sullivan* [2005] EWCA Civ 656, [2006] 1 WLR 172). This case held that where a clinical case manager attends a conference with legal advisers at which advice is being sought, the client can assert legal professional privilege, which can only be waived by the client. Conversely, where a clinical case manager enters into communications with an expert where obtaining legal advice is not the dominant purpose (see *Waugh v British Railways Board* [1980] AC 521), the occasion is not privileged, and the communications must be disclosed on standard disclosure.

ASSESSMENT OF DAMAGES

Cases where judgment is entered for damages to be decided by the court do not fall into the usual pattern of 'defended' cases. In such a case the court will make what is called a 'relevant order', which is defined by **PD 26, para. 12.1(1)**, as meaning any order or judgment which requires the amount of money that has to be paid to be decided by the court. This includes orders that require:

(a) the assessment of damages;
(b) the assessment of interest;
(c) the taking of an account;
(d) the making of an inquiry as to any sum due, but does not include an order for the assessment of costs.

According to **PD 26, para. 12.1(2)**, relevant orders may be made on entry of judgment in default, on entry of judgment on an admission, on the striking out of a statement of case, on a summary judgment application, on the determination of a preliminary issue or on a split trial as to liability, or even by consent or at trial.

When making a relevant order, the court will give directions, which may (**PD 26, para. 12.2(1)**):

(a) list the claim for a disposal hearing (see **42.68**);
(b) allocate or reallocate the claim to a track;
(c) direct the parties to file directions questionnaires by a specified date;
(d) stay the claim while the parties try to settle by ADR or other means.

Stays for settlement are dealt with as described at **42.62**.

The directions given when making a relevant order in a claim which is not stayed for ADR depend, principally, on whether the financial value of the claim is such that the claim would, if defended, be allocated to the small claims track (**PD 26, para. 12.3**). Normally, if a relevant order is made in a claim which would otherwise be a small claim but has not previously been allocated to a track, the court will allocate it to the small claims track and list it for a disposal hearing at which the amount payable will be decided. If the claim is not a small claim and the amount payable appears to be genuinely disputed on substantial grounds, or if the dispute is not suitable to be dealt with at a disposal hearing, the court will allocate the claim to an appropriate track for further hearing (see **42.69**). As a result, most personal injuries claims above the fast-track threshold, where there are arguments about causation or quantum, are allocated to a track rather than being dealt with at a disposal hearing.

Disposal hearings

A disposal hearing of a relevant order is a hearing which will not normally last longer than 30 minutes, but at which the court will decide and give judgment for the amount payable under the relevant order, or will give directions for the future conduct of the proceedings (**PD 26, para. 12.4(1) and (2)**). If a claim in which a relevant order has been made is a small claim, the

42.67

42.68

Commentary

amount payable under the order will normally be decided at a disposal hearing and the court may treat the disposal hearing as a final hearing for the purposes of **CPR, Part 27** (**PD 26, para. 12.4(3)**).

The court will not normally hear oral evidence at a disposal hearing (**PD 26, para. 12.4(1) (b)**). Evidence may, unless the court otherwise directs, be adduced under **CPR, r. 32.6** (see **PD 26, para. 12.4(4)**). This means that reliance may be placed on the matters set out in the particulars of claim (provided it is verified by a statement of truth) or by witness statement. The evidence relied upon must be served on the defendant at least three clear days before the disposal hearing.

Where the hearing is likely to exceed 30 minutes, or where the evidence is disputed, the court may allocate the case to a track and give assessment directions.

Assessment directions

42.69   If a relevant order is made by consent, the parties should file agreed directions with the draft consent order which they should invite the court to give (**PD 26, para. 12.2(3)**). For other relevant orders, other than those dealt with by stays for settlement or by way of a disposal hearing, the court will give directions, which may include allocating or reallocating the case to a case management track, directing that pre-trial checklists be filed within a stated period of time, and directing that the case be listed for a hearing or a further hearing (**para. 12.2(1)**). Allocating a case to the fast track or multi-track on making a relevant order should only happen if the amount payable is genuinely disputed on grounds that appear to be substantial, or if the dispute is not suitable to be dealt with at a disposal hearing (**para. 12.3**). If a claim has not been allocated to a track, and at the disposal hearing it becomes clear that its value is less than £10,000, in the ordinary case the small claims track costs regime should apply (*Voice and Script International v Alghafar* [2003] EWCA Civ 736, LTL 8/5/2003).

Hearing to assess damages

42.70   A Master or District Judge may decide the amount payable under a relevant order, irrespective of the financial value of the claim and of the track to which it has been allocated (**PD 26, para. 12.6**). But, when making a relevant order, the court may give directions specifying the level or type of judge who is to deal with the case (**para. 12.2(2)**). The designated Circuit Judge will from time to time set local guidelines for this purpose based on the value of the claim and the nature of any equitable relief sought. Hearings involving substantial damages or complex issues should usually be directed before a Circuit Judge or judge (*Sandry v Jones* (2000) *The Times*, 3 August 2000).

On an assessment of damages the defendant can raise any point which goes to quantification of the damage, provided that it is not inconsistent with any issue settled by the judgment (*Lunnun v Singh* [1999] CPLR 587). Where judgment for damages to be assessed was entered after the court rejected a defence that the claimant was guilty of gross misconduct disentitling him to any damages, it was still open for the defence to raise mitigation of damages on the assessment (*Pugh v Cantor Fitzgerald International* [2001] CPLR 271).

SUBSEQUENT CASE MANAGEMENT

42.71   Chapters 45, 46 and 47 deal in more detail with the further progress of cases on each of the three case management tracks following allocation. **Figure 42.1** shows the routes which cases may take from either a defence being filed or a 'relevant order' being made, up to the decision to allocate the case to a case management track. **Figure 42.2** shows in broad terms what happens to cases on the three case management tracks from the time they are allocated to a track until trial.

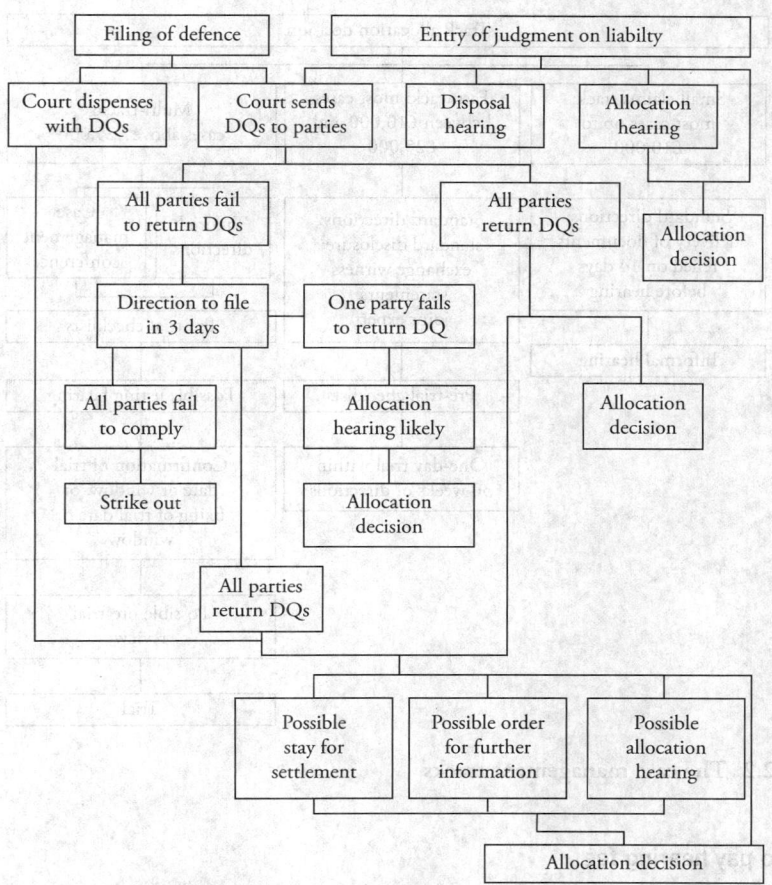

Figure 42.1 Routes to making track allocation decision
DQ = Directions questionnaire

Discussion on case management on the three tracks can be found in **chapters 45** to 47. The principal topics can be found as follows:

Case management conferences	**47.7**
Small claims track directions	**45.8–45.12**
Fast track directions	**46.14–46.21**
Multi-track directions	**47.3–47.6; 47.12–47.14**
Pre-trial checklists	**47.17**
Hearing fees	**45.13; 46.12; 47.21**
Hearing dates	**46.13; 47.16**
Pre-trial reviews	**47.23**
Small claims track costs	**45.28–45.32**
Fast track costs	**46.23; 70.16; 71.7**

Commentary

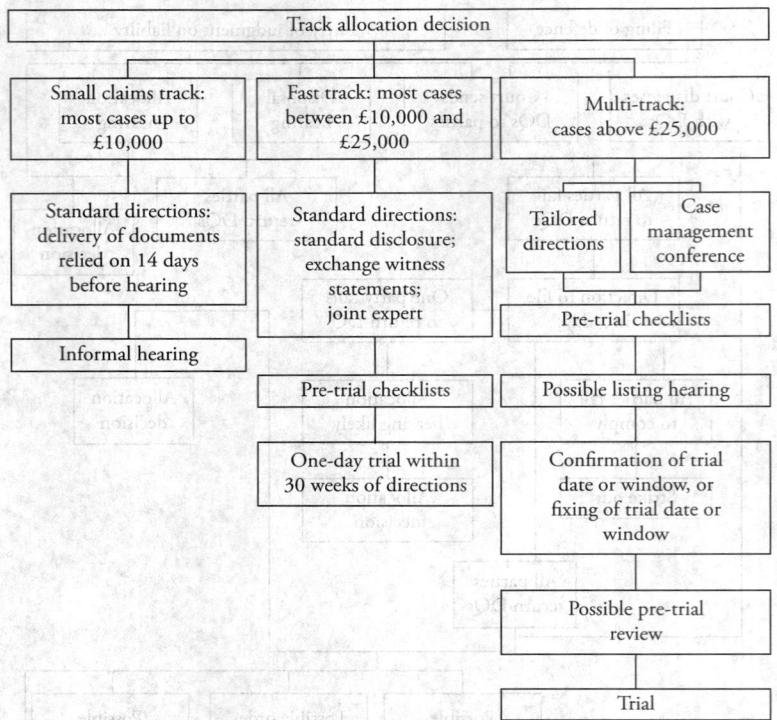

Figure 42.2 The case management tracks

Failing to pay hearing fee

42.72 **CPR, r. 3.7**, provides that claims will be struck out automatically if hearing fees are not paid after due warning, which the court gives by sending the claimant a form N173. Automatic striking out after due warning also covers non-payment of the issue and hearing fees for counterclaims, and dishonouring cheques used to pay fees (**rr. 3.7A** and **3.7B**). **PD 3B** says that if a claim is struck out, the court will send the defendant a notice which will explain the effect of **CPR, r. 25.11**, which provides that any interim injunction will cease having any effect after 14 days unless the claimant applies to reinstate the claim. This notice will prompt most defendants to apply for their costs against the defaulting claimant. Once the claim has been struck out the court retains a power to reinstate it (**r. 3.7(7)**), and on such an application the court will apply the criteria set out in **r. 3.9** relating to applications for relief from sanctions (see **chapter 48**). Non-payment of fees is always considered serious for the purposes of *Denton v T. H. White Ltd* [2014] EWCA Civ 906, [2014] 1 WLR 3926. Any order for reinstatement will be made conditional on either paying the fee or filing evidence of remission or part remission, of the fee (**r. 3.7(7)**). The time limit for payment or filing such evidence is two days from the date of the order if the claimant is present or represented, otherwise seven days from the date of service of the order (**r. 3.7(8)**).

Rules on remission and part remission of court fees can be found in **CPFO, sch. 2**.

Chapter 43   Costs Management

INTRODUCTION

Costs management involves the court in managing both the steps to be taken in proceedings **43.1** and the costs to be incurred by the parties, so as to further the overriding objective (**CPR, r. 3.12(2)**). This is done on the basis of detailed costs budgets prepared by the parties, which are agreed between the parties or approved by the court, and which are used as the basis for making decisions on the proportionate steps needed for preparing the case for trial.

Costs management is the central theme tying together many of the detailed reforms introduced on 1 April 2013. Under the Jackson reforms the courts need to take on an important role in managing costs as a necessary part of case management. As Sir Vivian Ramsey said in the 16th Implementation Lecture: 'It is no longer acceptable for questions of costs to be left to the end of litigation when the costs have been spent. Some control on the expenditure of costs needs to be implemented as part of the case management of cases. That control will now be provided by costs management.'

Need for costs management

Sir Rupert Jackson (*Preliminary Report* (2009), ch. 48, para. 3.12) concluded that the **43.2** development of costs capping and predictable costs (for which see **chapter 44**), together with the widespread use of summary assessments, meant that the judiciary were sufficiently familiar with costs to make cost management workable. Introducing costs management is not without its risks. There are two significant negative factors which point against using costs management (*Jackson Report*, ch. 40, para. 7.1):

(a) Costs management is an exercise that generates additional costs. It is only worth incurring these additional costs if there are net savings through the better management of the case as a result of the process.

(b) Costs management will impose additional demands on the limited resources of the court.

The counter-argument was first set out in the *Jackson Report* at ch. 40, paras 6.8 and 7.2 as follows:

(a) Litigation is in many instances a 'project', which both parties are pursuing for purely commercial ends.

(b) Any normal project costing thousands (or indeed millions) of pounds would be run on a budget. Litigation should be no different.

(c) The peculiarity of litigation is that at the time when costs are being run up, no one knows who will be paying the bill. There is sometimes the feeling that the more one spends, the more likely it is that the other side will end up paying the bill. This gives rise to a sort of 'arms race'.

(d) Under the present regime, neither party has any effective control over the (potentially recoverable) costs which the other side is running up.

(e) In truth both parties have an interest in controlling total costs within a sensible original budget, because at least one of them will be footing the bill.

(f) The parties' interests may, in truth, be best served if the court (i) controls the level of recoverable costs at each stage of the action, or alternatively (ii) makes less prescriptive orders (e.g. requiring notification when the budget for any stage is being overshot by, say, 20 per cent or more).

While in many cases litigation may be seen as a purely commercial project, it may be objected that in a great many it is not. The model fits well with the approach taken by many businesses, who weigh the expense and time commitment to litigation against its potential benefits. For many other litigants resort to the law is a matter of necessity or compulsion. An injured claimant does not enter litigation for purely commercial reasons, but to obtain the compensation they are entitled to as a matter of law. A business suing on unpaid invoices may do so for commercial purposes, but the main reason is to secure the assistance of the law in enforcing the payment obligations of customers who have not paid.

Point (b) in the list is, however, a compelling reason for having a budget of the anticipated costs of the contemplated litigation. The question remains as to how much time and effort should be devoted to developing and agreeing that budget. The force behind point (b) is that it is only fair to the client to ensure they have the information they need to make informed decisions about whether and how to pursue their legal remedies. Solicitors have professional responsibilities under the SRA Code of Conduct 2011, O 1.12 and O 1.13, and IB 1.14 to provide this form of information to their clients. Costs budgeting and costs management go further, because this information has to be shared with the other parties, and is subject to scrutiny and approval by the court.

Points (c) to (f) are well made. They do provide a justification for the further intervention of the courts, and are to be balanced against the negative factors mentioned above. There is not a great deal said about the second of those factors, the additional demands on court resources, but the *Jackson Report* at ch. 40, para. 7.15 says it is hoped that there will be a saving of judicial time through some cases settling earlier, given the parties' fuller understanding of their exposure on costs, and in more effective control of some of the present excesses of litigation. Research conducted in preparation for the *Jackson Report*, together with the experience gained from costs management pilot schemes in defamation claims (PD 51D) and in the Birmingham Mercantile Court and Technology and Construction Court (TCC), led to the conclusion that the benefits outweighed the risks.

Costs budgeting involves the ability to assess and estimate the likely costs in a claim in advance, so is a very different discipline from assessing costs after they have been incurred at the end of a case or on a summary assessment at an interim hearing. It is not even purely an exercise in estimating what costs might be incurred in the future. Costs budgets also need to comply with the requirements of reasonableness and proportionality (in **CPR, r. 44.3**).

ESSENTIAL FEATURES OF COSTS MANAGEMENT

43.3   The essential elements of costs management are that:

(a) the parties prepare and exchange litigation budgets or, as the case proceeds, amended budgets;

(b) the parties discuss and potentially agree each other's budgets;

(c) the court states the extent to which those budgets are approved;

(d) so far as possible, the court manages the case so that it proceeds within the approved budgets; and

(e) at the end of the litigation, the recoverable costs of the winning party are assessed in accordance with the approved budget.

From 1 April 2013 to 21 April 2014

For claims commenced from 1 April 2013 to 21 April 2014 (see Civil Procedure (Amendment   **43.4**
No. 4) Rules 2014 (SI 2014/867) r. 25(1), and CPR, r. 3.12(1) as in force at that time), costs management applied to all multi-track cases except:

(a) cases in the Admiralty and Commercial Courts;

(b) cases in the Chancery Division where the sum in dispute exceeded £2,000,000 excluding interest and costs; and

(c) cases in the TCC and the Mercantile Court where the sum in dispute exceeded £2,000,000 excluding interest and costs,

unless the proceedings were the subject of fixed costs or scale costs, or the court otherwise ordered. Rule r. 3.12(1) continued by saying that costs management also applied to any other proceedings or interim applications where the court so ordered.

High-value Chancery Division, TCC and Mercantile Court claims were excluded from costs management except where the court so ordered (pursuant to directions made under **r. 3.12(1)(b)** and **(c)** by the Chancellor of the High Court and by the President of the Queen's Bench Division on 18 February 2013).

From 22 April 2014 to 5 April 2016

For claims commenced on or after 22 April 2014, costs management applied by virtue of the   **43.5**
former CPR, r. 3.12(1), to all Part 7 multi-track cases, except:

(a) where the amount of money claimed as stated on the claim form was £10 million or more;

(b) where the proceedings were for a monetary claim which was not quantified or not fully quantified or were for a non-monetary claim, and the claim form contained a statement that the claim was valued at £10 million or more;

(c) where the proceedings were the subject of fixed costs or scale costs, or where the court otherwise ordered.

From 1 October 2015, the 81st Update also removed claims on the shorter trial pilot scheme unless the parties agreed that costs management should apply (**PD 51N, para. 2.58**).

From 6 April 2016

For claims commenced on or after 6 April 2016, costs management applies to all Part 7   **43.6**
multi-track cases, except:

(a) where the amount of money claimed as stated on the claim form is £10 million or more (**CPR, r. 3.12(1)(a)**);

(b) where the proceedings are for a monetary claim which is not quantified or not fully quantified or are for a non-monetary claim, and the claim form contains a statement that the claim is valued at £10 million or more (**r. 3.12(1)(b)**);

(c) where the proceedings include a claim on behalf of a child (and this exception continues to apply on the child reaching majority unless the court otherwise orders) (**r. 3.12(1)(c)**);

(d) where the proceedings are the subject of fixed costs or scale costs (**r. 31.12(1)(d)**). Fixed costs are laid down by **Part 45** and scale costs apply to cases in the Intellectual Property Enterprise Court (**rr. 45.30 to 45.36**);

(e) where the court otherwise orders (**r. 3.12(1)(e)**); and

Commentary

(f) Rolls Building cases within the shorter trials scheme, unless the parties agree that costs management should apply (**PD 51N, para. 2.58**, see **42.34**).

'Ordinarily' costs management is disapplied in claims where the claimant has severely impaired life expectation (five years or less) (**PD 3E, para. 2(b)**).

While the usual position is that costs management under **CPR, rr. 3.12 to 3.18**, applies only to multi-track claims, **r. 3.12(1A)** permits the court to bring other claims, such as fast track claims and high-value claims, into the costs management regime. Further, **r. 3.1(2)(ll)** gives the court the power to order any party to file and exchange a costs budget. These powers may be exercised by the court on its own initiative or on the application of a party (**PD 3E, para. 2**). In cases not normally covered by costs management, the parties should consider and, where practicable, discuss whether to apply for an order for the provision of costs budgets with a view to a costs management order being made (**para. 3**). There is a list in **para. 5** of cases which are outside **CPR, r. 3.12(1)**, which might be suitable for costs management. They include unfair prejudice petitions, company director disqualification proceedings, Part 8 claims involving substantial disputes of fact, and personal injury and clinical disputes with values of £10 million or more.

Fast track claims are most likely to be brought within the costs management rules where there are factors which give the court cause for concern, or where the likely costs mean that use of costs management is likely to be cost-efficient. Fast track claims will usually be far below £50,000, so costs management in these cases will frequently be based on one-page costs budgets (see **43.8**).

Under **r. 3.12(1)(d)** the court is given the power to exclude from the costs management rules multi-track claims that would normally be the subject of costs management.

COSTS BUDGETS

Filing costs budgets

43.7   Unless the court otherwise orders, all parties except litigants in person must file and exchange budgets with their directions questionnaires if the value of the claim is less than £50,000, otherwise not later than 21 days before the first case management conference (**CPR, r. 3.13(1)**). A litigant in person, even though not required to prepare a budget, must be provided with a copy of the budget of any other party (**PD 3E, para. 7.8**).

Format of costs budgets

43.8   By **PD 3E, para. 6(a)**, unless the court otherwise orders, a budget must be in the form of Precedent H (re-issued with effect from 3 October 2016, and annexed to **PD 3E**). It must be in landscape format with an easily legible typeface. In substantial cases the court may direct that budgets be limited initially to part only of the proceedings and subsequently extended to cover the whole of the proceedings. Costs budgeting requires each side to provide information on time costs and disbursements for the following phases in the litigation:

(a) pre-action costs;
(b) issue and statements of case;
(c) case management conference;
(d) disclosure;
(e) witness statements;
(f) expert reports;
(g) pre-trial review;

(h) trial preparation;

(i) trial;

(j) ADR/settlement discussions; and

(k) contingencies, which are anticipated costs not falling into the main categories, such as mediation, applications to amend, and applications for disclosure from non-parties. Contingencies should only be included if they are foreseen as more likely than not to be required (*Yeo v Times Newspapers Ltd (No. 2)* [2015] EWHC 209 (QB), [2015] 1 WLR 3031 at [71]).

Guidance on allocating costs to these phases is given in the guidance notes on Precedent H issued by the Ministry of Justice, which is reproduced in **figure 43.1**. Parties must follow this guidance in all respects (**PD 3E, para. 6(b)**).

Allowance must be made in each phase for advising the client, taking instructions and corresponding with other parties and the court (Guidance Note, para. 2). It may be assumed that the costs to be included in the budget should include the time costs for attendance on the client, and general project and strategy management for each stage. A note to this effect was included in the documentation used on the defamation proceedings cost management scheme, PD 51D. The 'contingency' phases should be used for anticipated costs which do not fall into any of the main categories (Guidance Note, para. 3). They include the trial of preliminary issues, and the costs of mediation. In substantial cases, the court may direct that budgets be limited initially to part only of the proceedings and subsequently extended to cover the whole proceedings. In cases where a party's budgeted costs do not exceed £25,000, or the value of the claim as stated on the claim form is less than £50,000, the parties must only use the first page of Precedent H (**PD 3E, para. 6(c)**).

A costs budget must be dated and verified by a statement of truth signed by a senior legal representative of the party (**PD 3E, para. 6(a)**; **PD 22, para. 2.2A**). A solicitor who signed a costs budget without the words of the statement of truth was regarded as having committed an error of form rather than substance in *Bank of Ireland v Philip Pank Partnership* [2014] EWHC 284 (TCC), [2014] 2 Costs LR 301. The form of the statement of truth was amended with effect from 22 April 2014 to remove the express reference to the indemnity principle (for which, see **71.30**), and is as follows:

This budget is a fair and accurate statement of incurred and estimated costs which it would be reasonable and proportionate for my client to incur in this litigation.

Failure to file a costs budget

Unless the court otherwise orders, any party which fails to file a budget despite being required   **43.9**
to do so will be treated as having filed a budget comprising only the applicable court fees (**CPR, r. 3.14**). This sanction is adjusted to the loss of 50 per cent of the defaulting party's costs if the defaulting party makes a successful Part 36 offer (**r. 36.23**).

Failing to file a costs budget is regarded as a serious breach of the CPR, because the court cannot manage the litigation and the costs to be incurred unless costs budgets are filed in good time before the first case management conference (*Mitchell v News Group Newspapers Ltd* [2013] EWCA Civ 1537, [2014] 1 WLR 795 at [30], apparently approved in *Denton v T. H. White Ltd* [2014] EWCA Civ 906, [2014] 1 WLR 3926 at [98]). It was further held that the sanction in **r. 3.14** applies both to situations where a party fails to file a costs budget at all and also where a party files a costs budget late. The mischief addressed by **rr. 3.13** and **3.14** is the last-minute filing of costs budgets. Lord Dyson MR also made a comment in *Mitchell* at [30] to the effect that under the main costs budgeting provisions that came into force on 1 April 2013 the need to discuss budgetary assumptions and the timetable is also an important requirement. This was an obligation under PD 51D, para. 4.1 (PD 51D was withdrawn as from 1 April 2013), but has not been included either in **CPR, rr. 3.12** to **3.18** or **PD 3E**.

Figure 43.1 Guidance Notes on Precedent H

1. This is the form on which you should set out your budget of anticipated costs in accordance with CPR Part 3 and Practice Directions 3E and 3F.
2. This table identifies where within the budget form the various items of work, **in so far as they are required by the circumstances of your case**, should be included. Allowance must be made in each phase for advising the client, taking instructions and corresponding with the other party/parties and the court in respect of matters falling within that phase.

Phase	Includes	Does NOT include
Pre-action	• Pre-Action Protocol correspondence • Investigating the merits of the claim and advising client • Considering ADR, advising on settlement and Part 36 offers • All other steps taken and advice given pre-action	Any work already incurred in relation to any other phase of the budget
Statements of case	• Preparation of Claim Form • Issue and service of proceedings • Preparation of Particulars of Claim, Defence, Reply, including taking instructions, instructing counsel and any necessary investigation • Considering opposing statements of case and advising client • Part 18 requests (request and answer) • Any conferences with counsel primarily relating to statements of case	Amendments to statements of case (see below)
CMC	• Completion of [Directions Questionnaires] • Arranging a CMC • Preparation of costs budget for first CMC and reviewing opponent's budget • Correspondence with opponents to agree directions and budgets, where possible • Preparation for, and attendance at, the CMC • Finalising the order	Subsequent CMCs
Disclosure	• Obtaining documents from client and advising on disclosure obligations • Reviewing documents for disclosure, preparing disclosure report or questionnaire response and list • Inspection • Reviewing opponent's list and documents, undertaking any appropriate investigations • Correspondence between parties about the scope of disclosure and queries arising • Consulting counsel, so far as appropriate, in relation to disclosure	• Applications for specific disclosure • Applications and requests for third party disclosure
Witness Statements	• Identifying witnesses • Obtaining statements • Preparing witness summaries • Consulting counsel, so far as appropriate, about witness statements • Reviewing opponent's statements and undertaking any appropriate investigations • Applications for witness summaries	Arranging for witnesses to attend trial (include in trial preparation)

Expert Reports	• Identifying and engaging suitable expert(s) • Reviewing draft and approving report(s) • Dealing with follow-up questions of experts • Considering opposing experts' reports • Meetings of experts (preparing agenda etc)	• Obtaining permission to adduce expert evidence (include in CMC or as separate application) • Arranging for experts to attend trial (include in trial preparation)
PTR	• [PTR] Bundle • Preparation of updated costs budgets and reviewing opponent's budget • Preparing and agreeing chronology, case summary and dramatis personae (if ordered and not already prepared earlier in case) • Completing and filing pre-trial checklists • Correspondence with opponents to agree directions and costs budgets, if possible • Attendance at the PTR	Assembling and/or copying the bundle (this is not fee earners' work)
Trial Preparation	• Trial bundles • Witness summonses, and arranging for witnesses to attend trial • Any final factual investigations • Supplemental disclosure and statements (if required) • Agreeing brief fee • Any pre trial conferences and advice from Counsel • Pre-trial liaison with witnesses	• Assembling and/or copying the trial bundle (this is not fee earners' work) • Counsel's brief fee and any refreshers
Trial	• Solicitors' attendance at trial • All conferences and other activity outside court hours during the trial • Attendance on witnesses during the trial • Counsel's brief fee and any refreshers • Dealing with draft judgment and related applications	• Preparation for trial • Agreeing brief fee
Settlement	• Settlement negotiations, including Part 36 and other offers and advising the client • Drafting settlement agreement or Tomlin order • Advice to the client on settlement (excluding advice included in the pre-action phase)	Mediation (should be included as a contingency)

3. The 'contingent cost' sections of this form should be used for **anticipated costs** which do not fall within the main categories set out in this form. Examples might be the trial of preliminary issues, a mediation, applications to amend, applications for disclosure against third parties or (in libel cases) applications re meaning. **Costs which are not anticipated** but which become necessary later are dealt with in paragraph 4.7 of the Practice Direction [in fact in **PD 3E, para 2.6**].

4. Any party may apply to the court if it considers that another party is behaving oppressively in seeking to cause the applicant to spend money disproportionately on costs and the court will grant such relief as may be appropriate.

Depriving a successful party of all its costs other than court fees is intended to be a draconian penalty for failing to comply with the requirement to file a costs budget. A court should only order otherwise in most cases on the same grounds as are relevant to a decision to grant relief from sanctions under **CPR, r. 3.9** (*Mitchell v News Group Newspapers Ltd* at [32]). This is sought by making an application in accordance with **Part 23** supported by evidence, see **32.12**. Unless the *Denton* criteria are satisfied, it is probable that relief will be refused (see **chapter 48**). If relief is granted it is also necessary to consider the terms to be imposed. In addition to paying the costs of and occasioned by the default, it is suggested that consideration should be given to disallowing all or part of the costs, apart from court fees, from the approved costs budget of the defaulting party for the period of the default.

Budget discussion reports

43.10 After receipt of costs budgets the parties (other than litigants in person) must discuss each other's budgets and compile a budget discussion report in Precedent R (**PD 3E, para. 6A**). This sets out agreed figures for each phase; identifies figures for phases that are not agreed; and contains a brief summary of the grounds of dispute. An agreed budget discussion report must be filed at court no later than seven days before the first case management conference (**CPR, r. 3.13(2)**).

AGREEMENT OR APPROVAL OF COSTS BUDGETS

43.11 The primary position is that costs budgets should be agreed by the parties. If the budgets or parts of the budgets are agreed between all parties, the court will record the extent of such agreement (**PD 3E, para. 7.3**). In so far as the budgets are not agreed, the court will review them and, after making any appropriate revisions, record its approval of the revised budgets (**para. 7.3**). Court approval is a forward-looking process, which deals with future costs yet to be incurred. Accordingly, the court may not approve costs incurred before the date of any budget as part of the costs management process. The court may, however, record its comments on those costs and should take those costs into account when considering the reasonableness and proportionality of all subsequent costs (**para. 7.4**).

Sales LJ in *Sarpd Oil International Ltd v Addax Energy SA* [2016] EWCA Civ 120, [2016] CP Rep 24 at [50] said that the case (or costs) management conference was the appropriate occasion on which issues between the parties on their respective budgets should be debated. The learned judge went on to explain that this applies both to future estimated costs and to already incurred costs. Thereafter, where the amount of costs is relevant on an interim application, such as an application for security for costs, the learned judge said it would be disproportionate to reopen the reasonableness and proportionality of the budgets, unless there was a material change of circumstances (see [51]). Such an interpretation was disapproved by the Briggs *Civil Courts Structure Review* (July 2016, Judiciary of England and Wales) at para. 5.26 as likely to undermine the efficient disposal of costs management conferences.

Sir Vivian Ramsey has said a court considering disputed costs budgets will look at both the total costs and the overall costs of each phase of the proceedings, but is not embarking on a detailed assessment in advance (16th Implementation Lecture, para. 21). It is the phase and total costs that need to be approved. It is not the role of the court in a cost management hearing to fix or approve the hourly rates claimed in a budget (**PD 3E, para. 7.10**). The underlying detail in the budget for each phase used by the party to calculate the totals claimed is provided for reference purposes only to assist the court in fixing the budget.

In doing so the court will apply the proportionality test in **CPR, r. 44.3(5)**, to the costs budget. The judge carrying out costs management will not only scrutinise the reasonableness of each party's budget, but will also stand back and consider whether the total sums on each side are proportionate in accordance with **r. 44.3(5)** (*Jackson Report*, ch. 40, para. 7.23). If the total figures are not proportionate, the judge will only approve budget figures for each party which are proportionate.

Thereafter both parties, if they choose to press on, will be litigating in part at their own expense, unless the conduct of the paying party results in a more generous assessment of costs.

After its budget has been approved, each party is required to re-file its budget in the form approved with recast figures, which shall be annexed to the order approving it (**PD 3E, para. 7.7**).

REVIEWS OF COSTS BUDGETS

Each party is required to revise its budget in respect of future costs upwards or downwards, if **43.12** significant developments in the litigation warrant such revisions (**PD 3E, para.** 7.6). This must be done in advance of the conclusion of the claim. An application to revise a costs budget at the end of a trial is too late (*Elvanite Full Circle Ltd v AMEC Earth and Environmental (UK) Ltd* [2013] EWHC 1643 (TCC), [2013] 4 All ER 765).

Amended budgets must be submitted to the other parties for agreement. In default of agreement, the amended budgets have to be submitted to the court, together with a note of (a) the changes made and the reasons for those changes and (b) the objections of any other party. The court may approve, vary or disapprove the revisions, having regard to any significant developments which have occurred since the date when the previous budget was approved or agreed.

The onus is on the parties to put forward revised budgets if significant developments in the litigation make this desirable (Sir Vivian Ramsey, 16th Implementation Lecture, para. 22). Solicitors may wish to diarise review dates for this purpose. As with the original budgets, a revised budget should initially be submitted to the other side for approval, and only referred to the court if this is not forthcoming. It may be necessary to hold a costs management conference for this purpose.

Anticipating possible events that will impact on costs estimates, such as unwanted interim applications by the other side, and including them in the original costs budget under 'contingencies', may avoid the need to return to court with revised costs budgets. If there were reasonable grounds for not including the costs of an interim application in a party's costs budget, the interim costs will be treated as additional to the approved budget (**PD 3E, para. 7.9**).

COSTS MANAGEMENT ORDERS

Nature of costs management orders

In addition to exercising its other powers, the court may manage the costs to be incurred by **43.13** any party in any proceedings (**CPR, r. 3.15(1)**). It may do so by making a 'costs management order' (**r. 3.15(2)**). By such order the court will:

(a) record the extent to which the budgets are agreed between the parties; or
(b) in respect of budgets or parts of budgets which are not agreed, record the court's approval after making appropriate revisions.

Where costs budgets have been filed and exchanged the court will make a costs management order unless it is satisfied that the litigation can be conducted justly and at proportionate cost in accordance with the overriding objective without such an order being made (**r. 3.15(2)**). This presumption applies also to cases outside the normal categories covered by **r. 3.12(1)**, because costs management is a necessary adjunct to proper case management and furthering the overriding objective. There will be circumstances, such as an impending mediation, that may justify postponing the decision to make a costs management order (16th Implementation Lecture, para. 18).

A court has to make a costs management order where it is not satisfied that the litigation is being conducted at proportionate cost (*Hegglin v Person(s) Unknown* [2014] EWHC 3793 (QB), [2015] 1 Costs LO 65). However, if the court refuses to approve costs budgets, it cannot go on to make a costs management order (*Willis v M. R. J. Rundell and Associates Ltd* [2013] EWHC 2923

(TCC), [2013] 6 Costs LR 924 at [25]), because **r. 3.15(2)** requires agreed or approved costs budgets as a precondition for a costs management order.

Judicial control of parties' budgets

43.14 If a costs management order has been made, the court will thereafter control the parties' budgets in respect of recoverable costs (**CPR, r. 3.15(3)**). The court may set a timetable or give other directions for future reviews of budgets (**PD 3E, para. 7.5**).

Costs management conferences

43.15 The court may convene a hearing which is solely for the purpose of costs management (for example, to approve a revised budget). Such a hearing is referred to as a 'costs management conference' (**CPR, r. 3.16(1)**). Where practicable, costs management conferences should be conducted by telephone or in writing (**r. 3.16(2)**), with points made in correspondence taking the place of formal skeleton arguments (*Yeo v Times Newspapers Ltd (No. 2)* [2015] EWHC 209 (QB), [2015] 1 WLR 3031 at [58]).

Costs relating to costs management

43.16 Ensuring that the costs involved in the process do not themselves add to the problem of excessive litigation costs has always been a concern. Save in exceptional circumstances, **PD 3E, para. 7.2** says:

(a) the recoverable costs of initially completing Precedent H shall not exceed the higher of £1,000 or 1 per cent of the approved budget; and

(b) all other recoverable costs of the budgeting and costs management process shall not exceed 2 per cent of the approved budget.

In so far as such costs exceed these limits they will have to be borne by the client or be absorbed in the firm's overheads.

CASE MANAGEMENT AND COSTS BUDGETS

43.17 The primary purpose for the introduction of costs budgeting is to provide an effective case management tool for judges when considering the directions that are best suited to the case in hand. When making any case management decision, the court will have regard to any available budgets of the parties and will take into account the costs involved in each procedural step (**CPR, r. 3.17(1)**). This is so whether or not a costs budgeting order has been made (**r. 3.17(2)**). This means that in deciding what directions to make, the court will have to consider the costs impact of those steps (16th Implementation Lecture, para. 17).

Examples given by Sir Vivian Ramsey in the 16th Implementation Lecture included:

(a) whether full electronic disclosure will result in disproportionate costs;

(b) whether it is proportionate to have standard disclosure, or whether the costs of more limited disclosure would be more proportionate; and

(c) the impact on costs of expert evidence and witness statements.

COSTS BUDGETS AND THE COSTS OF THE PROCEEDINGS

Costs management order or costs budget

43.18 A two-speed approach is contemplated when assessing costs in claims that are subject to costs management. A distinction is drawn between:

(a) claims where there has been a costs management order (in these cases the court will not depart from the receiving party's costs budget unless there is a good reason to do so); and

(b) claims where there have been costs budgets, but no costs management order (in these cases, a 20 per cent difference between the costs claimed in a detailed assessment and those shown on the budget may result in the excess costs being disallowed).

Assessment where there is a costs management order

In cases where a costs management order has been made, **CPR, r. 3.18**, provides that when **43.19**
assessing costs on the standard basis, the court:

(a) will have regard to the receiving party's last approved or agreed budget for each phase of
the proceedings; and

(b) will not depart from such approved or agreed budget unless satisfied that there is good
reason to do so.

In cases where there is a costs management order the parties will inevitably have filed costs budgets, so the provisions referred to at **43.20** and **43.21** also have to be complied with. On a detailed
assessment the receiving party must serve a breakdown in the form of Precedent Q in **PD 47** of
the costs claimed for each phase of the proceedings (**CPR, r. 47.6(1)(c)** and **(2)**). Where there has
been a costs management order, the need to show a good reason for departing from the budget
should reduce the area of dispute on the assessment of costs. In these cases the paying party will
have seen and considered the receiving party's budget from an early stage, so there are likely to be
fewer disputes than before the Jackson reforms about the amount of costs payable at the end of
the process (Sir Vivian Ramsey, 16th Implementation Lecture, para. 24). Where costs budgets
have been approved by the court and revised at regular intervals, the receiving party is unlikely to
persuade the court that costs incurred in excess of the budget are reasonable and proportionate
(*Henry v News Group Newspapers Ltd* [2013] EWCA Civ 19, [2013] CP Rep 20 at [28]).

Costs budgets whether or not there is a costs management order

In cases where costs budgets have been used, but there has been no costs management order, **43.20**
one of the factors the court will have regard to when assessing costs is the receiving party's last
approved budget (**CPR, r. 44.4(3)(h)**). This is mandatory. **PD 44, para. 3.4**, goes further, and
says that the court has a discretion to have regard to any other budget previously filed by the
receiving party. Cases where the court refuses to approve costs budgets fall into this category
(*Willis v M. R. J. Rundell and Associates Ltd* [2013] EWHC 2923 (TCC), [2013] 6 Costs LR 924). These
provisions apply to all assessments, both on the standard basis and on the indemnity basis, and
on summary and detailed assessments (**r. 44.4(1)**). Further provisions apply if the costs are
being assessed on a detailed assessment (**PD 44, para. 3.2**, see **43.21**). While there is no presumption against departing from the budget (unlike the position where there has been a costs
management order, see **43.18**), a 20 per cent discrepancy between the last costs budget and
the billed costs may be taken as evidence the costs claimed were unreasonable or disproportionate (**PD 44, para. 3.7**).

Detailed assessment where there has been a costs budget

On a detailed assessment (**PD 44, para. 3.2**), if there is a 20 per cent or more difference between **43.21**
the costs claimed by a receiving party and the costs shown in a costs budget filed by that party,
the receiving party must provide a statement of the reasons for that difference. If a paying party
claims to have reasonably relied on that budget, or if it wishes to rely on the budget to show the
costs claimed are unreasonable or disproportionate, the paying party must serve a statement setting out its case in its points of dispute (**para. 3.3**). Where there is a 20 per cent difference and:

(a) the court finds that the paying party reasonably relied on the budget, the court may
restrict the recoverable costs to such sum as is reasonable for the paying party to pay in the
light of that reliance (**para. 3.6**). This is so even if that sum is less than the amount of costs
reasonably and proportionately incurred by the paying party; or

(b) the court finds the receiving party has not provided a satisfactory explanation for the
difference, the court may regard the difference as evidence that the costs claimed are
unreasonable or disproportionate (**para. 3.7**).

Chapter 44   Costs Capping and Costs Protection

INTRODUCTION

44.1   The Jackson reforms have moved the provisions on costs capping orders, which limit the amount of costs a party may be ordered to pay to its opponent, from the relative obscurity in **CPR, Part 44**, to the mainstream of costs management within **Part 3**. These orders will be considered in this chapter, together with a number of other costs protection orders, namely:

(a) judicial review costs capping orders;
(b) protective costs orders;
(c) orders made in Aarhus Convention cases;
(d) costs limitation orders; and
(e) *Beddoe* orders.

Qualified one-way costs shifting is considered in **chapter 69**.

COSTS CAPPING

Nature of costs capping orders

44.2   A costs capping order is an order limiting the amount of future costs (including disbursements) which a party may recover pursuant to an order for costs subsequently made (**CPR, r. 3.19(1)(a)**). For this purpose 'future costs' are those incurred in respect of work done after the date of the costs capping order, but excluding the amount of any additional liability (**r. 3.19(1)(b)**).

Procedure for applying for a costs capping order

44.3   An application for a costs capping order may be made at any stage of the proceedings (**CPR, r. 3.19(5)**), although it should be made as soon as possible and preferably before the first case management hearing (**PD 3F, para. 1.2**). Where a costs capping order is sought in relation to trust funds, notice of the intention to apply for the order must be filed with the first statement of case or (in relation to Part 8 claims) with the evidence (**para. 5.5**). The application is made using the procedure in **CPR, Part 23** (**CPR, r. 3.20(1)**). The application notice must set out whether the order is sought in respect of the costs of the whole proceedings or on a particular issue which is ordered to be tried separately. It must be accompanied by a costs budget supported by a statement of truth setting out the costs incurred by the applicant to date and the likely future costs (**r. 3.20(2)**; **PD 3F, para. 2**; and see **43.8** for costs budgets). Directions may be made for dealing with the application, which may include filing schedules of costs, time estimates and whether the judge should sit with an assessor (**r. 3.20(3)**).

Requirements for making costs capping orders

By **CPR, r. 3.19(5)**, a costs capping order can only be made if:

(a) it is in the interests of justice to make the order;

(b) there is a substantial risk that without the order costs will be disproportionately incurred; and

(c) the risk of disproportionate costs cannot be adequately controlled by case management directions and orders or by the detailed assessment of costs.

If these conditions are made out, the court has a discretion whether to make the order, which it exercises taking into account all the circumstances of the case, but in particular (**r. 3.19(6)**):

(i) whether there is a substantial imbalance between the financial positions of the parties;

(ii) whether the costs of determining the amount of the cap are likely to be proportionate to the overall costs of the litigation;

(iii) the stage which the proceedings have reached; and

(iv) the costs which have been incurred to date and the future costs.

Discretion to make costs capping orders

The criteria for making costs capping orders set out in **44.4** demand a restrictive approach, and will be satisfied only in an exceptional case (**PD 3F, para. 1.1**; *Barr v Biffa Waste Services Ltd (No. 2)* [2009] EWHC 2444 (TCC), [2010] 3 Costs LR 317). This is in conflict with the statement in the *Jackson Report* at ch. 40, para. 7.18 that the intention was to remove the requirement for 'exceptional circumstances'. Delay weighs against making the order (**PD 3F, para. 1.2**).

Pre-*Jackson* cases were not very consistent on when costs capping orders might be appropriate. In *Smart v East Cheshire NHS Trust* [2003] EWHC 2806 (QB), [2004] 1 Costs LR 124 at [22], Gage J said:

The court should only consider making a costs cap order in cases where the applicant shows by evidence that there is a real and substantial risk that without such an order costs will be disproportionately or unreasonably incurred; and that this risk may not be managed by conventional case management and a detailed assessment of costs after a trial.

A different approach was adopted in *King v Telegraph Group Ltd* [2004] EWCA Civ 613, [2005] 1 WLR 2282 at [92] by Brooke LJ who said: '... it would be very much better for the court to exercise control over costs in advance, rather than to wait reactively until after the case is over and the costs are being assessed'. This is consistent with cases such as *Solutia UK Ltd v Griffiths* [2001] EWCA Civ 736, [2002] PIQR P16 and *Leigh v Michelin Tyre plc* [2003] EWCA Civ 1766, [2004] 1 WLR 846. The object of the order is to encourage the parties to plan the case in advance so as to ensure that costs are proportionate (*Jefferson v National Freight Carriers plc* [2001] EWCA Civ 2082, [2001] 2 Costs LR 313).

In *Henry v British Broadcasting Corporation* [2005] EWHC 2503 (QB), [2006] 1 All ER 154 a costs capping order was refused because the application was made at a very late stage, close to the trial. One of the reasons given in *Willis v Nicholson* [2007] EWCA Civ 199, [2007] PIQR P22 for refusing a cap beyond limiting the claimant to his latest estimate, rather than by a costs capping order, was a concern about the time and costs that would have been involved in having a costs judge decide what the costs cap should be.

44.4

44.5

Commentary

Form of costs capping orders

44.6   Costs capping orders are usually drafted to avoid an inflexible cap, while enabling the court to retain control over the amount of costs at any time. Either party may apply to vary the order, which may be allowed only if there has been a material change of circumstances or if there is some other compelling reason why a variation should be allowed (**CPR, r. 3.19(7)**). An application to vary is made in accordance with **CPR, Part 23** (**r. 3.21**), and should be supported by evidence and a revised costs budget. **Figure 44.1** is a typical costs capping order.

The future base costs of the [Claimant/Defendant] shall not without the permission of the court exceed the sum of £ (save that any costs awarded in favour of a party on any interim application shall not count towards the said £). Either party may apply without notice to increase the figure of £ and any such application shall be supported by a statement addressing the need for the increase and a revised costs budget calculated to trial.

Figure 44.1   Costs capping order

JUDICIAL REVIEW COSTS CAPPING

44.7   Judicial review costs capping came into force on 8 August 2016. It potentially applies where the judicial review claim form is filed from that date. Rather confusingly, the primary legislation calls this a 'costs capping order' (Criminal Justice and Courts Act 2015, s. 88(2)), but this is different from costs capping under **CPR, rr. 3.19** to **3.21**, a point made in the explanatory note to the Civil Procedure (Amendment No. 2) Rules 2016 (SI 2016/707) and in **CPR, r. 46.16(2)**. In the **CPR**, an order made under the Criminal Justice and Courts Act 2015, ss. 88 to 90, is called a 'judicial review costs capping order' (**CPR, r. 46.16(1)(a)**).

Applying for a judicial review costs capping order

44.8   An application for a judicial review costs capping order must normally be made in or accompany the claim form (**PD 46, para. 10.2**). It must be made on notice in accordance with **CPR, Part 23**, supported by written evidence (**r. 46.17(1)**). The evidence in support must set out why the order should be made, having regard to the requirements in the Criminal Justice and Courts Act 2015, s. 88(6)–(8), and the discretionary factors in s. 89(1). It must also include a summary of the applicant's financial resources complying with **PD 46, para. 10.1**, and must set out the costs and disbursements the applicant considers the parties are likely to incur in the future conduct of the proceedings. The court has a power to dispense with the financial statement (**CPR, r. 46.17(3)**), and may make a direction for additional information or evidence (**r. 46.17(4)**). The applicant must serve the application notice and supporting documents on every other party (**r. 46.17(2)**). Where the applicant is a body corporate, the court must consider giving directions for the provision of information about the ability of the applicant's members to provide financial support (**r. 46.18**).

Decision to make a judicial review costs capping order

44.9   Under the Criminal Justice and Courts Act 2015, s. 88(6), the court may make a judicial review costs capping order only if it is satisfied that:

(a) the proceedings are public interest proceedings;

(b) in the absence of the order, the applicant for judicial review would withdraw the application for judicial review or cease to participate in the proceedings; and

(c) it would be reasonable for the applicant for judicial review to do so.

By s. 88(7), proceedings are 'public interest proceedings' only if:

(a) an issue that is the subject of the proceedings is of general public importance;

(b) the public interest requires the issue to be resolved; and

(c) the proceedings are likely to provide an appropriate means of resolving it.

By s. 88(8), factors the court must take into account when determining whether proceedings are public interest proceedings include:

(a) the number of people likely to be directly affected if relief is granted to the applicant for judicial review;

(b) how significant the effect on those people is likely to be; and

(c) whether the proceedings involve consideration of a point of law of general public importance.

In exercising its discretion whether to make a judicial review costs capping order the court will take into account (s. 89(1)):

(a) the financial resources of the parties, including those of any person who may provide financial support to the parties;

(b) the extent to which the applicant for the order is likely to benefit if judicial review relief is granted;

(c) the extent to which any person who has provided, or may provide, the applicant with financial support is likely to benefit if relief is granted to the applicant for judicial review;

(d) whether legal representatives for the applicant for the order are acting free of charge; and

(e) whether the applicant for the order is an appropriate person to represent the interests of other persons or the public interest generally.

Under s. 89(2), a judicial review costs capping order that limits or removes the liability of the applicant for judicial review to pay the costs of another party to the proceedings if relief is not granted must also limit or remove the liability of the other party to pay the applicant's costs if judicial review is granted.

PROTECTIVE COSTS ORDERS

Under a PCO the applicant is given an immunity against paying the costs of the defendant. **44.10**
When first introduced, PCOs were most typically made in judicial review proceedings where the claimant would gain no personal benefit from a successful result. This function is now performed by judicial review costs capping orders (see **44.7** to **44.9**). Technically, PCOs have not been abolished (see **CPR, r. 3.19(2)**), but their ambit has been severely restricted.

Where a PCO has been made it may be inappropriate to require the parties to submit costs budgets because costs budgeting and PCOs have a similar effect (*Lumsdon v Legal Services Board* [2013] EWHC 3289 (Admin), LTL 5/11/2013).

Procedure for seeking a PCO

The procedure for seeking a PCO, according to *R (Corner House Research) v Secretary of State for* **44.11**
Trade and Industry [2005] EWCA Civ 192, [2005] 1 WLR 2600, is that:

(a) the claim form should on its face include the claim for the PCO;

(b) if the defendant intends to resist the application, reasons should be set out in the acknowledgment of service under **CPR, r. 54.8**;

(c) a judge will consider the application on the papers (if the order is granted, the defendant has the right to apply to have the order set aside, but has to show compelling reasons to alter the order (*R (Compton) v Wiltshire Primary Care Trust* [2008] EWCA Civ 749, [2009] 1 WLR 1436));

discretion is not necessarily restricted to those categories, and orders have been made in favour of a receiver in a company liquidation (*Re Wedstock Realizations Ltd* [1988] BCLC 354) and in favour of employees engaged in hostile litigation against their pension fund trustees (*McDonald v Horn* [1995] ICR 685).

A liquidator considering bringing proceedings for wrongful trading, preferences or in respect of transactions at an undervalue is not automatically entitled to the costs of those proceedings from the assets of the company (*Lewis v Commissioner of Inland Revenue* [2001] 3 All ER 499) and should consider making an application for a *Beddoe* order.

Where a derivative claim is made on behalf of a company, or other body capable of suing in its own name, that company or body may be ordered, under **CPR, r. 19.9E**, to indemnify the claimant against liability for costs. This was first established in *Wallersteiner v Moir (No. 2)* [1975] QB 373 and orders indemnifying claimants in derivative claims are sometimes called *Wallersteiner* orders.

Procedure for seeking a *Beddoe* order

44.16 The fact that a pre-emptive costs order is sought must be stated in the claim form (**PD 19C, para. 2(2)**). If an indemnity is also sought for the costs of the application for permission to continue the claim, that must be stated in the permission application (**PD 19C, para. 2(2)**).

Where trustees properly exercise a power vested in them to agree the costs of another party in relation to the administration of a trust there is no need for a court order, and the assessment of the costs can be dealt with under **CPR, r. 46.3**. Where the trustees have no such power, or decide against exercising it, an application will be necessary if a prospective costs order is to be made, and Practice Statement (Trust Proceedings: Prospective Costs Orders) [2001] 1 WLR 1082 applies. This sets out a model form of prospective costs order, and provides that in the absence of a dispute as to whether such an order is appropriate most such applications will be dealt with on the papers.

Where the application is made before proceedings are commenced, it is made by application notice in accordance with **CPR, r. 25.2**. Applications made during the course of existing proceedings are also made by application notice. In addition to asking for the indemnity as to costs mentioned above, the application normally also asks for directions whether the applicant should continue or defend the claim, and for any further or other relief. The application, in the usual case, is entirely domestic to the estate or trust concerned, so is often conducted in an informal manner, with material accepted on instructions without formal proof (*Re Evans* [1986] 1 WLR 101). On the first return day the court may adjourn the application so that letters may be sent to the beneficiaries of the fund informing them of the nature of the application and of their right to file evidence and appear on any further hearing of the application.

Decision whether to make a *Beddoe* order

44.17 When the court is considering making a pre-emptive costs order in favour of a person making a derivative claim for the benefit of a company, it is not an inflexible rule that an order will be refused if the company is jointly owned by the claimant and defendant (*Mumbray v Lapper* [2005] EWHC 1152 (Ch), [2005] BCC 990). It is better to say that when considering whether to make such an order the court will take into consideration the effect the order would have on the defendant's interests in the company: it may be unfair that a successful defendant who is not required to pay the unsuccessful claimant's costs should nevertheless have to bear a substantial loss in the value of his shares when the company pays the costs (*Halle v Trax BW Ltd* [2000] BCC 1020). Despite obiter indications to the contrary in *Halle v Trax BW Ltd*, there is no rule that a successful derivative claimant has a lien, on assets recovered in the claim, for costs (*Qayoumi v Oakhouse Property Holdings plc* [2002] EWHC 2547 (Ch), [2003] 1 BCLC 352).

A pre-emptive costs order was made in *Re Axa Equity and Life Assurance Society plc (No. 1)* [2001] 2 BCLC 447 in favour of an objector to a scheme of reorganisation of an insurance business which contained novel provisions and where the presence of the objector was necessary to test that the scheme was fair. Such orders will not be made where the litigation is really a hostile claim by one beneficiary against another (*Trustee Corporation Ltd v Nadir* [2001] BPIR 541). Nor will they be made where the litigation can be of no benefit to the trust (*Weth v Attorney General* [2001] EWCA Civ 263, LTL 23/2/2001).

Each application depends on its own facts and is essentially a matter for the discretion of the Master or judge who hears it. In exercising that discretion the court will take into account the following considerations:

(a) The importance of affording full and proper protection for the costs and expenses of trustees and personal representatives acting properly to protect the fund against adverse claims (*Re Turner* [1907] 2 Ch 126). Conversely, if after trial the court would be unlikely to make an order for payment of the trustee's costs out of the fund it would not be right to make a pre-emptive order (*Re Wedstock Realizations Ltd* [1988] BCLC 354), for example, as in the case of hostile litigation.

(b) The court has to form a view of the prospects of success or failure in the underlying action (*Re Dallaway* [1982] 1 WLR 756). In *National Anti-Vivisection Society Ltd v Duddington* (1989) *The Times,* 23 November 1989, Mummery J said that the fund in dispute should not be used to support contentions which were not made in good faith or on reasonable grounds. Obviously, the court should not be invited to conduct a mini-trial on the merits of the action. A weak claim against the fund would be a powerful reason for making an order in favour of the trustees (*Re Evans* [1986] 1 WLR 101 per Nourse LJ).

(c) A pre-emptive order should not be made if there is a real possibility of it operating unjustly. Where the beneficiaries are all adult, are not incapacitated and can make up their own minds whether the claim should be resisted or not, there must be countervailing considerations of some weight before it is right for the claim to be pursued or defended at the cost of the fund (*Re Evans* [1986] 1 WLR 101).

(d) Occasionally, there may be special factors to be weighed, for example where it is essential for a company administrator to obtain the court's decision because there is a large class of creditors who may be affected by the decision (*Re Exchange Securities and Commodities Ltd (No. 2)* [1985] BCLC 392).

Chapter 45 Small Claims

INTRODUCTION

45.1 The small claims track limit was raised from £5,000 to £10,000 on 1 April 2013. Detailed rules on allocating claims to the small claims track were considered at **42.28**. Despite the adjective 'small', the track is of immense significance to the civil justice system. Every year over 55,000 judicial determinations are made of cases in the small claims track representing over 75 per cent of all cases disposed of by way of final hearing.

The term 'small claim' is unfortunate given that the upper limit of the financial jurisdiction represents a sum which many would consider a large claim. Cases within the small claims track can range from very modest consumer disputes or arguments over dry-cleaning through to technically complex disputes over credit hire and factually complicated disagreements over building extensions. Many small claims relate to road traffic accidents.

The small claims track provides an entirely different type of dispute determination from that offered by the other two tracks. The basic 'no costs' rule positively encourages parties to represent themselves. Pre-hearing preparation is less formal than on the other case management tracks. Standard and menu disclosures do not apply. Witness statements are exchanged on the small claims track only where the nature of the case makes this desirable. There are severe restrictions on the use of expert evidence. At the hearing the District Judge may well adopt an interventionist approach designed to elicit the relevant information as quickly and as informally as possible.

For professional legal advisers the challenges are considerable. It is necessary to form a view of the merits of a case very quickly and often on the basis of a paucity of evidence. The client may not wish to incur the cost of legal representation at the hearing; in that case the role of the professional adviser is to advise on the merits of the case, to ensure that the client discloses copies of all the documents on which he intends to rely and to ensure that, if appropriate, the client's case is adequately set out in a witness statement. If necessary, the legal adviser may also assist in the preparation of an expert's report.

The European small claims procedure, which applies to cross-border civil and commercial cases which do not exceed €2,000, is considered at **45.33**.

SUMMARY JUDGMENT IN SMALL VALUE CLAIMS

It is open to a claimant or defendant to apply for summary judgment (see **chapter 34**). This **45.2** should normally be done before track allocation (**PD 26, para. 5.3(1)**). If summary judgment is given before allocation in a claim which is otherwise suitable for the small claims track, subject to **CPR, r. 46.13(3)**, the successful party can apply for costs in the ordinary way and is not subject to the rule providing for only modest fixed costs on the small claims track (see **45.28** and **68.34**).

ALLOCATION TO THE SMALL CLAIMS TRACK

Allocation rules

The rules governing allocation to the small claims track are considered in **chapter 42**, espe- **45.3** cially at **42.27** and **42.28**.

Remedy claimed

There is no restriction on the nature of remedies which can be granted on the small claims **45.4** track (**CPR, r. 27.3**). Thus injunctions, possession, restitution, specific performance and the like are available to the same extent as on the other tracks, though jurisdiction to grant search orders is restricted to the High Court (County Court Remedies Regulations 2014 (SI 2014/982), reg. 3).

DISTINCTIVE FEATURES OF THE SMALL CLAIMS TRACK

The important differences between small claims and the other tracks are: **45.5**

(a) Some rules and procedures have no application on the small claims track (see **45.6**).
(b) There is a Small Claims Mediation Service that may be used if all the parties indicate on their directions questionnaires that they agree to mediation (see **42.64**).
(c) The procedures after allocation are different (see **45.7** to **45.12**).
(d) Pre-trial checklists are not used on the small claims track.
(e) The procedure at the hearing is different (see **45.14** to **45.26**).
(f) The procedure on appeals (see **45.27**).
(g) Costs provisions are different (see **45.28** to **45.32**).

RESTRICTION ON APPLICATION OF THE CPR

CPR, r. 27.2, provides that on the small claims track the following parts of the CPR do not apply: **45.6**

(a) **Part 25** (interim remedies) except as it relates to interim injunctions.
(b) **Part 31** (disclosure and inspection).

(c) **Part 32** (evidence) except **r. 32.1**, which gives the court a general power to control evidence.

(d) **Part 33** (miscellaneous rules about evidence).

(e) **Part 35** (experts and assessors) except **r. 35.1**, which restricts the use of expert evidence, **r. 35.3**, which sets out the expert's overriding duty to the court and **rr. 35.7** and **35.8** (use of a single joint expert). **Rules 35.4(3A)** (only one expert) and **35.5(2)** (expert not to attend the hearing unless necessary) have express references to the small claims track, and are intended to apply to these cases, despite a drafting defect in **r. 27.2**.

(f) **Part 18** (further information), but see **45.16**.

(g) **Part 36** (offers to settle), but see **45.29**.

(h) **Part 39** (hearings) except **r. 39.2**, which is the general rule that hearings are to be in public.

In principle the other parts of the CPR apply to small claims except to the extent that any rule limits such application.

SMALL CLAIMS TRACK PROCEDURE

45.7   **Figure 45.1** is a flowchart of the small claims track procedure.

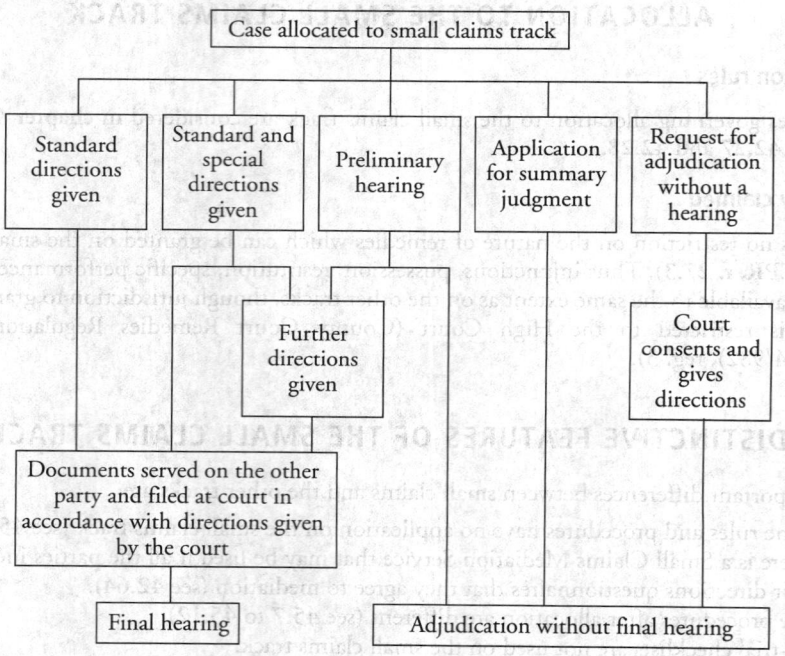

Figure 45.1 Small claims track procedure

Under **CPR, r. 27.4** once a case has been allocated to the small claims track the court has five options (described below) on how the case will be dealt with through to final disposal. Most small claims are given standard directions and a fixed hearing date (option 1). A party may ask the court to give particular directions (**PD 27, para. 2.4**), and should normally do so when returning the directions questionnaire. The court is given a general power under **CPR, r. 27.7**, to add to, vary or revoke directions.

Option 1: standard directions and fixed final hearing date

The court may give standard directions and fix a date for the final hearing (**CPR, r. 27.4(1)(a)**). **45.8**

By **r. 27.4(3)(a)**, read together with **PD 27, para. 2.2** and **app. B**, 'standard directions' means directions:

(a) that each party shall, at least 14 days before the date fixed for the final hearing, file and serve on every other party copies of all documents (including the letter before claim, any reply, and any expert's report) on which he intends to rely at the hearing;

(b) that the original documents must be brought to the hearing;

(c) fixing the hearing date and time allowed;

(d) encouraging the parties to contact each other with a view to trying to settle the claim or narrow the issues, and requiring the parties to notify the court immediately if the claim is settled; and

(e) informing the parties that they cannot rely on expert evidence at the hearing without a direction giving express permission to do so.

The relevant set of standard directions will be sent out by the court in the form of an order along with notification of the hearing date.

District Judges' experience will usually enable them to give a reasonable estimate of the length of hearing for routine cases. Most courts adopt a 'back-to-back' system for listing small claims cases so that, for example, two or more District Judges are jointly listed to hear many hours' worth of cases whose litigants are all instructed to attend court at 10.00 a.m. or 2.00 p.m. Experience shows that it is usually safe for the court to list twice or even three times the number of cases that could in fact be properly dealt with if all parties attended. Most small claim hearings take less than an hour; very few take more than one day.

Option 2: special directions and further directions

Instead of using the standard directions in **PD 27, app. B**, the court can give 'special directions' and consider what further directions are to be given no later than 28 days after giving special directions (**CPR, r. 27.4(1)(c)**). The power is seldom used. More usually a District Judge will either vary the standard directions, give special directions and fix a final hearing or alternatively fix a preliminary hearing. **45.9**

Option 3: special directions and fixed final hearing date

The court may give special directions and fix a date for the final hearing (**CPR, r. 27.4(1)(b)**). This will be appropriate where the District Judge can formulate special directions for the case without needing to hold a preliminary hearing. 'Special directions' are often based on the standard directions, although they can be completely tailor-made (**r. 27.4(3)(b)**). In formulating special directions, District Judges use their experience, the information and requests for directions in the directions questionnaires, and the guidance in **PD 27, app. A** (see **45.14**) on the information and documentation usually required for certain types of claim. **45.10**

Option 4: preliminary hearing

The court may fix a date for a preliminary hearing (**CPR, r. 27.4(1)(d)**). **45.11**

Consistent with the policy that the parties should attend court only when it is essential for them to do so, **r. 27.6** provides that the court may hold a preliminary hearing for the consideration of a small claim only in one of three situations:

(a) Where the court considers that special directions under **r. 27.4** are needed to ensure a fair hearing, and it appears necessary for a party to attend court to ensure that the party understands what must be done to comply with the special directions. This

Commentary

will be where the court considers (possibly from the content of the documents received) that it may be necessary to have the parties before the court to ensure that they understand what they must do in order that the case may be properly and efficiently progressed. Alternatively, it may be that special directions need to be considered, and that it would be inappropriate for the District Judge to make them without hearing the parties.

(b) To enable the court to dispose of the claim on the basis that one of the parties has no real prospect of success. This may be obvious from the documents, for example, where the claim is based on a cause of action not known to English law. In less clear-cut cases, particularly where the only witnesses are the parties themselves, the better course would often be to have the case listed for a short final hearing. That would permit the party with no apparent prospect of success an opportunity to present his evidence before the judicial decision is reached.

(c) To enable the court to strike out the whole or part of a statement of case where it discloses no reasonable grounds for bringing or defending the claim. This provision follows on from the one before. Alternatively, if the failure to disclose a cause of action or defence is due to sloppy drafting, an opportunity should be given to amend.

By r. 27.6(4), the court may treat a preliminary hearing as the final hearing of the claim if all parties agree. It is unlikely that this will commonly apply unless the point is a very short one, as it would otherwise mean that the preliminary appointment could take the same time as the substantive hearing.

After the preliminary hearing, the court will fix the date of the final hearing and inform the parties of the amount of time allowed, together with any other appropriate directions (r. 27.6(5)).

Option 5: proceeding without a hearing

45.12 The court may, if all parties agree, deal with a small claim without a hearing (CPR, r. 27.10). Rule 27.10 is infrequently used. It appears to give the court a discretion to refuse to deal with a claim on paper even if that is what the parties want. Dealing with a small claim without a hearing might be appropriate where, for example, one party is living outside the jurisdiction and is either unable or unwilling to return for an oral hearing. In such a case the District Judge would direct that copies of the relevant documents and witness statements be lodged; he would then give a written judgment.

HEARING FEE

45.13 Within 14 days of the date of dispatch of the notice (or the date when oral notice is given if no written notice is given) of the hearing date (or window), the claimant must pay the hearing fee (CPFO, fee 2.1). This is:

Value of claim	Hearing fee
Does not exceed £300	£25
£300.01 to £500	£55
£500.01 to £1,000	£80
£1,000.01 to £1,500	£115
£1,500.01 to £3,000	£170
Exceeds £3,000	£335

The hearing fee is payable by the defendant if the action is proceeding on the counterclaim alone. The fee for a case which exceeds the small claims track limit, but which is to be heard as a small claims track case, is £335 (rather than the fast track hearing fee of £545).

The hearing fee is refunded in full if the court receives notice in writing from the party who paid the fee, at least seven days before the date set for the hearing, that the case has been settled or discontinued.

SPECIAL DIRECTIONS

Information and documentation usually needed for particular types of claim

PD 27, app. A, sets out the type of information and documentation normally required for four types of claim frequently met on the small claims track. In the following lists, entries in square brackets have been added by the editors of this work. **45.14**

(a) Road traffic accident claims:
- witness statements, including from the parties themselves;
- invoices and estimates for repairs;
- agreements and invoices for any car hire costs;
- the police accident report;
- sketch plan, which should be agreed if possible;
- photographs of the scene of the accident and the damage.

(b) Building disputes, repairs, sale of goods, and similar contract claims:
- any written contract [or correspondence evidencing the contract, including any specification for the contract works];
- photographs;
- any plans;
- a list of the works complained of;
- [written complaints by the customer and any responses];
- a list of any outstanding works;
- any relevant estimate, invoice or receipt including any relating to repairs to each of the defects;
- invoices for work done or goods supplied;
- estimates for work to be completed;
- a valuation of work done to date.

(c) Landlord and tenant claims:
- a calculation of the amount of rent alleged to be owing, showing amounts received;
- details of breaches of an agreement which are said to justify withholding any deposit itemised showing how the total is made up and with invoices and estimates to support them;
- [the tenancy agreement, or correspondence evidencing the agreement];
- [contemporaneous documentation proving rent received];
- [documents showing complaints by the tenant];
- [documents showing work done on behalf of the landlord].

(d) Breach of duty cases (negligence, deficient professional services, etc). Details of the following:
- what it is said by the claimant was done negligently by the defendant;
- why it is said that the negligence is the fault of the defendant;
- what damage is said to have been caused;
- what injury or losses have been suffered and how any (and each) sum claimed has been calculated;
- the response of the defendant to each of the above.

Format of special directions

45.15 To assist court users, **PD 27, app. C**, sets out model special directions dealing with:

(a) further information to clarify a party's case;

(b) inspection of property;

(c) final hearing to take place at a location other than the court;

(d) requiring items to be brought to court;

(e) exchange of witness statements;

(f) warning that evidence will not be allowed if directions are not complied with;

(g) the form of an unless order;

(h) expert evidence;

(i) video evidence.

Requests for further information

45.16 The parties to a small claim are not permitted to make requests for further information under **CPR, Part 18**, see **r. 27.2(1)(f)**. This is subject to **r. 27.2(3)**, which says the court of its own initiative may order a party to provide further information if it considers it appropriate to do so. This is useful where the particulars of claim or defence are unclear and the court needs further information to clarify the case that the litigant intends to advance.

Documents

45.17 Parties to cases on the small claims track are not subject to the standard disclosure obligations of disclosing documents which adversely affect their case or support another party's case (**CPR, rr. 27.2(1)(b)** and **31.6**). Standard small claims directions do, however, require parties to file and serve, at least 14 days before the hearing, copies of the documents on which they intend to rely at the hearing (**r. 27.4(3)(a)**). When this is read together with the lists of documentation usually required in the types of cases considered in **PD 27, app. A**, it is clear that there is a fairly extensive obligation on the parties in small claims cases to provide documentation in support of their side of the dispute.

Witness statements

45.18 In deciding whether to make an order for the exchange of witness statements in a small claim, **PD 27, para. 2.5**, provides that the court must have regard to:

(a) whether either or both parties are represented;

(b) the amount in dispute;

(c) the nature of the matters in dispute. **PD 27, app. A**, says that witness statements will usually be required in road traffic accident claims. They may also be needed in more complex small claims, such as building disputes and holiday claims;

(d) whether the need for any party to clarify his case could better be dealt with by ordering him to provide further information under **PD 27, para. 2.3**;

(e) the need for the parties to have access to justice without undue formality, cost or delay.

By **CPR, r. 27.2(1)(c)**, the provisions of **rr. 32.2 to 32.19** (which include the provisions concerning the form and use of witness statements) do not apply to cases on the small claims track. Subject to the precise terms of the relevant direction, it is therefore permissible to use informal witness statements when these are ordered in small claims track cases.

Expert evidence

45.19 Most small claims can be resolved without expert evidence. The court is obliged to restrict expert evidence to that which is reasonably required to resolve the proceedings (**CPR, r. 35.1**), and normally only one expert may give evidence on a particular issue (**r. 35.4(3A)**). Where experts are required, permission must be expressly granted (**r. 27.5**). Usually the court will direct the evidence to be given through a written report of a jointly instructed expert (**PD 27, app. C; Guidance for Experts 2014, para. 34; CPR, rr. 35.7** and **35.8**, on the power to direct evidence to be given by a single joint expert, and on instructions to a single joint expert, apply to cases on the small claims track, see **r. 27.2(1)(e)**). A direction for the expert to attend the hearing will be given only if necessary in the interests of justice (**r. 35.5(2)**). The court will normally also give directions allowing the parties to put written questions to the expert. If the court allows each side to instruct an expert, any discussions between the experts should be by telephone or letter (**Guidance for Experts 2014, para. 74**). The costs which may be recovered by a successful party are limited to £750 for each expert (**PD 27, para. 7.3(2)**). While an expert on this track still owes an overriding duty to the court (**CPR, r. 35.3**), his or her report need not comply with all the requirements of **Part 35** (most of which is disapplied by **r. 27.2(1)(e)**). An informal letter from the expert will often suffice.

CONDUCT OF THE FINAL HEARING

The final hearing of a small claim will normally be before a District Judge. The hearing may be assigned to a Circuit Judge (**PD 27, para. 1**), with that judge's consent (**PD 2B, para. 11.2**), but this rarely happens, not least because any appeal would have to be taken to the High Court.   **45.20**

Hearings are informal, the strict rules of evidence do not apply, and expert evidence (whether written or oral) may be given only with the court's permission (**CPR, rr. 27.5** and **27.8**). The District Judge may well adopt an interventionist approach. In a small claim hearing the court will not always insist on the production of expert evidence, whereas it might be required for a similar case on one of the other tracks (*Bandegani v Norwich Union Fire Insurance Society Ltd* (1999) LTL 20/5/99, in which the claimant did not produce expert evidence for the value of a car which had been damaged in an accident).

Representation

By **PD 27, para. 3.2(1)**, at a hearing on the small claims track, a party's case may be presented: **45.21**

(a) by the party personally;
(b) by a lawyer; or
(c) by a lay representative.

A 'lawyer' means a barrister, a solicitor or legal executive employed by a solicitor (**para. 3.1(1)**). A 'lay representative' means any other person (**para. 3.1(2)**).

By **para. 3.2(2)** and **(3)**, the court's permission must be obtained for representation by a lay representative in the following circumstances:

(a) if the party being represented by the lay person is not present;
(b) if judgment has been given in the claim; or
(c) if the hearing is of an appeal against any decision made by the District Judge in the proceedings.

The court may refuse to hear a lay representative in any proceedings if it is of the opinion that he or she is acting in an unruly manner in those proceedings (Courts and Legal Services Act 1990, s. 11(4)). The court must specify the conduct which warranted its refusal (s. 11(5)).

An individual may be prohibited by an order of a County Court judge under s. 11(6) from acting as a lay representative. An order under s. 11(6) may be made where the judge has reason to believe that, in the present proceedings or any other proceedings, the individual has intentionally misled the court, or otherwise demonstrated unsuitability to exercise a right of audience. In *Paragon Finance plc v Noueiri* [2001] EWCA Civ 1402, [2001] 1 WLR 2357 (where a prohibition order was made by the Court of Appeal under its inherent jurisdiction), the representative's unsuitability was demonstrated by:

(a) his failure, or refusal, to understand crucial procedural rules;
(b) his bankruptcy, which meant that it would be futile to order him to pay wasted costs.

A corporate party is physically incapable of presenting its own case, but may be represented by a lawyer or a lay representative (*Avinue Ltd v Sunrule Ltd* [2003] EWCA Civ 1942, [2004] 1 WLR 634) or by any officer or employee (**PD 27, para. 3.2(4)**).

Public hearing

45.22 According to **PD 27, para. 4.1**, the hearing of a small claim will usually be in public, but the judge may decide to hold it in private if:

(a) the parties agree, or

(b) a ground mentioned in **CPR, r. 39.2(3)**, applies.

PD 27 goes on to say at **para. 4.2** that a hearing that takes place at the court will generally be in the judge's room, but it may take place in a courtroom. It may involve a site visit if the time involved is proportionate, though judgment will be given in the judge's room rather than on site.

Method of proceeding

45.23 **CPR, r. 27.8**, allows the court to adopt any method of proceeding at a small claims hearing that it considers to be fair. The hearings are informal, evidence need not be taken on oath (and in practice rarely is) and the court may limit cross-examination. **PD 27, para. 4.3**, provides that the judge may in particular:

(a) ask questions of any witness before allowing any other person to do so,

(b) ask questions of all or any of the witnesses before allowing any other person to ask questions of any witnesses,

(c) refuse to allow cross-examination of any witness until all the witnesses have given evidence-in-chief,

(d) limit cross-examination of a witness to a fixed time or to a particular subject or issue or both.

All the above is consistent with the interventionist approach. The District Judge will have pre-read all the papers and is thus able to focus on areas of evidence materially in dispute. Such an approach is favoured by most unrepresented parties although it remains important to ensure that every party has a reasonable opportunity to say or ask all they want to.

If both parties are legally represented, matters may proceed more efficiently if the usual sequence of a court trial is observed, with short opening speeches if of assistance, formal evidence given in chief (although a direction for witness statements to stand as evidence-in-chief may be useful), cross-examination, re-examination and closing speeches. With unrepresented litigants, the District Judge will assess the situation and the parties and decide what he or she needs to hear in order both to do justice and to ensure that the parties feel that within reason they have had their say. Although a District Judge may control cross-examination by the parties, it would not be appropriate to forbid cross-examination entirely (*Chilton v Saga Holidays plc* [1986] 1 All ER 841).

Hearings without the parties

45.24 Under **CPR, r. 27.9(1)**, a party to a small claim may request the court, by written notice given at least seven days before the hearing, to decide the claim without that party being present. A party who wishes to make use of this facility must serve every other party with copies of the documents filed at court at least seven days before the hearing (**r. 27.9(1)(b)**). If these steps are taken (and the party, as indicated, does not attend the hearing), the court will take into account the statement of case and any other documents filed by that party when deciding the claim (**r. 27.9(1)**).

If a *claimant* has not given notice under **r. 27.9(1)** but then does not attend the hearing, the court may, and usually will, strike out the claim (**r. 27.9(2)**).

The word 'may' in **r. 27.9(2)** gives the court a discretion and thus a party who has misunderstood the requirement to give seven days' notice and perhaps sends in a fax on the morning of the hearing, requesting the court to deal with the case on the basis of his written statements, will no doubt be given some indulgence. If the opposing party can demonstrate any prejudice caused by the lack of notice of the other party's non-appearance, an adjournment may be permitted. This may be, for example, because the party who is present needed to cross-examine the absent party about some feature of his case which would have demonstrated, e.g. the falseness of a particular piece of evidence, or that a certain document was not authentic. There may well also be a class of case where one party needs the other to attend in order to establish quantum, e.g. claims by former employees to commission payments based on sales. Generally speaking, a party who attends is likely to fare better than a party who does not attend.

If a *defendant* does not attend a hearing or give notice under **r. 27.9(1)**, and the claimant either does attend or has given the notice referred to, the court may, and usually will, decide the claim on the basis of the evidence of the claimant alone (**r. 27.9(3)**).

If *neither party* attends or gives notice, the court may strike out the claim and any defence and counterclaim (**r. 27.9(4)**).

Nothing in these provisions affects the general power of the court to adjourn a hearing for good reason, e.g. where a party who wishes to attend cannot do so because of illness.

Recording evidence and giving reasons

A court hearing of a small claim is tape-recorded by the court (**PD 27, para. 5.1**) and a party **45.25** may thereafter obtain a transcript on payment of the proper charges. The fact that a party is exempt from paying court fees does not mean that he or she can obtain a transcript without charge, since such charges are not made by Her Majesty's Courts and Tribunals Service directly.

The court must give reasons for its decision (**CPR, r. 27.8(6)**) and will do so 'as briefly and simply as the nature of the case allows' (**PD 27, para. 5.3(1)**). Reasons are normally given orally at the hearing although they may be given later, either in writing or at a hearing fixed for that purpose (**para. 5.3(2)**).

Where the judge decides the case without a hearing under **CPR, r. 27.10**, or a party who has given notice under **r. 27.9(1)** does not attend the hearing, the judge will prepare a note of his or her reasons and the court will send a copy to each party (**PD 27, para. 5.4**).

One practical difficulty is that of an impecunious and unrepresented party who is unable to afford the cost of a transcript. In such circumstances a Circuit Judge, before hearing an appeal or when deciding whether to give permission to appeal, may be of the opinion that a note from the District Judge setting out the main reasons for his decision would be of assistance; such a note from the District Judge to the Circuit Judge should be made available to all the parties.

Setting judgment aside and rehearing

A party to a small claim who was neither present nor represented at the hearing of the claim, **45.26** and who did not give written notice to the court under **CPR, r. 27.9(1)**, may apply for an order that judgment shall be set aside and the claim reheard (**r. 27.11(1)**).

To do this, application must be made not more than 14 days after the day on which notice of the judgment was served on that party (**r. 27.11(2)**). The court may then, by **r. 27.11(3)**, grant an application *only* if the applicant:

(a) had a good reason for not attending or being represented at the hearing or giving written notice to the court under **r. 27.9(1)**; and
(b) has a reasonable prospect of success at the hearing.

Commentary

Compare **r. 39.3(5)**, discussed in **62.2**, which applies to setting aside a judgment given in the absence of a party on the fast track or multi-track, but does not (by **r. 27.2(1)(h)**) apply to the small claims track.

A party may not apply to set judgment aside under **r. 27.11** if the court dealt with the claim without a hearing under **r. 27.10** (i.e. by an order of the court with the consent of the parties dispensing with the hearing (**r. 27.11(5)**).

A party who was deliberately absent from court without a proper reason has no right to have a rehearing, however strong that party's case may be. If the court concludes that there is good reason for the absence, there is still an obligation on the party applying to show a reasonable prospect of success. This may go beyond consideration of whatever documents have been previously filed and may lead to the court asking for written evidence or further documentary evidence.

If judgment is set aside, the court must fix a new hearing (**r. 27.11(4)(a)**). The new hearing may take place immediately after the hearing of the application to set aside the judgment and may be dealt with by the judge who set aside the judgment (**r. 27.11(4)(b)**).

APPEALS

45.27   The procedure for appeals is considered in **chapters** 74 and 75. An appeal against a court's order may be made only with the permission of that court or of the appeal court (**CPR, r. 52.3**). An appellant's notice in a small claim appeal must be in form N164 (**PD 27, para. 8A; PD 52B, para. 4.1**). A party to a case on the small claims track who wishes to appeal against an order made under **r. 27.10**, without a hearing, or in that party's absence in accordance with a request under **r. 27.9**, must apply to the appeal court for permission (**PD 27, para. 8.2**). When a decision has been made by a District Judge (as is usual on the small claims track), the 'appeal court' for these purposes is the Circuit Judge at the same County Court hearing centre (**PD 52A, para. 3.5** and **Table 1**). If permission to appeal has not been given by the District Judge, it must be requested in the appellant's notice (**CPR, r. 52.12(1)**).

The documents to be filed with the appellant's notice are a sealed copy of the order under appeal, any order granting or refusing permission to appeal, and the grounds of appeal (**PD 52B, para. 4.2**). There is no requirement to file a transcript of the District Judge's judgment in a small claims track appeal (**para. 6.2**). An appeal bundle must be filed within 35 days of filing the appellant's notice (**para. 6.3**), which must contain only those documents relevant to the appeal. Subject to any order by the appeal court, a list of documents that should be included in the appeal bundle is set out in **para. 6.4**.

If an appeal against an order made on the small claims track is allowed, the appeal court will, if possible, dispose of the case at the same time, rather than referring it back to the lower court or ordering a new hearing (**PD 27, para. 8.3**). The appeal court may dispose of the case without hearing further evidence (**para. 8.3**).

COSTS

Costs after allocation

45.28   After a claim has been allocated to the small claims track there are considerable restrictions on the costs that the successful party may recover. The restrictions apply both to the original proceedings and to any subsequent appeal (*Conlon v Royal Sun Alliance Insurance plc* [2015] EWCA

Civ 92, [2015] CP Rep 23). In principle (**CPR, r. 27.14(2)**) the court may not order a party to pay a sum to another party in respect of that other party's costs except:

(a) the fixed costs payable under **Part 45** (or which would be payable if **Part 45** applied) attributable to issuing the claim (**r. 27.14(2)(a)**);

(b) in proceedings which include a claim for an injunction or specific performance, an amount not exceeding £260 for legal advice and assistance relating to that claim (**r. 27.14(2)(b); PD 27, para. 7.2**);

(c) any court fees paid by the successful party (**r. 27.14(2)(c)**);

(d) expenses which a party or witness has reasonably incurred in travelling to or from a hearing or in staying away from home for the purposes of attending a hearing (**r. 27.14(2)(d)**);

(e) a sum not exceeding £90 a day for any loss of earnings or loss of leave by a party or witness due to attending a hearing or to staying away from home for the purpose of attending a hearing (**r. 27.14(2)(e); PD 27, para. 7.3**);

(f) a sum not exceeding £750 per expert for an expert's fees (**r. 27.14(2)(f); PD 27, para. 7.3**);

(g) such further costs as the court may assess by the summary procedure and order to be paid by a party who has behaved unreasonably;

(h) any unpaid Stage 1 and Stage 2 fixed costs under **CPR, r. 45.29**, pursuant to the RTA and EL/PL Protocols (see **8.29** to **8.60**) where the claimant reasonably believed the claim was valued at more than the small claims track limit and the defendant admitted liability; and

(i) in an appeal, the cost of any approved transcript reasonably incurred.

Unreasonable behaviour

Instead of the limited costs normally recoverable on the small claims track (see **45.28**), a successful party may seek to recover all of his costs from a party who has behaved unreasonably (**CPR, r. 27.14(2)(g)**). This inevitably involves the court exercising a wide discretion. The following may, it is suggested, be considered to be unreasonable:

45.29

(a) making a claim which the court has found to be wholly false;

(b) pursuing an untenable claim (*Memon v TNT UK Ltd* (2009) LTL 30/11/2009, claiming 30 days' loss of use of a car which was repaired in one day);

(c) failure to inform the court of the non-attendance of a witness;

(d) deliberate delay in dealing with an undeniable claim so as to force a party to issue proceedings;

(e) filing a spurious defence and then not attending the final hearing;

(f) paying the claim in full just before the final hearing;

(g) making unnecessary procedural applications;

(h) possibly, rejecting a Part 36 offer (see below).

A material factor may be that the rules in **Part 36** on offers to settle have no application in small claims proceedings (**r. 27.2(1)(g)**). **Rule 27.14(3)** provides that a party's rejection of an offer in settlement will not of itself constitute unreasonable behaviour under **r. 27.14(2)(g)**, but the court may take it into consideration when it is applying the unreasonableness test. A strong case should be required before the court holds that rejection of an offer is unreasonable behaviour.

When the court concludes that a party has behaved unreasonably, the court must conduct an immediate and summary assessment of the costs to be paid (**r. 27.14(2)(g)**). It will thus be important for a party who expects to be able successfully to press a claim for costs to have information available on the status of the fee earner, time claimed for attendances, correspondence, documents and so on, or even to have completed a formal statement of costs.

Costs after leaving the small claims track

If a case is reallocated from the small claims track to another track, the small claims costs provisions cease to apply after the claim has been reallocated and the fast track or multi-track rules will thereafter apply (**CPR, r. 27.15**).

45.30

Costs before reallocation to the small claims track

45.31   If a claim has been on some other track before being reallocated to the small claims track, the rules applicable to the first track will apply up to the date of reallocation and the small claims track rules will apply after that date, unless the court orders otherwise (**CPR, r. 46.13(2)**).

Allocation for assessment of damages

45.32   Claims may be allocated to the small claims track for determination of quantum after judgment has been entered for damages to be assessed. When this happens the limitation on costs in respect of the small claims hearing will apply, although costs of earlier stages will be based on the sums available on the track concerned. It is likely that if proceedings are to be transferred to the small claims track for the assessment of damages, the court will undertake a summary assessment of the costs incurred before the allocation to the small claims track.

EUROPEAN SMALL CLAIMS PROCEDURE

45.33   Regulation (EC) No. 861/2007 of 11 July 2007 (the 'ESCP Regulation') establishes a European small claims procedure ('ESCP') with effect from 1 January 2009. The Regulation applies, in cross-border cases, to civil and commercial matters, whatever the nature of the court or tribunal, where the value of a claim does not exceed €2,000 at the time when the claim form is received by the court or tribunal with jurisdiction, excluding all interest, expenses and disbursements (art. 2(1)). There are various excepted categories of claim in art. 2(1) and (2). The ESCP is intended to simplify and speed up litigation concerning small claims in cross-border cases, whilst reducing costs, by offering an optional tool in addition to the possibilities existing under the laws of the member States, which remain unaffected. The ESCP Regulation should also make it simpler to obtain recognition and to enforce a judgment given in the ESCP in another member State (recital 8).

There is a special ESCP claim form, which is completed and filed in accordance with the ESCP Regulation, in particular art. 4(1), and which has a declaration which is treated in England and Wales in the same way as a statement of truth (**CPR, r. 78.13**). ESCP claims must be commenced in the County Court (**High Court and County Courts Jurisdiction Order 1991 (SI 1991/724), art. 6B**). They are treated as if they are allocated to the small claims track (**CPR, r. 78.14(1)**), and the provisions of **Part 27** apply except for **r. 27.14** (costs in small claims track cases). There are also detailed procedural rules in the ESCP Regulation so these claims are primarily governed by the ESCP Regulation (**PD 78, para. 10**). Where the ESCP Regulation is silent, the CPR apply with necessary modifications. In particular, where the ESCP Regulation is silent on service, the Service Regulation and **CPR, Part 6**, apply as appropriate (**PD 78, para. 15**), and **CPR, Part 52**, applies to any appeals (**PD 78, para. 10**).

Although there are procedures in the ESCP Regulation for hearings, primarily this procedure is intended to provide a paper-based decision (art. 5(1)). An oral hearing will be convened only if the court considers this to be necessary or if a party so requests. The decision is ordinarily expected within 30 days of receipt of the response from the defendant (art. 7(1)), although it will be longer if there is an oral hearing. The unsuccessful party must bear the costs of the proceedings. However, the court or tribunal must not award costs to the successful party to the extent that they were unnecessarily incurred or are disproportionate to the claim (art. 16).

Chapter 46 Fast Track

INTRODUCTION

The fast track is intended to cover the majority of defended claims within the £10,000 to **46.1**
£25,000 monetary band. For proceedings issued before 6 April 2009, the upper limit of the
fast track bracket is £15,000 (**CPR, r. 26.6(4)(b)(ii)**), and for claims issued before 1 April
2013 the lower limit is £5,000. The fast track is also the track for non-monetary claims such
as injunctions, declarations and claims for specific performance which are unsuitable for the
small claims track and do not require the more complex treatment of the multi-track. The fast
track provides a 'no-frills' procedure for medium-sized cases that do not justify the detailed
and meticulous preparation appropriate for complex and important cases. Instead, a case
allocated to this track will be progressed to trial within a short timescale after the filing of a
defence. **CPR, r. 1.1(2)(c)**, provides that part of the overriding objective is that cases should
be dealt with proportionately, and it is this idea that underlies the whole concept of having a
fast track with limited costs. The intention is to increase access to justice by removing the
uncertainty faced by many litigants over the cost of litigating, and to provide a means of
obtaining justice speedily.

When claims are allocated to the fast track, directions will be given setting out the timetable
to be followed, with a fixed trial date or trial period no more than 30 weeks later. Such a timetable will be long enough for the parties to undertake the work necessary for preparing the
case for trial, but sufficiently tight to discourage elaboration. The court will use its case management powers (see **chapter 42**) and its power to impose sanctions (**chapter 48**) to provide
protection against oppressive or unreasonable behaviour, and in particular against a powerful
opponent driving up the costs so as to overwhelm a weaker litigant.

In contrast to the small claims track, the full range of procedures under the CPR is available
on fast track claims, together with traditional costs orders. There are adjustments to reflect the
relatively modest value of many cases on the fast track. These include being released from the
need to file a costs budget (see **43.5**, unless the court orders otherwise), limitations on expert
evidence (see **46.6**), and fixed (and reasonably modest) trial costs (see **71.6**) combined with
summary assessment of the costs of the proceedings (see **46.24**). Fixed costs for the entire
proceedings were introduced for most fast track personal injury claims by **CPR, rr. 45.29A to
45.29L**, see **70.17**.

ADVANCE PREPARATION

46.2   Once a case is allocated to the fast track and directions are given, there will be a limited period of no more than seven months in which to prepare the case for trial. Such is the importance of ensuring fast track claims are dealt with expeditiously that **PD 28, para. 3.12**, lays down a typical directions timetable providing for a trial 30 weeks after the notice of allocation. **Paragraph 3.13** envisages shortening this period in cases where some of the typical steps in the timetable are thought unnecessary. Claimants will therefore be well advised to ensure that their cases are in an advanced state of preparation before they issue proceedings, to make sure they do not fall behind schedule once the timetable starts running. They should ensure they have available for disclosure all disclosable documents, both on liability and the amount of damages. They should also have identified and if necessary traced all material witnesses, and preferably have reduced into writing at least draft statements for each witness. They should also have made some progress regarding obtaining any expert evidence that might be necessary. It is to be expected that in most fast track cases the court will direct that there should be joint instruction of experts. Prospective claimants will therefore be well advised to have identified possible experts to be instructed, and sought agreement with their prospective defendants for the joint instruction of agreed experts. Anything less than this will be storing up trouble for later on.

Defendants are in a similar, and sometimes more precarious, position. They too will easily find themselves in time difficulties later on unless they have completed at least some of the necessary preparation before the claim is issued. Full compliance with any relevant pre-action protocol will at least put them in a reasonably advanced state of preparedness. They should, at the very least, have available for disclosure their documentation on liability, and have draft statements from material witnesses. They should also be in the process of seeking agreement on the joint instruction of experts. Like claimants, failing to have these matters in hand will mean there will be little time to get the case ready before the trial arrives.

DIRECTIONS

46.3   When it allocates a case to the fast track, the court will at the same time give case management directions and set a timetable for the steps to be taken from that point through to trial (**CPR, r. 28.2(1)**). The directions given will be designed to ensure the issues are identified and the necessary evidence is prepared and disclosed (**PD 28, para. 3.3**). Usually the court will give directions of its own initiative without a hearing, and will take into account the respective statements of case, the directions questionnaires, and any further information provided by the parties. Occasionally it may hold a directions hearing, such as when it is proposing to make an unusual order, for example, to appoint an assessor (see **PD 28, para. 3.11**). It is the duty of the parties to ask for all directions that might be needed on any hearing that may be fixed (**para. 2.5**). If any direction or order is required that has not been provided for, it is the duty of the parties to make an application as soon as possible so as to avoid undue interference with the overall timetable (**para. 2.8**). If a directions hearing becomes necessary because of the default of any of the parties, the court will usually impose a sanction (**para. 2.3**).

Typically, by **CPR, rr. 28.2(2)** and **28.3**, the matters to be dealt with in directions given on allocation to the fast track will include:

(a)   disclosure of documents;
(b)   service of witness statements;

(c) expert evidence; and

(d) fixing a date for the trial, or a period (not exceeding three weeks) in which the trial is to take place.

Standard directions to be used in fast track cases are set out in the Appendix to **PD 28**. They include matters, such as orders for the provision of further information, which are not included in the basic list. This is because the directions given will be tailored by the procedural judge to the circumstances of each individual case. The time periods for taking the various steps will also be tailored to the requirements of each individual case, but a few indications of the probable times allowed for different steps will be given in the following paragraphs. Further directions may be given after consideration of pre-trial checklists (**CPR, r. 28.6(1)**, see **46.16** to **46.20**) or after failure to file or complete them (**r. 28.5(3)** to **(5)**, see **46.11**). The date for filing pre-trial checklists will be not more than eight weeks before the trial date or the beginning of the trial period (**r. 28.5(2)**). Further directions are usually given about four to six weeks before trial.

Disclosure

Disclosure is discussed fully in **chapter 50**. Disclosure in some form should have taken place before proceedings were issued in compliance with the pre-action protocols. Information about this should have been given with the directions questionnaire. Based on the respective statements of case and these questionnaires, the procedural judge may direct the parties to give standard disclosure as one of the directions made at this stage, or may direct that no disclosure need take place (where the parties confirm that disclosure has taken place and no further disclosure is required), or may specify the documents or classes of documents which the parties must disclose (**CPR, r. 28.3(2)**; **PD 28, para. 3**). The standard directions will provide for disclosure to be given by service of lists of documents, which must be delivered by a specified calendar date. It is also possible for disclosure to be given more informally without a list and with or without a disclosure statement. Disclosure is likely to be ordered for 28 days after service of the notice of allocation (**PD 28, para. 3.12**).

46.4

Witness statements

The exchange of witness statements is considered further in **chapter 51**. Standard directions will usually provide for simultaneous exchange by a specified calendar date of statements from all the factual witnesses on whose evidence each party intends to rely. Exchange is likely to be required about 10 weeks from the order for directions (**PD 28, para. 3.12**). By **CPR, r. 32.9(1)**, witness summaries may be used in circumstances where witness statements cannot be obtained for practical reasons, but such instances should be exceptional. **Rule 32.5(4)** points firmly in the direction of full witness statements, as witnesses will only be allowed to amplify their statements if there is 'good reason' not to confine them to their disclosed witness statements. Trial judges usually take a strict view against allowing additional questions in-chief seeking to introduce new matters or to insulate a witness against cross-examination under the guise of 'amplifying' an exchanged statement.

46.5

Expert evidence

For detailed consideration of directions about experts see **54.13** to **54.17**. Cases will not normally be on the fast track unless oral expert evidence at trial is limited to one expert per party in each expert field, and to two fields of expertise (**CPR, r. 26.6(5)**). It is difficult to see how any more experts could give evidence within the time limit for a fast track hearing. One of the powers available to the court is that of directing that the evidence on particular issues may be given by a single expert jointly instructed by the opposing parties (**r. 35.7**). Normally,

46.6

any permission will be for evidence from only one expert on any particular issue (**r. 35.4(3A)**). In order to keep down costs and to reduce the length of fast track trials, it will be usual for the court to make directions for the joint instruction of a single expert unless there is good reason for doing something else (**PD 28, para. 3.9(4)**). In addition, in fast track cases the court will not direct an expert to attend at trial unless it is necessary to do so in the interests of justice (**CPR, r. 35.5(2)**). It is expected that such directions will be rare.

If the parties are given permission to instruct their own experts, the court has a power under **r. 35.12** to direct a discussion between the experts with a view to producing an agreed statement of the issues on which they agree and the areas on which they are in disagreement. If the experts cannot reach agreement, the interests of justice are likely to be served only by allowing both parties to call their experts at the trial so the areas of disagreement can be adjudicated upon by the judge. In such cases it may not be possible to deal with the case in a single day, and the court may need to consider reallocating the case to the multi-track. This will be considered by the procedural judge on filing of pre-trial checklists by the parties.

Normally expert evidence should be prepared and/or exchanged about 14 weeks after the order giving directions (**PD 28, para. 3.12**). The standard fast track directions have several different options regarding expert evidence, as alternatives to the joint instruction of experts. Options provided within the standard directions are:

(a) Sequential service of experts' reports. Normally it will be the claimant who will serve first.

(b) Simultaneous exchange of reports on some issues, with sequential service on the others.

(c) Holding of a discussion between experts in cases where the other side's reports cannot be agreed within a short time (usually 14 days) after service. This form of direction provides for a specified calendar date by which the discussion must take place, and the filing of a joint statement of the agreed issues and those in dispute (with reasons for the lack of agreement) by another specified date (which will often be close to the date for filing pre-trial checklists).

(d) That expert evidence is not necessary and no party has permission to call or rely on expert evidence at the trial without permission expressly given by the court following an application.

(e) That the parties may rely on experts' reports at trial, but cannot call oral expert evidence.

(f) That the parties may rely on experts' reports, and the court will reconsider whether there is any need for experts to be called on consideration of the filed pre-trial checklists.

Questions to experts

46.7   The standard directions also make provision pursuant to the power given by **CPR, r. 35.6**, for written questions to be put to the experts for the purpose of clarifying their reports.

Questions should be sent, if at all, no later than 28 days after receiving the report (**r. 35.6(2)(b)**). Questions can be sent direct to the expert, but copies should be sent to the other side's solicitors. No time is laid down for the answers (although this may be done by a specific court order), but 28 days would seem to be reasonable. Sensible questions can only be asked if the party (or more commonly its solicitor) is guided by its own expert. If its own expert knows the answers, there will be little point in asking the questions in the first place, so it must be sensible to clear the written questions with the party's own experts first. It will take a little time for a party to receive the other side's expert reports, consider them, decide if it is a case where written questions should be put, contact its own expert and take its expert's advice about the written questions to be put, formulate the questions, and then serve them. Experts are often busy consultants and professionals with many calls on their time, so a period of 28 days for questions and answers may seem rather tight, but is necessary if a fast track timetable is to be met. Solicitors must send copies of directions orders to experts so they are aware of the court's timetable (**PD 35, para. 8**). Solicitors should also ensure that experts are aware of their rights and duties under **CPR, Part 35**, particularly **r. 35.14**, which allows an expert to file written requests for directions.

Further statements of case

When giving directions, the procedural judge may also direct that a party must file a further **46.8** statement of case, such as a reply or defence to counterclaim. The direction will specify a calendar date and time for doing so.

Requests for further information

Requests for further information are considered in more detail in **chapter 30**. Standard direc- **46.9** tions provide for two possible times for service of such requests (with either, both or neither being directed in any particular case):

(a) Within a short, specified, time after directions are given, where the request is based on the other side's statement of case. The direction will also specify the date by which the request must be dealt with. A response is usually required within 14 days.

(b) After disclosure or exchange of witness statements. The direction will lay down a limited time after disclosure or service of the statement within which the request must be served, and a limited time within which it must be dealt with.

PRE-TRIAL CHECKLISTS

Standard fast track directions provide for all parties to file completed pre-trial checklists, **46.10** previously known as listing questionnaires, no later than specific dates set out in the directions, unless the court considers the claim can be listed for trial without them. They are used to ensure the case is on course for being ready for trial, and to enable the procedural judge to set a trial timetable. If a party wants additional directions, the form has to be accompanied by an application notice and draft directions. Explanations must be given for witness dates to avoid. Information about experts includes whether opposing experts have signed a joint statement. If the time estimate has changed, the parties must say whether they have agreed a new estimate. When they are used, pre-trial checklists must be returned within the time specified by the court, which will be no later than eight weeks before the trial date or the beginning of the trial period (**CPR, r. 28.5(2)**).

Failure to file or complete pre-trial checklists

If no party files the completed pre-trial checklist by the date specified, the court will order **46.11** that unless a completed pre-trial checklist is filed within 7 days from service of that order, the claim, defence and any counterclaim will be struck out without further order of the court (**CPR, r. 28.5(3)**. If one party fails to file its pre-trial checklist, and if the court considers that a hearing is necessary to enable it to decide what directions to give in order to complete preparation of the case for trial, the court may give such directions as it considers appropriate (**CPR, r. 28.5(4)**). The court may require the parties to attend a hearing for this purpose, and if so will give at least three days' notice (unless abridged under **r. 3.1(2)(b)**) of the directions hearing using form N153 (**PD 28, para. 6.3**). Particularly where any of the parties are in default, the court may consider imposing sanctions and making 'unless' orders.

Notice of a pre-trial directions hearing will be in form N153.

HEARING FEES

46.12   With effect from 22 April 2014, the claimant is required to pay a hearing fee of £545 (**CPFO, fee 2.1**) at the same time as filing its pre-trial checklist. The former listing fee was discontinued with effect from 22 April 2014. Fee 2.1 is not payable in a case where the court fixed the hearing date on the issue of the claim. If the court fixes a trial date or trial week without requiring pre-trial checklists, fee 2.1 becomes payable within 14 days of the date of dispatch of the notice (or the date when oral notice is given if no written notice is given) of the trial date or week. The 'claimant' who has to pay the fees is the party making the relevant claim. Consequently, in *Penfold v Fuller* [2009] EWHC 1195 (Ch), LTL 8/6/2009, the original defendant had to pay the fees where the original claim had been compromised in a Tomlin order, and the hearing was to determine an application for specific performance of the Tomlin order brought by the original defendant. If the action is proceeding on a counterclaim alone, the fee is payable by the defendant. If the fee is not paid, the court will send a notice to pay in form N173, and failing payment within the time stated in the notice, the claim will be struck out (**CPR, r. 3.7**, see **42.72**).

As an incentive to settle, the hearing fee of £545 will be refunded in whole or in part on a sliding scale if the court receives notice in writing from the party who paid the fee that the case has been settled or discontinued. The refunds are:

Court notified more than 28 days before the hearing	100 per cent
Court notified between 15 and 28 days before the hearing	75 per cent
Court notified between 7 and 14 days before the hearing	50 per cent

FIXING THE DATE FOR TRIAL

46.13   When giving directions the court will fix the trial date or a period, not exceeding three weeks, in which the trial is to take place, and which will be specified in the notice of allocation (**CPR, r. 28.2(2) to (4)**). A trial window will usually be given at the allocation stage and the trial directions will be given on consideration of pre-trial checklists. A trial date or window may be altered, but only as a last resort or where it is necessary to avoid injustice (see **42.52**). Whichever course is taken, the court must give the parties at least three weeks' notice of the date of the trial unless, in exceptional circumstances, the court directs that shorter notice will be given (**r. 28.6(2)**).

Rule 28.2(4) provides that the 'standard' period between the giving of directions and the trial will be not more than 30 weeks. It is therefore open for procedural judges to lay down even tighter timetables, which depends on the complexity of the case and whether any of the usual steps have already been taken (**PD 28, para. 3.13**). There is also scope, if the procedural judge can be persuaded that it is necessary, for the timetable to be longer than the standard period. Factors such as those mentioned at **42.50** may influence the court when considering a longer timetable in an individual case.

STANDARD FAST TRACK TIMETABLE

46.14   Table 46.1 charts the progress of a fast track case from issue, through allocation to the fast track, up to trial. The case illustrated takes 39 weeks, or about nine months, from issue to trial. The various stages will vary from case to case (such as where there is a stay for negotiation or if the claimant effects service rather than the court) and, as mentioned in **46.13**, even the 30-week period between directions and trial may be considerably reduced in some cases. It will be obvious that the parties will have to be in a high state of preparedness before

Table 46.1 Progress of fast track case to trial

Week after allocation	Step in the proceedings	Time limit
	Issue of proceedings. Service by court (takes effect on second business day after posting)	Usual limitation period 4 months from issue (6 months if outside the jurisdiction)
	Acknowledgment of service or filing of defence	14 days after deemed service of the particulars of claim
	Provisional track allocation notice	On filing defence
	Possible transfer to defendant's home court	On filing defence
	Return of directions questionnaires and other documents required by the notice of proposed allocation	Not less than 28 days after service of the notice of proposed allocation
0	Allocation decision and directions given by the procedural judge	After return of directions questionnaires
4	Disclosure of documents	Usually 4 weeks after allocation
10	Exchange of witness statements	Usually 10 weeks after allocation
10	Service of hearsay notices	With exchanged witness statements
14	Experts' reports	Usually 14 weeks after allocation
(Say) 17	Written questions to experts	Between reports and pre-trial checklists
(Say) 19	Answers from experts	Usually 2 weeks from written questions
20	Service of pre-trial checklists (may be dispensed with)	Usually 20 weeks after
22	Return of pre-trial checklists	Usually 22 weeks after allocation
(Say) 24	Any directions arising out of the pre-trial checklists	Optional
(24)	Hearing if pre-trial checklists not returned	Only if parties in default
27	Confirmation of trial date	3 weeks before trial
27	Service of notice to admit	3 weeks before trial
28/29	Lodge trial bundle	3 to 7 days before trial
29	Service and filing of statements of costs	Not less than 2 days before the hearing
30	Trial	30 weeks after allocation

proceedings are issued in all but the very simplest of cases if they are to have any real prospect of adhering to such tight timetables without being forced on the mercy of the courts. Applications to vary the timetable are dealt with at **42.42** to **42.52**.

AGREED DIRECTIONS

The parties are encouraged to seek to agree suitable directions to be submitted to the court with their directions questionnaires. If this is done, the court will at least take them into account when giving directions, and if they are suitable, will simply approve them. To be approved the directions should essentially follow the above rules (see **PD 28, para. 3**), which means they must deal with disclosure, witness statements and expert evidence, lay down a timetable by calendar dates, and provide for a trial or trial period no more than 30 weeks after the start of the timetable.

46.15

PRE-TRIAL DIRECTIONS

46.16 On receipt of the pre-trial checklists, under **CPR, r. 28.6(1)**, the court will:

(a) Fix the date for the trial (or, if it has already done so, confirm the date).

(b) Give any further directions for the trial as may seem necessary, including setting a trial timetable. Standard directions for this stage are set out in the Appendix to **PD 28**.

(c) Specify any further steps that need to be taken before trial.

The parties should seek to agree directions, and they may submit a proposed order (**PD 28, para. 7.2(1)**). They should give reasons for any unusual directions. Usually directions will be made by the court without a hearing, but it may decide to hold a pre-trial directions hearing, giving the parties three clear days' notice (**PD 28, para. 6.3**).

Confirmation of expert directions

46.17 Pre-trial directions will confirm or make provision for the permission granted to the parties regarding reliance on written experts' reports and calling expert witnesses at trial. The direction will specify the experts by name, and say whether they can be called or whether it is only the expert's report that can be relied upon. Oral evidence from experts will only be allowed if the court believes it is necessary in the interests of justice (**PD 28, para. 7.2(4)**).

Trial timetable

46.18 The court may, if it considers that it is appropriate to do so, set a timetable for the trial. Setting a timetable is discretionary (**CPR, r. 28.6(1)(b)**), and is easier if the managing judge will be the trial judge. If it decides to set a timetable, the court must consult with the parties (**r. 39.4**). A trial timetable defines how much time the court will allow at trial for the various stages of the trial itself. A simple direction may limit the time to be spent by each party in calling its evidence and in addressing the court in closing submissions. More sophisticated timetables will define how much time will be allowed for each witness, or even for cross-examination and re-examination. If a timetable is set, it will usually provide for a five-hour trial, to include all stages including judgment and the summary assessment of costs.

Trial bundles

46.19 Standard pre-trial directions will provide that an indexed, paginated, bundle of documents contained in a ring binder must be lodged with the court not more than seven days or less than three days before the trial. Slightly inconsistently, the standard direction in the Appendix to **PD 28** provides that trial bundles must be lodged at least seven days before trial. The parties must seek to agree the contents of the trial bundle a reasonable time in advance, which in practical terms means no later than 14 days before the trial. For further details on the contents of the trial bundles, see **chapter 59**. The claimant is responsible for lodging the bundle. Lodgment at court is required so that the trial judge can read the case papers in advance of the trial. Judges are likely to take a very dim view if the bundle is not lodged in time. Identical bundles will be needed for each of the parties, with an additional bundle for the witness box.

Case summary

46.20 Standard pre-trial directions give the procedural judge the option of directing that a case summary should be included in the trial bundle. This document is intended to be non-partisan, and to be agreed if possible. It should usually be no more than 250 words, and should outline the matters in issue, referring where appropriate to the relevant documents in the trial bundle. Again, responsibility for this rests with the claimant.

FAST TRACK TRIALS

The trial of a fast track claim will usually take place in the County Court hearing centre where it is proceeding, but may take place in a civil trial centre or any other court if it is appropriate because of listing difficulties, the needs of the parties or for other reasons. The judge may be a District Judge or a Circuit Judge. The trial judge will generally have read the trial bundle and will usually dispense with opening speeches. Unless the trial judge otherwise directs, the trial will be conducted in accordance with any order previously made (see **46.18**), although the judge is free to set a fresh trial timetable (**PD 28, para. 8.3**). Given the time constraints and the need for proportionality, the trial judge will almost invariably order witness statements to stand as the evidence-in-chief and otherwise control the evidence to be presented. If a trial is not concluded on the day it is listed, the judge will normally sit on the following day to complete it (**PD 28, para. 8.6**; though this may not reflect reality). In such an event no further costs will be allowed to the parties.

46.21

COSTS IN FAST TRACK CASES

Fixed trial costs

CPR, r. 28.2(5), provides that the court's power to award trial costs is limited in accordance with **Part 45, Section VI**, which sets fixed amounts for the costs of a fast track trial depending on the amount recovered, with a small uplift if counsel is attended by a solicitor (**r. 45.38**; see **71.6**).

46.22

Fixed costs in fast track personal injury claims

Personal injuries claims that are started under either the RTA or EL/PL Protocol are subject to fixed costs as set out in **CPR, rr. 45.29A** to **45.29L** once they no longer continue under the relevant protocol (**r. 45.29A(1)**, see **70.17**).

46.23

Summary assessment in fast track claims

The general rule is that at the end of a fast track trial the court will make a summary assessment of the costs of the whole claim immediately after giving judgment (**PD 44, para. 9.2**). To assist the judge in assessing costs, the parties are required to file and serve, not less than two days before the trial, signed statements of their costs for the interim hearing in form N260. A statement of costs must, by **PD 44, para. 9.5(2)**, set out:

46.24

(a) the number of hours claimed;
(b) the hourly rate claimed;
(c) the grade of fee earner;
(d) the amount and nature of disbursements;
(e) the legal representative's costs for attending or appearing at the hearing;
(f) counsel's fees; and
(g) VAT on the above.

Any failure to file or serve a statement of costs, without reasonable excuse, will be taken into account in deciding the costs order to be made regarding the claim, the trial, and/or any detailed assessment hearing that might become necessary as a result of that failure (**PD 44, para. 9.6**; see **32.31**). Summary assessment (see **71.3**) is not permitted of an assisted party's costs, nor of the costs of a person under disability, unless the solicitor representing the person under disability waives the right to further costs (**PD 44, paras 9.8** and **9.9**).

Parties should try to ensure that their costs statements are realistic. The fact that a party's costs statement is inflated may well be used against that party by the court and the other side if costs are awarded to the other side. Underpricing a party's costs may assist in attacking its opponent's costs if it loses, but will be counterproductive if it is awarded costs.

The judge retains responsibility for ensuring that the costs claimed are not disproportionate or unreasonable, even if they are not disputed by the paying party (**PD 44, para. 9.10**). The fact that the paying party does not dispute the amount claimed can be taken as some indication that the amount is proportionate and reasonable.

Chapter 47   Multi-track

INTRODUCTION

A vast range of cases are allocated to the multi-track from simple contractual disputes involv- **47.1**
ing little more than £25,000, to complex commercial cases involving difficult issues of fact
and law with values of several million pounds, to cases where perhaps no money is at stake but
which raise points of real public importance. Case management on the multi-track reflects the
range of cases dealt with. Simpler cases are given standard directions without the need for
hearings, and the parties are expected to comply with those directions without complicating
or delaying matters. At the other end of the scale, the courts adopt a far more active approach,
possibly with several directions hearings in the form of case management conferences and
pre-trial reviews. The first case management conference is often an allocation and directions
hearing. The courts adopt a flexible approach to ensure each case receives the right amount of
case management input from the court (**PD 29, para. 3.2(2)**). Straightforward multi-track
cases may be given tight timetables from defence to trial that are similar to those on the fast
track. In such cases, the comments made in **46.1** apply with equal force about the need to be
well prepared before commencing proceedings, the main difference being on costs. Even in
complex multi-track cases it will be important for case preparation to be reasonably advanced
before issue, because under the CPR there is a great deal 'front loading', and the procedural
judge will want to be assisted by the parties in identifying the issues and the evidence required
at the first case management conference.

Cases on the multi-track will generally be dealt with either in the Royal Courts of Justice or
other civil trial centre (see **PD 29, paras 2** and **3.1**). The procedural judge may need to order
a transfer on first consideration or at an allocation hearing, see **42.7**. Case management will
generally be dealt with by Masters and District Judges (see **CPR, r. 2.4** and **PD 2B**), unless
the case has been selected for docketing (see **42.54**). It is the duty of the parties at all hearings
to consider whether any directions should be made, as this can avoid the need for additional
case management hearings later on (**PD 29, para. 3.5**).

Many of the civil justice reforms made in 2013 affect claims on the multi-track, and the case and costs management processes described in **chapters 42** and **43** need to be read together with this chapter.

CASE MANAGEMENT STAGES IN MULTI-TRACK CASES

47.2   Provisional track allocation takes place shortly after defences are filed (see **42.13**), but formal track allocation is decided by a procedural judge usually shortly after the return of directions questionnaires (see **42.26**) or at an allocation hearing (see **42.24**) or case management conference (see **42.25**). Once a case is allocated to the multi-track the court will give directions and hold such procedural hearings as may be appropriate in order to progress the case to trial or resolution by other means. **Figure 47.1** illustrates the main stages in the progress of a multi-track case to trial. Applications to vary the timetable are dealt with at **42.42** to **42.52**.

Directions on allocation

47.3   At the same time as a case is allocated to the multi-track the procedural judge will decide whether to give directions or to fix a case management conference or pre-trial review (or both

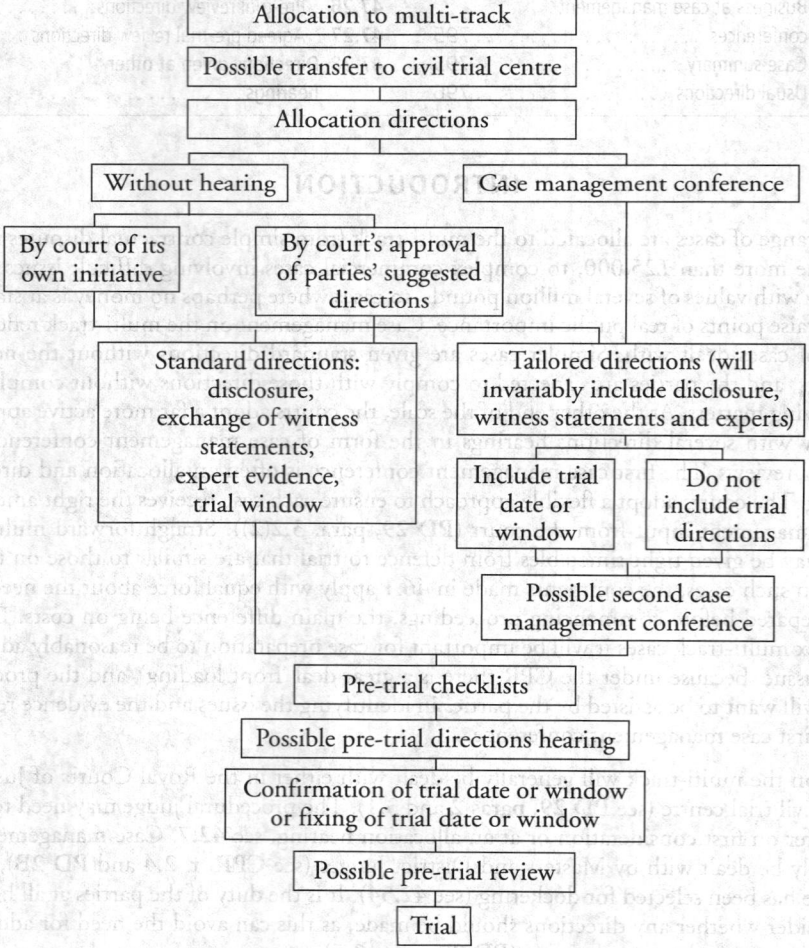

Figure 47.1 The multi-track

a case management conference and a pre-trial review) and such other directions as are thought fit (**CPR, r. 29.2(1)**). The procedural judge will therefore take a view as to the complexity of the case, and the amount of work required to get it ready for trial, and decide whether or not it is necessary to call the parties in before the court for a procedural hearing. The judge will also consider whether the case should be stayed while ADR procedures are attempted, see **42.61**.

The court will seek to tailor its directions to the needs of the case, and the steps the parties have already taken to prepare it for trial. It will also take into account the extent to which the parties have complied with any pre-action protocol (see **chapter 8**). The court's concern will be to ensure the issues between the parties are identified, and that the evidence required for the trial is prepared and disclosed (**PD 29, para. 4.3**).

Making an informed decision regarding directions

It is important that the court should be informed on the progress made by the parties in gathering the necessary evidence and in identifying the real issues in the case. It is in the interests of the parties to make sure that they provide all necessary information to the court. This will ensure the directions given are realistic and suitable for the case, and avoid the necessity for the court to ask for further information and perhaps impose sanctions. The information the court will act on may be gathered from:

47.4

(a) the claim form;
(b) the particulars of claim (if provided separately from the claim form);
(c) the defence;
(d) any documents (such as witness statements and experts' reports) filed with the particulars of claim or defence;
(e) the completed directions questionnaires;
(f) costs budgets and budget discussion reports filed by the parties;
(g) disclosure reports, electronic documents questionnaires, and proposed disclosure directions;
(h) any further documents filed with the directions questionnaires, provided these are agreed between the parties, or have been served on the other parties, with a statement to that effect (**PD 26, para. 2.2(2)**);
(i) any further information that the parties may be required to produce on an order by the court to clarify the matters in dispute or to give additional information; and
(j) any proposed directions, particularly where they have been agreed between the parties (**PD 29, para. 4.6**).

Inadequate information

From time to time parties in cases allocated to the multi-track provide little or no information other than that contained in their statements of case. In such cases the court may call a case management conference, and it may order the parties to provide further information about their cases pursuant to **CPR, r. 26.5(3)**. An order for further information at the allocation stage will be made on form N156. The order will set out the nature of the information and documentation required, and provide that copies must be sent to the court and other parties by a specified time. A note on form N156 warns that if an allocation hearing becomes necessary through a failure to provide the information ordered, the defaulting party may be ordered to pay the costs of that hearing.

47.5

However, it is perhaps more likely that the court will simply impose directions giving a tight timetable for trial (**PD 29, para. 4.10**). Doing so will put enormous pressure on the parties. They will either have to comply, or will find themselves in considerable difficulty unless they apply promptly for tailored directions. This is because the court will assume for the purposes of any later application (in the absence of any appeal or application within 14 days to vary)

Commentary

that the parties were content that the directions were correct in the circumstances then existing (**PD 29, para. 6.2(2)**).

The general approach in these cases where there is inadequate information is for directions along the following lines to be made by the court of its own initiative:

(a) filing and service of any further information required to clarify either party's case;

(b) standard disclosure between the parties (**para. 4.10(2)**, which is the source for this, has not been amended as part of the civil justice reforms of 2013, and may need to be reconsidered given the introduction of menu disclosure in multi-track claims. Standard disclosure is nevertheless a sensible fallback position. See **chapter 50**);

(c) simultaneous exchange of witness statements;

(d) for the appointment of a single expert unless there is good reason for not doing so;

(e) simultaneous exchange of experts' reports in cases or on issues where single expert directions have not been given (unless expert evidence is required on both liability and quantum, in which event the direction may be for simultaneous exchange on the liability issues, but sequential exchange on quantum issues);

(f) if experts' reports are not agreed, that there be a discussion between the experts for the purpose of identifying the expert evidence issues, and, if possible, reaching agreement between the experts, and the preparation of a statement setting out the issues on which they are agreed and a summary of their reasons on the issues where they disagree;

(g) listing a case management conference after the final date in the above directions;

(h) specifying a trial period; and

(i) if appropriate, directions for the parties to consider ADR.

An ADR direction may include provisions requiring the parties to file witness statements if they consider the case to be unsuitable for ADR giving their reasons for saying that the case is unsuitable (**PD 29, para. 4.10(9)**). This approach to ADR directions applies where the court does not hold a case management conference and where the court does not know what steps have been taken by the parties other than the exchange of statements of case, so is relatively unusual.

Avoiding the need for a directions hearing

47.6 Parties in a multi-track case must endeavour to agree appropriate directions for the management of the case, and must submit any agreed directions, or their respective proposals, to the court at least seven days before any case management conference. Where the court considers that the proposals are suitable, or if it issues its own directions, any case management conference will be vacated (**CPR, r. 29.4**; **PD 29, paras 4.6** and **4.7**). This is encouraged, as it obviously saves costs and court time. In order to obtain the court's approval the agreed directions should be based on the standard directions available on the Ministry of Justice website (**CPR, r. 29.1(2)**, and see **42.16**), and must:

(a) if appropriate, include a direction regarding the filing of a reply;

(b) if appropriate, provide for amending any statement of case;

(c) include provision about the disclosure of documents;

(d) include provision about both factual and expert evidence (the provision about expert evidence may be to the effect that no expert evidence is required);

(e) if appropriate, include dates for service of requests for further information and/or questions to experts, and when they should be answered;

(f) include a date or a period when it is proposed the trial will take place; and

(g) if appropriate, a date for a case management conference.

It will be seen that only items (c), (d) and (f) are obligatory in all cases, although the others will frequently arise in practice. Proposed agreed directions must lay down a timetable by reference to calendar dates. The court will scrutinise the timetable carefully, with particular attention to the proposals for the trial and case management conference, and will be astute to ensure these are no later than is reasonably necessary (**PD 29, para. 4.7(2)**). Ultimate responsibility for case management directions remains with the court, and it cannot be assumed that even agreed directions will always be approved.

By **PD 29, para. 4.7(3)** (which may need to be reconsidered given the introduction of menu disclosure in multi-track claims, see **chapter 50**), the provision in any agreed directions relating to disclosure may:

(a) limit disclosure to standard disclosure, or less than that; and/or

(b) direct that disclosure will take place by the supply of copy documents without a list of documents, but if so, it must say either that the parties must serve a disclosure statement with the copies, or that they have agreed to disclose in this way without a disclosure statement.

Under **PD 29, para.** 4.8(4), read together with **CPR, r.** 35.4(2), the provisions regarding factual and expert evidence should, if appropriate, deal with:

(a) whether the evidence should be disclosed simultaneously or sequentially;

(b) the use of a single expert;

(c) without prejudice discussions between the experts if a single expert is not going to be instructed;

(d) the field and issues which the expert evidence will address;

(e) if practicable, the name of the proposed expert; and

(f) the estimated costs of the proposed expert evidence.

The court is free to reject directions that have been agreed between the parties, but will take them into account when making its own directions (either without a hearing or on a case management conference). The ultimate responsibility for case management remains at all times with the court, and parties will be unwise to assume that agreed directions will be automatically approved.

Once directions have been made by consent, the court retains control, and can override them in the future if this is justified in the circumstances (*Re Debtors (Nos. 13-MISC-2000 and 14-MISC-2000)* (2000) *The Times,* 10 April 2000).

CASE MANAGEMENT CONFERENCES

Case management conferences are an integral part of the new system of active case management **47.7** by the courts. They are not simply directions hearings, but are intended to ensure that the real issues between the parties are identified. Side issues will be dispensed with either by agreement between the parties with due encouragement from the judge, or by means of summary judgment or striking-out determinations at an early stage. Case management conferences may be held immediately after a case is allocated to the multi-track or at any time thereafter through to the listing stage. They can be used as the vehicle for laying down directions at the allocation stage, or may be used later in order to assess how the case is progressing when the initial directions on allocation should have been completed. Normally the court has a discretion whether to call a case management conference. However, where it is contemplated that an order may be made either for the evidence on a particular issue to be given by a single expert, or that an assessor should be appointed, **PD 29, para. 4.13**, provides that a case management conference must be held unless the parties have consented to the order in writing. Some procedural judges use some case management conferences as mediation-style hearings to promote settlement. Judges adopting this practice will have extensive knowledge of the case, and will attempt to assist settlement so as to restrict and identify the issues to be tried. Whether this is a legitimate use of the judicial office, with the inherent pressure exerted by the presence of a judge and the lack of clear rules governing the roles of those present and how the hearing should be conducted, has yet to be decided.

Where a case management conference is or may be dealt with by the trial judge, no reference should be made to any Part 36 offers whether in the case management bundle or at the hearing (see **66.3**). **CPR, r. 36.16**, does not prevent disclosure to procedural judges who will not be conducting the trial.

Case management conferences will also be called in cases where the court feels it cannot properly give directions on its own initiative, and where no agreed directions have been filed which it feels can be approved (**PD 29, para. 4.12**).

By encouraging the parties to settle their dispute or resolve it outside the court system, and by forcing the parties into identifying the real issues at an early stage, case management conferences are a means of using court time to save more time.

Procedure before a case management conference

47.8   There is a commitment towards having case management conferences listed as promptly as possible (**PD 29, para. 4.12(2)**). The minimum period of notice the court will give to the parties of the date for the case management conference is three clear days (**CPR, r. 3.3(3); PD 29, para. 3.7**). In practice the parties need to anticipate the possibility of there being a case management conference some weeks in advance.

Matters to be addressed in advance of the first case management conference in multi-track claims include the following:

(a) Not less than 14 days before the first case management conference each party must file and serve a disclosure report complying with **r. 31.5(3)**, see **chapter 50**. Personal injuries claims are excepted from this requirement.

(b) The parties must seek to agree directions. This includes (in non-personal injuries claims) an obligation on the parties to meet or speak on the telephone at least seven days before the case management conference to seek to agree a proportionate proposal for disclosure of documents (**r. 31.5(5)**). In all multi-track claims there is a more general obligation to endeavour to agree all the appropriate directions for the case (**r. 29.1(2)**).

(c) Costs budgets should be served in accordance with **r. 3.13** (see **chapter 43**), unless one of the exceptions applies (see **43.6** and **43.7**).

(d) Discussion of costs budgets and filing of budget discussion reports (see **43.10**)

(e) A case management bundle for use at the case management conference.

(f) Possibly, a case summary (see **47.11**).

(g) In some specialist cases, preparation of lists of issues.

Attendance at case management conferences

47.9   If a case management conference is to be attended by a legal representative on behalf of a party, the representative must be someone familiar with the case (**CPR, r. 29.3(2)**). It is unacceptable to send a trainee with a two-page briefing note on such a hearing. Instead it will have to be the fee earner concerned, or someone (possibly counsel) who is fully familiar with the file, the issues and the proposed evidence, who must attend. They must be able to field the questions that are likely to be covered at the hearing, and have the authority to agree and/or make representations on the matters reasonably to be expected to arise. Where the inadequacy of the person attending or his or her instructions leads to the adjournment of the hearing, it will be normal for a wasted costs order to be made (**PD 29, para. 5.2(3)**), or even an order for indemnity-basis costs and interest on damages at a higher rate than usual (see *Baron v Lovell* [1999] CPLR 630). Where a direction is made for the attendance of the parties and one of the parties is a company, the order should be that individuals with knowledge of the history of the case should attend (*Tarajan Overseas Ltd v Kaye* [2001] EWCA Civ 1859, *The Times,* 22 January 2002).

In the Chancery Division, whenever possible, the advocates instructed or expected to appear at trial should attend case management conferences and other case management hearings (Chancery Guide, para. 17.21). In the Admiralty and Commercial Courts, case management conferences should be attended on behalf of each party both by the fee earner with conduct of the case and by at least one of the advocates retained (Admiralty and Commercial Courts Guide, para. D8.2). Case management conferences in complex cases in the Admiralty and Commercial Courts are regarded as particularly significant stages in the litigation, and are conducted by a designated judge who will manage the case, and will usually subsequently be the trial judge (paras D4.1, D4.2, D4.3 and D8.3).

Business at case management conferences

At a case management conference the court will, as stated by **CPR, rr. 3.12(2)** and **3.17, PD 3E, para. 7.3,** and **PD 29, para. 5.1:**   **47.10**

(a) make a thorough review of the steps the parties have taken to date in preparing the case for trial;

(b) consider the extent to which they have complied with any previous orders and directions;

(c) review any costs budgets that have not been agreed between all the parties, make appropriate revisions, and approve the revised budgets;

(d) decide on the directions needed to progress the action in accordance with the overriding objective and taking into account the costs budgets;

(e) ensure that reasonable agreements are made between the parties about the matters in issue and the future conduct of the claim; and

(f) record all such agreements.

To assist the court the legal representatives for all parties should ensure that all documents (and in particular witness statements and expert reports) the court is likely to ask to see are brought to court. The court may give directions for preparing a case management bundle. Legal representatives should consider whether the parties themselves should attend. If the witness statements and experts' reports have not been exchanged at the time of the case management conference, it should follow from *General Mediterranean Holdings SA v Patel* [2000] 1 WLR 272 that the only reports and statements that can legitimately be called for are those that have been disclosed or that may be voluntarily disclosed at the hearing.

It is not open to a judge to dismiss a claim at a hearing of an application for directions, particularly where dismissal of the claim is unprompted and without giving the parties advance notice so they can make representations (*Norbrook Laboratories Ltd v Carr* [2010] EWCA Civ 1108, LTL 14/10/2010).

Case summary

The parties must consider whether the court may be assisted by a written case summary (**PD 29, para. 5.6**). This should be a short document not exceeding 500 words which is designed to assist the court in understanding and dealing with the issues raised in the case (**para. 5.7**). It should give a brief chronology of the claim, and state the factual issues that are agreed and those in dispute, and the nature of the evidence needed to decide them. Responsibility for preparing the document rests with the claimant, and if possible it should be agreed by the other parties.   **47.11**

In the Admiralty and Commercial Courts, the legal representatives for each party must liaise for the purpose of preparing a short case memorandum, which will be included in the case management bundle. They must also prepare an agreed list of important issues (with a separate section dealing with matters which are common ground between all or some of the parties), and the claimant's solicitors must prepare the case management bundle (Admiralty and Commercial Courts Guide, paras D5.1, D6.1 and D7.1). The case management bundle must contain these documents, together with the claim form and statements of case (if a case summary has been prepared, the bundles must contain the summary rather than the relevant statement of case), and any orders etc. made so far (see para. D7.2), being careful to avoid any reference to interim payments and Part 36 offers (as the case management judge could well be the trial judge, see paras D5.4 and D7.4). The case management bundle must be lodged with the Listing Office at least seven days before the first case management conference (para. D7.5).

In the Technology and Construction Court, the court will fix a case management conference within 14 days of filing of the acknowledgment of service or defence or any order transferring the claim to the TCC (**PD 60, para. 8.1**). The court will then notify the parties of the date for the case management conference, and send them a case management information sheet and a case management directions form (see **PD 60, para. 8.2**, app. A and app. B). These should be completed and exchanged, and then filed by 4 p.m. two days before the case management conference (**para. 8.3**). The parties are encouraged to agree directions.

Usual directions

47.12   In all cases the court will set a timetable at the case management conference for the steps it decides are necessary for preparing the case for trial (**PD 29, paras** 5.3 and 5.4). Typically the court will consider giving directions on the following matters:

(a) Whether the claimant has made clear the claim that is being made and the amount being claimed, and whether the defence is no more than a bare denial or is otherwise unclear. Orders for amendment and/or for further information may be appropriate if the statements of case are insufficiently clear for the other side to understand the case that has to be met.

(b) The scope of disclosure of documents required.

(c) The nature of the expert evidence required, and how and when it should be obtained. The court will not give permission for the use of expert evidence unless it can identify each expert by name or field of expertise, and say whether each expert's evidence should be given orally or by use of a report. Further matters that may be considered are whether the evidence on a particular issue should be given by a single expert, or that an assessor should be appointed, and whether there should be discussions between the experts.

(d) Disclosure of witness statements and summaries.

(e) Whether further information should be provided on matters other than statements of case, such as witness statements.

(f) Arrangements for questions that may be put to experts.

(g) Whether it would be just and save costs to have split trials on liability and quantum, or whether there should be the trial of one or more preliminary issues.

(h) Whether to make a costs management order (see **chapter 43**).

(i) Whether there should be another case management conference, a costs management conference, or a pre-trial review.

(j) Whether to assign the case to a particular judge for case management (docketing, see **42.54**).

(k) Whether it is possible to fix a date for the trial, or to give a trial 'window'. The court will be anxious to comply with the rule that the trial should be fixed as soon as practicable (**CPR, r. 29.2(2)**).

(l) Whether the trial should be dealt with by a High Court judge, or by a specialist judge. If so, the court will also consider transferring the case to the appropriate court (**PD 29, para. 5.9**).

At case management conferences in Admiralty or Commercial Court cases the judge will, if practicable, fix the entire pre-trial timetable, or as much of it as practicable (see Admiralty and Commercial Courts Guide, para. D8.7). A standard set of directions is set out in the Admiralty and Commercial Courts Guide, app. 8. The same practice is followed where possible in the County Court, provided trial windows and the availability of judges are known. In a High Court District Registry, trial dates are fixed by liaising with the presiding judge through the diary manager. On each circuit the District Judges, designated civil judges and the presiding judge cooperate closely on timetabling issues.

Unusual directions

47.13   It is the duty of the parties to ensure that all interim matters are dealt with at the case management conference. If they want an order dealing with a matter that is not normally dealt with at a case management conference, such as an order for an interim payment or for specific disclosure, and they know the application is likely to be opposed, they should issue and serve an application notice (form N244) in time for it to be heard at the conference. If the time allowed for the conference is insufficient to deal also with the contested application, they must inform the court at once so that a fresh date can be fixed. Failure to take these steps may result in a costs sanction (**PD 29, para. 5.8**). PD 23A, para. 2.10, provides that where a party decides to make an application at a hearing that has already been fixed, but there is insufficient time to serve an application notice, it may be sufficient simply to give such written notice as is possible, and to make the application orally at the original hearing.

Other directions from those provided for by **CPR, r. 3.1(2)**, that may be considered in appropriate cases include:

(a) directing that part of the proceedings, such as a counterclaim, be dealt with as separate proceedings;
(b) staying the whole or part of the proceedings either generally or until a specified date or event;
(c) consolidating proceedings;
(d) trying two or more actions at the same time;
(e) deciding the order in which issues are to be tried; and
(f) excluding an issue from consideration.

Plans, photographs, models and video evidence

Generally a party intending to use photographs, plans, diagrams, models and similar items as evidence at trial must give notice to the other parties by the date for disclosing witness statements (**CPR, r. 33.6(4)**). The skeleton argument should refer to a document which must identify for the court all relevant features which appear in the maps, plans, diagrams or photographs to be used at the trial (*Hunte v E. Bottomley and Sons Ltd* [2007] EWCA Civ 1168, [2008] CP Rep 3). Video recordings fall into the wide definition of 'documents' for the purposes of **Part 31**, so the usual rules on disclosure and inspection apply (see **chapter 50**). Furthermore, there is an obligation to inform the court at the first opportunity that such evidence will be relied upon, as arrangements need to be made to ensure video equipment is available at trial, and extra time will be required for the trial for showing the evidence (*Rall v Hume* [2001] EWCA Civ 146, [2001] 3 All ER 248). **47.14**

Mesothelioma claims

Mesothelioma claims are governed by **PD 3D**. In these cases the claim form and particulars of claim must be marked either 'Living Mesothelioma Claim' or 'Fatal Mesothelioma Claim' (**para. 3.1**). On filing and serving the claim form and particulars of claim, or as soon as possible thereafter, and in any event at least seven days before the case management conference, the claimant must file and serve any witness statements about liability (**para. 3.2**). At the first case management conference, unless there is a good reason not to do so, the defendant must be prepared to show cause why judgment should not be entered on liability and why the defendant should not make a standard interim payment (**para. 6.2**). If liability remains in issue, directions will usually be made at the first case management conference for the defendant to file and serve outline submissions showing cause, and for a show-cause hearing (**para. 6.4**). **47.15**

If the defendant fails to show cause, or admits liability, judgment will normally be entered for a sum to be determined (see **42.67** to **42.70**), and for a standard interim payment. Otherwise, the court will give directions including setting the trial date or window (**paras 6.5** to **6.8**). In living mesothelioma claims the trial will generally not be more than 16 weeks after service of the claim form (**para. 7.1**), and will often decide that strict compliance with the pre-action protocols was unnecessary (**para. 9**).

FIXING THE DATE FOR TRIAL

The court will fix the trial date or the period in which the trial is to take place as soon as practicable (**CPR, r. 29.2(2)**). This may be possible when it gives allocation directions, but in complex cases (and also, perhaps, badly prepared cases and cases where the facts are developing, such as many personal injuries claims) this may have to be delayed, perhaps for a considerable period of time. Where fixing the trial date is postponed, it may be revisited either at a later case management conference, or on the application of the parties, or after further scrutiny by the court. **47.16**

Commentary

When the court fixes the date for trial (or lays down a trial period or 'window'), it will give written notice to the parties, and will also specify a date by which the parties must file pre-trial checklists (**r. 29.2(3)**). The court may alternatively make an order for an early trial on a fixed date and dispense with pre-trial checklists (**PD 29, para. 8.1(2)**), or may simply list the case for trial when it reconsiders the case at the time when pre-trial checklists would be sent out, dispensing with the need for checklists at that stage (**CPR, r. 29.6(1)**).

In Queen's Bench Division cases proceeding in the Royal Courts of Justice in London, other than cases in the Admiralty and Commercial Courts and the Technology and Construction Court, a direction will be given as early as practicable (often the first case management conference) identifying the trial window (see Queen's Bench Guide, para. 9.4.4). The trial window is the period of time within which the Queen's Bench Judges' Listing Officer is to arrange for the trial to take place (para. 9.1.1). The court will often direct that the claimant must by a stated date obtain a listing appointment with the Listing Officer and give notice of the appointment to the other parties (para. 9.4.5). At the listing hearing the claimant must bring any case summary, the particulars of claim and any orders relevant to listing, and all parties must have details of the dates of availability of their witnesses, experts and counsel. The Listing Officer will try to ensure the speedy disposal of the trial by arranging a firm trial date or trial period as soon as possible within the trial window, or, as the case may be, any 'not before' date directed by the court (para. 9.4.8). This will occasionally result in a fixed trial date, but more frequently a three-day or five-day trial period within the trial window on which or during which the trial will commence (para. 9.1.1).

Any party dissatisfied with a decision made by the Listing Officer can, within seven days of the decision and on giving one day's notice to all other parties, apply to the judge nominated to hear such applications. The application should be arranged through the Queen's Bench Listing Office (Queen's Bench Guide, para. 9.4.10).

The relevant listing office should be informed of any special needs of any witnesses prior to the hearing, so that suitable facilities, parking, access etc. can be dealt with (Queen's Bench Guide, para. 10.2.9; Chancery Guide, para. 9.11).

In most cases in the Admiralty and Commercial Courts, a fixed trial date will be given immediately after the pre-trial timetable has been set at the case management conference (Admiralty and Commercial Courts Guide, para. D16.1).

Fixed dates are given on the basis that if previous fixtures have been substantially underestimated, or urgent matters arise, the trial may be delayed for a few days. Where such a delay might cause particular inconvenience, the Clerk to the Commercial Court should be informed well in advance (para. D16.2).

In the Technology and Construction Court, the trial date is usually fixed at the first case management conference (**PD 60, para. 8.6**).

The power to adjourn the trial is considered at **61.9** to **61.14**, and listing and adjourning problems caused by the restricted availability of experts are discussed at **61.8**.

PRE-TRIAL CHECKLISTS

47.17 Pre-trial checklists, in form N170, will (unless dispensed with) be sent out to the parties by the court. These must be completed and returned by the date specified in the directions given when the court fixed the date or period for trial (**CPR, r. 29.6**). In multi-track claims directions for listing for trial are usually given on a case management conference at some stage after allocation. The forms should be served by the court at least 14 days before they must be returned. Each party is under an obligation to return a completed checklist before the specified date.

Purpose of checklists

47.18 Pre-trial checklists are used to check that earlier orders and directions have been complied with, and to provide up-to-date information to assist the court with deciding when to hold the trial and how long it will take, and in making trial timetable directions. Once all the checklists have been received, or the time limit has expired, the file will be placed before the procedural judge, who will make directions for trial along the same lines as those set out in **47.26**, or direct that there should be a pre-trial directions hearing or pre-trial review. A case management conference may be convened specifically to consider and limit issues.

Exchange of checklists

47.19 The CPR do not require the parties to exchange copies of their pre-trial checklists, but doing so may avoid the parties giving conflicting or incomplete information to the court (**PD 29, para. 8.1(5)**). Getting this right may avoid the need for a pre-trial directions hearing or pre-trial review.

Failure to file checklists

47.20 If no one returns a pre-trial checklist by the specified date, the court will order that unless a completed pre-trial checklist is filed within seven days from service of that order, the claim, defence and any counterclaim will be struck out without further order (**CPR, r. 29.6(3)**). Where only some of the parties file pre-trial checklists the court will fix a pre-trial directions hearing, under **r. 29.6(4)** (see **PD 29, para. 8.5**). It will also fix a directions hearing if any of the questionnaires do not provide the necessary information, or if the court considers that such a hearing is necessary to decide what further directions should be given to complete the preparations for trial (**CPR, r. 29.6(4)**).

HEARING FEES

47.21 A claimant is required to pay a hearing fee of £1,090 at the same time as filing the pre-trial checklist (**CPFO, fee 2.1**). Fee 2.1 is not payable if the court fixed the hearing date on the issue of the claim. If the court fixes a trial date or trial week without requiring pre-trial checklists, fee 2.1 becomes payable within 14 days of the date of dispatch of the notice (or the date when oral notice is given if no written notice is given) of the trial date or week. For discussion of who should pay these fees see **46.12**. If the fee is not paid, the court will send a notice to pay in form N173, and failing payment within the time stated in the notice, the claim will be struck out (**CPR, r. 3.7**, and see **42.72**).

As an incentive to settle, the hearing fee of £1,090 will be refunded in whole or in part on a sliding scale if the court receives notice in writing from the party who paid the fee that the case has been settled or discontinued. The refunds are:

Court notified more than 28 days before the hearing	100 per cent
Court notified between 15 and 28 days before the hearing	75 per cent
Court notified between 7 and 14 days before the hearing	50 per cent

PRE-TRIAL DIRECTIONS HEARINGS

47.22 Pre-trial directions hearings serve a similar purpose to pre-trial reviews, but concentrate on making the decisions relevant to fixing the date of the trial. They are fixed for dates as early as possible, and the parties are given at least three clear days' notice of the date. Even if a pre-trial directions hearing is fixed because some of the parties did not file their pre-trial checklists, the court will normally fix or confirm the trial date and make orders about the steps to prepare the case for trial (**PD 29, para. 8.3(2)**). The court is likely to make further directions similar to those set out in 47.28.

PRE-TRIAL REVIEW

47.23   If a pre-trial review (rather than a pre-trial directions hearing, see 47.22) is listed, it is likely to take place about eight to 10 weeks before trial. The pre-trial review gives the court a further opportunity to check that the parties have complied with earlier orders and directions, and may help in promoting settlement. Pre-trial reviews are not held in all cases, but only in those that merit the additional hearing. An example is *JN Dairies Ltd v Johal Dairies Ltd* [2010] EWCA Civ 348, LTL 31/3/2010, where shortly before the trial both sides disclosed evidence in support of allegations of discreditable conduct by the other side. It was held that both sides should have applied to the court to list a pre-trial review to deal with amendments, further disclosure and other directions. The intention is that pre-trial reviews should be conducted by the eventual trial judge.

Before the pre-trial review

47.24   In some cases a pre-trial review may be required by directions made by the court at an earlier stage, such as on allocation or at a case management conference. In other cases the court may decide to hold a pre-trial review of its own initiative, such as when it considers the pre-trial checklists. In this event it will give the parties at least seven clear days' notice of the hearing of a pre-trial review (**CPR, r. 29.7**).

In the Chancery Division the claimant should, seven days before the pre-trial review, circulate a list of matters to be considered at the pre-trial review, including proposals as to how the case should be tried. Other parties must respond at least two days before the hearing (Chancery Guide, para. 20.4). The claimant should deliver to the Chancery Judges' Listing Office, by 10 a.m. on the day before the hearing of the pre-trial review, a bundle containing the lists of matters to be considered and proposals on any matters which are not agreed, the trial timetable, together with the pleadings, orders, filed witness statements and experts' reports, and other reasonably necessary documents (para. 20.5).

In the Commercial Court the parties should have completed Commercial Court pre-trial checklists (in the form set out in the Admiralty and Commercial Courts Guide, app. 13) in accordance with the pre-trial timetable directions. Before the pre-trial review, the parties must discuss and, if possible, agree a draft written timetable for the trial (**PD 58, para. 11.3**). The claimant's solicitor must ensure that the case management bundle is up to date (**PD 58, para. 10.9**).

Attendance

47.25   The same rules about a fully informed representative being present apply to pre-trial reviews as apply to case management conferences (see 47.9) and in the specialist courts in particular they should be attended by the trial advocates.

Pre-trial review directions

47.26   At a pre-trial review the court will not readily change earlier directions, and will apply the same principles as are applied generally when the parties fail to apply within 14 days for variation of case management directions (**PD 29, paras 6 and 9.3**; see 47.5).

Perhaps the most important task on a pre-trial review is to determine the timetable for the trial itself. This can lay down time limits for examination and cross-examination of witnesses, and for speeches. Doing this is intended to force advocates to focus their preparation, and to produce well-managed trials. Other matters to be dealt with are:

(a) Evidence, particularly expert evidence. At this stage there should have been full disclosure and perhaps also discussions between the experts. It may be possible to make more rigorous directions about which experts really do need to be called at the trial, and which experts (or which parts of the expert evidence) can be taken from the experts' reports.

(b) A time estimate for the trial.

(c) Preparation and organisation of trial bundles.

(d) Fixing a trial date or week.

(e) Fixing the place of trial. This will normally be at a civil trial centre but may be at another court depending on the convenience of the parties and the availability of court resources (**PD 29, para. 10.1**).

Agreed pre-trial review directions

The parties are required to seek to agree the directions to be made on the pre-trial review, and   **47.27**
may file an agreed order (**PD 29, para. 9.2**). The court may then make an order in the terms agreed, or make some other order, or reject the proposals and continue with the pre-trial review.

DIRECTIONS GIVEN AT OTHER HEARINGS

The court is not restricted to making case management directions on the occasions described   **47.28**
above, but can do so on any occasion the case comes before the court (**PD 29, para. 3.4**). In fact, whenever there is a hearing it is the duty of the parties to consider whether any directions should be made, and to make any appropriate application on that occasion (**PD 29, para. 3.5**). Further, the court may hold a directions hearing on its own initiative on three clear days' notice whenever it appears necessary to do so. This can include situations where progress is delayed because one or other of the parties is in default of directions previously made (**PD 29, para. 3.6**). It can also occur because a party needs a direction not already in place, perhaps because a need to amend, or to ask for further information, has arisen since the last case management hearing. In such cases the application must be made as soon as possible so as to minimise the disruption to the original timetable (**PD 29, para. 3.8**).

Chapter 48   Non-compliance, Sanctions and Relief

INTRODUCTION

48.1   So that the court can ensure that its case management directions and orders are complied with, and to retain control over the conduct of litigation, it needs to be armed with suitable coercive powers. Once a court order is disobeyed, the imposition of a sanction is almost always inevitable if court orders are to continue to enjoy the respect which they ought to have (per Lord Neuberger of Abbotsbury PSC, *Global Torch Ltd v Apex Global Management Ltd (No. 2)* [2014] UKSC 64, [2014] 1 WLR 4495). Failure to enforce the rules of court will encourage parties to make tactical use of the legal process, which should not be allowed (*National Commercial Bank Jamaica Ltd v Olint Corporation Ltd* [2009] UKPC 16, [2009] 1 WLR 1405 at [15]).

Since the CPR came into force in April 1999 the courts have had a duty to manage cases actively (**CPR, r. 1.4**), and parties have been under a duty to help the court in furthering the overriding objective (**r. 1.3**). In practice the courts tolerated repeated breaches of directions, which resulted in a proliferation of interim applications and appeals over the consequences of non-compliance. Except in cases where a fair trial was no longer possible (*Taylor v Anderson* [2002] EWCA Civ 1680, [2003] RTR 305), or where there were repeated breaches amounting to a total disregard of court orders (*UCB Corporate Services Ltd v Halifax (SW) Ltd* [1999] CPLR 691), cases were rarely struck out for procedural default.

The most draconian sanction that may be imposed is striking out. **Rule 3.4(2)(c)** provides that the court may strike out the whole or part of a statement of case if it appears that there has been a failure to comply with a rule, practice direction or court order. In less serious cases of default or breach the court may be prepared to impose a sanction which, to use a phrase used in some of the cases under the old rules, 'fits the crime'.

It is to be expected that from time to time one or other of the parties to proceedings will be unable to keep to the directions timetable that will have been imposed by the court. This will not generally be a problem provided the parties cooperate and can still keep to the directions relating to the 'key dates' for filing directions questionnaires, case management conferences, pre-trial reviews, filing pre-trial checklists and trial (**rr. 26.3(6A), 28.4 and 29.5**). If the default is not serious or significant, or if it arises through events outside the control of the defaulting party, the normal expectation is that the parties will cooperate in compliance with **rr. 1.3** and **1.4(2)(a)** and resolve the difficulty by agreeing a new timetable that preserves the key dates (*Denton v T. H. White Ltd* [2014] EWCA Civ 906, [2014] 1 WLR 3926 at [41]). The time specified by any provision of the CPR or by the court for doing any act may be varied by the written agreement of the parties, unless there is an express prohibition on variation in the rules (**r. 2.11**). There are further restrictions on agreeing variations where a rule, practice direction or court order specifies a consequence for non-compliance (**r. 3.8(3)** and **(4)**).

In addition to situations where an innocent party applies for an order imposing a sanction for default, similar problems arise where a defaulting party fails to comply with the timetable prescribed by the CPR and practice directions. These often provide specific sanctions for default or (on one analysis) may impose implied sanctions in that a failure to secure an extension may result in adverse consequences.

Where a sanction is applied, it is possible for the defaulting party to apply for relief from the sanction (**r. 3.9**). A slack approach to compliance with procedural orders was recognised by Sir Rupert Jackson in the *Review of Civil Litigation Costs: Final Report* (2009), ch. 39, as a driver of excessive litigation costs. To combat this Sir Rupert Jackson recommended the replacement of r. 3.9, and that judges should take a more robust approach to case management. These changes, which came into force on 1 April 2013, have effected a revolution in civil procedure. While parties retain responsibility for progressing their claims, the timetable that they must adhere to is firmly under the control of the court. Compliance, and the consequences of breach, continue to depend on the circumstances of the particular case, but the primary concept is that rules and directions are made for the purpose of being obeyed.

The cases fall into a number of date categories. **Rule 3.9** was replaced on 1 April 2013, introducing a more robust regime less tolerant to non-compliance. *Mitchell v News Group Newspapers Ltd* [2013] EWCA Civ 1537, [2014] 1 WLR 795, was decided on 27 November 2013, and was widely interpreted as imposing a draconian approach. *Mitchell* was described as having been misunderstood and misapplied by Lord Dyson MR and Vos LJ in *Denton v T. H. White Ltd* [2014] EWCA Civ 906, [2014] 1 WLR 3926, which laid down the current guidelines on 4 July 2014. *Mitchell* has not been overturned (*Denton v T. H. White Ltd*, at [24], [98]), but 'clarified and amplified in certain respects' (at [3]), which is obvious code for substantially revised, while seeking to avoid problems with the doctrine of *stare decisis*. Cases on procedural default therefore have to be treated with a great deal of caution, with much depending on the date of the decision. This chapter includes pre-*Mitchell* and pre-*Denton* cases where they appear to have a continuing authority. For a detailed discussion of earlier authorities, see the 2014 edition of this work.

ORIGINAL SANCTION TOO HARSH

48.2   It is impermissible on an application for relief from sanctions to argue that the sanction imposed under an unless order is too harsh. **PD 28, para. 4.2(2)**, and **PD 29, para. 6.2(2)**, provide that the court will assume for the purposes of any later application that a party who did not appeal, and who made no application to vary under **CPR, r. 3.1(7)**, within 14 days of service of any order containing directions, was content that the directions were correct in the circumstances then existing. If there is any legitimate complaint about the seriousness of the sanction, the correct course is to appeal against the original order (*Fred Perry (Holdings) Ltd v Brands Plaza Trading Ltd* [2012] EWCA Civ 224, [2012] FSR 28 at [24]) or, exceptionally, by asking the court which made the original order to vary or revoke it under **r. 3.1(7)** (*Mitchell v News Group Newspapers Ltd* [2013] EWCA Civ 1537 at [44]; *Walsham Chalet Park Ltd v Tallington Lakes Ltd* [2014] EWCA Civ 1607, [2015] 1 Costs LO 157 at [44]). Proportionality of the proposed sanction has to be considered at the stage when the sanction is imposed, whereas on an application for relief from sanctions the court has to assume the sanction is proportionate (*Walsham Chalet Park Ltd v Tallington Lakes Ltd*). The reason the Supreme Court was able to entertain arguments about the proportionality of the original sanction in *Global Torch Ltd v Apex Global Management Ltd (No. 2)* [2014] UKSC 64, [2014] 1 WLR 4495 (at [22]–[27] and [40]) was that one of the five orders being appealed was the order of Norris J that originally imposed the sanction (see Lord Neuberger at [18]).

Once an order or direction has been made, the parties must comply, seek an extension, apply to vary or revoke the order, or appeal (see **42.42** to **42.52** and **chapter 74**). An application for relief from sanctions presupposes that the sanction was in principle properly imposed.

NON-COMPLIANCE

Non-compliance

48.3   Non-compliance may be obvious, for example, where nothing has been done by the deadline in a direction requiring a stated step to be taken by 4.00 p.m. on a stated day. It is important that a party's representatives are clear on what they have to do when directions or orders are made, and that they can comply within the time provided.

Doing something different from that required by the order is non-compliance. Having a disclosure statement signed by someone other than the party is a serious failure to comply with **CPR, r. 31.10(6)** (*Global Torch Ltd v Apex Global Management Ltd (No. 2)* [2014] UKSC 64, [2014] 1 WLR 4495). Where an order required the production of bank statements or other primary documents, there was a breach where secondary evidence was provided (*Sports Network Ltd v Calzaghe* [2008] EWHC 2566 (QB), LTL 3/11/2008). An order requiring a mandate for the release of medical records was breached in *Wahid v Skanska UK plc* [2014] EWHC 251 (QB), LTL 17/2/2014, where the claimant did not provide a signed mandate, even though his general practitioner did send the defendant the claimant's medical records. A further breach in *Wahid v Skanska UK plc* was in purporting to give specific disclosure of what had happened to certain documents that were no longer in the claimant's control, which was a failure to comply with the requirement in **CPR, r. 31.10(4)(b)**, to indicate what had happened to such documents when giving standard disclosure. The opposite problem arose in *E Group Ltd v Baker* [2008] EWHC 2349 (TCC), LTL 22/10/2008, where an order required a witness statement giving specific disclosure. There was an almost total disregard of the original order when the party only made minor amendments to a document (which was not a witness statement) which had previously been rejected by the court.

Purported compliance

Cases of purported compliance can cause considerable difficulty. It often happens that although documents are served by a deadline, the other side is far from content that they properly comply with the relevant order or direction. The first question is whether it is the order or the purported performance which is the problem. If the documents served technically comply with the terms of the order, the other side have either to accept the position or seek a more precise order from the court. There may be proportionality, delay or costs reasons against this. Where the view is that it is the performance which is defective, an application may be made for a sanction for breach.   **48.4**

The test is whether there has been complete compliance with the terms of the order, subject only to *de minimis* exceptions (*Jani-King (GB) Ltd v Prodger* [2007] EWHC 712 (QB), LTL 10/4/2007; *Hytec Information Systems Ltd v Coventry City Council* [1997] 1 WLR 1666). However, there is a reluctance to be drawn into disputes over what may appear to be a poor attempt at performance at the interim stage rather than leaving the question to trial, and it is not possible at the interim stage for adverse inferences to be drawn from, for example, the paucity of documents disclosed pursuant to an unless order for specific disclosure (*Rahamim v Reich* (2009) LTL 10/2/2009).

In considering purported performance a proportionate or balanced approach must be taken having regard to the practicalities of real life (*Sports Network Ltd v Calzaghe* [2008] EWHC 2566 (QB), LTL 3/11/2008, per Coulson J at [111]).

A party may be regarded as in breach where there has been only 'nominal' or 'purported' compliance (*Top Layers Interior Ltd v Azure Maritime Holdings SA* [2007] EWHC 2844 (QB), LTL 10/12/2007). Filing a directions questionnaire instead of a pre-trial checklist was regarded as a complete failure to comply in *British Gas Trading Ltd v Oak Cash and Carry Ltd* [2016] EWCA Civ 153, [2016] CP Rep 27. Where a party provides written evidence that it has complied, the court may reject that evidence if it finds it is incredible. There is no higher standard, such as 'plainly incredible' (*Lexi Holdings plc v Luqman* [2007] EWCA Civ 1501, LTL 7/8/2007).

RESPONDING TO THE OTHER SIDE'S DEFAULT

A party not in default faced with an opponent who has not complied with the court's directions is not entitled to try to make matters worse for the defaulting party by sitting back and waiting for the other side's default to get worse by the additional passage of time. Nor is the innocent party entitled to seek to take tactical advantage of technical breaches (*Denton v T. H. White Ltd* [2014] EWCA Civ 906, [2014] 1 WLR 3926 at [41]) or to jump the gun by making an immediate application for an order with sanctions.   **48.5**

Instead, the correct procedure is partly laid down in **PD 28, paras 5.1** to **5.3** (for fast track cases) and **PD 29, paras 7.1** to **7.3** (which are in identical terms and apply in multi-track cases). The innocent party should first write to the defaulting party referring to the default, asking for it to be rectified within a short reasonable period (usually seven or 14 days), and giving warning of an intention to apply for an order if the default is not remedied. Where the default carries a sanction, the maximum extension that can be agreed is 28 days (**CPR, r. 3.8(4)**). If there is continued default, the innocent party may apply for an order to enforce compliance or for a sanction to be imposed or both. Any application for such an order must be made without delay. If the innocent party does delay in making the application, the court

Commentary

may take the delay into account when it decides whether to make an order imposing a sanction or whether to grant relief from a sanction imposed by the relevant provision.

Last-minute applications to strike out for breach of orders, particularly applications made without notice for hearing on the day of trial, were discouraged by the Court of Appeal in *Whittaker v Soper* [2001] EWCA Civ 1462, LTL 28/9/2001.

APPROACH TO NON-COMPLIANCE

48.6   Courts dealing with non-compliance will usually take into account the nature of the default, the reasons for the non-compliance, whether the step has been taken before the application has been heard, the expected time for compliance if not, any prejudice caused to the other side, the impact of the non-compliance on costs and the trial date, and the impact on other court users and the court system. Based on its assessment of these factors, the court may view the default on any of five different levels of seriousness:

(a) Breaches that are neither serious nor significant are usually dealt with by allowing the defaulting party a limited period of time to comply, together with an adverse costs order in respect of any interim application needed to bring the matter before the court (*Colliers International Property Consultants v Colliers Jordan Lee Jafaar Sdn Bhd* [2008] EWHC 1524 (Comm), [2008] 2 Lloyd's Rep 368).

(b) If the default is more serious the court will make it plain it requires compliance by stating that a revised deadline is 'final', usually combined with an adverse costs order. Proportionality has to be kept in mind (*TIP Communications LLC v Motorola Ltd* [2009] EWHC 212 (Pat), LTL 23/2/2009, where a hearing just to badge an order as 'final' was regarded as contrary to the overriding objective). Breach of a final order usually results in a sanction being imposed on a further application to the court (*Sports Network Ltd v Calzaghe* [2008] EWHC 2566 (QB), LTL 3/11/2008).

(c) More serious defaults will be met by enforcing compliance by making an 'unless' order with a stated sanction in default, again usually combined with an adverse costs order (see **48.9**). Imposition of an unless order is itself viewed as a sanction (see **48.7**). Where the court decides against imposing an unless order, it will generally be wrong to impose a striking-out sanction without more if that order is breached (*Michael Wilson and Partners Ltd v Sinclair* [2015] EWCA Civ 774, [2015] 4 Costs LR 707). Breach of an unless order results in the immediate imposition of the stated sanction (see **48.24**).

(d) More serious defaults result in the immediate imposition of a sanction, which may restrict the evidence that may be adduced, or restrict the value of the claim, or even consist of striking out part or the whole of a party's statement of case with judgment for the innocent party.

(e) A trial date or trial window will only be vacated on account of procedural default if there are exceptional circumstances (see **42.52**).

The Court of Appeal in *Biguzzi v Rank Leisure plc* [1999] 1 WLR 1926, in affirming a decision to strike out for wholesale disregard of the court's rules, commented that striking out would not always be the correct approach. Under the CPR the court has wide powers to formulate suitable sanctions for breach of directions, which include making orders for indemnity costs, for paying money into court, and awarding interest at higher or lower rates. *Biguzzi v Rank Leisure plc* must not, however, be understood as promoting an unduly lenient approach to the imposition of sanctions. Doing justice involves ensuring proceedings are dealt with justly and at proportionate cost. A tough, robust approach to rule-compliance is insisted upon, in order to ensure that justice can be done in the majority of cases, and to ensure that court resources are not tied up in dealing with cases where parties are in default (*Mitchell v News Group Newspapers Ltd* [2013] EWCA Civ 1537, [2014] 1 WLR 795 at [38]).

There is a clear distinction between the initial imposition of a sanction and an application for relief from sanctions (*Michael Wilson and Partners Ltd v Sinclair*). Despite this, it has been said that the principles in *Mitchell* and *Denton v T. H. White Ltd* [2014] EWCA Civ 906, [2014] 1 WLR 3926 are 'relevant and important' not only on an application for relief from sanctions, but also at this earlier stage when the court is considering whether to impose a sanction for non-compliance (*Walsham Chalet Park Ltd v Tallington Lakes Ltd* [2014] EWCA Civ 1607, [2015] 1 Costs LO 157 at [44]). These are principles such as the need to enforce compliance with court orders and the spirit behind the *Mitchell* decision, such as taking into account the wider interests of other court users, and a robust but fair approach to non-compliance. It has been said that it is not wrong for a judge considering whether to impose a sanction to have regard to the three-stage *Denton* test (*Abdulle v Commissioner of Police of the Metropolis* [2015] EWCA Civ 1260, [2016] 1 WLR 898). Nevertheless, the ultimate question for the court in deciding whether to impose a sanction is materially different from that in deciding whether to grant relief from a sanction that has already been imposed (*Walsham Chalet Park Ltd v Tallington Lakes Ltd* per Richards LJ at [44]). When deciding whether to impose a sanction, proportionality of the sanction itself is in issue, whereas on an application for relief the court proceeds on the basis that the sanction was properly imposed.

Regarding proportionality, the approach taken by the Supreme Court in *Global Torch Ltd v Apex Global Management Ltd (No. 2)* [2014] UKSC 64, [2014] 1 WLR 4495 at [22]–[27] and [40] was to consider the nature of the breach, the number of opportunities the defaulting party was given to put it right, his continuing breach, whether the first-instance court or the Court of Appeal would have given relief if there had been late compliance, and the financial impact of the sanction. On the facts, a continuing breach had the effect of giving the defaulting party a tactical advantage in the litigation, which meant striking out in a $6 million claim was not disproportionate.

Unless orders

Applying the above principles, the court may take the view that the best way to ensure its directions are complied with by a defaulting party and that the trial date will be met, is to make an unless order. Unless orders should be reserved for situations where they are truly required to ensure litigation proceeds efficiently and at proportionate cost (*Denton v T. H. White Ltd* [2014] EWCA Civ 906, [2014] 1 WLR 3926 at [44]). Unless orders are hard to justify on the first occasion a step has to be taken in a case, where the automatic sanction is likely to be unduly harsh (*Kinsley v Commissioner of Police for the Metropolis* [2010] EWCA Civ 953, LTL 10/6/2010). It is likely to be appropriate to make an unless order where a party is in breach of an earlier order or direction, particularly where the earlier order was expressed to be 'final' (*Sports Network Ltd v Calzaghe*, at [114]). Where the reason advanced for non-compliance with an earlier order is regarded as little more than an excuse, an unless order may be the only way to impress on the defaulting party the importance of complying with the relevant orders (*D. Morgan plc v Mace and Jones* [2010] EWHC 697 (TCC), LTL 4/5/2010, where reliance on the claimant's managing director's illness was regarded as an excuse, primarily because he had not been ill throughout the entire period).

If the evidence is rejected, it is almost inevitable that an unless order will be made. In *Forrester Ketley and Co. v Brent* [2005] EWCA Civ 270, LTL 2/3/2005, it was held that the court below had been fully entitled to make unless orders, with striking out in default, on both the following grounds, where the defendant:

(a) had failed to provide a single document which clearly stated his case; and

(b) had failed to pay earlier interim costs orders.

Form of unless orders

An unless order gives the defaulting party a final opportunity to comply, and imposes a sanction in default. Often a costs sanction will be imposed at the same time. The period to be allowed by an unless order depends on the circumstances. Often 14 to 28 days will be appropriate. A stricter approach is taken where the court feels there is blameworthy conduct

48.7

48.8

than where a party is in default through events outside its control. A more generous period should be given for less contentious unless orders, such as for provision of security for costs (*Prince Radu of Hohenzollern v Houston* [2006] EWCA Civ 1575, *The Times*, 1 January 2007).

Like all other orders, orders with sanctions must specify the time within which the step under consideration must be taken by reference to a calendar date and a specific time (**CPR, r. 2.9**). The sanction part of the order may take the form of an unless provision. This is to the effect that if the terms of the order are breached, the other party may file a request for judgment to be entered and costs (**r. 3.5**). **PD 40B, para. 8.2**, lays down formulae for drafting unless orders. These are in the following forms (to be adapted as necessary):

(a) 'Unless the claimant serves his list of documents by 4.00 p.m. on Friday, 20 January 2017 his claim will be struck out and judgment entered for the defendant.' This is the preferred form.

(b) 'Unless the claimant serves his list of documents within 14 days of service of this order…' This should be used where the defaulting party did not attend the hearing where the order was made.

SANCTIONS

Sanctions available

48.9   The following is a non-exhaustive list of possible sanctions that may be imposed:

(a)   striking out the entire claim or defence (see **48.13**);

(b)   striking out part of the defaulting party's statement of case (see **48.16**);

(c)   debarring a party from amending or updating part of its statement of case or a schedule of future loss and expense (see **48.21**);

(d)   debarring a party from calling one or more witnesses, including expert witnesses (see **48.17**);

(e)   depriving a claimant who is in default of all or some of the interest that would otherwise have been awarded (see **48.10** and **64.27**);

(f)   increasing the rate of interest otherwise payable (if the default comprises non-compliance with a pre-action protocol) (see **8.4** and **48.10**);

(g)   requiring a defaulting party to pay all or some of the other party's costs of the proceedings (see **48.18**);

(h)   requiring the defaulting party to pay the costs of and occasioned by the application in which the default is considered;

(i)   ordering adverse costs orders to be paid on the indemnity basis (see **48.18**);

(j)   requiring adverse costs orders to be paid forthwith;

(k)   requiring the defaulting party to provide security as a condition for being allowed to continue with the proceedings (see **48.19**);

(l)   ordering security for costs (see **48.20**);

(m)   imposing a stay on proceedings in the event of non-compliance (*Summit Navigation Ltd v Generali Romania Asigurare Reasigurare SA* [2014] EWHC 398 (Comm), [2014] 2 Costs LR 367).

Non-compliance with applicable pre-action protocols

48.10   If, in the opinion of the court, there has been non-compliance with **PD Pre-action Conduct and Protocols** or any relevant pre-action protocol, the court will consider the extent of the parties' compliance (**PD Pre-action Conduct and Protocols, para. 13**) and the overall effect of the non-compliance on the other party when deciding whether to impose sanctions (**para. 16**). Minor or technical breaches are unlikely to result in sanctions (**para. 13**). An order may be made staying the proceedings while particular steps are taken to comply with the relevant protocol (**para. 15(b)**). By **para. 16** sanctions the court may impose include:

(a)   an order that the party at fault pay the costs of the proceedings, or part of the costs of the other party or parties;

(b)   an order that the party at fault pay those costs on an indemnity basis;

(c) if the party at fault is a claimant who has been awarded a sum of money, an order depriving that party of interest on that sum for a specified period, and/or awarding interest at a lower rate than would otherwise have been awarded;

(d) if the party at fault is a defendant, and the claimant has been awarded a sum of money, an order awarding interest on that sum for a specified period at a higher rate, not exceeding 10 per cent above base rate, than the rate which would otherwise have been awarded.

Sanctions prescribed by the CPR

Sanctions imposed by the CPR for various steps in litigation are set out in **table 48.1**.   48.11

Table 48.1 Sanctions prescribed by the CPR

Step in litigation	CPR provision	Prescribed sanction for default
Pre-action protocols	**PD Pre-action Conduct and Protocols, para. 16**	Range of sanctions, including costs and interest penalties
Serve claim form	**CPR, r. 7.6**	No extension = claim defeated
Serve particulars of claim	**r. 7.4**	None
Acknowledge service / serve defence	**r.12.3**	No automatic sanction, but claimant able to enter default judgment
Other statements of case / further information	**Part 16**	None
Directions questionnaires in County Court money claims	**r. 26.3(7A)**	Statement of case struck out
Directions questionnaires in High Court specified money claims	**r. 26.3(8)**	Court may: (a) order directions; (b) strike out the claim; (c) strike out the defence; or (d) list for a CMC
Directions questionnaires in non-money claims	**r. 26.3**	None
Disclosure reports	**r. 31.5(3)**	None
Costs budgets	**r. 3.14**	Limit costs to court fees
Inadequate attendance at CMC	**r. 29.3 / PD 29, para. 5.2(3)**	Normally a wasted costs order
Disclosure of documents relied upon	**r. 31.21**	Defaulting party cannot rely on the documents unless the court gives permission
Disclosure of documents helpful to other parties	**rr. 31.5 / 31.6**	None
Witness statements	**r. 32.10**	Witness may not be called to give oral evidence unless the court gives permission
Experts' reports	**r. 35.13**	Report may not be used or expert may not be called to give oral evidence unless the court gives permission
Short notice of interim application	**r. 23.4**	None. May be allowed to make the application orally (PD 23A, para. 2.10)

(continued)

Commentary

Step in litigation	CPR provision	Prescribed sanction for default
Non-payment of hearing fee	**rr. 3.7(4)**, **3.7A(6)**, **3.7B(3)**	Automatically struck out
Failing to lodge trial bundles	**r. 39.5**	None
Not ready for trial	**PD 28 para. 5.4**; **PD 29 para. 7.4**	Detailed guidance, but includes: (a) possibly depriving a party of right to raise or contest an issue or to rely on evidence (b) disallowing costs (c) refusing adjournment
Non-attendance of one party at trial	**r. 39.3**	Proceed in absence of the party, or strike out
Non-attendance of all parties at trial	**r. 39.3(1)(a)**	May strike out proceedings
Appeal out of time	**rr. 52.12** and **52.15**; **PD 52B**, **paras 3.1** to **3.3**	None
Schedule of costs for summary assessment	**PD 44, paras 9.5** and **9.6**	Taken into account in deciding what order to make about costs
Detailed assessment, commencement	**r. 47.8**	Loss of interest on costs (r. 47.8(3). If paying party applies for an order under r. 47.8(1), court may make an unless order (r. 47.8(2))

Failures to comply with the requirements for directions questionnaires and hearing fees are not the most serious defaults, but they attract striking out, the strongest sanction in the list. There is no prescribed sanction for failing to file a directions questionnaire in a non-money claim, but the breach is of the same nature as in a money claim. This cannot be because the Civil Procedure Rule Committee felt automatic striking out was a proportionate sanction for breach, but is a purely pragmatic approach of terminating claims if the relevant parties do not pay or comply, with relief being contemplated if and when they do.

Defaults that have the largest impact on costs include not being ready for trial, inadequate disclosure, and not complying with directions on witness statements and experts. The sanction in **r. 31.10** on disclosure only affects documents that the defaulting party wishes to rely on at trial. The most expensive defaults cover documents helpful to the innocent party, for which there is no prescribed sanction. While there are severe sanctions for breach of directions on witness statements and experts' reports, these apply unless the court otherwise orders, and are not as severe as striking out.

Sanctions arising from late service of witness statements and experts' reports take effect on expiry of the case management deadline, and not only at trial (*Chartwell Estate Agents Ltd v Fergies Properties SA* [2014] EWCA Civ 506, [2014] CP Rep 36 at [27]).

Where an expert fails to answer written questions by the time stated in directions (see **54.32**), the court may impose costs and other sanctions against the party instructing the expert or the expert (**Guidance for Experts 2014, paras 91** and **92**). If there is continued non-compliance, the court may debar a party from relying on the report or from calling the expert.

Implied sanction doctrine

48.12   Starting with *Sayers v Clarke Walker* [2002] EWCA Civ 645, [2002] 1 WLR 3095, the implied sanction doctrine is to the effect that where a party has not complied with a relevant rule or order, and if the court is unwilling to grant an extension of time, the consequence will be that the default provisions of the rule, or the original order, will stand. In such circumstances there is an implied sanction imposed by the rule or order, which then engages the principles in **CPR,**

r. 3.9 (see *Brooke LJ* at [21]). This principle has been applied in a series of cases dealing with applications to extend the time for bringing an appeal, including *YD (Turkey) v Secretary of State for the Home Department* [2006] EWCA Civ 52, [2006] 1 WLR 1646 and *Yeates v Aviva Insurance UK Ltd* [2012] EWCA Civ 634, LTL 16/5/2012, all of which held that the principles governing relief from sanctions apply by analogy even though there is no express sanction for default. The doctrine has also been applied to applications to extend time for serving respondents' notices in appeals (*Salford Estates (No. 2) Ltd v Altomart Ltd* [2014] EWCA Civ 1408, [2015] 1 WLR 1825) and to applications to amend appeal notices (*Lighting and Lamps UK Ltd v Clarke* (2016) LTL 4/3/2016).

It has also been relied upon in a number of cases dealing with applications to set aside default judgments (particularly *Hussain v Birmingham City Council* [2005] EWCA Civ 1570, LTL 25/11/2005 at [30]; *Regione Piemonte v Dexia Crediop SpA* [2014] EWCA Civ 1298, LTL 9/10/2014; and the cases cited at **20.14**). It was applied in *Gentry v Miller* [2016] EWCA Civ 141, [2016] 1 WLR 2696 where there were applications both to set aside a default judgment and to set aside judgment following non-attendance at trial. However, *Gentry v Miller* was not applied by a differently constituted Court of Appeal in *Mohun-Smith v TBO Investments Ltd* [2016] EWCA Civ 403, [2016] 1 WLR 2919 despite being cited in argument also on setting aside judgment following non-attendance at trial (see **62.6**).

It is likely that judges will be tempted to extend the doctrine into other situations. An example is *Elliott v Stobart Group Ltd* [2015] EWCA Civ 449, [2015] CP Rep 36, which in several ways is an unsatisfactory authority concerning a failure to comply with a direction for the disclosure of expert evidence.

In two Trinidad and Tobago appeals to the Privy Council (*Attorney General of Trinidad and Tobago v Matthews* [2011] UKPC 38, LTL 20/10/2011 and *Attorney General of Trinidad and Tobago v Universal Projects Ltd* [2011] UKPC 37, LTL 20/10/2011), Lord Dyson disapproved the implied sanction theory in the context of setting aside judgments entered in default. The principal reason was that the local provisions that are equivalent to, and in, for these purposes, the same terms as, **CPR, rr. 3.8** and **3.9**, are restricted to sanctions imposed by the very order, rule or practice direction that has been breached. This interpretation of **rr. 3.8** and **3.9** was adopted by the Court of Appeal in *Salford Estates (No. 2) Ltd v Altomart Ltd* [2014] EWCA Civ 1408, [2015] 1 WLR 1825 and *R (Hysaj) v Secretary of State for the Home Department* [2014] EWCA Civ 1633, [2015] 1 WLR 2472, but in the latter case Moore-Bick LJ concluded that the series of Court of Appeal authorities following *Sayers v Clarke Walker* meant it was now too well established, in relation to applications to extend time for appealing, for it to be overturned (at [36], see **74.22**).

One of the reasons given by Lord Dyson in *Attorney General of Trinidad and Tobago v Matthews* for rejecting the implied sanction doctrine was that it cannot have been intended by the Civil Procedure Rule Committee that, for example on an application to set aside a default judgment, the applicant would have to satisfy two sets of rules (in **rr. 13.3** and **3.9**). Cases such as *Mid-East Sales Ltd v United Engineering and Trading Co. (Pvt) Ltd* [2014] EWHC 1457 (Comm), [2014] 2 All ER (Comm) 623 apply a composite of the requirements of both tests. With respect, if there is any validity in the doctrine, it should be a two-stage process. At the first stage the court should apply the principles governing the particular situation (such as the rules on setting aside in **r. 13.3**). The second stage (relief from the implied sanction applying **r. 3.9**) should only arise if the court refuses to set aside, because it is only then that an implied sanction applies. However, the courts applying the doctrine seem to jump the gun and assume relief must be sought from the implied sanction at the same time as deciding whether to refuse (for example) to set aside the default judgment.

The importance of according finality to court decisions justifies importing by analogy the *Denton* principles to applications to extend time for bringing an appeal. It is submitted that this should be the limit on the implied sanction doctrine.

Commentary

STRIKING OUT

Whether striking out is appropriate

48.13 An applicant seeking a straight striking-out order has the burden of proof, whereas on an application for relief from sanctions (under **CPR, r. 3.9**, see **48.26**) after non-compliance with an unless order (see **48.7**, **48.8**) once the innocent party has established there is a default, the onus is on the defaulting party on the second and third stages (see **48.32**) of the *Denton* test (*Mitchell v News Group Newspapers Ltd* [2013] EWCA Civ 1537, [2014] 1 WLR 795 at [41]; *Denton v T. H. White Ltd* [2014] EWCA Civ 906, [2014] 1 WLR 3926 at [12]). Norris J at first instance in *Global Torch Ltd v Apex Global Management (No. 2)* [2013] EWHC 2818 (Ch), LTL 30/9/2013 at [8] said 'striking out of a statement of case is one of the most powerful weapons in the court's case management armoury and should not be deployed unless its consequences can be justified' (quoted with apparent approval by Lord Neuberger at [2014] UKSC 64, [2014] 1 WLR 4495 at [16] and by Richards LJ in *Walsham Chalet Park Ltd v Tallington Lakes Ltd* [2014] EWCA Civ 1607, [2015] 1 Costs LO 157 at [44]). Where a party is in persistent deliberate default (*Global Torch Ltd v Apex Global Management (No. 2)*), or where there has been a history of delay (*Necati v Metropolitan Police Commissioner* (2000) LTL 19/1/2001), there may come a point when the court will say it is right to apply the ultimate sanction of striking out, or that 'enough is enough' (*Duggan v Wood* [2001] EWCA Civ 1942, LTL 22/11/2001).

Prejudice

48.14 In *Axa Insurance Co. Ltd v Swire Fraser Ltd* [2000] CPLR 142 it was said that proof of prejudice is not a requirement for an order for striking out under **CPR, r. 3.4(2)(c)**. That said, prejudice to the innocent party is clearly an important factor, and where it is present, such as in *Purdy v Cambran* [1999] CPLR 843, where the defendant's expert died in the period of delay, it may fully justify striking out.

Fair trial

48.15 An important consideration is whether striking out is consistent with the European Convention on Human Rights, **art. 6**. The right to a fair trial in **art. 6** is a right to have a fair hearing within a reasonable time. In this context it is therefore important to note that the defendant, as well as the claimant, has rights under the article (*Circuit Systems Ltd v Zuken-Redac (UK) Ltd* [2001] BLR 253).

Where striking out is based on delay, it was held in *Taylor v Anderson* [2002] EWCA Civ 1680, [2003] RTR 305, that what is required is not considerable doubt, but a considerable risk or impossibility of a fair trial taking place.

LESSER SANCTIONS

Striking out part of a statement of case

48.16 Striking out the whole of a statement of case may not be proportionate. For example, a party may be in default of an order to provide further information on a single issue in a case where several issues are raised. A suitable sanction in such circumstances may be striking out the part of the statement of case dealing with that issue (see *QPS Consultants Ltd v Kruge Tissue (Manufacturing) Ltd* [1999] BLR 366).

Debarring a party from presenting part or all of its case

48.17 There are prescribed sanctions in CPR, **rr. 31.21** (disclosure), **32.10** (witness statements and witness summaries) and **35.13** (experts' reports) preventing parties in breach from making use of the evidence not disclosed in accordance with directions, unless the court gives permission. Similar sanctions can be imposed as part of the case management process. Where there is persistence in the disobedience of a direction that would lead to an unfair trial, Lord Neuberger in *Global Torch Ltd v Apex Global Management Ltd (No. 2)* [2014] UKSC 64, [2014] 1 WLR 4495 at [23] said that in the absence of special factors it would be almost inevitable that sanctions debarring the defaulting party from presenting or resisting the claim would be made and enforced.

Payment of costs

The normal costs order on a successful application to extend time or for relief from sanctions **48.18** is that the party in default pays the other side's costs, including the costs of and occasioned by the application. This is because default is seen as bringing such applications on the defaulting party's own head (*Axa Insurance Co. Ltd v Swire Fraser Ltd* [2000] CPLR 142). The normal costs order may be inadequate, particularly where granting relief from a default would result in the adjournment of a trial (*Denton v T. H. White Ltd* [2014] EWCA Civ 906, [2014] 1 WLR 3926 at [89]). Orders requiring a defaulting party to pay the costs of the proceedings to date as a sanction involve a substantial risk of impairing that party's right of access to the courts. Nevertheless, an order depriving the claimant of all her costs to date, and providing that the claimant would pay certain defence costs in any event, was made as an alternative to striking out in *Parnall v Hurst* [2003] EWHC 2164 (Ch), [2003] WTLR 997. Adverse costs orders covering all or part of the costs of the claim to date are not uncommon orders where the court allows a late amendment of a statement of case if the amendment makes a fundamental change to the nature of the case being advanced (*Beoco Ltd v Alfa Laval Co. Ltd* [1995] QB 137). Unreasonable opposition, however, may reverse the costs position (*Denton* at [41]–[43]).

Paying security

In *Grundy v Naqvi* (2001) LTL 1/2/2001 the defaulting party had some reason for not having complied (in that she wanted to amend her statement of case, which would have impacted the **48.19** content of the witness statements), albeit she was also guilty of delay in seeking permission to amend. An order was made requiring the defaulting party to pay £50,000 into court. The amount ordered must not be such that it will be impossible for the party to pay, because that would be the equivalent of striking out (see **20.21** and *Marstons plc v Charman* [2009] EWCA Civ 719, LTL 29/4/2009).

Security for costs as a condition

There is a power in **CPR, r. 3.1(3)**, to make an order subject to conditions. This is wide **48.20** enough to include making an order requiring the payment of money into court as security for the costs of the non-defaulting party (*Olatawura v Abiloye* [2002] EWCA Civ 998, [2003] 1 WLR 275). This power is not to be regarded as an easy way to obtain security for costs in situations where the conditions in **rr. 25.12** and **25.13** cannot be satisfied (*Huscroft v P & O Ferries Ltd* [2010] EWCA Civ 1483, [2011] 1 WLR 939). The purpose of **r. 3.1(3)** is to enable the court to grant relief on terms, and any condition imposed is only legitimate if it is a proportionate and effective means of achieving that purpose. In *Olatawura v Abiloye* factors to be taken into account when making an order tantamount to security for costs as a sanction were said to include:

(a) the ability of the respondent to pay;
(b) the respondent's conduct, including compliance with orders and pre-action protocols; and
(c) the apparent strength of the claim or defence (this is only to be taken into account where the defaulting party's case has no real prospect of success: *Ali v Hudson* [2003] EWCA Civ 1793, LTL 11/12/2003; *Global Torch Ltd v Apex Global Management Ltd (No. 2)* [2014] UKSC 64, [2014] 1 WLR 4495).

The court must be sensitive to the risk that it might be denying the respondent access to the court when making such an order (*Olatawura v Abiloye*). A distinction was drawn in *CIBC Mellon Trust Co. v Mora Hotel Corporation NV* [2002] EWCA Civ 1688, [2003] 1 All ER 564, between ordering security for costs incurred before the relevant default (which may be hard to justify if there is evidence that the defaulting party cannot afford to pay) and ordering security for the costs of the application, which may well be justifiable.

Depriving of interest and related sanctions

48.21   In *Walsh v Misseldine* [2000] CPLR 201 Stuart-Smith LJ made it clear that there is a real distinction between cases where liability is and is not in dispute. Where liability is admitted, depriving the claimant of interest or requiring the claimant to pay costs which can be set off against the damages award are effective sanctions for delay. They are not necessarily so if the claim turns out to be unsuccessful. A similar decision was reached in *Price v Price* [2003] EWCA Civ 888, [2003] 3 All ER 911, where the court allowed the claim to continue on condition that damages were restricted to the amount that might be substantiated by any medical report written before a stated date.

Substantive law and sanctions

48.22   Under the Housing Act 1988, s. 7(4), for example, in addition to establishing a statutory ground for possession, a possession order can only be made if the court considers it reasonable to do so. There is also a requirement to consider proportionality under the European Convention on Human Rights, **art. 8**. Concerns were raised by *Nelson v Circle Thirty Three Housing Trust Ltd* [2014] EWCA Civ 106, [2014] 3 Costs LO 355 at [14] about how these substantive law issues could be addressed if the tenant's defence was struck out as a sanction.

It is suggested that where there are overarching substantive law issues in a case, the court should be careful to ensure that those points are preserved even if the rest of the defaulting party's statement of case is struck out. This would require a careful analysis of the pleaded defence when the sanction is imposed. If the court fails to do this, the defaulting party should apply to vary the order under **CPR, r. 3.1(7)**, or (more appropriately) seek permission to appeal that order. Strictly, it is too late to raise such points even on an application under **r. 3.5(5)** (given that possession claims fall outside **r. 3.5(2)**) to obtain judgment following the striking out of the defence, because the sanction takes effect when the original order is breached (**r. 3.8(1)**).

BEFORE EXPIRY OF DEADLINE

48.23   A party which realises it will be unable to meet a case management deadline has a number of options:

(a) asking its opponent to consent to an extension of time (see 42.46);
(b) making an application for an extension of time before the deadline expires under **CPR, r. 3.1(2)(a)**; see 42.49);
(c) applying to vary or revoke the order imposing the deadline under **r. 3.1(7)** (see 42.42);
(d) appealing against the order imposing the deadline (see **chapter 74**); and
(e) serving a document in whatever form it may be at that time within the deadline.

Re Guidezone Ltd [2014] EWHC 1165 (Ch), [2014] 1 WLR 3728, recommended using options (a) or (b). Consent cannot be given to postpone a 'key date' (for which see 42.48), which includes the dates for filing directions questionnaires and pre-trial checklists, and the dates of case management conferences, pre-trial reviews and the trial. Nor can a party give consent to an extension of more than 28 days if there is a consequence attached to the relevant case management step (**r. 3.8(3)** and (4)). Any consent given pursuant to **r. 3.8(4)** has to be in writing, before expiry of the existing deadline, and cannot impinge on the date for any hearing. Attempts to sort out time problems consensually are to be encouraged (*Chartwell Estate Agents Ltd v Fergies Properties SA* [2014] EWCA Civ 506, [2014] CP Rep 36 at [47]). Consent should ordinarily be given where sensible reasons are given for a modest extension which neither imperils a hearing date nor disrupts the proceedings. A consent given in these circumstances complies with the requirement to co-operate in **rr. 1.3** and **1.4(2)(a)**, and is not a breach of the lawyer's duty to his client (*Hallam Estates Ltd v Baker* [2014] EWCA Civ 661, [2014] CP Rep 38 at [12]).

What a party must not do is to ignore a deadline, or take action short of obtaining consent or a court order granting an extension. Seeking to agree a revised timetable with the other side is not regarded as an adequate response to non-compliance with the case management timetable (*M. A. Lloyd and Sons Ltd v PPC International Ltd* [2014] EWHC 41 (QB), [2014] 2 Costs LR 256). Attempts by parties to set their own timetable after court-imposed deadlines had expired were described as a complete misunderstanding of the rules in *Chartwell Estate Agents Ltd v Fergies Properties SA*, at [47].

Option (e) was in effect recommended by *Chartwell Estate Agents Ltd v Fergies Properties SA* at [47], where it was said that witness statements could have been lodged at court as they stood at the deadline, even if they would need to be supplemented later when further evidence was available. In pragmatic terms, it is almost always more difficult to establish that compliance is inadequate than it is to establish that compliance is late. In *Nelson v Circle Thirty Three Housing Trust Ltd* [2014] EWCA Civ 106, [2014] 3 Costs LO 355, the court seemed to be content with substantial compliance. However, in *Global Torch Ltd v Apex Global Management Ltd (No. 2)* [2014] UKSC 64, [2014] 1 WLR 4495, the court concluded that filing a disclosure statement made by the personal assistant of one of the defendants failed to comply with an unless order that the disclosure statement be made by the defendant personally.

SANCTIONS TAKE EFFECT ON BREACH

An unless order takes effect on the day it is pronounced, except where the court specifies otherwise (**CPR, r. 40.7(1)**). An order must be complied with even if there is a delay in sealing it (*Rahamim v Reich* (2009) LTL 10/2/2009).   **48.24**

If a party fails to comply with a rule, practice direction or court order imposing any sanction, the sanction will take effect without the need for any further order unless the defaulting party applies for and obtains relief from the sanction (**CPR, r. 3.8**). **Rules 3.8(3)** and (4) impose restrictions on agreeing extensions between the parties (see **42.46**). Where a rule, practice direction or order uses the terms:

- 'shall be struck out or dismissed'; or
- 'will be struck out or dismissed',

the meaning is that the striking out or dismissal takes place automatically, and no further order from the court is necessary (**PD 3A, para. 1.9**).

In *Marcan Shipping (London) Ltd v Kefalas* [2007] EWCA Civ 463, [2007] 1 WLR 1864, it was held that if the innocent party applies for judgment under **r. 3.5**, the court's function is limited to deciding what order should properly be made to reflect the sanction which has already taken effect. The decision in *Langtree Group plc v Richardson* [2004] EWCA Civ 1447, LTL 14/10/2004, fails to give effect to **r. 3.8(1)**, and must be regarded as unsound. Failing to serve a schedule of special damages within the time stated by an unless order (which specified striking out of the special damages claim in default) resulted in the sanction taking effect automatically (*Tomer v Atlantic Cleaning Service Ltd* [2008] EWHC 1652 (QB), LTL 25/7/2008, applying *Marcan Shipping (London) Ltd v Kefalas*). Technical arguments to avoid this result, such as a purported voluntary

Commentary

withdrawal of the special damages claim, and the fact a schedule had never been served (so there never had been a special damages claim on which the unless order could bite), were rejected.

Procedure for entering judgment in default of an unless order

48.25   Where the court has made an order providing that a statement of case shall be struck out if a party does not comply with the order, **CPR, r. 3.5**, sets out the procedure for obtaining judgment on non-compliance with the order. This rule is intended to provide a quick and efficient way of entering judgment when a statement of case has been struck out after an unless order (*Apex Global Management Ltd v Fi Call Ltd* [2013] EWHC 3752 (Ch), LTL 9/12/2013 at [36]). A number of different situations are dealt with:

(a)   Where the party in default is the claimant and the order provides for the striking out of the whole of the particulars of claim, the defendant may enter judgment with costs by filing a request (there is no prescribed form) stating that the right to enter judgment has arisen because the court's order has not been complied with (**r. 3.5(2)(a) and (3)**).

(b)   Where the party in default is the defendant and the order provides for the striking out of the whole of the defence, and the claim is limited to one of the following forms of relief, namely, a specified sum of money, damages, and/or delivery of goods with the alternative of paying their value, the claimant may enter judgment with costs by filing a request (again there is no prescribed form) stating that the right to enter judgment has arisen because the court's order has not been complied with (**r. 3.5(2)(b) and (3)**).

(c)   Where neither (a) nor (b) applies, such as where the order provided for striking out of only part of a statement of case, or where the defendant is in default and the claimant has claimed equitable relief, the party seeking to enter judgment for non-compliance with the order must make an application in accordance with **Part 23** (**r. 3.5(4)**). This means that an application notice must be issued for a hearing on notice. As entering judgment for non-compliance with an order is not strictly an 'interim remedy', **r. 25.3(2)** does not apply and there is no specific requirement for evidence in support. However, particularly where equitable relief is sought, it will often be sensible to provide written evidence in support.

It is permissible to abandon non-common law heads of relief in order to be able to enter judgment by filing a request (*Apex Global Management Ltd v Fi Call Ltd* [2013] EWHC 3752 (Ch), LTL 9/12/2013 at [36]).

RELIEF FROM SANCTIONS

Procedure for seeking relief from sanctions

48.26   There are two mechanisms for seeking to retrieve the position once a sanction comes into effect:

(a)   Where judgment has been entered under **CPR, r. 3.5** (see **48.25**), following the striking out of a statement of case for breach of an unless order, the defaulting party may apply to set aside the judgment under **r. 3.6**.

(b)   A party in breach of any other rule, practice direction, or order imposing a sanction for non-compliance may apply for relief from the sanction (**r. 3.8(1)**).

In both types of application the court applies the principles governing relief from sanctions set out in **r. 3.9**, see **48.30**. Applications for relief from sanctions should be dealt with at a hearing rather than under **r. 23.8** without a hearing (*Collier v Williams* [2006] EWCA Civ 20, [2006] 1 WLR 1945; *Vernon v Spoudeas* [2010] EWCA Civ 666, LTL 6/5/2010).

The court has power to grant relief from a sanction without an application by the party in default by making an order on its own initiative extending time under **rr. 3.1(2)(a)** and **3.3** (*Keen Phillips v Field* [2006] EWCA Civ 1524, [2007] 1 WLR 686).

Pre-*Jackson* principles governing applications for relief

In its original form, CPR, r. 3.9(1), provided that on an application for relief from any **48.27** sanction imposed for a failure to comply with any rule, practice direction or court order, the court had to consider all the circumstances including the following nine factors:

(a) the interests of the administration of justice;

(b) whether the application for relief has been made promptly;

(c) whether the failure to comply was intentional;

(d) whether there is a good explanation for the failure;

(e) the extent to which the party in default has complied with other rules, practice directions, court orders and any relevant pre-action protocol;

(f) whether the failure to comply was caused by the party or his legal representative;

(g) whether the trial date or the likely trial date can still be met if relief is granted;

(h) the effect which any failure to comply had on each party; and

(i) the effect which the granting of relief would have on each party.

Evidence from solicitors set out in the *Jackson Report* was to the effect that there were frequent failures to comply with directions, but very few meaningful penalties were imposed. That was not the original intention. However, early authorities on r. 3.9(1) held it was essential for the judge to consider each of the factors listed in r. 3.9(1) systematically, and then to weigh the various factors in deciding whether granting relief would accord with the overriding objective (*Woodhouse v Consignia plc* [2002] EWCA Civ 275, [2002] 1 WLR 2558; and *RC Residuals Ltd v Linton Fuel Oils Ltd* [2002] EWCA Civ 911, [2002] 1 WLR 2782). This formalistic approach was disapproved by *Khatib v Ramco International* [2011] EWCA Civ 605, [2011] CP Rep 35, where it was said the judge had to identify the factors from the r. 3.9(1) list that were relevant to the circumstances of the particular case, and conduct an appropriate review and balancing exercise.

Use of the old rule 3.9 list

In *Thevarajah v Riordan (No. 1)* [2013] EWHC 3464 (Ch), LTL 12/8/2013, and *Rayyan Iraq Co. Ltd v Trans* **48.28** *Victory Marine Inc.* [2013] EWHC 2696 (Comm), [2013] 6 Costs LR 911, Hildyard J and Andrew Smith J respectively said that although the checklist of factors in CPR, r. 3.9(1), as in force before 1 April 2013 had been removed, those factors continued to be matters which needed to be considered as they enabled the court to assess whether relief from sanctions would be appropriate under the current **r. 3.9**.

These cases go too far in applying the old r. 3.9(1) factors (*Mitchell v News Group Newspapers Ltd* [2013] EWCA Civ 1537, [2014] 1 WLR 795 at [49]). Depending on the facts it may be appropriate to consider some or even all the old factors as part of 'all the circumstances of the case', while giving due weight to the two factors set out in the current **r. 3.9(1)** (the third stage (see **48.32**) of *Denton v T. H. White Ltd* [2014] EWCA Civ 906, [2014] 1 WLR 3926). Post-*Denton* authorities tend to avoid all mention of the old r. 3.9 factors.

Article 6 and relief from sanctions

Woodhouse v Consignia plc [2002] EWCA Civ 275, [2002] 1 WLR 2558 was authority for saying that **48.29** it had to be kept in mind that refusing relief deprives the defaulting party of access to the court, which has particular importance given **art. 6(1)** of the European Convention on Human Rights in the **Human Rights Act 1998, sch. 1.** It is submitted this remains the case after the reforms to **CPR, r. 3.9**, effected from 1 April 2013, and ideally, a judge dealing with an application for relief from sanctions under **CPR, r. 3.9**, should expressly state in his reasoning that he has considered the issues of legitimate aim and proportionality and the essence of the applicant's rights under **art. 6(1)** (*Al-Dawood Shipping Lines Ltd v Dynastic Maritime Inc.* [2010] EWCA Civ 104, LTL 19/2/2010). However, **art. 6(1)** does not feature prominently in the post-*Denton* cases, presumably on the basis that **CPR, r. 3.9**, combined with the *Denton* principles fully complies with the right to a fair trial.

Relief from sanctions from 1 April 2013

48.30   Jackson LJ in *Fred Perry (Holdings) Ltd v Brands Plaza Trading Ltd* [2012] EWCA Civ 224, [2012] FSR 28, said the previous culture of non-compliance and delay was injurious to the civil justice system and to litigants generally. Given the criticism, with effect from 1 April 2013, relief from sanctions is governed by a revised **CPR, r. 3.9**, which is in the following terms:

> On an application for relief from any sanction imposed for a failure to comply with any rule, practice direction or court order, the court will consider all the circumstances of the case, so as to enable it to deal justly with the application, including the need—
>
> (a) for litigation to be conducted efficiently and at proportionate cost; and
>
> (b) to enforce compliance with rules, practice directions and orders.

The revised **r. 3.9** sweeps away the old nine factors and replaces them with two concepts: the need for litigation to be conducted efficiently and at proportionate cost, and the need to comply with the timetable for the case. One of the objectives was plainly to remove the checklist approach to applications for relief from sanctions, and to free the courts from the growing jurisprudence on the old nine factors. Another was to set out the two primary considerations that have to be considered on applications for relief from sanctions. Courts are still required to consider all the circumstances of the case, but are now given clear guidance that efficient and proportionate conduct together with compliance with rules must weigh most heavily when balancing all the relevant circumstances.

In discussing the enforcement of rules and directions, the *Review of Civil Litigation Costs: Final Report* (2009) at para. 39.6.5 said:

> First, the courts should set realistic timetables for cases and not impossibly tough timetables in order to give the impression of firmness. Secondly, courts at all levels have become too tolerant of delays and non-compliance with orders. In doing so they have lost sight of the damage which the culture of delay and non-compliance is inflicting upon the civil justice system. The balance therefore needs to be redressed. However, I do not advocate the extreme course which was canvassed as one possibility in [the Preliminary Report] or any approach of that nature.

This new approach was referred to in a number of Court of Appeal decisions before 1 April 2013. An example is *Fred Perry (Holdings) Ltd v Brands Plaza Trading* [2012] EWCA Civ 224, [2012] FSR 28, per Lewison LJ, who specifically adopted the first four sentences of this quotation from the *Final Report*. The 'extreme course' referred to in the *Final Report* was that non-compliance with the rules or directions would not be tolerated unless there were 'exceptional circumstances' (*Review of Civil Litigation Costs: Preliminary Report* (2009), para. 43.4.21). This was rejected by *Denton v T. H. White Ltd* [2014] EWCA Civ 906, [2014] 1 WLR 3926.

The objective of **r. 3.9** is not simply discipline for its own sake. Rather, the objective of the rule is to achieve a just result, having regard not simply to the interests of the parties, but also to the wider interests of justice (*Chartwell Estate Agents Ltd v Fergies Properties SA* [2014] EWCA Civ 506, [2014] CP Rep 36 at [62]).

Mitchell v News Group Newspapers Ltd

48.31   *Mitchell v News Group Newspapers Ltd* [2013] EWCA Civ 1537, [2014] 1 WLR 795, is considered in some detail in Sime, 'Sanctions after *Mitchell*' [2013] CJQ 133, and there is a concise critique of the case by Professor Zander, 'A step too far' (2014) NLJ 16 May 2014, p. 7. The claimant filed a costs budget one day before a case management hearing, six days late under CPR, r. 3.13, as in force before 6 April 2016. The delay was caused by a combination of the senior associate solicitor who usually did the costs budgeting having left the firm, and the other fee earners with conduct of the case being heavily engaged on another case. A sanction was imposed treating the claimant as having filed a costs budget limited to court fees. An application for relief from that sanction was listed by vacating the half day which had been allocated to deal with claims by persons affected by asbestos-related diseases. Lord Dyson MR at [60] said that the decision was intended to send out a clear message that the civil justice reforms of 2013 have brought in a new robust approach to rule compliance. Rather than focusing on the interests of justice in the individual case, there is a shift to recognising that delay and the effect on the rest of the civil justice system are also important factors. A tough approach was needed to the problem of non-compliance.

The court in *Mitchell* said that on an application for relief from sanctions the following principles applied:

(1) The court must consider 'all the circumstances of the case, so as to enable it to deal justly with the application' as required by **r. 3.9(1)**, see [37]. This meant that the court:
  (a) must apply the overriding objective; and
  (b) must perform a balancing exercise taking into account the factors relevant to the application.

(2) The two paramount factors, with other circumstances being given less weight (see [36] and [37]) were:
  (a) the need for litigation to be conducted efficiently and at proportionate cost; and
  (b) the need to enforce compliance with rules, practice directions and orders.

(3) Relief from sanctions was unlikely to be granted unless either:
  (a) the breach is trivial (see [40]); or
  (b) there was a good reason for the non-compliance (at [42]), the burden being on the defaulting party to persuade the court to grant relief (at [41]); and
  (c) the application for relief is made promptly (see [40]).

(4) While relief from sanctions was unlikely unless the breach was trivial or there was a good reason, other factors might on occasion justify granting relief.

The *Denton* principles

The principles stated in *Mitchell v News Group Newspapers Ltd* [2013] EWCA Civ 1537, [2014] 1 WLR 795, caused considerable concern, and were revised by *Denton v T. H. White Ltd* [2014] EWCA Civ 906, [2014] 1 WLR 3926. In place of the triviality and good reasons principles, the Court of Appeal (at [24]) said a judge should approach an application for relief from sanctions in three stages: **48.32**

(a) The first stage is to identify and assess the seriousness and significance of the 'failure to comply with any rule, practice direction or court order' which engages **CPR r. 3.9(1)**. If the breach is neither serious nor significant, the court is unlikely to need to spend much time on the second and third stages.

(b) The second stage is to consider why the default occurred.

(c) The third stage is to evaluate 'all the circumstances of the case, so as to enable [the court] to deal justly with the application including [the factors in **r. 3.9(1)(a) and (b)**]'.

'Triviality' was recognised as having given rise to some difficulty, with semantic disputes on whether a substantial delay which had no effect on the conduct of a claim could be trivial. The first stage refocuses the inquiry on whether the breach is serious or significant. The second stage is not materially different from the *Mitchell* question of whether there is a good reason for the breach, but the court in *Denton* said the examples given in *Mitchell* 'are no more than examples' (at 30]).

It is the third stage that had often been ignored by judges seeking to apply *Mitchell*. It is made clear in *Denton* at [31]–[38] that even if there is a serious or significant breach and no good reason for the default, the court must then consider all the circumstances, and in particular the factors in **r. 3.9(1)(a) and (b)**. Even though there have been adverse findings at the first and second stages, it is possible to grant relief from sanctions after considering all the circumstances. The factors in **r. 3.9(1)(a) and (b)** need to be considered in every case and must be given particular (rather than 'paramount') importance when compared with such other factors as might be present (see [32]). This is essential to avoid the courts slipping back to a pre-*Jackson* lax approach to sanctions (at [38]). Also relevant at the third stage is whether the application for relief has been made promptly (see [36]) and any history of past breaches of other orders (also at [36]).

Proliferation of authorities on applications for relief from sanctions has been a long-term prob-lem. Lord Dyson MR in *Denton* expressed the hope at [24] that the guidelines would avoid the need in future to resort to the earlier authorities. Since *Denton* the flow of appellate decisions on sanctions has not abated. **Table 48.2** sets out the main authorities which were either approved in *Denton*, or which have been subsequently decided. While the *Denton* guidelines look coherent and consistent with the wording of **r. 3.9**, the outcomes of the cases in **table 48.2** lack consistency.

Table 48.2 Sanctions cases approved by or following *Denton v T. H. White Ltd*

Case	Default	Features	Decision
In time application			
Hallam Estates Ltd v Baker [2014] EWCA Civ 661, [2014] CP Rep 38 (*Denton* at [20]).	None.	6 days before deadline for points of dispute applied for 21-day extension.	Granted. Receiving party should have consented.
Statements of case			
Adlington v ELS International Lawyers LLP [2014] 1 Costs LR 105 (*Denton* at [14]).	Particulars of claim in 7 out of 134 claims in group litigation served in draft. Breach of unless order.	7 claimants on holiday. No adverse consequences to the litigation.	Relief granted. Breach one of form not substance.
Thevarajah v Riordan [2015] EWCA Civ 41, [2015] CP Rep 19.	Inadequate defence.	C wanted to rely on struck-out defence at trial on remedies for admissions.	Absurd to prevent this: increase C's burden at trial.
Amendment			
Hague Plant Ltd v Hague [2014] EWCA Civ 1609, [2015] CP Rep 14.	Re-amended particulars of claim 65 pages long.	Judge relied on *Mitchell* [17] (allocating fair share of court resources).	Valuable passage. Permission refused.
Costs budget			
Mitchell v News Group Newspapers Ltd [2013] EWCA Civ 1537, [2014] 1 WLR 795 (*Denton* at [9], [98]).	Costs budget 6 days late, 1 day before CMC.	Serious. No good reason. Impact on asbestosis claims.	Restrict budget to court fees. Order 'very tough' but within bounds [98].
Utilise TDS Ltd v Davies (in *Denton* at [67]–[80]).	Costs budget 45 minutes late. Also 13 days late in notifying court of ADR.	Not serious or significant. No good reason. Factors (a) and (b) did not point to refusal of relief. ADR breach (stage 3) did not make this serious.	Relief granted. D should have consented.
Disclosure			
Smailes v NcNally [2014] EWCA Civ 1299, LTL 31/7/2014.	Unless order for disclosure. C failed to include a category of documents. Clear failure to make reasonable search.	Omitted 22,000 pages. Previous failures to comply with disclosure directions involving 6 deadlines.	Breach of order, and claim struck out. Not an application for relief from sanctions.
Walsham Chalet Park Ltd v Tallington Lakes Ltd [2014] EWCA Civ 1607, [2015] 1 Costs LO 157.	Disclosure 4.5 months late. D complained disclosure inadequate.	Multiple prior disclosure deadlines. *Denton* relevant and import-ant at the stage when impo-sing a sanction is considered.	Relief 'in effect' given by revised directions.

Case	Default	Features	Decision
Global Torch Ltd v Apex Global Management Ltd (No. 2) [2014] UKSC 64, [2014] 1 WLR 4495.	Failing to sign disclosure statement in person. Unless order.	5 first-instance hearings. Jeopardy to overall fairness as other parties had signed.	Defence struck out. Not disproportionate [18]–[35].
Lakatamia Shipping Co. Ltd v Su [2014] EWHC 275 (Comm), [2014] 2 Costs LR 307 (*Denton* at [17]).	Disclosure 46 minutes late.	D had history of previous defaults.	Trivial; previous defaults did not make it serious. Relief granted.
McTear v Engelhard [2016] EWCA Civ 487, [2016] 4 WLR 108.	Late discovered documents exhibited to witness statements instead of disclosed immediately.	Both sides engaged in aggressive and uncoopera-tive correspondence; also witness statements served 50 minutes late.	Significant breach, but other side could deal with them properly at trial. Relief granted.
Suez Fortune Investments Ltd v Talbot Underwriting Ltd [2016] EWHC 1085 (Comm), LTL 16/5/2016.	Unless order for specific disclosure. Defaulting party alleged ownership of documents had passed to a former employee.	Knowingly put documents beyond their legal control without keeping copies.	Relief from sanctions refused.

Witness statements

Case	Default	Features	Decision
Denton v T. H. White Ltd [2014] EWCA Civ 906, [2014] 1 WLR 3926 at [46]–[57].	6 further witness statements served about 6 months late, about 6 weeks before trial.	Significant breach. No good reason. Factors (a) and (b) militated against relief. Trial not artificial basis because C still had 6 experts and numerous factual witnesses.	Not permitted to use the new witness statements.
Durrant v Chief Constable of Avon etc [2014] EWCA Civ1624 (*Denton* at [15]).	Unless order. 2 witness statements 1 day late; other witness statements later.	Trial adjourned as a result.	Refused permission to rely on any of the statements. Made more significant because of breach of previous orders.
Newland Shipping and Forwarding Ltd v Toba Trading FZC [2014] EWHC 210 (Comm), [2014] 2 Costs LR 279 (*Denton* at [16]).	Witness statements not provided even 5 months after deadline.	Provision of timely witness statements of obvious importance when there is a tight trial timetable.	Defence and counterclaim struck out.
Chartwell Estate Agents Ltd v Fergies Properties SA [2014] EWCA Civ 506, [2014] CP Rep 36 (*Denton* at [19]).	Both parties several weeks late in serving witness statements.	D taking tactical advantage because C had the burden of proof. Not trivial; no good reason.	Both sides given permission. No order for costs [60].
McTear v Engelhard [2016] EWCA Civ 487, [2016] 4 WLR 108.	Witness statements served 50 minutes late.	Both sides engaged in aggressive and uncooperative correspondence; also late disclosure of documents.	Not serious; no deliberate attempt to subvert the litigation process; relief granted.

(*continued*)

Case	Default	Features	Decision
Judge Sykes Frixou v Bhabra [2016] EWCA Civ 381, LTL 15/1/2016.	D sought to rely on witness statements the day before trial.	One of the statements had been used on an application under r. 13.3.	Permission refused. The r. 13.3 statement had been created for a different purpose.
Experts			
Elliott v Stobart Group Ltd [2015] EWCA Civ 449, [2015] CP Rep 36.	Report served 2 months late.	Lack of funds not a good reason.	Claim for damages struck out.
Freezing injunction			
Thevarajah v Riordan [2015] UKSC 78, [2016] 1 WLR 76.	Non-disclosure of assets; non-compliance with unless order.	Compliance after court refused relief from sanctions.	Belated compliance not a material change of circumstances.
Security for costs			
Summit Navigation Ltd v Generali Romania Asigurare Reasigurare SA [2014] EWHC 398 (Comm), [2014] 2 Costs LR 367 (*Denton* at [18]).	Security tendered 1 day late.	Trivial.	Relief granted. C should have consented.
Pre-trial checklist			
British Gas Trading Ltd v Oak Cash and Carry Ltd [2016] EWCA, [2016] CP Rep 27.	PTC filed 18 days after expiry of original order and 2 days after unless order.	Application not prompt, 31 days after breach, and loss of trial date.	If prompt, C should have consented to relief; as not prompt, relief refused.
Abdulle v Commissioner of Police of the Metropolis [2015] EWCA Civ 1260, [2016] 1 WLR 898.	PTC not filed 10 weeks after due date. Non-payment of hearing fee; default in preparing trial bundles.	Application to strike out (rather than for relief). Trial date was lost.	Judge's decision not to strike out within range of reasonable case management decisions.
Hearing fee			
Decadent Vapours Ltd v Bevan (in *Denton* at [58]–[66]).	Unless order to pay hearing and checklist fees. 3 weeks late.	Sent to arrive 1 day late. Lost in DX. Serious, but less so. C had previous breaches.	Not proportionate to strike out whole claim. D should have consented.
Appeal permission			
Altomart Ltd v Salford Estates (No. 2) Ltd [2014] EWCA Civ 1408, [2015] 1 WLR 1825.	Respondent's notice filed 31 days late.	Delay considerable. Little effect on the appeal. So not serious or significant. No good reason. Nothing against relief.	Extension allowed. Respondent to pay costs.
R (Hysaj) v Secretary of State for the Home Department [2014] EWCA Civ 1633, [2015] 1 WLR 2472.	1st appeal: notice of appeal 42 days late. 2nd appeal: 9 months late. 3rd appeal: 6 years late.	1st appeal: no prejudice to respondent. 2nd appeal: conflict with principle of finality. 3rd appeal: nothing exceptional to allow.	1st appeal: allowed. 2nd appeal: refused on balance. 3rd appeal: refused.

Case	Default	Features	Decision
Re D (Children) [2015] EWCA Civ 409, [2016] 1 FLR 249.	No grounds of appeal. Late.	Same rules apply to litigants in person.	Application for permission to appeal relisted.
Re H (Children) (Care Proceedings: Appeals out of Time) [2015] EWCA Civ 583, [2015] 1 WLR 5085.	Appellant's notice 20 days late. Failed to apply to renew permission application within 7 days.	Lawyers misunderstood when time started to run under FPR, r. 30.4(2). Not an adequate reason. Merits very strong.	Extension granted due to merits.
Appeal directions			
Patel v Mussa [2015] EWCA Civ 434, [2015] 1 WLR 4788.	Appeal bundle day before appeal. Skeleton argument morning of appeal.	Not trivial. No reasonable explanation. Judge entitled to refuse to hear case given late filing.	Refused to adjourn. Dismissed application to enforce order. 'Severe' but open to the judge.

Application to vary or revoke the original order

If an application for relief from sanctions is combined with an application to vary or revoke   **48.33**
the original order under **CPR, r. 3.1(7)** (for which, see **42.42**), the proper course is to consider
the application under **r. 3.1(7)** first, applying the *Tibbles v SIG plc* [2012] EWCA Civ 518, [2012] 1
WLR 2591 principles (*Mitchell v News Group Newspapers Ltd* [2013] EWCA Civ 1537, [2014] 1 WLR
795 at [44], [45]). If that application succeeds, there may be no breach and no sanction to be
relieved. If the **r. 3.1(7)** application is unsuccessful, the application for relief under **r. 3.9** has
to proceed on the basis that the original sanction was properly imposed.

Considered view of the Civil Procedure Rule Committee

In *Mitchell v News Group Newspapers Ltd* [2013] EWCA Civ 1537, [2014] 1 WLR 795, the Court of   **48.34**
Appeal held that the Master had been entitled to apply the sanction laid down by **CPR,
r. 3.14**, to disallow the claimant's costs other than court fees, by analogy. Although there was
no equivalent sanction provision in **PD 51D**, this sanction represented the considered view of
the Civil Procedure Rule Committee of what constituted a proportionate sanction for failure
to file a costs budget in time unless the court ordered otherwise. A court should only order
otherwise in most cases on the same grounds as are relevant to a decision to grant relief from
sanctions under **r. 3.9**.

This has been applied in other cases to mean that all the other sanctions set out in the CPR
are also to be taken as the considered view of the Civil Procedure Rule Committee of what
constitutes proportionate sanctions for the relevant instances of non-compliance. As stated by
Davis LJ in *Chartwell Estate Agents Ltd v Fergies Properties SA* [2014] EWCA Civ 506, [2014] CP Rep 36
at [24], there can be no available argument that the sanction prescribed by the CPR is of itself
unjust or disproportionate. With respect, even a cursory look at the table of sanctions prescribed by the CPR as set out in **table 48.1** will reveal that the prescribed sanctions have not
been laid down with a view to ensuring they provide a graduated system of proportionate
sanctions, but are instead a collection of pragmatic penalties lacking the benefit of an underlying coherent scheme.

Wheeler v Chief Constable of Gloucestershire Constabulary [2013] EWCA Civ 1791, LTL 18/12/2013, was
a case where both parties failed to file costs schedules in breach of **PD 44, para. 9.5(4)**. This
meant costs had to be referred to a detailed assessment rather than being summarily assessed
at the end of the appeal hearing. Applying *Mitchell v News Group Newspapers Ltd*, the successful

Commentary

Bad reasons

48.40   Bad reasons identified by the Master of the Rolls in *Mitchell v News Group Newspapers* [2013] EWCA Civ 1537, [2014] 1 WLR 795 at [41] included overlooking a deadline and failing to meet a deadline through other pressures of work (or will 'rarely' do so). In the case itself, pressures of work, a small firm, and unexpected delays with counsel did not amount to a good excuse for the default. Solicitors cannot take on too much work and expect to be relieved from sanctions if they fail to meet deadlines. Either they should refuse the work, or they should delegate the work to other fee earners in the firm. Misunderstanding the rules, resulting in not appreciating when time started to run, is not an acceptable excuse (*R (Hysaj) v Secretary of State for the Home Department* [2014] EWCA Civ 1633, [2015] 1 WLR 2472). Nor is shortage of money (*Hysaj* at [43]). Whether being a litigant in person can be a good reason for a particular failing depends on the circumstances, but generally being a litigant in person is not enough of itself (*Hysaj* at [44]). Protecting other persons from money laundering investigations was held to be a thoroughly bad reason in *Karbhari v Ahmed* [2013] EWHC 4042 (QB), [2014] 1 Costs LR 151. Delays while the clients disputed their solicitor's fees was regarded as a bad reason in *Newland Shipping and Forwarding Ltd v Toba Trading FZC* [2014] EWHC 210 (Comm), [2014] 2 Costs LR 279.

Durrant v Chief Constable of Avon and Somerset [2013] EWCA Civ 1624, [2014] 2 All ER 757, is regarded as a case involving a very late application for relief from the sanction in **CPR, r. 32.10**, which followed a sustained failure to comply with time limits for the exchange of witness statements imposed by a previous unless order, which necessitated the adjournment of the trial (*Chartwell Estate Agents Ltd v Fergies Properties SA* [2014] EWCA Civ 506, [2014] CP Rep 36 at [36], [53]). So analysed it is clearly a case with bad reasons for relief. The problem lurking within *Durrant v Chief Constable of Avon and Somerset* is that the Court of Appeal also refused relief relating to two of the witness statements that were served only one day late (albeit contrary to the unless order). While this can be justified on the basis that the application for relief was made very late, the main reasons relied on by the Court of Appeal related to the need for a robust approach to compliance. The proximity of the trial should be regarded as having been important, because breach of an unless order is not in itself always a bar to granting relief (*Adlington v ELS International Lawyers LLP* [2014] 1 Costs LR 105, approved in *Denton* at [13]).

Relief was refused in *SC DG Petrol SRL v Vitol Broking Ltd* [2013] EWHC 3920 (Comm), [2014] 2 Costs LR 205, for failure to comply with an unless order extending the time previously given to provide security for costs. The breach was not trivial. The reasons advanced related to problems in selling certain assets to raise the security that had been ordered, but failed to cover other means that might have been available to the claimant to raise funds from other sources. As such it had failed to establish a good reason for non-compliance. *D. Morgan plc v Mace and Jones* [2010] EWHC 697 (TCC), LTL 4/5/2010 was a case where reliance on the claimant's managing director's illness was regarded as an excuse, primarily because he had not been ill throughout the entire period.

All the circumstances of the case

48.41   At the third stage the court considers all the circumstances of the case, affording particular importance to 'factors (a) and (b)' from **CPR, r. 3.9(1)** (*Denton v T. H. White Ltd* [2014] EWCA Civ 906, [2014] 1 WLR 3926 at [35]). These are the need for litigation to be conducted efficiently and at proportionate cost, and the need to enforce compliance with rules, practice directions and orders. This is important because the old lax culture of non-compliance is no longer tolerated (at [34]). Other factors that might be relevant will vary from case to case (at [36]). Whether the application for relief is made promptly is taken into account (at [36]). A nuanced approach is required (at [38]), ensuring a robust but fair resolution is taken in the more serious cases. Judges must avoid an unreasonable approach that transforms rule compliance into trip wires (at [37]) in an inappropriate display of judicial musculature (at [19]). *Elliott v Stobart Group Ltd* [2015] EWCA Civ 449, [2015] CP Rep 36, falls into this trap.

Little time will be needed in considering the third stage if the breach was not serious or significant (*Denton* at [24]), but in other cases the more serious or significant the breach the less likely it is that relief will be granted (at [35]). Seriousness and significance are different but frequently connected concepts. The authorities may be analysed as showing that there is an ascending scale of seriousness depending on the circumstances:

(a) short delays, or minor imperfections in performance, which are remedied soon after the deadline;

(b) non-compliance caused by events outside the control of the party or his or her legal representative;

(c) non-compliance caused by 'bad' reasons, such as impecuniosity, overlooking a deadline, or misunderstanding the rules, which are remedied as soon as possible;

(d) non-compliance for reasons outside the party's control, but not rectified after an 'unless' order;

(e) non-compliance for blameworthy 'bad' reasons, such as covering up money laundering, or deliberate disobedience;

(f) repeated deliberate disobedience.

Significance is a measure of the impact of the breach on the litigation in question and on the wider administration of justice and other court users. A short delay may be at the upper end of the scale if it results in the need to adjourn the trial, as happened in *Durrant v Chief Constable of Avon and Somerset Constabulary* [2013] EWCA Civ 1624, [2014] 1 WLR 4313, or if other cases have to be vacated, as happened in *Mitchell v News Group Newspapers Ltd* [2013] EWCA Civ 1537, [2014] 1 WLR 795. A longer delay which has no impact on the particular case or other litigants will not be significant, as in the *Decadent* appeal in *Denton v T.H. White Ltd* (late payment of court fees) and *Salford Estates (No. 2) Ltd v Altomart Ltd* [2014] EWCA Civ 1408, [2015] 1 WLR 1825 (late filing of respondent's notice). There is a sliding scale between these extremes.

The *Decadent* appeal in *Denton v T.H. White Ltd* also shows that there may be a clear case for relief even if stages one and two are decided against the party in default. In *Chartwell Estate Agents Ltd v Fergies Properties SA* [2014] EWCA Civ 506, [2014] CP Rep 36, the claimant sought relief from the sanction in **CPR, r. 32.10**, for both parties for late service of witness statements. The application was issued two months after the deadline and three months before the trial. It was objected to by the defendant, who had calculated that if relief was refused, the claimant would lose the case. On the facts the two factors in **r. 3.9(1)(a)** and **(b)** were outweighed because:

(a) both parties were in default of the requirement to serve witness statements;

(b) granting relief did not put the trial date at risk;

(c) no significant extra cost would be occasioned if relief was granted; and

(d) refusal of relief effectively meant the end of the claim, because the burden of proof was on the claimant.

Reputational issues affecting witnesses in the case are regarded as having no more than a limited role to play on an application for relief from sanctions (*Durrant v Chief Constable of Avon and Somerset* [2013] EWCA Civ 1624, [2014] 1 WLR 4313 at [44]).

Client or solicitor at fault

Whether delay was the fault of the client or of its solicitor was one of the factors in the original **48.42** CPR, r. 3.9, as in force before 1 April 2013 (see **48.27**). There were inconsistent cases on the application of the old r. 3.9(1)(f). *Daryanani v Kumar and Co.* (2000) LTL 12/12/2000 held that it is inappropriate to draw a distinction or to apportion responsibility between the litigant himself and his advisers on the issue of delay. Conversely, in *Austin v Newcastle Chronicle and Journal Ltd*

[2001] EWCA Civ 834, LTL 18/5/2001, the court took into account that breach of a time limit was caused by an error of the solicitor in amending the wrong document. In *Mitchell v News Group Newspapers Ltd* [2013] EWCA Civ 1537, [2014] 1 WLR 795, the fact the default rested squarely with the legal representatives did not absolve the claimant in any degree. In *Michael v Middleton* [2013] 6 Costs LR 899 the claim was struck out despite the defaults occurring because of failures by the claimant's former solicitors.

Both parties in default

48.43   As shown by *Chartwell Estate Agents Ltd v Fergies Properties SA* [2014] EWCA Civ 506, [2014] CP Rep 36, both parties have obligations regarding compliance with court directions and the provisions of the CPR, and are required to cooperate with each other (**CPR, r. 1.4(2)(a)**). Where both sides are in breach of directions, it is difficult to justify imposing a sanction purely on the claimant, provided it is reasonably possible to have a fair trial notwithstanding the breach (*Western Trust and Savings Ltd v Acland and Lensam* (2000) LTL 19/6/2000). Some cases go further, pointing out that both sides have a duty to help the court to further the overriding objective (**r. 1.3**). Consequently it is inappropriate for defendants to sit back and let a claim go to sleep, and then complain about delay when the claimant resumes the claim (*Khalili v Bennett* [2000] EMLR 996; *Dainty v Reynolds* (2000) LTL 28/11/2000).

Merits of the case

48.44   Generally, the merits of the underlying case or appeal are irrelevant when the court is making directions or on an application for relief from sanctions (*Global Torch Ltd v Apex Global Management Ltd (No. 2)* [2014] UKSC 64, [2014] 1 WLR 4495 at [30]). Any investigation of the substantive merits on an application relating to directions would lead to an increase in the costs of the application and increased pressures on court time. It is therefore inherently undesirable and contrary to the ethos of the Woolf and Jackson reforms. Lord Neuberger of Abbotsbury PSC recognised it might be different in cases where a party had no real prospect of success (at [29]). Merits can be considered only if the party relying on them sets out that contention very clearly in advance (at [34]) and the court can be quickly persuaded that the merits are strong enough for summary judgment. Otherwise the court should refuse to consider the merits (at [31]).

Cases applying these principles in the context of applications to extend the time for bringing an appeal are considered at **74.22**.

Impact on other court users

48.45   In *SC DG Petrol SRL v Vitol Broking Ltd* [2013] EWHC 3920 (Comm), [2014] 2 Costs LR 205, Robin Knowles QC at [29], said:

I respectfully offer the observation that there are limits to the contribution that a party, especially a non-defaulting party, can usefully make in evidence or argument in respect of circumstances extending beyond the case in hand — for example on what is needed 'to enforce compliance with rules, practice directions and orders'. This is pre-eminently an area for the judge.

It is suggested that this misunderstands the impact on other litigants that judges are enjoined to consider by **CPR, r. 3.9(1)**, and *Mitchell v News Group Newspapers Ltd* [2013] EWCA Civ 1537, [2014] 1 WLR 795. This is really about the general effect on the civil justice system caused by a culture of non-compliance. The reference to the asbestos disease claims in *Mitchell v News Group Newspapers Ltd* was intended to be no more than an example of the deleterious effects of court time being taken up with hearings over non-compliance. It was not intended to impose an obligation on the court or the parties to adduce evidence of the direct impact of such hearings on other cases in the relevant court or in the diary of the particular judge. In any event, it would be quite wrong if one defaulting party were to be given relief from sanctions because it was their good fortune that the court happened to be free to hear the application for relief, whereas in an identical case of default relief were to be refused because there happened to be evidence that particular cases had to be relisted. It might also be mentioned that investigating and arguing over the actual effects on other litigants would be an additional unnecessary complication and expense, which is the last thing that applications for relief from sanctions need.

Prompt application for relief

One of the factors to be considered at the third stage is whether the application for relief from **48.46** sanctions was made promptly (*Denton v T. H. White Ltd* [2014] EWCA Civ 906, [2014] 1 WLR 3926 at [36]). See also *Mitchell v News Group Newspapers Ltd* [2013] EWCA Civ 1537, [2014] 1 WLR 795 at [40] and *Durrant v Chief Constable of Avon and Somerset Constabulary* [2013] EWCA Civ 1624, [2014] 1 WLR 4313 at [49]. This expression means acting with all reasonable celerity in the circumstances, but does not demand that the applicant has been guilty of no needless delay whatever (*Regency Rolls Ltd v Carnall* (2000) LTL 16/10/2000 at [45]). Greater expedition is required in cases where tight directions have been given to enable an early trial (*British Gas Trading Ltd v Oak Cash and Carry Ltd* [2016] EWCA Civ 153, [2016] CP Rep 27, where allowing 31 days to elapse, resulting in loss of the trial date, meant the application was not prompt).

Stays and sanctions

It was held in *Summit Navigation Ltd v Generali Romania Asigurare Reasigurare SA* [2014] EWHC 398 **48.47** (Comm), [2014] 1 WLR 3472, that there is an important difference between a stay of proceedings if security for costs is not provided, which is intended to be non-permanent, and sanctions intended to have a permanent effect, such as striking out. Leggatt J at [34] said these are different kinds of order, and at [36] said the broad language of **CPR, r. 3.9**, is quite capable of accommodating more than one approach to applications for relief from sanctions to take into account the nature of the sanction and the nature of the relief sought. As a result, at [37] Leggatt J felt that the factors in **r. 3.9(1)(a)** and **(b)** do not carry the same weight in an application to lift a stay as they do in the type of application dealt with in *Mitchell v News Group Newspapers Ltd* [2013] EWCA Civ 1537, [2014] 1 WLR 795.

Tactical advantage or legitimate opposition

Where a court finds that a party has attempted to take tactical advantage of a default **48.48** which is neither serious nor significant, or if there is a good reason for the default, or it is obvious that relief will be granted, the court may impose 'heavy costs sanctions' (*Denton v T. H. White Ltd* [2014] EWCA Civ 906, [2014] 1 WLR 3926 at [43]). These might include indemnity-basis costs, taking the misconduct into account in the final costs order under **CPR, r. 44.11**, and even freeing the winning party from the operation of **r. 3.18** in relation to costs budgets. The *Utilise* and *Decadent* appeals in *Denton v T. H. White Ltd* fell into this category as did *Hallam Estates Ltd v Baker* [2014] EWCA Civ 661, [2014] CP Rep 38, and *Summit Navigation Ltd v Generali Romania Asiguare Reasigurare SA* [2014] EWHC 398 (Comm), [2014] 1 WLR 3472, see **table 48.2**.

In *Chartwell Estate Agents Ltd v Fergies Properties SA* [2014] EWCA Civ 506, [2014] CP Rep 36, the defendant was criticised for taking tactical advantage of the claimant being two months late in serving its witness statements. In *Chilton v Surrey County Council* [1999] CPLR 525, the Court of Appeal took against the defendant partly because it seemed the defendant was attempting to take tactical advantage of a mistake by the claimant's solicitors in overlooking to serve a revised statement of past and future loss and expense rather than cooperating with the claimant's solicitors to put matters right. Both parties were criticised in *McTear v Engelhard*

[2016] EWCA Civ 487, [2016] 4 WLR 108 for engaging in aggressive and uncooperative correspondence over late disclosure and late service of witness statements. Conversely, in *M. A. Lloyd and Sons Ltd v PPC International Ltd* [2014] EWHC 41 (QB), [2014] 2 Costs LR 256, the defendant was criticised for being unduly timid following the claimant's non-compliance with an order for sequential service of witness statements, and it was said that an application to debar the claimant from raising the issue that should have been addressed by the witness statements was the appropriate response.

Sanctions in appeals

48.49 *Durrant v Chief Constable of Avon and Somerset* [2013] EWCA Civ 1624, [2014] 1 WLR 4313, was a case where an appeal against granting relief was allowed. This was not a case of trivial breaches, and there was no good reason for the default. While an appeal court will not lightly interfere with a case management decision (*Powell v Pallisers of Hereford Ltd* [2002] EWCA Civ 959, LTL 1/7/2002; *Mannion v Gray* [2012] EWCA Civ 1667, LTL 2/1/2013 at [18]; *Chartwell Estate Agents Ltd v Fergies Properties SA* [2014] EWCA Civ 506, [2014] CP Rep 36 at [62]), Richards LJ said it was vital that decisions under **CPR, r. 3.9**, which fail to follow the robust approach laid down by *Mitchell v News Group Newspapers Ltd* [2013] EWCA Civ 1537, [2014] 1 WLR 795, should not be allowed to stand. Failure to follow that approach constitutes an error of principle entitling an appeal court to interfere with the discretionary decision of the first-instance judge. It is likely also to lead to a decision that is plainly wrong, justifying intervention on that basis as well (at [38]).

Avoiding lesser sanctions by the back door

48.50 Sanctions falling short of striking out can create problems of defaulting parties avoiding the effects of the sanction by the back door. *Durrant v Chief Constable of Avon and Somerset* [2013] EWCA Civ 1624, [2014] 1 WLR 4313, was a case where a sanction prevented the defendant from calling witnesses. Richards LJ pointed out that the claim depended in part on the claimant's own credibility, which, despite the sanction, the defendant was entitled to challenge at trial. There was documentary material on the basis of which the defendant could properly mount such a challenge even though the defendant was unable to call any witnesses on his own behalf. It was probably wider than this. All the sanction did was to prevent the defendant from calling the police officers as witnesses. They had provided signed witness statements. These were hearsay evidence and hearsay is never rendered inadmissible purely on the ground that it is hearsay (Civil Evidence Act 1995, s. 1(1)). It is also not rendered inadmissible for failure to give due notice: the sanction in the Civil Evidence Act 1995, s. 2(4), is restricted to weight and costs.

Of course there is a discretionary power to exclude otherwise admissible evidence, but using **CPR, r. 32.1,** for this purpose would involve a considerable extension of its present ambit (see **49.8**) and would involve the need for a further interim application. In *Karbhari v Ahmed* [2013] EWHC 4042 (QB), [2014] 1 Costs LR 151, a replacement witness statement was disallowed. Turner J recognised that without going further it would be inevitable that cross-examination would afford the defendant the opportunity to introduce by the back door the evidence which the defendant wanted to introduce in chief. Patently false statements of truth gave the judge scope to prevent this by striking out the defence as an abuse of process.

Compliance after refusal of relief

48.51 Refusal of relief from sanctions is effectively a ruling that it is now too late for the defaulting party to comply. Subsequent 'compliance' is not, without additional facts, a material change of circumstances justifying reconsideration of the refusal (*Thevarajah v Riordan* [2015] UKSC 78, [2016] 1 WLR 76 per Lord Neuberger of Abbotsbury PSC at [21]).

SECOND CLAIMS AND ABUSE OF PROCESS

In many cases a claimant who cannot obtain relief from sanctions will be able to start fresh **48.52** proceedings alleging the same cause of action because the limitation period has not expired. Starting a second claim after earlier proceedings have been struck out may be an abuse of process. *Janov v Morris* [1981] 1 WLR 1389, a pre-CPR case, said that a second claim would normally be an abuse of process if striking out was for intentional and contumelious default, unless there was a satisfactory explanation for failing to obey the original order. *Icebird Ltd v Winegardner* [2009] UKPC 24, LTL 3/6/2009, which applies the *Janov v Morris* principles, is a Privy Council decision on an appeal from the Bahamas, where rules similar to the old RSC apply.

Whether this can be transplanted into the new code formed by the CPR may be doubtful (see **1.21** to **1.24** and *Dar Al Arkan Real Estate Development Co. v Al-Sayed Bader Hashim Al Refai* [2014] EWCA Civ 715, LTL 23/5/2014 at [36]). There may also be problems with consistency with the approach to second claim cases under the Limitation Act 1980, s. 33 (see **10.24**). However, the *Janov v Morris* principles were loyally applied in *Hall v Ministry of Defence* [2013] EWHC 4092 (QB), LTL 19/12/2013, where the second claim was restored on appeal because a failure to pay the costs ordered in the first claim was not intentional or contumelious, nor was this a case of wholesale disregard of court orders. Phillips J said there had to be something transforming the delay into an abuse of process for the purposes of **CPR, r. 3.4(2)(b)**, for example evidence that the claimant had lost interest in the claim. There is an obvious difference in the approach to the initial breach exemplified by *Mitchell v News Group Newspapers Ltd* [2013] EWCA Civ 1537, [2014] 1 WLR 795, and the *Janov v Morris* principles on striking out second claims. It may be that a stronger line could be taken by applying to strike out the second claim under **r. 3.4(2)(c)**, that there has been a failure to comply with a rule, practice direction or court order. This would require extending the accepted meaning of **r. 3.4(2)(c)**, which is traditionally regarded as referring to breaches within the present proceedings.

PROHIBITION FROM MAKING FURTHER APPLICATIONS

Where a litigant makes repeated applications of a similar nature, it is sometimes appropriate **48.53** to make a civil restraint order to the effect that no further applications of a specified type can be made by the named litigant without the permission of a judge (see **14.51** to **14.60**).

INORDINATE DELAY

Under the pre-CPR law, there were three bases on which claims could be struck out for delay: **48.54**

(a) On the ground of inordinate and inexcusable delay (also known as dismissal for want of prosecution, see *Birkett v James* [1978] AC 297). This was only available against a party in the position of a plaintiff; where there was inordinate and inexcusable delay; which had either given rise to a substantial risk that it would not be possible to have a fair trial, or which was likely to cause, or had caused, serious prejudice to the defendant; and, generally, the limitation period had to have expired.

(b) On the ground of non-compliance with a peremptory order. Guidelines for this type of case were laid down in *Hytec Information Systems Ltd v Coventry City Council* [1997] 1 WLR 1666 and other cases. These included the principle that unless orders were made as a last resort (which is no longer the case under the CPR) and a failure to comply would therefore usually result in the sanction being imposed; that late compliance would only be excused if there were compelling reasons, usually beyond the control of the defaulting parties: that a party who deliberately flouted an order ... ... that each case was considered on its own merits, with the ... ... interests of justice.

(e) On the ground that the delay amounted to an abuse of process ... ... 640; *Arbuthnot Latham Bank Ltd v* ... *... Ltd* [... defaulting party's conduct, which could be prolonged inactivity ... ... the court's process the court would be justified in striking out ... ... limitation period had not expired and even where the ... ... prejudice arising from the delay ...

Despite *Summers v Fairclough Homes* ... ... *Abermeadow Ltd* [2000] 2 BCLC 824 at pp. 835 and 836, it is ... ... and inexcusable delay has no application under the CPR ... ... Commonwealth jurisdictions. See, for example, ... *Ltd v* ... ... 3/5/2019 (Bahamas).

Chapter 49   General Law of Evidence

Commentary

FACTS OPEN TO PROOF

49.1   The only facts which are open to proof, or disproof, are facts in issue, relevant facts and collateral facts.

Facts in issue

49.2   In a civil trial, the facts in issue are those which the claimant must prove in order to succeed in his claim together with those which the defendant must prove in order to succeed in his defence. The facts in issue in a case are therefore determined partly by reference to the substantive law and partly by reference to what the parties allege, admit, do not admit and deny. They should be identifiable by reference to the statements of case, which should set out the issues on which the parties agree and disagree so that it is known in advance what facts have to be proved or disproved at trial. Under **CPR, r. 16.4(1)**, particulars of claim must include a concise statement of the facts on which the claimant relies, and under **r. 16.5(1)** a defence must state which of the allegations in the particulars of claim are denied or not admitted, and which are admitted, by the defendant. See further, as to the circumstances in which a party shall be taken to require that an allegation be proved or shall be taken to admit an allegation, **r. 16.5(3)** to **(5)**. However, the CPR make it clear that the court also has a role to play in determining what the facts in issue are in any given case. **Rule 32.1** provides that 'the court may control the evidence by giving directions as to—

(a) the issues on which it requires evidence;

(b) the nature of the evidence which it requires to decide those issues; and

(c) the way in which the evidence is to be placed before the court'.

This provision invests the court with an extraordinarily wide power whereby it can override the views of the parties not only as to the nature of the evidence appropriate to decide the issues in the case, and as to the way in which the evidence should be given, for example, in documentary form rather than orally, but also as to the very issues that do or do not call for evidence. Thus if the court is of the opinion, for example, that the parties have misunderstood the substantive law in such a way as to lead them to believe, erroneously, that a certain matter does or does not have to be proved, then it may give appropriate corrective directions.

Relevant facts

Relevant facts are facts from which the existence or non-existence of a fact in issue may be **49.3** inferred, and evidence of relevant facts is properly described as 'circumstantial evidence'. Some types of circumstantial evidence arise so often that they are referred to as presumptions of fact (see further, **49.22** to **49.24**). Typical examples of circumstantial evidence include evidence of motive to do a particular act, evidence of plans or other preparations for the performance of a particular act, evidence of opportunity, or lack of it, and evidence of identity. Concerning evidence of a person's motive to do an act, it does not become irrelevant simply because others may have the same motive (*Myers v The Queen* [2015] UKPC 40, [2016] AC 314). Another typical example of circumstantial evidence is evidence of lies told by a party, which may diminish credibility and make it harder for that party's case to be proved (see, for example, *MA (Somalia) v Secretary of State for the Home Department* [2010] UKSC 49, [2011] 2 All ER 65). Two final examples relate to the failure to give evidence or call witnesses, and standards of comparison.

Where one party fails to give evidence or call witnesses, the court may be justified in drawing all reasonable inferences from the evidence given by an opponent of the facts which the first party chose to withhold (per Lord Diplock in *British Railways Board v Herrington* [1972] AC 877 at p. 930). Thus inferences have been drawn from the unexplained absence of witnesses who were apparently available and whose evidence was crucial to the case (see *Lewis v Eliades* [2005] EWHC 488 (Ch), LTL 6/4/2005, affirmed in *Karis v Lewis* [2005] EWCA Civ 1637, LTL 22/12/2005; and *Baigent v Random House Group Ltd* [2006] EWHC 719 (Ch), [2006] EMLR 16 at [213]–[215]). In *Wisniewski v Central Manchester Health Authority* [1992] Lloyd's Rep Med 223 Brooke LJ derived the following principles from the authorities on the point:

(1) In certain circumstances a court may be entitled to draw adverse inferences from the absence or silence of a witness who might be expected to have material evidence to give on an issue in an action.
(2) If a court is willing to draw such inferences they may go to strengthen the evidence adduced on that issue by the other party or to weaken the evidence, if any, adduced by the party who might reasonably have been expected to call the witness.
(3) There must, however, have been some evidence, however weak, adduced to the former on the matter in question before the court is entitled to draw the desired inference: in other words, there must be a case to answer on that issue.
(4) If the reason for the witness's absence or silence satisfies the court then no such adverse inference may be drawn. If, on the other hand, there is some credible explanation given, even if it is not wholly satisfactory, the potentially detrimental effect of his/her absence or silence may be reduced or nullified.

Similarly, it has been held that a defendant who has, in breach of statutory duty, made it difficult or impossible for a claimant to adduce relevant evidence runs the risk of adverse factual findings (*Keefe v Isle of Man Steam Packet Co. Ltd* [2010] EWCA Civ 683, LTL 17/6/2010).

Where it is necessary to decide whether a person's conduct meets some objective standard, evidence of what others would do in the same circumstances is admissible to show what that standard is. See, for example, *Chapman v Walton* (1833) 10 Bing 57, where for the purpose of deciding whether a broker had exercised a reasonable degree of care, skill and judgment in the performance of his duties, evidence was received from other brokers as to what they would have done in the same circumstances. See also *Noble v Kennoway* (1780) 2 Doug KB 510, which concerned the practice of delaying the discharge of a ship's cargo, and *Fleet v Murton* (1871) LR 7 QB 126.

Collateral facts

Collateral facts are of three kinds. The first kind affects the credibility of witnesses, for **49.4** example, the fact that a witness is biased towards one of the parties or has made a previous inconsistent statement. The second type of collateral fact, often referred to as a preliminary

Commentary

fact, is a fact which must be proved as a condition precedent to the admissibility of an item of evidence. For example, under the Bankers' Books Evidence Act 1879, s. 4, a copy of an entry in a banker's book is only admissible under s. 3 of the Act if it is proved, *inter alia*, that the book was at the time of the making of the entry one of the ordinary books of the bank. See further at **49.80**. The third kind of collateral fact affects the competence of witnesses, for example, the fact that a potential expert witness is properly qualified in the subject calling for expertise.

RELEVANCE, ADMISSIBILITY AND THE DISCRETION TO EXCLUDE

49.5   The two governing principles underlying the English law of evidence are that:

(a) evidence must be sufficiently relevant in order to be admissible, but

(b) such evidence will only be admissible in so far as it is not excluded by the court either by virtue of a rule of law or in the exercise of its discretion.

However, there is no principle of law or practice which dictates that a judge cannot read or hear material that is actually or potentially inadmissible, especially if he or she is a judge of both law and fact (*Barings plc v Coopers and Lybrand* [2001] EWCA Civ 1163, [2001] CPLR 451). In that case, in which the judge, before the trial, was proposing to read background documentation by way of preparation for what was bound to be a long and complex case, it was held that there was no danger of his being so influenced by what he read that he would not decide the case only on the basis of the admissible evidence.

In general, disputes about the admissibility of evidence in civil proceedings are best resolved by the judge at the substantive hearing of an application or at the trial of a claim, rather than at a separate preliminary hearing, because the judge at a preliminary hearing will usually be less well informed about the case and preliminary hearings can cause unnecessary costs and delays (*Stroude v Beazer Homes Ltd* [2005] EWCA Civ 265, [2005] NPC 45).

The exclusionary rules of evidence, for example, the rules relating to opinion evidence and legal professional privilege, are covered elsewhere in this work. The following paragraphs consider relevance and discretionary exclusion.

Relevance

49.6   The word 'relevance' means that 'any two facts to which it is applied are so related to each other that according to the common course of events one either taken by itself or in connection with other facts proves or renders probable the past, present or future existence or non-existence of the other' (Stephen, *Digest of the Law of Evidence*, 12th edn., art. 1). Whether evidence is relevant is often a question of degree and determined not by strict logic but by common sense and experience.

Sometimes, evidence is plainly irrelevant. *Holcombe v Hewson* (1810) 2 Camp 391 concerned an alleged breach of covenant by the defendant, a publican, to buy his beer from the claimant, a brewer. The defence was that the claimant had previously supplied bad beer. Evidence purporting to rebut this, that the claimant had supplied other publicans with good beer, was held to be inadmissible because irrelevant: the issue was the quality of the beer supplied to the defendant, not the quality of different beer supplied to others. Similarly, in *Hollingham v Head* (1858) 27 LJ CP 241, where the defendant sought to establish that a contract was made on certain special terms, evidence that the claimant had entered into contracts with other customers on similar terms was held to be inadmissible because irrelevant: it afforded no reasonable inference as to the terms of the contract in question.

In other cases, relevance will be a question of degree. For example, evidence that after an accident the working practices of a defendant to a negligence action were altered and improved will not necessarily be relevant to the issue whether the accident was caused by negligence (see *Hart v Lancashire and Yorkshire Railway Co.* (1869) 21 LT 261). Conversely, in *Great Future International Ltd v Sealand Housing Corporation* [2002] EWCA Civ 1183, LTL 25/7/2002 evidence of an attempt by an employee (who was not called as a witness) of one of the claimants to persuade an expert retained for one of the defendants not to testify was held to be relevant to the question of mitigation of damage. In some cases evidence will be excluded because although it is undoubtedly of *some* relevance to the issues, it will give rise to a number of subsidiary issues which might well distract the court from the main issue. This may involve the court in a protracted investigation (see *Attorney General v Hitchcock* (1847) 1 Ex 91 at p. 105) or a difficult controversy of the same kind as that which it has to decide (see *Metropolitan Asylum District Managers v Hill* (1882) 47 LT 29). A good illustration is *Agassiz v London Tramway Co.* (1872) 21 WR 199, in which a passenger in an omnibus claimed damages for personal injuries suffered as a result of a collision alleged to have been caused by the negligence of the driver. After the accident another passenger had suggested to the conductor that the driver's conduct should be reported, to which the conductor had replied that the driver had been reported because he had been off the points five or six times that day. This evidence was held to have been properly excluded on the basis that it did not relate to the conduct of the driver at the relevant time and did not explain the cause of the collision, but gave rise to a multiplicity of side issues.

Evidence obtained unlawfully, improperly or unfairly

There is a general rule at common law that evidence is admissible notwithstanding that it has been obtained unlawfully, improperly or unfairly (*Helliwell v Piggott-Sims* [1980] FSR 582; *Calcraft v Guest* [1898] 1 QB 759; and *Goddard v Nationwide Building Society* [1987] QB 670) or has been created by an unlawful process (*Public Prosecution Service of Northern Ireland v Elliott* [2013] UKSC 32, [2013] 1 WLR 1611). There are three exceptions. The first relates to evidence obtained by torture. In *A v Secretary of State for the Home Department (No. 2)* [2005] UKHL 71, [2006] 2 AC 221, Lord Bingham of Cornhill held that, as a matter of constitutional principle, evidence obtained by torturing another may not lawfully be admitted against a party to proceedings in a British court, irrespective of where, or by whom, or on whose authority the torture was inflicted. The second exception is that evidence obtained by unjustifiable inhuman or degrading treatment contrary to the European Convention on Human Rights, art. 3, may also fall to be excluded (*Jalloh v Germany* (application 54810/00) (2006) 44 EHRR 32). The third exception relates to privileged documents. In civil proceedings, where a document protected by legal professional privilege, or secondary evidence of it, has been obtained by the wrongful act of the opponent of the party entitled to assert the privilege, that party may apply for an injunction to restrain the opponent from making any use of the confidential information (see **50.76** to **50.77**).

49.7

Discretion to exclude

Prior to the introduction of the CPR, a judge in a civil case had no discretion to exclude evidence admissible as a matter of law, and that principle applied even if the evidence in question had been obtained improperly or unlawfully (see per Lord Denning MR in *Helliwell v Piggott-Sims* [1980] FSR 582). On one view, there was an exception to this general rule whereby a judge could permit a witness, whether a party to the proceedings or not, to refuse to disclose information, typically information given and received under the seal of confidence, where disclosure would be a breach of some ethical or social value and non-disclosure would be unlikely to result in serious injustice in the case in which it was being claimed: see 16th Report of the Law Reform Committee, *Privilege in Civil Proceedings* (1967) Cmnd 3472, para. 1, and per Lords Hailsham of St Marylebone and Kilbrandon in *D v National Society for the Prevention of Cruelty to Children* [1978] AC 171. In that case, however, both Lord Simon of Glaisdale and Lord Edmund-Davies doubted the existence of such a wide discretionary power.

49.8

Commentary

CPR, r. 32.1(2), has introduced an exclusionary discretion of general application in civil cases, including claims allocated to the small claims track (see **CPR, r. 27.2(1)**). Under **r. 32.1(1)** the court may control the evidence by giving directions as to the issues on which it requires evidence, the nature of the evidence which it requires to decide those issues, and the way in which the evidence is to be placed before the court. **Rule 32.1(2)** provides that 'the court may use its power under this rule to exclude evidence that would otherwise be admissible' and **r. 32.1(3)** states that 'the court may limit cross-examination'. In exercising its powers under either **r. 32.1(2)** or **r. 32.1(3)**, the court must seek to give effect to the 'overriding objective' of the rules, to enable the court 'to deal with cases justly' (**r. 1.1**). The power conferred by **r. 32.1(2)** is extremely wide. Subject to **r. 1.1**, there are no express limitations as to the manner and extent of the exercise of the power (*Grobbelaar v Sun Newspapers Ltd* (1999) *The Times*, 12 August 1999). The court has always had the power to rule evidence inadmissible if it is of no more than marginal relevance (see **49.6**). **Rule 32.1(2)**, however, goes further: the court may exclude any type of otherwise admissible evidence, even if plainly relevant, although obviously the more relevant it is, the more reluctant the court is likely to be to exercise its power to exclude it. This was emphasised in *Great Future International Ltd v Sealand Housing Corporation* [2002] EWCA Civ 1183, LTL 25/7/2002, where it was said that the power under **r. 32.1(2)** has to be exercised with great circumspection. In *Post Office Counters Ltd v Mahida* [2003] EWCA Civ 1583, *The Times*, 31 October 2003, Hale LJ said, at [24], that the power to exclude admissible evidence under **r. 32.1(2)** is principally a case management power designed to allow the court to stop cases getting out of hand. This means the rule may be used by the court when managing cases with the aim of minimising the burden on litigants of slender means by excluding all peripheral material which is not essential to the just determination of the real issues between the parties and whose examination would be disproportionate to its importance to those issues (*McPhilemy v Times Newspapers Ltd* [1999] 3 All ER 775 per May LJ at p. 791). As to the exclusion of expert evidence by reason of non-compliance with **PD 35**, see *Stevens v Gullis* [2000] 1 All ER 527.

The court may also use **CPR, r. 32.1(2)**, to restrict the number of witnesses to be called, and to exclude any evidence thought to be superfluous.

In appropriate circumstances, the court may properly take the view that in order to give effect to the 'overriding objective' it should also exercise the discretion in **r. 32.1(2)** to exclude evidence that has been obtained illegally (for example, by a crime, tort or breach of contract or statute), improperly (for example, by trickery, deception, bribes, threats or inducements) or in breach of the right to respect for private and family life in the European Convention on Human Rights, **art. 8**, in the **Human Rights Act 1998, sch. 1** (for example, by covertly video-recording employees or claimants in personal injuries litigation). In *Jones v University of Warwick* [2003] EWCA Civ 151, [2003] 1 WLR 954, the defendant was allowed to use as evidence a video of the claimant obtained in breach of **art. 8** and by trespass, inquiry agents acting for the defendant's insurers having filmed the claimant without her knowledge after having gained access to her home by deception. Lord Woolf CJ held that the court had to consider two competing public interests: that in litigation the truth should be revealed and that the courts should not acquiesce in or encourage a party to use unlawful means to obtain evidence. Thus the judge's responsibility requires him, when exercising his discretion in accordance with the overriding objective, to consider not only the litigation before the court but also the effect of his decision on litigation generally. The weight to be attached to the two competing interests will vary according to the circumstances. The significance of the evidence will differ as will the gravity of the breach of **art. 8**. On the facts, it was held that it was not a case where the conduct of the insurers was so outrageous that the defence should be struck out and that it would be artificial and undesirable for the evidence to be excluded, which would have required the instruction of fresh medical experts. However, it was also stressed that the conduct of the insurers was improper and unjustified and that the trial judge should take it into account when deciding the appropriate order for costs. See also *Niemietz v Germany* (1992) 16 EHRR 97; *Halford v United Kingdom* (1997) 24 EHRR 523; *Tchenguiz v Imerman* [2010] EWCA Civ 908, [2011] 1 All ER 555.

CPR, r. 32.1(3), may be used by the court to impose limits on the time permitted for cross-examination of witnesses at trial (see, for example, *Rall v Hume* [2001] 3 All ER 248). The question for the judge in deciding whether or not to limit cross-examination is how long is it necessary for the cross-examination to last in the interests of justice, for both parties and for the witness in question and, concerning the last, account may be taken of the witness's medical condition (see *Three Rivers District Council v Bank of England* [2005] EWCA Civ 889, LTL 23/ 8/2005).

Rule 32.1(3) supplements the pre-existing discretionary powers of the judge to prevent questions in cross-examination which, in his or her opinion, are unnecessary, improper or oppressive. At common law, cross-examination should be conducted with restraint and with a measure of courtesy and consideration to the witness (see per Sankey LC in *Mechanical and General Inventions Co. Ltd v Austin* [1935] AC 346 at p. 360). Counsel should be restrained from embarking on lengthy cross-examination on matters that are not really in issue (*Mechanical and General Inventions Co. Ltd v Austin* at p. 359) or from framing questions in such a way as to invite argument rather than elicit evidence on the facts in issue (per Lord Hewart CJ in *R v Baldwin* (1925) 18 Cr App R 175). See also the Code of Conduct for barristers in the Bar Standards Handbook, r. C7.1: '…you must not make statements or ask questions merely to insult, humiliate or annoy a witness'.

In order to call into question a witness's credibility, the witness may be asked about his or her conviction for any offence, even if it is not one of dishonesty (see **49.68**), but the court may exercise its discretion under **CPR, r. 32.1(3)**, to limit such cross-examination to convictions for offences involving dishonesty. However, a judge sitting without a jury should be more hesitant to exclude otherwise relevant evidence and cross-examination, because a judge does not need to be protected from giving undue weight to evidence relating to a witness's credibility (*Watson v Chief Constable of Cleveland Police* [2001] EWCA Civ 1547, LTL 12/10/2001).

Circumstances vary infinitely, and for this reason it is submitted that it will normally be unnecessary and undesirable for the courts to provide general guidance, additional to that to be found in the inclusionary definition of 'dealing with a case justly' in **r. 1.1(2)**, on the way in which the discretionary powers under **r. 32.1(2)** and **(3)** should be exercised. For the same reason the exercise of these discretionary powers should only be open to appeal on the limited grounds discussed in **75.11**.

FORMAL ADMISSIONS

A fact which is formally admitted ceases to be in issue. Evidence of such a fact, being unnecessary, is inadmissible. Legal advisers owe a duty to their clients to consider whether any formal admissions can properly be made. Formal admissions should be made by a party in the case of facts as to which there is no serious dispute, thereby saving the other party to the case the unnecessary trouble and expense of proving them. A party may admit the truth of the whole or any part of another party's case (**CPR, r. 14.1(1)**), although once an admission has been made, the permission of the court is required to amend or withdraw it (**r. 14.1(5)**). A party who wishes to admit the truth of the whole or any part of another party's case before the commencement of proceedings may do so by giving notice in writing (see **r. 14.1A(1)**; see also **17.2** and **34.30**). A fact may be formally admitted in a variety of ways: by a defendant, in his or her defence, expressly (**r. 16.5(1)(c)**) or by default, i.e. by failing to deal with an allegation (**r. 16.5(5)**), and by either party in response to a notice to admit facts (**r. 32.18**) or in response to a written request, or court order, to give additional information (see **rr. 18.1** and **26.5(3)** and **PD 18**). Prior to the trial, a formal admission may also be made by a letter written by a legal adviser acting on behalf of a party (*Ellis v Allen* [1914] 1 Ch 904). According to **CPR, r. 14.1(2)**, a party may make an admission 'by giving notice in writing (such as in a statement of case or by letter)'. However, it would seem that it remains possible for a formal admission to be made by a party or a party's legal adviser orally, either at the trial itself (see *Urquhart v*

49.9

Commentary

Butterfield (1887) 37 ChD 357) or in interim proceedings, in which case the admission may subsequently be withdrawn, provided that the other party has not acted on it so as to give rise to an estoppel (*H. Clark (Doncaster) Ltd v Wilkinson* [1965] Ch 694).

PRESUMPTIONS

Introduction

49.10 There are numerous common law, equitable and statutory presumptions. The following paragraphs deal with some of the most important of them. The presumption of legal origin and the equitable presumptions of undue influence and advancement are not considered.

Rebuttable presumptions of law

49.11 Where a rebuttable presumption of law operates, on the proof or admission of basic or primary facts, and in the absence of further evidence, another fact must be presumed. The party relying on the presumption bears the burden of establishing the basic facts, and his adversary bears either an evidential burden to adduce some evidence in rebuttal of the presumed fact or, as the case may be, a legal burden to disprove the presumed fact. A rebuttable presumption which operates to put an evidential burden on the party against whom it operates is referred to as an evidential presumption. If the party relying on an evidential presumption proves the basic facts, the presumed fact will be treated as having been established unless his opponent adduces some evidence in rebuttal, but where the opponent discharges the evidential burden in the usual way (see **49.36**) the effect will be as if the presumption had never come into play at all: the party relying on the presumption bears the legal burden to prove on a balance of probabilities the fact that otherwise could have been presumed. It follows from this, of course, that if at the end of the day, on all the evidence before the court, the probability of the existence of the presumed fact is equal to the probability of its non-existence, the opponent will succeed. A rebuttable presumption which operates to put a legal burden on the party against whom it operates is referred to as a 'persuasive' or 'compelling' presumption. If a party relying on a persuasive presumption proves the basic facts, a legal burden is placed on the opponent to disprove the presumed fact. The opponent will therefore lose on the issue not only by adducing no evidence to disprove the presumed fact, but also where on all the evidence before the court the probability of the existence of the presumed fact is equal to the probability of its non-existence.

Some rebuttable presumptions, such as the presumption of mental capacity, operate without the proof or admission of basic facts, and in truth, therefore, are nothing more than rules relating to the incidence of the burden of proof that have been cast in the language pertaining to presumptions.

49.12 **Presumption of marriage**   There appear to be three types of presumption of marriage, a presumption of formal validity, a presumption of essential validity, and a presumption of marriage arising from cohabitation. They are considered here in outline only. (For a fuller treatment, see Keane, *The Modern Law of Evidence*, 8th edn. (Oxford: OUP, 2010) at pp. 654ff.)

The formal validity of a marriage depends upon the *lex loci celebrationis*. Under English law, for example, there are formal requirements, in the case of a Church of England marriage, to publish banns and to obtain a common licence, and in the case of other marriages to give due notice to the superintendent registrar. Under the presumption of the formal validity of a marriage, on the proof or admission of the basic facts that a marriage was celebrated between persons who intended to marry, the formal validity of the marriage will be presumed in the absence of sufficient evidence to the contrary. The presumption is a persuasive presumption. The leading authority relating to an English marriage is *Piers v Piers* (1849) 2 HL Cas 331, where a marriage performed in a private house was held to be formally valid despite the absence of evidence that the bishop of the diocese had granted the necessary special licence. For an example of the application of the presumption to a foreign marriage, see *Mahadervan v Mahadervan* [1964] P 233. It has been said that the standard of proof to be met by the party with the legal burden of disproving formal validity is high (see *Piers v Piers*), but it is submitted that under the modern law there is little likelihood of the courts applying the decision in *Mahadervan v Mahadervan*, where Sir Jocelyn Simon P held that the presumption can only be rebutted by evidence which satisfies beyond reasonable doubt that there was no valid marriage (see further at **49.41** to **49.44**).

Under the presumption of the essential validity of a marriage, on proof or admission of the basic facts that a formally valid marriage was celebrated, in the absence of sufficient evidence to the contrary, the essential validity of the marriage will be presumed, i.e. it will be presumed that the parties had the capacity to marry, and therefore, under English law, for example, were not related within the prohibited degrees, were aged 16 or over and were not already married (see *Tweney v Tweney* [1946] P 180). The presumption is probably a persuasive presumption. Evidence of a valid prior marriage will suffice to rebut the presumption (*Gatty v Attorney General* [1951] P 444; *Re Peete* [1952] 2 All ER 599), but not where the prior marriage is itself of doubtful validity (*Taylor v Taylor* [1967] P 25).

Under the persuasive presumption of marriage arising from cohabitation, on proof or admission of the basic fact that a man and woman have long cohabited as if man and wife, and have acquired the reputation of being husband and wife, it is presumed, in the absence of sufficient evidence to the contrary, that they were living together in consequence of a valid marriage (see *Sastry Velaider Aronegary v Sembecutty Vaigalie* (1881) 6 App Cas 364; *Al-Saedy v Musawi* [2010] EWHC 3293 (Fam), [2011] 2 FLR 287). The presumption applies even in the absence of evidence that a marriage ceremony has taken place (see *Re Taplin* [1937] 3 All ER 105 and *Re Taylor* [1961] 1 WLR 9). Evidence in rebuttal is required to meet a high standard (see *Re Taplin* and *Re Taylor*).

Presumption of legitimacy   Under the persuasive presumption of legitimacy, on proof or admission of the basic fact that a child was born or conceived during lawful wedlock, it is presumed, in the absence of sufficient evidence to the contrary, that the child is legitimate. The presumption applies where there is a maintenance order in force against the husband, unless it contains a non-cohabitation clause (*Bowen v Norman* [1938] 1 KB 689), where proceedings for divorce or nullity have commenced (*Knowles v Knowles* [1962] P 161) and where the parties are living apart, whether or not under a separation agreement (*Ettenfield v Ettenfield* [1940] P 96). The presumption does not apply where a decree of judicial separation or a magistrate's separation order is in force (see *Hetherington v Hetherington* (1887) 12 PD 112).   **49.13**

The presumption applies both where a child is born so soon after a marriage ceremony that premarital conception is indicated (*Poulett Peerage Case* [1903] AC 395) and where a child is born so soon after the mother's termination of her marriage that conception during the marriage is indicated (*Maturin v Attorney General* [1938] 2 All ER 214; *Re Heath* [1945] Ch 417). In *Re Overbury* [1955] Ch 122, six months after her first husband's death, a woman remarried, and two months later gave birth to a girl. It was held that the child was the legitimate daughter of the first husband, there being insufficient evidence to rebut the presumption.

The standard of proof to be met by the party seeking to rebut the presumption is governed by the Family Law Reform Act 1969, s. 26. It provides as follows:

Any presumption of law as to the legitimacy or illegitimacy of any person may in any civil proceedings be rebutted by evidence which shows that it is more probable than not that the person is illegitimate or legitimate as the case may be and it shall not be necessary to prove that fact beyond reasonable doubt in order to rebut the presumption.

Thus even weak evidence against legitimacy must prevail if there is no other evidence to counterbalance it, but where the evidence is such that legitimacy is as probable as illegitimacy, the party seeking to rebut the presumption will fail (see *S v S* [1972] AC 24 at p. 41, applied in *T (HH) v T (E)* [1971] 1 WLR 429).

The presumption of legitimacy may be rebutted by evidence that the husband and wife did not have sexual intercourse as a result of which the child was conceived (*Banbury Peerage Case* (1811) 1 Sim & St 153), evidence of the husband's impotence (*Legge v Edmonds* (1855) 25 LJ Ch 125), an admission of paternity by another man (*R v King's Lynn Justices, ex parte M* [1988] 2 FLR 79), evidence of the wife's cohabitation with another man for an appropriate period of time before the birth of the child (*Re Jenion* [1952] Ch 454), evidence of a DNA test excluding the husband as the father, coupled with evidence of the putative father's refusal to comply with an order for a blood test (*F v Child Support Agency* [1999] 2 FLR 244) or evidence of the conduct of the wife and illicit partner towards the child (*Kanapathipillai v Parpathy* [1956] AC 580). The inference of paternity to be drawn from a refusal to undergo DNA testing outweighs the presumption of legitimacy (*Secretary of State for Work and Pensions v Jones* [2003] EWHC 2163 (Fam), [2004] 1 FLR 282). Evidence in rebuttal may also take the form of evidence of non-access or the use of reliable contraceptives. Evidence of adultery on the part of the mother will not rebut the presumption unless accompanied by evidence that at the time of conception sexual intercourse between the husband and wife did not take place (*Gordon v Gordon* [1903] P 141).

49.14 **Presumption of death**   Under the presumption of death, if there is no acceptable affirmative evidence that a person was alive at some time during a continuous period of seven years or more, on the proof or admission of the basic facts that:

(a) there are persons who would be likely to have heard of him or her over that period,

(b) those persons have not heard of him or her, and

(c) all due enquiries have been made appropriate to the circumstances,

that person will be presumed to have died at some time within that period (per Sachs J in *Chard v Chard* [1956] P 259 at p. 272). The decision of the House of Lords in *Prudential Assurance Co. v Edmonds* (1877) 2 App Cas 487 suggests that this is an evidential presumption rebuttable by adducing sufficient evidence to raise the possibility of the existence of the absent person. As to the first of the basic facts, friends and relatives will not be treated as persons likely to have heard of the absent person where there are reasons which might have led the latter not to wish to be heard of by the former (see *Chard v Chard*) or where it is shown that the latter did not intend the former to hear of him or her (see *Watson v England* (1844) 14 Sim 28 and *Re Lidderdale* (1912) 57 SJ 3).

The authorities conflict on whether (c) above is among the basic facts to be proved or admitted before the presumption can arise (see *Willyams v Scottish Widows' Fund Life Assurance Society* (1888) 4 TLR 489; *Chipchase v Chipchase* [1939] P 391; and *Bradshaw v Bradshaw* [1956] P 274), the explanation for which is probably that in some cases the circumstances are such that it would not be appropriate to make any enquiries at all (see *Bullock v Bullock* [1960] 1 WLR 975).

Under the presumption of death, the court presumes only the fact of a person's death. Thus if it is sought to establish that the deceased died unmarried, childless or without next-of-kin, these additional facts require additional evidence (*Re Jackson* [1907] 2 Ch 354), although less evidence seems to be required than if the presumption had not applied (see *Dunn v Snowden* (1862) 32 LJ Ch 104; *Rawlinson v Miller* (1875) 1 ChD 52; *Greaves v Greenwood* (1877) 2 ExD 289). Additional evidence is also required to prove that the death took place at a particular period (per Giffard LJ in *Re Phené's Trusts* (1870) LR 5 App 139 at p. 144). As to the date on which one may presume the fact of death, the authorities are in conflict. *Re Phené's Trusts* was taken by the Privy Council in *Lal Chand Marwari v Mahant Ramrup Gir* (1925) 42 TLR 159 at p. 160 to be an authority for the proposition that the fact of death is presumed at the date of the proceedings. However, the decisions in *Re Westbrook's Trusts* [1873] WN 167 (criticised in *Re Rhodes* (1887) 36 ChD 586) and *Chipchase v Chipchase* [1939] P 391 are only consistent with the conflicting view that the fact of death may be presumed at the end of the continuous period of absence for seven years.

Presumption of regularity   Under this evidential presumption, often expressed in the maxim   **49.15**
omnia praesumuntur rite esse acta (all acts are presumed to have been duly done), on the proof or
admission of the basic fact that a person has acted in a public or official capacity, it is presumed,
in the absence of sufficient evidence to the contrary, that the person was regularly and properly
appointed and that the act was regularly and properly performed. Those presumed to have been
duly appointed have included a police officer (*R v Gordon* (1789) 1 Leach 515), an officer of the Post
Office (*R v Borrett* (1833) 6 Car & P 124), a judge (*R v Roberts* (1878) 38 LT 690) and an inspector of
the Health and Safety Executive (*Campbell v Wallsend Slipway and Engineering Co. Ltd* [1978] ICR
1015). In *R v Langton* (1876) 2 QBD 296 the presumption was used to establish the due incorporation of a company which had acted as such. In *R v Inland Revenue Commissioners, ex parte T. C.
Coombs and Co.* [1991] 2 AC 283 a tax inspector, with the consent of a General Commissioner, had
served notice under the Taxes Management Act 1970, s. 20, requiring stockbrokers to deliver
documentary information relevant to the tax liability of one of their former employees. It was
presumed, in the absence of evidence to the contrary, that both the inspector and the
Commissioner had acted within the limits of their authority, with honesty and discretion.

Presumption of mental capacity   The Mental Capacity Act 2005 deals with prospective   **49.16**
decision-making for living persons. Under s. 1(2) of the Act, a person must be assumed to
have capacity unless it is established that he lacks capacity; thus it is the party asserting mental
incapacity who bears the legal burden to prove it. This reflects the common law presumption
of mental capacity. At common law a party or witness is presumed to have mental capacity
until the contrary is proved, the burden of proving the contrary resting on the party asserting
incapacity (*Masterman-Lister v Brutton and Co. (Nos. 1 and 2)* [2002] EWCA Civ 1889, [2003] EWCA Civ
70, [2003] 1 WLR 1511). It has been held that if a prima facie case of incapacity is established,
the evidential burden shifts to the party asserting capacity (see, e.g., *Re Smith* [2014] EWHC 3926
(Ch), [2015] 4 All ER 329, where the authorities are reviewed). However, it is submitted that in
these circumstances the burden placed on the party asserting capacity is not the evidential
burden, but the provisional or tactical burden (see **49.36**) because the so-called 'presumption'
of mental capacity is nothing more than a rule relating to the incidence of the burden of proof
(see **49.11**). The court as a matter of practice should investigate the question of capacity
whenever there is reason to suspect its absence, even if the matter is not in contention. The
test is issue specific and depends on the nature and complexity of the transactions involved.
The test is whether the person was capable of understanding the issues on which his or her
consent or decision was necessary. However, although the decisions made are likely to be
important indicators of the existence or lack of understanding, a person is not to be regarded
as unable to make any rational decision merely because the decision made would not have
been made by a person of ordinary prudence and, conversely, is not to be regarded as having
mental capacity merely because his or her decision appears rational. The court must be astute
not to accept a plea of incompetence when the evidence does not suggest a lack of competence
(*Phillips v Symes* [2004] EWHC 1887 (Ch), LTL 18/8/2004).

Presumptions in testamentary cases   Under this evidential presumption, on the proof or   **49.17**
admission of the basic fact that a rational will has been duly executed, it is presumed, in the
absence of sufficient evidence to the contrary, that the testator was sane. Thus, in *Sutton v
Sadler* (1857) 3 CB NS 87, in which the heir-at-law brought an action against the devisee alleging
the insanity of the testator, it was held that the devisee bore the legal burden of proving that
he was the devisee under a duly executed will; that proof of the due execution of a rational will
gave rise to the presumption, placing an evidential burden on the heir-at-law; and that if the
heir-at-law had raised sufficient evidence for the issue of sanity to go before the tribunal of
fact, that tribunal should find against the devisee unless satisfied that he had discharged the
legal burden of proving on a balance of probabilities that the testator was sane.

There is a presumption of due execution on proof that a will contains the signatures of the
deceased, two witnesses and an attestation clause. Although this is an evidential presumption,
it can only be rebutted by the strongest evidence that the witness did not intend to attest the

deceased's signature (*Sherrington v Sherrington* [2005] EWCA Civ 326, [2005] WTLR 587). It is not rebutted merely because the attesting witnesses have no recollection of having signed (*Channon v Perkins* [2005] EWCA Civ 1808, LTL 1/12/2005).

49.18   **Principle of *res ipsa loquitur***   Under the principle of *res ipsa loquitur*, on proof or admission of the basic facts that some thing was under the management of the defendant or his or her employees and an accident occurred, being an accident which in the ordinary course of things does not occur if those who have the management of the thing use proper care, it may or must be presumed, in the absence of sufficient evidence to the contrary, that the accident was caused by the negligence of the defendant (see generally per Sir William Erle CJ in *Scott v London and St Katherine Docks Co.* (1865) 3 Hurl & C 596 at p. 601). This definition reflects the fact that in different cases the principle has been treated in different ways, as a persuasive presumption, as an evidential presumption (see **49.11**), and as a presumption of fact or provisional presumption (see **49.22**). In both *Woods v Duncan* [1946] AC 401 at pp. 419, 425 and 439 and *Barkway v South Wales Transport Co. Ltd* [1948] 2 All ER 460 at p. 471, it was treated as a persuasive presumption, shifting the onus of proof onto the defendant to show on the balance of probabilities that he was not negligent. See also per Lords Reid and Donovan in *Henderson v Henry E. Jenkins and Sons* [1970] AC 282 and also, it is submitted, *George v Eagle Air Services Ltd* [2009] UKPC 21, [2009] 1 WLR 2133 at [13]. In *The Kite* [1933] P 154, however, it was treated as an evidential presumption, so that if the defendant gives a reasonable explanation for the accident, which is equally consistent with the accident happening without his or her negligence as with it, then the burden of proof is on the claimant to show, as the claimant has to show from the beginning, that it was the negligence of the defendant that caused the accident. See also per Lord Pearson in *Henderson v Henry E. Jenkins and Sons*, per Lawton LJ in *Ward v Tesco Stores Ltd* [1976] 1 WLR 810, *Ng Chun Pui v Lee Chuen Tat* [1988] RTR 298 and *Dawkins v Carnival plc* [2011] EWCA Civ 1237, [2012] 1 Lloyd's Rep 1. Finally, there is authority that the principle of *res ipsa loquitur* is no more than a presumption of fact, so that proof of the basic facts gives rise to an inference of negligence which, in the absence of evidence to the contrary, may but need not be drawn (see per Greer LJ in *Langham v Wellingborough School Governors and Fryer* (1932) 101 LJ KB 513 at p. 518 and per Goddard LJ in *Easson v London and North Eastern Railway Co.* [1944] KB 421). There may be no anomaly in this diversity of approach. As it has been put elsewhere:

> Given that the facts calling for the application of the principle vary enormously from case to case so that in some the inference of negligence is slight, in others all but irresistible, efforts aimed at confining the principle to a single category seem ill-founded. At the risk of uncertainty, classification according to the facts of the case in question seems preferable. If the thing speaks for itself, it may do so with degrees of conviction. The hardship caused to the claimant may be remedied by placing the tactical, evidential or legal burden on the defendant depending on the strength of the basic facts in question. (Keane and McKeown, *The Modern Law of Evidence*, 10th edn. (2014), at p. 688.)

49.19   **Presumption that a time clause is not of the essence of a contract**   The Law of Property Act 1925, s. 41, contains a provision, first enacted in 1873, which fuses the common law and equitable rules on time in contracts. The effect is that, subject to three exceptions, a stipulation as to time in a contract (a time clause) is not deemed to be of the essence of the contract, and consequently it cannot be asserted that breach of such a stipulation repudiates the contract. The exceptions are:

(a) where the contract expressly states that time of performance is of the essence of the contract or must be strictly complied with;

(b) where the circumstances of the contract or its subject matter indicate that stipulations as to time must be strictly complied with; and

(c) where one party is guilty of undue delay and the innocent party gives notice that performance is required within a reasonable time.

There is a rebuttable presumption that stipulations as to time in rent review clauses are not of the essence of the contract (*United Scientific Holdings Ltd v Burnley Borough Council* [1978] AC 904). This presumption was rebutted in *Starmark Enterprises Ltd v CPL Distribution Ltd* [2001] EWCA Civ

1252, [2002] Ch 306, by a clause which stated that the tenant 'shall be deemed' to have agreed to an increased rent on failing to serve a counter-notice within one month of receipt of the rent notice. For a general discussion of when time is of the essence see *Re Gray* [2004] EWHC 1538 (Ch), [2005] 1 WLR 815.

Presumption that a fraudulent representation induced a contract   On proof of a fraudulent   **49.20**
representation of such a nature that it would be likely to have affected a reasonable person, it will be presumed that the representation induced the claimant to enter into the contract, unless the representor satisfies the court to the contrary. In *County NatWest Ltd v Barton* [2002] 4 All ER 494 it was held that the presumption alters the burden of proof, that the alteration remains unless and until the presumption is rebutted, and that the presumption continues to apply even if the representee gives evidence at the trial.

Irrebuttable presumptions of law

On the operation of an irrebuttable or conclusive presumption of law, on the proof or admis-   **49.21**
sion of basic or primary facts, another fact must be presumed and the party against whom the presumption operates is barred from adducing any evidence in rebuttal. For examples, see the Civil Evidence Act 1968, s. 13(1) (considered at **49.97**), and the State Immunity Act 1978, s. 21(a), under which a certificate issued by the Secretary of State for the Foreign and Commonwealth Office is conclusive evidence of whether any country is a State for the pur- poses of part 1 of the Act or of the person or persons to be regarded for those purposes as the head of government of a State (see, for example, *R (HRH Sultan of Pahang) v Secretary of State for the Home Department* [2011] EWCA Civ 616, *The Times*, 13 June 2011).

Presumptions of fact

On the operation of a presumption of fact, sometimes referred to as a provisional presump-   **49.22**
tion, on the proof or admission of basic or primary facts, another fact may be presumed in the absence of sufficient evidence to the contrary, so that the party against whom the pre- sumption operates bears a provisional or tactical burden in relation to the fact which may be presumed, not an evidential or legal burden. Presumptions of fact, therefore, are simply examples of circumstantial evidence, i.e. relevant facts, facts from which the existence or non-existence of a fact in issue may be inferred. In civil proceedings the only important examples of circumstantial evidence which have recurred so frequently as to be referred to as presumptions of fact are the presumption of continuance of life and the presumption of seaworthiness.

Presumption of continuance of life   On the operation of this presumption of fact, on the   **49.23**
proof or admission of the basic or primary fact that a person was alive on a certain date, it may be presumed, in the absence of sufficient evidence to the contrary, that he or she was alive on a subsequent date (*McDarmaid v Attorney General* [1950] P 218; *Re Peete* [1952] 2 All ER 599; *Chard v Chard* [1956] P 259). The strength of the presumption depends on the strength of the basic facts. If, for example, it were to be proved that a person was young and in good health on a certain date then, without more, the inference would be very strong that he or she was alive on the following day. If, on the other hand, it were to be proved that at a certain date a person was suffering from a terminal illness, then without more this would be unlikely to afford a reason- able inference that he or she was alive a year later (see *R v Lumley* (1869) LR 1 CCR 196 at p. 198).

Presumption of seaworthiness   On the operation of this presumption of fact, on the proof   **49.24**
or admission of the basic fact that a ship sank or became unable to continue her voyage shortly after putting out to sea, it may be presumed, in the absence of sufficient evidence to the con- trary, that she was unseaworthy on leaving port. It has been held that if, in the absence of evidence in rebuttal, the tribunal of fact were not to presume unseaworthiness, but were to find the contrary, then it would be such a finding against the reasonable inference to be drawn that it would amount to a verdict against the evidence (per Brett LJ in *Pickup v Thames and*

Commentary

Mersey Marine Insurance Co. Ltd (1873) 3 QBD 594 at p. 600; and see also *Ajum Goolam Hossen and Co. v Union Marine Insurance Co.* [1901] AC 362).

49.25 **Presumption of proper working order**   There is a presumption, which comes into operation without the need for proof or admission of any basic or primary facts, that in the absence of sufficient evidence to the contrary, mechanical or other instruments of a kind that are usually in proper working order, were in proper working order at the time of their use. The party against whom the presumption operates bears an evidential burden to adduce some evidence to the contrary. The presumption has been applied, e.g. in the case of speedometers (*Nicholas v Penny* [1950] 2 KB 466) and traffic lights (*Tingle Jacobs and Co. v Kennedy* [1964] 1 WLR 638).

Conflicting presumptions

49.26 Where two evidential or two persuasive presumptions are relied upon in the same case, and as a result the court finds itself obliged to draw two conclusions, the one in conflict with the other, then the two presumptions can be treated as having cancelled each other out, with the effect that the case can be decided on the basis of the ordinary rules pertaining to the burden of proof. This solution was adopted in *Monckton v Tarr* (1930) 2 BWCC 504, where the presumption of essential validity of marriage applied to two different ceremonies, but when a similar conflict arose in *Taylor v Taylor* [1967] P 25, the court preferred to preserve the existing marriage, rather than avoid it by virtue of an earlier effectively moribund one, an approach which suggests that the court may reach its decision not only on the basis of the comparative likelihood of the two presumed facts, but also having regard to policy considerations.

It is submitted that where two conflicting presumptions are relied upon in the same case, but they are of unequal strength, as when a rebuttable presumption of law conflicts with a presumption of fact, the conflict is more apparent than real, because the determinative factor will be the incidence of the legal burden of proof: the party bearing the legal burden will lose on the issue in question if he fails to discharge it to the requisite standard of proof. The outcome in *R v Willshire* (1881) 6 QBD 366 is consistent with this view. See also *Re Peatling* [1969] VR 214 (Supreme Court of Victoria).

JUDICIAL NOTICE

49.27 The doctrine of judicial notice takes two distinct forms, which were defined and distinguished by Lord Sumner in *Commonwealth Shipping Representative v Peninsular and Oriental Branch Service* [1923] AC 191 at p. 212: 'Judicial notice refers to facts, which a judge can be called upon to receive and to act upon, either from his general knowledge of them, or from enquiries to be made by himself for his own information from sources to which it is proper for him to refer'. These two forms of judicial notice require separate consideration. Consideration is also given to the extent to which, if at all, a judge may make use of his or her personal knowledge of facts in issue or of facts relevant to the facts in issue.

Judicial notice without inquiry at common law

49.28 If a fact is so notorious or of such common knowledge that it requires no proof, the judge, without recourse to any extraneous sources of information, may take judicial notice of it and thereby treat it as proved, notwithstanding that it has not been established by evidence. The doctrine may be illustrated by the following examples: the duration of the normal period of human gestation is about nine months (*Preston-Jones v Preston-Jones* [1951] AC 391); cats are ordinarily kept for domestic purposes (*Nye v Niblett* [1918] 1 KB 23); the streets of London are full of traffic (*Dennis v A. J. White and Co.* [1916] 2 KB 1); and a postcard is the sort of document which might be read by anyone (*Huth v Huth* [1915] 3 KB 32). In all of these examples, the doctrine was expressly applied, but in the case of facts beyond all serious dispute, for example, that Tuesday follows Monday, or that there are seven days in the week, it is common for judicial notice to be taken tacitly.

At common law, judicial notice is also taken of public Acts passed before 1851, but in the absence of express provision to the contrary, a private Act passed before 1851 must be proved by evidence, for which purpose production of a Queen's Printer's copy or an HMSO copy suffices (Evidence Act 1845, s. 3, and Documentary Evidence Act 1882, s. 2). Statutory instruments also call for proof, for which purpose Queen's Printer's or Stationery Office copies also suffice (see *R v Ashley* (1967) 52 Cr App R 42 and Documentary Evidence Act 1868, s. 2), but some have acquired such notoriety that judicial notice may be taken of them (see *R v Jones* (1968) 54 Cr App R 63).

As a general rule, foreign law, being a question of fact normally calling for expert evidence, cannot be the subject of judicial notice (*Brenan and Galen's Case* (1847) 10 QB 492 at p. 498). The exceptions to this general rule include:

(a) the common law of Northern Ireland (*Re Nesbitt* (1844) 14 LJ MC 30 at p. 33);
(b) Scots law in civil cases, of which judicial notice may be taken by the House of Lords; and
(c) a document purporting to bear the court's seal (**CPR, r. 2.6(3)**)

Judicial notice without inquiry pursuant to statute

Judicial notice of a fact, without inquiry, may be required by statute. Most of the statutory **49.29** provisions require judicial notice to be taken of the fact that a judicial or other official document has been signed by the person by whom it purports to have been signed or has been sealed by the court by which it purports to have been sealed. This applies in the case of:

(a) a judicial or official document purporting to have been signed by a judge of the Supreme Court (Evidence Act 1845, s. 2);
(b) a document purporting to bear the court's seal (**CPR, r. 2.6(3)**)

At common law, judicial notice is taken of public Acts passed before 1851 (see **49.79**). In the case of a UK statute (whether general, local and personal, or private) passed after 1850, the Interpretation Act 1978, s. 3, as supplemented by s. 22(1) and sch. 2, para. 2, requires judicial notice to be taken of it, unless the contrary is expressly provided by the Act. Evidence is therefore not required to prove either the contents of such an Act or that it has been duly passed by both Houses of Parliament. Judicial notice must also be taken of the European Community Treaties, the Official Journal of the Communities, and decisions of, or opinions by, the Court of Justice of the European Union (European Communities Act 1972, s. 3(2)).

Judicial notice after inquiry

If a fact is not sufficiently notorious to be the subject of judicial notice without inquiry, the **49.30** judge may take judicial notice of it and thereby treat it as proved, notwithstanding that it has not been established by evidence, after referring to reliable extraneous sources of information, such as certificates from ministers, learned treatises, works of reference and expert witnesses. The inquiry is distinct from proof by evidence because the rules of evidence do not apply, the results of the inquiry are not open to evidence in rebuttal, and the result constitutes a precedent, except in the case of facts lacking constancy, such as the status of a foreign government. There is obvious scope for abuse of the doctrine, but this has to be balanced against the reality that some facts are readily demonstrable by reference to sources of virtually indisputable authority and are likely to be in issue again, in other cases, so that proof in the normal way is undesirable, having regard to considerations of cost and the need for uniformity of decision. This may go some way towards explaining *McQuaker v Goddard* [1940] 1 KB 687, where it was held that judicial notice after inquiry could be taken of the fact that a camel is a domestic animal.

Commentary

Judicial notice after inquiry has usually been taken of three kinds of fact:

(a) facts which are readily demonstrable after reference to appropriate authoritative works of reference or learned treatises;

(b) customs and professional practices; and

(c) facts of a political nature.

49.31 **Readily demonstrable facts**   Examples include the day of the week on which a certain date fell, after reference to a diary or almanac; the longitude and latitude of a place, after reference to an atlas; and the date and place of a well-known historical event, after reference to an authoritative historical work.

49.32 **Customs and professional practices**   After consultation with suitably qualified expert witnesses, judicial notice may be taken of general customs and professional practices, such as the custom of the general lien of bankers on the securities of their customers (*Brandao v Barnett* (1846) 12 Cl & F 787; *George v Davies* [1911] 2 KB 445 at p. 448) and the practices of conveyancers (*Re Rosher* (1884) 26 ChD 801), ordnance surveyors (*Davey v Harrow Corporation* [1958] 1 QB 60) and accountants (*Heather v P-E Consulting Group Ltd* [1973] Ch 189).

49.33 **Political facts**   Judicial notice after inquiry has been taken of facts of a political nature such as the status of foreign governments, the membership of diplomatic suites and the extent of territorial sovereignty. The inquiry will usually be made of a minister, whose certificate will be treated as accurate because as a matter of public policy it is desirable to avoid a conflict between the courts and the executive on such issues. Examples include the fact that a country exists as an independent sovereign state (*Duff Development Co. v Government of Kelantan* [1924] AC 797, and see also *Mighell v Sultan of Johore* [1894] 1 QB 149 and *Carl Zeiss Stiftung v Rayner and Keeler Ltd (No. 2)* [1967] 1 AC 853); the fact that this country is in a state of war with another (*R v Bottrill, ex parte Kuechenmeister* [1947] KB 41); the membership of the staff of an ambassador (*Engelke v Mussmann* [1928] AC 433); and the classification 'secret' appearing on a document originating in a government office, meaning that the document contains information and material the unauthorised disclosure of which would cause serious injury to the interests of the nation (*Secretary of State for Defence v Guardian Newspapers Ltd* [1985] AC 339 per Lord Diplock at p. 354).

Personal knowledge

49.34 When a judge takes judicial notice of a notorious fact, he or she makes use of his or her general knowledge. The extent to which, if at all, a judge may make use of his or her personal and particular knowledge of facts in issue or relevant to the facts in issue, is unclear. There is certainly authority that a judge may use personal knowledge of matters within the common knowledge of people in the locality, but that is a principle which derives from cases decided under the Workmen's Compensation Acts, under which county court judges sat as arbitrators and took into account, in assessing compensation, personal knowledge of the labour market (see *Keane v Mount Vernon Colliery Co. Ltd* [1933] AC 309 and *Reynolds v Llanelly Associated Tinplate Co. Ltd* [1948] 1 All ER 140). In *Mullen v Hackney London Borough Council* [1997] 1 WLR 1103 the Court of Appeal held that a county court judge, in deciding which penalty to impose on the council for its failure to carry out an undertaking to the court, was entitled to take judicial notice of his own knowledge of the council's conduct in relation to previous undertakings. As to judicial notice, the facts in this case were clearly not notorious or of the kind of which judicial notice has been held to have been properly taken after inquiry. The Court of Appeal appears to have treated the principle deriving from cases such as *Keane v Mount Vernon Colliery Co. Ltd* as one of general application in any county court case (see Allen, *International Journal of Evidence and Proof* (1998) vol. 2, No. 1, 37).

THE BURDEN AND STANDARD OF PROOF

Legal burden

In this chapter, the phrase 'the legal burden' will be used to denote what has been variously described as 'the burden of proof', the 'probative burden', 'the ultimate burden', 'the burden of proof on the pleadings', 'the risk of non-persuasion' and 'the persuasive burden'. The legal burden is the obligation imposed on a party by a rule of law to prove (in some cases to negative or disprove) a fact in issue: a party which fails to discharge the burden will lose on the issue in question. In civil proceedings the standard of proof required to discharge the burden is proof on the balance of probabilities (see **49.41**). Whether a party has discharged the burden is decided by the tribunal of fact, whether judge or jury, once only, after the parties to the litigation have called all of their evidence. **49.35**

In exceptional cases, a judge may find it impossible to make a finding, one way or the other, on a disputed issue of fact, and therefore may decide the issue by resort to the legal burden. The principles to be derived from the authorities, in this respect, were summarised in *Stephens v Cannon* [2005] EWCA Civ 222, [2005] CP Rep 31 at [46] as follows:

(a) The situation in which the court finds itself before it can dispatch a disputed issue by resort to the burden of proof has to be exceptional.

(b) Nevertheless the issue does not have to be of any particular type.... It may be more likely to arise following an inquiry into, for example, the identity of the aggressor in an unwitnessed fight; but it can arise even after an inquiry, aided by good experts, into, for example, the cause of the sinking of a ship.

(c) The exceptional situation which entitles the court to resort to the burden of proof is that, notwithstanding that it has striven to do so, it cannot reasonably make a finding in relation to a disputed issue.

(d) A court which resorts to the burden of proof must ensure that others can discern that it has striven to make a finding in relation to a disputed issue and can understand the reasons why it has concluded that it cannot do so. The parties must be able to discern the court's endeavour and to understand its reasons in order to be able to perceive why they have won and lost. An appellate court must also be able to do so because otherwise it will not be able to accept that the court below was in the exceptional situation of being entitled to resort to the burden of proof.

(e) In a few cases the fact of the endeavour and the reasons for the conclusion will readily be inferred from the circumstances and so there will be no need for the court to demonstrate the endeavour and to explain the reasons in any detail in its judgment. In most cases, however, a more detailed demonstration and explanation in [the] judgment will be necessary.

Judges sometimes refer to the 'shifting' of a burden from a party to that party's opponent. In the case of the legal burden, this can only happen at common law on the operation of a rebuttable presumption of law of the persuasive variety: once the party relying on the presumption has proved the primary or basic facts giving rise to the presumption, the legal burden can be said to have shifted, in that the opponent will then bear the legal burden to disprove the fact that will otherwise be presumed (see **49.11**). When reference is made to the shifting of the burden in other circumstances, it is merely to signify that at a given moment in the course of the trial the burden appears to have been satisfied by the party on whom it lies, but in so far as this places a burden on the opponent, it is a tactical burden, not a legal or evidential burden (see per Mustill LJ in *Brady v Group Lotus Car Companies plc* [1987] 3 All ER 1050 at p. 1059): as already noted, whether a legal burden has been discharged is determined only once, at the end of the trial.

Evidential burden and right to begin

The evidential burden, sometimes referred to as 'the burden of adducing evidence' and 'the duty of passing the judge', is the obligation to adduce sufficient evidence of a fact to allow the **49.36** issue in question to go before the tribunal of fact. The burden is discharged when there is sufficient evidence to justify, as a possibility, a favourable finding by the tribunal of fact. Whether a party has discharged the burden is decided only once in the course of the trial, and is decided by the judge, as opposed to the tribunal of fact. Thus a claimant who bears the evidential and legal burden on a particular issue, and fails to discharge the evidential burden, necessarily fails on the issue, since the judge will refuse to let the issue go before the tribunal of fact. However, discharge of the evidential burden will not necessarily result in discharge of the legal burden: the issue goes to the tribunal of fact, which may or may not find in favour of the claimant, although a defendant who adduces no evidence in rebuttal clearly runs the risk of losing on the issue.

As with the legal burden, judges sometimes refer to the 'shifting' of the evidential burden. However, this can only happen at common law on the operation of a rebuttable presumption of law of the evidential variety: where the party relying on such a presumption adduces sufficient evidence of the primary or basic facts, the adversary will bear an evidential burden to adduce some evidence in rebuttal of the presumed fact (see **49.11**). When reference is made to the shifting of the evidential burden in other circumstances, it is to signify that at a given moment during the course of the trial, the burden appears to have been discharged by the party on whom it lies, but this is to place no more than a provisional or tactical burden, as opposed to an evidential burden, on his opponent, because as has been said, an opponent who adduces no evidence in rebuttal clearly runs the risk of losing on the issue in question (see *Sutton v Sadler* (1857) 3 CB NS 87).

The right to be the first party to adduce evidence is determined by the incidence of the evidential burden. Usually the claimant will adduce his evidence first, but where the evidential burden on all the issues in the action lies on the defendant, or one of the defendants, the defendant or that defendant is entitled to begin (see *Ponifex v Jolly* (1839) 9 Car & P 202 and *Re Parry* [1977] 1 WLR 93). In *Mercer v Whall* (1845) 14 LJ QB 267 a clerk brought an action for unliquidated damages for wrongful dismissal. The defendant admitted the dismissal but claimed justification on the grounds of the clerk's misconduct. Although the defendant would have had the right to begin if the claim had been for a liquidated sum, because then the only issue would have been the issue of misconduct, on which the defendant bore the evidential burden, it was held that the clerk had the right to begin because he bore the evidential burden in relation to damages.

Incidence of the legal and evidential burden

49.37   Subject to cases in which reliance is placed upon evidential presumptions (see **49.11** to **49.25**), the evidential burden in relation to any given fact in issue will lie on the party bearing the legal burden on that fact in issue. As to the incidence of the legal burden, this may be fixed by agreement of the parties, but otherwise falls to be determined by rules of law to be found in statutes and at common law, where the general guiding principle to be derived from the precedents is that 'he who asserts must prove'.

49.38   **By agreement**   The parties themselves may expressly agree upon the incidence of the legal burden (see, e.g. *Levy v Assicurazioni Generali* [1940] AC 791 and *Fred Chappell Ltd v National Car Parks Ltd* (1987) *The Times*, 22 May 1987), but where a written agreement such as an insurance policy contains no such express provision, the court may nonetheless have regard to the terms of the agreement and may treat the issue as a matter of construction. In *Munro, Brice and Co. v War Risks Association* [1918] 2 KB 78, a ship had disappeared for reasons unknown and a claim was made under a policy of insurance which covered the ship subject to an exemption in respect of loss by capture or in consequence of hostilities. The issue was whether the claimant had to prove that the ship was not lost by reason of enemy action. The court found for the claimant on the basis that it was for the defendant to prove that the facts fell within the exception, which they had failed to do. (Contrast, but question, *Hurst v Evans* [1917] 1 KB 352; and see also *Gorman v Hand-in-Hand Insurance Co.* (1877) IR 11 CL 224.) However, where a claimant in such a case relies upon a proviso to an exemption clause, the court may conclude that the claimant must prove that the facts fall within the proviso. This was the outcome in *The Glendarroch* [1894] P 226. In that case, an action in negligence for non-delivery of goods, the goods having been lost when the boat carrying them sank, the bill of lading contained a clause exempting the defendants in respect loss or damage caused by perils of the sea, provided that they were not negligent. It was held that it was for the claimants to prove the contract and non-delivery; for the defendants, if they relied upon the exemption clause (loss caused by perils of the sea), to prove that the facts fell within it; and for the claimants, if they relied upon the proviso to the exemption clause (negligence on the part of the defendants), to prove that the facts fell within that proviso.

By statute The incidence of the legal burden may be determined by statute. For example, under the Consumer Credit Act 1974, s. 140B(9), if a debtor or a surety alleges that the relationship between the creditor and the debtor is unfair to the debtor, within the meaning of s. 140A of that Act, it is for the creditor to prove the contrary. A further example is to be found in the Employment Rights Act 1996, s. 98: in a claim of unfair dismissal, it is for the former employee to prove that he or she was dismissed, but it is for the employer to show the reason for the dismissal and that it amounts to one of the five grounds set out and for which a dismissal is capable of being fair, failing which the dismissal is treated as automatically unfair. **49.39**

At common law As to the incidence of the legal burden at common law, the general guiding principle to be derived from the precedents is that 'he who asserts must prove, not he who denies' (*Joseph Constantine Steamship Line Ltd v Imperial Smelting Corporation Ltd* [1942] AC 154, per Lord Maugham at p. 174). For example, in *Wakelin v London and South Western Railway Co.* (1886) 12 App Cas 41, an action in negligence, brought by a widow under the Fatal Accidents Act 1846, in which the only evidence was that the husband had been found dead near a level crossing at the side of a railway line, it was held that the claim must fail: the widow bore the burden of proving that the death had been caused by the defendants' negligence, but the evidence adduced was as capable of indicating negligence on the part of the husband as on the part of the defendants (cf. *Jones v Great Western Railway Co.* (1930) 144 LT 194). The principle is most useful, as in *Wakelin v London and South Western Railway*, when the issues are straightforward. Thus in an action for negligence, the claimant bears the legal burden of proving duty of care, breach of the duty and consequential loss, and the defendant bears the burden of proving contributory negligence, *volenti non fit injuria*, or any other defence which goes beyond a bare denial of the claimant's allegations. Similarly, in an action for breach of contract, the claimant bears the legal burden of proving the contract, its breach and consequential loss, and the defendant bears the burden of proving any defence which goes beyond a bare denial of the claimant's allegations, e.g. discharge by agreement or frustration. **49.40**

The burden of proving a failure to mitigate rests on the defendant (*Geest plc v Lansiquot* [2002] UKPC 48, [2002] 1 WLR 3111, in which the Privy Council reviewed the authorities and agreed with both parties that the decision in *Selvanayagam v University of the West Indies* [1983] 1 WLR 585, that the burden lay on the claimant, cannot be relied upon).

In *BHP Billiton Petroleum Ltd v Dalmine SpA* [2003] EWCA Civ 170, [2003] BLR 271, it was held that in most cases the statements of case are likely to be a good guide to the incidence of the legal burden. The defendant manufactured and provided steel pipes used in the construction of a pipeline serving oil and gas fields in the Irish Sea. The pipeline failed after cracks developed in the welds which joined the pipes together. The defendant had fraudulently misrepresented that the pipes complied with the contractual specification, and the claimants, in reliance on this misrepresentation, had accepted and used the pipes which otherwise they would have rejected. On the question of causation, it was accepted by the claimants that they bore the burden of proving that the incorporation of non-compliant pipe caused the pipeline to fail and they succeeded in discharging this burden. However, the defendant in its defence averred

designed to produce one or more intermediate standards (per Richards LJ, giving the judgment of the court, in *R (N) v Mental Health Review Tribunal (Northern Region)* [2005] EWCA Civ 1605, [2006] QB 468 at [60]). However, the single civil standard is flexible. There is authority to support the view that, in the case of a serious allegation, the flexibility of the standard lies in an upward adjustment of the degree of probability required for the allegation to be proved (see, e.g. per Denning LJ in *Bater v Bater* [1951] P 35 at p. 37 and in *Hornal v Neuberger Products Ltd* [1957] 1 QB 247, considered at **49.42** and **49.43**). That approach, however, has now been repudiated.

Although there is a single civil *standard* of proof on the balance of probabilities, it is flexible in its *application*. In particular, the more serious the allegation or the more serious the consequences if the allegation is proved, the stronger must be the evidence before a court will find the allegation proved on the balance of probabilities. Thus the flexibility of the standard lies not in any adjustment to the degree of probability required for an allegation to be proved (such that a more serious allegation has to be proved to a higher degree of probability), but in the strength or quality of the evidence that will in practice be required for an allegation to be proved on the balance of probabilities. (*R (N) v Mental Health Review Tribunal (Northern Region)* at [62], approved by the House of Lords in *Re D* [2008] UKHL 33, [2008] 1 WLR 1499.)

Another formulation of the flexibility of the civil standard in the case of serious allegations is furnished by the following dictum of Morris LJ in *Hornal v Neuberger Products Ltd* [1957] 1 QB 247 at p. 266, approved and adopted by the House of Lords in *Khera v Secretary of State for the Home Department* [1984] AC 74 at pp. 113–14:

Though no court and no jury would give less careful attention to issues lacking gravity than to those marked by it, the very elements of gravity become a part of the whole range of circumstances which have to be weighed in the scale when deciding as to the balance of probabilities.

A further formulation of the flexibility of the civil standard relies upon the probability or otherwise of what is being alleged. In *Re Dellow's Will Trusts* [1964] 1 WLR 451, Ungoed-Thomas J said: 'The more serious the allegation the more cogent is the evidence required to overcome the unlikelihood of what is alleged and thus to prove it'. Similarly, in *Re H (Minors) (Sexual Abuse: Standard of Proof)* [1996] AC 563, concerning the standard of proof in care proceedings, it was held that where a serious allegation is made, the inherent probability or improbability of an event is itself a matter to be taken into account when weighing the possibilities and deciding whether, on balance, the event occurred (per Lord Nicholls of Birkenhead at p. 586). This approach was followed in *Secretary of State for the Home Department v Rehman* [2001] UKHL 74, [2003] 1 AC 153, where Lord Hoffmann said, at [55]:

It would need more cogent evidence to satisfy one that the creature seen walking in Regent's Park was more likely than not to have been a lioness than to be satisfied to the same standard of probability that it was an Alsatian.

However, it does not follow from the foregoing that serious allegations *necessarily* call for more cogent evidence. In *Re D* [2008] UKHL 33, [2008] 1 WLR 1499, Lord Carswell, in a judgment with which the other members of the House of Lords were in agreement, said, at [28]:

The seriousness of the allegation requires no elaboration: a tribunal of fact will look closely into the facts grounding an allegation of fraud before accepting that it has been established. The seriousness of consequences is another facet of the same proposition: if it is alleged that a bank manager has committed a minor peculation, that could entail very serious consequences for his career, so making it the less likely that he would risk doing such a thing. These are all matters of ordinary experience, requiring the application of good sense on the part of those who have to decide such issues. They do not require a different standard of proof or a specially cogent standard of evidence, merely appropriately careful consideration by the tribunal before it is satisfied of the matter which has to be established.

In that case, on the issue whether a prisoner released on licence was the person who had committed serious sexual offences against his nieces, it was held to be sufficient that the tribunal deciding the issue had given the necessary critical attention to the evidence adduced in support of such serious charges.

In *Re B (Children) (Care Proceedings: Standard of Proof)* [2008] UKHL 35, [2009] 1 AC 11, the House of Lords went even further. On the question of the standard of proof, in care proceedings, in relation to facts on which the court can conclude that a child is suffering, or is likely to suffer, significant harm, it was held that there is no room for the nostrum 'the more serious the allegation, the more cogent the evidence needed to prove it'. Baroness Hale, in a speech with which the other members of the House agreed, said, at [70]–[72]:

Neither the seriousness of the allegation nor the seriousness of the consequences should make any difference to the standard of proof to be applied in determining the facts. The inherent probabilities are simply something to be taken in account, where relevant, in deciding where the truth lies.

As to the seriousness of the consequences, they are serious either way. A child may find her relationship with her family seriously disrupted; or she may find herself still at risk of suffering serious harm. A parent may find his relationship with his child seriously disrupted: or he may find himself still at liberty to maltreat this or other children in the future.

As to the seriousness of the allegation, there is no logical or necessary connection between seriousness and probability. Some seriously harmful behaviour, such as murder, is sufficiently rare to be inherently improbable in most circumstances. Even then there are circumstances, such as a body with its throat cut and no weapon to hand, where it is not at all improbable. Other seriously harmful behaviour, such as alcohol or drug abuse, is regrettably all too common and not at all improbable. Nor are serious allegations made in a vacuum. Consider the famous example of the animal seen in Regent's Park. If it is seen outside the zoo on a stretch of greensward regularly used for walking dogs, then of course it is more likely to be a dog than a lion. If it is seen in the zoo next to the lions' enclosure when the door is open, then it may well be more likely to be a lion than a dog.

The reasoning in the final paragraph of this passage appears to be of general application, rather than confined to care proceedings, which suggests that there may be no room for the nostrum in question in the types of civil proceedings discussed in **49.42** to **49.44** or indeed in any civil proceedings of any kind. However, it has since been held, albeit at first instance, that in the case of deceit, the court does not readily find that dishonest conduct is established and requires more convincing evidence to establish it than to establish negligence or other kinds of civil liability, because the law considers it less likely that people behave dishonestly (*Maple Leaf Macro Volatility Master Fund v Rouvroy* [2009] EWHC 257 (Comm), [2009] 2 All ER (Comm) 287 at [327], relying on *Hornal v Neuberger Products Ltd* [1957] 1 QB 247 at p. 258, considered at **49.42**).

Allegations of crime or fraud

In *Hornal v Neuberger Products Ltd* [1957] 1 QB 247 the claimant claimed damages for breach of warranty or alternatively for fraud. The company had sold a lathe to the claimant. The issue was whether, as the claimant alleged, one of the directors of the defendant company had represented that the lathe had been reconditioned. If such a representation was made, there had been a fraudulent misrepresentation, because the director knew that the lathe had not been reconditioned. The trial judge was satisfied on a balance of probabilities, but not beyond reasonable doubt, that the representation was made and awarded damages for fraud, but dismissed the claim for damages for breach of warranty on the basis that the parties did not intend the representation to have contractual effect. On appeal, the Court of Appeal held that on an allegation of crime in civil proceedings, the standard was not the criminal standard, but the ordinary, and flexible, civil standard of proof, on a balance of probabilities. Although Denning LJ was of the view that the court requires a degree of probability proportionate to the allegation, that view has now been repudiated in favour of the approach of Morris LJ, that the very elements of gravity have to be weighed in the scale when deciding as to the balance of probabilities (see **49.41**).

49.42

Hornal v Neuberger Products Ltd was applied in *Re Dellow's Will Trusts* [1964] 1 WLR 451, where the issue was whether a woman had feloniously killed her husband, and also in *Post Office v Estuary Radio Ltd* [1967] 1 WLR 1396, which involved an allegation of a criminal offence under the

Wireless Telegraphy Act 1949. See also *Piermay Shipping Co. SA v Chester* [1979] 1 Lloyd's Rep 55 (an allegation of deliberately scuttling a ship), *Brazier v Bramwell Scaffolding (Dunedin) Ltd* [2001] UKPC 59, LTL 20/12/2001 (an allegation of conduct akin to fraud) and *Parks v Clout* [2003] EWCA Civ 1030, LTL 10/6/2003 (an allegation of obtaining letters of administration by fraud). Extreme and extraordinary allegations, such as asserting a conspiracy to pervert the course of justice, involving attempts to murder the appellant and fraud, will not be taken seriously without cogent supporting evidence (*R (Sivasubramaniam) v Wandsworth County Court* [2002] EWCA Civ 1738, [2003] 1 WLR 475).

Grounds of divorce

49.43   Prior to the Divorce Reform Act 1969, the old grounds for divorce were largely based on the concept of the matrimonial offence. For reasons of this kind, and because of the importance of divorce proceedings to both the parties and the state, the earlier authorities required the application of the criminal standard: see, in the case of allegations of cruelty, *Bater v Bater* [1951] P 35; in the case of allegations of adultery, *Ginesi v Ginesi* [1948] P 179, and also *Preston-Jones v Preston-Jones* [1951] AC 391 and *F v F* [1968] P 506, in both of which the finding of adultery would have rendered a child illegitimate; and see generally *Blyth v Blyth* [1966] AC 643. However, in *Bastable v Bastable* [1968] 1 WLR 1684, where adultery was in issue, Wilmer LJ and Winn LJ adopted as appropriate the dicta of Denning LJ in *Bater v Bater*, approved by the Court of Appeal in *Hornal v Neuberger Products Ltd* [1957] 1 QB 247, to the effect that the civil standard applies, but the court requires a degree of probability proportionate to the subject matter. Bearing in mind the present philosophy of divorce law, and the rejection of the view that in the case of serious allegations the degree of probability can be adjusted upwards, it is submitted that in all matrimonial causes the correct approach should be to consider the gravity of the allegation as part of the whole range of circumstances to be weighed in the scale when deciding on the balance of probabilities (see **49.41**).

Other cases

49.44   Other issues calling for flexibility in the application of the civil standard are set out below. In so far as some of the cases, on some of these issues, require, or seem to require, a standard at least as high as the criminal standard, it is submitted that they are unlikely to be followed, especially now that it is clear that the ordinary, flexible civil standard of proof is appropriate to allegations of crime in civil cases (see **49.42**).

(a) *Change of domicile*. A party seeking to prove an intention to change domicile must do so 'clearly and unequivocally' (*Moorhouse v Lord* (1863) 10 HL Cas 272 at p. 236; see also *Re Fuld (No. 3)* [1968] P 675 at p. 685).

(b) *Rebutting the presumption of the formal validity of a marriage*. The evidence in rebuttal of this strong common law presumption is required to be 'strong, distinct and satisfactory' (*Piers v Piers* (1849) 2 HL Cas 331 at p. 389) or 'evidence which satisfied beyond reasonable doubt that there was no valid marriage' (*Mahadervan v Mahadervan* [1964] P 233 at p. 246).

(c) *Rectification*. A party claiming rectification must prove his case by 'strong irrefragable evidence' (*Countess of Shelburne v Earl of Inchiquin* (1784) 1 Bro CC 338 at p. 341; and see also *Earl v Hector Whaling Ltd* [1961] 1 Lloyd's Rep 459).

(d) *Paternity*. The standard of proof required to make a finding of paternity is a heavy one, commensurate with the gravity of the issue, and although not the criminal standard, is more than the ordinary civil standard (*W v K* [1988] 1 FLR 86; and see also *Serio v Serio* (1983) 4 FLR 756).

(e) *Medical treatment for the mentally ill*. In order for a court to approve proposed medical treatment for an incompetent mentally ill patient without infringing the European Convention on Human Rights, **art. 3**, in the **Human Rights Act 1998, sch. 1**, it must be 'convincingly shown' that the treatment is medically necessary. This standard of proof may be met notwithstanding the existence of a responsible body of opinion against the proposed treatment (*R (N) v Dr M* [2002] EWCA Civ 1789, [2003] 1 WLR 562).

(f) *Continuing detention of mentally ill patients.* Cogent evidence will in practice be required in order to satisfy a tribunal, on the balance of probabilities, that the conditions for continuing detention under the Mental Health Act 1983, ss. 72 and 73, have been met (*R (N) v Mental Health Review Tribunal (Northern Region)* [2005] EWCA Civ 1605, [2006] QB 468).

WITNESSES: COMPETENCE, COMPELLABILITY, OATHS AND PROCEDURE

Competence and compellability — the general rule

The general rule may be put in the form of two propositions: **49.45**

(a) any person is competent in any proceedings; and

(b) all competent witnesses are compellable.

The only remaining exceptions to these two propositions relate to children, persons with a disorder or disability of the mind, the Sovereign, heads of other sovereign states, diplomats and, in prescribed circumstances, bankers. Many former categories of exception to the first proposition — non-Christians and atheists, those with criminal convictions or a pecuniary and proprietary interest in the outcome of the proceedings, and the parties to civil proceedings and their spouses — have been removed, over the centuries, mostly by statutory reform. Concerning the parties to the proceedings, the consequence is that any party to civil proceedings may give evidence and may compel any other party to those proceedings to give evidence. As to the spouses of the parties to proceedings, in *Monroe v Twistleton* (1802) Peake Add Cas 219 (followed in *O'Connor v Marjoribanks* (1842) 4 Man & G 435) it was held that a former spouse is incompetent following the termination of his or her marriage in so far as his or her evidence relates to events which occurred during the marriage. Reversal of this decision is plainly long overdue, although it is arguable that it can be ignored on the basis that the words 'husbands' and 'wives' in the Evidence Amendment Act 1853, by which the spouses of parties were rendered competent and compellable, can be taken to cover former husbands and wives (but cf. *Shenton v Tyler* [1939] Ch 620).

Children

The Children Act 1989, s. 96, provides as follows: **49.46**

(1) Subsection (2) applies where a child who is called as a witness in any civil proceedings does not, in the opinion of the court, understand the nature of an oath.

(2) The child's evidence may be heard by the court if, in its opinion —

   (a) he understands that it is his duty to speak the truth; and

   (b) he has sufficient understanding to justify his evidence being heard.

A child is a person under the age of 18 (s. 105). In deciding whether a child understands the nature of an oath, the courts are likely to be guided by the authorities which governed both civil and criminal cases before the law was changed, in criminal cases, by the Criminal Justice Act 1991, s. 52. Thus, in order to form an opinion on the issue, the judge will put preliminary questions to the child (see *R v Surgenor* (1940) 27 Cr App R 175), although whether the child warrants such an examination is a matter of judicial discretion. There is no fixed age at which a child should be treated as competent and below which he or she should be examined, but as a general working rule inquiry should be made of a child under the age of 14, although much depends on the type of child in question (*R v Khan* (1981) 73 Cr App R 190; and cf. *Bains v Director of Public Prosecutions* [1992] Crim LR 795). The watershed dividing children who are normally considered old enough to take the oath and those normally considered too young to do so probably falls between the ages of eight and 10 (see *R v Hayes* [1977] 1 WLR 234). The former practice was for judges to ask questions designed to discover whether the child was aware of the divine sanction of the oath, but in *R v Hayes* this practice was abandoned in favour of a secular approach. In that case, the Court of Appeal held that the important consideration is, 'whether the child has a sufficient appreciation of the solemnity of the occasion and the added responsibility to tell the truth, which is involved in taking an oath, over and above the duty to tell the truth which is an ordinary duty of social conduct'. If the child fails this secular test, then his or her evidence may be given unsworn if, in the opinion of the court, the conditions set out in the Children Act 1989, s. 96(2)(a) and (b), are met. It is submitted that 'the duty to speak the truth' to which s. 96(2)(a) refers, means the duty to tell the truth which is an ordinary duty of normal social conduct.

There is no presumption that a child should not give evidence in care proceedings. The court must weigh the possibility that the evidence will enable a better determination of the truth against the damage that may be done to the welfare of the child or any other child (*Re W (Children) (Family Proceedings: Evidence)* [2010] UKSC 12, [2010] 1 WLR 701).

Persons with a disorder or disability of the mind

49.47   In *R v Hill* (1851) 2 Den 254 it was established that if, in the opinion of the judge, a proposed witness, by reason of impaired intellect, does not understand the nature and sanction of an oath, he or she is incompetent to testify; and that a person of impaired intellect who does understand the oath may testify, in which case it will be for the tribunal of fact to attach such weight to his or her testimony as it sees fit, disregarding it altogether if it is so tainted with insanity as to be unworthy of credit. These propositions remain the law, except in one respect. The test to be applied should be the secular one adopted in *R v Hayes* [1977] 1 WLR 234 (see **49.46**): whether the proposed witness has a sufficient appreciation of the seriousness of the occasion and a realisation that taking the oath involves something more than the duty to tell the truth in ordinary day-to-day life (see *R v Bellamy* (1985) 82 Cr App R 222). The evidence of a witness with some history of mental illness should not be treated with caution in the absence of any medical foundation for regarding it as unreliable (*Milton v The Queen* [2015] UKPC 42, [2015] 1 WLR 5356).

The Sovereign, heads of State and diplomats

49.48   The Sovereign and heads of foreign sovereign States are competent but not compellable. Diplomats, consular officials, and various officers of prescribed international organisations also enjoy varying degrees of immunity from compellability (see the Diplomatic Privileges Act 1964, the Consular Relations Act 1968, the International Organisations Act 1968, the Diplomatic and other Privileges Act 1971, and the State Immunity Act 1978).

Bankers

49.49   The Bankers' Books Evidence Act 1879 provides for the admissibility of copies of entries in bankers' books as evidence of their contents (see **49.80**). Section 6 of the Act provides as follows:

A banker or officer of a bank shall not, in any legal proceeding to which the bank is not a party, be compellable to produce any banker's book the contents of which can be proved under this Act..., or to appear as a witness to prove the matters, transactions, and accounts therein recorded, unless by order of a judge made for special cause.

Oaths and affirmations

49.50   The general rule is that all witnesses must give sworn evidence, i.e. after having taken an oath or having made an affirmation. A judgment founded on unsworn evidence may be set aside as a nullity (*R v Marsham, ex parte Pethick Lawrence* [1912] 2 KB 362). In civil proceedings there are the following four exceptions to the general rule.

(a) In claims which have been allocated to the small claims track, the court need not take evidence on oath (**CPR, r. 27.8(4)**).

(b) Children under the age of 18 may be permitted to give their evidence unsworn (see **49.46**).

(c) A witness called only to produce a document may give unsworn evidence if the identity of the document is either not in dispute or is to be established by another witness (*Perry v Gibson* (1834) 1 Ad & El 48).

(d) Counsel may give unsworn evidence of the terms of a compromise reached by the parties (*Hickman v Berens* [1895] 2 Ch 638).

The form and manner of the administration of the oath in the case of Christians and Jews is governed by the Oaths Act 1978, s. 1(1). The officer administering the oath shall administer it in this form and manner without question unless the witness objects thereto, or is physically incapable of so taking the oath (s. 1(2)). For those of other religious belief, the oath shall be administered 'in any lawful manner' (s. 1(3)), upon such holy book as is appropriate. Whether an oath is administered in a lawful manner for these purposes depends on whether the oath appears to the court to be binding on the conscience of the witness and is one which the witness considers to be binding on his or her conscience, rather than on the intricacies of the witness's particular religion. Thus in *R v Kemble* [1990] 1 WLR 1111, an oath taken by a Muslim on the New Testament was held to have been administered in a lawful manner notwithstanding that under the strict tenets of Islam, an oath taken by a Muslim is only valid if taken on a copy of the Koran in Arabic. If the ground is properly laid for an expectation that a witness will take the oath on a particular holy book, but the witness affirms, the judge has a discretion to allow the reason why the witness did not take the oath on the holy book to be explored sensitively (*R v Mehrban* [2001] EWCA Crim 2627, [2002] 1 Cr App R 561). However, where a Muslim has affirmed, rather than having sworn on the Koran, cross-examining counsel should not be allowed to ask the witness whether he thinks that he is bound to tell the truth, except where there is good reason for such questioning and it has been approved by the judge (*R v Majid* [2009] EWCA Crim 2563, LTL 12/10/2009). Section 3 of the 1978 Act permits a person to be sworn with uplifted hand, in the form and manner in which an oath is usually administered in Scotland. Where an oath has been duly administered and taken, the fact that the person to whom it was administered had, at the time of taking it, no religious belief, shall not for any purpose affect its validity (s. 4(2)).

Any person who objects to being sworn shall be permitted to make his or her solemn affirmation instead (s. 5(1)), which shall be of the same force and effect as an oath (s. 5(4)). Where it is not reasonably practicable without inconvenience or delay to administer an oath in the manner appropriate to a person's religious belief, then he or she may be permitted, or required, to make his or her solemn affirmation instead (s. 5(2) and (3)).

Oral evidence, evidence by video link or other means and anonymous witnesses

Under **CPR, r. 32.2**, the general rule is that any fact which needs to be proved by the evidence of witnesses is to be proved:

(a) at trial, by their oral evidence given in public; and

(b) at any other hearing, by their evidence in writing.

As to the giving of evidence 'in public', a court has no common law power to extend the use of the closed material procedure beyond the use thus far sanctioned by Parliament. Under the closed material procedure a party is excluded from the closed part of the trial and therefore does not see the witnesses or see or read the closed documents, the submissions or the judgment. These flaws cannot be cured by a special advocate, who would be hampered by not being able to take instructions from his or her client. However, in some circumstances, a closed material procedure is necessary in order to achieve real justice and a fair trial, for example, in cases involving children, and in intellectual property proceedings where disclosure of confidential

49.51

material beyond 'confidentiality rings' would defeat the object of the proceedings brought to protect a commercial interest. Subject to these exceptions, the court should not sanction departure from the fundamental principles of open justice and natural justice. (*Al-Rawi v Security Service* [2011] UKSC 34, [2012] 1 AC 531). There is no additional exception in respect of extradition proceedings (*R (B) v Westminster Magistrates' Court* [2014] UKSC 59, [2015] AC 1195).

Under **r. 32.2(2)**, the general rule is subject:

(a) to any provision to the contrary contained in the CPR or elsewhere; or
(b) to any order of the court.

An example of the former is to be found in **r. 32.3**, which provides that the court may allow a witness to give evidence through a video link 'or by other means', e.g. by means of a telephone. No defined limit or set of circumstances should be placed upon this discretionary power, which is not restricted to cases in which the witness is seriously ill or cases of pressing need (*Rowland v Bock* [2002] 4 All ER 370). Lord Nicholls of Birkenhead in *Polanski v Condé Nast Publications Ltd* [2005] UKHL 10, [2005] 1 WLR 637, said that videoconferencing orders are readily available to all litigants in civil proceedings. This decision is discussed further at **58.11**. See also **PD 32, annex 3** and *Black v Pastouna* [2005] EWCA Civ 1389, *The Independent*, 2 December 2005, where Brooke LJ held that it is incumbent on those advising parties appearing before any court to take all the steps they can in accordance with **CPR, rr. 1.1** and **1.3**, to reduce the cost of the proceedings, including taking advantage of videoconferencing facilities whenever they are available and it is appropriate to use them. As to the use at trial of witness statements, see **chapter 51**. As to the power to direct that certain facts may not be proved by the oral evidence of proposed witnesses, see further at **49.52**, and generally at **49.8**.

The European Court of Human Rights has accepted, in the criminal context, that the Convention rights of witnesses include, where necessary, the preservation of their anonymity and has decided that such anonymity is not inconsistent with the right to a fair trial, provided that the need for anonymity is clearly established and, the ultimate test, the trial is fair. The jurisprudence of the European Court does not establish that a trial will inevitably be considered unfair simply because the evidence of an anonymous witness may be decisive to the outcome. However, a court should examine an application for anonymity with scrupulous care to ensure that it is necessary and that the witness is in genuine and justified fear of serious consequences if his true identify becomes known (*R v Davis* [2006] EWCA Crim 1155, [2006] 1 WLR 3130).

Directions in relation to witnesses

49.52   Before the CPR came into effect, the choice of witnesses to support a party's case, and the order in which they were to be called, were matters entirely for that party (*Briscoe v Briscoe* [1966] P 501). The judge had no right to call witnesses against the will of the parties (*Re Enoch and Zaretzky, Bock and Co.'s Arbitration* [1910] 1 KB 327), except in cases of civil contempt (*Yianni v Yianni* [1966] 1 WLR 120). Under **CPR, r. 32.1(1)**, the court may now control the evidence by giving directions as to not only the issues on which it requires evidence, but also as to the nature of the evidence which it requires to decide those issues and the way in which the evidence is to be placed before the court. Furthermore, under **r. 32.1(2)**, the court may use its power under the rule to exclude evidence that would otherwise be admissible. In exercising these powers, the judge must seek to give effect to the 'overriding objective'. **Rule 32.1(1)** does not empower the court to order a party to call a witness (*Society of Lloyd's v Jaffray* (2000) *The Times*, 3 August 2000). However, it is submitted that in appropriate circumstances a judge may take the view that in furtherance of the 'overriding objective' directions should be given under **r. 32.1(1)** as to the order in which witnesses should give their evidence, and as to which potential witnesses should not be called, on the basis either that the issue to which their evidence relates only requires evidence in written form or that their evidence, although admissible in law, should be excluded in the exercise of the judge's discretion. The judge also has the power to recall a witness called by a party (*Fallon v Calvert* [1960] 2 QB 201).

Judicial interventions

Interventions by a judge during the course of oral evidence inevitably carry the risk of depriv-   **49.53**
ing the judge of the advantage of calm and dispassionate observation. The greater the frequency of the interventions, the greater the risk, and where the interventions take the form of
lengthy interrogation of the witnesses, the risk becomes a serious one. The risk does not
depend on appearances or on what an objective observer of the process may think, but is that
the judge may so hamper his ability properly to evaluate and weigh the evidence as to impair
his judgement and, for that reason, render the trial unfair (*Southwark London Borough Council v
Kofi-Adu* [2006] EWCA Civ 281, [2006] HLR 33).

Time at which evidence should be adduced

As a general rule of practice, rather than law, a party should adduce all the evidence on   **49.54**
which he intends to rely before the close of his case. The authorities in this regard, which
are almost all criminal cases, indicate that there are two common law exceptions to the
general rule and a 'wider discretion' to be exercised outside the two exceptions only very
rarely. Under the first exception, evidence is allowed in rebuttal of matters arising *ex impro-
viso*, which no ingenuity could have foreseen (*R v Frost* (1839) 4 St Tr NS 85). Under this exception, it is for the judge, in the exercise of his or her discretion, to decide whether the
relevance of the evidence could reasonably have been anticipated (*R v Scott* (1984) 79 Cr App
R 49; *R v Day* (1940) 27 Cr App R 168). A party may rely on the exception where the evidence
in question was not at the outset clearly relevant, but only marginally, minimally or doubt-
fully relevant (*R v Levy* (1966) 50 Cr App R 198), or constituted fanciful and unreal statements,
e.g. allegations which were obviously ridiculous and untrue (*R v Hutchinson* (1985) 82 Cr App
R 51). Under the second exception, the judge has a discretion to admit evidence which has
not been adduced by reason of inadvertence or oversight. The evidence is usually of a formal
or uncontentious nature (see *v Waller* [1910] 1 KB 364; *Price v Humphries* [1958] 2 QB 353; and
Palastanga v Solman [1962] Crim LR 334), but sometimes relates to a matter of substance (see
Piggott v Sims [1973] RTR 15 and *Middleton v Rowlett* [1954] 1 WLR 831). It has been held that
the judge's discretion to admit evidence after the close of a party's case is not confined to the
two well-established exceptions, but the wider discretion should be exercised only on the
rarest of occasions (*R v Francis* [1991] 1 WLR 1264), as when an important witness arrives late
for reasons beyond his or her control (see, e.g. *James v South Glamorgan County Council* (1994)
99 Cr App R 321).

Although the exceptions to the general rule of practice are well established, more recent
authorities permit the court to take a generalised discretionary approach to admissibility, having regard to whether the defendant will be unfairly prejudiced (as when the defence would
have been conducted differently had the evidence in question been adduced at an earlier
stage). In *Jolly v Director of Public Prosecutions* [2000] Crim LR 471, applied in *Cook v Director of Public
Prosecutions* [2001] Crim LR 321, it was said to be 'beyond argument' that there is a general discretion to permit the prosecution to call evidence after closing its case. Before exercising the
discretion, the court would look carefully at the interests of justice overall and, in particular,
the risk of any prejudice whatsoever to the defence. The result is that the discretion would be
sparingly exercised, but it is doubtful whether it assists a court to speak in terms of 'exceptional circumstances'. Each case must be considered on its own facts. In civil cases, where
obviously regard must be had to the overriding objective, a broadly similar approach has been
adopted. In *Stocznia Gdanska SA v Latvian Shipping Co.* (2000) LTL 12/2/2001 the claimants, after the
close of the trial but before judgment had been handed down, sought to adduce further relevant evidence, namely, a document which ought to have been disclosed by one of the defendants and which the claimants could not have obtained by other means. It was held that the
claimants could rely on the document and that, in accordance with the overriding objective,
it would not be just to ignore it.

REFRESHING THE MEMORY

Refreshing memory in court

49.55   A witness who, in examination-in-chief, experiences difficulty in recollecting the events to which his or her evidence relates, may refer to a document such as a diary, log or other written statement, or, it seems, to a tape recording (see *R v Bailey* (2001) LTL 19/3/2001), in order to refresh his or her memory, provided that:

(a) it was made or verified by the witness at the time of the events to which it relates, or so shortly afterwards that the facts were still fresh in the witness's memory;

(b) it is produced for inspection by the court and opposite party; and

(c) it is, in prescribed cases, the original.

The principle operates not only where the witness does in fact refresh his or her memory, but also where the witness has no recollection of the events in question, but simply gives evidence as to the accuracy of the contents of the document. In both cases, however, it is the testimony of the witness, and not the document, which constitutes the evidence in the case. In *Maugham v Hubbard* (1828) 8 B & C 14 a witness called to prove that he had received a sum of money, looked at an unstamped acknowledgment that he had signed, and then gave evidence that he had no doubt that he had received the money, but had no recollection of having done so. It was held that his oral evidence sufficed to establish receipt of the money, the acknowledgment being incapable of being received in evidence because it was unstamped. In these circumstances, it is submitted that rather than preserve a fiction, it would be better to concede that the court is, in effect, admitting the written statement for the truth of its contents by way of exception to the hearsay rule. In fact the statement itself is admissible, with the permission of the court, as evidence of the truth of its contents, under the Civil Evidence Act 1995, s. 6(2) (a) (see **53.7**). Indeed, under the modern law, the scope for refreshing memory in court has been much reduced by reason of the existence of s. 6(2)(a) and the fact that in most cases it will be a witness's witness statement that stands as his or her evidence-in-chief (see **chapter 51**).

49.56   **Conditions**   The document 'must have been written either at the time of the transaction or so shortly afterwards that the facts were fresh in [the witness's] memory' (*Phipson on Evidence*, 11th edn., 1970, at p. 634, para. 1528), a definition which provides a measure of elasticity and should not be taken to confine witnesses to an over-short period (*R v Richardson* [1971] 2 QB 484). The question is obviously one of fact and degree, and for this reason the precedents are of limited, if any, value. The entry in the document may have been made or verified by the witness. As to the former, the document may be used even if based on earlier notes or jottings, provided that when written up, the facts were still fresh in the memory (*Attorney General's Reference (No. 3 of 1979)* (1979) 69 Cr App R 411). The witness may also refresh his or her memory from a copy of the original document, where the original has been destroyed, provided that the court is satisfied that the copy is accurate or substantially reproduces the original (*Topham v McGregor* (1844) 1 Car & K 320). See also *R v Mills* [1962] 1 WLR 1152 (notes written up by a witness with the assistance of a tape recording made by him but which was not itself admitted in evidence). The document may have been prepared by another, provided that the witness has verified it while the events were still fresh in his or her memory (*Burroughs v Martin* (1809) 2 Camp 112). Thus in *Anderson v Whalley* (1852) 3 Car & K 54, entries in a ship's log made by the mate and verified by the captain about a week later could be used by the latter to refresh his memory. A witness may also make use of a note dictated to another and then verified, whether by reading it personally or listening to it being read out, provided, in the latter case, that the other is called to prove that the note used in court is the note that was dictated and read back (*R v Kelsey* (1981) 74 Cr App R 213). In all cases, the document must be produced for inspection by the opposite party, who may wish to cross-examine the witness on its contents (*Beech v Jones* (1848) 5 CB 696). In cases, like *Maugham v Hubbard* (1828) 8 B & C 14, in which the witness has no recollection of the events in question but gives evidence as to the accuracy of what is recorded in the document, the original document must be produced (*Doe d Church and Phillips v Perkins* (1790) 3 TR 749), but where the original has been lost or destroyed, a verified or accurate copy will suffice (*Topham v McGregor* (1844) 1 Car & K 320).

Cross-examination on the document   Cross-examining counsel may inspect the document **49.57** without thereby making it evidence in the case. Counsel may also cross-examine on it without thereby making it evidence, but only if the cross-examination does not go beyond the parts used by the witness to refresh his or her memory. Cross-examination on other parts of the document entitles the party calling the witness to put the document in evidence and to let the tribunal of fact see the document on which the cross-examination has been based (*Gregory v Tavernor* (1833) 6 Car & P 280; *Senat v Senat* [1965] P 172 at p. 177). The document will then be admissible as evidence of the truth of its contents. The Civil Evidence Act 1995, s. 6, provides as follows:

(4) Nothing in this Act affects any of the rules of law as to the circumstances in which, where a person called as a witness in civil proceedings is cross-examined on a document used by him to refresh his memory, that document may be made evidence in the proceedings.

(5) Nothing in this section shall be construed as preventing a statement of any description referred to above from being admissible by virtue of section 1 as evidence of the matters stated.

It seems reasonably clear that the intention underlying these two subsections, when taken together, was to perpetuate the rule formerly stated with clarity in the Civil Evidence Act 1968, s. 3(2), that where a memory-refreshing document is made evidence in the proceedings, any statement made in the document will be admissible as evidence of the matters stated. It is submitted that the subsections should be construed in this way notwithstanding that whereas subsection (5) refers to 'a statement of any description referred to above', subsection (4) refers not to 'a statement', but to 'a document'.

Refreshing memory out of court

It is a common practice for a witness, before giving testimony, to refresh his or her memory **49.58** from statements or notes made by him or her at a time closer to the events in question, whether a private note or record, a proof of evidence, or a witness statement as such. Any rule to the contrary would be unenforceable, would make testimony more a test of memory than truthfulness, and would tend to create difficulties for honest witnesses, but be likely to do little to hamper dishonest witnesses (*R v Richardson* [1971] 2 QB 484). The conditions which apply in the case of a witness refreshing his memory while giving evidence do not apply to the witness who refreshes his or her memory outside the witness box (*R v Richardson*). However, as in the case of refreshing memory while giving evidence, cross-examining counsel is entitled to call for, inspect and cross-examine on a document which a witness has used to refresh his or her memory outside court but has not used while giving evidence, and if counsel cross-examines on material which has not been referred to by the witness, the party calling the witness may put the document in evidence, rendering it admissible as evidence of the matters it states (see *Owen v Edwards* (1983) 77 Cr App R 191 at p. 195, and the Civil Evidence Act 1995, s. 6(4) and (5), considered at **49.57**).

It is open to the judge, in the exercise of his or her discretion and in the interests of justice, to permit a witness who has begun to give his or her evidence, to withdraw and refresh his or her memory from a statement made by him or her closer to the time of the events in question, even if not made at the time of the events or so soon thereafter that the facts were fresh in the memory, if the following conditions are met:

(a) the witness says that he or she cannot now recall the details of the events because of the lapse of time;

(b) the witness made a statement much nearer the time of the event, the contents of which represented his or her recollection at that time;

(c) the witness did not read the statement before giving evidence; and

(d) the witness wishes to read the statement before continuing to give evidence.

The witness may withdraw from the witness box to read the statement, in which case there must be no communication with the witness, or the statement may be read by the witness in the witness box, but either way, the statement must be removed from the witness when he or she continues to give evidence, and the witness should not be permitted to refer to it again (see *R v Da Silva* [1990] 1 WLR 31). An alternative solution to the problem, in appropriate circumstances, would be for the party calling the witness to seek leave to admit the previous statement for the truth of its contents under the Civil Evidence Act 1995, s. 6(2)(a) (see further at **53.7**).

R v Da Silva has not created a rule of law that a witness, once in the witness box, can refer to a statement only if all four of the conditions specified in that case are met, because the court has a discretion whether to allow a witness to refresh his or her memory from a non-contemporaneous statement: see *R v South Ribble Magistrates, ex parte Cochrane* [1996] 2 Cr App R 544, where a witness who had read his statement before giving evidence, but had not taken it in properly, was allowed to refresh his memory. See also *R v Gordon* [2002] EWCA Crim 1, LTL 7/2/2002, where a witness, who was unable, because of dyslexia, to read his statement, adopted it after it was read out by counsel. It was held that there are no fixed and immutable rules to be followed before a witness can refresh memory by a document prepared when his or her memory was clearer, but there is a broad fact-sensitive judicial discretion to be exercised in the interests of fairness and justice.

PREVIOUS CONSISTENT STATEMENTS

The rule

49.59   At common law, as a general rule a previous consistent or self-serving statement of a witness is excluded as evidence of his or her consistency. Thus, a witness may not be asked in examination-in-chief about former oral or written statements made by him or her and consistent with the testimony which he or she is giving, and evidence about those statements should not be elicited from any other witness. The rule is usually justified on the basis that without it, a witness could manufacture evidence with ease (see, e.g. *R v Roberts* [1942] 1 All ER 187 at p. 191). In *Corke v Corke* [1958] P 93 a husband petitioned for divorce on the ground of adultery. One night he had accused his wife of having recently committed adultery with a lodger. The Court of Appeal held that the wife, who denied adultery, had been improperly permitted to give evidence that shortly after the husband's accusation, she had telephoned her doctor and asked him to examine herself and the lodger with a view to showing that there had been no recent sexual intercourse.

Exceptions

49.60   In civil proceedings, there are only three exceptions to the rule, under each of which the previous statement is admitted not only as evidence of consistency, but also as evidence of the facts it contains. They are:

(a) previous statements admissible, with the permission of the court, under the Civil Evidence Act 1995, s. 6(2);

(b) statements in documents used by a witness to refresh his or her memory, in cases in which cross-examination on the document has gone beyond the parts of it relied on by the witness, so that the document has become evidence in the case; and

(c) statements in rebuttal of allegations of recent fabrication.

The first two of these exceptions are considered at **53.7** and **49.57** respectively.

There is no general further exception to the effect that a witness who has been cross-examined to show inconsistencies, can be re-examined to show consistency by reference to a previous statement (*R v Beattie* (1989) 89 Cr App R 302 at p. 307). However, the court does have a residual discretion to permit such re-examination to ensure that the tribunal of fact is not positively misled by the cross-examination as to the existence of some fact or the terms of an earlier statement (*R v Ali* [2003] EWCA Crim 3214, [2004] 1 Cr App R 501).

Statements admissible to rebut allegations of recent fabrication

A previous consistent statement will not be admissible to bolster the credibility of a witness simply because his or her evidence was impeached in cross-examination, even if the impeachment took the form of showing a contradiction or inconsistency between his or her evidence and something he or she said on a previous occasion (see *R v Coll* (1889) 25 LR Ir 522 at p. 541 and *R v Beattie* (1989) 89 Cr App R 302 at pp. 306–7, and contrast, but question, *Ahmed v Brumfitt* (1967) 112 SJ 32). However, if in cross-examination it is suggested that a witness's version of events is a recent fabrication, evidence of his or her previous statements to the same effect will become admissible, and will normally be elicited in re-examination (*R v Oyesiku* (1971) 56 Cr App R 240; and see also *Flanagan v Fahy* [1918] 2 IR 361 and *Fox v General Medical Council* [1960] 1 WLR 1017). In *R v Oyesiku* the Court of Appeal adopted as a correct statement of the law the judgment of Dixon CJ in *Nominal Defendant v Clement* (1961) 104 CLR 476 (High Court of Australia), from which the following propositions derive:

49.61

(a) The exception requires a suggestion in cross-examination that the witness's account has been recently invented or reconstructed, even though not with conscious dishonesty.

(b) The previous statement is admissible if it was made contemporaneously with the event or at a time sufficiently early to be inconsistent with the suggestion of recent fabrication.

(c) The judge should exercise care to assure himself or herself that:

   (i) the account given is attacked on the ground of recent invention or reconstruction or a foundation for such an attack has been laid;

   (ii) the contents of the previous statement are to like effect as the account given in evidence; and

   (iii) the previous statement, having regard to the time and circumstances in which it was made, rationally tends to answer the attack.

The exception has no application where a cross-examination is on the basis that the witness's account was a fabrication from the outset, unless the effect of the cross-examination is in fact to create the impression of fabrication at a later stage (*R v Athwal* [2009] EWCA Crim 789, [2009] 1 WLR 2430).

In civil proceedings, a previous statement admissible under the exception is admissible not merely to confirm the witness's credit, but also as evidence of the facts contained in it. The Civil Evidence Act 1995, s. 6, provides as follows:

(2) A party who has called or intends to call a person as a witness in civil proceedings may not in those proceedings adduce evidence of a previous statement made by that person, except—

   ...

   (b) for the purpose of rebutting a suggestion that his evidence has been fabricated.

   ...

(5) Nothing in this section shall be construed as preventing a statement of any description referred to above from being admissible by virtue of section 1 as evidence of the matters stated.

A cross-examiner who is pursuing a suggestion of recent fabrication should not ask whether the witness told his or her solicitor or counsel what he or she now says is the truth, because such a question would require the witness either to waive legal professional privilege or to suffer criticism for not doing so; the witness may elect to open up the communication with the lawyer, but this will amount to waiver of the privilege (see *R v Seaton* [2010] EWCA Crim 1980, [2011] 1 WLR 623 at [43]).

Commentary

UNFAVOURABLE AND HOSTILE WITNESSES

Rule against attacking the credit of one's own witnesses

49.62   At common law, if a witness fails to come up to proof, or gives adverse evidence, such as evidence in support of the other party's version of the facts in issue, the general rule is that the party calling the witness is not thereby entitled to turn around and seek to impeach his or her credit or otherwise cross-examine the witness as if he or she were a witness for the opposite party: the party calling the witness will not be allowed, therefore, to question the witness about, or adduce evidence of, such matters as his or her bias or bad character, any previous convictions, or any previous inconsistent statements. The general rule, it seems, will not prevent the introduction of evidence of a witness's bad character so as to support some discrete part of the case of the party calling the witness, rather than to impeach the witness's credit in relation to his or her testimony (see *R v Ross* [2007] EWCA Crim 1457, [2008] Crim LR 306). The general rule has now been put on a statutory basis (see Criminal Procedure Act 1865, s. 3, at **49.64**). There are limited exceptions to this general rule in the case of hostile witnesses, but not in the case of witnesses who are merely unfavourable.

Unfavourable witnesses

49.63   An unfavourable witness is one who, displaying no hostility to the party calling him or her, fails to come up to proof or gives evidence unfavourable to that party. At common law, the party calling the witness is not permitted to impeach his or her credit, but may call other witnesses to give evidence of those matters as to which it was expected that the unfavourable witness would testify. In *Ewer v Ambrose* (1825) 3 B & C 746 a witness called by the defendant to prove a certain partnership, gave evidence to the contrary. It was held that the defendant, although not entitled to adduce general evidence to show that the witness was not to be believed on his oath, could contradict him by calling other witnesses. As Littledale J observed, were the rule otherwise, it would attach undue importance to the order in which witnesses are called: if a party with four witnesses to prove his case were to call first the one who happened to disprove it, he would be deprived of the evidence of the other three.

Hostile witnesses

49.64   A hostile witness is one who, in the opinion of the judge, shows no desire to tell the truth at the instance of the party calling him or her, to whom he or she displays a hostile animus (Stephen, *Digest of the Law of Evidence*, 12th edn., art. 147). In criminal cases, the prosecution may call a person as a witness even if that person has shown signs that he or she is likely to be a hostile witness, e.g. by retracting a statement or by making a second statement (see *R v Mann* (1972) 56 Cr App R 750 and *R v Dat* [1998] Crim LR 488). Similarly, in civil proceedings it seems that a party may call a witness who has indicated that he or she may be hostile, e.g. by refusing to make a statement or by refusing to testify having agreed to do so. (**CPR, r. 32.9**, under which a party unable to obtain a witness statement may seek permission to serve a witness summary instead, is discussed at **51.19**.)

At common law the judge has a discretion whether to treat a witness as hostile and allow the witness to be cross-examined by the party calling him or her, and the judge's decision will seldom be challenged successfully on appeal (*Rice v Howard* (1886) 16 QBD 681; *Price v Manning* (1889) 42 ChD 372). If a witness fails to give the evidence expected, or gives evidence contrary to an earlier statement, the judge should first consider inviting the witness to refresh his or her memory from material which can properly be used for that purpose, rather than simply proceeding to treat the witness as hostile, unless he or she displays such an excessive degree of hostility that that is the only appropriate course (*R v Maw* [1994] Crim LR 841). The judge will have regard to the attitude and demeanour of the witness, his or her willingness to cooperate, and any previous contradictory or inconsistent statements.

Under the Criminal Procedure Act 1865, s. 3, if a witness is treated as hostile, the party calling the witness may prove prior statements made by the witness and inconsistent with his or her evidence. Section 3 provides as follows:

A party producing a witness shall not be allowed to impeach his credit by general evidence of bad character, but he may, in case the witness shall, in the opinion of the judge, prove adverse, contradict him by other evidence, or, by leave of the judge, prove that he has made at other times a statement inconsistent with his present testimony; but before such last mentioned proof can be given the circumstances of the supposed statement, sufficient to designate the particular occasion, must be mentioned to the witness, and he must be asked whether or not he made such statement.

The word 'adverse', in s. 3, means hostile (*Greenough v Eccles* (1859) 5 CB NS 786, a decision under the Common Law Procedure (Amendment) Act 1856, s. 22, which was repealed but re-enacted by s. 3 of the 1865 Act). The first part of s. 3 applies to both unfavourable and hostile witnesses and is nothing more than a statutory re-statement of the common law rule against attacking the credit of one's own witnesses (see **49.62**). The next part of the section, which allows the party calling the witness to contradict him or her by other evidence, applies only to hostile witnesses, but has not affected the rule at common law that a party may contradict an *unfavourable* witness by calling other witnesses (*Greenough v Eccles*). The final part of the section, which permits proof of previous inconsistent statements, applies only in the case of hostile witnesses.

If a witness is treated as hostile, at common law the party calling the witness may ask him or her leading questions. Section 3 of the 1865 Act has not removed this right. Thus, where a witness has made a statement in favour of a party, but when called to testify, stands mute of malice and is treated as hostile, then although the case may not be governed by s. 3, because the witness has given no 'testimony', at common law he or she may be asked leading questions and the witness's previous statement may be put to him or her (*R v Thompson* (1976) 64 Cr App R 96, relying upon *Clarke v Saffery* (1824) Ry & M 126 and *Bastin v Carew* (1824) Ry & M 127). However, it is submitted that if, in these circumstances, the witness were to deny making the previous statement, it could not be proved at common law.

A hostile witness who is cross-examined on a previous inconsistent statement under s. 3 of the 1865 Act may or may not accept the truth of the contents of the statement. If its truth is accepted, the previous statement in effect becomes part of the witness's evidence and, subject to the assessment of his or her credibility, is capable of being accepted (*R v Maw* [1994] Crim LR 841; *R v Gibbons* [2008] EWCA Crim 1574, [2009] Crim LR 197). If its truth is not admitted by the witness, the previous statement is admissible as evidence of the matters stated by virtue of the Civil Evidence Act 1995, s. 6, which provides as follows:

(3) Where in the case of civil proceedings section 3...of the Criminal Procedure Act 1865 applies, which [makes] provision as to—
   (a) how far a witness may be discredited by the party producing him, ... this Act does not authorise the adducing of evidence of a previous inconsistent or contradictory statement otherwise than in accordance with those sections....
(5) Nothing in this section shall be construed as preventing a statement of any description referred to above from being admissible by virtue of section 1 as evidence of the matters stated.

It follows that if the witness does not admit the truth of the previous statement, the tribunal must decide whether to accept as true the contents of the previous statement or the evidence of the witness. The more recent criminal authorities suggest that there is no inflexible rule to the effect that a hostile witness's evidence should be regarded as unreliable where he or she is shown to have made previous inconsistent statements (see, e.g. *R v Pestano* [1981] Crim LR 397; *R v Governor of Pentonville Prison, ex parte Alves* [1993] AC 284 and *R v Goodway* [1993] 4 All ER 894 at p. 899; and contrast *R v Golder* [1960] 1 WLR 1169 at pp. 1172–3, approved in *R v Oliva* [1965] 1 WLR 1028). This more recent approach, it is submitted, has much to commend it, not least because in some cases the witness will be able to give a convincing explanation for the

Commentary

inconsistency. Whether the judge can give any credence to the witness, and if so, which parts of his or her evidence, if any, the judge should accept, are questions which fall to be resolved in the light of the particular circumstances of each case. Thus, where a hostile witness in the event proves not to be hostile and reverts to his original account, it may still be appropriate to approach his evidence with caution, in the light of the different accounts that he has given (*R v Greene* [2009] EWCA Crim 2282, *The Times,* 28 October 2009).

FAILURE TO CROSS-EXAMINE

49.65   A party who fails to cross-examine a witness on an issue in respect of which it is proposed to contradict his evidence-in-chief or impeach his credit by calling other witnesses, should not be permitted to invite the tribunal of fact to disbelieve the witness's evidence on the issue. The cross-examining party must lay a proper foundation by putting the matter to the witness so that he has an opportunity to give any explanation open to him (*Browne v Dunn* (1893) 6 R 67; and see also, to similar effect, the Code of Conduct for barristers in the Bar Standards Handbook, r. C7.2). It is not always necessary to put to the witness explicitly that he is lying, provided that the overall tenor of the cross-examination is designed to show that his account is not capable of belief (*R v Lovelock* [1997] Crim LR 821). However, there is a real danger in contradicting a young child witness that he will assent to what is being suggested simply to please or to bring the questioning to an end, or a speedier end, so that it can be very difficult to tell whether the child is truly changing his account or taking the line of least resistance (*R v W* [2010] EWCA Crim 1926, LTL 10/2/2011 at [28]–[31]).

FINALITY ON COLLATERAL ISSUES

The rule

49.66   The general rule at common law is that the answers given by a witness under cross-examination to questions on collateral issues, i.e. issues which are not directly relevant to the facts in issues in the case, must be treated as final, not in the sense that the tribunal of fact must accept the truth of the answers, but in the sense that the cross-examining party should not be allowed to call further evidence with a view to contradicting the witness. The rationale of the rule is to prevent the proliferation of issues of minimal or marginal relevance to the facts in issue, which would prolong the trial unnecessarily. Thus, it has been held that where a witness gives evidence through an interpreter and under cross-examination about his knowledge of English, denies that he is able to speak the language, the matter will normally be quite irrelevant to any matter directly in issue in the proceedings, and therefore evidence in rebuttal will normally be inadmissible (see *R v Burke* (1858) 8 Cox CC 44). In *Attorney General v Hitchcock* (1847) 1 Ex 91, in which a prosecution witness, under cross-examination, denied that he had made an out-of-court statement to a certain Cook to the effect that Excise officers had offered to give him £20 to give false evidence, it was held that the defence were not allowed to call Cook to give evidence in rebuttal, on the basis that it was irrelevant to the matters in issue that someone had thought fit to offer a bribe, which was not accepted, to give an untrue account of a transaction. The decision is not easily reconciled with *R v M* [2004] EWCA Crim 2085, LTL 6/7/2004. In that case, the sexual offences which formed the basis of the charge came to light when a private investigator and inquiry agents, being used by a man, S, whose wife had been having an affair with the accused, interviewed the victims. The accused said that S had induced the victims to give evidence against him by offers of financial reward, but all the victims denied any such financial inducement. It was held that the accused should have been allowed to call a witness to give evidence that she had been approached by the private investigator, and that when she had refused to give adverse information, had been told that S had unlimited funds for the right information. The court was of the view that although the witness's evidence, viewed in isolation, was collateral and 'borderline', it was relevant as showing that the victims might have been offered money or been influenced by the offer of money.

According to Pollock CB in *Attorney General v Hitchcock*, if the witness's answer is a matter on which the cross-examining party would be allowed to introduce evidence-in-chief, because of its connection with the issues in the case, then the matter is not collateral and may be rebutted. This test seems to be circular, and the cases show that it is not always easy to tell whether an issue is collateral. The explanation probably lies in the fact that relevance is a question of degree on which views may differ and the answer to which may turn on whether the matter which the cross-examining party seeks to prove is a single fact which is easy of proof or a broad issue involving a difficult and complex fact-finding task (see *R v S* [1992] Crim LR 307). Questions which go *merely* to the credit of the witness are clearly collateral, but it does not follow that questions on all other matters are not collateral. This is because in some cases the difference between questions going to credit and questions going to the issue will be barely discernible, if it can be said to exist at all. *R v Busby* (1981) 75 Cr App R 79 illustrates the point well. In that case, police officers under cross-examination denied two matters, that they had made up statements attributed to the accused and indicative of his guilt and that they had threatened W, a potential defence witness, to stop him from testifying. The Court of Appeal held that W should have been allowed to give evidence that he had been threatened by the officers, because it was evidence relevant to an issue in the case in that, if true, it showed that the police were prepared to go to improper lengths to secure a conviction, which would have supported the defence case that the statements attributed to him had been fabricated. Of this case, it has since been said that it has created a new exception to the general rule (see *R v Funderburk* [1990] 2 All ER 482 at p. 486), but it has also been said that the facts came within the exception of bias (see **49.69**) and that if the case cannot be explained on that basis, it is inconsistent with the general rule itself (*R v Edwards* [1991] 1 WLR 207 at p. 215).

To the general rule there are exceptions in the case of the previous convictions of a witness, his or her bias, a physical or mental disability affecting his or her reliability, and his or her reputation for untruthfulness. It is also convenient and usual to treat as an exception to the general rule proof of a witness's previous inconsistent statement, although strictly speaking such proof is not covered by the general rule, because permitted only where the statement is 'relative to the subject matter of the … proceeding' (Criminal Procedure Act 1865, ss. 4 and 5, considered at **49.67**).

Previous inconsistent statements

The proof of previous oral or written statements in civil proceedings is governed by the **49.67** Criminal Procedure Act 1865, ss. 4 and 5. Section 4 applies to both oral and written statements; s. 5 applies to written statements only (per Lord Taylor of Gosforth CJ in *R v Derby Magistrates' Court, ex parte B* [1996] AC 487 at pp. 498–9). They provide as follows:

4. If a witness, upon cross-examination as to a former statement made by him relative to the subject matter of the indictment or proceeding, and inconsistent with his present testimony, does not distinctly admit that he has made such a statement, proof may be given that he did in fact make it; but before such proof can be given, the circumstances of the supposed statement, sufficient to designate the particular occasion, must be mentioned to the witness, and he must be asked whether or not he made such statement.

5. A witness may be cross-examined as to previous statements made by him in writing or reduced into writing relative to the subject matter of the indictment or proceeding, without such writing being shown to him; but if it is intended to contradict such witness by the writing, his attention must, before such contradictory proof can be given, be called to those parts of the writing which are to be used for the purpose of so contradicting him; provided always, that it shall be competent for the judge, at any time during the trial, to require the production of the writing for his inspection, and he may thereupon make such use of it for the purposes of the trial as he may think fit.

Co. Ltd [1916] 1 KB 849, a claim for workmen's compensation by the father of a deceased stable boy who had been kicked by a horse and had been found nearby holding a halter, evidence that the boy had previously teased horses with a halter was admitted in rebuttal of the allegation that the accident had occurred in the course of the boy's employment. In *Jones v Greater Manchester Police Authority* [2001] EWHC Admin 189, [2002] ACD 4, in proceedings for a sex offender order under the Crime and Disorder Act 1998, s. 2, it was held that evidence of propensity to commit sexual offences is relevant and admissible, because the court seeks to predict the extent to which past events give rise to reasonable cause for believing that an order is necessary to protect the public from serious harm, and that the admission of such evidence breaches neither **art. 6** nor **art. 8** of the **European Convention on Human Rights**. See also *Barrett v Long* (1851) 3 HL Cas 395, *Osborne v Chocqueel* [1896] 2 QB 109 and *Sattin v National Union Bank* (1978) 122 SJ 367.

In *Mood Music Publishing Co. Ltd v De Wolfe Publishing Ltd* [1976] Ch 119, an action for infringement of copyright in which the defendants admitted the similarity between the musical work in which the claimants owned the copyright and the work which they had produced, but alleged that the similarity was coincidental, evidence was admitted to show that on other occasions the defendants had produced musical works bearing a close resemblance to works which were the subject of copyright. It was held that the evidence had been properly admitted to rebut the allegation of coincidence. Lord Denning MR added a gloss to the ordinary test of relevance, although in so far as it relates to giving the other party fair notice of the intention to adduce the evidence, under the current cards-on-the-table approach to civil litigation it is of little significance. He said (at p. 127): 'In civil cases, the courts will admit evidence of similar facts if it is logically probative, that is, if it is logically relevant in determining the matter which is in issue: provided that it is not oppressive or unfair to the other side: and also that the other side has fair notice of it and is able to deal with it' (cf. *EG Music v SF (Film) Distributors Ltd* [1978] FSR 121 and *Berger v Raymond and Son Ltd* [1984] 1 WLR 625). This dictum, however, only applies to civil cases tried by a judge alone, who is trained to distinguish between what is probative and what is not: where there is a jury, the court must be more careful about admitting the evidence (per Dillon LJ in *Thorpe v Chief Constable of Greater Manchester Police* [1989] 1 WLR 665 at p. 670).

The leading authority is *O'Brien v Chief Constable of South Wales* [2005] UKHL 26, [2005] 2 AC 534. The claimant was convicted of murder. After serving 11 years in prison, his case was referred to the Criminal Cases Review Commission and his appeal was allowed. He then brought proceedings against the Chief Constable for misfeasance in public office and malicious prosecution, alleging that he had been 'framed' by a Detective Inspector L and a Detective Chief Superintendent C, who was alleged to have approved some aspects of the misconduct alleged against L. The House of Lords held that evidence had properly been admitted to show that L had behaved with similar impropriety on two other occasions and that C had done so on one other occasion. The House of Lords held that the test of admissibility in civil cases is different from that which applies in criminal cases. There is no warrant for the automatic application of the criminal test in a civil suit. To do so would be to introduce an inflexibility which is inappropriate and undesirable. Lord Phillips of Worth Matravers said (at [53]–[56]):

[53] I would simply apply the test of relevance as the test of admissibility of similar fact evidence in a civil suit. Such evidence is admissible if it is potentially probative of an issue in the action.

[54] That is not to say that the policy considerations that have given rise to the complex rules... in the Criminal Justice Act 2003, ss. 100 to 106 [see generally *Blackstone's Criminal Practice 2017*, F13] have no part to play in the conduct of civil litigation. They are policy considerations which the judge who has the management of the civil litigation will wish to keep well in mind. CPR, r. 1.2, requires the court to give effect to the overriding objective of dealing with cases justly. This includes dealing with the case in a way which is proportionate to what is involved in the case, and in a manner which is expeditious and fair. Rule 1.4 requires the court actively to manage the case in

order to further the overriding objective. Rule 32.1 gives the court the power to control the evidence. This power expressly enables the court to exclude evidence that would otherwise be admissible and to limit cross-examination.

[55] Similar fact evidence will not necessarily risk causing any unfair prejudice to the party against whom it is directed...It may, however, carry such a risk. Evidence of impropriety which reflects adversely on the character of a party may risk causing prejudice that is disproportionate to its relevance, particularly where the trial is taking place before a jury. In such a case the judge will be astute to see that the probative cogency of the evidence justifies this risk of prejudice in the interests of a fair trial.

[56] Equally, when considering whether to admit evidence, or permit cross-examination, on matters that are collateral to the central issues, the judge will have regard to the need for proportionality and expedition. He will consider whether the evidence in question is likely to be relatively uncontroversial, or whether its admission is likely to create side issues which will unbalance the trial and make it harder to see the wood from the trees.

For an example of the potential application of these principles, in a case where the similar fact evidence related to facts subsequent to the facts in issue, see *Desmond v Bower* [2009] EWCA Civ 667, [2010] EMLR 5.

DOCUMENTARY EVIDENCE

Proof of contents

Proof of the contents of a document on which a party seeks to rely is now largely, but not exclusively, governed by the Civil Evidence Act 1995, ss. 8 and 9, which are considered in detail at **53.15** to **53.17**. Under s. 8, where a statement contained in a document is admissible in evidence in civil proceedings, it may be proved by the production of that document, or, whether or not that document is still in existence, by the production of a copy of that document or the material part of it, authenticated in such manner as the court may approve (s. 8(1)); and it is immaterial for this purpose how many removes there are between a copy and the original (s. 8(2)). Under s. 9, a document which is certified as forming part of the records of a business or public authority may be received in evidence without further proof (s. 9(1) and (2)); and the absence of an entry in the records of a business or public authority may be proved by the affidavit of an officer of the business or authority. A document, for the purposes of both sections, means 'anything in which information of any description is recorded' (s. 13), a definition wide enough to cover maps, plans, graphs, drawings, discs, audiotapes, soundtracks, photographs, negatives, videotapes and films; and for the purposes of s. 8, a copy, in relation to a document, means, 'anything onto which information recorded in the document has been copied, by whatever means and whether directly or indirectly' (s. 13).

49.75

Section 8 of the 1995 Act appears to be of general application, i.e. to apply to any statement contained in a document, and not merely statements admissible for the truth of their contents by virtue of the 1995 Act; and likewise s. 9 seems to apply to any document forming part of the records of a business or public authority. On this construction, these provisions have reversed the general common law rule (see **49.76**) that a party seeking to rely on the contents of a document must adduce primary evidence of those contents, i.e. usually the original. In any event, ss. 8 and 9 are permissive as to the means of proof. Section 14(2) of the Act provides that, 'Nothing in this Act affects the proof of documents by means other than those specified in section 8 or 9'. Sections 8 and 9, therefore, do not affect the operation of:

(a) the common law rule that where secondary evidence of the contents of a private document is admissible, it may take the form of oral evidence, which is not permitted under the 1995 Act;

(b) various statutory provisions, mostly relating to public and judicial documents, which provide for proof of their contents by copies which are required to take a particular form, such as an examined or certified copy (see **49.79**); or

(c) the Bankers' Books Evidence Act 1879, whereby copies of entries in bankers' books are admissible if certain conditions are met (see **49.80**).

Section 14(3) of the 1995 Act provides that nothing in the Act affects the operation of the following enactments:

(a) Documentary Evidence Act 1868, s. 2, which relates to the proof of certain official documents (see **49.79**);

(b) Documentary Evidence Act 1882, s. 2, which relates to documents printed under the superintendence of the Stationery Office (see **49.79**);

(c) Evidence (Colonial Statutes) Act 1907, which relates to proof of statutes of certain legislatures (see **49.101**);

(d) Evidence (Foreign, Dominion and Colonial Documents) Act 1933 (proof and effect of registers and official certificates of certain countries); and

(e) Oaths and Evidence (Overseas Authorities and Countries) Act 1963 (provision in respect of public registers of other countries).

Given the general saving in s. 14(2) of the 1995 Act, it is unclear why s. 14(3) refers to only some of the many pre-existing statutory provisions governing the proof of various specific types of document.

General rule at common law

49.76 The general rule at common law is that a party seeking to rely on the contents of a document must adduce primary evidence of the contents, that is:

(a) the original;

(b) an official copy, in the case of an enrolled document; or

(c) an informal admission.

As to originals, duplicates of a deed which have been executed by all parties are all originals (*Forbes v Samuel* [1913] 3 KB 706); a copy of a document which is signed or otherwise duly executed is an original; and a counterpart lease executed by the lessee alone is the original if tendered against him or her, and the other part is the original if tendered against the lessor (*Doe d West v Davis* (1806) 7 East 363). If a private document is required to be enrolled, i.e. officially filed in a court or other public office, the copy issued by the court or office is treated as the original. For example, where a grant of probate has been obtained, the probate copy of the will is treated as primary evidence of the contents of the will. Where a party to litigation makes an informal admission as to the contents of a document, it constitutes primary evidence of the contents and is admissible against him or her (*Slatterie v Pooley* (1840) 6 M & W 664; but see now the Civil Evidence Act 1995, s. 7(1), considered at **53.20** to **53.22**).

The general rule only applies where a party relies on the contents of the document. Thus whereas proof of the length of a tenancy or of the amount of rent due requires production of the lease, proof of the existence or fact of the tenancy, albeit created by a lease which defines its terms, may be proved by other means, such as parol evidence as to the payment of rent (see *Augustien v Challis* (1847) 1 Ex 279 (the amount of rent due) and *Twyman v Knowles* (1853) 13 CB 222 (the length of the tenancy); and cf. *R v Holy Trinity, Hull (Inhabitants)* (1827) 7 B & C 611 (the fact of a tenancy) and *Alderson v Clay* (1816) 1 Stark 405 (the fact of a partnership). Equally the rule does not apply where reference is made to a document merely for the purpose of establishing the bare fact of its existence (see *R v Elworthy* (1867) LR 1 CCR 103) or identifying it (see *Boyle v Wiseman* (1855) 11 Ex 360 at p. 367).

The general rule is well established, as are the common law exceptions to it, which are considered at **49.79** and **49.81** to **49.84**. However, the Court of Appeal in *Springsteen v Flute International Ltd* [2001] EMLR 654 appeared to reject the notion that, at common law, there is a general rule accompanied by a number of exceptions, in favour of a more generalised approach whereby the admissibility of secondary evidence of the contents of a document depends upon the weight to be attached to the secondary evidence. Observing 'with confidence' that the best evidence rule had finally expired, the court held that:

(a) Where the party seeking to adduce the secondary evidence could readily produce the document, it might be expected that, absent some special circumstances, the court would decline to admit the secondary evidence on the ground that it was worthless.

(b) At the other extreme, where that party genuinely could not produce the document, it might be expected that, absent some special circumstances, the court would admit the secondary evidence and attach such weight to it as it considered appropriate in the circumstances.

(c) In cases falling between these two extremes, it was for the court to make a judgment as to whether in all the circumstances any weight should be attached to the secondary evidence.

(d) Thus the admissibility of secondary evidence of the contents of documents is entirely dependent on whether or not any weight is to be attached to the evidence, which is a matter for the court to decide.

A similar approach was adopted in *Post Office Counters Ltd v Mahida* [2003] EWCA Civ 1583, *The Times*, 31 October 2003. The claimant had destroyed the primary documentary evidence proving the sums owed by the defendant, and relied on secondary evidence in the form of schedules drawn up by the claimant of the claims for payments and receipts submitted to it by the defendant. It was held to have been permissible to adduce this secondary evidence, but the judge had given it too much weight. The judge should have taken into account the claimant's delay in responding to the defendant's requests for the primary documents, and the claimant's failure to take proper care of that evidence.

Exceptions

Under the exceptions to the general rule, in the case of private documents, secondary evidence of the contents of a document may take the form of a copy, a copy of a copy (*Lafone v Griffin* (1909) 25 TLR 308), or oral evidence. Where a copy is produced, proof is required that it is a true copy of the original (see *R v Collins* (1960) 44 Cr App R 170).   **49.77**

It has been said that 'there are no degrees of secondary evidence' (per Lord Abinger CB in *Doe d Gilbert v Ross* (1840) 7 M & W 102), which means that although less weight may attach to inferior forms of secondary evidence, there is no obligation to tender the best type of secondary evidence available. For example, oral evidence of the contents of a document is admissible even if a copy of the document is available. To this principle, however, there are numerous exceptions: many public documents may be proved by oral evidence only if examined, certified or other types of copy are unavailable (see **49.79**); bankers' books are generally proved by examined copies (see **49.80**); and the contents of a will admitted to probate may not be proved by oral evidence if the original or probate copy exists.

Hearsay statements   Where the contents of a document, including a computer-produced document, are admissible by virtue of Civil Evidence Act 1995, they may be proved in accordance with ss. 8 and 9 of that Act (see **49.75** and generally at **53.15** to **53.17**).   **49.78**

Public and judicial documents   At common law, secondary evidence of the contents of public documents is admissible on the grounds that production of the originals would cause a high degree of inconvenience: see, e.g. *Mortimer v M'Callan* (1840) 6 M & W 58 (books   **49.79**

5. Verification of copy

A copy of an entry in a banker's book shall not be received in evidence under this Act unless it be further proved that the copy has been examined with the original entry and is correct.

Such proof shall be given by some person who has examined the copy with the original entry, and may be given either orally or by an affidavit sworn before any commissioner or person authorised to take affidavits. . . .

6. Case in which banker, etc., not compellable to produce book, etc.

A banker or officer of a bank shall not, in any legal proceeding to which the bank is not a party, be compellable to produce any banker's book the contents of which can be proved under this Act . . ., or to appear as a witness to prove the matters, transactions, and accounts therein recorded, unless by order of a judge made for special cause.

7. Court or judge may order inspection, etc.

On the application of any party to a legal proceeding a court or judge may order that such party be at liberty to inspect and take copies of any entries in a banker's book for any of the purposes of such proceedings. An order under this section may be made either with or without summoning the bank or any other party, and shall be served on the bank three clear days before the same is to be obeyed, unless the court or judge otherwise directs.

8. Costs

The costs of any application to a court or judge under or for the purposes of this Act, and the costs of anything done or to be done under an order of a court or judge made under or for the purposes of this Act shall be in the discretion of the court or judge, who may order the same or any part thereof to be paid to any party by the bank where the same have been occasioned by any default or delay on the part of the bank. Any such order against a bank may be enforced as if the bank was a party to the proceeding.

9. Interpretation of 'bank', 'banker', and 'bankers' books'

(1)   In this Act the expression 'bank' and 'banker' mean—

        (a) a deposit-taker;

        (c) the National Savings Bank.

(1A)   'Deposit taker' means—

        (a) a person who has permission under Part 4A of the Financial Services and Markets Act 2000 to accept deposits; or

        (b) an EEA firm of the kind mentioned in paragraph 5(b) of Schedule 3 to that Act which has permission under paragraph 15 of that Schedule (as a result of qualifying for authorisation under paragraph 12(1) of that Schedule) to accept deposits or other repayable funds from the public.

(1B)   But a person is not a deposit-taker if he has permission to accept deposits only for the purpose of carrying on another regulated activity in accordance with that permission.

(1C)   Subsections (1A) and (1B) must be read with—

        (a) section 22 of the Financial Services and Markets Act 2000;

        (b) any relevant order under that section; and

        (c) Schedule 2 to that Act.

(2)   Expressions in this Act relating to 'bankers' books' include ledgers, day books, cash books, account books and other records used in the ordinary business of the bank, whether those records are in written form or are kept on microfilm, magnetic tape or any other form of mechanical or electronic data retrieval mechanism.

10. Interpretation of 'legal proceeding', 'court', 'judge'

In this Act—

The expression 'legal proceeding' means any civil or criminal proceeding or inquiry in which evidence is or may be given, and includes—

(a) an arbitration;

(b) an application to, or an inquiry or other proceeding before, the Solicitors Disciplinary Tribunal or any body exercising functions in relation to solicitors in Scotland or Northern Ireland corresponding to the functions of that Tribunal; and

(c) an investigation, consideration or determination of a complaint by a member of the panel of ombudsmen for the purposes of the ombudsman scheme within the meaning of the Financial Services and Markets Act 2000;

The expression 'the court' means the court, judge, arbitrator, persons or person before whom a legal proceeding is held or taken;

The expression 'a judge' means with respect to England a judge of the High Court...

A judge of the county court may with respect to any action in such court exercise the powers of a judge under this Act.

In s. 9(2), the words 'other records used in the ordinary business of the bank' mean other records of the same type as ledgers, day books, cash books and account books, which are the means by which a bank records day-to-day financial transactions, and therefore records kept by the bank of conversations between its employees and customers or others or internal memoranda are not bankers' books (*Re Howglen Ltd* [2001] 1 All ER 376).

Paid cheques and paying-in slips retained by a bank after the conclusion of a banking transaction to which they relate are not bankers' books under the Act, because even if bundles of such documents can be treated as 'records used in the ordinary business of the bank', the addition of an individual cheque or paying-in slip cannot be regarded as making an 'entry' in those records (*Williams v Williams* [1987] 3 All ER 257). If such documents relate to the bank account of the other party to the action, an order for disclosure may be made and the bank, as agent holding the documents on that party's behalf, may then be required to disclose them. In other cases, the party seeking inspection may obtain a witness summons addressed to the appropriate officer of the bank and requiring him or her to attend at the hearing with all the relevant documents in the possession of the bank relating to the account in question.

An order under s. 7 of the Act is not a necessary precondition of producing evidence under s. 3 of the Act; the obtaining of an order under s. 7 enables bankers' books to be inspected and copied despite the duty of confidentiality owed by banker to customer and such an order is clearly unnecessary if, for instance, the customer waives his right to confidentiality and the bank agrees to inspection and copying of its books (*Wheatley v Commissioner of Police of the British Virgin Islands* [2006] UKPC 24, [2006] 1 WLR 1683, a decision relating to the equivalent British Virgin Islands statute).

Although s. 7 of the Act allows an application to be made without summoning the bank or any other party, there is much to be said for notice being given (per Widgery LJ in *R v Marlborough Street Magistrates' Court, ex parte Simpson* (1980) 70 Cr App R 291 at p. 294). An order may be made under s. 7 to inspect the account of a person who is not a party to the proceedings, even if that person is not compellable as a witness (*R v Andover Justices, ex parte Rhodes* [1980] Crim LR 644). However, an application under s. 7 in respect of the bank account of a third party will only be granted if:

(a) the court is satisfied that the account is in fact the account of the other party to the action or an account with which the other party is so much concerned that items in it would be admissible against him; and

(b) the applicant shows very strong grounds for suspicion, almost amounting to certainty, that there are items in the account which would be material evidence against the other party

(*South Staffordshire Tramways Co. v Ebbsmith* [1895] 2 QB 669 (a pre-trial application) and *D. B. Deniz Nakliyati TAS v Yugopetrol* [1992] 1 WLR 437 (an application against a judgment debtor)).

Save in exceptional circumstances, a foreign bank which is not a party to the proceedings should not be ordered to produce documents which are outside the jurisdiction and concern business transacted outside the jurisdiction, even if it carries on business within the jurisdiction, because an order under the 1879 Act is an exercise of sovereign authority to assist in the administration of justice and foreign banks owe their customers a duty of confidence

Commentary

regulated by their own laws (*MacKinnon v Donaldson Lufkin and Jenrette Securities Corporation* [1986] Ch 482). A party seeking to obtain documents from a foreign bank may apply to a Master under **CPR, r. 34.13**, for the issue of letters of request to the courts of the country in question, or may apply directly to such a court under the relevant local law, having first obtained the permission of the English court on a hearing with notice.

The 1879 Act may not be used to compel disclosure of incriminating material (see *Waterhouse v Barker* [1924] 2 KB 759 and *R v Bono* (1913) 29 TLR 635).

49.81   **Failure to produce after notice**   A party may produce the contents of a document by secondary evidence where the original is in the possession or control of another party to the proceedings who, having been served with a notice to produce it, has failed to do so (see *Dwyer v Collins* (1852) 21 LJ Ex 225). It is submitted that this rule subsists notwithstanding that the CPR make no provision for service of a formal notice to produce (see, formerly, RSC, ord. 24, r. 10). A notice to produce does not compel production of a document: a party who wishes to rely at the trial on the original of a document should serve a summons requiring a witness to produce the original to the court (see **CPR, r. 34.2**).

49.82   **Non-party's lawful refusal to produce**   Secondary evidence of the contents of a document will be admissible where the original is in the possession of a stranger to the litigation who, having been served with a witness summons requiring production of the document to the court (see **CPR, r. 34.2**), lawfully refuses to do so, e.g. by reason of a valid claim to privilege (*Mills v Oddy* (1834) 6 Car & P 728), diplomatic immunity (*R v Nowaz* [1976] 3 All ER 5) or because he cannot be compelled to produce it, being outside the jurisdiction (*Kilgour v Owen* (1889) 88 LT Jo 7). If the stranger unlawfully refuses to produce the original, secondary evidence is inadmissible (see, but doubt, *R v Llanfaethly (Inhabitants)* (1853) 2 El & Bl 940).

49.83   **Lost documents**   Secondary evidence of the contents of a document is admissible on proof that the original has been destroyed or cannot be found after due search, the quality of the proof required depending on the nature and value of the document in question (*Brewster v Sewell* (1820) 3 B & Ald 296).

49.84   **Production of original impossible**   Secondary evidence is obviously admissible where production of the original is impossible, either physically, e.g. because it is an inscription on a tombstone (per Alderson B in *Mortimer v M'Callan* (1840) 6 M & W 58), or legally, e.g. because a notice required by statute to be constantly affixed at a factory (*Owner v Bee Hive Spinning Co. Ltd* [1914] 1 KB 105) or a document in the custody of a foreign court (*Alivon v Furnival* (1834) 1 Cr M & R 277).

Proof of due execution

49.85   The general rule at common law is that a document will only be admitted in evidence on proof of due execution. A major exception exists in the case of public and judicial documents, proof of the contents of which are governed by statute: most of the relevant statutory provisions also exempt from proof of due execution (see **49.79**). As to private documents, proof of due execution is frequently formally admitted, and in certain circumstances may be presumed, but otherwise usually involves proving handwriting, a signature, or attestation. Some documents are also required to be stamped for the purposes of stamp duty.

49.86   **Presumptions**   It is provided in **CPR, r. 32.19(1)**, that a party to whom a document is disclosed under **Part 31** shall be deemed to admit its authenticity, unless he serves notice that he wishes the document to be proved at trial. Without such a notice, therefore, a party will be taken to admit that a document was printed, written, signed or executed as it purports to have been. Proof of due execution is also unnecessary where the document in question is in the possession of an opponent who has refused to comply with a notice to produce it (*Cooke v Tanswell* (1818) 8 Taunt 450). A document which is more than 20 years old and comes from proper custody is presumed to have been duly executed (see Evidence Act 1938, s. 4, whereby the period of 20 years was substituted for the 30-year period required at common law). Proper custody, for these purposes, does not require that the document comes from 'the best and most proper place of deposit', but if it is found elsewhere, the court must be satisfied that the other place was 'reasonable and natural' in the circumstances (*Meath (Bishop) v Marquis of Winchester* (1836) 3 Bing NC 183; cf. *Doe d Lord Arundel v Fowler* (1850) 14 QB 700).

There are three other common law presumptions relating to documents:

(a) that a document was made on the date which it bears (*Anderson v Weston* (1840) 6 Bing NC 296);

(b) that a deed was duly sealed (but see *Re Sandilands* (1871) LR 6 CP 411); and

(c) that an alteration or erasure in a deed was made before execution, but in a will was made after execution (per Lord Campbell CJ in *Doe d Tatum v Catomore* (1851) 16 QB 745).

Handwriting and signatures   Proof that a document was written or signed by the person by whom it purports to have been written or signed may be effected by the following means: **49.87**

(a) by the direct oral evidence of the author or signatory or by any witness to the execution of the document, or by admissible hearsay assertions to the same effect;

(b) by the opinion evidence of someone acquainted with the handwriting or signature (*Doe d Mudd v Suckermore* (1837) 5 Ad & El 703), although the weight to be attached to such evidence will obviously vary according to the circumstances; or

(c) by comparison of the disputed handwriting or signature with another document which is proved or admitted to have been written by the person in question, under Criminal Procedure Act 1865, s. 8, which provides as follows:

Comparison of a disputed writing with any writing proved to the satisfaction of the judge to be genuine shall be permitted to be made by witnesses; and such writings, and the evidence of witnesses respecting the same, may be submitted to the court and jury as evidence of the genuineness or otherwise of the writing in dispute.

The court need only be satisfied as to the genuineness of the specimen handwriting on a balance of probabilities. The judge, in comparing the disputed and specimen writing, may be assisted by an expert in handwriting or by someone who, although not an expert, is familiar with the handwriting in question (*Fitzwalter Peerage Claim* (1844) 10 Cl & F 193). A witness who has not seen the original of the 'disputed writing', e.g. because it is lost, is entitled to use a photocopy of it to make the comparison (*Lockheed-Arabia Corporation v Owen* [1993] QB 806).

Any of the above-mentioned means of proving handwriting may be used in the case of documents which, although not required by law to be attested, were in fact attested: the Criminal Procedure Act 1865, s. 7 provides that such a document may be proved as if there had been no attesting witness thereto.

Attestation   Except where probate is sought in common form, to prove the due execution of a will (or other testamentary document), one of the attesting witnesses, if available, must be called. Such witnesses are treated as the court's witnesses and may be cross-examined by the party seeking to prove due execution (*Oakes v Uzzell* [1932] P 19). Other evidence becomes admissible if the witness denies the execution (*Bowman v Hodgson* (1867) LR 1 P & D 362) or refuses to give evidence (*Re Ovens Goods* (1892) 29 LR Ir 451). If all the attesting witnesses are dead, insane, outside the jurisdiction or untraceable, proof is required of the handwriting of one of the attesting witnesses; and if, despite every effort to do so, it is impossible to prove such handwriting, other evidence of due execution becomes   **49.88**

Commentary

admissible, such as the evidence of a non-attesting witness to the execution (*Clarke v Clarke* (1879) 5 LR Ir 451).

Under the Evidence Act 1938, s. 3, except in the case of a will or other testamentary document, any document required by law to be attested may, instead of being proved by an attesting witness, be proved in the manner in which it might be proved if no attesting witness were alive (e.g. by evidence of the handwriting of an attesting witness or by the evidence of a non-attesting witness to the execution).

49.89   **Stamped documents**   A document requiring a stamp for the purposes of stamp duty shall not be given in evidence unless it is duly stamped in accordance with the law in force at the time when it was first executed or, the court having objected to the omission or insufficiency of the stamp, and the document being one which may be legally stamped after its execution, payment is made of the amount of unpaid duty, together with any penalty payable on stamping, and a further sum of one pound (Stamp Act 1891, s. 14). The parties cannot waive these rules (*Bowker v Williamson* (1889) 5 TLR 382). If a document requiring a stamp cannot be found or is in the possession of a party who refuses to comply with a notice to produce it, it is presumed to have been duly stamped; but if there is evidence to show that it was not duly stamped, then it is presumed, in the absence of sufficient evidence to the contrary, that this remained the case (*Closmadeuc v Carrel* (1856) 18 CB 36).

REAL EVIDENCE

Material objects and documents

49.90   Real evidence usually takes the form of a material object examined by the tribunal of fact as a means of proving its existence, condition or value; but subject to a formal admission by the party against whom it is tendered, and subject also to **CPR, r. 33.6** (which is considered at **49.94**), it needs to be accompanied by testimony to at least identify it or explain its provenance. A document may constitute real evidence, as when it is introduced not for the statements that it contains but as a material object, to show that it exists or the condition that it is in. There is no rule to the effect that oral evidence regarding a material object is inadmissible unless the object itself is produced, or its non-production excused (*Hocking v Ahlquist Brothers Ltd* [1944] 1 KB 120), but non-production of the object may affect the weight to be attached to the oral evidence and give rise to an inference adverse to the party failing to produce (see, e.g. *Armory v Delamirie* (1722) 1 Str 505).

Demeanour and appearance

49.91   The demeanour and attitude of a witness in the course of giving his or her evidence may be regarded as a form of real evidence which is relevant to the witness's credit and the weight to be attached to his or her evidence. Real evidence may also take the form of a person's physical appearance, as when injuries or scars are examined on a question of causation or quantum. The facial resemblance of a child to its alleged father and mother may be relevant on the question of legitimacy, although in many cases little weight should be attached to it (*C v C* (*Legitimacy: Photographic Evidence*) [1972] 1 WLR 1335; cf. *Slingsby v Attorney General* (1916) 33 TLR 120 at pp. 122–3). The appearance of an animal may also constitute real evidence, as in *Line v Taylor* (1862) 3 F & F 731, where a dog alleged to be of a vicious disposition was examined in court.

Printouts, photographs, videotapes and films

49.92   A computer printout (or photograph, videotape or film) is a document for the purposes of the Civil Evidence Act 1995 (see **53.15**) and under that Act may be used to prove the matters stated therein. They are also documents for the purposes of disclosure and inspection (see **chapter 50**). At common law, where a computer or other device is used as a calculator (i.e. as a tool which does not contribute its own knowledge, but merely performs a calculation, albeit sophisticated, which could have been performed manually), the resulting printout is not hearsay, but is treated as an item of real evidence. The actual proof and relevance of the printout depend on the evidence of the person using the computer, the computer programmer or other experts involved, who can testify as to such matters as the function and operation of the computer (see per Lord Lane CJ in *R v Wood* (1982) 76 Cr App R 23 at p. 26, in which a laborious mathematical process had been undertaken by a computer operated by chemists investigating the chemical composition of metal; and see also, in the case of a printout from a breathalyser, *Castle v Cross* [1984] 1 WLR 1372). The principle applies not only where the device in question processes information supplied to it, but also where it gathers information itself (*R v Spiby* (1990) 91 Cr App R 186, in which the printout came from a computerised machine used to monitor telephone calls and automatically record such information as the numbers to and from which calls were made, and the duration of the calls). In *R (O'Shea) v Coventry Magistrates' Court* [2004] EWHC 905 (Admin), [2004] Crim LR 948, automatically generated computer records of access and attempted access to web pages, including details matching O's credit card, email and home address, were admitted to show what had been recorded and not as evidence of the truth of what had been recorded. It was, therefore, real evidence and not hearsay. See also *R v Governor of Brixton Prison, ex parte Levin* [1997] AC 741.

In appropriate circumstances, the same principle applies in the case of photographs, video-tapes and films: see *R v Dodson* (1984) 79 Cr App R 220 (photographs taken by security cameras) and *Khan v Armaguard Ltd* [1994] 1 WLR 1204 (a videotape inconsistent with the claimant's claims about the nature of his injuries). It has been said that the photograph, together with the sketch and the photofit, are in a class of evidence of their own to which neither the rule against hearsay nor the rule against previous consistent statements applies (per Watkins LJ in *R v Cook* [1987] QB 417 at p. 425). In *The Statue of Liberty* [1968] 1 WLR 739, an action concerning a collision between two ships, a cinematograph film of radar echoes recorded by a shore radar station and produced mechanically and without human intervention was held to be admissible in evidence. Sir Jocelyn Simon P said (at p. 740):

If tape recordings are admissible, it seems that a photograph of radar reception is equally admissible—or indeed, any other type of photograph. It would be an absurd distinction that a photograph should be admissible if the camera were operated manually by a photographer, but not if it were operated by a trip or clock mechanism. Similarly, if evidence of weather conditions were relevant, the law would affront common sense if it were to say that those could be proved by a person who looked at a barometer from time to time, but not by producing a barograph record. So, too, with other types of dial recordings.

Regarding video recordings, there is an obligation to inform the court at the first opportunity that such evidence will be relied upon, as arrangements need to be made to ensure video equipment is available at trial, and extra time will be required for the trial for showing the evidence (*Rall v Hume* [2001] 3 All ER 248). Use of videos at trial takes two forms. They can be used as part of a party's affirmative case. In this event the videotapes may need to be played in their entirety. Alternatively, a party may wish to use a videotape in cross-examination of the opposing party by playing certain parts of the video for comment by the witness being cross-examined in order to undermine the witness. Use of a tape in this way will usually be legitimate, even if an application for such use is made quite close to the trial date. However, a direction is likely to be made limiting the footage to be shown (in *Rall v Hume* the limit was 20 minutes). Some inquiry agents are not very discriminating when shooting covert videos, and the court will be astute to ensure that the footage used does not infringe the European Convention on Human Rights, art. 8(1) (the right to private life).

Commentary

Views

49.93 A view is an inspection of a site or of an object that it is impossible or inconvenient to bring to court, e.g. an omnibus (see *London General Omnibus Co. Ltd v Lavell* [1901] 1 Ch 135). In some circumstances it will also be appropriate to conduct out-of-court demonstrations or re-enactments, before which, it is submitted, the demonstrator should take the oath and thereby offer himself or herself for cross-examination (see *Buckingham v Daily News Ltd* [1956] 2 QB 534; and cf. *Goold v Evans and Co.* [1951] 2 TLR 1189 at pp. 1191–2). Each of the parties must be given the opportunity of being present at a view, and a failure to do so may result in a re-trial (*Goold v Evans and Co.*). However, it has been said that the judge may visit the *locus in quo* in order to see that which has previously been represented to him or her in court by plan and photograph on his or her own and without reference to the parties at all (per Widgery LJ in *Salsbury v Woodland* [1970] 1 QB 324 at pp. 343–4). See also per Lord Denning LJ in *Goold v Evans and Co.* [1951] 2 TLR 1189 at p. 1191. Such an exception was doubted by Leveson LJ in *M v Director of Public Prosecutions* [2009] EWHC 752 (Admin), [2009] 2 Cr App R 12 at [20], having regard to the importance attached to the principle that justice must both be done and be seen to be done by all those concerned. In that case it was further held (at [31]) that:

> What is critical before any court embarks upon any view is that there is absolute clarity about precisely what is to happen..., about who is to stand in what position, about what (if any) objects should be placed in a specific position and about who will do what. None of this should happen at the scene of a view, which should be conducted without discussion.

Notice and inspection of plans, photographs, models, etc.

49.94 CPR, r. 33.6, governs the admissibility of evidence (such as a plan, photograph or model) which is not—

(a) contained in a witness statement, affidavit or expert's report;

(b) to be given orally at trial; or

(c) evidence of which prior notice must be given under r. 33.2 (hearsay evidence; see 53.9).

Unless the court orders otherwise, the evidence shall not be receivable at a trial unless the party intending to put it in evidence has given notice to the other parties of his intention and given each of them an opportunity to inspect it and to agree to its admission without further proof. In *Orford v Rasmi Electronics Ltd* [2002] EWCA Civ 1672, [2003] CPLR 213, one of the reasons for ordering a retrial was that a plan was not shown to the claimant until the morning of the trial, though it had been in existence for over five months. The rule is wide enough to cover not only the illustrations given, i.e. plans, photographs and models, but also films and video films and other varieties of real evidence. The rule also covers documents which may be received in evidence without further proof under the Civil Evidence Act 1995, s. 9 (see 53.16). Where the evidence forms part of expert evidence, the notice must be given when the expert's report is served on the other party (CPR, r. 33.6(6)). Subject to this, where the intention is to use the evidence as evidence of any fact, then notice must be given not later than the latest date for serving witness statements. If there are not to be witness statements, or the intention is to put the evidence in solely in order to disprove an allegation made in a witness statement, notice must be given at least 21 days before the hearing (r. 33.6(5)). Where the evidence is being produced to the court for any reason other than as part of factual or expert evidence, notice must also be given at least 21 days before the hearing (r. 33.6(7)). The court needs to be able to understand any map, plan, diagram or photograph relied upon. A section in the skeleton argument should explain all the relevant features to be seen from such evidence (*Hunte v E. Bottomley and Sons Ltd* [2007] EWCA Civ 1168, [2008] CP Rep 3).

JUDGMENTS AS EVIDENCE

In *Hollington v F. Hewthorn and Co. Ltd* [1943] KB 587 it was established that verdicts in criminal **49.95**
proceedings (or judgments in civil proceedings) are not admissible in subsequent proceedings
as evidence of the facts on which they were based. Thus, in that case, an action in negligence
against the driver of a car who had been convicted of careless driving at the time and place of
the accident in question, it was held that the conviction was inadmissible as evidence of negligence, being inadmissible as evidence of the fact that the driver had committed the offence.
The court was of the view that the civil court would know nothing of the evidence before the
criminal court, and the arguments that were addressed to it, and that the opinion of the criminal court was irrelevant. 'Irrelevant' means that the opinion of the first court is not a matter to
which a later court required to decide the issue should have regard, because it is the duty of the
later court to form its own opinion on the basis of the evidence put before it (*Rogers v Hoyle*
[2013] EWHC 1409 (QB), [2015] QB 265 at [93]). The modern foundation of the rule is the preservation of the fairness of the subsequent trial (*Rogers v Hoyle* [2014] EWCA Civ 257, [2015] QB 265 at
[40]). The rule in *Hollington v F. Hewthorn and Co. Ltd* understandably attracted much criticism
and, insofar as it applies not only to previous convictions, but also to findings of adultery and
paternity in previous civil proceedings, it has been reversed by the Civil Evidence Act 1968,
ss. 11 to 13.

Previous convictions

Civil Evidence Act 1968, s. 11   Section 11 of the Civil Evidence Act 1968 reverses the **49.96**
decision in *Hollington v F. Hewthorn and Co. Ltd* [1943] KB 587, and creates a persuasive presumption that the person convicted shall be taken to have committed the offence in question unless the contrary is proved. A claimant who wishes to rely on evidence of a
conviction under s. 11 must include in his or her particulars of claim a statement to that
effect and give details of the type of conviction and its date, the court or court-martial
which made it, and the issue in the claim to which it relates (**PD 16, para. 8.1**). Section 11
provides as follows:

(1) In any civil proceedings the fact that a person has been convicted of an offence by or before any
    court in the United Kingdom or by a court-martial there or elsewhere shall (subject to subsec-
    tion (3) below) be admissible in evidence for the purpose of proving, where to do so is relevant
    to any issue in those proceedings, that he committed that offence, whether he was so convicted
    upon a plea of guilty or otherwise and whether or not he is a party to the civil proceedings; but
    no conviction other than a subsisting one shall be admissible in evidence by virtue of
    this section.
(2) In any civil proceedings in which by virtue of this section a person is proved to have been con-
    victed of an offence by or before any court in the United Kingdom or by a court-martial there or
    elsewhere—
    (a) he shall be taken to have committed that offence unless the contrary is proved; and
    (b) without prejudice to the reception of any other admissible evidence for the purpose of
        identifying the facts on which the conviction was based, the contents of any document which
        is admissible as evidence of the conviction, and the contents of the information, complaint,
        indictment or charge-sheet on which the person in question was convicted, shall be admissible
        in evidence for that purpose.
(3) Nothing in this section shall prejudice the operation of section 13 of this Act or any other enactment
    whereby a conviction or a finding of fact in any criminal proceedings is for the purposes of any other
    proceedings made conclusive evidence of any fact.
(4) Where in any civil proceedings the contents of any document are admissible in evidence by virtue
    of subsection (2) above, a copy of that document, or of the material part thereof, purporting to be
    certified or otherwise authenticated by or on behalf of the court or authority having custody of that
    document shall be admissible in evidence and shall be taken to be a true copy of that document or
    part unless the contrary is shown.

(5) Nothing in . . .

(a) section 14 of the Powers of Criminal Courts (Sentencing) Act 2000 (under which a conviction leading to discharge is to be disregarded except as therein mentioned) . . . shall affect the operation of this section. . . .

(6) In this section 'court-martial' means a court-martial constituted under the Army Act 1955, the Air Force Act 1955 or the Naval Discipline Act 1957 or a disciplinary court constituted under section 52G of the said Act of 1957, and in relation to a court-martial 'conviction' means a finding of guilty which is, or falls to be treated as, the finding of the court, and 'convicted' shall be construed accordingly.

Section 18 provides that, for the purposes of s. 11, 'civil proceedings':

includes, in addition to civil proceedings in any of the ordinary courts of law—

(a) civil proceedings before any other tribunal, being proceedings in relation to which the strict rules of evidence apply; and

(b) an arbitration or reference, whether under an enactment or not,

but does not include civil proceedings in relation to which the strict rules of evidence do not apply.

A 'subsisting' conviction includes a conviction against which an appeal is pending, but not one which has been quashed on appeal; and therefore rather than finally dispose of civil proceedings in reliance on a conviction subsequently liable to be quashed, it is better to adjourn the civil proceedings pending the outcome of the appeal (see *Re Raphael* [1973] 1 WLR 998). Section 11 does not apply to foreign convictions (see *Union Carbide Corporation v Naturin Ltd* [1987] FSR 538). However, even if the rule in *Hollington v F. Hewthorn and Co. Ltd* covers foreign convictions, it will not apply where the issues in the criminal and civil proceedings are identical (*Director of the Assets Recovery Agency v Virtosu* [2008] EWHC 149 (QB), [2009] 1 WLR 2808 at [43], civil proceedings for a recovery order under the Proceeds of Crime Act 2002, s. 241). Foreign convictions may also be referred to in an affidavit in support of a freezing injunction where they are part of the narrative explanation of the case against the defendant and enable the claimant to comply with his or her duty to make full and frank disclosure to the court (*Arab Monetary Fund v Hashim (No. 2)* [1990] 1 All ER 673).

Section 11(2)(b) is 'without prejudice to the reception of any other admissible evidence for the purpose of identifying the facts on which the conviction was based'. Such other evidence could include a copy of the summing up, which would be admissible under the Civil Evidence Act 1995 (see *Brinks Ltd v Abu-Saleh (No. 2)* [1995] 1 WLR 1487, a decision under the Civil Evidence Act 1968), as would a transcript of the evidence given in the criminal case.

The authorities are in conflict as to when the pleadings of the subject of the criminal proceedings challenging the conviction can be struck out as an abuse of process. (On abuse of process generally, see **33.12** to **33.22**.) In *Brinks Ltd v Abu-Saleh* [1995] 1 WLR 1478 it was held, relying upon *Hunter v Chief Constable of West Midlands Police* [1982] AC 529, that such pleadings should be struck out in the absence of new evidence, not adduced at the criminal trial, that entirely changes the aspect of the case. In *J v Oyston* [1999] 1 WLR 694, on the other hand, Smedley J, although of the opinion that it may be unwise to say that there can never be an abuse where the subsequent civil proceedings are brought against the subject of the criminal proceedings, declined to follow *Brinks Ltd v Abu-Saleh*, pointing out that *Hunter v Chief Constable of West Midlands Police* was distinguishable, being a case where the subsequent civil proceedings were brought by the subject of the criminal proceedings. However, where a defendant in civil proceedings is entitled to challenge his conviction under s. 11(2), there may be an 'absence of realism' about his ability to prove that he did not commit the offence entitling the court to grant the claimant summary judgment: *CXX v DXX* [2012] EWHC 1535 (QB), 162 NLJ 806. (On summary judgment generally, see **chapter 34.**)

Section 11(2)(a) imposes on a party who wishes to 'go behind' a conviction the burden of proving, on the balance of probabilities, that the person convicted did not commit the offence, and therefore it is not sufficient to establish that the conviction is unsafe, that the judge in the criminal trial (or the Court of Appeal) made an error or that the prosecution was an abuse of process (*Raja v Van Hoogstraten* [2005] EWHC 1642 (Ch), LTL 22/8/2005).

There is a divergence of judicial opinion as to what weight should be attached to the conviction, in deciding whether a party has discharged the burden of proving 'the contrary' under s. 11(2)(a). In *Taylor v Taylor* [1970] 1 WLR 1148, Davies LJ was of the view that the standard to be met in order to upset the conviction was the balance of probabilities but that the verdict of the jury was entitled to very great weight (at p. 1152). Similar views were expressed by Lord Denning MR in *Stupple v Royal Insurance Co. Ltd* [1971] 1 QB 50. Lord Denning MR was of the opinion that the conviction does not merely shift the burden of proof, but is a weighty piece of evidence of itself (at p. 72). Buckley LJ, however, was of the view that the statutory presumption would give way to evidence establishing the contrary on the balance of probability without itself affording any evidential weight when deciding whether that onus had been discharged (at p. 76). See also, preferring the approach of Lord Denning, Moore-Bick J in *Phoenix Marine Inc. v China Ocean Shipping Co.* [1999] 1 All ER 138 at [143] and per Spencer J in *CXX v DXX* [2012] EWHC 1535 (QB), 162 NLJ 806 at [39]; and, preferring the view of Buckley LJ, per Stirling J in *Wright v Wright* (1971) 115 SJ 173. In *McIlkenny v Chief Constable of the West Midlands* [1980] QB 283 at p. 320 Lord Denning MR suggested, obiter, that a convicted man could only prove 'the contrary' under s. 11(2)(a) by proving that the conviction was obtained by fraud or collusion or by adducing fresh evidence which must be 'decisive' and 'conclusive'. On appeal, however, Lord Diplock disapproved the dictum, being of the opinion that the standard to be met, in proving 'the contrary' was proof on a balance of probabilities, but added that 'in the face of a conviction after a full hearing this is likely to be an uphill task' (*Hunter v Chief Constable of the West Midlands Police* [1982] AC 529 at p. 544).

Civil Evidence Act 1968, s. 13   Section 13 of the Civil Evidence Act 1968, which applies to   **49.97**
defamation proceedings, reverses the decision in *Hollington v F. Hewthorn and Co. Ltd* [1943] KB 587 (**49.95**) and creates a conclusive presumption, that the person convicted shall be conclusively taken to have committed the offence in question. Thus a defamation claim based on the defendant's statement that the claimant committed an offence in respect of which he has been convicted, will be struck out as an abuse of the process of the court, unless the statement also contains some other legally defamatory matter (*Levene v Roxhan* [1970] 1 WLR 1322). Section 13 provides as follows:

(1)   In an action for libel or slander in which the question whether the plaintiff did or did not commit a criminal offence is relevant to an issue arising in the action, proof that at the time when that issue falls to be determined, he stands convicted of that offence shall be conclusive evidence that he committed that offence; and his conviction thereof shall be admissible in evidence accordingly.

(2)   In any such action as aforesaid in which by virtue of this section the plaintiff is proved to have been convicted of an offence, the contents of any document which is admissible as evidence of the conviction, and the contents of the information, complaint, indictment or charge-sheet on which he was convicted, shall, without prejudice to the reception of any other admissible evidence for the purpose of identifying the facts on which the conviction was based, be admissible in evidence for the purpose of identifying those facts.

(2A) In the case of an action for libel or slander in which there is more than one plaintiff—

  (a)   the references in subsections (1) and (2) above to the plaintiff shall be construed as references to any of the plaintiffs, and

  (b)   proof that any of the plaintiffs stands convicted of an offence shall be conclusive evidence that he committed that offence so far as that fact is relevant to any issue arising in relation to his cause of action or that of any other plaintiff.

(3)   For the purposes of this section a person shall be taken to stand convicted of an offence if but only if there subsists against him a conviction of that offence by or before a court in the United Kingdom or by a court-martial there or elsewhere.

(4) Subsections (4) to (6) of section 11 of this Act shall apply for the purposes of this section as they apply for the purposes of that section, but as if in the said subsection (4) the reference to subsection (2) were a reference to subsection (2) of this section.

Previous findings of adultery and paternity

49.98 The Civil Evidence Act 1968, s. 12, reverses the rule in *Hollington v F. Hewthorn and Co. Ltd* [1943] KB 587 (**49.95**), in so far as it applied to previous findings of adultery and paternity, and creates two persuasive presumptions, that the person found guilty of adultery shall be taken to have committed the adultery, and that the person found to be the father of a child shall be taken to be, or have been, the father of the child. A claimant who wishes to rely on evidence under s. 12 of a finding or adjudication of adultery or paternity must include in his or her particulars of claim a statement to that effect and give details of the finding or adjudication and its date, the court which made it, and the issue in the claim to which it relates (**PD 16, para. 8.1**). Section 12 provides as follows:

(1) In any civil proceedings—
    (a) the fact that a person has been found guilty of adultery in any matrimonial proceedings; and
    (b) the fact that a person has been found to be the father of a child in relevant proceedings before any court in England and Wales or Northern Ireland or has been adjudged to be the father of a child in affiliation proceedings before any court in the United Kingdom; shall (subject to subsection (3) below) be admissible in evidence for the purpose of proving, where to do so is relevant to any issue in those civil proceedings, that he committed the adultery to which the finding relates or, as the case may be, is (or was) the father of that child, whether or not he offered any defence to the allegation of adultery or paternity and whether or not he is a party to the civil proceedings; but no finding or adjudication other than a subsisting one shall be admissible in evidence by virtue of this section.
(2) In any civil proceedings in which by virtue of this section a person is proved to have been found guilty of adultery as mentioned in subsection (1)(a) above or to have been found or adjudged to be the father of a child as mentioned in subsection (1)(b) above—
    (a) he shall be taken to have committed the adultery to which the finding relates or, as the case may be, to be (or have been) the father of that child, unless the contrary is proved; and
    (b) without prejudice to the reception of any other admissible evidence for the purpose of identifying the facts on which the finding or adjudication was based, the contents of any document which was before the court, or which contains any pronouncement of the court, in the other proceedings in question shall be admissible in evidence for that purpose.
(3) Nothing in this section shall prejudice the operation of any enactment whereby a finding of fact in any matrimonial or affiliation proceedings is for the purposes of any other proceedings made conclusive evidence of any fact.
(4) Subsection (4) of section 11 of this Act shall apply for the purposes of this section as if the reference to subsection (2) were a reference to subsection (2) of this section.
(5) In this section—
    'matrimonial proceedings' means any matrimonial cause in the High Court or a family court in England and Wales or in the High Court in Northern Ireland, any consistorial action in Scotland, or any appeal arising out of any such cause or action;
    'relevant proceedings' means—
    (a) proceedings on a complaint under section 42 of the National Assistance Act 1948 or section 26 of the Social Security Act 1986;
    (b) proceedings under the Children Act 1989;
    (c) proceedings which would have been relevant proceedings for the purposes of this section in the form in which it was in force before the passing of the Children Act 1989;
    (e) proceedings which are relevant proceedings as defined in section 8(5) of the Civil Evidence Act (Northern Ireland) 1971;
    'affiliation proceedings' means, in relation to Scotland, any action of affiliation and aliment; and in this subsection 'consistorial action' does not include an action of aliment only between husband and wife raised in the Court of Session or an action of interim aliment raised in the sheriff court.

As to the meaning of 'civil proceedings', see s. 18(1), which is considered at **49.96**. Under s. 12(2) the party seeking to disprove the adultery or paternity bears the legal burden of doing so, and the standard of proof required to discharge the burden is the ordinary civil standard of proof on a balance of probabilities (*Sutton v Sutton* [1970] 1 WLR 183).

Previous acquittals

Parliament rejected the Law Reform Committee's recommendation that in defamation proceedings evidence of an acquittal should be conclusive evidence of innocence (see 15th Report (1967) Cmnd 3391, para. 26 et seq.) The question still remains, however, whether the principle of *Hollington v F. Hewthorn and Co. Ltd* [1943] KB 587 (**49.95**) should apply to previous acquittals so as to render them inadmissible as evidence of innocence in subsequent civil proceedings. It is submitted that, on balance, the question should be answered in the affirmative because although it is desirable that a person acquitted of an offence should be granted some measure of immunity from assertions to the contrary, an allegation which was not proved beyond reasonable doubt may still be susceptible to proof on a balance of probabilities, as it was in *Loughans v Odhams Press* [1963] 1 QB 299, a libel suit arising out of the publication of a statement suggesting that the claimant had committed a murder in respect of which he had been acquitted. However, in *Packer v Clayton* (1932) 97 JP 14, a decision pre-dating *Hollington v F. Hewthorn and Co. Ltd*, Avory J expressed the opinion that in affiliation proceedings, the respondent's acquittal of a sexual offence against the applicant would be admissible to show that the jury were not convinced by her evidence. **49.99**

Other previous findings

The principle of *Hollington v F. Hewthorn and Co. Ltd* [1943] KB 587 would appear to apply, in civil proceedings, to all judicial findings in previous civil proceedings, except findings of adultery and paternity (see Civil Evidence Act 1968, s. 12, at **49.98**). In *Secretary of State for Trade and Industry v Bairstow* [2003] EWCA Civ 321, [2004] Ch 1, the Secretary of State began proceedings under the Company Directors Disqualification Act 1986, s. 8, seeking a disqualification order against B, the managing director of a company. By the time of the proceedings, B had been dismissed and his claim for damages for wrongful dismissal had been unsuccessful, both at first instance and on appeal. In the proceedings under the 1986 Act, the Court of Appeal held that the factual findings and conclusions of the judge at first instance in the wrongful dismissal proceedings were not admissible as evidence of the facts found in those proceedings. However, it was also held that the principle of abuse of process will prevent collateral attack on an earlier decision of a court of competent jurisdiction where relitigation of the same issues would be manifestly unfair or would bring the administration of justice into disrepute. See further at **33.12** to **33.21**. **49.100**

Parliament has established investigatory processes for providing the Secretary of State with reports, information or documents on which an opinion may be based that it is expedient in the public interest that a company should be wound up (Insolvency Act 1986, s. 124A(1)) or that a disqualification order should be made against a person (Company Directors Disqualification Act 1986, s. 8). It follows that the Secretary of State may use the relevant report etc. as evidence in support of a petition to wind up the company or an application for a disqualification order despite the rule in *Hollington v F. Hewthorn and Co. Ltd* (*Secretary of State for Business, Enterprise and Regulatory Reform v Aaron* [2008] EWCA Civ 1146, [2009] 1 BCLC 55).

The rule in *Hollington v F. Hewthorn and Co. Ltd* applies only to previous judicial findings as opposed to the opinions of an expert. Thus in a negligence claim arising out of a plane crash, the court may have regard to the contents of a report produced by the Air Accident Investigation Branch of the Department of Transport, including conclusions about the probable causes of the accident (*Rogers v Hoyle* [2014] EWCA Civ 257, [2015] QB 265).

Commentary

However, the principle in *Hollington v F. Hewthorn and Co. Ltd* does apply in relation to previous findings of inspectors appointed under what is now the Companies Act 1985, part 14 (*Savings and Investment Bank Ltd v Gasco Investments (Netherlands) BV* [1984] 1 WLR 271), an arbitration award, in later proceedings for the determination of a fair market rent (*Land Securities plc v Westminster City Council* [1993] 1 WLR 286) and the findings of Lord Bingham of Cornhill in his extra-statutory report into the collapse of BCCI (*Three Rivers District Council v Bank of England (No. 3)* [2001] UKHL 16, [2003] 2 AC 1). In *Hill v Clifford* [1907] 2 Ch 236 the Court of Appeal held that a finding by the General Medical Council that a dentist had been guilty of professional misconduct was admissible as prima facie evidence of the misconduct in subsequent civil proceedings concerning the dissolution of his partnership; but in these circumstances the court is entitled to reach its own view of the facts as previously found (*Clifford v Timms* [1908] AC 12). Similarly, the principle of *Hollington v F. Hewthorn and Co. Ltd* has been held to apply to findings of the Solicitors Disciplinary Tribunal that a solicitor has been dishonest (*Conlon v Simms* [2006] EWCA Civ 1749, [2008] 1 WLR 484). See also the discussion of this case at **33.17** on the device of using striking out to achieve a result sidestepping *Hollington v F. Hewthorn and Co. Ltd.* See also *Faulder v Silk* (1811) 3 Camp 126 (inquisitions in lunacy as prima facie evidence of a person's unsoundness of mind). As to statements contained in public documents, which at common law are admissible for the truth of their contents, see **53.24** to **53.26**. Although a person who was not a party to the earlier proceedings cannot be bound by the result, they can be affected by it.

FINDINGS ON QUESTIONS OF FOREIGN LAW

49.101   Points of foreign law are questions of fact, and therefore fall to be decided on the evidence adduced, normally expert evidence, except in the case of:

(a) points of foreign law which are formally admitted (see **49.9**) or of which judicial notice may be taken (see **49.28**) and

(b) the construction of provisions of foreign legislation admitted under the Evidence (Colonial Statutes) Act 1907, whereby copies of Acts, ordinances and statutes passed by the legislature of any part of Her Majesty's dominions exclusive of the United Kingdom and of orders, regulations and other instruments issued or made under the authority of any such Act, ordinance or statute, if purporting to be printed by the Government printer of the possession, shall be received in evidence by all courts in the United Kingdom without proof that the copies were so printed (see the authorities cited in *Jasiewicz v Jasiewicz* [1962] 1 WLR 1426).

Under the British Law Ascertainment Act 1859, English courts may state a case on a point of foreign law for the opinion of a superior court in another part of Her Majesty's dominions, and the opinion pronounced is admissible in evidence on the point. See also the Foreign Law Ascertainment Act 1861.

Points of foreign law must always be decided by the judge. Under the Senior Courts Act 1981, s. 69(5), where, for the purposes of disposing of any action or other matter which is being tried by a judge with a jury, it is necessary to ascertain the law of any other country which is applicable to the facts of the case, any question as to the effect of the evidence given with respect to that law shall, instead of being submitted to the jury, be decided by the judge alone. To like effect, see also the County Courts Act 1984, s. 68.

Foreign law will usually be established by the opinion evidence of an expert, who may refer to foreign statutes, decisions and texts. If the evidence of the experts conflicts, the judge is bound to look at the sources of knowledge upon which they have relied in order to reach a decision (see per Lord Langdale MR in *Earl Nelson v Lord Bridport* (1845) 8 Beav 527 at p. 537; and per

Scarman J in *Re Fuld (No. 3)* [1968] P 675 at pp. 700–3), but should not conduct his or her own research into those sources and rely on material not adduced in evidence in order to reject the expert testimony (per Lord Chelmsford in *Duchess di Sora v Phillipps* (1863) 10 HL Cas 624 at p. 640; and per Purchas LJ in *Bumper Development Corporation Ltd v Metropolitan Police Commissioner* [1991] 1 WLR 1362 at pp. 1368–71).

Although points of foreign law are questions of fact, if a point has been decided, and the same point arises again in a subsequent case, it does not necessarily need to be decided afresh on new expert evidence. The Civil Evidence Act 1972, s. 4, provides as follows:

(2) Where any question as to the law of any country or territory outside the United Kingdom, or of any part of the United Kingdom other than England and Wales, with respect to any matter has been determined (whether before or after the passing of this Act) in any such proceedings as are mentioned in subsection (4) below, then in any civil proceedings (not being proceedings before a court which can take judicial notice of the law of that country, territory or part with respect to that matter)—

(a) any finding made or decision given on that question in the first-mentioned proceedings shall, if reported or recorded in citable form, be admissible in evidence for the purpose of proving the law of that country, territory or part with respect to that matter; and

(b) if that finding or decision, as so reported or recorded, is adduced for that purpose, the law of that country, territory or part with respect to that matter shall be taken to be in accordance with that finding or decision unless the contrary is proved:

Provided that paragraph (b) above shall not apply in the case of a finding or decision which conflicts with another finding or decision on the same question adduced by virtue of this subsection in the same proceedings.

(3) Except with the leave of the court, a party to any civil proceedings shall not be permitted to adduce any such finding or decision as is mentioned in subsection (2) above by virtue of that subsection unless he has in accordance with rules of court given to every other party to the proceedings notice that he intends to do so.

(4) The proceedings referred to in subsection (2) above are the following, whether civil or criminal, namely—

(a) proceedings at first instance in any of the following courts, namely the High Court, the Crown Court, a court of quarter sessions, the Court of Chancery of the county palatine of Lancaster and the Court of Chancery of the county palatine of Durham;

(b) appeals arising out of any such proceedings as are mentioned in paragraph (a) above;

(c) proceedings before the Judicial Committee of the Privy Council on appeal (whether to Her Majesty in Council or to the Judicial Committee as such) from any decision of any court outside the United Kingdom.

(5) For the purposes of this section a finding or decision on any such question as is mentioned in subsection (2) above shall be taken to be reported or recorded in citable form if, but only if, it is reported or recorded in writing in a report, transcript or other document which, if that question had been a question as to the law of England and Wales, could be cited as an authority in legal proceedings in England and Wales.

'Civil proceedings', for the purposes of s. 4(2) and (3), means civil proceedings before any tribunal, in relation to which the strict rules of evidence apply, whether as a matter of law or by agreement of the parties (s. 5). **CPR, r. 33.7**, sets out the procedure which must be followed by a party who intends to put in evidence a finding under the Civil Evidence Act 1972, s. 4(2). He or she must give notice of his or her intention:

(a) if there are to be witness statements, not later than the latest date for serving them, or

(b) otherwise, not less than 21 days before the hearing;

and the notice must specify the question on which the finding was made and enclose a copy of a document where it is reported or recorded.

Section 4(2)(b) effectively raises a presumption that the earlier decision is correct. The weight to be attached to the earlier decision, however, is a matter for the trial judge, and although it is obviously desirable to reach consistent conclusions, the section is not to be construed as if it laid down a general rule that the presumption can only be displaced by particularly cogent evidence (*Phoenix Marine Inc. v China Ocean Shipping Co.* [1999] 1 Lloyd's Rep 682).

EVIDENCE OF CONSENT OF TRUSTEE TO ACT

49.102 A document purporting to contain the written consent of a person to act as trustee and to bear his or her signature, verified by some other person, is evidence of such consent (CPR, r. 33.8).

Chapter 50 Disclosure

Commentary

The following procedural checklists are relevant to this chapter:

INTRODUCTION

50.1 Disclosure is the formal process by which parties to claims give each other copies of the documents in their control which are material to the issues in the claim. Formal disclosure under **CPR, Part 31**, applies to claims on the fast track and multi-track, but not to claims on the small claims track (see **45.17**). Disclosure should take place in accordance with directions made by the court. In most fast track and multi-track claims directions for disclosure are made when the claim is allocated to a track (**rr. 28.2(1), 28.3, 29.2(1)(a); PD 29, para. 4**). Otherwise, directions are given at a case management conference (**CPR, r. 29.2(1)(b)**). The usual direction in fast track claims is for standard disclosure (see **50.4**), which covers documents in the control of the party making disclosure which that party intends to rely on at the trial, and also documents which adversely affect that party or which support the other side. Multi-track claims (other than claims for personal injuries) are governed by menu option disclosure (see **50.10**). Disclosure takes place in two stages. First, the parties exchange lists of documents using form N265 or electronic documents questionnaires using the form on the schedule to **PD 31B**. A list of documents identifies all the documents which support or adversely affect any of the parties to the claim, and also asserts any privilege claimed against disclosure in respect of identified documents or categories of documents (see **50.50 to 50.83**). Secondly, the parties allow their opponents to inspect the non-privileged disclosed documents. Usually this happens by providing photocopies, but there is provision for physical inspection of the originals and for disclosure in electronic form.

The disclosure system includes the following features:

(a) The potential for incurring disproportionate costs on disclosure. Many disputes generate large quantities of documentary evidence that needs to be disclosed.

(b) Disclosure traditionally extends to all materials on which information is recorded (see **50.17**) and materials that are relied upon, and also those that support another party or which might be adverse to any party. There is always a fear that the other side might not fully comply with their disclosure obligations.

(c) Disclosure obligations extend to electronic documents and even metadata. Disclosure of electronic documents at proportionate cost can be very challenging.

(d) To meet these challenges parties and the court need to tailor the approach to giving disclosure in complex claims to the circumstances of the case.

(e) Application of the principle of proportionality to limit the extent of the searches required to find disclosable documents.

(f) A requirement to include a 'disclosure statement' in the list of documents to the effect that the party giving disclosure has complied with its duties under **CPR, Part 31**.

(g) A requirement that litigants, rather than their lawyers, must sign the disclosure statement. This obligation is intended to bring home to litigants that it is their personal responsibility to give full disclosure (*Arrow Trading and Investments Est 1920 v Edwardian Group Ltd* [2004] EWHC 1319 (Ch), [2005] 1 BCLC 696).

Where an opponent fails to give disclosure in accordance with directions, the innocent party should still usually comply with its own disclosure obligations, but may apply for a sanction (usually an 'unless' order, see **chapter 48**) or for specific disclosure (see **50.41**). Deliberate destruction of documents to avoid the obligation to give disclosure, particularly after an unless order, is likely to result in a severe sanction, such as striking out (*Rybak v Langbar International Ltd* [2010] EWHC 2015 (Ch), LTL 24/8/2010).

Documents disclosed under **Part 31** are deemed to be authentic (see **50.43**), and if this is disputed, the party receiving the copies should serve a notice to prove. Disclosed documents are provided for the purposes of the present litigation and must not be used for any collateral purpose (**50.45**), although this protection is usually lost once the documents are referred to in open court.

DOCUMENTATION ON THE SMALL CLAIMS TRACK

The rules on disclosure in **CPR, Part 31**, do not apply at all to the small claims track (**r. 27.2(1)(b)**). On the small claims track, parties are required to disclose only the documents on which they intend to rely at trial (see **r. 27.4(3)(a)** and **45.17**).

50.2

FAST TRACK AND MULTI-TRACK DISCLOSURE

To ensure disclosure takes place in a proportionate manner, disclosure in fast track claims and personal injuries cases on the multi-track is usually made in accordance with standard disclosure (see **50.4**), whereas in most other multi-track claims the courts adopt menu option disclosure (discussed at **50.10**). More technically:

50.3

(a) fast track claims, multi-track personal injuries claims, and other multi-track claims where the court makes a specific direction to this effect, are governed by **CPR, r. 31.5(1)**, which starts from the position that the parties must give standard disclosure; and

(b) all other multi-track claims are governed by **r. 31.5(3) to (8)**, which lays down the scheme for menu option disclosure.

Commentary (side tab)

STANDARD DISCLOSURE

50.4   The procedure for standard disclosure is summarised in **procedural checklist 25**. In fast track and other claims in category (a) at **50.3** above, disclosure directions will usually expressly require standard disclosure, but a direction simply referring to disclosure in these cases means an order to give standard disclosure, unless the court directs otherwise (see **CPR, r. 31.5(1)(a)**). In these cases:

(i)   the court may alternatively dispense with or limit standard disclosure (**r. 31.5(1)(b)**); or

(ii) the parties may agree in writing to dispense with or to limit standard disclosure (**r. 31.5(1)(c)**).

In the exercise of its case management powers in furtherance of the overriding objective, the court may decide to make orders limiting or dispensing with standard disclosure, and it should not be assumed that an order for standard disclosure will simply be rubber-stamped by the court (see **50.37**).

Documents covered by standard disclosure

50.5   By **CPR, r. 31.6**, standard disclosure requires a party to disclose only:

(a)   the documents on which he relies; and

(b)   the documents which—

    (i)   adversely affect his own case;

    (ii)   adversely affect another party's case; or

    (iii) support another party's case; and

(c)   the documents which he is required to disclose by a relevant practice direction.

Although these categories do not include 'train of inquiry' documents (see **50.14**), they are nevertheless wide ranging, and many clients are surprised at the breadth of documentation that they are required to disclose. To ensure the system works fairly between the opposing parties, lawyers are under professional duties to advise their clients on their disclosure obligations (**50.31**), and clients must take personal responsibility by signing a disclosure statement (**50.22**).

While the categories set out in **r. 31.6** come close to the concept of relevance, that particular word is not used in **r. 31.6**, and is not the test (*Shah v HSBC Private Bank (UK) Ltd* [2011] EWCA Civ 1154, LTL13/10/2011). The category of documents upon which a party relies (**r. 31.6(a)**) is probably restricted to documents relied upon in support of that party's affirmative case or to rebut the case advanced by the other side. The fact a party does not intend to adduce a document as part of its evidence at trial is probably conclusive that the document does not fall into **r. 31.6(a)** (*Shah v HSBC Private Bank (UK) Ltd*). **Rule 31.6(a)** does not cover documents that may be referred to as a shield in cross-examination (*Favor Easy Management Ltd v Wu* [2010] EWCA Civ 1630, [2011] 1 WLR 1803 at [22]). **Rule 31.6(b)** is drafted in unqualified terms, and it is impermissible to read into it a qualification that it covers only documents that adversely affect another party's case 'as against another party' (*Serious Organised Crime Agency v Namli* [2011] EWCA Civ 1411, LTL 29/11/2011). The description 'documents which adversely affect [the disclosing party's] own case' (**r. 31.6(b)(i)**) is probably self-explanatory. **Rule 31.6(b)(ii)** is probably intended to cover documents in the control of party A in a multi-party claim which adversely affect the case of party B against party C (*Serious Organised Crime Agency v Namli* at [18]). If the other side does not have an affirmative case, there is nothing for **r. 31.6(b)(ii)** or **(iii)** to bite on (*Shah v HSBC Private Bank (UK) Ltd*). Whether a document falls into any of these categories is to be judged against the statements of case, and not by reference to matters raised elsewhere, even in exchanged witness statements (*Paddick v Associated Newspapers Ltd* [2003] EWHC 2991 (QB), LTL 12/12/2003). They do not cover documents which are relevant solely to credit (*Thorpe v Chief Constable of Greater Manchester*

Police [1989] 1 WLR 665, confirmed by *Favor Easy Management Ltd v Wu*), on the ground this helps to keep disclosure within reasonable and sensible bounds (*Thorpe v Chief Constable of Greater Manchester Police* per Neill LJ at p. 673).

Standard disclosure in personal injury claims

Annex C to the **Pre-action Protocol for Personal Injury Claims** contains detailed lists of categories of documents that should be disclosed in various types of personal injury claims. For example, in tripping cases the highway authority should disclose its records for the 12 months prior to the accident dealing with inspections of the relevant stretch of highway; maintenance including records of independent contractors working in the relevant area; minutes of highway authority meetings where maintenance or repair policy was discussed or decided; complaints about the state of highways; and other accidents on the relevant stretch of highway. Annex C has even more detailed lists for accidents at work. Standard disclosure imposes similar obligations, but will include claims-handling documents and party-and-party correspondence, and (although, because privileged, inspection will not be required) documents relating to legal advice on the claim.

50.6

The combined effect of **CPR, rr. 31.3, 31.6, 31.8** and **31.12(3)**, is to oblige a claimant in a personal injuries claim to disclose and give inspection of the claimant's GP and hospital records (*Bennett v Compass Group UK and Ireland Ltd* [2002] EWCA Civ 642, [2002] ICR 1177). This is so almost regardless of the nature of the dispute. The records will either confirm the claimant's injuries and their consequences, or will question those injuries or their extent, and will therefore support either the claimant's or the defendant's case (*OCS Group Ltd v Wells* [2008] EWHC 919 (QB), [2009] 1 WLR 1895). Where the claimant fails to cooperate in providing these records (which are under the claimant's control as defined by **r. 31.8(2)**), the court has the power to make an order that the claimant must provide the defendant with a signed authority for the release of the records, but such an order has to be carefully worded to ensure the claimant's rights are not infringed (*Bennett v Compass Group UK and Ireland Ltd*). This means that care should be taken to ensure the records to be disclosed are not wider (in terms of dates or nature of the document to be disclosed) than the nature of the case merits.

Standard disclosure in professional negligence claims

The solicitor's file under the original retainer is almost always, or always, covered by standard disclosure in a solicitors' professional negligence claim (*Martin v Triggs Turner Barton* [2008] EWHC 89 (Ch), [2008] WTLR 509). Where particulars of claim in a property valuation negligence claim set out the loss by reference to the price paid for the property, and the defence pleaded that the purchase was structured to obtain an unlawful tax saving, standard disclosure by the claimant had to include its tax returns (*KIS Lincoln v CB Richard Ellis Hotels Ltd* [2009] EWHC 2344 (TCC), [2010] PNLR 5).

50.7

Standard disclosure in commercial and contract claims

Contractual and commercial claims often generate considerable disclosable documentation. This will include the contractual documents, including the contract, tenders, offers, orders, shipping documents, delivery notes, invoices, documents recording or effecting payment, statements of account, and receipts; correspondence relating to forming the contract, its performance, and alleged breach; documents dealing with the effects of breach and any steps taken to mitigate damage; and often financial documentation, such as business accounts, tax records and financial records dealing with loss of profits or other heads of loss and damage.

50.8

A standard disclosure order is appropriate even in complex patent claims where there is likely to be a vast amount of potentially disclosable documentation, rather than putting the burden

Commentary

on the opposite party to make an application for specific disclosure. In cases with large volumes of documents, the costs of disclosure can be kept under control by cooperation between the parties over the extent of the searches that each should make (*Hospira Inc. v Amgen Inc.* [2010] EWHC 176 (Pat), LTL 25/2/2010).

In *Marlton v Tektronix UK Holdings Ltd* [2003] EWHC 383 (Ch), LTL 10/2/2003 there was a dispute about whether a contractual document was sent by email, so disclosure was ordered of the relevant hard disks, back-ups and server. Diaries containing business and personal details, which were relevant to establishing how much time a director had spent in managing a business, were ordered to be disclosed in *Re Cawgate Ltd* [2004] EWHC 1773 (Ch), LTL 30/6/2004. In an unfair prejudice case (see 85.9), where it was alleged the directors were receiving excessive remuneration, standard disclosure included financial documents such as accounts and budgets (*Arrow Trading and Investments Est 1920 v Edwardian Group Ltd* [2004] EWHC 1319 (Ch), [2005] 1 BCLC 696). In a patent infringement case there is no blanket immunity from standard disclosure concerning the obviousness of the patented invention, despite the objective nature of the question (*Nichia Corporation v Argos Ltd* [2007] EWCA Civ 741, [2007] Bus LR 1753). Seeking the names of employees who had made money laundering reports, whose names were redacted from the documents disclosed by a bank in a claim for breach of mandate, was held in *Shah v HSBC Private Bank (UK) Ltd* [2011] EWCA Civ 1154, LTL13/10/2011, to fall outside the categories in **r. 31.6** and to be a fishing expedition.

Standard disclosure in libel claims

50.9   A defendant who pleads justification is entitled to disclosure of all matters relating to the questions in issue as narrowed by the particulars (*Yorkshire Provident Life Assurance Co. v Gilbert and Rivington* [1895] 2 QB 148). The defendant was not entitled to disclosure of documents relating to unpleaded complaints by patients against the claimant doctor in *Taranissi v British Broadcasting Corporation* [2008] EWHC 2486 (QB), LTL 24/10/2008. A number of categories of documents were considered in the libel case of *Beckham v News Group Newspapers Ltd* [2005] EWHC 2252 (QB), LTL 25/10/2005:

(a)   Disclosure of documents relating to the claimants' public relations strategies was refused, because there was no sufficient foundation to the defendant's case that the claimants had presented a false image to the public.

(b)   Disclosure was also refused of documents relating to the claimants' move to Madrid, their commercial arrangements with a particular photographer, and the termination of an agency agreement with a public relations company.

(c)   Disclosure of tapes of a television documentary about the claimants, including all unedited versions, was dealt with by an order that the claimants must use their best endeavours to find out from those involved in making the documentary about incidents relied on by the defendant and to communicate such information to the defendant.

(d)   Disclosure of notes and tapes made by journalists when interviewing the claimants' former nanny was ordered. This was because the court needed to have regard to the totality of what the nanny said to the journalists, and because the items might be relevant to whether the nanny had appeared to be a credible source of information to the defendant's journalists.

MENU OPTION DISCLOSURE

50.10   In non-personal injuries multi-track claims, menu option disclosure applies unless the court otherwise orders (CPR, r. 31.5(2)). To the extent that the documents to be disclosed are electronic, the provisions of **PD 31B** (see 50.25) apply in addition to the menu option provisions (**r. 31.5(9)**). Menu option disclosure takes place in three stages.

Stage 1: Disclosure report

Not less than 14 days before the first case management conference (CMC) each party must **50.11**
file and serve a disclosure report in form N263 (**CPR, r. 31.5(3)**). This must be served with
their electronic documents questionnaire if this is required under **PD 31B (r. 31.5(4))**. A disclosure report must be verified by a statement of truth (**r. 31.5(3)**), and must:

(a) describe briefly what documents exist or may exist that are or may be relevant to the mat-
     ters in issue in the case;
(b) describe where and with whom those documents are or may be located;
(c) in the case of electronic documents, describe how those documents are stored;
(d) estimate the broad range of costs that could be involved in giving standard disclosure in
     the case, including the costs of searching for and disclosing any electronically stored docu-
     ments. This should be consistent with the party's costs budget, see **chapter 43**; and
(e) state which of the directions under **r. 31.5(6)** or (7) are to be sought.

Stage 2: Agree proposal for disclosure

Not less than seven days before the first CMC the parties must, at a meeting or by telephone, **50.12**
discuss and seek to agree a proposal in relation to disclosure that meets the overriding objective (**CPR, r. 31.5(5)**). A similar discussion must also be held on any other occasion as the
court may direct (**r. 31.5(5)**). Any agreed proposal should be filed at court. By **r. 31.5(6)**, if
the parties agree proposals for the scope of disclosure which the court considers are appropriate in all the circumstances, the court may approve them without a hearing and give directions
in the terms proposed.

Stage 3: CMC menu disclosure

If disclosure directions have not been made without a hearing under **CPR, r. 31.5(6)**, at the **50.13**
first or any subsequent CMC the court will decide on the appropriate orders to make about
disclosure. It will do so having regard to the overriding objective, the available costs budgets,
and the need to limit disclosure to that which is necessary to deal with the case justly
(**r. 31.5(7)**). The menu available under **r. 31.5(7)** comprises orders:

(a) dispensing with disclosure;
(b) that a party disclose the documents on which it relies (this concept was discussed at **50.5**),
     and at the same time request any specific disclosure it requires from any other party;
(c) directing, where practicable, the disclosure to be given by each party on an issue-by-issue
     basis;
(d) that each party disclose any documents which it is reasonable to suppose may contain
     information which enables that party to advance its own case or to damage that of any
     other party, or which leads to an inquiry which has either of those consequences (see
     50.14);
(e) for standard disclosure (see **50.4**);
(f) in whatever form the court considers appropriate (see **50.15**).

Train of inquiry documents

Disclosure of train of inquiry documents is permitted by **CPR, r. 31.5(7)(d)**. These are **50.14**
documents which are not themselves relevant, but which could provide information that
could lead to a train of inquiry resulting in finding relevant documents (*Compagnie Financiere
et Commerciale du Pacifique v Peruvian Guano Co.* (1882) 11 QBD 55). In this case Brett LJ said,
at p. 63:

every document relates to the matters in question in the action, which not only would be evidence upon
any issue, but also which, it is reasonable to suppose, contains information which *may*—not which
must —either directly or indirectly enable the party [seeking discovery] either to advance his own case or

to damage the case of his adversary...document can properly be said to contain information which may enable the party [seeking discovery] either to advance his own case or to damage the case of his adversary, if it is a document which may fairly lead him to a train of inquiry, which may have either of these two consequences.

Under the Rules of the Supreme Court 1965, the obligation to disclose 'train of inquiry' documents was a major cause of unnecessary costs and was a principal source of complaint by practitioners and litigants alike. In *O Co. v M Co.* [1996] 2 Lloyd's Rep 347 Colman J, out of frustration with the position under the RSC, stated, at pp. 350–1:

> The principle was never intended to justify demands for disclosure of documents at the far end of the spectrum of materiality which on the face of it were unrelated to the pleaded case of the plaintiff or defendant and which were required for purely speculative investigation...That formulation [Brett LJ's 'train of inquiry'] must not, in my judgment, be understood as justifying discovery demands which would involve parties to civil litigation being required to turn out the contents of their filing systems as if under criminal investigation merely on the off-chance that something might show up from which some relatively weak inference prejudicial to the case of the disclosing party might be drawn.

Train of inquiry documents are not covered by the definition of standard disclosure (see **50.4**), and are rarely required to be disclosed even in multi-track claims. A specific order to this effect must be obtained under the menu option if disclosure is to reach this far. Before making such an order the court will take into account all the circumstances of the case with particular regard to the overriding objective (**PD 31A, para. 5.4**). An order was made in *Commissioners of Inland Revenue v Exeter City AFC Ltd* [2004] BCC 519 for the disclosure of communications between the Inland Revenue and 20 to 30 football clubs connected to proposed and actual entry into insolvency of those football clubs. These were train of inquiry documents which could have advanced the defendant football club's case that the Inland Revenue had not been unfairly treated by the club's voluntary arrangement.

Key of the warehouse order

50.15   **CPR, r. 31.5(7)(f)**, allows the court to make any other order in relation to disclosure that the court considers appropriate. It allows the court, for example, to make a 'key of the warehouse' order. Such an order requires each party to hand over all its documents after removing any privileged documents, and the other side can then choose which documents it wishes to use in the litigation.

Disclosure directions

50.16   By **CPR, r. 31.5(8)**, the court may at any point give directions as to how disclosure is to be given, and in particular may direct:
   (a)   what searches are to be undertaken, of where, for what, in respect of which time periods and by whom and the extent of any search for electronically stored documents;
   (b)   whether lists of documents are required;
   (c)   how and when the disclosure statement is to be given;
   (d)   in what format documents are to be disclosed (and whether any identification is required);
   (e)   what is required in relation to documents that once existed but no longer exist; and
   (f)   whether disclosure shall take place in stages.

MATERIALS TO BE DISCLOSED

Documents

50.17   The regime for disclosure and inspection in **CPR, Part 31**, is concerned only with documents, and not any other type of evidence. A 'document' is defined in **r. 31.4** as 'anything in which information of any description is recorded' and 'copy' in relation to a document, means anything onto which information recorded in the document has been copied, by whatever means and whether directly or indirectly'. Thus a 'document' is not confined to paper, but includes electronic documents, audio and video cassettes, and other similar material.

Electronic documents include emails, messages on mobile telephones, word-processed documents and databases. In addition, the definition covers documents that are stored on servers and back-up systems and electronic documents that have been 'deleted'. It also extends to additional information stored and associated with electronic documents known as metadata (**PD 31A, para. 2A.1**). Disclosure of the metadata behind a record of an important meeting which had been created long after the event was ordered in *Hellard v Money* [2008] EWHC 2275 (Ch), LTL 29/4/2008.

Control of documents

By **CPR, r. 31.8(1)**, a party's duty to disclose documents is limited to documents which are now or have been previously within the party's control. **Rule 31.8(3)** provides that a document is or was in a party's control if: **50.18**

(a) it is or was in the party's physical possession;
(b) the party has or has had a right to possession of it; or
(c) the party has or has had a right to inspect or take copies of it.

There is control over documents if there is a prior or current practice of a party having access and inspection rights over documents in the possession of someone else (*Montpellier Estates Ltd v Leeds City Council* [2012] EWHC 1343 (QB), LTL 24/5/2012 at [33]). An employer or principal has a right to possession of documents in the hands of an employee in the course of the employee's employment or an agent in the course of the agency (*Fairstar Heavy Transport NV v Adkins* [2013] EWCA Civ 886, [2014] FSR 8). A company's documents may be under the control of a majority shareholder who has complete control over the company's affairs (*Re Tecnion Investments Ltd* [1985] BCLC 434) and it is possible for a subsidiary company's documents to be in the control of its parent company (*Lonrho Ltd v Shell Petroleum Co. Ltd* [1980] QB 358). Insurance claims documents in the possession of an insurer are in the control of the insured (*Mueller Europe Ltd v Central Roofing (South Wales) Ltd* [2012] EWHC 3417 (TCC), [2013] TCLR 2). While UK patients have control of their medical records by virtue of the Access to Health Records Act 1990, this depends on local legislation, so patients may not have control over medical records in other jurisdictions (*Favor Easy Management Ltd v Wu* [2010] EWCA Civ 1630, [2011] 1 WLR 1803).

Disclosure of copies

By **CPR, r. 31.9**, a copy of a document must be treated as a separate document, and therefore separately disclosed, if it contains a modification, obliteration or other marking or feature: **50.19**

(a) on which 'a party' (which clearly means the disclosing party) intends to rely; or
(b) which adversely affects the disclosing party's own case or supports another party's case.

So if, for example, several copies of a memorandum have been produced and some have been returned to the originator with other people's comments on them, and those comments are within (a) or (b) above, the copies must be disclosed. Otherwise it is not necessary to disclose the existence of copies of disclosed documents (**r. 31.9(1)**).

Reasonable search

CPR, r. 31.7 requires a party ordered to give standard disclosure to 'make a reasonable search for documents falling within r. 31.6(b) and (c)' (adverse material and documents specifically required by a practice direction). It is implicit in the obligation in **r. 31.7** that the search should be meaningful and effective (*Mueller Europe Ltd v Central Roofing (South Wales) Ltd* [2012] EWHC 3417 (TCC), [2013] TCLR 2). A search not carried out in good faith will not be reasonable (*Re* **50.20**

Commentary

Atrium Training Services Ltd [2013] EWHC 2882 (Ch), LTL 1/10/2013). The extent of the search must also be proportionate (**PD 31A, para. 2**). The searcher must search for the documents required by **CPR, r. 31.6(b)** and (**c**), but may make a policy decision not to search in places where the cost of searching could not be justified by the small chance of finding anything disclosable.

The duty to disclose under an order for standard disclosure is qualified by reasonableness. **CPR, r. 31.7(2)**, provides that the factors relevant in deciding the reasonableness of a search include the following:

(a) the number of documents involved;

(b) the nature and complexity of the proceedings;

(c) the ease and expense of retrieval of any particular document; and

(d) the significance of any document which is likely to be located during the search.

This list of factors is not intended to be exhaustive, and there may well be others which affect the reasonableness of disclosing documents. In applying these factors the court has to consider how central the documents are likely to be to the issues. It is particularly important to have contemporaneous documents where a case turns on the state of mind of a party (*Grace Shipping Inc. v C. F. Sharp and Co. (Malaya) Pte Ltd* [1987] 1 Lloyd's Rep 207), which may justify a wider search than might otherwise be the case (*Fiddes v Channel 4 Television Corporation* [2010] EWCA Civ 516, LTL 24/3/2010). If the documents could be described as secondary evidence (limited to being an aid in assessing the primary evidence), the extent of the search should be correspondingly limited (*Nichia Corporation v Argos Ltd* [2007] EWCA Civ 741, [2007] Bus LR 1753). In the first instance it is for the solicitor responsible for the disclosure process for each party to decide on what constitutes a reasonable search (**PD 31A, para. 2**). The rule does not demand that no stone be left unturned (*Abela v Hammonds Suddards* (2008) LTL 9/12/2008). A court asked to adjudicate on whether the search was sufficiently thorough might well be influenced by the diligence and conscientiousness displayed by the solicitor. Ultimately, it is for the court to decide whether the search was in fact reasonable (*Nichia Corporation v Argos Ltd*). This is not an exercise in reviewing the solicitor's decision (along the lines of judicial review), but of deciding what was reasonable.

A party who has not searched for a category or class of document on the grounds that to do so would be unreasonable, must state this in the disclosure statement (see **50.23**) and identify the category or class of document (**r. 31.7(3)**).

The extent of the search should be discussed by legal representative and client at all stages of litigation planning. Clients must provide their legal advisers with realistic information about the quantity of documents and the time and expense that may be involved in carrying out the search. It is the task of the lawyer to assess the legal significance and relevance of what might be disclosed if the search was extended, and all these factors must be taken into account and balanced against the value of the claim itself when deciding what kind of search would be reasonable.

LIST OF DOCUMENTS

50.21 When standard disclosure has been ordered, each party should make a list of the documents in its control which come within the categories set out in **CPR, r. 31.6** (see **50.5**). Lists of documents should be on form N265, and have to be served by the date stated in the court's directions on every other party (**r. 31.10(2)**; **PD 31A, para. 3.1**). Although a party will usually give disclosure in a list of documents, the requirement in **CPR, r. 31.2**, to disclose a document 'by stating that the document exists or has existed' can be satisfied by referring to a document's existence in a witness statement or expert's report (*SmithKline Beecham plc v Generics (UK) Ltd* [2003] EWCA Civ 1109, [2004] 1 WLR 1479 at [29]). On form N265, as required by **rr. 31.10(4)** and **31.19(4)**, the list is in three parts:

(a) Documents presently in the disclosing party's control which the controlling party does not object to being inspected.

(b) Documents presently in the disclosing party's control which the controlling party objects to being inspected, giving the reason for the objection. According to **PD 31A, para. 4.5**, a right or duty to withhold a document, or part of a document, from inspection must be claimed in writing with a statement of the grounds on which it is claimed, and, according to **para. 4.6**, should normally be included in the disclosure statement (see **50.23**), although form N265 is not laid out in that way.

(c) Documents that have been, but are no longer, in the disclosing party's control. The list must state when each document was last in the party's control and where each is now.

PD 31A, para. 3.2, provides that compliance with **CPR, r. 31.10(3)**, will be achieved by listing documents in chronological order, numbering them consecutively, and giving each of them a concise description, for example, 'letter, claimant to defendant, 19 Jan 2012'. Where there is a large number of documents which all fall into a particular category, the disclosing party is permitted to list those documents as a category, rather than individually, thus, for example: '50 bank statements relating to account number 1234546 at Anywhere Bank, September 2009–November 2013'.

Disclosure statement

The disclosing party's list of documents (form N265) must include a disclosure statement (**CPR, r. 31.10(5)**). The form of the statement, which is set out in the annex to **PD 31A**, is included in form N265 with a signature box. A disclosure statement is the statement of the disclosing party, or that party's insurer or the Motor Insurers' Bureau, rather than a legal representative (**CPR, r. 31.10(6)**). A disclosure statement is not a mere technicality. Its purpose is to impose a positive duty on each party to give full standard disclosure. Making a false disclosure statement may be punished as a contempt of court (**rr. 81.17** and **81.18**, see **chapter 81**). If there are several defendants in a case, each should sign a disclosure statement. Providing a single composite list of documents does not satisfy **r. 31.10** (*Arrow Trading and Investments Est 1920 v Edwardian Group Ltd* [2004] EWHC 1319 (Ch), [2005] 1 BCLC 696).

50.22

Where an insurer, or the Motor Insurers' Bureau, has a financial interest in the outcome of the proceedings, it may sign a disclosure statement on behalf of a party (**r. 31.10(9); PD 31A, para. 4.7**).

If the disclosing party is an individual, the disclosure statement is either the party's own statement, signed by the party or the party's litigation friend, or is the statement of the party's insurer or the Motor Insurers' Bureau.

If the disclosing party is not an individual, the disclosure statement must identify the person who is making and signing it and explain why he or she is considered an appropriate person to make it (**CPR, r. 31.10(7)**). It must state that person's name and address and the office or position he or she holds in the disclosing party (**PD 31A, para. 4.3**). The same rules apply when a disclosure statement is signed by an insurer or the Motor Insurers' Bureau (**PD 31A, para. 4.7**).

Having a disclosure statement signed by someone other than the party is a serious failure to comply with **CPR, r. 31.10(6)** (*Global Torch Ltd v Apex Global Management Ltd (No. 2)* [2014] UKSC 64, [2014] 1 WLR 4495). If a disclosure order requires a particular person to make disclosure on behalf of a party, that person cannot delegate the duty (*Carlco Ltd v Chief Constable of Dyfed-Powys Police* [2002] EWCA Civ 1754, LTL 18/11/2002). In *Carlco Ltd v Chief Constable of Dyfed-Powys Police* a disclosure order required disclosure to be made by the claimant company's 'officer', which meant it could only be signed by an officer who was an individual, and it could not be signed by a corporate director.

Contents of disclosure statement

By **CPR, r. 31.10(6)**, a disclosure statement must:

50.23

(a) set out the extent of the search that has been made to locate documents which are required to be disclosed;

(b) certify that the signatory understands the duty to disclose documents; and

(c) certify that to the best of his or her knowledge he or she has carried out that duty.

The disclosure statement certifies that a reasonable and proportionate search has been carried out to disclose all the documents required by the court's order.

PD 31A, para. 4.2, requires a disclosure statement expressly to state that the disclosing party believes the extent of the search to have been reasonable in all the circumstances; and **CPR, r. 31.7(3)**, requires a party who has not searched for a category or class of document on the grounds that to do so would be unreasonable, to state this in the disclosure statement, and identify the category or class of document not searched for. In the prescribed form of disclosure statement in **PD 31A, annex**, and form N265 the statement required by **CPR, r. 31.7(3)**, is turned into a description of the boundaries of a search:

I did not search for documents —

pre-dating —

located elsewhere than —

in categories other than—

for electronic documents (if electronic documents were searched for, further details must be given of the limits of the search)

In the disclosure statement the disclosing party should draw attention to any particular limitations which were adopted for proportionality reasons and give the reasons why the limitations were adopted (**PD 31A, para. 4.2(2)**).

The searcher must search for the documents required by **CPR, r. 31.6(b)** and (c), but may make a policy decision not to search in places where the cost of searching could not be justified by the small chance of finding anything disclosable.

Rule 31.3(2) requires a party who considers that it would be disproportionate to the issues in the case (see **50.36**) to permit inspection of a category or class of documents to state that fact in the disclosure statement.

PD 31A, para. 4.4, requires the legal representative of a disclosing party to endeavour to ensure that the individual making the disclosure statement understands the duty of disclosure under **CPR, Part 31**.

Dispensing with list of documents

50.24   **CPR, r. 31.10(8)**, provides that the parties may agree in writing to disclose documents without making a list, and to disclose documents without the disclosing party making a disclosure statement, but such agreement must be put into writing and lodged with the court (**PD 31A, para. 1.4**). Such agreements are comparatively uncommon, and form N265 is normally used.

ELECTRONIC DOCUMENTS

50.25   Disclosure of electronic documents is regulated by **PD 31B**, which was introduced on 1 October 2010. It applies to cases likely to be allocated to the multi-track (**PD 31A, para. 2A.2**), and provides a comprehensive and up-to-date set of rules governing the disclosure of electronic documents.

PD 31B, para. 6, sets out the following general principles:

(a) electronic documents should be managed efficiently in order to minimise the cost incurred;

(b) technology should be used in order to ensure that document management activities are undertaken efficiently and effectively;

(c) disclosure should be given in a manner which gives effect to the overriding objective;

(d) electronic documents should generally be made available for inspection in a form which allows the party receiving them the same ability to access, search, review and display the documents as the party giving disclosure; and

(e) disclosure of electronic documents which are of no relevance to the proceedings may place an excessive burden in time and cost on the party to whom disclosure is given.

In order to keep costs in proportion, the parties and their legal advisers are required to discuss the use of technology for the purposes of managing disclosure of electronic documents (**para. 8**). Particular topics to discuss are set out in **para. 9**, and include the tools to be used to reduce the burden and costs of disclosure, and the need to preserve electronic documents. In *Digicel (St Lucia) Ltd v Cable and Wireless plc* [2008] EWHC 2522 (Ch), [2009] 2 All ER 1094, the court ordered the parties' solicitors to meet to discuss the best way of restoring email accounts, in view of the possible cost of doing so.

Electronic documents questionnaire

An electronic documents questionnaire in the form in the schedule to **PD 31B** may be used   **50.26** to provide information relevant to the procedures for the disclosure of electronic documents. If used, the questionnaire has to be verified by a statement of truth (**PD 31B, para. 11**), and the questionnaire is treated as itself a disclosed document for the purpose of the collateral use rule in **CPR, r. 31.22**.

Directions for disclosure of electronic documents

Emphasis is placed on the importance of obtaining appropriate directions for disclosure at the   **50.27** first case management conference, which in turn requires cooperation between the parties (**PD 31B, paras 14 to 19**). One of the main difficulties in keeping costs under control in relation to electronic documents is the extent of the searches required under **CPR, r. 31.7**. **PD 31B, paras 20 to 27**, give guidance which includes a list of factors to be taken into account in deciding on the ambit of the search under **CPR, r. 31.7**. These factors include the nature and complexity of the proceedings, the ease of retrieval, and the availability of the documents or their contents from other sources. In *Fiddes v Channel 4 Television Corporation* [2010] EWCA Civ 516, LTL 24/3/2010, the technical costs of doing a search of backup tapes for deleted emails was estimated at £10,000. Even in the context of a case where the costs were already estimated at £1 million, and where the relevant respondent had changed her story from saying she had deleted her emails because her email account was full to saying she had not sent any emails in the relevant period, a finding that the documents in the proposed search were unlikely to be significant or relevant meant that a refusal to order the search was not overturned on appeal. **PD 31B, paras 25 to 27** deal with keyword searches for electronic documents. A search based on targeted keyword electronic searches was held to be inadequate in *Digicel (St Lucia) Ltd v Cable and Wireless plc*, where email accounts of specified individuals were required. Limited searches for electronic documents were regarded as reasonable in *Abela v Hammonds Suddards* (2008) LTL 9/12/2008.

Depending on the circumstances of the case, some of the following directions may be made to deal with disclosure of electronic documents:

(a) Arrangements for harvesting electronic documents. This involves identifying the individuals whose electronic documents should be brought into the disclosure exercise, which of their electronic devices (PCs, laptops, PDAs, mobile telephones etc.) should be included, the dates of the documents to be covered by the exercise, and whether the exercise includes deleted files and files from back-up storage devices.

(b) Providing the other side with the total number of documents harvested. Large numbers of documents usually mean that sophisticated search directions will be required.

(c) Whether harvested documents should be loaded onto an appropriate system (*Montpellier Estates Ltd v Leeds City Council* [2012] EWHC 1343 (QB), LTL 24/5/2012).

Commentary

(d) Arrangements for conducting a proportionate search of the harvested material. A discussion between the legal representatives of the parties may be ordered to seek agreement on how the search should be conducted.

(e) Applying keyword searches to identify relevant documents from those harvested. Parties should usually agree a list of keywords.

(f) Whether software should be used to decouple duplicates to reduce the number of documents to be disclosed (*Goodale v Ministry of Justice* (2009) LTL 9/9/2010).

(g) Whether a suitably qualified information technology consultant who is experienced in electronic disclosure should be retained to conduct the technical aspects of the search.

Inspection of electronic documents

50.28   Lists of documents may be provided in electronic form in CSV (comma-separated values) or other agreed format (**para. 30(2)**). **Paragraph 30(7)** is a reminder that any supplementary list should run sequentially from the last numbered entry in the previous list. Inspection may be given in electronic form, and may take the form of the provision of disclosure data electronically, or electronic copies of disclosed documents (**paras 31** and **32**). Unless otherwise agreed or ordered, electronic documents should be disclosed in their native form (i.e. preserving any metadata) (**para. 33**). If electronic documents are best accessed using technology which is not readily available to the other side, there is a duty to cooperate in making the documents available (**para. 36**).

ILLEGALLY OBTAINED DOCUMENTS

50.29   The Data Protection Act 1998, s. 55(1), provides that a person must not (and by s. 55(3) it is an offence to) knowingly or recklessly, without the consent of the data controller:

(a) obtain or disclose personal data or the information contained in personal data; or

(b) procure the disclosure to another person of the information contained in personal data.

Section 55(2)(a) provides that s. 55(1) does not apply to a person who shows that the obtaining, disclosing or procuring of the personal data or information:

(a) was necessary for the purpose of preventing or detecting crime; or

(b) was required or authorised by or under any enactment, by any rule of law or by order of a court.

In *Hughes v Carratu International plc* [2006] EWHC 1791 (QB), LTL 26/7/2006, the applicant became aware that the respondent professional investigator had come into possession of details relating to his bank account, which had been sent to it by a sub-agent. This was regarded as a possibly serious breach of the criminal law. The evidence in the case indicated that it was possible that the sub-agent was under the impression that such material would not be unwelcome to the respondent, nor possibly its principal (a well-known firm of solicitors). This was supported in part by the fact that something similar had happened in another case referred to the respondent by the same firm of solicitors. An order was made requiring the respondent to disclose all documents presently or formerly in its possession or control relating to the applicant's personal affairs, and disclosing the identities of the parties on whose behalf the information was gathered, and the identities of the parties who gathered that information. Removing documents from refuse sacks on the street outside a party's offices, copying them for use in litigation, and then returning the originals to the refuse sacks, was regarded as not giving rise even to a prima facie case of unlawfulness in *Consolidated Contractors International Co. SAL v Masri* [2011] EWCA Civ 21, [2011] CP Rep 20. Use of documents obtained using spyware on the other side's computer was reflected in an adverse costs order in *Walsh v Singh* [2011] EWCA Civ 80, [2011] 2 FLR 599.

In *Guidance Note (Illegally Obtained Evidence in Civil and Family Proceedings)* issued by the General Council of the Bar (September 2003), the following principles were set out for the guidance of the profession (which it is submitted are of equal relevance for solicitors):

(a) Legal representatives must never advise that evidence be obtained illegally, including by methods infringing the Data Protection Act 1998. Updating or clarifying such evidence is just as illegal as obtaining it in the first place.

(b) There is an important distinction between obtaining such data in the first place, which is illegal, and disclosure of such material in civil proceedings. If disclosure is compulsory, it is likely to be lawful. Standard disclosure under **CPR, r. 31.6**, is a rule of law within the meaning of the Data Protection Act 1998, s. 55(2)(a)(ii), and so will be regarded as compulsory for the purposes of s. 55.

(c) A party who has obtained relevant documents illegally is not entitled to claim legal professional privilege over them (see **50.53** and *Dubai Aluminium Co. Ltd v Al Alawi* [1999] 1 WLR 1964). In addition to the illegally obtained evidence, the source of the evidence and the letters of instruction to the person who obtained it must also be disclosed.

(d) If a client refuses to comply with these disclosure obligations, the legal representatives will be obliged to withdraw.

(e) If disclosure is made, the data can be used in evidence in the claim in the usual way.

(f) If there is doubt about the use of data, or the need to disclose it, the Guidance Note suggests a without notice application should be made to the court. The need for tactical secrecy may justify the application being made without notice. Any order made by the court for disclosure or use will provide the necessary compulsion within the last five words of s. 55(2)(a)(ii).

Tugendhat J in *Hughes v Carratu International plc* felt that the guidance in the Note is of equal relevance to solicitors (at [34]), but decided against formally endorsing the advice it contains (at [36]). Solicitors will be concerned that they are not put into difficult positions by the conduct of inquiry agents they instruct. To reduce the dangers exposed by *Hughes v Carratu International plc* it is suggested that:

(a) Standard letters of instruction should be settled for use by fee earners. These should expressly say that personal data or information contained in personal data must not be obtained illegally, or communicated to the firm, and that sub-agents must be told to take as much care in complying with the Data Protection Act 1998 as the main agent.

(b) Care should be taken over which inquiry agents are instructed. Agents known to use illegal methods should be avoided.

(c) Where there has been an infringement of the Data Protection Act 1998, consideration should be given to reporting the matter to the Information Commissioner and/or the Serious Organised Crime Agency.

Illegal access to documents in ancillary relief proceedings has for some time been governed by what are commonly called the *Hildebrand* rules (*Hildebrand v Hildebrand* [1992] 1 FLR 244). These were summarised in *White v Withers LLP* [2009] EWCA Civ 1122, [2010] 1 FLR 859, by Drake LJ at [37] as follows:

The family courts will not penalise the taking, copying and immediate return of documents but do not sanction the use of any force to obtain the documents, or the interception of documents or the retention of documents nor I would add, though it is not a feature of this case, the removal of any hard disk recording documents electronically. The evidence contained in the documents, even those wrongfully taken will be admitted in evidence because there is an overarching duty on the parties to give full and frank disclosure.

The '*Hildebrand* rules' were in fact a development from the original decision. *Hildebrand v Hildebrand*, as originally decided, was authority only as to the time when copies obtained unlawfully or clandestinely should be disclosed to a spouse.

In *Imerman - Tchenguiz* [2010] EWCA Civ 908, [2011] Fam 116, the wife's brothers accessed the husband's computer on nine occasions, downloaded electronic copies of his financial information and passed the electronic files to a forensic accountant for use in the wife's ancillary relief proceedings. The husband's computer had been password protected, with the files being stored on the wife's brothers' server. It was held that the wider *Hildebrand* rules are no longer good law, leaving just the narrow original decision in *Hildebrand v Hildebrand* as the surviving element of the rules. Instead, parties in ancillary relief proceedings who are concerned about spouses who may be attempting to salt away their assets should make use of freezing injunctions, search orders, preservation orders and the willingness of the courts to make adverse inferences against unforthcoming parties.

DUTIES ON PARTIES AND LAWYERS

Client's duty

50.30   The person responsible for making standard disclosure must certify, amongst other matters, that the duty to disclose is understood, and that to the best of his or her knowledge and belief, the duty has been discharged (**CPR, r. 31.10(6)(b)** and **(c)**). The certification is included in the disclosure statement required by **r. 31.10(5)** (see **50.19**) and has profound implications for the way in which a party should approach the whole disclosure process.

Standard disclosure requires disclosure of *only* the documents listed in **r. 31.6**, and so it is not sufficient to conduct an indiscriminate trawl through all documentation in the control of the party, extracting every single item which may have some relevance to the litigation. Whilst this may attract criticism as being expensive, or for 'front-loading' the costs of the case, it is submitted that the resultant saving in time and expense amply redresses the balance.

Under **r. 31.10(6)** and **PD 31A, para. 4.4**, it is clear that the person signing the disclosure statement must have an understanding of the duty to search and all that it entails, and also knowledge of the documents and issues in the case. The responsible person should normally be present at case management conferences and any other hearings where the issue of disclosure is likely to arise. For large corporate parties, or organisations such as local authorities, that person will normally be an in-house lawyer with responsibility for the case, but this situation can occasionally present problems. It may well be that the person with first-hand knowledge of the dispute is a departmental head who does not occupy a senior position in the organisation and who may, therefore, not be the appropriate person to sign the disclosure statement.

Almost every business will have a document archiving and destruction policy. This is absolutely proper. As was stated in *Beckett Bemrose and Hagen Solicitors v Future Mortgages Ltd* [2010] EWHC 1997 (QB), LTL 12/7/2010, it is common practice for files to be destroyed once they are more than six years old (the usual limitation period for most causes of action) as they occupy valuable space, and the same is true of electronic records.

Administrative problems may arise when documents that have to be disclosed emanate from different departments within the organisation. Organisations need to have sound and efficient document management systems. It may well be that 'documents officers' will have to be appointed within organisations for this purpose, as it is clear from the format of the disclosure statement that it cannot be signed by a legal representative. Parties may be well advised to seek legal advice on compliance with the duty.

Legal representative's duties to advise

50.31   At an early stage in a claim, a solicitor should advise his or her client of the obligations of standard disclosure (**PD 31B, para.** 7; *Rockwell Machine Tool Co. Ltd v E. P. Barrus (Concessionaires) Ltd* [1968] 1 WLR 693). The documents to be preserved include electronic documents which would otherwise be deleted in accordance with a document retention policy or otherwise deleted in the ordinary course of business (**PD 31B, para.** 7). Solicitors owe a duty to the court to ensure their clients make full disclosure. As Salmon J said in *Woods v Martins Bank Ltd* [1959] 1 QB 55 at p. 60:

It cannot be too clearly understood that solicitors owe a duty to the court, as officers of the court, carefully to go through the documents disclosed by their client to make sure, as far as possible, that no relevant documents have been omitted from their clients' affidavit [or list of documents].

It will often be sensible to give advice about keeping receipts and other documents commonly thrown away, and stopping routine destruction of documents. There may also be an obligation to advise a client to make an early and thorough search for documents which may need to be disclosed. It will often be sensible to explain the breadth of meaning of the word 'document' for this purpose (see **50.17**), emphasising that it includes emails and computer records. Solicitors (Law Society's Code for Advocacy, para. 5.1) and counsel (Code of Conduct of the Bar of England and Wales, guidance gC13) cannot continue to act for a client who refuses to authorise the disclosure of documents which should be disclosed to the other side.

LIST GENERALLY CONCLUSIVE

There is a general rule that statements by a party about the status of documents in his control **50.32** are conclusive at all stages up to the trial. In *Paddick v Associated Newspapers Ltd* [2003] EWHC 2991 (QB), LTL 12/12/2003, the claimant gave standard disclosure of extracts from two witness statements, and stated that the undisclosed parts were irrelevant. Disclosure of these parts was refused, the claimant's assertion as to relevance being conclusive. See also *Loutchansky v Times Newspapers* [2001] EWCA Civ 536, [2002] QB 321; *GE Capital Corporate Finance Group Ltd v Bankers Trust Co.* [1995] 1 WLR 172. Where a party credibly asserts that a category of documents is privileged, that assertion is also ordinarily a complete answer to an application for disclosure (*Beckham v News Group Newspapers Ltd* [2005] EWHC 2252 (QB), LTL 25/10/2005).

The purpose behind the general rule that statements on matters such as the privileged nature of documents withheld from disclosure are conclusive is the need to avoid mini trials at the interlocutory stage (*West London Pipeline and Storage Ltd v Total UK Ltd* [2008] EWHC 1729 (Comm), [2008] 2 CLC 258). While this is a very strong general rule, it is not absolute, because otherwise a party will be the judge in his own cause, and ultimately claims to privilege have to be proved. Beatson J referred to the following options where a claim to privilege is disputed:

(a) finding that the evidence before the court does not establish the privilege, and ordering inspection;

(b) ordering further evidence to be produced on oath on the claim to privilege;

(c) inspecting the documents under **CPR, r. 31.19** (for which see **50.35** and the principles laid down in *Atos Consulting Ltd v Avis Europe plc* [2007] EWHC 323 (TCC), [2008] Bus LR Digest D20); and

(d) ordering cross-examination of the witness making the claim to privilege under **r. 32.7**. This should be done only in an extreme case and where there is no alternative relief.

INSPECTION AND COPYING OF DOCUMENTS

The right of inspection of a disclosed document is contained in **CPR, r. 31.3**, which pro- **50.33** vides that a party to whom a document has been disclosed has a right to inspect it, except where:

(a) the document is no longer in the control of the party who disclosed it;

(b) the party disclosing the document has a right or duty to withhold inspection of it (see **50.50 to 50.82**);

(c) the disclosing party considers that it would be disproportionate to the issues in the case to permit inspection of documents within a category or class of document disclosed under **r. 31.6(b)** (adverse documents) (see **50.36**); or

(d) disclosure and inspection arises out of cross-border mediations to which **r. 78.26** applies (see **73.14**).

Written notice of a wish to inspect a document must be given to the party who disclosed it (**r. 31.15 (a)**) and inspection must be permitted not more than seven days after the date of receipt of that notice (**r. 31.15(b)**). A party may, instead of physical inspection, request a copy of the document, and, provided there is also an undertaking to pay reasonable copying costs, the party who disclosed the document must supply a copy not later than seven days after the date of receipt of the request (**r. 31.15(c)**). This rule is unclear, but it is submitted that the seven-day period in respect of supplying copies should begin when the undertaking to pay for the copies is given.

The parties should cooperate at an early stage in an endeavour to agree the format in which electronic documents should be inspected (**PD 31A, para. 2A.3**). In case of difficulty or disagreement, the matter should be resolved by directions, preferably at the first case management conference.

There is in general no duty of confidence between opposing parties in litigation, so no restrictions (beyond the undertaking not to use documents for collateral purposes, see **50.45**, and any confidentiality undertakings a party is prepared to give) will be imposed as to which individuals will be allowed to inspect the documents on the inspecting party's side (*Virgin Media Communications Ltd v British Sky Broadcasting Group plc* [2008] EWCA Civ 612, [2008] 1 WLR 2854). Despite this, it seems that it is appropriate to require solicitors to give individual confidentiality undertakings where disclosed documents are commercially sensitive (*Interdigital Technology Corporation v Nokia Corporation* [2008] EWHC 969 (Pat), LTL 19/5/2008, where the undertakings were that the documents would remain in the solicitor's premises except to the extent necessary for making applications to the court and delivering papers to counsel, but no undertaking was required from counsel).

Under **r. 31.12** the court may make an order for specific inspection, which is an order that a party permit inspection of a document, named in the order, which the party sought to exclude from inspection under **r. 31.2(2)** (permission to inspect would be disproportionate to the issues in the case, see **50.36**). An application for an order under **r. 31.12** must be made by application notice (see **50.41**).

Inspection of documents mentioned in statements of case etc.

50.34 Apart from the general right to inspect documents disclosed either by standard or specific disclosure (see **50.33**), a party has, under **CPR, r. 31.14(1)**, the right to inspect a document mentioned in:

(a) a statement of case;

(b) a witness statement;

(c) a witness summary; or

(d) an affidavit.

This particular right arises as soon as the document concerned is mentioned, even prior to it being listed in form N265. It is submitted that the limitations on inspection listed in **r. 31.3** (see **50.33**), apply here too. The word 'mentioned' in **r. 31.14** is as general as is possible. A document does not have to be relied on, or referred to, in any particular way or for any particular purpose, in order for it to be mentioned. It is enough if there is a direct allusion to it (*Rubin v Expandable Ltd* [2008] EWCA Civ 59, [2008] 1 WLR 1099). In *Rubin v Expandable Ltd* a witness statement said 'he wrote to me', which was held to be a direct allusion to the letter.

Normally the document has to be provided, unless there is a good reason for not doing so (*Co-operative Group Ltd v Carillion JM Ltd* [2014] EWHC 2253 (TCC), LTL 11/2/2014). Inspection may be objected to using the procedure in **r. 31.19** (see **50.35**), for example, on the ground that the document referred to is protected by privilege (*Rubin v Expandable Ltd*, where the fact that **r. 31.14** applied to the letter did not waive any right or duty to object to inspection on the ground of privilege or public interest). Further reasons for refusing inspection include length, volume, confidentiality and public interest immunity (*Tweed v Parades Commission for Northern Ireland* [2006] UKHL 53, [2007] 1 AC 650). If a party makes reference to a document which is not in its control, the appropriate course will be to seek to obtain the document by means of an order under **r. 31.17** (orders for disclosure against a person not a party), **r. 34.2(4)** and **(5)** (witness summons), or **r. 34.8** (evidence by deposition).

In *Bennett v Compass Group UK and Ireland Ltd* [2002] EWCA Civ 642, [2002] ICR 1177, it was held that the defendants were entitled to inspect the claimant's GP and hospital notes under **CPR, r. 31.14**, because they had been referred to in the medical report attached to the particulars of claim. This case was decided under the rule before it was amended on 25 March 2002. The current version of **r. 31.14**, by sub-para. (2), requires a court order for inspection of documents referred to in experts' reports. An expert's report must state the substance of all material instructions on which the report is based (**r. 35.10(3)**). However, in relation to those instructions, the court will not order disclosure of any specific document or permit any questioning in court other than by the party who instructed the expert, unless it is satisfied that there are reasonable grounds to consider that the statement of material instructions is inaccurate or incomplete (**r. 35.10(4)**).

REFUSAL TO DISCLOSE OR PERMIT INSPECTION

50.35

A person holding a document may dispute aspects of disclosure or inspection on a number of bases, namely:

(a) there may be factual disputes about the disclosability or existence of the document;

(b) there may be factual disputes about whether the document is or has ever been under the party's control;

(c) there may be a claim by a person under **CPR, r. 31.3(2)**, that it would be 'disproportionate' to the issues in the case to permit inspection of documents (see **50.36**);

(d) there may be a claim to withhold inspection on the basis of private privilege, i.e. professional legal privilege, litigation privilege, or the privilege against self-incrimination (see **50.50** to **50.79**);

(e) there may be a claim to withhold disclosure on the basis of public interest immunity (see **50.80** to **50.82**);

(f) where the disclosure of the identities of persons named in documents would interfere with their private lives (European Convention on Human Rights, **art. 8**, in the **Human Rights Act 1998, sch. 1**; *Webster v Ridgeway Foundation School Governors* [2009] EWHC 1140 (QB), [2009] ELR 439);

(g) where the disclosure of personal data is contrary to the Data Protection Act 1998 (see **50.96**); and

(h) where there is a claim that the documents contain confidential information (which rarely succeeds, see **50.66**).

Under **CPR, r. 31.19(3)**, a person who claims to have a right or a duty to withhold inspection of a document or part of a document must assert the right or duty in writing and state the grounds on which it is claimed. That assertion must be in the list in which the document is disclosed, or, if there has been no list, in a notice to the person wishing to inspect the document (**r. 31.19(4)**). Any party may then apply to the court under **r. 31.19(5)** to decide whether a claim made under **r. 31.19(3)** should be upheld. Thus an application for the court's decision on whether a claim to withhold inspection is justified may be made either by the party seeking inspection or the party resisting it. It is suggested in **PD 31A, para. 6.1**, that a claim to withhold inspection of a document does not require an application to the court, so that, generally speaking, it is the party who wishes to challenge that claim who must apply to the court. Although this is applicable in the case of disputes about private privilege, in the case of public interest immunity **r. 31.19(1)** provides that a person may apply to the court, without notice to other parties, for an order permitting disclosure of a document to be withheld on the ground that disclosure would damage the public interest. To decide an application under **r. 31.19(1)** or **(3)**, the court may require the person seeking to withhold inspection of a document to produce it to the court, and it may invite any person, whether or not a party, to make representations (**r. 31.19(6)**).

On a hearing under **r. 31.19**, *Atos Consulting Ltd v Avis Europe plc* [2007] EWHC 323 (TCC), [2008] Bus LR Digest D20, held that the correct procedure is:

(a) to consider the evidence produced on the application;

(b) to uphold the right to withhold inspection if this is established on the evidence and no sufficient grounds are put forward for challenging that right;

(c) to order inspection if the evidence does not establish a right to withhold the documents;

(d) to order further evidence to be produced if insufficient grounds have been shown for challenging the alleged right to withhold, or for the court to inspect the documents if there is no other means of deciding the matter; and

(e) to invite representations after any inspection.

On the facts, redacted parts of certain board minutes were irrelevant as they did not relate to the project in issue or related matters, so no inspection was ordered for these documents. Redacted parts of certain reports were alleged to contain privileged material, but the reports had been compiled by employees rather than lawyers, so there were sufficient grounds in the challenge to justify inspection. Disclosure of a redacted version of a document with the names of children removed did not amount to a concession that the whole of the document was relevant in *Webster v Ridgeway Foundation School Governors* [2009] EWHC 1140 (QB), [2009] ELR 439. In *Real Estate Opportunities Ltd v Aberdeen Asset Managers Jersey Ltd* [2006] EWHC 3249 (Ch), *The Times*, 23 January 2007, an order was made under **r. 31.19(5)** for inspection of interview transcripts supplied to one of the parties by the Financial Services Authority.

For the practice in anti-competition cases involving the Commission of the European Communities, see *Akzo Nobel Chemicals Ltd v Commission of the European Communities* (cases T-125 and T-253/03) [2008] Bus LR 348.

Inspection disproportionate to the case

50.36   Under CPR, **r. 31.3(2)**, a party who considers that it would be disproportionate to the issues in the case to permit inspection of documents within a category or class of document, is not required to permit inspection of those documents, but must state in the disclosure statement that inspection of those documents will not be permitted on the ground that to do so would be disproportionate.

Inspection of a redacted version of a school's database recording the behaviour of pupils, with the names of the pupils removed, was a very substantial task and regarded as disproportionate within the meaning of **r. 31.3(2)** in *Webster v Ridgeway Foundation School Governors* [2009] EWHC 1140 (QB), [2009] ELR 439.

ORDERS OR AGREEMENTS LIMITING OR AFFECTING DISCLOSURE

50.37   Standard disclosure may be dispensed with or limited by the court or by agreement between the parties under **CPR, r. 31.5(1)(b)**, or **(c)**, (standard disclosure), or under **r. 31.5(7)(a) or (f)**

(menu option disclosure). Any written agreement between the parties, should be lodged with the court (**PD 31A, para. 1.4**). These powers can also be used at a later stage, with the effect of varying the initial disclosure order, provided there has been a change of circumstances (*Serious Organised Crime Agency v Namli* [2011] EWCA Civ 1411, LTL 29/11/2011). On the fast track the court may decide not to direct standard disclosure, but may direct that no disclosure takes place, or specify the documents or classes of documents which the parties must disclose (**CPR, r. 28.3(2)**). This is likely to occur if, for example, whether in pursuance of a pre-action protocol or otherwise, there has already been substantial or total disclosure at some early stage.

The fact that the ultimate responsibility for case management rests with the court precludes the parties from agreeing a form of disclosure without approval. It may well be that the court will not be prepared to accept an agreement between the parties, in which event it will supplant the agreement with its own orders under **r. 28.3** in fast track cases or **r. 29.2** in cases on the multi-track (**r. 31.5**). Often this may be because the court, having scrutinised the documents before it, decides that it would be appropriate to limit standard disclosure to what it perceives to be the relevant issues. For example, where the respective statements of case make it clear that the whole litigation turns on whether a written contract was or was not subsequently varied by agreement between the parties, the court might limit disclosure to 'documents relevant to the issue as to whether or not the contract dated 25 February 2013 was varied in the course of correspondence between the parties, between 15 April and 8 May 2013'.

Staged disclosure

Under **CPR, r. 31.13**, the court may direct, or the parties may agree in writing, that disclosure **50.38** or inspection, or both, shall take place in stages. This may be appropriate, for example, in personal injuries claims if the court has ordered split trials of liability and quantum. It may also be appropriate in complex litigation, where to ensure the claim is managed efficiently the court may order the parties to disclose documents limited to selected issues, with a view to the case being reappraised at a later case management hearing. Although the rules are silent on the point, it is submitted that an agreement for staged disclosure should also be lodged with the court, in the same manner as an agreement for disclosure has to be lodged under **PD 31A, para. 1.4**.

Clarification of material

The court has the ability to order a party, under **CPR, Part 18**, to clarify any matter which is **50.39** in dispute in the proceedings, or to give additional information in relation to any such matter, whether or not the matter is contained or referred to in a statement of case (see **chapter 30**).

FAILURE TO DISCLOSE DOCUMENTS

Under **CPR, r. 31.21**, a party who has not disclosed, or not permitted inspection of, a docu- **50.40** ment may not rely on it, unless the court gives permission. An application for permission is considered applying the overriding objective. Key issues will include the importance of the documents, the reasons why they were not disclosed, the extent of any notice given to the other party of their contents, and the extent of any prejudice to the other party.

Failure to preserve documents covered by standard disclosure after the commencement of proceedings may result in adverse inferences being drawn (*Infabrics Ltd v Jaytex Ltd (No. 2)* [1985] FSR 75). Before the commencement of proceedings there is no duty on parties to preserve documents (*Douglas v Hello! Ltd (No. 2)* [2003] EWHC 55 (Ch), [2003] 1 All ER 1087). As a result, adverse inferences may be drawn in the case of destruction of documents before proceedings are commenced only if there is clear evidence that the destruction was deliberate and in anticipation of litigation (*Earles v Barclays Bank plc* [2009] EWHC 2500 (QB), [2010] Bus LR 566). Pre-action destruction of documents may be reflected in the order for costs even if adverse inferences cannot be drawn (*Earles v Barclays Bank plc*).

SPECIFIC DISCLOSURE

Jurisdiction and procedure

50.41   A party who wishes to obtain copies of particular documents which are believed to be in the custody of another party may make an application for specific disclosure under **CPR, r. 31.12**, and **PD 31A, para. 5.1**. Applications for specific disclosure are most frequently made after standard disclosure has been given, and the disclosed documents have been inspected. There is no restriction in this respect, and the court also has jurisdiction to order specific disclosure before standard disclosure has taken place (*Dayman v Canyon Holdings Ltd* (2006) LTL 11/1/2006). An early application may not accord with the overriding objective, particularly if its effect is to increase costs. Until an issue is pleaded specific disclosure will not be ordered (*Taranissi v British Broadcasting Corporation* [2008] EWHC 2486 (QB), LTL 24/10/2008). The procedure is summarised in **procedural checklist 26.**

If the application is made and granted, the court may make an order under **CPR, r. 31.12**, ordering a party to do one or more of the following:

(a) disclose documents or classes of documents specified in the order;

(b) carry out a search to the extent stated in the order;

(c) disclose any documents located as a result of that search.

Any application for an order under **r. 31.12** must be made by application notice, specifying the order that the applicant intends to ask the court to make, and must be supported by evidence (**PD 31A, para. 5.2**). The rules do not provide what this evidence should contain, but it is suggested that it should briefly explain the nature of the dispute, the stage reached in the proceedings, and the facts which lead the applicant to conclude that the documents sought exist, are disclosable and are within the control of the opposing party. The documents sought from the other side are commonly described in a schedule to the draft order. They must be described with reasonable precision. An application for disclosure of 'all documents relating to [the other side's] financial and tax affairs which are necessary to prove the quantum of his counterclaim' was held to be too imprecise in *Morgans v Needham* (1999) *The Times*, 5 November 1999.

PD 31A, para. 5.3, provides that 'the grounds on which the order is sought' may be set out in the application notice itself or in the evidence filed in support. **CPR, r. 31.12**, does not specify the form in which compliance with an order for specific disclosure should be undertaken. Form N265 (which is expressed to be for standard rather than specific disclosure) could be adapted, but it is likely that the court will want more formality and would require the party against whom the order is made to file evidence, or certify in some form whether the documents exist, and the extent of any search made.

The court may make an order for costs on such an application, or, where appropriate, may reserve the costs to abide the determination of the issue as to whether or not the documents disclosed are relevant.

Discretion to order specific disclosure

50.42   **PD 31A, para. 5.4**, provides that in deciding whether or not to make an order for specific disclosure, the court will take into account all the circumstances of the case, and in particular, the overriding objective. The overriding objective requires the parties, so far as possible and so far as economically reasonable, to have access to documents which might help their case (*Commissioners of Inland Revenue v Exeter City AFC Ltd* [2004] BCC 519). In this case extensive disclosure was ordered of Inland Revenue documents relating to voluntary arrangement cases involving about 20 to 30 other football clubs. The issue raised had national importance, and the costs of the exercise were not disproportionate. In *Chantrey Vellacott v Convergence Group plc* (2006) LTL 6/2/2006 specific disclosure, in the form of an order to conduct a proper search for emails and draft documents, was ordered primarily because the claim was likely to turn on the documents. In *Harrods Ltd v Times Newspapers Ltd* [2006] EWCA Civ 294, LTL 22/2/2006, the Court of Appeal said that a party was not permitted to go on a roving exercise (also sometimes called a fishing expedition). The defendant had criticised the claimant's employment practices, and had named two individual executives in a published article. It was held that an order for disclosure against the claimant should be limited to documents relating to the two named executives. *Simba-Tola v Elizabeth Fry Hostel* [2001] EWCA Civ 1371, LTL 30/7/2001, concerned an allegation of racial discrimination against the claimant by other residents at the hostel. The hostel had disclosed its file on the claimant and its log book. None of the alleged incidents were recorded in these documents. The claimant sought disclosure of the hostel's files on other residents to see whether the incidents were recorded on those files. The Court of Appeal held it would not be proportionate to make an order for disclosure that would result in duplication. Further, as the court had seen the disclosed file and log book, it was possible to conclude that the further files would not have any relevant information. Further disclosure was therefore refused.

Paragraph 5.4 concludes by warning that:

if the court concludes that the party from whom specific disclosure is sought has failed adequately to comply with the obligations imposed by an order for disclosure (whether by failing to make a sufficient search for documents or otherwise) the court will usually make such order as is necessary to ensure that those obligations are properly complied with.

This principle was applied in *Ovlas Trading SA v Strand (London) Ltd* [2009] EWHC 1025 (Ch), LTL 30/6/2009. Specific disclosure is not limited to documents covered by standard disclosure in **CPR, r. 31.6**, and it is possible, for example, to use **r. 31.12** to obtain disclosure of documents relevant solely to credit if sufficient grounds are shown (*Favor Easy Management Ltd v Wu* [2010] EWCA Civ 1630, [2011] 1 WLR 1803 at [20]).

Specific disclosure is often used to challenge the extent of the search made when giving standard disclosure (see **r. 31.12(2)(b)**; and see **50.20**). On such an application the court should take into account the factors in **r. 31.7(2)**, and (in relation to electronic documents) **PD 31B, para. 21**, in considering the reasonableness of the proposed search (*Fiddes v Channel 4 Television Corporation* [2010] EWCA Civ 516, LTL 24/3/2010).

AUTHENTICITY OF DOCUMENTS DISCLOSED

50.43 The authenticity of documents disclosed to a party under **CPR, Part 31**, is deemed to be admitted, unless the party serves notice requiring the document to be proved at trial (**r. 32.19**). A notice to prove a document (form N268) must be served by the latest date for serving witness statements, or within seven days of disclosure of the document, whichever is later (**r. 32.19(2)**).

CONTINUING DUTY TO DISCLOSE

50.44 The duty imposed by an order to give disclosure continues until the conclusion of the proceedings, that is, until the court gives its final judgment or order in the proceedings (which take effect when made: **CPR, r. 40.7**). If documents, to which a duty of disclosure extends, come to a party's notice at any time during the proceedings, every other party must be notified immediately (**r. 31.11(2)**). **PD 31A, para. 3.3**, provides that this should be done by a 'supplemental list', presumably in form N265. This further reinforces the suggestion made above that the duty of honest disclosure is precisely parallel to that under the previous rule.

COLLATERAL USE OF DISCLOSED DOCUMENTS

50.45   Following previous law and practice, it is provided in **CPR, r. 31.22**, that a party to whom a document has been disclosed may use such document only for the purposes of the proceedings in which it is disclosed. A similar restriction on collateral use applies to electronic documents questionnaires (**r. 31.22(4)**). There is a similar implied obligation on parties to an English arbitration not to disclose or use documents prepared for and used in the arbitration for any purpose outside the arbitration (*Ali Shipping Corporation v Shipyard Trogir* [1999] 1 WLR 314). There are exceptions in **r. 31.22(1)** where:

(a)   the document has been read to or by the court, or referred to, at a hearing that has been held in public; or

(b)   the court gives permission; or

(c)   the party who disclosed the document and the person to whom the document belongs, agree.

The court may, however, make an order restricting or prohibiting the use of a document which has been disclosed, even though that document has been read to or by the court, or referred to at a public hearing (**r. 31.22(2)**). An application for such an order may be made by a party or by any person to whom the document belongs (**r. 31.22(3)**).

This preserves the principle that, as one is required to complete disclosure with absolute honesty and thus confidential documents may be disclosed, it is right that a party should have the protection of knowing that the documents are to be used only for the current litigation. The rule, which evolved from *Riddick v Thames Board Mills Ltd* [1977] QB 881, is that a document disclosed in proceedings may not be used, for example, for unrelated commercial purposes, or as the basis on which to found another claim. Indeed, misuse of such documents will constitute a serious contempt of court. The prohibition against using material for collateral purposes does not apply to documents referred to in affidavits and witness statements, as these are regarded as having been voluntarily disclosed (*Cassidy v Hawcroft* [2000] CPLR 624).

Confidentiality clubs

50.46   Occasionally a party to litigation establishes a 'confidentiality club' (also known as a 'confidentiality ring'), which restricts the persons who can have access to documents disclosed under **CPR, Part 31**. The purpose is to reduce the risk of the documents, or the information they contain, being used for a purpose outside the present proceedings. Confidentiality club orders are exceptional, and should be made only if there are grounds for deciding that the restrictions on collateral use set out in **r. 31.22** are insufficient and that the justice of the case demands greater protection (*Roussel-Uclaf v ICI (No. 2)* [1990] RPC 45; *Porton Capital Technology Funds v 3M UK Holdings Ltd* [2010] EWHC 114 (Comm), LTL 8/2/2010). Such orders are usually inappropriate for small businesses, because all the directors and key personnel are likely to be involved in providing proper instructions to the relevant lawyers (*Croft House Care Ltd v Durham County Council* [2010] EWHC 909 (TCC), LTL 7/7/2010).

After use in a public hearing

50.47   The prohibition against collateral use of disclosed documents disappears once the documents have been used in a public hearing (**CPR, r. 31.22(1)**, although the words 'or referred to' in **r. 31.22(1)(a)** may cause some difficulty). In *SmithKline Beecham Biologicals SA v Connaught Laboratories Inc.* [1999] 4 All ER 498, documents pre-read by the judge and 'economically' referred to in court were held to be in the public domain. The phrase 'read to or by the court' has been interpreted as including documents made available to the judge with the reading list before *the trial starts* (*Derby v Weldon (No. 2)* (1988) *The Times*, 20 October 1988).

Once documents have been used in open court, an order restricting or prohibiting subsequent use will only be made if there are very good reasons for departing from the usual rule of publicity (*Lilly Icos Ltd v Pfizer Ltd* [2002] EWCA Civ 2, [2002] 1 WLR 2253). Merely asserting a document is confidential is insufficient. Specific reasons why a party would be damaged by subsequent use are required. Permission to use disclosed material will be refused where there is a very strong risk of dishonest or malicious use of the material (*Eronat v Tabbah* [2002] EWCA Civ 950, LTL 10/7/2002).

Permission for collateral use

An order may, in any event, be made by the court permitting a party to use a document for **50.48** other purposes, in its general discretion (**CPR, r. 31.22(1)(b)**). One example is *Apple Corps Ltd v Apple Computer Inc.* [1992] 1 CMLR 969, where documents, which had been disclosed in English proceedings, were required for the purposes of parallel proceedings before the European Commission, which constituted a cogent reason why the documents were permitted to be used outside the English proceedings. In relation to documents relating to an English arbitration, the High Court has jurisdiction to grant injunctions restraining and declarations that the confidentiality obligation does not apply (*Emmott v Michael Wilson and Partners Ltd* [2008] EWCA Civ 184, [2008] Bus LR 1361). Generally, arbitration documents should be kept confidential, unless disclosure is required in the interests of justice (*Ali Shipping Corporation v Shipyard Trogir* [1999] 1 WLR 314), such as where a court might be misled if it does not have access to the documents (*Emmott v Michael Wilson and Partners Ltd*). A material consideration in deciding whether to lift an order under **r. 31.22** is whether an order for non-party disclosure under **r. 31.17** (see **50.90**) could have been obtained (*SmithKline Beecham plc v Generics (UK) Ltd* [2003] EWCA Civ 1109, [2004] 1 WLR 1479 at [37]).

There are cases where the discretion has to be exercised by balancing competing public interests. In *Marlwood Commercial Inc. v Kozeny* [2004] EWCA Civ 798, [2005] 1 WLR 104, the competing interests were the due administration of justice of the civil claim and the investigation of an alleged serious fraud. Permission was granted. In *Tchenguiz v Serious Fraud Office* [2014] EWCA Civ 1409, LTL 31/10/2014, the competing public interests were the interests of justice as against the ordinary position that in the absence of special factors permission would not be given for collateral use, combined with the importance of not undermining cooperation between criminal investigation authorities in different jurisdictions. Permission to use the documents was refused.

Family proceedings documents

The general rule is that hearings in family proceedings are in private (Family Procedure Rules **50.49** 2010 (SI 2010/2955), r. 27.10). Part 12 of the Family Procedure Rules concerns proceedings relating to children (defined in rr. 12.1 and 12.2). Any information about proceedings relating to children held in private can be communicated only as permitted by rr. 12.72 to 12.75. The court may give permission for further disclosure (r. 12.73(1)(b)), but nothing in the rules permits communication to the public at large, or any section of the public (r. 12.73(2)). Other family proceedings are not automatically covered by secrecy even if heard in private. See *Clibbery v Allan* [2002] EWCA Civ 45, [2002] Fam 261, in which publication was allowed.

PRIVILEGE

Introduction

A disclosed document may be withheld from inspection if the disclosing party has a right or **50.50** duty to withhold it (**CPR, r. 31.3(1)(b)**). Such a right or duty is called a 'privilege'. A party asserting a privilege must do so in writing and state the grounds on which it is claimed (**r. 31.19(3)**). This must be done in the list in which the document is disclosed, if a list is given (**r. 31.19(4)**). Space is provided in the middle of the second page of form N265 for this purpose.

There are three heads of privilege: the privilege against self-incrimination (**50.51** and **50.52**); legal professional privilege (**50.53** to **50.63**); and 'without prejudice' communications (**50.68**). The three heads of privilege confer a right to withhold disclosure. Public interest immunity (**50.80** to **50.82**) arises from a duty to withhold disclosure. The burden of proof in a disputed claim for privilege rests on the person asserting the privilege (*West London Pipeline and Storage Ltd v Total UK Ltd* [2008] EWHC 1729 (Comm), [2008] 2 CLC 258; *Akzo Nobel Chemicals Ltd v Commission of the European Communities* (cases T-125 and T-253/03) [2008] Bus LR 348). When considering these different heads of privilege, it is worth bearing in mind the comment made by Lord Edmund-Davies in *Waugh v British Railways Board* [1980] AC 521 at p. 543:

> we should start from the basis that the public interest is, on balance, best served by rigidly confining within narrow limits the cases where material relevant to litigation may be lawfully withheld. Justice is better served by candour than by suppression.

The court will not order disclosure and/or inspection where disclosing and/or allowing inspection would be an offence under English criminal law, but the court has a discretion whether to order disclosure and/or inspection which would be an offence under a foreign law to which the disclosing party is subject (*Morris v Banque Arabe et Internationale d'Investissement SA* [2001] ILPr 37).

PRIVILEGE AGAINST SELF-INCRIMINATION

Common law rule

50.51 In *Blunt v Park Lane Hotel Ltd* [1942] 2 KB 253 Goddard LJ said, at p. 257:

> the rule is that no one is bound to answer any question [or to produce any document] if the answer thereto would, in the opinion of the judge, have a tendency to expose [him] to any criminal charge, penalty, or forfeiture which the judge regards as reasonably likely to be preferred or sued for.

The claimant had objected to answering questions in a slander claim on the ground that her answers would tend to expose her to the risk of ecclesiastical penalties. It was held that it was purely fantastic to suppose that in 1942 she would be subject to any ecclesiastical penalty if she admitted adultery, and permission was granted to ask the questions. In civil proceedings the right applies only as regards criminal offences under the law of any part of the United Kingdom and penalties provided for by such law (Civil Evidence Act 1968, s. 14(1)). Exposure to the risk of a penalty under EU legislation forming part of the law of the United Kingdom by virtue of the European Communities Act 1972 is a penalty for these purposes (*Rio Tinto Zinc Corporation v Westinghouse Electric Corporation* [1978] AC 547). A risk of exposure to a civil claim does not raise the privilege (Witnesses Act 1806). Statutory additional damages for breach of copyright are not penalties (*Rank Film Distributors Ltd v Video Information Centre* [1982] AC 380 at p. 425).

In *Rank Film Distributors Ltd v Video Information Centre* [1982] AC 380 it was held that where a criminal charge was more than a contrived, fanciful or remote possibility, the defendant could refuse to provide information by relying on the privilege. The privilege may arise, not only when answering might increase the risk of being prosecuted, but also where the prosecution may make use of the answer in deciding whether to prosecute, and where the prosecution may seek to rely on the answer in establishing guilt (*Den Norske Bank ASA v Antonatos* [1999] QB 271). Merely asserting there is a risk is not enough: the risk must be real and appreciable (*Rank Film Distributors Ltd v Video Information Centre*), and it is a matter for the court to determine the likelihood of a prosecution (*Rio Tinto Zinc Corporation v Westinghouse Electric Corporation* [1978] AC 547).

Subsequent committal proceedings for contempt of court are penal for this purpose (*Cobra Golf Inc. v Rata* [1998] Ch 109; *Memory Corporation plc v Sidhu* [2000] Ch 645), but disqualification proceedings under the Company Directors Disqualification Act 1986 are regulatory rather than penal (*Official Receiver v Stern* [2000] 1 WLR 2230). *Memory Corporation plc v Sidhu* discusses a possible exception to the privilege against incrimination where the risk of prosecution is for perjury arising out of the witness's conduct in the instant case. The cases on this exception are old and unsatisfactory, but the exception is probably good law. *Memory Corporation plc v Sidhu*, however, holds that even if the exception is good law relating to perjury, it does not extend to the risk of proceedings for contempt of court if the answers of a witness to an order requiring disclosure of assets are defective and hence a breach of the order.

The privilege extends to providing documents or answers that tend to expose the spouse or civil partner of the person asserting the privilege to criminal proceedings or proceedings for the recovery of a penalty (Civil Evidence Act 1968, s. 14(1)). As a corporation has legal personality it can claim the privilege (*Triplex Safety Glass Co. Ltd v Lancegaye Safety (1934) Glass Ltd* [1939] 2 KB 395). It may be necessary to distinguish between the corporation and its officers and employees, and to consider whether all or only some of them may be at risk of criminal proceedings (*Sociedade Nacional de Combustiveis de Angola UEE v Lundqvist* [1991] 2 QB 310).

The precise scope of the privilege has been modified as a result of the incorporation into UK law of the European Convention on Human Rights by the **Human Rights Act 1998**. In criminal cases the privilege may be claimed only after the witness has been sworn and a question has been put. The pre-Human Rights Act position that the privilege applied to incriminating documents and articles (*Rank Film Distributors Ltd v Video Information Centre* [1982] AC 380) as well as answers to questions, is no longer followed. In *C plc v P* [2007] EWCA Civ 493, [2008] Ch 1, it was held that the privilege does not apply to material that has an existence independent of the relevant order. The result was that free-standing evidence (in this case images of children found on a computer which had been imaged under the terms of a search order) which had not been created in compliance with the terms of the search order could be passed to the police. The distinction is between 'real' or 'independent' evidence, which is not protected by the privilege, and 'compelled testimony', which is (per Longmore LJ at [38]).

The privilege against self-incrimination may be lost by the turn of events. Obviously, there can be no adverse consequences from admitting a crime for which one has already been tried, convicted and sentenced (though there may be a question about whether what is to be admitted is what was found in the criminal trial). If the party has been acquitted, though, there may be a possibility of a further trial under the Criminal Justice Act 2003, s. 75. The party may be given a pardon, which again eliminates the risk of prosecution (*R v Boyes* (1861) 1 B & S 311). If the Crown Prosecution Service indicate in writing that they will not make use of the information sought for the purposes of any criminal proceedings against the party or the party's spouse or civil partner, and if a clause stating that no disclosure made in compliance with the order will be used in evidence in the prosecution of any offence committed by the party or spouse or civil partner is included in the order, the court may conclude there is no realistic risk of use by the prosecution, and hold that the privilege does not apply (*AT and T Istel Ltd v Tully* [1993] AC 45).

Statutory limitations on the rule

One of the consequences of the privilege against self-incrimination is that the risk of documents **50.52** being used against the party for the purposes of criminal proceedings is obviously greater in cases where the defendant is alleged to have been particularly dishonest, and the worse the conduct alleged the greater the prospect of a successful claim to the privilege. After *Rank Film Distributors Ltd v Video Information Centre* [1982] AC 380 there were fears that the privilege would operate to frustrate the use of search orders in intellectual property piracy claims, and Parliament intervened by enacting the Senior Courts Act 1981, s. 72, which has the effect of removing the privilege against self-incrimination in relation to claims involving the infringement of intellectual property rights and passing off, but also provides that the answers given shall not be used in any related criminal prosecution. Intellectual property has a wide meaning for this purpose (see s. 72(5)). Voicemail messages that contain both personal and commercially confidential material will come within the definition if the commercially confidential messages form a substantial proportion of the whole (*Phillips v News Group Newspapers Ltd* [2012] UKSC 28, [2013] 1 AC 1).

Similarly, where the information sought for the purposes of civil proceedings may lead to a prosecution under the Theft Act 1968, the privilege against self-incrimination has been removed by the Theft Act 1968, s. 31(1). The Fraud Act 2006, s. 13, removes the privilege for fraud offences under the Act and for related offences. In *Kensington International Ltd v Republic of Congo* [2007] EWCA Civ 1128, [2008] 1 WLR 1144, the claimant was experiencing difficulty in enforcing a money judgment against the Republic of Congo. It obtained a *Norwich Pharmacal* order (see **50.100**) against a company and an individual who had been engaged in oil trading with the Republic requiring them to disclose information about certain payments said to have been bribes. It was held that the *Norwich Pharmacal* application was a form of 'proceedings relating to property' as required by s. 13, because it was ancillary to the ongoing attempts to enforce the judgment debt, and the word 'property' includes 'money' (s. 13(3)). The corruption offences identified by the respondents were not offences under the Fraud Act 2006, but they were 'related offences' for the purposes of s.13, as they involved 'fraudulent conduct or purpose'. In addition to conspiracy to defraud, offences are 'related' within the meaning of s. 13(4) if they involve any form of fraudulent conduct or purpose, so are not limited to offences involving fraudulent intent. This is judged by reference to the essential character of the offence rather than the means by which it was committed. On this basis, an offence under the Proceeds of Crime Act 2002, s. 328, is a related offence even if, for example, the underlying offence relates to drug trafficking (*JSC BTA Bank v Ablyazov* [2009] EWCA Civ 1124, [2010] 1 WLR 976). These various provisions do not, of course, completely remove the privilege from civil proceedings. It still has an effect, for example, in civil assault cases, cases involving sexual offences, and in motoring claims.

LEGAL PROFESSIONAL PRIVILEGE

50.53   There are two classes of legal professional privilege: one arises out of the relationship of legal adviser and client, even where no litigation is contemplated (legal advice privilege, see **50.55**); and the other relates to communications connected with contemplated or pending litigation (see **50.60**). The privilege covers communications with a wide range of lawyers, including individuals who are not solicitors or barristers, but who are authorised persons for the purpose of providing advocacy, litigation, conveyancing or probate services (Legal Services Act 2007, s. 190). It covers in-house lawyers (*Alfred Crompton Amusement Machines Ltd v Commissioners of Customs and Excise (No. 2)* [1974] AC 405). It also extends to certain patent proceedings (Patents Act 1977, s. 103). It is, however, restricted to the legal profession and so does not apply to tax law advice provided by an accountant (*R (Prudential plc) v Special Commissioner of Income Tax* [2010] EWCA 1094, [2011] QB 669 or to doctors, priests or others entrusted with confidences (*Wheeler v Le Marchant* (1881) 17 Ch D 675). The privilege belongs to the client, not to the solicitor, though the solicitor is under a duty to the client to assert it unless it is waived by the client. A clinical case manager appointed to assist a severely disabled person who attends a conference or other occasion normally attracting legal professional privilege, is obliged to respect the claimant's privilege (*Wright v Sullivan* [2005] EWCA Civ 656, [2006] 1 WLR 172).

A number of cases in the House of Lords have described legal professional privilege as not merely a procedural right, but an important substantive right. Examples are *R (Morgan Grenfell and Co. Ltd) v Special Commissioner of Income Tax* [2002] UKHL 21, [2003] 1 AC 563 at [7]; *Three Rivers District Council v Bank of England (No. 6)* [2004] UKHL 48, [2005] 1 AC 610 at [25]; and *McE v Prison Service of Northern Ireland* [2009] UKHL 15, [2009] 1 AC 908 at [6]–[7]. Legal professional privilege is a fundamental human right long established in the common law (*R v Derby Magistrates' Court, ex parte B* [1996] AC 487). As Lord Taylor of Gosforth CJ said in this case, unless the privilege is waived by the client or abrogated it is absolute, so that:

legal professional privilege is thus much more than an ordinary rule of evidence, limited to the facts of a particular case. It is a fundamental condition on which the administration of justice as a whole rests.

The policy behind litigation privilege was described by Sir George Jessel MR in *Anderson v Bank of British Columbia* (1876) 2 ChD 644 as follows, at p. 649:

as, by reason of the complexity and difficulty of our law, litigation can only be properly conducted by professional men, it is absolutely necessary that a man, in order to prosecute his rights or to defend himself from an improper claim, should have recourse to the assistance of professional lawyers, and it being so absolutely necessary, it is equally necessary, to use a vulgar phrase, that he should be able to make a clean breast of it to the gentleman whom he consults with a view to the prosecution of his claim, or the substantiating his defence against the claim of others; that he should be able to place unrestricted and unbounded confidence in the professional agent, and that the communications he so makes to him should be kept secret, unless with his consent (for it is his privilege, and not the privilege of the confidential agent), that he should be enabled properly to conduct his litigation.

There is a slightly different policy justification for legal advice privilege, which is based on the sanctity of the rule of law. As Lord Scott of Foscote said in *Three Rivers District Council v Bank of England (No. 6)* [2004] UKHL 48, [2005] 1 AC 610 at [34]:

it is necessary in our society, a society in which the restraining and controlling framework is built upon a belief in the rule of law, that communications between clients and lawyers, whereby the clients are hoping for the assistance of the lawyers' legal skills in the management of their (the clients') affairs, should be secure against the possibility of any scrutiny from others, whether the police, the executive, business competitors, inquisitive busybodies or anyone else.

In recent times legal professional privilege has been regarded as part of the right of privacy guaranteed by the European Convention on Human Rights, art. 8 (*Campbell v United Kingdom* (1992) 15 EHRR 137) and part of EU law (*AM and S Europe Ltd v Commission of the European Communities* (case 155/79) [1983] QB 878). This is subject to art. 8(2), which means the privilege can be overridden for example where this is necessary in the interests of the welfare or protection of children (*Essex County Council v R* [1994] Fam 167).

Statutory exclusion of legal professional privilege

A statute will not exclude legal professional privilege unless it does so expressly or by necessary implication (*R (Morgan Grenfell and Co. Ltd) v Special Commissioner of Income Tax* [2002] UKHL 21, [2003] 1 AC 563). Following *R (Morgan Grenfell and Co. Ltd) v Special Commissioner of Income Tax*, it was held in *B v Auckland District Law Society* [2003] UKPC 38, [2003] 2 AC 736, that the statute in question did not override legal professional privilege either expressly or by necessary implication. Unlike questions relating to confidential documents, protection of legally privileged documents does not depend on balancing competing private and public interests, nor will the privilege be excluded by any common law right to compel production. Circumstances in which a statute will be held to have excluded legal professional privilege by necessary implication will be rare. The presumption against the removal of legal professional privilege is even stronger where general words in a statute merely delegate a power to legislate (*General Mediterranean Holdings SA v Patel* [2000] 1 WLR 272). **50.54**

Legal advice privilege

Confidential communications between a legal representative and client made for the giving or receiving of legal advice are protected by legal professional privilege. This is so whether or not litigation is contemplated. The privilege applies to communications between a client and his legal advisers, to documents evidencing such communications, and to documents intended to be such communications even if they are not in fact communicated. However, these are the limits of the privilege, and it is not open to the court to extend them (*Three Rivers District Council v Bank of England (No. 5)* [2003] EWCA Civ 474, [2003] QB 1556). **50.55**

The principle is that a client should be able to get legal advice in confidence. This raises issues as to who is the client (see **50.56**), and what is legal advice (see **50.57**), for this purpose. Another issue is whether obtaining legal advice must be the dominant purpose of the communication (see **50.58**). Examples are given at **50.59**.

50.56   **Client**   Where an individual seeks legal advice, it will usually be obvious that that individual is the client. The answer may not be so obvious where a litigation friend, trustee in bankruptcy, person acting under a power of attorney, or a personal representative is acting for someone else or an estate. In these cases the solicitor's retainer letter will or should make this clear. Where a solicitor is retained by a company or other corporation, it follows from *Three Rivers District Council v Bank of England (No. 5)* [2003] EWCA Civ 474, [2003] QB 1556, that the 'client' will be restricted to those personnel who have been authorised by the company or corporation to retain the services of the solicitor. On the facts the Bank had appointed three officials to deal with the Bank's communications with a private inquiry conducted by Lord Bingham of Cornhill as its 'Bingham Inquiry Unit', or 'BIU'. The BIU had sought legal assistance from a firm of solicitors. It was held that the BIU was the client for the purposes of legal advice privilege, so that communications between the solicitors and any other Bank official, even the Governor of the Bank, would not be protected. This decision may be too restrictive. There are hints in *Three Rivers District Council v Bank of England (No. 6)* [2004] UKHL 48, [2005] 1 AC 610, for example, at [118], that *Three Rivers District Council v Bank of England (No. 5)* might not survive if the matter were to be considered afresh by the House of Lords, but none of their lordships expressed a clear opinion on the issue.

As a practical consequence, corporate clients would be well advised to nominate a defined group of suitable employees or officers who will be the client when retaining a solicitor. To ensure that all sensitive communications are covered by the privilege, solicitors should ensure the legal context of the retainer is set out in clear terms in the retainer letter, and should advise the client that only employees and officers in the defined 'client' group prepare documents for use in seeking advice under the retainer.

50.57   **Legal advice**   'Legal advice' covers telling a client the law, and also includes advice as to what should prudently and sensibly be done in the relevant legal context (Taylor LJ in *Balabel v Air India* [1988] Ch 317 at p. 330). Advice will not be protected unless it is for a legal purpose (*McE v Prison Service of Northern Ireland* [2009] UKHL 15, [2009] 1 AC 908). To be protected the advice must be sought or given in a relevant legal context. So, if a solicitor becomes a client's 'man of business' with responsibility for advising the client on all matters of business, such as investment policy and financial matters, the privilege does not apply because without more there is no legal context (*Three Rivers District Council v Bank of England (No. 6)* [2004] UKHL 48, [2005] 1 AC 610 at [38]). In doubtful cases, according to Lord Scott of Foscote, there are two questions. First, did the advice sought relate to the rights, liabilities, obligations or remedies of the client under private law or under public law? Secondly, if so, did the occasion on which the communication took place and its purpose make it reasonable to expect that the privilege would apply? Putting it a different way, according to Lord Rodger of Earlsferry, the important question is whether the lawyer is being asked in his capacity as a lawyer to provide legal advice (at [58]).

In *Balabel v Air India*, approved in *Three Rivers District Council v Bank of England (No. 6)* at [111], Taylor LJ said the privilege is not restricted to specific requests for advice from clients and documents containing legal advice from solicitors. Where information is passed by the solicitor or the client to the other as part of a continuum aimed at keeping both informed, so that advice may later be given, privilege will attach. This is so even if there is no express reference to seeking advice (*Property Alliance Group Ltd v Royal Bank of Scotland plc* [2015] EWHC 3187 (Ch), [2016] 1 WLR 992). Further, legal advice is not confined to telling the client the law. It includes advice on what should prudently be done in the relevant legal context.

A preparatory document drawn up by a client, even if created without the intention of sending it to the lawyer, may be protected by legal advice privilege, although such a claim has to be considered restrictively (*Akzo Nobel Chemicals Ltd v Commission of the European Communities* (cases T-125 and T-253/03) [2008] Bus LR 348).

Advice given by a solicitor who is known by the client to be struck off is not protected by legal professional privilege (*Dadourian Group International Inc. v Simms* [2008] EWHC 1784 (Ch), LTL 1/8/2008).

Legal advice privilege and dominant purpose In *Three Rivers District Council v Bank of England (No. 5)* **50.58**
[2003] EWCA Civ 474, [2003] QB 1556, and *Three Rivers District Council v Bank of England (No. 6)* [2004] EWCA
Civ 218, [2004] QB 916, the Court of Appeal were of the view that seeking or giving legal advice
must be the dominant purpose of the communication if the occasion was to be protected by legal
advice privilege. One result was that each communication between the client and solicitor had to
be looked at before deciding whether the privilege applied on each occasion (*United States of
America v Philip Morris Inc.* [2004] EWCA Civ 330, [2004] 1 CLC 811). These Court of Appeal authorities
must be considered as wrongly decided on this point given the decision of the House of Lords in
Three Rivers District Council v Bank of England (No. 6) [2004] UKHL 48, [2005] 1 AC 610, and the approval
of the continuum of advice approach in *Balabel v Air India* [1988] Ch 317. Establishing a dominant
purpose of obtaining legal advice is, however, a requirement for litigation privilege, see **50.61**.

Examples of legal advice privilege Applying the above principles, legal advice privilege **50.59**
applies, for example, to the following:

(a) communications for the primary object of actual or contemplated civil or criminal proceedings (*Three Rivers District Council v Bank of England (No. 6)* [2004] UKHL 48, [2005] 1 AC 610 at [56]);
(b) conclusions reached by a solicitor from such communications (*Marsh v Sofaer* [2003] EWHC
   3334, [2004] PNLR 24);
(c) advice from the solicitor on matters such as the conveyance of property or drawing up of
   a will (*Three Rivers District Council v Bank of England (No. 6)* [2004] EWCA Civ 218, [2004] QB 916
   at [39]; [2004] UKHL 48, [2005] 1 AC 610 at [55]);
(d) confidential information given to a solicitor in the course of giving instructions relating to the
   drawing up of a will about matrimonial or financial difficulties, or about an anticipated inheritance (*Three Rivers District Council v Bank of England (No. 6)* [2004] UKHL 48, [2005] 1 AC 610 at [106]);
(e) confidential information given to a solicitor retained to give tax advice about family
   finances and family businesses (*Three Rivers District Council v Bank of England (No. 6)* [2004]
   UKHL 48, [2005] 1 AC 610 at [106]);
(f) advice or assistance from a lawyer to the promoter or opponent of a private Bill in Parliament
   (*Three Rivers District Council v Bank of England (No. 6)* [2004] UKHL 48, [2005] 1 AC 610 at [40]);
(g) advice from a solicitor on the best way to present evidence to a private, non-statutory
   inquiry, a coroner's inquest, a statutory inquiry or an ad hoc inquiry (*Three Rivers District
   Council v Bank of England (No. 6)* [2004] UKHL 48, [2005] 1 AC 610 at [44]);
(h) advice to a client about public law ramifications of a public inquiry (*Three Rivers District
   Council v Bank of England (No. 6)* [2004] UKHL 48, [2005] 1 AC 610);
(i) advice from in-house lawyers in the same circumstances as outside lawyers, provided the
   advice relates to legal as opposed to administrative matters (*Alfred Crompton Amusement
   Machines Ltd v Commissioners of Customs and Excise (No. 2)* [1974] AC 405); and
(j) instructions and briefs to counsel, and counsel's opinions, drafts and notes.

Legal advice privilege will not apply to the following:

(a) investment advice, or advice given by a solicitor as a patent or estate agent, because the
   advice is not given by the solicitor in his capacity as a solicitor;
(b) the actual conveyancing documents prepared by the solicitor (*R v Inner London Crown Court,
   ex parte Baines and Baines* [1988] QB 579, because they are not communications);
(c) a solicitor's client ledger accounts (*Nationwide Building Society v Various Solicitors* [1999] PNLR 53,
   because they are internal records, not communications dealing with advice);
(d) counsel's endorsement on a brief of the result of a hearing, because it is regarded as *publici
   juris* (*Nicholl v Jones* (1865) 2 Hem & M 588);
(e) documents prepared by the client's employees with the intention of sending them to the
   solicitors and in fact sent to the solicitors (*Three Rivers District Council v Bank of England (No.
   5)* [2003] EWCA Civ 474, [2003] QB 1556);
(f) documents prepared by the client's employees with the dominant purpose of obtaining
   legal advice, but which are not sent to the solicitor (*Three Rivers District Council v Bank of
   England (No. 5)*); or

proceedings does not become privileged (*Dubai Bank Ltd v Galadari* [1990] Ch 98; *Ventouris v Mountain* [1991] 1 WLR 607, CA). On the other hand, a selection of documents assembled or copied by a party's solicitor which would betray the trend of advice given to the party will be privileged (*Lyell v Kennedy (No. 3)* (1884) 27 ChD 1), provided the documents assembled were originally third-party, non-disclosable, documents. In principle, an assembly of translations of third-party documents will also be privileged if it will betray the trend of legal advice given. However, own-party documents (unprivileged documents disclosable by the party claiming privilege) are not protected by the *Lyell v Kennedy* principle (*Sumitomo Corporation v Credit Lyonnais Rouse Ltd* [2001] EWCA Civ 1152, [2002] 1 WLR 479). A lawyer's underlining or highlighting of documents (or the absence of such) does not give rise to legal professional privilege except in the unlikely event that the trend of advice may be revealed (*Imerman v Tchenguiz* [2009] EWHC 2902 (QB), LTL 20/11/2009). Counsel's annotations (which may separately be privileged) on documents may be redacted before the documents are disclosed.

Iniquity

50.63   Legal professional privilege does not apply where the purpose behind seeking legal advice is 'iniquitous', such as to devise a structure for a transaction to prejudice the interests of the client's creditors (see *Barclays Bank plc v Eustice* [1995] 1 WLR 1238). According to *Kuwait Airways Corporation v Iraqi Airways Co. (No. 6)* [2005] EWCA Civ 286, [2005] 1 WLR 2734:

(a) the fraud exception can apply both to litigation privilege and legal advice privilege;

(b) where the issue of fraud is one of the issues in the claim, there must be a very strong prima facie case of fraud;

(c) where fraud is not one of the issues in the claim, a prima facie case of fraud may be enough.

The privilege was lost on this ground in a case where a search order was obtained using information which had been gathered in breach of the Data Protection Act 1984 (*Dubai Aluminium Co. Ltd v Al Alawi* [1999] 1 WLR 1964). Communications in furtherance of a fraud or crime are not protected by privilege (*Finers v Miro* [1991] 1 WLR 35). It does not matter whether or not the solicitor was aware of the client's intent (*Gamlen Chemical Co. (UK) Ltd v Rochem Ltd* [1979] CA Transcript 777). The principle applies whether or not the claim is founded on the particular fraud in question (*Dubai Bank Ltd v Galadari (No. 6)* (1991) *The Times*, 22 April 1991). Where fraud between the solicitor and client is established in relation to the litigation itself, legal professional privilege is removed from all the relevant advice obtained in the litigation (*Dadourian Group International Inc. v Simms* [2008] EWHC 1784 (Ch), LTL 1/8/2008). Communications which are criminal in themselves, or intended to further a criminal purpose, are not covered by legal professional privilege. An affidavit setting out the details of an abusive telephone call (which was an offence contrary to the Telecommunications Act 1984, s. 43(1)(a)) and a threat to rip someone's throat out (which was a threat to kill contrary to the Offences against the Person Act 1861, s. 16) was held not to be privileged in *C v C (Privilege: Criminal Communications)* [2001] EWCA Civ 469, [2002] Fam 42.

Common interest privilege

50.64   Common interest privilege is a form of legal professional privilege, see *Buttes Gas and Oil Co. v Hammer (No. 3)* [1981] QB 223. It is a privilege in aid of anticipated litigation in which several persons have a common interest, and applies to cases where some only of the persons who have sought legal advice are eventually made parties to the litigation. For example, owners of adjoining houses complain of a nuisance which affects them both. Both take legal advice, and both exchange relevant documents. However, only one becomes a claimant (for whatever reasons). The various documents shared between the persons who took the legal advice will be privileged provided they had a common interest in advancing or defending the anticipated proceedings (*R v Trutch* [2001] EWCA Crim 1750, LTL 27/7/2001).

Joint privilege

For joint privilege to apply there must be a joint interest at the time of the communication. **50.65**
In *BBGP Managing General Partner Ltd v Babcock and Brown Global Partners* [2010] EWHC 2176 (Ch),
[2011] Ch 296 at [52] and [58], Norris J said:

I consider that the authorities establish that where a solicitor accepts a joint retainer from parties with
potentially conflicting interests one client cannot insist as against the other that legal professional privilege
attaches to any of what passes between the solicitor and that client during the currency and in the course
of the retainer: *Baugh v Cradocke* (1832) 1 Mood & R 182; *Perry v Smith* (1842) 9 M & W 681; *Shore v
Bedford* (1843) 5 Man & G 271; *Ross v Gibbs* (1869) LR 8 Eq 522 and *Re Konigsberg* [1989] 1 WLR 1257....
The right to confidentiality and privilege is a joint right of all the individual clients....No one [client]
can waive it.

The members of a partnership firm have joint privilege in legal advice about the firm's affairs, other
than advice sought in their sectional interest by some only of the partners. As it is a joint privilege,
none of the partners may disseminate or use the information contained in the advice in any legal
proceedings without the joint waiver of the other partners. Joint privilege does not apply if advice
is sought by one or more partners in respect of their sectional interest against other partners.

Other confidential situations

Confidentiality is only an element of the privilege, not its foundation. The fact that docu- **50.66**
ments may contain confidential information is not in itself a reason for withholding inspection (*Croft House Care Ltd v Durham County Council* [2010] EWHC 909 (TCC), LTL 7/7/2010, where the
documents were said to be commercially sensitive). Ultimately the question is whether inspection of the documents is necessary for disposing fairly of the proceedings, and in making that
decision the court should consider whether any special measure, such as redaction of the
documents, or holding hearings in private under **CPR, r. 39.2(3)**, should be adopted (*Science
Research Council v Nassé* [1980] AC 1028). Another approach is to preserve the confidentiality of
the documents at the disclosure stage, subject to review later to decide whether in the light of
the material then available the documents are required for disposing fairly of the proceedings
(*Mears Ltd v Leeds City Council* [2011] EWHC 40 (QB), LTL 19/1/2011).

The fact that a settlement agreement contains a confidentiality clause does not mean it cannot
be ordered to be disclosed in related litigation, as happened in *Cadogan Petroleum plc v Tolley* [2010]
EWHC 1107 (Ch), LTL 19/5/2010, where certain terms in a settlement between the claimant and
some of the defendants were relevant to the continuing litigation between the claimant and the
remaining defendants. While interviews with medical advisers are not covered by legal professional privilege, they are often treated as being *in pari materia* with legal advice. This is partly
because they may be covered by litigation privilege (see **50.60**), and partly because they are an
aspect of the right to respect for private life which is protected by the European Convention on
Human Rights, **art. 8**, in the **Human Rights Act 1998, sch. 1** (*McE v Prison Service of Northern
Ireland* [2009] UKHL 15, [2009] 1 AC 908 at [72]). A third party, whether official or unofficial, who
receives information in confidence with a view to matrimonial conciliation will not be compelled by the courts to disclose what was said without the parties' agreement (*McTaggart v
McTaggart* [1949] P 94; *D v National Society for the Prevention of Cruelty to Children* [1978] AC 171). This
privilege, which is based on the sanctity of marriage, also extends to proceedings under the
Children Act 1989 (*Re D (Minors) (Conciliation: Disclosure of Information)* [1993] Fam 231). A 'wish
letter' written at the same time as a discretionary trust was set up is a confidential document, but
the court may order it to be disclosed to the beneficiaries on an application for the court's sanction of a scheme of distribution where disclosure is in the best interests of the beneficiaries and
the due administration of the trust (*Breakspear v Acland* [2008] EWHC 220 (Ch), [2009] Ch 32).

Danger and confidentiality

A dilemma from time to time faced by professional people is whether they should alert the **50.67**
authorities to some danger when knowledge of the danger has come to them through a

confidential relationship. In *Re B (Children: Patient Confidentiality)* [2003] EWCA Civ 786, [2003] 2 FLR 813, it was held to be proper for a psychiatrist to report to the local authority child protection services information giving rise to a concern of child abuse. The Court of Appeal stated that the psychiatrist should have limited herself to making a report, and should not have gone further and provided a witness statement on the matter.

WITHOUT-PREJUDICE COMMUNICATIONS

50.68   Without-prejudice communications, whether oral or in writing, which are made with the intention of seeking a settlement of litigation, are privileged from disclosure, in both the present and subsequent proceedings (*Ofulue v Bossert* [2009] UKHL 16, [2009] AC 990). *Calderbank* offers, which are made without prejudice save as to costs, are considered at **66.57**. The policy is to encourage litigants to settle their differences rather than litigate them to the finish (see Lord Griffiths in *Rush and Tompkins Ltd v Greater London Council* [1989] AC 1280). Privilege does this by removing the potential embarrassment of concessions made in the course of negotiations being used at trial against the party who made them. So, on an application for costs, it is not permissible to adduce without-prejudice communications (other than *Calderbank* offers), without the joint consent of the parties, to establish whether a party unreasonably refused a proposal for ADR. Further, it is impermissible to draw adverse inferences from a party's reluctance to waive the joint privilege (*Reed Executive plc v Reed Business Information Ltd* [2004] EWCA Civ 887, [2004] 1 WLR 3026).

Without-prejudice protection applies to genuine attempts to negotiate a settlement of a dispute where the parties contemplate or might reasonably have contemplated litigation if they cannot agree. The question of proximity applies to the subject matter of the dispute, rather than the length of time before the threat or actual commencement of the contemplated litigation (*Barnetson v Framlington Group Ltd* [2007] EWCA Civ 502, [2007] 1 WLR 2443). It has been held to apply outside litigation to genuine settlement discussions between a bank and a regulator in relation to a regulatory investigation (*Property Alliance Group Ltd v Royal Bank of Scotland plc* [2015] EWHC 1557 (Ch), [2016] 1 WLR 361).

The privilege applies even if the words 'without prejudice' are not used, provided the purpose was to seek a settlement (*Chocoladefabriken Lindt & Sprungli AG v Nestlé Co. Ltd* [1978] RPC 287). It applies, for example, to joint settlement meetings, unless they are stated to be 'without prejudice save as to costs' (*Jackson v Ministry of Defence* [2006] EWCA Civ 46, LTL 12/1/2006). Without-prejudice privilege does not apply to apparently open correspondence which discusses repayment of an admitted liability, rather than negotiates the possible compromise of a disputed liability (*Bradford and Bingley plc v Rashid* [2006] UKHL 37, [2006] 1 WLR 2066). The question is whether the communication was genuinely intended to be a negotiating document (*Schering Corporation v Cipla Ltd* [2004] EWHC 2587 (Ch), [2005] FSR 25). In making this assessment the court must determine the author's intention, and must put itself in the position of a reasonable recipient to determine the message the communication conveyed (*South Shropshire District Council v Amos* [1986] 1 WLR 1271). Use of the words 'without prejudice' will not attach privilege to communications intended to prejudice the recipient or which are no more than an assertion of one party's rights (*Buckinghamshire County Council v Moran* [1990] Ch 623). A failure to use the words, coupled with a finding that the purpose of the communications was more administrative than with a view to settling a claim, meant that documents were not protected in *Prudential Assurance Co. Ltd v Prudential Insurance Co. of America* [2003] EWCA Civ 1154, [2004] ETMR 29. A letter marked 'without prejudice' proposing terms of a lease was not privileged, and the possibility of a dispute arising in the event the negotiations broke down was not sufficient to attract privilege (*Bath and North East Somerset District Council v Nicholson* (2002) LTL 22/2/2002).

Where the parties enter into 'without-prejudice' negotiations, continuing negotiations will be privileged until one party brings it home to the other party that the 'without-prejudice' basis of the negotiations is at an end. Thus, in *Cheddar Valley Engineering Ltd v Chaddlewood Homes Ltd* [1992] 1 WLR 820 it was held that prefacing one telephone offer with the word 'open' was insufficient to bring home the change in basis when further telephone negotiations and a letter did not repeat the word 'open'.

The public policy rationale of the privilege is, according to *Murrell v Healy* [2001] EWCA Civ 486, [2001] 4 All ER 345, directed solely to protecting admissions, and if documents are to be used for a different purpose, such as to show the amount of compensation paid for an earlier injury, they are admissible. This is not entirely consistent with *Unilever plc v Procter and Gamble Co.* [2000] 1 WLR 2436, and probably does not survive *Ofulue v Bossert* [2009] UKHL 16, [2009] AC 990, because it would create huge practical difficulties to dissect out identifiable admissions and withhold protection of the rest of without-prejudice communications. In *Re New Gadget Shop Ltd* [2005] EWHC 1606 (Ch), LTL 5/8/2005, the petitioner sought to dissect identifiable admissions out of without-prejudice communications, crafting its witness statements so as to include the alleged admissions but avoiding reference to any of the without-prejudice negotiations.

It was held that this approach was prohibited by *Unilever plc v Procter and Gamble Co.* [2000] 1 WLR 2436. The paragraphs seeking to achieve this were struck out.

A draft expert's report sent by the claimant 'without prejudice' in the early stages is inadmissible at trial on the question of deciding the amount of interest, even where the defendant is arguing that the award of interest should be reduced because of delays in formulating the value of the claim, and where the report dealt with quantifying the claim (*UYB Ltd v British Railways Board* (2000) *The Times*, 15 November 2000). This was not covered by legal professional privilege (in which event the claimant could have waived privilege), because the issue was when the defendant was first notified of the value of the claim.

In relation to mediated cross-border disputes governed by Directive 2008/52/EC, where a person seeks disclosure or inspection of mediation evidence in the control of a mediator or mediation administrator, an application must be made using the Part 23 procedure if there are pending proceedings, or using the Part 8 procedure if not (**CPR, r. 78.26(1)**). The mediator or mediation administrator must be made a respondent (**Part 23**) or party (**Part 8**). The evidence in support must include evidence that all parties to the mediation agree to the disclosure or inspection of the mediation evidence, or that disclosure is necessary for overriding considerations of public policy, or that disclosure is necessary to implement or enforce the mediation agreement (**r. 78.26(3)**).

Proof of settlement

Without-prejudice negotiations which result in a settlement are admissible to prove the terms **50.69** of the settlement (*Walker v Wilsher* (1889) 23 QBD 335). A party to without-prejudice negotiations can also rely on anything said in the course of them to show that the settlement agreement should be rectified (*Oceanbulk Shipping and Trading SA v TMT Asia Ltd* [2010] UKSC 44, [2011] 1 AC 662 at [33]). Such negotiations can also be relied upon, where they are relevant under the normal rules governing the interpretation of contracts (usually as part of the factual matrix or surrounding circumstances to show the true construction of the agreement), where those facts have a bearing on the meaning to be given to the words of the settlement (*Oceanbulk Shipping and Trading SA v TMT Asia Ltd* at [36]–[48]). In *Jackson v Thakrar* [2007] EWHC 271 (TCC), 113 Con LR 58, a chain of letters came into being without an intention to create legal relations, and at best amounted to an agreement to agree on a single topic. No settlement had been reached. In *Brown v Rice* [2007] EWHC 625 (Ch), [2008] FSR 3, an offer made in mediation did not deal with how the litigation should be disposed of, and had not been made in writing as previously stipulated. It was therefore incomplete, and there was no final settlement. Where the terms of settlement reached in without-prejudice communications are relevant in determining the extent of the liability of another person who is then sued by one of the parties to the settlement for a contribution towards the original liability, the privilege will not prevent inspection of the without-prejudice communications (*Gnitrow Ltd v Cape plc* [2000] 1 WLR 2327).

Abuse of without-prejudice rule

50.70   *Unilever plc v Procter and Gamble Co.* [2000] 1 WLR 2436 reiterated in a modern context the old rule that the without-prejudice rule will not protect statements made in circumstances where the rule is being unequivocally abused. Threats or other conduct which could be described as oppressive, dishonest or dishonourable could fall into this category. Thus, marking a letter 'without prejudice' will not protect the evidence of a threat of what will happen if an offer is not accepted (*Kitcat v Sharp* (1882) 48 LT 64).

A mere inconsistency between an admission made on a without-prejudice occasion and the pleaded case or the facts stated in a witness statement of the party making the admission will not result in the privilege being lost (*Savings and Investment Bank Ltd v Fincken* [2003] EWCA Civ 1630, [2004] 1 WLR 667). This is so even if persistence in the inconsistent position might lead to perjury. The strength of the public policy protecting without-prejudice communications is such that it should be lost only in truly exceptional circumstances (*Savings and Investment Bank Ltd v Fincken*) or where there is a very clear case of abuse of a privileged occasion (*Berry Trade Ltd v Moussavi* [2003] EWCA Civ 715, *The Times*, 3 June 2003). In *Berry Trade Ltd v Moussavi* the privilege was not lost where the alleged admissions were made orally in a lengthy without-prejudice meeting which was not tape-recorded or made the subject of a detailed note, and where the alleged admissions were small, selected parts of the discussion.

Use in interim applications

50.71   Without-prejudice correspondence is often used in interim applications, particularly applications seeking sanctions for default, or relief from sanctions (*Family Housing Association (Manchester) Ltd v Michael Hyde and Partners* [1993] 1 WLR 354). While the duty of full and frank disclosure might mean that a without-prejudice document, or the fact it existed, must be disclosed, it was held that there was no breach of the duty in *Linsen International Ltd v Humpuss Sea Transport Pte Ltd* [2010] EWHC 303 (Comm), LTL 1/3/2010. The defendant had deliberately chosen to withhold information about the without-prejudice negotiation, and neither the fact of the meeting nor what was discussed had any real bearing on the risk of dissipation of assets. Before using without-prejudice material the other side should be informed and given an opportunity to object, and before placing the material before the judge the court should be informed so it can react and rule on its use before the judge's knowledge is affected (*Berg v IML London Ltd* [2002] 1 WLR 3271). Use of without-prejudice material on an interim application by one party entitles the other party to use that material at trial, at least where the issues on the interim application included consideration of the underlying merits of the claim (*Somatra Ltd v Sinclair Roche and Temperley* [2000] 1 WLR 2453).

Use of without-prejudice material in subsequent proceedings

50.72   Once a document is protected by without-prejudice privilege, it will always (subject to the principles discussed in **50.68** to **50.70**) be privileged. Thus, an admission made in without-prejudice communications by one party will not be admissible in other proceedings against that party (*Rush and Tompkins Ltd v Greater London Council* [1989] AC 1280). If without-prejudice documents are used to found subsequent proceedings, those proceedings will be struck out as an abuse of process, unless the claimant in the subsequent proceedings can show that the statements relied upon were made improperly, or that there is some public interest favouring their subsequent use (*Unilever plc v Procter and Gamble Co.* [2000] 1 WLR 2436).

WAIVER OF PRIVILEGE

50.73   Legal professional privilege belongs to, and can be waived by, the client. The privilege against self-incrimination belongs to the witness, and can only be waived by him. The privilege in without-prejudice communications belongs to both sides jointly, and can only be waived if both sides consent (*Rush and Tompkins Ltd v Greater London Council* [1989] AC 1280). Adverse inferences will not be drawn from a refusal to waive privilege (*Sayers v Clarke Walker* [2002] EWCA Civ 910, LTL 26/6/2002; *Reed Executive plc v Reed Business Information Ltd* [2004] EWCA Civ 887, [2004] 1 WLR 3026).

Waiver of privilege may be given expressly, or implicitly such as by disclosing a privileged document to the other side. The public interest importance attached to legal advice privilege is such that something more than a reference to the effect of the advice is needed before any question of waiver can arise (*Brennan v Sunderland City Council* [2009] ICR 479). The underlying principle is that of fairness. There will be a waiver only if it would be unfair to allow the party making the disclosure not to reveal the whole of the relevant information because it may lead to the court or other parties having only a partial, and potentially misleading, impression of the material. In *R v Seaton* [2010] EWCA Crim 1980, [2011] 1 WLR 623, the defendant's evidence at trial differed in a significant way from the version of events in a statement presented to the police, through his solicitor, at interview. He explained the discrepancy by blaming his solicitor for getting the facts wrong. The solicitor was not called at trial. It was held that the defendant had waived his privilege, but only to the extent that was fair and necessary to avoid giving a misleading impression, and that the prosecution were entitled to comment in closing on the failure to call the defendant's solicitor to verify his explanation. From *Mac Hotels Ltd v Rider Levett Bucknall UK Ltd* [2010] EWHC 767 (TCC), LTL 28/4/2010, waiver of privilege through deployment of the privileged material in litigation has two elements:

(a) a clear reference to the existence of the privileged communications; and
(b) reliance on the privileged material for the purpose of making a particular point. If the reference to the privileged material is no more than mere narrative there is no waiver. If the content of the privileged material is used to support a point which the party deploying the material wishes to make, there will be a waiver of the privilege.

Examples include disclosure by service of a hearsay notice; by inclusion as an exhibit to a witness statement; by using the document to refresh the memory of a witness while giving evidence; and use of documents in re-examination to rebut an allegation of recent fabrication. In *Compagnie Noga d'Importation et d'Exportation SA v Australia and New Zealand Banking Group Ltd* [2007] EWHC 85 (Comm), LTL 5/2/2007, the defendant had made five affidavits, with the assistance of solicitors, about his assets pursuant to clauses in a freezing injunction. As a result he had waived any claim to privilege on the issue of disclosure of his assets. In *Re D (A Child)* [2011] EWCA Civ 684, [2011] 4 All ER 434, the mother of the child in interim care proceedings explained a change in her story between two witness statements by referring to various meetings with her solicitor and barrister, and setting out parts of what was discussed in those meetings. It was held that she had waived privilege in all the meetings with her solicitor and barrister over a five-week period leading up to the second witness statement. The references to the meetings with her lawyers were more than 'glancing references', which would not have amounted to a waiver, but had gone further and disclosed the nature of the advice she had received. Privilege was waived by the mother despite the fact her witness statement was drafted by her solicitor, and despite the fact that neither she nor her solicitor realised that the material in her second witness statement amounted to a waiver of privilege.

Use by both parties of incidents (or the denial of incidents) which are alleged to have occurred during mediation amounts to mutual waiver of privilege as both parties have chosen to plead privileged matter in public documents (*Hall v Pertemps Group Ltd* [2005] EWHC 3317 (Ch), *The Times*, 23 December 2005). A consent order in proceedings in Minnesota was held, on the wording of the order, not to be an implied waiver of privilege in *British American Tobacco (Investments) Ltd v United States of America* [2004] EWCA Civ 1064, LTL 30/7/2004. A party waives privilege for trial purposes by using materials in an interim application (*Derby and Co. Ltd v Weldon (No. 10)* [1991] 1 WLR 660).

In *Great Atlantic Insurance Co. v Home Insurance Co.* [1981] 1 WLR 529 the Court of Appeal held that where part of a document is used in counsel's opening, privilege in the whole of the document is waived unless it is a clearly separable document with different parts dealing with completely different subjects. A single letter can be a severable document if different parts of the letter are so distinct that they amount to different documents (*Pozzi v Eli Lilley and Co.* (1986) *The Times*, 3 December 1986). Where a document is severed, with privilege being asserted as to a part, the other parties must be informed that this has been done (*Nea Karteria Maritime Co. Ltd v Atlantic and Great Lakes Steamship Corporation (No. 2)* [1981] Com LR 138). If a document deals with a single subject matter, a party cannot waive privilege on a part, and assert privilege on the rest (*Great Atlantic Insurance Co. v Home Insurance Co.*). As Denning LJ said in *Burnell v British Transport Commission* [1956] 1 QB 187:

It would be most unfair that cross-examining counsel should use part of the document which was to his advantage and not allow anyone else, not even the judge or the opposing counsel, a sight of the rest of the document, much of which might have been against him.

Once privilege on a subject has been waived, the waiver will be taken to extend to any associated material (*Derby and Co. Ltd v Weldon (No. 10)*), but the court will seek to define the subject matter of the waiver quite restrictively (*General Accident Fire and Life Assurance Corporation Ltd v Tanter* [1984] 1 WLR 100). There are two questions that need to be addressed. The first is to define the transaction in relation to which disclosure has been made, which has to be considered objectively. It is not open to the disclosing party to define the transaction as limited to what he has chosen to disclose (*Fulham Leisure Holdings Ltd v Nicholson Graham and Jones* [2006] EWHC 158 (Ch), [2006] 2 All ER 599). The second question is whether further disclosure is required going beyond the strict limits of the transaction in order to avoid unfairness or misunderstanding of what has been disclosed (*Fulham Leisure Holdings Ltd v Nicholson Graham and Jones*). In *United Building and Plumbing Contractors v Kajla* [2002] EWCA Civ 628, LTL 26/4/2002, a party who put in evidence of meetings between the parties for settlement negotiations was held to have waived the privilege in the without-prejudice negotiations at those meetings.

Where a party allows documents which were protected by legal professional privilege to be used by a third party for a limited purpose, there is a limited waiver restricted to that purpose. A limited waiver does not destroy the privilege for all purposes (*B v Auckland District Law Society* [2003] UKPC 38, [2003] 2 AC 736).

Implied waiver

50.74   In a claim against the claimant's former solicitor the claimant's privilege over all documents concerned with the claim is impliedly waived to the extent necessary to enable the court to adjudicate the dispute fully and fairly. In *Lillicrap v Nalder and Son* [1993] 1 WLR 94 property developers sued their solicitors for negligently failing to advise them about a right of way over some land they purchased. The claimants had retained the solicitors to advise on a number of other transactions, and the solicitors said their files on those other transactions showed the claimants habitually ignored their warnings, so would have bought the land even if they had been properly advised. The Court of Appeal held that the previous transactions were relevant to an issue in the present proceedings, so the implied waiver extended to them as well as to the transaction in question. However, there are limits on the implied waiver of privilege in solicitors' negligence claims. In *Paragon Finance plc v Freshfields* [1999] 1 WLR 1183 the first firm of solicitors had acted for the finance company in relation to a number of mortgage transactions. The finance company made a number of claims against insurance policies entered into in relation to the mortgages, which the insurer disputed. The finance company then retained a second firm of solicitors to pursue outstanding insurance claims, and later sued the first firm of solicitors for professional negligence. A question arose as to whether the finance company had, by suing the first firm of solicitors, impliedly waived its privilege in respect of the work done by the second firm in pursuing the insurance claims. It was held that by suing the first firm of solicitors the finance company had only put its relationship with that firm into the public domain, and had not done so in respect of the work done by the second firm, and so had not waived its privilege in respect of the work done by the second firm.

Apart from professional negligence claims against the client's former solicitor, there is no general rule that privilege is waived by placing in issue events evidenced by privileged communications (*Farm Assist Ltd v Secretary of State for the Environment, Food and Rural Affairs* [2008] EWHC 3079 (TCC), [2009] BLR 80). Thus, privilege over the claimant's solicitor's files is not impliedly waived even where the contents of those files is highly relevant to the claimant's date of knowledge on an application under the Limitation Act 1980, s. 14 or s. 14A (*Mac Hotels Ltd v Rider Levett Bucknall UK Ltd* [2010] EWHC 767 (TCC), LTL 28/4/2010).

Secondary evidence

It was held in *Calcraft v Guest* [1898] 1 QB 759 that secondary evidence, such as a copy, of **50.75** otherwise privileged material is admissible at trial. In *Goddard v Nationwide Building Society* [1987] QB 670 Nourse LJ said that it makes no difference how the privileged material was obtained. Even if confidential documents have been obtained by theft, it is said that they will be admissible. However, the party who would otherwise be able to claim privilege may apply for an injunction to restrain use of such material if it has not yet been used in the litigation (*Goddard v Nationwide Building Society*). This was before the introduction of **CPR, r. 32.1(2)**, under which it is possible for the court to exercise its discretion to exclude stolen documents (see **49.8**). Alternatively, the court has always had a jurisdiction to grant an injunction to restrain use of privileged material which has fallen into the hands of another party, as long as the application is made before the material has been used in the litigation (*Goddard v Nationwide Building Society*).

Injunctions to restrain use of privileged material

In *ISTIL Group Inc. v Zahoor* [2003] EWHC 165 (Ch), [2003] 2 All ER 252, the claimant sought an **50.76** injunction to restrain the defendant from using documents which the claimant had sent to a person who then gave them to the defendant. The claimant alleged that the documents were protected by legal professional privilege. The defendant said that he should be allowed to use the documents because they came into existence as part of a scheme by the claimant to present a false case to the court. Unlike the situation considered at **50.50** to **50.72** (where the question is whether a party can successfully assert privilege), in the present situation the allegedly privileged documents are already in the hands of the other side. Here the court will balance the public interest in supporting legal professional privilege against the public interest in the administration of justice. On the facts there had been forgery and an attempt to place a misleading case before the court, so the injunction was refused.

The manner in which otherwise privileged materials came into the possession of the other party is important. If this happened illegally, the principles discussed at **50.29** apply. Alternatively, the circumstances may be taken as indicating that the party seeking to assert privilege has waived its privilege.

Waiver may arise inadvertently (*Great Atlantic Insurance Co. v Home Insurance Co.* [1981] 1 WLR 529). In *Guinness Peat Properties Ltd v Fitzroy Robinson Partnership* [1987] 1 WLR 1027 a privileged letter was inadvertently disclosed. The defendant allowed the claimant to inspect certain files before serving a list of documents. By accident, the letter was left in one of the files, and the claimant took a copy of it. The document later appeared in the defendant's list of documents, without a claim for privilege, and the claimant was again allowed to inspect it at the defendant's solicitors' office, but was not given a copy. Slade LJ said, at p. 1044:

Care must be taken by parties to litigation in the preparation of their lists of documents and no less great care must be taken in offering inspection of the documents disclosed. Ordinarily, in my judgment, a party to litigation who sees a particular document referred to in the other side's list, without privilege being claimed, and is subsequently permitted inspection of that document, is fully entitled to assume that any privilege which might otherwise have been claimed for it has been waived.

As Slade LJ said, this is ordinarily the position. It is subject to two exceptions:

(a) where a party or its solicitor procures inspection of the relevant document by fraud; and
(b) where a party or its solicitor realises on inspection that the document has been disclosed as a result of an obvious mistake.

Where either of these exceptions applies, Slade LJ in *Guinness Peat Properties Ltd v Fitzroy Robinson Partnership* said the court should ordinarily intervene, unless there is some equitable reason for not doing so, such as delay.

Guinness Peat Properties Ltd v Fitzroy Robinson Partnership was an example of an obvious mistake, as, being a trained lawyer, the claimant's solicitor must have realised the privileged nature of the letter as soon as he read it. Another, more obvious, example is *English and American Insurance Co. Ltd v Herbert Smith* [1988] FSR 232, where counsel's clerk allowed counsel's instructions and papers (including witness statements and counsel's written opinion) to be sent to the other side's solicitors. An injunction was granted restraining use being made of any of the information in the papers.

50.77   Principles governing applications for injunctions   In *Al Fayed v Commissioner of Police for the Metropolis* [2002] EWCA Civ 780, *The Times*, 17 June 2002, an injunction was refused because the recipient solicitors genuinely thought the other side's counsel's opinions had been disclosed on purpose. This case has a useful statement of the principles governing applications for injunctions to prevent use of privileged documents, which was approved in *Rawlinson and Hunter Trustees SA v Director of the Serious Fraud Office (No. 2)* [2014] EWCA Civ 1129, [2015] 1 WLR 797:

(a) A party giving inspection of documents has to decide what privileged documents to disclose before doing so.
(b) Although the privilege belongs to the client, the solicitor has ostensible authority to waive the privilege.
(c) A solicitor inspecting another party's documents owes no duty of care to the other party, and is generally entitled to assume that any privilege has been intentionally waived.
(d) Where privileged documents are given to the other side by mistake, it is generally too late thereafter to claim privilege by seeking an injunction to restrain use of those documents.
(e) Nevertheless, the court does have jurisdiction to grant such injunctions where justice requires.
(f) An injunction would be granted where documents were made available for inspection through an obvious mistake.
(g) A mistake was likely to be obvious where the receiving solicitor appreciated that a mistake had been made before making use of the documents or if it would have been obvious to a reasonable solicitor in the position of the receiving solicitor that a mistake had been made.
(h) In considering whether a mistake was obvious, it is relevant but not conclusive that a solicitor had considered the question and honestly concluded that the documents had not been made available by mistake.
(i) Even if there has been an obvious mistake, an injunction may be refused if it would be unjust or inequitable to grant an injunction.
(j) There are no rigid rules, because the court is exercising an equitable discretion.
(k) The same principles apply to the exercise of the discretion under **CPR, r. 31.20**.

The provisions of the CPR appear to reverse the common law position described above, with **r. 31.20** providing that where a party inadvertently allows a privileged document to be inspected, the party who has inspected the document may use it or its contents only with the permission of the court. Procedurally this means that there is no longer any need for the party making the inadvertent disclosure to apply for an injunction, and the onus must now be on the other party to seek an order giving permission to rely on the documents. However, in *Breeze v John Stacey and Sons Ltd* (1999) *The Times*, 8 July 1999, it was held that **r. 31.20** does no more than confirm the long-established principles set out above, and does not alter the law in any way.

Making use of an inadvertently disclosed document before seeking permission under **r. 31.20** may result in a sanction being imposed (*Property Alliance Group Ltd v Royal Bank of Scotland plc (No. 3)* [2015] EWHC 3341 (Ch), [2016] 4 WLR 3).

Different considerations apply where it is alleged that documents are protected by public interest immunity, see **50.80**, given the duty to protect the public interest (*Rawlinson and Hunter Trustees SA v Director of the Serious Fraud Office (No. 2)* [2014] EWCA Civ 1129, [2015] 1 WLR 797).

Documents *publici juris*

Notes of proceedings in open court and counsel's endorsement on the brief of the order of the court are *publici juris* (in the public domain) and are not privileged (*Nicholl v Jones* (1865) 2 Hem & M 588). Likewise, public records and documents are also *publici juris*. However, a collection of extracts or copies from public documents may be protected from production by legal professional privilege where the collection is a product of the professional knowledge, research and skill of a party's legal advisers (*Lyell v Kennedy (No. 3)* (1884) 27 ChD 1).   **50.78**

Beneficiaries and shareholders

There is a general rule that a *cestui que trust* (for which see *Tugwell v Hooper* (1847) 10 Beav 348) and a shareholder (for which see *W. Dennis and Sons Ltd v West Norfolk Farmers' Manure and Chemical Co-operative Co. Ltd* [1943] Ch 220) are entitled to see opinions from counsel and advice from solicitors paid for out of the fund or the assets of the company (respectively) for the purpose of administering the fund or the company. The rule is subject to an exception where the legal advice is sought by the trustees or company in hostile litigation against the beneficiary or shareholder in question. It applies to a company whether it is public or private and however many shareholders it has (*CAS Nominees Ltd v Nottingham Forest plc* [2001] 1 All ER 954). But where a company is merely a necessary but nominal defendant in proceedings between its shareholders and directors there is no 'hostile' litigation for this purpose, and the general rule applies (*Re Hydrosan Ltd* [1991] BCLC 418).   **50.79**

PUBLIC INTEREST IMMUNITY

General principles

Certain documents must be withheld from disclosure and/or inspection on the ground that revealing the existence and/or contents of the documents would be injurious to the public interest. Claims to public interest immunity are of two types: (a) claims that all documents of certain classes must be protected; (b) claims that individual documents need to be protected because of their particular 'contents'. Contents immunity attaches, for example, to diplomatic dispatches and documents relating to national security. There is a wide variation in the 'classes' of documents protected, from Cabinet minutes to more routine documents such as local authority social work records (*Re M (A Minor)* (1989) 88 LGR 841).   **50.80**

Ministerial certificates

The usual practice is that the responsible minister provides a certificate stating the grounds of the objection to disclosure and/or inspection, identifying the document in question. Such a certificate is not conclusive (*Conway v Rimmer* [1968] AC 910) and the court may require the document to be produced to it (**CPR, r. 31.19(6)**). It is, though, for the party seeking inspection to show that the claim to immunity should be rejected (*Air Canada v Secretary of State for Trade* [1983] 2 AC 394). A defective ministerial certificate may be amended (*R (Mohamed) v Secretary of State for Foreign and Commonwealth Affairs* [2008] EWHC 2100 (Admin), LTL 2/9/2008). If the party seeking disclosure establishes a counteracting interest to the claim for immunity, the court must balance the public interest in concealment against the public interest in the due administration of justice in favour of disclosure (see Lord Fraser of Tullybelton in the *Air Canada* case).   **50.81**

Procedure

Under **CPR, r. 31.19(1)**, a person (who need not be a party) may apply, without notice, for an order permitting him to withhold disclosure of a document on the ground that disclosure   **50.82**

Commentary

would damage the public interest. Usually the applicant for such an order is the Secretary of State for the government department asserting public interest immunity in the document. By **r. 31.19(2)**, unless the court otherwise orders, any order made under this rule must not be served on any other person, and must not be open to inspection by any other person. Claims for protection may alternatively be made in the list of documents served by a party (**r. 31.19(4)**), or may be insisted upon by the court of its own initiative.

It is questionable whether these procedures, particularly the procedure under **r. 31.19(1)**, comply with the European Convention on Human Rights, **art. 6(1)**, in the **Human Rights Act 1998, sch. 1**. In *Rowe v United Kingdom* (2000) 30 EHRR 1, the European Court of Human Rights considered the procedural aspects of withholding evidence in *criminal* trials on the grounds of public interest. It was held that to comply with **art. 6(1)** the accused had to be given information about the withheld information appropriate to the category of the evidence involved, and that it was for the trial judge (rather than a court on appeal) to decide whether the evidence should be withheld. **Rule 31.19** allows orders to be made without giving any information to the parties (or to just one side if one of the parties is the government department seeking to withhold disclosure), and for decisions to be made by judges other than the trial judge, which would seem to fall short of the safeguards contemplated by the European Court. In criminal trials there are the additional minimum rights given by **art. 6(3)**, which do not apply to civil cases, but this difference is unlikely to have a substantial effect on the implications of the decision in civil cases.

Closed material procedure

50.83   There are special procedures for permission to withhold closed material pursuant to the Terrorism Prevention and Investigation Measures Act 2011 and the Justice and Security Act 2013. See **CPR, Parts 80 and 82**. In these cases the overriding objective is modified to ensure that documents protected by public interest immunity, or which would be damaging to national security, are not disclosed (see **1.12**). Closed material procedures include notifying the Attorney General of proceedings, the appointment of special advocates, and the modification of the rules of evidence. They may also include permission to a party to set out part of its case in an open statement of case, and to deploy other material in closed statements of case, and in closed witness statements, with oral evidence at trial which would be kept secret from the other litigants, but made available to special advocates representing their interests. The court is then likely to deliver two judgments, one open and one closed.

Use of a statutory closed material procedure under the Employment Tribunals (Constitution and Rules of Procedure) Regulations 2004 (SI 2004/1861) in proceedings before an employment tribunal does not contravene the European Convention on Human Rights, **art. 6(1)**, in the **Human Rights Act 1998, sch. 1** (*Tariq v Home Office* [2012] UKSC 35, [2012] 1 AC 452).

Statutory intervention was required because at common law *Al Rawi v Security Service* [2011] UKSC 34, [2012] 1 AC 531, held that closed material procedures in civil proceedings would infringe the principles of natural justice that underpin civil justice, particularly the right to a fair trial, the right to be confronted by one's accusers, and the right to know the reasons for the outcome (per Lord Hope of Craighead DPSC at [72]).

CONFIDENTIAL DOCUMENTS

50.84   Confidentiality is not of itself a ground of privilege or public interest immunity, although it is an element in these concepts. Although there is a reluctance to order disclosure of confidential documents, if disclosure is necessary in the interests of the litigation, those interests override mere confidentiality (*Science Research Council v Nassé* [1980] AC 1028; *Three Rivers District Council v Bank of England (No. 5)* [2002] EWHC 2309 (Comm), LTL 8/11/2002, a point not dealt with on the appeal [2003] EWCA Civ 474, [2003] QB 1556). In such cases the court may consider whether confidentiality may be preserved while satisfying the needs of the litigation by ordering redactions, disclosure from other sources, and other appropriate means (*Science Research Council v Nassé; Wallace Smith Trust Co. Ltd v Deloitte Haskins and Sells* [1997] 1 WLR 257; *Three Rivers District Council v Bank of England*).

STATUTORY RESTRICTIONS ON DISCLOSURE

A statute may impose an express restriction on disclosure. Well-known examples are the **50.85** Contempt of Court Act 1981, s. 10, in relation to journalists' sources (see **50.86**), and the Official Secrets Act 1989. Other examples are the Anti-Terrorism, Crime and Security Act 2001, s. 19(2); the Serious Organised Crime and Police Act 2005, s. 33(1); and the Financial Services and Markets Act 2000, s. 348. It is also possible for a court to construe a statute to imply a restriction on disclosure (*Rowell v Pratt* [1938] AC 101). There is usually some reluctance to do this, because generally it is to be expected that a statute will contain an express exemption from disclosure if that is the intention (*Bank of Credit and Commerce International (Overseas) Ltd v Price Waterhouse (No. 2)* [1998] Ch 84), and in general clear words should be expected (*Tchenguiz v Director of the Serious Fraud Office* [2013] EWHC 2128 (QB), [2014] 1 WLR 1476).

Journalists' sources

The Contempt of Court Act 1981, s. 10 (which was enacted in response to *British Steel* **50.86** *Corporation v Granada Television Ltd* [1981] AC 1096), provides:

No court may require a person, nor is any person guilty of contempt of court for refusing to disclose, the source of information contained in a publication for which he is responsible, unless it be established to the satisfaction of the court that disclosure is necessary in the interests of justice or national security or for the prevention of disorder or crime.

The section provides a general protection to journalists' sources. It applies despite any proprietary claim for the delivery up of stolen documents if the documents could lead to the identification of the source (*Secretary of State for Defence v Guardian Newspapers Ltd* [1985] AC 339).

It also applies even if there has been no publication of the information, provided the information was supplied with a view to publication (*X Ltd v Morgan-Grampian (Publishers) Ltd* [1991] 1 AC 1). In *Totalise plc v Motley Fool Ltd* [2001] EMLR 750 a website operator was ordered to disclose the identity of a person who, it was alleged, had posted defamatory comments on the website. It was held that the Contempt of Court Act 1981, s. 10, had no application to the facts because the defendant took no responsibility for items posted on its website, since the section applied to information 'contained in a publication for which he is responsible'.

Disclosure of a journalist's source under one of the exceptions to s. 10 will only be ordered if 'necessary' for one of the exceptional reasons. The phrase 'interests of justice' is interpreted so 'that persons should be enabled to exercise important legal rights and to protect themselves from serious legal wrongs whether or not resort to legal proceedings in a court of law will be necessary to attain these objectives' (see Lord Bridge of Harwich in *X Ltd v Morgan-Grampian (Publishers) Ltd*). 'Prevention of crime' includes the detection and prosecution of crimes which are shown to have been committed and where detection and prosecution can sensibly be said to act as a practical deterrent to future criminal conduct of a similar type (see Lord Oliver of Aylmerton in *Re an Inquiry under the Company Securities (Insider Dealing) Act 1985* [1988] AC 660).

If one of the exceptions applies and is necessary, the court must then weigh the importance of disclosure for the exceptional reason against the importance of protecting the source of the information. Factors to be taken into account include the degree of confidentiality attaching to the information, the manner in which the information was obtained, the public interest in concealing journalists' sources, and whether the information brings to light iniquity on the part of the claimant. According to Lord Bridge in *X Ltd v Morgan-Grampian (Publishers) Ltd* disclosure should only be ordered if the balance is clearly on the side of disclosure, since

Commentary

otherwise the courts would be undermining the policy stated in the section. The interrelation between the Contempt of Court Act 1981, s. 10, the European Convention on Human Rights, **art. 10**, in the **Human Rights Act 1998, sch. 1** (freedom of expression), and *Norwich Pharmacal* orders was further considered in *Ashworth Hospital Authority v MGN Ltd* [2002] UKHL 29, [2002] 1 WLR 2033, and its sequel, *Mersey Care NHS Trust v Ackroyd* [2007] EWCA Civ 101, [2007] HRLR 19, decisions which almost certainly cannot be followed given the ruling in *Financial Times Ltd v United Kingdom* (application 821/03) (2009) 50 EHRR 46. Given the chilling effects of journalists being seen to assist in identifying anonymous sources, merely seeking to eliminate the threat of damage through future leaks of confidential information was regarded as insufficient to outweigh the public interest encapsulated in **art. 10**.

Data protection

50.87   The Data Protection Act 1998, s. 7, applies where personal data about an individual are held by a data controller. On making a request in writing and paying a fee (if applicable), the individual is entitled to have communicated to him in an intelligible form any personal data relating to him and any information about the source of that data. For this purpose 'data' means information which is processed automatically (generally by computer), and also information recorded as part of a filing system, or which forms part of an accessible record (which, by s. 68, means health, education and accessible public records). The selection of data from various manual and electronic files is not 'processing' for this purpose (*Johnson v Medical Defence Union (No. 2)* [2007] EWCA Civ 262, [2008] Bus LR 503). A manual filing system will only be regarded as 'data' within the meaning of the Data Protection Act 1998 if it is of sufficient sophistication to provide the same or similar ready accessibility as a computerised filing system. This means the files must be referenced or indexed in a way that makes it possible to identify with reasonable certainty and speed whether they contain personal data without having to leaf through the files themselves (*Durant v Financial Services Authority* [2003] EWCA Civ 1746, [2004] FSR 28). 'Personal data' is defined as meaning data relating to a living individual who can be identified from that data (or other information in the possession of the data controller), and includes expressions of opinion about the individual (s. 1(1)). According to *Durant v Financial Services Authority* information will come within this definition if:

(a)   the information is biographical in a significant sense, going beyond mere involvement in the events described in the file; and

(b)   the data subject (the applicant) is the focus of the information.

Thus, a file dealing with a complaint made to the Financial Services Authority by the applicant about a bank was not personal data because its focus was the complaint, not biographical information about the applicant.

There are various exemptions and further detailed provisions, such as a restriction on revealing information that would identify other individuals without their consent (s. 7(4)). When complying with a request for personal data which will also reveal details about other individuals, the data controller is required to balance the interests of the other individuals with the interests of the data subject. It may be permissible to redact the names of the other individuals if it is reasonable to do so.

The data controller is required to comply with a request promptly, and can be ordered to comply by the High Court or the County Court (ss. 7(9) and 15(1)). For the purpose of determining whether the applicant is entitled to the information under s. 7, the court may require the information to be made available for inspection by the court (but not the applicant, who will not be allowed to inspect the information until after a determination in his favour (s. 15(2)). On an application for an order under ss. 7(9) and 15(1), the court has an untrammelled discretion whether to grant an order, but the main factor is that access under the Act is mainly for the purpose of correcting inaccuracy (*Durant v Financial Services Authority*).

An individual who is refused an order under s. 7 on the ground that the information held is not personal data may subsequently be allowed access to the same information under any of the powers under **CPR, Part 31**, such as an application for specific disclosure (*Johnson v Medical Defence Union* [2004] EWHC 2509 (Ch), [2005] 1 WLR 750).

PRE-ACTION DISCLOSURE

The procedure for applying for an order for disclosure of documents before proceedings have **50.88** started is governed by **CPR, r. 31.16**. **Rule 31.17** deals with applications, after proceedings have started, for disclosure by a person who is not a party to the proceedings. These applications are made under the Senior Courts Act 1981, ss. 33(2) and 34, or the County Courts Act 1984, ss. 52(2) and 53. Until these sections were amended by the Civil Procedure (Modification of Enactments) Order 1998 (SI 1998/2940) such orders were available only in proceedings in respect of personal injury and wrongful death, but now they may be made in advance of any type of court proceedings.

Jurisdictional requirements for pre-action disclosure

Courts must follow a two-stage process on applications for pre-action disclosure (*Black v* **50.89** *Sumitomo Corporation* [2001] EWCA Civ 1819, [2002] 1 WLR 1562). At the first stage the jurisdictional requirements must be satisfied. If they are, at the second stage the court considers whether to exercise its discretion to make the order.

The jurisdictional requirements are:

(a) The respondent must be likely to be a party to subsequent proceedings (**CPR, r. 31.16(3)(a)**). The proceedings may be an additional claim as much as a Part 7 or 8 claim (*Moresfield Ltd v Banners* [2003] EWHC 1602 (Ch), LTL 3/7/2003), but not an arbitration (*EDO Corporation v Ultra Electronics Ltd* [2009] EWHC 682 (Ch), [2009] Bus LR 1306).

(b) The applicant must be likely to be a party to subsequent proceedings (**r. 31.16(3)(b)**).

(c) It must appear likely that relevant documents are or have been in the defendant's possession, custody or power (Senior Courts Act 1981, s. 33(2); County Courts Act 1984, s. 52(2)).

(d) An order can be made only if, had proceedings been started, the respondent's duty by way of standard disclosure set out in **CPR, r. 31.6**, would extend to the documents or classes of documents of which the applicant seeks disclosure (**r. 31.16(3)(c)**).

(e) By **r. 31.16(3)(d)**, the court may only make an order if disclosure before the proceedings have started is desirable in order:

   (i)   to dispose fairly of the anticipated proceedings;
   (ii)   to assist the dispute to be resolved without proceedings; or
   (iii) to save costs.

(f) The court may not make an order under these provisions if it considers that complying with the order would be injurious to the public interest (Senior Courts Act 1981, s. 35(1); County Courts Act 1984, s. 54(1)).

There has been controversy about the extent to which the merits of the underlying cause of action need to be established on an application for pre-action disclosure (requirements (a) and (b) above), which has been resolved by *Smith v Secretary of State for Energy and Climate Change* [2013] EWCA Civ 1585, [2014] 1 WLR 2283. In *Black v Sumitomo Corporation* [2001] EWCA Civ 1819, [2002] 1 WLR 1562, Rix LJ held that the word 'likely' in these requirements is intended to convey the idea that the applicant and the respondent to the application must be likely to be parties if subsequent proceedings are in fact issued. This is the key concept, and it means there is no requirement to establish a case on the merits at the first stage (*Smith v Secretary of State for Energy and Climate Change*; approved and applied in *Jet Airways (India) Ltd v Barloworld Handling Ltd* [2014] EWCA Civ 1311, [2015] CP Rep 4).

The court may, however, by **r. 46.1(3)**, make a different costs order, having regard to all the circumstances, which include the extent to which it was reasonable for the person against whom the order was sought to oppose the application, and whether the parties to the application have complied with any relevant pre-action protocol. As the starting point is that the applicant must pay the respondent's costs (**r. 46.1(2)**), it is not usually unreasonable for a respondent to resist the application (*SES Contracting Ltd v UK Coal plc* [2007] EWCA Civ 791, [2007] 5 Costs LR 758). It might be right to depart from the normal rule if the application were resisted in an unreasonable way, such as by using written evidence not backed up by contemporaneous documents (*SES Contracting Ltd v UK Coal plc*). It may be unreasonable where the respondent had an obligation to provide the documents in compliance with a pre-action protocol, or where the applicant has a contractual right to inspect the documents (*Moduleco Ltd v Carillion Construction Ltd* [2009] EWHC 250 (TCC), LTL 4/4/2009). Even where the respondent is regarded as acting unreasonably, costs against the respondent should be limited to the costs of the application, with the applicant still paying the costs of the exercise of disclosing the documents (*Bermuda International Securities Ltd v KPMG* [2001] CPLR 252).

Thus, as with all costs orders, the court will have regard to the general duty of cooperation between the parties and reasonableness of their conduct. In personal injury and clinical negligence cases, the protocols provide guidance as to reasonable pre-action behaviour, including the early exchange of information and documents. Any successful application for pre-action disclosure in such cases is almost certainly an indication that the pre-action protocols have not been complied with, and will therefore strongly suggest unreasonable behaviour on the part of the respondent, who should expect to be ordered to pay the applicant's costs.

DISCLOSURE BY NON-PARTIES

50.94 The procedure for applying for a non-party disclosure order is summarised in **procedural checklist 27**. Once proceedings have started, an application for an order for disclosure by a person who is not a party to the proceedings must be made in accordance with **CPR, Part 23** (see **chapter 32**), and must be supported by evidence (**r. 31.17(2)**). Notice of the application must be served on the respondent (**r. 23.4(1)**). The procedure enables the court to order a witness to produce relevant documents well before the trial, rather than having to wait until the trial and obtaining the documents from the witness under a witness summons. This can be extremely useful, as early disclosure can prevent the need to adjourn the trial.

The ability of the court to make an order for non-party disclosure in all types of cases will diminish, but not totally extinguish, the need for practices of the kind used in *Khanna v Lovell White Durrant* [1995] 1 WLR 121, in which the court invented the concept of the 'production appointment' for witnesses to attend under subpoena to bring documents to a hearing before the trial, in order that they could be photocopied for use in the proceedings (see **50.99**).

Requirements for non-party disclosure orders

50.95 An order for the disclosure of documents may be made against a non-party if:

(a) the documents sought are likely to support the case of the applicant or adversely affect the case of another party (**CPR, r. 31.17(3)**);

(b) the documents sought actually exist;

(c) disclosure is necessary for the purpose of disposing of the claim fairly or saving costs (**r. 31.17(3)**); and

(d) compliance would not be injurious to the public interest (Senior Courts Act 1981, s. 35(1); County Courts Act 1984, s. 54(1)).

'Likely' in this context means 'may well' support the applicant's case or adversely affect the case of another party (*Three Rivers District Council v Her Majesty's Treasury* [2002] EWCA Civ 1182, [2003] 1 WLR 210).

Disclosure against non-parties will only be granted where the documents sought are relevant (as opposed to disclosable under standard disclosure) (see *American Home Products Corporation v Novartis Pharmaceuticals UK Ltd* (2001) LTL 13/2/2001). The court should primarily consider relevance by a close analysis of the statements of case as they stand on the date of the application (*Flood v Times Newspapers Ltd* [2009] EWHC 411 (QB), [2009] EMLR 18). It should not embark on determining disputes of substance as to whether the documents are relevant (*Clark v Ardington Electrical Services* [2001] EWCA Civ 585, LTL 4/4/2001). There must be some evidential basis for the allegations in respect of which the documents are said to be relevant (*Re Skyward Builders plc* [2002] EWHC 1788 (Ch), [2002] 2 BCLC 750). The court is required to apply the test to each document sought, although the court is permitted to consider the documents on a sub-class by sub-class basis (*Three Rivers District Council v Her Majesty's Treasury* [2002] EWCA Civ 1182, [2003] 1 WLR 210).

Discretion to order non-party disclosure

Where the documents are relevant, it is then necessary to consider whether the court should refuse the order in its discretion, or impose some limit on disclosure, such as by ordering disclosure of documents only between stated dates. It will require a very exceptional case to justify ordering the disclosure of a non-party's confidential medical documents (*A v X* [2004] EWHC 447 (QB), LTL 6/4/2004). Further, the court will not make an order if it is not satisfied that the documents sought in fact exist. In *Re Howglen Ltd* [2001] 1 All ER 376 an application was made in general terms for documents against a non-party bank for bank records and interview notes. An order was made limited to the notes of three interviews identified in the evidence in support.   **50.96**

It will sometimes be possible to make an application under the Access to Health Records Act 1990, or the Bankers' Books Evidence Act 1879 (see **49.80**), as an alternative to making an application for non-party disclosure under the Senior Courts Act 1981, s. 34, or the County Courts Act 1984, s. 53.

An applicant for an order under **CPR, r. 31.17**, should consider carefully all alternative ways of obtaining the required documents. For example, it may be argued, in a particular case, that it is not necessary to see the document in advance of the trial, and that a witness summons or deposition will suffice. However, there will not be many cases in which the many documents sought will be sufficiently straightforward that they can be digested and properly dealt with by both parties on the morning of the trial, and without appearing in the trial bundle for pre-reading, and general principles of case management militate against last-minute surprises.

Form of order for non-party disclosure

An order for non-party disclosure must specify the documents or the classes of documents which the respondent must disclose, and require the respondent, when making disclosure, to specify any of these documents which are no longer in the respondent's control, or in respect of which the respondent claims a right or duty to withhold inspection (**CPR, r. 31.17(4)**). In addition, the court may order that the respondent be required to indicate what has happened to any documents now outside the respondent's control, and specify the time and place for disclosure and inspection (**r. 31.17(5)**).   **50.97**

The order may restrict access to the disclosed documents to the applicant's legal advisers and/ or experts (Senior Courts Act 1981, s. 34(2); County Courts Act 1984, s. 52(2)). This may be appropriate where the documents include trade secrets (*Premier Profiles Ltd v Tioxide Europe Ltd* (2002) LTL 25/9/2002).

The court may order the applicant to provide a sum of money to the respondent as a condition of compliance in advance of inspection (*Re Skyward Builders plc* [2002] EWHC 1788 (Ch), [2002] 2 BCLC 750, where the sum of £1,000 was ordered to be paid).

Costs of application for non-party disclosure

50.98   The rules on costs in **CPR, r. 46.1** (see **50.93**), apply equally to the costs of non-party disclosure as they do to the costs of pre-action disclosure. The presumption is that the court will award the non-party the costs of the application and of complying with the terms of any order made (**r. 46.1(2)**). However, the court has the power to make a different order to reflect what it may consider to be the reasonableness of the non-party's opposition to the application (**r. 46.1(3)**).

Additional powers to order pre-action and non-party disclosure

50.99   **CPR, r. 31.18**, provides that **rr. 31.16** and **31.17** do not limit any other power which the court may have to order disclosure before proceedings have started, or to order disclosure against a person who is not a party to the proceedings. This allows continuation of the practice in *Khanna v Lovell White Durrant* [1995] 1 WLR 121 of production appointments (see **50.94**) if considered preferable to an order for non-party disclosure. **Rule 31.18** also preserves the jurisdiction to make a *Norwich Pharmacal* order (see **50.100**). Additionally, orders may be made under the Data Protection Act 1998 (see **50.87**) and pursuant to the decision in *Bankers Trust Co. v Shapira* [1980] 1 WLR 1274 (see **50.104**).

NORWICH PHARMACAL ORDERS

50.100   In *Norwich Pharmacal Co. v Commissioners of Customs and Excise* [1974] AC 133 it was held that a person who, albeit innocently, became 'mixed up in the tortious acts of others so as to facilitate their wrongdoing' was under a duty to assist the person who had been wronged by giving that person full information and disclosing the identity of the wrongdoers.

The jurisdiction is based on the ancient Chancery bill of discovery, and is useful where a party has a cause of action but does not have the names and addresses of persons who should be named as the defendants. Using Lord Reid's terminology from *Norwich Pharmacal Co. v Commissioners of Customs and Excise*, the court may make an order compelling a person to provide information identifying wrongdoers if:

(a)   The respondent has become mixed up in the wrongdoing. There must be at least a good arguable case of wrongdoing by some person (in *R (Mohamed) v Secretary of State for Foreign and Commonwealth Affairs (No. 1)* [2008] EWHC 2048 (Admin), [2009] 1 WLR 2579, the word 'good' was dropped from this formulation at [67]). It has been held that an order can be made even if the underlying cause of action has not been clearly made out (*P v T Ltd* [1997] 1 WLR 1309). The respondent may be perfectly innocent, and may not even realise that there has been any wrongdoing (as in *Norwich Pharmacal Co. v Commissioners of Customs and Excise* itself). Where the respondent is a party to the wrongdoing it is usually named as defendant in the substantive claim, and is also under a duty to identify other wrongdoers (*British Steel Corporation v Granada Television Ltd* [1981] AC 1096). In cases of wilful evasion of court orders, it may be enough that the respondent has got mixed up in the affairs of the wrongdoer (*Mercantile Group (Europe) AG v Aiyela* [1994] QB 366).

(b)   The respondent has facilitated the wrongdoing. Involvement or participation in the wrongdoing may alternatively be sufficient (*Ashworth Hospital Authority v MGN Ltd* [2002] UKHL 29, [2002] 1 WLR 2033; *R (Omar) v Secretary of State for Foreign and Commonwealth Affairs* [2013] EWCA Civ 118, [2014] QB 112 at [38], [39]). Unwitting facilitation of the infringement of the claimants' patent by allowing infringing products into the country was sufficient in *Norwich Pharmacal Co. v Commissioners of Customs and Excise*. Providing information and questions to the security services of another country, which is then alleged to have used torture when questioning the claimant, was held to constitute the facilitation of arguable wrongdoing in

R (Mohamed) v Secretary of State for Foreign and Commonwealth Affairs (No. 1) [2008] EWHC 2048 (Admin), [2009] 1 WLR 2579. However, a person who has done nothing to facilitate the wrong-doing, and is a mere witness, is under no obligation to disclose the identity of the wrongdo-ers (*Ricci v Chow* [1987] 1 WLR 1658). Mann J turned the authorities on their heads in *Various Claimants v News Group Newspapers Ltd (No. 2)* [2013] EWHC 2119 (Ch), [2014] Ch 400, concluding that ultimately this element of the test is satisfied if the respondent is not a mere witness. In *Harrington v Polytechnic of North London* [1984] 1 WLR 1293 the claimant was a student who claimed he was prevented from attending the polytechnic by student pickets. Photographs were taken of the pickets, and the claimant sought an order compelling the lecturers to identify the pickets. It was held that the lecturers were mere witnesses when acting in their private capacities, but the polytechnic was ordered to provide the information as it had become mixed up in and facilitated the wrongdoing.

(c) The applicant has a sufficient interest. Generally this is satisfied by showing a genuine intention to bring legal proceedings against the wrongdoers. The condition will also be satisfied if the applicant has no intention to sue, but does intend to discipline employee wrongdoers (*Ashworth Hospital Authority v MGN Ltd* [2002] UKHL 29, [2002] 1 WLR 2033). Disclosure of the names of customers of someone alleged to be infringing the claimant's patent will not usually be ordered unless there is some real grievance or some significant purpose in doing so (*Smith Kline and French Laboratories Ltd v Doncaster Pharmaceuticals Ltd* [1989] FSR 407).

(d) Provision of the documents or information is necessary (*Ashworth Hospital Authority v MGN Ltd* [2002] UKHL 29, [2002] 1 WLR 2033 at [57]). Authorities such as *Mitsui and Co. Ltd v Nexen Petroleum UK Ltd* [2005] EWHC 625 (Ch), [2005] 3 All ER 511, which imposed a strin-gent test of necessity (requiring the evidence to be the final piece in the jigsaw, or *Norwich Pharmacal* orders to be a remedy of last resort), were deprecated in *R (Mohamed) v Secretary of State for Foreign and Commonwealth Affairs (No. 1)* [2008] EWHC 2048 (Admin), [2009] 1 WLR 2579. Rather, the court must consider all the circumstances, including the resources of the applicant, the urgency of the need for the information, and any public interest in satisfying the applicant's need for the information. The court will be very reluctant to order a bank to provide information under a *Norwich Pharmacal* order which involves a breach of confidence between a bank and its customer (*Koo Golden East Mongolia v Bank of Nova Scotia* [2007] EWCA Civ 1443, [2008] QB 717). In exercising its dis-cretion the court will, where appropriate, take into account the principles in the Data Protection Act 1998 and the right to free speech in the European Convention on Human Rights, **art. 10**, in the **Human Rights Act 1998, sch. 1** (*Totalise plc v Motley Fool Ltd* (No. 2) [2001] EWCA Civ 187, [2002] 1 WLR 1233; *Smith v ADVFN plc* [2008] EWHC 577 (QB), LTL 8/5/2008).

(e) The court exercises its discretion to make the order (the relief being equitable). Relevant factors include proportionality, expense, time, intrusion, any public policy considerations, the needs of the case and its seriousness (*R (Mohamed) v Secretary of State for Foreign and Commonwealth Affairs (No. 1)* [2008] EWHC 2048 (Admin), [2009] 1 WLR 2579 at [133] and [140]).

(f) The information sought is not protected by privilege, public interest, or State immunity. In *Koo Golden East Mongolia v Bank of Nova Scotia* [2007] EWCA Civ 1443, [2008] QB 717, the respondent was a central bank and was held entitled to claim State immunity under the State Immunity Act 1978, so relief was refused. In cases of possible privilege the court may alternatively grant the order, with the respondent taking the privilege point by way of objection to inspection under **CPR, r. 31.19**.

Scope of *Norwich Pharmacal* jurisdiction

The *Norwich Pharmacal* jurisdiction is not restricted to claims in tort, but is of general applica-tion, and applies to claims in breach of confidence and breach of contract (*British Steel*   **50.101**

Corporation v Granada Television Ltd [1981] AC 1096; *Ashworth Hospital Authority v MGN Ltd* [2001] 1 WLR 515 (CA); [2002] UKHL 29, [2002] 1 WLR 2033). The flexibility of the jurisdiction was emphasised in *R (Mohamed) v Secretary of State for Foreign and Commonwealth Affairs (No. 1)* [2008] EWHC 2048 (Admin), [2009] 1 WLR 2579 (disclosure of documents relevant to allegations of torture which were to be used to support an argument that confessions should be inadmissible in an overseas prosecution). In most cases where *Norwich Pharmacal* orders have been made it has been clear, or nearly so, that some tort or other civil wrong has been committed. *Re an Intended Claim, Carlton Film Distributors Ltd v VDC Ltd* [2003] EWHC 616 (Ch), LTL 21/3/2003 concerned an application for disclosure of information against an identified proposed defendant. The principle was extended in *Murphy v Murphy* [1999] 1 WLR 282, where an order was made against a settlor to disclose to a potential beneficiary the names and addresses of the trustees under a settlement, to enable the potential beneficiary to communicate with the trustees with a view to being considered for the distribution of trust property held on discretionary trusts. The trustees were obviously not wrongdoers for the purpose of the *Norwich Pharmacal* principle.

The Justice and Security Act 2013, s. 17, prevents *Norwich Pharmacal* orders being made in respect of 'sensitive information'. Broadly, sensitive information covers most material relating to the activities of the intelligence services (s. 17(3)). More generally, the *Norwich Pharmacal* jurisdiction will be excluded where it would be inconsistent with a statutory scheme governing the same area. On this basis it was held in *R (Omar) v Secretary of State for Foreign and Commonwealth Affairs* [2013] EWCA Civ 118, [2014] QB 112, that *Norwich Pharmacal* orders are not available for use in foreign criminal proceedings, which are governed by the Crime (International Co-operation) Act 2003.

Procedure for seeking *Norwich Pharmacal* orders

50.102   *Norwich Pharmacal* orders are usually sought by issuing a claim form against the facilitator, and then by issuing an application notice within that claim seeking the disclosure order. Applications have to be supported by witness statement evidence. It is possible in an urgent case to seek the order without giving notice (*Loose v Williamson* [1978] 1 WLR 639). The person from whom disclosure is sought may contact the person whose identity is sought and invite that person to submit reasons why disclosure should not be ordered; the court may require such contact to be made and may hear the person whose identity is sought (*Totalise plc v Motley Fool Ltd (No. 2)* [2001] EWCA Civ 187, [2002] 1 WLR 1233).

The order

50.103   While the court can order the respondent to provide 'full information' (*Norwich Pharmacal Co. v Commissioners of Customs and Excise* [1974] AC 133), this does not provide a general right to disclosure or for gathering information (*Arab Monetary Fund v Hashim (No. 5)* [1992] 2 All ER 911 at p. 914). The material to be disclosed should be confined to necessary information and documents, but this does not mean that it is limited to disclosure of the identity of the wrong doer or the 'final piece of the jigsaw'. What is necessary depends on the circumstances of each case (*R (Mohamed) v Secretary of State for Foreign and Commonwealth Affairs (No. 1)* [2008] EWHC 2048 (Admin), [2009] 1 WLR 2579 at [133], [134]).

Normally a successful applicant for a *Norwich Pharmacal* order should pay the costs of the party ordered to make disclosure, including the costs of making the disclosure (*Totalise plc v Motley Fool Ltd (No. 2)* [2001] EWCA Civ 1897, [2002] 1 WLR 1233). These costs may be recovered against the wrongdoer in the same or a subsequent claim (*Smith Kline and French Laboratories Ltd v R. D. Harbottle (Mercantile) Ltd* [1980] RPC 363). It may be appropriate to depart from the normal costs *rule where the* non-party is implicated in the wrongdoing (*JSC BTA Bank v Ablyazov* [2014] EWHC 2019 (Comm), [2015] 1 WLR 1547).

BANKERS TRUST ORDERS

In *Bankers Trust Co. v Shapira* [1980] 1 WLR 1274 a bank, which was a defendant in proceedings, **50.104** was ordered to disclose to the claimant certain confidential information, such as copies of correspondence, cheques, debit vouchers, transfer applications and internal memoranda, relating to two co-defendants, notwithstanding that those co-defendants had not yet been served with proceedings. The purpose of the order was to enable the applicant to trace the existence of and protect the assets claimed in the proceedings, in which, it was found, there was very strong evidence that the co-defendants had been guilty of fraud. Given the confidential nature of the documents to be disclosed, a party claiming an order of this kind must give an undertaking not to use the information obtained other than in the course of the proceedings. See also *Arab Monetary Fund v Hashim (No. 5)* [1992] 2 All ER 911 and *Omar v Omar* [1995] 1 WLR 1428.

DISCLOSURE ORDERS IN AID OF ARBITRATION

Where a dispute is referred to arbitration, the Arbitration Act 1996, s. 43, provides that court **50.105** procedures to procure documents or other material evidence may be used only with the permission of the arbitral tribunal or the agreement of the other parties. This provision does not prevent a court making a *Norwich Pharmacal* order (see **50.100**) in the period before a dispute has been referred to arbitration, where the power is used for preserving assets or remedies (*Glidepath Holding BV v Thompson* [2004] EWHC 2234 (Comm), [2005] 1 All ER (Comm) 434). Unless otherwise agreed by the parties, the court has under s. 44 five specified powers relating to the taking of evidence from witnesses, the preservation of evidence and making orders in relation to property (see **37.55**). These specified powers do not include orders for non-party disclosure under CPR, r. 31.17 (see **50.94**). Where there is a risk that documents may cease to exist or become unavailable, it may be possible to obtain an order for their preservation, such as by copying, under s. 44(2)(b), see *Assimina Maritime Ltd v Pakistan National Shipping Corporation* [2004] EWHC 3005 (Comm), [2005] 1 All ER (Comm) 460).

Whenever documents are referred to in a witness statement, strictly those documents should be exhibited unless there is a sufficient reason for not doing so, such as length, volume, confidentiality or public interest immunity (*Tweed v Parades Commission for Northern Ireland* [2006] UKHL 53; [2007] 1 AC 650).

The requirements for exhibits to affidavits, which are set out in **PD 32, paras 11.3 to 15.5**, apply to exhibits to witness statements (**para. 18.5**). Numbering of exhibits has already been referred to (see **51.3**). In the body of the witness statement exhibits must be introduced with the words:

I refer to the [description of exhibit] marked '[witness's initials and exhibit number]'

followed by a description of the exhibit. Exhibits must be kept separate from the witness statement. They should have a frontsheet having the same markings in the top right corner and heading as the witness statement. Where an exhibit contains several documents the frontsheet should list them with their dates, and/or state the nature of the documents exhibited (such as so many original letters and so many copy letters). The frontsheet needs to bear the correct exhibit mark, and needs to be signed by the maker of the statement.

Documents of a similar nature, such as correspondence, should be gathered together into a single exhibit, and arranged chronologically with the earliest document on top, and with each page numbered consecutively at the bottom centre. A convenient alternative, which is widely adopted by City firms, is to use a single comprehensive exhibit for each witness. The approach is to organise the material into sections, with each section containing documents of a similar nature in chronological order with the earliest on top. In complex applications this can be helpful, because having numerous exhibits, each with its own pagination system, can be confusing. It is permissible to use copy documents in exhibits, provided the originals are available at the hearing should they be needed (**para. 13.1**). Illegible pages should be followed with a typed version with an 'a' number.

Exhibits other than documents should be clearly marked with the appropriate exhibit number in such a manner that the mark cannot become detached from the exhibit. Small items may be placed in a container, with the container being appropriately marked (**para. 14**).

A common mistake is to exhibit court documents. This is unnecessary as sealed copies of these documents prove themselves (**CPR, r. 2.6(3)**, a point specifically made by **PD 32, para. 13.2**).

Exhibits must not be stapled, but should be securely fastened in a way that does not hinder the reading of the documents they contain (**para. 15.1(1)**).

Bulky exhibits

51.8 Where, on account of their bulk, the service of exhibits on other parties would be difficult or impracticable, directions should be sought dealing with arrangements for bringing the exhibits to the attention of the other parties and their custody pending trial (**PD 32, para. 15.4**).

Marginal references

51.9 A witness statement must 'give the reference to any document or documents mentioned either in the margin or in bold text in the body of the statement' (**PD 32, para. 19.1(7)**). It appears that this refers to the page references in the application or trial bundle, which will be added after the witness statement is signed. There is no objection to these references being added in manuscript (Admiralty and Commercial Courts Guide, app. 10, para. 3(i)). Time should be allowed for adding marginal references when preparing bundles.

STATEMENT OF TRUTH

51.10 A witness statement must include a signed statement that the witness believes the facts it contains are true. False statements may be punished as contempt of court (**CPR, rr.**

32.14, 81.17 and **81.18**; and see **23.15**). The form of statement of truth (see **PD 32, para. 20.2**) is:

I believe that the facts stated in this witness statement are true.

In *Aquarius Financial Enterprises Inc. v Certain Underwriters at Lloyd's Subscribing to Contract KD 970212* (2001) LTL 20/5/2001 there was evidence that one of the witness statements had been obtained by bullying, threats and inducements. Toulson J said that where a witness statement is prepared by someone other than the witness, there should be a written declaration by the person who prepared the statement giving information about its preparation, and certifying compliance with any appropriate code of practice. Whether this will become the practice remains to be seen. It is improper to put pressure on a witness to give anything other than his own account of the matters in question, and it is also improper to serve a witness statement which is known to be false or which it is known the maker does not in all respects believe to be true (Admiralty and Commercial Courts Guide, para. H1.3).

Witness unable to read or sign

Where a witness statement is made by a person who is unable to read or sign the statement, it must contain a certificate made by an 'authorised person' (**PD 22, para. 3A.1**). An authorised person is someone able to administer oaths and take affidavits, but need not be independent of the parties or their representatives. The certificate must be in the form set out in annex 1 to **PD 22**. It says that the witness statement has been read to the witness, who appeared to understand it and approved its contents, that the statement of truth has been read to the witness, that the witness appeared to understand it and the consequences of making a false statement, and that the witness signed or made his or her mark in the presence of the authorised person.

51.11

ALTERATIONS

Alterations to a witness statement must be initialled by the person taking the statement or, if the witness is unable to read or sign, by the 'authorised person' (see **51.11**) (**PD 32, para. 22.1**). A witness statement which contains an alteration that has not been initialled may be used in evidence only with the permission of the court (**para. 22.2**).

51.12

FAILURE TO COMPLY WITH PD 32

If a witness statement or exhibit fails to comply with **PD 32**, the court may refuse to admit it as evidence and may refuse to allow the costs arising out of its preparation (**PD 32, para. 25.1**). Permission to use a defective witness statement may be obtained from a judge (meaning judge, Master or District Judge: **CPR, r. 2.3(1)**) of the court.

51.13

Striking out witness statements

There is no specific power in the CPR equivalent to the old RSC, ord. 41, r. 6, providing for the striking out of written evidence which is scandalous, irrelevant or oppressive. The general exclusionary discretion in **CPR, r. 32.1**, is probably the source for the continuing power to control evidence which it would be embarrassing for the court to have to keep on file, although **r. 32.2(2) (b)** seems to have been relied upon in *Stroude v Beazer Homes Ltd* [2004] EWHC 676 (Ch), LTL 15/3/2004. That there is such a power under the CPR was regarded as beyond doubt in *Sandhurst Holdings Ltd v Grosvenor Assets Ltd* (2001) LTL 25/10/2001. According to *Anglo Continental Educational Group (GB) Ltd v Capital Homes (Southern) Ltd* [2009] EWCA Civ 218, [2009] NPC 44, a party who is served with a witness statement which is thought to include inadmissible evidence has three courses of action:

51.14

(a) Write to the other side asking for the basis on which the evidence is said to be admissible. If dissatisfied with the answer, apply to exclude the evidence before replying to it.

(b) Issue an application, to be heard at the trial, to exclude the allegedly inadmissible evidence. The problem with this approach is that it potentially increases the costs of the trial, and can lead to the detailed analysis of material which may be of minor importance.

(c) At a case management conference ask the court to direct the parties to identify in writing the precise point which they say the evidence establishes and why it is said that the evidence is admissible.

Sandhurst Holdings Ltd v Grosvenor Assets Ltd is authority for the proposition that the jurisdiction would be exercised sparingly, because the court's business would be seriously impeded if parties made striking-out applications as a matter of course whenever they perceived scandalous or irrelevant material was included in their opponents' evidence. A witness statement was ordered to be redacted to exclude inadmissible evidence of negotiations in *Stroude v Beazer Homes Ltd*. Likewise, in *Re New Gadget Shop Ltd* [2005] EWHC 1606 (Ch), LTL 5/8/2005, paragraphs in witness statements which used privileged material were struck out (see **50.68**).

FILING

51.15 If the court directs that a witness statement is to be filed, filing should be at the court (or Division of the court) where the case is or will be proceeding (**PD 32, para. 23.1**).

FOREIGN LANGUAGE

51.16 Where the court directs that a witness statement in a foreign language is to be filed, the party relying on it must have the statement translated, and the translator must make an affidavit verifying the translation, exhibiting both the translation and a copy of the foreign language witness statement. Both the original statement and the translator's affidavit must be filed (**PD 32, para. 23.2**). The importance of the witness first making and signing a statement in his own language, followed by a translation into English, rather than a statement being made in English, and then translated into the witness's language prior to signing, was reiterated in *Re Phoneer Ltd* [2002] 2 BCLC 241.

VOLUMINOUS WITNESS STATEMENTS AND EXHIBITS

51.17 The courts have for some time generally deprecated the use of voluminous written evidence. However, there are cases where it is inevitable, and then the witness statements and exhibits to be used should be put into separate bundles, with the pages numbered consecutively throughout (**PD 32, paras 15.3 and 18.5**).

DIRECTIONS FOR THE EXCHANGE OF WITNESS STATEMENTS

51.18 Witness statements are sometimes required in cases allocated to the small claims track (see **45.18**). Directions dealing with witness statements tend to be made only in the slightly more complex small claims. The technical rules on witness statements (in **CPR, Part 32**) do not apply to claims on the small claims track (**r. 27.2(1)(c)**), so the following discussion is largely limited to claims on the fast and multi-tracks. For these cases, directions for the exchange of witness statements are mandatory.

The court will order a party to serve on the other parties any witness statement of the oral evidence which the party serving the statement intends to rely on in relation to any issues of fact to be decided at the trial (r. 32.4(2)). Under r. 32.2(3), directions for the exchange of witness statements may:

(a) identify or limit the issues to which factual evidence may be directed;
(b) identify the witnesses who may be called or whose evidence may be read; and
(c) limit the length or format of witness statements.

When directions are made on allocating a case to the fast track or multi-track, or at a case management conference, the court will make provision for the date by when witness statements must be exchanged. The court may give directions as to the order in which witness statements are to be served, and whether or not they should be filed (r. 32.4(3)). Normally mutual exchange is required, and it usually takes place a few weeks after disclosure and inspection of documents. Part of the reason why witness statements are exchanged after disclosure of documents is that the witnesses may need to comment on some of the documentation in their statements. If a witness statement is not served within the time specified in the directions, the witness may only be called with permission.

WITNESS SUMMARIES

51.19 A party who is unable to obtain signed witness statements before the time prescribed for exchange may apply, without notice, for permission to serve witness summaries instead of witness statements (CPR, r. 32.9). A witness summary is simply a summary of the evidence that would have been included in a witness statement. A witness summary could be an unsigned draft statement or even just an indication of the issues it is hoped the witness could deal with. Permission to serve a witness summary can only be granted if the party is unable to obtain the relevant witness statement. Unless the court orders otherwise, a witness summary must be served within the period in which a witness statement would have had to be served.

LATE SERVICE OF WITNESS STATEMENTS

51.20 If a witness statement or witness summary for use at trial is not served in respect of an intended witness within the time specified by the court, the witness may not be called to give oral evidence unless the court gives permission (CPR, r. 32.10). The case law dealing with non-compliance with directions for the exchange of witness statements is discussed at 48.25.

USE OF WITNESS STATEMENTS AT TRIAL

51.21 A party who has served a witness statement, and wishes to rely at trial on the evidence of the witness who made the statement, must call the witness to give oral evidence, unless:

(a) an order has been made under CPR, r. 32.2(3)(b) that the witness statement is to be read; or
(b) the court orders otherwise under r. 32.5(1); or
(c) the statement is put in as hearsay evidence pursuant to r. 32.5(1) and the Civil Evidence Act 1995, see **chapter 53**.

There is also a power under CPR, r. 32.2(3)(a), to identify or limit the issues to which factual evidence may be directed. This is towards the extreme end of the court's powers. It should therefore be exercised, if at all, as early as possible, giving the parties liberty to apply as a safety valve, and only after considering less intrusive measures to control the evidence (*MacLennan v Morgan Sindall Infrastructure plc* [2013] EWHC 4044 (QB), [2014] 1 WLR 2462).

A party who has disclosed witness statements pursuant to directions cannot be ordered to call those witnesses at trial (*Society of Lloyd's v Jaffray* (2000) *The Times*, 3 August 2000), but should give prompt notice to the other parties that the witnesses will not be called. Despite the provisions of the Civil Evidence Act 1995, there are several reasons why judges tend to attach limited

Commentary

Chapter 52   Affidavits

INTRODUCTION

52.1   Affidavits are sworn written statements. They take much the same form as modern witness statements (see **chapter 51**), but they have a few formal differences (principally the commencement and jurat). They were formerly the main means by which evidence was placed before the court on interim applications. That role has now largely been taken over by the use of witness statements, although there are a small number of situations where affidavits must still be used in interim applications. Their remaining main use is for putting evidence before the court at the final hearings of certain types of proceedings, particularly matrimonial and family proceedings, insolvency proceedings, director disqualification proceedings and proceedings brought using **CPR, Part 8**.

FORM OF AFFIDAVITS

52.2   CPR, r. 32.16, provides that affidavits must be in the form set out in the appropriate PD, which is **PD 32, paras 2 to 16**. The form of an affidavit is broadly similar to that of a witness statement, described in **chapter 51**:

(a) An affidavit must be typed on one side only of consecutively numbered sheets of durable A4 paper with a 35 mm margin (**PD 32, para. 6.1(1), (2) and (4)**).

(b) It must have the same corner markings as witness statements (**PD 32, para. 3.2**; see **51.3**).

(c) It must be headed in the same way as witness statements (see **51.4**).

(d) After the heading and before the body of the affidavit there should appear a commencement (**PD 32, para. 4.1**). This should read:

I [full name] of [address, which can be a business address if sworn in the deponent's professional, business or occupational capacity] state on oath:

(e) The comments about the body of the text in witness statements at **51.5** apply equally to affidavits (**PD 32, paras 4.1 and 4.2**).

(f) The same provisions apply to exhibits to affidavits as apply to exhibits to witness statements (see **51.7** and **51.8**).

(g) The comments about marginal references in witness statements at **51.9** apply equally to affidavits (**PD 32, para. 6.1(7)**).

(h) Alterations need to be initialled by both the deponent and the person taking the affidavit (**PD 32, para. 8.1**).

(i) Instead of a statement of truth (see **51.10**), an affidavit ends with a jurat. The jurat must follow on from the body of the affidavit, and must not appear on a separate page. After giving the oath the affidavit has to be signed by all deponents (exceptionally an affidavit may be sworn by more than one person) and be completed by the person taking the affidavit. The person taking the affidavit must insert his or her full address, sign the jurat, and print his or her name and qualification under the signature (**PD 32, para. 5**).

QUALIFICATION OF PERSON TAKING AN AFFIDAVIT

52.3

A person who takes an affidavit must be duly qualified (solicitors, commissioners for oaths, magistrates, certain court officials and judges, British consuls and others authorised by statute, such as barristers), and independent of the parties and their representatives (**PD 32, para. 9**). For an affidavit taken by a court officer in the High Court or Court of Appeal, there is a £12 swearing fee, plus £2 per exhibit (**CPFO, fee 12**). But a commissioner for oaths may charge only £5 plus £2 per exhibit (Commissioners for Oaths (Fees) Order 1993 (SI 1993/2297)) and in the County Court no fee is charged.

AFFIRMATIONS

52.4

Affirmations are similar to affidavits, but the deponent will affirm rather than swear when executing the document. They can be used whenever an affidavit may or must be used. All the provisions in **PD 32** relating to affidavits apply also to affirmations (**PD 32, para. 16**). For affirmations the commencement should read:

I [full name] of [address] do solemnly and sincerely affirm:

In an affirmation, the word 'sworn' in the jurat is replaced by the word 'affirmed'.

INABILITY OF DEPONENT TO READ OR SIGN AN AFFIDAVIT

52.5

Where an affidavit is sworn by a person who is unable to read or sign it, the person before whom it is sworn must certify in the jurat that he or she has read the affidavit to the deponent and that the deponent appeared to understand it (**PD 32, para. 7.1(1) and (2)**). The person who took the affidavit must also certify that, in his or her presence, the deponent signed it or made his or her mark (**para. 7.1(3)**). Two versions of the form of the certificate appear in annex 1 to **PD 32**. If such a certificate is not included in the jurat, the affidavit may not be used unless the court is satisfied that it was read to the deponent and he or she appeared to understand it (**para. 7.2**).

FILING AND MISCELLANEOUS TOPICS

52.6

Identical provisions apply to filing of affidavits and affirmations, in relation to foreign language affidavits, and the use of voluminous affidavits and exhibits, as apply to witness statements (see **51.15** to **51.17**, and **PD 32, paras 10** and **15.3**). Likewise as regards failing to comply with **PD 32** (see **51.13** and **51.14**, and **PD 32, para. 25**).

SITUATIONS WHERE AFFIDAVITS MUST BE USED

52.7

Affidavits must be used whenever sworn evidence is required by an enactment, rule, order or practice directions (**PD 32, para. 1.4**). Examples include applications under the Protection from Harassment Act 1997, s. 3(5)(a), certain applications relating to confiscation and forfeiture in connection with criminal proceedings, and under the environmental control legislation. **PD 32** and **PD 25A** require affidavit evidence in support of applications for freezing injunctions and search orders and for orders to require an occupier to permit another to enter land. Verification of a translation of a witness statement or affidavit must be on affidavit (**PD 32,**

Commentary

paras 10.2 and **23.2**). Evidence in support of applications for judgment in default after service outside the jurisdiction without permission or against a State must be given on affidavit (**PD 12, para. 4.5**). Written evidence in support of or in opposition to a committal application or for permission to issue a writ of sequestration must be given by affidavit (**CPR, rr. 81.10, 81.11, 81.14** and **81.26; PD 81, para. 14.1**).

FALSE AFFIDAVITS

52.8 A witness swearing a false affidavit (or making a false affirmation) may be the subject of proceedings for contempt of court. **CPR, rr. 32.14, 81.17** and **81.18** (on false statements of truth, see **23.15**), have no application. The purpose behind **rr. 32.14, 81.17** and **81.18** is to provide jurisdiction to punish the makers of false statements used in proceedings in the absence of an oath. In respect of an affidavit or affirmation, there will be a contempt if the maker of the statement knew it was false, and that it was likely to interfere with the course of justice (*Malgar Ltd v R. E. Leach (Engineering) Ltd* [2000] FSR 393; *Hydropool Hot Tubs Ltd v Roberjot* [2011] EWHC 121 (Ch), LTL 11/2/2011). However, the maximum sentence that can be imposed for contempt of court is two years (Contempt of Court Act 1981, s. 14(1)), whereas courts have often regarded a longer sentence as appropriate for giving false evidence in court proceedings. It is therefore common for a giver of false evidence to be prosecuted either for perjury under the Perjury Act 1911, s. 1(1) (which, by s. 1(3), applies to statements in affidavits or affirmations made for the purposes of judicial proceedings as well as statements made in testimony during such proceedings), or for the common law offence of perverting the course of justice. The maximum sentence for perjury is seven years (Perjury Act 1911, s. 1(1)). The maximum sentence for a common law offence is life imprisonment.

Chapter 53   Hearsay Evidence

INTRODUCTION

The Civil Evidence Act 1995 gives effect to the main recommendations of the Law Commission   **53.1**
in its report, The Hearsay Rule in Civil Proceedings (Law Com. No. 216, Cm 2321, 1993).
These were as follows:

(a) The hearsay rule should be abolished.

(b) A party calling a person as a witness should not adduce evidence of a previous statement
     made by that person without the permission of the court.

(c) A party intending to rely on hearsay evidence should be required to give notice of that
     fact, if it is reasonable and appropriate to do so, but failure to do so should not render the
     evidence inadmissible, although it may detract from its weight and result in the imposi-
     tion of a costs sanction.

(d) A party should have the power to call a witness for cross-examination on his or her hearsay
     evidence.

(e) There should be guidelines to assist the court in assessing the weight of hearsay evidence.

(f) There should be no special conditions of admissibility or safeguards for business and other
     records, and the means of proving such records should be simplified.

(g) There should be no special conditions of admissibility or safeguards for statements
     contained in computer-produced documents: the potential for misuse of computers
     should be taken into account in considering the weight to be attached to such evidence.

The overall effect of the Civil Evidence Act 1995 has been to simplify the law and procedure
relating to hearsay in civil cases and to render admissible much that would have been

when he or she made the statement and, in cases in which the hearsay statement is to be proved by the statement of another (as when A's out-of-court oral statement is to be proved by B's written record of what was said), if that other person would have been competent to give evidence at the time when he or she made the statement. Section 5(1) provides as follows:

Hearsay evidence shall not be admitted in civil proceedings if or to the extent that it is shown to consist of, or to be proved by means of, a statement made by a person who at the time he made the statement was not competent as a witness.

For this purpose 'not competent as a witness' means suffering from such mental or physical infirmity, or lack of understanding, as would render a person incompetent as a witness in civil proceedings; but a child shall be treated as competent as a witness if he satisfies the requirements of section 96(2)(a) and (b) of the Children Act 1989 (conditions for reception of unsworn evidence of child).

The provisions of the Children Act 1989, s. 96(2)(a) and (b), are considered at **49.46**.

The burden of proof, under the Civil Evidence Act 1995, s. 5(1), is on the party seeking to exclude the hearsay evidence (*JC v CC* [2001] EWCA Civ 1625, LTL 25/10/2001).

PREVIOUS STATEMENTS

53.7   At common law, there is a general rule that a witness cannot be asked in examination-in-chief about former oral or written statements made by that witness and consistent with his or her evidence in the proceedings. In civil cases, the rule was subject to only two common law exceptions: statements admissible to rebut allegations of recent fabrication and memory-refreshing documents rendered admissible as a result of cross-examination. The general effect of s. 6 of the Civil Evidence Act 1995 has been to relax the rule, by providing that previous statements may be admissible with permission, and to preserve the two exceptions to the rule. As to the rule, s. 6 reflects the view that a requirement for permission is necessary in the case of the previous consistent statements of a person called as a witness in order to prevent the pointless proliferation of superfluous evidence, which would needlessly prolong trials and increase costs (Law Com. No. 216, para. 4.30). In fact, s. 6 goes further and imposes a requirement of permission in the case of *any* previous statement, i.e. whether consistent or merely relating to matters other than those as to which the witness will give evidence. However, the concluding words of the section make it clear that it cannot be used to prevent a witness statement from standing as the witness's evidence-in-chief under **CPR, r. 32.5(2)** (see **51.21**). As to the common law exceptions to the rule against previous consistent statements, they have been preserved by s. 6(2)(b) (statements in rebuttal of allegations of recent fabrication, considered at **49.61**) and s. 6(4) (memory-refreshing documents, considered at **49.57**).

Section 6 of the Act provides as follows:

(1) Subject as follows, the provisions of this Act as to hearsay evidence in civil proceedings apply equally (but with any necessary modifications) in relation to a previous statement made by a person called as a witness in the proceedings.

(2) A party who has called or intends to call a person as a witness in civil proceedings may not in those proceedings adduce evidence of a previous statement made by that person, except—

(a) with the leave of the court, or

(b) for the purpose of rebutting a suggestion that his evidence has been fabricated.

This shall not be construed as preventing a witness statement (that is, a written statement of oral evidence which a party to the proceedings intends to lead) from being adopted by a witness in giving evidence or treated as his evidence.

The question naturally arises as to when permission should be granted. It is submitted that where the witness is incapable of giving direct evidence on the matter in question, then provided that his or her statement is sufficiently relevant to the facts in issue and its admission would not be unjust to the other parties to the proceedings, permission should normally be granted. Typically, the witness will be incapable of giving direct evidence where he or she has no recollection of the matter at all or where, although the witness is not incapable of giving direct evidence on the matter, his or her evidence is of questionable reliability, inconsistent or not wholly intelligible by reason of partial loss of memory, lapse of time, age or physical or mental infirmity. Such an approach would be in line with that taken in *Morris v Stratford-on-Avon Rural District Council* [1973] 1 WLR 1059, a decision under the equivalent leave requirement of the Civil Evidence Act 1968 (s. 2(2)). In that case, a claim for damages against the Council for the alleged negligence of one its employees, the trial only began some five years after the cause of action had arisen. The employee gave confused and inconsistent evidence. At the conclusion of his examination-in-chief, counsel for the defendant was granted leave to admit in chief a written statement made by the employee and given to the defendant's insurers about nine months after the events in question. The Court of Appeal held that the trial judge had not erred in allowing the evidence to be admitted.

Where permission is given to admit a previous statement under s. 6, there are no restrictions as to when it may be introduced in evidence. In some cases, therefore, it may be appropriate to give evidence of the statement before or during the examination-in-chief of the witness, as when this might render more intelligible the direct evidence to be given.

ADVANCE NOTICE

The principal objectives of the notice provisions under the Civil Evidence Act 1995 are the same as they were in the case of the notice provisions under the Civil Evidence Act 1968: to deal with all issues arising out of the adduction of hearsay evidence pre-trial and therefore to avoid surprise at trial. The current provisions, however, are simpler and more flexible. They are based on the following principles (see generally Law Com. No. 216, paras 4.9 and 4.10): **53.8**

(a) The notice provision should require a party to give notice of the fact that he or she proposes to adduce hearsay, but should put the onus on the receiving party to demand such particulars as he or she requires in order to be able to make a proper assessment of the weight and cogency of the hearsay and to be in a position to respond to it adequately.

(b) Circumstances can arise in litigation rendering compliance with a notice requirement impracticable. For example, some hearings need to be arranged urgently. In other cases, albeit rarely, advance notification may carry a real risk of danger to the witness or someone else. For reasons of this kind, the new provisions make allowance for the possibility that in some circumstances it would be unreasonable and impracticable to give any notice at all.

(c) The notice provisions should be subject to rules of court to allow them to be disapplied in certain classes of proceedings if, as experience is gained, this is felt to be appropriate.

(d) The parties should be free to agree to exclude the notice provisions.

Section 2 of the 1995 Act provides as follows:

(1) A party proposing to adduce hearsay evidence in civil proceedings shall, subject to the following provisions of this section, give to the other party or parties to the proceedings—

    (a) such notice (if any) of that fact, and

    (b) on request, such particulars of or relating to the evidence, as is reasonable and practicable in the circumstances for the purpose of enabling him or them to deal with any matters arising from its being hearsay.

(2) Provision may be made by rules of court—

    (a) specifying classes of proceedings or evidence in relation to which subsection (1) does not apply, and

    (b) as to the manner in which (including the time within which) the duties imposed by that subsection are to be complied with in the cases where it does apply.

Commentary

(3) Subsection (1) may also be excluded by the agreement of the parties; and compliance with the duty to give notice may in any case be waived by the person to whom notice is required to be given.

Concerning s. 2(2), see also **53.11**.

Notice of intention to rely on hearsay evidence

53.9 The relevant rules on notice of intention to rely on hearsay evidence are to be found in **CPR, Part 33**, which does not apply to claims which have been allocated to the small claims track.

Under **r. 33.2(1)**, where a party intends to rely on hearsay evidence at trial and either that evidence is to be given by a witness giving oral evidence or is contained in a witness statement of a person who is not being called to give oral evidence, that party complies with s. 2(1)(a) of the Act by serving a witness statement on the other parties in accordance with the court's order. A party who intends to rely on a witness statement containing hearsay evidence without calling the maker of the statement, must, when serving the witness statement, inform the other parties that the witness is not being called to give oral evidence and give the reason why the witness will not be called (**r. 33.2(2)**). In all other cases where a party intends to rely on hearsay evidence at trial, for example where a party intends to rely on the contents of a letter or diary written by a person since deceased, or the contents of a computer printout, that party complies with s. 2(1)(a) of the Act by serving a notice on the other parties which:

(a) identifies the hearsay evidence;
(b) states that the party serving the notice proposes to rely on the evidence at trial; and
(c) gives the reason why the witness will not be called (**r. 33.2(3)**).

This notice must be served no later than the date for serving witness statements and, if the hearsay evidence is to be in a document, supply a copy to any party who requests him or her to do so (**r. 33.2(4)**). See further, in the case of documents which are shown to form part of the records of a business or public authority, **53.16**.

Consequences of failure to comply with the notice procedure

53.10 Section 2(4) of the 1995 Act provides as follows:

(4) A failure to comply with subsection (1), or with rules under subsection (2)(b), does not affect the admissibility of the evidence but may be taken into account by the court—
    (a) in considering the exercise of its powers with respect to the course of proceedings and costs, and
    (b) as a matter adversely affecting the weight to be given to the evidence in accordance with section 4.

Thus where a party does not give notice, when in all the circumstances of the case it would have been reasonable and practicable for him or her to have done so, or fails to give proper notice, or gives late notice, although the court may not refuse to admit the evidence, there are a number of other potential consequences:

(a) under s. 2(4)(a), the court, in the exercise of its powers with respect to the course of proceedings, may grant an adjournment in order to compel a party to give notice, to perfect an inadequate notice, or to allow the other party time to deal with the effect of late notification;
(b) under s. 2(4)(a), the court may also impose a costs sanction; and
(c) under s. 2(4)(b), the court may reduce the weight to be given to the evidence.

Circumstances in which notice of intention is not required

53.11 It is provided in CPR, **r. 33.3** that the duty to give notice of intention to rely on hearsay evidence does not apply:

(a) to evidence at hearings other than trials [i.e. on interim applications];
(aa) to an affidavit or witness statement which is to be used at trial but which does not contain hearsay evidence;

(b)   to a statement which a party to a probate claim wishes to put in evidence and which is alleged to have been made by the person whose estate is the subject of the proceedings; or

(c)   where the requirement is excluded by a practice direction.

Under **CPR, r. 33.3**, which is authorised by s. 2(2) of the 1995 Act (see **53.8**), the duty of notice to give intention to rely on hearsay evidence may be excluded by a practice direction. **PD 32, para.** 27 (considered at **59.7**) would appear to be an example of such exclusion. In *Charnock v Rowan* [2012] EWCA Civ 2, [2012] CP Rep 18 at [22]–[23] it was held, obiter, that **PD 32, para.** 27 reverses the notice requirement set out in s. 2(1) of the 1995 Act and that its effect is to treat the agreement of a bundle as the requisite notice, leaving it to the objecting party to serve a document-specific counter-notice.

POWER TO CALL WITNESSES FOR CROSS-EXAMINATION

Section 3 of the Civil Evidence Act 1995 provides as follows: **53.12**

3. Rules of court may provide that where a party to civil proceedings adduces hearsay evidence of a statement made by a person and does not call that person as a witness, any other party to the proceedings may, with the leave of the court, call that person as a witness and cross-examine him on the statement as if he had been called by the first-mentioned party and as if the hearsay statement were his evidence-in-chief.

The relevant rule of court is **CPR, r. 33.4**, which provides that where a party proposes to rely on hearsay evidence and does not propose to call the person who made the original statement to give oral evidence, the court may, on the application of any other party, permit that party to call the maker of the statement to be cross-examined on the contents of the statement. An application for permission to cross-examine under this rule must be made not more than 14 days after the day on which a notice of intention to rely on the hearsay evidence was served on the applicant (**r. 33.4(2)**).

In the normal case, **r. 33.4** applies where a party has served a witness statement but does not propose to call its maker as a witness. It also applies where a party neither calls the maker of one of its witness statements nor puts the statement in as hearsay, and another party, under **r. 32.5(5)** (see **51.23**), puts the witness statement in as hearsay, so that the first party may then, with the permission of the court, call the witness and cross-examine him on the statement (*Douglas v Hello! Ltd* [2003] EWCA Civ 332, [2003] EMLR 633).

WEIGHT TO BE GIVEN TO HEARSAY EVIDENCE

Section 4 of the Civil Evidence Act 1995 sets out the various matters to which the court shall   **53.13** or may have regard in estimating the weight, if any, to be given to hearsay evidence. The provision was introduced for two reasons. First, since the 1995 Act all but abolishes the hearsay rule, the courts need to be particularly vigilant in testing the reliability of such evidence. Secondly, such a provision can operate to deter parties from abusing abolition of the rule, for example, by deliberately failing to give notice, by giving late or inadequate notice, by relying on hearsay rather than calling a dubious witness who can give direct evidence, or by amassing hearsay statements on a point in an attempt to conceal an essential witness (see Law Com. No. 216, para. 4.19). Section 4 provides as follows:

(1)   In estimating the weight (if any) to be given to hearsay evidence in civil proceedings the court shall have regard to any circumstances from which any inference can reasonably be drawn as to the reliability or otherwise of the evidence.

(2)   Regard may be had, in particular, to the following—

(a)   whether it would have been reasonable and practicable for the party by whom the evidence was adduced to have produced the maker of the original statement as a witness;

Commentary

(b)   whether the original statement was made contemporaneously with the occurrence or existence of the matters stated;

(c)   whether the evidence involves multiple hearsay;

(d)   whether any person involved had any motive to conceal or misrepresent matters;

(e)   whether the original statement was an edited account, or was made in collaboration with another or for a particular purpose;

(f)   whether the circumstances in which the evidence is adduced as hearsay are such as to suggest an attempt to prevent proper evaluation of its weight.

Section 13 provides that, in relation to hearsay evidence, 'the original statement':

means the underlying statement (if any) by:

(a)   in the case of evidence of fact, a person having personal knowledge of that fact, or

(b)   in the case of evidence of opinion, the person whose opinion it is.

Section 4(2) is of particular importance in cases in which hearsay carries inherent dangers, making it difficult for the judge to assess the truth in the absence of the original maker of the statement, as when a defendant to a claim for a possession or anti-social behaviour order is faced in court with serious complaints made by anonymous or absent witnesses about matters that took place, if at all, many months earlier (*Moat Housing Group-South Ltd v Harris* [2005] EWCA Civ 287, [2006] QB 606, applied in *R (Cleary) v Highbury Corner Magistrates' Court* [2006] EWHC 1869 (Admin), [2007] 1 WLR 1272).

As to s. 4(2)(a), it is submitted that an inference as to unreliability may be drawn even if, had the maker of the original statement been called as a witness, the court would have granted leave under s. 6(2) to adduce evidence of the statement (see further at 53.7). However, it is also submitted that such an inference is unlikely to be drawn under s. 4(2)(a) where the other party or parties have not applied for permission to call the maker of the original statement for cross-examination under s. 3 (see further at 53.12).

Concerning s. 4(2)(d), the phrase 'any person involved' will cover not only the maker (or, in cases of collaboration, makers) of 'the original statement', but also, in all cases in which the statement is proved at trial other than by the maker of the original statement, the person who claims to have heard the statement or to have recorded it in a document, and, in all cases of multiple hearsay, the intermediaries through whom the information contained in 'the original statement' was supplied.

In estimating the weight to be attached to hearsay evidence contained in computer-generated documents, the courts are likely to use s. 4 to have regard to a variety of circumstances, in addition to those set out in s. 4(2), from which inferences can be drawn as to the reliability or otherwise of the evidence, including in particular the following circumstances:

(a)   the reliability or otherwise of the hardware and software;

(b)   the accuracy or otherwise with which data was input; and

(c)   the potential for misuse of the computer through the capacity to hack, corrupt and alter information.

IMPEACHING THE CREDIBILITY OF ABSENT WITNESSES

53.14   The general purpose of s. 5(2) of the Civil Evidence Act 1995 is to ensure that where the maker of 'the original statement' (see further at 53.13), or the maker of any statement relied upon to prove 'the original statement', is not called as a witness, evidence relating to his or her credibility is as admissible as it would have been if he or she had been called as a witness. Section 5(2) provides as follows:

(2)   Where in civil proceedings hearsay evidence is adduced and the maker of the original statement, or of any statement relied upon to prove another statement, is not called as a witness—

(a)   evidence which if he had been so called would be admissible for the purpose of attacking his credibility as a witness is admissible for that purpose in the proceedings; and

(b) evidence tending to prove that, whether before or after he made the statement, he made any other statement inconsistent with it is admissible for the purpose of showing that he had contradicted himself.

Provided that evidence may not be given of any matter of which, if he had been called as a witness and had denied that matter in cross-examination, evidence could not have been adduced by the cross-examining party.

The meaning of the phrase 'the maker ... of any statement relied upon to prove another statement' is unclear. It is submitted that the words 'another statement' should not be taken to mean a statement other than the original statement, but should be given a purposive construction so as to cover the statement of someone who has heard the original statement or recorded it in a document and, in the case of multiple hearsay, the statements of any intermediaries through whom the information contained in 'the original statement' was supplied. For example, if A makes an oral statement to B ('the original statement'), B tells C what A said, and C makes a written record of her conversation with B (by which means A's statement is to be proved), and if A, B and C are all unavailable to give evidence, it is submitted that for the purposes of s. 5(2), evidence relating to the credibility of A, B or C should be admissible.

The purpose of the proviso to s. 5(2) is to ensure that the rule on finality of answers to questions on collateral issues (see **49.66**) operates to restrict the evidence admissible under the subsection against the maker of the statement who is not called as a witness in the same way as it applies in relation to a person who is called as a witness. Evidence admissible for the purpose of attacking credibility under s. 5(2)(a) therefore includes the types of evidence admissible under exceptions to the rule on finality, namely evidence of bias, evidence of previous convictions, and evidence of mental or physical disability affecting reliability (see **49.68** to **49.70**). As to s. 5(2)(b), it seems that whereas a previous inconsistent statement of a person called as a witness is admissible not only to impugn his or her credibility but also as evidence of any matter stated (see s. 6(3) and (5) at **49.67**), a previous inconsistent statement of a maker of a statement not called as a witness and admissible under s. 5(2)(b) is admissible 'for the purpose of showing that he had contradicted himself', i.e. only for the purpose of impugning credibility.

By **CPR, r. 33.5**, a party who, in reliance on s. 5(2), wishes to call evidence to attack the credibility of 'the maker of the original statement', must give notice of intention to do so, to the party who proposes to give the hearsay statement in evidence, not more than 14 days after being served with the notice of intention to rely on the hearsay evidence. Somewhat curiously, there is no equivalent notice requirement where a party intends to attack the credibility of 'the maker ... of any statement relied upon to prove another statement'.

PROOF OF STATEMENTS CONTAINED IN DOCUMENTS

53.15 Documents certified as forming part of the records of a business or public authority are capable of being received in evidence without further proof (see **53.16**). Notarial acts and instruments may also be received in evidence without further proof (see **53.18**). The proof of statements contained in other documents is governed by s. 8 of the Civil Evidence Act 1995, which provides as follows:

(1) Where a statement contained in a document is admissible as evidence in civil proceedings, it may be proved—
  (a) by the production of that document, or
  (b) whether or not that document is still in existence, by the production of a copy of that document or of the material part of it,
  authenticated in such manner as the court may approve.
(2) It is immaterial for this purpose how many removes there are between a copy and the original.

A 'document', for the purposes of s. 8, means 'anything in which information of any description is recorded' (s. 13), a definition wide enough to embrace maps, plans, graphs, drawings, discs, CD-ROMs, computer-generated printouts, audiotapes, videotapes, negatives, photographs, films and microfilms. A 'copy', in relation to a document, means 'anything onto which information recorded in the document has been copied, by whatever means and whether directly or indirectly' (s. 13), a definition sufficiently wide to include transcripts of audiotapes. It is submitted that the requirement of 'authentication' at the end of s. 8(1) relates not to proof of the original of a document, but calls for authentication that a copy of a document is a true copy of the original (see *Ventouris v Mountain (No. 2)* [1992] 1 WLR 887, a decision under the Civil Evidence Act 1968). It is further submitted that, as under s. 6(1) of the 1968 Act, 'production' for the purposes of s. 8 of the 1995 Act refers not to counsel handing the document to the court, but to a witness who is qualified to do so in accordance with the rules producing the document and saying what it is (see per Staughton LJ in *Ventouris v Mountain (No. 2)* at p. 901). However, it seems that a statement contained in a document may also be proved by another hearsay statement. Thus, where it is sought to admit a statement which has been deliberately tape-recorded, but whose maker is unavailable to produce the tape and give direct evidence that it is the tape that he or she made, the tape may be proved by his or her out-of-court statements to the same effect (*Ventouris v Mountain (No. 2)*).

DOCUMENTS FORMING PART OF THE RECORDS OF A BUSINESS OR PUBLIC AUTHORITY

Entries in the records of a business or public authority

53.16   Record keeping within many organisations has largely been taken over by technology and there is often no one witness who can give direct evidence of all aspects of the way in which the records were compiled. For reasons of this kind, provision has been made for documents certified as forming parts of the records of a business or public authority to be received in evidence without further proof (see Law Com. No. 216, paras 3.12 and 4.39). Section 9 of the Civil Evidence Act 1995 provides as follows:

(1) A document which is shown to form part of the records of a business or public authority may be received in evidence in civil proceedings without further proof.

(2) A document shall be taken to form part of the records of a business or public authority if there is produced to the court a certificate to that effect signed by an officer of the business or authority to which the records belong. For this purpose—

    (a) a document purporting to be a certificate signed by an officer of a business or public authority shall be deemed to have been duly given by such an officer and signed by him; and

    (b) a certificate shall be treated as signed by a person if it purports to bear a facsimile of his signature.

'Records' means 'records in whatever form' (s. 9(4)), a definition which gives the courts scope to abandon the narrow definition of the word under the Civil Evidence Act 1968, for the purposes of which it was taken to mean 'records which a historian would regard as original or primary sources, that is documents which either give effect to a transaction itself or which contain a contemporaneous register of information supplied by those with direct knowledge of the facts' (see *H v Schering Chemicals Ltd* [1983] 1 WLR 143). Section 9(4) provides that '"business" includes any activity regularly carried on over a period of time, whether for profit or not, by any body (whether corporate or not) or by an individual', and '"public authority" includes any public or statutory undertaking, any government department and any person holding office under Her Majesty'. Not all businesses, as defined, will have 'officers' in the strict sense of that word, and so in s. 9(4) 'officer' is defined to include 'any person occupying a responsible position in relation to the relevant activities of the business or public authority or in relation to its records'.

Although business and other records can often be regarded as likely to be reliable, there are bound to be exceptions, and for this reason the court has been given the discretionary power to disapply the certification provisions in s. 9. Section 9(5) provides that:

(5) The court may, having regard to the circumstances of the case, direct that all or any of the above provisions of this section do not apply in relation to a particular document or record, or description of documents or records.

Unless the court orders otherwise, a document which may be received in evidence under s. 9 shall not be receivable at trial unless the party intending to put it in evidence has given notice to the other parties (**CPR, r. 33.6(2)** and **(3)**). A party intending to use a s. 9 document as evidence of any fact must give notice not later than the latest date for serving witness statements (**r. 33.6(4)**), unless the evidence forms part of expert evidence, in which case notice must be given when the expert's report is served on the other party (**r. 33.6(6)**). A party who has given notice of intention to put in evidence under s. 9 must give every other party an opportunity to inspect it and to agree to its admission without further proof (**r. 33.6(8)**).

Absence of an entry in the records of a business or public authority

At common law it seems that the non-existence of a fact can be inferred, without offending the **53.17** hearsay rule, by evidence of the absence of a recording of that fact in a record which, having regard to its compilation and custody, one would have expected that fact, had it existed, to have been recorded. Thus, it has been said that in order to prove that A is an illegal immigrant, an officer responsible for the compilation and custody of Home Office records of persons entitled to a certificate of registration in the UK, in which A's name does not appear, may give evidence that the method of compilation and custody of the records is such that if A's name is not there, he or she must be an illegal immigrant (per Bristow J in *R v Patel* [1981] 3 All ER 94 at p. 96, applied in *R v Shone* (1983) 76 Cr App R 72). Section 9(3) of the Civil Evidence Act 1995 facilitates the proof of the absence of an entry in the records of a business or public authority. It provides as follows:

(3) The absence of an entry in the records of a business or public authority may be proved in civil proceedings by affidavit of an officer of the business or authority to which the records belong.

In cases in which the court has any reason to suspect that the records are unlikely to be reliable, then it may direct that s. 9(3) does not apply by exercising its discretionary power under s. 9(5) (see **53.16**), in which case the absence of the entry will need to be proved either by calling the officer of the business or authority to give direct evidence or, if he or she cannot be called, by relying on a hearsay statement to the same effect.

NOTARIAL ACTS AND INSTRUMENTS

Notarial acts and instruments are bills of exchange which a notary has 'noted' or protested and **53.18** documents which a notary has authenticated in private or public form (see *Halsbury's Laws of England*, 4th edn., reissue, vol. 33, paras 728 and 732). At common law, it was necessary to call the notary or his clerk to prove authentication etc. (*Sutton v Gregory* (1797) Peake Add Cas 150). However, **CPR, r. 32.20**, provides as follows:

A notarial act or instrument may be received in evidence without further proof as duly authenticated in accordance with the requirements of law unless the contrary is proved.

HEARSAY FORMERLY ADMISSIBLE AT COMMON LAW

General

Section 9 of the Civil Evidence Act 1968 preserved and gave statutory force to a number of **53.19** common law exceptions to the rule against hearsay, without purporting to amend the law

Commentary

relating to those exceptions. The exceptions included informal admissions, works of reference, and public documents and records. The Civil Evidence Act 1995 perpetuates this state of affairs, except in the case of informal admissions, which are therefore now subject to the general provisions of the 1995 Act, including those relating to notice and weight. The other common law exceptions have been preserved for three reasons:

(a) statutory provisions such as the Evidence (Foreign, Dominion and Colonial Documents) Act 1933, s. 1, and the Oaths and Evidence (Overseas Authorities and Countries) Act 1963, s. 5, which are unaffected by the 1995 Act, presuppose the existence of the common law exceptions relating to public records;

(b) the procedural burden of the notice procedure should not be introduced where it has not been borne before; and

(c) the weight to be given to evidence admissible under the exceptions is rarely a matter for debate (see Law Com. No. 216, para. 4.33).

Informal admissions

53.20 Section 7(1) of the Civil Evidence Act 1995 provides that 'the common law rule effectively preserved by section 9(1) and (2)(a) of the Civil Evidence Act 1968 (admissibility of admissions adverse to a party) is superseded by the provisions of this Act'. 'Admissions adverse to a party' means informal admissions, i.e. statements by a party to the proceedings, or someone in privity with him or her, made other than while testifying in those proceedings, and adverse to his or her case. By virtue of s. 7(1), therefore, an informal admission shall not be excluded on the ground that it is hearsay (see s. 1(1) at **53.2**), but will be subject to the general provisions of the Act, including those relating to notice (s. 2) and weight (s. 4). The weight to be attached to an informal admission depends upon a variety of special considerations additional to those set out in s. 4 itself (see **53.13**). For example, regard should always be had to the whole statement, including any passages favourable to its maker which qualify, explain or even nullify those parts of the statement relied upon as an admission, because the favourable parts of the statement are as much evidence of the facts they state as the parts relied upon as constituting an admission. Equally, regard should be had to any contradictory evidence adduced by the maker of the statement at the trial. Regard should also be had to the circumstances in which the admission was made, including, for example, whether it was made as a result of some inducement or threat. There are two other important considerations: whether the admission contains facts of which its maker had personal knowledge, and whether the admission was vicarious, i.e. made by someone in privity with the party to the legal proceedings.

53.21 **Personal knowledge** There is no requirement under the 1995 Act that the hearsay statement tendered, in order to be admissible, must have been made by someone with personal knowledge of the matters stated. However, the weight to be attached to a statement containing facts of which its maker has no personal knowledge will vary according to the circumstances. For example, an admission made by a party as to his or her age is obviously not based on personal knowledge, but it concerns a matter as to which it is reasonable to suppose that he or she has been accurately informed (see *R v Turner* [1910] KB 346 and *Lustre Hosiery Ltd v York* (1936) 54 CLR 134 (High Court of Australia)). However, an admission made as to the countries of origin of certain imported goods made solely in reliance on the fact that the goods bear marks and labels indicating that they came from those countries, is likely to be evidentially worthless (see per Lord Hodson in *Comptroller of Customs v Western Electric Co. Ltd* [1966] AC 367 at p. 371).

53.22 **Vicarious admissions** Prior to the 1995 Act, an informal admission could only be received in evidence if it had been made by a party to the proceedings personally, or vicariously, i.e. by someone in privity with him. Under the 1995 Act, an out-of-court statement adverse to the case of a party may be admitted whether made by that party or by any other person. However, the weight to be attached to an admission made by someone who, at common law, would have been in privity with a party, is likely to be greater than an adverse statement made by someone else. Those in privity included the following:

(a) a predecessor in title of a party to proceedings, provided that the admission concerned title to the property and was made at a time when he or she had an interest in it (*Woolway v Rowe* (1834) 1 Ad & El 114);

(b) a partner, provided that the admission concerned the partnership affairs and was made in the ordinary course of its business (see the Partnership Act 1890, s. 15);

(c) a referee (*Williams v Innes* (1808) 1 Camp 364); and

(d) agents, provided that:

    (i) the admission was made at a time when the agency existed (*Edwards v Brookes (Milk) Ltd* [1963] 1 WLR 795);

    (ii) the communication in which it was made was authorised, expressly or by implication, by the principal (*Wagstaff v Wilson* (1832) 4 B & Ad 339; *G (A) v G (T)* [1970] 2 QB 643); and

    (iii) the admission was made in the course of a communication with some third party, as opposed to the principal (*Re Devala Provident Gold Mining Co.* (1883) 22 ChD 593).

At common law there was no privity between:

(a) spouses, merely by virtue of the marital relationship;

(b) parent and child, merely by virtue of that relationship (*G (A) v G (T)*);

(c) co-claimants or co-defendants; or

(d) a witness and the party calling him or her (*British Thomson-Houston Co. Ltd v British Insulated and Helsby Cables Ltd* [1924] 2 Ch 160).

Works of reference

It is provided in the Civil Evidence Act 1995, s. 7(2)(a), that: **53.23**

(2) The common law rules effectively preserved by section 9(1) and (2)(b) to (d) of the Civil Evidence Act 1968, that is, any rule of law whereby in civil proceedings—

    (a) published works dealing with matters of a public nature (for example, histories, scientific works, dictionaries and maps) are admissible as evidence of facts of a public nature stated in them...

shall continue to have effect.

The effect of s. 7(2)(a) is to preserve the common law rule that authoritative published works of reference dealing with matters of a public nature are admissible to prove, or to assist the court in deciding whether to take judicial notice of, facts of a public nature stated therein. Examples include:

(a) historical works concerning public facts (*Read v Bishop of Lincoln* [1892] AC 644);

(b) standard medical texts concerning the nature of a disease (*McCarthy v The Melita (Owners)* (1923) 16 BWCC 222);

(c) engineers' reports, within the common knowledge of engineers, on the nature of soil (*East London Railway Co. v Thames Conservators* (1904) 90 LT 347);

(d) Carlisle Tables, on average life expectancy (*Rowley v London and North Western Railway Co.* (1873) LR 8 Ex 221);

(e) dictionaries, on the meaning of English words (*Marchioness of Blandford v Dowager Duchess of Marlborough* (1743) 2 Atk 542; *R v Agricultural Land Tribunal, ex parte Benney* [1955] 2 QB 140); and

(f) published maps and plans concerning facts of geographical notoriety (*R v Orton* (1873) and *R v Jameson* (1896); *Stephen's Digest of the Law of Evidence*, 10th edn. at p. 48).

Public documents and records

It is provided in the Civil Evidence Act 1995, s. 7(2)(b) and (c), that: **53.24**

(2) The common law rules effectively preserved by section 9(1) and (2)(b) to (d) of the Civil Evidence Act 1968, that is, any rule of law whereby in civil proceedings—

    ...

(b) public documents (for example, public registers, and returns made under public authority with respect to matters of public interest) are admissible as evidence of the facts stated in them, or

(c) records (for example, the records of certain courts, treaties, Crown grants, pardons and commissions) are admissible as evidence of facts stated in them, shall continue to have effect.

53.25 **Examples**   This common law exception to the hearsay rule applies to a wide variety of documents made under public authority in relation to matters of public concern, and may be justified on the grounds of reliability and convenience. Examples include:

(a) recitals in public Acts of Parliament (*R v Sutton* (1816) 4 M & S 532);

(b) entries relating to acts of State and public matters in Parliamentary journals and governmental gazettes (*Attorney General v Theakston* (1820) 8 Price 89);

(c) entries in parish registers (and foreign registers) of baptisms, marriages and burials (see per Lord Selborne in *Lyell v Kennedy* (1889) 14 App Cas 437 at pp. 448–9);

(d) entries in the public books of a corporation relating to matters of public interest (*Shrewsbury v Hart* (1823) 1 Car & P 113);

(e) the contents of a file from the Companies Register containing the statutory returns made by a company (*R v Halpin* [1975] QB 907);

(f) entries in university records relating to degrees conferred (*Collins v Carnegie* (1834) 1 Ad & El 695);

(g) records of assessment by commissioners of land tax (*Doe d Strode v Seaton* (1834) 2 Ad & El 171); and

(h) findings of professional misconduct by the General Medical Council (*Hill v Clifford* [1907] 2 Ch 236).

53.26 **Conditions of admissibility**   The conditions of admissibility for statements in public documents vary to some extent according to the particular type of document in question. In general terms, however, a public document will only be admissible as evidence of the facts it contains if:

(a) it concerns a public matter;

(b) it was made by a public officer acting under a duty to inquire and record the results of his or her inquiry; and

(c) it was intended to be retained for public reference or inspection (see per Lord Blackburn in *Sturla v Freccia* (1880) 5 App Cas 623 at pp. 643–4).

As to the first of these conditions, 'public' must not be taken to mean the whole world: the matter in question may concern either the public at large or a section of the public (*Sturla v Freccia*; *Heath v Deane* [1905] 2 Ch 86). Under the second condition, the statement must have been made by a public officer, as opposed to a private individual, acting in discharge of a strict duty to inquire into, and satisfy himself or herself as to the truth of, the facts recorded (*Doe d France v Andrews* (1850) 15 QB 756; *White v Taylor* [1969] 1 Ch 150; *Wilton and Co. v Phillips* (1903) 19 TLR 390; *Brierly v Brierly* [1918] P 257; and cf. *Bird v Keep* [1918] 2 KB 692 at pp. 697–8 and 701 and *Re Stollery* [1926] Ch 284 at p. 322). In more recent times, however, it seems that strict compliance with the requirement of personal knowledge of the facts recorded is no longer required. Thus, where a duty is cast upon a company by statute to make accurate returns of company matters to the Registrar of Companies so that those returns can be filed and inspected by members of the public, all statements on the return are prima facie proof of the truth of their contents, notwithstanding that the relevant official at the Companies Register has no duty to inquire and satisfy himself or herself as to the truth of the recorded facts (*R v Halpin* [1975] QB 907).

The fact that the public official fails to record the matter in question promptly may affect the weight to be attached to the evidence, but does not affect its admissibility (*R v Halpin* at p. 916). The position is the same where the record in question was made by an interested party (*Irish Society v Bishop of Derry* (1846) 12 Cl & F 641, in which the Bishop's statements relating to advowsons in his diocese were admitted notwithstanding that some of them belonged to him).

Declarations as to pedigree or the existence of a marriage

At common law a declaration as to pedigree was admissible, after its maker's death, as evidence **53.27**
of the truth of its contents (see, e.g. *Johnson v Lawson* (1824) 2 Bing 86 and the *Berkeley Peerage Case* (1811) 4 Camp 401). Matters of pedigree concern the relationship by blood or marriage
between persons, including the fact and date of births, marriages and deaths, legitimacy, celibacy, failure of issue and intestacy. This exception to the hearsay rule would cover, for example, oral declarations by deceased parents that one of their children, whose legitimacy was in
issue, was born before their marriage, and written declarations such as entries in family Bibles
or pedigrees hung up in the family home. There was no requirement, on the part of the declarant, of personal knowledge of the facts stated, which might amount to nothing more than
reputation or family tradition handed down from one generation to another. Declarations as
to pedigree are now admissible pursuant to the Civil Evidence Act 1995, and s. 7(3) of that
Act provides as follows:

(3) The common law rules effectively preserved by section 9(3) and (4) of the Civil Evidence Act 1968,
     that is, any rule whereby in civil proceedings—
     ...
     (b) evidence of reputation or family tradition is admissible—
          (i)   for the purpose of proving or disproving pedigree or the existence of a marriage...
     shall continue to have effect in so far as they authorise the court to treat such evidence as proving
     or disproving that matter.
     Where any such rule applies, reputation or family tradition shall be treated for the purposes
     of this Act as a fact and not as a statement or multiplicity of statements about the matter in
     question.

In so far as s. 7(3) preserves the rule whereby evidence of reputation or family tradition is
admissible for the purpose of proving or disproving the existence of a marriage, it is to be
treated as applying in an equivalent way for the purpose of proving or disproving the existence
of a civil partnership (Civil Partnership Act 2004, s. 84(5)).

Evidence of reputation or family tradition is usually made up of a multiplicity of hearsay statements, but if it were to be treated as such, strict application of the provisions of the 1995 Act
relating to notice and weight would be impossible (see Law Com. No. 216, para. 4.34). For
this reason, s. 7(3) requires such evidence to be treated as evidence of fact. The effect is that
the party proposing to adduce such evidence, in complying with the notice requirement under
s. 2 of the Act (see **53.8** and **53.9**), will not be expected to give to the other parties particulars
of the person who had personal knowledge of the matters in question and of the intermediaries through whom the information was conveyed to him or her. A further effect is that the
court, in assessing the weight of the evidence under s. 4 of the Act (see **53.13**), will not be
expected to have regard to such matters as whether the person with personal knowledge of the
matters stated made the 'original statement' contemporaneously with the occurrence or existence of the matters stated.

Declarations as to public and general rights

At common law, a declaration as to the reputed existence of a public or general right was **53.28**
admissible, after its maker's death, as evidence of the existence of the right in question. Public
rights are those common to the public at large, such as rights to use paths (see *Radcliffe v
Marsden Urban District Council* (1908) 72 JP 475) or landing places on the banks of a river (*Drinkwater
v Porter* (1835) 7 Car & P 181). General rights are those common to a section of the public or a
considerable class of persons, such as the inhabitants of a parish or the tenants of a manor
(*Nicholas v Parker* (1805) 14 East 331n). Any person was competent to make a declaration as to
the reputed existence of a public right, and the fact that the declarant had no knowledge of
the subject went only to weight, not admissibility. A declaration as to general rights, however,
was only admissible if it was made by a person with some connection with or knowledge of

Commentary

the matters in question (see *Rogers v Wood* (1931) 2 B & Ad 245 and *Crease v Barrett* (1835) 1 Cr M & R 919). Declarations as to public and general rights are now admissible pursuant to the Civil Evidence Act 1995, and s. 7(3) of that Act provides as follows:

(3) The common law rules effectively preserved by section 9(3) and (4) of the Civil Evidence Act 1968, that is, any rule whereby in civil proceedings—

...

 (b) evidence of reputation or family tradition is admissible—...

 (ii) for the purpose of proving or disproving the existence of any public or general right or of identifying any person or thing,

shall continue to have effect in so far as they authorise the court to treat such evidence as proving or disproving that matter.

Where any such rule applies, reputation or family tradition shall be treated for the purposes of this Act as a fact and not as a statement or multiplicity of statements about the matter in question.

As to the rationale of the concluding part of s. 7(3), see **53.27**.

Chapter 54 Experts and Assessors

Commentary

INTRODUCTION

An 'expert' is a person who has been instructed to give or prepare expert evidence for the **54.1** purposes of proceedings (**CPR, r. 35.2(1)**). While it is not every case that needs expert evidence, the rule of evidence is that if a matter is outside the ordinary experience of the trial judge, not only is expert evidence admissible, but it is necessary because the judge has to make a ruling based on evidence (see **54.2** to **54.9**). A judge who happens to have special expertise is not entitled to apply it when acting judicially (*Rogers v Hoyle* [2014] EWCA Civ 257, [2015] QB 265 at [41]).

Practical issues about expert evidence include the fees that can be incurred, the need for other parties to know the expert evidence that is to be adduced (so they know the case they have to meet and can make informed decisions on seeking to compromise the dispute), and avoiding an unwarranted amount of court time being devoted to resolving apparent conflicts between opposing experts. The procedural rules described at **54.10** to **54.37** aim to address these issues and ensure cases are dealt with justly and at proportionate cost in accordance with **r. 1.1(1)**, while saving costs and promoting the principle of open trial preparation.

By **r. 35.1**, it is the duty of the court to restrict expert evidence to that which is reasonably required. It is the duty of the expert to help the court on matters within his or her expertise, a duty that overrides any obligation felt by the expert to whoever instructed him (**r. 35.3**). This is an overriding duty which liberates an expert from what may have been perceived previously as pressure to win the case for the party or parties from whom instructions are received.

Guidance for the Instruction of Experts in Civil Claims 2014, para. 11, expressly says that experts should not take it upon themselves to promote the point of view of the party instructing them or engage in the role of advocates or mediators. (Guidance for the Instruction of Experts in Civil Claims 2014 will be referred to here as Guidance for Experts 2014. It may be seen at http://www.judiciary.gov.uk.)

Furthermore, **CPR, r. 35.4(1)**, provides that no party may rely upon expert evidence without first having received the court's permission to do so. This applies to both the presentation of a written report and the calling of the expert to give oral evidence at trial. **Rule 35.7** gives the court the power, where both parties wish to rely upon expert evidence relating to a particular issue, to direct that evidence on that issue be given by one expert only. A direction for a 'single joint expert' generally eliminates the problem of the overtly biased expert.

The court's powers of case management, particularly the setting of timetables, and sanctions for non-observance, are designed to prevent delay in the filing and serving of experts' reports, and answers to written questions. Non-compliance with directions is discussed in **chapter 48**.

Instruction of experts before proceedings are issued is governed primarily by any relevant pre-action protocol, or by **PD Pre-action Conduct and Protocols** if the case is not governed by a specific protocol. Expert evidence obtained at this stage anticipates the directions that are likely to be made if the dispute results in a claim being issued. There is the risk that costs on expert evidence incurred before proceedings will be wasted if the court takes a different view on the nature of the expert evidence required, so there is a tendency towards caution at this stage. Key questions are:

(a) whether the case is likely to be allocated to the multi-track (where separate experts are more likely to be allowed) or the fast track (where joint selection or joint instruction are preferred methods);

(b) what expert evidence is required at this stage in order to ensure both sides are reasonably fully informed so they can make and consider proposals in settlement; and

(c) whether there is a need for the early instruction of an expert to preserve evidence.

Guidance for Experts 2014, para. 2, sets out the following objectives:

(a) to encourage the exchange of early and full information about the expert issues involved in the prospective legal claim;

(b) to enable the parties to avoid or reduce the scope of litigation by agreeing the whole or part of an expert issue before proceedings are started; and

(c) to support the efficient management of proceedings where litigation cannot be avoided.

CPR, Part 35, only applies where experts are instructed to give or prepare expert evidence for the purpose of court proceedings **r. 35.2(1)**. It does not refer to advice given which the instructing party does not intend to adduce as evidence in the proceedings (*Rogers v Hoyle* [2014] EWCA Civ 257, [2015] QB 265 at [62], [63]). **CPR, Part 35**, has to be supplemented, where applicable, by any relevant provisions from the various court guides and the rules and practice directions that apply in specialist proceedings (see **CPR, Parts 49** and **57 to 64**).

ADMISSIBILITY OF OPINION EVIDENCE

General rule

54.2   It is a general rule that opinion evidence is inadmissible. Under the general rule a witness may only attest to facts which are within his or her personal knowledge and is not permitted to draw inferences from those facts. There are two important exceptions to the rule:

(a) A lay witness may express an opinion on matters which can only realistically be conveyed in that way, such as when describing a person's age, or the speed of a vehicle, or the state of the weather. This exception is confirmed by the Civil Evidence Act 1972, s. 3(2), which provides:

It is hereby declared that where a person is called as a witness in any civil proceedings, a statement of opinion by him on any relevant matter on which he is not qualified to give expert evidence, if made as a way of conveying relevant facts personally perceived by him, is admissible as evidence of what he perceived.

(b) A properly qualified expert may state his or her opinion on matters falling within his or her particular area of expertise, if it is an expertise that is outside the ordinary expertise of the court (*Buckley v Thomas* (1554) Plowd 118 per Saunders J at p. 124; *Folkes v Chadd* (1782) 3 Doug KB 157).

Confirmation of this exception can be found in the Civil Evidence Act 1972, s. 3(1), which provides:

(1) Subject to any rules of court…where a person is called as a witness in any civil proceedings, his opinion on any relevant matter on which he is qualified to give expert evidence, shall be admissible in evidence.

Parliament has established investigatory processes for providing the Secretary of State with reports, information or documents on which an opinion may be based that it is expedient in the public interest that a company should be wound up (Insolvency Act 1986, s. 124A(1)) or that a disqualification order should be made against a person (Company Directors Disqualification Act 1986, s. 8). It follows that the Secretary of State may use the relevant report etc. as evidence in support of a petition to wind up the company or an application for a disqualification order despite the rule against opinion evidence (*Secretary of State for Business, Enterprise and Regulatory Reform v Aaron* [2008] EWCA Civ 1146, [2009] 1 BCLC 55). A copy of any report of inspectors appointed under the Companies Act 1985, part 14, certified by the Secretary of State to be a true copy, is admissible in any legal proceedings as evidence of the opinion of the inspectors in relation to any matter contained in the report (Companies Act 1985, s. 441(1)). Statutory reports are not always treated in the same way; see the discussion in *Rogers v Hoyle* [2014] EWCA Civ 257, [2015] QB 265 at [83]–[85].

Requirements for the admission of expert evidence

For expert evidence to be admissible in civil proceedings, the following requirements must be satisfied: **54.3**

(a) there must be a matter which is outside the ordinary experience of the tribunal of fact (see **54.4**);

(b) it must be a matter on which there is a recognised body of expertise governed by accepted rules and principles (see **54.5**);

(c) the witness put forward by the party seeking to rely on expert evidence must be suitably qualified to give expert testimony on the subject (see **54.6** to **54.7**); and

(d) the party seeking to rely on the expert's evidence must comply with the relevant rules of court under **CPR, Part 35**, including obtaining a direction granting permission to rely on the expert's evidence at trial under **r. 35.4(1)** (see **54.12** to **54.17**).

Greater latitude is given in small claims track cases, where the strict rules of evidence do not apply. See **45.19** and **45.20**.

Matter which is outside the ordinary experience of the judge

Typically, expert evidence will satisfy the first requirement if it addresses a matter of art or science beyond the experience of the tribunal of fact. Medical, engineering, valuation and accountancy issues are common examples. The rule is that if the matter is outside the ordinary experience of the tribunal of fact, expert evidence is admissible, and the converse is also true, that the tribunal of fact cannot reach a decision on that matter without the assistance of an   **54.4** expert because the court needs to act on evidence. In criminal law, the dividing line is illustrated by cases which have held that questions of intent (*R v Chard* (1971) 56 Cr App R 268) and provocation (*R v Turner* [1975] QB 834) are issues on which expert evidence is not admissible, because they are matters within the everyday experience of members of the jury. By way of contrast, the question of insanity or automatism (*R v Smith* [1979] 1 WLR 1445) are outside the normal experience of jurors, so expert evidence is required.

If the parties have used technical expressions in a contract, expert evidence is admissible to explain those technical expressions if they are outside the expertise of the judge (*Kingscroft Insurance Co. Ltd v Nissan Fire and Marine Insurance Co. Ltd* [2000] 1 All ER (Comm) 272). A case on the wrong side of this line was *J. F. Morgan Chase Bank v Springwell Navigation Corporation* [2006] EWHC 2755 (Comm), [2007] 1 All ER (Comm) 549 at [31]–[33].

Experts may not be called on matters which reasonably fall within the knowledge and experience of the tribunal of fact. Expert evidence is not usually admitted on questions of credibility of a witness, even where the witness under consideration is a child (*Re N (A Minor) (Sexual Abuse: Video Evidence)* [1997] 1 WLR 153, but contrast *Re M and R (Minors) (Sexual Abuse: Expert Evidence)* [1996] 4 All ER 239). Although an employment consultant may give expert evidence on the employment opportunities in an area, and the claimant's prospects of finding work, expert evidence is not admissible on a claimant's motivation for finding work (*Larby v Thurgood* [1993] ICR 66). In *esure Insurance Ltd v Direct Line Insurance plc* [2008] EWCA Civ 842, [2008] RPC 34, permission was refused to call an expert to give evidence about consumers' confusion over trademarks as the tribunal could form its own view. An accident reconstruction expert is permitted to give scientific evidence based on physical evidence of the road layout, vehicle positions, skid marks and the positions of debris, gouge and paint marks, and from that evidence to deduce minimum speeds and movements of the vehicles. However, such an expert is not permitted to analyse the witness statements and to draw conclusions as to what the drivers did, whether they should have seen each other, or taken avoiding action, as these are matters on which the trial judge does not need expert assistance (*Liddell v Middleton* [1996] PIQR P36).

In ordinary road traffic whiplash injuries there is no need for expert evidence on causation (*Casey v Cartwright* [2006] EWCA Civ 1280, [2007] 2 All ER 78, explaining *Kearsley v Klarfeld* [2005] EWCA Civ 1510, [2006] 2 All ER 303). It is only if the defendant contends that the nature of the collision, for example, at very low speed, makes it very unlikely that any injury was suffered in the accident, that medical evidence dealing with causation will be necessary. In such cases the defendant must satisfy the following formalities:

(a) within three months of receipt of the letter before claim, notify the other parties that the defendant contends this is a low impact case and that he intends to raise causation as an issue;
(b) the issue must be pleaded in the defence, and supported by a statement of truth; and
(c) within 21 days of serving the defence, the defendant must file and serve a witness statement clearly identifying the grounds on which the low impact issue is raised, making proper reference to the expert evidence on causation, including the circumstances of the impact and any resultant damage.

If the court is satisfied that the issue has been properly raised, it will generally give permission for the claimant to be medically examined on behalf of the defendant, and if the resultant report identifies a case on causation, it will generally give the defendant permission to rely on such evidence at trial.

Permission to adduce a report from a lawyer specialising in art law was refused in *Clarke v Marlborough Fine Art (London) Ltd* [2002] EWHC 11 (Ch), LTL 21/1/2002, because the report was unlikely to provide the court with material assistance on the issues (whether transactions were to the deceased's manifest disadvantage and whether the deceased had received independent legal advice). Experts may not be called on questions of English law, as this is within the expertise of the court (*Midland Bank Trust Co. Ltd v Hett, Stubbs and Kemp* [1979] Ch 384).

A medical report which was no more than a history of events as recounted by an asylum seeker was regarded as inadequate for its intended task of corroborating the claimant's account in *SA (Somalia) v Secretary of State for the Home Department* [2006] EWCA Civ 1302, LTL 10/10/2006, although it may be objected that it was not admissible at all.

Recognised body of expertise

The court must be satisfied by the party seeking to call the evidence that there is a body of **54.5** expertise governed by recognised standards or rules of conduct capable of influencing the court's decision on any of the issues which it has to decide, and that the witness has sufficient familiarity with and knowledge of the area of expertise to be of value to the court (see also *Liverpool Roman Catholic Archdiocesan Trustees Inc. v Goldberg (No. 3)* [2001] 1 WLR 2337).

Suitably qualified

In most situations the person tendered as an expert witness must possess suitable professional **54.6** qualifications and experience. These must be stated by the expert in his or her report (**PD 35, para. 3.2**). The minimum level of qualification and experience required depends on the issue being addressed. General practitioners may be suitably qualified to give expert evidence in simple personal injuries claims. Medical experts in multi-track claims will typically be consultants in the relevant field of medicine with many years of experience. Where an injury involves a number of areas of medical science, different experts will be required for each of those areas. A similar approach is taken with accountancy, engineering and valuation experts. Experts with national or international reputations may be needed in complex commercial and intellectual property cases, and claims involving issues at the forefront of current science.

In simple cases there is no requirement that the expertise must have been acquired in a professional capacity or in the course of the expert's business. An expert is a competent expert witness if the court considers that he or she has the necessary expertise, however it was obtained (*R v Silverlock* [1894] 2 QB 766). A person suitably qualified by his or her knowledge or experience is competent to give expert evidence on the law of a foreign jurisdiction, whether or not he or she has practised law in that jurisdiction (Civil Evidence Act 1972, s. 4(1)). In practical terms, despite s. 4, if the foreign law issue, or the case as a whole, is of significant importance it will be unwise to use a pure academic, and a leading practitioner in the relevant jurisdiction is likely to be a better witness.

Independence

It is important that expert evidence should be, and should be seen to be, the independent **54.7** product of the expert uninfluenced by the exigencies of the litigation (*Whitehouse v Jordan* [1981] 1 WLR 246 per Lord Wilberforce). A useful test for 'independence' is whether the expert would express the same opinion if given the same instructions by the opposite party (Guidance for Experts 2014, para. 11). Given that **CPR, r. 35.3**, provides that the expert has an overriding duty to the court rather than to the parties, an employee of a party involved in litigation can be an independent expert (*Field v Leeds City Council* [2000] 1 EGLR 54). A party proposing to use its employee's expert evidence should be given an opportunity to demonstrate that the employee has relevant experience and is aware of the primary duty to the court when giving expert evidence. It may help to demonstrate objectivity if training has been given to the employee on the special position of expert witnesses (*Field v Leeds City Council*). In *Liverpool Roman Catholic Archdiocesan Trustees Inc. v Goldberg (No. 3)* [2001] 1 WLR 2337 it was said that a professional relationship between a litigant and an expert prevented the expert from having the necessary independence to be called as an expert witness. This case was doubted, as being inconsistent with *Field v Leeds City Council* [2000] 1 EGLR 54, in *Admiral Management Services Ltd v Para-Protect Europe Ltd* [2002] EWHC 233 (Ch), [2002] 1 WLR 2722 at [33], and is probably wrong. It was also disapproved in *R (Factortame Ltd) v Secretary of State for Transport, Local Government and*

Commentary

the Regions (No. 8) [2002] EWCA Civ 932, [2003] QB 381, where Lord Phillips of Worth Matravers MR said at [70] the *Liverpool Roman Catholic Archdiocesan Trustees Inc.* case applied the wrong test (the test for apparent bias in a tribunal). In *DN v Greenwich London Borough Council* [2004] EWCA Civ 1659, [2005] LGR 597, an educational psychologist was held to be entitled to give expert evidence on his own behalf on why in his opinion his conduct did not fall below the relevant standard of care.

The mere fact that an expert has a conflict of interest does not prevent the expert being used as a witness (*Toth v Jarman* [2006] EWCA Civ 1028, [2006] 4 All ER 1276). Rather, the question is whether the conflict prevents the expert remaining independent. The presence of a conflict of interest may be a sufficient reason for the court refusing permission for the use of the expert. Where an expert has an interest in the proceedings, this should be disclosed to the court as soon as possible. Whether the expert's evidence should be allowed should be determined during the course of case management. In considering that question the judge will have to weigh the alternative choices available if the expert's evidence is excluded, having regard to the overriding objective (*R (Factortame Ltd) v Secretary of State for Transport, Local Government and the Regions (No. 8)* at [70]). A suggestion in *Toth v Jarman* that what is now the Guidance for Experts 2014 should be amended to require experts to state at the end of their report that they have no undisclosed conflict of interest has not been implemented. Instead, the Guidance for Experts 2014, para. 16(e), has a requirement that any expert instructed or appointed must have no potential conflict of interest.

Expert as factual witness

54.8 As a matter of practice, witnesses who are qualified to be experts are frequently called as witnesses of fact where they were personally involved in the matters relating to litigation. As factual witnesses, they are not subject to **CPR, Part 35**, and there is no requirement that permission be sought (see **54.12** to **54.15**). It is both inevitable and appropriate that a witness who happens to be a professional will give evidence of his actions based on his professional experience and expertise, because no professional person can explain or justify his actions and decisions save by reference to his training and experience (*ES v Chesterfield and North Derbyshire Royal Hospital NHS Trust* [2003] EWCA Civ 1284, [2004] Lloyd's Rep Med 90 at [31]). It would be intolerable if an architect suing for his fees had to adduce independent expert evidence as to what those fees should be (*Lusty Architects v Finsbury Securities Ltd* (1991) 58 BLR 66). A professional person is permitted to give evidence on his own conduct by reference to the professional literature reasonably available to him as a busy practitioner or by reference to his own professional experience. He may also rebut allegations made against him by the other side's expert as one professional person against another (*DN v Greenwich London Borough Council* [2004] EWCA Civ 1659, [2005] LGR 597 at [25]). The limit is that expressions of opinion from such a witness must be reasonably related to facts within his knowledge (*Multiplex Constructions (UK) Ltd v Cleveland Bridge UK Ltd* [2008] EWHC 2220 (TCC), LTL 2/10/2008). The lack of independence goes to weight rather than admissibility.

Abolition of ultimate issue rule

54.9 The Civil Evidence Act 1972, s. 3(3), provides:

(3) In this section 'relevant matter' includes an issue in the proceedings in question.

Section 3(1) is quoted at **54.2**. Section 3(3) abolishes what is often called the 'ultimate issue rule' in civil cases, which prohibited an expert from giving an opinion on 'the very issue which the court has to decide' (*Barings plc v Coopers and Lybrand* [2001] Lloyd's Rep (Bank) 85 at [54]). However, it is not for experts to attempt to make findings of fact. Instead, they should express their opinions on the basis of assumed facts which should be clearly identified and stated in their reports (*J. P. Morgan Chase Bank v Springwell Navigation Corporation* [2006] EWHC 2755 (Comm), [2007] 1 All ER (Comm) 549 at [21]).

DUTIES OF EXPERTS

In order to achieve impartiality of experts, **CPR, r. 35.3**, provides that:

54.10

(a) it is the duty of an expert to help the court on the matters within his or her expertise; and

(b) this duty overrides any obligation to the person from whom the expert has received instructions or by whom the expert is paid.

Practitioners should advise their clients of the expert's overriding duty to the court, so that the client understands that the expert will consider the matter objectively and not with a view to advancing the interests of the client. Deploying expert evidence that fails to comply with **Part 35** may leave the solicitor open to a wasted costs order (*Mengiste v Endowment Fund for the Rehabilitation of Tigray* [2013] EWCA Civ 1003, [2014] PNLR 4). It is sensible for solicitors to use standard letters for the instruction of experts, which should draw the expert's attention to the main duties imposed on experts by **Part 35**. Experts who may not be familiar with the requirements of the rules should be sent a copy of the Guidance for Experts 2014. Paragraphs 9 to 15 of the Guidance for Experts 2014 set out the duties of experts, and build on Cresswell J's statement of principle in *National Justice Compania Naviera SA v Prudential Assurance Co. Ltd* [1993] 2 Lloyd's Rep 68. The Guidance for Experts 2014 states that:

(a) Experts always owe a duty to exercise reasonable skill and care to those instructing them (Guidance for Experts 2014, para. 9).

(b) Experts must comply with any relevant professional code of ethics (Guidance for Experts 2014, para. 9).

(c) Experts have an overriding duty to help the court on matters within their expertise, and must not serve the exclusive interests of those instructing them (Guidance for Experts 2014, para. 9).

(d) Experts are obliged to assist the court in accordance with the overriding objective, which includes dealing with cases proportionately, expeditiously and fairly (Guidance for Experts 2014, para. 10). This includes an obligation to observe the court's directions and time limits, which is why **PD 35, para. 8**, requires the instructing party to provide copies of relevant orders for directions to the expert. An expert who is in any doubt may apply to the court for directions to assist him in carrying out his functions as an expert (**CPR, r. 35.14(1)**).

(e) Experts should provide independent opinions, and must not trespass into the role of the court in deciding facts or engaging in the role of advocates or mediators (Guidance for Experts 2014, para. 11).

(f) Experts should confine their opinions to matters which are material to the issues in the case, and must provide opinions only in relation to matters within their expertise. They should indicate without delay any questions or issues which are outside their expertise (Guidance for Experts 2014, para. 12).

(g) Experts should take into account all material facts before them. They should set out those facts and any literature in their reports. They should indicate whether any opinion expressed is provisional or qualified, and whether any additional information is required (Guidance for Experts 2014, para. 13).

(h) Experts should inform those instructing them without delay of any change in their opinions and the reasons for the change (Guidance for Experts 2014, para. 14).

In relation to points (f) and (g) above, experts should exercise caution when expressing their opinions in areas where the underlying science is in the process of development. In *R v Cannings* [2004] EWCA Crim 1, [2004] 1 WLR 2607 at [29], Judge LJ said that this is especially so where scientific knowledge on a topic is limited or incomplete. Experts in many fields will acknowledge the possibility that future research will undermine the accepted wisdom of the day, but that does not of itself provide a basis for rejecting expert evidence, or for conjuring up fanciful doubts about the possible impact of future research (at [178]).

Commentary

EXPERTS' IMMUNITY FROM SUIT

54.11   As a matter of public policy, lay witnesses have immunity from any civil proceedings brought in respect of the evidence they give in a court of law (see **51.26**). This immunity covers testimony in court, and also preparation for giving evidence in court, such as a proof, or Scottish precognition, or witness statement (*Watson v M'Ewan* [1905] AC 480). This immunity applies to a treating doctor, forensic scientist or other expert who is called to give factual evidence without having initially been retained by either party to the dispute, even if they are also asked for their professional opinion (*Jones v Kaney* [2011] UKSC 13, [2011] 2 AC 398 at [64]). All witnesses, including experts initially retained as experts in the case, are immune from suit in respect of claims in defamation (*Jones v Kaney* at [62]). Other than the above, the immunity from suit enjoyed by an expert witness, that is, someone who has been selected, instructed and paid for by a party, was abolished by *Jones v Kaney*. This means they may be sued in negligence or for breach of the implied term in the Supply of Goods and Services Act 1982, s. 13, to exercise reasonable skill and care, for example, if they are negligent in signing a joint statement without having read it. An expert's conduct may also justify a wasted costs order (*Phillips v Symes (No. 2)* [2004] EWHC 2330 (Ch), [2005] 1 WLR 2043; see **68.67**) or disciplinary proceedings by the expert's professional regulator (*Meadow v General Medical Council* [2006] EWCA Civ 1390, [2007] QB 462).

COURT CONTROL OVER EXPERT EVIDENCE

54.12   It is provided by **CPR, r. 35.4(1)**, that 'No party may call an expert or put in evidence an expert's report without the court's permission'. **Rule 35.1** provides that expert evidence shall be restricted to that which is reasonably required to resolve the proceedings. In deciding whether to grant permission the court will consider whether there is a cogent need for the expert evidence, and how helpful the evidence will be (*Mann v Chetty* [2001] CP Rep 24), and whether these benefits justify the cost involved (**r. 1.4(2)(h)**). In *J. P. Morgan Chase Bank v Springwell Navigation Corporation* [2006] EWHC 2755 (Comm), [2007] 1 All ER (Comm) 549, Aikens J warned against the natural tendency in complex litigation with voluminous documentation to resort to experts to assist in digesting the material, particularly in unusual areas of commercial practice. This can result in the judge being submerged by long and complicated reports which are expensive, time-consuming and possibly counterproductive. **Rule 35.1** can be used by the court to reject expert evidence if it is not reasonably required to resolve the proceedings. On the other hand, where there are complex issues outside the experience of the tribunal of fact it is impossible to do justice without expert evidence (*Mortgage Agency Services Number One Ltd v Edward Symmons LLP* [2013] EWCA Civ 1590, LTL 29/1/2014).

An 'expert' for the purposes of **CPR, Part 35**, is a person who has been instructed to give or prepare expert evidence for the purpose of civil proceedings (**rr. 35.2(1) and 2.1**). Expert evidence obtained for the purpose of other proceedings (for example, DNA evidence prepared for criminal proceedings) is still opinion evidence, and will be admissible in civil proceedings only if the requirements of **Part 35** are complied with (*Lavelle v Noble* [2011] EWCA Civ 441, LTL 18/4/2011). This is to be contrasted with other expert evidence, for example an air accident investigation report, which is not prepared for proceedings, and which is therefore outside **CPR, Part 35** (*Rogers v Hoyle* [2014] EWCA Civ 257, [2015] QB 265 at [62] and [63]).

A party applying for permission either to call an expert or to put in evidence an expert's report must identify (**r. 35.4(2)**):

(a) the field in which it is sought to rely on expert evidence; and

(b) where practicable, the name of the proposed expert.

If permission is granted under **r. 35.4**, it will be in relation only to the expert named or the field identified (**r. 35.4(3)**). Practitioners should apply in good time for permission to call an expert or such permission will not be granted. In *Calenti v North Middlesex NHS Trust* (2001) LTL

10/4/2001 the defendant was refused permission to call a medical expert two weeks prior to trial because to do so would work a significant injustice on the claimant.

The court has power to limit the amount of an expert's fees and expenses that the party who wishes to rely on the expert may recover from any other party (r. 35.4(4)). This rule was amended, with effect from 1 October 2009, to make clear that the power to restrict fees and expenses applies to costs recoverable between the parties but does not interfere with the contractual fees agreed between any party and its expert. The court may also exercise its discretion to terminate the expert's appointment in appropriate circumstances (*Kranidiotes v Paschali* (2001) EWCA 357, LTL 8/5/2001). This power is in addition to the court's general powers to restrict experts' fees on a subsequent detailed assessment of costs under **Part 44**. An expert who has caused significant expense to be incurred through flagrant, reckless disregard of his duties to the court may be ordered to pay those costs (*Phillips v Symes (No. 2)* [2004] EWHC 2330 (Ch), [2005] 1 WLR 2043). Where an expert adopts a biased or irrational approach, it may be appropriate for the judge to refer the witness's conduct to the relevant professional body, after giving the witness a suitable period of time to make representations (*Pearce v Ove Arup Partnership Ltd* (2001) LTL 8/11/2001).

In the absence of a duty of confidence, it is contrary to public policy for an expert to agree not to act for another party (*Lilly Icos LLC v Pfizer Ltd* (2000) LTL 26/1/2001).

Permission to use expert evidence

54.13 On the fast and multi-tracks, no expert may give evidence, whether written or oral, at a hearing without the permission of the court (**CPR, r. 35.4(1)**). When the parties apply for permission they must provide an estimate of the costs of the proposed experts (**r. 35.4(2)**). Permission is generally only granted for named experts in named fields. Directions may specify the issues the expert evidence should address (**r. 35.4(3)**). Where possible, matters requiring expert evidence should be dealt with by only one expert (**PD 35, para. 1**).

The first stage at which the court may give directions in relation to experts is at the allocation stage. By this time the parties to proceedings will have completed their directions questionnaires in form N180 or N181. Question E asks whether the party completing the form wishes to use expert evidence at the hearing and whether any expert reports have yet been copied to the other parties. The party completing the form is required to list the experts whose evidence it may wish to use, their fields of expertise, the justification for using the expert, and the estimated cost. A party must also indicate whether it will use a single joint expert in any field. These answers will assist the court in deciding on track allocation as well as the form of directions to be made on allocation.

Although the court has power to limit the expert evidence the parties may call at trial, and to limit the costs recoverable for the use of expert evidence, it does not have power to limit the experts a party can instruct. The court cannot impose a condition that a party must obtain the court's permission before instructing an expert (*Vasiliou v Hajigeorgiou* [2005] EWCA Civ 236, [2005] 1 WLR 2195). Where directions require an act to be done by an expert, or otherwise affect an expert, the party instructing the expert must serve a copy of the order on the expert (**para. 8**).

Experts are comparatively rare on the small claims track, see **45.19**. On the small claims track, expert evidence, whether written or oral, requires permission (**CPR, r. 27.5**). On this track only **rr. 35.1** (duty to restrict expert evidence), **35.3** (overriding duty of experts to the court), **35.7** (power to direct single joint expert) and **35.8** (instructions to single joint expert) apply (**r. 27.2(1)(e)**). **Rules 35.4(3A)** (only one expert) and **35.5(2)** (expert not to attend the hearing unless necessary) have express references to the small claims track, and are intended to apply to these cases, despite a drafting defect in **r. 27.2**. Experts' reports on this track can therefore be somewhat informal.

Where a claim has been allocated to the small claims track or the fast track, if permission is given for expert evidence, it will normally be given for evidence from only one expert on a particular issue (**r. 35.4(3A)**). On these two tracks the court will not direct an expert to attend a hearing unless it is necessary to do so in the interests of justice (**r. 35.5(2)**). In a soft tissue injury claim (defined by **RTA Protocol, para. 1.1(16A)**, see **8.40**) the claimant may not proceed unless the medical report served with the particulars of claim is a fixed cost medical report (**PD 16, para. 4.3A**) and permission to use expert evidence will normally be restricted to a single fixed cost medical report (**CPR, r. 35.4(3B)**).

Directions on the fast track

54.14 Where a case has been allocated to the fast track, **PD 28, para. 3.2**, provides:

The court will seek to tailor its directions to the needs of the case and the steps of which it is aware that the parties have already taken to prepare the case. In particular it will have regard to the extent to which PD Pre-action Conduct or any pre-action protocol has or (as the case may be) has not been complied with.

In most fast track claims the court will limit the expert evidence to one expert per party in relation to any field of expertise, and to expert evidence in no more than two expert fields (**CPR, r. 26.6(5)(b)**). Directions will be made for a single joint expert, unless there are good reasons for taking a different course (**PD 28, paras 3.7(4) and 3.9(4)**). Fast track claims should ordinarily be capable of being tried within one day (**CPR, r. 26.6(5)(a)**). It is therefore important to be able to identify at an early stage whether there is likely to be a significant conflict in the expert evidence, so that a decision can be made whether to reallocate the claim to the multi-track. In a suitable case, such as *Baron v Lovell* [1999] CPLR 630, a judge is entitled at a pre-trial review to direct that the medical evidence needed to determine the issues relating to the claimant's personal injury claim could be provided by the claimant's medical expert only.

It is also possible for the parties to agree the directions sought and if this is the case, the proposed directions should where necessary contain a provision regarding the use of a single joint expert, or in cases where the use of a single expert has not been agreed, the exchange and agreement of expert reports (including whether exchange is to be simultaneous or sequential) and without-prejudice discussions of the experts (**PD 28, para. 3.7**). It is possible that the court will not approve the directions submitted by the parties and will instead substitute its own directions, having regard to the parties' suggested directions (**PD 28, para. 3.8**). Alternatively, the court may hold an allocation hearing at which directions will be given.

According to **PD 28, para. 3.9(5)**, where a direction for a single joint expert is not given, the court's general approach will be:

(a) to direct disclosure of experts' reports by way of simultaneous exchange; and

(b) if experts' reports are not agreed, to direct a discussion between the experts for the purpose set out in **CPR, r. 35.12(1)** (identification of and agreement of the issues in the case) and the preparation of a report under **r. 35.12(3)** (see **54.31**).

Where expert reports are to be exchanged, generally this should be done within 14 weeks of the directions order (**PD 28, para. 3.12**).

The court will not direct an expert to attend a hearing of a fast track claim, unless it is necessary to do so in the interests of justice (**CPR, r. 35.5(2)**).

Directions on the multi-track

54.15 Paragraphs 4.2, 4.6, 4.7, 4.9 and 4.10 of PD 29 make virtually the same provision about directions on the multi-track concerning experts as those applicable on the fast track (see **54.14**). Proposed directions should take as their starting point the relevant model directions and standard directions available on the Ministry of Justice website (**CPR, r. 29.1(2)**). There is a greater willingness to allow the parties to instruct their own experts on the multi-track (*S (A Minor) v Birmingham Health Authority* (1999) LTL 23/11/99) and, as these claims are usually more complex than fast track claims, the time for exchanging experts' reports is likely to be longer than for fast track claims. There is also a greater willingness to allow experts to give oral evidence at trial in multi-track cases.

The spirit and effect of the rules mean that even in multi-track claims great care will be taken before making expert directions. For example, in claims relating to the alleged infringement of registered designs, expert evidence may not be useful (see *Oren v Red Box Toy Factory Ltd* [1999] FSR 785) and may well not be allowed (see *Thermos Ltd v Aladdin Sales and Marketing Ltd* (1999) *The Independent*, 13 December 1999). In *Mann v Chetty and Patel* (2000) LTL 26/10/2000 the Court of Appeal agreed that the judge had been right in a multi-track claim to refuse permission to call various experts, because the evidence would have been of minimal value, would not have been conclusive on the issues, and would have been disproportionate. In *Rawlinson v Cooper* [2002] EWCA Civ 392, LTL 11/3/2002, it was held that both an original report from a medical expert and a second report from the same witness, which included references to published papers on life expectancy and their application to the claimant's case, should be admitted in evidence. However, it is disproportionate to allow a party to call two experts in a single area (even if the expert was retained by the party in the matter in dispute, and so will be giving factual evidence as well) (*Carillion JM Ltd v Bath and North East Somerset Council* [2009] EWHC 166 (TCC), LTL 3/4/2009, architect in a construction case; *Beaumont v Ministry of Defence* [2009] EWHC 1258 (QB), LTL 18/6/2009, obstetrician in a clinical dispute). Calling two experts in such cases is permitted only if the circumstances are exceptional.

Directions for the exchange of scholarly information

In *Wardlaw v Farrar* [2003] EWCA Civ 1719, [2003] 4 All ER 1358, it was pointed out that there is a **54.16** standard direction dealing with disclosure of scholarly information used by medical experts for use in clinical disputes, based on the direction used by Masters Ungley and Yoxall, which should be followed in all courts dealing with medical negligence claims. The direction, which is set out below, can also be used in other categories of claim.

Any unpublished literature upon which any expert witness proposes to rely shall be served at the same time as service of his [report] together with a list of published literature and copies of any unpublished material. Any supplementary literature upon which any expert witness proposes to rely shall be notified to all other parties at least one month before trial. No expert witness shall rely upon any publications that have not been disclosed in accordance with this direction without [permission] of the trial judge on such terms as to costs as he deems fit.

Reports and privilege

Until an expert's report is disclosed to the other side, instructions to the expert and the **54.17** expert's report will be protected by legal professional privilege (see **50.60**). While privilege applies, the court will not make an order compelling disclosure, as that would run counter to the privilege (*Worrall v Reich* [1955] 1 QB 296). By disclosing a report, whether voluntarily or pursuant to directions, a party waives privilege (see **50.73**). Disclosing the final version of an expert's report does not waive privilege in earlier drafts of the report (*Jackson v Marley Davenport Ltd* [2004] EWCA Civ 1225, [2004] 1 WLR 2926). For privilege in respect of jointly instructed and jointly selected experts, see **54.19**. For experts instructed only to advise see **8.23** and **54.22**.

The status of instructions to experts once a report is disclosed is considered at **54.30**.

JOINT AND SEPARATE EXPERTS

Single joint expert

Under **CPR, r. 35.7**, where two or more parties wish to submit expert evidence on a particular **54.18** issue, the court has power to direct that evidence is to be given by a single joint expert only. A 'single joint expert' is an expert instructed to prepare a report for the court on behalf of two or more of the parties (including the claimant) (**r. 35.2(2)**). When considering whether to give permission for the parties to rely on expert evidence and whether that evidence should be from a single joint expert, **PD 35, para.** 7, provides that the court will take into account all the circumstances, and in particular whether:

(a) it is proportionate to have separate experts for each party on a particular issue with reference to:
  (i) the amount in dispute;
  (ii) the importance to the parties; and
  (iii) the complexity of the issue;

(b) the instruction of a single joint expert is likely to assist the parties and the court to resolve the issue more speedily and in a more cost-effective way than separately instructed experts;

(c) expert evidence is to be given on the issue of liability, causation or quantum;

(d) the expert evidence falls within a substantially established area of knowledge which is unlikely to be in dispute or there is likely to be a range of expert opinion;

(e) a party has already instructed an expert on the issue in question and whether or not that was done in compliance with any practice direction or relevant pre-action protocol;

(f) questions put in accordance with **CPR, r. 35.6,** are likely to remove the need for the other party to instruct an expert if one party has already instructed an expert;

(g) questions put to a single joint expert may not conclusively deal with all issues that may require testing prior to trial;

(h) a conference may be required with the legal representatives, experts and other witnesses which may make instruction of a single joint expert impractical; and

(i) a claim to privilege makes the instruction of any expert as a single joint expert inappropriate.

The parties for whom that person is a joint expert are called the 'relevant parties'. It may be that the relevant parties cannot agree on who that expert should be, in which case the court may:

(a) select the expert from a list prepared or identified by the relevant parties, or

(b) direct that the expert be selected in such other manner as the court may direct.

The court may give directions about the payment of a single joint expert's fees and expenses and about any inspection, examination or experiments which the expert may wish to carry out (**r. 35.8(3)**). Before a single joint expert is instructed the court may limit the amount that can be paid by way of fees and expenses to the expert and direct that the relevant parties pay that amount into court (**r. 35.8(4)**). In any event, where a single joint expert is instructed, the relevant parties are jointly and severally liable for the payment of the expert's fees and expenses, unless the court directs otherwise (**r. 35.8(5)**; Guidance for Experts 2014, para. 40). In this way, the parties will know in advance what their financial commitment is in the way of experts' fees.

The reasons for directing that a report be obtained from a single joint expert are that it saves time and costs and is usually proportionate to the issues in the case. It may be the case that in order to fulfil these objectives, it is simpler to use an employee of one of the parties, who is expert in the relevant discipline (see 54.7).

If a single joint expert's report is accepted by the parties, subject to receiving answers to written questions (see 54.32), it is inevitable that the report will be accepted at trial without needing to call the expert to give oral evidence. District Judges frequently make this clear when giving directions at the allocation stage.

Joint selection of expert

54.19 Joint selection is to be contrasted with joint instruction of experts. A jointly instructed expert receives instructions from both sides, who both contribute to the expert's fees, and both are entitled to the expert's report. A jointly selected expert is one who is chosen (usually by one side providing a list of proposed experts, and the other side deciding whether to object to any of those named) by both sides, but who is instructed by one side only. That party is entirely responsible for the expert's fees, and is, at least initially, entitled to assert legal professional privilege over the report (*Carlson v Townsend* [2001] EWCA Civ 511, [2001] 1 WLR 2415). *Carlson v Townsend* was interpreted by *Edwards-Tubb v J. D. Wetherspoon plc* [2011] EWCA Civ 136, [2011] 1 WLR 1373 at [14] as simply a decision that the expert in that case had been jointly selected and not jointly instructed. The court in *Edwards-Tubb v J. D. Wetherspoon plc* did not feel bound by the comments in *Carlson v Townsend* about the privileged nature of a jointly instructed expert's report, and felt that the need to prevent 'expert-shopping' overrides any absolute rule that a jointly selected expert's report is privileged unless privilege is waived. It accordingly held that where a party has obtained a report from a jointly selected expert, does not disclose that report, and then seeks to rely on the report of another expert, the court has a discretion, which it should usually exercise, to grant permission to rely on the new expert's evidence only on condition that the jointly selected expert's report is disclosed to the other side (at [31]). It is the same whether the joint instruction is pre-issue or post-issue. There are substantial practical and doctrinal problems with this decision, and there are questions over whether it will stand the test of time. Pre-action protocols often recommend joint selection of experts. Court directions tend to provide for joint instruction.

Joint expert or own experts

Whether a direction should be given for the instruction of a single joint expert depends on the nature of the issue being considered. Single joint experts are more appropriate where there is a settled and recognised body of expert knowledge. Separate experts are more suitable where it is known that there are different schools of thought in the area of expertise (*Oxley v Penwarden* [2001] CPLR 1), or where the opinions of the experts depend on issues of interpretation. Examples are issues as to appropriate surgical procedures, or disputes about outcomes in clinical dispute claims. In substantial claims where the central issues can only be resolved by expert evidence it is likely to be wrong for the court to insist on a single joint expert. In clinical disputes, it was suggested in *Peet v Mid-Kent Healthcare Trust* [2001] EWCA Civ 1703, [2002] 1 WLR 210, that the balance between proportionality and expense could be achieved by allowing the parties to call their own experts on the medical issues, but to direct the instruction of a joint expert on the non-medical issues. This is so even where the sums at stake are substantial. **54.20**

Challenging joint report

Where a single joint expert has been agreed by the parties and the court has directed that expert to report, a party who is unhappy with that expert's conclusions will not be permitted to call further expert evidence by way of their own expert unless it would be unjust pursuant to the overriding objective not to allow that evidence (*Daniels v Walker* [2000] 1 WLR 1382). *Daniels v Walker* also held that refusing an additional expert after a direction for a single joint expert did not infringe the European Convention on Human Rights, **art. 6(1)**, in the **Human Rights Act 1998, sch. 1**. In considering whether it would be unjust not to allow an additional expert, *Peet v Mid-Kent Healthcare Trust* [2001] EWCA Civ 1703, [2002] 1 WLR 210, held that good, not fanciful, reasons are required. A preliminary requirement if further expert evidence is to be allowed is whether there is any rational criticism of the joint expert's report. A significant discrepancy between the valuation evidence of a single joint expert and a second expert instructed by one of the parties may be a sufficient basis for allowing the second expert's evidence (*Marston v Lewis* [2004] EWHC 2833 (Ch), LTL 4/11/2004). There are cases where a pivotal issue depends on expert evidence and the jointly instructed expert's view is not easily capable of challenge in the absence of other expert opinion. If so, justice may require permission to be granted to seek a second opinion (*W v Oldham Metropolitan Borough Council* [2005] EWCA Civ 1247, [2006] 1 FLR 543, a family law case). **54.21**

Factors bearing on the exercise of the discretion to allow additional expert evidence after a jointly instructed expert has reported include the reasons for seeking another report, the nature of the case and the amount at stake, the effect of allowing another expert to report and its impact on delay and the trial (*Cosgrove v Pattison* [2001] CPLR 177). See also **54.38** for cross-examination of a joint expert.

If there is no basis for rational criticism of a joint expert's report, and if the joint report totally undermines one side's case, the court may enter summary judgment. Thus, in *Smith v Peter North and Partners* [2001] EWCA Civ 1553, [2002] PNLR 12, a joint expert reported in a claim for damages against a surveyor that the value of the property was the same with and without the defects. Summary judgment was entered for the defendant because there was no prospect of the claimant persuading the court that the cost of repairs was the correct measure of damages. Contrast *Layland v Fairview New Homes plc* [2002] EWHC 1350 (Ch), LTL 10/7/2002, in which, after considering various criticisms of a single jointly instructed valuation expert's report (which concluded the claimants had suffered no loss), Neuberger J allowed the claim to go to trial as there was material which could fruitfully be exploited in cross-examination.

Experts instructed only to advise

54.22 Parties on occasion instruct an expert with no present intention of using the expert's opinions in court proceedings. This may arise:

(a) in complex claims where a party to a dispute needs expert assistance as part of the investigative process; and

(b) where a litigant wants another expert to comment on a single joint expert's report.

In these circumstances, and while the report in question is not intended for use in the proceedings, neither **CPR, Part 35**, nor the Guidance for Experts 2014 applies (*Rogers v Hoyle* [2014] EWCA Civ 257, [2015] QB 265 at [62] and [63]). The expert's fees are unlikely to be recoverable as costs in the proceedings (Guidance for Experts 2014, para. 37). An expert who has advised in this way should only be proposed as a single joint expert if the other parties are given all relevant information about the previous involvement (para. 36).

Retaining an expert before directions are given

54.23 Retaining an expert without trying to agree a single joint expert with one's opponent carries the risk that the costs of the expert will not be allowed. Where it is necessary to instruct an expert before commencement of proceedings, the pre-action protocols encourage the joint instruction or joint selection of, and access to, experts (**PD Pre-action Conduct and Protocols, para. 7; Pre-action Protocol for Personal Injury Claims, para. 7.2**).

Retaining one's own expert may lead to the following consequences:

(a) The court may not grant permission for the expert's report to be used, so that the party who wishes to rely on the report may not recover the costs of instructing the expert.

(b) The court may order that a different, jointly instructed expert be used, so that the costs of the first expert are wasted.

(c) The court may allow the report to be used, but disallow the costs, and allow the opponent to instruct and call its own expert.

(d) An attempt to persuade one's opponent to use one's expert's report as the only report in the case may involve disclosing it earlier than might have been ordered by the court and the opponent may still not agree to its use.

There are, however, circumstances in which it is important to obtain an expert's report for the claimant, for example:

(a) In many cases, it may not be until an expert's report has been obtained that a claimant can be sure of having a case at all.

(b) There may be such lengthy waiting lists to get a report from the chosen expert that the claimant needs to initiate these procedures as soon as solicitors are instructed.

(c) In straightforward cases and given that the letter of instructions will be disclosed, if the expert who is instructed is well known and accepted as reputable by the opponent, time may be saved and the report may be accepted, perhaps subject to further questions being put by the opponent under **CPR, r. 35.6**.

It is nonetheless clear that the preferred approach is to communicate with one's opponent in an effort to agree on a mutually acceptable expert (*Carlson v Townsend* [2001] EWCA Civ 511, [2001] 1 WLR 2415).

INSTRUCTING EXPERTS

Appointment of experts

Before an expert is formally instructed, or the court's permission is sought, solicitors should establish (see Guidance for Experts 2014, para. 16): **54.24**

(a) that the expert is suitably qualified;
(b) that the expert is familiar with his or her duties as an expert in court proceedings;
(c) that the expert can provide a report, deal with questions and have discussions with other experts within a reasonable time and at a cost proportionate to the issues;
(d) whether the expert will be available for the trial;
(e) that there is no potential conflict of interest.

In practical terms, saying that availability for trial should be established can be a counsel of perfection, because in some fields there is a shortage of experts, and a measure of double-booking has to be tolerated. In these cases, a view has to be taken on the risks, including prospects that some cases might settle, or for some latitude within the trial window or trial timetables to allow double-booked cases to go ahead. Courts are, however, very reluctant to adjourn on this ground.

Terms of appointment should be agreed at the outset (para. 17). These should include the services required from the expert, time for delivery of the report, the basis of the expert's charges (which may be daily or hourly rates with an estimate of the time likely to be required, or a total fee for the services) including cancellation fees and fees for attending court, and arrangements for answering written questions. Cancellation fees (if any) depend on the nature of the work done by the expert, the length of notice given of any adjournment, and whether it is feasible for the expert to book other work given those circumstances. Agreement to delay payment of fees until the end of the case is permissible, but fees contingent on the nature of the expert's advice, or dependent on the outcome of the case, are strongly discouraged (para. 88).

Instructions

Solicitors must give clear instructions to retained experts (Guidance for Experts 2014, para. 20). When instructing an expert it is important to state that the retainer is on terms that the expert will perform the functions specified in the CPR. By doing so the expert will agree with his client that he will perform the duties that he owes to the court, with the result that there should be no conflict between the duty that the expert owes to his client (see **54.11**) and the duty he owes to the court (*Jones v Kaney* [2011] UKSC 13, [2011] 2 AC 398 at [49]). Instructions to the expert should include: **54.25**

(a) basic information, such as names, addresses, dates of birth, telephone numbers and dates of incidents;
(b) the nature and extent of the expertise called for;
(c) the purpose of the report, a description of what needs to be investigated and of the issues in the case;
(d) copies of the statements of case, witness statements and disclosed documents relevant to the report;
(e) where proceedings have not been commenced, whether that is the intention, and whether the expert is asked only for advice;
(f) an outline programme for all stages of the expert's work, consistent with good case management;

Commentary

(g) where proceedings have started, the dates of any hearings and details of matters such as the case management track for the case, together with copies of relevant court directions and orders.

The expert should confirm, without delay, whether he or she accepts the instructions, and should inform the instructing party without delay of any problems or insufficiency in the instructions (para. 22). Once instructions are accepted, the expert must not withdraw without first discussing the reasons with those who gave the instructions (para. 27), and should consider whether it might be more appropriate to seek directions under **CPR, r. 35.14**.

It may be the case that one or other of the parties has access to information which is not reasonably available to another party and which may assist an expert in preparing his or her report. In these circumstances, the court may direct the party who has such access to prepare and file a document recording the information and to serve a copy of that document on the other party (**r. 35.9**). The document must include sufficient details of all the facts, tests, experiments and assumptions which underlie any part of the information to enable the party on whom it is served to make, or to obtain, a proper interpretation of the information and an assessment of its significance (**PD 35, para. 4**).

Instructions to a single joint expert

54.26 Where a direction has been given by the court, in accordance with **CPR, r. 35.7**, for a single joint expert to be used, the parties should try to agree joint instructions, and should try to agree what documents should be included with the instructions (Guidance for Experts 2014, para. 38). They should also attempt to agree what assumptions the expert should be allowed to make. In the event of disagreement, they should try to agree where the areas of disagreement lie and their instructions should make this clear (para. 39). Where they cannot agree, each instructing party may give instructions to the expert (**CPR, r. 35.8(1)**), but must send a copy, at the same time, to the other instructing parties (**r. 35.8(2)**). There is no rule, and in fact it is contrary to the express terms of **r. 35.8(1)**, that a party should be bound to the instructions to a single joint expert proposed by the other side. The court should not order one side to sign instructions they object to (*Yorke v Katra* [2003] EWCA Civ 867, LTL 9/6/2003).

Single joint experts owe an equal duty to all parties, and must maintain independence, impartiality and transparency at all times (Guidance for Experts 2014, para. 43). They should keep all instructing parties informed of material steps they may take by copying correspondence to all parties (para. 42). A party will not be permitted to invite a jointly instructed expert to a conference without the written consent of the other parties or where the court has directed the meeting take place (*Peet v Mid-Kent Healthcare Trust* [2001] EWCA Civ 1703, [2002] 1 WLR 210).

WRITTEN REPORTS

Oral or written evidence at trial

54.27 Expert evidence is to be given in a written report, unless the court directs otherwise (**CPR, r. 35.5(1)**). A decision on attendance at trial may be made in the initial case management directions, or upon filing the pre-trial checklists, or on an application under **Part 23**. The court has a wide discretionary power on what expert evidence is adduced and in what form (**rr. 35.4 and 35.5**). If a claim is on the fast track, the court will not direct an expert to attend a hearing, unless it is necessary to do so in the interests of justice (**r. 35.5(2)**).

However, in the Commercial and Admiralty Courts a sole expert should be available to give oral evidence, unless his or her report is on discrete and substantially non-controversial matters collateral to the main issues (*Voaden v Champion* (2000) LTL 2/6/2000).

EXPERT'S RIGHT TO ASK COURT FOR DIRECTIONS

It is clear from **CPR, r. 35.3**, that it is an expert's duty to assist the court rather than the parties **54.33** from whom he or she has received instructions. Further, the court has control over an expert in respect of the issues on which he or she should report and has a power to give directions regarding any examination, inspection or experiment that an expert is to carry out. The court also has power to restrict the amount of fees and expenses to be paid to an expert. It would be wholly inappropriate, therefore, if an expert were to be unable to communicate with the court to clarify these matters from time to time. For example, an expert may find that it is necessary to carry out tests which had not been authorised by the court. Lines of communication between expert and court are opened by **r. 35.14**, and **PD 35, para. 8**. Under **CPR, r. 35.14**, an expert may file a written request for directions from the court, to assist the expert in carrying out his or her function as an expert. Under **PD 35, para. 8**, the instructing party is obliged to send copies of all the relevant orders to the expert. An expert who proposes to request directions under **CPR, r. 35.14**, must, unless the court orders otherwise, provide a copy of the proposed request to his or her instructing party at least seven days before filing it, and to all other parties at least four days before filing it (**r. 35.14(2)**). When the court gives directions to the expert, it may also order that a party be served with a copy of the directions (**r. 35.14(3)**). The wording of **r. 35.14(3)** is rather odd, stating that the court can order 'a party' to be served with a copy of the directions, but as the singular includes the plural, is to be interpreted as enabling the court to direct service on all the parties or such of the parties as may be specified in the directions.

INSPECTION, EXAMINATION AND TESTING OF PROPERTY

Invariably experts need to inspect, measure, examine and/or test the subject matter on which **54.34** they are asked to report. The expert may delegate these tasks, but where this is done the report must identify and state the qualifications of the person who did the delegated tasks, and say whether they were done under the supervision of the expert (**PD 35, para. 3.2(5)**).

The subject matter could be goods, land, buildings or machinery relevant to the issues in the claim. Where the subject matter is under the control of the party instructing the expert there should be no problem. Where it is under the control of the other side or a non-party, it will be necessary to secure their consent to the expert having access for the purpose of conducting any necessary inspection, examination, etc. If consent is not given, it is usually possible to obtain an order (usually on a case management conference) giving access, a subject dealt with in detail in **chapter 41**.

In *SKB plc v Apotex* (2003) LTL 4/2/2003, a patent claim, the court held that a confidentiality agreement between the parties had the effect that **CPR, r. 31.22** (undertaking not to use information disclosed for collateral purposes, see **50.45**), applied to the test results on samples of the defendant's products. It is possible that an implied undertaking in similar terms would be imposed even without a confidentiality agreement, although it is better for collateral use to be expressly dealt with when permission to inspect property is sought.

MEDICAL EXAMINATION

In personal injuries claims the defendant is entitled to test the severity of the claimant's **54.35** injuries by obtaining expert medical evidence on the claimant's history, present condition and prognosis. This is often done on a joint basis, particularly in claims suitable for the fast track, either in compliance with the **Pre-action Protocol for Personal Injury Claims** (see **8.23**) or as part of case management directions after proceedings are issued (see **46.6** and **54.12** to **54.15**). In these cases consent to the necessary medical examination is not usually an issue.

Where the parties intend to instruct competing experts, the defendant needs to request the claimant's consent to the medical examination by the defendant's experts. In practice, the defendant will usually provide a written consent form to be signed by the claimant for the release of the claimant's medical records at the same time. If the claimant fails to consent to the proposed medical examination, the court will not make a direct order requiring the claimant to comply. This is because any medical examination involves at least a technical assault on the patient, which is an infringement of the fundamental human right to liberty and security of person, and it is seen to be wrong to order a person to consent to an assault with the sanction of committal to prison in default. Instead, where a claimant refuses a reasonable request for a medical examination the court will make an order imposing a stay on the claim until the claimant submits to the examination (*Edmeades v Thames Board Mills Ltd* [1969] 2 QB 67). Where the medical examination relates to only part of a claim, it is likely that a limited stay will be imposed on the relevant issues only (*James v Baily Gibson and Co.* [2002] EWCA Civ 1690, LTL 30/10/2002).

In *Edmeades v Thames Board Mills Ltd* it was held that a stay will be imposed if it is just and reasonable in the circumstances. In *Starr v National Coal Board* [1977] 1 WLR 63 Scarman LJ said this has two elements:

(a) the defendant's request for the medical examination must be reasonable; and
(b) the claimant's refusal to consent to the examination, or consent subject to conditions, must be such as to prevent the just determination of the claim.

In complex claims it may be reasonable for the defendant to request the claimant to consent to examinations by experts in a number of different fields of medical science, and to consent to examinations for initial and updating reports.

A claimant is not allowed to consent to an examination by anyone other than certain experts (or even anyone other than a single named expert). The reason is that the claimant can go to anyone in the medical profession for a report, and the same freedom has to be allowed to the defendant (*Starr v National Coal Board* [1977] 1 WLR 63). Sometimes the claimant will refuse to consent because the proposed examination is particularly invasive, or even carries a risk of further injury. In these cases the court has to balance the need for the examination and proposed tests, for the proper preparation of the defendant's case, against the reasonableness of the claimant's objections based on the degree of pain, risk to health and inconvenience (*Prescott v Bulldog Tools Ltd* [1981] 3 All ER 869; see also *Aspinall v Sterling Mansell Ltd* [1981] 3 All ER 866).

Stays may also be imposed against defendants (*Cosgrove v Baker* (unreported) 14 December 1979); *Lacey v Harrison* [1993] PIQR P10) and in non-personal injuries claims (*Jackson v Mirror Group Newspapers Ltd* (1994) *The Times*, 29 March 1994, a libel claim) if the relevant party's medical condition is relevant to an issue in the case.

Conditions imposed by claimants

54.36   Claimants are entitled to require reasonable conditions to be met before consenting to a medical examination. Conditions usually regarded as reasonable include:

(a) that the defendant pays any loss of earnings incurred by the claimant in attending;
(b) that the defendant pays any out-of-pocket expenses incurred in attending;
(c) that the expert will not discuss or question the claimant about the accident except so far as is necessary for the purpose of compiling the medical report;
(d) that a friend, relative or legal representative attends with the claimant for moral support, unless that person will interfere with the examination (such as may happen in psychiatric consultations: *Whitehead v Avon County Council* (1995) 29 BMLR 152).

Disclosure of defendant's report

It has been held that it is never reasonable to insist that the defendant must disclose the report compiled after the examination as a condition of consenting to an examination (*Megarity v D. J. Ryan and Sons Ltd* [1980] 1 WLR 1237). This is because the report is protected by legal professional privilege, and would give the claimant an advantage not enjoyed by the defendant. An exception was recognised in *Hookham v Wiggins Teape Fine Papers Ltd* [1995] PIQR P392 where past delay in the claim or the proximity of the trial may justify such a condition in the particular circumstances. In *Beck v Ministry of Defence* [2003] EWCA Civ 1043, [2005] 1 WLR 2206, the defendant was required to disclose a copy of the first report it had commissioned on the claimant's injuries as a condition for being given permission to instruct a second expert.

54.37

CROSS-EXAMINATION

The substance of the instructions sent to an expert must be stated in his or her report (**CPR, r. 35.10(3)**; see **54.29**) and are not privileged against disclosure, but the court will not either order disclosure of any specific document or permit any questioning in court, other than by the party who instructed the expert, unless it is satisfied that there are reasonable grounds to consider the statement of instructions to be inaccurate or incomplete (**r. 35.10(4)**). If the court is so satisfied, it will permit cross-examination of the expert on the contents of his or her instructions where it appears to the court that it is in the interests of justice to do so (**PD 35, para. 5**).

54.38

In the normal course of things, a jointly instructed expert's report should be the evidence in the case on the issues covered by that report. Normally there should be no need for such a report to be amplified or tested by cross-examination (*Peet v Mid-Kent Healthcare Trust* [2001] EWCA Civ 1703, [2002] 1 WLR 210). It might be appropriate to order attendance for cross-examination where a single joint expert delivers his report shortly before the trial, or where the expert has not considered all the written questions put to him (*Coopers Payen Ltd v Southampton Container Terminal Ltd* [2003] EWCA Civ 1223, [2004] 1 Lloyd's Rep 331 at [41]). If, exceptionally, the expert is called at trial, any cross-examination should be restricted as far as possible (*Peet v Mid-Kent Healthcare Trust*).

CONCURRENT EVIDENCE ('HOT-TUBBING')

Directions may be made that some or all of the experts from like disciplines must give their evidence concurrently (**PD 35, para. 11.1**). Concurrent evidence directions can be made at any time, but typically at the first case management conference. Under this procedure, instead of going into the witness box at the trial on their own and being examined in chief, cross-examined and re-examined like other witnesses, the experts in a discipline will all give evidence together from the witness box or witness table.

54.39

Where a direction for concurrent evidence has been made the court may direct that the parties agree an agenda of points to be discussed by the experts at trial (**para. 11.2**). This is usually based upon the areas of disagreement identified in the experts' joint statement made pursuant to **CPR, r. 35.12** (see **54.31**).

At the trial, when the time comes for the experts to give their evidence, each of the relevant experts will take the oath or affirm (**para. 11.3**). Typically, unless the court orders otherwise, the judge will initiate the discussion by asking the experts, in turn, for their views on the items on the agenda (**para. 11.4(1)**). Once an expert has expressed a view the judge may ask questions about it. At one or more appropriate stages when questioning a

Commentary

particular expert, the judge may invite the other experts to comment or to ask that expert's own questions of the first expert. The parties' representatives may then question the experts (**para. 11.4(2)**). While such questioning may be designed to test the correctness of an expert's view, or seek clarification of it, it should not cover ground which has been fully explored already. In general a full cross-examination or re-examination is neither necessary nor appropriate. After questioning by counsel, the judge may summarise the experts' different positions on the issue and ask them to confirm or correct that summary (**para. 11.4(3)**).

ASSESSORS

54.40 CPR, r. 35.15, applies where the court appoints one or more persons as assessors under the Senior Courts Act 1981, s. 70, or the County Courts Act 1984, s. 63. The jurisdiction to sit with assessors extends to judicial review proceedings (*T-Mobile (UK) Ltd v Office of Communications* [2008] EWCA Civ 1373, [2009] 1 WLR 1565 at [35]). An assessor is someone who assists the court in dealing with a matter within his or her skill and expertise and who generally sits with the judge. Factors to be taken into account when considering whether to appoint an assessor include the complexity of the arguments and the amount in issue (*Agrimex Ltd v Tradigrain SA* [2003] EWHC 1656 (Comm), [2003] 2 Lloyd's Rep 537). While it is appropriate to appoint assessors in technically complex or detailed cases, such as nautical collision claims, the Technology and Construction Court did not need the assistance of an assessor in a compulsory purchase quantum case involving consideration of the relevant government department's Compensation Code (*Bacombe Group plc v London Development Agency* [2008] EWHC 1392 (TCC), LTL 3/7/2008).

Under **CPR, r. 35.15(3)**, an assessor shall take such part in the proceedings as the court may direct and, in particular, the court may direct the assessor to prepare a report for the court on any matter at issue in the proceedings and direct the assessor to attend the whole or any part of the trial to advise the court on any such matter. Where the assessor prepares the report for the court before the commencement of the trial, the court will send a copy to each of the parties enabling the parties to use the report at trial, although they are not permitted to question or cross-examine the assessor (**PD 35, para. 10.4**). To comply with the European Convention on Human Rights, **art. 6(1)**, in the **Human Rights Act 1998, sch. 1**, it is permissible for the judge to put questions to an assessor after discussion with counsel. The answers should then be disclosed to counsel, either orally or in writing, who are then permitted to make submissions to the judge on whether the advice of the assessor should be followed (*Bow Spring (Owners) v Manzanillo II (Owners)* [2004] EWCA Civ 1007, [2005] 1 WLR 144; *The Global Mariner* [2005] EWHC 380 (Admlty), [2005] 2 All ER (Comm) 389 at [14]).

Where it is intended to appoint an assessor to assist the court, at least 21 days before the appointment, the court will notify each party in writing of the name of the proposed assessor, of the matter in respect of which his or her assistance is sought and the qualifications of the assessor to give that assistance (**PD 35, para. 10.1**). An objection by a party to the appointment of an assessor, either on personal grounds or in relation to his or her qualifications, must be made in writing and filed with the court within seven days of receipt of the notification (**paras 10.2 and 10.3**). The court will consider any objections when deciding whether or not to make the appointment (**para. 10.3**).

Any consultation between assessors and the court must take place openly as part of the assembling of the evidence, and the parties are entitled to an opportunity to address the court on the assessor's advice (*Bow Spring (Owners) v Manzanillo II (Owners)*). The judge is not bound to accept the advice received from assessors (*Commissioners of the Admiralty v SS Ausonia (Owners)* (1920) 2 Ll L Rep 123 at p. 124).

The remuneration to be paid to the assessor for his or her services will be determined by the court and forms part of the costs of the proceedings (**CPR, r. 35.15(5)**). The court may order any party to deposit in the court office a specified sum in respect of the assessor's fees and, where it does so, the assessor will not be asked to act until the sum has been deposited (**r. 35.15(6)**), except in cases where the remuneration of the assessor is to be paid out of money provided by Parliament (**r. 35.15(7)**).

Commentary

PART K

Discontinuance and Stays

Chapter 55   Discontinuance

INTRODUCTION

From time to time a claimant may think better of having commenced proceedings, and will   **55.1**
want to discontinue without incurring all the costs of litigating to trial. It may be, for example, that after seeing the evidence available to the defendant it will be clear that the claim has limited prospects of success. A claimant in this situation may be able to negotiate a compromise with the defendant, who may agree terms which are not too onerous on the claimant. Before the CPR, a claimant could simply allow the case to go to sleep. Under the CPR it is very much more difficult to allow a case simply to go to sleep, given the active case management regime now in place. In most situations, a claimant who decides not to proceed should therefore now either seek to come to an accommodation with the defendant, or should discontinue. Any other course will almost certainly result in increased costs liabilities, particularly if there is a contested hearing.

A claimant who wishes to discontinue proceedings must file a notice of discontinuance. The general rule is that once a claim is discontinued, the claimant has to pay the defendant's costs of the claim.

DISTINCTION BETWEEN DISCONTINUING
AND ABANDONING

Discontinuance as a concept is restricted to causes of action. If a single cause of action gives   **55.2**
rise to more than one remedy (or more than one head of damages), some of the remedies or heads of damage may be abandoned without producing a formal discontinuance (**CPR, r. 38.1(2)**). A claimant abandoning some of the relief claimed simply has to comply with the rules on amendment (see **chapter 31**). The result is that if some of the relief claimed is abandoned, the claimant will almost certainly have to pay the costs of and arising from the amendments to the statements of case, but will incur no wider liability in relation to the costs of the claim.

WHAT MAY BE DISCONTINUED

A claimant may discontinue: **55.3**

(a) the whole claim (**CPR, r. 38.1(1)**); or
(b) part of the claim (i.e. some of the causes of action pleaded: **r. 38.1(1)**); and
(c) against all of the defendants (**r. 38.2(3)**); or
(d) against some of the defendants (**r. 38.2(3)**).

Arbitration claims under **Part 62** (see **chapter 72**) are also subject to the rules on discontinuance in **Part 38** (*Sheltam Rail Co. (Pty) Ltd v Mirambo Holdings Ltd* [2008] EWHC 829 (Comm), [2009] Bus LR 302).

PERMISSION TO DISCONTINUE

55.4   Generally, a claimant has the right to discontinue without seeking permission first (**CPR, r. 38.2(1)**). However, in some circumstances permission is required. These are:

(a) If an interim injunction has been granted in relation to the claim being discontinued, permission has to be sought from the court (**r. 38.2(2)(a)**).

(b) If any party has given an undertaking to the court in relation to the claim being discontinued, permission has to be sought from the court (**r. 38.2(2)(a)**).

(c) If the claimant has received an interim payment (whether by agreement or pursuant to a court order) in relation to the claim being discontinued, permission must be sought from the court or consent must be given in writing by the defendant (**r. 38.2(2)(b)**).

(d) Where there is more than one claimant, the claimant wishing to discontinue must either obtain permission to discontinue from the court, or must obtain consent in writing from all the other claimants (**r. 38.2(2)(c)**). In group litigation, permission to discontinue is not required where the claim form of the claimant who is seeking to discontinue only has a single named claimant (*Sayers v Smithkline Beecham plc* [2004] EWHC 1899 (QB), [2005] PIQR P8).

(e) Where a claim is brought by a person under a disability, and the discontinuance of the claim amounts to a settlement or a compromise, approval of the court is required under **r. 21.10** (see **14.22** and *Sayers v Smithkline Beecham plc*).

If consent is required, the signed consent(s) must be obtained before the claimant files the notice of discontinuance. If the court's permission has to be sought, a separate application for permission must be issued, and the claimant is only allowed to file the notice of discontinuance after the order granting permission is made. There may be greater reluctance to give permission to discontinue in probate claims (*Green v Briscoe* (2005) LTL 9/5/2005).

PROCEDURE FOR DISCONTINUING

55.5   A claimant discontinues all or part of the claim by filing a notice of discontinuance (form N279) with the court, and serving a copy on all other parties. Regarding contents:

(a) The notice of discontinuance that is filed at court must state that copies have been served on all other parties (**CPR, r. 38.3(2)**).

(b) In cases where the consent of another party is required, all copies of the notice of discontinuance must have copies of the consent annexed (**r. 38.3(3)**).

(c) In cases where there is more than one defendant, the notice of discontinuance must identify the defendants against whom the claim is being discontinued (**r. 38.3(4)**).

SETTING ASIDE NOTICE OF DISCONTINUANCE

55.6   A defendant may apply for an order setting aside a notice of discontinuance served without consent or permission, provided the application is made within 28 days of the notice (**CPR, r. 38.4**). A notice of discontinuance was set aside in *Fakih Brothers v A. P. Moller (Copenhagen) Ltd* [1994] 1 Lloyd's Rep 103, where it was served to avoid the imposition of an onerous term in a consent order, and in *Ernst and Young v Butte Mining plc* [1996] 1 WLR 1605, where it was served in order to pre-empt the effective service of a counterclaim.

EFFECT OF DISCONTINUANCE

Notice of discontinuance takes effect, and brings the proceedings to an end as against each **55.7** defendant, on the date it is served upon that defendant. This of course is subject to any right to apply to set aside the notice, and does not affect the court's power to deal with costs (**CPR, r. 38.5**).

Costs after discontinuing

Unless the court orders otherwise, the claimant is liable for the defendant's costs up to the date **55.8** of service of the notice of discontinuance (**CPR, r. 38.6(1)**). A costs liability taking effect by virtue of **r. 38.6(1)** is for costs on the standard basis. Alternatively, it is open to a defendant to seek an order for costs to be payable on the indemnity basis (*Jarvis plc v PricewaterhouseCoopers* [2000] 2 BCLC 368). The power to make some other order is exercised applying the factors set out in **r. 44.2** (see **68.5**) (*Longstaff International Ltd v Evans* [2005] EWHC 4 (Ch), LTL 26/1/2005). Unreasonably continuing a claim after it has become clear it is doomed to failure may justify an order for indemnity-basis costs from that date (*Wates Construction Ltd v HGP Greentree Allchurch Evans Ltd* [2005] EWHC 2174 (TCC), LTL 4/11/2005; and see **68.21**).

It may be appropriate to depart from the usual rule in favour of the claimant where there has been a change of circumstances since proceedings were issued making it uneconomic to continue (*Re Walker Wingsail Systems plc* [2005] EWCA Civ 247, [2006] 1 WLR 2194). The court can reverse the usual costs rule on a discontinuance where the claimant has in effect obtained all the relief sought in the proceedings (*Amoco (UK) Exploration Co. v British American Offshore Ltd* (2000) LTL 13/12/2000). On the facts of *Dooley v Parker* [2002] EWCA Civ 1188, it was ordered, following a discontinuance by the claimant, that the justice of the matter was best served by making no order as to costs up to service of the notice of discontinuance, and to award the claimant costs thereafter. Where notice of discontinuance is served primarily to avoid the costs of trial, there is no material to justify departing from the usual costs rule in **r. 38.6** (*Messih v McMillan Williams* [2010] EWCA Civ 844, LTL 22/7/2010). The correct approach is to consider all the matters relied upon as justifying departing from **r. 38.6**, and then to decide whether they are sufficient for that purpose.

Where a claim becomes academic through some act on the part of the defendant or a non-party, the court should apply the general discretionary factors set out in **r. 44.2**, on the question of costs, rather than **r. 38.6** (*Dhillon v Siddiqui* [2010] EWHC 1400 (Ch), LTL 17/6/2010). The fall-back order where an appeal from an Immigration Appeal Tribunal is discontinued before the hearing with the Secretary of State consenting to a rehearing of the decision being appealed is to make no order as to costs (*Sengoz v Secretary of State for the Home Department* [2001] EWCA Civ 1135, *The Times*, 13 August 2001). Patent claims are governed by the usual principles in **r. 38.6**, and what used to be known as *Earth Closet* orders (from *Baird v Moule's Patent Earth Closet Co. Ltd* (1881) 17 ChD 139) should no longer be made (*Fresenius Kabi Deutschland GmbH v Carefusion 303 Inc.* [2011] EWCA Civ 1288, [2012] 1 All ER 794). There are no costs consequences regarding discontinued small claims track cases (**r. 38.6(3)**).

If only part of the claim is discontinued, the claimant's liability is limited to the costs of the part of the claim that has been discontinued. Usually the claimant does not have to pay the defendant's costs following a partial discontinuance until the conclusion of the action. However, the court may in its discretion order these costs to be paid immediately, either after they have been agreed between the parties or after they have been assessed by the court (**r. 38.6(2)**). Where the claimant is required to pay the costs of the discontinued part of the claim straight away, the liability to do so arises 14 days after the relevant costs are agreed or assessed by the court. Failure to pay gives grounds for the court imposing a stay on the remainder of the proceedings until the costs are paid (**r. 38.8**).

Commentary

SUBSEQUENT PROCEEDINGS

55.9   A claimant who discontinues after a defence has been filed is not allowed to commence new proceedings against the same defendant arising out of the same or substantially the same facts as the original claim, unless the court first gives permission for the second claim to be issued (CPR, r. 38.7). If permission is granted, the court will normally give directions regarding issuing the substantive second claim (r. 25.2(3)).

Chapter 56   Stays

INTRODUCTION

By **CPR, r. 3.1(2)(f)**, the court has a general case management power to stay the whole or any **56.1**
part of any proceedings or judgment either generally or until a specified date or event. This
rule derives from the Senior Courts Act 1981, s. 49(3), which provides that nothing in the Act
affects the power of the High Court and Court of Appeal to stay proceedings where the court
thinks fit to do so, either of its own motion or on the application of any person, whether or
not a party to the proceedings. A stay may apply to only part of the proceedings, and where
this applies obviously the remaining parts of the proceedings will continue. A stay may be
lifted on proper grounds being shown (*Cooper v Williams* [1963] 2 QB 567).

The glossary to the CPR says a 'stay' imposes a halt on proceedings, apart from taking any
steps allowed by the CPR or the terms of the stay. Proceedings can be continued if the stay is
lifted. This is quite important, because in times past (particularly in the late nineteenth century) the courts were in the habit of ordering stays when nowadays they would strike out or
dismiss the proceedings. Old cases used to speak of absolute stays (meaning orders striking out
proceedings) and conditional stays (having the modern meaning of stays). This old misuse of
the word 'stay' should be a thing of the past.

Stays may be imposed in a great variety of different circumstances, and for widely varying
reasons.

STAY ON SETTLEMENT

For the stay of a claim when a Part 36 offer is accepted see 66.33. **56.2**
Ordinary consent orders following a compromise of a claim frequently provide for the stay of
the proceedings (see *Rofa Sport Management AG v DHL International (UK) Ltd* [1989] 1 WLR 902).
Similarly, a Tomlin order (see **63.16**) provides for the stay of the proceedings on the terms set
out in a schedule to the order, with liberty to apply.

STAYS FOR LITIGATION REASONS

There may be reasons relating to the efficient progress of the proceedings which make grant- **56.3**
ing a stay desirable. Examples are:

(a) Where there is no issue on liability in a personal injury case, but a clear prognosis will not
be possible for some time. This possibility is referred to in **PD 51A, para. 19(3)(b)**, where
the machinery referred to is an adjournment to determine prognosis.

Commentary

(g) A stay may be imposed to protect Parliamentary privilege and immunities (*R v Mote* [2007] EWCA Crim 3131, [2008] Crim LR 793, where the stay was lifted in respect of a prosecution of an MEP following a resolution by the European Parliament waiving the immunity).

EFFECT OF A STAY

56.6   While a stay is in place the proceedings remain alive, but no further steps may be taken to progress the claim other than applying to lift the stay. For some purposes time will continue to run during a stay, such as the limited period of validity for service of an originating process (*Aldridge v Edwards* [2000] CPLR 349). There is no need to apply to lift the stay imposed by a Tomlin order before making an application for a wasted costs order (*Wagstaff v Colls* [2003] EWCA Civ 469, [2003] PNLR 551). A stay on a judgment prevents any steps being taken to enforce it, until the stay is lifted.

PART L

Trial

Chapter 57   Witness Summonses

NATURE OF WITNESS SUMMONSES

A witness summons is a document issued by the court requiring a witness to attend court to **57.1**
give evidence or produce documents to the court (**CPR, r. 34.2(1)**). A witness summons must
be in form N20 (**r. 34.2(2)**) and there must be a separate witness summons for each witness
required to attend court (**r. 34.2(3)**). Two copies of the witness summons should be filed with
the court for sealing, one of which will be retained on the court file (**PD 34A, para. 1.2**).
A witness summons may, by **CPR, r. 34.2(4)**, require a witness to produce documents to the
court either:

(a) on the date fixed for a hearing; or
(b) on such date as the court may direct.

The only documents that a summons under **Part 34** can require a person to produce before a
hearing are documents which that person could be required to produce at the hearing
(**r. 34.2(5)**). This means that they must be relevant to the issues and otherwise admissible in
evidence at trial, and so is narrower than the scope of standard disclosure. **Rule 34.2(4)** may
be considered as an alternative to non-party disclosure. It also incorporates the device used by
the court in *Khanna v Lovell White Durrant* [1995] 1 WLR 121, in which the court invented the
concept of the 'production appointment' for witnesses to attend under summons to bring
documents to a hearing earlier than the trial, where, for example, the documents were required
by one or other party to prepare the case properly for trial and production on the morning of
the trial would have been insufficient.

ISSUE OF A WITNESS SUMMONS

A witness summons is issued on the date entered on the summons by the court (**CPR,** **57.2**
r. 34.3(1)). It must be issued by (**r. 34.3(3)**):

(a) the court where the case is proceeding; or
(b) the court where the hearing in question will be held.

The procedure is a simple one in which the party wishing to obtain a witness summons
attends at court with the completed summons in form N20, which the court then seals for
service. Where the witness summons is for the witness to attend at a trial, there is no requirement to obtain the court's permission, but permission must be obtained from the court under
r. 34.3(2) where a party wishes:

(a) to have a summons issued less than seven days before the date of the trial;
(b) to have a summons issued for a witness to attend court to give evidence or to produce
    documents on any date except the date fixed for trial; or

(c) to have a summons issued for a witness to attend court to give evidence or to produce documents at any hearing except the trial.

Thus the permission of the court is necessary where the witness summons is to be issued very close to the date of the trial, where a witness summons is required for attendance at an interim hearing or where a witness is required to attend to give oral evidence or produce documents at such a hearing. Applications for permission are made without notice to a District Judge or Master. There is no provision in **Part 34** for evidence in support of such applications and therefore it would seem sufficient to indicate orally, at the hearing of the application, the purpose for which the witness summons is sought.

Witness summons in aid of inferior court or tribunal

57.3   The High Court and the County Court have a discretion to issue a witness summons in aid of any court or tribunal that does not have power to issue a witness summons in relation to proceedings before it (**CPR, r. 34.4(1)**). For the applicable principles see *Inner West London Assistant Deputy Coroner v Channel 4 Television Corporation* [2007] EWHC 2513 (QB), [2008] 1 WLR 945. The court which issued a witness summons under this rule may set it aside (**r. 34.4(2)**). Such an application will be heard (**PD 34A, para. 2.3**):

(a) in the High Court by a Master at the Royal Courts of Justice or by a District Judge in a District Registry, and

(b) in the County Court by a District Judge.

Unless the court directs otherwise, the applicant on the application to set aside must give no less than two days' notice of the application to the party that issued the witness summons. The application to set aside will normally be dealt with at a hearing (**PD 34A, para. 2.4**).

SERVICE OF WITNESS SUMMONS

Time for serving a witness summons

57.4   The general rule, as set out in **CPR, r. 34.5(1)**, is that a witness summons is binding if it is served at least seven days before the date on which the witness is required to attend before the court or tribunal. However, the court has a discretion to direct that the witness summons is binding even though it will be served less than seven days before that date (**r. 34.5(2)**). **Rule 34.5(3)** provides that a witness summons which is served in accordance with **r. 34.5**, and requires the witness to attend court to give evidence, is binding until the conclusion of the hearing at which the attendance of the witness is required.

Service by the court or the party

57.5   A witness summons is served by the court unless it is indicated in writing, at the time of asking the court to issue the summons, that the party on whose behalf it is issued will serve it.

The usual practice is for the court to serve a witness summons either by post or by County Court Bailiff. Practitioners who wish to ensure certainty and expeditious service are likely to prefer to undertake service themselves.

Witness expenses

57.6   At the time of service of a witness summons the witness must be offered or paid a sum reasonably sufficient to cover his or her expenses in travelling to and from the court and compensation for loss of time (**CPR, r. 34.7**). The amount to be paid as compensation for loss of time is to be based on the sums payable to witnesses in the Crown Court (**PD 34A, paras 3.1 to 3.3**). These are determined by the Lord Chancellor under the Costs in Criminal Cases (General) Regulations 1986 (SI 1986/1335), reg. 17.

A witness required to produce documents under a witness summons will only be paid conduct money, so will not be compensated for the expense of producing the documents, unlike the position on an application for non-party disclosure under **CPR, rr. 31.17** and **48.1(2)** (see *Re Howglen Ltd* [2001] 1 All ER 376 at p. 384 and **50.96**). However, in *Individual Homes Ltd v Macbream Investments Ltd* (2002) *The Times,* 14 November 2002, an order was made joining the witness as a party for the purpose of making a costs order in its favour for complying with a witness summons to produce documents.

If the witness summons is to be served by the court, the sum for expenses must be deposited in the court office (**CPR, r. 34.6(2)**). If the witness summons is to be served by the party issuing it, the sum must be offered to the witness when the summons is served (**PD 34A, para. 3.4**).

FAILURE TO OBEY A WITNESS SUMMONS

County Court

A person who refuses or neglects, without sufficient cause, to appear, or produce documents, as required by a witness summons issued by the County Court may be fined up to £1,000 (County Courts Act 1984, s. 55(1) and (2)). A fine may also be imposed if a summoned witness attends court but refuses to be sworn or give evidence (s. 55(1)). A fine cannot be imposed unless witness expenses (see **57.6**) were paid or tendered at the time of serving the summons (s. 55(3)). A judge imposing a fine may, at his or her discretion, direct that all or part of it (after deducting costs) is to be applied to indemnifying the party injured by the refusal or neglect (s. 55(4)). These are statutory versions of the inherent powers of the High Court (see **57.8**), but the County Court has no power to issue a bench warrant for the arrest of a witness.

57.7

The power to impose a fine under s. 55 may be exercised by a Circuit Judge, District Judge, Assistant District Judge or Deputy District Judge (s. 55(1) and (4A)).

Before or after imposing a fine under s. 55 for disobeying a witness summons or refusing to give evidence or to be sworn, the court may give notice to the witness under **CPR, r. 81.36**. That notice must state that if the witness can demonstrate any reason why the fine should not, or should not have been, imposed, that person may give evidence by witness statement, affidavit or otherwise on the date specified in the notice (**r. 81.36(2)**). Although the rule is expressed to confer a discretion on the judge, it is clear that, in the light of the European Convention on Human Rights, **art. 6**, in the **Human Rights Act 1998, sch. 1**, a fine should not be imposed without giving the offender an opportunity of submitting a defence. A witness who attends the trial but refuses to give evidence may give an explanation there and then. Otherwise the judge should direct the court officer to issue a notice naming a day on which cause is to be shown by witness statement, affidavit or otherwise. Repayment may be ordered of part or all of any fine already paid if, on considering the cause shown, the judge decides that the fine should have been of a lesser amount, not imposed at all or not enforced.

If a fine imposed for failure to obey a witness summons is not paid, the court must report the matter to the Circuit Judge, who may, under the County Courts Act 1984, s. 129, order the fine to be enforced by any method available for the enforcement of a County Court judgment debt or a magistrates' court fine.

High Court

In the High Court failure to obey a witness summons is contempt of court (*Wyat v Wingford* (1729) 2 Ld Raym 1528), as is appearing in response to a summons but refusing to be sworn or to answer questions or to produce documents (*R v Daye* [1908] 2 KB 333). The procedure to be followed is laid down in **CPR, Part 81**, see **chapter 81**. No penalty may be imposed unless witness expenses (see **57.6**) were paid or tendered with the summons (*Fuller v Prentice* (1788) 1

57.8

H Bl 49; *Re Working Men's Mutual Society* (1882) 21 ChD 831). If disobedience was not wilful, no penalty will be imposed (*Horne v Smith* (1815) 6 Taunt 10; *Scholes v Hilton* (1842) 10 M & W 15) or enforcement of a penalty will be stayed (*R v Daye*). A person who has disobeyed a witness summons may be sued for damages by the party who obtained the summons, provided actual loss is proved (*Crewe v Field* (1896) 12 TLR 405; *Roberts v J. and F. Stone Lighting and Radio Ltd* (1945) 172 LT 240).

The High Court has an inherent power to issue a bench warrant for the arrest of a person required as a witness so as to secure his or her attendance in court (*Astrovlanis Compania Naviera SA v Linard (No. 2)* [1972] 2 Lloyd's Rep 187; *Zakharov v White* [2003] EWHC 2463 (Ch), *The Times*, 13 November 2003).

SETTING ASIDE OR VARYING A WITNESS SUMMONS

57.9 Under **CPR, r. 34.3(4)**, the court may set aside or vary a witness summons. This may be on the application of any party or by the witness. The presumption is that the interests of justice are best served by the grant of a witness summons (*Tilbury Consulting Ltd v Gittins* [2004] STC (SCD) 1). A witness summons may be set aside if the witness has no connection with the claim, or where the witness summons is used for tactical purposes, as was the case in *Harrison v Bloom Camillin* (1999) *The Independent*, 28 June 1999, in which it was found that the defendants were attempting to conduct a fishing expedition. A witness summons to produce documents was set aside in *Tajik Aluminium Plant v Hydro Aluminium AS* [2005] EWCA Civ 1218, [2006] 1 WLR 767, on the ground that it did not identify the documents required with sufficient certainty. The documents must be sufficiently described so as to leave no doubt in the mind of the witness what he is required to produce. It is not necessary to describe documents individually. A compendious description will suffice provided it enables the witness to know specifically what is covered. In *Peters v Skylet Andrew* [2009] EWHC 1511 (QB), LTL 2/7/2009, the court refused to set aside a witness summons to produce certain telephone accounts which were relevant to the dispute, as there was no other obvious way of obtaining the information.

Chapter 58   Giving Evidence without Attending Court

INTRODUCTION

At both the allocation and pre-trial checklist stages, the court will timetable certain events in **58.1** order to progress a case to trial, and at the pre-trial checklist stage in particular, the trial will be fixed for a date or period of time when it is thought that all the witnesses will be able to attend to give evidence. Prudent practitioners will have asked clients and witnesses to identify dates to avoid but it sometimes happens that, despite planning in advance, a witness is unable, physically, to attend court. On both the fast track and multi-track, the postponement of a trial is considered as an order of last resort (**PD 28, para. 5.4(6); PD 29, para. 7.4(6)**). Therefore, where a witness does have difficulties in attending court to give evidence in person, alternative means of giving evidence should be considered, in order that the trial is not postponed.

It may also be the case that in the period leading up to the trial, a hearing is necessary in respect of an interim remedy, for which a crucial witness is unable or refuses to provide a witness statement, without which the party wishing to make the application is unable to proceed.

One way of overcoming these difficulties is to take the witness's evidence by deposition.

DEPOSITIONS

CPR, r. 34.8, provides that a party to a claim may apply for an order for a person to be examined before the trial of the claim or an interim hearing takes place. The person from whom evidence is to be obtained is referred to as a deponent and the evidence itself is referred to as a deposition.

An order under **r. 34.8** is for the deponent to be examined on oath before either a judge, an examiner of the court or such other person as the court appoints (**r. 34.8(3)**). The order may also require the production of any document which the court considers is necessary for the purposes of the examination (**r. 34.8(4)**). Persons appointed by the Lord Chancellor as examiners of the court must be barristers or solicitor-advocates who have been practising for a period of at least three years (**r. 34.15**).

Witness expenses must be offered or paid when an order for examination is served (**r. 34.8(6)**) just as when a witness summons is served (see 57.6).

An order for a deposition to be taken may also order the party who obtained the order to serve a witness statement or witness summary in relation to the evidence to be given by the person to be examined (**r. 34.8(7)**).

The party who obtains an order for the examination of a deponent before an examiner of the court must (**PD 34A, para. 4.2**):

(a) apply to the Foreign Process Section of the Masters' Secretary's Department at the Royal Courts of Justice for the allocation of an examiner; and

(b) provide the allocated examiner with copies of all documents in the proceedings necessary to inform the examiner of the issues.

Conduct of examination

58.3   CPR, **r. 34.9**, provides details of the procedure to be adopted in conducting the examination of a deponent. Subject to any directions contained in the order for examination, the examination must be conducted in the same way as if the witness were giving evidence at a trial (**r. 34.9(1)**). If all the parties are present, the examiner may conduct the examination of a person not named in the order for examination if the parties and the person to be examined consent (**r. 34.9(2)**). Therefore, as all parties are present, they effectively have the right to ask questions under the usual rules of evidence, albeit via the examiner. If the examiner considers it appropriate, he or she may conduct the examination in private (**r. 34.9(3)**).

In ensuring that the deponent's evidence is recorded in full, as required by **r. 34.9(4)**, the court or the examiner may permit it to be recorded on audiotape or videotape, but the deposition must always be recorded in writing by the examiner or by a competent shorthand writer or stenographer (**PD 34A, para. 4.3**). If the deposition is not recorded verbatim, it must contain, as nearly as may be, the statement of the deponent; the examiner may record word for word any particular questions and answers, which appear to him or her to have special importance (**PD 34A, para. 4.4**).

PD 34A, para. 4.12, provides that once an examination is completed the examiner must sign the deposition, both the examiner and the deponent must initial any amendments to it, and it must be endorsed by the examiner with:

(a) a statement of the time occupied by the examination, and

(b) a record of any refusal by the deponent to sign the deposition and of his or her reasons for not doing so.

The examiner must send a copy of the deposition to the person who obtained the order for the examination of the witness, and to the court where the case is proceeding, for filing on the court file (**CPR, r. 34.9(5); PD 34A, para. 4.12(4)**). The party who obtained the order must then send each of the other parties a copy of the deposition received from the examiner (**CPR, r. 34.9(6)**).

Enforcing attendance for examination

58.4   If a person served with an order to attend before an examiner fails to attend or refuses to be sworn for the purpose of the examination or to answer any lawful question or produce any document at the examination, a certificate of that failure or refusal, signed by the examiner, must be filed by the party requiring the deposition (**CPR, r. 34.10(1)**).

If a deponent objects to answering any question or where any objection is taken to any question, the examiner must (**PD 34A, para. 4.5**):

(a) record in the deposition or a document attached to it:
   (i) the question,
   (ii) the nature of and grounds of the objection, and
   (iii) any answer given; and

(b) give his or her opinion on the validity of the objection and any question of costs arising from it.

By **CPR, r. 34.10(2)**, on the certificate of failure or refusal being filed, the party requiring the deposition may apply, without notice, to the court for an order requiring the deponent to attend or to be sworn or to answer any question or produce any document, as the case may be. The court may order the person against whom an order is made under this rule to pay any costs resulting from the failure or refusal.

Fees and expenses of examiner

An examiner of the court may charge a fee for an examination (**CPR, r. 34.14(1)**) and is not **58.5** required to send the deposition to the court unless the fee is paid (**r. 34.14(2)**). The examiner's fees and expenses must be paid by the party who obtained the order for examination (**r. 34.14(3)**) and if not paid within a reasonable time, the examiner may report that fact to the court (**r. 34.14(4)**).

The court may order the party who obtained on order for examination to deposit in the court office a specified sum in respect of the examiner's fees, and the examiner will not be asked to act until that sum has been deposited (**r. 34.14(5)**).

Use of deposition at a hearing

A deposition ordered under **CPR, r. 34.8**, may be given in evidence at a hearing unless the **58.6** court orders otherwise. A party intending to put a deposition in evidence at a hearing must serve notice of that intention on every other party at least 21 days before the day fixed for the hearing (**r. 34.11(1)**, **(2)** and **(3)**). Under **r. 34.11(4)** the court may require a deponent to attend the hearing and give evidence orally. Where a deposition is given in evidence at trial, it shall be treated as if it were a witness statement for the purposes of **r. 32.13** (availability of witness statement for inspection) (see **51.24**).

Restrictions on subsequent use of deposition taken for the purpose of any hearing except the trial

CPR, r. 34.12, provides that where the court orders a party to be examined about assets **58.7** (whether the party's or any other person's) for the purpose of any hearing except the trial, the deposition may be used only for the purpose of the proceedings in which the order was made. It may, however, be used for some other purpose:

(a) by the party who was examined;

(b) if the party who was examined agrees; or

(c) if the court gives permission.

Rule 34.12 is expressed to apply only to depositions relating to assets and will therefore be relevant to procedures concerning the enforcement of judgment, freezing orders, search orders and the like.

EXAMINATION OUT OF THE JURISDICTION

Requests to EU Regulation States

Regulation (EC) No. 1206/2001 on cooperation between the courts of Member States in the **58.8** taking of evidence in civil and commercial matters (the 'Taking of Evidence Regulation') provides for taking evidence in one EU State for use in civil proceedings in another EU State. It does not apply to Denmark (art. 1). Each Regulation State has designated courts where evidence can be taken (in England and Wales these are the Royal Courts of Justice and the court centres at Birmingham, Bristol, Cardiff, Manchester and Leeds, see **PD 34A, annex C**). Each Regulation State also has a central body (in England and Wales this is the Senior Master of the Queen's Bench Division, see **PD 34A, para. 9.2**) who is responsible for supplying information, seeking solutions to any difficulties that may arise, and, in exceptional cases, forwarding requests to the competent court.

A party to English civil proceedings seeking to obtain a deposition from a witness in a Regulation State must apply for an order for the issue of a request to a designated court in the Regulation State (**CPR, r. 34.23(2)**). The party seeking the order must undertake to be responsible for the costs sought by the requested court for fees for experts, interpreters and for the court's expenses (**r. 34.23(3)**). Requests for the taking of evidence under the Taking of Evidence Regulation need to be made in the official language of the requested court (art. 5), and must be in form A in the annex to the Taking of Evidence Regulation (art. 4). The request must include the questions to be put to the witness or a statement of the facts about which he is to be examined, and also include any request for the examination to be under oath or affirmation, and any special form to be used (such as recording the evidence in a deposition).

Within seven days of receipt of the request the requested court must send an acknowledgment to the requesting court (art. 7(1)). Where necessary, coercive measures (the local equivalent of a witness summons) may be applied by the requested court to secure the attendance of the witness (art. 13). A request should be executed within 90 days, failing which the requested court should inform the requesting court, stating the reasons for the delay (arts 10 and 15). Representatives of the requesting court should be able to be present when the evidence is taken if this is compatible with the law of the requesting court (art. 12), and representatives of the parties have the right to participate on such conditions as may be laid down by the requested court in accordance with local law (art. 11).

The requesting court can ask for use of communications technology, including videoconferencing and teleconferencing, for the purpose of taking the evidence (art. 10(4)). The party seeking the order must undertake to be responsible for the costs sought by the requested court for any communications technology used (**CPR, r. 34.23(3)**).

It is possible that Regulation (EC) No. 1206/2001 does not apply to applications for disclosure of assets orders against non-parties ancillary to freezing injunctions (see **38.25**). This is because there is no request for the taking of evidence in another member State (*Masri v Consolidated Contractors International (UK) Ltd (No. 4)* [2008] EWCA Civ 876, [2010] 1 AC 90; the decision in the House of Lords on the English law points meant this did not arise for decision on the appeal, [2009] UKHL 43, [2010] 1 AC 90).

Direct taking of evidence in Regulation States

58.9   A party can seek an order pursuant to **CPR, r. 34.23(5)**, for the submission of a request under art. 17 of the Taking of Evidence Regulation for the direct taking of evidence from a witness by the requested court. This involves the requesting court coming to this jurisdiction to take the witness's evidence itself. The party seeking the request must undertake to pay the court's expenses (**CPR, r. 34.23(6)(c)**). Direct taking of evidence is only permitted if it can be performed on a voluntary basis without the need for coercive measures (Taking of Evidence Regulation, art. 17(2)). The request must be in form I of the Taking of Evidence Regulation, and must be accompanied by a translation (**CPR, r. 34.23(6)(b)**). The central body of the requested court may only refuse the direct taking of evidence if the request does not fall within the scope of art. 1, or does not contain all the information required by art. 4, or if the direct taking of evidence is contrary to the fundamental principles of law of the requested State (art. 17(5)).

Non-EU countries: letters of request

CPR, r. 34.13, provides for a deposition to be taken from a witness in Denmark or a non-EU State **58.10** for use in English proceedings. The High Court, not the County Court, may order the issue of a letter of request to the judicial authorities of the country in which the proposed deponent is. All applications are dealt with at the RCJ. A letter of request is a request to a judicial authority to take the evidence of that person, or arrange for it to be taken (**r. 34.13(2)**). The High Court may make an order under this rule in relation to County Court proceedings (**r. 34.13(3)**).

An application for an order to issue a letter of request should be made by application notice in accordance with **Part 23** (**PD 34A, para. 5.2**). The documents listed in **CPR, r. 34.13(6)**, should be filed with the application notice, together with a draft order (**PD 34A, para. 5.3**). A draft letter of request should be in the form set out in **annex A** to **PD 34A**. The application will be dealt with by the Senior Master of the Queen's Bench Division of the High Court who will, if appropriate, sign the letter of request.

In exercising the discretion whether to order the issue of a letter of request the most important factor is the need to achieve justice. Thus, in *Banerji v Devi* (2005) LTL 29/6/2005 it was held to be wrong to refuse an order to take the evidence of a lawyer in India who had witnessed a signature which was alleged to have been forged, as the evidence was crucial on the forgery issue.

If the government of a country allows a person appointed by the High Court to examine a person in that country, the High Court may make an order appointing a special examiner (**CPR, r. 34.13(4)**), who may be the British consul or the consul-general or his or her deputy in the country where the evidence is to be taken (**PD 34A, para. 5.8**). If the country in question is not a party to a civil procedure convention providing for evidence to be taken, it will be necessary to obtain the Secretary of State's consent to the appointment of a consul.

Examination in a foreign country may be on oath or affirmation or in accordance with any procedure permitted in that country (**CPR, r. 34.13(5)**).

The procedural requirements set out in **PD 34A, paras 4.1 to 4.12**, relating to depositions taken in England and Wales for proceedings before courts in England and Wales apply to depositions to be taken abroad (**para. 5.9**).

The Criminal Justice (International Cooperation) Act 1990 empowers a judge in criminal proceedings to issue a letter of request to obtain evidence outside the United Kingdom. Section 3(7) provides that the evidence obtained shall not, without the consent of the appropriate authority, be used for any purpose other than that specified in the request. It was held in *BOC Ltd v Instrument Technology Ltd* [2001] EWCA Civ 854, [2002] QB 537, that, notwithstanding the apparently wide terms of s. 3(7), the provision is implicitly concerned only with the use of the evidence by the prosecuting authority or defendant in the criminal proceedings, and does not restrict use in civil proceedings.

Video links

A further means of presenting oral testimony from a witness who has difficulty in attending a **58.11** hearing or trial is to have the witness's evidence given by video link, or other means which the court may allow under **CPR, r. 32.3**. If a party wishes to use this method, it is advisable to ascertain from the court whether the necessary technical facilities are available.

Where the witness is in an EU State (other than Denmark), taking evidence by video link has to comply with the requirements of Regulation (EC) No. 1206/2001, which is discussed at **58.8**.

In *Polanski v Condé Nast Publications Ltd* [2005] UKHL 10, [2005] 1 WLR 637, the claimant brought libel proceedings in England, and sought permission to give evidence at the trial through a video link. In 1977 he had pleaded guilty in criminal proceedings in California, but had fled from the United States before sentence, and was living in France where he was safe from extradition. If he came to England to give evidence at his libel trial, there was a risk that he would be extradited to face the consequences of his United States conviction. Lord Nicholls of Birkenhead described videoconferencing facilities as being readily available to all litigants, and should not be denied to a party solely on the ground that he was a fugitive from justice. Indeed, the fact that he was a fugitive could be, and on the facts was, a sufficient reason for making a videoconferencing order. Videoconferencing directions were given in *Bank of Credit and Commerce International SA v Rahim* (2005) LTL 30/11/2005, where a witness in Pakistan was said to be in poor health (despite there being no medical evidence to this effect) and feared he might be arrested if he entered the United Kingdom. Other factors were the expense and inconvenience of bringing him from Pakistan, and the fact that as he was simply a witness, being outside the jurisdiction meant he could not be compelled to attend. Consideration should be given to allowing an expert to give evidence by video link where this is appropriate (**PD 35, annex, para. 19.2(c)**).

Detailed guidance on arranging and conducting videoconferencing is contained in **annex 3 to PD 32**. A list of the sites which are available for videoconferencing can be found at http://www.justice.gov.uk/guidance/courts-and-tribunals/courts/video-conferences/index.htm (**PD 32, para. 29.1**).

LETTERS OF REQUEST FROM FOREIGN COURTS

58.12 The statutory provisions on obtaining evidence for foreign courts are in the Evidence (Proceedings in Other Jurisdictions) Act 1975. The rules of court are in **CPR, rr. 34.16** to **34.21**, which should be read in conjunction with **PD 34A, paras 6.1 to 6.8**. To assist courts and practitioners there is an invaluable and very comprehensive *Treasury Solicitor's Guide to Letters of Request* produced by the Treasury Solicitor's Office.

Some letters of request from foreign courts are dealt with by officials and do not require action by legal representatives in England and Wales. Where a foreign court's letter of request cannot be dealt with in this way an application by an agent in England or Wales of a party to the foreign proceedings to give effect to the request should be made to the High Court by Part 8 claim form and should be supported by a witness statement or affidavit exhibiting the documents listed in **PD 34A, para. 6.3**. It may be made without notice being served on any other party (**CPR, r. 34.17(b)**).

A letter of request should be for the purpose of taking evidence on behalf of a foreign court. The High Court will not make an order for the examination of a witness where the letter of request is mainly of an investigatory nature. This is so even if the court is satisfied the witness can give some relevant and admissible evidence, unless it is possible to exclude the impermissible areas of the request without undue difficulty (*Re State of Norway's Application* [1987] QB 433; *United States of America v Philip Morris Inc.* [2003] EWHC 3028 (Comm), LTL 10/12/2003). It is very common for letters of request from the United States, where much wider discovery is permitted than in England and Wales, to be investigatory in nature, and sometimes oppressive. Such requests are often rejected, and have to be resubmitted in a truncated form, resulting in significant delays.

The order for the deponent to attend and be examined together with the evidence upon which the order was made must be served on the deponent (**PD 34A, para. 6.5**). Arrangements for the examination to take place at a specified time and place before an examiner of the court or such other person as the court may appoint shall be made by the applicant for the order and approved by the Senior Master (**CPR, r. 34.18**).

CPR, rr. 34.9 and 34.10, and PD 34A, paras 4.2 to 4.12, apply to examinations requested by foreign courts, except that the examiner must send the deposition to the Senior Master (PD 34A, para. 6.6).

Requests from Regulation States

Requests for the taking of evidence in England and Wales from other Regulation States under **58.13** the Taking of Evidence Regulation must be made to a designated court (the Royal Courts of Justice and the court centres at Birmingham, Bristol, Cardiff, Manchester and Leeds, see CPR, r. 34.24(2) and PD 34A, Annex C). The courts in England and Wales will act on requests in either English or French (PD 34A, para. 11.4), but otherwise translations are required. Once a request is received it is sent to the Treasury Solicitor (PD 34A, para. 11.2) who may apply on form N244 for an order for the evidence to be taken. The application is usually considered without notice (CPR, r. 34.24(2)(c)). The order and evidence in support must be served on the witness (PD 34A, para. 11.5). Arrangements for the taking of the evidence will be made by the Treasury Solicitor and approved by the court (para. 11.6), and the court will provide these details to the parties and the representatives of the foreign court (if they have indicated they wish to be present when the evidence is taken (para. 11.7). The evidence will be taken in accordance with CPR, rr. 34.9, 34.10 and 34.18, for which see 58.3 and 58.12 (r. 34.24(3)).

The examiner will send the deposition to the requested court for transmission to the requesting court, and a copy of the deposition to the Treasury Solicitor (r. 34.24(4)).

Collateral use of depositions

A deposition obtained under CPR, Part 34, is obtained subject to an undertaking, implied at **58.14** common law, not to use it for a collateral purpose without the consent of the witness or the permission of the requesting court. This includes depositions obtained under the Taking of Evidence Regulation. In exercising its discretion whether to grant permission for the collateral use of depositions, the court applies similar principles as apply in relation to the collateral use of disclosed documents (see 50.48). The court also takes into account the purpose of the relevant power to take evidence on deposition. Thus, in *Dendron GmbH v Regents of the University of California* [2004] EWHC 589 (Pat), [2005] 1 WLR 200, permission was granted for the use of depositions obtained under the Taking of Evidence Regulation in related proceedings in other Regulation States, but not for use in the United States.

Injunction restraining deposing witness

An injunction may be granted to restrain a party from deposing a witness for the purpose of **58.15** foreign proceedings (*Benfield Holdings Ltd v Richardson* [2007] EWHC 171 (QB), LTL 1/3/2007). The basis of the jurisdiction to do so is unconscionable conduct. It may be unconscionable where the pursuit of foreign proceedings was vexatious or oppressive or interfered with the due process of the court.

INJUNCTION TO RESTRAIN THREATS TO WITNESS OUTSIDE THE JURISDICTION

In *Masood v Zahoor* [2008] EWHC 328 (Ch), LTL 4/4/2008, an injunction was granted restraining **58.16** the defendant for the duration of the proceedings from threatening a witness with disciplinary proceedings or taking any step in the witness's country which might inhibit or prohibit the witness from giving evidence in the English proceedings.

Commentary

Large plans should be placed in an easily accessible file, which may have to be larger than the normal A4 format for trial bundles (Chancery Guide, para. 21.1). The skeleton argument should refer to a document which must identify for the court all relevant features which appear in the maps, plans, diagrams or photographs to be used at the trial (*Hunte v E. Bottomley and Sons Ltd* [2007] EWCA Civ 1168, [2008] CP Rep 3).

OTHER PROVISIONS DEALING WITH BUNDLES

59.6 Different requirements apply to bundles used in the following situations:

(a) interim applications in non-specialist proceedings (**32.17**);

(b) Chancery Division hearings (see Chancery Guide, paras 15.34 to 15.36 and 21.34 to 21.72);

(c) Admiralty and Commercial Court applications (see Admiralty and Commercial Courts Guide, paras F6 4 to F6.8 and F11 to F13 and app. 10);

(d) Admiralty and Commercial Court case management bundles (see **PD 58, para. 10.8**; Admiralty and Commercial Courts Guide, para. D7 and app. 10);

(e) Admiralty and Commercial Court trials (see Admiralty and Commercial Courts Guide, para. J3 and app. 10);

(f) Patents Court (see Patents Court Guide, section 14 and standard direction 19);

(g) appeals (see **PD 52, paras 5.6, 5.6A, 15.2 to 15.4 and 15.11**); and

(h) judicial review (see 77.47; **PD 52, para. 15.4**; and **PD 54A, paras 5.6 to 5.9**).

USE OF BUNDLES AT THE HEARING

59.7 All the documents in an agreed bundle (see **59.2**) are admissible at the hearing unless the court orders otherwise or if a party gives a written notice objecting to the admissibility of particular documents (**PD 32, para. 27.2**).

In *Gough v Mummery* [2002] EWCA Civ 1573, LTL 4/10/2002, the trial bundle contained one version of a letter from an expert, but a different (and more favourable) version (with the same date) was in the papers of counsel for the side relying on the letter. It was held that the trial judge's decisions to refuse an adjournment to investigate the differences between the two versions of the letter, and to refuse permission to rely on the version in counsel's papers, were discretionary matters and were not plainly wrong.

READING LISTS AND TIME ESTIMATES

59.8 In all Queen's Bench Division and Chancery Division claims where bundles must be lodged, the claimant or applicant must at the same time lodge:

(a) a reading list for the judge who will conduct the hearing;

(b) an estimated length of reading time; and

(c) an estimated length for the hearing.

This must be signed by all the advocates who will appear at the hearing. Each advocate's name, business address and telephone number must appear below his or her signature. In the event of disagreement about any of these matters, separate reading lists and estimates must be signed by the appropriate advocates. See Practice Direction (Royal Courts of Justice: Reading Lists and Time Estimates) [2000] 1 WLR 208.

Chapter 60   Trial by Jury

INTRODUCTION

Almost all civil trials nowadays are tried before a judge sitting alone. The last vestiges of the   **60.1**
former practice of conducting civil trials before juries are statutory rights in the County
Courts Act 1984, s. 66, and the Senior Courts Act 1981, s. 69, for trial by jury in actions in
deceit, malicious prosecution and false imprisonment. Libel and slander were removed from
this list from 1 January 2014 when the Defamation Act 2013, s. 11, was brought into force.
There are exceptions from the statutory rights to jury trial relating to cases involving prolonged examination of documents or accounts, or scientific or local investigations which cannot conveniently be made by a jury. Juries are not looked on favourably for a number of
reasons. These include the fact they do not give reasons for their decisions, the experience that
jury trials tend to take considerably longer than trials before a judge sitting alone, and the risk
that a jury will fail to reach even a majority verdict.

STATUTORY RIGHTS TO TRIAL BY JURY

The Senior Courts Act 1981, s. 69(1), provides: **60.2**

Where, on the application of any party to an action to be tried in the Queen's Bench Division, the court
is satisfied that there is in issue—
(a) a charge of fraud against that party; or
(b) a claim in respect of malicious prosecution or false imprisonment; or
(c) any question or issue of a kind prescribed for the purposes of this paragraph,
the action shall be tried with a jury, unless the court is of opinion that the trial requires any prolonged
examination of documents or accounts or any scientific or local investigation which cannot conveniently
be made with a jury.

The County Courts Act 1984, s. 66(3), is in essentially the same terms for County Court proceedings. The result is that the right to a jury only arises to claims proceeding in the Queen's
Bench Division of the High Court and the County Court, and not while a claim is in the
Chancery Division. Claims may be transferred to the Queen's Bench Division for the purpose
of securing trial by jury, if appropriate. Note also that the right to trial by jury in fraud cases is
only available to the defendant, but that either party has the right to a jury in claims for malicious prosecution and false imprisonment. 'Fraud' for this purpose is limited to claims in deceit
(*Stafford Winfield Cook and Partners Ltd v Winfield* [1981] 1 WLR 458).

In considering whether the proviso to the Senior Courts Act 1981, s. 69(1), applies, according
to *Phillips v Commissioner of Police of the Metropolis* [2003] EWCA Civ 382, [2003] CP Rep 48, three
questions must be asked:

(a) Would there be a prolonged examination of documents or any scientific investigation?
(b) If so, could the examination be conveniently made with a jury?
(c) If not, should the court nevertheless exercise its discretion to order trial with a jury?

In *Oliver v Calderdale Metropolitan Borough Council* (1999) *The Times,* 7 July 1999, it was said as a secondary ground for refusing a jury that a substantial dispute between the experts dealing with the psychological effects of an alleged malicious prosecution rendered the case unsuitable for trial by a jury. 'Documents' for the purpose of the proviso to s. 69 includes video footage. Whether the examination of that material could be made conveniently with a jury depends on factors such as the quality of the recordings and the quantity of material (*MacIntyre v Chief Constable of Kent* (2002) LTL 6/2/2002). In *Beta Construction Ltd v Channel Four Television Co. Ltd* [1990] 1 WLR 1042 Stuart Smith LJ made the point that some cases are inconvenient for juries because of the physical problems of jurors trying to follow documentation being taken from several files simultaneously, or trying to grapple with large plans within the confined space of most jury boxes. Where a case involves prolonged examination of documents which cannot conveniently be made with a jury, it is within the judge's case management discretion to order trial by judge of those issues, with jury trial for the rest (*Phillips v Commissioner of Police of the Metropolis*). In exercising the discretion under s. 69(4) whether to order selected issues to be tried by judge or jury, the court must assess the relative advantages and disadvantages of the different modes of trial without any predisposition in favour of either option (*Armstrong v Times Newspapers Ltd (No. 2)* [2006] EWCA Civ 519, [2006] 1 WLR 2462). Being a matter of discretion, it is unlikely that a successful appeal could be mounted against such a decision (*Gregson v Channel Four Television Corporation* [2002] EWCA Civ 941, LTL 4/7/2002).

TIME TO APPLY FOR TRIAL BY JURY

60.3   The Senior Courts Act 1981, s. 69(2), provides that an application for trial by jury must be made not later than such time before trial as may be prescribed. For claims other than libel and slander this is within 28 days after service of the defence (**CPR, r. 26.11(1)**). After this period the right to trial by jury is lost, with the judge having a discretion to order a jury trial on a late application which has to be exercised based on all the circumstances of the case (*Thornton v Telegraph Media Group Ltd* [2011] EWCA Civ 748, [2011] EMLR 29, where an order was made for trial by judge alone). For libel and slander claims an application for the court to exercise its discretion to order trial with a jury must be made at the first case management conference (**r. 26.11(2)**).

DISCRETION TO ORDER TRIAL BY JURY

60.4   In cases outside the categories where there is a right to a jury the court retains, in most cases, a discretion to make an order for jury trial. In the County Court there is no power to grant a jury even on a discretionary basis in certain proceedings under the Rent (Agriculture) Act 1976, the Rent Act 1977, the Protection from Eviction Act 1977 and the Housing Act 1988 (see the County Courts Act 1984, s. 66(1), which also refers to Admiralty proceedings for which the County Court no longer has jurisdiction).

In other categories of case both the High Court and the County Court have a discretion, which must be exercised judicially and in accordance with the overriding objective, to order trial by jury. However, the requirements of the **CPR, Part 1**, point strongly against the discretion being exercised particularly the need for expedition, saving costs, and the fact that a judge sitting alone gives a reasoned judgment (*Yeo v Times Newspapers Ltd* [2014] EWHC 2853 (QB), [2015] 1 WLR 971). Under the old rules before the CPR came into force it was in any event almost impossible to obtain a discretionary order for a jury, see *Ward v James* [1966] 1 QB 273, and *Williams v Beesley* [1973] 1 WLR 1295, and it was said in *Goldsmith v Pressdram Ltd* [1988] 1 WLR 64 that 'the emphasis now is against trial with juries, and the court should take this emphasis into account when exercising its discretion', per Lawton LJ.

JURY SELECTION

Juries must be selected randomly in accordance with the Juries Act 1974, ss. 2, 5 and 6 (*R v Tarrant* **60.5**
[1998] Crim LR 342). The former practice of allowing peremptory challenges to prospective jurors
has been abolished (Criminal Justice Act 1988, s. 118), but it is still possible to challenge for cause
(Juries Act 1974, s. 12).

RELEASING JURORS

Releasing jurors part way through a trial is inconvenient, and can lead to the need to discharge **60.6**
the entire jury and for the trial to start again. In an effort to avoid this happening, particularly
in lengthy trials, the trial judge should inquire of prospective jurors whether they will suffer
inconvenience or hardship through having to serve for the estimated length of the trial, and
excuse those who will be so affected (see Practice Direction (Juries: Length of Trial) [1981] 1
WLR 1129, which should be applied even under CPR).

During the course of the trial the judge may discharge a juror on the ground of evident necessity. An example from criminal proceedings is *R v Richardson* [1979] 1 WLR 1316, where the judge
discharged by telephone a juror whose husband had died during the night. It was held there
was no material irregularity in the trial despite the fact the decision to discharge the juror had
not been made in open court.

COMMUNICATIONS WITH THE JURY

All communications between the judge and jury should be conducted in open court and with **60.7**
the whole jury present (*R v Woods* (1987) 87 Cr App R 60).

SUMMING UP

It is not the function of the judge to embark on a fact-finding exercise when sitting with a jury. **60.8**
The judge must sum up the case, with an agreed list of issues where there is a conflict (*Balchin v
Chief Constable of Hampshire Constabulary* [2001] EWCA Civ 538, [2001] Po LR 92). Where an expert
in an assault claim against the police gave evidence which contradicted the account given by the
claimant, the judge had to give adequate assistance to the jury on how to approach the conflicting evidence (*Masters v Chief Constable of Sussex* [2002] EWCA Civ 1482, LTL 3/10/2002).

JURY VERDICTS

The jury should be told by the judge that they should deliberate on their verdict only when **60.9**
they are all together in the jury room (*R v Hastings* [2003] EWCA Crim 3730, *The Times,* 12 December
2003). A party who expressly asks for a question to be left to the jury cannot appeal against the
jury's decision on the grounds that it is perverse (*McPhilemy v Times Newspapers Ltd (No. 3)* [2001]
EMLR 832).

If, after being discharged, the jury indicate that they have given the wrong verdict, the judge
may invite them to retire again to reconsider their verdict and may accept a changed verdict if
it is in the interests of justice to do so (*Igwemma v Chief Constable of Greater Manchester Police*
[2001] EWCA Civ 953, [2002] QB 1012). In considering whether it is in the interests of justice, the
judge should take into account: the time that has elapsed since the original verdict was returned;
the reasons for seeking further assistance from the jury; and whether the jury may have been
persuaded to change their view by anything said or done since they gave their original verdict.

Majority verdicts

60.10 High Court civil juries have 12 members. County Court juries are eight strong. The jury must seek to reach a unanimous verdict, and the trial judge may only give a majority verdict direction where it appears that the jury has had such sufficient time for deliberation as the judge considers reasonable given the nature and complexity of the case (Juries Act 1974, s. 17(4)).

Permissible majority verdicts where there are not less than 11 jurors are 11:1, 10:2 and 10:1. Where there are only 10 jurors a 9:1 majority is permitted. In the County Court a majority of 7:1 is permissible. In addition, the court may accept a majority verdict with the consent of the parties (such as a simple majority verdict), and the parties may further agree to proceed with an incomplete jury (s. 17(5)).

Hung jury

60.11 Where the jury cannot reach a verdict, even a majority verdict, they should be discharged and the trial discontinued. The normal rule is that the costs of the inconclusive trial should be made to be in the case, so that whoever wins the subsequent trial recovers the costs of the first trial (*Camiller v Commissioner of Police of the Metropolis* (1999) *The Times*, 8 June 1999).

Chapter 61   Trial

The following procedural checklist is relevant to this chapter:

Procedural checklist 28   *Trial preparation*

INTRODUCTION

A key feature of the CPR is that the court must retain control of the progress of claims, and   **61.1**
one of the ways in which this is achieved is by giving the parties trial dates or windows at an

early stage. Trial directions are often given when a claim is allocated to a track, particularly in small claims and fast track claims. Small claims track cases are determined by District Judges at informal hearings where the strict rules of evidence do not apply. They are usually conducted in the District Judge's chambers. Hearings in small claims cases are discussed further in **chapter** 45. This chapter is principally concerned with trials in fast track and multi-track claims. The standard period between directions and the trial date or window in fast track claims is 30 weeks (**CPR, r. 28.2(4)**). Even in multi-track claims the court will fix a trial date or window as soon as practicable (**r. 29.2(2)**). Further ways in which the court maintains control, particularly over the trial process, include:

(a) holding pre-trial reviews in selected multi-track cases a few weeks before trial — these will usually be heard by the trial judge, and one of their main purposes is to decide how to conduct the trial in the most efficient manner;

(b) setting of trial timetables in advance, limiting the amount of time allowed for speeches and questioning of witnesses;

(c) an emphasis on written preparation;

(d) the use of Fridays as preparation days in long trials (although this is not set out anywhere in the CPR or practice directions, and is a matter for individual courts and judges).

PRE-TRIAL CHECKLISTS AND FIXING THE DATE OF TRIAL

61.2   These topics have already been considered in the context of the discussion of fast track cases (see **46.13** and **46.16**) and multi-track cases (see **47.16** and **47.17**). Essentially, directions made either on track allocation or at a case management conference or other directions hearing will fix a date for pre-trial checklists, and trial dates will be fixed as soon as possible. In fast track cases this means at the allocation stage. In multi-track cases, fixing the trial date as soon as possible may mean doing this at the allocation stage, but may mean doing so considerably later. If a trial date is given at an early stage it may be altered later, perhaps after the court considers the pre-trial checklists. Trial dates may either be fixtures, which obviously means that the trial will commence on a specific date, or may be given by means of a trial 'window' of up to three weeks.

Fast track listing

61.3   A trial date or a period in which the trial is to take place will usually be given in fast track cases as part of the standard directions at the track allocation stage. If a trial period is given, it should not exceed three weeks. The trial date or period should not be more than 30 weeks from the date of the directions. The trial date or period will be confirmed or altered at the listing stage, which is fixed as one of the standard fast track directions, and is usually about eight weeks before trial.

In his *Final Report*, ch. 3, para. 28, Lord Woolf said in relation to fast track listing, 'I attach great importance to trial dates being honoured and I know that the Court Service is already working towards developing an effective listing system to meet the needs of the fast track'. The report went on to explain the difficulties and delays that are likely if all cases are given fixed dates, which stem largely from the fact that most cases settle, and the probability that when this happens the courts will not be in use for a substantial part of the working week. It also identified a number of well-known problems. These include Her Majesty's Courts and Tribunals Service being unable to find a judge or court for some trials when they are listed; urgent applications being listed immediately before trials, resulting in trials being delayed or adjourned; the practice of the courts deliberately 'overbooking' in the hope that most of the *cases booked* for one particular day will settle; and 'block listing' a number of cases for the same time in circumstances where it is almost inevitable that the parties and witnesses in some of the cases blocked together will have to wait in court for a substantial time before their cases are reached. All these problems have a substantial impact on fast track cases. These cases are intended to be tried within a single day, and have restrictions on the costs recoverable, both of which may be rendered meaningless if listing shortcomings result in adjournments and part-heard trials.

As recognised by both the *Woolf Report* and the *Jackson Report*, ensuring fast track cases are tried as intended involves the cooperation of everyone involved. Practitioners are under an obligation to provide accurate information in their pre-trial checklists to enable hearing times to be calculated on a realistic basis. District Judges need to make realistic assessments of hearing times based on the information on the court files. Listing officers need to make provision for hearing urgent matters in ways that do not interfere with fast track trials, and must provide specific staggered times for hearings rather than block lists.

Multi-track listing

The key obligation in the CPR regarding fixing multi-track cases for trial is in **r. 29.2(2)**,   **61.4** which provides that the court must fix the trial date or period in which the trial will take place as soon as practicable. The trial date or window will be confirmed as soon as practicable after the parties have filed their pre-trial checklists, or after any listing hearing or pre-trial review (**r. 29.8(c)(ii)**). Given the wide variety of cases on the multi-track this will vary considerably from case to case. For some cases the trial date or period may be given in the directions made at the track allocation stage. In other cases it may not be possible until a considerable time later, perhaps in a case management conference or pre-trial review. Like fast track cases, there is a pre-trial checklist procedure in multi-track cases (see **47.17**). Directions for filing these checklists will be made at some stage in the directions process, normally with a view to the checklists being filed about 10 weeks before the intended trial. The trial date will be confirmed or altered at that stage.

As multi-track trials may sometimes stretch over several days or weeks, minor delays due to urgent applications being listed first are not so likely to have such an impact as in fast track cases, so the concerns noted in **61.3**, although still important, are not so fundamental.

It is interesting to note that if the court gives a trial window in a multi-track case instead of a fixture, the period should be just one week (**r. 29.8(c)(ii)**), rather than the possible three-week period for fast track cases.

Queen's Bench Division listing

In Admiralty, Commercial and Technology and Construction Court claims, trials are usually   **61.5** fixed at, or in consequence of, the first case management conference.

In other Queen's Bench Division claims in the Royal Courts of Justice the Queen's Bench Judges' Listing Officer (Room WG08, Royal Courts of Justice) is in general responsible for listing. There are three lists, namely the jury list, the trial list, and the interim hearings list (Queen's Bench Guide, para. 9.2). The trial list is for non-jury trials, preliminary issues and proceedings for contempt of court (para. 9.4.1). Listing arrangements are discussed at **47.16**. Most trials are assigned to a named judge when they appear in the daily cause list.

Chancery Division listing

There are three main Chancery Division lists called the trial list (for trials to be heard with   **61.6** witnesses), the interim hearings list (for interim applications and appeals from Masters), and the general list (for all other hearings) (Chancery Guide, paras 21.2 to 21.10). There is a warned list which is published on Fridays showing the cases liable to be heard in the following week. Chapter 21 of the Chancery Guide also deals with time estimates, appeals from Masters, and listing of bankruptcy applications and appeals, companies applications and petitions, bundles and adjournments.

Expedited hearing

61.7   In cases of real urgency the court may order an expedited hearing, exercising its power under **CPR, r. 3.1(2)(b)**. This is also known as 'speedy trial' and 'early hearing'. A Master or District Judge may only give directions for an expedited trial after consulting the Head of the relevant Division or a Judge nominated by the Head of Division (**PD 2B, para. 4.1**). An application for an expedited hearing, which of course involves leapfrogging over other litigants waiting to be heard, has to be supported by clear evidence of the need for a speedy trial (*Intervet (UK) Ltd v Merial* [2009] EWHC 1065 (Pat), LTL 21/5/2009). It can only be justified if there are very cogent reasons (*W. L. Gore and Associates GmbH v Geox SpA* [2008] EWHC 462 (Pat), LTL 7/4/2008). An argument that effective enforcement cannot be started until a final judgment has been obtained is not a convincing reason for expediting a trial (*Daltel Europe Ltd v Makki* [2004] EWHC 1631 (Ch), LTL 17/6/2004). Where the principal relief sought is money, or where declaratory relief is unlikely to resolve the dispute between the parties, it will be difficult to justify expediting the trial (*CPC Group Ltd v Qatari Diar Real Estate Investment Co.* [2009] EWHC 3204 (Ch), LTL 15/12/2009). A disputed claim for relief from forfeiture against a claim for delivery up of an aircraft may justify a speedy trial (*Celestial Aviation Trading 71 Ltd v Paramount Airways Private Ltd* [2009] EWHC 3142 (Comm), LTL 10/12/2009). Factors include any past delays, any prejudice to other parties, and the practicality of forcing parties to adhere to a tight timetable (*Law Debenture Trust Corporation plc v Elektrim SA* [2008] EWHC 2187 (Ch), LTL 1/10/2008). An example where an order was granted is *Wembley National Stadium Ltd v Wembley (London) Ltd* (2000) LTL 16/11/2000, where funding for a project which was dependent on the success of the proceedings was likely to be withdrawn within a limited time. The application should be made as early as possible (*Daltel Europe Ltd v Makki*). If the order is granted, the court will lay down a timetable with strict deadlines.

Availability of experts and listing

61.8   Two important concepts are that trials should be listed as soon as practicable, and once fixed should not be adjourned unless absolutely necessary. If a party wants to change experts in the run-up to trial, or to instruct an expert for the first time shortly before trial, they are obliged to instruct experts who will report in sufficient time and be available for the trial. In *Rollinson v Kimberly Clark Ltd* [1999] CPLR 581 an expert instructed about six months before trial was unable to attend trial. On an application made about three months before trial the judge refused to break the fixture, and her decision was upheld by the Court of Appeal. A decision of great practical importance is *Matthews v Tarmac Bricks and Tiles Ltd* [1999] CPLR 463. There had been some difficulty in fixing the trial, and the court convened a listing hearing which was attended by a young member of the Bar on behalf of the defendant. Counsel had been provided with a list of unavailable dates, which included 15 July. The judge asked why the defendant's two experts were unavailable on 15 July, to which counsel replied she had no instructions. The trial was then fixed for 15 July. The Master of the Rolls said it was not enough simply to tell the court which dates experts could not attend, but that reasons had to be given as well. Even if the actual reasons had been given, it did not follow that the court would not have still listed the case for 15 July. Experts have to be prepared to arrange their affairs to meet the commitments of the courts where that is practical. The case clearly underlines the importance of having someone familiar with the case and fully briefed attend at case management hearings (see **CPR, r. 29.3(2)**). However, it may be that the decision in this case turned on the history of difficulties in fixing the trial, and should not be seen as always applicable in other cases.

ADJOURNMENT

Power to adjourn

61.9 CPR, r. 3.1(2)(b), gives the court a general power to adjourn. Adjournments may be necessary due to shortages of court resources. They may be sought by a party on the ground of some event outside their control which prevents them from presenting their full case at the hearing. They are also, regrettably, sometimes sought because a party or their lawyers have failed to prepare the case in time, and adjournments in these circumstances are often attended by breaches of case management directions previously made by the court.

It is the duty of parties and their legal representatives to inform the court as soon as they become aware of any real prospect that a trial will not proceed so as to enable the court to reallocate its resources (*Albon v Naza Motor Trading Sdn Bhd (No. 5)* [2007] EWHC 2613 (Ch), [2008] 1 WLR 2380 at [12]).

In the Queen's Bench Division, a party seeking an adjournment must inform the Clerk of the Lists as soon as possible (Queen's Bench Guide, para. 9.8.2). If the application is by agreement, the parties should apply to the Clerk of the Lists in writing, who will consult the nominated judge who may grant the application and impose conditions, which usually include directions for a new trial date (para. 9.8.4). If the application is opposed, a hearing should be arranged through the Clerk of the Lists to be heard either by the nominated judge or the judge to whom the matter has been allocated. A short written summary of the reasons for the adjournment (formal evidence not being required) should be lodged with the Listing Office by 10.30 a.m. on the day before the application is heard (para. 9.8.5).

In the Chancery Division, a party seeking an adjournment must inform the Chancery Judges' Listing Officer as soon as possible (Chancery Guide, para. 21.32). The procedure is similar to that in the Queen's Bench Division, except that the summary of the reasons for seeking the adjournment in an opposed application should be lodged at the Chancery Judges' Listing Office by 12 noon on the day before the application is heard (para. 21.33).

In the County Court, agreed adjournments should be notified to the court office in writing as early as possible. Depending on the circumstances, the matter may be referred to the judge. If the adjournment is opposed, an application should be issued with the reasons for the adjournment being set out in the form N244.

There is greater reluctance to adjourn a fixed date trial than to put back a trial window (the effect of *Fitzroy Robinson Ltd v Mentmore Towers Ltd* [2009] EWHC 3070 (TCC), [2010] CP Rep 15; *Elliott Group Ltd v GECC UK* [2010] EWHC 409 (TCC), LTL 10/3/2010). Applications made immediately before the scheduled start of a trial should be avoided as they use up valuable court time, and often result in a waste of court resources and costs.

The power to grant an adjournment is discretionary, and should be exercised in accordance with the overriding objective (*Boyd and Hutchinson v Foenander* [2003] EWCA Civ 1516, [2004] BPIR 20). The court must ensure the parties are on an equal footing, that the case is dealt with proportionately, expeditiously and fairly, with an appropriate amount of the court's resources devoted to it taking into account the needs of other cases (*Fitzroy Robinson Ltd v Mentmore Towers Ltd* [2009] EWHC 3070 (TCC), [2010] CP Rep 15). Where an adjournment is sought for reasons outside the control of the party, it should usually be granted. Examples are where vital witnesses are unavoidably out of the country, or too ill to attend court. Adjourning to await the decision in an appeal in a different case on an issue raised in the present case is a pure case management matter, and the judge's decision is unlikely to be upset on appeal (*Corbett v South Yorkshire Strategic Health Authority* [2006] EWCA Civ 1797, LTL 6/12/2006).

Adjournments are unlikely to be granted where a party is not ready for trial through their own fault, or where they have been given a previous adjournment and are still not ready, unless the circumstances are exceptional.

An adjournment was refused in *Powell v Pallisers of Hereford Ltd* [2002] EWCA Civ 959, LTL 1/7/2002, where the defendant wanted more time to enable a third party to take part in the trial, but where an early trial date, which would ensure that the claim was tried by the time of the 2002 harvest, had been set because the claimant was a farmer in financial difficulties. A judge has a wide discretion whether to adjourn, and it is not easy for an appeal court to interfere with that discretion (*Roshdi v Thames Trains Ltd* [2002] EWCA Civ 284, LTL 20/2/2002).

Problems obtaining representation

61.10   The availability of counsel of choice, particularly where replacement counsel will have to spend a substantial amount of time reading into the case, or where the client reposes a great deal of confidence in existing counsel, is a factor to be taken into account (*Collins v Gordon* [2008] EWCA Civ 110 LTL 21/1/2008). Where the problem is self-induced, such as through dismissing solicitors shortly before the hearing, a short adjournment may be all that the court should grant (*Property Investor's Courses Ltd v Secretary of State for Trade and Industry* [2008] EWCA Civ 872, LTL 14/7/2008, where the court granted a two-day adjournment in a straightforward case). In *Bates v Croydon London Borough Council* [2001] EWCA Civ 134, LTL 23/1/2001, an adjournment should have been given as the appellant was awaiting a determination of an application for legal aid, and she had been served with the respondents' witness statements and other documents very shortly before the hearing. The court should respect the right of a party to seek public funding by granting adjournments where appropriate (*Berry Trade Ltd v Moussavi* [2002] EWCA Civ 477 [2002] 1 WLR 1910). An adjournment should have been granted in *Henry Butcher International Ltd v KG Engineering* [2004] EWCA Civ 1597, LTL 22/10/2004, to enable a party to obtain legal representation where the case had a complex history and raised complex legal issues. Similarly, in *Ghadami v Harlow District Council* [2004] EWCA Civ 891, LTL 21/6/2004, an adjournment should have been given where the date listed conflicted with an earlier direction and would have deprived a party of his counsel of choice. In *Joyce v King* (1987) *The Times*, 13 July 1987, the claimant was unable to obtain expert evidence without legal aid, and there were problems in obtaining legal aid. It was held that the trial should have been adjourned because it was not possible for the claimant to obtain justice without being given further time. An adjournment was granted in *Islam v Meah* [2005] EWCA Civ 1485, LTL 11/11/2005, where the defendant had limited understanding of English, and the adjournment was needed so he could obtain legal funding and legal representation.

Breach of case management directions

61.11   The general approach that will be adopted where an adjournment is sought after there has been a breach of case management directions is set out in **PD 28, para. 5.4** (fast track) and **PD 29, para. 7.4** (multi-track). These provide that the court will not allow a failure to comply with directions to lead to the postponement of the trial unless the circumstances of the case are exceptional. Litigants and lawyers must be in no doubt that the court will regard the postponement of a trial as an order of last resort. If practicable to do so, the court will exercise its powers in a manner that enables the case to come on for trial on the date or within the period previously set, and it may set a new, but tight, timetable, with sanctions for non-compliance (*Elliott Group Ltd v GECC UK* [2010] EWHC 409 (TCC), LTL 10/3/2010). Where it appears that one or more issues are or can be made ready for trial at the time fixed while others cannot, the court may direct that the trial will proceed on the issues that are or will then be ready, and order that no costs will be allowed for any later trial of the remaining issues or that those costs will be paid by the party in default. Where the court has no option but to postpone the trial it will do so for the shortest possible time and will give directions for the taking of the necessary steps in the meantime as rapidly as possible. In these cases the court may disallow costs as between solicitor and client, or order the person responsible to pay costs, or make any other order including ordering costs on the indemnity basis (Queen's Bench Guide, para. 9.8.7; Chancery Guide, para. 21.33). **PD 28, para. 5.4** and **PD 29, para. 7.4**, apply only where there has been a breach of case management directions, and not where an adjournment is sought on the basis of unavailability of counsel or witnesses (*Collins v Gordon* [2008] EWCA Civ 110, LTL 21/1/2008).

In *Gilbart v Thomas Graham* [2008] EWCA Civ 897, LTL 24/6/2008, the Court of Appeal overturned a decision to refuse an adjournment of the trial date, in order to give effect to the overriding objective. The defendant had applied for the adjournment 21 days before the date for the trial, on realising that the claimant had not disclosed crucial documents. 21 days was an unrealistically short time for the defendant to obtain specific disclosure from the claimant and to instruct an expert on a loss of profits claim. In *Ratiopharm (UK) Ltd v Alza Corporation* [2008] EWHC 1182 (Ch), LTL 1/5/2008, six months was regarded as enough time to prepare a patent infringement claim for trial (the party seeking to avoid the trial date having received a letter with the allegations in the litigation 13 months before the trial date). An adjournment of a fast track claim based on an argument that the claimant had suffered psychiatric injuries (which were not mentioned in the disclosed medical evidence) and that the claim should be reallocated to the multi-track was refused in *Taylor v Graham* (2000) LTL 25/5/2000, largely because evidence was not adduced substantiating the more complex nature of the claim justifying reallocation. Failing to prepare for trial because there were ongoing negotiations for a settlement is unlikely to be regarded as a sufficient reason for an adjournment (*Assiouti v Hosseini* (1999) LTL 26/11/99). An application to adjourn in *AC Electrical Wholesale plc v IGW Services Ltd* (2000) LTL 10/10/2000 based on a need to include a claim for loss of profits in a counterclaim was refused as there were no exceptional circumstances to explain why this had not been pleaded earlier.

Late applications to adjourn

According to *Fitzroy Robinson Ltd v Mentmore Towers Ltd* [2009] EWHC 3070 (TCC), [2010] CP Rep 15, **61.12** factors to be considered in eleventh-hour applications to adjourn include:

(a) the parties' conduct and the reasons for any delays;
(b) the extent to which the consequences of delays can be overcome before trial;
(c) the extent to which a fair trial may be prejudiced by the delays;
(d) specific matters affecting the trial such as illness of a crucial witness; and
(e) the consequences of an adjournment for the parties and the court.

The fact that a party has not applied to adjourn until the day of the trial, despite knowing for many weeks that it is in difficulties, may be a sufficient reason to refuse an adjournment (*National Westminster Bank plc v Aaronson* [2004] EWHC 618 (QB), LTL 9/3/2004). Where both parties are to blame for the failure to instruct an expert and in not informing the court of the need to adjourn until the last minute, it is wrong to refuse to adjourn if only one party will suffer detriment from the lack of adjournment (*Thomson v O'Connor* [2005] EWCA Civ 1533, LTL 7/11/2005). In *Alderson v Stillorgan Sales Ltd* [2001] EWCA Civ 1060, LTL 13/6/2001, the claimants were refused permission to call their own expert, and the court directed that the parties jointly instruct an expert, who was to report just over two weeks before the trial. The expert was late, and delivered his report, which was favourable to the defendants, five days before trial. The day before trial the claimants sought an adjournment, which was refused, and a renewed application on the day of the trial was also refused. On appeal it was held that waiting to the day before trial was inappropriate. The appeal was dismissed partly because the claimants should have appealed the original order, or applied to adjourn when the expert missed the date for delivering his report, and partly because their case was weak in any event.

Witness availability and medical reasons

61.13   Adjournments on the basis of witnesses being unavailable are decided applying the overriding objective. Factors to be considered, based on *Albon v Naza Motor Trading Sdn Bhd (No. 5)* [2007] EWHC 2613 (Ch), [2008] 1 WLR 2380, include:

(a)   court resources, particularly any court time lost through previous adjournments;

(b)   the history of past compliance with or breach of directions and orders;

(c)   whether there is medical evidence to the effect the witness cannot attend through ill-health;

(d)   whether that witness's evidence is reasonably necessary to ensure the party's case is properly presented. Primary witnesses are more likely to be regarded as needed in person than witnesses regarded as secondary. The court will bear in mind that the witness's witness statement is admissible in evidence under the Civil Evidence Act 1995, with the lack of cross-examination going to weight rather than admissibility. Even that may be offset if the witness is able to be cross-examined by video link;

(e)   the witness's availability at an adjourned hearing; and

(f)   whether the respondent will suffer prejudice which cannot be compensated by an award of costs or otherwise.

In *Green v Northern General Transport* (1970) 115 SJ 59 a new trial was ordered after the judge refused to adjourn despite a material witness being unavailable. In *Re A (A Child)* [2005] EWCA Civ 862, LTL 14/7/2005, the judge was held entitled to conclude that the medical evidence about the father's post-operative condition did not justify an adjournment of more than about a week. Justice is a two-way street, and the other parties are as entitled to a fair and expeditious hearing as the party seeking the adjournment. In *Khudados v Hayden* [2007] EWCA Civ 1316, LTL 13/12/2007, a general practitioner's letter commenting that the claimant had been up in the night with vomiting and nausea justified adjournments on the Friday and Monday, but was not sufficient for a further adjournment on the Tuesday. Vague medical notes do not have to be accepted at face value (*R (Copyright Canary City Ltd) v Thames Magistrates' Court* [2010] EWHC 2185 (Admin), LTL 17/9/2010). An adjournment was refused in *Ahmed v Butt* [2005] EWCA Civ 1448, LTL 1/11/2005, where a litigant in person complained of having a sore throat. The judge said he would reassess the matter as the hearing progressed, but allowed the hearing to continue even though the litigant in person became inaudible. It was held that the judge was entitled to refuse the initial application on this provisional basis, but erred in not adjourning when it became apparent the party was not capable of making himself heard.

Cold feet and tactical reasons

61.14   In *Skipsey v O'Rourke* [2005] EWCA Civ 912, LTL 30/6/2005, medical evidence that the claimant was 'not in a fit frame of mind' to attend was rightly held to be insufficient to justify an adjournment. (It later transpired that the doctor had understated the claimant's condition, and an adjournment was allowed on that basis.) The court felt in *Law Debenture Trust Corporation plc v Elektrim Finance BV* [2005] EWCA Civ 1354, LTL 8/11/2005, that an adjournment was sought in order to leave the present proceedings unresolved, so as to secure a forensic advantage in related proceedings in Poland. On that basis the adjournment was refused. An adjournment of a mortgage possession hearing was refused in *Cheval Bridging Finance Ltd v Hastings* (2008) LTL 12/12/2008 where there was no prospect of the defendant discharging the mortgage debt in a reasonable period.

SETTLEMENT BEFORE TRIAL

61.15   If a claim is settled, whether by agreement or acceptance of a Part 36 offer, or is discontinued, in the period between the giving of a trial date or 'window' and the commencement of the trial, it is the duty of the parties to notify the listing officer for the trial court immediately

Trial location

Normally trials will take place at the court where the case has been proceeding, but it may be **61.25** transferred to another court for trial if this is appropriate having regard to the convenience of the parties and the availability of court resources (**PD 28, para. 8.1**, for the fast track; **PD 29, para. 10.1**, for cases on the multi-track). Multi-track cases will generally have been transferred to civil trial centres when allocated to the multi-track (if commenced in a feeder court), but they may be allowed to proceed elsewhere if that is appropriate given the needs of the parties and the availability of court resources.

Allocation to judiciary

While District Judges in the County Court have trial jurisdiction in claims allocated to the **61.26** small claims and fast tracks (**PD 2B, para. 11.1(a)**), the general rule is that claims on the multi-track are tried by Circuit Judges (**paras 11.1(a) and 13**). Small claims will be tried by a Circuit Judge only with his or her consent (**para. 11.2(1)**). Assessments of damages may be conducted by District Judges without financial limit (**para. 11.1(c)**), and there is a list of proceedings under the landlord and tenant and other statutes in **para. 11.1** where District Judges have trial jurisdiction. **Paragraph 12** has a list of proceedings under various statutes, such as the Bankers' Books Evidence Act 1879, which have to be allocated to a Circuit Judge.

Trials in the Royal Courts of Justice are normally conducted by High Court judges and their deputies. Masters can conduct trials (**PD 2B**), but due to workload pressures this is unusual. In the Queen's Bench Division, trial before a Master will not usually be contemplated if it will last more than three days (Queen's Bench Guide, para. 10.1.1). In the Chancery Division, trial by Master is more likely for cases in Listing Category C (Chancery Guide, para. 17.31) or where the legal issues fall within the area of expertise of the Master, where the time estimate is not more than five days, taking into account other criteria set out in the Chancery Guide at para. 14.7.

Impartiality of judge

It has long been established that a judge must not sit in his or her own cause. The rule laid **61.27** down in *Dimes v Proprietors of Grand Junction Canal* (1852) 3 HL Cas 759 by Lord Campbell is now interpreted as not being confined to a claim in which the judge is a party, but applies also to a claim in which the outcome could, realistically, affect an interest of the judge. In *R v Bow Street Metropolitan Stipendiary Magistrate, ex parte Pinochet Ugarte (No. 2)* [2000] 1 AC 119 the House of Lords held that the principle that a judge is automatically disqualified from hearing a matter in his or her own cause is not limited to cases where the judge has a pecuniary interest in the outcome, but applies also to cases where the judge's decision would lead to the promotion of a cause in which the judge was involved together with one of the parties. The automatic disqualification rule is subject to the *de minimis* principle, in that some supposed financial interests are so small they can be ignored (*Locabail (UK) Ltd v Bayfield Properties Ltd* [2000] QB 451). The same principles apply to arbitrators (*AT and T Corporation v Saudi Cable Co.* [2000] 2 Lloyd's Rep 127).

Under the European Convention on Human Rights, **art. 6(1)**, in the **Human Rights Act 1998, sch. 1**, litigants are entitled to a fair hearing before an impartial tribunal. ECHR jurisprudence has established that there will be a breach where the existence of a legitimate reason or fear of a lack of impartiality is objectively justified. Before the implementation of the Convention, the House of Lords had held that a judge should not sit if there is a real danger of bias (*R v Gough* [1993] AC 646). A synthesis of the two tests was accomplished by the Court of Appeal in *Re Medicaments and Related Classes of Goods (No. 2)* [2001] 1 WLR 700, where the court laid down a two-stage test. In *Porter v Magill* [2001] UKHL 67, [2002] 2 AC 357,

Commentary

Lord Bingham of Cornhill approved this two-stage test, but said that the reference to 'a real danger' of bias in the test should be deleted. The words no longer serve any useful purpose and have not been used in the jurisprudence of the European Court of Human Rights. Following *Porter v Magill*, the test for bias can, according to *Taylor v Lawrence* [2002] EWCA Civ 90, [2003] QB 528, and *Lawal v Northern Spirit Ltd* [2003] UKHL 35, [2003] ICR 856, be formulated as follows:

The court must first ascertain all the circumstances which have a bearing on the suggestion that the judge was biased. It must then ask whether those circumstances would lead a fair-minded and informed observer to conclude that there was a real possibility that the tribunal was biased.

It was also said in *Taylor v Lawrence* that a judge should be circumspect about declaring the existence of a relationship where there is no real possibility of a fair-minded and informed observer regarding it as raising a possibility of bias. If it is clear that there is no possibility of bias being perceived, no purpose is served by mentioning the relationship. If it is clear that bias might be perceived, it is important that disclosure should be made. If the position is borderline, disclosure should be made so that the judge can consider, having heard the parties' submissions, whether to withdraw.

61.28 Application of the informed observer test An informed observer will be aware of the legal traditions and culture of this jurisdiction. In England and Wales judges are members of the legal profession and have regular contract with other members of the profession. The fact that a judge receives free legal services from the solicitors representing a party to a claim being heard by the judge would not, according to a five-judge Court of Appeal in *Taylor v Lawrence* [2002] EWCA Civ 90, [2003] QB 528, lead a fair-minded and informed observer to conclude that there was a real possibility that the judge was biased. Nor is there any apparent bias where the judge calls counsel into the judges' corridor to inform them that he thinks the case is weak and that the parties should consider a settlement (*Hart v Relentless Records Ltd* [2002] EWHC 1984 (Ch), [2003] FSR 36). There was no apparent bias in *Taylor v Williamsons* [2002] EWCA Civ 1380, [2003] CP Rep 20, where the judge forgot he had not heard final submissions, and had to withdraw his judgment when this was pointed out, and so could give judgment after considering final submissions.

Observing at the start of a trial that a party has no case gives the appearance of an inability to try the claim objectively (*Co-operative Group Ltd v International Computers Ltd* [2003] EWCA Civ 1955, [2004] Info TLR 25). It is unacceptable for a judge to form, or to give the impression of having formed, a firm view on the credibility of the evidence of one side before the other side has called any evidence (*Amjad v Steadman-Byrne* [2007] EWCA Civ 625, [2007] 1 WLR 2484). A judge should have recused himself in *Ealing London Borough Council v Jan* [2002] EWCA Civ 329, LTL 7/2/2002, having on a previous occasion twice stated in strong terms that he did not trust the defendant, even though the comments related to a different issue from the one to be determined in the subsequent hearing.

In *Re Medicaments and Related Classes of Goods (No. 2)* [2001] 1 WLR 700 one of the three members of the Restrictive Practices Court was an economist who had applied for a job during the course of the proceedings with a firm, one of whose members was providing expert evidence for one of the parties. When the member of the court realised the problem she immediately cancelled her job application and informed the parties, and the firm wrote stating that it had no jobs available in any event. It was held that a fair-minded observer would apprehend there was a real danger that the member of the court could not make an objective and impartial appraisal of the expert evidence. Before the start of a tribunal hearing in *Turner v Harada Ltd* [2001] EWCA Civ 599, LTL 6/4/2001, the chairman said: 'This is the seventh time that [Harada] have appeared here in the last six months…. [They] turn up with excuses and arguments to avoid matters going to trial…it is not as though [they] come here with a slate which is exactly clean'. It was held that a fair-minded observer would have concluded there was a real danger of bias. A judge who has decided a case is not precluded from reconsidering the case after it is remitted following a successful appeal (*Secretary of State for the Home Department v AF (No. 2)* [2007] EWHC 2828 (Admin), [2008] 2 All ER 67). In *Lawal v Northern Spirit Ltd* [2003] UKHL 35, [2003] ICR 856, it was held that the practice of leading counsel who have appeared as advocates before the Employment Appeal Tribunal being appointed to sit as part-time judges in the same tribunal did not infringe the bias rule. However, it tended to undermine public confidence in the system and should be discontinued.

There will be an injustice if the judge was predisposed or prejudiced against one party's case for reasons unconnected with the merits of the case (see *R v Inner West London Coroner, ex parte Dallaglio* [1994] 4 All ER 139). Guidance on situations where there may be a real danger of bias was given by the Court of Appeal in *Locabail (UK) Ltd v Bayfield Properties Ltd* [2000] QB 451, which is of particular relevance to cases dealt with by solicitor and barrister deputy judges. The Court of Appeal could not conceive of circumstances in which an objection could be soundly based on the religion (see also *Seer Technologies Inc. v Abbas* (2000) The Times, 16 March 2000), ethnic or national origin, gender, age, class, means or sexual orientation of the judge. Membership of the International Association of Jewish Lawyers and Jurists did not give rise to a real possibility of bias in a judge dealing with an immigration appeal by a Palestinian seeking asylum (*Helow v Secretary of State for the Home Department* [2008] UKHL 62, [2008] 1 WLR 2416). Nor, at least ordinarily, could there be a valid objection based on the judge's social, educational, service or employment background, nor that of any member of his or her family. Nor could an objection be based on previous political associations, membership of social, sporting or charitable bodies, or Masonic associations; previous judicial decisions; extra-curial utterances, whether in textbooks, lectures, speeches, articles (but see *Hoekstra v HM Advocate (No. 2)* 2000 JC 391 discussed in **91.48**), interviews, reports or responses to consultation papers; previous receipt of instructions to act for or against any party, solicitor or advocate engaged in the current case; or membership of the same Inn, circuit, local Law Society or chambers. By contrast, there might be a real danger of bias if there was personal friendship or animosity between the judge and anyone other than the lawyers involved in the present case; or if the judge was closely acquainted with a witness whose credibility was in issue; or if the judge had ruled against the credibility of a witness in a previous case in outspoken terms such as to cast doubt on whether the judge could deal with the witness in the current case with an open mind (but not if the judge had commented adversely on a party or witness in a previous case in temperate terms); or if the judge had expressed views on a matter also in issue in the present case in such extreme terms as to throw into doubt his or her ability to try the case objectively. If there is any doubt, it should be exercised in favour of refusing to sit.

Impartiality may be thrown into doubt where a judge has had a direct involvement in the passage of legislation or of executive rules relevant to the case (*McGonnell v United Kingdom* (2000) 30 EHRR 289, in which the European Court of Human Rights held there was an infringement of art. 6(1) of the European Convention on Human Rights in Guernsey).

An appearance of bias where a witness is well known to the judge cannot be removed, even by the party intending to call the witness deciding not to call him, and substituting alternative witnesses (*Morrison v AWG Group Ltd* [2006] EWCA Civ 6, The Independent, 25 January 2006). In such a case the safe course is to remove all possibility of apparent bias by recusal of the judge.

Bias and conflicting interests: procedure   Judges are obliged to mention any possible conflict when they become aware of its existence. Wherever possible this is done in advance of the commencement of the trial, so as to avoid the expense of an adjournment. If the matter becomes apparent at the commencement of a hearing (or during its course), the judge should mention it and the parties must consider whether they will waive the difficulty or ask the judge to decline to act or withdraw. Counsel should not seek to influence the decision of the   **61.29**

client, whether by referring to the judge's integrity or (surprisingly) the costs that would be thrown away (in a case where the costs would be met by a trade union) (*Smith v Kvaerner Cementation Foundations Ltd* [2006] EWCA Civ 242, [2007] 1 WLR 370). Any challenge based on apparent bias must be made when it arises, rather than awaiting the result of the hearing (*Amjad v Steadman-Byrne* [2007] EWCA Civ 625, [2007] 1 WLR 2484). The judge will give great weight to the parties' wishes, particularly if the hearing has already commenced (or if there is no other available judge). A judge who doubts his or her ability to be impartial will withdraw, even if the parties do not require it. If the parties waive their right to object, they cannot later raise the matter by way of appeal. See *Locabail (UK) Ltd v Bayfield Properties Ltd* [2000] QB 451.

Where proceedings are abandoned because of the appearance of bias on the part of a member of the court, the Lord Chancellor is not liable for any of the costs incurred at the wasted hearing (*Re Medicaments and Related Classes of Goods (No. 4)* [2001] EWCA Civ 1217, [2002] 1 WLR 269).

Rights of audience

61.30 Rights of audience and the right to conduct litigation are reserved legal activities within the meaning of the Legal Services Act 2007 (s. 12 and sch. 2). The only persons entitled to carry on these activities are regulated persons authorised to do so by an approved regulator and persons who are exempt in relation to the relevant activity (ss. 13 and 176). Approved regulators include the Law Society, the General Council of the Bar, the Chartered Institute of Legal Executives, the Council for Licensed Conveyancers and the Association of Law Costs Draftsmen (sch. 4). As a result, the following persons have rights of audience:

(a) litigants in person (who are exempt, sch. 3, para. 1(6)). 'Litigant in person' is the sole term to be used to describe individuals conducting proceedings on their own behalf (Practice Guidance (Litigants in Person: Terminology) [2013] 1 WLR 1318);
(b) counsel;
(c) solicitors;
(d) members of the Chartered Institute of Legal Executives;
(e) members of the Association of Law Costs Draftsmen;
(f) persons given express permission by the court in relation to the relevant proceedings (who are exempt, sch. 3, para. 1(2)); and
(g) persons given an express right of audience by statute (an example being the right given to local authority officers to present rent and possession claims on behalf of their employers under the County Courts Act 1984, s. 60).

A barrister who has not undertaken pupillage and who does not have a practising certificate (even if that person has appropriate professional indemnity insurance, provides details of his work to the Bar Council and makes his status clear to clients) is not authorised for the purpose of rights of audience in the courts (*R v K* [2008] EWCA Crim 1900, [2009] 1 WLR 694). Solicitors must comply with the Law Society advocacy qualifications before they can conduct High Court trials.

Members of the Association of Law Costs Draftsmen may be certified by the Association with rights of audience (Association of Law Costs Draftsmen Order 2006, SI 2006/3333). Unqualified costs negotiators are not properly instructed as agents of solicitors and therefore do not have rights of audience (*Ahmed v Powell* [2003] PNLR 22). A person with an enduring power of attorney does not have, in that capacity, a right of audience (*Gregory v Turner* [2003] EWCA Civ 183, [2003] 1 WLR 1149).

Practice Direction (Court Dress) (No. 4) [2008] 1 WLR 357 was made to ensure that solicitors and other authorised advocates are not precluded from wearing wigs when appearing in court.

Dress requirements for advocates appearing in the Senior Courts and in the County Court are:

(a) Queen's Counsel wear a short wig and a silk (or stuff) gown over a court coat;
(b) junior counsel wear a short wig and stuff gown with bands;

(c) solicitors and other authorised advocates wear a black solicitor's gown with bands, and they may wear short wigs in circumstances where they would be worn by Queen's Counsel or junior counsel.

Under Practice Direction (Court Dress) (No. 5) [2008] 1 WLR 1700, a civil judge must wear a gown without wig or bands when sitting in court, whether in public or private. The relevant Head of Division or the Senior Presiding Judge may agree for good reason that a gown should not be worn.

Legal representative prejudicing administration of justice   The court has a power to grant   **61.31**
an injunction to restrain a legal representative from appearing at a hearing if continued participation would lead to any order made being set aside on appeal (*Geveran Trading Co. Ltd v Skjevesland* [2002] EWCA Civ 1567, [2003] 1 WLR 912). Such applications are not governed by the same principles as apply regarding the impartiality of judges (see **61.27** to **61.28**), and the court must not be too ready to remove an advocate from a case. Advocates have no obligation not to be partisan. An advocate who is aware of a personal factor making his or her continued participation likely to prejudice the administration of justice or cause a procedural irregularity should withdraw, and must disclose to the other side any personal factor which might reasonably be regarded as open to objection.

McKenzie friends   The phrase McKenzie Friend ('MF') comes from *McKenzie v McKenzie*   **61.32**
[1971] P 33, and describes an unqualified person who assists a litigant who would otherwise be acting in person. Most MFs assist litigants who are individuals, but the court has inherent jurisdiction to permit a MF to assist a company (*Bank St Petersburg PJSC v Arkhangelsky (No. 2)* [2015] EWHC 2997 (Ch), [2016] 1 WLR 1081). The primary function of a MF is to provide moral support for a litigant at a hearing (a 'basic MF'). A MF is not permitted to conduct litigation or act as an advocate without the court's permission. Practice Note (McKenzie Friends: Civil and Family Courts) [2010] 1 WLR 1881 (the 'President's Guidance') sets out to provide guidance for all courts and is based on various decisions of the courts. The guidance provides that a MF may:

(a) provide moral support for the litigant;
(b) take notes;
(c) help with case papers; and
(d) quietly give advice on points of law or procedure, issues the litigant may wish to raise in court, and questions the litigant may wish to ask witnesses. The litigant is permitted to communicate any information, including filed evidence, to the MF for these purposes.

The President's Guidance says a MF:

(a) has no right to act on behalf of a litigant. It is the right of the litigant who wishes to receive reasonable assistance from a MF;
(b) has no right to address the court, or examine witnesses. Any person doing these is an advocate, and requires the grant of a right of audience (see **61.34**); and
(c) may not act as the litigant's agent in relation to the proceedings, nor manage the litigant's case outside court, such as by signing court documents.

There are different rules for small claims track hearings, see **45.21**.

Application to be a basic McKenzie friend   The President's Guidance says a litigant in per-   **61.33**
son intending to make a request for the assistance of a MF should make the application as soon as possible, indicating who the MF will be. The proposed MF should:

(a) provide a short curriculum vitae or other statement setting out his or her relevant experience;
(b) confirm that he or she has no interest in the case;
(c) confirm that he or she understands the role of a MF, and the duty of confidentiality.

The MF is entitled to attend the application, and to assist the litigant in making the application.

A litigant has a right to reasonable assistance from a lay person, and should be permitted to have a basic MF except where fairness and the interests of justice indicate that the assistance of a MF is not required. It is for the court or the objecting party to provide sufficient reasons why the litigant should not receive such assistance. There is a strong presumption in favour of permitting a basic MF, and it is for the objecting party to rebut this presumption. It will not be rebutted merely because the proceedings relate to a child or are to be heard in private or are confidential or that the court papers contain sensitive information about a family's affairs. Nor is it rebutted where the litigant appears to be capable of conducting the case alone, that the litigant is acting in person through choice, that the objecting party is unrepresented, that the hearing is for case management purposes, or that the proposed MF belongs to an organisation promoting a particular cause.

Reasons for denying a litigant the assistance of a MF (President's Guidance, para. 13) include where the assistance is being provided for an improper purpose, the assistance is unreasonable in degree or nature, the MF is subject to a civil proceedings order, the MF is using the litigant as a puppet, the MF is directly or indirectly conducting the litigation, and where the MF does not understand the duty of confidentiality.

A decision on permission for the assistance of a MF can be appealed by either party (the fourth bullet point in the President's Guidance, which says decisions granting permission should be regarded as final, deals with revisiting permission at a later stage, not appeals).

61.34 **Rights of audience for McKenzie friends** An application that a MF be permitted a right of audience must be made at the start of the hearing (*Clarkson v Gilbert* [2000] 2 FLR 839). The question for the court is whether in all the circumstances of the case the court should exercise its discretion under the Legal Services Act 2007, ss. 12 to 19. The court will be very slow to grant a MF a right of audience (*Paragon Finance plc v Noueiri* [2001] EWCA Civ 1402, [2001] 1 WLR 2357 at [67]). The way it was put in *R (Koli) v Maidstone Crown Court* [2011] EWHC 2821 (Admin), LTL 10/5/2011, was that rights of audience would only be granted in exceptional circumstances. This is because a person exercising a right of audience must ordinarily be properly trained, be under professional discipline (including an obligation to have professional liability insurance), and be subject to the overriding duty to the court (President's Guidance, para. 19). Decisions between 2000 and 2008 laying down an 'exceptional circumstances' test are per incuriam (*Re N (A Child) (McKenzie Friend: Rights of Audience)* [2008] EWHC Civ 2042 (Fam), [2008] 1 WLR 2743 at [21]).

In applying these principles, the court seeks to do justice bearing in mind that there is a spectrum between the 'professional' (but unqualified) MF (where the order will be made only in exceptional circumstances) and, at the other end, the spouse or partner of the litigant. The court will bear in mind the limited availability of public funding. An important factor is whether a right of audience is required to ensure the litigant receives a fair hearing (*Re N (A Child) (McKenzie Friend: Rights of Audience)* at [42]).

61.35 **Representation of companies at hearings** Paragraphs 5.2 to 5.6 of PD 39A deal with the representation of companies and corporations at hearings by employees (which is of some importance following the abolition of the rule that companies have to act by solicitors in the High Court). CPR, r. 39.6, provides that a company or corporation may appear at a hearing through a duly authorised employee provided the court gives permission. PD 39A, para. 5.3, says that permission should usually be given unless there is some particular and sufficient reason why it should be withheld. Additional factors, according to *Tracto Teknik GmbH v LKL International Pty Ltd* [2003] EWHC 1563 (Ch), [2003] 2 BCLC 519, are: whether the company is able to afford legal representation, the ability of the proposed representative to do the work required in the litigation, and whether the representative is able to understand and discharge the obligations (such as disclosure of documents) involved in the litigation.

Permission should generally be sought on an occasion prior to the hearing, but may be granted at the hearing itself. Permission may be sought informally. Like all representatives, the employee's status has to be included in the written statement of representatives pursuant to **PD 39A, para. 5.1**. In this case the statement must include the full name and registered number of the company or corporation, the employee's position within the company, and details of the board or other authorisation for the employee to act for the company.

In considering whether to grant permission for a company or other corporation to be represented by an employee, the matters to be taken into account include the complexity of the issues and the experience and position in the company or corporation of the proposed representative (**para. 5.3**). The trial judge in *Watson v Bluemoor Properties Ltd* [2002] EWCA Civ 1875, [2003] BCC 382, refused to permit a company to be represented by a former director who had been disqualified. The Court of Appeal said that the better course in such circumstances is to adjourn to give the company an opportunity to consider whether it wishes to continue, rather than entering judgment on the basis of non-attendance. Permission should not normally be granted in jury trials or contempt proceedings (**para. 5.6**). The Admiralty and Commercial Courts Guide, para. M3, says that, because of their complexity, in most Commercial Court cases it is not appropriate for a company litigant to be represented by an employee. See **45.21** for representation of companies in small claims track hearings.

CONDUCT OF THE TRIAL

Specific guidance for Chancery Division trials is given in the Chancery Guide, ch. 21, for the Queen's Bench Division in the Queen's Bench Guide, paras 10.2.1 to 10.2.8, and for Admiralty and Commercial Court trials by the Admiralty and Commercial Courts Guide, section J. The normal sequence of events in non-specialist cases is discussed in the following paragraphs and in **61.41** to **61.49**.
61.36

Before the hearing the court should be provided with a written statement of the name and professional address of each advocate, his or her qualification as an advocate, and the party he or she acts for (**PD 39A, para. 5.1**). This is usually done by advocates completing a slip provided by the court on the day of the hearing.

The rules give the courts a great deal of flexibility regarding how they will deal with trials. As previously discussed, the court can lay down trial timetables prescribing how the time available for the trial will be used, and allocating specified, limited times, for examination-in-chief, cross-examination and so on. The trial will then follow the timetable previously laid down, or laid down by the trial judge at the start, or will follow the traditional sequence of events.

Generally it will be the claimant who begins. However, it will be the defendant if the defendant has admitted all the issues on which the burden of proof rests on the claimant, so that the only live issues have to be proved by the defendant.

Summary disposal of issues and striking out at trial

The court has the power to strike out a claim or a severable part of a claim at the start or at any stage of a trial (**CPR, rr. 1.4, 3.3** and **3.4; PD 3A, para. 1.2**). Under **r. 1.4(2)(c)**, a trial judge has a power to make an order excluding certain issues from the trial. This power is additional to those for striking out (**chapter 33**) and summary judgment (**chapter 34**), but should be used sparingly and by applying the test of whether the issues in question have a real prospect of success. It can only be exercised after giving the parties an opportunity to make
61.37

representations (*Dunbar Assets plc v Dorcas Holdings Ltd* [2013] EWCA Civ 864, LT 12/7/2013). A failure by the trial judge to give the claimant sufficient notice of an intention to give summary judgment against the claimant at trial justified setting aside the judgment in *Orford v Rasmi Electronics Ltd* [2002] EWCA Civ 1672, [2003] CPLR 213.

In *Western Broadcasting Services v Seaga* [2007] UKPC 19, [2007] EMLR 18, these powers were assumed to be wide enough to encompass deciding in a summary fashion whether set-tlement negotiations had resulted in a binding agreement. However, given that a final decision was being made, doing so on the basis of written evidence alone was held to be unfair and outside the ambit of these powers, and the witnesses should have been called for cross-examination. In *Steenberg v Enterprise Inns plc* [2010] EWCA Civ 201, LTL 10/3/2010, on the second day of the trial, the judge proceeded to consider a preliminary issue based on the first day's evidence of the claimants' witnesses and the witness state-ments of the defendants' witnesses, and then struck out the claim. This procedure was regarded as so utterly flawed (involving accepting at face value disputed evidence from the defendants' witnesses) that the Court of Appeal commented that it should never be repeated. Similar criticism of summary disposal of claims at trial can be found in *Marson v Fattah* [2010] EWCA Civ 266, LTL 18/2/2010, and *Chasewood Park Residents Ltd v Kim* [2010] EWHC 579 (Ch), [2010] NPC 41. In most cases weak issues should be disposed of well before trial, and generally use of summary disposal at trial is deprecated as poten-tially time wasting and expensive (see *Royal Brompton Hospital NHS Trust v Hammond* [2001] BLR 297).

Concessions by advocates and abandonment of issues

61.38 In order to simplify the issues, or for tactical reasons, trial advocates may concede specified facts, issues, or legal arguments. In the absence of exceptional circumstances, failing to argue a point at a hearing which is raised in a party's statement of case or witness statements will result in the point being taken as abandoned (*Adams v Mason Bullock* [2004] EWHC 2910 (Ch), [2005] BPIR 241). The court has a discretion to allow a concession to be withdrawn. Where a party to an appeal seeks to withdraw a concession made in the court below, the appeal court has a discretion to permit this, but will be very cautious before granting permission (*Grobbelaar v News Group Newspapers Ltd* [2002] UKHL 40, [2002] 1 WLR 3024).

Permission to withdraw a concession was granted in *New Zealand Meat Board v Paramount Export Ltd* [2004] UKPC 45, [2005] 2 NZLR 447, where there was no possibility that the outcome would have been affected had the point been taken earlier.

Rulings by the judge

61.39 Trial judges frequently hear and determine all manner of procedural and evidential applica-tions during the course of a trial. After ruling on such matters the judge is *functus officio*. Subject to the rules discussed at **74.55**, advocates are not permitted to ask for such rulings to be reopened: if they wish to take the matter further they should seek permission to appeal (*R v Lashley* [2005] EWCA Crim 2016, *The Times*, 28 September 2005).

Daily trial transcripts

61.40 Her Majesty's Courts and Tribunals Service does not provide daily transcripts of the evidence and submissions made at hearings. Instead, hearings are recorded, and may be transcribed after the event. Requests for transcripts should be made to the court transcribing service. They are quite expensive, and tend to be used for appeal purposes (see **74.27**).

Sometimes one of the parties, particularly in important cases, will arrange for daily tran-scripts to be produced. Often these are purely for the use of the lawyers acting for the party who has arranged for the transcripts. Where copies are provided to the judge, they must also be provided to the other parties (*Lloyds Bank plc v Cassidy* [2004] EWCA Civ 1767, *The Times,* 11 January 2005).

Opening speech

The trial judge will generally have read the papers in the trial bundle before the trial. It will often be the case that in those circumstances there is no need for an opening speech, which may be dispensed with (**PD 28, para. 8.2**, for the fast track; **PD 29, para. 10.2**, for cases on the multi-track). In practice the claimant's advocate will normally begin the trial with a short opening speech, and the judge may allow the other parties to make short speeches (Queen's Bench Guide, para. 10.2.3; Chancery Guide, para. 21.90). In the Queen's Bench Division advocates should provide written summaries of their opening speeches if the points are not covered in their skeleton arguments. If an opening speech is allowed, counsel for the claimant will usually describe the nature of the claim, and will identify the issues to be tried by reference to the statements of case and/or the statement of issues. Some of the documentary evidence may be referred to. It sometimes happens that the judge will rise during the course of the opening to read some of the documents. The judge usually states at an early point in the trial how much pre-reading has been possible, and will deal with arrangements for additional reading. If there is a substantial amount of additional reading needed going beyond the filed reading lists, an additional list should be provided during the opening (Chancery Guide, para. 21.91).

61.41

It is usually convenient to deal with any outstanding procedural matters in the course of, or immediately after, the opening speeches (Queen's Bench Guide, para. 10.2.4; Chancery Guide, para. 21.92).

Claimant's case

After the claimant's opening speech evidence will be called on behalf of the claimant. Broadly, evidence adduced at trial will be real evidence (i.e. physical items), contemporaneous documentary evidence, views of the site, and the evidence of witnesses (see **chapter 49**).

61.42

Real evidence and documents admitted into evidence are made exhibits and are labelled with individual exhibits numbers. The judge has a discretion to inspect the *locus in quo* if there are compelling reasons to do so, outweighing the time and expense of a view. Inspections should generally be conducted in the presence of the parties.

There are occasions when evidence is adduced in a deposition, by affidavit or in the form of hearsay statements.

It is rather more usual for evidence from witnesses to be produced by calling the witnesses to give evidence from the witness box. Witnesses are sometimes asked to leave the court until they are called so they are not influenced by the evidence given by other witnesses, but they remain in court in the large majority of cases. Subject to any trial directions they may be called in any order. When called they are sworn or affirm in a manner they consider binding (Oaths Act 1978). A witness will be afforded anonymity, for example, by being allowed to give evidence behind a screen and without stating his or her name and address aloud, only in highly exceptional cases (*Re W (Children) (Care Proceedings: Witness Anonymity)* [2002] EWCA Civ 1626, [2003] 1 FLR 329).

Exhibits which are handed in and proved during the course of the trial will be recorded in an exhibit list and kept in the custody of the court until the conclusion of the trial, unless the judge directs otherwise (**PD 39A, para. 7**). At the conclusion of the trial the parties have the responsibility for taking away and preserving the exhibits pending any possible appeal.

Commentary

Examination-in-chief

61.43   Traditionally witnesses would give their evidence in answer to non-leading questions put to them by counsel for the party calling them. However, under the CPR witness statements of witnesses called at trial will stand as the evidence-in-chief unless the court otherwise orders (**r. 32.5(2)**). At least in the Chancery Division, witnesses are expected to have re-read their witness statements shortly before being called to give their evidence (Chancery Guide, para. 19.9). Technically, it is only possible to augment the evidence contained in the exchanged statements if, by virtue of **r. 32.5(3)** and **(4)**, the court considers there is good reason not to confine the witness to the contents of his or her witness statement, and for the purpose of either:

(a) amplifying the witness statement; or

(b) giving evidence in relation to new matters which have arisen since the witness statement was served on the other parties.

What will be regarded as a sufficiently 'good reason' to allow supplementary questions remains to be seen. There is a fear that different judges will take different views. Witness statements drafted in a deliberately concise way in accordance with the ethos of the *Woolf Report* as contemplated at ch. 12, paras 54 to 59, of avoiding elaborate over-drafting therefore may fall into the trap (which was also mentioned in the *Woolf Report* at chapter 12, para. 55) of encountering a trial judge who refuses to allow the witness to depart from or amplify his or her witness statement.

The trial judge is entitled to rely on additional or revised evidence on an unresolved issue from an expert based on further experiments conducted by the expert after a pre-trial meeting of the experts and before or during the hearing (*Aintree Hospitals NHS Trust v Sutcliffe* [2008] EWCA Civ 179, [2008] LS Law Medical 230).

Cross-examination

61.44   After being examined in chief, each witness may be cross-examined by counsel for the defendant. Where there is more than one defendant, they cross-examine in the order they appear on the court record. Cross-examination may be conducted using leading questions (i.e. questions which suggest the required answer). Cross-examination is permitted on the witness's statement, whether or not the statements are referred to in chief (**CPR, r. 32.11**). Cross-examination provides the other side the opportunity to test and seek to undermine the evidence given in chief. One of the main obligations on an advocate cross-examining a witness is to put his or her client's case. This means that the witness must be challenged and given an opportunity to comment on the points of conflict between the evidence he or she has given and the case being advanced by the cross-examining party. If this is not done, the court may decide that the witness's account is accepted. Peter Smith J gave a reminder of the importance of putting one's case positively to the other side's witnesses in *EPI Environmental Technologies Inc. v Symphony Plastic Technologies plc* [2004] EWHC 2945 (Ch), [2005] 1 WLR 3456. A failure to do so usually means the point cannot be taken against the witness in the closing speech. This has become even more important with witness statements usually standing as the examination-in-chief, as it allows the judge to assess the witness's response by reference to his or her demeanour and the overall context of the case. It was held in *Re Share* [2002] BPIR 194 that the judge was wrong to reject the evidence of two witnesses which had not been tested in cross-examination (the petitioner having elected not to cross-examine in order to save costs), even though there was documentary evidence which was flatly inconsistent with the oral testimony of those witnesses. For further discussion see **chapter 49**, particularly **49.8**.

A witness who has been cross-examined may be re-examined by counsel for the claimant on matters covered in cross-examination. Leading questions are not allowed.

Witness called by the judge

A witness who is not relied upon by either side may be called by the judge, who may conduct **61.45** the examination. As the witness is not called by another party, neither has a right to cross-examine, although the judge has a discretion to (and will usually) allow either or both parties to do so (*Fallon v Calvert* [1960] 2 QB 201).

Submissions of no case to answer

At the conclusion of the case for the claimant, the defendant may make a submission of no **61.46** case to answer. This is made on the basis that on the evidence adduced by the claimant the claim cannot succeed. In *Benham Ltd v Kythira Investments Ltd* [2003] EWCA Civ 1794, LTL 15/12/2003, it was said that a submission of no case to answer should rarely, if ever, be entertained in a civil case tried without a jury. As the judge is the trier both of law and fact, it is embarrassing for the judge to be asked to rule on the merits of the claim while the evidence is still incomplete. Further, if the judge's ruling were to be reversed on appeal, there would be the added cost of having a retrial. It has therefore been the practice that a defendant seeking to make a submission of no case to answer had to elect to call no evidence before making the submission (*Alexander v Rayson* [1936] 1 KB 169; *Young v Rank* [1950] 2 KB 510).

Under the CPR it remains the case that, in general, the judge may require a defendant to elect to call no evidence before making a submission of no case to answer (*Blinkhorn v Hall* (2000) LTL 13/4/2000; *Miller v Cawley* [2002] EWCA Civ 1100, [2003] CPLR 51). However, there may be circumstances where a submission may be entertained without putting the defendant to an election, as in *Mullan v Birmingham City Council* [2000] CP Rep 61. The power to dismiss on a submission of no case to answer without putting the defendants to their election whether to call evidence should be exercised with considerable caution (*Boyce v Wyatt Engineering* [2001] EWCA Civ 692, [2001] CP Rep 87).

Where the court allows a defendant to make a submission of no case to answer without being required to elect whether to call no evidence, the test by which the submission is determined is whether the claim has no real prospect of success (*Benham Ltd v Kythira Investments Ltd*). On the other hand, if the defendant is put to his election and decides to call no evidence, the submission of no case to answer is decided on the basis of whether the claimant has established the case on the balance of probabilities (*Miller v Cawley* [2002] EWCA Civ 1100, [2003] CPLR 51). It is a serious procedural irregularity for a judge to fail to put the defendant to its election on calling evidence, and then to decide a submission of no case to answer applying the balance of probabilities as the standard of proof (*Graham v Chorley Borough Council* [2006] EWCA Civ 92, [2006] PIQR P24). It is the judge's duty to survey the expert evidence together with that of the defendant before deciding to accede to a submission of no case to answer (*Youssif v Jordan* [2003] EWCA Civ 1852, *The Times*, 22 January 2004).

Defence case

Where the defence decide to call evidence, they may be allowed to make an opening speech **61.47** (though this is now rather unusual). They then call their evidence in the same way as the claimant. Where there is more than one defendant, they present their evidence in the order they appear on the record.

Closing speeches

Where the defence has called evidence, the defence closing speech is made before that of the **61.48** claimant. Speeches usually deal with how the evidence that has been adduced and the inferences that can be drawn from that evidence support the case for the party in question on the factual issues involved. Counsel also argue any legal points that arise, sometimes making use

Commentary

of skeleton arguments. In lengthy and complex cases, counsel should provide written summaries of their closing submissions (Chancery Guide, para. 21.93). Where a case has overrun, the judge may adjourn, or may take other measures, such as ordering closing submissions to be made in writing, to be followed by a written judgment (*Sleeman v Highway Care Ltd* (1999) *The Times,* 3 November 1999).

A judge who, after the close of evidence, realises he may decide the case on a new footing not addressed earlier in the trial, should give the parties a specific warning that this course may be taken, and invite them to make submissions on the matter (*Maersk Co. Ltd v Wilson* [2004] EWCA Civ 313, LTL 25/3/2004).

Role of the judge

61.49   During the course of the trial the judge may put questions to the witnesses, particularly if matters remain obscure after counsel's questions. Depending on the circumstances, it may be the judge's duty to ask questions, including leading questions, to ensure an accurate picture of the events is adduced (*Currey v Currey* [2004] EWCA Civ 1799, [2005] 1 FLR 952). This may include assisting litigants in person with the topics on which witnesses may be examined and cross-examined, and may include the judge putting questions to witnesses (**CPR, r. 3.1A(5)**). Judges should be careful to avoid interrupting the flow of counsel's questions, particularly during cross-examination (*Jones v National Coal Board* [1957] 2 QB 55, although the principles stated in this case might need to be re-evaluated because attitudes to interventions by the judge have changed since 1957, see *Almeida v CVC/Opportunity Equity Partners Ltd* [2006] UKPC 44, 2006 CILR 430). Frequent or intemperate interventions may give grounds for an appeal (*Re R (Children)* [2001] EWCA Civ 1880, LTL 7/12/2001, where there were interventions on average every 50 seconds, but compare *Priestley v Harrogate Healthcare NHS Trust* [2002] EWCA Civ 183, LTL 7/2/20029 and *Cairnstores Ltd v AB Hässle* [2002] EWCA Civ 1504, [2003] FSR 23, where appeals based on excessive intervention by the judge were dismissed). There is a more tolerant attitude to extensive judicial questioning of experts (particularly where the judge is trying to understand technical evidence) than of lay witnesses (*Manning v King's College Hospital NHS Trust* [2009] EWCA Civ 832, 110 BMLR 175). The question is whether a fair-minded and informed observer, having considered the facts, would conclude that there was a real possibility that the judge was biased (*Almeida v CVC/Opportunity Equity Partners Ltd*).

There are occasions when the judge needs to issue warnings to litigants to keep to the relevant issues and not to use intemperate language. Doing so gives no basis for the judge needing to recuse himself (*R (Riseborough) v Lands Tribunal* [2010] EWHC 1436 (Admin), LTL 25/6/2010).

The judge will have to rule on any applications and any objections to the admissibility of evidence or questions during the course of the trial.

Deciding the case

61.50   After hearing the evidence the judge must decide where the truth lies, decide any points of law, and give judgment. As Baroness Hale of Richmond said in *Re B (Children) (Care Proceedings: Standard of Proof)* [2008] UKHL 35, [2009] 1 AC 11 at [32], the judge is guided by any inherent probabilities, contemporaneous documentation or records, any circumstantial evidence tending to support one account or the other, and impressions made as to the character and motivations of the witnesses.

Generally, the judge is constrained by the pleadings, and has to make decisions on the pleaded issues, see **24.24**. There are limited exceptions. A judge should not be deterred from deciding a case on the correct basis where, through incompetent presentation, the underlying legal cause of action has not been identified by a party's representatives (*Watson v Durham University* [2008] EWCA Civ 1266, LTL 24/10/2008). The more usual course is to require the correct basis of the claim to be formulated through amended statements of case (see **chapter 31**), which can be done even at the end of closing speeches. The claimant has the burden of proof on a balance of probabilities. It is for the claimant to prove the case, and the judge should beware of too much speculative reconstruction (*Lynch v James Lynch and Sons (Transport) Ltd* (2000) LTL 8/3/2000). The law operates a binary system in which the only values are zero and one (*Re B (Children) (Care Proceedings: Standard of Proof)* per Lord Hoffmann at [2]). There is no halfway house for the judge who concludes there is a real possibility that a fact in issue took place (per Baroness Hale at [31], [32]). If the party with the burden of proof fails to discharge that burden, the fact is treated as not having happened. If the burden of proof is discharged, the court treats the fact as having happened.

Lord Hoffmann (at [3]) distinguished between:

(a) facts in issue. These are the facts which a legal rule requires to be proved in order to establish a legal right. These have to be proved on the balance of probabilities;

(b) facts used as a basis of making a prediction, which also have to be proved on the balance of probabilities (but compare *Secretary of State for the Home Department v Rehman* [2001] UKHL 47, [2003] 1 AC 153 at [56]); and

(c) facts which merely form part of the material from which a fact in issue may be inferred, which need not be proved to have happened.

Some facts are regarded as inherently improbable, so that strong evidence is required before the court can find them proved on the balance of probabilities. Examples are fraud, deliberate harm and child abuse. There is no necessary link between seriousness and probability. Instead, inherent probabilities have to be taken into account as a factor, 'to whatever extent is appropriate in the particular case' (*Re H (Minors) (Sexual Abuse: Standard of Proof)* [1996] AC 563 at p. 583; *Re B (Children) (Care Proceedings: Standard of Proof)* at [15], [72], [73]), but do not alter the balance of probabilities test.

In the absence of cross-examination (for example, where a witness statement is simply read to the court) the court cannot make findings against a party who denies what is alleged against him, unless the denial is self-evidently wrong, for example, because of other facts which are admitted or because the denial is plainly contradicted by reliable documents (*Re Hopes (Heathrow) Ltd* [2001] 1 BCLC 575). Some facts are so obvious they hardly require proof. An example is that closing windows in a house will reduce noise from outside (*Thornhill v Nationwide Metal Recycling Ltd* [2011] EWCA Civ 919, [2011] Env LR 33, and see judicial notice at **49.27**).

Deciding between witnesses

Cases are decided by the quality of the evidence adduced at the trial, not by weight of numbers **61.51** of witnesses on one side compared to the other (*Gurney Consulting Engineers v Gleeds Health and Safety Ltd* [2006] EWHC 43 (TCC) at [11]). In evaluating evidence given at trial, Peter Smith J in *EPI Environmental Technologies Inc. v Symphony Plastic Technologies plc* [2004] EWHC 2945 (Ch), [2005] 1 WLR 3456 at [74] gave the following guidance:

(a) It is essential to evaluate a witness's performance in the light of the entirety of his or her evidence. Witnesses can make mistakes, but those mistakes do not necessarily affect other parts of their evidence.

(b) Witnesses can regularly lie. However, lies themselves do not mean necessarily that the entirety of that witness's evidence is rejected. A witness may lie in a stupid attempt to bolster a case, but the actual case nevertheless remains good irrespective of the lie. Alternatively, a witness may lie because the case is a lie.

(c) It is essential that a witness is challenged with the other side's case. This involves putting the case positively. It is for the judge then to assess the witness's oral response and demeanour, and the likely veracity of the response in the overall context of the litigation.

In *Powell v Streatham Manor Nursing Home* [1935] AC 243, Lord Macmillan, referring to fraud cases, said, at p. 256, he found it essential to test the credibility of witnesses against objective facts proved independently, particularly the documents in the case. He also took into account their motives, and the overall probabilities of the case. In *Grace Shipping Inc. v C. F. Sharp and Co. (Malaya) Pte Ltd* [1987] 1 Lloyd's Rep 207 the Privy Council said witness evidence has to be assessed against the contemporaneous documents and the overall probabilities. A number of judges have said they find it almost impossible to tell whether a witness is telling the truth if they give evidence through an interpreter (Scrutton LJ in *Compañía Naviera Martiartu of Bilbao v Royal Exchange Assurance Corporation* (1922) 12 Ll L Rep 83 at p. 97; Lord Bingham of Cornhill in *The Business of Judging* (Oxford: OUP, 2000) at p. 11; also *Pacific Inter-Link Sdn Bhd v EFKO Food Ingredients Ltd* [2011] EWHC 923 (Comm), LTL 12/5/2011). Adopting a two-stage approach of making preliminary findings on the evidence of lay witnesses, and then testing those findings against the expert evidence, is likely to be wrong. In *Hall v Jakto Transport Ltd* [2005] EWCA Civ 1327, *The Times,* 28 November 2005, an engineering expert's evidence was relevant to how an accident might have happened. It was held that the judge should have considered the expert's evidence when reaching his conclusions on the credibility of the other witnesses, rather than making preliminary findings based only on the lay witnesses, then reassessing those findings in the light of the expert's evidence.

When faced with competing property valuations, the judge does not necessarily have to decide that one rather than the other is correct. An alternative approach is to seek to find the probable value of the property in the light of the evidence of both valuers (*Stephens v Cannon* [2005] EWCA Civ 222, [2005] CP Rep 31).

Adjudicating on expert evidence

61.52 It is common for judges to have to decide between conflicting expert evidence. When this happens the duty of the judge is to make findings of fact and resolve the conflict (*Sewell v Electrolux Ltd* (1997), *The Times,* 7 November 1997). In *Roadrunner Properties Ltd v Dean* [2003] EWCA Civ 1816, LTL 21/11/2003, the claimant's expert gave evidence that cracks in a party wall were caused by the defendants' use of a jackhammer. The Court of Appeal held the judge had been wrong to prefer the evidence of the defendants' expert, who advanced a hypothesis that the damage was due to climate change, a theory otherwise unsupported by evidence. The court commented that the trial judge had given too much credence to a comment by the defendants' expert that coincidence (that the claimant's damage occurred after use of the jackhammer) was not a forensic tool.

Where there is a conflict between an expert and lay witnesses, generally the judge should refuse to accept the lay evidence in preference to uncontradicted expert evidence (*Re B (A Minor) (Split Hearings: Jurisdiction)* [2000] 1 WLR 790). However, the judge is not obliged to accept expert evidence if there are sufficient grounds for rejecting it, such as where it does not speak to a relevant issue (see *R v Lanfear* [1968] 2 QB 77), or where the judge does not believe the expert or is otherwise unconvinced by the expert's evidence (*Dover District Council v Sherred* (1997) 29 HLR 864). In *Eckersley v Binnie* (1987) 18 Con LR 1, Henry LJ said: 'a coherent reasoned opinion by a suitably qualified expert should be the subject of a coherent reasoned rebuttal'. In *English v Emery Reimbold and Strick Ltd* [2002] EWCA Civ 605, [2002] 1 WLR 2409 at [20], Lord Phillips of Worth Matravers MR said this does not mean the judgment should contain a passage which suggests that the judge has applied the same, or even a superior, degree of expertise to that displayed by the expert. The judge simply has to provide an explanation as to why the evidence of one expert has been accepted over that of another. It may be that one expert's evidence accorded more satisfactorily with the facts found by the judge, or was more inherently credible than the other, or that one expert was better qualified or more objective. In *Coopers Payen Ltd v Southampton Container Terminal Ltd* [2003] EWCA Civ 1223, [2004] 1 Lloyd's Rep 331, Lightman J said at [67] that if there is no other direct evidence, the evidence given by a single joint expert is likely to be compelling. A judge may depart from it only in exceptional circumstances and after fully explaining the reasons. It is different if an expert, including a single joint expert, gives evidence on an issue of fact on which there is lay evidence. Where both the expert and the lay witness are credible, there is no rule of law or practice requiring the judge to prefer the evidence of the expert. The judge must consider whether the expert and lay evidence can be reconciled. If not, the judge must consider whether there is any explanation for the conflict or a possible error by a witness, and in the light of the circumstances, make a considered choice on which evidence to accept. The court in *Armstrong v First York Ltd* [2005] EWCA Civ 277, [2005] 1 WLR 2751, rejected the evidence of a jointly instructed expert who was called at the trial to give evidence in an emerging area of expertise (bio-mechanical accident reconstruction). Ultimately, litigation is conducted by trial by judge, not by experts (see Brooke LJ in *Armstrong v First York Ltd*).

The judge should not develop his own theory on a matter requiring expertise without recalling the experts for their guidance on the theory (*Deveron Joinery Co. Ltd v Perkins* [2003] EWCA Civ 1241, LTL 30/7/2003). In *Breeze v Ahmad* [2005] EWCA Civ 223, LTL 8/3/2005, the judge preferred the defendant's expert, who the judge said was 'compellingly supported' by the expert literature. None of the literature was introduced at the trial or shown to the claimant's expert. In fact it provided no support for the defendant's expert at all. The failure to adduce the literature was held to be a serious procedural irregularity, and a retrial was ordered. In *Re M (Child: Residence)* [2002] EWCA Civ 1052, [2002] 2 FLR 1059, it was held that it was not open to the judge to reject the uncontested evidence of three expert witnesses that the core personality of a father had been so damaged by childhood experiences as to make him unsuitable to be a child's primary carer simply on the basis of impressions while in the witness box. However, on issues such as future placement and parent-child attachment, a judge could depart from unanimous expert opinion. Also, there are cases where lay evidence may be preferred to expert evidence, such as where attesting witnesses are preferred to a handwriting expert over a contested will (*Fuller v Strum* (2000) *The Times*, 14 February 2001, reversed on other grounds [2001] EWCA Civ 1879, [2002] 1 WLR 1097).

Inadequate expert evidence

In *Woolley v Essex County Council* [2006] EWCA Civ 753, LTL 17/5/2006, a joint report by an **61.53** employment consultant considered the claimant's loss of earnings. The expert referred to the fact the claimant was a highly skilled glazier, and was likely to earn in the top centile of earnings for glaziers. However, the figures in the conclusion of the report used average earnings for glaziers. Neither side called the expert, or put questions to him. On appeal it was held it was incumbent on the judge to analyse the expert's report and consider whether the expert had inadvertently made a mistake. It was wrong for the judge to assume the expert was correct. As all the figures were available, the Court of Appeal substituted the correct award. In *Chambers v Excel Logistics Ltd* [2006] EWCA Civ 1031, LTL 7/6/2006, the medical expert said in his report that an injury had accelerated the claimant's back condition by three years. The claimant was off work on full pay for almost three years, and then retired. It was therefore unclear whether the expert meant that the relevant three years were those immediately after the accident, or whether the date he would have to retire was three years earlier than if he had not been injured. The expert was not called and no written questions were put to him, although it was essential that the point was clarified. The Court of Appeal had no material on which to resolve the issue, so the case was remitted back for reconsideration.

Resorting to the burden of proof

61.54   An appeal was allowed in *Cooper v Floor Cleaning Machines Ltd* [2003] EWCA Civ 1649, [2004] RTR 254, where the judge found that both drivers in a road traffic accident were not to be believed, and dismissed both the claim and counterclaim on the basis that neither side had proved its case on the balance of probabilities. Scott-Baker LJ said, at [3]:

It is, on any view, a wholly exceptional situation for a judge to conclude, particularly in a case concerning a road traffic accident, that a claim and counterclaim both fail on the basis of failure to discharge the burden of proof.

In *Stephens v Cannon* [2005] EWCA Civ 222, [2005] CP Rep 31, Wilson J laid down the following principles:

(a) There have to be exceptional circumstances before the court can be justified in deciding a disputed issue by resorting to the burden of proof.

(b) The circumstances will be exceptional where, despite striving to make a finding on the evidence, the court finds it is not reasonable to do so.

(c) A judge resorting to the burden of proof must analyse the evidence and set out in the judgment the steps taken to make a finding on the evidence, and the reasons why the judge has concluded this is not possible, unless these can readily be inferred from the circumstances of the case.

There have been exceptional cases which have been validly decided on the burden of proof. *Ashraf v Akram* [1999] EWCA Civ 640, for example, was a case where there were conflicting stories producing 'an intractable evidential tangle' such that resort to the burden of proof was permissible. In other cases, like *Baker v Market Harborough Industrial Co-operative Society Ltd* [1953] 1 WLR 1472, where two vehicles collided head-on in the middle of the road leaving no survivors, the proper inference may be that both drivers were equally to blame.

Judgment

61.55   Judgment is often given immediately, but in complicated cases may be reserved. Particularly in the High Court, there are cases where the judge will reserve judgment and provide the legal representatives with a written draft judgment usually about one day before the date fixed for pronouncing judgment (see Admiralty and Commercial Court Guide, para. J12; Chancery Guide paras 21.108 to 21.109; Queen's Bench Guide, paras 10.3.5 to 10.3.7). Such a judgment is not delivered until it is formally pronounced in court. Retaining the word 'draft' after a judgment is pronounced does not render the judgment invalid (*Birmingham City Council v Yardley* [2004] EWCA Civ 1756, *The Times*, 13 December 2004). The draft usually contains a confidentiality notice to the effect that it must not be communicated to clients until an hour before the hearing. Advocates should familiarise themselves with the draft and be ready to deal with any points that arise when judgment is delivered, and should refer any typographical errors to the judge's clerk not later than 12 noon on the day before pronouncement.

If judgment is reserved, the court retains the power to entertain further evidence, but will consider factors similar to those laid down in *Ladd v Marshall* [1954] 1 WLR 1489 (see **75.16**) in deciding whether allowing further evidence will accord with the overriding objective (*Townsend v Achilleas* (2000) LTL 6/7/2000; and see the discussion of reconsideration of judgments etc at **63.44** to **63.48**). The whole of any hearing, whether in the High Court or the County Court, will be recorded, unless the judge directs otherwise (**PD 39A, para. 6.1**). Unofficial tape-recording without permission (which will rarely be given) is a contempt of court. **Paragraphs 6.3** to **6.5** of PD 39A deal with obtaining transcripts of proceedings on payment of authorised charges.

Judges are required to give reasons for their judgments in order to comply with the European Convention on Human Rights, **art. 6(1)**, in the **Human Rights Act 1998, sch. 1** (*Torija v Spain* (application 18390/91) (1994) 19 EHRR 553 at [29]). Whether reasons are adequate depends on the nature of the case (*Flannery v Halifax Estate Agencies Ltd* [2000] 1 WLR 377). While it is desirable that a judgment should be comprehensible on first reading, that is not the test of whether reasons are adequate. This is tested in the context of understanding the pleadings, evidence and submissions at trial (*English v Emery Reimbold and Strick Ltd* [2002] EWCA Civ 605, [2002] 1 WLR 2409). There is no obligation to address every argument put forward by the parties, as long as they can see from the judgment the basis of the decision (*Eagil Trust Co. Ltd v Pigott-Brown* [1985] 3 All ER 119). Nor is it necessary to explain every factor the judge took into account in weighing the evidence. What the judge has to do is identify the issues which were vital to the decision, the manner in which the judge resolved them and record the matters which were critical to the decision (*English v Emery Reimbold and Strick Ltd* at [19]). Judgments need not be long. For example, it may be unnecessary to detail or even summarise items of evidence, provided the reasoning essential to the decision is clear to the parties.

It is counsel's duty to draw the judge's attention to any alleged deficiency in the judgment, and request clarification or a supplementary judgment on the issue, rather than raising the issue on an application for permission to appeal (*English v Emery Reimbold and Strick Ltd*; *Re S (Children)* [2007] EWCA Civ 694, [2007] CP Rep 37).

After judgment is given the court will deal with the question of costs, the form of the judgment, and any application for permission to appeal.

Further evidence after judgment and before order

The trial judge has a discretion to permit a party to adduce additional evidence after judgment has been handed down and before the final order has been made (*Navitaire Inc. v Easyjet Airline Co. Ltd* [2005] EWHC 282, [2006] RPC 4; and see **49.54**).   **61.56**

A distinction may be drawn between:

(a) requests to reopen a hearing before the judge delivers judgment. In this situation the application should probably be dealt with in accordance with the overriding objective of dealing with the case justly and at proportionate cost; and

(b) requests to reopen a hearing after judgment has been delivered, but before the judgment is drawn up (see **63.38**). Here the court will have regard to the *Ladd v Marshall* [1954] 1 WLR 1489 principles (see **75.16**), but with more flexibility than in appeals (*Navitaire Inc. v Easyjet Airline Co. Ltd*).

Particular emphasis is placed on the first of the *Ladd v Marshall* principles, and an application was refused in *Fisher v Cadman* [2005] EWHC 2424 (Ch), *The Times*, 23 June 2005, principally because the evidence could have been made available at the right time if the applicant had exercised reasonable diligence.

PRELIMINARY ISSUES

As a general rule, it is in the interests of the parties and the administration of justice that all issues arising in a dispute are tried at the same time. However, particularly in complex actions, costs and time can sometimes be saved if decisive, or potentially decisive, issues can be identified and ordered to be tried before or separately from the main trial. The court's decision on preliminary issues should be used by the parties as a basis for sensible discussions or negotiations. It should not be used as a platform from which the victor launches new, let alone   **61.57** unfounded, claims in order to transform its case on quantum (*Multiplex Constructions (UK) Ltd v Cleveland Bridge UK Ltd* [2008] EWHC 2220 (TCC), LTL 2/10/2008 at [1673]).

There are three types of order that can be made:

(a) for the trial of a preliminary issue on a point of law;
(b) for the separate trial of preliminary issues or questions of fact;
(c) for separate trials of liability and quantum.

The jurisdiction to make these orders derives from **CPR, r. 3.1(2)**.

Factors to be taken into account when deciding whether to order the determination of a preliminary issue were laid down by Neuberger J in *Steele v Steele* (2001) *The Times*, 5 June 2001, as follows:

(a) Whether the determination of the preliminary issue will dispose of the whole case or at least one aspect of the case.
(b) Whether the determination of the preliminary issue will significantly cut down the cost and the time involved in pre-trial preparation and in connection with the trial itself.
(c) If the preliminary issue is an issue of law, the amount of effort involved in identifying the relevant facts for the purposes of the preliminary issue.
(d) If the preliminary issue is an issue of law, whether it can be determined on agreed facts. If there are substantial disputes of fact it is unlikely to be safe to determine the legal issue until the facts are found.
(e) Whether the determination of the preliminary issue will unreasonably fetter either of the parties or the court in achieving a just result.
(f) The risk that an order will increase the costs or delay the trial, and the prospects that such an order may assist in settling the dispute.
(g) The more likely it is that the issue will have to be determined by the court the more appropriate it is to have it determined as a preliminary issue.
(h) The risk that the determination may lose its effect by subsequent amendment of the statements of case.
(i) Whether it is just and right to order the determination of the preliminary issue.

Procedure for trial of preliminary issues

61.58 Orders for the trial of preliminary issues are made either on the application of a party or by the court of its own initiative. It is rare for the court to make such an order without the concurrence of at least one of the parties. It is not possible to make such an order by consent. Normally the application is made at the allocation or listing stage, or on a case management hearing, although it is not unknown for an application to be made to the trial judge at the beginning of a trial.

Where an order for the preliminary trial of an issue of law or fact is made, the court must formulate the issue to be tried. It is important that the issue is defined with precision so as to avoid future difficulties of interpretation (*Avraamides v Colwill* [2006] EWCA Civ 1533, [2006] NPC 120). A preliminary issue should be decided against a schedule of agreed or assumed facts (*McLoughlin v Jones* [2006] EWCA Civ 1167, LTL 5/7/2006). If it is impossible to define the issue, no order should be made (*Allen v Gulf Oil Refining Ltd* [1981] AC 1001). If the issue is one of law, the court must further order the issue to be tried either:

(a) on the statements of case;
(b) on a case stated; or
(c) on an agreed statement of facts.

In *Keays v Murdoch Magazines (UK) Ltd* [1991] 1 WLR 1184, an issue as to whether words were capable of a defamatory meaning was ordered to be tried on the pleadings in conjunction with the copy of the magazine in which the offending article appeared.

Preliminary issues of law or fact

In *Allen v Gulf Oil Refining Ltd* [1981] AC 1001, Lord Roskill said: **61.59**

The preliminary point procedure can in certain classes of case be invoked to achieve the desirable aim of economy and simplicity. But cases in which invocation is desirable are few.

Situations identified by Lord Roskill as being suitable for trial as preliminary issues include:

(a) where a single issue of law can be isolated from the other issues in a case, and its decision may be finally determinative of the case as a whole;

(b) where the facts are agreed and the sole issue is one of law.

Neuberger J in *Re Bank of Credit and Commerce International SA, Banque Arabe Internationale d'Investissement SA v Morris* [2001] 1 BCLC 263 said that preliminary issues of law would not be ordered unless:

(a) they are so formulated that they can be answered without making artificial findings of fact (i.e. findings of fact which are not agreed and are disputed);

(b) they would, if determined one way, enable the court to dismiss at least one of the claims made in the proceedings; and

(c) the point can be formulated into a reasonably arguable issue.

In *Ashmore v Corporation of Lloyd's* [1992] 1 WLR 446, preliminary points of law were ordered to decide:

(a) whether Lloyd's owed a duty of care to the claimants who were 'names' (underwriting members of Lloyd's organised in syndicates); and

(b) whether Lloyd's had immunity from suit under the Lloyd's Act 1982, s. 14.

Issues raised in personal injuries cases as to the claimant's 'date of knowledge' under the Limitation Act 1980, s. 14, may be suitable for trial as preliminary issues. In *Keays v Murdoch Magazines (UK) Ltd* [1991] 1 WLR 1184, the issue whether the words published were capable of bearing a defamatory meaning was determined as a preliminary issue. One of the key factors is whether the procedure is likely to achieve a saving in costs, or whether it is likely to increase expense and delay.

The House of Lords has on several occasions disapproved the practice of making orders to determine points of law on assumed facts. As Lord Scarman said in *Tilling v Whiteman* [1980] AC 1, they are 'too often treacherous short cuts. Their price can be delay, anxiety and expense.' If the court finds against the point of law, the case will be no further advanced than when the order was made. If the facts are found or agreed first, the hearing on the preliminary issue should finally determine the proceedings.

There appears to be a slightly increased willingness to order the trial of preliminary issues under the CPR. The way it is put in the Chancery Guide, for example, at para. 21.27, is that costs can sometimes be saved by identifying decisive issues, or potentially decisive issues, and ordering that they be tried first. The decision of one issue, which in itself may not be decisive, may still be appropriate, because it may enable the parties to settle the remainder of their dispute.

Separate trials of liability and damages

Such orders are regarded as exceptional, and are only made where a clear demarcation line   **61.60** between the issues of liability and quantum can be drawn (*Marks v Chief Constable of Greater Manchester Police* (1992) *The Times*, 28 January 1992). Where certain items of evidence would need to be called at both trials, an order should not be made. In personal injuries cases where the long-term prognosis will only become clear some years after the event, unless quantum can be dealt with by provisional damages, it may be best for liability to be tried early while events are still relatively fresh, leaving quantum to be determined when the prognosis becomes clear (*Hawkins v New Mendip Engineering Ltd* [1966] 1 WLR 1341). If judgment is entered for damages to be assessed, it would be possible for the claimant to apply for an interim payment under **CPR, rr. 25.6** to **25.9** (see **chapter 36**). In these cases disclosure is normally initially limited to the issue of liability (*Baldock v Addison* [1995] 1 WLR 158).

A case where service failed to comply with **Part 6** was *Nelson v Clearsprings (Management) Ltd* [2006] EWCA Civ 1252, [2007] 1 WLR 962. The claim form was accidentally addressed to the defendant at 28 Brook Road, whereas the defendant lived at 26 Brook Road. As a result the defendant did not attend the hearing, and an order for possession was made. As this was a possession claim the judgment was not entered in default, but after a hearing under **Part 55**. This meant that the judgment could not be set aside under the default judgment provisions in **Part 13** (see **20.11** to **20.21**). Sir Anthony Clarke MR said that the intention cannot have been that a judgment entered when the defendant did not even know of the proceedings could only be set aside applying the criteria in **r. 39.3(5)**. Nor did it follow that such judgments would be set aside as of right. Instead:

(a) if the defendant can show he has not been served with the claim form at all, normally a judgment entered after a hearing would be set aside, with the claimant paying the costs;
(b) if the claimant could show there was no defence despite non-service, the claimant should cross-apply for summary judgment and an order dispensing with service of the claim form;
(c) if faced with such cross-applications, the court should make such order as is just; and
(d) if the defendant is guilty of inexcusable delay since learning of the judgment, that could of itself be a reason for refusing the application to set aside.

Both *Hackney London Borough Council v Driscoll* and *Nelson v Clearsprings (Management) Ltd* cite the pre-CPR case of *White v Weston* [1968] 2 QB 647, which held that an irregularly obtained judgment should be set aside as of right, with the claimant paying the costs. *White v Weston* was not cited in early editions of this work, because the wide, obligatory, rule it laid down has no place under the new code created by the CPR. It is no more than a non-binding illustration of what happened under the old system, and understood in that way it causes no harm.

Mandatory requirements for setting aside

CPR, r. 39.3(5), provides that orders to restore or set aside for non-attendance may only be **62.5** granted if the applicant:

(a) acted promptly on finding out about the order;
(b) had a good reason for not attending; and
(c) has a reasonable prospect of success at a reconvened trial.

These conditions are cumulative. If any of the conditions is not satisfied, there is no residual discretion to set aside (*Barclays Bank plc v Ellis* [2001] CP Rep 50). The general approach to be taken was stated by Lord Neuberger of Abbotsbury MR in *Bank of Scotland v Pereira* [2011] EWCA Civ 241, [2011] 1 WLR 2391 at [26] and adopted by Lord Dyson MR in *Mohun-Smith v TBO Investments Ltd* [2016] EWCA Civ 403, [2016] 1 WLR 2919 at [11]:

The strictness of this trio of hurdles is plain, but the rigour of the rule is modified by three factors. First, what constitutes promptness and what constitutes good reason for not attending is, in each case, very fact-sensitive, and the court should, at least in many cases, not be very rigorous when considering the applicant's conduct; similarly, the court should not pre-judge the applicant's case, particularly where there is an issue of fact, when considering the third hurdle. Secondly, like all other rules, r. 39.3 is subject to the overriding objective, and must be applied in that light. [The third point deals with the alternative of appealing.]

Unlike applications to set aside default judgments, where acting promptly is only a factor (see **r. 13.3(2)**), under **r. 39.3(5)** this is a mandatory precondition. Acting 'promptly' means acting with all reasonable celerity in the circumstances, but does not demand that the applicant has been guilty of no needless delay whatever (*Regency Rolls Ltd v Carnall* (2000) LTL 16/10/2000 at [45]). Applications issued 10–15 days (*Mohun-Smith v TBO Investments Ltd*) and six weeks (*Watson v Bluemoor Properties Ltd* [2002] EWCA Civ 1875, [2003] BCC 382) respectively after trial in complex claims were both regarded as 'prompt'. A delay of four months, even though the insurer did not have full knowledge at the date of the trial, meant the application in *Gentry v Miller* [2016] EWCA Civ 141, [2016] 1 WLR 2696 was not made promptly (at [40]).

The phrase 'good reason' in **r. 39.3(5)(b)** is sufficiently clear and does not need further definition (*Brazil v Brazil* [2002] EWCA Civ 1135, [2003] CP Rep 7. In this decision judgment was set aside because the applicant, who was illiterate, did not receive notice of the trial date.) The good reason requirement must be applied so as to give effect to the overriding objective (*Estate Acquisition and Development Ltd v Wiltshire* [2006] EWCA Civ 533, [2006] CP Rep 32). An application to set aside in *Neufville v Papamichael* (1999) LTL 23/11/99) was refused, primarily because there was no adequate explanation for the claimant, who failed to attend trial, not having kept in contact with his solicitors. There may be 'good reason' for non-attendance where there was no letter before claim, several of the court documents were not translated into the defendant's language, and the defendant thought the documents required his involvement as a witness rather than as a party (*Zambia v Meer Care and Desai* [2008] EWCA Civ 754, LTL 9/7/2008). The requirements of **r. 39.3** were held to be satisfied in *Thakerar v Northwich Park and St Mark's NHS Trust* [2002] EWCA Civ 617, LTL 24/4/2002, where the claimant had been admitted to hospital with a heart condition and was discharged during the course of the first day of the trial.

A 'reasonable' prospect of success has the same meaning as 'real' prospect of success (*E. D. and F. Man Liquid Products Ltd v Patel* [2003] EWCA Civ 472, [2003] CPLR 384, and see **34.10** to **34.26**). The fact there is a pleaded defence does not mean it has a reasonable prospect of success (*Sinclair v Johnson* [2008] EWCA Civ 667, LTL 23/5/2008). In contrast to *Bank of Scotland v Pereira* [2011] EWCA Civ 241, [2011] 1 WLR 2391, *Barclays Bank plc v Ellis* [2001] CP Rep 50 was a case where the court took a rigorous approach to the question of whether the party who failed to attend had a reasonable prospect of success at a reconvened trial.

Discretionary factors on setting aside for non-attendance

62.6 It is clear that if the mandatory conditions in **CPR, r. 39.3(5)** are met, the court must move to a second stage and consider whether to exercise its discretion to set aside the order (*Mohun-Smith v TBO Investments Ltd* [2016] EWCA Civ 403, [2016] 1 WLR 2919 at [37]). Once the mandatory requirements are met, Lord Neuberger of Abbotsbury MR in *Bank of Scotland v Pereira* [2011] EWCA Civ 241, [2011] 1 WLR 2391 at [25] said:

... it seems to me that it would be a very exceptional case where the court did not set aside the order. It is a fundamental principle of any civilised legal system, enshrined in the common law and in article 6 of the Convention for the Protection of Human Rights and Fundamental Freedoms, that all parties in a case are entitled to the opportunity to have their case dealt with at a hearing at which they or their representatives are present and are heard.

Until 2016 it was almost unheard of for an application to fail at the discretion stage.

Relief from sanctions after non-attendance

62.7 A different approach was suggested by *Gentry v Miller* [2016] EWCA Civ 141, [2016] 1 WLR 2696. After considering the mandatory requirements in **CPR, r. 39.3(5)**, Vos LJ suggested at [25] that the court must then consider the principles under **r. 3.9** for granting relief from sanctions (for which, see **48.32**). In considering the first stage of the principles in *Denton v T. H. White Ltd* [2014] EWCA Civ 906, [2014] 1 WLR 3926, the relevant sanction is the order granted when the applicant failed to attend the trial. Promptness in applying to set aside the resulting judgment, which is one of the mandatory requirements (**r. 39.3(5)(a)**), is also considered as part of all the circumstances under the third stage of the *Denton* principles (*Gentry v Miller* at [25]).

Gentry v Miller was a combined application to set aside a default judgment under **r. 13.3** and to set aside a judgment for non-attendance under **r. 39.3**. It was cited in argument in the Court of Appeal in *Mohun-Smith v TBO Investments Ltd* [2016] EWCA Civ 403, [2016] 1 WLR 2919, but was not referred to in any of the judgments. As discussed at **62.5** and **62.6**, *Mohun-Smith v TBO Investments Ltd* applied the accepted principles on the exercise of the discretion in **r. 39.3** applications, with no reference to the implied sanctions doctrine underpinning *Gentry v Miller*. It is therefore possible that *Gentry v Miller* will not be followed. Even if *Gentry v Miller* is right, arguably the relief from sanctions principles do not apply to cases where the non-attending party was not served with notice of the trial date, because there will have been no default by the non-attending party (see **62.4**).

Setting aside and appealing

Detailed guidance on the relationship between **CPR, r. 39.3**, and permission to appeal under **Part 52** was given by Lord Neuberger MR in *Bank of Scotland plc v Pereira* [2011] EWCA Civ 241, [2011] 1 WLR 2391. In *Tennero Ltd v Arnold* [2006] EWHC 1530 (QB), [2007] 1 WLR 1025, the defendant was taken ill while abroad, and sent evidence to the court to the effect he was too ill to attend the trial. The first County Court judge refused to adjourn the trial, and judgment was entered against him at the trial. On the advice of the Civil Appeals Office, the defendant made an application to set aside the judgment for non-attendance under **CPR, r. 39.3**. A second County Court judge refused to set aside the judgment. The defendant then brought the present appeal against the first judge's order refusing the adjournment. Jack J held that, having applied to the second County Court judge to set aside, it was thereafter no longer open to the defendant to appeal against the first County Court judge's refusal of the application to adjourn.

62.8

Setting aside on terms

In most cases the party who did not attend will be at fault, so usually will be ordered to pay the costs thrown away. If the non-attendance arose without fault, it may be appropriate to make some other order, such as costs in the case. In addition to setting aside the judgment, the court will invariably need to make consequential directions for further steps in the proceedings and setting a new trial date or window.

62.9

A counterclaim was reinstated in *Watson v Bluemoor Properties Ltd* [2002] EWCA Civ 1875, [2003] BCC 382, on terms that the party applying to reinstate made an interim payment and provided security for future costs.

Chapter 63   Judgments and Orders

INTRODUCTION

63.1   Although there is likely to be a delay between judgment being pronounced and the judgment being sealed and served, CPR, r. 40.7(1), provides that judgment in fact takes effect from the day it was given. Where a written judgment is sent in draft to the legal representatives of the parties under Practice Statement (Supreme Court: Judgments) [1998] 1 WLR 825, it is not given or made for the purposes of r. 40.7(1) until it is pronounced in court (*Prudential Assurance Co. Ltd v McBains Cooper* [2000] 1 WLR 2000). After a judgment or order has been pronounced by the court, the next step is to have it drawn up. In *Holtby v Hodgson* (1889) 24 QBD 103 Lord Esher MR said, at p. 107, 'Pronouncing judgment is not entering judgment; something has to be done which will be a record'. Given r. 40.7, on the question of compliance it is irrelevant that the order is not sealed until after the time specified for compliance (*Rahamim v Reich* (2009) LTL 10/2/2009).

The distinction between judgments and orders is that a judgment is the final decision which disposes of a claim (subject to appeal), whereas an order is an interim decision. However, there is no practical difference between the two, and both are enforceable in the same way.

A party seeking to dispute an order or judgment is usually limited to applying for permission to appeal (see **chapters** 74 and 75). There are exceptions where an application to review an order can be made back to the same judge as made the original order (or to a judge at the same or equivalent level) without appealing. Orders made without notice can be reviewed by applying to set aside or vary within seven days of service of the order (**r. 23.10**). Default judgments can be set aside using the procedure in **Part 13**. If there is a change of circumstances it may be possible to vary case management directions (see **47.32**). If there is an accidental slip or error in an order, it may be corrected under the slip rule (see **63.44**). Orders and judgments can be reviewed by the judge in the period between pronouncement and drawing up (see **63.45**). It may be right to refuse an application to set aside or vary an order where an appeal from that order is pending (*Barrie v J. Barrie (Plant Hire) Ltd* [2001] EWCA Civ 614, LTL 14/2/2001).

SETTLEMENTS

An offer to settle which is stated to be 'subject to contract' will not create a binding **63.2** contract until the parties have signed the contemplated agreement or award (*Morgan Walker Solicitors LLP v Zurich Professional and Financial Lines* [2010] EWHC 1352 (Ch), LTL 16/7/2010). Where the parties have agreed terms for settling the substantive issues in the claim, or on an interim application, they must also decide how those terms should be recorded. An important consideration in this regard is how the agreement can be enforced in the event of either party failing to abide by its terms. The simplest form of judgment provides for immediate payment of the sum agreed together with costs (often on the standard basis, to be the subject of a detailed assessment if not agreed). Enforcement proceedings can be taken on such a judgment on the same day as it is entered. Agreements are not always this simple. Five further ways of recording agreed terms were discussed by Slade J in *Green v Rozen* [1955] 1 WLR 741 (in the context of an agreement reached at the door of the court):

(a) Where a claim is settled on terms as to the payment of money, judgment may be entered for the agreed sum, subject to a stay of execution pending payment of stated instalments. If the instalments fall into arrears, the stay will be lifted, and the judgment creditor can immediately take enforcement proceedings.

(b) A consent order may be drawn up embodying the undertakings of both parties in a series of numbered paragraphs. If any of the terms are not complied with, enforcement may be possible immediately or on application to the court depending on the nature of the term in question.

(c) The agreement may be recorded in a Tomlin order. A Tomlin order has the effect of staying the proceedings save for the purpose of carrying the terms set out in a schedule to the order into effect. See **63.16**.

(d) A consent order may be drawn up staying all further proceedings upon the agreed terms. If the agreement is reached immediately before the hearing its terms will usually be endorsed on counsel's briefs and the court will be asked to make a consent order in those terms. Unlike Tomlin orders, the courts are very unwilling to remove the stay imposed by such orders, so enforcement can usually only be effected by bringing fresh proceedings for breach of the contract embodied in the compromise (see *Rofa Sport Management AG v DHL International (UK) Ltd* [1989] 1 WLR 902).

Commentary

(e) The court may be informed merely that the case has been settled upon terms endorsed on counsel's briefs. This is the most informal way of compromising a claim. Its effect is to supersede the existing claim with the compromise. Any breach can only be enforced by issuing fresh proceedings.

A sixth method was the subject of *Atkinson v Castan* (1991) *The Times*, 17 April 1991, where a consent order made 'no order' save as to costs, but set out the agreed terms in recitals. It was held that the claimants were entitled to enforce the terms stated in the recitals without the need to bring a fresh action.

Notifying court and effect of settling claim

63.3   Where terms are agreed in advance of a hearing, each party has a responsibility to inform the court so that the time set aside for the hearing can be reallocated to other litigants and the hearing fee may be refunded (**CPFO, fee 2.1**). However, as discussed above, it is usually desirable to incorporate the agreed terms in a judgment or order to facilitate enforcement in the event of breach. The options are largely as described above, except that entering the agreement on counsel's papers does not arise. Parties are under a continuing duty to keep the court informed if the prospects of settling the case may have an impact on listing for trial or on the pre-reading needed by the judge, see **61.15**. *Gurney Consulting Engineers v Gleeds Health and Safety Ltd (No. 2)* [2006] EWHC 536 (TCC), 108 Con LR 58, said that in the same way the court must be informed of settlement talks after the hearing and before judgment. This is to avoid the judge wasting time writing up a judgment which may not be needed.

Costs and terms of settlement

63.4   Settlements agreed after proceedings have been issued should deal with the costs of the parties and with the future status of the claim. Care should be taken to ensure the wording used reflects the parties' intentions, especially as regards any previous interim costs orders. Where there is existing litigation, agreement on costs is usually regarded as an essential term of any compromise agreement. Accordingly, agreement on all points on liability and remedies, but without being able to agree costs, means the compromise is incomplete and there is no settlement agreement (*BCT Software Solutions Ltd v C Brewer and Sons Ltd* [2002] EWCA Civ 1765; *Hutchinson v Grant* [2016] EWCA Civ 218, [2016] 2 Costs LR 189).

Options for dealing with the status of the claim include entering final judgment, dismissing the claim, granting a stay or discontinuing or withdrawing it. It should be kept in mind that if a claim is discontinued, the claimant is required to pay the defendant's costs unless specific provision is made to the contrary, and that the claimant is not necessarily barred from commencing fresh proceedings in respect of the same claim (see **chapter 55**). Care is also needed when drafting a consent order to ensure it reflects the parties' intentions on enforcement in the event of breach. For example, in landlord and tenant claims, a compromise may give the landlord a suspended possession order, which allows the landlord to proceed to enforcement by eviction if the tenant fails to comply. Alternatively, a compromise may reinstate the defendant as the lawful tenant, which merely allows the landlord to apply to the court to enforce compliance with any additional terms in the event of breach (*Gibb v Pubmaster Ltd* [2002] EWHC 2236 (Ch), LTL 9/10/2002).

ORDERS MADE AT HEARINGS

63.5   Counsel are under a duty to take notes of the court's judgment, and must endorse a note of the court's decision on the backsheet of their briefs. Instructing solicitors may use this as the basis for drawing up the court's order, so accuracy in noting is of great importance. If the orders are at all complex, counsel for both sides will often consult each other immediately after the hearing to ensure that both sides are clear on what the court has ordered. Counsel's endorsement of the order is not protected by legal professional privilege.

In addition, in interim applications the Master, District Judge or judge will either:

(a) initial the relevant paragraphs of the application notice or draft minutes of the order; or
(b) initial together with making amendments; or
(c) endorse the order on the affidavit, witness statement or application notice in abbreviated form or longhand.

Judgments in Queen's Bench Division trials are certified by the court associate.

The associate's function in this regard is to record what the judge said, and an order recording what the associate believed to be the judge's unexpressed intention was rectified in *Memminger-IRO GmbH v Triplite Ltd (No. 2)* (1992) *The Times*, 9 July 1992.

Remedies and findings beyond the statements of case

63.6 Remedies asked for by the claimant must be set out in the claim form (**CPR, r. 16.2(1)(b)**). Only exceptionally will relief be granted, without an amendment, where the relief claimed is based on implied allegations (*Kirin Amgen Inc. v Hoechst Marion Roussel Ltd* (2001) LTL 8/8/2001). Where the particulars of claim include a claim for 'further or other relief', unless the claimant obtains permission to amend, relief, according to *Kirin Amgen Inc. v Hoechst Marion Roussel Ltd*, will not normally be granted in respect of a claim which:

(a) is not pleaded; or
(b) is inconsistent with the relief specifically pleaded; or
(c) is not supported by the allegations in the pleaded case; or
(d) takes the defendant by surprise, unless there are exceptional circumstances.

The danger of a judge making findings of bad faith and giving false evidence when no bad faith had been pleaded is highlighted by *Co-operative Group Ltd v International Computers Ltd* [2003] EWCA Civ 1955, [2004] Info TLR 25, where an appeal was allowed partially on this ground.

FORM OF JUDGMENTS AND ORDERS

63.7 The heading of a judgment or order is the same as that for the claim, except that the name of the judge, Master or District Judge, if any, is included above the names of the parties (**CPR, r. 40.2(1)**). There then follow any recitals. These are followed by the body of the order, which may be short or may be complex, and should include the court's pronouncement on costs. Undertakings tend to be set out in schedules to orders. The terms of the orders must accurately reflect the pronouncement made by the court. Often it is necessary to amplify the court's words, or to put them in imperative form. The operative parts of a decision must be recorded in the judgment or order, which should be limited to the formal disposal of the application, trial or appeal. It is impermissible for the judge to make a direction that costs should be assessed by reference to guidance set out in specified paragraphs of the judgment (*Richardson Roofing Co. Ltd v Ballast plc* [2009] EWCA Civ 839, LTL 13/2/2009). It is also impermissible to include comments, for example, on the repugnant nature of a letter, in the formal order (*D'Silva v University College Union* [2009] EWCA Civ 1269, LTL 30/11/2009). To simplify this task and to ensure consistency, in both the High Court and the County Court there are many prescribed forms for judgments and orders. There are also model form orders contained in some of the practice directions, such as those for freezing injunctions and search orders in **PD 25A**. These must be used where applicable, with such variations as the circumstances of the case may require.

An order has to speak for itself, and extrinsic material, including earlier drafts, is not admissible as an aid to its proper construction (*Masri v Consolidated Contractors (Oil and Gas) Company SAL* [2009] EWCA Civ 36, [2009] 1 CLC 82, but contrast *Zipher Ltd v Markem Systems Ltd* [2009] EWCA Civ 44, [2009] FSR 14, discussed at **63.10**). In construing a court order the court is seeking to find the intention of the court that made the order (*Secretary of State for Business, Innovation and Skills v Feld* [2014] EWHC 1383 (Ch), [2014] 1 WLR 3396). The starting point is the natural and ordinary meaning of the words used in the light of the syntax, context and background of the order in accordance with *Investors Compensation Scheme Ltd v West Bromwich Building Society* [1998] 1 WLR 896 at pp. 912–13.

Every judgment and order must bear the date on which it was given or made, and be sealed by the court (**r. 40.2(2)**).

Where an application or appeal is dismissed, and the judge considers that it was totally without merit, this fact must be recorded in the order (and the judge must consider whether to make a civil restraint order). See **rr. 3.3(7), 3.4(6), 23.12, 52.4(3)** and **52.20(6)**, and the discussion of civil restraint orders at **14.55** to **14.60**.

Appeals against almost all interim orders can only be made with permission (**r. 52.3**). Usually permission must initially be sought from the lower court, with a right to renew the application for permission to the appeal court. Where a party has sought permission to appeal from the lower court, that court's order must by **r. 40.2(4)** state:

(a) whether an appeal lies from the judgment or order, and if so, to which appeal court (for which, see **74.4**), with an indication of the division of the High Court where the High Court is the appeal court;

(b) whether the lower court has given permission to appeal; and

(c) if not, the appeal court (including the appropriate division where relevant) to which any further application for permission to appeal may be made (this requirement is to assist litigants in person who are often confused about which court deals with appeals).

Time limits

63.8   Where an order imposes a time limit for doing any act, the date for compliance must be expressed as a calendar date, and must include the time of day by which the act must be done (**CPR, r. 2.9(1)**). Orders may be made subject to conditions, and may, at the court's discretion, specify the consequences of failing to comply (**r. 3.1(3)**).

Orders requiring an act to be done ('unless orders')

63.9   Orders requiring an act to be done, other than the payment of money, must specify the time within which the act must be done. The consequences of failing to comply with the order must also be set out (**PD 40B, paras 8.1** and **8.2**). There are two suitable forms of wording, and the first form should be used wherever possible. The second form should be used where the defaulting party does not attend:

Unless the claimant serves his list of documents by 4.00 p.m. on Friday, 12 November 2016, his claim will be struck out and judgment entered for the defendant.

Unless the defendant serves his list of documents within 14 days of service of this order . . .

Injunction orders and penal notice

63.10   Injunction orders, whether prohibitory or mandatory, are intended to have penal consequences and can be punished as a contempt of court. These orders need to be endorsed with a penal notice in form N77 (**CPR, rr. 81.4** and **81.9; PD 4**).

Undertakings in lieu of injunctions are also intended to have penal consequences, and can be punished as a contempt of court. While an undertaking can be enforced under **CPR, r. 81.4**, even if it does not contain a penal notice (**r. 81.9(2)**), it is the usual practice to reduce undertakings to writing using form N117, which must be served in accordance with **r. 81.7**. This includes a penal notice in the following terms:

If you do not comply with your promises to the court you may be held to be in contempt of court and imprisoned or fined, or your assets may be seized.

To ensure there is no doubt over the position, the court may refuse to accept an undertaking unless the person intending to give it personally signs the statement on the reverse of form N117 to the effect that they understand the undertaking they have given and the consequences of breach (**PD 81, para. 2.2**). This statement may alternatively be made in a separate letter which is filed at court (**para. 2.3**). If there is a dispute over whether an oral undertaking has been given (and in what terms), the Court of Appeal in *Zipher Ltd v Markem Systems Ltd* [2009] EWCA Civ 44, [2009] FSR 14, said:

(a) the relevant passages in the transcript of the hearing have to be read together and in their overall context;
(b) the court should avoid an overly semantic analysis of the words in the transcript;
(c) it is permissible to take into account what was said and done before and after the alleged undertaking to assist in resolving what was said and its effect; and
(d) if there is real doubt about the meaning or effect of what was said, it should be resolved in favour of the person who would be bound.

CONSENT ORDERS

Consent orders as contracts

Many orders are made 'by consent'. A true consent order is based on a contract between the parties. As such, the contract is arrived at by bargaining between the parties, perhaps in correspondence, and the consent order is simply evidence of that contract (*Wentworth v Bullen* (1840) 9 B & C 840). To be a true consent order there must be consideration passing from each side. If this is the case, then, unlike other orders, it will only be set aside on grounds, such as fraud or mistake, which would justify the setting aside of a contract (*Purcell v F. C. Trigell Ltd* [1971] 1 QB 358; *Centrehigh Ltd v Amen* (2001) LTL 18/7/2001). A common mistake of law can vitiate a consent order (applying the principles from *Kleinwort Benson Ltd v Lincoln City Council* [1999] 2 AC 349), but consent orders should not be set aside lightly. In *Brennan v Bolt Burdon* [2004] EWCA Civ 1017, [2005] QB 303, the claimant sought to set aside an agreement to discontinue a claim entered into on a mistaken view of the law before the law was clarified by *Anderton v Clwyd County Council (No. 2)* [2002] EWCA Civ 933, [2002] 1 WLR 3174. At the time of the agreement the law was in doubt, but the claimant entered into the agreement anyway, so there was no operative mistake. A consent order may be set aside on the ground that neither party intended to be bound by it (*Goodway v Zurich Insurance Co.* [2004] EWHC 137 (TCC), 96 Con LR 49). In theory a consent order may be void for uncertainty, but this applies only where it is legally or practically impossible to give the agreement any sensible content. This is likely to be extremely rare, because the court will lend its assistance in the working out of its orders or in their clarification (*Scammell v Dicker* [2005] EWCA Civ 405, [2005] 3 All ER 838). A consent order may have contractual effect, but leave the mechanics to be worked out by directions of the court, which may include giving one of the parties additional time to perform (*Chaggar v Chaggar* [2002] EWCA Civ 1637, LTL 30/10/2002). The court has jurisdiction to vary a consent order by discharging a term which is an unlawful restraint of trade while leaving the rest of the order in place (*Gerrard Ltd v Read* (2002) 152 NLJ 22).

63.11

Commentary

In *Green v Vickers Defence Systems* [2002] EWCA Civ 904, *The Times*, 1 July 2002, the deceased and the defendants entered into a consent order, settling a personal injuries claim arising out of the deceased having developed pleural plaques, under which the defendants paid a sum of money on a full-liability basis and on the assumption the deceased would not develop mesothelioma. It was held that the agreement meant that a subsequent claim based on the deceased developing mesothelioma would be paid on a full-liability basis. There is a common misapprehension that where a party fails to honour a term of a compromise agreement settling litigation the original claim is reopened. Although this can be the position where there are grounds for avoiding the contract, in most cases an agreement to compromise a claim brings proceedings on the claim to an end and replaces them with the contractual arrangements in the compromise. Breach of the compromise agreement gives rise to a new claim for breach of contract (*Lewis v Barnett* [2004] EWCA Civ 807, LTL 29/7/2004).

Tomlin orders made in commercial disputes are interpreted in the same way as other commercial agreements (*Sirius International Insurance Co. (Publ) v FAI General Insurance Ltd* [2004] UKHL 54, [2004] 1 WLR 3251). This means the court will seek to ascertain the contextual meaning of the language used. An objective approach is taken, with the court asking what a reasonable person would have understood the parties to have meant by the language used in the order.

See also **33.21**, on settlement acting as a bar to later proceedings.

Submission to consent order

63.12 There is a long-established distinction between a true consent order, which has contractual effect and cannot be appealed, and a situation where an order is marked 'by consent', but in reality is one where one side did no more than not object to the order being made (*Ropac Ltd v Inntrepreneur Pub Cc.* [2001] CP Rep 31, approved in *Pannone LLP v Aardvark Digital Ltd* [2011] EWCA Civ 803, [2011] 1 WLR 2275). In *Siebe Gorman and Co. Ltd v Pneupac Ltd* [1982] 1 WLR 185, Lord Denning MR said at p. 189:

It should be clearly understood by the profession that, when an order is expressed to be made 'by consent', it is ambiguous…. One meaning is this: the words 'by consent' may evidence a real contract between the parties. In such a case the court will only interfere with such an order on the same grounds as it would with any other contract. The other meaning is this: the words 'by consent' may mean 'the parties hereto not objecting'. In such a case there is no real contract between the parties. The order can be altered or varied by the court in the same circumstances as any other order that is made by the court without the consent of the parties.

In *Chanel Ltd v F. W. Woolworth and Co. Ltd* [1981] 1 WLR 485 a respondent was not permitted to reopen an interim order, previously disposed of by consent, on the ground that a subsequent authority had undermined the applicant's case. In *Di Placito v Slater* [2003] EWCA Civ 1863, [2004] 1 WLR 1605, the court refused permission to an applicant to be relieved from an undertaking previously given by consent. These cases were distinguished in *Kensington International Ltd v Republic of Congo* [2007] EWCA Civ 1128, [2008] 1 WLR 1144, where there was a clear difference between the matter previously disposed of by consent and the present application. The consent order had conceded that the respondent was under no obligation to disclose information about cargoes on a continuing basis from a stated date. The current application was for disclosure relating to two specific voyages, which was regarded as a different order made in different circumstances from the consent order.

These established principles have been called into question by *Safin (Fursecroft) Ltd v Badrig* [2015] EWCA Civ 739, [2016] L & TR 11, which held that the court has a 'real discretion' (per Sir Terence Etherton C at [43]) to grant extensions of time under **CPR, rr. 1.1** and **3.1(2)(a)**, in both types of consent order. An extension was allowed to permit late payment to avoid forfeiture of a lease despite the consent order encapsulating a genuine contract between the parties.

The problems with this decision are that it uses procedural law to rewrite substantive contract law; creates an unwarranted distinction between a compromise agreement simply recorded in writing and one written into a consent order; and fails to give effect to *Denton v T. H. White Ltd* [2014] EWCA Civ 906, [2014] 1 WLR 3926 on relief from sanctions, despite recognising (at [55]) the relevance of **r. 3.9** to the decision.

Marking of consent orders

Consent judgments and orders must be expressed as being 'by consent' (**CPR, r. 40.6(7)(b)**) and must be signed by the legal representatives for each party (or by the litigants in person where this is allowed, see **63.40** and **63.41**). **PD 40B, para. 3.4**, provides that the signatures of the legal representatives may be those of the solicitors or counsel acting for the parties. A Tomlin order (see **63.16**) should be headed 'Tomlin Order'. **63.13**

Consent orders in family proceedings

A further distinction relates to family proceedings. In these the legal effect of a consent order derives from the order, not the agreement of the parties. Consequently, there is no jurisdiction to vary a matrimonial consent order (*Thwaite v Thwaite* [1982] Fam 1). Where such an order was obtained by fraud, misrepresentation or mistake, the remedy is to appeal or bring fresh proceedings (*De Lasala v De Lasala* [1980] AC 546 per Lord Diplock). **63.14**

Consent orders as estoppels

A consent order can act as an estoppel which can be raised if fresh proceedings are brought alleging matters encompassed by the compromise (*Keith v Walcott* [1929] AC 482). However, whether this is the effect depends on what was agreed in the consent order, and it may be that one party has reserved the right to bring proceedings on certain allegations although they were raised in the compromised action (*Rice v Reed* [1900] 1 QB 54 and contrast *Jameson v Central Electricity Generating Board* [2000] 1 AC 455, where the terms of the settlement extinguished a claim against a concurrent tortfeasor). Particular care must be taken when entering into a consent order to compromise a claim for specific performance. Such a consent order may be construed as replacing the agreement on which the proceedings were based, or it may be construed as simply replacing the terms of the original contract expressly dealt with in the consent order, with the rest of the original contract still subsisting (as in *Paige v Webb* [2001] EWCA Civ 1220, LTL 26/7/2001). **63.15**

Tomlin orders

Tomlin orders are so named after Tomlin J who, in a Practice Note [1927] WN 290, laid down the procedure to be followed where terms of compromise are agreed and it is intended to stay the claim with the terms scheduled to an order. The modern form of Tomlin order should, according to a HMCTS Notice issued in September 2016, be worded: **63.16**

And, the parties having agreed to the terms set out in [the attached schedule] [a [confidential] schedule/ agreement dated ......, copies of which are held by the parties' solicitors/the solicitors for the [party]] [and to there being no order for costs]
IT IS BY CONSENT ORDERED that
(1) all further proceedings in this claim be stayed except for the purpose of carrying the terms of the agreement into effect.
AND for that purpose the parties have permission to apply [without the need to issue fresh proceedings].
(2) [any provision in respect of costs] (unless in preamble).

Tomlin orders are used where complex terms are agreed, or where the terms of a compromise go beyond the boundaries of the claim (for example, *E. F. Phillips and Sons Ltd v Clarke* [1970] Ch 322), or where it is sought to avoid publicity of the agreement. In the event of the scheduled

Commentary

terms being breached, enforcement is a two-stage process. First, the claim must be restored under the 'liberty to apply' clause, and an order obtained to compel compliance with the term breached. Secondly, if that order is itself breached, enforcement can follow in the usual way. In *Community Care North East v Durham County Council* [2010] EWHC 959 (QB), [2012] 1 WLR 338, it was held that:

(a) the court has power under **CPR, rr. 1.1, 1.4** and **3.7**, to vary the terms in the body of a Tomlin order. This might be appropriate where there has been a material change in circumstances (the same approach as for any other court order); and

(b) the terms in the schedule are a contract, so the court has no power to vary them under the CPR. The only basis for varying or revoking provisions in the schedule are those which apply in relation to contracts (e.g. fraud, undue influence, misrepresentation, mistake).

By **PD 40B, para. 3.5**, where a consent order is in the form of a stay of proceedings on agreed terms recorded in a schedule (a Tomlin order), any direction for the payment of money out of court or for the payment and assessment of costs must be contained in the body of the order and not the schedule. The reason is that these two forms of direction require action on the part of the court, and must therefore be included in the public part of the order and not concealed in the schedule. If the amount of costs has been agreed this can be included in the schedule.

JUDGMENTS

Money judgments and payment by instalments

63.17 A judgment for the payment of money (including costs) must be complied with within 14 days of the judgment, unless the court specifies some other date for compliance (**CPR, r. 40.11**). It may, for example, instead of requiring immediate payment, impose an order for payment by instalments. A judgment for payment by instalments must state the total amount of the judgment, the amount of each instalment, the number of instalments and the date on which each is to be paid, and to whom the instalments should be paid (**PD 40B, para. 12**). Variations in the date or rate of payment of money judgments in the County Court can be applied for by either the judgment creditor or the judgment debtor (**CPR, r. 40.9A**).

There is a general power to stay execution on the ground of matters that have occurred since the date of the judgment (**r. 40.8A**). There is also a power to stay execution on the ground of the judgment debtor's inability to pay (**r. 83.7**).

Judgments in foreign currency

63.18 Since *Miliangos v George Frank (Textiles) Ltd* [1976] AC 443, the general rule has been that in cases with a foreign element it has been possible to enter judgment in a foreign currency, and the date of conversion into sterling for enforcement purposes is the date of payment. As Lord Fraser said at p. 502:

Any conversion date earlier than the date of payment would, in my opinion, be open to the same objection as the breach date, *viz.* that it would necessarily leave a considerable interval of time between the conversion date and the date of payment. During that interval currency fluctuations might cause the sterling award to vary appreciably from the sum in foreign currency to which the creditor was entitled.... [Hence the date of conversion is] the date when the court authorises enforcement of the judgment.

Where judgment is given on a claim and a cross-claim in different currencies which are to be set off against each other (see **63.19**), the proper approach is to assess the principal amount payable on the claim and cross-claim, add interest to each, and then convert the smaller amount into the currency of the larger amount at the exchange rate prevailing at the date of the judgment (or agreement). The judgment should then set off the lesser from the greater, and provide for payment of the balance (*The Botany Triad* [1993] 2 Lloyd's Rep 259; *Fearns v Anglo-Dutch Paint and Chemical Co. Ltd* [2010] EWHC 2366 (Ch), [2011] 1 WLR 366).

For further discussion of the law on this subject, see *McGregor on Damages*.

Where a claimant intends to seek judgment in a foreign currency, the particulars of claim must specify the foreign currency, and must state why the claim is for payment in that currency, the sterling equivalent, and the source of the exchange rate relied upon (**PD 16, para. 9.1**). If the court orders a judgment to be entered in a foreign currency, by **PD 40B, para. 10**, the order must be in the following form:

It is ordered that the defendant pay the claimant [*state the sum in the foreign currency*] or the sterling equivalent at the time of payment.

The CPR contain no express provisions on the *enforcement* of judgments in foreign currency. In *Carnegie v Giessen* [2005] EWCA Civ 191, [2005] 1 WLR 2510, the Court of Appeal held that the relevant pre-CPR practice direction, Queen's Bench Masters' Practice Direction (11), is to be treated as remaining in force. The text of this practice direction, updated to comply with CPR terminology, appears in **appendix 1**.

Counterclaims

Where a cross-claim amounts to a set-off (see **34.37**) it operates as a defence to the claim. If **63.19** the set-off is successful, the amount assessed on the set-off must be deducted from the amount found due on the claim. If the set-off is less than the claim, judgment should be entered for the balance. If the set-off exceeds the claim, judgment should be entered for the defendant on the claim and, if the set-off has been pleaded as a counterclaim, judgment should be entered for the defendant on the counterclaim for the balance (*Hanak v Green* [1958] 2 QB 9). This should mean that the defendant is the successful party (subject to the discretion under the Senior Courts Act 1981, s. 51) on costs. The court has power to give separate judgments when dealing with cases where there are claims and counterclaims. It also has power to order a set-off between the two claims, and simply enter judgment for the balance (**CPR, r. 40.13(2)**). Where it does so, it retains power to make separate costs orders in respect of the claims and counterclaims (**r. 40.13(3)**).

According to *Fearns v Anglo-Dutch Paint and Chemical Co. Ltd* [2010] EWHC 2366 (Ch), [2011] 1 WLR 366, the courts also have inherent jurisdiction to allow cross-judgments in a single set of proceedings, or in different claims, to be set off against each other, even where the cross-judgment is not based on a cross-claim amounting to a set-off (*Edwards v Hope* (1885) 14 QBD 922; *Reid v Cupper* [1915] 2 KB 147; *Re a Debtor (No. 21 of 1950) (No. 2)* [1951] Ch 612). The survival of this inherent jurisdiction may be doubted given the terms of **r. 40.13**, see **1.2**. Set-off against judgments applies to judgments for damages and also to orders for costs (*Fearns v Anglo-Dutch Paint and Chemical Co. Ltd* at [37]). Ordering cross-judgments to be set off against each other is a matter of whether the court considers it just and equitable to exercise its discretion (*Fearns v Anglo-Dutch Paint and Chemical Co. Ltd* at [38]).

Set-off of judgments

There is a general discretion to permit a set-off between cross-judgments. This jurisdiction has **63.20** been codified for cases of cross-judgments in the County Court, and for cross-judgments in the County Court and the High Court, by the County Courts Act 1984, s. 72. In these cases the procedure on applications for permission to set off the judgments is governed by **CPR, r. 40.13A**, which includes provisions for identifying which court should deal with the application and for stays of execution pending the decision. There is no specific provision for situations where the cross-judgments are of the High Court, but the application is made using the Part 23 procedure.

The County Courts Act 1984, s. 72(2), provides that the set-off 'may be allowed in accordance with the practice for the time being in force in the High Court as to the allowance of set-off and in particular in relation to any solicitor's lien for costs'. In deciding whether to exercise the discretion to permit or refuse a set-off the court must consider all the circumstances of the case (*Reid v Cupper* [1915] 2 KB 147). As regards the practice of the High Court 'in relation to any solicitor's lien for costs', the practice has for many years been not generally to take it into account when deciding whether to order a set-off (*Re a Debtor (No. 21 of 1950)* [1951] Ch 612). In the absence of persuasive factors against permitting set-off, it is generally just to give permission. This is especially so where one party has no prospect of paying its debt (*Commissioners of HM Revenue and Customs v Xicom Systems Ltd* [2008] EWHC 1945 (Ch), [2009] 1 Costs LR 45).

Set-off of costs orders

63.21 Set-off of orders for costs was summarised by Scott LJ in five propositions in *Lockley v National Blood Transfusion Service* [1992] 1 WLR 492. Three of these related to public funding, but propositions 3 and 4 are of general application. The third proposition (although worded in the now discredited impeachment of title formula, see **34.37**), is to the effect that set-off is based on the principles of equitable set-off. In his fourth proposition Scott LJ said:

> Set-off of costs or damages to which one party is entitled against costs or damages to which another party is entitled depends upon the application of the equitable criterion [of equitable set-off] .... It is possible to regard all questions regarding costs [set-off of costs against costs is permitted by **CPR, r. 44.12**] as being subject to the statutory discretion conferred upon the court by section 51 of the [Senior Courts] Act 1981. But I would not have thought that a set-off of damages against damages could properly be described as a discretionary matter, nor that a set-off of costs against damages could be so described.

This last proposition does not address set-off of damages against costs, which possibly is covered by s. 51 (*Fearns v Anglo-Dutch Paint and Chemical Co. Ltd* at [73]). There is in any event a wider discretion to order set-off between money judgments and costs orders based on the authorities discussed at **63.19** where this would be just and equitable.

It is the amounts agreed or assessed under cross-costs orders that should be set off against each other, not the percentages in cross-percentage-based costs orders, because each side's costs will almost always be in differing amounts (*Amin v Amin* [2010] EWHC 827 (Ch), LTL 20/4/2010).

State benefits recoupment

63.22 In personal injuries cases where some or all of the damages are subject to recovery under the Social Security (Recovery of Benefits) Act 1997, the judgment should include a preamble setting out the amounts awarded under each head of damage, and the amount by which it has been reduced in accordance with the Act (**PD 40B, para. 5.1**). The judgment should then provide for entry of judgment and payment of the balance.

Interim payments

63.23 Detailed rules for the form of judgments given in cases where there have been interim payments are laid down in **PD 25B**. Further details are provided by **PD 40B, paras 5.1** and **5.1A**, for orders involving recoverable benefits or lump sum awards affected by the Social Security (Recovery of Benefits) Act 1997. In a preamble to the judgment in such a case there should be set out the total amount awarded and the amounts and dates of all interim payments. The total amount awarded should then be reduced by the total amount of the interim payments, with judgment being given for the balance. If the interim payments exceed the amount awarded at trial, by virtue of **CPR, r. 25.8(2)**, the judgment should set out any orders made for repayment, reimbursement, variation or discharge, and any award of interest on the over-paid interim payments.

Provisional damages

At common law an award of damages had to be by way of a single lump sum. This did not always produce a just result in personal injuries cases involving a risk of the claimant suffering some future deterioration related to the original injury. Although the court would increase the damages awarded to take into account the risk of the future deterioration, the uplift would only be a fraction of the true loss if it occurred, and the claimant would be overcompensated if it did not occur. To remedy this shortcoming, the courts have been given power to award provisional damages by the Senior Courts Act 1981, s. 32A, and the County Courts Act 1984, s. 51.

63.24

These sections provide that an award of provisional damages may be made in an:

action for damages for personal injuries in which there is proved or admitted to be a chance that at some definite or indefinite time in the future the injured person will, as a result of the act or omission which gave rise to the cause of action, develop some serious disease or suffer some serious deterioration in his physical or mental condition.

A provisional damages award has two elements:

(a) immediate damages in respect of the existing injuries, calculated on the assumption that the claimant will not develop the future disease or that the future deterioration will not be suffered; and

(b) an entitlement to return to court to apply for further damages if the disease develops or the deterioration is suffered.

Conditions for awarding provisional damages   There are four conditions:

63.25

(a) The particulars of claim must include a claim for provisional damages (**CPR, r. 41.2(1)(a)**).

(b) The future disease or deterioration must be to the claimant's physical or mental condition. A risk that the claimant may be discharged from long-term state-paid hospital care, with the result that he would then need a great deal of private medical care, is not a 'disease or deterioration' (*Adan v Securicor Custodial Services Ltd* [2004] EWHC 394 (QB), [2005] PIQR P79). An injury suffered in a second accident resulting from the injury suffered in the accident for which the defendant is responsible may be a 'deterioration' for these purposes (see *Hughes v Cheshire County Council* (unreported, 2 March 1989), mentioned in and doubted by *Willson v Ministry of Defence* [1991] 1 All ER 638).

(c) The future disease or deterioration must be 'serious'. According to Scott Baker J in *Willson v Ministry of Defence*, this connotes something beyond the ordinary or commonly experienced consequences of the injury in question. It is relevant to consider the effect on the particular claimant, for example, a hand injury will be more serious to a concert pianist than to most other claimants. One matter particularly considered in *Willson v Ministry of Defence* was whether possible future osteoarthritis could be the subject of a provisional damages award. An increased risk of the onset of osteoarthritis is a common factor where an accident victim has suffered fractured bones. As such, it is not beyond the ordinary, and Scott Baker J took the view that even if the future risk of osteoarthritis involved a possible need for surgery or a change in employment it would not be 'serious'.

(d) There must be a 'chance' that the future deterioration 'will' be suffered. If this is not admitted by the defendant, it must be proved on the balance of probabilities. The 'chance' that must be proved is one that is measurable as opposed to being fanciful. In *Patterson v Ministry of Defence* [1987] CLY 1194, Simon Brown J found that the claimant had about a 5 per cent risk of developing further pleural thickening, and decided there was a 'plain' chance of that happening for the purposes of making a provisional damages award.

63.26 **Discretion to award provisional damages**   Once the above conditions have been established, the court has a discretion whether to make a provisional damages award as opposed to a conventional lump-sum award. The most important factor in the exercise of this discretion would appear to be one of balancing the desirability of putting an end to litigation against the possibility of doing better justice by reserving the claimant's right to return to court for further damages. Provisional damages are more appropriate where the risk of the future deterioration is high and the nature of the possible future deterioration is very serious (for example, a future risk of severe epilepsy). Provisional damages are also more likely to be awarded if the claimant can point to some clear-cut future event that will trigger the entitlement to return to court for further damages.

63.27 **Provisional damages orders**   A provisional damages order:

(a) must specify the disease or type of deterioration in respect of which an application may be made for further damages as a future date;

(b) must specify the period within which that application may be made. The period for applying for further damages may be extended; and

(c) may be made in respect of more than one disease or type of deterioration, and may, in respect of each disease or type of deterioration, specify a different period for applying for further damages.

A model form of provisional damages judgment is set out in **PD 41A**. This includes the filing of a case file of documents to be preserved until the expiry of the period (or any extension) during which the claimant is entitled to apply for further damages if the specified disease develops or the specified deterioration is suffered. The documents that will usually be included in the case file are the judgment, the statements of case, a transcript of the judge's oral judgment, all medical reports relied upon, and a transcript of the claimant's own evidence in so far as the judge regards it as necessary (**PD 41A, para. 3.2**). The fact there may be a few 'loose ends' where the parties cannot agree does not prevent the court making a provisional damages award (*Hurditch v Sheffield Health Authority* [1989] QB 562).

Other matters dealt with in **PD 41A** are the entering of consent orders for provisional damages (**para. 4**) and default judgments (which can only be entered with the court's permission, with the Master or District Judge having to decide whether the case is an appropriate one for a provisional damages award, **para. 5**).

63.28 **Applying for further damages**   If the deterioration occurs, an application for further damages should be made within the period specified in the order (as extended from time to time). Only one application for further damages can be made in respect of each disease or deterioration specified in the order. The claimant must give 28 days' notice of the intention to ask for further damages. Within 21 days of the expiry of the 28 days' notice the claimant has to apply to the court for directions.

Structured settlements

63.29 By virtue of an agreement between the Inland Revenue and the Association of British Insurers in 1987, periodic payments made under certain settlements are deemed to be instalments of antecedent debts. The result is that the payments are capital and not income and therefore are not taxable. This tax advantage is obtained by using the whole or a part of the lump sum which would otherwise be available on settling a personal injury claim to purchase an annuity. There are four types of annuity which qualify under the scheme:

(a) a basic term annuity, which runs for a fixed number of years;

(b) an index-linked (i.e. one which rises with inflation) fixed-term annuity;

(c) an annuity for life or for a minimum number of years (which survives for the claimant's beneficiaries);

(d) an index-linked life or minimum-term annuity.

Annuities are bought from life offices. A life office will quote a price of an annuity if given certain details about the claimant (age, sex, medical reports, level of income required, etc.). A quotation will normally only remain open for a limited time. The basic idea is that the tax advantage should be shared between the parties, so that the claimant obtains a more favourable settlement which will provide more income than that obtainable under a lump-sum award, and the defendant will pay less for the annuity than the conventional award. Both parties need to agree on a settlement being structured, and it is generally thought that structuring is only viable where damages run into six figures.

Periodical payments

In addition to the established structured settlements, the court can make an award in the form of periodical payments (Damages Act 1996, s. 2, as substituted by the Courts Act 2003, s. 100, from 1 April 2005). In deciding whether to make a periodical payment order, and in what form, the court's overall aim is to make whatever order objectively best meets the claimant's needs (*Thompstone v Tameside and Glossop Acute Services NHS Trust* [2008] EWCA Civ 5, [2008] 1 WLR 2207). An agreement between the parties to an award for periodical payments, even where they are of full age and capacity, does not bind the court, which has to make its own decision (**CPR, r. 41.7; PD 41B;** *Morton v Portal Ltd* [2010] EWHC 1804 (QB), LTL 30/7/2010). The court performs an inquisitorial role in doing this, in which there are no legal burdens of proof. An award in the form of periodical payments can be made where both parties agree, or may be ordered by the court where it awards damages for future pecuniary loss in respect of personal injuries.

63.30

Commentary

Such an award can only be made if the court is satisfied the continuity of payments under the order is reasonably secure (Damages Act 1996, s. 2(3)). Continuity problems involving the status of NHS foundation trusts were resolved in *YM (A Child) v Gloucestershire Hospitals NHS Foundation Trust* [2006] EWHC 820 (QB), [2006] PIQR P27, by arrangements being agreed and implemented between the National Health Service Litigation Authority and the Department of Health, which were, subject to conditions, agreed to by the Trust. Rules on continuity of payments are in s. 2(4), **CPR, r. 41.9,** and **PD 41B, para. 3.** The report in the PIQR includes a model form of Tomlin order for use in similar cases.

In *Thompstone v Tameside Hospital NHS Foundation Trust* [2008] EWHC 2948 (QB), [2009] PIQR P153, the court set out a model periodical payments order which needs to be adapted to meet the requirements of individual cases, but any departure in future cases will need to be justified before being approved by the court.

In a personal injuries claim, either side may state in its statement of case whether it considers periodical payments or a lump sum is the more appropriate form for all or part of any award of damages (**CPR, r. 41.5**). The Damages Act 1996, s. 2(8), provides that an order for periodical payments is to be treated as providing for the amount of the payments to vary by reference to the retail prices index at such times and in such manner as might be determined or in accordance with the CPR. This may be disapplied or modified by the court under s. 2(9). There are no restrictions on the types of modifications that may be made under s. 2(9)(b). They may include using a measure based on annual earnings and converted into an index in place of the retail prices index (*Thompstone v Tameside and Glossop Acute Services NHS Trust* [2008] EWCA Civ 5, [2008] 1 WLR 2207 at [40]–[43]). In deciding on a suitable index (see [52]–[58]), the court considers:

(a) the accuracy of the match of the particular data series to the loss and expenditure being compensated;
(b) the authority of the collector of the data;
(c) statistical reliability;
(d) accessibility;

(e) consistency over time;

(f) reproducibility in the future; and

(g) simplicity and consistency in application.

After judgment was entered for damages to be assessed, directions were made in *Flora v Wakom (Heathrow) Ltd* [2005] EWHC 2822 (QB), [2006] PIQR Q95, requiring the claimant to file a statement of case and expert financial evidence dealing with whether a periodical payments order should be made, and whether the court should depart from the usual retail price index under s. 2(9). The defendant was then required to file a statement of case in response and any expert evidence relied upon. The court is under a duty to consider and indicate to the parties its view on the matter as soon as practicable (**CPR, r. 41.6**). In considering whether periodical payments might be appropriate, and whether to make a periodical payments award, the court must have regard to all the circumstances of the case, and which form of award will best meet the claimant's needs (**r. 41.7**). Factors to take into account include, by **PD 41B, para. 1**:

(a) the scale of the annual payments taking into account any contributory negligence;

(b) the claimant's preference, including his reasons for that preference and the nature of any financial advice received; and

(c) the defendant's preference, and his reasons for that preference. In considering the defendant's preference, usually it is sufficient if this is indicated to the court on instructions, without the need to call expert evidence. There is no absolute bar on a defendant adducing the evidence of a financial advice expert (to oppose that of the claimant), but it would be rare for permission to be granted (*Thompstone v Tameside and Glossop Acute Services NHS Trust* [2008] EWCA Civ 5, [2008] 1 WLR 2207 at [109]–[112]).

A periodical payments award must specify the annual amount of the award, how each payment is to be made and at what intervals, and the amounts of the main heads of loss (**CPR, r. 41.8(1)**). There are further requirements where the court orders the award to continue after death for the benefit of the claimant's dependents, where the award is to increase or decrease, and where there is an award for substantial capital purchases (**r. 41.8(2) to (4)**, supplemented by **PD 41B, para. 2**). Variations may be permitted pursuant to the Damages (Variation of Periodical Payments) Order 2005 (SI 2005/841). Where the court is satisfied under the Damages Act 1996, s. 2(6)(a), that special circumstances make an assignment or charge of periodical payments necessary, it must also take into account whether the capitalised value of the assignment or charge represents value for money, whether the assignment or charge is in the claimant's best interests, and how the claimant will be financially supported thereafter (**CPR, r. 41.10 and PD 41B, para. 4**).

As a result of the Damages Act 1996, s. 2, there are special rules on making Part 36 offers where a personal injuries claim includes damages for future pecuniary loss (**CPR, r. 36.18**, see **66.11**).

Where a claim which includes damages for future pecuniary loss is settled on behalf of a claimant under a disability, the usual rules in **Part 21** have to be complied with (see **14.22**), and also the rules in **PD 21, para. 6.3**. Where court approval is sought for a compromise, the court must be satisfied that the parties have considered whether there should be periodical payments (**para. 6.2**). Where the settlement includes periodical payments, the draft consent order must comply with **CPR, rr. 41.8 and 41.9** (see above). The court must be supplied with an opinion on the merits of the settlement or compromise given by counsel or the solicitor acting for the child or protected party (except in very clear cases), and a copy or record of any financial advice (**PD 21, para. 6.4**).

Fatal accidents claims

63.31   With effect from 6 April 2007, **CPR, r. 41.3A**, applies where a claim includes claims under the **Fatal Accidents Act 1976** and the **Law Reform (Miscellaneous Provisions) Act 1934** and where a claim under the Fatal Accidents Act 1976 is made by or on behalf of more than one person. In such cases, if a single sum of money is ordered or agreed to be paid in satisfaction of the claim, the court must apportion the money between the different claims or between the persons entitled to the money.

Fundamentally dishonest personal injury claims

With effect from 13 April 2015, the Criminal Justice and Courts Act 2015, s. 57, provides that **63.32** the court must dismiss a claim for damages for personal injuries, even if the court finds that the claimant is entitled to damages in respect of the claim, if the court is satisfied on the balance of probabilities that the claimant has been fundamentally dishonest in relation to the primary claim or a related claim (s. 57(2)). This includes a duty to dismiss any element of the personal injury claim in respect of which the claimant has not been dishonest (s. 57(3)). Damages that would have been awarded must still be recorded in the court's order (s. 57(4)), and these are deducted from any costs the claimant is ordered to pay to the defendant (s. 57(5)).

Part-owners in relation to claims for the detention of goods

In a claim by a person who is one of several people with interests in goods which are the sub- **63.33** ject of proceedings for wrongful interference and which is not based on a right to possession, any judgment can only be for damages unless every other part-owner gives written authority to the claimant to bring the claim on the part-owner's behalf as well as on the claimant's (**CPR, r. 40.14**).

Miscellaneous technical requirements in orders

A number of technical provisions for different types of judgment are contained in PD 40B. **63.34** Paragraph 14 gives examples of forms that can be used for judgments, and lays down certain matters to be included in the preamble of a judgment, such as the questions put to a jury and their findings, any orders made during the trial regarding the use of evidence, and the findings of the judge in respect of each head of damage in a personal injury case.

RESERVED JUDGMENTS

Judgment may be delivered extempore, or the judge may decide to reserve judgment to a later **63.35** occasion, usually in order to provide a written judgment. When reserving judgment the judge may indicate the overall result, with the reasons to follow in the written judgment. What a judge should not do is to deliver a reasoned extempore judgment, followed by a written judgment developing the reasons (even if the decision remains the same). See *McTear v Engelhard* [2016] EWCA Civ 487, [2016] 4 WLR 108 at [15].

PD 40E applies to all reserved judgments in all courts (**para. 1.1**). Where judgment is reserved, a copy will normally be provided to the parties' legal representatives by 4 p.m. on the second working day before the day listed for handing down the judgment (**para. 2.3**). This is done to enable parties to spot typographical, spelling and minor factual errors, and to give them the opportunity to agree costs and consider an appeal. In *R (Edwards) v Environment Agency* [2008] UKHL 22, [2008] 1 WLR 1587, Lord Hoffmann said, at [66], that sending a 27-paragraph memorandum of submissions commenting on draft speeches was an abuse of process. The purpose of disclosing draft speeches is to obtain the help of counsel in correcting inadvertent errors and ambiguities. It is not to enable counsel to reargue the case. Any proposed corrections should be sent to the clerk of the judge, with a copy to the other parties (**para. 3.1**). Only in the most exceptional circumstances is it appropriate to ask the judge to reconsider a point of substance. Examples are where counsel feels the judge has not given adequate reasons, or has decided the case on a point not sufficiently argued, or has relied on an authority that was not considered. See *Egan v Motor Services (Bath) Ltd* [2007] EWCA Civ 1002, [2008] 1 WLR 1589. A further example given by Lord Judge CJ in *R (Mohamed) v Secretary of State for Foreign and Commonwealth Affairs (No. 2)* [2010] EWCA Civ 158, [2011] QB 218, is where a judgment contains detrimental observations about an individual or the lawyers which are not necessary to the judgment and which appear to be based on a misunderstanding of the evidence, or a concession, or a submission. In such cases the appropriate course is to reconvene the hearing, or for counsel to provide written submissions by 12 noon on the working day before handing down (**para. 4.4**).

The draft judgment must be kept confidential until the judgment is formally handed down. Premature publication of a handed down judgment is a contempt of court (*Re The Lawyer* [2006] EWHC 1131 (Ch), *The Times*, 24 May 2006). During the two-day period between circulation and handing down, the draft judgment can be shown, in confidence, to the parties (**para. 2.4**) and the legal team with immediate conduct of the case (*Director of Public Prosecutions v P (No. 2)* [2007] EWHC 1144 (Admin), [2008] 1 WLR 1024). Neither the judgment nor its substance may be disclosed to any other person, and no action may be taken on it other than internally (**para. 2.4**). This means that while it is appropriate for junior solicitors to consult with their immediate supervising solicitor (and vice versa), wider circulation within chambers or the firm is impermissible. It is just as much a breach of **para. 2.4** to circulate a letter or email from counsel making suggestions for alterations to a draft judgment as it is to circulate the judgment itself (*R (Mohamed) v Secretary of State for Foreign and Commonwealth Affairs (No. 2)* at [11]). If a solicitor is in doubt as to the propriety of a particular disclosure, a request should be made by email to the judge's clerk or the presiding judge for permission (*Director of Public Prosecutions v P (No. 2)* at [15]; **PD 40E, para. 2.7**). The court has the power to waive the confidentiality on a formal interim application to that effect (*R (Mohamed) v Secretary of State for Foreign and Commonwealth Affairs (No. 2)*).

The parties should consider whether they can agree a draft order based on the circulated draft judgment. If they can, they should fax or email a copy to the clerk to the judge or presiding judge, and file four copies (with completed backsheets) in the relevant court office by 12 noon on the working day before handing down (**para. 4.2**). If consequential orders are agreed, there is no need for advocates to attend when judgment is handed down, and costs may be disallowed if they do (**paras 5.1 and 5.2**). Where consequential orders cannot be agreed, the application must be made by filing written submissions with the clerk to the judge or presiding judge by 12 noon on the working day before handing down (**para. 4.4**). Unless the court orders otherwise, the application will be determined without a hearing if in an appeal court, or at a hearing if at first instance (**para. 4.5**).

REDACTED AND ANONYMISED JUDGMENTS

Redacted judgments

63.36 The fact that a judgment contains personal information not otherwise available is not in itself a reason for redacting the judgment (*Kazeminy v Siddiqi* [2010] EWHC 201 (Comm), LTL 2/3/2010). Where a judgment includes passages that may be protected by public interest immunity (see **50.80** to **50.82**), the court may issue a redacted judgment after considering the strong public policy in favour of open justice and the material in support of immunity. Cogent reasons are required before the court will go behind a ministerial certificate seeking immunity (*R (Mohamed) v Secretary of State for Foreign and Commonwealth Affairs (No. 2)* [2010] EWCA Civ 65, [2011] QB 218 at [130]). Genuinely secret material will be protected (see [56]), and in this case the Divisional Court protected a great deal of material relevant to the workings of the security service in a closed judgment, which was not the subject of the appeal (see [50]). However, the Court of Appeal refused to redact a number of paragraphs from an open judgment, and the judgments in the Court of Appeal give careful consideration to the range of factors that may be relevant. Lord Judge LCJ said a redaction order will be made only in extreme circumstances (at [40]).

Anonymised judgments

There is a broad power to order the non-disclosure of the identity of any party if this is **63.37** necessary to protect the interests of that party (**CPR, r. 39.2(4)**). Courts have a duty to apply an intense focus on the particular circumstances (*Ivereigh v Associated Newspapers Ltd* [2008] EWHC 339 (QB)), and then to strike a balance between the interests of open justice and publicity for court proceedings, and the interests of a party or third person in protecting personal data (*Z v Finland* (application 22009/93) (1997) 25 EHRR 371; and see the European Convention on Human Rights, **arts 6(1)** and **8**, in the **Human Rights Act 1998, sch. 1**). The right to respect for private life under the European Convention on Human Rights, **art. 8**, is only engaged in this context if specific effects are identified by the applicant (*Karakó v Hungary* (application 39311/05) ECHR 28 April 2009). If they are, the court must consider whether there is sufficient general public interest in publishing a report of the proceedings which identifies the applicant to justify any resulting curtailment of his right, and his family's right, to respect for their private and family life (*Re Guardian News and Media Ltd* [2010] UKSC 1, [2010] 2 AC 697). It will only rarely be necessary for the identity of a child involved in proceedings to be revealed (*Ivereigh v Associated Newspapers Ltd*). Often the reasons for holding a hearing in private also justify anonymising any judgment, as do defamation claims of a sensitive nature (*Commissioners of HM Revenue and Customs v Banerjee (No. 2)* [2009] EWHC 1229 (Ch), [2009] 3 All ER 930 at [16], [28]). Otherwise, exceptional circumstances are required to justify anonymising a judgment (*Commissioners of HM Revenue and Customs v Banerjee (No. 2)* at [34]), and once material has been revealed in open court, it enters the public domain (*Commissioners of HM Revenue and Customs v Banerjee (No. 2)* at [38]).

ACCOUNTS AND INQUIRIES

At any stage of proceedings, on application by a party or of its own initiative, the court may **63.38** make an order directing accounts to be taken or inquiries to be made (**CPR, r. 25.1(1)(o)**). The practice on taking such accounts and conducting such inquiries is dealt with in **PD 40A**. When making such an order the court may also at the same time or later give directions as to how the account is to be taken or the inquiry conducted (**PD 40A, para. 1.1**). Among the directions that may be made are the following:

(a) that the relevant books of account shall be evidence of their contents, subject to the parties having the right to make objections (**para. 1.2**);

(b) that an account must be made out and verified by an accounting party by exhibiting it to an affidavit or witness statement (**para. 2(1)**);

(c) that, if appropriate, and at any stage in the proceedings, the parties must serve points of claim and points of defence (**para. 5**);

(d) that the matter should be advertised (**para. 10**);

(e) (in an account of debts or other liabilities) that a party examine the claims of those alleging they are owed money, and to file written evidence on his findings and reasons (**para. 11.1(1)**); and

(f) (in an inquiry for next of kin or unascertained beneficiaries) that a party examine the claims made and file written evidence with his findings and reasons (**para. 11.1(3)**).

Unless the court orders otherwise, accounts and inquiries are conducted by Masters or District Judges (**para. 9**). The court may direct the inquiry to be investigated in any manner, and direct the person making the claim to give further details, file written evidence and attend court (**para. 12**).

A party alleging that an account drawn by an accounting party is inaccurate (or making similar allegations) must give written notice of the objections to the accounting party (**para. 3.1**). These objections must give full particulars, specify the grounds on which it is alleged the account is inaccurate and be verified by a statement of truth (or exhibited to an affidavit or witness statement).

DRAWING UP ORDERS AND JUDGMENTS

63.39   CPR, **rr. 40.2(2)**, **40.3(1)** and **60.7**, provide that all judgments and orders have to be drawn up and sealed by the court, unless it dispenses with the need to do so. Normally the court will take responsibility for drawing up, but:

(a) unless otherwise ordered, every judgment or order in the Queen's Bench Division, including the Admiralty and Commercial Courts, and the Technology and Construction Court (but not the Administrative Court) must be drawn up by the parties;

(b) the court may order a party to draw up an order; or

(c) a party may, with the permission of the court, agree to draw up an order; or

(d) the court may direct a party to draw up the order subject to checking by the court before it is sealed; or

(e) the court may direct the parties to file an agreed statement of the terms of the order before the court itself draws up the order; or

(f) the order may be entered administratively by consent, in which event the parties will submit a drawn up version of their agreement for entry.

A party who is required to draw up a judgment is allowed seven days to file the relevant document, together with sufficient copies for all relevant parties, failing which any other party may draw it up and file it for sealing (**CPR, rr. 40.3(3)** and **40.4(1)**).

Every judgment or order (apart from judgments on admissions, default judgments, consent judgments and orders made by court officers under **rr. 70.5** and **71.2**) must state the name and judicial title of the judge who made it (**r. 40.2(1)**). Where a party has asked for permission to appeal, the lower court's order should, by **CPR, r. 40.2(3)** and **(4)** include:

(a) whether the judgment is final or not (see **74.6**);

(b) whether an appeal lies, and if so, to which court (see **74.4**);

(c) whether permission to appeal is granted; and

(d) if not, the appropriate court for making a renewed application for permission to appeal.

Once an order has been drawn up the court will serve sealed copies on the applicant and respondent, and also on any other person the court may order to be served (**r. 40.4(2)**). It will be the court that effects service unless one of the exceptions set out in **r. 6.21(2)** applies. The court is given a specific power by **r. 40.5** to order service on a litigant as well as the litigant's solicitor.

Entering administrative consent orders

63.40   In order to save time and costs, **CPR, r. 40.6**, allows certain types of consent orders to be entered by a purely administrative process without the need for obtaining the approval of a judge. However, this process may not be used if any of the parties is a litigant in person (**r. 40.6(2)(b)**). The types of orders covered are:

(a) judgments or orders for the payment of money;

(b) judgments or orders for the delivery up of goods (other than specific delivery);

(c) orders to dismiss the whole or part of the proceedings;

(d) orders for stays on agreed terms which dispose of the proceedings, including Tomlin orders;

(e) orders setting aside default judgments;

(f) orders for the payment out of money in court;

(g) orders for the discharge from liability of any party; and

(h) orders for the payment, waiver or assessment of costs.

The consent order has to be drawn up in the agreed terms, has to bear the words 'By Consent', and be signed by the solicitors or counsel acting for each of the parties. In cases where terms are annexed in a schedule, provisions dealing with the payment of money out of court and for the payment and assessment of costs should be contained in the body of the order rather than in the schedule (**PD 40B, para. 3.5**).

Where it is proposed to submit a Tomlin order (see **63.16**) to a Court Associate for sealing in the Rolls Building, the request must include a signed solicitors' certificate saying:

We certify that the only relief sought in this claim/counterclaim is the payment of money including an interest and costs, and that no ancillary relief has been sought at any stage.

Consent orders approved by the court

If an order is agreed between the parties, but includes a provision going beyond the types **63.41** of orders referred to in **63.40**, or if one of the parties is a litigant in person, it will have to be approved by a judge (often a District Judge or Master). It will be drawn up as above. The name of the judge will not be known, so the draft will have to include a space for the judge's details to be inserted (**PD 23A, para. 10.3**). If all the parties write to the court expressing their consent, the court will treat that as sufficient signing of the consent order (**PD 23A, para. 10.2**). The court will not necessarily make the order in accordance with the agreement between the parties, as the court retains ultimate control, particularly over case management matters. However, it will always take the terms agreed between the parties into account in whatever order it decides to make (see, for example, **PD 28, para. 3.8**).

In cases where the court's approval must be sought, either party may make the application for approval, and the application may be dealt with without a hearing (**CPR, r. 40.6(5) and (6)**). A court cannot make a consent order without the valid consent of the parties (*Sharland v Sharland* [2015] UKSC 60, [2015] 3 WLR 1070 at [29]). Nor can it make an order it does not have the power to make, even if the terms are agreed by the parties. For example, the court cannot order the parties 'to agree' (that is for the parties themselves), nor can the court order the claimant to discontinue. Instead, in these situations, an order may set out the terms the parties have agreed, or it might record an undertaking by the claimant to discontinue.

Chancery Division orders

Generally, in the Chancery Division the parties are responsible for providing the court with **63.42** an order in a form which may be approved and sealed without amendment (Chancery Guide, para. 22.1). Draft orders should usually be lodged with the court in Word format, thereby allowing the court to make minor adjustments without needing to retype the document (para. 22.2). There are guidelines for drawing up different forms of order (paras 22.3 to 22.16). Orders should be drawn in neutral terms reflecting what was understood to have been the intention of the court. They are then sent by email to the relevant judge's clerk or to Masters' Appointments, all within two working days of the hearing, copying in the other parties (para. 22.22).

REVIEW OF JUDGMENT

63.43   Appealing (see **chapters** 74 and 75) is the main way of impugning a decision. In limited circumstances a judgment or order may be corrected under the slip rule (**63.44**), or may be reconsidered (**63.45**) or recalled (**63.47**) before it is drawn up. There is also an exceptional power to reopen the whole proceedings where no appeal is possible (**63.48**).

Slip rule

63.44   The court has power to correct any accidental slip or omission in any judgment (**CPR, r. 40.12(1)**). The slip rule can be used to amend an order to give effect to the intention of the court (*Swindale v Forder* [2007] EWCA Civ 29, [2007] 1 FLR 1905). It cannot be used to enable the court to have second or additional thoughts (*Bristol-Myers Squibb Co. v Baker Norton Pharmaceuticals Inc. (No. 2)* [2001] RPC 913), or to add an undertaking which no one had in mind (*SmithKline Beecham plc v Apotex Europe Ltd* [2006] EWCA Civ 658, [2007] Ch 71), or to correct a substantive issue (*Markos v Goodfellow* (2002) LTL 11/10/2002), or to correct provisions which have been deliberately included in an order (*Leo Pharma A/S v Sandoz Ltd* [2010] EWHC 1911 (Pat), [2010] FSR 41). It cannot be used to correct matters of substance, for which the appropriate avenue is to appeal (*R+V Versicherung AG v Risk Insurance and Reinsurance Solutions SA* [2007] EWHC 79 (Comm), *The Times*, 26 February 2007). An order in *Gesek v Nazdrowicz-Woodley* (1998) LTL 13/11/98 appointing a representative for a deceased claimant referred to 'proceedings to be instituted'. In fact the relevant proceedings had already been issued. It was held that the order should be corrected under the slip rule, even though the correction was sought at trial. **Paragraphs 4.1 to 4.5 of PD 40B** deal with applications to correct errors in judgments and orders. If the error is obvious the court may deal with the application without notice. Opposed applications will normally be listed before the judge who gave the judgment or made the order.

Reconsideration before judgment is drawn up

63.45   The court may reconsider a judgment after it has been pronounced provided this is done before it is drawn up. During this period factual errors can be corrected (*Spice Girls Ltd v Aprilia World Service BV (No. 3)* (2000) *The Times*, 12 September 2000). The Court of Appeal may reconsider a judgment in the period between draft judgments being sent to the parties and formal delivery in court (*Royal Brompton Hospital NHS Trust v Hammond* [2001] BLR 317; see also the power to reopen an appeal under **CPR, r. 52.30**, discussed at **74.55**, and the inherent power to a similar effect in the Supreme Court, see **76.28**). The power to reconsider a judgment is not affected by **r. 40.7**, which provides that a judgment takes effect from the time of pronouncement (*Stewart v Engel* [2000] 1 WLR 2268). Reconsideration can be sought up to the time the judgment is sealed, a position that is not affected by **r. 52.12(2)(b)** (time for filing an appellant's notice runs from pronouncement) (*Paulin v Paulin* [2009] EWCA Civ 221, [2009] 3 All ER 88).

Reconsideration should be sought only in exceptional circumstances (*Re Barrell Enterprises* [1973] 1 WLR 19, as affirmed by *Stewart v Engel* and *Taylor v Lawrence* [2002] EWCA Civ 90, [2003] QB 528). The examples of exceptional circumstances justifying reconsideration of interim decisions, given by Neuberger J in *Re Blenheim Leisure (Restaurants) Ltd (No. 3)* (1999) *The Times*, 9 November 1999 (see **32.42**), would also justify reconsideration of a final judgment (*Stewart v Engel*). The fact that the party against whom judgment has been pronounced has a change of mind about not pursuing a particular cause of action is not an exceptional circumstance justifying reconsideration (*Stewart v Engel*). It would be a misuse of the jurisdiction to argue that a judge should reconsider an issue which was in dispute and already argued: that would be to subvert the appeal process (*Compagnie Noga* *d'Importation et d'Exportation SA v Abacha* [2001] 3 All ER 513). It is also an abuse of the procedure to advance points which were not argued before judgment was given (*Sheikh v Dogan* [2009] EWHC 2935 (Ch), LTL 24/11/2009).

Varying or revoking orders

It may sometimes, due to a change of circumstances, be appropriate for one judge to recon- **63.46**
sider case management directions made on a previous occasion by another judge of coordinate
jurisdiction. There is accordingly a power to vary or revoke previous orders (**CPR, r. 3.1(7)**),
which is considered fully at **42.42** to **42.45**.

There is a conflict in the cases over whether the power to revoke given by **r. 3.1(7)** applies to
final orders and judgments such as orders to approve settlements of persons under a disability
(*Roult v North West Strategic Health Authority* [2009] EWCA Civ 444, [2010] 1 WLR 487, where it was
held it did not extend to final orders). It was held in *Kojima v HSBC Bank plc* [2011] EWHC 611
(Ch), [2011] 3 All ER 359, that there is no jurisdictional ban on using **r. 3.1(7)** to revoke or vary
a final order. In this case it was held that the public interest in finality in litigation will generally mean that something more than a material change of circumstances or the judge having
been misled will be needed before the power is exercised. It was also used to vary a final costs
order to include a non-party costs order (see **68.61**) in *Latimer Management Consultants Ltd v
Ellingham Investments Ltd* [2006] EWHC 3662 (Ch), [2007] 1 WLR 2569, where it was discovered after
judgment that a litigant's costs were being funded by another person. In *Mid Suffolk District
Council v Clarke* [2006] EWCA Civ 71, [2006] Env LR 38, it was said that great caution is needed if
the court is asked to vary an order made at trial. An order was revoked under **r. 3.1(7)** in
Edwards v Golding [2007] EWCA Civ 416, The Times, 22 May 2007, rather than requiring an appeal
by a misjoined party.

Recalling judgment

A judge is under a positive obligation to recall a draft judgment sent to the legal repre- **63.47**
sentatives of the parties in advance of formal pronouncement (see **61.56**) if it becomes
clear that the draft is wrong (*Robinson v Bird* [2003] EWCA Civ 1820, [2004] WTLR 257). In *Taylor
v Williamsons* [2002] EWCA Civ 1380, [2003] CP Rep 20, after hearing evidence on a preliminary
issue, the case was adjourned with directions for the exchange and filing of written submissions. Before the deadline, and before receiving the claimant's submissions, the judge
issued a written judgment dismissing the claim. When the mistake was discovered, the
judge recalled his judgment, refused to recuse himself, and again gave judgment for the
defendant. An appeal by the claimant was dismissed. It was held that a judge has a wide
discretion to amend a judgment before it is perfected and to recall such a judgment, and
there was no reason to think the judge in this case had not reconsidered the case fairly in
the light of the further submissions.

Reopening proceedings

Like the Court of Appeal (*Taylor v Lawrence* [2002] EWCA Civ 90, [2003] QB 528, see **74.55**), the **63.48**
High Court has jurisdiction to reopen proceedings after they have been concluded to hear
more evidence or further argument (*Seray-Wurie v Hackney London Borough Council* [2002] EWCA
Civ 909, [2003] 1 WLR 257). The power should only be exercised where there has been a significant injustice and where there is no alternative remedy. There may be no alternative remedy
where an appeal court has refused permission to appeal (see **74.16** and the **Access to Justice
Act 1999, s. 54(4)**, which is a point made at **CPR, r. 52.30(7)**). Applications for permission
to reopen should be made on paper (*Taylor v Lawrence*).

The decisions referred to in the previous paragraph were both based on the court's inherent
jurisdiction. This means they have no direct relevance to the question of whether there is

Commentary

jurisdiction for a Circuit Judge to reopen a decision (*Seray-Wurie v Hackney London Borough Council*, a point which appears to be confirmed by **r. 52.30(3)**).

Functus officio

63.49 A judgment may be reconsidered or recalled in the period between delivery and drawing up (**63.45** to **63.48**). Subject to the slip rule (**63.44**), once the judgment has been drawn up into an order the judge is *functus officio*, which operates as a bar to further alterations by the judge (*Earl of Malmesbury v Strutt and Parker* [2007] EWHC 2199 (QB), [2007] 42 EG 294 (CS)).

REGISTER OF JUDGMENTS

63.50 Under the Courts Act 2003, s. 98, a register of money judgments from the High Court and the County Court, and also criminal fines, may be kept either by a body corporate in accordance with terms agreed with the Lord Chancellor, or it may be kept by the Lord Chancellor (Register of Judgments, Orders and Fines Regulations 2005, SI 2005/3595, regs 6 and 7). The relevant register is operated by Registry Trust Ltd. Appropriate officers in the High Court and County Court are required to provide the registrar with periodic returns of judgments and orders for the payment of money (reg. 8(1) and the definition of 'judgment' in reg. 3). The following are, by reg. 9, exempt from registration:

(a) judgments in family proceedings;

(b) judgments in the Administrative Court;

(c) judgments in the Technology and Construction Court;

(d) judgments under appeal, until the appeal has been determined;

(e) broadly, judgments in contested proceedings, until an order or application is made for payment by instalments, or the judgment creditor takes any step to enforce the judgment; and

(f) broadly, orders for the payment of money in claims for the recovery of land, until the judgment creditor takes any step to enforce the order.

Details given by the appropriate officer to the registrar include the debtor's full name, date of birth (which explains why this information is required in acknowledgments of service and defences), and the amount of the judgment debt (reg. 10). The amount may be increased, for example, after the assessment of costs (reg. 20). Registrations are removed after six years in any event (reg. 26). Registration may be cancelled if the judgment is satisfied within one month from the date of the judgment, or if it is set aside or reversed (reg. 11(2)). If the judgment is satisfied more than a month after judgment, the appropriate officer should notify the registrar who will endorse the entry with the fact the judgment has been satisfied (reg. 11(3)).

Records of judgments and orders

63.51 Official copies of court documents prove themselves (Senior Courts Act 1981, s. 132; **PD 32, para. 13.2**). This means, for example, that there is no need (and it is wrong) to exhibit a sealed judgment or order to a witness statement.

The Lord Chancellor may by regulations made by statutory instrument provide for the keeping of records of and in relation to proceedings of the County Court (County Courts Act 1984, s. 12(1)). A certified copy of an entry in a book or other document kept for this purpose is admissible in evidence without further proof as evidence of the entry and of the proceeding referred to and the regularity of that proceeding (s. 12(2)). The position is similar in the High

Court (Senior Courts Act 1981, s. 136). Where primary evidence of a court record has been destroyed or lost, secondary evidence is admissible to prove the existence of the originals (*Miller-Foulds v Secretary of State for Constitutional Affairs* (2008) LTL 20/11/2008).

A request for a certificate of any judgment or order of the County Court can be made in accordance with the procedure set down in **CPR, r. 40.14A.**

Commentary

Chapter 64 Interest

INTRODUCTION

64.1 Until *Sempra Metals Ltd v Commissioners of Inland Revenue* [2007] UKHL 34, [2008] 1 AC 561, the law on awarding interest was confused and based on the misapplication of principles (see [92]). The underlying problem was that the courts, following decisions in the eighteenth and nineteenth centuries, restricted the circumstances in which interest could be awarded, and generally restricted awards to simple as opposed to compound interest. This is contrary to economic reality. Money is not available commercially in return for simple interest only. This is true whether money is borrowed on overdraft or credit cards or mortgages, or when depositing money with banks or building societies (Lord Nicholls of Birkenhead at [52]). *Sempra Metals Ltd v Commissioners of Inland Revenue* reinterprets the leading authorities on awards of interest, and lays down a coherent set of principles which are consistent with the law on remoteness in contract and tort, and the modern law of restitution.

Statutory interest

64.2 The most straightforward way of claiming interest in a claim for money is to seek interest pursuant to the County Courts Act 1984, s. 69, or the Senior Courts Act 1981, s. 35A. See **64.9** to **64.12**. Although such awards are technically discretionary, they are usually made as a matter of course, and can be made in the absence of evidence of actual loss through being kept out of the principal sum. Under these provisions the court is restricted to awarding simple interest. While the rate of interest is in the court's discretion, the starting point is 8 per cent per annum (the rate under the Judgments Act 1838). These provisions do not apply to debt claims which are paid before proceedings are commenced. Despite these restrictions, claiming interest under these statutory provisions will often be the most convenient and cost-effective method of seeking interest.

There is a slightly more complicated statutory right to interest under the Late Payment of Commercial Debts (Interest) Act 1998 (see **64.15**). This again provides for simple interest only, but at a rate of 8 per cent over the Bank of England's official dealing rate. It does this by implying a term to pay interest, so it will be considered with contractual cases below. This Act applies only to claims for the contract price for the supply of goods or services where both the purchaser and supplier are acting in the course of a business. Where it applies this Act gives a right to interest, and at a better rate than under the County Courts Act 1984, s. 69, and the Senior Courts Act 1981, s. 35A.

Various other statutory powers to award interest are mentioned at **64.13**.

Contractual interest

Being contractual, such interest is payable as of right. It may provide for a high rate of interest, **64.3** which may be either simple or compound as agreed by the parties. The main problems with contractual interest relate to proving the relevant term and interpreting it, although it is also possible for such a term to be struck down as extortionate. See **64.14**.

Special jurisdiction to award interest

Equity cases are considered at **64.16**.   **64.4**

Interest as part of the principal award

Interest can be awarded as part of the claimant's damages in claims in contract and tort, as part **64.5** (or the whole) of the claimant's primary award in restitution, and in Admiralty cases. An award of interest as damages in contract or tort is subject to the usual rules on proof of loss, causation, remoteness and mitigation of damage. The award may include an element of compound interest. In restitution, the award is based on the benefit received by the defendant through the unjust use of the claimant's money. This is the main importance of *Sempra Metals Ltd v Commissioners of Inland Revenue* [2007] UKHL 34, [2008] 1 AC 561. While compound interest may be awarded, most of the key elements of the claim for interest have to be proved by the claimant (the exception is the rate of interest, where the burden of proof is on the defendant). Establishing interest as a head of damages or a restitutionary award is therefore likely to be complicated and costly. See **64.18** to **64.20**.

Statutory interest in addition to interest as damages or restitution

In *Sempra Metals Ltd v Commissioners of Inland Revenue* [2007] UKHL 34, [2008] 1 AC 561, the compound **64.6** interest awarded as the main restitutionary remedy covered the period from when the claimant made certain mistaken payments until the dates when those mistaken payments were offset against tax legitimately payable. The court also awarded statutory interest under the Senior Courts Act 1981, s. 35A, on the restitutionary interest from the dates of the offsets to the date of the hearing.

Pleading interest

Any claim for interest must be pleaded in the particulars of claim (or counterclaim), see **64.21**.   **64.7**

Conflict of laws

For the purposes of the conflict of laws, the right to interest on damages for personal injuries **64.8** under the Senior Courts Act 1981, s. 35A, is a remedy, not a substantive cause of action (*Maher v Groupama Grand Est* [2009] EWCA Civ 1191, LTL 12/11/2009).

STATUTORY INTEREST

Statutory interest on claims for damages

Statutory authority for adding interest to any sum recovered by way of damages is provided by **64.9** the Senior Courts Act 1981, s. 35A(1), and by the County Courts Act 1984, s. 69(1), which are in identical terms (except for referring to the High Court and County Court respectively). The County Courts Act 1984, s. 69(1), provides:

Subject to rules of court, in proceedings (whenever instituted) before [the County Court] for the recovery of a debt or damages there may be included in any sum for which judgment is given simple interest, at such rate as the court thinks fit or as may be prescribed, on all or any part of the debt or damages in respect of which judgment is given, or payment is made before judgment, for all or any part of the period between the date when the cause of action arose and—
(a) in the case of any sum paid before judgment, the date of the payment; and
(b) in the case of the sum for which judgment is given, the date of the judgment.

Interest on damages is therefore discretionary, and may be awarded on all or part of the amount recovered, and for such period and at such rates as the court may think fit. However, it is a discretion which is usually exercised in favour of the party obtaining judgment. The way it was expressed by Gloster J in *Socimer International Bank Ltd v Standard Bank London Ltd* [2006] EWHC 2896 (Comm), LTL 8/12/2006, was that statutory interest should be awarded unless there is a good reason for departing from the usual rule. The principle on which the courts act is that interest should be paid to compensate the claimant for being kept out of the money which the judgment shows should have been paid at an earlier time (*Wentworth v Wiltshire County Council* [1993] QB 654). Since the time at which the money should have been paid, the claimant will have been forced either to borrow money, or to use funds which could have been employed profitably for other purposes, or have been deprived of the use of the money awarded by the judgment. An award of interest compensates for this loss. While statutory interest may be lost in an exceptional case where there is a delay in commencing proceedings (*Kuwait Airways Corporation v Kuwait Insurance Co. SAK* [2000] Lloyd's Rep IR 678), it is wrong to disallow interest to take into account conduct in relation to offers and negotiations (*Benedetti v Sawiris* [2010] EWCA Civ 1427, LTL 16/12/2010). The latter can be dealt with by the order as to costs.

The statutory provisions only allow the court to award simple interest. It is therefore wrong in principle to award damages for things such as bank interest if an award of statutory interest on the other heads of damage is made, as that would amount to double recovery (*Wentworth v Wiltshire County Counci.* [1993] QB 654).

In personal injuries claims it is even clearer that interest should ordinarily be awarded in addition to damages. The Senior Courts Act 1981, s. 35A(2), and the County Courts Act 1984, s. 69(2), both provide:

In relation to a judgment given for damages for personal injuries or death which exceed £200 subsection (1) shall have effect—
(a) with the substitution of 'shall be included' for 'may be included'; and
(b) with the addition of 'unless the court is satisfied that there are special reasons to the contrary' after 'given', where first occurring.

The Senior Courts Act 1981, s. 35A(7), and the County Courts Act 1984, s. 69(6), state that the term 'personal injuries' includes any disease or impairment of a person's physical or mental condition.

Statutory interest on debt claims

64.10 The main provisions in the Senior Courts Act 1981, s. 35A(1), and the County Courts Act 1984, s. 69(1) (see 64.9), by their terms apply to debt claims as well as claims for damages. Accordingly, the court is given a general discretion to award simple interest on judgments for debts at such rates and for such periods as the court thinks fit. Restitution claims, and claims for sums of money subject to an obligation, no matter how they arise, are 'debt' claims within the meaning of the Senior Courts Act 1981, s. 35A, and the County Courts Act 1984, s. 69. They therefore attract discretionary simple interest (see *R (Kemp) v Denbighshire Local Health Board* [2006] EWHC 181 (Admin), [2007] 1 WLR 639).

In addition, s. 35A(3) of the 1981 Act and s. 69(3) of the 1984 Act (both of which are in the same terms apart from references to the High Court and County Court respectively) provide for the recovery of simple interest on debt claims which are paid after the commencement of proceedings even in the absence of a judgment. The County Courts Act 1984, s. 69(3), provides:

Subject to rules of court, where—
(a) there are proceedings (whenever instituted) before [the County Court] for the recovery of a debt; and
(b) the defendant pays the whole debt to the [claimant] (otherwise than in pursuance of a judgment in the proceedings),

the defendant shall be liable to pay the [claimant] simple interest, at such rate as the court thinks fit or as may be prescribed, on all or any part of the debt for all or any part of the period between the date the cause of action arose and the date of payment.

These provisions do not apply if interest is payable on the debt for some other reason (see **64.13**), because s. 35A(4) of the 1981 Act and s. 69(4) of the 1984 Act provide:

Interest in respect of a debt shall not be awarded under this section for a period during which, for whatever reason, interest on the debt already runs.

Payment before judgment

64.11 The reason why subsection (3) is in the Senior Courts Act 1981, s. 35A, and the County Courts Act 1984, s. 69, is that payment in full of a debt extinguishes the debt, and so subsection (3) is required to preserve a right to interest despite payment of the principal before judgment (see *Edmunds v Lloyds Italico & l'Ancora Compagnia di Assicurazione e Riassicurazione SpA* [1986] 1 WLR 492). On the other hand, payment of the sum claimed in a damages case does not extinguish the cause of action, and the court may still enter judgment for damages (even though full credit will be given so that no further damages will be paid) and interest. Consequently, there is no need for an equivalent provision to subsection (3) in relation to damages claims (*Edmunds v Lloyds Italico & l'Ancora Compagnia di Assicurazione e Riassicurazione SpA* [1986] 1 WLR 492).

Interest is not payable by virtue of s. 35A of the 1981 Act or s. 69 of the 1984 Act unless proceedings have been commenced (*President of India v La Pintada Compania Navigacion SA* [1985] AC 104; *Sempra Metals Ltd v Commissioners of Inland Revenue* [2007] UKHL 34, [2008] 1 AC 561 at [83]), though interest may be payable under other provisions (see **64.13** and **64.14**). In a damages claim there is nothing to stop the claimant insisting on an element representing interest to be included in any agreed settlement before proceedings are issued. In a debt claim where there is no defence, the debtor is well advised to pay the whole sum due before proceedings are commenced so as to avoid an order to pay interest as well. Once proceedings are commenced, interest may be claimed for the periods both before and after issue.

'Proceedings'

64.12 Statutory interest under the Senior Courts Act 1981, s. 35A, and the County Courts Act 1984, s. 69, applies 'in proceedings (whenever instituted)'. This normally means that a claim form has to be issued. In judicial review proceedings, the trigger point is when the judicial review claim form is submitted (*R (Kemp) v Denbighshire Local Health Board* [2006] EWHC 181 (Admin), [2007] 1 WLR 639).

Miscellaneous statutes

64.13 In addition to the general provisions in the Senior Courts Act 1981, s. 35A, and the County Courts Act 1984, s. 69, there are other statutes giving rights to interest. Examples are:

(a) The Bills of Exchange Act 1882, s. 57, which provides:

Where a bill is dishonoured, the measure of damages, which shall be deemed to be liquidated damages, shall be as follows:
(1) The holder may recover from any party liable on the bill and the drawer who has been compelled to pay the bill may recover from the acceptor, and an indorser who has been

compelled to pay the bill may recover from the acceptor or from the drawer, or from a prior indorser:

(a) The amount of the bill:

(b) Interest thereon from the time of presentment for payment if the bill is payable on demand, and from the maturity of the bill in any other case:

(c) The expenses of noting, or, when protest is necessary, and the protest has been extended, the expenses of protest.

[(2) Repealed]

(3) Where by this Act interest may be recovered as damages, such interest may, if justice require it, be withheld wholly or in part, and where a bill is expressed to be payable with interest at a given rate, interest as damages may or may not be given at the same rate as interest proper.

(b) In a claim against a carrier under the Convention on the Contract for the International Carriage of Goods by Road, the claimant is entitled to claim interest at 5 per cent per annum (Carriage of Goods by Road Act 1965, sch., art. 27).

(c) Under the Partnership Act 1890, s. 24(3), a partner who contributes more capital than the partnership agreement calls for is entitled to interest at 5 per cent per annum on the additional contribution from the date of payment, unless otherwise agreed.

(d) Under the Solicitors' (Non-contentious Business) Remuneration Order 1994 (SI 1994/2616), art. 14, a solicitor may charge interest at a rate not exceeding that payable on judgments on the amount of his or her unpaid costs in respect of non-contentious business or common form probate business, plus disbursements and VAT, subject to various conditions set out in the Order.

(e) Various revenue statutes provide for the payment of interest, such as the Taxes Management Act 1970, ss. 86 to 92.

CONTRACT CASES

Interest pursuant to contract

64.14   Interest may be payable under the express terms of a contract between the parties. Where this is the case, the interest is payable as of right, and is not a matter for the court's discretion. The only exception is where the rate of interest is extortionate within the meaning of the Consumer Credit Act 1974. Mortgage agreements and many other forms of credit agreement purport to give the lender an unfettered discretion to vary the rate of interest charged. Dyson LJ in *Paragon Finance plc v Nash* [2001] EWCA Civ 1466, [2002] 1 WLR 685, said that such a discretion is subject to an implied term that it is not to be exercised dishonestly, capriciously, arbitrarily or for an improper purpose. Express terms for the payment of interest often also provide that interest at the agreed rate shall be payable before and after proceedings, and even before and after judgment, until actual payment. The latter type of clause presents some difficulty over the form any judgment should take. One school of thought is to the effect that the judgment should only include contractual interest to the date of the judgment, leaving the creditor to bring a second action (if thought fit) to recover the post-judgment interest. The other school of thought would allow the court to make a judgment to include the interest to the date of judgment together with continuing interest at the contractual daily rate to payment.

Interest has also been awarded in cases where money has been lent on terms that it should be repaid on a set date with interest being payable until then. Where the loan is not repaid on the due date, the courts have awarded interest from the due date for repayment as damages (see *Cook v Fowler* (1874) LR 7 HL 27). As the award has been for damages, the courts have not always used the original interest rate as the measure of the damages for late payment.

Late payment of commercial debts

64.15   The Late Payment of Commercial Debts (Interest) Act 1998 was passed in compliance with Directive 2000/35/EC on combating late payment. Section 1(1) makes it an implied term in a contract to which the Act applies that any qualifying debt created by the contract carries simple interest subject to the terms of ss. 1 to 6 of the Act. The Act applies to contracts for the sale of goods and for the supply of services and related matters (s. 2), and a 'qualifying debt' is an obligation to pay the price under such a contract (s. 3(1)). In cross-border cases, the Act does not apply to contracts governed by the law of a part of the United Kingdom if there is no significant connection between the contract and that part of the United Kingdom and, but for the choice of law, the applicable law would be a foreign law (s. 12(1), and see *Martrade Shipping & Transport GmbH v United Enterprises Corporation* [2014] EWHC 1884 (Comm), [2015] 1 WLR 1).

With the exception of advance payments, interest runs from 30 days after the supplier performs its obligations under the contract, or 30 days after invoice or other notification of the price (s. 4(2), (4) and (5)). There is a maximum payment period of up to 30 days where the purchaser is a public authority, and in other cases a period of up to 60 days or longer as otherwise agreed (s. 4(3A) to (3C)). Where the payment period is longer than 60 days, the period must not be grossly unfair to the supplier (s. 4(3C)(b)). Where two invoices were used to bill the sum claimed, interest ran from the second invoice (*Ruttle Plant Hire Ltd v Secretary of State for the Environment, Food and Rural Affairs (No. 3)* [2008] EWHC 730 (TCC), [2009] 1 All ER (Comm) 73).

The rate of interest is as prescribed by statutory instrument (s. 6); see the Late Payment of Commercial Debts (Rate of Interest) (No. 3) Order 2002 (SI 2002/1675), which sets the rate at 8 per cent over the Bank of England's official dealing rate. That rate is referred to as the 'UK clearing bank base lending rate' and is published every day (except on Sundays) in *The Financial Times*. Until August 2006 it was known as the 'Repo', since repos or sale and repurchase agreements are one type of monetary policy instrument used by the Bank of England. It is currently known as the Official Bank Rate. The relevant rates can be seen on the Bank of England website http://www.bankofengland.co.uk, click on 'statistics', then 'interest and exchange rates data', and are shown in **table 64.1**.

Table 64.1 Bank of England Official Dealing Rates

Date	Interest (%)
	Repo Rate
8 October 1998	7.25
5 November 1998	6.75
10 December 1998	6.25
7 January 1999	6.00
4 February 1999	5.50
8 April 1999	5.25
10 June 1999	5.00
8 September 1999	5.25
4 November 1999	5.50
13 January 2000	5.75
10 February 2000	6.00
8 February 2001	5.75
5 April 2001	5.50
10 May 2001	5.25
2 August 2001	5.00
18 September 2001	4.75
4 October 2001	4.50
8 November 2001	4.00
6 February 2003	3.75

(continued)

Commentary

Date	Interest (%)
	Repo Rate
10 July 2003	3.50
6 November 2003	3.75
5 February 2004	4.00
6 May 2004	4.25
10 June 2004	4.50
5 August 2004	4.75
4 August 2005	4.50
	Official Bank Rate
3 August 2006	4.75
9 November 2006	5.00
10 May 2007	5.50
5 July 2007	5.75
6 December 2007	5.50
7 February 2008	5.25
10 April 2008	5.00
8 October 2008	4.50
4 December 2008	2.00
8 January 2009	1.50
6 November 2008	3.00
5 February 2009	1.00
5 March 2009	0.50

The rate of interest may be reduced in the interests of justice on account of any misconduct by the supplier (s. 5).

The 1998 Act has been brought into effect as follows:

Phase	Applies to contracts from	Scope
1	1 November 1998	Small businesses can claim statutory interest for late payment from large businesses and most public-sector bodies.
2	1 November 2000	Small businesses can claim statutory interest from small businesses, large businesses and most public-sector bodies.
3	7 August 2002	All businesses and public-sector bodies can claim statutory interest.

A payment is deemed to be late when an agreed credit period has expired, or, if there is none, 30 days after the later of:

(a) delivery of the goods or performance of the services under the contract; and
(b) the date the purchaser was notified of the amount of the debt.

There are special rules for advance payments. Where the parties have a system of payment by the end of the month following the month in which the invoice is received, payment will be late for the purposes of the legislation at the end of the month following the month in which the invoice was received.

A seller making use of the legislation must notify the purchaser. Notification may be oral, but written notice is preferable in the event of a dispute. The notice should state the amount owed, what it is owed for, how the statutory interest is calculated, should quote the original invoice number, and state to whom and where payment should be made, by what date and by what method.

The Bank of England base rate on 31 December will be the 'reference rate' for the following 1 January to 30 June. Base rate on 30 June will be the reference rate for the period 1 July to

31 December. Statutory interest under the late payment legislation is 8 per cent above the appropriate reference rate. So, if the reference rate is 1.5 per cent p.a., the rate payable under the late payment legislation would be simple interest at 9.5 per cent p.a. (but fluctuating every six months with any variations in Bank of England base rate).

In addition, a seller is entitled to charge statutory compensation on late payments (s. 5A). The amount of compensation varies with the amount of the debt, as follows:

Size of unpaid debt	Amount of compensation
Up to £999.99	£40.00
£1,000 to £9,999.99	£70.00
Over £9,999.99	£100.00

If the reasonable costs of the supplier in recovering the debt are not met by the fixed compensation, the supplier is also entitled to a sum equivalent to the difference between the fixed sum and those costs (s. 5A(2A)).

Parties to a contract can contract out of the late-payment legislation, provided they make their own arrangements for contractual interest. To prevent abuse, contractual interest must be 'substantial', otherwise it will be void and the late-payment legislation will apply. In considering whether a contractual remedy is substantial, the court must consider all the circumstances, including the rate of interest applicable to late payments and the length of credit periods. If the credit period is considered excessive, the court can strike it down and replace it with a 30-day default period. 'Representative bodies' are given standing to challenge contractual terms which are grossly unfair on behalf of small and medium-sized enterprises (SMEs). SMEs are independent enterprises which have fewer than 250 employees and either a turnover of less than 40 million euro or an annual balance sheet total not exceeding 27 million euro.

EQUITY CASES

There is a long-established practice of awarding interest in the Chancery Division ancillary to **64.16** equitable remedies such as the taking of an account or specific performance. Interest has been awarded in claims where defendants owing fiduciary duties have been found to have misapplied or withheld money, or been guilty of fraud (*Johnson v R* [1904] AC 817). It was not equitable to award interest on a loan where the loan deed neither mentioned interest nor stated a repayment date (*Destine Estates Ltd v Muir* [2014] EWHC 4191 (Ch), LTL 19/12/2014).

EXCEPTIONAL CASES WHERE INTEREST IS NOT AWARDED

Interest is not normally awarded on awards in libel cases, nor in claims for wrongful arrest or false **64.17** imprisonment (*Holtham v Commissioner of Police for the Metropolis* (1987) *The Independent*, 26 November 1987). In *Saunders v Edwards* [1987] 1 WLR 1116 it was held that interest should not have been awarded on a sum for inconvenience and disappointment made in a misrepresentation claim.

INTEREST AS PART OF THE PRINCIPAL AWARD

Interest as damages

At common law, the rule was that a court had no power, in the absence of any agreement, **64.18** to award interest as compensation for the late payment of a debt or damages (*London,*

Chatham and Dover Railway Co. v South Eastern Railway Co. [1893] AC 429). This decision was seen to be inconsistent with the general principles for the assessment of damages. It was interpreted by *President of India v La Pintada Compania Navigacion SA* [1985] AC 104 as applying to prevent claims to interest as damages where the loss fell within the first limb of *Hadley v Baxendale* (1854) 9 Exch 341, but not where it came within the second limb. The result was that where it was plain to everyone that interest loss would be suffered in the event of non-payment (the first limb), it could not be recovered. However, if the interest loss came about from circumstances known only to the contracting parties (the second limb), it was recoverable (*President of India v Lips Maritime Corporation* [1985] 2 Lloyd's Rep 180 at p. 185). This unsatisfactory position was swept away by *Sempra Metals Ltd v Commissioners of Inland Revenue* [2007] UKHL 34, [2008] 1 AC 561.

The present position is that, subject to the ordinary rules of remoteness, causation and mitigation of loss, any loss that is proved by the claimant arising as a result of the late payment of money is recoverable (*Sempra Metals Ltd v Commissioners of Inland Revenue* at [16], [92], [94]–[97], [165]). As Lord Hope of Craighead said, at [16]:

> The reality is that every creditor who is deprived of funds to which he is entitled and which he needs to run his business will have to incur an interest-bearing loan or employ other funds which could themselves have earned interest. It is a short step to say that interest losses will arise 'in the ordinary course of things' in such circumstances.

London, Chatham and Dover Railway Co. v South Eastern Railway Co. has not been overruled, but is confined to its own facts. It therefore applies only to claims at common law for unparticularised and unproven interest losses as damages for breach of a contract to pay a debt and claims for payment of a debt with interest (*Sempra Metals Ltd v Commissioners of Inland Revenue*, per Lord Nicholls of Birkenhead at [96]). In these cases, the claimant will usually be best advised to claim statutory interest under either the County Courts Act 1984, s. 69, or the Senior Courts Act 1981, s. 35A (see **64.9** to **64.12**). In fact, in any case where a party chooses not to prove his interest losses the remedy is to be found in the statutory interest provisions (*Sempra Metals Ltd v Commissioners of Inland Revenue* at [97]).

Admiralty cases

64.19   In the Admiralty Court there is a long-established practice of awarding interest as damages in claims arising out of collisions at sea and in salvage awards (*The Aldora* [1975] QB 748; *The Rilland* [1979] 1 Lloyd's Rep 455).

Restitution claims

64.20   The ancient position was that interest could not be awarded in a claim for money had and received (*Walker v Constable* (1798) 1 Bos & P 306). This was unprincipled, and stemmed from a misunderstanding of earlier authorities. Before *Sempra Metals Ltd v Commissioners of Inland Revenue* [2007] UKHL 34, [2008] 1 AC 561, it was recognised that awards in restitution were debts for the purposes of the Senior Courts Act 1981, s. 35A, and the County Courts Act 1984, s. 69 (see **64.10**). As a result, simple interest at the Judgments Act 1838 rate can be sought under the Senior Courts Act 1981, s. 35A, or the County Courts Act 1984, s. 69, on these awards without the claimant needing to prove his interest losses.

In *Sempra Metals Ltd v Commissioners of Inland Revenue* the principal sum claimed was for the loss of use over time of sums the claimant had paid to the Revenue in the mistaken belief that it had to pay those sums in tax. Departing from the decision in *Westdeutsche Landesbank Girozentrale v Islington London Borough Council* [1996] AC 669, it was held that there is jurisdiction to award compound interest as substantive restitutionary relief. Different views were expressed on whether this was at common law (Lord Hope of Craighead, Lord Nicholls of Birkenhead and Lord Scott of Foscote) or in the exercise of the court's equitable jurisdiction (Lord Walker of Gestingthorpe and Lord Mance), although the result was the same under both routes.

PLEADING INTEREST

Under **CPR, r. 16.4(2)**, if the claimant is seeking interest, the particulars of claim must: **64.21**

(a) state whether the claim is:
  (i)   under the terms of a contract; or
  (ii) under an enactment, and if so which; or
  (iii) on some other basis, and if so which basis;

(b) if the principal claim is for a specified sum of money, the particulars of claim must:
  (i)   state the percentage rate claimed for the interest and the date from which it is claimed;
  (ii) contain an interest calculation, giving a date (which should be no later than the date of issue of the claim form) to which past interest is calculated; and
  (iii) the daily rate at which future interest accrues.

If the claim is for an unspecified amount of money (as most damages claims are), it is sufficient, in addition to stating the basis on which interest is claimed, to say in the particulars of claim that interest is sought at such rates and for such periods on the sums found due to the claimant as the court may think fit, to be decided by the court. A claim to contractual interest requires the contractual term to be pleaded in the particulars of claim, together with an interest paragraph and a claim for the interest in the prayer. In claims for interest and statutory compensation under the Late Payment of Commercial Debts (Interest) Act 1998, the statutory implied term under s. 1(1) (and its extension to statutory compensation under s. 5A(3)) must be pleaded, together with an interest paragraph and a claim for the interest in the prayer. Where interest is sought as a primary remedy (see **64.18** to **64.20**), the claim to interest is set out in the loss and damage or remedies paragraphs in the particulars of claim, and also in the prayer.

RATE OF INTEREST

General rules

Interest pursuant to contract should be at the contract rate. Some statutes (such as the Partnership   **64.22**
Act 1890) lay down specific rates for interest recoverable. Under the Late Payment of Commercial Debts (Interest) Act 1998, interest is at 8 per cent above Bank of England base rate. Otherwise, the rate of interest is in the discretion of the court. Where this is so, in practical terms the starting point in most classes of case is the Judgments Act 1838 rate, which has been 8 per cent a year since 1 April 1993 (see **table 64.2**). There are other methods of determining the rate of interest to be paid. The court may assess interest by reference to the rates provided by index-linked government stock, or by reference to the base rate of the Bank of England (see **table 64.1**), or one of the clearing banks (usually adding a number of percentage points to that rate).

Commercial claims

In commercial cases and claims on bills of exchange, traditionally interest has been awarded at   **64.23**
1 per cent above base rate. The same applies in Admiralty claims (*Polish Steam Ship Co. v Atlantic Maritime Co.* [1985] QB 41). However, this is no more than a practice, and may be displaced by evidence showing that the rate is unfair to either party (*Shearson Lehman Hutton Inc. v Maclaine Watson and Co. Ltd (No. 2)* [1990] 3 All ER 723). Interest at the actual rate paid by the successful party on loans to pay their legal costs was awarded in *F and C Alternative Investments (Holdings) Ltd v Barthelemy* [2011] EWHC 2807 (Ch), *The Times,* 1 December 2011, where the court also awarded indemnity-basis costs. Where an interest loss is awarded as damages for breach of contract, the loss (and hence the rate) depends on the circumstances of the case, and what the claimant can prove. The loss may be the cost to the claimant of borrowing money, or the claimant's loss of the opportunity to invest the promised money, or loss in some other form. It is a head of loss and damage, and has to be proved in the normal way (*Sempra Metals Ltd v Commissioners of Inland*

Table 64.2 Judgments Act 1838 and Special and Basic Account rates of interest

Date (from)	Judgments Act 1838 rate	Special Account rate	Basic Account rate
1.4.1984	12% (from 10.11.1982)	12%	8%
16.4.1985	15%	12%	8%
1.8.1986	15%	11.5%	7.5%
1.1.1987	15%	12.25%	8.5%
1.4.1987	15%	11.75%	8.5%
1.11.1987	15%	11.25%	8.5%
1.12.1987	15%	11%	8%
1.5.1988	15%	9.5%	7.5%
1.8.1988	15%	11%	9%
1.11.1988	15%	12.25%	10.25%
1.1.1989	15%	13%	10.75%
1.11.1989	15%	14.25%	11.25%
1.4.1991	15%	12%	9.5%
1.10.1991	15%	10.25%	8%
1.2.1993	15%	8%	6%
1.4.1993	8%	8%	6%
1.8.1999	8%	7%	5.25%
1.2.2002	8%	6%	4%
1.2.2009	8%	3%	2%
1.6.2009	8%	1.5%	1%
1.7.2009	8%	0.5%	0.3%

Revenue [2007] UKHL 34, [2008] 1 AC 561 at [95]). In *Jaura v Ahmed* [2002] EWCA Civ 210, *The Times*, 18 March 2002, the court recognised that borrowing costs for small businesses are higher than those available to first-class borrowers, and awarded interest at 3 per cent above base rate. A rate of 2 per cent above base rate was applied in *Adinstone Ltd v Gatt* (2008) LTL 18/6/2008, being the rate established by the evidence as being the rate on the claimant's overdraft facility, and the rate anyone dealing with the claimant might have expected it to pay. In *McGlinn v Waltham Contractors Ltd (No. 5)* [2007] EWHC 698 (TCC), [2008] Bus LR 278, interest at 1 per cent above base rate was awarded against a builder in respect of defective building work.

Personal injury claims

64.24   In personal injuries claims, interest on damages for pain, suffering and loss of amenity has in recent years been awarded at 2 per cent a year from the date proceedings are issued (*Wright v British Railways Board* [1983] 1 AC 352). Despite the decision in *Wells v Wells* [1999] 1 AC 345, the rate applied remains at 2 per cent (*Lawrence v Chief Constable of Staffordshire* [2000] PIQR Q349). Past special damages (such as loss of earnings and out-of-pocket expenses) usually attract interest at half the appropriate rate of interest (to reflect the fact that the losses will usually be ongoing between the date of the accident and the trial, the court adopting a broad-brush approach to the precise dates when individual losses were incurred). The 'appropriate rate' for this purpose is the average rate allowed for money in the Special Account (formerly the short-term investment account) (see **table 64.2**). The Special Account rate is applied by the Court Funds Office to Court of Protection clients' accounts and children's funds accounts. There is also a Basic Account rate (see **table 64.2**), which is applied by the Court Funds Office to County Court and Queen's Bench claims involving adults only. Where the bulk of the losses were incurred a long time before trial, it may be appropriate to award interest on special damages at a higher (and perhaps the full) rate (see *Dexter v Courtaulds Ltd* [1984] 1 WLR 372; *Prokop v Department of Health and Social Security* [1985] CLY 1037). Interest is recoverable in full on past loss of earnings despite the recoupment of State benefits under the Social Security (Recovery of Benefits) Act 1997 (see *Wisely v John Fulton (Plumbers) Ltd* [2000] 1 WLR 820). Obviously, no interest is allowed on future loss and expense or loss of earning capacity. A claim in professional negligence against a solicitor based on mishandling of a personal injuries claim will usually attract ordinary interest at the Judgments Act 1838 rate rather than under the rules discussed in this paragraph (*Pinnock v Wilkins and Sons* (1990) *The Times*, 29 January 1990).

Restitution claims

Where interest is awarded as a remedy in restitution (see **64.20**), it will be at conventional   **64.25**
rates. This avoids the need for evidence on the matter of rates. The conventional rate is the reasonable cost the defendant would have incurred in borrowing the amount in question for the relevant period (*Sempra Metals Ltd v Commissioners of Inland Revenue* [2007] UKHL 34, [2008] 1 AC 561 at [103]). It is the cost to the defendant rather than the claimant because, unlike claims in contract and tort, restitutionary remedies are based on the gain made by the defendant (at [28]). The reasonable cost is the market value of the benefit the defendant acquired by having the use of the money. Different types of organisations can borrow money at different rates, so the conventional rate is the usual cost to organisations of the defendant's type (at [49] and [128]).

These usual rules can be displaced by evidence that there was no (or reduced) actual benefit to the defendant (at [48] and [118]), for example, where the money is placed by the defendant in a non-interest-bearing current account. There was a divergence of view on where the onus of proof lies, but the better view is that it rests on the defendant because it is a matter unlikely to be within the claimant's knowledge (see the cases at **49.40** and *Sempra Metals Ltd v Commissioners of Inland Revenue* at [47]).

Claimants' Part 36 offers and breach of protocols

Interest, including ordinary statutory interest under the Senior Courts Act 1981, s. 35A, or   **64.26**
County Courts Act 1984, s. 69, at a rate up to 10 per cent above base rate (see **table 64.1**) may be awarded where the claimant has made a successful claimant's Part 36 offer (see **CPR, r. 36.17(4)**), or where the defendant has failed to comply with **PD Pre-action Conduct and Protocols** or a relevant pre-action protocol (**PD Pre-action Conduct and Protocols, para. 16(d)**). In deciding whether to award interest as high as 10 per cent above base rate under **CPR, r. 36.17(4)**, the court should evaluate whether doing so would itself work an injustice or result in a disproportionate advantage to the claimant, or a disproportionate disadvantage to the defendant (*Little v George Little Sebire and Co.* (1999) *The Times*, 17 November 1999).

COMPOUND INTEREST

Until *Sempra Metals Ltd v Commissioners of Inland Revenue* [2007] UKHL 34, [2008] 1 AC 561, the   **64.27**
general rule has been that awards of interest are for simple interest. Simple interest is expressly provided for by the Senior Courts Act 1981, s. 35A, and the County Courts Act 1984, s. 69. As from 6 April 2008, interest on default sums payable under regulated agreements by the debtor or hirer is only payable if it is simple interest (Consumer Credit Act 1974, s. 86F, to be inserted by the Consumer Credit Act 2006, s. 13). However, to mark the court's disapproval in cases of breach of fiduciary duty the courts of equity would (and the Chancery Division will continue to) award compound interest with yearly (or such other as may seem appropriate) rests (*Wallersteiner v Moir (No. 2)* [1975] QB 373). Further it is the common practice of banks to

Commentary

charge their customers compound interest, and they are entitled to judgment at their usual compounded rates up to judgment or earlier payment (*National Bank of Greece SA v Pinios Shipping Co. (No. 1)* [1990] 1 AC 637). A deed of priority between two mortgagees giving priority to one mortgagee in the sum of £160,000 'together with interest thereon' was construed as meaning compound interest in *Whitbread plc v UCB Corporate Services Ltd* [2000] 3 EGLR 60. While the practice in most EU States is to award simple interest on awards of damages, compound interest is available in Germany, Poland and the Netherlands. Compound interest is the European Commission's method of choice in cases such as the infringement of EC competition rules and breach of obligations relating to state aid (see *Sempra Metals Ltd v Commissioners of Inland Revenue* [2007] UKHL 34, [2008] 1 AC 561 at [37]–[40]).

In *Sempra Metals Ltd v Commissioners of Inland Revenue* the House of Lords said that an element of compound interest is available where interest is claimed as damages for breach of contract or in tort (at [17], [95], [154]). It held that ordinarily compound interest would be awarded where an interest loss is the substantive relief in restitution (at [33], [34], [103] and [154]).

PERIOD OF INTEREST

64.28   Interest normally runs from the date the cause of action accrued until judgment or earlier payment. In the case of a claim on an unpaid invoice, the terms of the contract will determine when the invoice matured. In the absence of other evidence the practice is to take the date of maturity as being 30 days after the date of the invoice. In a contract for the sale of land, interest runs from the contractual date for completion notwithstanding the transfer has not been stamped or that the vendor was unable to comply with a request from the purchaser to register the transfer (*P & O Overseas Holdings Ltd v Rhys Braintree Ltd* [2002] EWCA Civ 296, [2002] 2 P & CR 27). Interest on property damaged by negligence is payable from the date of the repairs (or when a decision was made to write off the property damaged). See also *BP Exploration Co. (Libya) Ltd v Hunt (No. 2)* [1979] 1 WLR 783. In *McGlinn v Waltham Contractors Ltd (No. 5)* [2007] EWHC 698 (TCC), [2008] Bus LR 278, interest was awarded from the date of issue of proceedings against a builder in respect of defective building work.

Where either party is guilty of unjustifiable delay, the court may increase or reduce the rate of interest, or alter the period over which interest is payable, to reflect this fact (*Birkett v Hayes* [1982] 1 WLR 816; *Spittle v Bunney* [1988] 1 WLR 847). In *Beahan v Stoneham* (2001) LTL 16/5/2001 it was held that the judge had been wrong not to reduce the interest awarded on the claim for damages as the claimant had been guilty of delay. It is unnecessary for the defendant to establish prejudice. The starting point is to decide when the case could reasonably have been brought to trial. Interest for two years was disallowed. Reducing interest, even in the event of gross delay, may be unjust and give the defendant an unwarranted windfall if the defendant has been holding on to money that should have been paid to the claimant (*Adcock v Cooperative Insurance Society Ltd* [2000] Lloyd's Rep IR 657). In a case where there was unreasonable delay for two years, during which time there were high interest rates, the claimants were awarded interest at half the usual rate during the period of the delay (*Quorum AS v Schramm* [2002] CLC 77). Ultimately the decision is one within the discretion of the trial judge. The Senior Courts Act 1981, s. 35A(5), and the County Courts Act 1984, s. 69(5), provide that interest under the respective Acts may be calculated at different rates in respect of different periods.

INTEREST ON JUDGMENTS IN FOREIGN CURRENCY

64.29   Where judgment is given in a foreign currency, the rate of interest will be that appropriate for the relevant country (usually the rate at which money could be borrowed in that country). Evidence of the rate contended for should be adduced. See *Miliangos v George Frank (Textiles) Ltd*

(No. 2) [1977] QB 489. In *Braspetro Oil Services Co. v FPSO Construction Inc.* [2007] EWHC 1359 (Comm), [2007] 2 All ER (Comm) 924, it was held that factors to be considered include:

(a) The place where the claimant is incorporated and carries on business.

(b) The financial markets available to a person in the position of the claimant for the purposes of borrowing the currency in question. The markets may be global or local.

(c) Where the claimant is a member of a group of companies, the relationship between the claimant and other companies in the group.

(d) The stability of the currency of account and the claimant's currency. If the currency of account is more stable than the claimant's currency, delay in payment by the defendant means the claimant has to borrow at higher rates pending payment (*Helmsing Schiffahrts GmbH & Co. KG v Malta Drydocks Corporation* [1977] 2 Lloyd's Rep 444).

(e) The claimant's standing as a borrower (good standing resulting in lower rates, see *Kuwait Airways Corporation v Kuwait Insurance Co. SAK (No. 2)* [2000] 1 All ER (Comm) 972).

INTEREST ON JUDGMENT DEBTS

64.30 The Judgments Act 1838, s. 17, and the County Courts Act 1984, s. 74, are general provisions which allow simple interest, currently at 8 per cent a year, on all High Court money judgments and on relevant County Court money judgments (see below). An arbitration award registered as a judgment under the Arbitration Act 1996, s. 100, also attracts interest at the usual Judgments Act 1838, s. 17, rate (*Gater Assets Ltd v NAK Naftogaz Ukrainiy* [2008] EWHC 1108 (Comm), [2008] 2 Lloyd's Rep 295). Interest is payable from the date on which judgment is given unless the court orders otherwise under **CPR, r. 40.8(1)(b).** The Judgments Act 1838, s. 17, provides:

(1) Every judgment debt shall carry interest at the rate of 8 per cent per annum from such time as shall be prescribed by rules of court, until the same shall be satisfied, and such interest may be levied under a writ of execution on such judgment.

(2) Rules of court may provide for the court to disallow all or part of any interest otherwise payable under subsection (1).

Interest on a judgment runs from the date it is pronounced, not the date it might be drawn up (*Erven Warnink BV v J. Townend and Son (Hull) Ltd (No. 2)* [1982] 3 All ER 312). It is inappropriate to seek to evade the 8 per cent a year rate of interest on judgment debts by adjusting the date from which interest is to run (*Schlumberger Holdings Ltd v Electromagnetic Geoservices AS* [2009] EWHC 773 (Pat), LTL 7/5/2009). In the case of a judgment for damages to be decided by the court, Judgments Act 1838 interest runs on the damages from the date the damages are finally decided. Until then, the claimant can only claim interest on damages under the ordinary principles (which, in a personal injuries case, will be at considerably lower rates). See *Hunt v R. M. Douglas (Roofing) Ltd* [1990] 1 AC 398.

The County Courts Act 1984, s. 74, on the other hand, is an enabling provision allowing the Lord Chancellor to make orders that County Court judgments shall carry interest at such rates and for such periods as the rules may prescribe. The relevant rules are the County Courts (Interest on Judgment Debts) Order 1991 (SI 1991/1184), which provide that 'relevant judgments' are those for not less than £5,000 and those which are qualifying debts for the purposes of the Late Payment of Commercial Debts (Interest) Act 1998 (see **64.15**), and that interest at the Judgments Act 1838 rate (SI 1991/1184, art. 5) shall be payable from the date the judgment was given (art. 2(1)). However, there are exceptions. Interest is not payable:

(a) on claims based on regulated agreements under the Consumer Credit Act 1974 (SI 1991/1184, art. 2(3)(a));

(b) on judgments granting suspended orders for possession of dwelling houses, where the order is in favour of a landlord or mortgagee (art. 2(3)(b));

(c) in the case of a judgment deferring payment, until the date specified for payment (art. 3(a)); and

(d) in the case of a judgment payable by instalments, until instalments are in arrears, and then only on the arrears (art. 3(b)) (the same applies to High Court judgments, see *Caudery v Finnerty* (1892) 66 LT 684 and *Morse v Muir* [1939] 2 KB 106).

Where a judgment creditor takes enforcement proceedings on a relevant County Court judgment, accrual of interest ceases from that point unless the enforcement proceedings fail (art. 4). For these purposes applying for a charging order is not regarded as proceeding for enforcement.

INTEREST ON COSTS

64.31   Under the **CPR, r. 40.8**, interest on costs runs from the date the judgment is given, unless a rule or practice direction provides otherwise, or the court orders otherwise. Interest on costs where judgment has been entered for damages to be assessed therefore generally runs from the date of the liability judgment, but the court has a discretion to award interest on costs from some other date. This discretion may be exercised to reflect the periods over which the costs in assessing damages were in fact incurred (**r. 44.2(6)(g)**; *Powell v Herefordshire Health Authority* [2002] EWCA Civ 1786, [2003] 3 All ER 253). As regards interest on costs after a claim is automatically struck out for non-payment of the fees payable at the allocation or listing stages, or after acceptance of an offer to settle, or after a claim is discontinued, by virtue of **r. 44.9** interest runs from the date of the event giving rise to the entitlement to costs (i.e. the date of striking out, acceptance, or the date of service of the notice of discontinuance).

Conducting litigation for commercial reasons regardless of the rights and wrongs of the claim, with much of that party's evidence being rejected followed by a resounding defeat, was said in *Amoco (UK) Exploration Co. v British American Offshore Ltd* [2002] BLR 135 to give grounds for awarding interest on costs for the period before judgment from the time those costs were paid.

The conventional rate of interest on costs until the date of assessment before the costs judge is 1 per cent above base rate (*National Westminster Bank plc v Rabobank Nederland (No. 2)* [2007] EWHC 1742 (Comm), [2008] 1 All ER (Comm) 243). It is for the paying party to introduce evidence that some other rate should be applied. Expert evidence will be required if it is asserted that a body with the financial substance of the receiving party could borrow money below this rate. Second-hand expressions of understanding are not a safe basis for departing from the conventional rate (*National Westminster Bank plc v Rabobank Nederland (No. 2)*).

A rate of 1 per cent above base rate was applied to an order for the repayment of an interim payment in respect of costs in *Multiplex Construction Ltd v Cleveland Bridge Ltd* [2008] EWCA Civ 133, 118 Con LR 16. The power to award interest in this situation derives from CPR, **rr. 44.2(6)(g)** and **44.2(8)**.

PART M

Costs

Chapter 65   Solicitor and Own Client Costs

Commentary

INTRODUCTION

The purpose of this chapter is to deal with some of the core issues which arise in relation to   **65.1** solicitor and own client billing. It is somewhat remarkable in this market-driven age that the legal profession is still regulated in how it charges for its services. The primary regulatory scheme governing the solicitor and client relationship is in the Solicitors Act 1974, which is supported by the Solicitors (Non-contentious Business) Remuneration Order 1994 (SI 1994/2616), the Non-contentious Probate Rules 1987 (SI 1987/2024) and **CPR, Parts 44** to **48**, in relation to contentious business. In this context the Solicitors Act 1974, supported by the SRA Code of Conduct 2011, regulates the arrangement between the solicitor and client, and provides machinery for finalising the amount of the solicitor's fees if they cannot be agreed. This chapter will concentrate on contentious business.

By tradition the profession, in observing the statutory framework, had generally grown used to basing charges for services upon an expense rate for the particular grade of fee-earner plus a mark-up for care and conduct, the latter being determined by reference to what used to be RSC, ord. 62, app. 1, part 1, generally known as the 'seven pillars of wisdom'. There was a growing resistance in the marketplace to the application of the variable percentage uplift on expense rates, particularly from those who were volume buyers of legal services. They preferred to agree that solicitors' charges would be based on a composite hourly rate or rates per grade of fee-earners. This also reflected the more general public mood that there should be more transparency and certainty in solicitors' charges. Solicitors are required to give detailed costs information to their clients (see 65.3 to 65.6) to ensure a client is fully aware of how the solicitor will charge for the work done.

AGREEING SOLICITORS' CHARGES

The contract of retainer between the client and solicitor may be oral or written, but often will   **65.2** be partly oral and partly written or evidenced by writing. Client care letters, costs estimates and costs budgets tend to be the most important documents, particularly for consumer clients, although formal written contracts may be essential for clients providing bulk or high-cost work. Being a contract for the provision of services, the retainer will be subject to the Supply of Goods and Services Act 1982, which means that, by s. 15, the price of the solicitor's services will either be determined by the contract, left to be determined in a manner agreed by the contract or by the course of dealing between the parties, or be subject to an implied term that the client will pay a reasonable charge. What is a reasonable charge is a question of fact (s. 15(2)). Often charges will be based on hourly rates dependent on the status of the fee earner (see **71.47**), plus disbursements (see **71.53**), and will be subject to assessment under the provisions of the Solicitors Act 1974 (see **65.7**). Given the provisions of s. 15, it was held in *Mastercigars Direct Ltd v Withers LLP* [2007] EWHC 2733 (Ch), [2009] 1 WLR 881, to be unnecessary to imply a term into the retainer that the solicitors had to comply with the Solicitors' Costs Information and Client Care Code (now the SRA Code of Conduct 2011; see **65.3** to **65.6**). This case also held that while the solicitor had made a contractual promise to provide the client with updated costs estimates (see **65.6**), doing so was not a condition precedent to recovering charges which exceeded an earlier costs estimate.

It is of the utmost importance that the client responsible for giving instructions and incurring the liability for costs is clearly identified as being responsible for payment of those costs. This is of particular concern, for example, where acting for companies or a group of clients. A solicitor instructed to act for a company must make certain that the person giving instructions has proper authority to incur the costs which ultimately the company will be liable to pay. In *Lygoe v Ilsley* [2008] EWHC 831 (QB), LTL 28/4/2008, the court found the solicitor's case, that an individual was personally liable for the firm's fees for work done for various companies, was implausible in the absence of an agreement in writing. When acting for a group of clients it is necessary to determine how the costs are to be discharged and by whom.

Where solicitors are retained by executors to deal with non-contentious business, it is best practice for the solicitor to obtain prior agreement for the proposed charges not only from the executors, but also from any residuary beneficiary who is a statutory entitled party under the Solicitors' (Non-Contentious Business) Remuneration Order 1994 (SI 1994/2616) (*Jemma Trust Co. Ltd v Liptrott* [2003] EWCA Civ 1476, [2004] 1 WLR 646).

A written retainer from the client is always advisable and nearly always required by the SRA Code of Conduct 2011, O 1.13 and IB 1.13 to IB 1.20. These require clear explanations about fees, and the provision of information in a clear and accessible form that is appropriate for the client. Having a clear written agreement on charges should reduce the risk to the solicitor at a later stage when a bill of costs is rendered for the services provided. Indeed, with regard to contentious business, it is the duty of the solicitor to obtain a written authority from the client before a claim is commenced. Such authority must be signed by the party responsible for the solicitor's bill of costs and it must clearly identify the work to be carried out and extent of the retainer. This has long been the recognised position, see *Allen v Bone* (1841) 4 Beav 493.

CLIENT CARE

65.3   The SRA Code of Conduct 2011 provides that solicitors should:

(a) discuss whether the potential outcomes of the client's matter are likely to justify the expense or risk involved, including any risk of having to pay someone else's legal fees (IB 1.13);

(b) agree an appropriate level of service with the client, for example the type and frequency of communications (IB 1.1);

(c) explain the solicitor's responsibilities and those of the client (IB 1.2); and

(d) ensure that the client is told, in writing, the name and status of the person(s) dealing with the matter and the name and status of the person responsible for its overall supervision (IB 1.3).

For example, the frequency of reports on progress to the client should be agreed, and options such as the use of ADR should be considered. Where the person dealing with the matter leaves the firm, the client should be informed of the changeover arrangements, preferably in advance.

If there are any limitations or conditions on the retainer resulting from the solicitor's relationship with a third-party funder or introducer, these should be explained to the client (IB 1.5). Some constraints are proper and do not require disclosure to the client. Examples are service standards relating to dealing with client inquiries within a specified period of time, the use of specified computer software, telecommunications systems, or particular training provisions. Constraints such as not issuing proceedings without the consent of the funder are proper provided they do not operate against the client's best interests, but must be disclosed to the client. Constraints which impair the solicitor's independence are improper and cannot be cured by disclosure to the client. If such a relationship involves sharing any client information with a third party, the solicitor must inform the client and obtain the client's consent. Failure to do so will be a breach of the client confidentiality rule (O 4.1), and may be a breach of the Data Protection Act 1998.

Clients must be informed in writing at the outset of their matter of their right to complain and how complaints can be made (O 1.9). Firms must have written complaints procedures, which are brought to the attention of clients at the commencement of a retainer (IB 1.22), which must be provided to a client on request (IB 1.23). In the event that a client makes a complaint, they must be provided with all necessary information concerning the handling of the complaint (IB 1.24). Clients must also be informed in writing, both at the time of engagement and at the conclusion of the firms' complaints procedure, of their right to complain to the Legal Ombudsman, the time frame for doing so and be given full details of how to contact the Legal Ombudsman (O 1.10). Clients must not be charged the costs of handling complaints (IB 1.22(f)).

Information about costs

The SRA Code of Conduct 2011, O 1.13, says that clients must receive the best possible information, both at the time of engagement and when appropriate as their matter progresses, about the likely overall cost of their matter. Such information is likely to include: **65.4**

(a) advising the client of the basis and terms of the firm's charges;
(b) advising the client if the charges are to be increased;
(c) advising the client of likely payments which the client may need to make to others;
(d) discussing with the client how the client will pay, and in particular, whether they are eligible for public funding, whether the client's costs are covered by insurance, and whether they might be paid by someone else, such as an employer or trade union;
(e) advising the client that there are circumstances where the firm will be entitled to a lien;
(f) advising the client of their potential liability for the other side's costs;
(g) discussing with the client whether the liability for the other side's costs may be covered by existing or specially purchased insurance.

The purpose of O 1.13 is to ensure the client is given relevant costs information and that it is expressed clearly and in a way appropriate for the client. All costs information should be given in writing and regularly updated. The duty to advise means that the client must be informed of the implications involved in the various options available. It is often impossible to advise on the overall costs at the outset. In such cases the client should be given as much information as possible, told the reasons, and given either a ceiling or review dates. As the case progresses the client should be given updates on costs. Particular care is needed when advising a client on an offer to settle under **CPR, Part 36** (see **chapter 66**), to ensure the client understands the costs implications of the different options available (SRA Code of Conduct 2011, IB 1.13).

The actual terms of the retainer are a matter for negotiation between the firm and the client. There is no need for the client to be separately advised on the costs agreement unless the arrangement is unusual (such as the firm being paid by being issued with shares in a new company).

Additional duties in CFA and publicly funded cases

65.5 Where the firm is acting under a CFA (including a collective CFA), or any other method of funding governed by statute, there are additional duties under the SRA Code of Conduct 2011, IB 1.17, to give the client all relevant information relating to that arrangement. These are likely to include:

(a) the circumstances in which the client may be liable for the firm's costs and whether the firm will seek these costs from the client if it is entitled to do so;

(b) the right to an assessment of the firm's costs (if there is an intention to seek payment of all or part of the firm's costs from the client);

(c) if applicable, any obligation on the firm under a fee-sharing agreement to pay to a charity any fees received.

Where the client is publicly funded, there are additional duties under IB 1.18 to explain how their publicly funded status affects the costs. The following points must usually be covered:

(a) the circumstances in which the client will be liable for the firm's costs;

(b) the effect of the statutory charge (see **7.19**);

(c) the client's duty to pay any fixed or periodic contribution assessed and the consequences of failing to do so;

(d) that even if the publicly funded client is successful, the other side may not be ordered to pay costs or may not be in a position to pay them.

Client care letter and client estimates

65.6 The document generally referred to as a 'client care letter' has achieved a greater status in more recent times. In *Bailey v IBC Vehicles Ltd* [1998] 3 All ER 570 Judge LJ stated that 'in the ordinary case in which a "client care letter" has been provided the hourly rate claimed in the bill of costs should coincide with the terms of that letter' and further that 'in future, copies of the relevant documents (where they exist) or a short written explanation of the kind eventually provided in this case in September 1997, should normally be attached to the bill of costs'. In compliance with the SRA Code of Conduct 2011, O 1.13, in providing costs information for clients particular regard needs to be given to any estimates given. This is of vital importance, for example, where hourly rates are agreed with the client at the outset. Where the litigation is likely to span a number of years the solicitor should make provision for annual revision of those hourly rates. However, the client must be informed of any increase made on an annual review.

This has been given effect by **PD 47, para. 13.2(i)** which stipulates that where there is a dispute as to the receiving party's liability to pay costs to the solicitors who are acting for the receiving party, any letter or other written information provided by the solicitor to his or her client, explaining how the solicitor's charges are to be calculated, is to be lodged at court with the request for a detailed assessment hearing. The relevance of client care letters was further reinforced by *General of Berne Insurance Co. v Jardine Reinsurance Management Ltd* [1998] 1 WLR 1231 in the context of contentious business agreements.

It is advisable, but not an absolute requirement, that a solicitor acting for a client who may join in group litigation should say in the client care letter that some of the work done would be for the benefit of the group, and the individual client will be liable only for his share (*Brown v Russell Young and Co.* [2007] EWCA Civ 43, [2008] 1 WLR 525). Where several solicitors act for different parties in group litigation, the agreements between the solicitors should clearly define the arrangements for sharing the costs of generic work for the group. It is also sensible for careful records to be kept of the number of clients each solicitor is acting for at any specific time.

A breach of the former Solicitors' Practice Rules 1990 was a breach of subordinate legislation (*Swain v Law Society* [1983] 1 AC 598) which might have an effect on the solicitor's right to remuneration. Failing to send the client a client care letter does not prevent recovery, under a costs order, of the fees and disbursements incurred in fighting a claim (*Ghadami v Lyon Cole Insurance*

Group Ltd [2010] EWCA Civ 767, LTL 13/7/2010). In *Garbutt v Edwards* [2005] EWCA Civ 1206, [2006] 1 WLR 2907, the solicitors representing the successful party failed to provide their client with any costs estimate in breach of the Solicitors' Costs, Information and Client Care Code (now the SRA Code of Conduct 2011, O 1.13). The Court of Appeal held this did not render the retainer unlawful or unenforceable, so was not a knock-out blow to the assessment of the successful party's costs. Although this did not arise on the facts, the court said the paying party may be able to obtain a reduction in the amount payable if the costs incurred would have been lower if the solicitor had complied with the Code of Conduct. In *Mastercigars Direct Ltd v Withers LLP* [2007] EWHC 2733 (Ch), [2009] 1 WLR 881, the court characterised the costs information given by the solicitors as an estimate rather than a quotation or a document fixing an upper limit on the costs the firm would charge. Applying *Garbutt v Edwards*, it was a factor in assessing reasonableness. Disapproving a passage in *Cook on Costs* (London: Butterworths, 2007), the court held that exceeding the estimate without informing the client did not mean the solicitors were unable to recover the excess.

A requirement for greater transparency is shown in *Ralph Hume Garry v Gwillim* [2002] EWCA Civ 1500, [2003] 1 WLR 510, in which the court considered what constituted a bill for assessment under the Solicitors Act 1974. A bill may be for a gross sum (see **65.13**), but it must contain sufficient narrative to identify what the client is being charged for and to enable the client to decide whether to ask for detailed assessment (*Haigh v Ousey* (1857) 7 El & Bl 578). Nowadays it is common for solicitors to record all work done in a computerised time costing system. Where this happens, the least that a client is entitled to is a printout of that record suitably redacted (*Ralph Hume Garry v Gwillim*). A bill can only charge for the services which the client contracted to pay for. Thus, where a client asked for a solicitor but was represented by a legal executive, the solicitors were not entitled to any fee as the client had not received the representation he contracted for (*Pilbrow v Peerless De Rougemont and Co.* [1999] 3 All ER 355; *Adrian Alan Ltd v Fuglers* [2002] EWCA Civ 1655, [2003] PNLR 305).

SOLICITORS ACT 1974

Sections 59 to 71 of the Solicitors Act 1974 regulate contentious business.   **65.7**

Section 59 permits solicitors to enter into written agreements, called 'contentious business agreements', concerning remuneration for contentious business (see **65.11**).

Sections 67 to 70 deal with the situation where there is no contentious business agreement with the client and the requirements for delivery of a bill of costs, proceedings to recover costs by the solicitor and applications by the client or the solicitor for the detailed assessment of the bill of costs.

Section 69 provides that no action shall be brought to recover any costs due before the expiration of one month from the date on which a signed bill of costs was delivered to the party to be charged (s. 69(2A) and (2C)). A bill of costs sent by an agent solicitor to the principal solicitor for the purpose of assisting the principal in negotiating costs with a paying party is not a bill within the meaning of s. 69 (*Kingston Solicitors v Reiss Solicitors* [2014] EWCA Civ 172, [2014] 6 Costs LR 998). The requirement for delivery a month before bringing a claim is subject to two exceptions. If the client is about to quit the jurisdiction, become bankrupt or compound with creditors, or is about to do any other act which would prevent or delay the solicitor obtaining payment, the High Court may, upon application, permit the solicitor to commence an action to recover his or her costs and may also order that those costs be referred to detailed assessment.

Application for detailed assessment

Section 70 of the Solicitors Act 1974 provides for detailed assessment upon application of the   **65.8**
party chargeable or the solicitor. If before the expiration of one month from delivery of a bill

of costs, an application is made by the party chargeable, the court shall, without requiring any sum to be paid into court, order detailed assessment of the bill and that no claim be commenced until the assessment is completed. If no such application is made before expiration of the one-month period, the court may order detailed assessment on such terms, if any, as it thinks fit, but not terms as to costs of the assessment. Where an application is made by the party chargeable with the bill more than 12 months from its delivery, or after judgment has been obtained for recovery of the costs, or after the bill has been paid, no order for detailed assessment may be made except in special circumstances and, if an order is made, it may contain such terms as regards the costs of the detailed assessment as the court may think fit. The party chargeable with a bill is unable to obtain a detailed assessment under the Solicitors Act 1974 after 12 months from payment of the bill (s. 70(4)).

In *Connollys v Harrington* (2002) LTL 27/8/2002 it was held that the High Court has an inherent jurisdiction to order detailed assessment, even where the provisions of the Solicitors Act 1974 have not been complied with, and that the specific provisions in the Act do not oust that jurisdiction. Whether any such inherent jurisdiction exists in parallel with the Act is dubious and is inconsistent with *Harrison v Tew* [1990] 2 AC 523.

Two cases heard by the Court of Appeal have permitted detailed assessment more than 12 months after delivery of the bill (*Thomas Watts and Co. v Smith* (1998) 2 Costs LR 59 and *Turner and Co. v O. Palomo SA* [2000] 1 WLR 37). In each case the clients were entitled to challenge the solicitor's claim on the grounds that the fees claimed were unreasonably high even though the time for detailed assessment had expired. The statutory right to seek an order for detailed assessment was held not to exclude any other common law right to challenge the bills.

Section 71 provides that where a person other than the party chargeable with the bill has paid, or is or was liable to pay, a solicitor's bill, that person may apply for a detailed assessment of the bill as if that person were the party chargeable with it, and the court may make the same order as it might have made had the application been made by the party chargeable with the bill. However, where the court has no power to make an order, except in special circumstances, it may in considering whether there are special circumstances sufficient to justify the making of an order, take into account circumstances which affect the applicant but do not affect the party chargeable with the bill. The prohibition against a party chargeable with a bill seeking a detailed assessment more than 12 months after paying the bill in s. 70(4) does not apply in applications under s. 71, where the passing of time after payment is simply a factor to be taken into account in exercising the discretion in s. 71(3) whether to order the assessment of the bill (*McIlwraith v McIlwraith* [2002] EWHC 1757 (Ch), LTL 1/8/2002).

Conduct of detailed assessment

65.9   The procedure for seeking orders under the Solicitors Act 1974, part 3, leading up to the possible detailed assessment of the solicitor's charges, is laid down by **CPR, r. 46.10** and **Part 67**, and **PD 46, paras 6.4** to **6.19**; see **71.18**. The detailed assessment may deal with the profit costs or disbursements or both and the court may allow a claim to be commenced or to be continued for any costs not being challenged (s. 70(6)). The CPR apply in determining the amounts recoverable, see **65.18**.

CONTENTIOUS AND NON-CONTENTIOUS BUSINESS

65.10   It is important to remember that contentious and non-contentious costs must not be intermingled and put in one bill (see *Re a Solicitor* [1955] 2 QB 252). Essentially, contentious and non-contentious business are each governed by different sections of the Solicitors Act 1974 and in the case of non-contentious business additionally by the Solicitors (Non-contentious Business) Remuneration Order 1994 (SI 1994/2616). A solicitor conducting non-contentious business is entitled to charge both for the time spent on an hourly basis and a separate fee based on the value of the transaction or estate (*Jemma Trust Co. Ltd v Liptrott* [2003] EWCA Civ 1476, [2004] 1 WLR 646).

The definition of 'contentious business' in the Solicitors Act 1974, s. 87(1), uses the phrase 'in or for the purposes of proceedings'. This is to be construed as a composite whole (*Bilkus v Stockler Brunton* [2010] EWCA Civ 101, [2010] 1 WLR 2526). It covers pending proceedings and future proceedings. Enforcement proceedings are clearly proceedings. Other work done after the conclusion of proceedings is merely in consequence of those earlier proceedings. Nevertheless, work done by a firm for a client in valuing shares in a company which were ordered to be bought out by the respondents in an unfair prejudice petition under what is now the Companies Act 2006, s. 994, was carried out under a court order and pursuant to directions given by the court. It was therefore contentious business, and could not attract a value element.

CONTENTIOUS BUSINESS AGREEMENTS

A contentious business agreement made under the Solicitors Act 1974, s. 59, is not subject to a detailed assessment unless the agreement provides for the solicitor's remuneration to be by reference to an hourly rate (**s. 60(1)**). A contentious business agreement may provide that the solicitor be remunerated by a gross sum, an hourly rate or rates, salary or otherwise and at a higher or lower rate than the solicitor would ordinarily be entitled to (s. 59(1)). Sections 59 to 63 do not enable a solicitor to purchase an interest in the whole or part of the proceedings.

65.11

Any agreement pursuant to s. 59 must be in writing. An agreement will be a contentious business agreement if it satisfies the requirements of s. 59. There is no need for it to be expressly stated to be a 'contentious business agreement' (*Re Wilson Properties UK Ltd, Wilson v Specter Partnership* [2007] EWHC 133 (Ch), LTL 9/2/2007). The existence of a contentious business agreement does not affect the amount of, or any rights or remedies for recovery of, any costs payable by the client to, or to the client by, any person other than the solicitor, and that person may, unless bound by an agreement to the contrary, require the costs to be referred to detailed assessment (s. 60(2)). The client is not entitled to recover from any other person under an order for payment of any costs to which the contentious business agreement relates more than the amount payable by the client to the solicitor (s. 60(3); this is the indemnity principle — see **71.30**).

Since 2 June 2003 it has been possible for a solicitor to enter into a non-indemnity CFA under which the solicitor's costs are limited to those recoverable from the losing party. The paying party will no longer be able to use the indemnity principle to defeat such an agreement.

Enforcement of contentious business agreements

The Solicitors Act 1974, s. 61, provides that no action shall be brought to enforce a contentious business agreement, but on application a party to the agreement, or representative of a party, or a person who is liable to pay, or to be paid, the costs due, may apply to the court to enforce or set aside the agreement and determine its validity and effect. On any application, the court may enforce the agreement if it considers the same to be fair and reasonable or, if the contrary view is taken, may refer the agreement to detailed assessment.

65.12

If on a detailed assessment of any costs, a contentious business agreement is relied upon by the solicitor and the client objects, but does not allege that the agreement is unfair or unreasonable, the costs officer may review and consider the number of hours claimed by the solicitor and whether the number of hours claimed are excessive (s. 61(4B)).

Commentary

Contentious business agreements have become more attractive in recent years particularly because they bring some certainty to the solicitor on the question of hourly rates and remove the entitlement to a detailed assessment, unless the court considers that the agreement is not fair and reasonable. The client also benefits from certainty on the question of hourly rates.

ASSESSMENT WHERE THERE IS NO CONTENTIOUS BUSINESS AGREEMENT

65.13   Section 64 of the Solicitors Act 1974 stipulates that a solicitor's bill of costs may, at the option of the solicitor, be either a bill containing detailed items or a gross sum bill. A client who receives a gross sum bill may, at any time before being served with proceedings for recovery of the costs included in the bill and before the expiration of three months from the date on which the bill was delivered, require the solicitor to replace it with a bill containing detailed items and upon making such request the gross sum bill will be of no effect (s. 64(2)). Where proceedings are commenced on a gross sum bill, the court will, if requested by the party chargeable with the bill before the expiration of one month from service, order that the bill be referred to detailed assessment and that the solicitor shall provide the court with such further details of the costs as the costs officer may require (s. 64(3) and (4)).

PERIODIC BILLING

65.14   The modern trend is to bill clients on a more regular periodic basis. At the very least this helps the cash flow of the solicitor and keeps the client informed about the costs of the matter.

However, there are pitfalls for the unwary. There must be an agreement with the client at the outset that interim or periodic bills will be delivered and become payable, otherwise there is no right to render an interim bill, unless it coincides with a natural break in the litigation. It is important also to distinguish between two classes of bills which can be rendered during the course of litigation:

(a) an interim bill which is final for the period of work covered by it; and
(b) an interim bill which is on account of a final bill which is yet to be delivered.

A bill of type (a) is covered by the Solicitors Act 1974 and can be referred to detailed assessment and sued by the solicitor for non-payment. A bill of type (b) cannot be referred to detailed assessment nor can the solicitor issue proceedings for recovery. This interpretation of the two classes of bill was dealt with in *Davidsons v Jones-Fenleigh* (1980) 124 SJ 204.

BILL OF COSTS

65.15   It has long been established that any bill to a client must be a complete bill containing sufficient information to enable the client to obtain advice about its detailed assessment (see *Haigh v Ousey* (1857) 7 El & Bl 578). The purpose of the Solicitors Act 1974, ss. 64 and 69, is to protect the innocent or ignorant client by providing adequate information to justify the amount charged. It is not to provide an unscrupulous client with an unmeritorious defence. The detail required in the narrative of a bill therefore varies from case to case, and deficiencies in the detail provided in a bill can be made good from the client's own knowledge and documents sent with the bill and other information already in the possession of the client (*Ralph Hume Garry v Gwillim* [2002] EWCA Civ 1 500, [2003] 1 WLR 510). To prevent disputes it may be sensible to provide clients with printouts of accounts department records, see 65.6.

A bill of costs must include an adequate description of the work carried out coupled with the dates within which the services were rendered. Disbursements must relate to the period in question otherwise upon any detailed assessment there is a risk that any disbursements outside the scope of the period in question will be struck out and become irrecoverable.

There is a tendency not to pay much attention to the subject of billing and there is sometimes a remarkable lack of care and attention to detail, which is not lost on an astute client. Very often, the solicitor's bill of costs is the final professional service that the client receives on a particular matter and it represents the last opportunity that a firm has to promote itself positively. A sloppily composed bill of costs containing errors or incorrect information will leave the wrong impression with the client. There is also the temptation to add unnecessary narrative or explanation to the bill, in order, it would seem, to justify the fee. The majority of clients, and particularly commercial clients, can see through this. If there is an agreement to render interim bills, they should be delivered on the due dates.

DISBURSEMENTS

Only expenses which a solicitor incurs in order to provide his or her professional service are **65.16** disbursements which can be so described in a bill of costs to the client (see **71.53**). Any other amounts paid on the client's behalf, such as payments into court, payments of damages and payment of other side's costs, should form part of the cash account which should accompany a bill of costs.

It is also important to ensure that any disbursements which are not paid as at the date of rendering the bill of costs, are described as 'not yet paid'. Otherwise, there is a real risk that these disbursements will not be recoverable.

INTEREST

Interest is recoverable for costs for non-contentious business, provided sufficient notice is **65.17** given as required by the Solicitors (Non-contentious Business) Remuneration Order 1994 (SI 1994/2616). For contentious business, the opposite is the case. Ordinarily, a solicitor is not entitled to interest unless it is specified and agreed with the client at the inception of the retainer. Upon detailed assessment under the Solicitors Act 1974, if application is made to the costs officer, interest will be granted only upon disbursements already paid out by the solicitor.

As well as allowing interest to be charged on outstanding bills, the initial retainer may provide for the solicitor to receive a share of any interest to which the client may become entitled under the Judgments Act 1838, s. 17 (*Hunt v R. M. Douglas (Roofing) Ltd* [1990] 1 AC 398).

DETAILED ASSESSMENT

CPR, r. 46.9, sets out the basis of detailed assessment of solicitor and own client costs and **65.18** applies to every assessment of a solicitor's bill to his or her client except a bill which is to be paid out of the Community Legal Service Fund. The Solicitors Act 1974, s. 74(3), applies unless the solicitor and client have entered into a written agreement which expressly permits payment of an amount of costs greater than that which could be recovered from another party to proceedings in the County Court. Section 74(3) does not limit the costs between solicitor and client to the amount assessed between the parties (*Lynch v Paul Davidson Taylor* [2004] EWHC 89 (QB), [2004] 1 WLR 1753).

Pursuant to CPR, r. 46.9(3), costs payable to a solicitor by his or her client are to be assessed on the indemnity basis. They are presumed to have been reasonably incurred if they were incurred with the expressed or implied approval of the client, to be reasonable in amount if the amount is expressly or impliedly approved by the client and to have been unreasonably incurred if they are of an unusual nature or amount and the solicitor did not tell the client that it might not be possible to recover all of them from the other parties. Questions of proportionality do not arise.

The assessment procedure is prescribed in CPR, r. 46.10 (see 71.20).

Chapter 66   Part 36 Offers

Commentary

The following procedural checklist is relevant to this chapter:

Procedural checklist 29   Offer to settle

INTRODUCTION

66.1   In order to encourage parties to settle their dispute, **CPR, Part 36**, lays down a system for making formal offers having costs consequences if they are unreasonably refused. It has long been recognised that there is a public interest in parties seeking to settle their disputes rather than allowing their claims to be litigated through to trial. Settlements bring disputes to a swift conclusion, avoid most of the costs involved in protracted litigation, save court time, and avoid a great deal of the antagonism that often underlies litigation. A party who receives a realistic formal offer will ordinarily accept that offer, thereby compromising the claim. If a formal offer is refused, the litigation will continue, but the principle is that the offeror will be awarded its costs from the date the offer expired if the offeree fails to do better than the terms of the offer when the claim is finally determined.

The fundamental function of a **Part 36** offer is to put the offeree on risk as to costs if, as a result of the contingencies of litigation, it later transpires that the terms of the offer were at least as advantageous as the eventual outcome (*Matthews v Metal Improvements Co. Inc.* [2007] EWCA Civ 215, [2007] CP Rep 27).

This chapter describes the effect of **Part 36** as it applies to offers to settle made on or after 6 April 2015. This is the third version of **Part 36**. The first was in the original CPR and the second was introduced on 6 April 2007. **Part 36** is drafted as a self-contained procedural code (**CPR, r. 36.1(1)**; *Gibbon v Manchester City Council* [2010] EWCA Civ 726, [2010] 1 WLR 2081, per Moore-Bick LJ at [5]). It contains a carefully constructed and highly prescriptive set of rules dealing with formal offers to settle which have specific consequences. It prescribes in some detail the manner in which a Part 36 offer is to be made, and in some respects, particularly **rr. 36.11(2)** and **36.17(4)**, departs quite markedly from the normal concepts governing the law of contract. While the basic concepts of offer and acceptance underpin **Part 36**, it does not follow that all the rules of law governing the formation of contracts are imported into **Part 36**. The way it was put by Moore-Bick LJ at [6] was that:

Certainty is as much to be commended in procedural as in substantive law, especially, perhaps, in a procedural code which must be understood and followed by ordinary citizens who wish to conduct their own litigation. In my view, Part 36 was drafted with these considerations in mind and is to be read and understood according to its terms without importing other rules derived from the general law, save where that was clearly intended.

This approach is a recipe for disaster. **Part 36** is either a self-contained code or it is not. Saying the general rules of contract do not apply 'save where that was clearly intended' begs the question of where, within **Part 36**, these exceptions are clearly intended. If Moore-Bick LJ's principle was laid down to promote certainty, which is the stated objective, leaving a total lack of clarity over when contractual principles apply signally fails to achieve the objective. Litigants in person, the group the principle is stated to be aimed at protecting, will have no realistic hope of being able to understand the rules, and will be at the mercy of parties who are able to say things in correspondence that do not have the stated effect. While the rider stated by Moore-Bick LJ is not included in **r. 36.1(1)**, the rule expressly says it is a 'procedural' code. Presumably this means the general law of contract would need to be resorted to, for example, if the terms of a settlement under **Part 36** were illegal or if implementing the terms of a **Part 36** offer was frustrated. Various procedural concepts, such as compromising when a party is a child or protected party and recoverable pre-action costs, are referred to in **Part 36** but not defined within **Part 36** (**rr. 36.11** and **36.13**), and presumably should be interpreted consistently with procedural law outside **Part 36**.

One particular problem is that the construction of **Part 36** adopted by *Gibbon v Manchester City Council* and subsequent cases gives rise to results that are not intended by the parties. Holding that a claim has (or has not) been settled contrary to the intentions of either or both parties is difficult to justify, and appears to be contrary to the overriding objective of dealing with cases justly. It places a premium on establishing that an offer is technically an offer to settle within **Part 36**, which (given there is no obligation to use form N242A when making a Part 36 offer) will inevitably lead to semantic arguments over whether differently worded offers come within **Part 36**. Another practical problem is that the decision in *Gibbon v Manchester City Council* that a Part 36 offer remains open for acceptance until formally withdrawn in accordance with **r. 36.9** will be a potential trap in every case where there is a change in the person dealing with a claim on behalf of a client. Unless all the paperwork relating to the case is provided to the representative with current conduct of the case, there is a danger that the current representative will be unaware of a 'live' offer on the file of the former representative. This is a real problem when cases are transferred from insurers to solicitors, and when clients change solicitors where the former solicitor asserts a lien over the papers.

ADVISING ON PART 36 OFFERS

Advising on the terms to offer under **CPR, Part 36**, requires a great deal of professional judgment. Likewise, advising on whether an offer should be accepted requires a balancing of a number of factors, including risks on liability (including any contributory negligence and counterclaim or set-off) and risks on the amount of damages, as well as considering the likely level of interest that might be awarded. In claims where the prospects turn on whether evidence might be allowed in or disallowed, either in a future application or at trial, assessing the risks is even more difficult. Clients must be fully informed of the costs implications of the offer. This will include the amount that will be deducted by the adviser's firm in respect of costs, how that sum is calculated, and the client's right to the assessment of the firm's costs (SRA Code of Conduct 2011, O 1.13 and O 1.14). A legal adviser will be expected to give reasons for advice on whether offers should be accepted, and should concentrate on giving clear advice that can be readily understood by the client. Legal advisers are not required, particularly if advice is being given on the day of a trial, to engage in defensive advocacy by giving their clients a catalogue of every factor that might have a bearing on whether an offer should be accepted (*Moy v Pettman Smith* [2005] UKHL 7, [2005] 1 WLR 581).

66.2

NON-DISCLOSURE

Non-disclosure of Part 36 offers

There are restrictions on disclosure of Part 36 offers. **CPR, r. 36.16(1)**, provides that a Part 36 offer will be treated as 'without prejudice except as to costs'. The fact that a Part 36 offer has been made is not to be communicated to the trial judge until the case has been decided (**r. 36.16(2)**). Similar restrictions apply to appeals (see **r. 52.22(1)**). The restriction on disclosure in **r. 36.16(2)** applies to the trial judge, so does not prevent the offer being referred to the judge dealing with an application for summary judgment or striking out on the question of costs arising from that application, even if remedies have yet to be decided (*Experience Hendrix v Times Newspapers Ltd* [2008] EWHC 458 (Ch), LTL 14/3/2008). If this happens, other without-prejudice correspondence may be referred to in order to ensure the judge is not given a distorted picture (*Experience Hendrix v Times Newspapers Ltd*). In advance of trial a request should be made to the court office to remove all references to any offers to settle under **Part 36**

66.3

(and interim payments) from the court file to avoid accidental disclosure to the trial judge. However, **r. 36.16(2)** will not apply where (**r. 36.16(3)**):

(a) the defence of tender before claim has been raised;
(b) the proceedings have been stayed under **r. 36.14** following acceptance of a Part 36 offer;
(c) where the offeror and offeree agree in writing that it should not apply; or
(d) there has been a split trial (see **66.5**).

The embargo in **r. 36.16** on disclosing the existence of Part 36 offers to the judge until the case has been decided means that they are only relevant in deciding orders as to costs. They cannot be used on questions relating to the date for assessing damages or on the amount of interest to allow (*Johnson v Gore Wood and Co. (No. 2)* [2004] EWCA Civ 14, [2004] CP Rep 27).

If there is an inadvertent disclosure of a Part 36 offer, the judge has a discretion whether to order a new trial, but may continue if satisfied that no injustice will be done (*Millensted v Grosvenor House (Park Lane) Ltd* [1937] 1 KB 717). *Millensted v Grosvenor House (Park Lane) Ltd* was approved by *Garratt v Saxby* [2004] EWCA Civ 341, [2004] 1 WLR 2152. If, after inappropriate disclosure of a Part 36 offer, the judge thinks it proper or necessary for the due administration of justice, he may refuse to hear the trial any further and direct that it be tried by another judge. However, the judge should not be too ready to adopt this course, and if satisfied that no injustice will be done, may continue with the trial. Relevant considerations include the overriding objective, saving expense and dealing with claims justly and proportionately. If a new trial is ordered, the court will almost certainly consider making a wasted costs order against the legal representative at fault.

Disclosure of a Part 36 offer outside the proceedings in a way which will not come to the judge's attention does not harm or infringe the integrity of the court's process and requires no action by the court (*Re a Company (No. 007466 of 2003)* [2004] EWHC 35 (Ch), [2004] 1 WLR 1357).

Applications and non-disclosure to the trial judge

66.4 Much of the activity relating to making and accepting Part 36 offers is done without needing court permission. Applications to the court are necessary for a number of purposes:

(a) where a Part 36 offer is to be accepted by a child or a protected party, where court approval must be sought (see **66.34**);
(b) where there is an acceptance of an offer made by some of several defendants, or there are further deductible benefits, or an apportionment is required in a Fatal Accidents Act case (see **66.33** and **66.35**);
(c) where an acceptance is after the start of a trial (**CPR, r. 36.11(3)(d)**; see **66.32**);
(d) where the offeree seeks to withdraw or reduce an offer during the offer period (see **66.18**); and
(e) where the offeree seeks an order clarifying a Part 36 offer (see **66.23**).

In situation (a) above, if proceedings have not been commenced, the application is made by issuing a Part 8 claim (see **PD 8A, para. 3.1**). All other types of application relating to Part 36 offers (including situation (a) after the substantive claim has been issued) are made under the usual interim procedure in **Part 23** or at the trial or other hearing (**PD 36, paras 2.2** and **3.2**). In order to preserve the integrity of the offer in the event that the application is refused, such applications must be dealt with by a judge other than the judge (if any) allocated in advance to conduct the trial, unless the parties agree that such judge can hear the application (**CPR, r. 36.3(f)** and **PD 36, paras 2.2** and **3.2**).

Split trials and Part 36 offers

66.5 Whether a Part 36 offer can be disclosed to the court at the end of a split trial where part of a claim, or any issue in the claim, has been decided, is governed by **CPR, r. 36.16(3)(d)** and **(4)**. Where the Part 36 offer relates only to the parts or issues that have been decided, the Part 36 offer can be disclosed in full, and taken into account by the court on the question of costs of the relevant hearing (**r. 36.16(3)(d)**). Where the Part 36 offer is wider than the parts or issues that have been decided, the trial judge at the split trial may be told there is a Part 36 offer that is not restricted to the parts or issues that have been decided, but must not be told the terms of the offer (unless one of the other exceptions in **r. 36.16(3)(a)** to **(c)** applies (**r. 36.16(4)**). Under the version of Part 36 in effect before 6 April 2007, *HSS Hire Services Group plc v BMB Builders Merchants Ltd* [2005] EWCA Civ 626, [2005] 1 WLR 3158 held that other than in the most exceptional case, the question of costs of the split trial should be reserved until determination of quantum. The court may also take the view that costs should be reserved even in respect of costs which should be unaffected by any Part 36 offer, because there could be a set-off of costs (*Tullett Prebon plc v BGC Brokers LP* [2010] EWHC 989 (QB), [2010] 6 Costs LR 891; see **63.22**).

The rules in **r. 36.16** on non-disclosure of Part 36 offers in split trials probably do not extend to interim hearings which have the effect of disposing part of a claim or some of the issues in a claim. This is because the embargo on disclosure only applies to the trial judge (**r. 36.16(2)** and **(4)**), a term defined in **r. 36.3(f)** as: 'includes the judge (if any) allocated in advance to conduct a trial'. 'Trial' is defined to mean any trial in a case, whether it is a trial of all issues or a trial of liability, quantum or some other issue in the case (**r. 36.3(c)**). Whether the word 'includes' in **r. 36.3(f)** allows the rules on non-disclosure to extend to judges dealing with strike-out and summary judgment applications may have to be decided by the courts.

For accepting a Part 36 offer after a split trial, see **66.24**.

OFFERS TO SETTLE UNDER PART 36

Offers to settle

An offer to settle within the meaning of **CPR, Part 36** (a 'Part 36 offer'), must be made in writing and comply with the formalities described at **66.7**. One basic set of formalities applies to all Part 36 offers, although there are additional requirements dealing with particular circumstances. There is no requirement to pay money into court. The party making the offer is called the 'offeror', and the party to whom the offer is made is the 'offeree' (**r. 36.3(a)** and **(b)**).

66.6

A Part 36 offer may be made at any time, including before the commencement of proceedings (**r. 36.7(1)**) or in appeal proceedings (**r. 36.4**). It may be made in respect of the whole claim, or part, or any issue, and may cover the claim, any counterclaim or other additional claim (**r. 36.2(3)**). A Part 36 offer only has the consequences set out in **r. 36.17** (see **66.39** to **66.52**) in relation to the costs of the proceedings in respect of which it is made, and not in relation to any appeal from the final decision in those proceedings (**r. 36.4(1)**). Parties are not obliged to use the Part 36 format when making an offer to settle, but if they do not, the consequences in **rr. 36.13**, **36.14** and **36.17** do not apply (**r. 36.2(2)**). Instead, the fact that a party has made an admissible offer which does not comply with Part 36 is one of the matters that the court is obliged to take into account when having regard to all the circumstances in exercising its general discretion on costs in **r. 44.2(4)** (the note in parenthesis after **r. 36.2(2)** erroneously omits the word 'admissible').

A Part 36 offer remains open for acceptance until the offeror serves notice of withdrawal on the offeree (**r. 36.11(2)**; see **66.18** to **66.21**). According to *Gibbon v Manchester City Council* [2010] EWCA Civ 726, [2010] 1 WLR 2081, there is no objection to a party having more than one 'live' Part 36 offer at any one time (see Moore-Bick LJ at [32]–[33]). Strictly this is obiter as there was only one valid Part 36 offer in question in the case before his Lordship. On the basis of the reasoning in this judgment, multiple current Part 36 offers can arise:

(a) through the deliberate choice of the offeror. This might be done in a claim for non-monetary relief where differently formulated offers may be seen as a good way of protecting the costs position of the offeror. In a money claim it may be that, with the passage of time and increasing costs in the claim, the defendant might decide to keep on the table an earlier Part 36 offer of, say, £10,000, and make a later Part 36 offer for, say, £12,000 with its slightly different costs consequences; or

(b) through accident. This may occur where, for example, the defendant makes a Part 36 offer which is rejected, and, without formally withdrawing that offer, makes a later Part 36 offer. As the earlier Part 36 offer has not been withdrawn it is still 'live' even though it was rejected by the offeree (see 66.22). Another example is where the offeror intends to vary a Part 36 offer under r. 36.9(4), with terms less advantageous to the offeree (without changing the effective date of the original offer), but fails to do so clearly enough so that the new terms are interpreted as a new offer rather than a variation (*Gibbon v Manchester City Council* at [32]).

If a Part 36 offer is withdrawn (see 66.18 to 66.21) the offeror loses the costs and interest effects of a subsisting Part 36 offer (r. 36.17(7)(a)).

Formalities governing Part 36 offers: basic contents

66.7   A Part 36 offer intended to take effect in accordance with Part 36 must comply with the formalities set out in CPR, r. 36.5:

(a) It must be in writing (r. 36.5(1)(a)). Although a Part 36 offer may be made in a letter, it is better to use form N242A (see PD 36, para. 1.1).

(b) It must make clear that it is made pursuant to Part 36 (r. 36.5(1)(b)).

(c) If made at least 21 days before trial, it must specify a period of not less than 21 days within which the defendant will be liable for the claimant's costs in accordance with rr. 36.13 or 36.20 if the offer is accepted (r. 36.5(1)(c) and (3)).

(d) It must state whether it relates to the whole of the claim or part of it or to an issue that arises in the claim, and if so, which part or issue (r. 36.5(1)(d)). A defendant's offer to settle liability with a stated percentage deduction for contributory negligence is an offer on liability and is not an offer on part of a claim for the purposes of r. 36.13(2) or r. 36.14(3) (*Onay v Brown* [2009] EWCA Civ 775, LTL 10/8/2009).

(e) It must state whether it takes into account any counterclaim (r. 36.5(1)(e)).

In addition, a Part 36 offer needs to state the terms of the proposed compromise, which should be sufficiently precise and certain for an effective contract to be formed if the offer is accepted. In cases involving the enjoyment of land and interests in land, often it is prudent to include a marked-up scale plan as an attachment to the offer. In all cases it is important to be clear whether the offer is in full and final settlement of all causes of action between the parties, or defined causes of action or issues between the parties, and whether the offer takes into account any cross-claim or previous interim payment.

A developing question is the extent to which there must be strict compliance with these formalities and consistency with the other requirements of Part 36 for an offer to be a Part 36 offer to settle, a topic discussed at 66.17.

Terms as to costs

66.8   There is a long-standing distinction, when it comes to costs, between disputes where proceedings have and have not been issued. If proceedings have been issued, the court has jurisdiction to award costs as the court seised of the proceedings. If there are no proceedings, costs can only be payable by agreement (see the Senior Courts Act 1981, s. 51(1), and 68.2). CPR, r. 36.5(1)(c), provides that a Part 36 offer must specify a period of not less than 21 days within which the defendant will be liable for the claimant's costs in accordance with r. 36.13 or 36.20 if the offer is accepted. In the version of Part 36 which applied from 6 April 2007 to 5 April 2015, the former r. 36.10(1) said that if a Part 36 offer was accepted, the claimant would be entitled to the costs of the proceedings up to the date on which notice of acceptance was served, which was assumed to have the effect of entitling the claimant to standard-basis costs whether the acceptance was before or after proceedings were issued. The equivalent provision in the current **Part 36** is **r. 36.13(1)**, which also says that on acceptance of a Part 36 offer the claimant will be entitled to the costs of the proceedings, but adds in parenthesis 'including their recoverable pre-action costs'. If the acceptance occurs after proceedings are issued, pre-action costs are recoverable as costs incidental to the proceedings within the meaning of the Senior Courts Act 1981, s. 51(1). Technically, in the absence of express agreement about costs, there will be no 'recoverable' pre-action costs in a case where a pre-action Part 36 offer is accepted before proceedings are issued. The effect is that a pre-action Part 36 offer changes in character when a claim is issued, because after issue pre-action costs become recoverable (*Thompson v Bruce* [2011] EWHC 2228 (QB), LTL 1/7/2011).

In practical terms the requirement in **CPR, r. 36.5(1)(c)**, that on acceptance the defendant will be liable for the claimant's costs can make it impossible for a defendant to make a workable Part 36 offer once the costs in the case have built up (an example is *Walker Construction (UK) Ltd v Quayside Homes Ltd* [2014] EWCA Civ 93, [2014] BLR 215). In such a situation a non-Part 36 *Calderbank* offer may provide the best protection.

A claimant making a Part 36 offer should not include or make any reference to uplift interest under **r. 36.17(4)(a)**, as this is a discretionary consequence of non-acceptance (*Ali Reza-Delta Transport Co. Ltd v United Arab Shipping Co. SAG (No. 2)* [2003] EWCA Civ 811, [2004] 1 WLR 168). The same should apply to the additional amount in **r. 36.17(4)(d)**.

Money claims: additional requirements

A Part 36 offer made by a defendant in a claim for money must offer to pay a single sum of money (**CPR, r. 36.6(1)**). This rule is subject to two exceptions, see **66.11** and **66.12**. An offer to pay all or part of a sum of money at a date later than 14 days following the date of any acceptance is not treated as a Part 36 offer unless the offeree accepts the offer (**r. 36.6(2)**).

66.9

The single sum required by **r. 36.6(1)** is by **r. 36.5(4)** treated as inclusive of all interest until:

(a) the end of the period stated in the offer during which the defendant will be liable to pay the claimant's costs if the offer is accepted, in cases where the Part 36 offer is made at least 21 days before the trial; or

(b) the date 21 days after the date the offer was made if it was made less than 21 days before the trial.

Under the current version of **Part 36** there is no need for the detailed terms approved by *Crouch v King's Healthcare NHS Trust* [2004] EWCA Civ 1332, [2005] 1 WLR 2015, for Part 36 offers made by NHS trusts.

Personal injuries claims: deduction of benefits

When making a Part 36 offer in a claim for damages for personal injuries, the defendant should state (**CPR, r. 36.22(3)**) either:

66.10

(a) that the offer is made without regard to any liability for recoverable amounts; or

(b) that the offer is intended to include any deductible amounts.

A defendant who makes a compensation payment in a personal injuries claim is liable to pay the Secretary of State the amount of recoverable benefits paid to the claimant (see the Social Security (Recovery of Benefits) Act 1997, ss. 1, 8 and sch. 2) and also any recoverable lump sum payments as defined in the Social Security (Recovery of Benefits) (Lump Sum Payments) Regulations 2008 (SI 2008/1596), regs 4 and 12 (see the Social Security (Recovery of Benefits) Act 1997, s. 1A, the Pneumoconiosis etc. (Workers' Compensation) Act 1979, and the Mesothelioma Lump Sum Payments (Conditions and Amounts) Regulations 2008 (SI 2008/1963)). Recoverable State benefits arise in a great many personal injury claims, but only payments in pneumoconiosis and mesothelioma claims are recoverable lump sum payments (see the Social Security (Recovery of Benefits) Act 1997, s. 1A(2)). The term 'lump sum' in these provisions must not be confused with the same expression used in relation to periodical payments in **66.11**. As a result, most offers made by defendants are stated to include deductible amounts (see point (b) above). Before making such a Part 36 offer, the defendant must apply for a certificate which will provide details of recoverable benefits and recoverable lump sum payments (**CPR, r. 36.22(5)**). Once the certificate is received, the defendant will be able to comply with **r. 36.22(6)**, which requires the Part 36 offer to state:

(a) the amount of gross compensation;

(b) the name and amount of any deductible amount which will reduce the gross amount; and

(c) the net amount of compensation.

In a case where the offeror makes a Part 36 offer after a certificate has been applied for but before it is received, the offeror must within seven days of receipt of the certificate clarify the offer by stating the details required by **r. 36.22(6)** (**r. 36.22(7)**).

Permission is required to accept a Part 36 offer where further deductible benefits have accrued since the date of the offer, see **66.33**. The rules relating to success and liability for costs in personal injuries claims with recoverable benefits are discussed at **66.41**.

Personal injuries claims for future pecuniary loss

66.11 Claims for future pecuniary loss in personal injury claims are governed by the Damages Act 1996, s. 2(1), see **63.33**. **CPR, r. 36.18(3)**, provides that a Part 36 offer to settle a claim which is or includes a claim for future pecuniary loss (whether by the claimant or the defendant) may contain an offer to pay or accept:

(a) the whole or part of the damages for future pecuniary loss in the form of either:

    (i)   a lump sum (which must be a single sum of money: **rr. 36.18(5)** and **36.6**); or

    (ii)   periodical payments; or

    (iii)   both a lump sum and periodical payments;

(b) the whole or part of any other damages in the form of a lump sum.

Rule 36.18(4) lays down a number of compulsory and optional details to be included in a Part 36 offer to settle a personal injury claim involving damages for future pecuniary loss.

Compulsory elements are that the offer must:

(a) state the amount of any offer to pay the whole or part of any damages in the form of a lump sum (**r. 36.13(4)(a)**);

(b) state what part of the offer relates to damages for future pecuniary loss to be paid or accepted in the form of periodical payments (**r. 36.18(4)(c)**), and must specify:

    (i)   the amount and duration of the periodical payment;

    (ii)   the amount of any payments for substantial capital purchases and when they are to be made; and

    (iii)   that each amount is to vary by reference to the retail prices index (or some other named index, or that it is not to vary by reference to any index); and

(c) state either that any damages in the form of periodical payment will be funded in a way that ensures that continuity of payment is reasonably secure, or how continuity of payment is to be secured (**r. 36.18(4)(d)**).

Optional elements are (**r. 36.18(4)(b)**) that the offer may:

(a) state what part of the lump sum, if any, relates to damages for future pecuniary loss; and

(b) state what part relates to other damages to be accepted in the form of a lump sum.

An offer comprising a lump sum and periodical payments can only be accepted as a whole (**r. 36.18(6)**). If the offeree accepts an offer which includes payment of any part of the damages through periodical payments, the claimant must within seven days of the acceptance apply to the court for an award of damages in accordance with **rr. 41.4** to **41.10** and **PD 41B** (see **CPR, r. 36.18(7)**).

Offers in provisional damages claims

Provisional damages are considered at **63.24** to **63.28**. A Part 36 offer made in a claim which includes a claim for provisional damages must specify whether the offer includes an award of provisional damages (**CPR, r. 36.19(2)**). A provisional damages offer must state a single sum in respect of the immediate damages element in respect of the claimant's existing injuries, calculated on the assumption that the claimant will not develop the disease or suffer the deterioration justifying a claim for further damages (**rr. 36.19(4)** and **36.6**). The offer must by **r. 36.19(3)** also state:

66.12

(a) that the sum offered is in satisfaction of the claim for damages on the assumption that the claimant will not develop the disease or suffer the deterioration specified in the offer; and

(b) that the offer is subject to the condition that the claimant must make any claim for further damages within a specified period.

If the offeree accepts a Part 36 offer for provisional damages, the claimant must within seven days of the acceptance apply to the court for an award of provisional damages in accordance with **r. 41.2** and **PD 41A** (see **r. 36.19(5)**).

Defence of tender before claim

A defendant who wishes to rely on a defence of tender before claim must make a payment into court of the amount said to have been tendered (**CPR, r. 37.2**). The defence of tender before claim is not available until this has been done (**r. 37.2(2)**). The payment in should be paid at the time of filing the defence (*Greening v Williams* [2000] CP Rep 40). Usually the payment will be made by cheque, which must be made payable to the Accountant General of the Supreme Court (**PD 37, para. 1.1(1)(a)**). A litigant in person without a current account may, if the claim is proceeding in the County Court or a District Registry, lodge cash rather than using a cheque (**para. 1.2**). The payment must be accompanied by a copy of the defence and by Court Funds Office form 100. Notice of the payment in must be served on every other party, and a certificate of service (in form N215) must be filed in respect of each such notice (**CPR, r. 37.1**).

66.13

Money paid into court in support of a defence of tender before claim may not be paid out without the court's permission, except where a Part 36 offer is accepted without needing permission and the defendant agrees that the sum in court can be used to satisfy the offer (**r. 37.1**). If the claimant is willing to accept the sum in court, it usually means that the defendant has succeeded on his defence of tender before claim, in which event the claimant should pay the defendant's costs from the date of the pre-claim tender.

The rule that Part 36 offers must not be communicated to the trial judge does not apply to tenders before claim (**r. 36.16(3)(a)**).

Date a Part 36 offer is made

A Part 36 offer is made when it is served on the offeree (**CPR, r. 36.7(2)**). This wording removes the decision in *Charles v NTL Group Ltd* [2002] EWCA Civ 2004, LTL 13/12/2002, which held that the strict rules on service in Part 6 (see **chapter 15**), did not apply to Part 36 offers. The effect is that provided one of the prescribed methods of service in **r. 6.20** is used, there is no need for the offeree to prove receipt because of the irrebuttable presumption of service in **r. 6.26**. The intention appears to be that the provisions of Part 6 apply even to Part 36 offers made before proceedings are commenced.

66.14

Commentary

Where the offeree is legally represented, the offer must be served on the legal representative (PD 36, para. 1.2).

Relevant period for acceptance of a Part 36 offer

66.15   A Part 36 offer must specify a period of not less than 21 days within which the defendant will be liable for the claimant's costs in accordance with **CPR, r. 36.13** or **r. 36.20**, if the offer is accepted (**r. 36.5(1)(c)**). There is no provision within Part 36 for suspension of the relevant period while the offeree investigates the offer (*Martin v Randall* [2007] EWCA Civ 1155, LTL 22/10/2007). If the offeree wants more time, a time application should be made (in the absence of consent) under **r. 3.1(2)(a)**.

In the case of an offer made not less than 21 days before a trial, the period stated under **r. 36.5(1)(c)**, or such longer period as the parties may agree, is 'the relevant period' for the purposes of Part 36 (**r. 36.3(g)**).

In the case of a Part 36 offer made less than 21 days before a trial, 'the relevant period' is the period up to the end of the trial or such other period as the court has determined (**r. 36.3(g)**). In order for a Part 36 offer made less than 21 days before trial to have the full consequences in the event of non-acceptance set out in **r. 36.17**, it is necessary to obtain an order abridging the relevant period (see **rr. 3.1(2)(a) and 36.17(7)(c)**).

Time-limited Part 36 offers

66.16   In *C v D* [2011] EWCA Civ 646, [2012] 1 WLR 1962, it was held that a time-limited offer was inconsistent with the version of Part 36 in effect from 6 April 2007 to 5 April 2015. In particular it was inconsistent with the provisions now in **r. 36.11(2)** that a Part 36 offer can be accepted at any time unless it is withdrawn, and those now in **r. 36.17(3), (4) and (7)**, for costs and interest sanctions where judgment is at least as advantageous as a Part 36 offer unless the offer is withdrawn. This was always regarded as an unattractive result, and has been reversed by the current **r. 36.9(4)(b)**, which allows a Part 36 offer to be automatically withdrawn in accordance with its terms.

Defects in a Part 36 offer

66.17   An offer which does not comply with the technical requirements of **CPR, r. 36.5**, does not have the consequences on acceptance or following judgment set out in **rr. 36.13, r. 36.14** and **r. 36.17** (see **r. 36.2(2)**). The requirements referred to in **r. 36.5** are the formal requirements which apply to all Part 36 offers (see **66.7**), and also the specific requirements which apply in personal injuries claims relating to damages for future pecuniary loss (**r. 36.18**; see **66.11**), provisional damages (**r. 36.19**; see **66.12**), and deduction of benefits (**r. 36.22**; see **66.10**).

Part of the intention behind replacing **Part 36** in 2015 was to reduce disputes over whether offers comply with these technical requirements. Merely requiring the offer to make it clear it is made pursuant to **Part 36** (**r. 36.5(1)(b)**) is less prescriptive than the former requirement that the offer had to state on its face that it was intended to have the consequences of Part 36, Section I. Permitting time-limited Part 36 offers (**r. 36.9(4)(b)**) removes another technical objection. In considering whether an offer alleged to be a Part 36 offer is defective, and the extent of any defect, it was held before *Gibbon v Manchester City Council* [2010] EWCA Civ 726, [2010] 1 WLR 2081, that the offer should be interpreted as it would be read by a reasonable solicitor (*Onay v Brown* [2009] EWCA Civ 775, LTL 10/8/2009).

Serious departures from Part 36 will almost certainly mean the offer is not a Part 36 offer. Thus an offer specifically excluding the claimant from recovering all or part of its costs, or only offering a fixed sum in respect of costs, does not comply with **rr. 36.5(1)(c) and 36.13**, so will not be a Part 36 offer (*Howell v Lees-Millais* [2011] EWCA Civ 786, [2011] WTLR 1795). A letter offering an interim payment is not to be construed as a Part 36 offer (*Ali v Stagecoach* [2011] EWCA Civ 1494, LTL 28/10/2011).

The best way of avoiding making defective Part 36 offers is by using form N242A. A measure of protection may also be gained by including a request to the other side to notify the offeror of any defect as soon as possible (see *Seeff v Ho* [2011] EWCA Civ 401, [2011] 4 Costs LR 443).

It is arguable that an offer which complies with the technical requirements of Part 36, but is inconsistent with other provisions of Part 36 falls outside Part 36. In *C v D* at first instance ([2010] EWHC 2940 (Ch), [2011] 1 WLR 331) at [26] Warren J suggested that an offer to settle that said an acceptance would only be valid if hand-delivered would not stop the offer being a Part 36 offer. With respect, this ignores the provisions now in **rr. 36.7(2), 36.9(2)** and **36.11(1)**, which provide that offers, acceptances and withdrawals of offers take effect on 'service'. Service is regulated by Part 6, and so these provisions must import all the means of service permitted by Part 6. Either Warren J's conclusion at [26] is wrong (in the interests of certainty within a self-contained code as explained by *Gibbon v Manchester City Council* [2010] EWCA Civ 726, [2010] 1 WLR 2081), or it is necessary to differentiate between material and non-material departures from the scheme in Part 36. If so, any material departure from the scheme in Part 36 will mean the offer is not governed by Part 36. For example, providing that the defendant will be liable for the claimant's indemnity-basis costs if the offer is accepted in the relevant period would presumably be a material departure from Part 36.

A question arises as to whether minor defects in any of these requirements can be put right using the power to cure errors of procedure in **r. 3.10**. This rule provides that errors of procedure do not invalidate steps taken in proceedings unless the court so orders. It is suggested that this means that **r. 3.10** does not apply to a defective offer, because **r. 36.2(2)** says that nothing in Part 36 prevents a party from making an offer to settle in whatever form he chooses. A defective offer is not therefore without validity in any event. It simply does not have the consequences set out in **rr. 36.13, 36.14** and **36.17**. As the note to **r. 36.2** says, the court still has to take into account an offer that does not comply with **r. 36.5** when deciding the question of costs (**r. 44.2**). The implication is that this will not necessarily be in the same terms as if the offer had complied with **r. 36.5**, but it depends on the extent of the defect. In *Huntley v Simmonds* [2009] EWHC 406 (QB), LTL 6/3/2009, the Part 36 offer was defective in that it omitted the statement required in future pecuniary loss cases by **r. 36.18(4)(d)** (see **66.11**), that continuity of payments would be assured. It was held that while there would be cases where the court would not rectify formal defects, in this case there was no prejudice and the claimant understood the offer, so the court applied **r. 44.2(4)** and accorded the offer the same effect as one that complied with Part 36. This is discussed further at **66.51**.

A party who realises that his or her offer does not fully comply with Part 36 should replace the offer, before acceptance, with an offer that does comply. The consequences set out in **rr. 36.13, 36.14** and **36.17** will then apply from that time.

DEALING WITH THE OFFER

Withdrawing or changing a Part 36 offer during the relevant period

Before the expiry of the relevant period (see **66.15**), a Part 36 offer may be withdrawn or its terms changed in a way less advantageous to the offeree, but the withdrawal or change only takes effect at the end of the relevant period and provided the offeree has not served notice of acceptance within that period (**CPR, r. 36.10**). There is no prescribed form for withdrawing   **66.18** or changing a Part 36 offer. Any withdrawal must, however, comply strictly with the requirements of **r. 36.9(2)** if it is to be effective (*Gibbon v Manchester City Council* [2010] EWCA Civ 726, [2010] 1 WLR 2081 at [17]). It must be in writing, and should include an express reference to the date of the Part 36 offer and its terms, together with some words making it clear that the offer is being withdrawn (at [17]).

If the offeree serves notice of acceptance of the original offer before the expiry of the relevant period, the acceptance has effect unless the offeror applies to the court for permission to withdraw or change the offer within seven days of the notice of acceptance (or, if earlier, before the first day of the trial (**r. 36.10(2)(b)**). Permission to withdraw a Part 36 offer during the relevant period is sought by making an application in accordance with Part 23, and must be dealt with by a judge other than the trial judge (**PD 36, para. 2.2**).

On an application for permission to withdraw or change a Part 36 offer under **r. 36.10(2)(b)** the court will consider whether there has been a change of circumstances since the making of the original offer and whether it is in the interests of justice to give permission (**r. 36.10(3)**). Sufficient changes in circumstances may include:

(a) the discovery of further evidence puts a wholly different complexion on the case. However, merely receiving an expert's report contradicting the evidence of the claimant's expert is unlikely to be a sufficient change of circumstances (*Flynn v Scougall* [2004] EWCA Civ 873, [2004] 1 WLR 3069) or

(b) there has been a change in the legal outlook brought about by a judicial decision.

It might be in the interests of justice to permit an offer to be withdrawn or changed if the original offer was induced by fraud, or if there has been a mistake affecting the terms of the offer.

Withdrawing or changing a Part 36 offer after the relevant period

66.19 After expiry of the relevant period and provided the offeree has not previously served notice of acceptance, the offeror may withdraw the offer or change its terms to be less advantageous to the offeree without the permission of the court (**CPR, r. 36.9(1)**). The offeror withdraws or changes a Part 36 offer by serving written notice on the offeree (**r. 36.9(2)**); and see **66.18**. If a non-time limited Part 36 offer is not withdrawn, it may be accepted even after the relevant period (**r. 36.11(2)**).

A change in the terms of a Part 36 offer (whether it is an improved offer or one which is less advantageous to the offeree) takes effect when written notice of the change is served on the offeree (r. 36.9(2)).

Changing an offer to more advantageous terms

66.20 A Part 36 offer can be changed to make it more advantageous to the offeree at any time, during or after the relevant period. An improved offer is treated, not as withdrawing the original offer, but as making a new Part 36 offer on the improved terms (**CPR, r. 36.9(5)(a)**). In such a case the 'relevant period' for the purposes of **r. 36.5(1)(c)** is 21 days from service of the improved offer, or such longer period as may be stated in the notice of change (**r. 36.9(3)(b)**).

Effect of a withdrawn Part 36 offer

66.21 A withdrawn Part 36 offer does not have the effect on costs and interest (as laid down in **CPR, r. 36.17(3)** and (4)) of a subsisting Part 36 offer (**r. 36.17(7)(a)**). A note to **r. 36.17** points out that **r. 44.2(4)(c)** requires the court to consider any admissible offer to settle which does not have the costs consequences set out in Part 36 in deciding what order to make about costs. Without prejudice offers (see **50.68**) are not admissible, whereas open offers and offers made without prejudice save as to costs are admissible on the question of costs. This gives the court a wide scope on costs, to be exercised applying the overriding objective. In a suitable case the court can even treat the withdrawn Part 36 offer has having the same costs consequences as if it had not been withdrawn (see *Trustees of Stokes Pension Fund v Western Power Distribution (South West) plc* [2005] EWCA Civ 854, [2005] 1 WLR 3595, discussed at **66.51**).

Rejection of a Part 36 offer

66.22 There is no need for the offeree to give an express rejection of a Part 36 offer. In most cases the offeree will keep his options open by not responding to a Part 36 offer (see **66.28**). It was held in *Gibbon v Manchester City Council* [2010] EWCA Civ 726, [2010] 1 WLR 2081 at [16]–[17] that the rejection of a Part 36 offer by the offeree has no effect on its continuing validity. Likewise, there is no concept of an implied withdrawal of a Part 36 offer, such as where the offeror rejects a counter-offer from the offeree in terms similar to the terms of the offeror's offer. This is because the only way in which a non-time limited Part 36 offer ceases to be live (in the absence of an acceptance or the final disposal of the claim) is by the offeror formally withdrawing its offer under **CPR, r. 36.9(2)**. This means that the rejected offer can be accepted as of right by the offeree (even after the relevant period has expired), which was the actual decision in the first appeal in *Gibbon v Manchester City Council*.

Making a counter-offer does not operate as a rejection of a Part 36 offer. (**CPR, r. 36.11(2)** says a Part 36 offer may be accepted at any time 'whether or not the offeree has subsequently made a different offer', thereby reversing the effect of *Hawley v Luminar Leisure plc* [2006] EWCA Civ 30, [2006] 5 Costs LR 687, a decision under the version of Part 36 in effect before 6 April 2007.)

Clarification of a Part 36 offer

66.23 It may happen that a party makes a Part 36 offer, but that its terms are not clear to the offeree. This may occur where the claim raises more than one cause of action, or where there are joint claimants. It may also occur where the Part 36 offer fails to make clear what is included. In such cases, the offeree may request the offeror to clarify the offer, but the request must be made within seven days of the offer being made (**CPR, r. 36.8(1)**). The time when an offer or payment is made is defined as the date it is served (see **r. 36.7(2)**). If the offeror fails to give clarification as requested within seven days of receiving the request, the offeree may apply for an order that this be done, unless the trial has started (**r. 36.8(2)**). An application for an order requiring clarification should be made in accordance with Part 23 and the application notice should state the respects in which the terms of the Part 36 offer are said to require clarification.

Where the Part 36 offer fails to make clear what it includes, an order to clarify will almost certainly be made, in accordance with the overriding objective. Cases where the claimant or claimants want a global offer broken down between the respective claimants are less clear cut. Under the RSC, the court could order a defendant to break down a global payment in on the ground that it was 'embarrassing'. **CPR, r. 36.8**, uses the term 'clarification', and is almost certainly intended to lay down a different test. It is arguable that the court only has jurisdiction under **r. 36.8** where the Part 36 offer is unclear. This would mean that, provided the offer gives the details required by Part 36, and states clearly whether it covers the whole claim, or which parts, and whether it includes interest and any counterclaim etc., no further breakdown can be ordered. The alternative argument that **r. 36.8** gives the court a wide discretion to order a more detailed breakdown, for example, into different heads of damages, or to give details of dates and rates applied, is

Commentary

whether it had been reasonable for the claimant not to have accepted the offer based on the information available to the claimant at the time it was made. Part 36 offers are designed to put the claimant on risk as to costs if, as a result of the contingencies of litigation, it later transpires that the claimant is unable to beat the terms of the offer. A reduction in the value of the claim after the offer was made due to the onset of a non-accident-related medical condition provided no basis for departing from the position stated in r. 36.13(5). Where it is a claimant's offer that is accepted after the relevant period, there is no presumption that the post-relevant period costs awarded to the claimant will be on the indemnity basis, and unless the claimant can demonstrate the necessary conduct under r. 44.2, those costs will be ordered on the standard basis (*Fitzpatrick Contractors Ltd v Tyco Fire and Integrated Solutions (UK) Ltd* [2009] EWHC 274 (TCC), [2009] BLR 144). It may, however, be appropriate to award enhanced interest on the post-relevant period costs (in *Fitzpatrick Contractors Ltd v Tyco Fire and Integrated Solutions (UK) Ltd* such interest was awarded at 1 per cent above base rate).

66.29   **Acceptance of Part 36 offer covering part of the claim**   Where a defendant's Part 36 offer relates to only part of the claim, and either it is accepted without the claimant abandoning the balance of the claim, or it is accepted after expiry of the relevant period, the parties may agree the liability for costs, but if they do not, the court will make an order for costs (**CPR, r. 36.13(4)(c)**).

Acceptance in Warsaw/Montreal Convention cases

66.30   The Warsaw Convention 1929, art. 22(4) (as amended by The Hague Convention 1955), which is set out in the schedule to the Carriage by Air Act 1961, provides:

The limits prescribed in this article shall not prevent the court from awarding, in accordance with its own law, in addition, the whole or part of the court costs and of the other expenses of the litigation incurred by the plaintiff. The foregoing provision shall not apply if the amount of damages awarded... does not exceed the sum which the carrier has offered in writing to the plaintiff within a period of six months from the date of the occurrence causing the damage, or before the commencement of the action, if that is later.

The equivalent provision in the Montreal Convention 2004 is art. 22(6).

In *GKN Westland Helicopters Ltd v Korean Air* [2003] EWHC 1120 (Comm), [2003] 2 All ER (Comm) 578, the defendant made an offer within six months of the issue of the claim, then made a Part 36 payment in a slightly larger amount. The Part 36 payment was accepted. It was held that because the Part 36 payment was higher than the Warsaw Convention offer, the normal rule in what is now **CPR, r 36.13**, applied, and the defendant was liable to pay the claimant's costs of the claim. It was recognised that there is a latent conflict between r. 36.13 and art. 22 of the Convention where a claimant accepts a Part 36 offer which is less than a previous Warsaw Convention offer. The better view is that in such circumstances the Warsaw Convention should prevail, and the defendant should be awarded its costs from the date of the Warsaw Convention offer.

Acceptance of offer of amends in defamation cases

66.31   Under the Defamation Act 1996, s. 2(1), a person who has published a statement alleged to be defamatory of another may offer to make amends, by making a suitable correction and a sufficient apology, which are to be published in a reasonable and practicable manner, and to pay such compensation and costs as may be agreed or determined (s. 2(4)). Such an offer must be in writing and comply with the requirements of s. 2(3). A party accepting such an offer may not bring or continue defamation proceedings (s. 3(2)), although the aggrieved party may apply to the court for an order that the other side fulfil his offer (s. 3(3)), and if compensation is not agreed, it shall be determined by the court (s. 3(5)). An offer of amends, if not accepted, may in certain circumstances act as a defence, and may be relied upon in mitigation of damages (s. 4).

In *Warren v Random House Group Ltd* [2008] EWCA Civ 834, [2009] QB 600, the defendant made an offer of amends which was accepted by the claimant. Before compensation had been decided under s. 3(5), the defendant sought to withdraw the offer and to plead justification. As in the case of accepted Part 36 offers, the court felt that an accepted offer of amends does not create a contract in the strict sense, because the agreement contains express provisions as to what should or should not happen next, and the court retains a role (Clarke MR at [17]). This means that the agreement can be set aside on the usual grounds on which a contract can be set aside, and also where there are special or exceptional circumstances, applying the same principles as apply on seeking to be released from an uncertaking (see **37.64**).

Permission to accept

Acceptance while a trial is in progress   The court's permission is required for an acceptance **66.32** of a Part 36 offer while a trial is in progress (**CPR, r. 36.11(3)(d)**). This covers the period up to judgment being given or handed down (**r. 36.3(d)**). It is suggested that the principles enunciated in *Capital Bank plc v Stickland* [2004] EWCA Civ 1677, [2005] 1 WLR 3914, are a useful guide to how the discretion should be exercised under **r. 36.11(3)(d)**. This case concerned the late acceptance of a claimant's Part 36 offer under the version of Part 36 in effect before 6 April 2007.

In the majority of cases permission will be granted, with the only question being as to costs (*Cumper v Pothecary* [1941] 2 KB 58 at p. 67, quoted with approval by Longmore LJ in *Capital Bank plc v Strickland* at [17]). However, the court has a wide discretion, and may refuse permission, for example, where the acceptance is made very late, where there is a doubt about the availability of the money, or where there has been a change of circumstances (at [16]).

If late acceptance is allowed by consent or with the court's permission, the usual rule is that the claimant recovers costs up to the end of the relevant period, and the defendant recovers costs thereafter. This is subject to the court's discretion, and there may be reasons for making some other costs order. For example, the claimant may have accepted the offer after late disclosure of evidence or late amendment by the defendant which has had a material effect on the claimant's prospects. If the change is just an excuse for late acceptance, the usual costs rule will be applied, but where the change has had a real impact the court may allow the claimant to recover costs of the claim up to some later point, even the date of acceptance (*Factortame Ltd v Secretary of State for the Environment, Transport and the Regions* [2002] EWCA Civ 22, [2002] 1 WLR 2438). In exercising its discretion on costs, the court is not restricted to considering the circumstances surrounding the offer, and should consider all the circumstances relevant under **r. 44.2**, including the parties' willingness to participate in proposed mediation (*Chaudry v Yap* [2004] EWHC 3380 (Ch), LTL 28/10/2004).

Other cases where permission to accept is required   In addition to the situation where a **66.33** Part 36 offer is accepted after the start of the trial (see **66.32**), permission to accept is required where:

(a) The Part 36 offer is made by some, but not all, of a number of defendants and **CPR, r. 36.15(4)**, applies (**r. 36.11(3)(a)**, see **66.35**).

(b) The claim is for damages for personal injuries, the offer is intended to include any deductible amounts, and further deductible amounts have been paid to the claimant since the date of the offer (**r. 36.11(3)(b)**). In this situation the application must state the net amount offered in the Part 36 offer, the deductible amounts accrued at the date of the offer, and those that have subsequently accrued. The application must be accompanied by a copy of the current certificate of recoverable benefits and any recoverable lump sum (**PD 36, para. 3.3**). If permission to accept is granted, the court may direct that the amount of the offer payable to the offeree shall be reduced by a sum equivalent to the deductible amounts paid to the claimant since the date of the offer (**CPR, r. 36.22(9)**).

(c) An apportionment is required under **r. 41.3A** (Fatal Accidents Act claims) (**r. 36.11(3)(c)**).

(d) Any of the parties is a child or protected party (**r. 21.10**, see **66.34**). In this situation the stay on acceptance only takes effect when approval has been given (**r. 36.14(4)**).

66.34   **Acceptance by or on behalf of a child or protected party**   CPR, **r. 21.10(1)**, provides that no settlement or compromise relating to a claim by or on behalf of, or against, a child or protected party shall be valid without the approval of the court. In such a case there is no binding agreement until the proposed settlement is approved by the court under **r. 21.10**. This means that until that time either party may repudiate the settlement (*Dietz v Lennig Chemicals Ltd* [1969] 1 AC 170; *Drinkall v Whitwood* [2003] EWCA Civ 1547, [2004] 1 WLR 462).

66.35   **Acceptance of Part 36 offer made by some of the defendants**   In cases where a claimant wishes to accept a Part 36 offer made by some of a number of defendants, there are three situations that need to be distinguished:

(a) If the defendants are sued jointly or in the alternative, the claimant may accept the Part 36 offer if he discontinues the claim against the other defendants and those other defendants give written consent to the acceptance of the offer (**CPR, r. 36.15(2)**).

(b) If the defendants are alleged to have a several liability, the claimant may accept the offer and continue his claims against the other defendants (**r. 36.15(3)**).

(c) In all other cases the claimant must apply to the court for an order permitting him to accept the Part 36 offer (**r. 36.15(4)**).

Other consequences of acceptance

66.36   **Stay on acceptance**   If a Part 36 offer is accepted, the claim will be stayed (**CPR, r. 36.14(1)**). The stay will be on the terms of the offer where the Part 36 offer relates to the whole claim (**r. 36.14(2)**). If the Part 36 offer only related to part of the claim the claim is stayed as to that part on the terms of the offer (**r. 36.14(3)**). As **Part 36** is a self-contained code, it is impermissible for the claimant to enter judgment in the terms of the offer, which would then trigger the enhanced costs, interest and additional damages in **r. 36.17(4)**, because the effects of acceptance are those set out in **rr. 36.11** to **36.15** (*Jolly v Harsco Infrastructure Services Ltd* [2012] EWHC 3086 (QB), [2013] 1 Costs LR 115).

While an accepted Part 36 offer appears to form a contract, the better view is that it does not, because the court retains a role under the terms of **Part 36**. See *Flynn v Scourgall* [2004] EWCA Civ 873, [2004] 1 WLR 3069; *Scammell v Dicker* [2001] 1 WLR 631; *Orton v Collins* [2007] EWHC 803 (Ch), [2007] 1 WLR 2953; and *Warren v Random House Group Ltd* [2008] EWCA Civ 834, [2009] QB 600 at [21]. Where the terms of the acceptance include the disposition of an interest in land, the court has the power to order the parties to sign a single document incorporating the terms of the settlement (*Orton v Collins* [2007] EWHC 803 (Ch), [2007] 1 WLR 2953).

66.37   **Time for payment**   Unless the parties agree otherwise in writing, where a Part 36 offer to pay money is accepted, payment must be made within 14 days of the acceptance (**CPR, r. 36.14(6)(a)**). In the case of provisional damages awards and periodical payments awards, the 14 days run from the date of the court order, unless the court orders otherwise (**r. 36.14(6)(b)**). If the sum is not paid within these time limits, the claimant may enter judgment for the unpaid sum (**r. 36.14(7)**).

66.38   **Enforcement of agreed terms**   A stay under **CPR, r. 36.14** (see **66.36**), does not affect the power of the court to enforce the terms of the Part 36 offer, nor to deal with any question of costs or interest on costs relating to the proceedings (**r. 36.14(5)**). Enforcement of a term for the payment of money is effected by entering judgment followed by use of the normal procedures for enforcing judgments (see **chapter 79**). Terms other than for the payment of money can be enforced by making an interim application to the court, there being no need to commence a new claim (**r. 36.14(8)**).

CONSEQUENCES OF NON-ACCEPTANCE

Failing to obtain a judgment more advantageous than a Part 36 offer

The main reason for making a Part 36 offer is to gain the costs, damages and interest benefits set out in **CPR, r. 36.17**. These consequences apply (**r. 36.17(1)**), unless the court considers that their application would be unjust, where a Part 36 offer is not accepted and either: **66.39**

(a) a claimant fails to obtain a judgment more advantageous than a Part 36 offer made by a defendant; or

(b) judgment is entered against a defendant which is at least as advantageous to the claimant as the proposals set out in a Part 36 offer made by the claimant.

Deciding whether a judgment is more advantageous than a Part 36 offer has proved controversial. For money claims, and for the money element of a claim, a judgment is 'more advantageous' where it is better than the Part 36 offer in money terms by any amount, however small (**r. 36.17(2)**). Rule 36.17(2) is intended to provide a clear-cut dividing line (*Fox v Foundation Piling Ltd* [2011] EWCA Civ 790, [2011] 6 Costs LR 961). If the judgment is even by the smallest margin better than a Part 36 offer then, subject to the discretion in **r. 44.2**, the claimant should be awarded its costs. This is so, particularly in personal injuries claims, even where the judgment is substantially lower than the amount claimed. In these cases the defendant should have protected itself by making a realistic, albeit modest, Part 36 offer (*Morgan v UPS* [2008] EWCA Civ 1476, [2009] 3 Costs LR 384). *Fox v Foundation Piling Ltd* recognised there is a distinction between:

(a) cases where a claimant recovers more damages than a defendant's Part 36 offer, but with a substantial reduction on account of exaggeration. In these cases **r. 36.17(2)** applies, and the claimant should be awarded all its standard-basis costs; and

(b) cases where the claimant has been dishonest, where under **r. 44.2** different considerations apply.

Rule 36.17(2) overrules the decision in *Carver v BAA plc* [2008] EWCA Civ 412, [2009] 1 WLR 113, which held that 'more advantageous' in **r. 36.17(1)** is a more open-textured concept than the phrase 'fails to better' used in the version of Part 36 in effect before 6 April 2007. *Carver v BAA plc* appeared to hold that the court is entitled to decide that a judgment that exceeds a Part 36 offer by a small margin might not be more advantageous to a claimant given factors such as the costs of litigating a claim through to trial and the emotional stress of taking a case to trial.

Like must be compared with like. Where a Part 36 offer includes interest, the court must recalculate its award of interest to the date of the Part 36 offer in order to determine whether the judgment exceeds the terms of the offer (*Blackham v Entrepose UK* [2004] EWCA Civ 1109, [2005] 1 Costs LR 68). A gloss on this was applied in *Gibbon v Manchester City Council* [2010] EWCA Civ 726, [2010] 1 WLR 2081 at [36], where the trial judge had awarded interest at 8 per cent per annum, but the Court of Appeal recalculated the award applying an interest rate of 4 per cent per annum. The stated reason was that no more than 4 per cent per annum 'could have been expected' when the Part 36 offer was made. An award of interest is just as much a part of a judgment as the principal sum, and it is, with respect, very difficult to understand why this element of uncertainty (guessing what is a reasonable rate of interest, as opposed to the actual rate of interest awarded by the judge) should be grafted on to the calculations that have to be made under Part 36.

In a defamation claim, comparing the terms of an offer with the eventual judgment may, depending on the terms of the offer and the events at trial, involve considering the terms and value of any apology and any damage to the reputation of the claimant arising from the evidence given at the trial (*Jones v Associated Newspapers Ltd* [2007] EWHC 1489 (QB), [2008] 1 All ER 240).

Consistently with *Mitchell v James* [2002] EWCA Civ 997, [2004] 1 WLR 158, the court should ignore any terms in a claimant's Part 36 offer relating to indemnity-basis costs or enhanced interest (see **66.44**) in deciding whether the offer exceeds the judgment (*Ali Reza-Delta Transport Co. Ltd v United Arab Shipping Co. SAG (No. 2)* [2003] EWCA Civ 811, [2004] 1 WLR 168).

For non-money claims on and after 1 October 2011, it is submitted the approach suggested by Bingham MR in *Poache v News Group Newspapers Ltd* [1998] EMLR 161 at pp. 168–9 (cited with approval in *Carver v BAA plc*) has a continuing validity in deciding whether a judgment is more advantageous than a Part 36 offer:

> The judge must look closely at the facts of the particular case before him and ask: who, as a matter of substance and reality, has won? Has the [claimant] won anything of value which he could not have won without fighting the action through to the finish? Has the defendant substantially denied the [claimant] the prize which the [claimant] fought the action to win?

It is a fundamental error to make a costs order that penalises a party for failing to achieve a better result at trial than the terms of its own Part 36 offer (*Rolf v De Guerin* [2011] EWCA Civ 78, [2011] BLR 221).

Cases where rule 36.17 consequences do not apply

66.40   The consequences in **CPR, r. 36.17**, do not apply:

(a) where the court considers this would be unjust (**r. 36.17(3)** to **(5)**, see **66.47**);

(b) where the Part 36 offer has been withdrawn, or changed to terms less advantageous to the offeree than the judgment (**r. 36.17(7)(a)**, **(b)**, see **66.19**);

(c) if the Part 36 offer was made less than 21 days before trial (unless the court abridges time) **r. 36.17(7)(c)**;

(d) where qualified one-way costs shifting applies (see **chapter 69**); or

(e) where an admissible offer does not comply with the technical requirements of Part 36.

It is wrong in principle to apply the intentionally draconian consequences set out in **r. 36.17** to offers that do not comply with **Part 36**. In these cases the offer is simply taken into account in deciding on the order for costs under **r. 44.2(4)(c)** (*F and C Alternative Investments (Holdings) Ltd v Barthelemy (No. 3)* [2012] EWCA Civ 843, [2013] 1 WLR 548).

Personal injuries claims: success and deductible amounts

66.41   The format of Part 36 offers in personal injuries claims with deductible State benefits and recoverable lump sum payments was discussed at **66.10**. **CPR, r. 36.17(1)(a)**, applies for the purpose of determining whether the claimant has failed to obtain a judgment more advantageous than such an offer (including a lump sum offered under **r. 36.18**, for which, see **66.11**). The question is whether the claimant has failed to recover, after taking away deductible amounts, a sum greater than the net amount stated in the Part 36 offer in compliance with **r. 36.22(6)(c)**. Comparison of the award with the net sum in the Part 36 offer is intended to be compliant with the Social Security (Recovery of Benefits) Act 1997, s. 8 and sch. 2. It solves the problem identified in *Williams v Devon County Council* [2003] EWCA Civ 365, [2003] PIQR Q68, where the version of Part 36 in effect before 6 April 2007 required the court to compare the judgment with the gross sum (**r. 36.23(4)** in effect before 6 April 2007).

In comparing the judgment with the net sum under **r. 36.22(8)**, care still needs to be taken to ensure compliance with the rules in the Social Security (Recovery of Benefits) Act 1997 on recouping benefits against appropriate heads of damages and, in relation to recoverable lump sums, between different dependants.

Successful defendant's Part 36 offer

Assuming the claimant has won on liability, but fails to obtain a judgment more advantageous than a Part 36 offer made by a defendant, unless the court considers it unjust to do so, the court will order: **66.42**

(a) the defendant to pay the claimant's costs up to the expiry of the relevant period applying the usual principle that costs follow the event (**CPR, r. 44.2(2)(a)**);

(b) the claimant to pay the defendant's costs (including any recoverable pre-action costs) from the expiry of the relevant period (**r. 36.17(3)(a)**); and

(c) the claimant to pay interest on the defendant's costs (**r. 36.17(3)(b)**). There is no power to award interest at an enhanced rate on a defendant's costs (*Excelsior Commercial and Industrial Holdings Ltd v Salisbury Hamer Aspden and Johnson* [2002] EWCA Civ 879, [2002] CP Rep 67; *J. Murphy and Sons Ltd v Johnston Precast Ltd* [2008] EWHC 3104 (TCC), LTL 22/12/2008).

Successful claimant's Part 36 offer

CPR, r. 36.17(4), provides that unless the court considers it unjust to do so, where judgment is entered against a defendant which is at least as advantageous to the claimant as the proposals set out in a claimant's Part 36 offer, the court will order that the claimant is entitled to: **66.43**

(a) Interest on the whole or part of the sum of money (excluding interest) awarded at a rate not exceeding 10 per cent above base rate for some or all of the period starting with the date on which the relevant period expired. Enhanced interest cannot be ordered in respect of heads of damages that do not attract awards of interest. This applies to defamation claims (*McPhilemy v Times Newspapers Ltd (No. 2)* [2001] EWCA Civ 933, [2002] 1 WLR 934, see **64.17**) and to awards for future loss in personal injuries claims (*Pankhurst v White* [2010] EWCA Civ 1445, [2011] 3 Costs LR 392). An order running from the date of the offer rather than the expiry of the relevant period will be corrected on appeal (*Martin v Randall* [2007] EWCA Civ 1155, LTL 22/10/2007). Where interest is also awarded on the same sum for the same period under any other power (such as the County Courts Act 1984, s. 69, or the Senior Courts Act 1981, s. 35A), the total rate of interest may not exceed 10 per cent above base rate (**CPR, r. 36.17(6)**).

(b) His costs on the indemnity basis (see **71.44**) from the date on which the relevant period expired and ending with the trial or other final disposal of the claim. It does not extend to post-judgment applications, such as an application for a non-party costs order (see **68.61** and *Chantrey Vellacott v Convergence Group plc* (2007) LTL 3/10/2007).

(c) Interest on those indemnity basis costs at a rate not exceeding 10 per cent above base rate. The purpose of an order for interest on indemnity costs is to compensate for the cost of money, or loss of the use of money, borne before trial in relation to payments made on account of costs (*KR v Bryn Alyn Community (Holdings) Ltd* [2003] EWCA Civ 383, [2003] CP Rep 49; *Chantrey Vellacott v Convergence Group plc* (2007) LTL 3/10/2007).

(d) An additional amount not exceeding £75,000 calculated in accordance with **r. 36.17(4)(d)** (see **66.45**).

Enhanced interest

The court should not start with the assumption that it should award the maximum enhanced interest under **CPR, r. 36.17(4)(a)**) but must stand back and ensure that the enhanced **66.44** interest does not provide a disproportionate benefit (*Earl v Cantor Fitzgerald International (No. 2)* (2001) LTL 3/5/2001). Full 10 per cent above base rate interest was awarded in *Blue Sphere Global Ltd v Commissioners of HM Revenue and Customs* [2010] EWCA Civ 1448, LTL 16/12/2010. At first instance in *Pankhurst v White* [2010] EWHC 311 (QB), [2010] 3 Costs LR 402, enhanced interest on damages in a personal injuries claim was awarded at 10 per cent per annum on past losses (instead of the then current 6 per cent special account rate), and at 4 per cent per annum (instead of 2 per cent) on damages for pain, suffering and loss of amenity.

Additional amount

66.45 Sir Rupert Jackson's *Review of Civil Litigation Costs* (Ministry of Justice, December 2009) felt that CPR, r. 36.14(3), as in effect before 6 April 2007 did not go far enough in rewarding a claimant making a successful Part 36 offer, and recommended that a claimant making a successful Part 36 offer should be awarded an extra 10 per cent on the damages award (recommendation 94). This was implemented on 1 April 2013 through the enactment of the Legal Aid, Sentencing and Punishment of Offenders Act 2012, s. 55, the Offers to Settle in Civil Proceedings Order 2013 (SI 2013/93), and amendments to what is now **CPR, r. 36.17(4)**.

The additional amount is, in effect, a further head of damages, and is intended to provide a reward with real value to a claimant who makes a successful claimant's Part 36 offer. It can be awarded only once in a claim (**r. 36.17(4)(d)**). By SI 2013/93 and **CPR, r. 36.17(4)(d)**, slightly different approaches are taken in money and non-money claims:

(a) in money claims the additional amount is 10 per cent on the first £500,000 of the sum awarded to the claimant, plus 5 per cent on any sum awarded above £500,000 and up to £1,000,000 up to a maximum additional amount of £75,000; and

(b) in non-money claims the additional amount is calculated at 10 per cent for the first £500,000 and 5 per cent on the next £500,000 of the costs awarded to the claimant.

The additional amount in **r. 36.17(4)(d)** was seen by Sir Rupert Jackson as being an integral part of the civil justice reforms of 2013, which included abolishing the recoverability of CFA success fees and other additional liabilities. As stated in the tenth implementation lecture, abolition of success fees, increasing damages by 10 per cent, and the ability of claimants to augment their damages by a further 10 per cent by making an effective Part 36 offer, are parts of a balanced package. The balance in the package of reforms will only be maintained if the courts are ready to impose awards of the additional amount where the claimant has made a successful claimant's Part 36 offer.

Costs sanction on failing to file costs budget

66.46 In cases where costs budgeting applies, failure to file a costs budget on time results in being treated as having filed a costs budget limited to court fees (**CPR, r. 3.14**) unless relief from sanctions is granted. A party in this position would have very little incentive to make a Part 36 offer. To ameliorate the situation **r. 36.23** provides that such a party will be awarded half its costs for periods when otherwise it would have been awarded its costs in relation to late acceptance of Part 36 offers or if it has made a successful Part 36 offer for the purposes of **r. 36.17**.

Unjust to make orders under rule 36.17

66.47 In considering whether it would be unjust to make an order under **CPR, r. 36.17(3)** or (4) (see **66.42** and **66.45**), the court will, by **r. 36.17(5)**), take into account all the circumstances of the case, including:

(a) the terms of any Part 36 offer;

(b) the stage in the proceedings when any Part 36 offer was made, and in particular the period between the offer and the start of the trial;

(c) the information available to the parties at the time when the Part 36 offer was made;

(d) the conduct of the parties with regard to giving or refusing to give information for the purposes of enabling the offer to be made or evaluated. Conduct includes any failure by the claimant to give adequate disclosure to enable the defendant to assess the validity of the claim (*Mamidoil-Jetoil Greek Petroleum Co. SA v Okta Crude Oil Refinery AD (No. 2)* [2002] EWHC 2462 (Comm), [2003] 1 Lloyd's Rep 42). A lack of clarification of costs is a relevant consideration (*Thinc Group Ltd v Kingdom* [2013] EWCA Civ 1306, [2014] CP Rep 8); and

(e) whether the offer was a genuine attempt to settle the claim.

In *Huck v Robson* [2002] EWCA Civ 398, [2003] 1 WLR 1340, the claimant in a personal injuries claim made a Part 36 offer to settle a dispute on the basis that the defendant was 95 per cent liable. At trial the judge found for the claimant with no deduction for contributory negligence, and the claimant asked for indemnity-basis costs. It was held that while an offer based on marginally less than full liability might be illusory, that was not so in the present case, and the fact that no trial judge would make a finding of only 5 per cent contributory negligence was irrelevant. It was not unjust for the defendant to have to pay indemnity-basis costs and enhanced interest.

Other factors that have been held to be relevant include:

(a) whether the offeree had a good reason for rejecting the offer, such as a reasonable belief in its prospects of success based on the law as it then stood (*Mamidoil-Jetoil Greek Petroleum Co. SA v Okta Crude Oil Refinery AD (No. 2)*);

(b) whether the basis on which the case was decided was raised at a late stage (*Feltham v Freer Bouskell* [2013] EWHC 3086 (Ch), [2014] 1 Costs LO 29);

(c) unclear prognosis for the claimant's injuries at the time the Part 36 offer was made (*Rehill v Rider Holdings Ltd* [2014] EWCA Civ 42, [2014] 3 Costs LR 405);

(d) deliberate exaggeration (*Painting v University of Oxford* [2005] EWCA Civ 161, [2005] PIQR Q5); and

(e) a combination of recovering only a small fraction of the amount claimed, and partial success on the issues tried (*Walker Construction (UK) Ltd v Quayside Homes Ltd* [2014] EWCA Civ 93, [2014] BLR 215).

In *Hall v Stone* [2007] EWCA Civ 1354, [2008] CP Rep 263, Smith LJ at [82] said:

In these days where both sides are expected to conduct themselves in a reasonable way and to seek agreement where possible, it may be right to penalise a party to some degree for failing to accept a reasonable offer or for failing to come back with a counter-offer.

The fact that the offeror is funded under a CFA is irrelevant when deciding whether to make an order under r. 36.17(4) (*CEL Group Ltd v Nedlloyd Lines (UK) Ltd* [2003] EWCA Civ 1871, [2004] 1 Lloyd's Rep 388).

Awarding indemnity-basis costs after a successful claimant's Part 36 offer implies no misconduct on the defendant (*McPhilemy v Times Newspapers Ltd (No. 2)* [2001] EWCA Civ 933, [2002] 1 WLR 934), its practical effect being to ensure that the claimant does not recover any less than the costs he has in fact incurred (*Petrotrade Inc. v Texaco Ltd* [2002] 1 WLR 947). Indemnity costs and enhanced interest on those costs can be awarded even where the claimant is publicly funded (*Earl v Cantor Fitzgerald International (No. 2)* (2001) LTL 3/5/2001). The enhanced rate of interest on indemnity-basis costs runs from the date upon which the work was done or liability for disbursements was incurred, and runs until judgment. Thereafter, interest on costs is payable under the Judgments Act 1838, s. 17, in the usual way (*McPhilemy v Times Newspapers Ltd (No. 2)*).

Failing to exceed a withdrawn Part 36 offer

66.48 A withdrawn Part 36 offer does not have the costs consequences set out in **CPR, r. 36.17** (see **r. 36.17(7)(a)**). It may nevertheless have an effect on the orders the court makes on costs (**rr. 36.2(2)** and **44.2**). Where a withdrawn offer made by the defendant is more advantageous than the judgment, according to *Garner v Cleggs* [1983] 1 WLR 862 (approved by Longmore LJ in *Capital Bank plc v Stickland* [2004] EWCA Civ 1677, [2005] 1 WLR 3914 at [21]), the principled approach on costs is:

(a) for the claimant to be awarded costs up to the end of the relevant period;

(b) for the defendant to be awarded costs from the end of the relevant period to the date of any relevant change of circumstances affecting the risks in the litigation; and

(c) for the claimant to be awarded costs thereafter.

It may well be that the new scheme introduced with effect from 6 April 2015 will mean this will no longer be followed. In particular, point (b) above was based on the position before 6 April 2007 that Part 36 payments could only be withdrawn with the court's permission, whereas under the current provisions there is a right to withdraw a Part 36 offer after the relevant period has expired (**r. 36.9(1)**).

Departing from the normal rule on costs

66.49   The normal rule on costs described at **66.42** and **66.43** has been departed from where:

(a) a party was late in disclosing important evidence (*Ford v GKR Construction Ltd* [2000] 1 WLR 1397);

(b) a party has been unwilling to participate in proposed mediation (*Re Midland Linen Services Ltd* [2004] EWHC 3380 (Ch), LTL 28/10/2004);

(c) a claimant has deliberately exaggerated the claim (*Painting v University of Oxford* [2005] EWCA Civ 161, [2005] PIQR Q5).

Traditionally, the courts have taken a strict line that the normal rule should be followed even when the judge had been considering a slightly higher award (*Wagman v Vare Motors Ltd* [1959] 1 WLR 853). In *Jackson v Ministry of Defence* [2006] EWCA Civ 46, LTL 12/1/2006, the Court of Appeal approved a modest percentage reduction in the costs order to reflect the fact the claimant had only just beaten a Part 36 offer. Other factors may persuade a judge to depart from the normal rule, but there is great reluctance in countenancing such departures. Thus, in *Jones v Jones* (1999) *The Times*, 11 November 1999, there had been an offer of £120,000, and the claimant only recovered damages of £111,000. The amount of damages awarded was probably depressed by a third medical report served by the defendant some six months after the offer. These events occurred before the CPR came into force. The Court of Appeal held that the judge erred in principle in awarding the claimant costs up to the disclosure of the last medical report. Translated into CPR terms the Court of Appeal's substituted order would mean that the claimant would only recover her costs to the expiry of the relevant period. This decision may be at variance with the ethos of the CPR, and in particular with **r. 44.2**, which gives the court wide powers to take into account conduct on questions of costs. The case should be contrasted with *Ford v GKR Construction Ltd*, in which the Court of Appeal affirmed a decision to award the entire costs of the claim to the claimant who was awarded £85,000 despite an offer of £95,000. This was because her award was depressed below the level of the offer by virtue of video surveillance evidence introduced in the period of an adjournment between the first and second days of the trial, which was criticised as being late.

In *Painting v University of Oxford* the claimant pleaded loss and damage in excess of £400,000 on the basis that she suffered a long-term debilitating injury, and the defendant made an offer of £10,000. The judge found that the claimant had intentionally exaggerated her injuries, and awarded her £23,331. The Court of Appeal held that the essential question at trial was whether the claimant was exaggerating her injuries. The claimant's intentional exaggeration, combined with her failure to negotiate, justified making an order for the defendant to pay the claimant's costs to the expiry of the relevant period, and for the claimant to pay the defendant's costs thereafter, despite the judgment exceeding the amount in court.

An exaggeration of a claim was regarded in *Widlake v BAA Ltd* [2009] EWCA Civ 1256, [2010] PIQR P4, as an 'allegation' for the purposes of **r. 44.2(5)(b)** as well as being expressly part of **r. 44.2(5)(d)**, and so forms part of the conduct of the claimant in deciding what order to make on costs. Cases involving exaggeration are very fact-sensitive, as shown by *Allison v Brighton and Hove City Council* [2005] EWCA Civ 548, LTL 22/4/2005. Here the claim was for £45,000, but judgment was for £4,000. The claimant was awarded only 25 per cent of his costs in the period prior to an effective offer. Percentage costs orders of this type have been increasingly common since the introduction of the CPR.

In *Daniels v Commissioner of Police for the Metropolis* [2005] EWCA Civ 1312, [2006] CP Rep 9, the claimant was a serving police officer who was injured when thrown from her horse in a training session. She made a number of claimant's Part 36 offers, but the defendant refused to negotiate. At trial the claim was dismissed. The question on appeal was whether the refusal to negotiate was 'unreasonable' conduct in the *Halsey v Milton Keynes General NHS Trust* [2004] EWCA Civ 576, [2004] 1 WLR 3002, sense (see **68.19**). The Court of Appeal said it was difficult to imagine circumstances where rejecting a Part 36 offer could be characterised as unreasonable if the party who rejected the offer then won the case. That was particularly so on the facts, where the defendant routinely faced unmeritorious claims.

A decision illustrating the point that **r. 44.2** rarely overrides the usual rule where there has been a Part 36 offer exceeding the damages awarded is *Burgess v British Steel* (2000) The Times, 29 February 2000. In this case the Court of Appeal overturned a decision to award the claimant costs to the final date for accepting the offer (which was in the sum of £220,000), and to award no costs thereafter. Before making the offer the defendant had disclosed a medical report which asserted that the claimant was malingering and which implied the claimant was pursuing a bogus claim. At trial the claimant established that the claim was genuine, but only recovered £161,000. On appeal it was held this did not justify departing from the usual rule, and the second part of the costs order was altered so that the defendant recovered costs from the expiry of the relevant period.

Subject to the discussion at **66.39**, where the award at trial exceeds a Part 36 offer the court should not depart from the usual rule by examining whether the Part 36 offer was reasonable, nor by reason of the claimant having made a claimant's Part 36 offer which was higher than the award at trial (*Quorum AS v Schramm* [2002] CLC 77). In *Johnsey Estates (1990) Ltd v Secretary of State for the Environment* [2001] EWCA Civ 535, LTL 11/4/2001, the defendant made a first Part 36 offer of £200,000, followed by a second Part 36 offer of £250,000. At trial the judge awarded £200,000 plus interest of £36,000 to the date of the first Part 36 offer. The Court of Appeal overturned the judge's award of costs to the defendant from the date of the first Part 36 offer because this failed to take into account the award of interest, and substituted an award (apart from on one issue) to the claimant of its costs to the date of the second Part 36 offer, with the defendant recovering costs thereafter.

Awarding a defendant indemnity-basis costs

A defendant making a successful Part 36 offer will usually be awarded costs on the standard basis. An award of costs on the indemnity basis is normally reserved to cases where the court wishes to show its disapproval, but may extend to some cases where an offer has been made and rejected. Indemnity-basis costs may be appropriate where the claim is dismissed at trial, if the court also finds that the case was going to fail from the outset of the trial (*Reid Minty v Taylor* [2001] EWCA Civ 1723, [2002] 1 WLR 2800). In *Kiam v MGN Ltd (No. 2)* [2002] EWCA Civ 66, [2002] 1 WLR 2810, the Court of Appeal said that *Reid Minty v Taylor* decided no more than that conduct falling short of conduct deserving moral condemnation could still be so unreasonable as to justify an order of indemnity-basis costs. In *Kiam v MGN Ltd (No. 2)* it was held that such conduct needed to be unreasonable to a high degree, and the refusal of a settlement offer (not being a claimant's Part 36 offer) would rarely attract such an order.

66.50

Costs where the offer fails to comply with Part 36

66.51   By **CPR, r. 36.2(2)**, nothing in **Part 36** prevents a party from making an offer to settle in whatever way he chooses, but if that offer is not made in accordance with **Part 36**, it will not have the consequences set out in **Part 36**. As mentioned at **66.17**, the note to **r. 36.2** says the court still has to take into account an offer that does not comply with **r. 36.5** when deciding the question of costs (**r. 44.2**). The implication is that this will not necessarily be in the same terms as if the offer had complied with **r. 36.5**. The following discussion is based on cases decided under r. 36.1(2) as in effect before 6 April 2007. At that time the rule allowed the court to give full Part 36 effect to an offer that did not comply with Part 36 as in force then, so these cases probably disclose a rather over-indulgent approach to non-compliance.

In *Amber v Stacey* [2001] 1 WLR 1225 the defendant made a written offer that did not comply with Part 36 as in effect before 6 April 2007, but which was more generous than the award eventually made by the court. It was held to be wrong in principle to treat the offer in the same way as if it had been a Part 36 offer for the purposes of costs. However, it was taken into account when considering costs, with the result that the defendant was awarded half his costs from the date of the offer, the court being influenced by the claimant's intemperate response to the written offer. In *Mitchell v James* [2002] EWCA Civ 997, [2004] 1 WLR 158, a claimant's Part 36 offer failed to comply with r. 36.5(6)(b) as in effect before 6 April 2007 in that it did not state that after 21 days the defendant could only accept it if costs liability was agreed or if the court gave permission. It was said that if this had been the only defect in the offer, the court would have waived it as a mere technicality (see **r. 3.10**).

In *Hardy v Sutherland* [2001] EWCA Civ 976, LTL 13/6/2001, the defendant made a Part 36 offer and, some time later, a Part 36 payment. The claim was for money, so the earlier Part 36 offer did not comply with r. 36.3 as in effect before 6 April 2007. It was held that proper recognition of the offer would be accorded by depriving the claimant of a percentage of his costs up to the date for acceptance of the Part 36 payment (after which the defendant recovered costs from the claimant).

Perhaps the most radical decision is *Trustees of Stokes Pension Fund v Western Power Distribution (South West) plc* [2005] EWCA Civ 854, [2005] 1 WLR 3595. This was a claim for damages of £780,000. The defendant made a written offer before proceedings of £35,000, but did not pay in after proceedings were started as required by r. 36.10 as in effect before 6 April 2007. The defendant later paid in £20,000 and informed the claimant that the earlier offer was withdrawn. At trial the claimant recovered £25,000. On appeal the £35,000 written offer was treated as a payment in because the following four conditions were satisfied:

(a) the written offer was expressed in clear terms, stating whether it took into account any counterclaim and interest, in line with r. 36.5(2) as in effect before 6 April 2007;

(b) it was expressed to be open for acceptance for at least 21 days and generally accorded with the form of Part 36 offers;

(c) it was a genuine offer, not a sham; and

(d) the defendant was clearly good for the money when the offer was made.

The fact the defendant withdrew the £35,000 offer was held to be irrelevant because there was no evidence the claimant would have accepted the offer at a later stage if it had remained open. The Court of Appeal substituted an order that the claimant had to pay the defendant's costs from 21 days after the written offer.

Cases such as *Trustees of Stokes Pension Fund v Western Power Distribution (South West) plc* are instances of the court using its discretion under r. 36.1(2) as in effect before 6 April 2007 to treat offers which did not comply with the strict requirements of Part 36 as if they were Part 36 offers. Being discretionary, the court had a wide ambit in deciding on the appropriate consequences. It was regarded as an error of principle to treat an offer which did not comply with Part 36 as having either full or no effect, without considering intermediate positions (*Codent Ltd v Lyson Ltd* (2005) LTL 8/12/2005). In *Farag v Commissioner of Police of the Metropolis* [2005] EWCA Civ 1814, LTL 1 5/12/2005, the claim raised eight causes of action against the police. An offer to settle was refused, then withdrawn two years before the trial. All but one of the causes of action failed. The Court of Appeal took the offer into account in deciding to make no order as to costs. In *Codent Ltd v Lyson Ltd* an offer was made less than 21 days before trial and in the form of a Part 36 offer, whereas it should have been a Part 36 payment. The claimant was awarded 70 per cent of its costs up to the first day of the trial, and the defendant was awarded its costs thereafter.

Incomplete or unclear offers

An offer to settle made before the commencement of proceedings in *Phyllis Trading Ltd v 86* **66.52**
Lordship Road Ltd [2001] EWCA Civ 350, [2001] 2 EGLR 85, did not refer to costs. Thorpe LJ said that an offeree takes a real risk in rejecting such an offer out of hand, and has an obligation to state what is acceptable and to seek clarification. It was held that the offeree had to pay the costs from the date of the offer.

What is required is a 'clear and concise' offer to settle (*Amber v Stacey* [2001] 1 WLR 1225), so the judge is entitled to disregard a letter which is only an offer to negotiate (*Press v Chipperfield* [2003] EWCA Civ 484, LTL 25/3/2003). There were complex proceedings in *Rio Properties Inc. v Gibson Dunn and Crutcher* [2005] EWCA Civ 534, LTL 22/4/2005. The claimant purported to make a claimant's Part 36 offer in respect of the costs of various interim applications. It was held that it was open to the judge to decide the offer was difficult to evaluate and therefore should be disregarded on the question of costs.

PART 36 OFFERS IN APPEALS

Part 36 and appeals

A Part 36 offer which is made before trial has effect in relation to the costs of the proceedings **66.53**
up to the final disposal of the proceedings at first instance (**CPR, r. 36.4(1)**). A party intending to obtain costs protection for appeal proceedings needs to make a separate Part 36 offer in the appeal proceedings (**r. 36.4(2)**). Rule 36.4 also applies to statutory appeals (*Blue Sphere Global Ltd v Commissioners of HM Revenue and Customs* [2010] EWCA Civ 1448, LTL 16/12/2010).

A respondent in an appeal who makes an offer to accept all but a small fraction of the amount awarded by the court below will generally be regarded as having made a genuine offer to settle, and will usually be awarded indemnity costs (and possibly also enhanced interest) under **r. 36.17(4)**. As discussed in *CEL Group Ltd v Nedlloyd Lines (UK) Ltd* [2003] EWCA Civ 1871, [2004] 1 Lloyd's Rep 388, a respondent cannot reasonably be expected to give up a substantial part of the judgment under appeal, particularly where the appeal raises an all-or-nothing point.

PAYMENT UNDER COURT ORDER

CPR, r. 37.1, deals with payments into court under court orders. The party making the **66.54**
payment in must send the payment to the Court Funds Office. Usually the payment will be made by cheque, which must be made payable to the Accountant General of the Senior Courts (**PD 37, para. 1.1(1)(a)**). Lodgment of a cheque with the Court Funds Office is the effective date for making the payment (*ENE Kos 1 Ltd v Petróleo Brasileiro SA* [2009] EWCA Civ 1127, [2010] 1 WLR 1361). A litigant in person without a current account may, if the claim is

proceeding in the County Court or a District Registry, lodge cash rather than using a cheque (**para. 1.2**). The payment must be accompanied by a sealed copy of the court order and by Court Funds Office form 100. Notice of the payment in must be served on every other party, and a certificate of service (in form N215) must be filed in respect of each such notice (**CPR, r. 37.1**).

By **r. 37.3**, permission is in most cases required for the payment out of money paid into court under a court order. Permission is obtained by making an application in accordance with Part 23 (**PD 37, para. 3.2**). The application notice must state the grounds on which the order for payment out is sought, and it is often necessary to file a witness statement in support. Where the court gives permission, it will include a direction for the payment out of the money in court, including accrued interest (**para. 3.3**).

Permission for payment out is not required where:

(a) a Part 36 offer is accepted without needing the permission of the court (which is governed by **CPR, r. 36.11**, see **66.32** to **66.35**); and
(b) the defendant paid the sum in court and agrees that such sum should be used to satisfy the whole or part of the offer.

Where permission is not required for payment out of money in court, the requesting party should file a request in Court Funds Office form 201 with the Court Funds Office, which must state the details set out in **PD 37, para. 3.5**. The request must be accompanied by a statement that the defendant agrees to the money being used to satisfy a Part 36 offer, using Court Funds Office form 202 (**para. 3.4**). Interest on the money in court up to the date of acceptance is paid to the defendant (**para. 3.6**). The principal sum is in most cases paid by bank transfer to the legal representative of the party making the request (**para. 3.8(1)**). Exceptions are that payments in cases of unrepresented parties with public funding are made to the Legal Services Commission (**para. 3.8(2)**), and that parties can request payment out by cheque (**para. 3.7**).

PAYMENTS INTO COURT PURSUANT TO STATUTE

66.55 There are special provisions (made under **CPR, r. 37.4**) for payments into court pursuant to:

(a) the Life Assurance Companies (Payment into Court) Act 1896 (**PD 37, paras 4.1 to 5.2**);
(b) the Trustee Act 1925, s. 63 (**PD 37, paras 6.1 to 7.2**); and
(c) the Vehicular Access across Common and Other Land (England) Regulations 2002 (SI 2002/1711) (**PD 37, paras 8.1 to 8.5**).

RTA AND EL/PL PROTOCOL OFFERS TO SETTLE

66.56 Part 36 offers for RTA, employer's liability (EL) and public liability (PL) claims being dealt with under the RTA and EL/PL Protocols are governed by **CPR, rr. 36.24 to 36.30**, which in their original form came into effect on 30 April 2010 (RTA claims) and 31 July 2013 (EL and PL claims). An offer to settle in a relevant Protocol case must be set out in the court proceedings pack (part B) form (**r. 36.25(2)(a)**). It should contain the final total amount of the offers from both sides (in accordance with e.g. the **RTA Protocol, para. 7.64**). These amounts are treated as exclusive of all interest (**CPR, r. 36.27(a)**). A relevant Protocol offer is deemed to be made on the first business day after the court proceedings pack (parts A and B) is sent to the defendant. It must not be communicated to the court until the claim is determined, at which point the court will examine the relevant Protocol offer (**r. 36.28(1)**). There is an absolute prohibition on any other form of offer being communicated to the court (**r. 36.28(2)**).

There are costs consequences for non-acceptance of relevant Protocol offers by virtue of **r. 36.29(1)** in three different situations:

(a) where the determination of the court is less than or equal to the amount of the defendant's relevant Protocol offer (**r. 36.29(1)(a)**), the court must order the claimant to pay the fixed costs under **r. 45.26** and interest on those fixed costs from the first business day after the deemed date of the relevant Protocol offer (**r. 36.29(2)**);

(b) where the determination of the court is more than a defendant's relevant Protocol offer, but less than the claimant's relevant Protocol offer (**r. 36.29(1)(b)**), the court will order the defendant to pay the fixed costs under **r. 45.20** (**r. 36.29(3)**);

(c) where the determination of the court is equal to or more than the claimant's relevant Protocol offer (**r. 36.29(1)(c)**), the court will order the defendant to pay interest on the whole of the damages at a rate not exceeding 10 per cent above base rate for all or part of the period from the deemed date of the relevant Protocol offer, fixed costs under **r. 45.20**, and interest on those costs at a rate not exceeding 10 per cent above base rate.

Rule 36.30 is similar to **r. 36.22(8)**, and provides that the amount of a judgment is less than a relevant Protocol offer where the judgment is less than the offer once deductible amounts identified in the judgment are deducted. Where a claim no longer continues under a relevant Protocol, costs are governed by **r. 36.21**.

CALDERBANK OFFERS

A '*Calderbank* offer' is a written offer to settle stated to be 'without prejudice save as to costs'   **66.57**
(*Calderbank v Calderbank* [1976] Fam 93). Provided it is made in a genuine attempt to settle a dispute, such an offer will be protected from disclosure to the court without the joint consent of both parties until all questions on liability and remedies have been decided. Being without prejudice 'save as to costs' means that the communication can then be relied upon on the question of costs. This is confirmed by **CPR, r. 44.2(4)(c)**, which says that in deciding what order if any to make about costs, one of the circumstances that must be taken into account is any admissible offer to settle which is not a Part 36 offer.

Calderbank offers operate on a quite distinct basis from Part 36 offers. Although there is a wide discretion (*Coward v Phaestos Ltd* [2014] EWCA Civ 1256, [2015] CP Rep 2), failing to beat a *Calderbank* offer may result in the winner having to pay some or even all the offeror's costs from when the winner should have responded to the offer (*Walker Construction (UK) Ltd v Quayside Homes Ltd* [2014] EWCA Civ 93, [2014] BLR 215).

TRANSITIONAL PROVISIONS

Transitional provisions for Part 36 offers made before 6 April 2015 can be found in the Civil   **66.58**
Procedure (Amendment No. 8) Rules 2014 (SI 2014/3299), r. 18. The current rules generally only apply to Part 36 offers made on or after 6 April 2015.

Commentary

Chapter 67   Security for Costs

INTRODUCTION

67.1 Generally, the question of who pays for the costs of a claim is not determined until the claim is finally disposed of, whether by consent, interim process or trial. This is because the usual rule is that the successful party recovers costs from the loser and the outcome on the merits is only known when judgment is obtained. It is for this reason that the parties are not generally allowed to anticipate the eventual costs order by asking for interim orders that their opponents provide funds as security to pay for the costs of the action. Despite this, it is accepted that there have to be exceptions for cases where there is a significant risk of defendants suffering the injustice of having to defend proceedings with no real prospect of being able to recover costs if they are ultimately successful.

An order for security for costs can only be made: (a) before judgment (*Penny v Penny* [1996] 1 WLR 1204), or (b) for the costs of an appellant, or of a respondent to an appeal who also appeals (**CPR, r. 25.15**). Once security is given it may be retained, subject to the court's discretion, pending an appeal. An order for security for costs usually requires the claimant to pay money into court as security for the payment of any costs order that may eventually be made in favour of the defendant, and staying the claim until the security is provided. On the application three matters arise:

(a) whether there are grounds for ordering security for costs;

(b) if so, whether the court's discretion should be exercised in favour of making the order; and

(c) if so, how much security should be provided.

Each of these three matters will be considered after first looking at the procedure for making the application and the capacity of the respondent to the application.

PROCEDURE

67.2

A defendant may apply under **CPR, rr. 25.12** to **25.15**, for an order requiring the claimant to give security for costs. It is submitted that, like an application for an interim remedy, an application for security for costs may be made at any time after the defendant has filed an acknowledgment of service or a defence (see **r. 25.2(2)(c)**). The first application for security should normally be made at the first case management conference (see Admiralty and Commercial Courts Guide, app. 16, para. 1). It is made using the usual Part 23 procedure of issuing an application notice supported by written evidence (**r. 25.12(2)**). The written evidence should deal with the grounds on which security is sought, and with any factors relevant to the exercise of the court's discretion. These include the location of the claimant's assets, and any practical difficulties in enforcing any order for costs (see Admiralty and Commercial Courts Guide, app. 16, para. 3). It also needs to include an estimate of the defendant's likely costs of defending the claim, which should usually be given in the form of a costs budget in precedent H (see **chapter 43**).

Invariably the application should be made on notice to the claimant, and should be served on the claimant at least three clear days before the day appointed for hearing the application (**CPR, r. 23.7(1)(b)**). Applications against companies etc. under **r. 25.13(2)(c)** (see **67.12**), are in the first instance given hearings in private (**PD 39A, para. 1.5(8)**).

Applications for security for costs will be inappropriate in cases on the small claims track because of the restrictions on the recovery of costs in these claims. In fast track and multi-track claims it is the duty of the parties to make any application that may be appropriate at any hearing that has been fixed (**PD 28, para. 2.5** (fast track); **PD 29, para. 3.5** (multi-track)), so in many cases an application for security for costs should be made at the first case management hearing.

THE RESPONDENT

Claimants

67.3

Security for costs is generally available only against a claimant or a party in the position of being a claimant (**CPR, r. 25.12(1)**). An order for security for costs may be obtained against a person other than a claimant if that person assigned the claim under an arrangement designed to avoid the possibility of a costs order, or has contributed or agreed to contribute to the claimant's costs in return for a share of any property recovered in the proceedings (**r. 25.14**).

An order for security for costs should not be made against a claimant in proceedings to enforce a foreign award where the defendant objects to registration of the judgment on the ground of fraud. Enforcement of foreign awards (see **chapter 80**) is intended to be quasi-administrative. In substance it is the defendant who is attacking rather than defending, and it is wrong in principle to award security to such a defendant (*Gater Assets Ltd v NAK Naftogaz Ukrainiy* [2007] EWCA Civ 988, [2008] Bus LR 388).

By **r. 20.3**, the provisions on security for costs in **rr. 25.12** to **25.15** apply to an additional claim as if it were a claim. So a party bringing an additional claim may be ordered to give security for the costs of the additional claim in just the same way as an original claimant may be ordered to give security for the costs of the original claim. Under the old Rules of the Supreme Court it was held that if a defendant makes an additional claim against a person other than the claimant, the defendant to that additional claim cannot obtain an order for security against the original claimant, unless, as a result of directions given in the additional claim (for which see **29.9**), the defendant to the additional claim is given permission to defend jointly with the original defendant (see *Taly NDC International NV v Terra Nova Insurance Co. Ltd* [1985] 1 WLR 1359 per Parker LJ). The question is one of capacity in the main claim. There is therefore no jurisdiction to order a defendant to provide security for the costs of any interim application it may make (*Taly NDC International NV v Terra Nova Insurance Co. Ltd*).

Where a counterclaim is an entirely separate cross-claim, with an independent validity of its own, it is treated as a separate claim and security for the costs of the counterclaim may be ordered (*Hutchison Telephone (UK) Ltd v Ultimate Response Ltd* [1993] BCLC 307; *Newman v Wenden Properties Ltd* [2007] EWHC 336 (TCC), 114 Con LR 95). This needs to be distinguished from set-offs, where it has been held that security will not usually be ordered (*Neck v Taylor* [1893] 1 QB 560). The reason for this distinction is that a set-off, if established, amounts to a defence to the claim, so a defendant raising a set-off is for this purpose regarded as simply defending and not as advancing a claim. The distinction between set-offs and other types of counterclaim was considered at 34.36 and 34.37. Similarly, it will not be fair or just to order a defendant to provide security for costs of a counterclaim which sets out contentions which are in substance the mirror image of the allegations in the particulars of claim (*Samuel J. Cohl Co. v Eastern Mediterranean Maritime Ltd* [1980] 1 Lloyd's Rep 371; *Anglo Irish Asset Finance plc v Flood* [2011] EWCA Civ 799, LTL 11/7/2011). Where a defendant is counterclaiming, the question to be asked is whether, as a matter of substance, the position of the defendant can fairly be equated with that of a claimant, or whether, in truth, it does not go beyond that of a defendant (*Pimlott v Meregrove Holdings Ltd* [2003] EWHC 1766 (QB), [2003] All ER (D) 325 (Jun), in which it was held that the costs of pursuing the counterclaim would not add to the costs of defending the claim so there should be no security). Conversely, in *L/M International Construction Inc. v Circle Partnership Ltd* [1995] CLY 4010 the claimant sued for £1,000,000 and the defendant counterclaimed for £15,000,000. The court found that the defendant was in the position of a claimant and ordered it to give security.

If the issues raised on the counterclaim are wider than those raised by the claim, security for costs may be ordered against the defendant. The amount depends on the facts of the case. In *Petromin SA v Secnav Marine Ltd* [1995] 1 Lloyd's Rep 603 there was a significant claim and counterclaim based on identical facts. The court ordered the defendant to give security for the full amount of the claimant's costs on the counterclaim and not just the increase occasioned by defending the counterclaim. In *Kazakhstan Investment Fund Ltd v Aims Asset Management Sdn Bhd* (2002) LTL 23/5/2002 the court limited the costs to those of defending the counterclaim.

Parties other than claimants

67.4 Security for costs may be ordered against any party in the position of a claimant, even if they are not strictly 'claimants'. An example would be a petitioner on an unfair prejudice petition under the Companies Act 2006, s. 994 (*Re Unisoft Group Ltd (No. 1)* [1993] BCLC 1292). Another example is an appellant to an appeal (or a respondent who cross-appeals), see CPR, r. 25.15. By r. 25.14, an order for security for costs may also be made against someone other than a claimant if the court is satisfied that the person against whom the order is sought either:

(a) assigned the claim to the claimant with a view to avoiding the possibility of a costs order being made against him; or

(b) has contributed or agreed to contribute to the claimant's costs in return for a share of any money or property which the claimant may recover in the proceedings.

Foreign governments

67.5 An order for security for costs may be made against a foreign government (*Government of Sierra Leone v Davenport* [2003] EWHC 1913 (Ch), LTL 4/4/2005).

CONDITIONS FOR ORDERING SECURITY FOR COSTS

Security for costs can only be ordered if, having regard to all the circumstances of the case, it **67.6** is just to make the order (**CPR, r. 25.13(1)(a)**), and if one or more of the conditions set out in **r. 25.13(2)**, is satisfied. The conditions are:

(a)　the claimant is—
　　(i)　resident out of the jurisdiction; but
　　(ii)　not resident in a Brussels Contracting State, a State bound by the Lugano Convention or a Regulation State, as defined in s. 1(3) of the Civil Jurisdiction and Judgments Act 1982;

[(b)　revoked]

(c)　the claimant is a company or other body (whether incorporated inside or outside Great Britain) and there is reason to believe that it will be unable to pay the defendant's costs if ordered to do so;

(d)　the claimant has changed his address since the claim was commenced with a view to evading the consequences of the litigation;

(e)　the claimant failed to give his address in the claim form, or gave an incorrect address in that form;

(f)　the claimant is acting as a nominal claimant, other than as a representative claimant under Part 19, and there is reason to believe that he will be unable to pay the defendant's costs if ordered to do so;

(g)　the claimant has taken steps in relation to his assets that would make it difficult to enforce an order for costs against him.

There are some statutory restrictions on the availability of security for costs. For example, reg. 12 of the Civil Legal Aid (Costs) Regulations 2013 (SI 2013/611) provides that where a legally aided party is required to give security for costs, the amount of security must not exceed the amount, if any, which would be reasonable having regard to all the circumstances, including the legally aided party's financial resources and his or her conduct in the proceedings. Security for costs cannot be ordered against a national of a contracting State in proceedings arising out of the Convention on the Contract for the International Carriage of Goods by Road (Carriage of Goods by Road Act 1965, sch., art. 31(5)).

Security for costs as a sanction or condition

The conditions for ordering security for costs in the RSC were regarded as a complete and **67.7** exhaustive code of circumstances in which security could be ordered (see *Condliffe v Hislop* [1996] 1 WLR 753). The court now has wider powers under the CPR.

Under a combination of **CPR, rr. 3.1(2)(f), 3.1(3)(a)** and **3.1(5)**, the court may stay the whole or part of the proceedings as a condition for failing to comply with an order to pay a sum into court where a party has failed to comply with a rule, practice direction or pre-action protocol. Using these provisions an order may be made which is tantamount to an order for security for costs (*Olatawura v Abiloye* [2002] EWCA Civ 998, [2003] 1 WLR 275).

Under **r. 3.1(3)(a)** any order of the court may be made subject to a condition to pay a sum of money into court. The **r. 3.1(3)(a)** power cannot be used independently: it can only be used to attach a condition to an order made in the exercise of another power of the court. However, a stay can be ordered under **r. 3.1(2)(f)** 'in any appropriate case' (*CIBC Mellon Trust Co. v Mora Hotel Corporation NV* [2002] EWCA Civ 1688, [2003] 1 All ER 564 at [20]) and a condition for security for costs can then be added (at [21]).

The court should exercise its powers under **r. 3.1(3)(a)** and **(5)** to require a payment into court only in limited circumstances, and should only do so in the absence of good faith on the part of the party against whom the order is sought (*CIBC Mellon Trust Co. v Mora Hotel Corporation NV* at [38]). In *CIBC Mellon Trust Co. v Mora Hotel Corporation NV* an order for a stay of an application to set aside a default judgment was made subject to a condition that the stay would be lifted if security for the costs of the application was given and this part of the order was upheld by the Court of Appeal. Security for costs may be ordered as part of a conditional order on an application for summary judgment (*Allen v Bloomsbury Publishing plc* [2011] EWCA Civ 943, LTL 15/7/2011) or in relation to permission to appeal (*Shlaimoun v Mining Technologies International Inc.* [2012] EWCA Civ 772, LTL 21/6/2012). In *Shlaimoun v Mining Technologies International Inc.* the Master of the Rolls said that one of the conditions in **r. 25.13** would have to be satisfied.

An order for payment in should not be made without first giving the unsuccessful party three days' notice and an opportunity to file evidence as to their means. Such notice can be informal in the form of a letter from one party to another (*Anglo-Eastern Trust Ltd v Kermanshahchi* [2002] EWCA Civ 198, [2002] CP Rep 36). An order for security for costs imposed when granting an adjournment at the request of the party obtaining the benefit of the security was set aside in *Dardana Ltd v Yukos Oil Co.* [2002] EWCA Civ 543, [2002] 1 All ER (Comm) 819.

Resident outside the jurisdiction

67.8 Condition (a) in **CPR, r. 25.13(2)**, applies to a claimant, whether a natural or legal person, who is resident out of the jurisdiction and outside the States covered by the EU's **recast Brussels I Regulation** and the Brussels and Lugano Conventions (see **16.1**). In *Levene v Commissioners of Inland Revenue* [1928] AC 217 Viscount Cave LC quoted with approval the *Oxford English Dictionary* definition of 'reside' as 'To dwell permanently or for a considerable time, to have one's settled or usual abode, to live, in or at a particular place'. There is no general principle that a claimant outside the jurisdiction will be ordered to provide security if he fails to disclose where his assets are located (*Somerset-Leeke v Kay Trustees* [2003] EWHC 1243 (Ch), [2004] 3 All ER 406).

Applications for security on the ground of residence outside the jurisdiction almost always turn on the exercise of the court's discretion. The general factors considered are discussed at **67.16** to **67.20**. Factors particularly relevant on this ground are discussed at **67.21** to **67.23**.

67.9 **EU residents**   There has been some controversy over whether making an order for security for costs against a national of another EU country on the ground of residence outside the jurisdiction offends against the Treaty on the Functioning of the European Union, art. 18, which provides: 'Within the scope of application of the Treaties, and without prejudice to any special provisions contained therein, any discrimination on grounds of nationality shall be prohibited'. As nearly all EU nationals protected by art. 12 reside in Regulation or Convention States, this should no longer be a major issue. At one time it was held that there was a valid distinction between residence, which founds the jurisdiction to order security for costs, and nationality (see *Berkeley Administration Inc. v McClelland* [1990] 2 QB 407). This stance is now discredited, and the current approach, based on the CJEU decision of *Mund & Fester v Hatrex Internationaal Transport* (case C-398/92) [1994] ECR I-467, is that an English court should never exercise its discretion to order security for costs against an individual who is a national of and resident in another member State of the EU.

Security for costs can be ordered where the claimant is resident in a State outside the scope of the **recast Brussels I Regulation** or the Conventions, even if the claimant has assets within such a State (*De Beer v Kanaar and Co.* [2001] EWCA Civ 1318, [2003] 1 WLR 38).

67.10 **Companies resident outside Great Britain**   Although most companies reside in the country where they are incorporated, strictly they reside where their central control and management are. This is a question of fact. In *Re Little Olympian Each Ways Ltd* [1995] 1 WLR 560 Lindsay J identified the following as matters to be considered: the contents of the company's objects clause, its place of incorporation, where its real trade or business is carried on, where its books are kept, where its administrative work is done, where its directors meet or reside, where it 'keeps house', where its chief office is situated, and where its secretary resides.

Impecunious British companies can be ordered to provide security for costs under **CPR, r. 25.13(2)(c)** (see 67.12), so ordering an impecunious company registered in another EU country to provide security for costs does not offend against the Treaty on the Functioning of the European Union, art. 18 (*Chequepoint SARL v McClelland* [1997] QB 51).

Joint claimants   Security for costs may be ordered where there are joint claimants, some of whom are resident outside the jurisdiction. According to Lord Donaldson of Lymington MR in *Corfu Navigation Co. v Mobil Shipping Co. Ltd* [1991] 2 Lloyd's Rep 52 the basic principle underlying **CPR, r. 25.13(2)(a)**, is that it is prima facie unjust for a foreign claimant, who is in practical terms almost immune from the enforcement of any costs order that may be made, to be allowed to proceed with a claim without making funds available within the jurisdiction against which such an order can be enforced. Thus in *Okotcha v Voest Alpine Intertrading GmbH* [1993] BCLC 474 the court ordered security against a Nigerian company even though it was wholly owned by the co-claimant who would proceed with the claim in any event. It would, however, be appropriate to refuse to order security where it is probable that each of the joint claimants will be held to be liable for all the defendant's costs if the action is unsuccessful, provided the English claimants are likely to be able to pay those costs (see *Winthorp v Royal Exchange Assurance Co.* (1755) 1 Dick 282 as explained in *Slazengers Ltd v Seaspeed Ferries International Ltd* [1987] 1 WLR 1197 and in the light of *Corfu Navigation Co. v Mobil Shipping Co. Ltd*). Conversely, security may well be ordered where the English claimants are joined for the purpose of defeating an application for security (*Jones v Gurney* [1913] WN 72), or where it is impossible to predict the likely outcome on costs, or where each claimant is likely to be liable for only a portion of the defendant's costs (*Slazengers Ltd v Seaspeed Ferries International Ltd* [1987] 1 WLR 1197, [1988] 1 WLR 221).

67.11

Impecunious company or other body

Impecuniosity is no ground for ordering security for costs against an individual claimant, the principle being that individuals should not be prevented from seeking justice through want of means. Companies and other artificial persons need no such protection. With the repeal, as from 1 October 2009, of the Companies Act 1985, s. 726(1), by the Companies Act 2006, the jurisdiction to order security against impecunious corporations is now based solely on **CPR, r. 25.13(2)(c)**. This covers companies and also other bodies (whether incorporated inside or outside Great Britain). From this it is clear that the jurisdiction to order security for costs is available against unlimited companies, and also companies with a single member (*Jirehouse Capital v Beller* [2008] EWCA Civ 908, [2009] 1 WLR 751).

67.12

The question of whether there is 'reason to believe' a company would not be able to pay an order for costs is one of evaluating the risk, and does not have to be established on the balance of probabilities. No gloss (such as the phrase 'in significant danger' used in *Re Unisoft Group Ltd (No. 2)* [1993] BCLC 532) should be put on the words of the test in the rule (*Jirehouse Capital v Beller*). A company in liquidation will meet the test (*Hart Investments Ltd v Larchpark Ltd* [2007] EWHC 291 (TCC), [2008] 1 BCLC 589).

Applications based on **r. 25.13(2)(c)** usually require a comparison between the company's assets and the likely costs. The crucial question is whether the company will be able to meet the costs order at the time when the order has to be paid (*Re Unisoft Group Ltd (No. 2)* [1993] BCLC 532 at p. 534). A net asset balance is not therefore determinative of whether a company can pay a costs liability when it falls due: the court must consider the nature and liquidity of the company's assets (*Thistle Hotels Ltd v Gamma Four Ltd* [2004] EWHC 322 (Ch), [2004] 2 BCLC 174; *Longstaff International Ltd v Baker and McKenzie* [2004] EWHC 1852 (Ch), [2004] 1 WLR 2917). The judge is entitled to look behind the accounts at the reality of the situation, and to bear in mind the costs the company would have to pay for its own representation (*Autoweld Systems Ltd v Kito Enterprises LLC* [2010] EWCA Civ 1469, LTL 17/12/2010).

Inability to pay may be inferred from evidence that the claimant has declared unusually large dividends after the dispute arose (*Frost Capital Europe Ltd v Gathering of Developers Inc. Ltd* (2002) LTL 20/6/2002). Evidence of these matters should be included in the written evidence in support of the application. For example, in *Cheffick Ltd v JDM Associates* (1988) 43 BLR 52, the company's assets amounted to £1.2 million, and the defendant's costs were assessed at £800,000. Clearly, the claimant also had a large potential liability in costs to its own solicitors. It was held to be wrong in principle to order security against the company in view of its substantial assets. An offer undertaking to pay any costs ordered against the claimant by a related company was treated as a concession that the claimant was unable to pay the defendant's costs in *Longstaff International Ltd v Baker and McKenzie*. It may not be right to order security against a company which has no assets but which can meet the costs out of income (*Kim Barker Ltd v Aegon Insurance Co. (UK) Ltd* (1989) The Times, 9 October 1989).

An impecunious company ordinarily resident in Northern Ireland may be ordered to provide security under **r. 25.13(2)(c)** (*Re Dynaspan (UK) Ltd* [1995] 1 BCLC 536).

Nominal claimant

67.13   The court can order security against a nominal claimant (other than a representative appointed under **CPR, Part 19**) if there is reason to believe that he will be unable to pay the defendant's costs if ordered to do so (**r. 25.13(2)(f)**). The court is required to look at the reality of the situation. The fact that others will benefit from the claim does not render the claimant a nominal one. In *Farmer v Moseley (Holdings) Ltd* [2001] 2 BCLC 572 Neuberger J said that, in determining whether a claimant is a nominal claimant, assistance may be gained by looking 'with circumspection' at pre-CPR authorities (see **1.21** to **1.24**). In the 19th century the requirement for a nominal claimant to give security was primarily intended to deal with a claimant who assigned a cause of action to a person of no means, but in fact under the claimant's control, so as to avoid liability for costs (this situation is now specifically provided for in **r. 25.14**). In some cases under the old Rules of the Supreme Court security was ordered when a claimant became insolvent, so that the claimant's creditors would be the recipients of the fruits of the claim (for example, *Lloyd v Hathern Station Brick Co. Ltd* (1901) 85 LT 158; *Semler v Murphy* [1968] Ch 183). In more recent cases it has been stressed that security will not be ordered unless there is something more than the mere existence of others who will benefit from the fruits of the claim but who will not be liable if the claim fails (*Envis v Thakkar* [1997] BPIR 189; *Farmer v Moseley (Holdings) Ltd*). In *Envis v Thakkar* Kennedy LJ said that in his view, 'before a person can be branded as a nominal [claimant] ... there must be some element of deliberate duplicity or window-dressing which operates and probably was intended to operate to the detriment of the defendant'.

Change of address

67.14   CPR, **r. 25.13(2)(d)**, is aimed at the claimant who seeks to go to ground to avoid the possibility of having to pay the defendant's costs (*Aoun v Bahri* [2002] EWHC 29 (Comm), [2002] 3 All ER 182). **Rule 25.13(2)(d)** may be engaged where a claimant changes address more than once, so that the relevant change is not from the address stated on the claim form. In *Aoun v Bahri* the claimant was resident outside the jurisdiction when proceedings were issued, and subsequently moved to an address in England. Doing this to prevent an order for security for costs under **r. 25.13(2)(a)** would have given grounds for ordering security under **r. 25.13(2)(d)**. On the facts it was held that the move had been for personal reasons.

Taken steps to avoid enforcement

67.15 CPR, r. 25.13(2)(g), is not concerned with the claimant's motivation. It does not use the phrase 'with a view to' which can be found in r. 25.13(2)(d), so it is an objective test, and motive is irrelevant (*Bush v Bank Mandiri (Europe) Ltd* (2014) LTL 11/2/2014). This condition will be satisfied where the effect of the steps taken by the claimant with his assets is to make it more difficult to enforce an order for costs against him (*Aoun v Bahri* [2002] EWHC 29 (Comm), [2002] 3 All ER 182). On the facts, the sale of the claimant's home in Australia made it more difficult to enforce a costs order against him, and security was ordered. However, there has to be some connection between the steps alleged to have been taken to avoid enforcement and the proceedings. Examples are *Paragon Investments Inc. v Sharma* [2002] EWHC 2643 (Ch), LTL 22/11/2002, where the assets were moved several years before the proceedings, and *Somerset-Leeke v Kay Trustees* [2003] EWHC 1243 (Ch), [2004] 3 All ER 406, where the claimant had moved to Monaco many years before the events involved in the claim.

EXERCISE OF THE COURT'S DISCRETION

Factors to be taken into consideration

67.16 Once it has been established that the case comes within one of the conditions set out in **67.6**, the court has a general discretion whether to grant an order for security. In exercising this discretion the court will have regard to all the circumstances of the case and consider whether it would be just to make the order (see **CPR, rr. 25.13(1)(a) and 25.14(1)(a)**). There is a conflict in the Court of Appeal authorities on whether it is appropriate to consider the pre-CPR cases on the exercise of the discretion to award security for costs. It is submitted that the better view, which is consistent with the CPR being a new procedural code, is that stated in *Nasser v United Bank of Kuwait* [2001] EWCA Civ 556, [2002] 1 WLR 1868, which is that the substantial body of pre-CPR case law on the subject is consigned to history. Instead, the discretion has to be exercised applying the overriding objective, and by affording a proportionate protection against the difficulty identified by the ground relied upon as justifying security for costs in the case in question. The contrary view is supported by *Vedatech Corporation v Seagate Software Information* [2001] EWCA Civ 1924, LTL 29/11/2001, where an appeal was allowed because the judge had failed to take into account the fact that a Part 36 offer had been made, with particular reliance being placed on pre-CPR cases such as *Sir Lindsay Parkinson and Co. Ltd v Triplan Ltd* [1973] QB 609.

Thus, where security is sought against a claimant outside the EU and Lugano Convention States, the order should reflect the obstacles in the way, or the costs of, enforcing an English judgment for costs against the particular claimant or in the particular country concerned. In the context of applications against impecunious limited liability companies, it is suggested that one of the key factors will be that it is generally unjust for a defendant to have to defend with no realistic prospect of recovering its costs even if successful, but that security should not be in an amount that would stifle an apparently genuine claim. It is further suggested that the following factors should be taken into account:

(a) The risk of not being able to enforce a costs order, and/or the difficulty or expense of being able to enforce a costs order, if the defendant is awarded costs.

(b) The merits of the claim, where this can be investigated without holding a mini-trial (*Porzelack KG v Porzelack (UK) Ltd* [1987] 1 WLR 420; *Swain v Hillman* [2001] 1 All ER 91). This has an impact on the risk of needing to enforce a costs order against the claimant.

(c) Whether the defendant may be able to recover costs from someone other than the claimant.

(d) The impact on the claimant of having to give security. In some cases a substantial order for security will effectively deprive the claimant of the ability to take the claim to trial. Where the claimant is sheltering in a tax haven the court is unlikely to be very sympathetic, but where the claimant's inability to pay has been caused by the defendant's conduct complained of in the claim, a substantial order may unjustly stifle the claim.

(e) Whether the claimant's difficulty (if any) in being able to provide security has been caused by the defendant's activities. If so, security may well be refused (*Interoil Trading SA v Watford Petroleum Ltd* [2003] EWHC 1806 (Ch), LTL 16/7/2003).

(f) Delay in making the application. Generally the application should be made shortly after proceedings are commenced, and delay may be reflected either in refusing the application or reducing the amount of security ordered.

(g) Suspicions about the claimant's financial position if the claim is lost are material (*Frost Capital Europe Ltd v Gathering of Developers Inc. Ltd* (2002) LTL 20/6/2002, where the person in control of the claimant company refused to provide a guarantee for the costs).

Human rights considerations

67.17   An order which requires a litigant to pay a sum which the litigant cannot afford may amount to a breach of the right of access to a court guaranteed by the European Convention on Human Rights, **art. 6(1)**, in the **Human Rights Act 1998, sch. 1**. For a full discussion see **91.45**. See also **67.19** on the court's reluctance to make an order for security which would stifle a genuine claim.

See also the discussion in **67.22** of potential discrimination contrary to arts 6(1) and 14 of the Convention when making orders for security against persons not resident in Regulation or Convention States.

Prospects of success

67.18   There is no doubt that the prospect of success at trial is one of the matters that may sometimes be taken into account on the application (*Frost Capital Europe Ltd v Gathering of Developers Inc. Ltd* (2002) LTL 20/6/2002). If this is taken too far, an application for security may be blown up to an investigation similar to a trial. Robert Walker LJ in *Zappia Middle East Construction Co. Ltd v Clifford Chance* [2001] EWCA Civ 946 and also in *Antonelli v Allen* [2001] EWCA Civ 1563 said that evidence as to the merits of the claim or appeal is seldom helpful in an application for security for costs, and is rarely decisive unless it makes out an exceptionally strong case that a meritorious claim or appeal is likely to be stifled if security for costs is ordered. In a passage approved by the Court of Appeal in *Trident International Freight Services Ltd v Manchester Ship Canal Co.* [1990] BCLC 263, Browne-Wilkinson V-C in *Porzelack KG v Porzelack (UK) Ltd* [1987] 1 WLR 420 said at p. 423:

Undoubtedly, if it can clearly be demonstrated that the [claimant] is likely to succeed, in the sense that there is a very high probability of success, then that is a matter that can properly be weighed in the balance. Similarly, if it can be shown that there is a very high probability that the defendant will succeed, that is a matter that can be weighed. But for myself I deplore the attempt to go into the merits of the case, unless it can clearly be demonstrated one way or another that there is a high degree of probability of success or failure.

In the Commercial Court investigation of the merits is strongly discouraged (Admiralty and Commercial Courts Guide, app. 16, para. 4). Courts will keep control of applications in the interest of litigants in other actions by excluding evidence and making penal costs orders where the parties transgress the line and seek to delve into the merits in too much detail.

If there is no defence to the claim, it will almost certainly be unjust to order security. In such a case the defendant is highly unlikely to recover costs in any event, and ordering security often has the practical effect of preventing the claimant from proceeding with the claim. Lord Denning MR in *Sir Lindsay Parkinson and Co. Ltd v Triplan Ltd* [1973] QB 609 said at p. 627:

I am quite clear that a payment into court, or an open offer, is a matter which the court can take into account. It goes to show that there is substance in the claim: and that it would not be right to deprive the company of it by insisting on security for costs.

In *Vedatech Corporation v Seagate Software Information* [2001] EWCA Civ 1924, LTL 29/11/2001, the Court of Appeal set aside an order for security, holding that the judge had been wrong in not taking into account the fact that the defendant had made a substantial Part 36 offer. The decision in *Simaan General Contracting Co. v Pilkington Glass Ltd* [1987] 1 WLR 516, where Judge Newey QC held that the public policy protecting without-prejudice negotiations prevented their use in security for costs applications in assessing the claimant's prospects of success, is inconsistent with *Vedatech Corporation v Seagate Software Information* and (from a different context) *Family Housing Association (Manchester) Ltd v Michael Hyde and Partners* [1993] 1 WLR 354, and it is submitted that Judge Newey's decision should not be followed.

Stifling a genuine claim

Where the claimant's claim has a good chance of success (there being no need for anything   **67.19** higher), the court will hesitate before making an order which will have the practical effect of preventing the claimant from proceeding. The claimant has the burden of satisfying the court that ordering security for costs will stifle a genuine claim. In *Kuenyehia v International Hospitals Group Ltd* [2007] EWCA Civ 274, LTL 27/2/2007, the claimant, who produced misleading documentation and made inconsistent statements about the assets available for funding the claim, was held to have failed to discharge this burden. The essential policy is that the need to protect the defendant has to yield to the claimant's right of access to the courts to litigate the dispute if it is a genuine claim (*Hamilton v Al Fayed (No. 2)* [2002] EWCA Civ 665, [2003] QB 1175, a case on costs orders against non-parties, where the importance of the European Convention on Human Rights, **art. 6(1)**, in the **Human Rights Act 1998, sch. 1** was stressed). If the case is one where the court feels that security should be ordered, it can fix the amount of the security at a level which will not stifle the claimant in proceeding further (*Innovare Displays plc v Corporate Broking Services Ltd* [1991] BCC 174). In deciding whether a claim is likely to be stifled by an order for security for costs, the court is entitled to take into account any ability the claimant might have of raising money from friends, relatives, or if it is a company, its directors, shareholders, or other backers or interested persons. As this information is likely to be entirely within the claimant's knowledge, it is generally for the claimant to satisfy the court how and why other sources of funding are not available to fund the claim (*Flender Werft AG v Aegean Maritime Ltd* [1990] 2 Lloyd's Rep 27; *Newman v Wenden Properties Ltd* [2007] EWHC 336 (TCC), 114 Con LR 95), though there are cases where the court will be prepared to infer that the company will be prevented from pursuing its claim if security is ordered (*Trident International Freight Services Ltd v Manchester Ship Canal Co.* [1990] BCLC 263 as interpreted in *Keary Developments Ltd v Tarmac Construction Ltd* [1995] 3 All ER 534).

Delay in applying

Applications for security for costs should be made at an early stage in the proceedings. Lateness   **67.20** may of itself be a reason for refusing an order (*PR Records Ltd v Vinyl 2000 Ltd* [2002] EWHC 2860 (Ch), LTL 9/12/2002). There have been cases where security has been refused because the application was made just a few days or even a few hours before the trial. In *Innovare Displays plc v Corporate Broking Services Ltd* [1991] BCC 174 the trial was fixed for 25 January 1991, the application seeking security was issued on 21 December 1990 and was heard on 17 and 24 January 1991. The claimants were in financial difficulties, and throughout had encountered problems in raising money to fight the action. The defendants sought to excuse their late application by saying that it was not until mid-December that the claimants confirmed that the action would proceed. They did not want to waste money making applications if there was a chance that the action would not proceed. Once they were told that it would, they acted with proper dispatch. However, their solicitors had written to the claimants' solicitors in November 1990 warning that if agreement to provide security for their costs was not forthcoming by 15 November 1990, an application for security would be made. It was held that they had not acted with all due expedition, but they were not so dilatory that they had to be deprived entirely of security. A reduced order was made.

Lateness is regarded even more seriously when the application for security is made in a pending appeal to the Court of Appeal. Thus, an application for security was dismissed solely because of its lateness in *A Co. v K Ltd* [1987] 1 WLR 1655 when it was made 14 days before the hearing. In that case Sir John Donaldson MR mentioned that 'proportionality' may have a bearing on the discretion whether to grant security. The claimants had obtained judgment for $US2.6 million, and it seemed the defendants' only asset in the jurisdiction was $US830,000 which was in court. The costs of the appeal were £20,000, which the Master of the Rolls regarded as quite a tiny sum in proportion to the other sums at stake.

An order for security for costs made shortly before trial may be made in an 'unless' form rather than in the usual form of staying the claim until security is provided (*Vedatech Corporation v Crystal Decisions (UK) Ltd* [2002] EWCA Civ 357, LTL 28/1/2002). Care must be taken that any such order does not act oppressively or disproportionately, and consequently it may not be right to order a large sum to be paid into court within a short period of time.

Claimant resident outside Regulation and Convention States

67.21 In *Porzelack KG v Porzelack (UK) Ltd* [1987] 1 WLR 420 Browne-Wilkinson V-C said:

> The purpose of ordering security for costs against a [claimant] ordinarily resident outside the jurisdiction is to ensure that a successful defendant will have a fund available within the jurisdiction of this court against which it can enforce the judgment for costs....
>
> [The court has] an entirely general discretion either to award or refuse security, having regard to all the circumstances of the case.... The question is what, in all the circumstances of the case, is the just answer.

In *De Bry v Fitzgerald* [1990] 1 WLR 552 Lord Donaldson of Lymington MR said that the rationale of **CPR, r. 25.13(2)(a)**, is that a defendant should be entitled to security if there is reason to believe that, in the event of succeeding and being awarded the costs of the claim, there will be real difficulty in enforcing the order. If the difficulty arises from where the claimant chooses to live and the location of the claimant's assets, so that an order for costs will be unenforceable or only enforceable with a significant expenditure of time or money, the defendant should be entitled to security. Despite the strength of the language used by Lord Donaldson, there is no presumption that an order for security should be made merely based on the fact the claimant resides in a non-Convention country (*Prince Radu of Hohenzollern v Houston* [2006] EWHC 231 (QB), LTL 15/3/2006, unaffected on this point by the appeal, [2006] EWCA Civ 1575, [2007] 5 Costs LR 671). It is difficulty in enforcing in the place where the assets are likely to be, rather than enforcement in the country where the respondent happens to live, that has to be considered (*Aims Asset Management Sdn Bhd v Kazakhstan Investment Fund Ltd* [2002] EWHC 3225 (Ch), LTL 23/5/2002).

67.22 **Country of residence**   Given that ease of enforcement is an important consideration, much turns on the actual country where the claimant's assets are situated.

'Outside the jurisdiction' (in **CPR, r. 25.13(2)(a)(i)**) means outside England and Wales. There is unchallenged authority that security for costs will not be ordered against a resident of another part of the United Kingdom (*Raeburn v Andrews* (1874) LR 9 QB 118), because English judgments can be enforced in Scotland and Northern Ireland by mere registration under the Judgments Extension Act 1868. It is for similar reasons, combined with the effect of the Treaty on the Functioning of the European Union, art. 18, that security for costs will not be granted against a person against whom an English judgment can be enforced under the **recast Brussels I Regulation** (the Brussels I Regulation for proceedings instituted before 10 January 2015) or the Brussels or Lugano Conventions (**CPR, r. 25.13(2)(a)(ii)**; *Bunzl v Martin Bunzl International Ltd* (2000) *The Times*, 19 September 2000). Security for costs is therefore unavailable on the ground of residence against most claimants living in Europe.

The next category of countries is those with which there is a reciprocal enforcement convention, to which the Foreign Judgments (Reciprocal Enforcement) Act 1933 applies, see **chapter 80**. Denning J rejected an attempt to extend *Raeburn v Andrews* to such cases in *Kohn v Rinson and Stafford (Brod) Ltd* [1948] 1 KB 327. Nevertheless, a claimant can seek to defeat an application for security by adducing written evidence that any order for costs may be cheaply and easily enforced in the claimant's country of residence. The onus is on the claimant. Orders have been refused on account of the ease of enforcement in Monaco (*Somerset-Leake v Kay Trustees* [2003] EWHC 1243 (Ch), [2004] 3 All ER 406) and the British Virgin Islands (*Longstaff International Ltd v Baker and McKenzie* [2004] EWHC 1852 (Ch), [2004] 1 WLR 2917). Ease of enforcement is not the sole or decisive factor, and may be outweighed by other matters (*Thune v London Properties Ltd* [1990] 1 WLR 562).

The final category comprises the rest of the world. In these cases the court will do what is just in the circumstances (*Leyvand v Barasch* (2000) *The Times*, 23 March 2000). Any order for security for costs must be objectively justified, and not be discriminatory (*Nasser v United Bank of Kuwait* [2001] EWCA Civ 556, [2002] 1 WLR 1868; *Zappia Middle East Construction Co. Ltd v Clifford Chance* [2001] EWCA Civ 946). **CPR, r. 25.13(2)(a)**, does not mean that a claimant can be ordered to provide security for costs merely because of not residing in a Regulation or Convention State: that would be discrimination in providing access to the courts, contrary to the European Convention on Human Rights, **arts 6(1)** and **14**, in the **Human Rights Act 1998, sch. 1**. An order for security for costs under **CPR, r. 25.13(2)(a)**, should reflect the obstacles in the way, or the costs of, enforcing an English judgment for costs against the particular claimant or in the particular country concerned (*Nasser v United Bank of Kuwait*). As Gross J said in *Texuna International Ltd v Cairn Energy Ltd* [2004] EWHC 1102 (Comm), [2005] 1 BCLC 579, the court has to decide whether the claimant's country is:

(a) one where the obstacles to enforcement are so great that the claimant should be required to give security for the whole costs of the claim; or

(b) one where enforcement is simply more expensive than in England and Wales. In these cases the security should reflect the likely additional expense.

Security may be ordered where it is obvious that enforcement will be difficult and costly, particularly where the claimant is a one-ship company resident in, say, Panama or Liberia (see the judgment of Parker LJ in *Berkeley Administration Inc. v McClelland* [1990] 2 QB 407; *Aims Asset Management Sdn Bhd v Kazakhstan Investment Fund Ltd* [2002] EWHC 3225 (Ch), LTL 23/5/2002). A finding that a costs order is likely to be unenforceable in another State (here Sudan) does not breach any principle of international comity (*Al-Koronky v Time-Life Entertainment Group Ltd* [2006] EWCA Civ 1123, [2007] 1 Costs LR 57).

Factors where claimant resident outside Regulation and Convention States   Since the effect-   **67.23**
iveness of enforcement is the most important consideration, the following factors need to be taken into account if present:

(a) Whether the claimant has substantial assets within the jurisdiction. If it has this is a weighty factor against ordering security (*De Bry v Fitzgerald* [1990] 1 WLR 552). Assets within the jurisdiction include damages which the claimant hopes to recover in other proceedings (*Cripps v Heritage Distribution Corporation* [1999] CPLR 858). The fact the claimant has ATE insurance covering the defendant's costs is important, but may be counterbalanced by insurance law restrictions. In *Al-Koronky v Time-Life Entertainment Group Ltd* [2006] EWCA Civ 1123, [2007] 1 Costs LR 57, security was ordered despite the presence of ATE insurance because the policy was voidable if the claimant lost, after not telling the truth. The court felt that if the claimant lost, it was likely to be for a reason enabling the insurer to avoid the policy.

(b) The degree of fixity or permanence of those assets, and whether the claimant has a substantial connection with this country (*Leyvand v Barasch* (2000) *The Times*, 23 March 2000).

(c) Whether the claimant is impecunious. In *Thune v London Properties Ltd* [1990] 1 WLR 562 the bankruptcy of the claimants outweighed the ease of enforcement in Norway, where the claimants were resident.

(d) The ability of the claimant to transfer assets around the world, as in *Berkeley Administration Inc. v McClelland* [1990] 2 QB 407.

(e) Any lack of information, or refusal to provide information, about the claimant's assets (*Paragon Investments Inc. v Sharma* (2002) LTL 22/11/2002; *Zappia Middle East Construction Co. Ltd v Clifford Chance* [2001] EWCA Civ 946).

(f) Any evidence of misapplication of the claimant's assets (*Paragon Investments Inc. v Sharma*).

Claimant an impecunious company or other body

67.24 As with foreign claimants, the rationale behind ordering security against an impecunious company is to safeguard the defendant against the prospect of encountering real difficulty in enforcing any order for the costs of the action. Describing the effects of what is now **CPR, r. 25.13(2)(c)**, Megarry V-C in *Pearson v Naydler* [1977] 1 WLR 899 said, at p. 906:

> It is inherent in the whole concept of the [rule] that the court is to have power to order the company to do what it is likely to find difficulty in doing, namely to provide security for the costs which *ex hypothesi* it is likely to be unable to pay. At the same time, the court must not allow the [rule] to be used as an instrument of oppression, as by shutting out a small company from making a genuine claim against a large company.

A start-up company bringing a large and complex claim can expect to be required to provide substantial security for the defendant's costs (*Automotive Latch Systems Ltd v Honeywell International Inc.* [2006] EWHC 2340 (Comm), LTL 27/9/2006). One factor mentioned by Lord Denning MR in *Sir Lindsay Parkinson and Co. Ltd v Triplan Ltd* [1973] QB 609 is whether the company's want of means has been brought about by any conduct by the defendant, such as, in an action for breach of contract, delay in payment or the defendant's delay in performing its part of the contract.

AMOUNT

67.25 *Procon (Great Britain) Ltd v Provincial Building Co. Ltd* [1984] 1 WLR 557 establishes the principle that any security should be such as the court thinks fit in all the circumstances. The amount ordered should be neither illusory nor oppressive (*Hart Investments Ltd v Larchpark Ltd* [2007] EWHC 291 (TCC), [2008] 1 BCLC 589). The court needs assistance on the amount of costs the defendant is likely to incur in the claim, and for this reason it is usual to exhibit a summary statement of costs to the defendant's evidence in support. Security may be ordered for the entire costs of the proceedings, or up to a future point in the claim, and may include past as well as future costs. While security for costs can include pre-action costs, the court should be slow to exercise its discretion to include these as there is a risk that such an order could become penal in nature (*Lobster Group Ltd v Heidelberg Graphic Equipment Ltd* [2008] EWHC 413 (TCC), [2008] 2 All ER 1173). There is no rule of practice that the court will always reduce the defendant's estimate by a third (*Procon (Great Britain) Ltd v Provincial Building Co. Ltd*), but it is usual to make a deduction from the defendant's costs estimate to take into account any likely reduction on assessment of costs, and also to make an arbitrary discount in respect of future costs to take account of the chances of settling. In applications under **CPR, r. 25.13(2)(a)**, the amount is usually limited to the additional costs which would be incurred by reason of having to enforce any judgment for costs in the overseas jurisdiction (*Relational LLC v Hodges* [2011] EWCA Civ 774, [2012] ILPr 4).

In suitable cases the court may sit with a costs officer as an informal assessor (see Admiralty and Commercial Courts Guide, app. 16, para. 7).

As was mentioned at **67.19** and **67.20**, relevant factors going to the court's discretion which are in the claimant's favour, but which are not strong enough to deprive the defendant of an order for security, may be taken into account when deciding the amount of security to order. Thus, in *Innovare Displays plc v Corporate Broking Services Ltd* [1991] BCC 174, which was discussed at **67.20**, the lateness of the application and the difficulty faced by the claimants in providing security were taken into account by ordering the claimants to provide security in the sum of £10,000 when the defendant's estimated costs were £147,000. In contrast, it is wrong in principle to order merely nominal security on the ground that the defendant has known all along that the claimant is a company of limited means (*Roburn Construction Ltd v Williams Irwin (South) and Co. Ltd* [1991] BCC 726, where the judge's order for security in the sum of £5,000 out of estimated costs of £150,000 was increased to £40,000).

Security may be ordered in respect of the 'defendant's costs'. This may, according to *Noterise Ltd v Haseltine Lake and Co.* [1992] BCC 497, if the circumstances merit it, include costs the defendant may incur as against a co-defendant in contribution or indemnity proceedings.

Cases dealing with calculating the costs occasioned by bringing a counterclaim are considered at **67.3**.

ORDER

67.26 Orders for security for costs should follow form PF 44 (**PD 4**). It is usual to require security to be given by payment into court, although bonds and guarantees are alternatives, as are solicitors' undertakings. Security for costs will not usually be allowed in the form of a charge on real property. If the property is valuable, there should be no difficulty in obtaining a bank guarantee or money to pay into court. If no bank would lend against the property, it follows that the security is inadequate (*AP (UK) Ltd v West Midlands Fire and Civil Defence Authority* [2001] EWCA Civ 1917, [2002] CPLR 57). ATE insurance is unlikely to provide a satisfactory alternative to the usual forms of security (*Belco Trading Co. v Kondo* [2008] EWCA Civ 205, LTL 4/6/2008).

Until security is given the claim will be stayed. If the claimant fails to provide security in compliance with the order, the defendant can apply for the claim to be struck out (*Speed Up Holdings Ltd v Gough and Co. (Handly) Ltd* [1986] FSR 330), or the order may provide that the claim will be struck out automatically if security for costs is not provided within the time stated in the order (*Zappia Middle East Construction Co. Ltd v Clifford Chance* [2001] EWCA Civ 946; *Antonelli v Allen* [2001] EWCA Civ 1563). The Court of Appeal in *Prince Radu of Hohenzollern v Houston* [2006] EWCA Civ 1575, [2007] 5 Costs LR 671, questioned whether an unless order, having a similar effect to that in *Zappia Middle East Construction Co. Ltd v Clifford Chance*, was appropriate. A security for costs order is a special form of order which is intended to give the claimant a proper choice as to whether to put up the security and continue with the claim, or to withdraw the claim. It is not intended to be a weapon to be used by a defendant to obtain a speedy judgment without a trial. *Prince Radu of Hohenzollern v Houston* does not lay down an absolute rule, and there are cases where unless orders for security for costs are appropriate (*Allen v Bloomsbury Publishing plc* [2011] EWCA Civ 943, LTL 15/7/2011, where the claim was very weak). Nevertheless, in the light of *Prince Radu of Hohenzollern v Houston* it is doubtful that *Rajvel Construction Ltd v Bestville Properties Ltd* [2011] EWHC 2669 (TCC), LTL 8/9/2011, which decided the court has the power to grant a freezing injunction in support of an order for security for costs, is correct.

Summit Navigation Ltd v Generali Romania Asigurare Reasigurare SA [2014] EWHC 398 (Comm), [2014] 1 WLR 3472, if correct, renders most of the previous paragraph redundant by holding that a normal stay pending provision of security is a sanction within the meaning of **CPR, rr. 3.8** and 3.9. This would mean that the claimant will need to apply for relief from sanctions to get the stay lifted if he or she is late in providing security, with the restrictions in **r. 3.8** on the defendant consenting to lifting the stay.

If security is provided, the claim continues. After trial, the defendant, if successful, will have a secured fund from which its costs can be paid.

In the Admiralty and Commercial Courts defendants are sometimes required to give undertakings in damages if security is ordered (Admiralty and Commercial Courts Guide, app. 16, para. 5), and instead of ordering a stay it is more usual to give a time for providing the security with liberty to apply for dismissal of the claim in the event of default (para. 6).

Applications to vary

67.27   An application to vary an order for security for costs may be made if there is a material change in circumstances since the order was made (*Gordano Building Contractors Ltd v Burgess* [1988] 1 WLR 890). An application to vary will be refused if it depends on evidence which was available at the time of the hearing at which the original order was made (*Gordano Building Contractors Ltd v Burgess*).

An agreement on the amount of security is not in itself an agreement not to seek further security at a later stage, so an application to increase the amount of security will be considered on the usual material change of circumstances test (*Kazakhstan v Istil Group Inc.* [2005] EWCA Civ 1468, [2006] 1 WLR 596). An agreement may include a term that the agreed security for costs will not be increased even if there is a material change in circumstances. In such a case the court retains a residual discretion to allow an increase, but only if the circumstances are wholly exceptional (*Kazakhstan v Istil Group Inc.*).

It is common for the court to order security for costs up to a certain stage in the proceedings, for example, a pre-trial review, at which point a further order may be made. Otherwise a party applying for variation of an order must show a relevant change. The courts will be astute to avoid an appeal dressed up as a further application and there will be a heavy burden on a party seeking a further order.

SUCCESS BY THE CLAIMANT

67.28   In cases where the claimant is successful, the trial judge will normally accede to an application on the claimant's behalf for the security money in court to be repaid to the claimant, or for the release of any other security. If the defendant wishes to appeal, however, the court has a discretion whether to impose a stay on the release of the security so as to provide continued security for the costs up to trial in the event that the defendant's appeal succeeds (*Stabilad Ltd v Stephens and Carter Ltd* [1999] 1 WLR 1201). The stay is simply to preserve the security for the costs to trial.

SECURITY FOR COSTS OF AN APPEAL

67.29   The respondent to an appeal may make an application under CPR, **r. 25.15**, for security for the costs of the appeal or for the retention of existing security policy pending determination of the appeal. This rule only applies where permission to appeal has been granted, and does not apply where there is a pending application for permission to appeal, even if the appeal is to follow immediately if the application is granted (*Kevythalli Design Ltd v Ice Associates Ltd* [2010] EWCA Civ 379, LTL 28/4/2010). In considering whether to make an order under **r. 25.15**, in *Stabilad Ltd v Stephens and Carter Ltd* [1999] 1 WLR 1201, Auld LJ said that the fact the claimant had succeeded at first instance was irrelevant. Factors to be considered were the risks of the claimant being unable to pay the costs to trial if the security was released, the claimant's need for the money provided as security for fighting the appeal, and the prospects of the appeal succeeding. The court should also consider whether ordering security might stifle a genuine appeal, but an appellant raising this question is under an obligation to put before the court full and frank evidence of its means (*Mahan Air v Blue Sky One Ltd* [2011] EWCA Civ 544, LTL 11/5/2011). A failure to disclose assets permits the court to infer that assets have been put out of the reach of creditors (*Dubai Islamic Bank PJSC v PSI Energy Holding Co BSC* [2011] EWCA Civ 761, LTL 4/7/2011).

Normally, the amount of security ordered under **r. 25.15** should not exceed an approximate pre-estimate of the respondent's costs of the appeal (*Moore v Moore* [2009] EWCA Civ 433, [2009] 2 FLR 957). By a combination of the Senior Courts Act 1981, s. 15(3), and **CPR, rr. 25.12, 25.13** and **52.20**, it was held in *Dar International FEF Co. v Aon Ltd* [2003] EWCA Civ 1833, [2004] 1 WLR 1395, that the Court of Appeal has jurisdiction to order a claimant who was successful at first instance to provide security for the costs of the proceedings in the court below. It will be unusual for such an order to be made, not least because, if the claimant is based overseas, the order may be unenforceable.

Chapter 68   Costs Orders

INTRODUCTION

Orders for costs are made both at the end of the trial or appeal and at the end of any interim **68.1** hearings and enforcement proceedings made in the course of, or after judgment in, the proceedings. The costs of enforcement proceedings are often added to the judgment obtained in the action. The relationship between interim costs orders and the overall costs of the proceedings is considered at **68.26**.

The CPR set out a complete code on costs. Pre-CPR cases have no place in seeking to establish categories of claim where special rules on costs apply (*Cheltenham Borough Council v Laird* [2010] EWCA Civ 847, LTL 4/2/2010, where the Court of Appeal refuted the idea that there is any special rule on costs in fraud claims).

Legal costs will be incurred on behalf of a litigant from the time a solicitor is first consulted until the solicitor's retainer is terminated, perhaps after enforcement of any judgment that is obtained. The client (or the Legal Aid Agency (LAA) if the client is legally aided) bears the primary responsibility for paying its own solicitor's bill. The bill comprises the solicitor's remuneration for the work done on the case, together with counsel's and any experts' fees, court fees, and any other charges, expenses and disbursements.

Although each client is primarily responsible for its own solicitor's costs, it is usual for the successful party in proceedings to be awarded an order for costs against the unsuccessful party. This is sometimes known as 'costs shifting', a principle which is deeply embedded in the ethos of civil procedure and seems to have survived the root-and-branch review of costs conducted by Sir Rupert Jackson (*Review of Civil Litigation Costs* (Ministry of Justice, December 2009)). Recommendations of the *Review* included:

- Defining 'proportionality' (see **71.38**) by reference to the sum in issue (or value of the case), complexity, conduct, client reputation and public importance, and applying the concept globally (recommendation 1).
- Abrogating the indemnity principle (see **71.30**; recommendation 4), which has not been implemented.
- Repealing the Access to Justice Act 1999 provisions on the recoverability of ATE insurance premiums (recommendation 7) and repealing the Courts and Legal Services Act 1990, s. 58A(6) (costs orders to include fees payable under a CFA with a success fee) (recommendation 9). This was implemented with effect from 1 April 2013 (Legal Aid, Sentencing and Punishment of Offenders Act 2012, ss. 44 and 46–48).
- Referral fees in personal injuries claims should be banned (recommendation 20). This was implemented with effect from 1 April 2013 (Legal Aid, Sentencing and Punishment of Offenders Act 2012, ss. 56–60).
- There should be 'qualified one-way costs shifting' in favour of categories of litigants who merit protection against party-and-party costs orders (recommendations 8 and 19). This was implemented as part of the civil justice reforms of 2013, see **chapter 69**.
- Contingency fees should be allowed, but only after taking independent advice, and should not be recoverable from the other side (recommendations 14 and 15). These are called damages-based agreements (DBAs), and were implemented by the Legal Aid, Sentencing and Punishment of Offenders Act 2012, s. 45.
- Detailed recommendations for different categories of claims designed to reduce the cost of litigating (recommendations 22 to 69). Most of these have not been implemented.
- Detailed recommendations on aspects of general litigation, such as disclosure, experts, case management and appeals, again designed to reduce the cost of litigating (recommendations 70 to 94). These have been implemented by detailed amendments to the CPR that came into effect on 1 April 2013, and are discussed in the relevant chapters of this work.
- Recommendations on court administration and information technology (recommendations 95 to 103).

- More information to be provided on the N260 schedule of costs (see **71.4**) for trials and appeals to assist judges with summary assessments (recommendation 105). A more detailed form N260 was introduced with effect from 1 April 2013.
- New format for bills of costs (see **71.13**) to cut out boilerplate entries, and to produce a more informative document (recommendation 106), which was introduced on 1 April 2013.
- Development of software for time recording which will be able to produce the necessary information for summary assessments and detailed assessments (obviously this would be a complex and expensive project) (recommendation 107).
- A package of other proposals for detailed assessments (recommendation 108, chapter 45, section 5), which was implemented as part of the complete re-issue of **CPR, Parts 44 to 48** and **PD 44** to **PD 48** on 1 April 2013.

The civil justice reforms broadly came into force on 1 April 2013. There are detailed transition arrangements set out in the Civil Procedure (Amendment) Rules 2013 (SI 2013/262), Updates 60 and 61, relevant commencement orders, and the other relevant statutory instruments implementing aspects of the civil justice reforms. These are discussed in *Blackstone's Guide to the Civil Justice Reforms 2013*, Sime and French (Oxford: OUP, 2013), ch. 2. Slightly different transitional provisions apply to different aspects of the reforms. Among the most important are that the old law continues to apply to funding agreements entered into up to 31 March 2013, and the new law applies to funding agreements entered into on or after 1 April 2013. The new proportionality test in standard-basis assessments does not apply to claims commenced before 1 April 2013 (**CPR, r. 44.3(7)**). Most of the other amendments apply to existing claims as from 1 April 2013. This chapter sets out the law as it applies from 1 April 2013.

CONTENTIOUS AND NON-CONTENTIOUS COSTS

68.2   Solicitors' costs are divided into contentious and non-contentious costs, the distinction being that contentious costs relate to cases where proceedings have been begun before a court (see the Solicitors Act 1974, s. 87(1)); but see **65.10**.

CPR, r. 46.14, applies where the parties have compromised the substantive dispute and agreed which party is 'to pay the costs', but they have failed to agree 'the amount of those costs' **PD 46, para. 9.4**, says that unless the court orders otherwise **Part 45, section II** (fixed costs) applies, the relevant costs in a **r. 46.14** application will be treated as being claimed on the standard basis. This implies that they are treated as contentious costs because standard-basis assessments do not apply to non-contentious costs.

Most litigators who negotiate a settlement of a civil dispute without proceedings being issued would regard it as obvious that if they have agreed that one side will pay 'the reasonable' costs of the other side, those costs will be quantified as though they were contentious costs and on the standard basis. Unless there is something very unusual in the circumstances this is likely to be held to be the common intention of both sides, and an implied term will be found to that effect. Cautious litigators may feel it appropriate to set this out expressly, such as by agreeing: '[ ] shall pay the reasonable costs of [ ], to be quantified as if they were contentious costs on the standard basis'.

This chapter is mainly concerned with the rules relating to contentious costs.

GENERAL PRINCIPLES

68.3   The two main principles when it comes to deciding which party should pay the costs of an application or of the whole proceedings are:

(a) the costs payable by one party to another are in the discretion of the court (Senior Courts Act 1981, s. 51; **CPR, r. 44.2(1)**); and

(b) the general rule, as now stated in **r. 44.2(2)**, is that the unsuccessful party will be ordered to pay the costs of the successful party ('costs follow the event' in the old terminology).

The rule that costs usually follow the event is regarded as being reasonable for the purposes of the European Convention on Human Rights, **First Protocol, art. 1**, in the **Human Rights Act 1989, sch. 1**, because it may act as a disincentive to unnecessary litigation (*Antoniades v United Kingdom* (application 15434/89) (1990) 64 DR 232; *Hoare v United Kingdom* (application 16261/08) (2011) 53 EHRR SE1 at [57]).

Costs shifting between the parties is achieved, if at all, through the party-and-party costs order. There is a general rule that a party cannot bring subsequent proceedings seeking the costs of earlier proceedings between the same parties by way of damages (*Carroll v Kynaston* [2010] EWCA Civ 1404, [2011] QB 959). Also, once the trial judge has made a costs order, it is not open to the costs judge to vary or rescind it (*Drew v Whitbread plc* [2010] EWCA Civ 53, [2010] 1 WLR 1725). Waller LJ, at [26]–[28], pointed out that the functions of **CPR, r. 44.2** and **r. 44.4**, are different. **Rule 44.2** enables the court to make orders for costs when proceedings are finally disposed of, with the decision being based on all the circumstances of the case, including factors such as conduct, any exaggeration of the value of the claim etc. set out in **r. 44.2(4)** and **(5)**.

On an assessment of costs (see **chapter 71**) the costs judge must have regard to all the circumstances and to the factors set out in **r. 44.4(3)**, which include conduct, the value of the claim etc. On the face of it both the trial judge under **r. 44.2** and the costs judge under **r. 44.4** are required to consider many similar factors. If the trial judge makes an express ruling on any of those factors, that will bind the costs judge. For example, it may be appropriate for the trial judge to make a ruling that calling a particular witness was unnecessary, which will bind the costs judge (*Drew v Whitbread plc*, at [36]). The trial judge may alternatively help the costs judge on a point by giving some indication of the trial judge's view, which will guide but not bind the costs judge. This may be useful where the trial judge is in a good position to comment on the point. A party seeking such an indication should expressly make a request to the trial judge (at [35], [37]). Failing to raise a point relevant to assessment of costs under **r. 44.4** with the trial judge does not preclude a party raising the point with the costs judge (at [35]).

Range of possible costs orders

Under **CPR, r. 44.2(6)**, there are seven possible variations from the main rule that the unsuccessful party should pay the whole of the successful party's costs. These variations are: **68.4**

(a) that a party must pay only a proportion of another party's costs;
(b) that a party must pay a specified amount in respect of the other side's costs;
(c) that a party must pay costs from or until a certain date only;
(d) that a party must pay costs incurred before proceedings have begun;
(e) that a party must pay costs relating only to particular steps taken in the proceedings;
(f) that a party must pay costs relating only to a distinct part of the proceedings, although an order of this type can only be made if an order in either of the forms set out at (a) or (c) would not be practicable (**r. 44.2(7)**);
(g) that a party must pay interest on costs from or until a certain date, including a date before judgment.

All these variations restrict the amount of costs that a winning party may recover from the loser. They would seem appropriate, therefore, to mark the court's displeasure at some conduct on the part of the winning party, or to reflect a partial rather than a full win.

In the following situations (which are set out in **r. 44.9(1)**) a costs order will be deemed to have been made with costs payable on the standard basis:

(a) in favour of a defendant where a claim is struck out for non-payment of court fees under **r. 3.7** or for dishonouring a cheque tendered in payment of court fees under **r. 3.7B**;
(b) in favour of a claimant on accepting a Part 36 offer under **r. 36.10**; and
(c) in favour of a defendant where a claim is discontinued, under **r. 38.6**.

Commentary

Discretion on costs

68.5   The discretion granted by the Senior Courts Act 1981, s. 51(1), is very wide, and the courts
are opposed to limitations being imposed on it by implication or rigid rules of practice (see
Aiden Shipping Co. Ltd v Interbulk Ltd [1986] AC 965; *Bankamerica Finance Ltd v Nock* [1988] AC 1002).
The court has full power to determine by whom and to what extent the costs of an action are
to be paid (*Singh v Observer Ltd* [1989] 2 All ER 751). However, like any discretion, it must be
exercised judicially and on reasons connected with the case (see *Donald Campbell and Co. Ltd v
Pollock* [1927] AC 732, and the speech of Viscount Cave LC, which continues to represent the
law after the introduction of the CPR, see *Groupama Insurance Co. Ltd v Aon Ltd* [2003] EWCA Civ
1846, [2004] 1 All ER (Comm) 893).

In exercising its discretion on costs the court is required to have regard to all the circumstances, and in particular to the following matters (**CPR, r. 44.2(4) and (5)**):

(a) the conduct of all the parties, which means primarily, if not exclusively, their conduct in
relation to the litigation (*Bontoft v East Lindsey District Council* [2008] EWHC 2923 (QB), LTL
18/12/2008). Conduct includes:

    (i)   the extent to which the parties followed **PD Pre-action Conduct and Protocols** or
any relevant pre-action protocol;

    (ii) the extent to which it was reasonable for the parties to raise, pursue or contest each
of the allegations or issues;

    (iii) the manner in which the parties pursued or defended the action or particular
allegations or issues;

    (iv) whether the successful party exaggerated the value of the claim;

(b) whether a party was only partly successful; and

(c) any payment into court or admissible offer to settle.

Factor (a)(i) is one of the methods by which pre-action protocols will be enforced, albeit indirectly (others include a less tolerant attitude on applications by defaulting parties for more time
and for relief from sanctions and the interest sanctions discussed in **chapter 48**). **PD Pre-action
Conduct and Protocols, para. 16**, provides that the court will look at the overall effect of any
non-compliance with the protocols when deciding whether to impose sanctions. These may
include ordering the defaulting party to pay all or part of those costs, or to pay those costs on
an indemnity basis. In *Straker v Tudor Rose* [2007] EWCA Civ 368, [2008] Costs LR 205, the defendant
solicitors acted for both sides in a proposed transaction to purchase two properties off-plan,
conditional on obtaining finance by a particular date. The claimant sued the solicitors for failing
to seek an extension to that date when the finance was not available in time. The solicitors
made a Part 36 offer to the effect that the claimant would in any event only have obtained
finance for one of the properties. At trial the claimant won in respect of only the one property,
but recovered damages exceeding the amount offered by the solicitors. The judge awarded the
claimant only limited pre-action costs, and no costs from issue, on the ground that the claimant
had failed to negotiate, on the theory that if he had done so, the defendant would have improved
the offer above the amount awarded at trial. This was held to be so seriously wrong that it was
outside the generous ambit of the discretion on costs. Partial success on the claim justified a
one-third or one-quarter reduction in the claimant's costs. Adding a proportionate further
discount for non-compliance with the protocol (not negotiating), the Court of Appeal substituted an overall award of 60 per cent of the claimant's post-issue costs.

Factors (a)(ii) and (c) allow the court to take into account the extent to which the overall winner was in fact successful on the various issues, heads of claim etc. raised in the case, when
dealing with costs. This is intended to support the aspects of the overriding objective relating
to identifying the real issues in the case, and only pursuing those issues to trial (see **CPR,
r. 1.4(2)(b) and (c)**). Factor (a)(iii), which covers unreasonable conduct, could also be used
against parties who fail to conduct litigation in accordance with the overriding objective, such

as those who are unreasonably uncooperative (see **r. 1.4(2)(a)**). Factors (a)(ii) and (a)(iii) seem to have been important in justifying reducing the costs ordered against the unsuccessful party in *Mansfield v Wright* (2000) LTL 17/7/2000, where both sides failed to act on an indication by the trial judge to attempt to negotiate a settlement when the trial was adjourned part heard.

Exaggeration of the value of a claim (factor (a)(iv)) will obviously be relevant where the claim is inflated for the purpose of bringing it in the High Court or to have the case allocated to a higher track than it deserves. Overestimating the value of a genuine claim does not amount to exaggeration within the meaning of **r. 44.2(4)(c)** (*Morton v Portal Ltd* [2010] EWHC 1804 (QB), LTL 30/7/2010). There will only be exaggeration where there is inflation of the claim meriting criticism (*Morton v Portal Ltd*). In *Midland Packaging Ltd v HW Chartered Accountants* [2010] EWHC B16 (Mercantile) (BAILII), LTL 10/8/2010, although the judge considered exaggeration in terms of money (recovery of only one-third of the amount of the claim), it is reasonably clear from the judgment that the real exaggeration that resulted in an adverse costs order took the form of exaggerated evidence. At [52] the problem identified was that the claimant had a tendency to exaggerate on very significant aspects of his case, and that this took up a considerable amount of time and costs at trial. It could also be used in cases where exaggeration of the claim makes it difficult for the defendant to assess its true value for the purposes of making an offer to settle. *Painting v University of Oxford* [2005] EWCA Civ 161, [2005] PIQR Q5, and *Allison v Brighton and Hove City Council* [2005] EWCA Civ 548, LTL 22/4/2005, cases involving exaggeration in relation to Part 36 offers, are discussed at **66.49**. In *Hooper v Biddle* [2006] EWHC 2995 (Ch), LTL 11/10/2006, the original claim was for £3.75 million, the proceedings claimed £350,000, but judgment was for £38,000. Given the degree of exaggeration, the court made no order as to costs. A failed accusation of exaggeration may warrant an indemnity costs order (*Clarke v Maltby* [2010] EWHC 1856 (QB), LTL 27/7/2010).

Shirley v Caswell [2001] Costs LR 1 is a decision on its facts, and does not lay down a principle that orders for payment of a proportion of the other side's costs should not be made in certain circumstances (such as after service of notice of discontinuance). See *Dooley v Parker* [2002] EWCA Civ 1188, LTL 5/7/2002.

Costs follow the event

The rule that costs follow the event generally means that the successful party will obtain a costs order against the loser. So the first question is which party has been successful. The judge must consider the underlying realities of the litigation (*Onay v Brown* [2009] EWCA Civ 775, LTL 10/8/2009). A claimant who establishes liability and recovers more than a Part 36 offer is successful for this purpose (*Jackson v Ministry of Defence* [2006] EWCA Civ 46, LTL 12/1/2006, see **66.49**; *Widlake v BAA Ltd* [2009] EWCA Civ 1256, [2010] PIQR P4). Likewise, a claimant who establishes liability subject to a 25 per cent reduction for contributory negligence is the successful party (*Onay v Brown*). Even where the claimant insists on 100 per cent liability, a finding of 20 per cent contributory negligence (which was less than the 25 per cent offered in the defendant's Part 36 offer) will not, of itself, amount to 'conduct' within **CPR, r. 44.2(5)**, to justify depriving the claimant of part of its costs (*Sonmez v Kebabery Wholesale Ltd* [2009] EWCA Civ 1386, LTL 22/10/2009).

While in general a claimant who establishes liability and the right to more than nominal damages will be the successful party, there are cases where the damages recovered are so minimal that the defendant is the victor for the purposes of costs. An example is *Marcus v Medway Primary Care Trust* [2011] EWCA Civ 750, [2011] PIQR Q4, where a claimant recovered £2,000 on a claim alleged to be worth £525,000, and was ordered to pay 75 per cent of the defendants' costs. In a case primarily about regulating the future relations between the parties as opposed to seeking damages for past events, there is a reduced significance in any money judgment forming part of the overall relief in deciding which party is successful (*L'Oréal SA v Bellure NV* (2010) LTL 27/7/2010, where no order for costs was appropriate because in commercial terms the result was a draw).

68.6

Applying the general rule, in *Islam v Ali* [2003] EWCA Civ 612, LTL 26/3/2003, the court reversed the trial judge's costs order where he had failed to give due regard to the fact that the defendant had won in principle. See also *Adamson v Halifax plc* [2002] EWCA Civ 1134, [2003] 1 WLR 60. Having determined which party has won, the starting point is that the winner should recover its costs as against the unsuccessful party, although there are factors which may lead to a different order and they are discussed below. In *Scherer v Counting Instruments Ltd* [1986] 1 WLR 615 the Court of Appeal set out the following principles for the award of costs:

(a) The normal rule is that costs follow the event. The party who turns out to have unjustifiably either brought another party before the court, or given another party cause to have recourse to the court to obtain his rights, is required to recompense that other party in costs; but

(b) The judge has, under the Senior Courts Act 1981, s. 51, an unlimited discretion to make what order as to costs he considers that the justice of the case requires.

(c) Consequently a successful party has a reasonable expectation of obtaining an order for his costs to be paid by the opposing party, but has no right to such an order, for it depends upon the exercise of the court's discretion.

(d) This discretion is not one to be exercised arbitrarily; it must be exercised judicially, that is to say, in accordance with established principles and in relation to the facts of the case.

(e) The discretion cannot be well exercised unless there are relevant grounds for its exercise, for its exercise without grounds cannot be a proper exercise of the judge's function.

(f) The grounds must be connected with the case. This may extend to any matter relating to the litigation, but no further. In relation to an interim application, 'the case' is restricted to the application, and does not extend to the whole of the proceedings (*Hall v Rover Financial Services (GB) Ltd* [2002] EWCA Civ 1514, [2003] 1 Costs LR 70).

(g) If a party invokes the jurisdiction of the court to grant him some discretionary relief and establishes the basic grounds therefor, but the relief sought is denied in the exercise of discretion, as in *Dutton v Spink and Beeching (Sales) Ltd* [1977] 1 All ER 287 and *Ottway v Jones* [1955] 1 WLR 706, the opposing party may properly be ordered to pay his costs. But where the party who invokes the court's jurisdiction wholly fails to establish one or more of the ingredients necessary to entitle him to the relief claimed, whether discretionary or not, it is difficult to envisage a ground on which the opposing party could properly be ordered to pay his costs.

Under the CPR, in *Johnsey Estates (1990) Ltd v Secretary of State for the Environment* [2001] EWCA Civ 535, LTL 11/4/2001, the court repeated the above principles but added that:

(a) A judge may make different orders in relation to discrete issues in the case and should do so where a party has been successful in relation to some issues and unsuccessful on others.

(b) A party which has behaved unreasonably in relation to the litigation may be deprived of some or all of its costs.

It is incumbent on a judge to give reasons for departing from the usual rule that costs follow the event (*Brent London Borough Council v Aniedobe (No. 2)* (1999) LTL 23/11/99; *Aspin v Metric Group Ltd* [2007] EWCA Civ 922, LTL 25/9/2007). See also *Bellamy v Central Sheffield University NHS Trust* [2003] EWCA Civ 1124, LTL 2/7/2003. The approach, stated in *English v Emery Reimbold and Strick Ltd* [2002] EWCA Civ 605, [2002] 1 WLR 2409, to appeals against judgments with inadequate reasons (see **75.10**) applies also in this context (*Gould v Armstrong* [2002] EWCA Civ 1159, LTL 23/7/2002).

A court is not required to order costs. **CPR, r. 44.2(2)**, begins with the words 'If the court decides to make an order for costs'. Where a court feels that the appropriate exercise of the discretion leads to no order for costs, it may decline to make any order (*English v Emery Reimbold and Strick Ltd*). If there is no overall winner, an alternative achieving much the same result is to make an express order that there be no order for costs (*Cantor Gaming Ltd v Gameaccount Global Ltd* [2007] EWHC 2381 (Ch), LTL 25/9/2007).

Re Elgindata Ltd (No. 2) [1992] 1 WLR 1207 is authority for the proposition that a successful party is in normal circumstances entitled to have an order for costs against the loser, subject to limited exceptions such as where a successful party recovers no more than nominal damages or where the successful party has acted improperly or unreasonably. The Court of Appeal interfered with a costs order in *Alpha Chauffeurs Ltd v Citygate Dealership Ltd* [2002] EWCA Civ 207, LTL 21/2/2003, which placed the main burden of the costs on a party which had been broadly successful, and substituted an order complying with the principle that costs follow the event. It is different where a claimant wins on one issue, but the defendant is in reality the winner: in such a case it may be right to order the claimant to pay the defendant's costs (*HLB Kidsons v Lloyd's Underwriters Subscribing to Lloyd's Policy No. 621/PKID00101* [2007] EWHC 2699 (Comm), LTL 5/12/2007). Although *Re Elgindata Ltd (No. 2)* pre-dates the CPR it has been applied in a number of cases under the CPR (for example, *AEI Rediffusion Music Ltd v Phonographic Performance Ltd* [1999] 1 WLR 1507) and the starting point in most applications for costs is that the loser should pay the winner's costs. *Re Elgindata Ltd (No. 2)* provides a useful guide to the court's approach, but it cannot fetter the general discretion the court has under **r. 44.2**. As Lightman J put it in *Bank of Credit and Commerce International SA v Ali (No. 4)* (1999) 149 NLJ 1734, 'The straitjacket imposed on the court by *Re Elgindata Ltd (No. 2)*... is gone, and the search for justice is untrammelled by constraints beyond those laid down by the new code [i.e. the CPR] itself'.

Pre-CPR authorities must be treated with caution. The introduction of the CPR has encouraged parties to narrow issues and focus their attention on the points of dispute in a proportionate way. The courts have been encouraged to examine the degree of success and to tailor their orders to reflect that success and the justice of the case. Courts will also consider in detail the conduct of the parties. This has led to courts making issue-based orders and percentage orders (see *Johnsey Estates (1990) Ltd v Secretary of State for the Environment* and *Gwembe Valley Development Co. Ltd v Koshy (No. 2)* (2000) The Times, 30 March 2000, though some difficulties in making such orders were identified in *Shirley v Caswell* [2002] Lloyd's Rep PN 955; see **68.11** to **68.14**).

Material change in successful party's case　When the basis of a party's case is changed, that **68.7** party usually has to amend their statement of case, which usually results in an order that they pay the costs of and occasioned by the amendments (see **68.31** and **PD 19A**). Sometimes the court goes further and makes an order for costs covering all or part of the proceedings (*Beoco Ltd v Alfa Laval Co. Ltd* [1995] QB 137). It is a frequent occurrence that the case that emerges at trial is not exactly the same as that set out in the statements of case. It is a question of degree whether this will require the statements of case to be amended, and in practice it is only substantial changes which justify such a course. Likewise, it is a question of degree whether any difference between the pleaded case and the facts as they emerge at trial justify departing from the general rule that costs follow the event. It is wrong to depart from the general rule where any differences are small (*Alli v Luton and Dunstable NHS Trust* [2005] EWCA Civ 551, LTL 27/4/2005). Where the differences are material, and particularly where the losing party may have been misled, it would be appropriate to deprive the successful party of some or all of their costs.

Where there is no 'event'　Where honours are broadly even the starting point is no order as **68.8** to costs (*Taylor v Burton* [2014] EWCA Civ 63, LTL 6/2/2014). In *Dearling v Foregate Developments (Chester) Ltd* [2003] EWCA Civ 913, LTL 9/6/2003, at the invitation of the judge the parties had negotiated a commercial settlement with the defendant making a modest payment to the claimant. In the circumstances the settlement did not reflect the merits of the case, and it was impractical for the court to look into the facts. It was held that in the absence of any good reason for making some other order, the fall-back position was to make no order as to costs. Contrast *BCT Software Solutions Ltd v C. Brewer and Sons Ltd* [2003] EWCA Civ 939, LTL 11/7/2003, where an apportionment of costs by the trial judge after the claim was compromised, but with costs to be determined by the judge, was upheld on appeal. A judge limited to determine costs may legitimately decide there is no complete agreement to compromise a claim if the parties have not agreed the question of costs (see *BCT Software Solutions Ltd v C. Brewer and Sons Ltd*).

Success and State benefits

68.9   In *McCaffery v Datta* [1997] 1 WLR 870, the claimant was given judgment in a personal injuries case for £22,373. There had been a payment into court (which, under the CPR, would be a Part 36 offer to settle) of £2,500 (the maximum exempt sum under the former provisions of the Social Security Administration Act 1992) some time before trial. The amount of recoupable benefits under the Act was £25,419. The effect was that all the damages awarded had to be paid by the defendant to the compensation recovery unit of the Department of Social Security, leaving the claimant with nothing. In those circumstances the defendant contended that it should recover its costs from the date of the payment in. The Court of Appeal held that although the claimant had recovered nothing in the action, it could not be said that the defendant, who had to pay £22,373, was successful. The judge's costs order was therefore varied so as to award the claimant the costs of the action.

The general costs rules where there has been a Part 36 offer to settle are considered at **66.39** to **66.52**. How those rules relate to benefits recoupment was considered in *Bajwa v British Airways plc* [1999] PIQR Q152. In this case the defendant paid into court the sum of £2,500 at a time when the CRU certificate was in the sum of £2,573.34. It was held that the effective payment in was these two sums added together, that is, £5,073.34. At trial the claimant recovered £4,874.43. An appeal against the CRU certificate resulted in the recoupable benefits being reduced to £142.80. The defendant therefore had to pay £142.80 to the Secretary of State and £4,731.63 to the claimant. However, the important figures for costs purposes were the judgment (£4,874.43), which was less than the effective payment in (£5,073.34). The correct order on costs was that the claimant should recover her costs to the last date for accepting the payment in, but had to pay the defendant's costs thereafter.

Nominal damages

68.10   A claimant who has claimed substantial damages, but has only recovered nominal damages, will normally be ordered to pay the defendant's costs (*Texaco Ltd v Arco Technology Inc.* (1989) *The Times*, 13 October 1989; *Mappouras v Waldrons Solicitors* [2002] EWCA Civ 842, LTL 30/4/2002; for an exceptional case in which no order as to costs was made see *Bank of Credit and Commerce International SA v Ali (No. 4)* (1999) 149 NLJ 1734). Where a claimant recovers more than nominal damages, but only a small proportion of the amount claimed, costs should follow the event unless this conflicts with some other established principle (*Gupta v Klito* (1989) *The Times*, 23 November 1989), for example, that costs will be reduced if a claim has been exaggerated (see **68.15**).

Partial success

68.11   **Partial success to be taken into account**   The conduct that has to be taken into account in deciding orders as to costs includes whether the claimant has succeeded in whole or in part (**CPR, r. 44.2(4)(b)**), and also includes whether it was reasonable for a party to raise, pursue or contest a particular allegation or issue (**r. 44.2(5)(b)**). It may therefore be wrong in principle to allow a party all its costs where it has been unsuccessful on some issues, and hence such an order may in some circumstances be overturned on appeal (*Winter v Winter* (2000) LTL 10/11/2000; *Darougar v Belcher* [2002] EWCA Civ 1262, LTL 25/7/2002).

Before the introduction of the CPR, an 'issue' for this purpose was a matter which in itself either gave a right to relief or constituted a defence. Thus, in running-down actions it was held that liability and quantum were separate issues (see *Wagstaffe v Bentley* [1902] 1 KB 124), but negligence and contributory negligence were not (see *Quirk v Thomas* [1916] 1 KB 516). There is no rule that costs must be awarded in the same percentages as the decision on contributory negligence (*Horth v Thompson* [2010] EWHC 1674 (QB), LTL 7/7/2010). The CPR avoid the word 'issue' and the phrase 'cause of action', and instead refer to a party being successful 'on part of its case' (**r. 44.2(4)(b)**). This is certainly a deliberate move away from the old technical cases

Commentary

with what would now be Part 36 offers to settle). The question is whether a point on which the successful party lost is of such significance that it would be just for the court to make a separate costs order in respect of it (D. *Pride and Partners v Institute for Animal Health* [2009] EWHC 1617 (QB), LTL 14/7/2009). A slightly different formulation, based on *SmithKline Beecham plc v Apotex Europe Ltd (No. 2)* [2004] EWCA Civ 1703, [2005] Costs LR 293, is whether the successful party has lost on a discrete issue and whether the case is sufficiently exceptional to justify depriving the winner of some of its costs.

The result is that the court may reflect partial success in the order for costs whenever as a matter of reality the overall winner has not been totally successful, whether or not the partial failure was on a matter constituting of itself a right to relief or defence. Merely failing to recover as much as had been claimed does not give grounds for reducing the winner's costs (*Hall v Stone* [2007] EWCA Civ 1354, [2008] CP Rep 263). In general, a claimant who succeeds on primary liability is regarded as the overall winner, despite a finding of contributory negligence (*Krysia Maritime Inc. v Intership Ltd* [2008] EWHC 1880 (Admlty), [2008] 2 Lloyd's Rep 707, where it was also held the principle is the same in the Admiralty Court). There may be exceptions where the primary issue is the degree of contributory negligence, or where there is a finding of very substantial contributory negligence. A failure to mitigate may be reflected in a percentage reduction in the costs recovered (*Walsh v Singh* [2011] EWCA Civ 80, [2011] 2 FLR 599; *Abbott v Long* [2011] EWCA Civ 874, [2012] RTR 1).

The starting point on final costs orders is that the winner should be awarded the whole of its costs of the proceedings, even if there are issues on which he had been unsuccessful (*Actavis Ltd v Merck and Co. Inc.* [2007] EWHC 1625 (Pat), LTL 7/8/2007). However, depriving the winner of a percentage of his costs does not rest on a need to find unreasonable or improper conduct. Where the successful party had lost on a large number of issues the court was justified in making no order for costs (*Peer International Corporation v Editora Musical de Cuba* [2008] EWCA Civ 1260, LTL 26/11/2008).

Winter v Winter (2000) LTL 10/11/2000 made the point that the CPR have changed the position regarding awarding the whole costs to a party meeting with 'substantial success'. In *Stocznia Gdanska SA v Latvian Shipping Co.* (2001) *The Times*, 25 May 2001, Thomas J said that the reasonableness of raising an issue which was lost by the party who was the overall winner is not necessarily relevant to the question of depriving the successful party of part of its costs under r. 44.2(4)(b). In *National Westminster Bank plc v Kotonou* [2007] EWCA Civ 223, LTL 26/2/2007, the defendant sought to have a guarantee set aside on five grounds, four of which were unsuccessful. The Court of Appeal held that the case called for a percentage costs order, and said it would have been a surprise if the judge had awarded the claimant the whole of its costs. Each side was ordered to pay 50 per cent of the other side's costs.

68.12 **Principles** It is suggested that the following principles emerge from the authorities:

(a) The courts are likely to concentrate on whether a party was successful on an issue not the reasonableness of raising the issue in the first place (*AEI Rediffusion Music Ltd v Phonographic Performance Ltd* [1999] 1 WLR 1507; *Stocznia Gdanska SA v Latvian Shipping Co. (No. 2)* [1999] 3 All ER 822).

(b) A party which abandons issues, either prior to, or during, a trial, may be taken to have lost on those issues, which may be reflected in the order as to costs (*English v Emery Reimbold and Strick Ltd* [2002] EWCA Civ 605, [2002] 1 WLR 2409; *Carver v Hammersmith and Queen Charlotte's Health Authority* (2000) LTL 7/3/2001).

(c) There will often be an overlap in the evidence relating to issues upon which a party is successful and those upon which it fails. This has to be taken into account. In such circumstances it may be appropriate to award the successful party a proportion of its costs taking into account the fact that the paying party will have to pay its lawyers for the entire costs of the proceedings (*Liverpool City Council v Rosemary Chavasse Ltd* (1999) LTL 19/8/99, in which the court discounted the successful party's costs to 75 per cent).

(d) The award of costs to the successful party may be tempered by the manner in which it took the points, hence late amendment may lead to the loss of some or all of the costs up to the point of amendment and, in extreme cases, the award of the costs of the claim up to amendment against the successful party (for example, *Antonelli v Allen* (2000) *The Times*, 8 December 2000).

(e) Whether the issues on which the successful party lost materially contributed to the costs of the proceedings. If they had a negligible impact on overall costs, it may be appropriate to award the successful party all its costs (*Fleming v Chief Constable of Sussex* [2004] EWCA Civ 643, LTL 5/5/2004).

(f) It is not an argument that the party with overall success had to take certain bad points in order to obtain ATE insurance (*Kew v Bettamix Ltd* [2006] EWCA Civ 1535, [2007] PIQR P210).

(g) Where it is clear there has been partial success, but (as happens sometimes when costs are reconsidered on appeal) there is inadequate material on which to decide on an apportionment, no order as to costs may be the appropriate order (*Hackney London Borough Council v Campbell* [2005] EWCA Civ 613, LTL 28/4/2005).

The above points can only represent a guide, and there is a danger that too much can be read into any single case. The courts are anxious to preserve a wide degree of flexibility and discretion in the award of costs. As Lightman J put it in *Bank of Credit and Commerce International SA v Ali (No. 4)* (1999) 149 NLJ 1734:

My task is...to take an overview of the case as a whole...and reach a considered conclusion on two questions, first who succeeded in the action, and second (taking into account the answer to the first issue) what order for costs justice requires.

68.13   Percentage or issues-based costs orders   Where both parties are successful on some, but not all, of the issues in a case, the court may, instead of awarding the whole costs of the action to the ultimately successful party, award the costs of proving some of the issues to the unsuccessful party. The usual approach in the event of partial success is to award the successful party a percentage of its costs rather than an 'issues-based' order (see **CPR, r. 44.2(7)**, which says that an issues-based order should only be made when other forms of order are impracticable). In *English v Emery Reimbold and Strick Ltd* [2002] EWCA Civ 605, [2002] 1 WLR 2409 at [115], Lord Phillips of Worth Matravers MR said that making issues-based orders create difficulties at the stage of assessing costs because the costs judge has to master the issues in detail before determining whether individual items are attributable to issues which have been allowed or disallowed. It is for this reason that percentage orders are generally to be preferred.

It may be appropriate to make an issues-based costs order (rather than a percentage order) where there is a substantial imbalance between the amount of costs incurred by the different parties (*Research in Motion UK Ltd v Visto Corporation* [2008] EWHC 819 (Pat), LTL 22/4/2008). Such orders are unusual, though, because it is highly undesirable to make a costs order which results in the assessment of both sides' costs, and the disparity has to be substantial before this can be justified (*Abbott Laboratories Ltd v Evysio Medical Devices ULC* [2008] EWHC 1083 (Pat), LTL 21/5/2008). There is a well-established 'double deduction' rule when making a percentage costs order (e.g. *Earl of Malmesbury v Strutt and Parker* [2008] EWHC 424 (QB), 118 Con LR 68). Under this, if the claimant wins, but the defendant is successful on an issue representing 7.5 per cent of the claimant's costs, the claimant would be awarded 85 per cent of its costs (the 15 per cent deduction covering the 7.5 per cent of the claimant's costs on the issue he lost, and 7.5 per cent of the defendant's costs attributable to that issue which the claimant ought to pay). This rule is not applied mechanically. It is not a matter of simply calculating how many hours of the trial were taken up with the lost issue compared with the whole trial, or counting pages of the trial transcript (*Abbott Laboratories Ltd v Evysio Medical Devices ULC*). Often the judge needs to take into account work done before trial, the relative expense of the evidence required on the different issues, and the degree of overlap in investigating the successful and unsuccessful issues.

In most cases an essentially broad-brush approach is adopted in arriving at the figure for a percentage-based costs order (*HTC Corporation v Yozmot 33 Ltd* [2010] EWHC 1057 (Pat), LTL 8/6/2010). In a case where on cross-appeals the respondent succeeded on six out of the seven grounds of appeal, but where the appellant succeeded in reducing the judgment from £6 million to £3 million, as the greater proportion of the costs of the appeal was spent on the issues on which the respondent succeeded, the respondent was awarded 25 per cent of its costs, the discount reflecting the degree of financial success enjoyed by the appellant (*Cleveland Bridge UK Ltd v Multiplex Constructions (UK) Ltd* [2010] EWCA Civ 449, [2010] CILL 2863).

68.14 Success on liability, refusal of relief   Related problems arise in cases where the claimant succeeds in proving the pleaded cause of action, but is not awarded any relief or remedy. Obviously, if damage is part of the cause of action, as in negligence, then the defendant succeeds and should get the costs of the action. Where, conversely, relief is refused on discretionary grounds, further investigation or analysis may be necessary before the question of costs can be decided. If it should have been clear to the claimant that no relief would be granted, costs should be awarded to the defendant. If the matter preventing the court from granting the remedy sought arose during the course of the litigation, such as the appointment of an administrator preventing the court granting relief under an unfair prejudice petition under the Companies Act 2006, s. 994, probably the best result would be for the claimant to be awarded costs up to the date of the event preventing relief being granted, and for the defendant to be awarded costs thereafter. See *Re a Company (No. 008126 of 1989)* [1992] BCC 542.

68.15 Opponent's case unclear   In *Sengoz v Secretary of State for the Home Department* [2001] EWCA Civ 1135, *The Times*, 13 August 2001, an appeal from a tribunal was discontinued when the Secretary of State agreed to the matter being reheard before the tribunal. The court accepted that, until the grounds of appeal were fully considered, the Secretary of State was not in a position to decide on the appropriate course to take. In the circumstances there was no order as to costs.

Misconduct by the successful party

68.16 Principles   Misconduct by the successful party may result in costs not following the event (CPR, r. 44.2(4)(a)). Misconduct for this purpose must relate to the proceedings, and exterior dishonest conduct is not a basis for depriving a successful party of its costs (*Hall v Rover Financial Services (GB) Ltd* [2002] EWCA Civ 1514, [2003] 1 Costs LR 70, albeit a decision which was regarded as no more than a statement of practice in *Groupama Insurance Co. Ltd v Aon Ltd* [2003] EWCA Civ 1846, [2004] 1 All ER (Comm) 893). The court can take into account conduct before, as well as during, the proceedings, and in particular the extent to which the parties followed any relevant pre-action protocol. It can also take into account the manner in which a party pursued or defended the claim or a particular issue or allegation, and whether the claim was exaggerated by the claimant (r. 44.2(5)(d)). In *Hobbs v Marlowe* [1978] AC 16 the successful claimant was deprived of all of his costs apart from the issue fee because he had exaggerated his claim to avoid the action being referred to small arbitration.

68.17 Misconduct and final costs orders   Much depends on the nature of the misconduct and its consequences. Misconduct which might justify depriving the successful party of its costs would not necessarily be sufficient to justify an order requiring the successful party to pay the unsuccessful party's costs (see *Scherer v Counting Instruments Ltd* [1986] 1 WLR 615 at p. 622). A successful defendant was deprived of half the costs of the hearing in *Cable v Dallaturca* (1977) 121 SJ 795 for failing to serve an expert's report in accordance with the rules of court. In *Liverpool City Council v Rosemary Chavasse Ltd* (1999) LTL 19/8/99 (discussed at 68.12) the successful council had acted in flagrant disregard for the approach embodied in the CPR, and left

Commentary

matters to the last minute. This resulted in a costs order being reduced from 75 per cent to 50 per cent. In *Wright v HSBC Bank plc* [2006] EWHC 1473 (QB), LTL 30/6/2006, the unsuccessful claimant raised several arguments for disallowing all or part of the defendant's costs (21 months for the case to get to trial; failing to negotiate; and failing to inform the claimant of the true basis of her claim). None of these were meritorious points, but £5,000 was disallowed from the defendant's costs to reflect a failure to give full disclosure. In *Grupo Torras SA v Al-Sabah* [1999] CLC 1 a claim had been made against a number of defendants in conspiracy, dishonest assistance in breach of trust and related causes of action. The claims against the fourth, sixth and tenth defendants failed because the claimant failed to prove the essential element of dishonesty as against them. Mance LJ, who was the trial judge, held the fourth defendant would only recover 50 per cent of his costs because, although he did not realise there was a fraud, he was involved in deliberately backdating relevant documentation. The sixth defendant only recovered one-third of his costs. He was the finance director of one of the companies, and had deliberately deceived the auditors and gave untrue evidence at trial. The tenth defendant was a professional man who had created false documentation, misled the auditors and gave untruthful evidence at trial. He too only recovered one-third of his costs. Repeated lies by the successful defendant justified depriving her of two-thirds of her costs in *AXA Insurance plc v Sulaman* [2009] EWCA Civ 1331, [2010] CP Rep 19 (where it was emphasised that judges must be careful about relying on the facts of previous cases when deciding costs issues). In *Groupama Insurance Co. Ltd v Aon Ltd* [2003] EWCA Civ 1846, [2004] 1 All ER (Comm) 893, a second defendant which had to some extent brought the proceedings on itself by its conduct, but which succeeded at trial, recovered 90 per cent of its costs from the unsuccessful first defendant.

In *Smiths Ltd v Middleton (No. 2)* [1986] 1 WLR 598 the defendant had made a payment into court exceeding the amount recovered by the claimants, but the judge made no order as to costs after the payment in, because the defendant had brought the action on himself through keeping incomplete accounting records. A claimant who would have lost on the original statements of case, but who won on the basis of an amendment made at a very late stage was ordered to pay the defendant's costs of the action in *Anglo-Cyprian Trade Agencies Ltd v Paphos Wine Industries Ltd* [1951] 1 All ER 873.

68.18   Misconduct and interim costs orders   A failure to make full and frank disclosure which was not sufficiently serious to justify discharging a without notice order was nevertheless used to justify depriving the successful party of 25 per cent of the costs of an interim application to discharge the order in *Re Industrial Services Group Ltd (No. 1)* [2003] BPIR 392. In *R (Teleos plc) v Commissioners of Customs and Excise* [2005] EWCA Civ 200, [2005] 1 WLR 3007, the claimant issued an interim payment application which came on for hearing seven days later. The defendant's evidence was largely an analysis of material supplied by the claimant and was served about the day before the hearing. Skeleton arguments were exchanged on the day before the hearing. The application was dismissed. In those circumstances the Court of Appeal held the judge had been wrong to make no order as to costs. There was insufficient time to negotiate (so as to avoid the need for a hearing), due to the short period secured by the claimant for the hearing. Although the defendant's evidence was technically late, there was no prejudice. An order for costs to follow the event under **CPR, r. 44.2(2)(a)**, was substituted.

In *Jones v University of Warwick* [2003] EWCA Civ 151, [2003] 1 WLR 954, an inquiry agent tricked his way into the claimant's home posing as a market researcher and covertly filmed the claimant carrying out functions inconsistent with her claimed disability. The court allowed the video evidence but ordered the insurer to pay the costs of the admissibility hearing to mark the court's disapproval of the defendant's conduct.

68.19   Refusal to participate in ADR   A successful party may be deprived of its costs for unreasonably refusing to participate in arbitration or mediation procedures. In *Dunnett v Railtrack plc* [2002] EWCA Civ 303, [2002] 1 WLR 2434, a successful appellant was deprived of its costs when it refused mediation because it was not prepared to pay the claimant any further sum and was confident that it would succeed in its appeal. In depriving the successful party of its costs the court stated that parties and their lawyers should ensure that they are aware that it is one of their duties fully to consider ADR, especially when the court has suggested it, and not merely to turn it down flatly. In *Leicester Circuits Ltd v Coates Industries plc* [2003] EWCA Civ 333, LTL 5/3/2003, a successful appellant was deprived of costs when it withdrew from mediation shortly before the trial.

An order depriving a successful party of its costs is an exception to the rule that costs follow the event. The burden is on the unsuccessful party to establish that the rule should be departed from on the ground of an unreasonable refusal to agree to ADR (*Halsey v Milton Keynes General NHS Trust* [2004] EWCA Civ 576, [2004] 1 WLR 3002). The *Halsey* principle is not engaged through failing to initiate proposals for mediation (*Vale of Glamorgan Council v Roberts* [2008] EWHC 2911 (Ch), LTL 8/12/2008). Where a failure to mediate was caused by unreasonable attitudes taken by both sides, it is not open to the losing party to use the winner's failure as a basis for an adverse costs order (*Earl of Malmesbury v Strutt and Parker* [2008] EWHC 424 (QB), 118 Con LR 68). A party who agrees to mediation and takes an unreasonable stance in the mediation is in the same position as a party who unreasonably refuses to mediate at all (*Earl of Malmesbury v Strutt and Parker*). However, proof of conduct during mediation and other ADR processes is often impossible because of the rules relating to without prejudice and confidentiality.

Factors relevant to the question of whether a refusal to agree to ADR was unreasonable include, but according to Dyson LJ are not limited to:

(a) the nature of the dispute;
(b) the merits of the case (it may not be reasonable for a party with a weak case to insist on use of ADR);
(c) the extent to which other settlement methods had been attempted;
(d) whether the costs of the ADR procedure would be disproportionately high;
(e) whether any delay in setting up and attending the ADR procedure would be prejudicial; and
(f) whether it would be just to impose a costs sanction.

Silence in the face of an offer to participate in ADR is, as a general rule, of itself unreasonable (*PGF II SA v OMFS Co. 1 Ltd* [2013] EWCA Civ 1288, [2014] 1 WLR 1386). There is no presumption in favour of mediation or other forms of ADR. Each case depends on its own circumstances. A public authority is treated in the same way as any other category of party, and is under no additional responsibility to agree to the use of ADR.

Where a party reasonably declines mediation it will not be penalised in costs (*Société Internationale de Télécommunications Aéronautiques SC v Wyatt Co. (UK) Ltd* [2002] EWHC 2401 (Ch), LTL 15/11/2002). In *Hurst v Leeming* [2002] EWHC 1051 (Ch), [2003] 1 Lloyd's Rep 379, Lightman J held that a refusal to mediate was only justified if it would have no reasonable prospect of success. Refusing to negotiate after receiving Part 36 offers is unlikely to be unreasonable; see *Daniels v Commissioner of Police for the Metropolis* [2005] EWCA Civ 1312, [2006] CP Rep 9, discussed at 66.49. Small building disputes are one kind of case for which mediation is suitable (*Burchell v Bullard* [2005] EWCA Civ 358, [2005] BLR 330).

See also 73.13.

Other costs sanctions

68.20 As well as disallowing costs, the court has various other powers that may be exercised to reflect a finding of misconduct against either party. These powers include:

(a) Ordering costs to be paid on the indemnity basis rather than the standard basis. This is discussed in more detail at 68.21.
(b) Ordering payment of interim costs forthwith, rather than requiring the party obtaining the costs order to wait until after trial for payment (CPR, r. 44.2(1)(c)). Note that an

order stating the amount payable in respect of costs (such as a summary assessment) must be complied with within 14 days (**r. 44.7**).

(c) Ordering payment of interest on costs from or until a certain date, including a date before judgment (**r. 44.2(6)(g)**). The normal rule is that Judgments Act 1838 rate interest (currently 8 per cent a year simple interest) is payable on costs arising from court orders and judgments from the date of the judgment on liability.

(d) Ordering interest on costs at a rate different from the Judgments Act 1838 rate (e.g. **PD Pre-action Conduct and Protocols, para. 16(d)**, which allows the court to impose interest on costs at a rate up to 10 per cent above base rate in cases where there has been non-compliance with **PD Pre-action Conduct and Protocols** or a relevant pre-action protocol).

Indemnity-basis costs to reflect misconduct

68.21   One of the circumstances in which the court may order one party to pay another party's costs on the indemnity basis (see **71.44**) is where the court wishes to penalise the paying party for its misconduct in relation to the proceedings. On an application for indemnity-basis costs of the proceedings, it is necessary to consider the criticised conduct in the context of the entire litigation. It is not the character of the misconduct which engages the court's discretion, but the justice of the circumstances in which the receiving party became involved in the proceedings. There is an important difference between mere errors of judgment in the conduct of a case and behaviour resulting in the overall unreasonable or unsatisfactory conduct of the litigation (*National Westminster Bank plc v Rabobank Nederland (No. 2)* [2007] EWHC 1742 (Comm), [2008] 1 All ER (Comm) 243). Where the losing party has acted consistently throughout, the absence of proportionality on an indemnity-basis assessment is a factor in favour of awarding costs on the standard basis (*Simms v Law Society* [2005] EWCA Civ 849, [2005] ACD 98).

The Court of Appeal has declined to set out principles on which the discretion to award indemnity-basis costs is to be exercised, beyond stating that an indemnity costs order will be appropriate where the facts of the case or the conduct of the parties removes it from the norm (*Excelsior Commercial and Industrial Holdings Ltd v Salisbury Hamer Aspden and Johnson* [2002] EWCA Civ 879, [2002] CP Rep 67). It follows that the following list can only be taken as indicative of situations where an indemnity costs order might be made:

(a) Where the claim is an abuse of the court's process. In *R (Taha) v Lambeth London Borough Council* (Administrative Court, 7 February 2002), the defendant council had failed to process a housing benefit application for eight months. It then sought possession on the basis of eight weeks' rent arrears. It was ordered to pay the tenant's costs on an indemnity basis. See also *Sodeca SA v NE Investments Inc.* [2002] EWHC 1700 (QB), LTL 27/8/2002.

(b) Where a party is involved in dishonesty, or has acted in such a way as deserves condemnation (*Sea Wanderer Ltd v Nigel Burgess Ltd* (CA, May 1990); *Wailes v Stapleton Construction and Commercial Services Ltd* [1997] 2 Lloyd's Rep 112). In *esure Services Ltd v Quarcoo* [2009] EWCA Civ 595, LTL 30/6/2009, it was held to be wrong not to award indemnity-basis costs against a party who dishonestly brought a claim.

(c) Where the party's conduct of the litigation has removed it from the usual and made it appropriate for an indemnity order to be made. In *Cooper v P & O Stena Line Ltd* [1999] 1 Lloyd's Rep 734 the court condemned an allegation of malingering as one of fraud which should be pleaded as such. In fact there was no evidence to support the allegation and indemnity costs were ordered. See also *Craig v Railtrack plc* [2002] EWHC 168 (QB), LTL 18/2/2002, and *Kiam v MGN Ltd (No. 2)* [2002] EWCA Civ 66, [2002] 1 WLR 2810, in which it was said that indemnity-basis costs would be justified if the conduct of the claim was unreasonable to a high degree. Unreasonable pre-action conduct combined with bringing the claim on a misguided basis justified an indemnity costs order in *Noorani v Calver (No. 2)* [2009] EWHC 592 (QB), LTL 27/3/2009.

(d) Flagrant breaches of court orders, including unless orders (*Baron v Lovell* [1999] CPLR 630).

(e) Unreasonable pursuit of a weak claim or defence. See, for example, *Amoco (UK) Exploration Co. v British American Offshore Ltd* [2002] BLR 135. There must be something to mark the case out as unusual (*Shaina Investment Corporation v Standard Bank London Ltd* [2002] CPLR 14). It was not unreasonable for two drivers to maintain their denials of liability through to trial in a claim brought by the passengers in one of the vehicles where the witness statements left open the possibility of blame resting with one or other of the drivers or being shared between them (*Burton v Kingsley* [2005] EWHC 1034 (QB), [2006] PIQR P2). Despite a resounding defeat in *Balmoral Group Ltd v Borealis (UK) Ltd* [2006] EWHC 2531 (Comm), LTL 24/10/2006, the claim did have a solid basis, so it was not a suitable case for an indemnity-basis costs order. A weak case does not justify an indemnity-basis costs order, but having a case doomed to failure may do so. In *Wates Construction Ltd v HGP Greentree Allchurch Evans Ltd* [2005] EWHC 2174 (TCC), LTL 4/11/2005, an indemnity-basis costs order was made from the point, after the exchange of witness statements, when the claimant knew or ought to have known the case would fail.

(f) Where a stay or anti-suit injunction is granted for breach of an arbitration or jurisdiction clause (*A v B (No. 2)* [2007] EWHC 54 (Comm), [2007] 1 All ER (Comm) 633). Other first-instance cases making indemnity-basis costs orders for breach of jurisdiction, anti-suit and arbitration clauses are *Kyrgyz Mobil Tel Ltd v Fellowes International Holdings Ltd* [2005] EWHC 1314 (Comm) and *National Westminster Bank plc v Rabobank Nederland (No. 3)* [2007] EWHC 1742 (Comm), [2008] 1 All ER (Comm) 266. A similar approach was adopted when a party took an unmeritorious point over jurisdiction in an adjudication case (*Harris Calnan Construction Co. Ltd v Ridgewood (Kensington) Ltd* [2007] EWHC 2738 (TCC), [2008] Bus LR 636). In *C v D* [2007] EWCA Civ 1282, [2008] Bus LR 843, Longmore LJ declined to come to a definitive conclusion on the proper approach on this question (at [32]), and made a standard-basis costs order on the facts of the case (which was based on the doctrine that agreement on the seat of an arbitration was analogous to an exclusive jurisdiction clause, as opposed to being an actual jurisdiction clause). In some cases the claimant will be able to formulate a claim for an anti-suit injunction as a separate claim for breach of a jurisdiction clause or anti-suit clause. In these cases the successful party may have a claim for damages representing the costs of defending any proceedings brought in breach of the clause, and may also be entitled to the costs of the English proceedings for the injunction. The costs as damages claim is assessed on the indemnity basis (*National Westminster Bank plc v Rabobank Nederland (No. 3)*).

(g) Failure to send a letter before claim (*Phoenix Finance Ltd v Fédération Internationale de l'Automobile* [2002] EWHC 1242 (Ch), *The Times*, 27 June 2002).

(h) Where litigation has been pursued for extraneous motives. In *Amoco (UK) Exploration Co. v British American Offshore Ltd* the claimant conducted itself on the basis that its commercial interests took precedence over all other considerations.

The above examples all suggest some degree of turpitude and condemnation from the court, but this is not a necessary prerequisite for an indemnity costs order (*Reid Minty v Taylor* [2001] EWCA Civ 1723, [2002] 1 WLR 2800). Indemnity-basis costs may be awarded where rejection of a Part 36 offer is held to have been highly unreasonable: see **66.50**. There are other special cases where indemnity-basis costs will be ordered because of the nature of the litigation (see **68.46** and **68.47**).

Indemnity costs in favour of a publicly funded party   There has been debate about whether **68.22** it is appropriate to make an indemnity costs order in favour of a party in receipt of public funding. The award of costs is compensatory and the litigant should not profit from any costs order made. In normal circumstances an indemnity costs order will ensure that the receiving party will receive more of their costs from the paying party (see **71.44**). However, a party in receipt of public funding has no obligation to pay costs. Thus the lawyer may receive a windfall, being the difference between a public funding assessment and an indemnity assessment. This reason for not awarding indemnity costs was rejected in *Brawley v Marczynski (No. 2)* [2002] EWCA Civ 1453, [2003] 1 WLR 813, in which it was held that an indemnity costs order can be made in favour of a publicly funded party where the court intends to mark its disapproval of the paying party's conduct.

Claims wrongly commenced in the High Court

68.23   Where a claim has been commenced in the High Court which should have been commenced in the County Court in accordance with the Courts and Legal Services Act 1990, s. 1, or any other enactment, the court must take that error into account when quantifying costs (Senior Courts Act 1981, s. 51(8)). Usually this will result in a reduction in the costs which would otherwise be allowed, but such reduction must not be in excess of 25 per cent.

Costs of unnecessary attendance

68.24   A party should not be ordered to pay the costs of another party who need not have attended a hearing (*Cullen v Paterson* [2002] EWCA Civ 339, LTL 8/3/2002). Respondents who file written submissions or attend on applications for permission to appeal are in particular danger of being deprived of their costs, even if permission to appeal is refused (*Jolly v Jay* [2002] EWCA Civ 277, *The Times*, 3 April 2002; **PD 52C, para. 20(1)**).

INFORMING THE CLIENT

68.25   Where a costs order is made against a legally represented client who is not present in court when the order is made, the solicitor representing the client is under a duty to inform the client of the costs liability within seven days of the order being made (**CPR, r. 44.8**). The 'client' includes anyone, such as an insurer, trade union, the LSC or Lord Chancellor, which has instructed the solicitor or is liable for the solicitor's fees (**PD 44, para. 10.1**). At the same time as informing the client about the order, the solicitor should explain why it was made. The court has the power to order the solicitor to produce evidence that reasonable steps were taken to comply with the duty to notify the client (**PD 44, para. 10.3**).

INTERIM COSTS ORDERS

68.26   At the end of almost every interim application, and when almost any interim application is disposed of by consent, an order will be made or agreed declaring which party should pay the costs of that application. This includes without notice applications (*Mackay v Ashwood Enterprises Ltd* [2013] EWCA Civ 959, [2013] 5 Costs LR 816). Costs of interim applications are in the discretion of the court, but the discretion is usually (but not always) exercised in favour of the party who was successful in the application. Success may be established either by winning a contested application, or by showing that the need to make the application arose through the default of the other party. In deciding on 'success' the court may take into account the correspondence, and in particular whether an adequate response was made to the letter before claim (if relevant) (*Fox Gregory Ltd v Hamptons Group Ltd* [2006] EWCA Civ 1544, LTL 4/10/2006). It is usual to order costs of the proceedings in favour of a successful applicant in a summary judgment or striking-out application, even if remedies are left over to be determined later (*Experience Hendrix v Times Newspapers Ltd* [2008] EWHC 458 (Ch), LTL 14/3/2008). If an application is merited, but is discontinued when the respondent takes steps (such as filing an amended statement of case) to meet the issue, the applicant is the successful party, and should be awarded its costs of the interim application (*Finning UK Ltd v Inveresk plc* [2006] EWHC 2031 (QB), LTL 18/9/2006). Likewise, a party who consents to an interim order at the last minute will almost certainly have to pay the costs of the application (see *Law Society v Hadcroft* [2009] EWHC 947 (Ch), LTL 28/5/2009). Other types of application are essentially of a case management nature, so there is no 'winner', and in these applications the costs are usually treated as part of the general costs of the claim. Conversely, if a case management matter is unreasonably opposed, the applicant should be awarded its interim costs (*Finning UK Ltd v Inveresk plc*). To cater for these various possibilities (and situations where neither party is entirely successful) the courts can resort to a wide selection of different interim costs orders.

It is usual to reserve costs in applications for interim injunctions (*Picnic at Ascot Inc. v Derigs* [2001] FSR 2). This is not an invariable rule (*Albon v Naza Motor Trading Sdn Bhd (No. 4)* [2007] EWCA Civ 1124, [2008] 1 All ER (Comm) 351 at [21]), particularly where the interim injunction is granted on an issue which is unlikely to be determined at trial.

PD 44, para. 4.1, provides that the court may make an order about costs at any stage in a case, and in particular it may make interim costs orders when it deals with interim applications.

After proceedings have been dismissed the court still has jurisdiction to make an order concerning the costs of an application in the proceedings (*Re Ryan Developments Ltd* [2002] EWHC 1121 (Ch), [2002] 2 BCLC 792). Unless costs are reserved (see term 13 in **table 68.1**) at the first hearing, the court on a second hearing (unless it is an appeal) in the same claim has no jurisdiction to make a costs order in respect of the first hearing. In *Griffiths v Commissioner of Police of the Metropolis* [2003] EWCA Civ 313, LTL 5/3/2003, there was an interim hearing at which the judge ordered that a wasted costs order (see **68.67**) in respect of the costs of the interim hearing against the claimant and his solicitor be considered at the trial. This order was defective because it made no provision for who should pay the costs of the interim hearing, which meant that each side had to bear its own costs (see term 18 in **table 68.1**), whereas the judge plainly intended the claimant to have to pay the defendant's costs. On appeal it was held that the trial judge had no jurisdiction to make an order as to the costs of the interim hearing.

Summary assessment of interim costs

The costs of an interim hearing which has lasted less than a day ought to be dealt with by way of summary assessment there and then (**PD 44, para. 9.2**). There are exceptions where there is good reason not to assess summarily (**para. 9.2**). These might include: **68.27**

(a) where there are substantial grounds for disputing the sum claimed;
(b) where there is insufficient time to carry out the summary assessment;
(c) where there are complex legal arguments (*R v Cardiff City Council, ex parte Browne* (QBD, 11 August 1999));
(d) where the claim is a mortgage possession claim (**para. 9.3**);
(e) where the receiving party (as opposed to the paying party) is publicly funded (**para. 9.8**);
(f) where the receiving party (as opposed to the paying party) is under a disability (**para. 9.9**;
(g) where no statement of costs is served in time (see **32.30**, but see *MacDonald v Taree Holdings Ltd* [2000] CPLR 439, in which it was held that it may be permissible to conduct the summary assessment if time is given to the paying party to consider any schedule produced on short notice);
(h) in the early stages of continuing complex litigation (*Roundstone Nurseries Ltd v Stephenson Holdings Ltd* [2009] EWHC 1431 (TCC), [2009] 5 Costs LR 787 at [56]–[57]).

Where the court makes a summary assessment of interim costs, those costs will be stated in the order made by the court and will be payable in such period as the court decides (**CPR, r. 44.2(1)(c)**). Where the court does not specify a time for the payment of the costs, they are payable within 14 days (**r. 44.7**). Any application for an extension of time in which to pay such costs should be supported by evidence (*Pepin v Watts* [2001] CPLR 9).

Detailed assessment of interim costs

Orders for costs will be treated as requiring detailed assessment unless the order specifies the sum to be paid or states that fixed costs are to be paid (**PD 44, para. 8.2**). Detailed assessments generally take place after the proceedings are concluded (**CPR, r. 47.1**). The court may order, or the parties may agree in writing to treat the proceedings as concluded for this purpose **68.28**

(**PD 47, para. 1.2**), and the court may make an order allowing detailed assessment proceedings to commence where there is no realistic prospect of the claim proceeding (**para. 1.4**).

MEANINGS OF COSTS ORDERS

68.29   Various standard forms of wording are regularly used by the courts to express the decision on the incidence of costs. Usually it will be apparent from the whole of the document recording the order whether the costs provision covers the whole proceedings, or just some part of the claim (such as the costs of an interim application). Some of the forms used can apply to both final and interim costs, and some of the commonly occurring decisions can be expressed using more than one form of words, so some care is needed. **Table 68.1** sets out the meanings of the most commonly used forms of costs orders. More technical definitions for most of the terms can be found in **PD 44, para. 4.2**.

Table 68.1   Meanings of common costs orders

Term	Meaning
1. Claimant's costs	As a final order, the claimant is entitled to recover its costs of the proceedings from the defendant.
2. Defendant's costs	As a final order, the defendant is entitled to recover its costs of the proceedings from the claimant.
3. Claimant's costs	In an interim application, the claimant is entitled to recover its costs of the application from the defendant.
4. Defendant's costs	In an interim application, the defendant is entitled to recover its costs of the application from the claimant.
5. Claimant's costs in any event	Identical meaning to 1 and 3 above.
6. Defendant's costs in any event	Identical meaning to 2 and 4 above.
7. Costs in the case	This is an order made on interim applications and hearings, often where the court makes case management decisions or otherwise where there is no obvious winner of the interim application. The order means the interim costs form part of the general costs of the proceedings, so the party awarded its costs of the proceedings on the final disposal of the claim will be entitled to be paid its costs of the interim application.
8. Costs in the application	Identical meaning to 7 above.
9. Claimant's costs in case	This is an order half-way between 3 and 7 above. It is typically used where the claimant has met with partial success on an interim application. It means that if the claimant is awarded its costs of the proceedings on the final disposal of the claim, it will be entitled to be paid its costs of the interim application, but if the defendant is awarded costs on the final disposal of the claim, each party bears its own costs of the interim application.
10. Claimant's costs in application	Identical meaning to 9 above.
11. Defendant's costs in case	This is the reverse of 9 above. If the defendant is awarded its costs of the proceedings on the final disposal of the claim, it will be entitled to be paid its costs of the interim application, but if the claimant is awarded costs on the final disposal of the claim, each party bears its own costs of the interim application.

Term	Meaning
12. Defendant's costs in application	Identical meaning to 11 above.
13. Costs reserved	This is an interim costs order deferring the decision on costs to a later hearing, when the judge will usually make orders relating to both hearings. If the judge dealing with the second hearing does not make an order relating to the first hearing, the costs of that hearing are treated as being in the case (see 7 above), unless the judge does not address his mind to the issue, in which event the costs may be determined on an appeal (*Taylor v Burton* [2014] EWCA Civ 21, LTL 23/1/2014). This form of order should not be used if nothing further can happen at the second hearing (which may be the trial) to affect the costs of the first hearing (*Elvee Ltd v Taylor* [2001] EWCA Civ 1943, [2002] FSR 48).
14. Costs thrown away	Broadly similar to 3 and 4 above. It is typically made when a judgment or order is set aside, such as on a successful application to set aside a default judgment. In such a case the order entitles the claimant to recover from the defendant the costs of: • preparing for and attending any hearing relating to making the original order or judgment that is now being set aside; • preparing for and attending any hearing to set aside the original order or judgment; • preparing for and attending any adjourned relevant hearing; and • any steps to enforce the original order or judgment.
15. Costs of and occasioned by	This is the usual order made when the court allows an application to amend a statement of case. See further 68.31. This order requires the party making the amendment to pay the other party's costs of: • preparing for and attending any hearing seeking permission to amend; and • any consequential amendments to its own statement of case.
16. No order as to costs	Each party bears its own costs of the application or proceedings.
17. Each party to pay its own costs	Identical to 16 above.
18. Order silent on costs	The general rule is that neither side can recover costs (**CPR, r. 44.10(1)(a); PD 23A, para. 13.2**). Exceptions cover: • trustees and personal representatives who can always recover their costs out of the fund (**CPR, r. 44.10(1)(b)**); • parties entitled to recover costs pursuant to a lease, mortgage or other security, who continue to be entitled to recover their costs under a provision of the contract (**r. 44.10(1)(b)**); and • orders granting permission to appeal, orders granting permission to apply for judicial review, and orders and directions made on applications without notice. These are deemed to include an order for the applicant's costs in the case (**r. 44.10(2)**). Any party affected by such a deemed order for costs may apply at any time to vary the order (**r. 44.10(3)**).
19. Costs here and below	This is an order often made on disposal of appeals. The party who is successful on the appeal is by this order entitled to recover its costs both of the appeal and in the court below. See 68.36.
20. Detailed assessment of the costs of the [Claimant] which are payable by the Lord Chancellor	Order authorising the court to assess the costs payable from public funds of a litigant (whether they are successful or not) with the benefit of public funding. This is the modern form of what used to be called a 'legal aid taxation'.

Commentary

Fit for counsel

68.30   **PD 44, para. 5.1,** allows the court when making a costs order for detailed assessment (including both interim costs orders and final costs orders made at trial) to state an opinion as to whether or not the hearing was fit for representation by one or more counsel. This will generally only be done where the paying party challenges the use of counsel, where the court wishes to record its opinion that the case was not fit for counsel, or where more than one counsel appeared for a party (**para. 5.1(2)**).

COSTS OF PARTICULAR TYPES OF PROCEEDINGS

Amendment

68.31   The costs of and arising from any amendment to a statements of case are, unless the court orders otherwise, borne by the party making the amendment (see notes to **PD 19A**). An order for payment of the costs of an amendment will also require payment of the costs of making consequential amendments to other documents.

It is possible to ask for a less onerous costs order where, for example, the need to amend cannot be characterised as being the fault of the party seeking permission. Unreasonably refusing to consent to proposed amendments may result in the respondent being ordered to pay the applicant's costs of the application (although in principle, the applicant should remain responsible for the costs of and occasioned by the actual amendments). See *La Chemise Lacoste SA v Sketchers USA Ltd* (2006) LTL 24/5/2006. Another point is that if permission is sought at a very late stage to make amendments having a fundamental effect on the way the case is set out, particularly where the other side are prejudiced, such as by being unable to make an effective Part 36 offer to settle, the court may impose very stringent costs terms when granting permission to amend. Thus in *Beoco Ltd v Alfa Laval Co. Ltd* [1995] QB 137 permission to amend was granted on terms that the claimant paid the defendant's costs up to the date of the amendment, and 85 per cent of the defendant's costs thereafter. Such a penal approach is not always correct. In *Professional Information Technology Consultants Ltd v Jones* [2001] EWCA Civ 2103, *The Independent*, 28 January 2002, the claim succeeded on the basis of a late amendment, but this was reflected by simply reducing the costs of the claim recovered by the claimant by one-third.

Costs of pre-commencement disclosure and disclosure against non-parties

68.32   Applications for pre-commencement disclosure and for orders against persons who are not parties for disclosure of documents were considered in **chapter 50**. The general rule is that the court must award the costs of the application to the person against whom the order is sought (**CPR, r. 46.1**). The practice has been to add the costs of the application as a head of damages in the case of pre-commencement disclosure. This may no longer be necessary as under the CPR the pre-commencement application is made in the same action as the main claim, whereas under the old system the application formed a separate action commenced by its own originating process. In the case of disclosure against a non-party the costs will be part of the costs of the claim, and should be dealt with by a specific costs order between the parties. The court retains a discretion to make a different costs order in a particular case, having regard to all the circumstances, including the extent to which it may have been reasonable for the respondent to have opposed the disclosure application (**r. 46.1(3)**). This may be the case where the respondent has failed to honour its obligations under the Access to Health Records Act 1990 (which applies to most medical records compiled since 1 November 1991) or under any applicable pre-action protocol (which will potentially apply to many applications for pre-commencement disclosure against likely defendants).

Costs after transfer

Subject to any order that may have been made by the original court, if proceedings are trans- **68.33** ferred from one court to another, the court to which they are transferred will deal with all questions as to costs, including the costs incurred before the transfer (County Courts Act 1984, s. 45; **CPR, r. 44.10(5)**).

Costs before track allocation or where the claim has never been allocated

The special rules relating to costs in cases on the small claims track and fast track do not apply **68.34** until a claim is allocated to one of these tracks (**CPR, r. 46.11(1) and (2); PD 46, para. 7.1(1)**). Once a claim is allocated to either of these tracks the special rules relating to that track will apply to work done before as well as after allocation, with the exception that any costs orders made before a claim is allocated to one of these two tracks are not affected by any subsequent allocation (**PD 46, para. 7.1(2)**). This means, for example, that where default judgment is entered on a small-value claim, the costs restrictions in **CPR, Part 27**, do not apply, although the fixed costs rules in **Part 45** would be applied instead.

Where a claim has not been allocated to a track the court retains a general discretion as to costs, but will attach considerable weight to the track that the matter would have been allocated to. In particular, the court may restrict the assessed costs to the costs that would have been allowed on the track to which the claim would have been allocated if allocation had taken place (**r. 46.13(3)**). Thus in *Voice and Script International v Alghafar* [2003] EWCA Civ 736, LTL 8/5/2003, a failure to allocate the case to the small claims track did not preclude the court from awarding the costs as if it had been. Conversely in *Woodings v British Telecommunications plc* (2003) LTL 17/3/2003 several related claims were settled, without issuing proceedings, for less than £1,000 per claimant. Although this would normally have indicated that the claims were small claims, the court was persuaded that, because of the extent of the technical and medical evidence required, they would have been allocated to the multi-track and accordingly costs could be awarded as for that track.

Reallocation from the small claims track

Before making an order to reallocate a claim from the small claims track to another track, the **68.35** court must decide whether any party is to pay costs to any other party down to the date of the reallocation order (**PD 46, para. 8.1**). Such costs must be those payable under **CPR, Part 27**, which in effect means that they are limited to fixed costs and any further costs which may be ordered for unreasonable behaviour (**r. 27.14**). If a costs order is made on reallocation, the court should make an immediate summary assessment of those costs (**PD 46, para. 8.1**). Fast track or multi-track costs rules will apply from the date of reallocation (**CPR, r. 27.15**).

Costs after an appeal

A court dealing with a case on appeal can make orders relating to the costs of the proceedings **68.36** giving rise to the appeal as well as the appeal itself (**CPR, r. 44.10(4)**). If an appeal is successful, the appeal court may order the losing party to pay the costs 'here and below', or may make different orders relating to the proceedings at the two levels, or may leave the costs order of the court below undisturbed while making whatever order may be appropriate for the costs of the appeal. It may be appropriate to deprive a party of its costs if the decision on the appeal turned on points not raised below, or on points not raised in the notice of appeal, or where the appeal is only partly successful or where the court's time has been wasted.

Wills cases

In a case involving a disputed will, costs normally follow the event. An alternative costs order **68.37** may be made where the testator or those interested in the residue of the estate had been the cause of the litigation or if the circumstances led reasonably to an investigation. Applying these principles in *Re Good* [2002] EWHC 640 (Ch), *The Times*, 22 May 2002, Rimer J ordered the unsuccessful parties to pay only half the claimant's costs. In contentious probate cases, if the testator, or the person interested in the residue, is the real cause of the need for the litigation, costs usually come out of the estate (*Kostic v Chaplin* [2007] EWHC 2909 (Ch), [2008] 2 Costs LR 271). If the circumstances led reasonably to an investigation of the matter, costs are usually borne by those who incur them (*Spiers v English* [1907] P 122; *Re Cutcliffe's Estate* [1959] P 6). In probate claims, a defendant requiring the will to be proved in solemn form (see **CPR, r. 57.7(5)**) will not be ordered to pay costs unless there is no reasonable ground for opposing the will (Senior Courts Costs Office Guide 2013, para. 2.8(e)).

Winding-up petitions

68.38   If a company is ordered to be wound up, unless otherwise stated, the petitioner will be entitled to his costs as a claim in the winding up. The supporting creditors may also be awarded one set of costs to be shared among them, provided they have given notice of intention to appear or been given permission to appear (see **82.72**). Where a petition is adjourned, unless the contrary is said, the costs will generally be in the petition (para. 2.14). See **82.77** to **82.87**.

Judicial review and public law proceedings

68.39   Government departments are not exempt from costs orders (*R (Bahta) v Secretary of State for the Home Department* [2011] EWCA Civ 895, [2011] CP Rep 43). Costs in judicial review and other public law proceedings generally follow the event. However, an unsuccessful claimant in judicial review proceedings is not usually ordered to pay more than one set of costs where there are interested parties in addition to the defendant (*Bolton Metropolitan District Council v Secretary of State for the Environment* [1995] 1 WLR 1176). A second set of costs may be ordered where the interested party deals with a separate issue not dealt with by the defendant. An unsuccessful party is more likely to be ordered to pay a second set of costs at first instance than on an appeal (when the issues should have crystallised, and so there is less likelihood of a second party having a separate interest that needs to be represented), and paying a third set of costs will in any event be rarely justified (*Bolton Metropolitan District Council v Secretary of State for the Environment*). An order that the claimant pays the defendant's costs includes both the costs to the final hearing and the costs before the grant of permission (*R (Davey) v Aylesbury Vale District Council* [2007] EWCA Civ 1166, [2008] 1 WLR 878).

Whether a coroner, inferior court or tribunal should be ordered to pay or recover its costs in proceedings to challenge its jurisdiction or decision largely depends on the stance it takes in the High Court. In *R (Davies) v HM Deputy Coroner for Birmingham* [2004] EWCA Civ 207, [2004] 1 WLR 2739, the Court of Appeal stated the following principles:

(a)   The established practice is to make no order for costs where the inferior court or tribunal does not appear in the High Court (see also *Moore's (Wallisdown) Ltd v Pensions Ombudsman* [2002] 1 WLR 1649), unless there has been a flagrant instance of improper behaviour, or where the court or tribunal unreasonably refuses to sign a consent order.

(b)   Where the inferior court or tribunal takes an active part, costs usually follow the event. Where the inferior court or tribunal loses, the costs it is usually ordered to pay are not limited to the amount by which the costs of other parties were increased by its participation (*Moore's (Wallisdown) Ltd v Pensions Ombudsman*).

(c)   Where the inferior court or tribunal plays a neutral role, assisting the High Court on matters of jurisdiction or procedure, the established practice is to make no order for costs for or against it. This is subject to the court's overall discretion on costs, which may make it just for the applicant to be compensated in costs out of public funds through a costs order against the inferior court or tribunal.

The general principles governing costs when proceedings are discontinued, including *Sengoz v Secretary of State for the Home Department* [2001] EWCA Civ 1135, *The Times*, 13 August 2001, in relation to judicial review, are considered at **55.8**. If the court can with confidence conclude that an applicant would have won had the matter proceeded to a full hearing, the applicant can be awarded his costs (*R (G) v Worcestershire County Council* [2005] EWHC 2332 (Admin); *DB v Worcestershire County Council* [2006] EWHC 2613 (Admin), LTL 3/11/2006). Where the public body concedes and an application for judicial review is withdrawn by consent, it is wrong not to award the claimant its costs (*Mendes v Southwark London Borough Council* [2009] EWCA Civ 594, [2010] HLR 3). Likewise, where the public body fails to provide reasons for a decision on having been invited to do so under the pre-action protocol, and provides reasons following a reference to the CJEU (*R (Mellor) v Secretary of State for Communities and Local Government* [2009] EWCA Civ 1201, LTL 18/11/2009).

Review proceedings concerning various environmental matters must not be prohibitively expensive (Directive 85/337/EEC, art. 10(a); Directive 96/61/EC, art. 15(a)). This is a matter that has to be addressed by the court as opposed to the costs judge (*R (Edwards) v Environment Agency (No. 2)* [2010] UKSC 57, [2011] 1 WLR 79). This should be done in the early stages of the proceedings. It may be addressed by making a protective costs order or a costs capping order (see **chapter 44**), and may need to be revisited at the end of the proceedings. It was recognised in *Venn v Secretary of State for Communities and Local Government* [2014] EWCA Civ 1539, [2015] 1 WLR 2328 at [34] that the costs protection regime introduced by **CPR, r. 45.41** is not Aarhus-compliant, but that reform is for Parliament.

With effect from 13 April 2015, the applicant or defendant in proceedings for judicial review may not be ordered to pay the costs of an intervener unless there are exceptional circumstances making this appropriate (Criminal Justice and Courts Act 2015, s. 87). This restriction on costs orders applies to proceedings in the High Court and Court of Appeal, but not in the Supreme Court (s. 87(3)). An applicant or defendant in judicial review proceedings may apply under **CPR, r. 46.15**, for an order for costs against an intervener if one of the four conditions set out in Criminal Justice and Courts Act 2015, s. 87(6), is satisfied. These include cases where the intervener's evidence and representations have not been of significant assistance to the court, or where the intervener has behaved unreasonably.

MISCELLANEOUS SITUATIONS IN WHICH COSTS DO NOT FOLLOW THE EVENT

The following are situations where costs orders usually do not follow the event: **68.40**

(a) The costs of any application to extend time are borne by the party making the application.

(b) A party failing to make admissions of facts or in relation to documents after service of a notice to admit facts or documents, or after service of a list of documents, is usually responsible for paying the costs of proving those matters.

(c) In a claim for defamation concerning words which impute unchastity or adultery to a woman or girl, costs must not exceed the damages awarded, unless the court is satisfied there were reasonable grounds for bringing the claim (Slander of Women Act 1891, s. 1).

(d) If successive actions are brought against persons jointly or otherwise liable for the same damage, costs will be ordered in favour of the claimant in the first action only unless there were reasonable grounds for bringing the later actions (**Civil Liability (Contribution) Act 1978, s. 4**).

MULTIPLE PARTIES AND CLAIMS

Multiple defendants

Where a claimant succeeds against joint tortfeasors, costs will be ordered against each defend-   **68.41**
ant, and the claimant can then recover costs against any one (or more) of the defendants

(*Niru Battery Manufacturing Co. v Milestone Trading Ltd* [2003] EWHC 1032 (Comm)). Any defendant paying such costs can then seek a contribution from the others under the **Civil Liability (Contribution) Act 1978**. If successful defendants are separately represented, the claimant should be liable for any additional costs only if the separate representation was reasonable. An example of what can happen where joint defendants are successful is *Korner v H. Korner and Co. Ltd* [1951] Ch 10. Eight defendants were jointly represented, and seven of them were successful in the action. It was held that generally the defence costs should be regarded as incurred by each defendant equally, which would in this case have resulted in the claimant paying seven-eighths of the total defence costs. However, as different defences had been delivered for each defendant, each successful defendant was awarded one-eighth of the general costs of the proceedings, together with such costs and counsel's fees as were attributable to their own defence.

Bullock and *Sanderson* orders

68.42   Where a claimant claims against two defendants in the alternative, and succeeds against one only, the court may, in its discretion, make a special order that the unsuccessful defendant must pay the successful defendant's costs (*Irvine v Commissioner of Police for the Metropolis* [2005] EWCA Civ 129, LTL 3/2/2005). These orders cannot be made where the claim fails against both defendants (*McGlinn v Waltham Contractors Ltd (No. 5)* [2007] EWHC 698 (TCC), [2008] Bus LR 278) or where the defendants succeed in defending a large part of the claim (*Whitehead v Searle* [2007] EWHC 2046 (QB), LTL 11/9/2007). It is clear that in this area the court has a wide measure of discretion (*Goldsworthy v Brickell* [1987] Ch 378). That said, from *Besterman v British Motor Cab Co.* [1914] 3 KB 181, it is apparent that, in deciding whether to make a special order, the court must first look at all the facts the claimant knew or could reasonably have discovered as at the date the defendants were joined and consider whether the joinder was reasonable. Factors bearing on this, according to the Court of Appeal in *Irvine v Commissioner of Police for the Metropolis*, include:

(a) whether the claims against the various defendants are made 'in the alternative';
(b) the nature of the evidence and allegations against the defendants who were eventually successful;
(c) whether the causes of action are connected with each other; and
(d) whether the unsuccessful defendant had blamed the other defendants.

If it was not reasonable to join the two defendants, costs should follow the event. In such a case the successful defendant will recover its costs from the claimant and the claimant will recover the costs of the claim against the unsuccessful defendant from the unsuccessful defendant. The unsuccessful defendant is not required to reimburse the claimant for the costs the claimant has to pay to the successful defendant.

If, on the other hand, it was reasonable to join the two defendants, the court has a choice of two special orders, the choice being in the court's discretion (per Lord Brandon of Oakbrook in *Bankamerica Finance Ltd v Nock* [1988] AC 1002). The special orders are known as *Bullock* orders, from *Bullock v London General Omnibus Co.* [1907] 1 KB 264, and *Sanderson* orders, from *Sanderson v Blyth Theatre Co.* [1903] 2 KB 533.

For the purposes of exposition, assume that the claim of the claimant ('C') against the first defendant ('D1') is dismissed, but that C obtains judgment against the second defendant ('D2'). In a *Bullock* order, C would be ordered to pay D1's costs, but would recover its own costs and would be reimbursed in respect of the costs it has had to pay to D1 from D2. The difference between a *Bullock* order and the usual rule that costs follow the event is that if costs followed the event C would not be reimbursed by D2 for the costs C had to pay D1. In a *Sanderson* order, D2 has to pay C's costs, and D2 also has to pay D1's costs direct. C has no liability to pay D1's costs. Provided all parties are solvent, the eventual effect of *Bullock* and *Sanderson* orders is the same. However, the *Bullock* form is more usual because it most closely follows the rule that costs follow the event. Traditionally, the *Sanderson* form has been said to be appropriate where C is either legally aided or insolvent, because in those circumstances only a *Sanderson* order adequately protects the successful D1. Despite the traditional view, a *Sanderson* order was upheld by the House of Lords in *Bankamerica Finance Ltd v Nock* [1988] AC 1002 where D2, not C, was insolvent, the judge having decided to make a *Sanderson* order because it tended to spread the hardship caused by irrecoverable costs most fairly between C and D1, the success-ful defendant.

Multiple claimants

Problems are not so likely to be caused through having different judgments in respect of dif-ferent claimants because actions with joint claimants are only allowed to proceed if the claim-ants are jointly represented. It is implicit in this that there must be a large degree of identity of interest between the joint claimants, so split judgments must be very rare.

68.43

Counterclaims

For set-off of costs orders see **63.20**. Where the claim and counterclaim are unrelated, it may be appropriate to award the winner on the claim the costs of the claim and the winner on the counterclaim the costs of the counterclaim. The effect of this form of order was considered in *Medway Oil and Storage Co. Ltd v Continental Contractors Ltd* [1929] AC 88, where the House of Lords decided that this form of judgment entitled the defendant to all its costs of the action save those costs exclusively referable to the counterclaim. Under this principle there is no apportionment of costs, but items of costs common to both the claim and counterclaim, such as counsel's brief fee, may be divided between the claim and counterclaim. The distinction between apportionment and division is rather technical. Different courts vary in their willing-ness to apply the *Medway Oil* principles. They were applied in *Hay v Szterbin* [2010] EWHC 1967 (Ch), LTL 2/8/2010, where a Tomlin order merely referred to costs that 'relate exclusively' to the claim against one of three defendants. Conversely, in *Bateman v Joyce* [2008] EWHC 90100 (Costs), LTL 26/6/2008, the court said it would apply the principles only if the order used words such as 'for the avoidance of doubt the principle in *Medway Oil* applies'.

68.44

The net effect of *Medway Oil and Storage Co. Ltd v Continental Contractors Ltd* is, if the issues on the claim and counterclaim are similar, that the party recovering costs of the claim obtains by far the largest share. Even before the introduction of the CPR it was recognised that this does not always produce a just result (per Denning LJ in *Chell Engineering Ltd v Unit Tool and Engineering Co. Ltd* [1950] 1 All ER 378). While the court continues to have the power to order a party to pay the costs relating to a distinct part of the proceedings (**CPR, r. 44.2(6)(f)**), it should only do so if it is not practicable to make an order for payment of a proportion of the other side's costs or costs from a certain date only (**r. 44.2(7)**). Where the claim and counterclaim are related to each other, the costs order should usually award a percentage of the total costs of claim and counterclaim to the party who has achieved overall success (*English v Emery Reimbold and Strick Ltd* [2002] EWCA Civ 605, [2002] 1 WLR 2409; *Burchell v Bullard* [2005] EWCA Civ 358, [2005] BLR 330).

Another refinement is typified by *Box v Midland Bank Ltd* [1981] 1 Lloyd's Rep 434. The claimant recovered £5,000, and the defendant established a £39,000 equitable set-off. The Court of Appeal held that the judge should have made no order for costs. The approach exemplified by *Medway Oil and Storage Co. Ltd v Continental Contractors Ltd* was recognised by the Court of Appeal in *Universal Cycles plc v Grangebriar Ltd* [2000] CPLR 42 as being the usual form of order where the claimant is successful on the claim and the defendant is successful on a counterclaim. Where there is a set-off, the Court of Appeal in *Universal Cycles plc v Grangebriar Ltd* approved the *Chell Engineering* approach of awarding the overall winner either the entire costs of the claim, or a proportion of those costs. In *Universal Cycles plc v Grangebriar Ltd* itself the claim was for the price of goods sold and delivered, and there was a counterclaim alleging the goods were not of satisfactory quality and not fit for their purpose, it being further alleged that the value of the counterclaim exceeded that of the claim. At trial judgment was given to the claimant for £109,000, and judgment for the defendant on the counterclaim for £25,000. Neither party wanted a costs order in the *Medway Oil* form. The

Commentary

judge awarded the claimant its costs to the date of the defence and counterclaim, and required the claimant to pay half the defendant's costs thereafter. The Court of Appeal held that the judge had erred in placing too much emphasis on the amount of time spent on the substantive issues on which the respective parties had succeeded, and too little emphasis on the fact that the claimant had been the overall winner and on the late service by the defendant of its schedule of loss. Further, the order made by the judge stepped over the well-known line that a successful party should not, in the absence of a Part 36 offer and save perhaps in very exceptional cases, be ordered to pay any of the losing party's costs. An order was substituted for the defendant to pay all the claimant's costs, apart from the costs of the trial itself. In *Williams Corporate Finance plc v Holland* [2001] EWCA Civ 1526, LTL 22/10/2001, the claim consisted of seven heads, totalling £40,000. Most of the heads of claim were defeated, and the defendant succeeded on his counterclaim, but there was a net finding in favour of the claimant of about £2,500. The judge awarded the claimant its costs, but on appeal no order as to costs was substituted.

Additional claims under Part 20

68.45   Where a claimant succeeds in an action against a defendant, and the defendant successfully claims an indemnity from an additional party under **Part 20**, here referred to as a third party, the third party should be ordered to pay all the defendant's costs, including the costs the defendant will have been ordered to pay the claimant (*Jablochkoff Co. v McMurdo* [1884] WN 84). In such a case, if the defendant proves to be insolvent, the claimant will be unable to recover its costs from the third party, because it has no direct order against the third party. Therefore, it may, in a proper case, be appropriate to make an order akin to a *Sanderson* order requiring the third party to pay the claimant's costs directly (*Edginton v Clark* [1964] 1 QB 367). If a claimant succeeds against a defendant who succeeds against a third party, but the court considers that the defendant has defended the claim for reasons which provided no benefit to the third party, the third party will be ordered to pay the costs of the additional claim only (*Blore v Ashby* (1889) 42 ChD 682).

It is wrong to order the defendant to pay the third party's costs where the original claim and additional claim are partially successful (*Burchell v Bullard* [2005] EWCA Civ 358, [2005] BLR 330). A percentage order is more appropriate.

When considering costs orders between a defendant and a third party where the main proceedings fail with the result that the additional claim also fails, the usual rule is that costs follow the event under **CPR, r. 44.2(2)(a)**. This means that the court should usually ignore the incidence of costs in the main proceedings. A successful third party should recover its costs from the defendant even if the claimant in the main proceedings is impecunious (*Arkin v Borchard Lines Ltd (Nos. 2 and 3)* [2005] EWCA Civ 655, [2005] 1 WLR 3055 at [77]). As between the claimant and defendant when both the claim and additional claim fail, it may be appropriate to order the claimant to pay the defendant's costs on the claim and to reimburse the defendant in respect of the costs of both sides on the additional claim. This may be appropriate where the nature of the claim made the additional claim both inevitable and reasonable (*Arkin v Borchard Lines Ltd (Nos. 2 and 3)*), or where the main and additional claims are based on interconnected facts with the additional claim being contingent on the result in the main proceedings (*Green v Sunset and Vine Productions Ltd* [2009] EWHC 1610 (QB), LTL 10/11/2009). In an appropriate case the court may make such order as to costs as between claimants, defendants and third parties as may be just in accordance with the overriding objective (see *Arkin v Borchard Lines Ltd (Nos. 2 and 3)* at [75] and [77]). In this case the defendants and third parties were alleged to have collective responsibility for alleged anti-competitive activities. Costs orders were therefore made to share the costs burden equally among them (at [78] and [79]). A claimant who discontinues will normally have to pay the costs both of the defendant and the third party, unless the parties agree that the costs in the additional claim should be considered by the court, and the court finds, for example, that the additional claim would have failed (*Young v J. R. Smart (Builders) Ltd (No. 2)* (2000) LTL 7/2/2000).

Additional claims and Part 36 offers to settle

In *Alpha Chauffeurs Ltd v Citygate Dealership Ltd* [2002] EWCA Civ 207, LTL 21/2/2003, judgment was given **68.46** for the claimant in the sum of £47,862 against the first defendant. Judgment was given to the first defendant in the sum of £41,219 against the third party, and a counterclaim made by the first defendant against the claimant was dismissed. The third party was also joined as a second defendant, with the claimant recovering nominal damages of £2 against the third party (as a second defendant). The third party had made what would now be a Part 36 offer to settle in respect of the sum claimed by the claimant, but no Part 36 offer to the defendant. Applying the rule that costs follow the event:

(a) The claimant should have been ordered to pay the third party's costs in its capacity as second defendant, applying the usual rule discussed at **68.10** where nominal damages are recovered.

(b) The first defendant was ordered to pay the claimant's costs of bringing its claim against the first defendant and in defending the first defendant's counterclaim.

(c) The third party was ordered to pay the first defendant's costs of the additional claim and the first defendant's costs of defending the main claim.

(d) The third party was ordered to reimburse the first defendant for the costs it was ordered to pay the claimant under point (b) for bringing the main claim against the first defendant, but not the costs of either the claimant or the first defendant in relation to the counterclaim.

SPECIAL CASES

Litigants under a disability

Generally, where money is ordered or agreed to be paid to, or is ordered to be paid by, a child **68.47** or protected party, the court must order a detailed assessment of the costs payable by that party to his solicitor (**CPR, r. 46.4(1) and (2)**), including costs payable out of money belonging to the person under disability. On an assessment under **r. 46.4(2)**, the court must also assess any costs payable to the parties under disabilities (**r. 46.4(2)(b)**) unless:

(a) the court has issued a default costs certificate (see **71.15**) in relation to those costs; or

(b) the case is a road traffic accident claim where fixed costs are payable under **Part 45, Section II** (see **70.8** to **70.15**).

Exceptional cases where the court need not order the assessment of the costs payable by a party under a disability to his solicitor are set out in **PD 46, para. 2.1**. These cover cases where there is no need to protect the child or protected party by ordering an assessment. An example is where another party has agreed to pay a specified sum in respect of the child or protected party's costs and the solicitor waives the right to further costs (**para. 2.1(b)**). In personal injury claims where the damages do not exceed £25,000 (**CPR, r. 21.12(1A)**), where the costs payable comprise only the success fee or balance of the payment due to the child or protected person's legal representative under a CFA or DBA, the court may direct a summary assessment (**r. 46.4(5)**).

An order for costs can be made against the litigation friend acting for a claimant who is a person under disability by virtue of the undertaking to pay the costs that may be ordered against the person under disability required by **r. 21.4(3)(c)**. A successful party seeking such an order must apply promptly after judgment. The litigant normally indemnifies the litigation friend, but will not be required to do so where the litigation friend has acted for his or her own personal benefit (*Huxley v Wooton* (1912) 29 TLR 132) or if the litigation friend is guilty of some misconduct in relation to the proceedings.

Trustees, personal representatives and estates

Trustees and personal representatives are, in so far as costs are not recovered from another **68.48** party, entitled to recover their costs out of the fund. The court may, however, order otherwise and may do so where the party otherwise entitled to the costs has acted unreasonably. A trustee or personal representative who has acted substantially for his or her own benefit is likely to be treated like any other party. This may be the case where the proceedings are adversarial in nature (see *Holding and Management Ltd v Property Holding and Investment Trust plc* [1989] 1 WLR 1313; *Shovelar v Lane* [2011] EWCA Civ 802, [2011] 4 All ER 669).

On an unsuccessful challenge to the validity of a will, provided the challenge is a reasonable one and is based on an error which occurred in the drafting or execution of the will, the court will often order that all parties' costs are paid from the estate (*Marley v Rawlings (No. 2)* [2014] UKSC 51, [2015] AC 157 at [6]). This is more likely where the estate is very substantial (at [11]) and may be affected by other considerations, such as funding arrangements and whether the litigation is regarded as hostile.

Contractual rights to costs

68.49   Leases and other forms of contract sometimes have express terms that one party to the contract will pay the other's costs if the parties become involved in litigation. Costs orders in these cases tend to be made having regard to the contractual term on costs, as recognised by **CPR, r. 44.5.** The *Gomba Holdings (UK) Ltd v Minories Finance Ltd (No. 2)* [1993] Ch 171 principles (see **68.50**) are applied to other contractual rights to costs (*Church Commissioners for England v Ibrahim* [1997] 1 EGLR 13; *Chaplair Ltd v Kumari* [2015] EWCA Civ 798, [2015] CP Rep 46). A costs order will usually be made in accordance with contractual terms even in claims on the small claims track (*Chaplair Ltd v Kumari*).

Mortgagees' rights to costs

68.50   It is an established principle that a mortgagee is entitled to add any properly incurred costs, charges or expenses to the secured debt. Many mortgages make express provision for this, but even if they do not such a term will be implied (*Cottrell v Stratton* (1872) LR 8 Ch App 295). A court may disallow any costs, charges or expenses which were not 'properly incurred', unless the mortgage makes express provision to alter this (although a mortgage deed that purported to entitle the mortgagee to add improperly incurred costs might be open to question on public policy grounds: *Gomba Holdings (UK) Ltd v Minories Finance Ltd (No. 2)* [1993] Ch 171).

As an exception to the established principle, a mortgagee will not be permitted to add its costs to the security where a stranger impugns the title to the mortgage, or the enforcement or exercise of some right or power accruing to the mortgagee under the mortgage, even if the costs have been reasonably and properly incurred by the mortgagee (*Parker-Tweedale v Dunbar Bank plc (No. 2)* [1991] Ch 26).

In *Gomba Holdings (UK) Ltd v Minories Finance Ltd (No. 2)* [1993] Ch 171, the Court of Appeal laid down the following principles:

(a) Where there is a contractual right to costs, the discretion in the Senior Courts Act 1981, s. 51, should ordinarily be exercised so as to reflect that right.

(b) The power to disallow a mortgagee from adding its costs to the security derives from the power of the courts of equity to fix the terms on which redemption will be allowed.

(c) A decision by the court to refuse costs, in whole or in part, to a mortgagee litigant may be a decision in the exercise of the discretion under the Senior Courts Act 1981, s. 51, or in the exercise of its power to fix the terms on which redemption will be allowed, or a decision on the extent of the mortgagee's contractual right to add its costs to the security or a combination of these.

(d) A mortgagee is not to be deprived of a contractual or equitable right to add costs to the security merely by reason of an order for payment of costs made without reference to the mortgagee's contractual or equitable rights and without any adjudication of whether or not the mortgagee should be deprived of those costs.

(e) The contractual basis of assessing costs under most mortgages will be the indemnity basis (see **71.44** and **CPR, r. 44.5**).

The principles laid down in *Gomba Holdings (UK) Ltd v Minories Finance Ltd (No. 2)* are reflected by **PD 44, paras 7.1** to **7.3**, which are to the effect that generally the court will not assess a mortgagee's costs, because the mortgagee can simply add its indemnity-basis costs to the security. If the mortgagor wishes to object to the amount added to the security in this way, the mortgagor may apply for the taking of an account as to whether items added to the security were unreasonably incurred or were of an unreasonable amount. If the order is made, the account will be conducted before a costs officer.

Restrictive covenants

A claimant seeking a declaration of freedom from restrictive covenants under the Law of **68.51** Property Act 1925, s. 84(2), is seeking for his own benefit the protection of a court order against the existence of possible adverse rights. For the declaration to be effective it is necessary for the claimant to join as defendants everyone who might have such an adverse right. The policy adopted by the courts is that defendants joined in this type of claim should be able to participate without risks as to costs until they can make an informed decision on whether to oppose the application. Guidelines laid down by *University of East London Higher Education Corporation v Barking and Dagenham London Borough Council (No. 2)* [2004] EWHC 2908 (Ch), [2005] Ch 354 (applying *Re Jeffkins' Indentures* [1965] 1 WLR 375 and *Re Wembley Park Estate Co. Ltd's Transfer* [1968] Ch 491) are:

(a) the claimant must pay each defendant's costs on the indemnity basis up to the point when an informed decision could be made; and

(b) thereafter, any defendant opposing the application unsuccessfully must pay his own costs, but not those of the claimant.

GROUP LITIGATION

Where a claim is proceeding under a group litigation order (GLO), there will be 'indi- **68.52** vidual costs' which are specific to that particular claim, and 'common costs', which will be those incurred on the GLO issues, the costs of a claim proceeding as a test claim, and the lead solicitor's costs in administering the group litigants (**CPR, r. 46.6(2)**). If the group loses, the general rule is that the common costs will be divided equally among group members, who will have several liability for them (**r. 46.6(3)**). The individual costs of a particular claim will be that claimant's liability. A group litigant who loses will usually be ordered to pay the winning side's costs, and will also be liable for the costs of his own claim and an equal proportion, together with all the other group litigants, of the common costs (**r. 46.6(4)**). When making costs orders at hearings involving group and individual issues, the court will apportion the costs between the group and individual issues (**r. 46.6(5)**). Where a party joins the group register late, or leaves early, the court may make an order covering that party's responsibility for the common costs to date (**r. 46.6(6) and (7)**).

The appropriate costs orders to be made in group litigation in respect of the costs of individual claimants who settle or discontinue during the course of the proceedings were considered in *Sayers v Merck SmithKline Beecham plc* [2001] EWCA Civ 2027, [2002] 1 WLR 2274. It might be likely that the costs of common issues will be ordered to follow the determination of those issues rather than awaiting the individual fate of each claimant's claim, it would be wrong to say this is the presumptive position. Claimants who settle should deal with all aspects of costs, including common costs, as part of the settlement negotiations. In relation to discontinuing claimants, the costs of common issues should be determined following the trial of the common issues.

Care needs to be taken to control the costs in group litigation, with one particular concern being the considerable amount of administrative time often expended in these cases (*Solutia UK Ltd v Griffiths* [2001] EWCA Civ 736, [2001] CPLR 419).

Generic costs incurred in what was intended to be group litigation, but which was settled before proceedings were issued (and hence before a GLO was made), are recoverable in a detailed assessment following a Part 8 application under **r. 46.14** (*Brown v Russell Young and Co.* [2007] EWCA Civ 43, [2008] 1 WLR 525).

PUBLICLY FUNDED LITIGANTS

Successful publicly funded litigants

68.53   If a legally aided party or an LSC funded client (together referred to as 'publicly funded litigants') is successful, the court will make an order for costs on exactly the same principles as apply in unassisted claims. The publicly funded litigant has no beneficial interest in the costs, which must be paid to his or her solicitor to obtain a valid discharge. The recovered costs are used to pay the publicly funded costs. Any damages or property recovered or preserved in the proceedings will be subject to the Lord Chancellor's first charge under the Legal Aid, Sentencing and Punishment of Offenders Act 2012, s. 25, or the **Access to Justice Act 1999, s. 10(7)**, in respect of any shortfall between the solicitor's charges and the costs recovered from the paying party, and contributions from the publicly funded litigant.

Costs against a publicly funded litigant

68.54   **Cost protection**   Many publicly funded litigants will be protected against adverse costs orders if they are unsuccessful. 'Cost protection' applies to assisted parties under the Legal Aid, Sentencing and Punishment of Offenders Act 2012, by virtue of s. 26, and to LSC funded clients (see the Community Legal Service (Costs) Regulations 2000 (SI 2000/441)).

A litigant who obtains public funding by fraud does not obtain cost protection (*Jones v Congregational and General Insurance plc* [2003] EWHC 1027 (QB), [2003] 1 WLR 3001).

68.55   **Determining costs payable by assisted party**   Where cost protection applies, the Legal Aid, Sentencing and Punishment of Offenders Act 2012, s. 26(1), and the **Access to Justice Act 1999, s. 11(1)**, both provide that, except in prescribed circumstances, any costs ordered to be paid by the publicly funded litigant shall not exceed the amount (if any) which is reasonable having regard to all the circumstances including:

(a) the financial resources of all the parties to the proceedings; and
(b) their conduct in connection with the dispute to which the proceedings relate.

Exclusions from cost protection are provided for by the Civil Legal Aid (Costs) Regulations 2013, SI 2013/611, reg. 6, so that it does not apply to help at court, and in certain circumstances to legal help, help with family mediation and family help (lower). Unless they have competing interests in the proceedings, the publicly funded client's partner's resources are treated as the resources of the funded party (reg. 13(3)). However, the first £100,000 of the value of the publicly funded client's home is ignored (reg. 13(1)). Also ignored is the value of the publicly funded client's clothes and household furniture, unless the circumstances are exceptional (reg. 13(2)). The court can take into account any damages recovered by a funded party who fails to beat a Part 36 offer to settle, and any resulting costs liability under s. 26 has priority over the Lord Chancellor's first charge (*Cook v Swinfen* [1967] 1 WLR 457).

The court is required to consider whether, but for cost protection, it would have made a costs order against the publicly funded party, and, if so, whether it would have specified the amount payable (reg. 15(1)). If so (or if the court decides to make a reasonably modest order), and if the court considers it has enough information to do so, the court can immediately make an order under s. 26 specifying the amount the publicly funded party shall pay (reg. 15(2) and (3)). Usually, the 'reasonable' sum that a publicly funded litigant should pay will be relatively modest, or nothing. It may be a sum payable by instalments (*Williams v Walkett* [1994] CLY 3587) or a set-off against sums awarded in favour of the assisted party. Often the judge will be guided by the level of contribution payable by the publicly funded party under the Legal Aid, Sentencing and Punishment of Offenders Act 2012, s. 23 (*Mercantile Credit Co. Ltd v Cross* [1965] 2 QB 194), but must not do so blindly, because the test at this stage is not the same as the rules governing the level of contribution (*Gooday v Gooday* [1969] P 1).

If the court does not make an immediate order under s. 26, but decides it would have ordered costs against the publicly funded party but for the cost protection rule, the non-funded party has three months to request a hearing to determine the costs payable by the publicly funded party (reg. 16(2)). Regulation 16 lays down a detailed procedure for the determination of the amount, if any, payable.

Form of order   The normal order where a party is publicly funded is for a detailed assessment **68.56** of costs (*South Somerset District Council v Hughes* [2009] EWCA Civ 1245, LTL 15/7/2009). The court will be slow to depart from this position. An opposing party seeking a variation (with the effect that part of the costs of the publicly funded litigant will have to be paid by that party) should be on written notice supported by a short letter setting out the basis of the application and stating the source of the alleged jurisdiction for making the order and the rules relied upon.

Under the Legal Aid Act 1988, it was common to make orders that were colloquially known as 'football pools orders', providing that the assisted party was to pay the other side's costs, not to be enforced without the permission of the court. These were intended to allow the non-assisted party to return to court in the event of the assisted party coming into money at a later date. Under the traditional wording, the non-assisted party could return to court during the six years following the order, but a more sophisticated wording was approved in *Parr v Smith* [1995] 2 All ER 1031, which allowed an indefinite time for the application. Under the Legal Aid, Sentencing and Punishment of Offenders Act 2012 once a s. 26 order has been made, the non-funded party should generally apply within the next three months. Any later application can be entertained only up to six years from the order, and only on the grounds of significant change in the funded party's circumstances, or material additional information coming to light about the funded party's resources, or other good reasons (Civil Legal Aid (Costs) Regulations 2013, SI 2013/611, reg. 19).

A court may make orders in favour of both parties on different issues, even where one party is publicly funded, which will be set off against each other without infringing the principle of cost protection (*Hill v Bailey* [2003] EWHC 2835 (Ch), [2004] 1 All ER 1210). In relation to interim costs orders against publicly funded litigants, the court may make an order that the costs shall be set off against any future award in the claim of damages or costs against the non-funded party (*Lockley v National Blood Transfusion Service* [1992] 1 WLR 492; *R (Burkett) v Hammersmith and Fulham London Borough Council (No. 2)* [2004] EWCA Civ 1342, [2005] CP Rep 11).

An unsuccessful party who has been publicly funded for only part of the time during which litigation has been pending obtains the benefit of cost protection (if applicable) only for the period during which public funding was in place (*Dugon v Williamson* [1964] Ch 59). The same result applies where, as in *Turner v Plasplugs Ltd* [1996] 2 All ER 939, proceedings continue beyond a limitation in a certificate without the certificate being amended to cover future stages of the litigation. Cost protection is lost where a certificate is discharged on the date of giving notice of acting in person or change of solicitor (*Burridge v Stafford* (1999) 149 NLJ 1474). The effect of revocation of a certificate is that the party is treated as never having cost protection. In *DEG-Deutsche Investitions- und Entwicklungsgesellschaft mbH v Koshy* [2001] EWCA Civ 79, [2001] 3 All ER 878 the Court of Appeal held that revocation of a certificate is arguably the most significant change that could happen to a person's circumstances, and justified the court varying earlier costs orders previously covered by cost protection.

Costs against the Lord Chancellor

68.57 Under the Legal Aid, Sentencing and Punishment of Offenders Act 2012, s. 26(6)(d), and the Civil Legal Aid (Costs) Regulations 2013 (SI 2013/611), reg. 10, a court deciding a claim in favour of a non-publicly funded litigant as against one who is publicly funded may make an order requiring the Lord Chancellor to pay the non-publicly funded litigant's costs. Before such an order can be made, the following conditions must be satisfied:

(a) The proceedings must be finally decided in favour of the non-publicly funded litigant (reg. 10(1)). Where an appeal may be brought, any order against the Lord Chancellor will not take effect until the time limit for seeking permission to appeal has elapsed without permission being granted, or, if no permission is required, no appeal is brought within the time limit for bringing an appeal (reg. 10(5)). Where an appeal is brought by the publicly funded party, a fresh application may be brought in the appeal court.

(b) The non-publicly funded litigant must make the application for a costs order against the Lord Chancellor within three months of the making of a costs order (reg. 16(2)). A late application can be made where there is a good reason for the delay (reg. 10(3)(b)(ii)).

(c) The court must be satisfied that it is just and equitable in the circumstances that provision for the costs should be made out of public funds (reg. 10(3)(d)). It will normally be just and equitable that the Lord Chancellor should stand behind the client unless the costs judge is aware of facts rendering that result unjust or inequitable (*R (Gunn) v Secretary of State for the Home Department* [2001] EWCA Civ 891, [2001] 1 WLR 1634).

Further, in respect of costs incurred in proceedings at first instance, the following additional conditions (in reg. 10(3)(c)) must be satisfied:

(i) The proceedings must have been instituted by the publicly funded litigant.

(ii) The applicant must be an individual.

(iii) It must be shown that the non-publicly funded litigant will suffer financial hardship if the order is not made.

The Divisional Court is not a court of first instance when reviewing the decision of a court or tribunal (*R v Leeds County Court, ex parte Morris* [1990] 1 QB 523), but is a court of first instance when reviewing the decision of a person or body other than a court or tribunal (*R v Greenwich London Borough Council, ex parte Lovelace (No. 2)* [1992] QB 155). Where the assisted party receives public funding for only part of the proceedings, an order under the Legal Aid, Sentencing and Punishment of Offenders Act 2012, s. 26(6)(d), is restricted to the costs attributable to the part that is funded (SI 2013/611, reg. 10(4)). 'Attributed' was construed as covering costs in a 14-week hiatus not covered by the claimant's legal aid certificates when she changed solicitors in *Murphy v Rayner* [2013] EWHC 3878 (Ch), [2014] 1 WLR 677.

68.58 **Claim finally decided in favour of the assisted person** Proceedings are finally decided in favour of an unassisted person (condition (a) in **68.57**) when no appeal lies, or if the time for appealing has expired. In *Kelly v London Transport Executive* [1982] 1 WLR 1055 the unassisted defendant had made what would now be a Part 36 offer to settle exceeding the damages awarded to the claimant. The Court of Appeal held that the defendants had been substantially successful and that the action had been finally decided in its favour for these purposes.

68.59 **Financial hardship** In *Hanning v Maitland (No. 2)* [1970] 1 QB 580, decided when the final condition required severe financial hardship, Lord Denning MR said the term should not be restrictively construed 'so as to exclude people of modest income or modest capital who would find it difficult to bear their own costs', but should exclude commercial concerns in a considerable way of business, insurance companies and 'wealthy folk' who would not feel the costs of the litigation. Public bodies, including government departments, could (under the pre-2001 Regulations) suffer severe financial hardship (*R (Gunn) v Secretary of State for the Home Department* [2001] EWCA Civ 891, [2001] 1 WLR 1634). In *Adams v Riley* [1988] QB 372 it was explained that the unassisted party's spouse's financial resources are not to be aggregated with those of the unassisted party in determining whether the unassisted party will suffer severe financial hardship if an order against the Lord Chancellor is refused, but are to be taken into account in that an unassisted party with a financially independent spouse is better placed than a party with a dependent spouse. In *Adams v Riley* the court determined the amount that the defendant could pay towards his costs without suffering financial hardship, and made an order that the rest should be paid from public funds.

Both parties publicly funded

An order cannot be made against the Lord Chancellor where both parties are publicly funded (see condition (a) at **68.57**). This can produce rather harsh results, as in *Almond v Miles* (1992) *The Times*, 4 February 1992. In this case a publicly funded defendant successfully resisted a claim by a publicly funded claimant to a share in the equity of the defendant's flat. Under what is now the Legal Aid, Sentencing and Punishment of Offenders Act 2012, s. 25, the defendant's costs of £18,000 were a first charge on her flat, which had been 'preserved' in the proceedings. The claimant had the benefit of cost protection, but was required to pay certain instalments towards the defendant's costs. Although the defendant had been financially prejudiced by the proceedings, the court could not make an order against public funds, because the defendant was herself publicly funded. **68.60**

NON-PARTY COSTS ORDERS

In *Aiden Shipping Co. Ltd v Interbulk Ltd* [1986] AC 965 the House of Lords decided that the Senior Courts Act 1981, s. 51, confers a sufficiently wide discretion on the court on the question of costs to allow it to award costs against non-parties. In the case before the House of Lords two separate sets of proceedings were commenced. In the first, a shipowner made a claim against the charterers of the ship. In the second, essentially the same dispute was litigated between the charterers and their subcharterers. The actions were not consolidated. The House of Lords upheld the judge's order that the unsuccessful shipowner should pay the charterer's costs, such costs to include any costs the charterers had to pay the subcharterers in the second action. **68.61**

The basic principle is that such an order will only be made where it is in accordance with the requirements of reason and justice. In *Re Land and Property Trust Co. plc* [1991] 1 WLR 601, Nicholls LJ said 'the circumstances in which it will be just to make a costs order against a person who is not a party to the proceedings will be exceptional'. 'Exceptional' means outside the ordinary run of cases where non-parties pursued or defended claims for their own benefit and at their own expense. Even if there is some exceptional feature present, an order will be refused if there is no causation (*Hamilton v Al Fayed (No. 2)* [2002] EWCA Civ 665, [2003] QB 1175).

Costs orders against non-parties can be made in cases where there is 'no order as to costs' between claimant and defendant (*Myatt v National Coal Board (No. 2)* [2007] EWCA Civ 307, [2007] 1 WLR 1559). A costs order against a non-party may be made even where the non-party is domiciled outside the jurisdiction, and without the need to comply with the rules in (for example) the **recast Brussels I Regulation, art. 4** (see **16.16**) (*National Justice Compañía Naviera SA v Prudential Assurance Co. Ltd (No. 2)* [2000] 1 WLR 603).

Non-parties who substantially control proceedings or who will benefit from them will ordinarily be ordered to pay the successful party's costs (*Dymocks Franchise Systems (NSW) Pty Ltd v Todd* [2004] UKPC 39, [2004] 1 WLR 2807). Substantial involvement by a non-party in a claim that was without merit and without justification was enough for a non-party costs order in *Systemcare (UK) Ltd v Services Design Technology Ltd* [2011] EWCA Civ 546, [2012] 1 BCLC 14. Personal satisfaction in defeating an opponent as a means of settling a score is a sufficient personal interest (*Latimer Management Consultants Ltd v Ellingham Investments Ltd* [2006] EWHC 3662 (Ch), [2007] 1 WLR 2569).

Commentary

Non-party costs orders may possibly be made:

- against an outsider who was funding the litigation on behalf of the unsuccessful party (*Singh v Observer Ltd* [1989] 2 All ER 751), doubted in *Symphony Group plc v Hodgson* [1994] QB 179;
- against an outside insurer which accepts it is liable to indemnify its insured who is the losing party in the litigation (*Marley v Rawlings (No. 2)* [2014] UKSC 51, [2015] AC 157);
- against directors of a company who improperly cause the other side to incur costs in a winding-up petition (*Re a Company (No. 004055 of 1991)* [1991] 1 WLR 1003), although it is not necessary to find impropriety before making a non-party costs order (*BE Studios Ltd v Smith and Williamson Ltd* [2005] EWHC 2730 (Ch), [2006] 2 All ER 811; *Goodwood Recoveries Ltd v Breen* [2005] EWCA Civ 414, [2006] 1 WLR 2723);
- against a shareholder who was instrumental in commencing or defending proceedings for his own benefit (*CIBC Mellon Trust Co v Stolzenberg (No. 3)* [2005] EWCA Civ 628, [2005] 2 BCLC 618); and
- where the non-party has been found, under the law concerning maintenance and champerty, to have maintained the claim (*McFarlane v E. E. Caledonia Ltd (No. 2)* [1995] 1 WLR 366).

Personal costs orders were made in winding-up proceedings against a director who treated companies as extensions of himself (*Re North West Holdings plc* [2001] EWCA Civ 67, [2001] 1 BCLC 468), and where a director contested proceedings against the company for his personal reasons (*Re Aurum Marketing Ltd* [2000] 2 BCLC 645). Normally, however, if litigation is conducted in the name of a company in good faith, it is contrary to the principles of separate corporate personality and limited liability to make any person other than the company itself liable to pay another party's costs because the company loses (*Taylor v Pace Developments Ltd* [1991] BCC 406; *Floods of Queensferry Ltd v Shand Construction Ltd* [2002] EWCA Civ 918, [2003] Lloyd's Rep IR 181, where the circumstances in which a director maintained a company's litigation were described by the trial judge as 'extraordinary'). A non-party costs order is unlikely to be made against a liquidator funding litigation in the name of the company (*Eastglen Ltd v Grafton* [1996] 2 BCLC 279).

Non-party costs orders against third party funders

68.62   The essential policy is that the need to protect the successful party by granting an effective costs order has to yield to the right of access to the courts to litigate the dispute in the first place (*Hamilton v Al Fayed (No. 2)* [2002] EWCA Civ 665, [2003] QB 1175; European Convention on Human Rights, **art. 6(1)**, in the **Human Rights Act 1998, sch. 1**). It is in the public interest that funding for litigation should be available, provided the real motivation is to enable a party to litigate what the funders perceive to be a genuine case. A pure funder of litigation should not ordinarily be liable to a non-party costs order, and it is only if there is something exceptional in the circumstances that such an order can be justified (*Gulf Azov Shipping Co Ltd v Idisi* [2004] EWCA Civ 292, LTL 15/3/2004).

The motivation of any outside funder will be a relevant consideration. In *Hamilton v Al Fayed (No. 2)* the court drew the distinction between 'pure funders' who fund litigation out of philanthropic or charitable motives and 'professional' funders who are normally contractually bound to fund litigation. The court held that it would be rare for pure funders to be exposed to a costs order where they acted out of altruistic motives and had reasonable grounds for believing that the party was acting properly. If pure funders were regularly exposed to costs orders, there was a real risk that the funds would dry up and that access to justice would be reduced. Regarding professional funders, *Arkin v Borchard Lines Ltd (Nos. 2 and 3)* [2005] EWCA Civ 655, [2005] 1 WLR 3055, said a balance has to be struck between the need not to discourage professional funding of claims brought by persons otherwise unable to afford litigation, and the fair application of the principle that costs follow the event. It was held that the professional funder should ordinarily (in the absence of champerty and unreasonable conduct) be liable up to the amount it contributed to the unsuccessful party's costs.

Non-party costs orders against solicitors

Non-party costs orders may be made in the case of wanton and officious intermeddling with litigation falling short of champerty in the strict sense (*Nordstern Allgemeine Versicherungs AG v Internav Ltd* [1999] 2 Lloyd's Rep 139). There is no jurisdiction to make a non-party costs order against a lawyer solely on the ground that he conducted the case without taking a fee (*Tolstoy-Miloslavsky v Aldington* [1996] 1 WLR 736). In that case Rose LJ at p. 745 said there are only three categories of conduct which can give rise to an order for costs against a solicitor:

68.63

(a) where the case comes within the wasted costs jurisdiction (see **68.67**);

(b) where the solicitor is in breach of duty to the court in circumstances that, even before the Judicature Acts, such an order might be made. Examples are where the solicitor acts without authority or in breach of an undertaking (even if this is done unwittingly); and

(c) if the solicitor acts outside the role of a solicitor, for example in a private capacity or as a true third-party funder for someone else.

Cases in the second and third categories are very fact-sensitive. A lawyer who funds litigation knowing the client has acted unlawfully and has no defence will fall into the second category (*Gulf Azov Shipping Co Ltd v Idisi* [2004] EWCA Civ 292, LTL 15/3/2004). A non-party costs order was made in *Adris v Bank of Scotland plc* [2010] EWHC 941 (QB), [2010] 4 Costs LR 598, because the solicitor promised to pay for ATE cover in its advertising but failed to do so in a case where the clients would not have brought the claim if they knew there was no ATE cover. It is probably the same if the solicitor fails to obtain ATE cover in breach of the client's express instructions to do so (*Flatman v Germany* [2013] EWCA Civ 278, [2013] 1 WLR 2676).

A solicitor will come within the third category where litigation was pursued entirely or substantially for the benefit of the solicitor, such that the solicitor is the real party in very important and critical respects (*Myatt v National Coal Board (No. 2)* [2007] EWCA Civ 307, [2007] 1 WLR 1559). A solicitor who funds disbursements on behalf of a client on the basis these will be recovered from the other side if the claim succeeds does not on that account become the real party within the third category (*Flatman v Germany*). Nor does a solicitor become the real party through committing an act of negligence (on the facts, failing to advise on obtaining ATE cover) and thereby coming into a conflict of interest with the client (*Heron v TNT (UK) Ltd* [2013] EWCA Civ 469, [2014] 1 WLR 1277).

Procedure on non-party costs applications

An application for a costs order against a non-party follows a summary procedure. The fact that costs proceedings may take some time to determine does not stop them being summary (*Robertson Research International Ltd v ABG Exploration BV* [1999] CPLR 756). This is a different approach to that adopted in wasted costs applications (see **68.67**). However, if the application is speculative or bound to fail, the court should summarily dismiss it (*Bristol and West plc v Bhadresa (No. 2)* [1999] CPLR 209). The person against whom the costs order is sought must be joined as a party for the purposes of costs only, and must be given a reasonable opportunity to attend the hearing to give reasons why the court should not make the order (**CPR, r. 46.2**). An application to join a non-party should ordinarily be acceded to (*PR Records Ltd v Vinyl 2000 Ltd* [2007] EWHC 1721 (Ch), LTL 25/7/2007). The court has a power under the Senior Courts Act 1981, s. 51(3), to determine by whom, and to what extent, costs are to be paid, and it therefore has an ancillary power to order a party to disclose who its funders were (*Raiffeisen Zentralbank Österreich AG v Crossseas Shipping Ltd* [2003] EWHC 1381 (Comm), LTL 13/6/2003, in which the successful claimant found that the defendant was impecunious and was granted an order to discover who was funding the defendant).

68.64

Commentary

The strict rules of evidence will not apply when the court considers whether to make the order. The court should limit the issues to be considered and, if necessary, the length of cross-examination and submissions. An order may accordingly be refused if the non-party against whom the application is made has not been provided with the basic safeguards required by natural justice, such as being informed in advance of the trial that the application will be made, and the issue against the non-party being accurately framed by statements of case (*Symphony Group plc v Hodgson* [1994] QB 179). In *Shah v Karanjia* [1993] 4 All ER 792 an application for costs against a brother of the claimant was refused principally because he had not been separately represented at the trial, the claim against him had not been formulated against him until after the trial, and he had been asked questions in cross-examination at trial with a view to obtaining information for the application for costs against him.

Costs orders against experts

68.65   In *Phillips v Symes (No 2)* [2004] EWHC 2330 (Ch), [2005] 1 WLR 2043, it was held, by extension of the jurisdiction to order costs against non-parties, that the court has power to order costs to be paid by expert witnesses. Such an order may be made where an expert breaches his or her duties to the court and as a result significant costs are incurred, or where an expert produced a report without having examined the property in question (*Admiral Insurance Services Ltd v Daniels* (2007 Cambridge County Court) LTL 14/6/2007). A similar procedure to that discussed at **68.64** should be followed. The expert should be given a warning, and orders should follow the two-stage process of first considering whether there is a case to answer, followed by a hearing to allow the expert to appear and give reasons why an order should not be made.

Costs order in favour of non-party

68.66   In *J v Oyston* [2002] EWHC 819 (QB), [2002] CPLR 563, an order for costs was made in favour of the Solicitors' Indemnity Fund, a non-party which had taken over conduct of proceedings in the name of the claimant whom it had agreed to indemnify and in which it was successful. Such an order can be made under the Senior Courts Act 1981, s. 51, provided the court finds there are exceptional circumstances. The Fund would have been liable for the defendant's costs if he had won, and it would be unreasonable, unjust and extraordinary if the defendant were not to be ordered to pay the Fund's costs if he lost.

WASTED COSTS ORDERS

68.67   The court has a power under the Senior Courts Act 1981, s. 51(6), to make a legal representative liable for any wasted costs. This can take one of two forms:

(a) disallowing the costs of a party and ordering the legal representative to indemnify his or her client against the costs; and/or

(b) ordering the legal representative to pay the costs of another party.

Where the court makes a wasted costs order it must inform the relevant approved regulator and/or the Director of Legal Aid Casework (s. 51(7A)). The term 'wasted costs' is defined in s. 51(7) to mean any costs incurred by a party:

(a) as a result of any improper, unreasonable or negligent act or omission on the part of any legal or other representative or any employee of such a representative; or

(b) which, in the light of any such act or omission occurring after they were incurred, the court considers it unreasonable to expect that party to pay.

The phrase 'improper, unreasonable or negligent' was considered by the Court of Appeal in *Ridehalgh v Horsefield* [1994] Ch 205, which is the leading authority in this field. Whether an act or omission is 'improper' is to be judged by the standards of the consensus of professional, including judicial, opinion and is not limited to breaches of the professional code. 'Unreasonable' includes behaviour that is:

vexatious, designed to harass the other side rather than advance the resolution of the case, and it makes no difference that the conduct is the product of excessive zeal and not improper motive....The acid test is whether the conduct admits of a reasonable explanation.

'Negligent':

should be understood in an untechnical way to denote failure to act with the competence reasonably to be expected of ordinary members of the profession.

'Negligent' requires something more than mere negligence (*Persaud v Persaud* [2003] EWCA Civ 394, [2003] PNLR 519). Negligent handling of a client's case is not enough: the lawyer's conduct must also be a breach of duty to the court (*Radford and Co. v Charles* [2003] EWHC 3180 (Ch), [2004] PNLR 25). A wasted costs order will only be made if there is something akin to a legal representative being guilty of an abuse of process. A failure to address the Bar Council guidance on advising in publicly funded cases was regarded in *Persaud v Persaud* as a breach of duty to the legal aid authorities and not a breach of duty to the court, and was an insufficient basis for a wasted costs order.

The test to be applied to determine whether an act or omission justifies a wasted costs order is the same whether or not the party is publicly funded (*Filmlab Systems International Ltd v Pennington* [1995] 1 WLR 673). There must be a causal link between the legal representative's behaviour and the waste of costs (**PD 46, para. 5.5(b)**; *Ridehalgh v Horsefield*; *Brown v Bennett (No. 2)* [2002] 1 WLR 713).

It is appropriate for the court to make a wasted costs order only if it is just in all the circumstances to make a legal representative compensate a party for wasted costs (**PD 46, para. 5.5(c)**).

'Legal representative' includes solicitor and counsel. Acts or omissions by counsel which may lead to costs which may be the subject of a wasted costs order include both pre-trial paperwork and conduct during the trial (*Ridehalgh v Horsefield*; *Brown v Bennett 'No. 2)*). Solicitors cannot avoid their responsibility to the parties and the court by slavishly following counsel's advice. It is incumbent on them to exercise an independent judgment (*Davy-Chiesman v Davy-Chiesman* [1984] Fam 48; *Locke v Camberwell Health Authority* (1991) 2 Med LR 249; *Ridehalgh v Horsefield*).

An application for a wasted costs order can be made against one's own legal representative and that of one's opponent (*Medcalf v Mardell* [2002] UKHL 27, [2003] 1 AC 120). An order will not be made against former solicitors who ceased to act before proceedings were issued (*Byrne v Sefton Health Authority* [2001] EWCA Civ 1904, [2002] 1 WLR 775). An application can be made against a non-party (*Lubrizol Ltd v Tyndallwoods Solicitors* (1998) LTL 10/4/98).

The courts must be astute to ensure that wasted costs applications do not become another form of satellite litigation. They will be reserved for exceptional cases where a party was injured by the unjustified behaviour of a legal representative (*Ridehalgh v Horsefield*). They should be confined to matters that are susceptible to summary disposal on agreed facts or after brief investigation. Complex, time-consuming inquiries are to be avoided. Compensation of a party who has suffered at the hand of a legal representative is only one of a number of competing interests to be considered (*Re Merc Property Ltd* [1999] 2 BCLC 286; *Wall v Lefever* [1998] 1 FCR 605; *Medcalf v Mardell*).

The legal representative against whom an application for a wasted costs order is made must be given an opportunity to respond before the court makes the order (**CPR, r. 46.8(2)**; *Re Wiseman Lee (Solicitors) (Wasted Costs Order) (No. 5 of 2000)* [2001] EWCA Crim 707, *The Times*, 5 April 2001). The court should not make an order against the legal representative of a party who is unable or unwilling to waive privilege, unless the court is satisfied that, if unconstrained, the legal representative could say nothing to resist the order and also that it is fair and just to make the order in the circumstances (*Medcalf v Mardell*).

Commentary

Procedure on wasted costs applications

68.68 An application for a wasted costs order should be made to the judge who tried the matter (*Re P* [2002] 1 Cr App R 207). In certain limited circumstances it is possible for another court to have jurisdiction, such as where it is impracticable for the trial judge to deal with the matter, or where the parties agree to another judge dealing with it. Unless such an exception applies, a District Judge has no jurisdiction to make a wasted costs order after a claim has been tried by a Circuit Judge (*Gray v Going Places Leisure Travel Ltd* [2005] EWCA Civ 189, LTL 7/2/2005). The fact that the trial judge has already criticised the conduct complained of will not necessarily mean that the judge is biased and should not hear the application (*Bahai v Rashidian* [1985] 1 WLR 1337).

Although an application can be made at any stage of proceedings, it should normally be made after trial (**PD 46, para. 5.2**; *Filmlab Systems International Ltd v Pennington* [1995] 1 WLR 673). An application can be made at any time up to and including the detailed assessment of costs (**PD 46, para. 5.2**; *Melchior v Vettivel* [2002] CP Rep 24). It can be made after the main proceedings have been stayed by consent following a Tomlin order (*Wagstaff v Colls* [2003] EWCA Civ 469, [2003] PNLR 561). The award of costs as between the parties and the making of a wasted costs order are two distinct functions (*Melchior v Vettivel*).

A party to proceedings may apply for a wasted costs order either orally or by filing an application notice under **CPR, Part 23** (**PD 46, para. 5.5**). The court can make an order of its own initiative (**PD 46, para. 5.3**). It should be slow to do so as the inquiry will necessarily involve a party in additional expense. Where application is made under **Part 23**, a copy of the application notice must be served, with a copy of the written evidence and a draft order, at least three days before the application is to be heard (**CPR, r. 23.7**). The application notice and evidence in support must (**PD 46, para. 5.9**) identify:

(a) what the legal representative is alleged to have done or failed to do; and
(b) the costs which the legal representative may be ordered to pay or which are sought to be paid.

Where the court initiates the inquiry it is incumbent on the judge to ensure that the order shows clearly the breach alleged so that the legal representative has sufficient information upon which to respond.

The application will generally be considered in two stages (**PD 46, para. 5.7**). In the first stage, the court must be satisfied:

(a) that it has before it evidence or other material which, if unanswered, would be likely to lead to a wasted costs order being made; and
(b) the wasted costs proceedings are justified notwithstanding the likely costs involved.

At the second stage (even if the court is satisfied at stage 1) the court will consider, after giving the legal representative an opportunity to give reasons why the court should not make a wasted costs order, whether it is appropriate to make a wasted costs order.

Elaborate proceedings, disclosure or requests for further information are not generally appropriate given the summary nature of the investigation (*Re Merc Property Ltd* [1999] 2 BCLC 286). The court has no power to direct that privileged documents must be disclosed (*General Mediterranean Holdings SA v Patel* [2000] 1 WLR 272; see *Medcalf v Mardell* [2002] UKHL 27, [2003] 1 AC 120, and *Brown v Eennett (No. 2)* [2002] 1 WLR 713 for the consequences of this).

The court will approach the application by considering the three points stated in **PD 46, para. 5.5**:

(a) Has the legal representative acted improperly, unreasonably or negligently?
(b) Has the legal representative's conduct caused a party to incur unnecessary costs (see *R v Secretary of State for the Home Department, ex parte Mach* [2001] EWCA Civ 645, LTL 27/4/2001)?

(c) Is it just in all the circumstances to order the legal representative to compensate that party for the whole or part of those costs?

It is submitted that there is no burden on the representative to exculpate him or herself.

The court can direct a costs judge or a District Judge to decide the amount of costs to be disallowed or paid (**CPR, r. 46.8(3)(b)**).

Examples of wasted costs

The wasted costs powers against lawyers and other parties are compensatory in nature.   **68.69**

Conduct justifying a wasted costs order may include failing to attend an appointment, failing to comply with the court's orders, negligent mispleading of the case, inefficient presentation of the case at trial through being ill-prepared, and pressing on with a claim after it has become hopeless (for example, through failing to read the materials disclosed by the other side on disclosure). Pleading an unjustified allegation of fraud in breach of the Bar Code of Conduct may be 'improper' conduct (*Medcalf v Mardell* [2002] UKHL 27, [2003] 1 AC 120, where an order was refused). A solicitor who swears an affidavit in support of a winding-up petition in circumstances where he knows that the petition, if fought on the merits, will fail, acts unreasonably and may be the subject of a wasted costs order (*Re a Company (No. 006798 of 1995)* [1996] 1 WLR 491). A solicitor is not entitled to abdicate all responsibility for a case by instructing counsel, but the more specialist the area the more reasonable it is to follow counsel's advice. Thus in *R v Horsham District Council, ex parte Wenman* [1995] 1 WLR 680 a solicitor was absolved from liability when acting on counsel's advice in judicial review proceedings. A finding that a claim had a less than 50 per cent chance of success is not enough. The requirements for wasted costs orders in weak cases are that the claim was hopeless and a breach of the solicitor's duty to the court (*Patel v Air India Ltd* [2010] EWCA Civ 443, LTL 14/5/2010). In *Ridehalgh v Horsefield* the Court of Appeal expressed the view that, largely because of the 'cab rank rule' whereby barristers (and to some extent solicitors) are not entitled to pick and choose their clients, it is not improper for a lawyer to represent a client who is bound to lose. However, pursuing a case which amounts to an abuse of process would be 'improper'. The distinction is largely one of degree. The Court of Appeal also made a point of deprecating the practice of making threats to apply for wasted costs orders as a means of unacceptable intimidation, although there is a distinction between that and giving proper notice that an application will be made in the case of persistent improper, unreasonable or negligent conduct.

Chapter 69   Qualified One-way Costs Shifting

INTRODUCTION

69.1   Unless a litigant has BTE insurance (such as in a motor insurance policy or household insurance), abolishing the recoverability of ATE insurance premiums means there is little incentive to insure the risk of having to pay the other side's costs if the claim is unsuccessful. There is nothing to stop a litigant taking out ATE cover, but premiums are often prohibitively expensive. Under the pre-Jackson system, a litigant reasonably confident of winning, but aware there is a risk of losing, was often prepared to pay a substantial ATE premium because, when the claim succeeded, the premium was repaid under the costs order by the losing party.

Sir Rupert Jackson recognised that removing CFA success fees, and abolishing the recoverability of ATE insurance premiums, brought the balance too far against claimants, and particularly individual claimants. This is addressed in the *Jackson Report* by recommendation 19 for the introduction of qualified one-way costs shifting ('QOCS'), together with recommendations 10 and 65 for an uplift of 10 per cent in awards of damages for pain and suffering, loss of amenity, physical inconvenience and discomfort, and social discredit as implemented by *Simmons v Castle* [2012] EWCA Civ 1039, [2012] EWCA Civ 1288, [2013] 1 WLR 1239.

NATURE OF QOCS

69.2   'Costs shifting' describes the usual rule that costs follow the event or that costs are otherwise paid by one side to the other (**CPR, r. 44.2(2)(a)**). The costs incurred by the successful party are 'shifted' to the losing party under the usual costs order. QOCS adjusts this traditional position by saying that the usual costs order should only be made in favour of one party, typically the claimant. This means that if the claimant wins, the defendant should be ordered to pay the claimant's costs in the usual way. However, if the claimant loses, QOCS means that while the claimant remains liable to pay its own lawyers' costs, the claimant will not also have to pay the successful defendant's costs under the usual order for costs to follow the event.

Under QOCS a claimant therefore has a valuable protection against paying the defendant's costs. As a result, there should be no need for a claimant who will have the benefit of QOCS to take out ATE insurance, because normally they will not be required to pay the defendant's costs even if they lose.

QOCS is 'qualified' one-way costs shifting, because this protection to the claimant is not absolute. It is recognised that if it was an invariable rule, it would be open to abuse, with some claimants indulging in costs-inflating practices secure in the knowledge they would never be brought to account. Accordingly, under the QOCS scheme that was introduced from 1 April 2013 there are exceptions for different types of misbehaviour, and no protection against the enforcement of adverse costs orders against damages and interest recovered in the proceedings.

CATEGORIES OF CASE COVERED BY QOCS

Transitional provisions governing QOCS

As from 1 April 2013, QOCS applies to personal injury and clinical negligence cases (**CPR, r. 44.13**). QOCS does not apply to proceedings in which the claimant has entered into a pre-commencement funding arrangement (as defined by **r. 48.2**, see **r. 44.17**). A pre-commencement funding arrangement is a funding arrangement as defined by **r. 43.2(1)(k)(i)**, as in force before 1 April 2013 (CFAs with success fees), where:

69.3

(a) the agreement was entered into before 1 April 2013 specifically for the purposes of the provision to the person by whom the success fee is payable of advocacy or litigation services in relation to the matter that is the subject of the proceedings in which the costs order is to be made; or

(b) the agreement was entered into before 1 April 2013 and advocacy or litigation services were provided to that person under the agreement in connection with that matter before 1 April 2013 (**r. 48.2(1)(a)(i)**).

This means that if the claimant, for example, entered into a CFA with a success fee before 1 April 2013, QOCS will not apply.

Personal injuries claims governed by QOCS

Under **CPR, r. 44.13**, the provisions on QOCS in **rr. 44.14 to 44.16** apply to proceedings which include a claim for damages:

69.4

(a) for personal injuries;

(b) under the Fatal Accidents Act 1976; or

(c) which arises out of death or personal injury and survives for the benefit of an estate by virtue of the **Law Reform (Miscellaneous Provisions) Act 1934, s. 1(1)**.

A claim against the Motor Insurers' Bureau under the Motor Vehicles (Compulsory Insurance) (Information Centre and Compensation Body) Regulations 2003 (SI 2003/37), reg. 13, is a claim for a civil debt rather than for damages for personal injuries. It is therefore not covered by QOCS (*Howe v Motor Insurers' Bureau (No. 2)* [2016] EWHC 884 (QB), [2016] 1 WLR 2751).

Applications for disclosure before proceedings start, pursuant to the Senior Courts Act 1981, s. 33, or the County Courts Act 1984, s. 52 (and see also **CPR, r. 31.16**), are excluded from the scope of QOCS (**r. 44.13(1)**, proviso).

There is an extended definition of 'claimant' for the purposes of the rules on QOCS in **r. 44.13(2)**, namely:

In this Section, 'claimant' means a person bringing a claim to which this Section applies or an estate on behalf of which such a claim is brought, and includes a person making a counterclaim or an additional claim.

This is intended to mean that it does not matter whether the personal injuries claim is brought by an original claimant or in a defence and counterclaim or in an additional claim, such as a third-party claim, under **Part 20**. It probably achieves that aim by the use of the phrase 'person bringing a claim to which this Section applies' (**r. 44.13(2)**), being an implicit reference back to the personal injuries claims spelt out in **r. 44.13(1)**. In *Wagenaar v Weekend Travel Ltd* [2014] EWCA Civ 1105, [2015] 1 WLR 1968, the claimant sued the defendant for damages for personal injuries, and the defendant brought in a third party under Part 20 to seek an indemnity or contribution. At trial the claim and third party claim were defeated. QOCS protected the claimant, but it was held that QOCS did not protect the defendant on the Part 20 claim, because the defendant was not itself bringing a claim for personal injuries.

Sir Rupert Jackson primarily recommended QOCS for personal injuries claims, but also said that it should be considered for other categories of claim, particularly those where traditionally there is an inequality of arms between claimants and defendants (*Jackson Report*, Executive Summary, para. 2.7), and proposed that QOCS should be applied to defamation claims (recommendation 65). Extending the categories of case covered by QOCS is a matter for the future.

No financial eligibility requirement

69.5   At one stage it was proposed that QOCS would not be available to the very wealthy (Reforming Civil Litigation Funding and Costs in England and Wales — Implementation of Lord Justice Jackson's Recommendations: The Government Response (Cm 8041, March 2011), para. 11). An obvious problem with that proposal was when and how the claimant's financial resources would be assessed for that purpose. As the financial means exception was only intended to apply to a very small number of 'very wealthy' claimants, the costs of making that assessment in all cases far outweighed its value. It has therefore been decided that QOCS will apply to all claimants whatever their means, so there is no financial test to determine eligibility.

EFFECT OF QOCS

69.6   One-way costs shifting is achieved by **CPR, r. 44.14(1)**, in a somewhat obscure fashion. This provides:

> Subject to rr. 44.15 and 44.16, orders for costs made against a claimant may be enforced without the permission of the court but only to the extent that the aggregate amount in money terms of such orders does not exceed the aggregate amount in money terms of any orders for damages and interest made in favour of the claimant.

Claimant loses the case

69.7   If the claimant loses the case with no award of damages, the effect is that no costs will be payable by the claimant, because the aggregate amount referred to in **CPR, r. 44.14(1)**, is nil. The rule does not prevent an adverse costs order being made against the unsuccessful claimant, but instead provides that any costs order that is made is not enforceable against the claimant. It is therefore rather like the costs protection granted to legally aided parties, and the familiar 'football pools' orders that have been made for many years (which provide that costs being ordered against an assisted party are not to be enforced without the court's permission). Although **r. 44.14(1)** is similar to a football pools order in effect, it is not the same. Under **r. 44.14(1)** all the court has to do is to make a normal adverse costs order against the unsuccessful claimant. The order may but need not say that it may not be enforced without the court's permission. **Rule 44.14(1)** then applies with the effect that (as nothing has been recovered in the litigation) nothing is payable by the claimant towards the defendant's costs. Procedures that apply in legal aid cases for seeking permission to enforce the costs order on the basis that the claimant's financial circumstances have improved do not apply, because under **r. 44.14(1)** the financial exposure of the claimant is limited to the money award in the actual proceedings.

Claimant partially successful

69.8   In cases where the claimant is partially successful, **CPR, r. 44.14(1)**, operates in a slightly different way. First, the court will have to decide what costs order to make given the respective degrees of success of the parties and the other factors set out in **r. 44.2**. If the court makes a full or partial costs award in favour of the claimant, **r. 44.14** has no application. However, if the court makes an adverse costs order against the claimant (whether a full costs order in favour of the defendant, or a percentage costs order in favour of the defendant), **r. 44.14(1)** applies to restrict the amount of costs that the defendant can recover from the claimant to the aggregate amount in money terms of any orders for damages and interest made in favour of the claimant. In such a case QOCS does not provide full costs protection for the claimant, because the money award may be eaten up by the costs order in favour of the defendant, but the claimant is protected in the sense that taking into account such sums as they were awarded in the case, the claimant will not have to pay anything beyond the total award to the defendant under the defendant's costs order.

QOCS and defendants' Part 36 offers

The main reason for the Byzantine wording of **CPR, r. 44.14(1)**, is to deal with split costs orders under **r. 36.17(3)** where the defendant has made a Part 36 offer and the claimant has failed to achieve a judgment more advantageous than that offer. Assuming the claimant with the benefit of QOCS has succeeded on liability and obtained a money award, **r. 36.17(3)** says that unless the court considers it unjust to do so, it will award costs to the claimant up to the end of the relevant period as defined by **r. 36.3(g)** and award the defendant its costs thereafter. **69.9**

The two costs orders can be set off against each other (**r. 44.12**). The net effect, especially if the Part 36 offer was made in the early stages of the claim, is that there is often a net costs liability due from the claimant to the defendant under an order made under **r. 36.17(3)**. By virtue of **r. 44.14(1)**, that net costs liability can be enforced without permission against the awards in favour of the claimant for damages and interest, up to the extent of reducing those figures to zero.

QOCS and interim costs orders

Interim costs orders against a claimant with QOCS protection are dealt with in a similar way to Part 36 offers. Liability under such adverse interim costs orders can only be enforced against the claimant up to the amount the claimant eventually recovers by way of damages and interest (**CPR, r. 44.14(1)**). To ensure this happens, interim costs orders cannot be enforced against claimants with QOCS protection until the end of the case (**r. 44.14(2)**; see **69.11**). **69.10**

Time for enforcing costs orders against claimants

An order for costs made against a claimant may be enforced only after the proceedings have been concluded and the costs have been assessed or agreed (**CPR, r. 44.14(2)**). This is particularly relevant where there have been interim costs orders against a claimant with QOCS protection (see **69.10**). It allows the court to set off the main costs order in the proceedings against the adverse interim costs orders under **r. 44.12**, and to apply the QOCS protection rule in **r. 44.14(1)** to the balance to avoid any costs liability of the claimant exceeding the aggregate of the money award in damages and interest. **69.11**

Credit scoring

An order for costs which is enforced only to the extent permitted by **CPR, r. 44.14(1)**, shall not be treated as an unsatisfied or outstanding judgment for the purposes of any court record (**r. 44.14(3)**). **69.12**

Commentary

MISBEHAVIOUR UNDER CPR, PART 44, SECTION II

69.13   CPR, r. 44.15, provides:

> Orders for costs made against the claimant may be enforced to the full extent of such orders without the permission of the court where the proceedings have been struck out on the grounds that—
> (a) the claimant has disclosed no reasonable grounds for bringing the proceedings;
> (b) the proceedings are an abuse of the court's process; or
> (c) the conduct of—
>   (i)   the claimant; or
>   (ii) a person acting on the claimant's behalf and with the claimant's knowledge of such conduct,
> is likely to obstruct the just disposal of the proceedings.

With respect to the Civil Procedure Rule Committee, this comes nowhere near implementing the idea in the *Jackson Report*. Claimants who lose the protection granted by QOCS should be those who have forfeited the right to costs protection through either:

(a) advancing a fraudulent claim; or
(b) abusing the court system.

The expression used in point (b) above is deliberately not the same as the term 'abuse of process', which is used in **r. 3.4(2)(b)**. This is because claims are struck out regularly under **r. 3.4(2)** for all sorts of reasons that are not blameworthy, and do not amount to abusing the civil justice system. The genesis of the problem is no doubt the use of **r. 3.4(2)** phraseology in the Ministerial Statement of 17 July 2012 by the Parliamentary Under-Secretary of State, Ministry of Justice (Jonathan Djanogly) on the Implementation of Part 2 of the Legal Aid, Sentencing and Punishment of Offenders Act 2012: Civil Litigation Funding and Costs. What seems to have happened is that **r. 44.15** has faithfully reproduced the wording used in that statement, but has not necessarily enacted the intention behind it.

Claims that have been struck out

69.14   What CPR, **r. 44.15**, has done is largely to replicate the wording of **r. 3.4(2)**. Adopting the same words as are used in **r. 3.4(2)** means that the courts will inevitably apply the same principles in interpreting **r. 44.15** as they have done for many years in interpreting **r. 3.4(2)**. It means that costs protection will be lost under **r. 44.15** in, among others, the following situations:

(a) Where a claim is struck out due to drafting errors by the claimant's legal representatives or the claimant if acting in person. Striking out in such cases is on the ground the claim discloses no reasonable cause of action. It does not necessarily mean it is not a genuine claim.

(b) Where a claim is struck out on the basis that it is seeking to extend the situations where there is a duty of care, perhaps because the law is not yet ready to make the necessary extension. It would mean that many of the cases that have formulated the boundaries of the law of negligence are ones where costs protection under QOCS would not apply.

(c) Where a claim is time-barred. Time-barred claims are struck out on the basis that they are an abuse of process, because limitation is only a procedural defence, which does not determine whether there were reasonable grounds for bringing the claim. Many strike-out applications engaging the Limitation Act 1980, ss. 14 and 33, are very difficult to predict, and it seems bizarre that if they are successful then costs protection is lost. What is also strange is that costs protection under QOCS will not be lost under **r. 44.15** if, instead of the limitation point being taken on a striking-out application, it is taken as a preliminary issue, because **r. 44.15** only applies if the claim is struck out.

(d) A claim may be struck out as an abuse of process even if the strict rules of *res judicata* do not apply, but on the basis that the claim could and should have been brought in earlier proceedings (*Henderson v Henderson* (1843) 3 Hare 100; *Johnson v Gore Wood and Co.* [2002] 2 AC 1).

This may be a little more blameworthy than the other examples, but the cases in this area show that often incredibly tight distinctions are made in these applications (for example, *Jameson v Central Electricity Generating Board* [2000] 1 AC 455).

In all these cases costs protection will be lost. However, costs protection will not be lost if instead of taking a point on a striking-out application, judgment is obtained against the claimant, either on an application for summary judgment or on the trial of a preliminary issue. Where a claim has been struck out on any of the stated grounds, an order for costs against the claimant may be enforced to the full extent of the order without the permission of the court (**r. 44.15**). It seems from the wording that there is no discretion to reimpose QOCS costs protection in these cases.

There are plenty of other situations where claims are struck out under **r. 3.4(2)** where the claimant fully deserves to lose their costs protection under QOCS. Claims which are totally without merit, claims deliberately aimed at abusing the court's process, and fraudulent claims will fall into this category. A practical solution would be to adopt the first of these as being the test for automatic loss of QOCS protection under **r. 44.15**: that costs protection is lost if a claim is struck out under **r. 3.4(2)** with the court recording in the order that it considers that the claim was totally without merit under **r. 3.4(6)**. This could be extended to equivalent situations, such as refusing permission to appeal, striking out an appellant's notice, or dismissing an appeal that is totally without merit under **r. 52.20(5), (6)**.

Loss of QOCS costs protection: fraudulent claims

The second problem with **CPR, r. 44.15**, is that it only applies if the claim has actually been struck out. Many fraudulent claims will not come within **r. 44.15** because it is extremely difficult to strike out a claim on the basis it is fraudulent. The nature of such an allegation means it is rarely going to be a suitable issue to decide on an interim application, and so it will usually be left to be determined at trial. If the case proceeds through to trial, there are various reasons why it will not then be struck out even if fraud is found (*Summers v Fairclough Homes Ltd* [2012] UKSC 26, [2012] 1 WLR 2004, see **33.14**). In these cases the defendant may make an application for permission to remove the claimant's QOCS costs protection under **r. 44.16(1)**. For **r. 44.16(1)** to apply the court needs to find on the balance of probabilities that the claim was fundamentally dishonest.

While there are examples of actual striking-out orders being made in fraudulent claims (in which event costs protection under QOCS is lost automatically under **r. 44.15**), this is unusual. In most cases of alleged fraud the court will need to conduct a hearing to decide whether the required level of dishonesty can be established to the civil standard of proof. Usually this should be done at trial (**PD 44, para. 12.4(a)**), but it follows from *Summers v Fairclough Homes Ltd* that it will only rarely be appropriate to strike out the claim at that stage.

Allegations of fundamental dishonesty in settled and discontinued claims

Unless there are exceptional circumstances, the court will not inquire into whether the claim was fundamentally dishonest if the proceedings have been settled (**PD 44, para. 12.4(b)**). Under **CPR, r. 38.6(1)**, unless the court orders otherwise, a claimant who discontinues is liable for the costs of the defendant. Where a personal injuries claim has been discontinued, the effect of **CPR, r. 44.14(1)**, is that generally the claimant has costs protection under QOCS which overrides the usual costs position under **r. 38.6(1)**. However, the court may in such a case inquire into whether the claim was fundamentally dishonest under **r. 44.16(1)**, and can do so even if the notice of discontinuance has not been set aside (**PD 44, para. 12.4(c)**).

69.15

69.16

Proceedings for the financial benefit of another

69.17   The court may grant permission to enforce a costs order against a claimant who would otherwise have costs protection under QOCS if the proceedings include a claim which is made for the financial benefit of another person (**CPR, r. 44.16(2)**). Examples are subrogated claims and claims for credit hire (**PD 44, para. 12.2**), but do not include the provision of personal services rendered gratuitously for things like personal care, domestic assistance etc. (**PD 44, para. 12.3**). In such a case the court may also make a non-party costs order under the Senior Courts Act 1981, s. 51, and **CPR, r. 46.2**, against that other person (**r. 44.16(3)**), and in fact usually will do so (**PD 44, para. 12.5**).

Chapter 70   Fixed Costs etc.

INTRODUCTION

Fixed costs provide a means of ensuring certainty over how much litigation will cost a losing party under a party-and-party costs order, and a method by which the government can limit costs as a matter of policy. Certainty is obtained at the expense of flexibility, and while losing parties are protected by modestly calibrated fixed costs, successful parties have to meet any shortfall between the fixed amounts and their actual costs from their own resources. Part of the policy in using fixed costs is to put pressure on legal representatives to deliver the legal services covered by the fixed costs regime within the financial constraints laid down in the rules.   **70.1**

As part of the civil justice reforms of 2013 the whole of **CPR, Part 45**, on fixed costs was re-issued with substantial alterations with effect from 1 April 2013. This chapter deals with the post-1 April 2013 system. Fixed costs apply to simple steps in the litigation process, most fast track personal injury claims, and trial costs in fast track claims (for which, see 71.7). There is also a scale costs system for patent claims in the Intellectual Property Enterprise Court, which covers substantial claims in a complex area of law, and a rule limiting costs in environmental law claims.

SOURCE OF THE FIXED COSTS REGIME

The term 'fixed costs' means costs the amounts of which are fixed by the CPR, whether or not   **70.2**
the court has a discretion to allow some other or no amount, and includes the costs fixed by **CPR, rr.** 45.1 to 45.8, 45.11, 45.18, 45.21, 45.37 and 45.38 (**r.** 44.1(1)). These fixed costs are adopted by **r.** 27.14(2)(a) for all claims decided on the small claims track.

SITUATIONS WHERE FIXED COSTS APPLY

CPR, Part 45, and various other provisions lay down the situations where fixed costs apply,   **70.3**
broadly as follows:
(a) where the only claim is a claim for a specified sum of money which is more than £25 and judgment is given after the defendant admits all or part of the claim (**r.** 45.1(2)(a)(ii) and (iii));

(b) where the only claim is a claim for a specified sum of money which is more than £25 and judgment is entered by default (**r. 45.1(2)(a)(i)**);

(c) where the only claim is a claim for a specified sum of money which is more than £25 and summary judgment is entered (**r. 45.1(2)(a)(iv)**);

(d) where the only claim is a claim for a specified sum of money which is more than £25 and the claim succeeds after the defence is struck out as disclosing no reasonable grounds for defending the claim (**r. 45.1(2)(a)(v)**);

(e) where the only claim is for a specified sum of money and the defendant pays it together with the fixed commencement costs within 14 days of service of the particulars of claim (**rr. 45.1(2)(a)(vi)** and **45.3**; **r. 45.1(2)(a)(vi)** mistakenly refers to **r. 45.4** instead of **r. 45.3**);

(f) where judgment is given on a fixed date claim (see **r. 7.9** and **PD 7B**) for delivery of goods, worth more than £25 (**CPR, rr. 45.1(2)(b)** and **45.4**);

(g) in possession claims (with or without a money claim), including claims under **Part 55**, where the defendant gives up possession and pays the amount claimed with fixed commencement costs stated on the claim form (**rr. 45.1(2)(c)** and **45.5**);

(h) in possession claims based on non-payment of rent where the court gives a fixed date for the hearing when it issues the claim and judgment is given without the defendant denying liability (beyond making proposals for paying arrears of rent) (**rr. 45.1(2)(d)** and **45.5**);

(i) in accelerated possession claims of land let on assured shorthold tenancies under **Part 55, Section II**, where possession orders are made without the defendant denying liability (**rr. 45.1(2)(e)** and **45.5**);

(j) in successful demotion claims under **Part 65, Section III** (**rr. 45.1(2)(f)** and **45.5**);

(k) where a judgment creditor takes steps to enforce a judgment or order under **Parts 70** to **73** (**rr. 45.1(2)(g)** and **45.8**);

(l) on the issue of a default costs certificate (**PD 47, paras 10.7** and **10.8**); and

(m) on the determination of a small claims track claim (**CPR, r. 27.14(2)(a)**), and **PD 45, para. 1.2**.

The fixed costs regime in **Part 45, Section I** (**rr. 45.1** to **45.8**), applies unless the court orders otherwise (**r. 45.1(1)**). In the small claims track, **r. 27.14(2)(g)** permits the court to order further costs to be paid by a party who has behaved unreasonably (see **45.29**).

The fixed costs regime does not apply where the value of a claim for money or goods does not exceed £25 (**r. 45.1(3)**). Fixed costs usually apply to enforcement proceedings without the £25 minimum value, but the £25 threshold does apply to enforcement under **r. 70.5(4)** of awards made by tribunals other than the High Court and the County Court, and in relation to warrants of control and warrants of delivery under **r. 83.15** (**r. 45.8, Table 5**).

The amounts fixed are intended to deliver a moderate and predictable scheme of costs where there are no unusual factors and no real contest. It follows that the court is likely to depart from this regime where it is clear that it will not deliver proper remuneration for cases outside the norm. It is suggested that the court will have in mind the factors listed in **r. 44.4** (factors to be taken into account in deciding the amount of costs) in deciding whether to depart from fixed costs. For example, the court is unlikely to confine a successful claimant to fixed costs on a contested application for summary judgment, but a court may restrict a claimant to fixed costs on a straightforward rent arrears possession claim.

SUMS INCLUDED IN FIXED COSTS

70.4 Where the fixed costs regime of **CPR, Part 45, Section I** (**rr. 45.1** to **45.8** covering tables 1 to 5), applies, the costs are incremental, with each increment corresponding to a step in the proceedings:

(a) commencement (table 1 or 3);

(b) entry of judgment (table 2);

(c) exceptional forms of service (table 4);

(d) enforcement (table 5).

In addition, the successful litigant is entitled to recover the relevant court fee, for example, the issue fee or (in the case of summary judgment) the application fee (**r. 45.1(4)**).

Because the scheme is incremental, the amount that can be entered or that will be awarded will be the aggregate of the applicable sums.

Amounts allowed

There are 13 tables in **CPR, Part** 45, setting out the amounts allowed by way of fixed costs. **70.5** These are:

Table 1	Fixed costs on commencement of a claim for the recovery of money or goods (**r. 45.2**)
Table 2	Fixed costs on entry of judgment in a claim for the recovery of money or goods (**r. 45.4**)
Table 3	Fixed costs on commencement of a claim for the recovery of land or a demotion claim (**r. 45.5**, and see **rr. 65.11** to **65.20**)
Table 4	Miscellaneous fixed costs (**r. 45.7**)
Table 5	Fixed enforcement costs (**r. 45.8**)
Table 6	Fixed costs in relation to the RTA protocol (**r. 45.18**, and see **8.29** to **8.59**)
Table 6A	Fixed costs in relation to the EL/PL Protocol (**r. 45.18**, and see **8.60**)
Table 6B	Fixed costs where a claim no longer continues under the RTA Protocol (**r. 45.29C**, and see **70.17**)
Table 6C	Fixed costs in employers' liability claims where a claim no longer continues under the EL/PL Protocol (**r. 45.29E**, and see **70.17**)
Table 6D	Fixed costs in public liability claims where a claim no longer continues under the EL/PL Protocol (**r. 45.29E**, and see **70.17**)
Table 7	Fixed costs on commencement of a County Court claim conducted by an HMRC officer (**r. 45.34**)
Table 8	Fixed costs on entry of judgment in a County Court claim conducted by an HMRC officer (**r. 45.35**)
Table 9	Fixed fast track trial costs (**r. 45.38**, see **71.7**)

Rule 45.6(1) provides for fixed costs under **r. 45.1(2)(d)** and **(f)** of £57.25 for entering judgment in possession claims and demotion claims. Where an order for possession is made in an accelerated possession claim, the fixed costs under **r. 45.1(2)(e)** for preparing and filing the claim form, the documents that accompany the claim form, and the request for possession, total £79.50 (**r. 45.6(2)**).

PD 47, para. 10.7, provides for fixed costs of £80 plus the appropriate court fee to be included in default costs certificates.

ENTERING FIXED COSTS ON THE CLAIM FORM

Where fixed costs are recoverable they should be inserted on the claim form or application (for **70.6** example, simple claims for the recovery of money or possession of land, or where the party is seeking to enforce a tribunal award under **CPR, r. 70.5**) or the request for the enforcement process. At the bottom right-hand corner of the general claim form (N1) there is a box for entering a number of figures, including the issue fee and fixed costs for commencing the proceedings. In claims where fixed costs do not apply (i.e. most damages claims and claims for equitable relief), the relevant box on the claim form should be marked 'to be assessed' (**PD 45, para. 1.3**).

Commentary

SMALL CLAIMS TRACK FIXED COSTS

70.7   It is provided in CPR, r. 27.14(2)(a)(ii), that the fixed costs payable in small claims track cases are those which are payable under Part 45, or would be payable under Part 45 if that Part applied to the case. This provision is necessary because the fixed costs rules in Part 45 do not apply, for example, to unspecified money claims (most damages claims), and the plain intention behind r. 27.14(2)(a) is that the same fixed costs should be recoverable in all types of small claims track cases. This is confirmed by PD 45, para. 1.2, which says the fixed costs to be awarded in small claims track cases are the sum of the fixed commencement costs calculated in accordance with table 1 in r. 45.2 and the appropriate court fees paid by the claimant.

PREDICTABLE COSTS IN ROAD TRAFFIC ACCIDENT CLAIMS

Disputes covered by the scheme

70.8   CPR, Part 45, Section II (rr. 45.9 to 45.15), provides a scheme (which originally came into force on 6 October 2003) for predictable costs for certain road traffic claims that settle before the issue of proceedings and (from 1 April 2005), proceedings for the approval of a settlement or compromise under r. 21.10(2). The rules are supplemented by PD 45, paras 2.1 to 2.10.

The provisions apply only to disputes arising out of road traffic accidents occurring on or after 6 October 2003. A road traffic accident is defined as 'an accident resulting in bodily injury to any person or damage to property caused by, or arising out of, the use of a motor vehicle on a road or other public place in England and Wales' (CPR, r. 45.9(4)). A motor vehicle is a mechanically propelled vehicle intended for use on roads (r. 45.9(4)) and a road is any highway and any other road to which the public has access, including bridges over which a road passes (r. 45.9(4)). Where a claim arises from a road traffic accident, such as where a passenger is injured when alighting from a coach, the predictable costs scheme in rr. 45.9 to 45.15 applies and is not displaced by pleading the claim under the Occupiers' Liability Act 1957 or on any other legal basis (*Green v Kis Coaches and Taxis Ltd* (2008) LTL 13/5/2008 (Plymouth County Court)).

The provisions are confined to claims which settle before issue of proceedings (PD 45, para. 2.1) for agreed damages which do not exceed £10,000 (CPR, r. 45.9(2)(c)) and for which the small claims track would not have been appropriate (r. 45.9(2)(d)). The agreed damages must include damages in respect of personal injury and/or damage to property (r. 45.9(2)(b)). They must, by PD 45, para. 2.3, be calculated including:

(a)   general and special damages and interest;

(b)   interim payments;

but after deducting:

(c)   an amount attributable to agreed contributory negligence;

(d)   any amount which the compensating party is required by statute to pay directly to a third party (such as compensation recovery payments and National Health Service expenses).

Provided the above conditions are satisfied, there is no further requirement that the costs sought fall within the indemnity principle (see 71.30). It is enough that the conditions are satisfied (*Nizami v Butt* [2006] EWHC 159 (QB), [2006] 1 WLR 3307).

Amount recoverable

70.9   The amount which can be allowed in costs-only proceedings relating to a dispute within CPR, Part 45, Section II (see 70.8), is limited by r. 45.10 to:

(a)   fixed recoverable costs related to the amount of the agreed damages prescribed by r. 45.11(1) (see 70.10);

(b) VAT on item (a) (**r. 45.11(3)**);

(c) disbursements (**r. 45.12(1)**), limited to the items listed in **r. 45.12(2)** (see **70.13**). Where there is more than one claimant in relation to a single accident, damages will be agreed in relation to them individually and costs will be calculated in relation to each of them accordingly (**PD 45, para. 2.7**).

Where the costs limit specified in **r. 45.10** is acceptable there is no need for costs-only proceedings. If it is considered that there are exceptional circumstances justifying a greater recovery, costs-only proceedings may be brought under **r. 45.13** (see **70.14**).

Fixed recoverable costs

The fixed recoverable costs which are to be allowed in relation to a dispute within **CPR, Part 45, Section II** (see **70.8**), are, by **r. 45.11(1) and (2)**:   **70.10**

(a) £800, plus

(b) 20 per cent of the damages agreed up to £5,000, plus

(c) 15 per cent of the damages agreed between £5,000 and £10,000, plus

(d) 12.5 per cent London weighting, where available (see **70.12**).

VAT can be added (**r. 45.11(3)**).

If the court considers that there are exceptional circumstances, it may entertain a claim for more than the fixed recoverable costs (**r. 45.13(1)**; see **70.14**).

Examples   If agreed damages are £3,500 and no London weighting is available, the fixed recoverable costs are: **70.11**

£800 + 20% of £3,500 = £800 + £700 = £1,500

If a London weighting is available, the amount is increased by 12.5 per cent (12.5% of £1,500 is £187.50) to £1,687.50.

If agreed damages are £8,500 and no London weighting is available, the fixed recoverable costs are:

£800 + 20% of £5,000 + 15% of £3,500 = £800 + £1,000 + £525 = £2,325

The London weighting on £2,325 is 12.5% of £2,325, which is £290.62, giving a total of £2,615.62.

London weighting   The 12.5 per cent London weighting is available under **CPR, r. 45.11(2)**, if the claimant lives or works in the area described by **PD 45, para. 2.6**, and instructs solicitors practising in that area. The designated area consists of the area served by the County Court hearing centres at: Barnet, Bow, Brentford, Bromley, Central London, Clerkenwell and Shoreditch, Croydon, Dartford, Edmonton, Gravesend, Ilford, Lambeth, Mayor's and City of London, Romford, Uxbridge, Wandsworth, Willesden, and Woolwich.   **70.12**

Disbursements

By **CPR, r. 45.12**, only the following disbursements can be recovered under the scheme: **70.13**

(a) the cost of obtaining medical records;

(b) the cost of obtaining a medical report;

(c) the cost of obtaining a police report;

(d) the cost of obtaining an engineer's report;

(e) the cost of a search of the records of the Driver and Vehicle Licensing Agency;

(f) where the claimant is a child or protected party, necessarily incurred counsels' and court fees for a court application for approval of the settlement;

(g) any other disbursement which has arisen due to a 'particular feature' of the dispute.

Commentary

Claim for more than the fixed recoverable costs

70.14 If the court considers that there are exceptional circumstances, it may entertain a claim, in costs-only proceedings, for more than the fixed recoverable costs (**CPR, r. 45.13(1)**). If it considers the claim is appropriate, it may either assess the costs or make an order for them to be assessed (**r. 45.13(2)**). However, if the assessed figure is not 20 per cent or more above the fixed costs, the claimant will only be able to recover the fixed costs or, if they are less, the assessed costs (**r. 45.14**). If an application for an assessment is unsuccessful, or results in an assessment which is less than 20 per cent above the fixed costs, the claimant must pay the defendant's costs of defending the costs-only proceedings, and the court cannot make any order in respect of the claimant's costs of those proceedings (**r. 45.15**).

Practical implications

70.15 When a road traffic accident claim is within **CPR, Part 45, Section II**, a solicitor will simply be able to agree the costs set out in **rr. 45.10 to 45.12**, dispensing with any assessment of costs. It is hoped that this will enhance the cash flow for firms representing claimants and provide transparency and predictability for defendant insurers. It should also lead to a reduction in costs-only proceedings for relatively minor cases, as exemplified by the approach in *Nizami v Butt* [2006] EWHC 159 (QB), [2006] 1 WLR 3307 (see **70.8**).

Naturally there will be a temptation for the receiving party to bring costs-only proceedings in the hope of achieving a better level of remuneration from a detailed assessment. The scheme therefore places a considerable costs risk on a claimant who seeks to adopt this route (see **70.14**). The provisions of **Part 36** and **r. 47.20** concerning offers to settle apply. In addition the assessment must beat the predictable costs by 20 per cent or more before anything extra is payable (**r. 45.15**). This creates something of an anomaly. The costs officer or costs judge will be able to work out from **r. 45.11** the predictable costs and will know when the critical 20 per cent is achieved. It might be suggested that **r. 45.14** is akin to an assessment hearing. Given the level of costs that can arise on costs-only proceedings, the receiving party will be at significant risk in commencing such proceedings.

RTA AND EL/PL PROTOCOL FIXED COSTS

70.16 **CPR, rr. 45.16 to 45.28**, set out the code dealing with fixed costs recoverable in RTA and EL/PL Protocol claims (see **8.29 to 8.60**). The only costs allowed (**r. 45.17**) are:

(a) fixed costs under **r. 45.18**, which are set out in tables 6 and 6A in **Part 45**;
(b) disbursements in accordance with **r. 45.19**;
(c) fixed costs for additional advice on quantum for claims over £10,000 in accordance with
    r. 45.23B;

The Stage 1 fixed costs for RTA claims up to £10,000 are £200, and the Stage 2 fixed costs are £300. For RTA claims over £10,000 and up to £25,000, Stage 1 fixed costs are £200 and Stage 2 fixed costs are £600.

For EL and PL claims up to £10,000 Stage 1 fixed costs are £3,000 and Stage 2 fixed costs are £600. For EL and PL claims over £10,000 and up to £25,000 these figures are £300 (Stage 1) and £1,300 (Stage 2).

In all RTA and EL/PL Protocol claims, at Stage 3 the advocate's costs (Type B fixed costs) are £250, and the costs of any advice on quantum where the claimant is a child (Type C) is £150. Type C fixed costs are also available where the claim is worth more than £10,000 and advice on quantum from a specialist solicitor or from counsel is reasonably required to value the claim (**r. 45.23B**). From 1 October 2014 there are fixed costs for medical reports in whiplash claims under the RTA Protocol (**r. 45.19(2A)**).

CLAIMS LEAVING THE RTA AND EL/PL PROTOCOLS

From 31 July 2013, RTA and EL/PL Protocol claims that continue outside the relevant Protocol are governed by the fixed costs rules in **CPR, rr. 45.29A to 45.29L**. Table 6B sets out the fixed costs for RTA claims. EL claims are governed by table 6C, and PL claims by table 6D. In each table the fixed costs are divided into claims between £1,000 and £5,000; more than £5,000 up to £10,000; and more than £10,000 up to £25,000. Each table also fixes costs depending on whether the claim is settled before issue of proceedings; or between issue and before trial; or if the claim is disposed of at trial. A further fixed amount is allowed for trial advocacy fees. A 12.5 per cent London weighting is allowed (**rr. 45.29C(2)** and **45.29E(2)**) in the same circumstances as described at **70.12**. Recoverable disbursements are dealt with by **r. 45.29I** and **PD 45, para. 2A.1**. There is a power to exceed the fixed amounts where there are exceptional circumstances **r. 45.29J**. From 1 October 2014 there are fixed costs for medical reports in whiplash claims leaving the RTA Protocol (**r. 45.29I(2A)**).

70.17

SCALE COSTS IN THE INTELLECTUAL PROPERTY ENTERPRISE COURT

CPR, rr. 45.30 to 45.32, lay down rules for scale costs in proceedings in the Intellectual Property Enterprise Court. Scale costs do not apply where the court considers a party to have behaved in a manner that amounts to an abuse of the court's process, or where the claim concerns infringement or revocation of a patent or registered design the validity of which has been certified by a court in earlier proceedings (**r. 45.30(2)**).

70.18

The maximum amount of scale costs that the court will award for each stage of an Intellectual Property Enterprise Court claim are set out in **PD 45, para. 3.3**. This has two tables, table A for each stage up to determination of liability, and table B for each stage in an inquiry as to damages or an account of profits. Each entry in the tables is the maximum (to which VAT should be added, **r. 45.31(5)**) for that stage. For example, the maximum for particulars of claim is £6,125, and the maximum for making or defending an application is £2,500. Whatever the sums allowed under the various stages in tables A and B, **r. 45.31(1)** provides that in any event the total scale costs cannot exceed:

(a) £50,000 on the final determination on liability; and
(b) £25,000 on an inquiry as to damages or account of profits.

Fixed Revenue and Customs costs

CPR, rr. 45.33 to 45.36, set out fixed costs rules for commencing and entering judgment in County Court debt claims brought by HMRC Officers under the Commissioners for Revenue and Customs Act 2005, s. 25(1A).

70.19

ENVIRONMENTAL LAW CASES

CPR, rr. 45.41 to 45.44, provide rules to limit the costs of environmental law judicial review claims governed by the Aarhus Convention 1998. Claimants opt into the costs limitation

70.20

rules in these cases by stating the claim is an Aarhus Convention claim in the claim form (**r. 45.44(1)**), although the defendant can object, in which case the court will determine whether the Convention applies. A claimant can opt out of the cost limitation rules by not stating that the claim is an Aarhus Convention claim in the claim form (**r. 45.42(a)**). Where it applies, the claimant's liability for costs is limited to £5,000 if they are an individual and not a business, and £10,000 in other cases (**PD 45, para. 5.1**). Costs liability of defendants is limited to £35,000 (**para. 5.2**).

Chapter 71   Assessment of Costs

The following procedural checklist is relevant to this chapter:

Procedural checklist 30   Summary assessment of costs

INTRODUCTION

71.1 Once a costs order has been made, it is necessary to determine how much should be allowed in respect of those costs, that is, how much the paying party must pay to the receiving party. A similar determination must be made when a solicitor bills a client and when a solicitor is seeking to recover costs from the State in a publicly funded claim. The costs of and incidental to the proceedings are, by the Senior Courts Act 1981, s. 51(1), in the discretion of the court. It follows from this that once proceedings are started, a costs order will ordinarily cover pre-commencement costs as well as costs incurred from the date proceedings were issued. By **CPR, r. 44.1(1)**, 'costs' includes fees, charges, disbursements, expenses, remuneration, reimbursement allowed to a litigant in person under **r. 46.5**, and any fee or reward charged by a lay representative for acting on behalf of a party in proceedings allocated to the small claims track. Whether costs incurred in mediation are included is discussed at **8.6**. Generally, the costs incurred by a party in seeking funding for litigation do not form part of the costs of the claim (*National Westminster Bank plc v Kotonou* [2009] EWHC 3309 (Ch), LTL 17/12/2009, the exception being where the costs in seeking funding form the subject matter of the litigation).

There is no rule that the costs of one set of proceedings cannot be recovered as costs which are 'of and incidental to' another set of proceedings within the meaning of the Senior Courts Act 1981, s. 51(1) (*Roach v Home Office* [2009] EWHC 312 (QB), [2010] QB 256). It may therefore be possible to recover the costs of attending an inquest as incidental to subsequent civil proceedings. Relevant factors are:

(a) the purpose of the attendance at the inquest;
(b) the relevance of the attendance to the subsequent proceedings; and
(c) the reasonableness and proportionality of the costs incurred.

In **chapter 70** the system of fixed costs applicable to certain situations in litigation was considered. This chapter will deal with assessment of costs by the courts.

All references in this chapter, other than in **71.39** and **71.56** to **71.63**, are to the CPR and practice directions in force from 1 April 2013 (and as subsequently amended) following the civil justice reforms of 2013.

METHODS OF QUANTIFICATION OF COSTS

71.2 It is open to the parties to agree the amount of costs to be paid under a costs order. Alternatively, costs may be assessed by the court. **CPR, r. 44.6**, provides that when the court makes a costs order it may either:

(a) make a summary assessment of the costs; or
(b) order a detailed assessment by a costs officer.

A 'costs officer' is defined by **CPR, r. 44.1(1)**, to mean a costs judge (which in turn means a taxing master of the Senior Courts), a District Judge or an authorised court officer (i.e. a civil servant, in a District Registry, the Family Court, the Senior Courts Costs Office or the County Court, who is authorised by the Lord Chancellor to assess costs).

AGREEING AMOUNT OF COSTS

Parties may agree the amount of costs to be paid when they settle a claim or when agreeing a **71.3** consent order. If the agreement is to be drawn up in a consent order or judgment, the draft order should include a term that one party shall pay the agreed sum in costs to the other (**PD 47, para. 9.3**). If the agreement is reached after the order or judgment is made, either party may apply for a costs certificate in the amount agreed (**CPR, r. 47.10(1)**, and see **71.28**). Such an application is made under **r. 40.6**, and may be dealt with by a costs officer (**PD 47, para. 9.1**). The court will not give its approval to disproportionate or unreasonable costs. So, when the amount of costs has been agreed between the parties, any court order must state that the order is made by consent (**PD 44, para. 9.10**).

SUMMARY ASSESSMENT

Summary assessment involves a short assessment of a party's costs. Because it is a summary **71.4** procedure it will not involve the lengthy consideration of items which is reserved for a detailed assessment. Thus in *Gould v Armstrong* [2002] EWCA Civ 1159, LTL 23/7/2002, the court approved a robust summary assessment as an effective and proportionate means of avoiding the cost and delay associated with a detailed assessment.

The procedure for summary assessment of costs is summarised in **procedural checklist 30**.

Summary assessment of costs generally arises at the conclusion of a fast track trial or other hearings which do not last more than one day (**PD 44, para. 9.2**) (see **32.31, 46.22** and **68.27**). There are situations where it will not be appropriate to conduct a summary assessment of costs even though the conditions of **para. 9.2** are met (for a list of these see **68.27**). Conversely there is nothing to prevent the court from summarily assessing the costs even where the conditions in **para. 9.2** are not met, for example, when the trial lasts for more than one day (*Q v Q (Family Proceedings: Costs Order)* [2002] 2 FLR 668). Summary assessment is not required where the parties have agreed the amount of the costs, in which event the order must state the order is by consent (**para. 9.10**).

Summary assessment is preceded by the service of a statement of costs on form N260 not less than 24 hours before the time fixed for the hearing (or two days before a fast track trial) (**para. 9.5(4)**). At first sight the wording of this provision suggests that the requirement to serve the costs statement is mandatory and that failure would lead to the loss of all costs or alternatively to a detailed assessment. This approach was rejected by the court in *MacDonald v Taree Holdings Ltd* [2000] CPLR 439. Instead, any failure to serve the statement of costs without reasonable cause will be taken into account in deciding what order to make about the costs of the claim, and about the costs of any further hearing or detailed assessment hearing (**para. 9.6**). In *Wheeler v Chief Constable of Gloucestershire Constabulary* [2013] EWCA Civ 1791, LTL 18/12/2013, a failure to file a statement of costs resulted in the court ordering a detailed assessment, which was penalised by ordering the successful party to pay the costs of the detailed assessment.

Statement of costs

A statement of costs must be in form N260 and must, by **PD 44, para. 9.5(2)**, address the **71.5** following matters:

(a) The number of hours claimed, divided into detailed component parts of the work done as set out in the statement of costs form (N260).
(b) The hourly rate claimed. Practitioners may wish to consider **tables 71.2, 71.3** and **71.4**, which set out the guideline rate for each court in the country, based on figures from the Guide to the Summary Assessment of Costs published by the Senior Courts Costs Office (SCCO).

(c) The grade of fee earner. The name and grade of the fee earners working on the case must be entered on form N260, together with their hourly rates. It is important to refer to the four categories of fee earner found at the foot of the form N260 and to appreciate that they are experience based. Thus the term 'partner' has no place in the form N260, whereas a solicitor with over eight years' post-qualification experience in litigation is an acceptable description.

(d) The amount and nature of disbursements. Work which is outsourced should normally appear in the body of the bill as if carried out by the firm (*Smith Graham v Lord Chancellor's Department* (1999) 149 NLJ 1433). There is some concern as to whether a solicitor should be able to recover for work outsourced to agents. While there is no appellate authority on the issue, Judge Michael Cook found that such items could be allowed on an assessment, provided there is sufficient information to allow the judge to ascertain whether they were reasonably incurred and reasonable in amount (*Stringer v Copley* (2002) LTL 17/10/2002).

(e) The amount of the legal representative's costs for attending or appearing at the hearing.

(f) Counsel's fees.

(g) VAT on the above. Practitioners must be vigilant to ensure that VAT is included in the bill only if it is properly claimed. Costs are compensatory and thus VAT can only be charged if the receiving party will lose the VAT. Most VAT-registered parties will be able to reclaim VAT and thus it will not represent an overall loss. Hence VAT should not generally be claimed where the party is registered for VAT. (See **PD 44, paras 2.3** and **2.4** and **71.54**.)

(h) The statement of costs must be signed (**PD 44, para. 9.5(3)**). The signature is not an empty formality, it is a certificate given by an officer of the court that the statement is accurate and that there is no infringement of the indemnity principle. It affords a presumption of trust to the paying party (*Bailey v IBC Vehicles Ltd* [1998] 3 All ER 570). Where a solicitor failed to sign a statement of costs the court has been prepared to stay the issue of the costs order (*Wilson v Howard Pawnbrokers* [2002] EWHC 1489 (Ch), LTL 19/8/2002).

Quantifying costs on a summary assessment

71.6 Courts sometimes develop conventional figures for summarily assessed costs for certain types of proceeding, such as the costs awarded for straightforward landlord and tenant possession proceedings. Although this may be acceptable in straightforward possession claims, it is contrary to principle in the majority of claims. On a summary assessment of costs the court must focus on the detailed breakdown of costs actually incurred by the party in question as shown on its statement of costs. The court is entitled to draw on its general experience of costs in comparable cases, and it may be helpful to draw on that experience when comparing the total from its assessment of the costs on the schedule to see whether those costs were reasonable and proportionate. What the court cannot do is to use a judicial tariff for different categories of claims (*1-800 Flowers Inc. v Phonenames Ltd* [2001] EWCA Civ 721, [2001] 2 Costs LR 286). For the same reasons it is an error for a court to fix a figure for costs at what the judge considers to be the upper reasonable limit for cases of that type without considering the actual costs on an item-by-item basis (*Morgan v Spirit Group Ltd* [2011] EWCA Civ 68, [2011] PIQR P9). The court can call for whatever evidence is available at the time in deciding on the figure to allow, such as looking at counsel's brief to see the brief fee, as well as looking at the costs statements and hearing the advocates on the work involved in the matter.

In *Edwards v Devon and Cornwall Constabulary* [2001] EWCA Civ 388, LTL 13/3/2001, on a summary assessment after a fast track trial, the judge reduced the claimant's costs schedule from £7,500 to £2,500 and did not allow counsel to address him on the reduction. After disbursements this gave the claimant's solicitors £620 in a non-straightforward personal injuries claim. The Court of Appeal substituted its own summary assessment of the claimant's costs. In *Contractreal Ltd v Davies* [2001] EWCA Civ 928, LTL 17/5/2001, the appellant's costs were reduced from £21,000 to £1,750 on a summary assessment. On appeal it was held that the judge had placed too much weight upon the size of the bill in comparison with the amount in issue when considering proportionality, and had failed to distinguish between pre and post-CPR costs (proportionality only applies to the latter), and the court ordered a detailed assessment.

Where costs are assessed summarily they are payable within 14 days unless the court in its discretion thinks fit to order otherwise (**CPR, rr. 44.2 and 44.7**). A party seeking such a direction must apply for it and, where appropriate, must back up the application with evidence. The court can, of its own initiative, postpone the date of payment, where it considers there are appropriate reasons (*Pepin v Watts* [2001] CPLR 9 at [29]).

FAST TRACK TRIAL COSTS

Fixed trial costs

There is a system of fixed trial costs in fast track claims. The amounts allowed depend on the   **71.7**
value of the claim and whether the claim is governed by the fixed costs regime for claims leaving the RTA or EL/PL Protocols, and are set out in **CPR, rr. 45.29C, 45.29E and 45.38**; see **table 71.1**. Claims not covered by these two protocols are identified as 'Non-PI' in the table. There is also a system of fixed costs for the claim in cases governed by the RTA and EL/PL Protocols, see **70.16** and **70.17**.

For a successful claimant the value of the claim is the amount of the judgment excluding interest, costs and any reduction for contributory negligence, whereas for a successful defendant it is the amount the claimant specified on the claim form (or the maximum amount that could have been recovered on the pleaded case) (**r. 45.38(3)**). If there is a counterclaim and both parties succeed, the relevant amount is the difference between the value of the two claims (**r. 45.39(6)**). If there is a counterclaim with a greater value than the claim, and the claimant succeeds on the claim and defeats the counterclaim, the relevant amount is the value of the counterclaim (**r. 45.38(6)**). There are detailed rules dealing with cases where there are several claimants or several defendants, including whether more than one party can be awarded fast track trial costs, which are set out in **r. 45.40**. Claims for non-monetary remedies are deemed to have a value between £3,000 and £10,000, but the court has a discretion to make some other order, see **r. 45.38(4)**.

The court is not permitted to award more or less than the set figures for trial costs, unless it decides not to award any fast track trial costs or **r. 45.39** applies (**r. 45.38(2)**). Guidance given by the Senior Costs Judge to the Designated Civil Judges Conference on 24 November 2000 is to the effect that this means that unless a **r. 45.39** factor applies, the court must allow the standard trial costs even if the brief fee is lower than the standard amount. This is so notwithstanding the indemnity principle (see **71.30**).

The additional allowance for a solicitor attending with counsel is only available in cases not governed by the RTA and EL/PL Protocols (**r. 45.39(2)**; there is no equivalent in **rr. 45.29A to 45.29L**). This £345 sum will only be payable if the court awards fast track trial costs and if the court considers that it was necessary for a legal representative to attend to assist counsel (**r. 45.39(2)**).

Table 71.1 Fast track fixed trial costs

Value of claim	Non-PI	RTA	EL/PL
No more than £3,000	£485	£500	£500
£3,000 to £10,000	£690	£710	£710
£10,000 to £15,000	£1,035	£1,070	£1,070
£15,000 to £25,000	£1,650	£1,705	£1,705

Value of claim	Non-PI	RTA	EL/PL
Attendance by solicitor with counsel	£345	N/A	N/A
Non-monetary relief	£690	N/A	N/A

Abortive preparation, split trials and misconduct

71.8   If a fast track claim settles before the start of the trial, costs may be allowed in respect of the advocate preparing for trial, but the amount allowed cannot be more than the above figures (**CPR, r. 46.12**). In deciding the amount to be allowed for the abortive preparation, the court will take into account when the claim settled and when the court was notified of that fact.

If there are split trials, such as on liability and quantum, it is possible to be awarded a second tranche of fast track trial costs, but the second award should not exceed two thirds of the amount payable under the first award, subject to a minimum award of £485 (**r. 45.39(3)** and **(4)**).

A successful party may, by **r. 45.39(7)**, be awarded less than the above fixed fast track trial costs for unreasonable or improper behaviour during the trial, and the losing party may be ordered to pay an additional amount if it is guilty of behaving improperly during the trial (**r. 45.39(8)**).

INTERIM PAYMENT ON ACCOUNT OF COSTS

71.9   The court has a power to make an order for an amount to be paid on account of costs which will be assessed at some later stage (**CPR, r. 44.2(8)**). In the ordinary course, an order for an interim payment on account will be made (**r. 44.2(8)**), applying the overriding objective (*Berntsen v Tait* [2013] EWCA Civ 1520, LTL 2/10/2013). An important factor in exercising the discretion under **r. 44.2(8)** is that the receiving party should not be kept out of moneys that will almost certainly be found to be payable under the costs order (*Blakemore v Cummings* [2009] EWCA Civ 1276, [2010] 1 WLR 983). Other relevant circumstances, which will vary from case to case, include any uncertainty over the amount likely to be assessed, a relatively short time to the detailed assessment hearing, delay, the likelihood of an appeal, and the financial means of the paying party. An order for an interim payment on account of costs may be made even where the receiving party is late in commencing detailed assessment proceedings (*Allason v Random House UK Ltd* (2002) LTL 28/2/2002, where a payment of £140,000 was ordered in respect of costs said to amount to at least £175,000). An interim payment on account of costs may be ordered even where there is no detailed breakdown of the costs (*Simms v Law Society* [2005] EWCA Civ 849, [2005] ACD 98).

Where there has been a full trial, the successful party should normally be awarded an interim payment on account of costs under **r. 44.2(8)** in an amount up to the minimum sum which is almost certain to be awarded on a detailed assessment (*Mars UK Ltd v Teknowledge Ltd* [1999] IP & T 26). It is for the successful party to justify the court making an order, and, bearing in mind **r. 47.16**, it may be inappropriate even to make an interim payment in the minimum sum the successful party will inevitably recover in a detailed assessment (*Dyson Ltd v Hoover Ltd (No. 4)* [2003] EWHC 624 (Ch), [2004] 1 WLR 1264).

If the paying party fails to pay an interim payment on account of costs, the court has jurisdiction to make an order debarring that party from taking part in the detailed assessment (*Days Healthcare UK Ltd v Pihsiang Machinery Manufacturing Co. Ltd* [2006] EWHC 1444 (QB), [2006] 4 All ER 233). Langley J said that the assessment hearing would still proceed, but simply without the paying party, as it would be wrong to rubber-stamp the bill without any adjudication by the costs judge.

A stay on payment of an interim payment on account of costs may be ordered where immediate payment runs the risk that justice will not be done, for example, where there is an appeal (*Renewable Power and Light plc v Renewable Power and Light Services Inc.* (2008) LTL 7/4/2008).

DETAILED ASSESSMENT

Unlike summary assessment, a detailed assessment is not generally conducted until the conclusion of the proceedings (**CPR, r. 47.1**). Proceedings are concluded when the court has finally determined the matters in issue in the claim, whether or not there is an appeal (**PD 47, para. 1.1**). However, the court retains a power to order an assessment at an earlier stage. An order may be made allowing detailed assessment proceedings to be commenced if there is no realistic prospect of the claim continuing (**PD 47, para. 1.5**).

71.10

Appropriate office

All applications and requests in detailed assessment proceedings must be made to or filed at the 'appropriate office' (**CPR, r. 47.4**). In High Court cases this is usually the Senior Courts Costs Office (SCCO). If the court dealing with the case when the judgment or order was made or when the event occurred which gave rise to the right to assessment, or to which the case has subsequently been transferred, is the Family Court or a District Registry or the County Court then that registry, court or hearing centre is the appropriate office (**PD 47, para. 4.1**). The County Court normally deals with detailed assessments from tribunals and similar bodies (**para. 4.1(b)**). County Court hearing centres may make a direction that another hearing centre is to be the appropriate office (**CPR, r. 47.4(3)**). Any court can direct that the SCCO is to be the appropriate office (**CPR, r. 47.4(2)**), but should only do so having regard to the size of the bill of costs, its difficulty, length of hearing and costs to the parties (**PD 47, para. 4.3(2)**). An order transferring a bill to another court or to the SCCO can be made on the application of a party or on the court's own initiative.

71.11

Detailed assessments in London County Court hearing centres (Barnet, Bow, Brentford, Central London, Clerkenwell and Shoreditch, Croydon, Edmonton, Ilford, Lambeth, Mayor's and City of London, Romford, Wandsworth, Willesden and Woolwich) will take place in the SCCO unless the court orders otherwise (**PD 47, para. 4.2**). However, default costs certificates and applications to set aside default costs certificates should be issued and heard in the relevant County Court hearing centre (**para. 4.2(2)(b)**), and appeals are lodged at the Central London Civil Justice Centre (**para. 4.2(2)(c)**).

Commencement of detailed assessment proceedings

Detailed assessment proceedings must be commenced within three months of the judgment, order, award or other determination giving rise to the right to costs (**CPR, r. 47.7**). The period may be extended or shortened by agreement between the parties (**PD 47, para. 6.1**). A similar three-month period is laid down in respect of cases terminated by discontinuance, dismissal or acceptance of Part 36 offers (**CPR, r. 47.7**). Detailed assessment proceedings are commenced by serving on the paying party a notice of commencement (form N252) together with a copy of the bill of costs and, if a costs management order has been made (see **43.13**), a breakdown of the costs claimed for each phase of the proceedings (**r. 47.6(1)**) using Precedent Q in **PD 47**. The receiving party is also required to serve copies of counsel's fee notes and experts' fee invoices, written evidence for all disbursements exceeding £500, and a statement giving the name and address for service of any person upon whom the receiving party intends to serve the notice of commencement (**PD 47, para. 5.2**). The persons referred to in the previous sentence are known as 'relevant persons', who are defined by **PD 47, para. 5.5**, as persons who took part in the proceedings and who are directly liable

71.12

to pay the costs under a costs order, and also persons who have given notice that they have a financial interest in the outcome of the assessment and any other person the court may direct to be treated as a relevant person. Relevant persons must also be served with the notice of commencement, the bill of costs and any breakdown in Precedent Q (**CPR, r. 47.6(2)**). They are thereafter regarded as being parties to the assessment proceedings.

Assessment of costs payable out of the legal aid fund is commenced by filing a request for a detailed assessment (Form N258A), which must be served on the assisted person (**r. 47.18(3)**). This must be done within three months from the date when the right to detailed assessment arose (**r. 47.18(2)**). In assessments of publicly funded costs, in addition to the documents referred to in the previous paragraph, the request for a detailed assessment must, by **PD 47, para. 17.2**, be accompanied by the legal aid certificates, LSC certificates, certificates recording the determinations of the Director of Legal Aid Casework, any relevant amendments and authorities, and any certificate of discharge, revocation or withdrawal.

The relevant papers in support of the bill described in **PD 47, para. 13.12**, have to be lodged only if requested by the costs officer (**para. 17.2(2)**). Names and addresses of any person with financial interests in the assessment, and of the assisted person, if he or she wishes to attend, must be provided.

The effect of failing to commence proceedings for the detailed assessment of costs within the prescribed time limit is considered at **71.25**.

Bill of costs

71.13   There are four model forms of bill of costs set out in the schedule to **PD 47**, precedents A to D. See also the New Bill of Costs Pilot Scheme in **PD 51L** for assessments in the SCCO, which operated in its original form between 1 October 2015 and 2 October 2016, and in its revised form from 3 October 2016, with a view to establishing a mandatory form of bill of costs for all work from 1 October 2017. **PD 47, paras 5.7** and **5.12**, provide that a bill of costs may consist of such of the following sections as may be appropriate:

(a) a title page;
(b) background information;
(c) items of costs claimed under the following headings:
    (i)   attendances on the court and on counsel up to the date of the notice of commencement;
    (ii)   attendances on and communications with the receiving party;
    (iii) attendances on and communications with witnesses including expert witnesses;
    (iv) attendances to inspect any property or place for the purposes of the proceedings;
    (v)   attendances on and communications with other persons, including offices of public records;
    (vi) communications with the court and with counsel;
    (vii) work done on documents;
    (viii) attendances on and communications with London and other agents and work done by them;
    (ix) other work done which was of or incidental to the proceedings and which is not already covered in the heads listed above.
(d) a summary showing the total costs claimed on each page of the bill;
(e) schedules of time spent on non-routine attendances; and
(f) appropriate certificates as set out in precedent F in the schedule to **PD 47**.

The bill may be divided into two or more parts to distinguish between times when the receiving party was acting in person and between times before and during the continuance of legal aid (**PD 47, para. 5 8(1)** and **(4)**). Different parts must also be used where there are different paying parties (**para. 5.8(5)**) and to distinguish between costs for work done before and after 1 April 2013 (**para. 5.8(7)**). Where a costs management order has been made, with the receiving party's costs budget having been agreed or approved, the bill must be divided into separate parts corresponding to each phase in the budget (**para. 5.8(8)**), with a separate part for the costs of the costs management process (**para. 5.8(9)**).

Where the receiving party was represented by different legal representatives during the course of proceedings, the bill should be divided into different parts so as to distinguish between the costs payable in respect of each legal representative (**PD 47, para. 5.8(3)**). If the receiving party fails to do this, and the costs judge completes the assessment and issues a final certificate, the receiving party cannot claim a further assessment of the omitted costs (*Moat Housing Group-South Ltd v Harris (No. 2)* [2007] EWHC 3092 (QB), [2008] 1 WLR 1578). If one of the firms' costs are omitted from the bill, and the parties agree the costs in the bill, whether the bill can be amended depends on the construction of the agreement, and whether the receiving party has communicated an intention to make a later claim for the costs incurred by the other solicitors.

Each item in the bill must be consecutively numbered (**PD 47, para. 5.15**). The bill may be organised into five columns, headed 'Item', 'Amount claimed', 'VAT', with the last two left blank, but headed 'Amount allowed' and 'VAT' (**PD 47, para. 5.17** and precedents A to C).

Points of dispute

In a detailed assessment of costs the paying party and others served with the notice of commencement may dispute any item in the bill by serving all the other parties with points of dispute. Points of dispute should be short and to the point, and should follow as closely as possible precedent G in the schedule to PD 47 (**PD 47, para. 8.2**; Senior Courts Costs Office Guide 2013, para. 6.2). They must:

    71.14

(a) identify any general points or matters of principle which require decision before the individual items in the bill are addressed; and
(b) identify specific points, stating concisely the nature and grounds of the dispute.

Once a point has been made it should not be repeated, but the item numbers where the point arises should be inserted in the left hand box as shown in precedent G (**para. 8.2**). Copies of the points of dispute should also be served on other persons appearing on the statement of persons whom the receiving party intended to serve with the notice of commencement. These must be served within 21 days after service of the notice of commencement (see **CPR, r. 47.9(2)**).

Default costs certificate

If the paying party fails to serve points of dispute within the permitted time, the receiving party may, on filing a request (form N254), obtain a default costs certificate (**CPR, rr. 47.9(4)** and **47.11**; Senior Courts Costs Office Guide 2013, sect. 7), which means that all the costs in the bill are allowed. A default certificate includes an order to pay the relevant costs (**r. 47.11(2)**; see forms N255 and N255HC). The right to a default certificate is lost if the receiving party delays making the request until after the paying party serves points of dispute, albeit late. A party who serves points of dispute late will not be heard on the assessment hearing, unless the court so permits (**r. 47.9(3)**). There is a power to set aside a default costs certificate on the ground of there being good reason to do so. The court will also be concerned to see a draft of the proposed points of dispute and will take into account whether the application to set aside was made promptly (**r. 47.12; PD 47, paras 11.1 to 11.3**).

    71.15

Reply

The receiving party has the right, but is not obliged, to serve a reply to any points of dispute. Any reply should be served on the party who served the points of dispute within 21 days after service (**CPR, r. 47.13**). A reply must, whenever possible, be set out in the form of Precedent G in the schedule to PD 47 (**PD 47, para. 12.2**). Filing a reply does not

    71.16

Commentary

receiving party any further costs as being too draconian, and substituted an order that the claimant receive 80 per cent of her assessed costs. (See also *Tanfern Ltd v Cameron-MacDonald* [2000] 1 WLR 1311 and **71.25**.)

Misconduct

71.26   **CPR, r. 44.11**, deals with cases where there has been a failure to conduct detailed assessment proceedings in accordance with the rules, and where the court finds that the conduct of a party or a legal representative before or during the proceedings was unreasonable or improper. The word 'unreasonable' in **r. 44.11(1)(b)** has to be construed narrowly (*Haji-Ioannou v Frangos (No 2)* [2006] EWCA Civ 1663, [2008] 1 WLR 144; *Lahey v Pirelli Tyres Ltd* [2007] EWCA Civ 91, [2007] 1 WLR 998). Improper conduct includes steps likely to prevent or inhibit the court from furthering the overriding objective (**PD 44, para. 11.2**). In any of these cases the court has a power to disallow all or part of the costs being assessed, or to order the party or legal representative in default to pay any other party's costs incurred because of the misconduct. Before making such an order the court must give the party or legal representative a reasonable opportunity to attend a hearing and give reasons why the proposed order should not be made (**PD 44, para. 11.1**). The court's approach can be seen from three cases, *Q v J* [2003] EWHC 251 (Fam), LTL 14/5/2003, *Tanfern Ltd v Cameron-MacDonald* [2000] 1 WLR 1311 and *MacDonald v Taree Holdings Ltd* [2000] CPLR 439. In each case the court was being asked to take action that would have resulted in the successful party being deprived of all or a substantial portion of its costs. Although such an approach may have been within the ambit of the CPR, it was felt that the court had to act proportionately. Dressing up an application complaining of late commencement (see **71.25**) as an application based on misconduct, even after eight years' delay, is unlikely to be successful (*Botham v Niazi* [2004] EWHC 2602 (QB), LTL 18/11/2004). In *Haji-Ioannou v Frangos (No 2)* [2006] EWCA Civ 1663, [2008] 1 WLR 144, it was held that the key to the apparent tension between **rr. 44.11** and **47.8** lies in the word 'misconduct'. While non-compliance with a rule, practice direction or court order is the only jurisdictional requirement before **r. 44.11** is engaged, it will usually be necessary to consider the extent of the misconduct as a matter of discretion before costs (as opposed to interest) are disallowed under **r. 44.11**. A bad breach, for example, inordinate and inexcusable delay combined with prejudice, might come into that category, whereas inordinate delay without prejudice might not. On the facts there was a five-year delay, but no prejudice, so the court only disallowed interest.

Interim costs certificate

71.27   Although the court has a general power to order costs on account (see **CPR, rr. 44.2(8)** and **71.9**), there is also a power to issue an interim costs certificate under **r. 47.16**. This power only arises once the receiving party has lodged a request for a detailed assessment. Generally the order will require that the payment under the interim certificate will be made to the receiving party within 14 days, although there is a power to order the sum to be paid into court. Application is made on notice in the usual way in accordance with **Part 23**. The court has a general discretion and there does not have to be any agreement on the amount to be paid. In practice the court takes into account the matters revealed by the points of dispute and it is good practice to be able to tell the judge the amount that is undisputed.

Final costs certificate

71.28   Within 14 days after the end of the detailed assessment hearing the receiving party must complete the bill and return it to the court (**CPR, r. 47.17(2)**) together with receipted fee notes and accounts (**PD 47, para. 16.4**). Once the completed bill is filed at the court, a final costs certificate, which includes an order to pay the costs to which it relates, will be served by the court on all the parties to the assessment proceedings (**CPR, r. 47.17(3) and (5)**).

Appeals against assessment decisions

There are special rules dealing with appeals from decisions made by authorised court offi-   **71.29**
cers in detailed assessment proceedings (see **CPR, rr. 47.21** to **47.24,** and **PD 47, paras 20.1**
to **20.6**). Appeals from assessment decisions by District Judges, Masters, costs judges,
Circuit Judges etc. follow the usual rules for appeals described in **chapters 74** and **75.** This
paragraph deals with appeals from authorised officers. These appeals are made to a costs
judge or a District Judge of the High Court (**CPR, r. 47.22**). There is no requirement to
seek permission or for written reasons (**PD 47, para. 20.2**). The appellant must file an
appellant's notice in form N161 within 21 days after the decision appealed against (**CPR,
r. 47.23**(1)). The appellant's notice should be accompanied by a suitable record of the decision appealed against (**PD 47, para. 20.5**), which may be the official transcript, or the
officer's comments written on the bill, or the advocates' notes of the reasons given. On
receipt of the appeal notice the court will serve copies on the parties together with notice of
the appeal hearing (**CPR, r. 47.23**(2)). The appeal takes the form of a rehearing of the
assessment proceedings (**r. 47.24**).

INDEMNITY PRINCIPLE

The 'indemnity principle' is that a party cannot be liable to pay more to the other side in costs   **71.30**
than the winner is liable to pay its own lawyers. This principle underlies the decision in *Marley v
Rawlings (No. 2)* [2014] UKSC 51, [2015] AC 157 (see **6.16**), where it was deployed at the earlier
stage when the court was making the costs order, rather than at the usual stage when those costs
are assessed. Once it is established that solicitors were acting for a receiving party there is a presumption that the client is liable to pay the solicitor, and the onus is on the paying party to rebut
that presumption. In order to rebut the presumption it has to be shown there are no circumstances in which the solicitor would look to the client for payment (*Meretz Investments NV v ACP
Ltd* [2007] EWHC 2635 (Ch), LTL 21/11/2007). Thus, if the lawyers representing the successful party
have intimated that their client need 'not worry' about paying their fees, there is a prospect that
the court will hold the loser has no liability in costs (*British Waterways Board v Norman* (1993) 26
HLR 232). However, this decision has to be compared with *Times Newspapers Ltd v Burstein* [2002]
EWCA Civ 139, 28/11/2002. The receiving party's lawyers produced evidence of a valid retainer to
pay their fees. In reply the paying party produced evidence to show that the receiving party was
impecunious and did not have the wherewithal to pay his solicitors. The receiving party thus
argued that the retainer was, in truth, an illegal CFA, that there was no valid retainer and that
there was no liability on the paying party to pay his lawyers. The Court of Appeal relied on the
fact that there was a retainer in rejecting the receiving party's argument.

For a short time it was thought that the indemnity principle had passed into history after the
decision in *Thai Trading Co. v Taylor* [1998] QB 781. However, subsequent developments such as
Hughes v Kingston upon Hull City Council [1999] QB 1193, *Awwad v Geraghty and Co.* [2001] QB 570,
amendments made to the Solicitors' Practice Rules 1990, r. 8(1) (made pursuant to the
Solicitors Act 1974, s. 31), and the Solicitors Act 1974, s. 60(3) (which provides that a client
of a solicitor is not entitled to recover from any other person under an order for the payment
of any costs to which a contentious business agreement relates more than the amount payable
to the solicitor in respect of those costs under the agreement), have made it clear that the
indemnity principle is still adhered to. The **Access to Justice Act 1999, s. 31,** amended the
Senior Courts Act 1981, s 51(2), by adding that rules of court may provide that the amount
awarded to a party in respect of costs need not be limited to the amount that would have been
payable by the party if costs had not been awarded. This is primarily aimed at enabling the
CPR to provide for a losing party to pay all the costs where the successful party has entered
into a conditional fee arrangement (which was implemented by the now revoked CPR,
r. 44.3A), but also permits removal of part or even the entire operation of the indemnity

Commentary

principle. The *Jackson Report* recommended the abolition of the indemnity principle (recommendation 4) but this has not been implemented.

A CFA in the prescribed form 'shall not be unenforceable' as being champertous (see **Courts and Legal Services Act 1990, s. 58**, as amended by the Legal Aid, Sentencing and Punishment of Offenders Act 2012). This means that CFAs that do not comply with the requirements of **s. 58** (see **6.6** to **6.9**) are unenforceable (*Times Newspapers Ltd v Burstein* [2002] EWCA Civ 1739, LTL 28/11/2002). Where a solicitor acts for an impecunious client without a CFA, if it is alleged there has been an infringement of the indemnity principle, it is necessary for the court to determine the true nature of the retainer.

Between 2 June 2003 and 31 October 2005, the Conditional Fee Agreements Regulations 2000 (SI 2000/692), reg. 3A, allowed a client to enter into a CFA with a legal representative which provided that the client would be liable to pay the lawyer's fees and expenses only if and to the extent that costs were recovered in the proceedings. This in effect abrogated the indemnity principle for this type of CFA. Predictable costs under **rr. 45.9** to **45.15** (see **70.8** to **70.15**) are not affected by the indemnity principle (*Nizami v Butt* [2006] EWHC 159 (QB), [2006] 1 WLR 3307).

If the arrangement between the solicitor and the client amounts to an unlawful agreement to conduct litigation on a contingency basis (without complying with the requirements for damages-based agreements in the Legal Aid, Sentencing and Punishment of Offenders Act 2012, s. 45, and the Damages-Based Agreements Regulations 2013, SI 2013/609), the client will not be entitled to seek an order for costs even if successful (*Hughes v Kingston upon Hull City Council* [1999] QB 1193). In *General of Berne Insurance Co. v Jardine Reinsurance Management Ltd* [1998] 1 WLR 1231 it was held that the indemnity principle has to be applied on an item-by-item basis rather than on a global basis. This means that if the client would not have been liable to pay an individual item in the solicitor's bill, it will be disallowed between the parties simply on the indemnity principle, even if the client is liable to pay the rest of the bill. In *Nederlandse Reassurante Groep Holding NV v Bacon and Woodrow* (1998) LTL 9/6/98 it was held that the item-by-item approach applies whether or not the receiving party and its solicitor have entered into a contentious business agreement.

In *Bailey v IBC Vehicles Ltd* [1998] 3 All ER 570 it was held that the court has the power to order disclosure of documents and the provision of information to check whether the indemnity principle has been infringed, but went on to say that the jurisdiction to do so should not be over-enthusiastically deployed.

For older cases, the principle derived from *R v Miller* [1983] 1 WLR 1056 is that there is a presumption that a solicitor's client is personally liable for the costs incurred by the solicitor. The presumption can be rebutted if it is established that there is a clear express or implied agreement that the client would not have to pay the solicitor's costs in any event. Further, statements of costs and bills of costs have to be signed by the solicitor acting for the receiving party. The signature is no empty formality. It operates as a certificate by an officer of the court that the receiving party's solicitors are not seeking to recover in relation to each item more than they have agreed to charge their client (see per Henry LJ in *Bailey v IBC Vehicles Ltd* [1998] 3 All ER 570 at p. 575) The indemnity principle is not infringed where the firm invoices the client in euros, even where the costs order is in sterling (*Schlumberger Holdings Ltd v Electromagnetic Geoservices AS* [2009] EWHC 775 (Pat), LTL 16/4/2009).

Since September 1999 there has been a professional requirement that solicitors must provide a client care letter for every case setting out the charging arrangements between them and their client (see **5.3**). That letter, or any other written arrangement affecting the costs payable between solicitor and client, must be filed with the court as part of any detailed assessment if liability to pay the receiving party's solicitor is disputed by the receiving party (**PD 47, para. 13.2(i)**). For the effect of breach of these requirements see **65.6**. Further, the bill of costs used in any detailed assessment must set out a short but adequate explanation of any agreement or arrangement between the solicitor and client which affects the costs claimed against the paying party. Underlining the continuing importance of the indemnity principle, a costs budget must contain a statement of truth which must be signed by a senior legal representative of the party in the form set out in **PD 22, para. 2.2A**, which includes a statement to the effect that the costs incurred do not exceed the costs the client is liable to pay.

Proving infringement of the indemnity principle

If the issue of whether the indemnity principle has been infringed is raised, the receiving party can **71.31** ask the costs judge to rule on whether there is a genuine issue. If not, that is the end of the matter. If a genuine issue is raised (or the receiving party accepts that a genuine issue is raised without asking for a ruling on this preliminary point), the costs judge will have to rule on whether the indemnity principle has in fact been infringed. This will almost certainly require the receiving party to adduce documents such as the client care letter, the terms of any retainer contract, and any bills sent to the client. **PD 47, para. 13.13**, and the Senior Courts Costs Office Guide 2013, sect. 12, provide that the court may direct the receiving party to produce any document which, in the opinion of the court, is necessary to enable it to reach its decision. These documents will in the first instance be produced to the court, but the court may ask the receiving party to elect whether to disclose the particular document to the paying party in order to rely on the contents of the document, or whether to decline disclosure and instead rely on other evidence.

Where there is a substantial dispute about whether the indemnity principle has been infringed and/or whether confidential documents should be produced, it may be appropriate to seek directions for split hearing dates or times (Senior Courts Costs Office Guide 2013, para. 12.5).

Costs of pro bono representation

Under the Legal Services Act 2007, s. 194(3), the court may order any person to make a pay- **71.32** ment to the prescribed charity in respect of pro bono representation of a party. The prescribed charity is the Access to Justice Foundation (s. 194(8); Legal Services Act 2007 (Prescribed Charity) Order 2008 (SI 2008/2680)). In considering whether to order a payment to the prescribed charity, and the terms of such an order, the court must have regard to whether it would, apart from s. 194, have made an order in favour of the party with the pro bono representation and the terms of the order it would have made (s. 194(4)). Such an order cannot be made in respect of representation before 1 October 2008 (s. 194(11)). Nor can it be made against another person with pro bono representation, or a person with public funding (s. 194(6)).

An order under s. 194(3) must be for fixed costs where **CPR, Part 45**, would otherwise apply (**r. 46.7(1)(a)**). Where **Part 45** does not apply, the court may by **r. 46.7(1)(b)** determine the amount of the payment (other than a sum equivalent to fixed costs) to be made by the paying party to the prescribed charity by:

(a) making a summary assessment; or

(b) making an order for detailed assessment,

of a sum equivalent to all or part of the costs the paying party would have been ordered to pay to the party with pro bono representation in respect of that representation had it not been provided free of charge.

Under **PD 44, para. 9.2** and **PD 46, para. 4.1**, the general rule is that the court will make a summary assessment of costs in the circumstances unless there is good reason not to do so. To assist the court in making a summary assessment of the amount payable to the prescribed charity, the party who has pro bono representation must prepare, file and serve, in accordance with **PD 44, para. 9.5(2)**, a written statement of costs of the sum equivalent to the costs that party would have claimed for that legal representation had it not been provided free of charge (**PD 46, para. 4.1**).

Where there is an order for detailed assessment and the receiving party had pro bono representation for part only of the proceedings, the bill of costs must be divided into different parts to differentiate between the different periods of funding (**PD 47, para. 5.8**). The bill of costs must not include a claim for VAT in respect of the pro bono costs (**PD 44, para. 2.14**).

An order under the Legal Services Act 2007, s. 194(3), must specify that the payment by the paying party must be made to the prescribed charity (**r. 46.7**). The receiving party is required to keep the prescribed charity informed by sending it copies of relevant orders and certificates (**r. 46.7(3)**, order under s. 194(3); **r. 47.11(4)**, default costs certificate; **r. 47.12(3)**, order setting aside or varying default costs certificate; **r. 47.17(6)**, final costs certificate).

Documents and information relating to funding

71.33   In *Dickinson v Rushmer* (2002) 152 NLJ 58 it was held that if confidential documents are shown to the costs judge, they should also be disclosed to the paying party. Alternatively, the receiving party can maintain legal professional privilege in these documents, and rely on secondary evidence of the retainer (although this might be difficult or impossible if the assessment hearing is being dealt with by a costs draftsman). In *South Coast Shipping Co. Ltd v Havant Borough Council* [2002] 3 All ER 779 Pumfrey J said that in the great majority of cases the paying party would be content to agree that the costs judge alone should see privileged documents, and it is only where it is necessary and proportionate that the receiving party should be put to an election whether to allow privileged documents to be disclosed to the paying party. In *Giambrone v JMC Holidays Ltd* [2002] EWHC 495 (QB), LTL 25/3/2002, it was held the costs judge had been wrong not to follow **PD 47, para. 13.13**, the costs judge having ordered the receiving party's solicitor to serve a witness statement on the paying party exhibiting the relevant documents on whether the indemnity principle had been infringed, as this deprived the receiving party of the right to claim privilege in the documents.

In *Hutchings v British Transport Police Authority* [2006] EWHC 90064 (Costs) (BAILII), LTL 4/12/2006, there was no evidence the receiving party had BTE insurance. There was a complete statement of prior advice which said there was none, which was repeated in the correspondence. The paying party raised a request for further information under **CPR, Part 18**, containing 13 questions aimed at discovering whether, despite the signature on the bill, there was in fact BTE cover available to the receiving party. The District Judge regarded the whole exercise as a fishing expedition. On appeal it was held:

(a) The starting point is the overriding objective and deprecating satellite litigation over costs issues.

(b) A paying party is entitled to know the case against it and to challenge items felt unreasonable or disproportionate.

(c) It was permissible to ask by way of a request for further information:
   (i)   Do you have insurance?
   (ii) With whom?
   (iii) Do you have any legal expenses insurance?

Any other points that the paying party may want to raise should be by way of points of dispute, not a request for further information.

Similarly, in *Arroyo v BP Exploration Co. (Colombia) Ltd* (2010) LTL 4/6/2010, a request for further information for the disclosure of the claimant's ATE cover was refused, and disclosure of the ATE policy was held to fall outside both standard disclosure and 'train of inquiry' disclosure, and was in any event privileged.

CFAs and the indemnity principle

71.34   Even after the abolition of recoverability of success fees and additional liabilities connected with CFAs with effect from 1 April 2013, it is still open to a paying party to argue that infringements of the requirements as to form of CFAs (discussed in **chapter 6**) render the retainer illegal with the result that there was no payment obligation on the CFA-funded client, and hence no costs liability on the unsuccessful party by reason of the indemnity principle (see **71.30**). A number of related issues were brought together in *Hollins v Russell* [2003] EWCA Civ 718, [2003] 1 WLR 2487. The Court of Appeal came to the following conclusions:

(a) The presumption that the bill is accurate afforded by the solicitor's signature on the bill does not apply where the point of substance relates to compliance with the legal require-ments for an effective CFA.

(b) The funding agreement is a privileged document and its production cannot be compelled. However, on a standard-basis assessment, the receiving party will have to show compli-ance. Thus in practice the CFA will normally be produced, suitably redacted if it contains sensitive commercial information. Other memoranda and documents should not gener-ally be produced. Partial disclosure in accordance with *Hollins v Russell* is difficult to justify, unless it is regarded as a limited waiver (see **50.73**).

(c) Not every breach of the Regulations will lead to a breach of the indemnity principle. The costs judge should ask the following question:

Has the particular departure from a regulation or requirement in the Courts and Legal Services Act 1990, s. 58, either on its own or in conjunction with any other such depar-ture in this case, had a materially adverse effect either upon the protection afforded to the client or upon the proper administration of justice?

(d) Even where the indemnity principle does work in favour of the paying party, disburse-ments and any insurance premium will still be payable.

(e) Costs officers must be astute to ensure that issues over the indemnity principle do not develop into time-consuming and expensive satellite litigation (*Times Newspapers Ltd v Burstein* [2002] EWCA Civ 139, LTL 28/11/2002).

BASIS OF QUANTIFICATION

The two bases

Costs may be quantified either on the standard or the indemnity basis. Under the old system before the CPR came into force there was a twofold test to be applied when decid-ing whether to allow costs on either basis. Costs would only be recoverable if, first, they were reasonably incurred and secondly, to the extent that they were reasonable in amount. These concepts were approached from opposite directions under the two different bases, with doubts resolved in favour of the paying party on the standard basis, and in favour of the receiving party under the indemnity basis. Under the CPR it still is necessary to con-sider both whether individual items of costs should have been incurred, and whether they should be allowed in full or reduced. However, to tie in with the overriding objective, on an assessment on the standard basis the court is required to consider not only concepts of reasonableness, but also of proportionality. **71.35**

Standard basis

On an assessment on the standard basis, **CPR, r. 44.3(2)**, provides that the court will: **71.36**

(a) only allow costs which are proportionate to the matters in issue. Costs which are dispro-portionate in amount may be disallowed or reduced even if they were reasonably or necessarily incurred; and

(b) resolve any doubt which it may have about whether costs were reasonably and proportionately incurred or were reasonable and proportionate in amount in favour of the paying party.

Principles for determining reasonableness

71.37   In deciding whether costs were reasonably incurred or were reasonable and proportionate in amount, the court is to have regard to all the circumstances. Under the old system the court was assisted in this task by what were called the 'seven pillars', which included the complexity of the item or the action, and the difficulty or novelty of the questions involved. The 'seven pillars' were set out in RSC, ord. 62, appendix 2, para. 1. In the **CPR, r. 44.4(3)** provides for eight matters to be taken into account. They echo the former position, but have been expanded to include the conduct of the parties before as well as during the proceedings (and thus take into account compliance, or otherwise, with any applicable pre-action protocol) and their efforts to resolve the dispute. The matters to be taken into account omit the old third pillar, which required the court to have regard to the number and importance of the documents prepared or perused However, time spent on documentation can still be charged for as is plain from **PD 47, para. 5.12(7)**, which includes work on documents. Any costs budgets will be taken into account under **CPR, r. 44.4(3)(h)**, as more fully explained at **43.18** to **43.21**.

A costs judge has the power to disallow entire sections of costs if they are held to be 'unreasonably incurred', or to reduce items to reasonable amounts, which is a sufficient safeguard against excess in most circumstances. Where there has been unreasonable or improper conduct, the costs judge also has the powers described at **71.26**. However, a costs judge does not have jurisdiction to vary a costs order, even one deemed to be made after acceptance of an offer to settle under **CPR, Part 36**, by making a percentage reduction in the costs payable before starting a detailed assessment (*Lahey v Pirelli Tyres Ltd* [2007] EWCA Civ 91, [2007] 1 WLR 998).

Proportionality

71.38   One of the main aims of the CPR is to provide a system of civil justice which is affordable and proportionate to the importance of the claim. The overriding objective requires the court to deal with claims justly and at proportionate cost. This includes ensuring claims are conducted in ways that will save expense and which are proportionate to the nature of the case (**CPR, r. 1.1(2)**). The parties are required to cooperate in achieving this aim, which means they must conduct themselves in ways that do not involve unnecessary costs, or costs which are not really justified by the nature or importance of the claim. The court will not give its approval to disproportionate or unreasonable costs (see **PD 44, para. 9.10**).

Former guidance on the practice to be adopted when deciding whether costs are proportionate on standard basis assessments given in *Lownds v Home Office* [2002] EWCA Civ 365, [2002] 1 WLR 2450 (see **71.39**) has been swept away by the amendments to what are now **CPR, rr. 44.3** and **44.4** made with effect from 1 April 2013. The new proportionality test applies to claims commenced on or after 1 April 2013 (see **71.35** and **71.40**). For cases governed by the new rule, cases like *Hoare v United Kingdom* (application 16261/08) (2011) 53 EHRR SE1, which said at [60] that costs of £770,000 in a personal injury claim arising out of criminal conduct were described as substantial but not unreasonable, can no longer be relied upon.

Pre-1 April 2013 proportionality test

71.39   The discussion in **71.39** applies to claims commenced before 1 April 2013, and references here are to the provisions of the CPR and practice directions in force immediately before that day. In a case where proportionality is an issue, a preliminary judgment on the proportionality of the costs as a whole should be made at the outset. This is done having particular regard to the factors in CPR, r. 44.5(3). If the judge concludes that the costs are not disproportionate, the various items of costs are then considered one by one, applying the reasonableness tests in r 44.4(2). If the judge concludes that the costs as a whole may be disproportionate, each item will be scrutinised applying both the reasonableness and necessity tests (for the latter, see below). A failure to follow the two-stage process laid down in *Lownds v Home Office* resulted in the assessment being set aside in *Morgan v Spirit Group Ltd* [2011] EWCA Civ 68, [2011] PIQR P9.

In applying the test of proportionality on a standard-basis assessment under r. 44.4(2), it is said in PD 43–48, para. 11.1, that the relationship between the total costs incurred and the financial value of the claim is not always a reliable guide. Still less can the court simply apply a fixed percentage to the value of the claim and say that any costs above that percentage are disproportionate (para. 11.1).

The key to proportionality, according to the Court of Appeal in *Lownds v Home Office* [2002] EWCA Civ 365, [2002] 1 WLR 2450 at [26]–[28], was to be found in PD 43–48, para. 11.2, which stated that: 'In any proceedings there will be costs which will inevitably be incurred and which are *necessary* for the successful conduct of the case' (emphasis added). If the appropriate conduct of the proceedings made costs necessary then the requirement of proportionality did not prevent recovery of those costs. The threshold required to meet necessity was higher than that of reasonableness, but Lord Woolf CJ in *Lownds v Home Office* at [37] said it was still a standard which a competent solicitor should be able to achieve without undue difficulty, and the courts should be careful not to impose too high a standard with the benefit of hindsight. Solicitors were not obliged to conduct litigation at uneconomic rates, which meant that in modest claims the proportion of costs was likely to be higher than in larger claims (PD 43–48, para. 11.2). The time spent on an issue at trial may not be an accurate guide to the amount of time properly spent in preparing that issue for trial (para. 11.3). The court would have regard to whether the appropriate level of fee earner and counsel were employed, whether offers to settle had been made, whether unnecessary experts had been instructed, and the other matters set out in CPR, r. 44.5(3). Regard should also be had to the amount which it was reasonable for the receiving party to believe might be recovered. For a claimant this was the sum it was reasonable for him to believe he might recover at the time the claim was made (*Lownds v Home Office* at [39]). For a defendant this was likely to be the sum claimed. In deciding what was necessary, the paying party's conduct was highly relevant, because cooperation can reduce costs, and being uncooperative can increase costs.

Counsel spending 12 days preparing for a striking-out application was regarded as being disproportionate in *Orwin v British Coal Corporation* [2003] EWHC 757 (Ch), LTL 24/4/2003, and the fee was reduced by two-thirds. Costs of £770,000 in a personal injury claim arising out of criminal conduct were described as substantial but not unreasonable in *Hoare v United Kingdom* (application 16261/08) (2011) 53 EHRR SE1 at [60].

Proportionality from 1 April 2013

For claims commenced from 1 April 2013 proportionality is defined in CPR, r. 44.3(5), as **71.40** follows:

Costs incurred are proportionate if they bear a reasonable relationship to—
(a) the sums in issue in the proceedings;
(b) the value of any non-monetary relief in issue in the proceedings;
(c) the complexity of the litigation;
(d) any additional work generated by the conduct of the paying party; and
(e) any wider factors involved in the proceedings, such as reputation or public importance.

On a standard basis assessment the court will not allow costs which have been unreasonably incurred or are unreasonable in amount (r. 44.3(1)). A key amendment made with effect from 1 April 2013 to r. 44.3(2)(a) (see 71.35), is that costs which are disproportionate in amount may be disallowed or reduced even if they were reasonably or necessarily incurred. Also new is the reference to proportionality in resolving doubts in r. 44.3(2)(b). 'Proportionality' under the new r. 44.3(2) is intended to come into play on those occasions when an assessment of 'reasonable' costs will result in an excessive figure. As stated in the *Jackson Report* at ch. 40, para. 7.22, in essence proportionality trumps reasonableness.

A deliberate decision has been made not to elaborate on the new proportionality test by including detailed guidance in the relevant practice direction. As stated in the third implementation lecture at para. 2.1, the rule as drafted is sufficiently clear. Simplicity is felt to promote certainty and the avoidance of technical satellite litigation (para. 2.3, and which is part of the purpose behind recommendation 2 of the *Jackson Report*).

Operation of the new proportionality test

71.41 This was discussed in the third implementation lecture at para. 2.2. What Sir Rupert Jackson envisaged was that the proportionality test would be applied in different ways in different situations. They may be categorised as follows:

(a) Cases where it is obvious at the outset that the costs claimed are proportionate. In these cases the only issue to consider under **CPR, r. 44.3** is the reasonableness of the individual items on the bill of costs.

(b) Cases where it is obvious from the outset that the costs claimed are disproportionate. In these cases the costs judge will have to consider the reasonableness of each item on the bill. The judge will also have to consider how to reduce the bill to a proportionate level. This may be achieved by reducing particular items, or by reducing the overall total to reach a proportionate figure.

(c) Borderline cases where it is unclear whether the bill is disproportionate until after the costs judge has dealt with the reasonableness of the individual items in the bill. In these cases the costs judge should not be constrained, whether by a practice direction or anything else, on how to approach the task of ensuring the costs allowed are both reasonable and proportionate.

In *Walker Construction (UK) Ltd v Quayside Homes Ltd* [2014] EWCA Civ 93, [2014] BLR 215, the successful defendant was awarded £10,885 on its counterclaim. On appeal it was held that it had been plainly wrong and disproportionate to award the defendant the whole of its costs of £345,000. A decision that has generated some surprise is *Willis v M. R. J. Rundell and Associates Ltd* [2013] EWHC 2923 (TCC), [2013] 6 Costs LR 924, where it was held that the fact the combined costs budgets of both sides came to £1.6 million in a claim with a value of £1.1 million meant that the costs budgets were disproportionate.

Case planning

71.42 Increasingly the courts are expecting to see evidence of case planning. The aspiration was set out in *Jefferson v National Freight Carriers plc* [2001] EWCA Civ 2082, LTL 4/10/2001, when Lord Woolf CJ cited with approval the following extract of the trial judge's comments:

In modern litigation, with the emphasis on proportionality, it is necessary for parties to make an assessment at the outset of the likely value of the claim and its importance and complexity, and then to plan in advance the necessary work, the appropriate level of person to carry out the work, the overall time that would be necessary and [the] appropriate spend on various stages in bringing the action to trial, and the likely overall cost. While it was not unusual for costs to exceed the amount in issue, it was, in the context of modern litigation such as the present case, one reason for seeking to curb the amount of work done, and the cost by reference to the need for proportionality.

It follows that the courts are increasingly expecting to see evidence that the issue of costs and proportionality was addressed at the outset of the case rather than the amount of costs simply developing as the case progressed. Consideration of the costs budgets and reference to a case plan will assist the judge in deciding on how the case should be managed (see **CPR, r. 3.17**) and whether the costs are proportionate for the purposes of **r. 44.3**.

Costs based on track appropriate for trial result

A costs judge is not permitted to reopen the costs order made by the trial judge or recorded in **71.43** an interim or consent order (*O'Beirne v Hudson* [2010] EWCA Civ 52, [2010] 1 WLR 1717 at [16]; *Drew v Whitbread plc* [2010] EWCA Civ 53, [2010] 1 WLR 1725, and see the discussion at **68.4**). If the costs order provides for assessment on the standard basis, it is therefore not open to the costs judge to conduct the assessment of costs on the small claims track basis (*O'Beirne v Hudson*), or on the fast track basis (with fixed fast track trial costs) if the claim has been allocated to the multi-track (*Drew v Whitbread plc*).

While the costs judge is not permitted to rewrite the costs order in the manner described in the previous paragraph, the costs judge is entitled to take into account all the circumstances of the case (**CPR, r. 44.4(1)**), which may include the fact that the claim 'would almost certainly have been allocated to the small claims track if it had been allocated' (**r. 46.13(3)**; *O'Beirne v Hudson* per Waller LJ at [16]). At that stage the costs judge may consider whether it was reasonable for the paying party to pay the costs of a lawyer. The costs judge would not be bound to disallow the costs of retaining a lawyer, but the fact the claim would have been allocated to the small claims track is a highly material circumstance in deciding what to allow on the assessment (*O'Beirne v Hudson* per Waller LJ at [17]). In making that decision the costs judge should give the items on the bill very anxious scrutiny to see whether the costs of each item were necessarily or reasonably incurred, and thus whether it is reasonable for the paying party to pay more than would be recoverable in a case that was allocated to the small claims track (*O'Beirne v Hudson* per Waller LJ at [19] and [22]).

An apparently similar approach was taken in *Drew v Whitbread plc* in relation to a case which had been allocated to the multi-track, but where the damages awarded at trial were less than the multi-track threshold. It is not permissible to assess costs on the fast track basis in such a case, because that would be rescinding an order that provided for the assessment of standard-basis costs. However, if the claim 'was in reality a fast track case' (see *Drew v Whitbread plc* at [39]), it may be reasonable to allow only fast track fixed trial costs. The difficulty with the application of this principle in *Drew v Whitbread plc* is that, unlike *O'Beirne v Hudson*, in this case there was an order allocating the case to the multi-track. While the approach of the Court of Appeal may avoid rescinding the trial judge's order for costs, it is hard to see how it is not rescinding the procedural judge's allocation order. This would only be permissible if there had been a material change of circumstances, pursuant to **r. 3.1(7)**.

A similar case of quasi-revisiting of the track allocation decision is *Morgan v Spirit Group Ltd* [2011] EWCA Civ 68, [2011] PIQR P9, see **71.6**, where judgment was given for £14,000 in a claim valued at £40,000. These cases may be seen as a welcome discipline for claimants who may be tempted to overvalue their claims for costs reasons. It is submitted that the cases are in fact unprincipled (because they directly or indirectly overturn allocation decisions in the absence of an appeal), and are likely to give rise to further satellite litigation. Values given to claims at the allocation stage are given before disclosure and the exchange of witness and expert evidence. Allocation decisions should stand or fall based on the evidence available at that time, rather than on the fuller evidence available at trial. Deciding that an allocation decision can be circumvented because 'it almost certainly' would or should have been made differently invites a contest between the parties, possibly with the need to adduce evidence of the state of knowledge of the value of the claim of at least the claimant's solicitors at the date of allocation. Instead, inflation of a claim for track allocation purposes should be dealt with under **r. 44.2(5)(d)**, which covers exaggeration, or, if the costs are out of proportion to the value of the claim, by applying the proportionality rules discussed at **71.40**.

Commentary

Indemnity basis

71.44   On an assessment on the indemnity basis there is no reference to proportionality, and any doubts on whether costs were reasonably incurred or were reasonable in amount is resolved in favour of the receiving party (**CPR, r. 44.3(3)**).

Choice of basis

71.45   Costs orders should identify the intended basis of quantification. Unless the phrase 'indemnity basis' is used, quantification will be on the standard basis (**CPR, r. 44.3(4)**). Inclusion of the word 'reasonable' in an order that provides for payment of the claimant's 'reasonable costs and disbursements on the standard basis' adds nothing, and the assessment is simply on the standard basis (*O'Beirne v Hudson* [2010] EWCA Civ 52, [2010] 1 WLR 1717). The usual rule in contentious litigation is that costs are payable on the standard basis. Indemnity basis costs are normally used only where there is some misconduct deserving such a course (*Reid Minty v Taylor* [2001] EWCA Civ 1723, [2002] 1 WLR 2800). Parties who act in the capacity of trustee, personal representative or mortgagee are in general entitled to costs on the indemnity basis, but the court may order otherwise if the party has acted otherwise than for the benefit of the fund (**r. 46.3**).

Assessments between solicitor and own client (other than in publicly funded cases and where there is a conditional fee agreement) are by virtue of **r. 46.9** dealt with on the indemnity basis, but subject to the following presumptions:

(a) that costs were reasonably incurred if they were incurred with the express or implied approval of the client;

(b) that costs were reasonable in amount if the amount was expressly or impliedly approved by the client; and

(c) that costs were unreasonably incurred if they are unusual in nature or amount and the solicitor did not tell the client that for that reason they might not be recoverable from the other side.

AMOUNT TO BE ALLOWED

Hourly rates

71.46   Before the Woolf reforms, one of the most common methods for computing the cost of a solicitor's time in conducting litigation was to apply the direct cost to the firm of the fee earner engaged in the matter to the amount of time spent, and then to add a 'mark-up' to reflect imponderable factors, such as general supervision, skill, responsibility and commercial profit. Most local courts developed conventional hourly rates for their courts, which were sometimes refined by applying different hourly rates to different grades of fee earners. It was extremely difficult to persuade a District Judge to depart from the conventional figures for his or her court. However, in theory different rates could be applied if an individual firm could show the direct cost for its fee earners was different from the conventional rate. The mark-up percentage could vary for different items on the bill. In *Johnson v Reed Corrugated Cases Ltd* [1992] 1 All ER 169 it was suggested that an uplift starting at 50 per cent was appropriate for ordinary cases, and in *Brush v Bower Cotton and Bower* [1993] 1 WLR 1328 it was suggested that 35 per cent was the appropriate uplift for interim applications where the solicitor sat behind counsel. For more complex cases higher levels of mark-up were appropriate, up to 100 or even 120 per cent for complex commercial or clinical dispute claims. Non-straightforward interim applications dealt with by a solicitor without the assistance of counsel might justify a mark-up of 60 per cent or more.

The modern approach is to apply a single hourly rate to the work done by the solicitor. Clients find this less confusing, and, by applying a suitable rate, it is not difficult to find a figure which provides the same rate of remuneration as the old system of direct cost plus mark-up. It is also the modern approach to provide different rates for different grades of fee earner.

Category of fee earner

Her Majesty's Courts and Tribunals Service has published guideline hourly rates for the summary assessment of costs. They are commonly used in detailed assessments as well. The rates have a built-in 50 per cent uplift (*Various Ledward Claimants v Kent and Medway Health Authority* [2003] EWHC 2551 (QB), LTL 4/11/2003). Various locations in England and Wales have been divided into three bands (see **table 71.2**), and different hourly rates have been laid down (from January 2003, and with inflation-related revisions from January 2005, January 2007 and January 2009) for four grades of fee-earner (see **table 71.3**). There is a separate table of guideline rates for London-based firms (see **table 71.4**). The figures given in **tables 71.3** and **71.4** are guidelines, and it is open to the designated civil judge to lay down more exact guidelines for rates in his area. It is also open for a firm to seek to establish a different rate (either generally or for individual claims where the notional 50 per cent uplift is inappropriate), and for this purpose the costs estimate for the paying party may be relevant evidence (see further at **71.48**).

71.47

Table 71.2 Solicitors' hourly rates: areas covered by the three provincial bands

Band one (January 2003)

Aldershot, Farnham, Bournemouth; Birmingham Inner; Cambridge City Centre; Canterbury, Maidstone, Medway and Tunbridge Wells; Cardiff (Inner); Kingston, Guildford, Reigate, Epsom; Leeds Inner (within 1 km of the City Art Gallery); Lewes; Liverpool, Birkenhead; Manchester Central; Newcastle City Centre (within 2 miles of St Nicholas Cathedral); Norwich; Nottingham City; Southampton, Portsmouth; Swindon, Basingstoke.

Band two (January 2003)

Bath, Cheltenham and Gloucester; Bristol; Bury; Chelmsford North, Cambridge County, Peterborough, Bury St Edmunds, Norfolk; Essex and East Suffolk; Lowestoft; Chelmsford South; Hampshire, Dorset, Wiltshire, Isle of Wight; Hull (City); Leeds Outer, Wakefield and Pontefract; Leigh; Luton, Bedford, St Albans, Hitchin and Hertford; Manchester Outer, Oldham, Bolton, Tameside; Milton Keynes and Aylesbury; Oxford (Inner/Outer), Reading, Slough; Sheffield and South Yorkshire; Southport; St Helens; Stockport, Altrincham, Salford; Swansea, Newport, Cardiff (Outer); Watford; Wigan; York, Harrogate.

Band three (January 2003)

Accrington, Burnley, Blackburn, Rawtenstall and Nelson; Birmingham Outer; Bradford (Dewsbury, Halifax, Huddersfield, Keighley and Skipton); Chester and North Wales; Coventry, Rugby, Nuneaton, Stratford and Warwick; Cumbria; Devon, Cornwall, Exeter, Taunton and Yeovil; Grimsby; Hull Outer; Kidderminster; Lincoln; Newcastle (other than City Centre); Northampton and Leicester; Nottingham and Derbyshire; Plymouth; Preston, Lancaster, Blackpool, Chorley; Scarborough and Ripon; South and West Wales; Stafford, Stoke, Tamworth; Teesside; Trowbridge; Weston-super-Mare; Wolverhampton, Walsall, Dudley and Stourbridge; Worcester, Hereford, Evesham and Redditch; Shrewsbury, Telford, Ludlow, Oswestry.

Band one (January 2005 and January 2007)

Aldershot, Farnham, Bournemouth (including Poole); Birmingham Inner; Bristol; Cambridge City, Harlow; Canterbury, Maidstone, Medway and Tunbridge Wells; Cardiff (Inner); Chelmsford South, Essex and East Suffolk; Fareham, Winchester; Hampshire, Dorset, Wiltshire, Isle of Wight; Kingston, Guildford, Reigate, Epsom; Leeds Inner (within 2 km of the City Art Gallery); Lewes; Liverpool, Birkenhead; Manchester Central; Newcastle City Centre (within 2 miles of St Nicholas Cathedral); Norwich City; Nottingham City; Oxford, Thames Valley; Southampton, Portsmouth; Swindon, Basingstoke; Watford.

Band two (January 2005 and January 2007)

Bath, Cheltenham and Gloucester, Taunton, Yeovil; Bury; Chelmsford North, Cambridge County, Peterborough, Bury St Edmunds, Norfolk, Lowestoft; Chester and North Wales; Coventry, Rugby, Nuneaton, Stratford and Warwick; Exeter, Plymouth; Hull (City); Leeds Outer, Wakefield and Pontefract; Leigh; Lincoln; Luton, Bedford, St Albans, Hitchin, Hertford; Manchester Outer, Oldham, Bolton, Tameside; Newcastle (other than City Centre); Nottingham and Derbyshire; Sheffield, Doncaster and South Yorkshire; Southport; St Helens; Stockport, Altrincham, Salford; Swansea, Newport, Cardiff (Outer); Wigan; Wolverhampton, Walsall, Dudley and Stourbridge; York, Harrogate.

Band three (January 2005 and January 2007)

Birmingham Outer; Bradford (Dewsbury, Halifax, Huddersfield, Keighley and Skipton); Cumbria; Devon, Cornwall; Grimsby, Skegness; Hull Outer; Kidderminster; Northampton and Leicester; Preston, Lancaster, Blackpool, Chorley, Accrington, Burnley, Blackburn, Rawtenstall and Nelson; Scarborough and Ripon; Stafford, Stoke, Tamworth; Teesside; Worcester, Hereford, Evesham and Redditch; Shrewsbury, Telford, Ludlow, Oswestry; South and West Wales.

Band one (January 2008)

Aldershot, Farnham, Bournemouth (including Poole); Birmingham Inner; Bristol; Cambridge City, Harlow; Canterbury, Maidstone, Medway and Tunbridge Wells; Cardiff (Inner); Chelmsford South, Essex, East Suffolk; Chester; Fareham, Winchester; Hampshire, Dorset, Wiltshire, Isle of Wight; Kingston, Guildford, Reigate, Epsom; Leeds Inner (within 2 km of the City Art Gallery); Lewes; Liverpool, Birkenhead; Manchester Central; Newcastle — City Centre (within 2 miles of St Nicholas Cathedral); Norwich City; Nottingham City; Oxford, Thames Valley; Southampton, Portsmouth; Swindon, Basingstoke; Watford

Band two (January 2008)

Bath, Cheltenham and Gloucester, Taunton, Yeovil; Bury; Chelmsford North, Cambridge County, Peterborough, Bury St Edmunds, Norfolk, Lowestoft; Cheshire and North Wales; Coventry, Rugby, Nuneaton, Stratford and Warwick; Exeter, Plymouth; Hull (City); Leeds Outer, Wakefield and Pontefract; Leigh; Lincoln; Luton, Bedford, St Albans, Hitchin, Hertford; Manchester Outer, Oldham, Bolton, Tameside; Newcastle (other than City Centre); Nottingham and Derbyshire; Sheffield, Doncaster and South Yorkshire; Southport; St Helens; Stockport, Altrincham, Salford; Swansea, Newport, Cardiff (Outer); Wigan; Wolverhampton, Walsall, Dudley and Stourbridge; York, Harrogate

Band three (January 2008)

Birmingham Outer; Bradford (Dewsbury, Halifax, Huddersfield, Keighley and Skipton); Cumbria; Devon, Cornwall; Grimsby, Skegness; Hull Outer; Kidderminster; Northampton and Leicester; Preston, Lancaster, Blackpool, Chorley, Accrington, Burnley, Blackburn, Rawtenstall and Nelson; Scarborough and Ripon; Stafford, Stoke, Tamworth; Teesside; Worcester, Hereford, Evesham and Redditch; Shrewsbury, Telford, Ludlow, Oswestry; South and West Wales

Table 71.3 Guideline hourly charging rates

	Grade			
	A	B	C	D
Band one				
January 2003	175	155	130	95
January 2005	184	163	137	100
January 2007	195	173	145	106
January 2008	203	180	151	110
January 2009	213	189	158	116
1 April 2010	217*	192	161	118
Band two				
January 2003	165	145	120	90
January 2005	173	152	126	95
January 2007	183	161	133	101
January 2008	191	168	139	105
January 2009	198	174	144	109
1 April 2010	201*	177	146	111
Band three				
January 2003	150	135	115	85

January 2005	158	142	121	90
January 2007	167	150	128	95
January 2008	174	156	133	99
January 2009	198	174	144	109
1 April 2010	201*	177	146	111

* An hourly rate in excess of the guideline figures may be appropriate for Grade A fee earners in substantial and complex litigation where other factors, including the value of the litigation, the level of complexity, the urgency or importance of the matter as well as any international element would justify a significantly higher rate to reflect higher average costs.

Table 71.4 London hourly rates

	Grade			
	A	B	C	D
London 1				
City of London Jan 2003	342*	247	189	116
City of London Jan 2005 EC1, EC2, EC3, EC4	359	259	198	122
City of London Jan 2007 EC1, EC2, EC3, EC4	380	274	210	129
City of London Jan 2008 EC1, EC2, EC3, EC4	396	285	219	134
City of London Jan 2009	402	291	222	136
City of London 1 April 2010 EC1, EC2, EC3, EC4	409*	296	226	138
London 2				
Central London Jan 2003	263	200	163	105
Central London Jan 2005 W1, WC1, WC2, SW1	276	210	171	110
Central London Jan 2007 W1, WC1, WC2, SW1	292	222	181	116
Central London Jan 2008 W1, WC1, WC2, SW1	304	231	189	121
Central London Jan 2009	312	238	193	124
Central London 1 April 2010 W1, WC1, WC2, SW1	317*	242	196	126
Outer London Jan 2003 (including Bromley, Croydon, Dartford, Gravesend, Uxbridge)	189–221	142–189	137	100
Outer London Jan 2005 (All other London postcodes: W, NW, N, E, SE, SW and Bromley, Croydon, Dartford, Gravesend and Uxbridge)	198–232	149–198	144	105
Outer London Jan 2008 (All other London postcodes: W, NW, N, E, SE, SW and Bromley, Croydon, Dartford, Gravesend and Uxbridge)	219–256	165–219	158	116
Outer London Jan 2009	225–263	169–255	162	119
Outer London 1 April 2010 (All other London postcodes: W, NW, N, E, SE, SW and Bromley, Croydon, Dartford Gravesend and Uxbridge)	229–267*	172–229	165	121

* An hourly rate in excess of the guideline figures may be appropriate for Grade A fee earners in substantial and complex litigation where other factors, including the value of the litigation, the level of complexity, the urgency or importance of the matter as well as any international element would justify a significantly higher rate to reflect higher average costs.

The four grades of fee earner are:

A   Solicitors with over eight years' post-qualification experience including at least eight years' litigation experience.

B   Solicitors and legal executives (i.e. fellows of the Chartered Institute of Legal Executives) with over four years' post-qualification experience including at least four years' litigation experience.

C   Other solicitors and legal executives and fee earners of equivalent experience.

D   Trainee solicitors, paralegals and fee earners of equivalent experience.

Fee earners who are not fellows of the Chartered Institute of Legal Executives are not entitled to call themselves legal executives. Unqualified clerks may fall into grades B, C or D depending on their experience. Legal executives generally spend two years in a solicitor's office before passing their Part 1 general examinations, then take a further two years before passing their Part 2 specialist examinations, then complete a further two years in practice before being able to become fellows. Unqualified fee earners need to have equivalent experience if they are to be regarded as coming into grades B or C.

Many High Court cases justify category A fee earners, but specific tasks within the proceedings, such as sitting behind counsel at interim hearings, may only justify a fee earner in a lower category. A complex, high-value clinical negligence claim in *Higgs v Camden and Islington Health Authority* [2003] EWHC 15 (QB), LTL 22/1/2003, justified the employment of a senior partner (a category A fee earner), and the client was entitled to expect no less. In the County Court, the nature and complexity of the various items of work will dictate the level of fee earner that will be reasonable. In *Bensusan v Freedman* (2001) LTL 6/11/2001 the work was of a type typically dealt with by grade B fee earners, so the hourly rate was reduced from the amount claimed to the appropriate grade B rate. It is recognised that it is often more economical to brief counsel than for a solicitor to act as the advocate. Where having a solicitor advocate leads to an increase in costs the court will consider whether the increase can be justified.

Exceeding a guideline rate

71.48   The rates in **tables 71.3** and **71.4** are no more than a guide and can be exceeded where the nature of the case warrants it. When considering whether the guideline rate provides proper remuneration, the court will take into account the factors set out in **CPR, r. 44.4(3)**, which include the conduct of the parties, the amount involved, any complexity or novelty, the skill, effort and specialist knowledge required, the time spent on the case, any international element and the place where and the circumstances in which the work was done. Thus in *Higgs v Camden and Islington Health Authority* [2003] EWHC 15 (QB), LTL 22/1/2003, the appellate court upheld a rate of £300 per hour where the case involved a child who was brain-damaged from birth. The court indicated that the SCCO guideline figures were not intended to replace the experience and knowledge of those familiar with the local area and with the field generally.

London solicitors

71.49   Whether it is reasonable to instruct expensive London solicitors rather than more economical provincial solicitors involves an objective element of reasonableness which nevertheless has to be considered in the context of the particular circumstances of the particular clients (*Wraith v Sheffield Forgemasters Ltd* [1998] 1 WLR 132; *Truscott v Truscott* [1998] FLR 265). The list of factors in *Wraith v Sheffield Forgemasters Ltd* was a list prepared for that case, and, although useful, other factors are likely to be relevant in other cases (*Higgins v Ministry of Defence* [2010] EWHC 654 (QB), [2010] 6 Costs LR 867). In *A v Chief Constable of South Yorkshire* [2008] EWHC 1658 (QB), [2008] 6 Costs LR 935, it was held that it was unreasonable for a claimant in Sheffield to instruct specialist London solicitors for a complex personal injuries claim against the police. In *Solutia UK Ltd v Griffiths* [2001] EWCA Civ 736, [2001] CPLR 419, it was held to be reasonable to have instructed London solicitors in litigation which could have been handled far more cheaply by provincial solicitors where the London solicitors had previously conducted related, and more complex litigation, arising out of the same facts. Likewise, in *Higgins v Ministry of Defence* [2010] EWHC 654 (QB), [2010] 6 Costs LR 867, it was held to have been reasonable for an 82-year-old claimant living in Broadstairs, Kent, to instruct a central London firm on an asbestosis claim. In *Ryan v Tretol Group Ltd* (2002) Supreme Court Costs Office Case Summaries No. 10 of 2002 it was held to have been reasonable to change from provincial to London solicitors in an asbestosis claim after the fee earner dealing with the claim (who was an asbestosis expert) left the provincial firm. The London firm had been recommended by an asbestosis support organisation, and it was not apparent that there were any firms with experience of asbestosis claims in the local area. In *Gazley v Wade* [2004] EWHC 2675 (QB), LTL 25/11/2004, it was held to have been unreasonable to instruct specialist London solicitors for a libel claim. Although it was not a 'Norfolk case', the claimant was living in Norwich, there was evidence that local non-specialist firms had the necessary competence, and any technical advice could have been sought from specialist members of the Bar.

Retaining two firms simultaneously

A party will not recover costs which are duplicated by instructing two firms of solicitors, even **71.50** if the second firm is based overseas in a claim with an international dimension (*Bühler AG v FP Spomax SA* [2008] EWHC 1109 (Pat), LTL 7/7/2008).

Correspondence and attendances

Routine letters out and emails out (those which by reason of their simplicity should not be **71.51** regarded as items of substance) and routine telephone calls (which cannot properly amount to an attendance) will in general be allowed on a unit basis of six minutes each, the charge being calculated by reference to the appropriate hourly rate. The unit charge for letters and emails out will include perusing and considering the relevant letters or emails in, and no separate charge should be made for incoming letters and emails. The court may, in its discretion, allow an actual time charge for preparation of electronic communications other than emails sent by solicitors, which properly amount to attendances, provided that the time taken has been recorded (**PD 47, para. 5.22(2)**). Local travelling expenses incurred by solicitors (normally within 10 miles of the court) will not be allowed. Travelling and waiting time is usually allowed at the rate agreed between solicitor and client. The cost of postage, couriers, outgoing telephone calls, fax and telex messages will in general not be allowed unless unusually heavy. Nor will the cost of making copies normally be allowed, unless the documents to be copied were unusually numerous. Agency charges as between a principal solicitor and his or her agent will be dealt with normally on the basis that the charges form part of the principal solicitor's charges (**PD 47, para. 5.22(6)**).

Counsel's fees

Counsel's fees are based on a judgment taking into account all the relevant circumstances, **71.52** including:

(a) the seniority of counsel;
(b) the amount of time reasonably spent on the work;
(c) the number of documents perused and their importance and technicality (even if brief);
(d) the specialist knowledge and skill of counsel;
(e) the complexity of the work undertaken;
(f) the difficulty or novelty of the questions involved;
(g) the value of the claim and its importance;
(h) the responsibility involved;
(i) the place and circumstances where the work is performed; and
(j) whether there is any overlap with other work performed by counsel which reduces the work that would otherwise have been necessary.

Matthews v Dorkin (2C00) LTL 10/11/2000 is an interesting example of an appeal dealing with several different fees of counsel of nine years' call in a substantial personal injuries claim. For example, a fee of £875 was allowed for a written advice and schedule of loss and damage reasonably taking seven hours. A fee of £335 was allowed for a 24-minute telephone conference which required two hours and 15 minutes' preparation. A fee of £750 was allowed for a 4½ hour conference with experts at the solicitor's office which required three hours' preparation.

In *Matthews v Dorkin* brief fees were allowed of £350 on an application to break a fixture on account of the unavailability of experts, £525 on a 30-minute hearing requiring two and a half hours' preparation, and trial brief fees (at 50 per cent of those of leading counsel) of £4,000 with refreshers of £600 per day. The general approach is that junior counsel are allowed between 50 and 67 per cent of the leader's brief fees. Where there are several counsel on one side, their respective fees should reflect their seniority and responsibility in the conduct of the case (*Loveday v Renton (No. 2)* [1992] 3 All ER 184 at p. 194).

In *Hornsby v Clark Kenneth Leventhal* [2000] 4 All ER 567 it was held, in relation to counsel's fees for an appeal to the Court of Appeal, that the first stage is to assess the fee for the skeleton argument. This is assessed largely by reference to the time reasonably spent in reading the documents, researching the law and drafting the skeleton. Next the brief fee should be assessed applying the guidance in *Loveday v Renton (No. 2)* at p. 194 (which essentially identified the factors set out in points (a) to (j) above). In so far as preparation for the skeleton argument reduced the amount of preparation required for the hearing, that should not be included in the brief fee. The third stage is to aggregate the fees for the skeleton and the brief, to cross-check that the total is not too large or too small, and to adjust accordingly.

The Senior Courts Costs Office has also published figures for counsel's fees based on run-of-the-mill cases in the Queen's Bench and Chancery Divisions. These are set out in **table 71.5**. They are regarded as a useful starting point when assessing counsel's fees. The appropriate figure does not depend wholly on counsel's seniority, but also the level of counsel merited by the application and the circumstances of the individual case.

Table 71.5 Guidelines for counsel's fees

	Jan 2003, 1 hour	hearings of ½ day	Jan 2005, 1 hour	hearings of ½ day	Jan 2007, 1 hour	hearings of ½ day
Queen's Bench Division						
Junior up to 5 years call	220	385	245	425	259	450
Junior 5–10 years call	330	655	365	725	386	767
Junior 10+ years call	500	1,000	550	1,100	582	1,164
Chancery Division						
Junior up to 5 years call	250	475	275	525	291	556
Junior 5–10 years call	425	800	470	880	497	931
Junior 10+ years call	650	1,200	715	1,320	757	1,397
Administrative Court						
Junior up to 5 years call	325	500	360	550	381	582
Junior 5–10 years call	600	1,000	660	1,100	698	1,164
Junior 10+ years call	850	1,500	935	1,650	989	1,746

Disbursements

Disbursements are payments made by a solicitor for goods or services other than items which **71.53** enable the solicitor to render its service to the client. Office overheads therefore are not disbursements. It was held in *Crane v Canons Leisure Centre* [2007] EWCA Civ 1352, [2008] 1 WLR 2549, that the distinction is between charges by the solicitors for work that they do themselves or are directly responsible for (which are base costs), and expenses they incur for the client and which they pass to the client at cost (which are disbursements). The distinction does not depend on whether the solicitors do the work themselves or delegate it, but rather whether the solicitors remain in control and responsible for the work. Work delegated to another solicitor or to a costs draftsman or costs consultant is therefore part of the solicitor's base costs, not a disbursement.

Expenses legitimately claimed as disbursements are shown and charged separately on the solicitor's bill, and the client is not charged with VAT on these items. *The VAT Guide* (February 2011) (HMRC Notice 700) at para. 25.1 sets out eight conditions that must be satisfied if an item is to be treated as a disbursement:

(a) the solicitor must have acted as the agent for the client when paying the third party;
(b) the client must have actually received and used the goods or services provided by the third party (this condition usually prevents the solicitor's travelling and subsistence expenses, telephone bills and postage being treated as disbursements);
(c) the client must be responsible for paying the third party;
(d) the client must have authorised the solicitor to make the payment on the client's behalf;
(e) the client must have known the goods or services would be provided by a third party;
(f) the solicitor's outlay must be separately itemised in the bill (or invoice);
(g) the solicitor can only recover the exact amount paid to the third party; and
(h) the goods or services must be clearly additional to the supplies which the solicitor has made to the client on his own account.

Further guidance is given in **PD 44, para. 2.11**. Examples of valid disbursements are court fees, fees on affidavits, estate duty and stamp duty payable by clients, fees for experts' reports and services such as reproducing photographs. A referral fee (see now the Legal Aid, Sentencing and Punishment of Offenders Act 2012, ss. 56 to 60) paid by a claims handling company to its subsidiary was held not to be a disbursement in *Sharratt v London Central Bus Co. Ltd (No. 2)* [2004] EWCA Civ 575, [2004] 3 All ER 325, because it related to work done before the solicitor's retainer came into existence. Generally, it is only advantageous to treat a payment as a disbursement for VAT purposes where no VAT is chargeable on the supply by the third party, or where the client is not entitled to reclaim the VAT as input tax.

Counsel's fees are not technically disbursements because they are part of the services provided by the solicitor. They should therefore be included in the solicitor's services part of the bill and charged with VAT. This is so even if the barrister is not VAT registered. However, there is a long-standing HMRC concession which allows solicitors to readdress non-VAT-registered barristers' fee notes to the client, who pays counsel directly or provides a separate cheque for the barrister's fees. When this is done, the fees payable to counsel do not appear in the solicitor's bill at all (and are not included in the solicitor's quarterly VAT return).

VALUE ADDED TAX

Every statement, bill of costs, fee sheet, account or voucher on which VAT is included must **71.54** state the VAT registration number of the provider (**PD 44, para. 2.2** and **PD 47, para. 5.10(3)**). VAT should not be included in a claim for costs if the receiving party is able to recover the VAT as input tax (**PD 44, para. 2.3**) or if the receiving party is a government department in respect of the costs of services rendered by its legal staff (**para. 2.13**). Where

Commentary

there is a dispute about whether the receiving party is VAT registered, the receiving party's solicitors or auditors must provide a certificate in the form of precedent F in the schedule to **PD 47 (PD 44, para. 2.5)**.

Whenever there is a dispute about whether a service is zero rated, reference should be made to HM Revenue and Customs so that the official view can be made known at the assessment **(PD 44, para. 2.6)**. Medical reports prepared for the purposes of litigation are liable to VAT if the expert is VAT registered (Directive 77/388/EEC; *d'Ambrumenil v Commissioners of Customs and Excise* (case C-307/01) [2003] ECR I-13989). Petty or general disbursements, such as postage, fares, telephone charges and costs of telegraphic transfers are normally treated as part of the solicitor's overheads, included in the firm's profit costs, and charged to VAT **(PD 44, para. 2.11)**.

The summary in a bill of costs must show the total profit costs and disbursements separately from the total VAT claimed **(PD 47, para. 5.20)**. Where there is a change to the rate of VAT during the course of proceedings, the bill should be divided into separate parts to distinguish work done at the different rates **(para. 5.8**, but see also **PD 44, paras** 2.7 and 2.8 on electing to charge the lower rate, and **para. 2.9** on apportionment where there is a lump-sum charge for work spanning both periods).

APPORTIONMENT BETWEEN JOINT PARTIES

71.55   In the absence of express agreement, the general rule is that costs incurred by joint parties are to be divided equally between them (*Meretz Investments NV v ACP Ltd* [2007] EWHC 2635 (Ch), LTL 21/11/2007). This will be displaced where specific costs are shown to be attributable to a particular party.

CONDITIONAL FEE AGREEMENTS

71.56   The discussion in **71.56** to **71.63** concerns CFAs entered into before 1 April 2013 and CFAs entered into after that date in relation to insolvency-related proceedings, publication and privacy proceedings or mesothelioma claims. For these CFAs, the provisions of CPR, Parts 43 to 48, relating to funding arrangements, and the attendant provisions of the old PD 43–48, as in force immediately before 1 April 2013, continue to apply (see the current **CPR, Part 48**, and **PD 48**). All references to the CPR and practice directions in the following paragraphs of **71.56** to **71.63** are to rules and directions in force immediately before 1 April 2013.

Where a party is funded under a CFA (a funding arrangement as defined in CPR, r. 43.2), there will be two elements to that party's costs: the 'base costs' and the 'additional liability'. 'Costs' recoverable under a party and party costs order include any additional liability incurred under a funding arrangement (r. 43.2(1)(a)). The base costs are those that are charged in the usual way to reflect the solicitor's basic remuneration and are defined as costs other than the amount of any additional liability (PD 43–48, para. 2.1). The 'additional liability' means the percentage increase that a lawyer may charge to reflect his or her involvement in the case, any insurance premium charged or any amount in respect of provision made by a membership organisation (CPR, r. 43.2(1)(o)). This reflects the three most common forms of funding conditional fee litigation. In some cases the solicitor may charge an uplift expressed as a percentage of the base costs. Either additionally or alternatively the client may insure to cover its own costs, or both sides' costs, or indeed any one of a number of permutations of costs orders that may be made. Subject to the points below, this premium can be charged to the paying party. A litigant may enter into an agreement with one of a number of approved membership organisations (such as trade unions) to meet his legal costs. An amount to secure this benefit may be recovered from the paying party.

In *MGN Ltd v United Kingdom* (application 39401/04) (2011) 53 EHRR 5, a newspaper publisher applied to the European Court of Human Rights complaining that the 95 per cent and 100 per cent success fees payable for a hearing in the House of Lords were an interference with the newspaper's right to freedom of expression under the European Convention on Human Rights, art. 10. It was held that paying success fees at this level was plainly an interference with the newspaper's right to freedom of expression (at [192]). Given the statutory scheme under-pinning CFAs, they were clearly prescribed by law (at [194]), and they performed a legitimate aim in that they promoted the widest public access to legal services for civil litigation funded by the private sector, and thus the protection of the rights of others within the meaning of art. 10(2) (at [197]). Nevertheless, the court decided the requirement that the applicant pay suc-cess fees to the claimant was a violation of art. 10 because paying the success fees was not necessary in a democratic society, was disproportionate having regard to the legitimate aims sought to be achieved and exceeded even the broad margin of appreciation accorded to the government in such matters.

While the court may summarily assess base costs at various stages during the case, there will be no assessment of the additional liability until the conclusion of the case or the part of the case to which a funding arrangement relates (r. 44.3A(1)). The parties can by agreement pro-vide for an earlier assessment if they so wish.

Procedure for assessing an additional liability

Assessment of an additional liability is commenced in the same way as any other detailed **71.57** assessment, save that the receiving party has to serve on the paying party and any other rele-vant persons relevant details of the additional liability (PD 43–48, para. 32.4). What consti-tutes 'relevant details' is set out fully at para. 32.5. Otherwise the assessment proceeds in the usual way to assess both base costs and any additional liability. The consideration of each of the two elements must be separate (para. 11.5).

Recovering additional liabilities from the paying party

CPR, r. 44.3B(1), provided that, unless the court otherwise orders, additional liabilities are **71.58** not recoverable under a party-and-party costs order in favour of a CFA litigant:

(a) in respect of the percentage increase relating to the cost to the legal representative of the postponement of payment;

(b) in respect of the cost of a membership organisation exceeding the likely premium for an equivalent insurance policy;

(c) during a period when the receiving party has failed to provide information about the funding arrangement;

(d) in respect of a percentage increase where there has been a failure to state the reasons for setting the percentage increase at the level stated in the CFA; and

(e) in respect of an insurance premium where the receiving party has failed to provide information about the insurance policy in question by the time required by a rule, practice direction or court order.

In relation to the last three matters a party who has entered into a funding arrangement is obliged to give notice to its opponents of the fact at the earliest opportunity. This is done by serving a notice in form N251 (CPR, r. 44.15; PD 43–48, paras 19.1 to 19.5; PD Pre-action Conduct, para. 9.3). A party which has failed to serve the form N251 or has otherwise trans-gressed is precluded (unless the court orders otherwise) from claiming the additional liability for the period when the notice was not served or there was any other default (**CPR, r. 44.3B(1)**). As with any other sanction, the court should address the factors set out in **r. 3.9** and *Denton v T. H. White Ltd* [2014] EWCA Civ 906, [2014] 1 WLR 3926, see *Mishcon de Reya v Caliendo* [2015] EWCA Civ 1029, [2016] CP Rep 3.

In *Crane v Canons Leisure Centre* [2007] EWCA Civ 1352, [2008] 1 WLR 2549, a collective CFA defined base costs as 'charges for work done by or on behalf of the Solicitors which would have been payable if this agreement did not provide for a success fee, calculated on the basis of the fees allowable for that work in the court in which the [claim] in question is conducted or would be conducted if proceedings were to be issued'. The costs of the detailed assessment, which was actually conducted by costs consultants engaged by the solicitors, were held to be part of the solicitors' base costs, and to attract the success fee on the same footing as the base costs on the substantive claim.

Assessing the percentage uplift

71.59 Guidance on the court's approach to assessing an additional liability was given in PD 43–48, section 11. In respect of any additional liability, the court will view matters as they reasonably appeared to the practitioner at the time that he entered into the agreement (para. 11.7). If the success fee was reasonable at that time, the court cannot substitute different rates for different periods of the proceedings as the risks change when more information becomes available (*U v Liverpool City Council* [2005] EWCA Civ 475, [2005] 1 WLR 2657).

In deciding whether a percentage increase is reasonable, relevant factors to be taken into account include (para. 11.8):

(a) the risk that the circumstances in which the costs, fees or expenses would be payable might or might not occur;

(b) the legal representative's liability for any disbursements;

(c) what other methods of financing the costs were available to the receiving party.

The costs officer has a power to allow different percentages to cover different items of costs or different periods. So different percentages may be applied for any protocol period, up to the issue of proceedings and for the trial. It is also acceptable to have a particular percentage applicable to one possible outcome (for example, settling within the protocol period) and another to cover a different eventuality (the case being contested to trial). See *Callery v Gray* [2001] EWCA Civ 1117, [2001] 1 WLR 2112.

A percentage increase will not be disallowed on the basis that the total of the additional liability and the base costs seems disproportionate (PD 43–48, para. 11.9). Doing so might run the risk of penalising a solicitor for entering into a funding arrangement, by allowing a lesser sum than might be permitted to a non-funded party.

Amounts allowed

71.60 The appellate courts have been reluctant to give guidance on the amount that a court will grant by way of uplift for the good reason that each case will turn on its own facts. The predictable costs rules for road traffic claims in accidents from 6 October 2003 (**CPR, Part 45, Sections II and III**), and for employers' liability claims in accidents from 1 October 2004 (**Part 45, Section IV**), lay down fixed success fees for these types of claim. See the discussion at **70.8** to **70.20**. These provide for two-stage success fees. Broadly, 100 per cent uplifts are applied to claims which are taken to trial, but 12.5 per cent (road traffic) and 25 per cent (employers' liability) uplifts apply where the claim is disposed of before trial. These figures should be seen as some guidance for other types of claim. Two-stage success fees are encouraged for all types of case (*Atack v Lee* [2004] EWCA Civ 1712, [2005] 1 WLR 2643). Other categories of case may involve substantially greater risks, and may justify significantly higher success fees for cases which do not go to trial.

Before the introduction of **Part 45, Sections II to IV**, there were a number of decisions on rates for success fees, mainly dealing with straightforward road traffic claims. In *Callery v Gray* [2001] EWCA Civ 1117, [2001] 1 WLR 2112, Lord Woolf CJ said that every case has some risk. Experience suggests that at least 90 per cent of straightforward road traffic claims settle without the need to issue proceedings. For this type of claim an uplift of 20 per cent is the maximum that could reasonably be agreed. Naturally if there are other factors then this limit might be exceeded. The court was also of the view that it is permissible to set a success fee on the basis that the matter fought to trial (say 100 per cent) but to rebate that down to 20 per cent if the case settled in the protocol period. The court stressed that this was an indication given on the basis of the present evidence and that it might be appropriate to refine the figures later.

In *Halloran v Delaney* [2002] EWCA Civ 1258, [2003] 1 WLR 28, the court felt that an increase of 5 per cent was appropriate for cases that settled before the issue of proceedings, and that the 5 per cent would be appropriate for any Part 8 costs-only proceedings. In *Re Claims Direct Test Cases* [2003] EWCA Civ 136, [2003] 4 All ER 508, the court said that *Halloran v Delaney* was not a case intended to give general guidance, that it was only intended to refer to the most straightforward of cases where the prospect of success is virtually 100 per cent, and that solicitors would be well advised to adopt the two-tier approach to the success fee advocated in *Callery v Gray*. Faced with these difficult authorities there is still a regrettable lack of certainty about percentage uplifts, even in the most straightforward cases. It is suggested that a case which settles in the protocol period (or before the issue of proceedings) may still attract a 5 per cent success fee or even the 12.5 per cent success fee allowed under the predictable costs regime (see **70.9**), provided there is no suggestion to the solicitor that there is anything unusual about the case. To cater for such dangers lurking under the limpid pools of otherwise tranquil litigation a solicitor would be well advised to adopt the two-stage approach outlined in *Callery v Gray*.

It is suggested that it would be wrong in principle to extrapolate from the above cases any general propositions applicable to other areas of litigation. It has to be understood that the cases are predicated on very straightforward litigation where statistics suggest there is a 90 per cent settlement rate. To take this conclusion into another area of litigation, for example, clinical negligence, is to ignore this aspect of the above cases. It is sometimes suggested that *Bensusan v Freedman* (2001) LTL 6/11/2001 is an authority for the contrary proposition. In that case an uplift of 20 per cent was permitted for a case that settled after the defendant had denied liability and asserted contributory negligence. This is a first-instance decision which fails to give due weight to the risks in contested litigation and it is suggested that it may well not be followed.

Assessing an insurance premium

The **Access to Justice Act 1999, s. 29**, enabled a successful client to claim the premium from the unsuccessful opponent. It provided: **71.61**

Where in any proceedings a costs order is made in favour of any party who has taken out an insurance policy against the risk of incurring a liability in those proceedings, the costs payable to him may, subject in the case of court proceedings to rules of court, include costs in respect of the premium of the policy.

In general the same considerations apply to insurance premiums as apply to percentage uplifts. A 'premium' for this purpose is the sum paid by the client to the insurer (*Re Claims Direct Test Cases* [2003] EWCA Civ 136, [2003] 4 All ER 508). A fee charged by a claims handling company for a basket of services is not converted into a 'premium' simply by describing it as such (*Sharratt v London Central Bus Co. Ltd (No. 2)* [2004] EWCA Civ 575, [2004] 3 All ER 325). In this case the Court of Appeal upheld the costs judge's approach of finding how much the company had paid to its underwriters, and making adjustments to that figure to find the premium recoverable under the **Access to Justice Act 1999, s. 29**. The specific considerations relating to insurance cover are in PD 43–48, para. 11.10:

In deciding whether the cost of insurance cover is reasonable, relevant factors to be taken into account include:
(1) where the insurance cover is not purchased in support of a CFA with a success fee, how its cost compares with the likely cost of funding the case with a CFA with a success fee and supporting insurance cover;

(2) the level and extent of the cover provided;
(3) the availability of any pre-existing insurance cover;
(4) whether any part of the premium would be rebated in the event of early settlement;
(5) the amount of commission payable to the receiving party or his legal representatives or other agents.

Where there is a dispute about the insurance premium in a staged policy (within the meaning of PD 43–48, para. 19.4(3A)), it will normally be sufficient for the receiving party to set out in any reply (see 71.16) the reasons for choosing the particular insurance policy and the basis on which the insurance premium is rated, whether block rated or individually rated (PD 43–48, para. 39.2). There is an evidential burden on the paying party to adduce at least some material to support the argument that the premium is unreasonably high (*Rogers v Merthyr Tydfil County Borough Council* [2006] EWCA Civ 1134, [2007] 1 WLR 808). An objection can only be sustained on the basis of evidence and analysis, not by assertion (*Kris Motor Spares Ltd v Fox Williams LLP* [2010] EWHC 1008 (QB), LTL 13/5/2010).

In *Callery v Gray* [2001] EWCA Civ 1117, [2001] 1 WLR 2112, and *Callery v Gray (No. 2)* [2001] EWCA Civ 1246, [2001] 1 WLR 2142, the Court of Appeal considered whether an ATE insurance premium is recoverable in a case that settles prior to the issue of proceedings. The court held that it could be recovered as 'insurance . . . against the risk of incurring a liability' within the **Access to Justice Act 1999, s. 29.** Provided the premium is reasonable, it will usually be recoverable against an unsuccessful defendant even though it is taken out soon after the solicitor is retained, and before the defendant's response is known. On the facts of that decision the premium of £350 was recoverable.

The decisions in *Callery v Gray* and *Callery v Gray (No. 2)* were affirmed by the House of Lords in *Callery v Gray (Nos. 1 and 2)* [2002] UKHL 28, [2002] 1 WLR 2000, in which it was held that it is for the Court of Appeal to lay down principles in this area.

The question of when an ATE insurance policy should be taken out was considered further by the Senior Costs Judge, Chief Master Hurst, in *Re Claims Direct Test Cases* (2002) LTL 29/7/2002. He found that where an incident occurred, particularly a minor road traffic accident causing slight injury, and where liability was accepted at the outset, it would be generally disproportionate and unreasonable to take out an ATE policy. That is likely to have a substantial impact upon the insurance market. Bulk providers generally insist that all cases from panel solicitors are insured, even if liability is, or is very likely to be, accepted. This allows a fixed premium to be set, with the stronger cases subsidising the weaker ones. If the stronger cases are filtered out because the premium is not recoverable, premiums are likely to rise. The Chief Master held that only the insurance element of the package of products included in the Claims Direct contract was recoverable, and allowed £621.13 (against the £1,525 claimed). The claimant's appeal was dismissed (*Re Claims Direct Test Cases* [2003] EWCA Civ 136, [2003] 4 All ER 508).

Some ATE insurers have sought to set their premium by reference to the amount of damages actually awarded. In *Pirie v Ayling* (2003) LTL 5/3/2003 the premium was stated to be 20 per cent of the damages awarded. Chief Master Hurst held that the agreement was not champertous, as there was no real danger that the purity of justice might be offended: the insurance company makes its profit from the insurance not from the litigation, the litigation simply provides the means of satisfying the insured's liability for the premium. However, the effect of the agreement was that the premium was £2,600. That was held not to be reasonable or proportionate in a road traffic accident case worth £13,000. In line with *Callery v Gray (No. 2)* [2001] EWCA Civ 1246, [2001] 1 WLR 2142, the premium allowed was £350.

PD 43–48, para. 11.10, requires the court to consider whether there was an existing policy of insurance (before-the-event or BTE insurance) and whether it would be reasonable for the successful party to have used that policy rather than obtaining fresh ATE insurance. This was considered in *Sarwar v Alam* [2001] EWCA Civ 1401, [2002] 1 WLR 125. The court held that a solicitor is under a duty to make reasonable inquiries to ascertain whether there is a BTE policy. Often such policies are linked to housing or motor insurance. Where there is such a policy, it is unlikely to be reasonable to incur a fresh premium for ATE insurance. However, there may be circumstances where it is inappropriate for the BTE insurance policy to be used. Where, for example, a passenger is covered by the driver's BTE policy, but wants to sue the driver. This might be particularly the case where the policy allows the driver's BTE insurer full control over the claim.

In more complex litigation the courts seem to be taking a more generous stance. In *Ashworth v Peterborough United Football Club Ltd* (2002) LTL 4/7/2002 the SCCO considered the reasonableness of an ATE insurance premium taken out in a multi-track commercial dispute. By consent the defendant was ordered to pay Mr Ashworth £66,000 in damages plus his costs on the standard basis. The bill of costs came to £104,858, of which £45,937.50 was the ATE premium. The defendant contended that the premium was unreasonable because the insurance could have been taken earlier, that it was disproportionate and excessive and that the claimant did not disclose the amount of the expected premium before it was taken out. The Master held that on the evidence available, insurance was probably not available at the outset, and that the defendant could not show that it was disproportionate to the matter in issue (not just as against the sum insured). Further it was not reasonable to have expected the claimant to obtain cover elsewhere given the restrictive market conditions at the time. It was not unlawful for the claimant to obtain retrospective own-cost cover, and the claimant gave as much information to the defendant as he was obliged to give.

In *Inline Logistics Ltd v UCI Logistics Ltd* [2002] EWHC 519 (Ch), [2002] 2 Costs LR 304, the amount paid as an ATE premium (£40,000 plus £2,000 tax) was not disputed, though there was an unsuccessful argument that the premium was not recoverable (see **5.13**). Unfortunately the report does not record the level of cover purchased for that sum.

In *Sarwar v Alam* (2003) LTL 23/3/2003 the claimant appealed an important test case to the Court of Appeal having lost before both the District Judge and the Circuit Judge. The claimant took out an ATE policy with a limit of indemnity of £125,000. The premium was £62,500 subject to a 50 per cent no-claims bonus. The full amount was paid in advance. The discount only applied if the paying party made no challenge to the amount of the premium, to the frustration of the defendant. However, Master Rogers allowed the premium in full, saying:

I have come to the conclusion that although the premium was high, it was unlikely that the claimant's advisers could have obtained an alternative quotation at a lower rate. They tried but were unsuccessful. Law and practice were in a state of flux and insurers were understandably reluctant to commit themselves on a large potential liability.

Assessing a fee to a membership organisation

A court assessing the reasonableness of a fee to a membership organisation has to consider how **71.62** this form of funding compares with the alternatives. PD 43–48, para. 11.11, requires:

Where the court is considering a provision made by a membership organisation, CPR, r. 44.3B(1)(b), provides that any such provision which exceeds the likely cost to the receiving party of the premium of an insurance policy against the risk of incurring a liability to pay the costs of other parties to the proceedings is not recoverable. In such circumstances the court will, when assessing the additional liability, have regard to the factors set out in para. 11.10 [see **71.61**], in addition to the factors set out in r. 44.5.

This will require the court to construe each document as different CFAs may differ in their wording. In *Arkin v Borchard Lines Ltd* (2001) LTL 19/6/2001, interim costs orders had been made in favour of the claimant and the defendant respectively on different interim applications. The claimant had entered into a CFA, and wished to set off the two sets of interim costs. Colman J held that the terms of the CFA in question, which said the lawyers were successful if they 'recover[ed] costs... or interim awards during the litigation', meant that the costs award in favour of the claimant did not infringe the indemnity principle (see **71.30** to **71.34**). It was held to be unarguable that the word 'recover' in the CFA meant that actual receipt was necessary. The two costs orders could therefore be set off against each other. Further, where one costs order is summarily assessed, and the competing costs order is directed to be subject to a detailed assessment, the court could legitimately preserve the set-off by varying the time for payment of the summarily assessed costs.

Application to assess

71.63   A client who retains a solicitor under a CFA may apply to the court for it to assess the base costs (i.e. the costs other than the percentage increase) or the percentage increase (i.e. the percentage increase pursuant to the CFA either between the solicitor and client or between the solicitor and counsel, and otherwise sometimes known as the success fee) or both (Solicitors Act 1974, part 3; CPR, rr. 48.8 and 48.10; Senior Courts Costs Office Guide 2013, sect. 30). Base costs are assessed on the indemnity basis as if there was no CFA. The percentage increase may be reduced if the court considers it disproportionate having regard to all the relevant factors as they appeared to the solicitor or counsel when the CFA was entered into. This is discussed in detail at **6.12** to **6.17** and **6.19** to **6.21**.

LITIGANTS IN PERSON

71.64   A litigant in person may be awarded costs (Litigants in Person (Costs and Expenses) Act 1975), which may be quantified either by summary or detailed assessment in the court's discretion. When quantifying these costs, **CPR, r. 46.5(2)**, provides that the litigant will not recover more than two thirds of the costs and all the disbursements which would have been allowed if the litigant had been represented by a legal representative. In quantifying the costs for time spent on the litigation, the litigant in person will be allowed his or her financial loss for doing the work on the case. A copy of the evidence proving the financial loss must be served on the paying party at least 24 hours before the assessment hearing (**PD 46, para. 3.2**). A litigant who cannot establish any such loss will be allowed an amount in respect of time spent reasonably doing the work at a rate of £9.25 per hour until 30 September 2011, and £18 per hour from 1 October 2011 (**PD 46, para. 3.4**). A litigant in person is not entitled to a witness allowance for his or her own attendance at court.

By **CPR, r. 46.5(6)**, a company acting without a legal representative is regarded as a litigant in person, as is a barrister, solicitor, solicitor's employee or authorised litigator who is acting for him or herself (*Khan v Lord Chancellor* [2003] EWHC 12 (QB), [2003] 1 WLR 2385; *Boyd and Hutchinson v Joseph* [2003] EWHC 413 (Ch), [2003] 3 Costs LR 358). Similarly a qualified barrister as a litigant will have to show good reason for employing another barrister (*Jackson v Lord Chancellor* [2003] EWHC 626 (QB), LTL 31/3/2003). A solicitor who, instead of acting personally, is represented by his or her firm or by him or herself in his or her firm name, is not regarded as a litigant in person (*Malkinson v Trim* [2002] EWCA Civ 1273, [2003] 1 WLR 463).

In a complex case a litigant in person may need to spend an extremely long time researching matters. In *R (Wulfsohr) v Legal Services Commission* [2002] EWCA Civ 250, LTL 8/2/2002, the Court of Appeal accepted that a litigant in person had spent 1,200 hours in preparation for five hearings, and took into account that a firm of solicitors had estimated the costs if they had been retained at £15,000 to £20,000. Applying the cap of two-thirds of the amount which would have been allowed if the client had been represented by lawyers (**CPR, r. 46.5(2)**), the court allowed £10,460. See also the Senior Courts Costs Office Guide 2013, sect. 22.

Litigation work done by litigant's employees

71.65   The general rule is that work done by a litigant personally in the course of instructing his solicitor is not recoverable as costs (*Re Nossen's Letter Patent* [1969] 1 WLR 638). Nor, in general, are costs recoverable for work done by a litigant who happens to be an insolvency officeholder, such as a liquidator or administrator (*Sisu Capital Fund Ltd v Tucker* [2005] EWHC 2321 (Ch), [2006] 1 All ER 167). The original rule (for which, see *London Scottish Benefit Society v Chorley* (1884) 13 QBD 872) extended to all costs incurred by litigants in person, other than a solicitor acting for himself. As discussed at **71.64**, the old rule has been removed for litigants in person by the Litigants in Person (Costs and Expenses) Act 1975, and for companies acting without legal representatives by **CPR, r. 46.5(6)**. The general rule continues to apply to prevent work done by a litigant in instructing his lawyers from being recoverable as costs (*Admiral Management Services Ltd v Para-Protect Europe Ltd* [2002] EWHC 233 (Ch), [2002] 1 WLR 2722).

By way of exception to the general rule, work done by specialists employed by a litigant may be recoverable as costs, provided:

(a) the staff have a sufficient level of expertise to qualify as experts (*Admiral Management Services Ltd v Para-Protect Europe Ltd*);

(b) the work done was of an expert nature, not merely factual (*Richards and Wallington (Plant Hire) Ltd v Monk and Co. Ltd* (1984) Costs LR (Core Vol) 79); and

(c) the amount recovered is limited to a reasonable sum for the actual and direct costs of the work done by the specialists, and does not include any element for the general overheads of the business (*Re Nossen's Letter Patent*).

Litigation work done by unauthorised persons

There is no jurisdiction to allow a party to recover the fees of a person who is not legally quali- **71.66**
fied who has assisted in the preparation and presentation of a claim (*United Building and Plumbing Contractors v Kajla* [2002] EWCA Civ 628, LTL 26/4/2002). Rights to conduct litigation are governed by the Legal Services Act 2007, see **61.30**. Where a client retains an unauthorised person to act on his behalf in litigation, the client is regarded for costs purposes as acting as a litigant in person (*Agassi v Robinson (No. 2)* [2005] EWCA Civ 1507, [2006] 1 WLR 2126). A successful party represented by an unauthorised person cannot recover the cost of work which it was not lawful for the unauthorised person to perform. If the unauthorised person is a specialist with expertise in the area, it may be that the expense of some of the work done can be recovered as disbursements under **CPR, r. 46.5(3)(a)(ii)** (*Agassi v Robinson (No. 2)*).

COSTS-ONLY PROCEEDINGS

Settling before proceedings are issued

It frequently happens that disputes are resolved before proceedings are issued on the basis that **71.67**
one side shall do or abstain from doing something (often it is simply the payment of compensation) and shall also pay the other side's reasonable costs. Ideally, the parties will at the same time, or soon afterwards, agree the amount of those costs. If they cannot agree the amount of the costs payable, several problems may arise. One analysis of the situation is that there is no complete agreement between the parties. This may be so because a term such as 'reasonable costs' used between the parties may not be sufficiently precise to constitute a contract of compromise. It is submitted that the term 'reasonable costs' has been in use for several decades, and is understood by almost the entire profession as meaning 'standard basis costs, to be agreed between the parties, failing which such amount as would be assessed by the court on a detailed assessment'. However, there are problems. One is that as proceedings have not been issued, the costs of the receiving party are arguably non-contentious costs (Solicitors Act 1974, s. 87(1)). In *Bilkus v Stockler Brunton* [2010] EWCA Civ 101, [2010] 1 WLR 2526, it was held that work 'for the purposes of proceedings' in s. 87(1) includes costs for the purpose of future proceedings. This may assume the future proceedings have to be issued for such costs to (become) contentious, but if not, the problem identified here disappears. Standard basis

Commentary

assessments only arise in the context of contentious costs, so there is a technical problem in the accepted meaning of the term 'reasonable costs' in settlements reached before proceedings are issued. Further, there is scope for disagreement as to what should happen if the parties cannot agree the amount of the receiving party's costs.

Assuming the terms of the settlement are held to be sufficiently precise to amount to a contract, the next problem is how to get an adjudication of the amount of costs payable if the parties cannot agree the amount that should be paid. The traditional method, which can still be used (**PD 46, para. 9.12**), is for the receiving party to issue proceedings using a Part 7 claim form for breach of the compromise agreement seeking damages in the amount of their reasonable costs. Assuming liability was not disputed, the court would enter judgment for damages to be assessed, or for a specified sum in respect of costs. If judgment was entered for damages to be assessed, the court would then convene a hearing to assess damages (rather than a hearing for a detailed assessment), at which hearing the court would assess the amount of costs that was reasonable in accordance with the compromise agreement. This in turn would (potentially) raise difficulties as to the intention of the parties on the question of the basis on which the reasonableness of the receiving party's costs should be judged.

Part 8 claim for an order for costs

71.68   In an attempt to avoid most of the difficulties identified in 71.67, CPR, r. 46.14, provides that where parties to a dispute have a written agreement on all matters in dispute, except the amount of costs to be paid, either party to the compromise agreement may start Part 8 proceedings seeking an order for costs. If such an order is made, there will then be a court order for costs (**CPR, r. 46.14(5)**) which can form the basis of assessment proceedings. A claim form issued under **CPR, r. 46.14** must identify the claim or dispute giving rise to the compromise, state the date and terms of the compromise, state the amount of costs claimed and whether they are claimed on the standard or indemnity basis, and a draft order (**PD 46, para. 9.3**). The written evidence in support has to include copies of documents relied upon to prove the defendant's agreement to pay costs (**para. 9.5 and CPR, r. 46.14(4)**).

The former rule that the court had to dismiss the claim if it was opposed has been removed as has the former restriction that only a detailed assessment could be ordered. Instead, when the time for acknowledging service has expired, unless the defendant indicates an intention to defend the claimant can make a request in writing for an order for a detailed or summary assessment of its costs (**PD 46, para. 9.7**). The general rule is that an order will be made for a detailed assessment, but if the court is in a position to make a summary assessment it should generally do so (**para. 9.9**). Costs of the Part 8 claim are an extra layer of costs, and should also be dealt with (*Tasleem v Beverley* [2013] EWCA Civ 1805, [2014] 1 WLR 3567). The claim may be dealt with without being allocated to a track (**para. 9.11**). A defendant may oppose the claim by filing a witness statement in accordance with **CPR, r. 8.5(3)** (**PD 46, para. 9.10**). The court will then give directions, which may include a direction that the claim proceeds as a Part 7 claim. If a defendant acts unreasonably in forcing a claimant into using the Part 7 procedure rather than the procedure under **r. 46.14**, the court can award costs of the Part 7 claim on the indemnity basis (*Bensusan v Freedman* (2001) LTL 6/11/2000).

PAYMENT OF COSTS TO CLIENT

71.69   Normally the costs agreed or assessed will be paid to the solicitor representing the receiving party. A former solicitor for the receiving party will have a lien for any unpaid costs. That lien may be defeated by a compromise if it is fairly entered into (*Snell's Equity* 32nd edn. (London: Sweet & Maxwell, 2010), para. 44-033). To protect a solicitor's claim, particularly after the solicitor is dis-instructed and the client is acting in person, the court will intervene (*Khans Solicitors v Chifuntwe* [2013] EWCA Civ 481, [2014] 1 WLR 1185 at [33]) if:

(a) the paying party is colluding with the client to cheat the solicitor of his fees; or

(b) the paying party is on notice that the receiving party's solicitor has a claim on the funds for outstanding fees.

To avoid having to pay twice in cases where there is any doubt, either the former solicitor or the paying party may apply to the court for an order to pay the sum due into court pending allocation by the court. This may be achieved through a stakeholder claim using **CPR, Part 86.**

PART N

Alternative Dispute Resolution

Chapter 72 Arbitration Claims

The following procedural checklist is relevant to this chapter:

Procedural checklist 31   Arbitration claim

INTRODUCTION

Arbitration claims are governed by **CPR, Part 62**, and **PD 62**.   **72.1**

CPR, Part 62, is part of 'a new procedural code with the overriding objective of enabling the court to deal with cases justly' (**r. 1.1(1)**). However, when dealing with applications under the Arbitration Act 1996, the court must observe the general principles in s. 1 of that Act. These are:

(a) the object of arbitration is to obtain the fair resolution of disputes by an impartial tribunal without unnecessary delay or expense;

(b) the parties should be free to agree how their disputes are resolved, subject only to such safeguards as are necessary in the public interest;

(c) in matters governed by part 1 of the Act the court should not intervene except as provided by that part.

In *Kalmneft JSC v Glencore International AG* [2002] 1 All ER 76, the Commercial Court heard an application under **CPR, r. 3.1(2)(a)**, to extend the 28-day time limit specified in the Arbitration Act 1996, s. 70(3), for making applications under ss. 67 and 68. Colman J held that, in exercising its discretion under **CPR, r. 3.1(2)(a)**, the court must take into consideration both the general principles of the 1996 Act and the overriding objective of the CPR, and held that the most significant factor is the need, stated in s. 1(a) of the 1996 Act, to avoid unnecessary delay. The application in this case was made before **CPR, Part 62**, came into force, but it is submitted that the replacement of PD 49G by **CPR, Part 62**, should make no difference to the approach taken by Colman J, given the fundamental importance of the principles in the Arbitration Act 1996, s. 1, to arbitrations in England and Wales. This approach was endorsed in *Gold Coast Ltd v Naval Gijon SA* [2006] EWHC 1044 (Comm), [2006] 2 Lloyd's Rep 400 and in *Interprods Ltd v De La Rue International Ltd* [2013] EWHC 3971 (Comm), LTL 16/1/2014.

CPR, Part 62, is very similar to the old PD 49G. Accordingly, it is likely that case law under PD 49G and its predecessor, RSC, ord. 73, would be considered relevant in determining cases arising out of it. In deciding *Vale do Rio Doce Navegação SA v Shanghai Bao Steel Ocean Shipping Co. Ltd* [2000] 2 Lloyd's Rep 1, Thomas J stated, at p. 8:

It seems to me clear that the principles applicable to the approach to the former RSC, ord. 73, and PD 49G are the same, as the principles are premised on the nature of an arbitration.

Although the judge said that it should generally be unnecessary to consider cases under the old law, he considered previous law extensively when deciding how best to interpret the provisions of what is now **CPR, r. 62.5(1)**. His reason for doing so was that: 'the underlying rationale in those cases remains applicable' (at p. 7).

Part 62 is divided into three sections. Section I deals with claims under the Arbitration Act 1996, Section II deals with claims under the old law and Section III applies to all enforcement proceedings other than by an action or claim on the award.

CLAIMS UNDER THE ARBITRATION ACT 1996

Starting the claim

72.2   An arbitration claim must be brought using the arbitration claim form, form N8. It should be issued using the standard **CPR, Part 8**, procedure (see **chapter 13**; **CPR, r. 62.3(1)**; **PD 62, para. 2.2**). An application for an interim remedy under the Arbitration Act 1996, s. 44, must be made using an arbitration claim form (**PD 62, para. 8.1**). However, an application to the court to stay legal proceedings in favour of arbitration should be made by application notice to the court dealing with those proceedings, using form N244 (or in the Commercial Court N244(CC)) (**CPR, r. 62.3(2)**).

An arbitration claim form may be issued in one of the following (**PD 62, para. 2.3(1)**):

(a) The Admiralty and Commercial Registry at the Royal Courts of Justice, London. The arbitration claim will be entered into the Commercial List.
(b) The Technology and Construction Court Registry at St Dunstan's House, London. The arbitration claim will be entered into the TCC List.
(c) A District Registry of the High Court where a Mercantile Court has been established (see **2.19**). The arbitration claim will be entered into the list of the Mercantile Court.
(d) A District Registry of the High Court with the arbitration claim form marked 'Technology and Construction Court' in the top right-hand corner. The arbitration claim will be entered into the TCC List.

However, if the arbitration claim relates to a landlord and tenant or partnership dispute, it must be issued in the Chancery Division of the High Court (**PD 62, para. 2.3(2)**).

A claimant should have regard to the principles set out in the High Court and County Courts (Allocation of Arbitration Proceedings) Order 1996 (SI 1996/3215) in determining where an arbitration claim is to be issued (**PD 62, para. 2.1**). Pursuant to SI 1996/3215, art. 5(4), the following criteria should be taken into account:

(a) the financial substance of the dispute, including the value of any claim or counterclaim;
(b) the nature of the dispute, for example, whether it arises out of a commercial or business transaction or relates to engineering, building or other construction work;
(c) whether the proceedings are otherwise important and, in particular, whether they raise questions of importance to persons who are not parties; and
(d) whether the balance of convenience points to having the proceedings taken in the Central London Civil Justice Centre Mercantile List.

Where the financial substance of the dispute exceeds £200,000, the proceedings are to be taken in the High Court unless they do not raise questions of general importance to persons who are not parties.

The principles contained in **CPR, r. 30.5(3)**, relating to transfer between Divisions and to and from a specialist list apply with the effect that the High Court, or a judge of the Technology and Construction Court, may order arbitration claims to be transferred to another Division or specialist list (**CPR, r. 62.3(4)**).

The Admiralty and Commercial Courts Guide, paras O19.1 and O19.2, state that an arbitration claim which raises no significant point of arbitration law or practice will normally be transferred from the Commercial Court:

(a) to the Chancery Division, if it is a rent-review arbitration;
(b) to the Technology and Construction Court, if it is a construction or engineering arbitration; or
(c) to the Admiralty Court, if it is a salvage arbitration.

Contents of arbitration claim form

72.3

An arbitration claim form must include a concise statement of the remedy claimed and (where appropriate) any questions on which the claimant seeks the decision of the court (**CPR, r. 62.4(1)(a)**). A reference in the arbitration claim form to a witness statement or affidavit filed in support of the claim is not sufficient to comply with the requirements of **r. 62.4(1)(a)** (Admiralty and Commercial Courts Guide, para. O3.2).

Where the claimant is challenging an arbitration award, the part or parts of the award being challenged must be identified and the grounds of the challenge must be specified. The claimant must identify the defendants against whom any claim for costs is made. The claimant must also specify the section of the Arbitration Act 1996 under which the application is brought and show that any statutory requirements laid down by the Act for the application being brought have been satisfied (**CPR, r. 62.4(1)(b) to (e)**).

An arbitration claim form must give the names and addresses of the persons on whom it is to be served. It must state their role in the arbitration and whether they are defendants. If the arbitration claim is being made without notice in an urgent application pursuant to the Arbitration Act 1996, s. 44(3) (order for the preservation of evidence or assets), that fact must be stated and the grounds relied upon should be specified (**CPR, r. 62.4(1)(f)**).

Service of arbitration claim form

72.4

Unless the court orders otherwise, the claimant must serve an arbitration claim form within one month from the date of issue (**CPR, r. 62.4(2)**). A claimant may apply to extend the time for service in accordance with the provisions of **r. 7.6** (see **15.30** to **15.33**).

A certificate of service (**r. 6.17**) must be filed within seven days of service of an arbitration claim form by the claimant (**PD 62, para. 3.2**). The court may exercise its powers under **CPR, r. 6.15**, to permit service of an arbitration claim form at the address of a party's solicitor or representative acting for that party in the arbitration (**PD 62, para. 3.1**).

Service of arbitration claim form out of the jurisdiction

72.5

The court may give permission to serve an arbitration claim form out of the jurisdiction in the following circumstances (**CPR, r. 62.5(1)**):

(a) When the claimant seeks to challenge an arbitration award or to appeal to the court on a question of law arising out of an award. For the court to be able to give permission in these circumstances the award must have been made in England and Wales.
(b) If the claim is for an order under the Arbitration Act 1996, s. 44 (court powers exercisable in support of arbitral proceedings; see **37.55**). The court may give permission for service out of the jurisdiction notwithstanding that the only remedy sought is in respect of arbitral proceedings which are taking (or will take) place outside of England and Wales.

(c) Any other situation where the claimant seeks a remedy or requires a question to be determined by the court which affects an arbitration (whether started or not), an arbitration agreement or an arbitration award. However, for this general provision to apply, the seat of the arbitration must be in England and Wales. If this is not the case, the court may give permission nonetheless as long as the seat has not been designated or if, by reason of a connection with England and Wales or Northern Ireland, the court is satisfied that it is appropriate to do so in line with the Arbitration Act 1996, s. 2(4)(b). *Steamship Mutual Underwriting Association (Bermuda) Ltd v Sulpicio Lines Inc.* [2008] EWHC 914 (Comm), [2008] 2 Lloyd's Rep 269, is an example of the existence of extraterritorial jurisdiction being confirmed in the context of **CPR, r. 62.5(1)(c)**. In *Enercon GmbH v Enercon (India) Ltd* [2012] EWHC 689 (Comm), [2012] 1 Lloyd's Rep 519, Eder J held that, because the claimant had participated in parallel proceedings in the Indian courts, it was for an Indian court to determine the proper seat of the arbitration and it would therefore be inappropriate for the English court to grant permission to serve the claim form out of the jurisdiction, even though he would have held that the seat was England and Wales.

In *Vale do Rio Doce Navegação SA v Shanghai Bao Steel Ocean Shipping Co. Ltd* [2000] 2 Lloyd's Rep 1 Thomas J decided that these provisions as set out in the former PD 49G only apply to claims brought by and against parties to an arbitration. The court did not consider an application by or against a non-party (e.g. a witness) to be something 'affecting an arbitration'. Accordingly, service of an arbitration claim form outside the jurisdiction would not be permitted in such a case. This decision was followed in *Starlight Shipping Co. v Tai Ping Insurance Co. Ltd, Hubei Branch* [2007] EWHC 1893 (Comm), [2008] 1 All ER (Comm) 593, where Cooke J held that a person who is not a party to an arbitration agreement cannot take advantage of the rule, a position followed in *Cruz City 1 Mauritius Holdings v Unitech Ltd* [2014] EWHC 3704 (Comm), [2015] 1 All ER (Comm) 305. However, other recent cases have confirmed that permission may be granted to serve an arbitration claim out of the jurisdiction on a third party in certain circumstances under **CPR, r. 62.5(1)(b)** (*Tedcom Finance Ltd v Vetabet Holdings Ltd* [2011] EWCA Civ 191, [2011] Arb LR 8; *JSC AMC Ingosstrakh Investments v BNP Paribas SA* [2012] EWCA Civ 644, [2012] 1 Lloyd's Rep 649; *PJSC Vseukrainskyi Aktsionernyi Bank v Maksimov* [2013] EWHC 3203 (Comm), LTL 31/10/2013).

An application for the grant of permission must be supported by written evidence stating the grounds on which the application is made. The evidence must also show in what place or country the person to be served is or probably may be found (**r. 62.5(2)**). In *Bitumex (HK) Co. Ltd v IRPC Public Co. Ltd* [2012] EWHC 1065 (Comm), [2012] 2 All ER (Comm) 1131, HHJ Mackie QC granted an application for a retrospective order for alternative service out of the jurisdiction on the basis that the case was exceptional because it concerned the service of an arbitration claim form.

The provisions of **rr. 6.40 to 6.46**, which regulate the service of claim forms abroad, apply to the service of arbitration claim forms out of the jurisdiction (**r. 62.5(3)**).

As an alternative to service out of the jurisdiction, the Commercial Court has allowed arbitration claim forms to be served on solicitors within the jurisdiction who represent a defendant in an underlying arbitration seated within England and Wales. This 'invariable practice' (*Kyrgyz Republic Ministry of Transport Department of Civil Aviation v Finrep GmbH* [2006] EWHC 1722, [2007] Bus LR D17) was followed in *JSC AMC Ingosstrakh Investments v BNP Paribas SA* [2012] EWCA Civ 644, [2012] 1 Lloyd's Rep 649, and confirmed in *Cruz City 1 Mauritius Holdings v Unitech Ltd* [2013] EWHC 1323 (Comm), [2013] 2 All ER (Comm) 1137. In the latter case, the judge held that this practice could be followed where there was 'good reason' for service to take place more quickly than under the applicable service convention and that this criterion would be satisfied in 'the vast majority of cases'.

Notice

72.6 Some provisions of the Arbitration Act 1996 require an application to be made on notice. On an application to remove an arbitrator (Arbitration Act 1996, s. 24), to consider and adjust the amount of fees and expenses for which the parties are liable (s. 28), or to determine the fees and expenses payable to the arbitrators where the arbitrators have withheld the award pending payment (s. 56), the arbitrators concerned must be made defendants to the application (**CPR, r. 62.6(1)**). In this way the statutory requirement for notice is fulfilled by serving the arbitration claim form on them together with any written evidence in support (**r. 62.6(2)**). Where the Arbitration Act 1996 requires an application to the court to be made on notice to any other party to the arbitration, that notice must be given by making that party a defendant (**CPR, r. 62.6(3)**).

Supply of documents from court records

An arbitration claim form may only be inspected with the permission of the court (**PD 62, para. 5.1** which overrides **CPR, r. 5.4**). In *Glidepath BV v Thompson* [2005] EWHC 818 (Comm), [2005] 2 Lloyd's Rep 549, a third party made an application under **r. 5.4(5)** requesting copies of certain documents on the court file following a successful application for a stay under the Arbitration Act 1996, s. 9. The applicant, to assist him in presenting an employment tribunal case, sought access to the particulars of claim, notices of application in respect of a freezing injunction and a *Norwich Pharmacal* application made before the proceedings were stayed. The Commercial Court refused to order production of the documents requested as neither the specific interest of the applicant in establishing his alleged rights before the employment tribunal, nor the interests of justice generally, could justify the granting of access to the documents. The court stated that it must be clearly established that the document sought will play an essential part in establishing the right of defence in question. 'To set the reasonable necessity threshold no higher than a requirement of evidential relevance would represent a most undesirable invasion by the courts of the confidentiality of arbitration in this country' (at [27]).

72.7

Acknowledgment of service

A defendant to an arbitration application may acknowledge service by completing form N15 or, as an alternative in the Commercial Court, form N210(CC) (Admiralty and Commercial Courts Guide, para. O5.1(b)). The general rule is that the defendant must acknowledge service within 14 days after service of the arbitration claim form (**CPR, r. 10.3(1)(b)**). If the court authorises service of the arbitration claim form out of the jurisdiction in accordance with **r. 62.5(1)** (see 72.5), it will set a time limit for acknowledgment of service (**r. 62.5(4)**).

72.8

An arbitrator (or ACAS) who is sent a copy of an arbitration claim form for his information may apply to be made a defendant. Such an application must be served on the claimant but need not be served on any other party. Alternatively an arbitrator (or ACAS), without becoming a party to the arbitration claim, may make representations by filing written evidence or in writing to the court (**PD 62, paras 4.1 to 4.3**).

Case management

All arbitration claims are allocated to the multi-track (although **CPR, Part 29**, does not apply). There is no requirement to file a directions questionnaire (**CPR, r. 62.7(1) to (3)**).

72.9

The following directions apply automatically unless the court orders otherwise (**CPR, r. 62.7(4)**; **PD 62, para. 6.1**):

(a) A defendant who wishes to rely on evidence before the court must file and serve his written evidence within 21 days after the date by which he was required to acknowledge service or, if an acknowledgment of service is not required, within 21 days after service of the arbitration claim form (**PD 62, para. 6.2**).

(b) A claimant who wishes to put evidence before the court in reply to written evidence filed under (a) above must file or serve his written evidence within seven days after service of the defendant's evidence (**PD 62, para. 6.3**).

(c) Agreed indexed and paginated bundles of all the evidence and other documents to be used at the hearing must be prepared by the claimant (**PD 62, para. 6.4**).

(d) Not later than five days before the hearing date, estimates for the length of the hearing must be filed together with a complete set of the documents to be used (**PD 62, para. 6.5**).

(e) Not later than two days before the hearing date the claimant must file and serve:
    (i)   a chronology of the relevant events cross-referenced to the bundle of documents;
    (ii)   where necessary, a list of persons involved; and
    (iii) a skeleton argument which lists succinctly:
        (1) the issues which arise for decision;
        (2) the grounds for relief (or opposing relief) to be relied upon;
        (3) the submissions of fact to be made with references to the evidence; and
        (4) the submissions of law with references to the relevant authorities (**PD 62, para. 6.6**).

(f) Not later than the day before the hearing date the defendant shall file and serve a skeleton argument which lists succinctly:
    (i)   the issues which arise for decision;
    (ii)   the grounds for relief (or opposing relief) to be relied upon;
    (iii) the submissions of fact to be made with the references to the evidence; and
    (iv) the submissions of law with references to the relevant authorities (**PD 62, para. 6.7**).

However, where an application is likely to last more than half a day the defendant's skeleton argument should be served one clear day before the hearing date, consistently with the Commercial Court practice for heavy applications (Admiralty and Commercial Courts Guide, para. O6.6(b)).

The Admiralty and Commercial Courts Guide, para. O6.2, states that claimants should apply for a hearing date as soon as possible after issuing an arbitration claim form or, in the case of an appeal, obtaining permission to appeal.

In the Commercial Court an application for directions in a pending arbitration claim should be made by application notice under **CPR, Part 23** (Admiralty and Commercial Courts Guide, para. O6.5).

Where an arbitration application involves recognition and/or enforcement of an agreement to arbitrate and that application is challenged on the grounds that the parties to the application were not bound by an agreement to arbitrate, it will usually be necessary for the court to resolve that issue in order to determine the application. For this purpose it may be necessary for there to be disclosure of documents and/or factual and/or expert evidence. In that event, it is the responsibility of those advising the applicant to liaise with the other party and to arrange with the Listing Office for a case management conference to be listed as early as possible to enable the court to give directions as to the steps to be taken before the hearing of the application (Admiralty and Commercial Courts Guide, para. O6.5).

Application for stay of legal proceedings

72.10 An application for a stay of legal proceedings under the Arbitration Act 1996, s. 9, is governed by **CPR, Part 62**; there is no indication that **Part 11** applies in relation to such proceedings (*Bilta (UK) Ltd v Nazir* [2010] EWHC 1086 (Ch), [2010] Bus LR 1634). An application notice seeking a stay of legal proceedings under the Arbitration Act 1996, s. 9, must be served on all parties to the relevant proceedings who have given an address for service (**CPR, r. 62.8(1)**). It should also be served on any party to those legal proceedings who has not given an address for service by sending a copy of the application notice to his last known address or at a place where it is likely to come to his attention. This can be done whether or not the party is within the jurisdiction (**r. 62.8(2)**).

On an application for a stay where a question arises as to whether an arbitration agreement has been concluded or as to whether the particular dispute which is the subject matter of the proceedings falls within the terms of an arbitration agreement, the court may determine that question. See, for example, *City of London v Sancheti* [2008] EWCA Civ 1283, [2008] 2 CLC 730, in which the Court of Appeal upheld a county court's refusal to grant a stay where the applicant was not a party to the relevant arbitration agreement, subsequently followed in *J & W Sanderson Ltd v Fenox (UK) Ltd* [2014] EWHC 4322 (Ch), LTL 29/12/2014. Alternatively it may give directions for its determination. The court may order proceedings to be stayed pending its decision (r. 62.8(3)).

Securing the attendance of witnesses

The Arbitration Act 1996, s. 43, allows a party to an arbitration to use court proceedings to **72.11** secure the attendance of witnesses at an arbitration. A party wishing to invoke this procedure may apply for a witness summons in accordance with **CPR, Part 34** (see **chapter 57**) (**PD 62, para. 7.1**). The application should be made to the Admiralty and Commercial Registry, or, if the attendance of the witness is required within the district of a District Registry, to that Registry (**PD 62, para. 7.2**). This power is only available if the witness is in the United Kingdom and if the arbitral proceedings are being conducted in England and Wales or Northern Ireland (Arbitration Act 1996, s. 43(3)). The courts may also, under s. 44, issue an order about taking evidence of witnesses in support of arbitral proceedings. Section 2(3) provides the discretion to use s. 44 in relation to arbitrations seated outside England and Wales, provided that the foreign seat does not make a witness summons inappropriate (*Commerce and Industry Insurance Co. of Canada v Certain Underwriters at Lloyd's of London* [2002] 1 WLR 1323). The s. 44 powers are available only to the extent that the arbitral tribunal does not possess these powers or is unable to act (s. 44(5)) (*ASM Shipping Ltd v TTMI Ltd (No. 2)* [2007] EWHC 927 (Comm), [2007] 2 Lloyd's Rep 155).

The applicant must file an affidavit or witness statement showing that the application is made with the permission of the tribunal or the agreement of the other parties (**PD 62, para. 7.3**).

This process was used in *Tajik Aluminium Plant v Hydro Aluminium AS* [2005] EWCA Civ 1218, [2006] 1 WLR 767. To ensure the attendance of witnesses at an arbitration, the claimants had obtained the consent of the tribunal to make an application to court under the Arbitration Act 1996, s. 43, to obtain a witness summons to compel third parties to attend the official hearing and to produce documents. The Court of Appeal held that documents so requested had to be specifically identified or at least described in some compendious manner that enabled the individual documents falling within the scope of the witness summons to be clearly identified. The Court of Appeal upheld the order to set aside the witness summonses on the ground that the schedules contained broad descriptions of documents but failed to identify them in a sufficiently certain manner.

Time limit for challenges to or appeals from awards

The Arbitration Act 1996, s. 70(3), provides that any challenge to or appeal from an award **72.12** brought under ss. 67 to 69 must be brought within 28 days of the date of the award. However, as long as the time limit has not expired, a claimant may apply without notice on a Part 23 application notice for an order extending that time limit (**CPR, r. 62.9(1) and (2); PD 62, para. 11.1(1)**). The Admiralty and Commercial Courts Guide, para. O9.2, states that any challenge to an award should be made without delay and the court will require cogent reasons for extending time. The court will generally make its decision without a hearing (**PD 62, para. 10.2**). Where the court makes an order extending the time limit, the defendant must file his written evidence within 21 days from service of the order (**PD 62, para. 10.2**).

If the time limit has already expired, a claimant is not precluded from applying retrospectively for an extension of time. In such circumstances the claimant must set out in a separately identified part in the arbitration claim form the grounds why an order extending time should be made (**CPR, r. 62.9(3)(a); PD 62, para. 11.1(2)**). Any defendant who wishes to oppose the extension of time application may file written evidence in opposition within seven days after service of the arbitration claim form (**CPR, r. 62.9(3)(b)**). If the court makes an order extending the time limit, each defendant's time for acknowledging service and serving evidence shall start to run as if the arbitration claim form had been served on the date when the court's order is served on that defendant (**r. 62.9(3)(c)**).

In *Kalmneft JSC v Glencore International AG* [2002] 1 All ER 76 Colman J held that applications both for an extension of the 28-day time limit provided by the Arbitration Act 1996, s. 70(3), and for challenging an award under ss. 67 to 69 are governed by s. 80(5). This provides that such applications are governed by the provisions of the CPR for extending periods of time. Colman J stated that in exercising any discretion available under **CPR, r. 3.1**, the court should have in mind the general principles set out in the Arbitration Act 1996, s. 1. These differ from the overriding objective of the CPR, because they emphasise the principles of party autonomy and finality of awards and restrict the supervisory role of the courts. Accordingly much weight must be accorded to the avoidance of delay at all stages of an arbitration, both before and after an interim or final award. This was stated to be a distinct public policy factor to be given due weight in the discretionary balance. Other factors emphasised by Colman J were:

(a) whether the claimant had acted reasonably in all the circumstances;
(b) whether the defendant or the arbitrator had caused or contributed to the delay;
(c) whether the defendant would suffer irremediable prejudice;
(d) whether the arbitration had proceeded during the period of delay and, if so, what impact on the progress of the arbitration or the costs incurred in respect of it the determination of the application by the court might now have;
(e) the strength of the application; and
(f) whether in the broadest sense it would be unfair to the claimant for him to be denied the opportunity of having the application determined.

The principles laid down in *Kalmneft JSC v Glencore International AG* [2002] 1 All ER 76 were applied by the Court of Appeal in *Nagusina Naviera v Allied Maritime Inc.* [2002] EWCA Civ 1147, LTL 10/7/2002. Mance LJ identified the 'primary factors' in considering an application as being delay, reasonableness and causation. In his Lordship's view factor (c) was not 'an essential pre-condition' and factor (d) was a relatively minor consideration. The principles were also applied in *Peoples' Insurance Company of China, Hebei Branch v Vysanthi Shipping Co. Ltd* [2003] EWHC 1655 (Comm), LTL 18/7/2003, with the important gloss that the Arbitration Act 1996, s. 67, expressly draws attention to the fact that parties might lose the right to object if they fail to make a challenge within the requisite time. *Dulwich Estate v Baptiste* [2007] EWHC 410 (Ch), *The Times*, 22 February 2007 held that a 21 or 31-day delay was not in itself determinative of the application. However, in *Nestor Maritime SA v Sea Anchor Shipping Co. Ltd* [2012] EWHC 996 (Comm), [2012] 2 Lloyd's Rep 144, the claimant's delay of six months after the expiry of the 28-day deadline in making an application to extend time for a challenge under s. 68 weighed heavily in the court's decision to refuse the application. The judge, referring to the principles laid down in *Kalmneft JSC v Glencore International AG*, was also swayed by the weakness of the underlying challenge and the fact that it was 'doomed to fail' under s. 73 due to the claimant's continued participation in the arbitral proceedings. *Terna Bahrain Holding Co. WLL v Al Shamsi* [2012] EWHC 3283 (Comm), [2013] 1 All ER (Comm) 580 confirmed that the strength of a challenge application will impact on the court's willingness to allow an extension of time application. This case also emphasised that the applicant must be prepared to give full and frank evidence of the reasons for the delay. However, despite weak challenges under s. 67 and s. 68, the court allowed an extension of time in *Interprods Ltd v De La Rue International Ltd* [2013] EWHC 3971, LTL 16/1/2014. In *DDT Trucks of North America Ltd v DDT Holdings Ltd* [2007] EWHC 1542 (Comm), [2007] 2 Lloyd's Rep 213, the court stated that the *Kalmneft* principles should be applied more strictly in relation to s. 67 applications where the jurisdiction of the arbitrator is challenged. Notable in this case also was the court's willingness to take into account the fact that the defendants' conduct of the proceedings depended upon the existence of a conditional fee agreement (CFA). Cooke J concluded that the grant of an extension of time would inevitably result in the protraction of proceedings, and the need to conclude further CFAs. This amounted to relevant prejudice to the defendants for these purposes.

Permission to appeal against the decision of a court under the Arbitration Act 1996, ss. 67 to 69, can only be granted by the trial judge (s. 67(4); *Athletic Union of Constantinople v National Basketball Association (No. 2)* [2002] EWCA Civ 830, [2002] 1 WLR 2863). However, the Court of Appeal retains a residual jurisdiction to ensure a fair hearing of an application for permission to appeal so that it can intervene in cases of procedural unfairness or where the decision of the trial judge is not a true decision (*North Range Shipping Ltd v Seatrans Shipping Corporation* [2002] EWCA Civ 405, [2002] 1 WLR 2397). Such applications, which involve applying to the Court of Appeal for permission to appeal (*Michael Wilson and Partners Ltd v Emmott* [2015] EWCA Civ 1285, [2016] 1 WLR 857), are 'only very rarely going to succeed' (*Republic of Kazakhstan v Istil Group Inc.* [2007] EWCA Civ 471, [2007] 2 Lloyd's Rep 548).

Challenging the substantive jurisdiction of the tribunal

A challenge to substantive jurisdiction can be brought to the court under the Arbitration Act **72.13** 1996, s. 32, 67 or 72.

Section 32(1) gives the parties to the dispute the right to apply to the courts to rule on a preliminary question as to the substantive jurisdiction of the arbitral tribunal prior to the handing down of the award. The application should be made upon notice to the other parties (s. 32(1)). The application also requires either the written agreement of all the parties to the proceedings (s. 32(2)(a)) or the permission of the tribunal and the court's satisfaction that (i) the determination will result in substantial cost savings, (ii) the application has been made without delay, and (iii) there is a good reason for the matter to be decided by the court (s. 32(2)(b)(i) to (iii)).

A party may, under s. 67, challenge an award made by an arbitral tribunal on the ground that the tribunal did not have substantive jurisdiction. The application should be made on notice to the other parties and to the tribunal (s. 67(1)). A party may challenge an award or seek an order declaring the award, in whole or in part, to be of no effect on the basis of the tribunal's lack of substantive jurisdiction (s. 67(1)(b)). A party may lose the right to object under s. 67 if they continue to take part in an arbitration without having raised a jurisdictional objection before the tribunal, provided they knew or could, with reasonable diligence, have known of the grounds for the objection (s. 73(1)). The court may (a) confirm the award, (b) vary the award, or (c) set aside the award in whole or in part (s. 67(3)). *Integral Petroleum SA v Melars Group Ltd* [2016] EWCA Civ 108, LTL 1/3/2016 has confirmed that the relief under s. 67 is discretionary and the court is entitled to decide not to grant any relief, even if it finds that the arbitrator lacked jurisdiction.

A court hearing a s. 67 arbitration claim may examine the arguments already addressed to the tribunal in a far wider manner than a court hearing a challenge to an award under the Arbitration Act 1996, ss. 68 and 69, and where a party alleges that he has not submitted to the arbitrator's jurisdiction, he is entitled to a full judicial determination on evidence of an issue of jurisdiction before the English court under s. 67, or under s. 72 if he has taken no part in the arbitration (*Dallah Real Estate and Tourism Holding Co. v Ministry of Religious Affairs of the Government of Pakistan* [2010] UKSC 46, [2011] 1 AC 763).

In *Dallah* the jurisdiction of the tribunal was challenged as part of resisting enforcement of an award made in France, pursuant to s. 103 rather than by way of a challenge to the award under s. 67. The Supreme Court, however, held that the standard of review of a tribunal's finding on jurisdiction should not differ depending on whether the review is carried out by the courts of the seat or the courts where enforcement of the award is sought. As to the review, the tribunal's own view of its jurisdiction has no legal or evidential value. The starting point for a challenge must be an independent investigation, and a full rehearing by the court is appropriate because the court should not be placed in a worse position than the arbitrator in determining the issue which in a given case might turn on contested issues of fact. Whilst the court may have regard to the reasoning and findings of the tribunal if they are helpful, the court is neither bound nor restricted by those findings. The parties will be allowed to introduce additional evidence which was not before the arbitrator. The grounds of objection to jurisdiction taken in an arbitration are not to be examined as closely as in a statement of case, so a party may, taking a broad view, be permitted to adduce new evidence in support of a new or different argument, coming within the existing 'grounds of objection' raised before the arbitrators, on an appeal under s. 67 (*Primetrade AG v Ythan Ltd* [2005] EWHC 2399 (Comm), [2006] 1 All ER 376; confirmed in *Habaş Sınai ve Tıbbi Gazlar İstihsal Endüstrisi AŞ v VSC Steel Co. Ltd* [2013] EWHC 4071 (Comm), [2014] 1 Lloyd's Rep 479).

Permission of the High Court is required for an appeal against a decision of the High Court regarding the substantive jurisdiction of an arbitral tribunal under s. 67(1) (s. 67(4)). For the limited jurisdiction of the Court of Appeal to review a refusal of permission, see the cases discussed at **72.15**.

Section 72 gives a person alleged to be a party to the dispute, but who has no wish to take part in the proceedings, the right to apply to the court for a declaration or injunction or other appropriate relief to determine the question of whether: (a) there is a valid arbitration agreement, (b) whether the tribunal is properly constituted or (c) what matters have been submitted in accordance with the arbitration agreement (s. 72(1)(a) to (c)). In *Broda Agro Trade (Cyprus) Ltd v Alfred C. Toepfer International GmbH* [2010] EWCA Civ 1100, [2011] 1 Lloyd's Rep 243, the applicant applied for a ruling under s. 72 that there was no valid arbitration agreement and that the original award on jurisdiction was not binding on it. The applicant argued that although it had participated in the arbitration proceedings, it had done so only on the merits whilst it continued to deny the arbitral tribunal's jurisdiction, and had not participated in the separate arbitral proceedings on jurisdiction. The Court of Appeal, however, saw no basis for an implied restriction of the statute's words 'takes no part in the proceedings' to the proceedings relating to determining the arbitral tribunal's jurisdiction. Accordingly, where a party participates in any part of the arbitral proceedings, that party no longer has recourse to an application under s. 72.

The Court of Appeal in *Broda Agro Trade (Cyprus) Ltd v Alfred C. Toepfer International GmbH* also stated that the restrictions in ss. 67 and 72 on challenges to the jurisdiction of an arbitral tribunal cannot be circumvented by making a claim at common law. The jurisdiction of the court to make a declaration regarding an arbitration agreement is subject to the restrictions in the Arbitration Act 1996. Accordingly, the applicant's request for a common law declaration as to the effect of the arbitration agreement added nothing. This statement from the Court of Appeal casts doubt on the possibility of requesting the court to make a declaration concerning an arbitration agreement using its inherent jurisdiction. Accordingly, the analysis in *British Telecommunications plc v SAE Group Inc.* [2009] EWHC 252 (TCC), [2009] BLR 231, should be treated with caution. In *British Telecommunications plc v SAE Group Inc.* (which was not cited in *Broda*) an application was made for a declaration that there was no valid and binding arbitration agreement. The applicator sought a declaration using the court's inherent jurisdiction, or, in the alternative, pursuant to ss. 32 or 72 of the Act. Ramsey J found on the facts that there was no valid arbitration agreement, and applied an analysis which resulted in the relief being granted pursuant to the court's inherent jurisdiction, rather than by the powers granted by the Arbitration Act 1996.

Challenging an award for serious irregularity

72.14   There are directions relating to challenging an award for serious irregularity under the Arbitration Act 1996, s. 68, in the Admiralty and Commercial Courts Guide, paras O8.6 to O8.10. Such applications are only appropriate where there are grounds for thinking both:

(a) that an irregularity has occurred; and
(b) that that irregularity has caused or will cause substantial injustice to the party making the challenge (para. O3.6(a)).

An application challenging an award on the grounds of serious irregularity should not therefore be regarded as an alternative to, or as a means of supporting, an application for permission to appeal (para. O8.6(b)).

A challenge to an award must be supported by evidence of the circumstances on which the claimant relies as giving rise to the irregularity complained of and the nature of the injustice which has been or will be caused to him (para. O8.7). If the nature of the challenge itself or the evidence filed in support of it leads the court to consider that the claim has no real prospect of success, the court may exercise its powers under **CPR, r. 3.3(4)**, to dismiss the application without a hearing. A respondent who intends to invite the court to deal with the application without a hearing should within 21 days file a respondent's notice to that effect together with a skeleton argument (not exceeding 15 pages) and any evidence relied upon. The applicant may file a skeleton/evidence in reply within seven days of service of the respondent's notice and skeleton argument. Where the court makes an order dismissing the application without a hearing the applicant will have the right to apply to the court to set aside the order and to seek directions for the hearing of the application. If such an application is made and dismissed after a hearing, the court may consider whether it is appropriate to award costs on an indemnity basis (Admiralty and Commercial Courts Guide, para. O8.8).

If the arbitration claim form includes both a challenge to an award by way of an appeal and a challenge on the grounds of serious irregularity, the applications should be set out in separate sections of the arbitration claim form and the grounds on which they are made should be separately identified (para. O8.9). The papers will be placed before a judge to consider how the applications may most appropriately be disposed of. It will usually be more appropriate to dispose of the application to set aside or remit the award before considering the application for permission to appeal (para. O8.10).

Failing to ensure that experienced counsel understood a point taken by the other side is not a serious irregularity, unless the arbitrator was aware of the misunderstanding (*Bandwidth Shipping Corporation v Intaari* [2007] EWCA Civ 998, [2008] Bus LR 702). Likewise, it is not a serious irregularity within the Arbitration Act 1996, s. 68(2), for an arbitrator to fail to point out arguments that one or other side may have missed in support of their case. An arbitrator has no duty to do so (under s. 33) (*E. D. and F. Man Sugar Ltd v Belmont Shipping Ltd* [2011] EWHC 2992 (Comm), LTL 1/12/2011). An arbitrator's decision not to hold an oral hearing, which might have caused the arbitrator to reach a different conclusion, did not amount to serious irregularity but rather the exercise of the arbitrator's discretion pursuant to s. 34(2)(h) (*O'Donoghue v Enterprise Inns plc* [2008] EWHC 2273 (Ch), [2008] NPC 103). *Interprods Ltd v De La Rue International Ltd* [2014] EWHC 68 (Comm), [2014] 1 Lloyd's Rep 540, confirmed that certain active case management steps taken by an arbitrator did not constitute a serious irregularity, nor did appointment of the arbitrator by the LCIA in two other cases where one of the parties was represented by the same firm of solicitors as was representing the respondent. There is no obligation to address a dissenting arbitrator's concerns, and a failure to do so would not amount to a serious irregularity within s. 68(2) where there is no reason to suppose that the majority would have reached a different view had they specifically addressed the dissenter's concerns (*Ispat Industries Ltd v Western Bulk Pte Ltd* [2011] EWHC 93 (Comm), LTL 4/2/2011). A further issue raised in *Bandwidth Shipping Corporation v Intaari* also appeared in *Compañía Sud-Americana de Vapores SA v Nippon Yusen Kaisha* [2009] EWHC 1606 (Comm), [2010] 1 Lloyd's Rep 436. Where a challenge is made on the grounds of serious irregularity, the reasoning to be applied requires that the court ask whether, but for the irregularity which caused the tribunal to reach its decision, the tribunal would have reached the same conclusion. This reasoning appears to run contrary to that which appears in *Van der Giessen-de Noord Shipbuilding Division BV v Imtech Marine & Offshore BV* [2008] EWHC 2904 (Comm), [2009] 1 Lloyd's Rep 273, where it was held, *inter alia*, that in determining whether there had been a substantial injustice, it was not for the court to decide what would have happened in the arbitration had there been no irregularity. The case gave further guidance in relation to challenges for serious irregularity. First, the power to set aside an award in whole or in part was not available simply because the tribunal had made a mistake, whether of fact or law. Furthermore, this power was not available merely because the arbitrators did not deal with all the points made or arguments advanced, or because they did not set out each step by which they reached their conclusion. Second, a failure to deal with an issue was not deemed to be the same as a failure to set out the reasoning for rejecting a particular argument.

This approach was applied in *Petrochemical Industries Co. (KSC) v Dow Chemical Co.* [2012] EWHC 2739 (Comm), [2012] 2 Lloyd's Rep 691, where Andrew Smith J gave useful guidance on whether a particular question was an 'issue' within the meaning of s. 68(2)(d), whether that issue was 'put to' the tribunal, and whether the tribunal failed to 'deal with' it. The judge rejected a number of previous tests for determining what an 'issue' is and preferred instead to give that phrase its ordinary meaning. He did, however, distinguish between 'issues' on the one hand and 'arguments', 'points', 'lines of reasoning' or 'steps' in an argument on the other. As to whether the tribunal 'dealt with' an issue, Andrew Smith J confirmed that this depends on a consideration of the award but a tribunal does not have to set out every step by which it reaches its conclusion or deal with each point made by the parties.

As noted above, it is not sufficient that there has been a serious irregularity of the kinds listed in s. 68. The irregularity must also be of a kind the court considers has caused or will cause substantial injustice to the applicant. This was highlighted in *CNH Global NV v PGN Logistics Ltd* [2009] EWHC 977 (Comm), [2009] 1 CLC 807, a case that arose out of what Burton J referred to as a 'howler' by the arbitral tribunal (a failure to award interest) which the tribunal had corrected by a subsequent addendum to the award issued pursuant to what is now the ICC Arbitration Rules (2012) art. 35. Article 35 covers the correction of a 'clerical, computational, or typographical error, or any errors of similar nature'. The claimant challenged the addendum on the basis that the error it corrected was not of that nature and that by issuing the addendum the tribunal had exceeded its powers (one of the categories of serious irregularity listed in the Arbitration Act 1996, s. 68(2)(b)). Burton J agreed that the error corrected was not a clerical or computation error, and that the tribunal did not have any power to correct it at all. The addendum was therefore beyond its powers and an irregularity falling within s. 68(2)(b). However, as the addendum was simply correcting 'the original howler' which had in turn caused substantial injustice to the defendant, and its effect on the claimant was only to remove a wholly undeserved windfall, Burton J concluded it could not possibly be argued that the addendum caused substantial injustice to the applicant and therefore dismissed the s. 68 application. For relevant considerations on whether to remit to the arbitral tribunal or to set aside the award, see *Secretary of State for the Home Department v Raytheon Systems Ltd* [2015] EWHC 311 (TCC), [2015] Bus LR 626.

Applications for permission to appeal

72.15 The Arbitration Act 1996, s. 69, provides that in certain circumstances, unless otherwise agreed by the parties, a party to arbitral proceedings may appeal to the court on a question of law arising out of an award. Exclusion of s. 69 can be achieved only by sufficiently clear wording: the phrase 'final, conclusive and binding' in an arbitration agreement is not sufficient (*Shell Egypt West Manzala GmbH v Dana Gas Egypt Ltd* [2009] EWHC 2097 (Comm), [2010] 1 Lloyd's Rep 109). An appeal under s. 69 cannot be entertained where the law applied by the arbitrators was not the law of England and Wales (Arbitration Act 1996, s. 82(1)(a); *Schwebel v Schwebel* [2010] EWHC 3280 (TCC), 161 NLJ 29).

The question must be a question of law, not fact. The classic examination of what amounts to a question of law is that of Mustill J in *Finelvet AG v Vinava Shipping Co. Ltd* [1983] 1 WLR 1469:

(1) The arbitrator ascertains the facts. This process includes the making of findings on any facts which are in dispute.

(2) The arbitrator ascertains the law. This process comprises not only the identification of all material rules of statute and common law, but also the identification and interpretation of the relevant parts of the contract, and the identification of those facts which must be taken into account when the decision is reached.

(3) In the light of the facts and the law so ascertained, the arbitrator reaches his decision.

An appeal on a point of law is possible only in relation to matters falling within (2). The question of law must arise out of an award made in arbitral proceedings to which the appellant was party. A party cannot appeal on a new point of law which was not raised before the tribunal (see, for example, *STX Pan Ocean Co. Ltd v Ugland Bulk Transport AS* [2007] EWHC 1317 (Comm), [2008] 1 Lloyd's Rep 210).

Unless the claimant can obtain the agreement of all the other parties to the proceedings, an appeal cannot be brought without the permission of the court (s. 69(2)).

PD 62, para. 12.6(2), does not say whether the reasons relied on by the respondent in opposing the grant of permission to appeal under the Arbitration Act 1996, s. 69, need to be points of law. This was considered in *CTI Group Inc. v Transclear SA (No. 2)* [2007] EWHC 2340 (Comm), [2008] 1 All ER (Comm) 203, by Field J. He concluded that s. 69 grounds 'must be based on a point or points of law' and that deciding a question of mixed fact and law would go against the clear policy of the Arbitration Act 1996 to restrict grounds on which arbitral awards may be challenged. Further, even if an agreement between the parties exists which would allow an appeal on questions of fact, such an agreement cannot expand the jurisdiction of the court to entertain such an appeal under s. 69, and it is very doubtful whether the courts have any inherent jurisdiction to entertain such an appeal (*Guangzhou Dockyards Co Ltd v ENE Aegiali I* [2010] EWHC 2826 (Comm), [2011] 1 Lloyd's Rep 30).

According to criteria set out in the Arbitration Act 1996, s. 69(3), permission to bring an appeal will only be granted if:

(a) the determination of the question will substantially affect the rights of one or more of the parties;

(b) the question is one which the tribunal was asked to determine;

(c) on the basis of the findings of fact in the award:

   (i) the decision of the tribunal on the question is obviously wrong; or

   (ii) the question is one of general public importance and the decision of the tribunal is at least open to serious doubt; and

(d) despite the agreement of the parties to resolve the matter by arbitration, it is just and proper in all the circumstances for the court to determine the question.

On an application for permission, the arbitration claim form must identify the question of law, state the grounds (but not the argument) on which the claimant alleges that permission should be granted, be accompanied by a skeleton argument and have the award appended (**PD 62, para. 12.1**). The claimant should file written evidence in support of the application with the claim form only if it is necessary to show (insofar as it is not apparent from the award itself) that the matters set out in s. 69(3) have been satisfied and to satisfy the court that permission should be granted (**para. 12.4**). Unless there is a dispute as to whether the question raised in the appeal is one which the tribunal was asked to determine, no documents adduced in or produced for the purposes of the arbitration may be put before the court other than the award and any document (such as the contract) referred to in the award which the court needs in order to determine the point of law arising out of the award (**para. 12.5**).

If the defendant wishes to oppose the grant of permission, it must file a respondent's notice setting out the grounds (but not the argument) on which the defendant opposes the application (**para. 12.6(1)**).

The respondent's notice should also specify whether the defendant wishes to contend that the award should be upheld for reasons not expressed (or not fully expressed) in it. The reasons for any such contentions should be stated (**para. 12.6(2)**). The respondent's notice should be accompanied by a skeleton argument (**para. 12.7**) and evidence that complies with the requirements of para. 12.4 (**para. 12.8**). The claimant may file and serve evidence or argument in reply only if it is necessary to do so and any such evidence must be as brief as possible (**para. 12.9**). In *CMA CGM SA v Beteiligungs-Kommanditgesellschaft MS 'Northern Pioneer' Schiffahrtsgesellschaft mbH & Co.* [2002] EWCA Civ 1878, [2003] 1 WLR 1015, the Court of Appeal emphasised that the written material should be capable of being read and digested by the judge within 30 minutes. *Morris Homes (West Midlands) Ltd v Keay* [2013] EWHC 932 (TCC), [2013] BLR 370 clarified that, while it might not always be possible to deal with such an application in half an hour, the process of determining a s. 69 application is summary. A failure to comply with **paras 12.1** to **12.9** may carry costs consequences for the party or their representative (**para. 12.11**). An oral hearing is not normally required to decide such an application for leave to appeal and it can be determined entirely on paper (**para. 12.12**; see *BLCT (13096) Ltd v J Sainsbury plc* [2003] EWCA Civ 884, [2004] 1 CLC 24 and *HMV UK Ltd v Propinvest Friar LP* [2011] EWCA Civ 1708, [2012] 1 Lloyd's Rep 416).

The judge should give brief reasons on refusing permission to appeal, which need to be sufficient to identify which of the statutory tests has not been met (**para. 12.14**; *North Range Shipping Ltd v Seatrans Shipping Corporation* [2002] EWCA Civ 405, [2002] 1 WLR 2397). It is sufficient to say 'for the reasons given by the arbitrators' if that is the judge's reason. In some cases it is necessary to go further, but reasons should still be brief. The Court of Appeal has confirmed that it has a residuary discretion to review decisions of the first instance court to refuse leave to appeal where there was clear unfairness in the process. However, in *CGU International Insurance plc v AstraZeneca Insurance Co. Ltd* [2006] EWCA Civ 1340, [2007] Bus LR 162, the Court of Appeal found no reason to believe that the judge's refusal was perverse or arbitrary. The Court also confirmed that *North Range Shipping Ltd v Seatrans Shipping Corporation* had not been decided per incuriam. The same residuary discretion applies to applications for leave to appeal under the Arbitration Act 1996, s. 68(4) (*ASM Shipping Ltd v TTMI Ltd* [2006] EWCA Civ 1341, [2006] 2 CLC 471).

The residuary discretion recognised by *CGU International Insurance plc v AstraZeneca Insurance Co. Ltd*, to review a judge's decision to refuse permission, is strictly limited. It may be used where there has been procedural unfairness in the judge's decision, or if there has been a failure to engage with the arguments on the limited question of an appeal (*Kazakhstan v Istil Group Ltd (No. 2)* [2007] EWCA Civ 471, [2008] Bus LR 878). The refusal of a first-instance judge to grant permission to appeal under s. 69 does not affect the jurisdiction of the Court of Appeal to hear an appeal on whether there was an exclusion agreement in relation to the right to appeal, and s. 69(6) does not apply so the court's permission is not required (*Sumukan Ltd v Commonwealth Secretariat* [2007] EWCA Civ 243, [2007] Bus LR 1075). These limited rights of access to the courts to challenge an award are compliant with the European Convention on Human Rights, **art. 6(1)**, in the **Human Rights Act 1998, sch. 1**. The High Court judge in effect operates as a second-tier appeal court, because, under the Arbitration Act 1996 an objection to jurisdiction is normally made first to the arbitrator(s). It is therefore a proportionate and legitimate restriction to provide in most cases that the High Court judge rather than the Court of Appeal, is the final appeal court (*Kazakhstan v Istil Group Ltd (No. 2)*). Even where there were serious administrative failings by the court in dealing with an application for permission to appeal, this may not have impinged on the decision-making process in refusing permission to appeal (*Philip Hanby Ltd v Clarke* [2013] EWCA Civ 647, LTL 4/7/2013).

Hearings

72.16 The general rule in **CPR, r. 39.2(1)**, providing for all hearings to be held in public, is displaced in the case of arbitration claims (**r. 62.10(1)** and **(2)**). Although the court has a discretion to order that an arbitration claim be heard either in public or in private, the presumption is that all arbitration claims are to be heard in private. However, arbitration claims concerning the determination of a preliminary point of law under the Arbitration Act 1996, s. 45, or an appeal under s. 69 on a question of law arising out of an award will be heard in public unless the court orders otherwise (**CPR, r. 62.10(3)**). This exception does not apply to hearings to determine the preliminary question of whether the court, on an application to determine a preliminary point of law, is satisfied that the determination of the question is likely to produce substantial savings on costs and was made without delay. It also does not apply to applications for permission to appeal on a point of law (**r. 62.10(4)(a) and (b)**).

Rule 62.10 was considered in *Department of Economics, Policy and Development of the City of Moscow v Bankers Trust Co.* [2004] EWCA Civ 314, [2005] QB 207. The Court of Appeal noted that **r. 62.10** introduced a starting point of privacy for arbitration claims which differs from the usual position prevailing under the CPR. However, this is not a blanket rule and in every case, while it is appropriate to start the hearing in private, the court should be ready to hear representations from one or other party that the hearing should continue in public, and should, if appropriate, raise the possibility with the parties. In *Glidepath BV v Thompson* [2005] EWHC 818 (Comm), [2005] 2 Lloyd's Rep 549, the Commercial Court referred to *Bankers Trust* and confirmed, at [17], that the 'character of confidentiality is further reflected in CPR, r. 62.10'.

However, that presumption may shift where an arbitration claim is heard before the Court of Appeal. In *C v D* [2007] EWCA Civ 1282, [2008] Bus LR 843 at [34] the Court of Appeal made clear that 'It is not the practice of this court to sit in private on arbitration (or indeed any other) appeals unless there is a special reason to do so. That is the case even though parties to arbitrations can legitimately expect that arbitrations are themselves confidential to the parties.' The court emphasised that any application for privacy or anonymity (for arbitration appeals) should be supported by written evidence in the form of a statement from someone at managerial level explaining the need for privacy or anonymity.

APPLICATIONS UNDER THE OLD LAW

CPR, rr. 62.11 to 62.16, deal with the procedure to be adopted on applications to the court to which the 'old law', as specified in the Arbitration Act 1996, s. 107, applies. These applications are becoming increasingly rare, and will not be considered further.   **72.17**

ENFORCEMENT OF AWARDS

Action on the award

CPR, Part 62, does not apply to enforcement of awards by bringing a claim on the award (**r. 62.17**). A party enforcing an award in such a manner, rather than using the simpler statutory methods of enforcement, should commence the claim under **Part 8**. Such proceedings would not be an arbitration claim and the usual provisions of the CPR would apply.   **72.18**

Statutory enforcement

Applications for permission to enforce awards under the statutory regime (Arbitration Act 1996, ss. 66 and 101; Arbitration Act 1950, s. 26; or Arbitration Act 1975, s. 3(1)(a)) may be made without notice as an arbitration claim using form N8 (see **72.2**; **CPR, r. 62.18(1)**).   **72.19**

On an application for permission to enforce, the court may direct that the arbitration claim form be served on such parties to the arbitration as it may specify (**r. 62.18(2)**). With the permission of the court, the arbitration claim form may be served out of the jurisdiction irrespective of where the award was, or is treated as having been, made (**r. 62.18(4)**). If the court directs that the arbitration form be served on the parties to the arbitration, the parties

Commentary

on whom it is served must acknowledge service and the enforcement proceedings will continue as if they were an arbitration claim governed by all applicable rules of **Part 62** (**r. 62.18(3)**).

On an application for permission to enforce an agreed award (Arbitration Act 1996, s. 51(2)), the arbitration claim form must state that the award is an agreed award. Any order made by the court must also contain such a statement (**CPR, r. 62.18(5)**).

An application for permission to enforce an award must be supported by written evidence exhibiting the arbitration agreement and the original award (or copies thereof). If the application is to enforce a New York Convention award under the Arbitration Act 1996, s. 101, or the Arbitration Act 1975, s. 3(1)(a), the duly authenticated original award and the original arbitration agreement (or duly certified copies) must be exhibited (**CPR, r. 62.18(6)(a)**). However, in *Lombard-Knight v Rainstorm Pictures Inc.* [2014] EWCA Civ 356, [2014] Bus LR 1196 the Court of Appeal held that, where the parties had clearly agreed that photocopies of the arbitration agreements attached to the claim form were true copies, any failure to properly certify the copies was immaterial. If the New York Convention award or agreement is in a foreign language, a translation certified by an official or sworn translator or by a diplomat or consular agent must be provided.

The written evidence must state the name and the usual or last-known place of residence or business of the claimant and of the person against whom it is sought to enforce the award (**r. 62.18(6)(b)**). It must also state that the award has not been complied with or, alternatively, the extent to which it has not been complied with at the date of the application (**r. 62.18(6)(c)**).

The Admiralty and Commercial Courts Guide, para. O18.4, states that two copies of the draft order must accompany the application. If the claimant wishes to enter judgment, the form of the judgment must correspond to the form of the award.

The claimant must draw up the order giving permission. It must be served by delivering a copy to the defendant personally or by sending a copy to the defendant's usual or last-known place of residence or business (**CPR, r. 62.18(7)**). The court's permission is not required for the order to be served out of the jurisdiction and any order to be served outside the jurisdiction should be served in accordance with **rr. 6.40** to **6.46** as if the order were an arbitration claim form (**r. 62.18(8)**). If an order giving permission to enforce is made on an application without notice, the application will have to be served with the order. If service is to be outside the jurisdiction, the provisions of the CPR are somewhat contradictory, with **rr. 62.16(2)** and **62.18(4)** indicating permission is needed to serve out the claim form and **r. 62.18(8)** specifying no permission is needed to serve out the court's order. In practice, the court will require the parties to seek permission to serve out the claim form, even though the order with which it is served does not require the same permission. Any application to set aside the order must be brought within 14 days after service and the award cannot be enforced until this period has expired. If the defendant applies within this period, the award cannot be enforced until after the application is finally disposed of. If the order is to be served out of the jurisdiction, the court may fix some other time limit within which the defendant must apply to have it set aside (**r. 62.18(9)**).

In *Colliers International Property Consultants v Colliers Jordan Lee Jafaar Sdn Bhd* [2008] EWHC 1524 (Comm), [2008] 2 Lloyd's Rep 368, a draft order for a claim served in Malaysia had led the judge to give a deadline of 14 days for an application to set it aside rather than 24 days, which was the appropriate time limit for that jurisdiction. However, since no steps had been taken to enforce the judgment, no prejudice had been suffered by the applicant and the application was therefore dismissed.

The order served on the defendant must contain a statement of the right to make an application to set it aside. It must also state the fact that the award cannot be enforced until after the time limit has expired or until after the application is finally disposed of, should the defendant make an application to set aside the order (**r. 62.18(10)**).

If the defendant is a body corporate, the arbitration claim form and any order giving permission to enforce should be served at its registered or principal address (**r. 62.18(11)**).

In *Gater Assets Ltd v NAK Naftogaz Ukrainiy* [2007] EWCA Civ 988, [2008] Bus LR 388 the Court of Appeal considered whether an order for security for costs could be made against a claimant seeking to enforce a New York Convention arbitration award. The three Lords Justice each arrived at a different conclusion as to whether, and in what circumstances, the court had jurisdiction to award security against an award creditor. However, the majority concluded that as a matter of principle the court should be reluctant, save in an exceptional case, to order security for costs against an award creditor, even if the power to do so should be technically available (followed in *Diag Human SE v Czech Republic* [2013] EWHC 3190 (Comm), [2014] 1 All ER (Comm) 605).

The court may refuse to recognise or enforce a foreign arbitral award in a number of circumstances specified in the Arbitration Act 1996, s. 103, mirroring those set out in the New York Convention 1958, art. V. One ground specified in s. 103(2)(f) is that the award has not yet become binding on the parties, or has been set aside or suspended by a competent authority of the country in which, or under the law of which, it was made. In *Svenska Petroleum Exploration AB v Lithuania (No. 2)* [2006] EWCA Civ 1529, [2007] QB 886, the claimant had applied to strike out the respondent's application to set aside an order giving permission to enforce an ICC interim award in England under the Arbitration Act 1996, s. 103(1). On appeal to the Court of Appeal, one of the grounds upon which the respondent continued to object was that the award was not final and conclusive. The determination of whether an award is final and binding depends on its status in the country where it was made. The interim award was issued in Denmark and, under Danish law, an arbitral award on jurisdiction is reviewable by the Danish courts. Initially, the learned deputy judge held that the award was not final and binding since the right to challenge the award under Danish law had not been lost irretrievably. Following a hearing on this point, however, Gloster J concluded that the award was in fact final, because any right to challenge the award had most likely been lost through delay. This decision was upheld by the Court of Appeal although it was confirmed that the finality of an award depends upon the laws of the country in which it was rendered.

In *Yukos Capital Sàrl v OJSC Rosneft Oil Co.* [2012] EWCA Civ 855, [2013] 1 All ER 223, the Court of Appeal held that the English courts were not barred by the act of State doctrine from investigating and potentially refusing recognition of decisions by the Russian courts setting aside two ICC awards handed down in Russia, on the basis that those decisions were alleged to be 'partial and dependent'. Moreover, an earlier decision to this effect by the Dutch courts did not raise an issue estoppel in the English proceedings because the Dutch decision was based on Dutch public policy while the English decision would be based on English public policy, and the two might be different. In *Malicorp Ltd v Egypt* [2015] EWHC 361 (Comm), [2015] 1 Lloyd's Rep 423 the court confirmed that the proper approach is to give effect to a foreign court decision setting aside an arbitral award unless it offends basic principles of honesty and natural justice and domestic concepts of public policy. In this case, there was no suggestion that the Egyptian court decision setting aside the award was perverse. The award had also granted the claimant remedies on a basis which had not been pleaded or argued, thereby denying the defendant the right to present its case. As a result, enforcement of the award was not permitted. In *IPCO (Nigeria) Ltd v Nigerian National Petroleum Corporation* [2008] EWCA Civ 1157, [2009] 1 Lloyd's Rep 89, the court confirmed, in relation to a New York Convention award, that it can order partial enforcement of arbitral awards. The Court of Appeal has also confirmed that the court has the power to enter judgment in terms of a declaratory award under s. 66 (*West Tankers Inc. v Allianz SpA* [2012] EWCA Civ 27, [2012] Bus LR 1701).

As discussed at **72.13**, the Supreme Court in *Dallah Real Estate and Tourism Holding Co. v Ministry of Religious Affairs of the Government of Pakistan* [2010] UKSC 46, [2011] 1 AC 763, held that where a court is asked to enforce an award, and an application is made to resist enforcement under the Arbitration Act 1996, s. 103, on the basis that the tribunal did not have jurisdiction, a party is entitled to a full determination on evidence of the issue of jurisdiction. The standard of review does not differ depending on whether the review is carried out at the courts of the seat of the arbitration (domestic and pursuant to s. 67) or the courts where enforcement is sought. See 72.13 for further discussion of the appropriate standard of review.

Interest on award

72.20   An applicant seeking to enforce an award of interest where the whole or any part of the interest relates to a period after the date of the award must file a statement giving the following particulars (**CPR, r. 62.19(1)**):

(a) whether simple or compound interest was awarded;

(b) the date from which interest was awarded;

(c) whether rests were provided for, in which case they should be specified;

(d) the rate of interest awarded; and

(e) a calculation showing the total amount claimed up to the date of the certificate. Any sums which will become due thereafter should be shown on a daily-rate basis.

Such a statement must be filed whenever the amount of interest has to be quantified for the purpose of obtaining a judgment or order for the enforcement of an award (Arbitration Act 1996, s. 66) or enforcing such a judgment or order (**CPR, r. 62.19(2)**).

Chapter 73   Alternative Dispute Resolution

INTRODUCTION

The introduction of the CPR began a process designed to reform court procedures to make them **73.1** more effective and more affordable. However, whatever changes are introduced, a fair trial of complex issues will always be expensive. By its nature, adversarial litigation may not be able to provide a resolution to the parties' dispute which is truly in their best interests. Accordingly, recognising the limits of litigation, Lord Woolf noted in his *Interim Report* (ch. 18, paras 1 and 2) that:

In recent years there has been, both in this country and overseas, a growth in alternative dispute resolution (ADR) and an increasing recognition of its contribution to the fair, appropriate and effective resolution of civil disputes. The fact that litigation is not the only means of achieving this aim, and may not in all cases be the best, is my main reason for including ADR in an Inquiry whose essential focus is on improving access to justice through the courts. My second reason is to increase awareness still further among the legal professional and the general public, of what ADR has to offer.... From the point of view of the Court Service, ADR has the obvious advantage of saving scarce judicial and other resources. More significantly, in my view, it offers a variety of benefits to litigants or potential litigants.

While the courts were not to become involved in administering ADR, Lord Woolf recommended that the two systems worked together:

Where there is a satisfactory alternative which offers a prospect of resolving a dispute in a way which is to the advantage of the litigants, then the court should encourage the use of this alternative. This is a responsibility which the courts should accept. It is in their interest that they should do so. (*Interim Report*, ch. 18, para. 31.)

Since the CPR were introduced the courts have been balancing their support for ADR with the right of access to the courts. The leading case is now the Court of Appeal decision in *Halsey v Milton Keynes General NHS Trust* [2004] EWCA Civ 576, [2004] 1 WLR 3002. The central message of this case (at [11]) is that:

Parties sometimes need to be encouraged by the court to embark on an ADR. The need for such encouragement should diminish in time if the virtue of ADR in suitable cases is demonstrated even more convincingly than it has been thus far. The value and importance of ADR have been established

1289

within a remarkably short time. All members of the legal profession who conduct litigation should now routinely consider with their clients whether their disputes are suitable for ADR. But we reiterate that the court's role is to encourage, not to compel. The form of encouragement may be robust.

For an example of robust encouragement, see *Egan v Motor Services (Bath) Ltd* [2007] EWCA Civ 1002, [2008] 1 WLR 1539. Here the Court of Appeal expressed its dismay ('completely cuckoo') at seeing legal costs of more than £100,000 being spent on a dispute over £6,000.

Judicial support for alternative dispute resolution

73.2   In *R (Cowl) v Plymouth City Council* [2001] EWCA Civ 1935, [2002] 1 WLR 803, Lord Woolf restated his support for ADR judicially. He spoke of 'the paramount importance of avoiding litigation whenever this is possible' and how both sides must 'be acutely conscious of the contribution alternative dispute resolution can make to resolving disputes in a manner which both meets the needs of the parties and the public and saves time, expense and stress'.

Judicial support for alternative dispute resolution was extended to holding that agreements to mediate, entered into before a dispute has arisen, are enforceable. This contrasts with the usual English law position that agreements to negotiate are unenforceable. In *Cable and Wireless plc v IBM United Kingdom Ltd* [2002] EWHC 2059 (Comm), [2002] 2 All ER (Comm) 1041, Colman J stated that 'for the courts now to decline to enforce contractual references to ADR on the grounds of intrinsic uncertainty would be to fly in the face of public policy as expressed in the CPR'. However, the Court of Appeal declined to follow this decision in *Sulamerica Cia Nacional de Seguros SA v Enesa Engenharia SA* [2012] EWCA Civ 638, [2013] 1 WLR 102 where the court held that a relatively detailed mediation provision was incapable of giving rise to a binding obligation because it failed to define a mediation process. *Sulamerica* was applied in *Tang Chung Wah v Grant Thornton International Ltd* [2012] EWHC 3198 (Ch), [2013] 1 Lloyd's Rep 11. This case arose out of a dispute within an international accountancy network. Before commencing arbitration proceedings the relevant agreement called for disputes to be referred to the Chief Executive and thereafter to a Panel of Board Members for resolution. The court relied on *Sulamerica* in finding that the process was too nebulous and equivocal to be enforceable. It also laid down a test whereby the court should assess (1) whether there is a sufficiently clear and unequivocal commitment to commence a process, (2) whether the steps a party should take to commence the process can be discerned and (3) whether the process itself is sufficiently clearly defined to allow the court to determine the minimum required of the parties in terms of participation in a process and when or how the process can be terminable without breach.

These authorities, together with authorities from other jurisdictions, were reviewed in *Emirates Trading Agency LLC v Prime Mineral Exports Private Ltd* [2014] EWHC 2104 (Comm), [2015] 1 WLR 1145. The court concluded that a dispute resolution clause that required the parties to seek to resolve their disputes by friendly discussions in good faith and within a limited period was enforceable.

In appropriate circumstances, the courts will impose costs sanctions on parties they perceive to have insufficiently explored the possibilities of alternative dispute resolution (see **73.23**).

There is no official framework or rules for ADR in the CPR. However, the CPR are framed so that ADR is always to be considered as an alternative to pursuing a claim through the courts. There are a number of provisions whereby court proceedings intersect with ADR. These are described at **73.9** to **73.23**.

WHAT IS ADR?

73.3   ADR is understood to mean any alternative process to litigation through the courts. The various types of ADR broadly fall into two main categories. The first category involves processes that are, similar to litigation, adjudicatory. These result in a final and binding determination on the parties. The second category includes procedures that facilitate a negotiated settlement between the disputing parties within a structured framework. These, the non-adjudicative processes, usually involve some kind of third-party involvement.

ADJUDICATIVE ADR

The adjudicative procedures include such processes as arbitration and expert determination where a final and binding determination is made on the dispute. These types of ADR are widely used in commercial contracts. Arbitration is often used for the resolution of cross-border, high-value disputes and, domestically, for rent review disputes under commercial leases. Expert determination is often included in energy contracts for disputes that relate to specific technical accounting matters. In such cases, an expert accountant will be nominated by the parties to make a determination on the matters in dispute.

73.4

Adjudication under the Housing Grants, Construction and Regeneration Act 1996

In common with certain other jurisdictions, the various United Kingdom jurisdictions have imposed by statute a quasi-judicial process for certain construction disputes. The Housing Grants, Construction and Regeneration Act 1996 created a right to refer to adjudication a dispute arising under any agreement which is a construction contract, entered into after that date. The Act applies to England, Wales and Scotland, and there is equivalent legislation for Northern Ireland. To be covered by the Act, a construction contract must comply with certain statutory requirements. Contracts with residential occupiers are not included (s. 106). Certain matters which would normally be called construction work (including most oil and gas, process plant and utility construction work) are outside the scope of statutory adjudication as a result of the detailed definition of 'construction operations' in the Act (s. 105). Other types of contract (including leases, contracts relating to shares and guarantees) are exempted by regulations made by the Secretary of State (the Construction Contracts (England and Wales) Exclusion Order 1998 (SI 1998/648) and its Scottish and Northern Irish counterparts).

73.5

In the absence of a compliant adjudication provision in a construction contract a statutory scheme applies as a term of the contract implied by statute. The scheme is set out in sch. 1 to the Scheme for Construction Contracts (England and Wales) Regulations 1998 (SI 1998/649) made under the Act. Under para. 12 of the scheme an adjudicator is obliged to act impartially, reach his decision in accordance with the relevant contract terms and the law applicable to the contract and 'avoid incurring unnecessary expense'. Absent any agreement between the parties on the appointment of an adjudicator, a nominating body, for example, the Royal Institute of Chartered Surveyors (RICS), may make an appointment at the request of one of the parties.

The Act lays down a framework for the conduct of adjudication: for example, the adjudicator must reach a decision within 28 days of the dispute having been referred to him or such longer period as the parties may agree (s. 108(2)). Within this broad outline, the parties are free to agree more detailed express terms, and often do so by reference to published sets of rules.

Adjudication is a fast and often effective mechanism for resolving construction disputes. The adjudicator's decision is binding until 'the dispute is finally determined by legal proceedings, by arbitration…or by agreement' (s. 108(3)). The parties can agree that the adjudicator's decision will be final and binding. Enforcement is by way of an application to court for sums owing under the contract. Speed is the critical factor in adjudication proceedings as most parties want to have a determination of the dispute as quickly as possible without having to resort to litigation or arbitration.

Expert determination

Expert determination is where the parties choose to refer a particular type of dispute to an independent third party to decide the matter applying his own expertise. The third party is

73.6

chosen by the parties and usually possesses expertise and technical knowledge relevant to the subject of the dispute, but need not be a lawyer. It is important that the contract sets out a default appointment process to be used if the parties are unable to agree who is to act as expert. It is usual to provide that an industry body (such as the Institute of Chartered Accountants in England and Wales (ICAEW) or the Law Society) or a third-party body (such as the Centre for Effective Dispute Resolution (CEDR), the London Court of International Arbitration (LCIA), the International Chamber of Commerce (ICC), the International Centre for Expertise, the City Disputes Panel or the Expert Witness Institute) is to make the appointment. This type of process is most suitable for determining technical aspects of a complex dispute. Provisions for expert determination, to resolve financial or technical issues, are also common in long-term contracts or where there is an ongoing commercial relationship between the parties. An expert is only vested with the powers prescribed in the relevant contract. It is therefore advisable to set out clearly the manner in which the expert determination should proceed to avoid any delay at the time the dispute arises. There are no procedural restrictions on the parties, although if a speedy outcome is sought a simpler process is preferable. It is useful to include a provision in the contract allowing the parties to agree the procedure for the expert determination or to apply standard terms or rules of a third-party body regarding expert determination. If the parties cannot so agree, a default arrangement should provide for the expert himself to determine the process. This can prevent time being wasted on agreeing a procedure once a dispute has arisen and is referred to expert determination. An expert does not, unless there is a provision to the contrary, have to receive formal submissions from the parties, either oral or written. He may reach his final decision based on his own investigations and expertise. However, in practice, it is generally accepted that each party will make at least written submissions on the matters in dispute. The parties and the expert agree terms of reference, setting out the procedure to be followed and the expert's terms of engagement.

Expert determination is particularly useful for resolving technical issues, for example, accounting disputes, valuation of corporate shareholdings and the calculation of sums paid under oil and gas joint operation agreements. The decision of an expert is final and the parties can and usually do expressly agree in the contract to be bound by the decision of the expert. The exceptions to such finality are fraud and manifest error. An expert's determination cannot be enforced in the same way as an arbitration award. The Arbitration Act 1996 does not apply to expert determination so enforcement is a matter of implementing the contract provisions. The English courts will recognise the expert's determination as final and binding save in cases of fraud or if the expert has exceeded his mandate.

An expert differs from an arbitrator in that an expert can be sued for negligence by the parties, though experts usually seek to limit such liability in their terms of reference. An arbitrator is immune under the Arbitration Act 1996, s. 29, unless the alleged act or omission was shown to be committed in bad faith. A clause in a contract may not always be clear as to which type of dispute resolution is being used, expert determination or arbitration. The dispute resolution provision in a contract does not need to refer to an arbitrator or arbitration for it to fall into that category. Accordingly, parties need to be careful when drafting their dispute resolution clause to ensure that their intention is clear. In *David Wilson Homes Ltd v Survey Services Ltd* [2001] EWCA Civ 34, [2001] 1 All ER (Comm) 449, the Court of Appeal confirmed that in interpreting the dispute clause 'the important thing is that there should be an agreement to refer disputes to a person other than the court who is to resolve the dispute in a manner binding on the parties to the agreement' (at [11]). Despite the lack of any reference to arbitration, the Court of Appeal confirmed it was in fact an arbitration clause and not expert determination. Many expert determination clauses clearly state that the expert is acting as an expert and not as an arbitrator to avoid any such confusion. Usually the scope and remit of the expert is narrower than that of an arbitral tribunal and does not involve determinations on questions of law.

Arbitration

Arbitration is a private, usually contractual, dispute resolution option where an impartial **73.7** tribunal issues a final and binding award on the matters in dispute. It is consensual in nature and it must be clear from the parties' agreement that they intended to arbitrate. All signatory states to the Convention on the Recognition and Enforcement of Foreign Arbitral Awards 1958 (the New York Convention) will recognise an agreement to arbitrate and stay litigation proceedings. Prima facie evidence of an agreement to arbitrate is required unless the national court finds that the arbitration agreement is 'null and void, inoperative, or incapable of being performed' (art. II(3)). In general, the courts in England and Wales will order a stay of litigation proceedings under the Arbitration Act 1996, s. 9, and give a benevolent construction in favour of arbitration. For examples of cases considering whether a stay should or should not be granted see *Kruppa v Benedetti* [2014] EWHC 1887 (Comm), [2014] 2 All ER (Comm) 617, and *Lombard North Central plc v GATX Corporation* [2012] EWHC 1067 (Comm), [2012] 2 All ER (Comm) 1119.

The cornerstone of arbitration is party autonomy. Subject to any mandatory requirements under the Arbitration Act 1996, the parties are free to agree exactly how any disputes should be resolved in arbitral proceedings. The Arbitration Act 1996 gives effect to this principle by reducing the intervention of the courts to a minimum. They have a purely supportive and supervisory role in arbitration proceedings. The courts can assist the arbitration process, for example, by ordering witnesses to attend hearings, but cannot review the merits of an award. There are limited mandatory grounds of appeal should an aggrieved party wish to challenge the tribunal's award.

There are two main options available to commercial entities considering incorporating an arbitration clause into a contract: ad hoc arbitration or institutional arbitration.

In ad hoc arbitration, there is no administering body so the parties are free to agree the type of arbitration procedure that best suits their needs. Should they be unable to do so, the tribunal will determine the process. The parties in ad hoc arbitration will pay for the tribunal's costs but will not pay an arbitral institution a fee to help administer the arbitration.

In reality, it is recommended that when drafting an ad hoc clause the parties choose an appointing authority to help with the constitution of the tribunal (which will cost a small fee). In the absence of an arbitral institution carrying out the administrative function, the chairman of an ad hoc tribunal may seek the parties' agreement to nominate a secretary to the tribunal to assist in the smooth running of the case. This may reduce the perceived cost benefit of an ad hoc arbitration. Parties in ad hoc arbitration often apply the United Nations Commission on International Trade Law (UNCITRAL) Arbitration Rules which provide some guidance for the tribunal on procedure.

The second option, institutional or administered arbitration, is where the parties incorporate into the contract the rules of a designated international arbitration institution. Examples of such arbitral institutions are the London Court of International Arbitration (LCIA), the Stockholm Chamber of Commerce (SCC), the Hong Kong International Arbitration Centre (HKIAC) and the International Chamber of Commerce (ICC). Each of the international institutions has its own set of rules and they have varying degrees of regulation. Some (like the LCIA) are considered to have more of a 'light touch' administration, while others (including the ICC) are viewed as having a higher level of regulation throughout the process. This includes scrutiny and approval of an award by the ICC Court before it is issued by the tribunal. In contrast, other institutions may rely more heavily on the tribunals to produce well-crafted and enforceable awards. Parties often prefer to choose institutional arbitration in their contracts because of the administrative and procedural support offered. Anecdotally, the involvement of an arbitral institution in ensuring the procedural integrity of the arbitration and quality of the award may also aid enforcement.

There are certain types of international disputes that are referred to particular institutions. Investment disputes, for example, between an investor and a host State, are often referred to the International Centre for Settlement of Investment Disputes (ICSID) at the World Bank in Washington. About 9–13 per cent of the ICC's cases each year involve a State or State entity. Some of these investment disputes arise under concession contracts that have specific arbitration clauses. In other cases, the investor will base its claim on a relevant bilateral or multilateral investment treaty. These types of international arbitrations are not contractual but rely on the State's standing offer to arbitrate certain types of disputes set out in the relevant treaty.

Domestically, the best-known arbitration institute is the Chartered Institute of Arbitrators. It plays a leading role in training arbitrators and promoting the process generally. It also promulgates arbitration rules and administers more than 100 bespoke arbitration schemes for consumer and commercial markets.

The parties to an arbitration agreement can choose the number of tribunal members. Although a sole arbitrator is the default position under the Arbitration Act 1996, s. 15(3), and under a number of institutional rules, parties often prefer to be able to nominate one member each of a three-member tribunal. Three-member tribunals are commonly chosen for high-value disputes or where the issues are legally or factually complex. The parties can also agree the procedure for the arbitration including limiting document production to clear and specific categories. In international arbitration there is usually only limited document disclosure. The International Bar Association (IBA) Rules on the Taking of Evidence are often referred to by arbitrators to ensure that full common law-style discovery is avoided. Parties can, if they so wish, expressly include these IBA Rules into their contract, in whole or in part, as a means of reducing uncertainty in the procedure to be applied by the tribunal should a dispute arise in the future.

The flexibility and private nature of arbitration makes it a popular option in commercial contracts. In addition, the finality of the award provides commercial certainty. **CPR, r. 62.18(1)**, requires that an application must be made to the court for permission to enforce an award. Once this permission has been granted, an English-seated arbitral award is enforceable in England and Wales under the Arbitration Act 1996, s. 66, as if it were a court judgment. If necessary, an English-seated award can also be enforced abroad in all of the contracting States to the New York Convention on the Recognition and Enforcement of Foreign Arbitral Awards 1958. Foreign awards may be enforced in the English courts in accordance with part 3 of the Arbitration Act 1996.

Arbitration is used in a huge range of commercial transactions from sport to construction. Certain types of transactions have given rise to their own specialised arbitration procedures. A good example of this is 'baseball arbitration', or last offer arbitration. This type of arbitration was first used in the United States by sports clubs in negotiations over professional athletes' salaries. It is now more widely used, for example, in reinsurance contracts, and where parties have an ongoing relationship. The arbitrator's ability to determine quantum in the case is restricted. After making their submissions to the tribunal both parties must recommend a figure that they believe would settle the dispute. The arbitrator can only choose the figure which he finds is closest to what he would have awarded. There are therefore only two possible outcomes in a baseball arbitration. Clearly both sides will try to be reasonable in their proposed figure as they would not wish to alienate the tribunal forcing it to choose the other party's suggestion. This type of arbitration is only appropriate where the parties agree sums are due and payable under a contract, but the actual amount is disputed. There are clear risks in this type of arbitration, but as the parties are forced to make reasonable quotes it often encourages settlement.

Trade arbitration

73.8 London is an international centre for commodity disputes, from maritime to metals. Each commodity association has its own distinct set of arbitration rules, many of which contain an appellate body system. Examples include GAFTA (Grain and Feed Trade Association) and FOSFA (Federation of Oils Seeds and Fats Association). The London Metal Exchange is the world's leading market for base metals. Any disputes arising under a metal contract must be referred to arbitration under the LME Arbitration Rules. The same is true for the Refined Sugar Association (RSA), originally founded in 1891. Although each association has its own rules these arbitrations do add to the jurisprudence under the Arbitration Act 1996. In *Rustal Trading Ltd v Gill & Duffus SA* [2000] 1 Lloyd's Rep 14, for example, the High Court had to decide whether one of the arbitrators in an RSA arbitration was biased as he had been involved in an earlier dispute involving one of the parties. This argument was dismissed as the previous dispute was two years earlier and in any event the court did not find it out of the ordinary that the parties in such trade arbitrations may have had previous experience with each other.

Commodity trade arbitration is a specialist form of arbitration. Nevertheless, maritime arbitration under the LMAA (London Maritime Arbitrators Association) has generated a large number of cases before the English courts. The fundamental principles that govern these arbitrations are the same for general commercial matters, and the Arbitration Act 1996 applies when the seat of the arbitration is in England.

NON-ADJUDICATIVE ADR

A wide range of processes fall into the category of non-adjudicative ADR. These procedures are often used to assist parties to ongoing litigation or arbitration to reach a settlement or as a precursor to adjudicative processes. They are widely used in England in labour relations and family law disputes, and throughout the commercial sector. They can cut short a dispute and save time and money if an amicable settlement can be agreed. This type of ADR involves the intervention of an independent, neutral third party. The flexibility of procedure and informality allowed may lend itself to a positive outcome. Parties can control exactly how the process will take place and can be more forthright in their discussions as non-adjudicative ADR is a confidential process and the result is non-binding and usually unenforceable without a subsequent settlement agreement. **73.9**

Conciliation/negotiation

Negotiation is often a useful form of ADR in commercial disputes where the relationship between the parties is ongoing. The parties can use the time of negotiation as a cooling-off period to try to resolve their dispute quickly and cheaply. In many contracts, negotiation is a precondition to arbitration or litigation. Many commercial contracts have a multi-tiered dispute resolution clause that will impose an obligation to try to reach an amicable settlement through negotiation. Usually a certain time period is designated for this purpose, for example, seven or 15 days. There are not the same negative costs implications in failure to engage in pre-agreed forms of ADR followed by arbitration as exist for litigation (see **73.23**). **73.10**

Negotiation can take place with just the parties present or an independent third party can be involved. The role of the negotiator is purely to facilitate the parties in reaching a resolution. He does not take sides although he can have separate caucus meetings with each side to see if he can bring them any closer to reaching an amicable settlement. A conciliation process takes place in a similar way. A neutral conciliator will also try to assist the parties in finding a mutually satisfactory resolution to the dispute. The procedure in the negotiation or conciliation is driven by the parties and flexibility is essential. It is unlikely there will be any formal written or oral submissions, but they can be used to enable each party to get a better understanding of the issues in dispute.

Negotiation is also used during an ongoing arbitration or litigation. Having commenced formal proceedings, the parties may be more willing to reach a compromise solution once they

Commentary

have seen the opposing arguments articulated in the initial pleadings. Many cases are settled successfully in this way. A party should take care in using arbitration as a tool to force a respondent to negotiate a settlement. Once an arbitration is commenced it cannot be unilaterally withdrawn. The consent of both parties is required. If no negotiated settlement is reached, the arbitration will continue, whether the party chooses to participate or not. It is therefore worth making a genuine attempt to reach a negotiated settlement prior to any formal proceedings being commenced.

Mediation

73.11   **What kind of cases are suitable for mediation?**   Virtually all civil disputes can be resolved by mediation. The remedies available in mediation are potentially far wider than those which can be obtained through litigation as the parties to a mediation can agree, or be guided to, any resolution of their dispute which they wish. However, mediation may be less suitable in cases where:

(a) a party is contemplating or facing a large number of similar claims for which it seeks to set some kind of legal precedent;

(b) a party is confident it can swiftly vindicate its legal rights and obtain full relief by proceeding to summary judgment; or

(c) a party requires speedy injunctive relief.

The fact that a dispute raises complicated issues of fact or law, involves more than two parties or has given rise to an acrimonious relationship between the litigants, should be no barrier to mediation. In all these cases mediation may ultimately provide the parties with a more satisfactory resolution to their dispute than the courts can provide.

73.12   **What happens at the mediation?**   The venue for a mediation will generally consist of one large room where the parties and the mediator can meet together and private rooms for the parties either to meet separately with the mediator or to discuss the matter alone when the mediator is with the other party or parties.

At the start of the mediation, the parties will usually meet in the presence of the mediator and briefly explain their case. In some mediations the parties will have had the opportunity, before the mediation meeting begins, to provide the mediator with a written submission outlining their positions and with copies of documents they believe to be relevant.

Having made their opening presentations the parties will retire to their private rooms and the mediator will move between them trying to help them reach an agreement. The mediator will be able to influence the parties during this stage by controlling the flow of information, deciding on how to present a party's evidence to the other side and ultimately by suggesting or influencing the architecture of any settlement.

The mediation can end at any time as the parties and the mediator are under no obligation to remain. If a settlement is reached, it will normally be recorded in writing at the mediation.

The mediation process is confidential and without prejudice. If the mediation does not lead to settlement, a party will not generally be able to make use of information it obtained during the mediation in the continuing court proceedings. The nature of confidentiality, privilege and the without-prejudice principle in relation to mediation was considered in *Farm Assist Ltd v Secretary of State for the Environment, Food and Rural Affairs (No. 2)* [2009] EWHC 1102 (TCC), [2009] BLR 399. The claimant had served a witness summons on a mediator to procure her attendance to give evidence in relation to a claim that the agreement reached at mediation had been procured through duress. The mediator applied to set aside the witness summons. The court concluded that mediation proceedings are confidential both as between the parties and as between the parties and the mediator. However, where necessary in the interests of justice for evidence to be given of confidential matters, the court could order evidence to be given. Further, the proceedings are covered by without-prejudice privilege. This privilege exists between the parties and does not belong to the mediator. Accordingly, the parties can waive this privilege. There is also a further 'privilege', which arises other than the mediator's right to confidentiality in relation to the mediation proceedings. Nonetheless, in the interests of justice, the court ordered the mediator to give evidence of what was said and done in the mediation.

Usually, the mediator's and mediation institution's fees will be divided equally, and each party bears its own costs of attending the mediation. Mediation costs were considered by the SCCO in *National Westminster Bank plc v Feeney* [2006] EWHC 90066 (Costs). The parties had engaged in mediation using standard CEDR terms. These provided for the costs of the mediation to be shared equally. In contrast, the wording of the Tomlin order settling the claim provided for the claimant to pay the defendant's costs. The court held that the parties' costs of attending the mediation did not fall within the Tomlin order and thus would not be payable by the claimant to the defendant. However, the costs of the mediator should be included in the Tomlin order undertaking to pay the other party's costs. It is submitted that the logic of this distinction is not apparent.

Costs of mediation were again considered in *Lobster Group Ltd v Heidelberg Graphic Equipment Ltd* [2008] EWHC 413 (TCC), [2008] 2 All ER 1173. The court held that costs incurred in a pre-action mediation would not form part of an order for security for costs for the main proceedings. This was because mediation costs which failed to prevent the commencement of proceedings over two years later could not be described as 'costs of and incidental to the proceedings' within the Senior Courts Act 1981, s. 51(1). Additionally, in any event, the parties had agreed in the mediation agreement to bear their own costs, and it would be a breach of that agreement to allow a party to recover its share of the mediation costs by way of an order for security. In *Roundstone Nurseries Ltd v Stephenson Holdings Ltd* [2009] EWHC 1431 (TCC), [2009] 5 Costs LR 787, the court made an order in respect of costs incurred during a mediation on the basis that the mediation took place as part of the pre-action protocol process.

Does mediation work?   There is much speculation as to whether mediation does, as its supporters claim, lead to settlements in most cases in which it is used. A report by Professor Hazel Genn, published by the Lord Chancellor's Department in 2002, assessed the impact of ADR orders made in the Commercial Court (*Court-based ADR Initiatives for Non-family Civil Disputes* (Research Paper 1/2002)). The paper is based upon data collected from court files and interviews with solicitors relating to 233 ADR orders made between July 1996 and June 2000. **73.13**

Professor Genn found that ADR was undertaken in just over half of the cases in which an ADR order was made. However, the figures showed an increasing use of ADR towards the end of her review period. Of the cases in which ADR was attempted, 52 per cent settled through ADR and a further 20 per cent settled some time after the conclusion of the ADR procedure. Only 5 per cent continued to trial. Where ADR was not attempted, 15 per cent went to trial and 63 per cent settled, with about one-fifth of the cases that settled attributing the settlement to the making of an ADR order.

How will the European Mediation Directive change the mediation landscape?   Directive 2008/52/EC (the Mediation Directive) aims to promote and regulate the development of mediation throughout the EU. The Mediation Directive applies to cross-border disputes in civil and commercial matters, save for rights and obligations which are not at the parties' disposal under the relevant applicable law (for example, in the context of family law or employment law matters). **73.14**

The Mediation Directive is implemented in England and Wales by **CPR, Part 78, Section III**.

Section III only applies to mediated cross-border disputes that are within the scope of the Mediation Directive. Perhaps the most pertinent aspect of **Section III** is that it provides for the enforcement of a mediation settlement agreement. To enforce a mediation settlement, the parties,

Commentary

or one party with the explicit consent of the others, may make an application in accordance with **Part 23** (where there are existing proceedings in England and Wales) or in accordance with **Part 8** (where there are no existing proceedings in England and Wales). The mediation settlement agreement must be annexed to the application notice or claim form when it is filed. Where only one party makes the application, evidence of the explicit consent of the other parties must also be included with the application. The court will make an order making the mediation settlement enforceable, without the need for a hearing (unless the court directs otherwise).

The other aspects of **Section III** relate to the disclosure or inspection of mediation evidence that is within the control of the mediator or the mediation administration, and where a party wishes to obtain mediation evidence from a mediator or mediation administration. In support of such an application, the party seeking disclosure or inspection, or evidence of a witness, must include evidence that all parties to the mediation agree to the application, or that the mediation evidence is necessary for overriding considerations of public policy, or that the mediation evidence is necessary to implement or enforce the mediation settlement agreement.

The mediation of cross-border disputes, to which the Mediation Directive (and **CPR, Part 78, Section III**) apply, probably represents only a small percentage of the UK mediation workload. The impact of the Mediation Directive in England and Wales appears to have been relatively limited to date. On 18 September 2015, the European Commission launched a public consultation on the application of the Directive across Europe, asking whether the Directive has met its objectives and how effectively each provision has been implemented.

Early neutral evaluation

73.15   Early neutral evaluation aims to provide parties with an early and frank evaluation by an independent party of the merits of their claim. It usually takes place at a much earlier stage than arbitration, although, like negotiation and conciliation, it can be used at any time during a dispute. The concept of early neutral evaluation was conceived in the United States as a mechanism to reduce the costs of litigation. Early neutral evaluation can be carried out by a third-party evaluator and several ADR centres offer advice on appointing an appropriate evaluator, for example CEDR (http://www.cedr.com). All courts in England and Wales should also be able to offer to hear an early neutral evaluation with the aim of helping the parties to settle the case (**CPR, r. 3.1(2)(m)**). The Commercial Court offers an early evaluation scheme, where a judge can give an assessment of the merits of the claims (Admiralty and Commercial Courts Guide, para. G2). Although this is non-binding it has not been widely used.

The assessment of the judge or third-party evaluator is non-binding on the parties but often works to ensure that the parties reach a settlement before expending time and resources on litigation or arbitration proceedings. The assessment will focus on the central issues involved in the dispute and the relevant law. The evaluation is usually issued in written form to the parties. The costs involved in the process are a lot less than arbitration or litigation and the entire procedure takes place quite quickly.

Mini-trial or executive trial

73.16   The mini or executive trial is not in reality a trial. It is a structured settlement process where the parties make summary submissions on the particular dispute. The executives of the parties attend the meeting with an independent adviser, often nominated by an appropriate dispute resolution institution. The executives having heard the summary submissions try to reach an agreement. If this is not possible, the neutral adviser issues an advisory opinion. This is not binding on the parties, but usually a further meeting between the executives is held after the *opinion* has been given in a final attempt to reach an amicable settlement. The mini-trial was introduced to meet a business need. It is a fast and efficient means of resolving a dispute where the control rests exclusively with the business executives.

Med-arb

A hybrid form of dispute resolution is mediation-arbitration or 'med-arb'. Originally conceived   **73.17**
in the 1970s med-arb was thought to provide disputing parties with the best of both options.
Each stage of the process is kept separate. The mediation process takes place first and if that fails
to produce a solution to the dispute, arbitration proceedings will commence with the mediator
sitting as arbitrator. One of the main disadvantages of med-arb is that parties may be less open
during the mediation process as they know that if the mediation is unsuccessful they will have
the same independent third party acting as an arbitrator with the power to issue a final and binding award. This drawback has given rise to debate on whether the process itself is fundamentally
flawed at law. Can a person who has already acted as a mediator and been privy to certain confidential information from the parties in private caucus meetings really be an independent unbiased arbitrator? The Arbitration Act 1996, s. 24(1), requires the tribunal to be impartial and a
legitimate concern may be raised as to whether a person who has acted as a mediator first necessarily complies with this obligation. A similar obligation of impartiality and independence exists
under the European Convention on Human Rights. In any event, med-arb is used quite extensively throughout Asia, for example in China International Economic and Trade Arbitration
Commission (CIETAC) and Singapore International Arbitration Centre (SIAC) arbitrations,
without any such issues being a problem. Parties seem to be happy that the independent third
party is familiar with the dispute from the outset and, if an agreed settlement cannot be reached
after the initial mediation, for him to continue to act as arbitrator.

CONTRACT TERMS

The type of dispute resolution clause in any particular contract will depend on the type of   **73.18**
transaction, the parties to the contract, the forum and the applicable law. Choice of any form
of adjudicative ADR will determine an issue definitively whereas non-adjudicative ADR provides a forum within which the parties can reach an agreed settlement.

When drafting a contract particular care and attention should be given to the dispute resolution clause. A decision must be made about which type of ADR should be chosen or whether
a range of options is required under the contract. Unfortunately, at the time of drafting a contract most parties do not envisage anything going wrong so it can be difficult to discuss in any
detail the significance of the type of ADR chosen. It is always essential to consider the preferred
dispute resolution option of each client. It is best to explain the implications of each option so
that there are no unrealistic expectations should a dispute arise under the contract in the future.

Contract terms should be drafted clearly to avoid any controversy or disagreement as to the
scope and extent of the dispute resolution clause. This is particularly true if the contract provides
for hybrid or bifurcated dispute resolution provisions, under which different procedures apply
to particular types of dispute. For example, technical issues may be referred to an expert accountant, with all other disputes under the contract being referred to arbitration. Option clauses
providing one party with a choice of dispute resolution options, but limiting the choice of the
other party, are becoming increasingly common, particularly in finance transactions. These types
of clauses can be problematic in certain jurisdictions and local advice should be sought before
entering into them.

It has also become quite common to include several different forms of dispute resolution
provisions in a multi-tiered clause. In this way, parties seek to minimise their time and costs
spent on any future dispute. The options provided in these clauses usually start with mandatory negotiations, move to mediation and then on to arbitration or litigation depending on
the will of the parties. The most important consideration for such a multi-tiered clause is to
include time limits for each of the non-binding dispute resolution options. Otherwise one
party could use them as a mere dilatory tactic rather than a genuine attempt at resolution.

Commentary

Such time limits can range from 15 days to 90 days depending on the type of contract. Clearly the final option of arbitration or litigation cannot be so prescribed. Arbitration can have rigorous time limits imposed in a contract, often referred to as fast-track arbitration. It must, however, be left open to the parties to agree an extension if necessary, otherwise the tribunal's jurisdiction may expire.

The decisions in *Sulamerica Cia Nacional de Seguros SA v Enesa Engenharia SA* [2012] EWCA Civ 638, [2013] 1 WLR 102 and *Tang Chun Wah v Grant Thornton International Ltd* [2012] EWHC 3198 (Ch), [2013] 1 Lloyd's Rep 11 mentioned at 73.2 give guidance to contract drafters seeking to craft enforceable ADR provisions as a precursor to litigation or arbitration. It seems that the safest course will be to adopt model clauses promulgated by the mediation institutions (a list of the most active UK institutions appears at 73.24), but anyone wanting to draft an enforceable ADR provision should start with the guidance offered by the court in *Tang Chun Wah*.

RELATIONSHIP BETWEEN THE COURTS AND ADR

73.19   In his *Final Report* (ch. 1, para. 7(d)) Lord Woolf stated how ADR should be among the tools used by the court to resolve disputes at an early stage:

> Two other significant aims of my recommendations need to be borne in mind: that of encouraging the resolution of disputes before they come to litigation, for example by greater use of pre-litigation disclosure and of ADR, and that of encouraging settlement, for example by introducing plaintiffs' offers to settle, and by the disposing of issues so as to narrow the dispute. All these are intended to divert cases from the court system or to ensure that those cases which do go through the court system are disposed of as rapidly as possible. I share the view, expressed in the Commercial Court Practice Statement of 10 December 1993, that although the primary role of the court is as a forum for deciding cases it is right that the court should encourage the parties to consider the use of ADR as a means to resolve their dispute. I believe that the same is true of helping the parties to settle a case.

ADR received further judicial support in the *Jackson Report* (January 2010). Although this did not recommend any rule changes in order to promote ADR, two primary recommendations were made. First, there should be a 'serious campaign to ensure that all litigation lawyers and judges are properly informed of how ADR works, and the benefits that it can bring'. Secondly, that an 'authoritative handbook' should be prepared to provide practical guidance on all aspects of ADR. This has been realised in *The Jackson ADR Handbook*, now in its 2nd edition (Oxford: OUP, 2016). The *Handbook* has received judicial support, for example by Briggs LJ, who referred to it in his judgment in *PGF II SA v OMFS Co. 1 Ltd* [2013] EWCA Civ 1288, [2014] 1 WLR 1386.

The courts' encouragement of mediation forces litigation practitioners to familiarise themselves with ADR processes. This familiarity leads to an increased demand for mediation. The courts' attitude also goes some way to removing the concern that by suggesting ADR a party could be taken to lack confidence in the strength of its case.

ADR and active case management

73.20   Encouraging ADR is part of the court's active case management role, which in turn is how the court furthers the overriding objective. **CPR, r. 1.4**, includes 'encouraging the parties to use an alternative dispute resolution procedure if the court considers that appropriate and facilitating the use of such procedure' among the matters expressly included within active case management.

CPR, r. 1.3, which requires the parties to help the court to further the overriding objective, places the parties under a duty in relation to ADR. Practically, this will require the parties to be aware of ADR and to consider seriously the possibility of using it to resolve their dispute.

The extent of a party's obligation to consider ADR was considered in detail by the Court of Appeal in *Halsey v Milton Keynes General NHS Trust* [2004] EWCA Civ 576, [2004] 1 WLR 3002. The court made reference to the judgment of Brooke LJ in *Dunnett v Railtrack plc* [2002] EWCA Civ

303, [2002] 1 WLR 2434, who had emphasised how 'skilled mediators are now able to achieve results satisfactory to both parties in many cases which are quite beyond the power of lawyers and courts to achieve'. However, the court rejected the submission that there should be a presumption in favour of mediation. It also emphasised that any compulsion of ADR would be an unacceptable constraint on the right of access to the court and therefore a violation of the European Convention on Human Rights, **art. 6**, in the **Human Rights Act 1998, sch. 1**.

In the Glossary to the CPR, 'alternative dispute resolution' is broadly defined as a:

collective description of methods of resolving disputes otherwise than through the normal trial process.

The well-advised litigant will consider the possibility of resorting to ADR at the earliest possible stage, even before proceedings are initiated. **PD Pre-action Conduct and Protocols, paras 8** to **11**, require all parties, in accordance with the overriding objective, to try to avoid the necessity for starting proceedings and to consider whether some form of alternative dispute resolution procedure would be more suitable than litigation. This may include conducting genuine and reasonable negotiations with a view to settling the claim economically. Court guides also actively encourage parties to consider the use of ADR. See Admiralty and Commercial Court Guide, ch. G, Chancery Guide, para. 17.1, Queen's Bench Guide, para. 6.6, and TCC Guide, s. 7.

In certain circumstances the court will use its powers under other provisions of the CPR to assist the parties to mediate. For example, in *Arrow Trading and Investments Est 1920 v Edwardian Group Ltd* [2004] EWHC 1319 (Ch), [2005] 1 BCLC 696, the court granted advance disclosure of documents relating to quantum to put the claimant in a position whereby it could meaningfully mediate the dispute.

The court's encouragement of mediation has even extended to proceedings which the parties have agreed to conduct outside of the usual court processes. In *C v RHL* [2005] EWHC 873 (Comm), LTL 12/5/2005, the court was only asked to issue an anti-suit injunction preventing a party from continuing court proceedings in Russia in breach of an agreement to arbitrate. Instead of issuing the injunction, the court directed the parties to mediate and issued a standard ADR order.

ADR and the directions questionnaire

CPR, r. 26.4(1), provides that a party filing a directions questionnaire may request the proceedings be stayed while the parties try to settle the case by ADR or other means. Where all parties request a stay, the court will direct that the proceedings be stayed for one month (**r. 26.4(2)**). If the court otherwise considers that such a stay would be appropriate, it will direct that the proceedings, either in whole or in part, be stayed for one month, or for such other period as it considers appropriate (**r. 26.4(2A)**). **73.21**

In a complex case before the TCC, the judge refused to order a window in the trial preparation directions for the parties to engage in ADR. The judge noted the delay to the timetable that would result and stated that the period between key stages, such as disclosure and exchange of witness statements, should be sufficient to enable the parties to reflect and consider their positions (*CIP Properties (AIPT) Ltd v Galliford Try Infrastructure Ltd* [2014] EWHC 3546, 156 Con LR 202).

If only one party requests a stay, the court is likely to try to ascertain why the other party is refusing (this may be a matter addressed at a case management conference).

ADR and case management conferences

The subject of ADR may be raised at the case management conference, especially if the judge believes that the parties have not previously considered it themselves. The judge may 'invite' the parties to try ADR (see, for example, the Admiralty and Commercial Courts Guide, paras G1.3 and G1.6 to G1.8 and appendix 7 for a draft ADR order; Chancery Guide, para. 17.3). **73.22**

The draft ADR order set out in app. 7 to the Admiralty and Commercial Courts Guide provides for the parties to inform the court of the steps they have taken towards ADR, should ADR not be successful. Without prejudice to matters of privilege, they have to inform the court why such steps have failed. Accordingly, while the court cannot ask the parties to provide details of their attempts to settle (questions such as 'How much is between you now?' would be off-limits), the parties can expect to be asked whether they agreed to attend a mediation. If they refused, this may have to be justified. Similarly, a party who did something to frustrate the mediation, such as sending a representative without authority to settle, may have to justify its actions.

Consequences of refusing to consider ADR

73.23   A party which does not take its duty to consider ADR seriously is likely to be penalised when the court looks to the question of costs. In exercising its discretion as to the award of costs, the court is obliged to have regard to the conduct of the parties (**CPR, r. 44.2(4)**). This includes considering:

The manner in which a party pursued or defended his case or a particular allegation or issue (**CPR, r. 44.2(5)(c)**).

Accordingly a winning party may find its recovery of costs reduced by reason of a failure to cooperate in relation to ADR. An unsuccessful defendant who refused to consider ADR to try to settle the case before trial could be liable for interest on costs (perhaps running from a date before judgment) (**CPR, r. 44.2(6)(g)**) or indemnity costs.

The Court of Appeal in *Halsey v Milton Keynes General NHS Trust* [2004] EWCA Civ 576, [2004] 1 WLR 3002, stated that a party who refuses even to consider ADR is always at risk of an adverse costs order. The court set out a number of factors which may be relevant in considering whether a party has acted unreasonably in refusing ADR. These include, but are not limited to:

(a) the nature of the dispute;
(b) the merits of the case (it may not be reasonable for a party with a weak case to insist on the use of ADR);
(c) the extent to which other settlement methods have been attempted;
(d) whether the costs of ADR would be disproportionately high;
(e) whether any delay in setting up and attending the ADR would have been prejudicial; and
(f) whether the ADR had a reasonable prospect of success.

The Court of Appeal also stated that the unsuccessful party should have the burden of showing that mediation would have had a reasonable prospect of success.

The Court of Appeal has subsequently applied the *Halsey* principles both to uphold a party's refusal to mediate (*Reed Executive plc v Reed Business Information Ltd* [2004] EWCA Civ 887, [2004] 1 WLR 3026) and to characterise a refusal as unreasonable (*Burchell v Bullard* [2005] EWCA Civ 358, [2005] BLR 330). In *Reed Executive plc v Reed Business Information Ltd* the court was guided by the fact that the offer to mediate came late and the successful party reasonably believed itself to have a good case. Delays in setting up or proposing mediation were also considered a reasonable factor in a defendant's refusal to take part in mediation in *ADS Aerospace Ltd v EMS Global Tracking Ltd* [2012] EWHC 2904 (TCC), 145 Con LR 29.

In *Burchell v Bullard* the court favoured mediation in a case where the amounts in dispute were dwarfed by the legal costs. It also stated that a party cannot rely on its own obstinacy to assert that mediation had no reasonable prospect of success. In *Earl of Malmesbury v Strutt and Parker* [2008] EWHC 424 (QB), 118 Con LR 68, the court was critical of a claimant who attended a mediation but adopted a position that 'was plainly unrealistic and unreasonable'. Such an approach was characterised as being not dissimilar in effect to an unreasonable refusal to engage in mediation. This was stated to be something the court should take account of when applying the principles considered in *Halsey*.

Commentary

Halsey was applied by the Court of Appeal in *Swain-Mason v Mills and Reeve LLP* [2012] EWCA Civ 498, [2012] STC 1760. The defendant solicitors' firm had prevailed in a claim brought against it by a former client. The trial judge had penalised the defendant for refusing to mediate in the belief, which proved to be correct, that the claim against it was without merit. The Court of Appeal reversed this decision. A reasonable refusal to mediate did not become unreasonable just because it was maintained over a long period. Further, if a party with a reasonable belief in the strength of its case was to be compelled to mediate, it could not be said that mediation was a voluntary process. To punish a defendant in such a position would be making mediation compulsory for all. In *Mann v Mann* [2014] EWHC 537 (Fam), [2014] 1 WLR 2807, the court reiterated that it could not compel parties to engage in mediation, but it could encourage them by means of an 'Ungley order', which obliges a party that considers its case unsuitable for resolution by ADR to (a) file a witness statement giving reasons upon which it relied for saying the case was unsuitable before the commencement of the proceedings and (b) justify that decision at the conclusion of the proceedings.

In *Northrop Grumman Mission Systems Europe Ltd v BAE Systems (Al Diriyah C4I) Ltd* [2014] EWHC 3148 (TCC), 156 Con LR 141, the court found that a party had acted unreasonably in rejecting an offer to mediate, even though it reasonably considered that it had a strong case. There, the court was persuaded by the fact that the cost of mediation would not have affected the litigation, was not disproportionately high and would have had a reasonable prospect of success. However, the court did not modify the general rule on costs. However, in *Garritt-Critchley v Ronnan* [2014] EWHC 1774 (Ch), [2015] 3 Costs LR 453, the court awarded indemnity costs to the claimant because the defendant's failure to engage with mediation was unreasonable. Interestingly, in that case the court suggested that the sort of case that by its nature would rule out mediation would be where the party wished to resolve a point of law, or considered that a binding precedent would be useful, or where injunctive or other relief was essential to protect the parties.

In *Laporte v Commissioner of Police of the Metropolis* [2015] EWHC 371 (QB), [2015] 3 Costs LR 471 the court awarded a successful defendant only two thirds of its costs on the basis that it had failed adequately to justify its failure to engage in ADR which had a reasonable prospect of success. In *Reid v Buckinghamshire Healthcare NHS Trust* [2015] EWHC B21 (Costs) the court held that costs sanctions for an unreasonable refusal to mediate may be applied where the party refusing to mediate is the losing party.

A further significant holding in *Reed Executive plc v Reed Business Information Ltd* was that the court cannot compel production of without-prejudice material in order to assess whether a failure to mediate was unreasonable. The court would have to base any assessment on material that was either open or marked 'without prejudice subject to costs'.

A 'modest extension' to the *Halsey* principles was made by *PGF II SA v OMFS Co. 1 Ltd* [2013] EWCA Civ 1288, [2014] 1 WLR 1386, to cover the situation where a party receives an invitation to participate in ADR and is completely silent in response. In that case, the defendant was heavily penalised in costs, as the court held that its silence was prima facie unreasonable in itself. This will be the case regardless of whether a refusal to participate in ADR might have been justified by the identification of reasonable grounds.

USEFUL ADDRESSES

ADR Group   **73.24**
160 Fleet Street
London
EC4A 2DQ
United Kingdom
Tel: 44 (0)203 600 50 50
Fax: +44 (0)203 600 50 50
Email: info@adrgroup.co.uk
Web: www.adrgroup.co.uk

Centre for Effective Dispute Resolution
International Dispute Resolution Centre
70 Fleet Street
London EC4Y 1EU
United Kingdom
Tel: +44 (0)20 7536 6000
Fax: +44 (0)20 7536 6001
Email: info@cedr.com
Web: www.cedr.com/solve/dispute-resolution-services/

The Chartered Institute of Arbitrators
International Arbitration and Mediation Centre
12 Bloomsbury Square
London WC1A 2LP
United Kingdom
Tel: +44 (0)20 7421 7444
Fax: +44 (0)20 7900 2917
Email: info@arbitrators.org
Web: www.ciarb.org

ICC International Chamber of Commerce
33–43 avenue du Président Wilson
75116 Paris
France
Tel: +33 (0)1 49 53 29 05
Fax: +33 (0)1 49 53 29 33
E-mail: arb@iccwbo.org
Web: www.iccwbo.org/products-and-services/arbitration-and-adr/

LCIA
International Dispute Resolution Centre
70 Fleet Street
London
EC4Y 1EU
United Kingdom
Tel: +44 (0)20 7936 6200
Fax: +44 (0)20 7936 6211
Email: lcia@lcia.org
Web: www.lcia.org

RICS Dispute Resolution Service
Surveyor Court
Westwood Way
Coventry
CV4 8JE
United Kingdom
Tel: +44 (0)20 7334 3806
Email: drs@rics.org
Web: www.rics.org/uk/join/member-accreditations-list/dispute-resolution-service/

PART O

Appeals, Judicial Review and EU References

INTRODUCTION

74.1   From time to time decisions are made in error, and the system of appeals is designed to ensure that these are corrected. There is a strong public interest in regarding judicial decisions as final and binding, and an open-ended appeals system would undermine this by encouraging unsuccessful litigants to have 'another bite at the cherry'. Striking a balance between encouraging finality and correcting mistakes is not easy, and explains some of the complications that arise in the area of appeals.

Careful thought must be given before embarking on an appeal. In his annual review of 1989–90, in considering appeals to the Court of Appeal, Lord Donaldson of Lymington MR said:

> The question which the adviser may ask himself is whether, looking at the matter objectively, there are sufficient grounds for believing not only that the case should have been decided differently, but that in all the circumstances it can be demonstrated to the satisfaction of the Court of Appeal that there are grounds for reversing the judge's findings. In considering this question the adviser must never forget the financial risk which an appellant undertakes of having not only to pay his own costs of the appeal, but those of his opponent and, for this purpose, the adviser has two clients if the litigant is [publicly funded]. Nor must he underrate the effect upon his client of the emotional and other consequences of a continued state of uncertainty pending an appeal. In a word, one of the most important duties of a professional legal adviser is to save his clients from themselves and always to remember that, whilst it may well be reasonable to institute or to defend particular proceedings at first instance, a wholly new and different situation arises once the claim has been fully investigated by the court and a decision given.

The law relating to appeals comes from various statutory sources, and **CPR, r. 52.1(4)**, recognises that its provisions have to yield to other rules, enactments and practice directions setting out special rules for particular categories of appeals. This chapter describes the procedure for bringing appeals in force from 3 October 2016. The current **CPR, Part 52**, applies where an appellant's notice was issued on or after 3 October 2016 (Civil Procedure (Amendment No. 3) Rules 2016 (SI 2016/788), r. 16). The most important changes are the abolition of the distinction between interim and final appeals, and adjustments to the procedure for seeking permission to appeal to the Court of Appeal. For a full discussion of the previous law, see *Blackstone's Civil Practice 2016*, ch. 74.

DECISIONS SUSCEPTIBLE TO APPEAL

74.2   The Court of Appeal has jurisdiction to hear appeals from High Court 'judgments' and 'orders' (Senior Courts Act 1981, s. 16(1)) and County Court 'determinations' (County Courts Act 1984, s. 77(1)). The term used in the Access to Justice Act 1999 (Destination of Appeals) Order 2016 (SI 2016/917) is 'decision', which is defined to include any judgment, order or direction of the High Court or County Court (art. 2). This means that a party is not entitled to appeal against the reasons for a decision given in his favour (*Compagnie Noga d'Importation et d'Exportation SA v Australia and New Zealand Banking Group Ltd* [2002] EWCA Civ 1142, [2003] 1 WLR 307), nor against findings of fact unless they concern the issue on which the whole case was decided, or if they are the subject of a declaration (*Re M (Children)* [2013] EWCA Civ 1170, LTL 4/10/2013). A witness who is criticised in findings of fact cannot appeal against those findings (*Re B and H (Children)* [2009] EWCA Civ 228, LTL 8/4/2009). The practice and procedure to be followed in appeals within the County Court and the High Court are governed by the CPR (Civil Procedure Act 1997, s. 1(1)). Although the County Courts Act 1984, s. 77(1A), says that such rules may provide for any appeal 'from the exercise by a judge of the [County Court] of any power', given by any enactment, to be to another judge of the County Court, it is submitted that these appeals are restricted in the same way as appeals to the Court of Appeal.

APPELLANT

An 'appellant' is a person who brings or seeks to bring an appeal (**CPR, r. 52.1(3)(d)**). A per-   **74.3**
son who was not a party to the proceedings in the lower court can be an 'appellant' for this
purpose (*George Wimpey UK Ltd v Tewkesbury Borough Council* [2008] EWCA Civ 12, [2008] 1 WLR
1649). In deciding whether to grant permission to appeal to such a person the court will take
into account whether any application was made to add the person in the lower court, and
whether the person has a real interest in the appeal.

ROUTES OF APPEAL

The basic civil appeals structure is, by the **Access to Justice Act 1999 (Destination of Appeals)**   **74.4**
Order 2016 (SI 2016/917) (the **Destination of Appeals Order**), PD 52A, and the
Constitutional Reform Act 2005, as follows:

(a) Decisions of County Court District Judges may be appealed to the County Court Circuit Judge.
(b) Decisions of High Court Masters, District Judges and Registrars may be appealed to a
    High Court judge.
(c) Decisions of County Court Circuit Judges may be appealed to a High Court judge.
(d) Decisions of High Court judges may be appealed to the Court of Appeal.
(e) Court of Appeal decisions may be appealed to the Supreme Court.

Tables of appeal routes are set out in **PD 52A, para. 3.5**, and are summarised in **table 74.1**. For
these purposes the **Destination of Appeals Order, arts** 4 and 5 define which members of the judiciary fall into each category by reference to the lists in the primary legislation. For County Court
District Judges this is the County Courts Act 1984, s. 5(1)(b) and (2)(m) and (r) to (v) (as substituted by the Crime and Courts Act 2013, sch. 9, para. 4). County Court Circuit Judges include
the various members of the judiciary set out in the County Courts Act 1984, s. 5(1)(a) and (2)(a)
to (l) and (n) to (q) (as substituted by the Crime and Courts Act 2013, sch. 9, para. 4). Masters
include all the offices listed in the Senior Courts Act 1981, sch. 2, part 2, and also District Judges
of the High Court (**Destination of Appeals Order, art. 4(1)(b)**). These basic routes of appeal also
apply in relation to deputy judges and their equivalents, such as Deputy District Judges (**Destination
of Appeals Order, arts** 4(1)(c) and 5; County Courts Act 1984, s. 5(2)(m)). Decisions of Recorders
sitting as County Court Circuit Judges need to be appealed to a Designated Civil Judge authorised
under para. 5 of the Table in the Senior Courts Act 1981, s. 9 (**PD 52A, para. 4.4(b)**).

Table 74.1 Structure of the civil appeals system

Decision appealed from	Appeal to	Period for commencing appeal	Whether permission is required
Magistrates' court licensing matters	Crown Court	21 days from decision (liquor) or notification (others)	No
Magistrates' court Children Act 1989 cases	Family Division single judge	14 days from determination	No
Magistrates' court interim maintenance	Family Division Divisional Court	6 weeks from order	No
Inferior court on point of law or jurisdiction	QBD Divisional Court	21 days after decision	No
Inferior court by way of judicial review	QBD Divisional Court	3 months from ground arising	Yes, from Divisional Court
Statutory appeals	High Court	Depends on statute. Often 28 days	Depends on statute

Commentary

Decision appealed from	Appeal to	Period for commencing appeal	Whether permission is required
Judicial review appeals	Court of Appeal	7 days	Yes
County Court District Judge (other than Companies Acts)	County Court Circuit Judge	21 days from decision 21 days from decision	Yes Yes
County Court District Judge non-insolvency Companies Act decision	High Court judge		
County Court Circuit Judge first instance decision	High Court judge	21 days from decision	Yes
County Court Circuit Judge appeal decision	Court of Appeal	21 days from decision	Yes
High Court Master, District Judge or Registrar	High Court judge	21 days from decision	Yes
Leapfrog appeal from Master	Court of Appeal	21 days from decision	Yes
IPEC District Judge	Enterprise Judge	21 days from decision	Yes
IPEC Enterprise Judge	Court of Appeal	21 days of decision	Yes
Authorised officer in detailed assessment	District Judge	21 days from decision	No
County Court legal adviser	District Judge	14 days after service	No
High Court judge	Court of Appeal	21 days from decision	Yes
Court of Appeal	Supreme Court	28 days from decision (14 days in contempt appeals)	Yes
Leapfrog appeal from High Court	Supreme Court	14 days from decision	Yes, from both High Court judge and Supreme Court

Unusual appeal routes

74.5   As a general rule an appeal has to be made to the next most senior level of the court system. Special cases are:

(a) **Small claims track** Appeals in these cases are considered at **45.27**.

(b) **Companies Acts** In proceedings brought pursuant to the Companies Acts 1985, 1989 and 2006 which are not insolvency proceedings, an appeal from a County Court District Judge has to be made to a High Court Judge (**Destination of Appeals Order, art. 5(4)**).

(c) **Insolvency** Appeal routes in insolvency proceedings are set out in **PD 52A, para. 3.5, Table 2**. This provides, for example, that appeals in individual insolvency from County Court District Judges must be brought to a High Court judge (see **84.14**).

(d) **Intellectual Property Enterprise Court (IPEC)** Appeals from District Judges in the IPEC are made to an Enterprise Judge (**Destination of Appeals Order, art. 4(2)**).

(e) **Costs officers** Appeals from decisions by costs officers under **CPR, r. 47.21**, are made to Masters or District Judges (**PD 2B, para. 3.1(e)**).

(f) **County Court legal advisers** A decision by a County Court legal adviser may be reconsidered by a County Court District Judge (**PD 51K, para. 3.2**).

(g) *Leapfrog appeals from Masters* Appeals from High Court masters etc. can be diverted to the Court of Appeal (see **Access to Justice Act 1999, s. 57(1)**, discussed at **74.7**).

(h) **Leapfrog appeals to the Supreme Court** are discussed at **76.3**.

(i) **Special statutory rights of appeal** There are a number of specific statutes dealing with appeals in particular cases, which as a result fall outside the **Destination of Appeals Order** (see **art. 3(b)**). An example is an appeal to the Court of Appeal from the Patents Court under the Patents Act 1977, s. 97(3), which is a specific procedure for patent appeals. This means, for example, that such appeals are not governed by the restrictions on second-tier appeals in **Access to Justice Act 1999, s. 55** (see **74.6**; *Smith International Inc. v Specialised Petroleum Services Group Ltd* [2005] EWCA Civ 1357, [2006] 1 WLR 252).

(j) **Contempt of Court** An appeal against an order or decision to punish for contempt of court, where the appellant is the defendant (or, in relation to an application for committal or attachment, the applicant), is made to the Court of Appeal (Administration of Justice Act 1960, s. 13(2)).

Second-tier appeals

Where the appeal is a second appeal, the appeal is taken to the Court of Appeal, even though   **74.6** the decision being appealed was that made by a Circuit Judge (**Destination of Appeals Order, art. 6**). Typically this will cover decisions by County Court District Judges, which are appealed to the Circuit Judge. If a second appeal is taken, under this exception it must be taken to the Court of Appeal.

In *Southern and District Finance plc v Turner* [2003] EWCA Civ 1574, LTL 7/11/2003, a County Court District Judge dismissed an application to set aside a possession order. Eight months later the defendant brought an appeal against that decision, but omitted to seek permission to appeal out of time (see **74.21**). The Circuit Judge dismissed the appeal on the ground that no permission to extend time for appealing had been included in the appellant's notice. An appeal from the Circuit Judge's refusal to consider extending time (whether this was on the basis of the judge deciding he had no jurisdiction to extend time, or a decision not to extend time) was held to be a first appeal, not a second appeal coming within **art. 6**, so should have been taken to a High Court judge under **art. 4(1)**. In *Convergence Group plc v Chantrey Vellacott* [2005] EWCA Civ 290, *The Times*, 25 April 2005, there was an application to amend a statement of case. The Master refused permission for certain amendments, but did not deal with others through lack of time. The application was taken to the judge, who refused all the proposed amendments. It was held that an appeal to the Court of Appeal was a first appeal, because the appeal in relation to the amendments which had not been considered by the Master was a first appeal, and the others could be regarded as raising common issues. This case must be treated with caution. Its logic could be reversed, producing the opposite result. It also misapplies *Uphill v BRB (Residuary) Ltd* [2005] EWCA Civ 60, [2005] 1 WLR 2070, a case discussed at **74.15**.

The principles governing obtaining permission to appeal in second-tier appeals are considered at **74.15**.

Leapfrog appeals to the Court of Appeal

If the normal route for a first appeal from a decision of a District Judge or Master would be to   **74.7** a Circuit Judge or to a High Court judge, either the lower court or the appeal court may order the appeal to be transferred to the Court of Appeal. This may be done if it is considered that the appeal will raise an important point of principle or practice or there is some other compelling reason for the Court of Appeal to hear it (**CPR, r. 52.23(1)**). There may be a compelling reason where the case was not allocated to the multi-track because of an administrative error (*Ollivierre v Chief Constable of Thames Valley* [2011] EWCA Civ 1733, LTL 1/12/2011). Where the judge in the lower court refuses permission to appeal, he cannot make an order under **r. 52.23**, because, until permission to appeal is granted, there is no appeal to be transferred (*7E Communications Ltd v Vertex Antennentechnik GmbH* [2007] EWCA Civ 140, [2007] 1 WLR 2175). The Master of the Rolls has a similar power to divert appeals to the Court of Appeal (**Access to Justice Act 1999, s. 57(1)**).

Commentary

Order of lower court: identification of appeal route

74.8   Where a party has asked for permission to appeal, the lower court's order should by **CPR, r. 40.2(3)** and **(4)**, include a number of details, including identifying the appeal court (and where relevant, the Division of the High Court). Where permission to appeal is refused, the order must also specify the level of judge who should consider a renewed application for permission (**r. 52.3(3)(b)**). Judges and court staff in the appeal court have to determine whether their court has jurisdiction simply by looking at the face of the order being appealed, and are not required to consider the background of the case. A party who believes an order has not been drawn up correctly can apply for it to be corrected under the slip rule (see **63.44**). Any refusal to correct the order can itself be a ground of appeal, but does not change the court having jurisdiction to hear the appeal (*Scribes West Ltd v Relsa Anstalt* [2004] EWCA Civ 965, [2005] 1 WLR 1839).

Appeal centres

74.9   Appeals within the County Court, appeals from the County Court, and appeals within the High Court to a judge of the High Court must be brought in the appropriate appeal centre (**PD 52B, para. 2.1**). There are two lists of appeal centres for each of the six circuits and District Registry appeals in **PD 52B**. The venue for an appeal within the County Court is determined by the Designated Civil Judge, and may be different from the appeal centre (**para. 2.1**).

The Court of Appeal is located at the Royal Courts of Justice, and its administrative office is known as the Civil Appeals Office. The Civil Appeals Office staff include a number of lawyers who, among other tasks, ensure that the Court of Appeal has jurisdiction to consider prospective appeals and that permission to appeal is sought where necessary.

Judicial review of County Court decisions

74.10   There are only very limited circumstances in which a claim may be made for judicial review of a decision of the County Court, as an appeal court, on an application for permission to appeal. The **Access to Justice Act 1999, s. 54(4)** (see **74.16**), which prevents appeals against decisions on permission to appeal, does not impliedly remove the High Court's jurisdiction of judicial review of County Court decisions (*R (Sivasubramaniam) v Wandsworth County Court* [2002] EWCA Civ 1738, [2003] 1 WLR 475). Permission to claim judicial review will, however, normally be refused where there is a suitable alternative procedure, such as a statutory appeal procedure (*R (Sivasubramaniam, v Wandsworth County Court*). Judicial review is confined to very rare cases where the County Court has acted without jurisdiction or failed to afford the appellant a fair hearing (*R (Mahon) v Taunton County Court* [2001] EWHC 1078 (Admin), [2002] ACD 192; *Gregory v Turner* [2003] EWCA Civ 183, [2003] 1 WLR 1149). Cases where the County Court judge had simply got it wrong, even extremely wrong, on the law or facts are not sufficiently exceptional to justify judicial review. Suitable cases include those where the County Court embarked on an inquiry where it lacked power, or failed to adjudicate on a matter which it had an unequivocal duty to address, and cases where there has been a clear frustration or corruption of the judicial process (*Strickson v Preston County Court* [2007] EWCA Civ 1132, LTL 9/11/2007).

PERMISSION TO APPEAL

When permission is required

74.11   There is a general requirement in **CPR, r. 52.3**, for permission to appeal from any decision of a judge in the County Court or the High Court except for appeals against:

(a)   orders, listed in **r. 52.3(1)(a)**, which affect individuals' liberty (see **74.12**);

(b) decisions of authorised court officers in detailed assessment proceedings (**rr. 47.21, 47.22 and 52.1(2)**). Appeals under **r. 47.21** may be heard by a Master or District Judge (**PD 2B, para. 3.1(e)**);

(c) decisions granting or refusing an application for refusal of recognition or enforcement of a judgment under the **recast Brussels I Regulation** (**CPR, r. 74.7A(3)**); and

(d) some statutory appeals, depending on the wording of the relevant statute.

There is also a right to have a decision by a legal adviser under **PD 51K**, the County Court Legal Advisers Pilot Scheme, reconsidered by a District Judge (**para. 3.2**). A request for reconsideration must be filed within 14 days of service of the decision (**para. 3.3**).

Appeals affecting liberty

CPR, r. 52.3(1)(a), provides that permission is not required for an appeal: **74.12**

(a) by a contemnor against an order for committal to prison, whether immediate or suspended (**r. 52.3(1)(a)(i)**). Appeals against fines and sequestration orders require permission (*Masri v Consolidated Contractors International Co. SAL* [2011] EWCA Civ 898, [2012] 1 WLR 223). An appeal against a committal order where the contemnor is the respondent requires permission (*Poole Borough Council v Hambridge* [2007] EWCA Civ 990, [2008] CP Rep 1);

(b) against refusal to grant habeas corpus (**r. 52.3(1)(a)(ii)**);

(c) against a secure accommodation order made under the Children Act 1989, s. 25 (**CPR, r. 52.3(1)(a)(iii)**).

Permission to appeal is not required for a first appeal from a committal order made by a Circuit Judge. 'Committal orders' are orders which commit a person to prison. Permission is required for any other order or decision of a Circuit Judge made in the exercise of the jurisdiction to punish for contempt (*Barnet London Borough Council v Hurst* [2002] EWCA Civ 1009, [2002] 4 All ER 457). Permission is required on appeals by claimants asserting that the lower court was wrong to find that a defendant had purged his contempt, or that the lower court imposed an unduly light penalty for contempt of court (*Government of Sierra Leone v Davenport* [2002] EWCA Civ 230, [2002] CPLR 236). Second appeals in contempt proceedings apparently always require permission, see **r. 52.7** and *Barnet London Borough Council v Hurst*. The guidance given in *Barnet London Borough Council v Hurst* about appeals in contempt proceedings from decisions of District Judges is probably wrong as it appears to overlook the fact that the word 'judge' in **r. 52.3** is defined in **r. 2.3(1)** as meaning, unless the context requires otherwise, a judge, Master or District Judge or a person authorised as such, and is not restricted to Circuit Judges.

Seeking permission

Generally, permission to appeal may be sought either from the lower court at the hearing at   **74.13**
which the decision to be appealed was made or from the appeal court (**CPR, r. 52.3(2)**). Permission from the appeal court must be sought by filing an appellant's notice at the appeal court within 21 days after the decision of the lower court (**r. 52.12(2)(b)**). This period may be extended either by the lower court or appeal court, see **74.20**. However, **r. 52.7(1)** provides that permission is required from the Court of Appeal for all appeals to that court from a decision of the County Court or the High Court (or from the family court or the Upper Tribunal) which was itself made on appeal. Where the lower court refuses an application for permission to appeal, a further application for permission to appeal may be made to the appeal court (**r. 52.3(3)(a)**). The order will specify the court to which any further application should be made, and the level of the judge who should hear the application (**r. 52.3(3)(b)**).

Applications for permission to appeal sought from the lower court are made orally at the end of the hearing, usually as the last item of business after costs have been determined. A party who needs more time to decide whether to appeal can ask the lower court to adjourn, in which event the application for permission can be made to the lower court at the relevant hearing, albeit at a later date. If permission is not sought at the hearing in the lower court (perhaps because of a change of mind), the only option, given the wording of r. 52.3(2), is to seek permission from the appeal court (*Balmoral Group Ltd v Borealis (UK) Ltd* [2006] EWHC 2228 (Comm), LTL 6/9/2006).

Permission that is sought from the appeal court is asked for initially by seeking permission in writing in the appellant's notice (r. 52.3(2)(b)); PD 52A, para. 4.2) and is normally considered on paper without a hearing (CPR, rr. 52.4(1) and 52.5(1)). Short reasons are usually all that is given on an application for permission to appeal. Just because they are short does not mean they infringe the requirement for a reasoned decision in the European Convention on Human Rights, art. 6, in the Human Rights Act 1998, sch. 1 (*Hyams v Plender* [2001] 1 WLR 32 at [17]).

An appellant is under a duty to inform the Civil Appeals Office in writing of any facts affecting the giving or refusing of permission to appeal (*Walbrook Trustees (Jersey) Ltd v Fattal* [2008] EWCA Civ 427, LTL 11/3/2008). If such facts arise after permission is granted, the appellant should write to the Civil Appeals Office and seek directions.

Test for granting permission on first appeals

74.14   CPR, r. 52.6(1), provides that on first appeals permission to appeal may be given only where either:

(a) the court considers that the appeal would have a real prospect of success; or
(b) there is some other compelling reason why the appeal should be heard.

Lord Woolf MR said in *Swain v Hillman* [2001] 1 All ER 91 that a 'real' prospect of success means that the prospect of success must be realistic rather than fanciful. The court considering a request for permission is not required to analyse whether the grounds of the proposed appeal will succeed, but merely whether there is a real prospect of success (*Hunt v Peasegood* (2000) *The Times*, 20 October 2000). Its function is limited to a review of the decision of the court below (see 75.5) to see whether a prospective appellant has an arguable case, fit to present to the full court on appeal, that the decision below was plainly wrong or unjust through a serious irregularity (see 75.6 and *Re W (Children) (Permission to Appeal)* [2007] EWCA Civ 786, [2007] Fam Law 897). Even hopeless appeals may be allowed to proceed where the area of law in question is the subject of considerable controversy (*Beedell v West Ferry Printers Ltd* [2001] EWCA Civ 400, [2001] ICR 962).

A failure by a judge to address an issue may be a compelling reason within r. 52.6(1) (*Sofola v Lloyds TSB Bank* [2005] EWHC 1335 (QB), LTL 5/7/2005). There may be a compelling reason for the appeal where the lower court's decision has been overtaken by a subsequent authority, but there is unlikely to be a compelling reason if the lower court was not informed of a binding authority due to a failure by the appellant's advocate (*Sofola v Lloyds TSB Bank*). Apparently, the court should take into account an appellant's strong feelings of injustice when considering whether to grant permission, at least where those feelings are arguably objectively justified (*Malcolm v MacKenzie* [2004] EWCA Civ 584, LTL 18/5/2004).

There is some reluctance in giving permission to appeal against case management decisions, such as disclosure orders and orders dealing with the timetable of the claim. In these cases the court will also consider whether the issue is of sufficient significance to justify the costs of an appeal; the procedural consequences of an appeal (such as losing a trial date); and whether it would be more convenient to determine the point at or after trial (PD 52A, para. 4.6).

Second appeals to the Court of Appeal

As discussed at **74.13**, generally permission to appeal may be sought from either the lower court or from the appeal court. Second appeals are in a different category. The **Access to Justice Act 1999, s. 55(1)**, and **CPR, r. 52.7(1)**, provide that permission is required from the Court of Appeal (and cannot be given by the lower court) for any appeal to that court from a decision of the County Court or the High Court which was itself made on appeal. The question of what amounts to a second-tier appeal is considered at **74.6**. By **r. 52.7(2)**, the Court of Appeal will not give permission unless it considers that either:

74.15

(a) the appeal would have a real prospect of success and also would raise an important point of principle or practice; or

(b) there is some other compelling reason for the Court of Appeal to hear it.

Under **r. 52.7(2)(a)(ii)**, the point of principle or practice must be an important one. It is not enough that the grounds of appeal may have a real prospect of success. An issue can fall within **r. 52.7(2)(a)(ii)** only when it has not yet been determined by previous authority. An appeal based on whether an established point has been correctly applied does not come within the rule (*Uphill v BRB (Residuary) Ltd* [2005] EWCA Civ 60, [2005] 1 WLR 2070). The decision on the first appeal will therefore often be the final decision, with second appeals being something of a rarity (see *Tanfern Ltd v Cameron-MacDonald* [2000] 1 WLR 1311).

The *Uphill v BRB (Residuary) Ltd* approach means that even if the lower court's decision is plainly wrong there is no compelling reason for granting permission for a second appeal (*GB v RJB* [2009] EWCA Civ 545, [2009] 2 FLR 632). The same principle applies even if the would-be appellant won at first instance, but lost on a first appeal. It is increasingly felt that this may be unjust, as there is a real difference between an appellant who has lost twice but wants a third chance to win, and one who, having won at first instance, loses a first appeal on grounds which the single judge in the Court of Appeal feels are arguably wrong (*Farmer v Wilkinson* [2009] EWCA Civ 1143, LTL 16/11/2009). Future reform on this point is merited.

Veitch v Avery (2002) LTL 26/7/2002 was an appeal for which permission was granted under what is now **r. 52.7(2)(b)**. No point of practice or principle was raised in the second appeal, but the judge dealing with the first appeal had allowed an appeal from a District Judge and struck out the claim based on the original particulars of claim despite there being amended particulars which raised an arguable claim. Conversely, permission was refused in *Uphill v BRB (Residuary) Ltd* where it was emphasised that 'compelling' is a very strong word. Dyson LJ said that even if the prospects of success on the appeal are very high there may not be a compelling reason. However, where there has been a procedural irregularity rendering the first appeal unfair, there may be a compelling reason even if the overall prospects are not very high. Embarking on a mini-trial in an appeal from a summary judgment decision was not a compelling reason in *Miller v Garton Shires* [2006] EWCA Civ 1386, LTL 31/10/2006.

Refusal of permission to appeal

There is no appeal from a decision of the appeal court, made at an oral hearing or on the papers, to allow or refuse permission to appeal to that court (**Access to Justice Act 1999, s. 54(4)**). The ban in **s. 54(4)** prevents the Court of Appeal from reviewing a High Court judge's refusal of permission to appeal from the decision of a costs judge, and there is no residual inherent jurisdiction to hear such an appeal (*Riniker v University College London* [2001] 1 WLR 13).

74.16

Instead of refusing permission on the papers, the judge may make an order adjourning the application for permission into court for an oral hearing. It has not been unusual for an application that is adjourned into court to include an order for the substantive appeal to follow immediately if permission is granted. This latter practice was described as normally undesirable by Lord Neuberger MR in *Shlaimoun v Mining Technologies International Inc.* [2012] EWCA Civ 772, LTL 21/6/2012 at [8]. It requires the court to set aside as much time as is required for the full appeal and means the parties have to prepare (and incur costs) for the full appeal as well as addressing the arguments on granting permission.

A judge faced with an application for permission to appeal made out of time may come to the conclusion that the appeal is both weak on the merits and that time should not be extended. By reason of the **Access to Justice Act 1999, s. 54(4)**, refusing permission to appeal will result in an end to the appeal process. Taking the easier course of refusing permission to extend time will not, as the appellant can apply for permission to appeal the refusal of the extension, which can be renewed to the Court of Appeal. This difference should be kept in mind when deciding which course to take (*Foenander v Bond Lewis and Co.* [2001] EWCA Civ 759, [2002] 1 WLR 525).

Reconsideration of whether to grant permission

74.17 Reconsideration of a refusal of permission to appeal is not an appeal against refusal, which is not permitted (see 74.16). Reconsideration applications in appeals to the County Court and to the High Court are governed by **CPR, r. 52.4**. Subject to r. 52.4(3) and any other rule or practice direction that provides otherwise, where the appeal court, without a hearing, refuses permission to appeal, the person seeking permission may request a reconsideration of the decision at an oral hearing (**r. 52.4(2)**; *Cassie v Ministry of Defence* [2002] EWCA Civ 838, LTL 17/4/2002). A request for reconsideration must be filed within seven days after service of the notice that permission has been refused (**r. 52.4(6)**). The documents that must be filed with the appellant's notice in an appeal to the County Court or High Court are listed in **PD 52B, para. 4.2**, and include the sealed order under appeal and the grounds of appeal. An appeal bundle must be filed within 35 days of the appellant's notice (**para. 6.3**). Where a judge of the High Court, or a Designated Judge or a Specialist Circuit Judge refuses permission without a hearing and considers the application is totally without merit, an order can be made to the effect that the application cannot be reconsidered at a hearing (**r. 52.4(3)**).

In appeals to the Court of Appeal, the judge considering the application on the papers may direct that the application be determined at an oral hearing (**r. 52.5(2)**). This rule further provides that the judge must so direct if of the opinion that the application cannot be fairly determined on paper without an oral hearing. This rule therefore revokes the former right vested in the appellant to seek reconsideration of a refusal of permission to appeal, and vests the decision in the single judge of the Court of Appeal. Unless the court directs otherwise, an oral hearing directed under **r. 52.5(2)** must be listed no later than 14 days after the direction, and will be heard by the judge who made the direction (**r. 52.5(3)**). A direction under **r. 52.5(2)** may identify the issues that should be focused on at the oral hearing, may direct the respondent to serve and file written submissions (see 74.18), and may direct the respondent to attend the oral hearing (**r. 52.5(4)**).

On applications for permission to appeal to the Court of Appeal, within 14 days of filing the appellant's notice the appellant must lodge a core bundle (and if necessary a supplementary bundle) complying with **PD 52C, para. 27** (see **para. 14**).

There is a recognised principle in the Court of Appeal that permission hearings will not be adjourned for the convenience of counsel, the view being that these can be readily dealt with by junior counsel (*Bracknell Forest Borough Council v N* [2006] EWCA Civ 1562, [2007] Fam Law 121).

Notice of permission hearing to respondent

74.18 In County Court and High Court appeals a copy of an appellant's request for reconsideration of the question of permission at an oral hearing must be served on the respondent at the same time as it is filed (**PD 52B, para.** 7.4(a)). The respondent will also have been served with the appellant's notice and skeleton argument shortly after they were filed (**paras 6.5** and **8.3**; see **74.23** and **74.28**). The court will give notice of the permission hearing to the respondent, but the respondent is not required to attend unless the court so orders or requests (**para. 8.1(a)**). Requiring these documents to be served ensures the respondent is informed of the landmarks in the appeal process. A respondent will not be awarded its costs for attending a permission hearing unless one of the reasons in **para. 8(1)** applies, such as being ordered to attend, or where the substantive appeal is ordered to follow on from the permission hearing. Proceeding to determine the substantive appeal on this hearing, in the absence of the respondent, is a serious procedural irregularity for the purposes of **CPR, r. 52.21(3)(b)** (*Howard v Stanton* [2011] EWCA Civ 1481, LTL 16/11/2011, and see **75.14**).

Respondents in appeals to the Court of Appeal may be directed by **r.** 52.5(4)(b), and if not, should consider whether (**PD 52C, para. 19**) to file and serve a short (up to three-page) statement dealing with:

(a) any reasons why permission to appeal should be refused, directed to the threshold test for granting permission to appeal. It may also be appropriate to point to any material inaccuracy in the papers placed before the court (*Jolly v Jay* [2002] EWCA Civ 277, *The Times*, 3 April 2002);

(b) arguments for limiting the issues on the appeal under **CPR, r. 52.6(2)(a)**;

(c) arguments for imposing any conditions on the appeal under **r.** 52.6(2)(b); and

(d) any reasons for refusing any additional application being made by the appellant, or why any such application should only be allowed on terms. Evidence in support by the respondent should either be included in the written statement and verified by a statement of truth, or filed and served separately (**PD 52C, para. 19(2)(b)**).

A respondent's statement under **PD 52C, para. 19** must be filed and served on all other parties within 14 days of service of the appellant's notice or, if later, the appellant's skeleton argument (**para.** 19(1)(a)). Normally there will be no order for recovery of the costs of the respondent's statement (**para. 20(1)**).

Respondents in appeals to the Court of Appeal are not expected to attend the permission hearing unless the court so directs, and a respondent who voluntarily attends will not normally be awarded their costs (**paras 16(1)** and **20**). If the court requests the respondent's attendance at the permission hearing, the appellant must supply the respondent with a copy of the skeleton argument and any documents to which the appellant intends to refer (**para. 16(2)**). Where the court requests submissions or attendance, normally the respondent will be awarded costs if permission is refused (**para. 20(2)**).

Limiting the issues on granting permission

By **CPR, r. 52.6(2)**, an order giving permission to appeal may limit the issues to be heard and be made subject to conditions. If the court confines its permission to some issues only, it should expressly refuse permission on any remaining issues, or adjourn the question of permission on any remaining issues to the appeal court (**PD 52C, para. 18(1)**). In **para. 18(1)**, the expression the 'court' is the lower court, so the power to revisit under this provision is restricted to situations where the lower court limits the issues on granting permission to appeal. If the question of permission on an issue is adjourned to the appeal court, the appellant must, within 14 days after service of the court's order, inform the appeal court and the respondent in writing whether the reserved issue is to be pursued (**para. 18(2)**).

In a County Court or High Court appeal, an appellant can make a request, following the procedure in **74.17**, for the reconsideration at an oral hearing of permission on any issues for which permission is refused by the appeal court if the refusal was on the papers. In the Court of Appeal there is no provision for reconsideration of a decision to limit the issues on the

74.19

appeal where permission is granted on the papers, but that may be a reason for listing the application for an oral hearing under **CPR, r. 52.5(2)**. In all appeals, a decision of the appeal court to limit the issues cannot be reopened if this was decided at a hearing (**Access to Justice Act 1999, s. 54(4)**). Where the issues are limited by the appeal court on an application for permission, the appeal court cannot revisit the issues to be considered at the final hearing of the appeal (*Fieldman* / *Markovitch* [2001] CP Rep 119). Where a party is given a choice between proceeding with an appeal on a limited basis, or starting a fresh claim, choosing to proceed with the appeal does not amount to an election, but does mean that starting a fresh claim will be an abuse of process (*Koshy v DEG-Deutsche Investitions- und Entwicklungsgesellschaft mbH* [2008] EWCA Civ 27, LTL 5/2/2008).

TIME FOR APPEALING

Time limits

74.20   An appellant must normally initiate an appeal (by filing an appellant's notice in form N161) no later than 21 days from the date of the decision of the lower court (**CPR, r. 52.12(2)(b)**). The appellant's notice may be filed online in the Court of Appeal by following the guidance at http://www.justice.gov.uk/courts/rcj-rolls-building/court-of-appeal/civil-division/filing.

The lower court may direct some other period for filing a notice of appeal (which may be longer or shorter than 21 days) (**r. 52.12(2)(a)**). An extension should be granted by the lower court only in exceptional circumstances (*Aujla v Sanghera* [2004] EWCA Civ 122, LTL 23/1/2004). The reason for this restrictive approach is that the appeal court exercises the main jurisdiction on granting extensions of time in appeals (see **74.21** and **74.22**). This means that stronger grounds are required to justify an enlargement of the usual 21 days than mere pressure on a prospective appellant's solicitors caused by the 21-day time limit (*City Television v Conference and Training Office Ltd* [2001] EWCA Civ 1770, LTL 16/11/2001). Judgments and orders take effect from the date they are given or made, or such other date as the court may specify (**CPR, r. 40.7(1)**). Delays in formally drawing up the order do not, therefore, delay time running for the purposes of appeals. During the course of a detailed assessment of a bill of costs in *Kasir v Darlington and Simpson Rolling Mills Ltd* (2001) LTL 1/5/2001 the costs judge made a number of decisions, which the appellant wished to appeal. He did not appeal until the detailed assessment process was completed five months later. It was held that time started running in respect of each decision when it was made, and permission to appeal was refused.

Where the lower court judge announces a decision and reserves the reasons for the judgment until a later date, it may be appropriate for the judge to exercise the power under **r. 52.12(2)(a)** in fixing the period for filing a notice of appeal to take account of the delay in giving reasons. A lower court judge can exercise the power under **r. 52.12(2)(a)**, even after the 21-day appeal period has expired, but should not do so after an appellant's notice has been lodged with the appeal court (*Aujla v Sanghera*).

Extending time for appealing

74.21   The court may extend or shorten the time for compliance with any rule, practice direction or court order, even if an application for extension is made after the time for compliance has expired (**CPR, r. 3.1(2)(a)**). The time for bringing an appeal may be extended under this power. By **r. 52.15(1)**, an application to vary the time limit for filing an appellant's notice must be made to the appeal court. The parties may not (by **r. 52.15(2)**) agree between themselves to extend any date or time limit for the purposes of appealing.

Permission to extend time for appealing is sought by including an application for more time in the appellant's notice (**PD 52B, para. 3.2; PD 52C, para. 4(1)**). The notice should state the reason for the delay and the steps taken prior to the application being made (PD 52B, para. 3.2; PD 52C, para. 4(2)). Bringing an appeal out of time without seeking permission in the appellant's notice to extend time is an irregularity, which the court has jurisdiction to cure under CPR, r. 3.10 (*Southern and District Finance plc v Turner* [2003] EWCA Civ 1574, LTL 7/11/2003).

Where an extension is sought and permission to appeal is given (usually the respondent is not given an opportunity to make representations on whether permission to appeal should be granted, see 74.18), the respondent has the right to be heard on whether an extension of time should be allowed. However, a respondent who unreasonably opposes an extension of time runs the risk of being ordered to pay the appellant's costs of the application to extend time (PD 52C, para. 4(3)(b)).

Principles for granting extensions of time

The principles laid down for applications for relief from sanctions by *Denton v T. H. White Ltd* **74.22** [2014] EWCA Civ 906, [2014] 1 WLR 3926, are applied on applications to extend time for appealing (*R (Hysaj) v Secretary of State for the Home Department* [2014] EWCA Civ 1633, [2015] 1 WLR 2472). Technically, the provisions in CPR, rr. 3.8 and 3.9, only apply where a sanction is imposed by the very rule that the applicant is said to have breached (*Salford Estates (No. 2) Ltd v Altomart Ltd* [2014] EWCA Civ 1408, [2015] 1 WLR 1825, per Moore-Bick LJ at [10]). **Rule 52.12(2)(b)**, which prescribes the 21-day time limit for bringing an appeal, does not include any express sanction for breach. It is said there is an implied sanction for breach in that if permission to extend time is refused the appeal cannot be brought. In a series of cases starting with *Sayers v Clarke Walker* [2002] EWCA Civ 645, [2002] 1 WLR 3095, it has been held that the relief from sanctions principles should be applied by analogy. The original reasons for adopting this approach were the need for consistency and avoiding the use of judge-made checklists (per Brooke LJ at [21]). It is now clear that the justification is based on the implied sanctions doctrine (see 48.13; *R (Hysaj) v Secretary of State for the Home Department*). The same approach applies also to applications to extend time for service of a respondent's notice (*Salford Estates (No. 2) Ltd v Altomart Ltd*); appeals governed by the Family Procedure Rules 2010 (*Re D (Children)* [2015] EWCA Civ 409, [2016] 1 FLR 249); and applications to extend time for reconsideration of a permission application (under r. 52.4(2), see *Re H (Children) (Care Proceedings: Appeals out of Time)* [2015] EWCA Civ 583, [2015] 1 WLR 5085, a decision under the equivalent Family Procedure Rules 2010, r. 30.3(6)).

Permission will be considered using the three-stage test in *Denton*, see 48.32. The same principles apply to litigants in person (*Re D (Children)*). Each application must be viewed by reference to the criterion of justice, and it is important to bear in mind that time limits are there to be observed, and that justice may be seriously defeated if there is any laxity in this regard (*Southern and District Finance plc v Turner* [2003] EWCA Civ 1574, LTL 7/11/2003). In *Salford Estates (No. 2) Ltd v Altomart Ltd* issuing a respondent's notice 36 days late was regarded as a substantial delay, but not a serious or significant breach because it had little effect on the progress of the appeal (at [21]–[22]). While there was no persuasive reason for the delay, permission was granted in accordance with *Denton* because of the finding at stage one. There were three applications in *R (Hysaj) v Secretary of State for the Home Department*. In the first appeal the notice of appeal was filed 42 days late. An extension of time was granted, but only after careful analysis of exactly what was done in this period, such as seeking permission to appeal and seeking funding. A failure to appreciate that time for filing the appellant's notice runs from the decision of the lower court despite the clear wording of r. 52.12(2)(b) was regarded as a poor reason for the delay. A suggestion that a large number of practitioners thought time runs from obtaining permission to appeal met with no sympathy at [22] because it is the responsibility of practitioners to make themselves familiar with the provisions of the CPR. In the second appeal the delay was nine months, and permission was

must lodge a core bundle (and if necessary a supplementary bundle) within 14 days of filing the appellant's notice (**PD 52C, para. 14**). Assuming permission to appeal to the Court of Appeal is granted, the Court of Appeal will issue a listing window application. Within 14 days thereafter the appellant must serve every respondent with a proposed index for the core appeal bundle and any supplementary bundle (timetable in **PD 52C, para. 21**). Appeal bundles need to be agreed within 49 days after the date of the listing window notification, the appellant must serve a final bundle index with page numbers no later than 63 days after the listing window notification, and the appeal bundles must be lodged no later than 42 days before the appeal hearing.

An appeal bundle must contain only those documents relevant to the appeal (**PD 52B, para. 6.3; PD 52C. para. 27(2)**). Bundles must be paginated and in chronological order, and must contain an index (**PD 52C, paras 27(13) and (14)**). Subject to any order made by the court:

(a) in an appeal to the County Court or High Court, the appeal bundle must contain the documents listed in **PD 52B, para. 6.4(1)**;

(b) the core bundle in an application for permission to appeal to the Court of Appeal must only contain the documents listed in the relevant core bundle index on the Justice website at http://www.justice.gov.uk/courts/rcj-rolls-building/court-of-appeal/civil-division/core-bundle-indices (**PD 52C, para. 27(1)**);

(c) a supplementary bundle in an application for permission to appeal to the Court of Appeal should only contain documents that are relevant to the grounds of appeal and necessary for the court to read for the purpose of determining whether to grant permission to appeal (**para. 27(2)**);

(d) the core bundle in a substantive appeal to the Court of Appeal must contain the final (replacement) versions of the skeleton arguments cross-referenced to the pagination in the bundles, the documents from the core bundle on the application for permission to appeal, and the documents listed in **para. 28(8)(d)**;

(e) supplementary bundles in a substantive appeal to the Court of Appeal may only contain documents relevant to the grounds of appeal which will be necessary for the court to read in preparation for the appeal hearing, and must be certified by the advocate responsible for arguing the case (**para. 27(9)(c)**).

Compulsory documents include a copy of the appellant's notice, a copy of any skeleton arguments, and a copy of the order under appeal. Documents to be included if relevant include statements of case, application notices, witness statements and key contemporaneous documents which the appellant or respondent consider to be relevant to the appeal.

The key to deciding what to include in the appeal bundle is having a clear grasp of the real issues raised by the appeal. What the appeal court does not want is an appeal bundle put together in an unthinking manner, including the whole trial bundle and miscellaneous superfluous documents, such as solicitors' correspondence, unless these materials go to the issues raised by the appeal (*Scribes West Ltd v Relsa Anstalt (No. 1)* [2004] EWCA Civ 835, [2005] CP Rep 2 at [11]). No more than a single copy of each document should be included unless there is a good reason for doing so.

In complex appeals, particularly where several related appeals are to proceed together, bundles may need to be put together in chronological files (with the documents usually identifying their original file numbers) even though this may not comply with the terms of **PD 52B** or **52C**. Agreement should be attempted between the parties, and, if achieved, a consent order should be sought from the Deputy Master or supervising Lord Justice, on paper (*Leofelis SA v Lonsdale Sports Ltd* [2008] EWCA Civ 640, [2008] ETMR 63).

In appeals to the County Court and High Court, a respondent who has been served with an appeal bundle and who considers that relevant documents have been omitted may file and serve on all other parties a respondent's supplementary appeal bundle (**PD 52B, para. 8.2**). This bundle must be filed and served as soon as practicable after service of the appeal bundle, but in any event not less than seven days before the hearing.

In appeals to the Court of Appeal, if there is no agreement about particular documents, they must be placed in a separate unagreed documents bundle. An application under **CPR, Part 23**, supported by a statement not exceeding three pages, must be made not less than 42 days before the appeal hearing to seek the court's permission to rely on unagreed documents. Such an application is normally heard at the appeal hearing (**PD 52C, para. 27(12)**).

Appeal bundles: format

Appeal bundles must be copied single-sided, and in exactly the same form with no extra markings other than pagination as those given to the judge at the hearing below (Civil Appeals Form 204, paras 5.5 and 5.6). All staples, clips etc. must be removed. Every page in the appeal bundle must be paginated consecutively, in bold figures at the bottom of the page, but differently from the form of pagination used in the hearing below. Statements of case must appear in 'chapter' form, with the claim followed by particulars of claim, and further information following the relevant statement of case. Statements of case overtaken by amendments should be excluded. Documents within categories should appear chronologically.

74.26

Documents should be copies, not originals. Originals can be provided at the hearing if necessary. Copies of photographs should be in colour and of good quality (**PD 52C, para. 27(14)**). The pages, other than transcripts, must be placed in lever arch files, ring binders or robust plastic folders, filled sensibly (not too many or few pages for the binder), with the Court of Appeal reference and case name appearing clearly on the spine and front of each file. 300 pages is a good guide to not overfilling files (*Leofelis SA v Lonsdale Sports Ltd* [2008] EWCA Civ 640, *The Times*, 23 July 2008). In the Court of Appeal, no supplementary bundle, whether for permission to appeal or on the substantive appeal, may exceed one lever arch file of 350 pages unless the court gives permission (**para. 27(11)**). An index must be included at the front of the bundle (**PD 52B, para. 6.3**); **PD 52C, para. 27(1)**. Where several files are needed, experience dictates that colour-coded files help at the hearing (*Scribes West Ltd v Relsa Anstalt (No. 1)* [2004] EWCA Civ 835, [2005] CP Rep 2 at [16]).

Pages sent to the court to be added to the appeal bundle must be sent already punched and paginated for immediate inclusion in the existing binders. They should be filed as soon as practicable, and in any event no less than seven days before the hearing (**PD 52B, para. 6.6**).

Core bundles

Before 3 October 2016, core bundles were cut-down versions of the full appeal bundles, typically used in heavy appeals with a great deal of documentation. Since 3 October 2016, all appeals to the Court of Appeal need two core bundles, one for the permission application, and the other for the substantive appeal. Both core bundles have defined contents, as discussed at 74.26.

74.27

Skeleton argument: procedural requirements

In appeals to the County Court and High Court, subject to any order of the court, **PD 52B, para. 8.3** says the parties to an appeal should file and serve skeleton arguments only where:

74.28

(a) the complexity of the issues of fact or law in the appeal justify them; or
(b) skeleton arguments would assist the court in respects not readily apparent from the papers in the appeal.

In appeals to the Court of Appeal the appellant must file a skeleton argument at the same time as filing the appellant's notice (**PD 52C, para. 3(3)(g)**). A skeleton argument in an application for permission to appeal must be served with the appellant's notice (**PD 52C, para. 7.1A**). A respondent who files a respondent's notice must file and serve its skeleton argument within 14 days after filing the respondent's notice (**PD 52C, para. 21, Timetable 1**).

Respondents must serve the appellant with replacement skeleton arguments with cross-references to the appeal bundle no later than 70 days after the listing window notification (**PD 52C, para. 21, Timetable 1**). All replacement skeleton arguments must be included in the core appeal bundle, which must be lodged no later than 42 days before the appeal hearing (**para. 21, Timetable 2**, and **para. 27(8)**). The court may refuse to hear argument on a point not included in a skeleton argument filed within the prescribed time (**para. 31(4)**).

Skeleton arguments: contents

74.29   Form N163 should be used (or used as a cover sheet) for the skeleton arguments. The purpose of a skeleton argument is to assist the court by setting out as concisely as practicable the arguments upon which a party intends to rely (**PD 52A, para. 5.1(1)**). By **para. 5.1(2)** a skeleton argument must:

   (a) be concise;
   (b) both define and confine the areas of controversy;
   (c) be set out in numbered paragraphs;
   (d) be cross-referenced to any relevant document in the bundle;
   (e) be self-contained and not incorporate by reference material from previous skeleton arguments; and
   (f) not include extensive quotations from documents or authorities.

Documents to be relied on must be identified (**para. 5.1(3)**). Where it is necessary to refer to an authority, a skeleton argument must state the proposition of law the authority demonstrates, and identify the parts of the authority that support the proposition (**para. 5.1(4)**). If more than one authority is cited in support of a given proposition, the skeleton argument must briefly state why. In the case of questions of fact, the skeleton should state briefly the basis on which it is contended that the Court of Appeal can interfere with the finding of fact concerned, with cross-references to the passages in the transcript or notes of evidence which bear on the point (Practice Direction (Court of Appeal: Procedure) [1995] 1 WLR 1191).

For appeals to the Court of Appeal, skeleton arguments must not normally exceed 25 pages and must be printed on A4 paper in not less than 12 point font and 1.5 line spacing (**PD 52C, para. 31(1)**). Each skeleton argument should be labelled as appropriate (e.g. appellant's PTA skeleton; appellant's replacement skeleton; respondent's supplementary skeleton) and dated on its front sheet. In the past it has been said that for a one-day appeal on a point of law 10 pages should be enough. Length obscures the points that are germane to the resolution of an appeal (*Tchenguiz v Director of the Serious Fraud Office* [2014] EWCA Civ 1333, [2015] 1 WLR 838). Skeleton arguments should not be prepared as verbatim scripts or as footnoted theses. They are aids to oral advocacy, not substitutes. A skeleton argument in *D. Pride and Partners v Institute for Animal Health* [2009] EWHC 1617 (QB), LTL 14/7/2009, was criticised for resembling the style of a textbook.

Any statement of costs must show the amount claimed for the skeleton argument separately (**PD 52A, para. 5.3**). The court may disallow the cost of preparing a skeleton argument that does not comply with the requirements of **PD 52A** and **PD 52C** (**PD 52C, para. 31(5)**), a point reiterated by *Standard Bank plc v Via Mat International Ltd* [2013] EWCA Civ 490, [2013] 2 All ER (Comm) 1222. A skeleton argument that does not comply may be rejected by the Civil Appeals Office. If it is re-filed out of time an application must be made under **CPR, Part 23**, for permission to rely on it (**PD 52C, para. 31(2)(b)**).

Detailed guidance was given by the Court of Appeal in *Raja v Van Hoogstraten (No. 9)* [2008] EWCA Civ 1444, [2009] 1 WLR 1143 at [126]–[128]:

126. We remind practitioners that skeleton arguments should not be prepared as verbatim scripts to be read out in public or as footnoted theses to be read in private. Good skeleton arguments are tools with practical uses: an agenda for the hearing, a summary of the main points, propositions and arguments to be developed orally, a useful way of noting citations and references, a convenient place for making cross-references, a time-saving means of avoiding unnecessary dictation to the court and laborious and pointless note-taking by the court.

127. Skeleton arguments are aids to oral advocacy. They are not written briefs which are used in some jurisdictions as substitutes for oral advocacy. An unintended and unfortunate side effect of the growth in written advocacy (written opening and closing submissions and 'speaking notes', as well as skeleton arguments) has been that too many practitioners, at increased cost to their clients and diminishing assistance to the court, burden their opponents and the court with written briefs. They are anything but brief. The result is that there is no real saving of legal costs, or of precious hearing, reading and writing time . . . .

128. The skeletal nature of written advocacy is in danger of being overlooked. In some cases we are weighed down by the skeleton arguments and when we dare to complain about the time they take up, we are sometimes told that we can read them 'in our own time' after the hearing. In our judgment, this is not what appellate advocacy is about, or ought to be about, in this court.

Record of the judgment of the lower court

If the judgment of the lower court was recorded, an application for an approved transcript should be made as soon as possible, and in any event within seven days after filing the appellant's notice (**PD 52B, para. 6.2**). Photocopies are not acceptable. If there is no official transcript, the next best is the lower court judge's written judgment signed by the judge. If the lower court's judgment was oral and not recorded, the advocates should confer and submit, if possible, an agreed note of the judgment to the judge for signature. If the note cannot be agreed, both versions should be submitted with a covering letter explaining the situation. These points are important, because appeals, even from District Judges and Masters, can only succeed by attacking the decision-making process in some way, and injustice may result if no reliable record is available of what was said in the lower court.

74.30

A request may be made for the provision of transcripts at the public expense on the ground of poor financial circumstances, and this should wherever possible be made to the lower court when asking for permission to appeal. Applications can be made in the Court of Appeal (in the appellant's notice: **PD 52C, para. 6(2)**) to a Deputy Master, with a right of review to a judge of the Court of Appeal (see *Hyams v Plender* [2001] 1 WLR 32 at [28], where comments are made by Brooke LJ suggesting that similar arrangements should be made for appeals to the High Court). An order for provision of transcripts at public expense was refused in *Perotti v Westminster City Council* [2005] EWCA Civ 581, [2005] CP Rep 38. In this case the litigant said the transcript was needed for formulating his grounds of appeal, but he had tape recorded the judgment, and could have asked for the note of judgment made by the respondent's advocate.

Transcripts or notes of the evidence (as opposed to the judgment) are not generally needed on applications for permission to appeal, but may become necessary if permission is granted for the purposes of the substantive appeal.

SERVICE ON THE RESPONDENT

74.31   By **CPR, r. 52.12(3)**, unless the appeal court orders otherwise, an appellant's notice must be served on each respondent as soon as practicable, and in any event not later than seven days, after it is filed. A certificate of service must be filed (**PD 52B, para. 6.1**).

If permission to appeal is not required, or was given by the lower court, a copy of the appeal bundle must be served on each respondent at the same time as the appeal bundle is filed (**para. 6.5(a)**).

If the appellant is asking the appeal court for permission to appeal, the appeal bundle generally has to be served as soon as practicable after notification, and in any event within 14 days of permission being granted (**para. 6.5(b)**). Where the appeal court directs that the application for permission be heard on the same occasion as the appeal, the appeal bundle must be served as soon as practicable, and in any event within 14 days after notification of the hearing date (**para. 6.5(c)**).

AFTER PERMISSION TO APPEAL IS GIVEN

Notification

74.32   In cases where permission to appeal has to be obtained from the appeal court, the appeal court will send the parties copies of the order granting permission and any other directions given by the court.

If permission to appeal is granted, and if the appeal court is not the Court of Appeal, the appeal court will send the parties notification of the hearing or the period during which the appeal is likely to be heard ('the listing window'). Appeals in the Court of Appeal are given a listing window notification. The hear-by date is the last day of the listing window (**PD 52C, para. 22**). Listing in the Court of Appeal is considered at **74.35**.

Service of appeal papers

74.33   The normal rule is that service must be effected by the parties (**PD 52B, para. 6.1**; **PD 52C, para. 7.1**).

Appeal questionnaires

74.34   For Court of Appeal cases, at the same time as giving the parties a listing window notification, the Civil Appeals Office will send the appellant an appeal questionnaire. This must be returned within 14 days, and must include the appellant's advocate's time estimate for the hearing, confirmation that the transcript of evidence given at the lower court's hearing has been requested, confirmation that appeal bundles are being prepared (though this should be unnecessary, as appeal bundles should have been filed with the appellant's notice before permission was granted), and confirmation that copies of the questionnaire and appeal bundle have been served on the respondents (**PD 52C, para. 23**). A respondent who disagrees with the time estimate must inform the court within seven days of service of the questionnaire (**para. 24**). Where the appeal court is the High Court, use of appeal questionnaires is optional.

Court of Appeal listing

74.35   Appeals to the Court of Appeal are divided into seven categories, or lists.

These are:

(a) The applications list. This includes all applications for permission to appeal, as well as applications for interim remedies in pending appeals.

(b) The appeals list. These are cases where permission to appeal has been given and cases where an appeal lies without needing permission.

(c) The expedited list. This includes applications and appeals where the Court of Appeal has directed an expedited hearing in accordance with the practice laid down in *Unilever plc v Chefaro Proprietaries Ltd* [1995] 1 WLR 243. Asylum appeals, appeals where rights might be irrevocably conferred on third parties, and cases where unlawful material is about to be published, may typically be allocated to this list.

(d) The stand-out list. This is for appeals and applications which are not ready for hearing and which have, for good reasons, been stood out by judicial direction.

(e) The special fixtures list, which is a subdivision of the appeals list, where there is a need to list cases before particular judges, or in a particular order, or at a particular location or time.

(f) The second fixtures list. Appeals designated as 'second fixtures' are given hearing dates on the express basis that the list is fully booked for the period in question, and therefore they will only be heard if a suitable gap occurs in the list.

(g) The short warned list. This is for appeals which the court considers may be prepared for hearing by an advocate other than the one originally instructed on either a half day's notice, or, if the court so directs, 48 hours' notice. An appeal or application on this list may be called on at any time with the appropriate short notice. Further details are given in Practice Note (Court of Appeal: Listing) [2001] 1 WLR 479. An objection to being included in this list may be made to a Lord Justice or the Master of the Court of Appeal, but will be granted only for the most compelling reasons. An example would be where the appeal cannot be mastered by a substitute advocate within the contemplated time. If the original advocate cannot deal with the hearing because of prior commitments, he or she is under a professional duty to take all practicable measures to ensure the lay client is represented at the hearing by an advocate who is fully instructed and able to argue the appeal. A failure in this duty may be visited by a wasted costs order. There has been a short warned list for many years, and surprisingly few complaints have been made about it despite the fact there are occasions when appeals are handed over to an advocate who has had no prior involvement with the case on very short notice.

In addition, the Court of Appeal sits at various times at a number of provincial trial centres. Partly this is for the convenience of parties, but it also serves a number of wider public interest purposes relating to access to justice and informing the public and senior judiciary (purposes which can be traced back to Magna Carta 1215, ss. 17 and 18). There is great reluctance in breaking fixtures for hearings in provincial centres, even where counsel of choice is unavailable for such a hearing through being pre-booked (*Newport City Council v Charles* [2008] EWCA Civ 893, *The Times*, 29 July 2008).

Practice Guidance: Court of Appeal (Civil Division) Hear-by Dates (2015) sets out periods from issue of the appellant's notice to when the Court of Appeal will strive to hear the appeal. Interim appeals where permission is granted on the papers have nine-month hear-by dates; for final appeals where permission is granted at a hearing it is 19 months. Arrangements for dealing with applications for expedition and for a hearing beyond a hear-by date are described in Practice Note (Court of Appeal: Listing Windows) [2001] 1 WLR 1517.

SHORT HEARINGS BY VIDEOCONFERENCING

Where appropriate and available, parties should use technology, such as videoconferencing, to reduce costs. In *Black v Pastouna* [2005] EWCA Civ 1389, *The Independent*, 2 December 2005, it was said that the additional costs of travelling a long distance to court may be disallowed on short (up to 30-minute) appeals if videoconferencing facilities are available. **74.36**

RESPONDENT'S NOTICE AND OTHER DOCUMENTS

Respondent's notice

74.37   In any appeal a respondent may file and serve a respondent's notice (**CPR, r. 52.13(1)**). The respondent's notice may be filed online in the Court of Appeal by using the online form. By **CPR, r. 52.13(2)**, a respondent's notice must be filed by a respondent who:

(a) is seeking permission to appeal from the appeal court; or

(b) wishes to ask the appeal court to uphold the order of the lower court for reasons different from or additional to those given by the lower court.

Respondents accordingly fall into three broad categories:

(a) Respondents who simply wish to uphold the decision of the court below for the same reasons as given by the judge below. Such a respondent need not serve a respondent's notice.

(b) Respondents who wish to uphold the decision of the court below for reasons different from or additional to those given by the lower court. Such a respondent is not appealing as such, so there is no question of seeking permission to cross-appeal. However, a respondent's notice is required for the purpose of setting out the different or additional reasons (**PD 52C, para. 8(3)**). A respondent who does not file a respondent's notice is not entitled to address the appeal court on any reason not relied on in the judgment of the lower court, unless the appeal court gives permission. It is not a legitimate exercise of the lower court judge's discretion to make a declaration in terms of factual findings in order to convert what would otherwise be reasons for the primary decision into 'judgments' or 'orders' or 'determinations' within the meaning of the Senior Courts Act 1981, s. 15(1), or the County Courts Act 1984, s. 77(1), if the only purpose is to force the respondent to seek permission under **CPR, r. 52.3(1)**, for what would otherwise be a purely defensive respondent's notice. See *Compagnie Noga d'Importation et d'Exportation SA v Australia and New Zealand Banking Group Ltd* [2002] EWCA Civ 1142, [2003] 1 WLR 307.

(c) Respondents who wish to ask the appeal court to vary the order of the lower court are cross-appealing, and permission to appeal must be sought on the same basis as for an appellant (**PD 52C, para. 8(3)**). A respondent's notice is required for setting out the grounds on which it is to be argued that the order of the court below should be varied.

A respondent's notice is similar to an appellant's notice (see **74.23**) and must be in form N162. Together with appellants' notices they are called 'appeal notices' in the **CPR (r. 52.1(3) (f))**. A respondent who seeks permission to cross-appeal from the appeal court must do so in the respondent's notice (**r. 52.13(3)**).

Filing and serving a respondent's notice

74.38   Generally, a respondent's notice must be filed within such period as may be directed by the lower court. Where the court makes no such direction, the notice must be filed within 14 days after the date laid down by **CPR, r. 52.13(5)**, relevant to the circumstances of the appeal. This date will be either:

(a) the date the respondent was served with the appellant's notice in cases where permission to appeal was given by the lower court, or permission to appeal was not required; or

(b) the date the respondent was served with notification that the appeal court gave the appellant permission to appeal; or

(c) the date the respondent was served with notification that the application for permission to appeal and the appeal itself are to be heard together.

Unless the appeal court orders otherwise, a respondent's notice must be served on the appellant and any other respondent as soon as practicable, and in any event not later than seven days after it is filed (**r. 52.13(6)**). Extending time for service of a respondent's notice is discussed at **74.22**.

Respondent's skeleton argument

A respondent who files a respondent's notice in an appeal to the Court of Appeal must lodge **74.39** and serve a skeleton argument (**PD 52C, para. 9**). It should conform to the principles applicable to appellants' skeletons (see **74.29**), but should also seek to answer the arguments in the appellant's skeleton. A respondent in an appeal to the Court of Appeal who does not file a respondent's notice (see **74.37**) must lodge and serve his skeleton argument no later than 35 days after the date of the listing window notification (**para. 21, Timetable 1**). An unrepresented respondent need not file a skeleton argument (**para. 13(1)**).

Respondent's documents

A respondent's notice must, by **PD 52C, para. 10**, be lodged with: **74.40**
(a) two additional copies of the respondent's notice for the appeal court; and
(b) one copy of the respondent's notice for each appellant and any other respondents.

Supplementary skeleton argument

PD 52C, para. 32, lays down a timetable for supplementary skeleton arguments in the **74.41** Court of Appeal. Supplementary skeleton arguments may become necessary sometimes when new advocates are appointed, or when the law has moved on, or where there is a need to respond to a point raised in an opponent's skeleton argument. An appellant in this situation must file and serve its supplementary skeleton argument as soon as practicable together with a request for permission to rely on it (**para. 32(2)**). Permission will be granted only where this is strictly necessary (**para. 32(1)**). Only exceptionally will the court allow the use of a supplementary skeleton argument if lodged less than seven days before the hearing (**para. 32(3)**).

Copies of skeleton arguments for law reporters

In appeals to the Court of Appeal, legal representatives must supply two additional copies of **74.42** their skeleton arguments, including any supplementary skeleton arguments, to the usher before the commencement of the hearing (**PD 52C, para. 33**). These are for accredited law reporters and accredited media reporters. Any application to lift or vary this requirement is made orally at the commencement of the hearing.

COMPLIANCE WITH DEADLINES

Before 3 October 2016, **PD 52C, para. 21**, contained a final deadline for appeals to the Court **74.43** of Appeal, that all the papers needed for the appeal had to be filed and served at least seven days before the hearing. If the seven-day deadline could not be met, both the court and the other parties had to be informed. Any party who failed to comply could be required to attend before the presiding Lord Justice to explain what was being done, and seek permission to proceed with or to oppose the appeal (*Jeyapragash v Secretary of State for the Home Department* [2004] EWCA Civ 1260, [2005] 1 All ER 412). Since the civil justice reforms of 2013 all deadlines are regarded as essential (see **chapter 48** for sanctions), and deadlines in appeals have a particular importance because they are required for effective pre-reading by the judges. See also **74.49** to **74.50** for the jurisdiction of appeal courts to impose sanctions and to dismiss appeals for non-compliance.

APPLICATIONS WITHIN APPEALS

74.44   Notice of an application made to the appeal court for a remedy incidental to the appeal (such as an application for security for costs) should be included in the appellant's notice (**PD 52B, para. 4.3; PD 52C, para. 3(3)(c)**), or may be made by an ordinary application notice under **CPR, Part 23**.

The applicant must file the following documents with the application:

(a)   one additional copy of the application notice for the appeal court and one copy for each of the respondents;

(b)   where applicable, a sealed copy of the order which is the subject of the main appeal; and

(c)   a bundle of documents, which should include the application notice and any written evidence in support of the application.

An application notice may be filed online in the Court of Appeal. In the Court of Appeal, interim applications within appeals are often determined by a single Lord Justice. Short, half-hour, applications to the Court of Appeal may be suitable for hearing through video link. Details can be obtained through the Civil Appeals Office. Costs may be disallowed where counsel travel unnecessary distances instead of using this facility (*Babbings v Kirklees Metropolitan Borough Council* [2004] EWCA Civ 1431, *The Times*, 4 November 2004).

The Master of the Rolls may designate an eligible officer to be the Court of Appeal Master to exercise judicial authority under **CPR, r. 52.24**, to deal with matters incidental to appeals, matters where there is no substantial dispute, and dismissal of appeals and applications for procedural default. There are also Deputy Masters. However, Masters and deputies cannot give permission to appeal, grant stays (other than temporary stays of the decision of the lower court over a period when the Court of Appeal is not sitting or cannot conveniently be convened) or grant injunctions (**r. 52.24(3)**). A party is entitled, within seven days of being served with notice of the decision, to request that any decision by a court officer be reviewed by a single judge (**r. 52.24(5), (6) and (7)**). A single judge may refer any matter for a decision by a court consisting of two or more judges (**r. 52.24(8)**).

AMENDMENT OF AN APPEAL NOTICE

74.45   By **CPR, r. 52.21(5)**, a party to an appeal may not rely at the hearing of the appeal on a matter not contained in their appeal notice unless the appeal court gives permission. Similarly, the Court of Appeal may refuse to hear argument on a point not included in the skeleton argument (**PD 52C, para. 31(4)**). Failing to make clear the real basis for challenging the decision below is unfair on the appeal court (whose pre-reading is wasted) and unfair on respondents, who will not know the case they have to meet (*IS Innovative Software Ltd v Howes* [2004] EWCA Civ 275, *The Times*, 10 March 2004).

Normally, an appellant seeking to change the basis of its case should apply for permission to amend the grounds of appeal (**CPR, r. 52.17**). These applications are governed by the principles in *Swain Mason v Mills and Reeve LLP* [2011] EWCA Civ 14, [2011] 1 WLR 2735 and *Ketteman v Hansel Properties Ltd* [1987] AC 189 on late amendments (see **31.6** to **31.9**), and also by the relief from sanctions principles from *Denton v T. H. White Ltd* [2014] EWCA Civ 906, [2014] 1 WLR 3926. See *Lighting and Lamps UK Ltd v Clarke* (2016) LTL 4/3/2016. At the first stage the court considers the seriousness of the delay in place of the seriousness of the breach (*Lighting and Lamps UK Ltd v Clarke*).

An application for permission to amend will normally be dealt with at the hearing of the appeal, unless that course would cause unnecessary expense or delay, in which case a request should be made for the application to amend to be heard in advance (**PD 52C, para. 30(3)**). It will almost certainly also be necessary to seek permission to file a supplementary skeleton argument (for procedure, see **para. 32**).

STAY OF EXECUTION

Initiating an appeal does not have the automatic effect of staying execution on any judgment **74.46** obtained in the lower court. By **CPR, r. 52.16**, an appeal will operate as a stay of any order or decision of the lower court only if:

(a) the appeal court or the lower court so orders; or

(b) the appeal is from the Immigration and Asylum Chamber of the Upper Tribunal.

The basic rule is that a litigant is entitled to enjoy the fruits of its success (*BMW AG v Commissioners of HM Revenue and Customs* [2008] EWCA Civ 1028, LTL 7/10/2008). This means that enforcement should be allowed to proceed unless in all the circumstances of the case and having regard to the risk of injustice to the parties a stay ought to be imposed (*Gater Assets Ltd v NAK Naftogaz Ukrainiy* [2008] EWCA Civ 1051, LTL 8/10/2008). The court has an unfettered discretion to impose a stay of execution if the justice of the case so demands (*BMW AG v Commissioners of HM Revenue and Customs*). Relevant questions are (*Hammond Suddard Solicitors v Agrichem International Holdings Ltd* [2001] EWCA Civ 2065, [2002] CP Rep 21 per Clarke LJ at [22]):

(a) If a stay is refused, what are the risks of the appeal being stifled?

(b) If a stay is granted and the appeal fails, what are the risks that the respondent will be unable to enforce the judgment?

(c) If a stay is refused and the appeal succeeds, and the judgment is enforced in the meantime, what are the risks of the appellant being able to recover what has been paid to the respondent?

Proudman J in *Hall v Elia* (2016) LTL 11/3/2016 said *Hammond Suddard Solicitors v Agrichem International Holdings Ltd* has been overtaken by *Thevarajah v Riordan* [2015] UKSC 78, [2016] 1 WLR 76 (see **42.44**). The effect is that on a renewed application for a stay of execution in an appeal the appellant needs to establish either a material change of circumstances or a serious mistake in the earlier stay decision.

The appeal court also has a discretion to suspend an order for possession pending the appeal (*Admiral Taverns (Cygnet) Ltd v Daniel* [2008] EWHC 1688 (QB), [2008] NPC 86).

Evidence in support of an application for a stay must be full, frank and clear (*Hammond Suddard Solicitors v Agrichem International Holdings Ltd*).

INTERIM INJUNCTIONS IN PENDING APPEALS

On an application for an interim injunction in a pending appeal the following principles were **74.47** laid down by *Novartis AG v Hospira UK Ltd* [2013] EWCA Civ 583, [2014] 1 WLR 1264 at [41]:

(a) The court must be satisfied that the appeal has a real prospect of success.

(b) Beyond showing a real prospect of success, it will not usually be useful to attempt to form a view as to how much stronger the prospects of appeal are, or to attempt to give weight to that view in assessing the balance of convenience.

(c) It does not follow automatically from the fact that an interim injunction has or would have been granted pre-trial that an injunction pending appeal should be granted. The court must assess all the relevant circumstances including the period of time before the appeal can be heard and the balance of hardship between the parties.

(d) Granting injunctions is not limited to cases where the appeal would be rendered nugatory: that represents the extreme end of the spectrum.

Commentary

(e) The court should endeavour to find the solution that is best able to do justice between the parties once the appeal has been heard.

REVOKING PERMISSION, STRIKING OUT, IMPOSING CONDITIONS

74.48   By CPR, r. 52.18(1), an appeal court has the following powers: it may strike out the whole or part of an appeal notice; it may set aside permission to appeal in whole or in part; or it may impose or vary conditions upon which an appeal may be brought. These powers may be exercised only where there is a compelling reason (r. 52.18(2)). In *Angel Airlines SA v Dean and Dean* [2006] EWCA Civ 1505, [2007] 3 Costs LR 355, permission to appeal to the Court of Appeal had been granted by Gloster J in the High Court. Rix LJ, at [29], said that in the circumstances the power to revoke the permission granted by Gloster J under r. 52.18 was vested in the High Court. This misunderstands the phrase 'the appeal court' as it appears in r. 52.18(1), which is defined in r. 52.1(3)(b) to mean the court to which an appeal is made. In any event *Angel Airlines SA v Dean and Dean* held that the Court of Appeal has power to revoke permission to appeal, either under r. 52.20 (which says the appeal court has all the powers of the lower court, see 75.19) or in the court's inherent jurisdiction. In addition to its powers under r. 52.18, an appeal court may impose conditions under its general case management powers in rr. 2.1 and 3.1, which can be exercised even after an application to impose conditions has been refused by the judge in the court below (*Contract Facilities Ltd v Rees's Estate* [2003] EWCA Civ 1105, LTL 24/7/2003). Applications to set aside or impose conditions on the grant of permission to appeal should be made within 14 days of service of the order granting permission (*Mamidoil-Jetoil Greek Petroleum Company SA v Okta Crude Oil Refinery AD (No. 3)* [2003] EWCA Civ 617, [2003] 2 Lloyd's Rep 645).

It is recognised that the power to strike out an appeal notice 'is one that is just as capable of abuse as is the power to put in hopeless notices of appeal' (*Burgess v Stafford Hotel Ltd* [1990] 1 WLR 1215 per Glidewell LJ). Requiring a 'compelling reason' for the exercise of the powers under r. 52.18(1) deliberately sets a high standard, in part in order to comply with the requirement in the European Convention on Human Rights, **art. 6(1)**, in the **Human Rights Act 1998, sch. 1**, of ensuring appellants have a fair trial of their appeals (*Dadourian Group International Inc. v Simms* [2009] EWCA Civ 169, [2009] 1 Lloyd's Rep 601). There may be a compelling reason where the appeal is being brought to secure some collateral advantage, or where the application will achieve a substantial saving of time. This may be so where there are cogent grounds demonstrating the appeal had no prospects of success. Otherwise, in all ordinary circumstances the granting of permission to appeal is conclusive (*Hunt v Peasegood* (2000) *The Times*, 20 October 2000). A party who was present at the hearing at which permission was given may not subsequently apply for an order that the court exercise its powers to set aside permission or to impose conditions (r. 52.18(3)).

Sanctions and conditions in appeals

74.49   *Bell Electric Ltd v Aweco Appliance Systems GmbH & Co. KG* [2002] EWCA Civ 1501, [2003] 1 All ER 344, which said there is a wholly unfettered discretion under CPR, r. 52.18(1)(c), to impose and vary conditions upon which appeals may be brought, should be understood as referring to the width of the conditions that may be imposed, rather than the circumstances in which conditions may be imposed, which require a compelling reason (r. 52.18(2)). In this case the appellant was found to have disregarded the orders of the court below in a deliberate and cynical manner, and ordered that unless the appellant complied with the terms of the order below within the next 14 days the appeal would be stayed. The need for a compelling reason in r. 52.18(2) may not add much to the analysis when an appeal court is considering imposing a sanction, but must be borne in mind (*Michael Wilson and Partners Ltd v Sinclair* [2015] EWCA Civ 774, [2015] CP Rep 45).

A condition requiring an appellant to pay the costs whether he won or lost was held to be excessive in *King v Daltray* [2003] EWCA Civ 808, LTL 4/6/2003. An order that there be no order as to costs on the appeal was substituted. In *Masri v Consolidated Contractors International (UK) Ltd* [2007] EWCA Civ 702, LTL 31/7/2007, a condition was imposed requiring payment of an interim payment and costs ordered in the court below, with a sanction of striking out the appeal in the event of default. A condition requiring a payment into court may be varied on the ground that the appellant cannot afford to make the payment, but evidence will be required that the amount is such as to prevent the appellant funding the appeal (*Branch Empire Ltd v Coote* [2003] EWHC 1674, LTL 16/6/2003). In *R (Medical Justice) v Secretary of State for the Home Department* [2011] EWCA Civ 269, [2011] 1 WLR 2852, the Secretary of State was granted permission to appeal by Silber J on condition that, whatever the outcome of the appeal, the Secretary of State would pay the costs of the hearing in the lower court and the respondent's costs of the appeal. An appeal by the Secretary of State against these conditions was dismissed on the ground there was no jurisdiction by virtue of the **Access to Justice Act 1999, s. 54(4)** (see **74.16**). Permission to appeal is a composite decision. An appellant who objects to conditions set by the lower court can abandon the prospective appeal, accept the conditions, or make a fresh application for permission from the appeal court under r. 52.3(3) (see **74.13**).

DISMISSAL FOR NON-COMPLIANCE

The rules on lodging documents, skeleton arguments etc. are of a case management nature. **74.50** Failing to comply may result in sanctions, even dismissal of the appeal (*Patel v Mussa* [2015] EWCA Civ 434, [2015] 1 WLR 4788). In the Court of Appeal such cases may be considered by the Head of the Civil Appeals Office or by a Deputy Master. The court sees it as its duty to protect the interests of respondents, who already have a decision of a competent authority in their favour, by insisting on all reasonable expedition and strict compliance with the timetable laid down. See *Hyams v Plender* [2001] 1 WLR 32. An order imposing a sanction may itself be appealed independently of the substantive appeal (*Patel v Mussa*).

DISPOSAL OF APPEALS BY CONSENT

Where the parties to an appeal have reached a settlement disposing of the appeal, they may **74.51** make a joint request asking for the appeal to be dismissed by consent (**PD 52A, para. 6.3**). An appellant who does not wish to pursue an appeal may make a request to the appeal court for the appeal to be dismissed. If granted, this will usually be on terms that the appellant pays the costs (**para. 6.1**), but may be on the basis of no order as to costs if the respondent's representative signs a consent to that effect (**para. 6.2**). An appeal may be allowed by consent, but the appeal court must first be satisfied that the lower court's decision was wrong (**para. 6.4**). Appeals and applications settled where one of the parties is under a disability require the court's approval (**para. 6.5**). In these cases the proposed consent order should be supported by an opinion from the advocate acting for the child advising on whether the terms are for the benefit of the child or protected party.

Solicitors and counsel have a duty to inform the court, by letter if possible, as soon as it is known that an appeal which has been listed for hearing will not proceed (*Red River UK Ltd v Sheikh* [2009] EWCA Civ 643, [2009] CP Rep 41). Even if a case settles very late in the day steps must be taken through the Royal Courts of Justice switchboard to notify the appeal court judges' clerks, to prevent unnecessary preparation (*Tasyurdu v Immigration Appeal Tribunal* [2003] EWCA Civ 447, [2003] CPLR 343; *Yell Ltd v Garton* [2004] EWCA Civ 87, [2004] CP Rep 29).

AUTHORITIES

Cases

74.52 In the High Court lists of authorities should be provided to the Head Usher by 5.30 p.m. on the working day before the appeal hearing. In the County Court it is usually necessary to have photocopies of reports available at the hearing.

For Court of Appeal hearings (only), bundles of authorities containing photocopies of the principal authorities each side will be relying upon must be lodged no later than seven days before the hearing (**PD 52C, para. 21, Timeline 2; para. 29**). Obviously, this can only be done after conferring with the advocate for the respondent. There is no need to provide authorities for propositions not in dispute. Normally, the bundle should contain no more than 10 authorities with the relevant passages marked for pre-reading. **Paragraph 29(4)(b)** recognises that the scale of the appeal may warrant more extensive citation. The bundle must include a certificate signed by the advocates that the requirements of **para. 29** on citing and marking up authorities has been complied with.

The *Law Reports* published by the Incorporated Council of Law Reporting for England and Wales should be cited in preference to other reports, as they contain counsel's arguments and are readily available (**Practice Direction: Citation of Authorities** (2012)). Next best are the *Weekly Law Reports* and *All England Law Reports* if a case is not, or not yet, reported in the official *Law Reports*. Other reports, even obscure reports, may be used for sufficient reason, but advocates should provide photocopies (of the title page and relevant pages only). Occasionally it is useful to refer to more than one source if there are discrepancies between reports. There are restrictions on using certain authorities, discussed in Practice Direction (Citation of Authorities) [2001] 1 WLR 1001, see **32.19**. If unreported decisions are relied upon, the official transcript should be produced rather than the handed-down text of the judgment (**Practice Direction: Citation of Authorities** (2012), para. 10), and they should only be used if they contain statements of principle not found in reported authorities (**Practice Direction: Citation of Authorities** (2012), para. 10). Excessive citation of authorities, and reliance on summaries of cases not prepared by a professional lawyer, will not be tolerated (*Hamblin v Field* [2000] BPIR 621).

Use of *Hansard* extracts

74.53 It was decided in *Pepper v Hart* [1993] AC 593 that Parliamentary material may be used as an aid to determining the true intention of the legislature where:

(a) the legislation is ambiguous or obscure or the literal meaning leads to an absurdity;
(b) the material relied upon consists of statements by a minister or promoter of the Bill and such other material as is necessary to understand those statements; and
(c) the statements relied on are clear.

It is permissible to have recourse to ministerial statements and explanatory notes prepared by the relevant government department while the Bill was proceeding through Parliament, where doing so complies with the principles in *Pepper v Hart*. However, reference to debates in Parliament is contrary to the Bill of Rights (1688), art. 9, so cannot be justified as an aid to interpretation in court (see *Wilson v First County Trust Ltd (No. 2)* [2003] UKHL 40, [2004] 1 AC 816). Even where use of ministerial statements and explanatory notes is permissible, the court must be careful not to give these documents determinative effect, as Members of Parliament may not have generally agreed with the stated reasons or conclusions (*Wilson v First County Trust Ltd (No. 2)*). In *McDonnell v Congregation of Christian Brothers Trustees* [2003] UKHL 63, [2003] 1 AC 1101, Lord Bingham of Cornhill said he would need much persuasion, save possibly in exceptional circumstances, that it is proper to depart from a previous decision of the House of Lords on the basis that the previous decision is inconsistent with the will of Parliament as discovered from *Hansard*. Lord Steyn in the same case said there is a view that *Pepper v Hart* allows the court to treat the intentions of government revealed in debates in Parliament as reflecting the will of Parliament. That view raises serious conceptual and constitutional difficulties. The better view is that it has been decided by *Wilson v First County Trust Ltd (No. 2)* that use of debates from *Hansard* is not permissible.

Any party intending to refer to extracts from *Hansard* in accordance with the principles laid down in *Pepper v Hart* must give reasonable advance notice to the court and other parties. In the Court of Appeal the extracts should be included in the bundle of authorities (see 74.52).

FORM OF APPEAL ORDERS

The general rules relating to drawing up orders (see **chapter 63**) apply to orders made after appeal hearings. However, to assist the Civil Appeals Office in sifting applications for permission to bring a second appeal (see 74.15 for the restrictions on such appeals), orders made on first appeals must (see *Tanfern Ltd v Cameron-MacDonald* [2000] 1 WLR 1311) comply with the requirements of **CPR, rr. 40.2** and **52.3(3)** (see 74.8), including a statement of the name and status of the judge in the lower court.   **74.54**

Commentary

REOPENING APPEALS

Confirming the decision in *Taylor v Lawrence* [2002] EWCA Civ 90, [2003] QB 528, it is provided in **CPR, r. 52.30**, that the Court of Appeal and High Court may reopen an appeal (or application for permission to appeal: **PD 52A, para.** 7.1 and *Barclays Bank plc v Guy (No. 2)* [2010] EWCA Civ 1396, [2011] 1 WLR 681) in exceptional circumstances. This power derives from the court's inherent jurisdiction, and so is not available to a Circuit Judge in the County Court (**CPR, r. 52.30(3)**). An appeal may be reopened (see **r. 52.30(1)**) if all of the following three conditions are satisfied: **74.55**

(a) It is necessary to do so to avoid real injustice (such as where new facts come to light after the court makes its decision, as in *Taylor v Lawrence*, or where the appeal court was misled by false evidence into an erroneous conclusion, as in *Feakins v Department for Environment Food and Rural Affairs* [2006] EWCA Civ 699, [2006] NPC 66).
(b) The circumstances are exceptional and make it appropriate to reopen the appeal. A case is exceptional if it is possible a significant injustice will occur and there is no effective alternative remedy (*Re Uddin (A Child)* [2005] EWCA Civ 52, [2005] 1 WLR 2398). This might be found where the integrity of the earlier process has been critically undermined. The admission of fresh evidence (see 75.16), or establishing that the decision was wrong, will not be enough. Nor will pointing to mistakes by the party's legal representatives (*R (Nicholas) v Upper Tribunal Administrative Appeals Chamber* [2013] EWCA Civ 799, LTL 5/7/2013). It is necessary to show the decision was arrived at by a corrupted process, such as fraud or bias (*Guy v Barclays Bank plc* [2010] EWCA Civ 1396, [2011] 1 WLR 681). Appeal decisions alleged to have been obtained through fraud should, save in the most exceptional circumstances, be brought by way of fresh proceedings (*Jaffray v Society of Lloyd's* [2007] EWCA Civ 586, [2008] 1 WLR 75; see 75.18). Exceptional cases are those where there is incontestable, admissible, evidence of the fraud.
(c) There is no alternative effective remedy (so if the injustice could be remedied by a readily available further appeal, the court will not reopen the present appeal).

Procedure for reopening appeals

Permission is required to reopen an appeal, even if permission was not required for the initial appeal (**CPR, r. 52.30(4)**). An application for permission is made by application notice (in   **74.56** form N244) supported by written evidence (**PD 52A, para.** 7.2), and is made to the court whose decision the applicant wishes to reopen (**para.** 7.1). There is no right to an oral hearing unless the judge so directs (**CPR, r.** 52.30(5)), and the application must not be served on any other party, again unless the court otherwise directs (**PD 52A, para.** 7.2). An application cannot be granted unless the judge makes a direction for service on the other party and gives them an opportunity to make representations (**CPR, r.** 52.30(6)). The respondent has 14 days from being served to file and serve written evidence in reply (**PD 52A, para.** 7.3). There is no right of appeal or review from a decision on an application for permission to reopen, which is final (**CPR, r.** 52.30(7); *Meghani v Nessfield Ltd* [2008] EWHC 2827 (Ch), LTL 19/12/2008).

RESIDUAL APPELLATE JURISDICTION

74.57   In *Aden Refinery Co. Ltd v Ugland Management Co. Ltd* [1987] QB 650, Mustill LJ said that an appeal court has power to intervene in cases where the judge in the court below in truth never reached a decision at all, whether by reason of bias, chance, whimsy or personal interest. This was relied upon in *North Range Shipping Ltd v Seatrans Shipping Corporation* [2002] EWCA Civ 405, [2002] 1 WLR 2397, to create a residual appellate jurisdiction which may apply generally. *North Range Shipping Ltd v Seatrans Shipping Corporation* was an appeal against an arbitral award on a point of law. There are stringent restrictions on these appeals to the courts, one of which is that any second appeal from the decision of a High Court judge can only be brought with the permission of the High Court judge (Arbitration Act 1996, s. 69(8)). Tuckey LJ held that the Court of Appeal has a residual jurisdiction to hear such appeals on the grounds of misconduct or unfairness, justifying the decision on the basis that the jurisdiction is directed to the integrity of the decision-making process or the decision maker rather than being a direct attack on the decision itself. This was refined by *CGU International Insurance Co. plc v AstraZeneca Insurance Co. Ltd* [2006] EWCA Civ 1340, [2007] Bus LR 162, where Rix LJ at [79] said that an appeal on this basis will only succeed if the unfairness is of such a quality that it invalidates the decision.

While the residual appellate jurisdiction was recognised in *Patel v Mussa* [2015] EWCA Civ 434, [2015] 1 WLR 4788, the reasoning doubts whether it can be applied in appeals from the County Court, which has no inherent jurisdiction. Appeals from the County Court calling into question the decision-making process should instead be brought by way of judicial review, and then only in exceptional cases (see 74.10).

APPEALS BY WAY OF CASE STATED

74.58   A number of statutes provide that appeals may be brought to the High Court by way of case stated. Among the most well known are the Magistrates' Courts Act 1980, s. 111, and the Senior Courts Act 1981, s. 28. These provide for appeals by case stated from decisions made by magistrates' courts and the Crown Court on the ground they are wrong in law or in excess of jurisdiction. See *Blackstone's Criminal Practice 2017*, paras D29.17 to D29.24 and D29.37 to D29.39. A decision of the High Court on an appeal by case stated under either of these provisions is final, subject to the right of appeal in criminal cases to the Supreme Court under the Administration of Justice Act 1960 (see Senior Courts Act 1981, s. 28A(4), where, at least in the text at www.legislation.gov.uk, the description of the effect of the 1960 Act mistakenly refers to appeals to the Senior Courts instead of the Supreme Court because of the unintended effect of blanket amendments made by the Constitutional Reform Act 2005, s. 59(6), and sch. 11, para. 26).

Consequently, in a civil case the Court of Appeal has no jurisdiction to entertain a further appeal from the High Court's decision (*Westminster City Council v O'Reilly* [2003] EWCA Civ 1007, [2004] 1 WLR 195).

PD 52E applies to cases where enactments provide for appeals to be by way of case stated and to cases where a question of law may be referred to the court by way of case stated. In these cases the general provisions of **CPR, Part 52**, apply, subject to certain amendments. **PD 52E, paras 2.1** to **2.4**, apply to appeals by way of case stated from the Crown Court or magistrates' courts. In these appeals the appellant's notice must be filed in the High Court within 10 days after receipt of the stated case (**para. 2.2**). **Paragraphs 3.1** to **3.14** apply to appeals from ministers, government departments, tribunals and other persons by way of case stated. In these cases the appellant's notice and the stated case must be filed and served within 14 days after stating the case (**para. 3.6**). The minister or government department is entitled to attend the appeal hearing and to make representations (**para. 3.10**).

STATUTORY APPEALS

PD 52D applies to all statutory appeals, and to other appeals which are subject to special   **74.59**
provision, but not to appeals by way of case stated (for which see **74.58**). These appeals are governed by the main provisions of **CPR, Part 52**, but with certain refinements.

Where any statute prescribes a period within which an appeal must be filed, unless the statute provides otherwise, the appeal court may not extend that period (**PD 52D, para. 3.5**). Where the appellant wishes to appeal against a decision of the Administrative Appeals Chamber of the Upper Tribunal, the appellant's notice must be filed within 28 days of the date on which the Upper Tribunal's decision on permission to appeal to the Court of Appeal is sent to the appellant (**para. 3.3**). Where the appellant wishes to appeal against a decision of any other Chamber of the Upper Tribunal, the appellant's notice must be filed within 28 days of the date on which the Upper Tribunal's decision on permission to appeal to the Court of Appeal is given (**para. 3.3(2)**). Where a statement of reasons for a decision is given later than the notice of that decision, the deadline for filing the appellant's notice is calculated from the date on which the statement of reasons is sent to the appellant (**para. 3.3A**).

The appellant is required to serve the appellant's notice on the chairman of the tribunal, minister of State, government department or other person from whose decision the appeal is brought, in addition to the respondents (**para. 3.4(1)**). In a statutory appeal any person may apply for permission to file evidence or make representations in the appeal (**CPR, r. 52.25**). Such an application must be made promptly (**r. 52.25(2)**). An application for permission must be made by letter to the relevant court office, identifying the appeal, explaining who the applicant is and indicating why and in what form the applicant wants to participate in the hearing (**PD 52D, para. 3.7**).

A clear distinction must be made between the provisions which provide the court with jurisdiction in a statutory appeal, and the provisions in **CPR, Part 52**, and **PD 52D** which govern the conduct of the appeal thereafter. **CPR, Part 52**, and **PD 52D** do not impose a requirement for seeking permission to appeal for statutory appeals where otherwise the right of appeal is unrestricted (*Colley v Council for Licensed Conveyancers* [2001] EWCA Civ 1137, [2002] 1 WLR 160). Once seised of an appeal, **CPR, Part 52**, applies, which means, for example, that an appellant's notice is required even in appeals by way of case stated (*Woodpecker v Commissioners of HM Revenue and Customs* [2009] EWHC 3442 (Ch), LTL 21/10/2009). Conditions upon which a statutory appeal may be brought may be imposed under **r. 52.18**, which applies both to appeals requiring permission and those which can be brought as of right (*Calltel Telecom Ltd v Commissioners of HM Revenue and Customs* [2008] EWHC 2107 (Ch), [2009] Bus LR 513).

Commentary

Costs in statutory appeals etc.

74.60   For costs against inferior courts, coroners etc. see **68.39**.

For orders limiting appeal costs in appeals from non-costs jurisdictions, see **75.22**.

Special appeal provisions

74.61   Section 4 of PD 52D contains a large number of special rules applicable to various categories of specialist appeals. These include appeals from various tribunals to the Court of Appeal (such as appeals from the Immigration and Asylum Chamber of the Upper Tribunal), and appeals to the High Court under various statutory provisions, most of which are highly specialised. For appeals under the Trade Marks Act 1938, s. 18, see *E. I. Dupont de Nemours and Co. v S. T. Dupont* [2003] EWCA Civ 1368, [2006] 1 WLR 2793. Appeals under the Party Wall etc. Act 1996 were considered in *Zissis v Lukomski* [2006] EWCA Civ 341, [2006] 1 WLR 2778, which also considered how technical errors in bringing a statutory appeal could be cured by amendment or by invoking the overriding objective.

CPR powers, for example, to dispense with service, do not apply to time limits laid down in primary legislation for bringing statutory appeals (*Mucelli v Government of Albania* [2009] UKHL 2, [2009] 1 WLR 276, see **15.24**). *Mucelli v Government of Albania* was a decision under the Extradition Act 2003, but the same principle applies to a range of other statutory appeals (*Massan v Secretary of State for the Home Department* [2011] EWCA Civ 686, LTL 30/6/2011, an application to extend time for filing the appellant's notice in an appeal under the Asylum and Nationality Act 2006; *R (Harrison) v General Medical Council* [2011] EWHC 1741 (Admin), LTL 8/6/2011, an appeal under the Medical Act 1983; *R (Modaresi) v Secretary of State for Health* [2011] EWCA Civ 1359, LTL 23/11/2011, an appeal under the Mental Health Act 1983).

74.62   **Housing Act 1996, ss. 204 and 204A**   Appeals under both ss. 204 and 204A of the Housing Act 1996 should be included in one appellant's notice, unless this is not possible because of urgency (**PD 52D, para. 28.1(2)**). An appeal under s. 204 was held in *Van Aken v Camden London Borough Council* [2002] EWCA Civ 1724, [2003] 1 WLR 684, to have been brought within the 21-day time limit laid down by s. 204(2) where the documents were put through the court's letter box after the court had closed on the 21st day.

74.63   **Law of Property Act 1922**   Appeals against decisions of the Secretary of State under the Law of Property Act 1922, sch. 15, para. 16, lie to the High Court (**CPR, r. 52.26**).

74.64   **Osteopaths Act 1993**   Substantive appeals under the Osteopaths Act 1993 lie to the High Court under **CPR, Part 52**, and so do appeals against interim suspension orders pending resolution of substantive appeals. Unless the High Court forms the view that the substantive appeal is bound to succeed, it should be slow to allow an appeal against an interim suspension order because it will not be in a position to assess whether the decision was wrong within the meaning of **r. 52.21(3)(a)** (*Moody v General Osteopathic Council* [2007] EWHC 2518 (Admin), [2008] 2 All ER 532).

74.65   **Pension Schemes Act 1993 and Pensions Act 2004**   Appeals from determinations of the Pensions Ombudsman under the Pension Schemes Act 1993, s. 151(4), or the Pension Protection Fund Ombudsman, under the Pensions Act 2004, s. 217(1), lie to the High Court (**CPR, r. 52.29**).

74.66   **Planning legislation**   An appeal, on a point of law, against the Secretary of State's decision on an appeal against an enforcement notice, a notice under the Town and Country Planning Act 1990, s. 207, or a listed building enforcement notice, lies to the High Court (**CPR, r. 52.28**). Where permission to apply for a planning statutory review has been refused at a hearing in the High Court (for which, see **PD 8C**), permission to appeal may be sought from the Court of Appeal (**CPR, r. 52.10**).

Tribunals and Inquiries Act 1992   Decisions of a limited list of tribunals can be challenged   **74.67**
on points of law either by appealing to the High Court or by requesting the tribunal to state
and sign a special case for the opinion of the High Court. See the Tribunals and Inquiries Act
1992, s. 11(1), and **CPR, r. 52.27**.

Chapter 75   Hearing of Appeals

INTRODUCTION

75.1   This chapter will discuss the nature of appeal hearings, and the grounds on which an appeal court may overturn the decision of the court below. References to **CPR, Part 52**, are to the version in force from 3 October 2016.

COMPOSITION OF THE COURT

75.2   An appeal from a County Court District Judge will be to a County Court Circuit Judge. An appeal from a High Court Master or District Judge will be to a High Court judge. The same is true with appeals from County Court Circuit Judges (other than appeals from final decisions in multi-track and specialist jurisdiction proceedings, where the appeal is to the Court of Appeal).

The Senior Courts Act 1981, s. 54(2), provides that the Court of Appeal shall be duly constituted for the purposes of exercising any of its jurisdiction if it consists of one or more judges. Section 54(3) provides that the Master of the Rolls may give directions about the minimum number of judges required for different descriptions of proceedings and, by s. 54(4) the Master of the Rolls or any designated Lord Justice can determine the number of judges who will sit in any particular proceedings. In the absence of special circumstances, there is nothing wrong with a judge who refused permission to appeal on the papers being one of the judges hearing the substantive appeal after permission is granted on a renewed application (*Sengupta v Holmes* [2002] EWCA Civ 1104, 99 (39) LSG 39). Normally, two Lords Justices sit on interim appeals, and three sit on final appeals. Where a two-judge court is equally divided, either party may apply for a rehearing before a three-judge court.

Occasionally an appeal court will sit with assessors, as in some appeals on costs issues.

THE HEARING

75.3   Normally it is unnecessary for the advocate for the appellant to open the appeal, as the judges usually do fairly extensive pre-reading. In most cases the judges will have pre-read the appeal bundle and skeleton arguments, and usually will have read the core authorities bundle (if there is one). The judge (or presiding judge in a multi-member court) usually indicates the extent of the pre-reading that has been done. In appeals to the Court of Appeal, if it is felt that it would be helpful for the appellant's advocate to open the appeal, the presiding judge will notify the advocates in advance. The intention is that court time is spent dealing with the substance of the arguments and that time should not be wasted in extensive reading from documents.

PART 36 OFFERS

The fact that a Part 36 offer has been made must not be disclosed to the court on any applica-   **75.4**
tion for permission to appeal or on any appeal until all questions (other than costs) have been determined (**CPR, r. 52.22(1)**). This is for the same reason (the risk of unfairly influencing the court) as applies at trial (see **r. 36.16**). However, the embargo does not apply if the Part 36 offer is relevant to the substance of the appeal, or if the fact that a Part 36 offer has been made is properly relevant to the matter to be decided (**r. 52.22(2) and (3)**).

REVIEW OF THE DECISION BELOW

Review not rehearing

By **CPR, r. 52.21(1)**, every appeal will be limited to a review of the decision of the lower   **75.5**
court unless:

(a) a practice direction makes different provision for a particular category of appeal; or
(b) the court considers that in the circumstances of an individual appeal it would be in the interests of justice to hold a rehearing.

There are very few exceptions. The power to conduct an appeal by way of rehearing is to be exercised in rare cases where necessary in order for justice to be done. The fair trial require-ments of the European Convention on Human Rights, **art. 6**, in the **Human Rights Act 1998, sch. 1** do not compel the court to conduct rehearings in appeals from without-notice decisions (*Dyson Ltd v Registrar of Trademarks* [2003] EWHC 1062 (Ch), [2003] 1 WLR 2406). The exceptional nature of holding a rehearing rather than a review on an appeal was stressed in *Lewis v Secretary of State for Trade and Industry* [2001] 2 BCLC 597. It had been submitted that a rehearing was appro-priate because the lower court had not stated reasons for its decision. Neuberger J said that even in such cases the appeal should be by way of review unless the court below had been asked to give its reasons and had refused to do so, or there was some good reason for not asking the lower court to give its reasons. The limited circumstances in which an appeal should take the form of a rehearing rather than a review, particularly where the decision appealed against is one based on discretion, were stressed in *Audergon v La Baguette Ltd* [2002] EWCA Civ 10, [2002] CPLR 192. In *Richardson v Ealing London Borough Council* [2005] EWCA Civ 1798, [2006] CP Rep 19, the Court of Appeal reiterated the practice requiring an exceptional case before conducting an appeal as a rehearing. In *McFaddens Solicitors v Chandrasekaran* [2007] EWCA Civ 220, LTL 26/2/2007, the appeal court could only have fulfilled its task in an appeal against a summary judgment decision by reference to all the material put before the Master. While this looks like a rehearing, it was to be regarded as a review within the meaning of **CPR, r. 52.21**. *Bank of Ireland v Robertson* (2003) LTL 21/2/2003 was an exceptional case where an appeal was conducted by way of rehearing. The appellant was a litigant in person, had been unable to attend the hearing, and this was the first occasion on which he had been able to present his case.

Grounds for allowing appeals

The restriction of an appeal court's function to a review of the lower court's decision means   **75.6**
that for almost all appeals, the appeal court will allow an appeal only where (**CPR, r. 52.21(3)**) the decision of the lower court was:

(a) wrong; or
(b) unjust because of a serious procedural or other irregularity in the proceedings in the lower court.

In addition, a decision will only be wrong or unjust if the matter of complaint would have made a difference to the decision of the lower court (*Ebden v Richardson* [2008] EWCA Civ 1589, LTL 10/11/2008).

Duty to take point in lower court

75.7   An appellant is not allowed to present a totally new argument that is not stated in the grounds of appeal and was not taken in the court below (*Gover v Propertycare Ltd* [2006] EWCA Civ 286, [2006] ICR 1073). This obligation was infringed in *City and General (Holborn) Ltd v Royal and Sun Alliance Insurance plc* [2010] EWCA Civ 911, [2010] BLR 639, where in the court below both parties argued for an all-or-nothing approach on whether the claim was time-barred under the Limitation Act 1980, but on appeal the claimant sought to argue that there were three causes of action, each with a different date of accrual. There is a discretion to permit a new point to be taken on an appeal if there is a sufficient reason. This may arise where there has been a recent legal development, although in *Thorne v Lass Salt Garvin* [2009] EWHC 100 (QB), LTL 5/2/2009, the court refused permission where the 'recent' authority forming the basis of the new point had been reported several months before the hearing in the lower court, but the legal representatives of the appellant had not appreciated its relevance to the case in hand.

It is counsel's duty in the lower court to draw the judge's attention to any alleged deficiency in a judgment, and request clarification or a supplementary judgment on the issue. It is not open to counsel to keep quiet and then raise the issue on an application for permission to appeal (*Re S (Children)* [2007] EWCA Civ 694, *The Times*, 2 July 2007). See also the discussion on handed-down judgments at **63.35** and **75.20**.

Wrong decisions

75.8   'Wrong' in CPR, r. 52.21(3)(a), means unsustainable (*Abrahams v Lenton* [2003] EWHC 1104 (QB), LTL 20/5/2003). An insubstantial point, even if a technical error, does not render a decision wrong (*Orford v Rasmi Electronics Ltd* [2004] EWCA Civ 809, LTL 4/8/2004). An arithmetical error in computing damages may be sufficient (*Pope v Energem Mining (IOM) Ltd* [2011] EWCA Civ 1043, LTL 6/9/2011). The strength of the other evidence at trial may mean that, despite an error, the decision below was not wrong (*Daly v Sheikh* [2004] EWCA Civ 119, LTL 13/2/2004). In *DEG-Deutsche Investitions- und Entwicklungsgesellschaft mbH v Koshy* [2001] EWCA Civ 79, [2001] 3 All ER 878, Robert Walker LJ at [24] rejected a submission that there is no power to allow an appeal where the lower court's decision was correct on the law and evidence as it stood before the lower court, even though a change in the law, or fresh evidence, or supervening events, show it (with hindsight) to have been wrong. The Court of Appeal seems to have gone even further in *Law v St Margarets Insurance Ltd* [2001] EWCA Civ 30, LTL 18/1/2001, where the appeal was allowed on the basis of furthering the overriding objective rather than holding that the lower court's discretion fell outside the generous ambit given to discretionary decisions. Similarly, in *Ayonrinde v Oyemomilara* [2001] EWCA Civ 1296, LTL 17/7/2001, it was difficult to say that the lower court's decision was wrong on the material before the judge below. However, the decision in the lower court caused injustice to the appellant, and the case was treated as an exceptional case which justified setting aside the decision below.

Questions of fact

75.9   The trial judge sees the demeanour of witnesses, and can assess their intelligence and credibility in a way that an appeal court cannot, even with the benefit of a transcript. It is accordingly very difficult to succeed on an appeal based on arguments that findings of fact by the court below were wrong (*Orford v Rasmi Electronics Ltd* [2004] EWCA Civ 809, LTL 4/8/2004). A decision may be plainly wrong where it cannot be reasonably explained or justified, and so is one which no reasonable judge could have made (*Henderson v Foxworth Investments Ltd* [2014] UKSC 41, [2014] 1 WLR 2600). Appeal courts are often more comfortable if they are invited to allow an appeal based on the inferences that may be drawn from the evidence (see **75.12**) rather than a direct attack on the findings of fact.

The appeal court's function is to review the decision of the court below. It is not to embark on making original findings of fact (*Designer Guild Ltd v Russell Williams (Textiles) Ltd* [2000] 1 WLR 2416). An appeal court has to accept the findings of fact of the court below on an interim appeal, and is not entitled to take a different view of the facts on which the decision below was founded (*Momson v Azeez* [2009] EWCA Civ 202, LTL 18/3/2009).

A trial finding of fact can be upset on appeal if there was no evidence to support that finding, or if the finding was against the weight of the evidence as a whole (*Bank of Credit and Commerce International (Overseas) Ltd v Akindele* [2001] Ch 437). An appeal on a question of fact was allowed in *George Ralph Architects v Lazarowicz* (2000) LTL 27/10/2000, where the judge found an agreement by preferring one side's witnesses, but where the agreement was not referred to in the contemporaneous documents.

Failure to give reasons

The definition of issues, marshalling of evidence and giving reasons are the building blocks of the reasoned judicial process. See **61.55**. An analysis of the judgment in *Glicksman v Redbridge Healthcare NHS Trust* [2001] EWCA Civ 1097, LTL 12/7/2001, showed that the judge below had made findings expressed as conclusions without giving reasons for the implicit rejection of testimony going the other way. Further, there were no findings on the secondary issues on which counsel had relied. The judgment was set aside with an order for a retrial. A case just on the other side of the line was *Harris v CDMR Purfleet Ltd* (2008) LTL 20/11/2008), where although there were doubts as to the judge's reasons, it was reasonably clear why the judge had reached his decision, and his conclusions were clear. A judge must address the main evidential conflicts, and identify why (for example) certain witnesses have been found to be truthful and others to be untruthful or inaccurate (*Baird v Thurrock Borough Council* [2005] EWCA Civ 1499, *The Times*, 15 November 2005). Making findings in a column in a Scott schedule is no substitute for a reasoned judgment on the issues (*Habib Bank Ltd v Liverpool Freeport (Electronics) Ltd* [2004] EWCA Civ 1062, LTL 29/7/2004). In *Clifford v Grimley* [2001] EWCA Civ 1658, LTL 23/10/2001, the judge failed to weigh up many of the issues, which were dealt with in a robust manner which was cursory and superficial. Nevertheless, the short analysis did not sufficiently undermine the findings of fact to justify interference on appeal. Further, in a well-known area an experienced judge is not expected to spell out every nuance of the principles that are being applied in coming to the decision (*Novus Aviation Ltd v Onur Air Taşımacılık AŞ* [2009] EWCA Civ 122, [2009] 1 Lloyd's Rep 576).

75.10

Commentary

An unsuccessful party should not seek to upset a judgment on the ground of inadequate reasons unless, despite considering the judgment in the light of the evidence and submissions at trial, they are unable to understand why the judge had decided against them (*English v Emery Reimbold and Strick Ltd* [2002] EWCA Civ 605, [2002] 1 WLR 2409). It is the advocate's duty to draw the judge's attention to any ambiguity or alleged deficiency in the judge's reasoning (*Re A and L (Children)* [2011] EWCA Civ 1205, [2012] 1 FLR 134). When an application for permission to appeal is made to the trial judge on the ground of inadequate reasons, the trial judge should consider whether his judgment was defective. If so, the judge should seek to remedy this by giving additional reasons, and refuse permission to appeal as the problem is thereby remedied. Where an appeal court finds a renewed application for permission on this ground to be well founded, it should consider adjourning the application and remitting the case to the trial judge with an invitation to provide additional reasons for the decision. If the application proceeds to an appeal hearing, the appeal will only succeed if the reasons cannot be discerned even in the context of the evidence and submissions at the trial (*English v Emery Reimbold and Strick Ltd*). There is no obligation to deal with every argument advanced by the parties, provided the basis of the decision is sufficiently clear (*Hague Plant Ltd v Hague* [2014] EWCA Civ 1609, [2015] CP Rep 14 at [4]). A failure to address an issue was not sufficient to justify interference on appeal where the judgment was otherwise a careful one in *Powell v Pallisers of Hereford Ltd* [2002] EWCA Civ 959,

LTL 1/7/2002. The practice of giving no reasons for decisions on costs could only comply with the European Convention on Human Rights, **art. 6(1)**, in the **Human Rights Act 1998, sch. 1**, if the reason for the decision is implicit from the circumstances (*English v Emery Reimbold and Strick Ltd*).

Discretion

75.11   The most important statement on the role of an appellate court in a discretionary matter is that of Lord Diplock in *Hadmor Productions Ltd v Hamilton* [1983] 1 AC 191. This was a case dealing with an appeal in respect of an interim injunction, but his lordship's comments are equally applicable in other types of interim appeals. His lordship said, at p. 220:

> Upon an appeal from the judge's grant or refusal of an [interim] injunction the function of an appellate court, whether it be the Court of Appeal or your lordships' House, is not to exercise an independent discretion of its own. It must defer to the judge's exercise of his discretion and must not interfere with it merely upon the ground that the members of the appellate court would have exercised the discretion differently. The function of the appellate court is initially one of review only. It may set aside the judge's exercise of his discretion on the ground that it was based upon a misunderstanding of the law or of the evidence before him or upon an inference that particular facts existed or did not exist, which, although it was one that might legitimately have been drawn upon the evidence that was before the judge, can be demonstrated to be wrong by further evidence that has become available by the time of the appeal; or upon the ground that there has been a change of circumstances after the judge made his order that would have justified his acceding to an application to vary it. Since reasons given by judges for granting or refusing [interim] injunctions may sometimes be sketchy, there may also be occasional cases where even though no erroneous assumption of law or fact can be identified the judge's decision to grant or refuse the injunction is so aberrant that it must be set aside upon the ground that no reasonable judge regardful of his duty to act judicially could have reached it. It is only if and after the appellate court has reached the conclusion that the judge's exercise of his discretion must be set aside for one or other of these reasons, that it becomes entitled to exercise an original discretion of its own.

Robust and fair case management decisions will be supported, even if the appeal court would have decided the case in the opposite way if it had been dealing with the application at first instance (*Chartwell Estate Agents Ltd v Fergies Properties SA* [2014] EWCA Civ 506, [2014] CP Rep 36). This applies, for example, to decisions for and against striking out and for and against granting relief from sanctions (*Abdulle v Commissioner of Police of the Metropolis* [2015] EWCA Civ 1260, [2016] 1 WLR 898). An appeal against a case management decision can only succeed if it was one the judge could not properly have made (*Global Torch Ltd v Apex Global Management Ltd (No. 2)* [2014] UKSC 64, [2014] 1 WLR 4495 at [13]). Thus, discretionary decisions may be reversed on appeal where the judge below erred in principle in his approach, or left out of account or took into account some feature he should not have considered, or that his decision was wholly wrong because he failed to balance the various factors fairly in the scale (*Adamson v Halifax plc* [2002] EWCA Civ 1134 [2003] 1 WLR 60). The way it was put by Lord Fraser of Tullybelton in *G v G (Minors: Custody Appeal)* [1985] 1 WLR 647 is that the appeal court 'should only interfere when it considers that the judge of first instance has not merely preferred an imperfect solution which is different from an alternative imperfect solution which the Court of Appeal might or would have adopted, but has exceeded the generous ambit within which a reasonable disagreement is possible'.

Any conclusion reached at a case management conference is made at the judge's discretion, and, unless the judge has clearly erred by failing to fulfil the overriding objective, there is a distinct reluctance to interfere on an appeal (*Powell v Pallisers of Hereford Ltd* [2002] EWCA Civ 959, LTL 1/7/2002). There may be an even greater reluctance to interfere with a discretion exercised by a trial judge (*Swain-Mason v Mills and Reeve LLP* [2011] EWCA Civ 14, [2011] 1 WLR 2735 at [78]). In *Raja v Van Hoogstraten (No. 9)* [2008] EWCA Civ 1444, [2009] 1 WLR 1143 at [119], Mummery LJ said that an appeal court will not interfere with the wide discretion of the judge on costs unless there was some error of principle or some other reason why the judge's decision was plainly wrong. In *Straker v Tudor Rose* [2007] EWCA Civ 368, [2008] 2 Costs LR 205, Waller LJ at [2], [10], pointed out that appeal courts are loath to interfere with the discretion exercised by a judge in any area, and particularly so in the area of costs. A number of Court of Appeal authorities had been cited to the court, and Waller LJ commented:

I do not gain much assistance from them. In the area of costs, where all cases are different and fact specific, I would suggest that authorities apart from those that lay down clear principles are of little assistance. It is to the Rules that one should go, and it is by reference to the Rules that one should test whether the judge has gone wrong in any particular case.

Strictly, a decision based on evaluation is not an exercise of discretion. An evaluation requires the court to consider and weigh a number of factors, but ultimately this will produce a single correct answer. An appeal court will only interfere with the lower court's evaluation if the judge applied some wrong principle, or failed to take a relevant matter into account, or took into account an irrelevant matter, or if the judge was plainly wrong. See the cases referred to in *Sarpd Oil International Ltd v Addax Energy SA* [2016] EWCA Civ 120, [2016] CP Rep 24 at [14].

Inferences

It takes a strong case before an appeal court will decide that a decision was wrong on the basis of inferences drawn by the trial judge from eyewitness evidence; the question being whether the inferences could fairly be drawn from the evidence (*Silverlink Trains Ltd v Collins-Williamson* [2009] EWCA Civ 850, LTL 31/7/2009). An appeal court may draw its own inferences of fact which it considers justified on the evidence (**CPR, r. 52.21(4)**). This includes inferences to be drawn from the facts found by the judge in the lower court and inferences to be drawn from the documents (*The Mouna* [1991] 2 Lloyd's Rep 221).

75.12

New point of law

On an appeal it is possible to raise a new point of law that was not presented to the court below. There is some reluctance to allow this, and normally permission will be granted only if there is no possibility of any injustice occurring, such as through the failure to raise the point of law at first instance affecting the conduct of the trial, the evidence, or the evaluation of the evidence. There is even greater reluctance to allow a point of mixed law and fact to be raised for the first time on an appeal. A mixed point will almost certainly require an amendment to the appellant's statement of case, which will not be granted where permission to amend would have been refused if the point had been raised at trial (*Jones v Environcom Ltd* [2011] EWCA Civ 1152, [2012] PNLR 5, and see **31.6** and **31.13**).

75.13

Serious procedural irregularities

Procedural irregularities include misdirections to the jury (in jury trials) and the improper admission or non-admission of evidence. By **CPR, r. 52.21(3)**, a procedural irregularity is a valid ground for appeal only if it was a serious one and it caused an unjust decision in the lower court (*Tanfern Ltd v Cameron-MacDonald* [2000] 1 WLR 1311). An appeal on this ground is an onerous one, and the procedural irregularity must have caused an injustice to the appellant (*Keith Davy (Crantock) Ltd v Ibatex Ltd* [2001] EWCA Civ 740, LTL 2/5/2001). While not providing the opposite party with a letter sent to the judge, and thereby failing to give the other side an opportunity to respond to it, was held to be a serious procedural irregularity in *National Westminster Bank plc v Rushmer* [2010] EWHC 554 (Ch), [2010] 2 FLR 362, it only affected an alternative case, and so did not render the entire decision unjust. There are cases where an appeal will be allowed on the ground of serious procedural irregularity despite the appeal court forming the view that nevertheless the lower court's decision was right (*Dunbar Assets plc v Dorcas Holdings Ltd* [2013] EWCA Civ 864, LTL 12/7/2013).

75.14

Examples of serious procedural irregularity

Allowing one party to adduce additional evidence but not the other, and restricting the cross-examination of a key witness, amounted to a serious procedural irregularity in *Hayes v*

75.15

Commentary

Transco plc [2003] EWCA Civ 1261, LTL 17/9/2003. Refusing permission to call a witness who would have made no difference was insufficient in *Wade v Varney* [2003] EWCA Civ 1279, LTL 22/9/2003. In *Aberavon and Port Talbot Rugby Football Club v Welsh Rugby Union Ltd* [2003] EWCA Civ 584, LTL 9/4/2003, it was held that the appellant had been given sufficient opportunity in the court to make representations by being given the opportunity to make written representations.

Arguments that the judge in the lower court was predisposed against the appellant, often because of previous decisions, are frequently made but there is rarely any material to support such an allegation (*Hicks v Russell Jones and Walker* [2008] EWCA Civ 340, LTL 3/3/2008). In *Taylor v Williamsons* [2002] EWCA Civ 1380, [2003] CP Rep 20, discussed at **63.47**, an appeal was dismissed despite the judge issuing a written judgment before receiving the submissions from one of the parties. The judge had recalled the judgment, and given a new judgment after hearing submissions. An appeal may be based on excessive delay in delivering judgment where this impedes the judge's recollection of the evidence (*Manning v King's College Hospital NHS Trust* [2009] EWCA Civ 832, (2009) 110 BMLR 175, where eight months' delay in a complex case was forgiven; *Cobham v Frett* [2001] 1 WLR 1775 where a 12-month delay was regarded as excessive; *Bond v Dunster Properties Ltd* [2011] EWCA Civ 455, LTL 21/4/2011, where a 22-month delay did not make the decision unsafe). A delay of three months calls for some explanation (*Habib Bank Ltd v Liverpool Freeport (Electronics) Ltd* [2004] EWCA Civ 1062, LTL 29/7/2004). In appeals based on delay, the appellate court should consider the quality of the judge's notes, and carefully scrutinise the findings of fact and the reasons given by the judge. It is only if there are errors possibly attributable to the delay that an appeal should be allowed on this ground (*Cobham v Frett*).

Fresh evidence

75.16   By CPR, r. **52.21(2)**, unless it orders otherwise, the appeal court will not receive oral evidence or any evidence which was not before the lower court. Before the CPR came into force a restrictive approach was taken to the introduction of fresh evidence on appeals, the guiding principles being laid down in *Ladd v Marshall* [1954] 1 WLR 1489 (see **75.17**). The rule in *Ladd v Marshall* applied to appeals from trials and final determinations, and reflected the policy of requiring parties to advance their entire case at trial, and not deliberately leaving over points for the purpose of appeals (and thereby obtaining a 'second bite at the cherry'). With the introduction of the CPR, the discretion to admit fresh evidence on an appeal has to be exercised in accordance with the overriding objective (*Evans v Tiger Investments Ltd* [2002] EWCA Civ 161, [2002] 2 BCLC 185). However, the *Ladd v Marshall* principles remain relevant as matters which must necessarily be considered, although not as strict rules (*Banks v Cox* (2000) LTL 17/7/2000). Strong grounds have to be shown before fresh evidence will be admitted, and the *Ladd v Marshall* principles will be looked at with considerable care (*Hertfordshire Investments Ltd v Bubb* [2000] 1 WLR 2318). The Court of Appeal has to be particularly cautious where the appellant seeks to put further questions to witnesses (whether lay or expert) where the witness has been cross-examined at trial (*Riyad Bank SAL v Ahli United Bank (UK) plc* [2005] EWCA Civ 1419, *The Times*, 16 December 2005). It will be a rare case where the *Ladd v Marshall* conditions are not satisfied but the court nevertheless admits fresh evidence on an appeal (*Shaker v Al-Bedrawi* [2002] EWCA Civ 1452, [2003] 1 BCLC 157 at [88]). An example is where the appeal court receives an undertaking from a party (*Sharab v Prince Al-Waleed bin Talal bin Abdal-Aziz-Al-Saud* [2009] EWCA Civ 353, [2009] 2 Lloyd's Rep 160). On the facts the undertaking was declined by the appeal court because it effectively would have created a different situation, so would have required the appeal court to exercise its own discretion rather than reviewing that of the judge below.

Ladd v Marshall concerns applications to adduce fresh evidence after trial. A more flexible approach is adopted in appeals against procedural decisions (*Anglo Irish Asset Finance plc v Flood* [2011] EWCA Civ 799, LTL 11/7/2011). On an interim appeal fresh evidence might be admitted if there has been a material change of circumstances (*R (Iran) v Secretary of State for the Home Department* [2005] EWCA Civ 982, [2005] Imm AR 535).

Applications for permission to adduce fresh evidence can be made to the Master of the Court of Appeal, but they are often directed to be listed for hearing at the same time as the appeal (Practice Direction (Court of Appeal: Procedure) [1995] 1 WLR 1191). A separate bundle should be prepared for the further evidence application, so that it can be kept separate from the main appeal bundles.

Ladd v Marshall principles

Under *Ladd v Marshall* [1954] 1 WLR 1489 fresh evidence would be allowed on an appeal against **75.17** a final decision only if the evidence:

(a) could not have been obtained with reasonable diligence for use at the hearing in the lower court;
(b) would probably have an important influence on the result; and
(c) was apparently credible.

In considering whether evidence could have been obtained with reasonable diligence, no distinction is to be made between the knowledge of the lay client and that of the solicitor (*Evans v Tiger Investments Ltd* [2002] EWCA Civ 161, [2002] 2 BCLC 185). Evidence from a witness who was not called at trial will not satisfy condition (a) if the witness (although uncooperative) had given enough information for a draft witness statement to be prepared, as the draft statement could have been adduced as hearsay (see **chapter 53**) and the witness could have been compelled to attend the trial (see **chapter 57**) (see *Transview Properties Ltd v City Site Properties Ltd* [2009] EWCA Civ 1255, LTL 24/11/2009). The *Ladd v Marshall* test will rarely be satisfied where the fresh evidence goes merely to credit (*Hamilton v Al Fayed (No. 1)* [2001] EMLR 394). Where the new evidence is credible and there has been a clear attempt to deceive the court, the requirements of justice would point strongly towards admitting the evidence (*Daly v Sheikh* [2002] EWCA Civ 1630, LTL 24/10/2002). A relaxation of the strict *Ladd v Marshall* principles may be appropriate where it is in the public interest that fraudulent road traffic claims are exposed (*Singh v Habib* [2011] EWCA Civ 599, LTL 12/4/2011). In *Singh v Habib* once certain items of credible fresh evidence were identified, other, less convincing, evidence which formed part of the whole picture of the case, was also admitted. Evidence obtained after trial in *Arundel Corporation v Khokher* [2003] EWCA Civ 491, LTL 9/4/2003, from the respondent's solicitor's former employees contradicted evidence given at trial by the respondent and his solicitor. Permission to adduce the evidence was granted, because the evidence was credible and raised a prima facie case that the finding at trial should be reversed. There may be other reasons for refusing permission to adduce new evidence. In *Sadrolashrafi v Marvel International Food Logistics Ltd* [2004] EWHC 777 (Ch), [2004] BPIR 729, permission was refused because the new evidence was entirely contrary to the evidence given by the appellant at the hearing below and which the appellant knew was untrue. Evidence produced at a very late stage (Thursday for an appeal heard the following Monday) was disallowed in *Rakusens Ltd v Baser Ambalaj Plastik Sanayi Ticaret AS* [2001] EWCA Civ 1820, [2002] 1 BCLC 104, on the ground that it was completely unreasonable to expect the other side to deal with the evidence on such short notice.

Judgment obtained by fraud

Where the judge has been wilfully deceived by fraudulent evidence, justice requires a retrial **75.18** (*Prentice v Hereward Housing Association* [2001] 2 All ER (Comm) 900). Likewise where there is a risk that a fraud has been perpetrated on the court below (*Couwenbergh v Valkova* [2004] EWCA Civ 676, LTL 27/5/2004). There are two lines of authority on how a judgment obtained by fraud should be dealt with:

(a) remit for retrial: *Hamilton v Al-Fayed (No. 4)* [2001] EMLR 15; or
(b) bring fresh proceedings: *Kuwait Airways Corporation v Iraqi Airways Co.* [2001] 1 WLR 429.

The difference between them is that remitting for retrial is appropriate in cases where the fraud is admitted or incontrovertible, but fresh proceedings are appropriate where the allegation of fraud is contested (*Owens v Noble* [2010] EWCA Civ 224, [2010] 1 WLR 2491). It is permissible, and may be more efficient, in cases which are to be remitted for the case to be remitted to the trial judge (*Owens v Noble* [2010] EWCA Civ 284, LTL 18/3/2010).

Where a claim has been settled in a Tomlin order, it is permissible to start fresh proceedings claiming damages on the ground that the settlement was induced by fraud or misrepresentation. Such fresh proceedings are not an abuse of process or barred by *res judicata* (*Zurich Insurance Co. plc v Hayward* [2011] EWCA Civ 641, [2011] CP Rep 39). On the trial of such a fraud claim it is necessary to prove that the claimant must have been influenced by the misrepresentation (*Zurich Insurance Co. plc v Hayward* [2016] UKSC 48, [2016] 3 WLR 637). This is a question of fact. Accordingly, such a claim may succeed even if the party bringing the fraud claim might not have believed the representation (that the claimant on the facts had permanent injuries), but believed that those injuries would be presented to the court as true, and that there was a real risk that the court would make findings based on accepting the representations, which would result in a higher award. Damages were awarded based on the difference between the real value of the original claim and the damages agreed in the Tomlin order.

GENERAL POWERS VESTED IN THE APPEAL COURT

75.19   By CPR, **r. 52.20(1)**, in relation to an appeal the appeal court has all the powers of the lower court. In particular, by **r. 52.20(2)**, the appeal court has power to do any of the following things:

(a) Affirm, set aside or vary any order or judgment made or given by the lower court. The power to vary does not extend to making a different type of order from the order the court below had been asked to make (*King v Telegraph Group Ltd* [2004] EWCA Civ 613, [2005] 1 WLR 2282). Where the appeal court allows an appeal against the exercise of a discretion and substitutes its own discretionary decision, it should do so on the basis of the material that was before the court below and normally nothing else. Otherwise, a successful appellant will often find that having complied with the now overturned earlier decision will make it difficult for the appeal court to exercise the discretion in his favour (*Swain-Mason v Mills and Reeve LLP* [2011] EWCA Civ 14, [2011] 1 WLR 2735 at [102]).

(b) Refer any claim or issue for determination by the lower court (**r. 52.20(2)(b)**). This power is stated in general terms, and allows the court to refer back a point to the trial judge which is only contingently relevant in the present appeal (*Hicks v Russell Jones and Walker* [2007] EWCA Civ 844, [2009] 1 WLR 487). The judge in the lower court may give directions for written submissions or further evidence to assist with this. Where the appeal court refers such a question to the lower court for a supplementary judgment, permission to appeal may be set aside where the supplementary judgment results in the appeal having no real prospect of success (*Hicks v Russell Jones and Walker* [2008] EWCA Civ 340, LTL 3/3/2008).

(c) Order a new trial or hearing, which is a last resort (*White v White* [2001] EWCA Civ 955, LTL 21/6/2001). If an appeal court orders a rehearing, it should make it clear on the face of its order whether the rehearing should be at appeal court level, or whether the case should be remitted back to the lower court for the rehearing (*Fowler de Pledge v Smith* [2003] EWCA Civ 703, *The Times*, 27 May 2003).

(d) Make orders for the payment of interest.

(e) Make a costs order.

In rare cases, the Court of Appeal has jurisdiction to take a point of general importance of its own motion which was not raised in the court below (*Bulale v Secretary of State for the Home Department* [2008] EWCA Civ 806, [2009] QB 536).

By **r. 52.20(3)**, in an appeal from a claim tried with a jury, the Court of Appeal may, instead of ordering a new trial, make an order for damages or the award made by the jury. If the appeal court refuses permission to appeal, strikes out an appellant's notice, or dismisses an appeal, and it considers the matter was totally without merit, that fact must be recorded in the court's order, and the court must consider whether to make a civil restraint order (**r. 52.20(5) and (6)**; see **14.55**).

HANDED-DOWN JUDGMENTS

75.20

Below the Court of Appeal, it is usual for the court to give judgment immediately after the arguments, although occasionally judgment will be reserved. This is rather more common in the Court of Appeal. The procedure for handing down reserved judgments in writing is set out in **PD 40E** (see **63.35**). On an appeal, an application for a consequential order is determined without a hearing (**PD 40E, para. 4.5(a)**).

COSTS

75.21

Under **CPR, r. 52.20(2)(e)**, the appeal court has power to make costs orders in relation to the appeal hearing and for the proceedings in the lower court.

Costs of appeals are likely to be summarily assessed if the hearing lasts not more than one day (see **PD 44, para. 9.2(b)**).

Appeal costs in appeals from no-costs jurisdictions

75.22

An appeal from a tribunal decision will involve moving from a no-costs jurisdiction to a costs-shifting jurisdiction in the appeal court. Protective costs orders (for which, see **44.10**) are available only in limited circumstances, and will not be available if the claim is not made in public law litigation (*Eweida v British Airways plc* [2009] EWCA Civ 1025, [2010] CP Rep 6). In that case an alternative application for a costs capping order (for which, see **44.2**) was refused largely on the ground that, even if there was a risk of costs being disproportionately incurred by the other side, that could be controlled by the costs judge on assessment. *Eweida v British Airways plc* seems to have been accepted by *Unison v Kelly* [2012] EWCA Civ 1148, [2012] IRLR 951, where an alternative route to providing costs protection was found by granting permission to appeal on condition that no costs were sought from the respondent. The unsatisfactory result in these cases has been addressed by **CPR, r. 52.19**, which provides that in any proceedings in which costs recovery is normally limited or excluded at first instance, an appeal court may make an order that the recoverable costs of an appeal will be limited to the extent which the court specifies. In making such an order the court will have regard to:

(a) the means of both parties;
(b) all the circumstances of the case; and
(c) the need to facilitate access to justice.

An application for such an order must be made as soon as practicable and will be determined without a hearing unless the court orders otherwise (**r. 52.19(4)**).

Commentary

Chapter 76   Appeals to the Supreme Court

INTRODUCTION

76.1 By the Constitutional Reform Act 2005, ss. 23–60, the Supreme Court of the United Kingdom replaced the Appellate Committee of the House of Lords as the highest court in the land with effect from 1 October 2009 (see the Constitutional Reform Act 2005 (Commencement No. 11) Order 2009 (SI 2009/1604)), which is the date the Supreme Court came into operation. One of the reasons for the change was to provide greater clarity in the country's constitutional arrangements by continuing the process of separating the judiciary from the legislature.

The Supreme Court is a superior court of record (Constitutional Reform Act 2005, s. 40(1)) and is intended to:

- be the final court of appeal for all United Kingdom civil cases, and criminal cases from England, Wales and Northern Ireland;
- hear appeals on arguable points of law of general public importance;
- concentrate on cases of the greatest public and constitutional importance; and
- maintain and develop the role of the highest court in the United Kingdom as a leader in the common law world.

The Supreme Court Rules 2009 (SI 2009/1603) ('SCR') were made under the Constitutional Reform Act 2005, s. 45, and govern the procedure of the Supreme Court. The overriding objective of the SCR is to secure that the Supreme Court is accessible, fair and efficient (r. 2(2), reflecting s. 45(3)). The SCR came into force on 1 October 2009, together with 14 practice directions:

General Note and the Jurisdiction of the Supreme Court (PD 1 Supreme Court)
The Registry of the Supreme Court (PD 2 Supreme Court)
Applications for Permission to Appeal (PD 3 Supreme Court)
Notice of Appeal (PD 4 Supreme Court)
Papers for the Appeal Hearing (PD 5 Supreme Court)
The Appeal Hearing (PD 6 Supreme Court)
Applications, Documents, Forms and Orders (PD 7 Supreme Court)

Miscellaneous Matters (bankruptcy, grouping or linking appeals, cross-appeals, death of a party, dispute between parties being settled, exhibits, fees and security for costs, interveners, new submissions, opposed procedural applications, patents, public funding and legal aid, specialist advisers and advocates to the Court, stay of execution, transcription, withdrawal of appeals and applications, broadcasting, and enforcement of orders made by the Supreme Court) (PD 8 Supreme Court)
The Human Rights Act 1998 (PD 9 Supreme Court)
Devolution Jurisdiction (PD 10 Supreme Court)
The European Court of Justice (PD 11 Supreme Court)
Criminal Proceedings (PD 12 Supreme Court)
Costs (PD 13 Supreme Court)
Filing Documents in the Registry of the Supreme Court by Electronic Means (PD 14 Supreme Court)

The SCR and Practice Directions can be accessed at the Supreme Court website, http://supremecourt.uk/.

JURISDICTION

The jurisdiction of the Supreme Court is defined by the Constitutional Reform Act 2005, **76.2** s. 40. Its jurisdiction corresponds to that of the House of Lords in its judicial capacity under the Appellate Jurisdiction Acts 1876 and 1888 (which are repealed) together with devolution matters under the Scotland Act 1998, the Northern Ireland Act 1998 and the Government of Wales Act 2006, which are transferred to the Supreme Court from the Judicial Committee of the Privy Council. It is specifically provided that an appeal lies to the Supreme Court from any order or judgment of the Court of Appeal in England and Wales in civil proceedings (Constitutional Reform Act 2005, s. 40(2)), and the Supreme Court assumes the jurisdiction previously exercised by the House of Lords under various statutes set out in sch. 9 (see s. 40(4)). This chapter will concentrate on the civil jurisdiction of the Supreme Court.

The Supreme Court has power to determine any question necessary to be determined for the purpose of doing justice in an appeal (s. 40(5)). This, together with s. 40(2) and the overriding objective of ensuring it is accessible, fair and efficient, permit the Supreme Court to adopt procedures even if they are not specifically stated in the SCR. On this basis the Supreme Court held it had power to adopt a closed material procedure in *Bank Mellat v HM Treasury (No. 2)* [2013] UKSC 38, [2014] AC 700.

LEAPFROG APPEALS

Very exceptionally, a direct appeal from the decision of a High Court judge to the Supreme **76.3** Court is possible under the Administration of Justice Act 1969, ss. 12 to 15 (as amended by the Criminal Justice and Courts Act 2015, s. 63, with effect from 13 April 2015). There are the following conditions:

(a) a sufficient case for an appeal to the Supreme Court must be made out to justify an application for permission to bring such an appeal;
(b) the appeal must involve a point of law of general public importance;
(c) the point of law must either relate to the construction of an Act of Parliament or statutory instrument, or else be a point on which the judge at first instance is bound by a decision of the Court of Appeal or of the House of Lords or the Supreme Court (s. 12(3));
(d) alternatively to (c), under s. 12(3A) either:
  (i) the proceedings must entail a decision relating to a matter of national importance or consideration of such a matter;

(ii)   the result of the proceedings must be so significant that a hearing by the Supreme Court is justified; or

(iii) the benefits of earlier consideration by the Supreme Court outweigh the benefits of consideration by the Court of Appeal;

(e) the trial judge must certify, either immediately at the end of the trial or within the next 14 days, that the case is a suitable one for a direct appeal to the Supreme Court;

(f) the Supreme Court must grant permission to bring the appeal direct on an application made by any of the parties within one month of the date of the judge's certificate.

When the Criminal Justice and Courts Act 2015, ss. 64 to 66, are brought into force, there are similar requirements for leapfrog appeals from the Upper Tribunal, the Employment Appeal Tribunal and the Special Immigration Appeals Commission.

Detailed procedural requirements are in PD 3 Supreme Court, paras 3.6.1 to 3.6.16.

In *R (Jones) v Ceredigion County Council* [2007] UKHL 24, [2007] 1 WLR 1400, an appellant with two grounds of appeal was given permission to use the leapfrog procedure on only one ground. The permission to use the leapfrog procedure is couched in terms of a proposal. If taken up, the appellant is limited to the terms of the proposal, and so in this case would have had to abandon the other ground. As it had refused the proposal, it was able (with the appropriate permission) to take both grounds to the Court of Appeal. What is to be avoided is allowing a party to bring appeals in parallel to both the Court of Appeal and Supreme Court on different issues arising from the same order.

APPEALS FROM THE COURT OF APPEAL

Permission to appeal

76.4   An appeal from the Court of Appeal can only be made with permission from the Court of Appeal or the Supreme Court (Constitutional Reform Act 2005, s. 40(6)), but this is subject to any restriction on such an appeal in any enactment. The most important general restriction on rights of appeal is the **Access to Justice Act 1999, s. 54(4)** (see **74.16**). The effect of this provision is that the Supreme Court may not entertain any appeal against an order of the Court of Appeal refusing permission for an appeal to the Court of Appeal from a lower court.

This means, for example (as explained by PD 1 Supreme Court, para. 1.2.21, in relation to appeals in judicial review cases), that if the Court of Appeal refuses permission to appeal to it against the Administrative Court's refusal of permission to apply for judicial review, there is no appeal to the Supreme Court. The Supreme Court has no jurisdiction to entertain such an appeal (*R v Secretary of State for Trade and Industry, ex parte Eastaway* [2000] 1 WLR 2222, applying *Lane v Esdaile* [1891] AC 210). However, if the Court of Appeal grants permission to appeal to it against the Administrative Court's refusal of permission to apply for judicial review, but then itself refuses permission to apply for judicial review, the Supreme Court does have jurisdiction to hear an appeal against the Court of Appeal's refusal of permission to apply for judicial review (*R (Burkett) v Hammersmith and Fulham London Borough Council* [2002] 1 WLR 1593).

Permission from the Court of Appeal

76.5   The initial application for permission to appeal should be made to the Court of Appeal immediately after judgment has been pronounced (SCR, r. 10(2)). Procedures dealing with seeking permission in the Court of Appeal were formerly contained in PD 52, paras 15.13 to 15.21 (now deleted). Those paragraphs are referred to here as they may continue to provide some guidance. They provided that the Court of Appeal can deal with an application for permission to

CROSS-APPEALS

A respondent who wishes to argue that the order appealed from should be upheld on grounds **76.12** different from those relied on by the court below, must state that clearly in the respondent's written case (but need not cross-appeal, see SCR, r. 25(1)). Other than for appeals as of right, a respondent who wishes to argue that the order appealed from should be varied must obtain permission to cross-appeal (r. 25(2)). This is sought from the Supreme Court and can be filed only after permission to appeal has been granted to the original appellant (PD 8 Supreme Court, para. 8.3.2). A similar procedure is followed to that on seeking permission to appeal, with such modifications as are appropriate.

SERVICE AND FILING

Service

Documents in Supreme Court appeals are served (SCR, r. 6(1)) by any of the following methods: **76.13**

(a) personal service;
(b) first class post (or an alternative service which provides for delivery on the next working day);
(c) (with the consent of the party to be served) through a document exchange;
(d) (with the consent of the party to be served or at the direction of the Registrar) by electronic means in accordance with the relevant practice direction.

A document served by first class post or through a document exchange will be taken to have been served on the second day after it was posted or left at the document exchange, as the case may be (not including days which are not business days) (r. 6(3)). Where the address of the person on whom a document is to be served is unknown, the Registrar may direct that service is to be effected by an alternative method (r. 6(2)).

Filing

SCR, r. 7(1), permits a document to be filed by any of the following methods: **76.14**

(a) personal delivery;
(b) first class post (or an alternative service which provides for delivery on the next working day);
(c) through a document exchange;
(d) (with the consent of the Registrar) by electronic means in accordance with PD 14 Supreme Court.

Except with the consent of the Registrar, SCR, r. 7(3), provides that the contents of documents:

(a) filed in hard copy must also be provided to the Registry by electronic means, and
(b) filed by electronic means must also be provided to the Registry in hard copy.

PROCEDURAL APPLICATIONS

Any procedural application must be made in form SC002 (SCR, r. 30(2); PD 7 Supreme **76.15** Court, para. 7.1.2) and must (SCR, r. 30(2); PD 7 Supreme Court, para. 7.1.3):

(a) state the order the applicant is seeking;
(b) set out the reasons for making the application; and
(c) where necessary, be supported by written evidence.

There is a prescribed fee of £350 on filing an application (Supreme Court Fees Order 2009, fee 3.3). A copy of the application must be served on every other party before it is filed (SCR, r. 30(3)). The original must be filed together with three copies and a certificate of service.

1355

A party who wishes to oppose an application must, within seven days after service, file notice of objection in form SC003 together with three copies, and must (before filing) serve a copy on the applicant and any other parties (r. 30(4)). There is a prescribed fee of £150 (Supreme Court Fees Order 2009, fee 3.4).

Applications are dealt with without a hearing wherever possible. Unless the Registrar directs otherwise, opposed procedural applications are referred to a panel of Justices and may be decided with or without an oral hearing (PD 7 Supreme Court, para. 7.1.6).

NOTICE OF APPEAL

76.16   Where permission to appeal is granted by the Supreme Court, the application for permission to appeal will stand as the notice of appeal and the grounds of appeal are limited to those on which permission has been granted (SCR, r. 18(1)). The appellant must, within 14 days of the grant of permission to appeal, file notice under r. 18(1)(c) that he intends to proceed with the appeal. When the notice is filed, the application for permission to appeal will be resealed and the appellant must then serve a copy on each respondent, on any intervener whose submissions have been taken into account under r. 15, and on any intervener in the court below. After service, the appellant must file the original notice of appeal and three copies (r. 18(2); PD 4 Supreme Court, para. 4.1.1) together with a certificate of service.

In any other case an appellant must serve and then file a notice of appeal in form SC001 (with three copies) together with a certificate of service (SCR, rr. 18(3), 19(1) and 20). Filing must take place within 42 days of the date of the order or decision of the court below (r. 19(2)).

There is a further prescribed fee at this stage, which is £800 (Supreme Court Fees Order 2009, fee 2.1) in cases where notice to proceed is filed, and £1,600 in cases where there is notice of appeal (fee 2.2).

ACKNOWLEDGMENT BY RESPONDENT

76.17   Each respondent who intends to participate in the appeal must, within 14 days after service of the notice of appeal under SCR, rr. 18(2)(a) or 20, serve and then file notice of objection/ acknowledgment in form SC003, together with a certificate of service (r. 21). A respondent who does not file notice will not be permitted to participate in the appeal, will not be given notice of its progress (r. 21(3)), and will not obtain an order for costs (PD 4 Supreme Court, para. 4.6.4).

There is a prescribed fee of £320 (Supreme Court Fees Order 2009, fee 2.4).

DOCUMENTS

76.18   Multiple copies of the documents required on appeals to the Supreme Court must be produced, partly to inform the other parties, partly for use of the Justices dealing with the appeal, and partly for records purposes. The minimum numbers laid down in the practice directions do not include the copies required for the party's own use, and may need to be increased where there are multiple parties in the appeal. The basic requirements are summarised in **table 76.1**.

Statement of facts and issues

76.19   A statement of facts and issues is a single document, which is drafted initially by the appellant but must be submitted to, and agreed with, every respondent before being filed (SCR, r. 22(2)). The statement must set out the relevant facts and, if the parties cannot agree on

Table 76.1 Copies of documents to be filed in the Registry and served on other parties

Document	Copies for Registry	Copies for other parties
By the appellant		
Notice of appeal	Original and 3 copies	1
Statement of facts and issues	Original and 7 copies	As arranged
Appendix Part 1	8	1
Appendix Part 2 and any subsequent Parts	10	1
Appellant's case	Original and 7 copies	As arranged
Core volumes	10	As arranged
Authorities volumes	10	As arranged
By the respondent and interveners		
Respondent's acknowledgment	Original and 3 copies	1
Respondent's (intervener's) case	Original and 7 copies	As arranged; 10 for core volumes
Respondent's authorities	Nil	10 for joint set of authorities
Respondent's additional documents	10	As arranged
Applications		
Application in form SC002	Original and 3 copies	1
Notice of objection	Original and 3 copies	1
Oral hearing: affidavits, witness statements and other documents	8	1

any matter, the statement should make clear what items are disputed. The statement should contain references to every law report of the proceedings below, and should state the duration of the proceedings below. It should be signed by counsel for all parties (PD 5 Supreme Court, para. 5.1.2). It must be filed within 112 days after filing the notice of appeal (SCR, r. 22(1)).

Appendix

The documents to be included in the appendix are, by PD 5 Supreme Court, para. 5.1.5:   **76.20**

(a) the order appealed against;
(b) if separate from the order at (a) above, the order refusing permission to appeal to the Supreme Court;
(c) the official transcript of the judgment of the court below;
(d) the final order(s) of all other courts below;
(e) the official transcript of the final judgment(s) of all other courts below;
(f) (where they are necessary for understanding the legal issues and the argument) the relevant documents filed in the courts below; and
(g) (where they are necessary for understanding the legal issues and the argument) the relevant documents and correspondence relating to the appeal.

The appendix should contain only such material as is necessary for understanding the legal issues and the argument to be presented to the Supreme Court (SCR, r. 22(2)). It should not contain documents which were not in evidence below, nor should it contain transcripts of the proceedings or evidence below unless they are essential to the legal argument (PD 5 Supreme Court, para. 5.1.4). If necessary, the appendix should be prepared in several parts, with only the most essential documents being included in part 1. It is only part 1 that will be included in the core volumes (see **76.22**). The appendix must be submitted to, and agreed with, every respondent before being filed (SCR, r. 22(2)), with the deadline for filing being 112 days after filing the notice of appeal (r. 22(1)).

Appellants' and respondents' cases

76.21   After the Registrar has informed the parties of the date fixed for the hearing (see **76.25**), the appellant and every respondent (and any intervener and advocate to the court) must sequentially exchange their respective written cases and file them (SCR, r. 22(4)). A 'case' is the statement of a party's argument in the appeal (PD 6 Supreme Court, para. 6.3.1). There is no prescribed maximum length, but the Supreme Court favours brevity, and a case should be a concise summary of the submissions to be developed. The case should be confined to the heads of argument that counsel propose to submit at the hearing, and omit material contained in the statement of facts and issues (para. 6.3.2). It must conclude with a numbered summary of the reasons upon which the argument is founded, and must be signed by counsel. Its purpose is to enable counsel to concentrate their arguments on the real issues in the appeal (*M. V. Yorke Motors v Edwards* [1982] 1 WLR 444). Unreported cases should be cited only if they are binding on the Court of Appeal and if the substance of the decision is not to be found in any fully reported case (*Roberts Petroleum Ltd v Bernard Kenny Ltd* [1983] 2 AC 192). Any intention to invite the Supreme Court to depart from one of its (or the House of Lords') earlier decisions must be clearly stated in a separate paragraph in the case.

There is further guidance in PD 6 Supreme Court, paras 6.3.3 to 6.3.13. The appellant must file seven copies of its case at least five weeks before the hearing, and the respondent must file seven copies of its case at least three weeks before the hearing (paras 6.3.9 and 6.3.10).

Core volumes

76.22   As soon as the parties' cases have been exchanged and in any event not later than 14 days before the date fixed for the hearing, the appellant must file 10 copies of the core volumes and, if necessary, additional volumes containing further parts of the appendix (SCR, r. 23; PD 6 Supreme Court, para. 6.4.3). The core volumes contain:

(a) the notice of appeal or the resealed application for permission to appeal;
(b) notice of cross-appeal (if any);
(c) statement of facts and issues;
(d) appellants' and respondents' cases, with cross-references to the appendix and authorities volume(s);
(e) case of the advocate to the court or intervener, if any;
(f) part 1 of the appendix; and
(g) index to the authorities volume(s).

Authorities

76.23   The volumes of authorities that may be referred to during the hearing must be prepared in accordance with PD 6 Supreme Court, paras 6.5.1 to 6.5.8, and 10 copies of the volumes of authorities must be filed by the appellant at the same time as the core volumes (SCR, r. 24; PD 6 Supreme Court, para. 6.5.1). These should be a joint set of authorities, which should appear in alphabetical order and be divided into domestic, Strasbourg (ECHR), foreign and academic material. The appellants have the initial responsibility for producing the authorities volumes and for filing them at the Registry but, to enable the appellants to file the volumes, the respondents must provide the appellants with 10 copies of any authorities which the respondents require but which the appellants do not, or arrange with the appellants for their photocopying.

Exhibits

Parties who require exhibits to be available for inspection at the hearing must apply to the   **76.24**
Registrar for permission in advance of the hearing (PD 8 Supreme Court, para. 8.6.1).

FIXING THE HEARING

A prescribed fee of £4,820 is payable when the appellant files the statement of relevant facts   **76.25**
and issues and appendix (Supreme Court Fees Order 2009, fee 2.5). Within seven days thereafter, every party must notify the Registrar that the appeal is ready for listing, and provide a
time estimate from counsel (SCR, r. 22(3)). The Registrar will then inform the parties of the
date fixed for the hearing, which takes the form of a provisional date agreed with the parties
(see PD 6 Supreme Court, para. 6.6.1). Any request for an expedited hearing should be made
to the Registrar (SCR, r. 31(1)). Wherever possible the views of all parties should be obtained
before a request is made (r. 31(2); PD 4 Supreme Court, para. 4.8.1).

THE HEARING

The Supreme Court has a President, Deputy President, and 10 Justices of the Supreme Court.   **76.26**
At the request of the President of the Supreme Court, the Constitutional Reform Act 2005,
s. 38, allows the following to be appointed as acting judges of the Court:

(a) a person who holds office as a senior territorial judge (as defined in s. 38(8), including
     Court of Appeal judges);
(b) a member of the supplementary panel under s. 39 (recently retired Supreme Court
     Justices).

The Supreme Court sits with an uneven number of judges, being at least three in number
with a majority being permanent Justices (s. 42(1)). The Justices should be addressed as 'My
Lord' or 'My Lady' (PD 6 Supreme Court, para. 6.6.8). Hearings are conducted in accordance with PD 6 Supreme Court and any directions given by the Court (SCR, r. 27(4)). These
may limit oral submissions to a specified duration. Counsel must assume the Justices have
read the printed cases and judgment under appeal, but not all the papers that have been filed
(para. 6.6.7).

No more than two counsel will be heard on behalf of a party, or a single counsel for an intervener (para. 6.6.5). Counsel briefed to appear in the Supreme Court are expected to be present at and throughout the hearing. Hearings in the Supreme Court take precedence over
hearings in lower courts, and counsel should not ordinarily accept instructions to appear in
the Supreme Court on a hearing for a fixed date if they already have a conflicting engagement.
If through unforeseen circumstances counsel will find it difficult or embarrassing to appear in
the Supreme Court, they should write to the presiding Justice and seek leave to be absent. This
will ordinarily be given if sufficient reason is shown. See Practice Statement (House of
Lords: Appearance of Counsel) [2008] 1 WLR 1143.

Supreme Court proceedings are exempted from the prohibitions on broadcasting and photography (Constitutional Reform Act 2005, s. 47), but visitors to the Supreme Court are
prohibited from taking photographs or filming its proceedings. Legal representatives and
members of the public are, however, permitted to use text-based communications from the
court provided these are silent and avoid disruption (Practice Guidance (Court Proceedings:
Live Text-based Communications) (No. 2) [2012] 1 WLR 12). Exceptions relate to cases
with reporting restrictions, cases involving children, and where there is an order against
reporting to avoid influencing a lower court.

Commentary

JUDGMENT AND COSTS

76.27 Judgment is usually delivered in open court, but may be promulgated by the Registrar (SCR, r. 28). One junior counsel may attend when judgment is delivered in open court (PD 6 Supreme Court, para. 6.8.2). The Supreme Court has all the powers of the court below (SCR, r. 29(1)) and may:

(a) affirm, set aside or vary any order or judgment made or given by that court;

(b) remit any issue for determination by that court;

(c) order a new trial or hearing;

(d) make orders for the payment of interest;

(e) make a costs order (for which see rr. 46 to 53; PD 6 Supreme Court, paras. 6.3.7, 6.7.1, 6.7.2 and 6.9.5; and PD 13 Supreme Court). The fees of two counsel only are allowed on assessment unless the court orders otherwise on application on the hearing of the appeal (PD 6 Supreme Court, para. 6.3.7).

In an appropriate case the Supreme Court can overrule the order below and substitute its own order (*Manchester City Council v Pinnock (Nos. 1 and 2)* [2011] UKSC 6, [2011] 2 AC 104).

An order of the Supreme Court may be enforced in the same way as an order of the court below (SCR, r. 29(2); see 79.2).

SETTING ASIDE SUPREME COURT DECISION

76.28 There is no equivalent in the SCR to CPR, r. 52.30 on reopening final appeals (discussed at **63.45** and **63.48**). Nevertheless, the Supreme Court has inherent jurisdiction to set aside a previous decision made by itself or the House of Lords in order to correct a probable significant injustice, in circumstances where there is no alternative effective remedy (*R (Edwards) v Environment Agency (No. 2)* [2010] UKSC 57, [2011] 1 WLR 79 at [35]; *R (Bancoult) v Secretary of State for Foreign and Commonwealth Affairs (No. 4)* [2016] UKSC 35, [2016] 3 WLR 157). This jurisdiction will not be exercised merely because it is thought the earlier decision was wrong (*R v Bow Street Metropolitan Stipendiary Magistrate, ex parte Pinochet Ugarte (No. 2)* [2000] 1 AC 119 at p. 132). What is required is that, without their own fault, a party has been subjected to an unfair procedure. This might arise where:

(a) costs are awarded without giving the parties a fair opportunity to address argument on the issue (*Broome v Cassell and Co. Ltd (No. 2)* [1972] AC 1136);

(b) another party has failed to disclose relevant documentation (*R (Bancoult) v Secretary of State for Foreign and Commonwealth Affairs (No. 4)* at [8]); or

(c) fresh evidence has been discovered after judgment.

Chapter 77   Judicial Review

The following procedural checklist is relevant to this chapter:

Procedural checklist 34   Claim for judicial review

INTRODUCTION

77.1 Judicial review is the means by which the courts control administrative action by public bodies (including inferior courts and tribunals). It is a supervisory jurisdiction which reviews administrative action rather than being an appellate jurisdiction.

The primary legislation dealing with judicial review is the Senior Courts Act 1981.

The principal rules of court governing claims for judicial review are in **CPR, Part 54**, supplemented by **PD 54A. CPR, r. 54.1(2)(a)**, defines a claim for judicial review as:

a claim to review the lawfulness of—
(i)   an enactment; or
(ii) a decision, action or failure to act in relation to the exercise of a public function.

Although other remedies may be sought, the characteristic remedies in judicial review claims are the prerogative mandatory, prohibiting and quashing orders (see 77.53 to 77.60), which the County Court does not have power to grant (County Courts Act 1984, s. 38(3)(a)). Judicial review claims are assigned to the Queen's Bench Division in the High Court by the Senior Courts Act 1981, sch. 1, para. 2(b), and are dealt with in the Administrative Court.

A judicial review claim may be transferred to the Upper Tribunal if the conditions in the Senior Courts Act 1981, s. 31A, are met. In addition, challenges to a decision of the Secretary of State for the Home Department not to entertain an asylum or human rights claim are dealt with by the Upper Tribunal under the Tribunals, Courts and Enforcement Act 2007, ss. 15 and 18.

There are two conditions necessary to determine whether a decision by a body is judicially reviewable:

(a) the decision or action must be made by a public body (see 77.3 and 77.4); and
(b) the public body must make a public law decision or take a public law action (see 77.5).

BODIES OPEN TO JUDICIAL REVIEW

77.2 Any body performing public law duties or powers is susceptible to judicial review. Historically, the most important factor considered by the courts in identifying activities subject to judicial review was the source of the power being exercised by the decision-maker whose decision was sought to be challenged. However, the courts have recognised that such an approach is too restrictive and they are now influenced by the type of function performed by the decision-maker (*R v Panel on Take-overs and Mergers, ex parte Datafin plc* [1987] QB 815).

The essential elements which comprise a public law body are (1) a 'public element' (which can take many different forms); and (2) the exclusion of bodies whose sole source of power is consensual submission to their jurisdiction (per Sir John Donaldson MR in *R v Panel on Take-overs and Mergers, ex parte Datafin plc*).

Central government and statutory bodies

77.3 Central government and bodies which derive authority from statute are susceptible to judicial review. Central government's powers derive from the prerogative (as to which see below) or statute. The range of statutory bodies which have been held to be reviewable also includes inferior courts, local authorities, tribunals and inquiries and regulators with a statutory basis. Ministers acting on behalf of the Crown are also subject to judicial review (*Re M* [1994] 1 AC 377). The Parliamentary Commissioner for Standards has been held not to be reviewable because he or she is one of the means by which the Select Committee on Standards and Privileges carries out its functions, and those functions form part of the proceedings of Parliament (*R v Parliamentary Commissioner for Standards, ex parte Al Fayed* [1998] 1 WLR 669) and the courts will not intervene in the affairs of Parliament.

Other courts and tribunals susceptible to judicial review include magistrates' courts, coroners' courts, local election courts (*R v Cripps, ex parte Muldoon* [1984] QB 68 (DC), [1984] QB 686 (CA)), the old patents appeal tribunals which were replaced by the Patents Court (*Baldwin and Francis Ltd v Patents Appeal Tribunal* [1959] AC 663), the County Court (save where it performs the functions of a superior court) and statutory tribunals in certain circumstances (where a High Court judge does not sit, and dependent upon their powers and relationship with the High Court according to its enabling statute) (*R v Cripps, ex parte Muldoon* [1984] QB 686). Judicial review does not lie against the High Court or the Court of Appeal, but only against the decisions of inferior courts. The decision of a District Judge under the Extradition Act 2003 is deemed to be a decision of the High Court for these purposes and therefore not amenable to judicial review (*R (Okandeji) v Bow Street Magistrates' Court* [2005] EWHC 2925 (Admin), [2006] 1 WLR 674). The High Court did have jurisdiction to judicially review the decision of the County Court in refusing permission to appeal (*R (Sivasubramaniam) v Wandsworth County Court* [2002] EWCA Civ 1738, [2003] 1 WLR 475). However, where the claimant had sought judicial review of the original decision, and had not sought permission to appeal it, judicial review was not available since the proper remedy was to seek permission to appeal the decision of the County Court in the first instance. It would only be in rare cases that judicial review would be permitted against the decision of the County Court to refuse permission to appeal (*Sivasubramaniam*). Examples of such rare cases would include where the lower court had fundamentally departed from the correct procedures, where it could be said that the judicial process itself had been frustrated or corrupted or where the lower court had acted in complete disregard of its duties (*Strickson v Preston County Court* [2007] EWCA Civ 1132, LTL 9/11/2007).

Following the creation of a single tribunal structure by the Tribunals, Courts and Enforcement Act 2007, it has been held by the Supreme Court that a decision of the Upper Tribunal is subject to judicial review only if there is an important point of practice or principle or some other compelling reason for the case to be reviewed (*R (Cart) v Upper Tribunal* [2011] UKSC 28, [2012] 1 AC 663). See also *R (NB (Algeria)) v Secretary of State for the Home Department* [2012] EWCA Civ 1050, [2013] 1 WLR 31. Any historical exceptions relating to judicial review of immigration and asylum decisions identified in *R (Sivasubramaniam) v Wandsworth County Court* [2002] EWCA Civ 1738, [2003] 1 WLR 475, cannot now apply to the centralised tribunal system (*R (Rana) v Upper Tribunal (Immigration and Asylum Chamber)* [2010] EWHC 3558 (Admin), LTL 20/1/2011).

The Senior Courts Act 1981, s. 29(3), enables the High Court to make prerogative orders against the Crown Court to the same extent as it may against an inferior court other than in relation to the Crown Court's jurisdiction in trial on indictment matters. Trial on indictment includes decisions as to sentence, such as confiscation and compensation orders, as they are an integral part of the trial process and therefore outside the scope of judicial review (*R (Faithfull) v Crown Court at Ipswich* [2007] EWHC 2763 (Admin), [2008] 1 WLR 1636).

Nationalised industries are also subject to judicial review. For example, the British Coal Corporation has been held to be reviewable in respect of its decision to close coal pits (*R v British Coal Corporation, ex parte Vardy* [1993] ICR 720).

It is possible for a statute to confer on a private body public functions and therefore, at least in relation to the performance of those functions, such a body could be subject to judicial review. Therefore professional bodies incorporated by royal charter or under the Companies Act 2006 may have statutory powers and duties conferred upon them, and be judicially reviewable in respect of the exercise of those powers and duties.

Non-statutory bodies

77.4   Non-statutory bodies which carry out public law functions will also be susceptible to judicial review. Bodies concerned with the regulation of commercial and professional activities to ensure compliance with proper standards, e.g. the Law Society and the Institute of Chartered Accountants, may be susceptible to judicial review whether or not their powers derive from statute or royal charter. Other self-regulating organisations and other private institutions may also perform some types of public function.

The Panel on Takeovers and Mergers was held in *R v Panel on Take-overs and Mergers, ex parte Datafin plc* [1987] QB 815 to be judicially reviewable despite the fact that it had no direct statutory authority. The Court of Appeal was influenced by the fact that the Panel 'oversees and regulates a very important part of the United Kingdom financial market' without any legal support. It considered that if the body in question exercised public law functions or the exercise of its functions had public law consequences, this would be sufficient to make it reviewable. The Panel clearly exercised public functions.

Following *R v Panel on Take-overs and Mergers, ex parte Datafin plc* the Advertising Standards Authority was found to be a public body upon the basis that, in the absence of a self-regulatory body such as the Authority, its function would be exercised by the Director General of Fair Trading (*R v Advertising Standards Authority, ex parte Insurance Service plc* (1990) 2 Admin LR 77). Similarly, although financial services self-regulating organisations lack statutory underpinning (but were contemplated by the Financial Services Act 1986), they have been found to be reviewable (*R v Life Assurance Unit Trust Regulatory Organisation Ltd, ex parte Ross* [1993] QB 17), as has the London Metal Exchange, which is a recognised investment exchange (*R v London Metal Exchange, ex parte Albatros Warehousing BV* (2000) LTL 31/3/2000).

However, the decisions of bodies set up by self-regulating organisations pursuant to regulatory powers are not also automatically reviewable. Bodies will not be reviewable where their source of authority is contractual or consensual, or if they do not exercise governmental powers (for example *R v Association of British Travel Agents, ex parte Sunspell Ltd* [2001] ACD 16) and this can be the case even though in relation to a particular industry or activity the person concerned effectively has no choice other than to sign up to a contract to be bound by a body's rules or regulations (for example *R v Panel of the Federation of Communication Services Ltd, ex parte Kubis* (1999) 11 Admin LR 43 concerning dealers in the mobile telephone industry).

The Insurance Ombudsman Bureau (a body recognised by LAUTRO as performing a complaints investigation function for the purposes of the Financial Services Act 1986 and with voluntary membership) has been held to possess power over its members which was solely derived from contract and was not therefore regarded as a public body (*R v Insurance Ombudsman Bureau, ex parte Aegon Life Assurance Ltd* [1994] COD 426).

Lloyd's, which has powers derived from a private Act (initially the Lloyd's Act 1871) and which does not extend to any persons other than those who wish to operate in the section of the market governed by Lloyd's and who have to commit themselves by entering into Lloyd's uniform contract, has been held not to be a public body for the purposes of judicial review (*R v Lloyd's of London, ex parte Johnson* (unreported, 16 August 1996)). However, certain of Lloyd's functions have been held to be public law functions and amenable to judicial review, although relations between Lloyd's and its names not involving the exercise of regulatory or disciplinary functions are governed by private law (*Doll-Steinberg v Society of Lloyd's* [2002] EWCA Civ 996).

The Court of Appeal has held it arguable that the Press Complaints Commission is a body subject to judicial review (*R v Press Complaints Commission, ex parte Stewart-Brady* (1997) 9 Admin LR 274).

Bodies exercising monopolistic powers may be reviewable. Reviewability was accepted by the Privy Council in the case of a bulk electricity supplier in New Zealand (*Mercury Energy Ltd v Electricity Corporation of New Zealand Ltd* [1994] 1 WLR 521).

A housing association, as a registered provider of social housing, is amenable to judicial review in respect of its functions in managing and allocating its housing stock (*R (Weaver) v London and Quadrant Housing Trust* [2009] EWCA Civ 587, [2010] 1 WLR 363 at [83]).

The courts have taken a restrictive approach in some instances. In *R v Chief Rabbi, ex parte Wachmann* [1992] 1 WLR 1036, Simon Brown J stated that, 'To attract the court's supervisory jurisdiction there must be not merely a public but potentially a governmental interest in the decision-making power in question'. Sports bodies not backed by statute are generally outside the scope of judicial review. In *R v Disciplinary Committee of the Jockey Club, ex parte Aga Khan* [1993] 1 WLR 909 the Court of Appeal required the existence of governmental and not simply 'public' functions and possibly actual (as opposed to potential) governmental intervention. Therefore the Jockey Club was held to fall outside the scope of the court's supervisory jurisdiction because it did not form part of a system of governmental control. The court was also influenced by the fact that the Club's source of power was contractual and that a private law remedy was available to the claimant (see 77.5; see also *R (Mullins) v Appeal Board of the Jockey Club* [2005] EWHC 2197 (Admin), [2006] ACD 2; and *R v Football Association Ltd, ex parte Football League Ltd* [1993] 2 All ER 833).

In some instances both public law and private law rights may be protected. For example, the Court of Appeal has accepted that for certain functions the Institute of Chartered Accountants is a public body and that its members might also have contractual rights against it (*Andreou v Institute of Chartered Accountants in England and Wales* [1998] 1 All ER 14).

Decisions of leaders of particular faiths on disciplinary issues have consistently been held not to be judicially reviewable (*R v Chief Rabbi, ex parte Wachmann*; *R v Imam of Bury Park Jame Masjid Luton, ex parte Sulaiman Ali* [1994] COD 142). However, the consistory courts of the Church of England have been deemed to be within the jurisdiction of the High Court because of their regulation by measures which have the effect of Acts of Parliament and therefore form part of the fabric of the State (*R v Chancellor of the Chichester Consistory Court, ex parte News Group Newspapers* [1992] COD 48). The position with the Provincial Court of the Church of Wales was held to be different in that, following its disestablishment under the Welsh Church Act 1914, its legal authority arises solely from consensual submission to its jurisdiction and it is therefore analogous to other religious bodies not established as part of the State (*R v Provincial Court of the Church in Wales, ex parte Williams*).

The university visitor, whose authority is based upon common law, is subject only to limited review. The House of Lords has held that the jurisdiction of a university visitor is reviewable only in circumstances where the university visitor acts outside his or her jurisdiction or if the university visitor abuses his or her power in a manner wholly incompatible with his or her judicial role or in breach of the rules of natural justice (*Page v Hull University Visitor* [1993] AC 682). Therefore only certain of the visitor's decisions are reviewable on the basis that he or she is in a unique position where it is highly desirable that there should be finality of decisions. This decision has been followed upon the same limited basis (*R v Visitors to the Inns of Court, ex parte Calder* [1994] QB 1). (See also *R (Varma) v Visitor to Cranfield University* [2004] EWHC 1705 (Admin), [2004] ELR 616.)

Decisions concerning pupils made by a non-maintained school for children with special educational needs were not amenable to judicial review even though the school received most of its funding from a local education authority (*R v Muntham House School, ex parte R* [2000] LGR 255).

On the other hand, a decision by managers of a private psychiatric hospital to change the focus of one of its wards is an act of a public nature susceptible to judicial review (*R (A) v Partnerships in Care Ltd* [2002] EWHC 529 (Admin), [2002] 1 WLR 2610).

A defendant private limited company, set up by a local authority to manage local farmers' markets, and having as directors stallholders of those markets, was a public body amenable to judicial review. The defendant owed its existence to the authority, which had set it up using its statutory powers, the defendant had effectively stepped into the authority's shoes and the authority had assisted the defendant in many respects (*R (Beer) v Hampshire Farmers Market Ltd* [2003] EWCA Civ 1056, [2004] 1 WLR 233).

A private company limited by guarantee, operating on a mutual basis, whose members were healthcare professionals who were afforded the right to request certain discretionary benefits, such as professional indemnity or insurance cover, in exchange for an annual fee, was not amenable to judicial review. Its relevant functions were not governmental, but rather those of an insurance company. The company was not woven into the fabric of public regulation just because it operated in the healthcare sphere or because there was a public interest in patients being indemnified against negligent treatment (*R (Moreton) v Medical Defence Union Ltd* [2006] EWHC 1948 (Admin), [2007] LS Law Medical 180). These examples demonstrate the fact-specific nature of the question of when a body is judicially reviewable.

DECISIONS OPEN TO JUDICIAL REVIEW

77.5 Primary legislation may be reviewed to determine its compatibility with European Union (EU) law. Where national law conflicts with any directly effective provision of EU law, the rule of national law must be set aside and EU law applied (*R v Secretary of State for Transport, ex parte Factortame Ltd (No. 2)* [1991] 1 AC 603). As to the reviewability of primary legislation for compatibility with the European Convention on Human Rights in the **Human Rights Act 1998, sch. 1**, see **chapter 91**.

Subordinate legislation which has been debated in and approved by affirmative resolution of both Houses of Parliament is susceptible to judicial review (*R (Asif Javed) v Secretary of State for the Home Department* [2001] EWCA Civ 789, [2002] QB 129).

The exercise of prerogative powers (i.e. non-statutory acts of executive government) may be amenable to judicial review (*R v Criminal Injuries Compensation Board, ex parte Lain* [1967] 2 QB 864). In *Council of Civil Service Unions v Minister for the Civil Service* [1985] AC 374 the House of Lords held that prerogative powers were reviewable, but Lord Roskill listed six examples of prerogative powers which he thought would not be reviewable, i.e. treaty making, defence of the realm, prerogative of mercy, grant of honours, dissolution of Parliament and the appointment of ministers. The prerogative of mercy has subsequently been held to be judicially reviewable (*R v Secretary of State for the Home Department, ex parte Bentley* [1994] QB 349). The prerogative power of colonial governance does not enjoy immunity from judicial review (*R (Bancoult) v Secretary of State for Foreign and Commonwealth Affairs (No. 2)* [2008] UKHL 61, [2009] 1 AC 453). The exclusion of existing treaties from the scope of judicial review has been confirmed given their non-binding status in domestic law which means they are unable to form the basis of a judicial review challenge (*R (Corner House Research) v Director of the Serious Fraud Office* [2008] UKHL 60, [2009] 1 AC 756). However, in *R (Wheeler) v Office of the Prime Minister* [2008] EWHC 1409 (Admin), [2008] ACD 70, the issue of political promises made in relation to the government entering into a treaty was within the scope of judicial review, although it was found that in the specific circumstances there had been no breach of legitimate expectation by the government's decision not to hold a referendum before entering into the Lisbon Treaty.

The High Court has reviewed the exercise of prerogative powers by the Crown in certain instances, including a decision of the Foreign Secretary to refuse to issue an applicant with a passport (*R v Secretary of State for Foreign and Commonwealth Affairs, ex parte Everett* [1989] QB 811) and the residual power of the Home Secretary to depart from immigration rules (*R v Secretary of State for the Home Department, ex parte Beedassee* [1989] COD 525). Judicial review would lie against a refusal of the Foreign Office to render diplomatic assistance to a British national in a foreign State but the expectation which an individual could legitimately hold of a response to a request for assistance would be limited (*R (Abbasi) v Secretary of State for Foreign and Commonwealth Affairs* [2002] EWCA Civ 1598, [2003] UKHRR 76).

The court will not adjudicate on the legality, validity or acceptability of the sovereign acts of a foreign State save in exceptional circumstances. In principle such exceptional circumstances might exist in cases where the acts were in breach of clearly established rules of international law, contrary to English principles of public policy or involved a grave infringement of human rights. However, as a matter of discretion the court will generally be reluctant to sit in judgment on the acts of a foreign sovereign State (*R (Noor Khan) v Secretary of State for Foreign and Commonwealth Affairs* [2014] EWCA Civ 24, [2014] 1 WLR 872). Where, however, a jurisdiction is a Crown dependency rather than a fully independent State in international law, such as the Channel Islands, the UK government has a responsibility to ensure compliance with international law and therefore the UK courts may judicially review decisions of the relevant authorities such as an Order in Council made on the advice of the UK government (*R (Barclay) v Lord Chancellor and Secretary of State for Justice (No. 2)* [2014] UKSC 54, [2015] AC 276).

Only decisions or actions which are made in a public law context are subject to judicial review. Even if a body may in some circumstances be susceptible to judicial review, not every decision will be reviewable. There must be a decision with a public law element sufficient to justify judicial review (*R v British Broadcasting Corporation, ex parte Lavelle* [1983] 1 WLR 23).

However, even where there is a private law cause of action, judicial review may still be appropriate where there is a sufficiently public issue. For example, judicial review was appropriate where the question was whether the Secretary of State had exceeded his powers in granting consent to a market authority to grant leases (*R (Corporation of London) v Secretary of State for the Environment, Food and Rural Affairs* [2004] EWCA Civ 1765, [2005] 1 WLR 1286, reversed on another point [2006] UKHL 30, [2006] 1 WLR 1721). Similarly, even though declarations can be granted in private law proceedings on the construction of private law contracts without the affected party being a party to the proceedings, where the dispute concerned the construction of a planning agreement under the Town and Country Planning Act 1990, s. 106, in reality the document was about the planning objectives of a planning authority, which were therefore public law matters which ought to be dealt with in judicial review proceedings with the local planning authority as a party (*Milebush Properties Ltd v Tameside Metropolitan Borough Council* [2011] EWCA Civ 270, [2011] PTSR 1654). The existence of a contractual relationship or a decision based upon the consent of the parties will always make it difficult to establish that the decision is amenable to judicial review (*R v Criminal Injuries Compensation Board, ex parte Lain* [1967] 2 QB 864; *R v National Joint Council for the Craft of Dental Technicians (Dispute Committee), ex parte Neate* [1953] 1 QB 704). However, it will not necessarily follow that every situation where the source of power is contractual is not amenable to judicial review. The overriding question will usually be the function being exercised, rather than the source of power. Where the function is set in the context of voluntary, contractual arrangements, that will be relevant to considering whether there is a sufficient public law element (*R (Holmcroft Properties Ltd) v KPMG LLP* [2016] EWHC 323 (Admin), [2016] ACD 67).

Thus ordinary employment cases are generally deemed to be governed by private law. Clearly cases relating purely to the construction of contractual terms and conditions of employment are not reviewable (*McClaren v Home Office* [1990] ICR 808). A disciplinary tribunal set up by the BBC in relation to the dismissal of an employee depended solely upon the contract of employment between the claimant and the BBC and was therefore a procedure of a merely private or domestic character and so not judicially reviewable (*R v British Broadcasting Corporation, ex parte Lavelle* [1983] 1 WLR 23). The terms of a senior nursing officer's employment have been regarded as a matter of private law notwithstanding that they incorporated the NHS Whitley Council agreement on conditions of service, a form of statutory negotiation between employers' and employees' representatives (*R v East Berkshire Health Authority, ex parte Walsh* [1985] QB 152). (See also *R (Tucker) v Director-General of the National Crime Squad* [2003] EWCA Civ 2, [2003] ICR 599; *Skidmore v Dartford and Gravesham NHS Trust* [2003] UKHL 27, [2003] ICR 721.)

However, public law issues may arise where an employer exercises a power which is not wholly contract-based. A decision to suspend a claimant in breach of a code of discipline which had statutory force was reviewable (*R v Secretary of State for the Home Department, ex parte Attard* (1990) 2 Admin LR 641). The employment conditions of police constables are underpinned by statute and accordingly reviewable (*Chief Constable of North Wales Police v Evans* [1982] 1 WLR 1155). A decision is reviewable if it involves a constitutional or public law principle such as the appointment of Crown prosecutors (*R v Crown Prosecution Service, ex parte Hogg* (1994) 6 Admin LR 778). Public law issues arise where the question is whether the public body had authority to enter into the contract, but not where the only issue is whether or not there is a breach by a public authority of its own internal procedures or standing orders (as was the case in *R v Lambeth London Borough Council, ex parte Thompson* [1996] COD 217). The Court of Appeal has left open the question whether a decision of the Civil Service Board that a claimant had not been unfairly dismissed from his position as a civil servant was reviewable on the basis that he had no contract of employment and there was a sufficient public law element involved (*R v Civil Service Appeal Board, ex parte Bruce* [1989] 2 All ER 907).

A body exercising a public function which makes a promise that it would behave in a certain way in the future is making a representation which has the character of a contract, but a breach of that promise may still be amenable to judicial review if the breach amounts to an abuse of power (*R v North and East Devon Health Authority, ex parte Coughlan* [2001] QB 213).

Public procurement exercises give rise to particular issues. The current position in considering the availability of judicial review in cases involving public procurement appears to be as follows:

(a) if it is shown that the tendering process is subject to mandatory statutory provisions then judicial review will be available;

(b) in order to establish whether the process is subject to statutory requirements, it is necessary to look at the wording, scheme and purpose of the relevant statute;

(c) in order to allege breach of the principles of natural justice in the tendering process, the claimant must be able to spell out the procedural requirements from the statute by express wording or necessary implication; and

(d) even if the tendering process is not carried out under a mandatory statutory provision, if there is a sufficient public law element to the decision it may still be reviewable (see *R v Bridgend County Borough Council, ex parte Jones* [2002] 2 LGLR 361 and *Cookson and Clegg Ltd v Ministry of Defence* [2005] EWCA Civ 811, [2006] Eu LR 1092).

A number of cases establish that public procurement procedures by public authorities can be the subject of judicial review proceedings, e.g. where a local authority boycotted products in order to pressurise companies to withdraw their interests in South Africa (*R v Lewisham London Borough Council, ex parte Shell UK Ltd* [1988] 1 All ER 938; and note *R v Derbyshire County Council, ex parte The Times Supplements Ltd* (1991) 3 Admin LR 241). A more restrictive approach was adopted in relation to tendering for shorthand writers' contracts (*R v Lord Chancellor's Department, ex parte Hibbit and Saunders* [1993] COD 326) and concerning tenders under part 2 of the Environmental Protection Act 1990 (*Mass Energy Ltd v Birmingham City Council* [1994] Env LR 298).

However, in *R v Legal Aid Board, ex parte Donn and Co.* [1996] 3 All ER 1 the court held that the decision of a Legal Aid Committee, in awarding a contract to solicitors for the conduct of a multi-party action, was justiciable in public law, first, because the nature and purpose of the selection process and its consequences were one indivisible whole and, secondly, in view of the function exercised by the Committee, the purpose for which the Committee was empowered to act, and the consequences of the decision-making process. Similarly, in *R (Bevan and Clarke LLP) v Neath Port Talbot County Borough Council* [2012] EWHC 236 (Admin), [2012] BLGR 728, a local authority decision on rates paid to private-sector operators of residential care homes was in principle amenable to judicial review, although the court should be cautious of providers wishing to improve their contractual negotiating position by recourse to public law principles and bear in mind the alternative remedial structure in competitive tendering for contracts with public authorities.

It has been held that breach of the Public Contracts Regulations 2006 (SI 2006/5, since replaced by the Public Contracts Regulations 2015 (SI 2015/102)) in relation to public procurement can give rise to public law as well as private law remedies where the claimant is affected by the departure in some way or where the departure is of such gravity that it justifies the public law remedy in any event (*R (Chandler) v Secretary of State for Children, Schools and Families* [2009] EWCA Civ 1011, [2010] PTSR 749). See also *R. (Unison) v NHS Wiltshire Primary Care Trust* [2012] EWHC 624 (Admin), [2012] ACD 84.

Procedural exclusivity

Where the invalidity of a decision arises as a collateral issue in a claim for infringement of **77.6** a private law right of the claimant, the issue should be resolved as a private law matter (per Lord Diplock in *O'Reilly v Mackman* [1983] 2 AC 237). Consequently, an action for damages against a local planning authority for negligence comprises a private law action (*Davy v Spelthorne Borough Council* [1984] AC 262); a reduction in a general practitioner's practice allowance by a family practitioner committee was a private law issue (*Roy v Kensington and Chelsea and Westminster Family Practitioner Committee* [1992] 1 AC 624); a claim in respect of inordinate delay in paying compensation for handguns surrendered under the Firearms (Amendment) Act 1997 was a private law matter (*Steed v Secretary of State for the Home Department* [2000] 1 WLR 1169); but an action against a local authority in respect of an alleged breach of its duties under the Housing (Homeless Persons) Act 1977 was a public law matter which should have proceeded by way of judicial review (*Cocks v Thanet District Council* [1983] 2 AC 286); a defendant was unable to challenge the validity of an enforcement notice under s. 87 of the Town and Country Planning Act 1971 on the basis that such matters should have been raised by way of judicial review and were not suitable for decision by a criminal court (*R v Wicks* [1998] AC 92); but, subject to clear Parliamentary intention to the contrary, the legality of a decision made pursuant to a by-law could be raised as a defence to a criminal charge (*Boddington v British Transport Police* [1999] 2 AC 143); and an ordinary action was held to be the more appropriate procedure to deal with an action against a local authority to recover sums due under improvement grants (*Trustees of the Dennis Rye Pension Fund v Sheffield City Council* [1998] 1 WLR 840). A defendant may raise a public law defence to private law proceedings where there has been an infringement of a pre-existing private law right (*Wandsworth London Borough Council v Winder* [1985] AC 461; *Wandsworth London Borough Council v A* [2000] 1 WLR 1246).

Although the courts will not strike out a private law claim simply on the grounds that it would have been more appropriate to use judicial review, they will do so if it amounts to an abuse of process. It is therefore important for a claimant to select the correct route of challenge. In deciding whether using a private law claim for a public law issue amounts to an abuse of process the court will consider whether the private law route has been used to take advantage of a longer limitation period, in view of the short time limits for judicial review claims (see 77.36), or whether other judicial review rules have been flouted (*Clark v University of Lincolnshire and Humberside* [2000] 1 WLR 1988). It has been held that where a litigant has a claim which could be brought either by judicial review or by an ordinary action the choice of either might amount to an abuse of process. The exercise of the jurisdiction to strike out the claim on this ground would depend on a consideration of all the relevant circumstances, including any matters occurring before the proceedings were instituted and which remedy would be more appropriate (*Phonographic Performance Ltd v Department of Trade and Industry* [2004] EWHC 1795 (Ch), [2004] 1 WLR 2893; see also *Jones v Powys Local Health Board* [2008] EWHC 2562 (Admin), [2009] 12 CCL Rep 68). For example, proceedings commenced by a landowner seeking declarations in respect of a breach of condition notice in the planning context should have been brought by judicial review since service of a breach of condition notice was a purely public law act, and therefore could not be challenged by private law proceedings (*Trim v North Dorset District Council* [2010] EWCA Civ 1446, [2011] 1 WLR 1901).

The practical consequences of the choice made between public and private law should be considered rather than merely technical questions concerning the distinction between public and private rights (*Trustees of the Dennis Rye Pension Fund v Sheffield City Council*). A similar approach has been taken where the factual circumstances of cases are such that they may fall into both public law and private law (*Andreou v Institute of Chartered Accountants in England and Wales* [1998] 1 All ER 14 — a finding of the Disciplinary Committee of the Institute of Chartered Accountants).

GROUNDS OF JUDICIAL REVIEW

77.7   Judicial review is not an appeal mechanism, but a review of public law functions (*R v Richmond upon Thames London Borough Council, ex parte JC* (2000) *The Times*, 26 April 2000 (QBD); [2001] LGR 146 (CA)). There are a number of classifications of the grounds upon which a decision by a public authority may be found to be invalid. A commonly used classification is the tripartite distinction in *Council of Civil Service Unions v Minister for the Civil Service* [1985] AC 374 between:

(a) illegality,
(b) irrationality, and
(c) procedural impropriety.

This classification is not set in stone. Within each of the three heads are a number of grounds which are capable of being characterised in more than one way. In addition, many factual situations can be analysed in more than one way. For example, where a statute lays down a procedure with which a public authority needs to comply, a failure to follow the wording of the statute could fall under both the illegality head (see **77.8** to **77.11**) and the procedural impropriety head (see **77.22** to **77.29**).

Illegality

77.8   Illegality arises where a decision-maker who must understand correctly the law that regulates his or her decision-making power and must give effect to it fails to do so (Lord Diplock in *Council of Civil Service Unions v Minister for the Civil Service* [1985] AC 374). Illegality also includes acts done beyond the powers of the person or body performing or authorising the act ('*ultra vires*'). It also includes an act performed or authorised in error as to what the law authorising the person or body permits that person or body to do. An error in relation to a precedent (jurisdictional) fact is also often placed under the illegality heading. An action or decision is said to be tainted by illegality if:

(a) it was purportedly taken under legislation which does not contain the requisite power; or
(b) it was purportedly taken under legislation which contains precise limits on the circumstances in which a power or duty can be used, and the action or decision in question either exceeds these limits or fails to perform the power or duty in a proper way.

'Illegal' could also be used to describe a statutory instrument which conflicts with primary legislation, or an Act of Parliament which is incompatible with EU law. Where a particular area falls within the scope of EU law then legislation may be challenged on principles of EU law, such as the principle of effectiveness (*R (Unison) v Lord Chancellor* [2015] EWCA Civ 935, [2016] ICR 1).

One particular aspect of illegality is an allegation of a breach of Convention rights under the **Human Rights Act 1998** (see **chapter 91**). Similarly, where a public body fails to comply with the public sector equality duty imposed by the Equality Act 2010, s. 149, its decision will be susceptible to review. However, this duty is not to be treated as a tick box exercise; the court should ask whether as a matter of substance there has been compliance (*R (Greenwich Community Law Centre) v Greenwich London Borough Council* [2012] EWCA Civ 496, [2012] Eq LR 572).

Ultra vires **acts**   Whether or not a decision is *ultra vires* depends upon the relevant primary   **77.9**
or secondary legislation and its interpretation on the particular facts and circumstances of each case. Therefore few general rules can be laid down. The permitting legislation should be considered in order to establish what the body exercising the public function is entitled to do and what limits there are on the steps that may be taken in performance of the function. Where the relevant body either exceeds the stipulated function or purports to perform the function in a manner not permitted by the legislation, its powers will have been exceeded and the decision will therefore be open to review.

Errors of law   An alternative way of analysing illegality is as an error of law. This is where a   **77.10**
public body makes a decision based upon an incorrect interpretation of the law. For example, the House of Lords has held that the defendant borough council misinterpreted s. 4(2)(b) of the Housing (Homeless Persons) Act 1977 in holding that the immigrant claimant became 'intentionally homeless' by bringing his homeless family to the United Kingdom to live with him (*Re Islam (Tafazzul)* [1983] 1 AC 688).

Precedent (jurisdictional) fact/error of fact   Although error of fact has not historically been   **77.11**
regarded as a ground for judicial review (*R v Hillingdon London Borough Council, ex parte Puhlhofer* [1986] AC 484), the courts will review instances where the public body has failed to establish a vital fact which triggers its power and makes the exercise of its powers lawful, e.g. the requirement to establish that a person is an 'illegal entrant' before the power of deportation can lawfully arise under the Immigration Act 1971 (*Khera v Secretary of State for the Home Department* [1984] AC 74). Factual aspects of a decision may be reviewed in some limited circumstances (see per Lords Slynn of Hadley, Nolan and Clyde in *R (Alconbury Developments Ltd) v Secretary of State for the Environment, Transport and the Regions* [2001] UKHL 23, [2003] 2 AC 295).

For there to be a sufficient mistake of fact giving rise to unfairness the following criteria need to be fulfilled:

(a) there must be a mistake as to an existing fact, including mistake as to the availability of evidence;

(b) the fact or evidence must now be uncontentious and objectively verifiable;

(c) the claimant or his advisers must not have been responsible for the mistake of fact; and

(d) the mistake must have played a material (but not necessarily decisive) part in the Tribunal's reasoning (*E v Secretary of State for the Home Department* [2004] EWCA Civ 49, [2004] QB 1044). (See also *R (Ross) v West Sussex Primary Care Trust* [2008] EWHC 2252 (Admin), [2008] 11 CCL Rep 787; *Connolly v Secretary of State for Communities and Local Government* [2009] EWCA Civ 1059, [2009] NPC 114; and *R (March) v Secretary of State for Health* [2010] EWHC 765 (Admin), [2010] Med LR 271.)

There is a distinction to be made between cases where an appeal court is satisfied, on new evidence, that a minister or inferior body or tribunal took a decision on the basis of a belief as to the existence of a material fact that has now been demonstrated to be plainly wrong, and cases where it took its decision in the mistaken belief that there was in fact no apparently cogent evidence to refute a material finding it had made (see *Shabana Shaheen v Secretary of State for the Home Department* [2005] EWCA Civ 1294, [2006] Imm AR 57, where, on the facts, the Court of Appeal held that the Immigration Appeal Tribunal had not made an error of law).

Commentary

Irrationality

77.12   A decision may be tainted by irrationality where the decision-making body allegedly:

(a) acted for an improper purpose;

(b) acted with bad faith;

(c) fettered its discretion;

(d) improperly delegated its functions;

(e) reached a conclusion that no body properly directing itself on the relevant law and acting reasonably could have reached;

(f) failed to take into account relevant matters or took into account irrelevant matters;

(g) abused its powers or infringed a legitimate expectation; or, possibly,

(h) acted in a disproportionate manner; or

(i) did not act consistently.

The **Human Rights Act 1998** may also provide a backdrop to claims based upon the ground of irrationality. When scrutinising an executive decision which interferes with human rights, the court will ask, applying an objective test, whether the decision-maker could reasonably have concluded that the interference was necessary to achieve one or more of the legitimate aims recognised by the Convention (*R (Mahmood) v Secretary of State for the Home Department* [2001] 1 WLR 840). The proportionality of any interference will now be an issue in any review by the courts of the decision of a public authority (*R (Daly) v Secretary of State for the Home Department* [2001] 2 AC 532) in a case raising the **Human Rights Act 1998**.

77.13   **Improper purpose**   In cases where a power granted to a public body for one purpose is exercised by it for a different purpose, that power is deemed not to have been validly exercised, e.g. where a local authority decided to avoid the products of a company in order to put pressure upon its parent companies to withdraw their interests from South Africa (*R v Lewisham London Borough Council, ex parte Shell UK Ltd* [1988] 1 All ER 938); or where a transaction by a local council was for the improper purpose of circumventing its restrictions on borrowing and spending (*Crédit Suisse v Allerdale Borough Council* [1997] QB 306).

Generally the interpretation by the courts of the purpose of a statutory provision involves a search for the 'natural and ordinary meaning' of the word or term. Although reference may be made to Parliamentary records to aid the construction of legislation which is ambiguous or obscure (*Pepper v Hart* [1993] AC 593) this principle is not applicable in relation to the determination of the general purpose of a statutory scheme, but only to resolve ambiguity in a statutory provision. Where the statutory purpose is clearly ascertainable, there must be a rational connection between that purpose and the practical effect of the legislation in question, otherwise the measure may be unlawful for incompatibility with the statutory purpose (*R (Ben Hoare Bell Solicitors) v Lord Chancellor* [2015] EWHC 523 (Admin), [2015] 1 WLR 4175).

77.14   **Bad faith**   A decision is made in bad faith if it has been affected by motives such as fraud, malice, or personal self-interest. A power is deemed to have been exercised fraudulently where the decision-maker had an intention to achieve an object other than that which it claimed to be seeking, e.g. the promotion of another public or private interest. A power is regarded as exercised maliciously if an action or decision is motivated by a personal animosity towards those who are directly affected by its exercise, e.g. the decision by a county council to cease advertising in journals controlled by Times Newspapers (which had written an article criticising a councillor) was explicitly held to be motivated by bad faith and declared invalid (*R v Derbyshire County Council, ex parte The Times Supplements Ltd* (1991) 3 Admin LR 241).

77.15   **Fettering of discretion**   Where a public body maintains a rigid policy with no exceptions it thereby fetters its discretion. Although a public authority can have a policy, it must consider particular cases rather than fetter its discretion by always following its stated policy blindly. Thus, for example, a rule of the Board of Trade which excluded grants for items costing less than £25 each was only permissible provided that the Board was always willing to listen to anyone with something new to say (*British Oxygen Co. Ltd v Board of Trade* [1971] AC 610); a policy formulated on the premises that amusement arcades would be harmful to young persons was unlawful (*Sagnata Investments Ltd v Norwich Corporation* [1971] 2 QB 614); a policy to restrict access to a solicitor by a person remanded in custody was unlawful (*R v Chief Constable of South Wales, ex parte Merrick* [1994] 1 WLR 663); the policy of a licensing committee which provided that an applicant for a betting office licence must have a legal interest in the premises was unlawful (*R v Forest Betting Licensing Committee, ex parte Noquet* (1988) *The Times*, 21 June 1988).

The courts may be prepared to scrutinise closely the conduct of a decision-maker in assessing whether or not he or she has unlawfully fettered his or her discretion, e.g. a course of conduct involving the consistent rejection of applications belonging to a particular class may justify an inference that the public body has adopted a policy to refuse them all. However, it is unlikely that the courts will deem a decision-maker to have fettered his or her discretion in circumstances where he or she afforded those individuals affected the ability to make representations, e.g. decisions of local authorities in relation to the disposition of planning appeals or proposals for the compulsory acquisition of land have been upheld in circumstances where the decision was made after a public inquiry (*Franklin v Minister of Town and Country Planning* [1948] AC 87; *Stringer v Minister of Housing and Local Government* [1970] 1 WLR 1281).

Improper delegation   In general a public law function must be exercised only by the body to whom it has been given. When a power is provided to a person in circumstances indicating that trust is being placed in his or her individual judgment and discretion, that person must exercise that power personally unless he or she has been expressly empowered to delegate it to another. Public bodies which exercise functions analogous to the judiciary are precluded from delegating their powers of decision unless there is express authority to that effect (*General Council of Medical Education and Registration of the United Kingdom v Dental Board of the United Kingdom* [1936] Ch 41).

77.16

Where an authority vested with discretionary powers affecting private rights then empowers one of its committees, members or officers to exercise those powers independently without any supervisory control, the exercise of those powers is likely to be held invalid. Thus, for example, a delegation by the Director of Public Prosecutions to non-qualified lawyers of the power to review prosecutions in order to decide whether there was sufficient evidence to proceed was held to be unlawful because the statute giving the power to the Director clearly contemplated that it would only be delegated to a member of the Crown Prosecution Service who was a lawyer (*R v Director of Public Prosecutions, ex parte Association of First Division Civil Servants* (1988) *The Times*, 24 May 1988).

However, in the case of local authorities, s. 101 of the Local Government Act 1972 expressly permits some delegation. The degree of control maintained by the delegating authority is an important factor in determining the validity of the delegation. The control must be close enough for the decision to be identified as that of the delegating authority (*Hall v Manchester Corporation* (1915) 84 LJ Ch 732). Clearly it is improper for an authority to delegate wide discretionary powers to another authority over which it is incapable of exercising direct control, unless it is expressly permitted so to delegate. Also relevant to the proper delegation of powers are the nature of the power and the impact of its exercise upon individual interests.

The courts have recognised that duties imposed upon and powers granted to government ministers are normally exercised under the authority of ministers by responsible officials of the department (*Carltona Ltd v Commissioners of Works* [1943] 2 All ER 560). Thus, decisions taken in this manner will not have involved an impermissible delegation. This principle has been applied to the Benefits Agency, which was held to be part of the Department of Social Security, and the Agency staff therefore were regarded as part of the Civil Service (*R v Secretary of State for the Home Department, ex parte Sherwin* (1996) 32 BMLR 1). There may, however, be matters of such importance that the minister is legally required to address them personally. The presumption in relation to ministers may be expressly excluded by legislation (e.g. as in the Immigration Act 1971).

77.17   *Wednesbury* unreasonableness   Lord Greene MR stated in *Associated Provincial Picture Houses Ltd v Wednesbury Corporation* [1948] 1 KB 223:

> it may be still possible to say that, although the local authority have kept within the four corners of the matters which they ought to consider, they have nevertheless come to a conclusion so unreasonable that no reasonable authority could ever have come to it.

In order to prove '*Wednesbury* unreasonableness' something overwhelming must be proved but this test has been fulfilled in a number of cases, e.g. a local authority resolution to ban a rugby club from its property for not putting pressure upon three of its players not to participate in a tour of South Africa (*Wheeler v Leicester City Council* [1985] AC 1054); a justices' clerk's refusal to supply duplicate legal aid orders (*R v Liverpool Justices, ex parte R. M. Broudie and Co.* (1994) 7 Admin LR 242); and the Lottery Commission's refusal to allow a bidder one month to allay its concerns about the bid (*R v National Lottery Commission, ex parte Camelot Group plc* [2001] EMLR 3).

77.18   **Failure to take account of relevant considerations**   A further limb of the ground of irrationality comprises failure to take account of relevant considerations or the taking into account of an irrelevant consideration. For example, the court held that a borough council took into account irrelevant (philanthropic) considerations in deciding to overpay its staff, and also failed to take into account relevant considerations of comparable wages and the costs of living (*Roberts v Hopwood* [1925] AC 578).

Guidance or circulars may also be material considerations that should be taken into account when making decisions on how to implement legislation, although they cannot override legislation. Failure to take such guidance contained in circulars into account was an error of law amenable to judicial review and also breached the claimant's legitimate expectation that such guidance would be taken into account (*R (Jeeves) v Gravesham Borough Council* [2006] EWHC 1249 (Admin), [2007] 1 P & CR 15).

A statute may expressly or impliedly make clear considerations to which regard must or must not be had. There may also be considerations to which the decision-maker may have regard in the exercise of his discretion subject to normal public law principles (*CREEDNZ Inc. v Governor-General* [1981] 1 NZLR 172).

A failure to assess the evidence properly, resulting in a decision which appears to be unsupported by the evidence, can also be characterised as a failure to take account of relevant considerations. This may arise where the court is unable to identify the evidence to support a decision, in which event the decision will be flawed in law (*AJ (Liberia) v Secretary of State for the Home Department* [2006] EWCA Civ 1736, LTL 15/12/2006).

It is not necessary to prove that the influence of irrelevant factors was the chief or main influence upon the decision made or action taken. As a general rule it is enough to prove that the influence was material or substantial (*R v Inner London Education Authority, ex parte Westminster City Council* [1986] 1 WLR 28). Where a decision-maker leaves out of account some relevant matter, the key question is whether that factor might realistically have caused the decision-maker to reach a different conclusion (*W v Special Educational Needs Tribunal* (2000) *The Times*, 12 December 2000). If the challenge is based upon a claim that relevant considerations were not taken into account, the courts will therefore normally try to assess the actual or potential importance of the factor that was overlooked, even though this may involve a degree of speculation.

Examples of decisions challenged under this ground include the unlawful expenditure of public funds by a board of guardians in cancelling a series of loans to miners without taking into

Civ 744, [2005] Imm AR 608, there has been some doubt cast on the development of the law in this area. Abuse of power should not be seen as a magic ingredient able to achieve remedial results which other forms of illegality cannot match. It is not a special and more extreme category of illegality, but rather a general concept underlying other particular forms. However, in extreme cases it is accepted that a court could hold that unfairness is so obvious and the remedy so plain that there is only one way in which the Secretary of State could reasonably exercise his discretion (R (S) v Secretary of State for the Home Department [2007] EWCA Civ 546, [2007] ACD 94).

The public law concepts of legitimate expectation and abuse of power, rather than the private law concept of estoppel, have been held to be relevant to planning law. Situations could therefore arise in the planning field where it would be a breach of legitimate expectation and therefore an abuse of power for a public body to act in a particular way (R (Reprotech (Pebsham) Ltd) v East Sussex County Council [2002] UKHL 8, [2003] 1 WLR 348) but such situations will be rare (Henry Boot Homes Ltd v Bassetlaw District Council [2002] EWCA Civ 983, [2003] 1 P & CR 23).

The doctrine of estoppel can offer no more protection than the principle of legitimate expectation (R (Capital Care Services (UK) Ltd) v Secretary of State for the Home Department [2012] EWCA Civ 1151, LTL 24/7/2012). However, cause of action estoppel, rather than the public law concept of legitimate expectation, will still be relevant in the context of enforcement notice appeals (R (East Hertfordshire District Council) v First Secretary of State [2007] EWHC 834 (Admin), [2007] JPL 1304).

Proportionality   Proportionality is a concept central both to EU law and to the European   **77.20**
Convention on Human Rights and means that remedies or measures should be proportionate to the legitimate aim that is sought to be achieved or the state of affairs they are intended to redress, and thus the administrative process should be in proportion to the outcome of the process (see **91.13**). The conventional view is that proportionality is simply a facet of irrationality/Wednesbury unreasonableness (see **77.17**) and there is no separate ground of proportionality within the domestic context (R v Secretary of State for the Home Department, ex parte Brind [1991] 1 AC 696). However, it is clear that the tests of proportionality and Wednesbury unreasonableness do not always yield the same results but are moving closer together (R (Association of British Civilian Internees: Far East Region) v Secretary of State for Defence [2003] EWCA Civ 473, [2003] QB 1397). Although there is an overlap between the traditional grounds of judicial review and the approach of proportionality, the intensity of review is greater under the proportionality approach (R (Daly) v Secretary of State for the Home Department [2001] UKHL 26, [2001] 2 AC 532). Proportionality has been raised in the context of personal liberty (R v Secretary of State for the Home Department, ex parte Pegg [1995] COD 84) and has also been applied where a sentencing decision is susceptible to judicial review (R v Highbury Corner Justices, ex parte Uchendu (1994) 158 JP 409).

The failure of a decision-maker expressly to refer to proportionality in a decision does not necessarily render the decision liable to be quashed. Where a decision-maker has taken account of all material considerations, there is no 'straitjacket' imposed requiring the presence of the word in the final decision (Lough v First Secretary of State [2004] EWCA Civ 905, [2004] 1 WLR 2557).

Administrative consistency   There is a general principle, as one aspect of irrationality as a   **77.21**
ground for review, that like cases should be treated alike (but clearly where cases are not alike this may justify differential treatment).

Where the Agricultural Wages Board established a new category of worker whose minimum wage was lower than that of a standard worker, but excluded mushroom harvesters from those who could be paid this rate, this exclusion was found to infringe the principle of public administration that all persons in a similar situation should be treated similarly (R (Middlebrook Mushrooms Ltd) v Agricultural Wages Board of England and Wales [2004] EWHC 1447 (Admin), The Times, 15 July 2004).

Commentary

Similarly, where a policy which applied to Iraqi Kurds was not applied to a claimant who could show a direct comparison with two other Iraqi Kurds who were in precisely the same position as the claimant, and who had both been granted refugee status under this policy, the court found that the application of unequal treatment to refugees in a like position was so unfair as to amount to a misuse of governmental power (*R (Rashid) v Secretary of State for the Home Department* [2005] EWCA Civ 744, [2005] Imm AR 608). The principle of consistency also required that categorisation of prisoners should not depend on subjective differing professional judgments of various prison governors in different prisons, but should be dealt with on a consistent basis (*R (Lowe) v Governor of Liverpool Prison* [2008] EWHC 2167 (Admin), [2009] Prison LR 197). However, where one party's subsidy was lower than competitors' because it was based on information that was more up to date and accurate than the older figures used to calculated competitors' subsidies, it was simply 'bad luck' for the particular company because to have allowed that company to benefit from an increased subsidy based on out-of-date information would have resulted in an unjustified windfall and would not have been in the public interest (*Tate and Lyle Sugars Ltd v Secretary of State for Energy and Climate Change* [2011] EWCA Civ 664, [2011] ACD 92).

Procedural impropriety

77.22   Procedural impropriety is concerned with the procedure by which a decision is reached, not the ultimate outcome. In order to prove procedural impropriety the claimant must show that the decision was reached in an unfair manner. If there is no statutory framework which expressly stipulates the relevant procedural requirements, there are two applicable common law rules under this head, namely:

(a) the rule against bias, which requires the public body to be impartial and to be seen to be so; and

(b) the right to a fair hearing whereby those affected by a decision of a public body are entitled to know what the case is against them and to have a proper opportunity to put their case forward.

Infringement of express procedural rules

77.23   A decision made or action taken by a public body should not infringe express procedural rules outlined in primary or secondary legislation, e.g. a notice of school closure was quashed where there was a failure to consult under s. 184 of the Education Act 1993 and a government circular (*R v Lambeth London Borough Council, ex parte N* [1996] ELR 299); procedural codes are laid out in the town and country planning legislation which set out the procedure for an appeal or a full structured inquiry. Courts may be called upon to adjudicate upon the extent to which the statutory procedure is fulfilled. The courts will also supplement an express statutory scheme to ensure that the minimum common law standards of procedural fairness are met (see for instance *Bank Mellat v HM Treasury (No. 2)* [2013] UKSC 38, [2014] AC 700).

Implied procedural rules

77.24   The requirement to comply with express procedural rules is supported by the common law obligation to provide a fair hearing. The rules of natural justice embody a duty to act fairly. Whenever a public function is performed there is an inference, in the absence of an express requirement to the contrary, that the function is required to be performed fairly. This is more compelling in the case of any decision which may adversely affect a person's rights or interests (e.g. *R v Liverpool Corporation, ex parte Liverpool Taxi Fleet Operators' Association* [1972] 2 QB 299) but will not apply to situations which are too remote to qualify for a fair hearing.

The two fundamental common law rules set out in 77.22 also apply where there is no statutory procedural code.

Bias

In cases where the decision-maker has a direct personal or proprietary interest in the outcome **77.25**
of a matter, he or she should always be disqualified from adjudicating upon the issue. However,
when the interest is indirect, the courts generally apply the following test. First, the court
should ascertain all the circumstances which have a bearing on the suggestion that the tribunal
is biased. Secondly, it should ask whether those circumstances would lead a fair-minded and
informed observer to conclude that there is a real possibility that the tribunal is biased (*Porter
v Magill* [2001] UKHL 67, [2002] 2 AC 357; see also **91.48**). See also *Bolkiah v Brunei Darussalam*
[2007] UKPC 62, LTL 9/11/2007.

The House of Lords has held a judge in the House of Lords involved with Amnesty
International to be automatically disqualified because his participation in a case where
Amnesty was an intervener offended the fundamental principle that a man may not be a judge
in his own cause. Although this principle normally applies only in cases where the judge has a
pecuniary interest, the court confirmed that it could and did extend to cases where the judge
has a non-pecuniary interest (sufficient to amount to an interest in the outcome of the pro-
ceedings) in one of the parties thereto (*R v Bow Street Metropolitan Stipendiary Magistrate, ex parte
Pinochet Ugarte (No. 2)* [2000] 1 AC 119, subsequently applied in *Locabail (UK) Ltd v Bayfield Properties
Ltd* [2000] QB 451 and *East Northamptonshire District Council v Secretary of State for Communities and
Local Government* [2012] EWHC 4377 (Admin), (2012) 156 (47) SJLB 31).

Even where a judge has made findings adverse to a party in the substantive hearing, it is only
in exceptional circumstances that he will be required to recuse himself from dealing with the
consequential issues as to costs. In *Mengiste v Endowment Fund for the Rehabilitation of Tigray*
[2013] EWCA Civ 1003, [2014] CP Rep 5, it was held that such exceptional circumstances existed
during a wasted costs application because the judge made findings in the substantive hearing
which were only relevant to costs, expressed his criticism in absolute terms with no possibility
of the appellant solicitors explaining themselves, and made extreme and unbalanced criticisms. These factors amounted to apparent bias, requiring the judge to recuse himself.

In considering the question of apparent bias it is necessary to look beyond pecuniary or personal interests and to consider in addition whether, from the point of view of the fair-minded
and informed observer, there is a real possibility that the decision-maker is biased in the sense
of approaching the decision with a closed mind and without impartial consideration of all
relevant issues (*Georgiou v Enfield London Borough Council* [2004] EWHC 779 (Admin), [2004] LGR
497). The two concepts of automatic disqualification and apparent bias can also be analysed as
two strands of a single overarching requirement that judges or tribunal members should not sit
or should face disqualification where there is a real possibility, assessed by a fair-minded and
informed observer, that the tribunal objectively appears to be or could be biased. Taking this
approach it could be said that the automatic disqualification test deals with cases where the
personal interests of the judge concerned can be deemed to constitute apparent bias. It is not
always necessary therefore to choose between the two doctrines in the analysis of the case (*R
(Darsho Kaur) v Institute of Legal Executives Appeal Tribunal* [2011] EWCA Civ 1168, [2012] 1 All ER 1435).

In relation to the apparent bias of advisers to decision-making bodies, the correct question is
whether the observer, knowing the composition and remit of both the advisory body and the
deciding body, would perceive a real possibility both of bias in the advice and of its infecting
the decision (*R (Royal Brompton and Harefield NHS Foundation Trust) v Joint Committee of Primary Care
Trusts* [2012] EWCA Civ 472, (2012) 126 BMLR 134).

The question of independence should be tested by reference to the fair-minded and informed
observer's knowledge of all the information which could have been ascertained by a fair-minded
outside observer (*Re P (A Barrister)* [2005] 1 WLR 3019). The fair-minded observer would not
reach a conclusion without seeking to obtain the full facts (*Virdi v Law Society* [2010] EWCA Civ
100, [2010] 1 WLR 2840). However, the information to be attributed to the fair-minded and

informed observer includes that which would be apparent to the court upon investigation and is not restricted to that available to a hypothetical observer at an original hearing (*National Assembly for Wales v Condron* [2006] EWCA Civ 1573, [2006] NPC 127). The attributes of the fair-minded and informed observer include reserving judgment until she has seen and fully understood both sides of an argument, taking the trouble to inform herself on all relevant matters, taking a balanced approach to any information she is given, being able to put material into social, political or geographical context, knowing that judges like anyone else have their weaknesses but knowing that fairness requires judges to be, and be seen to be, unbiased (*Helow v Secretary of State for the Home Department* [2008] UKHL 62, [2008] 1 WLR 2416, subsequently applied in *Competition Commission v BAA Ltd* [2010] EWCA Civ 1097, [2011] UKCLR 1).

A public body should not allow decisions to be made by people who have a financial interest in the decision or a family/business connection with any party. However, it has been held that no bias arose in the case of a grant of planning permission to develop a rugby club's land where it was subsequently discovered that the club had an interest in acquiring land belonging to the chairman of the planning authority (*R v Secretary of State for the Environment, ex parte Kirkstall Valley Campaign Ltd* [1996] 3 All ER 304), nor where a planning officer had to consider various development proposals, including one put forward by her husband's company, since her decision was actually adverse to that company (*R (Persimmon Homes Ltd) v Vale of Glamorgan Council* [2010] EWHC 535 (Admin), LTL 22/3/2010). Bias may also arise because of a personal business relationship between the adjudicator and one of the parties, or because of partisanship by the adjudicator in relation to the issues to be resolved. Where a decision-maker takes part in the determination of an appeal against one of his or her own decisions (unless he or she is expressly authorised to do so by statute) it will be tainted by apparent bias, e.g. a clerk to a statutory tribunal could not act as clerk to the appeal tribunal hearing the appeal against that decision (*R v Salford Assessment Committee, ex parte Ogden* [1937] 2 KB 1). See also *R (Al-Hasan) v Secretary of State for the Home Department* [2005] UKHL 13, [2005] 1 WLR 688.

However, membership of the freemasons should not prevent a member of local government from making decisions whenever another freemason had an interest in the outcome of the decision, based on the true nature of freemasonry whereby freemasons were required to obey the law and were not required to be partial to any other freemason. A fair-minded observer informed of the facts in connection with freemasonry which had been placed before the court would not have concluded that there was a real possibility of bias in these circumstances (*R (Port Regis School Ltd) v North Dorset District Council* [2006] EWHC 742 (Admin), [2006] LGR 696). In appointing members to the Northern Ireland Parades Commission it was important to ensure that the Commission would be accepted as independent, objective and impartial in its approach. Therefore the appointment of two loyalists who were prominent and outspoken in their views was unlawful (*Re Duffy* [2008] UKHL 4, [2008] NI 152).

It is acceptable for decision-makers not acting in a judicial or quasi-judicial capacity to come to a decision with their own views, as long as there is no predetermination, they are open to new arguments right up to the moment of the decision, and make that decision based on the merits of the particular situation. In the planning context, therefore, a planning permission was not rendered unlawful simply because the planning committee members were all of a single political group and had previously expressed views on planning issues, as there was little evidence to suggest that they were any more politically motivated than would normally be expected from elected policy makers (*R (Lewis) v Redcar and Cleveland Borough Council* [2008] EWCA Civ 746, [2009] 1 WLR 83).

Local authority councillors were entitled to have regard to and apply policies that they had voiced support for in local elections and which had formed part of their manifesto, such as planning or land disposal policies. The court could not interfere in the political process in this way. Evidence of proper observations or apparent favouring of a particular decision was not enough for the court to quash a decision: there would need to be positive evidence that the local authority had approached the decision with a closed mind (*R (Island Farm Development Ltd) v Bridgend County Borough Council* [2006] EWHC 2189 (Admin), [2006] NPC 100).

It is important to distinguish between the concepts of predetermination, i.e. approaching a matter with a closed mind, and appearance of bias. Bias is concerned with appearances whereas predetermination concerns what in fact happened. The test of apparent bias relating to predetermination is a difficult one to satisfy (*R (Persimmon Homes Ltd) v Vale of Glamorgan Council* [2010] EWHC 535 (Admin), LTL 22/3/2010). However, where an interim inquiry report contained such strongly worded allegations that a fair-minded observer would conclude that the author had already made up his mind and would not be approaching the remainder of the inquiry with an open mind, that was held to amount to apparent bias (*Mitchell v Georges* [2014] UKPC 43, LTL 2/1/2015).

There is no absolute rule that knowledge of prejudicial publicity (such as knowledge of previous convictions) is fatal to the fairness and impartiality of the proceedings (*R (Mahfouz) v Professional Conduct Committee of the General Medical Council* [2004] EWCA Civ 233, [2004] Lloyd's Rep Med 389). Bias or apparent bias is not to be equated with knowledge of inadmissible and potentially prejudicial information. However, the effect of this knowledge has to be considered in the context of the proceedings as a whole, including the likely impact of the oral evidence and the legal advice available. Where the tribunal was made up of experienced and sophisticated members it could be assumed they would understand the proper approach and the need to disregard irrelevant material. Similarly, where members of an administrative decision-making board looking into alleged financial irregularities were appointed by a government minister who had made public comments about the irregularities, there was no reason to think that the appointees, as professional men who had sworn an oath to perform their functions conscientiously, would not do so. There was therefore no appearance of bias (*Belize Bank Ltd v Attorney General of Belize* [2011] UKPC 36, LTL 20/10/2011).

A party may waive its objections to a decision-maker who may otherwise have been disqualified on the ground of bias (*R (Giant's Causeway etc. Tramway Co.) v Antrim Justices* [1895] 2 IR 603). Any objection may be deemed to have been waived if the party or its legal representative knew of the disqualification and agreed to take part in the proceedings by failing to raise an objection at the earliest opportunity. For example, a claimant waived his right to complain that a decision not to grant him British citizenship was, or appeared to have been, prejudged following a newspaper article reporting that the decision-maker would not grant the application, because he had not objected to that decision-maker continuing to deal with the application and making the decision (*R v Secretary of State for the Home Department, ex parte Al Fayed* [2001] Imm AR 134). Clearly there is no presumption of waiver if there is no complete disclosure of an interest or if the party was not aware of the interest. Statutes may also provide an express exemption in certain instances.

In the absence of bias in respect of an earlier decision which had been remitted, or an expressed view from which it was impossible to depart, a decision-maker could rehear a remitted matter rather than recuse himself and have the matter determined by a different decision-maker (*Jones v Department of Transport Welsh Traffic Office* [2005] EWCA Civ 58, 102 (11) LSG 31). (See also *Secretary of State for the Home Department v AF (No. 2)* [2007] EWHC 2828 (Admin), [2008] 2 All ER 67, reversed on another point in *Secretary of State for the Home Department v AF (No. 2)* [2008] EWCA Civ 117, [2008] 1 WLR 2528.)

The common law rules on bias are now applied in the context of the requirement in **art. 6(1) of the European Convention on Human Rights** that civil rights and obligations (and criminal charges) must be determined by 'an independent and impartial tribunal' (see **91.48**).

Right to a fair hearing

The right to a fair hearing embodies the idea of even-handedness between the parties in relation to obtaining information which is made available, and the provision of an opportunity to

77.26

Commentary

make representations. The concept of a fair hearing varies from case to case. For example, there may be an entitlement to an oral hearing in cases where the livelihood or liberty of the claimant is at stake, whereas such an entitlement will not be deemed necessary in relation to more minor matters with less potentially adverse consequences. The two main elements of procedural fairness are:

(a) the right to know the opposing case; and

(b) a fair opportunity to answer that case.

The overall test is what a reasonable man would consider to be fair in the particular circumstances (*Ridge v Baldwin* [1964] AC 40). (For the right to fairness and information in relation to consultation see **77.29**.)

The right to information on the case against an individual includes entitlement to notice of the allegations made against him or her so that the individual has an adequate opportunity to prepare his or her own case, arrange for representation (if necessary) and appear at any hearing. The right to notice includes, by implication, provision of sufficient detail of the opposing case to provide a fair opportunity to prepare one's own case, e.g. a rating assessment which was determined upon a valuer's report which had not been disclosed to the other party was quashed (*R v Westminster Assessment Committee, ex parte Grosvenor House (Park Lane) Ltd* [1941] 1 KB 53). However, the use of anonymous witness statements by a governing body considering whether to exclude a pupil from school was considered to be fair in the particular circumstances of that case (*R (T) v Elliott School Head Teacher* [2002] EWCA Civ 1349, [2003] ELR 160; *R (A) v North Westminster Community School Head Teacher* [2002] EWHC 2351, [2003] ELR 378).

The procedure required to satisfy the requirements of a fair hearing will depend to a large extent on the nature of the decision-making body in question. The necessity for an oral hearing will depend upon the seriousness of the circumstances of the case and the subject matter being dealt with. In many instances an opportunity to make written representations will be sufficient, provided that the demands of fairness are met, e.g. the Army Board of the Defence Council could deal with a complaint of racial discrimination by way of written representations (*R v Army Board of the Defence Council, ex parte Anderson* [1992] QB 169). By contrast, in some situations express procedural rules may provide a right to an oral hearing, by way of oral representations. For example, in the homelessness context a right to make oral representations (although not the right to a full hearing with third-party witnesses and cross-examination) is provided by express regulations in advance of decisions to terminate tenancies and obtain possession, whereas the same requirement is not expressly set out in advance of administrative decisions concerning the provision of new accommodation. The difference in effect of the decisions makes the difference in process entirely understandable (*Makisi v Birmingham City Council* [2011] EWCA Civ 355, [2011] PTSR 1545). This illustrates that the exact requirements of a fair hearing will depend on the context.

For example, in *R (Smith) v Parole Board (No. 2)* [2005] UKHL 1, [2005] 1 WLR 350, the House of Lords held that, while the common law duty of procedural fairness did not require the Parole Board to hold an oral hearing in every case, the Parole Board's duty was not as constricted as previously assumed. The prisoner should have the benefit of a procedure which fairly reflected, on the facts of his particular case, the importance of what was at stake for him and for society. The Parole Board might be assisted in its task of assessing risk by having some exposure to the prisoner. See also *R (Hammond) v Secretary of State for the Home Department* [2005] UKHL 69, [2006] 1 AC 603.

In *Re Reilly's Application for Judicial Review* [2013] UKSC 61, [2014] AC 1115, the Supreme Court held that it was not possible to define exhaustively when an oral hearing would be required, but that oral hearings would be required in cases where:

(a) important facts were in dispute or the prisoner advanced significant explanation or mitigation that had to be heard orally to be disposed of fairly;

(b) it was maintained on tenable grounds that an oral hearing was necessary to enable the prisoner to put his case effectively;

(c) it would be unfair for a decision to be made on the papers; or

(d) the Parole Board could not otherwise fairly make an independent assessment of risk, or the means by which that risk should be managed.

An oral hearing had to be held whenever it appeared on the papers that the prisoner was potentially suitable for release, although oral hearings might also be appropriate in other circumstances.

On the other hand, where on the facts of the case it is thought that an oral hearing would be a mere formality, there is no absolute right to a public and oral hearing at every stage in proceedings where the prisoner has had a fair and public hearing at his original trial. To provide for oral hearings in every case would cause delay and it has not been shown that any good purpose would be served by adopting such a procedure generally (*R (Dudson) v Secretary of State for the Home Department* [2005] UKHL 52, [2006] AC 245). It may be sufficient for the prisoner to be given the opportunity to make written representations (*R v Secretary of State for the Home Department, ex parte Doody* [1994] 1 AC 531). See also *R (Thompson) v Law Society* [2004] EWCA Civ 167, [2004] 1 WLR 2522; *Naraynsingh v Commissioner of Police* [2004] UKPC 20, 64 WIR 392. There is no clear entitlement to legal representation. Again, this will depend upon the seriousness or complexity of the charges made. The courts have held that prisoners charged with serious disciplinary offences have no general right to legal representation under the rules of natural justice, but the Boards of prison visitors have a discretion whether to allow it in the individual circumstances of each case (*R v Secretary of State for the Home Department, ex parte Tarrant* [1985] QB 251; *R v Board of Visitors of HM Prison, the Maze, ex parte Hone* [1988] AC 379). See also *R (S) v Knowlsey NHS Primary Care Trust* [2006] EWHC 26 (Admin), [2006] Lloyd's Rep Med 123; and *Kulkarni v Milton Keynes Hospital NHS Foundation Trust* [2009] EWCA Civ 789, [2010] ICR 101.

As long as the claimant is given an opportunity to set out his case at some stage during the proceedings, it does not appear to be contrary to the right to a fair hearing for a decision to be made without the claimant or his legal representative being present (e.g. *Auburn Court Ltd v Kingston and Saint Andrew Corporation, Building Surveyor* [2004] UKPC 11, 64 WIR 210).

In addition to the right to legal representation, in some circumstances a fair hearing may require that a party be allowed to adduce expert evidence. Where expert evidence is not permitted, a party may be deprived of an adequate opportunity to present its case (*Cummings v Weymouth and Portland Borough Council* [2007] EWHC 1601 (Admin), [2007] 2 P & CR 25).

Practical limitations may be placed upon the right to a fair process. For example, although the presence of an interpreter and/or representative in an interview in respect of an asylum claim provides a practical safeguard against faulty record-keeping and protects the claimant's interests to ensure the requisite standard of fairness, where such a safeguard is no longer practically available due to changes in public funding, a tape recording of the interview would be the only sensible method of redressing the imbalance of the Secretary of State being able to rely on a document without an adequate opportunity for the claimant to refute it (*R (Dirshe) v Secretary of State for the Home Department* [2005] EWCA Civ 421, [2005] 1 WLR 2685).

Reasons

There is no general duty under English law upon a decision-maker to give reasons for his or her decisions although statute does provide for such a duty in certain instances (e.g. Housing Act 1985, s. 64). However, in *R v Civil Service Appeal Board, ex parte Cunningham* [1992] ICR 816 Lord Donaldson MR stated that:

77.27

I do not accept that, just because Parliament has ruled that some tribunals should be required to give reasons for their decisions, it follows that the common law is unable to impose a similar requirement upon other tribunals, if justice so requires.

In *R v Ministry of Defence, ex parte Murray* [1998] COD 134, the Divisional Court confirmed that although the law did not at that time recognise a general duty to give reasons, there was a perceptible trend towards an insistence on greater transparency in decision-making. Where a statute conferred a power to make decisions affecting individuals, the court would readily apply necessary additional procedural safeguards so as to ensure the attainment of fairness. The Court of Appeal has acknowledged that it might be the trend for requirements to give reasons to become the norm rather than the exception, but despite this there remains no general duty at common law to give reasons for an administrative decision. Indeed the Court of Appeal considered that the Freedom of Information Act 2000 was Parliament's considered statutory framework for the disclosure of information held by public authorities, and its enactment therefore militated against the incremental imposition by the judiciary of a common law general duty to give reasons (*Hasan v Secretary of State for Trade and Industry* [2008] EWCA Civ 1312, [2009] 3 All ER 539).

Reasons should therefore be given where either:

(a) a decision without reasons was insufficient to achieve justice; or
(b) the decision appeared aberrant.

In determining whether reasons should be given, relevant considerations include the absence of any right of appeal, the importance of an effective means of detecting the kind of error which would entitle the court to intervene, and whether the body in question exercises a judicial function. Factors which militate against such a duty include the placing of an undue burden on decision-makers, considerations of public interest, or inexpressible value judgments. Therefore the requirement of fairness may require the giving of reasons in circumstances where there is no express statutory authority stipulating this. The position is influenced by the fact that there is an obligation at common law, and also in accordance with the European Convention on Human Rights, **art. 6**, in the **Human Rights Act 1998, sch. 1**, at least to give a short statement of the reasons for a decision when determining civil rights and obligations or criminal charges.

Cases suggest that a duty to give reasons arises in cases where the body departs from its usual policy or practice (*R v Islington London Borough Council, ex parte Rixon* [1997] ELR 66), and where a failure to give reasons or the giving of inadequate reasons would lead to the quashing of the decision in question (*R v Westminster City Council, ex parte Ermakov* [1996] 2 All ER 302).

Circumstances may require reasons to be given even if there is no specific requirement. Although neither the Medical Act 1983 nor its rules of procedure expressly or impliedly imposed on the Council a duty to state reasons for its decisions, this did not exclude an obligation to give reasons where the common law would require reasons to be given (*Stefan v General Medical Council* [1999] 1 WLR 1293; *Selvanathan v General Medical Council* [2001] Lloyd's Rep Med 1). Although there is no general obligation upon the Director of Public Prosecutions to give reasons for a decision not to prosecute, it has been held that he would, in the absence of compelling reasons to the contrary, be expected to do so where his refusal concerned a death in custody, in respect of which a properly directed jury had returned a verdict of unlawful killing (*R v Director of Public Prosecutions, ex parte Manning* [2001] QB 330). Similarly, where an immigrant had her application for indefinite leave to remain on the grounds of domestic violence refused, fairness required that the tribunal should have given proper reasons for its rejection of the evidence on domestic violence (*AG (India) v Secretary of State for the Home Department* [2007] EWCA Civ 1534, LTL 5/12/2007) and proper reasons should also be given for an immigration judge's findings on the credibility of a particular witness (*MO (Iraq) v Secretary of State for the Home Department* [2008] EWCA Civ 995, LTL 24/7/2008).

However, reasons are less important when a decision is essentially a matter of judgment. Upon the challenge of a planning decision, a local authority was entitled to repeat its statement of a pure value judgment when an inspector disagreed with that judgment (*Welsh Development*

Agency v Carmarthenshire County Council (1999) 80 P & CR 192). When deciding against an application for a capital grant, the Millennium Commission had only to say that another application was preferred and did not have to elucidate further (*R (Asha Foundation) v Millennium Commission* [2002] EWHC 916 (Admin), [2002] ACD 79; [2003] EWCA Civ 88, [2003] ACD 50).

Where reasons are required, such as reasons for a decision to grant planning permission, they need only be intelligible and adequate, and need only refer to the main issues in the dispute and not to every material consideration (*South Bucks District Council v Porter (No. 2)* [2004] UKHL 33, [2004] 1 WLR 1953). Although reasons need only be brief, they must be sufficient to explain the decision. They must be clear and adequate and deal with the substantial issues in the case but what are good reasons in any particular case depends on the circumstances of the case (*R v Immigration Appeal Tribunal, ex parte Jebunisha Kharvaleb Patel* [1996] Imm AR 161). An adjudicator refusing permission to appeal against a refusal to grant asylum was not required to address every point raised at length. Rather, sufficient reasons should be given to enable an appellant or other relevant person to see why a claimant had lost on any particular issue. If this test is satisfied, usually a more schematic approach would not be necessary (*R (Bahrami) v Immigration Appeal Tribunal* [2003] EWHC 1453 (Admin), LTL 4/6/2003 and *R (Macrae) v County of Herefordshire District Council* [2012] EWCA Civ 457, [2012] LLR 720). See also **91.49**.

Reasons must include the findings of fact in relation to each aspect of the decision and why they lead to the particular conclusion. Where insufficient reasons were given by the Conduct and Competence Committee of the Health Professions Council the decision was quashed and remitted to a freshly constituted committee (*Ryell v Health Professions Council* [2005] EWHC 2797 (Admin), [2007] Imm AR 81).

Where a fact-finding tribunal notes discrepancies in evidence its job is to evaluate them in making its decision. Usually it will need to do no more than describe them and state the conclusion reached. However, in some cases the inconsistencies would be such that the conclusion reached would require an explanation, for example, where the decision-maker decided the inconsistencies were insignificant. A failure to do this would amount to inadequate reasoning for the decision (*AK v Secretary of State for the Home Department* [2006] EWCA Civ 1117, [2007] Imm AR 81).

Where a number of reasons were given for the rejection of evidence, the fact that some of the reasons did not bear analysis was not enough to justify setting aside the decision. However, in an exceptional case where little of the reasoning could survive the scrutiny of the appellate court, the reasoning was sufficiently defective overall to justify the conclusion that the decision could not be upheld on that basis and the decision should therefore be remitted for fresh determination (*HK v Secretary of State for the Home Department* [2006] EWCA Civ 1037, *The Independent*, 27 July 2006). A trial judge must address evidential conflicts and assess that evidence to explain the judgment he reached. A failure to do so renders the decision inadequate and the finding of the trial judge should be quashed (*Baird v Thurrock Borough Council* [2005] EWCA Civ 1499, *The Times*, 15 November 2005).

The Court of Appeal does not have the power to invite a decision-maker to give supplementary reasons for its decision. Rather, in the rare cases where the appellant could not understand why the particular finding had been made and where the decision-maker appeared to have taken an erroneous approach to the evidence, the case should be remitted for reconsideration (*Hatungimana v Secretary of State for the Home Department* [2006] EWCA Civ 231, *The Times*, 2 March 2006).

Where there is a statutory duty to give reasons as part of the notification of the decision, the court will only accept subsequent evidence of the reasons in exceptional circumstances. In other cases, the court will be cautious about accepting late reasons. Relevant considerations which the court will take into account include: whether the new reasons are consistent with

the original reasons, whether the new reasons are the original reasons of the whole tribunal, whether there is a real risk that the later reasons were composed subsequently in order to support the tribunal's decision, and the circumstances in which the later reasons are put forward. The degree of scrutiny and caution to be applied by the court to subsequent reasons is dependent on the subject matter of the administrative decision in question. Furthermore, the court will bear in mind the qualifications and experience of the persons on the tribunal (*R (Nash) v Chelsea College of Art and Design* [2001] EWHC 538 (Admin), *The Times*, 25 July 2001).

Procedural legitimate expectation

77.28   A procedural legitimate expectation arises in circumstances where a decision deprived the claimant of:

some benefit or advantage which either (i) he had in the past been permitted by the decision-maker to enjoy and which he can legitimately expect to be permitted to continue to do until there has been communicated to him some rational grounds for withdrawing it on which he has been given an opportunity to comment; or (ii) he has received assurance from the decision-maker that it will not be withdrawn without giving him first an opportunity of advancing reasons for contending that they should not be withdrawn. (Lord Diplock in *Council of Civil Service Unions v Minister for the Civil Service* [1985] AC 374).

The concept of procedural legitimate expectation has been applied to ensure that no adverse decision will be taken without first giving the affected party an opportunity of making representations.

An expectation will be derived from an express promise or representation or an implied representation based upon past actions. In order for a promise to have this effect it must be clear and unambiguous and the claimant must have made full relevant disclosure prior to obtaining it (*R v Commissioners of Inland Revenue, ex parte MFK Underwriting Agencies Ltd* [1990] 1 WLR 1545) (see **77.19**). The court has acknowledged that the concept of legitimate expectation will only be protected where there is no contrary public interest (*R v North and East Devon Health Authority, ex parte Coughlan* [2001] QB 213).

Examples of legitimate expectations are that taxi drivers had a legitimate expectation of consultation prior to the issue of licences in circumstances where such consultation had been expressly promised (*R v Liverpool Corporation, ex parte Liverpool Taxi Fleet Operators' Association* [1972] 2 QB 299); civil servants had a legitimate expectation of consultation prior to the removal of trade union rights, subject to considerations of national security (*Council of Civil Service Unions v Minister for the Civil Service* [1985] AC 374); coal miners' unions had a legitimate expectation of consultation on pit closures (*R v British Coal Corporation, ex parte Vardy* [1993] ICR 720); illegal immigrants had a legitimate expectation of an opportunity to state their case prior to deportation (*R v Attorney General of Hong Kong, ex parte Ng Yuen Shiu* [1983] 2 AC 629); residents had a legitimate expectation of being consulted about all the options in respect of a traffic order (*R (Montpeliers and Trevors Association) v City of Westminster* [2005] EWHC 16 (Admin), [2006] LGR 304).

Consultation

77.29   A public authority may be under an express or implied obligation to consult. An obligation to consult also arises where a failure to do so would be so unfair as to amount to an abuse of power (*R (Dudley Metropolitan Borough Council) v Secretary of State for Communities and Local Government* [2012] EWHC 1729 (Admin), [2013] BLGR 68).

In many areas consultation is playing an increasingly important role. For example, in the context of environmental decisions, consultation is particularly significant given the Government's obligations under the Convention on Access to Information, Public

Participation in Decision-Making and Access to Justice in Environmental Matters 1998 (the Aarhus Convention). There are four basic requirements of an adequate consultation:

(a) It must be at a time when proposals are still at a formative stage.
(b) The proposer must give sufficient reasons for any proposal to allow intelligent consideration and response.
(c) Adequate time must be given for consideration and response.
(d) The product of consultation must be conscientiously taken into account in finalising any proposals.

See *R v North and East Devon Health Authority, ex parte Coughlan* [2001] QB 213, adopting the formulation of Stephen Sedley QC in *R v Brent London Borough Council, ex parte Gunning* (1985) 84 LGR 168. Where it is alleged that a consultation process is unfair, it must be shown that there is a clear error precluding proper consultation, although it is sufficient to show that the unfairness affects only a group of the persons affected by the consultation (*R (Royal Brompton and Harefield NHS Foundation Trust) v Joint Committee of Primary Care Trusts* [2012] EWCA Civ 472, (2012) 126 BMLR 134).

On the issue of new-build nuclear power plants, the court found that the government's consultation paper had been inadequate in that it contained no proposals as such, the information given was insufficient, there was no discussion of the public considerations that would apply to the issue, the period given for consultation was inadequate and it could not be said that the decision eventually made would have been reasonably foreseeable by those consultees who took the consultation document at face value and relied upon it (*R (Greenpeace Ltd) v Secretary of State for Trade and Industry* [2007] EWHC 311 (Admin), [2007] Env LR 29). What a fair consultation requires depends on the circumstances of the case. In the context of a statutory duty to consult on proposals to establish a unitary local authority, the Boundary Committee had a degree of flexibility as to the way in which the consultation should be carried out, although this was subject to the need to comply with the general requirements set out in *R v North and East Devon Health Authority, ex parte Coughlan* (see above) and in particular to publish sufficient material in a form which members of the public could understand, in order to enable all those interested to respond intelligently (see *R (Breckland District Council) v Boundary Committee* [2009] EWCA Civ 239, [2009] BLGR 589).

In circumstances where a decision-maker is discharging an important public function which engages a strong public interest, fairness and the right to information mean that the consultation process should involve a high degree of transparency and disclosure. This may even necessitate outlining alternative options in addition to the decision-maker's preferred option to ensure meaningful public participation if consultees are unlikely to have significant background knowledge (*R (Moseley and Stirling) v Haringey London Borough Council* [2014] UKSC 56, [2014] 1 WLR 3947, but cf. *R (United Co. Rusal plc) v London Metal Exchange* [2014] EWCA Civ 1271, [2015] 1 WLR 1375, where different circumstances were such that there was no need to consult on options the decision-maker had already discarded). Failure to disclose the fully executable version of an economic model that was central to the decision-making process was therefore unfair, as without it consultees could not properly review and test the model and therefore they were unable to make properly informed representations on it. The additional cost and time involved in releasing the fully executable version of the model should not weigh heavily in the balance in deciding whether fairness required disclosure (*R (Eisai Ltd) v National Institute for Health and Clinical Excellence* [2008] EWCA Civ 438, 101 BMLR 26). However, consultation with each affected individual would not be practicable where an urgent and difficult decision is required (*R (Legal Remedy UK) v Secretary of State for Health* [2007] EWHC 1252 (Admin), 96 BMLR 191).

Although there is a duty to re-consult if the final proposal is significantly different from what has been consulted upon, this duty does not arise if the differences are very slight and

Commentary

clearly not such as to impose a duty of fairness on the body to re-consult, or where the final proposal itself has emerged from the consultation exercise (*R v East Kent Hospital NHS Trust, ex parte Smith* [2002] EWHC 2640 (Admin), LTL 9/12/2002). The duty to consult while proposals are still at a formative stage does not mean that there must be a first round of consultation on whether the possible options should be reduced to one and then a second round of consultation on that last option. A limited consultation may be considered fair in circumstances where a full and formal consultation has recently been carried out (*R (Milton Keynes Council) v Secretary of State for Communities and Local Government* [2011] EWCA Civ 1575, [2012] JPL 728). Whether there can be said to have been a legitimate expectation as to the extent of the consultation will depend on the context and evidence in each particular case (*R (Tinns) v Secretary of State for Transport* [2006] EWHC 193 (Admin), LTL 11/1/2006).

There will still be circumstances where fairness does not require consultation, for example, where legislation has prescribed a particular procedure for a rule-making process which is subject to other control mechanisms and which does not include an express duty to consult (*R (Bapio Action Ltd) v Secretary of State for the Home Department* [2008] UKHL 27, [2008] 1 AC 1003). Alternatively there may be situations where the statutory scheme is such that a court is bound to follow a particular process even in the face of a failure to consult, contrary to a procedural legitimate expectation. This is an extension of the general principle that a legitimate expectation cannot override the law (see 77.19).

ALTERNATIVE REMEDIES TO JUDICIAL REVIEW

77.30   Generally, any alternative remedies should be exhausted before resorting to judicial review in cases where the alternative remedy is adequate to resolve the complaint (*R v Sandwell Metropolitan Borough Council, ex parte Wilkinson* (1998) 31 HLR 22). Although the jurisdiction of the court to grant relief by way of judicial review is not ousted by the existence of an alternative remedy, it may exercise its discretion to refuse relief, refuse to grant permission or adjourn the case until after the alternative remedy has been used.

In particular, there should not in commercial disputes be two sets of parallel proceedings based on the same facts and seeking the same remedies, with two sets of costs and duplication of the time, effort and resources of both the parties and the court (see *Cookson and Clegg Ltd v Ministry of Defence* [2005] EWCA Civ 811, [2006] Eu LR 1092, where the judicial review claim was dismissed).

Where there is an alternative remedy available that is more suitable, a judicial review will not be permitted to continue in the Administrative Court. For example, where a matter concerning the lawfulness of the arrest and detention of various individuals could have instead been brought in private law as false imprisonment, and where there were complex factual issues and disputes of fact involved which were wholly inappropriate for judicial review proceedings, the matter should have been addressed in an ordinary Queen's Bench claim (*Sher v Chief Constable of Greater Manchester* [2010] EWHC 1859 (Admin), [2011] 2 All ER 364). Claims involving complex disputes of facts are not well suited to resolution in the Administrative Court and may instead need to be transferred and dealt with as a Part 7 claim (*R (SS) v Secretary of State for the Home Department* [2015] EWCA Civ 652, LTL 26/6/2015).

A number of cases have indicated that judicial review is to be regarded as a remedy of last resort. For example, permission to apply for judicial review of a decision of the Law Society was set aside because of the existence of an alternative remedy in the form of an appeal to the Master of the Rolls (*R v Law Society, ex parte Kingsley* [1996] COD 59); permission to apply for judicial review was set aside where a claimant had a statutory right of appeal to the Secretary of State under the Town and Country Planning Act 1990, s. 78, against a grant of planning permission subject to conditions (*R v Secretary of State for the Home Department, ex parte Watts*

[1997] COD 152); judicial review of a decision of the Customs and Excise Commissioners was refused because the claimant should have invoked a statutory right of recourse to a value added tax and duties tribunal (*R v Commissioners of Customs and Excise, ex parte Bosworth Beverages Ltd* (2000) *The Times*, 24 April 2000); judicial review of a decision of the Secretary of State for the Home Department to issue a notice of liability to a civil penalty under the Immigration and Asylum Act 1999, s. 35, was refused on the basis that the claimant's remedy was to defend civil proceedings brought by the Home Secretary after the expiry of the time prescribed for payment of the penalty (*R (Balbo B & C Auto Transporti Internazionali) v Secretary of State for the Home Department* [2001] EWHC 195 (Admin), [2001] 1 WLR 1556); a challenge to the service of prohibition notices by the FSA should have been by way of appeal to the Financial Services and Markets Tribunal rather than by way of judicial review (*R (Davies) v Financial Services Authority* [2003] EWCA Civ 1128, [2004] 1 WLR 185).

Even in a case where there was a public law element, because it was a dispute under a tenancy agreement with a registered social landlord, it was held that the matter could have been brought either as a claim for breach of contract or under the housing legislation since it was essentially a contractual relationship that happened to possess a public law dimension. Judicial review is a remedy of last resort and should not be used where other remedies, including private law remedies, are available and have not been used (*R (McIntyre) v Gentoo Group Ltd* [2010] EWHC 5 (Admin), 154(2) SJLB 829). This principle will not apply where the two claims are separate and 'profoundly different', even if the same relief is being sought. Where a claimant was seeking to advance claims before the Administrative Court that could not be advanced before the First-Tier Tribunal, there was no reason to force a stay of the judicial review proceedings pending the resolution of the tax appeal (*R (Veolia ES Ltd) v Revenue and Customs Commissioners* [2015] EWCA Civ 747, [2015] BTC 23).

It is possible to depart from this principle in exceptional circumstances, e.g. an urgent case where interim relief is required which would not be available in the appeal or complaint. Factors which the courts have taken into account in order to decide whether the circumstances are exceptional include: the speed of the appeal, whether it is convenient, whether the matter demands a particular or technical knowledge, and whether the alternative remedy is one which the claimant could first be expected to use, e.g. the delay in instituting disciplinary charges against police officers was such a serious breach of police regulations that the officers need not first exercise a right of appeal to the Secretary of State (*R v Chief Constable of Merseyside Police, ex parte Calveley* [1986] QB 424). Gross procedural unfairness in an appeal may be regarded as an exceptional case, so that it would be permissible to allow judicial review of an interim decision by an immigration judge, despite there being an alternative remedy available under the relevant legislation (*R (AM (Cameroon)) v Asylum and Immigration Tribunal* [2007] EWCA Civ 131, *The Times*, 11 April 2007). However, truly exceptional reasons must be given in order to bypass any statutory appeal procedure in favour of judicial review. Despite the apparent bias of a governing body which decided to exclude two pupils from school, any resulting unfairness could be remedied by the Independent Appeals Panel and any unfairness at an earlier stage in the proceedings was not so serious as to have contaminated an appeal (*R (A) v Kingsmead School Governors* [2002] EWCA Civ 1822, [2003] ELR 104).

Where there is an avenue for an appeal from an inferior court or tribunal to the Court of Appeal or High Court the claimant should appeal rather than seek a judicial review of the inferior court's decision in the Administrative Court. Where that avenue has been followed by the claimant and the appeal has been dismissed or the claimant has been refused permission to appeal, the claimant will not normally be permitted to re-litigate the same matter by way of judicial review, because that would be an abuse of the process of the court (see *R (Sivasubramaniam) v Wandsworth County Court* [2002] EWCA Civ 1738, [2003] 1 WLR 475). However, in exceptional cases, such as where the judicial process itself has been frustrated or corrupted and there has been a substantial denial of the right to a fair trial, judicial review may be permitted despite permission to appeal the decision of the lower court being refused (*Strickson v Preston County Court* [2007] EWCA Civ 1132, LTL 9/11/2007; see also **77.3**). This may also be the case where the tribunal has acted outside its jurisdiction (*R (Rana) v Upper Tribunal (Immigration and Asylum Chamber)* [2010] EWHC 3558 (Admin), LTL 20/1/2011). However, only in the case of the clearest provision will a court conclude that judicial review is excluded (*Leech v Deputy Governor of Parkhurst Prison* [1988] AC 533).

PERMISSION TO PROCEED WITH A CLAIM FOR JUDICIAL REVIEW

Pre-action protocol

77.31   The **Pre-action Protocol for Judicial Review** sets out a code of good practice and contains the steps which the parties should generally follow before making a claim for judicial review. Litigants should also note the general **PD Pre-Action Conduct and Protocols**, which applies to judicial review.

All claimants must consider whether they should follow the protocol, depending upon the circumstances of their case. For example the protocol is unlikely to be appropriate in very urgent cases. Where the protocol applies, the court will normally expect all parties to comply with it and will take into account compliance or non-compliance when giving directions for case management proceedings or when making orders for costs (e.g. *Aegis Group plc v Commissioners of Inland Revenue* [2005] EWHC 1468 (Ch), [2006] STC 23; see also **PD Pre-action Conduct and Protocols**). The protocol makes it clear that it does not affect the need to comply with the short time limits for commencing judicial review proceedings, which cannot be extended by agreement between the parties, but the court will take into account any agreement by one party not to 'take a time point' against the other in respect of delay while complying with the protocol.

The protocol requires that, before making a claim, the claimant should send a letter to the defendant. The purpose of the letter is to identify the issues in dispute and establish whether litigation can be avoided. The letter should normally contain the details of any interested parties known to the claimant. A copy of the letter before claim should be sent to all interested parties for information. The defendant should normally respond within 14 days to the letter before claim. Failure to do so will be taken into account by the court and sanctions may be imposed unless there are good reasons. Public body defendants, including government departments with limited resources, are not exempt from the general rules on costs, and if a claimant sends an adequate letter of claim, it is unacceptable for a defendant not to give an adequate response. In particular, if the claimant then issues proceedings and seeks relief, there would be an expectation that the claimant would be entitled to costs (*R (Bahta) v Secretary of State for the Home Department* [2011] EWCA Civ 895, [2011] CP Rep 43). The response should be sent to all interested parties identified by the claimant and contain details of any other parties whom the defendant considers also have an interest. Standard form letters of claim and response can be found in the annexes to the pre-action protocol.

One of the purposes of the protocol is to identify the extent to which the exchange of information can lead to the avoidance of litigation. However, requests for documents at this pre-action stage should be proportionate and limited to what is necessary. The protocol includes consideration of alternative dispute resolution (**Pre-action Protocol for Judicial Review, para. 3.1**). This links with the approach of the Court of Appeal, which has stipulated that courts should ask parties to judicial review proceedings to explain what steps they have taken to resolve the dispute, and why a complaints procedure or some other form of alternative dispute resolution has not been used to resolve or reduce the issues in dispute (*R (Cowl) v Plymouth City Council* [2001] EWCA Civ 1935, [2002] 1 WLR 803; Practice Statement (Administrative Court: Administration of Justice) [2002] 1 WLR 810).

Test for permission

77.32 Permission to proceed with a claim for judicial review must be obtained from a High Court judge (usually one of the Queen's Bench Division who has been assigned to hear matters listed in the Administrative Court Office List) (**CPR, r. 54.4**; Senior Courts Act 1981, s. 31(3)). To grant permission the court has to be satisfied that:

(a) there is an arguable case for review;
(b) the claimant has a 'sufficient interest' (see 77.35); and
(c) there has not been 'undue delay' (see 77.36).

Traditionally the test for the grant of permission has been that a claimant must demonstrate to the court upon 'a quick perusal of the papers' that there is an arguable case for granting relief (*R v Commissioners of Inland Revenue, ex parte National Federation of Self-Employed and Small Businesses Ltd* [1982] AC 617).

Permission should be granted if on the material available the court considers, without going into the matter in depth, that there is an arguable case for granting the relief claimed by the claimant. The Court of Appeal has held that the test to be applied in deciding whether to grant permission is whether the judge is satisfied that there is a case fit for further investigation at a full with-notice hearing of a substantive claim for judicial review (*R v Secretary of State for the Home Department, ex parte Begum* [1990] COD 107). However, some judges seem to apply more stringent criteria and require a claimant to demonstrate something approaching a reasonable prospect of success or a strong prima facie case.

The court will generally, in the first instance, consider the question of permission without a hearing (**PD 54A, para. 8.4**). In the event of a hearing, neither the defendant nor any other interested party need attend, unless the court directs otherwise (**para. 8.5**). If, for example, on considering the papers, the judge cannot decide whether there is an arguable case, he or she may invite the proposed defendant to attend the hearing of the permission application and make representations as to whether permission should be granted.

Permission will be refused where an application is frivolous, vexatious or hopeless; or a claim is made by 'busybodies with misguided or trivial complaints of administrative error' (*R v Commissioners of Inland Revenue, ex parte National Federation of Self-Employed and Small Businesses Ltd* [1982] AC 617); or a claim is misconceived, unarguable or groundless. Rigorous examination by the judge is required at the permission stage of a judicial review claim so as to restrict the exploitation of judicial review as a commercial weapon by rival property developers (*R (Noble Organisation Ltd) v Thanet District Council* [2005] EWCA Civ 782, [2006] Env LR 8). Permission will also be refused if there is a more appropriate alternative procedure (see 77.30); or a claim for judicial review is an inappropriate procedure, e.g. because the matter relates to private law and should therefore be commenced by way of a claim form under **CPR, Part 7**.

In addition the High Court may consider at the permission stage whether the outcome for the applicant would have been substantially different if the conduct complained of had not occurred, and must consider that issue where asked to do so by the defendant. If the court concludes it is highly likely that the outcome for the applicant would not have been substantially different, the court must refuse permission unless it certifies that there are reasons of exceptional public interest (Senior Courts Act 1981, s. 31, as amended by the Criminal Justice and Courts Act 2015).

Procedure on an application for permission

77.33 A claim for judicial review may be commenced either at the Administrative Court Office at the Royal Courts of Justice in London or at one of the Regional Offices in Birmingham, Cardiff, Leeds and Manchester. Where the claim is in an excepted class as set out in

PD 54D, para. 3, however, proceedings must be started in London. The excepted classes of claim are:

(1) proceedings to which Part 76 or Part 79 applies:
    (a) proceedings relating to control orders under Part 76;
    (b) financial restriction proceedings under Part 79;
    (c) proceedings relating to terrorism or allegations of terrorism; and
    (d) proceedings in which a special advocate is, or is to be, instructed;
(2) proceedings to which CPR, sch. 1, RSC, ord. 115, applies;
(3) proceedings under the Proceeds of Crime Act 2002;
(4) appeals to the Administrative Court under the Extradition Act 2003;
(5) proceedings which must be heard by a Divisional Court; and
(6) proceedings relating to the discipline of solicitors.

The following documents must be filed when seeking permission to proceed with a claim for judicial review:

(a) a claim form (form N461);
(b) written evidence in support of the claim;
(c) a copy of any order that the claimant seeks to have quashed;
(d) where the claim for judicial review relates to a decision of a court or tribunal, an approved copy of the reasons for reaching that decision;
(e) copies of any documents on which the claimant proposes to rely;
(f) copies of any relevant statutory material; and
(g) a list of essential documents for advance reading by the court.

Where it is not possible to file all of these documents, the claimant must indicate which documents have not been filed and the reasons why they are not currently available (**PD 54A, para. 5.8**).

The claim form should set out a detailed statement of the claimant's grounds for bringing the claim and the facts which the claimant will seek to rely on (**PD 54A, para. 5.6**). It should state the claimant's name and description, the relief sought and the grounds on which it is sought, the name and address of the claimant's solicitor (if any) and the claimant's address for service. The claim form must also include or be accompanied by any application to extend the time limit for filing the claim form and any application for directions (**PD 54A, para. 5.6**). The claim form must also state the name and address of any person the claimant considers to be an interested party, that the claimant is requesting permission to proceed with a claim for judicial review, and any remedy (including any interim remedy) sought (**CPR, r. 54.6(1)**). Where the claimant seeks to raise any issue under the **Human Rights Act 1998**, or seeks any remedy available under that Act, the claim form must include the information required by **PD 16, para. 15** (**PD 54A, para. 5.3**). Where the claimant intends to raise a devolution issue, the claim form must specify that the claimant wishes to raise a devolution issue and identify the relevant provisions of the Government of Wales Act 2006, the Northern Ireland Act 1998 or the Scotland Act 1998, and contain a summary of the facts, circumstances and points of law on the basis of which it is alleged that a devolution issue arises (**PD 54A, para. 5.4**).

The written evidence to be filed with the claim form will generally be in witness-statement form. The evidence in support must verify the facts relied upon in support of the application, establish a sufficient interest by the claimant in the subject matter of the claim, exhibit a copy of the decision challenged and make full and frank disclosure of all relevant facts, even those not in the claimant's favour. The witness statement should ideally be signed by someone having first-hand personal knowledge of the facts. If permission is obtained upon the basis of false statements or the suppression of material facts, the court may set aside permission or refuse the relief sought at the substantive hearing (*R v Kensington Income Tax Commissioners, ex parte Princess Edmond de Polignac* [1917] 1 KB 486; *R v Jockey Club Licensing*

Committee, ex parte Wright [1991] COD 306). On filing a claim form for judicial review, the claimant's solicitor must also lodge two copies of a paginated indexed bundle containing all the documents referred to above (**PD 54A, para. 5.9**) and a further bundle of the relevant legislative provisions and statutory instruments required for the proper consideration of the application (Practice Direction (Crown Office List: Legislation Bundle) [1997] 1 WLR 52).

Urgent cases procedure

The Administrative Court has issued guidance on the procedure to be followed for cases **77.34** which are urgent or which include applications for interim injunctions in Practice Statement (Administrative Court: Listing and Urgent Cases) [2002] 1 WLR 810.

A claimant seeking urgent consideration must complete form N463 stating the reasons for urgency, the proposed timescale for consideration of the permission application, and the date by which the full hearing of the merits should take place if permission is granted. A claimant who applies for an interim injunction must also provide a draft order and a statement of the grounds on which the injunction is sought. The application must be served by fax and post, along with the claim form, on the defendant and interested parties. The defendant and interested parties must be advised that they may make representations on the application.

Each day a judge will act as the 'urgent judge' to hear urgent applications on that day. A judge will consider the application within the time requested, and may order that an oral hearing should take place. The judge will then make such order as is appropriate.

The court has become increasingly vigilant in ensuring that the out-of-hours process is not abused by parties. As judges dealing with an urgent application might be wholly unfamiliar or only have passing familiarity with the case, the court expects parties making applications to ensure that the judge is fully apprised of the relevant facts, including by making material disclosure beyond merely ensuring that the documents contain reference to material matters and drawing the judge's attention specifically to those facts or aspects of the law which might tell against the application or affect the judge's view of its merits. Further, those who obtain an injunction on an undertaking to do something 'forthwith' have a personal obligation to ensure that what is required is done, and if not seek relief from the court at the earliest possible opportunity (*R (Kozlowski) v Serious Organised Crime Agency* [2013] EWHC 1741 (Admin), LTL 23/5/2013). Anyone making an out-of-hours application must also make an appropriate application the next working day, and counsel or solicitors making the application give their own personal undertaking to file the application and pay the requisite fee (*Rehman v Secretary of State for the Home Department* [2013] EWHC 2658 (Admin), LTL 3/9/2013).

Standing of the claimant

Section 31(3) of the Senior Courts Act 1981 provides that the court will not grant permission **77.35** to proceed with a claim for judicial review 'unless it considers that the [claimant] has a sufficient interest in the matter to which the [claim] relates'.

The phrase 'sufficient interest' has been given a wide interpretation by the courts. They will assess the extent of the claimant's interest against the factual and legal circumstances of the claim. The test for deciding whether a claimant has sufficient interest was considered by the House of Lords in *R v Commissioners of Inland Revenue, ex parte National Federation of Self-Employed and Small Businesses Ltd* [1982] AC 617. The court held that not only was standing a ground in itself upon which permission could be refused, it should also be considered at the substantive hearing after the relevant law and facts were examined in full. The court added that there are different tests for standing at the permission and the substantive stages. At the former stage it is merely a 'threshold' question for the court, designed to weed out frivolous or vexatious cases. However, at the substantive hearing the claimant must be able to show a strong case on the merits, judged in relation to the claimant's own concern with the subject matter of the claim (*R v Monopolies and Mergers Commission, ex parte Argyll Group plc* [1986] 1 WLR 763).

Since *R v Commissioners of Inland Revenue, ex parte National Federation of Self-Employed and Small Businesses Ltd*, the courts have adopted a broad and flexible approach to this test. The more important the issue and the stronger the merits of the claim, the more ready will the courts be to grant permission, notwithstanding the limited personal involvement of the claimant. Standing will normally extend to individuals affected by the decision or action in question, e.g. a person threatened with deportation, or an individual with a direct financial or legal interest. For example, an elector and taxpayer was deemed to have sufficient standing to claim that a government undertaking to pay a contribution to the European Community was *ultra vires* (*R v HM Treasury ex parte Smedley* [1985] QB 657); a taxpayer was permitted to challenge a decision of the Inland Revenue on its method of valuation of a rival company's profits (*R v Attorney General, ex parte Imperial Chemical Industries plc* [1987] 1 CMLR 72); an owner of land within the green belt in the vicinity of a proposed development had sufficient standing, even though not directly affected by the development (*R v Selby District Council, ex parte Samuel Smith Old Breweries* [2001] PLCR 6); an inhabitant of Rugby (although temporarily homeless at the time) had standing to challenge the grant of a permit to a cement company with a plant near Rugby town centre because as an inhabitant he would be affected by any adverse impact on the environment (*R (Edwards) v Environment Agency* [2004] EWHC 736 (Admin), [2004] 3 All ER 21) and it was not necessary for him to have been active in a campaign on the issue to have an interest; a Palestinian living in the Occupied Territories had sufficient interest to bring judicial review proceedings in relation to the Secretary of State's decision to grant licences for the export of military items to Israel (*Hasan v Secretary of State for Trade and Industry* [2007] EWHC 2630 (Admin), [2008] ACD 10).

Even where a claimant had been active in a matter, appearing as an objector at a public inquiry, where the compulsory purchase orders in question raised no issue as to any right or interest of the claimant, and where the orders did not deprive the claimant of anything, his application could not succeed as the court's role was to decide disputes between parties and not to pronounce on hypothetical questions, however interesting, where there was no dispute to be resolved (*R (Murley) v Secretary of State for Transport* [2005] EWHC 2324 (Admin), LTL 10/1/2006).

Standing also extends to representative groups. For example, the Child Poverty Action Group was held to have standing sufficient to commence proceedings relating to the interpretation of social security legislation (*R v Secretary of State for Social Services, ex parte Child Poverty Action Group* [1990] 2 QB 540); the Law Society in a challenge to the Lord Chancellor's cuts to legal aid eligibility (*R v Lord Chancellor, ex parte Law Society (No. 2)* (1994) 6 Admin LR 833); the Royal College of Nursing in a challenge to a government circular advising on abortion-related work for nurses (*Royal College of Nursing of the United Kingdom v Department of Health and Social Security* [1981] AC 800); and the National Union of Mineworkers in relation to the reduction of supplementary benefits to striking workers (*R v Chief Adjudication Officer, ex parte Bland* (1985) *The Times*, 6 February 1985).

Pressure groups acting in the public interest have also been granted standing. For example, Greenpeace were held to have sufficient interest to seek judicial review of the Inspectorate of Pollution's decision to vary authorisations for the discharge of radioactive waste from Sellafield (*R v Inspectorate of Pollution, ex parte Greenpeace Ltd* [1994] 1 WLR 570). The judge was influenced by the fact that, if the claim failed on its merits, the persons whom Greenpeace represented might not have an effective way to bring these issues before the court. He held that the issue of whether an interest group or other representative body had sufficient standing should be decided on the facts of each individual case as a matter of discretion. The World Development Movement was held to have standing to challenge a decision of the Foreign Secretary to use overseas aid money to fund the Pergau Dam project in Malaysia (*R v Secretary of State for Foreign and Commonwealth Affairs, ex parte World Development Movement Ltd* [1995] 1 WLR 386). The Divisional Court took into account factors such as the importance of the issue raised, the likely absence of any other responsible challenger, and the prominent role of the claimants in giving advice on overseas aid. However, a company set up specifically to save a theatre did not have sufficient standing to challenge the Secretary of State's refusal to list the theatre site as an ancient monument (*R v Secretary of State for the Environment, ex parte Rose Theatre Trust Co.* [1990] 1 QB 504).

It would be misconceived at the permission stage to elevate the question of standing 'above the elementary level of excluding busybodies and troublemakers and to demand something akin to a special private interest in the subject matter' (*R v Somerset County Council, ex parte Dixon* [1997] COD 323). There is no authority for the proposition that a court is compelled to refuse permission where the interest of the claimant is shared with the generality of the public.

The 'sufficient interest' standing test differs from the test under the **Human Rights Act 1998**, which provides that the claimant must be a 'victim' of the alleged violation of the Convention: that is, the claimant must have a personal interest in the claim (**Human Rights Act 1998, s.** 7(1)). **Section** 7(3) of the Act makes clear that it is the victim test which must prevail in human rights judicial review proceedings. This excludes judicial review challenges by representative bodies or pressure groups on human rights issues which are of general, rather than individual, importance.

Timescales for commencement

In a claim for judicial review the claim form must normally be filed promptly, and in any event not later than three months after the grounds to make the claim first arose (**CPR, r.** 54.5(1)). However, the deadline is shortened to six weeks from the date on which the grounds arose in judicial reviews relating to a decision under the Town and Country Planning Act 1990, the Planning (Listed Buildings and Conservation Areas) Act 1990, the Planning (Hazardous Substances) Act 1990 and the Planning (Consequential Provisions) Act 1990, and to 30 days from the date on which the claimant first knew or ought to have known that grounds had arisen in relation to a decision governed by the Public Contracts Regulations 2006 (SI 2006/5) (**CPR, r.** 54.5(5) and (6)). These shorter deadlines are intended to bring judicial review into line with the timescales for bringing statutory challenges to planning and procurement decisions. These shorter limits are strictly applied and the court does not have jurisdiction to hear a claim lodged even one day past the relevant time limit, meaning the exact wording of the relevant time limit must be considered as there is an important distinction between claims having to be issued within a certain period 'from' a particular date or 'starting with' that date (*R (Williams) v Secretary of State for Energy and Climate Change* [2015] EWHC 1202 (Admin), [2015] JPL 1257). Even where the court does have the discretion to extend time, there has been a trend towards stricter enforcement of timescales and procedural rules generally to mirror that trend in private law civil proceedings (*R (Kigen) v Secretary of State for the Home Department* [2015] EWCA Civ 1286, [2016] 1 WLR 723). See also below for the different position in relation to EU claims.

77.36

The time limit may not be extended by agreement between the parties (**r.** 54.5(2)). Where the High Court considers that there has been undue delay in making a claim for judicial review, the court may refuse to grant permission or any relief sought in the claim if it considers that the grant of the relief sought would be 'likely to cause substantial hardship to, or substantially prejudice the rights of, any person or would be detrimental to good administration' (Senior Courts Act 1981, s. 31(6)). Time taken to comply with the **Pre-action Protocol for Judicial Review** is not a good excuse for failing to issue judicial review proceedings promptly (see Introduction to the protocol).

The wide discretion granted to the courts in relation to the grant or refusal of relief is restricted by the Senior Courts Act 1981, s. 31(7), and by **CPR, r.** 54.5(3), which provide that s. 31(6) and **r.** 54.5(1) are without prejudice to any other statutory provisions which have the effect of limiting the time within which a claim for judicial review must be made.

Commentary

1395

Section 7(5) of the **Human Rights Act 1998** introduces a general time limit of one year for proceedings based upon a Convention right. However, this time limit is expressly stated to be without prejudice to stricter time limits, such as those that usually apply in judicial review proceedings.

A claimant seeking judicial review must file the claim form promptly and is not necessarily entitled to wait up to three months before commencing proceedings. In certain situations the utmost promptitude is expected, particularly where third parties may be adversely affected by the overturning of a decision, e.g. *R v Independent Television Commission, ex parte TVNi* [1996] JR 60. Grounds for a judicial review application in respect of a planning permission first arise for the purposes of **CPR, r. 54.5(1)**, from the date of the grant of permission, not from the earlier date when the planning committee passed a resolution authorising one of the authority's officers to grant outline permission on fulfilment of conditions precedent (*R (Burkett) v Hammersmith and Fulham London Borough Council* [2002] UKHL 23, [2002] 1 WLR 1593). Permission may be granted where a challenged decision was made in circumstances where the claimant for judicial review did not know of its susceptibility to challenge until long after the interveners had incurred most or all of the expense and effort upon which they relied to establish the prejudice in opposition to the grant of permission (*R v Licensing Authority, ex parte Novartis Pharmaceuticals Ltd* [2000] COD 232).

A claimant who has failed to bring proceedings within the time limit may apply to the court for an extension (under **CPR, r. 3.1(2)(a)**) of the time limit for filing the claim form. A claim form filed after the time limit set by **CPR, r. 54.5(1)**, must be accompanied by an application to extend the limit (**PD 54A, para. 5.6**). The onus is on the claimant to show that there is a good reason for extending time for applying for judicial review (*R v Warwickshire County Council, ex parte Collymore* [1995] ELR 217). Examples of 'good reasons' which have been accepted include:

(a) the claimant's lack of knowledge (it has been held that delay is no bar to relief when material matters were not known to the claimant until a later point in time, e.g. *R v Department of Transport, ex parte Presvac Engineering Ltd* (1992) 4 Admin LR 121);

(b) sensible and reasonable behaviour by the claimant which has caused no prejudice (*R v Commissioner for Local Administration, ex parte Croydon London Borough Council* [1989] 1 All ER 1033);

(c) exhaustion of all alternative remedies by the claimant prior to commencing proceedings (e.g. *R v Rochdale Metropolitan Borough Council, ex parte Cromer Ring Mill Ltd* [1982] 3 All ER 761);

(d) delay by the claimant in securing legal aid — provided that the application for legal aid has been expeditiously pursued on the part of the claimant (e.g. *R v Stratford-on-Avon District Council, ex parte Jackson* [1985] 1 WLR 1319);

(e) issues in the public interest (*R v Secretary of State for the Home Department, ex parte Ruddock* [1987] 1 WLR 1482, which concerned the challenge by a member of CND of the defendant's decision to tap her telephone; *R v Secretary of State for Trade and Industry, ex parte Greenpeace Ltd* [2000] 2 CMLR 94, which related to the incomplete and unlawful implementation by the United Kingdom of an EC Directive and the defendant's legally erroneous approach to the Directive);

(f) ongoing negotiations between the parties (*R v Greenwich London Borough Council, ex parte Patterson* (1994) 26 HLR 159);

(g) poor legal advice — courts have in particular sought to protect the interests of individual claimants in housing and immigration cases where it may not be possible to compensate the claimant by way of a damages award (e.g. *R v Secretary of State for the Home Department, ex parte Oyeleye* [1994] Imm AR 268);

(h) in certain circumstances, awaiting the decision of the Secretary of State on whether to call in a grant of planning permission (*R (Burkett) v Hammersmith and Fulham London Borough Council* [2002] UKHL 23, [2002] 1 WLR 1593).

An extension of time has been granted in circumstances where the claim was in substance the same as an earlier discontinued claim that had been brought for the benefit of a wider group (*R (SDR) v Bristol City Council* [2012] EWHC 859 (Admin), LTL 5/4/2012). However, the grant of an extension of time involves an exercise of discretion on the part of the court and there is no guarantee that an extension will be given in any particular case.

The courts have not been persuaded by arguments for an extension of time in circumstances where: there is a risk of prejudice to third parties (e.g. *R v Independent Television Commission, ex parte TVNi* [1996] JR 60); an extension of time would adversely affect market dealings which have been undertaken in good faith (*R v Independent Television, ex parte TVNi*); an intention had been expressed by the claimant to bring proceedings but a significant period of time elapsed before anything was done (*R v Independent Television Commission, ex parte White Rose Television Ltd* (unreported, 24 January 1992)).

Where an issue of EU law is involved, only the three-month limit applies and the additional requirement for promptness does not apply, because it does not meet the criteria of certainty and effectiveness which must be met when transposing EU Directives (*R (Buglife) v Medway Council* [2011] EWHC 746 (Admin), [2011] Env LR 27, applying *Uniplex (UK) Ltd v NHS Business Services Authority* (case C-406/08) [2010] PTSR 1377; see also *R (U and Partners (East Anglia) Ltd) v Broads Authority* [2011] EWHC 1824 (Admin), [2011] JPL 1583 and *R (Berky) v Newport City Council* [2012] EWCA Civ 378, [2012] 2 CMLR 44).

As to compatibility of the judicial review time limit with the Human Rights Act 1998 see **91.42**. The claim form must be served on the defendant and any person the claimant considers to be an interested party (unless the court directs otherwise) within seven days after the date of issue (**CPR, r. 54.7**). Where the claim for judicial review relates to proceedings in a court or tribunal, any other parties to those proceedings must be named in the claim form as interested parties and therefore served with the claim form (**PD 54A, para. 5.1**).

Acknowledgment of service

Any person who has been served with a claim form commencing proceedings for judicial **77.37** review and who wishes to take part in the proceedings must file an acknowledgment of service (form N462) (**CPR, r. 54.8(1)**). The acknowledgment of service must be filed not more than 21 days after service of the claim form and must be served on the claimant and any other person named in the claim form as soon as practicable and, in any event, not later than seven days after it is filed (**r. 54.8(2)**). These time limits may not be extended by agreement between the parties (**r. 54.8(3)**).

If the intention is to contest the claim, the acknowledgment of service must set out a summary of the grounds for doing so, and must also state the name and address of any person whom the person filing the acknowledgment considers to be an interested party (**r. 54.8(4)**). The acknowledgment of service may also include or be accompanied by an application for directions. A defendant who succeeds at the substantive hearing is in principle entitled to recover the costs of submitting an acknowledgment of service (*R (Leach) v Local Commissioner for Administration* [2001] EWHC 455 (Admin), [2001] CP Rep 97).

A person served with a judicial review claim form who does not acknowledge service in accordance with **r. 54.8** may not, without the court's permission, take part in the hearing to decide whether permission to proceed should be given (**r. 54.9(1)(a)**). However, if the person complies with **r. 54.14** (filing and service of a response by the defendant or any other person served with the claim form) or any other direction of the court regarding filing and service of detailed grounds for contesting the claim or supporting it on additional grounds, and any written evidence, he may take part in the judicial review hearing (**r. 54.9(1)(b)**).

Where a person takes part in the judicial review hearing, the court may take his failure to file an acknowledgment of service into account when deciding what order to make about costs (r. 54.9(2)).

Under the rules on non-party access to documents in **Part 5**, a non-party to judicial review has a right to have sight of the claim form, acknowledgment of service and detailed grounds, the latter falling within the CPR definition of defence (*R (Corner House Research) v Director of the Serious Fraud Office* [2008] EWHC 246 (Admin), [2008] ACD 63).

If a defendant does not wish to participate actively in the proceedings, for example because of restraints on resources, it may still need to consider putting a witness statement or documents before the court, serving an outline defence or having a representative at the hearing in order to fulfil its duty of candour and assist the court in disposing of the matter fairly (*R (Midcounties Co-operative Ltd v Forest of Dean District Council* [2015] EWHC 1251 (Admin), [2015] BLGR 829).

Relevant considerations in deciding whether or not to grant permission

77.38   If the court considers that there has been undue delay in claiming judicial review, permission to proceed with the claim, or relief at the substantive hearing, may be refused if it would be likely to lead to substantial hardship or prejudice or detriment to good administration (Senior Courts Act 1981, s. 31(6)). For example, in *R v Secretary of State for Health, ex parte Furneaux* [1994] 2 All ER 652 relief was refused because of prejudice to a rival pharmacy, but in other cases with serious consequences for a party or third party, relief has not been refused, e.g. in *R v Port Talbot Borough Council, ex parte Jones* [1988] 2 All ER 207 the grant of relief required the defendant to leave her home, and in *R v Secretary of State for the Environment, ex parte Chichester District Council* [1993] 2 PLR 1 relief caused a third party to face criminal proceedings.

In *R v Dairy Produce Quota Tribunal, ex parte Caswell* [1990] 2 AC 738 the House of Lords held that matters of particular importance in determining whether or not there is detriment to good administration, apart from the length of time itself, will be the extent of the effect of the relevant decision, and the impact which would be felt if it were to be reopened. Section 31(6) of the Senior Courts Act 1981 requires affirmative evidence of detriment, i.e. the foreseen consequences of granting the relief sought must be positive harm to good administration, or at least evidence from which it can properly be inferred, and in considering detriment the court can take into account the effect on other potential claimants and the consequences if their claims were successful.

The effect of *R v Criminal Injuries Compensation Board, ex parte A* [1998] QB 659 (CA), [1999] 2 AC 330 (HL), is that permission to proceed and the substantive hearing should be regarded as two distinct stages. Permission should not be granted if:

(a) the claim form for judicial review was not filed promptly and in any event within three months and there is no good reason to extend time (**CPR, rr. 3.1(2)(a) and 54.5(1)**); or

(b) relief would be likely to cause substantial hardship, substantial prejudice or detriment to good administration (Senior Courts Act 1981, s. 31(6)).

At the substantive hearing delay may again be considered but the defendant will be permitted to recanvass an issue of promptness which was decided at the permission stage in the claimant's favour only if any of the following conditions are satisfied:

(a) if the judge hearing the original application expressly so indicated;

(b) if new and relevant material was introduced at the substantive hearing;

(c) if, exceptionally, the issues as they had developed at the full hearing put a different aspect on the question of promptness; or

(d) if the first judge had plainly overlooked some relevant matter or otherwise reached a decision per incuriam.

See *R (Lichfield Securities Ltd) v Lichfield District Council* [2001] EWCA Civ 304, 3 LGLR 35.

It has been held that there is nothing in EU law which prevents the court from applying the Senior Courts Act 1981, s. 31(6), even in the case of an alleged breach of EU law by the defendant (*R v North West Leicestershire District Council, ex parte Moses* [2000] Env LR 443). Only in exceptional circumstances will the court entertain a judicial review claim that has become purely academic by the withdrawal of the original decision by the public body. Such circumstances may arise where there are allegations of bad faith (*R (K) v Entry Clearance Officer, Tashkent* [2012] EWHC 2875 (Admin), LTL 5/10/2012).

Amendment of application for permission

A judicial review claim form may be amended in accordance with the general principles of **77.39** CPR, **Part 17**, discussed in **chapter 31**. In general, amendments will be allowed for the purpose of putting the claimant's case fully before the court, provided that the defendant is not unfairly prejudiced as a result.

DETERMINATION OF THE APPLICATION FOR PERMISSION

Once a judicial review claim form and supporting evidence have been filed, the general rule is **77.40** that, in the first instance, the court will consider the question of permission to proceed with the claim without a hearing (**PD 54A, para. 8.4**). Where this rule applies, the papers are passed to a judge to read and to make a decision without hearing oral arguments.

If permission to proceed is given, the court may also give directions (**CPR, r. 54.10(1)**), which may include a stay of proceedings to which the claim relates (**r. 54.10(2)**).

The court may give permission to proceed subject to conditions, or on certain grounds only (**r. 54.12(1)(b)**). This was not possible before the CPR (*R v Criminal Injuries Compensation Board, ex parte A* [1998] QB 659).

The court will serve its order giving or refusing permission to proceed with a claim for judicial review, and any directions, on the parties and any other person who filed an acknowledgment of service (**r. 54.11**). The order will be accompanied by the court's reasons if it refuses permission or gives permission to proceed either subject to conditions or on certain grounds only (**r. 54.12(2)**).

The claimant may not appeal against a refusal of permission to proceed, or against permission given subject to conditions or on certain grounds only, but may normally request that the decision be reconsidered at a hearing (**r. 54.12(3)**). A request for reconsideration of a decision must be filed within seven days after service of the court's reasons for the decision (**r. 54.12(4)**). The parties and any other person who has filed an acknowledgment of service will be given at least two days' notice of the hearing date (**r. 54.12(5)**).

However, where the court considers the application to be 'totally without merit' on the papers, a request for oral reconsideration will not be entertained (**r. 54.12(7)**) and any application to the Court of Appeal will also be decided on the papers without an oral hearing (**r. 52.15(1A)(b)**). The term 'totally without merit' means simply 'bound to fail' (*R (Grace) v Secretary of State for the Home Department* [2014] EWCA Civ 1091, [2014] 1 WLR 3432). *GR (Albania) v Secretary of State for the Home Department* [2013] EWCA Civ 1286 involved a permission application which had been certified as 'totally without merit' at first instance. This is a different, higher, test than the usual permission threshold of whether a matter is 'arguable'. In view of the removal of the right to an oral renewal hearing, no case should be certified as 'totally without merit' unless a judge is confident that it is truly bound to fail, and judges are encouraged to give reasons for any such certification (*R (Wasif) v Secretary of State for the Home Department* [2016] EWCA Civ 82, [2016] 1 WLR 2793). On the permission to appeal, Underhill LJ considered the case on the papers and ordered that the application be considered by the

Court of Appeal in an expedited oral hearing. However, at that hearing Moses and Gloster LLJ held that in light of the CPR, the Court of Appeal had no power to order such an oral hearing, and remitted the case to Underhill LJ to consider on the papers. Neither the defendant nor any other person served with the claim form may apply to set aside an order giving permission to proceed with a claim for judicial review (r. 54.13).

If, contrary to the general rule, the court, in its discretion, decides that there should be an oral hearing of an application for permission to proceed with a claim for judicial review, the Administrative Court Office will fix a hearing date without any intervening consideration of the papers. The application is made to a judge in open court unless the court directs that it should be made in private or to a Divisional Court. The defendant and other interested parties are not required to attend, unless the court directs otherwise (PD 54A, para. 8.5). If the defendant or any other party does attend, the court will not generally order the claimant to pay their costs of doing so (para. 8.6) (R (Mount Cook Land Ltd) v Westminster City Council [2003] EWCA Civ 1346, [2004] CP Rep 12; Payne v Caerphilly County Borough Council [2004] EWCA Civ 433, LTL 17/3/2004). In Practice Statement (Judicial Review: Costs) [2004] 2 All ER 994 it was confirmed that a grant of permission to pursue a claim for judicial review would be deemed to contain an order that costs of that application be costs in the case. A different costs order can be specifically made by the judge granting permission.

Normally no witnesses attend a permission hearing and the claimant is not required to be there in person. An application for permission to proceed with a claim for judicial review is listed on the basis that the application will take no more than 20 minutes, and any reply by a defendant who attends will take no more than 10 minutes (Practice Direction (Crown Office List) (No. 2) [1991] 1 WLR 280). If permission is granted, any applications for interim relief or special directions are considered. If permission is refused, the decision can be appealed to the Court of Appeal with that court's permission (CPR, r. 52.15(1)).

An appeal to the Court of Appeal after permission is refused in an oral application will be heard by a full Court of Appeal (rather than a single Lord Justice). An application for permission to appeal against the High Court's refusal to permit a claim for judicial review to proceed must be made within seven days of the High Court's decision (r. 52.15(2)). The appellant's notice must be accompanied by the documents specified in PD 52C, para. 3(3). A copy of it must be served on all respondents to the appeal in accordance with CPR, r. 52.4(3) (PD 52C, paras 3(1) and 7.2). Instead of granting permission to appeal, the Court of Appeal may proceed directly to give the permission to proceed with the claim which was initially sought (CPR, r. 52.15(3)) and the case will be returned to the High Court, unless the Court of Appeal orders otherwise (r. 52.15(4); see R (Werner) v Commissioners of Inland Revenue [2002] EWCA Civ 979, [2002] STC 1213 at [30]–[33]). The Court of Appeal should be cautious about retaining the substantive proceedings (R (AA) v Secretary of State for the Home Department [2012] EWCA Civ 23, The Times, 5 March 2012), but this would be appropriate where, for example, the High Court is bound by authority or, for some other reason, a further appeal to the Court of Appeal would be inevitable (PD 52C, para. 15.3). If permission has been refused by the Court of Appeal, the court of first instance may, nevertheless, subsequently grant permission if there have been developments of which the Court of Appeal was unaware (R v Radio Authority, ex parte Wildman [1999] COD 255). If the Court of Appeal refuses permission there is generally no appeal or possibility of renewing the application to the Supreme Court (Re Poh [1983] 1 WLR 2; R v Secretary of State for Trade and Industry, ex parte Eastaway [2000] 1 WLR 2222). Where, however, the Court of Appeal grants permission to appeal but then refuses permission for judicial review (for example, on the grounds of delay), the Supreme Court has jurisdiction to grant permission to appeal against this decision (R (Burkett) v Hammersmith and Fulham London Borough Council [2002] UKHL 23, [2002] 1 WLR 1593).

A claimant who no longer requires any substantive relief but wishes the claim to go forward to test the lawfulness of the defendant's procedures in general must inform the defendant that he wishes the court to scrutinise the defendant's practices and procedures (*R (Tshikangu) v Newham London Borough Council* [2001] EWHC 92 (Admin), [2001] NPC 33). The parties should consider whether a test case is appropriate, and if so what that case should be. If they are not agreed, application should be made to the court for it to consider the matter before the costs of a substantive hearing are incurred.

PROCEDURE ONCE PERMISSION HAS BEEN GRANTED

Defendant's evidence and evidence in reply

If permission is given to proceed with a claim for judicial review, the order granting permission will be served on the defendant and any other person who filed an acknowledgment of service (**CPR, r. 54.11**). Any of those persons who wish to contest the claim, or to support it on additional grounds, must, within 35 days after service of the permission order, file and serve the detailed grounds for contesting or supporting and their written evidence (**r. 54.14(1)**). If it is intended to rely on documents not already filed, a paginated bundle of the new documents must be filed with the detailed grounds (**PD 54A, para. 10.1**). In judicial review proceedings, **CPR, r. 54.14(1)**, applies instead of **r. 8.5(3)** to (6) (**r. 54.14(2)**). The 35-day time limit can be extended or shortened on application to a master of the Administrative Court Office or a High Court judge (**r. 3.1(2)(a)**). The 35-day time limit applies both to written evidence and to detailed grounds for contesting the claim or supporting it on additional grounds (*R (J) v Newham London Borough Council* [2001] EWHC 992 (Admin), *The Independent*, 10 December 2001). Failure to serve within the time limit may be dealt with by the general discretion of the court to extend time, subject to the overriding objective. Any evidence in reply should include details of the facts which the defendant intends to rely upon, its answers to issues raised by the claimant, a response to the claimant's evidence, and should exhibit all documents relevant to the decision challenged which have not been exhibited with the claimant's evidence and which the defendant wishes to rely upon at the substantive hearing. The written evidence should also make clear if there is any factual conflict between the claimant and the defendant. The written evidence should be filed in the Administrative Court Office. Note the obligation on the defendant to consider whether evidence should be filed even if not actively participating in the proceedings (see 77.37).

77.41

Permission to proceed with a judicial review claim is permission to proceed on specified grounds only. The claimant will not be able to rely on other grounds without further permission from the court (**r. 54.15**). Notice of intention to rely on additional grounds must be given to the court, and to any other person served with the claim form, no later than seven clear days before the hearing (or the warned date if one has been given) (**PD 54A, para. 11.1**). Where there is good reason to allow argument on an additional ground, permission should be granted. Each case should be considered on its facts. In exercising discretion, a judge should bear in mind that if permission to rely on a ground is refused, the Court of Appeal on an appeal from the hearing at first instance would not be able to consider it (*R (Smith) v Parole Board* [2003] EWCA Civ 1014, [2003] 1 WLR 2548). Cf. the approach in *Opoku v Principal of Southwark School* [2002] EWHC 2092 (Admin), [2003] 1 WLR 234).

The service of written evidence in reply by the claimant may be considered necessary where there is a factual dispute, where new circumstances have arisen since applying for permission to proceed, or in order to comment upon documents disclosed by the defendant.

Interim remedies

Although most forms of interim remedies are available in judicial review proceedings, obtaining interim remedies is more restricted than in private law actions. Generally the most appropriate time to apply for interim remedies is at the stage of applying for

77.42

permission but a court may grant interim remedies to any of the parties during the course of judicial review proceedings. (If interim remedies are sought after the substantive application has been dismissed, pending appeal, it will be necessary to show that the appeal has a good prospect of success.)

A claim form for judicial review must state any interim remedy which is claimed. In particular, it may ask for the court, when giving permission for the claim to proceed to direct (under **CPR, r. 54.10(2)**) a stay of proceedings to which the claim relates. A stay under **r. 54.10(2)** has the effect that the public body's decision or procedure which is the subject of challenge should not continue or take effect until the judicial review challenge is determined. In considering whether to grant a stay, the court will take into account the effect on third parties and may refuse a stay notwithstanding a grant of permission to proceed with the claim for judicial review, applying balance of convenience considerations. A stay is available as a remedy against all public bodies against whom permission has been granted, including the Crown in the form of a government department or minister (*R v Secretary of State for Education, ex parte Avon County Council* [1991] 1 QB 558). A cross-undertaking for damages to a party to the action may be made a condition of a stay (*R v Inspectorate of Pollution, ex parte Greenpeace Ltd* [1994] 1 WLR 570).

The court may also at any time grant in the proceedings interim remedies in accordance with **CPR, Part 25**. The general principles governing the grant of interim remedies apply also in relation to judicial review proceedings (*R v Ministry of Agriculture, Fisheries and Food, ex parte Monsanto plc* [1999] QB 1161). However, these have to be applied in the context of the public law questions raised in such proceedings (see 77.58). **Rule 25.1** lists the interim remedies which include an interim injunction (**r. 25.1(1)(a)**), interim declaration (**r. 25.1(1)(b)**), freezing injunction (**r. 25.1(1)(f)**), search order (**r. 25.1(1)(h)**), and an order for the detention and inspection of relevant property (**r. 25.1(1)(c)**). Generally, notice of an application for an interim remedy should be given to all parties (**r. 25.3(1)**).

Injunctions are the main type of interim relief ordered in judicial review proceedings. To obtain an interim injunction in a civil case, it must be established that the claimant has a serious issue to be tried on the merits and that the 'balance of convenience' favours the making of an interim order (*American Cyanamid Co. v Ethicon Ltd* [1975] AC 396; see **chapter 37**). The balance of convenience test involves the court considering whether there is an adequate alternative remedy in damages, the interests of the general public to whom the duties are owed, the importance of upholding the law of the land, and the duty upon certain authorities to enforce the law in the public interest. There is a presumption in favour of a cross-undertaking in damages (**PD 25A, para. 5.1(1)**). The court must also consider whether to require an undertaking by the applicant to pay damages sustained by a person other than the respondent, including another party to the proceedings or any other person who may suffer a loss as a consequence of the injunction (**para. 5.1A**). Before ordering a cross-undertaking in damages with respect to the respondent or any other person's damages in Aarhus Convention claims, however, the court must also have regard to ensuring that the claim is not prohibitively expensive for the applicant and make directions to ensure that the case is heard promptly (**para. 5.1B**).

The approach to applications for interim injunctions in judicial review proceedings is similar to that adopted in applications for interim injunctions in private law claims (*R v Kensington and Chelsea Royal London Borough Council, ex parte Hammell* [1989] QB 518). However, where public bodies are concerned the balance of convenience may be more difficult to make out — i.e. ordinary financial considerations may be qualified by recognition of the interests of the general public (*Smith v Inner London Education Authority* [1978] 1 All ER 411). Usually an application is for a prohibitory injunction to prevent a public body from doing something. Where a mandatory injunction is sought, the order will not be granted unless the court has a high degree of assurance of the merits of the case.

An interim injunction is available against a government minister but will only be granted in limited circumstances, i.e. where it is necessary for the court to have power to prevent irreparable harm to the citizen by unauthorised governmental action (*Re M* [1994] 1 AC 377). An interim injunction has been granted against a minister of the Crown to restrain him from implementing a new regime authorised by an Act of Parliament where there was a strong prima facie case that the Act was in breach of EU law (*R v Secretary of State for Transport, ex parte Factortame Ltd (No. 2)* [1991] 1 AC 603). The Court of Justice of the European Union ruled that where a national court was seised of a case involving EU law issues and it was necessary to grant interim relief in order to ensure the full effectiveness of the rights claimed under directly applicable EU law, any rule of national law preventing the grant of such interim relief must be set aside. A reference to the Court of Justice of the European Union is required to establish whether domestic or EU law is applicable when a domestic court is asked to grant an injunction to restrain the government from making regulations during the implementation period pursuant to an EC Directive (*R v Secretary of State for Health, ex parte Imperial Tobacco Ltd* [2001] 1 WLR 127). EU law permits applications for an injunction in the domestic courts in support of an application to the domestic court challenging the validity of an EC Directive. In order to grant an injunction, serious doubts are required as to the validity of the EU measure and the need to avoid serious and irreparable damage (which is not purely financial) to the party seeking the injunction.

CPR, r. 25.1(1)(b), provides for the grant of an interim declaration. Prior to the introduction of the CPR the existence of such a remedy was uncertain. Interim declarations are granted on a similar basis to interim injunctions. The decision whether or not to grant an interim injunction or declaration is a matter of discretion for the court of first instance, with which the Court of Appeal will not interfere unless there is an error of law or plain error of fact or assessment. In deciding whether to grant an interim remedy, the court should have regard to the 'threshold condition' that legislation ought to be fulfilled in all but exceptional cases. Thereafter, considering the balance of convenience, the concurrent elements are the strength of the case and the parties' respective losses if the declaration were granted or refused (*R v Secretary of State for Trade and Industry, ex parte Trades Union Congress* [2000] IRLR 565). An interim declaration of unlawfulness has been granted in respect of arrangements for the control of pesticides made under regulations which were made by statutory instrument, pending determination by the Court of Justice of the European Union of a reference made in another case concerning interpretation of the Directive which the regulations were made to implement (*R v Ministry of Agriculture, Fisheries and Food, ex parte British Agrochemicals Association Ltd (No. 2)* [2000] 1 CMLR 826). However, the grant of an interim declaration to render national legislation inoperative pending the decision of the Court of Justice of the European Union will be rare, as there is a presumption in favour of the national law being applicable (*R v Secretary of State for Trade and Industry, ex parte Trades Union Congress* [2001] 1 CMLR 8).

Interim applications

An interim application may be made to any judge or to a Master of the Queen's Bench Division. **77.43** However, a Master or District Judge outside London may not grant most types of interim relief other than orders by consent (see **PD 2B, paras 2** and **3**) although he or she may deal with applications for interim procedural relief by case management. Where the application for judicial review is to be heard by a Divisional Court, any appeal from a decision of a Master will lie to the Divisional Court itself. Contested interim applications are normally heard by a judge nominated to hear Administrative Court Office List cases. Uncontested interim applications are dealt with by the Administrative Court without the need for attendance (Practice Direction (Administrative Court: Uncontested Proceedings) [2008] 1 WLR 1377).

CPR, Part 23, and **PD 23A** apply to interim applications in judicial review proceedings. **Part 23** requires that all applications are to be made by filing and serving an application notice (**r. 23.3(1)**). An application will not necessarily result in a hearing even if one is requested (**r. 23.8**).

Interim applications may have to be made seeking the exercise of the court's general powers of management under **r. 3.1(2)**, e.g. to extend or shorten the time for compliance with any rule, practice direction or court order (**r. 3.1(2)(a)**), consolidation in order that two or more matters be tried at the same time (**r. 3.1(2)(h)**), or to adjourn or expedite a hearing (**r. 3.1(2)(b)**).

Disclosure

77.44   The court has jurisdiction to order cross-examination of witnesses and disclosure in judicial review proceedings but the assumption is that disclosure is not required unless the court orders otherwise (**PD 54A, para. 12.1**).

There is no automatic right to disclosure of documents in judicial review proceedings, but this is because there is already a separate duty of candour on the part of defendants who must set out fully what they did and why, so far as is necessary, fully and fairly to meet the challenge (*R v Lancashire County Council, ex parte Huddleston* [1986] 2 All ER 941). Disclosure will only be ordered where it is required to ensure the justice of the case and to dispose fairly of the matter (*R v Commissioners of Inland Revenue, ex parte J. Rothschild Holdings plc* [1987] STC 163). The courts have held (Lord Scarman in *R v Commissioners of Inland Revenue, ex parte National Federation of Self-Employed and Small Businesses Ltd* [1982] AC 617):

Upon general principles, discovery should not be ordered unless or until the court is satisfied that the evidence reveals reasonable grounds for believing that there has been a breach of public duty; and it should be limited strictly to documents relevant to the issue which emerges from the affidavits.

Where an application for judicial review involves a consideration of the proportionality of the defendant's actions, the disclosure of documents will be ordered more readily than in an application where no issues of proportionality arise. However, whether disclosure should be ordered will depend on the balancing of several factors, of which proportionality is only one, albeit a significant one. In cases where disclosure is ordered, it should always be carefully limited to the issues which require it in the interests of justice (*Tweed v Parades Commission* [2006] UKHL 53, [2007] 1 AC 650).

The courts will not permit the claimant to obtain disclosure to go behind an assertion in the defendant's written evidence and check its accuracy unless the claimant has some evidence that the contents are false or not accurate (*R v Secretary of State for the Environment, ex parte Islington London Borough Council* [1992] COD 67). A successful application for disclosure is less likely at the permission stage (where the claimant could always point to the lack of full disclosure to strengthen its argument for permission to be granted) than at the substantive hearing where the issues are considered in greater detail (*Sky Blue Sports and Leisure Ltd v Coventry City Council* [2013] EWHC 3366 (Admin), [2014] BLGR 34).

Disclosure and inspection may be withheld on the grounds of public interest immunity. In addition, where there may be sensitive material disclosed in the course of proceedings there is the possibility of using the closed material procedure provided for under the Justice and Security Act 2013 (see *R (Sarkandi) v Secretary of State for Foreign and Commonwealth Affairs* [2015] EWCA Civ 687, LTL 14/7/2015, for an example of closed material procedure being used in judicial review). There may also be the possibility of the use of a confidentiality ring (*R (Serdar Mohammed) v Secretary of State for Defence* [2012] EWHC 3454 (Admin), [2014] 1 WLR 1071); *R (National Association of Probation Officers) v Secretary of State for Justice* [2014] EWHC 4349 (Admin), LTL 28/11/2014.

The courts will order disclosure where the defendant public body has not included documents which might have been expected to be provided or an explanation for the absence of documents (*R (Bredenkamp) v Secretary of State for Foreign and Commonwealth Affairs* [2013] EWHC 2480 (Admin), [2013] Lloyd's Rep FC 690). The court may also come under particular pressure to order disclosure in **Human Rights Act 1998** cases, which may involve a factual examination of the merits of a case (see **chapter 91**). In *R (Al-Sweady) v Secretary of State for Defence* [2009] EWHC 2387 (Admin), [2010] HRLR 2, the High Court held that where the outcome of a judicial review application might depend upon the determination of a factual dispute, the court should give urgent consideration to ordering disclosure and cross-examination. Similarly in *R (National Association of Probation Officers) v Secretary of State for Justice* [2014] EWHC 4349 (Admin), LTL 28/11/2014, the court noted that a claim involving Convention rights required an assessment of the merits and therefore, applying the *Tweed* test, the court may require specific documentation, disclosure of which should be ordered unless there is evidence demonstrating a specific reason or public interest against disclosure. It is envisaged that such orders might occur with increasing regularity in cases involving crucial factual disputes relating to human rights issues.

The duty of candour does not amount to a general duty of disclosure on a public body. There is a very high duty on public authorities to assist the court with a full and accurate explanation of all the relevant facts where it is not possible for the court to assess the merits of an issue unless the public authority provides the court with information which it alone can provide (*Secretary of State for Foreign and Commonwealth Affairs v Quark Fishing Ltd* [2002] EWCA Civ 1409, LTL 30/10/2002) (note that this obligation may exist even if the defendant chooses not to participate in the proceedings, see 77.37). However, the duty of candour should not be used to transfer to the public authority the onus of proving matters which the claimant is under a duty and in a position to prove, such as the reasonableness or otherwise of the decision (*Marshall v Deputy Governor of Bermuda* [2010] UKPC 9, *The Times*, 7 June 2010).

The CPR do not explicitly allow the court to order pre-action disclosure in judicial review proceedings. It has been held that the court does in principle have such powers, although in general pre-action disclosure in judicial review is undesirable and the court will only depart from the normal judicial review procedures in exceptional circumstances (*British Union for the Abolition of Vivisection v Secretary of State for the Home Department* [2014] EWHC 43 (Admin), [2014] ACD 69). Further, in the case of pre-action disclosure there is the practical issue for a potential claimant of needing to apply for permission to seek judicial review promptly and the timescale may make it impractical to seek pre-action disclosure first.

It is extremely difficult to obtain an order to provide clarification or further information in judicial review proceedings. Claimants who wish defendants to answer a request for further information should first serve them informally, requesting a response within a reasonable time, prior to making an application to the court (**PD 18, para. 1.1**).

Interested parties and interveners

A claimant seeking judicial review is under a duty to serve a copy of the claim form upon any person the claimant considers to be an interested party, unless the court directs otherwise (**CPR, r. 54.7**). 'Interested party' is defined as any person (other than the claimant and the defendant) who is directly affected by the claim (**r. 54.1(2)(f)**). The meaning of persons 'directly affected' was considered by the House of Lords in *R v Rent Officer Service, ex parte Muldoon* [1996] 1 WLR 1103. It was suggested (per Lord Keith of Kinkel at p. 1105), 'That a person is directly affected by something connotes that he is affected without the intervention of any intermediate agency'. The Secretary of State for Social Security was held to be only indirectly affected by a judicial review claim which challenged a failure to determine claims for housing benefit, as it was the local authority which would have to pay the claimants if the claim were successful. Similarly, the courts have refused to regard tobacco companies as 'directly affected' by a claim for judicial review of a refusal by the Legal Aid Board to grant the claimants legal aid to bring proceedings against the tobacco company (*R v Legal Aid Board, ex parte Megarry* [1994] COD 468).

The role of an interested party is restricted to making submissions in relation to the main claim and therefore there is jurisdiction for them to be heard only where they are directly affected by that main claim. There is no provision allowing an interested party to advance

77.45

a different claim against the defendant, and a person who is not seeking the same relief as the claimant will not be directly affected by the claim and therefore cannot be heard as an interested party (*R (McVey) v Secretary of State for Health* [2010] EWHC 1225 (Admin), [2010] ACD 95).

Any person served with the claim form who wishes to take part in the judicial review must file an acknowledgment of service in accordance with **r. 54.8**. Failure to file an acknowledgment of service means that the permission of the court will be required to take part in a hearing to decide permission to proceed with the claim (**r. 54.9(1)(a)**).

An interested party who has not acknowledged service cannot take part in the substantive hearing without filing and serving detailed grounds for contesting the claim or supporting it on additional grounds, and any written evidence (**r. 54.9(1)(b)**).

Filing an acknowledgment of service entitles an interested party to be served with the court's order giving or refusing permission to proceed and any directions (**r. 54.11**). If the claimant requests that a refusal of permission be reconsidered at a hearing, any person who has filed an acknowledgment of service will be given at least two days' notice of the hearing (**r. 54.12(5)**). Any person served with the claim form may not apply to set aside an order giving permission to proceed (**r. 54.13**).

No interested party need attend a hearing on the question of permission to proceed unless the court directs otherwise (**PD 54A, para. 8.5**). Where the defendant or any other party does attend a hearing, the court will not generally make an order for costs against the claimant (**para. 8.6**).

Any person served with the claim form who wishes to contest the claim or support it on additional grounds must file and serve detailed grounds for contesting or supporting the claim and any written evidence within 35 days after service of the order giving permission to proceed (**CPR, r. 54.14(1)**).

Any person may apply for permission to file evidence or to make representations at the substantive judicial review hearing, and those granted such permission are known as interveners (**r. 54.17(1)**). Such an application must be made promptly (**r. 54.17(2)**) since it will usually be essential not to delay the hearing (**PD 54A, para. 13.5**). An application for permission to file evidence or make representations at the hearing of the judicial review claim should be made by letter to the Administrative Court Office, identifying the claim, explaining who the applicant is and indicating why and in what form the applicant wants to participate in the hearing (**para. 13.3**). If the applicant is seeking a prospective order as to costs, the letter should say what kind of order and on what grounds (**para. 13.4**). Where all the parties consent, the court may deal with such an application without a hearing (**para. 13.1**). Where the court gives permission for a person to file evidence or make representations at the substantive hearing, it may do so on conditions and may give case management directions (**para. 13.2**).

There is no general right for a third party to be heard on appeal, although the Court of Appeal may exercise its discretion to permit this.

The court will rarely grant two sets of costs in judicial review proceedings to two parties who appear in the same interest (*R v Industrial Disputes Tribunal, ex parte American Express Co. Inc.* [1954] 1 WLR 1118; *Bolton Metropolitan District Council v Secretary of State for the Environment* [1995] 1 WLR 1176). However, in exceptional circumstances the court may grant two sets of costs, e.g. where the issues are complex or important or the interests of the two parties concerned are divergent (*R v Registrar of Companies, ex parte Central Bank of India* [1986] QB 1114).

Parties to the proceedings may not be ordered by the High Court or the Court of Appeal to pay the costs of any intervener, but a party may apply for costs from an intervener in certain circumstances set out in the Criminal Justice and Courts Act 2015, s. 87 (see **68.39**).

SUBSTANTIVE HEARING

Listing the hearing

The court may decide a claim for judicial review without a hearing if all the parties agree **(CPR, r. 54.18)**. The effect of this rule is that once permission has been granted for judicial review the claim can only be substantively disposed of by an oral hearing, unless all parties agree. It is not possible to deal with the matter in any other way (*R (Parsipoor) v Secretary of State for the Home Department* [2011] EWCA Civ 276, [2011] 1 WLR 3187). If the parties agree about the final order to be made in a claim for judicial review, the claimant must file at the court two copies of a document signed by all the parties setting out the terms of the proposed agreed order, together with a short statement of the matters relied upon as justifying the proposal and copies of any authorities or statutory provisions relied on **(PD 54A, para. 17.1)**. The court will consider the documents and will make the order if satisfied that the order should be made **(para. 17.2)**. If the court is not satisfied that the order should be made, a hearing date will be set **(para. 17.3)**. Where the agreement relates to an order for costs only, the parties need only file a document signed by all the parties setting out the terms of the proposed order **(para. 17.4)**. Where a claim is entered for hearing it must be entered in the Administrative Court Office List in accordance with Practice Direction (Crown Office List) [1987] 1 WLR 232. All claims for judicial review are included within the Administrative Court Office List which is divided into five parts. These are:

Part A: cases not ready to be heard, i.e. permission has not yet been obtained or the time limits for the filing of evidence have not yet expired.

Part B: cases ready to be heard, i.e. the warned list. All applications are entered in Part B once all relevant time limits have expired, i.e. usually after the 35-day period for service of the defendant's written evidence has ended. When a case enters Part B the claimant or the claimant's solicitors will be informed of this by letter and must duly inform their counsel, the defendant and any other interested parties of the likelihood of the case being listed at short notice. Applications for adjournments will be granted only in exceptional circumstances (Practice Direction (Crown Office List: Preparation for Hearings) [2000] 2 All ER 896).

Part C: cases stood out, i.e. where a case appears in Part B or Part E and any party is not ready to be heard, the case may be stood out of the list into Part C upon application to the master of the court office, and may be appealed to a judge or the Divisional Court by a court application.

Part D: the expedited list, i.e. cases listed to be heard as soon as practicable. An application to be entered in Part D should initially be made to the master of the Administrative Court Office, and may be appealed to a Divisional Court or judge by a court application.

Part E: cases listed for hearing, i.e. cases where a date for the substantive hearing has been fixed. When a case is about to be listed under Part E, the Administrative Court Office will send a letter to the claimant's solicitors asking them to confirm that the case is still active and informing them that it will be listed shortly. If the claimant does not confirm within two weeks that the case is still active, the case may be put before the court and struck out for want of prosecution. The listing policy of the Administrative Court in fixing substantive hearings, the operation of the short warned list and vacating fixtures is set out in Practice Statement (Administrative Court: Listing and Urgent Cases) [2002] 1 WLR 810.

Documentation

Skeleton arguments are mandatory in all cases in the Administrative Court Office List. The claimant's counsel is required to file a skeleton argument with the Administrative Court Office and serve a copy on counsel for the defendant at least 21 working days before the date of the

77.46

77.47

Commentary

hearing or warned date (**PD 54A, para. 15.1**). The defendant and any other party wishing to make representations at the substantive hearing must file and serve a skeleton argument not less than 14 working days before the date of the hearing or the warned date (**para. 15.2**). If the application is to be heard by a Divisional Court, two copies of the skeleton argument must be lodged. The skeleton arguments may be supplemented up to one working day before the hearing (Practice Direction (Crown Office List: Preparation for Hearings) [1994] 1 WLR 1551). The skeleton arguments must quote the Administrative Court Office reference number and the warned/fixed date, provide a time estimate for the complete hearing (including delivery of judgment), and must also contain a list of issues, a list of the legal points to be taken (together with any relevant authorities with page references to the passages relied on), a chronology of events (with page references to the bundle of documents to be filed), a list of essential documents for the advance reading of the court (with page references to the passages relied on) (if different to that filed with the claim form), a time estimate for that reading, and a list of persons referred to (**PD 54A, para. 15.3**). Time estimates will be required from each party once the application is entered in Part B of the List. Great care must be taken by counsel to provide a well-judged and realistic time estimate for the hearing (Practice Direction (Crown Office List: Estimated Length of Hearing) [1987] 1 All ER 1184). The obligations upon counsel in the practice directions apply equally to a solicitor advocate.

For the use of extracts from *Hansard* under the rule in *Pepper v Hart* [1993] AC 593 see the guidance at **74.53**. Where this is permitted, the party must serve upon all other parties and the Administrative Court Office the relevant extract together with a brief summary of the argument based on the extract at least five working days before the hearing (Practice Direction (*Hansard*: Citation) [1995] 1 WLR 192).

The claimant's solicitor is responsible for preparing a paginated and indexed bundle of documents which must be lodged in the Administrative Court Office at the same time as the skeleton argument is filed (**PD 54A, para. 16.1**). The bundle must also include documents required by the defendant and any other party who is to make representations at the hearing (**para. 16.2**). If the claim is to be heard by a Divisional Court, two copies of each bundle must be lodged. The bundles must contain copies of the claim form, the decision complained of (if not separately exhibited), any relevant correspondence between the parties and any orders made in the course of the proceedings, and the written evidence filed by both parties. Where possible, the parties' solicitors should agree the contents of the bundles.

If the obligation to lodge a proper bundle is not complied with, the application for judicial review may be struck out and the costs imposed upon the claimant or the claimant's solicitor (*R v Home Secretary, ex parte Meyer-Wulff* [1986] Imm AR 258).

Oral evidence

77.48   In judicial review proceedings the Administrative Court may, either under **CPR, r. 32.1**, or its inherent jurisdiction, hear oral evidence and order the cross-examination of witnesses (*R (G) v Ealing London Borough Council* [2002] EWHC 250 (Admin), [2002] ACD 48). In practice, the courts very rarely allow cross-examination in judicial review cases on the basis that it is not usually required in the interests of justice (*Khera v Secretary of State for the Home Department* [1984] AC 74; *George v Secretary of State for the Environment* (1979) 77 LGR 689). Generally, applications to cross-examine will be successful only where they are necessary in relation to disputes over the factual circumstances, in particular, applications based upon procedural impropriety where there is a material conflict of evidence about the procedure followed by the defendant, or where bad faith and/or bias is alleged against the defendant. In *R (Bancoult) v Secretary of State for Foreign and Commonwealth Affairs* [2012] EWHC 2115 (Admin), LTL 27/7/2012, cross-examination of two witnesses of the defendant in relation to confidential documents sent between Washington and London was exceptionally permitted, as the proceedings could not be fairly determined without resolving the claimant's allegation based on those documents. In the absence of cross-examination the defendant's evidence of the facts must be assumed to be correct, unless there are documents which show that this evidence cannot be correct. Therefore, the proper course of action for a claimant who wishes to challenge the defendant's evidence is to apply for cross-examination of the relevant witness, despite the general practice of not permitting cross-examination (*R (McVey) v Secretary of State for Health* [2010] EWHC 1225 (Admin), [2010] ACD 95).

A court considering making an order for compulsory treatment of a detained person under the Mental Health Act 1983 which might involve breaches of his rights under the European Convention on Human Rights should fully review the merits of the proposed treatment and, for that purpose, allow cross-examination of the specialists instructed on both sides (*R (Wilkinson) v Responsible Medical Officer Broadmoor Hospital* [2001] EWCA Civ 1545, [2002] 1 WLR 419). However, this approach should not be used as a charter for routine applications to the court for oral evidence in human rights cases generally. The decision whether to allow cross-examination will depend largely on the nature of the right that has allegedly been breached and the nature of the alleged breach. It should not be overlooked that the court's role is essentially one of review (*R (N) v Dr M* [2002] EWCA Civ 1789, [2003] 1 WLR 562; see also *R (Al-Sweady) v Secretary of State for Defence* [2009] EWHC 2387 (Admin), [2010] HRLR 2).

Expert evidence

The general approach to evidence in judicial review proceedings is that fresh evidence can only be adduced in very limited circumstances (*R v Secretary of State for the Environment, ex parte Powis* [1981] 1 WLR 584). However, in some cases fairness may require that new expert evidence is used, although such cases will be very rare. Expert evidence will be allowed only to explain technical processes, and not to give an opinion on the reasonableness of the expert tribunal's decision, which would amount to an attempt to challenge the technical judgment of the tribunal on the merits of the case (*R (Lynch) v General Dental Council* [2003] EWHC 2987 (Admin), [2004] 1 All ER 1159).

77.49

Constitution of the court

A claim for judicial review in a civil matter should be made to a judge sitting in open court, unless the court directs that it should be made to a judge in private or to a Divisional Court of the Queen's Bench Division.

77.50

Substantive judicial review applications in civil matters are therefore generally heard by a single judge sitting in open court. There may be cases involving regulatory issues in which a private hearing may be ordered in the light of **CPR, r. 39.2(3)(a)** or **(c)**, in circumstances involving confidential information of significance or where there is a special reason to fear that reporting of the case may be unbalanced (*R (Amvac Chemical UK Ltd) v Secretary State for the Environment, Food and Rural Affairs* [2001] EWHC 1011 (Admin), [2002] ACD 219). A substantive application in a civil case is heard by the Divisional Court only in exceptional circumstances, such as where the application raises questions of difficulty, complexity or importance. Occasionally, the hearing may be before a judge in chambers. In exceptional cases the Court of Appeal may, where it deals with an appeal against refusal to give permission to proceed with a claim for judicial review (see 77.40), hear the substantive application (e.g. as in *British Airways Board v Laker Airways Ltd* [1984] QB 142). However, usually the substantive hearing is heard by a different judge or court from that which granted permission.

Transfer of proceedings

CPR, Part 30, applies to transfers to and from the Administrative Court (r. 54.20). The court may order a claim to continue as if it had not been started under **Part 54**, and where it does so it may give directions about the future management of the claim. **PD 54A, para. 14.1** draws attention to **CPR, r. 30.5**, which provides that the High Court may order proceedings in any Division of the High Court to be transferred to another Division and to or from a

77.51

Commentary

specialist list. An application for the transfer of proceedings to or from a specialist list must be made to a judge dealing with claims in that list (**r. 30.5(3)**).

In deciding whether a claim is suitable for transfer to the Administrative Court, the court will consider whether it raises issues of public law to which **Part 54** should apply (**PD 54A, para. 14.2**).

The court may, if it thinks appropriate where a claim for damages is included in an application for judicial review, determine the public law issues and then order issues relating to private law liability to proceed as if commenced under **CPR, Part 7**. Alternatively, the court may award damages at the judicial review hearing and leave quantum to be assessed by the court subsequently. However, it is likely that where the only remedies sought are public law remedies the court will not allow the matter to proceed as if commenced under **Part 7**. In order to permit the transfer of a case under **r. 54.20** it is likely that the court would require that the issues be sufficiently clearly defined, and at least some of the claims that are sought to be pursued in a **Part 7** claim must already be in existence (*R v East Berkshire Health Authority, ex parte Walsh* [1985] QB 152).

A claim in contract will not be struck out because it could more appropriately be made under **Part 54**, unless there is an abuse of process, for example delay in starting proceedings (*Clark v University of Lincolnshire and Humberside* [2000] 1 WLR 1988).

Settlement, withdrawal or discontinuance

77.52   Settlement, withdrawal or discontinuance of proceedings is dealt with by Practice Direction (Administrative Court: Uncontested Proceedings) [2008] 1 WLR 1377. This provides that draft orders and statements signed by all parties should be presented to the court for consideration in the case of settlement. Where matters are to be withdrawn or discontinued and there is a need for the leave of the court or an order as to costs, again a statement and draft order signed by all parties should be put before the court. The order will then be made without the need for parties to attend court. Where no leave or costs order is required the claimant should simply notify the court and all other parties of the discontinuance using the procedure in **CPR, Part 38** (see **chapter 55**).

REMEDIES

77.53   All the remedies available in judicial review proceedings are subject to the discretion of the court, so that even if a case is proved the court may refuse any or all of the remedies sought by the claimant. The High Court may exercise its discretion under the Senior Courts Act 1981, s. 31, to make the prerogative mandatory, prohibiting and quashing orders and provide the private law remedies of injunction, declaration, damages, restitution or the recovery of any sum due. The Administrative Court may make a declaration of incompatibility under the **Human Rights Act 1998, s. 4**. These remedies may be sought individually (except that a judicial review claim may not seek a money remedy alone: **CPR, r. 54.3(2)**), alternatively or in combination. Declaratory and injunctive relief are obtainable in proceedings for judicial review even when one of the prerogative orders is capable of being granted (*R v Secretary of State for Employment, ex parte Equal Opportunities Commission* [1995] 1 AC 1).

The High Court must refuse to grant any relief if it appears to the court to be highly likely that the outcome for the applicant would not have been substantially different if the conduct complained of had not occurred, unless it certifies there are reasons of exceptional public interest which warrant the grant of relief (Senior Courts Act 1981, s. 31, as amended by the Criminal Justice and Courts Act 2015). The intended purpose of this rule is to prevent unnecessary time and cost on litigation where there have been only minor procedural defects. For examples of the operation of this rule, see *R (Logan) v Havering London Borough Council* [2015] EWHC 3193 (Admin), [2016] PTSR 603; *Bokrosova v London Borough of Lambeth* [2015] EWHC 3386 (Admin),

[2016] PTSR 355 and *R (Spitalfields Historic Trust Ltd) v Mayor of London* [2016] EWHC 1006 (Admin), LTL 17/5/2016. The **CPR, Part 54**, procedure must be used for a judicial review claim seeking a prerogative order or an injunction under the Senior Courts Act 1981, s. 30, restraining a person from acting in an office in which he or she is not entitled to act (**CPR, r. 54.2**). It may be used for a judicial review claim seeking a declaration or an injunction, but must be used if a declaration or injunction is sought in addition to a prerogative order or an injunction under the Senior Courts Act 1981, s. 30 (**CPR, r. 54.3(1)**).

The discretionary nature of remedies

All public law remedies are discretionary, i.e. even though the claimant has standing to commence judicial review proceedings, the decision or action in question is reviewable, and the grounds for review are proved, the court may yet decide not to award the claimant all or part of the remedies requested. The court has withheld remedies on a number of grounds.   **77.54**

The court may refuse to grant the relief requested if suitable alternative remedies have not been pursued (e.g. *R v Secretary of State for the Home Department, ex parte Swati* [1986] 1 WLR 477) (see **77.30**).

A court may refuse relief because of the claimant's conduct or motives, for example, where the claimant suppressed or misrepresented material facts in presenting the claim (*R v Kensington Income Tax Commissioners, ex parte Princess Edmond de Polignac* [1917] 1 KB 486), or delayed in commencing proceedings. The time limits set out in **CPR, r. 54.5(1)** and the Senior Courts Act 1981, s. 31, must be adhered to strictly and therefore undue delay may result in the refusal of any relief (see **77.36**). The court may also refuse to grant relief if it believes the likely effect of a remedy will serve no practical purpose, e.g. in cases where the public body has already remedied its position to meet the claimant's demands (*R v Gloucestershire County Council, ex parte P* [1994] ELR 334), or where the court is satisfied that there was no real possibility that the relevant issue could have affected the substantive outcome (*Secretary of State for Communities and Local Government v South Gloucestershire Council* [2016] EWCA Civ 74). The quashing of a challenged planning permission may be withheld where it is impossible to sever the part to which the claimant's challenge relates from the rest of the planning permission, which was lawfully granted. In those circumstances relief would simply take the form of a declaration that the local authority had failed to consult properly before granting planning permission (*R (Guiney) v Greenwich London Borough Council* [2008] EWHC 2012 (Admin), [2009] JPL 211). Breach of a statutory provision may have such an insignificant effect that the court may refuse relief (as in *R v Dairy Produce Quota Tribunal, ex parte Davies* [1987] 2 CMLR 399). In exercising its discretion, the court will take into account whether others will be directly or indirectly affected by its decision — e.g. a decision which has the potential to affect a large number of individuals such as an inquiry into a new motorway. Therefore reliance upon a decision by third parties may also induce the court not to grant the remedy claimed.

If an issue is theoretical, then in ordinary civil proceedings this may be a compelling factor against the grant of relief. Occasionally the court may grant an advisory opinion, e.g. in the form of a declaration, where it is desirable that it should do so (*R v Secretary of State for Employment, ex parte Equal Opportunities Commission* [1995] 1 AC 1). However, the court will be wary of going beyond the proper exercise of judicial power by giving advisory opinions, particularly in cases where they relate to hypothetical facts divorced from any concrete situation rather than matters of pure law (*R (Smith) v Oxfordshire Assistant Deputy Coroner* [2010] UKSC 29, [2011] 1 AC 1; *R (Rusbridger) v Attorney General* [2003] UKHL 38, [2004] 1 AC 357).

Quashing order

A quashing order deprives the decision which is being reviewed of all legal effect and the decision challenged is therefore effectively set aside. Until a decision is quashed, it is deemed to   **77.55**

Commentary

possess a 'presumption of validity' and is disobeyed at the claimant's risk pending the substantive judicial review hearing (*F. Hoffmann-La Roche & Co. AG v Secretary of State for Trade and Industry* [1975] AC 295).

A quashing order is available to quash the decisions of inferior courts or tribunals and any other public body 'having legal authority to determine questions affecting the rights of subjects, and having the duty to act judicially' (per Lord Atkin in *R v Electricity Commissioners, ex parte London Electricity Joint Committee Co. (1920) Ltd* [1924] 1 KB 171). The courts have subsequently accepted that a quashing order is not confined to the review of decisions of a judicial nature (*R v Hillingdon London Borough Council, ex parte Royco Homes Ltd* [1974] QB 720). The court will consider the nature of the power exercised in order to determine whether this test has been satisfied. A quashing order may be claimed against a broad range of administrative decision-makers, e.g. local authorities, legal committees and ministers of the Crown and may relate to administrative decisions and delegated legislation.

Where a quashing order is sought and the court is satisfied that there are grounds for quashing the decision it may in addition remit the matter to the decision-maker and 'direct it to reconsider the matter and reach a decision in accordance with the judgment of the court' (**CPR, r. 54.19(2)(a)**). This power may be used to ensure that a decision is reconsidered and a new decision made. However, there is no guarantee that a different result will be reached: the decision-maker is justified in reaching the same result again provided that the matter is reconsidered in accordance with the law. Where the court considers that there is no purpose to be served in remitting the matter to the decision-maker, it may, subject to any statutory provision, take the decision itself (**r. 54.19(2)(b)**). (However, where a power is given by statute to a tribunal, person or other body, it may be the case that the court cannot take the decision itself.)

Prohibiting order

77.56   A prohibiting order prevents the decision-maker from acting or continuing to act in excess of jurisdiction. Therefore, if a public body threatens to make an unlawful decision which could be quashed had it been made, the court may make a prohibiting order to prevent the decision being made. For example, a local council was prohibited from increasing the number of taxi licences in breach of an undertaking to consult the local professional association (*R v Liverpool Corporation, ex parte Liverpool Taxi Fleet Operators' Association* [1972] 2 QB 299).

If a want of jurisdiction is apparent, a prohibiting order may be claimed immediately. If it is not apparent, the claimant must wait until the tribunal has stepped outside its jurisdiction or is undoubtedly about to do so (*Zohrab v Smith* (1848) 17 LJ QB 174). Doubts have been expressed about the power to claim a prohibiting order for an anticipatory excess of jurisdiction (*Re Ashby* [1934] OR 421). A prohibiting order is not granted lightly (*Governors of Queen Anne's Bounty v Pitt-Rivers* [1936] 2 KB 419). A prohibiting order is not available against a public body which has already completed the acts complained of (*Yates v Palmer* (1849) 6 Dowl & L 283). A prohibiting order is also not available to review a finding of fact made by an inferior court for the purpose of assuming jurisdiction (*Joseph v Henry* (1850) 19 LJ QB 369). It may be refused in a case of laches (see **10.40**) or misconduct by the applicant (*Parochial Church Council of St Magnus-the-Martyr v Chancellor of London* [1923] P 38).

Mandatory order

77.57   A mandatory order requires an inferior court or tribunal or a person or body of persons charged with a public duty to carry out its judicial or other public duty. A mandatory order may compel a court or tribunal to state its case (*R v Watson, ex parte Bretherton* [1945] KB 96) and to give reasons for its decision where it was required to do so by statute (*Brayhead (Ascot) Ltd v Berkshire County Council* [1964] 2 QB 303). This includes the provision of adequately intelligible reasons (*Earl Iveagh v Minister of Housing and Local Government* [1964] 1 QB 395). A mandatory order can compel a public body to exercise its discretion in accordance with the law, though the court is reluctant to use the remedy in this way (e.g. *R v Barnet London Borough Council, ex parte Nilish Shah* [1983] 2 AC 309).

It is preferable that the claimant is able to say that performance of the duty has been demanded and that the performance has been refused by the authority obliged to discharge it (*State (Modern Homes (Ireland) Ltd) v Dublin Corporation* [1953] IR 202). Therefore, before applying for judicial review, a claimant should make a specific demand or request to the authority to perform the duty imposed upon it. This corresponds with the requirement upon a claimant to write an appropriate 'letter before action' prior to claiming judicial review (see 77.31).

The court has a wide discretion to refuse to make a mandatory order. One will not be granted unless the defendant has an absolute duty, or has already decided in the claimant's favour all factors necessary to render it subject to a duty, to do that which the claimant seeks. A mandatory order cannot be made against the Crown (Crown Proceedings Act 1947, s. 40) but can be made against ministers.

Injunctions

Under the Senior Courts Act 1981, s. 31(2), in judicial review proceedings the court may **77.58** make a declaration or grant an injunction if it considers that it would be just and convenient having regard to:

(a) the nature of the matters in respect of which a remedy may be granted by way of a mandatory, prohibiting or quashing order;
(b) the nature of the persons and bodies against whom a remedy may be granted by way of such an order; and
(c) all the circumstances of the case.

In a claim for judicial review a final injunction can be granted in order to restrain a public body from acting unlawfully, restrain the implementation of an unlawful decision or compel a public authority to comply with its statutory duties. Injunctive relief does not lie against the Crown itself (Crown Proceedings Act 1947, ss. 21 and 38) but injunctions can be granted against ministers and other officers of the Crown in their official as well as their private capacities (*Re M* [1994] 1 AC 377) and, in particular, an injunction may be granted against a minister of the Crown in order to give a remedy in favour of a party invoking rights derived from directly applicable EU law (*R v Secretary of State for Transport, ex parte Factortame Ltd (No. 2)* [1991] 1 AC 603).

The discretion conferred upon the court under the conditions stipulated in the Senior Courts Act 1981, s. 31(2), is broad but must be exercised in accordance with recognised principles. An injunction will be refused if the injury complained of is very trivial or if it has ceased and there is no likelihood of its recurrence. Further, a court will not order an injunction to do something which is impossible, or where the grant of an injunction would be oppressive.

A final injunction, although granted at the conclusion of the proceedings, need not be expressed to have perpetual effect, i.e. it may be awarded for a fixed period. However, a mandatory injunction will not be granted to ensure the performance of a continuing series of acts which the court cannot supervise although the court may award a prohibitory injunction to restrain the discontinuance of a public service.

Declarations

A declaration may be granted in judicial review proceedings in the circumstances set out in **77.59** the Senior Courts Act 1981, s. 31(2) (see 77.58).

Commentary

Declaratory relief and any other private law remedy may be granted by a court even if none of the prerogative remedies is available, provided the case is within the realm of public law.

The court has a broad discretion to grant declaratory relief (*Barnard v National Dock Labour Board* [1953] 2 QB 18). Declarations may be sought in order to challenge the legality of decisions taken or policies adopted by a public body, to challenge delegated legislation, to determine the ambit of public law obligations, to pronounce upon questions of law and the compatibility of primary legislation with EU law (*R v Secretary of State for Employment, ex parte Equal Opportunities Commission* [1995] 1 AC 1).

The court may consider granting relief because of any public interest element involved (*R v HM Treasury, ex parte Smedley* [1985] QB 657) or as a means of securing a private law entitlement (*Roy v Kensington and Chelsea and Westminster Family Practitioner Committee* [1992] 1 AC 624). The court may grant a declaration in relation to future rights (*R v HM Treasury, ex parte Smedley*). However the circumstances must be appropriate for the grant, e.g. not too complex or uncertain. The courts are also willing to grant a negative declaration, e.g. a declaration of no right or no liability.

There are some limitations upon the scope of declaratory relief. Declaratory relief does not lie in respect of claims which are legally unenforceable (*Mutasa v Attorney General* [1980] QB 114); *intra vires* errors of law appearing on the face of the record (*Punton v Minister of Pensions and National Insurance (No. 2)* [1964] 1 WLR 226); and matters which are academic or hypothetical. Courts should not make general declarations which are unnecessary and irrelevant for the particular claimant in the case, especially in circumstances where a claimant has been persuaded to bring a claim for judicial review by those who wish to challenge an issue generally (*R (Burke) v General Medical Council* [2005] EWCA Civ 1003, [2006] QB 273). The civil courts are also reluctant to grant declaratory relief if a declaration could interfere with criminal proceedings (*R v Medicines Control Agency, ex parte Pharma Nord Ltd* (1997) 10 Admin LR 646).

Damages

77.60   Damages arising from any matter to which a judicial review claim relates may be awarded if the court is satisfied that they would have been awarded in an ordinary claim started at the same time as the judicial review claim (Senior Courts Act 1981, s. 31(4)).

A person who has suffered loss as a result of unlawful administrative conduct has to claim and establish liability under a recognised cause of action to claim damages. This will usually be a tort claim, e.g. negligence, negligent misstatement, breach of statutory duty (including breach of Convention rights under the **Human Rights Act 1998**), misfeasance in public office.

There are circumstances in which a public law breach of EU law gives rise to a claim for damages in judicial review proceedings. The Court of Justice of the European Union has held that member States must pay compensation for harm caused to an individual for failure to implement an EU Directive (*Francovich v Italy* (cases C-6 and 9/90) [1995] ICR 722). The CJEU has subsequently held that a right to compensation from member States is a universal principle and exists where three conditions are met:

(a)   the rule of law infringed must be intended to confer rights on individuals;
(b)   the breach must be sufficiently serious; and
(c)   there must be a direct causal link between the breach and the damage sustained (*Brasserie du Pêcheur SA v Germany* (cases C-46 and 48/93) [1996] QB 404).

Subsequent cases have applied these principles (e.g. *R v HM Treasury, ex parte British Telecommunications plc* (case C-392/93) [1996] QB 615; *R v Ministry of Agriculture, Fisheries and Food, ex parte Hedley Lomas (Ireland) Ltd* (case C-5/94) [1997] QB 139; *R v Secretary of State for Transport, ex parte Factortame Ltd (No. 5)* [2000] 1 AC 524).

However, damages are not available simply because an application for judicial review is successful (*R v Metropolitan Borough of Knowsley, ex parte Maguire* [1992] COD 499).

CPR, Part 16, applies to making a claim for damages in a judicial review claim, i.e. the normal rules as to statements of case apply and the loss or damage suffered must be fully particularised.

Suspension of the effect of orders

The Supreme Court has held that it should not lend itself to procedures designed to obfuscate   **77.61**
the effect of its judgments. In *HM Treasury v Ahmed* [2010] UKSC 5, [2010] 2 AC 534, the court
declined to temporarily suspend the effect of its judgment declaring certain freezing orders
aimed at terrorists *ultra vires* in order to allow the Treasury to address the effects of the order.
Despite the substantial public policy reasons in favour of such a suspension, to do so would
have required the court to enforce regulations that it had found to be unlawful.

Appeals

An appeal against the decision of the High Court in a substantive hearing of a judicial review   **77.62**
claim lies to the Court of Appeal and thereafter to the Supreme Court in the normal way. The
procedure for substantive appeals is discussed in **chapters 75** and **76**. Appeals from decisions
to refuse permission to apply for judicial review were considered at **77.40**.

When considering whether to grant permission to appeal from a substantive hearing for judicial review, the court will consider whether there is a prima facie case that an error has been made; whether there is an issue of legal principle involved (*R v Secretary of State for the Environment, ex parte Kirkstall Valley Campaign Ltd* [1996] 3 All ER 304); whether the issue is one which should be examined by the Court of Appeal in the public interest; and whether the appeal raises an issue where the law requires clarification (*Smith v Cosworth Casting Processes Ltd* [1997] 1 WLR 1538). The task of the Court of Appeal in a judicial review appeal is to resolve genuine questions of law: it does not reconsider the original decision-maker's findings of fact where the original tribunal disbelieved the claimant (*R (Nine Nepalese Asylum Seekers) v Immigration Appeal Tribunal* [2003] EWCA Civ 1892, *The Independent*, 21 January 2004). A further appeal to the Supreme Court may be entertained in a public law matter (provided it is otherwise a suitable case for an appeal to the Court) even in cases where there is no longer any *lis* between the parties (*R v Secretary of State for the Home Department, ex parte Salem* [1999] 1 AC 450), although academic appeals will only be heard if there are good reasons in the public interest for doing so.

Planning Court

Judicial reviews and statutory challenges started from 6 April 2014 onwards which relate to   **77.63**
any of the planning matters specified in **CPR, r. 54.21(2)(a)**, will be allocated to the Planning
Court. Pre-existing cases could also be transferred to the Planning Court. Cases which will be
allocated to the Planning Court include (but are not limited to) challenges to planning permission and development consents, compulsory purchase orders, EU environmental legislation and domestic transpositions of such legislation (including assessments for development consents, habitats, waste and pollution control) and planning policy documents. The objective is for Planning Court cases to be heard by specialist judges.

In addition, parties may apply for a Planning Court case to be classed as 'significant'. A case may be significant where it has a significant economic impact locally or beyond its immediate locality, raises important points of law, generates significant public interest, or by virtue of the nature or volume of technical material is best dealt with by judges with significant experience of handling such matters (**PD 54E, para. 3.2**). Shortened timescales apply to cases classed as significant. For judicial reviews, applications for permission are to be dealt with within three

Commentary

weeks of the deadline for filing the acknowledgment of service, oral renewals of applications for permission are to be heard within one month of the application, and substantive hearings are to take place within 10 weeks of the deadline for the defendant to submit its detailed grounds (**PD 54E, para. 3.4**). Under the previous regime for planning cases in the Administrative Court (the 'Planning Fast Track'), the court took the target timescales seriously and in particular there was an indication that counsel's unavailability should not be accepted as a reason for the case to be listed significantly outside the target timescale (*London and Henley (Middle Brook Street) Ltd v Secretary of State for Communities and Local Government* [2013] EWHC 4207 (Admin), LTL 9/1/2014). The Planning Court has continued this approach.

Chapter 78 References to the Court of Justice of the European Union

INTRODUCTION

An English court faced with a question of European Union law may sometimes decide it itself, **78.1** or may refer it to the Court of Justice of the European Union (CJEU) in Luxembourg for a preliminary ruling. If a reference is made, the English proceedings will be stayed, at least in relation to the issue concerned, pending the ruling of the CJEU. Once it is made, the ruling is binding on the English court, but it is only a preliminary ruling, in that the English court is left to apply the ruling to the facts of the case and to give judgment. The general policy is that EU law should be applied consistently in all member States.

QUESTIONS WHICH MAY BE REFERRED

References may be made: **78.2**

(a) under art. 267 of the Treaty on the Functioning of the European Union (TFEU); or

(b) on the interpretation of any of the instruments referred to in the Civil Jurisdiction and Judgments Act 1982 (1982 Act), s. 1(1), or the Contracts (Applicable Law) Act 1990, s. 1.

Article 267 TFEU provides in its first paragraph:

The Court of Justice of the European Union shall have jurisdiction to give preliminary rulings concerning:

(a) the interpretation of the Treaties;

(b) the validity and interpretation of acts of the institutions, bodies, offices or agencies of the Union.

'The Treaties' are the TFEU and the Treaty on European Union (art. 1(2) TFEU). Under para. (b) of art. 267 the CJEU can rule on the validity or interpretation of Regulations, Directives and Decisions of the Council or Commission. Although the CJEU can give rulings on the interpretation of the Brussels Convention, the Brussels I Regulation and the **recast Brussels I Regulation** (see **chapter 16**), it cannot do so on the modified version of the Brussels Convention set out in sch. 4 to the 1982 Act governing allocation of jurisdiction within the United Kingdom (*Kleinwort Benson Ltd v Glasgow City Council* (case C-346/93) [1996] QB 57; *Cook v Virgin Media Ltd* [2015] EWCA Civ 1287, [2016] 1 WLR 1672).

Questions referred for preliminary rulings must concern only the interpretation or validity of a provision of EU law, since the CJEU does not have jurisdiction to interpret national law or to assess its validity, although the CJEU does have jurisdiction to provide the national court with all the guidance as to the interpretation of EU law necessary to enable that court to rule on the compatibility of national rules with EU law (*CHEZ Razpredelenie Bulgaria AD v Komisia za zashtita ot diskriminatsia* (case C-83/14) [2016] 1 CMLR 14). It is for the referring court to apply the relevant provision of EU law to the case (CJEU Recommendations to national courts and tribunals in relation to the initiation of preliminary ruling proceedings ([2012] OJ C338, p. 1), para. 7 ('Recommendations to national courts'); see e.g. *R (Newby Foods Ltd) v Food Standards Agency* [2016] EWHC 408 (Admin), LTL 1/4/2016).

The Charter of Fundamental Rights of the EU was given direct effect by the coming into force of the Lisbon Treaty in December 2009 and binds member States when implementing EU law. Some claimants are now relying on the rights in the Charter in addition to or instead of the European Convention on Human Rights. The relationship between the Charter and the Convention is likely to continue to draw attention and has, for example, been the subject of a reference to the CJEU in the context of the rights of asylum seekers (*R (NS (Afghanistan)) v Secretary of State for the Home Department* (case C-411/10) [2013] QB 102). The Grand Chamber's ruling on the preliminary reference in this case was explained by the Supreme Court in *R (EM (Eritrea)) v Secretary of State for the Home Department* [2014] UKSC 12, [2014] AC 1321 per Lord Kerr at [56] and [66].

REFERRING COURT OR TRIBUNAL

78.3   It is a matter for the CJEU to decide whether a body is a court or tribunal for the purposes of art. 267 TFEU, and the categorisation of that body under national law is not conclusive (*Politi v Italy* (case 43/71) [1971] ECR 1039; *Corbiau v Administration des Contributions* (case C-24/92) [1993] ECR I-1277). The CJEU will take a number of factors into account when making this determination, including: whether the body is established by law, whether it is permanent, whether its jurisdiction is compulsory, whether its procedure is *inter partes*, whether it applies rules of law, and whether it is independent (*Dorsch Consult Ingenieurgesellschaft mbH v Bundesbaugesellschaft Berlin mbH* (case C-54/96) [1997] ECR I-4961; *Denuit v Transorient—Mosaïque Voyages et Culture SA* (case C-125/04) [2005] ECR I-923). For example, a Dutch body, called the Appeals Committee for General Medicine, which operated with the consent of the public authorities and with their cooperation, and which, after an adversarial procedure, delivered decisions, which were recognised as final, was considered as a court or tribunal within the meaning of art. 267 (*Broekmeulen v Huisarts Registratie Commissie* (case 246/80) [1981] ECR 2311). By contrast, a Bulgarian body, the Commission for Protection against Discrimination (Komisia za zashtita ot diskriminatsia), established by statute and dealing with claims under, and enforcing the terms of, the law on protection against discrimination, was considered not to fall within art. 267 on the basis that the decision it was called on to give at the end of proceedings before it was similar in substance to an administrative decision and did not have a judicial nature within the meaning of the case law of the CJEU relating to the concept of 'court or tribunal' (*Belov v CHEZ Elektro Balgaria AD* (case C-394/11) [2013] 2 CMLR 29). Also, the court or tribunal making the reference must be in a member State. Whether an arbitral court or tribunal can be regarded as an emanation of a member State will depend on the nature of the arbitration in question. The fact that the arbitral body gives a judgment according to law, and that the award is binding between the parties, will not, however, be sufficient. There must be a closer link between the arbitration procedure and the ordinary court system in a member State for the body to be considered as a court or tribunal of a member State (*Nordsee Deutsche Hochseefischerei GmbH v Reederei Mond Hochseefischerei Nordstern AG & Co. KG* (case 102/81) [1982] ECR 1095).

MANDATORY REFERENCES

Article 267 TFEU provides: **78.4**

Where any such question is raised in a case pending before a court or tribunal of a member State against whose decisions there is no judicial remedy under national law, that court or tribunal shall bring the matter before the Court.

Accordingly, references are mandatory in courts of last instance. In England this is generally the Supreme Court, unless by statute or rule some lower court is the final court of appeal. However, even in the Supreme Court there must be a 'question' that needs to be referred. The national court has the sole responsibility for deciding whether there is a need for a reference (*X v Inspecteur van Rijksbelastingdienst* (case C-72/14) [2016] 1 CMLR 27). If a point is covered by considerable and consistent authority from the CJEU such that its answer is obvious, there is no 'question' within the meaning of art. 267 (per Lord Diplock in *Garland v British Rail Engineering Ltd* [1983] 2 AC 751 at p. 771; *Srl Cilfit v Ministry of Health* (case 283/81) [1982] ECR 3415). If a lower national court has made a reference to the CJEU concerning the same legal issue, it is for the national court or tribunal against whose decisions there is no judicial remedy under national law to decide whether a further reference is necessary in light of the existing reference. However, that court is not required to wait until an answer to the question referred by the lower court has been given (*X v Inspecteur van Rijksbelastingdienst*). If it is not necessary to decide either whether EU law applies or the scope of its application to the present case, the reference procedure is not available even in the Supreme Court (*R v Secretary of State for Health, ex parte Imperial Tobacco Ltd* [2001] 1 WLR 127).

DISCRETIONARY REFERENCES

For courts below the Supreme Court, art. 267 TFEU provides: **78.5**

Where such a question is raised before any court or tribunal of a member State, that court or tribunal may, if it considers that a decision on the question is necessary to enable it to give judgment, request the Court to give a ruling thereon.

Two questions arise in such cases:

(a) whether a decision on the question of EU law is necessary to enable the court to give judgment; and
(b) if so, whether the court should in the exercise of its discretion order that a reference be made.

Guidelines on both questions were given by the Court of Appeal in *H. P. Bulmer Ltd v J. Bollinger SA* [1974] Ch 401 by Lord Denning MR at pp. 422–5. Whether to make a discretionary reference, and the extent of the questions to be posed to the CJEU, are essentially case management matters which are unlikely to be overturned on appeal (*Evans v Secretary of State for the Environment, Transport and the Regions* [2001] EWCA Civ 32, [2001] 2 CMLR 10). Further, permission to appeal on the ground that a reference to the CJEU should have been made should not be given simply for the purpose of making a reference (*Ministry of Justice v O'Brien* [2015] EWCA Civ 1368).

Guidelines for discretionary references

In *H. P. Bulmer Ltd v J. Bollinger SA* [1974] Ch 401 Lord Denning MR laid down four guidelines as   **78.6**
to whether a decision from the European Court is necessary. They are no more than guidelines, and cannot be considered as binding (*Lord Bethell v SABENA* [1983] 3 CMLR 1).

Whether the point will be conclusive   Article 267 TFEU provides that the court must con-   **78.7**
sider whether 'a decision on the question is necessary to enable it to give judgment'. Lord Denning's view was that the point must be such that, whichever way it is decided, it will be

conclusive of the case. This is probably too onerous. Ormrod LJ in *Polydor Ltd v Harlequin Record Shops Ltd* [1980] 2 CMLR 413 said it was sufficient if the point was 'reasonably necessary', and Bingham J in *Customs and Excise Commissioners v ApS Samex* [1983] 1 All ER 1042 said that the question must be 'substantially, if not quite totally, determinative of the litigation'.

78.8   **Previous ruling**   As Lord Denning said in *H. P. Bulmer Ltd v J. Bollinger SA* [1974] Ch 401:

> In some cases…it may be found that the same point—or substantially the same point—has already been decided by the European Court in a previous case. In that event it is not necessary for the English court to decide it. It can follow the previous decision without troubling the European Court.

This is subject to the proviso that, with changing social and economic factors, the CJEU is not bound by its earlier decisions.

78.9   *Acte claire*   No reference needs to be made if the correct application of EU law is so obvious as to leave no scope for any reasonable doubt (*Ministry of Justice v O'Brien* [2015] EWCA Civ 1368). Lord Denning MR (in *H. P. Bulmer Ltd v J. Bollinger SA* [1974] Ch 401) commented that in this event, 'there is no need to interpret the Treaty but only apply it'. This should be read in the light of Lord Diplock's comment in *R v Henn* [1981] AC 850 at p. 906 that the court should not be 'too ready to hold that because the meaning of the English text (which is one of [nine] of equal authority) seems plain no question of interpretation can be involved'. A point may be *acte claire* after considering the text, together with decisions of the CJEU and relevant *travaux préparatoires* (*Lucasfilm Ltd v Ainsworth* [2009] EWCA Civ 1328, [2010] Ch 503 at [114], [129]; reversed in part on another point [2011] UKSC 39, [2012] 1 AC 208). However, if a point turns on the *travaux préparatoires* alone, it is unlikely to be *acte claire* (*Draco AB's SPC Application* [1996] RPC 417). Where a question has been referred to the CJEU by another member State and as such cannot be regarded as *acte claire*, the national court may nevertheless proceed on the basis that the issue is *acte claire* and apply it to the facts of the case (*Re N (Children) (Adoption: Jurisdiction)* [2016] UKSC 15, [2016] 2 WLR 1103).

78.10   **Deciding the facts first**   It is for the national court to decide at what stage it is necessary to make a reference to the CJEU. In general, it is best to decide the facts before making a reference, because it should then be clear if the question of EU law is necessary, and it enables the CJEU to take into account all the relevant facts when making its ruling. In any event, it is usually best not to make the reference at least until it is possible to define the factual and legal context of the question. It is also usually best not to make a reference until both sides have been heard (Recommendations to national courts, paras 18 and 19) (*Eli Lilly and Co. v Human Genome Sciences Inc.* [2012] EWHC 2290 (Pat), LTL 8/8/2012). 'Necessity' relates to the court's ability to give judgment, not a party's case management strategy or decisions (*ViiV Healthcare UK Ltd v Teva UK Ltd* [2015] EWHC 1074 (Ch), LTL 29/4/2015).

78.11   **Amending questions**   An English court may amend the questions set out in an order for reference to the CJEU by exercising its power under **CPR, r. 3.1**(7). However, the court may refuse an application to amend the wording of questions which have been referred to the CJEU, particularly in circumstances where there is (a) no finding that the court has made the order on a false basis, and (b) no material change of circumstances since the order (*SAS Institute Inc. v World Programming Ltd* [2010] EWHC 3012 (Ch), [2011] FSR 12).

Factors relevant to the discretion

78.12   General guidance has been provided by the CJEU on when it is appropriate to refer matters. The following factors were identified by Lord Denning MR in *H. P. Bulmer Ltd v J. Bollinger SA* [1974] Ch 401 as being relevant in the exercise of the court's discretion:

(a)   delay in obtaining a ruling from the CJEU (delays have been reduced in recent years);

(b)   the importance of not overloading the CJEU;

(c)   expense to the parties;

(d) the wishes of the parties. Although clearly relevant, the court can nevertheless make a reference even if both parties object, and, also, there is no such thing as a reference by consent. Ultimately the decision is that of the judge;

(e) difficulty and importance, for example, where a case raised a vital question as to the limit of EU competences conferred by the Treaties and a tension between fundamental principles of national security and basic procedural fairness which was not straightforward (*ZZ v Secretary of State for the Home Department* [2011] EWCA Civ 440, LTL 19/4/2011). Simple points should be decided by the English court;

(f) questions involving the comparison of texts in the different languages of the member States are best decided by the CJEU (*Customs and Excise Commissioners v ApS Samex* [1983] 1 All ER 1042);

(g) questions requiring a panoramic view of the EU and its institutions, the functioning of the Internal Market or a broad view of the orderly development of the EU should be decided by the CJEU (*Customs and Excise Commissioners v ApS Samex*);

(h) whether the application for a reference is made in bad faith so as to delay judgment being given (*Customs and Excise Commissioners v ApS Samex*).

Additionally, where the arguments of the parties and the material facts are not sufficiently clear for the court to confidently frame clear and precise questions, the court may decline to make a reference (*Dr Reddy's Laboratories (UK) Ltd v Warner-Lambert Co LLC* [2012] EWHC 1791 (Pat), [2012] Eu LR 747).

Questioning the validity of institutional acts

Where a national court intends to question the validity of an act of an institution, body, office   **78.13**
or agency of the EU or where the validity of an institutional act is brought into issue by the parties, it must refer the question to the CJEU (*Foto-Frost v Hauptzollamt Lübeck-Ost* (case 314/85) [1987] ECR 4199; *R (International Air Transport Association) v Department for Transport* (case C-344/04) [2006] ECR I-403). Where the national court has serious doubts about the validity of an institutional act on which a national measure is based, the national court may, in an exceptional case, suspend or grant interim relief in respect of the national measure, but it must refer the question of validity to the CJEU (*Zuckerfabrik Süderdithmarschen AG v Hauptzollamt Itzehoe* (cases C-143/88 and C-92/89) [1991] ECR I-415; Recommendations to national courts, paras 16 and 17). The right to question the validity of institutional acts does not extend to the preparatory acts of European institutions (*Conex Banninger Ltd v European Commission* [2010] EWHC 1978 (Ch), [2011] Eu LR 100).

PROCEDURE IN ENGLAND

An order referring a question to the CJEU may be made at any stage of the proceedings, and   **78.14**
may be made by the court of its own initiative or on an application made by a party in accordance with **CPR, Part 23** (see **rr. 68.1(c)** and **68.2(1)**). An order for a reference (a request to the CJEU for a preliminary ruling: **r. 68.1(d)**) cannot be made by consent, and should not normally be made by a Master or District Judge (**r. 68.2(2)**). Although it can be made at any stage, it is usual for a reference to be made at trial after the facts have been found (see **78.10**). However, once the English court has given final judgment in a claim and its order has been drawn up it is *functus officio* and has no power at that stage to order a reference (*Chiron Corporation v Murex Diagnostics Ltd (No. 8)* [1995] FSR 309).

A person who has been granted permission to intervene in domestic proceedings will not necessarily be a 'party' in the subsequent reference proceedings and whether he or she should be made a party will depend on various factors including his or her interest in the overall outcome and what he or she might contribute in terms of expertise and experience (*R (Philip Morris Brands*

Sàrl) v Secretary of State for Health [2014] EWHC 3669 (Admin), LTL 19/11/2014; *R (British American Tobacco UK Ltd) v Secretary of State for Health* [2014] EWHC 3515 (Admin), [2015] 1 CMLR 35).

Where the English court decides to make a reference, the request for the preliminary ruling of the CJEU has to be set out in a schedule to the court's order (**r. 68.2(4)**). It must contain the matters specified in the Rules of Procedure of the Court of Justice and comply with the Recommendations to national courts (**r. 68.2(3)**): see the CJEU's website, http://curia.europa.eu. Often the applicant will prepare a draft, or the court may direct one of the parties to do so, but the order will be settled finally by the court (**PD 68, para. 1.1**).

As it will need to be translated into the other official languages, each question on which a ruling is sought must be expressed as clearly and succinctly as possible (**PD 68, para. 1.2**), avoiding superfluous detail (Recommendations to national courts, para. 21). The question should be stated in a general form, and not in a specific form tied to the facts of the case in hand. The questions on which a ruling of the CJEU is sought should appear in a separate and clearly identified section of the schedule to the order making the reference, preferably at the beginning or end (Recommendations to national courts, para. 26). They must be capable of being understood in their own terms without referring to the statement of the grounds of the request (Recommendations to national courts, para. 26).

All relevant information should be provided to give the CJEU and interested persons a clear understanding of the factual and legal context of the main proceedings. This can normally be done in about 10 pages (Recommendations to national courts, para. 22). A reference in excess of 20 pages in length (including the order and the schedule) will be summarised by the CJEU for the purposes of translation (**PD 68, para. 1.5**).

A request for a preliminary ruling should, in addition to the text of the questions referred (Recommendations to national courts, paras 22 to 26; Rules of Procedure of the Court of Justice, art. 94; **PD 68, para. 1.3**):

(a) give the full name of the referring court;

(b) identify the parties;

(c) summarise the nature and history of the proceedings as determined by the referring court, or at least an account of the facts on which the questions referred are based;

(d) set out the tenor of the relevant rules of national law, and where appropriate, the relevant national case law;

(e) state the reasons which prompted the referring court to inquire about the interpretation or validity of the provisions of EU law, and the relationship between those provisions and national law;

(f) identify the provisions of EU law which the CJEU is being requested to interpret;

(g) contain a brief summary of the relevant arguments of the parties; and

(h) if it considers itself able to do so, state the referring court's view on the answer to the questions referred to the CJEU.

The parties must also prepare a bundle of key documents to be sent direct to the Registrar of the CJEU (**PD 68, para. 2.2**).

Unless the court orders otherwise, the English proceedings will be stayed pending the ruling of the CJEU (**CPR, r. 68.5**). The only exception contemplated by the Recommendations to national courts (para. 29) is where protective measures need to be ordered by the national court. There is jurisdiction under **CPR, r. 19.2(2)(a)**, to add parties to the English proceedings as claimants solely for the purpose of enabling them to take part in the reference to the CJEU (*Football Association Premier League Ltd v QC Leisure* [2008] EWHC 2897 (Ch), [2009] 1 WLR 1603). In that case, as the additional claimants had no other interest in the proceedings, conditions were imposed requiring them to provide the defendants 28 days' advance notice of any written observations they intended to make, and to limit their oral submissions in the CJEU to 15 minutes each (see [21]).

The Senior Master sends a copy of the order making the reference to the Registrar of the CJEU (**r. 68.4(2)**). Unless the court orders otherwise, the Senior Master will send the papers to the CJEU even if the time for appealing has not expired or any application for permission to appeal or any appeal is yet to be determined (**r. 68.4(3)**).

The domestic court making the reference to the CJEU can request the President of the CJEU to consider whether there are special circumstances which would justify a case being given priority under the Rules of Procedure of the Court of Justice, art. 53(3), and whether the case raises matters of exceptional urgency under art. 107 of those Rules. In *R (International Air Transport Association) v Department for Transport* [2004] EWHC 1721 (Admin), [2004] 3 CMLR 20, such a request was made when the Administrative Court found that there was evidence to show a significant risk that low-cost airline operators would suffer serious damage and be liable to criminal proceeding if they became liable to the provisions of a Regulation due to come into force in the next year.

Urgent preliminary rulings

The CJEU has an expedited preliminary ruling procedure (Rules of Procedure of the Court of Justice, art. 105) as well as the urgent preliminary ruling procedure in art. 107. Further guidance on these procedures can be found in the Recommendations to national courts, paras 36 to 44. Any request to use these procedures must state which provision is relied upon, and the matters of fact and law on which the application is based, together with an indication of the proposed answers to the questions referred (**CPR, r. 68.3(2)**). If the CJEU rejects urgency, it may nevertheless decide to give a case priority under the Rules of Procedure of the Court of Justice, art. 53(3) (*A v B* (case C-489/14) [2016] ILPr 10).   **78.15**

PROCEDURE IN THE CJEU

The Registrar of the CJEU notifies the parties, member States and the Commission of any reference filed. A notice is published in the *Official Journal* indicating the names of the parties involved and a summary of the questions on which a preliminary ruling is being sought. The procedure of the court generally comprises a written part and an oral part (Rules of Procedure of the Court of Justice, art. 53.1).   **78.16**

After the oral hearing (if any) the case is adjourned, during which the advocate general delivers an opinion, followed by the judgment of the court. The CJEU Registry stays in contact with the national court until judgment is given, and sends various documents to the national court, including written observations, report of the hearing, opinion of the advocate general, and the judgment of the CJEU. The ruling binds the domestic court on the interpretation of the provision of EU law in question, but the domestic court has to apply the ruling to the facts of the case in which it arose. It is for the domestic court alone to find the facts, and the domestic court is entitled to disregard any conclusion reached by the CJEU in so far as it is based on a factual background inconsistent with the findings of the domestic court (*Arsenal Football Club plc v Reed (No. 2)* [2003] EWCA Civ 696, [2003] 3 All ER 865). Where the CJEU makes a finding of fact which is inevitable in the circumstances but a domestic judge misconstrues the CJEU's ruling as inconsistent with his or her own findings, the domestic court should follow the ruling of the CJEU (*Arsenal Football Club plc v Reed (No. 2)*).

Individual concern

Article 263 TFEU provides that the CJEU may review the legality of legislative acts, of acts of the Council, of the Commission and of the European Central Bank, other than recommendations and opinions, and of acts of the European Parliament and of the European   **78.17**

Council intended to produce legal effects vis-à-vis third parties. It shall also review the legality of acts of bodies, offices or agencies of the European Union intended to produce legal effects vis-à-vis third parties. Such proceedings may be brought by a member State, the European Parliament, the Council or the Commission. Proceedings may also be brought by a natural or legal person to whom the regulation or decision under review is addressed or is of direct and individual concern. This is usually interpreted as meaning that the applicant, if not a State or the Council or Commission, must be affected by the measure by reason of certain attributes peculiar to the applicant or a factual situation which differentiates the applicant from all other persons and distinguishes it individually (*Plaumann & Co. v Commission* (case 25/62) [1963] ECR 95, affirmed in *Inuit Tapiriit Kanatami v European Parliament* (case C-583/11 P) [2014] QB 648).

Individuals are therefore not permitted to challenge decisions which are not addressed to them personally (*Unión de Pequeños Agricultores v Council of the European Union* (case C-50/00 P) [2003] QB 893, where it was held that the CJEU did not have jurisdiction to examine in an individual case whether national procedural rules permitted a challenge to the legality of EU measures).

As a result of the Treaty of Lisbon, TFEU, art. 263, now provides that a natural or legal person may also institute proceedings against any regulatory act which is of direct concern to them and does not entail implementing measures. In *Inuit Tapiriit Kanatami v European Parliament* the CJEU held that 'regulatory act' does not include legislative acts. Individuals will therefore only have standing to challenge legislative acts if the direct and individual concern test is satisfied.

COSTS

78.18   The costs of the parties in seeking a preliminary ruling from the CJEU are always reserved to the domestic court (Recommendations to national courts, para. 31; Rules of Procedure of the Court of Justice, art. 102). Costs in direct actions are provided for under Title IV, Chapter 6 of the Rules of Procedure.

PART P

Enforcement

Chapter 79 Enforcement

INTRODUCTION

Entering judgment does not provide a litigant with the remedy sought in the proceedings. **79.1** Parties may well refuse to comply with the judgments and orders of the court. Public confidence in the legal system would be eroded if the courts were without powers to enforce compliance. In fact, a range of enforcement procedures are available, each being designed to deal with different situations. Where a number of procedures are available, a judgment creditor can choose whichever one seems likely to be the most effective, and can use more than one method of enforcement either at the same time or one after another (**CPR, r. 70.2(2)(b)**, but see **79.28** for an exception) Largely, the procedures are similar in both the High Court and the County Court. The major exception is that attachment of earnings orders (**79.25**) are generally only available in the County Court.

There has been a long-standing project to modernise the law relating to enforcement. Primary legislation for the latest changes can be found in the Tribunals, Courts and Enforcement Act

2007, and the relevant provisions came into force on 6 April 2014. They replace the law on enforcement against goods with enforcement through taking control of goods, and replace bailiffs with enforcement agents for this purpose. It is the law as it stands after the commencement of these changes that is dealt with in this chapter. Enforcement of final foreign judgments is dealt with in **chapter 80**. Interim enforcement in the High Court in support of foreign proceedings is also possible using the powers conferred by the **Civil Jurisdiction and Judgments Act 1982** s. **25** (see **37.16**).

A failure of the judicial system to enforce a judgment at all may amount to a breach of the right to a fair trial in the European Convention on Human Rights, art. **6(1)**, in the **Human Rights Act 1998, sch.** 1 (*Van de Hurk v Netherlands* (application 16034/90) (1994) 18 EHRR 481). As explained in *Hornsby v Greece* (application 18357/91) (1997) 24 EHRR 250 at [40], the right to a fair trial 'would be illusory if a Contracting State's domestic legal system allowed a final, binding judicial decision to remain inoperative to the detriment of one party'. Likewise, excessive delays in the system for enforcing judgments will be a breach of the right to a fair trial (*Immobiliare Saffi v Italy* (application 22774/93) (1999) 30 EHRR 756). Systemic failings of the kinds encountered in the European case law are not a feature of enforcement in England and Wales, and the fact that English law leaves the initiative on enforcement to the parties cannot in itself be a violation of art. 5.

TRANSFER OF PROCEEDINGS

79.2   A case may need to be transferred or sent to another hearing centre before enforcement proceedings are taken.

(a) A County Court claim (other than one under the Consumer Credit Act 1974) will have to be transferred to the High Court if enforcement by taking control of goods is sought of a judgment exceeding £5,000 (**High Court and County Courts Jurisdiction Order 1991 (SI 1991/724), art. 8(1)(a)**). While the County Court has unlimited jurisdiction to make charging orders, enforcement of a charging order by sale (see **79.33**) must take place in the High Court if the amount owing exceeds £350,000 (County Courts Act 1984, s. 23(c); County Court Jurisdiction Order 2014 (SI 2014/503), art. 3).

(b) A High Court claim will have to be transferred to the County Court if:

(i) enforcement by taking control of goods is sought of a judgment under £600 (**High Court and County Courts Jurisdiction Order 1991, art. 8(1)(b)**);

(ii) a charging order is sought where the judgment debt is under £5,000 (Charging Orders Act 1979, s. 1(2); SI 2014/503, art. 3); or

(iii) an attachment of earnings order is sought (Attachment of Earnings Act 1971, s. 1).

(c) An application for a third party debt order must generally be issued in the court which made the judgment or order that is being enforced (**CPR, r. 72.3(1)(b)**). There are exceptions where the claim has already been transferred (**r. 72.3(1)(b)(i)**) and for claims in the County Court Money Claims Centre, which may be enforced at any County Court hearing centre (**r. 72.3(1)(b)(ii)**) and **PD 70, para. 2.3**).

(d) Applications for attachment of earnings orders and County Court charging orders (other than charging orders over interests in funds in court) are made centrally to the County Court Money Claims Centre (**CPR, rr. 89.3 and 73.3(2)**). Hearings in these applications are usually dealt with by transferring the case to the judgment debtor's home court.

(e) A possession claim against trespassers (see **CPR, Part 55, and chapter 35**) may be enforced either in the High Court or the County Court (**High Court and County Courts Jurisdiction Order 1991, art. 8B**).

(f) An application for a judgment summons must be made at the County Court hearing centre serving the address where the judgment debtor resides or carries on business (**CPR, sch. 2, CCR, ord. 28, r. 1**).

(g) Subject to the above, an application to enforce a judgment in the County Court may be made at any County Court hearing centre, unless an enactment, rule or practice direction provides otherwise (**PD 70, para. 2.3**).

A judgment creditor seeking to enforce a County Court judgment or order in the High Court should issue an application to transfer the claim to the High Court under the County Courts Act 1984, s. 42, and should then apply for a certificate of judgment under **CPR, r. 40.14A**. The request for the certificate is made in writing, must state it is needed for the purpose of enforcement by taking control of goods (if this is the case) and confirm that the application to transfer has been made, attaching a copy of the application. Granting the certificate operates as an order to transfer the proceedings to the High Court (**r. 83.19**).

Normally, a judgment creditor wishing to enforce a High Court judgment or order in the County Court must apply to the High Court for an order transferring the proceedings in accordance with **r. 70.3(1)**. Once a transfer order has been obtained, **PD 70, para. 3.1**, requires the judgment creditor to file at the County Court:

(a) a copy of the judgment or order which is being enforced;
(b) a copy of the order transferring the proceedings;
(c) a certificate verifying the amount due under the judgment or order being enforced;
(d) a copy of any enforcement officer's return if a writ of control has been issued; and
(e) an application notice or request for enforcement in the County Court.

Where it is sought to enforce a High Court judgment in the County Court by warrant of control or warrant of delivery, it appears from **CPR, rr. 70.3(1), 83.17(1) and 83.17(3)** (which are obscurely worded on the question of permission and orders for transfers in this situation) that permission to enforce may be granted by either the High Court or the County Court.

ENFORCEMENT OF AWARDS BY TRIBUNALS ETC.

Statutes provide that certain decisions of courts (other than the High Court and the County Court), tribunals and other bodies, and certain compromises, are enforceable as though they were court orders, or that the amount payable under such a decision or compromise is recoverable as if payable under a court order. In these cases, the decision or compromise can be enforced using the procedures in **CPR, Parts 71 to 73, 81, 83 and 84** (information against debtors, third party debt orders and charging orders, by taking control of goods, enforcement against land, attachment of earnings, judgment summons or committal (**CPR, r. 70.5(1) and (2A)**). Where the enactment provides that a sum of money is recoverable as if it were payable under a County Court order:

79.3

(a) it must be enforced in the County Court if it is for less than £600;
(b) it may be enforced in either the County Court or the High Court if it is for £600 or more but less than £5,000; and
(c) it must be enforced in the High Court if it is for £5,000 or more (**High Court and County Courts Jurisdiction Order 1991 (SI 1991/724), art. 8(2)**. There are exceptions in **SI 1991/724, art. 8(3)**, relating to enforcement under the Employment Tribunals Act 1996, ss. 15(1) and 19A(3). **CPR, r. 70.5**, does not apply to arbitration awards, confiscation and forfeiture proceedings, or traffic enforcement (all of which have their own special rules relating to enforcement, see **r. 70.5(2)**).

Enforcement of a 'conditional compromise', which is one where the person to whom money is payable under a compromise agreement has to do something in addition to discontinuing or not starting proceedings, must be commenced by making an application on notice (**r. 70.5(4A)**).

Applications to enforce other awards under **r. 70.5** are made without notice, with the application being filed in the court for the district where the judgment debtor resides or carries on business, unless the court orders otherwise (**r. 70.5(4)**). The application is made on form N332B (**PD 70, para. 4.1**) and must include the information set out at **para. 4.3**. If the enactment provides that decisions or compromises are enforceable only if a court so orders, the application is made using form N332A, and a copy of the decision or compromise must be filed with the application notice (**CPR, r. 70.5(6)**). If the enactment requires registration in the High Court, an application to the head clerk of the Action Department at the RCJ must be made in accordance with **r. 70.5(8)** and **PD 70, paras 5.1** and **5.2**.

An order of the Supreme Court (**chapter 76**) may be enforced by applying to make it an order of the High Court using the procedure in **PD 40B, paras 13.1** to **13.3**. An application needs to be issued using the Part 23 procedure in the High Court supported by the evidence set out in **PD 40B, para. 13.2**. The application is usually heard without notice by the procedural judge.

CRIMINAL CONFISCATION ORDERS

79.4   Confiscation orders made by the criminal courts are discussed in *Blackstone's Criminal Practice 2017* at E19. The result of an all assets confiscation order will be that there will be nothing available for a civil judgment creditor. If there is a single loser in the criminal proceedings who has also obtained a civil judgment, it may be appropriate for the criminal court to quash a confiscation order under the Criminal Justice Act 1988 to allow the judgment creditor to enforce its civil judgment (*R v Silvester* [2009] EWCA Crim 2182, LTL 9/11/2009).

STAY OF EXECUTION

79.5   A judgment debtor who is unable to pay or who alleges that it is otherwise inexpedient to enforce an order may apply for a stay of execution (**CPR, r. 83.7**). Such an application must be made in accordance with **Part 23**, and must be supported by a witness statement substantiating the grounds relied on, and disclosing the debtor's means. Often the result of a successful application will be a stay of execution or suspension of a warrant pending payment of the judgment by instalments.

ORDERS TO OBTAIN INFORMATION
FROM JUDGMENT DEBTORS

79.6   Where little is known about a judgment debtor's finances, application may be made without notice for an order to obtain information from the judgment debtor. Where the judgment debtor is a company or other corporation, an officer of that body may be required to attend court to provide information about the judgment debtor's means or any other matter to assist with enforcement (**CPR, r. 71.2(1)(b)**). 'An officer of that body' includes a director of the judgment debtor, but not a director of a corporate director of the judgment debtor (*Masri v Consolidated Contractors International (UK) Ltd (No. 4)* [2008] EWCA Civ 876, [2010] 1 AC 90; a point not overturned on the appeal, [2009] UKHL 43, [2010] 1 AC 90) or a former officer (*Vitol SA v Capri Marine Ltd* [2008] EWHC 378 (Comm), [2009] Bus LR 271). The House of Lords in *Masri v Consolidated Contractors International (UK) Ltd (No. 4)* held that, where a company is a judgment debtor, **r. 71.2** does not permit an order to be made for the examination of an officer of the company who is domiciled outside the jurisdiction. It is different if the judgment debtor is an individual, against whom an order may be made under **r. 71.2** together with permission to serve abroad under **Part 6**.

An application for an order to obtain information under **Part 71** must be made using the prescribed application notice (form N316). This must state the debtor's name and address, identify the judgment and state the amount presently owing under the judgment (**PD 71, para. 1.2**). If the creditor wishes the debtor to be questioned before a judge (which will only be allowed if there are compelling reasons: **para. 2.2**) or to produce specific documents (such as bank statements and other financial material), these matters must be stated in the application notice (**para. 1.2**). If the application complies with these requirements, it will be dealt with by a court officer without a hearing (**CPR, r. 71.2**), and the officer will make an order requiring the debtor to attend court, produce documents and answer questions. That order must be served personally on the judgment debtor not less than 14 days before the hearing (**r. 71.3**), with service usually being effected by the creditor rather than the court (**PD 71, para. 3**). Once served, the debtor has seven days to ask the judgment creditor for a reasonable sum to cover the debtor's travelling expenses to court, which must be paid (**CPR, r. 71.4**). The judgment creditor must swear an affidavit (a witness statement being insufficient) giving details of service of the order, any request for and payment of travelling expenses, and how much of the judgment remains unpaid. This affidavit must be filed two days before the hearing or produced at the hearing (**r. 71.5**).

At the hearing the court officer will ask a set of standard questions which are set out in form EX140 for the examination of individuals, and EX141 for officers of companies or corporations. The judgment creditor may ask questions, or may request the court officer to ask additional, written questions (**PD 71, para. 4.2**). If the hearing takes place before a judge, the judgment creditor must attend (**CPR, r. 71.6**) and the questioning is conducted by the creditor or the creditor's legal representative (**PD 71, para. 5.1**). 'The examination is not only intended to be an examination, but to be a cross-examination, and that of the severest kind' (per James LJ in *Republic of Costa Rica v Stronsberg* (1880) 16 ChD 8). The basic policy is to prevent a judgment debtor defeating a judgment by dissipating or concealing assets. Accordingly, the debtor is required to answer all questions fairly directed to establishing the debtor's financial circumstances, including amounts, names, account and policy numbers. The evidence is recorded and signed by the debtor.

If the debtor fails to attend or otherwise fails to comply, the court usually makes a suspended committal order, which gives the debtor a second chance to comply (**PD 71, para. 7.1**). If the debtor again fails to comply, a committal order can be made by the judge (**CPR, r. 71.8**).

ENFORCEMENT OFFICERS AND AGENTS

79.7 High Court enforcement is carried out by enforcement officers authorised under the Courts Act 2003. An enforcement officer is an individual authorised to act as such by the Lord Chancellor or a person acting on his behalf (Courts Act 2003, sch. 7, para. 2(1)). Enforcement officers are appointed under the High Court Enforcement Officers Regulations 2004 (SI 2004/400). Once assigned to a district, an enforcement officer must undertake enforcement action for all writs of control which are to be executed at addresses within that district (SI 2004/400, reg. 7).

County Court enforcement is carried out by enforcement agents authorised under the Tribunals, Courts and Enforcement Act 2007, ss. 63 and 64. Applications for certificates under s. 64 must be made to the County Court Business Centre (**CPR, r. 84.18**) and must be supported by evidence that the applicant satisfies the requirements in the Certification of Enforcement Agents Regulations 2014 (SI 2014/421), reg. 3.

Commentary

TAKING CONTROL OF GOODS

Introduction

79.8 Taking control of goods involves an enforcement officer or enforcement agent taking control of the judgment debtor's goods and selling them to recover the sum owed under a judgment debt (Tribunals, Courts and Enforcement Act 2007, s. 62(1)). The 'TCG procedure' is the statutory procedure for taking control of goods and selling them to recover a sum in accordance with the statutory scheme in the Tribunals, Courts and Enforcement Act 2007, sch. 12, and regulations made under that Act (**CPR, r. 83.1(2)(h)**). The legislative framework is:

(a) The principal primary legislation can be found in the Tribunals, Courts and Enforcement Act 2007, ss. 62 to 87. Detailed provisions on the nature of the process and the powers of enforcement agents are set out in sch. 12, and it is sch. 12 that is the central part of the statutory scheme. Schedule 12 has been amended by the Crime and Courts Act 2013. There is also primary legislation in the County Courts Act 1984.

(b) More detailed provisions on the process, supplementing those in the Tribunals, Courts and Enforcement Act 2007, sch. 12, are to be found in the Taking Control of Goods Regulations 2013 (SI 2013/1894).

(c) Consequential amendments to existing legislation (several of which are quite significant) are to be found in the Tribunals, Courts and Enforcement Act 2007, sch. 13, with more in the Tribunals, Courts and Enforcement Act 2007 (Consequential, Transitional and Saving Provision) Order 2014 (SI 2014/600).

(d) Provisions dealing with the appointment of High Court enforcement officers are in the Courts Act 2003 and the High Court Enforcement Officers Regulations 2004 (SI 2004/400).

(e) For County Court judgments, certification of enforcement agents is dealt with by the Tribunals, Courts and Enforcement Act 2007, ss. 63 and 64; the Certification of Enforcement Agents Regulations 2014 (SI 2014/421); and **CPR, rr. 84.17 to 84.20**. Applications are made using form EAC1.

(f) Court procedures relating to taking control of goods can be found in **CPR, Parts 83, 84** and **85**, together with other relevant provisions, such as **Part 70** and **rr. 40.8A** and **40.14A**.

(g) Replacements for the court forms for writs and warrants of control were introduced on 6 April 2014 (PF Nos 53, 54, 56, 57, 58, 62, 63, 66, 66A and 71 for the High Court, and forms N42, N323, N326, N327 and N444 for the County Court). Templates for the forms to be used by enforcement agents in giving notice for various purposes to judgment debtors, and for controlled goods agreements, are set out in the schedule to SI 2014/421.

(h) Fees that may be charged are set out in the Taking Control of Goods (Fees) Regulations 2014 (SI 2014/1). This provides partly for fixed fees for different stages in the enforcement process, and partly for fees based on the amounts recovered.

The relevant legislation came into force on 6 April 2014, replacing writs of *fieri facias* and warrants of execution and most of the pre-existing law relating to enforcement against goods (and the related subject of distraint by landlords). About half the provisions in the Courts Act 2003 relating to High Court enforcement against goods remain in force. The Courts Act 2003 had already revoked the provisions relating to writs of *fieri facias* that used to be found in the Senior Courts Act 1981, ss. 138 to 138B. While paras 8 to 11 of the Courts Act 2013, sch. 7, no longer apply after 6 April 2014, the rest of sch. 7 continues in force. While an enforcement officer has the duties, powers, rights, privileges and liabilities that a sheriff of a county would have had at common law (sch. 7, para. 4(2)), this is subject to the Tribunals, *Courts and Enforcement Act 2007*, sch. 12, in the case of a writ conferring power to use the sch. 12 procedure (Courts Act 2003, sch. 7, para. 4(1A)).

Also encompassed within the scheme is the writ of *fieri facias de bonis ecclesiasticis*. This is an ancient procedure for seizing a debtor's ecclesiastical property to satisfy a High Court judgment after what is now a writ of control has been returned unsatisfied. It is directed to the bishop of the diocese and executed by diocesan officers of the bishop (**CPR, r. 83.11**).

A warrant of control is not available if the judgment is payable by instalments, and the instalments are up to date (**r. 83.15(10)**), nor is it available where the debtor is a child under 16 (SI 2013/1894, reg. 10).

Responsibility for execution of warrants of control

Under the County Courts Act 1984, s. 123, County Court District Judges were responsible for the acts and defaults of the bailiffs attached to their court. In order to remove any potential conflict between the District Judge's role as High Bailiff and his judicial responsibilities, such as in relation to the suspension of warrants, s. 123 has been repealed, and s. 85(2) has been amended. Responsibility for issuing warrants of control in the County Court is now given to 'any person authorised by or on behalf of the Lord Chancellor'. In practice this is the court manager.   **79.9**

Issue of writ or warrant of control

Issue is usually purely a matter of producing the correct documents. In the High Court these are a signed request to issue the writ or warrant, the judgment or order being enforced, any order giving permission if required, and paying a fee (**CPR, r. 83.9**). In the County Court again a request is required, and the creditor must certify the amount remaining outstanding on the judgment or order, and, where there is an order to pay by instalments, that the whole or part of any instalment remains unpaid, and paying a fee (**r. 83.15**). The writ or warrant is issued by being sealed (**r. 83.9(2)**). Permission is required in a number of situations set out in **r. 83.2**. These include where more than six years have elapsed since the date of the judgment or order, and where there has been any change in the parties.   **79.10**

A writ or warrant of control is then served on an enforcement officer (High Court) or an enforcement agent (County Court). A writ or warrant of control is valid for a period of 12 months, but the court can order it to be extended for a further 12 months (Taking Control of Goods Regulations 2013 (SI 2013/1894), reg. 9).

Enforcement after six years

Where six years have elapsed since the date of the judgment or order, permission to enforce is required (**CPR, r. 83.2(3)(a)**). The six-year period is regarded as a hurdle rather than a limit (*Society of Lloyd's v Longtin* [2005] EWHC 2491 (Comm), [2005] 2 CLC 774). While the exercise of the court's discretion is directed at doing justice between the parties in all the circumstances of the case (*Good Challenger Navegante SA v Metalexportimport SA* [2003] EWCA Civ 1668, [2004] 1 Lloyd's Rep 67), the court will only extend the six-year period where it is demonstrably just to do so. The burden of proof is on the judgment creditor to establish that it is just (*Duer v Frazer* [2001] 1 WLR 919).   **79.11**

Notice of enforcement

Before taking control of the debtor's goods the enforcement agent must give the judgment debtor notice of enforcement in the prescribed form. This must be served on the debtor at the address where he usually lives or carries on business at least seven clear days before the enforcement agent takes control of the goods (Taking Control of Goods Regulations 2013 (SI 2013/1894), regs 6 and 8). This gives the debtor a chance to pay off the judgment before his goods are seized.   **79.12**

Commentary

Gaining entry

79.13 At common law the sheriff was not permitted to use force to gain initial access to a dwelling house (*Semayne's Case* (1604) 5 Co Rep 91a). Forcible entry was permitted in the case of commercial or business premises (*Hodder v Williams* [1895] 2 QB 663) or after the sheriff or his officers had been forcibly ejected. Forced entry in other situations was held to be illegal in *McLeod v Butterwick* [1998] 1 WLR 1603.

Under the new scheme, the only premises that may be entered without an entry warrant are premises where the debtor usually lives or carries on a trade or business (Tribunals, Courts and Enforcement Act 2007, sch. 12, para. 14(6)). Enforcement officers and enforcement agents executing a writ or warrant of control are as a result limited to enforcement at a specified address (*Huntress Search Ltd v Canapeum Ltd* [2010] EWHC 1270 (QB), 160 NLJ 841). An entry warrant may be sought from the court if there is reason to believe the debtor has goods on other premises (sch. 12, para. 15). Enforcement by taking control of goods can be effected on any day of the week, but only between the hours of 6 a.m. and 9 p.m., unless the court orders otherwise (Taking Control of Goods Regulations 2013 (SI 2013/1894), regs 12 and 13).

Entry must be through a door or other usual means of access, such as through French doors or a loading bay (reg. 20). Reasonable force may be used to effect entry or to do anything for which entry is authorised if this is necessary (Tribunals, Courts and Enforcement Act 2007, sch. 12, para. 17) in the following situations:

(a) where the enforcement agent has power to enter the premises under paras 14, 15 or 16; these powers cover the place the debtor usually lives or carries on a trade or business, and other premises covered by an entry warrant (para. 18);

(b) where enforcement is at a place at which the enforcement agent reasonably believes the debtor carries on a trade or business (para. 18A);

(c) where the enforcement agent has a power of re-entry under para. 16 and the enforcement agent reasonably believes the debtor carries on a trade or business on the premises (para. 19); and

(d) where the enforcement agent has taken control of the goods by entering into a controlled goods agreement, and the debtor has failed to comply with any provision of the controlled goods agreement relating to payment of the debt, provided the debtor is given notice of the enforcement agent's intention to re-enter (para. 19A).

In addition, the enforcement agent can apply for a warrant permitting the use of reasonable force to execute against goods on the highway or to effect re-entry (SI 2013/1894, regs 28 and 29).

These enhanced powers to use force to effect entry or re-entry overturn the position established by *McLeod v Butterwick*. They are intended to be balanced by the regulatory and complaints processes also enacted under the Tribunals, Courts and Enforcement Act 2007 and the Certification of Enforcement Agents Regulations 2014 (SI 2014/421).

Seizing goods

79.14 By the Tribunals, Courts and Enforcement Act 2007, sch. 12, para. 13, taking control of goods involves doing one of the following:

(a) Securing the goods on the premises. This may be by locking them in a cupboard or outbuilding, or immobilising them.

(b) Securing them on the highway.

(c) Removing them and securing them elsewhere. Unless there are exceptional circumstances, they must be secured within a reasonable distance from where they were seized. The debtor must be provided with an inventory of the removed goods as soon as reasonably practicable, and the enforcement agent has a duty to take reasonable care of the removed goods (paras 34 and 35).

(d) Entering into a controlled goods agreement.

Unless the goods seized are goods on the highway (typically a car or van), the enforcement agent may not take control of goods whose aggregate value is more than the amount outstanding (para. 12). It is only goods that belong to the debtor and which are in the place where the debtor usually lives or carries on business that may be seized (paras 9(a), 10 and 14(6)). Exempt goods may not be seized (para. 11). Exempt goods are defined by the Taking Control of Goods Regulations 2013 (SI 2013/1894), regs 4 and 5 to include:

(a) items or equipment used personally by the debtor in his employment, business, trade, profession, study or education, up to a value of £1,350;

(b) clothing, bedding, furniture, household equipment, items and provisions as are reasonably required to satisfy the basic domestic needs of the debtor and every member of the debtor's household;

(c) assistance dogs;

(d) vehicles with disabled persons' badges;

(e) goods which happen to be the debtor's home, such as a houseboat.

Priorities

It sometimes happens that more than one creditor will seek to enforce by taking control of a debtor's goods at about the same time. The priority of a writ of control is determined by reference to the time it is received by the enforcement officer, whereas the priority of a warrant of control is determined by reference to the date it is issued (**CPR, r. 83.4(5)**). **79.15**

A related problem is in establishing whether a purchaser of any of the judgment debtor's goods will take them free of the claims of the judgment creditor under a writ or warrant of control. The property in the judgment debtor's goods is bound by the writ or warrant of control from the point the issued writ or warrant is received by the enforcement officer or enforcement agent (Tribunals, Courts and Enforcement Act 2007, sch. 12, paras 4 and 5). From that point any transfer or assignment of any interest in the debtor's goods is subject to the creditor's right to enforce against those goods, unless the third party purchaser bought the goods in good faith, for valuable consideration, and without notice of the writ or warrant. The enforcement officer or enforcement agent is required to endorse the writ or warrant of control with the time and date of receipt, which is to provide evidence of the point in time when the writ or warrant was received for this purpose (Courts Act 2003, sch. 7, para. 7; County Courts Act 1984, s. 99).

Controlled goods agreement

Under a controlled goods agreement the debtor is permitted to retain custody of the goods, but acknowledges that the enforcement agent is taking control of them, and agrees not to remove or dispose of them, or permit anyone else to do so, before the debt is paid (Tribunals, Courts and Enforcement Act 2007, sch. 12, para. 13(4)). It can be entered into between the enforcement agent and the debtor, or an adult authorised to do so by the debtor, or someone with apparent authority if the premises are used for a trade or business (Taking Control of Goods Regulations 2013 (SI 2013/1894), reg. 14). The agreement must be in writing, and comply with the requirements in reg. 15. Subject to the court authorising shorter notice, the enforcement agent has to give the debtor two days' advance notice in writing of any intention to re-enter the premises (usually because the enforcement agent now intends to remove the seized goods) (regs 23 to 27). **79.16**

Sale

Often, the threat of sale is sufficient incentive to persuade the debtor to pay. On payment the execution is superseded and the goods are released (Tribunals, Courts and Enforcement Act 2007, sch. 12, para. 6(3)(a)). Otherwise, the enforcement agent must make or obtain a **79.17** valuation of the controlled goods, and must sell or dispose of them for the best price that can reasonably be obtained (paras 36 and 37). The debtor must be given seven clear days' notice in writing of the arrangement for sale (para. 40). Unless the court orders otherwise, the goods will be sold by public auction (para. 41). The auction must be publicly advertised and must be conducted by a qualified auctioneer or on an online auction or internet auction site (Taking Control of Goods Regulations 2013 (SI 2013/1894), reg. 43). After the sale the debtor is given a detailed account in writing of the sale, and the proceeds are used to pay the amount outstanding on the judgment. Purchasers of the goods acquire good title (Tribunals, Courts and Enforcement Act 2007, sch. 12, paras 50 and 51).

ADMINISTRATION ORDERS

79.18 By virtue of the County Courts Act 1984, s. 112, and **CPR, sch. 2, CCR, ord. 39**, the County Court may make an administration order in respect of an individual debtor's debts listed in a schedule to the order if the debtor is unable to pay forthwith the amount of a judgment debt and the debtor's whole indebtedness (including the judgment) is no more than £5,000. An administration order may be made of the court's own initiative, on consideration of information provided under **CPR, Part 71**, or on the application of the debtor. The order has the immediate effect of restricting creditors named in the order from joining in bankruptcy petitions against the debtor. The order will usually provide for the debtor to make specified payments by instalments, with periodic dividends being paid to the named creditors.

The Tribunals, Courts and Enforcement Act 2007, s. 106, provides for a substantially revised administration order scheme, but it has not been brought into force.

THIRD PARTY DEBT ORDERS

79.19 Third party debt orders (formerly called garnishee proceedings) have the effect of transforming a debt payable by a third party (the garnishee under the old terminology) to the judgment debtor into an obligation to pay the debt to the judgment creditor. Third party debt orders are a particularly effective method of enforcement where the debt to be attached is owed by a responsible body, such as a bank or building society. They are not restricted to such bodies.

Third party debt orders can be made where there is a 'debt due or accruing due to the judgment debtor from a third party' (**CPR, r. 72.2(1)(a)**). This rule applies in a simple and mechanistic way only to debts owed to the judgment debtor, and not to debts owed to other persons even if connected to the judgment debtor (*Continental Transfert Technique Ltd v Federal Government of Nigeria* [2009] EWHC 2898 (Comm), LTL 18/11/2009). Contingent liabilities are not debts for this purpose (*Kier Regional Ltd v City and General (Holborn) Ltd* [2008] EWHC 2454 (TCC), [2008] CILL 2639), nor is money in a joint bank account (*Hirschon v Evans* [1938] 2 KB 801). A court could and should, in the absence of contrary indications, accept as sufficient for this purpose evidence that the judgment debtor previously held an account at a bank which appears to have been in credit at that time (*Alawiye v Mahmood* [2006] EWHC 277 (Ch), [2007] 1 WLR 79). Lindsay J also said that evidence that in the past a bank account was overdrawn might be enough if there is nothing to indicate that overall the bank is owed money by the judgment debtor (see [8]). A third party debt order was made against a bank account in the name of an unincorporated association in *Huntingdon Life Sciences Group plc v Stop Huntingdon Animal Cruelty* [2005] EWHC 2233 (QB), [2005] 4 All ER 899. A third party debt order can be made against a third party who owes a judgment debt to the judgment debtor in unrelated proceedings. This is so even where the earlier judgment debt is covered by a public funding statutory charge, but the third party debt order in such a case has to provide for payment to the judgment debtor's provider in the earlier proceedings, in accordance with what is now the Civil Legal Aid (Statutory Charge) Regulations 2013 (SI 2013/503), reg. 13 (*Beechwood Construction Ltd v Afza* [2008] EWHC 2671

(Ch), LTL 6/11/2008). It is essential that there is a relationship of creditor and debtor between the judgment debtor and the third party. If the evidence goes no further than showing that the judgment debtor might ultimately have a beneficial interest in money in a bank account held by a trustee there is no such relationship. In such a case a third party debt order will be refused (*AIG Capital Partners Inc. v Republic of Kazakhstan* [2005] EWHC 2239 (Comm), [2006] 1 WLR 1420).

Application for an interim order

Third party debt orders follow a two-stage process. The first stage is commenced by a without **79.20** notice application (**CPR, r. 72.3**) verified by a statement of truth in form N349 containing the information prescribed by **PD 72, para. 1.2**. The required information includes details of the judgment debtor, the judgment, and details of the third party debt. Speculative applications will be rejected, and orders will only be made if there is evidence substantiating a belief that the debtor has (say) an account with a specific bank or building society (**PD 72, para. 1.3**). The application is considered by a judge without a hearing (**CPR, r. 72.4(1)**), with most applications being dealt with by Masters and District Judges. *Thakerar v Lynch Hall and Hornby (No. 2)* [2005] EWHC 2752 (Ch), [2006] 1 WLR 1513, held that a bankruptcy registrar has jurisdiction to deal with an application made in insolvency proceedings.

If satisfied there is a debt due or accruing due to the judgment debtor, the judge may make an interim third party debt order directing the third party not to make any payment which reduces the amount he owes the judgment debtor to less than the amount specified in the order. The judge will also fix a hearing to consider making the order final. The amount specified will be the total outstanding on the judgment or order being enforced, together with fixed costs (**r. 72.4(3)**).

Service of the interim order

An interim order must be served on the third party who owes money to the judgment debtor **79.21** not less than 21 days before the date fixed for the hearing to consider making the order final (**CPR, r. 72.5(1)(a)**), and is binding on the third party when it is served on the third party (**r. 72.4(4)**). If the third party is a bank or building society it must carry out a search to identify all accounts held by the judgment debtor, and must disclose to the court and the judgment creditor the account numbers, whether they are in credit, and, if so, whether the balance is sufficient to cover the amount specified in the interim order, or the amount in the account if insufficient (**r. 72.6(1) and (2)**). It must also state if it asserts any right to the money in the account, for example, by set-off, giving details of the ground for that assertion (**r. 72.6(2)(c)(iii)**). A third party which is not a bank or building society has seven days after service to notify the court and the judgment creditor in writing if nothing is owed to the judgment debtor or the amount owed is less than the amount specified in the interim order (**r. 72.6(4)**).

The interim order must also be served on the judgment debtor. This needs to be done not less than seven days after service on the third party, and not less than seven days before the date fixed for the hearing (**r. 72.5(1)(b)**). Where service is effected by the judgment creditor, a certificate of service must be filed not less than two days before the hearing, or must be produced at the hearing (**r. 72.5(2)**). A judgment debtor who is an individual and who is suffering hardship in meeting ordinary living expenses as a result of the interim order may apply for a *hardship payment order permitting one or more payments out of the account* (**r. 72.7; PD 72, paras 5.1 to 5.6**).

Application for final third party debt order

The second stage is when the court considers whether to make a final third party debt order **79.22** on the date fixed when the interim order was made. A judgment debtor or third party objecting to the final order, or who knows or believes someone else has a claim to the money, must file and serve written evidence stating the grounds of any objection or details of the other claim not less than three days before the hearing (**CPR, r. 72.8**). If the court is notified that another person has a claim to the money it will serve notice of the application and the hearing on that person (**r. 72.8(5)**). At the hearing the court may make a final third party debt order, discharge the interim order, decide any issues or direct a trial of any issues (**r. 72.8(6)**). A final third party debt order is enforceable as an order to pay money. By **r. 72.9(2)**, to the extent of the amount paid under the final order, the third party's debt to the judgment debtor is discharged.

Attachable money

79.23 It is possible to obtain a third party debt order only over debts due to the judgment debtor. Examples are money in a bank account, trade debts, judgment debts, and rent due to a landlord. Conversely, claims for damages, matrimonial maintenance orders, and salary not presently payable are not attachable. Most conditions imposed by banks and building societies restricting the right to withdraw money from the judgment debtor's account are disregarded once a third party debt order is made (Senior Courts Act 1981, s. 40; County Courts Act 1984, s. 108; **CPR, r. 72.2(3)**).

Discretion to make third party debt orders

79.24 A third party debt order may be refused if it would be inequitable to grant it. The onus of proof is on the judgment debtor to show why an interim third party debt order should not be made final (*Westacre Investments Inc. v Yugoimport SDPR* [2008] EWHC 801 (Comm), [2009] 1 All ER (Comm) 780). It is a fundamental feature of a third party debt order that the third party must be discharged from its liability to the judgment debtor in the amount that the third party pays to the judgment creditor. If the third party is located in a jurisdiction which will not recognise such a discharge, a court in England or Wales should not make a third party debt order (*Société Eram Shipping Co. Ltd v Compagnie Internationale de Navigation* [2003] UKHL 30, [2004] 1 AC 260; *Kuwait Oil Tanker Co. SAK v Qabazard* [2003] UKHL 31, [2004] 1 AC 300). The insolvency of the judgment debtor is a sufficient reason for refusing to make an order, because its effect may be to prefer the judgment creditor over the general body of creditors (*Roberts Petroleum Ltd v Bernard Kenny Ltd* [1983] 2 AC 192). Conversely, if a judgment creditor secured a charging order or third party debt order in competition with other creditors who had not been so quick off the mark, that should not affect the court's discretion to make the order final (*Reed v Oury* (2000) LTL 12/2/2001). The burden of proof remains on the judgment debtor in cases where the third party debt order is sought more than six years after the judgment, the lapse of time being no more than one of the factors to be considered in making the decision. Arguments that the judgment creditor could have discovered the third party debt sooner, or that a few months beyond six years have elapsed, are unlikely to be significant factors (*Westacre Investments Inc. v Yugoimport SDPR* [2008] EWHC 801 (Comm), [2009] 1 All ER (Comm) 780).

ATTACHMENT OF EARNINGS

79.25 Where a judgment debtor is employed, but has no other substantial assets, the most effective method of enforcement is by obtaining an attachment of earnings order. Such an order can only be made, unless the application is by the debtor, if the debtor has failed to make one or more payments as required by the relevant adjudication (Attachment of Earnings Act 1971, s. 3(3)). The Attachment of Earnings Act 1971, s. 6(1), provides:

An attachment of earnings order shall be an order directed to a person who appears to the court to have the debtor in his employment and shall operate as an instruction to that person—
(a) to make periodical deductions from the debtor's earnings . . . and

(b)   at such times as the order may require, or as the court may allow, to pay the amounts deducted to the collecting officer of the court, as specified in the order.

The High Court has no jurisdiction to make attachment of earnings orders. All civil applications for attachment of earnings orders have to be made in the County Court Money Claims Centre (**CPR, r. 89.3**).

Earnings attachable

An attachment of earnings order may be made in respect of wages, salaries, fees, bonuses, commission and overtime payable under a contract of service, including occupational pensions and statutory sick pay. An order cannot be made in respect of self-employed income, nor State pensions, benefits or allowances (Attachment of Earnings Act 1971, s. 24). Disputes over whether particular payments are earnings are determined under **CPR, r. 89.12**. **79.26**

Procedure for applying for an attachment of earnings order

An application for an attachment of earnings order is made by filing a request in a standard form with a certificate of the amount of money remaining due under the judgment and that the whole or part of any instalment remains unpaid (**CPR, r. 89.4(1)**), and paying a fee. The court then serves the debtor with the application together with a reply form in form N56, together with an instruction to the debtor to complete and file the reply form within eight days after service (**r. 89.5**). A copy of the reply form is sent to the judgment creditor. The reply form is considered by an administrative officer of the court, who may make an attachment of earnings order if there is sufficient information to do so (**r. 89.7(1)**). If the court officer decides not to make an order, the application is referred to the District Judge who may determine the application without a hearing, or transfer the application to the debtor's home court (**r. 89.7(7)**). Either party may object to an order made by a court officer or District Judge by making an application within 14 days after service of the order (**r. 89.7(3) and (9)**), in which event the application must be transferred to the debtor's home court for hearing (**r. 89.7(4) and (10)**). The parties must be given at least two days' notice of the hearing (**r. 89.7(5) and (11)**). **79.27**

At the hearing the District Judge confirms that the debtor is not unemployed or self-employed. Provided the debtor is employed, the District Judge will consider the debtor's income and regular outgoings, and will fix:

(a)   The debtor's protected earnings rate. This is the amount the debtor is considered to need to maintain his or her family, each week or month, and any deductions made under the order will not reduce the debtor's income below this level.

(b)   The debtor's normal deduction rate. This is the amount, subject to the protected earnings rate, which is deducted from the debtor's earnings each week or month.

Costs may be fixed and allowed without a detailed assessment (**r. 89.10**). Normally, the order will then be served on the debtor's employer (**r. 89.11**), who will make the deductions specified and pay the money deducted to the court. Alternatively, the court may make a suspended attachment of earnings order, which will only be served on the employer if the debtor fails to pay agreed instalments promptly. A debtor with several creditors may be ordered to file a list of creditors with a view to making an administration order (see **79.18**) or a consolidated attachment of earnings order (**rr. 89.18 to 89.22**).

Supplementary points

While an attachment of earnings order is in force, permission of the court is required before a warrant of control will be issued for the judgment debt (Attachment of Earnings Act 1971, s. 8(2)(b)). Also, during the currency of the order the debtor is under a duty (enforceable by imprisonment or a fine: s. 23) to notify the court of any change in his or her employment (s. 15). **79.28**

Commentary

CHARGING ORDERS

79.29   A charging order is defined by the Charging Orders Act 1979, s. 1(1), as an order 'impos-ing on any such property of the debtor as may be specified in the order a charge for secur-ing the payment of any money due or to become due under [a] judgment or order'. In addition to money judgments, a charging order can be made in respect of assessed costs, but not unassessed costs (*Monte Developments Ltd v Court Management Consultants Ltd* [2010] EWHC 3071 (Ch), [2011] 1 WLR 1579). A charging order secures a judgment debt: it does not of itself produce any money. By s. 3(4) a charge imposed by a charging order has the same effect, and is enforceable in the same way, 'as an equitable charge created by the debtor by writing under his hand'. It may therefore be enforced either by sale (see **79.33**) or through the appointment of a receiver (see **79.40**) (*Midland Bank plc v Pike* [1988] 2 All ER 434). It is possible to obtain a charging order in respect of a judgment payable by instalments even where the instalments are not in arrears (s. 1(6) and (7) in force from 1 October 2012). The Lord Chancellor may impose a minimum threshold below which a charging order cannot be made (s. 3A). A charging order of course takes effect subject to any prior charges or mortgages. Once obtained and registered at the Land Registry, a charging order can give a measure of long-term security, which is necessary if there is no immediate prospect of recovery by other methods. It was held in *Ezekiel v Orakpo* [1997] 1 WLR 340, that a charging order extends to cover the judgment debt, interest and costs even if it does not expressly say so. As a charging order is simply security for payment, it is possible to make an order for payment by instalments as well as a charging order (*Robaigealach v Allied Irish Bank plc* (2001) LTL 12/11/2001).

Exceptionally, it may be possible to enforce the charge by bringing sale proceedings (see **79.33**), or the charge may result in the judgment being paid if the charged property is sold by the judgment debtor and the purchaser wishes (as is usual) to purchase it clear of encum-brances. Neither LA 1980, s. 20 (mortgages), nor s. 24 (judgments) applies to enforcement of a charging order, with the result there is no limitation period (*Ezekiel v Orakpo; Yorkshire Bank Finance Ltd v Mulhall* [2008] EWCA Civ 1156, [2009] 2 All ER (Comm) 164).

Chargeable property

79.30   A charge may be imposed by the Charging Orders Act 1979 only on the types of property listed in s. 2 of the Act. These are the judgment debtor's interest in land, securities and partnership property. Section 2(1) allows a charging order to be made on the interest of a beneficiary under a trust for sale. If land is held by the judgment debtor alone, any charg-ing order should be expressed to attach to his legal and beneficial interest in the land. Likewise, if there are joint debtors who own the entire beneficial interest, the charging order should cover their whole legal and beneficial interests (*Clark v Chief Land Registrar* [1994] Ch 370). Where there is one judgment debtor who is a co-owner of land, the charg-ing order should secure his beneficial interest in the land (*National Westminster Bank Ltd v Stockman* [1981] 1 WLR 67). It may be possible to obtain a charging order against a company which is an organ of a State which is a judgment debtor (*Kensington International Ltd v Republic of Congo* [2005] EWHC 2684 (Comm), [2006] 2 BCLC 296; *Walker International Holdings Ltd v Republic of Congo* [2005] EWHC 2813 (Comm), LTL 16/12/2005; *Continental Transfert Technique Ltd v Federal Government of Nigeria* [2009] EWHC 2898 (Comm), LTL 18/11/2009), although the law on this is evolving. In *Habib Bank Ltd v Ahmed* [2004] EWCA Civ 805, *The Independent*, 30 June 2004, the debtor sought to put real property out of the reach of a charging order by transferring title to members of his family. The transfers were set aside under the Insolvency Act 1986, s. 423, as transactions at an undervalue, and the charging order was made abso-lute. Likewise, transfers of industrial units from the judgment debtor to related compan-ies, between judgment and the assessment of costs, were set aside under s. 423 so that charging orders could be made in *Beckenham MC Ltd v Centralex Ltd* [2004] EWHC 1287 (Ch), [2004] 2 BCLC 764. In *Walker International Holdings Ltd v Congo* [2005] EWHC 2813 (Comm), LTL 16/12/2005, it was held that shares nominally owned by one company were in reality owned through a second company by the judgment debtor, with the result that an interim charging order was properly made in respect of the shares.

An application for a charging order under the Solicitors Act 1974, s. 73, is not precluded by the standard restriction in precedent L (**PD 46, para. 6.5**) or the Solicitors Act 1974, s. 70(2)(b), precluding proceedings to enforce a solicitor's bill until detailed assessment proceedings are concluded (*Mastercigars Direct Ltd v Withers LLP* [2007] EWHC 2733 (Ch), [2009] 1 WLR 881).

Procedure on applying for a charging order

Subject to the transfer rules discussed at 79.2, both the High Court and County Court may make charging orders. However, County Court applications for charging orders must be made to the County Court Money Claims Centre unless the application is for a charging order over an interest in a fund in court, in which case the application is made to the court where the judgment was made (**CPR, r. 73.3(2) and (3)**). **79.31**

There is a two-stage process for obtaining charging orders. The first stage is to apply for an interim charging order by issuing an application notice in form N379 (land) or N380 (securities) verified by a statement of truth (**CPR, r. 73.3(5)**) containing the information prescribed by **PD 73, para. 1.2**. The required information includes details of the judgment debtor, the judgment, and the property which it is intended to charge. Evidence of the property where it is sought to charge the debtor's interest in land is usually provided by an office copy entry obtained from the Land Registry under the Land Registration Act 1988.

Slightly different procedures apply depending on whether the application is made to the County Court Money Claims Centre. Where this is so, the application is initially dealt with without a hearing, usually by a court officer (**CPR, r. 73.4(2) and (3)**). The court officer may make an interim charging order (**r. 73.4(5)**), or may refer the application to a judge, who may make an interim charging order or transfer the application to the debtor's home court for a hearing to consider whether to make a final charging order (**r. 73.4(6)**). An interim order made by a court officer may be reconsidered if a request is made within 14 days of service of the order (**r. 73.5**). The interim order, application notice and any documents filed in support must be served by the creditor on the debtor and other persons listed in **r. 73.7(7)** within 21 days of the interim order. Certificates of service relating to each person served, and a statement of the amount due including interest and costs, must then be filed by the creditor within 28 days of the interim order (**r. 73.7(2)**).

Charging order applications in venues other than the County Court Money Claims Centre are initially dealt with by a judge without a hearing (**r. 73.6(2)**). The judge may make an interim order charging the debtor's interest in the relevant asset and fixing a hearing to consider making a final charging order (**r. 73.6(3)**). The creditor must effect service not less than 21 days before the final hearing (**r. 73.7(5) and (7)**), and must either file certificates of service not less than two days before the final hearing, or produce the certificates at the hearing (**r. 73.7(6)**).

Service of an interim charging order effectively prevents dealings with the assets charged pending the final hearing (**rr. 73.8 and 73.9**). If the interim order relates to registered land, it is usual, as a precaution, to protect it by entering a unilateral or agreed notice under the Land Registration Act 2002, ss. 32 and 34. Applications for charging orders are expressly stated to be writs or orders affecting land by the Charging Orders Act 1979, s. 3(2). Protection by notice is not available in cases excluded by the Land Registration Act 2002, s. 33, which include interests under a trust of land and settlements under the Settled Land Act

ENFORCEMENT OF JUDGMENTS FOR THE DELIVERY OF GOODS

79.37 Enforcement of judgments for the delivery of goods is by means of warrants (or, in the High Court, writs) of delivery. There are two types, corresponding with the forms of relief stated in the Torts (Interference with Goods) Act 1977, s. 3. The first is known as a warrant (or writ) of specific delivery. It requires the enforcement officer or enforcement agent to seize the goods specified in the judgment, with no alternative of recovering their value. The second is known as a warrant (or writ) of delivery. It requires the enforcement officer or enforcement agent to seize either the goods specified in the judgment, or their value.

As with enforcement by taking control of goods (**79.10**), issue is simply a matter of the creditor filing a request accompanied by the judgment (High Court), and paying the court fee. At least seven days before enforcement is levied the debtor must be served with a written notice warning of the warrant (**CPR, r. 83.24**).

ENFORCEMENT OF JUDGMENTS FOR THE POSSESSION OF LAND

Procedure on writ or warrant of possession

79.38 In the High Court permission is required before a writ of possession will be issued (**CPR, r. 83.13(2)**). In the County Court an application to issue a warrant of possession may be made without notice (**r. 83.26(2)**), but the application must be accompanied by a certificate that the land has not been vacated (**r. 83.26(4)**) and, where the land is a dwelling-house subject to a mortgage, a certificate that notice has been given in accordance with the Dwelling Houses (Execution of Possession Orders by Mortgagees) Regulations 2010 (SI 2010/809) (**CPR, r. 83.26(5)**, and see **87.48** to **87.57**). By way of exception, permission is not required if the possession claim was against trespassers and no more than three months have expired from the date of the order (**rr. 83.13(3)** and **83.26(10)** and **(11)**). It is always of the utmost importance that the land is adequately described.

The police are often informed of the time when possession will be enforced, as entry may be gained by force if necessary. The claimant will also usually need to attend to change the locks and make the premises secure after possession is obtained. When enforcing the warrant or writ, the enforcement officer or enforcement agent is required to turn out everyone on the premises, even if they are not parties (*R v Wandsworth County Court, ex parte Wandsworth London Borough Council* [1975] 1 WLR 1314). However, there is a divergence of practice regarding goods in the premises. In the High Court, these too must be removed by the enforcement officer, but in the County Court this is unnecessary (County Courts Act 1984, s. 111(1)).

Warrants and writs of restitution

79.39 It sometimes happens that persons ejected when a warrant or writ of possession is enforced regain entry at some later date. Such persons may be removed a second time under a warrant (County Court) or writ (High Court) of restitution. These is a species of warrant (or writ) in aid of a primary warrant (or writ). Permission is required for the issue of such warrants or writs (**CPR, r. 83.26(8)**). The application is made using the **CPR, Part 23**, procedure, but the application notice need not be served on the respondent unless the court otherwise directs. The application must be supported by evidence by witness statement or affidavit giving evidence of wrongful re-entry. The court looks for a plain and sufficient nexus between the original recovery of possession and the need to effect further recovery of the same land (*Wiltshire County Council v Frazer (No. 2)* [1986] 1 WLR 109).

RECEIVERS BY WAY OF EQUITABLE EXECUTION

Nature of receivership

Courts are empowered to appoint receivers by the Senior Courts Act 1981, s. 37 (powers of **79.40** the High Court regarding receivers), and the County Courts Act 1984, ss. 38 (remedies available in the County Court) and 107 (receivers by way of equitable execution) where this is just and convenient. *Masri v Consolidated Contractors International (UK) Ltd (No. 2)* [2008] EWCA Civ 303, [2009] QB 450, established that the jurisdiction under s. 37 is not limited to the circumstances where a receiver could have been appointed in 1873 (the date of the Supreme Court of Judicature Act 1873), and that a receiver by way of equitable execution may be appointed over an asset whether or not the asset is at that time amenable to execution at law. The law governing the jurisdiction is capable of being developed incrementally to new situations. It extends to enable the appointment of a receiver by way of equitable execution over a power to revoke a discretionary trust vested in the judgment debtor where the objects of the trust include the judgment debtor (*Tasarruf Mevduati Sigorta Fonu v Merrill Lynch Bank and Trust Company (Cayman) Ltd* [2011] UKPC 17, [2011] 4 All ER 704). A receivership order has the effect of appointing some responsible person to receive rents, profits and moneys receivable in respect of the judgment debtor's interest in certain property, and to apply that income in specified ways, including payment of a judgment debt. According to *Maclaine Watson and Co. Ltd v International Tin Council* [1988] Ch 1, such an order can only be made where:

(a) it is impossible to enforce using any of the other methods of enforcement; and
(b) the appointment of a receiver will be effective.

These conditions are not always applied rigidly (*Manchester and Liverpool District Banking Co. Ltd v Parkinson* (1889) 22 QBD 173). Enforcement of a judgment outside the EU may be sufficiently difficult in practical terms as to justify the appointment of a receiver (*Masri v Consolidated Contractors International Co. SAL* [2008] EWHC 2492 (Comm), LTL 28/10/2008). An appointment of a receiver by way of equitable execution operates *in personam*, so the extraterritorial restrictions relating to applications for third party debt orders (for which see **79.24**) do not apply (*Masri v Consolidated Contractors International (UK) Ltd (No. 2)* [2008] EWCA Civ 303, [2009] QB 450).

On the question whether the appointment of a receiver will be effective, the Senior Courts Act 1981, s. 37(1), provides that an appointment can only be made if it is just and convenient. Under **PD 69, para. 5**, when considering an application for the appointment of a receiver as a method of enforcing a judgment, the court must have regard to the amount claimed by the judgment creditor, the amount likely to be obtained by the receiver, and the probable costs of the appointment.

A receiver might be appointed where the judgment debtor has some valuable right not in the nature of a debt (and hence not amenable to a third party debt order). A receiver might also be appointed to receive rents from a number of tenants who are suing their landlord for failing to maintain the premises, and to apply the money in effecting necessary repairs (*Hart v Emelkirk Ltd* [1983] 1 WLR 1289).

Procedure for seeking the appointment of a receiver

An application for the appointment of a receiver in existing proceedings is made using the **79.41** **CPR, Part 23**, procedure, and must be supported by two witness statements or affidavits. The first explains the reasons why the appointment is required, gives details of the property which it is proposed that the receiver should get in or manage, estimates the value of the property and amount of income likely to be produced, gives details of the judgment or order being enforced and the extent to which the judgment debtor has failed to comply with it and why judgment cannot be enforced in any other way (**PD 69, para. 4.1**). It should also give the

Commentary

name, address and position of the proposed receiver ('the nominee', **para. 4.2(1)**). The second witness statement should be by a person who knows the nominee, and needs to state a belief that the nominee is a suitable person to be appointed, and the basis of that belief (**para. 4.2(2)**). The written evidence must be accompanied by a signed consent from the nominee (**para. 4.2(3)**).

Order appointing a receiver

79.42   The order appointing a receiver may:

    (a) require the receiver to provide security, usually by bond (in the case of insolvency practitioners) or guarantee (**CPR, r. 69.5; PD 69, para. 7.2**) — the security is usually fixed at twice the annual income from the property;

    (b) allow the receiver proper remuneration (**CPR, r. 69.7; PD 69, paras 9.1 to 9.6**);

    (c) require the receiver to submit periodic accounts (**CPR, r. 69.8; PD 69, paras 10.1 to 10.3**);

    (d) require moneys received to be paid into court (**PD 69, para. 6.3(3)**);

    (e) authorise the receiver to carry on an activity or incur an expense (**PD 69, para. 6.3(4)**).

ENFORCEMENT OF MANDATORY ORDERS

79.43   If a mandatory order is not complied with, the court may direct that the act required by the injunction be done by another person, with the expense of doing so being borne by the disobedient party (**CPR, r. 70.2A**).

ENFORCEMENT AGAINST PARTICULAR TYPES OF PARTY

Partnerships

79.44   With effect from 2 October 2006, a judgment or order made against a partnership may be enforced without permission against:

    (a) any property of the partnership within the jurisdiction (**PD 70, para. 6A.1**);

    (b) any person who was within the jurisdiction when the claim form was issued and who is not a limited partner, if that person acknowledged service of the claim form as a partner, or having been served as a partner with the claim form, failed to acknowledge service of it, or admitted in his statement of case that he is or was a partner at the material time, or was found by the court to have been a partner at the relevant time (**PD 70, para. 6A.2**); or

    (c) any person who was ordinarily resident outside the jurisdiction when the claim form was issued and who is not a limited partner, if that person acknowledged service of the claim form as a partner, or was served within the jurisdiction as a partner, or who was served outside the jurisdiction as a partner with permission under **CPR, Part 6, Section III** (**PD 70, para. 6A.3**).

A judgment or order may be enforced against a person not falling into the categories set out in points (a) to (c) above only with the court's permission (**PD 70, para. 6A.4**). This will include limited partners, and other partners who do not come within PD 70, paras 6A.2 or 6A.3.

There are special provisions dealing with service and appearance at court by a partnership in relation to enforcement by:

    (a) attaching debts due or accruing due to a judgment creditor by a partnership (see **PD 72, paras 3A.1 to 3A.3**); and

(b) charging order or interim charging order against property within the jurisdiction belonging to a judgment debtor that is a partnership (see **PD 73, paras 4A.1** to **4A.3**).

Representative parties

If a claim is brought or ordered to be continued against a representative party under **CPR, r. 19.6(1)**, any judgment or order given in the claim is binding on all persons represented, unless the court orders otherwise (**r. 19.6(4)**). However, the judgment or order cannot be enforced against a person who is not a party to the claim unless the court gives permission (**r. 19.6(4)**). The same applies to a claim in which the court has, under **r. 19.7(2)**, appointed a representative of persons who cannot be ascertained (**r. 19.7(7)**). **79.45**

The Crown

A successful claimant may not enforce a judgment against the Crown by process of execution (Crown Proceedings Act 1947, s. 25(4)). None of the provisions of **CPR, rr. 40.8A** and **70.2A** and **Parts 69** to **73, 81, 83, 84** and **89** or **CPR, sch. 2, CCR, ord. 28**, apply to the Crown (**CPR, r. 66.6**). The Crown, on the other hand, may enforce a judgment in its favour against a private litigant in the normal way (Crown Proceedings Act 1947, s. 26(1)). **79.46**

In order to obtain satisfaction of orders against the Crown, a successful claimant must follow the procedure set out in the Crown Proceedings Act 1947, s. 25. It is as follows:

(a) The claimant should apply to the court, at least 21 days after the date of the order, for a certificate in form No. 95 or No. 96 in the High Court, or form N293A in the County Court.
(b) The certificate must set out full particulars of the order made, including, where appropriate, the amount payable by the Crown.
(c) Once obtained, the certificate should be served on the solicitors acting for the Crown.
(d) The Crown will then make payment.

The Crown Proceedings Act 1947 gives no deadline for payment of the amount due by the Crown. The court may order that payment be suspended pending appeal (s. 25(3)).

Attaching Crown debts

A person who has obtained judgment against a defendant who is owed money by the Crown may obtain an order under the Crown Proceedings Act 1947, s. 27(1), directing payment of the money to the judgment creditor instead of the judgment debtor. The application is made by application notice using the Part 23 procedure, supported by written evidence setting out the facts giving rise to the application, stating the name and last known address of the person to be restrained, identifying the order to be enforced and the amount outstanding under it, and identifying the debt owed by the Crown in respect of which the application is made (**CPR, r. 66.7**). **79.47**

Chapter 80   Enforcement of Foreign Judgments

INTRODUCTION

80.1 English law provides for enforcement of foreign judgments under common law and under five different enforcement regimes based upon international instruments (Administration of Justice Act 1920, Foreign Judgments (Reciprocal Enforcement) Act 1933, Brussels and Lugano Conventions, Brussels I Regulation/**recast Brussels 1 Regulation** (for proceedings instituted on or after 10 January 2015), Hague Convention on Choice of Court Agreements). The choice of the appropriate mechanism will depend on the country of origin of the judgment.

The common law and the statutory schemes are not mutually exclusive. However, where a statutory scheme is available, it should be preferred because its regime is generally more favourable to the party seeking enforcement.

COMMON LAW

80.2 At common law, a foreign judgment creates an implied contract to pay, which can be enforced in England subject to certain defences (*Grant v Easton* (1883) 13 QBD 302). The party seeking to enforce the foreign judgment must commence proceedings in the appropriate English court based on this implied contract to pay. This party will usually seek to obtain summary judgment on the basis that the defendant has no reasonable prospect of defending the claim.

Foreign court must have had jurisdiction over the defendant

80.3 The foreign court must have had jurisdiction over the defendant according to English conflict of laws rules (*Sirdar Gurdyal Singh v Rajah of Faridkote* [1894] AC 670). The position of the foreign court is relevant and admissible but not conclusive and the question of whether there has been a submission is considered in an international context and in the light of an objective assessment of all the facts (*Rubin v Eurofinance SA* [2012] UKSC 46, [2013] 1 AC 236 at [160] per Lord Collins). There are four circumstances or cases in which a foreign court has jurisdiction to give a judgment *in personam* (*Rubin v Eurofinance SA* at [7] per Lord Collins approving Dicey, Morris and Collins, *Conflict of Laws*, 15th edn (London: Sweet & Maxwell, 2012), para. 14R-054, where the grounds are summarised). The defendant, at the date of the commencement of the proceedings, must have been present in the foreign country (*Adams v Cape Industries plc* [1990] Ch 433). Alternatively, the defendant must have submitted, or agreed to submit, to the jurisdiction of the foreign court. Actual submission includes filing a claim or counterclaim in the proceedings or any other voluntary appearance in the foreign court other than for disputing jurisdiction. This has included where the defendant has agreed to a consent order dismissing the claims and cross-appeals on the merits (*Adams v Cape Industries plc* at p. 461) and where the defendant has entered a conditional appearance in order to set aside proceedings on jurisdictional grounds where the application to set aside has been dismissed (*Harris v Taylor* [1915] 2 KB 580). In *Spliethoff's Bevrachtingskantoor BV v Bank of China Ltd* [2015] EWHC 999 (Comm), [2016] 1 All ER (Comm) 1034, the fact that the defendant had chosen to fully defend claims against it after the dismissal of its jurisdictional challenges meant that it had submitted to the jurisdiction. Agreement to submit includes contractual non-exclusive and exclusive jurisdiction clauses as well as clauses relating to acceptance of service of process. An actual agreement to submit might arise through an implied term (*Vizcaya Partners Ltd v Picard* [2016] UKPC 5, [2016] Bus LR 413). Submission to the jurisdiction of the foreign court in one set of proceedings may amount to submission to the jurisdiction in relation to claims concerning the same subject matter or related claims (*Murthy v Sivajothy* [1999] 1 WLR 467). The court will not permit enforcement of a foreign judgment against a person who was not present in the foreign jurisdiction when the proceedings were commenced and has not submitted to the jurisdiction of the foreign court (*Rubin v Eurofinance SA* [2012] UKSC 46, [2013] 1 AC 236).

Conditions relating to the foreign judgment

To be enforceable at common law, the judgment of the foreign court must be conclusive on   **80.4**
its merits. In particular, the foreign court must have ruled it had jurisdiction and accordingly decided on the cause of action, without the possibility of its decision being varied, reopened or set aside by that court (*The Sennar (No. 2)* [1985] 1 WLR 490). A right to appeal the foreign judgment to a higher court does not prevent it from being conclusive (*Nouvion v Freeman* (1889) 15 App Cas 1). The claim must be for a definite sum or for a sum ascertainable by a simple calculation (*Beatty v Beatty* [1924] 1 KB 807). Foreign judgments for the enforcement of penal (*United States of America v Inkley* [1989] QB 255) or revenue (*Re Visser* [1928] Ch 877) laws may not be enforced in the English courts. Revenue debts due in other EU States may be recovered under the Finance Act 2011, s. 87 and sch. 25.

Defences to an enforcement claim

In addition to the conditions set out at **80.3** and **80.4**, a defendant can resist the claim by   **80.5**
raising a number of defences. The defendant may argue that the foreign judgment was obtained by fraud (*Jet Holdings Inc. v Patel* [1990] 1 QB 335) whether on the part of the foreign court or the successful party. The fraud must have been operative in obtaining the foreign judgment, in the sense that without such fraud the judgment would not have been made, or there is a real possibility that it would not have been made (*Gelley v Shepherd* [2013] EWCA Civ 1172, [2014] 1 P & CR DG5). The foreign court's view of the fraud is not conclusive (*Jet Holdings Inc. v Patel* [1990] 1 QB 335) and the fraud may be either extrinsic or collateral to the dispute or cause of action before the foreign court, or may affect the conduct of the foreign court's proceedings (*Owens Bank Ltd v Bracco* [1992] 2 AC 443). The defendant may claim that the judgment is contrary to public policy (*Soleimany v Soleimany* [1999] QB 785). In *JSC 'Aeroflot-Russian Airlines' v Berezovsky* [2012] EWHC 3017 (Ch), LTL 9/11/2012, the judge summarily dismissed a

claim for enforcement of a foreign judgment on the ground that there was a complete defence of public policy by reason that the foreign judgment infringed the finality principle by interfering with a prior judgment. However, the appeal against summary judgment was allowed because the question of whether a foreign judgment is final and binding was found to be a matter of the relevant foreign law which required the court to make findings of fact which it could only do at trial. The court held that the correct test for the purposes of the finality principle is whether the earlier foreign judgment would have precluded the unsuccessful party from bringing fresh proceedings in the jurisdiction ([2014] EWCA Civ 20, LTL 16/1/2014). In *JSC VTB Bank v Skurikhin* [2014] EWHC 271 (Comm), LTL 19/2/2014, the court considered whether the public policy exception applies to 'penalties'. The court refused to grant summary judgment in relation to those parts of the judgments that were characterised as penalties. The court held that it was at least arguable that the award of a certain interest rate by the foreign court ran contrary to English public policy. But this decision pre-dates the Supreme Court's consideration of the public policy on penalties in *Cavendish Square Holding BV v Makdessi* [2015] UKSC 67, [2015] 3 WLR 1373.

The defendant may contend that the proceedings leading to the foreign judgment were contrary to natural or substantive justice (*Adams v Cape Industries plc* [1990] Ch 433). The English court will not recognise a decision of a foreign court which offends against basic principles of honesty, natural justice and domestic concepts of public policy (*Yukos Capital Sàrl v OJSC Oil Company Rosneft* [2014] EWHC 2188 (Comm), [2014] 2 Lloyd's Rep 435). In deciding whether to recognise a foreign judgment, an English court would have regard to its obligation to act in a manner consistent with the right to a fair trial guaranteed by the European Convention on Human Rights, **art. 6**, in the **Human Rights Act 1998, sch. 1** (*Al-Bassam v Al-Bassam* [2004] EWCA Civ 857, [2004] WTLR 757). A default judgment for enforcement of a foreign judgment may not be set aside on the ground that the foreign judgment sought to be enforced has been set aside if the English court finds that, in setting aside the foreign judgment, the foreign court had breached the European Convention on Human Rights, **art. 6** (*Merchant International Co. Ltd v Natsionalna Aktsionerna Kompaniia Naftogaz Ukrainy* [2012] EWCA Civ 196, [2012] 1 WLR 3036). For multiple damages see 80.6.

COMMONWEALTH JUDGMENTS

80.6 Under the Administration of Justice Act 1920 (the '1920 Act') a without-notice application can be made for the registration of a judgment of a superior court of a Commonwealth country in the High Court within 12 months of the date of the judgment in question or such longer period as may be allowed by the court (s. 9(1)). No judgment shall be registered if it falls within one of categories listed in s. 9(2) (which include many of the defences available at common law). In all other cases, the High Court has a discretion whether to register the judgment.

The 1920 Act applies to judgments of superior courts of those parts of Her Majesty's dominions outside the United Kingdom that are specified in the Reciprocal Enforcement of Judgments (Administration of Justice Act 1920, Part II) (Consolidation) Order 1984 (SI 1984/129) as amended and as affected by the Foreign Judgments (Reciprocal Enforcement) Act 1933, s. 7(2), under which the 1920 Act ceased to apply to Newfoundland (now Newfoundland and Labrador) and Saskatchewan when the 1933 Act was applied to those provinces. Also Regulation (EC) No. 44/2001 (Regulation (EU) No. 1215/2012 for proceedings commenced on or after 10 January 2015) has superseded the 1920 Act's application to Cyprus and Malta.

A foreign judgment for multiple damages will not be registered under either the Administration of Justice Act 1920 or the Foreign Judgments (Reciprocal Enforcement) Act 1933, and it is a defence to proceedings at common law for the recovery of any sum payable under such a judgment (Protection of Trading Interests Act 1980, s. 5(1)). A judgment arrived at by multiplying the amount assessed as compensation is a judgment for multiple damages (s. 5(3)). Where a foreign judgment consists of identifiable compensatory damages and multiple damages, it is only the multiple damages part of the judgment which is not enforceable (*Lewis v Eliades* [2003] EWCA Civ 1758, [2004] 1 WLR 692).

RECIPROCAL ENFORCEMENT ARRANGEMENTS

Under the Foreign Judgments (Reciprocal Enforcement) Act 1933 (the '1933 Act') an application **80.7** can be made for the registration of judgments of recognised courts and tribunals of States with which this country has entered into reciprocal enforcement arrangements, provided the application is made within six years of the judgment. The 1933 Act considerably increased the circumstances in which foreign judgments can be registered, but enforcement is subject to a wide range of defences similar to those available at common law. The circumstances in which a registered judgment must or may be set aside are set out in s. 4. For multiple damages see **80.6**.

The 1933 Act is applied, as a result of reciprocal enforcement conventions concluded with individual countries, by Orders in Council under s. 1, to judgments of recognised courts in Australia, Canada, Guernsey, India, the Isle of Man, Israel, Jersey, Pakistan, Suriname and Tonga. It also applies to judgments of recognised courts in Austria, Belgium, France, Germany, Italy, the Netherlands and Norway which are not covered by the Brussels I Regulation or **recast Brussels I Regulation** or, in the case of Norway, the Lugano Convention.

BRUSSELS CONVENTION JUDGMENTS

Under the Civil Jurisdiction and Judgments Act 1982, s. 4, a judgment of a court of another **80.8** contracting State to the Brussels Convention (i.e. Aruba and the French overseas departments) may be registered in the courts of this country. The same applies to a judgment of a Gibraltar court (Civil Jurisdiction and Judgments Act 1982 (Gibraltar) Order 1997 (SI 1997/2602)). When registered, such a judgment has the same force and effect as if the judgment had been given in this country. Articles 27 and 28 of the Convention set out a number of defences to registration, such as recognition being contrary to public policy, the defendant not having been duly served with the document instituting the foreign proceedings, the judgment being irreconcilable with another judgment and the judgment conflicting with provisions of the Convention which determine which courts will have jurisdiction in various defined circumstances. However, art. 29 provides that there cannot, under any circumstances, be a review of the substance of such a judgment.

A judgment will not be registered in England and Wales if the nature of the judgment is unclear (*La Caisse Régionale du Crédit Agricole Nord de France v Ashdown* [2007] EWCA Civ 574, LTL 15/5/2007 in which it was not clear whether the judgment of the foreign court was enforceable as a money judgment or represented a sum fixed by the court merely for the purposes of a liquidation).

Third-party debt orders are a means of enforcement of a judgment *in rem* against the debt. Accordingly, exclusive jurisdiction for enforcement by this method is given to the courts where the debt is situated (*Kuwait Oil Tanker Co. SAK v Qabazard* [2003] UKHL 31, [2004] 1 AC 300 in relation to the Lugano Convention 1988, art. 16(5), which is identical with art. 16(5) of the Brussels Convention).

A default judgment, or a judgment entered after striking out for breach of an unless order, can be registered under the Brussels Convention. Recognition of such a judgment (or any other judgment) may be refused on public policy grounds under art. 27 of the Convention if such recognition is contrary to public policy in the member State in which recognition is sought.

1453

Recourse to the public policy defence is available only where recognition or enforcement of the judgment would be at variance to an unacceptable degree with the legal order of the member State in which enforcement is sought. The infringement would have to constitute a manifest breach of a rule of law regarded as essential in the legal order of the member State in which enforcement is sought or of a right recognised as being fundamental within that legal order (*Gambazzi v DaimlerChrysler Canada Inc.* (case C-394/07) [2009] 1 Lloyd's Rep 647). Recognition of a Dutch judgment which had been obtained in manifest contravention of **art. 6(1)** of the European Convention on Human Rights was refused as being contrary to public policy under art. 27(1) of the Brussels Convention in *Maronier v Larmer* [2002] EWCA Civ 774, [2003] QB 620. *TSN Kunststoffrecycling GmbH v Jurgens* [2002] EWCA Civ 11, [2002] 1 WLR 2459 involved a judgment entered in default in Germany which was registered for enforcement in England. The judgment debtor alleged that the 14-day period for responding to the claim provided by the German rules of procedure was insufficient, and argued that under art. 27(2) the judgment should not be recognised because he had not been served in sufficient time to be able to arrange for his defence. It was held that to ensure effective enforcement of judgments, the exception provided by art. 27(2) should not be expanded further than reasonably necessary to protect the judgment debtor's right to a fair trial. It was found that five weeks had elapsed between service and entry of the default judgment, so registration was not set aside.

BRUSSELS I REGULATION AND LUGANO CONVENTION 2007

80.9   For proceedings initiated from 1 March 2002 (or 1 July 2007 in the case of Denmark) up to and including 9 January 2015, Regulation (EC) No. 44/2001, the 'Brussels I Regulation', replaced the provisions on enforcement under the Brussels Convention in all EU countries. The Lugano Convention 2007 (which applies to Iceland, Norway and Switzerland) is in the same terms. The principles are almost identical to those applicable under the Brussels and the previous Lugano 1988 Conventions. For legal proceedings instituted on or after 10 January 2015, Regulation (EC) No. 44/2001 is replaced by **Regulation (EU) No. 1215/2012**, the 'recast Brussels I Regulation'.

Conditions for application of the Brussels I Regulation or the Lugano Convention 2007

80.10   To obtain registration, the claimant must show that three conditions are fulfilled:

(a) The foreign judgment must fall within the scope of the Regulation, that is, the subject matter of the dispute must be commercial or civil (Brussels I Regulation, art. 1(1) and (2)).

(b) The proceedings must have been instituted on or after 1 March 2002. Earlier proceedings will be enforced under the Regulation if instituted after the entry into force of the Brussels and Lugano Conventions in the State of origin and the State of enforcement and if judgment is given on or after the date of entry into force of the Regulation in both the member State of origin and the member State addressed (art. 66; *Wolf Naturprodukte GmbH v SEWAR spol sro* (case C-514/10) [2012] ILPr 37). The Regulation will also apply if the jurisdiction of the court of origin of the foreign judgment was founded upon rules which accorded with those provided for in Chapter II of the Regulation or in a convention concluded between the member State of origin and the member State addressed which was in force when the proceedings were instituted (art. 66(2)(b) of the Regulation). A judgment of a court of the Republic of Cyprus should be recognised and enforced in other member States even where it relates to land in Northern Cyprus. Recognition and enforcement is not precluded by the fact that the application of EU law is suspended in those areas of Cyprus in which the government of the Republic of Cyprus does not exercise effective control (*Apostolides v Orams* (case C-420/07) [2009] ECR I-3571; *Orams v Apostolides* [2010] EWCA Civ 9, [2011] QB 519).

(c) The ruling for which enforcement is sought must be a judgment given by a court or tribunal of a member State, whatever the judgment may be called, including a decree, order, decision or writ of execution, as well as the determination of costs or expenses by an officer of the court (art. 32).

Authentic instruments and court settlements are also enforceable. A document formally drawn up or registered as an authentic instrument and which is enforceable in one Regulation State must be registered as a foreign judgment (arts 57 and 58).

The conditions to be fulfilled under the Lugano Convention 2007 are the same as those in the Regulation (Lugano Convention 2007, arts 1(1) and (2), 32, 57, 58 and 63).

The Brussels I Regulation and the Lugano Convention 2007 do not apply to arbitration (art. 1(2)(d) of both).

Grounds of defence

A defendant may raise one of four grounds of defence set out in the Brussels I Regulation, **80.11** art. 34. Recognition of a foreign judgment may be refused because it is manifestly contrary to public policy of the member State in which recognition is sought (art. 34(1)). The judgment will not be recognised where it was given in default of appearance, if the defendant has not been served with the document instituting proceedings in sufficient time and in such a way as to enable him to arrange his defence, unless the defendant failed to commence proceedings to challenge the judgment when it was possible for him to do so (art. 34(2)). 'Service' in art. 34(2) has the same meaning as in art. 30 (now **recast Brussels I Regulation, art. 32**; see **16.38**) and Regulation (EC) No. 1393/2007 (see **16.62**) (*Tavoulareas v Tsavliris* [2006] EWCA Civ 1772, [2007] 1 WLR 1573). Mere notification of proceedings is not service. 'Default of appearance' has two meanings, encompassing both failing to comply with procedures involving returning a formal document to the court and actual physical attendance at court (*Tavoulareas v Tsavliris (No. 2)*). A defendant will only have been able to challenge the judgment for the purposes of the proviso to the Brussels I Regulation, art. 34(2), if the judgment was served on him in sufficient time to enable him to arrange his defence in the courts of the State in which the judgment was given (*ASML Netherlands BV v Semiconductor Industry Services GmbH* (case C-283/05) [2007] 1 All ER (Comm) 949). Whether the defendant has been able to arrange his or her defence is a question of substance, not form, and it is not sufficient to show that the method of service was effected in accordance with local law (*Reeve v Plummer* [2014] EWHC 4695 (QB), [2015] ILPr 19). In that case, it was held that none of the defendants had had the opportunity to arrange for their defence within the meaning of art. 34(2). However, two of the defendants could not rely on art. 34(2) as they had failed to take steps to challenge the judgment in Belgium after they had been served with the default judgment. Their attempt to challenge recognition therefore failed.

Where the defendant claims that he was not served with the document instituting the proceedings, the court of the State in which enforcement is sought has jurisdiction to verify that the information in relation to service specified in a certificate issued by a court of the State in which the judgment was given is consistent with the evidence (*Trade Agency Ltd v Seramico Investments Ltd* (case C-619/10) ECLI:EU:C:2012:531).

A judgment will also not be recognised where it is irreconcilable with a judgment given in a dispute between the same parties in the State in which recognition is sought (art. 34(3)). The same applies to a judgment that is irreconcilable with an earlier judgment given in another Regulation State or in a third State involving the same cause of action and between the same parties (art. 34(4)). Article 34(4) does not cover irreconcilable judgments of the courts of the same State (*Salzgitter Mannesmann Handel GmbH v SC Laminorul SA* (case C-157/12) [2014] 1 WLR 904).

Where an ordinary appeal has been lodged, the court of the country in which recognition is sought may stay the enforcement proceedings (art. 37).

Recast Brussels 1 Regulation

80.12   The **recast Brussels 1 Regulation** applies to legal proceedings instituted, authentic instruments formally drawn up or registered and to court settlements approved or concluded on or after 10 January 2015. The Brussels 1 Regulation will continue to apply to judgments given in legal proceedings instituted, to authentic instruments formally drawn up or registered and to court settlements approved or concluded before 10 January 2015 which fall within its scope (**recast Brussels 1 Regulation, art. 66**).

In addition to the temporal requirement, in order for the **recast Brussels 1 Regulation** to apply, the subject matter of the foreign judgment must fall within its scope, that is, the subject matter of the dispute must be commercial or civil, subject to specified exceptions. Matters that are expressly excluded from its scope include the liability of a State for acts and omissions in the exercise of State authority, bankruptcy, arbitration, maintenance obligations arising from a family relationship, and wills and succession (**art. 1(1) and (2)**).

The **recast Brussels 1 Regulation** applies to any ruling for which enforcement is sought which is a judgment given by a court or tribunal of a member State, as defined in **art. 2(a)**, whatever the judgment may be called. This includes provisional measures ordered by a court or tribunal with jurisdiction as to the substance of the matter (**art. 2(a)**). The **recast Brussels I Regulation** does not apply to arbitration. The scope of the arbitration exception in the Brussels I Regulation has been clarified in the **recast Brussels I Regulation**: a ruling given by a court of a Member State as to whether or not an arbitration agreement is null and void, inoperative or incapable of being performed is not enforceable under the **recast Brussels I Regulation**. However, a judgment on the substance of a matter made after such a ruling shall be recognised and enforced under the **recast Brussels I Regulation**, without prejudice to the competence of the court to decide on the recognition and enforcement of arbitral awards in accordance with the New York Convention 1958, which takes precedence over the Regulation (**art. 1(2)(d) and recital 12**).

A judgment falling within the scope of the **recast Brussels 1 Regulation** that is enforceable in the member State in which it is given will be enforceable in other member States without any declaration of enforceability being required (**art. 39**). Subject to the provisions of the **recast Brussels 1 Regulation**, judgments of other member States will be enforced under the same conditions as a judgment given in the enforcing State (**art. 41**).

A copy of the judgment and a certificate issued by the court of origin certifying that the judgment is enforceable must be provided to the relevant enforcement authority and served on the judgment debtor before the first enforcement measure is initiated (**arts 42 and 43**). Where necessary, the relevant enforcement authority may require the applicant to provide a translation of the contents of the certificate and/or a translation of the judgment (**art. 42(3) and (4)**). A judgment debtor domiciled in a member State other than the member State of origin may request a translation of the judgment (if not already provided) in order to contest the enforcement. In this case no measures of enforcement may be taken other than protective measures until the translation has been provided (**art. 43(2)**).

The defences to recognition and declaration of enforceability available under the Brussels I Regulation, art. 34 (see **80.11**), are available under the **recast Brussels 1 Regulation** as defences to recognition and enforcement (**arts 45 and 46**). In the event of an application for refusal of enforcement, the court may, on the application of the judgment debtor, limit the enforcement proceedings to protective measures; make enforcement conditional on the provision of security; or suspend the enforcement proceedings (**art. 44**).

The court must decide on an application for refusal of enforcement without delay (**art. 48**). The decision on the application for refusal of enforcement may be appealed against by either party (**art. 49**).

Changes to **CPR, Part 74**, and **PD 74A** to take into account the provisions of the **recast Brussels 1 Regulation** came into force on 10 January 2015 (Civil Procedure (Amendment No. 7) Rules 2014 (SI 2014/2948)). However, the previous provisions of CPR 74 and PD 74A apply to proceedings commenced before 10 January 2015. The updated CPR now refer to the **recast Brussels 1 Regulation** as 'the Judgments Regulation' and the Brussels 1 Regulation as 'the previous Judgments Regulation'. In particular:

(a) **CPR, r. 74.4A**, requires a person seeking the enforcement of a judgment under the **recast Brussels 1 Regulation** to provide the documents required by **art. 42** of the Regulation, except in the case of protective measures falling within **art. 43(3)**. This rule therefore applies the simplified procedure for enforcement, as a registration order is no longer required.

(b) **CPR, r. 74.7A**, deals with applications under the **recast Brussels 1 Regulation, art. 45** or **46**, that the court should refuse to recognise or enforce a judgment. The application must be made in accordance with **CPR, Part 23**, to the court in which the judgment is being enforced or, if the judgment debtor is not aware of any proceedings relating to enforcement, the High Court. An appeal against a decision granting or refusing an application for refusal of recognition or enforcement must be made in accordance with **Part 52**. However, permission is not required to appeal or put in evidence (**r. 74.7A(3)**). The judgment debtor must serve copies of any order made under the **recast Brussels 1 Regulation, art. 45** or **46**, or in any appeal under **art. 49** on all other parties, any other person affected by the order, any court in which proceedings relating to enforcement of the judgment are pending in England and Wales and any enforcement agent or officer as soon as practicable (**CPR, r. 74.7A(4)**). The court may require the judgment creditor to disclose to the judgment debtor the court(s) in which any proceedings relating to enforcement of the judgment are pending in England and Wales (**r. 74.7A(5)**).

(c) **CPR, r. 74.7B**, addresses relief against enforcement under the **recast Brussels 1 Regulation, art. 44**. An application must be made in accordance with **CPR, Part 23**, to the court in which the judgment is being enforced or, if the judgment debtor is not aware of any enforcement proceedings, to the High Court (**r. 74.7B(1)**). The judgment debtor must serve copies of any order made on all other parties, any other person affected by the order, any court in which proceedings relating to enforcement of the judgment are pending in England and Wales and any enforcement agent or officer as soon as practicable (**r. 74.7B(2)**).

(d) Under **CPR, r. 74.7C**, the court may suspend proceedings under the **recast Brussels 1 Regulation, art. 38**, either on its own initiative or on the application of any party. The requirements of the application are identical to applications made under **CPR, r. 74.7B**.

HAGUE CONVENTION ON CHOICE OF COURT AGREEMENTS 2005

The Hague Convention on Choice of Court Agreements 2005 (the '2005 Hague Convention') **80.13** came into force on 1 October 2015. It applies in international cases where there is an exclusive choice of court agreement concluded in a civil or commercial matter. Examples of what constitutes an exclusive choice of court agreement are given in the Explanatory Report on the 2005 Hague Convention. It applies to exclusive choice of court agreements concluded after its entry into force for the State of the court chosen in the parties' agreement, and does not apply to proceedings instituted before its entry into force for the State of the court seised. Interim measures are not governed by the 2005 Hague Convention (art. 7).

A judgment given in a Contracting State designated in an exclusive choice of court agreement shall be recognised and enforced in other Contracting States without 'review of the merits of the judgment given by the court of origin' (art. 8(2)). The enforcing court is 'bound by findings of fact on which the court of origin based its jurisdiction, unless the judgment is given by default' (art. 8(2)).

Under the Civil Jurisdiction and Judgments Act 1982 (the 1982 Act), s. 4B, a judgment of a court of another 2005 Hague Convention State (i.e. the member States of the EU excluding Denmark, and Mexico) which is required to be recognised and enforced under the 2005

Hague Convention must be registered in the courts of this country without delay on completion of the formalities of art. 13 of the Convention 'if the registering court considers that it meets the condition for recognition in art. 8(3) of the Convention, without any review of whether a ground for refusal under art. 9 applies' (1982 Act, s. 4B(1) and (3)). Article 8(3) of the Convention provides that a judgment shall be recognised only if it has effect in the State of origin, and shall be enforced only if it is enforceable in the State of origin.

When registered, such a judgment has the same force and effect as if the judgment had been given in this country (1982 Act, s. 4B(6)).

Recognition or enforcement 'may be postponed or refused if the judgment is the subject of review in the State of origin or if the time limit for seeking ordinary review has not expired' (2005 Hague Convention, art. 8(4)).

A party against whom enforcement is sought is not entitled to make any submission on the application for registration (1982 Act, s. 4B(4)), but can appeal against registration of a judgment (s. 6B). The court must refuse or revoke registration only if certain circumstances apply (s. 6B(3)). These include that one or more of the grounds for refusal of recognition and enforcement in art. 9 of the Convention apply (1982 Act, s. 6B(3)(c)). In summary, these grounds are: that the agreement was null and void under the law of the State of the chosen court (2005 Hague Convention, art. 9(a)); lack of capacity (art. 9(b)); deficiencies in the notification or service of the claim (art. 9(c)); the judgment was obtained by fraud (art. 9(d)); recognition or enforcement would be incompatible with the public policy of the requested State, including fundamental principles of procedural fairness (art. 9(e)); an inconsistent judgment in the requested State in a dispute between the same parties (art. 9(f)); an inconsistent earlier judgment in another State between the same parties on the same cause of action, provided that earlier judgment fulfils the conditions for recognition in the requested State (art. 9(g)).

The relationship between the Brussels Convention, the **recast Brussels 1 Regulation**, the Lugano Convention (and any other international instruments concluded before or after the 2005 Hague Convention) and the 2005 Hague Convention, in relation to international exclusive choice of court agreements is determined by the 2005 Hague Convention, art. 26 (**1982 Act, s. 1(4)(c)**). The 2005 Hague Convention, art. 26(1), provides that the Convention shall be interpreted insofar as possible to be compatible with other treaties in force for Hague Convention Contracting States. Where all the parties are resident in a Contracting State which is party to another treaty, the Hague Convention shall not affect the application by a Contracting State of that other treaty (2005 Hague Convention, art. 26(2)). Accordingly, where all parties are within the EU, or one or more parties are outside the EU but the choice of court in the agreement is an EU court, the **recast Brussels 1 Regulation** will apply. Further, the 2005 Hague Convention does not affect the application by a Contracting State of a treaty that was concluded before the 2005 Hague Convention entered into force for that Contracting State, if applying it would be inconsistent with the obligations of that Contracting State to a non-Contracting State (2005 Hague Convention, art. 26(3)).

The CPR have been updated to reflect the coming into force of the 2005 Hague Convention. In particular, the Convention is now within the scope of **CPR, Part 74**, and **r. 74.3** has been amended to refer to the 1982 Act, s. 4B, which in turn refers to registration of a Hague Convention judgment. Consequential amendments have been made to **CPR, Part 74** and **PD 74A** (see **80.16** and **80.19**).

NORTHERN IRISH AND SCOTTISH JUDGMENTS

80.14 Under the Civil Jurisdiction and Judgments Act 1982 (the '1982 Act'), s. 18, judgments of the courts of Northern Ireland and Scotland can be enforced in England and Wales by a simple process of registration of a certificate of the judgment in question. The only defences are that the procedure has not been complied with or that there has been an earlier judgment dealing with the same matter. The procedure is set out in **CPR, rr. 74.14 to 74.18.**

REGISTRATION IN ENGLAND AND WALES OF FOREIGN JUDGMENTS

80.15

CPR, rr. 74.2 to 74.11, set out the procedure for registering judgments under:

(a) the Administration of Justice Act 1920 (the '1920 Act'; see **80.6**);
(b) the Foreign Judgments (Reciprocal Enforcement) Act 1933 (the '1933 Act'; see **80.7**);
(c) the Civil Jurisdiction and Judgments Act 1982 (the '1982 Act'; see **80.8**);
(d) the Brussels I Regulation or the Lugano Convention 2007 (see **80.9**).

There is no requirement for registration of judgments under the **recast Brussels I Regulation.**

For the purpose of the registration procedure, a 'judgment' means any judgment of a foreign court or tribunal, whatever it may be called, and includes decrees, orders, decisions, writs of execution, writs of control and costs determinations (**CPR, r. 74.2(1)(c)**).

Applications for registration must be made to the Queen's Bench Division of the High Court (**r. 74.3(2); PD 74A, para. 4.1**). Applications may be made without notice (**CPR, r. 74.3(2)**) in accordance with Part 23 (**PD 74A, para. 4.4**) and must be supported by written evidence complying with **CPR, r. 74.4** (see **80.16 to 80.20**).

Common requirements for evidence under the 1920, 1933 and 1982 Acts

80.16

Applications for registration under the 1920, 1933 and 1982 Acts (but not the Brussels I Regulation or the Lugano Convention 2007, for which see **80.20**) must, by **CPR, r. 74.4(1)** and (**2**), be supported by written evidence which:

(a) states the name of the judgment creditor and an address for service within the jurisdiction;
(b) states the name and address of the judgment debtor;
(c) states the grounds on which the judgment creditor is entitled to enforce the judgment;
(d) states the amount outstanding (if a money judgment);
(e) states details of any interest recoverable on the judgment, including the rate, dates and amounts;
(f) exhibits the judgment or a verified or certified or otherwise authenticated copy of the judgment; and
(g) exhibits a translation of the judgment (if not in English) into English certified by a notary public or other qualified person, or which is confirmed to be accurate.

Evidence under the 1920 Act

80.17

In addition to the matters set out at **80.16**, the evidence in support of an application for registration under the 1920 Act must, by **CPR, r. 74.4(3)**:

(a) state that the judgment is not a judgment which under the 1920 Act, s. 9, cannot be registered (**r. 74.4(3)(a)**);
(b) state that the judgment is not one to which the Protection of Trading Interests Act 1980, s. 5, applies (**r. 74.4(3)(b)**).

In *Standard Chartered Bank Ltd v Zungeru Power Ltd* [2014] EWHC 4714 (QB), LTL 17/11/2014, the High Court considered whether to uphold an order permitting registration of a Nigerian freezing order under the Administration of Justice Act 1920. The High Court allowed the claimant's application to set aside the order on the basis that the judgment, in the form of a freezing order, did not qualify for registration as it was not a money judgment. There was nothing about the circumstances of the case which meant that there could be a different inter-pretation of the 1920 Act. The court also refused to register an ancillary disclosure order under s. 9(2)(b) of the 1920 Act because the party to whom the order was directed was neither carrying on business nor ordinarily resident in Nigeria and had not agreed to submit to the Nigerian court's jurisdiction.

Evidence under the 1933 Act

80.18   In addition to the matters set out at **80.16**, the evidence in support of an application for reg-istration under the 1933 Act must, by **CPR, r. 74.4(4)**, state that it is a money judgment, confirm that it can be enforced by execution in the State of origin, and deal with various other matters. These include providing any further evidence as to the enforceability of the judgment in the State of origin, and the law of that State under which any interest has become due under the judgment, which may be required under the relevant Order in Council extending part 1 of the 1933 Act to that State.

Evidence under the 1982 Act

80.19   In addition to the matters set out at **80.16**, the evidence in support of an application for registration under the 1982 Act must, by **CPR, r. 74.4(5)**, exhibit documents showing that under the law of the State of origin the judgment is enforceable against the judgment debtor and has been served, and, where the judgment was entered in default, documents proving service of the originating process and, where appropriate, a document showing that the judgment creditor was in receipt of legal aid from the State of origin.

Evidence in support of an application for registration of a 2005 Hague Convention judgment under the 1982 Act, s 4B, must, by **CPR, r. 74.4(5A)**, include any evidence required by art. 13 of the 2005 Hague Convention, which deals with documents to be produced by the party seeking recognition or applying for enforcement.

Evidence under the Brussels I Regulation or the Lugano Convention 2007

80.20   Written evidence in support of applications for registration in the High Court of judgments under the Brussels I Regulation and the Lugano Convention 2007 must comply with:

(a) **CPR, r. 74.4(6)**;
(b) **PD 74A, paras 6.1** to **6.5** (in relation to the Brussels I Regulation) or **6A.1** to **6A.5** (in relation to the Lugano Convention 2007); and
(c) the Brussels I Regulation, arts 40, 53, 54 and 55, or the same articles of the Lugano Convention 2007.

The evidence must, in particular:

(a) state an address for service within the jurisdiction (Brussels I Regulation, art. 40(2); Lugano Convention 2007, art. 40(2));
(b) state details of any interest recoverable on the judgment, including the rate, dates and amount accrued up to the date of the application (**CPR, r. 74.4(6)**);
(c) exhibit a copy of the judgment in a form establishing its authenticity (Brussels I Regulation, art. 53(1); Lugano Convention 2007, art. 53(1));
(d) exhibit a certificate in the form set out in Annex V to the Regulation or the Convention (Brussels I Regulation, art. 53(2); Lugano Convention 2007, art. 53(2));
(e) exhibit a certified translation of the certificate (Brussels I Regulation, art. 55(2); Lugano Convention 2007, art. 55(2)); and
(f) exhibit a translation of the judgment (if not in English) into English certified by a notary public or other qualified person, or accompanied by written evidence confirming its accuracy (**CPR, r. 74.4(6)**).

REGISTRATION ORDERS

Where a judgment must be registered (and therefore not where the **recast Brussels 1 Regulation** applies), an order granting permission to register a judgment must be drawn up by the judgment creditor and served on the judgment debtor (**CPR, r. 74.6(1)**). The order must give full particulars of the original judgment, and the name and address for service within the jurisdiction of the judgment creditor. It must also set out the rights to apply to set aside (under the 1920 and 1933 Acts) or to appeal against the registration (under the 1982 Act, the Brussels I Regulation or the Lugano Convention 2007), the time for making such application or appeal, and that no enforcement measures will be taken until the end of that period (**CPR, r. 74.6(3)** and see **r. 74.9**). Registration serves as a decision that the judgment is recognised for the purposes of the 1982 Act, and the Brussels I Regulation or the Lugano Convention 2007 (**CPR, r. 74.10**). The Central Office of the Senior Courts at the Royal Courts of Justice keeps registers of foreign judgments ordered to be enforced under the 1920, 1933 and 1982 Acts, the Brussels I Regulation and the Lugano Convention 2007 (**PD 74A, para. 3(1)**). **80.21**

Service of registration orders

Service of a registration order must be effected by the judgment creditor on the judgment debtor by delivering the order personally, or by serving a company in accordance with the Companies Act 2006 or as directed by the court (**CPR, r. 74.6(1)**). Permission is not required for service outside the jurisdiction (**r. 74.6(2)**). **80.22**

TIMING OF ENFORCEMENT

A party seeking to enforce a judgment to which the **recast Brussels I Regulation** applies, must comply with **art. 43** of the Regulation (**CPR, r. 74.9(1)**). For judgments registered under the 1920 or 1933 Act, no steps to enforce judgment can be taken before the end of the period in which a party can apply to have registration set aside including a period extended by the court (**CPR, r. 74.9(2)(a)**). For judgments registered under the 1982 Act or the Lugano Convention 2007, no steps to enforce judgment can be taken before the end of the period in which a party can appeal against a registration order including a period extended by the court (**CPR, r. 74.9(2)(a)**). Where there is an application to set aside registration or an appeal against a registration order no steps to enforce judgment can be taken until the application or appeal has been determined (**r. 74.9(2)(b)**). A party seeking to enforce a judgment after registration must file evidence of service of the registration order and any other relevant court order (**r. 74.9(3)**). **80.23**

Applications to set aside under the 1920 and 1933 Acts

Applications to set aside under the 1920 and 1933 Acts must be made within the time allowed in the registration order (**CPR, r. 74.7(1)**). This time limit can be extended by a court, but an application for an extension must be made before the end of the period as originally fixed or extended (**r. 74.7(2)**). The court hearing an application may order any issue between the parties to be tried (**r. 74.7(3)**). **80.24**

Appeals under the 1982 Act, the Brussels I Regulation and the Lugano Convention 2007

Appeals against the granting or refusal of registration under the 1982 Act, the Brussels I Regulation or the Lugano Convention 2007 are made in accordance with **CPR, Part 52**, but no permission to appeal is required (**r. 74.8(1)** and **(2)**). The appellant's notice must be **80.25**

Commentary

trial allegations of extensive failure to comply with interim orders, the court may select some allegations for hearing, leaving others to be pursued on another occasion (*JSC BTA Bank v Ablyazov (No. 7)*). It is desirable that all extant allegations are considered on a single occasion, particularly because the maximum term of committal on any one occasion is two years (Contempt of Court Act 1981, s. 14(1)), but there is no fixed rule (*JSC BTA Bank v Ablyazov (No. 7)* at [29]).

A committal application may not be discontinued without the permission of the court (**PD 81, para. 16.3**). The court may not dispose of a committal application without a hearing (**para. 13.3**).

Striking out

81.14   **PD 81, para. 16.1**, states that the court may, either on the application of the respondent or of its own initiative, strike out a committal application on the following grounds:

(a)   The committal application and the evidence served in support of it disclose no reasonable ground for alleging that the respondent is guilty of contempt of court.

(b)   The committal application is an abuse of the court's process or, if made in existing proceedings, is otherwise likely to obstruct the just disposal of those proceedings.

(c)   There has been a failure to comply with a rule, practice direction or court order.

This is equivalent to **CPR, r. 3.4(2)**, which is discussed in **chapter 33**. Disputes about facts or law will not be determined on an application to strike out. If there are such disputes which ought to be determined at a substantive hearing, the committal application will not be struck out (*Masri v Consolidated Contractors International Co. SAL* [2010] EWHC 2458 (Comm), [2011] Bus LR D55).

A committal application is an abuse of process if it is not made for a proper purpose (*Sectorguard plc v Dienne plc* [2009] EWHC 2693 (Ch), LTL 10/11/2009). Committal proceedings are appropriate, albeit as a last resort, for seeking to obtain compliance with a court order or an undertaking to the court, or for bringing to the court's attention serious, but not technical and certainly not involuntary, breaches of an order or undertaking (*Sectorguard plc v Dienne plc* at [47]). Proceedings relating to purely technical breaches, or not directed at obtaining compliance, will be struck out (*Sectorguard plc v Dienne plc* at [47]).

An applicant's failure to comply with a rule or practice direction may not be fatal to the application. **PD 81, para. 16.2**, provides that any procedural defect in the commencement or conduct by the applicant of a committal application may be waived by the court if the court is satisfied that no injustice has been caused to the respondent by the defect.

HEARING A COMMITTAL APPLICATION

General

81.15   Although they are civil proceedings (*Daltel Europe Ltd v Makki* [2006] EWCA Civ 94, [2006] 1 WLR 2704), committal proceedings for a civil contempt of court are treated as criminal proceedings for the purposes of the European Convention on Human Rights, **art. 6** in the **Human Rights Act 1998, sch. 1**, so that **art. 6(3)** applies (*Berry Trade Ltd v Moussavi* [2002] EWCA Civ 477, [2002] 1 WLR 1910 at [31]; *Raja v Van Hoogstraten* [2004] EWCA Civ 968, [2004] 4 All ER 793) and are criminal proceedings for the purposes of legal aid (*King's Lynn and West Norfolk Borough Council v Bunning* [2013] EWHC 3390 (QB), [2015] 1 WLR 531). An allegation of civil contempt of court must be proved beyond reasonable doubt (**PD 81, para. 9**). However, a finding that a person has committed a civil contempt does not give that person a criminal record (*Director of the Serious Fraud Office v O'Brien* [2014] UKSC 23, [2014] AC 1246 at [38]).

In an appropriate case the court may deal with a committal application in the absence of the respondent (*Re P (A Child)* [2006] EWCA Civ 1792, [2007] 1 FLR 1820). In *Navig8 Chemicals Pool Inc. v Nu Tek (HK) Pvt Ltd* (2016) LTL 27/6/2016 the court determined whether a committal application should be heard without the respondent by applying the checklist for criminal trials in *R v Hayward* [2001] EWCA Crim 168, [2001] QB 862 at [22], which was modified by the House of Lords in *R v Jones* [2002] UKHL 5, [2003] 1 AC 1 at [13]–[15].

A committal application should be heard separately from any other application in the proceedings (*Lexi Holdings plc v Luqman* [2007] EWHC 1508 (Ch), LTL 9/7/2007 at [4]). It should certainly not be dealt with in the course of a substantive hearing of the case in which the disobeyed order was made (*Inplayer Ltd v Thorogood* [2014] EWCA Civ 1511, LTL 25/11/2014 at [41]).

Open justice is a fundamental principle. The general rule is that all committal hearings must be listed and heard in public (Practice Direction (Committal for Contempt: Open Court) [2015] 1 WLR 2195, paras 3 and 5). If it is not possible to include the case in the public court list the day before the hearing, notification should be given in accordance with para. 6 of the practice direction. A court can decide not to hear all or part of a committal application in public only in exceptional circumstances where strictly necessary to secure the proper administration of justice and can do so only as far as is strictly necessary to achieve that purpose (para. 4). A court considering departing from the principle of open justice in relation to a committal hearing must notify national media through the Press Association and, at the outset of the committal hearing, hear submissions from the parties and/or the media on whether to impose the proposed derogation (para. 8). Derogation from open justice should not be granted simply because the parties consent (para. 12; *H v News Group Newspapers Ltd* [2011] EWCA Civ 42, [2011] 1 WLR 1645 at [12]). The fact that the committal application is being made in proceedings relating to a child does not of itself justify the application being heard in private (para. 9). The fact that the hearing may involve disclosure of material which ought not to be published does not of itself justify hearing the application in private if such publication can be restrained by an appropriate order (para. 9). Whenever a court decides to exercise its discretion to sit in private it must, before continuing the hearing in private, sit in public in order to give a reasoned public judgment setting out why it is doing so (para. 10). Prescribed information about a committal order private must be given whether it was made in public or in private (see **81.17**).

To show that a person is in contempt, it must be established that his or her conduct was intentional and that he or she knew of all the facts which made that conduct a breach of the order, but it is not necessary to prove that he or she appreciated that the conduct did breach the order (*Heaton's Transport (St Helens) Ltd v Transport and General Workers' Union* [1973] AC 15; see also *Adam Phones Ltd v Goldschmidt* [1999] 4 All ER 486 on the view that it should be necessary to prove intention to breach the order). If it is impossible to comply with an order, failure to comply with it may be breach of the order but is not contempt (*Sectorguard plc v Dienne plc* [2009] EWHC 2693 (Ch), LTL 10/11/2009 at [33]). This means that if impossibility is an issue, the onus is on the applicant to prove that the respondent could comply (*Re A (A Child) (Removal from Jurisdiction: Contempt of Court)* [2008] EWCA Civ 1138, [2009] 1 WLR 1482; *Re L-W (Enforcement and Committal: Contact)* [2010] EWCA Civ 1253, [2011] 1 FLR 1095 at [34]; but see *Re J (Children)* [2015] EWCA Civ 1019, [2016] 2 FCR 48 for controversy).

Where more than one breach is alleged, the court must consider whether each of them has been proved beyond reasonable doubt, but in deciding whether the breaches justify committal, the court must consider the whole picture to see whether it portrays a respondent seeking to comply with the orders of the court or one bent on flouting them (*Gulf Azov Shipping Co. Ltd v Idisi* [2001] EWCA Civ 21, LTL 16/1/2001 at [18]).

At the end of the applicant's case, the respondent may make a submission of no case to answer (*Shadrokh-Cigari v Shadrokh-Cigari* [2010] EWCA Civ 21, [2010] 1 WLR 1311 at [24]). This need not necessarily be on the basis of adducing no evidence if the submission fails (*Templeton Insurance Ltd v Motorcare Warranties Ltd* [2012] EWHC 795 (Comm), LTL 11/4/2012 at [24]). See **61.46**.

For appeals in contempt proceedings see **74.5** and **74.12**; the Administration of Justice Act 1960, s. 13; and **CPR, sch. 1, RSC, ord. 109.**

Evidence

81.16   Written evidence in support of or in opposition to a committal application must be given by affidavit (**PD 81, para. 14.1**) and, unless the court directs otherwise, must be filed (**para. 14.2**). The court may give directions requiring the attendance for cross-examination of a witness who has given written evidence (**CPR, r. 81.28(4)**).

The following rules do not apply to committal applications (**PD 81, para. 14.3**):

(a) **CPR, r. 35.7** (court's power to direct that evidence is to be given by a single joint expert);
(b) **r. 35.8** (instructions to single joint expert); and
(c) **r. 35.9** (power of court to direct a party to provide information).

Unless the court hearing a committal application otherwise permits, the applicant may not rely on (**r. 81.28(1)**):

(a) any grounds other than those set out in the application notice; or
(b) any evidence unless it has been served in accordance with **r. 81.10** and **PD 81**.

A respondent is not a compellable witness (*Re B (A Minor) (Contempt of Court: Affidavit Evidence)* [1996] 1 WLR 627) and should be warned that he or she is not obliged to give evidence (*Re K (Return Order: Failure to Comply: Committal: Appeal)* [2014] EWCA Civ 905, [2015] 1 FLR 927 at [61]). The court must ensure that a respondent is made aware of the right to remain silent and also of the risk that adverse inferences may be drawn from silence (*Inplayer Ltd v Thorogood* [2014] EWCA Civ 1511, LTL 25/11/2014 at [40]). A respondent may give oral evidence at the hearing, despite not filing or serving any written evidence (**CPR, r. 81.28(2)(a)**). A respondent who gives oral evidence may be cross-examined (**r. 81.28(2)(a)**). The respondent, even if unrepresented, must be allowed to give evidence first before being cross-examined (*Re K (Return Order: Failure to Comply: Committal: Appeal)* at [61]). The respondent may call a witness to give evidence at the hearing even though that witness has not made an affidavit or witness statement, provided the court gives permission (**r. 81.28(2)(b)**). Orders for further information under **r. 18.1** may not be made against a respondent to a committal application (**PD 81, para. 14.4**). Additional information should not be necessary in committal applications where the breaches are listed in the application notice and it is a matter for the court to determine whether those breaches are made out. For appropriate orders and undertakings to prevent prejudicial use of information obtained by a receiver appointed to enforce the respondent's compliance see *Milsom v Ablyazov* [2011] EWHC 1846 (Ch), [2012] Lloyd's Rep FC 98.

The court may require or permit any party or other person (other than the respondent) to give oral evidence at the hearing (**CPR, r. 81.28(3)**).

The admission of hearsay evidence is governed by the Civil Evidence Act 1995, because committal proceedings are civil proceedings despite being treated as criminal proceedings for the purposes of the European Convention on Human Rights, art. 6 in the **Human Rights Act 1998, sch. 1** (*Daltel Europe Ltd v Makki* [2006] EWCA Civ 94, [2006] 1 WLR 2704).

ORDERS THE COURT MAY MAKE

Committal

81.17   A court may commit a contemnor to prison for up to two years (Contempt of Court Act 1981, s. 14(1)).

A committal order must adequately particularise the breaches which have been proved and for which the sentence has been imposed (*Nicholls v Nicholls* [1997] 1 WLR 314). It should expressly state what the breaches were rather than refer to an application notice or claim form (*Nicholls v Nicholls*). A judge signing a committal order has a duty to ensure that it is properly drawn (*Nicholls v Nicholls*).

Any court which decides to make an order of committal (including a suspended order) must sit in public and state (**CPR, r. 81.28(5)**; Practice Direction (Committal for Contempt: Open Court) [2015] 1 WLR 2195, para. 13(1)):

(a) the name of the respondent;
(b) in general terms the nature of the contempt of court in respect of which the committal order is being made; and
(c) the punishment being imposed.

These details must be provided to the national media and to the Judicial Office for publication on its website. There are never any circumstances in which anyone may be committed to custody without these matters being stated by the court sitting in public (para. 13(2)). The court must either produce a written judgment setting out its reasons or ensure that any oral judgment is transcribed on an expedited basis (para. 14). Copies of the written judgment or transcript must be provided to the parties and the national media, and to the Judicial Office and BAILII for publication on their websites (para. 15). In the County Court, where it is not the usual practice to give reasoned judgments because it is not a court of record, the judgment should set out the information required by para. 13(1) with short, written, reasons why the court arrived at its decision (Practice Guidance: Committal for Contempt of Court — Open Court, para. 6; a pro forma is provided in annex 1 to the Guidance).

There is no jurisdiction to remand a contemnor in custody to await sentencing (*Delaney v Delaney* [1996] QB 387), except in the case of an injunction to which a power of arrest has been attached under the Housing Act 1996, s. 153C or s. 153D (s. 155(2)(b) and (5) and sch. 15), or the Police and Justice Act 2007, s. 27 (see **88.15**), or the Policing and Crime Act 2009, s. 36 (see **88.34**), or in respect of which a warrant for arrest has been issued under the Housing Act 1996, s. 155(3) or the Policing and Crime Act 2009, s. 36.

A committal order is an order for the issue of a warrant of committal (**CPR, r. 81.30(1)**). A copy of the committal order must be served on the respondent either before or at the time of executing the warrant (**r. 81.30(2)(a)**). Alternatively, if the warrant has been signed by the judge, the order may be served at any time within 36 hours after the warrant is executed (**r. 81.30(2)(b)**). A warrant of committal cannot be executed more than two years after it is issued without a further order of the court (**r. 81.30(3)**).

If a committal order has been made in the respondent's absence, the court may, on its own initiative, fix a date and time when the respondent is to be brought before the court (**r. 81.28(6)**). It may order the respondent's solicitor to disclose contact details given in confidence so that the respondent may be apprehended to serve the sentence (*JSC BTA Bank v Solodchenko (No. 3)* [2011] EWHC 2163 (Ch), [2013] Ch 1). But such an order will not be made if it is foreseeable that it would deprive the respondent of access to legal advice (*JSC BTA Bank v Ablyazov* [2012] EWHC 1252 (Comm), LTL 17/5/2012). If a committal order is made in the respondent's absence for failure to comply with an interim order, the court may bar the respondent from taking any further part in the proceedings unless he or she surrenders to custody (*JSC BTA Bank v Ablyazov (No. 8)* [2012] EWCA Civ 1411, [2013] 1 WLR 1331). But an appeal against the committal order itself should not be subject to such a condition (*JSC BTA Bank v Ablyazov* [2012] EWCA Civ 639, LTL 16/5/2012). Such a condition is a means of persuading a contemnor to comply rather than a further punishment for the contempt (*JSC BTA Bank v Ablyazov* [2012] EWCA Civ 1411 per Maurice Kay LJ at [201]–[202]).

A person aged under 21 may not be committed to prison (Powers of Criminal Courts (Sentencing) Act 2000, s. 89(1)(b)). A contemnor who is at least 18 but under 21 may be committed to be detained under s. 108 of the 2000 Act and the Secretary of State will direct where the person is to be detained (s. 108(5)). Committal for detention under s. 108 may not be ordered unless the court is of the opinion that no other method of dealing with the person is appropriate (s. 108(3), which lists matters which the court must take into consideration).

Commentary

The minimum age for imprisonment will be lowered to 18 when the Criminal Justice and Court Services Act 2000, s. 61, is brought into force, and then the provision for committal for detention of persons aged 18 to 20 will be repealed. An injunction should not be made against a person aged under 18, as it cannot be enforced by committal, and the person is unlikely to have assets which could be used to pay a fine or which could be sequestrated (*Wookey v Wookey* [1991] Fam 121). Threats or fears of indirect consequences of disobedience do not justify an injunction (*Harrow London Borough Council v G* [2004] EWHC 17 (QB), LTL 23/1/2004).

Other punishments

81.18 In addition to, or instead of, committing to prison, the court may impose a fine (Contempt of Court Act 1981, s. 14), take security (a recognisance) for good behaviour, make a summary award of damages (*Midland Marts Ltd v Hobday* [1989] 1 WLR 1148), make a sequestration order or deliver a reprimand. Nothing in **CPR, Part 81** detracts from the court's power to fine a person or require security (a recognisance) for good behaviour (**r. 81.2(2)**). If a fine rather than committal is the appropriate order, it is wrong to order committal (even if it is suspended) on the ground that the contemnor could not afford to pay a fine (*Re M (Children)* [2005] EWCA Civ 615, [2005] 2 FLR 1006).

Sentencing decision

81.19 In *Crystal Mews Ltd v Metterick* [2006] EWHC 3087 (Ch), 2006 WL 3739209 at [13], Lawrence Collins J listed the following matters which may be taken into account in determining sentence: (a) whether the applicant has been prejudiced by virtue of the contempt and whether the prejudice is capable of remedy; (b) the extent to which the contemnor has acted under pressure; (c) whether the breach of the order was deliberate or unintentional; (d) the degree of culpability; (e) whether the contemnor has been placed in breach of the order by reason of the conduct of others; (f) whether the contemnor appreciates the seriousness of the deliberate breach; (g) whether the contemnor has cooperated. In *Asia Islamic Trade Finance Fund Ltd v Drum Risk Management Ltd* [2015] EWHC 3748 (Comm), LTL 22/12/2015 Popplewell J added: (h) whether there has been any acceptance of responsibility, any apology, any remorse or any reasonable excuse put forward.

A sentence of imprisonment for contempt of court must be for a fixed term of not more than two years (Contempt of Court Act 1981, s. 14(1)), but the court has a power to discharge a committed contemnor (see **81.22**), which will be done on acceptance by the court that the contemnor's contempt has been purged. In any case, a person who is committed to a term of imprisonment for contempt of court must be released unconditionally after serving half of the term (Criminal Justice Act 2003, s. 258). The court may order suspension of a committal order (see **81.20**).

Committal for any period is always a sanction of last resort (*Ansah v Ansah* [1977] Fam 138 per Ormrod LJ at p. 144; *Gulf Azov Shipping Co. Ltd v Idisi* [2001] EWCA Civ 21, LTL 16/1/2001 at [70]). It is only appropriate where there has been 'some extra obstinate or obstructive dimension' to the contemnor's breach of the court's order (*Broomleigh Housing Association Ltd v Okonkwo* [2010] EWCA Civ 1113, [2011] HLR 5 at [22]). This extra dimension is often described as 'contumacy'.

In every case the court must consider whether committal is necessary, what is the shortest period of imprisonment necessary, and whether a sentence of imprisonment can be suspended or dispensed with altogether (*Templeton Insurance Ltd v Thomas* [2013] EWCA Civ 35, LTL 5/2/2013 at [42]).

Breach of a freezing order is such an attack on the administration of justice that it usually merits an immediate term of imprisonment of some not insubstantial amount (*Templeton Insurance Ltd v Thomas*, at [42]).

The two-year maximum should not be exceeded on any single occasion, even if the judge is dealing with the activation of a suspended sentence as well as a more recent contempt (*Villiers v Villiers* [1994] 1 WLR 493). Nevertheless, if a contemnor has served a maximum sentence for not complying with a court order and still refuses to comply, the court may make a new order in the same terms and impose a further maximum sentence for not complying with the new order. It is for the court to decide whether this course is both necessary and proportionate (*Wilkinson v Anjum* [2011] EWCA Civ 1196, [2012] 1 WLR 1036).

Suspension

A court making an order of committal may also order that its execution will be suspended for **81.20** such period, or on such terms or conditions, as the court may specify (**CPR, r. 81.29(1)**). A court imposing a sentence of imprisonment for contempt should always expressly consider whether the sentence might properly be suspended (*Slade v Slade* [2009] EWCA Civ 748, [2010] 1 WLR 1262 at [25]). If, as is usual, committal is suspended so as to give the contemnor a chance to comply with the court's order, the court must specify the period of suspension and the terms or conditions of the suspension (*Bluffield v Curtis* [1998] 1 FLR 170 at p. 173). Where the execution of a committal order is suspended, the applicant for the committal order must, unless the court directs otherwise, serve a copy of the suspension order on the respondent (**r. 81.29(2)**). In the County Court form N79 must be used (**PD 4, Table 3**) and failure to use it is a fundamental defect which will invalidate the order so that it cannot be activated (*Couzens v Couzens* [2001] 2 FLR 701). The standard of proof for breach of a suspension condition is the civil standard of balance of probabilities (*Alfa Laval Tumba AB v Pacy* [2010] EWHC 674 (Ch), LTL 30/3/2010). Care must be taken to distinguish between an allegation that a condition for suspension of committal has been breached and an allegation that there has been a further act of contempt (*Phillips v Symes* [2003] EWCA Civ 1769, LTL 5/12/2003).

Criminal proceedings for the same act

An act which contravenes a court order in civil proceedings may be both a civil contempt of court **81.21** and a criminal offence. There is no abuse of process in bringing both criminal proceedings and proceedings for civil contempt in respect of the same act (*Director of Public Prosecutions v Tweddell* [2001] EWHC 188 (Admin), [2002] 2 FLR 400), though the court hearing the second proceedings should take into account any punishment already imposed (*Lomas v Parle* [2003] EWCA Civ 1804, [2004] 1 WLR 1642) and the contemnor must not be sentenced twice for the same conduct. This means that even if the second court considers that the first court's sentence for that conduct was inadequate, it cannot impose a further punishment (*Slade v Slade* [2009] EWCA Civ 748, [2010] 1 WLR 1262). If the second court is sentencing for contempt, it must confine itself to sentencing for:

(a) other aspects of the contemnor's conduct that breached the court's order; and
(b) the fact, irrelevant to the criminal proceedings, that particular conduct which had been punished in the criminal court was also a civil contempt (*Slade v Slade* at [22]).

In relation to point (b), the civil court's task is to sentence only for the fact of the contempt and not for its content, though it may take into consideration the seriousness of the contempt (*Slade v Slade* at [23]). Putting this into practice may be very difficult indeed.

Use of both civil contempt and criminal proceedings is forbidden by statute in the case of non-molestation orders (Family Law Act 1996, s. 42A(3) and (4)) and anti-harassment injunctions (Protection from Harassment Act 1997, s. 3(7) and (8); see **88.24**).

Discharge

A person committed to prison for contempt of court may apply to the court to be discharged **81.22** (**CPR, r. 81.31**). The application is made in writing attested by the governor of the prison (or any other officer of the prison not below the rank of principal officer) showing that the

statutory power to attach a power of arrest to an order, as such a power cannot be attached to an undertaking.

An ambiguity in an undertaking should be construed in favour of the person sought to be committed (*Haddonstone Ltd v Sharp* [1996] FSR 767 per Rose and Stuart-Smith LJJ; *Jobsearch Ltd v Relational Designers Ltd* [2004] EWHC 661 (Ch), [2004] FSR 36).

The court may decline to accept an undertaking unless the party giving it has made a signed statement to the effect that the party understands the terms of the undertaking and the consequences of failure to comply with it (**PD 81, para. 2.2**). That statement may be endorsed on the order containing the undertaking or may be filed in a separate document such as a letter (**para. 2.3**). In County Court proceedings, form N117 may be used (**para. 2.4**). The court may decline to consider proceedings for contempt of court for disobeying an undertaking which was not accompanied by such a statement (**para. 2.2**).

The procedure for committing for breach of an undertaking is the same as that relating to breach of court orders and judgments (see 81.4 to 81.24) with such modifications as are necessary (**CPR, r. 81.4(4)**, applying **rr. 81.4 to 81.11** so far as applicable).

Rules 81.5 and 81.6 do not apply to undertakings. Instead, **r. 81.7(1)** provides that when a court accepts an undertaking it will deliver, to the person who gave the undertaking, a copy of a document recording it:

(a) by handing a copy to that person before he or she leaves the court building; or
(b) where that person's place of residence or business is known, by posting a copy to that address; or
(c) by posting a copy to that person's solicitor.

Where delivery cannot be effected in this way, the court officer must deliver a copy of the document to the party for whose benefit the undertaking is given, and that party must serve it personally as soon as is practicable (**r. 81.7(2)**).

If an undertaking has been given by a company or other corporation, it cannot be enforced against a director or other officer unless he or she has been served with 'a copy of the judgment or order' (**r. 81.7(3)**), meaning, presumably, a judgment or order which refers to or incorporates the undertaking.

There are occasions when a solicitor is required to give an undertaking to the court, for example, when an application is made as a matter of urgency and there has not been time to issue the proceedings in which the application is made. An application for committal for breach of a solicitor's undertaking cannot be made without the court's permission (**r. 81.11(1)**). Application for permission must be made by application notice under **Part 23** (**r. 81.11(2)**). It must be supported by an affidavit setting out the grounds on which committal is sought (**r. 81.11(3)**). It may be made without notice (**r. 81.11(4)**) and **r. 23.9** (service after disposal of without-notice application) and **r. 23.10** (setting aside or variation) do not apply (**r. 81.11(5)**). If permission is given, it must be acted on within 14 days (**r. 81.11(6)**). See further **21.19 and 21.20**.

COURT'S POWER TO ORDER COMMITTAL OF ITS OWN INITIATIVE

81.26   Nothing in **CPR, Part 81** affects the power of the High Court or the Court of Appeal to make an order of committal of its own initiative against a person guilty of contempt of court (**r. 81.2(3)**). A judge has power to initiate committal proceedings personally for breach of an order of the court, in the absence of an application. However, in these circumstances another judge should try the matter (*Re M (A Minor) (Contempt of Court: Committal of Court's Own Motion)* [1999] Fam 263).

SEQUESTRATION

Nature of sequestration

A writ of sequestration appoints sequestrators who are empowered to enter the contemnor's **81.27**
land and to seize the contemnor's personal property, which they will hold until the contempt
is purged and their remuneration and expenses are paid. A writ of sequestration must be in
form No. 67 (**CPR, r. 81.27**). The court may order the sale of sequestrated assets (*Richardson
v Richardson* [1989] Fam 95).

Rules of court concerning sequestration have only ever been provided for the High Court (see
now **r. 81.19**). Nevertheless, the County Court may order sequestration of assets to enforce
compliance with an order it has made and it is unnecessary to transfer the proceedings to the
High Court for this purpose (*Rose v Laskington Ltd* [1990] 1 QB 562).

Rules

For the purposes of **CPR, Part 83**, a writ of sequestration is a writ of execution (**r. 83.1(2)(l)(iii)**) **81.28**
and is subject to the rules in **Part 83** (see **79.8** to **79.11**). However, an application for permission
to issue a writ of sequestration must be made in accordance with **Part 81, Section 7** (**r. 83.2A**).

Generally, the rules in **Part 81, Section 7** make the same provision for sequestration as the
rules in **Part 81, Section 2** concerning committal.

Rule 81.20 on the circumstances in which a judgment, order or undertaking may be enforced
by a writ of sequestration against a person's property is in the same terms as **r. 81.4** (see **81.4**),
except that the Debtors Acts 1869 and 1878 are not relevant and there is no exception for an
order for delivery of goods or payment of their value, because sequestration is one of the permitted means of enforcing such an order (**CPR, r. 83.14(2)(c)**).

Rules 81.21, 81.22 and **81.24** on service of judgments and orders are in the same terms as
rr. 81.5, 81.6 and **81.8** (see **81.5**). **Rule 81.23** on service of undertakings is in the same terms
as **r. 81.7** (see **81.25**).

Rule 81.25 (penal notice) is in the same terms as **r. 81.9**, and **PD 81, para. 1** is applied by
para. 6 (see **81.6**).

Application for permission to issue writ of sequestration

A writ of sequestration can be issued only with the court's permission (**CPR, r. 81.20(1)**). An **81.29**
application for permission must be made by filing an application notice under **Part 23**
(**rr. 81.26(2)** and **83.2A**). It must be made (**r. 81.26(1)**):

(a) to a single judge of the Division of the High Court in which the proceedings were
   commenced or to which they have subsequently been transferred; or

(b) in any other case, to a single judge of the Queen's Bench Division.

Rule 81.26(3) (contents of application notice) is in the same terms as **r. 81.10(3)**, and **PD 81,
paras 13.1** and **13.2** apply (see **81.9**). **PD 81, paras 15.1** and **15.2** (hearing date), apply (see
81.10). **Rule 81.26(4)** and **(5)** (service) are in the same terms as **r. 81.10(4)** and **(5)** (see
81.11). All the provisions of **CPR, Part 81** and **PD 81** discussed at **81.13** to **81.16** apply.

Dies non

A writ of sequestration may not be executed on a Sunday, Good Friday or Christmas Day **81.30**
(**CPR, r. 83.6(3); PD 81, para. 7.1**) unless:

(a) the court orders otherwise (**CPR, r. 83.6(3); PD 81, para. 7.1**); or

(b) it enforces a judgment, order or undertaking in an Admiralty claim *in rem* (CPR, r. 83.6(1)(c); PD 81, para. 7.2).

Renewal after 12 months

81.31 For the purposes of **CPR, r. 83.3**, which requires renewal of a writ of execution if it has not been wholly executed within 12 months, a writ of sequestration is wholly executed either when the sequestrators have effectively seized all the contemnor's assets or when there is compliance with the court's order. If those objectives have been achieved within 12 months, the sequestrators may deal with consequential matters without renewal of the writ (*H v N* [2009] EWHC 640 (Fam), [2009] 1 WLR 2335).

ACTS IN OTHER PROCEEDINGS TREATED AS CONTEMPT

81.32 Various statutes provide that if a person fails to cooperate with various tribunals and investigative processes, that fact may be certified to the High Court which may punish the person as for contempt of court. **PD 81, para. 3**, identifies some provisions to that effect. There is a much longer list in appendix F to the Law Commission's consultation paper on Contempt of Court (Consultation Paper 209). The procedure for certifying or applying is set out in **CPR, r. 81.15**, and the general rules for committal and sequestration proceedings considered in this chapter apply.

PART Q

Insolvency Proceedings and Companies Matters

Chapter 82 Winding Up and Administration of Registered Companies

Commentary

The following procedural checklist is relevant to this chapter:

Procedural checklist 35   Application by a creditor whose debt is presently payable to wind up a company incorporated in England and Wales

NATURE OF WINDING UP AND ADMINISTRATION

Winding up

82.1   The Insolvency Act 1986 confers on the High Court and County Court a jurisdiction to order the winding up of virtually any kind of business, other than one conducted by a sole trader.

Sole traders are excluded from the winding-up jurisdiction because they are subject to bankruptcy law (see **chapter 83**). The making of a winding-up order is discretionary.

In practice the great majority of applications for winding up are to wind up companies which have been incorporated by registration with the Registrar of Companies in England and Wales under the Companies Act 2006 or its predecessors. These include private limited companies and plcs. They are often referred to as 'registered companies', though in the legislation they are simply called 'companies'.

The winding-up provisions of the Insolvency Act 1986 are primarily drafted to apply to registered companies, which are the subject of part 4 of the Act (ss. 73 to 219). Part 4 is applied in various ways to other business entities, for example, to societies registered, or deemed to be registered, under the Co-operative and Community Benefit Societies Act 2014 (s. 123 of that Act), building societies (Building Societies Act 1986, ss. 86 to 103 and sch. 15), incorporated friendly societies (Friendly Societies Act 1992, ss. 22 and 23 and sch. 10), insolvent partnerships (Insolvent Partnerships Order 1994 (SI 1994/2421)) and limited liability partnerships (Limited Liability Partnerships Regulations 2001 (SI 2001/1090), reg. 5). Part 4 of the Insolvency Act 1986 is also extended by part 5 of the Act to the winding up of what it calls 'unregistered companies', which include companies formed outside the United Kingdom. The present chapter concentrates on the winding up of registered companies.

The winding up of a company by order of the court is known as a 'compulsory' winding up to contrast it with a winding up effected without a court order, which is called a 'voluntary' winding up (as in the Insolvency Act 1986, s. 84(2)).

The procedure for compulsory winding up serves three principal purposes:

(a) It enables unsecured creditors of an insolvent company to have it liquidated for their benefit (and in this respect compulsory liquidation has some affinity with bankruptcy, which is discussed in **chapter 83**).

(b) It enables members of a solvent company to have it liquidated for their benefit. (The Insolvency Act 1986 is misleadingly titled: it applies to the winding up of solvent as well as insolvent companies. In the special jargon of insolvency, the members of a company are referred to as 'contributories', see **82.59**.)

(c) It enables the Secretary of State and other public officials to have a company liquidated in the public interest.

The winding up or liquidation (the terms are used interchangeably) of a company is carried out by its liquidator. The provisions of the Insolvency Act 1986, ss. 136 to 140, ensure that a company has a liquidator as from the time that a court makes an order for it to be wound up. Initially the liquidator is the official receiver (see **82.16**), but if the assets are sufficient, an insolvency practitioner, who must be qualified to act in relation to the company (see **82.15**), may be appointed.

The liquidator of a company being wound up by the court entirely displaces the company's directors and performs his or her duties as an officer of the court subject to its control. The task of the liquidator of a company is to remove the company from all its legal relationships. Its contracts must be completed, transferred or otherwise brought to an end; it must cease carrying on its business except so far as may be necessary for its beneficial winding up; its liabilities (including post-liquidation interest) must be paid, as far as possible; and its legal disputes must be settled.

The members are entitled to benefit from any property remaining unless the company's constitution provides otherwise. Surplus non-cash assets may be sold and the proceeds distributed to the members or, if the company's constitution provides, the property may be distributed in kind.

The liquidation of a registered company is completed by dissolving it, which means removing its name from the Register of Companies so that it ceases to exist as a juristic person.

Winding up is a process undertaken for the collective benefit of a company's creditors and members. A winding-up order is said to operate 'in favour of all the creditors and of all contributories of the company' (Insolvency Act 1986, s. 130(4)).

Administration

82.2 For an insolvent registered company, administration is an alternative to both winding up and the appointment of an administrative receiver. An administrator of a company manages its affairs, business and property in accordance with a proposal approved by creditors and usually does so in the interests of all the company's creditors (Insolvency Act 1986, sch. B1, paras 1(1) and 3(2)). The statute law on administration is in the Insolvency Act 1986, part 2 (s. 8) and sch. B1.

A company enters administration when the appointment of an administrator takes effect (Insolvency Act 1986, sch. B1, para. 1(2)). Until 14 September 2003, only the court could appoint an administrator. Now an administrator of a company may be appointed out of court by the company itself or its directors or by the holder of a qualifying floating charge in respect of the company's property (sch. B1, paras 14 and 22), though such an appointment does not take effect until notice of appointment is filed in court (sch. B1, paras 18, 19, 29 and 31). Persons who are entitled to appoint an administrator out of court may alternatively apply to the court to make an appointment, by means of an administration order under sch. B1, para. 10 (see **82.90** to **82.105**), and in certain circumstances (see **82.91**) must do so. An application for an administration order may also be made by certain persons, such as creditors who do not hold qualifying floating charges, who are not entitled to make an appointment out of court (see **82.91**). The making of an administration order is discretionary.

An administrator of a company is asked to formulate, if possible, proposals for achieving the purpose of administration (see **82.93**). The proposals must be submitted, within 10 weeks of the administrator's appointment, to the company's unsecured creditors for approval (sch. B1, para. 51). If the proposals are approved, the administrator must manage the affairs, business and property of the company in accordance with them (sch. B1, para. 68).

The administrator of a company is required to report to the Secretary of State if it appears to the administrator that the conduct of any person who has been a director of the company makes that person unfit to be concerned in the management of a company, and an application may then be made for a disqualification order (Company Directors Disqualification Act 1986, ss. 6 and 7) (see **chapter 86**).

PROCEDURAL RULES

Insolvency Rules 1986

82.3 Applications for winding-up and administration orders are proceedings under the Insolvency Act 1986 and are therefore 'insolvency proceedings' for the purpose of the Insolvency Rules 1986 (SI 1986/1925) (IR 1986), by r. 13.7 of those rules. IR 1986, r. 7.51A(2), provides that all provisions of the CPR (including related practice directions) which are not either specifically applied or expressly excluded apply to proceedings under the Insolvency Act 1986 or IR 1986 with any necessary modifications, except so far as inconsistent with IR 1986.

The IR 1986 also govern bankruptcy proceedings, which are considered in **chapter 83**. Applications and appeals in relation to insolvency proceedings are considered in **chapter 84**. The CPR and IR 1986 are supplemented by **PD Insolvency Proceedings**, which is reproduced in **appendix 1**.

Work has been in progress for several years on new rules to replace IR 1986. When this edition was being prepared it was expected that the new rules would be made in Autumn 2016 and would come into force in April 2017. However, it was not possible to include coverage of them in this edition.

As the requirement that an application for a winding-up order or bankruptcy order must be made by petition is imposed by statute, the court has no power under the CPR to waive a failure to comply with it (*Re Osea Road Camp Sites Ltd* [2004] EWHC 2437 (Ch), [2005] 1 WLR 760).

Track allocation

All insolvency proceedings, including winding-up and bankruptcy petitions and admin-   **82.4** istration applications, are allocated to the multi-track by IR 1986, r. 7.51A(3), and so the provisions of the CPR concerning directions questionnaires and track allocation do not apply.

Forms

The forms contained in sch. 4 to IR 1986 must be used in and in connection with insol-   **82.5** vency proceedings, whether in the High Court or County Court (IR 1986, r. 12A.30(1)). The forms must be used with such variations, if any, as the circumstances may require (r. 12.A.30(2)).

Forms can be downloaded from the Insolvency Service website: https://www.gov.uk/government/organisations/insolvency-service.

Time limits

Where by any provision of the Insolvency Act 1986 or the IR 1986 about winding up, the   **82.6** time for doing anything is limited, the court may extend the time, either before or after it has expired, on such terms, if any, as it thinks just (IR 1986, r. 4.3). (The same provision is made in relation to bankruptcy proceedings by the Insolvency Act 1986, s. 376.) The court may also, under **CPR, r. 3.1(2)(a)**, as applied by IR 1986, r. 12A.55(2), extend or shorten the time for compliance with anything required or authorised to be done by the IR 1986, even if an application for extension is made after the time for compliance has expired. An application to extend or abridge time in winding-up proceedings is made to the member of court staff in charge of the winding-up list in the RCJ or a District Judge in a District Registry or the County Court (**PD Insolvency Proceedings, paras 12.1** and **12.2**).

IR 1986, r. 12A.55(1), provides that the provisions of **CPR, r. 2.8** (see **chapter 3**), apply, as regards computation of time, to anything required or authorised to be done by IR 1986.

Meaning of 'business day'

In IR 1986, 'business day' means (by r. 13.13(1)) any day other than a Saturday, a Sunday,   **82.7** Christmas Day, Good Friday or a day which is a bank holiday in any part of England and Wales under or by virtue of the Banking and Financial Dealings Act 1971.

WHICH COURT?

Subject to Regulation (EC) No. 1346/2000, art. 3 (see **82.9**), the High Court has jurisdiction   **82.8** to wind up any company incorporated by registration in England and Wales (Insolvency Act 1986, s. 117(1) and (7)).

High Court proceedings under the enactments relating to companies are assigned to the Chancery Division by the Senior Courts Act 1981, sch. 1, para. 1. Specific Chancery Division judges are designated to deal with company matters and there is a separate registry for such matters. This administrative arrangement is known as the Companies Court.

Subject to Regulation (EC) No. 1346/2000, art. 3 (see **82.9**), if the amount of a registered company's share capital paid up or credited as paid up does not exceed £120,000, the County Court has concurrent jurisdiction with the High Court to wind up the company (Insolvency Act 1986, s. 117(2)). But if the company's registered office is in the London insolvency district, winding-up proceedings can be commenced only in the High Court (s. 117(2A); High Court and County Courts Jurisdiction Order (SI 1991/724), art. 6C).

The London insolvency district comprises the areas served by the following County Court hearing centres: Barnet, Bow, Brentford, the County Court at Central London, Clerkenwell and Shoreditch, Edmonton, Lambeth, Mayor's and City of London Court, Wandsworth, West London, and Willesden (London Insolvency District (County Court at Central London) Order 2014 (SI 2014/818), art. 3, which has not been amended to reflect the closure of the West London (later renamed Hammersmith) hearing centre).

If, in the six months immediately preceding presentation of a petition to wind up a company, it has had different addresses for its registered office then it is the place which has longest been its registered office in that period which is its situation for these purposes (Insolvency Act 1986, s. 117(2A); SI 1991/724, art. 6C).

In the County Court, a petition to wind up a company may only be commenced in the County Court hearing centre outside the London insolvency district which serves the area in which the company's registered office is situated (Insolvency (Commencement of Proceedings) and Insolvency Rules 1986 (Amendment) Rules 2014 (SI 2014/817), r. 2(1)), unless, for that hearing centre, SI 2014/817, sch. 1, lists an alternative hearing centre, in which case the listed alternative hearing centre must be used (SI 2014/817, r. 2(2)). If, in the six months immediately preceding presentation of a petition to wind up a company, it has had different addresses for its registered office, it is the place which has longest been its registered office in that period which determines the hearing centre to be used (SI 2014/817, r. 2(3)). SI 2014/817, sch. 1, lists all hearing centres, including those in the London insolvency district. The schedule identifies the hearing centres in which winding-up proceedings cannot be commenced and shows where they should be brought instead, either at an alternative hearing centre or, in the London insolvency district, in the High Court.

A court in England and Wales does not have jurisdiction to wind up a company registered in Scotland (*Re Helene plc* [2000] 2 BCLC 249). A petition to wind up a Scottish registered company must be presented to the Court of Session or a sheriff court.

Regulation (EC) No. 1346/2000 and Regulation (EU) 2015/848

82.9 The jurisdiction of English courts in relation to winding up companies is, by the Insolvency Act 1986, s. 117(7), subject to Regulation (EC) No. 1346/2000, art. 3. The same applies to jurisdiction in relation to the bankruptcy of individuals (Insolvency Act 1986, s. 265(3)). The Regulation applies to the winding up of a company only if the winding up is on the ground of insolvency. A revised version of Regulation 1346/2000 comes into effect on 26 June 2017. That revised version is Regulation (EU) 2015/848. At the time of going to press, consequential amendments had not been made to UK legislation.

The scheme of Regulations 1346/2000 and 2015/848 is that the main insolvency proceedings in the European Union (apart from Denmark which has opted out of applying the Regulations) in relation to a debtor should be opened in the EU State where the debtor's 'centre of main interests' (COMI, see **82.10**) is located (art. 3(1) of both Regulations). Those main insolvency proceedings should be universal, that is, they should deal with all the debtor's assets wherever they are located.

If a debtor with a COMI in one EU State has an establishment (see **82.11**) in another EU State, insolvency proceedings may be opened in that State, but must be limited to dealing with the assets in that State (art. 3(2)), and are known as 'territorial proceedings' if main proceedings have not been opened (art. 3(4)) or 'secondary proceedings' if main proceedings have been opened (art. 3(3)).

The Regulations do not apply to insolvency proceedings relating to a debtor whose COMI is in Denmark or outside the European Union. But the Regulations apply to a company whose COMI is in an EU State other than Denmark, even if the company is incorporated in Denmark or outside the European Union (*Re BRAC Rent-A-Car International Inc.* [2003] EWHC 128 (Ch), [2003] 1 WLR 1421).

Regulation (EU) 2015/848, art. 4, introduces a new rule, that 'A court seised of a request to open insolvency proceedings shall of its own motion examine whether it has jurisdiction pursuant to art. 3'. The court's judgment opening proceedings must specify the grounds on which its jurisdiction is based and, in particular, whether jurisdiction is based on art. 3(1) (main proceedings) or art. 3(2) (territorial or secondary proceedings).

Centre of main interests

Recital 13 in the preamble to Regulation (EC) No. 1346/2000 states that the 'centre of main interests' (COMI) of a debtor should correspond to the place where the debtor conducts the administration of his interests on a regular basis, and asserts that this should be ascertainable by third parties, but the term is left undefined in the body of the Regulation. A debtor can have only one COMI (*Re BRAC Rent-A-Car International Inc.* [2003] EWHC 128 (Ch), [2003] 1 WLR 1421 at [23]), but may move it at will (*Shierson v Vlieland-Boddy* [2005] EWCA Civ 974, [2005] 1 WLR 3966). A court must not take any account of movement of a debtor's COMI to another jurisdiction after a request to open insolvency proceedings in respect of the debtor has been filed (*Staubitz-Schreiber* (case C-1/04) [2006] ECR I-701, overruling on this point *Shierson v Vlieland-Boddy*).

82.10

The COMI of a company is presumed to be where its registered office is, in the absence of proof to the contrary (art. 3(1)). The registered office of a company registered in England and Wales must be in England and Wales (Companies Act 2006, s. 9(6)(a)).

Recital 13 and art. 3(1), reflect an intention 'to attach greater importance to' the place where a company has its central administration as the criterion for jurisdiction (*Interedil Srl v Fallimento Interedil Srl* (case C-396/09) [2012] Bus LR 1582 at [48]). It is also of great importance that the COMI can be ascertained by third parties. The presumption that the COMI is at the company's registered office (art. 3(1)) reflects the fact that this normally corresponds to the head office and is also readily ascertainable by third parties, as every company must state the location of its registered office in letters and order forms, whether in paper form or in any other medium, and on its websites (Directive 2009/101/EC, art. 5, implemented in the United Kingdom by the Company, Limited Liability Partnership and Business (Names and Trading Disclosures) Regulations 2015 (SI 2015/17), regs 24 and 25).

The location of a debtor's COMI is a question of fact to which the usual civil standard of proof on balance of probabilities applies (*Shierson v Vlieland-Boddy*). In the case of a company, this is subject to the presumption that the COMI is at its registered office. That presumption can be displaced only if 'factors which are both objective and ascertainable by third parties enable it to be established that an actual situation exists which is different from' that presumption (*Re Eurofood IFSC Ltd* (case C-341/04) [2006] Ch 508 at [34]; *Re Stanford International Bank Ltd* [2010] EWCA Civ 137, [2010] Bus LR 1270 at [56]). Those factors must be assessed in a comprehensive manner, taking account of the particular circumstances of each case (*Rastelli Davide e C Snc v Hidoux* (case C-191/10) [2012] All ER (EC) 239 at [36]). What is ascertainable by third parties is what is in the public domain and what they would learn in the ordinary course of business with the company, not what can be ascertained only on inquiry (*Re Stanford*

In practice, the most important classes of petitions are those by creditors and those by contributories (and about 95 per cent of petitions are by creditors). The noticeable difference between these two classes of petitions is that, in general, creditors petition to wind up insolvent companies, whereas contributories petition to wind up solvent companies. The procedure for contributories' petitions is not the same as the procedure on other types of petition and is considered separately in **82.62** to **82.69**. For procedural purposes a petition to wind up a company presented at the instance of the company's administrator or by the supervisor of a voluntary arrangement in force for the company is treated as a contributory's petition.

Effect of voluntary arrangement and administration moratoriums

82.18 A petition for a company to be wound up by the court cannot be presented while a moratorium under the Insolvency Act 1986, s. 1A (moratorium when directors propose a voluntary arrangement), is in force in relation to the company (sch. A1, para. 12(1)(a)).

While a company is in administration, and while an interim moratorium is in force when an administration application has been presented or notice of intention to appoint an administrator out of court has been filed, the court may not make a winding-up order, except on a public interest petition presented by the Secretary of State or the Financial Conduct Authority or Prudential Regulation Authority (sch. B1, paras 42 and 44). When the court makes an administration order it must dismiss any outstanding winding-up petition (para. 40(1)(a)).

A petition for the winding up of a company must be 'suspended' while the company is in administration following an appointment out of court by the holder of a floating charge (sch. B1, para. 40(1)(b)), unless it is a public interest petition (para. 40(2)). During the suspension, s. 127(1) (avoidance of property dispositions) does not apply to anything done by the administrator (s. 127(2)). It is clear that the suspension automatically comes to an end when the administration comes to an end.

FORM AND CONTENTS OF WINDING-UP PETITION

Prescribed form

82.19 Under r. 4.7 of the IR 1986 the prescribed form of petition for the winding up of a company, if the petitioner is not a contributory, is form 4.2 in sch. 4 to the Rules. (Rule 4.7 does not apply to contributories' petitions, by r. 4.2(2).)

Heading

82.20 A winding-up petition must be entitled, 'In the matter of [the company sought to be wound up] and in the matter of the Insolvency Act 1986'.

A petition can refer to only one company because a winding-up order can refer to only one company (*Re Shields Marine Insurance Co., Lee and Moor's Case* (1867) 17 LT 308). In order to wind up a group of companies it is necessary to present a separate petition for each company in the group (*Re a Company* [1984] BCLC 307). However, the rules permit the petitioner to provide one statement of truth verifying several petitions (IR 1986, r. 4.12(7); see **82.24**).

Prescribed paragraphs

82.21 The prescribed paragraphs of a petition (form 4.2) to wind up a registered company state:

(1) The full name, registered number and date of incorporation of the company, and which Companies Act it was registered under.

(2) The address of its registered office.

(3)   Its nominal capital (otherwise known as authorised share capital) and how that is divided into shares, and its paid-up capital. **PD Insolvency Proceedings, para. 11.2(5)**, says that what should be given is:

(a)   In the case of companies incorporated under any of the Companies Acts prior to the Companies Act 2006, a statement of the nominal capital of the company, the manner in which its shares are divided up and the amount of the capital paid up or credited as paid up.

(b)   In the case of any other companies, a statement of the known issued share capital of the company, the manner in which its shares are divided up and the amount of the capital paid up or credited as paid up.

(4)   The principal objects of the company. **PD Insolvency Proceedings 2014, para. 11.2(6)**, says that what should be given is:

(a)   In the case of companies incorporated under any of the Companies Acts prior to the Companies Act 2006, brief details of the principal objects for which the company was established followed, where appropriate, by the words 'and other objects stated in the memorandum of association of the company'.

(b)   In the case of companies incorporated under the Companies Act 2006, either:

(i)   a statement confirming that its objects are unrestricted pursuant to the Companies Act 2006, s. 31(1); or alternatively

(ii)   a statement confirming that its objects are restricted by its articles of association and brief details of such restrictions.

(5)   The 'grounds on which a winding-up order is sought'. In the case of a creditor's petition, this paragraph must state that the company is unable to pay its debts, which is shown by the fact that it has not paid the petitioner's debt. Details should then be given of how that debt arose, including the nature of the transaction, order number and date, invoice number and date, and interest claimed.

(6)   A statement of whether the company is or is not one of the types of company to which Regulation (EC) No. 1346/2000 does not apply (see **82.12**).

(7)   A statement that, for the reasons stated in the written evidence filed in support of the petition, it is considered that Regulation (EC) No. 1346/2000 will or will not apply, and, if the Regulation does apply, whether the proceedings will be main, secondary or territorial proceedings (see **82.9**). When petitioning for the winding up of a company registered in England and Wales, we recommend that this paragraph should be completed as follows. If it has been identified in para. (6) that the Regulation does not apply, or if the COMI of the company is in Denmark or is outside the European Union, or if the petition is on a ground other than insolvency, state that the Regulation does not apply. Otherwise, state that the Regulation does apply and identify the proceedings as 'main proceedings', unless the centre of the company's main interests is in another EU State apart from Denmark. If the centre of the company's main interests is in another EU State (apart from Denmark) and main proceedings have not been opened there, identify the petition proceedings as 'territorial proceedings'. If main proceedings have been opened in the State where the COMI is located, identify the petition proceedings as 'secondary proceedings'.

(7A)   A statement, if applicable, that the reasons why more than four months have elapsed since a statutory demand was served on the company are set out in the statement of truth filed in support of the petition.

(8)   A statement that: 'In the circumstances it is just and equitable that the company should be wound up'.

There is then a prayer that the company named may be wound up by the court under the provisions of the Insolvency Act 1986 or that such other order may be made as the court thinks fit.

It is very important that items (1) to (3) correspond exactly with the data on the company's file at Companies House.

The prescribed form of petition ends with a section headed 'endorsement'. This has spaces to be filled in by a court official with the venue for hearing the petition (see **82.25**) and spaces to be filled in with the name, address and telephone number of the petitioner's solicitors and their reference number and equivalent details of their London agents. The information about the petitioner's solicitors must be completed before the petition is filed.

Grounds on which a winding-up order is sought

82.22 A petition for a winding-up order must allege the existence of one or more of the circumstances in which the court may make a winding-up order and state the facts from which it may be concluded that the alleged circumstance or circumstances exist.

The circumstances in which a registered company may be wound up by the court are listed in the Insolvency Act 1986, s. 122(1):

A company may be wound up by the court if—

(a) the company has by special resolution resolved that the company be wound up by the court,

(b) being a public company which was registered as such on its original incorporation, the company has not been issued with a trading certificate under section 761 of the Companies Act 2006 (requirement as to minimum share capital) and more than a year has expired since it was so registered,

(c) it is an old public company, within the meaning of Schedule 3 to the Companies Act 2006 (Consequential Amendments, Transitional Provisions and Savings) Order 2009 [SI 2009/1941],

(d) the company does not commence its business within a year from its incorporation or suspends its business for a whole year,

(e) [*repealed*]

(f) the company is unable to pay its debts,

(fa) at the time at which a moratorium for the company under section 1A comes to an end, no voluntary arrangement approved under Part 1 has effect in relation to the company,

(g) the court is of the opinion that it is just and equitable that the company should be wound up.

A petition is bound to fail if it does not allege any facts from which it may be concluded that at least one of the prescribed circumstances exists (*Securum Finance Ltd v Camswell Ltd* [1994] BCC 434, in which it was said that such a petition would be an abuse of process).

Evidence that company is unable to pay its debts

82.23 By far the most common type of petition is a creditor's petition alleging that the company is unable to pay its debts. The Insolvency Act 1986, s. 123, provides several means of proving that circumstance in the case of a registered company:

(1) A company is deemed unable to pay its debts—

(a) if a creditor (by assignment or otherwise) to whom the company is indebted in a sum exceeding £750 then due has served on the company, by leaving it at the company's registered office, a written demand (in the prescribed form) requiring the company to pay the sum so due and the company has for three weeks thereafter neglected to pay the sum or to secure or compound for it to the reasonable satisfaction of the creditor, or

(b) if, in England and Wales, execution or other process issued on a judgment, decree or order of any court in favour of a creditor of the company is returned unsatisfied in whole or in part, or

(c) if, in Scotland, the induciae of a charge for payment on an extract decree, or an extract registered bond, or an extract registered protest, have expired without payment being made, or

(d) if, in Northern Ireland, a certificate of unenforceability has been granted in respect of a judgment against the company, or

(e) if it is proved to the satisfaction of the court that the company is unable to pay its debts as they fall due.

(2) A company is also deemed unable to pay its debts if it is proved to the satisfaction of the court that the value of the company's assets is less than the amount of its liabilities, taking into account its contingent and prospective liabilities.

Unlike the position in bankruptcy proceedings, it is not necessary for a creditor of a company to present a statutory demand or issue execution before presenting a winding-up petition. In practice, it is common for a creditor petitioner to rely on the fact that the company has not paid a debt owed to the petitioner as proof (under s. 123(1)(e)) of the company's inability to pay its debts (see *Taylors Industrial Flooring Ltd v M and H Plant Hire (Manchester) Ltd* [1990] BCLC 216 at p. 219; *Re a Company (No. 003079 of 1990)* [1991] BCLC 235 at pp. 235–6).

If a statutory demand is used, it must be in the prescribed form, which is form 4.1 in sch. 4 to the IR 1986. A statutory demand can be served only for an amount due for payment at the time of service: it cannot, for example, be served for a contingent debt where the contingency has not occurred (*JSF Finance and Currency Exchange Co. Ltd v Akma Solutions Inc.* [2001] 2 BCLC 307). Unlike bankruptcy, there is no procedure for obtaining a court order setting aside a statutory demand served on a company.

Only an undisputed creditor of a company has standing to petition for it to be wound up: if there is a dispute on substantial grounds about the existence of the petitioner's debt, the petition will be dismissed (see **82.29**).

Verification of the petition

A petition must be verified by a statement of truth (IR 1986, rr. 4.7(1) and 4.12(1)) in accordance with **CPR, Part 22** (IR 1986, r. 13.13(17)). IR 1986, r. 4.12(8), requires the statement of truth to state: **82.24**

(a) whether, in the opinion of 'the person making the application', Regulation (EC) No. 1346/2000 will apply; and

(b) if so, whether the proceedings will be main proceedings or territorial proceedings.

For advice on these statements see the commentary in **82.21** on para. 7 of the prescribed form of petition. That paragraph of the prescribed form of petition states that the supporting statement of truth states the reasons for these opinions, but r. 4.12(8) requires only the opinions to be stated.

Rule 4.12(4) provides that the statement of truth must be authenticated by:

(a) the petitioner (or if there are two or more petitioners, any one of them); or

(b) some person such as a director, company secretary or similar company officer, or a solicitor, who has been concerned in the matters giving rise to the presentation of the petition; or

(c) some responsible person who is duly authorised to make the affidavit or witness statement and has the requisite knowledge of those matters.

In cases (b) and (c) the person verifying the petition must state the capacity in which, and the authority by which, he or she does so, and the means of knowing the matters contained in the written evidence (IR 1986, r. 4.12(5)). In r. 4.12(4)(b) 'solicitor' does not include a body recognised by the Law Society under the Administration of Justice Act 1985, s. 9, as suitable to carry on legal services (Solicitors' Recognised Bodies Order 1991 (SI 1991/ 2684), arts 2(1) and 4(a) and sch. 1).

If there are simultaneous petitions to wind up several companies (e.g. all companies in a group), it is permissible to make one statement of truth referring to all the companies and submit a photocopy with each petition (IR 1986, r. 4.12(7)). There must be a photocopy for each petition and the statement of truth must refer to all the companies by name.

FILING OF PETITION AND FIXING OF VENUE

82.25 A petition for the winding up of a company must be filed in court together with copies to be served on the company and sent to other persons. A court officer seals all copies of the petition and fixes a venue for hearing the petition which is endorsed on all copies of the petition (IR 1986, r. 4.7).

Unless the petition is presented by the company itself, it must be accompanied by a copy for service on the company (r. 4.7(3)). (If the company is the petitioner, service on the company is not required.)

Rule 4.7(4) requires additional copies of the petition in the following circumstances:

(a) if the company is in course of being wound up voluntarily, and a liquidator has been appointed, one copy of the petition to be sent to the voluntary liquidator;
(b) if the company is in administration, one copy to be sent to the administrator;
(c) if an administrative receiver has been appointed in relation to the company, one copy to be sent to that administrative receiver;
(d) if there is in force for the company a voluntary arrangement under part 1 (ss. 1 to 7) of the Insolvency Act 1986, one copy for the supervisor of the arrangement;
(e) if a member State liquidator has been appointed in main proceedings in relation to the company, one copy to be sent to that liquidator.

There are also special provisions when the company sought to be wound up is a bank (r. 4.7(4)(e)), an insurance company (Financial Services and Markets Act 2000, s. 369(1)) or an open-ended investment company (Open-Ended Investment Companies Regulations 2001 (SI 2001/1228), reg. 31(3)).

FEE AND DEPOSIT

82.26 On filing a winding-up petition, a court fee of £280 must be paid (**CPFO, fee 3.3**). The petitioner must deposit £1,600 (£5,000 for a public interest petition) as security for the administration fee which will become payable to the official receiver on the making of a winding-up order (Insolvency Act 1986, s. 414(4); Insolvency Proceedings (Fees) Order 2016 (SI 2016/692), arts 2 and 4(2)–(4)). A petition cannot be filed unless the receipt for the deposit is produced (IR 1986, r. 4.7(2)). The deposit will be used to discharge the official receiver's administration fee to the extent that the company's assets are insufficient (SI 2016/692, art. 4(4)); the administration fee is £5,000 (£7,500 for a public interest petition) (sch. 1). The court will transmit the deposit to its official receiver (art. 4(3)). If a winding-up order is made, any part of the deposit which is not required to pay the administration fee must be returned (art. 4(5)). If the petition is dismissed or withdrawn, the deposit must be repaid less an administration fee of £50 (art. 4(9)). The court fee is not repayable.

STOPPING PRESENTATION OF, OR PROCEEDING WITH, PETITION

Introduction

82.27 Presentation of a petition for the winding up of a company may cause it considerable disruption. The provisions of the Insolvency Act 1986, s. 127, for the control of transactions while a petition is pending mean that the company's bank account will be frozen. Gazetting of the petition is taken up by credit reference agencies and may damage the company's business and reputation. Despite the great inconvenience that can be caused by the presentation of an unsuccessful winding-up petition, a petitioner is never required to give an undertaking in damages unless there is an application for the appointment of a provisional liquidator (*Re Highfield Commodities Ltd* [1985] 1 WLR 149).

If the court considers that a petition to wind up a company is an abuse of process, it will:

(a) if the petition has not already been presented, restrain presentation of the petition;
(b) if the petition has been presented, restrain gazetting of the petition and strike it out.

An application to restrain presentation of a petition to wind up a company must be made to a court having jurisdiction to wind up the company (IR 1986, r. 4.6A(a)). It must be listed before a judge (**PD Insolvency Proceedings, para. 3.2(3)**). Applications to stop proceedings on a petition that has already been presented are made by application in those proceedings. The procedure on applications is described in **84.1** to **84.6**.

An order made by the court on an application to restrain presentation of a petition is not made in the exercise of its jurisdiction to wind up companies, and therefore cannot be reviewed, rescinded or varied by it under IR 1986, r. 7.47 (*Re Portedge Ltd* [1997] BCC 23 at p. 27).

In any proceedings to prevent the prosecution of a petition for the compulsory winding up of a company, the company must prove that the petition or proposed petition would constitute an abuse of process by showing, for example:

(a) That it is bound to fail because it is a disputed debt or cross-claim petition (see **82.29** and **82.30**).
(b) That it is an abuse of process because it is oppressive or unfair (*Cadiz Waterworks Co v Barnett* (1874) LR 19 Eq 182 at pp. 194–7).
(c) That it is an abuse of process because it has been presented for a collateral purpose and not for the benefit of creditors generally (or the benefit of contributories if it is a contributory's petition) (*Cadiz Waterworks Co v Barnett* (1874) LR 19 Eq 182 at pp. 195–6).
(d) That it is an abuse of process or is bound to fail, because the petitioner is seeking to wind up the company instead of pursuing an alternative and more appropriate remedy (*Charles Forte Investments Ltd v Amanda* [1964] Ch 240). This reason is most often found in relation to contributories' petitions, where the suitable alternative remedy may be an unfair prejudice petition under the Companies Act 2006, s. 994, or a fair offer to purchase the petitioner's shares. When a creditor's petition is based on an undisputed, unpaid debt, it cannot be objected that there is a suitable alternative remedy (*Cornhill Insurance plc v Improvement Services Ltd* [1986] 1 WLR 114 at p. 118). In particular, if there are no substantial grounds for disputing the petitioner's debt, the petitioner is not required to obtain judgment for it before presenting a winding-up petition (*Cornhill Insurance plc v Improvement Services Ltd* [1986] 1 WLR 114; *Re a Company (No. 003079 of 1990)* [1991] BCLC 235 at pp. 235–6).
(e) In the case of a petition that has already been presented, that it is bound to fail as a matter of law or because of lack of evidence (*Charles Forte Investments Ltd v Amanda* [1964] Ch 240).

A contractual obligation of a creditor not to apply for winding up (or administration) will be enforced by the court, if necessary by striking out, and is not contrary to public policy (*Re a Company (No. 00928 of 1991)* [1991] BCLC 514; *Re COLT Telecom Group plc* [2002] EWHC 2815 (Ch), LTL 20/12/2002). But a company's articles of association cannot remove its members' statutory right to apply as contributories for it to be wound up (*Re Peveril Gold Mines Ltd* [1898] 1 Ch 122).

Improper purpose

A winding-up order operates in favour of all creditors and contributories of the company (Insolvency Act 1986, s. 130(4)). It is an abuse of process for a person to petition for a

82.28

1499

company's compulsory liquidation otherwise than for the purpose of providing for all its creditors and contributories the benefits that the liquidation will produce (though no doubt self-interest will be the petitioner's primary concern) (*Re a Company (No. 001573 of 1983)* [1983] BCLC 492). In *Re Southbourne Sheet Metal Co. Ltd* [1992] BCLC 361 Harman J said, at p. 364:

a winding-up petition is not a *lis inter partes* [lawsuit between parties] for the benefit of A as against B. It is the invoking by A of a class remedy for the benefit of himself and other members of the class. Nonetheless, it is (a) based upon a commercial interest of the person invoking the remedy, and (b) it is for the benefit of himself, amongst other members of the class.

If other members of the petitioner's class take the view that it is not expedient to pursue the petition, the court will consider their views when deciding whether to exercise its discretion to make a winding-up order. The idea of a petitioner as a representative of a class applies primarily to creditors' petitions.

Disputed debts

82.29   If there is a dispute about the existence of a petitioner's debt then, as a matter of practice, it is usual, on the company's application, to strike out the petition (*Re a Company (No. 0013734 of 1991)* [1993] BCLC 59). A disputed debt petition is prevented from proceeding even if the company sought to be wound up is insolvent (*Mann v Goldstein* [1968] 1 WLR 1091). However, the petition may be adjourned on the assumption that another creditor will apply to be substituted as petitioner (*Re R. A. Foulds Ltd* (1986) 2 BCC 99,269).

A disputed debt petition is prevented from proceeding because proceedings on a creditor's winding-up petition are not suited to determining a dispute about the debt on which the petition is based. A dispute about a debt should be tried as an ordinary claim. A disputed debt petition will not be prevented from proceeding if the court decides that it would be proper for the dispute to be determined in the proceedings on the winding-up petition (*Re Claybridge Shipping Co. SA* [1997] 1 BCLC 572).

If the fact that a company is indebted to a creditor is not disputed, but the amount to be paid, and/or the time at which it is to be paid, is disputed (in particular, if only part of the petitioner's debt is disputed) then the petitioner's standing is not in question and the petition will not be struck out (*Re Tweeds Garages Ltd* [1962] Ch 406).

If it is found that only part of the debt is disputed and there is no evidence of the company's ability to pay the undisputed part, the petition may be adjourned for a short time to allow the company to pay the undisputed debt if it can (*Re Javelin Promotions Ltd* [2003] EWHC 1932 (Ch), LTL 30/9/2003).

In practice it may be difficult to distinguish between a dispute about existence and a dispute about quantum (see *Re a Company (No. 003729 of 1982)* [1984] 1 WLR 1090; *Re R. A. Foulds Ltd* (1986) 2 BCC 99,269).

It is irrelevant that the company has not paid money to the person who is petitioning or threatening to petition in response to a statutory demand for the disputed amount claimed: the fact that the claim is disputed means that the company has a reasonable excuse for not complying with the statutory demand and so has not 'neglected' to comply with it, and so is not deemed to be unable to pay its debts (*Re London and Paris Banking Corporation* (1874) LR 19 Eq 444; *Re a Company (No. 003729 of 1982)* [1984] 1 WLR 1090).

The court will not prevent a disputed debt petition proceeding unless it is satisfied that 'the debt is disputed on some substantial ground (and not just on some ground which is frivolous or without substance and which the court should, therefore, ignore)' (*Mann v Goldstein* [1968] 1 WLR 1091 per Ungoed-Thomas J at p. 1096). In *Stonegate Securities Ltd v Gregory* [1980] Ch 576 Goff LJ, at p. 589, expressed the court's task as distinguishing 'whether there is a bona fide dispute or whether it is insubstantial or trumped up'. A bona fide belief that there is a dispute is not enough in itself because it does not prove that there is substance in the dispute (Re a Company (No. 001946 of 1991) [1991] BCLC 737).

It is for the court hearing the petition to decide whether the dispute is substantial enough to justify dismissing the petition. The question is not decided by the continuance of other proceedings brought by the petitioner to recover the debt, even if an application by the petitioner for summary judgment in those proceedings has failed (Re Welsh Brick Industries Ltd [1946] 2 All ER 197). The same applies to a failure to get an appeal against a tax assessment struck out (Commissioners of HM Revenue and Customs v Changtel Solutions UK Ltd [2015] EWCA Civ 29, [2015] BCC 317). If the court hearing the petition decides there is not a substantial dispute then the petition must continue even if other proceedings are also continuing (James Dolman and Co. Ltd v Pedley [2003] EWCA Civ 1686, LTL 25/9/2003).

Cross-claim against petitioner

If a creditor of a company presents a petition for the compulsory winding up of the company, but the company claims from the petitioner a sum which is greater than or equal to the petitioner's debt, or falls short of it by £750 or less, the practice is to treat the petition in the same way as a disputed debt petition (Re Portman Provincial Cinemas Ltd [1999] 1 WLR 157; Re LHF Wools Ltd [1970] Ch 27; Re Bayoil SA [1999] 1 WLR 147). Unless there are special circumstances, the petition will be prevented from proceeding. **82.30**

If the company's cross-claim against the petitioner is less than the petitioner's debt and it is shown that the company is unable to pay its debts, a winding-up order will be made (Blue Star Security Services (Scotland) Ltd 1992 SLT (Sh Ct) 80).

According to Nourse LJ in Re Bayoil SA [1999] 1 WLR 147 at p. 155, the company has the burden of proving:

(a) that its cross-claim is larger than the admitted debt of the petitioner or falls short of it by £750 or less (Greenacre Publishing Group v The Manson Group [2000] BCC 11);

(b) that its cross-claim has substance (per Lord Denning MR in Re Portman Provincial Cinemas Ltd [1999] 1 WLR 157), or is 'genuine and serious' (Re Bayoil SA [1999] 1 WLR 147 per Nourse LJ at p. 155 and Ward LJ at p. 156) or is 'genuine, serious and of substance' (Orion Media Marketing Ltd v Media Brook Ltd [2002] 1 BCLC 184 at p. 191); provided the cross-claim meets this standard, it does not matter that it is disputed.

The fact that there has been delay in taking steps to establish a cross-claim by arbitration or litigation may show that the cross-claim is not based on substantial grounds (Re a Debtor (No. 544/SD/98) [2000] 1 BCLC 103 per Robert Walker LJ at p. 114; Guardi Shoes Ltd v Datum Contracts [2002] CILL 1934). But it is wrong to require a company to prove that it has been unable to litigate a cross-claim as a condition for preventing presentation of, or proceeding with, a creditor's winding-up petition (Bolsover District Council v Dennis Rye Ltd [2009] EWCA Civ 372, [2009] 4 All ER 1140 at [23]; Accessory People Ltd v Rouass [2010] EWCA Civ 302, LTL 13/4/2010).

Costs of proceedings to stop a petition

Orders as to costs of proceedings for preventing a petition are at the discretion of the court but will normally follow the event (Cannon Screen Entertainment Ltd v Handmade Films (Distributors) Ltd (1988) 5 BCC 207). Abuse of process by presenting a petition to put pressure on a solvent company to pay a disputed debt is 'a high risk strategy', and the petitioner may be ordered to pay the company's costs on an indemnity basis (Re a Company (No. 0012209 of 1991) [1992] 1 WLR 351). **82.31**

Commentary

COMMENCEMENT OF WINDING UP, GOING INTO LIQUIDATION, ETC.

82.32   The Insolvency Act 1986, s. 129(2), provides that if an order for the winding up of a company is made on a petition presented when the company was not in voluntary liquidation, the winding up by the court is deemed to have commenced at the time when the petition was presented. This is not at the beginning of the day on which the petition was presented but at the moment of presentation, because s. 129(2) refers to the time rather than the date of presentation of the petition (*Re London and Devon Biscuit Co.* (1871) LR 12 Eq 190; *Re Blackburn Industries Pty Ltd* [1980] QdR 211 per D. M. Campbell J at p. 217 and Dunn J at p. 224; see also the latter case on appeal sub nom. *Wilde v Australian Trade Equipment Co. Pty Ltd* (1981) 145 CLR 590).

If a winding-up order is made on an administration application (see **82.104**), the winding up commences on the making of the order (s. 129(1A)).

If an order for the winding up of a registered company is made on a petition presented after a resolution for voluntary winding up has been adopted, the winding up is deemed to have commenced at the time when that resolution was adopted (s. 129(1)).

The Insolvency Act 1986 also uses the phrase, 'to go into liquidation'. By s. 247(2), a company goes into liquidation when it adopts a resolution for voluntary winding up or when an order for its winding up is made (unless it had already passed a resolution for voluntary winding up, in which case the date of that resolution is the date of going into liquidation).

SERVICE OF PETITION

General rule

82.33   Unless a petition to wind up a company is presented by the company itself, a copy of the petition must be served on the company (IR 1986, r. 4.8(1)). It must be served at least seven business days *before* it is notified in the *London Gazette* (see **82.39**), and the *Gazette* notice must appear at least seven business days before the hearing date (IR 1986, r. 4.11(4)(b)). 'Business day' is defined in r. 13.13(1) (see **82.7**). Service is the responsibility of the petitioner and will not be undertaken by the court (**PD Insolvency Proceedings, para. 6.2**).

Service at the registered office

82.34   The petition must be served at the company's registered office, if it has one (IR 1986, r. 4.8(2)). A petition may be served at the company's registered office in any of the following ways (IR 1986, r. 4.8(3)):

(a) it may be handed to a person who there and then acknowledges him or herself to be — or to the best of the server's knowledge, information and belief is — a director or other officer, or employee, of the company; or

(b) it may be handed to a person who there and then acknowledges him or herself to be authorised to accept service of documents on the company's behalf; or

(c) in the absence of any such person as is mentioned in (a) or (b), it may be deposited at or about the registered office in such a way that it is likely to come to the notice of a person attending at the office.

It is clear from r. 4.8(6) that service at the registered office may not be effected in any other way (for example, by post) without the court's approval or direction.

Service at principal place of business or on officer of company

82.35 IR 1986, r. 4.8(4), specifies methods for serving a winding-up petition on the company sought to be wound up if:

(a) service at its registered office is not practicable, or

(b) the company has no registered office.

In either of those cases the petition may be served by:

(a) leaving it at the company's last known principal place of business in such a way that it is likely to come to the attention of a person attending there; or

(b) delivering it to the secretary or some director, manager or principal officer of the company, wherever that person may be found.

Option (a) only authorises service at a place of business within the jurisdiction (*Re Tea Trading Co. K. and C. Popoff Brothers* [1933] Ch 647 at p. 651).

Order for alternative service

82.36 If for any reason it is impracticable to effect service as provided by IR 1986, r. 4.8(2) to (4) (see **82.34** and **82.35**), the petition may be served in such other manner as the court may approve or direct (r. 4.8(6)). An application for the court's approval or direction under r. 4.8(6) may be made without notice to other parties (r. 4.8(7)). An application must be accompanied by a witness statement setting out what steps have been taken to comply with r. 4.8(2) to (5) and the reasons why it is impracticable to effect service as provided in those paragraphs (r. 4.8(7)).

Certificate of service

82.37 Service of a winding-up petition must be proved by a certificate of service (IR 1986, r. 4.9A(1)). This must be sufficient to identify the petition served and must specify the matters set out in r. 4.9A(2). If substituted service has been ordered, the certificate of service must have attached to it a sealed copy of the order (r. 4.9A(3)). A certificate of service must be verified by a statement of truth (r. 13.13(16)) in accordance with **CPR, Part 22** (IR 1986, r. 13.13(17)). The certificate of service must be filed in court as soon as reasonably practicable after service, and in any event not less than five business days (see **82.7**) before the hearing of the petition (r. 4.9A(4)).

Copies for other persons

82.38 If a petition is presented to wind up a company which has a voluntary liquidator, an administrator, a supervisor of a voluntary arrangement and/or an administrative receiver, a copy of the petition must be sent to that officer on the next business day after the petition is served on the company (IR 1986, r. 4.10(1), (2), (3) and (5)). 'Business day' is defined in r. 13.13(1) (see **82.7**).

If a winding-up petition asks for the opening of secondary proceedings against a company which is already the subject of main insolvency proceedings in another EU State (see **82.9**), a copy of the petition must be served on a member State liquidator appointed in the main proceedings (see **82.17**) unless that liquidator is the petitioner (IR 1986, r. 4.10(3A)).

PUBLICISATION OF PETITION

Need for and timing of notice

82.39 A winding-up order is a collective remedy and the order operates in favour of all creditors and contributories (Insolvency Act 1986, s. 130(4)), who can all appear at the hearing of the petition to support or oppose it. Therefore, unless the court otherwise directs, notice of a winding-up petition must be given by the petitioner (IR 1986, r. 4.11(1)). The notice must be given by 'gazetting' (r. 4.11(2)), that is, by one advertisement in the *London Gazette* (r. 13.13(4) and (4A)). If gazetting is not reasonably practicable, notice must be given in such other manner as the court thinks just (r. 4.11(3)). The notice serves to invite creditors and contributories to appear on the hearing of the petition and submit their views to the court: the notice is a substitute for, and renders unnecessary, service of the petition on them (*Re National Credit and Exchange Co. Ltd* (1862) 7 LT 817; *Re Marlborough Club Co.* (1865) LR 1 Eq 216; *Re New Gas Co.* (1877) 5 ChD 703). The contents of the notice of a winding-up petition in the *London Gazette* are specified in IR 1986, rr. 4.11(5), 12A.33, 12A.34 and 12A.36 (see r. 13.13(4B)(a)). The prescribed form of an advertisement is form 4.6 in sch. 4 to the IR 1986.

Notice of a petition must appear at least seven business days *before* the date appointed for the hearing, and, unless the company itself is the petitioner, must not appear until at least seven business days *after* service of the petition on the company (IR 1986, r. 4.11(4)). 'Business day' is defined in r. 13.13(1) (see **82.7**).

If notice of a winding-up petition is not given in accordance with r. 4.11, the petition may be dismissed (r. 4.11(6)). Rule 4.11(6) applies where no notice at all is given and it applies to notice that is given for the purpose of complying with r. 4.11, but is given at the wrong time or is wrongly worded. It does not apply to any notification of the petition that is not made for the purpose of complying with r. 4.11 (see **82.41**).

The period of seven days between service of the petition on the company and notification of the petition is required so that the company may, depending on the circumstances:

(a) apply for the petition to be struck out;

(b) pay the debt on a creditor's petition;

(c) consider its position generally with regard to the petition;

(d) if necessary, make an application under the Insolvency Act 1986, s. 127, for an anticipatory validation order (*Re Signland Ltd* [1982] 2 All ER 609 at p. 609; *Re a Company (No. 0013925 of 1991)* [1992] BCLC 562 at p. 564).

The power to dismiss a prematurely advertised petition to wind up a company is a discretionary disciplinary power and might not be exercised on the company's application if the company does not show that it has been prejudiced, e.g. by showing on a creditor's petition that it could have paid the debt (*Re Roselmar Properties Ltd* (1986) 2 BCC 99,156; *Re Corbenstoke Ltd* [1989] BCLC 496; *Re Garton (Western) Ltd* [1989] BCLC 304).

Equally, the timely advertisement of a creditor's petition is important to ensure that the class remedy of winding up by the court is available to all creditors, and is not used as a means of putting pressure on the company to pay the petitioner's debt or costs (**PD Insolvency Proceedings, para. 11.5.1**). The court may, under IR 1986, r. 4.11(6), dismiss a petition if there has been a failure to advertise it without good reason accepted by the court (**PD Insolvency Proceedings, para. 11.5.1**).

A company may apply for a direction that a petition for it to be wound up should not be gazetted. It is for the company to show sufficient reason for departure from the normal practice of gazetting petitions other than contributories' petitions (*Re a Company (No. 007946 of 1993)* [1994] Ch 198; *Re a Company (No. 007923 of 1994)* [1995] 1 WLR 953), but it is not necessary for the company to show that the petition is bound to fail (*Re a Company (No. 007923 of 1994)* [1995] 1 WLR 953). If the company has not obtained an order under the Insolvency Act 1986, s. 127, validating dispositions in the ordinary course of the company's business, the court will not direct that the petition should not be gazetted, other than in exceptional circumstances (*Applied Data Base Ltd v Secretary of State for Trade and Industry* [1995] 1 BCLC 272 at pp. 274–5).

Provision of copies of the petition

82.40 When a petition has been presented for the winding up of a company, the petitioner (or the petitioner's solicitor, if there is one) must, on request, supply to any director, contributory or creditor of the company a copy of the petition. A copy must be supplied within two days of being applied for and a fee of 15p per A4 or A5 page (30p per A3 page) may be charged (IR 1986, rr. 4.13 and 13.11(b)).

Other publicisation of the petition

82.41 Publicity for a winding-up petition, given otherwise than for the purpose of complying with IR 1986, r. 4.11, is not 'notice' for the purposes of that rule and, in particular, r. 4.11(6) (which provides a power to dismiss a petition for failure to comply with r. 4.11) does not apply (*Re a Company (No. 0013925 of 1991)* [1992] BCLC 562; *SN Group plc v Barclays Bank plc* [1993] BCC 506; *Secretary of State for Trade and Industry v North West Holdings plc* [1999] 1 BCLC 425, overruling *Re a Company (No. 001127 of 1992)* [1992] BCC 477). However, in *Re FSA Business Software Ltd* [1990] BCLC 465 Warner J said, at p. 829: 'It is at least a breach of the spirit of the rules of this court for publicity to be given to a winding-up petition before it has been advertised'.

The court may dismiss a petition if its existence is notified before the expiry of seven business days from service on the company and the notification was designed to put pressure on the company: such conduct is an abuse of process (*Re a Company (No. 0013925 of 1991)* [1992] BCLC 562; *Re a Company (No. 001127 of 1992)* [1992] BCC 477). In *SN Group plc v Barclays Bank plc* [1993] BCC 506 it was found that the publicisation of the petition was not designed to put pressure on the company (which was found to be insolvent) and the company's application to have the petition dismissed was rejected.

Publicisation of an intention to present a petition may be an abuse of process which may be punished by striking out the petition when it is presented (*Re Doreen Boards Ltd* [1996] 1 BCLC 501).

Errors in notice

82.42 If there is an error or inaccuracy in notice of a winding-up petition then, unless the court waives it, the person who was responsible for giving the notice must, as soon as reasonably practicable, give fresh notice for the purpose of correcting the error or inaccuracy (IR 1986, r. 12A.37(3)). The court has a discretion to waive an error (*Re Worthing Royal Sea House Hotel Co.* [1872] WN 74).

In *Re Vidiofusion Ltd* [1974] 1 WLR 1548 the advertisement incorrectly gave the company's name as 'Videofusion Ltd' ('e' instead of 'i'). Megarry J waived the mistake and said that, normally, an error would be waived if four conditions are satisfied:

(a) There must be no other company on the register with a similar name.
(b) The true name and the misspelt name should have substantially the same pronunciation.
(c) There should be no marked visual difference between the true name and the misspelt name (so that 'Jaxen' for 'Jackson' would not be waived despite the similarity of pronunciation).
(d) The error must not materially affect the alphabetical order of the names.

It is submitted that it is no longer appropriate to waive errors in spelling, now that there are over 3 million British registered companies and now that banks and other persons checking whether they deal with companies which are the subject of winding-up petitions use computer searches which are usually not capable of recognising such errors.

CONTROL OF TRANSACTIONS AND LITIGATION
WHILE PETITION IS PENDING

82.43   If a winding-up order is made against a company, the winding up is deemed to have commenced at the time when the petition was presented, or the time the company went into voluntary liquidation, if earlier (Insolvency Act 1986, s. 129). The general principle of winding up is that all non-preferential unsecured creditors are treated equally. So the Act makes provision to prevent specific unsecured creditors recovering payment of debts at the expense of the other unsecured creditors. (The winding up of a company does not, in general, affect security interests in the company's property.) Provision is made for the stay of other proceedings against the company while the petition is pending (Insolvency Act 1986, s. 126, see **84.20**), for all dispositions of the company's property to be invalid unless sanctioned by the court (s. 127), and for avoidance of attachments, sequestrations, distresses and executions against the company's property (s. 128). The company itself and its directors may not appoint an administrator out of court (sch. B1, para. 25(a)), though a holder of a qualifying floating charge may do so unless a provisional liquidator has been appointed (para. 17(a)). The Act also prevents alterations in the status of the company's members without the approval of the court (s. 127).

APPOINTMENT OF A PROVISIONAL LIQUIDATOR

Function of a provisional liquidator

82.44   A provisional liquidator of a company may be appointed by the court under the Insolvency Act 1986, s. 135. An appointment may be made at any time in the period between presentation of a petition for the compulsory winding up of the company and the court's disposal of the petition (by making a winding-up order, dismissing the petition or striking it out) (Insolvency Act 1986, s. 135(1) and (2); *Re a Company (No. 00315 of 1973)* [1973] 1 WLR 1566).

The usual object of the appointment is that an independent person will take charge of the company's affairs, maintain the status quo and prevent prejudice either to those supporting the winding-up petition or to those against it, pending the court's decision on the petition (per Lord President Clyde in *Levy v Napier* 1962 SC 468 at p. 477; per Street J in *Re Carapark Industries Pty Ltd* (1966) 86 WN (Pt 1) (NSW) 165 at p. 171). Provisional liquidators are independent persons operating under the direction of the court for a purpose that is entirely one of preservation during an interim period: a provisional liquidator does not represent any one group of creditors (*Re Bank of Credit and Commerce International SA (No. 2)* [1992] BCLC 579). The name 'provisional liquidator' is misleading because the one thing that a provisional liquidator of a company does not do is carry out the liquidation of the company.

The appointment of a provisional liquidator of a company terminates the powers of the directors as effectively as does the making of a winding-up order (*Re Mawcon Ltd* [1969] 1 WLR 78). The directors do, however, have standing to apply for the provisional liquidator's appointment to be discharged (*Re Union Accident Insurance Co. Ltd* [1972] 1 WLR 640) or apply for an administration order to be made in relation to the company (*Re Gosscott (Groundworks) Ltd* [1988] BCLC 363 per Mervyn Davies J at p. 366).

Who may apply for a provisional liquidator to be appointed

82.45   When a petition has been presented for the compulsory liquidation of a company, an application to appoint a provisional liquidator may be made by (IR 1986, 4. 25(1)):

(a)   the petitioner,

(b)   a creditor of the company,

(c) a contributory of the company,

(d) the company itself,

(e) the Secretary of State,

(f) a temporary administrator (see **82.17**),

(g) a member State liquidator appointed in main proceedings (see **82.17**),

(h) any person who would, under any enactment, be entitled to present a petition to wind up the company.

Application procedure

An application to the court for the appointment of a provisional liquidator of a company   **82.46**
must be supported by a witness statement stating (IR 1986, r. 4.25(2)):

(a) The grounds for the appointment.

(b) If the proposed provisional liquidator is not the official receiver, that the person proposed has consented to act and that he or she is, to the best of the applicant's knowledge, a qualified insolvency practitioner.

(c) Whether or not the official receiver has been informed of the application and, if so, whether a copy of the application has been sent to the official receiver. Whether or not it is proposed that the official receiver should be the provisional liquidator, a copy of the application and supporting affidavit must be sent to the official receiver, who may attend the hearing and make representations (r. 4.25(3)). If it is not possible to send these copies, the official receiver must at least be informed of the application in time to attend the hearing (r. 4.25(3)).

(d) Whether, to the applicant's knowledge:

(i)   there has been proposed, or is in force, for the company a voluntary arrangement;

(ii)   an administrator or administrative receiver is acting in relation to the company;

(iii) a voluntary liquidator has been appointed.

(e) The applicant's estimate of the value of the assets in respect of which the provisional liquidator is to be appointed.

Application without notice to other parties

As it is not inevitable that a winding-up order will be made after the appointment of a   **82.47**
provisional liquidator, if an application for such an appointment is made without notice
to the company and the court has no opportunity to hear the company's views, the court
will not make the appointment unless the applicant gives an undertaking in damages (i.e.
undertakes that if winding up is not ordered the applicant will compensate the company
for any loss it suffers as a result of the appointment: the company would not be able to sue
for damages because the damage would have been caused by court order). However, if an
application is made in those circumstances by the Crown in connection with a public
interest winding-up petition, an undertaking in damages will not be required (*Re Highfield
Commodities Ltd* [1985] 1 WLR 149). An undertaking in damages is not usually required if the
company had an opportunity to give the court its views on the application (*Re Highfield
Commodities Ltd* at p.155).

According to Hoffmann J in *Re First Express Ltd* [1991] BCC 782 at p. 785 and *Re Secure and
Provide plc* [1992] BCC 405, an order should not be made without notice to other parties unless:

(a) giving the company an opportunity to be heard appears likely to cause injustice to the applicant, because of:

(i)   the delay involved, or

(ii) action which it is likely will be taken before the order can be made; and

(b) the court is satisfied that any damage which the company may suffer from the appointment of the provisional liquidator may be compensated through the applicant's undertaking in damages or that the risk of incompensable loss is clearly outweighed by the risk of injustice to the applicant if the order is not made.

Form of order

82.48 The order appointing a provisional liquidator of a company should be in form 4.15 in sch. 4 to the IR 1986 and it must specify the functions to be carried out by the provisional liquidator in relation to the company's affairs (IR 1986, r. 4.26(1)). The appointment of a provisional liquidator may be made on such terms as the court thinks just (r. 4.25(4)).

Transmission of order

82.49 Having made an order appointing a provisional liquidator of a company, the court will send a sealed copy of the order to the person appointed as provisional liquidator, and (if the person appointed is not the official receiver) to the official receiver, and to the company's administrative receiver, if there is one (IR 1986, r. 4.26(2) and (3)). Further copies are provided to the provisional liquidator to be sent to the company (or to its voluntary liquidator, if there is one) and to Companies House (r. 4.26(2) and (3)).

Public notification

82.50 A provisional liquidator must notify Companies House of his or her appointment (IR 1986, r. 4.26(2) and (3)) and, unless the court orders otherwise, gazette it (r. 4.25A(3)).

Joint provisional liquidators

82.51 If two or more persons are appointed joint provisional liquidators of a company, the order of appointment must state whether any act required or authorised under any enactment to be done by the provisional liquidator is to be done by all or any one or more of the persons for the time being holding the office (Insolvency Act 1986, s. 231).

Deposit for the official receiver's remuneration and expenses

82.52 On applying for the official receiver to be appointed provisional liquidator of a company, the applicant must deposit with the official receiver such sum as the court directs to cover remuneration and expenses (IR 1986, r. 4.27(1)). Alternatively, security for the amount may be given if the official receiver agrees (r. 4.27(1)).

From time to time the official receiver may apply to the court to order a further amount to be deposited or secured, and if the order is not complied with within two days of service, the court may discharge the official receiver's appointment as provisional liquidator (r. 4.27(2)).

Control of litigation after provisional liquidator appointed

82.53 The Insolvency Act 1986, s. 130(2), provides that when a provisional liquidator has been appointed, no action or proceeding shall be proceeded with or commenced against the company or its property, except by permission of the court and subject to such terms as the court may impose. See 84.21. No one may appoint an administrator out of court (sch. B1, paras 17(a) and 25(a)).

CERTIFICATE OF COMPLIANCE

82.54 Before the date appointed for the hearing of a winding-up petition, the petitioner or the petitioner's solicitor must file in court a certificate of compliance with the rules relating to service and advertisement (IR 1986, r. 4.14(1)). The prescribed form of certificate is form 4.7 in IR 1986, sch. 4. A certificate must (r. 4.14(2)):

(a) state the date of presentation of the petition;

(b) state the date fixed for hearing it;

(c) state the date or dates on which the petition was served and notice of it was given in compliance with the rules;

(d) be accompanied by a copy of the notice. If filing a copy of the notice is not reasonably practicable, a description of the form and content of any notice given is to be filed.

Rule 4.14(1) requires the certificate of compliance to be filed at least five business days (see **82.7**) before the hearing of the petition.

Failure to file a certificate of compliance is a ground on which the court may, if it thinks just, dismiss the petition (r. 4.14(3)). In *Re J. Lang and Co. Ltd* (1892) 36 SJ 271 North J thought that a petition should not be dismissed for failure to file a certificate of compliance unless the failure had caused substantial injustice which could not be remedied by an order of the court.

A copy or description of the notice must be filed with the certificate even if it was defective in some way, for example, because it was published at the wrong time or omitted or misprinted important words (**PD Insolvency Proceedings, para. 11.5.2**). If the petition has not been notified because of an order forbidding notification, the prescribed form of certificate should be adapted to state that the petition was served but that notification has been forbidden by the court (see *Re a Company (No. 002791 of 1986)* [1986] 2 BCC 99,281). Failure to notify a petition in pursuance of such an order is not in itself a ground for dismissing the petition (*Re Five Oaks Construction Ltd* (1968) 112 SJ 86).

A petitioner who has given notice of the petition but has decided not to pursue it should nevertheless file a copy or description of the notice (**PD Insolvency Proceedings, para. 11.5.2**) and a certificate of compliance so as to be entitled to costs.

PERMISSION TO WITHDRAW A PETITION

Under IR 1986, r. 4.15, a person petitioning for a company to be wound up may apply to the court without notice to other parties for permission to withdraw the petition. The following conditions must be satisfied:

(a) The petition must not have been advertised and no notices with reference to the petition (whether in support of or in opposition to it) must have been received by the petitioner, either under r. 4.16 (see **82.72**) or otherwise (*Re Wavern Engineering Co. Ltd* (1986) 3 BCC 3).

(b) The company must consent to the court giving permission to withdraw the petition.

(c) The parties must have agreed who is to pay costs. If there has been no agreement, the petition must be heard so that the court can make an order, but then the petition must be advertised (*Re Shusella Ltd* [1983] BCLC 505).

(d) The application must be made at least five business days (see **82.7**) before the day fixed for hearing the petition.

An application for permission to withdraw a petition is heard by the member of court staff in charge of the winding-up list in the RCJ or a District Judge in a District Registry or the County Court (**PD Insolvency Proceedings, paras 12.1** and **12.2**). The prescribed form of order for permission to withdraw a petition is form 4.8 in sch. 4 to the IR 1986.

SUBSTITUTION OF PETITIONER

Circumstances in which a substitution may be made

When a winding-up petition is pending, IR 1986, r. 4.19, permits the substitution of a new petitioner if the original petitioner:

(a) is subsequently found not entitled to petition;

(b) fails to advertise the petition, within the time prescribed by IR 1986 (see **82.39**) or such extended time as the court may allow;

82.55

82.56

the petition has been gazetted, the petition will be dismissed and the company will be ordered to pay the petitioner's costs (*Re Nowmost Co. Ltd* [1996] 2 BCLC 492). However, the court may make no order as to part or all of the petitioner's costs as a penalty for unreasonable pre-action behaviour (**CPR, r. 44.2(4)(a) and (5)(a)**) or unreasonable rejection of an offer of payment (*Holmes v Mainstream Ventures Ltd* [2009] EWHC 3330 (Ch), [2010] 1 BCLC 651). Such a penalty may be reduced because of the company's own unreasonable behaviour (*Holmes v Mainstream Ventures Ltd*).

The company

82.81   **Successful petition**   The 'usual compulsory order' made on a winding-up petition includes provision for the payment of the company's costs of preparing for and appearing at the hearing of a successful winding-up petition as an expense of the liquidation (*Re Bostels Ltd* [1968] Ch 346 at p. 350). However, the company's assets available for distribution to its creditors should not be expended unjustifiably. If the company has unjustifiably opposed the petition or tried to prevent it proceeding, the court may order the person who instigated the company's opposition to pay its costs (*Re a Company (No. 004055 of 1991)* [1991] 1 WLR 1003). There must be an opportunity for the person against whom such a costs order is sought to submit a defence and, if necessary, put in evidence, before the order is made (*Re a Company (No. 004055 of 1991)*).

82.82   **Unsuccessful petition**   The company's costs of opposing an unsuccessful winding-up petition must be paid by the petitioner unless there are exceptional circumstances (*Re Fernforest Ltd* [1990] BCLC 693). A petition is not unsuccessful if it results in payment of the petitioner's debt (see **82.80**). The company will be awarded its costs against the petitioner if the petition is dismissed for failure to file a certificate of compliance (*Re Royal Mutual Benefit Building Society* [1960] 1 WLR 1143).

Supporting creditors and contributories

82.83   **Successful petition**   When a winding-up order is made, creditors who appeared to support the petition will be awarded one set of costs between them to be paid as an expense of the liquidation, and a second set of costs will be awarded on the same basis to supporting contributories (*Re Bostels Ltd* [1968] Ch 346 at p. 350). It is an invariable rule that only one set of costs is awarded to successful supporting creditors even if several persons legitimately appear to present separate views (*Re Esal (Commodities) Ltd* [1985] BCLC 450). The creditors and contributories must arrange among themselves how to divide up the costs.

Costs ordered to be paid to supporting creditors and contributories rank equally with the petitioner's costs in the order of priority of payments set out in IR 1986, r. 4.218 (where they are item (h)).

82.84   **Unsuccessful petition**   Supporters of an unsuccessful petition are not entitled to costs (*Re Humber Ironworks Co.* (1866) LR 2 Eq 15).

Opposing creditors and contributories

82.85   **Successful petition**   Creditors or contributories appearing to oppose a successful petition are not entitled to costs (*Re Bathampton Properties Ltd* [1976] 1 WLR 168 at p. 171).

82.86   **Unsuccessful petition**   Creditors who appear to oppose an unsuccessful petition may be given one set of costs between them from the petitioner and so may opposing contributories if their interests are distinct from the company's (*Re Peckham etc. Tramways Co.* (1888) 57 LJ Ch 462 per Chitty J at p. 463). A contributory whose interests are not distinct from the company's will not be awarded costs (*Re Times Life Assurance and Guarantee Co., ex parte Nunneley* (1870) LR 5 Ch App 381).

Assessment

The court may order costs of proceedings on a winding-up petition to be decided by detailed **82.87** assessment (IR 1986, r. 7.34A(5)). If costs of a successful petition to wind up a company are payable as an expense out of the insolvent estate, they must be decided by detailed assessment unless agreed between the liquidator and the person entitled to payment (r. 7.34A(1)). In the absence of agreement, the liquidator may serve notice requiring detailed assessment proceedings to be commenced by the person entitled to payment (r. 7.34A(2)(a)). Such a notice must be served if required by the liquidation committee (r. 7.34A(2)(b)). Detailed assessment proceedings must be commenced in the court to which the winding-up proceedings are allocated (r. 7.34A(3)).

NOTICE TO OFFICIAL RECEIVER AND PERFECTION OF THE ORDER

When a winding-up order is made the court gives notice to its official receiver forthwith (IR **82.88** 1986, r. 4.20(1)).

The petitioner, and every person who appeared on the hearing of the petition, must, not later than the business day after the order is made, leave at the court all documents necessary to enable the order to be completed (r. 4.20(2)). 'Business day' is defined in r. 13.13(1) (see **82.7**). It is not normally necessary to appoint a time for settlement of the order (r. 4.20(3)). The court will draw up the order (**PD Insolvency Proceedings, para. 8.1**).

When a winding-up order has been made, the court sends three sealed copies to the official receiver (IR 1986, r. 4.21(1)). The official receiver sends one of those copies by post to the company at its registered office (r. 4.21(2)). (If there is no registered office the company's copy may be sent to the company's principal, or last known principal, place of business, or be served on such person or persons as the court directs: r. 4.21(2).) A second copy is forwarded to the registrar of companies (r. 4.21(3)) who must enter it in his records relating to the company (Insolvency Act 1986, s. 130(1)) and officially notify receipt of it in the *London Gazette* (Companies Act 2006, ss. 1077 and 1078(1) and (2)).

If a winding-up order made against a registered company has been erroneously made against the wrong company, it may be rescinded and the registrar of companies may be ordered to correct the records at Companies House (*Re Calmex Ltd* [1989] 1 All ER 485).

Having received copies of a winding-up order the official receiver must forthwith cause the order to be gazetted and may also advertise notice of the order in such other manner as he or she thinks fit (IR 1986, r. 4.21(4)).

A copy of the *Gazette* containing the notice of the order may, in any proceedings, be produced as conclusive evidence that the order was made on the date specified in the notice (IR 1986, r. 12A.37(2)).

If a winding-up order that has been gazetted is varied by the court, the official receiver must cause the variation of the order to be gazetted (r. 12A.37(3)). If an order has been erroneously or inaccurately gazetted, the official receiver must cause a further entry to be made in the *Gazette* for the purpose of correcting the error or inaccuracy (r. 12A.37(3)).

CORRECTION OF ERRORS

An application for permission to amend an error in a petition discovered after the winding-up **82.89** order has been made should be made to the member of court staff in charge of the winding-up

PROCEDURAL RULES

83.2   A creditor's application for an order making an individual bankrupt must be made by petition (a 'bankruptcy petition') presented to the court under the Insolvency Act 1986, s. 264. An individual subject to bankruptcy proceedings is usually referred to as a 'debtor'. As a bankruptcy petition is a proceeding under the Insolvency Act 1986 it is an insolvency proceeding for the purposes of the Insolvency Rules 1986 (SI 1986/1925) (IR 1986), by r. 13.7 of those rules. The scope of the IR 1986 and general rules on track allocation, forms, time limits and the meaning of 'business day' are described in **82.3** to **82.7**.

JURISDICTION

Scope of English bankruptcy law

83.3   Only debtors with a sufficient connection with England and Wales can be made bankrupt under English law. The required connection is specified in the Insolvency Act 1986, ss. 263I (adjudicator's jurisdiction over a debtor's application) and 265 (conditions for presenting a creditor's petition), which are in the same terms. A debtor may be made bankrupt if either the debtor's centre of main interests (COMI) is in England and Wales or the COMI is outside the European Union or is in Denmark and:

(a) the debtor is domiciled in England and Wales; or

(b) at any time within the three years ending with the day the petition is presented or the application is made, the debtor:

    (i) has been ordinarily resident, or has had a place of business, in England and Wales; or

    (ii) has carried on business in England and Wales.

It is sufficient, for the purposes of condition (b)(ii), that the debtor was a member of a firm or partnership carrying on business, or that an agent or manager carried on the business for the debtor or for a firm or partnership of which the debtor was a member.

Section 263I and the current wording of s. 265 are the result of amendments made by the Enterprise and Regulatory Reform Act 2013, sch. 18 and sch. 19, para. 17. Explanatory notes to that Act state that the intention was to clarify but not change the rules on jurisdiction. However, it seems that under the new wording, a debtor whose COMI is in any part of the European Union other than England, Wales or Denmark, but who has an establishment in England and Wales cannot now be made bankrupt here in secondary or territorial proceedings, even though s. 264(1)(c) continues to provide for a petition to be presented in respect of such a debtor (see **83.5**).

Where domicile is in dispute, the onus is on the petitioner to establish that the debtor is domiciled in England and Wales, but if the petitioner establishes that England and Wales is the debtor's domicile of origin, the onus is on the debtor to prove a change of domicile (*Henwood v Barlow Clowes International Ltd* [2007] EWHC 1579 (Ch), [2007] BPIR 1329).

Under Regulation (EC) No. 1346/2000, an individual's COMI ought to be the place where he or she can be contacted by creditors (*Skjevesland v Geveran Trading Co. Ltd* [2002] EWHC 2898 (Ch), [2003] BCC 391 at [60]).

From 26 June 2017 Regulation 1346/2000 is replaced by Regulation (EU) 2015/848. Article 3 of the new Regulation adds new rules for determining an individual's COMI. In the case of an individual exercising an independent business or professional activity, the COMI shall be presumed to be that individual's principal place of business in the absence of proof to the contrary. But that presumption shall only apply if the individual's principal place of business has not been moved to another member State within the three-month period prior to the request for the opening of insolvency proceedings. In the case of any other individual, the COMI shall be presumed to be the place of the individual's habitual residence in the absence of proof to the contrary. This presumption shall only apply if the habitual residence has not been moved to another member State within the six-month period prior to the request for the opening of insolvency proceedings.

Appropriate court

Both the High Court and County Court have bankruptcy jurisdiction (Insolvency Act 1986, **83.4** s. 373(1)). Most bankruptcy petitions must be presented in the County Court. In order to determine which court is the appropriate one for presentation of a bankruptcy petition, it is necessary to establish:

(a) whether the proceedings are allocated to the London insolvency district (see **82.8**) by IR 1986, r. 7.10ZA;

(b) whether the debtor is resident in England and Wales. If the petitioner is unable to ascertain the place where the debtor resides or, if the debtor carries on business in England and Wales, both where the debtor resides and where the debtor carries on business, the petition is allocated to the London insolvency district (r. 7.10ZA(c)(i)) and must be presented to the High Court (r. 6.9A(2)).

A bankruptcy petition in respect of a debtor who is resident in England and Wales is allocated by r. 7.10ZA to the London insolvency district if, within the six months immediately preceding the presentation of the petition:

(a) the debtor carried on business within the area of the London insolvency district:

   (i) for the greater part of those six months; or

   (ii) for a longer period in those six months than in any other insolvency district (r. 7.10ZA(a)(i)); or

(b) the debtor did not carry on business in England and Wales but resided within the area of the London insolvency district for:

   (i) the greater part of those six months; or

   (ii) a longer period in those six months than in any other insolvency district (r. 7.10ZA(a)(ii)).

Such a petition must be presented to the High Court if the petition debt is £50,000 or more, or to the County Court at Central London if it is less than £50,000 (r. 6.9A(1)). The District Judges assigned to bankruptcy work in the County Court at Central London sit in the Thomas More Building of the Royal Courts of Justice.

A bankruptcy petition in respect of a debtor who is not resident in England and Wales is allocated to the London insolvency district if, within the six months immediately preceding the presentation of the petition:

(a) the debtor carried on business within the area of the London insolvency district (r. 7.10ZA(a)(iii)); or

(b) the debtor did not carry on business in England and Wales but resided within the area of the London insolvency district (r. 7.10ZA(a)(iv)); or

(c) the debtor neither carried on business nor resided in England and Wales (r. 7.10ZA(a)(v)).

In circumstances (a) and (b) the petition must be presented to the High Court if the petition debt is £50,000 or more, or to the County Court at Central London if it is less than £50,000 (r. 6.9A(1)). In circumstance (c) the petition must be presented to the High Court (r. 6.9A(2)).

Bankruptcy proceedings allocated to the London insolvency district when they are commenced in the County Court may only be commenced in the County Court at Central London (Insolvency (Commencement of Proceedings) and Insolvency Rules 1986 (Amendment) Rules 2014 (SI 2014/817), r. 3(1)).

If proceedings are not allocated to the London insolvency district, the petition must be presented to 'the debtor's own County Court hearing centre' if the debtor is resident in England and Wales (IR 1986, r. 6.9A(3)).

For a debtor who has carried on business in England and Wales within the six months immediately preceding the presentation of the petition, the debtor's own County Court hearing centre is the hearing centre which serves the insolvency district where for the longest period during those six months:

(a) the debtor carried on business, or
(b) the principal place of business was located, if business was carried on in more than one insolvency district (r. 6.9A(4)(a)).

For a debtor who has not carried on business in England and Wales within the six months immediately preceding the presentation of the petition, the debtor's own County Court hearing centre is the hearing centre which serves the insolvency district where the debtor resided for the longest period during those six months (r. 6.9A(4)(b)).

If a debtor is not resident in England and Wales, but was resident or carried on business here within the six months before presentation of the petition, unless proceedings are allocated to the London insolvency district, the petition may be presented either to the debtor's own County Court hearing centre or to the High Court (r. 6.9A(5)).

No insolvency districts have been designated by the Lord Chancellor (under the Insolvency Act 1986, s. 374) other than the London insolvency district. SI 2014/817, r. 3 and sch. 1, are drafted on the basis that, outside the London insolvency district, the area served by a County Court hearing centre is its insolvency district. In the County Court, outside the London insolvency district, a bankruptcy petition that IR 1986 requires to be presented to the debtor's own County Court hearing centre may only be presented there (SI 2014/817, r. 3(2)), unless, for that hearing centre, SI 2014/817, sch. 1, lists an alternative hearing centre, in which case the listed alternative hearing centre must be used (SI 2014/817, r. 3(3)).

The debtor's own County Court hearing centre can be found by entering the postcode of the place where the debtor carried on business or resided, as appropriate, and selecting 'bankruptcy' in the Court and Tribunal Finder at https://courttribunalfinder.service.gov.uk/.

There are special rules for a petition presented by a minister of the Crown or a government department (rr. 6.9A(1) and 7.10ZA(b)) and for members of partnerships which are subject to winding-up proceedings (rr. 6.9A(2) and 7.10ZA(c)(ii)).

A bankruptcy petition which is presented at a time when an IVA is in force for the debtor must be presented to the court or County Court hearing centre in which proceedings relating to the IVA have been taken (r. 6.9A(6)).

A bankruptcy petition must contain sufficient information to establish that it is presented in the appropriate court or County Court hearing centre (r. 6.9A(7)). See para. 2 of the prescribed forms of petition (forms 6.7, 6.8, 6.9 and 6.10).

WHO MAY PRESENT A BANKRUPTCY PETITION?

83.5 By the Insolvency Act 1986, s. 264(1), a petition for an order making an individual bankrupt may be presented by:

(a) one of the individual's unsecured creditors, or by two or more unsecured creditors jointly (see **83.6** to **83.27**); or
(b) the supervisor of, or any person (other than the individual) who is for the time being bound by, an approved IVA (see **83.32**).

In addition, s. 264(1)(c) continues to provide that office holders in main insolvency proceedings elsewhere in the European Union (apart from Denmark) concerning the individual can petition for his or her bankruptcy in England and Wales. However, as pointed out in **83.3**, it seems that such an individual (whose COMI would be in the EU State in which the main proceedings were opened) cannot now be made bankrupt in England and Wales. What is said in **82.17** about who may apply for a winding-up order in England and Wales in relation to an English company whose COMI is in another EU State (apart from Denmark) applies equally to applying for the bankruptcy of an English debtor in that situation, with the Insolvency Act 1986, s. 264, rather than s. 124 being the applicable English legislation.

A bankruptcy order which is made on a creditor's petition in accordance with the Insolvency Act 1986 meets the requirements of **art 1.** of the First **Protocol** to the European Convention on Human Rights in the **Human Rights Act 1998, sch. 1**, and is not, provided the insolvency law is properly applied by the court, a disproportionate exercise of power (*Shrimpton v Darbys Solicitors LLP* [2011] EWHC 3796 (Ch), [2012] BPIR 631).

CREDITOR'S PETITION

Who may petition as a creditor?

For the purposes of the law of bankruptcy, the term 'creditor' is given a very wide definition in the Insolvency Act 1986, s. 383 (which must be read with s. 382). However, a bankruptcy petition can be filed only in respect of a debt for a liquidated sum payable to the petitioning creditor (or one or more of joint petitioners) immediately or at some certain, future time (s. 267(2)(b)) and the debt must be at least £5,000 (s. 267(2)(a) and (4)).

83.6

The term 'liquidated sum' is not defined in the legislation. A debt for a liquidated sum 'must be a pre-ascertained liability under the agreement which gives rise to it' (*McGuinness v Norwich and Peterborough Building Society* [2011] EWCA Civ 1286, [2012] BPIR 145 at [36]). A contractual liability is for a liquidated sum if the amount due is to be ascertained in accordance with a contractual formula or machinery which will produce a figure (*McGuinness v Norwich and Peterborough Building Society* at [36]). A claim in tort is invariably unliquidated, because a judicial process is required to ascertain the damages due (*McGuinness v Norwich and Peterborough Building Society* at [36]). A claim for liquidated damages is a debt for a liquidated sum (*McGuinness v Norwich and Peterborough Building Society* at [37]–[41]). Whether a claim under a guarantee of another person's debt is a debt for a liquidated sum depends on the wording of the guarantee, as discussed in detail in *McGuinness v Norwich and Peterborough Building Society*.

A judgment debt is a debt for a liquidated sum. For discussion of whether a bankruptcy petition should be adjourned because of an application to appeal against the petition judgment debt see *Society of Lloyd's v Beaumont* [2006] BPIR 1021.

For the purpose of determining standing to petition for bankruptcy, a solicitor's bill is for an unliquidated sum, unless the amount of the bill is liquidated by judicial assessment or determination or by the client's agreement (*Truex v Toll* [2009] EWHC 396 (Ch), [2009] 1 WLR 2121; see *Phillips and Co. v Bath Housing Cooperative Ltd* [2012] EWCA Civ 1591, [2013] BPIR 102). The fact that the period of 12 months for applying for assessment of the bill has passed without an application being made is irrelevant. A mere acknowledgment by the client is not an agreement sufficient to make the debt liquidated: there must be an agreement from which the client is bound not to resile.

A secured creditor cannot petition (s. 267(2)(b)) unless the petition states that if a bankruptcy order is made, the creditor will surrender the security for the benefit of all creditors (s. 269(1)(a)). A partially secured creditor may divide the debt into a secured and an unsecured part and petition in respect of the unsecured part (s. 269(1)(b) and (2)).

Commentary

In r. 6.5(4)(a) the terms 'counterclaim' and 'cross-demand' comprehend counterclaims and cross-demands that are not legal or equitable set-offs, and a statutory demand based on dishonour of a cheque or other bill of exchange may be set aside if the debtor has a counterclaim or cross-demand, even if it would not be a defence to the claim on the bill or cheque (*Hofer v Strawson* [1999] 2 BCLC 336). A contractual bar to asserting a set-off cannot prevent the court granting an application under r. 6.5(4)(a) (*Stone v Vallance* [2008] BPIR 236). If a court has already dismissed proceedings brought by the debtor advancing the counterclaim etc. which is said to equal or exceed the debt claimed in a statutory demand, the bankruptcy court may nevertheless set aside the statutory demand if persuaded that an appeal against the first decision has a realistic, as opposed to fanciful, prospect of success (*Society of Lloyd's v Bowman* [2003] EWCA Civ 1886, [2004] BPIR 324).

The test for setting aside a bankruptcy statutory demand when the debtor claims to have a counterclaim, set-off or cross-demand, or disputes the debt, is whether, in the court's opinion, the debtor has raised a 'genuine triable issue' (**PD Insolvency Proceedings, para. 13.3.4**; *Kellar v BBR Graphic Engineers (Yorks) Ltd* [2002] BPIR 544; *Crossley-Cooke v Europanel (UK) Ltd* [2010] EWHC 124 (Ch), [2010] BPIR 561). The court cannot find that a triable issue is 'genuine', or that the grounds of a dispute appear to be 'substantial' (IR 1986, r 6.5(4)(b)), simply by finding that the debtor's case is arguable. There has to be something to suggest that the debtor's assertion is sustainable, and this may mean that the 'genuine triable issue' criterion is the same as having a real prospect of success (*Collier v P. and M. J. Wright (Holdings) Ltd* [2007] EWCA Civ 1329, [2008] 1 WLR 643 per Arden LJ at [21]).

Rule 6.5(4)(c) does not apply if the statutory demand states that the creditor will release security for the benefit of all the creditors if a bankruptcy order is made (referring to the Insolvency Act 1986, s. 269(1)(a); see **83.6**) (*1st Credit Finance Ltd v Bartram* [2010] EWHC 2910 (Ch), [2011] BPIR 1). Under r. 6.5(4)(d) a statutory demand will be set aside if no bankruptcy order would be made on a petition based on not complying with it, for example, because it is for an unprovable debt (*Levy v Legal Services Commission* [2001] 1 All ER 895).

If the amount of the debt is overstated in the demand, the debtor will be deemed to have complied with it if the correct amount is paid within the time allowed (IR 1986, r. 6.25(3)).

A creditor's petition in respect of a debt or debts cannot be presented at a time when there is an outstanding application to set aside a statutory demand served in respect of the debt or any of the debts (Insolvency Act 1986, s. 267(2)(d)). An application made out of time, and for which the court has not extended time, does not count for the purposes of s. 267(2)(d) (*Re Chohan* (2000) LTL 7/11/2000), nor does an appeal against a dismissed application (*Hurst v Bennett* (2001) *The Independent*, 9 April 2001). After the court has made an order dismissing an application to set aside a statutory demand, a petition may be presented either from a time stated in the court's order (as required by IR 1986, r. 6.5(6)) or, if no time is specified, as soon as reasonably practicable (*Darbyshire v Turpin* [2013] EWHC 954 (Ch), [2013] BPIR 558).

Usually, a court's decision to set aside a statutory demand does not determine any substantive dispute about the existence or size of the debt demanded. It follows that on an appeal against a decision to set aside, further evidence concerning that dispute may be admitted even if it does not satisfy the tests established in *Ladd v Marshall* [1954] 1 WLR 1489 (see **75.16** and **75.17**) (*Heavy Duty Parts Ltd v Anelay* [2004] EWHC 960 (Ch), [2004] BPIR 729). The court should consider: (a) the importance of the evidence to the party seeking to adduce it, (b) the reasons for not adducing it in the court below, (c) the extent of any prejudice which its admission would cause the opposing party, and (d) the overriding objective (*Sadrolashrafi v Marvel International Food Logistics Ltd* [2004] EWHC 777 (Ch), [2004] BPIR 834 at [16]).

If the person who served the statutory demand ought to have known of the circumstances which would lead to it being set aside, the costs of applying under r. 6.4 may be awarded on an indemnity basis (*Re Kirkman-Moeller* [2005] EWHC 205 (Ch), LTL 19/1/2005).

On an application to set aside a statutory demand, the court may make a consent order dismissing the application, setting aside the demand, or giving permission to withdraw the application, without the attendance of the parties (**PD Insolvency Proceedings, para. 16.3(1)**). Such orders may be made with or without an order for costs as may be agreed. A consent order dismissing an application to set aside a statutory demand will give permission to present a petition on or after the seventh day after the date of the order, unless a different date is agreed.

Form and contents of creditor's petition

There are three prescribed forms for a creditor's petition (forms 6.7, 6.8 and 6.9 in IR **83.9** 1986, sch. 4). Form 6.7 is used when the petition is based on failure to comply with a statutory demand for a liquidated sum payable immediately. Form 6.8 is used when the petition is based on failure to comply with a statutory demand for a liquidated sum payable at a future date. Form 6.9 is used for a petition based on partially or wholly unsatisfied execution.

If the petition is based on failure to comply with a statutory demand and more than four months have elapsed since the demand was served, the petition must include a statement explaining the reasons for the delay (r. 6.12(7)).

There is detailed advice on creditors' bankruptcy petitions in **PD Insolvency Proceedings, paras 14.1 to 14.7.**

Verification of creditor's petition

A creditor's petition must be verified by a statement of truth (IR 1986, rr. 6.10(1) and 6.12(1)) **83.10** using form 6.13A in IR 1986, sch. 4. The statement of truth must repeat the reasons given in the petition for waiting more than four months to rely on a statutory demand and must add an explanation of the circumstances which have contributed to late presentation of the petition.

Rule 6.12(4) provides that the statement of truth must be authenticated by:

(a) the petitioner (or if there are two or more petitioners, any one of them); or

(b) some person such as a director, company secretary or similar company officer, or a solicitor, who has been concerned in the matters giving rise to the presentation of the petition; or

(c) some responsible person who is duly authorised to make the affidavit or witness statement and has the requisite knowledge of those matters.

In cases (b) and (c) the person authenticating the statement of truth must state the capacity in which, and the authority by which, he or she does so, and the means of knowing the matters verified (r. 6.12(5)).

Filing of creditor's petition and fixing of venue

A creditor's bankruptcy petition must be filed in court together with one copy for service on **83.11** the debtor (IR 1986, r. 6.10(1) and (3)). A court officer seals all copies of the petition and fixes a venue for hearing it, which is endorsed on all copies (r. 6.10(3) and (5)).

The court must forthwith send notice of the petition to the Chief Land Registrar to be noted in the register of pending actions (r. 6.13). If the petition is dismissed, or withdrawn with the court's permission, the court must order the registration of the petition as a pending action to be vacated (r. 6.27). Damages cannot be recovered for breach of the duty imposed by r. 6.13 (or, it is submitted, r. 6.27) (*Poulton's Trustee v Ministry of Justice* [2010] EWCA Civ 392, [2011] Ch 1).

Fee and deposit

83.12   On filing a creditor's bankruptcy petition, a court fee of £280 must be paid (**CPFO, fee 3.1(b)**). The petitioner must deposit £990 as security for the administration fee which will become payable to the official receiver on the making of a bankruptcy order (Insolvency Act 1986, s. 415(3); Insolvency Proceedings (Fees) Order 2016 (SI 2016/692), arts 2 and 4(2)–(4)). A petition cannot be filed unless the receipt for the deposit is produced (IR 1986, r. 6.10(2)). For details of the payment procedure see **PD Insolvency Proceedings, para. 14.4**. The deposit will be used to discharge the official receiver's administration fee and must be used to discharge that fee to the extent that the assets in the bankrupt's estate are insufficient (SI 2016/692, art. 4(4)); the administration fee is £2,775 (sch. 1). The court will transmit the deposit to its official receiver (art. 4(3)). If a bankruptcy order is made, any part of the deposit which is not required to pay the administration fee must be returned (art. 4(5)). If the petition is dismissed or withdrawn, the deposit must be repaid less an administration fee of £50 (art. 4(9)). The court fee is not repayable.

Service of creditor's petition

83.13   The debtor must be served personally with a sealed copy of a creditor's petition (IR 1986, r. 6.14(1)). If the court is satisfied by written evidence that prompt personal service cannot be effected because the debtor is avoiding service, or for any other cause, it may make an order for substituted service to be effected in such manner as it thinks just (r. 6.14(2)). **PD Insolvency Proceedings, para. 13.2.4**, sets out what must normally be done to justify an order for substituted service. If the debtor dies before service of the petition, the court may order it to be served on the deceased's personal representatives, or on such other persons as it thinks just (IR 1986, r. 6.16).

If a bankruptcy petition asks for the opening of secondary proceedings against a debtor who is already the subject of main insolvency proceedings in another EU State (see **83.5**), a copy of the petition must be sent to a member State liquidator appointed in the main proceedings (IR 1986, r. 6.14(5)). Rule 6.14(5) does not make allowance for the member State liquidator being the petitioner.

Proof of service

83.14   Service of a creditor's bankruptcy petition must be proved by a certificate of service (IR 1986, r. 6.15A(1)) using form 6.17A (personal service) or form 6.18A (substituted service) in IR 1986, sch. 4. The certificate of service must be filed in court as soon as reasonably practicable after service, and in any event not less than five business days (see **82.7**) before the hearing of the petition (r. 6.15A(4)).

Control of transactions and litigation while petition is pending

83.15   If a bankruptcy order is made, all dispositions of the debtor's property since the bankruptcy petition was presented (or application was made) are void unless made with the consent of the court or subsequently ratified by the court (Insolvency Act 1986, s. 284). For control of litigation while a bankruptcy petition or application is pending see **84.27**.

Appointment of interim receiver

83.16   At any time after the presentation of a bankruptcy petition, but before a bankruptcy order is made, the court may, under the Insolvency Act 1986, s. 286, appoint the official receiver (or, from 6 April 2017, an insolvency practitioner) as interim receiver of the debtor's property. It must be shown that the appointment is necessary for the protection of the debtor's property (s. 286(1)).

An application for the appointment of an interim receiver may be made by the debtor or any creditor, or, if the proceedings are secondary proceedings (see **83.5**), a temporary administrator or member State liquidator appointed in the main proceedings (IR 1986, r. 6.51(1)). The application (see **84.1** to **84.6**) must be supported by a witness statement showing (r. 6.51(2)):

(a) the grounds for the appointment;
(b) whether or not the official receiver has been informed of the application and has been provided with a copy of it;
(c) whether, to the applicant's knowledge, an IVA has been proposed or is in force;
(d) the applicant's estimate of the value of the property or business in respect of which the interim receiver is to be appointed.

The applicant must send copies of the application and evidence to the official receiver (r. 6.51(4)), who may attend the hearing of the application and make representations (r. 6.51(5)). If it is not possible to send these copies, the official receiver must at least be informed of the application in time to attend the hearing (r. 6.51(4)).

The court may make the appointment applied for, on such terms as it thinks just, if satisfied that sufficient grounds are shown for the appointment (r. 6.51(6)).

Before an order appointing the official receiver as interim receiver of a debtor may be issued, the applicant must deposit with the official receiver such sum as the court directs to cover remuneration and expenses (r. 6.53(1)). Alternatively, security for the amount may be given if the official receiver agrees (r. 6.53(1)).

From time to time the official receiver may apply to the court to order a further amount to be deposited or secured, and if the order is not complied with within two days of service, the court may discharge the official receiver's appointment as interim receiver (r. 6.53(2)).

The court's order of appointment must state the nature of and describe the property to which the appointment relates and state what duties are to be performed in relation to the debtor's affairs (r. 6.52(1)). For control of litigation against a debtor when an interim receiver has been appointed see **84.28**.

Permission to withdraw a petition

A bankruptcy petition cannot be withdrawn without the court's permission (Insolvency Act 1986, s. 266(2)). Permission to withdraw a creditor's petition will not be given until the petition is heard (IR 1986, r. 6.32(3)). If a creditor has given notice of intention to appear at the hearing, or if the court so orders, a witness statement must be filed specifying the grounds of the application and the circumstances in which it is made (r. 6.32(1)). If any payment has been made to the petitioner since the petition was filed, the witness statement must include the information set out in r. 6.32(2), which will reveal whether the payment might be avoided under the Insolvency Act 1986, s. 284, if another creditor were to be substituted as petitioner (see **83.20**) and a bankruptcy order made. **83.17**

If the petition has not been served and either form 6.21 (see **83.19**) or a statement that no notices have been received from supporting or opposing creditors is given by or on behalf of the petitioning creditor, the court may make a consent order, giving permission to withdraw the petition (with no order for costs), without the attendance of the parties (**PD Insolvency Proceedings, para. 16.3(2)**).

Opposition by debtor

If the debtor intends to oppose a creditor's bankruptcy petition, a notice specifying the grounds of objection must be filed in court at least five business days (see **82.7**) before the day fixed for the hearing (IR 1986, r. 6.21). A copy must be sent to the petitioner or the petitioner's solicitor (r. 6.21). **83.18**

Notice of appearance

83.19   By IR 1986, r. 6.23, any creditor wishing to appear on the hearing of a creditor's bankruptcy petition must send notice to the petitioner to arrive not later than 4 p.m. on the business day (see **82.7**) before the date appointed for the hearing (or the date of an adjournment).

A notice of appearance must be in form 6.20 in IR 1986, sch. 4, and must state whether the appearance will be to support or oppose the petition (r. 6.23(2)(b)). The notice must also state the name and address of the person giving it, and any telephone number and reference which may be required for communication with that person or with any other person (to be also specified in the notice) authorised to speak or act on behalf of the person giving the notice (r. 6.23(2)(a)). The notice must also state the amount and nature of the debt claimed by the person giving the notice (r. 6.23(2)(c)).

The petitioner must prepare for the court a list of persons who have given notice of intention to appear, stating whether they support or oppose the petition, and must hand a copy of the list to the court before the commencement of the hearing (IR 1986, r. 6.24; prescribed form is form 6.21 in sch. 4).

A person who has not given notice in accordance with r. 6.23 may appear on the hearing of the petition only with the permission of the court (r. 6.23(4)).

The petitioner must add to the list required by r. 6.24 the name of anyone given permission by the court to appear without having given proper notice (r. 6.24(4)).

Substitution of petitioner

83.20   When a bankruptcy petition is pending, IR 1986, r. 6.30, permits the substitution of a new petitioner if the original petitioner:

(a) is subsequently found not entitled to petition;

(b) consents to withdraw the petition;

(c) consents to allow the petition to be dismissed;

(d) consents to an adjournment of the petition;

(e) fails to appear in support of the petition when it is called on in court on the day originally fixed for the hearing or on a day to which it is adjourned; or

(f) appears when the petition is called on in court but does not apply for an order in the terms of the prayer of the petition.

Any creditor who has (a) given notice of intention to appear on the hearing, (b) is desirous of prosecuting the petition, and (c) would have been in a position to petition for the debtor's bankruptcy on the date on which the present petition was presented, may be substituted as petitioner (IR 1986, r. 6.30(2)).

If a bankruptcy petition asks for the opening of secondary proceedings (see **83.5**), and the member State liquidator appointed in the main proceedings is not the petitioner, that member State liquidator may be substituted as petitioner if he or she is desirous of prosecuting the petition (r. 6.239).

It is also possible to make a change of carriage order at the hearing of the petition (see **83.26**).

Change of venue

83.21   **Extension of time for hearing**   If a creditor's bankruptcy petition has not been served, the petitioner may apply under IR 1986, r. 6.28, for the court to appoint another venue for the hearing. The application (see **84.1** to **84.6**) must state the reasons why the petition has not been served (r. 6.28(2)). If another date is appointed, the petitioner must forthwith notify any creditor who has given notice of intention to appear on the hearing.

Adjournment If the court adjourns the hearing of a creditor's bankruptcy petition, the **83.22** petitioner must (unless the court otherwise directs) notify the debtor and any creditor who has given notice of intention to appear on the hearing (IR 1986, r. 6.29).

Expedited hearing Normally the hearing of a creditor's bankruptcy petition cannot take **83.23** place until 14 days after it was served on the debtor (IR 1986, r. 6.18(1)). However, the court may, under r. 6.18(2), hear the petition at an earlier date if:

(a) it appears that the debtor has absconded;
(b) the court is satisfied that it is a proper case for an expedited hearing; or
(c) the debtor consents.

HEARING A CREDITOR'S PETITION
AND MAKING THE ORDER

Orders the court may make

On the hearing of a creditor's bankruptcy petition, the court may make a bankruptcy order if **83.24** satisfied that the statements in the petition are true, and that the debt on which it is founded has not been paid, or secured or compounded for (or, if it is a future debt, that the debtor has no reasonable prospect of being able to pay when it falls due) (Insolvency Act 1986, s. 271(1); IR 1986, r. 6.25(1)). The payment referred to in the Insolvency Act 1986, s. 271(1), is a payment which is unconditional in the sense that it is not liable to be avoided under s. 284(1) if a bankruptcy order is made (*Smith v Ian Simpson and Co.* [2001] Ch 239). The court will normally be satisfied that a debt has not been paid, or secured or compounded for if a certificate (known as a certificate of continuing debt) is provided in the form set out in **PD Insolvency Proceedings, para. 14.5**.

If the petition is in respect of a judgment debt, or a sum ordered to be paid by a court, the court may stay or dismiss the petition if an appeal is pending from the judgment or order, or if execution of the judgment has been stayed (IR 1986, r. 6.25(2)). On a petition in respect of a judgment debt, if there is no appeal against or application to stay judgment, the only grounds on which the correctness of the judgment may be challenged are that: (a) it was obtained fraudulently, (b) it was obtained by collusion between the debtor and the claimant, or (c) there was a miscarriage of justice (*Dawodu v American Express Bank* [2001] BPIR 983).

A petition will not be dismissed on the ground that the amount of the debt was overstated in a statutory demand, unless the debtor notified the creditor, within the three weeks allowed for complying with the demand, that he or she disputed its validity (r. 6.25(3)).

Ordinarily, a debtor will not be permitted to re-argue, on the hearing of a petition, a contention that the statutory demand was invalid if that contention has already been rejected on a substantive hearing of an application to set aside the statutory demand (*Turner v Royal Bank of Scotland plc* [2000] BPIR 683). The same applies if a contention advanced in preparation for an application to set aside was abandoned (*Adams v Mason Bullock* [2004] EWHC 2910 (Ch), [2005] BPIR 241). The question may be reopened if there has been a change of circumstances (*Turner v Royal Bank of Scotland* at p. 294). The principle does not apply if there has been no reasoned determination at all at the earlier stage (*Commissioners of Inland Revenue v Lee-Phipps* [2003] BPIR 803; *Vaidya v Wijayawardhana* [2010] EWHC 716 (Ch), [2010] BPIR 1016). If no reasons were given for dismissing the application to set aside the statutory demand without a hearing, the court cannot infer that a particular contention of the debtor had been considered and rejected (*Vaidya v Wijayawardhana*).

If either form 6.21 (see **83.19**) or a statement that no notices have been received from supporting or opposing creditors is given by or on behalf of the petitioning creditor, the court

Commentary

may make a consent order, dismissing the petition, with or without an order for costs as may be agreed, without the attendance of the parties (**PD Insolvency Proceedings, para. 16.3(2)**).

Non-appearance of creditor

83.25   If the petitioning creditor fails to appear on the hearing of the petition, no subsequent petition against the same debtor may be presented by the same creditor in respect of the same debt, unless the court to which the first petition was presented gives permission (IR 1986, r. 6.26). There is detailed consideration of r. 6.26 in *Omgate Ltd v Gordon* [2001] BPIR 909.

Change of carriage of creditor's petition

83.26   At the hearing of a creditor's petition, the court may, under IR 1986, r. 6.31, give another creditor carriage of the petition if it appears that the petitioning creditor:

(a) intends by any means to secure the postponement, adjournment or withdrawal of the petition; or

(b) does not intend to prosecute the petition, either diligently or at all.

After a change of carriage order the petition is still based on the original petitioner's debt, unlike the position where there is a substitution of petitioner.

Settlement and transmission of bankruptcy order

83.27   If a bankruptcy order is made on a creditor's petition, the court will settle it (IR 1986, r. 6.33(1)). Two sealed copies will be sent to the official receiver, who will forthwith send one to the bankrupt (r. 6.34(1)).

The official receiver will send a notice to the Chief Land Registrar for registration in the register of writs and orders affecting land, cause the order to be gazetted, cause prescribed information to be entered in the individual insolvency register, and may also advertise notice of the order in such other manner as he or she thinks fit (rr. 6.34(2) and 6A.4). However, the bankrupt or a creditor may apply to the court for an order requiring the official receiver not to do these things pending a further order by the court (r. 6.34(3)). An application for such an order (see **84.1** to **84.6**) must be supported by a witness statement stating the grounds for applying (r. 6.34(3)). If the order is made, the applicant must deliver it forthwith to the official receiver (r. 6.34(4)).

For control of litigation against a bankrupt see **84.29**.

DEBTOR'S APPLICATION

83.28   An individual may apply to an adjudicator to be made bankrupt in accordance with the Insolvency Act 1986, ss. 263H–263O (s. 263H(1)). The only ground for such an application is that the individual is unable to pay his or her debts (s. 263H(2)). The contents of the application are specified in IR 1986, r. 6.38, sch. 2A and sch. 2B. It must be submitted electronically (r. 6.39).

The debtor must pay an adjudicator's administration fee of £130 and a deposit of £550 for the official receiver's administration fee (which is £1,900) (Insolvency Proceedings (Fees) Order 2016 (SI 2016/692), art. 2 and sch. 1). The rules on how the deposit is applied or repaid are the same as for a creditor's petition (see **83.12**).

The adjudicator must determine the application within the determination period (r. 6.42(1)), which is 28 days from the date the application is made (r. 6.43(1)). This can be extended by 14 days if the adjudicator requests further information from the debtor (r. 6.43(2)). Failure to make a determination within the determination period is a refusal (r. 6.43(3)). The

an interim order and will refuse one if it is clear that bankruptcy will be preferable to an IVA (*Hurst v Kroll Buchler Phillips Ltd* [2002] EWHC 2855 (Ch), [2003] BPIR 872).

If there is no application for an interim order, and the fast-track procedure is not being used, the nominee reports to the debtor's creditors in accordance with the Insolvency Act 1986, s. 256A, and IR 1986, r. 5.14A.

In the fast-track procedure, if the official receiver agrees to act as nominee, the proposal is not reported to the court. Instead the official receiver invites creditors to vote by post on the proposal (IR 1986, rr. 5.39 to 5.43).

Approval of voluntary arrangement

If a meeting of creditors is held, its chairman must report the result to the court (Insolvency Act 1986, s. 259(1); IR 1986, r. 5.27).   **83.31**

If the result is that the creditors have declined to approve the proposal, the court may discharge any interim order (Insolvency Act 1986, s. 259(2)).

If the creditors accept the proposal, the IVA will take effect as if made at the meeting (s. 260(1) and (2)) and any interim order will cease to have effect 28 days after the chairman's report is made to the court (s. 260(4)). The chairman must report the approval of the IVA to the Secretary of State for entry in the register of IVAs (IR 1986, rr. 5.28 and 5.29). If a bankruptcy petition is pending against the debtor, it is deemed to have been dismissed when the interim order ceases to have effect, unless the court orders otherwise (Insolvency Act 1986, s. 260(5)). If the debtor is an undischarged bankrupt, the court must annul the bankruptcy order on an application made by the bankrupt or by the official receiver (s. 261; IR 1986, rr. 5.51 to 5.56, 5.60 and 5.61).

It is unnecessary to obtain the court's approval of an IVA which has been approved by a creditors' meeting, but a dissentient creditor may apply to the court under s. 262 to revoke or suspend the approval because the creditor's interests are prejudiced by the IVA and/or the meeting was vitiated by a material irregularity. Such an application must be made within 28 days after the chairman's report is made to the court. For the procedure if a revocation or suspension order is made see IR 1986, r. 5.30. An application under the Insolvency Act 1986, s. 262, may also be made by the nominee, the official receiver or the debtor. If the meeting declined to approve the proposal, those persons can also apply under s. 262 for an order directing a further meeting to reconsider the proposal on the ground that there was a material irregularity in the first meeting.

In the fast-track procedure, the official receiver must notify the Secretary of State whether the proposal has been approved or rejected by the creditors (s. 263C). If the official receiver reports approval, the IVA takes effect (s. 263D(1) and (2)) and the court must annul the bankruptcy order on the application of the official receiver (s. 263D(3); IR 1986, rr. 5.57 to 5.61). Section 263F provides for revocation of a fast-track IVA by the court on an application made within 28 days of notification under s. 263C. The procedure if a revocation order is made is in IR 1986, r. 5.46.

BANKRUPTCY PETITION ALLEGING DEFAULT IN CONNECTION WITH VOLUNTARY ARRANGEMENT

A bankruptcy petition may be presented against a debtor who has entered into an approved   **83.32**
IVA, but the court will not make a bankruptcy order unless it is satisfied that one of the circumstances listed in the Insolvency Act 1986, s. 276(1), exists. Those circumstances are failure by the debtor to comply with his or her obligations under the IVA, provision of false or misleading information to procure approval of the IVA, and failure of the debtor to cooperate

with the IVA supervisor. It is possible to make a bankruptcy order even though a default has been remedied (*Carter-Knight v Peat* [2000] BPIR 968). A petition may be presented by the supervisor of, or any person (other than the debtor) who is for the time being bound by, the IVA (s. 264(1)(c)) and is subject to the same rules as a creditor's petition (IR 1986, r. 6.6). If the petitioner is not the supervisor of the IVA, an extra copy of the petition must be filed for service on the supervisor (IR 1986, rr. 6.10(3) and 6.14(4)).

DEBT RELIEF ORDERS AND ADMINISTRATION ORDERS

83.33   A debtor may obtain an order dealing with specified debts within fairly low financial limits. The two forms of order are:

(a) debt relief orders (DROs) (Insolvency Act 1986, ss. 251A to 251X);

(b) administration orders (AOs) (County Courts Act 1984, ss. 112 to 117).

A DRO is made by an official receiver and normally there is no court involvement. An application must be made through an approved intermediary designated by the Secretary of State. A DRO has the same effect on debts as a bankruptcy order but applies only to the debts listed in the DRO, which can only be unsecured debts for liquidated sums payable either immediately or at a certain future time (Insolvency Act 1986, s 251A). A DRO is available only to a debtor whose finances are within the following limits: maximum total debts for liquidated sums £20,000, maximum surplus income £50 a month, maximum total value of property £1,000 (Insolvency Act 1986, sch. 4ZA, paras 6 to 8; Insolvency Proceedings (Monetary Limits) Order 1986 (SI 1986/1996), sch., part 2).

An AO is a court-administered debt management scheme for an individual with total debts of no more than £5,000, one of which must be a judgment debt. The order is made by the County Court and requires periodic instalments to pay all, or a realistic proportion, of specified debts. An AO may be made on the debtor's application, or by the court on consideration of information provided under **CPR, Part 71**. See **79.18**.

Chapter 84   Insolvency Applications and Appeals

APPLICATIONS IN INSOLVENCY PROCEEDINGS

Procedural rules

Applications in insolvency proceedings are governed by rr. 7.1 to 7.10 of the Insolvency Rules 1986 (SI 1986/1925) (IR 1986). Rules 7.1 to 7.10 apply, according to r. 7.1, to any application made to the court under the Insolvency Act 1986 or IR 1986, apart from a petition for a winding-up order or an administration application (see **chapter 82**) and a bankruptcy petition (see **chapter 83**). However, the Insolvency Rules 1986 were not made for the purposes of all provisions of the Insolvency Act 1986. By ss. 411(1) and 412(1), they could have been made only for the purposes of parts 1 to 11 (ss. 1 to 385) of the Act. Accordingly IR 1986,   **84.1** rr. 7.1 to 7.10, do not apply, for example, to the provisions in the Insolvency Act 1986, part 16, for reversing transactions defrauding creditors (*Re Banco Nacional de Cuba* [2001] 1 WLR 2039 at p. 2048). This chapter outlines the general procedural rules relating to applications in insolvency proceedings and discusses in some detail applications to stay, commence or continue litigation against persons who are the subject of insolvency proceedings.

Form and content

84.2   The prescribed form for an application in insolvency proceedings is form 7.1A (application notice) in IR 1986, sch. 4. It is necessary to state on this form whether or not the application is in insolvency proceedings which are already before the court. Applications that are not in proceedings already before the court include an application for an order forbidding the presentation of a winding-up petition (see **82.27**), an application under the Insolvency Act 1986, s. 252, for an interim order, if the applicant is not an undischarged bankrupt (see **83.30**), an application under s. 35 by a receiver or manager of a company's property, appointed out of court, for directions, and any application in a voluntary winding up (*Re Continental Assurance Co. of London plc (No. 2)* [1998] 1 BCLC 583).

Applications that are made in insolvency proceedings which are already before the court include any interim application while a petition for a winding-up, administration or bankruptcy order is pending.

Where there are two joined matters between the same parties, one of which is an insolvency application and the other requires a different form of originating process, both may be commenced by the insolvency application (**CPR, r. 7.3**; *Re Prestige Grindings Ltd* [2005] EWHC 3076 (Ch), [2006] 1 BCLC 440).

An application must state the matters set out in IR 1986, r. 7.3(1). It must be authenticated by the applicant, if acting in person, or by, or on behalf of, the applicant's solicitor (r. 7.3(3)).

Filing and fee

84.3   An insolvency application must be filed with the court, accompanied by one copy in any event, plus enough copies for service on every person who is to be served (IR 1986, r. 7.4(1)).

If an application is not in insolvency proceedings which are already before the court, the court fee is £280 (**CPFO, fee 3.5**). The court fee for an application in proceedings which are before the court is £50 if the application is by consent or without notice (**fee 3.11**), or £155 if it is with notice (**fee 3.12**).

Venue, directions, track allocation

84.4   When an application is filed, the court must fix a venue for it to be heard unless (IR 1986, r. 7.4(2)):

(a) it considers it not appropriate to do so — the court may, for example, direct that no venue is to be fixed before service and may set a time limit for service (*Re Continental Assurance Co. of London plc (No. 2)* [1998] 1 BCLC 583);

(b) the rule under which the application is brought provides otherwise; or

(c) the relevant provisions of IA 1986 or IR 1986 do not require service of the application on, or notice of it to be given to, any person, in which case the court may either fix a venue or hear the application as soon as reasonably practicable without fixing a venue (r. 7.5A).

Any application should be made, in the High Court, to the Registrar, and in the County Court, to the District Judge, unless (r. 7.6A(2) and (3)):

(a) a direction to the contrary has been given; or

(b) the Registrar or District Judge does not have power to make the order required (see **PD 2B**).

In the RCJ a general direction has been given that applications relating to the matters listed in **PD Insolvency Proceedings, para. 12.1**, are to be heard by the member of court staff in charge of the winding-up list. If the Registrar or District Judge thinks that the matter should properly be decided by the judge, it may be referred up (IR 1986, r. 7.6A(4)).

The court may at any time give such directions as it thinks just concerning service or notice of the application, the procedure on the application, and evidence (rr. 7.4(4) and 7.10(2) and (3)).

All insolvency proceedings are allocated to the multi-track by IR 1986, r. 7.51A(3), and so the provisions of the CPR concerning directions questionnaires and track allocation do not apply.

The hearing of an application is in open court, unless the court orders otherwise (IR 1986, r. 7.6A(1)). For the circumstances in which a hearing may be in private see **CPR, r. 39.2** and **PD 39A, paras 1.1 to 1.15**.

The Registrars and District Judges operate urgent applications lists for urgent and time-critical applications and may be available to hear urgent applications at other times (**PD Insolvency Proceedings 2014, para. 9.1**). A party asking for an application to be dealt with in the urgent applications list or urgently at any other time must complete the certificate set out in **para. 9.1**. Appropriate sanctions may be imposed for misuse of this service (**para. 9.1**).

Service

A sealed copy of an insolvency application must be served on the respondent named in it (IR   **84.5**
1986, r. 7.4(3)) at least 14 days before the date fixed for the hearing, unless (r. 7.4(5)):

(a) the provision of IA 1986 or IR 1986 under which the application is made specifies a different period; or
(b) the application is urgent, in which case the court may hear it immediately, even without notice to, or attendance by, other parties, or may authorise a period of service shorter than 14 days (r. 7.4(6)).

CPR, Part 6 (service of documents), apart from **rr. 6.30 to 6.47** (service of the claim form and other documents out of the jurisdiction) and **rr. 6.48 to 6.51** (service of documents from foreign courts or tribunals), applies to service in England and Wales with such modifications as the court may direct (IR 1986, rr. 7.51A(1), 12A.16(1) and 12A.17), treating an application against a respondent as a claim form (r. 12A.16(3)).

If it is necessary to serve an application outside England and Wales, the court must be asked to direct how **CPR, Part 6**, excluding **rr. 6.30 to 6.47** (service of the claim form and other documents out of the jurisdiction), is to apply (IR 1986, rr. 7.51A(1), 12A.16 and 12A.20), treating an application against a respondent as a claim form (r. 12A.16(3)). Before the CPR came into force, the insolvency court's discretion in this respect was held to be more extensive than under RSC, ord. 11, and the practice of the courts in dealing with applications under RSC, ord. 11, was irrelevant to applications in insolvency proceedings (*Re Busytoday Ltd* [1992] 1 WLR 683). In particular, it was not necessary for service in a foreign jurisdiction to be effected in accordance with the law of that jurisdiction (*Re Busytoday Ltd*; see now **CPR, r. 6.40(3)(c) and (4)**, and *Habib Bank Ltd v Central Bank of Sudan* [2006] EWHC 1767 (Comm), [2007] 1 WLR 470).

Where there are joint office-holders in insolvency proceedings service on one of them is to be treated as service on all of them (IR 1986, r. 12A.19).

Insolvency express trials (IET) pilot

For two years from 1 April 2016, a pilot scheme is in operation for express trials of proceedings   **84.6**
before the Bankruptcy Registrars in the Bankruptcy and Companies Courts (**PD 51P, para. 1.1(1)**). The scheme applies to any simple application made to a Registrar which can be disposed of in no

more than two days, which requires only limited directions (rather than case management) and disclosure, and where each party's costs will not exceed £75,000 (**para. 1.1(2)**). The application form (form 7.1A) must be marked 'IET' clearly in bold on the first page (**para. 2.1(a)**). The application must end with statements that the case is suitable for the IET list (**para. 2.1(b)**) and that the respondent is entitled to object to the use of the IET procedure (**para. 2.1(c)**; the procedure for objecting to IET is in **para. 2.6**). The application should be no longer than 15 pages (**para. 2.4**, which specifies page and font size) and deal with the matters set out in **para. 2.2**. Evidence to be filed in support of the application is specified in **para. 2.3**. On issue, the court will set a date for the directions hearing no more than 45 days after the date of issue (**para. 2.5**) at which a date for the final hearing will be set between three and six months after that hearing (**para. 3.1**). A costs cap of £75,000 will be imposed and the CPR provisions for costs management will not apply (**para. 3.4**). The trial date may not be vacated by consent and an adjournment will be granted only in exceptional circumstances (**para. 4.1**). Judgment will generally be given at trial or within four weeks after (**para. 5**). The court may assess costs summarily or ordered detailed assessment (**para. 4.2**).

REVIEW, RESCISSION AND VARIATION OF AN ORDER MADE IN INSOLVENCY PROCEEDINGS

Statutory provision

84.7 Rule 7.47(1) of IR 1986 provides:

Every court having jurisdiction for the purposes of Parts 1 to 4 of the [Insolvency Act 1986] and Parts 1 to 4 of the [IR 1986] may review, rescind or vary any order made by it in the exercise of that jurisdiction.

An equivalent provision in relation to bankruptcy jurisdiction is made by the Insolvency Act 1986, s. 375(1). These provisions apply to orders at first instance and on appeal (*Re Cahillane* [2015] EWHC 62 (Ch), [2016] 1 WLR 45).

Jurisdiction

84.8 Any Chancery Division judge may review, rescind or vary an order made by another Chancery Division judge, because the legislation provides that 'the court' may review etc. its decisions (*Re W. and A. Glaser Ltd* [1994] BCC 199 at p. 206). The Registrars in bankruptcy do not form a separate court within the Chancery Division (*Re Rolls Razor Ltd (No. 2)* [1970] Ch 576 at pp. 590–1) and a decision of a Registrar may be reviewed etc. by the Registrar or by a judge. This means that when an order has been made by a Registrar it is possible both to apply to the judge to rescind or review the order and to appeal against it, though this should be rare (*Re Piccadilly Property Management Ltd* [1999] 2 BCLC 145).

In *Re a Debtor (No. 32 of 1991) (No. 2)* [1994] BCC 524 at p. 528 Vinelott J said that the procedure for review etc.:

should not be resorted to in place of the ordinary process of appeal, save in cases where the court is satisfied that there has been something amounting to a miscarriage of justice which cannot be corrected by the ordinary process of appeal.

Nature of process

84.9 The power to review, rescind or vary is unfettered but must be exercised judicially (*Mond v Hammond Suddards* [2000] Ch 40 per Chadwick LJ at p. 49). It is not to be used in order to hear an appeal against a decision of a judge of coordinate jurisdiction, save in the most exceptional circumstances (*Mond v Hammond Suddards* [2000] Ch 40 at p. 49). Such an exceptional circumstance might be where the court is satisfied that there has been something amounting to a

miscarriage of justice which cannot be corrected by the ordinary process of appeal (*Re a Debtor (No. 32 of 1991) (No. 2)* [1994] BCC 524 per Vinelott J at p. 528).

The distinction between an appeal and an application to review, rescind or vary is that the question on an appeal against a decision is whether the decision was right or wrong or was otherwise unjust through a serious procedural or other irregularity, whereas the question on an application to review, rescind or vary is whether the original order ought to remain in force in the light either of changed circumstances or further evidence (per N. Millett J in *Re a Debtor (No: 32-SD-1991)* [1993] 1 WLR 314 at p. 319; *Mond v Hammond Suddards* [2000] Ch 40 per Chadwick LJ at p. 49; CPR, r. 52.21(3)). It is submitted that further evidence should be admitted on an application to review, rescind or vary a decision on the same basis as it would be admitted on an appeal against the decision (see 75.16 and 75.17).

An application to review, rescind or vary a decision must not be used merely to obtain a rehearing (*Egleton v Commissioners of Inland Revenue* [2003] EWHC 3226, [2004] BPIR 476) or merely to restate the applicant's case in what is hoped to be a more persuasive way (*RWH Enterprises Ltd v Portedge Ltd* [1998] BCC 556; *Re Thirty-eight Building Ltd (No. 2)* [2000] 1 BCLC 201; *Papanicola v Humphreys* [2005] EWHC 335 (Ch), [2005] 2 All ER 418 at [26]).

The court's approach

84.10 In *Papanicola v Humphreys* [2005] EWHC 335 (Ch), [2005] 2 All ER 418 at [25], Laddie J summarised the principles on which the court will exercise its wide discretion to review, rescind or vary orders in insolvency proceedings. Among the points made by his Lordship are:

(2) The onus is on the applicant to demonstrate the existence of circumstances which justify exercise of the discretion [to review, rescind or vary] in his favour.

(3) Those circumstances must be exceptional.

(4) The circumstances relied on must involve a material difference to what was before the court which made the original order. In other words there must be something new to justify the overturning of the original order.

(5) There is no limit to the factors which may be taken into account. They can include, for example, changes which have occurred since the making of the original order and significant facts which, although in existence at the time of the original order, were not brought to the court's attention at that time.

(6) Where the new circumstances relied on consist of or include new evidence which could have been made available at the original hearing, that, and any explanation... the applicant gives for the failure to produce it then or any lack of such explanation, are factors which can be taken into account in the exercise of the discretion.

In relation to point (4), there is a material difference if the party seeking review etc. of an order was not present or represented when the order was made, but is now *Holtham v Kelmanson* [2006] EWHC 2588 (Ch), [2006] BPIR 1422).

RESCISSION OF A WINDING-UP ORDER

84.11 An application under IR 1986, r. 7.47(1), for a winding-up order to be rescinded must be made within five business days of the date on which the order was made (r. 7.47(4)) though this time limit may be extended by the court under r. 4.3 as in *Re Calmex Ltd* [1989] 1 All ER 485 and *Re Virgo Systems Ltd* [1990] BCLC 34. An extension of time is unlikely to be granted if liquidators have incurred expense in investigating the company's insolvency (*Re Mid East Trading Ltd* [1997] 3 All ER 481 at p. 489, in which the application was about 14 months late).

Applications for rescission of winding-up orders are regulated by PD Insolvency Proceedings, **para. 11.7.** An application must be accompanied by written evidence of assets and liabilities to demonstrate solvency. An application may be made only by a creditor or a contributory

Commentary

(though the company may join in the application) (*Re Mid East Trading Ltd* [1997] 3 All ER 481) and the costs of an unsuccessful application will be paid by the creditor or contributory applicant even when the company has been joined.

The hearing of an application to rescind a winding-up order is a rehearing of the petition on which the order was made and that petition is restored to the court. Accordingly, any person who might have been heard on the hearing of the petition may appear on the hearing of the application to rescind, and IR 1986, r. 4.16 (which requires notice of intention to appear or the permission of the court — see 82.72), applies (*Re Dollar Land (Feltham) Ltd* [1995] 2 BCLC 370).

An applicant for rescission of a winding-up order must adduce new material which tends to show that the original order ought not to have been made, and which was not before the court on the making of the order (*Re Mid East Trading Ltd* [1997] 3 All ER 481 at p. 490).

APPEALS IN INSOLVENCY PROCEEDINGS

Procedural rules

84.12 PD Insolvency Proceedings, para. 20.9.3, specifies that the procedural rules and practice which apply to appeals in insolvency proceedings are CPR, Part 52 (IR 1986, r. 7.49A(3); see chapters 74 and 75), and PD 52A, PD 52B and PD 52C, except for (PD Insolvency Proceedings, para. 20.9.4):

(a) PD 52A, paras 4.3, 4.4 and 4.5 (judges hearing appeals; for the provision that is made in this regard see IR 1986, r. 7.47(2) (corporate insolvency proceedings) and PD Insolvency Proceedings 2014, paras 20.7 and 20.8); and

(b) PD 52B, section II (venue for appeals and filing of notices; see IR 1986, sch. 2D (corporate insolvency proceedings) and PD Insolvency Proceedings, paras 20.5 and 20.6).

Unless the lower court directs otherwise, the time limit for filing an appellant's notice is 21 days from the date of the decision being appealed (IR 1986, r. 7.49A(2); CPR, r. 52.12).

Permission to appeal

84.13 An appeal against a decision at first instance in insolvency proceedings cannot be brought unless permission to appeal has been given either by the court which made the decision or the court which has jurisdiction to hear the appeal (IR 1986, r. 7.49A(1)).

Destination of appeals

84.14 **From a County Court decision** In a civil matter in proceedings under the Insolvency Act 1986, parts 1–4, and IR 1986, parts 1–4 (corporate insolvency), an appeal from a decision of a District Judge in the County Court must be made in accordance with IR 1986, sch. 2D, which specifies, according to the location of the County Court hearing centre in which the decision was made, whether the appeal is to a High Court Judge sitting in a District Registry or to a Registrar in Bankruptcy of the High Court (IR 1986, r. 7.47(2)(a)). An appeal from a decision of a Circuit Judge sitting in the County Court in corporate insolvency proceedings must be made to a High Court Judge (r. 7.47(2)(b)(i)). In individual insolvency proceedings, an appeal from a decision of the County Court lies to a single Judge of the High Court (Insolvency Act 1986, s. 375(2)). An appeal against a decision made by the County Court in insolvency proceedings cannot be made in any other way (IR 1986, r. 7.47(3) (corporate insolvency); Insolvency Act 1986, s. 375(3) (individual insolvency)).

84.15 **From a first-instance decision by a High Court District Judge, Master or Registrar** An appeal from an order made by a district judge sitting in a district registry, by a Chancery

Division Master or at first instance by a Registrar in Bankruptcy of the High Court is to a High Court judge (IR 1986, r. 7.47(2)(b)(ii)–(iv) (corporate insolvency); Insolvency Act 1986, s. 375(2) (individual insolvency)).

From a first-instance decision by a High Court judge   An appeal from an order made by a High Court judge is to the Court of Appeal in the normal way (IR 1986, r. 7.47(2)(d)).   **84.16**

Further appeal   A decision by a High Court judge or Registrar on a first appeal may be appealed to the Court of Appeal, but only with the permission of that court (IR 1986, r. 7.47(2)(c) and (d); **Access to Justice Act 1999, s. 55; CPR, r. 52.7**).   **84.17**

Stay of proceedings in a winding up pending appeal

It has been said that it is not the practice of the court to stay proceedings in the winding up of a company pending determination of an appeal against the winding-up order (*Re A and BC Chewing Gum Ltd* [1975] 1 WLR 579 at pp. 592–3; *Re Calahurst Ltd* [1989] BCLC 140 at p. 141). However, there are several reported cases on appeals which incidentally mention that the winding up was stayed, so the practice is not invariable (see, for example, *Re Westbourne Galleries Ltd* [1971] Ch 799 at p. 813 (contributory's petition); *Re Industrial and Commercial Securities plc* (1988) 5 BCC 320 (where the petitioner's debt had been paid after the winding-up order was made and it may be that this payment would, in itself, have justified a stay of proceedings); *Re Dollar Land (Feltham) Ltd* [1995] 2 BCLC 370 at p. 378).   **84.18**

LITIGATION AGAINST PERSONS SUBJECT TO INSOLVENCY PROCEEDINGS

Introduction

One of the objectives of winding up a company or administering a debtor's estate in bankruptcy is to distribute the insolvent person's free assets to unsecured creditors equally. The amount of each creditor's claim is to be settled by the liquidator or trustee in bankruptcy, subject to appeal to the court. Accordingly legal proceedings against the estate, including proceedings to execute judgments, must not be taken without the court's permission (see **84.22** and **84.29**), which will always be refused if the proceedings will upset the orderly administration and distribution of the estate (see **84.33**). Similarly the administration of a company is intended to manage the company in accordance with a plan agreed by the majority of unsecured creditors, and so legal proceedings against a company in administration can only be taken with the court's permission or the administrator's consent, so that particular creditors cannot gain any advantage over others (see **84.25**).   **84.19**

Litigation against companies and individuals is also controlled while preparations are made for winding up, administration, bankruptcy, and company and individual voluntary arrangements. The different insolvency procedures are subject to two types of control:

(a) An optional power given to an insolvent person and, in the case of companies, to creditors to ask for proceedings to be stayed, either by the court in which the proceedings are pending or by the court controlling the insolvency proceedings. This power is available when:
   (i) a winding-up petition is pending (see **84.20**);
   (ii) an application for an interim order allowing for preparation of an individual voluntary arrangement is pending (see **84.26**);
   (iii) a bankruptcy application or petition is pending (see **84.27**);
   (iv) a bankruptcy order is in force (see **84.29**), except in relation to creditors (see (b)(vi)).

Commentary

(b) A prohibition on proceedings being brought or continued without the permission of the court which is controlling the insolvency procedure. This applies when:
  (i) a provisional liquidator has been appointed (see **84.21**);
  (ii) a winding-up order has been made (see **84.22**);
  (iii) a moratorium is in force allowing preparation of a company voluntary arrangement (see **84.24**);
  (iv) an administration application is pending or notice has been filed of the appointment of an administrator out of court, or a company is in administration (see **84.25**);
  (v) an interim order is in force allowing preparation of an individual voluntary arrangement (see **84.26**);
  (vi) a bankruptcy order is in force or an interim receiver has been appointed, in relation to a creditor only (see **84.29**).

An optional power to ask the court which controls the winding up to stay proceedings is available in the voluntary liquidation of a company (see **84.23**).

Although the CPR treat a claim against a partnership as being against the firm as a single defendant, permission should be sought if any member of the partnership is subject to an insolvency proceeding (*Bank of Scotland v Breytenbach* [2012] BPIR 1 at [7]–[8]).

There are no provisions for the control of litigation against a company when an administrative receiver is appointed.

While a winding-up petition is pending

84.20 After a petition has been presented asking for the compulsory winding up of a company, but before the final hearing of the petition, an application may be made, by the company, or any creditor or contributory, for any claim or proceeding against the company to be stayed (Insolvency Act 1986, s. 126).

Applications under s. 126 to stay or restrain a pending claim or proceeding against the company are made as follows:

(a) Where the claim or proceeding is pending in the High Court, the application is for a stay and is made using form N244. It must be made to the Master or District Judge in the division or District Registry (or specialist court) in which the matter is proceeding (*Re People's Garden Co.* (1875) 1 ChD 44; *Garbutt v Fawcus* (1875) 1 ChD 155; *Re Morriston Patent Fuel and Brick Co.* [1877] WN 20; *Re Artistic Colour Printing Co.* (1880) 14 ChD 502; *Re General Service Co-operative Stores* [1891] 1 Ch 496).

(b) Where the pending proceeding is an appeal in the High Court or to the Court of Appeal, the application is for a stay and is made to the court to which the appeal is made (Insolvency Act 1986, s. 126(1)(a)). In the Court of Appeal, Civil Division, the application may be included in a respondent's notice (**PD 52C, para. 11**).

(c) Where the pending action or proceeding is in any other tribunal (including the County Court and magistrates' courts), the application is for an order to restrain further proceedings in the action or proceeding (Insolvency Act 1986, s. 126(1)(b)). The application is made to the court having jurisdiction to wind up the company. As it is an application for an injunction it must be listed before a judge (**PD Insolvency Proceedings, para. 3.2(3)**).

An order under the Insolvency Act 1986, s. 126, may be made on an application made without notice to other parties if the applicant gives an undertaking in damages (see **37.24** to **37.26**) (*Re London and Suburban Bank Ltd* (1871) 25 LT 23; *Masbach v James Anderson and Co. Ltd* (1877) 37 LT 440).

In *Bowkett v Fullers United Electric Works Ltd* [1923] 1 KB 160 Bankes LJ said, at pp. 163–4:

> The general policy of the court in exercising this jurisdiction, when a petition has been presented which may result in a winding-up order or a scheme, is to secure that no creditor shall thenceforward gain priority over others of his class, and when an application is made to stay proceedings under [s. 126] very exceptional circumstances must exist to justify the court in refusing to accede to the application, because if the plaintiff's action is not stayed he will get payment in full while if his action is stayed he will take his place properly among other creditors of his class.... No doubt the court has a discretion whether it will stay a plaintiff's action, but it is against the policy of the court to exercise that discretion by allowing a plaintiff to proceed except in very special circumstances.

When a provisional liquidator is appointed

84.21 If, while a winding-up petition is pending against a company, a provisional liquidator is appointed, the effect on claims or proceedings against the company is the same as when a winding-up order is made, that is, they cannot proceed without the permission of the winding-up court (Insolvency Act 1986, s. 130(2); see **84.22**).

When a winding-up order has been made

84.22 When a winding-up order has been made against a company no claim or proceeding may be proceeded with or commenced against the company except by permission of the court, and subject to such terms as the court may impose (Insolvency Act 1986, s. 130(2)).

The court by which permission must be given under s. 130(2) is the court which made the winding-up order (*Wilson v Natal Investment Co.* (1867) 36 LJ Ch 312; *Thames Plate Glass Co. v Land and Sea Telegraph Construction Co.* (1871) LR 6 Ch App 643). That court will issue an injunction to prevent the continuance of any proceedings which it will not sanction (*Re Waterloo Life etc. Insurance Co. (No. 2)* (1862) 31 Beav 589; *Re International Pulp and Paper Co.* (1876) 3 ChD 594). Any judge of the High Court may exercise its jurisdiction in this respect (*Fabric Sales Ltd v Eratex Ltd* [1984] 1 WLR 863).

Permission will not be given on an application made without notice to the company (*Western and Brazilian Telegraph Co. v Bibby* (1880) 42 LT 821) other than in exceptional cases where permission is urgently required (*Fabric Sales Ltd v Eratex Ltd* [1984] 1 WLR 863 at p. 866).

When a company is in voluntary liquidation

84.23 In the voluntary liquidation of a company, an application may be made under the Insolvency Act 1986, s. 112, for the court to exercise its power to restrain or stay proceedings against the company (*Re Keynsham Co.* (1863) 33 Beav 123; *Re Life Association of England Ltd* (1864) 34 LJ Ch 64; *Re Peninsular etc. Banking Co.* (1866) 35 Beav 278; *Re East Kent Shipping Co. Ltd* (1868) 18 LT 748; *Re Paraguassu Steam Tramroad Co., Black and Co.'s Case* (1872) LR 8 Ch App 254 at p. 263). An application may be made by the liquidator or any creditor or contributory (s. 112(1)). If satisfied that it will be just and beneficial to restrain or stay the proceedings, the court may accede wholly or partially to the application on such terms and conditions as it thinks fit, or may make such other order on the application as it thinks just (s. 112(2)). An application under s. 112 concerning the voluntary winding up of a company should be made to a court having jurisdiction to wind up the company. However, it is not entirely clear whether the statutory power of the court which is invoked by an application to restrain proceedings is the s. 126 or the s. 130 power. Older cases support the view that where a claim is proceeding in the Court of Appeal or the High Court against a company in voluntary liquidation, an application under s. 126, using the CPR, Part 23, procedure may be made to the Court of Appeal or the High Court Division in which the claim is proceeding (*Walker v Banagher Distillery Co. Ltd* (1875) 1 QBD 129; *Needham v Rivers Protection and Manure Co.* (1875) 1 ChD 253).

Commentary

Moratorium in force in relation to a company

84.24   While a moratorium under the Insolvency Act 1986, s. 1A (moratorium when directors propose a voluntary arrangement), is in force in relation to a company, no proceedings and no execution or other legal process may be commenced or continued against the company or its property, except with the permission of the court (sch. A1, para. 12(1)(h)).

While a moratorium is in force in relation to a company no petition for the company to be wound up by the court may be presented, other than by the Secretary of State or the Financial Services Authority (sch. A1, para. 12(1)(a), (4) and (5)), and no administration application may be made (sch. A1, para. 12(1)(d)).

Administration and preparation for administration

84.25   While a company is in administration, no legal process (including legal proceedings, execution and distress) may be instituted against the company or its property except with the consent of the administrator or the permission of the court (Insolvency Act 1986, sch. B1, para. 43(1) and (6)). This protection is known as a moratorium. The same protection applies (except that only the court can give permission) during the following periods of preparation for administration (para. 44):

(a)   from when an application is made to the court for an administration order until the court's administration order takes effect or the application is dismissed;

(b)   from when the holder of a floating charge files with the court a notice of intention to appoint an administrator until the appointment takes effect, provided this is within five business days;

(c)   from when a notice of intention to appoint an administrator is filed with the court by the company or its directors until the appointment takes effect, provided this is within 10 business days.

Protection under para. 44 is known as an interim moratorium. It does not prevent or require the court's permission for (para. 44(7)):

(a)   the presentation of a public-interest winding-up petition by the Secretary of State or the Financial Services Authority;

(b)   the appointment of an administrator by the holder of a floating charge;

(c)   the appointment of an administrative receiver;

(d)   the carrying out by an administrative receiver of his or her functions.

Interim order in respect of an individual voluntary arrangement

84.26   While an interim order is in force, under the Insolvency Act 1986, s. 252, in respect of an individual, a moratorium is imposed so that a voluntary arrangement may be prepared for approval by creditors. The effect is that no bankruptcy petition, other proceedings, execution or other legal process may be commenced or continued against the individual, or his or her property, except with the permission of the court (s. 252(2)). Application for permission is by application in the voluntary arrangement proceedings.

While an application for an interim order in respect of an individual is pending, the court to which the application has been made may stay any action, execution or other legal process against the property or person of the individual (s. 254(1)). An application for a stay should be made by application in the voluntary arrangement proceedings. Alternatively a court in which other proceedings are pending may stay them, or allow them to continue on such terms as it thinks fit, on proof that an application for an interim order has been made by the defendant (s. 254(2)). An application under s. 254(2) should use the CPR, Part 23 procedure.

While a bankruptcy application or petition is pending

84.27   After a bankruptcy petition has been presented against an individual, but before the final hearing of the petition, the court in which the petition is pending may stay any action, execution or other legal process against the property or person of the individual (Insolvency Act 1986, s. 285(1)). The same applies when proceedings on a bankruptcy application are ongoing, but then the application is to be made, it seems, to the court to which a bankruptcy petition against the individual should be presented (see **83.4**). Application for a stay under s. 285(1) is by application in the bankruptcy proceedings. Alternatively a court in which other proceedings are pending may stay them, or allow them to continue on such terms as it thinks fit, on proof that a bankruptcy application has been made or a bankruptcy petition has been presented in respect of the defendant (s. 285(2)). An application under s. 285(2) should use the CPR, Part 23 procedure.

When an interim receiver has been appointed

When an interim receiver of an individual's property has been appointed under the Insolvency Act 1986, s. 286, the effect on other proceedings against the individual is the same as if a bankruptcy order had been made against the individual (s. 286(6); see **84.29**). **84.28**

When a bankruptcy order has been made

The Insolvency Act 1986, s. 285(3), provides that, once an individual has been adjudicated bankrupt, a person who is a creditor in respect of a debt provable in the bankruptcy: **84.29**

(a) does not have any remedy against the property or person of the bankrupt in respect of the debt;

(b) until the individual's discharge from bankruptcy, may not commence any claim or other legal proceedings against the bankrupt, except with the permission of the court and on such terms as the court may impose.

In addition, the provisions of s. 285(1) and (2) (see **84.27**) continue to apply after a bankruptcy order has been made. A claim for possession of property let to the bankrupt, on the ground that rent is in arrears, is not a remedy in respect of the arrears, and so is not taken away by s. 285(3) (*Sharples v Places for People Homes Ltd* [2011] EWCA Civ 813, [2012] 1 All ER 582). The debts that are provable in bankruptcy are defined in IR 1986, r. 12.3.

General principles governing the exercise of discretion to grant permission

The following paragraphs discuss the general principles which apply when permission is sought to commence or continue proceedings against a defendant who is subject to insolvency proceedings. **84.30**

Existence of discretion   Whether or not a claimant is given permission to proceed is a matter for the discretion of the court (*Thames Plate Glass Co. v Land and Sea Telegraph Construction Co.* (1871) LR 6 Ch App 643; *Re Atlantic Computer Systems plc* [1992] Ch 505 at p. 523), which is free to make such order as is 'right and fair in the circumstances' (*Re Aro Co. Ltd* [1980] Ch 196 at p. 209; *Re Exchange Securities and Commodities Ltd* [1983] BCLC 186). **84.31**

Onus   The onus is on the applicant to show a case for giving permission (*Re Lancashire Cotton Spinning Co., ex parte Carnelley* (1887) 35 ChD 656; *Re Higginshaw Mills and Spinning Co.* [1896] 2 Ch 544). However, on an application to restrain or stay proceedings against a company in voluntary liquidation the onus is on the applicant to show why the order should be made (*Currie v Consolidated Kent Collieries Corporation Ltd* [1906] 1 KB 134). **84.32**

Purpose of the provisions   In *Re David Lloyd and Co.* (1877) 6 ChD 339 James LJ said, at p. 344, that the provisions in winding-up and bankruptcy legislation enabling the court to interfere with claims: **84.33**

were intended, not for the purpose of harassing, or impeding, or injuring third persons, but for the purpose of preserving the limited assets of the company or bankrupt in the best way for distribution among all the persons who have claims upon them. There being only a small fund or a limited fund to

1553

be divided among a great number of persons, it would be monstrous that one or more of them should be harassing the company with actions and incurring costs which would increase the claims against the company and diminish the assets which ought to be divided among all the creditors.

See also *Langley Constructions (Brixham) Ltd v Wells* [1969] 1 WLR 503 at p. 508; *Re J. Burrows (Leeds) Ltd* [1982] 1 WLR 1177 at p. 1181.

84.34   Substantiality of claim   The court should not be asked to order a liquidator or trustee in bankruptcy to waste the assets he or she is administering on defending insubstantial claims (*Re Hartlebury Printers Ltd* [1992] ICR 559). Permission will not be given to commence proceedings if there is no prospect that the court would grant the relief claimed (*Re Polly Peck International plc (No. 2)* [1998] 3 All ER 812). The test is the same as on an application for summary judgment (see **34.10**) (*Enron Metals and Commodity Ltd v HIH Casualty and General Insurance Ltd* [2005] EWHC 485 (Ch), *The Times*, 6 April 2005). The old practice was to require an affidavit from an applicant seeking permission to commence or continue proceedings verifying the claim made in the proceedings (*Re St Cuthbert's Lead Smelting Co. (No. 2)* [1866] WN 154). This practice would seem to be unnecessary now that **CPR, r. 22.1** requires every statement of case to be verified by a statement of truth. The court does not examine the merits of the applicant's case, provided it is satisfied that the claim is not clearly unsustainable (*Bristol and West Building Society v Trustee of the Property of Back* [1998] 1 BCLC 485). The question of the substantiality of the applicant's case is decided on the material presented by the applicant: the company or debtor or trustee in bankruptcy will not be granted an order for disclosure of documents to test the applicant's case (*Re Bank of Credit and Commerce International SA (No. 4)* [1994] 1 BCLC 419). It is open to the court to limit permission initially to issue of the claim form and particulars of claim and service of defence, after which it can assess the nature of the claim (as in *Thames Plate Glass Co. v Land and Sea Telegraph Co.* (1870) LR 11 Eq 248).

84.35   Appropriateness of forum   The procedure for making a claim against an insolvent person in liquidation or bankruptcy is by submitting a proof to the liquidator or trustee and, if necessary, appealing to the court in charge of the insolvency against the liquidator or trustee's decision. The advantages of this procedure to those interested in the insolvency are that claims are generally dealt with quickly and at a low cost. Usually, the essential question on an application to commence or proceed with an action or proceeding is whether the action or proceeding is a better way of dealing with the matter. Permission will not be given to bring or continue proceedings if the question at issue can just as well be resolved in the winding-up or bankruptcy proceedings (*Re St Cuthbert Lead Smelting Co.* (1866) 35 Beav 384; *Re Exchange Securities and Commodities Ltd* [1983] BCLC 186). Determining the appropriate method of dealing with the applicant's claim is the essential question on an application for permission to commence or continue proceedings against an insolvent person (*Re Bank of Credit and Commerce International SA (No. 4)* [1994] 1 BCLC 419).

Proceedings in respect of a claim for which the claimant has already put in a proof in the winding up or bankruptcy will not be allowed to continue because the claimant has elected to have the matter dealt with in the insolvency (*Craven v Blackpool Greyhound Stadium and Racecourse Ltd* [1936] 3 All ER 513).

84.36   Insolvent person necessary party to proceedings against others or where claim is insured   Permission will normally be given for a claim or proceeding against an insolvent person if that person is a necessary defendant to a claim against another person, or the claim is insured, and the claimant undertakes not to enforce any order obtained in the claim against the insolvent person, without the insolvency court's permission (*McEwen v London Bombay and Mediterranean Bank Ltd* (1866) 15 LT 495; *Re Breech Loading Armoury Co.* [1867] WN 75; *Bristol and West Building Society v Trustee of the Property of Back* [1998] 1 BCLC 485).

Retrospective permission

There has been some uncertainty about whether retrospective permission can be given to **84.37**
commence a claim against a company after a provisional liquidator has been appointed or
a winding-up order made, or against an undischarged bankrupt. However, in the most
recent reported cases, retrospective permission has been granted (*Bank of Scotland v Breytenbach*
[2012] BPIR 1 (bankruptcy); *Bank of Ireland v Colliers International UK plc* [2012] EWHC 2942 (Ch),
[2013] Ch 422 (winding up)). In both cases the judges stated that their judgments are
intended to resolve uncertainties and to establish the principle that retrospective permission may be given and so may be cited despite being given on applications which only one
party attended.

Defending claim by the insolvent person

If a person who has issued a claim pursues it while subject to insolvency proceedings, a defend- **84.38**
ant does not require permission to take essentially defensive steps in the proceedings (*Cook v
Mortgage Debenture Ltd* [2016] EWCA Civ 103, [2016] 1 BCLC 479). For example, permission is not
required to pursue an appeal against a judgment in favour of an insolvent person in a claim
which that person has proceeded with since a winding-up or bankruptcy order (*Humber and
Co. v John Griffiths Cycle Co.* (1901) 85 LT 141). Permission is not required for a counterclaim to
the extent that the counterclaim is a defence, such as a set-off (*Dominion Trust Co. v Brydges*
(1920) 28 BCR 451; *Standard Trust Co. v Turner Crossing Inc.* (1992) 15 CBR (3d) 75), but if judgment
is sought on the counterclaim for an amount exceeding the insolvent's claim, permission is
required (*Langley Constructions (Brixham) Ltd v Wells* [1969] 1 WLR 503).

Permission is also not required to take, in existing proceedings in which an insolvent person
is a party, steps which have none of the character of legal proceedings against the insolvent
party (*Cook v Mortgage Debenture Ltd*, application to be joined but not seeking any relief against
the insolvent party).

How does a party 'proceed with' a claim?

In Australia it has been held that 'not everything that happens in litigation involves a person **84.39**
who proceeds with litigation' (*FAI Workers Compensation (NSW) Ltd v Philkor Builders Pty Ltd* (1996)
20 ACSR 592 at p. 595): the test is whether what is done moves the litigation 'from an incipi-
ent stage to consummation' (*FAI Workers Compensation (NSW) Ltd v Philkor Builders Pty Ltd* at
p. 596). So a person who has commenced proceedings against an insolvent person does not
proceed with them by applying to have them dismissed (*FAI Workers Compensation (NSW) Ltd v
Philkor Builders Pty Ltd* at p. 596; *Re DIM Furniture Wholesale (NSW) Pty Ltd* (1998) 28 ACSR 407),
even though the application may result in the defendant being ordered to pay costs (*FAI
Workers Compensation (NSW) Ltd v Philkor Builders Pty Ltd*). An application for permission to proceed with a claim is not itself a 'fresh proceeding' in the claim, because it does not, if successful, advance the claim towards completion: it merely removes a bar against taking further
steps (*Re M and M Outdoor Centre Pty Ltd* (1996) 135 FLR 179).

Costs

The costs of a successful application to proceed with a claim should be added to the costs of **84.40**
the claim (*Re Aro Co. Ltd* [1980] Ch 196 at p. 211). However, the costs of an application for
retrospective permission must normally be paid by the applicant who failed to obtain permission at the proper time (*Re Wanzer Ltd* [1891] 1 Ch 305).

If proceedings against a company in liquidation are necessary in order to establish and/or
quantify a claim against the company, any costs which the company is ordered to pay must
be proved for dividend in the winding up (*Re Poole Firebrick and Blue Clay Co.* (1873) LR 17 Eq 268;

Commentary

Re Thurso New Gas Co. (1889) 42 ChD 486; *Re British Gold Fields of West Africa* [1899] 2 Ch 7). But if the company is ordered to pay the costs of proceedings which the liquidator has chosen to carry on in the hope of benefiting the company then the costs are payable in full as an expense of the liquidation (*Re Trent and Humber Ship-building Co., Bailey and Leetham's Case* (1869) LR 8 Eq 94; *Re Wenborn and Co.* [1905] 1 Ch 413). The principles are the same whether the winding up is voluntary or by the court (*Re Pacific Coast Syndicate Ltd* [1913] 2 Ch 26). The costs that are recoverable in full include costs incurred before the commencement of the winding up (*Re London Drapery Stores* [1898] 2 Ch 684; *Norglen Ltd v Reeds Rains Prudential Ltd* [1999] 2 AC 1 at p. 21).

When proceedings by a creditor are halted by the Insolvency Act 1986, s. 130(2), the creditor is entitled to prove for the costs of the proceedings up to the time that s. 130(2) took effect (*Re Welsh Potosi Mining Co., ex parte Tobin* (1858) 28 LJ Ch 44).

LITIGATION IN WINDING UP

84.41   As far as possible, litigation by or against a company being wound up is to be conducted within the winding-up proceedings. A claim against the company must be submitted to the liquidator, who will decide whether to accept it in whole or part, subject to appeal to the court. The Insolvency Act 1986, ss. 212 (see **84.42**), 213 and 214 (see **84.43**), and sch. B1, para. 75 (see **84.42**), allow some claims of a company in liquidation to be brought by application in the winding-up proceedings, with a consequent saving in court fees, and authorise the company's liquidator and other persons to make such an application.

Misfeasance proceedings

84.42   The Insolvency Act 1986, s. 212 and sch. B1, para. 75, provide that some claims by a company which is being wound up may be pursued by an application in the winding-up proceedings. Applications under these provisions are known as 'misfeasance proceedings' and they are an optional alternative to an ordinary claim. There are limits on which defendants and which causes of action may be pursued in misfeasance proceedings.

By s. 212(1), the only persons against whom misfeasance proceedings may be taken under s. 212 are persons who:

(a) are, or have been, officers of the company;

(b) have acted as liquidator or administrative receiver of the company; or

(c) are, or have been, concerned, or have taken part, in the promotion, formation or management of the company.

The only causes of action which may be pursued in s. 212 misfeasance proceedings are those which allege that the defendant has misapplied or retained, or become accountable for, any money or other property of the company, or has been guilty of any misfeasance or breach of any fiduciary or other duty in relation to the company (s. 212(1)). Where the defendant has acted as liquidator of the company, this includes any misfeasance or breach of duty in connection with the carrying on of his or her functions as liquidator (s. 212(2)).

Schedule B1, para. 75, makes the same provision in relation to proceedings against a person who:

(a) is, or purports to be, the administrator of the company; or

(b) has been, or has purported to be, its administrator (sch. B1, para. 75(1)).

An application under s. 212 may be made by the official receiver, the company's liquidator or any creditor or contributory of the company (s. 212(3)). An application under sch. B1, para. 75, may be made by any of those persons or by the company's administrator (sch. B1, para. 75(2)), and may be made if the company is in administration without being wound up.

The permission of the court must be obtained for an application:

(a) by a contributory under s. 212 (but not under sch. B1, para. 75) (s. 212(5));
(b) against a liquidator or administrator who has been released or discharged from liability (s. 212(4); sch. B1, para. 75(6)).

If a claim in the name of a company in liquidation is brought against an officer etc. of the company, the court may convert it into misfeasance proceedings by substituting the liquidator (or other authorised applicant) for the company as claimant, under **CPR, r. 19.2(4)**, and allowing consequential amendments (*Parkinson Engineering Services plc v Swan* [2009] EWCA Civ 1366, [2010] Bus LR 857). In *Parkinson Engineering Services plc v Swan* the claim was against a former administrator and the court made the substitution after the expiry of the limitation period, as the claim could not properly be continued because it was barred by the previous discharge of the administrator under what is now the Insolvency Act 1986, sch. B1, para. 98, and that bar could be disapplied only in misfeasance proceedings (sch. B1, para. 75(6)). It was crucial to the exercise of the power under **CPR, r. 19.5(3)(b)** that the switch from Part 7 claim to misfeasance proceedings involved no change in the cause of action or the facts to be asserted.

Fraudulent and wrongful trading

84.43 The Insolvency Act 1986, ss. 213 and 214, provide causes of action which can be asserted only in the course of the winding up of a company, and only by an application by the liquidator. An application under s. 213 may be made against any persons who were knowingly parties to the carrying on of any business of the company with intent to defraud creditors (of the company or any other person), or for any fraudulent purpose. An application under s. 214 may be made against a person if (s. 214(2)):

(a) the company has gone into insolvent liquidation (defined in s. 214(6));
(b) at some time before the commencement of the winding up of the company, that person knew or ought to have concluded that there was no reasonable prospect that the company would avoid going into insolvent liquidation; and
(c) that person was a director of the company at that time.

s. 448(3) (warrant to seize documents requisitioned under part 14 of the 1985 Act), either on its own or as extended by s. 50 of the 2001 Act (power to seize material so as to assess whether it is what is sought or which is inseparable from material which is sought). These proceedings are the subject of **PD 49A, para. 26**.

Proceedings in relation to companies' affairs are brought not only under the Companies Acts, but also under the Insolvency Act 1986 under a completely separate set of rules, which have their own forms of originating process (see **chapters 82 and 84**). The court's jurisdiction to deal with a company's affairs on an application under the Companies Acts or the Insolvency Act 1986 arises only by virtue of the statutes and is limited to the matters mentioned in the various provisions authorising applications to be made. Any claim by or against a company which is not within those provisions must be pursued by some other form of litigation, such as a claim in equity, contract or tort.

PROCEEDINGS UNDER THE COMPANIES ACTS

Commencement under Part 7 or Part 8

85.4   All proceedings to which PD 49A applies must be commenced by Part 8 claim form (**PD 49A, para. 5(1)**), except for the following, which must be commenced by Part 7 claim form:

(a) an application under the Companies Act 2006, s. 370 (claim by members of a company in its name for a remedy for breach of the provisions requiring members' approval of political donations and expenditure) (**PD 49A, para. 11**);

(b) an application under the Companies Act 2006, s. 955 (for an order to secure compliance with the City Code or with a requirement under s. 947 to disclose documents or information to the Panel on Takeovers and Mergers) (**PD 49A, para. 16**);

(c) an application under the Companies Act 2006, s. 968(6) (for compensation for breach of an agreement which has been invalidated by a takeover bid because the company is opted into the provisions overriding takeover barriers) (**PD 49A, para. 17**).

In the High Court the claim form must be issued out of the office of the Companies Court Registrar or a Chancery District Registry; in the County Court it will be issued out of the County Court office (**para. 5(2)**).

For proceedings started by Part 8 claim form, the provisions of **CPR, Part 8** apply, except where modified by **PD 49A** or any other practice direction (**PD 49A, para. 5(1)(b)**).

Title of proceedings

85.5   Every claim form starting proceedings to which PD 49A applies (except proceedings under the Criminal Justice and Police Act 2001) must be entitled in the matter of the company in question and in the matter of the relevant Act (**PD 49A, para. 4(1)**). The same applies to all affidavits, witness statements, notices and other documents in the proceedings.

Where a company changes its name in the course of proceedings, the title must be altered by substituting the new name for the old, and inserting the old name in brackets at the end of the title (**PD 49A, para. 4(2)**).

Parties

85.6   If the company concerned is not the claimant in a claim under the Companies Act 2006, it should be made a defendant to the claim, unless the court orders otherwise (**PD 49A, para. 7(1)**). Where an application is made in proceedings to which the company concerned is, or is required to be, a defendant, the company must be made a respondent to the application unless the court orders otherwise (**para. 7(2)**). **Paragraph 7** does not apply where different provision is made by any other enactment, the CPR or another practice direction.

A claim commenced by the company concerned need not have a defendant if it is under:

(a) the Companies Act 2006, part 26 (arrangements and reconstructions) or part 27 (mergers and divisions of public companies) (**PD 49A, para. 15**);
(b) Regulation (EC) No. 2157/2001, art. 25 or art. 26 (**PD 49A, paras 19(4) and 21(2)**);
(c) the Companies (Cross-Border Mergers) Regulations 2007 (SI 2007/2974), reg. 6 or reg. 16 (**PD 49A, paras 23(2) and 25(3)**).

Service

The parties are responsible for service of documents in proceedings to which **PD 49A** applies (**PD 49A, para. 28**).   **85.7**

For some types of claim, **PD 49A** requires notification of the claim to specific persons. This means that, unless the court orders otherwise, the person must be sent a copy of the claim form as soon as reasonably practicable after the claim form has been issued (**PD 49A, para. 5(3)**). The proceedings concerned are:

(a) an application for an order under the Companies Act 2006, s. 169(5) (**PD 49A, para. 8**);
(b) an application for an order under the Companies Act 2006, s. 295 or 317 (**PD 49A, para. 10**);
(c) an application for a declaration under the Companies Act 2006, s. 456(1) (**PD 49A, para. 12**);
(d) an application for an order under the Companies Act 2006, s. 511(6), 514(7), 515(7) or 518(9) (**PD 49A, para. 13**);
(e) an application for an order under the Companies Act 2006, s. 527(5) (**PD 49A, para. 14**).

An application under the Companies Act 2006, s. 1132 (production and inspection of books where offence suspected), may be made without notice to any person against whom an order is sought (**PD 49A, para. 18**).

Other rules for specific types of claim

There are specific rules relating to: **85.8**

(a) an application for an order under the Companies Act 2006, part 26 or part 27, to sanction a compromise or arrangement (**PD 49A, para. 15**);
(b) an application to confirm a reduction in capital (**PD 49A, para. 27**).

UNFAIR PREJUDICE

Statutory provision

The Companies Act 2006, s. 994, entitles a member of a company to apply to the court by petition for an order giving relief in respect of conduct of the company's affairs which is unfairly prejudicial to the interests of its members generally or of some part of its members (including at least the petitioner), or any actual or proposed act which is or would be so prejudicial.   **85.9**

Procedural rules

The Companies (Unfair Prejudice Applications) Proceedings Rules 2009 (SI 2009/2469) apply to all proceedings under the Companies Act 2006, s. 994. The CPR apply to proceedings on an unfair prejudice petition, with any necessary modifications, except so far as they are inconsistent with the Companies Act 2006 or SI 2009/2469 (SI 2009/2469, r. 2(2)). The procedure provided by SI 2009/2469 follows the procedure for contributories' winding-up petitions (see **82.62** to **82.70**). An unfair prejudice petition may seek a winding up by the   **85.10** court as an alternative remedy, though **PD 49B, para. 1**, says that it is undesirable to do that as a matter of course: 'The petition should not ask for a winding-up order unless that is the relief which the petitioner prefers or it is thought that it may be the only relief to which the petitioner is entitled'.

The requirement that an application under the Companies Act 2006, s. 994, must be made by petition is imposed by statute and so the court has no power under the CPR to waive a failure to comply with it (*Re Osea Road Camp Sites Ltd* [2004] EWHC 2437 (Ch), [2005] 1 WLR 760).

Form and contents of petition

85.11   The prescribed form for a petition under the Companies Act 2006, s. 994, is set out in the schedule to SI 2009/2469 and is to be used with such variations, if any, as the circumstances may require (SI 2009/2469, r. 3(1)). The petition must specify the grounds on which it is presented and the nature of the relief which is sought by the petitioner (SI 2009/2469, r. 3(2)). The extensive powers of the court to make orders on an unfair prejudice petition are set out in the Companies Act 2006, s. 996. The relief sought must be appropriate to the conduct of which the petition complains (*Re J. E. Cade and Son Ltd* [1992] BCLC 213 at p. 223), though it need not be directed solely towards remedying the particular things that have happened (*Re Hailey Group Ltd* [1993] BCLC 459 at p. 472). The court is required to make the order that is appropriate at the time of the hearing (*Re Hailey Group Ltd* at p. 472).

If a winding-up order is asked for, the petition must comply with **PD 49B** on orders under the Insolvency Act 1986, s. 127, sanctioning transactions by the company while the petition is pending.

The petition must state the names of persons on whom it is intended to serve the petition (known as the 'respondents'), one of whom will be the company itself.

There is no provision for verification of an unfair prejudice petition by affidavit or statement of truth.

Filing the petition and fixing a return day

85.12   An unfair prejudice petition must be delivered to the court for filing with copies for service on all the respondents (including the company itself) named in the petition (SI 2009/2469, r. 3(2)). The court will fix a hearing for a day (called the 'return day') on which, unless the court otherwise directs, the petitioner and any respondent (including the company) must attend for directions to be given in relation to the procedure on the petition (SI 2009/2469, r. 3(3)).

A fee of £280 must be paid on filing a petition (**CPFO, fee 3.3**).

Service of the petition

85.13   The petitioner must, at least 14 days before the return day, serve a sealed copy of the petition on all respondents named in the petition (including the company itself) (SI 2009/2469, r. 4). The applicable rules on service are those of **CPR, Part 6**. If the petition also prays for a winding up, there must be personal service in accordance with **CPR, rr. 6.5(3) and 6.22(3)** (see **82.66**).

Directions

85.14   SI 2009/2469, r. 5, requires the court, on the return day, or at any time after it, to give such directions as it thinks appropriate with respect to the following matters:

(a) service of the petition, whether in connection with the venue for a further hearing, or for any other purpose;

(b) whether particulars of claim and defence are to be delivered;

(c) whether, and if so by what means, the petition is to be advertised;

(d) the manner in which any evidence is to be adduced at any hearing before the judge and in particular:

   (i) the taking of evidence wholly or in part by affidavit or witness statements or orally;

   (ii) the cross-examination of any deponents to affidavits or witness statements;

   (iii) the matters to be dealt with in evidence;

(e) any other matter affecting the procedure on the petition or in connection with the hearing and disposal of the petition;

(f) such orders, if any, including a stay for any period, as the court thinks fit, with a view to mediation or other form of alternative dispute resolution.

The Registrar should consider directing the parties and/or their advisers to meet with a view to narrowing the issues, identifying what issues are really important, what issues are really in dispute, how those issues are to be resolved or proved, and resolving and narrowing any other matters which in the context of the particular petition could reasonably be expected to be narrowed (*Re Rotadata Ltd* [2000] 1 BCLC 122 at p. 127).

Interim orders

85.15 The court will grant interim injunctions to preserve the status quo if, but only if, departure from the status quo might affect the remedy sought in an unfair prejudice petition (*Callard v Pringle* [2007] EWCA Civ 1075, [2008] 2 BCLC 505). See, for example, *Re a Company (No. 002612 of 1984* [1985] BCLC 80; *Re Sticky Fingers Restaurant Ltd* [1992] BCLC 84; *Re a Company (No. 003061 of 1993)* [1994] BCC 883; *Incasep Ltd v Jones* [2002] EWCA Civ 961, [2003] BCC 226. An interim injunction will not be granted unless the court considers that the petition has a real prospect of success (*Re X Ltd* (2001) *The Times*, 5 June 2001).

In proceedings on an unfair prejudice petition the court does not have jurisdiction to order an interim payment under CPR, **Part 25** (*Re a Company (No. 004175 of 1986*) [1987] 1 WLR 585; *Re a Company (No. 004502 of 1988)* [1991] BCC 234). The court will not make a freezing order against any party to an unfair prejudice petition, unless it alleges what amounts to a cause of action against that party (*Re Premier Electronics (GB) Ltd* [2002] 2 BCLC 634). An interim injunction prohibiting the company from paying a director remuneration which has not been authorised may be made without joining the director as a party (*Riener v Gershinson* [2004] EWHC 76 (Ch), [2004] 2 BCLC 376).

A minority member of a company who is petitioning under the Companies Act 2006, s. 994, may also be frustrating the holding of general meetings, by refusing so to attend so that any meeting will be inquorate, so as to prevent prejudicial resolutions being adopted. The majority may apply under s. 306 for an order convening a meeting with the usual quorum rules suspended. The court hearing the s. 306 application will take into account the existence of s. 994 proceedings when deciding whether to make an order under s. 306 (*Re Sticky Fingers Restaurant Ltd*).

Unlike a winding-up petition, it is not necessary to strike out an unfair prejudice petition where there is a dispute about the petitioner's standing; an unfair prejudice petition may be stayed to enable the petitioner to establish standing (*Re Starlight Developers Ltd* [2007] EWHC 1660 (Ch), [2007] BCC 929).

Stay in favour of arbitration

85.16 The Court of Appeal has upheld the effectiveness of an arbitration agreement which covers the disputes giving rise to an unfair prejudice petition (*Fulham Football Club (1987) Ltd v Richards* [2011] EWCA Civ 855, [2012] Ch 833). This means a party to the arbitration agreement who is made a party to the proceedings on the petition can apply to the court under the Arbitration

Act 1996, s. 9, for proceedings on the petition to be stayed so that the dispute can be dealt with by arbitration instead of by the court. The Court of Appeal held that an arbitrator is capable of deciding whether there has been unfair prejudice (at [77]). However, it is possible that in some cases an arbitrator will not be able to order suitable remedies, particularly if they involve persons who are not party to the arbitration agreement. In such a case it would be necessary to make an application to the court to make suitable orders in the light of the arbitrator's findings.

Amendment

85.17 An unfair prejudice petition may be amended to add an instance of alleged prejudicial conduct which has occurred since the petition was presented (*Cobden Investments Ltd v RWM Langport Ltd* [2007] EWHC 3048 (Ch), LTL 4/1/2008).

Costs

85.18 It is a misapplication of the company's money to pay any costs of proceedings on an unfair prejudice petition (other than as ordered by the court), except for those necessarily incurred in representing the company as a separate person (*Re Kenyon Swansea Ltd* [1987] BCLC 514; *Re Elgindata Ltd* [1991] BCLC 959). The court may order the company to indemnify the petitioner for the costs of obtaining an order in favour of the company as a separate person (*Clark v Cutland* [2003] EWCA Civ 810, [2004] 1 WLR 783). The company may provide a qualifying third party indemnity, as permitted by the Companies Act 2006, s. 234, to a director who successfully defends an allegation of negligence, default, breach of duty or breach of trust contained in an unfair prejudice petition (*Branch v Bagley* [2004] EWHC 426 (Ch), LTL 10/3/2004).

The court will issue an interim injunction to prevent misapplication of the company's assets on funding a defence to a petition. It may also restrain expenditure on other proceedings started against the petitioner which concern the same issues, if they were started in response to the petition (*Pollard v Pollard* (2007) LTL 26/9/2007).

Court's order

85.19 If the court is satisfied that the applicant's petition is well founded it is empowered by the Companies Act 2006, s. 996(1), to make such order as it thinks fit for giving relief in respect of the matters complained of. More particularly, under s. 996(2), the court may:

(a) regulate the conduct of the company's affairs in the future; this could include ordering an alteration of the company's memorandum or articles or preventing the company from making any, or any specified, alteration to the memorandum or articles without the court's permission;

(b) require the company to refrain from doing or continuing an act complained of by the petitioner or to do an act which the petitioner has complained it has omitted to do;

(c) authorise civil proceedings to be brought in the name and on behalf of the company by such person or persons and on such terms as the court may direct;

(d) require the company not to make any, or any specified, alterations in its articles without the leave of the court;

(e) provide for the purchase of the shares of any members of the company by other members or by the company itself and, in the case of a purchase by the company itself, the reduction of the company's capital accordingly.

The court has jurisdiction to make orders against persons who are not members of the company or who are not involved in the conduct complained of (provided they have been made parties to the proceedings), but it is inconceivable that the court would order a person who was not a member of the company to buy the petitioner's shares (*Re Little Olympian Each-ways Ltd* [1994] 2 BCLC 420).

The court has a power under s. 996(1) to make such orders as it considers will enable the company, for the future, to be properly run, and for its affairs to be under the conduct of somebody who the shareholders generally can be confident will conduct the affairs of the company properly (*Re a Company (No. 00789 of 1987)* [1990] BCLC 384 per Harman J at p. 395, followed in *Re Hailey Group Ltd* [1993] BCLC 459).

The rule that he who comes to equity must come with clean hands does not apply to unfair prejudice petitions. In other words, a petitioner's own misconduct is not in itself a reason for rejecting the petition, though it may show that the petitioner was not unfairly prejudiced or may affect the remedy given by the court (*Re London School of Electronics Ltd* [1986] Ch 211; *Richardson v Blackmore* [2005] EWCA Civ 1356, [2006] BCC 276).

The most common order is that the majority shareholders must buy the petitioner's shares. Exceptionally, in *Re Brenfield Squash Racquets Club Ltd* [1996] 2 BCLC 184 the majority shareholder was ordered to sell its shares to the petitioner.

If it is plain that the appropriate solution to the situation which the petitioner is complaining about is sale of the petitioner's shares, if other members of the company are willing to buy them, and if the articles provide a procedure for determining the price to be paid on a sale from one member to another, that procedure should be adopted, instead of petitioning under s. 994. A petition is appropriate, for the purpose of obtaining the court's valuation of the shares, if there is any risk that the procedure provided by the articles will undervalue them (*Re a Company (No. 00330 of 1991)* [1991] BCLC 597). However, if an offer is made which proposes a genuinely independent valuation, the court will strike out the petition as an abuse of process: the petitioner is not entitled to insist on the court carrying out a valuation which can be performed more cheaply by an accountant (*Re a Company (No. 00836 of 1995)* [1996] 2 BCLC 192).

There is a helpful discussion of what counts as a reasonable offer to purchase a petitioner's shares in *O'Neill v Phillips* [1999] 1 WLR 1092 at pp. 1107–8. An offer is not reasonable if the offeror cannot finance it (*West v Blanchet* [2000] 1 BCLC 795). In many cases the petitioner contends that the value of the shares has been diminished by the conduct complained of in the petition and some way has to be found for a valuer to take this into account. If the value of the shares depends on the answer to a question of law, the question should be left for the court to decide (*North Holdings Ltd v Southern Tropics Ltd* [1999] 2 BCLC 625).

A Tomlin order (see **63.16**) should not be made if the petition asked alternatively for the winding up of the company (*Re a Company (No. 003324 of 1979)* [1981] 1 WLR 1059). It is suggested that this difficulty may be overcome by obtaining permission to amend the petition to remove the prayer for winding up.

Notification of the court's order

If the court considers that an order it has made in unfair prejudice proceedings **85.20** should be advertised, it must give directions as to the manner and time of advertisement (SI 2009/2469, r. 6).

Chapter 86 Director Disqualification

STATUTORY PROVISIONS

Nature of a disqualification order

86.1 The Company Directors Disqualification Act 1986 (CDDA 1986) enables the civil and criminal courts to protect the public by making disqualification orders which ban persons from acting as company directors when it is shown that they are unfit to do so.

By CDDA 1986, s. 1(1), the main practical effect of a disqualification order is that the person against whom the order is made must not, without permission of a court (see **86.39**), be a director of a company or in any way, whether directly or indirectly, be concerned or take part in the management of a company, for the duration of the order. The person is also banned from being concerned or taking part, in any way, whether directly or indirectly, in the promotion or formation of a company, from acting as receiver of a company's property and from acting as an insolvency practitioner.

A disqualification undertaking (see **86.4**) has the same effect as a disqualification order but is made without court proceedings.

The acts which a disqualified person is prohibited from doing are listed in two paragraphs in s. 1(1), but the only form of disqualification order which may be made is one disqualifying a person from doing all the things listed: it is not possible to disqualify from only a selection of them (*Official Receiver v Hannan* [1997] 2 BCLC 473). It is not possible to make a disqualification order limited to a particular class of companies, such as public companies (*R v Ward* [2002] BCC 953).

Acting in contravention of a disqualification order is an offence triable either way (CDDA 1986, s. 13). In addition a person who contravenes a disqualification order by being a director of a company, or being concerned, whether directly or indirectly, or taking part, in the management of a company, may be made personally liable for all debts and liabilities of the company incurred while so acting (CDDA 1986, s. 15(1)(a), (3)(a) and (4)). A person liable under s. 15 is jointly and severally liable with the company itself and with any other person who is also jointly and severally liable for the debts (whether under s. 15 or some other provision) (CDDA 1986, s. 15(2)).

In CDDA 1986, 'company' means not only registered companies, but all unregistered companies capable of being wound up under part 5 of the Insolvency Act 1986 (see **82.1**) (CDDA 1986, s. 22(2) and (9)). This includes partnerships (Insolvent Partnerships Order 1994 (SI 1994/2421)) and it is submitted that it was wrong for Rattee J to suggest in *Secretary of State for Trade and Industry v Barnett* [1998] 2 BCLC 64 at p. 70 that a disqualified person could run a business in partnership with his wife. CDDA 1986 is applied, with modifications, to limited liability partnerships by the Limited Liability Partnerships Regulations 2001 (SI 2001/1090), reg. 4(2).

Grounds for disqualification

The circumstances in which a disqualification order may be made are summarised in **table 86.1**.   **86.2**

The vast majority of disqualification orders are made under CDDA 1986, s. 6, and this chapter will concentrate on applications under s. 7 for orders under s. 6 and applications under s. 8 (which have many similarities to those under s. 7).

In ss. 6 and 7, 'director' includes a shadow director (s. 6(3C)) and 'shadow director' is defined in s. 22(5) in the same way as it is defined in the Companies Act 2006, s. 251. The definition of shadow director is discussed in *Secretary of State for Trade and Industry v Deverell* [2001] Ch 340.

CDDA 1986 also extends to directors and officers of building societies (s. 22A), incorporated friendly societies (s. 22B) and NHS foundation trusts (s. 22C), to committee members and officers of registered societies (s. 22E), to charity trustees of charitable incorporated organisations (s. 22F), to officers of insolvent partnerships (Insolvent Partnerships Order 1994, art. 16 and sch. 8), and to members of limited liability partnerships (Limited Liability Partnerships Regulations 2001 (SI 2001/1090), reg. 4(2)(g)).

Purpose of disqualification under sections 6 and 8

In *Re Sevenoaks Stationers (Retail) Ltd* [1991] Ch 164 Dillon LJ said, at p. 176:   **86.3**

It is beyond dispute that the purpose of CDDA 1986, s. 6, is to protect the public, and in particular potential creditors of companies, from losing money through companies becoming insolvent when the directors of those companies are people unfit to be concerned in the management of a company.

Protection is not necessarily limited to the British public (*Re Westminster Property Management Ltd (No. 2)* [2001] BCC 305 at p. 358).

A further, related purpose is to raise standards of responsibility among those who make use of limited liability (per Nicholls V-C in *Secretary of State for Trade and Industry v Ettinger* [1993] BCLC 896 at p. 899). This was described by Scott V-C in *Re Barings plc* [1998] BCC 583 at p. 590 as subsidiary to the main purpose of protection of the public.

Table 86.1 Circumstances in which a disqualification order may be made

Section of CDDA 1986	Circumstance	Court which may make order	Who may apply for order	Period of disqualification
s. 2	Conviction of an indictable offence in connection with the promotion, formation, management, liquidation or striking off of a company, with the receivership of a company's property or with being an administrative receiver of a company.	(a) Convicting court, or (b) court with jurisdiction to wind up any company in relation to which offence was committed.	(a) Court's own motion. (b) See note 1.	Up to 15 years (five if made by magistrates' court).
s. 3	Persistent default in filing returns, accounts or other documents	Court with jurisdiction to wind up any company in relation to which default committed.	See note 1.	Up to five years.
s. 4	Fraud or fraudulent trading revealed in winding up.	Court with jurisdiction to wind up any company in relation to which fraud was committed.	See note 1.	Up to 15 years.
s. 5	Three convictions for failure to file documents with registrar.	Convicting court.	Court's own motion.	Up to five years.
s. 5A	Conviction abroad of offence relating to company management etc.	High Court.	Secretary of State.	Up to 15 years.
s. 6	Conduct while director of a company which has become insolvent shows unfitness.	See 86.6.	Secretary of State, see note 2.	Two to 15 years.
s. 8	Director found to be unfit.	High Court.	Secretary of State.	Up to 15 years.
s. 8ZA	Instructing unfit director disqualified under s. 6.	As for s. 6.	Secretary of State, see note 3.	Two to 15 years.
s. 8ZD	Instructing unfit director disqualified under s. 8.	High Court.	Secretary of State.	Up to 15 years.
s. 9A	Competition disqualification order.	High Court.	CMA or a specified regulator.	Up to 15 years.
s. 10	Participation in wrongful trading.	Court which finds wrongful trading.	Court's own motion.	Up to 15 years.

Note 1. The persons who may apply for an order under s. 2, 3 or 4 are (by s. 16(2)) the Secretary of State or the official receiver, or the liquidator or any past or present member or creditor of any company in relation to which the offence or other default was committed or is alleged to have been committed. An applicant must have a legitimate interest in having the defendant disqualified (Re Adbury Park Estates Ltd [2003] BCC 696).

Note 2. The application is made under s. 7. If the company which became insolvent is being or has been wound up by the court, the Secretary of State may direct the official receiver to apply (s. 7(1)).

Note 3. The application is made under s. 8ZB. If the application for disqualification of the unfit director was made by the official receiver, the Secretary of State may direct the official receiver to apply (s. 8ZB(1)(b)).

In *Re Blackspur Group plc* [1998] 1 WLR 422 the Court of Appeal said, at p. 426:

The purpose of [CDDA 1986] is the protection of the public, by means of prohibitory remedial action, by anticipated deterrent effect on further misconduct and by encouragement of higher standards of honesty and diligence in corporate management, from those who are unfit to be concerned in the management of a company.

See also per Sir Andrew Park in *Re Morija plc* [2007] EWHC 3055 (Ch), [2008] 2 BCLC 313 at [33]. Other judges at first instance have taken raising standards to be the primary purpose of disqualification: see Lawrence Collins J in *Re Bradcrown Ltd* [2001] 1 BCLC 547 at p. 550 (apparently misreading the mention of it in *Re Westmid Packing Services Ltd* at p. 129 as a statement by the court of the law whereas in fact it was only a summary of counsel's argument) and Peter Smith J in *Re J. A. Chapman and Co. Ltd* [2003] EWHC 532 (Ch), [2003] 2 BCLC 206 at [9]. That this is the primary purpose may be indicated by the rule that, if unfitness is proved, a disqualification order must be made under s. 6 (which requires a disqualification period of at least two years), whether or not the court thinks that the defendant is a danger to the public (*Re Grayan Building Services Ltd* [1995] Ch 241).

The purpose of a disqualification order is not to mete out retribution for aggrieved creditors (*Re Cubelock Ltd* [2001] BCC 523 at p. 536).

DISQUALIFICATION UNDERTAKINGS

86.4 Instead of applying to the court for an order under CDDA 1986, s. 5A, 6, 8, 8ZA or 8ZD, disqualifying a person from being a director, the Secretary of State may accept from the person a disqualification undertaking, if expedient in the public interest (ss. 5A(4), 7(2A), 8(2A), 8ZC and 8ZE). Instead of applying under s. 9A for a competition disqualification order, the Competition and Markets Authority or a specified regulator may, under s. 9B, accept a disqualification undertaking. A disqualification undertaking is an undertaking by a person not to do any of the things which are prohibited by a disqualification order, for a specified period of time. (ss. 1A and 9B). Sections 13 and 15 apply to disqualification undertakings as well as disqualification orders, so that the penalties for breaching an undertaking are the same as for acting contrary to a disqualification order.

Giving a disqualification undertaking because of inability to fund a trial is not the result of a violation of the European Convention on Human Rights, **art. 6(1)**, in the **Human Rights Act 1998, sch. 1**, and is not a ground for setting aside the undertaking (*Secretary of State for Trade and Industry v Davies* [2006] EWHC 299 (Ch), [2006] 2 BCLC 489).

The Secretary of State refuses to accept a disqualification undertaking unless it is accompanied by an agreed statement of the facts which showed the person's unfitness to be a director, and the Secretary of State is entitled to insist on such a statement (*Re Blackspur Group plc (No. 3)* [2001] EWCA Civ 1595, [2002] 2 BCLC 263).

PROCEDURAL RULES

86.5 All applications under CDDA 1986, s. 5A, 7, 8, 8ZB, 8ZD or 9A, for a disqualification order are governed by the Insolvent Companies (Disqualification of Unfit Directors) Proceedings Rules 1987 (SI 1987/2023). SI 1987/2023, r. 2(1), provides that the CPR and any relevant practice direction apply in respect of any application to which SI 1987/2023 applies except where SI 1987/2023 makes provision to inconsistent effect.

The most relevant practice direction is **PD Directors Disqualification Proceedings**, which, by **para. 1.3**, applies to applications for disqualification orders under any section of the CDDA 1986, applications to act as a director despite being disqualified and any application under **CPR, Part 23**, in connection with such proceedings.

Commentary

Disqualification proceedings are not insolvency proceedings and the Insolvency Rules 1986 (SI 1986/1925) do not apply to them (*Dobson v Hastings* [1992] Ch 394) except in relation to appeals (see **86.37** and **86.39**).

MAKING THE APPLICATION

Court to which application is to be made

86.6   An application under CDDA 1986, s. 7, for a disqualification order under s. 6, alleges:

(a) that the defendant is, or has been, a director or shadow director of a company (known as the 'lead company') which has at any time become insolvent (whether while the defendant was a director or subsequently), and

(b) that the defendant's conduct as a director or shadow director of the lead company (either taken alone or taken together with conduct as a director or shadow director of any other company — known as a 'collateral company') makes the defendant unfit to be concerned in the management of a company.

For these purposes a company 'becomes insolvent' if (s. 6(2)):

(a) the company goes into liquidation (see **82.32**) at a time when its assets are insufficient for the payment of its debts and other liabilities and the expenses of the winding up (s.6(2)(a)); or

(b) the company enters administration (s. 6(2)(b)); or

(c) an administrative receiver of the company is appointed (s. 6(2)(c)).

For the purposes of s. 6(2)(a), post-liquidation interest, either payable or receivable, cannot be taken into account, but the liquidator's remuneration, if properly approved, must be (*Official Receiver v Moore* [1995] BCC 293).

The court to which a s. 7 application for a disqualification order must be made depends on the type of insolvency procedure to which the lead company is subject when the proceedings commence, or has been subject to in the past.

If the lead company is being, or has been, wound up compulsorily, the disqualification application must be made to the court which is carrying out, or has carried out, the winding up (s. 6(3)(a)).

If the lead company is being, or has been, wound up voluntarily, the application must be made to a court which has (or had) jurisdiction to wind it up (s. 6(3)(b)). The rules on jurisdiction in winding up are set out in **82.8**. The Insolvency Act 1986, s. 117(2A) (only the High Court has jurisdiction in the London insolvency district) is to be read with the reference to presentation of the petition for winding up replaced by a reference to the passing of the resolution for voluntary winding up (CDDA 1986, s. 6(3A)(a)). No equivalent provision is made with respect to the Insolvency (Commencement of Proceedings) and Insolvency Rules 1986 (Amendment) Rules 2014 (SI 2014/817), r. 2(3), in relation to County Court hearing centres outside the London insolvency district.

If the lead company has never been in liquidation but has at any time been in administration or administrative receivership, the disqualification application must be made to a court which has jurisdiction to wind it up (s. 6(3)(c)), meaning the court which had jurisdiction at the time the administrator or administrative receiver was appointed (*Secretary of State for Trade and Industry v Arnold* [2007] EWHC 1933 (Ch), [2008] 1 BCLC 581). In that situation, the Insolvency Act 1986, s. 117(2A), is to be read with the reference to presentation of the petition for winding up replaced by a reference to the appointment of the administrator or (as the case may be) the appointment of the administrative receiver (CDDA 1986, s. 6(3A)(b)).

Jurisdiction is not affected by dissolution of the lead company (*Re Working Project Ltd* [1995] 1 BCLC 226).

By s. 6(3B), nothing in s. 6(3) invalidates disqualification proceedings by reason of their being taken in the wrong court.

An application under s. 8 alleges that the defendant's conduct in relation to one or more companies makes the defendant unfit to be concerned in the management of a company. An application under s. 8 must be made to the High Court or to the Court of Session in Scotland, whichever has jurisdiction to wind up the company or companies concerned (s. 8(3); *Re Helene plc* [2000] 2 BCLC 249).

An application may be made in respect of two or more lead companies (*Re Surrey Leisure Ltd* [1999] 2 BCLC 457). *Re Surrey Leisure Ltd* concerned s. 7 applications, but it was conceded in *Re Helene plc* that the decision applies to s. 8 applications as well.

Proper claimant

An application under CDDA 1986, s. 7 or s. 8, must be made by the Secretary of State, who **86.7** must consider that it is expedient in the public interest that a disqualification order should be made. Decisions on when to apply for disqualification orders are taken in the Disqualification Unit of the Insolvency Service, which is an executive agency of the Department for Business, Innovation and Skills (http://www.insolvency.gov.uk).

If the lead company in an application under s. 7 is being or has been wound up by the court, the Secretary of State may direct the official receiver to make the application (s. 7(1)). If the lead company has never been in compulsory liquidation (for example, if it is in administration), the official receiver does not have standing to make an application, which can only be made by the Secretary of State. The court may order a substitution of claimant if proceedings are started by the wrong claimant (*Re NP Engineering and Security Products Ltd* [1998] 1 BCLC 208).

Permission of the court after two/three years

An application under CDDA 1986, s. 7, may be made without the permission of the court **86.8** if it is made within three years of the date on which the lead company became insolvent (s. 7(2); but two years for companies which became insolvent before 1 October 2015). The date of becoming insolvent is the date when one of the events mentioned in s. 6(2) occurred. If more than one of them occurred, it is the date when the first of them occurred (*Re Tasbian Ltd (No. 1)* [1991] BCLC 54). An application is made when the claim form is received by the court (**PD 7A, para. 5.1**; *Secretary of State for Trade and Industry v Vohora* [2007] EWHC 2656 (Ch), [2008] Bus LR 161). If the court office is closed on the last day of the permission-free period, that period is extended to the next day on which the office is open (*Re Philipp and Lion Ltd* [1994] 1 BCLC 739).

When the permission-free period has expired an application may be made only with the permission of the court (s. 7(2)). Permission is applied for by application notice under **CPR, Part 23**, as amplified by **PD Directors Disqualification Proceedings, paras 17 and 19**.

The permission-free period is not properly described as a limitation period after which a person is immune from a claim: the need to obtain the permission of the court should be seen as an additional condition which applies after the permission-free period (*Secretary of State for Trade and Industry v Davies* [1996] 4 All ER 289 per Millett LJ at pp. 298–9).

According to Scott LJ in *Re Probe Data Systems Ltd (No. 3)* [1992] BCLC 405 at p. 416, in considering whether to give permission to make an application after the permission-free period the court should take account of all relevant circumstances, including, but not limited to:

(a) the length of the delay,
(b) the reasons for the delay,

(c) the gravity of the charges against the defendant, and

(d) the degree of prejudice caused to the defendant by the delay.

An important factor in favour of granting permission is that disqualification proceedings are brought, not to vindicate a private right, but to protect the public from the actions of a person alleged to be unfit to be a director of a company (*Secretary of State for Trade and Industry v Davies* per Millett LJ at pp. 296–7).

The applicant must explain why the application for permission is necessary, which necessarily involves giving reasons for the delay (*Secretary of State for Trade and Industry v Davies* at p. 299). However, there is no rule that an application for permission will not be considered unless the applicant gives a satisfactory reason for the delay: the satisfactoriness of the reason is just one of the factors to be taken into account by the court when exercising its discretion (*Secretary of State for Trade and Industry v Davies*).

Warning notice

86.9 By CDDA 1986, s. 16(1), any person intending to apply to the County Court or the High Court for the making of a disqualification order must give not less than 10 days' notice of that intention to the person against whom the order is sought. An application made without giving the correct period of notice is not a nullity (*Secretary of State for Trade and Industry v Langridge* [1991] Ch 402), but may be an abuse of process, for which one possible sanction would be to strike out the claim (*Re Finelist Ltd* [2003] EWHC 1780 (Ch), [2004] BCC 877 at [93]).

Use of Part 8 procedure, track allocation, form of application

86.10 An application under CDDA 1986 for a disqualification order must be made using the procedure in **CPR, Part 8** (see **chapter 13**) (SI 1987/2023, r. 2(2)), and must use form N500 (**PD Directors Disqualification Proceedings, para. 4.2**).

In the High Court the claim form must be issued out of the office of the Companies Court Registrar or a Chancery District Registry; in the County Court it will be issued out of a County Court office (**PD Directors Disqualification Proceedings, para. 4.1A**). The County Court or a High Court District Registry cannot be used for an application under CDDA 1986, s. 9A.

All disqualification proceedings are allocated to the multi-track by **PD Directors Disqualification Proceedings, para. 2.1**, and so the provisions of the CPR relating to track allocation and directions questionnaires do not apply.

When the claim form is issued, the court will fix a date for the first hearing of the claim, which must not be less than eight weeks from the date of issue of the claim form (SI 1987/2023, r. 7(1)).

In disqualification proceedings the court's power to allow a Part 8 claim to continue as a Part 7 claim (**CPR r. 8.1(3)**) is disapplied and Part 20 claims are not permitted (SI 1987/2023, r. 2(3)).

The title for the claim form and all affidavits, notices and other documents in the proceedings is, 'In the matter of [the company or companies in question] and in the matter of the Company Directors Disqualification Act 1986' (**PD Directors Disqualification Proceedings, para. 5.1**). In an application under CDDA 1986, s. 7, only the lead company or companies should be named in the heading (**PD Directors Disqualification Proceedings, para. 5.1**).

CPR, r. 8.2 (contents of Part 8 claim form), does not apply (SI 1987/2023, r. 2(3)). Instead **PD Directors Disqualification Proceedings, para. 6.1**, requires the claim form to include the information required by SI 1987/2023, r. 4, augmented with information relevant to applications under CDDA 1986, ss. 2 to 5. Form N500 has been designed to comply with these requirements. An important feature is that the claim form must identify the section of the Act under which the application is made and an endorsement on the form spells out the maximum periods of disqualification under each section.

The claim form must be verified by a statement of truth.

Case against the defendant

When the claim form is issued, evidence in support of the application must be filed in court (SI 1987/2023, r. 3(1)). It must be in the form of one or more affidavits and must include a statement of the matters by reference to which the defendant is alleged to be unfit to be concerned in the management of a company (r. 3(2) and (3)). These matters are commonly referred to as 'charges' (see **86.22**). If the official receiver is making the application, the evidence can be in the form of an official receiver's report (with or without affidavits from other persons), which shall be treated as if it had been verified by affidavit by the official receiver and shall be prima facie evidence of any matter contained in it (SI 1987/2023, r. 3(2)). Exhibits must be lodged with the court, where they will be retained until the conclusion of the proceedings (**PD Directors Disqualification Proceedings, para. 9.3(2)**).

86.11

The applicant may subsequently file further evidence, provided the defendant has an adequate opportunity to deal with it (*Secretary of State for Trade and Industry v Andrews* [2005] EWHC 3513 (Ch), LTL 27/1/2005).

In *Re Pinemoor Ltd* [1997] BCC 708 Chadwick J asked persons preparing affidavits in support of disqualification applications to be careful to distinguish between the facts which they are able to establish by direct evidence, the inferences which they invite the court to draw from those facts, and the matters which are said to amount to unfitness on the part of the defendant. This would help defendants to concentrate on the factual matters which they need to address in their own affidavits.

In practice a relatively short affidavit is prepared by an official in the Disqualification Unit of the Insolvency Service referring to charges which are specified in a detailed report prepared by the insolvency practitioner who has investigated the company. In *Secretary of State for Trade and Industry v Hickling* [1996] BCC 678 Judge Weeks QC said, at p. 690, that the investigative report should not omit significant available evidence in favour of a defendant. It should attempt to deal with any explanation the defendant has already offered. Where there are several defendants, it should endeavour to apportion responsibility. It should avoid sweeping statements for which there is no evidence.

The applicant has a duty to present the case against the defendant fairly (*Re Finelist Ltd* [2003] EWHC 1780 (Ch), [2004] BCC 877). The defendant should have been invited to comment on the proposed charges before the claim was issued (*Re Finelist Ltd*).

An allegation of dishonesty must be made 'fairly and squarely' in the affidavit (*Secretary of State for Trade and Industry v Goldberg* [2003] EWHC 2843 (Ch), [2004] 1 BCLC 597 at [53]).

Service

The claim form and a copy of the case against the defendant must be served on the defendant (SI 1987/2023, rr. 3(1) and 5(1)). Service may be by first-class post to the

86.12

defendant's last known address, in which case the date of service will, unless the contrary is shown, be deemed to be the seventh day next following that on which the claim form was posted (r. 5(1)). Service may be effected in some other way (*Official Receiver v Hodgkinson* (2000) LTL 13/10/2000). Apart from the deemed date of service by post, **CPR, Part 6, Sections I, II and III,** apply (**PD Directors Disqualification Proceedings, para. 7.2**). The court will not serve the claim form (**para. 7.1**). Provision for service out of the jurisdiction is made by SI 1987/2023, r. 5(2), and **PD Directors Disqualification Proceedings, para. 7.3. CPR, r. 10.3(2)** (period for acknowledgment of service of claim form served out of the jurisdiction), is disapplied by **PD Directors Disqualification Proceedings, para. 8.1**.

Acknowledgment of service

86.13   The claim form must be accompanied by form N502, acknowledgment of service (SI 1987/2023, r. 5(3), which disapplies **CPR, r. 8.3(2)** (contents of **Part 8** acknowledgment of service); **PD Directors Disqualification Proceedings, para. 8.1**). This form complies with SI 1987/2023, r. 5(4), by asking the defendant to indicate the grounds on which it is intended to dispute the claim.

The defendant must file the acknowledgment of service not more than 14 days after service of the claim form and serve it on the claimant and any other party (**PD Directors Disqualification Proceedings, para. 8.3**). A defendant who fails to file an acknowledgment in time may attend the hearing of the application but may not take part unless the court gives permission (**para. 8.4**).

Exchange of evidence

86.14   Any affidavit evidence which the defendant wishes the court to take into consideration in opposition to the application must be filed within 28 days of service of the claim form (SI 1987/2023, r. 6(1)). Copies must be served on the claimant and any other defendant (r. 6(1); **PD Directors Disqualification Proceedings, paras 9.4** and **9.5**). Rule 6(1) of SI 1987/2023 means that all the evidence which the defendant wishes the court to take into consideration must ordinarily be by affidavit: oral evidence-in-chief at the trial of the application will be allowed only in exceptional circumstances (*Re Rex Williams Leisure plc* [1994] Ch 350). Since disqualification proceedings are penal in nature, the defendant cannot be required to give evidence, but a defendant who chooses to file his or her own affidavit may be ordered to attend for cross-examination on it (*Re Dominion International Group plc* [1995] 1 WLR 649). If the defendant is not cross-examined, the court cannot find a charge proved if the defendant's affidavit denies it, unless the denial is self-evidently wrong, for example, because of other facts which are admitted or because it is plainly contradicted by reliable documents (*Re Hopes (Heathrow) Ltd* [2001] 1 BCLC 575).

Defendants have been criticised for filing evidence, for example, from accountants, which goes way beyond what is permissible in expert evidence (*Re Oakfame Construction Ltd* [1996] BCC 67; *Re Dominion International Group plc (No. 2)* [1996] 1 BCLC 572 at p. 600).

Once the defendant has filed evidence, the claimant then has 14 days in which to file further evidence (SI 1987/2023, r. 6(2); **PD Directors Disqualification Proceedings, para. 9.6**). Before the first hearing the parties may vary these time limits by written agreement, but after the first hearing extension of time for filing evidence is governed by **CPR, rr. 2.11** and **29.5** (**PD Directors Disqualification Proceedings, para. 9.7**). **PD Directors Disqualification Proceedings, para. 9.8**, asks for all evidence to be filed before the first hearing, so far as is possible.

In *Secretary of State for Trade and Industry v Davies* [1996] 4 All ER 289 Millett LJ said, at p. 299, that an application for extension of the time for filing evidence should be considered in the same way as an application for permission to commence proceedings after the two-year time limit (see **86.8**). His lordship went on to say:

But it must be more difficult to justify a failure even to issue the originating process within the time limit than to justify the failure to serve adequate supporting evidence at the same time; and the fact that the process has been issued within time must be a relevant factor to be taken into account, particularly if it is accompanied, as it was in the present case, with a statement of the grounds upon which the Secretary of State alleges that the [defendant] is unfit to be a director of a company.

Disclosure

Any material which would be of assistance to the defendant's case in disqualification pro- **86.15** ceedings should be disclosed, as in criminal proceedings (*Secretary of State for Trade and Industry v Baker* [1998] Ch 356; *Re Astra Holdings plc* [1998] 2 BCLC 44). A report made to the Secretary of State under CDDA 1986, s. 7(3) or (4), by an official receiver, liquidator, administrator or administrative receiver is not privileged (*Secretary of State for Trade and Industry v Baker*).

Delay, effect of other proceedings

A claim for the making of a disqualification order may be struck out if there is delay in pro- **86.16** ceeding to trial and the delay has substantially damaged the possibility of a fair trial or has otherwise prejudiced the defendant, as long as striking out would not be contrary to the public interest (*Re Noble Trees Ltd* [1993] BCLC 1185; *Official Receiver v B Ltd* [1994] 2 BCLC 1; *Re Manlon Trading Ltd* [1996] Ch 136). The type of delay which justifies striking out is usually described as inordinate and inexcusable, but in *Re Abermeadow Ltd* [2000] 2 BCLC 824 the court continued to consider whether to strike out a claim even after finding that the delay was excusable.

A disqualification claim against a person need not be adjourned to await the outcome of civil proceedings against the person in relation to matters relied on as evidence of unfitness (*Re Rex Williams Leisure plc* [1994] Ch 350). Formerly it was usual to adjourn a disqualification claim to await the conclusion of criminal proceedings against the same defendant, if the same facts would be in issue in the two proceedings, so as to avoid prejudicing the criminal trial. However, such adjournments are less necessary now that CDDA 1986, s. 20, has been amended to provide that a statement made by a person in pursuance of a requirement imposed by or under ss. 6 to 10 cannot be used by the prosecution in criminal proceedings against that person (except for proceedings for perjury in making the statement itself). This provision covers statements made in the defendant's affidavits in opposition to a disqualification claim and statements made in cross-examination at the hearing of the claim (*Secretary of State for Trade and Industry v Crane* [2001] 2 BCLC 222).

Delay does not mean that proceedings must be dismissed, unless there can no longer be a fair hearing or it would otherwise be unfair for proceedings to continue (*Secretary of State for Trade and Industry v Davies* [2006] EWHC 299 (Ch), [2006] 2 BCLC 489).

If a criminal court has convicted a person of an offence, but did not consider making a dis- qualification order, it is not an abuse of process for an application to be made in civil proceed- ings for a disqualification order based on the conduct for which the person was convicted in the criminal court (*Re Denis Hilton Ltd* [2002] 1 BCLC 302).

If a criminal court disqualifies a person under CDDA 1986, s. 2, after conviction for an offence in relation to a company, it is not necessarily an abuse of process to apply for a further

1575

FACTORS WHICH THE COURT CONSIDERS IN AN APPLICATION UNDER SECTION 6 OR 8

Unfitness must be proved

86.21   The court cannot disqualify a person under CDDA 1986, s. 6, unless it is satisfied that the person's conduct as a director or shadow director of a particular company — either taken alone or taken in conjunction with conduct as director or shadow director of any other company — makes that person unfit to be concerned in the management of a company. This means unfit to be concerned in the management of companies generally, though not necessarily every company in the country (*Re Polly Peck International plc (No. 2)* [1994] 1 BCLC 574; *Re Barings plc (No. 5)* [2000] 1 BCLC 523 at p. 535): it is possible to give permission for a disqualified person to manage a particular company (see **86.39**). If the court does find that the defendant's past conduct renders the defendant unfit, it must make a disqualification order for at least two years, regardless of subsequent reform of character (*Re Grayan Building Services Ltd* [1995] Ch 241). Subsequent reform of character may be taken into account when fixing the length of the disqualification period (see **86.32**).

The court's approach should not be that it will make a disqualification order if unfitness is proved, unless there are exceptional circumstances. The court should instead consider whether all the evidence, including evidence of extenuating circumstances, proves unfitness (*Cathie v Secretary of State for Business, Innovation and Skills* [2012] EWCA Civ 739, LTL 1/6/2012).

On an application under s. 8, the court may, at its discretion, disqualify a defendant whose conduct in relation to a particular company demonstrates unfitness to be concerned in the management of a company. There is no minimum period of disqualification under s. 8, but otherwise the principles which the court applies in deciding cases are the same as for s. 6 (*Secretary of State for Trade and Industry v Hollier* [2006] EWHC 1804 (Ch), [2007] Bus LR 352 at [50] and [59]). The two sections are compared and contrasted in *Re J. A. Chapman and Co. Ltd* [2003] EWHC 532 (Ch), [2003] 2 BCLC 206 at [2]–[9].

In *Re Sevenoaks Stationers (Retail) Ltd* [1991] Ch 164 Dillon LJ said, at p. 176:

The test laid down in s. 6 — apart from the requirement that the person concerned is or has been a director of a company which has become insolvent — is whether the person's conduct as a director of the company or companies in question 'makes him unfit to be concerned in the management of a company'. These are ordinary words of the English language and they should be simple to apply in most cases. It is important to hold to those words in each case.

Evidence

86.22   The matters by reference to which the defendant is alleged to be unfit (commonly known as the 'charges') must be specified by the claimant in a statement filed with the claim form (SI 1987/2023, r. 3(3)). Whatever other evidence is before the court, its reasons for making a disqualification order must be limited to proved charges: this ensures the defendant knows what case has to be answered (*Re Deaduck Ltd* [2000] 1 BCLC 148 at pp. 159 and 164–5). Only proved charges may be taken into account when setting the period of disqualification (*Re Sevenoaks Stationers (Retail) Ltd* [1991] Ch 164 at p. 177). But other evidence may show the context in which the proved misconduct occurred and may influence the court's assessment of its gravity, either when deciding whether the proved charges demonstrate unfitness (*Re Deaduck Ltd* at pp. 159 and 164–5) or (at least in so far as it provides mitigation) when determining the period of disqualification (*Re Sevenoaks Stationers (Retail) Ltd* at p. 177).

The r. 3(3) statement need not be treated like an indictment in a criminal trial. The court has a discretion whether to allow the claimant to add to or alter the charges made in the r. 3(3) statement, the paramount requirement being that the defendant must know the charges that have to be met (*Re Sevenoaks Stationers (Retail) Ltd* at p. 177; *Re Stephenson Cobbold Ltd* [2000] 2 BCLC 614; *Kappler v Secretary of State for Trade and Industry* [2006] BCC 845).

Whether a defendant is unfit is a question of fact (*Re Sevenoaks Stationers (Retail) Ltd* at p. 176). Determining that question:

involves the evaluation of the seriousness of the charges which have been proved and a judgment of the trial judge as to whether, taking all the circumstances into account, including all matters of mitigation and extenuation, the director is or is not unfit. (*Re Hitco 2000 Ltd* [1995] 2 BCLC 63 at p. 65.)

Charges must be viewed cumulatively, so that it is no defence to say that no individual instance of misconduct merits disqualification (*Re Barings plc (No. 5)* [2000] 1 BCLC 523 at p. 535). Circumstances which may be taken into account include the defendant's health at the time of the alleged misconduct (*Re CEM Connections Ltd* [2000] BCC 917). It is irrelevant that some other remedy has been or might be obtained for the misconduct (*Re Grayan Building Services Ltd* [1995] Ch 241). General evidence of character is irrelevant (*Re Dawes and Henderson (Agencies) Ltd* [1997] 1 BCLC 329) though it may be relevant in determining the period of disqualification (*Re Westmid Packing Services Ltd* [1998] 2 All ER 124 at p. 133).

Parliament has established investigatory processes for providing the Secretary of State with reports, information or documents on which an opinion may be based that it is expedient in the public interest that a disqualification order should be made against a person (CDDA 1986, s. 8). It follows that the Secretary of State may use the relevant report etc. as evidence in support of an application for a disqualification order despite the rules against evidence of opinion and findings of fact (*Re Barings plc (No. 2)* [1998] 1 BCLC 590; *Re Barings plc (No. 5)* [1999] 1 BCLC 433; *Secretary of State for Business, Enterprise and Regulatory Reform v Aaron* [2008] EWCA Civ 1146, [2009] 1 BCLC 55). This is so whether the application is for disqualification under s. 6 or s. 8 (*Secretary of State for Trade and Industry v Ashcroft* [1998] Ch 71). A copy of any report of inspectors appointed under the Companies Act 1985, part 14, certified by the Secretary of State to be a true copy, is admissible in any legal proceedings as evidence of the opinion of the inspectors in relation to any matter contained in the report (Companies Act 1985, s. 441(1)). However, the rules against evidence of opinion and findings of fact apply to other material, including other court proceedings (*Secretary of State for Trade and Industry v Bairstow* [2003] EWCA Civ 321, [2004] Ch 1). In *Secretary of State for Trade and Industry v Bairstow* the conduct of Mr Bairstow which was in issue in disqualification proceedings had also been in issue in a claim by Mr Bairstow for wrongful dismissal which he had lost. It was held (following *Hollington v F. Hewthorn and Co. Ltd* [1943] KB 587; see **49.100**) that the judgments given in the wrongful dismissal claim were not admissible evidence of the facts found in that claim. It was also held that it was not an abuse of process for Mr Bairstow to require the Secretary of State to prove those facts by admissible evidence. The test is whether the relitigation (a) would be manifestly unfair to a party to the disqualification proceedings or (b) would bring the administration of justice into disrepute. In this case it was clearly not unfair to any party and it was necessary in the interests of justice for the Secretary of State's serious charges to be proved to the satisfaction of the court by legally admissible evidence. On the other hand, in *Secretary of State for Business, Innovation and Skills v Potiwal* [2012] EWHC 3723 (Ch), LTL 8/1/2013, it was unfair to require the Secretary of State to spend a large quantity of public money (£400,000) on proving again aspects of the defendant's character which had already been ruled on by a tribunal in proceedings between the defendant's company and HMRC. There was no issue estoppel (see **33.16**), because while there was privity between the defendant and the company of which he was sole director and 40 per cent shareholder, there was no privity between HMRC and the Secretary of State.

For the purposes of the European Convention on Human Rights, **art. 6**, in the **Human Rights Act 1998, sch. 1**, directors disqualification proceedings in civil courts under CDDA

1986, ss. 6 to 10, are civil rather than criminal proceedings (*DC v United Kingdom* (application 39031/97) [2000] BCC 710). The safeguards required to protect the defendant are therefore less than in criminal proceedings. In particular, it may be allowable to use in evidence the defendant's own admissions of wrongdoing made under threat of punishment for not providing information to, for example, an insolvency office holder under the Insolvency Act 1986, s. 235 (*DC v United Kingdom*; *Official Receiver v Stern* [2000] 1 WLR 2230). The European Court of Human Rights has so far accepted that it is fair to use compulsorily obtained evidence in directors disqualification proceedings only where the evidence is not contested and is not a significant part of the case (*DC v United Kingdom*). The Court of Appeal has said that it is generally best for the trial judge to decide questions of fairness, either at a pre-trial review or in the course of the trial, having regard to all relevant factors (*Official Receiver v Stern* [2000] 1 WLR 2230). So far, the court has not accepted that hearing a claim for a disqualification order when the defendant is unable to pay for professional representation, even in a complex case, is a breach of **art. 6** (*Secretary of State for Trade and Industry v Davies* [2006] EWHC 299 (Ch), [2006] 2 BCLC 489; *Re City Truck Group Ltd* [2007] EWHC 350 (Ch), [2007] 2 BCLC 649).

The standard of proof is the civil standard of balance of probabilities. It is not an abuse of process to allege, in director disqualification proceedings, misconduct that would constitute a criminal offence, even though the criminal standard of proof is not required (*Re Mea Corporation Ltd* [2006] EWHC 1846 (Ch), [2007] 1 BCLC 618).

A court hearing a director disqualification claim must consider:

(a) what the defendant did (see **86.23**);
(b) whether the defendant's actions were due to the defendant's lack of probity or incompetence or both (see **86.24**);
(c) whether the case against the defendant is serious enough to warrant disqualification (see **86.24**).

What the defendant did

86.23   The limitations on the conduct from which charges may be formulated are considered at **86.25** to **86.28**.

The court must have regard to matters specified in CDDA 1986, sch. 1 (see **86.29**). It may take into account matters not listed in sch. 1 (*Re Bath Glass Ltd* [1988] BCLC 329 at p. 332; *Re Sykes (Butchers) Ltd* [1998] 1 BCLC 110 at p. 125) and the fact that they are not in the schedule does not mean that they are less significant than the matters that are in the schedule. Any allegation of unfitness must be considered on its merits irrespective of whether it is in the schedule (*Re Amaron Ltd* [2001] 1 BCLC 562 at p. 568). The contrary view accepted in *Secretary of State for Trade and Industry v Goldberg* [2003] EWHC 2843 (Ch), [2004] 1 BCLC 597 at [11], without reference to *Re Amaron Ltd*, must be wrong. In practice there are recurring themes in cases, notably the way in which defendants have financed trading while insolvent by using money owed to unsecured trade creditors and involuntary creditors such as HM Revenue and Customs (see **86.30**). In *Re Firedart Ltd* [1994] 2 BCLC 340 Arden J said, at p. 351:

there are a number of matters which if proved would generally lead me to the conclusion that a director was unfit to be concerned in the management of a company. They include: trading while insolvent; taking personal benefits over and above any proper remuneration; failing to keep proper accounting records.

For trading while insolvent see **86.30**. Arden J's reference to taking personal benefits is echoed by Lindsay J in *Re Polly Peck International plc (No. 2)* [1994] 1 BCLC 574, who said that any breach of duty designed to benefit the defendant who owed the duty is likely to be regarded as serious enough to warrant disqualification, but a breach of duty which was not intended to benefit the defendant might not warrant disqualification (see also *Re Deaduck Ltd* [2000] 1 BCLC 148 at p. 160). On failure to keep proper accounting records see per Nicholls V-C in *Secretary of State for Trade and Industry v Ettinger* [1993] BCLC 896 at p. 900.

In *Secretary of State for Trade and Industry v McTighe (No. 2)* [1996] 2 BCLC 477 Morritt LJ said that persistent failure to cooperate with the liquidator and the official receiver would demonstrate unfitness.

Seriousness of case

In *Re Grayan Building Services Ltd* [1995] Ch 241 Hoffmann LJ said, at p. 253, that the court must decide whether the defendant's conduct,   **86.24**

viewed cumulatively and taking into account any extenuating circumstances, has fallen below the standards of probity and competence appropriate for persons fit to be directors of companies.

As the minimum period of disqualification under CDDA 1986, s. 6, is two years, a disqualification order should not be made at all if the defendant's misconduct is not serious enough to merit two years' disqualification (*Re Polly Peck International plc (No. 2)* [1994] 1 BCLC 574).

Although the mere fact that a defendant's misconduct is neither dishonest nor contrary to the law does not mean that it cannot render the director unfit (*Re Deaduck Ltd* [2000] 1 BCLC 148 at p. 167), the courts have generally been more ready to disqualify for lack of probity than for incompetence. In *Re Lo-Line Electric Motors Ltd* [1988] Ch 477 Browne-Wilkinson V-C said, at p. 486:

Ordinary commercial misjudgment is in itself not sufficient to justify disqualification. In the normal case, the conduct complained of must display a lack of commercial probity, although I have no doubt that in an extreme case of gross negligence or total incompetence disqualification could be appropriate.

In *Re McNulty's Interchange Ltd* (1988) 4 BCC 533 Browne-Wilkinson V-C repeated that commercial misjudgment does not demonstrate unfitness and went on to say that an application for a disqualification order should not be made where all that is alleged is mere mismanagement. In *Re Sevenoaks Stationers (Retail) Ltd* [1991] Ch 164 Dillon LJ said, at p. 184, that he did not think it was necessary for incompetence to be 'total', as suggested by Browne-Wilkinson V-C in *Re Lo-Line Electric Motors Ltd*, to render a director unfit: incompetence or negligence 'in a very marked degree' was sufficient in the case before him. In *Re Barings plc (No. 5)* [1999] 1 BCLC 433 Jonathan Parker J, at pp. 483–4, reconciled the two approaches by saying:

Where... [the claimant's] case is based solely on allegations of incompetence...the burden is on [the claimant] to satisfy the court that the conduct complained of demonstrates incompetence of a high degree.

On appeal in *Re Barings plc (No. 5)* [2000] 1 BCLC 523 the Court of Appeal, at p. 535, said that it wished to emphasise what Jonathan Parker J had said. The Court of Appeal went on to suggest that it is unnecessary to require an exaggerated degree of incompetence to justify the penalty of disqualification, given that the court can give permission to act during a period of disqualification (see **86.39**). But it is surely better to adopt the view of Lindsay J in *Re Polly Peck International plc (No. 2)* that the court's power to give permission is not something to be taken into account when deciding whether to disqualify. It is not right to deal with misconduct that is not serious enough to warrant the minimum period of two years' disqualification by disqualifying and then giving permission to act despite being disqualified: the right course is not to disqualify at all. In *Re Cubelock Ltd* [2001] BCC 523 Park J said, at p. 536, that 'the Court of Appeal [in *Re Barings plc (No. 5)*] did not to any appreciable extent diminish the level of incompetence which would be required to justify a disqualification'. Jonathan Parker J's formulation has been followed in *Re Bradcrown Ltd* [2001] 1 BCLC 547 and *Secretary of State for Trade and Industry v Walker* [2003] EWHC 175 (Ch), [2003] 1 BCLC 363. For examples of incompetence of such seriousness as to amount to unfitness see *Re Barings plc* [1998] BCC 583 and *Re Barings plc (No. 5)*.

De facto directorships included

86.25   The past conduct that the court considers is conduct as a director whether properly appointed as such or not (*Re Lo-Line Electric Motors Ltd* [1988] Ch 477). In *Re Lo-Line Electric Motors Ltd* Browne-Wilkinson V-C said that Parliament's plain intention was to have regard to the conduct of a person acting as a director, whether validly appointed, invalidly appointed or just assuming to act as a director without any appointment at all. (A person who acts as a director without being properly appointed is known as a de facto director.) It may be very difficult to decide whether what a person has done amounts to acting as a director so as to make the individual liable to disqualification, though in practice the question may be inextricably linked with whether what he or she has done in itself merits disqualification — see *Secretary of State for Trade and Industry v Tjolle* [1998] 1 BCLC 333. In *Re Kaytech International plc* [1999] 2 BCLC 351 the Court of Appeal refused to lay down a definition of de facto director, but found that in the case before it an individual had acted as a director. *Re Sykes (Butchers) Ltd* [1998] 1 BCLC 110 is another case in which a defendant was found to have been a de facto director. There is a full review of the authorities in *Secretary of State for Trade and Industry v Hollier* [2006] EWHC 1804 (Ch), [2007] Bus LR 352. See also the list of points which are of general practical importance in determining who is a de facto director given by Arden LJ in *Smithton Ltd v Naggar* [2014] EWCA Civ 939, [2015] 1 WLR 189, at [33]–[45].

Geographical coverage

86.26   The court may consider conduct that occurred outside England and Wales, and persons who are not British subjects or are not domiciled in England and Wales may be disqualified under CDDA 1986, s. 6 (*Re Seagull Manufacturing Co. Ltd (No. 2)* [1994] Ch 91).

Lead and collateral companies

86.27   An application to disqualify a person under CDDA 1986, s. 6, arises because the person has been a director of a company which has become insolvent (s. 6(1)(a)), but, under s. 6(1)(b), the court may consider the person's conduct as director both of that company (the 'lead company') and one or more other companies or overseas companies ('collateral companies'). Any conduct in relation to collateral companies which tends to show that the director is unfit may be considered: the court is not restricted to considering conduct which arises from or is in some way connected with the affairs of the lead company (*Secretary of State for Trade and Industry v Ivens* [1997] 2 BCLC 334). Conduct in relation to a collateral company may be considered even though it became insolvent more than two years before proceedings commenced (*Secretary of State for Trade and Industry v Ivens*). But if there is in fact nothing in the director's conduct in relation to the lead company which shows that the director is unfit, the court cannot consider anything done in relation to collateral companies (*Secretary of State for Trade and Industry v Ivens*).

Conduct in relation to other companies can only be considered for the purpose of proving unfitness. A finding that a defendant's conduct in relation to the lead company demonstrates unfitness cannot be negatived by consideration of his or her conduct in relation to other companies (*Re Bath Glass Ltd* [1988] BCLC 329 at pp. 331–2).

It is possible to apply in respect of two or more lead companies (*Re Surrey Leisure Ltd* [1999] 2 BCLC 457).

Conduct in relation to the insolvency

For the purposes of CDDA 1986, s. 6, conduct as a director of a company includes, where the **86.28** company has become insolvent, conduct in relation to any matter connected with or arising out of the insolvency of that company (s. 6(2)). This includes conduct in relation to the director disqualification claim itself (*Secretary of State for Trade and Industry v Reynard* [2002] EWCA Civ 497, [2002] 2 BCLC 625).

Statutory list of matters to be considered

When considering whether a person's conduct in relation to a company makes the person **86.29** unfit to be a director, the court is required by CDDA 1986, s. 9, to have regard in particular to the matters mentioned in part 1 of sch. 1 to the Act as in force before 1 October 2015. For conduct occurring on or after 1 October 2015, s. 9 is replaced by s. 12C and there is a new sch. 1. The fact that particular matters are listed in sch. 1 does not mean that the court may not have regard to other matters (see **86.23**).

Taking unwarranted risks with creditors' money

In *Secretary of State for Trade and Industry v Creegan* [2002] 1 BCLC 99 it was held that unfitness is **86.30** not demonstrated merely by allowing a company to trade while knowing it to be insolvent: it must also be shown that the defendant knew or ought to have known that there was no reasonable prospect of meeting creditors' claims. The phrase 'taking unwarranted risks with creditors' money' is used in some of the cases to describe this kind of misconduct (see, for example, *Re Living Images Ltd* [1996] 1 BCLC 348).

A policy of not paying on time creditors who do not press for payment may demonstrate unfitness, especially where the money is used to finance trading while insolvent (*Re Sevenoaks Stationers (Retail) Ltd* [1991] Ch 164). A non-payment policy may demonstrate unfitness even if it is not shown that the defendant intended that the creditors would never be paid (*Secretary of State for Trade and Industry v McTighe (No. 2)* [1996] 2 BCLC 477; *Re Structural Concrete Ltd* [2001] BCC 578), but the mere fact that debts are routinely paid late may not show unfitness (*Re Funtime Ltd* [2000] 1 BCLC 247). A non-payment policy may demonstrate unfitness if adopted while the company is solvent (*Re Hopes (Heathrow) Ltd* [2001] 1 BCLC 575). Although it is often so-called Crown debts (especially value added tax and employees' national insurance and tax contributions) that are the subject of a non-payment policy, the identity of the creditor is not the crucial factor demonstrating unfitness, and the court must consider the significance of the non-payment policy and whether the defendant was taking unfair advantage of the creditor's forbearance (*Re Sevenoaks Stationers (Retail) Ltd* at p. 183; *Re Amaron Ltd* [2001] 1 BCLC 562 at pp. 571–3).

MAKING THE ORDER

Absence of defendant

On hearing an application for a disqualification order, the court may make the order even if **86.31** (SI 1987/2023, r. 8(1)):
(a) the defendant has not acknowledged service of the claim form;
(b) the defendant has not filed evidence;
(c) the defendant has not appeared at the hearing.

However, a disqualification order made in the absence of the defendant may be set aside or varied by the court on such terms as it thinks just (r. 8(2)).

A person subject to a compensation order or undertaking may ask the court to reduce the amount payable or revoke the order (s. 15C(1)). The court must hear the Secretary of State on such an application (s. 15C(2)).

APPEAL

Procedure

86.37   Appeals in disqualification proceedings are governed by the rules governing appeals in corporate insolvency proceedings discussed at **84.12** to **84.17** (*Re Tasbian Ltd (No. 2)* [1991] BCLC 59, CA; *Re Probe Data Systems Ltd (No. 3)* [1992] BCLC 405 (in which the Court of Appeal held that *Re Tasbian Ltd (No. 2)* is not manifestly wrong)). This is so whether the proceedings concerned a company in liquidation (as in *Re Tasbian Ltd (No. 2)*) or subject to another insolvency procedure (*Secretary of State for Trade and Industry v Jones* [1999] BCC 336).

Stay pending appeal

86.38   The High Court and the Court of Appeal have inherent jurisdiction to stay a disqualification order pending an appeal (*Secretary of State for Trade and Industry v Bannister* [1996] 1 WLR 271, in which a stay was refused and which left open the question whether the County Court could grant a stay).

PERMISSION TO ACT DURING A PERIOD OF DISQUALIFICATION

86.39   A person subject to a disqualification order or undertaking may apply for permission to do any of the things which it prohibits, apart from acting as an insolvency practitioner (CDDA 1986, ss. 1(1) and 1A(1)).

Permission may be given at the same time as a disqualification order is made under s. 6 or s. 8. A person facing disqualification proceedings who envisages applying for permission if disqualified should do so in those proceedings so that the application can be heard by the judge who makes the disqualification order (*Secretary of State for Trade and Industry v Collins* [2000] 2 BCLC 223) and the application should be made by application notice under **CPR, Part 23** (**PD Directors Disqualification Proceedings, para. 20.2**). After a disqualification order has been made under CDDA 1986, s. 6 or s. 8, an application to do any of the things prohibited by the order must be made to the court which made the order (s. 17(1)) and the application should be made by claim form under **CPR, Part 8** (form N208). If there are two or more orders, the application should be made to the court which made the last of them (s. 17(4)).

An application to do anything prohibited by a disqualification undertaking accepted under s. 7(2A) or s. 8(2A) may be made to any court to which, if the undertaking had not been accepted, the Secretary of State could have applied for a disqualification order (CDDA 1986, s. 17(3)).

The title for the application notice or claim form and all affidavits, notices and other documents in the proceedings is 'In the matter of [the company or companies in question] and in the matter of the Company Directors Disqualification Act 1986' (**PD Directors Disqualification Proceedings, para. 21.1**).

Evidence in support of an application must be by affidavit (**PD Directors Disqualification Proceedings, para. 22.1**). Clear evidence is required of the precise role the applicant is to play in the company in question together with up-to-date and adequate information about the company (*Secretary of State for Trade and Industry v Collins* [2000] 2 BCLC 223). If the applicant's disqualification was made under the summary *Carecraft* procedure, the applicant should not be permitted to offer evidence about his or her past behaviour in addition to that contained in the agreed *Carecraft* statement, unless asked to do so by the court (*Secretary of State for Trade and Industry v Collins* [2000] 2 BCLC 223). The same applies to the agreed statement of facts in a disqualification undertaking (*Re Morija plc* [2007] EWHC 3055 (Ch), [2008] 2 BCLC 313).

The application notice or claim form and supporting evidence must be served on the Secretary of State (**para. 23.1**). Service of an application notice will not be undertaken by the court (**para. 26.1**). The Secretary of State must appear on a hearing of an application for permission, in order to call the court's attention to any relevant matters, and may give evidence or call witnesses (CDDA 1986, s. 17(5)). The matters which the Secretary of State may raise on the application for permission are not limited to those which were considered when making the disqualification order, though the disqualified person must be given adequate notice of new matters, which will not be possible if the application for permission is heard immediately after the disqualification order is made (*Re Westminster Property Management Ltd (No. 2)* [2001] BCC 305 at 355). The Secretary of State's appearance is required only because of the disqualified person's wish to act as a director etc. despite disqualification, and so the disqualified person should be ordered to pay the Secretary of State's costs (*Secretary of State for Trade and Industry v Collins* [2000] 2 BCLC 223).

Applications for permission are allocated to the multi-track by **PD Directors Disqualification Proceedings, para. 2.1,** and so the provisions of the CPR relating to track allocation and directions questionnaires do not apply.

In *Re Westminster Property Management Ltd (No. 2)* [2001] BCC 305 at 355 Lloyd J said, at p. 361, that the applicant's burden of showing justification for being allowed to act as a director or be concerned in the management of a company:

is likely only to be satisfied if it can be shown that the corporate body in question has a need for the services of the person in question, that there is no risk to the public from the person in question acting as a director, and further that to allow the person in question to act as a director would not subvert or reduce the effect of the disqualification order, even if only in its deterrent effect.

Permission will be given only if there is a need for it (*Re Cargo Agency Ltd* [1992] BCLC 686) and that must be the company's need for the disqualified person's services, not that person's desire to manage companies (*Re Gibson Davies Ltd* [1995] BCC 11). When the person who is applying for permission to manage a company is substantially the only person interested in the company's equity capital, it is difficult to find any company need that is separate from the applicant's. In those circumstances the question is, according to Rattee J in *Secretary of State for Trade and Industry v Barnett* [1998] 2 BCLC 64 at p. 72:

whether it is necessary for [the applicant] to be a director of a company in order to protect some legitimate interest of [the applicant] himself, or of any third party, which it is in all the circumstances of the case reasonable that the court should seek to protect. If it is so necessary, then the next question is whether that need can be met without infringing the protection of the public secured by the disqualification order.

Saving tax may be a legitimate interest for this purpose (*Re Dawes and Henderson (Agencies) Ltd (No. 2)* [1999] 2 BCLC 317).

The principles to be applied when deciding whether to grant permission were reviewed by Scott V-C in *Re Barings plc (No. 3)* [2000] 1 WLR 634. His lordship said that permission should never be granted without serious consideration (at p. 641). If permission is granted, the reasons for doing so must be consistent with the reasons for making the disqualification order (at p. 640). In particular the court should ask whether the situation in which the disqualified person would be given permission to act would risk recurrence of the particular faults for which he or she had been disqualified (at p. 641).

Adequate protection of the public must be provided. For example, an independent chartered accountant or solicitor must act as co-director (*Re Majestic Recording Studios Ltd* [1989] BCLC 1; *Secretary of State for Trade and Industry v Palfreman* [1995] 2 BCLC 301). In *Re Gibson Davies Ltd* 10 protective undertakings were given. The court does not tolerate imperfect compliance with such undertakings (*Re Brian Sheridan Cars Ltd* [1996] 1 BCLC 327), but this raises the question of who is to check that the undertakings are being observed. In *Re Hennelly's Utilities Ltd* [2004] EWHC 34 (Ch), [2005] BCC 542, the court required the finance director, of the company which the disqualified person was applying to manage, to provide quarterly reports to the Department of Trade and Industry on the disqualified person's compliance with undertakings he had given. The learned deputy judge said, at [63]:

> the court has to balance any need for the director to act against the protection of the public from the conduct that led to the disqualification order. But the protection of the public (i.e. creditors, employees, lenders, investors and all those with whom the company will do business) is...paramount.

See further, D Milman, 'Partial disqualification orders' (1991) 12 Co Law 224; Robert Goddard, 'Leave to act and the disqualified director: *Re Hennelly's Utilities Ltd*' (2004) 25 Co Law 222. The practice of granting permission subject to conditions was criticised in *Re TLL Realisations Ltd* [2000] BCC 998 by Ferris J, who said that 'If it is felt that [permission] should not be unconditional this may suggest that the better view is that it should not be granted at all'. The court must bear in mind that the purpose of a disqualification order or undertaking is to protect the public (a) from misconduct by the disqualified person, (b) by deterring others from doing what the disqualified person did and (c) by maintaining and improving standards of integrity of directors (*Re Morija plc* [2007] EWHC 3055 (Ch), [2008] 2 BCLC 313 at [33]). The more serious the misconduct which led to the disqualification order or undertaking, the greater the risk of future misconduct and the greater the need to maintain disqualification as a deterrent to others (*Re Morija plc* at [35]).

It is not the policy of the Act to prevent a disqualified director from earning his or her living, only from doing so with the insulation from liability available to company directors. Being a member of an unlimited company imposes unlimited liability when the company is wound up and so an application to be a director of an unlimited company of which the applicant will be substantially the only interested member may be looked on favourably by the court, provided there are undertakings to maintain the company's unlimited status (*Re Dawes and Henderson (Agencies) Ltd (No. 2)*).

Appeals against decisions on applications for permission are governed by the rules governing appeals in corporate insolvency proceedings discussed at **84.12** to **84.17** (*Re Britannia Homes Centres Ltd* [2001] 2 BCLC 63 and see **86.37**).

VARIATION OF DISQUALIFICATION UNDERTAKING

86.40   A person who has given a disqualification undertaking may apply under CDDA 1986, s. 8A, for an order reducing or ending the period for which the undertaking is to be in force. The application may be made to any court to which, if the undertaking had not been accepted, the Secretary of State could have applied for a disqualification order (s. 8A(3)). The application must be made under **CPR, Part 8**, using form N501 (**PD Directors Disqualification Proceedings, para. 30.2**). The Secretary of State must be made the defendant to the application (**para. 30.5**), which must be served by the applicant, by first-class post, on the Treasury Solicitor (**para. 30.6**). On the hearing of the application, the Secretary of State must appear, in order to call the court's attention to any relevant matters, and may give evidence or call witnesses (CDDA 1986, s. 8A(2)). **PD Directors Disqualification Proceedings, paras 29** to **34**, give full details of the procedure to be followed, which has much in common with the procedure for applying for a disqualification order.

Disqualification undertakings were created in order to avoid court proceedings, so variation of an undertaking should be ordered only where circumstances have arisen since the undertaking was given which could not have been foreseen or which were not intended to be covered by the undertaking (*Re INS Realisations Ltd* [2006] EWHC 135 (Ch), [2006] 1 WLR 3433 at [39]–[40]). An application for variation should not normally be made just because the undertaking was given without legal advice or because other directors of the company were given shorter disqualification periods by the court (*Re INS Realisations Ltd* at [43]).

Commentary

PART R

Mortgage Possession Claims

Chapter 87   Mortgage Possession Claims

The following procedural checklists are relevant to this chapter:

Procedural checklist 37   Residential mortgage possession claims
Procedural checklist 38   Enforcement of possession orders

NATURE OF MORTGAGES

Rights to possession

87.1 A legal mortgage of a freehold or leasehold estate is a charge created by deed to secure financial liabilities owed by the borrower (or 'mortgagor') to the lender (or 'mortgagee') (Law of Property Act 1925, ss. 85 and 86). Part 3 of the 1925 Act sets out a framework of rights, powers and obligations of parties to a mortgage. These are subject to the terms of the mortgage deed itself. The lender has a legal estate in the charged property and at common law has an immediate right to possession of the property (*Four-Maids Ltd v Dudley Marshall (Properties) Ltd* [1957] Ch 317 at p. 320). Mortgage deeds usually make exercise of this right conditional on default by the borrower. Rights to possession or to sell may also be conferred on other grounds, such as the insolvency or death of the borrower.

In practice, a lender wishing to realise its security will require possession so as to sell the mortgaged property under its statutory power of sale (see ss. 101 to 103 of the 1925 Act). In order to be able to take possession of mortgaged property against the wishes of the borrower or anyone else occupying the property, a lender must obtain a court order for possession, which can be enforced by a warrant of possession.

Types of mortgage

87.2 Most mortgages granted by financial institutions are instalment mortgages, under which the borrower agrees to repay capital, and accrued interest, over a set term of years by regular instalments. If the borrower pays all the instalments, the mortgage debt will be discharged at the end of the term.

Some mortgages only require the borrower to repay the accrued interest during the term of the mortgage. An 'interest-only' mortgage leaves the capital sum outstanding at the end of the mortgage term. The borrower may repay the capital sum by maintaining a life assurance policy which matures on expiry of the term; or through other means such as remortgage or sale of the property. Failure to pay the outstanding debt at the end of the term will be a breach of an express or implied covenant in the mortgage agreement, giving rise to a separate ground for possession by the lender.

A small number of mortgages operate as overdrafts on a current account. Rather than paying a monthly instalment, the borrower must reduce the overdraft debt to a stated amount by an agreed date, with the aim of repaying the overdraft in full by the end of the term. A failure to do so is a breach of the mortgage agreement, but this should be distinguished from arrears of monthly instalments under a repayment mortgage and again gives rise to a separate ground for possession.

Some mortgage deeds are expressed as 'all money' charges. Such charges grant security not just for the mortgage debt but also for all other liabilities owed by the borrower to the lender, including any unsecured loans and shortfall debts following the sale of other secured property.

'Buy-to-let' mortgages, where the lender allows the borrower to let the property to tenants, are essentially commercial in nature and are subject to lighter regulation. Lenders have no right to possession against tenants living in the property in accordance with the lender's letting conditions, even where the borrower is in breach of the mortgage agreement. In such circumstances lenders must appoint a Law of Property Act (or 'fixed charge') receiver, who becomes the agent of the borrower and may serve notice to terminate the tenancy in the capacity of landlord.

Until March 2016 a distinct regime covered second charge lending and secured loans by financial institutions regulated by the Office of Fair Trading under the Consumer Credit Act 1974. Regulation has now been assumed by the Financial Conduct Authority.

This chapter focuses on possession claims based on arrears under a first charge mortgage of residential property.

COMMENCEMENT OF PROCEEDINGS

Pre-action protocol

The **Pre-action Protocol for Possession Claims Based on Mortgage or Home Purchase Plan Arrears in Respect of Residential Property** (the **Mortgage Protocol**) initially came into force on 19 November 2008 and was substantially amended on 6 April 2015. Its aim is to encourage initial communication between the parties and out-of-court resolution of disputes. That notwithstanding, there will be cases where a possession order is necessary. The **Mortgage Protocol** contains no specific sanctions for non-compliance. However, non-compliance may be indicative of unreasonable conduct, which may entitle the court to disallow certain costs (see **87.28**) or adjourn or stay the proceedings (see **87.29**). This is consistent with **PD Pre-action Conduct and Protocols, paras 15** and **16**. | **87.3**

Practitioners should refer to the specific requirements of the **Mortgage Protocol**. In essence, when a borrower falls into arrears there are obligations on mortgage lenders to provide full financial statements, to attempt discussion with the borrower about the causes of the problem, to consider changes to the monthly payment date or proposals to sell the mortgaged property, to respond promptly to borrowers' proposals, and to check who is in occupation of the property. If an agreement is breached, 15 business days' written notice must be given of the intention to start a possession claim (**para. 5.8**).

Lenders should, before starting a claim, allow the borrower an opportunity to make a claim to the Department for Work and Pensions (DWP) for support for mortgage interest or universal credit, or for a payment from the local authority or a welfare or charitable organisation (**para. 6.1(a)** and **(b)**). The borrower is required to provide to the lender all the evidence required to process such a claim (**para. 6.1(a)(iv)**).

If the borrower can demonstrate reasonable steps have been or can be taken to sell the property at an 'appropriate' price in accordance with reasonable professional advice, the mortgage lender must consider postponing starting a claim. But the borrower must reciprocate, by actively marketing the property and keeping the mortgage lender informed (**paras 6.2** and **6.3**). If the lender decides against postponing issuing (perhaps because of negative equity, or an errant co-owner) it must inform the borrower of the reasons five business days before starting proceedings (**para. 6.4**).

Lenders should seek information about whether the property is occupied by an authorised tenant (**para. 5.2**).

Starting a possession claim is a last resort which normally must not be used unless all other reasonable attempts to resolve the position have failed. Claims must not normally be started when settlement is being actively explored. Lenders are encouraged to consider a wide range of options, including extending the term, changing the type of mortgage, deferring interest, capitalising arrears or making use of government forbearance initiatives (**para. 7.1**). Further restrictions operate if an apparently genuine complaint has been made to the Financial Ombudsman (**para. 8.1**). However there is no compulsion on lenders to adopt any particular solution. Compliance with the **Mortgage Protocol** is evidenced at the hearing by production of a standard-form checklist in form N123 (see **87.24**). Lenders and their solicitors should complete the checklist and consider compliance with the **Mortgage Protocol** before the issue of proceedings in order to avoid any later adverse costs consequences.

Mortgage lenders should take into account the Good Practice Awareness Guidelines for Consumers with Mental Health Problems and Debt issued by the Money Advice Liaison Group, which since 21 March 2016 is a regulatory obligation under the FCA's Mortgage Conduct of Business source book (MCOB), r. 13.3.1D. This guidance does not mean that a lender has to ignore the payment record of the borrower in deciding whether to bring proceedings (*Graves v Capital Home Loans Ltd* [2014] EWCA Civ 1297, [2014] CTLC 233).

Procedural framework

87.4 A possession claim brought by a mortgage lender must follow the procedure set out in **CPR, Part 55** and **PD 55A**. However, a judgment creditor seeking to enforce a charging order by sale, even if also seeking possession, uses the procedure in **CPR, Part 73** (**r. 73.10**; see **79.33**).

Other pre-issue considerations

87.5 A lender should check all relevant terms of the mortgage contract when contemplating possession proceedings. The mortgage deed rarely reflects the entire arrangement negotiated between lender and borrower. A mortgage deed is usually in short form, incorporating the lender's then current printed standard conditions. Further terms, such as the amount of the loan and the initial interest rate, may appear in an offer letter. Lenders should ensure that the right to possession has arisen under the particular terms and conditions of the mortgage.

Care should be taken, particularly with flats, or new properties where the estate conveyancing may have used plot numbers, to identify the correct parcel of land and postal address of the property, including postcode. Specific inquiry should be made by solicitors of their lender client as to what its records show as the last known address of the proposed defendants. When joint borrowers separate, the deserted partner may supply the lender with the other's new address. Lenders and their solicitors should not divulge the address details of one separated borrower to another without consent, particularly where any suggestion of domestic abuse may have arisen.

Office copy Land Registry entries should be obtained, a matrimonial homes search made, and instructions taken on them for the material to be included in the claim form and particulars of claim. Where the property is leasehold the lease should be obtained and the lease plan should be checked against the title plan in the office copy entries.

The limitation period for the enforcement of a mortgage made by deed is governed by the Limitation Act 1980, s. 20. In relation to the principal it is 12 years from the date the cause of action accrued; for interest it is six years (*Bristol and West plc v Bartlett* [2002] EWCA Civ 1181). In arrears cases the cause of action will usually accrue on the date on which two instalments fell into arrears. Despite the long limitation period, the date of the last payment should always be checked.

If a possession order in existing proceedings has been suspended on condition that defined payments were made, even if all the arrears the subject of that order have been cleared, there is no need to start new proceedings if fresh arrears accrue (*Bank of Scotland plc v Zinda* [2011] EWCA Civ 706, [2012] 1 WLR 728). Instead, the existing order can simply be enforced and the **Mortgage Protocol** need not be followed. Further, the court will only consider whether indeed fresh arrears have accrued, and any arguments in opposition to possession, if an application for permission to issue the warrant is required or an application to suspend the warrant is made by the borrower or occupiers.

Status of those with registered interests

87.6 The Land Registry search and entries may identify others with relevant rights in the property, and their status must be considered. Although all borrowers and any guarantor should be parties to the action, it is unwise to add unnecessary parties. Those with registered matrimonial homes rights are entitled to be joined, and must be notified (**PD 55A, para. 2.5(1)**), ideally by sending copies of the proceedings.

If the borrower is already subject to insolvency proceedings, it may be necessary to obtain permission to commence or continue a claim (see **84.19** to **84.40**). However, the rights of a secured lender to pursue possession action are generally unaffected by the bankruptcy of the borrower and are not subject to the general moratorium on claims (Insolvency Act 1986, s. 285(4)). A bankrupt borrower is a proper defendant. He or she is entitled to be heard on the question of possession of the property, even though it is part of the estate vested in the trustee, who should be served with a copy of the proceedings.

CPR, r. 55.10(2), requires the claimant to give notice of the hearing to other registered charge holders (see **87.17**). This may forestall proceedings by another secured lender or facilitate case management by the court of existing claims affecting the same property (see **r. 1.4**). Since 21 March 2016 there is a new regulatory obligation under MCOB, r. 13.4A.2, to give notice to 'each person having a legal or equitable mortgage in the relevant property over which the firm has security'. This is arguably wider than **CPR, r. 55.10(2)**. Further, MCOB, r. 13.4A.3, states that 'a firm should make reasonable efforts to discover the existence of other charge holders at the start of the...litigation process'.

Venue

Possession claims should be commenced in the County Court hearing centre serving the address of the mortgaged property, which may be found by entering the postcode at https://courttribunalfinder.service.gov.uk/search/postcode. Claim form N5 must be used and separate particulars of claim must be filed and served with it. A claim may be commenced in the High Court only if a certificate is filed with the claim form stating the reasons for bringing the claim in that court (**CPR, r. 55.3(2); PD 55A, para. 1.3**). Factual or legal complexity, or points of law of general importance may indicate a High Court case: value alone does not (**PD 55A, paras 1.3 and 1.4**). Alternatively claims may be issued via the electronic web-based PCOL (Possession Claim Online) system, covered by **PD 55B** (see **87.11** to **87.14**), which will automatically select the appropriate hearing centre.

87.7

PARTICULARS OF CLAIM

Content of particulars of claim

The content of the particulars of claim in a possession claim generally (including possession claims against tenants and trespassers) is prescribed by **PD 55A, para. 2.1**. Form N120 should be used. **CPR, r. 55.4** reminds the claimant to comply with the often ignored **Part 16** (statements of case), the mortgage being a contract in writing (see **PD 16, para. 7.3**). This is reinforced by the specific provisions of **PD 55A, para. 2.1**. In all possession claims the particulars must:

87.8

(a) identify the land in question;
(b) indicate whether the claim includes residential property;
(c) state the ground for possession, e.g. arrears;
(d) state full details of the relationship between the parties — to be noted if any original party to the deed has transferred their interest;
(e) identify all persons who, to the best of the claimant's knowledge and belief, are in possession. If the mortgage is buy-to-let and authorised tenants are in the property, their status will have to be disclosed to the court in the pre-action checklist.

Form N120 requires the claimant to identify the relief sought. In practice the choice is whether also to seek a money judgment for the outstanding balance (see **87.26**). The claim form and the particulars of claim must each be verified by a statement of truth.

Extra information for mortgage claims

87.9 There are additional requirements for particulars of claim in mortgage possession cases (**PD 55A, paras 2.5 and 2.5A**):

(a) Matrimonial homes rights must be identified (**para. 2.5(1)**).

(b) The state of the mortgage account must be set out, showing the amount of the advance (and further advances), periodic repayments and regular payments of interest due (**para. 2.5(2)(a)**).

(c) There must be a statement of the amount necessary to redeem the mortgage on a projected date less than 14 days after issue, separately showing costs and administration fees (**para. 2.5(2)(b)**).

(d) If the secured loan is a regulated consumer credit agreement, that fact must be stated (**para. 2.5(2)(c)**) together with the dates of any default or termination notices under the Consumer Credit Act 1974, ss. 76 or 87, and, if appropriate, why the loan is not subject to s. 141 (which requires such claims to be brought in the County Court) (**PD 55A, para. 2.5(4) and (5)**).

(e) If the claim is based on instalment arrears, there must be a schedule giving details of dates and amounts of payments due and made under the mortgage for the preceding two years, or since the first date of default if later (thus demonstrating how the arrears have accumulated since the account was last up to date). It is imperative that the schedule carries a running total of the arrears, and is intelligible to both average borrower and judge. The temptation to attach a spreadsheet produced for other purposes should be resisted, unless clearly charting the arrears pattern. Also the schedule must show other payments due under the mortgage, and whether they fall within the contractual payments and are in arrears (**para. 2.5(3)**).

(f) If relying on over two years' arrears, a full schedule must be exhibited to a witness statement (**para. 2.5A**).

(g) Relevant information about the defendant's circumstances must be provided, in particular about social security benefits payable to the defendant or directly to the mortgage lender (**para. 2.5(6)**). Relevant information includes details of bankruptcy, or the belief that the defendant receives rents sufficient, say, to pay the mortgage.

(h) Previous steps taken to recover the debt secured by the mortgage must be stated. Past proceedings must be disclosed, quoting their outcome. Their existence may be relevant to how the court exercises any discretion to adjourn, or to suspend any order (**para. 2.5(8)**).

Service

87.10 After issue, the court will serve the proceedings, in accordance with **CPR, Part 6**. The norm is postal service at the last known address of the defendant, which may not be the property address. For service outside England and Wales see **chapter 16**.

POSSESSION CLAIM ONLINE (PCOL)

PCOL

87.11 Mortgage possession claims can now be brought online, with a reduced issue fee of £325 (**CPFO, fee 1.4(c)**). Their progress can be monitored at any time. The procedure is regulated by **CPR, r. 55.10A**, and **PD 55B**.

Availability of PCOL

87.12 PCOL is available for mortgage possession claims brought by claimants with UK addresses, solely on the grounds of arrears. The conventional procedure must be adopted if another breach of covenant is alleged or if the relief sought is other than possession and a money judgment for the balance, interest and costs. If any defendant has an address for service outside England and Wales, or the claimant cannot provide a postcode for the mortgaged property, PCOL is not available (**PD 55B, para. 5.1**). PCOL is not to be used if the defendant is known to be a child or protected party (**para. 5.2**).

Access to PCOL

Claimants request the issue of a claim electronically by accessing the PCOL website at https://www.possessionclaim.gov.uk/pcol/. It is important to access the website for further information generally and in particular to identify how to monitor and progress the claim. PCOL users access the site by complying with a customary security system of username and password, and make fee payments for PCOL applications by debit or credit card or, for frequent users, by an account system. The website is clearly claimant orientated, and whilst in theory defendants can use the site, there are practical difficulties, not least for defendants who wish to make applications requiring fees remission (**PD 55B, para. 4.2**).

87.13

Procedure

The claimant requests issue of the claim form by completing an online form and paying the fee through the website, or in another approved way (**PD 55B, para. 6.1**). PCOL differs from the conventional procedure principally in that the particulars of claim must be included in the online form and not filed separately (**para. 6.2**). There is no need to file a copy mortgage deed (**para. 6.2**). If the claimant has already provided the defendant with a full schedule of arrears, the particulars can be abbreviated (**PD 55B, paras 6.3A and 6.3B**).

87.14

If there is only an arrears summary in the particulars, the claimant must serve within seven days of issue the full arrears history containing the information required under **para. 6.3**. The claimant must also either make a confirmatory witness statement dealing with the full arrears history, or verify compliance by way of oral evidence and produce the arrears history.

Acknowledgment of receipt by the court of the claim form is not confirmation of either issue or service (**para. 6.5**). An online claim is 'brought' for limitation purposes when the online claim form is received by the court's computer system (**para. 6.6**).

Upon issue, the court serves a printed version of the claim form, and a defence form for completion by the defendant, and sends notice of issue to the claimant (**para. 6.7**). The claim is deemed to be served on the fifth day after issue, whether a business day or not (**para. 6.8**).

PCOL issues the proceedings in the appropriate County Court hearing centre, based on the postcode of the mortgaged property, as provided by the claimant (**para. 6.11**). That hearing centre then has jurisdiction to hear the claim and enforce the judgment (**para. 6.11**). If an error caused by mistyping the postcode or computer glitches is spotted, that hearing centre may transfer to the correct one. Non-local cases are likely to be transferred, both for the convenience of the defendant and to aid enforcement of any possession order.

Each claim form carries a unique customer identification number or password enabling the defendant to access it on the PCOL website (**para. 6.10**).

A defendant may file an electronic defence to a PCOL claim, in which case a hard copy should not also be filed (**para. 7**). The requirement for statements of case (and application notices) to be verified by statement of truth and the method of online signature (by entry of the name) are addressed in **PD 55B, paras 8 and 9**. A form which is required to be signed by a person is deemed to be signed if that person's name is entered in the form online. Sanctions for abuse are in **CPR, r. 32.14**.

Commentary

PRE-HEARING STEPS

Date of hearing

87.15   When issuing a claim form in a mortgage possession case, the court will fix a hearing date not less than 28 days from issue (**CPR, r. 55.5**). The standard period between issue and hearing is not more than eight weeks (**r. 55.5(3)(b)**). The defendant must be served with the claim form and particulars of claim not less than 21 days before the hearing (**r. 55.5(3)**). If service is to take place outside the jurisdiction, the standard time may be exceeded. The court may, under **r. 3.1(2)(a)**, vary the time for compliance with any rule.

Defence

87.16   When the court effects service, it sends, with the claim form and particulars, a pack including notes for guidance (N7) and a defence form (N11M). That seeks, in questionnaire style, details of the defendant's financial position, as well as providing space for specific reasons to oppose the making of a possession order.

No acknowledgment of service is required (**CPR, r. 55.7(1)**) nor is there any real sanction if the defendant fails to file a defence within the time specified in **r. 15.4**. Defendants ideally should include in their defence all the evidence relied upon, including, if applicable, details of housing benefit claims.

Notice to tenants and others

87.17   To comply with **CPR, r. 55.10**, not less than five days after receiving notification of the hearing date, the claimant must send a notice: (a) to the property, addressed to 'the tenant or occupier', (b) to the housing department of the local authority in whose area the property is situated, and (c) to the proprietor of any other registered charge. The notice must state that the claim has been commenced in respect of the property, quoting its full address, the name and address of claimant and defendant, and the court issuing the claim form, plus date, time and place of hearing. 'Send' means dispatch, not serve. Customarily the notice is given in a standard-form letter. Care should be taken to ensure the accuracy of the property address. If the court is not satisfied with compliance, the hearing will be adjourned. **MCOB, r. 13.4A.2**, requires notice of the hearing to be given to each person having a legal or equitable mortgage in the relevant property (see **87.6**).

Claimant's evidence

87.18   **CPR, r. 55.8(4)**, provides that all witness statements must be filed and served at least two days before the hearing. Any fact to be proved at the hearing may be proved by witness statement, unless there is a genuine dispute of fact (**PD 55A, para. 5.4**). Usually, the only evidence before the court is a claim form, verified by statement of truth, and an updating claimant's witness statement. Despite the requirements of **PD 55A, para. 5.1**, to the effect that the claimant should, wherever possible, include in its statement of case all its evidence, in practice this rarely happens because of the need to comply with **CPR, r. 55.10** (see **87.17**). The statement of the claimant should be made by a person with knowledge of the mortgage account, and of suitable seniority and delegated authority. Its timing is delicate: if too close to the hearing, a defendant may seek an adjournment to take advice. The ideal is about 14 days before the hearing.

Contents of the claimant's witness statement

87.19   The claimant's evidence should deal specifically with the following:

(a) matters not dealt with in the particulars of claim and changes to any facts stated therein;

(b) in PCOL cases, and if not earlier produced, a copy of the mortgage deed, terms and conditions and any default notices under Consumer Credit Act 1974;

(c) the term of the mortgage;

(d) the amount of the arrears, both at the statement date and those potentially existing at the hearing date, assuming no further payments — if there is more than one mortgage account, the figures for the accounts should be separately stated, and totalled;

(e) the outstanding balance(s) on the mortgage account(s);

(f) the date the next instalment is due;

(g) the date of the last payment;

(h) compliance with **CPR, r. 55.10**, if not dealt with by filing a separate certificate;

(i) up-to-date evidence of title; and

(j) a Land Registry search (or Land Charges search if unregistered land) in form HRR (obtained using form HR3) to discover the existence of any registered family law rights. A spouse, cohabitant or civil partner, present or past, not a party, may apply to be joined to the proceedings.

Evidence of compliance with the **Mortgage Protocol** is covered at the hearing by form N123 (see **87.24**), which has its own statement of truth. Guidance notes in the form may assist in completing it.

Land Registry entries

Evidence of title involves the production of office or electronic Land Registry copies ideally not more than a month old. These reveal any changes to registered entries, such as further charges, transfers of the legal estate, or notes of bankruptcy orders. The Land Registration Act 2002, s. 67(1), provides that an official copy ('the office copy') of the register, part thereof or any filed document, is admissible to the same extent as the original. In the exceedingly rare case of unregistered title, the original mortgage must be produced, together with a Land Charges search.

87.20

Change of lender

It is increasingly common for financial institutions to refinance their 'mortgage books', which may mean that a claimant lender has assigned its interest before the hearing. Usually this will happen where an existing claim has stood adjourned for some time. If the borrower defaults on an arrangement, the new lender will wish to continue with the claim. Before doing so it must apply to be substituted as the new claimant in the action, in accordance with **CPR, r. 19.2(4)**. The application to substitute will need to include evidence of the transfer, notice of the assignment served on the borrower and updated official copies showing the change in title of the registered charge holder. The solicitors conducting the claim, and the advocate appearing for the claimant at the hearing, must be instructed by the new lender. The previous lender no longer has standing to proceed with the claim or enforcement of any order. To do so may amount to an abuse of process and leave any order made in its favour liable to be set aside or the claim struck out.

87.21

Pre-hearing adjournments

In cases where the arrears have been repaid after a possession claim has been commenced, but before a possession order has been made, the correct approach is for the claim to be adjourned generally with permission to restore. This is because once the right to possession has arisen it crystallises. There is no need to start a new claim even if the arrears are cleared but later accrue again, as the original cause of action remains. If further arrears do accrue, the lender can apply to restore the claim and continue with the original proceedings (*Greyhound Guarantee v Caulfield* [1981] CLY 1808; *Halifax plc v Taffs* [1999] CLY 4385).

87.22

In practice secured lenders will commonly seek adjournment of a possession claim where arrears have been reduced to less than two months.

It has become common for courts to adjourn the claim generally on the basis that if not restored by a certain date (commonly 12 months from the date of order) it will be struck out. This does not preclude the lender later instituting proceedings for fresh arrears. Following such an order, the lender should monitor the situation and take action if necessary to restore before the strike-out date.

The inherent powers of the court to adjourn at the request of the borrower are very limited. In practice, a degree of pragmatism exists. If a defendant writes indicating a hospital appointment on the hearing date, there is little point in the claimant urging upon the court the making of a possession order. It begs an application to set aside the order under **CPR, r. 3.1(2)(m)**, causing added delay and costs. Likewise if the claimant has failed to comply with an aspect of procedure, application of the overriding objective leads the court usually to adjourn rather than dismiss. So, short purposive adjournments exist in practice.

Pre-hearing adjournments: procedure

87.23   Because there is no prejudice to the borrower, most courts adjourn on the written application of the lender only. Because of lack of time, a consent application for an adjournment signed by both sides in advance of the hearing is rarely lodged.

Most lenders write seeking an adjournment and pay the application fee of £100 (**CPFO, fee 2.5(a)**). This fee can be added to the borrower's account. No fee is payable if the application to adjourn is by consent and is received by the court at least 14 days before the date set for the hearing (**CPFO, notes to fee 2.5**). Others ask for the letter to be put before the District Judge at the hearing, who will then make the order. The latter approach may save the fee, but does not vacate the hearing in advance so the lender will still have to pay the advocate's fee. As the court may not prepare and send the adjournment order in sufficient time to reach the parties before the hearing, the lender should confirm with the borrower what it has done, to save the borrower wasting time attending an aborted hearing. Letters to the court should emphasise in the heading the hearing date and time.

An adjourned case can be restored by complying with any provisions of the order granting the earlier adjournment. Even if not ordered, an updating witness statement will be required dealing with the current arrears.

If, whatever the arrears, the lender's policy is to support any payment arrangement with a suspended possession order, the hearing must proceed.

FIRST HEARING

Matters to be considered

87.24   All court hearings dealing with mortgage possession cases are in private (**PD 39A, para. 1.5**). The hearing normally takes place before a District Judge. Customarily only a few minutes are allocated. Within this time, the court must be satisfied that all formalities have been complied with, and will receive from the claimant's solicitor, up-to-date Land Registry entries, fresh search in form HRR, and (if not filed) copy mortgage documents. The form N123 checklist must be handed in, with a copy for the defendant, evidencing compliance with the **Mortgage Protocol**. Although form N123 must only be handed to the court at the possession hearing, it relates to the conduct of the parties prior to the issue of the claim. Up-to-date information on attempts by the parties since issue to reach an arrangement should be included with the advocate's instructions. An oral update on the crucial figures (last payment, existing arrears and balance outstanding) is given. These figures should have been checked with the lender that day and be at the advocate's fingertips. Advocates should tell the court the length of the term and type of mortgage, and indicate any unusual features of the case. They must be succinct.

Usually the facts and figures are not disputed. If a defendant attends, it is usually to propose a payment plan, or seek time to make a proposal, and oppose an outright possession order. It is rare for a defence to be filed beforehand. The court must identify any issues in the case. The court will usually have insufficient time then to resolve any but the most straightforward problems, because there will be many other cases waiting to be heard. The court will adjourn to a longer hearing, and may give interim directions, such as to file a defence, or clearer defence, to encapsulate what is raised for the first time at the hearing.

ORDERS FOR POSSESSION

Types of order

If the court is satisfied on all the formalities, and there are no substantial areas of dispute, it will proceed to make an order for possession. Two types of order are available: **87.25**

(a) A 'straight' order for possession, which usually requires the borrower to give the lender possession after 28 days. Upon expiry of the 28-day period, the lender is free to apply for a warrant of possession. The court has discretion to extend or reduce the period stated in the order. If extending (for instance to allow additional time for the borrower to move out), a 56-day order is common; more unusually the court may make a 'forthwith' order which may be enforced immediately.

(b) A 'suspended' order for possession. As with a straight order, possession will usually be ordered in 28 days. However, enforcement of the order is suspended on payment by the borrower of the current instalments as they fall due, plus defined regular sums off the stated arrears. A first payment date, normally when the next contractual instalment is due, should be specified. The circumstances in which a court will consider making a suspended order are set out below.

Money judgment

The lender has the choice of including a claim for a money judgment in its particulars of claim. **87.26** If it does so and proceeds with the claim, it will be entitled to judgment for the outstanding balance due at the hearing date (*Cheltenham and Gloucester Building Society v Grattidge* (1993) 25 HLR 454). The money judgment is usually expressed not to be enforceable without the court's permission, and will only be relied on by the lender in the event that the proceeds of sale of the property are insufficient to discharge the outstanding mortgage balance at the date of sale. Between the date of the hearing and the date of sale, the lender will usually incur significant further costs in enforcing the order, and then managing, marketing and selling the property. These costs will be added to the mortgage debt but will not be reflected in the money judgment. One alternative is therefore to include a claim for a money judgment in the possession proceedings, but adjourn it generally. The money claim can then be restored if required after sale of the property, and judgment will be entered at that time for the full amount of the shortfall debt.

The lender's further alternative is not to include a money claim at all. If after the sale of the repossessed property there is a shortfall, a fresh money claim may be brought for the shortfall debt. The limitation period runs from the date of default by the borrower, not the date of sale of the property, and is 12 years (six years for accrued interest) (see **87.5**). Court fees for money claims increased significantly in April 2015, and are now capped at £10,000 for claims of £200,000 or more (**CPFO, fee 1.1**). By contrast a money claim in possession proceedings only attracts the possession claim issue fee (**CPFO, note to fee 1.4**), which is £355 or £325 on PCOL (**CPFO, fees 1.4(b) and (c)**). Court fees are set out in Form EX50.

Commentary

Costs: general approach

87.27   Lenders can reimburse themselves out of the mortgaged property for all costs, charges and expenses reasonably and properly incurred in enforcing or preserving their security (*Parker-Tweedale v Dunbar Bank plc (No. 2)* [1991] Ch 26). Conventionally mortgages contain clauses that the borrower will pay the costs of the lender, both of proceedings under the mortgage, and those properly incurred in preserving the security.

Lenders generally should not seek costs within possession proceedings, which will be assessed by the court. As a result most possession orders are silent as to costs. The range of options available to secured lenders is set out in **PD 44, paras 7.1 to 7.3.**

Costs orders

87.28   Suppose the lender makes a mistake, causing additional hearings? Its costs have been unreasonably incurred. But if a borrower needs time to assemble cogent evidence of a payment plan or proposed sale, an adjournment of perhaps six weeks to the next available date is helpful, and justice is done if the order remains silent on costs.

Gomba Holdings (UK) Ltd v Minories Finance Ltd (No. 2) [1993] Ch 171 established certain principles (see **68.50**). Although costs orders are discretionary, the discretion should normally be exercised to reflect any contractual right to costs. The power of the court to disallow a lender's costs sought to be added to the security derives from the court's equitable jurisdiction to fix the terms of redemption of a mortgage and not from the Senior Courts Act 1981, s. 51. A lender is not to be deprived of the right to add costs to the security merely because of a costs order made without reference to the contractual provisions.

A borrower succeeding on an issue may be entitled to costs against the lender. The court can make such an order, and one depriving the lender of the right to add both costs it has to pay the borrower, and its own costs, to the security. Also, the court may decide that it should limit the contractual entitlement to costs as to part because the lender has acted unreasonably.

Any *Gomba Holdings* order should specify precisely what costs are involved, e.g. 'the costs of preparing the witness statement of AB shall not be added to the security'.

UNDEFENDED CASES: DELAYING POSSESSION

Suspended orders under the Administration of Justice Act 1970, s. 36

87.29   At common law, unless the lender consented, the court's only power to delay possession was to afford the borrower a brief opportunity to redeem the entire mortgage (*Birmingham Citizens Permanent Building Society v Caunt* [1962] Ch 883). The position was altered radically by the Administration of Justice Act 1970, s. 36. This gives the court power to adjourn the proceedings, or make a possession order but stay, suspend or postpone the date for possession, if satisfied the sums due can be paid within a reasonable period of time. Section 36 provides that:

(1) Where the mortgagee under a mortgage of land which consists of or includes a dwelling-house brings an action in which he claims possession of the mortgaged property, ... the court may exercise any of the powers conferred on it by subsection (2) below if it appears to the court that in the event of it exercising the power the mortgagor is likely to be able within a reasonable period to pay any sums due under the mortgage or to remedy a default consisting of a breach of any other obligation arising under or by virtue of the mortgage.

(2) The court:

   (a) may adjourn the proceedings, or

(b) on giving judgment, or making any order, for delivery of possession of the mortgaged property, or at any time before the execution of such judgment or order, may:
  (i) stay or suspend execution of the judgment or order, or
  (ii) postpone the date for delivery of possession,
for such period or periods as the court thinks reasonable.

The Administration of Justice Act 1973, s. 8, clarified that where failure to pay an instalment triggers an obligation to pay the entire mortgage balance, 'any sums due' under s. 36 is to be treated as the arrears of instalments only, not the outstanding balance.

These provisions apply only if the security includes a dwelling-house. By the Administration of Justice Act 1970, s. 39(1), this includes any building or part of a building which is used as a dwelling (*Royal Bank of Scotland plc v Miller* [2001] EWCA Civ 344, [2002] QB 255).

There are two issues for the court:

(a) whether there is sufficient evidence to support the borrower's proposals; and
(b) whether the timescale proposed for discharge of the arrears is reasonable.

The provisions do not apply to regulated agreements under the Consumer Credit Act 1974 (Administration of Justice Act 1970, s. 38A). Instead the court can make a 'time order' pursuant to the Consumer Credit Act 1974, s. 129. A time order changes the contractually agreed terms, providing for payment of any sums owed on such terms as the court considers just and reasonable.

The section 36 discretion: evidence needed to satisfy the court

In *Cheltenham and Gloucester Building Society v Grant* (1994) 26 HLR 703 a practical approach was **87.30** adopted. The Court of Appeal declined to lay down rigid rules for busy first-instance judges. They must be allowed to act without hearing evidence. It is for the judge to decide whether to act on the basis of informal material, thereby allowing a first-instance court to accept evidence that does not comply with **CPR, Part 32**. The effect of the *Grant* case is that if the lender submits the court should not accept what it is told by the borrower, the consequence may be an adjournment.

A common-sense approach is favoured. The borrower may be present: he could be put on oath if required; much of the information tendered, as to future earnings and expenses, will be incapable of ready challenge. If applying at a warrant stage, information may be in the application notice, verified by a statement of truth, as required by **Part 22**. If a borrower attends court and explains reasons for past default and hopes for future improvement, it is rare for the representative of the lender to seek to ask questions. With an offer of remortgage, it can be more effective for submissions to be made on that offer letter, pointing out its deficiencies, than directly to challenge the borrower, or require the author of the letter to attend court.

It is helpful for a borrower to produce to the court a full financial statement to show that there genuinely is the scope to make payments. Citizens Advice Bureaux, and other debt-counselling agencies, produce good examples, which, typed and totalled, offer the hard-pressed judge easy-to-digest evidence of ability, or inability, to pay.

The section 36 discretion: a reasonable period to pay the arrears

The Court of Appeal in *Cheltenham and Gloucester Building Society v Norgan* [1996] 1 WLR 343 held **87.31** that it is reasonable to take account of the whole of the remaining part of the original term of the mortgage. Although the *Norgan* case was on a warrant, the same principles apply to the initial decision whether and on what basis to suspend any order. Having identified the amount of the arrears, the following are potentially relevant to the exercise of discretion:

(a) the amount the borrower could reasonably afford to pay, now and in the future;
(b) the duration of any temporary financial crisis;

(c) the reason for the accumulation of arrears;

(d) the nature of the security;

(e) the length of the remaining term;

(f) the type of mortgage and relevant contractual provisions, for example, date of repayment of the principal;

(g) whether it is a case under the Administration of Justice Act 1973, s. 8; and

(h) the period over which it is reasonable to expect the lender to recoup arrears of interest, or whether it is reasonable to capitalise them.

Consideration of these factors lies at the heart of the argument on terms for suspension. If the outstanding balance is close to the current value of the property, a much shorter repayment period may be indicated. The means of the borrower may dictate a modest monthly payment can be made off the arrears. If the court has sufficient available material to indicate a potential improvement to finances (for example, if the partner will be going back to work part-time when the youngest child goes to school), it can either make a stepped order increasing the instalments off arrears at fixed future dates, or bring the case back for review. The existence of a future review date does not preclude enforcement if the order is breached in the interim.

The problem faced by many borrowers is convincing the court to exercise discretion in their favour. If someone has failed to make instalment payments in the past, how can they persuade the court that they are now likely to be able to pay both monthly instalments and something off the arrears? If the borrower can point to a period of limited earnings during ill-health, or a period of redundancy, it will help. A chequered payment history must be explained to show why matters will improve.

Intended sale

87.32 A common plea by those who have exhausted every other avenue of keeping their home is for time to sell. Better they should sell the house, as owner-occupier, than the lender take possession, when with the windows boarded up and garden unkempt, purchasers seek a knock-down price. Lenders must take reasonable care to ensure they obtain the best price they reasonably can (*Michael v Miller* [2004] EWCA Civ 282, [2004] 2 EGLR 151), but few householders trust the lender to sell for as much as they believe they can obtain. The concerns are not one-sided. The lender fears a deliberate delay, the borrower wanting to link the sale to obtaining fresh accommodation, or trying to achieve an unreasonably high price. Whether the lender should itself sell or adopt the borrower's proposed sale is an argument explored in a number of cases. All these cases should now be considered in the light of the **Mortgage Protocol, para. 6.2.**

In *Target Home Loans v Clothier* [1994] 1 All ER 439 it was decided that if there is a prospect of an early sale, the court must ask if it is better for all parties that it is conducted by the borrower or the lender. If the view is that, for both borrower and lender, the prospects of an early sale are best served by deferring an order for possession, that is a solid reason for making a suspended order. But deferment should be short. In the *Clothier* case it was for three months. *National and Provincial Building Society v Lloyd* [1996] 1 All ER 630 suggested that on clear evidence of completion of the sale 'in six or nine months, or even a year', that was a reasonable period. This was rejected as a general proposition in *Bristol and West Building Society v Ellis* (1997) 29 HLR 282. In the *Ellis* case a proposal to discharge arrears of £11,000 at £10 per month until sale in three to five years' time met no favour. There were doubts that the proceeds would cover the mortgage debt and arrears, and insufficient evidence that the borrower would really sell. What is a reasonable period depends on the facts of each case. The arrears level and extent of the security are factors. Letters from estate agents giving likely sale prices should be treated with reserve.

The position where there is negative equity was considered in *Cheltenham and Gloucester Building Society v Krausz* [1997] 1 WLR 1558. The Administration of Justice Act 1970, s. 36, cannot be used to delay possession simply to enable borrowers to sell, if they will not give good title at completion, because of inability to discharge the mortgage.

Firm evidence of particular sale

The historic stance of many lenders that, without firm evidence, they should not be prevented   **87.33** from gaining possession to exercise their power of sale, must now be viewed in the light of the **Mortgage Protocol, para. 6.2,** and pre-2008 cases should be treated with caution. When a potential sale is proposed by the borrower the mortgage lender should provide reasons before rejecting the proposal (**para. 6.4**). An adjournment to investigate may be required.

That aside, the court will assist if there is an exchange of contracts with an arm's-length purchaser, and will postpone possession, if necessary staying a warrant, to enable completion of the sale. The court will suspend if comprehensive proposals (see **87.34**) are approved. Beyond that, the more compelling the evidence of likely sale and the larger the equity, the longer will be the likely postponement. In practice, any order giving 56 days or less is unlikely to be worth appealing. Any initial suspension period is, in reality, a window for the borrower to exchange contracts unconditionally.

Comprehensive proposals

The court may be able to look favourably on a mixed package of proposals by the borrower.   **87.34** Perhaps the borrower can, in the short term, by calling in favours and delaying payment to less pressing creditors, afford the current instalments plus a small amount off the arrears monthly for, say, three months. In principle, that proposal, plus an as yet loosely formulated plan to sell, may be a basis for a suspended order with review.

ISSUES AND POSSIBLE DEFENCES

Outstanding issues with one of the defendants

Generally the court should not make a possession order against one borrower until it is satis-   **87.35** fied that a right to possession has also arisen against any co-borrowers. So, if there are two borrowers and one of them has not been served, or claims to have a defence, it is inappropriate to make an order at this stage. In *Albany Homes Ltd v Massey* [1997] 2 All ER 609 it was held that possession proceedings should be adjourned until the outstanding issues with one of the defendants, involving undue influence, had been determined. An order for possession against one borrower would be pointless if, immediately it was complied with, the co-borrower remaining in possession simply granted the other joint borrower a licence to re-occupy.

Overriding interests

Although form N120 (particulars of claim) requires the claimant in a mortgage possession   **87.36** claim to have inquired of those in occupation of the property before issue, occupants' rights must be considered, and the notice required by **CPR, r. 55.10** is intended to give them an opportunity to attend the hearing of the claim. The equitable interest of an occupier, often as a result of capital contributions to the property, may have priority over the lender if both the interest and the occupation predate the mortgage (Land Registration Act 2002, sch. 3, para. 2). For a discussion of these issues see *Lloyds Bank plc v Rosset* [1991] 1 AC 107 and *Abbey National Building Society v Cann* [1991] 1 AC 56.

If a tenancy pre-dates the mortgage and the tenant's rights have not been postponed in writing to those of the lender at the time of the mortgage, the tenancy will constitute an overriding interest which is binding on the lender (*Woolwich Building Society v Dickman* [1996] 3 All ER 204). As such the tenant will be entitled to resist a possession order.

Commentary

Overriding interests have been considered by the Supreme Court in the context of sale and rent back ('SARB') agreements (*Southern Pacific Mortgages Ltd v Scott* [2014] UKSC 52, [2015] AC 385). Briefly, home owners were persuaded to sell their properties to purchasers who promised to grant them tenancies, with the intention of allowing them to remain in their homes for many years after the sale. The purchasers bought the properties with the help of mortgages, without disclosing the SARB arrangement to the lender. The purchasers subsequently defaulted on their mortgage payments. The question in the case was whether the sellers/ tenants had any interest in the property which was binding on the lenders, preventing them from taking possession action.

The Supreme Court decided that the purchasers were only able to grant a proprietary right to the seller/tenant after the completion of the purchase. Where a mortgage is used to support the purchase, the transfer to the purchaser and the grant of the charge are one indivisible transaction. The effect of this is that there is no moment in time when the purchaser is able to grant an interest to the seller/tenant free of the mortgage. As a result, any interest the seller/tenant acquires takes effect after the mortgage and cannot constitute an overriding interest against the lender.

Tenants generally

87.37   Tenants are at real risk in a mortgage possession claim. Frequently, if the borrower does not attend, there is no evidence before the court of the existence, let alone status, of a tenant. The claimant's solicitor should be prepared to assist the court in this regard, if only to forestall future applications. As well as the **CPR, r. 55.10** notice (see **87.17**), the form N123 checklist now requires lenders to state (at para. 7) what steps they have taken to check whether there is a tenant of the borrower in occupation, whether that tenant was authorised by the lender, and what order the lender is seeking in the light of the information obtained.

Tenancies created prior to the mortgage may constitute overriding interests and are considered at **87.36**.

For tenancies created after the mortgage, a distinction must be drawn between those authorised by the lender, which will be binding on it, and those which are not authorised, which will not. The lender must act in good faith in seeking possession, and the court will look at the actual, rather than the formal relationship of the parties (*Quennell v Maltby* [1979] 1 WLR 318). Before considering joining a tenant to the proceedings under **CPR, Part 19**, the court must identify whether that tenancy can potentially operate as a defence to the claim. Joinder gives a right to disclosure of all the documents in the action and may have costs implications.

Unauthorised tenants

87.38   Generally it is a condition of residential mortgages that the borrowers must reside at the mortgaged property and the property must not be let. If a tenancy was created by the borrower after the mortgage, without the consent of the lender, the tenancy is unauthorised, and is no bar to a possession order (*Britannia Building Society v Earl* [1990] 1 WLR 422). The tenant need not be joined to the claim, as a possession order operates against the land, and serves to deprive any occupier of the right to remain.

Since 1 October 2010, the Mortgage Repossessions (Protection of Tenants etc.) Act 2010 and the Dwelling Houses (Execution of Possession Orders by Mortgagees) Regulations 2010 (SI 2010/1809) have given some limited protection to unauthorised tenants, defined as persons occupying under assured, protected, or statutory tenancies, whose tenancies do not bind the mortgagee. **CPR, r. 55.10(4A)**, enables applications to be made to the court by such tenants, although not parties to the action. By virtue of s. 1(2) of the 2010 Act, when making a possession order the court may, on the application of the tenant, postpone the date for delivery of possession for a period not exceeding two months. Under the 2010 Act the court will take account of the tenant's circumstances and any breach of the tenancy. There is a power to direct rental payments to the lender during the period of postponement without thereby creating any fresh tenancy. More commonly, unauthorised tenants will apply to suspend the warrant at enforcement stage, rather than seek to postpone the effective date of the possession order (see 87.52).

Authorised tenants

With 'buy-to-let' mortgages, the borrower is expressly authorised to let the property subject to the letting conditions set out in the mortgage offer. Commonly this will provide for tenancies to be assured shorthold tenancies with an initial fixed period of no more than 12 months, to non-corporate privately funded tenants. A possession order should not be made if the tenant is authorised and remains lawfully in occupation.   **87.39**

Some mortgage conditions require the borrower to seek the lender's consent to each new tenancy granted, although this rarely happens in practice. The issue of implied permission remains unclear. On the one hand lenders are aware that the nature of the mortgage product is to encourage the property to be let; on the other, lenders will argue that they are not bound by individual tenancies to which they did not expressly consent. Decisions will turn on the facts of each case and the applicable conditions.

Sometimes where the mortgage is a residential product, the lender may expressly consent in writing to a letting part way through the term. In such cases the tenant is authorised in the same way as if the mortgage were 'buy-to-let'.

In *Paratus AMC Ltd v Fosuhene* [2013] EWCA Civ 827, [2014] HLR 1, payments made without court authority by a tenant directly to a lender were held not to bind the lender, as the payer had not identified herself as a tenant. As such the lender did not accept the payments as rent and there was no implied consent to the tenancy.

The **Mortgage Protocol, para 5.2**, states that the lender should seek information about whether the property is occupied by an authorised tenant, and this information must be included in the form N123 checklist. **Paragraph 7.2** states that where there is an authorised tenant in occupation of the property, at the possession hearing the court will consider whether (a) further directions are required; (b) to adjourn the possession claim until possession has been recovered against the tenant (i.e. by the borrower or a receiver); or (c) to make an order conditional upon the tenant's right of occupation. The result of this is that lenders should generally not commence a mortgage possession claim where they are aware that an authorised tenant is in the property.

Appointment of a receiver

If there is an authorised tenant in the property, the lender should not seek a possession order against the borrower in mortgage possession proceedings, but should instead appoint a receiver of the income from the property under the Law of Property Act 1925, s. 101(1)(iii). A receiver appointed under the 1925 Act is known as an 'LPA receiver', and has the limited powers conferred by s. 109 of the Act. More commonly, the mortgage conditions will provide for the appointment of a receiver with both the powers under s. 109 and further contractual powers conferred by the mortgage conditions. Such a receiver is properly a 'fixed-charge receiver'.   **87.40**

The lender may appoint a receiver at any time after its power of sale has arisen under s. 103 of the Act (s. 109(1)). Although the receiver is appointed by the lender, once appointed they become the agent of the borrower (s. 109(2)). As such the receiver can take action as landlord against the authorised tenant, serving the appropriate statutory notices to terminate the tenancy and take possession. If terminating the tenancy gives the receiver vacant possession, the mortgage lender can sell without further order, as in *Horsham Properties Group Ltd v Clark* [2008] EWHC 2327 (Ch), [2009] 1 P & CR 8.

Undue influence

87.41   Sometimes the reason for the inability to sustain the contractual payments is family breakdown. One party, often the wife or female partner, wishes to challenge the mortgage, or a further advance. Perhaps one of two joint owners used the security of the property to raise business funds. The other may raise the defence of undue influence, contending that the charge, or further advance, be set aside.

The leading case is *Barclays Bank plc v O'Brien* [1994] 1 AC 180. If there is nothing to put the lender on notice, undue influence cannot operate as a defence to possession, no matter what other remedies the disadvantaged homeowner may have against his or her former partner.

Since the *O'Brien* case, banks have developed practices to prevent undue influence defences succeeding. They now regularly obtain a letter from the joint borrower's solicitor confirming that the effect of the transaction has been explained to him or her. In *Royal Bank of Scotland plc v Etridge (No. 2)* [2001] UKHL 44, [2002] 2 AC 773, the House of Lords explained *O'Brien* and added detailed guidance. As a result of banks following this guidance, the flow of like cases has substantially diminished.

Forgery and *non est factum*

87.42   If the signature of one of two joint borrowers on the mortgage deed has been forged, the aggrieved party has the right to set aside the mortgage so as not to be bound by it. Forgery may take place when one borrower wishes to raise additional funds without the knowledge of his or her co-owner. Misrepresentation is a necessary foundation for a plea of *non est factum* ('not my deed'). See *Destine Estates Ltd v Muir* [2014] EWHC 4191 (Ch), LTL 19/12/2014.

A forged legal charge may still operate as an equitable charge on the beneficial interest of the forging borrower; equally if both borrowers signed the mortgage application but one did not execute the deed, an equitable charge on both borrowers' beneficial interests may be created as a result of a written agreement to create a legal charge (Law of Property Act 1925, s. 53(1)(c)). An equitable charge may be enforced by way of application for an order for sale under s. 90 of the 1925 Act.

Where the advance under the forged mortgage was used to discharge a prior charge to which both borrowers consented, rights of subrogation may exist.

Misrepresentation

87.43   Misrepresentations given by or on behalf of the lender, inducing a borrower to enter into the transaction, may afford a potential defence to a possession claim. If the misrepresentation was by an agent of the lender such as a broker, the borrower must prove that it was made in the course of the agency so as to make the lender vicariously liable.

Unfair terms

87.44   Unfair terms in non-individually negotiated mortgage contracts do not bind consumer borrowers. See the Unfair Terms in Consumer Contracts Regulations 1999 (SI 1999/2083) for contracts before 1 October 2015, and the Consumer Rights Act 2015 since that date. However, main terms concerning the price paid and the value of the mortgage product are exempt from control if set out in plain intelligible language (SI 1999/2083, reg. 6(2); 2015 Act, s. 64). If a mortgage can continue without the offending term, that term can be severed and the mortgage can still be enforced.

Technical defences

87.45   A mortgage contract made by a lender without the necessary regulatory authorisation or exemption is unenforceable against a borrower (Financial Services and Markets Act 2000, ss.

19, 26 and 27), unless the court considers it just and equitable (s. 28). However, breach of the MCOB sourcebook rules does not render a mortgage unenforceable (*Thakker v Northern Rock (Asset Management) plc* [2014] EWHC 2107 (QB), LTL 6/2/2014). Breaches of the technical requirements of the Consumer Credit Act 1974 on default notices or otherwise may offer defences. Occupation by the borrower for 12 years since the last mortgage payment offers a potential defence under the Limitation Act 1980 (*Ashe v National Westminster Bank plc* [2008] EWCA Civ 55, [2008] 1 WLR 710).

A common argument by borrowers is that as the mortgage deed is only signed by the borrower and not signed by the lender it has not been validly executed. This argument relies on the Law of Property (Miscellaneous Provisions) Act 1989, s. 2, which requires a contract for the disposition of an interest in land to be in writing and signed by all parties. However, a legal charge is a disposition; not an agreement for a disposition, and is not therefore within s. 2 (*The Mortgage Business Plc v Lamb* (Preston County Court, 12 July 2013, unreported)).

Challenging arrears

Even if the mortgage is admitted, there may be a dispute over the figures contended for by the lender. Payments may go astray, sometimes into the holding accounts of the lender, awaiting tracing and allocating, or take longer in clearance than expected. The court should not treat as a dispute of substance every case where the arrears statement is not agreed. The lender claimant will not want this, because of the delay; the borrower defendant may gain time, but end up paying for the litigation. The preferable course is to adjourn for a short period to enable the parties to try to narrow the issues. This may result in the need to try only a discrete issue, such as whether the arrears are £2,000 or £3,000, or the making of an order based on a minimum agreed arrears figure. **87.46**

It is important to distinguish between arrears and other payments due under the mortgage. These should have been separately identified in the statement annexed to the particulars (**PD 55A, para. 2.5(3)**). A lender may make payments to protect its security, such as the property insurance premium or ground rent or service charges due under the borrower's lease. Such payments may correctly be debited to the mortgage account, meaning that the mortgage cannot be redeemed without the borrower repaying them with accrued interest. The mortgage conditions may allow the lender to capitalise these sums, and adjust the monthly payment accordingly, or to demand reimbursement. However, any claim would form a separate cause of action.

There may be challenges to how the lender has calculated the monthly instalment, or whether payments made by the borrower in reduction of capital have been correctly attributed. In *Bank of Scotland plc v Rea* [2014] NI Master 11, a case in the High Court in Northern Ireland, the court criticised the lender for adding the arrears to the outstanding balance and increasing the current monthly instalment, so that the arrears would be repaid by the end of the term, but continuing to treat the arrears as outstanding for the purpose of possession proceedings.

It is possible that the contractual terms of the loan permit the lender to vary the rate of interest payable by reference to a bank base rate, or even to vary the percentage over base rate that is payable (*Alexander v West Bromwich Mortgage Co. Ltd* [2015] EWHC 135 (Comm), [2015] 2 All ER (Comm) 224).

Track allocation

If disputed matters remain unresolved, and a defence has been filed, case management directions given under **CPR, r. 55.8(1)(b)**, will include track allocation. Allocation principles are dealt with in **r. 55.9**. The court has to consider all the normal factors set out in **r. 26.8**, as applicable to a case of this nature: the amount of the arrears, the importance to the defendant of retaining possession of the land and the importance to the claimant of vacant possession. **87.47**

The level of arrears alone may be under the small claims limit, but the value of the property, and usually the balance outstanding under the mortgage (often claimed in the action) will substantially exceed the fast track limit. The perceived advantages of the fast track are speed and limitation of trial costs. Given the usual costs covenant in mortgage deeds, the latter consideration is less relevant. Allocation to the multi-track is usually appropriate, and, save in the most complex of cases, speedy trial can be achieved by fixing a trial window near to, or sooner than, the 30 weeks for a fast track case. Once allocated to the fast track or multi-track, unless the court otherwise directs, all the evidence will be orally tested, in accordance with **Part 32**.

ENFORCEMENT OF COUNTY COURT POSSESSION ORDERS

Warrants of possession

87.48　If a borrower breaches a suspended order, or fails to vacate to comply with a straight order, enforcement is by paper application for a bailiff's warrant (form N325). Permission is needed if the order is more than six years old or there has been a change in the parties such as a transfer by the lender or the death of the borrower (**CPR, r. 83.2(3)**). The warrant is initially valid for one year, but may be extended. When the warrant is executed the bailiff must evict everyone in the property (*R v Wandsworth County Court, ex parte Wandsworth London Borough Council* [1975] 1 WLR 1314). The bailiff usually visits the property prior to the actual eviction appointment and will report to the court anything that requires its attention. It may be necessary to invoke the assistance of others to execute the warrant, for example, the police if a breach of the peace is feared. The lender is given adequate notice, so it can secure the premises once the bailiff has obtained possession.

Further postponement of possession

87.49　Until completion of execution of a warrant of possession, the court retains its powers under the Administration of Justice Act 1970, s. 36. Any change in the circumstances of the borrower affecting ability to pay the mortgage arrears may found a further application, usually for suspension of the warrant. A stay normally connotes a brief delay in the enforcement procedure, whereas a suspension will be granted for a longer term. In either case conditions may be imposed.

There is no theoretical limit to the number of successive applications for suspension. The facts behind a failed application should not found a further one, but be the subject of appeal. In practice the line is blurred. Slight changes to the factual matrix found fresh applications. It is often speedier to allow the court to adjudicate on a further application than to appeal. If there is a mix of rehearing and new facts, the appellate court may direct a rehearing. It may not disturb the original exercise of discretion. Accordingly lenders may decide against challenging the jurisdiction to hear what appears to be a 'similar facts' application. If the target is speedy possession, taking some technical points may be self-defeating.

Available orders

87.50　It is common for borrowers to wait until the last minute before applying to suspend a warrant of possession, delaying the application in the hope of a change in their circumstances. Often the evidence produced is less than convincing, but dismissal of the application may only beg an appeal or fresh application. The court may instead, using its general case-management and listing powers, adjourn for a short period to test the promises or aspirations of the borrower. An applicant saying that his purchaser will exchange tomorrow may not later persuade a court to suspend, if that promise has been broken. The dangers of failing properly to formulate proposals to pay until the appeal stage, and the need then to satisfy the court that in the light of past failures there is a realistic prospect of payment, were highlighted in *Jameer v Paratus AMC*

[2012] EWCA Civ 1924, [2013] HLR 18, applying *Bank of Scotland plc v Zinda* [2011] EWCA Civ 706, [2012] 1 WLR 728.

If satisfied on the borrower's application, the warrant will be suspended on payment of the arrears at a determined rate, identifying the date of next payment. If further information is required, the court may adjourn for a short period, staying the warrant during the adjournment and directing that certain payments be made in the interim. In a borderline case there appears no reason in principle why the court cannot direct that, notwithstanding the stay, the lender can immediately obtain a new date for the warrant to be executed, provided it is after the return date.

Discouraging repeated applications

A lender at the 'warrant suspension' stage, wishing to inhibit unmeritorious applications, each **87.51** causing successive warrant execution appointments to be vacated, may consider various pragmatic solutions:

(a) On dismissal of the borrower's application, it may ask for an order that no further application be made without the permission of the court. This does not preclude the borrower from applying for permission, and the court suspending the warrant, without notice, pending the hearing for permission.
(b) In preference to a short adjournment or stay, the court may dismiss the application, having there and then refixed the warrant execution date sufficiently distant to meet the borrower's minimum requirements. This solution is useful when the borrower raises compassionate grounds of questionable legal merit.
(c) Reserving the case to the same judge may signal that the court will view with scepticism an identical argument being revisited.
(d) Although the application is dismissed, the warrant is ordered to lie in the court and not actually be executed, for a few days.
(e) Cases of misuse of the court's procedures may be met by a civil restraint order (see **14.55** to **14.60**).

Unauthorised tenants

Since 1 October 2010 a mortgagee of a dwelling-house must give written notice to tenants **87.52** and occupiers that it intends to apply for a warrant of possession (Mortgage Repossessions (Protection of Tenants etc.) Act 2010; Dwelling Houses (Execution of Possession Orders by Mortgagees) Regulations 2010 (SI 2010/1809); **CPR, r. 83.26(5)**). A warrant cannot be executed before the end of the prescribed period of 14 days beginning with the day of service of that notice (2010 Act, s. 2(2); SI 2010/1809, reg. 3). The notice must be in the form set out in the schedule to SI 2010/1809 (reg. 4). It may be given (reg. 5):

(a) by first class or registered post, addressed to a tenant by name, or otherwise to 'the tenant or occupier';
(b) by leaving it at or affixed to the property; or
(c) by personal service on an apparent resident.

Giving this notice may spark a last-minute reaction by the tenant.

Section 1(4) of the 2010 Act provides that the court may, on the application of any unauthorised tenant, stay or suspend execution of a possession order for a period not exceeding two months if:

(a) the court did not postpone the date for possession under s. 1(2) when making the possession order or, if it did, the applicant was not the tenant when it exercised those powers;
(b) the applicant has asked the lender to give an undertaking in writing not to enforce the order for two months beginning with the date the undertaking is given; and
(c) the lender has not given such an undertaking.

In considering the exercise of its powers the court must take into account the circumstances of the tenant and the nature of any breach of the tenancy agreement, and can impose terms (s. 1(5), (6) and (7); see also **87.38**).

In *Bank of Scotland plc v Ashraf* (Romford County Court, 5 October 2010, unreported) the court decided that the request for an undertaking should be read disjunctively from the other provisions of s. 1(4). This results in an unauthorised tenant being able to apply to postpone execution without necessarily having requested an undertaking from the mortgage lender.

While a court can, under **CPR, r. 23.8**, deal on paper with applications under the 2010 Act, it will usually do so at a hearing. Until an applicant appears before the court, it is difficult to ascertain his or her true standing. The applicant may be a licensee, an unauthorised tenant, or even a tenant whose interest would have defeated the claim to possession and who would be entitled to joinder (see **87.39**). Frustrating as it is for lenders, the result may be the cancellation of a warrant appointment, as the court will almost inevitably, upon receipt of the application, stay the warrant pending an oral hearing on the application.

Party unaware of proceedings

87.53   Sometimes in family breakdown situations one partner hides from the other both non-payment of the mortgage, and the possession proceedings themselves. Although the original service of proceedings may have been good (service to last known address), the unsuspecting partner has a right to apply to set aside the possession order or warrant. A **Part 55** hearing is not a trial (*Forcelux Ltd v Binnie* [2009] EWCA Civ 854, [2010] HLR 20) and any application is under **CPR, r. 3.1(2)(m)**. The court must consider all the circumstances under **r. 3.9**, giving precedence to the requirements of **r. 39.3(5)** (*Hackney London Borough Council v Findlay* [2011] EWCA Civ 8, [2011] HLR 15, decided under r. 3.9 as in force before 1 April 2013). If the applicant shows the potential for a different order, if only a suspension on less onerous terms, that may suffice, provided the application has been made promptly.

Paying the arrears

87.54   If after a warrant issues, a sufficient payment is made so that the lender is willing to allow the borrower to remain in occupation on the basis of the existing suspended possession order, the warrant can be withdrawn by letter. If the borrower again defaults, and the warrant has neither expired nor been formally discharged, a fresh eviction date can be sought by letter. If the basis of agreement is that, despite a straight order, there is now to be a suspended arrangement, a variation order is important. If the entire arrears are paid, so that the mortgage account is brought fully up to date, it should be remembered that the original suspended order remains in full force, if only as an obligation to pay the contractual mortgage instalments, and a fresh warrant can thereafter issue for subsequent arrears (*Bank of Scotland plc v Zinda* [2011] EWCA Civ 706, [2012] 1 WLR 728).

Completion of execution

87.55   It is the borrower's responsibility to deliver up vacant possession. However, it is unnecessary to remove all the furniture and belongings of the borrower to complete execution under a County Court warrant (County Courts Act 1984, s. 111(1)). In practice, lenders allow borrowers an opportunity within a fortnight to make arrangements to collect their effects. Standard mortgage terms usually allow the lender then to dispose of personal possessions without liability. Once in possession, the lender becomes an involuntary bailee, and its rights under the mortgage conditions are subject to an obligation to do what is right and reasonable in the circumstances (*Da Rocha-Afodu v Mortgage Express Ltd* [2014] EWCA Civ 454, [2014] 2 P & CR DG10). There comes a point when it is reasonable for the lender to sell or throw away the goods (*Campbell v Redstone Mortgages Ltd* [2014] EWHC 3081 (Ch), [2015] 1 P & CR DG18).

Once execution is complete, the court has no further powers to stay or suspend the warrant. The borrower's only option is to apply to set aside the warrant, and possibly also the possession order, on the grounds that one or both were obtained by fraud, or there has been abuse of process or oppressive conduct. An example of oppressive conduct is where a lender agrees to suspend only if all arrears are paid immediately, and advises the borrower that if that is impossible, they should not bother making an application to suspend (*Cheltenham and Gloucester Building Society v Obi* (1996) 28 HLR 22; see more recently *Jayashankar v Lloyds TSB plc* [2011] EW Misc 9 (CC)).

Forcible re-entry

If a borrower evicted lawfully by execution of a bailiff's warrant forcibly re-enters, the remedy **87.56** is a warrant of restitution (**CPR, r. 83.26(8)**; see **79.39**). Permission to apply for the warrant is needed. The application is without notice, under **Part 23**, supported by a witness statement, establishing the wrongful re-entry was undertaken by or on behalf of a party to the proceedings. The court staff should be invited to refer the file immediately to the District Judge for the warrant to issue.

Redemption of the mortgage

Execution of a warrant of possession does not of itself extinguish the proprietary rights of a **87.57** borrower. A borrower who redeems the mortgage, even when out of occupation, can re-enter.

Commentary

PART S

Anti-social Behaviour and Harassment

Chapter 88   Anti-social Behaviour and Harassment

INTRODUCTION

This chapter deals with the powers of the civil courts to make orders controlling behaviour **88.1** which causes distress, nuisance or annoyance. The powers considered in this chapter arise under the following Acts:

(a) the Anti-social Behaviour, Crime and Policing Act 2014;
(b) the Police and Justice Act 2006, s. 27 (power of arrest added to local authority's injunction) (**88.15**);
(c) the Anti-social Behaviour Act 2003, ss. 26A, 26B and 26C (parenting orders) (**88.16** to **88.19**);
(d) the Protection from Harassment Act 1997, ss. 3 and 3A (**88.20** to **88.26**);
(e) the Policing and Crime Act 2009, part 4 (injunctions to prevent gang-related violence) (**88.29** to **88.39**).

Powers (a) to (c) and (e) are exercised in the public interest on the application of bodies exercising public functions. Power (d) is a private law remedy, though it can be used to protect large groups of people.

The legal devices employed are injunctions (powers (a) and (d)), injunctions enhanced by a power of arrest (powers (a) and (b)) and orders of the civil courts which it is a criminal offence to disobey (powers (c) and (d)). Compliance with an injunction may be enforced by committal (see **chapter 81**). Powers of arrest are used to bring to court people who have breached injunctions so that applications to commit them may be heard. If a power of arrest is not attached to an injunction, it may be possible to obtain a warrant for arrest (powers (a) and (d)).

In some cases, more than one statutory power will apply to a particular case. It is for the applicant to choose which statute to proceed under. The judge will then exercise his or her discretion to make whatever order seems most appropriate in the circumstances, provided that the statutory conditions are satisfied. There is no 'closest fit' principle requiring the court to consider all other available statutory provisions (*Birmingham City Council v James* [2013] EWCA Civ 552, [2014] 1 WLR 23).

Before 23 March 2015, when the relevant provisions of the Anti-social Behaviour, Crime and Policing Act 2014 came into force, orders and injunctions could be made under the following provisions:

(a) the Housing Act 1996, part 5, ch. 3 (anti-social behaviour injunctions and injunctions against unlawful use of premises);

(b) the Crime and Disorder Act 1998, ss. 1B and 1D (anti-social behaviour orders, ASBOs);

(c) the Violent Crime Reduction Act 2006, ss. 1 to 14 (drinking banning orders).

This legislation has all been repealed, but applications for orders under these provisions made, but not resolved, before 23 March 2015 continue to be governed by the repealed legislation, which also continues to apply to all orders made under the repealed provisions (Anti-social Behaviour, Crime and Policing Act 2014, s. 21(1) and (2)), though any orders still in force after five years will be treated as injunctions under s. 1 of the 2014 Act (s. 21(5) and (6)). For full details of the repealed provisions, see the 2015 edition of *Blackstone's Civil Practice*.

INJUNCTIONS UNDER THE ANTI-SOCIAL BEHAVIOUR, CRIME AND POLICING ACT 2014

Power to grant injunctions

88.2   The court has power to grant injunctions against a person aged 10 or over if two conditions are satisfied:

(a) the court is satisfied, on the balance of probabilities, that the respondent has engaged or threatens to engage in anti-social behaviour; and

(b) the court considers it just and convenient to grant the injunction for the purpose of preventing the respondent from engaging in anti-social behaviour (Anti-social Behaviour, Crime and Policing Act 2014, s. 1(1) to (3)).

Any injunction granted must state the period for which it has effect, or state that it has effect until further order (s. 1(6)). If the injunction is granted before the respondent reaches the age of 18, a period must be specified and it must be no more than 12 months.

For the purpose of preventing the respondent from engaging in anti-social behaviour, the injunction may prohibit the respondent from doing or require the respondent to do anything described in the injunction (s. 1(4)). However, prohibitions and requirements, must, so far as practicable, be such as to avoid any interference with the times, if any, at which the respondent normally works or attends school or any other educational establishments and any conflicts with any other court order or injunction to which the respondent may be subject (s. 1(5)). The injunction can specify periods for which particular prohibitions or requirements have effect (s. 1(7)).

The application must be made to a youth court if the respondent is aged under 18, and to the High Court or the County Court in all other cases.

If the respondent is under 18 at the time of the application, the applicant must consult the local youth offending team about the application (but need not do so for a without-notice application) for an injunction, or any application for variation or discharge of the injunction (s. 14(1)(a) and (3)(a)). The applicant must also do this if the application is adjourned before the first on-notice application (s. 14(2)(a)) or if an application is made for variation or discharge (s. 14(3)(b)). The applicant must also inform any other body or individual that the applicant thinks appropriate that an application is to be made or a without-notice application is adjourned (s. 14(1)(b) and (2)(b)).

The Youth Justice and Criminal Evidence Act 1999, part 2, ch. 1 (special measures for vulnerable and intimidated witnesses), applies to proceedings under the Anti-social Behaviour, Crime and Policing Act 2014, part 1, but with the modifications set out in s. 16 of the 2014 Act. The reporting restrictions in respect of children and young persons set out in the Children and Young Persons Act 1933, s. 49, do not apply to applications for an injunction made under part 1 of the 2014 Act (s. 17).

An application for an injunction under part 1 of the 2014 Act is subject to the Part 8 procedure as modified by **CPR, r. 65.43** and **PD 65**. The application must be made by form 16A, which is treated as a Part 8 claim form (**PD 65, para. 1.1**). The claim form must set out the matters required by **CPR, r. 8.2**, and the terms of the injunction applied for (**r. 65.43(3)**). An application can be made at any County Court hearing centre and must be supported by a witness statement which is filed with the claim form (**r. 65.43(2)**). If the application is made without notice, the witness statement must also explain why notice has not been given (**r. 65.43(4)(a)**). Applications made on notice must be personally served on the respondent, together with the evidence in support (**r. 65.43(5)**). If the application on notice is to be heard before the time expires for filing an acknowledgment of service under **r. 8.3**, service must be effected by the claimant not less than two days before the hearing, and the defendant can take part in the hearing whether or not an acknowledgment of service has been filed (**r. 65.43(6)**).

If the application is made on notice, but at a County Court hearing centre which does not serve the address at which the claimant or the respondent resides or carries on business, the application will be issued there and transferred to the hearing centre serving the relevant address (**r. 65.43(2A)**; **PD 65, para. 1.1(2)**). An applicant should consider the potential delay that might occur if the application is not made at the appropriate County Court hearing centre in the first instance.

Any proceedings started in a youth court will be transferred to the High Court or the County Court hearing centre which serves the address where the respondent resides after the respondent reaches the age of 18, and any order of the youth court will continue to have effect as if it were an order of the High Court or County Court (**PD 65, para. 1A.1**).

Meaning of anti-social behaviour

'Anti-social behaviour' is defined by the Anti-social Behaviour, Crime and Policing Act 2014, s. 2, to mean: **88.3**

(a) conduct that has caused, or is likely to cause, harassment, alarm or distress to any person (s. 2(1)(a));
(b) conduct capable of causing nuisance or annoyance to a person in relation to that person's occupation of residential premises (s. 2(1)(b)); or
(c) conduct capable of causing housing-related nuisance or annoyance to any person (s. 2(1)(c)).

'Housing-related' means conduct which directly or indirectly relates to the housing management functions of a housing provider or a local authority (s. 2(3)). The housing management functions of a housing provider include functions conferred on it under an enactment and its powers and duties as the holder of an estate or interest in housing accommodation (s. 2(4)).

It was held that the court's jurisdiction under the previous provisions for injunctions prohibiting housing-related anti-social conduct (Housing Act 1996, s. 153A) was to be regarded as broad rather than narrow. Provided the respondent's conduct taken as a whole was 'housing-related' in that it directly or indirectly related to or affected the local authority's housing management functions, an injunction could be granted. In particular, there was no requirement that a respondent had to be a tenant or an occupier of property owned by the local authority before an injunction could be granted under s. 153A (*Swindon Borough Council v Redpath* [2009] EWCA Civ 943, [2010] BLGR 28).

In deciding whether to grant an injunction under s. 1, the court may take into account conduct occurring up to six months before the commencement date of 23 March 2015 (s. 21(7)).

An interim injunction was granted under the 2014 Act on the application of the police authority, prohibiting the leader and deputy leader of a registered political party who held anti-Muslim views from entering any mosque or Islamic cultural centre in a particular town without prior invitation, but the court did not consider it appropriate to prevent them from entering the town altogether (*Chief Constable of Bedfordshire v Golding* [2015] EWHC 1875 (QB), LTL 7/7/2015).

Contents of injunctions

88.4   If an injunction granted under the Anti-social Behaviour, Crime and Policing Act 2014, s. 1, imposes a requirement, it must also specify the person who is to be responsible for supervising that requirement. That person can be an individual or an organisation (s. 3(1)). The court must receive evidence from this person about the suitability and enforceability of the proposed requirement before the requirement is included in the injunction (s. 3(2)). Before including two or more requirements in an injunction, the court must first consider their compatibility with each other (s. 3(3)). The person responsible for supervising the requirements must make any necessary arrangements in relation to the requirements and promote the respondent's compliance with them, and report compliance or non-compliance with the requirements to the applicant and the appropriate chief officer of police as defined in s. 3(5) (see s. 3(4)).

A respondent who is subject to a requirement included in an injunction must keep in touch with the supervising person in relation to that requirement and act in accordance with any instructions given by that person from time to time, and notify that person of any change of address (s. 3(6)). These requirements have effect as requirements of the injunction.

Power of arrest

88.5   A court granting an injunction under the Anti-social Behaviour, Crime and Policing Act 2014, s. 1, may, under s. 4(1), attach a power of arrest to a prohibition or a requirement of the injunction (apart from a requirement that has the effect of requiring the respondent to participate in particular activities) if it thinks that:

(a)   the anti-social behaviour in which the respondent has engaged or threatens to engage consists of or includes the use or threatened use of violence against other persons; or

(b)   there is a significant risk of harm to persons other than the respondent.

'Harm' includes serious ill-treatment or abuse, whether physical or not (s. 20(1)).

A power of arrest can be specified for a shorter period than the requirement or prohibition to which it relates (s. 4(2)).

An application seeking a power of arrest to be attached to any provision of the injunction must be made in the proceedings seeking the injunction by claim form or application under **CPR, Part 23** (**r. 65.49(1)**) and it must be supported by written evidence, and the application notice and the evidence in support must be served personally on the respondent not less than two days before the hearing (**r. 65.49(3)**). Where the injunction contains a provision to which a power of arrest is attached, each relevant provision must be set out in a separate paragraph, and the claimant must deliver a copy of the relevant provisions to any police station for the area in which the conduct occurred. If the injunction was granted without notice, the respondent must be served with the injunction order before a copy is delivered to the relevant police station (**r. 65.44(2)** and **(3)**).

Applications for injunctions

An injunction under the Anti-social Behaviour, Crime and Policing Act 2014, s. 1, can be **88.6** granted on the application of a wide range of interested parties. These include local authorities, housing providers (although a housing provider can only make an application if it concerns anti-social behaviour that directly or indirectly relates to or affects its housing management functions), the chief officer of police for a police area, the Chief Constable of the British Transport Police, the Environment Agency and the Secretary of State exercising security management arrangements under the National Health Service Act 2006, s. 195(3) (Anti-social Behaviour, Crime and Policing Act 2014, s. 5).

Only a housing provider, a local authority or the chief officer of police can apply for an injunction in respect of anti-social behaviour arising out of a person's occupation of residential premises under s. 2(1)(b). A 'housing provider' means a housing trust, a housing action trust, a non-profit private registered provider of social housing, a Welsh body registered as a social landlord, and any other body that is a landlord under a secure tenancy within the meaning of the Housing Act 1985, s. 79 (Anti-social Behaviour, Crime and Policing Act 2014, s. 20(1)). 'Local authority' means a district council, a county council, a London Borough council, the Common Council of the City of London or the Council of the Isles of Scilly, and in relation to Wales, a county council or a county borough council (s. 20(2)).

Applications without notice

An application for an injunction can be made without notice to the respondent (Anti-social **88.7** Behaviour, Crime and Policing Act 2014, s. 6(1)), but if this occurs, the court must either adjourn the proceedings and grant an interim injunction under s. 7, or adjourn the proceedings without granting an interim injunction, or dismiss the application (s. 6(2)). Where an application is made without notice, the evidence in support must state the reasons why notice was not given.

In *Moat Housing Group-South Ltd v Harris* [2005] EWCA Civ 287, [2006] QB 606 at [72], the Court of Appeal stated the following principles governing the making of orders without notice (in the context of the former Housing Act 1996, s. 153A). An order may be made without notice only if there are exceptional circumstances. An example of an exceptional circumstance is that there is a risk of significant harm to some person or persons attributable to the conduct of the defendant if the order is not made immediately. The order must not be wider than is necessary and must be proportionate as a means of avoiding the apprehended harm.

In *KY v DD (Without-Notice Applications)* [2011] EWHC 1277 (Fam), [2011] Fam Law 797, the court set out additional guidance which should be followed when making without-notice applications. Such applications should only be made in cases of genuine urgency. The information put before the court to substantiate a without-notice order should be closely scrutinised. If the applicant is not present to verify it in person, it should be substantiated by the production of a contemporaneous note of the instructions. If additional information is put before the court orally, there should be a direction for the filing of evidence to confirm that information within a very short period of time. It is incumbent on those considering the making of a without-notice application to consider carefully whether it is justified and to be clear about the evidential basis for it.

Interim injunctions

If the court adjourns the application for an injunction (whether it is made with or without **88.8** notice), it can grant an interim injunction lasting until the final hearing of the application or until further order, if it thinks it just to do so (Anti-social Behaviour, Crime and Policing Act 2014, s. 7(1)). An interim injunction granted on a without-notice application cannot require the respondent to participate in particular activities (s. 7(3)). Otherwise the court has the same powers, including the power of arrest, which it would have on a final injunction.

Variation or discharge of injunctions

88.9   The court may vary or discharge an injunction on the application of the applicant or the respondent. The application should be made to the court which granted the injunction, or the County Court if the injunction was granted by a youth court but the respondent is now 18 or over (Anti-social Behaviour, Crime and Policing Act 2014, s. 8(2)). The court can vary an injunction by including an additional prohibition or requirement, attaching a power of arrest, or extending the period for which a prohibition, requirement or a power of arrest has effect (s. 8(3)). If an application for variation or discharge is dismissed, the applicant can make no further application without the consent of the court or the other party (s. 8(4)).

An application to vary or discharge an injunction must be made in accordance with **CPR, Part 23**. If the application is made without notice, the application must state the reasons why notice has not been given (**r. 65.45(3)**). Where an order is made varying or discharging any provision to which a power of arrest is attached, the claimant must immediately inform the police station to which a copy of the injunction order was delivered and deliver a copy of the order to any police station so informed (**r. 65.44(4)**).

Breach of injunction

88.10   **Arrest without warrant**   Where a power of arrest is attached to a provision of an injunction, a constable may arrest the respondent without a warrant if he or she has reasonable cause to suspect that the respondent is in breach of the provision (Anti-social Behaviour, Crime and Policing Act 2014, s. 9(1)). The applicant must be informed. Within the period of 24 hours beginning with the arrest, the arrested person must be brought before a judge of the court which granted the injunction (except that the relevant court is the County Court if the injunction was granted by a youth court but the respondent is now aged 18 or over, or a justice of the peace if the person is under 18) (s. 9(3)). In calculating the period of 24 hours, Christmas Day, Good Friday and any Sunday are to be disregarded (s. 9(4)). The court has power to remand the respondent if the matter cannot be disposed of immediately, and if the respondent is brought before a justice of the peace, the respondent must be remanded to appear before the youth court that granted the injunction (s. 9(6)).

88.11   **Issue of arrest warrant**   If the applicant believes that the respondent is in breach of the terms of the injunction, the applicant can apply for the issue of a warrant of arrest. The application must be made in accordance with **CPR, Part 23**, and may be without notice (**r. 65.46(1)**). An affidavit must be filed with the application notice setting out grounds for the application. Alternatively, oral evidence of the grounds for the application can be given at the hearing and where this occurs, the applicant must produce a written record of that evidence which must be served on the person arrested at the time of the arrest (**r. 65.46(2) and (3)**). A warrant for arrest will not be issued unless the application is substantiated on oath and the judge has reasonable grounds to believe that the respondent has failed to comply with the injunction (**PD 65, para. 2.1**).

The application is made before a judge of the court which granted the injunction except that if the injunction was granted by a youth court and the respondent is below the age of 18, the application is made to a justice of the peace, and if the respondent is now over 18, the application is made to a judge of the county court (Anti-social Behaviour, Crime and Policing Act 2014, s. 10(1) and (2)).

The judge can only issue the warrant if there are reasonable grounds for believing that the respondent is in breach of the injunction. The warrant will require the respondent to be brought before the court that issued the warrant, except that a warrant granted by a justice of the peace will require the respondent to be brought before the youth court if the respondent is aged under 18, but if the respondent is aged 18 or over, the warrant will require the respondent to be brought to the County Court (s. 10(4) to (6)).

The court has power to remand the respondent, and once the respondent is arrested the applicant must be informed (s. 10(7) and (8)).

Proceedings following arrest   Where a person is arrested pursuant to a power of arrest **88.12** attached to a provision of an injunction order, or a warrant of arrest, the judge before whom the person is brought can deal with the matter or adjourn the proceedings. If the proceedings are adjourned and the arrested person is released, the matter must be dealt with within 28 days of the date on which the arrested person appears in court and the arrested person must be given at least two days' notice of the hearing (**CPR, r. 64.47(3)**). An application notice seeking the committal of the arrested person can be issued even if the arrested person is not dealt with within the 28-day period. If an application for committal is made, **Sections** 2 and **8** of **Part 81** apply, but the references to a judge include references to a district judge (**r. 65.47(5)**). See *Brown v Haringey London Borough Council* [2015] EWCA Civ 483, [2015] HLR 30 for guidance issued by the Court of Appeal on the route to be taken when applying for legal aid for representation in committal proceedings.

Remands   If a respondent is remanded, the Anti-social Behaviour, Crime and Policing Act **88.13** 2014, sch. 1, has effect. This contains provisions for grants of bail and the taking of recognisances, and remands for medical examinations and reports. If the court fixes the amount of any recognisance, with a view to it being taken subsequently, it can be taken by a judge, a justice of the peace, a justice's clerk, a police officer of the rank of inspector or above, or in charge of a police station, or, where the arrested person is in custody, the governor or keeper of the prison (**CPR, r. 64.48**). Bail applications can be made orally or in an application notice, in which case the application notice must state the requirements set out in **PD 65, para. 3.2**.

The powers exercisable on a breach of an injunction in respect of anyone under the age of 18 are set out in sch. 2 to the 2014 Act.

Exclusion from home

An injunction under the Anti-social Behaviour, Crime and Policing Act 2014, s. 1, which **88.14** excludes someone from the place where he or she normally lives can only be granted if (s. 13):

(a) the person is aged 18 or over;
(b) the applicant is a local authority, the chief officer of police for the police area that the premises are in, or a housing provider where the premises are owned or managed by a housing provider. A housing provider owns a place if it is entitled to dispose of the fee simple of the place, whether in possession or in reversion and it is entitled to the rents and profits under a lease that was for a term of not less than three years when it was granted (see s. 13(2));
(c) the court thinks that the anti-social behaviour in which the respondent has engaged or threatens to engage consists of or includes the use or threatened use of violence against other persons or there is a significant risk of harm to other persons from the respondent.

POWER OF ARREST ADDED TO LOCAL AUTHORITY'S INJUNCTION

The Local Government Act 1972, s. 222, enables a local authority to bring, defend or appear **88.15** in proceedings for the promotion or protection of the interests of inhabitants of its area. However, s. 222 should not be used to obtain, in effect, an anti-social behaviour order under the court's general discretion to grant injunctions under the Senior Courts Act 1981, s. 37.

The authority should instead seek an anti-social behaviour order under the relevant statutes so that the detailed checks and balances developed by Parliament and in the decided cases will apply (*Birmingham City Council v Shafi* [2008] EWCA Civ 1186, [2009] 1 WLR 1916). See also *Birmingham City Council v James* [2013] EWCA Civ 552, [2014] 1 WLR 23, at **88.1**. In *A Local Authority v DL* [2010] EWHC 2675 (Fam), [2011] Fam Law 26, it was held that the High Court has an inherent jurisdiction to make a non-molestation order against the son of elderly vulnerable parents, on the application of a local authority, despite the fact that the parents did not lack capacity to bring their own proceedings. An order could be made under the court's jurisdiction even if an ASBO or injunction order could not be obtained under the Crime and Disorder Act 1998 or the Housing Act 1996, s. 153A. If the facts warrant an injunction order under the court's inherent jurisdiction, they also warrant an order under the Local Government Act 1972, s. 222. The two stand or fall together.

Where an injunction is obtained by a local authority by virtue of the Local Government Act 1972, s. 222, which prohibits conduct capable of causing nuisance or annoyance to a person (the potential victim), the court may attach a power of arrest to any provision of the injunction (Police and Justice Act 2006, s. 27(2)). By the Police and Justice Act 2006, s. 27(2) and (3), the court may attach a power of arrest if it thinks that either:

(a) the conduct being prohibited consists of or includes the use or threatened use of violence, or

(b) there is a significant risk of harm to the potential victim — harm being defined in s. 27(12) as including serious ill-treatment or abuse (whether physical or not).

An application for a power of arrest to be attached to an injunction must be made in the proceedings seeking the injunction. It may be made in the claim form, the acknowledgment of service, the defence or counterclaim in a Part 7 claim, or an application under **CPR, Part 23** (**r. 65.9(1)**). It must be supported by written evidence (**r. 65.9(2)**). If the application is made on notice, the local authority must serve it, with a copy of the evidence, personally on the person against whom the injunction is sought, not less than two days before the hearing (**r. 65.9(3)**).

If a power of arrest is added, under the Police and Justice Act 2006, s. 27, to any provision of an injunction obtained by a local authority, the claimant must deliver a copy of the provisions to which the power is attached (each of those provisions must be in a separate paragraph) to any police station for the area where the conduct occurred (**CPR, rr. 65.4(1)** and (2) and **65.10(1A)(a)**). If the injunction was granted without notice, delivery to a police station cannot be done until the injunction has been served on the defendant (**rr. 65.4(3)** and **65.10 1A)(a)**).

If a provision of an injunction to which a power of arrest is attached is varied or discharged, the claimant must immediately inform the police station to which it delivered the copy of the provision and deliver a copy of the order which varies or discharges it (**rr. 65.4(4)** and **65.10(1A)(a)**).

Where a power of arrest is added, under the Police and Justice Act 2006, s. 27, to any provision of an injunction obtained by a local authority, a constable may arrest, without warrant, a person whom he has reasonable cause for suspecting to be in breach of that provision (s. 27(4)). After making an arrest, the constable must, as soon as is reasonably practicable, inform the local authority (s. 27(5)). The arrestee must be brought before the court within 24 hours of arrest, excluding Christmas Day, Good Friday or any Sunday (s. 27(6)(a) and (7)). When the arrestee is first brought before a judge, that judge may deal with the matter or adjourn proceedings (**CPR, r. 65.6(2)** applied by **r. 65.10(1A)(b)**). If the matter is not disposed of forthwith, the arrestee may be remanded (Police and Justice Act 2006, s. 27(6)(b)), either in custody or on bail, in accordance with sch. 10. The procedure for applying for bail is in **CPR, r. 65.7**, and **PD 65, paras 3.1 to 3.3**, as applied by **para. 4A.1**.

There is also a power under the Police and Justice Act 2006, s. 27(9), (10) and (11), to remand for a medical report or a report on mental condition (see **PD 65, paras 4.1** and **4A.2**).

An arrestee who is released when proceedings are adjourned must be dealt with (whether by the same or another judge) within 28 days of the first court appearance (**CPR, rr. 65.6(4)(a)** and **65.10(1A)(b)**) and must be given at least two days' notice of the hearing (**rr. 65.6(4)(b)** and **65.10(1A)(b)**). 'Must' in **r. 65.6(4)(a)** is directory rather than mandatory, as it is provided in **r. 65.6(5)** that failure to meet the 28-day deadline does not invalidate any application notice seeking committal for contempt.

PARENTING ORDERS

The Anti-social Behaviour Act 2003, ss. 26A, 26B and 26C, enable local authorities and relevant housing providers to seek parenting orders from the court. 'Relevant housing provider' means a non-profit registered provider of social housing or a registered social landlord (ss. 25B(1A) and 29(1)).

A magistrates' court or, where s. 26C applies, the County Court may make a parenting order, under s. 26A (on the application of a local authority) or s. 26B (on the application of a relevant housing provider), in respect of a parent of a child or young person, if it is satisfied:

(a) that the child or young person has engaged in anti-social behaviour; and
(b) that making the order would be desirable in the interests of preventing the child or young person from engaging in further anti-social behaviour.

An individual is a child if aged under 14, a young person if aged 14 or over but under 18 (Crime and Disorder Act 1998, s. 117(1), applied by the Anti-social Behaviour Act 2003, s.29(1)).

A parenting order is an order which requires the parent:

(a) to comply, for a period not exceeding 12 months, with such requirements as are specified in the order (ss. 26A(3)(a) and 26B(3)(a)); and
(b) to attend, for a concurrent period not exceeding three months, such counselling or guidance programme as may be specified in directions given by the responsible officer (defined in s. 26A(8) and s. 26B(9) and (10)).

Requirement (b) may, but need not, be included if another parenting order has been obtained under s. 26A, s. 26B or any other enactment in respect of the same parent on a previous occasion (s. 26A(3)(b) and (4); s. 26B(3)(b) and (4)). A counselling or guidance programme may be, or include, a residential course (ss. 26A(5) and 26B(5)), but only if the court is satisfied that the attendance of the parent at a residential course is likely to be more effective than attendance at a non-residential course in preventing the child or young person from engaging in further anti-social behaviour (ss. 26A(6) and 26B(6)). Also the court must be satisfied that any interference with family life which is likely to result from the attendance of the parent at a residential course is proportionate in all the circumstances (ss. 26A(7) and 26B(7)).

A relevant housing provider must not make an application for a parenting order without first consulting the local authority in whose area the child or young person in question resides or appears to reside (s. 26B(8)). If the child or young person resides or appears to reside in a place which is within the area of a county council and a district council, then each local authority must be consulted (s. 26B(8A)).

Parenting orders incidental to County Court proceedings

The Anti-social Behaviour Act 2003, s. 26C, provides for parenting orders under s. 26A or s. 26B to be made in County Court proceedings. The provisions are similar to those under which ASBOs may be made.

88.16

88.17

A 'relevant authority' may apply for a parenting order to be made, in County Court proceedings to which it is a party (s. 26C(1)). A relevant authority may apply to be joined to proceedings for the purpose of making an application (s. 26C(2)). If it is a party to County Court proceedings, it may apply for an individual to be joined in those proceedings so that it may apply for a parenting order, provided it considers that a child or young person of which that person is a parent has engaged in anti-social behaviour that is material to those proceedings (s. 26C(3)). No person under 18 may be joined (**PD 65, para. 16.3**).

For parenting orders the relevant authorities are local authorities and relevant housing providers (Anti-social Behaviour Act 2003, s. 26C(1)).

Procedure

88.18   Any application for a parenting order to be made under the Anti-social Behaviour Act 2003, s. 26A or s. 26B, must be accompanied by written evidence (**CPR, r. 65.41**). If the application is by a relevant housing provider, there must be evidence that it has consulted the relevant local authority in accordance with the Anti-social Behaviour Act 2003, s. 26B(8) (**PD 65, para. 16.1**). An application should be made as soon as possible after the relevant authority becomes aware of the circumstances which lead it to apply for a parenting order (**CPR, rr. 65.38(2), 65.39(2)(a)** and **65.40(1)(b)**). The application must normally be on notice to the person against whom the parenting order is sought (**rr. 65.38(3), 65.39(2)(b)** and **65.40(4)**).

If a relevant authority wishes to apply as a party to County Court proceedings for a parenting order to be made against another party, it should make the application in its claim form or, if it is a defendant, in an application notice filed with the defence (**r. 65.38(1)**). If the relevant authority only becomes aware at a later stage of the need for a parenting order, it must apply for one as soon as possible by application notice (**r. 65.38(2)**).

An application to be joined to County Court proceedings so as to apply for a parenting order to be made against one of the existing parties is an application for addition of a party and so must be made under **Part 19, Section I** (**r. 65.39(1)(a)**). It should be made in the same application notice as the application for the parenting order (**r. 65.39(1)(b)**).

An application to join a person to County Court proceedings so that a parenting order may be made is an application for addition of a party and must be made under **Part 19, Section I**, but **r. 19.2** does not apply (**r. 65.40(2)**). It should be made in the same application notice as the application for the parenting order (**r. 65.40(1)(a)**). It must contain the authority's reasons for claiming the anti-social behaviour of the child or young person is material in relation to the proceedings, and details of the behaviour alleged (**r. 65.40(3)**).

Service

88.19   A parenting order made under the Anti-social Behaviour Act 2003, s. 26A or s. 26B, must be served personally on the defendant (**PD 65, para. 16.2**).

PROTECTION FROM HARASSMENT ACT 1997

88.20   The Protection from Harassment Act 1997 prohibits a person knowingly pursuing a course of conduct which amounts to harassment of another (s. 1(1)) or, in certain circumstances, a course of conduct which involves harassment of two or more persons (s. 1(1A)). The definition of harassment is considered in more detail in **88.21** to **88.23**. The Act provides both criminal (ss. 2, 2A, 4, 4A and 5) and civil (ss. 3 and 3A) sanctions. Civil proceedings are considered in **88.24** to **88.26**.

Commentary

Conduct amounting to harassment

88.21 The Protection from Harassment Act 1997, s. 1(1), provides that a person must not pursue a course of conduct which amounts to harassment of another and which he or she knows or ought to know amounts to harassment of the other. By s. 1(1A) a person must not pursue a course of conduct which involves harassment of two or more persons and which he or she knows, or ought to know, involves harassment of those persons and by which he or she intends to persuade any person not to do something which that person is entitled to do or to do something which that person is not under any obligation to do. Section 1(1A) will be particularly useful in cases where a campaign of harassment is carried out by pressure groups in respect of a business or property, and there is no 'course of conduct' against any one victim for the purposes of s. 1(1), because no individual is affected twice (see **88.22**).

By s. 1(2), a person ought to know that conduct amounts to or involves harassment if a reasonable person in possession of the same information would think that the course of conduct amounted to or involved harassment. Whether or not an individual has contravened this prohibition is determined objectively by considering whether a reasonable person would think that what the individual did amounted to harassment (*R v Colohan* [2001] EWCA Crim 1251, [2001] 2 FLR 757). In civil proceedings the standard of proof of contravention of s. 1(1) is the civil standard on the balance of probabilities (*Hipgrave v Jones* [2004] EWHC 2901 (QB), [2005] 2 FLR 174).

It appears that the definition of harassment has been left deliberately imprecise. The interpretation section (s. 7(2)) defines harassing a person as including 'alarming the person or causing the person distress', but Lord Phillips of Worth Matravers MR said in *Thomas v News Group Newspapers Ltd* [2001] EWCA Civ 1233, [2002] EMLR 4 at [29]–[30]:

There are many actions that foreseeably alarm or cause a person distress that could not possibly be described as harassment. It seems to me that s. 7 is dealing with that element of the offence which is constituted by the effect of the conduct rather than with the types of conduct that produce that effect.

... 'Harassment' is a word which has a meaning which is generally understood. It describes conduct targeted at an individual which is calculated to produce the consequences described in s. 7 and which is oppressive and unreasonable.

It is not necessary to prove an intention to alarm or distress: it is sufficient that the conduct is liable to produce those consequences (*Banks v Ablex Ltd* [2005] EWCA Civ 173, [2005] IRLR 357).

Newspaper articles likely to incite racial hatred of an individual may be harassment of that individual (*Thomas v News Group Newspapers Ltd* [2001] EWCA Civ 1233, [2002] EMLR 4). Damage to the claimant's shop windows, obstructing their customers and sending offensive letters and materials constituted harassment in *Silverton v Gravett* (2001) LTL 31/10/2001.

By s. 7(4) 'conduct' includes speech, which seems common sense given the nature of the distress which the 1997 Act is intended to relieve.

Course of conduct

88.22 The Protection from Harassment Act 1997, s. 1, prohibits a 'course of conduct'. By s. 7(3), in the case of conduct in relation to a single individual, this must involve conduct on at least two occasions in relation to that individual (*Banks v Ablex Ltd* [2005] EWCA Civ 173, [2005] IRLR 357). In the case of conduct in relation to two or more persons (see s. 1(1A)), a course of conduct must involve conduct on at least one occasion in relation to each of those persons (s. 7(3)(b)). The two or more incidents of harassment do not therefore need to be against the same person in a case which is brought under s. 1(1A).

'The requirement of a course of conduct shows that Parliament was conscious that it might not be in the public interest to allow the law to be set in motion for one boorish incident' (Lord Hoffmann in *Wainwright v Home Office* [2003] UKHL 53, [2004] 2 AC 406 at [46]).

Two separate incidents may amount to a course of conduct, if they are shown to be motivated by a common purpose of harassment (compare *Baron v Crown Prosecution Service* (2000) LTL 13/6/2000, in which two letters, clearly intended as harassment, amounted to a course of conduct, with *Lau v Director of Public Prosecutions* [2000] 1 FLR 799, in which no connection was proved between two incidents six months apart). Even if there are two or more incidents, they may not all be sufficiently serious to amount to harassment within the meaning of the 1997 Act. The gravity of the misconduct has to be sufficiently serious to sustain criminal liability under s. 2 (*Sunderland City Council v Conn* [2007] EWCA Civ 1492, [2008] IRLR 324; *Lipscombe v Forestry Commission* [2008] EWHC 3342 (QB), LTL 4/2/2009). In *Pratt v Director of Public Prosecutions* (2001) *The Times*, 22 August 2001, the Administrative Court emphasised that the fewer and wider spread the incidents put in evidence, the less likely they would be found to constitute a course of conduct (see also *R v Nitin Patel* [2004] EWCA Crim 3284, [2005] 1 Cr App R 27; *James v Crown Prosecution Service* [2009] EWHC 2925 (Admin), [2010] Crim LR 580). A gift of a plant, sending a letter and redirecting a misdirected package could not themselves amount to harassment, but when combined with secretly filming the victim and going through her rubbish, they could (*King v Director of Public Prosecutions* (2000) *The Independent*, 31 July 2000). Computer-generated bills and communications from a company may amount to a course of harassment (*Ferguson v British Gas Trading Ltd* [2009] EWCA Civ 46, [2009] 3 All ER 304). In *Roberts v Bank of Scotland plc* [2013] EWCA Civ 882, LTL 11/6/2013, the Court of Appeal held that the judge at first instance had been entitled to award damages of £7,500 to a claimant for harassment by the Bank which consisted of making repeated and numerous telephone calls (over 547) over the course of a year) to the claimant about the state of her account. The Bank's conduct amounted to harassment both because of the number of the calls and their content, some of which were intimidatory.

An alleged act of harassment which occurred around 18 months after the previous acts of harassment, and in a different place under different circumstances, did not form part of a course of conduct when considered with the previous incidents (*Marinello v Edinburgh City Council* [2010] CSOH 17, 2010 SLT 349).

An act which occurred during the course of proceedings and after the issue of the claim form can be relied upon to establish a course of conduct (*Iqbal v Dean Manson Solicitors* [2011] EWCA Civ 123, [2011] CP Rep 26). The commencement and service of civil proceedings may amount to harassment as they may be a form of conduct that might well cause anxiety, alarm and distress, particularly where such proceedings were vexatious (*Apsion v Dilnot* [2013] EWHC 2428 (QB), LTL 11/4/2013). The prevention of harassment is a legitimate social objective that may justify a restriction on the respondent's rights under the European Convention on Human Rights, art. 6, in the Human Rights Act 1998, sch. 1 (*R (on the application of Waxman) v Crown Prosecution Service* [2012] EWHC 133 (Admin), 176 JP 121.

Posting threatening communications on the internet and by email can amount to a course of conduct' (*XY v Facebook Ireland Ltd* [2012] NIQB 96, LTL 24/12/2012). See also *WXY v Gewanter* [2012] EWHC 496 (QB), LTL 15/3/2012, [2013] EWHC 589 (QB), LTL 21/3/2013, *AMP v Persons Unknown* [2011] EWHC 3454 (TCC), [2011] Info TLR 25, and *QRS v Beach* [2014] EWHC 3057 (QB), LTL 29/9/2014).

An allegation of harassment by publication is likely to engage the defendant's rights under the European Convention on Human Rights, art. 10. Accordingly, the test in the **Human Rights Act 1998, s. 12(3)**, as explained in *Cream Holdings Ltd v Banerjee* [2004] UKHL 44, [2005] 1 AC 253, should be applied. An applicant for an interim injunction must establish that they are 'likely' to succeed at trial in obtaining permanent relief in respect of the harassment, and the court should grant an interim injunction only if that test is satisfied (*Neocleous v Jones* [2011] EWHC 3459 (QB), [2011] Info TLR 39). See also *Law Society v Kordowski* [2011] EWHC 3185 (QB), LTL 14/12/2011, and *ZAM v CFW* [2011] EWHC 476 [2011], LTL 9/3/2011. The fact that statements are true and can be justified at trial will not necessarily prevent the conduct from being harassment, or prevent a court from granting an injunction at an interlocutory stage. The court will scrutinise the conduct carefully before deciding if the line has been crossed, and any relief granted has

to be no more that is absolutely necessary in interfering with **art. 10** rights (*Merlin Entertainments LPC v Cave* [2014] EWHC 3036 (QB), [2015] EMLR 3).

False allegations made to neighbours and to the police about a claimant which led to many police visits to the claimant's house were held to be a course of conduct amounting to harassment in *Mitton v Benefield* [2011] EWHC 2098 (QB), LTL 4/8/2011. On the other hand, six incidents over a nine-month period, all of which included an element of violence, during a close and affectionate relationship were held not to amount to a course of conduct or harassment in *R v Widdows* [2011] EWCA Crim 1500, [2011] 2 FLR 869. Statements made by a witness are protected by witness immunity under the rule in *Westcott v Westcott* [2008] EWCA Civ 818, [2009] QB 407. Accordingly a harassment claim cannot be brought in respect of such statements (*Crawford v Jenkins* [2014] EWCA Civ 1035, [2015] 1 All ER 476).

A course of conduct which amounts to stalking is an offence under s. 2A or, where it involves a fear of violence or serious alarm or distress, s. 4A (inserted by the Protection of Freedoms Act 2012, s. 111, with effect from 25 November 2012).

Excluded situations

The Protection from Harassment Act 1997, s. 1, does not apply if the person who pursued what **88.23** would otherwise have been a course of conduct amounting to harassment, shows that it was pursued for the purpose of preventing or detecting crime (s. 1(3)(a)), or under any enactment or rule of law, or duty imposed by an enactment (s. 1(3)(b)), or that in the particular circumstances the pursuit of the course of conduct was reasonable (s. 1(3)(c)). A person's explanation of the purpose of their conduct is part of the evidence of all of the circumstances which the court must assess in ascertaining whether that conduct came within s. 1(3). In order to come within the exception in s. 1(3)(a), it must be shown that the alleged harasser acted rationally. Rationality is not the same as reasonableness. Reasonableness is an external, objective standard applied to the outcome of a person's thoughts or intentions. The question is whether a notional hypothetically reasonable person in the alleged harasser's position would have engaged in the relevant conduct for the purpose of preventing or detecting crime. A test of rationality, by comparison, applies a minimum objective standard to the relevant person's mental processes. It imports a requirement of good faith, a requirement that there should be some logical connection between the evidence and the ostensible reasons for the decision, and an absence of arbitrariness, of capriciousness or of reasoning so outrageous in its defiance of logic as to be perverse. The relevant purpose must be the dominant purpose (*Hayes v Willoughby* [2013] UKSC 17, [2013] 1 WLR 935). The mere fact that the alleged conduct occurred in the context of police work is not enough (*Dowson v Chief Constable of Northumbria* [2009] EWHC 907 (QB), LTL 7/5/2009). If a course of conduct was pursued partly to prevent or detect crime and partly for other reasons, a person might claim the protection of s. 1(3)(c) and show that their conduct was reasonable in the circumstances. If a person invokes both s. 1(3)(a) and (c), the court should first determine whether the sole purpose of the conduct was to prevent or detect crime. If the detection or prevention of crime was not the dominant purpose of the conduct, then the court should consider whether the conduct was in any event reasonable under s. 1(3)(c) (*Hayes v Willoughby*). Where the conduct complained of involves the publication of articles, in deciding whether the conduct was reasonable under s. 1(3)(c), the court has to balance the claimant's rights under **art. 8** in the **Human Rights Act 1998, sch. 1**, against the defendant's **art. 10** rights and must decide whether a continuing future public interest in publication outweighs the claimant's **art. 8** rights (*Ware v McAllister* [2015] EWHC 3086 (QB), LTL 27/7/2015). Where the defendant has no reasonable prospect of establishing that a campaign of harassment was justified under s. 1(3), the court may grant an interim injunction (*Cheshire West and Chester Council v Pickthall* [2015] EWHC 2141 (QB), LTL 17/8/2015).

Section 1 also does not apply to any act, by a specified person, which is certified by the Secretary of State to have been related to national security, the economic well-being of the United Kingdom, or the prevention or detection of serious crime (s. 12).

Civil proceedings

88.24   Section 3(1) of the Protection from Harassment Act 1997 provides that an actual or apprehended breach of s. 1(1) may be the subject of a claim in civil proceedings by the victim or potential victim. On such a claim, damages may be awarded for (among other things) any anxiety and/or any financial loss caused by the harassment (s. 3(2)).

The claimant does not need to establish that any injury or loss sustained by the harassment was foreseeable. Section 1 is concerned with deliberate conduct of a kind which the defendant knew or ought to have known would amount to harassment of the claimant. Once that is proved, the defendant is responsible (by s. 3) for damages for the injury and loss which flowed from that conduct. There is nothing in the language of the statute to import an additional requirement of foreseeability (*Jones v Ruth* [2011] EWCA Civ 804, [2012] 1 All ER 490).

A corporation cannot make a claim under s. 3 (*Daiichi Pharmaceuticals UK Ltd v Stop Huntingdon Animal Cruelty* [2003] EWHC 2337 (QB), [2004] 1 WLR 1503). If a campaign against a company involves harassment under s. 1(1) of individuals who are employees, directors or shareholders of the company, each of those individuals may take action under s. 3. In *Emerson Developments Ltd v Avery* [2004] EWHC 194 (QB), LTL 26/1/2004, one individual, who was a director and employee of a company, sued as a representative of all employees of the company under **CPR, r. 19.6**, and this is now usual in such cases.

An employer may be held vicariously liable under the Protection from Harassment Act 1997, s. 3, for harassment by one of its employees acting in the course of his or her employment (*Majrowski v Guy's and St Thomas's NHS Trust* [2006] UKHL 34, [2007] 1 AC 224; *Green v DB Group Services (UK) Ltd* [2006] EWHC 1898 (QB), [2006] IRLR 764). Vicarious liability for harassment may be established either by proving that one employee, on at least two occasions, pursued a course of conduct which amounted to harassment, or that there have been acts of harassment by more than one employee, each acting on different occasions in furtherance of some joint design (*Daniels v Commissioner of Police of the Metropolis* [2006] EWHC 1622 (QB), LTL 12/7/2006).

A claim under s. 3 must use the **CPR, Part 8**, procedure (see **chapter 13**) (r. 65.28(a)). In the High Court it must be commenced in the Queen's Bench Division; otherwise it must be commenced in a County Court hearing centre. If the application is commenced in a hearing centre which does not serve the place where (a) the defendant or (b) the claimant resides or carries on business, the claim will be issued by the County Court hearing centre where the claim is commenced, and sent to the hearing centre serving the claimant or defendant's address or place of business as appropriate (r. 65.28(2)).

A civil claim for breach or apprehended breach of the Protection from Harassment Act 1997, s. 1, may ask for an injunction to restrain future breach. In the County Court an injunction may be granted by a District Judge (**PD 2B, para. 8.1(c)**). Contravention of such an injunction without reasonable excuse is a criminal offence (Protection from Harassment Act 1997, s. 3(6) and (9)). Alternatively, breach of an injunction can be punished by committal (see **chapter 81**) and s. 3 provides for a warrant for arrest to be issued to bring a person who breaches such an injunction to court to consider an application for committal (see **88.25**). Committal for contempt and criminal proceedings are mutually exclusive alternatives (s. 3(7) and (8)).

An injunction may create an exclusion zone if that is reasonably necessary for the protection of the claimant's legitimate interests (*Burris v Azadani* [1995] 1 WLR 1372; *Church of Jesus Christ of Latter-Day Saints v Price* [2004] EWHC 3245 (QB)). See also *Slade v Slade* [2009] EWCA Civ 748, [2010] 1 WLR 1262.

If claimant and defendant are within the jurisdiction, an injunction may be granted to restrain harassment of the claimant when abroad (*Potter v Price* [2004] EWHC 781 (QB), LTL 28/7/2004).

Under s. 3A, where there is an actual or apprehended breach of s. 1(1A) (course of conduct involving harassment of two or more persons), an injunction may be granted restraining the relevant person from pursuing any conduct which amounts to harassment in relation to any person or persons mentioned or described in the injunction. An application for an injunction under s. 3A may be made to the High Court or the County Court by any person who is or may be the victim of the course of conduct in question, or any person who is or may be a person falling within s. 1(1A)(c) (a person whom the wrongdoer intends to persuade not to do something he is entitled to do or to do something which he is not under any obligation to do). A company may apply for an injunction under s. 3A in circumstances where the company falls within s. 1(1A)(c). 'Person' in s. 1(1A)(c) is not limited to individuals and may be a body corporate (*SmithKline Beecham plc v Avery* [2009] EWHC 1488 (QB), LTL 1/7/2009; see also *Monarch Airlines Ltd v Yaqab* [2016] EWHC 1003 (QB), LTL 14/3/2016 where a company obtained a permanent injunction against its former employee under ss. 1(1A) and 3A preventing him from sending offensive emails to its employees following his dismissal from the company). Section 3A(3) applies s. 3(3) to (9) (sanctions for breach of an injunction order) to an order granted under s. 3A.

Although s. 3A has widened the scope of the Act to encompass victims who are not parties, where a representative defendant has been appointed under **CPR, r. 19.6**, the provisions of **r. 19.6(4)(b)** cannot be circumvented (*AGC Chemicals Europe Ltd v Stop Huntington Animal Cruelty* [2010] EWHC 3674 (QB), LTL 11/6/2010). **Rule 19.6(4)(b)** requires the court's permission for enforcement of an order against a person who is not a party (see *Astellas Pharma v Stop Huntingdon Animal Cruelty* [2011] EWCA Civ 752, *The Times*, 11 July 2011). Permission to enforce an order against unidentified non-parties may not be granted in the order itself (*SmithKline Beecham plc v Avery* [2007] EWHC 948 (QB), LTL 9/5/2007; *Huntingdon Life Sciences Group plc v Stop Huntingdon Animal Cruelty (SHAC)* [2007] EWHC 522 (QB), LTL 19/4/2007). Therefore, it is not possible to declare in the order that any represented person not named in the order is a 'defendant' for the purposes of the Protection against Harassment Act 1997, s. 3(3) (warrant for arrest) or s. 3(6) (contravention of order is an offence) (*AGC Chemicals Europe Ltd v Stop Huntington Animal Cruelty* [2010] EWHC 3674 (QB), LTL 11/6/2010).

Warrant for arrest

88.25 Where the court grants an injunction for the purpose of restraining the defendant from pursuing any conduct which amounts to harassment, and the claimant considers that the defendant is in breach, the claimant may apply for a warrant for the defendant's arrest (Protection from Harassment Act 1997, s. 3(3) and s. 3A(3)). Such application may be to a High Court judge if the injunction was granted by that court (s. 3(4)(a)), or to a judge of the County Court (s. 3(4)(b)). Such a warrant can only be issued if the application is substantiated on oath (i.e. it must be supported by an affidavit or sworn testimony), and the judge has reasonable grounds for believing that there may have been a breach of the injunction (s. 3(5)(a) and (b)). The evidence must set out the grounds of the application, state whether the claimant has informed the police of the conduct of the defendant as described in the affidavit, and state whether, to the claimant's knowledge, criminal proceedings are being pursued (**CPR, r. 65.29(2)**).

Dealing with arrestee

88.26 Where a person is arrested in execution of a warrant issued under the Protection from Harassment Act 1997, s. 3(3), the judge before whom the person is first brought may deal with the matter or adjourn proceedings (**CPR, r. 65.30(1)**). An arrestee who is released when proceedings are adjourned must be dealt with (whether by the same or another judge) within 28 days of the first court appearance (**r. 65.30(2)(a)**) and must be given at least two days' notice of the hearing (**r. 65.30(2)(b)**).

Conviction for the offence of doing something prohibited by an anti-harassment injunction precludes punishment of the same act as a civil contempt of court (Protection from Harassment Act 1997, s. 3(7)). Conversely, a person cannot be criminally convicted for conduct which has been punished as contempt of court (s. 3(8)).

BEHAVIOUR CONTROL AND HUMAN RIGHTS

Relevant Convention rights

88.27   Orders granted under the Anti-social Behaviour, Crime and Policing Act 2014 (**88.2** to **88.14**), the Police and Justice Act 2006, s. 27(2) (**88.15**) or the Protection from Harassment Act 1997 (**88.20** to **88.26**) may potentially infringe an individual's rights under the European Convention on Human Rights in the **Human Rights Act 1998, sch. 1**. This is particularly so in cases of harassment arising from the acts of protest groups. An order which seeks to ban an individual from particular premises or a particular area may infringe his **art. 8** right to a private or family life. An order preventing an individual speaking or publishing specified words may contravene his **art. 10** right to freedom of expression. An order that prevents an individual from associating with other named individuals or specified groups or organisations, or prevents him from demonstrating, for example, against an animal testing laboratory, could infringe his **art. 11** right to freedom of assembly and to freedom of association with others.

An individual's rights under each of these articles are limited and restrictions can be placed on them which are prescribed by law and are necessary in a democratic society for the prevention of disorder or crime, for the protection of health or morals, or for the protection of the rights of others (**arts 8(2), 10(2)** and **11(2)**). **Article 11** also does not prevent the imposition of lawful restrictions on the exercise of the rights of freedom of assembly and association by members of the armed forces, the police or the administration of the State (**art. 11(2)**).

Impact of Convention rights in harassment and anti-social behaviour cases

88.28   The courts have shown no reluctance in granting orders discussed in this chapter if the individual has acted in a way which causes harassment, alarm or distress to others. However, the orders granted must be proportionate in the sense of being commensurate with the risk to be guarded against, particularly where the order will interfere with a right protected by the **Human Rights Act 1998** (*R v Boness* [2005] EWCA Crim 2395, [2006] 1 Cr App R (S) 120; *Percy v Director of Public Prosecutions* [2001] EWHC 1125 (Admin), [2002] Crim LR 835). A parenting order (see **88.16** to **88.19**) with a residential course for counselling or guidance may be made only if any interference with family life (**art. 8**) is proportionate in all the circumstances (Anti-social Behaviour Act 2003, ss. 26A(7) and 26B(7)).

While most restrictions on freedom of expression or assembly will be granted only if there is a risk or threat of violence, an injunction to prevent harassment is not limited to acts which place the victim in fear of violence but can be granted when rights of protest and expression amount to harassment (*EDO MBM Technology Ltd v Campaign to Smash EDO* [2005] EWHC 837; *SmithKline Beecham plc v Avery* [2009] EWHC 1488 (QB), LTL 1/7/2009; *Law Society v Kordowski* [2011] EWHC 3185 (QB), LTL 14/12/2011).

The common law of nuisance and the Protection from Harassment Act 1997 can limit an individual's right to freedom of expression and manifestation of his religious belief under the European Convention on Human Rights, **art. 9**, in the **Human Rights Act 1998, sch. 1**, in the interests of public order and for the protection of others, and an exclusion order can be granted even if it interferes with the defendant's lawful actions and right to move freely along the highway (*Church of Jesus Christ of Latter-Day Saints v Price* [2004] EWHC 3245 (QB)).

A fair balance should be struck between the rights of the defendant and the proper protection of the claimants. Such a balance was struck by the court in *Hall v Save Newchurch Guinea Pigs (Campaign)* [2005] EWHC 372 (QB), *The Times*, 7 April 2005, where the claimants sought and obtained injunctive relief under the Protection from Harassment Act 1997 against animal rights activists, even though the defendants' conduct was not of itself tortious or unlawful in that it amounted to a peaceful demonstration, as an injunction was reasonably necessary for the protection of the claimant's legitimate interests. The court also imposed an exclusion zone around the premises. To strike a balance between the rights of the claimants and the rights of the demonstrators, the court provided that the defendants would be entitled to protest once per week between certain hours, although it limited the number of protesters who could be present at each demonstration.

A similar balance was struck in the order made against animal rights protesters in *Huntingdon Life Sciences Group plc v Stop Huntingdon Animal Cruelty (SHAC)* [2007] EWHC 522 (QB), LTL 19/4/2007, where an injunction was granted in favour of the claimants although the terms of the order specified the maximum number of protesters, the requirement to give notice to the police prior to a demonstration, provision for parking and delivery of protesters to and from a designated protest area, a ban on the use of megaphones and restriction of protest processions to one every three months. See also *RWE Npower plc v Carrol* [2007] EWHC 947 (QB), LTL 9/5/2007; *SmithKline Beecham plc v Avery* [2007] EWHC 948 (QB), LTL 9/5/2007; *Bayer Cropscience Ltd v Stop Huntingdon Cruelty (SHAC)* [2009] EWHC 3289 (QB), LTL 8/3/2010. In *Novartis Pharmaceuticals UK Ltd v Stop Huntington Animal Cruelty* [2009] EWHC 2716 (QB), LTL 6/11/2009, the court had to balance the rights, of freedom of assembly and association and freedom of expression, of animal rights activists against the right to respect for private and family life of the pharmaceutical company's employees. The court held that any restrictions on the freedom of expression or freedom of assembly or both had to be: convincingly established, justified by compelling reasons, subject to careful scrutiny, proportionate and no more than necessary. The giving of notice to the police in relation to demonstrations and compliance with police conditions were reasonable and acceptable, but the balance of convenience was strongly against making an order prohibiting protesters from wearing blood-splattered clothing or costumes as it was likely to be practically unenforceable and was not proportionate. It was not so easy to decide where the balance lay in relation to the prohibition sought in relation to the wearing of balaclavas, face coverings and masks. Although ghoulish masks had the potential to cause anxiety and distress and could be used to disguise the identity of someone intent on harassing conduct, given the late application for such a provision, the practical difficulties it would cause for the police, the risk of it raising tensions and the interference it would cause to those who wished to wear inoffensive masks, such an order was not made in the circumstances of that case. A permanent injunction was granted preventing demonstrations by animal rights groups at the applicant's medical laboratory together with an order banning photography, balaclavas and masks. A balance was achieved between the applicant's **art. 8** rights and the protesters' **arts 10** and **11** rights by allowing the protesters to demonstrate opposite the premises once a week for three hours, although the number of protesters was limited to 25 and they were required to give 24 hours' advance notice of a demonstration to the police and the applicant, and by giving them the right to a larger demonstration of up to 100 people once a year (*Harlan Laboratories UK Ltd v Stop Huntingdon Animal Cruelty (SHAC)* [2012] EWHC 3408 (QB), LTL 11/12/2012).

The court is also, in appropriate circumstances, prepared to look at the human rights of an individual protester separately from those of a larger group. In *Mayor of London v Hall* [2010] EWCA Civ 817, [2011] 1 WLR 504, the Court of Appeal remitted for reconsideration to the High Court the question whether it was proportionate to grant an order for possession and an injunction against a protester in respect of his protest and camping on Parliament Square Gardens as his human rights had not been considered separately from the group of protesters. The individual was in a different position from the other protestors. He had been demonstrating for far longer, his demonstration pitch was in a different part of Parliament Square Gardens and his demonstration had not put off visitors or damaged the flora. The judge should consider his individual rights under the European Convention on Human Rights, **arts 10** and **11**. The High Court held that the orders were proportionate and the interference with rights under **arts 10** and **11** was justified (*Mayor of London v Haw* [2011] EWHC 585 (QB), LTL 24/3/2011). The court granted an order for possession of land occupied by protesters who set up camps next to St Paul's Cathedral and other injunctive relief as the protesters were occupying the land to the exclusion of the landowners and the extent and duration of the obstruction was causing a public nuisance and interfering with the **art. 9** rights of worshippers and visitors to the Cathedral. Any interference the orders caused to the rights of the protesters under **arts 10 and 11** were lawful, necessary and proportionate to safeguard the rights of the landowners and the rights and freedoms of others, the interests of public health and safety, the prevention of disorder and crime and to protect the environment within the City of London. Determining the limits to the **art. 10** and **11** rights of lawful assembly on the highway is fact-sensitive and relevant factors include the extent to which the continuation of the protest breaches domestic law, the importance of the precise location of the protesters, the duration of the protest, the degree to which the protesters occupy the land and the extent to which the protest interferes with the rights of others, including the owners of the land and members of the public (*City of London Corporation v Samede* [2012] EWCA Civ 160, [2012] PTSR 1624). See also *Islington London Borough Council v Jones* [2012] EWHC 1537 (QB), LTL 1/6/2012).

The rights of freedom of expression and assembly are qualified rights and must give way, where it is necessary and proportionate, to the rights of others. An order preventing protesters from entering or remaining without consent on land intended for the 2012 London Olympic Games was granted where the protest was obstructing the rights of the person with exclusive rights of possession to the site (*Olympic Delivery Authority v Persons Unknown* [2012] EWHC 1012 (Ch), LTL 3/5/2012). It will only be in an exceptional case that a trespasser's **art. 8** rights would prevail over a landowner's rights under **art. 1** of the First Protocol (*Manchester Ship Canal Developments Ltd v Persons Unknown* [2014] EWHC 645 (Ch), LTL 17/3/2014).

In *Othman v English National Resistance* [2013] EWHC 1421 (QB), LTL 26/2/2013, the court granted injunctions preventing protesters from demonstrating within 500 metres of the family home of a radical Muslim cleric and restrained them from releasing personal information about his family, including young children of the family. His wife and children (who applied for the injunction) suffered extreme distress when the demonstrations took place and they became prisoners in their home. Granting the injunctions did not breach the protestors' rights under **arts 9, 10, 11** or **14**. The injunctions were restrictions imposed by law and were necessary in a democratic society for the protection of public order and the rights and freedoms of others, and the children's rights under **art. 8** had to be given particular weight.

The provisions in the Police Reform and Social Responsibility Act 2011, part 3, which conferred powers on the police and authorised officers of the local authority to stop protesters from erecting and using tents for the purposes of sleeping or staying in Parliament Square did not infringe the protesters' rights of freedom of expression and assembly. The provisions are of limited effect and relate only to sleeping and do not impede or prevent any other form of protest or demonstration in Parliament Square at any time of the day or night (*R (Gallastegui) v Westminster City Council* [2013] EWCA Civ 28, [2013] 2 All ER 579).

In relation to relief which might interfere with the Convention right to freedom of expression, the **Human Rights Act 1988, s. 12(3)**, provides that no relief is to be granted so as to restrain publication before trial unless the court is satisfied that the applicant is likely to establish that publication should not be allowed. 'Likely' means 'more likely than not' (*Cream Holdings Ltd v Banerjee* [2004] UKHL 44, [2005] 1 AC 253). See also *Neocleous v Jones* [2011] EWHC 3459 (QB), LTL 5/1/2012, and *EWQ v GDF* [2012] EWHC 2182 (QB), LTL 3/8/2012.

On an application for an injunction to prevent harassment by publication of newspaper articles and photographs, an individual's **art. 8** rights did not prevail over a newspaper's **art. 10** rights of freedom of expression where, because of the applicant's association with a public figure, she had no reasonable expectation of privacy (*Trimingham v Associated Newspapers Ltd* [2012] EWHC 1296 (QB), [2012] 4 All ER 717). On the other hand, in *SKA v CRH* [2012] EWHC 2236 (QB), LTL 3/8/2012, an injunction was granted preventing the respondent from disclosing private information about the applicants and harassing them because their **art. 8** rights substantially outweighed the respondent's rights under **art. 10**. See also *Othman v English National Resistance*.

Many of the remedies for anti-social behaviour and harassment arise in a criminal context, such as orders under the Public Order Act 1986 or orders to disperse groups under the Antisocial Behaviour Act 2003, s. 30. Protests are not excluded from those powers, and no fundamental Convention rights will be overridden, provided the use of the powers is proportionate. The question to ask is whether the making of a dispersal order for the protection of the public from harassment, alarm or distress was disproportionate having regard to the defendant's rights under the **Human Rights Act 1998** (*R (Singh) v Chief Constable of the West Midlands* [2005] EWHC 2840 (Admin), [2006] Crim LR 442).

In *R (Catt) v Association of Chief Police Officers of England, Wales and Northern Ireland* [2015] UKSC 9, [2015] AC 1065, the Supreme Court held that the retention of records of a person's peaceful participation in demonstrations from 2005 organised by an extremist protest group was proportionate under **art. 8**, as the records were held with the objective of securing public safety or preventing crime or disorder. The inclusion of the individual's details on the database had minimal impact on the individual's private life and did not carry any stigma of guilt.

INJUNCTIONS UNDER THE POLICING AND CRIME ACT 2009

Injunctions to prevent gang-related violence

Either the High Court or the County Court can grant an injunction to prevent gang-related violence or gang-related drug-dealing activity under the provisions of part 4 (ss. 34 to 50) of the Policing and Crime Act 2009. Something is 'gang-related' if it occurs in the course of, or is otherwise related to, the activities of a group that consists of at least three people and has one or more characteristics that enable its members to be identified by others as a group. 'Violence' includes a threat of violence. 'Drug-dealing activity' means the unlawful production, supply, importation, or exportation of a controlled drug. An injunction cannot be made against a person aged under 14 (s. 34(1)).   **88.29**

The application

An application for an injunction under the Policing and Crime Act 2009, s. 34, can be made by (s. 37):   **88.30**

(a) the chief officer of police for a police area; or
(b) the chief constable of the British Transport Police Force; or
(c) the local authority (meaning a district council, a county council, a London borough council, the Common Council of the City of London, the Council of the Isles of Scilly, or in Wales, a county council or a county borough council).

Before applying for an injunction, the applicant must consult any local authority, any chief police officer or any other body or individual that the applicant thinks it is appropriate to consult (s. 38).

If the respondent is under the age of 18, the applicant must also consult the youth offending team in the area in which the respondent resides and if it appears that the respondent resides in the area of two or more youth offending teams, the applicant must consult the teams that he thinks appropriate (s. 38(2)(aa) and (3)).

The application must be made by form N16A (**PD 65, para. 1.1**) and may be made at any County Court hearing centre. If the claim is made on notice at a County Court hearing centre which does not serve the address where (a) the defendant resides or carries on business or (b) the claimant resides or carries on business, the application will be issued by the County Court hearing centre where the application is made and sent to the hearing centre serving the address where the defendant resides or the conduct complained of occurred (**CPR, r. 65.43(2) and (2A); PD 65, para. 1.1(2)**). Where the application is made without notice, it can be made

Commentary

at any County Court hearing centre and will be heard at the hearing centre where the application is made and, at any stage of the proceedings, it may be transferred to either the hearing centre serving the address where the defendant resides or carries on business or where the conduct complained of occurred, or any other hearing centre which the court considers appropriate (**CPR, r. 65.43(4)**). Unless the court otherwise orders, an application on notice under **r. 65.43** must be made at one of the County Court hearing centres set out in **PD 65, para. 1.2**. Form N16A must state the matters required by **CPR, r. 8.2**, and the terms of the injunction applied for (**r. 65.43(3); PD 65, para. 1.1**). The application must be supported by a witness statement which is filed with the claim form (**CPR, r. 65.43(2)(c)**). The application must be served, together with a copy of the witness statement, by the claimant on the defendant personally (**r. 65.43(5)**). An application made on notice can be listed for hearing before the expiry of the time for the defendant to file an acknowledgment of service under **r. 8.3**. In such a case, the claimant must serve the application notice and witness statement on the defendant not less than two days before the hearing and the defendant may take part in the hearing whether or not he has filed an acknowledgment of service (**r. 65.43(6)**).

Without-notice application

88.31   An application for an injunction under the Policing and Crime Act 2009, s. 34, can be made without giving notice to the respondent (s. 39). If a without-notice application is made, the applicant need not comply with the consultation requirements in s. 38. Where a without-notice application is made, the witness statement in support of the application must state the reasons why notice has not been given (**CPR, r. 65.43(4)**).

The court cannot make an order immediately on a without-notice application. It must either dismiss the application or adjourn it (Policing and Crime Act 2009, s. 39(4)). If the court adjourns the proceedings, the applicant must comply with the consultation requirements before the date of the full hearing on notice (s. 39(5)).

Applications for an injunction which includes a power of arrest

88.32   If an application for an injunction under the Policing and Crime Act 2009, s. 34, made with or without notice, includes an application for a power of arrest to be attached to any provision of the injunction, it must be made in the proceedings seeking the injunction by claim form or an application under **CPR, Part 23**, and every application must be supported by evidence (**r. 65.49(1)**). Every application made on notice must be served personally by the applicant on the respondent, together with a copy of the written evidence, not less than two days before the hearing (**r. 65.49(3)**).

The injunction order

88.33   The court can grant an injunction under the Policing and Crime Act 2009, s. 34, if two conditions are met (s. 34(2) and (3)):

(a) the court must be satisfied on the balance of probabilities that the respondent has engaged in, or has encouraged or assisted, gang-related violence or gang-related drug activity; and

(b) the court must think that it is necessary to grant the injunction for either or both of the following purposes:

    (i)   to prevent the respondent from engaging in, or encouraging or assisting, gang-related violence or gang-related drug activity;

    (ii) to protect the respondent from gang-related violence or gang-related drug activity.

The prohibitions that can be included in the injunction (see s. 35(2)) may, in particular, have the effect of prohibiting the respondent from:

(a) being in a particular place (place includes an area: s. 35(7));

(b) being with particular persons in a particular place;

(c) being in charge of a particular species of animal in a particular place;

(d) wearing particular descriptions of articles of clothing in a particular place;

(e) using the internet to facilitate or encourage violence or drug-dealing activity.

The requirements that can be included in the injunction (see s. 35(3)) may, in particular, have the effect of requiring the respondent to:

(a) notify the person who applied for the injunction of the respondent's address and of any change of that address;

(b) be at a particular place between particular times on particular days, although this cannot require the respondent to be at a particular place for more than eight hours in any day (s. 35(4));

(c) present himself or herself to a particular person at a place where he or she is required to be between particular times on particular days;

(d) participate in particular activities between particular times on particular days.

The prohibitions and requirements included in the injunction must, so far as is practicable, be such as to avoid any conflict with the respondent's religious beliefs, and any interference with the times at which the respondent works or attends any educational establishment (s. 35(5)).

The court cannot include a prohibition or requirement that has effect after the end of the period of two years beginning with the day the injunction is granted (s. 36(2)).

The court will apply the civil standard of proof in deciding whether to grant an injunction under s. 34, and neither this nor the use of hearsay evidence on such applications violates the defendant's rights under **art. 6** in the **Human Rights Act 1998, sch. 1** (*Chief Constable of Lancashire v Wilson* [2015] EWHC 2763 (QB), LTL 7/3/2016). Once there is a serious issue to be tried as to whether the individual was a member of the gang responsible for the violence complained about, the court is not confined to restraining the particular conduct attributed to the individual, but can impose orders restraining the individual from engaging in conduct attributable to the gang as a whole. The court should take care to consider whether, on the facts, any particular individual might be restrained to a lesser extent than the others (*Murray v Chief Constable of Lancashire* [2015] EWCA Civ 1174, LTL 18/11/2015).

Power of arrest

When making an injunction under the Policing and Crime Act 2009, s. 34, the court can **88.34** attach a power of arrest to any prohibition or requirement in the injunction, other than one which has the effect of requiring the respondent to participate in particular activities (s. 36(6)). If the court attaches a power of arrest, it may specify that the power is to have effect for a shorter period than the prohibition or requirement to which it relates (s. 36(7)). If an injunction contains one or more provisions to which a power of arrest is attached ('the relevant provisions'), each relevant provision must be set out in a separate paragraph of the injunction and the claimant must deliver a copy of the relevant provisions to any police station for the area where the conduct occurred (**CPR, r. 65.44(1)** and **(2)**). If the injunction has been granted without notice, the claimant must not deliver a copy of the relevant provisions to any police station before the defendant has been served with the injunction containing the relevant provisions (**r. 65.44(3)**).

If a power of arrest is attached to a provision of an injunction, a constable can arrest without warrant a person whom he has reasonable cause to suspect to be in breach of the injunction (s. 43(2)). If an arrest is made, the constable must inform the person who applied for the injunction (s. 43(3)).

The person who applied for an injunction can also apply to a relevant judge for a warrant for the arrest of the respondent if the respondent is in breach of the terms of the injunction

(s. 44(2)). The relevant judge can issue a warrant on such an application only if there are reasonable grounds for believing that the respondent is in breach of any provision of the injunction (s. 44(3); **PD 65, para. 2.1(2)**). If a person is brought before the court under a warrant issued under s. 44(3), but the matter is not disposed of, the court may remand the person (s. 44(4)).

An application for a warrant of arrest must be made in accordance with **CPR, Part 23**, and may be made without notice. An application for a warrant of arrest must be supported by an affidavit (which must be filed with the application notice) setting out the grounds for the application or the applicant must give oral evidence of the grounds for the application at the hearing (**r. 65.46(2); PD 65, para. 2.1**). If oral evidence is given at the hearing, the applicant must produce a written record of that evidence, which must be served on the person arrested at the time of the arrest (**CPR, r. 65.46(3)**).

A person arrested must be brought before a relevant judge within the period of 24 hours beginning with the time of the arrest (Policing and Crime Act 2009, s. 43(4)). In calculating the period of 24 hours, Christmas Day, Good Friday and any Sunday are to be disregarded (see s. 43(6)). The relevant judge means a judge of the court that granted the injunction, except that where the respondent is aged 18 or over but the injunction was granted by a youth court, it means a judge of the County Court (s. 43(7)).

If a person is arrested pursuant to a power of arrest attached to a provision of an injunction or a warrant of arrest, the judge before whom a person is brought following his arrest can either deal with the matter or adjourn the proceedings (**CPR, r. 65.47(1) and (2)**). If the matter is not disposed of when the person is brought before the court, the judge may remand the person (Policing and Crime Act 2009, s. 43(5)). If the proceedings are adjourned and the arrested person is released, the matter must be dealt with (whether by the same or another judge) within 28 days of the date on which the arrested person appears in court and the arrested person must be given not less than two days' notice of the hearing (**CPR, r. 65.47(3)**). An application notice seeking the committal for contempt of court of the arrested person may be issued even if the arrested person is not dealt with within the 28-day period (**r. 65.47(4)**). The person arrested can apply for bail either orally or by an application notice (**PD 65, para. 3.1**). An application notice seeking bail must comply with the requirements in **PD 65, para. 3.2**.

Remand

88.35 The provisions of the Policing and Crime Act 2009, sch. 5, apply to the remand of a person. Only a person aged 18 or over can be remanded in custody. If, in accordance with sch. 5, para. 2(2)(b), the court fixes the amount of any recognisance with a view to it being taken subsequently, the recognisance may be taken by any of the persons set out in **CPR, r. 65.48(1)**, with the same consequences as if it had been entered into before the court. The person having custody of an applicant for bail must release that person if satisfied that the required recognisances have been taken (**r. 65.48(2)**).

The court also has power to remand a person who has been brought before the court under the Policing and Crime Act 2009, s. 43 or s. 44, for the purposes of enabling a medical examination to take place and a report to be made (s. 45(2)). If a person is remanded in custody for that purpose, the adjournment may not be for more than three weeks at a time (s. 45(3)). If the person is remanded on bail for that purpose, the adjournment may not be for more than four weeks at a time (s. 45(4)).

Section 36(4A) provides that where the respondent is under the age of 18 on the injunction date, and any prohibition or requirement in the injunction is to have effect after the respondent reaches that age and for at least the period of four weeks beginning with the respondent's 18th birthday, the court must order the applicant and the respondent to attend a review hearing on a specified date within that period. This does not apply if a variation is made within or at any time after the period of four weeks ending with the respondent's 18th birthday (s. 42(4A)).

Breach of an order by a person under the age of 18

The Policing and Crime Act 2009, s. 46A and sch. 5A, contain detailed provisions about the **88.36** power of the court in relation to breach of an injunction by a respondent under the age of 18. Schedule 5A provides that the court may make supervision (if necessary, with electronic monitoring requirements) or detention orders in such cases.

Review of the injunction order

A court which has made an injunction under the Policing and Crime Act 2009, s. 34, has **88.37** power to order the applicant and the respondent to attend one or more review hearings on a specified date or dates to review whether the injunction should be varied or discharged (s. 36(3) and (5)).

If any prohibition or requirement in the injunction is to have effect after the end of the period of one year beginning with the injunction date, the court must order the applicant and the respondent to attend a review hearing on a specified date within the last four weeks of the one-year period (s. 36(4)).

Variation or discharge of the injunction order

The court can vary or discharge an injunction made under the Policing and Crime Act 2009, **88.38** s. 34, if a review hearing is held, or an application to vary or discharge the injunction can be made by the applicant or the respondent (s. 42(1) and (2)). Before making such an application, the applicant or respondent must first consult with any local authority, chief police officer or any other body or individual that the applicant or respondent thinks it appropriate to consult (s. 42(5)).

An application to vary or discharge an injunction must be made in accordance with **CPR, Part 23** (**r. 65.45(1)**). The application should normally be made on notice, but if the application is made without giving notice, the application notice must state why notice has not been given (**r. 65.45(2) and (3)**).

The power to vary an injunction includes (Policing and Crime Act 2009, s. 42(3)) power to:

(a) include an additional prohibition or requirement in the injunction;
(b) extend the period for which a prohibition or requirement in the injunction has effect, provided this does not extend beyond the period of two days beginning with the day on which the injunction is granted;
(c) attach a power of arrest or extend the period for which a power of arrest attached to the injunction has effect.

If an application to vary or discharge an injunction is dismissed, no further application to vary or discharge it may be made by any person without the consent of the court (s. 42(6)).

If an order is made varying or discharging any provision which contains a power of arrest, the claimant must immediately inform the police station to which the relevant provision was delivered and deliver a copy of the order varying or discharging that provision to that police station (**CPR, r. 65.44(4)**).

Interim injunction orders

If an application for an injunction under the Policing and Crime Act 2009, s. 34, has been **88.39** made on notice to the respondent and the court adjourns the hearing of the application, the court may grant an interim injunction if it considers that it is just and convenient to do so

Commentary

(s. 40(1) and (2)). If an interim injunction is granted, the court has power to attach any of the provisions to the injunction which it has power to include in an injunction granted under s. 34, including a power of arrest (s. 40(3)).

However, if an application is made without notice and the proceedings are adjourned, the court can make an interim injunction only if it is necessary to do so (s. 41(2)). This is intended to be a more onerous test to satisfy in order to provide an additional safeguard for interim injunctions granted without notice. In such cases, the court can only grant an injunction if it is necessary rather than it being merely just and convenient to do so. The provisions that can be attached to an interim injunction granted without notice to the respondent are more limited than those that can be attached to an interim injunction which has been made after notice as an interim injunction granted without notice cannot require the respondent to participate in particular activities (s. 41(3)).

From 1 June 2015, youth courts are given power to grant gang-related violence injunctions in respect of anyone under the age of 18, and 'the court' in the case of anyone under 18 means the youth court (Crime and Courts Act 2013, s. 18).

PART T

Sale of Goods and Unfair Contracts

Chapter 89   Sale of Goods

INTRODUCTION

The principal statute governing contracts for the sale of goods is the Sale of Goods Act 1979   **89.1**
(SoGA 1979), itself based on an 1893 predecessor which sought to consolidate the law. It has
been described as a 'Code' (*Re Wait* [1927] 1 Ch 606), although rules of common law which are
not inconsistent with its provisions are expressly preserved (SoGA 1979, s. 62(2)). SoGA
1979 was heavily amended in 1994, 1995, 2002 and most recently in 2015. From 1 October
2015 the Consumer Rights Act 2015 (CRA 2015) modifies the law of supply of goods where
the supplier is a 'trader' and the other party is a 'consumer' (CRA 2015, s. 1(1)). A trader is a
person acting for purposes relating to that person's trade, profession or business (s. 2(2)).
A consumer is an individual acting for purposes that are wholly or mainly outside that
individual's trade, profession or business (s. 2(3)). The burden of proving that an individual is
not a consumer is on the trader (s. 2(4)). So there are now three principal sources of sale of
goods law. SoGA 1979 presumptively applies to all contracts for the sale of goods, is the
relevant statute for all business to business sales, and other sales which are not consumer
supply contracts, and governs issues such as the transfer of ownership for all sales. CRA 2015
is wider as it is concerned with all consumer supply contracts, including hire, hire-purchase,
and the supply of services and digital content. Part 2 of chapter 1 of CRA 2015 modifies

SoGA 1979 in respect of consumer sales, with its provisions principally concerned with the standard terms of the contract, risk and remedies. The modifications are expressly indicated in the relevant section (SoGA 1979, s. 1(5) and (6)). Lastly, the common law applies where not inconsistent with either enactment.

A sale of goods contract is one by which the seller transfers or agrees to transfer the ownership or property in goods to the buyer for a money consideration called the price (SoGA 1979, s. 2(1) and 61(1); CRA 2015, s. 4(1) and 5). This covers the usual situation where goods are sold and where ownership of the goods is simultaneously transferred to the buyer. The related situation where the transfer of the property in the goods is to take place at a future date, or subject to some condition (such as payment of the price at some time in the future), is called an agreement to sell (SoGA 1979, s. 2(4)). Transactions which do not transfer property are not sales of goods (*PST Energy 7 Shipping LLC v OW Bunker Malta Ltd* [2016] UKSC 23, [2016] 2 WLR 1193).

The modifications to the common law of contract made by SoGA 1979 and CRA 2015 are wide ranging, covering most aspects of the transaction. The Acts lay down general rules governing matters such as the obligations to deliver the goods and pay for them, when property and risk passes from the seller to the buyer, quality and fitness for purpose of the goods, and remedies for breach. Many of the general rules set out in SoGA 1979 are subject to the express or implied intention of the parties, although there are restrictions on contracting out of some provisions in the Unfair Contract Terms Act 1977 for business to business sales, and part 2 of the CRA 2015 for business to consumer sales (see further **chapter 90**).

GENERAL RULES AND DEFINITIONS

Sale of goods or supply of services

89.2   In some cases it is difficult to decide whether what is being provided is goods or a service. Under CRA 2015 the distinction is of less importance where the supplier is a trader and the other party a consumer. The distinction is essentially that in a contract for the sale of goods the principal consideration provided by the seller is the transfer of ownership of the goods, whereas in a contract for the supply of services, which could include supplying goods, the principal consideration provided by the supplier is the work done in providing the service, rather than the value of any goods supplied in the course of providing the service. For example, in a building contract the main consideration provided by the builder is usually the value of the work done, rather than the value of the bricks, cement, plaster, wood, nails and other materials supplied. Such a contract is therefore one for the supply of services, but with the incidental supply of goods. It is not a contract for the sale of goods within the meaning of SoGA 1979. Where the party engaging the builder is not a consumer, the supply of services aspect of the building contract would, however, be subject to the provisions of the Supply of Goods and Services Act 1982 (SoGSA 1982), part 2, and the materials supplied under the contract would be subject to the provisions of SoGSA 1982, part 1.

In deciding whether a contract is for the sale of goods or for services, the main tests to be applied can be summarised as follows:

(a) if there is a sale of goods which are later to be fixed to chattels or land as a subsidiary obligation, the contract will be for the sale of goods;

(b) if there is an agreement to fix goods to land or to another chattel to which the sale of the goods is a subsidiary obligation, the contract will be for supply of services;

(c) if the principal obligation is the supply of goods with any work to them being incidental, then the contract will be for sale of goods; and

(d) if the customer supplies materials which are to be worked on (with or without other materials) by the supplier, the contract will be for the supply of services.

Even in business to business contracts the distinction is no longer as important as it once was, as the statutory implied terms about the quality of goods are very similar to those for the quality of services. There are some differences. For example, the property in goods sold under SoGA 1979 generally passes, in the absence of a term dealing with the matter, in accordance with the rules in SoGA 1979, s. 18 (see **89.12**). Property often passes in accordance with these rules when the contract for the sale of goods is made. Different considerations apply in contracts for the supply of goods and services, and property in goods supplied may not pass until they are fixed (such as to the land of the customer: *Tripp v Armitage* (1839) 4 M & W 687; *Wincanton Group Ltd v Garbe Logistics UK 1 Sàrl* [2011] EWHC 905 (Ch), LTL 19/4/2011) or even until the completion of the work of installation (*Seath v Moore* (1886) 1 App Cas 350). Another example is the effect of the buyer defaulting at some time after having paid a sum on account. In a contract for the sale of goods, such a sum will usually be recoverable by the defaulting buyer, subject to a set-off by the seller for damages for the buyer's default. In a contract for the supply of goods and services, such an advance may not be recoverable at all by the defaulting buyer (*Hyundai Heavy Industries Co. Ltd v Papadopolos* [1980] 1 WLR 1129).

Under CRA 2015 the distinction is now of little or no relevance with contracts for work and materials falling within the definition of contracts for a transfer of goods (CRA 2015, s. 8) and special provision being made, where installation falls within the scope of the contract, that goods do not conform until they are installed correctly (s. 15). Contracts to supply services to consumers are governed by CRA 2015, part 1, chapter 4.

Sales distinguished from other contracts

The concept of 'bailment' covers a number of situations. It includes situations where the owner of goods (the 'bailor') delivers them to another who looks after them for the bailor; where the bailor loans goods to the bailee, either gratuitously or for hire; where the bailor pledges goods by delivering them to another as security for money borrowed by the bailor; where the bailor delivers goods to a carrier for the purpose of having the goods transported somewhere; and where the bailor delivers goods to a tradesman for something to be done to the goods (often repairs or improvements). Bailments are obviously not sales of goods. Even bailments with an option to purchase (such as hire purchase agreements) are not sales of goods (*Helby v Matthews* [1895] AC 471). The hirer under such an agreement has not 'bought or agreed to buy' the goods within the meaning of SoGA 1979, s. 25(1). Where the hirer under either a contract of hire or hire-purchase is a consumer, CRA 2015, part 1, chapter 2, applies to the contract as one to supply goods (s. 3(2)(b) and (c), (4) and (7)). For other contracts the Supply of Goods (Implied Terms) Act 1973 provides implied terms analogous to those in SoGA 1979.

89.3

If the contract is intended to operate by way of mortgage, charge, pledge or other security it is not a sale of goods (SoGA 1979, s. 62(4)) or a contract to supply goods (CRA 2015, s. 3(3)(c)). A pledge can exist at common law and under the Consumer Credit Act 1974, and is an actual or constructive delivery and bailment of the goods by the debtor to the creditor to be kept until the debt has been discharged. Property in the goods does not pass, but the pledgee has a right to sell the goods.

A common form of transaction is a 'sale and lease back' where the owner sells the goods to a finance company and then leases those same goods back. A genuine transaction will be upheld as a sale of the goods rather than a charge over them, the test being the true intention of the parties rather than the legal form (*North Central Wagon Finance Co. v Brailsford* [1962] 1 WLR 1288).

Definition of 'goods'

The definition of 'goods' appears both in SoGA 1979, s. 61(1), where it includes all personal chattels other than things in action and money, and CRA 2015, s. 2(8), where it embraces tangible movable items, including water, gas and electricity if they are put up for supply in a

89.4

Commentary

limited volume or set quantity. Things in action are rights to procure the payment of money through court proceedings, such as debts and rights under insurance policies. The main definition means that although computer disks, being physical objects, are 'goods', a software programme is not (*St Albans City and District Council v International Computers Ltd* [1996] 4 All ER 481). This was considered in *Southwark London Borough Council v IBM UK Ltd* [2011] EWHC 549 (TCC), 135 Con LR 136, where Akenhead J at [96], [97], said it depends on what is being sold. If it is software under licence, there are no goods. Conversely, if it is a compact disc on which software is impressed that is sold, the sale is of goods. This line of authority is becoming less relevant as software is now invariably intangible, and not subject to SoGA 1979 or the common law rules based on the concept of possession (*Your Response Ltd v Datastream Business Media Ltd* [2014] EWCA Civ 281, [2015] QB 41). The issue is of no relevance where digital content is supplied to a consumer, either under a contract or gratuitously, because CRA 2015 sets out the rights and obligation in part 1, chapter 3.

Goods may be classified as existing goods or future goods (SoGA 1979, s. 5(1)). 'Existing goods' are those already owned or possessed by the seller. 'Future goods' are goods to be manufactured or acquired by the seller after making the contract.

SoGA 1979 also divides goods into specific goods and unascertained goods. This is principally relevant to the passing of property. 'Specific goods' are defined as goods identified and agreed on at the time a contract of sale is made and includes an undivided share of goods identified and agreed on (SoGA 1979, s. 61(1)). Most everyday consumer sales involve specific existing goods as the buyer selects the product on display which he or she wishes to buy. The definition of specific goods is wide enough to also include identified goods not owned by the seller at the time of the contract but which the seller intends to acquire in order to transfer them to the buyer, and even to a contract for the sale of potatoes to be grown in a particular field (*Howell v Coupland* (1876) 1 QBD 258). The term 'unascertained goods' is not defined, but means all goods which are not specific goods, that is, not identified and agreed on as the contract goods at the point of formation. Most commercial sales of goods by description will be for unascertained goods.

Money consideration

89.5 There must be a money consideration for a contract for the sale of goods. A gift is not provided for money consideration. Promotional gifts are unlikely to give rise to a sale of goods as the consideration is usually the purchase of other goods and not money (*Esso Petroleum Co. Ltd v Customs and Excise Commissioners* [1976] 1 WLR 1). A simple exchange of goods or barter is not a sale of goods. A common difficulty exists when goods (usually motor vehicles) are part exchanged. The court has to decide whether there is an exchange of goods (with or without some balancing payment) or whether there are there two separate, back-to-back, sale of goods transactions with only any credit balance being paid in money. The test is: what is the contractual intention? Each case will turn on its own facts: compare *G. J. Dawson (Clapham) Ltd v H. and G. Dutfield* [1936] 2 All ER 232 and *Forthright Finance Ltd v Ingate* [1997] 4 All ER 99.

Formation of the contract

89.6 There must be a binding consensual contract between the buyer and the seller. That is determined applying the usual rules of contract law. There are few rules on formation in the Act save for auction sales (SoGA 1979, s. 57), so the question is one for general contractual rules. Since the abolition in 1954 of the requirement for writing in contracts for the sale of goods over £10, there have been no formalities for a sale of goods contract (see now SoGA 1979, s. 4). Capacity to enter into the contract is governed by the general law. A reasonable price must be paid for necessaries sold and delivered to children, or to persons who are incompetent by reason of mental incapacity or drunkenness (s. 3(2)).

Between parties of full capacity, there will be no contract unless the essential terms are agreed (*May and Butcher v R* [1934] 2 KB 17n). This does not preclude there being a valid and binding contract for the sale of goods where no price is agreed for the goods. The price may be fixed in a manner agreed between the parties or may be determined by a course of dealing between the parties (SoGA 1979, s. 8(1)). Alternatively, the price may be left unstated and not capable of being determined in accordance with s. 8(1), in which event a reasonable price is payable (s. 8(2)). Finally, s. 9 provides for the unusual cases where the price for the goods is to be fixed by a third party identified in the contract. If the third party does not make the valuation, the contract is avoided, but if any of the goods have been delivered the buyer must pay a reasonable price for them.

MAIN OBLIGATIONS IN A CONTRACT FOR THE SALE OF GOODS

Under a contract for the sale of goods, the seller agrees to transfer ownership in goods to the buyer, and the buyer agrees to accept them and pay the agreed price. The buyer will want to be able to make use of the goods (either personally or by way of resale), and an important question is that of the contractual responsibility for delivering the goods. A related question is the determination of when risk passes to the buyer, which is important if the goods are lost in transit or otherwise before they are received by the buyer. These various matters are discussed at **89.8** to **89.15**.   **89.7**

Delivery in non-consumer sales

It is necessary to distinguish consumer sales from other sales. Under SoGA 1979 the seller's primary obligation is to deliver the goods to the buyer, and the buyer's to accept and pay for them in accordance with the terms of the contract (SoGA 1979, s. 27). The contract may define (expressly or by implication) the place where the goods should be delivered. This may be the seller's place of business, or those of the buyer, or some other place (such as a construction site where the goods are to be used, or the place of business of a carrier or a ship to be used to transport the goods to the buyer). In the absence of agreement the default rule is that the place of delivery is the seller's place of business if he has one (s. 29(1) and (2)). That is, the default rule in business to business sales is 'ex works' or 'ex warehouse', and most commercial items are sold and priced on that basis. SoGA 1979, s. 61(1), defines 'delivery' as the voluntary transfer of possession from one person to another. Often this is done by the seller handing the goods to the buyer, or the buyer selecting them from the stock of the seller, and paying for them. There are more difficult situations. 'Possession', which is a key concept in the definition of delivery, is not defined in SoGA 1979, and is notoriously difficult to define. A seller may transfer possession, for example, by giving the buyer the means of access to goods, such as by handing over the keys to the warehouse where they are stored (*Hilton v Tucker* (1888) 39 ChD 669). There are four further common situations that should be noted: **89.8**

(a) Where the goods are in the possession of a third person (such as a warehouseman), delivery takes place when that third person acknowledges to the buyer that the goods are held on behalf of the buyer (SoGA 1979, s. 29(4)). This is known as 'attornment'.

(b) A seller can deliver goods for the purposes of a contract for the sale of goods by delivering to the buyer a document of title to the goods. Delivery takes place on delivery of a document of title even if the goods are in the possession of a third person and even if the third person has not attorned to the buyer. This method of delivery is very common in international sales. Documents of title are defined in the Factors Act 1889, s. 1(4), as being any bill of lading, dock warrant, warehouse keeper's certificate, a warrant or order for the delivery of goods, and any other document used in the ordinary course of business as proof of possession or control of goods. Delivery orders, warehouse keepers' receipts and warrants for goods are not, or not always, regarded as documents of title.

(c) Delivery of goods to a carrier for transmission to the buyer is prima facie deemed to be delivery to the buyer (SoGA 1979, s. 32(1)).

(d) In a sale and lease-back transaction, the seller makes constructive delivery of the goods to the buyer, which then leases the goods back to the seller, even though the goods never leave the seller's possession (*Michael Gerson (Leasing) Ltd v Wilkinson* [2001] QB 514).

The definition of 'delivery' was extended as from 18 September 1995 by amendments made by the Sale of Goods (Amendment) Act 1995, s. 2, so that delivery, in relation to sales from a bulk under SoGA 1979, ss. 20A and 20B, includes such appropriation of goods to the contract as results in property in the goods being transferred to the buyer. Sections 20A and 20B are considered at **89.13**.

Delivery is to be distinguished from the passing of property in the goods, as property can pass before delivery, at the time of delivery or after delivery. The obligation to deliver the goods may be separate from the obligation to pay for them, but in the absence of agreement they are concurrent conditions (SoGA 1979, s. 28). SoGA 1979, s. 29, sets out the rules for delivery; SoGA 1979, s. 30, and CRA 2015, s. 26, deal with deliveries of the wrong quantity; SoGA 1979, s. 31, and CRA 2015, s. 26, deal with instalments; and SoGA 1979, s. 33, deals with deliveries to the buyer at a distant place.

Delivery in consumer sales

89.9   Where the sale of goods is to a consumer, and unless otherwise agreed, the contract is treated as including a term that the trader must deliver the goods to the consumer (CRA 2015, s. 28(2)). Unless the time or period is agreed, the contract is treated as including a term that the trader must deliver the goods without undue delay and in any event within 30 days (s. 28(3)). Further detailed provision is made with the consumer entitled to treat the contract at an end where the trader is in default (s. 28(6), (8)). These rules cannot be contracted out of (s. 31(1)(j)).

Payment

89.10   The obligation upon the buyer is to make payment in accordance with the terms of the contract between the parties (SoGA 1979, s. 27). The price will usually be fixed by the contract, but may be ascertained in a manner agreed by the contract or by a course of dealing between the parties (s. 8(1)). Otherwise the buyer must pay a reasonable price, which is a question of fact depending on all the circumstances of the particular case (s. 8(2) and (3)). Section 28 of SoGA 1979 provides that unless otherwise agreed, delivery of the goods and payment of the price are concurrent conditions, and the seller must be ready and willing to give possession of the goods to the buyer in exchange for the price and the buyer must be ready and willing to pay the price in exchange for possession of the goods. The default rule is that the time of payment is not of the essence of the contract, so unless it appears that a different intention appears (by use of the language of 'condition' or expressly making time of payment 'of the essence') the seller is not entitled to terminate the contract merely by reason of late payment (SoGA 1979, s. 10(1)).

Place and method of payment

89.11   The place of payment may be specified in the contract in which case the payment must be made at that place. Where there is no express provision in the terms of the contract, the intention of the parties may be determined from the surrounding circumstances, or from the method of payment provided for. If the intention of the parties cannot be ascertained then, by

SoGA 1979, ss. 28 and 29(2), the obligation seems to be to make payment at the seller's place of business or residence.

In default of agreement between the parties, the manner of payment is cash. Payment by post will be at the seller's risk of loss or delay only if payment by that method is expressly or impliedly authorised by the contract. The defence of tender before claim, which is available to the buyer in an action by the seller for the price, depends upon tender having taken place in cash unless the contract otherwise provides or unless the seller has waived the right to demand cash payment. Tender before claim is a CPR glossary term, and now applies to claims for specified amounts and unspecified amounts. The defence of tender before claim must be included in the statement of case (usually the defence), and the defence is only available if the money is paid into court (**CPR, r. 37.3**).

Passing of property

When goods are sold, three things pass to the buyer: ownership or property, possession, and risk. **89.12** Although they are connected, they are distinct concepts. 'Property' or 'ownership' is used in the sense of title, or the general property in the goods, as opposed to a special property, such as the interest of a pledgee (SoGA 1979, s. 61(1), and CRA 2015, s. 4(1)). Consumer sales follow the same rules as other sales (CRA 2015, s. 4(2)). The over-arching rule is that property passes when it is intended to pass (SoGA 1979, s. 17(1)). Property cannot pass until goods are ascertained as the contract goods. In the very nature of things property cannot pass in wholly unascertained goods (SoGA 1979, s. 16; *Re London Wine Co. (Shippers) Ltd* 1986 PCC 121; *Re Goldcorp Exchange Ltd* [1995] 1 AC 74). This is now modified in relation to an undivided share in an identified bulk (SoGA 1979, ss. 20A and 20B, considered at **89.13**). Property may be transferred before delivery, at delivery or after delivery (e.g. on payment). In ascertaining intention, regard may be had to the terms of the contract, the conduct of the parties and the circumstances of the case (s. 17(2)). If the intention of the parties cannot be ascertained then s. 18 contains a number of general default rules to be applied to determine when property is to pass.

The rules in SoGA 1979, s. 18, are as follows (r. 5 is subdivided into four sub-rules, set out at (e) to (h), with the order of sub-rules (1) and (2) reversed for ease of exposition):

(a) Where there is an unconditional contract for the sale of specific goods in a deliverable state, the property in the goods passes to the buyer when the contract is made, and it is immaterial whether the time of payment or the time of delivery or both be postponed (SoGA 1979, s. 18, r. 1). An 'unconditional' contract is not defined in SoGA 1979, but means that there are no later conditions which must be fulfilled (e.g. payment of the price) before property passes. Goods will be in a 'deliverable state' if they are in such a condition that the buyer would under the contract be bound to take delivery of them (s. 61(5)). The rule of simultaneous contract and conveyance has not proved convenient or appropriate for either business or consumer sales. Accordingly the courts are very ready to infer that property only passes upon payment or delivery on very little evidence (*R. V. Ward Ltd v Bignall* [1967] 1 QB 534; *Kulkarni v Manor Credit (Davenham) Ltd* [2010] EWCA Civ 69, [2010] 2 All ER (Comm) 1017).

(b) Where there is a contract for the sale of specific goods and the seller is bound to do something to the goods for the purpose of putting them into a deliverable state, the property does not pass until the thing is done and the buyer has had notice that it has been done (s. 18, r. 2). The key event is that the seller has given notice that the goods are now in a deliverable state.

(c) Where there is a contract for the sale of specific goods in a deliverable state, but the seller is bound to weigh, measure, test, or do some other act or thing with reference to the goods for the purpose of ascertaining the price, the property does not pass until the act or thing is done and the buyer has had notice that it has been done (s. 18, r. 3). The obligation to weigh, measure, test or do some other act must be on the seller, and the act must be for the purpose of ascertaining the price of goods already in the deliverable state. As with r. 2, the key event is that notice must be given to the buyer that the step has been taken.

(d) When goods are delivered to the buyer on approval or on sale or return or other similar terms, the property in the goods passes to the buyer:
 (i) when the buyer signifies approval or acceptance to the seller or does any other act adopting the transaction;
 (ii) if the buyer does not signify approval or acceptance to the seller but retains the goods without giving notice of rejection, then, if a time has been fixed for the return of the goods, on the expiration of that time, and, if no time has been fixed, on the expiration of a reasonable time (s. 18, r. 4). Sales on approval and transactions involving sale or return are common, and this rule will govern the passing of title if the parties have not reached some other agreement.
(e) Where, in pursuance of the contract, the seller delivers the goods to the buyer or to a carrier or other bailee (whether named by the buyer or not) for the purpose of transmission to the buyer, and does not reserve the right of disposal, the seller is to be taken to have unconditionally appropriated the goods to the contract for the purposes of s. 18, r. 5(1), so that property passes at that time (s. 18, r. 5(2)). So unless there is a retention of title clause, property will generally pass on delivery to the buyer, or prior to that, upon delivery by the seller to the first carrier for transmission to the buyer.
(f) Where there is a contract for the sale of unascertained or future goods by description, and goods of that description and in a deliverable state are unconditionally appropriated to the contract, either by the seller with the assent of the buyer or by the buyer with the assent of the seller, the property in the goods passes to the buyer; and the assent may be express or implied, and may be given either before or after the appropriation is made (s. 18, r. 5(1)). While expressed to be the principal rule for passing of property in unascertained goods, in practice this sub-rule is only engaged where it is alleged that property has passed prior to delivery to the buyer, or a carrier or bailee for the purpose of transmission to the buyer. It is a difficult rule to satisfy (*Carlos Federspiel and Co. SA v Charles Twigg and Co. Ltd* [1957] 1 Lloyd's Rep 240).
(g) Where there is a contract for the sale of a specified quantity of unascertained goods in a deliverable state forming part of a bulk which is identified either in the contract or by subsequent agreement between the parties, and the bulk is reduced to (or to less than) that quantity, then, if the buyer under that contract is the only buyer to whom the goods are then due out of the bulk:
 (i) the remaining goods are to be taken as appropriated to that contract at the time when the bulk is so reduced; and
 (ii) the property in those goods then passes to the buyer (s. 18, r. 5(3)).
(h) Rule 5(3) also applies where the bulk is reduced to (or to less than) the aggregate of the quantities due to a single buyer under separate contracts relating to that bulk and that buyer is the only buyer to whom goods are then due out of that bulk (s. 18, r. 5(4); *Karlshamns Olje Fabriker v Eastport Navigation Corporation* [1982] 1 All ER 208).

Rules 5(1) to 5(4) deal with the unconditional appropriation of deliverable goods to the contract by express or implied agreement. 'Appropriation' is not defined in SoGA 1979, but means an intention to attach the contract irrevocably to those goods so that those goods and no others are the subject of the sale and become the property of the buyer. Sales of goods forming part of a bulk are now governed by ss. 20A and 20B (**89.13**).

Sales of goods held in bulk

89.13   A contract may provide for the sale of (say) 100 tonnes of wheat from a cargo of 2,000 tonnes presently on board a named ship. This would be a sale of a specified quantity of unascertained goods forming part of a bulk which is identified in the agreement between the parties. Once the buyer pays the price for some or all of the 100 tonnes subject to the contract, SoGA 1979, s. 20A, applies (see s. 20A(1)). If the section applies, by s. 20A(2):
(a) property in an undivided share in the bulk is transferred to the buyer; and
(b) the buyer becomes an owner in common of the bulk.

The rest of s. 20A deals with calculating the size of the undivided share of the buyer, particularly where the bulk is insufficient for all the purchasers, and with the situation where a buyer has paid only part of the price. When s. 20A applies, the buyer is deemed to consent to other purchasers taking delivery of their shares out of the bulk, and the section does not impose an obligation on a buyer from the bulk to compensate any other buyer for any shortfall in the goods delivered (s. 20B).

Passing of possession

The concept of possession, and some of the situations encountered in sale contracts, were considered at **89.8**. Normally, possession passes on physically handing over the goods to the buyer. **89.14**

Passing of risk in non-consumer sales

Risk is important in cases where goods are damaged or lost and in deciding who has an insurable interest in goods. It is not defined in SoGA 1979 but means the risk of loss of, or damage to, the goods which is not attributable to a breach of duty by either seller or buyer, whether a breach of contractual duty or a breach of duty as a bailee (SoGA 1979, s. 20(3)). So risk operates where loss or damage is attributable to third parties to the sale contract (such as carriers or warehouse-keepers) or to natural events. In non-consumer sales, unless otherwise agreed, risk is presumed to pass with property (SoGA 1979, s. 20(1)). Risk may be transferred to the buyer before delivery if, for example, property passes before delivery. More commonly commercial sellers will wish to pass risk as soon as possible, and to delay the passing of property for as long as possible, or at least until they are paid or have an adequate assurance of payment. **89.15**

Risk in transit is primarily governed by the contract between the parties. In international sales this is usually provided for expressly, or by reference to well-known forms of international sale agreement — such as under 'CIF' contracts ('cost, insurance, freight'), where risk passes on shipment or as from shipment (*Comptoir d'Achat et de Vente du Boerenbond Belge SA v Luis de Ridder Ltda* [1949] AC 293), and 'FOB' sales ('free on board'), where risk passes on shipment (*Pyrene Co. Ltd v Scindia Navigation Ltd* [1954] 2 QB 402).

Some aspects of risk in transit are dealt with by ss. 32 and 33. If the seller fails to make a reasonable contract with a carrier having regard to the nature of the goods and the other circumstances of the case, the buyer may decline to treat delivery to the carrier as a delivery to the buyer (s. 32(2)). The result would be that goods damaged in transit would be treated as not delivered to the buyer, so the seller would retain ownership of the goods (presumably lost or damaged), and would be liable to the buyer for non-delivery. Unless otherwise agreed, where goods are sent by the seller by sea transport in circumstances where it is usual to insure, the seller must give the buyer sufficient notice to enable the buyer to insure the goods during transit. If the seller fails to give such notice, the goods remain at the risk of the seller during the transit by sea (s. 32(3)).

Passing of risk in consumer sales

In relation to consumer contracts the goods remain at the trader's risk until they come into the physical possession of the consumer or a person identified by the consumer to take physical possession (SoGA 1979, s. 20(4); CRA 2015, s. 29(1) and (2)). Where a carrier is used in a consumer contract, delivery to the carrier is not delivery to the consumer unless the carrier is commissioned by the consumer and is not a carrier the trader named as an option (CRA 2015, s. 29(3) and (4)). These rules cannot be contracted out of (s. 31(1)(k)). **89.16**

TERMS OF THE CONTRACT

As discussed at **89.6**, there are no legal formalities required for a contract for the sale of goods. A great many contracts for the sale of goods are simply entered into orally, or even without any **89.17** words being exchanged, such as where uncommunicative customers present goods for payment at a cash till, and the sales assistant simply processes the transaction without saying anything. Usually such a contract will be evidenced by writing in the form of the sales receipt produced by the cash till and handed to the customer. In such contracts the main obligations will take place there and then, with the goods having been selected by the customer, and with delivery, acceptance and payment all taking place on the spot. Where the customer pays in cash, the transaction will be a simple sale of goods governed by SoGA 1979 and CRA 2015. Beyond the main obligations just mentioned, the relevant Acts will also incorporate such of the statutory terms discussed at **89.28** to **89.35** as are appropriate into the contract. If the transaction is paid for by credit card and the customer is an individual, the shop in fact looks to the credit card company for payment and the transaction has Consumer Credit Act 1974 ramifications. Where the customer pays by cheque, the contract will be a simple sale of goods, but with a secondary contract based on the cheque. If the cheque is dishonoured, the shop can take advantage of the simple method of obtaining summary judgment on the cheque discussed at **34.40**.

Although it is possible for detailed contractual terms to be agreed orally, it is far more common for people agreeing oral terms to restrict themselves to matters such as the description of the goods, price, and time and place for delivery. There are plenty of other issues that could be included as terms in a contract of sale. These include insurance of the goods until they are delivered; which party bears the loss if the goods are stolen, damaged or destroyed before delivery; the consequences of minor or major defects in the goods; the arrangements for effecting repairs to rectify defects present when the goods are delivered, including where the repairs should take place; liabilities to third parties arising out of the performance of the contract; limitations in the liability of the parties for consequential losses (particularly loss of profits) in the event of breach and other exclusions of liability; the effect of events outside the control of either party; and choice of law and jurisdiction in the event of litigation. These (and other detailed terms) can often be found in contractual documents. Occasionally, detailed terms will be negotiated between the parties, and reduced to writing in a contract specifically drawn up for the purpose. Far more commonly, detailed terms are found in the small print on the reverse of order forms, confirmation of order forms, invoices, delivery documents and other documents used by the parties. Sometimes such standard terms are simply referred to, such as the quotation form which says it is made on 'our standard terms of trading which are available on request'.

The law relating to the incorporation of express terms into contracts is discussed at **89.18** to **89.20**. The consequences of the classification of different types of terms are discussed at **89.21** to **89.27**. The statutory terms in sale of goods contracts are discussed at **89.28** to **89.35**. Breach of the main provisions in sale of goods contracts is discussed at **89.36** to **89.43**.

Incorporation of terms: signed contracts

89.18   If the contract is in writing and has been signed by a party, that party will be bound by those written terms even if he or she has not read them (*L'Estrange v F. Graucob Ltd* [1934] 2 KB 394), or was unable to understand them (*The Luna* [1920] P 22). This clear rule is qualified by the following requirements and exceptions:

(a) The party signing must be aware that the document being signed contains or refers to some written terms.

(b) The terms referred to must actually be present or available so that, for example, where documents sent by facsimile refer to terms stated on the back which are not stated or otherwise communicated that gives rise to a cogent inference that the terms were not intended to apply (*Poseidon Freight Forwarding Co. Ltd v Davies Turner Southern Ltd* [1996] CLC 1264).

(c) The party signing must be given reasonably sufficient notice of the exact terms relied upon by the other side — a concept which the courts apply particularly to unusual or onerous terms (see **89.20**).

(d) Where a complete contract already existed rather than mere negotiations between the parties, subsequent signing of a document including new terms will not bind either party unless there is a variation (for which consideration will be required) or a novation.

(e) Terms cannot be relied upon where the contract is void or unenforceable as a result of a mistake.

(f) An exception exists under the doctrine of *non est factum*, which is a rare and special category of mistake which applies only where a party to the contract has been misled into signing a contract without being negligent (*Saunders v Anglia Building Society* [1971] AC 1004).

(g) Terms cannot be relied on where there has been a misrepresentation of the terms or effect of a clause (*Curtis v Chemical Cleaning and Dyeing Co. Ltd* [1951] 1 KB 805).

(h) Terms cannot be relied on where the contract is voidable as a result of duress (*Atlas Express Ltd v Kafco (Importers and Distributors) Ltd* [1989] QB 833). However, not every form of pressure will amount to duress (*CTN Cash and Carry Ltd v Gallagher Ltd* [1994] 4 All ER 714 and *Alf Vaughan and Co. Ltd v Royscot Trust plc* [1999] 1 All ER (Comm) 856).

The fact that a signed written contract exists will not normally prevent there being other express terms of that contract which have not been put into the signed document, provided they are not inconsistent with the written terms. However, many written contracts contain an 'entire agreement' clause which seeks to exclude the existence of other terms. Such clauses are not always wholly effective and their meaning is a question of contractual construction. If the 'entire agreement' clause excludes misrepresentations or implied terms then it will be subject to the statutory rules limiting the effectiveness of such clauses. See *AXA Sun Life Services plc v Campbell Martin Ltd* [2011] EWCA Civ 133, [2012] Bus LR 203.

Standard terms of trading

In commercial transactions there is often a dispute as to which set of standard terms applies to the contract. This is usually resolved by examining the events chronologically looking for the offer or counter-offer which has actually been accepted (often by performing the contract) which means that the party firing the last shot in the negotiations will usually succeed in showing that the last terms are the basis for the contract (*British Road Services Ltd v Arthur V. Crutchley and Co. Ltd* [1968] 1 WLR 811). However, sometimes the last shot is construed as an acceptance of the previous terms sent by the other side, with the effect that the other side's standard terms apply to the contract (*Butler Machine Tool Co. Ltd v Ex-Cell-O Corporation (England) Ltd* [1979] 1 WLR 401). It is also noteworthy that a clause purporting to provide that those standard terms shall prevail over the terms of the other party, is ineffective if the other side then respond by sending their standard terms in the usual situation where this is regarded as the making of a counter-offer (*Butler Machine Tool Co. Ltd v Ex-Cell-O Corporation (England) Ltd*). **89.19**

Incorporation of terms: onerous or unusual terms

If a contract contains some particularly onerous or unusual terms the court will look with great care to see whether the onerous term has been incorporated into the contract at all. This approach is at variance with the general approach that a party is bound by the terms which that party is aware are in a written agreement, despite not reading them (see **89.18**). This exception is limited to unusual or onerous terms. The most striking description of this rule is to be found in the judgment of Denning LJ in *J. Spurling Ltd v Bradshaw* [1956] 1 WLR 461 at p. 466, where he said, 'Some clauses I have seen would need to be printed in red ink on the face of the document with a red hand pointing to it before the notice could be held to be sufficient'. The importance of this rule has been slightly reduced by the statutory control of exemption clauses. Nevertheless it remains an important way of challenging onerous or unusual express terms of a written contract. It is still being applied today with important consequences for the parties: see, for example, the decisions of the Court of Appeal in *Interfoto Picture Library Ltd v Stiletto Visual Programmes Ltd* [1989] QB 433 and *AEG (UK) Ltd v Logic Resource Ltd* [1996] CLC 265. **89.20**

Commentary

Classification of terms

89.21   Contract terms are usually divided into conditions or warranties. Breach of a condition discharges the innocent party from further performance of the contract and damages may be claimed for loss caused by the breach. Breach of a warranty gives the innocent party only a right to claim damages (SoGA 1979, s. 11(3)), the measure of damages being defined in SoGA 1979, s. 53.

A term is a condition if it is expressly made such by statute. What is less clear is the effect of a label given to the obligation in the contract itself. It seems that a term need not be a condition merely because it is so described in the contract (*Wickman Machine Tool Sales Ltd v L. Schuler AG* [1974] AC 235, although contrast *Lombard North Central plc v Butterworth* [1987] QB 527, where the clause provided that terms in the contract had 'the property that any breach of them is treated as going to the root of the contract'). Whether a term is a condition (breach of which may give rise to a right to treat the contract as repudiated), or a warranty (breach of which may give rise to a claim for damages but not to a right to reject the goods and treat the contract as repudiated) depends in each case on the construction of the contract and a clause may be a condition, even though called a warranty in the contract (SoGA 1979, s. 11(3)).

There is also a further category of terms known as intermediate terms, where the nature and seriousness of the breach will determine whether the innocent party is discharged from further performance or merely entitled to damages.

Construing written contracts

89.22   The object of the rules of construction of written terms is always to discover the intention of the parties from the words used in the contract, in the light of the surrounding circumstances.

The function of the court is to decide the objective intention of the parties. The question is not what the parties understood the words or document to mean but the meaning which the document would convey to a reasonable person having all the background knowledge which would reasonably have been available to the parties in the situation in which they were at the time of the contract (*Investors Compensation Scheme Ltd v West Bromwich Building Society* [1998] 1 WLR 896).

A common problem is the poorly drafted written contract. There are no special rules of construction, but in applying the rules set out above, in *Antaios Compania Naviera SA v Salen Rederierna AB* [1984] AC 676, Lord Diplock said: 'if a detailed semantic syntactical analysis of words in a commercial contract is going to lead to a conclusion that flouts business common sense, it must yield to business common sense'. This is an important reflection of the purpose of all rules of construction, namely to ascertain the intention of the parties. It has been said that if there are two tenable interpretations of a clause in a commercial contract the one more consistent with business common sense should be preferred (*Rainy Sky SA v Kookmin Bank* [2011] UKSC 50, [2011] 1 WLR 2900). However, it has been stressed that the principal obligation of the court is loyalty to the contractual language (*Arnold v Britton* [2015] UKSC 36, [2015] AC 1619).

The principles of construction also embrace a number of subsidiary rules:

(a) the conventional meaning should be given to the words used unless:

   (i) there is some well-known trade custom or trade practice which means that a special meaning is to be given to words (probably the best known example being a 'baker's dozen' meaning 13), or

   (ii) there is some custom or usage which means words have a particular meaning in that locality or trade, or

(iii) the words are technical words, in which case the normal accepted technical meaning should be applied;

(b) words should be construed so as to avoid absurd or inconsistent provisions as the parties cannot have intended that the contract should be absurd or inconsistent;

(c) the whole contract will be considered so that individual words or phrases are considered in their context, and any recitals may be used as a guide to the interpretation of the operative parts of a contract;

(d) in written contracts, as in statutes, general words which follow several specific words are to be construed in a similar manner — the *eiusdem generis* rule; and

(e) a written contract is construed more strongly against its grantor or maker — the *contra proferentem* rule. This only arises where there remains an ambiguity which has not been resolved by the application of the earlier rules.

Evidence of earlier drafts of the contract or negotiations cannot be admitted (save where the court is being asked to rectify the text of the agreement). However, this will not prevent evidence being admitted of the customary meaning of words in a particular trade or of a special technical meaning of words (see **49.32**).

Exemption and indemnity clauses

Special rules of construction apply to exemption clauses which seek to exempt one party from the consequences of some breach of contract and to indemnity clauses which require the innocent party to indemnify the party in breach against claims from third parties. The burden of proof is upon the party claiming that some liability is excluded to show that the particular liability falls within the ambit of the particular clause. The party making this claim should therefore set it out in the statement of case (**CPR, r. 16.5(2)(b)**). When ascertaining the intention of the parties: **89.23**

(a) an exemption clause must be clear so that a clause which effectively absolves one party from any performance at all may be held to be meaningless as it could not have been the intention of the parties that there were no mutual obligations (*Tor Line AB v Alltrans Group of Canada Ltd* [1984] 1 WLR 48); and

(b) when considering exemption clauses excluding liability for negligence the three tests in *Canada Steamship Lines Ltd v The King* [1952] AC 192 are applied, namely:

   (i) if the clause plainly excludes such liability then (subject to statutory control) effect will be given to it;

   (ii) if the clause is unclear it will be construed contra proferentem; and

   (iii) if the clause covers liabilities other than negligence (e.g. damage by lightning) then it will be held not to cover negligence.

Force majeure clauses

Force majeure clauses are intended to deal with the consequences of one or other of the parties being unable to perform the contract through the intervention of government action or other circumstances outside the party's control. There is no general concept of *force majeure* in English law. Sale of goods contracts often contain express *force majeure* clauses which limit the seller's liability in circumstances anticipated by the clause with or without provision for notice to be given to the buyer. The true effect of a *force majeure* clause is to limit the seller's obligation to perform and it is not therefore an exemption clause which excludes liability for breach of contract as no breach will have occurred. An important consequence is that such terms may not be required to satisfy the test of reasonableness under the Unfair Contract Terms Act 1977. The burden of proving that the clause applies is upon the party seeking to rely upon it, usually the seller. A party making this claim should therefore set it out in its statement of case (**CPR, rr. 16.4 and 16.5**).   **89.24**

Liquidated damages and penalty clauses

89.25   A sum of money which is payable, under a provision of a contract by a party who is in default of contractual obligations in some stated way or ways, may be either an agreed or liquidated damages clause or a penalty. Incentives for early performance or payment will not be classified as a penalty. Thus a clause, properly incorporated into the contract, which provides for a 10 per cent discount on the agreed price if it is paid within 28 days will be upheld. Even an acceleration clause, saying that the whole of a sum outstanding shall become due and payable forthwith on default of any payment, is not a penalty (*Wallingford v Mutual Society* (1880) 5 App Cas 685).

A common problem is 'default interest' payable under a contract. Default interest in regulated agreements is controlled by the Consumer Credit Act 1974, s. 93. Default interest is also controlled at common law as a possible penalty. In *Patel v Zubowski* [1996] GCCR 2173 interest of 80 per cent which was payable if money owed to a solicitors' firm was not paid on the due date was held to be a penalty and wholly irrecoverable. A provision for 'default interest' in a consumer contract will not necessarily be an unfair contract term, particularly if it is expressed fully, clearly and legibly, and contains no concealed pitfalls or traps (*Director General of Fair Trading v First National Bank plc* [2001] UKHL 52, [2002] 1 AC 481).

A clause which provides for the payment of a sum of money on the happening of a certain event which is not itself a breach of contract by either party will not be a liquidated damages or penalty clause (*Export Credits Guarantee Department v Universal Oil Products Co.* [1983] 1 WLR 399).

There are no special rules of construction for liquidated damages or penalty clauses in contracts, and thus the onerous clauses rule and the *contra proferentem* rule are often of practical importance. If the sum stipulated in the contract is a penalty, the clause will not be enforced. The label given by the parties to the clause is a guide, but is not determinative, of whether it is a penalty or a liquidated damages clause (*Dunlop Pneumatic Tyre Co. Ltd v New Garage and Motor Co. Ltd* [1915] AC 79).

The common law penalty rule has been restated by the Supreme Court. A provision is penal if it was a secondary obligation (arising upon breach of a primary obligation) which imposed a detriment out of all proportion to any legitimate interest of the innocent party in the enforcement of primary obligations. The fact that a provision was not a genuine pre-estimate of loss or that it operated as a deterrent does not necessarily mean it is penal, because the legitimate interest of the innocent party might extend beyond the recovery of compensation for loss. There is a strong presumption in commercial cases that the parties were the best judges of what it was legitimate to provide for in provisions concerning the consequences of breach (*Cavendish Square Holding BV v Makdessi* [2015] UKSC 67, [2015] 3 WLR 1373).

Forfeiture clauses

89.26   Forfeiture clauses where a sum, usually the deposit, is forfeited on breach of contract by the buyer, or clauses providing for the withholding of payments or the transfer of property are now subject to the penalty rule as restated (*Cavendish Square Holding BV v Makdessi* [2015] UKSC 67, [2015] 3 WLR 1373). A majority of the Supreme Court also considered that the penalty rule and the equitable jurisdiction to relieve against forfeiture might both be engaged, as they operated at different points, with different effects.

Timing of delivery

89.27   A common issue is whether the stipulation as to time for delivery is a condition or warranty or intermediate term (see **89.21**). SoGA 1979, s. 10(2), provides that whether time is of the essence (i.e. is a condition) depends upon the terms of the contract. It is open to the parties to make time of the essence (*Bunge v Tradax Export* [1981] 1 WLR 711).

STANDARD INCIDENTS

The statutory terms in non-consumer contracts

The traditional common law method for plugging gaps in the express provisions of the **89.28** contract is the implied term, but the traditional concern that terms should only be implied where it is necessary to do so (and not on the basis of a lower threshold of reasonableness) has recently been reaffirmed (*Marks and Spencer plc v BNP Paribas Securities Services Trust Co. (Jersey) Ltd* [2015] UKSC 72, [2016] AC 742). Implied terms arise either as a matter of fact or are implied as a matter of law. Terms may be implied in fact into a contract in at least three ways:

(a) to reflect the common intentions of the parties — the 'officious bystander' test (*Shirlaw v Southern Foundries (1926) Ltd* [1939] 2 KB 206, affirmed [1940] AC 701);
(b) to give business efficacy to the agreement — the terms which are necessary to make the contract work (*Luxor (Eastbourne) Ltd v Cooper* [1941] AC 108); and
(c) because that is what the contract, read as a whole against the background, would have been reasonably understood to mean (*Attorney General of Belize v Belize Telecom Ltd* [2009] UKPC 10, [2009] 1 WLR 2900; although that formulation was treated with caution by the Supreme Court in *Marks and Spencer plc v BNP Paribas Securities Services Trust Co. (Jersey) Ltd*).

Terms implied by law arise not as a result of the presumed intention of the parties, but as a result of general considerations of policy, such as the implied duty of trust and confidence in employment contracts. So too in this context, the statutory implied terms in SoGA 1979, ss. 12 to 15, see **89.30** to **89.35**.

The principal terms implied in non-consumer contracts by SoGA 1979 are:

(a) implied terms about title, etc. (s. 12);
(b) the implied term where there has been a sale by description (s. 13);
(c) implied terms about quality or fitness (s. 14); and,
(d) implied terms where there is a sale by sample (s. 15).

Those implied terms can be varied or excluded by express agreement between the parties, by course of dealings between the parties or by such usage as binds both parties to the contract (SoGA 1979, s. 55(1)). These statutory implied terms are considered further at **89.30** to **89.35**.

Liability for breach of the implied terms is strict (*Slater v Finning Ltd* [1997] AC 473 per Lord Steyn), so there is no scope for any finding of contributory negligence (*Hi-Lite Electrical Ltd v Wolseley UK Ltd* [2011] EWHC 2153 (TCC), [2011] BLR 629).

Standard terms in consumer contracts

The CRA 2015 abandons the language of implied terms and instead speaks of the contract **89.29** being treated as including particular terms, apparently for reasons of intelligibility. The reformulation of the standard incidents of consumer supply contracts (including hire, hire-purchase and work and materials) reflects in part the requirements of the EU Consumer Sales Directive, 99/44/EC (previously incorporated into SoGA 1979), and in part domestic public policy.

The main terms imposed for consumer supply contracts by CRA 2015 are:

(a) satisfactory quality (s. 9);
(b) fitness for a particular purpose (s.10);
(c) goods to be as described (s. 11);
(d) other pre-contract information (s. 12);
(e) goods to match a sample (s. 13);
(f) goods to match a model (s. 14);

1659

(g)   installation as part of conformity (s. 15);

(h)   digital content as part of conformity (s. 16); and

(i)   trader having the right to supply the goods (s. 17).

The classification of terms into conditions and warranties is irrelevant to the available remedies in CRA 2015. While *caveat emptor* is the notional starting point (s. 18), these represent a significant suite of obligations which cannot be contracted out of (s. 31). The Act is also clear about the consumer's various rights to enforce these mandatory terms (s. 19).

Title and right to supply

89.30   For non-consumer contracts SoGA 1979, s. 12(1), creates an implied condition (s. 12(5A)) on the part of the seller that in the case of a sale the seller has the right to sell the goods, and in the case of an agreement to sell the seller will have that right at the time when the property is to pass. By the Unfair Contract Terms Act 1977, s. 6(1)(a), this condition cannot be excluded or restricted by reference to any contract term. The right to sell involves two concepts. First, the buyer must be able to pass good title. Secondly, the sale must not be unlawful (e.g. an infringement of a trade mark). SoGA 1979, s. 12(2), creates two implied warranties (s. 12(5A)) on the part of the seller that:

(a)   the goods are free, and will remain free until the time when property is to pass, from any charge or encumbrance not disclosed or known to the buyer before the contract is made; and

(b)   the buyer will enjoy quiet possession of the goods except in so far as it may be disturbed by the owner or other person entitled to the benefit of any charge or encumbrance so disclosed or known.

For consumer contracts equivalent provisions are made by imposing similar standard incidents in supply contracts, using the language of the trader having the right to supply the goods (CRA 2015, s. 17; SoGA 1979, s. 12(7)). These terms cannot be contracted out of (CRA 2015, s. 31(1)(i)).

Sales by description

89.31   Where there is a non-consumer contract for sale by description there is an implied term, which is a condition (SoGA 1979, s. 13(1A)), that the goods will correspond to the description (s. 13(1)). Further, where there is a non-consumer contract for sale by sample there is an implied term, which is a condition (s. 15(3)), that the bulk will correspond to the sample (s. 15(2(a))). If the sale is by sample and description, the goods must correspond to the description as well as to the sample (s. 13(2)). A sale is not prevented from being by description merely because being exposed for sale or hire the goods are selected by the buyer (s. 13(3)). In non-consumer sales, liability under s. 13 can be restricted or excluded only in so far as the term satisfies the test of reasonableness (Unfair Contract Terms Act 1977, s. 6(1A)).

Sales by description are a common type of contract for the sale of goods. All sales of unascertained goods will be by description, as will all sales of goods which the buyer has not seen at all, and many sales by sample. This implied condition can be extremely important in practice. If the seller is not acting in the course of a business, such as in private sales of second-hand cars, the statutory terms about quality and fitness will not be implied. The only remedy for the buyer may be to rely upon a breach of this condition.

For consumer contracts equivalent provisions are made by imposing similar standard incidents in supply contracts, using the language that the goods will match the description (CRA 2015, s. 11; SoGA 1979, s. 13(5)). It is further provided that any information provided by the trader about the goods which is information mentioned in the Consumer Contracts (Information, Cancellation and Additional Charges) Regulations 2013 (SI 2013/3134), sch. 1, para. (a), or sch. 2, para. (a), is to be treated as included as a term of the contract. These provide for mandatory information to be provided in a clear and comprehensible manner for both on-premises and off-premises contracts about 'the main characteristics of the goods or services, to the extent appropriate to the medium of communication and to the goods or services'. It is also provided that where SI 2013/3134, regs 9, 10 or 13, require the trader to provide information additional to that in sch. 1, para. (a), or sch. 2, para. (a), any of that information provided is to be treated as included as a term of the contract (CRA 2015, s. 12). The information requirements are set out in detail in SI 2013/3134, sch. 1 and sch. 2. These terms cannot be contracted out of (CRA 2015, s. 31(1)(c) and (d)).

Quality and fitness

In respect of non-consumer contracts SoGA 1979, s. 14, implies terms that goods sold should **89.32** be of satisfactory quality and reasonably fit for their purpose. These are the implied terms which arise in most sale of goods litigation. These implied terms are conditions (s. 14(6)). The previous standard of merchantable quality was replaced (from 3 January 1995) by the concept of satisfactory quality (see **89.33**). The implied terms apply where the seller sells the goods in the course of a business (s. 14(2)). In non-consumer sales, liability can be restricted or excluded only in so far as the term satisfies the test of reasonableness (Unfair Contract Terms Act 1977, s. 6(1A)). For consumer contracts equivalent provisions are made by imposing similar standard incidents in supply contracts (CRA 2015, ss. 9 and 10; SoGA 1979, s. 14(9)). These terms cannot be contracted out of (CRA 2015, s. 31(1)(a) and (b)).

Satisfactory quality

'Satisfactory quality' means the standard that a reasonable person would regard as satisfactory, **89.33** taking account of any description of the goods, the price (if relevant) and all other relevant circumstances (SoGA 1979, s. 14(2A)). Quality of goods includes their state and condition and the following (among others) are in appropriate cases aspects of the quality of goods:

(a) fitness for the purpose for which goods of the kind in question are commonly supplied;
(b) appearance and finish;
(c) freedom from minor defects;
(d) safety; and
(e) durability (s. 14(2B)).

The implied term of satisfactory quality does not, by s. 14(2C), extend to any matter making the goods unsatisfactory:

(a) which is specifically drawn to the buyer's attention before the contract is made;
(b) where the buyer examines the goods before the contract is made, which that examination ought to reveal; or
(c) in the case of a contract for sale by sample, which would have been apparent on a reasonable examination of the sample.

Pre-1995 cases need to be treated with caution in the light of the change in the test from 'merchantable quality' to 'satisfactory quality'. Compare *Rogers v Parish (Scarborough) Ltd* [1987] QB 933. Nevertheless, the following cases decided under the 'merchantable quality' test would be decided in the same way under the current test. Coalite delivered with an explosive substance accidentally included in the delivery (and which blew up in the claimant's fireplace) was not of merchantable quality (*Wilson v Rickett Cockrell and Co. Ltd* [1954] 1 QB 598). Nor was a bun which contained a stone (*Chaproniere v Mason* (1905) 21 TLR 633). In *Mash and Murrell Ltd v Joseph I. Emmanuel Ltd* [1961] 1 WLR 862 (at first instance, reversed on other grounds) Diplock J held that potatoes were not of merchantable quality as they were not loaded on board a ship for transportation to the buyer in a state that they would endure the normal sea voyage and arrive in a merchantable condition. (See also *KG Bominflot Bunkergesellschaft für Mineraloele mbH & Co. KG v Petroplus Marketing AG* [2010] EWCA Civ 1145, [2011] 1 Lloyd's Rep 442.)

Commentary

There will be a breach of the condition of satisfactory quality when a new car is sold with a number of minor defects (as in a case under the merchantable test, *Rogers v Parish (Scarborough) Ltd* [1987] QB 933, where the car had minor bodywork defects and also minor mechanical problems that resulted in it misfiring and being excessively noisy). More tolerance is given to sellers of second-hand cars, having regard to the fact they are described as second-hand, and also the fact that prices will be considerably lower than for new vehicles of the same kind. In *Business Appliances Specialists Ltd v Nationwide Credit Corporation Ltd* [1988] RTR 332 it was stressed that merchantability in relation to second-hand goods is not restricted to safety (or in the case of cars, roadworthiness). A second-hand car may of course be sold for ordinary motoring purposes, or for scrap, or as a source for spare parts. More will be expected if the car is bought and sold with the intention that it is still roadworthy. Further, more will be expected of a car that is not very old and with a relatively low mileage, than from a car sold at a lower price near the end of its useful life. The fact that a vehicle breaks down soon after being sold may be evidence that it was defective at the time of purchase (*Crowther v Shannon Motor Co.* [1975] 1 WLR 30).

In *Business Appliances Specialists Ltd v Nationwide Credit Corporation Ltd* the buyer purchased a second-hand Mercedes for £14,850 with 37,000 miles recorded on the clock. After a further 800 miles it broke down with excessive wear evident in its valves (well beyond that expected in a car of that age). It was held there was no breach of the merchantability test, second-hand cars being expected to have ordinary wear and tear. If the valve defect really was ordinary wear and tear, no doubt this decision would be the same today, but the expert evidence in the case indicated it was worse than that, and it is submitted that the case would be decided differently under the present satisfactory quality test. A second-hand vehicle that was in fact a rebuilt insurance write-off would be sold in breach of the merchantability test, even in the absence of any specific defects, if the fact it had been rebuilt was not disclosed (*Shine v General Guarantee Corporation Ltd* [1988] 1 All ER 911). The description used when the item is sold is of considerable importance. In *Bartlett v Sydney Marcus Ltd* [1965] 1 WLR 1013, a second-hand car was sold with a defective clutch. Before the sale there was a discussion between the buyer and seller, and the seller indicated that if the buyer wanted the seller to repair the clutch the price would be £25 more. The buyer decided to have it repaired elsewhere, and it cost £84. It was held there was no breach of the merchantability test, the case really being one where the repairs turned out to be more expensive than anticipated.

The current statutory test of satisfactory quality was considered by the Court of Appeal in *Clegg v Andersson* [2003] EWCA Civ 320, [2003] 1 All ER (Comm) 721. The test is not whether a reasonable person would find the goods acceptable but is an objective comparison of the state of the goods with the standard which a reasonable person would find acceptable. Thus, for a high-priced quality product, the customer may be entitled to expect that it is free from even minor defects, in other words perfect or very nearly so. Contrast the unsatisfactory decision in *Egan v Motor Services (Bath) Ltd* [2007] EWCA Civ 1002, [2008] 1 WLR 1589.

For consumer contracts equivalent provisions are made by imposing similar standard incidents in supply contracts (CRA 2015, s. 9; SoGA 1979, s. 14(9)). The relevant circumstances for the application of the satisfactory quality test also specifically include any public statements on the specific characteristics of the goods made by the seller, the producer or his representative, particularly in advertising or labelling (CRA 2015, s. 9(5) and (6)) unless one of the limited exceptions applies (s. 9(7)). These terms cannot be contracted out of (s. 31(1)(a)).

As the principal test for conformity of the goods, CRA 2015, s. 9, may need in appropriate cases to be considered alongside two of the new standard incidents of consumer supply contracts. First, that if installation of the goods by the trader or someone for whom he is responsible forms part of the contract the goods must be installed correctly before the goods can conform (s. 15). Liability under s. 15 cannot be contracted out of (s. 31(1)(g)). Secondly, where the goods are an item which includes digital content, the digital content must conform before the goods can conform (s. 16). This will be relevant to the supply of many consumer electronic devices, including smartphones, tablets and games consoles. Liability under s. 16 cannot be contracted out of (s. 31(1)(h)).

Fitness for particular purpose

In non-consumer contracts a term of fitness for a particular purpose is implied where the seller sells in the course of a business and the buyer makes known any particular purpose for which the goods are being bought, except where the circumstances show that the buyer does not rely or that it is unreasonable for the buyer to rely on the skill or judgment of the seller (SoGA 1979, s. 14(3)). The particular purpose for which the goods are bought may be made known to the seller either expressly or by implication (*Jewson Ltd v Boyhan* [2003] EWCA Civ 1030, [2004] 1 Lloyd's Rep 505). Where a seller knew the buyer had already bought plumbing components of a particular type for a building project, it was held in *BSS Group plc v Makers (UK) Ltd* [2011] EWCA Civ 809, [2011] TCLR 7, to be an inescapable inference that the seller knew that valves it later sold to the buyer had to be compatible with the previously purchased components. A seller's only obligation under s. 14(3) is to ensure the goods are fit for the purpose they will ordinarily be used for, unless the buyer makes known to the seller any abnormal feature or idiosyncrasy which will put additional demands on the goods (*Slater v Finning Ltd* [1997] AC 473). The particular purpose for which goods may have been bought may in fact be the only usual purpose for those goods (see *Priest v Last* [1903] 2 KB 148, where the goods were a hot-water bottle). If a buyer of goods for installation in a house relies on the seller's skill and judgment, the goods will be in breach of s. 14(3) if they breach building or other regulations, even if they are supplied in strict conformity to the contract (*Lowe v W. Machell Joinery Ltd* [2011] EWCA Civ 794, [2012] 1 All ER (Comm) 153).

The wording of s. 14(3) shows that the burden of proving that the section does not apply on the ground that the buyer has not, or that it was unreasonable for him to rely, on the seller's skill or judgment rests on the seller (*Slater v Finning Ltd* per Lord Steyn). Normally, it will be taken to be the case that a buyer, simply by going to a retailer to buy something, relies on that retailer to exercise skill and judgment in selecting suitable stock (*Grant v Australian Knitting Mills Ltd* [1936] AC 85). Where the seller is also the manufacturer, it is nigh on impossible to rebut the presumption of reliance (*Kendall v Lillico* [1969] AC 31). The presumption also applies where both parties are traders, but of course it is easier to rebut it. In cases where a buyer intends to use the goods in another country, it will usually be the case that the presumption will be rebutted in so far as the issue may be whether the goods are reasonably fit for use in that other country, because usually it will be the buyer who will be best placed to know this (*Teheran-Europe Co. Ltd v S. T. Belton Ltd* [1968] 2 QB 545).

If the buyer has some unusual susceptibility to contaminants found in the goods sold, it is a question of fact and degree whether the goods breach the condition. *Griffiths v Peter Conway Ltd* [1939] 1 All ER 685 has been described as a highly special case (in *Ashington Piggeries Ltd v Christopher Hill Ltd* [1972] AC 441), but in this case it was held that there was no breach of the condition where a buyer contracted dermatitis from a coat sold by the seller, the buyer having an unusually sensitive skin, and the coat not being such as to harm any normal purchaser. On the other hand, in *Ashington Piggeries Ltd v Christopher Hill Ltd* animal meal was contaminated with a trace of a toxic substance that was harmful to many animals, but which was peculiarly harmful to the buyer's mink. It was held there was a breach of the condition.

For consumer contracts equivalent provisions are made by imposing similar standard incidents in supply contracts (CRA 2015, s. 10; SoGA 1979, s. 14(9)). These terms cannot be contracted out of (CRA 2015, s. 31(1)(b)).

Sale by sample or model

In non-consumer sales the implied conditions in a contract of sale by sample are:

(a) that the bulk will correspond to the sample in quality (SoGA 1979, s. 15(2)(a)); and

89.34

89.35

Commentary

(b) that the goods will be free from any defect making their quality unsatisfactory which would not be apparent on reasonable examination of the sample (s. 15(2)(c)).

In non-consumer sales liability can be restricted or excluded only in so far as the term satisfies the test of reasonableness (Unfair Contract Terms Act 1977, s. 6(1A)).

For consumer contracts equivalent provisions are made by imposing similar standard incidents in supply contracts requiring goods to match a sample (CRA 2015, s. 13; SoGA 1979, s. 15(5)) and also for goods to match a model seen or examined (CRA 2015, s. 14). The latter is a new term, tracking more faithfully the language of the EU Consumer Sales Directive, 99/44/EC. Its language would be broad enough to extend to purchasing a television from an electrical outlet store having examined the showroom display model. These terms cannot be contracted out of (CRA 2015, s. 31(1)(e) and (f)).

REMEDIES FOR BREACH

Remedies for breach of consumer contracts

89.36   Additional remedies for consumer buyers based on the Consumer Sales Directive, 99/44/EC, were originally inserted as part 5A of SoGA 1979, which has now been deleted and replaced by CRA 2015, ss. 19 to 24. These provisions form a new and complex code based on the four European remedies of repair, replacement, rejection and reduction of the price. In order to achieve clarity and certainty the new provisions provide separately for an explicit 'short-term' right to reject, and a final right of rejection. Rather than breach, the provisions speak of the conformity, or otherwise, of the goods (s. 19(1) and (2)).

CRA 2015, s. 19, provides the key to the following provisions, establishing which remedies are applicable in respect of the statutory rights in ss. 9 to 17.

If the goods do not conform to the contract at any time within six months after delivery, they must be taken not to have conformed at the date of delivery (s. 19(14)) unless:

(a) it is established that they did so conform on that day; the burden of proof must be on the seller (s. 19(15)(a)) or;
(b) the rule is incompatible with the nature of the goods or how they fail to conform with the contract (s. 19(15)(b)).

Both the short-term and the final right to reject also entail treating the contract as at an end (ss. 19(14) and 20(4)), and there is complex provision for consequential rights to a refund (ss. 20(9) to (19) and 24(8) to (11)). The principal rule is that the trader can make no deduction from the refunded price to take account of the consumer's use of the goods if the final right to reject is exercised in the first six months (s. 24(10) to (11)). There are special rules on partial rejection (s. 21).

In outline the new short-term right to reject is available for breaches of the statutory rights in ss. 9 to 17, save for the installation term and right to supply term (s. 19(3)). For installation under s. 15 and breach of other requirements stated in the contract the other remedies, including the final right to reject, are available (s. 19(4)). For breach of the right to supply in s. 17(1) the right to reject is unlimited, in line with the existing law (ss. 19(6) and 20(3)). In essence the short-term right to reject must be exercised within 30 days of ownership transferring and delivery or installation (s. 22(3)). Provision is made for perishable goods (s. 22(4)). If the consumer requests or agrees repair or replacement the clock stops until the repaired or replacement item is supplied, and if they do not conform, the consumer can reject if the original time limit (ignoring the time waiting for repair or replacement) has not expired or within seven days of supply of the repaired or replacement item (s. 22(6) to (8)).

The notorious decision in *Bernstein v Pamson Motors (Golders Green) Ltd* [1987] 2 All ER 220 (right to reject new car lost after 140 miles' use, and less than four weeks' ownership) which had previously been expressly stated not to survive the 1995 amendments to SoGA 1979 (*Clegg v Andersson* [2003] EWCA Civ 320, [2003] 1 All ER (Comm) 721) is also clearly incompatible with the new short-term right to reject for consumer buyers.

There is a right to require the seller to repair or replace the goods (ss. 19(3)(b) and (4) and 23) save where that would be impossible or disproportionate in comparison to the other of those remedies (s. 23(3)). The repair or replacement must be within a reasonable time and without significant inconvenience to the buyer and at the cost of the seller (s. 23(2)).

There is a separate right to a reduction in the purchase price up to the full amount of the price or, alternatively, to exercise the final right of rejection (ss. 19(3)(c) and (4), 20(2) and 24). Either right can be exercised where:

(a) after one repair or one replacement the goods do not conform;
(b) the buyer cannot require repair or replacement because of s. 23(3): or
(c) where the consumer has required the trader to repair or replace the goods, but the trader is in breach of the requirement in s. 23(2)(a) to do so within a reasonable time and without significant inconvenience to the buyer (s. 24(5)).

The reduction in price is 'by an appropriate amount' (s. 24(1)(a)), which is not defined. It is, presumably, a reduction to the price which would have been paid for the goods in their actual state.

Other common law or equitable remedies, including specific performance or damages and termination for breach of an express term are largely preserved (s. 19(9) to (12)).

Remedies for breach of non-consumer contracts: breach by the seller

Termination   The principal self-help remedies in non-consumer sales for supply of non-conforming goods are rejection of the goods and termination of the contract for breach of a condition, or in the language of the Act, treating the contract as repudiated (SoGA 1979, s. 11(3)), including the statutory conditions in ss. 12 to 15. This is now qualified by the restriction on termination for slight breaches in s. 15A. It is also possible to terminate for a sufficiently serious breach of an innominate term in a sale of goods contract (*Cehave NV v Bremer Handelsgesellschaft mbH* [1976] QB 44). **89.37**

The buyer's right to terminate will be lost where the buyer is held to have accepted the goods (SoGA 1979, ss. 11(4) and 35). Acceptance is deemed to have occurred when it is intimated by the buyer to the seller, or when the goods have been delivered and the buyer does any act in relation to them which is inconsistent with the seller's ownership (s. 35(1)). Once goods are delivered, if the buyer has not previously examined them, acceptance is not deemed to have occurred until the buyer has had a reasonable opportunity of examining them for the purpose of ascertaining whether they are in conformity with the contract (s. 35(2)(a)). Acceptance is also deemed to have occurred when after a lapse of a reasonable time the buyer retains the goods without intimating to the seller that they have been rejected (s. 35(4)). In determining whether the buyer has had the goods for a reasonable time, the court will take into account whether the buyer has had a reasonable opportunity of examining the goods for the purpose of ascertaining whether they conform with the contract (s. 35(5)).

By s. 35(6), a buyer is not deemed to have accepted the goods merely because:

(a) the buyer asks for, or agrees to, their repair by or under an arrangement with the seller; or
(b) the goods are delivered to another under a sub-sale or other disposition.

Where the buyer elects to keep non-conforming goods, or is deemed to have accepted them he is nevertheless entitled to damages for breach of contract, usually calculated by reference to the difference between the value of the goods as delivered and the value they would have had if there had been no breach (s. 53).

89.38   **Non-delivery**   Where the seller fails to deliver in accordance with the contract the recoverable sums are:

(a) damages for non-delivery (s. 51); and

(b) any special damages and interest (s. 54).

Alternatively, the buyer may sue for specific performance if the goods were specific or ascertained goods (s. 52), but this jurisdiction is rarely exercised and only in cases of unique goods or goods otherwise having a special value. The damages recoverable under s. 51 are the estimated loss directly and naturally resulting, in the ordinary course of events, from the seller's breach of contract (s. 51(2)). Where there is an available market for the goods the measure of damages is usually the difference between the contract price and the market or current price of the goods at the time or times when they ought to have been delivered (s. 51(3)).

An outright refusal by the seller to perform his or her obligations will amount to a repudiatory breach of contract unless the seller's obligations under the contract were limited, or the contract has become frustrated. The ordinary contract law concepts of repudiatory breach, the need for acceptance of that breach, and of anticipatory breach, will apply. If a repudiatory breach exists and is accepted by the buyer, the buyer will have the following remedies:

(a) a claim in restitution for the money paid, on a total failure of consideration; or

(b) a claim for damages for non-delivery; or

(c) a claim for specific performance if the goods are specific goods or are ascertained goods.

89.39   **Delay in delivery**   If the time for delivery is of the essence, or more than a reasonable time for the delivery has passed and the seller has not delivered the goods, the seller will be in repudiatory breach of contract (*Hartley v Hymans* [1920] 3 KB 475). The buyer will then be able:

(a) to accept the repudiatory breach and claim damages for non-delivery; or

(b) rarely, to seek specific performance of the contract.

Remedies for breach of non-consumer contracts: breach by the buyer

89.40   The buyer's duty is to accept the goods and pay for them in accordance with the terms of the contract. Where the parties have a number of separate contracts it is important to note that (in the absence of express terms in each contract) a claim arising under one contract will not give rise to a defence in another (*B. Hargreaves Ltd v Action 2000 Ltd* [1993] BCLC 1111).

89.41   **Late payment**   Many written contracts provide for interest to be charged on late payments. In litigation interest can be claimed under the Senior Courts Act 1981, s. 35A, or the County Courts Act 1984, s. 69. In contracts covered by the Late Payment of Commercial Debts (Interest) Act 1998 a statutory implied term is inserted into the contract that the debt carries simple interest at the prescribed statutory rate.

89.42   **Failure to take delivery**   If the buyer wrongfully fails to take delivery of the goods, the seller can maintain an action for the price if property in the goods has passed to the buyer or where the price is payable irrespective of delivery (SOGA 1979, s. 49). However, s. 49 is not a complete code of situations in which the price may be recovered under a contract of sale, and the price may be recoverable on the express terms of the contract (*PST Energy 7 Shipping LLC v OW Bunker Malta Ltd* [2016] UKSC 23, [2016] 2 WLR 1193). The more usual course is to sue for damages occasioned by the refusal of delivery and a reasonable charge for care of the goods under s. 37. Damages for non-acceptance are governed by s. 50. The measure of damages is the estimated loss directly and naturally resulting from the buyer's breach of contract. If there is an available market for the goods, the seller must resell the goods and the damages will be:

(a) the difference between the contract price and the market or current price when the goods ought to have been accepted; and

(b) the reasonable costs of sale.

The best evidence of market value is the price of the last actual market transaction before the time for acceptance (*Glencore Energy UK Ltd v Cirrus Oil Services Ltd* [2014] EWHC 87 (Comm), [2014] 1 All ER (Comm) 513). If there is no available market for the goods, the best evidence might be based on expert evidence of comparable market prices. An action for the price has obvious advantages where it may be difficult to prove any loss has been suffered, or where arguments over mitigation of loss may arise.

Seller's rights in the goods   The seller's rights in the goods can be of particular importance if **89.43** the buyer is insolvent. Retention of title clauses until payment are now common. Where there are no contract terms, if property has passed, the unpaid seller (defined in SoGA 1979, s. 38) usually has, by virtue of s. 39:

(a) a statutory lien on the goods;
(b) a right of stoppage in transit in case of insolvency; and
(c) a right of resale.

The statutory right of resale arises under s. 48. If property has not passed, the seller may have a claim for delivery up of the goods and damages for wrongful interference with the goods against the buyer and any other person in possession.

SALES BY NON-OWNERS

The traditional rule remains that no one can pass better title than that person possesses: *nemo* **89.44** *dat quod non habet*. There are nine main exceptions to this rule:

(a) Estoppel — where the owner is precluded by conduct from denying the seller's authority to sell (SoGA 1979, s. 21(1)).
(b) Sales under the Factors Act 1889 — sales by mercantile agents who are in possession of the goods or documents of title to the goods with the consent of the true owner who sell in the ordinary course of their business to a person acting in good faith without notice will, pass title (SoGA 1979, s. 21(2)(a); Factors Act 1889).
(c) Sales under special powers — this exception covers a large group of sales such as sales of goods distrained upon, sales by mortgagors, receivers and under bills of sale and sale of uncollected goods under the Torts (Interference with Goods) Act 1977, ss. 12 and 13 (SoGA 1979, s. 21(2)(b)).
(d) Sales under voidable title — where a sale of goods contract is voidable (e.g. by mis-representation, undue influence, mistake or duress), the buyer's title will be voida-ble and a sale on of the goods to someone in good faith without notice of the defect in title can pass title (SoGA 1979, s. 23).
(e) Sales by seller in possession — this is a very similar situation to sales under the Factors Act 1889, s. 8, so that a seller who remains in possession of goods or the documents of title, can sell goods a second time to someone else acting in good faith and without notice of the first sale and will pass title (SoGA 1979, s. 24; *Michael Gerson (Leasing) Ltd v Wilkinson* [2001] QB 514).
(f) Sales by buyer in possession — this is similar to the Factors Act 1889, s. 9, and renders valid a sale by the buyer who has possession of the goods or the documents of title and sells on the goods which he or she does not yet own to any person acting in good faith and without notice of a lien or other right of the original seller (SoGA 1979, s. 25).
(g) Sales of motor vehicles within part 3 of the Hire Purchase Act 1964 — motor vehicles which are hired under hire purchase agreements or agreed to be sold under conditional sale agreements and are sold by the hirer to a private purchaser in good faith without notice of the hire purchase or conditional sale agreement will pass title in the motor vehicle. Where a fraudster obtains a vehicle from a dealer by purporting to enter into a hire purchase agreement, the hire purchase company (which obtains title by buying the vehicle from the dealer) remains the legal owner of the vehicle, and is not defeated by

s. 27, if the fraudster then sells the car to an innocent purchaser. This is because the fraudster is not a 'debtor' under the hire purchase agreement within the meaning of s. 29(4) (*Shogun Finance Ltd v Hudson* [2003] UKHL 62, [2004] 1 AC 919).

(h) Sales by agents can also pass title under the ordinary rules of agency if the agent has actual or apparent authority to bind his or her principal as the ordinary rules of agency apply (SoGA 1979, s. 62(2)).

(i) Under the Torts (Interference with Goods) Act 1977 payment of damages under s. 5 will extinguish the title of the original owner enabling the person paying damages to pass title in those goods.

Chapter 90   Unfair Contracts

INTRODUCTION

Statutory control limiting the normal freedom to contract upon any terms which the parties **90.1** agree is not new. Even many centuries ago there was legislation, such as the Statute of Frauds 1677 and the usury laws. There are two principal enactments. First, the Unfair Contract Terms Act 1977 (UCTA 1977) which is now exclusively concerned with business-to-business contracts. Secondly, the Consumer Rights Act 2015 (CRA 2015), part 2 of which consolidates rules on unfair terms in business-to-consumer contracts previously found in UCTA 1977 and in the now repealed Unfair Terms in Consumer Contracts Regulations 1999 (SI 1999/2083, the 1999 Regulations).

The main policy behind the modern legislation is to provide essential safeguards against the worst excesses of the principle of freedom of contract. The law is particularly concerned to protect consumers as they are often in a weak bargaining position compared to large retailers and other large businesses, and cannot realistically enter into contracts other than on the terms insisted upon by the businesses they are dealing with. The law is also concerned to curb the worst excesses of the use of standard terms of trading. However, the approach is somewhat limited. The legislation is reasonably effective in limiting exclusions of liability (particularly in relation to breaches causing personal injuries or death, and in relation to the statutory implied terms in contracts for the sale of goods and the supply of services), and limiting terms allowing a party to render no performance or a performance substantially different from that reasonably expected. However, there is no general requirement that terms must be fair. Nor does the legislation do anything to protect customers who feel they have been charged an unfair price.

The main statutory provisions are:

(a) UCTA 1977, which introduced important controls on exclusion clauses and standard terms in contracts, and which limits the right to contract out of the statutory terms under the Sale of Goods Act 1979 (SoGA 1979) (see **chapter 89**) and the Supply of Goods (Implied Terms) Act 1973.

(b) Part 2 of CRA 2015, which prohibits terms and notices excluding or limiting liability for negligently caused death and personal injury, makes other unfair terms in consumer contracts subject to a requirement of fairness, requires terms to be in plain and intelligible language, and gives powers of investigation and enforcement to consumer groups and the Competition and Markets Authority (CMA). Part 2 implements the EU Directive on unfair contract terms, 93/13/EEC.

UNFAIR TERMS IN BUSINESS CONTRACTS

Application of the Act

90.2 UCTA 1977 came into force on 1 February 1978. It does not apply to contracts made before that date, but does apply to any loss or damage which is suffered on or after that date (s. 31). Its provisions apply only to business liability (s. 1(3)). 'Business' includes a profession and the activities of any government department or local or public authority (s. 14). 'Business liability' is liability for breach of an obligation or duty arising from things done or to be done by a person in the course of a business (whether that person's own or another's) (s. 1(3)). It does not matter whether any breach of duty or obligation is inadvertent or intentional, or whether liability arises directly or vicariously. 'Person' is not defined and so includes a body of persons corporate or unincorporate (Interpretation Act 1978, sch. 1). UCTA 1977 does not apply to terms in consumer contracts or consumer notices (defined in s. 14) which are now governed by CRA 2015, part 2 (UCTA 1977, ss. 2(4), 3(3), 6(5), and 8(4A)).

Negligence liability

90.3 By UCTA 1977, s. 1(1), 'negligence' means the breach of:

(a) any obligation arising from the express or implied terms of a contract to take reasonable care or exercise reasonable skill in the performance of the contract;

(b) any common law duty to take reasonable care or exercise reasonable skill (but not any stricter duty); and

(c) the duty of care imposed by the Occupiers' Liability Act 1957.

UCTA 1977 prevents contract terms or notices which exclude or restrict liability for personal injury or death from being effective at all (s. 2(1)). Loss or damage (other than for personal injury or death) can only be excluded or restricted in so far as a clause satisfies the test of reasonableness (s. 2(2)). Knowledge of or agreement to a contract term or notice which excludes or restricts liability is not of itself to be taken as indicating acceptance of any risk (s. 2(3)).

Contract terms

90.4 Before considering whether a purported term may fall foul of UCTA 1977, it is first necessary to determine whether it was in fact a term of the contract (see **89.23**: this is a point specifically mentioned also in UCTA 1977, s. 11(2)), and secondly whether the term purports to apply on the facts of the case. If the term appears to apply, it will also be necessary to consider whether it may be cut down by UCTA 1977.

Where one party deals on another's written standard terms of business, there can be no exclusion or restriction of liability in respect of a breach by that other person save where the term satisfies the test of reasonableness (UCTA 1977, s. 3(2)(a)). Similarly, a person dealing on standard terms cannot claim to be contractually entitled to render a contractual performance substantially different from that reasonably expected, or no performance at all, unless the contract terms satisfies the test of reasonableness (s. 3(2)(b)).

Statutory implied terms

90.5 Prohibitions on excluding liability for breach of the statutory implied terms under SoGA 1979 and the Supply of Goods (Implied Terms) Act 1973 (SoGITA 1973) are contained in UCTA 1977, s. 6. The restrictions may be summarised as follows:

(a) an absolute prohibition on excluding or restricting the implied terms about title in SoGA 1979, s. 12, and SoGITA 1973, s. 8; and

(b) a qualified prohibition in non-consumer cases on excluding or restricting the implied terms in SoGA 1979, ss. 13 to 15, and the SoGITA 1973, ss. 9 to 11, so that to be effective an exclusion or restriction must satisfy the test of reasonableness (which is provided for by UCTA 1977, s. 11 and sch. 2).

Misrepresentations

Similar protection to that provided under UCTA 1977 is provided under the **Misrepresentation Act 1967, s. 3(1)**, in relation to the exclusion of liability in respect of misrepresentations. A term purporting to exclude or restrict liability for any misrepresentation made before contract, or to exclude or restrict any remedies available by reason of such misrepresentations, is of no effect except in so far as the term satisfies the test of reasonableness set out in UCTA 1977, s. 11. The 1967 Act does not apply to terms in consumer contracts, which are now governed by CRA 2015, part 2 (**Misrepresentation Act 1967, s. 3(2)**).   **90.6**

Reasonableness

The test of reasonableness is set out in UCTA 1977, s. 11. By s. 11(1), the requirement of reasonableness for the purposes of UCTA 1977 and the **Misrepresentation Act 1967, s. 3(1)**, is that the term must have been a fair and reasonable one to be included having regard to the circumstances which were, or ought reasonably to have been, known to or in the contemplation of the parties when the contract was made. It is for those claiming that a contract term or notice satisfies the test of reasonableness to show that it does (UCTA 1977, s. 11(5)). In *Sheffield v Pickfords Ltd* [1997] CLC 648 the Court of Appeal held that any claim concerning standard terms of business implicitly raises the question whether those terms are reasonable, and it is not essential for the party seeking to enforce the terms to assert in a statement of case that they are reasonable. It was also held that particulars of any specific fact or matter relied upon could be given before any issue is raised.   **90.7**

Particular situations are governed by the following additional provisions:

(a) In determining for the purposes of non-consumer contracts governed by UCTA 1977, s. 6 (sale of goods and hire-purchase) and s. 7 (miscellaneous contracts, other than sale and hire-purchase, under which ownership or possession of goods passes), whether a contract term satisfies the test of reasonableness, the court must have regard to the matters set out in sch. 2 to the Act (see **90.8**) (s. 11(2)).

(b) In relation to a notice (not being a notice which has contractual effect, such as a notice purporting to restrict or exclude liability in respect of theft), the requirement of reasonableness is that it should be fair and reasonable to allow reliance on it, having regard to all the circumstances obtaining when the liability arose or (but for the notice) would have arisen (s. 11(3)).

(c) Where the question arises whether a term or notice seeking to restrict a person's liability to a specified sum or money satisfies the requirement of reasonableness, regard shall be had (in the case of contract terms) to the matters mentioned in (a) above, and in all cases to:

  (i) the resources which that person could expect to have available for the purpose of meeting the liability should it arise; and

  (ii) how far it was open to that person to obtain insurance cover for the liability (s. 11(4)).

Reasonableness guidelines

The guidelines set out in UCTA 1977, sch. 2, may be considered in relation to an attempt to exclude or restrict liability for breach of the implied terms about conformity with description or sample or about quality or fitness in a sale of goods, hire-purchase or similar transaction (UCTA 1977, ss. 6(3), 7(3) and (4)). In deciding whether the exclusion or restriction is reasonable, sch. 2 requires regard to be had to: **90.8**

(a) the strength of the bargaining position of the parties relative to each other, taking into account (amongst other things) alternative means by which the customer's requirements could have been met;

(b) whether the customer received an inducement to agree to the term, or in accepting it had an opportunity of entering into a similar contract with other persons, but without having to accept such a term;

(c) whether the customer knew or ought reasonably to have known of the existence of the term (having regard, amongst other things, to any custom of the trade and any previous course of dealings between the parties);

(d) where the term excludes or restricts any relevant liability if some condition is not complied with, whether it was reasonable at the time of the contract to expect that compliance with that condition would be practicable;

(e) whether the goods were manufactured, processed or adapted to the special order of the customer.

In *St Albans City and District Council v International Computers Ltd* [1995] FSR 686, the council suffered a £1.3 million loss due to an error made by the computer company. The company sought to rely on a clause in its contract restricting its liability to £100,000. Scott Baker J took into account the following factors: (a) the parties were of unequal bargaining power; (b) the defendant had not justified the figure of £100,000, which was small in relation to the potential risk; (c) the defendant was insured in an aggregate figure of £50 million worldwide; (d) whether it was better for the risk to fall on a council or an international computer company. Despite the facts that both parties were free to make their own bargains, that the council entered into the contract with its eyes open, that such restrictions were commonplace in the computer industry, and that the software involved was a developing technology, it was held that the defendant had failed to discharge its burden of proof. The term was therefore unreasonable and unenforceable.

The fact that a contract is the result of negotiations between substantial companies is likely to indicate that the court should not find that its terms are unreasonable. In *Watford Electronics Ltd v Sanderson CFL Ltd* [2001] 1 All ER (Comm) 696 Peter Gibson LJ quoted with approval the following remarks of Judge Thayne Forbes in *Salvage Association v CAP Financial Services Ltd* [1995] FSR 654:

Generally speaking, where a party well able to look after itself enters into a commercial contract and, with full knowledge of all relevant circumstances, willingly accepts the terms of the contract which provides for apportionment of the financial risks of that transaction, I think it is very likely that those terms will be held to be fair and reasonable.

In *Watford Electronics Ltd v Sanderson CFL Ltd* Chadwick LJ said, at [55]:

Where experienced businessmen representing substantial companies of equal bargaining power negotiate an agreement, they may be taken to have had regard to the matters known to them. They should in my view be taken to be the best judge of the commercial fairness of the agreement which they have made; including the fairness of each of the terms in that agreement.

Terms in a standard-form contract are more likely to be held to be reasonable if they were negotiated between trade associations (as opposed to standard terms simply imposed by one party), as in such cases there is no substantial difference in bargaining power (see *R. W. Green Ltd v Cade Bros Farms Ltd* [1978] 1 Lloyd's Rep 602, and compare *George Mitchell (Chesterhall) Ltd v Finney Lock Seeds Ltd* [1983] 2 AC 803, where standard conditions were used by seed merchants without objection from farmers). The guidelines in sch. 2 are not exhaustive of the circumstances that may be considered. So, in *R and B Customs Brokers Co. Ltd v United Dominions Trust Ltd* [1988] 1 WLR 321 it was said that the court could take into account the question whether the party seeking to rely on an exclusion or restriction had an opportunity to discover the defect covered by the term.

Reasonableness in other contracts

90.9   In cases where terms are subject to the test of reasonableness under UCTA 1977, but the guidelines in sch. 2 (see **90.8**) do not apply (for example, if the term does not purport to restrict the statutory implied terms, or if the dispute concerns the exclusion of liability for misrepresentations, or the contract is not one involving the sale etc. of goods), the court must apply the general test of reasonableness set out at **90.7**. However, the court can apply the sch. 2 guidelines by analogy (*Singer Co. (UK) Ltd v Tees and Hartlepool Port Authority* [1988] 2 Lloyd's Rep 164).

As regards insurance (UCTA 1977, s. 11(4)(b)), the court will consider the availability of insurance rather than the actual insurance cover of the defendant (*Singer Co. (UK) Ltd v Tees and Hartlepool Port Authority*). Limitation of liability may well be reasonable for a person who stores or carries another's goods without being informed of their value, particularly if the goods could be more cheaply insured by the owner (*Singer Co. (UK) Ltd v Tees and Hartlepool Port Authority*).

In *Smith v Eric S. Bush* [1990] 1 AC 831 the question arose as to whether it was reasonable for surveyors instructed by the mortgagee to exclude or restrict liability in relation to their survey reports prepared in connection with the sale of ordinary houses. The House of Lords held, having regard to the relative expense to the purchaser of buying a house, and the high rates of interest charged to borrowers, that it was not reasonable to throw the risk of loss flowing from the incompetence or carelessness of the surveyor on to the purchaser, and exclusion clauses were held to be unenforceable. On the other hand, in relation to very expensive houses, and industrial property, it was said that prudent purchasers would obtain their own survey reports, and it may well be reasonable for surveyors to exclude their liability, or at least to restrict it to the amount of their insurance cover.

Excluded contracts

Certain contracts are excluded either in whole or in part from the provisions of UCTA 1977 by sch. 1. The provisions on negligence liability (s. 2) and liability in contract (s. 3) do not apply to the types of contract listed in sch. 1, para. 1. These exclusions may be summarised as contracts relating to insurance, creation or transfer of an interest in land, intellectual property, formation or dissolution of a company or its constitution, and the creation or transfer of securities. Special provisions exist in relation to certain marine and hovercraft contracts (paras 2 and 3). The exclusions of negligence liability in s. 2(1) and (2) only apply to employment contracts in favour of the employee (sch. 1, para. 4).   **90.10**

In *Commerzbank AG v Keen* [2006] EWCA Civ 1536, [2007] IRLR 132, the Court of Appeal rejected as unarguable that general provisions of UCTA 1977 applied to contracts of employment. Moses LJ observed that:

> It is all too easy in analysing authority and discussion of the application of the 1977 Act to contracts of employment to overlook the impact of the words 'consumer' and 'business' used in ss. 3 and 12 of the Act. An employee does not deal with an employer as a consumer. A bank's business is not entering into contracts of employment with its employees.

Practice

In *Sheffield v Pickfords Ltd* [1997] CLC 648 the Court of Appeal held that it was not essential for a party relying on contract terms or standard terms to assert that those terms are reasonable. That allegation is implicit if a party relies in a statement of case on terms which have to satisfy the test of reasonableness. However, the better practice is to make at least a general assertion of reasonableness of such contract or standard terms in the statement of case. Further information can then be sought or ordered of the facts and matter relied on as showing reasonableness, if necessary.   **90.11**

UNFAIR TERMS IN CONSUMER CONTRACTS

Scope

90.12 CRA 2015 came into force on 1 October 2015, replacing the Unfair Terms in Consumer Contracts Regulations 1999 (SI 1999/2083). CRA 2015, part 2, differs from UCTA 1977 in that it applies to consumer contracts. The Arbitration Act 1996 extends CRA 2015, part 2, to arbitration agreements within s. 89(1) of that Act and, in relation to those agreements only, a consumer does not have to be a natural person (Arbitration Act 1996, s. 90).

CRA 2015, part 2, applies to all contracts concluded between a trader and a consumer, which are dubbed 'consumer contracts', as well as 'consumer notices' (CRA 2015, s. 61(1)). 'Consumer' has the standard European definition, based on Directive 93/13/EEC, art. 2(b). A 'consumer' is defined as an individual acting for purposes that are wholly or mainly outside that individual's trade, business or profession (CRA 2015, ss. 2(3) and 76(2)). A 'seller or supplier' is any natural or legal person who, in the contract, is acting for purposes relating to his trade, business or profession, whether publicly owned or privately owned (ss. 2(2) and 76(2)). The burden of proving that an individual is not a consumer is on the trader (ss. 2(4) and 76(3)).

For the purposes of Directive 93/13/EEC, art. 2(b), the term 'consumer' must be given an autonomous European meaning which does not depend on national laws (*Turner and Co. (GB) Ltd v Abi* [2010] EWHC 2078 (QB), [2011] 1 CMLR 17). An individual who enters into a contract appointing an agent to sell shares in a company, where the individual is a full-time working director of the company, does so for the purposes of his or her trade, business or profession and is not a consumer (*Turner and Co. (GB) Ltd v Abi*). The decision of the Court of Appeal in *R and B Customs Brokers Co. Ltd v United Dominions Trust Ltd* [1988] 1 WLR 321 on the meaning of 'consumer' in the original version of UCTA 1977 is no longer good law.

The requirement of transparency

90.13 A trader must ensure that any written term of a consumer contract or consumer notice is transparent; that is, it must be expressed in plain, intelligible language and must be legible (CRA 2015, s. 68). The main sanction for breach of this requirement is that, in legal proceedings between the seller or supplier and the consumer, if there is doubt about the meaning of a written term, the interpretation which is most favourable to the consumer shall prevail (CRA 2015, ss. 69(1)). In addition, being in plain and intelligible language is a condition for the exemption of terms defining the subject matter or price from the fairness requirement.

The requirement of fairness

90.14 A term in a consumer contract or consumer notice excluding or restricting liability for death or personal injury resulting from negligence is prohibited (CRA 2015, s. 65). Any other term in a consumer contract or consumer notice is unfair if, contrary to the requirement of good faith, it causes a significant imbalance in the parties' rights and obligations arising under the contract, to the detriment of the consumer (CRA 2015, s. 62(4) and (6)).

CRA 2015, sch. 2, part 1, provides an indicative and non-exhaustive list of terms which may be regarded as unfair. In *Director General of Fair Trading v First National Bank plc* [2001] UKHL 52, [2002] 1 AC 481, Lord Bingham of Cornhill said, at [17]:

The requirement of significant imbalance is met if a term is so weighted in favour of the supplier as to tilt the parties' rights and obligations under the contract significantly in his favour. This may be by the granting to the supplier of a beneficial option or discretion or power, or by the imposing on the consumer of a disadvantageous burden or risk or duty. The illustrative terms set out in sch. 3 to the regulations provide very good examples of terms which may be regarded as unfair; whether a given term is or is not to be so regarded depends on whether it causes a significant imbalance in the parties' rights and obligations under the contract. This involves looking at the contract as a whole. But the imbalance must be to the detriment of the consumer; a significant imbalance to the detriment of the supplier, assumed to be the stronger party, is not a mischief which the regulations seek to address. The requirement of good faith in this context is one of fair and open dealing. Openness requires that the terms should be expressed fully, clearly and legibly, containing no concealed pitfalls or traps. Appropriate prominence should be given to terms which might operate disadvantageously to the customer. Fair dealing requires that a supplier should not, whether deliberately or unconsciously, take advantage of the consumer's necessity, indigence, lack of experience, unfamiliarity with the subject matter of the contract, weak bargaining position or any other factor listed in or analogous to those listed in sch. 2 of the regulations. Good faith in this context is not an artificial or technical concept; nor, since Lord Mansfield was its champion, is it a concept wholly unfamiliar to British lawyers. It looks to good standards of commercial morality and practice.

The factors which must be taken into account in assessing the unfairness of a contract term are:

(a) the nature of the subject matter of the contract;
(b) all the circumstances existing when the term was agreed; and
(c) all the other terms of the contract or of another contract on which it is dependent (CRA 2015, s. 62(5); s. 69(7) makes provision for contractual notices).

But in so far as a term is transparent and prominent, the assessment of its fairness must not extend to:

(a) the specification of the main subject matter of the contract; or
(b) the appropriateness of the price payable under the contract by comparison with the goods, digital content or services supplied under it (s. 64).

Terms concerned with the matters specified in s. 64 are usually called 'core terms'. Payments to be made if the consumer defaults are not part of the price or remuneration for this purpose (*Director General of Fair Trading v First National Bank plc*). But bank charges levied on personal current account customers in respect of unauthorised overdrafts were held to be part of the price or remuneration for the banking services provided (*Office of Fair Trading v Abbey National plc* [2009] UKSC 6, [2010] 1 AC 696).

Consequence of unfairness

An unfair term in a consumer contract or an unfair consumer notice is not binding on the consumer (CRA 2015, s. 62(1) and (2)). The contract will continue to have effect in every other respect so far as practicable (s. 67). The consumer is not prevented from enforcing the unfair term or notice against the trader (s. 62(3)).   **90.15**

Enforcement

The CMA and other regulators responsible for enforcing the law on unfair contract terms may apply for an injunction (including an interim injunction) against any person appearing to be using, or recommending use of, an unfair term drawn up for general use in contracts concluded with consumers (CRA 2015, s. 70 and schs 3 and 5). An injunction may prevent enforcement of an unfair term in existing contracts as well as preventing its use in future contracts (*Office of Fair Trading v Foxtons Ltd* [2009] EWCA Civ 288, [2010] 1 WLR 663).   **90.16**

Practice

A new requirement obliges the court to consider the fairness of a contract term even if none of the parties to the proceedings has raised that issue or indicated that it intends to raise it (CRA 2015, s. 71).   **90.17**

If a consumer wishes to allege that a term is not in plain intelligible language, that fact ought to be specifically asserted in the consumer's statement of case, particularly if there is to be a challenge to a core term (which can only be challenged if it is not in plain intelligible

Commentary

language). An allegation by a consumer that a term is unfair ought to appear in the consumer's statement of case. However, in the light of the court's duty, the failure to assert unfairness does not prevent the court refusing to enforce the term, as an unfair term is not binding on the consumer.

UNFAIR RELATIONSHIPS

90.18   The Consumer Credit Act 1974, ss. 140A to 140D, which were inserted by the Consumer Credit Act 2006 and came into force on 6 April 2007, introduced the concept of 'unfair relationships' between creditors and debtors arising out of credit agreements. For the purposes of these sections, a credit agreement is any agreement between an individual (the 'debtor') and any other person (the 'creditor') by which the creditor provides the debtor with credit of any amount (s. 140C(1)). The sections apply to agreements whether or not they are otherwise regulated by the Act. They replace earlier provisions for reopening extortionate credit bargains.

Concept of unfair relationship

90.19   The Consumer Credit Act 1974, s. 140A(1), provides that the court may exercise its powers under s. 140B (see **90.20**) if it determines that the relationship between the creditor and debtor, arising out of a credit agreement, is unfair to the debtor because of one or more of the following:

(a) any terms of the agreement or any related agreement;

(b) the way in which the creditor has exercised or enforced any of his rights;

(c) any other thing done (or not done) by or on behalf of the creditor either before or after the making of the agreement or any related agreement.

The court is to have regard to all matters it thinks relevant. There is limited guidance on the extremely wide concept of an unfair relationship, but the jurisdiction was examined by the Supreme Court in *Plevin v Paragon Personal Finance Ltd* [2014] UKSC 61, [2014] 1 WLR 4222. In *Patel v Patel* [2009] EWHC 3264 (QB), LTL 16/12/2009, the court found that a consolidating loan was part of an unfair relationship and reduced the amount payable under s. 140B. The non-disclosure of a startling level of commission earned by the creditor on the sale of payment protection insurance may give rise to an unfair relationship (*Plevin v Paragon Personal Finance Ltd*; overruling *Harrison v Black Horse Ltd* [2011] EWCA Civ 1128, [2012] Lloyd's Rep IR 521).

Where an allegation is made that an unfair relationship exists, it is for the creditor to prove the contrary (s. 140B(9)).

Powers available

90.20   If the court decides that there is or was an unfair relationship, arising out of a credit agreement, it can exercise the following powers under the Consumer Credit Act 1974, s. 140B:

(a) require the creditor to repay any sum;

(b) require the creditor to do or not to do anything specified in the order;

(c) reduce or vary any sum payable;

(d) direct the return to any surety of any property provided by him as security;

(e) set aside in whole or in part any duty imposed on the debtor or surety;

(f) alter the terms of the agreement;

(g) direct accounts to be taken.

These powers can be exercised:

(a) on an application by the debtor or surety (s. 140B(2)(a)), which must be made to the County Court (s. 140B(4)(a)); or

(b) at the instance of the debtor or surety in enforcement proceedings (s. 140B(2)(b)) or any other proceedings where the amount paid or payable is relevant (s. 140B(2)(c)).

The procedure to be adopted is set out in **PD 7B, para. 10**.

Transitional provisions

There are transitional provisions in the Consumer Credit Act 2006, sch. 3, paras 14 to 16.   **90.21** The court has power to make an order under the Consumer Credit Act 1974, s. 140B, in connection with an agreement made before 6 April 2007, but only:

(a) on an application by the debtor or surety, under s. 140B(2)(a), made after 6 April 2008, or, under s. 140B(2)(b) or (c), in proceedings commenced before that date to enforce the agreement or any related agreement or in which the amount payable or paid is relevant; and
(b) if the agreement did not become a completed agreement before that date.

In determining whether or not an agreement is a related agreement, it is immaterial when the agreement was made.

Commentary

PART U

Human Rights and Civil Procedure

Chapter 91   Human Rights and Civil Procedure

Commentary

INTRODUCTION

91.1   On 2 October 2000 most provisions of the **Human Rights Act 1998** came into force in England and Wales and much of the European Convention on Human Rights was incorporated into English law. As a consequence, public authorities are required to comply with Convention rights such as the right to a fair hearing and freedom of expression. Individuals and companies are able to rely on the Convention directly in cases against the government and other public authorities. Also, courts and tribunals fall within the Act's definition of public authorities and so must comply with the Act.

In 1951, the United Kingdom was amongst the first countries to ratify the European Convention on Human Rights. However, it was not until 2 October 2000 that the Convention could be directly relied upon in the English and Welsh courts. An individual who alleges an infringement of the Convention can still apply to the European Court of Human Rights in Strasbourg notwithstanding the right to rely on the Convention in the domestic courts. However, an application to Strasbourg may only be brought once all domestic remedies, including court and appeal hearings, have been exhausted. Proceedings may then be brought against the United Kingdom government, alleging a failure to ensure that national law is in accordance with the Convention (e.g. *Pretty v United Kingdom* (application 2346/02) (2002) 35 EHRR 1).

Until the **Human Rights Act 1998** came into force the role of the Convention in the English courts was restricted to, for example, being used to resolve an ambiguity (*R v Secretary of State for the Home Department, ex parte Brind* [1991] 1 AC 696) and being relied upon where the rules of common law or equity were uncertain (*R v Secretary of State for the Environment, ex parte NALGO* (1993) 5 Admin LR 785). Earlier legislation must be interpreted in accordance with the Convention (see **91.3**).

In *Locabail (UK) Ltd v Waldorf Investment Corporation (No. 4)* [2000] UKHRR 592, the applicant applied in the High Court for a stay of execution of a warrant of possession while the European Court of Human Rights considered her complaint that she had been denied her right to a fair trial. The argument that success in Strasbourg would render the initial possession order unlawful did not succeed: the European Court of Human Rights is not a further court of appeal from the domestic courts.

Since the European Court of Human Rights is not an appellate court in the English jurisdiction, the English courts, in deciding whether to enforce their own judgments, do not have to take into account any ruling which the European Court might in the future give on an application regarding the circumstances of liability (*Westminster City Council v Porter* [2002] EWHC 1589 (Ch), [2003] Ch 436).

In relation to overseas territories, the Convention will only apply to nationals of that territory if the governing State has notified the Council of Europe of such intention under art. 56(1). The same principle will apply to protocols enacted under the Convention. Unless there is a specific extension to another territory for whose international relations a contracting State is responsible, actions affecting individuals in that territory will not be subject to the Convention (*R (Quark Fishing Ltd) v Secretary of State for Foreign and Commonwealth Affairs* [2005] UKHL 57, [2006] 1 AC 529). Furthermore, a national of a contracting State who is outside of the jurisdiction of that State cannot rely on the Convention or the Act if his rights are breached in a non-contracting State (see *R (Abbasi) v Secretary of State for Foreign and Commonwealth Affairs* [2002] EWCA Civ 1598, [2003] UKHRR 76, concerning a British national captured by United States forces in Afghanistan and detained in Guantánamo Bay in Cuba and note also *R (Al Rawi) v Secretary of State for Foreign and Commonwealth Affairs* [2006] EWCA Civ 1279, [2008] QB 289).

Where the United States government sought to have a confiscation order made in the United States registered in the United Kingdom so that it could be enforced against the appellant's United Kingdom assets, it was accepted that the order would have constituted a breach of **art. 6** if it had taken place in a Convention State. However, given the territorial limitation on the reach of the Convention the House of Lords found that it was difficult to see how registration of the enforcement order in the United Kingdom could constitute a breach of the Convention. **Article 6** was therefore not engaged. Only a case of extreme unfairness (which this was not) would justify using the exception to the principle of territoriality so as to give indirect effect to the Convention (*Barnette v United States of America* [2004] UKHL 37, [2004] 1 WLR 2241). See also *United States of America v Montgomery (No. 2)* [2004] UKHL 37, [2004] 1 WLR 2241.

However, actions taken abroad by United Kingdom diplomatic or consular officials who exercise the authority of the State will be governed by domestic human rights law and therefore could be the subject of a claim under the **Human Rights Act 1998** (*R (B) v Secretary of State for Foreign and Commonwealth Affairs* [2004] EWCA Civ 1344, [2005] QB 643). This exception also extends to United Kingdom vessels, aircraft and even a British military prison operating in Iraq where the victim was within the jurisdiction of the United Kingdom for the purposes of **art. 1** of the Convention (*R (Al-Skeini) v Secretary of State for Defence* [2007] UKHL 26, [2008] 1 AC 153; confirmed by *Al-Skeini v United Kingdom* (application 55721/07) (2011) 53 EHRR 18). United Kingdom troops on active service overseas are within United Kingdom jurisdiction for the purposes of **art. 1** only when they are on a United Kingdom military base (*R (Smith) v Secretary of State for Defence* [2010] UKSC 29, [2011] 1 AC 1). Where British forces exercised complete control, both by force and in law, over premises in Iraq, prisoners detained by them were under the United Kingdom's jurisdiction for the purposes of **art. 1**; see European Court of Human Rights decision on admissibility, *Al-Saadoon v United Kingdom* (application 61498/08) (2010) 51 EHRR 9 and *Al-Skeini v United Kingdom*). There is a further exception to the principle of territoriality where the State party has 'effective control' of an area (either lawfully or unlawfully), but this does not apply in territories outside the regional sphere of the party States of the Convention.

Even where an act is carried out under authority of international law, that will not necessarily displace obligations under the **Human Rights Act 1998** since UN Resolutions, for example, should be interpreted with a presumption that they would not conflict with member States' obligations under human rights law. Where a UN Resolution authorised British forces to take any measures necessary for stability and security in Iraq this did not justify a breach of **art. 5** since it did not specifically authorise internment (*Al-Jedda v United Kingdom* (application 27021/08) (2011) 53 EHRR 23).

The Charter of Fundamental Rights of the European Union came into force with the Treaty of Lisbon in December 2009. The Charter is based on the Convention, other international instruments and the national law of member States. Charter provisions that correspond to Convention provisions have the same scope and meaning as understood for the Convention provision (Charter, art. 52(3)). The Charter also contains a number of economic and social provisions which are not included in the Convention. In view of this, the United Kingdom and Poland entered into Protocol 7 of 2007 which was interpreted by some parties as providing these member States with an 'opt-out' from the Charter. However, the Court of Justice of the European Union has since held that notwithstanding the Protocol, the United Kingdom and Poland are obliged to comply with the Charter (*R (NS (Afghanistan)) v Secretary of State for the Home Department* (case C-411/10) [2013] QB 102). As such, the Charter, including those provisions which are not in the Convention, forms part of domestic law (*R (AB) v Secretary of State for the Home Department* [2013] EWHC 3453 (Admin), [2014] 2 CMLR 22). It is worth noting that many of the Charter's provisions are understood as principles which may be relied on only when the court is considering the interpretation of legislation and executive acts implementing the principle (Charter, art. 52(5)) and are therefore not directly justiciable rights. However, some rights

Commentary

will have direct effect, such as those reflecting general principles of EU law and not requiring definition in national law to take effect, and may therefore require disapplication of national legislation which is in breach of Charter rights (*Benkharbouche v Embassy of the Republic of Sudan* [2015] EWCA Civ 33, [2016] QB 347).

MAIN PROVISIONS OF THE HUMAN RIGHTS ACT 1998

Sources of European human rights law

91.2   By virtue of the **Human Rights Act 1998, s. 2(1)**, a court or tribunal determining a question which has arisen in connection with a Convention right must take into account any judgment, decision, declaration or advisory opinion of the European Court of Human Rights. The court or tribunal must also take into account any opinion or decision of the Commission or decision of the Committee of Ministers, whenever made or given, so far as, in the opinion of the court or tribunal, it is relevant to the proceedings in which that question has arisen. The words 'take into account' were chosen deliberately to make it clear that these decisions are to be used as guidance and are not intended to operate as binding precedent.

The House of Lords has explained that:

Under the Convention, the United Kingdom is bound to accept a judgment of the Strasbourg court as binding. But a court adjudicating in litigation in the United Kingdom about a domestic 'Convention right' is not bound by a decision of the Strasbourg court. It must take it into account. (*Re McKerr* [2004] UKHL 12, [2004] 1 WLR 807, per Lord Hoffmann at [66].)

However, Lord Rodger of Earlsferry, also in the House of Lords, has said:

while the decisions of the European Court of Human Rights on the interpretation of the Convention are not binding, they provide authoritative guidance which courts have to take into account when interpreting the rights in domestic law. (*R (S) v Chief Constable of the South Yorkshire Police* [2004] UKHL 39, [2004] 1 WLR 2196 at [66].)

Where there is a clear and consistent line of Strasbourg authority it would require some special reason to depart from that line of authority. Lord Bingham of Cornhill has commented that:

This reflects the fact that the Convention is an international instrument, the correct interpretation of which can be authoritatively expounded only by the Strasbourg court. From this it follows that a national court subject to a duty such as that imposed by s. 2 should not without strong reason dilute or weaken the effect of the Strasbourg case law. (*R (Ullah) v Secretary of State for the Home Department* [2004] UKHL 26, [2004] 2 AC 323 at [20].)

Although the non-binding status of Strasbourg authority is accepted, the usual approach seems to be that a clear line of authority or a Grand Chamber judgment should be treated as authoritative unless it is apparent that Strasbourg had misunderstood or overlooked some significant feature of English law or practice which would lead it to review its interpretation when applied to English circumstances (see, for example, Lord Neuberger in *Manchester City Corporation v Pinnock* [2010] UKSC 45, [2011] 2 AC 104 and Lord Mance in *R (Chester) v Secretary of State for Justice* [2013] UKSC 63, [2014] AC 271). However, there is some flexibility to this and in certain cases, where the result produced would be one the courts do not consider acceptable, the Supreme Court is able to decline to follow a decision of the European Court of Human Rights (*R (Kaiyam) v Secretary of State for Justice* [2014] UKSC 66, [2015] AC 1344).

Where there are 'mixed messages' in the Strasbourg case law, the domestic court will have to make a choice about the scope and application of the relevant Convention right (*R (Hicks) v Commissioner of Police of the Metropolis* [2014] EWCA Civ 3, [2014] 1 WLR 2152). National courts are also given a margin of appreciation in some areas, for example, where the Strasbourg court had decided previously that national courts could in general determine the rules for extinction of title and adverse possession and that the United Kingdom legislative provisions were

Convention compliant in this area. Once such a margin of appreciation has been granted it applies to all cases and it is not open to the domestic court not to follow it because a case is distinguishable on the facts (*Ofulue v Bossert* [2008] EWCA Civ 7, [2009] Ch 1, affirmed on other grounds [2009] UKHL 16, [2009] 1 AC 990). Where the extent of the margin of appreciation has not been tested, domestic courts should not be inhibited from going further than the current state of authority of the Strasbourg court given the general margin of appreciation member States have in matters of delicate social policy. Therefore domestic courts are free to give what they consider to be a principled and rational interpretation in deciding that discrimination on the grounds of marital status would be likely to violate **art. 14**, notwithstanding that the matter has not yet been decided upon by the Strasbourg court (*Re G (Adoption: Unmarried Couple)* [2008] UKHL 38, [2009] 1 AC 173).

There may be cases where the Strasbourg jurisprudence is not entirely clear and the domestic courts may have difficulty in identifying clear principles from it. In *N v Secretary of State for the Home Department* [2005] UKHL 31, [2005] 2 AC 296, Lord Hope of Craighead expressed the view, at [25], that:

It is not for us to search for a solution...which is not to be found in the Strasbourg case law. It is for the Strasbourg court, not for us, to decide whether its case law is out of touch with modern conditions and to determine what further extensions, if any, are needed to the rights guaranteed by the Convention. We must take the case law as we find it, not as we would like it to be.

The duty to take into account decisions of the Strasbourg court does not displace the doctrine of precedent in domestic law, even where domestic authority appears to be inconsistent with Strasbourg case law. There is a clear duty to give practical recognition to the principles laid down by the Strasbourg court as governing the Convention rights. However, a court faced with an apparent inconsistency between a domestic decision of a higher court and a Strasbourg decision should still follow the domestic decision, under the normal rules of precedent, and should deal with the inconsistency by expressing a view on this and giving leave to appeal. By doing so the domestic court will have discharged its duty under the **Human Rights Act 1998** (*Kay v Lambeth London Borough Council* [2006] UKHL 10, [2006] 2 AC 465).

Interpretation of legislation

The interpretation of legislation is dealt with in the **Human Rights Act 1998, s. 3(1)**, which provides that so far as it is possible to do so, primary and subordinate legislation must be read and given effect in a way which is compatible with the Convention rights. **Section 3** applies to primary and subordinate legislation whenever enacted but does not affect the validity, continuing operation or enforcement of any incompatible primary legislation, or of any incompatible subordinate legislation if primary legislation prevents removal of the incompatibility (**s. 3(2)**). The courts are free to give a new meaning to legislation which they have interpreted previously where the earlier interpretation was in conflict with a Convention right. However, they will be reluctant to do so if the new interpretation of that legislation would affect transactions that have created rights and obligations on which the parties intend to rely. If interpreting legislation in line with **s. 3** would mean that the rights and obligations of the parties to an agreement entered into before 2 October 2000 would be different now to what they were at the time the agreement was entered into then this would result in unfairness to one or another of the parties (*Wilson v First County Trust Ltd (No. 2)* [2003] UKHL 40, [2004] 1 AC 816; *Law v Society of Lloyd's* [2003] EWCA Civ 1887, *The Times*, 23 January 2004).

Section 3 will sometimes require the adoption of an interpretation which linguistically may appear strained. The techniques to be used will not only involve the reading down of express language in a statute, but also the implications of provisions (*R v A (No. 2)* [2001] UKHL 25, [2002] 1 AC 45). However, a reading of legislation which 'departs substantially from a fundamental feature of an Act of Parliament is likely to have crossed the boundary between interpretation and amendment' (*Re S (Minors) (Care Order: Implementation of Care Plan)* [2002] UKHL 10, [2002]

91.3

2 AC 291, per Lord Nicholls of Birkenhead at [40]). The courts will not interpret legislation in a way which would effectively amend it. It must be possible to give the provision as it stands the Convention-compatible interpretation required by **s. 3** (*R (Wilkinson) v Commissioners of Inland Revenue* [2005] UKHL 30, [2005] 1 WLR 1718).

However, the House of Lords has held that the courts have in the past concentrated excessively on the linguistic features of the particular statute. Their lordships rejected a literal approach and instead emphasised a broad approach, which concentrated in a purposive way on the importance of the fundamental right involved (*Ghaidan v Godin-Mendoza* [2004] UKHL 30, [2004] 2 AC 557).

Declaration of incompatibility

91.4 Under the **Human Rights Act 1998, s. 4**, where the court is satisfied that a provision in primary legislation is incompatible with a Convention right, it may make a declaration of incompatibility. Such a declaration may also be made in proceedings in which a court considers that a provision of subordinate legislation, made in the exercise of a power conferred by primary legislation, is incompatible. Declarations of incompatibility may only be made in respect of subordinate legislation where the court is satisfied that (disregarding any possibility of revocation) the primary legislation concerned prevents removal of the incompatibility. A person cannot apply for a declaration of incompatibility unless he is adversely affected by the legislation in question (*Taylor v Lancashire County Council* [2005] EWCA Civ 284, [2005] 1 WLR 2668).

A declaration of incompatibility may be made only by the High Court, Court of Appeal or Supreme Court (**s. 4(5)**). Such a declaration is not binding on the parties to the proceedings in which it is made and does not affect the validity, continuing operation or enforcement of the provision in respect of which it is given (**s. 4(6)**). A declaration of incompatibility does, however, enable Parliament to amend the relevant legislation through a fast-track procedure.

The court may not make a declaration of incompatibility unless 21 days' notice, or such other period of notice as the court directs, has been given to the Crown. Where notice has been given to the Crown, a minister or other person permitted by the Act shall be joined as a party on giving notice to the court (**CPR, r. 19.4A(2)**). The Crown should be joined to the proceedings in advance of any appeal hearing in which an issue is raised which might lead the Supreme Court to consider making a declaration of incompatibility (*R v A* [2001] 1 WLR 789).

A number of declarations of incompatibility have been made by the courts, including declarations in respect of:

(a) the Mental Health Act 1983, s. 73, which placed the burden of proof on a restricted patient to show that he was no longer suffering from a mental disorder warranting detention in order to satisfy the mental health review tribunal that he was entitled to discharge, contrary to **art. 5** of the Convention (*R (H) v Mental Health Review Tribunal, North and East Region* [2001] EWCA Civ 415, [2002] QB 1);

(b) part 2 of the Immigration and Asylum Act 1999, which penalised carriers of illegal immigrants into the United Kingdom, in breach of **art. 6** of the Convention (*International Transport Roth GmbH v Secretary of State for the Home Department* [2002] EWCA Civ 158, [2003] QB 728);

(c) the Social Security Contributions and Benefits Act 1992, ss. 36 to 38, which applied a different treatment of benefits as between widows and widowers, contrary to **art. 8** of the Convention (*R (Hooper) v Secretary of State for Work and Pensions* [2005] UKHL 29, [2005] 1 WLR 1681);

(d) the Matrimonial Causes Act 1973, s. 11(c), which requires a marriage to be between a man and a woman in order for it to be valid, contrary to **arts 8** and **12** of the Convention (in the context of post-operative transsexuals applying for a marriage declaration) (*Bellinger v Bellinger* [2003] UKHL 21, [2003] 2 AC 467);

(e) the Housing Act 1996, s. 185(4), which had the effect that a person who had been subject to immigration control was not afforded the same priority need for accommodation as a comparable person who had not been subject to immigration control, thus infringing **art. 14** in conjunction with **art. 8** (*R (Morris) v Westminster City Council* [2005] EWCA Civ 1184, [2006] 1 WLR 505);

(f) the Care Standards Act 2000, s. 82(4)(b), pursuant to which care workers could be provisionally listed as unsuited to working with vulnerable adults, without giving them an opportunity to answer the allegations, contrary to **arts 6(1)** and **8(1)** (*R (Wright) v Secretary of State for Health* [2009] UKHL 3, [2009] 1 AC 739).

It appears that the declaration of incompatibility procedure cannot extend to breaches of positive rights. That is, the absence of a provision guaranteeing a particular Convention right in statute does not in itself mean that the statute is incompatible with **art. 6(1)** of the Convention, but rather signifies at most the existence of a lacuna in the statute (see Lord Nicholls of Birkenhead in *Re S (Minors) (Care Order: Implementation of Care Plan)* [2002] UKHL 10, [2002] 2 AC 291 at p. 322).

Statement of compatibility

Since 24 November 1998, under the **Human Rights Act 1998, s. 19**, a minister of the Crown **91.5** in charge of a Bill in either House of Parliament has been required before the second reading of the Bill:

(a) to make a statement to the effect that in his or her view the provisions of the Bill are compatible with Convention rights ('a statement of compatibility'); or

(b) to make a statement to the effect that although he or she is unable to make a statement of compatibility the government nevertheless wishes the House to proceed with the Bill.

This statement must be in writing and be published in such manner as the minister making it considers appropriate. The statement of compatibility is designed to minimise the number of domestic statutes that are incompatible with Convention rights.

Obligations of public authorities

The **Human Rights Act 1998, s. 6**, requires public authorities to act in a way which is com- **91.6** patible with Convention rights. **Section 6(1)** provides that: 'It is unlawful for a public authority to act in a way which is incompatible with a Convention right'. An 'act' includes a failure to act but, by **s. 6(6)**, does not include a failure: (a) to introduce in, or lay before, Parliament a proposal for legislation; or (b) to make any primary legislation or remedial order.

The Act provides no exhaustive definition of a public authority. Bodies such as government departments, local authorities, the police and health authorities will clearly be considered public authorities. In addition to these traditional public authorities, the definition of a public authority also includes bodies 'certain of whose functions are functions of a public nature' (**s. 6(3)**) and these are known as quasi-public authorities. Traditional public organisations must act in accordance with the Convention in respect of all their functions — whether under public or private law — but quasi-public authorities are only required to conform to the Convention in relation to public functions and not private law matters. For example, doctors in general practice will be considered as public authorities in relation to their National Health Service functions, but not in relation to their private patients.

A housing association generally is not a public authority for the purposes of **s. 6** (*R (Heather) v Leonard Cheshire Foundation* [2001] EWHC Admin 429, [2002] 2 All ER 936) nor is a private-sector service provider which has a contractual relationship with a local authority to supply residential accommodation (*R (Servite Houses) v Goldsmith* (2001) 33 HLR 35). However, a housing association may be deemed to be a public authority if it was created by a local authority which controls it and has an integrated relationship with it (*Poplar Housing and Regeneration Community*

Association Ltd v Donoghue [2001] EWCA Civ 595, [2002] QB 48). Similarly, a private limited company set up by a local authority to manage local farmers' markets and having as directors, stallholders in those markets, was a public authority since the company owed its existence to the authority and initially worked alongside it (*R (Beer) v Hampshire Farmers Market Ltd* [2003] EWCA Civ 1056, [2004] 1 WLR 233).

In all cases it is necessary to look at the context and the basis on which a private law body acted, with the ultimate focus on the nature of the functions undertaken. The State can in some circumstances remain responsible for the conduct of a private body to which it has delegated State powers, but the mere possession of special powers conferred by Parliament does not of itself mean that the body has functions of a public nature. Equally there could be bodies without special statutory powers that fall within the definition of public authority. Where a body acted as a private, profit-making company, that motivation would point against treating it as a body with functions of a public nature (see *YL v Birmingham City Council* [2007] UKHL 27, [2008] 1 AC 95, where it was decided that a private care home, when providing care to a resident pursuant to agreements made with a local authority under the relevant legislation, was not performing functions of a public nature within the meaning of s. 6(3)(b)). On the other hand, in *R (Weaver) v London and Quadrant Housing Trust* [2009] EWCA Civ 587, [2010] 1 WLR 363, it was held that a registered social landlord was performing a public function for the purposes of s. 6(3)(b) when it terminated a tenancy. The Court of Appeal found that the function of allocating and managing subsidised housing was a governmental function and that the act of termination was so inextricably linked to that function that it was also a public act. It was found that it would severely limit the significance of identifying certain bodies as hybrid or quasi-public authorities if the fact that the relevant act was contractual meant that it was necessarily a private act falling within s. 6(5).

Bodies which have been held not to be a public authority for the purposes of s. 6 include: a parochial church council in the context of its service of notices on lay rectors, living in church property, requiring them to fund necessary repairs to the chancel (*Aston Cantlow and Wilmcote with Billesley Parochial Church Council v Wallbank* [2003] UKHL 37, [2004] 1 AC 546); the RSPCA in the context of its intention to adopt a policy to exclude from membership persons whose application was for the real or predominant purpose of bringing about a change in RSPCA policy in respect of field sports (*Royal Society for the Prevention of Cruelty to Animals v Attorney General* [2002] 1 WLR 448); an adjudicator exercising functions under the Housing Grants, Construction and Regeneration Act 1996 (*Austin Hall Building Ltd v Buckland Securities Ltd* [2001] BLR 272); the Jockey Club (*R (Mullins) v Appeal Board of the Jockey Club* [2005] EWHC 2197 (Admin), [2006] ACD 2) and Railtrack (*Cameron v Network Rail Infrastructure Ltd* [2006] EWHC 1133 (QB), [2007] 1 WLR 163).

Section 6(2) may provide a defence to an allegation of a breach of the Convention under s. 6(1) either if the public authority could not have acted differently under the relevant statute (s. 6(2)(a)) or if the public authority was acting so as to give effect to the relevant legislation (s. 6(2)(b)) (e.g. *R (Hooper) v Secretary of State for Work and Pensions* [2005] UKHL 29, [2005] 1 WLR 1681).

Section 6(3) expressly includes courts and tribunals as public authorities. Courts and tribunals therefore will be bound to act in a manner that is compatible with the Convention. Unless legislation explicitly states otherwise, judges need to be mindful of the Convention in all proceedings, even those involving only private parties. The Act is therefore developing a degree of *horizontal effect* between private individuals and companies as well as the intended *vertical effect* between public authorities and individuals, both because of s. 6 and because of the Convention's influence on the common law, as in *Douglas v Hello! Ltd* [2001] QB 967. It has been held that s. 6 does not require an appellate court to determine afresh issues relating to Convention rights, but only to conduct a review of the lower court's decision. Review of a purely discretionary decision will be conducted on the basis of whether the lower court exceeded the generous ambit within which reasonable disagreement is possible, whereas the test for an evaluative decision (such as the proportionality of a care order) is whether the lower court was wrong (*Re B (A Child) (Care Proceedings: Appeal)* [2013] UKSC 33, [2013] 1 WLR 1911).

Both Houses of Parliament are outside the definition of public authority (**s. 6(3)**).

Victims

Proceedings alleging a breach of Convention rights may only be brought by a 'victim' (**Human Rights Act 1998, s. 7**). The term 'victim' in this context has a more restrictive definition than that used to establish standing in judicial review. Companies and individuals are able to invoke the Convention. Although the point has not been fully argued, it seems that parents of a minor whose human rights have been breached do have standing to complain as victims under **s. 7** (*R (Holub) v Secretary of State for the Home Department* [2001] 1 WLR 13590). However, public-interest and pressure groups are unable to bring claims based on the **Human Rights Act 1998** unless a 'victim' is found to act as a figurehead applicant (e.g. *Greenpeace Schweiz v Switzerland* (application 27644/95) (1997) 23 EHRR CD 116). A trade association is not a victim for this purpose (*Re Medicaments and Related Classes of Goods (No. 4)* [2001] EWCA Civ 1217, [2002] 1 WLR 269). A local authority cannot be a victim for the purposes of **s. 7** (*R (Westminster City Council) v Mayor of London* [2002] EWHC 2440 (Admin), [2003] LGR 611), nor can an NHS trust (*Grampian University Hospitals NHS Trust v Napier* 2004 JC 117). The expected recipient of a pending decision is not a victim for the purposes of **s. 7** because no act or decision capable of being the subject of judicial review has taken place (*R (Hirst) v Secretary of State for the Home Department* [2002] EWHC 1592 (Admin)).

91.7

Time limits

Cases against public bodies alleging a breach of the Convention must be brought within one year of the date on which the relevant act took place (**Human Rights Act 1998, s. 7(5)**). This time limit may be extended where the court considers it equitable to do so, weighing in the balance all the circumstances of the case including the culpable delay in bringing proceedings, the length of the delay, the degree of prejudice to the defendant, the issue of proportionality and the issue of overall fairness (*Bedford v Bedfordshire County Council* [2013] EWHC 1717 (QB), [2014] PTSR 351). For instance, the court has granted an extension in circumstances where the cause of the delay is out of the claimant's hands and the balance of potential prejudice lies in the claimant's favour in the context of a well-founded claim alleging serious shortcomings that need to be properly explored (*D v Commissioner of Police of the Metropolis* [2012] EWHC 309 (QB), LTL 23/2/2012). However, the time limit would not be extended where the claimant had known about the relevant matters for some time, no adequate reason had been given for the delay and where a trial date had been set and may well be jeopardised by an extension allowing further claims to be made (*XYZ v Chief Constable of Gwent* [2014] EWHC 1448 (QB), LTL 3/4/2014). Where another rule imposes a shorter time limit (e.g. the judicial review time limit) the shorter time limit prevails (**s. 7(5)**).

91.8

Remedies

The **Human Rights Act 1998, s. 8**, provides that in relation to any act (or proposed act) of a public authority which the court finds is (or would be) unlawful, it may grant such relief or remedy or make such order within its powers as it considers just and appropriate. A court may grant any remedy which it deems appropriate provided that it has jurisdiction to grant that remedy (**s. 8(1)**).

91.9

Damages may be awarded only by a court which has power to make such an award, or to order the payment of compensation, in civil proceedings **s. 8(2)**. No award may be made unless the court is satisfied that such an award is necessary to 'afford just satisfaction to the person in whose favour it is made' **s. 8(3)** and in considering an award, a court must take into account all the circumstances of the case including:

(a) any other relief or remedy granted, or order made, in relation to the act in question (by that or any other court); and

(b) the consequences of any decision (of that or any other court) in respect of that act.

In determining whether to award damages or the amount of an award, the court must take into account the principles applied by the European Court of Human Rights in relation to the award of compensation under art. 41 of the Convention. Article 41 also proceeds on the basis of affording 'just satisfaction'. There is no automatic entitlement to an award of damages and the Strasbourg court's decision is guided by the particular circumstances of each case having regard to equitable considerations. The European Court of Human Rights often holds that no award of damages should be made since a finding of violation may itself constitute sufficient 'just satisfaction' (e.g. *R (Greenfield) v Secretary of State for the Home Department* [2005] UKHL 14, [2005] 1 WLR 673). Otherwise, the court's awards of damages are usually modest although in some cases, particularly relating to an infringement of property rights, such as expropriation, substantial damages may be awarded. Although the court may be asked to consider detailed factual issues of quantum, given the inherently public law nature of human rights claims, such matters are still suitable to be dealt with by the Queen's Bench Division rather than needing to be transferred to the Commercial Court (*Breyer Group v Department for Energy and Climate Change* [2016] EWHC 763 (Comm), LTL 29/2/2016).

Where an individual was detained under powers conferred by the Mental Health Act 1983, and then later applied for the Mental Health Review Tribunal to review the detention, delays occurring in the hearings of those applications were held to constitute an infringement of **art. 5(4)** and an award for damages under **art. 5(5)** would be made 'where necessary' if on the facts the distress and frustration that occurred justified such an award (*R (B) v Mental Health Review Tribunal* [2002] EWHC 1553 (Admin), [2003] MHLR 19). Similarly, in relation to custodial sentences damages should ordinarily be awarded where it is established that the prisoner was detained longer than he otherwise would have been, with the frustration and delay which is presumed to arise from delay generally requiring a modest award of damages (*R (Faulkner) v Secretary of State for Justice* [2013] UKSC 23, [2013] 2 AC 254). See also *R (Hester) v Secretary of State for Justice* [2011] EWHC 3926 (Admin), LTL 20/12/2011. There may even be occasions where aggravated damages under **art. 5** will be appropriate. In *R (M) v Secretary of State for the Home Department* [2011] EWHC 3667 (Admin), [2012] ACD 34, the Secretary of State's behaviour in removing the claimant family on an erroneous ground, failing to notify them in advance of their removal and her subsequent delay in admitting the unlawful nature of the detention and removal justified such a remedy.

In assessing quantum an English court should derive assistance from similar Strasbourg cases rather than from English decisions in analogous cases (*van Colle v Chief Constable of the Hertfordshire Police* [2007] EWCA Civ 325, [2007] 1 WLR 1821; reversed on another point [2008] UKHL 50, [2009] 1 AC 225). See also *Anufrijeva v Southwark London Borough Council* [2003] EWCA Civ 1406, [2004] QB 1124 and *Gas and Electricity Markets Authority v Infinis plc* [2013] EWCA Civ 70, [2013] JPL 1037. In respect of damages for a breach of **art. 8**, damages need not be limited to compensation for distress caused but may also include an element to compensate for the misuse of victims' private information (*Gulati v MGN Ltd* [2015] EWCA Civ 1291, [2016] 2 WLR 1217). Damages may be awarded for future infringement of rights under the **Human Rights Act 1998** (*Marcic v Thames Water Utilities Ltd (No. 2)* [2001] EWHC Technology 394, [2002] QB 1003; although on the facts there was no infringement: *Marcic v Thames Water Utilities Ltd* [2003] UKHL 66, [2004] 2 AC 42).

An individual applicant in judicial review proceedings is not entitled to claim damages under the **Human Rights Act 1998** in respect of a local authority's conduct in breach of the European Convention on Human Rights, on the basis that proceedings for judicial review are not brought 'by or at the instigation of a public authority' under the **Human Rights Act 1998, s. 22(4)** (*R (Ben-Abdelaziz) v Haringey London Borough Council* [2001] EWCA Civ 803, [2001] 1 WLR 1485).

The Strasbourg court also has the power to make a costs order.

Judicial acts

Courts and tribunals are public authorities for the purposes of the **Human Rights Act 1998** (by **s. 6(3)**) but **s. 9** provides that proceedings in respect of a judicial act may be brought only: **91.10**

(a) by exercising a right of appeal;
(b) on an application for judicial review; or
(c) in such other forum as may be prescribed by rules.

Any rule of law which prevents a court from being the subject of judicial review is not affected (**s. 9(2)**). Where proceedings are brought in respect of a judicial act done in good faith, damages may be awarded to compensate the victim only to the extent required by **art. 5(5)** of the Convention (which provides that everyone who has been the victim of arrest or detention in contravention of the provisions of **art. 5** shall have an enforceable right to compensation) (**s. 9(3)**). For these purposes there is no clear definition of bad faith, but a judge will be considered to have been acting in bad faith if he or she was acting for a purpose ulterior to his or her judicial function (*Webster v Lord Chancellor* [2015] EWCA Civ 742, [2016] QB 676).

A claim in respect of a judicial act maybe brought only in the High Court (**CPR, r. 7.11(1)**). Where a claim is in respect of a judicial act which is alleged to have infringed the claimant's **art. 5** rights and which is based on a finding by a court or tribunal that the claimant's Convention rights have been infringed, the court hearing the claim (a) may proceed on the basis of the finding of that other court or tribunal that there has been an infringement but it is not required to do so, and (b) may reach its own conclusion in the light of that finding and of the evidence heard by that other court or tribunal (**CPR, r. 33.9**).

Where a claim is made under the **Human Rights Act 1998** for damages in respect of a judicial act that claim must be set out in the statement of case or the appeal notice; and notice must be given to the Crown. Where the appropriate person has not applied to be joined as a party within 21 days, or such other period as the court directs, after the notice is served, the court may join the appropriate person as a party (**CPR, r. 19.4A**).

Proceedings affecting the right to freedom of expression

The **Human Rights Act 1998, s. 12**, applies where a court (or tribunal) is considering granting relief in civil proceedings which might affect the exercise of the right to freedom of expression (**s. 12(1) and (5)**). The court must not grant such relief if the person against whom the application is made (the respondent) is not present, unless the court is satisfied that the applicant has taken all practicable steps to notify the respondent or there are compelling reasons why the respondent should not be notified (**s. 12(2)**). No relief is to be granted so as to restrain publication before trial, unless the court is satisfied that the applicant is likely to establish that publication should not be allowed (**s. 12(3)**). This means that an applicant's prospects of success at trial must be sufficiently favourable to justify an order being made in the particular circumstances of the case and a court will be 'very slow' to make an interim restraint order unless satisfied that the applicant is more likely than not to succeed at trial, but there will be cases where a lesser degree of likelihood will suffice (*Cream Holdings Ltd v Banerjee* [2004] UKHL 44, [2005] 1 AC 253 and see, e.g. *E v Channel Four* [2005] EWHC 1144 (Fam), [2005] 2 FLR 913). The court must have 'particular regard' to the importance of the right of freedom of expression (**s. 12(4)**). If the proceedings relate to journalistic, literary or artistic material the court is required by **s. 12(4)** to have particular regard to two conflicting factors: **91.11**

(a) the extent to which the material has, or is about to, become available to the public, or it is, or would be, in the public interest for the material to be published; and
(b) any relevant privacy code.

Commentary

CONVENTION RIGHTS

Derogation from Convention rights

91.12   The Convention rights which are incorporated into domestic law are set out in the **Human Rights Act 1998, sch. 1**. The articles detailing the Convention rights fall into three broad groups: those which are absolute, those which may be derogated from and those which are qualified. Those that are absolute must never be infringed by any of the Convention States. An example is **art. 3**, which prohibits torture or inhuman or degrading treatment. Some rights may be derogated from, for example, in times of war or other emergency which threatens a State. The United Kingdom entered a derogation, which was set out in **sch. 3** to the Act, from **art. 5** of the Convention (right to liberty and security) so that foreign nationals who were suspected international terrorists thought to be a risk to national security could be detained indefinitely to await deportation but this was held by the House of Lords to be disproportionate and discriminatory (*A (FC) v Secretary of State for the Home Department* [2004] UKHL 56, [2005] 2 AC 68) and has been withdrawn.

Certain rights are qualified in order to balance the competing interests of individuals as against the public interest or, indeed, the interests of other individuals. Qualified rights are, therefore, rights with which a State may legitimately interfere in the interests of the protection of others or of the State itself. Qualified rights are set out in **arts 8 to 11**, all of which provide that interference with the rights must be in accordance with the law and pursuant to a legitimate aim.

In addition, any interference with a qualified Convention right must be necessary in a democratic society and consequently 'correspond to a pressing social need' (*Dudgeon v United Kingdom* (1981) 4 EHRR 149) and 'be proportionate to the legitimate aim pursued' (*Silver v United Kingdom* (applications 5947/72, 6205/73, 7052/75, 7061/75, 7107/75, 7113/75, 7136/75) (1983) 5 EHRR 347). State intervention in the lives of individuals should be minimal, and the duty of the State to protect legitimate aims does not permit it to restrict disproportionately the rights of individuals. When considering whether or not a measure is proportionate the court is to conduct a balancing exercise 'between the demands of the general interests of the community and the requirement of the protection of the individual's fundamental rights' (*Soering v United Kingdom* (application 14038/88) (1989) 11 EHRR 439).

Proportionality

91.13   When considering whether Convention rights have been breached, the European Court of Human Rights has employed the principle of 'proportionality'. Proportionality is established if the legislative objective is sufficiently important to justify limiting a fundamental right, the measures designed to meet the legislative objective are rationally connected to that objective, and the means used to impair the right are no more than necessary to accomplish the legitimate objective (*De Freitas v Permanent Secretary of Ministry of Agriculture, Fisheries, Lands and Housing* [1999] 1 AC 69; *Bank Mellat v HM Treasury (No. 2)* [2013] UKSC 39, [2014] AC 700; and see, e.g. *R (Countryside Alliance) v Attorney General* [2005] EWHC 1677 (Admin), [2005] NPC 107; [2006] EWCA Civ 817, [2007] QB 305; [2007] UKHL 52, [2008] 1 AC 719).

The proportionality of any interference may now be an issue in any consideration by the courts of certain articles of the Convention. Proportionality has to be considered in two distinct stages, first to ask whether the objective of the measure could be achieved by means involving less interference with an individual's rights, and secondly, to ask whether the measure has an excessive or disproportionate effect on the interests of affected persons. In deciding this last question, the Strasbourg Court assesses whether a fair balance has been struck between the individual's rights and those of the State (*R (Samaroo) v Secretary of State for the Home*

Department [2001] UKHRR 1150). The question of whether a fair balance has been struck between the rights of the individual and the rights of the community as a whole is an important one which should never be overlooked in assessing proportionality (*Huang v Secretary of State for the Home Department* [2007] UKHL 11, [2007] 2 AC 167, citing *R (Razgar) v Secretary of State for the Home Department* [2004] UKHL 27, [2004] 2 AC 368). See also **77.20**. A measure may be disproportionate by reason of its being discriminatory in some respect which is incapable of objective justification (*Bank Mellat v HM Treasury (No. 2)*). An objective justification would require that the discrimination is itself proportionate (*Humphreys v Commissioners of HM Revenue and Customs* [2012] UKSC 18, [2012] 1 WLR 1545).

Where Convention rights are in question as part of a judicial review, therefore, the court must not simply exercise a review function but should instead consider for itself whether the relevant Convention rights have been violated (*Secretary of State for the Home Department v Nasseri* [2009] UKHL 23, [2010] 1 AC 1). However, the level of judicial scrutiny will depend on the significance of the right, the degree of interference and the factors capable of justifying the interference. The court has to test the adequacy of the factual basis of the decision, consider whether the objective was necessary and review the rationality of the decision as a means of achieving the objective. While the court is the ultimate arbiter of the appropriate balance between the Convention rights engaged and the justifications for interfering with the rights, it should not remake a decision reasonably open to the decision-maker and the court is entitled to attach special weight to the judgement of a decision-maker with special institutional competence (*R (Lord Carlile of Berriew) v Secretary of State for the Home Department* [2014] UKSC 60, [2015] AC 945).

Margin of appreciation

When considering whether Convention rights, particularly qualified rights, have been breached, the European Court of Human Rights has employed the concept of the 'margin of appreciation', which permits a State latitude in the manner in which it takes and enforces public policy decisions. This makes allowances for each country's cultural and political identities as it adopts and adapts to this international treaty. For example, what might constitute free speech in one country could be interpreted as an invasion of privacy in another. However, the doctrine cannot directly be applied to cases where United Kingdom courts interpret Convention rights under the **Human Rights Act 1998** because domestic courts can be expected to have a better understanding of domestic issues than the Strasbourg court. The domestic application of this doctrine was examined by Lord Hope of Craighead in *R v Director of Public Prosecutions, ex parte Kebilene* [2000] 2 AC 326. He recognised that in certain areas (e.g. economic and social policy) the executive will be given an area of judgment within which the judiciary will defer to the decision in question.

91.14

ARTICLES OF THE CONVENTION INCORPORATED INTO THE HUMAN RIGHTS ACT 1998

Article 2: right to life

Article 2 establishes a country's positive duty to take steps to safeguard the lives of its citizens, and sets out the limited exceptions to the right to life. These centre on the maintenance of law and order and focus on curbing violence and controlling criminals and prisoners. The overriding objective is to limit the level of permissible force to that which is 'absolutely necessary'.

91.15

Article 3: prohibition of torture

Article 3 prohibits torture and inhuman or degrading treatment or punishment. This article cannot be derogated from even in times of war and public emergency. **Article 3**, together with

91.16

Commentary

the common law position and other international conventions, requires that evidence obtained by torture should be inadmissible as unreliable, unfair and offensive to ordinary standards of humanity and decency. Whether and in what circumstances this rule could be overridden must be left to the legislature, and would require nothing short of an express legislative provision. Evidence should not be admitted where it is concluded on a balance of probabilities that it was obtained by torture. If there is doubt as to whether the evidence was obtained by torture or not, then it should be admitted but the doubt should be borne in mind when evaluating the evidence (*A v Secretary of State for the Home Department (No. 2)* [2005] UKHL 71, [2006] 2 AC 221). Also inherent in **art. 3** is the obligation on the State to conduct an investigation into allegations of ill-treatment by private individuals, although the nature of that obligation varies depending on the seriousness of the alleged breach (*D v Commissioner of Police of the Metropolis* [2015] EWCA Civ 646, [2016] QB 161).

Article 4: prohibition of slavery and forced labour

91.17 There can be no derogation from this article under any circumstances.

Article 5: right to liberty and security of person

91.18 Article 5 aims to ensure that no one is deprived of liberty in an arbitrary fashion. It provides that a person can be deprived of liberty only in limited cases.

Article 6: right to a fair trial

91.19 Article 6(1) provides:

> In the determination of his civil rights and obligations or of any criminal charge against him, everyone is entitled to a fair and public hearing within a reasonable time by an independent and impartial tribunal established by law. Judgment shall be pronounced publicly but the press and public may be excluded from all or part of the trial in the interest of morals, public order or national security in a democratic society, where the interests of juveniles or the protection of the private life of the parties so require, or to the extent strictly necessary in the opinion of the court in special circumstances where publicity would prejudice the interests of justice.

91.20 **Scope of article 6(1)**   In addition to court and arbitration hearings, **art. 6(1)** will cover other proceedings which determine rights or obligations. For example, **art. 6(1)** applies to disciplinary proceedings which determine the right of someone to practise a profession (*Le Compte v Belgium* (applications 6878/75 and 7238/75) (1982) 4 EHRR 1). On the other hand, for example, a reprimand or the imposition of a fine following a disciplinary hearing held in private by a domestic tribunal of the Law Society does not involve a determination of civil rights and obligations and therefore **art. 6** is not engaged (*R (Thompson) v Law Society* [2004] EWCA Civ 167, [2004] 1 WLR 2522). **Article 6(1)** has no relevance to an investigation under the Companies Act 1985, part 14, which makes a critical report, as this does not determine the criticised person's rights (*Fayed v United Kingdom* (application 17101/90) (1994) 18 EHRR 393). An assessment of refugee status does not amount to civil proceedings for the purposes of **art. 6** (*HH (Iran) v Secretary of State for the Home Department* [2008] EWCA Civ 504, LTL 14/4/2008). The right to accommodation given by the Children Act 1989, s. 20, is (probably) not a civil right for the purposes of **art. 6** (*R (A) v Croydon London Borough Council* [2008] EWCA Civ 1445, [2009] 1 FLR 1325; [2009] UKSC 8, [2009] 1 WLR 2557 at [45] and [65]). Indeed, any situations where the award of services or benefits depends on a series of evaluative judgments by the provider, rather than being rights of which the applicant could consider himself the holder, would not give rise to 'civil rights' and therefore would not engage **art. 6(1)**. Rights to accommodation under the Housing Act 1993 fall within this category (*Ali v Birmingham City Council* [2010] UKSC 8, [2010] 2 AC 39). If there is no exercisable right in domestic law then there will be no right to a determination under **art. 6** (*R (Kehoe) v Secretary of State for Work and Pensions* [2005] UKHL 48, [2006] 1 AC 42).

'Civil rights and obligations' are given an autonomous meaning. For example, the right to practise medicine was held to be a civil right despite its domestic categorisation as public (*König v Germany* (application 6232/73) (1979–80) 2 EHRR 170).

The classification of proceedings as 'civil' will not conclusively determine whether a matter should be regarded as civil. When considering whether a matter is civil or criminal (with the additional safeguards which attach to the latter) the European Court of Human Rights looks at three factors: (a) how the proceedings are classified in domestic law; (b) the nature of the offence; and (c) the possible sanctions (*Engel v Netherlands* (applications 5100/71, 5101/71, 5102/71, 5354/72 and 5370/72) (1979–80) 1 EHRR 647). For example, proceedings to obtain an anti-social behaviour order are civil (*Clingham v Kensington and Chelsea Royal London Borough Council* [2002] UKHL 39, [2003] 1 AC 787).

The European Court of Human Rights has held that substantive tax matters are outside the scope of **art. 6** (*Ferrazzini v Italy* [2001] STC 1314). Although the imposition of tax surcharges does not determine any civil rights or obligations within **art. 6** (*Bancroft v Crutchfield* [2002] STC 347), a VAT assessment has been held to determine a civil right, but not a criminal charge, on the basis that it is civil in nature and there is no penal or deterrent element (*Ali v Commissioners of Customs and Excise* (2002) LTL 15/7/2002). Proceedings brought in a magistrates' court for condemnation of goods seized by customs officers are civil not criminal (*R (Mudie) v Dover Magistrates' Court* [2003] EWCA Civ 237, [2003] QB 1238) and the same classification applies to an application for restoration of goods seized by customs officers (*Gora v Commissioners of Customs and Excise* [2003] EWCA Civ 525, [2004] QB 93). Determinations of penalties by the Commissioners of Inland Revenue (*King v Walden* [2001] STC 822) and the imposition of penalties by Customs and Excise for dishonest evasion of VAT (*Han v Commissioners of Customs and Excise* [2001] EWCA Civ 1040, [2001] 1 WLR 2253) have been held to be criminal but the imposition of a fixed penalty of £50 for a failure to supply documents and information pursuant to a notice was held to be civil (*Sharkey v Commissioners of HM Revenue and Customs* [2006] EWHC 300 (Ch), [2006] STC 2026).

It is possible for a party to expressly or impliedly waive rights under **art. 6**. Where criminal proceedings were found to be incompatible with the offenders' rights under **art. 6** but the offenders had delayed by more than two years in objecting to those proceedings, this was held to be acquiescence to the resulting convictions and sentences (*Ruddy v Procurator Fiscal* [2006] HRLR 16). Parties who enter into arbitration agreements are contracting into the restricted supervisory regime of the Arbitration Act 1996. These restricted provisions are not inconsistent with the Convention. Equally if they mutually agreed to exclude a right of appeal altogether, that would not be contrary to **art. 6** as they had preferred the 1996 process and could not therefore be permitted to rely on **art. 6** (*Sumukan Ltd v Commonwealth Secretariat* [2007] EWCA Civ 243, [2007] Bus LR 1075). A party could be taken to have waived his right to go to court under **art. 6** in favour of the arbitral process (*Stretford v Football Association Ltd* [2007] EWCA Civ 238, [2007] Bus LR 1052). However, if there was duress or undue influence which invalidated the arbitration agreement, there would be no waiver of relevant rights under **art. 6** (*El Nasharty v J. Sainsbury plc* [2007] EWHC 2618 (Comm), [2008] 1 Lloyd's Rep 360).

Rights protected by article 6   The **art. 6(1)** requirement to provide a fair hearing breaks down into various rights: **91.21**

(a)   The right of access to a court, which is an integral part of **art. 6(1)** despite not being expressly set out there (*Jones v Ministry of the Interior of Saudi Arabia* [2004] EWCA Civ 1394, [2005] UKHRR 57 reversed in part, although not on this point, [2006] UKHL 26, [2007] 1 AC 270). The right of access is not absolute, but limitations must be proportionate and legitimate, and should not restrict or reduce the access in such a way that the essence of the right is impaired (*Jones v United Kingdom* (applications 34356/06 and 40528/06) (2014) 59 EHRR 1). For example, the **Fatal Accidents Act 1976, s. 2(3)** (which provides that not more than one action should lie for and in respect of the same subject matter of complaint), has been construed in such a way as to safeguard the right of access to a court (*Cachia v Faluyi* [2001] EWCA Civ 998, [2001] 1 WLR

1966). The State Immunity Act 1978 was also considered incompatible with the right of access to a court in seeking to prevent employment law claims being brought against embassies, and a declaration of incompatibility was made in this regard (*Benkharbouche v Embassy of the Republic of Sudan* [2015] EWCA Civ 33, [2016] QB 347) but note the contrary conclusion was reached in *Ogelegbanwei v President of the Federal Republic of Nigeria* [2016] EWHC 8 (QB), LTL 22/1/2016 where the court considered the relevant provisions of the State Immunity Act 1978 to be a proportionate method of pursuing a legitimate aim.

(b) A hearing in one's own presence. There is a right to an oral hearing although in a civil trial a party has the right to be present only if the tribunal is required to carry out an appraisal of his or her personal character (*Muyldermans v Belgium* (application 12217/86) (1993) 15 EHRR 204).

(c) Equality of arms. In putting its case, a party must not be put at a substantial disadvantage as regards the opposing party. Thus, for example, each party must have the same opportunity to summon witnesses and each party must have an opportunity to oppose the arguments advanced by the other side. Both the common law and the Convention regard fairness as including the need for the court to know, before it reaches its conclusion, what the parties have to say about the issues and the evidence that the court has before it. Where the judge in an Admiralty claim has sought advice from nautical assessors, for example, that advice should be disclosed to the parties for them to make their own representations as to whether the judge should accept the advice (*Bow Spring (Owners) v Manzanillo II (Owners)* [2004] EWCA Civ 1007, [2005] 1 WLR 144).

(d) Prejudicial publicity. There should be no commentary which prejudges the accused in a criminal trial.

(e) Reasoned judgment. Judgments must be supported by reasoning. The extent and substance of the reasons depend upon the circumstances. They need not be elaborate or lengthy, but they should be such as to tell the parties in broad terms why the decision was reached (*Stefan v General Medical Council* [1999] 1 WLR 1293).

(f) A public hearing. An oral public hearing must be available unless exceptional circumstances dictate otherwise (*Werner v Austria* (application 21835/93) (1998) 26 EHRR 310). This is not absolute but can be limited only to the extent that is 'strictly necessary...in special circumstances'.

(g) A hearing within a reasonable time. Numerous factors will have a bearing on what constitutes a reasonable time from the commencement of proceedings to the final determination of the case, for instance, the importance of the subject matter, the difficulties of the case, whether they be legal or factual, and the behaviour of the individual and the public body (e.g. *EDC v United Kingdom* [1998] BCC 370 concerning the length of time taken to deal with directors disqualification proceedings).

(h) An independent and impartial tribunal. To assess independence, it is necessary to have regard to the manner of appointment of a tribunal's members, their term of office, the existence of guarantees against outside pressures and whether the body presents an appearance of independence (*Bryan v United Kingdom* (application 19178/91) (1996) 21 EHRR 342). The appearance of independence of any tribunal is to be assessed on an objective basis. 'Impartial' means lack of prejudice or bias (*Piersack v Belgium* (application 8692/79) (1983) 5 EHRR 169). A tribunal and its members are to be presumed impartial unless proved otherwise (*Le Compte v Belgium* (applications 6878/75 and 7238/75) (1982) 4 EHRR 1). The court will examine the actual prejudices, if any, the tribunal holds and also whether undertakings given by the tribunal are sufficient to exclude doubts over impartiality (see further **61.27** and **77.25**).

(i) A tribunal established by law. The de facto doctrine validates the acts as well as the office of a judge, where he mistakenly presides over a court without proper authority, when the world at large believes that he has proper authority (*Coppard v Commissioners of Customs and Excise* [2003] EWCA Civ 511, [2003] QB 1428).

91.22 **Specific guarantees in criminal cases**   Article 6(2) preserves the principle that the accused is innocent until proved guilty. It does not, however, prevent a burden being placed on the accused to prove a defence. Nor does it prohibit presumptions of law or fact. Strict liability offences are acceptable under **art. 6(2)** so long as they still require the prosecution to establish the elements of the offence (*Salabiaku v France* (application 10589/83) (1991) 13 EHRR 379).

Article 6(3) guarantees five further rights in criminal cases. These lay down the minimum requirements for procedural fairness in a criminal trial. They are not exhaustive. Indeed, **art. 6(1)** may require further protection to be given than is provided for by **art. 6(3)**. The **art. 6(3)** rights are the right to be informed of a charge, adequate time and facilities for the preparation of a defence, legal representation including legal aid, attendance and examination of witnesses and free translation. In *Kulkarni v Milton Keynes Hospital NHS Foundation Trust* [2009] EWCA Civ 789, [2010] ICR 101, the Court of Appeal suggested that the right to legal representation may extend to internal disciplinary proceedings where the consequence of such proceedings would be the end of an individual's professional career.

Article 7: no punishment without lawful authority

Article 7 protects citizens against retrospective criminal laws. A defendant may not be convicted in a criminal case when the relevant action was not illegal at the time it was carried out. **91.23**

Article 8: right to respect for private and family life

Article 8(1) provides that 'Everyone has the right to respect for his private and family life, his **91.24** home and his correspondence'. This article imposes primarily negative obligations on the State not to disclose or delve into personal matters confidential to an individual.

Private life has been held to have a broad definition including the protection of corporeal rights, personal identity, private space, and respect for sexual orientation (*Dudgeon v United Kingdom* (1982) 4 EHRR 149). As a result, for instance, compulsory blood (*X v Austria* (1979) 18 DR 154) and urine (*Peters v Netherlands* (1994) 77-A DR 75) tests and severe corporal punishment (*B v United Kingdom* (1998) 5 BHRC 137) have been found to violate **art. 8**. Not only does respect for the home include a residence but it can also include an office and business premises (*Niemietz v Germany* (application 13710/88) (1993) 16 EHRR 97). However, it is unclear whether or not a company can have a right to a private life. In *R v Broadcasting Standards Commission, ex parte British Broadcasting Corporation* [2001] QB 885 it was held that the BBC's actions in surreptitiously filming on a company's premises constituted an unwarranted infringement of the company's privacy under the Broadcasting Act 1996. However, Lord Woolf MR emphasised that the meaning of privacy in this context was not the same as under **art. 8** of the Convention. Lord Mustill, whilst concurring on the facts, regarded privacy as an 'essentially human and personal concept' and could not see how it could apply to a company, 'which has no sensitivities to wound, and no selfhood to protect'. However, the decision of the European Court of Human Rights in *Société Colas Est v France* (application 37971/97) (2004) 39 EHRR 17 suggests that a company may have **art. 8** rights. Although the case concerned the question of whether the protection offered by **art. 8** covered the right to respect for a company's registered office, branches or other business premises, building on the *Niemietz* case, the Court also noted that:

Building on its dynamic interpretation of the Convention, the Court considers that the time has come to hold that in certain circumstances the rights guaranteed by art. 8 of the Convention may be construed as including the right to respect for a company's registered office, branches or other business premises.

This is supported by *R (Amro International SA) v Financial Services Authority* [2010] EWCA Civ 123, [2010] Bus LR 1541, in which the court commented that **art. 8** 'is or may be engaged' in respect of documents being obtained in a corporate context and therefore proportionality must be considered. A definitive ruling on whether a company can claim under **art. 8** is, however, still awaited.

Commentary

The definition of family life is broad including family relationships between husband and wife and parent and child (*Johansen v Norway* (application 17383/90) (1997) 23 EHRR 33). Ties between unmarried couples (*Kroon v Netherlands* (application 18535/91) (1995) 19 EHRR 263), parents and their illegitimate children (*Johnston v Ireland* (application 9697/82) (1987) 9 EHRR 203) and grand-parents and grandchildren (*Marckx v Belgium* (application 6833/74) (1979–80) 2 EHRR 330) have also fallen into this category.

Unauthorised settlement on one's own land (in a caravan occupied without planning permission) falls within the concept of 'home' under art. 8 (*Buckley v United Kingdom* (application 20348/92) (1997) 23 EHRR 101).

Article 8(1) is qualified by **art. 8(2)**. Any interference by a public authority with the exercise of the rights guaranteed by **art. 8(1)** must both be in accordance with the law and also be necessary in a democratic society in the interests of national security, public safety or the economic well-being of the country, for the prevention of disorder or crime, for the protection of health or morals, or the protection of the rights and freedoms of others. No interference with the right under **art. 8(1)** may be greater than is necessary to achieve its intended objective.

Rights under **art. 8** may be violated when the State obtains personal and private details about an individual without his or her consent and without statutory authority. For example, the making of non-party disclosure orders for witness evidence given to the police in proceedings can raise **art. 8** issues such that the court must conduct a proper balancing exercise taking into account all the circumstances and objections (*Mitchell v News Group Newspapers Ltd* [2014] EWHC 879 (QB), LTL 2/4/2014). In *Halford v United Kingdom* (application 20605/92) (1997) 24 EHRR 523 it was established that interference with private telephone calls made at work in a private office on a personal line was a breach of **art. 8**. See also *Khan v United Kingdom* (application 35394/97) (2001) 31 EHRR 45, where **art. 8** was held to be infringed by the police obtaining evidence using a covertly installed listening device at the applicant's home, and *Armstrong v United Kingdom* (application 48521/99) (2003) 36 EHRR 30. A statutory framework for the interception of communications and covert surveillance by security, law enforcement and other public authorities is provided by the Regulation of Investigatory Powers Act 2000. The government believes that action taken in accordance with that Act will be 'in accordance with the law' for the purposes of **art. 8(2)**.

It appears that **art. 8(1)** has effectively given rise to a limited cause of action generating rights to equitable remedies and damages for breach of confidence, albeit there is no freestanding cause of action for breach of privacy (see *Wainwright v Home Office* [2003] UKHL 53, [2004] 2 AC 406; but cf. *Wainwright v United Kingdom* (application 12350/04) (2007) 44 EHRR 40; see also **91.55**). **Article 8** is also capable of being infringed by noise resulting from schemes implemented by public authorities if it seriously affects an individual's private life. The absence of any possibility of a grant to help protect against the noise, or any compensation, is capable of negativing any justification for interference with the **art. 8** right (*Andrews v Reading Borough Council* [2004] EWHC 970 (Admin), [2004] UKHRR 599).

Article 9: freedom of thought, conscience and religion

91.25   **Article 9** establishes the right to manifest religion and beliefs, rather than simply to hold particular views. For example, a parent's religious convictions are a relevant consideration for a local education authority when considering the admission of a child to a particular school (*R (K) v Newham London Borough Council* [2002] EWHC 405 (Admin), [2002] ELR 390). **Article 9(2)** provides that this freedom may be limited by law where necessary in a democratic society in the interests of public safety, for the protection of public order, health or morals or for the protection of the rights and freedoms of others (see, for example, *R (Shabina Begum) v Denbigh High School* [2006] UKHL 15, [2007] 1 AC 100).

Article 10: freedom of expression

Article 10(1) provides that: **91.26**

Everyone has the right to freedom of expression. This right shall include freedom to hold opinions and to receive and impart information and ideas without interference by public authority and regardless of frontiers. This Article shall not prevent States from requiring the licensing of broadcasting, television or cinema enterprises.

The term 'expression' has been given a broad definition and includes words, works of art (*Müller v Switzerland* (application 10737/84) (1991) 13 EHRR 212), images (*Chorherr v Austria* (application 13308/87) (1994) 17 EHRR 358) and dress (*Stevens v United Kingdom* (1986) 46 DR 245). The types of expression covered include political, journalistic, artistic and commercial expression. All legal entities including companies are protected by **art. 10** (*Autronic AG v Switzerland* (application 12726/87) (1990) 12 EHRR 485). The right to freedom of expression also includes the right to be provided with information (*Open Door Counselling and Dublin Well Woman v Ireland* (applications 14234/88 and 14235/88) (1993) 15 EHRR 244).

Generally, **art. 10(1)** is qualified by **art. 10(2)** in that it:

may be subject to such formalities, conditions, restrictions or penalties as are prescribed by law and are necessary in a democratic society, in the interests of national security, territorial integrity or public safety, for the prevention of disorder or crime, for the protection of health or morals, for the protection of the reputation or rights of others, for preventing the disclosure of information received in confidence, or for maintaining the authority and impartiality of the judiciary.

In practice, commercial and artistic expression have tended to receive less protection from the Strasbourg court than political or journalistic expression, although the court requires a strong justification for interfering with the right to freedom of expression and will need to be satisfied that the restriction is 'prescribed by law' and that a pressing 'social need' is 'convincingly established' (*Handyside v United Kingdom* (application 5493/72) (1979–80) 1 EHRR 737). The right to freedom of expression carries with it certain responsibilities which include avoiding expression which does not contribute to public debate and which is gratuitously offensive to others (*Otto-Preminger Institute v Austria* (application 13470/87) (1995) 19 EHRR 34). Additionally, when an individual agrees or contracts to limit his or her freedom of expression, generally actions by the State will not be interpreted as an interference (*Vereniging Rechtswinkels Utrecht v Netherlands* (1986) 46 DR 200).

Article 11: freedom of assembly and association

Article 11 provides not only the freedom of peaceful assembly but also guarantees the right to   **91.27** public processions and meetings both in private and in public and includes the right to form and join trade unions. The right in **art. 11** can be limited by restrictions prescribed by law which are necessary in a democratic society in the interests of national security or public safety, for the prevention of disorder or crime, for the protection of health or morals or for the protection of the rights and freedoms of others.

Article 12: right to marry

Article 12 provides the right to marry and found a family. **Article 12** rights apply to those   **91.28** already married and those intending to marry. The legislation concerning adoption of children falls within **art. 12**.

Article 14: prohibition of discrimination in enjoyment of Convention rights

Article 14 establishes the principle of equality of application of the Convention. The rights   **91.29** and freedoms protected by the Convention must be available to everyone regardless of sex, race, colour, language, religion, political or other opinion, national or social origin, association with a national minority, property, birth or other status.

The following test is guidance for the application of **art. 14**:

(a) Do the facts of the case fall within the ambit of one or more of the substantive Convention provisions?

(b) Is there different treatment as respects the Convention right between the complainant on the one hand and other persons put forward by comparison ('the chosen comparators') on the other?

(c) Are the chosen comparators in an analogous situation to the complainant's situation?

(d) If so, does the difference have an objective and reasonable justification, or, otherwise stated, does it pursue a legitimate aim, and does the differential treatment bear a reasonable relationship of proportionality to the aim sought to be achieved?

(e) Is the difference in treatment based on one or more of the grounds prescribed, expressly or by inference, in **art. 14**?

(See also *Ghaidan v Godin-Mendoza* [2004] UKHL 30, [2004] 2 AC 557; *A v Secretary of State for the Home Department* [2004] UKHL 56, [2005] 2 AC 68.)

However, it is not always necessary to follow the sequential analysis set out in *Michalak v Wandsworth London Borough Council* (see *R (Carson) v Secretary of State for Work and Pensions* [2005] UKHL 37, [2006] 1 AC 173, where the House of Lords recognised that the *Michalak* questions did not suit every case and context, although they may be useful in some cases; and note *Carson v United Kingdom* (application 42184/05) (2009) 48 EHRR 41).

In deciding whether a comparator enjoying preferential treatment is in an analogous or relevantly similar situation it is pertinent to have regard to the purpose of the measure in question. The ground for differential treatment must amount to status in the sense of a personal characteristic concerning what a person is, rather than historical fact or what he was doing or what had been done to him (*R (S) v Chief Constable of the South Yorkshire Police* [2004] UKHL 39, [2004] 1 WLR 2196; *R (RJM) v Secretary of State for Work and Pensions* [2008] UKHL 63, [2009] 1 AC 311). A personal characteristic cannot be defined by the differential treatment of which a person complains. The length of sentence to be served by a prisoner was not found to fall within the 'other status' ground of **art. 14**, as it depended not on a personal characteristic but on what the prisoner had done (*R (Clift) v Secretary of State for the Home Department* [2006] UKHL 54, [2007] 1 AC 484). Overall a generous meaning should be given to the term 'other status' and the term 'personal characteristic' simply requires concentration on what somebody is, rather than what he is doing or what is done to him. Therefore homelessness is a personal characteristic and an 'other status' for the purposes of **art. 14**, despite being a voluntary choice, not being a legal status and not having previously been recognised as a status by the European Court of Human Rights (the issue never having been raised before that court) (*R (RJM) v Secretary of State for Work and Pensions*). Being a prisoner is also accepted as an 'other status' (*Shelley v United Kingdom* (application 23800/06) (2008) 46 EHRR SE16). However, whereas discrimination on any of the core or primary grounds listed in **art. 14**, such as sex or race, is regarded as 'suspect' and therefore requires intense scrutiny, discrimination on other grounds merely requires some rational justification (*Stewart v Secretary of State for Work and Pensions* [2011] EWCA Civ 907, [2011] UKHRR 1048). Discrimination on the grounds of disability, which is not among the core grounds listed in **art. 14**, has received special treatment in this regard. The court has accepted that disability discrimination may fall into the 'suspect' group of grounds because of its recognition in domestic law and numerous international instruments (*AM (Somalia) v Entry Clearance Officer* [2009] EWCA Civ 634, (2009) UKHRR 1073).

In matters of general economic and social policy, the court will apply a wide margin of appreciation and only interfere where the policy is 'manifestly without reasonable foundation', even in relation to the core grounds listed in **art. 14** (*Humphreys v Commissioners of Revenue and Customs* [2012] UKSC 18, [2012] 1 WLR 1545). Further, the court has found that in cases of indirect discrimination the proportionality review must be conducted by way of the usual rather than enhanced standard (*Burnip v Birmingham City Council* [2012] EWCA Civ 629, [2013] PTSR 117).

Administrative convenience cannot be a sufficient justification for discrimination without some other justification as to why those in analogous or relevantly similar situations are being excluded (*Francis v Secretary of State for Work and Pensions* [2005] EWCA Civ 1303, [2006] 1 WLR 3202). It is accepted, however, that seeking to clear a backlog of cases to allow subsequent cases to be dealt with more efficiently is a legitimate aim for any administrative system. With that overall aim in mind it was acceptable to apply different treatment to young adults with parents (whose right to family life was engaged) and young adults who were without parents (where the only right engaged was the private life of the young adults in question), given that there was not differential treatment in relation to exactly the same Convention right (*AL (Serbia) v Secretary of State for the Home Department* [2008] UKHL 42, [2008] 1 WLR 1434).

The trigger for the application of **art. 14** is whether the facts in issue 'fall within the ambit' of one or more of the other Convention provisions (see *Secretary of State for Work and Pensions v M* [2006] UKHL 11, [2006] 2 AC 91), but the finding of a violation under **art. 14** is not dependent on first establishing a violation of some other Convention right (*Michalak v Wandsworth London Borough Council* [2002] EWCA Civ 271, [2003] 1 WLR 617).

Article 16: restrictions on political activity of aliens

Article 16 establishes that nothing in **arts 10** (freedom of expression), **11** (freedom of assembly and association) and **14** (prohibition against discrimination) shall prevent governments from imposing restrictions on the political activities of aliens (a term which includes stateless persons). **91.30**

Article 17: prohibition of abuse of rights

Article 17 states that the Convention may not be interpreted as allowing any State, group or person any right to participate in any activities aimed at the destruction of any of the rights and freedoms set out in the Convention. **91.31**

Article 18: limitation on use of restrictions of rights

Article 18 states that restrictions on rights under the Convention cannot be applied for any purposes other than those for which those restrictions have been prescribed. **Article 18** (like **art. 14**) may not be used individually but only in conjunction with a claim for a breach of some other article of the Convention. **91.32**

Article 1 of the First Protocol: protection of property

Article 1 of the First Protocol provides that: **91.33**

Every natural or legal person is entitled to the peaceful enjoyment of his possessions. No one shall be deprived of his possessions except in the public interest and subject to the conditions provided for by law and by the general principles of international law.

However, this provision does not in any way impair the right of a State to enforce such laws as it deems necessary to control the use of property in accordance with the general interest or to secure the payment of taxes or other contributions or penalties.

A diverse number of economic interests are included within this article, including not only tangible interests such as a house, but shares, patents, the entitlement to a pension, the right to exercise a profession and even a legal claim, so long as it is concrete and adequately specified.

According to the European Court of Human Rights in *Sporrong v Sweden* (applications 7151/75 and 7152/75) (1983) 5 EHRR 35, in order to show that **art. 1** of the First Protocol has been violated, it must be demonstrated that:

(a) the peaceful enjoyment of the applicant's possessions has been interfered with by the State; or

(b) the applicant has been deprived of possessions by the State; or

(c) the applicant's possessions have been subjected to control by the State.

These rights are to be balanced against the State's rights to interfere with the peaceful enjoyment of property in the public interest or to control use of property in accordance with the general interest. There is a wide margin of appreciation although an interference with property, including raising taxes, must be proportionate.

Any deprivation under **art. 1** of the First Protocol must be necessary and proportionate. In the context, necessary means reasonably necessary, rather than strictly or absolutely necessary. The test of what is necessary is driven by a balancing exercise, rather than by a requirement to use the approach which is least intrusive of Convention rights (*R (Clays Lane Housing Co-operative Ltd) v Housing Corporation* [2004] EWCA Civ 1658, [2005] 1 WLR 2229).

Failure by a sewerage undertaker to carry out works to bring an end to repeated flooding to the claimant's property did not constitute an unjustifiable interference with the claimant's rights under **art. 1** of the First Protocol and **art. 8** of the Convention (*Marcic v Thames Water Utilities Ltd* [2003] UKHL 66, [2004] 2 AC 42). By contrast, the imposition of financial penalties upon lorry drivers and haulage companies under the Immigration and Asylum Act 1999, as persons responsible for clandestine entrants into the United Kingdom, was incompatible with both **art. 6** of the Convention and **art. 1** of the First Protocol (*International Transport Roth GmbH v Secretary of State for the Home Department* [2002] EWCA Civ 158, [2003] QB 728).

Retrospective legislation will not of itself necessarily be incompatible with **art. 1** of the First Protocol but special justification, beyond being necessary to achieve the aims of the legislation, is required for retrospective changes which affect or upset legitimate expectations (*Re Recovery of Medical Costs for Asbestos Diseases (Wales) Bill* [2015] UKSC 3, [2015] AC 1016).

Article 2 of the First Protocol: right to education

91.34   **Article 2** of the First Protocol establishes that no one shall be denied the right to education and that the State shall respect the right of parents to ensure such education and teaching is in conformity with their own religious and philosophical convictions. Education has been defined to include primary and secondary education, and the European Commission of Human Rights has accepted that access to university education may be limited. The United Kingdom has made a reservation adopting this Article only 'so far as it is compatible with the provision of efficient instruction and training, and the avoidance of unreasonable public expenditure'.

Article 3 of the First Protocol: right to free elections

91.35   **Article 3** of the First Protocol provides that States must hold elections at regular intervals which will allow the free expression of the opinion of the people in choosing the legislature.

Thirteenth Protocol: abolition of the death penalty

91.36   **Article 1** of the Thirteenth Protocol abolishes the death penalty and provides that no one shall be condemned to such penalty or executed.

IMPACT OF THE HUMAN RIGHTS ACT 1998
ON CIVIL LITIGATION

91.37   Although **Human Rights Act 1998** points may be raised in civil litigation, they need to be raised carefully and only in appropriate circumstances. There have been a number of cases where bad arguments have been raised and there has been judicial comment about taking a responsible attitude to when it is right to raise a **Human Rights Act 1998** point. For example, Lord Woolf MR was critical of such points being raised in a case management context (*Daniels v Walker* [2000] 1 WLR 1382) and Mummery LJ has also said that the temptation to turn a court hearing into an international human rights seminar should be resisted (*Williams v Cowell* [2000] 1 WLR 187). In instances where the European Convention on Human Rights has been cited in domestic law, judges have been reluctant to accept 'the deployment of generalised propositions from the Convention' (*R v North West Lancashire Health Authority, ex parte A* [2000] 1 WLR 977) and simply referring to the Convention without specific case law is regarded as unhelpful to the court in doing justice to an argument (*Barclays Bank plc v Ellis* [2001] CP Rep 50). However, the Court of Appeal has accepted that the **Human Rights Act 1998** provides the courts with an extra tool for interpreting the language of a rule of court so as to produce a just result and avoid any question of the violation of a litigant's right to a fair trial under **art. 6** of the Convention (*Goode v Martin* [2001] EWCA Civ 1899, [2002] 1 WLR 1828).

The manner and formalities by which evidence is provided to the court to permit it to take account of European Court of Human Rights judgments, decisions, declarations or opinions are set out in rules which specify the law reports or other versions of cases which may be used and require that parties give the court and other parties three days' notice of the authorities they intend to cite (**PD 39A, para. 8.1**).

RIGHT TO A FAIR AND PUBLIC HEARING AND CIVIL LITIGATION

Presence of litigant

In order to comply with the requirements of **art. 6** of the Convention, an adjournment will **91.38** usually have to be granted for a litigant whose presence is needed for the fair trial of a case but who is unable to attend through no fault of his own, although the applicant for the adjournment must be able to demonstrate that the inability to attend is genuine (*Teinaz v Wandsworth London Borough Council* [2002] EWCA Civ 1040, [2002] ICR 1471).

The right to attend a civil trial and give evidence is not an absolute right. The question in every individual case is whether, viewed as a whole, the trial process is fair. It is unlikely that any party has an absolute right to be present throughout proceedings; this would need to be balanced against the interests of other parties (*Zambia v Meer Care and Desai* [2006] EWCA Civ 390, [2006] 1 CLC 436). See also *Dhillon v Asiedu* [2012] EWCA Civ 1020, [2012] CP Rep 44; *Three Mile Inn Ltd v Daley* [2012] EWCA Civ 970, LTL 27/8/2012.

Equality of arms

Courts are bound to give effect to the overriding objective set out in **CPR, r. 1.1(1)**, 'to deal **91.39** with cases justly' and are given guidelines in **r. 1.1(2)** as to how this might be achieved. **Article 6** of the European Convention on Human Rights introduces the principle of equality of arms. It has been held that notwithstanding these principles, the court has no power to veto a party's choice of legal representative. In *Maltez v Lewis* (1999) 16 Const LJ 65, a party who could only afford less experienced representation than her opponent, who had instructed leading counsel, argued that this was against the 'level playing field envisaged by the CPR. As a consequence, it was submitted that her opponent should be debarred from instructing such experienced counsel. It was held that the court could not interfere with a party's choice of legal representative, but that any imbalance could be dealt with in other ways, for example, by allowing a smaller firm of solicitors more time to carry out work or requiring a larger firm to prepare bundles for the court. The principle of equality of arms should not affect the approach adopted in *Maltez v Lewis*. In *R v Bow County Court, ex parte Pelling* [1999] 1 WLR 1807 the refusal to allow the claimant to act as a McKenzie friend was held not to contravene **art. 6(1)**.

Equality of arms was considered in *R v Secretary of State for the Home Department, ex parte Quaquah* [2000] HRLR 325, in which the Secretary of State was not allowed to remove the claimant from the United Kingdom while he was pursuing an outstanding claim for damages for malicious prosecution against the Home Office. The claimant was entitled to have adequate time and facilities to pursue his tort claim.

Limitation periods

91.40   Limitation periods must be considered in the light of the right of access to a court. Although the effect of a limitation period is to prevent a claimant having a hearing, this does not infringe **art. 6(1)** of the European Convention on Human Rights, provided the limitation period is proportionate (*Pérez de Rada Cavanilles v Spain* (application 28090/95) (2000) 29 EHRR 109). Limitation periods fulfil legitimate aims, including certainty and conclusiveness and prevent courts being forced to consider claims where evidence is either no longer available or not reliable. Where the time limit reflects a proportionate pursuit of these aims, it will be acceptable. However, a particularly strict application of a three-day time limit for requesting a judgment to be set aside was held to be contrary to **art. 6** (*Pérez de Rada Cavanilles v Spain* (application 28090/95) (2000) 29 EHRR 109). Conversely in *Stubbings v United Kingdom* (applications 22083/93 and 22095/93) (1997) 23 EHRR 213 the European Court of Human Rights endorsed the application of a six-year limitation period so as to bar a claim arising out of alleged sexual abuse (but see now *A v Hoare* [2008] UKHL 6, [2008] 1 AC 844). A 14-day time limit to challenge the valuation of livestock was held to be compatible with **art. 6** (*J. and P. M. Dockeray v Secretary of State for the Environment, Food and Rural Affairs* [2002] EWHC 420 (Admin), [2002] HRLR 27) and a two-month time limit under **CPR, r. 74.8**, for filing a notice of appeal was held to be compliant with **art. 6**, notwithstanding that the court had jurisdiction under **r. 3.1(2)(a)** to extend time (*Citibank NA v Rafidian Bank* [2003] EWHC 1950 (QB), [2003] 2 All ER (Comm) 1054). In circumstances where the time limit cannot be extended for good reason or where the ability to extend is extremely limited, issues may arise.

There is doubt about whether the obligation to apply 'promptly' in judicial review is sufficiently certain to comply with **art. 6** (*R (Burkett) v Hammersmith and Fulham London Borough Council* [2002] UKHL 23, [2002] 1 WLR 1593). However, the European Court of Human Rights has dismissed a complaint that the judicial review time limit of 'promptly and in any event within three months' is misleading and contrary to the principles of legal certainty because of the inconsistent and discretionary views taken by the domestic courts of the applicable time limits. The European Court of Human Rights regarded the time limit as a strict procedural requirement which served a public-interest purpose, namely, the need to avoid prejudice being caused to third parties who may have altered their situation on the strength of administrative decisions. The time limit is not contrary to **art. 6** (*Lam v United Kingdom* (application 41671/98) decision 5 July 2001).

As a consequence of **art. 6**, substitution of parties to a claim so that a new party is being sued may be allowed even after a limitation period has expired. Where the claimant sought to substitute an individual named solicitor for a firm of solicitors as defendant, it was clear that she had always intended to sue this solicitor, indeed he was mentioned by name in her particulars of claim. There was no cause of action against the firm but only against the individual solicitor. The approach to be taken in light of **art. 6** was to interpret rules of court so as to produce a just result and avoid unjustifiable infringement of a litigant's right of access to court. Substitution should be allowed even though the limitation period had expired (*Kesslar v Moore and Tibbits* [2004] EWCA Civ 1551, [2005] PNLR 17).

CPR, r. 17.4 (which prohibits amendment of a statement of case to include a new claim for which the limitation period has expired if the new claim does not arise out of the same facts as the original claim), has been interpreted broadly in the light of the right of access to a court (*Goode v Martin* [2001] EWCA Civ 1899, [2002] 1 WLR 1828; see **31.25**).

Strike-out applications and default and summary judgment

The court has a duty actively to manage cases (**CPR, r. 1.4** and **Part 26**). This includes decid-   **91.41**
ing promptly which issues need full investigation and trial and accordingly disposing summarily of the others (**r. 1.4(2)(c)**). The power to make orders for summary disposal of issues
includes the power to strike out a statement of case in whole or in part under **r. 3.4**, in addition to the power to give summary judgment under **Part 24**, where a claimant or defendant
has no reasonable prospect of success. These powers may be exercised on the court's own initiative, without hearing the parties or giving them an opportunity to make representations
(**r. 3.3(4)**).

One issue is whether striking out for failure to comply with procedural rules or orders is a
denial of the right of access to a court. In *Canada Trust Co. v Stolzenberg* (unreported, 14 October
1998) a party who failed to comply with an unless order unsuccessfully claimed he had been
deprived of the right to a fair trial contrary to **art. 6** of the European Convention on Human
Rights. The court held that he had deprived himself of that right by his own non-compliance.
Similarly, in *JSC BTA Bank v Ablyazov (No. 8)* [2012] EWCA Civ 1411, [2013] 1 WLR 1331, the appellant was found to have absconded after he had been found guilty of contempt of court, and
the court made an unless order striking out his defence unless he surrendered to court. In
circumstances where the appellant had forfeited the opportunity for trial by his non-compliance
with an order which was entirely within the power of the court to make, there could be no
breach of his rights. However, in *Re Swaptronics Ltd* (1998) *The Times*, 17 August 1998, and *Arrow
Nominees Inc. v Blackledge* [2000] 1 BCLC 709 (point not considered on appeal) it was held that
striking out as a penalty for contempt of court could only be consistent with **art. 6** if the
contempt led to a 'real risk' that a fair trial could not happen. In relation to abuse of process,
it has been held that the modern doctrine on this subject is compliant with **art. 6**, and further
that a litigant's right under **art. 6** does not confer immunity from the normal disciplines of
civil procedure (*Barnett v Nigel Hall Menswear Ltd* [2013] EWHC 91 (QB), LTL 5/2/2013).

A defendant's right to a fair trial was not violated by the operation of **CPR, rr. 6.5(6)** and **6.7**,
as they were worded before 1 October 2008, which deemed that the claim form and particulars of claim had been served even though he had not received them (*Akram v Adam* [2004]
EWCA Civ 1601, [2005] 1 WLR 2762). The judge had found that the defendant had no defence,
and there was therefore no need to set aside the judgment in default and make the claimant
apply for summary judgment, with all the time and expense that would involve. **Article 6** does
not, as of right, entitle the defendant to a trial or oblige the claimant to show on some other
occasion that the defendant has no arguable defence.

Refusal to set aside a judgment entered in default of compliance of an unless order raises an
art. 6 issue as the losing party would be deprived of a trial of his defence on the merits, but the
State can impose restrictions on the right of access to a court provided they serve a legitimate
aim, are proportionate and do not destroy the very essence of the right. The legitimate aim of
imposing the sanction of judgment in default of compliance is to secure compliance with court
orders (*CIBC Mellon Trust Co. v Stolzenberg* [2004] EWCA Civ 827, *The Independent*, 2 July 2004).
However, this needs to be balanced with the fundamental right to a fair trial and therefore in
some circumstances a party will still be given the opportunity properly to present his or her case
and evidence despite failure to comply with orders of the court (*Apex Global Management Ltd v Fi
Call Ltd* (2014) LTL 2/12/2014).

The summary judgment procedure has been held to be compliant with **art. 6(1)** (*Monsanto plc
v Tilly* [2000] Env LR 313; *S v Gloucestershire County Council* [2001] Fam 313). Care must be taken
where the grant of summary judgment would interfere with the right of a journalist to freedom of expression (*Al Misnad v Azzaman Ltd* [2003] EWHC 1783, LTL 22/7/2003).

Convention rights may also be relevant where claims are struck out on the ground that there
is no cause of action. This question has arisen in the context of claims against public

Commentary

authorities in negligence. In *Osman v United Kingdom* (application 23452/94) (2000) 29 EHRR 245 the European Court of Human Rights held that it was a breach of the applicant's **art. 6(1)** right of access to a court to strike out a negligence claim on the basis that the imposition of a duty of care would not be fair, just or reasonable. However, in its subsequent judgments in *TP v United Kingdom* (application 28945/95) [2001] 2 FLR 549 and *Z v United Kingdom* (application 29392/95) [2001] 2 FLR 612 the European Court of Human Rights effectively overruled *Osman* and held that there was no violation of the right of access to a court in such cases. The European Court of Human Rights did, however, hold that in striking out negligence claims arising from local authorities' exercise of their child protection functions, the English courts had denied the claimants an effective remedy for violations of certain substantive Convention rights, contrary to **art. 13** of the Convention (which has not been incorporated into United Kingdom law). These decisions might suggest that the courts should not strike out negligence claims which affect substantive Convention rights, but since an apparently effective remedy is now available under the **Human Rights Act 1998**, the right of access under **art. 6** is likely to have a very limited application to the striking out of negligence claims or other civil claims.

Although *Osman* can no longer be regarded as correct, the effect of English decisions since *Osman* is that some cases which might previously have been the subject of a strike-out application will instead have to proceed to trial (*Barrett v Enfield London Borough Council* [2001] 2 AC 550). Although Lord Woolf MR held in *Kent v Griffiths* [2001] QB 36 at p. 51, that cases should still be struck out when the position is clear, many English judges now seem to regard questions about the existence of a duty of care in negligence as difficult matters which should generally be decided only after careful consideration of the evidence at trial (e.g. Lord Browne-Wilkinson in *Barrett*; Otton LJ in *L (A Child) v Reading Borough Council* [2001] 1 WLR 1575; and see *D v East Berkshire Community Health NHS Trust* [2005] UKHL 23, [2005] 2 AC 373; note also *Matthews v Ministry of Defence* [2003] UKHL 4, [2003] 1 AC 1163).

Time limits and delay

91.42   The CPR aim at dispensing justice without delay and provide sanctions where parties have failed to comply with time limits imposed for carrying out steps in litigation (see **r. 3.4(2)** and **chapter 48**). **Article 6(1)** of the European Convention on Human Rights requires the hearing of the merits of a claim to take place within a reasonable time. It is possible to invoke **art. 6(1)** when opposing applications for time extensions, although delay in proceedings will not of itself violate **art. 6(1)**, unless the delay is found to be unreasonable (*Darnell v United Kingdom* (application 15058/89) (1994) 18 EHRR 205; *Re Swaptronics Ltd* (1998) *The Times*, 17 August 1998). Civil proceedings will only be struck out as an abuse of process by reason of the claimant's delay where it would no longer be possible for the defendant to receive a fair trial (*Re McHugh Southern Ltd* [2002] EWHC 3069 (Ch), *The Times*, 30 January 2003).

However, where criminal proceedings, from the time of the initial arrest to the time when the applicant was finally refused leave to appeal to the House of Lords, lasted eight years and five months, of which there were four years and three months of almost total inactivity, that amounted to breach of **art. 6(1)**, particularly considering that the applicant's liberty was involved. The relevant factors to have regard to are the complexity of the case, the conduct of the applicant and the relevant authorities and the importance of what was at stake for the applicant (*Crowther v United Kingdom* (application 53741/00) (2005) *The Times*, 11 February 2005). See also *Minshall v United Kingdom* (application 7350/06) (2012) 55 EHRR 36. Similarly, where it took four years to deal with costs questions there was a violation of **art. 6(1)** (*Robins v United Kingdom* (application 22410/93) (1998) 26 EHRR 527).

When considering whether to stay proceedings (for example, until the determination of parallel disciplinary proceedings), the court must consider the significance of taking any step which impinges on a litigant's right to have issues determined by a court within a reasonable time under **art. 6(1)**. The burden is on the applicant seeking a stay to demonstrate through cogent evidence that there are sound reasons for granting a stay (*Wakefield v Channel Four Television Corporation* [2005] EWHC 2410 (QB), LTL 4/11/2005).

A breach of the right in **art. 6** to a hearing within a reasonable time might ground a claim to a just and appropriate remedy but would not entitle a defendant to a stay or dismissal of the proceedings against him unless there could no longer be a fair hearing or it would otherwise be unfair to continue with the proceedings against him (*Secretary of State for Trade and Industry v Davies* [2006] EWHC 299 (Ch), [2006] 2 BCLC 489; see also *Eastaway v Secretary of State for Trade and Industry* [2007] EWCA Civ 425, [2008] 1 BCLC 153).

The principle that it is not possible to rebut, by evidence of the actual date of receipt, the presumption that service of a claim form occurred on the day deemed by CPR, r. 6.7, as it was worded before 1 October 2008, is compatible with **art. 6** (*Anderton v Clwyd County Council (No. 2)* [2002] EWCA Civ 933, [2002] 1 WLR 3174).

Directions and evidence

As part of its case management powers, the court has power to exclude an issue from considera- **91.43** tion (**CPR, r. 3.1(2)(k)**) and power to control evidence by giving directions about the issues on which it requires evidence, the nature of the evidence which it requires to decide those issues and the way in which the evidence is to be placed before the court, as well as the power to limit cross-examination (**r. 32.1**). The court's failure properly to exercise its case management powers may be a breach of **art. 6**. In *Re M (A Child)* [2012] EWCA Civ 1905, LTL 22/11/2012 the court considered a fact-finding hearing which had concluded that the father of the child was responsible for her non-accidental injuries. The failure of the judge at that hearing to allow the father, who had a low IQ and limited cognitive abilities, to benefit from recommended protective measures when giving his evidence was a breach of his Convention rights. As a general principle, parties in family proceedings should be represented (*P v United Kingdom* (application 56547/00) (2002) 35 EHRR 31). Where a father's solicitors had stopped acting shortly before a hearing relating to his application for contact with his daughter, and fresh evidence showed that the father was a vulnerable applicant, the judge's refusal to grant an adjournment to allow new counsel to be appointed was in breach of **art. 6** (*Re L (A Child) (Application Hearing)* [2013] EWCA Civ 267, [2013] 2 FLR 1444). Receipt of hearsay evidence, consisting of statements made by someone who cannot be cross-examined, does not inevitably prevent a fair trial under **art. 6** (*Clingham v Kensington and Chelsea Royal London Borough Council* [2002] UKHL 39, [2003] 1 AC 787). However, failure by the prosecution to lay evidence before the trial judge and thus permit him to rule on the question of disclosure is contrary to **art. 6** (*Atlan v United Kingdom* (application 36533/97) (2002) 34 EHRR 33). The court's refusal to permit a party to give evidence by way of video link in order to avoid the risk of being arrested on warrant should he return to the United Kingdom was held not to pay sufficient regard to **art. 6** and the need to ensure that the parties were on an equal footing (*Rowland v Bock* [2002] EWHC 692 (QB), [2002] 4 All ER 370). Taking a child's evidence by video link in a criminal case did not contravene the defendant's right to a fair trial under **art. 6** (*R (D) v Camberwell Green Youth Court* [2005] UKHL 4, [2005] 1 WLR 393).

The rules on the use of experts encourage the use of a single joint expert and permit the court to control the manner in which the expert investigates the issues as well as limiting the amount which the expert may be paid for his or her services (**CPR, r. 35.8(3)(b) and (4)(a)**).

These rules must be seen in the context of the right to a fair trial in **art. 6(1)** of the European Convention on Human Rights. **Article 6(1)** does not guarantee the right to call expert evidence, save where it is necessary to ensure the fairness of the proceedings. **CPR, r. 35.1**, requires the court to restrict expert evidence, and **r. 35.7** allows it to direct that evidence shall be given by a single joint expert instructed by both parties. The appointment of a single joint expert will not be contrary to **art. 6(1)**, although the right to a fair trial may demand that the parties participate equally in the preparation of the expert's report, including attending interviews and examining the documents on which the report is based (*Mantovanelli v France* (application 21497/93) (1997) 24 EHRR 370). In *Daniels v Walker* [2000] 1 WLR 1382 the judge refused to allow a defendant, who was dissatisfied with the instructions to a joint expert and the resulting report, to instruct another expert of his own. Lord Woolf MR accepted that additional questions could be put to the expert, but rejected the defendant's argument that the procedure conflicted with **art. 6(1)**. The overriding objective of the CPR, which requires the court to deal with cases 'justly', enables it to ensure that all CPR procedures operate in accordance with **art. 6**.

The power of a court to regulate its own procedures is subject to limitations. There is no power in the CPR, nor any common law power, to adopt a procedure in ordinary civil litigation whereby one party would not be allowed access to evidence and would be excluded from part of the trial (a closed material procedure). Where a trial involves evidence that is sensitive, for example, on national security grounds, the public interest immunity test exists, which is consistent with the right to a fair trial since it does not exclude one party and there is therefore no unfairness or inequality of arms. Any departure from the ordinary principles of open and natural justice, which a closed material procedure would be, must be explicitly authorised by Parliament (*Al-Rawi v Security Service* [2011] UKSC 34, [2012] 1 AC 531).

Following this decision, Parliament has enacted part 2 of the Justice and Security Act 2013 which allows a closed material procedure to be used in civil proceedings in relation to material the disclosure of which would be damaging to the interests of national security. **CPR, Part 82**, sets out the rules governing the closed material procedure, under which the material is withheld from the other party and disclosed only to the court and the special advocate appointed to represent the interests of the excluded party.

A public body may also withhold disclosure of documents injurious to the public interest under public interest immunity, so that the documents are excluded from the evidence. The coexistence of the closed material procedure alongside public interest immunity has been described by the court as 'uneasy' (*CF v Security Service* [2013] EWHC 3402 (QB), [2014] 1 WLR 1699).

Injunctions

91.44 It is arguable that there are ample safeguards by virtue of the undertakings to be provided by the applicant as set out in the draft orders in the annex to **PD 25A** and the normally short return date given by the court to enable the case for the respondent to be put (*Chappell v United Kingdom* (application 10461/83) (1990) 12 EHRR 1). However, before granting an injunction without notice, the court will have regard to all the circumstances of the case and take account of **art. 6(1)** of the European Convention on Human Rights. In particular, there may be an issue under **art. 6** where an order requires answers to questions. Further, the court has discharged freezing and search orders on the basis of material non-disclosure, namely, failure by the applicant to disclose the fact that evidence relied upon in a without notice application was obtained in breach of **art. 8(1)** of the Convention (*St Merryn Meat Ltd v Hawkins* [2001] CP Rep 116).

It was found to be inconsistent with **art. 6(3)** rights for a judge to proceed to a hearing on an application to commit for contempt of court for breach of a freezing and disclosure order without giving the breaching party an opportunity to be heard where the judge knew that the absent party wished to be heard in person, but was prevented from being present by matters over which he had no control (*Raja v Van Hoogstraten* [2004] EWCA Civ 968, [2004] 4 All ER 793).

Financial constraints on access to justice

91.45 Financial burdens placed on parties to litigation, such as security for costs orders or court fees must be considered in the light of the right of access to a court.

The Convention is intended to guarantee practical and effective rights, particularly with regard to the right of access to a court. It is central to the concept of a fair trial, in civil as in criminal proceedings, that a litigant is not denied the opportunity to present his case effectively before the court and that he is able to enjoy equality of arms with the opposing side. However, **art. 6(1)** leaves the State with a free choice as to the means to be used to guarantee litigants these rights. The right of access to a court is not absolute and may be subject to restrictions, provided that they pursue a legitimate aim and are proportionate. Moreover, it is not incumbent on the State to ensure total equality of arms between the assisted party and the opposing side, as long as each side is given a reasonable opportunity to present his case under conditions that do not place him at a substantial disadvantage.

Under **CPR, r. 3.1(5)**, the court may order a party to pay a sum of money into court if that party has, without good reason, failed to comply with a rule, practice direction or a relevant pre-action protocol. Such an order may be made against a claimant or a defendant and the sum of money will be security for any sum payable by that party to any other party in the proceedings (**r. 3.1(6A)**). Before making such an order, the court must have regard to the amount in dispute, the costs incurred and the costs to be incurred (**r. 3.1(6)**).

In deciding whether to require security, the court may anticipate the arguments likely to be put forward on an application under **r. 3.9** for relief from sanctions, including the effect which the granting of relief would have on each party.

The court must, under **art. 6(1)** of the European Convention on Human Rights, take into account inability to pay where that would result in a party being unable to proceed with a claim. In *Tolstoy Miloslavsky v United Kingdom* (application 18139/91) (1995) 20 EHRR 442, the European Court of Human Rights found that an order for security for costs in relation to appellate proceedings would not infringe **art. 6(1)**, but there could be a violation if an order for security denies access to a court of first instance (*Aït-Mouhoub v France* (application 22924/93) (2000) 30 EHRR 382). In *Federal Bank of the Middle East Ltd v Hadkinson* [2000] 1 WLR 1695 the Court of Appeal found no contravention of **art. 6(1)** by an order requiring security for the costs of an appeal from a summary judgment. An order for security for costs against a claimant was not upheld where the claimant was not represented at the hearing of the application (*Nasser v United Bank of Kuwait* [2001] EWCA Civ 556, [2002] 1 WLR 1868).

The right to a fair trial pursuant to **art. 6** also requires that a conditional order as to costs, imposed as a condition of defending a claim, should be reasonable on the basis that, in circumstances where a party cannot comply with such an order, the effect of the order extends beyond limiting his right of access to the court and impairs the very essence of the right (*Anglo-Eastern Trust Ltd v Kermanshahchi* [2002] EWCA Civ 198, [2002] CP Rep 36).

A litigant who wishes to instruct counsel and solicitors to defend an application in committal proceedings but has insufficient means to do so has a right to apply for public funding which should be respected by the courts (*Berry Trade Ltd v Moussavi* [2002] EWCA Civ 477, [2002] 1 WLR 1910).

It may be possible to argue that there is a breach of **art. 6(1)** if public funding is not available (*Airey v Ireland* (application 6289/73) (1979–80) 2 EHRR 305; and see *Perotti v Collyer-Bristow* [2003] EWCA Civ 1521, [2004] 2 All ER 189). The question of whether legal aid is necessary to guarantee a fair hearing must be determined on the particular facts of each case and will depend on the importance of what is at stake for the applicant in the proceedings, the complexity of the relevant law and procedure and the applicant's capacity to represent himself effectively. The Convention guarantees effective, not theoretical, rights and therefore the question is whether the applicant's appearance before the tribunal in question without a lawyer is effective; whether the proceedings taken as a whole are fair, and appear to be fair; and whether equality of arms has been guaranteed. The critical question is whether an unrepresented litigant was able to present his or her case effectively and without obvious unfairness. It is not the case that **art. 6** will require funding in only rare and extreme cases (*R (Gudanaviciene) v Director of Legal Aid Casework* [2014] EWCA Civ 1622, [2015] 1 WLR 2247). In unusually lengthy and complicated defamation proceedings, where the applicants were of very limited means and were represented pro bono whereas their opponents were one of the most wealthy companies in the world and employed substantial experienced legal teams, it was found that the denial of legal aid deprived the applicants of the opportunity to present their case effectively and contributed to an unacceptable inequality of arms (*Steel v United Kingdom* (application 68416/01) (2005) 41 EHRR 22). Where legal aid was refused for an appeal on the grounds that there was no reasonable prospect of success and where the costs of the claim would have been disproportionate to the sum at stake, the refusal of legal aid was not contrary to **art. 6** (*Stewart-Brady v United Kingdom* (applications 27436/95) and 28406/95 (1997) 24 EHRR CD 38). However, the withdrawal of a claimant's public funding soon before trial on the basis that it appeared that neither of the defendants had sufficient assets to satisfy any judgment against them was a breach of **art. 6(1)** (*R (Alliss) v Legal Services Commission* [2002] EWHC 2079 (Admin), [2003] ACD 16). In family law proceedings where the parties lack capacity, the importance of the issues and potential consequences may well mean that not only the availability of legal aid but also the length of time taken and the complexity of the application process for legal aid themselves raise **art. 6** issues (*Re D (A Child) (No. 2)* [2015] EWFC 2, [2015] 1 FLR 1247). Where public funding is not available in family law proceedings, other case management options such as questioning by the judge should be considered to ensure that proper cross examination and a fair hearing are achieved (*Re K (Children)* [2015] EWCA Civ 543, [2015] 1 WLR 3801).

Article 6 does not require the Criminal Injuries Compensation Authority to pay a claimant's costs of representation (*C v Secretary of State for the Home Department* [2003] EWHC 1295 (QB), LTL 22/5/2003). Funding for the representation of the family of a deceased person may be required to be provided where an inquiry into the cause of death is required by **art. 2** if there is a sufficient degree of State responsibility for the death (*R (Khan) v Secretary of State for Health* [2003] EWCA Civ 1129, [2004] 1 WLR 971; *R (Amin) v Secretary of State for the Home Department* [2003] UKHL 51, [2004] 1 AC 653) and if the involvement of the next of kin in the process is necessary to safeguard their legitimate interests (*R (Letts) v Lord Chancellor* [2015] EWHC 402 (Admin), [2015] 2 Costs LR 217). However, where the primary cause of death was not State involvement, such as a rail accident caused by a private individual, but the State was still responsible for a framework of rail safety, there would not necessarily be a requirement for relatives of the deceased to be funded to enable them to have full legal representation at the inquest, particularly where the court found that the coroner could carry out a full investigation into the deaths without the benefit of full legal representation from the family (*R (Main) v Minister for Legal Aid* [2007] EWCA Civ 1147, [2008] HRLR 8).

The scheme chosen by Parliament to allow success fees in CFAs to be recoverable from the losing party in an action for defamation is compatible with **art. 10** and therefore the threat of liability to pay such a sum does not infringe the defendant's right to freedom of expression. It is a proportionate measure chosen by Parliament to provide other litigants access to justice (*Campbell v MGN Ltd (No. 2)* [2005] UKHL 61, [2005] 1 WLR 3394). This remains the position in the United Kingdom despite a contrary ruling from the European Court of Human Rights on the issue (*MGN Ltd v United Kingdom* (application 39401/04) [2011] 1 Costs LO 84) and in the absence of any exceptional circumstances the UK House of Lords decision remains binding on lower courts (*Miller v Associated Newspapers Ltd* [2016] EWHC 397 (QB), [2016] 2 Costs LR 195). Similar considerations apply to the recovery of ATE (after the event) insurance premiums (*Eight Representative Claimants v MGN Ltd* [2016] EWHC 855 (Ch), [2016] 3 Costs LO 413).

In addition, recovery of all elements of a CFA (including success fees and ATE insurance) in line with the Access to Justice Act 1999 was compatible with **art. 6** and **art. 1** of the First Protocol since it was a rational and coherent scheme for providing access to justice and was not disproportionate (*Lawrence v Fen Tigers Ltd (No. 3)* [2015] UKSC 50, [2015] 1 WLR 3485).

Vexatious litigants

The Senior Courts Act 1981, s. 42, which restricts vexatious proceedings, does not infringe **91.46** the European Convention on Human Rights or the **Human Rights Act 1998** (*Ebert v Official Receiver* [2001] EWCA Civ 340, [2002] 1 WLR 320). Further, a fair and reasonable opportunity to put one's case before the court does not involve an unlimited and uncontrolled opportunity to address the court (*Attorney General v Covey* [2001] EWCA Civ 254, *The Times*, 2 March 2001).

This is on the basis that there is inherent in the Convention the need to balance the interests of the individual against the interests of the community, and if litigants were given unlimited time to make oral submissions, this would prejudice other litigants waiting to have their cases heard, and result in unnecessary expense to the justice system. See also *Attorney General v D'Souza* (2004) 148 SJLB 1061.

Oral public hearing

CPR, r. 39.2(1), provides that, as a general rule, hearings are to be in public. This includes **91.47** the trial. **Article 6(1)** of the European Convention on Human Rights provides that every person is entitled to a public hearing, although there are some very limited exceptions. The cases where hearings must be heard in private should be covered by the exceptions in **art. 6(1)**. These exceptions broadly reflect the common law exceptions and the national courts have a margin of appreciation (*A v British Broadcasting Corporation* [2014] UKSC 25, [2015] AC 588).

Witnesses may only rely on **art. 2** to avoid giving evidence in public where they can demonstrate that to do so would pose an objectively verifiable real and immediate risk to their lives (*Deripaska v Cherney* [2012] EWCA Civ 1235, [2013] CP Rep 1).

Article 6(1) states that judgment should be pronounced publicly, even where the hearing has been in private, and this may cause more difficulty. However, where a hearing in private is strictly necessary because publicity would prejudice the interests of justice, judgment need not be pronounced publicly (*Re Trusts of X Charity* [2003] EWHC 1462 (Ch), [2003] 1 WLR 2751). **PD 39A, para. 1.11**, provides that when a hearing takes place in public, members of the public may obtain a transcript of any judgment given or a copy of any order made, upon payment of the appropriate fee. However, where the judgment is given or an order made in private, anyone who seeks a transcript of the judgment or copy order must seek the judge's permission (**PD 39A, para. 1.12**).

Although in some cases, particularly sentencing cases, fairness might not require an oral hearing, there must still be the possibility of an oral hearing where it is considered necessary for fairness. Where a prisoner faced the prospect of lengthy imprisonment and fairness required an oral hearing, this was not an entitlement of which he should be lightly deprived. A rule which denied a sentencing judge any possibility of holding a fair hearing is therefore incompatible with **art. 6** (*R (Hammond) v Secretary of State for the Home Department* [2005] UKHL 69, [2006] 1 AC 603).

It is not a requirement of **art. 6** that there should be an oral hearing of an application for permission to appeal under the Arbitration Act 1996, s. 69, unless the circumstances are exceptional (*BLCT (13096) Ltd v J. Sainsbury plc* [2003] EWCA Civ 884, [2004] 1 CLC 24).

Independent and impartial tribunal

The guarantee of a fair hearing in **art. 6(1)** of the European Convention on Human Rights **91.48** includes the right to an independent and impartial tribunal.

The requirement of an independent and impartial tribunal cast doubt on the position of temporary sheriffs in Scotland trying criminal cases, where they did not have sufficient

Commentary

security of tenure (*Starrs v Ruxton* 2000 JC 208) but note the position of a temporary judge (*Kearney v HM Advocate* [2006] HRLR 15). Lack of security of tenure need not be a problem when trying a case to which the State is not a party (*Clancy v Caird* 2000 SC 441).

In *Hoekstra v HM Advocate (No. 2)* 2000 JC 391 it was held that the test of impartiality is both subjective and objective. A judge, who had, with two other judges, just heard an appeal in which issues relating to the application of the Convention were raised, wrote an article for a national newspaper that was highly critical of the Convention and its incorporation into national law. It was held that this did not pass the objective test of impartiality. The judgment in the appeal in question had to be set aside as it had been given by a court which was not properly constituted by three impartial judges.

In the same way the objective test of impartiality may not be fulfilled where a judge is called upon to rule judicially on the effect of legislation that he or she has drafted or promoted during the parliamentary process. The fair-minded and informed observer might conclude that there was a real possibility that the judge would subconsciously strive to avoid reaching a conclusion which would undermine the very clear assurances he had given to Parliament as to the effect of the legislation (*Davidson v Scottish Ministers* [2004] UKHL 34, [2009] 2 All ER 501).

In some circumstances the requirement of an independent and impartial tribunal can be satisfied by the possibility of a judicial review of a decision of the Secretary of State even when the Secretary of State is not impartial and independent, having formulated the policy which related to the decision under challenge (*R (Alconbury Developments Ltd) v Secretary of State for the Environment, Transport and the Regions* [2001] UKHL 23, [2003] 2 AC 295).

In some cases 'full jurisdiction' would necessitate jurisdiction over findings of primary fact and in others it would not. A local authority's administrative decision that accommodation offered to the homeless claimant was suitable, combined with judicial review, guaranteed compliance with **art. 6(1)** (*Runa Begum v Tower Hamlets London Borough Council* [2003] UKHL 5, [2003] 2 AC 430; see also *Ali v Birmingham City Council* [2008] EWCA Civ 1228, [2009] 2 All ER 501, affirmed [2010] UKSC 8, [2010] 2 AC 39). However, the right for asylum seekers to apply for judicial review did not remedy the procedural unfairness of the system operated by the Secretary of State in deciding whether asylum seekers had made their claims as soon as reasonably practicable after arrival in the United Kingdom. Judicial review did not allow sufficiently close review of determinations of fact to satisfy **art. 6**. However, the Court of Appeal held that if the Secretary of State were to remedy the deficiencies in procedure the combination of his decision-making process and judicial review of that process would then satisfy the requirements of **art. 6(1)** (*R (Q) v Secretary of State for the Home Department* [2003] EWCA Civ 364, [2004] QB 36). This was also the approach taken in *Tsfayo v United Kingdom* (application 60860/00) (2009) 48 EHRR 18, where the European Court of Human Rights held that, where a first-instance tribunal decision is essentially a finding of fact, judicial review is not sufficient to protect **art. 6** rights as the court does not have the power to make fresh findings of fact. See also *R (Bono) v Harlow District Council* [2002] EWHC 423 (Admin), [2002] 1 WLR 2475; *Adan v Newham London Borough Council* [2001] EWCA Civ 1916, [2002] 1 WLR 2120; *R (S) v Brent London Borough Council* [2002] EWCA Civ 693, [2002] ACD 90; *Secretary of State for Health v Personal Representative of Christopher Beeson* [2002] EWCA Civ 1812, [2003] UKHRR 353; *Feld v Barnet London Borough Council* [2004] EWCA Civ 1307, [2005] HLR 9.

The courts have reconciled the domestic law on apparent bias (see **77.25**) with the jurisprudence of the European Court of Human Rights by applying the following test. First, the court should ascertain all the circumstances which have a bearing on the suggestion that the judge is biased. Second, it should ask whether those circumstances would lead a fair-minded and informed observer to conclude that there is a real possibility that the tribunal is biased (*Porter v Magill* [2001] UKHL 67, [2002] 2 AC 357).

There is a real possibility of bias where the adjudicator has had a number of private conversations with one party and thus appears to have taken into account submissions from that party which were not made available to the other party (*Discain Project Services Ltd v Opecprime Development Ltd* [2001] BLR 285); where the judge's brother was chairman of a company with whom the defendant had been in (an unrelated) dispute (*Perot Systems Europe Ltd v Johnson* [2003] EWHC 1635 (QB), LTL 4/6/2003); where a potential witness was well known to the judge, even where that witness did not give evidence at the trial, as he was still involved in the case and replacement witnesses may have given the evidence that he would have given (*AWG Group Ltd v Morrison* [2006] EWCA Civ 6, [2006] 1 WLR 1163); where a part-time judge of the Employment Appeal Tribunal appeared as an advocate before that Tribunal, chaired by another judge sitting with two lay members, one or both of whom had previously sat with that part-time judge (*Lawal v Northern Spirit Ltd* [2003] UKHL 35, [2003] ICR 856); where the chairman of an employment tribunal had commented before any evidence was called that the appellant faced an uphill struggle with the case, indicating that the tribunal had prejudged the matter before hearing the relevant evidence (*Project v Hutt* (2006) 150 SJLB 702); where a judge had had previous dealings with a partner in a firm of solicitors, in relation to him joining the firm, which had ended acrimoniously, and the judge was then due to hear an application in which another partner in the same firm was involved (*Howell v Millais* [2007] EWCA Civ 720, [2007] NPC 88); where a judge had commented to counsel in chambers before hearing all the evidence that he believed one party's evidence and could not see how the other party could win, because it indicated that he had prematurely closed his mind to the possibility that the other party's evidence might change his mind (*Amjad v Steadman-Byrne* [2007] EWCA Civ 625, [2007] 1 WLR 2484); and where a judge had made numerous hostile and disparaging interventions giving the impression that her annoyance with counsel for one of the parties had influenced the approach taken to the case (*Re G (a Child)* [2015] EWCA Civ 834, LTL 28/7/2015).

There has been held to be no real possibility of bias in the following circumstances: if a judge sits on a substantive appeal after refusing permission to appeal on paper (*Sengupta v Holmes* [2002] EWCA Civ 1104, (2002) 99 (39) LSG 39); where a memory lapse caused a judge to write and circulate his judgment before having the opportunity of considering the closing submissions of the parties' legal advisers, but said he would subsequently consider the judgment in the light of the submissions (*Taylor v Williamsons* [2002] EWCA Civ 1380, [2003] CP Rep 20); where an employment tribunal indicated to the parties before the evidence was completed that the respondent's treatment of the applicant had been 'appalling', because the views expressed were only preliminary (*Southwark London Borough Council v Jiminez* [2003] EWCA Civ 502, [2003] ICR 1176); where a judge had acted as a legal member of a mental health review tribunal after sentencing the patient to the sentence that was being reviewed, as a fair-minded and informed observer would take account of various factors including the fact that the tribunal had no power to question the validity of the original sentence and that a judge would not be reluctant to change his mind if and when there was a rational basis for doing so — the decision facing the tribunal was different from the one the judge had made earlier (*R (M) v Mental Health Review Team* [2005] EWHC 2791 (Admin), 90 BMLR 65); where the judge had intervened and asked numerous questions throughout the hearing, including during examination of witnesses, in particular of one party against whom he had become increasingly hostile, since it was found that despite the judge's conduct it was inevitable that any judge would have reached the same conclusion — even if the trial had been fair, the result would have been the same (*Mortgage Credit Ltd v Kalli* [2007] EWCA Civ 1156, LTL 15/10/2007); where there had been a significant amount of intervention by the recorder, but where the interventions were justified, there was no attempt to take over the examination or cross-examination of the witness and where there was no suggestion in the transcript that the appellant's counsel had not been able to put his case properly (*Jemaldeen v A-Z Law Solicitors* [2012] EWCA Civ 1431, [2013] CP Rep 8); and where a chief registrar had made interruptions and references to not being honest during the evidence from a litigant in person which were held to have been for the purposes of

Commentary

focusing the litigant in person rather than demonstrating bias or pre-determination (*Michael v Official Receiver* [2014] EWCA Civ 1590, LTL 14/11/2014).

Courts should be careful not to accede to applications by people who do not want a case to be heard by a particular judge unless there are sufficient grounds for such recusal (*Phillips v Symes* [2004] EWHC 490 (Ch), LTL 21/3/2005; see also *Dobbs v Triodos Bank NV* [2005] EWCA Civ 468, [2006] CP Rep 1). A judge hearing an application which relied on his own previous findings should not recuse himself unless he either considered that he genuinely could not give one party a fair hearing or that a fair-minded and informed observer would conclude that there was a real possibility that he would not do so, as it was important that judges did not recuse themselves too readily in long and complex cases in view of the convenience of having a single judge in charge of both the procedural and substantial parts of the case (*Otkritie International Investment Management Ltd v Urumov* [2014] EWCA Civ 1315, [2015] CP Rep 6). Mere complaint about the conduct of a chairman of an employment tribunal does not give rise to an automatic decision to recuse. The substance of the allegations should be addressed and analysed (*Ansar v Lloyds TSB Bank plc* [2006] EWCA Civ 1462, [2007] IRLR 211). For example, where a judge had been sent a letter making serious allegations about the other party, to say that the judge might have been biased was an artificial way of putting the complaint. The true complaint was that the party had not received a fair trial because she had not been given the opportunity to defend herself against damaging allegations going to her credit (*Diedrichs-Shurland v Talanga-Stiftung* [2006] UKPC 58, LTL 7/12/2006).

A judge has to be free from any actual or apparent bias, but counsel has no such duty. The court should prevent an advocate from acting only where there is a risk of disclosure of relevant confidential information or in very exceptional circumstances (*Geveran Trading Co. Ltd v Skjevesland* [2002] EWCA Civ 1567, [2003] 1 WLR 912). Similarly, art. 6 does not impose any requirement as to the independence or impartiality of the prosecutor in and of itself, although if a lack of such independence and impartiality results in unfairness to a defendant that might be a violation of **art. 6(1)** (*R (Haase) v Independent Adjudicator* [2008] EWCA Civ 1089, [2009] QB 550).

Further the test of apparent bias is not relevant to whether or not an expert witness should be permitted to give evidence, although the duties of an expert witness are to give an objective and unbiased opinion (*Saunder v Birmingham City Council* (EAT 21 May 2008) LTL 12/6/2008).

Where an allegation of bias had been dealt with at a public and impartial hearing and the decision reached that although there had been apparent bias the irregularity had been waived by the party failing to make a timely application to remove the umpire, there was no apparent contravention of **art. 6. Article 6** does not contain an overarching principle that an award tainted by apparent bias must be set aside. It is for national courts to decide whether to set the decision aside or not, the critical question being whether the decision of the court on the bias question discloses any violation of **art. 6**. Where the judge had then refused permission to appeal under the Arbitration Act 1996, the Court of Appeal would only have a residual jurisdiction to grant permission to appeal if there was unfairness in the decision-making process or a contravention of **art. 6**, which in this case there was not (*ASM Shipping Ltd v TTMI Ltd* [2006] EWCA Civ 1341, [2006] 2 CLC 471).

There was nothing untoward in an arbitrator considering the question of his own jurisdiction. It is not uncommon for arbitrators to consider the issue of whether they are competent to act by reason of bias. There was therefore no reason to restrain an arbitrator from holding a hearing to consider his own jurisdiction where the parties, each receiving independent legal advice, had expressly agreed that their dispute should be resolved by the arbitrator, according to the principles of the law of international arbitration. It would require exceptional circumstances before an English court would interfere with that agreement and infringe those principles (*Weissfisch v Julius* [2006] EWCA Civ 218, [2006] 1 Lloyd's Rep 716). If one arbitrator has withdrawn on the grounds of apparent bias, there is no invariable rule, nor is it necessarily the case, that the other two arbitrators would be affected second hand by apparent bias and therefore should recuse themselves or be excluded from the proceedings (*ASM Shipping Ltd v Bruce-Harris* [2007] EWHC 1513 (Comm), [2008] 1 Lloyd's Rep 61).

Reasoned judgment

Article 6 of the European Convention on Human Rights requires reasons to be given for any **91.49** decision on the merits and where permission to appeal is not given in order that the parties are aware of the grounds on which the decision was reached. The extent of reasoning required by the European Court of Human Rights does not go any further than that which is required under domestic law (*English v Emery Reimbold and Strick Ltd* [2002] EWCA Civ 605, [2002] 1 WLR 2409). Where there are legitimate restraints on a right of appeal, such as the need for a matter to be of general importance, it is sufficient for the court to refer to those limitations. **Article 6** does not require reasons to be given for refusing permission to appeal against arbitral awards (*Mousaka Inc. v Golden Seagull Maritime Inc.* [2002] 1 WLR 395). In refusing leave to appeal under the Arbitration Act 1996, s. 69, adequate reasons would in almost all cases be given by identifying the threshold test or tests which the applicant has failed, without explaining why the relevant test had been failed (*North Range Shipping Ltd v Seatrans Shipping Corporation* [2002] EWCA Civ 405, [2002] 1 WLR 2397). Where the tribunal's decision is not obviously wrong or open to serious doubt, it might not always be enough simply to refer to the statutory test but it would be enough for the judge to uphold the arbitrator's reasons. Otherwise it might be necessary to go further, but any further reasons need only be brief so as to show the losing party why he had lost (see also 77.27).

Inattentive tribunal

There may not be a fair trial, as required by the European Convention on Human Rights, **art. 6,** **91.50** if the tribunal does not give full attention to the case. In *Stansby v Datapulse plc* [2003] EWCA Civ 1951, [2004] ICR 523, a hearing by an employment tribunal was unfair because a lay member fell asleep having consumed alcohol. Conversely in *R v Betson* [2004] EWCA Crim 254, [2004] 2 Cr App R 52, a criminal trial by jury was not unfair, even though the judge fell asleep during counsel's speeches to the jury, because the judge's summing up could not be criticised and the jury were apparently not influenced by his lapse.

Enforcement of foreign judgments and restraining foreign proceedings

Where a party has not received a fair trial in another jurisdiction contrary to **art. 6(1)** of the **91.51** Convention, it would be contrary to public policy for the United Kingdom to enforce the judgment (*Maronier v Larmer* [2002] EWCA Civ 774, [2003] QB 620).

However, the domestic courts will not refuse to register or enforce a foreign judgment or order just because some aspect constituted a breach of **art. 6** where it is not contrary to the overall interests of justice to register the order (*Barnette v United States of America* [2004] UKHL 37, [2004] 1 WLR 2241). Only a flagrant denial of the right to a fair trial would make it contrary to the interests of justice to enforce the foreign order (*United States of America v Montgomery (No. 2)* [2004] UKHL 37, [2004] 1 WLR 2241). While there is a strong presumption that courts in Convention States will be in compliance with their obligations under the Convention, the domestic court is still entitled to consider whether this is the case on the particular facts. In *Merchant International Co. Ltd v Natsionalna Aktsionerna Kompanii Naftogaz Ukrainy* [2012] EWCA Civ 196, [2012] 1 WLR 3036, a judgment of the Ukrainian court was a flagrant breach of the principle of legal certainty and the English court was entitled to refuse to recognise it; see also *JSC 'Aeroflot-Russian Airlines' v Berezovsky* [2014] EWCA Civ 20, [2014] 1 CLC 53.

Although a foreign judgment given in proceedings which in the view of an English court do not meet the requirements of a fair trial will not be recognised in England, it is not for the English court to restrain a party in proceedings before it from suing in another jurisdiction where that country is not itself bound by the Convention (*Al-Bassam v Al-Bassam* [2004] EWCA Civ 857, [2004] WTLR 757). The fear as to the fairness of the foreign proceedings and the enforceability of the foreign judgment in England should not be considered until the foreign judgment has been given. Limited interim restraint of the right to sue in another jurisdiction may, however, be necessary to protect the process of the English court from misuse.

RIGHT TO PRIVACY AND CONFIDENTIALITY
AND CIVIL LITIGATION

91.52   **Article 8** of the European Convention on Human Rights provides a right to confidentiality in communications passing between a lawyer and his or her client. In *General Mediterranean Holdings SA v Patel* [2000] 1 WLR 272 it was contended that the former CPR, r. 48.7(3), was *ultra vires* the Civil Procedure Rule Committee. This provided that for the purposes of determining an application for a wasted costs order, the court could direct the disclosure of privileged documents to the court and, if the court so directed, to the other party to the application. It was held that the general words, 'may modify the rules of evidence' in the Civil Procedure Act 1997, sch. 1, para. 4, did not give the rule-makers power to abrogate or limit a person's right to legal confidentiality. To the extent that r. 48.7(3) diminished the substantive right to legal confidentiality it was *ultra vires*.

Toulson J also addressed the human rights issue and said that, as a matter of discretion, the court would not have ordered disclosure under r. 48.7(3) because the defendants had a right of confidentiality under **art. 8** of the European Convention in respect of their communications with their solicitors unless there was justification for the court to interfere with that right under **art. 8(2)**. Adjudicating an application for a wasted costs order did not justify such interference.

Legal professional privilege is not impliedly overridden by the Inland Revenue's power under the Taxes Management Act 1970, s. 20(1), to require delivery of documents in a person's possession or power (*R (Morgan Grenfell and Co. Ltd) v Special Commissioner of Income Tax* [2002] UKHL 21, [2003] 1 AC 563). This decision highlighted the importance of legal professional privilege as 'a fundamental human right long established in the common law' as well as part of the right to privacy guaranteed by **art. 8** of the Convention, but note *McE v Prison Service of Northern Ireland* [2009] UKHL 15, [2009] 1 AC 908. The protection of legal advice privilege under **art. 8** has been further recognised by the Supreme Court (*R (Prudential plc) v Special Commissioner of Income Tax* [2013] UKSC 1, [2013] 2 AC 185).

CPR, r. 35.10, requires an expert's report to state the substance of his or her material instructions and effectively removes any privilege which would have attached to those instructions. It is arguable (though not likely) that this requirement might infringe a party's right to privacy under **art. 8**, although in a case concerning communications with experts who were instructed solely for the purpose of related criminal proceedings, the High Court has held that a witness should neither volunteer, nor be compelled to disclose, such privileged communications unless the privilege has been waived (*S County Council v B* [2000] Fam 76). The without-prejudice rule should be applied with restraint and only in cases in which the public interest plainly justifies its use (*Prudential Assurance Co. Ltd v Prudential Insurance Co. of America* [2003] EWCA Civ 1154, [2004] ETMR 29).

The refusal of the defendant local authority to supply the claimant with confidential information, in order to assist her decision whether to apply to remove the defendant as guardian of a child in care, constituted a breach of the claimant's rights under **arts 6** and **8** on the basis that a balance was required to be struck between the public and private interest in maintaining the confidentiality of the information and the public and private interest in permitting its disclosure for certain purposes (*R (Stevens) v Plymouth City Council* [2002] EWCA Civ 388, [2002] 1 WLR 2583).

Other areas where **art. 8** might be infringed are:

(a) in applications seeking disclosure of medical records; and

(b) surveillance evidence particularly in personal injury claims and covert videos of employees at work (see *Halford v United Kingdom* (application 20605/92) (1997) 24 EHRR 523).

However, the actions of the defendant insurers in *Jones v University of Warwick* [2003] EWCA Civ 151, [2003] 1 WLR 954 in filming the claimant covertly at home in order to vitiate her personal injury claim did not necessarily render the evidence inadmissible. The Convention does not decide what is to be the consequence of evidence being obtained in breach of **art. 8(1)**, but rather it is for the domestic court to decide whether or not admitting the evidence would be in keeping with **art. 8(2)**. Such evidence is admissible under **art. 8(2)**, provided that the inquiries made and the surveillance carried out were reasonable and proportionate in the circumstances and necessary in a democratic society (see also *Martin v McGuiness* 2003 SLT 1424).

Admitting as evidence a covert video recording made by a childcare employee, depicting the unwanted sexual advances made towards her by her employer in front of his child, engaged the child's **art. 8** rights to respect to his private life. However, where that interference is necessary to protect a claimant's right to a fair trial under **art. 6**, the court will allow such evidence to be produced. The employment tribunal was directed to view the video in private to protect the child's rights as much as possible (*XXX v YYY* [2004] EWCA Civ 231, [2004] IRLR 471). In contrast where the police covertly filmed a person in a custody suite for identification purposes and used the videotape in the prosecution against him, such interference was not in accordance with the law, because the police had failed to comply with the procedures set out in relevant Codes of Practice under the Police and Criminal Evidence Act 1984, s. 66 (*Perry v United Kingdom* (application 63737/00) (2004) 39 EHRR 3).

When considering a search order, the court ought to have regard to the **art. 8** right to respect for home life and this can extend to an individual's office (*Niemietz v Germany* (application 13710/88) (1993) 16 EHRR 97).

RIGHT TO FREEDOM OF EXPRESSION AND CIVIL LITIGATION

One particular issue concerning the right to freedom of expression is the extent to which it **91.53** sometimes has to be balanced against the qualified Convention rights of others, such as whether the right of an individual to a fair trial will be prejudiced by the publication of information about the proceedings (*Observer v United Kingdom* (application 13585/88) (1992) 14 EHRR 153) and the effect on the right to privacy of others (e.g. *Lingens v Austria* (application 9815/82) (1986) 8 EHRR 407). For example, racist material does not enjoy the protection of **art. 10** because it breaches the rights of others (*Thomas v News Group Newspapers Ltd* [2001] EWCA Civ 1233, [2002] EMLR 4). Where the right to freedom of expression conflicts with the unqualified rights (such as **art. 3**) of litigants or others there can be no derogation from the unqualified right, although care must be taken to ensure the extent of interference with freedom of expression is no greater than necessary (*A v British Broadcasting Corporation* [2014] UKSC 25, [2015] AC 588).

Cases on the interrelation of the right to freedom of expression and libel need to be reappraised in the light of the Defamation Act 2013. The principle of strict liability for unintentional defamation was an interference with freedom of expression under **art. 10** (*O'Shea v MGN Ltd* [2001] EMLR 943). So too was a ban on the defendant in libel proceedings relying at all on leaked confidential documents crucial to the former defences of justification and

Reynolds public interest (*Commissioner of Police of the Metropolis v Times Newspapers Ltd* [2011] EWHC 2705 (QB), [2014] EMLR 1). The old repetition and conduct rules in defamation were not incompatible with **arts. 6** and **10** (*Berezovsky v Forbes Inc.* [2001] EWCA Civ 1251, [2001] EMLR 45). It was held that **art. 10** does not affect the principles underlying the former defence of justification (*Chase v News Group Newspapers Ltd* [2002] EWCA Civ 1772, [2003] EMLR 11). In *Times Newspapers Ltd (Nos. 1 and 2) v United Kingdom* (applications 3002/03 and 23676/03) [2009] EMLR 14, the European Court of Human Rights held that there had been no violation of **art. 10** by the 'internet publication rule', whereby each internet publication of a defamatory statement gave rise to a separate cause of action. For corporate claimants, the principle that libel was actionable without proof of special damage did not infringe **art. 10** (*Jameel v Wall Street Journal Europe Sprl* [2005] EWCA Civ 74, [2005] QB 904, reversed on another point [2006] UKHL 44, [2007] 1 AC 359). **Article 10** of the European Convention on Human Rights was cited successfully in reducing excessive damages awarded by a jury in a defamation case (*Tolstoy Miloslavsky v United Kingdom* (application 18139/91) (1995) 20 EHRR 442). The **Human Rights Act 1998** has rendered the courts more likely to entertain a submission that pursuit of a libel claim is an abuse of process, particularly where the publications that took place in England did not amount to a real and substantial tort and the costs of the proceedings would be disproportionate to the damage and vindication that would result from a judgment in the claimant's favour (*Jameel v Dow Jones and Co. Inc.* [2005] EWCA Civ 75, [2005] QB 946).

The High Court has the power to impose a cost-capping regime in appropriate cases, such as defamation cases where extravagant claimant's costs might inhibit the defendant's exercise of his right to freedom of expression (*King v Telegraph Group Ltd* [2004] EWCA Civ 613, [2005] 1 WLR 2282). The usual costs rules may also be altered in privacy and defamation cases where the right to freedom of expression might otherwise be violated, so that where the defendant's case was not entirely without merit, the costs had far exceeded the damages awarded and the claimant was a wealthy celebrity, a requirement on an unsuccessful defendant to pay a substantial success fee was disproportionate (*MGN Ltd v United Kingdom* (application 39401/04) (2011) 53 EHRR 5).

The 'public interest' exception to press freedom has been raised in a number of cases concerning protection of a journalist's source. For example, in *Goodwin v United Kingdom* (application 17488/90) (1996) 22 EHRR 123 the European Court of Human Rights considered that on the facts the case for disclosing a source neither outweighed the need to protect democratic freedoms nor satisfied the requirement of proportionality. In the later case of *Camelot Group plc v Centaur Communications Ltd* [1999] QB 124 the Court of Appeal considered that where there was a continuing threat of leaks the 'interests of justice' as specified in s. 10 of the Contempt of Court Act 1981 outweighed the need to protect press freedoms. The court justified its approach by impliedly equating the 'interests of justice' with the public interest exception in **art. 10(2)** (see also *John v Express Newspapers* [2000] 1 WLR 1931, *Ashworth Hospital Authority v MGN Ltd* [2002] UKHL 29, [2002] 1 WLR 2033; cf. *Mersey Care NHS Trust v Ackroyd* [2003] EWCA Civ 663, [2003] Lloyd's Rep Med 379; *Mersey Care NHS Trust v Ackroyd* [2007] EWCA Civ 101, [2007] HRLR 19; *Malik v Crown Court at Manchester* [2008] EWHC 1362 (Admin), [2008] 4 All ER 403). On the other hand, in *Financial Times Ltd v United Kingdom* (application 821/03) (2010) 50 EHRR 46), emphasising the chilling effect of journalists being seen to assist in the identification of anonymous sources, the European Court of Human Rights found that there had been a violation of **art. 10** by virtue of a disclosure order made against newspapers in relation to the source of leaked information. The public interest in the protection of journalists' sources was sufficient to outweigh any threat of damage through the future dissemination of a company's confidential information or any possibility of obtaining damages for past breaches of confidence. The Supreme Court has noted the parallels between the *Reynolds* public interest defence to defamation and the balancing exercise between **arts. 8** and **10**, and has reiterated the importance of **art. 10** in ensuring press freedom to publish matters of genuine public interest (*Flood v Times Newspapers Ltd* [2012] UKSC 11, [2012] 2 AC 273).

The Code of Practice of the Advertising Standards Authority was held to be compliant with the European Convention on Human Rights, **art. 10(2)** in *R v Advertising Standards Authority Ltd, ex parte Matthias Rath BV* [2001] EMLR 22.

PRIVACY, FREEDOM OF EXPRESSION AND INJUNCTIONS

The key provisions in relation to privacy, freedom of expression and injunctions are **arts 8** and **10** of the European Convention on Human Rights and s. 12 of the **Human Rights Act 1998** (see **91.11**).

91.54

Article 8

Article 8 informs the right of personal privacy under the equitable doctrine of breach of confidence (*Douglas v Hello! Ltd* [2001] QB 967). It may, for example, be relied upon in order to prevent publication of photographs of the interior of a party's home for security reasons (*Beckham v MGN Ltd* (2001) LTL 30/7/2001; see also *A v B plc* [2002] EWCA Civ 337, [2003] QB 195). However, there is no separate cause of action in England for invasion of privacy (*Wainwright v Home Office* [2003] UKHL 53, [2004] 2 AC 406; cf. *Wainwright v United Kingdom* (application 12350/04) (2007) 44 EHRR 40). **Article 8** may be engaged in the sense that information could relate to family life without it necessarily following that there was a reasonable expectation of privacy (which would be required for a breach of **art. 8** in this context) (*Hutcheson v News Group Newspapers Ltd* [2011] EWCA Civ 808, [2012] EMLR 2).

91.55

Article 8 has also been relied upon to prevent the publication of photographs of the claimant, a children's television presenter, visiting a brothel on the basis that freedom of expression was outweighed by the 'peculiar degree of intrusion into the integrity of the claimant's personality' by their publication (*Theakston v MGN Ltd* [2002] EWHC 137 (QB), [2002] EMLR 22). The broad test has been said to be 'whether disclosure of the information about the individual would give substantial offence to a person of ordinary sensibilities assuming that person was placed in similar circumstances' (*Campbell v Mirror Group Newspapers Ltd* [2004] UKHL 22, [2004] 2 AC 457 per Lord Hope of Craighead at [92]). Pictures of the claimant's attendance at Narcotics Anonymous and the details of her treatment were private information and imported a duty of confidence as the claimant had a reasonable expectation that this information would be kept confidential, although it was justifiable to publish the fact that she was misleading the public when she said she did not take drugs. There was also a reasonable expectation of privacy in relation to sexual activities carried on between consenting adults on private property, and serious reasons would need to exist before interference with this expectation could be justified. In the circumstances, exposure could not be justified in the public interest and amounted to a breach of confidence and a breach of **art. 8** rights (*Mosley v News Group Newspapers Ltd* [2008] EWHC 1777 (QB), [2008] EMLR 20). See also *Lady Archer v Williams* [2003] EWHC 1670 (QB), [2003] EMLR 38; *McKennitt v Ash* [2006] EWCA Civ 1714, [2008] QB 73; and *PJS v News Group Newspapers Ltd* [2016] UKSC 26, [2016] 2 WLR 1253.

Once it has been decided that the information is confidential and of a private nature, the test to be applied when considering whether it is necessary to restrict freedom of expression in order to prevent disclosure is not simply whether the information is a matter of public interest but whether in all the circumstances it is in the public interest that the duty of confidence should be breached. In applying the test of proportionality the nature of the relationship that gave rise to the duty of confidentiality might be important. Where an employee of the Prince of Wales had disclosed his journals, it was relevant that there was an important public interest in employees respecting the obligations of confidence they had assumed. The public interest in disclosure of the journals' contents did not ultimately outweigh the confidential nature of the information and the relationship of confidence under which it had been received (*Prince of*

Wales v Associated Newspapers Ltd [2006] EWCA Civ 1776, [2008] Ch 57). However, the mere fact that information was imparted in the course of a relationship of confidence does not create an expectation of privacy. It is a question to be decided on a case-by-case basis following a detailed examination of the circumstances, including the nature of the information and the circumstances in which it had been imparted or obtained (*Lord Browne of Madingley v Associated Newspapers Ltd* [2007] EWCA Civ 295, [2008] QB 103). Private correspondence attracts the protection of **art. 8** not only when in the hands of the writer or during transmission, but also once received by the recipient or in someone else's hands (*Warner v Verfides* [2008] EWHC 2609 (Ch), [2009] Bus LR 500). Even where material has already been sent to a media organisation in such a way that private information could easily be accessed (such as in circumstances where redaction carried out was ineffective), the redacted material still attracts the protection of **art. 8** and an injunction to restrain publication would still be appropriate as the only way to stop the people who had received the material from reading and publishing it (*Ambrosiadou v Coward* [2011] EWCA Civ 409, [2011] 2 FLR 617).

A photograph taken of an infant child on the street in a public place could arguably breach the reasonable expectation of privacy. The fact that the subject is a child is of great significance as the law should protect the children of parents who are in the public eye from intrusive media attention. Whether or not there is a breach will depend on the circumstances. It is not possible to draw a general distinction between activities that are part of a person's private recreation time (which are protected from intrusion) and other activities such as walking down the street or a trip to the shop to buy milk. Since it is not necessarily the case that such routine activities should not attract a reasonable expectation of privacy, it will depend on the circumstances (*Murray v Express Newspapers plc* [2008] EWCA Civ 446, [2009] Ch 481).

Generally, when a court is deciding where the balance lies between **art. 8** and **art. 10** rights, it should accord particular weight to the rights of children likely to be affected by any publication, but the interests of those children cannot be treated as overriding and the public interest in disclosure must still be weighed against the likely harm done through the interference with privacy rights (*ETK v News Group Newspapers Ltd* [2011] EWCA Civ 439, [2011] 1 WLR 1827).

In cases relating to vulnerable individuals, the public interest in favour of publication and freedom of expression can usually be satisfied without any need to identify the individuals in question. Where the BBC had produced a television programme about adoption which would have constituted a massive intrusion into the privacy of the subject of the programme, to the extent that it would undermine her dignity as a human being and mean there was a risk that she would be greeted with a hostile and abusive reaction from viewers who might recognise her following the broadcast, the value of the broadcaster's expression under **art. 10** could not be proportionate to the violation of her privacy. The programme could still be broadcast but without identifying the subject or her child (*T v British Broadcasting Corporation* [2007] EWHC 1683 (QB), [2008] 1 FLR 281).

One of the essential features of the protection of private law under **art. 8** is that it enables people to live freely according to their own choices. However, the courts have stated that while the freedom to live as one chooses is a valuable freedom, so also is the freedom to criticise (within the limits of the law) the conduct of other members of society as being harmful or wrong. Where the substance of an application to restrict publication of details about a personal relationship was essentially aimed at protecting the applicant's business relationship, it was likely that newspapers would publish the story in a way that was capable of being defended in accordance with the law of defamation. Therefore the applicant was not likely to succeed in a claim for breach of confidence or misuse of private information, and as such no injunction could be granted (*LNS v Persons Unknown* [2010] EWHC 119 (QB), [2010] 2 FLR 1306).

Similarly, the courts are reluctant to allow individuals to hide behind **art. 8** to avoid a complainant's attempt to seek redress. While sexual activity would normally lead to a reasonable expectation of privacy therefore, this could not be the case where the activity amounted to sexual harassment (*BUQ v HRE* [2012] EWHC 774 (QB), [2012] IRLR 653).

Where the identity of the applicant has already been revealed in local and national media in an unjustified manner, contrary to **art. 8**, the actions of the applicant in attracting further publicity as the victim of such interference do not nullify his claim. The disclosure by a local authority of closed circuit television footage and photographs of a person during a suicide bid to local and national media without taking adequate steps to ensure that his identity was masked was held to be a disproportionate and therefore unjustified interference with his private life (*Peck v United Kingdom* (application 44647/98) (2003) 36 EHRR 41).

A third party, who knows or ought to be aware that an individual has information which is private or personal to which he can properly deny access to third parties and from which he intends to profit commercially, will be in breach of duty if he uses or publishes the material without authority to the detriment of the owner. However, such material is only protected by the law of confidence and is not treated as property that can be owned or transferred. The publisher who has the right to publish the material has no right of confidence in unauthorised publication of that material by a third party and has no cause of action in that respect (*Douglas v Hello! Ltd (No. 3)* [2005] EWCA Civ 595, [2006] QB 125).

Article 8 does not impose a positive requirement on the press to notify individuals in advance of an intention to publish potentially private information so as to give them the opportunity to seek an injunction. The imposition of such a requirement might give rise to a chilling effect on freedom of expression, and would be difficult to give effect to in practice where, for example, a public interest exception would probably be required (*Mosley v United Kingdom* (application 48009/08) (2011) 53 EHRR 30).

Article 10

The principle of open justice is fundamental in civil litigation, and applies once the parties step into the public forum by invoking the assistance of the court (*R (Willford) v Financial Services Authority* [2013] EWCA Civ 674, [2013] CP Rep 43. However, the principle is not absolute and the court has the power to permit the identity of a party or witness to be withheld from public disclosure where necessary in the interests of justice. Even where Convention rights are engaged, the starting point is the common law principle of open justice, the application of which would normally meet the requirements of the Convention. However, where Convention and common law principles conflict, effect has to be given to the former (*A v British Broadcasting Corporation* [2014] UKSC 25, [2015] AC 588).   **91.56**

Injunctions to protect information which might lead to the identification of the claimants have been granted on the basis that the claim fell within the exceptions to the **art. 10(1)** right of freedom of expression on a narrow interpretation of all the criteria within **art. 10(2)** of the Convention. Those criteria were, first, the grant of an injunction had to be in accordance with the law. Second, there had to be a strong and pressing need for confidentiality to be protected. If the relevant information has become generally accessible and in the public domain such that it has ceased to be confidential information then no injunction will be granted (*BBC v HarperCollins Publishers Ltd* [2010] EWHC 2424 (Ch), [2011] EMLR 6). Third, the remedy sought had to be proportionate to the legitimate aim pursued (*Venables v News Group Newspapers Ltd* [2001] Fam 430, where **art. 10** was overridden by **arts. 2** and **3**, and see also *X, a Woman Formerly Known as Mary Bell v S* [2003] EWHC 1101 (QB), [2003] FSR 850).

The wide availability of information on the internet has thrown issues of anonymity into sharper relief. Although the court would usually make an anonymity order in such cases, it should be recognised that the press also have a legitimate interest and their views should also be considered (*X v Dartford and Gravesham NHS Trust* [2015] EWCA Civ 96, [2015] 1 WLR 3647).

Commentary

Greater protection may be available to data subjects given the decision in *Google Spain SL v Agencia Española de Protección de Datos (AEPD)* (case C-131/12) [2014] QB 1022, [2014] QB 1022 on the right to require search engine operators to remove links under the Data Protection Directive 95/46/EC.

In criminal proceedings, given the weight traditionally given to the importance of open reporting of criminal proceedings in particular, it is appropriate in carrying out the balancing exercise to begin by acknowledging the force of the argument under **art. 10** before considering whether the right under **art. 8** is sufficient to outweigh it. Where an injunction was sought to protect the identity of a child who was not itself directly involved in proceedings, but whose mother was the defendant, the **art. 8** right was held not to outweigh the strong rule in favour of unrestricted publicity of any proceedings in a criminal trial (*Re S (A Child) (Identification: Restrictions on Publication)* [2004] UKHL 47, [2005] 1 AC 593; see also *Re Press Association* [2012] EWCA Crim 2434, [2013] 1 WLR 1979). However, a local authority was entitled to an injunction restraining the publication of the identity of a defendant and victim in a criminal trial and their HIV status, to protect the privacy of their children who were not involved in the trial but were the subject of care proceedings. In the circumstances knowledge of the identity was not essential in order to give the public an adequate understanding of the issues for the purposes of open justice or general discussion. The naming of the parents was likely to inflict substantial damage on the children's **art. 8** rights (*A Local Authority v W* [2005] EWHC 1564 (Fam), [2006] 1 FLR 1).

The right to reputation is protected by **art. 8** and may in certain circumstances, where allegations are particularly serious given the position of the individual and where he has clearly been caused severe distress, mean that it is necessary for the identity of parties to litigation to be withheld to avoid an unjustifiable interference with his private life. However, the importance attached to open justice will generally be greater than that attached to the right to reputation. Clear and cogent reasons will be needed before the principle of open justice is derogated from, and media speculation is not sufficient (*Gray v UVW* [2010] EWHC 2367 (QB), LTL 25/10/2010; *Global Torch Ltd v Apex Global Management Ltd* [2013] EWHC 223 (Ch), LTL 18/2/2013, affirmed by the Court of Appeal [2013] EWCA Civ 819, [2013] 1 WLR 2993). Where, however, the proceedings concerned financial information relating to the value of private assets in a trust, the beneficiaries of which were minors who had not been told about the extent of the wealth and where there were concerns about the effect that such disclosure might have on their lives, the court considered the use of reporting restrictions and anonymisation to be appropriate, rather than a private hearing (*V v T* [2014] EWHC 3432 (Ch), [2015] WTLR 173). Similarly where proceedings concerning financial remedies involved evidence of an individual's financial interests, reporting restrictions would be the appropriate way of protecting his or her **art. 8** rights (*Cooper-Hohn v Hohn* [2014] EWHC 2314 (Fam), [2015] 1 FLR 19). See also **61.21**.

Even in child care proceedings, reporting restrictions should not be too wide where the parents of the child in question wish there to be publicity. The **art. 10** rights of the parents should not be disproportionately interfered with, particularly in light of the fundamental principle that justice should be administered in public, and particularly in relation to alleged miscarriages of justice where it is essential that there be open and public debate in the media in order to promote public confidence in the judicial process and to deter abuses of power (*Re Webster* [2006] EWHC 2733 (Fam), [2007] EMLR 7). Similarly there is a public interest in publishing a judgment which completely proscribed the operation of parental responsibility for a lengthy period of time, and withholding publication entirely would be a disproportionate response to the risk of identification of the family. Instead a reporting restriction would suffice to prevent the publication of further details about the family (*H v A (No. 2)* [2015] EWHC 2630 (Fam), [2016] 1 FCR 338). See also *Re British Broadcasting Corporation* [2009] UKHL 34, [2010] 1 AC 145. There is to be a gradual transition in the family justice system to greater openness, rather than it being exceptional to publish decisions. However, judgments on the issue of publication should be short with only basic reasons being given (*Re C (A Child)* [2015] EWCA Civ 500, [2015] Fam Law 781).

Where it was in the public interest for there to be open debate concerning the use of freezing orders on suspected terrorists, that public interest justified the interference with the applicant's private life by revealing his identity, particularly where the evidence as to the effect on his private life had been general and therefore not compelling. Without identifying a relevant individual, stories in the media are less compelling and given less importance by editors, and therefore public debate and information would in fact suffer by not identifying him, meaning that in this case there was a powerful public interest in allowing the suspect to be identified (*Re Guardian News and Media Ltd* [2010] UKSC 1, [2010] 2 AC 697). In fact, the court has recognised the legitimate interests of the press and suggested that their representations should be taken into account before making anonymity orders (*X v Dartford and Gravesham NHS Trust* [2015] EWCA Civ 96, [2015] 1 WLR 3647; but note *Secretary of State for the Home Department v AP (No. 2)* [2010] UKSC 26, [2010] 1 WLR 1652, where there was no evidence of the strong public interest in open media reporting before the court and therefore anonymity was granted in proceedings relating to a control order).

It is important to recognise that in applications for anonymity orders each case is likely to turn on its own facts and much will depend on the evidence before the court as to the extent of the damage to private life as compared to the evidence of the public interest in disclosure (see, for example, *AMM v HXW* [2010] EWHC 2457 (QB), 160 NLJ 1425, and *KJH v HGF* [2010] EWHC 3064 (QB), LTL 26/11/2010). Even in civil proceedings involving patients subject to compulsory powers under the Mental Health Act 1983, there is no presumption of an anonymity order. Each case must be considered on its own facts with the public's right to know balanced against the effect on the individual patient. Where there was a real risk that a patient's integration into the community would not be successful, an anonymity order was necessary (*R (C) v Secretary of State for Justice* [2016] UKSC 2, [2016] 1 WLR 444). Generally, however, it is likely that if an individual is identified, significant other information about the proceedings would have to be withheld from disclosure, whereas if the party were to remain anonymous, greater details of the matter could be published, which may better serve the public interest (*H v News Group Newspapers Ltd* [2011] EWCA Civ 42, [2011] 1 WLR 1645).

Another alternative is an order under the Children and Young Persons Act 1933, s. 39, prohibiting the identification of a child in newspaper reports, since this would protect the rights of a vulnerable child but interfere less with the principle of open justice and freedom of expression and be less restrictive than a full anonymity order (*A (A Child) v Cambridge University Hospitals NHS Foundation Trust* [2011] EWHC 454 (QB), [2011] EMLR 18). Note *R(Y) v Aylesbury Crown Court* [2012] EWHC 1140 (Admin), [2012] EMLR 26.

Article 10 requires the provision of full and public reasons for decisions of the court, which are also required under **art. 6**. There is no reason to prevent publication of a judge's full reasons in circumstances where the relevant information has already been published so that it is no longer confidential in any event (*Long Beach Ltd v Global Witness Ltd* [2007] EWHC 1816 (QB), LTL 2/8/2007).

A defendant protester's right to freedom of expression under **art. 10** would be interfered with in granting an injunction to make him cease his protest and remove placards which encroached on to the public highway but did not interfere with the public's right to pass and repass on the highway (*Westminster City Council v Haw* [2002] EWHC 2073).

The provisions of the Copyright, Designs and Patents Act 1988 fulfil the requirements of **art. 10(2)** of the Convention in that the needs of a democratic society include the recognition and protection of private property including intellectual property. Rare circumstances could arise where the right to freedom of expression under **art. 10** conflicts with the protection

Commentary

afforded by the 1988 Act, notwithstanding the express exceptions in the Act (*Ashdown v Telegraph Group Ltd* [2001] EWCA Civ 1142, [2002] Ch 149). In those circumstances the court is bound to apply the 1988 Act in a manner which accommodates the right of freedom of expression, which requires the court to look closely at the facts of individual cases. Usually this can be achieved by declining the discretionary relief of an injunction.

Interim injunctions

91.57   The **Human Rights Act 1998** has not substantially altered the test for the grant of interim injunctions in *American Cyanamid Co. v Ethicon Ltd* [1975] AC 396. Although the requirement in the **Human Rights Act 1998, s. 12(3)**, that the applicant 'is likely to establish' at trial that publication should not be allowed is slightly higher in the scale of probability than 'a real prospect' of success, the difference between the two is so small that there would not be many, if any, cases that would proceed under *American Cyanamid* but fail under **s. 12(3)** (*Imutran Ltd v Uncaged Campaigns Ltd* [2001] 2 All ER 385).

The right of an author and publisher to freedom of expression under **art. 10** is secondary to the countervailing public interest within **art. 10(2)**, namely, the public policy exemplified in the law of contract whereby the courts regularly enforce provisions for the restriction of competition provided they are reasonable and proportionate. Accordingly, an interim injunction was granted to restrain publication until trial of a claim that the defendant publisher had induced or procured a breach of contract between another publisher and the claimant (*Psychology Press Ltd v Flanagan* [2002] EWHC 1205 (QB), LTL 24/6/2002).

Where the potential consequences of not granting injunctive relief may be grave this will be a factor in the court's decision as to whether to grant relief. Where the claimant sought an interim injunction restraining the defendants from pursuing conduct that amounted to harassment of the claimant's employees, the court found that there was a serious likelihood that in the absence of injunctive relief the employees would suffer unlawful harassment of a serious nature and therefore it was just and convenient to afford protection to them when the claimant had established a real prospect of success at trial (*Emerson Developments Ltd v Avery* [2004] EWHC 194 (QB), LTL 26/01/2004).

Where the public interest justifies the publication of information, it is less likely that an injunction will be granted. The public interest justified the disclosure of undercover filming in a food production company that supplied the NHS by an investigative journalist posing as an employee. The public interest in disclosure was not qualified by the need to give the owner of the information a right to respond. Furthermore, the court was not convinced that this was in fact confidential information at all. Mann J stated that there had to be something more than an employee filming the workplace to have the quality of confidential information, and it was not made confidential simply because of the confidentiality provisions in the employee's contract (*Tillery Valley Foods Ltd v Channel Four Television Corporation* [2004] EWHC 1075 (Ch), [2004] 101 (22) LSG 31).

The body of case law building up under the **Human Rights Act 1998** regarding the need to balance the competing interests in **art. 8** and **art. 10** relates to breach of confidence, and is not equally applicable to interim injunction applications in the law of defamation. Where a claimant sought an interim injunction in libel proceedings and relied on the **Human Rights Act 1998, s. 12(3)**, as interpreted in *Cream Holdings Ltd v Banerjee* [2004] UKHL 44, [2005] 1 AC 253, to argue that the test for restraint of publication should be whether the claimant was able to demonstrate at this stage that she would be more likely than not to establish at trial that publication should not be allowed, the court held that the test to be applied in defamation proceedings is that the claimant must demonstrate that it is clear that the alleged libel is untrue and that the plea of justification is bound to fail (*Bonnard v Perryman* [1891] 2 Ch 269). This test is still good law. The authorities put forward by the claimant dealt with protection of confidential information, and had not changed the law of defamation (*Greene v Associated Newspapers Ltd* [2004] EWCA Civ 1462, [2005] QB 972). However, in trade mark infringement actions involving comparative advertising it has been held that the general rule is that in *Cream Holdings Ltd v Banerjee*, so an interim injunction will not be granted unless it is shown that the claimant will probably succeed at trial (*Boehringer Ingelheim Ltd v Vetplus Ltd* [2007] EWCA Civ 583, [2007] Bus LR 1456).

Commentary

PART V

Terminology

Chapter 92   Changes in Terminology Made by the CPR

The reforms of civil procedure begun by the CPR in 1998 have introduced new terminology.   **92.1**
Sometimes this is a straightforward change of name, for example, from plaintiff to claimant.
Often the change of terminology reflects a change of procedure, for example, discovery has
been replaced by disclosure of documents. Very little legislation dating from before the CPR
has been amended to use the new terminology. For example, there are still several references
in the County Courts Act 1984 to 'plaintiffs' and none to 'claimants'. **Table 92.1** is a brief
guide to the changes in terminology, which will aid in translating older legislation, cases and
textbooks.

Table 92.1 New terminology

Old term	New term
action	claim
affidavit of service	certificate of service
amicus curiae	advocate to the court
Anton Piller order	search order
assessment (of costs)	summary assessment
bailiff	enforcement agent (in relation to enforcement of judgments)
Calderbank letter (or offer)	admissible offer to settle
certiorari, order of	quashing order
close of pleadings	(no equivalent)
conditional leave to defend	conditional order
costs in the cause	costs in the case
counterclaim	a counterclaim is an additional claim but the term 'counterclaim' is also still in use
county courts	the County Court, and hearing centres
Crown Office	Administrative Court Office
discovery	disclosure
distress	taking control of goods
entering an appearance	acknowledgment of service
ex parte	without notice (to other parties)
garnishee order	third party debt order
Grepe v Loam order	civil restraint order
guardian *ad litem*	litigation friend
home court	claimant's preferred court
in camera	in private
in open court	in public
inter partes hearing	hearing with notice (or hearing on notice) (to other parties)
interlocutory	interim
interlocutory judgment for damages to be assessed	judgment for an amount to be decided by the court
interpleader	stakeholder claim
interrogatory	request for further information
leave	permission
legal aid taxation	detailed assessment of costs payable by the Lord Chancellor under Part 1 of the Legal Aid, Sentencing and Punishment of Offenders Act 2012
mandamus, order of	mandatory order
Mareva injunction (or order)	freezing injunction
minor	child
motion (in Chancery)	judge's application

Old term	New term
motions day (in Chancery)	applications day
next friend	litigation friend
not admitted	required to prove
oral examination	obtaining information from judgment debtor
originating application	Part 8 claim form (application notice in insolvency proceedings)
originating summons	Part 8 claim form
payment in	Part 36 offer (in most situations)
patient	protected person
plaintiff	claimant
pleading	statement of case
preliminary act (Admiralty proceedings)	collision statement of case
prohibition, order of	prohibiting order
rebutter	(no equivalent)
rejoinder	(no equivalent)
request for further and better particulars	request for further information
schedule of special damages	schedule of past and future loss and expense
setting down (for trial)	listing (for trial)
sheriff	enforcement officer
small claims arbitration	small claims track
specific discovery	specific disclosure
statement of claim	particulars of claim
subpoena	witness summons
substituted service	alternative service
summons for directions	case management conference
summons (for interim application)	application notice
summons (to commence proceedings in a county court)	claim form
Supreme Court Taxing Office	Senior Courts Costs Office
surrebutter	(no equivalent)
surrejoinder	(no equivalent)
taxation (of costs)	detailed assessment
taxing master	costs judge
third-party proceedings	additional claim
triable issue	real prospect of success
warrant of distress	warrant of control
warrant of execution	warrant of control
writ (to commence proceedings)	claim form (writs are still used in execution of judgments)
writ of *fieri facias*	writ of control (but writ of *fieri facias de bonis ecclesiasticis* is unchanged)

Index

This is a subject index to the contents of the **procedural checklists** (PC) and **chapters 1** to **92** of *Blackstone's Civil Practice: The Commentary*.

Each heading in **chapters 1** to **92** is numbered. The first heading in **chapter 2** is **2.1**, the second is **2.2**, and so on. This index refers to headings by their numbers.